THE

TREASURY OF DAVID:

CONTAINING

AN ORIGINAL EXPOSITION OF THE BOOK OF PSALMS;

A COLLECTION OF ILLUSTRATIVE EXTRACTS FROM THE WHOLE
RANGE OF LITERATURE;

A SERIES OF HOMILETICAL HINTS UPON ALMOST EVERY VERSE;

AND LISTS OF WRITERS UPON EACH PSALM.

IN TWO VOLUMES

BY

C. H. SPURGEON.

VOLUME II
PSALM LXXXVIII TO CL

THE OLD-TIME GOSPEL HOUR
Lynchburg, Virginia

ISBN 52256

Published in Nashville, Tennessee, by Thomas Nelson, Inc., Publishers
and distributed in Canada by Lawson Falle, Ltd.,
Cambridge, Ontario.
Manufactured in the United States of America.

1 2 3 4 5 6 7 8 9 10 – 85 84

PREFACE

THE labour of compiling the notes of this volume may be judged of from the fact that upon my writing to one of the most scholarly men of this age for a little assistance in my researches upon that well-known Psalm, the 103rd I received a note commencing, "I have hunted through my books, and have been surprised to find that, with the exception of what is universally known, there is so little about Psalm 103." This most generous-hearted brother had the warmest zeal and love to stimulate his investigations, yet this was the result, and had I repeated the experiment upon other Biblical students, and changed the Psalm, I should in very few instances have received any other reply. Hence, gentle reader, your patience has been exercised in waiting for Vol. IV. of the Treasury, and my toil has been correspondingly increased. Here, however, is the volume, as portly as its fellows, and I hope not inferior to any of them; at least, I can honestly say, if it be so, it is not the fault of my endeavours, for I have bated no jot of energy, spared no cost, and withheld no time, though this last has been a very precious commodity with me, and has frequently been snatched from rest which fatigue demanded, and which prudence might have wisely yielded.

Nor is this the only reason for the time which this volume has occupied, though we judge it to be quite sufficient, but we have desired to complete this work at our best, and not to allow the close of it to exhibit signs of fatigue and decline. We have often sat down to write our comment upon a Psalm, and have risen from the task because we did not feel at home at it. It is of no use compelling the mind, its productions in such a case are like forced fruits, disappointing and devoid of flavour. We like to write after the manner of JOHN BUNYAN, who said, "As I pulled, it came," and we prefer that the pulling should be as gentle as possible. So it has happened that we have lingered for months over a Psalm, feeling quite unfit to enter upon it. Especially was this the case over the hundred and ninth Psalm, which we sometimes think we never should have been able to handle at all if it had not been for the Bulgarian massacres, which threw us into such a state of righteous indignation that while we were musing the fire burned, and we melted the sentences, and wished that we could pour them boiling hot upon the monsters. Later tidings make us feel that the other side might well be favoured with similar visitations. Other Psalms have had their difficulties, though none to be compared with CIX. The grand *Cosmos* of Psalm CIV. was not to be dismissed in a few days; even now, after laying our best efforts at its feet, we feel dissatisfied with the poor result. However, we have done our best, and have grappled honestly with all hard places. We are so far through our labour, and look for a full deliverance. If some of our friends have had to wait, we hope they will be gainers by obtaining fruit all the riper and better from coming in due season. The book is finished, however, and with it two-thirds of my allotted task, for which may God be praised.

I am the more surprised at the general paucity of sermons and comments upon this portion of the book of Psalms, because it contains some of the more notable compositions, such as Psalms 84, 90, 91, 92, and 103. These and some of the others are so rich that, had several volumes existed illustrating any one of them, it would not have been a matter of wonder. When I have found one sermon upon a passage, it has generally been easy to collect a score upon the same ; preachers evidently run so much in ruts that they leave a large portion of the Scriptures without exposition. This suggests many thoughts, which, as they will naturally occur to every thoughtful reader, I need not enlarge upon in a mere preface, but this much may be said, we trust, without giving offence—if the habit of expounding the passages of Scripture which are read in public worship should ever become more common, the preparation for doing this in an interesting and instructive manner would greatly tend to enlarge the range of texts discussed from the pulpit, and would almost inevitably lead to the people's receiving from their teachers more of God's word and less of man's, and this would be no small benefit.

In this volume, as in all the rest, we have had the indefatigable assistance of Mr. J. L. KEYS, who, in addition to a vast amount of copying, has visited various libraries and museums to select from rare works which could not be found in any other places. Our venerable friend, the Rev. GEORGE ROGERS, has all along contributed his invaluable sermon-outlines, for which we are deeply grateful. Mr. GRACEY, the classical tutor of the Pastors' College, assisted us through the earlier Psalms of this volume in making selections from the Latin authors, and when he was obliged to decline, owing to the pressure of his engagements, his place was ably filled by the Rev. E. T. GIBSON, late of Crayford, to whom we also owe certain notes from German authors. I think it right to repeat the intimation that I am not to be understood as endorsing all the passages quoted from other authors. The names are given, and each writer bears his own responsibility.

Only one word of self-defence shall further delay the courteous reader. A critic has so greatly mistaken my meaning as to find in the title to the Sermon Notes a specimen of human vanity. I am amazed at his discovery. I do not pretend to be entirely free from that vice, but no trace of it is discoverable there by my keenest and most conscientious inspection ; on the contrary, I called those outlines " Hints to the Village Preacher,"* because I did not think those of them which are my own to be good enough to offer to my brethren in the regular ministry, but hoped that they might aid those

---

* This was the original heading.

good men, engaged all the week in business, who are generally, but I think incorrectly, called *lay-preachers*, and are not supposed to have the facilities of time and books which fall to the lot of the regular ministry. I thought this somewhat modest on my part, and did not see how it could be misunderstood. Our village ministers are among the most thoughtful and usefu of our brotherhood, and I never dreamed of casting a slur upon them ; as, however, I have been misunderstood, I will now, without altering the title, take higher ground, and say that I trust the hints may be useful to any preachers in city or country ; for the other day I met one of the most eminent metropolitan divines, and he most kindly thanked me for having suggested to him by a hint in the Treasury a sermon which he hoped had been most acceptable to his congregation, and he remarked that there was no need to be so very bashful about the aforesaid " hints." I have followed his advice, and may now, perhaps, be misunderstood again. It is a small matter to be unjustly censured, but still I would not even seem to despise brethren in more obscure spheres, for it is the last thing in my heart.

For the generous reviews which the former volumes have received on all hands I am deeply grateful. I commit this fourth volume to the press, praying that it may, according to the Lord's will, tend to the upbuilding of his church and his own glory.

C. H. Spurgeon

INDEX

OF AUTHORS QUOTED OR REFERRED TO.

PSALM LXXXVIII.

TITLE.—A Song or Psalm for the sons of Korah. *This sad complaint reads very little like a Song, nor can we conceive how it could be called by a name which denotes a song of praise or triumph; yet perhaps it was intentionally so called to show how faith " glories in tribulations also." Assuredly, if ever there was a song of sorrow and a Psalm of sadness, this is one. The sons of Korah, who had often united in chanting jubilant odes, are now bidden to take charge of this mournful dirge-like hymn. Servants and singers must not be choosers.* To the chief Musician. *He must superintend the singers and see that they do their duty well, for holy sorrow ought to be expressed with quite as much care as the most joyful praise; nothing should be slovenly in the Lord's house. It is more difficult to express sorrow fitly than it is to pour forth notes of gladness.* Upon Mahalath Leannoth. *This is translated by Alexander, " concerning afflictive sickness," and if this be correct, it indicates the mental malady which occasioned this plaintive song.* Maschil. *This term has occurred many times before, and the reader will remember that it indicates an instructive or didactic Psalm :—the sorrows of one saint are lessons to others; experimental teaching is exceedingly valuable.* Of Heman the Ezrahite. *This, probably, informs us as to its authorship; it was written by Heman, but which Heman it would not be easy to determine, though it will not be a very serious mistake if we suppose it to be the man alluded to in 1 Kings iv. 31, as the brother of Ethan, and one of the five sons of Zerah (1 Chron. ii. 6), the son of Judah, and hence called " the Ezrahite : " if this be the man, he was famous for his wisdom, and his being in Egypt during the time of Pharaoh's oppression may help to account for the deep bass of his song, and for the antique form of many of the expressions, which are more after the manner of Job than David. There was, however, a Heman in David's day who was one of the grand trio of chief musicians, " Heman, Asaph, and Ethan " (1 Chron. xv. 19), and no one can prove that this was not the composer. The point is of no consequence; whoever wrote the Psalm must have been a man of deep experience, who had done business on the great waters of soul trouble.*

SUBJECT AND DIVISIONS.—*This Psalm is fragmentary, and the only division of any service to us would be that suggested by Albert Barnes, viz.—A description of the sick man's sufferings (verses 1—9), and a prayer for mercy and deliverance (10—18). We shall, however, consider each verse separately, and so exhibit the better the incoherence of the author's grief. The reader had better first peruse the Psalm as a whole.*

EXPOSITION.

O LORD God of my salvation, I have cried day *and* night before thee :

2 Let my prayer come before thee : incline thine ear unto my cry ;

3 For my soul is full of troubles : and my life draweth nigh unto the grave.

4 I am counted with them that go down into the pit : I am as a man *that hath* no strength :

5 Free among the dead, like the slain that lie in the grave, whom thou rememberest no more : and they are cut off from thy hand.

6 Thou hast laid me in the lowest pit, in darkness, in the deeps.

7 Thy wrath lieth hard upon me, and thou hast afflicted *me* with all thy waves. Selah.

8 Thou hast put away mine acquaintance far from me ; thou hast made me an abomination unto them : *I am* shut up, and I cannot come forth.

9 Mine eye mourneth by reason of affliction : LORD, I have called daily upon thee, I have stretched out my hands unto thee.

10 Wilt thou shew wonders to the dead ? shall the dead arise *and* praise thee ? Selah.

11 Shall thy lovingkindness be declared in the grave ? *or* thy faithfulness in destruction ?

12 Shall thy wonders be known in the dark ? and thy righteousness in the land of forgetfulness ?

13 But unto thee have I cried, O LORD ; and in the morning shall my prayer prevent thee.

14 LORD, why castest thou off my soul ? *why* hidest thou thy face from me ?

15 I *am* afflicted and ready to die from *my* youth up : *while* I suffer thy terrors I am distracted.

16 Thy fierce wrath goeth over me ; thy terrors have cut me off.

17 They came round about me daily like water ; they compassed me about together.

18 Lover and friend hast thou put far from me, *and* mine acquaintance into darkness.

1. "*O Lord God of my salvation.*" This is a hopeful title by which to address the Lord, and it has about it the only ray of comfortable light which shines throughout the Psalm. The writer has salvation, he is sure of that, and God is the sole author of it. While a man can see God as his Saviour, it is not altogether midnight with him. While the living God can be spoken of as the life of our salvation, our hope will not quite expire. It is one of the characteristics of true faith that she turns to Jehovah, the saving God, when all other confidences have proved liars unto her. "*I have cried day and night before thee.*" His distress had not blown out the sparks of his prayer, but quickened them into a greater ardency, till they burned perpetually like a furnace at full blast. His prayer was personal—whoever had not prayed, he had done so ; it was intensely earnest, so that it was correctly described as a cry, such as children utter to move the pity of their parents ; and it was unceasing, neither the business of the day nor the weariness of the night had silenced it : surely such entreaties could not be in vain. Perhaps, if Heman's pain had not been incessant his supplications might have been intermittent ; it is a good thing that sickness will not let us rest if we spend our restlessness in prayer. Day and night are both suitable to prayer ; it is no work of darkness, therefore let us go with Daniel and pray when men can see us ; yet, since supplication needs no light, let us accompany Jacob and wrestle at Jabbok till the day breaketh. Evil is transformed to good when it drives us to prayer. One expression of the text is worthy of special note ; "*before thee*" is a remarkable intimation that the Psalmist's cries had an aim and a direction towards the Lord, and were not the mere clamours of nature, but the groanings of a gracious heart towards Jehovah, the God of salvation. Of what use are arrows shot into the air ? The archer's business is to look well at the mark he drives at. Prayers must be directed to heaven with earnest care. So thought Heman—his cries were all meant for the heart of his God. He had no eye to onlookers as Pharisees have, but all his prayers were before his God.

2. "*Let my prayer come before thee.*" Admit it to an audience ; let it speak with thee. Though it be *my* prayer, and therefore very imperfect, yet deny it not *thy* gracious consideration. "*Incline thine ear unto my cry.*" It is not music save to the ear of mercy, yet be not vexed with its discord, though it be but a cry, for it is the most natural expression of my soul's anguish. When my heart speaks, let thine ear hear. There may be obstacles which impede the upward flight of our prayers—let us entreat the Lord to remove them ; and as there may also be offences which prevent the Lord from giving favourable regard to our requests—let us implore him to put these out of the way. He who has prayed day and night cannot bear to lose all his labour. Only those who are indifferent in prayer will be indifferent about the issue of prayer.

3. "*For my soul is full of troubles.*" I am satiated and nauseated with them. Like a vessel full to the brim with vinegar, my heart is filled up with adversity till it can hold no more. He had his house full and his hands full of sorrow ; but, worse than that, he had his heart full of it. Trouble in the soul is the soul of trouble. A little soul trouble is painful ; what must it be to be sated with it ? And how much worse still to have your prayers return empty when your soul remains full of grief.

"*And my life draweth nigh unto the grave.*" He felt as if he must die, indeed he thought himself half dead already. All his life was going, his spiritual life declined, his mental life decayed, his bodily life flickered ; he was nearer dead than alive. Some of us can enter into this experience, for many a time have we traversed this valley of death-shade, ay ! and dwelt in it by the month together. Really to die and be with Christ will be a gala day's enjoyment compared with our misery when a worse than physical death has cast its dreadful shadow over us. Death would be welcomed as a relief by those whose depressed spirits make their existence a living death. Are good men ever permitted to suffer thus ? Indeed they are ; and some of them are even all their life-time subject to bondage. O Lord, be pleased to set free thy prisoners of hope ! Let none of thy mourners imagine that a strange thing has happened unto him, but rather rejoice as he sees the footprints of brethren who have trodden this desert before.

4. "*I am counted with them that go down into the pit.*" My weakness is so great that both by myself and others I am considered as good as dead. If those about me have not ordered my coffin they have at least conversed about my sepulchre, discussed my estate, and reckoned their share of it. Many a man has been buried before he was dead, and the only mourning over him has been because he refused to fulfil the greedy expectations of his hypocritical relatives by going down to the pit at once. It has come to this with some afflicted believers, that their hungry heirs think they have lived too long. "*I am as a man that hath no strength.*" I have but the name to live ; my constitution is broken up ; I can scarce crawl about my sick room, my mind is even weaker than my body, and my faith weakest of all. The sons and daughters of sorrow will need but little explanation of these sentences, they are to such tried ones as household words.

5. "*Free among the dead.*" Unbound from all that links a man with life, familiar with death's door, a freeman of the city of the sepulchre, I seem no more one of earth's drudges, but begin to anticipate the rest of the tomb. It is a sad case when our only hope lies in the direction of death, our only liberty of spirit amid the congenial horrors of corruption. "*Like the slain that lie in the grave, whom thou rememberest no more.*" He felt as if he were as utterly forgotten as those whose carcases are left to rot on the battle-field. As when a soldier, mortally wounded, bleeds unheeded amid the heaps of slain, and remains to his last expiring groan unpitied and unsuccoured, so did Heman sigh out his soul in loneliest sorrow, feeling as if even God himself had quite forgotten him. How low the spirits of good and brave men will sometimes sink. Under the influence of certain disorders everything will wear a sombre aspect, and the heart will dive into the profoundest deeps of misery. It is all very well for those who are in robust health and full of spirits to blame those whose lives are sicklied o'er with the pale cast of melancholy, but the evil is as real as a gaping wound, and all the more hard to bear because it lies so much in the region of the soul that to the inexperienced it appears to be a mere matter of fancy and diseased imagination. Reader, never ridicule the nervous and hypochondriacal, their pain is real ; though much of the evil lies in the imagination, it is not imaginary. "*And they are cut off from thy hand.*" Poor Heman felt as if God himself had put him away, smitten him and laid him among the corpses of those executed by divine justice. He mourned that the hand of the Lord had gone out against him, and that he was divided from the great Author of his life. This is the essence of wormwood. Man's blows are trifles, but God's smitings are terrible to a gracious heart. To feel utterly forsaken of the Lord and cast away as though hopelessly corrupt is the very climax of heart-desolation.

6. "*Thou hast laid me in the lowest pit, in darkness, in the deeps.*" What a collection of forcible metaphors, each one expressive of the utmost grief. Heman compared his forlorn condition to an imprisonment in a subterranean dungeon, to confinement in the realms of the dead, and to a plunge into the abyss. None of the similes are strained. The mind can descend far lower than the body, for there are bottomless pits. The flesh can bear only a certain number of wounds and no more, but the soul can bleed in ten thousand ways, and die over and over again each hour. It is grievous to the good man to see the Lord whom he loves laying him in the sepulchre of despondency ; piling nightshade upon him, putting out all his candles, and heaping over him solid masses of sorrow : evil from so good a hand seems evil indeed, and yet if faith could but be allowed to speak she would remind the depressed spirit that it is better to fall into the hand of the Lord than into the hands of man, and moreover she would tell the despondent heart that

God never placed a Joseph in a pit without drawing him up again to fill a throne : that he never caused a horror of great darkness to fall upon an Abraham without revealing his covenant to him ; and never cast even a Jonah into the deeps without preparing the means to land him safely on dry land. Alas, when under deep depression the mind forgets all this, and is only conscious of its unutterable misery ; the man sees the lion but not the honey in its carcase, he feels the thorns but he cannot smell the roses which adorn them. He who now feebly expounds these words knows within himself more than he would care or dare to tell of the abysses of inward anguish. He has sailed round the Cape of Storms, and has drifted along by the dreary headlands of despair. He has groaned out with one of old—" My bones are pierced in me in the night season ; and my sinews take no rest. I go mourning without the sun. Terrors are turned upon me, they pursue my soul as the wind." Those who know this bitterness by experience will sympathise, but from others it would be idle to expect pity, nor would their pity be worth the having if it could be obtained. It is an unspeakable consolation that our Lord Jesus knows this experience, right well, having, with the exception of the sin of it, felt it all and more than all in Gethsemane when he was exceeding sorrowful even unto death.

7. " Thy wrath lieth hard upon me." Dreadful plight this, the worst in which a man can be found. Wrath is heavy in itself ; God's wrath is crushing beyond conception, and when that presses hard the soul is oppressed indeed. The wrath of God is the very hell of hell, and when it weighs upon the conscience a man feels a torment such as only that of damned spirits can exceed. Joy or peace, or even numbness of indifference, there can be none to one who is loaded with this most tremendous of burdens. " And thou hast afflicted me with all thy waves," or all thy breakers. He pictures God's wrath as breaking over him like those waves of the sea which swell, and rage, and dash with fury upon the shore. How could his frail barque hope to survive those cruel breakers, white like the hungry teeth of death ? Seas of affliction seemed to rush in upon him with all the force of omnipotence ; he felt himself to be oppressed and afflicted like Israel in Egypt, when they cried by reason of their afflictions. It appeared impossible for him to suffer more, he had exhausted the methods of adversity and endured all its waves. So have we imagined, and yet it is not really quite so bad. The worst case might be worse, there are alleviations to every woe ; God has other and more terrible waves which, if he chose to let them forth, would sweep us into the infernal abyss, whence hope has long since been banished.

" Selah." There was need to rest. Above the breakers the swimmer lifts his head and looks around him, breathing for a moment, until the next wave comes. Even lamentation must have its pauses. Nights are broken up into watches, and even so mourning has its intervals. Such sorrowful music is a great strain both on voices and instruments, and it is well to give the singers the relief of silence for a while.

8. " Thou hast put away mine acquaintance far from me." If ever we need friends it is in the dreary hour of despondency and the weary time of bodily sickness ; therefore does the sufferer complain because divine providence had removed his friends. Perhaps his disease was infectious or defiling, so that he was legally separated from his fellow men, perhaps their fears kept them away from his plague-stricken house, or else his good name had become so injured that they naturally avoided him. Most friends require but small excuse for turning their backs on the afflicted. The swallows offer no apology for leaving us to winter by ourselves. Yet it is a piercing pain which arises from the desertion of dear associates ; it is a wound which festers and refuses to be healed. " Thou hast made me an abomination unto them." They turned from him as though he had become loathsome and contaminating, and this because of something which the Lord had done to him ; therefore, he brings his complaint to the prime mover in his trouble. He who is still flattered by the companions of his pleasure can little guess the wretchedness which will be his portion should be become poor, or slanderously accused, for then one by one the parasites of his prosperity will go their way and leave him to his fate, not without cutting remarks on their part to increase his misery. Men have not so much power to bless by friendship as to curse by treachery. Earth's poisons are more deadly than her medicines are healing. The mass of men who gather around a man and flatter him are like tame leopards ; when they lick his hand it is well for him to remember that with equal gusto they would drink his blood. " Cursed is he that trusteth in man." " I am shut up, and I cannot come forth." He was a

prisoner in his room, and felt like a leper in the lazaretto, or a condemned criminal in his cell. His mind, too, was bound as with fetters of iron ; he felt no liberty of hope, he could take no flights of joy. When God shuts friends out, and shuts us in to pine away alone, it is no wonder if we water our couch with tears.

9. " *Mine eye mourneth by reason of affliction.*" He wept his eyes out. He exhausted the lachrymal glands, he wore away the sight itself. Tears in showers are a blessing, and work our good ; but in floods they become destructive and injurious. " *Lord, I have called daily upon thee.*" His tears wetted his prayers, but did not damp their fervour. He prayed still, though no answer came to dry his eyes. Nothing can make a true believer cease praying ; it is a part of his nature, and pray he must. " *I have stretched out my hands unto thee.*" He used the appropriate posture of a supplicant, of his own accord ; men need no posture-maker, or master of the ceremonies, when they are eagerly pleading for mercy, nature suggests to them attitudes both natural and correct. As a little child stretches out its hands to its mother while it cries, so did this afflicted child of God. He prayed all over, his eyes wept, his voice cried, his hands were outstretched, and his heart broke. This was prayer indeed.

10. " *Wilt thou shew wonders to the dead ?* " Wherefore then suffer me to die ? While I live thou canst in me display the glories of thy grace, but when I have passed into the unknown land, how canst thou illustrate in me thy love ? If I perish thou wilt lose a worshipper who both reverenced, and in his own experience illustrated, the wonders of thy character and acts. This is good pleading, and therefore he repeats it. " *Shall the dead arise and praise thee ?* " He is thinking only of the present, and not of the last great day, and he urges that the Lord would have one the less to praise him among the sons of men. Shades take no part in the quires of the Sabbath, ghosts sing no joyous psalms, sepulchres and vaults send forth no notes of thanksgiving. True the souls of departed saints render glory to God, but the dejected Psalmist's thoughts do not mount to heaven but survey the gloomy grave : he stays on this side of eternity, where in the grave he sees no wonders and hears no songs.

" *Selah.*" At the mouth of the tomb he sits down to meditate, and then returns to his theme.

11. " *Shall thy lovingkindness be declared in the gₗₐve ?* " Thy tender goodness —who shall testify concerning it in that cold abode where the worm and corruption hold their riot ? The living may indite " Meditations among the Tombs," but the dead know nothing, and therefore can declare nothing. " *Or thy faithfulness in destruction ?* " If the Lord suffered his servant to die before the divine promise was fulfilled, it would be quite impossible for his faithfulness to be proclaimed. The poet is dealing with this life only, and looking at the matter from the point of view afforded by time and the present race of men ; if a believer were deserted and permitted to die in despair, there could come no voice from his grave to inform mankind that the Lord had rectified his wrongs and relieved him of his trials, no songs would leap up from the cold sod to hymn the truth and goodness of the Lord ; but as far as men are concerned, a voice which loved to magnify the grace of God would be silenced, and a loving witness for the Lord removed from the sphere of testimony.

12. " *Shall thy wonders be known in the dark ?* " If not here permitted to prove the goodness of Jehovah, how could the singer do so in the land of darkness and deathshade ? Could his tongue, when turned into a clod, charm the dull cold ear of death ? Is not a living dog better than a dead lion, and a living believer of more value to the cause of God on earth than all the departed put together ? " *And thy righteousness in the land of forgetfulness ?* " What shall be told concerning thee in the regions of oblivion ? Where memory and love are lost, and men are alike unknowing and unknown, forgetful and forgotten, what witness to the divine holiness can be borne ? The whole argument amounts to this—if the believer dies unblest, how will God's honour be preserved ? Who will bear witness to his truth and righteousness ?

13. " *But unto thee have I cried, O Lord ;* " I have continued to pray for help to thee, O Jehovah, the living God, even though thou hast so long delayed to answer. A true-born child of God may be known by his continuing to cry ; a hypocrite is great at a spurt, but the genuine believer holds on till he wins his suit. " *And in the morning shall my prayer prevent thee.*" He meant to plead on yet, and to increase his earnestness. He intended to be up betimes, to anticipate the daylight, and

begin to pray before the sun was up. If the Lord is pleased to delay, he has a right
to do as he wills, but we must not therefore become tardy in supplication. If we
count the Lord slack concerning his promise we must only be the more eager to
outrun him, lest sinful sloth on our path should hinder the blessing.

> "Let prayer and holy hymn
>   Perfume the morning air ;
> Before the world with smoke is dim
>   Bestir thy soul to prayer.
> While flowers are wet with dew
>   Lament thy sins with tears,
> And ere the sun shines forth anew
>   Tell to thy Lord thy fears."

14. " *Lord, why casteth thou off my soul ?* " Hast thou not aforetime chosen
me, wilt thou now reject me ? Shall thine elect ones become thy reprobates ?
Dost thou, like changeable men, give a writing of divorcement to those whom thy
love has espoused. Can thy beloveds become thy cast-offs ? " *Why hidest thou
thy face from me ?* " Wilt thou not so much as look upon me ? Canst thou not
afford me a solitary smile ? Why this severity to one who has in brighter days
basked in the light of thy favour ? We may put these questions to the Lord, nay,
we ought to do so. It is not undue familiarity, but holy boldness. It may help
us to remove the evil which provokes the Lord to jealousy, if we seriously beg him
to shew us wherefore he contends with us. He cannot act towards us in other
than a right and gracious manner, therefore for every stroke of his rod there is a
sufficient reason in the judgment of his loving heart ; let us try to learn that reason
and profit by it.

15. " *I am afflicted and ready to die from my youth up.* " His affliction had now
lasted so long that he could hardly remember when it commenced ; it seemed to
him as if he had been at death's door ever since he was a child. This was no doubt
an exaggeration of a depressed spirit, and yet perhaps Heman may have been born
under the cypress, and have been all his days afflicted with some chronic disease
or bodily infirmity ; there are holy men and women whose lives are a long apprenticeship to patience, and these deserve both our sympathy and our reverence,—
our reverence we have ventured to say, for since the Saviour became the acquaintance
of grief, sorrow has become honourable in believers' eyes. A life-long sickness
may by divine grace prove to be a life-long blessing. Better suffer from childhood
to old age than be let alone to find pleasure in sin.

" *While I suffer thy terrors I am distracted.* " Long use had not blunted the
edge of sorrow, God's terrors had not lost their terror ; rather had they become
more overwhelming and had driven the man to despair. He was unable to collect
his thoughts, he was so tossed about that he could not judge and weigh his own
condition in a calm and rational manner. Sickness alone will thus distract the
mind ; and when a sense of divine anger is added thereto, it is not to be wondered
at if reason finds it hard to hold the reins. How near akin to madness soul-depression
sometimes may be, it is not our province to decide ; but we speak what we do know
when we say that a feather-weight might be sufficient to turn the scale at times.
Thank God, O ye tempted ones who yet retain your reason ! Thank him that the
devil himself cannot add that feather while the Lord stands by to adjust all things.
Even though we have grazed upon the rock of utter distraction, we bless the infinitely gracious Steersman that the vessel is seaworthy yet, and answers to her
helm : tempest-tossed from the hour of her launch even to this hour, yet she mounts
the waves and defies the hurricane.

16. " *Thy fierce wrath goeth over me.* " What an expression, " fierce wrath,"
and it is a man of God who feels it ! Do we seek an explanation ? It seemed so
to him, but " things are not what they seem." No punitive anger ever falls upon
the saved one, for Jesus shields him from it all ; but a father's anger may fall upon
his dearest child, none the less but all the more, because he loves it. Since Jesus
bore my guilt as my substitute, my Judge cannot punish me, but my Father can
and will correct me. In this sense the Father may even manifest " fierce wrath "
to his erring child, and under a sense of it that dear broken-down one may be laid
in the dust and covered with wretchedness, and yet for all that he may be accepted
and beloved of the Lord all the while. Heman represents God's wrath as breaking
over him as waves over a wreck. " *Thy terrors have cut me off.* " They have made
me a marked man, they have made me feel like a leper separated from the congre-

gation of thy people, and they have caused others to look upon me as no better than dead. Blessed be God this is the sufferer's idea and not the very truth, for the Lord will neither cast off nor cut off his people, but will visit his mourners with choice refreshments.

17. "*They came round about me daily like water.*" My troubles, and thy chastisements poured in upon me, penetrating everywhere, and drowning all. Such is the permeating and pervading power of spiritual distress, there is no shutting it out ; it soaks into the soul like the dew into Gideon's fleece ; it sucks the spirit down as the quicksand swallows the ship ; it overwhelms it as the deluge submerged the green earth. "*They compassed me about together.*" Griefs hemmed him in. He was like the deer in the hunt, when the dogs are all around and at his throat. Poor soul ! and yet he was a man greatly beloved of heaven !

18. "*Lover and friend hast thou put far from me.*" Even when they are near me bodily, they are so unable to swim with me in such deep waters, that they stand like men far away on the shore while I am buffeted with the billows ; but, alas, they shun me, the dearest lover of all is afraid of such a distracted one, and those who took counsel with me avoid me now ! The Lord Jesus knew the meaning of this in all its wormwood and gall when in his passion. In dreadful loneliness he trod the wine-press, and all his garments were distained with the red blood of those sour grapes. Lonely sorrow falls to the lot of not a few ; let them not repine, but enter herein into close communion with that dearest lover and friend who is never far from his tried ones. "*And mine acquaintance into darkness,*" or better still, *my acquaintance is darkness.* I am familiar only with sadness, all else has vanished. I am a child crying alone in the dark. Will the heavenly Father leave his child there ? Here he breaks off, and anything more from us would only spoil the abruptness of the unexpected FINIS.

[*We have not attempted to interpret this Psalm concerning our Lord, but we fully believe that where the members are, the Head is to be seen pre-eminently. To have given a double exposition under each verse would have been difficult and confusing ; we have therefore left the Messianic references to be pointed out in the* Notes, *where, if God the Holy Ghost be pleased to illustrate the page, we have gathered up more than enough to lead each devout reader to behold Jesus, the man of sorrows and the acquaintance of grief.*]

EXPLANATORY NOTES AND QUAINT SAYINGS.

Title.—"*Mahalath Leannoth.*" I lean to the idea, that the words *Mahalath Leannoth* are intended to denote some musical instrument of the plaintive order, and in this opinion KIMCHI and other Jewish writers perfectly agree. They assert that it was a wind-instrument, answering very much to the flute, and employed mainly in giving utterance to sentiments of grief, upon occasions of great sorrow and lamentation. With this view of the title, I should look for no new translation, but should just read it substantially as our translators here : " A Song or Psalm for the sons of Korah, to the giver of victory, upon Mahalath Leannoth, an instruction for Heman, the Ezrahite.—*John Morison.*

Title.—"*Leannoth*" is variously rendered, according as it is derived from עָנָה, *anah, to suffer, be afflicted,* or from עָנָה, *anah, to chant, sing.* Gesenius, De Wette, Dr. Davies, and others take the latter view ; while Mudge, Hengstenberg, Alexander, and others take the former. Mudge translates, *to create dejection* ; Alexander renders, *mahalath leannoth, concerning afflictive sickness* ; Hengstenberg reads, *upon the distress of oppression.* The Septuagint (ἀποκριθῆναι) and the Vulgate (*respondendum*) indicate a *responsive* song, and Houbigant translates the words in question, *for the choirs, that they may answer.* Many etymologists consider the primary idea of עָנָה, *anah, to sing,* that of *answering.* The tone of the psalm in question, however, being decidedly that of *sadness and dejection,* it appears more probable that *leannoth* denotes the strictly elegiac character of the performance, and the whole title may read therefore, " *A Song or Psalm, for the sons of Korah, to the chief musician, upon the flutes* [*or the hollow instruments*], *to afflict* [*or cause dejection*], *a didactic Psalm of Heman, the Ezrahite.*"—*F. G. Hibbard, in " The Psalms chronologically arranged, with Historical Introductions." New York,* 1856.

Title.—The explanation :—to be performed mournfully with subdued voice, agrees with the mournful contents, whose tone is even more gloomy than that of Ps. lxxvii.—*From " The Psalms, By C. B. Moll."* [*Lange's Series of Commentaries.*]

Title.—" *Heman.*" 1. David was not the only man acquainted with sad exercise and affliction of spirit, for here is another, to wit, *Heman the Ezrahite*, as deep in trouble of spirit as he or any other beside. 2. They are not all men of weak minds and shallow wits who are acquainted with trouble of spirit, and borne down with the sense of God's wrath ; for here is *Heman*, one amongst the wisest of all Israel (and inferior to none for wisdom, except to Solomon alone), under the heaviest exercise we can imagine possible for a saint. 3. When it pleaseth God to exercise a man of parts, of great gifts and graces, he can make his burden proportionable to his strength, and give him as much to do with the difficulties he puts him to, as a weaker man shall find in his exercise, as appeareth in the experience of *Heman*. 4. Wise men in their trouble must take the same course with the simpler sort of men ; that is, they must run to God as others do, and seek relief only in his grace, who as he distributeth the measures of trouble, can also give comfort, ease, and deliverance from them, as the practice of *Heman* doth teach us. 5. What trouble of wounded spirit some of God's children have felt in former times, others dear to God may find the like in after ages, and all men ought to prepare for the like, and should not think the exercise strange when it cometh, but must comfort themselves in this, that other saints whose names are recorded in Scripture, have been under like affliction ; for the Psalm is appointed " to give instruction " ; it is " *Maschil of Heman.*" 6. What is at one time matter of mourning to one of God's children, may become matter of joy and singing afterward, both to himself and to others, as this sad anguish of spirit in *Heman* is made a song of joy unto God's glory, and the comfort of all afflicted souls, labouring under the sense of sin and felt wrath of God, unto the world's end ; it is " *A Song, a Psalm for the sons of Korah.*" 7. Such as are most heartily afflicted in spirit, and do flee to God for reconciliation and consolation through Christ, have no reason to suspect themselves, that they are not esteemed of and loved as dear children, because they feel so much of God's wrath : for here is a saint who hath drunken of that cup (as deep as any who shall read this Psalm), here is one so much loved and honoured of God, as to be a penman of Holy Scripture, and a pattern of faith and patience unto others ; even *Heman the Ezrahite.*—*David Dickson.*

Whole Psalm.—" We have in this Psalm the voice of our suffering Redeemer," says Horne ; and the contents may be thus briefly stated—

1. *The plaintive wailing* of the suffering one, verses 1, 2. It strongly resembles Ps. xxii. 1, 2.

2. *His soul exceeding sorrowful, even unto death*, verses 3, 4, 5. The word *"free"* in our version, is חפש, properly denoting separation from others, and here rendered by Junius and Tremellius, " set aside from intercourse and communication with men, having nothing in common with them, like those who are afflicted with leprosy, and are sent away to separate dwellings." They quote 2 Chron. xxvi. 21.

3. *His feelings of hell*, verses 6, 7. For he feels God's prison, and the gloom of God's darkest wrath. And " *Selah* " gives time to ponder.

4. *His feelings of shame and helplessness*, verse 8. " His own receive him not."

5. *The effects of soul-agony upon his body*, verse 9.

6. *His submission to the Lord*, verse 9. It is the very tone of Gethsemane, " Nevertheless. *not my will !* "

7. *The sustaining hope of resurrection*, verses 10 (with a solemn pause, " Selah "), 11, 12. The " *land of forgetfulness*," and " *the dark*," express the unseen world, which, to those on this side of the vail, is so unknown, and where those who enter it are to us as if they had for ever been forgotten by those they left behind. God's wonders shall be made known there. There shall be victory gained over death and the grave : God's " *lovingkindness* " to man, and his " *faithfulness*," pledge him to do this new thing in the universe. Messiah must return from the abodes of the invisible state ; and in due time, Heman, as well as all other members of the Messiah's body, must return also. Yes, God's *wonders* shall be known at the grave's mouth. God's *righteousness*, in giving what satisfied justice in behalf of Messiah's members, has been manifested gloriously, so that resurrection must follow, and the land of forgetfulness must give up its dead. O morning of surpassing bliss, hasten on ! Messiah has risen ; when shall all that are his arise ? Till that day dawn, they must take up their Head's plaintive expostulations, and remind their

God in Heman's strains of what he has yet to accomplish. " *Wilt thou shew wonders to the dead?*" etc.

8. *His perseverance in vehement prayer*, verses 13, 14.

9. *His long-continued and manifold woes*, verses 15, 16, 17.

10. *His loneliness of soul*, verse 18. Hengstenberg renders the last clause of this verse more literally—" The dark kingdom of the dead is instead of all my companions." What unutterable gloom ! completed by this last dark shade—all sympathy from every quarter totally withdrawn ! Forlorn indeed ! Sinking from gloom to gloom, from one deep to another, and every billow sweeping over him, and wrath, like a tremendous mountain, " *leaning* " or resting its weight on the crushed worm. Not even Psalm xxii. is more awfully solemnising, there being in this deeply melancholy Psalm only one cheering glimpse through the intense gloom, namely, that of resurrection hoped for, but still at a distance. At such a price was salvation purchased by him who is the resurrection and the life. He himself wrestled for life and resurrection in our name—and that price so paid is the reason why to us salvation is free. And so we hear in solemn joy the harp of Judah struck by Heman, to overawe our souls not with his own sorrows, but with what Horsley calls " The lamentation of Messiah," or yet more fully, *The sorrowful days and nights of the Man of Sorrows.—Andrew A. Bonar.*

*Whole Psalm.—*This Psalm stands alone in all the Psalter for the unrelieved gloom, the hopeless sorrow of its tone. Even the very saddest of the others, and the Lamentations themselves, admit some variations of key, some strains of hopefulness ; here only all is darkness to the close.—*Neale and Littledale.*

*Whole Psalm.—*The prophecy in the foregoing Psalm of the conversion of all nations is followed by this Passion-Psalm, in order that it may never be forgotten that God has purchased to himself an universal church, by the precious blood of his dear Son.—*Christopher Wordsworth.*

*Whole Psalm.—*All the misery and sorrow which are described in this Psalm, says Brentius, have been the lot of Christ's people. We may therefore take the Psalm, he adds, to be common to Christ and his church.—*W. Wilson.*

Verse 1.—" My." That little word " *my* " opens for a moment a space between the clouds through which the Sun of righteousness casts one solitary beam. Generally speaking, you will find that when the Psalm begins with lamentation, it ends with praise ; like the sun, which, rising in clouds and mist, sets brightly, and darts forth its parting rays just before it goes down. But here the first gleam shoots across the sky just as the sun rises, and no sooner has the ray appeared, than thick clouds and darkness gather over it ; the sun continues its course throughout the whole day enveloped in clouds ; and sets at last in a thicker bank of them than it ever had around it during the day. " Lover and friend hast thou put far from me, and mine acquaintance into darkness." In what a dark cloud does the sun of Heman set !—*J. C. Philpot.*

Verse 1.—" Before thee." He had not recklessly poured forth his complaints, or cast them to the winds, as many are wont to do, who have no hope in their calamities ; but he had always mingled with his complaining prayers for obtaining deliverance, and had directed them to God, where faith assured him his prayers would be seen again. This must be attentively noted, since herein is seen of what kind the complaints of the saints are.—*Mollerus.*

Verse 1.—" Before thee." Other men seek some hiding place where they may murmur against God, but the Psalmist comes into the Lord's presence and states his grievances. When a man dares to pour out his complaint before the Lord's own face, his woes are real, and not the result of petulance or a rebellious spirit.—*C. H. S.*

Verses 1, 2.—" Before thee." Not seeking to be seen by human eye, but by God alone, therefore, " *let my prayer come before thee*," that is, let it be acceptable before thee, after the similitude of ambassadors who are admitted to audience ; and when my prayer has entered " *incline thine ear unto my cry*," because thou hearest the desire of the afflicted.—*Richardus Hampolus.*

Verse 2.—" Incline thine ear," etc. It is necessary that God should incline his ear unto our prayer, else it would be in vain to come before Him. The prodigal did not venture to present his prayer before the father ran and fell upon his neck and kissed him. For then he said, Luke xv. 21, "Father, I have sinned against heaven, and in thy sight," etc., and so he obtained mercy. Esther did not present her prayer to Ahasuerus before he descended from his throne and inclined himself to her. Esth. v. 2, etc.—*Le Blanc.*

Verse 3.—" *My soul is full of troubles.*" The Lord Jesus emptied himself of glory, that he might be full of trouble. His soul, which was free from human sin, was full of human troubles, that we who are full of sin might be free from trouble ; his life drew nigh to the terrors of the unseen world, that we might not be its spoil and prey.—" *Plain Commentary.*"

Verse 3.—" *My soul is full of troubles.*" Hear into what a depth of spiritual distress three worthy servants of God in these later times were plunged and pressed down under the sense of God's anger for sin. Blessed *Mistress Brettergh* upon her last bed was horribly hemmed in with the sorrows of death ; the very grief of hell laid hold upon her soul ; a roaring wilderness of woe was within her, as she confessed of herself. She said, her sin had made her a prey to Satan ; and wished that she had never been born, or that she had been made any other creature rather than a woman. She cried out many times, woe, woe, woe, etc. ; a weak, a woful, a wretched, a forsaken woman ; with tears continually trickling from her eyes. *Master Peacock*, that man of God, in that his dreadful visitation and desertion, recounting some smaller sins, burst out in these words : " And for these," saith he, " I feel now a hell in my conscience." Upon other occasions he cried out, groaning most pitifully, " Oh me, wretch ! Oh mine heart is miserable ! Oh, oh, miserable and woful ! The burden of my sin lieth so heavy upon me, I doubt it will break my heart. Oh how woful and miserable is my state that I am hunted by hell-hounds ! " When by-standers asked if he would pray, he answered, " I cannot." Suffer us, say they, to pray for you. " Take not," replied he, " the name of God in vain, by praying for a reprobate."

What grievous pangs, what sorrowful torments, what boiling heats of the fire of hell that blessed saint of God, *John Glover*, felt inwardly in his spirit, saith Foxe, no speech outwardly is able to express. Being young, saith he, I remember I was once or twice with him, whom partly by his talk I perceived, and partly by mine own eyes saw to be so worn and consumed by the space of five years, that neither almost any brooking of meat, quietness of sleep, pleasure of life, yea, and almost no kind of senses was left in him. Upon apprehension of some backsliding, he was so perplexed, that if he had been in the deepest pit of hell, he could almost have despaired no more of his salvation ; in which intolerable griefs of mind, saith he, although he neither had, nor could have any joy of his meat, yet was he compelled to eat against his appetite, to the end to defer the time of his damnation so long as he might ; thinking with himself, but that he must needs be thrown into hell, the breath being once out of his body. I dare not pass out of this point, lest some child of God should be here discouraged, before I tell you that every one of these three was at length blessedly recovered, and did rise most gloriously out of their several depths of extremest spiritual misery, before their end.

Hear, therefore, *Mistress Brettergh's* triumphant songs and ravishments of spirit, after the return of her well-beloved : " O Lord Jesu, dost thou pray for me ? O blessed and sweet Saviour, how wonderful ! How wonderful are thy mercies ! Oh thy love is unspeakable, thou hast dealt so graciously with me ! O my Lord and my God, blessed be thy name for evermore, which hast shewed me the path of life. Thou didst, O Lord, hide thy face from me for a little season, but with everlasting mercy thou hast had compassion on me. And now, blessed Lord, thy comfortable presence is come ; yea, Lord, thou hast had respect unto thine hand-maid, and art come with fulness of joy, and abundance of consolation. O blessed be thy name, my Lord and my God. O the joys that I feel in my soul ! They be wonderful. O Father, how merciful and marvellously gracious art thou unto me ! yea, Lord, I feel thy mercy and I am assured of thy love ; and so certain am I thereof, as Thou art the God of truth, even so sure do I know myself to be thine, O Lord my God, and this my soul knoweth right well. Blessed be the Lord that hath thus comforted me, and hath brought me now to a place more sweet unto me than the garden of Eden. Oh the joy, the delightsome joy that I feel ! O praise the Lord for his mercies, and for this joy which my soul feeleth full well ; praise his name for evermore.

Hear with what heavenly calmness and sweet comforts *Master Peacock's* heart was refreshed and ravished when the storm was over : " Truly, my heart and soul," saith he, (when the tempest was something allayed) " have been far led and deeply troubled with temptations, and stings of conscience, but I thank God they are eased in good measure. Wherefore I desire that I be not branded with the note of a cast-away or reprobate. Such questions, oppositions, and all tending thereto, I renounce. Concerning mine inconsiderate speeches in my temptation, I humbly and heartily ask mercy of God for them all." Afterward by little, and little, more light did arise in his heart, and he brake out into such speeches as these : " I do, God be praised, feel such comfort from that, what shall I call it ? " " Agony," said one that stood by. " Nay," quoth he, " that is too little ; that had I five hundred worlds, I could not make satisfaction for such an issue. Oh, the sea is not more full of water, nor the sun of light, than the Lord of mercy ; yea, his mercies are ten thousand times more. What great cause have I to magnify the great good- ness of God, that hath humbled such a wretched miscreant, and of so base condition, to an estate so glorious and stately. The Lord hath honoured me with his goodness ! I am sure he hath provided a glorious kingdom for me. The joy that I feel in mine heart is incredible." For the third, (namely, *John Glover*) hear Mr. Foxe : " Though this good servant of God suffered many years so sharp temptations, and strong buffettings of Satan ; yet the Lord, who graciously preserved him all the while, not only at last did rid him out of all discomfort, but also framed him thereby to such mortification of life, as the like lightly hath not been seen ; in such sort, as he being like one placed in heaven already, and dead in this world both in word and meditation, led a life altogether celestial, abhorring in his mind all profane doings—*Robert Bolton* (1572—1631), *in* " *Instructions for a right Comforting afflicted Consciences.*"

Verse 3.—" *My life.*" The Hebrew word rendered *life* is in the plural number, as in Gen. ii. 7 ; iii. 14, 17 ; vi. 17 ; vii. 15 ; *et al.* *Why* the plural was used as applicable to life cannot now be known with certainty. It *may* have been to accord with the fact, that man has *two* kinds of life ;—the animal life,—or life in common with the inferior creation ; and intellectual, or higher life,—the life of the *soul.* The meaning here is, that he was about to die ; or that his *life* or *lives* approached that state when the grave closes over us ; the extinction of the mere animal life ; and the separation of the soul—the immortal part—from the body.—*Albert Barnes.*

3. " *The grave.*" The word which is rendered " *hell* " in the Prayer Book trans- lation, and " *the grave* " in the Bible version, and which is usually translated either as *hell* or *the grave*, is in the Hebrew שׁאל and in the Greek " *Hades.*" " *Hades* " signifies " the unseen world." The word " *Sheol* " is literally " the Devouring, or the Insatiable." (Compare Hab. ii. 5, " who enlargeth his desire as hell, and is as death, and cannot be satisfied ; " and also Prov. xxx. 15, 16.) " *Sheol* " seems to have presented itself to the thoughts of the ancient Hebrews as a gloomy, silent, inevitable, and mysterious abode, situated within the earth, whither the souls of the departed were compelled to repair and to dwell, upon their being separated from the body. (Isa. xiv. 9—20). They believed that the spirits of all human kind were contained there in a state of waiting, and there especially dwelt the souls of the giants before the flood (1 Pet. iii. 19, 20), and of the great ones of old, the *Rephaim*, whom they pictured to themselves as fearful and gigantic spectres (Com- pare Prov. ii. 18). These ideas became modified and developed with the increasing clearness of divine teaching ; and they divided the abode of the dead into different states of hope and comfort, which they called Abraham's bosom and paradise (Luke xvi. 22, 23 ; xxiii. 43) ; and of misery and suffering (Wisdom iii. 1). Life and immortality were brought to light by the Saviour, and also judgment and Hell— the *Gehenna* of everlasting punishment, as distinguished from the Unseen World. (Compare Rev. xx. 13, 14.) From these speculations of Jewish Rabbis respecting *Sheol* the church of Rome appears to have developed the doctrine of Purgatory. It should be added that it was a received opinion among the followers of Rabbinical teaching, that all of the seed of Abraham, though they would be dwellers in *Sheol* before the general resurrection, would finally escape the *Gehenna* of everlasting fire. The rich man (Luke xvi. 23) is in Hades in torments when he calls to Abraham his father.—" *Plain Commentary.*"

Verse 4.—" *I am counted with them that go down into the pit.*" Not only myself, says he, but others also now despair of my life, and number me with those whose corpses are borne forth to burial. For now all my powers have failed and my vital spirits become quenched. He uses the word גֶּבֶר which indicates fortitude rather than אָדָם or אִישׁ in order to show how great the severity of these evils was, and the vehemence of his griefs, which had broken even a most robust man.—*Mollerus.*

Verse 4.—"*I am counted with them that go down into the pit.*" Next to the troubles of Christ's soul, are mentioned the disgrace and ignominy to which he submitted : He who was the fountain of immortality, from whom no one could take his life, who could in a moment have commanded twelve legions of angels to his aid, or have caused heaven and earth, at a word speaking, to fly away before him, he was *counted among them that go down into the pit ;* he died, to all appearance, like the rest of mankind ; nay, he was forcibly put to death, as a malefactor ; and seemed, in the hands of his executioners, *as a man that had no strength,* no power, or might, to help and save himself. His strength went from him ; he became weak, and like another man. The people shook their heads at him, saying, " He saved others, himself he cannot save."—*Samuel Burder.*

Verse 4.—There is in the original an antithesis, which cannot be conveyed by mere translation, arising from the fact that the first word for *man* is one implying strength.—*J. A. Alexander.*

Verse 5.—" *Free among the dead.*" In the former verse he had said that he had approached very near to death, now he is plainly dead : there he was about to be buried, here he is laid in the sepulchre : thus had his sufferings increased. *Free* is to be understood of the affairs of this life, as when it is said, Job iii. 19, " And the servant is free from his master."—*Martin Bucer,* 1491—1551.

Verse 5.—" *Free among the dead.*" בַּמֵּתִים חָפְשִׁי *bammethim chophshi,* I rather think, means *stripped among the dead.* Both the *fourth* and *fifth* verses seem to allude to a *field of battle :* the *slain* and the *wounded* are found scattered over the plain ; the *spoilers* come among them, and strip, not only the *dead,* but those also who appear to be *mortally wounded* and cannot recover, and are so feeble as not to be able to *resist.* Hence the Psalmist says, " *I am as a man that hath no strength,*" verse 4.—*Adam Clarke.*

Verse 5.—" *Free.*" There is no immunity so long as we are in the flesh, there is no truce, but constant unrest distracts us. Liberty, therefore, is given to us after death, because we rest from our labours.—*Franciscus Vatablus.*

Verse 5.—" *Cut off from thy hand.*" Beware how you ever look upon yourself as *cut off* from life and from enjoyment ; you are not cut off, only taken apart, laid aside, it may be but for a season, or it may be for life ; but still you are part of the body of which Christ is the Head. Some must suffer and some must serve, but each one is necessary to the other, " the whole body is fitly framed together by that which every joint supplieth," " the eye cannot say to the hand, I have no need of thee : nor again the head to the feet, I have no need of you : " Eph. iv. 16 ; 1 Cor. xii. 21. Your feet may be set fast ; they may have run with great activity, and you sorrow now, because they can run no more. But do not sorrow thus, do not envy those who are running ; you have a work to do ; it may be the work of the head, or of the eye, it surely is whatever work God gives to you. It may be the work of lying still, of not stirring hand or foot, of scarcely speaking, scarcely showing life. Fear not : if He your heavenly Master has given it to you to do, it is *His* work, and He will bless it. Do not repine. Do not say, *This* is work, and, this is *not* ; how do you know ? What work, think you, was Daniel doing in the lions' den ? or Shadrach, Meshach, and Abednego in the fiery furnace ? Their work was " glorious, laudable, and honourable," they were glorifying God in suffering.—*From " Sickness, its Trials and Blessings."* [Anon.] 1868.

Verse 6.—" *Thou hast laid me in the lowest pit,*" etc. He expands his meaning by another similitude. For he compares himself to a captive who has been cast into a deep, foul, dark, and slimy pit, where he is shut up and plunged in filth and darkness, having not a remnant of hope and life ; after the manner of Jeremiah's sufferings, chap. xxxvii. By this simile he means that he was in the greatest anxieties and sorrows of mind, destitute of every hope and sense of consolation, and that the terrors of death continually increased and augmented.—*Mollerus.*

Verse 6.—When a saint is under terrible impressions of Jehovah's infinite wrath, he cannot but be under great horror of conscience, and in perplexing depths of mental trouble. The sense which he hath of avenging wrath, occasions a conflict in his spirit, inexpressibly agonizing and terrible. When his troubled conscience is inflamed, by a sense of the fiery indignation of God almighty, the more he thinks of him as his infinite enemy, the more he is dismayed : every thought of *him*, brings doleful tidings, and pours oil upon the raging flame. Trouble of conscience for sin, is indeed very disquieting ; but, a sense of the vindictive wrath of God, kindled in the conscience, is still more dreadful. No words can express the direful anguish, which the disconsolate soul then feels. The Christian cannot at that time think so much as one quieting, one cheering thought. What he first thinks of is tormenting to his wounded spirit : he changes that thought for another, and that is still more tormenting. He finds himself entangled, as in the midst of a thicket of thorns ; so that, which way soever he turns himself, he is pierced and grieved afresh. This dismal thought often arises in his troubled mind,—That if death were, in his present condition, to surprise and cut him off, he should sink for ever and ever, under the intolerable wrath of the infinite Jehovah. The most exquisite torment of body is almost nothing, in comparison of the anguish of his spirit at such times. Oh ! how inconceivable is the anguish, the agony, especially of a holy soul, when it is conflicting with the tremendous wrath of the eternal God ! The bodily torture even of crucifixion, could not extort from the holy Jesus the smallest sigh or complaint ; but the sense of his Father's wrath in his soul, wrung from him that doleful outcry, " My God, my God, why hast thou forsaken me ! "— *John Colquhoun, in " A Treatise on Spiritual Comfort,"* 1814.

Verse 7.—" *Thy wrath lieth hard upon me.*" Others read, *sustains itself*, or *bears up itself upon me*, which is as if a giant should with his whole weight stay himself upon a child.—*Thomas Goodwin.*

Verse 7.—There are some that feel the wrath of God on their souls and consciences, and yet are not under wrath, but are true saints of God. Examples ye have in Paul, that chosen vessel of God to bear the name of Jesus among the Gentiles, he had fightings without and terrors within. Heman the Ezrahite said, ' The waves of the Lord's indignation are gone over my head, so that they are like to drown me ; I suffer terrors and doubtings from my very youth, so that I can never be quit of them.' And both these were the dear children of God. Now, if thou feelest nothing but wrath, and thou dost ask how thou shalt judge of thy state when thou art bearing such a wrath, that put all the sand of the sea in balance with it, it would overweigh it ; and when thou hast such a fire in thy conscience, that, put iron and brass in that fire, it would melt them, for they were not able to abide it : how then shalt thou know, in this case, that thou art loved of God, and that he hath chosen thee to eternal life ? I tell thee, if thou art the chosen child of God, and a vessel of mercy, under a sense of wrath, in this estate this will be thy disposition. First, Thou wilt hate and detest thy sin, which is the cause of thy misery, and hath brought thee to this pain. Secondly, Thou wilt have some dolour and sorrow for thy sin, and thou wilt lament because thou hast provoked God to anger against thee. Thirdly, Thou wilt have a desire to be reconciled to God ; and thou wouldst gladly be at peace with him, that thy sins may be taken away out of his sight. Fourthly, There will be hunger and thirst for the blood of Christ to quench that wrath, and for his righteousness to cover thy soul. Fifthly, There will be a patient waiting upon the Lord's deliverance, and when thou canst not get to this persuasion, then there will be a hope above hope, and thou wilt say with Job, xiii. 15, ' Lord, I will trust in thee, though thou shouldst slay me.'— *John Welch.*

Verse 8.—There are times when an unspeakable sadness steals upon me, an immense loneliness takes possession of my soul, a longing perchance for some vanished hand and voice to comfort me as of old, a desolation without form and void, that wraps me in its folds, and darkens my inmost being. It was not thus in the first days of my illness. Then all was so new and strange, that a strange spiritual strength filled my soul, and seemed to bear me up as with angel hands. The love and kindness that my sickness called forth, came to me with a sweet surprise ; tender solicitude made my very pain into an occasion of joy to me ; and hope was strong and recovery was near, only a few brief weeks between me and returning health, with nothing of sickness remaining, but the memory of all that love and sympathy, like a line of light my Saviour's feet had left, as he walked with me on the troubled sea. But now that hope is deferred, and returning health seems to loiter by the way, and recovery is delayed, and the trial lengthens out like an ever-lengthening chain, my soul begins to faint and tire, and the burthen to grow heavier. Even to those who love me most, my pain and helplessness is now an accustomed thing, while to me it keeps its keen edge of suffering, but little dulled by use. My ills to them are a tedious oft-told tale which comes with something of a dull reiterance. It has become almost a matter of course that in the pleasant plan I should be left out, that in the pleasant walk I should be left behind; a matter of course that the pleasures of life should pass me by with folded hand and averted face; and sickness, and monotonous days, and grey shadows should be my portion. . . .

And O my God, my spirit sometimes faints beneath a nameless dread that this loneliness will grow deeper and deeper, if it be thy will that my sickness should continue, or recovery be long delayed. I can no longer be the companion of those I love; shall I be as dear to them as if I could have kept by their side, and been bound up with all their active interests and pleasures? I have to see others take my place, and do my work for them; shall I not suffer loss in their eyes, and others enter into the heritage of love which might have been mine? Will they not grow weary of me, weary of the same old ills, oft repeated, but ever new, and turn with an unconscious feeling of relief, to brighter hearts, and more joyous lives?

My God, my God, to whom can I turn for comfort but unto thee, thou who didst drink the bitter cup of human loneliness to the dregs that thou mightest make thyself a brother to the lonely, a merciful and faithful High Priest to the desolate soul; thou who alone canst pass within, the doors being shut to all human aid, into that secret place of thunder, where the tempest-tossed soul suffers and struggles alone; thou who alone canst command the winds and tempests, and say unto the sea, " Be still ! " and unto the wind, " Blow not ! " and there shall be a great calm.

As a child alone in the dark, my heart cries out for thee, cries for thine embracing arms, for thy voice of comfort, for thy pierced heart on which to rest my aching head, and feel that Love is near.—*From " Christ the Consoler. A Book of Comfort for the Sick."* [Anon.] 1872.

Verse 8.—" *Thou hast put away mine acquaintance.*" This tempest of afflictions is all the heavier, because, First, all my acquaintance departed far from me, like swallows in winter time: Prov. xiv. 20. *The poor is hated even of his own neighbour, but the rich hath many friends.* Seneca wisely admonishes : *Flies follow honey, wolves corpses, ants food, the mob follows the pay, not the man.* Job said, Chap. xix. 13, He hath put my brethren far from me, and mine acquaintance are verily estranged from me. My kinsfolk have failed, and my familiar friends have forgotten me. Secondly, Not only do they often depart from the afflicted, but they themselves add to his trouble, and precipitate his falling fortune. A rich man beginning to fall is held up by his friends ; but a poor man being down, is thrust away by those who once pretended to love him.—*Le Blanc.*

Verse 8.—" *Thou hast made me an abomination unto them : "* lit, " abominations," as if I were one great mass of abominations. (Gen. xlvi. 34 ; xliii. 32.) As Israel was an abomination to the Egyptians, so Messiah, the antitypical Israel, was to the world.—*A. R. Fausset.*

Verse 8.—" *An abomination.*" As one who is unclean,—excluded from social intercourse ; Gen. xlvi. 34. Compare Job ix. 31 ; xix. 19 ; xxx. 10. " *I cannot come forth.*" The man suspected of leprosy was " shut up seven days : " Levit. xiii. 4.—*William Kay.*

Verse 9.—" *Mine eye mourneth,*" . . . " *I have called.*" Weeping must not hinder praying ; we must sow in tears : " *Mine eye mourns,*" but " *I cry unto thee daily.*" Let prayers and tears go together, and they shall be accepted together : " I have heard thy prayers, I have seen thy tears."—*Matthew Henry.*

Verse 9.—The first clause seems literally to mean the soreness and dimness of sight caused by excessive weeping, and is so taken by many of the commentators, and Lorinus aptly quotes a Latin poet, *Catullus,* in illustration :—

Mœsta neque assiduo tabescere lumina fleto
Cessarent.

Nor my sad eyes to pine with constant tears
Could cease.

—Neale's Commentary.

Verse 10.—He assureth himself God would not fail to comfort him before he died ; and again, that the Lord would rather miraculously raise him from the dead, than not glorify himself in his deliverance : and in this also he taketh a safe course, for he seeks for what he might expect, rather in an ordinary way, than by looking for miracles.—*David Dickson.*

Verse 10.—" *Shall the dead arise and praise thee ?* " So far from this being an argument against the resurrection, it is Messiah's own most powerful plea for it —that otherwise man would be deprived of salvation, and God of the praise which the redeemed shall give for it to all eternity. Thou canst not show wonders to *the dead* as such ; for " God is not the God of the dead, but of the living." (Matt. xxii. 32.) Or even if thou wert to show thy wonders, it is only by their rising to life again that they can duly praise thee for them.—*A. R. Fausset.*

Verse 10.—" *The dead.*" The word comes from a root which expresses what is weak and languid, and at the same time stretched out and long-extended, and which can accordingly be employed to describe the shadowy forms of the under world as well as the giants and heroes of the olden time.—*Carl Bernhard Moll, in Lange's Commentary.*

Verse 10.—" *The dead.*" An attentive consideration seems to leave little room for doubt that the dead were called Rephaim (as Gesenius also hints) from some notion of Scheol being the residence of the fallen spirits or buried giants.—*F. W. Farrar, in Smith's Dictionary of the Bible.*

Verses 10, 11.—Can my soul ever come to think I shall live in thy favour, in thy free grace and loving-kindness, to be justified by it, to apprehend myself a living man, and all my sins forgiven ? To do this, saith he, is as great a wonder as to raise a man up from death to life ; therefore he useth that expression, " *Wilt thou shew wonders to the dead ?* " He calleth it a wonder ; for of all works else, you shall find in Scripture the resurrection from the dead counted the greatest wonder.

The phrase in the 10th verse, as the Septuagint translates it, is exceeding emphatical. Saith he, " Wilt thou shew wonders to the dead ? Shall the physicians arise and praise thee ? " So they read it, and so some good Hebrecians read it also ; that is, Go send for all the college of physicians, all the angels out of heaven, all the skilful ministers and prophets that were then upon the earth, Gad and David, for he lived in David's time ; send for them all. All these physicians may come with their cordials and balms ; they will never cure me, never heal my soul, never raise me up to life again, except thou raise me ; for I am " free among the dead," saith he. Now then, to work faith in such a one ; for this poor soul, being thus dead, to go out of himself, and by naked and sheer faith to go to Jesus Christ alone, whom God raised from the dead, and to believe on him alone ; this is now as great a power as indeed to raise a man up from death to life.—*Thomas Goodwin.*

Verses 10—12.—In these verses we find mention made of four things on the part of God : " wonders," " loving-kindness," " faithfulness," and " righteousness." These were four attributes of the blessed Jehovah which the eyes of Heman had been opened to see, and which the heart of Heman had been wrought upon to feel. But he comes, by divine teaching, into a spot where these attributes seem to be completely lost to him ; and yet, (so mysterious are the ways of God !) that spot was made the very place where those attributes were more powerfully displayed, and made more deeply and experimentally known to his soul.

The Lord led the blind by a way that he knew not into these spots of experience, that in them he might more fully open up to him those attributes of which he had already gained a glimpse ; but the Lord brought him in such a mysterious way, that all his former knowledge was baffled. He therefore puts up this inquiry to the Lord, how it was possible that in those spots where he now was, these attributes could be displayed or made known ?

1. He begins—" *Wilt thou shew wonders to the dead ?* " He is speaking here of his own experience ; *he* is that " dead " person to whom those " wonders " are to be shown. And being in that state of experience, he considered that every act of mercy shown to him where he then was, must be a " wonder." " *Shall the dead arise and praise thee ?* " What ! the dark, stupid, cold, barren, helpless soul, that cannot lift up one little finger, that cannot utter one spiritual word, that cannot put forth one gracious desire, that cannot lift up itself a hair's breadth out of the mass that presses it down—" Shall it *arise ?* " and more than that, " *praise thee ?* " What ! can lamentation ever be turned into praise ? Can complaint ever be changed

into thanksgiving? Can the mourner ever shout and sing? Oh, it is a wonder of wonders, if "the dead" are to "arise," if "the dead" are to "praise thee;" if the dead are to stand upon their feet, and shout victory through thy blood!— *J. C. Philpot.*

Verse 11.—"*In the grave.*" Here is a striking figure of what a living soul feels under the manifestations of the deep corruptions of his heart. All his good words, once so esteemed; and all his good works, once so prized; and all his prayers, and all his faith, and hope, and love, and all the imaginations of his heart, are not merely paralysed and dead, not merely reduced to a state of utter helplessness, but also in soul-feeling turned into rottenness and corruption. When we feel this we are spiritually brought where Heman was, when he said, "Shall thy lovingkindness be *declared* in the grave?" What! wilt thou manifest thy love to a stinking corpse? What! is thy love to be shed abroad in a heart full of pollution and putrefaction? Is thy lovingkindness to come forth from thy glorious sanctuary, where thou sittest enthroned in majesty, and holiness, and purity,—is it to leave that eternal abode of ineffable light and glory, and enter into the dark, polluted, and loathsome "grave"? What! is thy lovingkindness to come out of the sanctuary into the charnel-house? Shall it be "declared" *there*—revealed there—spoken there—manifested there— made known there? For nothing else but the *declaration* of it there will do. He does not say, "Shall thy lovingkindness be declared in the Scriptures?" "Shall thy lovingkindness be declared in Christ?" "Shall thy lovingkindness be declared by the mouth of ministers?" "Shall thy lovingkindness be declared in holy and pure hearts?"—but he says, "Shall thy lovingkindness be *declared,*" uttered, spoken, revealed, manifested, "in the *grave*?" where everything is contrary to it, where everything is unworthy of it,—the last of all places fit for the lovingkindness of an all-pure God to enter.—*J. C. Philpot.*

Verse 11.—"*Thy faithfulness in destruction.*" You will see God's faithfulness to have been manifested most,—in destruction. You will see God's faithfulness to his covenant most clearly evidenced in destroying your false religion, in order to set up his own kingdom in your soul; in destroying everything which alienated and drew away your affections from him, that he alone might be enshrined in your hearts; and you will say, when the Lord leads you to look at the path he has led you, in after years, "Of all God's mercies his greatest have been those that seemed at the time to be the greatest miseries; the richest blessings which he has given us, are those which came wrapped up in the outside covering of curses; and his faithfulness has been as much or more manifested in destruction, than in restoration."—*J. C. Philpot.*

Verse 11.—It is not by leaving man in the "destruction" which sin and death produce, that God will declare his "faithfulness" to his promises which have flowed out of his "loving-kindness;" for instance, his promise that the woman's seed should bruise the serpent's head (Gen. xiii. 15; and Hos. xiii. 14).—*A. R. Fausset.*

Verse 12.—"*Wilt thou show thy righteousness in the land of forgetfulness?*"— where I have forgotten thee, where I turned aside from thee, where I have let slip out of my memory all thy previous dealings with me—and shall thy righteousness be manifested even there? Wilt thou prove thine equity in showing forth mercy, because for me a sacrifice has been offered, thy righteousness running parallel with the atoning stream of Christ's blood? When I have forgotten thee and forsaken thee, and turned my back upon thee, can thy righteousness be there manifested? What! righteousness running side by side with mercy! and righteousness still preserving all its unbending strictness, because this very backsliding of heart, this very forgetfulness of soul, this very alienation of affection, this very turning my back upon thee, have all been atoned for; and righteousness can be still shown "in the land of forgetfulness," because all my sins committed in the land of forgetfulness have been atoned for by redeeming blood!—*J. C. Philpot.*

Verse 13.—"*But,*" etc. That "*but*" seems to come in as an expression of his resolution hitherto, that though these were his apprehensions of his condition, yet he had sought the Lord, and would go on to do the same. Suppose thou findest no relish in the ordinances, yet use them; thou art desperately sick, yet eat still, take all that is brought thee, some strength will come of it. Say, "Be I damned or saved, hypocrite or no hypocrite, I resolve to go on."—*Thomas Goodwin.*

Verse 13.—" *In the morning shall my prayer prevent thee.*" The morning prayer is the best. . . . In the morning God gave various gifts. First, the manna, Exod. xvi. 13, *And in the morning the dew lay round about the host:* He who is in the camp of God, and bravely fights, receives from God dew and consolation, if in the morning, that is, in the beginning of temptation, he prays. In the evening flesh was given, whence death overtook them, but in another case in the morning the manna was given, whereby life was sustained, until they came into the land of promise. Secondly, the law was given in the morning, Exod. xix. 16, *And it came to pass on the third day in the morning, that there were thunders and lightnings, and a thick cloud upon the mount, and the voice of the trumpet exceeding loud.* In morning devotion the thunders of God, that is, his judgments, are more distinctly heard; his lightnings, that is, his divine enlightenments, are best seen; the thick cloud upon the mount, that is, the divine overshadowing of the soul, is perceived; and the voice of the trumpet is best heard, that is, inspiration then with greater force moves the mind. Thirdly, in the morning, very early, the children of Israel went forth from Egypt; for in the middle of the night God smote all the first-born in the land of Egypt, Exod. xii. 29. . . . In the morning pray, and you shall conquer your daily and nightly foes; and the Red Sea itself, that is, the place of temptation, shall be to thee a field of glory, of victory and exultation, and all things shall go well with thee.—*Le Blanc.*

Verse 13.—" *Unto thee have I cried, O Lord.*" There is something concomitant with the Christian's present darkness of spirit, that distinguisheth it from the hypocrite's horror; and that is the lively working of grace, which then commonly is very visible, when his peace and former comfort are most questioned by him; the less joy he hath from any present sense of the love of God, the more abounding you shall find him in sorrow for his sin that clouded his joy; the further Christ is gone out of his sight, the more he clings in his love to Christ, and vehemently cries after him in prayer, as we see in Heman here. O the fervent prayers that then are shot from his troubled spirit to heaven, the pangs of affection which are springing after God, and his face and favour! Never did a banished child more desire admittance into his angry father's presence, than he to have the light of God's countenance shine on him, which is now veiled from him.—*William Gurnall.*

Verse 14.—" *Why hidest thou thy face from me?*" Numerous are the complaints of good men under this dark cloud; and to a child of light it is indeed a darkness that may be felt; it beclouds and bewilders the mind; the brightest evidences are in a great measure hid; the Bible itself is sealed, and fast closed; we see not our signs, nor our tokens for good; every good thing is at a distance from us, behind the cloud, and we cannot get at it; there is a dismal gloom upon our path; we know not where we are, where to step, nor which way to steer; which way God is gone we know not, but he knoweth the way that we take; and such a prayer as this suits us well,—Seek thy servants, for we are lost. Christ is hid, and there is a frowning cloud upon the sweet countenance of God, in which he hides his blessed face; or, as he did to the disciples, holds our eyes, that we should not see him. But, though this is often the case with believers, and they cannot see one beam of light before them; though all evidences are hid, and the light of the Lord's countenance is withdrawn; though no signs nor love tokens appear; and though the life-giving commandment is hid from them, and he shows them no wonders out of his law; yet these Israelites have light in their dwellings—they have light to see the corruptions of their own hearts; to see the workings of unbelief, legal pride, enmity, rebellion, the double diligence of Satan, and the wretched advantages he takes of them in these dark seasons.—*William Huntington.*

Verse 15.—" *I am afflicted.*" (Vulg. *Pauper sum ego.*) God more readily hears the poor, and gives himself wholly to them. First, his eyes, to behold them, Ps. xi. 5, " *His eyes behold the poor.*" Secondly, his ears, to hear them, Ps. x. 17, " *Thou wilt prepare their hearts, thou wilt cause thine ears to hear.*" Thirdly, his hand, to help, Ps. cvii. 41, " *Yet setteth he the poor on high from his affliction.*" Fourthly, his breast and his arms, to receive the fugitives and those in peril, Ps. lx. 9, " *The Lord also will be a refuge for the oppressed.*" Fifthly, memory to recollect for them, Ps. ix. 18, " *The needy shall not alway be forgotten.*" Sixthly, intellect, to care for them, and watch over their comfort, Ps. xl. 17, " *But I am poor and needy; yet the Lord thinketh upon me.*" Seventhly, goodwill, to love their prayers, Ps. xxii. 24, " *For he hath not despised nor abhorred the affliction of the afflicted, neither hath he hid his face from him."* Eighthly and lastly, he gives himself wholly to them, to preserve them, Ps. lxxii. 13, " *He shall save the souls of the needy."—Le Blanc.*

Verse 15.—" I am afflicted and ready to die from my youth up." How much some suffer ! I have seen a child, who at the age of twenty months had probably suffered more bodily pain than the whole congregation of a thousand souls, where its parents worshipped. Asaph seems to have been of a sad heart. Jeremiah lived and died lamenting. Heman seems to have been of the same lot and of the same turn of mind.—*William S. Plumer.*

Verse 15.—(First clause). We found the heat more oppressive this day than we had yet experienced it. The hillocks of sand between which we were slowly moving at the usual camel's pace, reflected the sun's rays upon us, till our faces were glowing as if we had been by the side of a furnace. . . . Perhaps it was through this part of the desert of Shur that Hagar wandered, intending to go back to her native country ; and it may have been by this way that Joseph carried the young child Jesus when they fled into the land of Egypt. Even in tender infancy the sufferings of the Redeemer began, and he complains, " *I am afflicted and ready to die from my youth up."* Perhaps these scorching beams beat upon his infant brow, and this sand-laden breeze dried up his infant lips, while the heat of the curse of God began to melt his heart within. Even in the desert we see the suretyship of Jesus.—*R. M. McCheyne's " Narrative of a Mission of Inquiry to the Jews."*

Verse 15.—" From my youth up." That is, for a long time ;—so long, that the remembrance of it seems to go back to my very childhood. My whole life has been a life of trouble and sorrow, and I have not strength to bear it longer. It may have been literally true that the author of the Psalm had been a man always afflicted ; or, this may be the language of strong emotion, meaning that his sufferings had been of so long continuance that they seemed to him to have begun in his very boyhood.—*Albert Barnes.*

Verse 15.—" While I suffer thy terrors I am distracted." The word doth not signify properly the distraction of a man that is mad, but the distraction of a man that is in doubt. It is the distraction of a man who knows not what to do, not of a man who knows not what he doth, and yet that distraction doth often lead to a degree of this ; for a man who is much troubled to know what to do, and cannot know it, grows at last to do he knows not what.—*Joseph Caryl.*

Verse 15.—" While I suffer thy terrors I am distracted." The Psalm hath this striking peculiarity in it, namely, that it not only hath reference to the Lord Jesus Christ, and him alone ; but that he himself is the sole speaker from the beginning to the end. And although the whole of the Psalms are of him, and concerning him, more or less, and he is the great object and subject of all ; yet, secondarily and subordinately we meet with many parts in the Psalms where his church is also noticed, and becomes concerned, from union with him, in what is said. But in this Psalm there is allusion to no other.* All is of him and his incommunicable work. All is of the Son of God in our nature. It contains an account of the cries of the Lord Jesus " when in the days of his flesh he offered up prayers and supplications, with strong crying and tears."

The soul-agonies of Christ even from the moment of his incarnation to his death, may be contemplated, or read, from the sacred records of Scripture, but cannot come within the province of any created power to conceive, much less unfold. It is remarkable that whatever the Lord meant to convey by the phrase, " *I am distracted,"* this is the only place in the whole Bible where the word " *distracted"* is used. Indeed the inspired writers have varied their terms of expression, when speaking of Christ's sufferings, as if unable to convey any full idea. Matthew renders it that the Lord Jesus said : " *My soul is exceeding sorrowful, even unto death !* " (Matt. xxvi. 38.) Mark describes him as " being sore amazed, and very heavy ! " (Mark xiv. 33.) And Luke : his " being in an agony ! " (Luke xxii. 44.) But here we must rest, in point of apprehension, for we can proceed no further.—*Robert Hawker.*

*Verse 15.—*O Lord, the monotony of my changeless days oppresses me, the constant weariness of my body weighs me down. I am weary of gazing on the same dull objects : I am tired of going through the same dull round day after day ; the very inanimate things about my room, and the patterns on the walls, seem

---

* We differ from Dr. Hawker in his exclusion of the saints from this Psalm. Where the Head is the members are never far away.—Ed.

quickened with the waste of my life, and, through the power of association, my own thoughts and my own pain come back upon me from them with a dull reverberation. My heart is too tired to hope ; I dare not look forward to the future ; I expect nothing from the days to come, and yet my heart sinks at the thought of the grey waste of years before me ; and I wonder how I shall endure, whether I shall faint by the way, before I reach my far-off home.—*From " Christ the Consoler."*

Verse 16.—*" Thy fierce wrath goeth over me."* Like a sea of liquid fire ; (xlii. 7). —*Heb. "* Thy hot *wraths." LXX. αἱ ὀργαί σου.—William Kay.*

Verse 16.—*" Thy terrors have cut me off."* In the Hebrew verb the last syllable is repeated for the purpose of putting vehemence into the expression. The word נפצ signifies, to shut up and press into some narrow place, in order that one may not breathe or escape. . . . In this sense Gregory Nazianzen in his first oration concerning peace, calls grief δεσμον καρδιας (the prison of the heart.)—*Mollerus.*

Verse 17.—*" Like water ; "*—not merely because it drowns, but because it searches every crevice, goes to the very bottom, and makes its way on all sides when once it obtains an entrance, thus fitly denoting the penetrating force of temptation and trouble.—*Hugo Cardinalis.*

Verse 18.—*" Lover and friend hast thou put far from me,"* etc. Next to the joys of religion, those of friendship are most rational, sublime, and satisfactory. But they, like all other earthly joys, have their mixtures and alloys, and are very precarious. We are often called to weep with our friends, and sometimes to weep over them. Grief and tears for their death are the sad tribute we pay for loving and being beloved, and living long in this world. This seems to have been the case with the author of this melancholy Psalm, where our text is. He was exercised with great afflictions of body, and deep distress of mind. " His soul was full of troubles, and his life drew nigh to the grave. He was shut up and confined by weakness and pain, and could not go forth," to his business or pleasure, to the social or solemn assembly, ver. 3—8. He adds, that " he had been afflicted and ready to die from his youth up," v. 15 ; which seems to intimate that he was now an old man. Some of his acquaintance and friends had deserted him, and he was " become an abomination to them," v. 8. They would not assist him, nor afford him the comfort of a friendly visit, and the cheap kindness of a soft, compassionate word. Others of them, who would have been faithful and kind to him in his distress, were taken out of the world ; and this at a time when, through age and infirmities, he peculiarly needed their company and assistance. To this he refers in the text ; and with this he concludes the Psalm, as the heaviest stroke of all, " *Lover and friend hast thou put far from me, and mine acquaintance into darkness."* This is a common case ; and frequently the case of the aged. It is no unusual thing for old people to outlive their nearest relations ; the companions of their lives ; their children, and sometimes their grandchildren too ; and they are, as the Psalmist expresseth it, " like a sparrow alone upon the house-top." . . .

What chiefly afflicted the Psalmist, and will afflict every generous heart, was, that his friends and lovers were removed into " *darkness ; "* that is, to the grave, which is called in Scripture, " the land of darkness and the shadow of death, without any order or succession ; and where the light is as darkness." Job x. 21, 22. They were put so far from him, that he could see them no more ; were dead and buried out of his sight ; neither would one of their friends on earth any more behold them. Thus are our friends put into darkness. The eyes that used to sparkle with pleasure, when we met after a long absence, are closed in death. The voice that used to delight and edify us is sealed up in everlasting silence. There is no conversing with them personally nor by letters. Not lands and seas divide us from them, but regions of vast, unknown space, which we cannot yet pass over ; and which they cannot and indeed would not tread back, as much as they loved us. We have no way of conveying intelligence to them or receiving it from them. Perhaps they were put far away from us in their youth, or in the midst of their days and usefulness ; when we promised ourselves many years of pleasure in their friendship and converse, and expected many years of service from them, for their families, for the church, and the world. Alas ! one awful, fatal stroke hath broken down all the pleasing fabric of love and happiness.

But these are reflections which must not be dwelt upon. When they begin to grow very painful, as they soon will, it is time to turn our thoughts to that which is the second thing observable in the text ; namely, the Psalmist's devout acknowledgment of the hand of God in this affliction. *" Thou hast put them far from me."* This good man, through the whole Psalm, ascribeth all his afflictions, and particularly the death of his friends, to the hand of God. He takes no notice of their diseases ; he neither blames them for imprudence and delay, nor those who attended them for neglect or misapplication ; but looks beyond all second causes to the great Lord of all ; owns him as the supreme sovereign of every life, and disposer of every event. And we shall do well to make this idea of the blessed God familiar to our minds, as it is at once most instructive and most comfortable.

The holy Scriptures confirm the dictates of reason upon this subject ; assuring us that God " maketh peace and createth evil ; " that " out of the mouth of the Lord proceedeth evil and good ; " that the most casual events are under his direction, so that " not a sparrow falleth to," nor lighteth on, " the ground without him ; " much less do his rational creatures and children die without his notice and appointment. By whatever disease or casualties they die, it is God who " taketh away their breath, changeth their countenance, and sendeth them into darkness." With awful majesty God claimeth this as his prerogative ; " I wound, and I heal : neither is there any that can deliver out of my hand." (Deut. xxxii. 39.) He removeth our friends who hath a right to do it. They were our friends, but they are his creatures ; and may he not do what he will with his own ? He gave them life of his free goodness, and he hath a right to demand it when he pleaseth. Dear as they were to us, we must acknowledge they were sinners ; and, as such, had forfeited their lives to the justice of God : and shall not he determine when to take them away ? They were our friends ; but do we not hope and believe that, by repentance, faith in Christ, and sanctifying grace, they were become his friends too ; dear to him by many indissoluble ties ? Hath he not then a superior claim to them, and a greater interest in them ? Is it not fit that he should be served first ? May he not call home his friends when he pleaseth ? Shall he wait for, or ask, our consent first ? He doth it, whom we cannot, dare not, gainsay. " Behold, he taketh away, who can hinder him ? who will say unto him, what doest thou ? " (Job. ix. 12.) He doth it, who is infinitely good and wise ; and doth everything in the best time and manner. His knowledge is perfect and unerring ; his goodness boundless and never-failing. Though his judgments are a great deep, and his schemes utterly unsearchable by us ; yet we may reasonably believe that he consulteth the happiness of his servants in what is most mysterious and most grievous ; and his word giveth us the strongest assurance of it. So that whether we exercise the faith of Christians or the reason of men, we must acknowledge the hand of God, yea, his wisdom and goodness, in removing our acquaintance into darkness.—*Job Orton*, 1717—1783.

Verse 18.—" *Mine acquaintance into darkness.*" Rather, *my acquaintanceship is darkness*, that is, darkness is all I have to converse with ; my circle of acquaintance is comprised in blank darkness.—*Ernest Hawkins.*

Verse 18.—To be discountenanced or coldly treated by Christian friends, is often a consequence of a believer's having forfeited his spiritual comfort. When the Lord is angry with his rebellious child, and is chastening him, he not only giveth Satan leave to trouble him, but permitteth some of the saints who are acquainted with him, to discountenance him, and by their cold treatment of him, to add to his grief. When the father of a family resolves the more effectually to correct his obstinate child, he will say to the rest of the household, " Do not be familiar with him ; shew him no countenance ; put him to shame." In like manner, when the Lord is smiting, especially with spiritual trouble, his disobedient child, he, as it were, saith to others of his children, " Have for a season no familiarity with him ; treat him with coldness and neglect ; in order that he may be ashamed, and humbled for his iniquity." Job, under his grievous affliction, complained thus, " He hath put my brethren far from me, and mine acquaintance are verily estranged from me," etc. (ch. xix. 13—19). And likewise Heman, " *Thou hast laid me in the lowest pit, in darkness.*" When the favour of God to the soul is clouded, the comfort of Christian society is also obscured. When He frowns on one, his children commonly appear to frown likewise ; and when he makes himself strange to one, so for the most part do they. If a holy man, then, under trouble of spirit, begins to be treated with disregard, and even with contempt, by some of his Christian brethren, he ought not to be surprised ; neither should he take occasion to be angry, or to quarrel with them ; but he should look above them, and take the afflictive dispensation, only out of the hand of the Lord, as a necessary part of the chastisement intended for him. He ought to say with respect to them, as David concerning Shimei, " The Lord hath bidden them ; " or, as Heman did, " Thou *hast put away mine acquaintance far from me.*"—*John Colquhoun.*

Verse 18.—The very rhythm of the last line shows that the piece is not complete. The ear remains in suspense ; until the majestic lxxxixth shall burst upon it like a bright Resurrection-morning.—*William Kay.*

HINTS TO PREACHERS.

Verse 1.—I. Confidence in prayer,—" God of my salvation." II. Earnestness in prayer,—" I have cried." III. Perseverance in prayer,—" Day and night."—*G. R.*

Verse 2.—Prayer as an ambassador. I. An audience sought, or the benefit of access. II. Attention entreated, or the blessing of success. III. The Process explained, or prayer comes and God inclines.

Verse 3.—I. A good man is exposed to inward troubles. 1. To soul troubles. 2. To the soul full of troubles. II. To outward troubles. " My life," etc. 1. From outward persecutions. 2. From inward griefs. III. To both inward and outward troubles at the same time. " Soul full," etc., " *and* my life," etc.—*G. R.*

Verse 4 (*last clause*).—Conscious weakness, painfully felt, at certain times, in various duties. Intended to keep us humble, to drive us to our knees, and to bring greater glory to God.

Verses 4, 5.—I. The resemblance of the righteous man to the wicked. 1. In natural death. 2. In bodily infirmities. II. His difference from them. He is " counted with them " but is not of them. 1. He experiences natural death only. 2. His strength is perfected in weakness. 3. For him to die is gain.—*G. R.*

Verses 6, 7.—1. What the afflictions of the people of God appear to be to themselves. 1. Extreme,—" laid me in the lowest pit." 2. Inexplicable,—" in darkness." 3. Humiliating,—" in the deeps." 4. Severe,—" thy wrath lieth hard." 5. Exhaustive,—" afflicted with all thy waves." II. What they are in reality. 1. Not extreme, but light. 2. Not inexplicable, but according to the will of God. 3. Not humiliating, but elevating. " Humble yourselves under," etc. 4. Not severe, but gentle. Not in anger, but in love. 5. Not exhaustive, but partial. Not all thy waves, but a few ripples only. The slight motion in the harbour when there is a boisterous ocean beyond.—*G. R.*

Verse 8 (*last clause*).—This may describe us when despondency is chronic, when trouble is overwhelming, when sickness detains us at home, when we feel restrained in Christian labour, or hampered in prayer.

Verse 9.—I. Sorrow before God,—" Mine eye," etc. II. Prayer to God,—" I have called," etc. III. Waiting for God,—" called daily." IV. Dependence on God,—" I have stretched," etc. These hands can do nothing without thee.—*G. R.*

Verses 10—12.—I. The supposition. 1. That a child of God should be wholly dead. 2. That he should remain for ever in the grave. 3. That he should be destroyed. 4. That he should always remain in darkness. 5. That he should be entirely forgotten, as though he had never existed. II. The consequences involved in this supposition. 1. God's wonders to them would cease. 2. His praise from them would be lost. 3. His lovingkindness to them would be unknown. 4. His faithfulness destroyed. 5. His wonders to them would be lost to others. 6. His former righteousness to them would be forgotten. III. The plea founded upon these consequences,—" Wilt thou," etc. It cannot be that thy praise for grace shown to thy people can be lost, and none can render it but themselves. " Then what wilt thou do unto thy great name ? "—*G. R.*

Verse 13.—I. Blessings delayed to prayer,—" Unto thee," etc. II. Blessings anticipated by prayer,—" In the morning," etc. Daily mercies anticipated by morning prayers.—*G. R.*

Verse 13 (*last clause*).—The advantages of early morning prayer-meetings.

Verse 14.—I. Afflictions are mysterious though just. II. Just though mysterious. —*G. R.*

Verse 14.—Solemn enquiries, to be followed by searching examinations, by sorrowful confessions, stern self-denials, and sweet restorations.

Verse 15.—I. The afflictions of the righteous may be long continued though severe. " I am afflicted, etc., from my youth up." II. Severe though long continued. 1. Painful,—" afflicted." 2. Threatening,—" ready to die." 3. Terrific,— " suffer thy terrors." 4. Distracting,—" I am," etc.—*G. R.*

Verse 15.—The personal sufferings of Christ for the salvation of his people.— *Sermon by Robert Hawker.* Works, Vol. IV. p. 91.

Verse 16.—I. Good men are often tried men. II. Tried men frequently misjudge the Lord's dealings. III. The Lord does not take them at their word, he is better than their fears.—*G. R.*

Verse 18.—The loss of friends intended to remind us of our own mortality, to wean us from earth, to lead us to more complete trust in the Lord, to chasten us for sin, and to draw us away to the great meeting place.

Verse 18.—The words of our text will lead us to remark that, I. The happiness of life greatly depends on intimate friendships. II. The trial of parting with intimate friends is exceedingly painful. III. In this, as indeed in every affliction, the best consolation is drawn from a belief in, and meditation upon, God's governing providence.—*Joseph Lathrop*, 1845.

PSALM LXXXIX.

We have now reached the majestic Covenant Psalm, *which, according to the Jewish arrangement, closes the third book of the Psalms. It is the utterance of a believer, in presence of great national disaster, pleading with his God, urging the grand argument of covenant engagements, and expecting deliverance and help, because of the faithfulness of Jehovah.*

Title.—Maschil. *This is most fitly called a Maschil, for it is most instructive. No subject is more important or is so fully the key to all theology as that of the covenant. He who is taught by the Holy Spirit to be clear upon the covenant of grace will be a scribe well instructed in the things of the kingdom; he whose doctrinal theory is a mingle-mangle of works and grace is scarcely fit to be teacher of babes.* Of Ethan the Ezra-hite : *perhaps the same person as Jeduthun, who was a musician in David's reign; was noted for his wisdom in Solomon's days, and probably survived till the troubles of Rehoboam's period. If this be the man, he must have written this Psalm in his old age, when troubles were coming thick and heavy upon the dynasty of David and the land of Judah ; this is not at all improbable, and there is much in the Psalm which looks that way.*

Division.—*The sacred poet commences by affirming his belief in the faithfulness of the Lord to his covenant with the house of David, and makes his first pause at verse 4. He then praises and magnifies the name of the Lord for his power, justice, and mercy, 5—14. This leads him to sing of the happiness of the people who have such a God to be their glory and defence, 15—18. He rehearses the terms of the covenant at full length with evident delight, 19—37, and then mournfully pours out his complaint and petition, 38—51, closing the whole with a hearty benediction and a double Amen. May the Holy Spirit greatly bless to us the reading of this most precious Psalm of instruction.*

EXPOSITION.

I WILL sing of the mercies of the Lord for ever : with my mouth will
I make known thy faithfulness to all generations.

2 For I have said, Mercy shall be built up for ever : thy faithfulness
shalt thou establish in the very heavens.

3 I have made a covenant with my chosen, I have sworn unto David my
servant,

4 Thy seed will I establish for ever, and build up thy throne to all generations. Selah.

1. " *I will sing of the mercies of the Lord for ever.*" A devout resolve, and very commendable when a man is exercised with great trouble on account of an apparent departure of the Lord from his covenant and promise. Whatever we may observe abroad or experience in our own persons, we ought still to praise God for his mercies, since they most certainly remain the same, whether we can perceive them or not. Sense sings but now and then, but faith is an eternal songster. Whether others sing or not, believers must never give over ; in them should be constancy of praise, since God's love to them cannot by any possibility have changed, however providence may seem to frown. We are not only to believe the Lord's goodness, but to rejoice in it evermore ; it is the source of all our joy ; and as it cannot be dried up, so the stream ought never to fail to flow, or cease to flash in sparkling crystal of song. We have not one, but many *mercies* to rejoice in, and should therefore multiply the expressions of our thankfulness. It is *Jehovah* who deigns to deal out to us our daily benefits, and he is the all-sufficient and immutable God ; therefore our rejoicing in him must never suffer diminution. By no means let his exchequer of glory be deprived of the continual revenue which we owe to it. Even time itself must not bound our praises—they must leap into eternity ; he blesses us with eternal mercies—let us sing unto him *for ever.* "*With my mouth will I make known thy faithfulness to all generations.*" The utterances of the present

23

will instruct future generations. What Ethan sung is now a text-book for Christians, and will be so as long as this dispensation shall last. We ought to have an eye to posterity in all that we write, for we are the schoolmasters of succeeding ages. Ethan first spoke with his mouth that which he recorded with his pen—a worthy example of using both means of communication ; the mouth has a warmer manner than the pen, but the pen's speech lives longest, and is heard farther and wider. While reading this Psalm, such is the freshness of the style, that one seems to hear it gushing from the poet's mouth ; he makes the letters live and talk, or, rather, sing to us. Note, that in this second sentence he speaks of *faithfulness*, which is the mercy of God's mercies—the brightest jewel in the crown of goodness. The grace of an unfaithful God would be a poor subject for music, but unchangeable love and immutable promises demand everlasting songs. In times of trouble it is the divine faithfulness which the soul hangs upon ; this is the bower anchor of the soul, its holdfast, and its stay. Because God is, and ever will be, faithful, we have a theme for song which will not be out of date for future generations ; it will never be worn out, never be disproved, never be unnecessary, never be an idle subject, valueless to mankind. It will also be always desirable to make it known, for men are too apt to forget it, or to doubt it, when hard times press upon them. We cannot too much multiply testimonies to the Lord's faithful mercy—if our own generation should not need them others will : sceptics are so ready to repeat old doubts and invent new ones that believers should be equally prompt to bring forth evidences both old and new. Whoever may neglect this duty, those who are highly favoured, as Ethan was, should not be backward.

2. " *For I have said, Mercy shall be built up for ever.*" His heart was persuaded of it, and he had affirmed it as an indisputable truth. He was certain that upon a sure foundation the Lord intended to pile up a glorious palace of goodness— a house of refuge for all people, wherein the Son of David should for ever be glorified as the dispenser of heavenly grace. " *Thy faithfulness shalt thou establish in the very heavens.*" This divine edifice, he felt assured, would tower into the skies, and would be turreted with divine faithfulness even as its foundations were laid in eternal love. God's faithfulness is no thing of earth, for here nothing is firm, and all things savour of the changes of the moon and the fickleness of the sea : heaven is the birthplace of truth, and there it dwells in eternal vigour. As the blue arch above us remains unimpaired by age, so does the Lord's truth ; as in the firmament he hangs his covenant bow, so in the upper heavens the faithfulness of God is enthroned in immutable glory. This Ethan said, and this we may say ; come what will, mercy and faithfulness are built up by " the Eternal Builder," and his own nature is the guarantee for their perpetuity. This is to be called to mind whenever the church is in trouble, or our own spirits bowed down with grief.

3. " *I have made a covenant with my chosen, I have sworn unto David my servant.*" This was the ground of the Psalmist's confidence in God's mercy and truth, for he knew that the Lord had made a covenant of grace with David and his seed, and confirmed it by an oath. Here he quotes the very words of God, which were revealed to him by the Holy Spirit, and are a condensation of the original covenant in 2 Samuel vii. Well might he write in the former verse, " I have said," when he knew that Jehovah had said, " I have sworn." David was the Lord's elect, and with him a covenant was made, which ran along in the line of his seed until it received a final and never-ending fulfilment in " the Son of David." David's house must be royal : as long as there was a sceptre in Judah, David's seed must be the only rightful dynasty ; the great " King of the Jews " died with that title above his head in the three current languages of the then known world, and at this day he is owned as king by men of every tongue. The oath sworn to David has not been broken, though the temporal crown is no longer worn, for in the covenant itself his kingdom was spoken of as enduring for ever. In Christ Jesus there is a covenant established with all the Lord's *chosen*, and they are by grace led to be the Lord's *servants*, and then are ordained kings and priests by Christ Jesus. How sweet it is to see the Lord, not only making a covenant, but owning to it in after days, and bearing witness to his own oath ; this ought to be solid ground for faith, and Ethan, the Ezrahite, evidently thought it so. Let the reader and writer both pause over such glorious lines, and sing of the mercies of the Lord, who thus avows the bonds of the covenant, and, in so doing, gives a renewed pledge of his faithfulness to it. " *I have*," says the Lord, and yet again " *I have*," as though he himself was nothing loath to dwell upon the theme. We also would lovingly linger over the *ipsissima*

verba of the covenant made with David, reading them carefully and with joy. They are thus recorded in 2 Sam. vii. 12—16 : "And when thy days be fulfilled, and thou shalt sleep with thy fathers, I will set up thy seed after thee, which shall proceed out of thy bowels, and I will establish his kingdom. He shall build an house for my name, and I will stablish the throne of his kingdom for ever. I will be his father, and he shall be my son. If he commit iniquity, I will chasten him with the rod of men, and with the stripes of the children of men : But my mercy shall not depart away from him, as I took it from Saul, whom I put away before thee. And thine house and thy kingdom shall be established for ever before thee : thy throne shall be established for ever." After reading this, let us remember that the Lord has said to us by his servant Isaiah, " I will make an everlasting covenant with you, even the sure mercies of David."

Verse 4.—" *Thy seed will I establish for ever.*" David must always have a seed, and truly in Jesus this is fulfilled beyond his hopes. What a seed David has in the multitude which have sprung from him who was both his Son and his Lord. The Son of David is the Great Progenitor, the second Adam, the Everlasting Father, he sees his seed, and in them beholds of the travail of his soul. " *And build up thy throne to all generations.*" David's dynasty never decays, but on the contrary, is evermore consolidated by the great Architect of heaven and earth. Jesus is a king as well as a progenitor, and his throne is ever being built up—his kingdom comes —his power extends.

Thus runs the covenant ; and when the church declines, it is ours to plead it before the ever faithful God, as the Psalmist does in the latter verses of this sacred song. Christ must reign, but why is his name blasphemed and his gospel so despised ? The more gracious Christians are, the more will they be moved to jealousy by the sad estate of the Redeemer's cause, and the more will they argue the case with the great Covenant-maker, crying day and night before him, " Thy kingdom come."

" *Selah.*" It would not be meet to hurry on. Rest, O reader, at the bidding of this Selah, and let each syllable of the covenant ring in thine ears ; and then lift up the heart and proceed with the sacred poet to tell forth the praises of the Lord.

5 And the heavens shall praise thy wonders, O Lord : thy faithfulness also in the congregation of the saints.

6 For who in the heaven can be compared unto the Lord ? *who* among the sons of the mighty can be likened unto the Lord ?

7 God is greatly to be feared in the assembly of the saints, and to be had in reverence of all *them that are* about him.

8 O Lord God of hosts, who *is* a strong Lord like unto thee ? or to thy faithfulness round about thee ?

9 Thou rulest the raging of the sea : when the waves thereof arise, thou stillest them.

10 Thou hast broken Rahab in pieces, as one that is slain ; thou hast scattered thine enemies with thy strong arm.

11 The heavens *are* thine, the earth also *is* thine : *as for* the world and the fulness thereof, thou hast founded them.

12 The north and the south thou hast created them : Tabor and Hermon shall rejoice in thy name.

13 Thou hast a mighty arm : strong is thy hand, *and* high is thy right hand.

14 Justice and judgment *are* the habitation of thy throne : mercy and truth shall go before thy face.

5. " *And the heavens shall praise thy wonders, O Lord.*" Looking down upon what God had done, and was about to do, in connection with his covenant of grace, all heaven would be filled with adoring wonder. The sun and moon, which had been made tokens of the covenant, would praise God for such an extraordinary display of mercy, and the angels and redeemed spirits would sing, " as it were, a new song." " *Thy faithfulness also in the congregation of the saints.*" By which is probably intended the holy ones on earth. So that the " whole family in heaven and earth " would join in the praise. Earth and heaven are one in admiring and adoring

the covenant God. Saints above see most clearly into the heights and depths of divine love, therefore, they praise its wonders ; and saints below, being conscious of their many sins and multiplied provocations of the Lord, admire his faithfulness. The heavens broke forth with music at the wonders of mercy contained in the glad tidings concerning Bethlehem, and the saints who came together in the temple magnified the faithfulness of God at the birth of the Son of David. Since that auspicious day, the general assembly on high and the sacred congregation below have not ceased to sing unto Jehovah, the Lord that keepeth covenant with his elect.

6. " For who in the heaven can be compared unto the Lord ; " therefore all heaven worships him, seeing none can equal him. " Who among the sons of the mighty can be likened unto the Lord ? "—therefore the assemblies of the saints on earth adore him, seeing none can rival him. Until we can find one equally worthy to be praised, we will give unto the Lord alone all the homage of our praise. Neither among the sons of the morning nor the sons of the mighty can any peer be found for Jehovah, yea none that can be mentioned in the same day ; therefore he is rightly praised. Since the Lord Jesus, both as God and as man, is far above all creatures, he also is to be devoutly worshipped. How full of poetic fire is this verse ! How bold is the challenge ! How triumphant the holy boasting ! The sweet singer dwells upon the name of Jehovah with evident exultation ; to him the God of Israel is God indeed and God alone. He closely follows the language long before rehearsed by Miriam, when she sang, " Who is like unto thee, O Jehovah, among the gods ? Who is like thee ? " His thoughts are evidently flying back to the days of Moses and the marvels of the Red Sea, when God was gloriously known by his incommunicable name ; there is a ring of timbrels in the double question, and a sound as of the twinkling feet of rejoicing maidens. Have we no poets now ? Is there not a man among us who can compose hymns flaming with this spirit ? O, Spirit of the living God, be thou the inspirer of some master minds among us !

7. " God is greatly to be feared in the assembly of the saints." The holiest tremble in the presence of the thrice Holy One ; their familiarity is seasoned with the profoundest awe. Perfect love casts out the fear which hath torment, and works in lieu thereof that other fear which is akin to joy unutterable. How reverent should our worship be ! Where angels veil their faces, men should surely bow in lowliest fashion. Sin is akin to presumptuous boldness, but holiness is sister to holy fear. " And to be had in reverence of all them that are about him." The nearer they are the more they adore. If mere creatures are struck with awe, the courtiers and favourites of heaven must be yet more reverent in the presence of the Great King. God's children are those who most earnestly pray " hallowed be thy name." Irreverence is rebellion. Thoughts of the covenant of grace tend to create a deeper awe of God, they draw us closer to him, and the more his glories are seen by us in that nearer access, the more humbly we prostrate ourselves before his Majesty.

8. " O Lord God of hosts, who is a strong Lord like unto thee ? " Or Jehovah, God of Hosts, who is like thee, Mighty Jah. Alexander remarks, that the infinite superiority of God to men and angels is here expressed, or rather indicated, by an accumulation of descriptive titles. Here we have the name which displays his self-existence, the title which denotes his dominion over all his creatures, and an adjective which sets forth the power with which he exercises his sovereignty. Yet this great and terrible God has entered into covenant with men ! Who would not reverence him with deepest love ? " Or to thy faithfulness round about thee." He dwells in faithfulness ; it is said to be the girdle of the loins of his only-begotten Son, who is the express image of his person. None in all creation is faithful as he is ; even his angels might prove faithless if he left them to themselves, but he cannot " lie unto David," or forget to keep his oath. Men often fail in truth because their power is limited, and then they find it easier to break their word than to keep it ; but the strong Jehovah is equal to all his engagements, and will assuredly keep them. Unrivalled might and unparalleled truth are wedded in the character of Jehovah. Blessed be his name that it is so.

9. " Thou rulest the raging of the sea." Always, even in the hour of ocean's maddest fury, the Lord controls it. At the Red Sea the foaming billows saw their God and stood upright in awe. " When the waves thereof arise, thou stillest them." None else can do this ; to attempt it would be madness, but the Lord's " hush " silences the boisterous storm. So did the Lord's Anointed calm the storms of Galilee, for he is Lord of all : so also does the great Ruler of Providence evermore

govern the fickle wills of men, and quiet the tumults of the people. As a mother stills her babe to sleep, so the Lord calms the fury of the sea, the anger of men, the tempest of adversity, the despair of the soul, and the rage of hell. "The Lord sitteth upon the floods : yea, the Lord sitteth King for ever," and in all his ruling and over-ruling he has respect unto his covenant ; therefore, although our house be not so with God as our hearts would wish, yet we will rejoice in his covenant ordered in all things and sure, and delight in him as all our salvation and all our desire.

10. " *Thou hast broken Rahab in pieces as one that is slain.*" Egypt was crushed like a corpse beneath the chariot wheels of the destroyer : its pomp and glory were broken like the limbs of the dead in battle. Egypt was Israel's ancient foe, and its overthrow was a theme to which devout minds constantly reverted, as to a subject fit for their most exulting songs. We, too, have seen our Rahab broken, our sins o'erthrown, and we cannot but unite in the ascription of praise unto the Lord. " *Thou hast scattered thine enemies with thy strong arm.*" Thy strength has strewn thy foes dead upon the plain, or compelled them to flee hither and thither in dismay. Jehovah has overthrown his enemies with his own right arm, unaided and alone. Proud Rahab, swelling in her fury like the sea, was utterly broken and scattered before the Lord of Hosts.

11. " *The heavens are thine, the earth also is thine.*" All things are alike God's —rebellious earth as well as adoring heaven. Let us not despair of the kingdom of truth ; the Lord has not abdicated the throne of earth or handed it over to the sway of Satan. " *As for the world and the fulness thereof, thou hast founded them.*" The habitable and cultivated earth, with all its produce, owns the Lord to be both its Creator and Sustainer, builder and upholder.

12. " *The north and the south thou hast created them.*" North and south, opposite poles, agree in this—that Jehovah fashioned them. " *Tabor and Hermon shall rejoice in thy name,*" that is to say, east and west are equally formed by thee, and therefore give thee praise. Turn to all points of the compass, and behold the Lord is there. The regions of snow and the gardens of the sun are his dominions : both the land of the dawning and the home of the setting sun rejoice to own his sway. Tabor was on the west of Jordan and Hermon on the east, and it seems natural to consider these two mountains as representatives of the east and west. Keble paraphrases the passage thus :—

> " Both Hermon moist, and Tabor lone,
> They wait on thee with glad acclaim."

13. " *Thou hast a mighty arm,*" omnipotence is thine in smiting or uplifting ; " *strong is thy hand,*" thy power to create and grasp is beyond conception great ; " *and high is thy right hand* "—thy skill is incomparable, thy favour ennobling, thy working glorious. The power of God so impressed the Psalmist that in many ways he repeated the same thought : and indeed the truth of God's omnipotence is so full of refreshment to gracious hearts that it cannot be too much dwelt upon, especially when viewed in connection with his mercy and truth, as in the following verse.

14. " *Justice and judgment are the habitation of thy throne.*" They are the basis of the divine government, the sphere within which his sovereignty moves. God as a sovereign is never unjust or unwise. He is too holy to be unrighteous, too wise to be mistaken ; this is constant matter for joy to the upright in heart. " *Mercy and truth shall go before thy face.*" They are the harbingers and heralds of the Lord ; he calls these to the front to deal with guilty and changeful man ; he makes them, in the person of the Lord Jesus, to be his ambassadors, and so poor, guilty man is enabled to endure the presence of his righteous Lord. If mercy had not paved the way, the coming of God to any man must have been swift destruction.

Thus has the poet sung the glories of the covenant God. It was meet that before he poured forth his lament he should record his praise, lest his sorrow should seem to have withered his faith. Before we argue our case before the Lord it is most becoming to acknowledge that we know him to be supremely great and good, whatever may be the appearance of his providence ; this is such a course as every wise man will take who desires to have an answer of peace in the day of trouble.

15 Blessed *is* the people that know the joyful sound : they shall walk, O Lord, in the light of thy countenance,

16 In thy name shall they rejoice all the day : and in thy righteousness shall they be exalted.

17 For thou *art* the glory of their strength : and in thy favour our horn shall be exalted.

18 For the LORD *is* our defence ; and the Holy One of Israel *is* our king.

15. " *Blessed is the people that know the joyful sound.*" He is a blessed God of whom the Psalmist has been singing, and therefore they are a blessed people who partake of his bounty, and know how to exult in his favour. Praise is a peculiarly joyful sound, and blessed are those who are familiar with its strains. The covenant promises have also a sound beyond measure precious, and they are highly favoured who understand their meaning and recognise their own personal interest in them. There may also be a reference here to the blowing of trumpets and other gladsome noises which attended the worship of Jehovah, who, unlike the gods of the heathen was not adored by the shrieks of wretched victims, or the yells and outcries of terror-stricken crowds, but by the joyful shouts of his happy people. " *They shall walk, O Lord, in the light of thy countenance.*" For them it is joy enough that Jehovah is favourable to them ; all day long this contents them and enables them with vigour to pursue their pilgrimage. Only a covenant God could look with favour upon men, and those who have known him in that relationship learn to rejoice in him, yea, to walk with him in fellowship, and to continue in communion with him. If we give God our ear and hear the joyful sound, he will shew us his face and make us glad. While the sun shines, men walk without stumbling as to their feet, and when the Lord smiles on us we live without grief as to our souls.

16. " *In thy name shall they rejoice all the day.*" And good cause they have for so doing, for to the soul which, in Christ Jesus, has entered into covenant with God, every attribute is a fountain of delight. There is no hour in the day, and no day in our life, in which we may not rejoice in the name, person, and character of the Lord. We need no other reason for rejoicing. As philosophers could make merry without music, so can we rejoice without carnal comforts ; the Lord All-sufficient is an all-sufficient source of joy. " *And in thy righteousness shall they be exalted.*" By the Lord's righteous dealings the saints are uplifted in due time, however great may have been the oppression and the depression from which they may have suffered. In the righteousness which the covenant supplies, which is entirely of the Lord, believers are set on high, in a secure and blessed position, so that they are full of sacred happiness. If God were unjust, or if he regarded us as being without righteousness, we must be filled with misery, but as neither of these things is so, we are exalted indeed, and would extol the name of the Lord.

17. " *For thou art the glory of their strength.*" Surely in the Lord Jehovah have we both righteousness and strength. He is our beauty and glory when we are strong in him, as well as our comfort and sustenance when we tremble because of conscious weakness in ourselves. No man whom the Lord makes strong may dare to glory in himself, he must ascribe all honour to the Lord alone ; we have neither strength nor beauty apart from him. " *And in thy favour our horn shall be exalted.*" By the use of the word *our* the Psalmist identifies himself with the blessed people, and this indicates how much sweeter it is to sing in the first person than concerning others. May we have grace to claim a place among those in covenant with God, in Christ Jesus, for then a sense of divine favour will make us also bold and joyous. A creature full of strength and courage lifts up its horn, and so also does a believer become potent, valiant, and daring. The horn was an eastern ornament, worn by men and women, or at least is so at this day, and by the uplifting of this the wearer showed himself to be in good spirits, and in a confident frame of mind : we wear no such outward vanities, but our inward soul is adorned and made bravely triumphant when the favour of God is felt by us. Worldly men need outward prosperity to make them lift up their heads, but the saints find more than enough encouragement in the secret love of God.

18. " *For the Lord is our defence.*" Whoever else may defend us, he is our ultimate Defender and Shield. " *And the Holy One of Israel is our king.*" He who protects should govern, our defender should be acknowledged as our king. Kings are called the shields of nations, and the God of Israel is both our Ruler and our Defence. Another sense may be that Israel's defender and king was of the Lord, belonging to him and sent by him ; even the protectors of the land being them-

selves protected by the Lord.   The title " the Holy One of Israel " is peculiarly delightful to the renewed heart.   God is one, we worship none beside.   He is holiness itself, the only being who can be called " the Holy One," and in his perfection of character we see the most excellent reason for our faith.   He who is holy cannot break his promises, or act unjustly concerning his oath and covenant.   Moreover, he is the Holy One *of Israel*, being specially the God of his own elect, ours by peculiar ties, ours for ever and ever.   Who among the saints will not rejoice in the God of election ?   Are they not indeed a people greatly blessed who can call this God their God for ever and ever ?

19 Then thou spakest in vision to thy holy one, and saidst, I have laid help upon *one that is* mighty ; I have exalted *one* chosen out of the people.

20 I have found David my servant ; with my holy oil have I anointed him :

21 With whom my hand shall be established : mine arm also shall strengthen him.

22 The enemy shall not exact upon him ; nor the son of wickedness afflict him.

23 And I will beat down his foes before his face, and plague them that hate him.

24 But my faithfulness and my mercy *shall be* with him : and in my name shall his horn be exalted.

25 I will set his hand also in the sea, and his right hand in the rivers.

26 He shall cry unto me, Thou *art* my father, my God, and the rock of my salvation.

27 Also I will make him *my* firstborn, higher than the kings of the earth.

28 My mercy will I keep for him for evermore, and my covenant shall stand fast with him.

29 His seed also will I make *to endure* for ever, and his throne as the days of heaven.

30 If his children forsake my law, and walk not in my judgments ;

31 If they break my statutes, and keep not my commandments ;

32 Then will I visit their transgression with the rod, and their iniquity with stripes.

33 Nevertheless my lovingkindness will I not utterly take from him, nor suffer my faithfulness to fail.

34 My covenant will I not break, nor alter the thing that is gone out of my lips.

35 Once have I sworn by my holiness that I will not lie unto David.

36 His seed shall endure for ever, and his throne as the sun before me.

37 It shall be established for ever as the moon, and *as* a faithful witness in heaven. Selah.

19. " *Then thou spakest in vision to thy holy one.*"   The Psalmist returns to a consideration of the covenant made with David.   The holy one here meant may be either David or Nathan the prophet, but most probably the latter, for it was to him that the word of the Lord came by night.   2 Sam. vii. 4, 5.   God condescends to employ his gracious ministers to be the means of communication between himself and his favoured ones,—even to King David the covenant was revealed by Nathan the prophet ; thus the Lord puts honour upon his ministers.   " *I have laid help upon one that is mighty.*"   The Lord had made David a mighty man of valour, and now he covenants to make him the helper and defender of the Jewish state.   In a far fuller sense the Lord Jesus is essentially and immeasurably mighty, and on him the salvation of his people rests by divine appointment, while his success is secured by divine strength being engaged to be with him.   Let us lay our faith where God has laid our help.   " *I have exalted one chosen out of the people.*"   David

was God's elect, elect out of the people, as one of themselves, and elect to the highest position in the state. In his extraction, election, and exaltation, he was an eminent type of the Lord Jesus, who is the man of the people, the chosen of God, and the king of his church. Whom God exalts let us exalt. Woe unto those who despise him, they are guilty of contempt of court before the Lord of Hosts, as well as of rejecting the Son of God.

20. " *I have found David my servant.*" David was discovered by the Lord among the sheepfolds and recognised as a man of gracious spirit, full of faith and courage, and therefore fit to be leader in Israel. " *With my holy oil have I anointed him.*" By the hand of Samuel, David was anointed to be king long before he ascended the throne. The verse must also be expounded of the Prince Emanuel; he became the servant of the Lord for our sakes, the Father having found for us in his person a mighty deliverer, therefore upon him rested the Spirit without measure, to qualify him for all the offices of love to which he was set apart. We have not a Saviour self-appointed and unqualified, but one sent of God and divinely endowed for his work. Our Saviour Jesus is also the Lord's Christ, or anointed. The oil with which he is anointed is God's own oil, and holy oil; he is divinely endowed with the Spirit of holiness.

21. " *With whom my hand shall be established,*" or, " with whom my hand shall ever be present." The almightiness of God abides permanently with Jesus in his work as Redeemer and Ruler of his people. " *Mine arm also shall strengthen him.*" The fulness of divine power shall attend him. This covenant promise ought to be urged in prayer before the Lord, for the great lack of the church at this time is power. We have everything except the divine energy, and we must never rest content until we see it in full operation among us. Jesus must be among us, and then there will be no lack of force in any of our church agencies.

22. " *The enemy shall not exact upon him;* " he shall not be vexed and persecuted as a helpless debtor by an extortionate creditor. " *Nor the son of wickedness afflict him.*" Graceless men shall no longer make his life a burden. David had in his earlier history been hunted by Saul like a partridge on the mountains, and though he had striven in all things to act justly towards Saul, because he was the Lord's anointed, yet Saul was never content with his displays of loyalty, but persecuted him relentlessly. The covenant, therefore, engaged that his life of hardship and oppression should come to an end for ever; it did so in David's own person, and more remarkably still in the life of Solomon his son. Who does not in all this see a type of the Lord Jesus, who though he was once seized for our debts, and also evil entreated by the ungodly, is now so exalted that he can never be exacted upon any more, neither can the fiercest of his enemies vex him again. No Judas can now betray him to death, no Pilate can deliver him to be crucified. Satan cannot tempt him, and our sins cannot burden him.

23. " *And I will beat down his foes before his face* "—crushing them and their plans. God himself thus fights the battles of his Son, and effectually overturns his foes. " *And plague them that hate him,*" or *smite his haters.* May none of us learn the terror of this threatening, which is surely being fulfilled upon all those unbelievers who have rejected the Son of God, and died in the hardness of their hearts. The prophecy is also having another fulfilment in the overthrow of systems of error, and the vexation caused to their promoters. There is no such plague to bad men as the prosperity of the cause of Jesus.

24. " *But my faithfulness and my mercy shall be with him.*" These were the two attributes of which the Psalmist began to sing in the first verse of the Psalm, doubtless because he saw them to be most prominent in the covenant which he was about to plead with God. To David and his seed, God was gracious and faithful, and though through their sin the literal kingdom lost all its glory and the dynasty became obscure, yet the line remained unbroken and more than all its former glory was restored by the enthronisation of him who is Prince of the kings of the earth, with whom the Lord's mercy and faithfulness remain for ever. All who are in Jesus should rejoice, for they shall prove in their own experience the faithful mercy of the Lord. " *And in my name shall his horn be exalted.*" Gloriously does the Lord Jesus lift up his head, raised to the highest place of honour by the mandate of the Father. David and Solomon in their dignity were but faint types of the Lord Jesus, who is far above all principalities and powers. The fullest exaltation of the horn of Jesus is yet to come in that millenial period which is hastening on,

25. " *I will set his hand also in the sea, and his right hand in the rivers.*" He

shall reach far beyond the little rivers which stand for boundaries in Palestine ; he shall by his power embrace all lands from sea to sea. He shall lave his hand in the ocean and his right hand in earth's mightiest streams. As monarchs hold in their hands a globe to set forth their dominion over the earth, he shall grasp the far more unconquerable sea, and be Lord of all. This power is to be given him of the Lord, and is to be abiding ; so we understand the words " *I will set.*" The verse has in it a voice of good cheer concerning sailors, and all dwellers on the waters ; the hand of Jesus is over them, and as he found his first apostles by the sea, so we trust he still finds earnest disciples there.

26. " *He shall cry unto me, Thou art my father.*" David's seed would be a praying race, and so in the main they were, and when they were not they smarted for it. The Lord Jesus was pre-eminent in prayer, and his favourite mode of address was " Father." Never was there a son more filial in his cries than " the Firstborn among many brethren." God had one Son without sin, but he never had a son who lived without prayer. " *My God,*" so our Lord called his Father when upon the cross. " *And the rock of my salvation.*" It was to his Father that he turned for help when in sore anguish in Gethsemane, and to him he committed his spirit in the article of death. In this filial crying the true sons should imitate him. This is the common language of the elect family : adoption, reverence, trust, must all speak in their turns, and will do if we are heirs according to promise. To say to God " Thou art my father " is more than learning and talent can teach us ; the new birth is essential to this. Reader, hast thou the nature of a child and the spirit of one who can cry, " Abba, Father " ?

27. " *Also I will make him my firstborn.*" Among the kings the seed of David were to be most favoured and indulged with most love and paternal regard from God : but in Jesus we see this in the highest degree verified, for he has pre-eminence in all things, inasmuch as by inheritance he has a more glorious name than any other, and is " *higher than the kings of the earth.*" Who can rival heaven's Firstborn ? The double portion and the government belong to him. Kings are honoured when they honour him, and those who honour him are kings ! In the millenial glory it shall be seen what the covenant stores up for the once despised Son of David, but even now faith sees him exalted as King of kings and Lord of lords. Lo, we bow before thee, thou Heir of all things ! Our sheaves do obeisance to thy sheaf. All thy mother's children call thee blessed. Thou art he whom thy brethren shall praise. Jesus is no servant of princes, nor would he have his bride, the church, degrade herself by bowing before kings and eating the bread of a pensioner at their hands. He and his kingdom are higher than the kings of the earth. Let the great ones of the earth be wise and submit to him, for he is Lord, and he is the governor among the nations.

28. " *My mercy will I keep for him for evermore.*" The kings of David's line needed mercy, and mercy prevented their house from utterly perishing until the Son of Mary came. He needs no mercy for himself, but he is a representative man, and the mercy of God is required for those who are in him : for such mercy is kept for ever. " *And my covenant shall stand fast with him.*" With Jesus the covenant is ratified both by blood of sacrifice and by oath of God ; it cannot be cancelled or altered, but is an eternal verity, resting upon the veracity of one who cannot lie. What exultation fills our hearts as we see that the covenant of grace is *sure* to all the seed, because it stands fast with *him* with whom we are indissolubly united.

29. " *His seed also will I make to endure for ever.*" David's seed lives on in the person of the Lord Jesus, and the seed of Jesus in the persons of believers. Saints are a race that neither death nor hell can kill. Rome and its priests, with their inquisition and other infernal cruelties, have laboured to exterminate the covenant seed, but " vain is their rage, their efforts vain." As long as God lives, his people must live. " *And his throne as the days of heaven.*" Jesus reigns on, and will reign till the skies shall fall, yea, and when the heavens shall pass away with a great noise, and the elements shall melt with fervent heat, his throne shall stand. What a blessed covenant is this ! Some commentators talk of conditions, but we fail to see any ; the promises are as absolute as they can possibly be, and if any conditions as to the conduct of the favoured individuals can be conceived, they are disposed of in the succeeding verses.

30. " *If his children forsake my law, and walk not in my judgments.*" It was possible, terribly possible, that David's posterity might wander from the Lord ; indeed they did so, but what then ? Was the mercy of God to pass away from David's

seed ?—far from it. So, too, the seed of the Son of David are apt to start aside, but are they therefore cast away ? Not a single word gives liberty for such an idea, but the very reverse. Expositors in their fear of Calvinistic doctrine shake off the fear of adding to the word of God, or else they would not have spent their time in talking about " the conditions " of this absolutely unconditional covenant.

31. " *If they break my statutes, and keep not my commandments.*" The dreadful " *if* " is suggested again, and the sad case is stated in other forms. But if it should be so, what then ? Death and rejection ? Ah, no ; Blessed be God, No ! If their sin be negative or positive, if it be forsaking or profanation ; if either judgments or commandments or both be violated, yet there is not a word as to final destruction, but the very reverse. Legalism will import its ifs, but the Lord slays the ifs as fast as they rise. Eternal shalls and wills make glorious havoc among the ifs and buts.

32. " *Then will I visit their transgression with the rod.*" Not with the sword, not with death and destruction ; but still with a smarting, tingling, painful rod. Saints must smart if they sin : God will see to that. He hates sin too much not to visit it, and he loves his saints too well not to chasten them. God never plays with his rod, he lays it well home to his children, he *visits* them with it in their houses, bodies, and hearts, and makes them know that he is grieved with their ways. He smites home and chastens " *their iniquity with stripes,*" which are either many or few in proportion as the heart is properly affected by them. The rod is a covenant blessing, and is meant to be used. As sin is so frequent, the rod never rests long together ; in God's family the rod is not spared, or the children would be spoiled.

33. " *Nevertheless.*" And a glorious nevertheless too ! " *Nevertheless my loving-kindness will I not utterly take from him.*" O glorious fear-killing sentence ! This crowns the covenant with exceeding glory. Mercy may seem to depart from the Lord's chosen, but it shall never altogether do so. Jesus still enjoys the divine favour, and we are in him, and therefore under the most trying circumstances the Lord's lovingkindness to each one of his chosen will endure the strain. If the covenant could be made void by our sins it would have been void long ere this ; and if renewed its tenure would not be worth an hour's purchase if it had remained dependant upon us. God may leave his people, and they may thereby suffer much and fall very low, but utterly and altogether he never can remove his love from them ; for that would be to cast a reflection upon his own truth, and this he will never allow, for he adds, " *nor suffer my faithfulness to fail.*" Man fails in all points, but God in none. To be faithful is one of the eternal characteristics of God, in which he always places a great part of his glory : his truth is one of his peculiar treasures and crown jewels, and he will never endure that it should be tarnished in any degree. This passage sweetly assures us that the heirs of glory shall not be utterly cast off. Let those deny the safety of the saints who choose to do so, we have not so learned Christ. We believe in the gospel rod, but not in the penal sword for the adopted sons.

34. " *My covenant will I not break.*" It is his own covenant. He devised it, drew up the draft of it, and voluntarily entered into it ; he therefore thinks much of it. It is not a man's covenant, but the Lord claims it as his own. It is an evil thing among men for one to be a " covenant-breaker," and such an opprobrious epithet shall never be applicable to the Most High. " *Nor alter the thing that is gone out of my lips.*" Alterations and afterthoughts belong to short-sighted beings who meet with unexpected events which operate upon them to change their minds, but the Lord who sees everything from the beginning has no such reason for shifting his ground. He is besides immutable in his nature and designs, and cannot change in heart, and therefore not in promise. A word once given is sacred ; once let a promise pass our lips and honesty forbids that we should recall it,—unless indeed the thing promised be impossible, or wicked, neither of which can happen with the promises of God. How consoling it is to see the Lord thus resolute. He, in the words before us, virtually reasserts his covenant and rehearses his engagements. This he does at such length, and with such reiteration, that it is evident he takes pleasure in that most ancient and solemn contract. If it were conceivable that he had repented of it, he would not be found dwelling upon it, and repeating it with renewed emphasis.

35. " *Once have I sworn by my holiness that I will not lie unto David.*" Because he could swear by no greater he swore by himself, and by that peculiar attribute which is his highest glory, being the subject of threefold adoration by all the hosts

of heaven. God here pledges the crown of his kingdom, the excellent beauty of his person, the essence of his nature. He does as good as say that if he ceases to be true to his covenant he will have forfeited his holy character. What more can he say ? In what stronger language can he express his unalterable adherence to the truth of his promise ? An oath is the end of all strife ; it ought to be the end of all doubt on our part. We cannot imagine that God could lie, yet he puts it so—that if the covenant were not kept by him, he would regard it as a lie. Here is ground for strong confidence ; may our faith be of such a nature as these assurances will warrant.

36. " *His seed shall endure for ever.*" David's line in the person of Jesus is an endless one, and the race of Jesus, as represented in successive generations of believers, shows no sign of failure. No power, human or Satanic, can break the Christian succession ; as saints die others shall rise up to fill their places, so that till the last day, the day of doom, Jesus shall have a seed to serve him. " *And his throne as the sun before me.*" In our Lord Jesus the dynasty of David remains upon the throne. Jesus has never abdicated, nor gone into banishment. He reigns, and must reign so long as the sun continues to shine upon the earth. A seed and a throne are the two great promises of the covenant, and they are as important to us as to our Lord Jesus himself ; for we are the seed who must endure for ever, and we are protected and ennobled by that King whose royalties are to last for ever.

37. " *It shall be established for ever as the moon.*" The kingdom may wax and wane to mortal eyes, but it shall still abide as long as the moon walks in her silver beauty. " *And as a faithful witness in heaven.*" The most stable part of the universe is selected as a type of Messiah's kingdom, and both sun and moon are made to be symbols of its long endurance. Whatever else there is in the sky which faithfully witnesses to the unbending course of nature is also called upon to be a sign of the Lord's truth. When heaven and earth witness, and the Lord himself swears, there remains no excuse for doubting, and faith joyfully reposes in confident expectation.

38 But thou hast cast off and abhorred, thou hast been wroth with thine anointed.

39 Thou hast made void the covenant of thy servant : thou hast profaned his crown *by casting it* to the ground.

40 Thou hast broken down all his hedges ; thou hast brought his strong holds to ruin.

41 All that pass by the way spoil him : he is a reproach to his neighbours.

42 Thou hast set up the right hand of his adversaries ; thou hast made all his enemies to rejoice.

43 Thou hast also turned the edge of his sword, and hast not made him to stand in the battle.

44 Thou hast made his glory to cease, and cast his throne down to the ground.

45 The days of his youth hast thou shortened : thou hast covered him with shame. Selah.

46 How long, Lord ? wilt thou hide thyself for ever ? shall thy wrath burn like fire ?

47 Remember how short my time is : wherefore hast thou made all men in vain ?

48 What man *is he that* liveth, and shall not see death ? shall he deliver his soul from the hand of the grave ? Selah.

49 Lord, where *are* thy former lovingkindnesses, *which* thou swarest unto David in thy truth ?

50 Remember, Lord, the reproach of thy servants ; *how* I do bear in my bosom *the reproach of* all the mighty people :

51 Wherewith thine enemies have reproached, O Lord ; wherewith they have reproached the footsteps of thine anointed.

52 Blessed *be* the Lord for evermore. Amen, and Amen.

38. " *But thou hast cast off and abhorred.*" The Lord had promised not to cast off the seed of David, and yet it looked as if he had done so, and that too in the most angry manner, as if he loathed the person of the king. God's actions may appear to us to be the reverse of his promises, and then our best course is to come before him in prayer and put the matter before him just as it strikes our apprehension. We are allowed to do this, for this holy and inspired man did so unrebuked, but we must do it humbly and in faith. " *Thou hast been wroth with thine anointed.*" He deserved the wrath, doubtless, but the Psalmist's point is, that this appeared to him to conflict with the gracious covenant. He puts the matter plainly, and makes bold with the Lord, and the Lord loves to have his servants so do ; it shows that they believe his engagements to be matters of fact.

39. " *Thou hast made void the covenant of thy servant.*" The dispensations of providence looked as if there had been a disannulling of the sacred compact, though indeed it was not so. " *Thou hast profaned his crown by casting it to the ground.*" The king had been subject to such sorrow and shame that his diadem had been as it were taken from his head, dashed on the earth, and rolled in the mire. He was a theocratic monarch, and the Lord, who gave him his crown, took it from him and treated it with contempt,—at least so it seemed. In these sad days also we may utter the same plaint, for Jesus is not acknowledged in many of the churches, and usurpers have profaned his crown. When we hear of kings and queens set up as " heads of the church," and a priest styled " The Vicar of Christ," while parliaments and courts take upon themselves to legislate for the church of God, we may bitterly lament that things should come to so wretched a pass. Few are there who will acknowledge the crown rights of King Jesus, the very subject is considered to be out of date. O Lord how long !

40. " *Thou hast broken down all his hedges.*" He was no longer sheltered from the slanderous assaults of contemptuous tongues ; the awe which should guard the royal name had ceased to separate him from his fellows. The " divinity which doth hedge a king " had departed. Hitherto, the royal family had been like a vine within an enclosure, but the wall was now laid low, and the vine was unprotected. It is sorrowfully true that in many places the enclosures of the church have been destroyed, the line of demarcation between the church and the world has almost vanished, and godless men fill the sacred offices. Alas, O Lord God, shall it be always so ? Shall thy true vine be deserted by thee, thou great Husbandman ? Set up the boundaries again, and keep thy church as a vineyard reserved for thyself. " *Thou hast brought his strongholds to ruin.*" The forts of the land were in the possession of the enemy and were dismantled, the defences of the kingdom were overthrown. Thus has it happened that precious truths, which were the bulwarks of the church, have been assailed by heresy, and the citadels of sound doctrine have been abandoned to the foe. O God, how canst thou suffer this ? As the God of truth, wilt thou not arise and tread down falsehood ?

41. " *All that pass by the way spoil him.*" Idle passers-by, who have nothing else to do, must needs have a pluck at this vine, and they do it without difficulty, since the hedges are gone. Woe is the day when every petty reasoner has an argument against religion, and men in their cups are fluent with objections against the gospel of Jesus. Although Jesus on the cross is nothing to them, and they pass him by without inquiring into what he has done for them, yet they can loiter as long as you will, if there be but the hope of driving another nail into his hands and helping to crucify the Lord afresh. They will not touch him with the finger of faith, but they pluck at him with the hand of malice. " *He is a reproach to his neighbours.*" David's successors had unneighbourly neighbours, who were a reproach to good fellowship, because they were so ready to reproach their neighbour. The Jews were much taunted by the surrounding Gentiles when at any time they fell into trouble. At this time the people of God, who follow the Lord fully, are subject to a thousand reproaches, and some of them of the most bitter kind. These reproaches are really the reproach of Christ, and, at bottom, are meant for him. Shall it always be so ? Shall he, who deserves to be universally adored, be subject to general scorn ? Where, then, O God, is thy faithfulness to thy covenant ?

42. " *Thou hast set up the right hand of his adversaries.*" Thou hast done it, *thou*, who hast sworn to give him help and victory, thou hast, instead thereof sided with his enemies, and lent them thy strength, so that they have gained the supremacy. " *Thou hast made all his enemies to rejoice.*" They are boasting over him, and are glorying in his defeat, and this is done by thyself. O God,—how

is this ? Where is the covenant ? Hast thou forgotten thine own pledges and promises ?

43. " *Also turned the edge of his sword.*" When he goes to war he is as unsuccessful as though his sword refused to cut, and gave way like a sword of lead. His weapons fail him. " *And hast not made him to stand in the battle.* His heart fails him as well as his sword—he wavers, he falls. This has happened even to naturally brave men—a terrible dread has unmanned them. At this present the church has few swords of true Jerusalem metal ; her sons are pliable, her ministers yield to pressure. We need men whose edge cannot be turned, firm for truth, keen against error, sharp towards sin, cutting their way into men's hearts. Courage and decision are more needed now than ever, for charity towards heresy is the fashionable vice, and indifference to all truth, under the name of liberal-mindedness, is the crowning virtue of the age. The Lord send us men of the school of Elias, or, at least, of Luther and Knox.

44. " *Thou hast made his glory to cease.*" The brightness of his reign and the prosperity of his house are gone, his fame is tarnished, his honour disgraced. " *And cast his throne down to the ground.*" He has lost his power to govern at home or to conquer abroad. This happened to kings of David's line, and, more grievous to tell, it is happening in these days to the visible kingdom of the Lord Jesus. Where are the glories of Pentecost ? Where is the majesty of the Reformation ? Where does his kingdom come among the sons of men ? Woe is unto us, for the glory has departed, and the gospel throne of Jesus is hidden from our eyes !

45. " *The days of his youth hast thou shortened.*" The time of the king's energy was brief, he grew feeble before his time. " *Thou hast covered him with shame.*" Shame was heaped upon him because of his premature decay and his failure in arms. This was very grievous to the writer of this Psalm, who was evidently a most loyal adherent of the house of David. In this our day we have to bemoan the lack of vigour in religion—the heroic days of Christianity are over, her raven locks are sprinkled with untimely grey. Is this according to the covenant ? Can this be as the Lord has promised ? Let us plead with the righteous Judge of all the earth, and beseech him to fulfil his word wherein he has promised that those who wait upon him shall renew their strength.

Selah. The interceding poet takes breath amid his lament, and then turns from describing the sorrows of the kingdom to pleading with the Lord.

46. " *How long, Lord ?*" The appeal is to Jehovah, and the argument is the length of the affliction endured. Chastisement with a rod is not a lengthened matter, therefore he appeals to God to cut short the time of tribulation. " *Wilt thou hide thyself for ever ?*" Hast thou not promised to appear for thy servant—wilt thou then for ever forsake him ? " *Shall thy wrath burn like fire ?*" Shall it go on and on evermore till it utterly consume its object ? Be pleased to set a bound ! How far wilt thou go ? Wilt thou burn up the throne which thou hast sworn to perpetuate ? Even thus we would entreat the Lord to remember the cause of Christ in these days. Can he be so angry with his church as to leave her much longer ? How far will he suffer things to go ? Shall truth die out, and saints exist no more ? How long will he leave matters to take their course ? Surely he must interpose soon, for, if he do not, true religion will be utterly consumed, as it were, with fire.

47. " *Remember how short my time is.*" If so brief, do not make it altogether bitter. If thine anger burn on it will outlast this mortal life, and then there will be no time for thy mercy to restore me. Some expositors ascribe these words, and all the preceding verses, to the state of the Lord Jesus in the days of his humiliation, and this gives an instructive meaning ; but we prefer to continue our reference all through to the church, which is the seed of the Lord Jesus, even as the succeeding kings were the seed of David. We, having transgressed, are made to feel the rod, but we pray the Lord not to continue his stripes lest our whole life be passed in misery. " *Wherefore hast thou made all men in vain ?*" If the Lord do not shine upon his work we live for nothing—we count it no longer life if his cause does not prosper. We live if the King lives, but not else. Everything is vanity if religion be vanity. If the kingdom of heaven should fail, everything is a failure. Creation is a blot, providence an error, and our own existence a hell, if the faithfulness of God can fail and his covenant of grace can be dissolved. If the gospel system can be disproved, nothing remains for us or any other of the sons of men, which can render existence worth the having.

48. " *What man is he that liveth, and shall not see death ?*" All must die. None

of our race can answer to the question here propounded except in the negative; there is none that can claim to elude the arrows of death. " *Shall he deliver his soul from the hand of the grave ?* " Neither by strength, wisdom, nor virtue can any man escape the common doom, for to the dust return we must. Since then we must all die, do not make this life all wretchedness, by smiting us so long, O Lord. Thy Son our covenant Head died, and so also shall we ; let us not be so deserted of thee in this brief span that we shall be quite unable to testify to thy faithfulness ; make us not feel that we have lived in vain. Thus the brevity of life and the certainty of death are turned into pleas with the Most High.

" *Selah.*" Here we rest again, and proceed to further pleadings.

49. " *Lord, where are thy former lovingkindnesses, which thou swarest unto David in thy truth ?*" Here he comes to grand pleading, hand to hand work with the covenant angel. We may remind the Lord of his first deeds of love, his former love to his church, his former favour to ourselves. Then may we plead his oath, and beg him to remember that he has sworn to bless his chosen ; and we may wrestle hard also, by urging upon him his own character, and laying hold upon his inviolable truth. When things look black we may bring forth our strong reasons, and debate the case with our condescending God, who has himself said, " Come now, and let us reason together."

50. " *Remember, Lord, the reproach of thy servants.*" By reason of their great troubles they were made a mock of by ungodly men, and hence the Lord's pity is entreated. Will a father stand by and see his children insulted ? The Psalmist entreats the Lord to compassionate the wretchedness brought upon his servants by the taunts of their adversaries, who jested at them on account of their sufferings. "*How I do bear in my bosom the reproach of all the mighty people.*" The Psalmist himself laid the scorn of the great and the proud to heart. He felt as if all the reproaches which vexed his nation were centred in himself, and therefore in sacred sympathy with the people he poured out his heart. We ought to weep with those that weep ; reproach brought upon the saints and their cause ought to burden us : if we can hear Christ blasphemed, and see his servants insulted, and remain unmoved, we have not the true Israelite's spirit. Our grief at the griefs of the Lord's people may be pleaded in prayer, and it will be acceptable argument.

There is one interpretation of this verse which must not be passed over ; the original is, " *Remember my bearing in my bosom all the many nations ;* " and this may be understood as a pleading of the church that the Lord would remember her because she was yet to be the mother of many nations, according to the prophecy of Ps. lxxvii. She was as it were ready to give birth to nations, but how could they be born if she herself died in the meanwhile ? The church is the hope of the world ; should she expire, the nations would never come to the birth of regeneration, but must abide in death.

51. " *Wherewith thine enemies have reproached, O Lord.*" Here is another forcible point ; the scoffers are the Lord's enemies as well as ours, and their reproach falls upon him as well as upon us ; therefore we cry for the Lord's interposition. When Jehovah's own name is in the quarrel, surely he will arise. " *Wherewith they have reproached the footsteps of thine anointed.*" Tracking him and finding occasion to blaspheme at every turn ; not only watching his words and actions, but even his harmless steps. Neither Christ nor his church can please the world, whichever way we turn scoffers will rail. Does this verse refer to the oft-repeated sarcasm— " Where is the promise of his coming ? " Is the reproach aimed at the delays of the Messiah, those long-expected footfalls which as yet are unheard ? O Lord, how long shall this thread-bare taunt continue ? How long ? How long ?

> " Come, for creation groans
>   Impatient of thy stay,
> Worn out with these long years of ill,
>   These ages of delay.
>
> " Come, in thy glorious might,
>   Come with the iron rod,
> Scattering thy foes before thy face.
>   Most Mighty Son of God."

52. " *Blessed be the Lord for evermore.*" He ends where he began ; he has sailed round the world and reached port again. Let us bless God before we pray, and while we pray, and when we have done praying, for he always deserves it of us.

If we cannot understand him, we will not distrust him. When his ways are beyond our judgment we will not be so foolish as to judge; yet we shall do so if we consider his dealings to be unkind or unfaithful. He is, he must be, he shall be, for ever, our blessed God. "*Amen, and Amen.*" All our hearts say so. So be it, Lord, we wish it over and over again. Be thou blessed evermore.

EXPLANATORY NOTES AND QUAINT SAYINGS

Whole Psalm.—The present Psalm makes a pair with the preceding one. It is a spiritual Allegro to that Penseroso . . . That Psalm was a dirge of Passion-Tide, this Psalm is a carol of Christmas.—*Christopher Wordsworth.*

Whole Psalm.—There are many passages in this Psalm which do clearly evidence that it is to be interpreted of Christ; yea, there are many things in this Psalm that can never be clearly, pertinently, and appositely applied to any but Jesus Christ. For a taste, see ver. 19, "*I have laid help upon one that is mighty,*" mighty to pardon, reconcile, to justify, to save, to bring to glory; suitable to that of the Apostle, Heb. vii. 25, "He is able to save to the uttermost"—that is, to all ends and purposes, perfectly, completely, fully, continually, perpetually. Christ is a thorough Saviour, a mighty Saviour: Isa. lxiii. 1, "Mighty to save." There needs none to come after him to finish the work which he hath begun: ver. 19, "*I have exalted one chosen out of the people,*" which is the very title given to our Lord Jesus: Isa. xlii. 1, "Behold my servant, whom I uphold; mine elect," or chosen one, "in whom my soul delighteth": ver. 20, "*I have found David my servant.*" Christ is very frequently called by that name, as being most dearly beloved of God, and most highly esteemed and valued by God, and as being typified by him both as king and prophet of his church: ver. 20, "*With my holy oil have I anointed him;*" suitable to that of Christ; Luke iv. 18, "The Spirit of the Lord is upon me, because he hath anointed me to preach the gospel to the poor;" and therefore we need not doubt of the excellency, authority, certainty, and sufficiency of the gospel: ver. 27, "*I will make him my first-born, higher than the kings of the earth.*" Christ is the first-born of every creature, and in all things hath the pre-eminence: ver. 29, "*His seed also will I make to endure for ever, and his throne as the days of heaven.*" This is chiefly spoken of Christ and his kingdom. The aspectable heaven is corruptible, but the kingdom of heaven is eternal; and such shall be Christ's seed, throne and kingdom: ver. 36, "*His seed shall endure for ever, and his throne as the sun before me.*" "Christ shall see his seed, he shall prolong his days, and the pleasure of the LORD shall prosper in his hand," Isa. liii. 10. "*And his throne as the sun before me*"; that is, perpetual and glorious, as the Chaldee explaineth it, "*shall shine as the sun.*" Other kingdoms and thrones have their times and their turns, their rise and their ruins, but so hath not the kingdom and throne of Jesus Christ. Christ's dominion is "an everlasting dominion," which shall not pass away; "and his kingdom that which shall not be destroyed," Dan. vii. 13, 14. I might give further instances out of this Psalm, but enough is as good as a feast. Now saith God, "I have made a covenant with him"; so then there is a covenant that God the Father hath made with Christ the Mediator; which covenant, the Father engages to the Son, shall stand fast, there shall be no cancelling or disannulling of it. God the Father hath not only made a covenant of grace with the saints in Christ, but he has also made a covenant of redemption, as we call it for distinction sake, with Jesus Christ himself: "My covenant shall stand fast with him;" that is, with Christ, as we have fully and clearly demonstrated.—*Thomas Brooks.*

Verse 1.—This one short verse contains the summary, pith, and argument of the whole long Psalm; wherein observe THE SONG'S DITTY, *the lovingkindness and truth of the Lord*, manifested unto the whole world generally, to David's house (that is, the church) especially. THE SINGER'S DUTY, *magnifying the mercies of God always, even from one generation to another.* And by all means; with his *mouth*, for that is expressed in this verse; with his *mind*, for that is implied in the next—"*I have said,*" etc., that is, believed in my heart, and therefore spake it with my tongue, Ps. cxvi. 10. "For out of the heart's abundance the mouth speaketh," Matt. xii. 34.—*John Boys.*

Verse 1.—"*I will sing.*" It is to be observed that he does not say, I will *speak* of the goodness of the Lord; but, I will sing. The celebration of the divine goodness has joined with itself the joy and exultation of a pious mind, which cannot be poured forth better than in song. That pleasantness and exuberance of a happy spirit, which by singing is instilled into the ears of the listeners, has a certain wonderful power of moving the affections ; so that not in vain were pious minds taught by the Holy Spirit to inculcate the wonderful work of God in songs composed for this purpose, to commit them to memory and to appoint them to be sung.—*Musculus.*

Verse 1.—" *I will sing.*"—The Psalmist has a very sad complaint to make of the deplorable condition of the family of David at this time, and yet he begins the Psalm with songs of praise ; for we must in every thing, in every state, give thanks. We think when we are in trouble we get ease by complaining : but we do more, we get joy, by praising. Let our complaints therefore be turned into thanksgiving ; and in these verses we find that which will be in matter of praise and thanksgiving for us in the worst of times, whether upon a personal or public account.—*Matthew Henry.*

Verse 1.—" *Sing of the mercies of the Lord for ever.*" S. Gregory the Great raises the question here as to how a perpetual singing of the *mercies* of God is compatible with unalloyed bliss in heaven, inasmuch as the thought of mercy connotes the memory of sin and sorrow, which needed mercy, whereas Isaiah saith that " the former troubles are forgotten," and " the former things shall not be remembered, nor come upon the heart " (ch. lxv. 16, 17). And he replies that it will be like the memory of past sickness in time of health, without stain, without grief, and serving only to heighten the felicity of the redeemed, by the contrast with the past, and to increase their love and gratitude towards God. And so sings the Cluniac :*

> " Their breasts are filled with gladness,
>   Their mouths are tuned to praise,
> What time, now safe for ever,
>   On former sins they gaze :
> The fouler was the error,
>   The sadder was the fall,
> The ampler are the praises
>   Of Him who pardoned all."

Note, too, that he says, " with *my* mouth," not with that of any deputy ; " *I will make known,*" not secretly or timidly, not in a whisper, but boldly preach, " *Thy faithfulness,*" or *truth,* not my own opinion, far less my own falsehood, but thy Truth, which is, thine Only-begotten Son.—*Gregory, Bernard, Hugo, and Augustine : quoted by Neale and Littledale.*

Verse 1.—" *Mercies.*" The word may be rendered *graces, kindnesses, goodnesses,* and designs the abundance of grace.—*John Gill.*

Verse 1.—" *The mercies.*" His manifold and sundry mercies : as if he should say, we have tasted of more than one, yea, we have felt all his mercies ; I will therefore praise the same for ever. I will sing his mercy for creating this universe, which is *macrocosmos,* a great world ; and for making man, which is *microcosmos,* a little world. 1. My song shall set forth his kindness, for that he gave me being. 2. For adding to my being, life, which he denieth unto stones. 3. To life, sense, which he denieth unto plants. 4. To sense, speech and understanding, which he denieth unto brute beasts. . . .

I am exceeding much bound unto God for creating me when I was not ; and for preserving me under his wings ever since I was : yet I am more bound to his mercy for redeeming me, for blessing me with all spiritual blessings in heavenly things in Christ his Son (Eph. 1, 3), for his electing of me, for his calling of me, for his justifying of me, for his sanctifying of me. These graces are the riches of his goodness and glory, *misericordiæ in æternum,* everlasting mercies, as reaching from everlasting predestination to everlasting glorification. O Lord, I will alway sing thy *mercies* in promising, and ever shew thy *truth* in performing thy promise made to David, thy chosen servant, concerning thy Son, my Saviour, saying, " Thy seed will I establish for ever." So the fathers expound our text : I will ever sing thy mercies, in vouchsafing to send thy Son to visit thy servants, sick to death in sin. First, I will ever sing of thy mercifulness, and then will ever be shewing thy faithfulness. *Neque enim exhiberetur veritas in impletione promissorum, nisi præcederet misericordia in remissione peccatorum.* (*For truth, in the fulfilment of the promises, would not be shown forth ; unless mercy, in the forgiveness of sins, should precede it.*) And what

* Bernard of Clairvaux.

is *God's mercy set up for ever, and his truth established in the heavens*, but that which Isaiah terms, " the sure mercies of David "; that is, aş Paul construeth Isaiah, the holy promise made to David : and the promise made to David, is briefly this, " Thy seed will I establish for ever, and set up thy throne from generation to generation." —*John Boys*.

Verse 1.—" *For ever*." I know some join *in æternum* to the noun *misericordias*, and not to the verb *cantabo*, making the sense to be this : I will alway sing thy mercies which endure for ever. But *always* is referred as well, if not better, unto the verb, " *I will sing* : " as who would say, Lord, thy mercies are so manifest, and so manifold, so great in their number, and so good in their nature, that I will always, so long as I have any being, sing praises unto thee. Haply some will object, " All flesh is grass, and the goodliness thereof is as the flower of the field : the grass withereth, the flower fadeth " (Isa. xl. 6, 7). David being persecuted by Saul, said, " There is but a step between me and death " (1 Sam. xx. 3). Nay, David, thy life is shorter than a stride, but " a span long," as thyself witnesseth, Ps. xxxix. 5. How can he then that begs his bread but for a day promise to spend his breath in magnifying the Lord for ever ? Answer is made, that the prophet will not only commend the mercies of the Lord in word, but also commit them unto writing. *Ut sciat hæc ætas, posteritasque legat* * (*that this age may know, and that posterity may read.*) As the tongue of the prophet is termed elsewhere " the pen of a writer ; " so the writing of the Prophet is here termed *his mouth*, as Euthymeus upon the place (Acts iv. 25), *Liber Psalmorum os David* (*The Book of Psalms is the mouth of David*). He doth intend to note the mercies of God, and to set forth his truth in a book, the which he will leave behind him (as an instrument) to convey the same *from generation to generation*, from the generation of Jews to the generation of Christians. Or from the Old Testament to the New : for the blessed Apostles in their sermons usually cite sentences out of the Psalms. S. Peter telleth us that the gospel was preached unto the dead (1 Peter iv. 6) ; so may we say, that the gospel is preached by the dead. For the most ancient fathers, and other judicious authors, who have spent their days in writing learned expositions and godly meditations upon the Holy Scriptures, although they be dead, yet they " sing alway the mercies of the Lord, and shew the truth of his word from one generation to another." It is reported in our chronicles of Athelstan, *parum ætati vixit, multum gloriæ* (*he lived but little of time, but much of glory*). So many zealous and industrious doctors have lived (in respect of their age) but a little, yet in respect of their acts, a great while, shining still in their works and writings, as lights of the world.

Or the prophet may be said to *sing ever* intentionally, though not actually. For as the wicked, if he could live alway, would sin alway, so the good man (if God should suffer him alway to breathe on earth) would sing alway the mercies of the Lord.—*John Boys*.

Verse 1.—" *With my mouth*." The author has heard continual praises from a tongue half eaten away with cancer. What use, beloved reader, are you making of your tongue ?—*Philip Bennett Power*.

Verse 2.—" *I have said*." The word אָמַרְתִּי, " *I have said*," is used, in the Book of Psalms, to express two things ; either a fixed purpose, or a settled opinion of the person speaking. The Psalmist, therefore, delivers the whole of this second verse in his own person, and introduces not God speaking till the next verse.—*Samuel Horsley*.

Verse 2.—" *I have said*," etc. The perpetuity of mercy is one eminent piece of this Psalm, for with that he begins : " *Mercy shall be built up for ever*," etc. And they are the sure mercies of our spiritual David (Christ), he means. Now, to set forth the perpetuity hereof, he first useth words that express firmitude, as " *established*," " *built up for ever*," ver. 2, 4. Then he uses such similitudes as are taken from things which are held most firm and inviolable amongst men, as verse 4, *fœdus incidi*, I have cut or engraven my covenant (so in the Hebrew), alluding to what was then in use, when covenants were mutually to be made, such as they intended to be inviolate, and never to be broken ; to signify so much, they did engrave and cut them into the most durable lasting matter, as marble, or brass, or the like. You may see this to have been the way of writing in use, as what was to last for ever : as Job xix. 23, 24. " Oh that my words were now written ! oh that they were

* Eobanus Hessus.

printed in a book! That they were graven with an iron pen and lead in the rock for ever!" And what is that rock or marble here? No other than the heart itself of our gracious and most merciful Jehovah, and his most unalterable and immovable purposes, truth and faithfulness. This is that foundation "*in the heavens*," whereon mercy is built up for ever, as ver. 2, which (as the Apostle says) "remains for ever;" and so they become "the sure mercies of David," Isai. lv. 3. Again, solemn oaths amongst men serve to ratify and make things sworn to perpetual. This also is there specified as having been taken by God: "Once have I sworn by my holiness," etc., and sworn by him that cannot lie, and sworn to that end, "to show the immutability of his counsel," Heb. vi. 17. And not only is the immutability of his mercy illustrated by these things taken from what is firm on earth, but he ascends up to the heavens, and first into the very highest heavens: ver. 2, "*For I have said, Mercy shall be built up for ever: thy faithfulness shalt thou establish in the very heavens:*" comparing them to an house built not on earth, or upon a foundation of earth, which thieves break through, and violence destroys, but in heaven, whither they cannot reach.—*Thomas Goodwin.*

Verse 2.—"*Mercy shall be built up for ever.*" What is this "mercy" that is "built up for ever"? but the glorious and the gracious scheme, the glorious and the gracious fabric, of our salvation, founded in the eternal purpose of God—carried into execution by the labours and the death of Jesus Christ—and then applied and brought home to the heart by the illuminating and converting power of the Holy Ghost? This is that "mercy" which is "built up for ever." It was planned from everlasting, and will know no ruin or decay, through the illimitable line of eternity itself. Who is the builder of this fabric? Not man's free-will. Not man's own righteousness or wisdom. Not human power nor human skill. Every true believer will here join issue with David, that it is God, and God alone, who builds up the temple of his Church; and who, as the builder of it, is alone entitled to all the glory.

The elect constitute and form one grand house of mercy: an house, erected to display and to perpetuate the riches of the Father's free grace, of the Son's atoning merit, and of the Holy Ghost's efficacious agency. This house, contrary to the fate of all sublunary buildings, will never fall down, nor ever be taken down. As nothing can be added to it, so nothing can be diminished from it. Fire cannot injure it; storms cannot overthrow it; age cannot impair it. It stands on a rock, and is immovable as the rock on which it stands—the three-fold rock of God's inviolable decree of Christ's finished redemption, and of the Spirit's never-failing faithfulness.—*Augustus Montague Toplady,* 1740—1778.

Verse 2—"*Built up.*" Mention of a building of mercy, presupposes miserable ruins, and denotes that this building is intended for the benefit of an elect world ruined by Adam's fall. Free grace and love set on foot this building for them, every stone in which, from the lowest to the highest, is mercy to them; from top to bottom, from the foundation-stone to the top-stone, all is free and rich mercy to them. And the ground of this glorious building is God's covenant with his chosen: "*I have made a covenant with my chosen.*"—*Thomas Boston.*

Verse 2.—"*Built up.*" Former mercies are fundamental to later ones. The mercies that we enjoy this day are founded upon the mercies of former days, such as we ought joyfully and thankfully to recount with delight and praise; remembering the years of the right hand of the Most High.—*John Howe.*

Verse 2 (*last clause*).—The meaning of this passage appears to be, that the constancy of the celestial motions, the regular vicissitudes of day and night, and alternations of the seasons, were emblems of God's own immutability.—*R. Warner,* 1828.

Verse 2.—

> "For I have said, Thy mercies rise,
> A deathless structure, to the skies:
> The heav'ns were planted by thy hand,
> And, as the heav'ns, Thy truth shall stand."
>   —*Richard Mant.*

Verse 3.—"*I have made a covenant with my chosen.*" We must ponder here with pious wonder how God has deigned to enter into a covenant with man, the immortal with the mortal, the most powerful with the weakest, the most just with the most unjust, the richest with the poorest, the most blessed with the most wretched. The prophet wonders that God is mindful of man, and visits the son of man. Of how much greater admiration, I say, is it worthy, that they are also joined together, and that not after a simple fashion, but by the ties of a covenant? If man had affirmed this of himself, that God was united and bound to him by a covenant, who is there that would not have condemned him of temerity? Now God himself is introduced affirming this very thing of himself, that he had made a covenant with man. What saint does not see in this thing, how great the φιλανθρωπία of God is!—*Musculus.*

Verse 3.—" *I have made a covenant with my chosen.*" On heaven's side is God himself, the party proposer. Though he was the party offended, yet the motion for a covenant comes from him. . . . The Father of mercies saith, " The lost creatures cannot contract for themselves; and if another undertake not for them, they must perish: they cannot choose an undertaker for themselves. I will choose one for them, and I will make a covenant with my chosen." On man's side is God's chosen, or *chosen One*, for the word of God is singular; the Son, *the last Adam.* Who else as fit to be undertaker on man's side? who else could have been the Father's choice for this vast undertaking? No angel nor man was capable of it, but " *the Mighty One* " (verse 19) whom the Father points out to us as his *chosen*, Isai. xlii. 1.—*Thomas Boston.*

Verses 3, 4.—" *I have made a covenant with my chosen,*" etc. Do you suppose that this was spoken to David, in his own person only? No, indeed; but to David as the antitype, figure, and forerunner of Jesus Christ. Hence, the Septuagint version renders it, *I have covenanted* τοις εκλεκτοις μου, *with my elect people*, or with my chosen ones: *i.e.* with them in Christ, and with Christ in their name. " *I have sworn unto David my servant,*" unto the Messiah, who was typified by David; unto my co-eternal Son, who stipulated to take on himself " the form of a servant "; thy seed, *i.e.* all those whom I have given to thee in the decree of election, all those whom thou shalt live and die to redeem, these " *will I establish for ever,*" so as to render their salvation irreversible and inamissable: " *and build up thy throne,*" thy mediatorial throne, as King of saints and covenant Head of the elect, " *to all generations* " : there shall always be a succession of favoured sinners to be called and sanctified, in consequence of thy fœderal obedience unto death; and every period of time shall recompense thy covenant-sufferings with an increasing revenue of converted souls, until as many as are ordained to eternal life are gathered in.

Observe, here, that when Christ received the promise from the Father concerning the establishment of his (*i.e.* of Christ's) throne to all generations, the plain meaning is, that his people shall be thus established; for, consider Christ in his divine capacity as the Son of God, and his throne was already established, and had been from everlasting, and would have continued to be established without end, even if he had never been incarnate at all. Therefore, the promise imports that Christ shall reign, not simply as a person in the Godhead (which he ever did, ever will, and ever must); but relatively, mediatorially, and in his office-character, as the deliverer and king of Zion. Hence it follows, that his people cannot be lost: for he would be a poor sort of a king who had or might have no subjects to reign over. Consequently, that " throne " of glory on which Christ sits is already encircled in part, and will at last be completely surrounded and made still more glorious, by that innumerable company, that general assembly and church of the first-born, who are written in heaven.—*Augustus Montague Toplady.*

Verse 5.—" *The heavens,*" etc. Now, for this kingdom of his, the heavens are said to praise his wonders, which is spoken of the *angels*, who are often called the heavens, from their place; as in Job it is said, " The heavens are not clean in his sight." And these knowing the wonders of that covenant of grace, they, even they are said to praise; " The heavens shall praise thy wonders, O Lord." In the Hebrew it is " thy wonder," or " thy miracle," in the singular number which, in Eph. iii. 10, the angels are said to adore: and in Luke i., to " sing glory to the Highest: " for his grace to man is that miracle. Now the material heavens do not praise the mercy of God, or the grace of God, or the covenant of grace, or the throne of grace that is established in the heavens. They understand nothing of Christ; no, they do not so much as materially give occasion to man to praise God for these; and therefore this is meant of the angels; and most interpreters understand the next words of them: " *Thy faithfulness also in the congregation of the saints,*" angels, and the holy ones made perfect, for there the great congregation is. For even in the heavens, who can be compared to the Lord, where all his angels thus do praise him? " *Who among the sons of the mighty,*" of all the powers of the earth, " *can be likened unto the*

Lord ? " for he is the " King of kings, and he is the Lord of lords : " God above all gods, even angels themselves, as elsewhere the Psalmist hath it. And he says not only, " *There is none like thee ;* " but, " Who is like unto thee ? " his excellency so exceeds. And in the 7th verse, he is there presented with all his saints and angels round about him, as one that is greatly to be feared, or that is terrible in himself, by reason of his greatness, in this his council and assembly of his saints, and to be had in reverence of all that are about him. For saints and angels, they are of his council in heaven (as might be shewn), and encompass the manifestation of his glory there round about.—*Thomas Goodwin.*

Verse 5.—" *Thy wonders,*" etc. As the heavens are a proof of God's power, in respect of his first framing them out of nothing ; so are they a pattern of God's faithfulness, in their constant and orderly motion according to his word since their framing : " *The heavens shall praise thy faithfulness also.*" However the power and faithfulness of God may be seen and heard in the work and speech of the heavens by all men, yet are they not observed and hearkened unto except in the Church by God's children : therefore saith he, " *They shall praise thy faithfulness also in the congregation of the saints.*"—*David Dickson.*

Verse 5.—" *Thy wonders.*" Thy wondrousness (*literally,* wonder), not " Thy wondrous works," but " Thy wonderful mysterious nature and being," as separate and distinct from all created beings.—*J. J. S. Perowne.*

Verse 5.—" *Thy wonders,*" etc. It is a wonderful salvation, it is such a salvation as the angels desire to pry into it ; and it is such a salvation, that all the prophets desire to pry into it ; it is almost six thousand years since all the angels in heaven fell into a sea of wonder at this great salvation ; it is almost six thousand years since Abel fell into a sea of wonder at this great salvation ; and what think ye is his exercise this day ? He is even wondering at this great salvation.—*Andrew Gray,* 1616.

Verse 6.—" *Who in the heaven ?* " Who in the sky ? Ainsworth reads it. In the clouds, *in nubibus, æquabitur,* is to be equalled, saith Calvin, to Jehovah, *Quis enim in superiore nube par æstimetur Jehova.* Who in the higher clouds is equal to Jehovah, so Tremellius reads it. " *Who in the heavens ?* " *i.e.,* say some, in the starry heavens, among the celestial bodies, sun, moon, or stars ; which were adored as gods, not only by the Persians, but also by some idolatrous Jews, because of their brightness and beauty, their lustre and glory. Which of all those famous lamps, and heavenly luminaries, is to be compared to the Father of lights, and Sun of righteousness ? They may glister like glowworms in the night of Paganism, among them who are covered with the mantle of darkness, but when this Sun ariseth, and day appeareth, they all vanish and disappear.

" *Who in the heavens ?* " *i.e.,* say others, in the heaven of heavens, the highest, the third heavens, among the celestial spirits, cherubims and seraphims, angels and archangels, principalities and powers, thrones and dominions ? Who among the innumerable company of angels ? who among those pure, those perfect spirits, who are the ancientest, the honourablest house of the creation, is to be compared to the Father of Spirits.—*George Swinnock.*

Verse 6.—" *Who can be compared ?* " The Dutch have translated these words, " Who can be shadowed with him ? " that is, they are not worthy to be accounted shadows unto such a comparison with him.—*Thomas Goodwin.*

Verse 6.—" *Who among the sons of the mighty.*" Literally, " *Who is he among the sons of* " Alim (or of Gods, as in Ps. xxix. 1), *i.e.,* according to Suicer, the powerful, the princes of the earth.—*Daniel Cresswell.*

Verse 7.—" *God is greatly to be feared.*" Ainsworth reads, " God is daunting terrible." The original word is נַעֲרָץ, from עָרַץ, *arats, he was broken, bruised, terrified.* " An epithet of God," says Bythner, " as though breaking all things."—*Editorial Note to Calvin in loc.*

Verse 7.—" *God is greatly to be feared.*" The worship of God is to be performed with great fear and reverence ; " *God is greatly to be feared.*" Piscator translates it, *Vehementer formidandus,* to be vehemently feared ; and opposes it to that formal, careless, trifling, vain spirit, which too often is found in those that approach the Lord in the duties of his worship.—*John Flavel.*

Verse 7.—" *God is greatly to be feared in the assembly of the saints.*" Those saints of his who walk close with him, have a daunting power in their appearance. I appeal to guilty consciences, to apostates, to professors who have secret haunts of wickedness : sometime when you come but into the presence of one who is a truly gracious godly man or woman whom your conscience tells you walks close with God, doth not even the very sight of such an one terrify you ? the very lustre of that holiness you see in such an one strikes upon your conscience. Then you think, such an one walks close with God indeed, but I have basely forsaken the Lord, and have had such a haunt of wickedness, I have brought dreadful guilt upon my soul since I saw him last. Ecclesiastical stories tell us of Basil, when the officers came to apprehend him, he being then exercised in holy duties, that there was such a majesty and lustre came from his countenance, that the officers fell down backward (as they did who came to apprehend Christ), they were not able to lay hold of him. Surely, when the saints shall be raised in their holiness, when every one of them shall have their hearts filled with holiness, it will cause abundance of fear even in all hearts of those that converse with them.—*Jeremiah Burroughs.*

Verse 8.—" *Thy faithfulness round about thee.*" For just as the tyrants of this world move abroad surrounded by impiety, avarice, contempt of God, and pride, as with a body-guard, so God sits on his exalted throne, surrounded with majesty, faithfulness, mercy and equal love to all his people, as with a vesture of gold.— *J. Baptista Folengius.*

Verse 8.—" *Thy faithfulness round about thee.*" Whatever he doth, he is mindful of his faithfulness and covenant, before and behind, and on each side ; he can look no way, but that is in his eye. And though he employ angels, and send them down into the world, and they stand round about him ; yet he hath better harbingers than these—mercy, and truth, and faithfulness, that wait round about him.— *Thomas Goodwin.*

Verse 9.—" *Thou rulest the raging of the sea.*" Surely the Spirit of God would have us to take notice, that though the sea be indeed such a giant, such a monster, as will make a heart of oak shake, or a heart of brass melt, yet what is it to God, but an infant ? he can bind it and lay it to sleep, even as a little child. And if the great sea be in the hand of God as a little child, what is great to God ! and how great is God ! What is strong to God ! and how strong is God ! What or who is too great, or too strong for God to deal with ?—*Joseph Caryl.*

Verse 9.—" *Thou rulest.*" Here under a figure taken from God's providential government, we have an exhibition of the power of God in defeating the efforts of the enemies of his Church. An instance of this, in the literal sense, we have in the appeasing of the storm by our Lord. " And he arose, and rebuked the wind, and said unto the sea, Peace, be still. And the wind ceased, and there was a great calm." Here we see that God reigns over the sea immediately, and alters or modifies the arrangements of nature according to his sovereign pleasure. That which Jesus did on one occasion is constantly done by the God of providence. He has not left the ocean to be disturbed at random by the winds, nor to be kept in peace by the laws of nature. He rules the raging of the sea. He raises the waves, and he stilleth them. This exhibits a continually working providence. And what he does in providence he does also in his kingdom of grace. He suffers the fury of the enemy to swell against his cause, but he stills it at his pleasure.—*Alexander Carson.*

Verse 10.—" *Broken ;*" " *scattered.*" God has more ways than one to deal with his and his church's enemies.—*Matthew Henry.*

Verse 10.—" *Rahab.*" The reason why *Egypt* is expressed in Scripture under this word, ariseth from the two significations of it ; first, it signifies *strength*, for Egypt was a very strong nation, and therefore the Israelites were reproved for going to them for help, and relying upon their strength, which though great in itself, yet should be to them but a broken reed ; secondly, it signifieth *pride*, or *the proud* ; men are usually proud of strength, and *Egypt* being a strong nation, was also a very proud nation.—*Joseph Caryl.*

Verse 11.—" *The heavens are thine, the earth also is thine.*" Therefore we praise thee, therefore we trust in thee, therefore we will not fear what man can do against us.—*Matthew Henry.*

Verse 12.—" *The north and the south thou hast created them,*" etc. The heights of Huttin, commonly fixed on by tradition as the Mount of Beatitudes, appear a little to the west of Tiberias. Over these the graceful top of Mount Tabor is seen, and beyond it the little Hermon, famous for its dews ; and still farther, and apparently higher, the bleak mountains of Gilboa, on which David prayed that there might fall no dew nor rain. A view of the position of Tabor and Hermon from such a situation as that which we now occupied, shewed us how accurately they might be reckoned the " umbilicus terræ "—the central point of the land, and led us to infer that this is the true explanation of the manner in which they are referred to in the 89th Psalm, 12th verse. It is as if the Psalmist had said, North, south, and *all that is between*—or in other words, The whole land from north to south, to its very centre and throughout its very marrow—shall rejoice in thy name.—*R. M. McCheyne.*

Verse 12.—" *Tabor and Hermon.*" These hills, the one to the east and the other to the west, in Canaan, were much frequented by the saints of God. David speaks of the sacred hill of *Hermon*, and compares brotherly-love to the dew of it. Pss. xlii. 6 ; cxxxiii. 3. And *Tabor*, yet more eminent for the memorable spot of Christ's transfiguration, and from whence God the Father proclaimed his perfect love and approbation of Jesus as his dear Son. Well might this hymn, therefore, in allusion to those glorious events, call even the holy hills to rejoice in Jehovah's name, Matt. xvii. 1—5.—*Robert Hawker.*

Verse 13.—" *Strong is thy hand* " ; even thy left hand ; as much as to say *tu polles utraque manu*, thou hast both hands alike powerful.—*John Trapp.*

Verse 14.—" *Justice and judgment are the habitation of thy throne.*" As if the Psalmist had said, " The ornaments with which God is invested, instead of being a robe of purple, a diadem, or a sceptre, are, that he is the righteous and impartial judge of the world, a merciful father, and a faithful protector of his people." Earthly kings, from their having nothing in themselves to procure for them authority, and to give them dignity, are under the necessity of borrowing elsewhere what will invest them therewith ; but God, having in himself all-sufficiency, and standing in no need of any other helps, exhibits to us the splendour of his own image in his righteousness, mercy, and truth.—*John Calvin.*

Verse 14.—" *Justice and judgment are the habitation of thy throne.*" The Holy Ghost alludeth to the thrones of earthly princes, which were underpropped with pillars, as Solomon's throne with lions, 1 Kings xix. 20, that were both a support and an ornament to it. Now, saith the Psalmist, justice and judgment are the pillars upon which God's throne standeth, as Calvin expoundeth it, the robe and diadem, the purple and sceptre, the regalia with which God's throne is adorned.—*George Swinnock.*

Verse 14.—" *Justice and judgment are the habitation of thy throne.*" Jehovah is here exhibited, by the sacred poet, under the character of a Sovereign, and of a Judge, he being presented to our adoring regard as on his *throne ;* the throne of universal empire, and absolute dominion ; as exercising his authority, and executing his laws, with an omnipotent but impartial hand. For " Justice and judgment are the *habitation*," the *preparation*, the *establishment*, or the *basis*, of this throne. Our textual translation is, *habitation ;* the marginal, *establishment ;* the Septuagint, *preparation ;* and, if I mistake not, our best modern interpreters render the original term, *basis* or *foundation ;* which, on the whole, seems most agreeable. The *basis*, then, of Jehovah's government, or that on which it rests, is " *justice and judgment.*" By " *justice,*" I conceive we are to understand the attribute so called ; and, by " *judgment,*" the impartial exercise of that attribute in the Divine administration. So that were not the Most High to administer impartial justice in his moral government, he might be considered, if it be lawful to use the expression, as abdicating his throne.—*Abraham Booth,* 1734—1806.

Verse 14.—" *Justice,*" which defends his subjects, and does every one right. " *Judgment,*" which restrains rebels, and keeps off injuries. " *Mercy,*" which shows compassion, pardons, supports the weak. " *Truth,*" that performs whatsoever he promiseth.—*William Nicholson.*

Verse 14.—" *Mercy and truth shall go before thy face.*" Note, 1. Mercy is said to go before the face of God, because God sends mercy before judgment, that he might find less to punish : so Bellarmine. 2. That God permits not his face to be seen before he has forgiven our sins through mercy : so Rickelius. 3. That no one comes to the knowledge of God, but he who has obtained mercy beforehand. 4. That

God comes to no one unless His grace go before Him. . . . . . . Truth goes before the face of God, because God keeps it ever before his eyes, to mould his actions thereby. Pindar calls truth θυγατερα Διος the daughter of God. Epaminondas the Theban general, cultivated truth so studiously, that he is reported never to have spoken a falsehood even in jest. In the courts of kings this is a rare virtue.—*Le Blanc.*

Verse 14.—" Mercy and truth."   Mercy in promising ; *truth* in performing. *Truth*, in being as good as thy word ; *mercy*, in being better.—*Matthew Henry.*

Verse 14.—" Shall go." In his *active going forth*, tender mercy and goodness announce him, and faithful truth will tell his people he is there when he comes forth. His activities are mercy and faithfulness, because his will is at work and his nature is love. Yet his throne still maintains justice and judgment.—*J. N. Darby.*

Verse 15.—" Blessed is the people that know the joyful sound." Not that *hear ;* for then the blessing were cheap indeed. Thousands *hear* the Gospel sound, but sometimes not ten of a thousand know it.—*Thomas James Judkin,* 1841.

Verse 15.—" Blessed is the people that know the joyful sound "—viz., of the trumpets sounded in token of joy at the great festivals, and chiefly on the first day of the seventh month, the feast of trumpets (Lev. xxiii. 24), and on extraordinary occasions, especially after the yearly atonement, on the day of jubilee, the tenth day of the seventh month of the fiftieth year, proclaiming liberty to bondmen, and restoration of their inheritance to them that had forfeited it (Lev. xxv. 8—10). As the jubilee joy did not come till after the atonement, so no Gospel joy and liberty are ours till first we know Christ as our atonement. " In the day of the people's gladness " they blew the trumpets over their sacrifices, " that they might be to them for a memorial before God " (Num. x. 10). David and Israel brought up the ark of the Lord to Zion " with shouting, and with the sound of the trumpet " (2 Sam. vi. 15). In Num. xxiii. 21, Balaam makes it the distinguishing glory of Israel, " The Lord his God is with him, and the shout of a king is among them," (Compare Ps. xcviii. 6 ; xxvii. 6. *margin*).—*A. R. Fausset.*

Verse 15.—" People that know the joyful sound." Here it is supposed that we have intelligence in respect of " *the joyful sound."* For there is knowledge not merely of the utterances and intonations, but of the sense and substance, of the thought and feeling, which they convey. And I suppose this to be the meaning of Christ when he says, " My sheep hear my voice, and they follow me ; and a stranger will they not follow, for they know not the voice of strangers." And I have often been surprised, to note the accuracy with which persons otherwise not very intelligent, not largely informed, not of critical acumen, will yet, when they hear a discourse, judge, discriminate, determine ; will be able to say at once—" Truth, clear, unmixed, without a cloud upon it ; " or—" Doctrine clouded, statements confused, not the lucid Gospel ; " or be able to say, if it be so—" No Gospel at all ; contradiction to the truth of Christ." They " *Know the joyful sound,"* as it rolls from the plentitude of God's own voice and bosom, in his august and blessed revelations ; as it is confirmed, authenticated and sealed by the precious blood of our Lord and Saviour Jesus Christ ; as it is witnessed to by the eternal Spirit ; " the joyful sound," that there is salvation for lost and ruined men by faith in the blood and in the obedience of him who died upon the tree, and is now enthroned in the highest place in heaven.— *James Stratten,* 1845.

Verse 15.—" They shall walk in the light of thy countenance." Surely, next to the love of God's heart, believers value the smiles of his face ; from which, as from the agency of the sun, arise the buddings of conscious joy, the leaves of unsullied profession, the variegated blossom of holy tempers, and the beneficent fruits of moral righteousness. They are totally mistaken who suppose that " *the light of God's countenance,"* and the privileges of the gospel, and the comforts of the Spirit, conduce to make us indolent and unactive in the way of duty. The text cuts up this surmise by the roots. For, it does not say, they shall *sit down* in the light of thy countenance ; or, they shall *lie down* in the light of thy countenance ; but " *they shall* WALK in the light of thy countenance." What is walking ? It is a progressive motion from one point of space to another. And what is that holy walking which God's Spirit enables all his people to observe ? It is a continued, progressive motion from sin to holiness ; from all that is evil, to every good word and work. And the self-same " light of God's countenance " in which you, O believer, are enabled to walk, and which at first gave you spiritual feet wherewith to walk, will keep you in a walking and in a working state, to the end of your warfare.—*Augustus Montague Toplady.*

Verse 15.—There is the dreadful and there is the joyful sound. The dreadful sound was at Mount Sinai. The joyful sound is from Mount Sion. When the people heard the former they were far from beholding the glory of God's face. Moses only was admitted to see his "back-parts;" the people were kept at a distance, and the light of God's glory that they saw was so terrible to them, that they could not abide it. But they that know the "joyful sound," they shall be admitted near, nearer than Moses, so as to see the glory of God's face or brightness of his countenance, and that not only transiently, as Moses saw God's back-parts, but continually. The light of God's glory shall not be terrible to them, but easy and sweet, so that they may dwell in it and walk in it ; and it shall be to them instead of the light of the sun ; for the sun shall no more be their light by day, nor the moon by night, but God shall be their everlasting light. Compare this with Isa. ii. 5, and Rev. xxi. 23, 24 and xxii. 4, 5.—*Jonathan Edwards.*

Verse 16.—"*And in thy righteousness shall they be exalted.*" In these words briefly we may notice, 1. The believer's promotion ; he is "*exalted.*" In the first Adam we were debased unto the lowest hell, the crown having fallen from our heads ; but in Christ, the second Adam, we are again exalted ; yea, exalted as high as heaven, for we "sit together with him in heavenly places," says the apostle. This is an incredible paradox to a blind world, that the believer who is sitting at this moment upon the dunghill of this earth, should at the same time be sitting in heaven in Christ, his glorious Head and representative, Eph. ii. 6. 2. We have the ground of the believer's preferment and exaltation ; it is "*in thy righteousness.*" It is not in any righteousness of his own ; no, this he utterly disclaims, reckoning it but "dung and loss," "filthy rags," dogs' meat : but it is in *thy* righteousness ; that is, the righteousness of God, as the apostle calls it : Rom. i. 17, Phil. iii. 9. The righteousness of God is variously taken in Scripture. Sometimes for the infinite rectitude and equity of his nature : Ps. xi. 7, "The righteous Lord loveth righteousness." Sometimes for his rectoral equity, or distributive justice which he exerciseth in the government of the world, rewarding the good and punishing evil-doers : Ps. xcvii. 2, "Righteousness and judgment are the habitation of his throne." Sometimes it is put for his veracity and faithfulness in accomplishing his word of promise, or in executing his word of threatening : Ps. xxxvi. 5, 6, "Thy faithfulness reacheth unto the clouds : thy righteousness is like the great mountains." Sometimes it is put for the perfect righteousness which Christ the Son of God, as our Surety and Mediator, brought in, by his obedience to the law, and death on the cross, for the justification of guilty sinners : and this as I said, is frequently called the righteousness of God ; and in this sense I understand it here in the text : "*In thy righteousness shall they be exalted.*"—*Ebenezer Erskine.*

Verse 17.—"*In thy favour our horn shall be exalted.*" A man of lofty bearing is said to carry his horn very high. To him who is proudly interfering with the affairs of another it will be said, "Why show your *kombu,*" "horn," "here ?" "See that fellow, what a fine horn he has ; he will make the people run." "Truly, my lord, you have a great horn." "Chinnan has lost his money ; ay, and his hornship too." "Alas ! alas ! I am like the deer, whose horns have fallen off."—*Joseph Roberts' "Oriental Illustrations."*

Verse 19 (*second clause*).—[New Translation] "*A mighty chief have I supplied with help.*" Literally, "I have equalized help," that is, I have laid or given sufficient help, "upon a mighty one." The verb denotes "to equalize," or "make one thing equal or equiponderant to another," as a means to the end, or vice versa.—*Richard Mant.*

Verse 19.—"*Chosen*" has here its strict sense, but not without allusion to its specific use as signifying a young warrior.—*J. A. Alexander.*

Verse 20.—"*With my holy oil have I anointed him.*" As the literal David was thrice anointed king, once by Samuel in Jesse's house at Bethlehem ; once at Hebron, after the death of Saul, as king over Judah ; and again at seven years' end, as ruler over all Israel : so also "God anointed Jesus of Nazareth with the Holy Ghost and with power" in his nativity at Bethlehem ; a second time over his Church at his resurrection, when the tyrant who sought his life was overcome, and then only over the small " confederation " (which *Hebron* means) of his Jewish disciples ; but a third time in his ascension to the heavenly Jerusalem, the Vision of Peace, where he, now crowned as King of Glory, was anointed over all heaven and earth, supreme over all the princes of God. He was thrice anointed in another sense also, once as Prophet, once as Priest, and once as King.—*Neale and Littledale.*

Verses 20—24.—" *I have* FOUND *David,*" God exclaims. When sin brought death into the world, and annihilated the hopes of mankind from the first covenant, I—the Almighty—in my care for them, *sought out* a Redeemer. I sought for him in the Divine Nature ; and I " *found* " him in my Only Son. I endowed him with ample powers, and I covenanted that, in the weakness of his Incarnation, " *my hand* " and " *arm* " should " *strengthen* " him. I declared that Satan " *the enemy* " should " *not exact upon him ;* " nor should Judas—" the son of wickedness "—be enabled to " *afflict him.*" The Jews, " *his foes,*" shall fall before him ; they shall be " *smitten down* " in their rejection of him ; they shall perish from off their land, and be dispersed abroad among the nations. My " *truth*" shall be ever with him ; and acting in my " *name* " and power, he shall be exalted and glorified amongst men.— *William Hill Tucker.*

Verse 22.—" *The enemy shall not exact upon him.*" The allusion appears to us to be made to a cruel and unjust creditor, who exacts not only his just debts, but some exaggerated demand, with usurious interest, which was not permitted.—*Williams, quoted by Ed. of Calvin.*

Verse 25.—" *I will set his hand also in the sea, and his right hand in the rivers.*" That is, he should reign from the Mediterranean to the Euphrates ; figuratively expressed by his left hand being extended to the sea, and his right hand to the rivers. A similar expression is used, according to Curtius, by the Scythian ambassadors to Alexander. " If," said they, " the gods had given thee a body as great as thy mind, the whole world would not be able to contain thee. Thou wouldst reach with one hand to the east, and with the other to the west."—*Kitto's Pictorial Bible.*

Verse 25.—" *I will set his hand also in the sea, and his right hand in the rivers.*" A certain artist was in the habit of saying that he should represent Alexander in such a manner, that in one hand he should hold a city and from the other pour a river. Christ is represented here as of immense stature, higher than all mountains, with one hand holding the earth, and the other the sea, while from Eastern sea to Western he extends his arms.—*Le Blanc.*

Verse 26.—" *He shall cry unto me, Thou art my father.*" When did David call God his Father ? It is striking that we do not find anywhere in the Old Testament that the patriarchs or prophets called God their Father. You do not find them addressing him as Father : they did not know him as such. This verse is unintelligible in reference to David ; but in regard to the True David it is exactly what he did say, —" My Father, and your Father ; my God, and your God." Never until Christ uttered these words, never until he appeared on earth in humanity as the Son of God, did any man or any child of humanity address God in this endearing character. It was after Christ said, " I ascend unto my Father, and your Father," that believers were enabled to look up to God and to say, " Abba, Father." Here you see distinctly that this applies to Christ. He was the first to say this : David did not say it. If there were no other proof in the whole Psalm, that one clause would be a demonstration to me that no other man than the Lord Jesus Christ can be here spoken of.—*Capel Molyneux,* 1855.

Verse 26.—" *My Father.*" Christ commenced his labours by referring to his Father, for in Luke ii. he says, " Wist ye not that I must be about my Father's business ? " and his last words were, " Father, into thy hands I commend my spirit ; " and through his whole life he most constantly addressed God as his Father. " *He shall cry unto me : Thou art my Father,*" as far as my divinity is concerned. " *My God,*" as far as my humanity is concerned ; " *the support of my salvation,*" as regards my mortality.—*Bellarmine.*

Verses 26—28. Christ had a command to be a sufferer, and a body prepared him for that purpose ; so he had likewise a command to be an advocate, and a life given him, and a throne prepared for him at the right hand of God to that end. This commission is contained in the words before us ; and this after his exaltation, ver. 24, 25. Yet for the full completing of it, ver. 27, the matter of the plea is there mentioned, " *Thou art the rock of my salvation*," the foundation, the first cause, of all thy salvation I have wrought in the world, being the first mover of it, and promising the acceptance of me in the performance of what was necessary for it. As he hath authority to cry to God, so he hath an assurance of the prevalency of his cry, in regard of the stability of the covenant of mediation, which shall stand fast with him, or be faithful to him ; " *my mercy will I keep for him for evermore*," ver. 28. The treasures of my mercy are reserved only to be opened and dispensed by him ; and the enjoying of his spiritual seed for ever, and the establishing of his own throne thereby, is the promised fruit of this cry, ver. 28.—*Stephen Charnock.*

Verse 27.—" *I will make him my first-born.*" First, because he is first in the order of predestination ; for it is through him, as through the head, that we are predestinated, as we read in Ephes. i. Secondly, because he is first in the second generation to life everlasting, whence he is called (Colos. i.) " *the firstborn from the dead* " ; and in Rev. i., " *the first-begotten of the dead* " ; and, thirdly, because he had the rights of the first-born ; for " *he was appointed heir of all things* " ; and he was made not only first-born, but also, " *high above the kings of the earth*" ; that is, Prince of the kings of the earth, and King of kings.—*Bellarmine.*

Verse 27.—" *Also I will make him my first-born, higher than the kings of the earth.*" This promise plainly implies superiority of a nature similar to what was enjoyed of old by the eldest son of a family—the birth-right privileges and blessings, which consisted principally in three important particulars : First, A double portion of the parent's earthly possessions, Deut. xxi. 17 ; Secondly, Rule or authority over the younger branches of the family, 2 Chron. xxi. 3 ; and, Thirdly, The exercise of the priesthood, because God claimed all the first-born as his, and in their stead he appointed the Levites to do the priest's office, Numb. viii. 14—17. But, whilst it is literally true that Jesus was the first-born son of his virgin mother, and on that account entitled to the customary privileges, the promise in the 89th Psalm gives intimation of something specific and unusual. David was the youngest son of Jesse, the lowest on the list of a numerous family,—the very last individual among them who could have expected exaltation over all others. But, notwithstanding these natural disadvantages, he was God's choice ; and by referring to the Scripture history it would be easy to show, in a variety of particulars, how the promise made to David, " *I will make him my first-born*," was literally and remarkably fulfilled in the son of Jesse. In like manner Jesus, to all human appearance, entering the world as heir-apparent only to the poverty of Mary and her espoused husband, was far removed from every prospect of realizing that combination of royal and sacerdotal prerogative, which nevertheless was made sure to him by the promise of his heavenly Father : " I will make him *my* first-born." The pronoun " *my* " gives great emphasis to the promise, but this word is interpolated ; and however truly it conveys an idea of the unspeakable superiority which belongs to Jesus Christ as the result of his relationship with God, still we shall find that, even without this important pronoun, the promise simply of being " *first-born* " has a sublimity and grandeur about it which needs neither ornament nor addition. The great Jehovah, the Maker and the Owner and the Ruler of the universe, hath said respecting his Christ, " I will make him my first-born " ; that is, I will constitute him the chief of all creatures, and the depository of all power, and the possessor of all privileges, and the heir of all creation. By way of excellence, *he* is *the* first-born, " higher than all the kings of the earth,"—enjoying priority in point of time, and precedence in point of place.—*David Pitcairn, in " The Anointed Saviour,"* 1846.

Verse 27.—" *My firstborn.*" In the Hebrew idiom all kings were *the sons of God :* but David is the chief of these, God's *first-born.* The Greeks had a similar mode of expressing themselves. Kings were the nurslings of Jupiter.—*Alexander Geddes.*

Verse 28.—" *My mercy will I keep for him for evermore.*" How will he keep his mercy for Christ for evermore ? Very simply, I think. Is not Christ the Fountain of all mercy to us ? Is it not the mercy of God the Father flowing to us through Christ that we enjoy ? Is he not the Depository of it all ? God says, then, I will keep it for him ; for ever and ever shall it be lodged in Christ, and his people shall enjoy it throughout eternity.—*Capel Molyneux.*

Verses 28—30.—Here is comfort to those who are true branches, and continue to bring forth fruit in the midst of all the trials that befall them, that God will not suffer them to be cut off by their corruption. If anything in them should provoke God to do it, it must be sin. Now for that, you see how Christ promiseth that God will take order therewith, and will purge it out of them. This is the covenant made with David (as he was a type of Christ, with whom the same covenant is made sure and firm), that " *if his seed forsake my law, and walk not in my judgments,*"—What ! presently turn them out of doors, and cut them off, as those he meant to have no more to do with ? What ! nothing but utter rejection ? Is there no means of reclaiming them ? Never a rod in the house ? Yes—" *then will I visit their transgression with the rod, and their iniquity with stripes,*" whip out their stubbornness and sinfulness ; " *but my lovingkindness will I not utterly take from him* " as I did from Saul, as it is in 1 Chron. xvii. 13.

Let the saints consider this, that they may return when they are fallen, and submit to him and his nature, and suffer him to do what he will with them, and endure cutting, and lancing, and burning, so long as he cuts them not off ; endure chastening, and all his dealings else, knowing that all the fruit is but to take away the sin, to make them " partakers of his holiness ; " and " if by any means," as Paul speaks of himself (Phil. iii. 11), be the means what it will, it is no matter. And God, if at any time he seems to cut thee off, yet it is but as the incestuous Corinthian was cut off, that ' the flesh might be destroyed, and the spirit saved.'—*Thomas Goodwin.*

Verse 29.—" *His seed* " and " *throne* " are coupled together, as if his *throne* could not stand if his *seed* did fail. If his subjects should perish, what would he be king of ? If his members should consume, what would he be head of ?—*Stephen Charnock.*

Verse 30.—" *If his children forsake my law.*" An objection is supposed : ' Suppose this seed who are included in the covenant fall into transgression, how shall the covenant stand fast then ? ' The covenant, with the seed, shall stand for ever, but the seed must be a holy seed. Then the objector supposes—' Suppose the seed become unholy ? ' Well, God explains—" If his children forsake my law, and walk not in my judgments "—that is, if the seed practically fall away—" If they break my statutes, and keep not my commandments ; then will I visit their transgression with the rod, and their iniquity with stripes. Nevertheless my lovingkindness will I not take from him, nor suffer my faithfulness to fail." Mark the case. What is it that God will do ? The case supposed is that the seed of Christ forsakes the law and breaks his statutes. I need not say to you that that is realized every day. These are not the ungodly or the unconverted that are spoken of, but God's own children. Do you say, ' Can they be guilty of breaking God's statutes, and forsaking God's law ? ' We do it every day. There is no single day of our lives that we do not do it. . . .

How astonished many would be, if they knew what the real case was of those perhaps whom they admire, and think highly advanced and exalted in the Divine life, if they were to know the falls, the wretched falls, falls in heart, in word and in practice ; if they were to know the deep distress that the children of God, who are far advanced as they suppose in the Divine life, are continually suffering from the effect of such transgression ! That is exactly what God says ; he comes and contemplates such a case, and he says, " If they break my statutes, and keep not my commandments, then "—what ? What will God do ? Some people say, " Then God will leave them." Those who object to the doctrine of final perseverance say this : " It is true he will preserve the believer from the toils of the Devil and the temptations of the world, but not from the breaking forth of his own natural evil. He may be betrayed by that, and finally lost." God exactly meets that case ; he contemplates the worst case—actual transgression. He says, " If a child of mine breaks my law." He does not say anything about the Devil, or the outward temptations of the world ; but he says, " If they forsake my law and break my statutes." Let us be instructed by God. He does not say he will leave them and forsake them. Mark what he will do ! He says—" I will visit their transgression with the rod, and their iniquity with stripes." That is the provision which God has made in his covenant : and it is delightful to see how God has contemplated our case to the uttermost. There is nothing in our history that God has not met in the covenant with Christ. If you are in union with Christ, and a partaker of the covenant, your case is met in every conceivable emergency. Nothing can befall you which is not contemplated— nothing which God has not provided for. Even if you fall, God has provided for it ; but take heed ; the provision involves much that will be terrible and desperately painful to your mind. There is nothing to encourage sin about it ; there is nothing to give us license, nothing to lead a man to boast, " I am safe at last." Be it so : but safe how ? How will God secure their safety ? " I will visit their transgression with the rod, and their iniquity with stripes."—*Capel Molyneux.*

Verse 30.—" *If his children forsake my law.*" If they fall into sins of commission ; if they shoot beyond the mark. " *And walk not in my judgments.*" If they fall into sins of omission, and shoot short. Where note that " *every transgression and disobedience* (that is, every commission and omission) *receiveth a just recompence of reward,*" Heb. ii. 2.—*John Trapp.*

Verse 30.—" *His children,*" בָּנָיו, *his sons, i.e.* Christians, born through the griefs of Christ on the cross, like the pangs of one in travail.—*Geier.*

Verse 30.—A man may forsake the doctrines of the Gospel. He may fall into great errors, great aberrations from Truth ; he may forsake the ordinances of the Lord's house, though he sees God's word is clear upon the point. He esteems those things as nothing worth, which the Lord esteems so well, that he has given them to his church as a sacred deposit, which she is to convey down to the latest posterity till time shall be no more. And what is still more—a man may forsake for a time the principles of the precious Gospel of the living God. But I can imagine a state still more solemnly affecting than even this. It is a part of God's wisdom, (and it is for our good that it is so—all God's wisdom is for his people's good)—it is a part of the wisdom of God, that sin should lead to sin ; that one neglect shall pave the way to another ; that that which is bad shall lead to that which is worse, and that which is worse shall prepare the way for that which is worst. . . . . The longer I live, the more I am brought to this—to know that there is not a sin that ever was committed, but I need the grace of God to keep me from it.—*James Harrington Evans.*

Verses 30—34.—God here says two things ; first, that he will chastise them, next, that he will not, on that account, cast them out of his covenant. O wonderful tempering of the kindness and severity of God ! in which he finds his own glory, and believers their safety ! The heavenly Father loves the blood and the marks of his Christ which he sees upon them, and the remains of faith and godliness which are preserved hidden in the depth of their heart ; this is why he will not cast them off. On the other hand, he considers that it accords neither with his wisdom nor his holiness to bestow his grace and salvation upon those who do not repent for having cast off his law and given themselves up to iniquity. In order to harmonize these opposite desires, he takes the rod, and chastises them, to arouse their conscience, and to excite their faith ; to restore them, by the repentance which his discipline produces, to such a state, as that he may be able to bestow upon them, without shame, the blessings he has promised to the children of his Son ; just as a wise parent, by moderate and judicious correction gradually draws back his son from those irregularities of life into which he has plunged ; and thereby preserves his honour, and himself the pleasure of being able to love and please him without misgiving. Or, as a skilful surgeon, by the pain which his knife, or cautery, or bitter potions, cause his patient, saves his life, and wards off death.—*Jean Daillé.*

Verses 30—34.—When our heavenly Father is, as it were, forced to put forth his anger, he then makes use of a father's rod, not an executioner's axe. He will neither break his children's bones, nor his own covenant. He lashes in love, in measure, in pity, and compassion.—*Thomas Lye,* 1621—1684.

Verse 32.—" *Then will I visit their transgression with the rod,*" etc. He does not simply say, I will smite them ; but, I will visit with the rod. It is one thing merely to smite, it is another thing to smite by visiting. For visitation implies oversight and paternal care. The metaphor is taken from those who undertake to watch over the sick, or train up children, or tend sheep. He does not say, I will visit *them* with the rod ; but, I will visit *their transgression* with the rod. We ought to think perpetually, what it is the rod of God visits in us, that we may confess our transgressions, and amend our lives.—*Musculus.*

Verse 33.—" *Nevertheless my lovingkindness,*" etc. Except the covenant of grace had this article in it for remission of sin and for fatherly correction, to drive unto repentance, that the penitent person coming to God by faith might have sin forgiven him and lovingkindness shown to him ; this covenant should fail us no less than the covenant of works.—*David Dickson.*

Verse 33.—" *I will not utterly take from him.*" Why " from *him*" ? Because all

God's lovingkindness to his people is centred in Christ. Does God love you ? it is because he loves Christ ; you are one with Christ. Your transgressions are your own ; they are separate from Christ ; but God's love is not your own ; it is Christ's : you receive it because you are one with him. How beautifully that is distinguished here—" If they transgress, I will punish *them* ; but my lovingkindness will I not take from *him* "—in whom alone they find it ; and in union with whom alone they enjoy it.— *Capel Molyneux.*

Verse 33.—" *From him.*" The words, " *Nevertheless my lovingkindness will I not utterly take from him,*" are worthy of consideration ; for the question being about those who are chastised, it would appear that he should have written, from *them*, and not from *him*. But the prophet has thus worded it, because, being the children and members of his Christ, the favours which God bestows upon us belong to him in some manner ; and it seems that the Psalmist wishes to show us hereby, that it is in Jesus Christ, and for love of him alone, that God bestows favours on us. And that which follows, in the 34th verse, agrees herewith,—" *My covenant will I not break*"—for it is properly to Jesus Christ, on account of his admirable obedience, that God the Father has promised to be merciful to our iniquities, and never to leave one of those to perish who are in covenant with him.—*Jean Daillé.*

Verse 33.—" *Nor suffer my faithfulness to fail.*" Man's faith may fail him sometimes, but God's faithfulness never fails him : *God will not suffer his faithfulness to fail.* God's operations may have an aspect that way ; the devil's temptations, and our unbelieving hearts, may not only make us think so, but persuade us it is so, whereas it cannot be so, for the Lord will not suffer it, he will not make a lie in his truth or faithfulness ; so the Hebrew is : he is a God that cannot lie, he is Truth, speaks truth, and not one of his promises can or shall fail ; which may afford strong consolation unto all that are under any promise of God.—*William Greenhill.*

Verse 34.—" *My covenant will I not break.*" He had said above, " *If the children of David break my statutes ;* " and now, alluding to that breach, he declares that he will not requite them as they requite him, "*. My covenant will I not break*," implying, that although his people may not altogether act in a manner corresponding to their vocation, as they ought to do, he will not suffer his covenant to be broken and disannulled on account of their fault, because he will promptly and effectually prevent this in the way of blotting out their sins by a gratuitous pardon.—*John Calvin.*

Verse 35.—" *Once have I sworn by my holiness.*" He lays here his holiness to pledge for the assurance of his promise, as the attribute most dear to him, most valued by him, as though no other could give an assurance parallel to it, in this concern of an everlasting redemption, which is there spoken of. He that swears, swears by a greater than himself. God having no greater than himself, swears by himself ; and swearing here by his holiness seems to equal that single to all his other attributes, as if he were more concerned in the honour of it than of all the rest. It is as if he should have said, Since I have not a more excellent perfection to swear by than that of my holiness, I lay this to pawn for your security, and bind myself by that which I will never part with, were it possible for me to be stripped of all the rest. It is a tacit imprecation of himself, If I lie unto David, let me never be counted holy, or thought righteous enough to be trusted by angels or men. This attribute he makes most of.— *Stephen Charnock.*

Verse 36.—" *His seed shall endure for ever.*" They shall continue for ever in three senses. *First.* In the succession of their race to the end of the world. It will never be cut off.—" The Church is in danger ! " *What* Church ? " Upon this rock," says he, " I will build *my* Church ; and the gates of hell shall not prevail against it." Yea, his people shall continue to increase in number and excellency. We shall leave the world better than we entered it : and so will our *children ;* till Jerusalem shall be established, and be made a praise in the whole earth. *Secondly.* In their religious character to the end of their own life. If left to themselves, we could not be sure of their persevering to the end of a day or an hour. But they are kept by the power of God, through faith, unto salvation. He upholdeth them with his hand. They shall hold on their way. In all their dangers they shall be more than conquerors. *Thirdly.* In their glorified state, through eternal ages. The world passeth away, and the lusts thereof ; but he that doeth the will of God abideth for ever. All other greatness is only for life : it is frequently less durable—at death it *ends.* But *then*, the Christian's greatness—I will not say, begins ; for it began the moment he prayed —but then it continues, increases, and is perfected.—*William Jay*.

Verse 37.—" *It shall be established for ever as the moon.*" This clause Kimchi expounds not only of the perpetuity, but of the quality and condition of David's Kingdom, after this fashion : If his children be good, they shall be like the moon, when full and shining ; if bad, like the moon waning and obscure. Nevertheless the kingdom itself shall not cease, just as the moon does not go out of existence, whilst it is obscure, but lasts perpetually.—*Musculus*.

Verse 37.—" *And as a faithful witness in heaven.*" [New Translation] " *And as the rainbow's faithful sign.*" The rainbow is not expressly mentioned in the original, which speaks only of " the faithful witness in heaven." Some commentators understand the " witness " thus mentioned to be no other than the moon itself. I prefer however the interpretation that fixes it on the rainbow, which God after the deluge appointed as a " sign " or "witness " of his mercy in Christ. Gen. ix. 12—17. Conformably to this appointment, the Jews, when they behold the rainbow, are said to bless God, who remembers his covenant and is faithful to his promise. And the tradition of this its designation to proclaim comfort to mankind was strong among the heathens : for, according to the mythology of the Greeks, the " rainbow " was the daughter of " wonder," " a sign to mortal men," and regarded, upon its appearance, as a messenger of the celestial deities. Thus Homer with remarkable conformity to the Scripture account speaks of the " rainbow." which " Jove hath set in the cloud, a sign to men."—*Richard Mant*.

Verse 38.—" *But thou hast cast off,*" etc. The complainings of the saints mean-while are so exaggerated, that carnal feeling makes itself more apparent in them, than faith . . . . Yet such is the goodness of God, he is not offended with these complaints, provided faith is not altogether extinguished, or succumbs.—*Mollerus*.

Verse 39.—" *Thou hast profaned his crown,*" etc. The *crown* of a king (like that of the high priest, on which was inscribed " holiness to the Lord ") (Exod. xxviii. 36) was a sacred thing, and therefore to cast it in the dust was to *profane* it.—*A. R. Fausset*.

Verse 40.—" *Hedges* " and " *strong holds.*" Both of these may refer to the appointments of a vineyard in which the king was the vine. It was usually fenced around with a stone wall, and in it was a small house or tower, wherein a keeper was set to keep away intruders. When the wall, or hedge, was thrown down, every passer by plucked at the fruit, and when the tower was gone the vineyard was left open to the neighbours who could do as they would with the vines. When the church is no longer separated from the world, and her divine Keeper has no more a dwelling-place within her, her plight is wretched indeed.—*C. H. S.*

Verse 43.—" *Thou hast also turned the edge of his sword,*" etc. The arms and military prowess of thy people are no longer of any use to them ; THOU art *against* them, and therefore they are fallen. In what a perilous and hopeless situation must that soldier be who, defending his life against his mortal foe, has his sword *broken*, or its *edge turned ;* or, in modern warfare, whose *gun misses fire !* The *Gauls*, when invaded by the Romans, had no method of *hardening iron ;* at every blow their swords *bended*, so that they were obliged, before they could strike again, to put them under their foot or over their knee, to straighten them ; and in most cases, before this could be done, their better armed foe had taken away their life ! The edge of their sword was turned, so that they could not stand in battle ; and hence the *Gauls* were conquered by the Romans.—*Adam Clarke*.

Verse 43.—" *Thou hast also turned the edge of his sword,*" that it cannot do execu-tion as it has done ; and what is worse, thou hast " turned the edge " of his spirit, and taken off his courage, and hast not made him " to *stand*," as he used to do, " *in the day of battle.*" The spirit of men is what the Father and Former of spirits makes them ; nor can we stand with any strength or resolution, farther than God is pleased to uphold us. If men's hearts fail them, it is God that dispirits them ; but it is sad with the church when those cannot stand that should stand up for it.—*Matthew Henry*.

Verse 45.—" *The days of his youth hast thou shortened.*" Our kings have not reigned half their days, nor lived out half their lives. The *four* last kings of Judea reigned but a short time, and either died by the sword or in captivity. *Jehoahaz* reigned only *three months*, and was led captive to Egypt, where he *died*. *Jehoiakim* reigned only *eleven years*, and was tributary to the Chaldeans, who *put him to death*, and cast his body into the common sewer. *Jehoiachim* reigned *three months and ten days*, and was led *captive* to Babylon, where he continued in prison to the time of Evil-merodach, who, though he loosed him from prison, never invested him with any power. *Zedekiah*, the last of all, had reigned only *eleven years* when he was taken, *his eyes put out*, was *loaded with chains*, and thus carried to Babylon. Most of these kings died a violent and *premature* death. Thus the " *days of their youth* "—of their power, dignity, and life, " *were shortened*," and they themselves " *covered with shame*." " *Selah;* " so it most incontestably is.—*Adam Clarke*.

Verse 45.—" *Thou hast covered him with shame. Selah*." Thou hast wrapped him up in the winding-sheet of shame. Lord, this is true.—*John Trapp*.

Verses 46, 47.—This undoubtedly sounds like the voice of one who knows no hereafter. The Psalmist speaks as if all his hopes were bound by the grave ; as if the overthrow of the united kingdom of Judah and Ephraim had bereft him of all his joy ; and as if he knew no future kingdom to compensate him with its hopes. But it would be doing cruel injustice to take him thus at his word. What we hear is the language of passion, not of sedate conviction. This is well expressed by John Howe in a famous sermon. " The expostulation (he observes) was somewhat passionate, and did proceed upon the sudden view of this disconsolate case, very abstractly considered, and by itself only ; and the Psalmist did not, at that instant, look beyond it to a better and more comfortable scene of things. An eye bleared with present sorrow sees not far, nor comprehends so much at one view, as it would at another time, or as it doth presently when the tear is wiped out and its own beams have cleared it up."

It would be unwarrantable, therefore, to infer from Ethan's expostulation, that the saints who lived under the early kings were strangers to the hope of everlasting life. I am inclined to go further, and to point to this very complaint as affording a presumption that there was in their hearts an irrepressible sentiment of immortality. The bird that frets and wounds itself on the bars of its cage shews thereby that its proper home is the free air. When inveterate sensuality has succeeded in quenching in a man's heart the hope of a life beyond the grave, the dreary void which succeeds utters itself, not in solemn complaints like Ethan's, but in songs of forced mirth— dismal Anacreontic songs : " Let us eat and drink for to-morrow we die."

> " 'Tis time to live if I grow old,
> 'Tis time short pleasures now to take,
> Of little life the best to make,
> And manage wisely the last stake." *

—*William Binnie*.

Verse 46.—" *Shall thy wrath burn like fire?* " an element that hath no mercy.— *William Nicholson*.

Verse 47.—" *Wherefore hast thou made all men in vain?* " If I should demand of any, for what cause especially man came into the world ; he would answer with the Psalmist, God did not create man in vain. Did He create man to heap up wealth together ? no, for the apostle saith, " we brought nothing into this world, and it is certain, that we can carry nothing out. And, having food and raiment, let us be therewith content." 1 Tim. vi. 6, 7, 8. Did he create him to hawk after power and principality ? no, for Nebuchadnezzar lusting after these, lost no less than a kingdom. Did he create him to eat, drink and play ? no, for Seneca, though an heathen saith, *major sum*, etc., I am greater, and born to greater things, than that I should be a vile slave of my senses. What then is the proper end of man ? That we should live to the praise of the glory of his grace wherewith he hath made us freely accepted in his Beloved. Eph. i. 6.—*William Pulley*.

Verse 47.—" *Wherefore hast thou made all men in vain?* " If we think that God hath made man " *in vain*," because so many have short lives, and long afflictions in this world, it is true that God " *hath made* " them so ; but it is not true, that therefore they are " made in vain." For those whose days are few and full of trouble, yet may

* Anacreon's *Age*, as translated by Cowley.

glorify God, and do some good, may keep their communion with God, and go to heaven, and then they are not made in vain. If we think that God has made men in vain, because the most of men neither serve him nor enjoy him, it is true, that as to themselves, they were made in vain, better for them they had not been born, than not be " born again " ; but it was not owing to God, that they were made in vain, it was owing to themselves ; nor are they made in vain as to him ; for he has " made all things for himself, even the wicked for the day of evil," and those whom he is not glorified by he will be glorified upon.—*Matthew Henry.*

Verse 47.—*" Wherefore hast thou made all men in vain ? "* When I add to the consideration of my short time, that of dying mankind, and behold a dark and deadly shade universally overspreading the world, the whole species of human creatures vanishing, quitting the stage round about me, and disappearing almost as soon as they show themselves ; have I not a fair and plausible ground for that (seemingly rude) challenge ? Why is there so unaccountable a phenomenon ? such a creature made to no purpose ; the noblest part of this inferior creation brought forth into being without any imaginable design ? I know not how to untie the knot, upon this only view of the case, or avoid the absurdity. It is hard sure to design the supposal, (or what it may yet seem hard to suppose), *" that all men were made in vain."—John Howe.*

Verse 47.—*" Wherefore hast thou made all men in vain ? "* Two thoughts crush us—*Man was made to mourn, and man was made in vain.* Yes, this thought is painfully pressed upon us,—man is " *made in vain !* " In how many particulars, especially when we survey that large range of characters to which we may give the denomination of *wasted lives ;* there to behold peerless *genius* frittering itself away upon unworthy attainments, upon worthless performances ; *imagination* that might adorn truth, if that *were* possible ; *wit*, that might select and discriminate the true from the false ; and *eloquence* that might enforce the true ;—where do we find these ? Unsatisfactory and miserable world, may we well exclaim, where nothing is real, and nothing is realised ; when I consider how our lives are passed in the struggle for existence ; when I consider the worry of life, where it is not a woe—the woe, where it is not a worry ; when I consider how the millions pass their time in a mere toil for sensual objects, and that those to whom the sad contradiction of life never comes, are the most wretched of all, did they but know it ; when I consider the millions of distorted existences ; and the many millions !—the greater number of the world by far— who wander Christless, loveless, hopeless, over the broad highway of it ; when I consider life in many of the awakened as a restless dream, as children beating the curtain and crying in the night ; when I consider how many questions recur for ever to us ; and will not be silenced, and cannot be answered ; when I consider the vanity of the philosopher's inquisitiveness, and the end of Royalty in the tomb ; when I look round on the region of my own joys, and know how short their lease is, and that their very ineffableness is a blight upon them ; when I consider how little the best can do, and that none can do anything well ; and, finally, when I consider the immeasurable immensity of thought within, unfulfilled, and the goading restlessness, I can almost exclaim with our unhappy poet [Byron]—

> " Count all the joys thine hours have seen,
>   Count all thy days from anguish free,
> And know, whatever thou hast been,
>   'Twere something better not to be."

—*E. Paxton Hood, in " Dark Sayings on a Harp,"* 1865.

Verses 47, 48.—In these verses, the fundamental condition of Israel's blessedness is found to be an acknowledgment of the total unprofitableness of the flesh. Resurrection is the basis upon which the sure mercies of David rest availably for faith (Acts xiii. 34). This is rather implied than directly stated in the present Psalm.— *Arthur Pridham.*

Verse 48.—*" What man."* Mi gheber, says the original ; it is not *Ishe*, which is the first name of man, in the scriptures, and signifies nothing but a *sound ;* a voice, a word, a musical air which dies, and evaporates ; what wonder if man, that is but *Ishe*, a *sound*, should die too ? It is not Adam, which is another name of man, and signifies nothing but *red earth ;* let it be earth red with blood, (with that murder which we have done upon ourselves,) let it be earth red with blushing, (so the word is used in the original,) with a conscience of our own infirmity, what wonder if man, that is but Adam, guilty of this self-murder in himself, guilty of this in-born frailty in himself, die too ? It is not *Enos*, which is also a third name of man, and signifies nothing but a *wretched and miserable creature ;* what wonder that man, that is but earth, that is a burden to his neighbours, to his friends, to his kindred, to himself, to whom all others, and to whom myself desires death, what wonder if he die ? But this question is framed upon more of these names ; not *Ishe*, not Adam, not Enos ; but it is *Mi gheber, Quis vir ;* which is the word always signifying a man accomplished in all excellences, a man accompanied with all advantages ; fame, and a good opinion justly conceived, keeps him from being *Ishe*, a mere sound, standing only upon popular acclamation ; innocency and integrity keeps him from being Adam, red earth, from bleeding, or blushing at anything he hath done ; that holy and religious art of arts, which St. Paul professed. *That he knew how to want, and how to abound*, keeps him from being Enos, miserable or wretched in any fortune ; he is *gheber*, a great man, and a good man, a happy man, and a holy man, and yet *Mi gheber, Quis homo*, this man must see death.—*John Donne.*

Verse 48.—This Psalm is one of those twelve that are marked in the forehead with *Maschil ;* that is, *a Psalm giving instruction.* It consisteth of as many verses as the year doth of weeks, and hath, like the year, its summer and winter. The summer part is the former ; wherein, the church having reaped a most rich crop (the best blessings of heaven and earth) the Psalmist breaketh forth into the praises of their gracious Benefactor, " *I will sing of the mercies of the Lord for ever* " : so he beginneth, and so he goeth on a great way. Who now would expect anything but mercies, and singing, and summer all the way ? But summer ceaseth, and winter commenceth, at verse 38 : " *But thou hast cast off and abhorred, thou hast been wroth with thine anointed.*" Mercies and singing are now turned into troubles and mourning. But nothing shall you hear but bitter querimonies and expostulations till you come to the last verse. There the good man's come to himself again. Though God were angry with his people, he cannot part with God in discontent. Though God had laden them with crosses, he lifts up his head, and presents God with blessing ; " *Blessed be the Lord for evermore. Amen, and Amen.*" He blesseth him as well for winter as for summer, for troubles as for mercies. And thus the last verse of the Psalm having as much affinity with the first in matter, as the last day of the year hath with the first in season ; if we circle the Psalm, and bring both ends together, we find a fit resemblance between the year and it.

The text is one of the Psalmist's winter-drops ; a black line from that pen, which erstwhile was so filled with joy, and wrote nothing but rubrics. He complaineth in the next precedent verse, of the brevity of his own life (it was like a winter's day, very short) ; in this, of the instability of man's life ; as though he had said, I am not the only mortal. Other men's lives, though haply clothed with more comforts than mine, are altogether as mortal as mine ; for his interrogations are equivalent to strong negations. As to *see sleep* is to sleep ; so to *see* or *taste death* is to die. There is no surviving such a sight. Death says, as God once to Moses, " There shall no man *see* me *and live.*" Exod. xxxiii. 20.—*Thomas Du-gard, in a Funeral Sermon,* 1648.

Verse 48.—Death spares no *rank*, no *condition* of men. Kings as well as subjects, princes as well as the meanest rustics are liable to this fatal stroke. The lofty cedars and low shrubs ; palaces and cottages are alike here. Indeed, we read that Julius Cæsar bid the master of the ship wherein he was sailing, take courage notwithstanding the boisterous tempest, because he had Cæsar and his fortunes embarked in his vessel, as much as to say, the element on which they then were could not prove fatal to an emperor, to so great a one as he was. Our William surnamed Rufus said, he never heard of a king that was drowned. And Charles the fifth, at the Battle of Tunis, being advised to retire when the great ordnance began to play, told them that it was never known that an emperor was slain with great shot, and so rushed into the battle. But this we are sure of, it was never known or heard that any king or crowned head escaped the blow of death at last. The sceptre cannot keep off ' the arrows that fly by day, and the sickness which wastes at noon-day ; ' it is no screen, no guard against the shafts of death. We have heard of great tyrants and usurpers who vaunted that they had the power of life and death, and as absolutely disposed of men as Domitian did of flies ; but we have heard likewise that in a short time (and generally the shorter the more furious they have been) their sceptres are fallen out of their hands ; their crowns are toppled off their heads, and they are themselves snatched away by the King of Terrors. Or, if we speak of those royal personages that are mild and gentle, and like Vespasian are the darlings and delight of the people, yet these no less than others have their fatal hour, and their regal honour and majesty are laid in the dust. *The King doth not die*, may be a Common-law maxim, but it is a falsehood according to the laws of God and Nature, and the established constitution of heaven. For God himself who hath said, " *Ye are gods*," hath also added, " *Ye shall die like men.*" In the *Escurial* the palace of the Kings of Spain, is their *cemetery* too ; there their royal ashes lie. So in the place where the kings and queens of England are crowned, their predecessors are entombed : to tell them, as it were, that their crowns exempt them not from the grave, and that there is no greatness and splendour that can guard them from the arrest of death. He regards the rich and wealthy no more than the poor and necessitous : he snatches persons out of their mansion-houses and hereditary seats, as well as out of almshouses and hospitals. His dominion is over masters as well as servants, parents as well as children, superiors as well as inferiors.—*John Edwards.*

Verse 48.—

" The boast of heraldry, the pomp of power,
    And all that beauty, all that wealth e'er gave,
Await alike th' inevitable hour—
    The paths of glory lead but to the grave.

" Can storied urn, or animated bust,
    Back to its mansions call the fleeting breath ?
Can Honour's voice provoke the silent dust,
    Or Flatt'ry soothe the dull cold ear of Death ? "

—*Thomas Gray*, 1716—1771.

Verse 50.—" *How I do bear in my bosom the reproach*," etc. I take the reproaches of thy servants and thine anointed, (1) as if they reproached me in mine own particular ; or, (2) in that they lie so heavy upon my heart ; or, (3) in that I am resolved quietly to endure them, and to swallow them down in silence, as not being indeed able to shake them off ; because in the eye of reason our condition is at present so contrary to what we waited for ; or, (4) in that their reproaches came not to his ears by hearsay only, but were openly to his face cast as it were into his bosom.—*Arthur Jackson.*

Verse 50.—" *I do bear in my bosom the reproach*," etc. The reproach of religion and of the godly doth lie near, and should lie near, the heart of every lively member of the church.—*David Dickson.*

Verse 51.—" *They have reproached the footsteps of thine anointed.*" This phrase is obscure in diction, and therefore variously interpreted : 1. Some by the *footsteps of Christ*, judge that his advent in the flesh is meant : others refer the words to David, and take the meaning to be, imitation of him. The first exposition yields this sense : Be mindful, O Lord, of the reproach of thy enemies, wherewith they insult our expectation of thy Anointed, and scoff at his advent as if it would never come. The second interpretation is this : Recollect, O Lord, what contempt thy enemies heap upon us on account of thy servant David, because we fondly cherish his memory and his example, and nourish the hope of thy Covenant with him, clinging tenaciously thereto. . . . Thirdly, this clause may be so interpreted that by עֲקֵבוֹת, that is, the heel, we may understand the extremities of the Kingdom of Christ, of David. Thus we may imagine the enemies of God threw this in the teeth of the people of Israel, that they had already come to the end and extremity of the Kingdom of David.— *Musculus.*

Verse 51 (second clause).—The *Chaldee* has : " They have scoffed at the tardiness of Thy Messiah's footsteps." So *Kimchi :* " He delays so long, they say He will never come." Compare 2 Peter iii. 4, 9. The Arabic *àqaba* is used in the sense of " delaying."—*William Kay.*

Verse 51.—" *The footsteps*," or *foot soles*, that is, the ways, life, actions, and sufferings, Pss. lvi. 6 and xlix. 5. This referred to Christ, respecteth the oracle, Gen. iii. 15, that the Serpent should bruise the foot-sole of the woman's seed ; referred to Christians which follow his footsteps, in suffering and dying with him, that we may be glorified with him (1 Pet. ii. 21 ; Rom. viii. 17) ; it noteth the scandal of the Cross of Christ, " to the Jews a stumbling block, and to the Greeks foolishness." (1 Cor. i.

23 ; 1 Pet. iv. 13, 14.) The Chaldee understands it of the slackness of the footsteps. —*Henry Ainsworth.*

Verse 52.—"*Blessed be the Lord for evermore. Amen, and Amen.*" Victory begins to shine in the phrase, *Blessed be Jehovah for evermore. Amen, and Amen.* Some think that these words are not the words of the Psalmist, because they are of opinion that they do not agree with the preceding, but were written by another, or added by the Collector of the Psalms as a concluding doxology ; or if the Psalmist wrote them, he did so merely in finishing his prayer. But it is a matter of the greatest moment ; for it indicates the victory of faith, since he observes that after that grief, the reproach of the heel is gloriously removed that the Messiah may remain a victor for ever, having bruised the serpent's head, and taken away from him in perpetuity all his power of hurting. That this should certainly take place, he adds the seal of faith again and again : "*Amen, and Amen.*"—*James Alling,* 1618—1679.

Verse 52.—This doxology belongs alike to all the Psalms of the Third Book, and ought not to be treated as if it were merely the last verse of the Psalm to which it adjoins. It ought to be set forth in such a shape as would enable and invite God's people to sing it as a separate formula of praise, or in connection with any other Psalm. —*William Binnie.*

Verse 52.—As to the words *Amen, and Amen,* I readily grant that they are here employed to mark the end of the third book of the Psalms.—*John Calvin.*

HINTS TO PREACHERS.

Verse 1.—I. Mercies celebrated. 1. When ?—"for ever." 2. By whom ?—by those who are the subjects of them. 3. Therefore they must live for ever to celebrate them. II. Faithfulness declared. 1. To our own generation. 2. To succeeding generations by its influence upon others.

Verse 2.—I. The Testimony. 1. To the constancy of Mercy. (1) It builds up its trophies every moment. (2) It preserves them for ever. 2. To the constancy of Faithfulness. It remains as the ordinances of heaven. II. Its Confirmation. "I have said," etc., said it, 1. Upon the ground of Scripture. 2. of experience. 3. of reason. 4. of observation of others.

Verses 3, 4. I. The Covenant made. 1. With whom ?—with David and in him with David's Lord and Son. The true David—the chosen one—the servant of the Father in redemption. 2. For what ?—(1) for his seed. He should have a seed and that seed should be established. (2) for himself, "his throne," etc. II. The Covenant confirmed. 1. By decree. "I have made," etc. 2. By promise. "I will establish." 3. By oath. "I have sworn."

Verse 6.—We have a comparison between God and the most excellent in heaven and earth—challenge both worlds. 1. The true God, sovereign of heaven and earth is incomparably great in his BEING and EXISTENCE ; (1) because his being is of himself *eternal* ; (2) because he is a *perfect* being ; (3) because he is *independent* ; (4) because he is unchangeable. 2. God is incomparably great in his ATTRIBUTES and PERFECTIONS. (1) In his *holiness* ; (2) in his *wisdom* and *knowledge* ; (3) in his *power* ; (4) in his *justice* ; (5) in his patience ; (6) in his *love* and *goodness*. 3. God is incomparably great in his WORKS—creation ; providence ; redemption, and human salvation.— *Theophilus Jones,* 1830.

Verse 6.—The Incomparableness of God, in his Being, Attributes, Works, and Word.—*Swinnock.* [Nichol's Edition of Swinnock's Works, Vol. IV., pp. 373—508.]

Verses 6, 7.—I. In creation God is far above other beings. Verse 6. II. In Redemption he is far above himself in creation. Verse 7.

Verses 9, 10.—God's present rule in the midst of confusion, and rebellion ; and his ultimate overthrow of all adverse forces.

Verse 11.—I. God's possession of heaven, the model of his possession of earth. II. God's possession of earth most certain, and its manifestation in the future most sure. III. The course of action suggested to his people by the two facts.

Verse 12.—The joy of creation in its Creator.

Verse 14.—I. The Equity of the divine government—" justice," etc. No creature can eventually be unjustly dealt with under his dominion, and his kingdom ruleth over all. II. The Sovereignty of the divine government. Truth before mercy. Mercy founded upon truth. " Thou wilt perform the truth to Jacob and the mercy to Abraham." The covenant made in mercy to Abraham is fulfilled in truth to Jacob.

Verse 15.—I. The gospel is a joyful sound. Good tidings, etc. II. It is a joyful sound to those who know it, hear it, believe it, love it, obey it. III. They to whom it is a joyful sound are blessed. " They shall walk," etc.

Verse 15.—1. There is a theoretical knowledge of the gospel. 2. An experimental knowledge, and, 3. A practical knowledge.—*W. Dransfield*, 1859.

Verse 16.—I. Exultation. 1. " In thy name," etc., as rich in mercy as the God of salvation—of all grace—of all consolation. 2. At what season—" all the day," morning, noon, and night. II. Exaltation. " In thy righteousness," etc. 1. How not exalted. Not in their own righteousness. 2. How exalted. " In *thy*," etc. Procured for them—by a divine person (*thy*)—imputed to them. Ours, though thine. The righteousness of God as God could not exalt us, but his righteousness as God-man can. Exalted above hell, above earth, above Paradise, above angels. Exalted to friends of God—children of God—one with God, to heaven.

Verse 16 (*second clause*).—Consider, I. What the believer is exalted *above* or *from*, by God's righteousness. I. It exalts him above the law. 2. Above the world. 3. Above the power and malice of Satan. 4. Above death. 5. Above all accusations (Rom. viii. 33, 34). II. *To* what happiness or dignity the believer is exalted by virtue of that righteousness. 1. To a state of peace and reconciliation with God. 2. To sonship. 3. To fellowship and familiarity with God, and access to him. 4. And finally, to a state of endless glory.—*E. Erskine*.

Verse 17.—I. The blessedness of the righteous. 1. Their internal glory. Reliance upon divine strength. 2. Their internal honour. " In thy favour," etc. II. The participation in that blessedness. The *their* of the people of God becomes *our*. Their strength our horn. Happy they, who, with respect to all the privileges of the saints, can thus turn *their* into *our*.

Verse 17.—1. Consider our natural weakness. 2. Consider our strength in God. 3. Give God the glory of it.

Verse 18.—I. Jehovah—his power, self-existence, and majesty—our defence. II. The Holy One of Israel—his character, covenant character, and unity—our government.

Verse 19.—I. The work required. " Help." 1. By whom ? By God himself. 2. For what ? To reconcile God to man, and man to God. II. The person selected for this work. 1. Human. " Chosen out of the people." 2. Divine. " Thy Holy One." III. His qualifications for the work. 1. His own ability for the office. " One that is mighty." 2. His appointment to it by God. " I have laid," etc. " I have chosen," etc.

Verse 19 (*last clause*).—Election, extraction, exaltation.

Verses 20, 21.—I. The Messiah would be of the seed of David. The true David. II. He would be a servant of the Father. " My servant." III. He would be consecrated to his office by God. " With my holy oil," etc. IV. He would perfectly fulfil it. " With whom my hand," etc. V. He would be sustained in it by the Father. " Mine arm," etc.

Verses 22, 23.—I. A prophecy of the conflict of the Messiah with Satan. Satan could not exact any debt or homage from him. II. Of his refutation of his enemies. " I will beat down," etc. The Scribes and Pharisees were beaten down before his face. III. Of the destruction of their city and nation. " And plague them," etc.

Verse 26.—Our Lord's filial spirit, and how it was displayed.

Verse 29.—I. The subjects of Messiah's reign. " His seed." 1. For union—*his* seed. 2. For resemblance. 3. For multitude. II. The duration of his reign. 1. They for ever one with him. 2. He for ever on the throne.

Verses 30—34.—I. The persons referred to. " His children." " Ye are all the children," etc. II. The supposition concerning them. " If his children forsake," etc. 1. They may possibly—may fall, though not fall away. 2. They will probably, because they are far from being perfect. 3. They have actually : as David himself and others. III. The threatening founded upon that supposition. 1. Specified— " the rod—stripes." They shall smart for it sooner or later. 2. Certified. " Then will I." IV. The qualification of the threatening. " Nevertheless," etc. 1. The nevertheless characterized. Loving-kindness not removed, etc. 2. Emphasized. The rod may seem to be in anger, nevertheless, etc.

There is, I. An if. II. A then. III. A nevertheless.

Verse 39.—I. Providences may often seem to be at variance with promises. II. Promises are never at variance with providences. It is the covenant of thy servant and his crown still.

Verse 39.—How the throne of King Jesus may be profaned.

Verse 40.—I. What God had done. " Broken down," etc. II. What he had not done. Not taken away sorrow for his departure and desire for his return.

Verse 43.—Cases in which the sword of the gospel appears to have its edge turned.

Verses 44, 45.—I. A prophecy that the Messiah would be meek and lowly. " Made his glory to cease." II. Would become a servant to the Father. " Cast his throne down," etc. III. Would be cut off in the midst of his days. " The days of his youth," etc. IV. That he would die an ignominious death. " Hast covered him," etc.

Verse 45.—The excellence of the first days of Christianity, and in what respect their glory has departed from us.

Verse 46.—The hand of God is to be acknowledged. I. In the nature of affliction. " Wilt thou hide thyself," etc. II. In the duration of affliction. " How long, Lord ? " III. In the severity of affliction. Wrath burning like fire. IV. In the issue of affliction. How long ? for ever ? In all these respects the words are applicable both to Christ and to his people.

Verse 46.—" *Remember.*" The prayer of the dying thief, the troubled believer, the persecuted Christian.

Verse 47.—I. An appeal to divine goodness. " Remember," etc. Let not my life be all trouble and sorrow. II. To divine wisdom. " Wherefore," etc. Was man made only to be miserable ? Will not man have been made in vain if his life be but short, and that short life be nothing but sorrow ?

Verse 52.—I. The voice. " Blessed," etc. In himself in all his works and ways— in his judgments as well as in his mercies—as the God and Father of our Lord Jesus Christ—" for evermore." II. The echo, " Amen and amen." Amen, says the church on earth—says the church in heaven—say the angels of God—says the whole holy and happy universe—says eternity past and eternity to come.

PSALM XC.

TITLE.—A Prayer of Moses the man of God. *Many attempts have been made to prove that Moses did not write this Psalm, but we remain unmoved in the conviction that he did so. The condition of Israel in the wilderness is so pre-eminently illustrative of each verse, and the turns, expressions, and words are so similar to many in the Pentateuch, that the difficulties suggested are, to our mind, light as air in comparison with the internal evidence in favour of its Mosaic origin. Moses was mighty in word as well as deed, and this Psalm we believe to be one of his weighty utterances, worthy to stand side by side with his glorious oration recorded in Deuteronomy. Moses was peculiarly a man of God and God's man ; chosen of God, inspired of God, honoured of God, and faithful to God in all his house, he well deserved the name which is here given him. The Psalm is called a prayer, for the closing petitions enter into its essence, and the preceding verses are a meditation preparatory to the supplication. Men of God are sure to be men of prayer. This was not the only prayer of Moses, indeed it is but a specimen of the manner in which the seer of Horeb was wont to commune with heaven, and intercede for the good of Israel. This is the oldest of the Psalms, and stands between two books of Psalms as a composition unique in its grandeur, and alone in its sublime antiquity. Many generations of mourners have listened to this Psalm when standing around the open grave, and have been consoled thereby, even when they have not perceived its special application to Israel in the wilderness and have failed to remember the far higher ground upon which believers now stand.*

SUBJECT AND DIVISIONS.—*Moses sings of the frailty of man, and the shortness of life, contrasting therewith the eternity of God, and founding thereon earnest appeals for compassion. The only division which will be useful separates the contemplation 1—11 from the prayer 12—17 : there is indeed no need to make even this break, for the unity is well preserved throughout.*

EXPOSITION.

LORD, thou hast been our dwelling place in all generations.

2 Before the mountains were brought forth, or ever thou hadst formed the earth and the world, even from everlasting to everlasting, thou *art* God.

3 Thou turnest man to destruction ; and sayest, Return, ye children of men.

4 For a thousand years in thy sight *are but* as yesterday when it is past, and *as* a watch in the night.

5 Thou carriest them away as with a flood ; they are *as* a sleep : in the morning *they are* like grass *which* groweth up.

6 In the morning it flourisheth, and groweth up ; in the evening it is cut down, and withereth.

7 For we are consumed by thine anger, and by thy wrath are we troubled.

8 Thou hast set our iniquities before thee, our secret *sins* in the light of thy countenance.

9 For all our days are passed away in thy wrath : we spend our years as a tale *that is told.*

10 The days of our years *are* threescore years and ten ; and if by reason of strength *they be* fourscore years, yet *is* their strength labour and sorrow; for it is soon cut off, and we fly away.

11 Who knoweth the power of thine anger ? even according to thy fear, *so is* thy wrath.

1. *" Lord, thou hast been our dwelling place in all generations."* We must consider the whole Psalm as written for the tribes in the desert, and then we shall see

the primary meaning of each verse. Moses, in effect, says—wanderers though we be in the howling wilderness, yet we find a home in thee, even as our forefathers did when they came out of Ur of the Chaldees and dwelt in tents among the Canaanites. To the saints the Lord Jehovah, the self-existent God, stands instead of mansion and rooftree; he shelters, comforts, protects, preserves, and cherishes all his own. Foxes have holes and the birds of the air have nests, but the saints dwell in their God, and have always done so in all ages. Not in the tabernacle or the temple do we dwell, but in God himself; and this we have always done since there was a church in the world. We have not shifted our abode. King's palaces have vanished beneath the crumbling hand of time—they have been burned with fire and buried beneath mountains of ruins, but the imperial race of heaven has never lost its regal habitation. Go to the Palatine and see how the Cæsars are forgotten of the halls which echoed to their despotic mandates, and resounded with the plaudits of the nations over which they ruled, and then look upward and see in the ever-living Jehovah the divine home of the faithful, untouched by so much as the finger of decay. Where dwelt our fathers, a hundred generations since, there dwell we still. It is of New Testament saints that the Holy Ghost has said, " He that keepeth his commandments dwelleth in God and God in him ! " It was a divine mouth which said, " Abide in me," and then added, " he that abideth in me and I in him the same bringeth forth much fruit." It is most sweet to speak with the Lord as Moses did, saying, " Lord, thou art our dwelling place," and it is wise to draw from the Lord's eternal condescensions reasons for expecting present and future mercies, as the Psalmist did in the next Psalm wherein he describes the safety of those who dwell in God.

2. " *Before the mountains were brought forth.*" Before those elder giants had struggled forth from nature's womb, as her dread firstborn, the Lord was glorious and self-sufficient. Mountains to him, though hoar with the snows of ages, are but new-born babes, young things whose birth was but yesterday, mere novelties of an hour. " *Or ever thou hadst formed the earth and the world.*" Here too the allusion is to a birth. Earth was born but the other day, and her solid land was delivered from the flood but a short while ago. " *Even from everlasting to everlasting, thou art God,*" or, " thou art, O God." God was, when nothing else was. He was God when the earth was not a world but a chaos, when mountains were not upheaved, and the generation of the heavens and the earth had not commenced. In this Eternal One there is a safe abode for the successive generations of men. If God himself were of yesterday, he would not be a suitable refuge for mortal men ; if he could change and cease to be God he would be but an uncertain dwelling-place for his people. The eternal existence of God is here mentioned to set forth, by contrast, the brevity of human life.

3. " *Thou turnest man to destruction,*" or " to dust." Man's body is resolved into its elements, and is as though it had been crushed and ground to powder. " *And sayest, Return, ye children of men,*" i.e., return even to the dust out of which ye were taken. The frailty of man is thus forcibly set forth ; God creates him out of the dust, and back to dust he goes at the word of his Creator. God resolves and man dissolves. A word created and a word destroys. Observe how the action of God is recognised ; man is not said to die because of the decree of fate, or the action of inevitable law, but the Lord is made the agent of all, his hand turns and his voice speaks ; without these we should not die, no power on earth or hell could kill us.

> "An angel's arm can't save me from the grave,
> Myriads of angels can't confine me there."

4. " *For a thousand years in thy sight are but as yesterday when it is past.*" A thousand years ! This is a long stretch of time. How much may be crowded into it,—the rise and fall of empires, the glory and obliteration of dynasties, the beginning and the end of elaborate systems of human philosophy, and countless events, all important to household and individual, which elude the pens of historians. Yet this period, which might even be called the limit of modern history, and is in human language almost identical with an indefinite length of time, is to the Lord as nothing, even as time already gone. A moment yet to come is longer than " yesterday when it is past," for that no longer exists at all, yet such is a chiliad to the Eternal. In comparison with eternity, the most lengthened reaches of time are mere points, there is, in fact, no possible comparison between them. " *And as a watch in the night,*" a time which is no sooner come than gone. There is scarce time enough in a thousand years for the angels to change watches ; when their millennium of service

is almost over it seems as though the watch were newly set. We are dreaming through the long night of time, but God is ever keeping watch, and a thousand years are as nothing to him. A host of days and nights must be combined to make up a thousand years to us, but to God, that space of time does not make up a whole night, but only a brief portion of it. If a thousand years be to God as a single night-watch, what must be the life-time of the Eternal!

5. *" Thou carriest them away as with a flood."* As when a torrent rushes down the river-bed and bears all before it, so does the Lord bear away by death the succeeding generations of men. As the hurricane sweeps the clouds from the sky, so time removes the children of men. *" They are as a sleep."* Before God men must appear as unreal as the dreams of the night, the phantoms of sleep. Not only are our plans and devices like a sleep, but we ourselves are such. " We are such stuff as dreams are made of." *" In the morning they are like grass which groweth up."* As grass is green in the morning and hay at night, so men are changed from health to corruption in a few hours. We are not cedars, or oaks, but only poor grass, which is vigorous in the spring, but lasts not a summer through. What is there upon earth more frail than we!

6. *" In the morning it flourisheth, and groweth up."* Blooming with abounding beauty till the meadows are all besprent with gems, the grass has a golden hour, even as man in his youth has a heyday of flowery glory. *" In the evening it is cut down, and withereth."* The scythe ends the blossoming of the field-flowers, and the dews at night weep their fall. Here is the history of the grass—sown, grown, blown, mown, gone; and the history of man is not much more. Natural decay would put an end both to us and the grass in due time; few, however, are left to experience the full result of age, for death comes with his scythe, and removes our life in the midst of its verdure. How great a change in how short a time! The morning saw the blooming, and the evening sees the withering.

7. This mortality is not accidental, neither was it inevitable in the original of our nature, but sin has provoked the Lord to anger, and therefore thus we die. *" For we are consumed by thine anger."* This is the scythe which mows and the scorching heat which withers. This was specially the case in reference to the people in the wilderness, whose lives were cut short by justice on account of their waywardness; they failed, not by a natural decline, but through the blast of the well-deserved judgments of God. It must have been a very mournful sight to Moses to see the whole nation melt away during the forty years of their pilgrimage, till none remained of all that came out of Egypt. As God's favour is life, so his anger is death; as well might grass grow in an oven as men flourish when the Lord is wroth with them. *" And by thy wrath are we troubled,"* or terror-stricken. A sense of divine anger confounded them, so that they lived as men who knew that they were doomed. This is true of us in a measure, but not altogether, for now that immortality and life are brought to light by the gospel, death has changed its aspect, and, to believers in Jesus, it is no more a judicial execution. Anger and wrath are the sting of death, and in these believers have no share; love and mercy now conduct us to glory by the way of the tomb. It is not seemly to read these words at a Christian's funeral without words of explanation, and a distinct endeavour to show how little they belong to believers in Jesus, and how far we are privileged beyond those with whom he was not well pleased, " whose carcases fell in the wilderness." To apply an ode, written by the leader of the legal dispensation under circumstances of peculiar judgment, in reference to a people under penal censure, to those who fall asleep in Jesus, seems to be the height of blundering. We may learn much from it, but we ought not to misapply it by taking to ourselves, as the beloved of the Lord, that which was chiefly true of those to whom God had sworn in his wrath that they should not enter into his rest. When, however, a soul is under conviction of sin, the language of this Psalm is highly appropriate to his case, and will naturally suggest itself to the distracted mind. No fire consumes like God's anger, and no anguish so troubles the heart as his wrath. Blessed be that dear substitute,

> " Who bore that we might never bear
> His Father's righteous ire."

8. *" Thou hast set our iniquities before thee."* Hence these tears! Sin seen by God must work death; it is only by the covering blood of atonement that life comes to any of us. When God was overthrowing the tribes in the wilderness he had their iniquities before him, and therefore dealt with them in severity. He could

not have their iniquities before him and not smite them. *" Our secret sins in the light of thy countenance."* There are no secrets before God; he unearths man's hidden things, and exposes them to the light. There can be no more powerful luminary than the face of God, yet, in that strong light, the Lord set the hidden sins of Israel. Sunlight can never be compared with the light of him who made the sun, of whom it is written, " God is light, and in him is no darkness at all." If by his countenance is here meant his love and favour, it is not possible for the heinousness of sin to be more clearly manifested than when it is seen to involve ingratitude to one so infinitely good and kind. Rebellion in the light of justice is black, but in the light of love it is devilish. How can we grieve so good a God? The children of Israel had been brought out of Egypt with a high hand, fed in the wilderness with a liberal hand, and guided with a tender hand, and their sins were peculiarly atrocious. We, too, having been redeemed by the blood of Jesus, and saved by abounding grace, will be verily guilty if we forsake the Lord. What manner of persons ought we to be? How ought we to pray for cleansing from secret faults?

It is to us a wellspring of delights to remember that our sins, as believers, are now cast behind the Lord's back, and shall never be brought to light again: therefore we live, because, the guilt being removed, the death-penalty is removed also.

9. *" For all our days are passed away in thy wrath."* Justice shortened the days of rebellious Israel; each halting place became a graveyard; they marked their march by the tombs they left behind them. Because of the penal sentence their days were dried up, and their lives wasted away. *" We spend our years as a tale that is told."* Yea, not their days only, but their *years* flew by them like a thought, swift as a meditation, rapid and idle as a gossip's story. Sin had cast a shadow over all things, and made the lives of the dying wanderers to be both vain and brief. The first sentence is not intended for believers to quote, as though it applied to themselves, for our days are all passed amid the lovingkindness of the Lord, even as David says in the twenty-third Psalm, " Surely goodness and mercy shall follow me all the days of my life." Neither is the life of the gracious man unsubstantial as a story-teller's tale; he lives in Jesus, he has the divine Spirit within him, and to him " life is real, life is earnest "—the simile only holds good if we consider that a holy life is rich in interest, full of wonders, chequered with many changes, yet as easily ordered by Providence as the improvisatore arranges the details of the story with which he beguiles the hour. Our lives are illustrations of heavenly goodness, parables of divine wisdom, poems of sacred thought, and records of infinite love; happy are we whose lives are such tales.

10. *" The days of our years are threescore years and ten."* Moses himself lived longer than this, but his was the exception not the rule: in his day life had come to be very much the same in duration as it is with us. This is brevity itself compared with the men of the elder time, it is nothing when contrasted with eternity. Yet is life long enough for virtue and piety, and all too long for vice and blasphemy. Moses here in the original writes in a disconnected manner, as if he would set forth the utter insignificance of man's hurried existence. His words may be rendered, " The days of our years! In them seventy years: " as much as to say, " The days of our years? What about them? Are they worth mentioning? The account is utterly insignificant, their full tale is but seventy." *" And if by reason of strength they be fourscore years, yet is their strength labour and sorrow."* The unusual strength which overleaps the bound of threescore and ten only lands the aged man in a region where life is a weariness and a woe. The strength of old age, its very prime and pride, are but labour and sorrow; what must its weakness be? What panting for breath! What toiling to move! What a failing of the senses! What a crushing sense of weakness! The evil days are come and the years wherein a man cries, " I have no pleasure in them." The grasshopper has become a burden and desire faileth. Such is old age. Yet mellowed by hallowed experience, and solaced by immortal hopes, the latter days of aged Christians are not so much to be pitied as envied. The sun is setting and the heat of the day is over, but sweet is the calm and cool of the eventide; and the fair day melts away, not into a dark and dreary night, but into a glorious, unclouded, eternal day. The mortal fades to make room for the immortal; the old man falls asleep to wake up in the region of perennial youth. *" For it is soon cut off, and we fly away."* The cable is broken and the vessel sails upon the sea of eternity; the chain is snapped and the eagle mounts to its native air above the clouds. Moses mourned for men as he thus sung; and well he might, as all his comrades fell at his side. His words are more nearly rendered,

" He drives us fast and we fly away ; " as the quails were blown along by the strong west wind, so are men hurried before the tempests of death. To us, however, as believers, the winds are favourable ; they bear us as the gales bear the swallows away from the wintry realms, to lands

> " Where everlasting spring abides
> And never withering flowers."

Who wishes it to be otherwise ? Wherefore should we linger here ? What has this poor world to offer us that we should tarry on its shores ? Away, away ! This is not our rest. Heavenward, Ho ! Let the Lord's winds drive fast if so he ordains, for they waft us the more swiftly to himself, and our own dear country.

11. " *Who knoweth the power of thine anger ?* " Moses saw men dying all around him : he lived among funerals, and was overwhelmed at the terrible results of the divine displeasure. He felt that none could measure the might of the Lord's wrath. " *Even according to thy fear, so is thy wrath.*" Good men dread that wrath beyond conception, but they never ascribe too much terror to it : bad men are dreadfully convulsed when they awake to a sense of it, but their horror is not greater than it had need be, for it is a fearful thing to fall into the hands of an angry God. Holy Scripture when it depicts God's wrath against sin never uses an hyperbole : it would be impossible to exaggerate it. Whatever feelings of pious awe and holy trembling may move the tender heart, it is never too much moved ; apart from other considerations the great truth of the divine anger, when most powerfully felt, never impresses the mind with a solemnity in excess of the legitimate result of such a contemplation. What the power of God's anger is in hell, and what it would be on earth, were it not in mercy restrained, no man living can rightly conceive. Modern thinkers rail at Milton and Dante, Bunyan and Baxter, for their terrible imagery ; but the truth is that no vision of poet, or denunciation of holy seer, can ever reach to the dread height of this great argument, much less go beyond it. The wrath to come has its horrors rather diminished than enhanced in description by the dark lines of human fancy ; it baffles words, it leaves imagination far behind. Beware ye that forget God lest he tear you in pieces and there be none to deliver. God is terrible out of his holy places. Remember Sodom and Gomorrah ! Remember Korah and his company ! Mark well the graves of lust in the wilderness ! Nay, rather bethink ye of the place where their worm dieth not, and their fire is not quenched. Who is able to stand against this justly angry God ? Who will dare to rush upon the bosses of his buckler, or tempt the edge of his sword ? Be it ours to submit ourselves as dying sinners to this eternal God, who can, even at this moment, command us to the dust, and thence to hell.

12 So teach *us* to number our days, that we may apply *our* hearts unto wisdom.

13 Return, O LORD, how long ? and let it repent thee concerning thy servants.

14 O satisfy us early with thy mercy ; that we may rejoice and be glad all our days.

15 Make us glad according to the days *wherein* thou hast afflicted us, *and* the years *wherein* we have seen evil.

16 Let thy work appear unto thy servants, and thy glory unto their children.

17 And let the beauty of the LORD our God be upon us : and establish thou the work of our hands upon us ; yea, the work of our hands establish thou it.

12. " *So teach us to number our days.*" Instruct us to set store by time, mourning for that time past wherein we have wrought the will of the flesh, using diligently the time present, which is the accepted hour and the day of salvation, and reckoning the time which lieth in the future to be too uncertain to allow us safely to delay any gracious work or prayer. Numeration is a child's exercise in arithmetic, but in order to number their days aright the best of men need the Lord's teaching. We are more anxious to count the stars than our days, and yet the latter is by far more practical. " *That we may apply our hearts unto wisdom.*" Men are led by reflections

upon the brevity of time to give their earnest attention to eternal things ; they become humble as they look into the grave which is so soon to be their bed, their passions cool in the presence of mortality, and they yield themselves up to the dictates of unerring wisdom ; but this is only the case when the Lord himself is the teacher ; he alone can teach to real and lasting profit. Thus Moses prayed that the dispensations of justice might be sanctified in mercy. " The law is our school-master to bring us to Christ," when the Lord himself speaks by the law. It is most meet that the heart which will so soon cease to beat should while it moves be regulated by wisdom's hand. A short life should be wisely spent. We have not enough time at our disposal to justify us in misspending a single quarter of an hour. Neither are we sure of enough of life to justify us in procrastinating for a moment. If we were wise in heart we should see this, but mere head wisdom will not guide us aright.

13. " *Return, O Lord, how long ?* " Come in mercy to us again. Do not leave us to perish. Suffer not our lives to be both brief and bitter. Thou hast said to us, " Return, ye children of men," and now we humbly cry to thee, " Return, thou preserver of men." Thy presence alone can reconcile us to this transient existence ; turn thou unto us. As sin drives God from us, so repentance cries to the Lord to return to us. When men are under chastisement they are allowed to expostulate, and ask " how long ? " Our fault in these times is not too great boldness with God, but too much backwardness in pleading with him. " *And let it repent thee concerning thy servants.*" Thus Moses acknowledges the Israelites to be God's servants still. They had rebelled, but they had not utterly forsaken the Lord ; they owned their obligations to obey his will, and pleaded them as a reason for pity. Will not a man spare his own servants ? Though God smote Israel, yet they were his people, and he had never disowned them, therefore is he entreated to deal favourably with them. If they might not see the promised land, yet he is begged to cheer them on the road with his mercy, and to turn his frown into a smile. The prayer is like others which came from the meek lawgiver when he boldly pleaded with God for the nation ; it is Moses-like. He here speaks with the Lord as a man speaketh with his friend.

14. " *O satisfy us early with thy mercy.*" Since they must die, and die so soon, the Psalmist pleads for speedy mercy upon himself and his brethren. Good men know how to turn the darkest trials into arguments at the throne of grace. He who has but the heart to pray need never be without pleas in prayer. The only satisfying food for the Lord's people is the favour of God ; this Moses earnestly seeks for, and as the manna fell in the morning he beseeches the Lord to send at once his satisfying favour, that all through the little day of life they might be filled there-with. Are we so soon to die ? Then, Lord, do not starve us while we live. Satisfy us at once, we pray thee. Our day is short and the night hastens on, O give us in the early morning of our days to be satisfied with thy favour, that all through our little day we may be happy. " *That we may rejoice and be glad all our days.*" Being filled with divine love, their brief life on earth would become a joyful festival, and would continue so as long as it lasted. When the Lord refreshes us with his presence, our joy is such that no man can take it from us. Apprehensions of speedy death are not able to distress those who enjoy the present favour of God ; though they know that the night cometh they see nothing to fear in it, but continue to live while they live, triumphing in the present favour of God and leaving the future in his loving hands. Since the whole generation which came out of Egypt had been doomed to die in the wilderness, they would naturally feel despondent, and therefore their great leader seeks for them that blessing which, beyond all others, consoles the heart, namely, the presence and favour of the Lord.

15. " *Make us glad according to the days wherein thou hast afflicted us, and the years wherein we have seen evil.*" None can gladden the heart as thou canst, O Lord, therefore as thou hast made us sad be pleased to make us glad. Fill the other scale. Proportion thy dispensations. Give us the lamb, since thou has sent us the bitter herbs. Make our days as long as our nights. The prayer is original, childlike, and full of meaning ; it is moreover based upon a great principle in providential good-ness, by which the Lord puts the good over against the evil in due measure. Great trial enables us to bear great joy, and may be regarded as the herald of extraordinary grace. God's dealings are according to scale ; small lives are small throughout ; and great histories are great both in sorrow and happiness. Where there are high hills there are also deep valleys. As God provides the sea for leviathan, so does he find a pool for the minnow ; in the sea all things are in fit proportion for the mighty monster, while in the little brook all things befit the tiny fish. If we have

fierce afflictions we may look for overflowing delights, and our faith may boldly ask for them. God who is great in justice when he chastens will not be little in mercy when he blesses, he will be great all through ; let us appeal to him with unstaggering faith.

16. " *Let thy work appear unto thy servants.*" See how he dwells upon that word *servants*. It is as far as the law can go, and Moses goes to the full length permitted him : henceforth Jesus calls us not servants but friends, and if we are wise we shall make full use of our wider liberty. Moses asks for displays of divine power and providence conspicuously wrought, that all the people might be cheered thereby. They could find no solace in their own faulty works, but in the work of God they would find comfort. " *And thy glory unto their children.*" While their sons were growing up around them, they desired to see some outshinings of the promised glory gleaming upon them. Their sons were to inherit the land which had been given them by covenant, and therefore they sought on their behalf some tokens of the coming good, some morning dawnings of the approaching noonday. How eagerly do good men plead for their children. They can bear very much personal affliction if they may but be sure that their children will know the glory of God, and thereby be led to serve him. We are content with the work if our children may but see the glory which will result from it : we sow joyfully if they may reap.

17. " *And let the beauty of the Lord our God be upon us.*" Even upon us who must not see thy glory in the land of Canaan ; it shall suffice us if in our characters the holiness of God is reflected, and if over all our camp the lovely excellences of our God shall cast a sacred beauty. Sanctification should be the daily object of our petitions. " *And establish thou the work of our hands upon us ; yea, the work of our hands establish thou it.*" Let what we do be done in truth, and last when we are in the grave ; may the work of the present generation minister permanently to the building up of the nation. Good men are anxious not to work in vain. They know that without the Lord they can do nothing, and therefore they cry to him for help in the work, for acceptance of their efforts, and for the establishment of their designs. The church as a whole earnestly desires that the hand of the Lord may so work with the hand of his people, that a substantial, yea, an eternal edifice to the praise and glory of God may be the result. We come and go, but the Lord's work abides. We are content to die, so long as Jesus lives and his kingdom grows. Since the Lord abides for ever the same, we trust our work in his hands, and feel that since it is far more his work than ours he will secure it immortality. When we have withered like grass, our holy service, like gold, silver, and precious stones, will survive the fire.

EXPLANATORY NOTES AND QUAINT SAYINGS.

Title.—The correctness of the title which ascribes the Psalm to Moses is confirmed by its unique simplicity and grandeur ; its appropriateness to his times and circumstances ; its resemblance to the Law in urging the connection between sin and death ; its similarity of diction to the poetical portions of the Pentateuch, without the slightest trace of imitation or quotation ; its marked unlikeness to the Psalms of David, and still more to those of later date ; and finally, the proved impossibility of plausibly assigning it to any other age or author.—*J. A. Alexander.*

Title.—" *A prayer of Moses.*" Moses may be considered as the first composer of sacred hymns.—*Samuel Burder.*

Title.—The Psalm is described in the title as a *prayer.* This description shews, as Amyraldus saw, that the kernel of the Psalm is the *second* part, and that the design of the first is to prepare the way for the second, and lay down a basis on which it may rest.—*E. W. Hengstenberg.*

Title.—" *A prayer of Moses.*" Moses was an old and much-tried man, but age and experience had taught him that, amidst the perpetual changes which are taking place in the universe, one thing at least remains immutable, even the faithfulness of him who is " from everlasting to everlasting God." How far back into the past may the patriarch have been looking when he spake these words ? The burning bush, the fiery furnace of Egypt, the Red Sea, Pharaoh with his chariots of war, and the weary march of Israel through the wilderness, were all before him ; and in all of them he had experienced that " God is the Rock, his work perfect, all his ways judgment " (Deut. xxxii. 4). But Moses was looking beyond these scenes of his personal history when he said, " Remember the days of old, consider the years of many generations" (Deut. xxxii. 7), and we may be sure that he was also looking beyond them when he indited the song, " *Thou hast been our dwelling place in all generations.*" Yes ; he was casting in his mind how God had been the refuge of Jacob and Isaac, of Abraham, Noah, and all the patriarchs. Moses could take a retrospect of above a thousand years, which had all confirmed the truth. I can do more. At this point of time I can look back to the days of Moses and Joshua and David, and descending thence to the days of the Son of God upon earth, and of Paul and Peter, and all the saints of the Church down to the present hour ; and what a thousand years avouched to Moses, three thousand now avouch to me : the Lord is the dwelling-place of those that trust in him from generation to generation. Yes ; and to him who was the refuge of a Moses and an Abraham, I too in the day of trouble can lift my hands. Delightful thought ! That great Being who, during the lapse of three thousand years, amidst the countless changes of the universe, has to this day remained unchanged, is MY God.—*Augustus F. Tholuck, in " Hours of Christian Devotion,"* 1870.

Whole Psalm.—Although some difficulties have been started, there seems no reason to doubt that this Psalm is the composition of Moses. From the remotest period his name has been attached to it, and almost every Biblical scholar, from Jerome down to Hengstenberg, has agreed to accept it as a prayer of that " man of God " whose name it has always carried. If so, it is one of the oldest poems in the world. Compared with it Homer and Pindar are (so to speak) modern, and even King David is of recent date. That is to say, compared with this ancient hymn the other Psalms are as much more modern as Tennyson and Longfellow are more modern than Chaucer. In either case there are nearly five centuries between.—*James Hamilton.*

Whole Psalm.—The 90th Psalm might be cited as perhaps the most sublime of human compositions—the deepest in feeling—the loftiest in theologic conception— the most magnificent in its imagery. True is it in its report of human life—as troubled, transitory, and sinful. True in its conception of the Eternal—the Sovereign and the Judge ; and yet the refuge and hope of men, who, notwithstanding the most severe trials of their faith, lose not their confidence in him ; but who, in the firmness of faith, pray for, as if they were predicting, a near-at-hand season of refreshment. Wrapped, one might say, in mystery, until the distant day of revelation should come, there is here conveyed the doctrine of Immortality ; for in the very plaint of the brevity of the life of man, and of the sadness of these, his few years of trouble, and their brevity, and their gloom, there is brought into contrast the Divine immutability ; and yet it is in terms of a submissive piety : the thought of a life eternal is here in embryo. No taint is there in this Psalm of the pride and petulance —the half-uttered blasphemy—the malign disputing or arraignment of the justice or goodness of God, which have so often shed a venomous colour upon the language of those who have writhed in anguish, personal or relative. There are few probably among those who have passed through times of bitter and distracting woe, or who have stood—the helpless spectators of the miseries of others, that have not fallen into moods of mind violently in contrast with the devout and hopeful melancholy which breathes throughout this ode. Rightly attributed to the Hebrew Lawgiver or not, it bespeaks its remote antiquity, not merely by the majestic simplicity of its style, but negatively, by the entire avoidance of those sophisticated turns of thought which belong to a late—a lost age in a people's intellectual and moral history. This Psalm, undoubtedly, is centuries older than the moralizings of that time when the Jewish mind had listened to what it could never bring into a true assimilation with its own mind—the abstractions of the Greek Philosophy.

With this one Psalm only in view—if it were required of us to say, in brief, what we mean by the phrase—" The Spirit of the Hebrew Poetry "—we find our answer well condensed in this sample. This magnificent composition gives evidence, not merely as to the mental qualities of the writer, but as to the tastes and habitudes of the writer's contemporaries, his hearers, and his readers ; on these several points— *first,* the free and customary command of a poetic diction, and its facile imagery ; so that whatever the poetic soul would utter, the poet's material is near at hand for his use. There is then that depth of feeling—mournful, reflective, and yet hopeful and trustful, apart from which poetry can win for itself no higher esteem than what we bestow upon other decorative arts, which minister to the demands of luxurious *sloth.* There is, moreover, as we might say, underlying this poem, from the first line to the last, the substance of philosophic thought, apart from which, expressed or understood, poetry is frivolous, and is not in harmony with the seriousness of human life : this Psalm is of a sort which Plato would have written, or Sophocles— if only the one or the other of these minds had possessed a heaven-descended Theology. —*Isaac Taylor.*

Verse 1.—" *Lord.*" Observe the change of the Divine names in this Psalm. Moses begins with the declaration of the Majesty of the Lord (*Adonai*), but when he arrives at ver. 13, he opens his prayer with the Name of grace and covenanted mercy to Israel—JEHOVAH ; and he sums up all in ver. 17, with a supplication for the manifestation of the *beauty* נֹעַם of " the Lord our God " (JEHOVAH, ELOHIM).— *Christopher Wordsworth.*

Verse 1.—" *Lord, thou hast been our dwelling place.*" Many seem to beg God's help in prayer, but are not protected by him : they seek it only in a storm, and when all other means and refuges fail them. But a Christian must maintain constant communication with God ; must dwell in God, not run to him now and then.— *Thomas Manton.*

Verse 1.—This exordium breathes life, and pertains to a certain hope of the resurrection and of eternal life. Since he calls God, who is eternal, our habitation, or to speak more clearly, our place of refuge, to whom fleeing we may be in safety. For if God is our dwelling-place, and God is life, and we dwellers in him, it necessarily follows, that we are in life, and shall live for ever. . . . For who will call God the dwelling-place of the dead ? Who shall regard him as a sepulchre ? He is life ; and therefore they also live to whom he is a dwelling-place. After this fashion Moses, in the very introduction, before he lets loose his horrible thunderings and lightnings, fortifies the trembling, that they may firmly hold God to be the living dwelling-place of the living, of those that pray to him, and put their trust in him.

It is a remarkable expression, the like of which is nowhere in Sacred Scripture, that God is a *dwelling-place.* Scripture in other places says the very opposite, it calls men temples of God, in whom God dwells ; " the temple of God is holy," says Paul, " which temple ye are." Moses inverts this, and affirms, we are inhabitants and masters in this house. For the Hebrew word מָעוֹן properly signifies a dwelling place, as when the Scripture says, " In Zion is his dwelling place," where this word (Maon) is used. But because a house is for the purpose of safety, it results, that this word has the meaning of a refuge or place of refuge. But Moses wishes to speak with such great care that he may show that all our hopes have been placed most securely in God, and that they who are about to pray to this God may be assured that they are not afflicted in this work in vain, nor die, since they have God as a place of refuge, and the divine Majesty as a dwelling-place, in which they may rest secure for ever. Almost in the same strain Paul speaks, when he says to the Colossians, " Your life is hid with Christ in God." For it is a much clearer and more luminous expression to say, Believers dwell in God, than that God dwells in them. He dwelt also visibly in Zion, but the place is changed. But because he (the believer) is in God, it is manifest, that he cannot be moved nor transferred, for God is a habitation of a kind that cannot perish. Moses therefore wished to exhibit the most certain life, when he said, God is our dwelling place, not the earth, not heaven, not paradise, but simply God himself. If after this manner you take this Psalm it will become sweet, and seem in all respects most useful. When a monk, it often happened to me when I read this Psalm, that I was compelled to lay the book out of my hand. But I knew not that these terrors were not addressed to an awakened mind. I knew not that Moses was speaking to a most obdurate and proud multitude, which neither understood nor cared for the anger of God, nor were humbled by their calamities, or even in prospect of death.—*Martin Luther.*

Verse 1.—" *Lord, thou hast been our dwelling place,*" etc. In this first part the prophet acknowledgeth that God in all times, and in all ages hath had a special care of his saints and servants, to provide for them all things necessary for this life ; for under the name of " *dwelling place,*" or *mansion house,* the prophet understandeth all helps and comforts necessary for this life, both for maintenance and protection. For the use of such houses was wont to be not only to defend men from the injury of the weather, and to keep safely, within the walls and under the roof all other things necessary for this life, and to be a place of abode, wherein men might the more commodiously provide for all other things necessary, and walk in some calling profitable to their neighbour and to the glory of God ; but also to protect them from the violence of brute beasts and rage of enemies. Now the prophet herein seems to note a special and more immediate providence of God ; (for of all kind of people they seemed to be most forsaken and forlorn) ; that whereas the rest of the world seemed to have their habitations and mansions rooted in the earth, and so to dwell upon the earth ; to live in cities and walled towns in all wealth and state ; God's people were as it were without house and home. Abraham was called out of his own country, from his father's house, where no doubt he had goodly buildings and large revenues, and was commanded by God to live as a foreigner in a strange country, amongst savage people, that he knew not ; and to abide in tents, booths, and cabins, having little hope to live a settled and comfortable life in any place. In like manner lived his posterity, Isaac, Jacob, and the twelve patriarchs, wandering from place to place in the land of Canaan ; from thence translated into the land of Egypt, there living at courtesy, and as it were tenants at will, and in such slavery and bondage, that it had been better for them to have been without house and home. After this for forty years together (at which time this Psalm was penned) they wandered up and down in a desolate wilderness, removing from place to place, and wandering, as it were in a maze. So that of all the people of the earth, God's own people had hitherto lived as pilgrims and banished persons, without house or home ; and therefore the prophet here professeth that God himself more immediately by his extraordinary providence, for many ages together had protected them, and been as it were a mansion house unto them ; that is, the more they were deprived of these ordinary comforts of this life, the more was God present with them, supplying by his extraordinary and .immediate providence what they wanted in regard of ordinary means. The due consideration of this point may minister matter of great joy and comfort to such children of God as are thoroughly humbled with the consideration of man's mortality in general, or of theirs whom they rely and depend upon in special.—*William Bradshaw*, 1621.

Verse 1.—" *Our dwelling place.*" God created the earth for beasts to inhabit, the sea for fishes, the air for fowls, and heaven for angels and stars, so that man hath no place to dwell and abide in but God alone.—*Giovanni della Mirandola Pico*, 1463—1494.

Verses 1, 2.—The comfort of the believer against the miseries of this short life is taken from the decree of their election, and the eternal covenant of redemption settled in the purpose and counsel of the blessed Trinity for their behoof, wherein it was agreed before the world was, that the *Word* to be incarnate, should be the Saviour of the elect : for here the asserting of the eternity of God is with relation to his own chosen people ; for " *Thou hast been our dwelling place in all generations,*" and, " *thou art God from everlasting to everlasting,*" is in substance thus much :— Thou art from everlasting to everlasting the same unchangeable God in purpose and affection toward us thy people, and so thou art *our God* from everlasting, in regard of thy eternal purpose of love, electing us, and in regard of thy appointing redemption for us by the Redeemer.—*David Dickson*.

Verses 1, 2.—If man be ephemeral, God is eternal.—*James Hamilton*.

Verses 1—6.—

"O Lord, thou art our home, to whom we fly,
     And so hast always been, from age to age ;
Before the hills did intercept the eye,
     Or that the frame was up of earthly stage,
         One God thou wert, and art, and still shall be ;
         The line of time, it doth not measure thee.

Both death and life obey thy holy lore,
     And visit in their turns as they are sent ;
A thousand years with thee they are no more
     Than yesterday, which, ere it is, is spent :
         Or as a watch by night, that course doth keep,
         And goes and comes, unwares to them that sleep.

Thou carryest man away as with a tide :
     Then down swim all his thoughts that mounted high ;
Much like a mocking dream, that will not bide,
     But flies before the sight of waking eye ;
         Or as the grass, that cannot term obtain,
         To see the summer come about again.

> At morning, fair it musters on the ground ;
> At even it is cut down and laid along :
> And though it spared were, and favour found,
> The weather would perform the mower's wrong :
> Thus hast thou hanged our life on brittle pins,
> To let us know it will not bear our sins."
>
> —*Francis Bacon.*

Verse 2.—" *The earth and the world.*" The word *earth* here is used to denote the world as distinguished either from heaven (Gen. i. 1), or from the sea (Gen. i. 10). The term " *world* " in the original is commonly employed to denote the earth considered as *inhabited*, or as capable of being inhabited, a dwelling-place for living beings.—*Albert Barnes.*

Verse 2.—" *From everlasting to everlasting, thou art God.*" The everlastingness of which Moses speaks is to be referred not only to the essence of God, but also to his providence, by which he governs the world. He intends not merely that he is, but that he is God.—*John Calvin.*

Verse 2.—Such a God (he says) have we, such a God do we worship, to such a God do we pray, at whose command all created things sprang into being. Why then should we fear if this God favours us ? Why should we tremble at the anger of the whole world ? If he is our dwelling-place, shall we not be safe though the heavens should go to wrack ? For we have a Lord greater than all the world. We have a Lord so mighty that at his word all things sprang into being. And yet we are so fainthearted that if the anger of a single prince or king, nay, even of a single neighbour, is to be borne, we tremble and droop in spirit. Yet in comparison with this King, all things beside in the whole world are but as the lightest dust which a slight breath moves from its place, and suffers not to be still. In this way this description of God is consolatory, and trembling spirits ought to look to this consolation in their temptations and dangers.—*Martin Luther.*

Verse 3.—" *Thou turnest man to destruction,*" etc. The prophet conceiveth of God as of a *potter*, that having of dust tempered a mass, and framed it into a vessel, and dried it, doth presently, within a minute or an hour after, dash it again in pieces, and beat it to dust, in passion as it were speaking unto it, " Get thee to dust again." The word here translated " *destruction,*" signifies a beating, or grinding, or pounding of a thing to powder. And the prophet seems to allude to the third of Genesis, where God speaks of Adam, " Dust thou art, and to dust thou shalt return," as if he should say, O Lord, thou that hast made and framed man of the dust of the earth, thou beatest him to dust again ; and as thou madest him by thy word alone, so with thy word thou suddenly turnest, and beatest him again to dust ; as a man that makes a thing, and presently mars it again. . . . He doth it with a word, against which is no resistance, when that word is once come out of his mouth ; it is not all the diet, physic, and help, and prayers in the world that can save the life. And this he can do suddenly, in the twinkling of an eye. And therefore we should, as we love our lives, fear him, and take heed how we offend and displease him that can with a word turn the strongest man into dust.—*William Bradshaw.*

Verse 3.—" *Thou turnest man to destruction,*" etc. The first word for " *man,*" signifies a man full of misery, full of sicknesses and infirmities, a miserable man, אֱנוֹשׁ. And the other word here used in the end of the verse, signifies a man made of *clay*, or of the very slime of the earth. From hence we learn what is the nature of all men, of all the sons of *Adam*, viz., a piece of living *clay*, a little piece of red earth. And besides that man is subject to *breaking* and *crushing*, every way a miserable man ; so is he of a brittle mould, a piece of red clay, that hath in it for a time a living soul, which must return to God that gave it ; and the body, this piece of earth, return to the earth from whence it came : and if we had no Scripture at all to prove this, daily experience before our eyes makes it clear how all men, even the wisest, the strongest, the greatest and the mightiest monarchs and princes in the world, be but miserable men, made of red earth, and quickly turn again to dust.—*Samuel Smith, in " Moses his Prayer," 1656.*

Verse 3.—" *Thou turnest man to destruction.*" Augustine says, We walk amid perils. If we were glass vases we might fear less dangers. What is there more fragile than a vase of glass ? And yet it is preserved, and lasts for centuries : we therefore are more frail and infirm.—*Le Blanc.*

Verse 3.—" *Return ye.*" One being asked what life was? made an answer answerless, for he presently turned his back and went his way.—*John Trapp.*

Verse 4.—" *A thousand years,*" etc. As to a very rich man a thousand sovereigns are as one penny; so, to the eternal God, a thousand years are as one day.—*John Albert Bengel, 1687—1752.*

Verse 4.—The Holy Ghost expresseth himself according to the manner of men, to give us some notion of an infinite duration, by a resemblance suited to our capacity. If a thousand years be but as a day to the life of God, then as a year is to the life of man, so are three hundred and sixty-five thousand years to the life of God; and as seventy years are to the life of man, so are twenty-five millions five hundred and fifty thousand years to the life of God. Yet still, since there is no proportion between time and eternity, we must dart our thoughts beyond all these, for years and days measure only the duration of created things, and of those only that are material and corporeal, subject to the motion of the heavens, which makes days and years.— *Stephen Charnock.*

Verse 4.—" *As yesterday when it is past, and as a watch in the night.*" He corrects the previous clause with an extraordinary abbreviation. For he says that the whole space of human life, although it may be very long, and reach a thousand years, yet with God it is esteemed not only as one day, which has already gone, but is scarcely equal to the fourth part of a night. For the nights were divided into four watches, which lasted three hours each. And indeed by the word *night*, it is meant that human affairs in this life are involved in much darkness, many errors, dangers, terrors and sorrows.—*Mollerus.*

Verse 4.—" *As a watch in the night.*" The night is wont to appear shorter than the day, and to pass more swiftly, because those who sleep, says Euthymius, notice not the lapse of time. On account of the darkness also, it is less observed; and to those at work the time seems longer, than to those who have their work done.— *Lorinus.*

Verse 4.—" *A watch in the night.*" Sir John Chardin observes in a note on this verse, that as the people of the East have no clocks, the several parts of the day and of the night, which are eight in all, are given notice of. In the Indies, the parts of the night are made known as well by instruments of music in great cities, as by the rounds of the watchmen, who with cries, and small drums, give them notice that a fourth part of the night is passed. Now as these cries awaked those who had slept all that quarter part of the night, it appeared to them but as a moment.—*Harmer's Observations.*

Verse 4.—The ages and the dispensations, the promise to Adam, the engagement with Noah, the oath to Abraham, the covenant with Moses—these were but watches, through which the children of men had to wait amid the darkness of things created, until the morning should dawn of things uncreated. Now is " the night far spent, and the day at hand."—*Plain Commentary.*

Verse 5.—" *Thou carriest them away as with a flood.*" זְרַמְתָּם (*zeram-tam*) *thou hast inundated them,* namely, the years of man, i.e., thou hast hurried them away with a flood, thou hast made them to glide away as water, *they will be as a sleep.*— Bythner's " *Lyre of David.*"

Verse 5.—" *Thou carriest them away as with a flood.*" Let us meditate seriously upon the swift passage of our days, how our life runs away like a stream of waters, and carrieth us with it. Our condition in the eyes of God in regard of our life in this world is as if a man that knows not how to swim, should be cast into a great stream of water, and be carried down with it, so that he may sometimes lift up his head or his hands, and cry for help, or catch hold of this thing and that, for a time, but his end will be drowning, and it is but a small time that he can hold out, for the flood which carries him away will soon swallow him up. And surely our life here if it be rightly considered, is but like the life of a person thus violently carried down a stream. All the actions and motions of our life are but like unto the strivings and strugglings of a man in that case: our eating, our drinking, our physic, our sports, and all other actions are but like the motions of the sinking man. When we have done all that we can, die we must, and be drowned in this deluge.—*William Bradshaw.*

Verse 5.—" *Away as with a flood.*" " A man is a bubble," said the Greek proverb, which Lucian represents to this purpose, saying, " All the world is a storm, and men rise up in their several generations like bubbles. Some of these instantly sink into the deluge of their first parent, and are hidden in a sheet of water, having no other business in the world but to be born, that they might be able to die; others float up and down two or three turns, and suddenly disappear, and give their place to others: and they that live longest upon the face of the waters are in perpetual motion, restless and uneasy, and being crushed in by a great drop from a cloud, sink into flatness and a froth; the change not being great; it being hardly possible that a bubble should be more a nothing than it was before."—*Jeremy Taylor.*

Verse 5 (first clause).—The most ancient mode of measuring small portions of time was by water flowing out of a vessel, the clepsydra of the Greeks and Romans; and Ovid has compared the lapse of time to the flowing of a river [Metam. xv. 180].—*Stephen Street.*

Verse 5.—" *They are as a sleep.*" For as in the visions of sleep, we seeing, see not, hearing we hear not, tasting or touching we neither taste nor touch, speaking we speak not, walking we walk not; but when we seem to employ movements and gestures, in no respect do we employ them, since the mind vainly forms without any real objects images of things that exist not, as if they existed. In this very way, the imaginations of those who are awake closely resemble dreams; they come, they go, they confront us and flee from us; before they are seized, they fly away.— *Philo, in Le Blanc.*

Verse 5.—" *They are as a sleep.*" Our life may be compared to sleep in four respects.   1. In regard of the shortness of it.   2. In regard of the easiness of being put out of it.   3. In regard of the many means to disquiet and break it off.   4. With regard to the many errors in it.

For the first three.   Sleep is but short, and the sweeter it is, the shorter it seems to be.   And as it is but short of itself, though it should last the full swing of nature; so the soundest sleep is easily broken; the least knock, the lowest call puts men out of it; and a number of means and occasions there be to interrupt and break it off. And is it not so with the life of man?   Is not the longest life short?   Is it not the shorter, the sweeter and fuller of contents it is?   And is it not easily taken away? Are there not many means to bring us unto our end?   even as many as there are to waken us out of sleep.

For the fourth.   How many errors are we subject to in sleep?   In sleep the prisoner many times dreams that he is at liberty; he that is at liberty, that he is in prison; he that is hungry, that he is feeding daintily; he that is in want, that he is in great abundance; he that abounds, that he is in great want.   How many in their sleep have thought they have gotten that which they shall be better for for ever, and when they are even in the hope of present possessing some such goodly matter, or beginning to enjoy it, or in the midst of their joy, they are suddenly awaked, and then all is gone with them, and their golden fancies vanish away in an instant.   So for evil and sorrow as well.   And is it not just so in the life of man?— *William Bradshaw.*

Verse 5.—" *They are like grass.*" In this last similitude, the prophet compares men to *grass*, that as *grass* hath a time of growing and a time of withering, even so has man. " *In the morning it flourisheth, and groweth up.*" In which words Moses compares the former part of man's life, which is the space of thirty-three years, to the time of growing of grass, and that is accounted the time of the perfection of man's strength and age; at which age, according to the course of nature, man flourisheth as grass doth; that is the time of a man's prime and flourishing estate.

But " *in the evening* "; that is, when the grass is ripe, and ready to be cut down, " *it withereth.*" Even so man, being once at his strength, and ripest age, doth not stand at a stay, nor continueth long so; but presently begins to decay, and to wither away, till old age comes, and he is cut down by the scythe of death.

Now, in that Moses useth so many similitudes, and all to show how frail this life of man is, we are taught, that the frailty, vanity, and shortness of man's life is such, that examples will scarcely shew it.   Death comes as a *flood*, violently and suddenly; we are as a *sleep*; we are as *grass*; our life is like a *dream*; we spend our days *as a tale that is told*, verse 9.   All these similitudes Moses hath in this Psalm, as if he wanted words and examples, how to express the vanity, frailty, and shortness thereof.—*Samuel Smith.*

Verse 6.—" *In the morning.*" This can hardly mean " in early youth," as some of the Rabbis explain. The words, strictly speaking, are a part of the comparison (" they are as grass which springeth afresh in the morning "), and are only thus placed first to give emphasis to the figure. In the East, one night's rain works a change as if by magic. The field at evening was brown, parched, arid as a desert; in the morning it is green with the blades of grass. The scorching hot wind (James i. 11) blows upon it, and again before evening it is withered.—*J. J. S. Perowne.*

Verse 6.—" *Cut down.*"

Stout and strong to-day,
To-morrow turned to clay.

This day in his bloom,
The next, in the tomb.

It is true that to some Death sends his grey harbingers before, and gives them timely warning of his approach. But in how many cases does he arrive unannounced, and, lifting up his scythe, mow down the lofty! On shipboard there is but a plank between us and death; on horseback, but a fall. As we walk along the streets, Death stretches a threatening finger from every tile upon the roofs! "He comes up into our windows, and enters into our palaces; he cuts off the children from without, and the young men from the streets." Jer. ix. 21. Our life is less than an handbreadth. How soon and how insensibly we slip into the grave!—*Augustus F. Tholuck.*

Verse 7.—" *For we are consumed by thine anger.*" This is a point disputed by philosophers. They seek for the cause of death, since indeed proofs of immortality that cannot be despised exist in nature. The prophet replies, that the chief cause must not be sought in the material, either in a defect of the fluids, or in a failure of the natural heat; but that God being offended at the sins of men, hath subjected this nature to death and other infinite calamities. Therefore, our sins are the causes which have brought down this destruction. Hence he says, *In thine anger we vanish away.*—*Mollerus.*

Verse 7.—" *For we are consumed by thine anger,*" etc. Whence we may first of all observe, how they compare their present estate in the wilderness, with the estate of other nations and people, and shew that their estate was far worse than theirs: for others died now one, and then one, and so they were diminished; but for them, they were hastily consumed, and suddenly swept away by the plague and pestilence which raged amongst them. Hence we may observe, first of all—That it is a ground of humiliation to God's people when their estate is worse than God's enemies'. Moses gathers this as an argument to humble them, and to move them to repentance and to seek unto God; viz., that because of their sins they were in a far worse case and condition than the very enemies of God were. For though their lives were short, yet they confess that theirs was far worse than the very heathen themselves, for they were *suddenly consumed by his anger.* When God is worse to his own church and people than he is to his enemies; when the Lord sends wars in a nation called by his name, and peace in other kingdoms that are anti-Christian; sends famine in his church, and plenty to the wicked; sends the plague and pestilence in his church, and health and prosperity to the wicked; oh, here is matter of mourning and humiliation; and it is that which hath touched God's people to the quick, and wounded them to the heart, to see the enemies of the church in better condition than the church itself.—*Samuel Smith.*

Verse 7.—" *By thy wrath are we troubled.*" The word used by Moses is much stronger than merely "troubled." It implies being cut off, destroyed—in forms moreover of overwhelming terror.—*Henry Cowles, in* " *The Psalms; with Notes.*" *New York,* 1872.

Verse 8.—God needs no other light to discern our sins by but the light of his own face. It pierceth through the darkest places; the brightness thereof enlighteneth all things, discovers all things. So that the sins that are committed in deepest darkness are all one to him as if they were done in the face of the sun. For they are done in his face, that shines more, and from which proceeds more light than from the face of the sun. So that this ought to make us the more fearful to offend; he sees us when we see not him, and the light of his countenance shines about us when we think ourselves hidden in darkness.

Our sins are not only then in his sight when they are a committing and whilst the deed is doing; but ever after, when the act is past and gone and forgotten, yet then is it before the face of God, even as if it were in committing : and how should this make us afraid to sin ! When our sins are not only in his sight while they are a committing, but so continue still for ever after they are past and done.

God *sets our sins before him ;* this shows he is so affected with them, he takes them so to heart, that he doth in a special manner continue the remembrance of them. As those that having had great wrong will store it up, or register it, or keep some remembrance of it or other, lest they should forget, when time shall serve to be quit with those that have wronged them : so doth God, and his so doing is a sign that he takes our sins deeply to heart ; which should teach us to fear the more how we offend him. When God in any judgment of death, or sickness, or loss of friends, shews his wrath, we should think and meditate of this ; especially when he comes nearest us : Now the Lord looks upon my sins, they are now before him ; and we should never rest till we have by repentance moved him to blot them out. Yea, to this end we should ourselves call them to remembrance. For the more we remember them, the more God forgets them ; the more we forget them, the more God remembers them ; the more we look upon them ourselves, the more he turneth his eyes from them.—*William Bradshaw.*

Verse 8.—It is a well known fact that the appearance of objects, and the ideas which we form of them, are very much affected by the situation in which they are placed in respect to us, and by the light in which they are seen. Objects seen at a distance, for example, appear much smaller than they really are. The same object, viewed through different mediums, will often exhibit different appearances. A lighted candle, or a star, appears bright during the absence of the sun ; but when that luminary returns, their brightness is eclipsed. Since the appearance of objects, and the ideas which we form of them, are thus affected by extraneous circumstances, it follows, that no two persons will form precisely the same ideas of any object, unless they view it in the same light, or are placed with respect to it in the same situation.

Apply these remarks to the case before us. The Psalmist addressing God, says, " *Thou hast set our iniquities before thee, our secret sins in the light of thy countenance.*" That is, our iniquities or open transgressions, and our secret sins, the sins of our hearts, are placed as it were, full before God's face, immediately under his eye ; and he sees them in the pure, clear, all-disclosing light of his own holiness and glory. Now if we would see our sins as they appear to him, that is, as they really are, if we would see their number, blackness and criminality, and the malignity and desert of every sin, we must place ourselves, as nearly as is possible, in his situation, and look at sin, as it were, through his eyes. We must place ourselves and our sins in the centre of that circle which is irradiated by the light of his countenance, where all his infinite perfections are clearly displayed, where his awful majesty is seen, where his concentrated glories blaze, and burn, and dazzle, with insufferable brightness. And in order to this, we must, in thought, leave our dark and sinful world, where God is unseen and almost forgotten, and where consequently, the evil of sinning against him cannot be fully perceived—and mount up to heaven, the peculiar habitation of his holiness and glory, where he does not, as here, conceal himself behind the veil of his works, and of second causes, but shines forth the unveiled God, and is seen as he is.

My hearers, if you are willing to see your sins in their true colours ; if you would rightly estimate their number, magnitude and criminality, bring them into the hallowed place, where nothing is seen but the brightness of unsullied purity, and the splendours of uncreated glory ; where the sun itself would appear only as a dark spot ; and there, in the midst of this circle of seraphic intelligences, with the infinite God pouring all the light of his countenance round you, review your lives, contemplate your offences, and see how they appear. Recollect that the God, in whose presence you are, is the Being who forbids sin, the Being of whose eternal law sin is the transgression, and against whom every sin is committed.—*Edward Payson.*

Verse 9.—" *For all our days go back again* (פנה) *in thy wrath.*" Hitherto he has spoken of the cause of that wrath of God which moveth him to smite the world with such mortality. Now here he further sets forth the same by the effects thereof in reference to that present argument he hath in hand. 1. That our days do as it were go backward in his wrath : that whereas God gave us being to live, our life and our being are nothing else but a going backward, as it were, to death and to nothing. Even as if a stranger being suddenly rapt and carried mid-way to his home, where are all his comforts, he should spend all the time that is behind, not in going forward to his home, but in going backward to the place from which he was suddenly brought. All the sons of Adam as soon as they have being and live are brought suddenly a great part of their way : and whereas they should go forward and live longer and longer, they from their first beginning to live go backward again to death and to nothing. This is the sum in effect of that which the Lord saith in the beginning of the Psalm, (ver. 3 :) " *Thou bringest men to destruction ; saying, Return again, ye sons of Adam :* " as if he should say, Thou makest a man, and when he is made, he in thy wrath doth haste to nothing else but destruction and to be marred again. Thus do our days as it were go backward, and we in them return from whence we came.— *William Bradshaw.*

Verse 9.—When I was in Egypt, three or four years ago, I saw what Moses himself might have seen, and what the Israelites, no doubt, very often witnessed :—a crowd of people surrounding a professed story-teller, who was going through some tale, riveting the attention and exciting the feelings of those who listened to him. This is one of the customs of the East. It naturally springs up among any people who have few books, or none ; where the masses are unable to read, and where, therefore, they are dependent for excitement or information on those who can address the ear, and who recite, in prose or verse, traditional tales and popular legends. I dare say this sort of thing would be much in repute among the Israelites themselves during their detention in the wilderness, and that it served to beguile for them many a tedious hour. It is by this custom, then, that we venture to illustrate the statement of the text.

The hearing of a story is attended by a rapid and passing interest—it leaves behind it a vague impression, beyond which comparatively but few incidents may stand out distinctly in the after thought. In our own day even, when tales are put into printed books, and run through three or four volumes, we feel when we have finished one, how short it appears after all, or how short the time it seemed to take for its perusal. If full of incident, it may seem sometimes long to remember, but we generally come to the close with a sort of feeling that says, " And so that's all." But this must have been much more the case with the tales " that were told." These had to be compressed into what could be repeated at one time, or of which three or four might be given in an evening or an hour. The story ended ; and then came the sense of shortness, brevity, the rapid flight of the period employed by it, with something like a feeling of wonder and dissatisfaction at the discovery of this. " For what is your life ? It is even as a vapour, that appeareth for a little time, and then vanisheth away."—*Thomas Binney.*

Verse 9.—" *As a tale.*" The grace whereof is *brevity.*—*John Trapp.*

Verse 9.—" *As a tale that is told.*" The Chaldee has it, *like the breath of our mouth in winter.*—*Daniel Cresswell.*

Verse 9.—The thirty-eight years, which after this they were away in the wilderness, were not the subject of the sacred history, for little or nothing is recorded of that which happened to them from the second year to the fortieth. After they came out of Egypt, their time was perfectly trifled away, and was not worthy to be the subject of a history, but only of " *a tale that is told ;* " for it was only to pass away time like telling stories, that they spent those years in the wilderness ; all that while they were in the consuming, and another generation was in the rising. . . . The spending of our years is like the telling of a tale. A year when it is past is like a tale when it is told. Some of our years are as a pleasant story, others as a tragical one ; most mixed, but all short and transient ; that which was long in the doing may be told in a short time.—*Matthew Henry.*

Verse 9.—" *We spend our years as a tale that is told,*" or, *as a meditation* (so some translate) suddenly or swiftly : a discourse is quickly over, whether it be a discourse from the mouth, or in the mind ; and of the two the latter is far the more swift and nimble of foot. A discourse in our thoughts outruns the sun, as much as the sun outruns a snail ; the thoughts of a man will travel the world over in a moment ; he that now sits in this place, may be at the world's end in his thoughts, before I can speak another word.—*Joseph Caryl.*

Verse 9.—" *We spend our years as a tale that is told.*" This seems to express both a necessary fact and a censure. The rapid consumption of our years—their speedy passing away, is inevitable. But they may be spent also in a trifling manner to little valuable purpose, which would complete the disconsolate reflection on them, by the addition of guilt and censure.—*John Foster,* 1768—1843.

Verse 9.—" *As a tale that is told.*" In the Hebrew it is כְּמוֹ־הֶגֶה, *sicut meditatio,* (*as a meditation*) and so we read it in the margin, as if all our years were little else than a continual meditation upon the things of this world. Indeed, much of man's time is spent in this kind of vain meditation, as how to deceive and play fast and loose for advantage ; such a meditation had they, Isaiah lix. 13, or meditating with the heart lying words ; the same word in the Hebrew as in my text ; or how to heap up riches, such a meditation had that covetous man in the gospel, Luke xii. 17 ; or how to violate the sacred bonds of religion and laws of God, such a meditation had they, Ps. ii. 1—3 ; and in such vain meditations as these do men spend their years " as a tale that is told." . . .

To close this point with Gregory Nazianzen.

What are we but a vain dream that hath no existence or being, a mere phantasm or apparition that cannot be held, a ship sailing in the sea which leaves no impression or track behind it, a dust, a vapour, a morning dew, a flower flourishing one day and fading another, yea, the same day behold it springing and withered, but my text adds another metaphor from the flying of a bird, " *and we fly away,*" not go and run but fly, the quickest motion that any corporeal creature hath. Our life is like the flight of a bird, 'tis here now and 'tis gone out of sight suddenly. The Prophet therefore speaking of the speedy departure of Ephraim's glory expresseth it thus, " It shall flee away like a bird," Hos. ix. 11 ; and Solomon saith the like of riches, " they make themselves wings and flee away like an eagle toward heaven "; Prov. xxiii. 5. David wished for the wings of a dove that he might flee away and be at rest, and good cause he had for it, for this life is not more short than miserable. . . .

Be it our care then not to come creeping and coughing to God with a load of diseases and infirmities about us, when we are at death's door and not before, but to consecrate the first fruits of our life to his service. It is in the spending our time (as one compares it) as in the distilling of waters, the thinnest and purest part runs out first and only the lees at last : what an unworthy thing will it be to offer the prime of our time to the world, the flesh, and the devil, and the dregs of it to God. He that forbad the lame and the blind in beasts to be sacrificed, will not surely allow it in men ; if they come not to present their bodies a living sacrifice, while they are living and lively too, ere they be lame or blind or deformed with extremity of age, it is even a miracle if it prove then a holy, acceptable, or reasonable service.—*Thomas Washbourne*, 1655.

Verse 9 (*second clause*).—The Hebrew is different from all the Versions. " *We consume our years* (כְמוֹ־הֶגֶה *kemo hegeh*) *like a groan.*" We live a dying, whining, complaining life, and at last a *groan* is its termination !—*Adam Clarke.*

Verse 9.—The Vulgate translation has, " *Our years pass away like those of a spider.*" It implies that our life is as frail as the thread of a spider's web. Constituted most curiously the spider's web is ; but what more fragile ? In what is there more wisdom than in the complicated frame of the human body ; and what more easily destroyed ? Glass is granite compared with flesh ; and vapours are rocks compared with life.—*C.H.S.*

Verse 10.—" *It is soon cut off, and we fly away.*" At the Witan or council assembled by Edwin of Northumbria at Godmundingham (modern name Godmanham), to debate on the mission of Paulinus, the King was thus addressed by a heathen Thane, one of his chief men :—" The present life of man, O King, may be likened to what often happens when thou art sitting at supper with thy thanes and nobles in winter-time. A fire blazes on the hearth, and warms the chamber ; outside rages a storm of wind and snow ; a sparrow flies in at one door of thy hall, and quickly passes out at the other. For a moment and while it is within, it is unharmed by the wintry blast, but this brief season of happiness over, it returns to that wintry blast whence it came, and vanishes from thy sight. Such is the brief life of man ; we know not what went before it, and we are utterly ignorant as to what shall follow it. If, therefore, this new doctrine contain anything more certain, it justly deserves to be followed.—*Bede's Chronicle.*

Verse 10.—*The time of our life is threescore years and ten* (saith Moses), or set it upon the tenters, and rack it to *fourscore*, though not one in every fourscore arrives to that account, yet can we not be said to live so long ; for take out, first, ten years for infancy and childhood, which Solomon calls the time of wantonness and vanity (Eccles. xi.), wherein we scarce remember what we did, or whether we lived or no ; and how short is it then ? Take out of the remainder a third part for sleep, wherein like blocks we lie senseless, and how short is it then ? Take out yet besides the time of our carking and worldly care, wherein we seem both dead and buried in the affairs of the world, and how short is it then ? And take out yet besides, our times of wilful sinning and rebellion, for while we sin, we live not, but we are " *dead in sin*," and what remaineth of life ? yea, how short is it then ? so short is that life which nature allows, and yet we sleep away part, and play away part, and the cares of the world have a great part, so that the true spiritual and Christian life hath little or nothing in the end.—*From a Sermon by Robert Wilkinson, entitled " A Meditation of Mortalitie, preached to the late Prince Henry, some few daies before his death,"* 1612.

Verse 10.—" *Threescore years and ten.*" It may at first seem surprising that Moses should describe the days of man as " *Threescore years and ten.*" But when it is remembered, that, in the second year of the pilgrimage in the wilderness, as related in Numbers xiv., God declared that all those who had been recently numbered at Sinai should die in the wilderness, before the expiration of forty years, the lamentation of Moses on the brevity of human life becomes very intelligible and appropriate ; and the Psalm itself acquires a solemn and affecting interest, as a penitential confession of the sins which had entailed such melancholy consequences on the Hebrew nation ; and as a humble deprecation of God's wrath ; and as a funeral dirge upon those whose death had been pre-announced by the awful voice of God.—*Christopher Wordsworth.*

Verse 10.—There have been several *gradual abbreviations* of man's life. Death hath been coming nearer and nearer to us, as you may see in the several ages and periods of the world. Adam, the first of human kind, lived nine hundred and thirty years. And seven or eight hundred years was a usual period of man's life before the Flood. But the Sacred History (which hath the advantage and pre-eminence of all other histories whatsoever, by reason of its antiquity) acquaints us that immediately after the Flood the years of man's life were shortened by no less than half. . . . *After the Flood* man's life was apparently shorter than it was before, for they fell from nine hundred, eight hundred, and seven hundred years to four hundred and three hundred, as we see in the age of Arphaxad, Salah, Heber : yea, they fell to two hundred and odd years, as we read of Peleg, Reu, Serug, and Tharah ; yea, they came down to less than two hundred years. In the space of a few years man's life was again cut shorter by almost half, if not a full half. We read that Abraham lived but one hundred and seventy-five years, so that man's age ran very low then. See the account given in Scripture of Nahor, Sarah, Ishmael, Isaac, Jacob, Joseph (who died at a hundred) which confirms the same. And again the *third time*, man's life was shortened by almost *another half*, viz., about the year of the World 2,500, in Moses' time. For he sets the bounds of man's life thus : " The days of our years are threescore years and ten ; and if by reason of strength they be fourscore years, yet is their strength labour and sorrow ; for it is soon cut off, and we fly away." Ps. xc. 10. Eighty years is the utmost limit he sets man's life at, *i.e.*, in the most ordinary and common account of man's life. Though some are of the opinion that these words do not give an account of the duration of man's life in general, but refer to the short lives of the Israelites in the wilderness, yet I do not see but it may take in both ; and Moses who composed the Psalm, lived a hundred and twenty years himself, yet he might speak of the common term of man's life, and what usually happened to the generality of men.—*John Edwards.*

Verse 10.—" *Their strength is labour and sorrow.*" Most commonly old age is a feeble estate ; the very grasshopper is a burden to it. Eccl. xii. 5. Even the old man himself is a burden, to his wife, to his children, to himself. As Barzillai said to David, " I am this day fourscore years old : and can I discern between good and evil ? can thy servant taste what I eat or what I drink ? can I hear any more the voice of singing men and singing women ? " 2 Sam. xix. 35. Old age, we say, is a good guest, and should be made welcome, but that he brings such a troop with him ; blindness, aches, coughs, etc. ; these are troublesome, how should they be welcome ? " *Their strength is labour and sorrow.*" If their very strength, which is their best, be labour and grief, what is their worst ?—*Thomas Adams.*

Verse 10.—" *Their strength is labour and sorrow.*"—

> Unnumbered maladies his joints invade,
> Lay siege to life, and press the dire blockade.
> —*Samuel Johnson, 1709—1784.*

Verse 10.—" *Their strength.*" Properly, " *the pride* " of the days of our life is labour and sorrow—*i.e.*, our days at their best.—*Barth's* " *Bible Manual.*"

Verse 10.—" *We fly away.*"

> Bird of my breast, away !
> The long-wish'd hour is come !
> On to the realms of cloudless day,
> On to thy glorious home !
>
> Long has been thine to mourn
> In banishment and pain,
> Return, thou wand'ring dove, return,
> And find thy ark again !
>
> Away, on joyous wing,
> Immensity to range ;
> Around the throne to soar and sing,
> And faith for sight exchange
>
> * * * * *
>
> Flee, then, from sin and woe,
> To joys immortal flee ;
> Quit thy dark prison-house below,
> And be for ever free !
>
> I come, ye blessed throng,
> Your tasks and joys to share ;
> O, fill my lips with holy song,
> My drooping wing upbear.

—*Henry Francis Lyte,* 1793—1847.

Verse 11.—" *Who knoweth the power of thine anger ?* " We may take some scantling, some measure of the wrath of man, and know how far it can go, and what it can do, but we can take no measure of the wrath of God, for it is unmeasurable.—*Joseph Caryl.*

Verse 11.—" *Who knoweth the power of thine anger ?* " None at all ; and unless the power of that can be known, it must abide as unspeakable as the love of Christ which passeth knowledge.—*John Bunyan.*

Verse 11.—Moses, I think, here means, that it is a holy awe of God, and that alone, which makes us truly and deeply feel his anger. We see that the reprobate, although they are severely punished, only chafe upon the bit, or kick against God, or become exasperated, or are stupefied, as if they were hardened against all calamities ; so far are they from being subdued. And though they are full of trouble, and cry aloud, yet the Divine anger does not so penetrate their hearts as to abate their pride and fierceness. The minds of the godly alone are wounded with the wrath of God ; nor do they wait for his thunder-bolts, to which the reprobate hold out their hard and iron necks, but they tremble the very moment when God moves only his little finger. This I consider to be the true meaning of the prophet.—*John Calvin.*

Verse 11.—" *Who knoweth the power of thine anger ?* " etc. The meaning is, What man doth truly know and acknowledge the power of thy anger, according to that measure of fear wherewith thou oughtest to be feared ? Note hence, how Moses and the people of God, though they feared God, yet notwithstanding confess that they failed in respect of that measure of the fear of God which they ought to have had ; for we must not think, but Moses and some of his people did truly fear God. But yet in regard of the power of God's anger, which was now very great and grievous, their fear of God was not answerable and proportionable ; then it is apparent that Moses and this people failed in respect of the measure of the fear of God which they ought to have had, in regard of the greatness and grievousness of the judgments of God upon them.

See, that the best of God's servants in this life fall short in their fear of God, and so in all graces of the Spirit ; in that love of God, in faith, in repentance, and in obedience, we come short all of us of that which the Lord requires at our hands. For though we do know God, and that he is a just God, and righteous, and cannot wink at sin ; yet what man is there that so fears before him as he ought to be feared ? what man so quakes at his anger as he should ; and is so afraid of sin as he ought to be ? We have no grace here in perfection, but the best faith is mixed with infidelity ; our hope with fear ; our joy with sorrow. It is well we can discern our wants and imperfections, and cry out with the man in the gospel, " I believe ; Lord, help my unbelief ! "—*Samuel Smith.*

Verse 11.—" *Who knoweth the power of thine anger ? "* No man knows the power of God's anger, because that power has never yet put itself forth to its full stretch. Is there, then, no measure of God's wrath—no standard by which we may estimate its intenseness ? There is no fixed measure or standard, but there is a variable one. The wicked man's fear of God is a measure of the wrath of God. If we take the man as he may be sometime taken, when the angel of death is upon him, when the sins of his youth and of his maturer years throng him like an armed troop, and affright and afflict him—when with all his senses keenly alive to the rapid strides of bodily decay, he feels that he must die, and yet that he is not prepared—why, it may come to pass, it does occasionally, though not always come to pass, that his anticipations of the future are literally tremendous. There is such a fear and such a dread of that God into whose immediate presence he feels himself about to be ushered, that even they who love him best, and charm him most, shrink from the wildness of his gaze and the fearfulness of his speech. And we cannot tell the man, though he may be just delirious with apprehension, that his fear of God invests the wrath of God with a darker than its actual colouring. On the contrary, we know that " *according to the fear, so is the wrath.*" We know that if man's fear of God be wrought up to the highest pitch, and the mind throb so vehemently that its frame-work threaten to give way and crumble, we know that the wrath of the Almighty keeps pace with this gigantic fear. . . .

If it has happened to you—and there is not perhaps a man on the face of the earth to whom it does not sometimes happen—if it has ever happened to you to be crushed with the thought, that a life of ungodliness must issue in an eternity of woe, and if amid the solitude of midnight and amid the dejections of sickness there pass across the spirit the fitful figures of an avenging ministry, then we have to tell you, it is not the roar of battle which is powerful enough, nor the wail of orphans which is thrilling enough, to serve as the vehicle of such a communication ; we have to tell you, that you fly to a refuge of lies, if you dare flatter yourselves that either the stillness of the hour or the feebleness of disease has caused you to invest vengeance with too much of the terrible. We have to tell you, that the picture was not overdrawn which you drew in your agony. " *According to thy fear, so is thy wrath.*" Fear is but a mirror, which you may lengthen indefinitely, and widen indefinitely, and wrath lengthens with the lengthening and widens with the widening, still crowding the mirror with new and fierce forms of wasting and woe. We caution you, then, against ever cherishing the flattering notion, that fear can exaggerate God's wrath. We tell you, that when fear has done its worst, it can in no degree come up to the wrath which it images. . . .

Now, it is easy to pass from this view of the text to another, which is in a certain sense similar. You will always find, that men's apprehensions of God's wrath are nicely proportioned to the fear and reverence which are excited in them by the name and the attributes of God. He will have but light thoughts of future vengeance, who has but low thoughts of the character and properties of his Creator : and from this it comes to pass, that the great body of men betray a kind of stupid insensibility to the wrath of Jehovah. . . . Look at the crowd of the worldly and the indifferent. There is no fear of God in that crowd ; they are " of the earth earthy." The soul is sepulchred in the body, and has never wakened to a sense of its position with reference to a holy and avenging Creator. Now, then, you may understand the absence of all knowledge of the power of God's wrath. " *Who knoweth the power of thine anger ? even according to thy fear, so is thy wrath.*"—*Henry Melvill.*

Verse 11.—" *Who knoweth the power of thine anger ? "* etc. This he utters, 1. By way of lamentation. He sighing forth a most doleful complaint against the security and stupor he observed in that generation of men in his time, both in those that had already died in their sins, as well as of that new generation that had come up in their room, who still lived in their sins ; oh, says he, ' Who of them knoweth the power of thine anger ? ' namely, of that wrath which followeth after death, and seizeth upon men's souls for ever ; that is, who considers it, or regards it, till it take hold upon them ? He utters it, 2. In a way of astonishment, out of the apprehension he had of the greatness of that wrath. " *Who knoweth the power of thine anger ? "* that is, who hath or can take it in according to the greatness of it ? which he endeavours to set forth, as applying himself to our own apprehension, in this wise, " *Even according to thy fear, so is thy wrath.*" Where those words, " *thy fear"* are taken *objective*, and so signify the *fear of thee*; and so the meaning is, that according to whatever proportion our souls can take in, in fears of thee and of thine anger, so great is thy wrath itself. You have souls that are able to comprehend vast fears and terrors; they are as extensive in their fears as in their desires, which are stretched beyond what this world or the creatures can afford them, to an infinity. The soul of man is a dark cell, which when it begets fears once, strange and fearful apparitions rise up in it, which far exceed the ordinary proportion of worldly evils (which yet also our fears usually make greater than they prove to be); but here, as to that punishment which is the effect of God's own immediate wrath, let the soul enlarge itself, says he, and widen its apprehension to the utmost; fear what you can imagine, yet still God's wrath, and the punishment it inflicts, are not only proportionable, but infinitely exceeding all you can fear or imagine. *"Who knoweth the power of thine anger?"* It passeth knowledge.—*Thomas Goodwin.*

Verse 12.—*" So teach us to number our days, that we may apply our hearts unto wisdom."* Moses who was learned in all the sciences of the Egyptians (among which arithmetic was one) desireth to learn this point of arithmetic only of thee, O Lord; and why? Is it because, as Job speaketh, thou hast determined the number of his days? Would Moses have thee reveal to every man the moment of his end? Such speculations may well beseem an Egyptian, an Israelite they do not beseem. Thy children, O Lord, know that it is not for them so to know times and seasons which thou keepest in thine own power, and are a secret sealed up with thee: we should not pry into that counting-house, nor curiously inquire into that sum. It is not then a mathematical numbering of days that Moses would be schooled in, but a moral; he would have God not simply to teach him to number, but to number " *so* "; and " *so* " points out a special manner, a manner that may be useful for the children of God. And indeed our petitions must bear this mark of profitable desires, and we should not ask aught of thee but that by which (if we speed) we may become the better; he that so studies his mortality learns it as he should, and it is only thou, O Lord, that takest him out such a lesson. But what is the use, O Moses, that thou wouldst have man make of such a knowledge? *" Even to apply his heart unto wisdom."* O happy knowledge, by which a man becomes wise; for wisdom is the beauty of a reasonable soul. God created him therewith, but sin hath divorced the soul and wisdom; so that a sinful man is indeed no better than a fool, so the Scripture calleth him; and well it may call him so, seeing all his carriage is vain, and the upshot of his endeavours but vexation of spirit. But though sin have divorced wisdom and the soul, yet are they not so severed but they may be reunited; and nothing is more powerful in furthering this union than this feeling meditation— that we are mortal.—*Arthur Lake.*

Verse 12.—*" So teach us,"* etc. Moses sends you to God for teaching. " Teach thou us; not as the world teacheth—teach thou us." No meaner Master; no inferior school; not Moses himself except as he speaks God's word and becomes the schoolmaster to bring us to Christ; not the prophets, not apostles themselves, neither " holy men of old," except as they " spake and were moved by the Holy Ghost." This knowledge comes not from flesh and blood, but from God. " So teach thou us." ' And so David says, " Teach me thy way, O Lord, and I will walk in thy truth." And hence our Lord's promise to his disciples, " The Holy Ghost, he shall teach you all things."—*Charles Richard Sumner,* 1850.

Verse 12.—*" Teach us to number our days."* Mark what it is which Moses here prays for, only to be taught to number his days. But did he not do this'already? Was it not his daily work this, his constant and continual employment? Yes, doubtless it was; yea, and he did it carefully and conscientiously too. But yet he thought he did it not well enough, and therefore prays here in the text to be taught to do better. See a good man, how little he pleaseth himself in any action of his life, in any performance of duty that he does. He can never think that he does well enough whatever he does, but still desires to do otherwise, and would fain do better. There is an affection of modesty and humility which still accompanies real piety; and every pious man is an humble, modest man, and never reckons himself a perfect proficient, or to be advanced above a teaching, but is content and covetous to be a continual learner; to know more than he knows and to do better than he does; yea, and thinks it no disparagement to his graces at all to take advice, and to seek instruction where it is to be had.—*Edm. Barker's Funeral Sermon for Lady Capell.* 1661.

Verse 12.—" *Teach us to number our days.*"

" Improve Time in time, while the Time doth last,
For all Time is no time, when the Time is past."

—*From Richard Pigot's " Life of Man, symbolised by the Months of the Year,"* 1866.

Verse 12.—" *Teach us to number our days.*" The proverbial oracles of our parsimonious ancestors have informed us that the fatal waste of fortune is by small expenses, by the profusion of sums too little singly to alarm our caution, and which we never suffer ourselves to consider together. Of the same kind is prodigality of life : he that hopes to look back hereafter with satisfaction upon past years, must learn to know the present value of single minutes, and endeavour to let no particle of time fall useless to the ground. An Italian philosopher expressed in his motto that time was his estate ; an estate, indeed, that will produce nothing without cultivation, but will always abundantly repay the labours of industry, and satisfy the most extensive desires, if no part of it be suffered to lie waste by negligence, to be overrun by noxious plants, or laid out for show rather than for use.—*Samuel Johnson.*

Verse 12.—" *To number our days,*" is not simply to take the reckoning and admeasurement of human life. This has been done already in Holy Scripture, where it is said, " *The days of our years are threescore years and ten ; and if by reason of strength they be fourscore years, yet is their strength labour and sorrow ; for it is soon cut off, and we fly away.*" Nor yet is it, in the world's phrase, to calculate the chances of survivorship, which any man may do in the instance of the aggregate, but which no man can do in the case of the individual. But it is to take the measure of our days as compared with the work to be performed, with the provision to be laid up for eternity, with the preparation to be made for death, with the precaution to be taken against judgment. It is to estimate human life by the purposes to which it should be applied, by the eternity to which it must conduct, and in which it shall at last be absorbed. Under this aspect it is, that David contemplates man when he says, " *Thou hast made my days as an handbreadth ; and mine age is as nothing before thee,*" Ps. xxxix. 5 ; and then proceeds to include in this comprehensive estimate even those whose days have been the longest upon earth : " Verily, every man at his best estate is altogether vanity.—*"Thomas Dale,* 1847.

Verse 12.—" *To number our days.*" Number we our days by our daily prayers—number we them by our daily obedience and daily acts of love—number we them by the memories that they bring of holy men who have entered into their Saviour's peace, and by the hopes which are woven with them of glory and of grace won for us !—*Plain Commentary.*

Verse 12.—" *Apply our hearts unto wisdom.*" Sir Thomas Smith, secretary to Queen Elizabeth, some months before his death said, That it was a great pity men knew not to what end they were born into this world, until they were ready to go out of it.—*Charles Bradbury.*

Verse 12.—" *Apply our hearts unto wisdom.*" St. Austin says, " We can never do that, except we number every day as our last day." Many put far the evil day. They refuse to leave the earth, when the earth is about to take its leave of them.—*William Secker.*

Verse 12.—" *Apply our hearts unto wisdom.*" Moses speaketh of *wisdom* as if it were physic, which doth no good before it be applied ; and the part to apply it to is the *heart*, where all man's affections are to love it and to cherish it, like a kind of hostess. When the heart seeketh it findeth, as though it were brought unto her, like Abraham's ram. Therefore God saith, " They shall seek me and find me, because they shall seek me with their hearts," Jer. xxix. 13 ; as though they should not find him with all their seeking unless they did seek him with their heart. Therefore the way to get wisdom is to apply your hearts unto it, as if it were your calling and living, to which you were bound 'prentices. A man may apply his ears and his eyes as many truants do to their books, and yet never prove scholars ; but from that day when a man begins to apply his heart unto wisdom, he learneth more in a month after than he did in a year before, nay, than ever he did in his life. Even as you see the wicked, because they apply their hearts to wickedness, how fast they proceed, how easily and how quickly they become perfect swearers, expert drunkards, cunning deceivers, so if ye could apply your hearts as thoroughly to knowledge and goodness, you might become like the apostle which teacheth you. Therefore, when Solomon sheweth men the way how to come by wisdom, he speaks often of the heart, as, " Give thine heart to wisdom," " let wisdom enter into thine heart," " get wisdom," " keep wisdom," " embrace wisdom," Prov. ii. 10, iv. 5, xiii. 8, as though a man went a wooing for wisdom. Wisdom is like God's daughter, that he giveth to the man that loveth her, and sueth for her, and meaneth to set her at his heart. Thus we have learned how to apply knowledge that it may do us good ; not to our ears, like them which hear sermons only, nor to our tongues like them which make table-talk of religion, but to our hearts, that we may say with the virgin, " My heart doth magnify the Lord," Luke i., and the heart will apply it to the ear and to the tongue, as Christ saith, " *Out of the abundance of the heart the mouth speaketh,*" Matt. xii. 34.—*Henry Smith.*

Verse 12.—Of all arithmetical rules this is the hardest—*to number our days.* Men can number their herds and droves of oxen and of sheep, they can estimate the revenues of their manors and farms, they can with a little pains number and tell their coins, and yet they are persuaded that their days are infinite and innumerable and therefore do never begin to number them. Who saith not upon the view of another, surely yonder man looketh by his countenance as if he would not live long, or yonder woman is old, her days cannot be many : thus we can number other men's days and years, and utterly forget our own, therefore this is the true wisdom of mortal men, to number their own days.—*Thomas Tymme.*

Verse 12.—Observe here, after that Moses had given us a description of the wrath of God, presently his thoughts are taken up with the meditation of death. The wrath of God thought on makes us think of death. . . . Let us often think of the wrath of God, and let the thought of it so far work upon us, as to keep us in a constant awe and fear of God ; and let this fear drive us to God by prayer, that fearing as we ought, we may pray as we are commanded, and praying, we may prevent the wrath of God. If our present sorrows do not move us, God will send greater ; and when our sorrows are grown too great for us, we shall have little heart or comfort to pray. Let our fears then quicken our prayers ; and let our prayers be such as are able to overcome our fears : so both ways shall we be happy, in that our fears have taught us to pray, and our prayers have made us to fear no more.— *Christopher Shute, in " Ars pie moriendi : or, The true Accomptant. A Sermon,"* etc., 1658.

Verse 12.—It is evident, that the great thing wanted to make men provide for eternity, is the practical persuasion that they have but a short time to live. They will not apply their hearts unto wisdom until they are brought to the numbering of their days. And how are you to be brought, my brethren ? The most surprising thing in the text is, that it should be in the form of a prayer. It is necessary that God should interfere to make men number their days. We call this surprising. What! is there not enough to make us feel our frailty, without an actual, super-natural impression ? What ! are there not lessons enough of that frailty without any new teaching from above ? Go into our churchyards—all ages speak to all ranks. Can we need more to prove to us the uncertainty of life ? Go into mourning families—and where are they not to be found ?—in this it is the old, in that it is the young, whom death has removed—and is there not eloquence in tears to persuade us that we are mortal ? Can it be that in treading every day on the dust of our fathers, and meeting every day with the funerals of our brethren, we shall not yet be practically taught to number our days, unless God print the truth on our hearts, through some special operation of his Spirit ? It is not thus in other things. In other things the frequency of the occurrence makes us expect it. The husbandman does not pray to be made believe that the seed must be buried and die before it will germinate. This has been the course of the grain of every one else, and where there is so much experience what room is there for prayer ? The mariner does not pray to be taught that the needle of his compass points towards the north. The needle of every compass has so pointed since the secret was discovered, and he has not to ask when he is already so sure. The benighted man does not pray to be made to feel that the sun will rise in a few hours. Morning has succeeded to night since the world was made, and why should he ask what he knows too well to doubt ? But in none of these things is there greater room for assurance than we have each one for himself, in regard to its being appointed to him once to die. Nevertheless, we must pray to be made to know—to be made to feel—that we are to die, in the face of an experience which is certainly not less than that of the parties to whom we have referred. This is a petition that we may believe, believe as they do : for they act on their belief in the fact, which this experience incontestably attests.

And we may say of this, that it is amongst the strangest of the strange things that may be affirmed of human nature, that whilst, in regard to inferior concerns, we can carefully avail ourselves of experience, taking care to register its decisions and to deduce from them rules for our guidance—in the mightiest concern of all we can act as though experience had furnished no evidence, and we were left without matter from which to draw inferences. And, nevertheless, in regard to nothing else is the experience so uniform. The grain does not always germinate—but every man dies. The needle does not always point due north—but every man dies. The sun does not cross the horizon in every place in every twenty-four hours—but every man dies. Yet we must pray—pray as for the revelation of a mystery hidden from our gaze—we must pray to be made to know—to be made to believe—that every man dies! For I call it not belief, and our text calls it not belief, in the shortness of life and the certainty of death, which allows men to live without thought of eternity, without anxiety as to the soul, or without an effort to secure to themselves salvation. I call it not belief—no, no, anything rather than belief. Men are rational beings, beings of forethought, disposed to make provision for what they feel to be inevitable ; and if there were not a practical infidelity as to their own mortality, they could not be practically reckless as to their own safety.—*Henry Melvill.*

Verse 12.—" *So teach us to number our days,*" etc. Five things I note in these words : first, that death is the haven of every man ; whether he sit on the throne, or keep in a cottage, at last he must knock at death's door, as all his fathers have done before him. Secondly, that man's time is set, and his bounds appointed, which he cannot pass, no more than the Egyptians could pass the sea ; and therefore Moses saith, " *Teach us to number our days,*" as though there were a number of our days. Thirdly, that our days are few, as though we were sent into this world but to see it ; and therefore Moses, speaking of our life, speaks of days, not of years, nor of months, nor of weeks ; but " *Teach us to number our days,*" shewing that it is an easy thing even for a man to number his days, they be so few. Fourthly, the aptness of man to forget death rather than anything else ; and therefore Moses prayeth the Lord to teach him to number his days, as though they were still slipping out of his mind. Lastly, that to remember how short a time we have to live, will make us apply our hearts to that which is good.—*Henry Smith.*

Verse 12.—" *Our hearts.*" In both the Scriptures of the Old and New Testament, the term " *heart* " is applied alike to the mind that thinks, to the spirit that feels, and the will that acts. And it here stands for the whole mental and moral nature of man, and implies that the whole soul and spirit, with all their might, are to be applied in the service of wisdom.—*William Brown Keer*, 1863.

Verse 12.—" *Wisdom.*" I consider this " *wisdom* " identical with the hypostatic *wisdom* described by Solomon, Prov. vii. 15—31, and ix. 1, 5, even Immanuel, the *wisdom*, righteousness, sanctification, and redemption of his people. The chief pursuit of life should be the attainment of an experimental knowledge of Christ, by whom " kings reign and princes decree justice ; whose delights are with the sons of men, and who crieth, Whoso findeth me findeth life, and shall obtain favour of the Lord ; come, eat of my bread and drink of the wine which I have mingled." David in the Psalms, and Solomon, his son, in the Proverbs, have predictively manifested Messiah as the hypostatic *wisdom*, " whose goings forth have been from of old, from everlasting."—*J. N. Coleman.*

Verse 13.—" *Let it repent thee.*" According to the not unfrequent and well known phraseology of Scripture, God is said to repent, when putting away men's sorrow, and affording new ground of gladness, he appears as it were to be changed.—*John Calvin.*

Verse 14.—" *O satisfy us with thy mercy.*" A poor hungry soul lying under sense of wrath, will promise to itself happiness for ever, if it can but once again find what it hath sometimes felt ; that is, one sweet fill of God's sensible mercy towards it.—*David Dickson.*

Verse 14.—" *O satisfy us.*" That is everywhere and evermore the cry of humanity. And what a strange cry it is, when you think of it, brethren ! Man is the offspring of God ; the bearer of his image ; he stands at the head of the terrestrial creation ; on earth he is peerless ; he possesses wondrous capacities of thought, and feeling, and action. The world, and all that is in it, has been formed in a complete and beautiful adaptation to his being. Nature seems to be ever calling to him with a thousand voices, to be glad and rejoice ; and yet he is unsatisfied, discontented, miserable ! This is a most strange thing—strange, that is, on any theory respecting man's character and condition, but that which is supplied by the Bible ; and it is not only a testimony to the ruin of his nature, but also to the insufficiency of everything earthly to meet his cravings.—*Charles M. Merry*, 1864.

Verse 14.—" *O satisfy us early with thy mercy ; that we may rejoice and be glad all our days.*" We pass now to this particular prayer, and those limbs that make up the body of it. They are many ; as many as words in it : satisfy, and satisfy us, and do that early, and do that with that which is thine, and let that be mercy. So that first it is a prayer for fulness ·and satisfaction,—*satisfy :* and then it is a prayer not only of appropriation to ourselves, satisfy me, but of a charitable dilation and extension to others, satisfy *us*, all us, all thy servants, all thy church ; and then thirdly it is a prayer of despatch and expedition, " Satisfy us *early ;* " and after that, it is a prayer of evidence and manifestation, satisfy us with that which is, and which we may discern to be *thine ;* and then lastly it is a prayer of limitation even upon God himself, that God will take no other way herein but the way of " *mercy.*" " *Satisfy us early with thy mercy.*" . . . . . . There is a spiritual fulness in this life of which St. Hierome speaks, *Ebrietas felix, satietas salutaris,* A happy excess and a wholesome surfeit ; *quæ quanto copiosius sumitur, majorem donat sobrietatem.* In which the more we eat, the more temperate we are, and the more we drink, the more sober. In which (as St. Bernard also expresses it in his mellifluence) *Mutua interminabili inexplicabili generatione, desiderium generat satietatem, et satietas parit desiderium,* By a mutual and reciprocal, by an undeterminable and inexpressible generation of one another, the desire of spiritual graces begets a satiety, and then this satiety begets a farther desire. This is a holy ambition, a sacred covetousness. Naphtali's blessing, " *O Naphtali, satisfied with favour, and full with the blessing of the Lord,*" Deut. xxxiii. 23 ; St. Stephen's blessing, " *Full of faith and of the Holy Ghost,*" Acts vi. 5 ; the blessed Virgin's blessing, " *Full of grace* " *;* Dorcas' blessing, " *Full of good works and of alms-deeds,*" Acts ix. 36 ; the blessing of him who is blessed above all, and who blesseth all, even Christ Jesus, " *Full of wisdom, full of the Holy Ghost, full of grace and truth.*" Luke ii. 40, Luke iv. 1, John i. 14. . . . . . . " *Satisfy us early with*" that which is thine, " *thy mercy ;* " for there are mercies (in a fair extent and accommodation of the word, that is refreshings, eases, deliverances), that are not *his* mercies, nor his satisfactions. . . . . . . It is not his mercy, except we go by good ways to good ends ; except our safety be established by alliance with his friends, except our peace may be had with the perfect continuance of our religion, there is no safety, there is no peace. But let me feel the effect of this prayer, as it is a prayer of manifestation, let me discern that that which is done upon me is done by the hand of God, and I care not what it be, I had rather have God's vinegar, than man's oil, God's wormwood, than man's manna, God's justice, than any man's mercy ; for therefore did Gregory Nyssen call St. Basil in a holy sense, Ambidextrum, because he took everything that came by the right handle, and with the right hand, because he saw it come from God. Even afflictions are welcome when we see them to be his : though the way that he would choose, and the way that this prayer entreats. be only mercy, " *Satisfy us early with thy mercy.*"—*John Donne.*

Verse 16.—" *And thy glory unto their children.*" That is to say, that our children may see the glorious fruit of this affliction in us, that so they may not be discouraged thereby to serve thee, but rather the more heartened, when they shall see what a glorious work thou hast wrought in and upon us by afflicting us.—*William Bradshaw.*

Verses 16, 17.—" *Thy work.*" " *The work of our hands.*" You will observe a beautiful parallelism between two things which are sometimes confounded and sometimes too jealously sundered : I mean *God's agency* and *man's instrumentality*, between man's personal activity and that power of God which actuates and animates, and gives it a vital efficacy. For forty years it had been the business of Moses to bring Israel into a right state politically, morally, religiously : *that* had been *his* work. And yet, in so far as it was to have any success or enduringness, it must be God's work. " The work of our hands" do thou establish ; and this God does when, in answer to prayer, he adopts the works of his servants, and makes it his own " work," his own " glory," his own " beauty."—*James Hamilton.*

Verses 16, 17.—There is a twofold Rabbinical tradition respecting this verse and the preceding one ; that they were the original prayer recited by Moses as a blessing on the work of making the Tabernacle and its ornaments, and that subsequently he employed them as the usual formula of benediction for any newly undertaken task, whenever God's *glorious Majesty* was to be consulted for an answer by Urim and Thummim.—*Lyranus, R. Shelomo, and Genebrardus, quoted by Neale.*

Verses 16, 17.—They were content to live and to die as pilgrims, provided only they could feel that in his sterner dealings with them God was, however slowly, preparing the way for that display of glorious blessedness which should be the lot of their descendants. In a similar spirit they ask God to establish the work of their hands, though they reckoned not that they should behold its results. Their comfort in sowing was the belief that their children would reap.—*Joseph Francis Thrupp.*

Verses 16, 17.—It is worthy of notice that this prayer was answered. Though the first generation fell in the wilderness, yet the labours of Moses and his companions were blessed to the second. These were the most devoted to God of any generation that Israel ever saw. It was of them that the Lord said, " I remember thee, the kindness of thy youth, the love of thine espousals, when thou wentest after me in the wilderness, in a land that was not sown. Israel was holiness unto the Lord, and the first fruits of his increase." It was then that Balaam could not curse, but, though desirous of the wages of unrighteousness, was compelled to forego them, and his curse was turned into a blessing. We are taught by this case, amidst temporal calamities and judgments, in which our earthly hopes may be in a manner extinguished, to seek to have the loss repaired by spiritual blessings. If God's work does but appear to us, and our posterity after us, we need not be dismayed at the evils which afflict the earth.—*Andrew Fuller.*

Verse 17.—" *Let the beauty of the Lord our God be upon us,*" etc. Let us try to look at our life's work in relation to the Lord's beauty. Our *work* and Divine *Beauty*, at first sight, how different ; yet, on deeper insight, how truly *one*, how inseparably united. There is light so beauty-giving, that nothing it touches is positively ugly. In our sea-girt island, with our fickle climate and grey atmosphere, we can only rarely imagine what magic power the serene skies, the balmy air, the sunny atmosphere of the South have over even the least interesting object in nature ; but from certain hours, in certain places, I think we may form an idea of the transforming faculty of light.

There is also spiritual light, so beauty-inspiring, that the plainest face within which it is born is illumined with singular loveliness, which wins its way into many a heart. Who of us has not marvelled at an unexpected light, in what we had always thought an uninteresting face ? Who has not beheld a light divine irradiate the human countenance, giving joy, and prophesying perfection, where we had least thought to find beauty ? May we not take these facts as emblems, albeit faint and imperfect, of what the " *Beauty of the Lord* " does for us, and our work ? You know what the natural light can do for material objects ; you know what mental and moral light can work for human faces ; rise from these, and know what spiritual light, Divine Light, can do for immortal beings and immortal works.—*Jessie Coombs, in " Thoughts for the Inner Life," 1867.*

Verse 17.—" *The beauty of the Lord.*" In the word נֹעַם (beauty) there is something like a deluge of grace. Thus far, he says, we have sought thy work, O Lord. There we do nothing, but are only spectators and recipients of thy gifts, we are merely passive. There thou showest thyself to us, and makest us safe, by thy work alone, which thou doest, when thou dost liberate us from that disease which Satan inflicted on the whole human race in Adam, to wit, Sin and Eternal death.—*Martin Luther.*

Verse 17.—God is glorified and his work advances when his church is beautiful. " *The beauty of the Lord* " is the beauty of holiness,—that beauty which in the Lord Jesus himself shone with lustre so resplendent, and which ought to be repeated or reflected by every disciple. And it is towards this that all amongst us who love the Saviour, and who long for the extension of his Kingdom, should very mainly direct their endeavours. Nothing can be sadder than when preaching or personal effort is contradicted and neutralized by the low or unlovely lives of those who pass for Christians ; and nothing can go further to insure success than when prayer is carried out and preaching is seconded by the pure, holy, and benevolent lives of those who seek to follow the Lamb whithersoever he goeth.—*James Hamilton.*

Verse 17.—" *The work of our hands.*" Jarchi interprets this of the work of the Tabernacle, in which the hands of the Israelites were employed in the wilderness ; so Arama of the Tabernacle of Bezaleel.—*John Gill.*

HINTS TO PREACHERS.

Verse 1.— The near and dear relation between God and his people, so that they mutually dwell in each other.

Verse 1.—The abode of the church the same in all ages; her relation to God never changes.

Verse 1.—I. The soul is at home in God. 1. Originally. Its birth-place—its native air—home of its thoughts, will, conscience, affections, desires. 2. Experimentally. When it returns here it feels itself at home : " Return unto thy rest," etc. 3. Eternally. The soul, once returned to this home, never leaves it : " it shall go no more out for ever." II. The soul is not at home elsewhere. " Our dwelling place," etc. 1. For all men. 2. At all times. He is ever the same, and the wants of the soul substantially are ever the same.—*G. R.*

Verse 2.—A Discourse upon the Eternity of God. S. **Charnock**. Works I. pp. 344—373, Nichol's Edition.

Verse 2 (*last clause*).—The consideration of God's eternity may serve, I. For the support of our faith ; in reference to our own condition for the future ; in reference to our posterity ; and to the condition of God's church to the end of the world. II. For the encouragement of our obedience. We serve the God, who can give us an everlasting reward. III. For the terror of wicked men.—*Tillotson's Sermon on the Eternity of God.*

Verse 3.—I. The cause of death—" thou turnest." II. The nature of death —" return." III. The necessities of death—reconciliation with God, and preparation to return.

Verse 4.—I. Contemplate the lengthened period with all its events. II. Consider what he must be to whom all this is as nothing. III. Consider how we stand towards him.

Verse 5.—Comparison of mortal life to sleep. See William Bradshaw's remarks in our Notes on this verse.

Verses 5, 6.—The lesson of the Meadows. I. Grass growing the emblem of youth. II. Grass flowering—or man in his prime. III. The scythe. IV. Grass mown—or man at death.

Verse 7.—I. Man's chief troubles are the effect of death. 1. His own death. 2. The death of others. II. Death is the effect of Divine anger : " We are consumed by," etc. III. Divine anger is the effect of sin. Death by sin.—*G. R.*

Verse 8.—I. The notice which God takes of sin. 1. Individual. "*Our* iniquities." 2. Universal notice—" iniquities "—not one only, but all. 3. Minute, even the most secret sins. 4. Constant : " Set them before " him—" in the light," etc. II. The notice which we should take of them on that account. 1. In our thoughts. Set them before us. 2. In our consciences. Condemn ourselves on account of them. 3. In our wills. Turn from them by repentance—turn to a pardoning God by faith.—*G. R.*

Verse 9.—I. Every man has a history. His life is as a tale—a separate tale— to be told. II. Every man's history has some display of God in it. All our days, some may say, are passed away in thy wrath—all, others may say, in thy love— and others, some of our days in anger and some in love. III. Every man's history will be told. In death, at judgment, through eternity.—*G. R.*

Verse 10.—I. What life is *to* most. It seldom reaches its natural limits. One half die in childhood : more than half of the other half die in manhood ; few attain to old age. II. What life is *at* most. " Threescore years," etc. III. What it is to most beyond that limit. " If by reason," etc. IV. What it is to all. " It is soon cut off," etc.—*G. R.*

Verse 11.—I. The anger of God against sin is not fully known by its effects in this life. " Who knoweth the power," etc. Here we see the hidings of its power. II. The anger of God against sin hereafter is equal to our greatest fears. "According to thy fear," etc. ; or, " the fear of thee," etc.—*G. R.*

Verse 12.—I. The Reckoning. 1. What their usual number. 2. How many of them are already spent. 3. How uncertain the number that remains. 4. How much of them must be occupied with the necessary duties of this life. 5. What afflictions and helplessness may attend them. II. The use to be made of it. 1. To " seek wisdom "—not riches, worldly honours, or pleasures—but wisdom ; not the wisdom of the world, but of God. 2. To " apply the heart " to it. Not mental merely, but moral wisdom; not speculative merely, but experimental; not theoretical merely, but practical. 3. To seek it at once—immediately. 4. To seek it constantly—" *apply* our hearts," etc. III. The help to be sought in it. " So teach us," etc. 1. Our own ability is insufficient through the perversion both of the mind and heart by sin. 2. Divine help may be obtained. " If any man lack wisdom," etc.—*G. R.*

Verse 12.—The Sense of Mortality. Show the variety of blessings dispensed to different classes by the right use of the sense of mortality. I. It may be an antidote for the sorrowful. Reflect, " there is an end." II. It should be a restorative to the labouring. III. It should be a remedy for the impatient. IV. As a balm to the wounded in heart. V. As a corrective for the worldly. VI. As a sedative to the frivolous.—*R. Andrew Griffin, in " Stems and Twigs,"* 1872.

Verse 13.—In what manner the Lord may be said to repent.

Verse 14 *(first clause).*—See " Spurgeon's Sermons," No. 513: " The Young Man's Prayer."

Verse 14.—I. The deepest yearning of man is for satisfaction. II. Satisfaction can only be found in the realization of Divine mercy.—*C. M. Merry,* 1864.

Verse 14.—" *O satisfy us early with thy mercy,"* etc. Learn, 1. That our souls can have no solid satisfaction in earthly things. 2. That the mercy of God alone can satisfy our souls. 3. That nothing but satisfaction in God can fill our days with joy and gladness.—*John Cawood,* 1842.

Verse 14.—I. The most cheerful days of earth are made more cheerful by thoughts of Divine mercy. II. The most sorrowful days of earth are made glad by the consciousness of Divine love.—*G. R.*

Verse 15.—I. The joy of faith is in proportion to the sorrow of repentance. II. The joy of consolation is in proportion to suffering in affliction. III. The joy of the returning smiles of God is in proportion to the terror of his frowns.—*G. R.*

Verse 15.—The Balance of life, or the manner in which our joys are set over against our sorrows.

Verse 16.—I. Our duty—" work," and our desire about it. II. Our children's portion—" glory," and our prayer in reference to it.

Verse 17.—The Right Establishment, or the work which will endure—why it will endure and should endure. Why we wish our work to be of such a nature, and whether there are enduring elements in it.

PSALM XCI.

This Psalm is without a title, and we have no means of ascertaining either the name of its writer, or the date of its composition, with certainty. The Jewish doctors consider that when the author's name is not mentioned we may assign the Psalm to the last-named writer ; and, if so, this is another Psalm of Moses, the man of God. Many expressions here used are similar to those of Moses in Deuteronomy, and the internal evidence, from the peculiar idioms, would point towards him as the composer. The continued lives of Joshua and Caleb, who followed the Lord fully, make remarkably apt illustrations of this Psalm, for they, as a reward for abiding in continued nearness to the Lord, lived on " amongst the dead, amid their graves." For these reasons it is by no means improbable that this Psalm may have been written by Moses, but we dare not dogmatize. If David's pen was used in giving us this matchless ode, we cannot believe as some do that he thus commemorated the plague which devastated Jerusalem on account of his numbering the people. For him, then, to sing of himself as seeing " the reward of the wicked " would be clean contrary to his declaration, " I have sinned, but these sheep, what have they done ? " ; and the absence of any allusion to the sacrifice upon Zion could not be in any way accounted for, since David's repentance would inevitably have led him to dwell upon the atoning sacrifice and the sprinkling of blood by the hyssop.

In the whole collection there is not a more cheering Psalm, its tone is elevated and sustained throughout, faith is at its best, and speaks nobly. A German physician was wont to speak of it as the best preservative in times of cholera, and in truth it is a heavenly medicine against plague and pest. He who can live in its spirit will be fearless, even if once again London should become a lazar-house, and the grave be gorged with carcases.

DIVISION.—On this occasion we shall follow the divisions which our translators have placed at the head of the Psalm, for they are pithy and suggestive. 1. The state of the godly. 3. Their safety. 9. Their habitation. 11. Their servants. 14. Their friend ; with the effects of them all.

EXPOSITION.

HE that dwelleth in the secret place of the most High shall abide under the shadow of the Almighty.

2 I will say of the LORD, *He is* my refuge and my fortress : my God ; in him will I trust.

1. " *He that dwelleth in the secret place of the most High.*" The blessings here promised are not for all believers, but for those who live in close fellowship with God. Every child of God looks towards the inner sanctuary and the mercy-seat, yet all do not *dwell* in the most holy place ; they run to it at times, and enjoy occasional approaches, but they do not habitually reside in the mysterious presence. Those who through rich grace obtain unusual and continuous communion with God, so as to abide in Christ and Christ in them, become possessors of rare and special benefits, which are missed by those who follow afar off, and grieve the Holy Spirit of God. Into the secret place those only come who know the love of God in Christ Jesus, and those only *dwell* there to whom to live is Christ. To them the veil is rent, the mercy-seat is revealed, the covering cherubs are manifest, and the awful glory of the Most High is apparent : these, like Simeon, have the Holy Ghost upon them, and like Anna they depart not from the temple ; they are the courtiers of the Great King, the valiant men who keep watch around the bed of Solomon, the virgin souls who follow the Lamb whithersoever he goeth. Elect out of the elect, they have " attained unto the first three," and shall walk with their Lord in white, for they are worthy. Sitting down in the august presence-chamber where shines the mystic light of the Sheckinah, they know what it is to be raised up together, and to be made to sit together with Christ in the heavenlies, and of them it is truly said that their conversation is in heaven. Special grace like theirs brings with it special immunity. Outer court worshippers little know what

belongs to the inner sanctuary, or surely they would press on until the place of nearness and divine familiarity became theirs.   Those who are the Lord's constant guests shall find that he will never suffer any to be injured within his gates ; he has eaten the covenant salt with them, and is pledged for their protection.

" *Shall abide under the shadow of the Almighty.*" The Omnipotent Lord will shield all those who dwell with him, they shall remain under his care as guests under the protection of their host.   In the most holy place the wings of the cherubim were the most conspicuous objects, and they probably suggested to the Psalmist the expression here employed.   Those who commune with God are safe with him, no evil can reach them, for the outstretched wings of his power and love cover them from all harm.   This protection is constant—they *abide* under it, and it is all-sufficient, for it is the shadow of *the Almighty*, whose omnipotence will surely screen them from all attack.   No shelter can be imagined at all comparable to the protection of Jehovah's own shadow.   The Almighty himself is where his shadow is, and hence those who dwell in his secret place are shielded by himself.   What a shade in the day of noxious heat !   What a refuge in the hour of deadly storm !   Communion with God is safety.   The more closely we cling to our Almighty Father the more confident may we be.

2. " *I will say of the Lord, He is my refuge and my fortress.*"   To take up a general truth and make it our own by personal faith is the highest wisdom.   It is but poor comfort to say ' the Lord is a refuge,' but to say he is *my* refuge, is the essence of consolation.   Those who believe should also speak—" I will *say*," for such bold avowals honour God and lead others to seek the same confidence.   Men are apt enough to proclaim their doubts, and even to boast of them, indeed there is a party nowadays of the most audacious pretenders to culture and thought, who glory in casting suspicion upon everything ; hence it becomes the duty of all true believers to speak out and testify with calm courage to their own well-grounded reliance upon their God.   Let others say what they will, be it ours to say of the Lord, " he is our *refuge.*"   But what we say we must prove by our actions, we must fly to the Lord for shelter, and not to an arm of flesh.   The bird flies away to the thicket, and the fox hastens to its hole, every creature uses its refuge in the hour of danger, and even so in all peril or fear of peril let us flee unto Jehovah, the Eternal Protector of his own.   Let us, when we are secure in the Lord, rejoice that our position is unassailable, for he is our *fortress* as well as our refuge.   No moat, portcullis, drawbridge, wall, battlement and donjon, could make us so secure as we are when the attributes of the Lord of Hosts environ us around.   Behold this day the Lord is to us instead of walls and bulwarks !   Our ramparts defy the leaguered hosts of hell.   Foes in flesh, and foes in ghostly guise are alike baulked of their prey when the Lord of Hosts stands between us and their fury, and all other evil forces are turned aside.   Walls cannot keep out the pestilence, but the Lord can.

As if it were not enough to call the Lord his refuge and fortress, he adds, " *My God ! in him will I trust.*"   Now he can say no more ; " my God " means all, and more than all, that heart can conceive by way of security.   It was most meet that he should say " in him will I trust," since to deny faith to such a one were wilful wickedness and wanton insult.   He who dwells in an impregnable fortress, naturally trusts in it ; and shall not he who dwells in God feel himself well at ease, and repose his soul in safety ?   O that we more fully carried out the Psalmist's resolve !   We have trusted in God, let us trust him still.   He has never failed us, why then should we suspect him ?   To trust in man is natural to fallen nature, to trust in God should be as natural to regenerated nature.   Where there is every reason and warrant for faith, we ought to place our confidence without hesitancy or wavering.   Dear reader, pray for grace to say, " In *him* will I trust."

3 Surely he shall deliver thee from the snare of the fowler, *and* from the noisome pestilence.

4 He shall cover thee with his feathers, and under his wings shalt thou trust : his truth *shall be thy* shield and buckler.

5 Thou shalt not be afraid for the terror by night ; *nor* for the arrow *that* flieth by day ;

6 *Nor* for the pestilence *that* walketh in darkness ; *nor* for the destruction *that* wasteth at noonday.

7 A thousand shall fall at thy side, and ten thousand at thy right hand ; *but* it shall not come nigh thee.

8 Only with thine eyes shalt thou behold and see the reward of the wicked.

3. " *Surely he shall deliver thee from the snare of the fowler.*" Assuredly no subtle plot shall succeed against one who has the eyes of God watching for his defence. We are foolish and weak as poor little birds, and are very apt to be lured to our destruction by cunning foes, but if we dwell near to God, he will see to it that the most skilful deceiver shall not entrap us.

> " Satan the fowler who betrays
> Unguarded souls a thousand ways,"

shall be foiled in the case of the man whose high and honourable condition consists in residence within the holy place of the Most High. " *And from the noisome pestilence.*" He who is a Spirit can protect us from evil spirits, he who is mysterious can rescue us from mysterious dangers, he who is immortal can redeem us from mortal sickness. There is a deadly pestilence of error, we are safe from that if we dwell in communion with the God of truth ; there is a fatal pestilence of sin, we shall not be infected by it if we abide with the thrice Holy One ; there is also a pestilence of disease, and even from that calamity our faith shall win immunity if it be of that high order which abides in God, walks on in calm serenity, and ventures all things for duty's sake. Faith by cheering the heart keeps it free from the fear which, in times of pestilence, kills more than the plague itself. It will not in all cases ward off disease and death, but where the man is such as the first verse describes, it will assuredly render him immortal where others die ; if all the saints are not so sheltered it is because they have not all such a close abiding with God, and consequently not such confidence in the promise. Such special faith is not given to all, for there are diversities in the measure of faith. It is not of all believers that the Psalmist sings, but only of those who dwell in the secret place of the Most High. Too many among us are weak in faith, and in fact place more reliance in a phial or a globule than in the Lord and giver of life, and if we die of pestilence as others die it is because we acted like others, and did not in patience possess our souls. The great mercy is that in such a case our deaths are blessed, and it is well with us, for we are for ever with the Lord. Pestilence to the saints shall not be noisome but the messenger of heaven.

4. " *He shall cover thee with his feathers, and under his wings shall thou trust.*" A wonderful expression ! Had it been invented by an uninspired man it would have verged upon blasphemy, for who should dare to apply such words to the Infinite Jehovah ? But as he himself authorised, yea, dictated the language, we have here a transcendent condescension, such as it becomes us to admire and adore. Doth the Lord speak of his feathers, as though he likened himself to a bird ? Who will not see herein a matchless love, a divine tenderness, which should both woo and win our confidence ? Even as a hen covereth her chickens so doth the Lord protect the souls which dwell in him ; let us cower down beneath him for comfort and for safety. Hawks in the sky and snares in the field are equally harmless when we nestle so near the Lord. " *His truth*"—his true promise, and his faithfulness to his promise " *shall be thy shield and buckler.*" Double armour has he who relies upon the Lord. He bears a shield and wears an all-surrounding coat of mail—such is the force of the word " buckler." To quench fiery darts the truth is a most effectual shield, and to blunt all swords it is an equally effectual coat of mail. Let us go forth to battle thus harnessed for the war, and we shall be safe in the thickest of the fight. It has been so, and so shall it be till we reach the land of peace, and there among the " helmed cherubim and sworded seraphim," we will wear no other ornament, his truth shall still be our shield and buckler.

5. " *Thou shalt not be afraid for the terror by night.*" Such frail creatures are we that both by night and by day we are in danger, and so sinful are we that in either season we may be readily carried away by fear ; the promise before us secures the favourite of heaven both from danger and from the fear of it. Night is the congenial hour of horrors, when alarms walk abroad like beasts of prey, or ghouls from among the tombs ; our fears turn the sweet season of repose into one of dread, and though angels are abroad and fill our chambers, we dream of demons and dire visitants from hell. Blessed is that communion with God which renders us im-

pervious to midnight frights, and horrors born of darkness. Not to be afraid is in itself an unspeakable blessing, since for every suffering which we endure from real injury we are tormented by a thousand griefs which arise from fear only. The shadow of the Almighty removes all gloom from the shadow of night : once covered by the divine wing, we care not what winged terrors may fly abroad in the earth. "*Nor for the arrow that flieth by day.*" Cunning foes lie in ambuscade, and aim the deadly shaft at our hearts, but we do not fear them, and have no cause to do so. That arrow is not made which can destroy the righteous, for the Lord hath said, "No weapon that is formed against thee shall prosper." In times of great danger those who have made the Lord their refuge, and therefore have refused to use the carnal weapon, have been singularly preserved ; the annals of the Quakers bear good evidence to this ; yet probably the main thought is, that from the cowardly attacks of crafty malice those who walk by faith shall be protected, from cunning heresies they shall be preserved, and in sudden temptations they shall be secured from harm. Day has its perils as well as night, arrows more deadly than those poisoned by the Indian are flying noiselessly through the air, and we shall be their victims unless we find both shield and buckler in our God. O believer, dwell under the shadow of the Lord, and none of the archers shall destroy thee, they may shoot at thee and wound thee grievously, but thy bow shall abide in strength. When Satan's quiver shall be empty thou shalt remain uninjured by his craft and cruelty, yea, his broken darts shall be to thee as trophies of the truth and power of the Lord thy God.

6. "*Nor for the pestilence that walketh in darkness.*" It is shrouded in mystery as to its cause and cure, it marches on, unseen of men, slaying with hidden weapons, like an enemy stabbing in the dark, yet those who dwell in God are not afraid of it. Nothing is more alarming than the assassin's plot, for he may at any moment steal in upon a man, and lay him low at a stroke ; and such is the plague in the days of its power, none can promise themselves freedom from it for an hour in any place in the infected city; it enters a house men know not how, and its very breath is mortal ; yet those choice souls who dwell in God shall live above fear in the most plague-stricken places—they *shall not be afraid of the "plagues which in the darkness walk.*" "*Nor for the destruction that wasteth at noonday.*" Famine may starve, or bloody war devour, earthquake may overturn and tempest may smite, but amid all, the man who has sought the mercy seat and is sheltered beneath the wings which overshadow it, shall abide in perfect peace. Days of horror and nights of terror are for other men, his days and nights are alike spent with God, and therefore pass away in sacred quiet. His peace is not a thing of times and seasons, it does not rise and set with the sun, nor does it depend upon the healthiness of the atmosphere or the security of the country. Upon the child of the Lord's own heart pestilence has no destroying power, and calamity no wasting influence : pestilence walks in darkness, but he dwells in light ; destruction wastes at noonday, but upon him another sun has risen whose beams bring restoration. Remember that the voice which saith "thou shalt not fear" is that of God himself, who hereby pledges his word for the safety of those who abide under his shadow, nay, not for their safety only, but for their serenity. So far shall they be from being injured that they shall not even be made to fear the ills which are around them, since the Lord protects them.

> "He, his shadowy plumes outspread,
> With his wing shall fence thy head :
> And his truth around thee wield,
> Strong as targe or bossy shield !
> Naught shall strike thee with dismay,
> Fear by night, nor shaft by day."

7. "*A thousand shall fall at thy side, and ten thousand at thy right hand.*" So terribly may the plague rage among men that the bills of mortality may become very heavy and continue to grow ten times heavier still, yet shall such as this Psalm speaks of survive the scythe of death. "*It shall not come nigh thee.*" It shall be so near as to be at thy side, and yet not nigh enough to touch thee ; like a fire it shall burn all around, yet shall not the smell of it pass upon thee. How true is this of the plague of moral evil, of heresy, and of backsliding. Whole nations are infected, yet the man who communes with God is not affected by the contagion ; he holds the truth when falsehood is all the fashion. Professors all around him are

plague-smitten, the church is wasted, the very life of religion decays, but in the same place and time, in fellowship with God, the believer renews his youth, and his soul knows no sickness. In a measure this also is true of physical evil; the Lord still puts a difference between Israel and Egypt in the day of his plagues. Sennacherib's army is blasted, but Jerusalem is in health.

> "Our God his chosen people saves
> Amongst the dead, amidst the graves."

8. "*Only with thine eyes shalt thou behold and see the reward of the wicked.*" The sight shall reveal both the justice and the mercy of God; in them that perish the severity of God will be manifest, and in the believer's escape the richness of divine goodness will be apparent. Joshua and Caleb verified this promise. The Puritan preachers during the plague of London must have been much impressed with this verse as they came out of their hiding-places to proclaim mercy and judgment to the dissolute age which was so sorely visited with the pest. The sight of God's judgments softens the heart, excites a solemn awe, creates gratitude, and so stirs up the deepest kind of adoration. It is such a sight as none of us would wish to see, and yet if we did see it we might thus be lifted up to the very noblest style of manhood. Let us but watch providence, and we shall find ourselves living in a school where examples of the ultimate reward of sin are very plentiful. One case may not be judged alone lest we misjudge, but instances of divine visitation will be plentiful in the memory of any attentive observer of men and things; from all these put together we may fairly draw conclusions, and unless we shut our eyes to that which is self-evident, we shall soon perceive that there is after all a moral ruler over the sons of men, who sooner or later rewards the ungodly with due punishment.

9 Because thou hast made the LORD *which is* my refuge, *even* the most High, thy habitation;

10 There shall no evil befall thee, neither shall any plague come nigh thy dwelling.

9, 10. Before expounding these verses I cannot refrain from recording a personal incident illustrating their power to soothe the heart, when they are applied by the Holy Spirit. In the year 1854, when I had scarcely been in London twelve months, the neighbourhood in which I laboured was visited by Asiatic cholera, and my congregation suffered from its inroads. Family after family summoned me to the bedside of the smitten, and almost every day I was called to visit the grave. I gave myself up with youthful ardour to the visitation of the sick, and was sent for from all corners of the district by persons of all ranks and religions. I became weary in body and sick at heart. My friends seemed falling one by one, and I felt or fancied that I was sickening like those around me. A little more work and weeping would have laid me low among the rest; I felt that my burden was heavier than I could bear, and I was ready to sink under it. As God would have it, I was returning mournfully home from a funeral, when my curiosity led me to read a paper which was wafered up in a shoemaker's window in the Dover Road. It did not look like a trade announcement, nor was it, for it bore in a good bold handwriting these words:—"*Because thou hast made the Lord, which is my refuge, even the most High, thy habitation; there shall no evil befall thee, neither shall any plague come nigh thy dwelling.*" The effect upon my heart was immediate. Faith appropriated the passage as her own. I felt secure, refreshed, girt with immortality. I went on with my visitation of the dying in a calm and peaceful spirit; I felt no fear of evil, and I suffered no harm. The providence which moved the tradesman to place those verses in his window I gratefully acknowledge, and in the remembrance of its marvellous power I adore the Lord my God.

The Psalmist in these verses assures the man who dwells in God that he shall be secure. Though faith claims no merit of its own, yet the Lord rewards it wherever he sees it. He who *makes* God his refuge shall find him a refuge; he who dwells in God shall find his dwelling protected. We must *make* the Lord our habitation by choosing him for our trust and rest, and then we shall receive immunity from harm; no evil shall touch us personally, and no stroke of judgment shall assail our household. The *dwelling* here intended by the original was only a tent, yet the frail covering would prove to be a sufficient shelter from harm of all sorts. It matters little whether our abode be a gipsy's hut or a monarch's palace if the soul has made the Most High its habitation. Get into God and you dwell in all good, and ill is banished far away. It is not because we are perfect or highly esteemed among men that we can hope for shelter in the day of evil, but because our refuge is the Eternal God, and our faith has learned to hide beneath his sheltering wing.

> " For this no ill thy cause shall daunt,
> No scourge thy tabernacle haunt."

It is impossible that any ill should happen to the man who is beloved of the Lord ; the most crushing calamities can only shorten his journey and hasten him to his reward. Ill to him is no ill, but only good in a mysterious form. Losses enrich him, sickness is his medicine, reproach is his honour, death is his gain. No evil in the strict sense of the word can happen to him, for everything is overruled for good. Happy is he who is in such a case. He is secure where others are in peril, he lives where others die.

11 For he shall give his angels charge over thee, to keep thee in all thy ways.

12 They shall bear thee up in *their* hands, lest thou dash thy foot against a stone.

13 Thou shalt tread upon the lion and adder : the young lion and the dragon shalt thou trample under feet.

11. " *For he shall give his angels charge over thee.*" Not one guardian angel, as some fondly dream, but all the angels are here alluded to. They are the body-guard of the princes of the blood imperial of heaven, and they have received commission from their Lord and ours to watch carefully over all the interests of the faithful. When men have a charge they become doubly careful, and therefore the angels are represented as bidden by God himself to see to it that the elect are secured. It is down in the marching orders of the hosts of heaven that they take special note of the people who dwell in God. It is not to be wondered at that the servants are bidden to be careful of the comfort of their Master's guests ; and we may be quite sure that when they are specially charged by the Lord himself they will carefully discharge the duty imposed upon them. " *To keep thee in all thy ways.*" To be a body-guard, a garrison to the body, soul, and spirit of the saint. The limit of this protection " in all thy ways " is yet no limit to the heart which is right with God. It is not the way of the believer to go out of his way. He keeps in the way, and then the angels keep him. The protection here promised is exceeding broad as to place, for it refers to *all* our ways, and what do we wish for more ? How angels thus keep us we cannot tell. Whether they repel demons, counteract spiritual plots, or even ward off the subtler physical forces of disease, we do not know. Perhaps we shall one day stand amazed at the multiplied services which the unseen bands have rendered to us.

12. " *They,*" that is the angels, God's own angels, shall cheerfully become our servitors. " *They shall bear thee up in their hands* " ; as nurses carry little children, with careful love, so shall those glorious spirits upbear each individual believer. " *Lest thou dash thy foot against a stone ;* " even minor ills they ward off. It is most desirable that we should not stumble, but as the way is rough, it is most gracious on the Lord's part to send his servants to bear us up above the loose pebbles. If we cannot have the way smoothed it answers every purpose if we have angels to bear us up in their hands. Since the greatest ills may arise out of little accidents, it shews the wisdom of the Lord that from the smaller evils we are protected.

13. " *Thou shalt tread upon the lion and adder.*" Over force and fraud shalt thou march victoriously ; bold opponents and treacherous adversaries shall alike be trodden down. When our shoes are iron and brass, lions and adders are easily enough crushed beneath our heel. " *The young lion and the dragon shalt thou trample under feet.*" The strongest foe in power, and the most mysterious in cunning, shall be conquered by the man of God. Not only from stones in the way, but from serpents also, shall we be safe. To men who dwell in God the most evil forces become harmless, they wear a charmed life, and defy the deadliest ills. Their feet come into contact with the worst of foes, even Satan himself nibbles at their heel, but in Christ Jesus they have the assured hope of bruising Satan under their feet shortly.

The people of God are the real " George and the dragon," the true lion-kings and serpent-tamers. Their dominion over the powers of darkness makes them cry, " Lord, even the devils are subject unto us through thy word."

14 Because he hath set his love upon me, therefore will I deliver him : I will set him on high, because he hath known my name.

15 He shall call upon me, and I will answer him : I *will be* with him in trouble ; I will deliver him, and honour him.

16 With long life will I satisfy him, and shew him my salvation.

14. Here we have the Lord himself speaking of his own chosen one. " *Because he hath set his love upon me, therefore will I deliver him.*" Not because he deserves to be thus kept, but because with all his imperfections he does love his God ; therefore not the angels of God only, but the God of angels himself will come to his rescue in all perilous times, and will effectually deliver him. When the heart is enamoured of the Lord, all taken up with him, and intensely attached to him, the Lord will recognise the sacred flame, and preserve the man who bears it in his bosom. It is love,—love set upon God, which is the distinguishing mark of those whom the Lord secures from ill. " *I will set him on high, because he hath known my name.*" The man has known the attributes of God so as to trust in him, and then by experience has arrived at a yet deeper knowledge, this shall be regarded by the Lord as a pledge of his grace, and he will set the owner of it above danger or fear, where he shall dwell in peace and joy. None abide in intimate fellowship with God unless they possess a warm affection towards God, and an intelligent trust in him ; these gifts of grace are precious in Jehovah's eyes, and wherever he sees them he smiles upon them. How elevated is the standing which the Lord gives to the believer. We ought to covet it right earnestly. If we climb on high it may be dangerous, but if God sets us there it is glorious.

15. " *He shall call upon me, and I will answer him.*" He will have need to pray, he will be led to pray aright, and the answer shall surely come. Saints are first called *of* God, and then they call *upon* God ; such calls as theirs always obtain answers. Not without prayer will the blessing come to the most favoured, but by means of prayer they shall receive all good things. " *I will be with him in trouble,*" or " I am with him in trouble." Heirs of heaven are conscious of a special divine presence in times of severe trial. God is always near in sympathy and in power to help his tried ones. " *I will deliver him, and honour him.*" The man honours God, and God honours him. Believers are not delivered or preserved in a way which lowers them, and makes them feel themselves degraded ; far from it, the Lord's salvation bestows honour upon those it delivers. God first gives us conquering grace, and then rewards us for it.

16. " *With long life will I satisfy him.*" The man described in this Psalm fills out the measure of his days, and whether he dies young or old he is quite satisfied with life, and is content to leave it. He shall rise from life's banquet as a man who has had enough, and would not have more even if he could. " *And shew him my salvation.*" The full sight of divine grace shall be his closing vision. He shall look from Amana and Lebanon. Not with destruction before him black as night, but with salvation bright as noonday smiling upon him he shall enter into his rest.

EXPLANATORY NOTES AND QUAINT SAYINGS.

Whole Psalm.—The Talmud writers ascribe not only the ninety-first Psalm, but the nine ensuing, to the pen of Moses ; but from a rule which will in no respect hold, that all the Psalms which are without the name of an author in their respective titles are the production of the poet whose name is given in the nearest preceding title. And though it is impossible to prove that this highly beautiful ode was not written by David, the general drift of its scenery and allusions rather concur in showing that, like the last, we are indebted for it to the muse of Moses : that it was composed by him during the journey through the wilderness, shortly after the plague of the fiery serpents ; when the children of Israel, having returned to a better spirit, were again received into the favour of JEHOVAH. Besides political enemies, the children of Israel in the wilderness had other evils in great numbers to encounter, from the nature and diseases of the climate, which exposed them to coups de soleil, or *sun smitings*, during the heat of the day ; and to pestilential vapours, *moon smitings*, during the damp of the night, so as to render the miraculous canopy of the cloud that hung over them in the former season, and the miraculous column of fire that cheered and purified them in the latter, equally needful and refreshing. In Egypt, they had seen so much of the plague, and they had been so fearfully threatened with it as a punishment for disobedience, that they could not but be in dread of its reappearance, from the incessant fatigues of their journeying. In addition to all which, they had to be perpetually on their guard against the insidious attacks of the savage monsters and reptiles of " that great and terrible wilderness," as Moses describes it on another occasion, " wherein were fiery serpents, and scorpions, and drought ; where there was no water " (Deut. viii. 15) ; and where, also, as we learn from other parts of Scripture, bears, lions, leopards or tigers, and " the wolf of the evening," as Jeremiah has beautifully expressed it, prowled without restraint. Now in the Psalm before us, and especially in the verses 6 to 13, we have so clear and graphic a description of the whole of these evils presented to us, as to bring its composition directly home to the circumstances and the period here pitched upon, and to render it at least needless to hunt out for any other occasion.—*J. M. Good's " Historical Outline of the Book of Psalms,"* 1842.

Whole Psalm.—It is one of the most excellent works of this kind which has ever appeared. It is impossible to imagine anything more solid, more beautiful, more profound, or more ornamented. Could the Latin or any modern language express thoroughly all the beauties and elegancies as well of the *words* as of the *sentences*, it would not be difficult to persuade the reader that we have no poem, either in *Greek* or *Latin*, comparable to this Hebrew ode.—*Simon de Muis.*

Whole Psalm.—Psalm XC. spoke of man withering away beneath God's anger against sin. Psalm XCI. tells of a Man, who is able to tread the lion and adder under his feet.—Undoubtedly the Tempter was right in referring this Psalm to " the Son of God " (Matthew iv. 6).

The imagery of the Psalm seems to be in part drawn from that Passover Night, when the Destroying Angel passed through Egypt ; while the faithful and obedient Israelites were sheltered by God.—*William Kay.*

Verse 1.—" *He,*" no matter who he may be, rich or poor, learned or unlearned, patrician or plebeian, young or old, for " God is no respecter of persons," but " he is rich to all that call upon him."—*Bellarmine.*

Verse 1.—" *He that dwelleth in the secret place of the Most High.*" Note, he who dwells in the secret place of the Most High is not he that conjures up one or two slight and fleeting acts of hope in him, but the man that places in him an assiduous and constant confidence. In this way he establishes for himself in God by that full trust, a home, a dwelling-place, a mansion, . . . The Hebrew for *he that dwelleth,* is יֹשֵׁב, that is, dwelling in quietude, and resting, enduring and remaining with constancy.—*Le Blanc.*

Verse 1.—" *He that dwelleth in the secret place of the most High.*" What intimate and unrestrained communion does this describe !—the Christian in everything making known his heart, with its needs and wishes, its thoughts and feelings, its doubts and anxieties, its sorrows and its joys, to God, as to a loving, perfect friend. And all is not on one side. This Almighty Friend has admitted his chosen one to his " *secret place.*" It is almost too wonderful to be true. It is almost too presumptuous a thought for such creatures as we are to entertain. But he himself permits it, *desires* it, teaches us to realise that it is *communion* to which he calls us. " The secret of the Lord is with them that fear him." And what is this " *secret* " ? It is *that* in God which the world neither knows, nor sees, nor cares to enjoy. It is his mind revealed to those that love him, his plans, and ways (" He made known his *ways* to *Moses,*" Ps. ciii. 7), and thoughts opened to them. Yea, and things hid from angels are manifest to the least of his friends, (1 Peter i. 12). He wishes us to know him, and by his Word and by his Spirit he puts himself before us. Ah ! it is not his fault if we do not know him. It is our own carelessness.—*Mary B. M. Duncan, in " Under the Shadow,"* 1867.

Verse 1.—By " *secret* " here is meant a place of refuge from the storms of the world under the secret of his providence, who careth for all his children. Also, by the " *secret of the most High,*" some writers understand the castle of his mighty defence, to which his people run, being pursued by enemies, as the wild creature doth to his hole or den for succour, when the hunter hath him in chase, and the dogs are near. This then being the meaning of that which the prophet calleth the "*secret place of the most High*," and our dwelling in it, by confidence in him; we learn, in all troubles, to cleave to *God* chiefly or only for help, and to *means* but as underlings to his providence. . . . .

That which is here translated "*dwelleth*," is as much in weight as sitteth, or is settled; and so, our dwelling in God's secret, is as much as our sitting down in it; the meaning is, we must make it our rest, as if we should say, Here will we dwell. From whence we learn, that God's children should not come to God's *secret-place* as guests to an inn, but as inhabitants to their own dwellings; that is, they should continue to trust in God, as well in want as in fulness; and as much when they *wither* in their root, as when they *flourish* in it.—*Robert Horn.*

Verse 1.—"*He that dwelleth*," etc. 1. " He dwells," therefore he shall " abide." He shall lodge quietly, securely. 2. "He dwells in the secret place," therefore he shall " abide under the shadow." In the cool, the favour, the cover from the heat. 3. " He dwelleth in the secret place of the Most High, therefore he shall abide under the shadow of the Almighty;" *i.e.*, of the all-powerful God, of the God of heaven; of that God whose name is Shaddai, All-sufficient.—*Adam Clarke.*

Verse 1.—"*Shall abide*." The Hebrew for "*shall abide*" is יִתְלוֹנָן, which signifies *he shall pass the night*. Abiding denotes a constant and continuous dwelling of the just in the assistance and protection of God. That help and protection of God is not like a lodge in a garden of cucumbers, or in a vineyard; which is destroyed in a moment, nor is it like a tent in the way which is abandoned by the traveller. It is a strong tower, a paternal home, wherein we spend all our life with the best, wealthiest, and mightiest of parents. *Passing the night* also denotes security and rest in time of darkness, temptations and calamities. With God Abraham passed the night, when He foretold to him the affliction of his descendants in Egypt, and their deliverance, Gen. xv. 12 seq. Then also God said to him (verse 1), *Fear not Abram, I am thy shield.* And leading him forth he showed him the glittering stars, and said, Tell the number of the stars, if thou be able; so shall thy seed be.—*Le Blanc.*

Verse 1.—"*The shadow*." The allusion of this verse may be to the awful and mystic symbols of the ark. Under the ancient ceremony, the high priest only could enter, and that but once a year, into the holy place, where stood the emblems of the divine glory and presence; but under the present bright and merciful dispensation, every true believer has access, with boldness, into the holiest of all; and he who now dwelleth in the secret place of prayer and communion with the God of salvation, shall find the divine mercy and care spread over him for his daily protection and solace.—*John Morison.*

Verse 1.—"*Under the shadow of the Almighty*." This is an expression which implies great nearness. We must walk very close to a companion, if we would have his shadow fall on us. Can we imagine any expression more perfect in describing the *constant presence* of God with his chosen ones, than this—they shall " *abide under his shadow* "? In Solomon's beautiful allegory, the Church in a time of special communion with Christ, says of him—" I sat down under his shadow with great delight " (Cant. ii. 3)—" sat down," desiring not to leave it, but to abide there for ever. And it is he who chooses to dwell in the secret place of the most High, who shall " abide under the shadow of the Almighty." There is a condition and a promise attached to it. The condition is, that we " dwell in the secret place,"—the promise, that if we do so we " shall abide under the shadow." It is of importance to view it thus. For when we remember the blessing is a *promised* blessing—we are led to feel it is a gift—a thing therefore to be prayed for in faith, as well as sought for by God's appointed means. Ah, the hopes that *this* awakens! My wandering, wavering, unstable heart, that of itself cannot keep to one course two days together, is to seek its perseverance from God, and not in its own strength. He will hold it to him if it be but seeking for stedfastness. It is not we who cling to him. It is he who keeps near to us.—*Mary B. M. Duncan.*

Verses 1—4; 9.—O you that be in fear of any danger, leave all carnal shifts, and carking counsels, and projects, and dwell in the rock of God's power and providence, and be like the dove that nestles in the holes of the rock; by faith betake yourselves unto God, by faith dwell in that rock, and there nestle yourselves, make your nests of safety in the clefts of this rock. But how may we do this thing, and what is the way to do it? Do this,—Set thy faith on work to make God that unto thee which thy necessity requires, pitch and throw thyself upon his power and providence, with a resolution of spirit to rest thyself upon it for safety, come what will come. See an excellent practice of this, Ps. xci. 1, " *He that dwelleth in the secret place of the most High shall abide under the shadow of the Almighty ;* " that is, he shall be safe from all fears and dangers. Ay, that is true, you will say, who makes any doubt of it ? But how shall a man come to dwell, and get into this secret place, within this strong tower ? See verse 2 : " *I will say of the Lord, He is my refuge and my fortress ;* " as if he had said, I will not only say, that he is a refuge ; but he is *my* refuge, I will say to the Lord ; that is, I will set my faith on work in particular, to throw, devolve, and pitch myself upon him for my safety. And see what follows upon this setting faith thus on work, verses 3, 4 : " *Surely he shall deliver thee from the snare of the fowler, and from the noisome pestilence. He shall cover thee with his feathers,*" etc. So confident the Psalmist is that upon this course taken, safety shall follow.

Our safety lies not simply upon this, because God is a refuge, and is an habitation, but " Because *thou hast made* the Lord which is my refuge, thy habitation, there shall no evil befall thee," etc. It is therefore the *making* of God our habitation, upon which our safety lies ; and this is the way to make God an habitation, thus to pitch and cast ourselves by faith upon his power and providence.—*Jeremiah Dyke.*

Verse 1.—We read of a stag that roamed about in the greatest security, by reason of its having a label on its neck, " *Touch me not, I belong to Cæsar* " : thus the true servants of God are always safe, even among lions, bears, serpents, fire, water, thunder, and tempests ; for all creatures know and reverence the shadow of God.— *Bellarmine.*

Verse 2.—" *My refuge, my fortress, my God." " My refuge.*" God is our " *refuge.*" He who avails himself of a refuge is one who is forced to fly. It is a quiet retreat from a pursuing enemy. And there are trials, and temptations, and enemies, from which the Christian does best to fly. He cannot resist them. They are too strong for him. His wisdom is to fly into the refuge of the secret place of his God—to rest in the shadow of the Almighty. His " strength is to sit still " *there.* Isai. xxx. 7. " *My fortress.*" The Psalmist says, moreover, that God is his " *fortress.*" Here the idea is changed—no longer a peaceful, quiet hiding-place, but a tower of defence— strong, manifest, ready to meet the attacks of all enemies, ready and able to resist them all. God is a Friend who meets every want in our nature, who can supply every need. So when we are weak and fainting, and unable to meet the brunt of battle, and striving against sin and sorrow and the wrath of man, he is our safe, quiet resting-place—our *fortress* also where no harm can reach us, no attack injure us. " *My God.*" Now the Psalmist, as a summing up of all his praises, says " I will say of him, He is . . . my God ! " Is there anything omitted in the former part of his declaration ? *Everything* is here—all possible ascription of honour, and glory, and power to him " *as God* "—" God over all, blessed for ever," and of love, reverence, trust, obedience, and filial relation towards him on the part of the Psalmist, as MY God . . . when reflecting on the refuge and strength which the Lord has always been to him, and recalling his blessed experiences of sweet communion with God—words fail him. He can only say (but oh, with what expression !) MY GOD !—*Mary B. M. Duncan.*

Verse 2.—" *My God.*" Specially art thou my God, first, on thy part, because of the special goodness and favour which thou dost bestow upon me. Secondly, on my part, because of the special love and reverence with which I cling to thee.— *J. Paulus Palanterius.*

Verses 2—4.—If the severity and justice of God terrify, the Lord offereth himself as *a bird with stretched out wings* to receive the supplicant, ver. 4. If enemies who are too strong do pursue, the Lord openeth his bosom as a *refuge*, ver. 2. If the child be assaulted, he becometh a fortress, ver. 2. If he be hotly pursued and enquired after, the Lord becometh a *secret place* to hide his child ; if persecution be hot, God giveth himself for a *shadow* ; if potentates and mighty rulers turn enemies, the Lord interposeth as the *Most High and Almighty Saviour*, ver. 1. If his adversaries be crafty like fowlers or hunters, the Lord promiseth to prevent and break the snares, ver. 3. Whether evils do come upon the believer night or day, secretly or openly, to destroy him, the Lord preserveth his child from *destruction* ; and if stumbling-blocks be laid in his child's way, he hath his instruments, his servants, his angels, prepared to keep the believer that he stumble not : " *He shall give his angels charge over thee* " ; not one angel only, but all of them, or a number of them.—*David Dickson.*

Verse 3.—" *He shall deliver thee from the snare of the fowler.*" Are we therefore beasts ? Beasts doubtless. *When man was in honour he understood not, but was like the foolish beasts.* [Ps. xlix.] Men are certainly beasts, wandering sheep, having no shepherd. Why art thou proud, O man ? Why dost thou boast thyself O smatterer ? See what a beast thou art, for whom the snares of the fowler are being prepared. But who are these *fowlers* ? The fowlers indeed are the worst and wickedest, the cleverest and the cruellest. The fowlers are they who sound no horn, that they may not be heard, but shoot their arrows in secret places at the innocent. . . . But lo ! since we know the fowlers and the beasts, our further enquiry must be, what this *snare* may be. I wish not myself to invent it, nor to deliver to you what is subject to doubt. The Apostle shows us this snare, for he was not ignorant of the devices of these fowlers. Tell us, I pray, blessed Paul, what this snare of the devil is, from which the faithful soul rejoices that it is delivered ? *They that will be rich* [in this world ?] says he, *fall into temptation and the snare* [of the devil ?] (1 Tim. 6). Are not the riches of this world, then, the snare of the devil ? Alas ! how few we find who can boast of freedom from this snare, how many who grieve that they seem to themselves too little enmeshed in the net, and who still labour and toil with all their strength to involve and entangle themselves more and more. Ye who have left all and followed the Son of man who has not where to lay his head, rejoice and say, *He hath delivered me from the snare of the fowlers.*— *Bernard.*

Verse 3.—" *Surely he shall deliver thee from the noisome pestilence.*" Lord Craven lived in London when that sad calamity, the plague, raged. His house was in that part of the town called Craven Buildings. On the plague growing epidemic, his Lordship, to avoid the danger, resolved to go to his seat in the country. His coach and six were accordingly at the door, his baggage put up, and all things in readiness for the journey. As he was walking through his hall with his hat on, his cane under his arm, and putting on his gloves, in order to step into his carriage, he overheard his negro, who served him as postillion, saying to another servant, " I suppose, by my Lord's quitting London to avoid the plague, that his God lives in the country, and not in town." The poor negro said this in the simplicity of his heart, as really believing a plurality of gods. The speech, however, struck Lord Craven very sensibly, and made him pause. " My God," thought he, " lives every-where, and can preserve me in town as well as in the country. I will even stay where I am. The ignorance of that negro has just now preached to me a very useful sermon. Lord, pardon this unbelief, and that distrust of thy providence, which made me think of running from thy hand." He immediately ordered his horses to be taken from the coach, and the baggage to be taken in. He continued in London, was remarkably useful among his sick neighbours, and never caught the infection.— *Whitecross's Anecdotes.*

Verses 3, 6.—" *Pestilence.*" It is from a word (דֶּבֶר) that signifies to speak, and speak out ; the pestilence is a speaking thing, it proclaims the wrath of God amongst a people. Drusius fetches it from the same root, but in *piel*, which is to decree ; showing that the pestilence is a thing decreed in heaven, not casual. Kirker thinks it is called דֶּבֶר, because it keeps order, and spares neither great nor small. The Hebrew root signifies to destroy, to cut off, and hence may the plague or pestilence have its name. The Septuagint renders it θάνατος, death, for ordinarily it is death ; and it is expressed by " *Death.*" Rev. vi. 8, he sat on the pale horse, and killed with sword, hunger, death, and beasts of the earth ; it refers to Ezek. xiv. 21, where the pestilence is mentioned. Pestilence may be from a word which signifies to spread, spoil, rush upon, for it doth so ; 2 Sam. xxiv. 15, seventy thousand slain in three days ; and plague, a πληγη from πλησσω, to smite, to wound, for it smites suddenly, and wounds mortally ; hence it is in Numb. xiv. 12, " I will smite them with the pestilence." This judgment is very grievous, it is called in verse 3 the " noisome pestilence," because it is infectious, contagious ; and therefore the French read it, " *de la peste dangereuse,*" from the dangerous pestilence, it doth endanger those that come near it : and Musculus hath it, *a peste omnium pessima,* from the worst pestilence of all : and others, the woful pestilence ; it brings a multitude of woes with it to any place or person it comes unto, it is a messenger of woful fears, sorrows, distractions, terrors, and death itself.—*William Greenhill.*

Verse 4.—" *He shall cover thee with his feathers,*" etc. Christ's wings are both for healing and for hiding (Mat. iv. 2), for curing and securing us ; the devil and his instruments would soon devour the servants of God, if he did not set an invincible guard about them, and cover them with the golden feathers of his protection.—*Thomas Watson.*

Verse 4.—" *He shall cover thee with his feathers,*" etc. This is the promise of the present life. For the promise of the life to come, who can explain? If the expectation of the just be gladness, and such gladness, that no object of desire in the world is worthy to be compared with it, what will the thing itself be which is expected? No eye, apart from thee, O God, hath seen what thou hast prepared for them that love thee. Under these wings, therefore, four blessings are conferred upon us. For under these we are *concealed*; under these we are *protected* from the attack of the hawks and kites, which are the powers of the air: under these a salubrious shade *refreshes* us, and wards off the overpowering heat of the sun; under these also we are *nourished* and cherished.—*Bernard.*

Verse 4.—" *He shall cover thee with his feathers,*" etc.

> His plumes shall make a downie bed,
> Where thou shalt rest; He shall display
> His wings of truth over thy head,
> Which, like a shield, shall drive away
> The feares of night, the darts of day.
>   *Thomas Cary.*

Verse 4.—" *His truth shall be thy shield and buckler.*" That which we must oppose to all perils is the truth, or Word of God; so long as we keep that, and ward off darts and swords by that means, we shall not be overcome.—*David Dickson.*

Verse 5.—The true remedy against tormenting fear is faith in God; for many terrible things may befall men when they are most secure, like unto those which befall men in the night: but for any harm which may befall the believer this way, the Lord here willeth him to be nothing afraid: " *Thou shalt not be afraid for the terror by night.*" Many sadder accidents may befall men when they are most watching and upon their guard, but the Lord willeth the believer to be confident that he shall not be harmed this way: " *Thou shalt not be afraid for the arrow that flieth by day.*" Many evils are men subject unto, which come upon them men cannot tell how, but from such evils the Lord assureth the believer he shall have no harm: " *Thou shalt not be afraid of the pestilence which walketh in darkness.*" Men are subject to many evils which come upon them openly, and not unawares, such as are calamities from enemies and oppressors; the Lord willeth the believer to be confident that he shall not be harmed this way: " *Thou shalt not be afraid for the destruction that wasteth at noonday.*"—*David Dickson.*

Verse 5.—" *Thou shalt not be afraid.*" Not only do the pious stand safe, they are not even touched with fear. For the prophet does not say, Thou shalt not be seized; but, Thou shalt not be afraid. Certainly such a confidence of mind could not be attributed to natural powers, in so menacing and so overwhelming a destruction. For it is natural to mortals, it is implanted in them by God the author and maker of nature, to fear whatever is hurtful and deadly, especially what visibly smites and suddenly destroys. Therefore does he beautifully join together these two things; the first, in saying, *Thou shalt not be afraid;* the second, by adding, *For the terror.* He acknowledges that this plague is terrible to nature; and then by his trust in divine protection he promises himself this security, that he shall not fear the evil, which would otherwise make human nature quail. Wherefore, in my judgment, those persons are neither kind (*humani*) nor pious who are of opinion that so great a calamity is not to be dreaded by mortals. They neither observe the condition of our nature, nor honour the blessing of divine protection; both of which we see here done by the prophet.—*Musculus.*

Verse 5.—Not that we are always actually delivered out of every particular danger or grievance, but because all will turn (such is our confidence in God) to our greater good; and the more we suffer the greater shall our reward and our glory be. To the same purpose is the expression of Isaiah: " When thou passest through the waters, I will be with thee; and through the rivers, they shall not overflow thee: when thou walkest through the fire, thou shalt not be burned; neither shall the flame kindle upon thee." Isai. xliii. 2. So also Habakkuk iii. 17, 18, " Although the fig tree shall not blossom," &c.; and Job v. 19, 20, etc. And therefore here is no ground, if the words be rightly understood, for any man absolutely to presume or conclude that he shall actually be delivered out of any particular danger ; much less upon such a presumption wilfully to run into dangers. If such figures, the ornament of all language ; such rhetorical, emphatical amplifications be allowed to human writers, and well enough understood in ordinary language ; why not to holy writers as well, who had to do with men, as well as others ; whose end also was to use such expressions as might affect and move ? That human writers have said as much of the security of good and godly men, I shall need to go no further than Horace his Ode, *Integer vitæ scelerisque purus*, &c. Most dangerous then and erroneous is the inference of some men, yea, of some expositors, here, upon these words of the Psalmist, that no godly man can suffer by the plague, or pestilence : nor is old Lactantius his assertion much sounder, *Non potest ergo fieri, quin hominem justum inter descrimina tempestatum*, &c., that no just man can perish by war, or by tempest. (Instit. 1, v., c. 18). Most interpreters conclude here, that the godly are preserved in time of public calamities ; which, in a right sense, may be true ; but withal they should have added, that all godly men are not exempted at such times ; to prevent rash judgments.—*Westminster Assembly's Annotations.*

Verse 5.—" *The arrow.*" The arrow in this passage probably means the pestilence. The Arabs denote the pestilence by an allusion to this flying weapon. " I desired to remove to a less contagious air. I received from Solyman, the emperor, this message ; that the emperor wondered what I meant, in desiring to remove my habitation ; *is not the pestilence God's arrow, which will always hit his mark ?* If God would visit me herewith, how could I avoid it ? is not the plague, said he, in my own palace, and yet I do not think of removing."—*Busbequiu's Travels.* " What, say they, is not the plague the dart of Almighty God, and can we escape the blow that he levels at us ? is not his hand steady to hit the persons he aims at ? can we run out of his sight, and beyond his power ? "—*Smith's Remarks on the Turks,* 1673. *Herbert* also speaking of Curroon, says, " That year his empire was so wounded with God's arrows of plague, pestilence, and famine, as this thousand years before was never so terrible." See Ezekiel v. 16.—*S. Burder's Scripture Expositor.*

Verses 5, 6.—Joseph Scaliger explains, in Epis. 9, these two verses thus, *thou shalt not fear,* מִפַּחַד *from consternation by night,* מֵחֵץ *, from the arrow flying by day,* מִדֶּבֶר *from pestilence walking at evening,* מִקֶּטֶב *, from devastation at noon.* Under these four he comprehends all the evils and dangers to which man is liable. And as the Hebrews divide the four-and-twenty hours of day and night into four parts, namely, evening, midnight, morning, and mid-day, so he understands the hours of danger to be divided accordingly : in a word, " that the man who has made God his refuge," is always safe, day and night, at every hour, from every danger.—*Bythner.*

Verse 6.—" *The pestilence that walketh in darkness ; the destruction that wasteth at noonday.*" The description is equally forcible and correct. The diseases of all hot climates, and especially where vegetation is highly luxuriant, and marshes and miry swamps are abundant, as in the wilderness here referred to, proceed from the accumulating vapours of the *night,* or from the violence of the sun's rays at *mid-day.* The Beriberi of Ceylon, the spasmodic cholera and jungle-fever of India, and the greater part of the fevers of inter-tropical climates, especially that called the yellow fever, chiefly originate from the first of these—" the *pestilence* that stalketh in darkness " ; while sun-strokes or coups de soleil, apoplexies, inflammations of the brain, and liver-complaints of most kinds, proceed from the second, " the *destruction* that wasteth at noonday." And it is in allusion to this double source of mischief that the Psalmist exclaims most beautifully on another occasion, cxxi. 6 : " The sun shall not smite thee by day, nor the moon by night." And hence the Israelites were miraculously defended against both during their passage through the wilderness by the pillar of a cloud in the day-time, to ward off the solar rays ; and by the pillar of fire by night, to dissipate the collecting vapours, and preserve the atmosphere clear, dry, and healthy.—*J. M. Good.*

Verse 6.—The putrid plague-fever often comes on in the night while the patient is asleep ; the solstitial disease seizes in heat of harvest upon a man in open air, and cuts him off, perhaps ere evening. It is safety from perils like these that is spoken of. All these blessings are derived from and rest on (verse 1) the position of him that claims them " *under the covert of the Most High.*"—*Andrew A. Bonar.*

Verse 6.—" *The pestilence that walketh in darkness.*" It walketh not so much in natural darkness, or in the darkness of the night, as in a figurative darkness, no man knowing where it walks, or whither it will walk, in the clearest light, whether to the poor man's house, or to the rich man's house, whether to the dwelling of the plebeian, or of the prince, till it hath left its own mark, and given a deadly stroke.—*Joseph Caryl.*

Verse 7.—" *Ten thousand.*" The word *myriad* would better represent the exact idea in the original, as the Hebrew word is different from that which is translated " a thousand." It is here put for any large number.—*Albert Barnes.*

Verse 7.—" *It shall not come nigh thee.*" Not nigh thee ? What ? when they die on this side and on that side, on every hand of a man, doth it not come nigh him ? Yes, nigh him, but not so nigh as to hurt him : *the power of God can bring us near to danger, and yet keep us far from harm.* As good may be locally near us, and yet virtually far from us, so may evil. The multitude thronged Christ in the Gospel, and yet but one touched him so as to receive good ; so Christ can keep us in a throng of dangers, that not one shall touch us to our hurt.—*Joseph Caryl.*

Verse 7.—" *It shall not come nigh thee.*" Not with a view of showing that all good men may hope to escape from the pestilence, but as proofs that some who have had superior faith have done so, I have collected the following instances from various sources.—*C. H. S.*

Before his departure from Isna [Isny], the town was greatly afflicted with the pestilence ; and he understanding that many of the wealthiest of the inhabitants intended to forsake the place, without having any respect or care of such as laboured with that disease, and that the houses of such as were infected, were commanded to be shut up by the magistrate, he openly admonished them, either to continue in the town, or liberally to bestow their alms before their departure, for the relief of such as were sick. And during the time of the visitation, he himself in person would visit those that were sick ; he would administer spiritual comfort unto them, pray for them, and would be present with them day and night ; and yet by the providence of God he remained untouched, and was preserved by the allpowerful hand of God.— *From the Life of Paulus Fagius, in T. Fuller's Abel Redevivus.*

In 1576, Cardinal Carlo Borromeo, Archbishop of Milan, the worthiest of all the successors of St. Ambrose, when he learnt at Lodi, that the plague had made its appearance in his city, went at once to the city. His council of clergy advised him to remain in some healthy part of his diocese till the sickness should have spent itself, but he replied that a bishop, whose duty it is to give his life for his sheep, could not rightly abandon them in time of peril. They owned that to stand by them was the higher course. " Well," he said, " is it not a bishop's duty to choose the higher course ? " So back into the town of deadly sickness he went, leading the people to repent, and watching over them in their suffering, visiting the hospitals, and, by his own example, encouraging his clergy in carrying spiritual consolation to the dying. All the time the plague lasted, which was four months, his exertions were fearless and unwearied, and what was remarkable was, that of his whole household only two died, and they were persons who had not been called to go about among the sick.—*From " A Book of Golden Deeds,"* 1864.

Although Defoe's history of the plague is a work of fiction, yet its statements are generally facts, and therefore we extract the following :—" The misery of the poor I had many occasions to be an eye-witness of, and sometimes also of the charitable assistance that some pious people daily gave to such, sending them relief and supplies both of food, physic, and other help, as they found they wanted. . . . Some pious ladies were transported with zeal in so good a work, and so confident in the protection of Providence in discharge of the great duty of charity, that they went about in person distributing alms to the poor, and even visiting poor families, though sick and infected, in their very houses, appointing nurses to attend those that wanted attending, and ordering apothecaries and surgeons . . . giving their blessing to the poor in substantial relief to them, as well as hearty prayers for them. I will not undertake to say, as some do, that none of those charitable people were suffered to fall under the calamity itself ; but this I may say, that I never knew anyone of them that came to any ill, which I mention for the encouragement of others in case of the like distress : and, doubtless, if they that give to the poor lend to the Lord, and he will repay them, those that hazard their lives to give to the poor, and to comfort and assist the poor in such misery as this, may hope to be protected in the work."— *Daniel Defoe's Journal of the Plague in London.*

Horne, in his notes on the Psalms, refers to the plague in Marseilles and the devotion of its bishop. There is a full account of him in the *Percy Anecdotes* from which we cull the following :—" M. de Belsunce, Bishop of Marseilles, so distinguished himself for his humanity during the plague which raged in that city in 1720, that the Regent of France offered him the richer and more honourable See of Laon, in Picardy ; but he refused it, saying, he should be unwilling to leave a flock that had been endeared to him by their sufferings. His pious and intrepid labours are commemorated in a picture in the Town Hall of Marseilles, in which he is represented in his episcopal habit, attended by his almoners, giving his benediction to the dying. . . . But perhaps the most touching picture extant of the bishop's humane labours, is to be found in a letter of his own, written to the Bishop of Soissons, Sept. 27, 1720. ' Never,' he says, ' was desolation greater, nor was ever anything like this. Here have been many cruel plagues, but none was ever more cruel : to be sick and dead was almost the same thing. What a melancholy spectacle have we on all sides ! we go into the streets full of dead bodies, half rotten through, which we pass to come to a dying body, to excite him to an act of contrition, and give him absolution.' " Notwithstanding exposure to a pestilence so fatal, the devoted bishop escaped uninjured.

While France justly boasts of " Marseilles' good Bishop," England may congratulate herself on having cherished in her bosom a clergyman who in an equally earnest manner discharged his pastoral care, and watched over the simple flock committed to his charge, at no less risk of life, and with no less fervour of piety and benevolence. The Rev. W. Mompesson was rector of Eyam in Derbyshire, in the time of the plague that nearly depopulated the town in the year 1666. During the whole time of the calamity, he performed the functions of the physician, the legislator, and the minister of his afflicted parish ; assisting the sick with his medicines, his advice, and his prayers. Tradition still shows a cavern near Eyam, where this worthy pastor used to preach to such of his parishioners as had not caught the distemper. Although the village was almost depopulated, his exertions prevented the spread of the plague to other districts, and he himself survived unharmed.

Verse 8.—" *Only with thine eyes shalt thou behold and see the reward of the wicked.*" First, indeed, because of thy own escape ; secondly, on account of thy complete security ; thirdly, for the sake of comparison ; fourthly, because of the perfect pre-eminence of justice itself. For then it will not be the time of mercy, but of judgment ; nor shall any mercy in any way be ever shown towards the wicked there, where no improvement can be hoped for. Far away will be that softness of human infirmity, which meanwhile charity nevertheless uses for salvation, collecting in the ample folds of her outspread net good and bad fishes, that is, pleasant and hurtful affections. But this is done at sea. On the shore she chooses only the good, and so rejoicing with them that do rejoice, it hence comes to pass that she weeps not with those that weep.—*Bernard.*

Verse 9.—Here commences the second half of the Psalm. And it is as though the Psalmist feared lest (as is too often the case with us) we should, in dwelling on the promises and blessings of God, and applying them to ourselves, forget the condition to which they are annexed—the character of those who are to receive them. He therefore pauses here to remind us of the opening verses of the Psalm, by repeating again their substance.—*Mary B. M. Duncan.*

Verse 9.—" *Because thou hast made the Lord,*" etc. What faith is this, what trust is that which God hath promised protection and deliverance to in the time of a plague ? What act of faith is it ? What faith is it ? I answer *first*, there is a faith of persuasion, called faith, whereby men are persuaded and verily believe that they shall not die, nor fall by the hand of the plague. This is well ; but I do not find in the 91st Psalm that this protection is entailed upon this persuasion, neither do I find this faith here mentioned.

There is also a faith of reliance, whereby a man doth rely upon God for salvation ; this is a justifying faith, true justifying faith ; this is true faith indeed : but I do not find in this Psalm, that this promise of protection and deliverance in the time of a plague is entailed upon this, nor that this is here mentioned.

But again, there is a faith, I may call it a faith of recourse unto God, whereby a man doth betake himself unto God for shelter, for protection as to his habitation : when other men do run one this way, another that way, to their hiding places : in the time of a plague for a man then to betake himself to God as to his habitation,

I think this is the faith here spoken of in this 91st Psalm : for do but mark the words of the Psalm : at the 1st verse, " He that dwelleth in the secret place of the Most High," in the hiding place of the Most High ; as if he should say, " When others run from the plague and pestilence and run to their hiding places," " He that dwelleth in the secret place of the Most High," that betakes himself to God as his hiding place and his habitation, he shall abide under the shadow of the Almighty, shall be protected ; and so at the 9th verse, " Because thou hast made the Lord which is my refuge, even the Most High thy habitation, there shall no evil befall thee, neither shall any plague come nigh thy dwelling ; " as if he should say to us, In time of a plague men are running and looking out for habitations and hiding places ; but because thou hast made the Lord thy habitation, and hast recourse to him as thy habitation, " no evil shall befall thee, neither shall the plague come nigh thy dwelling : " and again at the 11th verse it is said, " He shall give his angels charge over thee to keep thee in all thy ways," the ways of thy calling ; as if he should say, In the time of a plague men will be very apt to leave station and calling, and so run away from the plague and pestilence ; but saith he, " He shall give his angels charge over thee, to keep thee in all thy ways," the ways of thy calling and place ; that is, look when a man in the time of a plague shall conscientiously keep his station and place, and betake himself to God as his habitation ; this is the faith that is here spoken of, and this is the faith that God hath promised protection to, here in the 91st Psalm. . . . This promise of protection and deliverance is not made to a believer as a believer, but as acting and exercising faith ; for though a man be a believer, if he do not act and exercise his faith, this promise will not reach him, therefore if a believer die, not exercising faith and trusting in God, it is no disparagement to the promise.—*William Bridge.*

Verse 9.—No man can have two *homes*—two places of *constant* resort. And if the Lord be truly " *our habitation,*" we can have no other refuge for our souls, no other resting-place for our hearts.—*Mary B. M. Duncan.*

Verses 9, 10.—There is a threefold preservation which the church and the members of it may look for from divine providence. One from, another in, and a third by, dangers. *First,* from dangers, according to the promise in one of the Psalms, " Because thou hast made the Lord who is my refuge, even the Most High thy habitation : there shall no evil befall thee, neither shall any plague come nigh thy dwelling." Austin had appointed to go to a certain town to visit the Christians there, and to give them a sermon or more. The day and place were known to his enemies, who set armed men to lie in wait for him by the way which he was to pass, and kill him. As God would have it, the guide whom the people had sent with him to prevent his going out of the right way mistook, and led him into a by-path, yet brought him at last to his journey's end. Which when the people understood, as also the adversaries' disappointment, they adored the providence of God, and gave him thanks for that great deliverance.*

II. In dangers. So in Job v. 19, 20. " He shall deliver thee in six troubles, yea in seven there shall no evil touch thee. In famine he shall redeem thee from death ; and in war from the power of the sword." In time of famine the widow of Sarepta's store was made to hold out. The providence of God was with Daniel in the lion's den, shutting up the mouths of those furious beasts : and with the men in the fiery furnace, giving a prohibition to the fire that it should not burn, when they were in the jaws of danger, yea of death. The church hath always been a lily among thorns, yet flourishes still. This bush is yet far from a consumption, although it has seldom or never been out of the fire.

III. By danger. There is a preservation from greater evils by less. No poison but Providence knoweth how to make an antidote ; so Jonah was swallowed by a whale, and by that danger kept alive. Joseph thrown into a pit, and afterwards sold into Egypt, and by these hazards brought to be a nursing father to the church. Chrysostom excellently, Fides in periculis secura est, in securitate periclitatur.† Faith is endangered by security, but secure in the midst of danger, as Esther's was when she said, " If I perish I perish." God preserveth us, not as we do fruits that are to last but for a year, in sugar ; but as flesh for a long voyage in salt : we must expect in this life much brine and pickle, because our heavenly Father preserveth us as those whom he resolveth to keep for ever, in and by dangers themselves. Paul's

---

* Agnoscunt omnes miram Dei providentiam, cui ut liberatori gratias merito egerunt. Possidonius in vita August, chap. xii.

† Homil. xxvi. operis imperf. in Matt.

thorn in the flesh, which had much of danger and trouble in it, was given him on purpose to prevent pride, which was a great evil. " Lest I," said he, " should be exalted above measure through abundance of revelations, there was given me a thor ɩ in the flesh, the messenger of Satan to buffet me, lest I should be exalted abɔve measure." Elsewhere having commemorated Alexander the coppersmith's withstanding anɑ doing him much evil, yea Nero's opening his mouth as a lion against him, and the Lord's delivering of him thence, he concludeth as more than a conqueror. " And the Lord shall deliver me from every evil work, and will preserve me unto his heavenly kingdom ; to whom be glory for ever and ever, Amen." 2 Tim. iv. 14, 15, 17, 18.—*John Arrowsmith, (1602—1659.)*

Verses 9—14.—Dependence on Christ is not the cause of his hiding us, but it is the qualification of the person that shall be hid.—*Ralph Robinson.*

Verse 10.—" *There shall no evil befall thee,*" etc. It is a security in the very midst of evils. Not like the security of angels—safety in a world of safety, quiet in a calm ; but it is quiet in a storm, safety amid desolation and the elements of destruction, deliverance where everything else is going to wreck.—*Charles Bradley,* 1840.

Verse 10.—God doth not say no afflictions shall befall us, but no *evil.*—*Thomas Watson.*

Verse 10.—Sin which has kindled a fire in hell, is kindling fires on earth continually. And when they break out, every one is asking how they happened. Amos replies, " Shall there be evil in a city, and the Lord hath not done it ? " And when desolation is made by fire, Isaiah declares, The Lord hath " consumed us, because of our iniquities." Many years ago my house was oft threatened to be destroyed, but the Lord insured it, by giving me the 10th verse of the 91st Psalm ; and the Lord's providence is the best insurance.—*John Berridge.*

Verse 11.—" *He shall give his angels charge,*" etc. Charge ; charge is a strict command, more than a bare command ; as when you would have a servant do a business certainly and fully, you lay a charge upon him, I charge you that you do not neglect that business ; you do not barely tell what he should do, prescribe him his work, but you charge him to do it. So says the Lord unto the angels : My servants or children, now they are in the plague and pestilence, O my angels, I charge you stir not from their houses, I charge you, stir not from such an one's bed-side ; it is a charge, " He shall give his angels charge."

Further, he doth not only, and will not only charge his angel, but his angels ; not one angel charged with the safety of his people, but many angels ; for their better guard and security, " He shall give his angels charge." And again, " He will give his angels charge over *thee* to keep thee ; " to keep *thee* ; charge over *thee* and to keep thee ; not only over the whole church of God, but over every particular member of the church of God ; " He will give his angels charge over thee to keep thee ; " this is his marvellous care. Well, but besides this, " He will give his angels charge to keep thee *in all thy ways,*" not in some of thy ways, but in all thy ways. As God's providence is particular in regard of our persons, so it is universal in regard of our ways. " He will give his angels charge over thee, to keep thee," not in some but " in all thy ways."

But is this all ? No ; " They shall bear thee up in their hands," as every servant desires and loves to take up the young heir, or the young master into his arms, so the angels. It is a great matter that the Lord promiseth to pitch his tents. " And the angels of the Lord shall pitch their tents round about them that fear him ; " but here is more ; the angels shall not only pitch their tents, be their guard, but their nurses, to bear them up in their hands ; but why ? " That thou dash not thy foot against a stone." When children begin to go, they are very apt to fall and get many a knock ; to stumble at every little stone. Now there are many stones of stumbling that are in our way, and we are very apt to fall and miscarry ; but such is the goodness of God, the providence of God, the goodness of his providence, that as he hath provided his angels to be our guard, in opposition to all our foreign enemies, so he hath provided his angels to be our nurses, in opposition to all our weaknesses and infirmities, that we get no hurt, that we miscarry not in the least.

But what need God make use of angels to protect his people, he is able to do it alone ; and is it not for God's dishonour to make use of them for the protection of his people ? No, it is for the honour of God, for the more honourable the servants are, the instruments are, that a king or prince doth use for the protecting of his people, the more honourable is that king or prince. Now the angels, they are honourable creatures; frequently they are called gods; "Thou hast made him a little lower than the angels." . . . They are the fittest people in the world for this employment, fittest in regard of themselves, fittest in regard of the saints. They are fittest in regard of themselves, for *First*, they are an exceeding strong and potent people; who more fit to look to and care for the concernments of the saints and people of God, than those that are strong and potent? It is said of the angels in the ciii. Psalm, that they excel in strength. v. 20. . . . One angel you know destroyed a hundred and fourscore thousand of the host of Assyria in a night; as one constable will scare away twenty thieves, so one good angel invested with God's authority is able to drive away a thousand evil angels, devils: they are an exceeding strong and potent people. *Second*. As they are an exceeding strong and potent people, so they are a very knowing and a wise people; and who so fit to manage the affairs and concerns of the saints and people of God, and to protect and defend them, as a knowing and understanding people? You know what Joab said to David; "Thou art for wisdom as an angel of God." Says our Saviour, "No man knoweth that day and time, no, not the angels in heaven;" as if the angels in heaven knew every secret and were acquainted with every hidden thing: they are an exceeding knowing people, very prudent and very wise. *Third*. As they are an exceeding knowing and wise people, so they are also exceeding active and expeditious, quick in despatches. Who more fit to protect and defend the saints and people of God, than those that are active, expedite, and quick in their despatches? such are the angels. In the first of Ezekiel ye read that every one had four wings; why? because of their great activity and expedition, and the quick despatch they make in all their affairs. *Fourth*. As they are an active and expeditious people, so they are a people very faithful both to God and man; in the ciii. Psalm they are ready to do God's will, and not only ready to fulfil God's will, but they do it: "Bless the Lord all ye his angels that excel in strength (v. 20), that do his commandments, hearkening unto the voice of his word. Bless ye the Lord, all ye his hosts, ye ministers of his that do his pleasure." They are very faithful; and who so fit to do the work, to attend and look to the concernments of the saints and people of God, as those that are faithful? *Fifth*. As they are an exceeding faithful people, so they are a people that are very loving to the saints and children of God, very loving; otherwise they were not fit to be their nurses: what is a nurse without love? They are loving to the saints. "Do it not," (said the angel unto John), "I am thy fellow-servant;" do not give divine worship to me, I am thy fellow-servant; fellow-servants are loving to one another; they are fellow-servants with the saints. . . . It is recorded of Alexander that being in great danger and to fight next day with his enemies, he slept very soundly the night before; and he being asked the reason thereof, said, Parmenio wakes; meaning a great and faithful captain of his; Parmenio wakes, says he. The angels are called watchmen; they watch and are faithful, therefore you may be secure, quiet, and at rest: trust in the Lord for ever, upon this account, in this day trust in the Lord.

If these things be so, then, friends, why should we not stoop to any work commanded, though it lie much beneath us? Do not you think that the attending upon a sick man, a man that hath a plague sore running upon him, is a work that lies much beneath angels? yet the angels do it because it is commanded, though much beneath them yet they stoop to it because it is commanded: and what though a work lie much beneath you, yet if it be commanded, why should you not stoop to it? You will say, Such an one is much beneath me, I will not lay my hand under his shoes, he is much beneath me; ah, but the angels lay their hands under your shoes, and the work they do for you is much beneath them: why should we not be like our attendants? This is angelical obedience; the angels do you many a kindness, and never look for thanks from you, they do many a kindness that you are not aware of: why are you delivered sometimes you know not how? here is a hand under a wing, the ministration of angels is the cause of it. But I say the work they stoop to for you is much beneath them, and therefore why should we not stoop to any work commanded, though it lie much beneath us?—*William Bridge*.

Verse 11.—"*He shall give his angels charge over thee,*" etc. When Satan tempted Christ in the wilderness, he alleged but one sentence of Scripture for himself, Matthew iv. 6, and that Psalm out of which he borrowed it made so plain against him, that he was fain to pick here a word and there a word, and leave out that which went before, and skip in the midst, and omit that which came after, or else he had marred his cause. The Scripture is so holy, and pure, and true, that no word nor syllable thereof can make for the Devil, or for sinners, or for heretics : yet, as the Devil alleged Scripture, though it made not for him, but against him, so do the libertines, and epicures, and heretics, as though they had learned at his school.—*Henry Smith.*

Verse 11.—One angel armed with the power and glory of God is stronger than a whole country. Earthly princes are subject to many changes and great unsurety of life and estate. The reason is, their enemies may kill their watch, and corrupt their guard. But what men or kingdoms can touch the Church's watch ? what angels of gold are able to corrupt the angels of God ? and then how can that perish that is committed to keepers so mighty and faithful ? Secondly, the charge of us is given to those ministering spirits by parcels, not in gross and piece-meal, not in a lump : our members in a book, our hairs by tale and number. For it is upon record, and, as it were, delivered to them in writing in one Psalm, *They keep all our bones*, Ps. xxxiv. 20 ; in this, *they keep our very foot*, putting it in security (ver. 12) ; and elsewhere our whole man and every member. And can a charge so precisely and so particularly given and taken, be neglected ? Thirdly, their manner of keeping us, as it is set down in the text, cannot but promise great assurance ; for, is not the little child safe while the nurse carrieth it in her arms, or beareth it in her hands ? So while these nurses so bear us, can we be in danger ? but our nurses on earth may fall ; these nurses, the *angels*, cannot.—*Robert Horn.*

Verse 11.—"*His angels.*" Taking the word *angel* in its literal meaning, as *messenger*, we may look upon any agency which God employs to strengthen, protect, and help us, as *his angel* to us.—*Mary B. M. Duncan.*

Verse 11.—"*To keep thee in all thy ways.*" How should those heavenly spirits bear that man in their arms, like nurses, upon earth living ; or bear up his soul to heaven, like winged porters, when he dies, that refuseth the right way ? They shall keep us in all our ways. Out of the way it is their charge to oppose us, as to preserve us in the way. Nor is this more a terror to the ungodly, than to the righteous a comfort. For if an angel would keep even a Balaam from sinning, how much more careful are all those glorious powers to prevent the miscarriages of God's children ! From how many falls and bruises have they saved us ! In how many inclinations to evil have they turned us, either by removing occasions, or by casting in secretly good motions ! We sin too often, and should catch many more falls, if those holy guardians did not uphold us. Satan is ready to divert us, when we endeavour to do well ; when to do ill, angels are as ready to prevent us. We are in Joshua the high-priest's case, with Satan on the one hand, on the other an angel, Zech. iii. 1 : without this, our danger were greater than our defence, and we could neither stand nor rise.—*Thomas Adams.*

Verse 11.—"*To keep thee in all thy ways.*" Their commission, large as it is, reaches no further : when you leave that, you lose your guard ; but while you keep your way, angels, yea, the God of angels, will keep you. Do not so much fear losing your estate or your liberty or your lives, as losing your way, and leaving your way : fear that more than anything ; nothing but sin exposeth you to misery. So long as you keep your way, you shall keep other things ; or if you lose any of them, you shall get what is better : though you may be sufferers for Christ you shall not be losers by him.—*Samuel Slater (—1704), in "Morning Exercises."*

Verse 11.—"*In all thy ways.*" Your ways are God's ways, your way is the way commanded by God. If you be out of God's ways, you are out of your own way : if you be in your way, the angels shall keep you, even in the time of a plague, and bear you up in their hands that you dash not your foot against a stone ; but if you be out of your way, I will not insure your safety. When Balaam went upon the devil's errand an angel met him and scared his ass, and the ass ran his foot against the wall, dashed his foot against the wall. The promise is, " Thou shalt not dash thy foot against a stone " ; but he was out of his way, and the angel met him and scared his ass, and his ass made him rush his leg against the wall. Jonah went out of his way when he ran away from God ; God bade him go one way, and he went another. Well, what then ? were the angels with him for his protection ? the very sea would not be quiet till he was thrown overboard : instead of angels to protect him, he had a whale to devour him. I confess indeed, through the free grace and mercy of God, the belly of destruction was made a chamber of preservation to him, but he was out of his way ; and instead of an angel to keep him that he dash not his foot, his whole body was thrown overboard. Says Solomon, " As a bird from her nest, so is a man out of his place ": so long as the bird is in her nest it is free from the hawk, it is free from the birding-piece, it is free from the nets and gins and snares as long as it is in its nest; but when the bird is off her nest then she is exposed to many dangers. So, so long as a man is in his way, in his place and in his way, he is well and under protection; but when a man is off his nest, out of his place and out of his way, then is he exposed to all dangers: but be but in your way and then you may assure yourselves of divine protection, and of the management thereof by the hands of angels. Oh who would not labour always to be in that way which God hath appointed him to be in? Why should we not always consider with ourselves and say, But am I in my way? Old Mr. Dod being upon the water and going out of one boat into another, slipped between them, and the first word he spake was this, " Am I in my way? " so we should always be saying, But am I in my way? am I in my way? I am now idling away my time, but am I in my way? Oh my soul, am I in my way? I am in my calling this day without prayer in the morning and reading the Scriptures; but am I in my way? Oh my soul, am I in my way? I am now in such frothy company where I get no good, but hurt; but am I in my way? Ever consider this, Am I in my way? You may expect the Lord's protection and the angels' attendance, if you be in your way, but not else.—*William Bridge.*

Verse 11.—We have the safeguard of the empire; not only the protection of the King, from which the wicked as outlaws are secluded; but also the keeping of angels, to whom he hath given a charge over us, to keep us in all his ways. So nearly we participate of his divine things, that we have his own guard royal to attend us.—*Thomas Adams.*

Verse 11.—" *He shall give his angels charge over thee,"* etc.

> And is there care in heaven, and is there love
> In heavenly spirits to these creatures base,
> That may compassion of their evils move?
> There is, else much more wretched were the race
> Of men than beasts. But oh, the exceeding grace
> Of highest God, that loves his creatures so,
> And all his works with mercy doth embrace,
> That blessed angels he sends to and fro,
> To serve us wicked men, to serve his wicked foe!
>
> How oft do they their silver bowers leave,
> To come to succour us that succour want!
> How oft do they with golden pinions cleave
> The flitting skies, like flying pursuivant,
> Against foul fiends to aid us militant!
> They for us fight, they watch and duly ward,
> And their bright squadrons round about us plant;
> And all for love and nothing for reward.
> Oh, why should heavenly God to man have such regard!
> —*Edmund Spenser,* 1552—1599.

Verses 11, 12.—It is observable that Scripture is the weapon that Satan doth desire to wield against Christ. In his other ways of dealing he was shy, and did but lay them in Christ's way, offering only the occasion, and leaving him to take them up; but in this he is more confident, and industriously pleads it as a thing which he could better stand to and more confidently avouch. The care of his subtlety herein, lay in the misrepresentation and abuse of it, as may be seen in these particulars: (1) In that he urged this promise to promote a sinful thing, contrary to the general end of all Scripture, which was therefore written ' that we sin not.' (2) But more especially in his clipping and mutilating of it. He industriously leaves out that part of it which doth limit and confine the promise of protection to lawful undertakings, such as this was not, and renders it as a general promise of absolute safety, be the action what it will. It is a citation from Ps. xci. 11, 12 which there runs thus, " He shall give his angels charge over thee, *to keep thee in all thy ways."* These last words, " *in all thy ways,"* which doth direct to a true understanding of God's intention in that promise, he deceitfully leaves out, as if they were needless and unnecessary parts of the promise, when indeed they were on purpose put there by the Spirit of God, to give a description of those persons and actions, unto whom, in such cases, the accomplishment of the promise might be expected; for albeit the word in the original, which is translated "*ways*"—דְּרָכִים—doth signify any kind of way or action in the general, yet in this place it doth not ; for then God were engaged to an absolute protection of men, not only when they unnecessarily thrust themselves into dangers, but in the most abominably sinful actions whatsoever, which would have been a direct contradiction to those many scriptures wherein God threatens to withdraw his hand and leave sinners to the danger of their iniquities ; but it is evident that the sense of it is no more than this, ' God is with you, while you are with him.' We have a paraphrase of this text, to this purpose, in Prov. iii. 23, " Then shalt thou walk in thy way safely, and thy foot shall not stumble ; " where the condition of this safety, pointed to in the word " then," which leads the promise, is expressly mentioned in the foregoing verses, " My son, let them "— that is, the precepts of wisdom—" not depart from thine eyes . . . Then "—not upon other terms—" shalt thou walk in thy way safely." The "*ways*" then in this promise cited by Satan, are the ways of duty, or the ways of our lawful callings. The fallacy of Satan in this dealing with Scripture is obvious, and Christ might have given this answer, as Bernard hath it, That God promiseth to keep him in his ways, but not in self-created dangers, for that was not his way, but his ruin ; or if a way, it was Satan's way, but not his. (3) To these two, some add another abuse, in a subtle concealment of the following verse in Ps. xci. : " *Thou shalt tread upon the lion and adder.*" This concerned Satan, whose cruelty and poisonous deceits were fitly represented by the lion and the adder, and there the promise is also explained to have a respect to Satan's temptations—that is—God would so manage his protection, that his children should not be led into a snare.—*Richard Gilpin.*

Verses 11, 12.—There is, to my mind, a very remarkable coincidence of expression between the verses of this Psalm, about the office of God's angels, and that passage in Isaiah where Christ's sympathy and presence receive the same charge attributed to them without interposition. In Isaiah lxiii. 9, we read, " In all their affliction he was afflicted, and the angel of his presence saved them." And again, " They shall bear thee up in their hands, lest thou dash thy foot against a stone," compared with, " And he bare them, and he carried them all the days of old." Christ in us, by sympathy with our nature—Christ in us, by the indwelling of his Spirit in each individual heart—thus he knows all our needs. Christ with us, in every step, all-powerful to make all work for good, and with love and pity watching over our interests—thus his presence saves us, and *all* things are made his messengers to us.—*Mary B. M. Duncan.*

Verse 12.—" Angels . . . shall bear thee up . . . lest thou dash thy foot against a stone." Angels are introduced as bearing up the believer in their hands, not that he may be carried in safety over some vast ocean, not that he may be transported through hostile and menacing squadrons, not that, when exposed to some extraordinary danger, he may be conveyed to a place of refuge, but, as bearing him up in their arms, " *lest at any time he hurt his foot against a stone.*" . . . Angels, the topmost beings in creation, the radiant, the magnificent, the powerful—angels are represented as holding up a righteous man, lest some pebble in the path should make him trip, lest he hurt his foot against a stone.

Is there, after all, any want of keeping between the agency and the act, so that there is even the appearance of angels being unworthily employed, employed on what is beneath them, when engaged in bearing us up, lest at any time we hurt the foot against a stone ? Nay, the hurting the foot against a stone has often laid the foundation of fatal bodily disease : the injury which seemed too trifling to be worth notice has produced extreme sickness, and ended in death. Is it different in spiritual respects, in regard of the soul, to which the promise in our text must be specially applied ? Not a jot. Or, if there be a difference, it is only that the peril to the soul from a slight injury is far greater than that to the body : the worst spiritual diseases might commonly be traced to inconsiderable beginnings. . . .

It can be no easy thing, this keeping the foot from being hurt against a stone, seeing that the highest of created beings are commissioned to effect it. Neither is it. The difficulty in religion is the taking up the cross " daily," rather than the taking it up on some set occasion, and under extraordinary circumstances. The serving God in little things, the carrying religious principle into the details of life, the discipline of our tempers, the regulation of our speech, the domestic Christianity, the momentary sacrifices, the secret and unobserved self-denials ; who that knows anything of the difficulties of piety, does not know that there is greater danger of his failing in these than in trials of apparently far higher cost, and harder endurance ; if on no other account, yet because the very absence of what looks important, or arduous, is likely to throw him off his guard, make him careless or confident, and thereby almost insure defect or defeat ?—*Henry Melvill.*

Verse 12.—To carry them in their hands is a metaphor, and signifies a perfect execution of their custody, to have a special care of them, and therefore is rather expressed so, than carrying them on their shoulders.   That which one carries on their hand they are sure to keep.   The Spaniards have a proverb when they would signify eminent favour and friendship, ' they carry him upon the palms of their hands,' that is, they exceedingly love him, and diligently keep him.   " *Lest thou dash thy foot against a stone.*"   He persists in the metaphor : children often stumble and fall, unless they be led and carried in hands and arms.   By *stones* are meant all difficulties, objections, perils, both to the outward and inward man, as Christ is said to take care of hairs and sparrows, that is, of every thing even to a hair.   Now we know what this charge is, saving that Zanchy adds also the metaphor of school-masters, and says that we are poor rustic people, strangers ; but being adopted into the household of God, he gives his most noble ministers, *the angels*, charge, first of our nursing, and then of our education ; when we are weaned, to instruct us, to admonish, to institute, to correct us, to comfort us, to defend us, to preserve us from all evil, and to provoke us to all good.   And these angels, seeing we are so dear to God, that for our sakes he spared not his own Son, take this charge with all their hearts upon them, and omit nothing of their duty from our birth to the end of our life.—*Henry Lawrence, in " A Treatise of our Communion and Warre with Angells,* 1646.

Verse 13.—" *Thou shalt tread upon the lion and adder, the young lion and the dragon shalt thou trample under feet.*"   What avails a human foot among these ? What force of human affection can stand fast among such terrible monsters ?   These are spiritual wickednesses, and are designated by not incongruous titles. . . . One is an *asp*, another a basilisk, a third a *lion*, and a fourth a *dragon*, because each in his own invisible way variously wounds,—one by his bite, another by his look, a third by his roar or blow, and a fourth by his breath. . . . .

Consider this also, whether perchance we are able to meet these four temptations with four virtues.   The lion roars, who will not fear ?   If any there be, he shall be *brave*.   But when the lion is foiled, the dragon lurks in the sand, in order to excite the soul with his poisonous breath ; breathing therein the lust of earthly things. Who, think you, shall escape his wiles ?   None but the *prudent*.   But perhaps whilst you are careful in attacking these, some annoyance vexes you ; and lo ! the asp is upon you forthwith.   For he seems to have found for himself a reasonable moment.   Who is he that shall not be exasperated by this asp ?   Certainly the man of *temperance* and modesty, who knows how to abound, and to suffer want. On this opportunity, I think, the Evil Eye with its wicked allurements may determine to fascinate thee.   Who shall turn away his face ?   Truly the *just* man, who not only desires not to take to himself the glory due to God, but not even to receive what is presented by another : if yet he is a just man, that justly executes what is just, who performs not his righteousness before men, who, lastly, although he is just, lifts not up his head.   For this virtue consists specially in humility.   This purifies the intention, this also obtains merit all the more truly and effectually, because it arrogates less to itself.—*Bernard.*

Verse 13.—" *Adder.*"   The *pethen* is classed with the lion as being equally to be dreaded by the traveller. . . . There is no doubt that the Egyptian cobra is the *pethen* of Scripture.—*J. G. Wood.*

Verse 13.—" *Dragon.*"   The expression is used (1) for " sea-monsters," (2) for serpents, (3) for wild beasts or birds characteristic of desolate places, and (4) it is used figuratively to represent the enemies of the Lord, and especially Pharaoh, as head and representative of the Egyptian power, and Nebuchadnezzar, the head and representative of the Chaldean monarchy.   The term is thus a general one, signifying any monstrous creature, whether of the land or of the water, and is to be set down with the one or the other, according as the context indicates.—*John Duns, in " Biblical Natural Science.*"

Verse 13.—" *Thou shalt tread upon ; " " thou shalt trample under feet.*"   Thou shalt tread upon them, not accidentally, as a man treads upon an adder or a serpent in the way ; but his meaning is, thou shalt intentionally tread upon them like a conqueror, thou shalt tread upon them to testify the dominion over them, so when the Lord Jesus gave that promise (Luke x. 19) to his disciples, that they should do great things, he saith, *You shall tread upon serpents ;* that is, you shall have power to overcome whatsoever may annoy you : serpentine power is all hurtful power, whether literal or mystical. As the Apostle assures all believers (Rom. xvi. 20), " *God shall tread down Satan* (that old serpent) *under your feet shortly.*"—*Joseph Caryl.*

Verse 13 *(second clause).*—But what is said unto Christ ? " *And thou shalt tread on the lion and dragon.*" *Lion,* for overt wrath ; *dragon* for covert lurking.—*Augustine.*

Verse 14.—" *Because he hath set his love upon me.*" Vulg. " *Because he hath hoped in me.*" Whatever is to be done, whatever is to be declined, whatever is to be endured, whatever is to be chosen, thou O Lord art my hope. This is the only cause of all my promises, this the sole reason of my expectation. Let another pretend to merit, let him boast that he bears the burden and heat of the day, let him say that he fasts twice on the Sabbath, let him finally glory that he is not as other men ; for me it is good to cleave unto God, to place my hope in the Lord God. Let others hope in other things, one in his knowledge of letters, another in his worldly-wisdom, one in his nobility, one in his dignity, another in some other vanity, for thy sake I have made all things loss, and count them but dung ; since thou, Lord, art my hope.—*Bernard,* quoted by *Le Blanc.*

Verse 14 *(first clause).*—As there is a *because* and a *therefore* in the process of the law, in concluding death for sin, so there is a *because* and a *therefore* in the process of grace, and of the *gospel,* which doth reason from one grace given to infer another grace to be given, even grace for grace ; and such is this here : " *Because he hath set his love upon me, therefore will I deliver him.*"—*David Dickson.*

Verse 14.—He does not say, Because he is without sin, because he has perfectly kept all my precepts, because he has merit and is worthy to be delivered and guarded. But he produces those qualities which are even found in the weak, the imperfect, and those still exposed to sin in the flesh, namely, adhesion, knowledge of his name, and prayer.—*Musculus.*

Verse 14.—" *He hath set his love upon me.*" In the love of a divinely illuminated believer there is (1) the sweet property of *gratitude.* The soul has just and enlarged views of the salvation which he has obtained through the name of Jesus. The evils from which he is saved ; the blessings in hand, and the blessings in hope ; the salvation in time, and the salvation through eternity, which can and shall be enjoyed through the name of Jesus, excites feelings of the most ardent gratitude in the soul of the Christian. (2) Another delightful ingredient in this settled love is, *admiration.* Everything in the scheme and execution of God's redeeming plan is an object of admiration. All that the Lord Jesus is in himself ; all that he has done ; all that he does at the present ; and all that he has promised to do for his people, deserves the warmest admiration. This holy feeling is experienced in the breast of the man to whom the Lord can say, " *He hath set his love upon me.*" (3) Another ingredient in the illuminated love of the believer is *delightful complacency.* Nothing can afford complacent delight in any excellency unless we are persuaded that we either do possess, or may possess it. I may go to the palace of the greatest monarch in the world, and be deeply struck with astonishment and admiration at the wonder beheld, but there will not be one thrill of complacency felt in my bosom at the view of the astonishing objects which crowd upon my vision. Why ? Because I neither have, nor can have any interest in them ; they are not mine, nor ever can be ; therefore, I cannot take complacent delight in them. But the love of the Christian is a delightful love, (as Mr. Baxter called it,) because there is in the Lord everything that is worthy of infinite and eternal admiration ; and then there is the thought which produces a thrill of pleasure,—whatever I admire I can, in some measure, possess. The illuminated eye of God's favourite sees everything in the Lord to supply his necessities ; everything to satisfy his desires, all his own ; which makes the soul delight itself in the Lord, and he rests in his love. Therefore, the Lord says of the object of his lovingkindness, " He hath set his love upon me "— he hath renounced sin as the greatest abomination ; he hath taken off the heart from all idolatrous attachment to the creature, and placed it fixedly and supremely upon God.—*William Dawson, Methodist Preacher* (1773—1841).

Verse 14.—" *He hath set his love upon me.*" We have a similar expression in daily use, which means the bending of all our energies to one end—a ceaseless effort after one object. We say, "I have set my heart on such a thing." This is what God will have from us—an intense, single-hearted love. We must love him "with all our heart, and with all our soul, and with all our strength, and with all our mind," so that, like Jesus, we may "delight to do his will." Just let us think of the way in which setting our heart on anything affects us, head, hands, time, thought, action—all are at work for its attainment. How we sacrifice everything else to it! Comfort, ease, present advantage, money, health, nay, our very selves, go freely for the sake of our cherished wish.

Have I so "set my heart upon" God? Temperaments differ. This may be an overdrawn picture of the way in which some of us seek a cherished object. But each knows his own capability in this way. God also knows our frame, and requires his best at every man's hand.

There is one thing in this verse which may encourage us very much. It is not because of *perfect* love that God will deliver. It is to the will to love and serve—it is to the *setting* the heart, that the promise is made—to the "full purpose of heart" that is *set* to cleave unto the Lord.—*Mary B. M. Duncan.*

Verse 14.—"*I will set him on high.*" That is, in an inaccessible, or lofty place, I will set him, which means, I will deliver him. When men truly know God to be a deliverer, they both put confidence in him, and call upon him. Then God exalts and delivers him that calls.—*Franciscus Vatablus.*

Verse 14.—"*I will set him on high, because he hath known my name.*" There is a great deal of safety in the knowledge of God, in his attributes, and in his Christ. A man's safety we see lies in his running to the tower (Prov. xxiii. 10); he runs and is safe. And it is the knowledge of this tower that sets a man a running to it. Hence we find safety attributed to the knowledge of the Lord. "*I will set him on high,*" I will exalt him, and so he shall be safe. Why so? "*Because he hath known my name*"; for the knowing of God aright was that which made him run, and so he is exalted and set on high. Then a man is safe when he hath got this tower to be his tower, when he hath gotten God to be his God. Now when we know God, we get him to be our God, and make this tower our tower, Jer. xxiv. 7: "I will give them an heart to know me, and I will be their God."—*Jeremiah Dyke, in "The Righteous Man's Tower,"* 1639.

Verses 14—16.—"*He hath known my name.*" From this text I would introduce to your notice the most desirable character under the sun; and I would exhibit him before you to excite each one to seek, until you obtain the same blessedness. The character that I shall exhibit is GOD'S FAVOURITE, one who is an object of the "loving-kindness of the Lord"; and in reading this passage there are two things which strike our attention concerning such a character. *First,* what the Lord says *of* him. *Second,* what the Lord says *to* him.

Now, then, my brethren—LOOK! There stands before you GOD'S FAVOURITE!

I. Listen to *what God says* OF *him.* 1. He says of him, "*He knows my name.*" The first principle of the life of God in the fallen soul of man is knowledge; spiritual, divine knowledge. The first operation of the Holy Ghost in the work of salvation, is a conviction of the character and perfections and relations of God. The Lord says, "he knows my name." He knows my name as Omniscient, Omnipresent, Holy, Just and True. (1) He first knows my name as a sin-hating, sin-avenging God; and this knowledge was a means of leading him to a deep sense of his own personal corruption, guilt, and danger as a sinner. (2) But the favourite of the Lord knows his name as revealed to Moses, as "The Lord, the Lord God, merciful and gracious, longsuffering, and abundant in goodness and truth, keeping mercy for thousands, forgiving iniquity, and transgression, and sin." He knows the name of the Lord as concentrated in the name of Jesus, who "shall save his people from their sins." By the *white* beams of God's holiness, (if I may so speak), the sinner sees his corruption, guilt and deformity: by the *red* beams of God's justice he sees his unspeakable danger: by the *mild* beams of God's mercy, he discovers a ground of hope—that there is pardon for his aggravated crimes. But it is in the face of our Lord Jesus Christ, that God appears most delightful. Hence we can say to every saved soul, as Paul did to the Corinthians:—" God, who commanded the light to shine out of darkness, hath shined in our hearts, to give the light of the knowledge of the glory of God in the face of Jesus Christ." As all the colours of the rainbow meet in one sunbeam, so all the perfections of God as perfectly unite, and more beautifully shine forth, in the person and offices of Jesus Christ, upon the soul of the penitent believer. This saving knowledge is always vital, active, and powerful.—*William Dawson.*

Verse 14.—" *He hath known my name.*" May we not get some light on this expression from the custom of the Jews, keeping the name JEHOVAH sacred to their own use, regarding it as too holy even to be pronounced by them in common use, and thus preserving it from being taken in vain by the heathen around? Thus it was known to Jews only. . . . But whatever be the origin of the expressions, to " know *his name,*" to " trust in *his name,*" to " believe in *his name,*" it evidently in all these cases means whatever is revealed concerning him—all that by which he maketh himself known. His Word, his Providence, above all, his Son, are included thus in his *name,* which we must know, believe in, and trust. So that to " know his name " is to know himself, as revealed in the Gospel.—*Mary B. M. Duncan.*

Verse 14 (*last clause*).—Sound love to God, floweth from and is joined with sound knowledge of God, as his Majesty is declared unto us in Scripture : the believer who hath set his *love* upon God, " *hath known my name,*" saith he.—*David Dickson.*

Verse 15.—" *I will answer him.*" I think we sometimes discourage ourselves by a misconception of the exact meaning of the expression, " *answer,*" taking it to mean only *grant.* Now, an answer is not necessarily an acquiescence. It may be a refusal, an explanation, a promise, a conditional grant. It is, in fact, simply *attention to our request expressed.* In this sense, before we call he will answer, and while we are yet speaking he will hear, Isaiah lxv. 24.—*Mary B. M. Duncan.*

Verse 15.—" *I will be with him in trouble.*" *I will be with him in trouble,* says God : and shall I seek meanwhile anything else than trouble ? It is good for me to cleave unto God. Not only so, but also to put my hope in the Lord : because *I will deliver him,* he says, *and honour him. I will be with him in trouble. My delights,* he says, *are with the sons of men.* Emanuel God with us. *Hail,* thou art *highly favoured,* says the Angel to Mary, *the Lord is with thee.* In the fulness of grace he is with us, in the plentitude of glory we shall be with him. He descends in order to be near to those who are of a troubled heart, that he may be with us in our trouble. . . . . . . It is better for me, O Lord, to be troubled, whilst only thou art with me, than to reign without thee, to feast without thee, to be honoured without thee. It is good rather to be embraced by thee in trouble, to have thee in this furnace with me, than to be without thee even in heaven. For what have I in heaven, and without thee what do I desire upon earth ? The furnace tries the gold, and the temptation of trouble just men.—*Bernard.*

Verse 15.—" *I will be with him in trouble.*" God hath made promises of his special presence with his saints in suffering. If we have such a friend to visit us in prison, we shall do well enough ; though we change our place, we shall not change our keeper. " *I will be with him.*" God will hold our head and heart when we are fainting ! What if we have more afflictions than others, if we have more of God's company ? God's honour is dear to him ; it would not be for his honour to bring his children into sufferings, and leave them there ; he will be with them to animate and support them ; yea, when new troubles arise. Job v. 19. " He shall deliver thee in six troubles."—*Thomas Watson.*

Verse 15.—" *I will be with him in trouble.*" Again God speaks and acts like a tender-hearted mother towards a sickly child. When the child is in perfect health she can leave it in the hands of the nurse ; but when it is sick she will attend it herself ; she will say to the nurse, " You may attend a while to some other business, I will watch over the child myself." She hears the slightest moan ; she flies to the cradle ; she takes it in her arms ; she kisses its lips, and drops a tear upon its face, and asks, " What can I do for thee, my child ? How can I relieve thy pain and soften thy sufferings ? Don't weep and break my heart ; it is thy mother's arms that are around thee ; it is thy mother's lap on which thou art laid ; it is thy mother's voice that speaks to thee ; it is thy mother that is with thee ; fear not." So the Lord speaks to his afflicted children. " *I will be with him in trouble.*" No mother can equally sympathise with her suffering child ; as the Lord does with his suffering people. No ! could all the love that ever dwelt in all the mothers' hearts that ever existed, be united in one mother's heart, and fixed on her only child, it would no more bear a comparison with the love of God to his people than the summer midnight glow-worm is to be compared to the summer mid-day sun.

Oh, that delightful sentence ! " *I will be with him in trouble.*" At other times God will leave them in the hands of angels : " I will give them charge over them, to keep them in all their ways ; they bear them up lest at any time they dash their feet against a stone." But when they are in trouble, I will say to the angels, " Stand aside, I will take care of them myself." " *I* will be with them in trouble." So he speaks to his people : " When thou passest through the waters, I will be with thee ; and through the rivers, they shall not overflow thee : when thou walkest through the fire, thou shalt not be burned ; neither shall the flame kindle upon thee. For I am the Lord thy God, the Holy One of Israel, thy Saviour." When languishing in sickness, he will make his bed, and his pillow ; when travelling through the valley of the shadow of death, the Lord will be with him, and enable him to sing, "I will fear no evil : for thou art with me ; thy rod and thy staff they comfort me." Thus he is with them as their physician and nurse, in pain and sickness ; as their strength in weakness ; as their guide in difficulty ; their ease in pain ; and as their life in death. " *I will be with him in trouble.*"—*William Dawson.*

Verse 16.—" *With long life will I satisfy him.*" Saint Bernard interprets this of *heaven ;* because he thought nothing long that had an end. This, indeed, is the emphasis of heaven's joy ; those blessed souls never sin, never weep more ; they shall not only be with the Lord, but ever with the Lord. This is the accent which is set on the eulogies given to heaven in Scripture. 'Tis " an inheritance," and that an " incorruptible one, that fadeth not away ; " it is " a crown of glory," and that a weighty one, yea, " an exceeding great and eternal weight of glory." When once it is on the saint's head it can never fall, or be snatched off ; it is a feast, but such a one that hath a sitting down to it but no rising up from it.—*William Gurnall.*

Verse 16.—" *With long life will I satisfy him.*" Observe the joyful contrast here to the mournful words in the foregoing Psalm. " We spend our years as a tale that is told. The days of our years are threescore years and ten," (xc. 9, 10.) The life of Israel in the wilderness was shortened by Disobedience. The Obedience of Christ in the wilderness has won for us a blessed immortality.—*Christopher Wordsworth.*

Verse 16.—" *With long life will I satisfy him,*" etc. The margin here is " length of days ; " that is, days lengthened out or multiplied. The meaning is, I will give him length of days as he desires, or until he is satisfied with life ;—implying (1) that it is natural to desire long life ; (2) that long life is to be regarded as a blessing (comp. Prov. iii. 2, 16 ; Ex. xx. 12) ; (3) that the tendency of religion is to lengthen out life ; since virtue, temperance, regular industry, calmness of mind, moderation in all things, freedom from excesses in eating and drinking,—to all of which religion prompts,— contribute to health and to length of days ; and (4) that a time will come, even under this promised blessing of length of days, when a man will be " *satisfied* " with living ; when he will have no strong desire to live longer ; when, under the infirmities of advanced years, and under his lonely feelings from the fact that his early friends have fallen, and under the influence of a bright hope of heaven, he will feel that he has had *enough* of life here, and that it is better to depart to another world. " *And shew him my salvation.*" In another life, after he shall be satisfied with this life.—*Albert Barnes.*

Verse 16.—" *With long life will I satisfy him.*" This promise concerning length of life contains a gift of God by no means to be despised. Many enemies indeed will plot against his life, and desire to extinguish him as suddenly and as quickly as possible ; but I shall so guard him that he shall live to a good old age and be filled with years, and desire to depart from life.—*J. B. Folengius.*

Verse 16.—" *With long life will I satisfy him.*"

> We live in deeds, not years ; in thoughts, not breaths ;
> In feelings, not in figures on a dial.
> We should count time by heart-throbs. He most lives
> Who thinks most, feels the noblest, acts the best.
>   *Philip James Bailey, in " Festus."*

Verse 16.—" *Long life.*"

> They err who measure life by years,
>   With false or thoughtless tongue ;
> Some hearts grow old before their time ;
>   Others are always young.
>
> 'Tis not the number of the lines
>   On life's fast filling page,
> 'Tis not the pulse's added throbs,
>   Which constitute their age.

Some souls are serfs among the free
While others nobly thrive ;
They stand just where their fathers stood
Dead, even while they live.

Others, all spirit, heart, and sense,
Theirs the mysterious power,
To live in thrills of joy or woe,
A twelvemonth in an hour !

Bryan W. Procter.

Verse 16.—" *Long life.*"

He liveth long who liveth well !
All other life is short and vain :
He liveth longest who can tell
Of living most for heavenly gain

He liveth long who liveth well !
All else is being flung away ;
He liveth longest who can tell
Of true things truly done each day.

Horatius Bonar.

Verse 16.—" *I will shew him my salvation.*" The last, greatest, climax of blessing, including and concluding all ! What God does is perfectly done. Hitherto has his servant caught glimpses of the " great salvation." The Spirit has revealed step by step of it, as he was able to bear it. The Word has taught him, and he has rejoiced in his light. But all was seen *in part* and known *in part.* But when God has satisfied his servant with length of days, and time for him is over, eternity begun, he will " *shew him his salvation.*" All will be plain. All will be known. God will be revealed in his love and his glory. And we shall know all things, even as we are known ! —*Mary B. M. Duncan.*

HINTS TO PREACHERS.

Verse 1.—I. The secret dwelling-place. There is the dweller in the dark world, in the favoured land, in the holy city, in the outer court ; but the holy of holies is the " secret place "—communion, acceptance, etc. II. The protecting shadow— security, peace, etc.; like hamlets of olden time clustered beneath castle walls.— *Charles A. Davis.*

Verse 1.—I. *The person.* One who is in intimate, personal, secret, abiding communion with God, dwelling near the mercy-seat, within the veil. II. The Privilege. He is the guest of God, protected, refreshed, and comforted by him, and that to all eternity.

Verses 1, 2.—Four names of God. I. We commune with him reverently, for he is the Most High. II. We rest in him as the Almighty. III. We rejoice in him as Jehovah or Lord. IV. We trust him as EL, the mighty God.

Verse 2.—I. Observe the nouns applied to God—refuge from trouble, fortress in trouble, God at all times. II. Observe the pronouns applied by man—" *I* " will say, " *my* refuge, my fortress," etc.—*G. R.*

Verse 2.—The power, excellence, fruit, reasonableness, and open avowal of personal faith.

Verse 3.—Invisible protection from invisible dangers ; wisdom to meet cunning, love to war with cruelty, omnipresence to match mystery, life to baffle death.

Verse 3.—SURELY, or reasons for assured confidence in God's protection.

Verses 3—7.—Pestilence, panic, and peace ; (for times of widespread disease).— *Charles A. Davis.*

Verses 3, 8, 9.—I. Saints are safe—" *surely,*" (verse 3). II. The evil is bounded —" *only,*" (verse 8). III. The Lord has reasons for preserving his own—" *because,*" (verse 9).

Verse 4.—I. The compassion of God. II. The confidence of saints. III. The panoply of truth.

Verses 5, 6.—I. The exposure of all men to fear. 1. Continually, day and night. 2. Deservedly : " conscience doth make cowards of us all." II. The exemption of some men from fear. 1. Because of their trust. 2. Because of the divine protection.

Verse 7.—How an evil may be near but not nigh.

Verse 8.—What we have actually seen of the reward of the wicked.

Verses 9, 10.—I. God our spiritual habitation. II. God the keeper of our earthly habitation. III. General truth that the spiritual blesses the temporal.

Verse 10.—I. The Personal Blessing. II. The Domestic Blessing. III. The connection between the two.

Verses 14—16.—The six " I wills."

Verses 11, 12.—A " wrested " Scripture righted. I. Satan's version—presumptuousness. II. The Holy Spirit's version—trustfulness.—*Charles A. Davis.*

Verses 11, 12.—I. The Ministry of Angels as employed by God. 1. Official : " he shall give," etc. 2. Personal : " over thee." 3. Constant : " in all thy ways." II. As enjoyed by man. 1. For preservation : " shall bear thee," etc. ; tenderly but effectually. 2. Under limitation. They cannot do the work of God, or of Christ, or of the Spirit, or of the word, or of ministers, for salvation ; " are they not all ministering spirits," etc.—*G. R.*

Verse 12.—Preservation from minor evils most precious because they are often most grievous, lead to greater evils, and involve much damage.

Verse 13.—The believer's love set upon God.

Verse 13.—I. Every child of God has his enemies. 1. They are numerous : " the lion, adder, young lion, dragon." 2. Diversified : subtle and powerful—" lion and adder ; " new and old—" young lion " and the " old dragon." II. He will finally obtain a complete victory over them—" Thou shalt tread," etc. ; " shall put thy foot," etc. ; " the Lord shall bruise Satan," etc.—*G. R.*

Verse 14.—Here we have, I. Love for love : " Because," etc. 1. The fact of the saints' love to God. There is, first, love in God without their love, then love for their love. 2. The evidence of his love to them : " I will deliver him "—from sin, from danger, from temptation, from every evil. II. Honour for honour. 1. His honouring God. " He hath known my name " and made it known ; God honouring him ; " I will set him on high "—high in honour, in happiness, in glory.—*G. R.*

Verses 15, 16.—Observe, I. The exceeding great and precious promises. 1. Answer to prayer : " he shall call," etc. 2. Comfort in trouble : " I will be with him." 3. Deliverance from trouble : " I will deliver him." 4. Greater honour after trouble : deliver " and honour him." 5. Length of days ; life long enough to satisfy him. 6. God's salvation : " shew him my salvation ; " far beyond what man could think or desire. II. To whom these promises belong ; who is the *he* and the *him* to whom these promises are made. He " calls upon God," says the fifteenth verse ; he " hath known my name," says the verse preceding ; he " hath set his love upon me," says the former part of the same verse ; he " has made the Lord his habitation," says the ninth verse ; he " dwelleth in the secret place of the most High," says the first verse. Hannah More says, " To preach privileges without specifying to whom they belong is like putting a letter in the post-office without a direction." It may be very good and contain a valuable remittance, but no one can tell for whom it is intended. All the promises of Scriptures are plainly directed to those to whom they belong. The direction put upon the promises of this Psalm is unmistakably clear and often repeated.—*G. R.*

PSALM XCII.

TITLE.—A Psalm or Song for the Sabbath-day. *This admirable composition is both a Psalm and a Song, full of equal measures of solemnity and joy; and it was intended to be sung upon the day of rest. The subject is the praise of God; praise is Sabbatic work, the joyful occupation of resting hearts. Since a true Sabbath can only be found in God, it is wise to meditate upon him on the Sabbath day. The style is worthy of the theme and of the day, its inspiration is from the "fount of every blessing"; David spake as the Spirit gave him utterance. In the church of Christ, at this hour, no Psalm is more frequently sung upon the Lord's day than the present. The delightful version of Dr. Watts is familiar to us all—*

> *"Sweet is the work, my God, my King,*
> *To praise thy name, give thanks, and sing;*
> *To shew thy love by morning light,*
> *And talk of all thy truth at night."*

The Sabbath was set apart for adoring the Lord in his finished work of creation, hence the suitableness of this Psalm; Christians may take even a higher flight, for they celebrate complete redemption. No one acquainted with David's style will hesitate to ascribe to him the authorship of this divine hymn: the ravings of the Rabbis who speak of its being composed by Adam, only need to be mentioned to be dismissed. Adam in Paradise had neither harps to play upon, nor wicked men to contend with.

EXPOSITION.

*I*T is a good *thing* to give thanks unto the LORD, and to sing praises unto thy name, O most High:

2 To shew forth thy lovingkindness in the morning, and thy faithfulness every night,

3 Upon an instrument of ten strings, and upon the psaltery; upon the harp with a solemn sound.

4 For thou, LORD, hast made me glad through thy work: I will triumph in the works of thy hands.

1. "*It is a good thing to give thanks unto the Lord,*" or JEHOVAH. It is good ethically, for it is the Lord's right; it is good emotionally, for it is pleasant to the heart; it is good practically, for it leads others to render the same homage. When duty and pleasure combine, who will be backward? To give thanks to God is but a small return for the great benefits wherewith he daily loadeth us; yet as he by his Spirit calls it a good thing, we must not despise it, or neglect it. We thank men when they oblige us, how much more ought we to bless the Lord when he benefits us. Devout praise is always good, it is never out of season, never superfluous, but it is especially suitable to the Sabbath; a Sabbath without thanksgiving is a Sabbath profaned. "*And to sing praises unto thy name, O most High.*" It is good to give thanks in the form of vocal song. Nature itself teaches us thus to express our gratitude to God; do not the birds sing, and the brooks warble as they flow? To give his gratitude a tongue is wise in man. Silent worship is sweet, but vocal worship is sweeter. To deny the tongue the privilege of uttering the praises of God involves an unnatural strain upon the most commendable promptings of our renewed manhood, and it is a problem to us how the members of the Society of Friends can deprive themselves of so noble, so natural, so inspiring a part of sacred worship. Good as they are, they miss one good thing when they decline to sing praises unto the name of the Lord. Our personal experience has confirmed us in the belief that it is good to sing unto the Lord; we have often felt like Luther when he said, "Come, let us sing a Psalm, and drive away the devil."

2. "*To shew forth thy lovingkindness in the morning.*" The day should begin with praise: no hour is too early for holy song. Lovingkindness is a most appropriate theme for those dewy hours when morn is sowing all the earth with orient pearl.

116

Eagerly and promptly should we magnify the Lord ; we leave unpleasant tasks as long as we can, but our hearts are so engrossed with the adoration of God that we would rise betimes to attend to it. There is a peculiar freshness and charm about early morning praises ; the day is loveliest when it first opens its eyelids, and God himself seems then to make distribution of the day's manna, which tastes most sweetly if gathered ere the sun is hot. It seems most meet that if our hearts and harps have been silent through the shades of night, we should be eager again to take our place among the chosen choir who ceaselessly hymn the Eternal One. " *And thy faithfulness every night.*" No hour is too late for praise, the end of the day must not be the end of gratitude. When nature seems in silent contemplation to adore its Maker, it ill becomes the children of God to refrain their thanksgiving. Evening is the time for retrospect, memory is busy with the experience of the day, hence the appropriate theme for song is the divine *faithfulness*, of which another day has furnished fresh evidences. When darkness has settled down o'er all things, " a shade immense," then there comes over wise men a congenial, meditative spirit, and it is most fitting that they should take an expanded view of the truth and goodness of Jehovah—

> " This sacred shade and solitude, what is it ?
> 'Tis the felt presence of the Deity."

" *Every night,*" clouded or clear, moonlit or dark, calm or tempestuous, is alike suitable for a song upon the faithfulness of God, since in all seasons, and under all circumstances, it abides the same, and is the mainstay of the believer's consolation. Shame on us that we are so backward in magnifying the Lord, who in the daytime scatters bounteous love, and in the night season walks his rounds of watching care.

3. " *Upon an instrument of ten strings ;* " with the fullest range of music, uttering before God with the full compass of melody the richest emotions of his soul. " *And upon the psaltery ;* " thus giving variety to praise : the Psalmist felt that every sweet-sounding instrument should be consecrated to God. George Herbert and Martin Luther aided their private devotions by instrumental music ; and whatever may have been the differences of opinion in the Christian church, as to the performance of instrumental music in public, we have met with no objection to its personal and private use. " *Upon the harp with a solemn sound,*" or upon *meditation with a harp ;* as much as to say, my meditative soul is, after all, the best instrument, and the harp's dulcet tones come in to aid my thoughts. It is blessed work when hand and tongue work together in the heavenly occupation of praise.

> " Strings and voices, hands and hearts,
> In the concert bear your parts :
> All that breathe, your God adore,
> Praise him, praise him, evermore."

It is, however, much to be feared that attention to the mere mechanism of music, noting keys and strings, bars and crochets, has carried many away from the spiritual harmony which is the soul and essence of praise. Fine music without devotion is but a splendid garment upon a corpse.

4. " *For thou, Lord, hast made me glad through thy work.*" It was natural for the Psalmist to sing, because he was glad, and to sing unto the Lord, because his gladness was caused by a contemplation of the divine work. If we consider either creation or providence, we shall find overflowing reasons for joy ; but when we come to review the work of redemption, gladness knows no bounds, but feels that she must praise the Lord with all her might. There are times when in the contemplation of redeeming love we feel that if we did not sing we must die; silence would be as horrible to us as if we were gagged by inquisitors, or stifled by murderers. " *I will triumph in the works of thy hands.*" I cannot help it, I must and I will rejoice in the Lord, even as one who has won the victory and has divided great spoil. In the first sentence of this verse he expresses the unity of God's *work*, and in the second the variety of his *works ;* in both there is reason for gladness and triumph. When God reveals his work to a man, and performs a work in his soul, he makes his heart glad most effectually, and then the natural consequence is continual praise.

5 O Lord, how great are thy works ! *and* thy thoughts are very deep.
6 A brutish man knoweth not ; neither doth a fool understand this

5. "*O Lord, how great are thy works!*" He is lost in wonder. He utters an exclamation of amazement. How vast! How stupendous are the doings of Jehovah! Great for number, extent, and glory and design are all the creations of the Infinite One. "*And thy thoughts are very deep.*" The Lord's plans are as marvellous as his acts; his designs are as profound as his doings are vast. Creation is immeasurable, and the wisdom displayed in it unsearchable. Some men think but cannot work, and others are mere drudges working without thought; in the Eternal the conception and the execution go together. Providence is inexhaustible, and the divine decrees which originate it are inscrutable. Redemption is grand beyond conception, and the thoughts of love which planned it are infinite. Man is superficial, God is inscrutable; man is shallow, God is deep. Dive as we may we shall never fathom the mysterious plan, or exhaust the boundless wisdom of the all-comprehending mind of the Lord. We stand by the fathomless sea of divine wisdom, and exclaim with holy awe, " O the depth !"

6. "*A brutish man knoweth not; neither doth a fool understand this.*" In this and the following verses the effect of the Psalm is heightened by contrast; the shadows are thrown in to bring out the lights more prominently. What a stoop from the preceding verse; from the saint to the brute, from the worshipper to the boor, from the Psalmist to the fool! Yet, alas, the character described here is no uncommon one. The boorish or boarish man, for such is almost the very Hebrew word, sees nothing in nature; and if it be pointed out to him, his foolish mind will not comprehend it. He may be a philosopher, and yet be such a brutish being that he will not own the existence of a Maker for the ten thousand matchless creations around him, which wear, even upon their surface, the evidences of profound design. The unbelieving heart, let it boast as it will, does not know; and with all its parade of intellect, it does not understand. A man must either be a saint or a brute, he has no other choice; his type must be the adoring seraph, or the ungrateful swine. So far from paying respect to great thinkers who will not own the glory or the being of God, we ought to regard them as comparable to the beasts which perish, only vastly lower than mere brutes, because their degrading condition is of their own choosing. O God, how sorrowful a thing it is that men whom thou hast so largely gifted, and made in thine own image, should so brutify themselves that they will neither see nor understand what thou hast made so clear. Well might an eccentric writer say, " God made man a little lower than the angels at first, and he has been trying to get lower ever since."

7 When the wicked spring as the grass, and when all the workers of iniquity do flourish; *it is* that they shall be destroyed for ever :

8 But thou, LORD, *art most* high for evermore.

9 For, lo, thine enemies, O LORD, for, lo, thine enemies shall perish ; all the workers of iniquity shall be scattered.

7. "*When the wicked spring as the grass,*" in abundance, and apparent strength, hastening on their progress like verdant plants, which come to perfection in a day, "*and when all the workers of iniquity do flourish;*" flowering in their prime and pride, their pomp and their prosperity; "*it is that they shall be destroyed for ever.*" They grow to die, they blossom to be blasted. They flower for a short space to wither without end. Greatness and glory are to them but the prelude of their overthrow. Little does their opposition matter, the Lord reigns on as if they had never blasphemed him; as a mountain abides the same though the meadows at its feet bloom or wither, even so the Most High is unaffected by the fleeting mortals who dare oppose him : they shall soon vanish for ever from among the living. But as for the wicked—how can our minds endure the contemplation of their doom " *for ever.*" Destruction " *for ever* " is a portion far too terrible for the mind to realise. Eye hath not seen, nor ear heard, the full terror of the wrath to come!

8. "*But thou, Lord, art most high for evermore.*" This is the middle verse of the Psalm, and the great fact which this Sabbath song is meant to illustrate. God is at once the highest and most enduring of all beings. Others rise to fall, but he is the Most High to eternity. Glory be to his name! How great a God we worship! Who would not fear thee, O thou High Eternal One! The ungodly are destroyed for ever, and God is most high for ever; evil is cast down, and the Holy One reigns supreme eternally.

9. *" For, lo, thine enemies, O Lord."*   It is a wonder full of instruction and warning, observe it, O ye sons of men ; *" for, lo, thine enemies shall perish ; "* they shall cease from among men, they shall be known no more.   In that the thing is spoken twice it is confirmed by the Lord, it shall surely be, and that speedily.   *" All the workers of iniquity shall be scattered ; "* their forces shall be dispersed, their hopes broken, and themselves driven hither and thither like chaff before the tempest.   They shall scatter like timid sheep pursued by the lion, they will not have the courage to remain in arms, nor the unity to abide in confederacy.   The grass cannot resist the scythe, but falls in withering ranks, even so are the ungodly cut down and swept away in process of time, while the Lord whom they despised sits unmoved upon the throne of his infinite dominion.   Terrible as this fact is, no true-hearted man would wish to have it otherwise.   Treason against the great Monarch of the universe ought not to go unpunished ; such wanton wickedness richly merits the severest doom.

10 But my horn shalt thou exalt like *the horn of* an unicorn : I shall be anointed with fresh oil.

11 Mine eye also shall see *my desire* on mine enemies, *and* mine ears shall hear *my desire* of the wicked that rise up against me.

10. *" But my horn shalt thou exalt like the horn of an unicorn."*   The believer rejoices that he shall not be suffered to perish, but shall be strengthened and enabled to triumph over his enemies, by the divine aid.   The unicorn may have been some gigantic ox or buffalo now unknown, and perhaps extinct—among the ancients it was the favourite symbol of unconquerable power ; the Psalmist adopts it as his emblem.   Faith takes delight in foreseeing the mercy of the Lord, and sings of what he will do as well as of what he has done.   *" I shall be anointed with fresh oil."*   Strengthening shall be attended with refreshment and honour.   As guests were anointed at feasts with perfumed unguents, so shall the saints be cheered and delighted by fresh outpourings of divine grace ; and for this reason they shall not pass away like the wicked.   Observe the contrast between the happiness of the brutish people and the joy of the righteous, the brutish men grow with a sort of vegetable vigour of their own, but the righteous are dealt with by the Lord himself, and all the good which they receive comes directly from his own right hand, and so is doubly precious in their esteem.   The Psalmist speaks in the first person, and it should be a matter of prayer with the reader that he may be enabled to do the same.

11. *" Mine eye also shall see* MY DESIRE *on mine enemies."*   The words, "my desire," inserted by the translators, had far better have been left out.   He does not say what he should see concerning his enemies, he leaves that blank, and we have no right to fill in the vacant space with words which look vindictive.   He would see that which would be for God's glory, and that which would be eminently right and just.   *" And mine ears shall hear* MY DESIRE *of the wicked that rise up against me."*   Here, again, the words " my desire " are not inspired, and are a needless and perhaps a false interpolation.   The good man is quite silent as to what he expected to hear ; he knew that what he should hear would vindicate his faith in his God, and he was content to leave his cruel foes in God's hands, without an expression concerning his own desire one way or the other.   It is always best to leave Scripture as we find it.   The broken sense of inspiration is better let alone than pieced out with additions of a translator's own invention ; it is like repairing pure gold with tinsel, or a mosaic of gems with painted wood.   The holy Psalmist had seen the beginning of the ungodly, and expected to see their end ; he felt sure that God would right all wrongs, and clear his Providence from the charge of favouring the unjust ; this confidence he here expresses, and sits down contentedly to wait the issues of the future.

12 The righteous shall flourish like the palm tree : he shall grow like a cedar in Lebanon.

13 Those that be planted in the house of the LORD shall flourish in the courts of our God.

14 They shall still bring forth fruit in old age ; they shall be fat and flourishing ;

15 To shew that the LORD *is* upright : *he is* my rock, and *there is* no un-righteousness in him.

12. The song now contrasts the condition of the righteous with that of the grace-less. The wicked " spring as the grass," but " *The righteous shall flourish like the palm tree,*" whose growth may not be so rapid, but whose endurance for centuries is in fine contrast with the transitory verdure of the meadow. When we see a noble palm standing erect, sending all its strength upward in one bold column, and growing amid the dearth and drought of the desert, we have a fine picture of the godly man, who in his uprightness aims alone at the glory of God ; and, independent of outward circumstances, is made by divine grace to live and thrive where all things else perish. The text tells us not only what the righteous is, but what he shall be ; come what may, the good man shall flourish, and flourish after the noblest manner. " *He shall grow like a cedar in Lebanon.*" This is another noble and long-lived tree. " As the days of a tree are the days of my people," saith the Lord. On the summit of the mountain, unsheltered from the blast, the cedar waves its mighty branches in per-petual verdure, and so the truly godly man under all adversities retains the joy of his soul, and continues to make progress in the divine life. Grass, which makes hay for oxen, is a good enough emblem of the unregenerate ; but cedars, which build the temple of the Lord, are none too excellent to set forth the heirs of heaven.

13. " *Those that be planted in the house of the Lord shall flourish in the courts of our God.*" In the court-yards of Oriental houses trees were planted, and being thoroughly screened, they would be likely to bring forth their fruit to perfection in trying seasons ; even so, those who by grace are brought into communion with the Lord, shall be likened to trees planted in the Lord's house, and shall find it good to their souls. No heart has so much joy as that which abides in the Lord Jesus. Fellowship with the stem begets fertility in the branches. If a man abide in Christ he brings forth much fruit. Those professors who are rooted to the world do not flourish ; those who send forth their roots into the marshes of frivolous pleasure cannot be in a vigorous condition ; but those who dwell in habitual fellowship with God shall become men of full growth, rich in grace, happy in experience, mighty in influence, honoured and honourable. Much depends upon the soil in which a tree is planted ; everything, in our case, depends upon our abiding in the Lord Jesus, and deriving all our supplies from him. If we ever really grow in the courts of the Lord's house we must be planted there, for no tree grows in God's garden self-sown ; once planted of the Lord, we shall never be rooted up, but in his courts we shall take root downward, and bring forth fruit upward to his glory for ever.

14. " *They shall still bring forth fruit in old age.*" Nature decays but grace thrives. Fruit, as far as nature is concerned, belongs to days of vigour ; but in the garden of grace, when plants are weak in themselves, they become strong in the Lord, and abound in fruit acceptable with God. Happy they who can sing this Sabbath Psalm, enjoying the rest which breathes through every verse of it ; no fear as to the future can distress them, for their evil days, when the strong man faileth, are the subject of a gracious promise, and therefore they await them with quiet expect-ancy. Aged believers possess a ripe experience, and by their mellow tempers and sweet testimonies they feed many. Even if bedridden, they bear the fruit of patience ; if poor and obscure, their lowly and contented spirit becomes the admiration of those who know how to appreciate modest worth. Grace does not leave the saint when the keepers of the house do tremble ; the promise is still sure though the eyes can no longer read it ; the bread of heaven is fed upon when the grinders fail ; and the voice of the Spirit in the soul is still melodious when the daughters of music are brought low. Blessed be the Lord for this ! Because even to hoar hairs he is the I AM, who made his people, he therefore bears and carries them.

" *They shall be fat and flourishing.*" They do not drag out a wretched, starveling existence, but are like trees full of sap, which bear luxuriant foliage. God does not pinch his poor servants, and diminish their consolations when their infirmities grow upon them ; rather does he see to it that they shall renew their strength, for their mouths shall be satisfied with his own good things. Such an one as Paul the aged would not ask our pity, but invite our sympathetic gratitude ; however feeble his outward man may be, his inner man is so renewed day by day that we may well envy his perennial peace.

15. This mercy to the aged proves the faithfulness of their God, and leads them " *to shew that the Lord is upright* " by their cheerful testimony to his ceaseless goodness.

We do not serve a Master who will run back from his promise. Whoever else may defraud us, he never will. Every aged Christian is a letter of commendation to the immutable fidelity of Jehovah. "*He is my rock, and there is no unrighteousness in him.*" Here is the Psalmist's own seal and sign manual : still was he building upon his God, and still was the Lord a firm foundation for his trust. For shelter, for defence, for indwelling, for foundation, God is our rock ; hitherto he has been to us all that he said he would be, and we may be doubly sure that he will abide the same even unto the end. He has tried us, but he has never allowed us to be tempted above what we are able to bear : he has delayed our reward, but he has never been unrighteous to forget our work of faith and labour of love. He is a friend without fault, a helper without fail. Whatever he may do with us, he is always in the right ; his dispensations have no flaw in them, no, not the most minute. He is true and righteous altogether, and so we weave the end of the Psalm with its beginning, and make a coronet of it, for the head of our Beloved. "*It is a good thing to sing praises unto the Lord,*" for "*he is my rock, and there is no unrighteousness in him.*"

EXPLANATORY NOTES AND QUAINT SAYINGS.

Title.—This is entitled "*A Psalm to be sung on the day of the Sabbath.*" It is known that the Jews appropriated certain Psalms to particular days. R. Selomo thinks that it refers to the future state of the blessed, which is a perpetual sabbath. Others pretend that it was composed by Adam, on the seventh day of the creation. It might, with more probability, have been supposed to be put, by a poetic fiction, into the mouth of Adam, beholding, with wonder and gratitude, the recent creation. But ver. 2 seems to refer to the morning and evening sacrifice, which the Psalmist considers as most proper for prayer and praise.—*D. Cresswell.*

Title.—"*For the Sabbath day.*" Perchance, as *Lud. de Dieu* remarks on this place, every day of the week had its allotted Psalms, according to what is said in the *Talmud,* lib. קדשים. The songs which the Levites formerly sang in the sanctuary are these : on the first day, Ps. xxiv. ; on the second, Ps. xlviii. ; on the third, Ps. lxxxii. ; on the fourth, the 104th ; on the fifth, the 81st ; on the sixth, the 93rd ; on the seventh, the 92nd, the beginning of which is, *a Psalm or a Canticle for the Sabbath day,* that is to say, for the future age, which will be altogether a sabbath.—*Martin Geier.*

Title.—"*For the Sabbath.*"—It is observable that the name JEHOVAH occurs in the Psalm seven times—the sabbatical number (1, 4, 5, 8, 9, 13, 15).—*C. Wordsworth.*

Verse 1.—"*It is a good thing.*" It is *bonum, honestum, jucundum, utile ;* an honest, pleasant, and profitable good. The altar of incense was to be overlaid with pure gold, and to have a crown of gold round about it. Which (if we may allegorically apply it) intimateth unto us, that the spiritual incense of prayers and praises is rich and precious, a golden, and a royal thing.—*Henry Jeanes, in " The Works of Heaven upon Earth,"* 1649.

Verse 1.—"*It is a good thing to give thanks,*" etc. Giving of thanks is more noble and perfect in itself than petition ; because in petition often our own good is eyed and regarded, but in giving of thanks only God's honour. The Lord Jesus said, " It is more blessed to give than to receive." Now, a subordinate end of petition is to receive some good from God, but the sole end of thanks is to give glory unto God.— *William Ames* (1576—1633), *in " Medulla Theologica."*

Verse 1.—"*Give thanks ;*" "*praises.*" We thank God for his benefits, and praise him for his perfections.—*Filliucius, out of Aquinas.*

Verse 1.—"*To sing praises.*" 1. *Singing is the music of nature.* The Scriptures tell us, the mountains sing (Isai. xliv. 23) ; the valleys sing (Psalm lxv. 13) ; the trees of the wood sing (1 Chron. xvi. 33). Nay, the air is the birds' music-room, where they chant their musical notes.

2. *Singing is the music of ordinances.* Augustine reports of himself, that when he came to Milan and heard the people sing, he wept for joy in the church to hear that pleasing melody. And Beza confesses, that at his first entrance into the congregation, and hearing them sing Ps. xci., he felt himself exceedingly comforted, and did retain the sound of it afterwards upon his heart. The Rabbis tell us, that the

Jews, after the feast of the Passover was celebrated, sang Psalm cxi., and the five following Psalms ; and our Saviour and his apostles " sang an hymn " immediately after the blessed supper, (Matt. xxvi. 30).

3. *Singing is the music of saints.* (1.) They have performed this duty in their greatest numbers, (Psalm cxlix. 1). (2.) In their greatest straits, (Isai. xxvi. 19). (3.) In their greatest flight, (Isai. xlii. 10, 11). (4.) In their greatest deliverances, (Isai. lxv. 14). (5.) In their greatest plenties. In all these changes singing hath been their stated duty and delight. And indeed it is meet that the saints and servants of God should sing forth their joys and praises to the Lord Almighty ; every attribute of him can set both their song and their tune.

4. *Singing is the music of angels.* Job tells us, " The morning stars sang together," (Job xxxviii. 7). Now these morning stars, as Pineda tells us, are the angels ; to which the Chaldee paraphrase accords, naming these morning stars, *aciem angelorum,* " a host of angels." Nay, when this heavenly host was sent to proclaim the birth of our dearest Jesus, they delivered their message in this raised way of duty, (Luke ii. 13). They were αἰνούντων, delivering their messages in a " laudatory singing," the whole company of angels making a musical choir. Nay, in heaven, there is the angels' joyous music, they there sing hallelujahs to the Most High, and to the Lamb who sits upon the throne, (Rev. v. 11, 12).

5. *Singing is the music of heaven.* The glorious saints and angels accent their praises this way, and make one harmony in their state of blessedness ; and this is the music of the bride-chamber, (Rev. xv. 3). The saints who were tuning here their Psalms, are now singing hallelujahs in a louder strain, and articulating their joys, which here they could not express to their perfect satisfaction. Here they laboured with drowsy hearts, and faltering tongues ; but in glory these impediments are removed, and nothing is left to jar their joyous celebrations.—*John Wells* (—1676), *in* " *The Morning Exercises.*"

Verse 2.—" *In the morning.*" When indeed the mind after the rest of the night is more active, devoted and constant. In other parts of the day, as at noon, or in the afternoon, many sounds of business disturb, and greater lassitude oppresses. Compare Pss. v. 4, lix. 17, lxiii. 2, lxxxviii. 14, cxix. 147, 148, where this same part of the day is celebrated as the fittest for sacred meditations. However, this ought not to be taken exclusively, as if, in the morning alone, and not also at noon or in the evening, it was suitable to celebrate divine grace.—*Martin Geier.*

Verse 2.—" *In the morning.*" The Brahmins rise three hours before the sun, to pray. The Indians would esteem it a great sin to eat in the morning before praying to their gods. The ancient Romans considered it impious if they had not a little chamber in their house, appropriated to prayer. Let us take a lesson from these Turks and heathen ; their zealous ardour ought to shame us. Because we possess the true light, should their zeal surpass ours ?—*Frederic Arndt, in " Lights of the Morning,*" 1861.

Verse 2.—" *To shew forth thy lovingkindness in the morning.*" Our praise ought to be suitably arranged. In the time of prosperity or the *morning* we should declare thy lovingkindness, because whatever of prosperity we have proceeds from the mercy and grace of God ; and in the time of adversity or *night*, we should declare thy justice or faithfulness, because whatever adversity happens to us is ordained by the just judgment of God.—*J. Turrecremata.*

Verse 2.—God's " *mercy* " is itself the *morning ray*, which scatters away darkness (xxx. 5, lix. 16) ; his " *faithfulness* " the guardian, that assures us against *night* peril.—*F. Delitzsch.*

Verse 2.—" *In the morning, and . . every night.*" God is Alpha and Omega. It is fit we should begin and end the day with his praise, who begins and ends it for us with mercy. Well, thou seest thy duty plainly laid before thee. As thou wouldst have God prosper thy labour in the day, and sweeten thy rest in the night, clasp them both together with thy morning and evening devotions. He that takes no care to set forth God's portion of time in the morning, doth not only rob God of his due, but is a thief to himself all the day after, by losing the blessing which a faithful prayer might bring from heaven on his undertakings. And he that closeth his eyes at night without prayer, lies down before his bed is made.—*William Gurnall.*

Verse 2.—" *Thy faithfulness* (Vulg. ' *veritas*,') *every night.*" Truth can be taken in its proper signification. Thus St. Jerome on our Psalm takes it, and says : " The truth of the Lord is announced in the night, as if it were wrapped up in some verbal obscurities. In an enigma it is spoken, and in parables ; that seeing, they should not see, and hearing, they should not understand. Moses ascended mount Sinai, Exod. xxiv., and passed into the tempest and into the blackness and darkness, and there spake with the Lord." Thus Jerome. Christ brings back the light to us, as Lactantius teaches. Shall we wait, says he, till Socrates shall know something ? Or Anaxagoras find light in the darkness ? Or Democritus draw forth the truth from a well ? Or till Empedocles expands the paths of his soul ? Or Ascesilas and Carneades see, feel, and perceive ? Behold a voice from heaven teaches us the truth, and reveals it more clearly to us than the sun himself. . . . . . In the night truth is to be shown forth, that the night may be turned into day.—*Le Blanc.*

Verse 3.—" *Upon an instrument of ten strings.*" Eusebius, in his comment on this Psalm, says : " *The psaltery of ten strings* is the worship of the Holy Spirit performed by means of the *five* senses of the body, and by the *five* powers of the soul." And to confirm this interpretation, he quotes the apostle, 1 Cor. xiv. 15 : " I will pray with the spirit, and with the understanding also ; I will sing with the spirit, and with the understanding also." " As the mind has its influence by which it moves the body, so the spirit has its own influence by which it moves the soul." Whatever may be thought of this gloss, one thing is pretty evident from it, that *instrumental music* was not in use in the church of Christ in the time of Eusebius, which was near the middle of the *fourth* century. Had any such thing then existed in the Christian Church, he would have doubtless alluded to or spiritualized it ; or, as he quoted the words of the apostle above, would have shown that *carnal usages* were substituted for *spiritual exercises.*—*Adam Clarke.*

Verse 3.—In Augustine to Ambrose there is the following passage bearing on this same subject :—" Sometimes, from over jealousy, I would entirely put from me and from the church the melodies of the sweet chants that we use in the Psalter, lest our ears seduce us ; and the way of Athanasius, bishop of Alexandria, seems the safe one, who, as I have often heard, made the reader chant with so slight a change of voice, that it was more like speaking than singing. And yet, when I call to mind the tears I shed when I heard the chants of thy church in the infancy of my recovered faith, and reflect that I was affected, not by the mere music, but by the subject brought out as it were by clear voices and appropriate tune, then, in turn, I confess how useful is the practice."

Verse 3.—We are not to conceive that God enjoyed the harp as feeling a delight like ourselves in mere melody of sounds ; but the Jews, who were yet under age, were restricted to the use of such childish elements. The intention of them was to stimulate the worshippers, and stir them up more actively to the celebration of the praise of God with the heart. We are to remember that the worship of God was never understood to consist in such outward services, which were only necessary to help forward a people, as yet weak and rude in knowledge, in the spiritual worship of God. A difference is to be observed in this respect between his people under the Old and under the New Testament ; for now that Christ has appeared, and the church has reached full age, it were only to bury the light of the Gospel, should we introduce the shadows of a departed dispensation. From this, it appears that the Papists, in employing instrumental music, cannot be said so much to imitate the practice of God's ancient people, as to ape it in a senseless and absurd manner, exhibiting a silly delight in that worship of the Old Testament which was figurative, and terminated with the gospel.—*John Calvin.*

Verse 3.—Chrysostom says, " Instrumental music was only permitted to the Jews, as sacrifice was, for the heaviness and grossness of their souls. God condescended to their weakness, because they were lately drawn off from idols ; but now instead of organs, we may use our own bodies to praise him withal." Theodoret has many like expressions in his comments upon the Psalms and other places. But the author under the name of Justin Martyr is more express in his determination, as to matter of fact, telling us plainly, " that the use of singing with instrumental music was not received in the Christian churches as it was among the Jews in their infant state, but only the use of plain song."—*Joseph Bingham.*

Verse 3.—Instrumental music, the more I think of it, appears with increasing evidence to be utterly unsuited to the genius of the gospel dispensation. There was a glare, if I may so express it, which characterized even the divine appointments of Judaism. An august temple, ornamented with gold and silver, and precious stones, golden candlesticks, golden altars, priests in rich attire, trumpets, cymbals, harps ; all of which were adapted to an age and dispensation when the church was in a state of infancy. But when the substance is come, it is time that the shadows flee away. The best exposition of harps in singing is given by Dr. Watts—

> "Oh may my heart in tune be found,
> Like David's harp of solemn sound."

> —*Andrew Fuller.*

Verse 3 (*last clause*).—" *On meditation with a harp.*" [New translation.] By a bold but intelligible figure, *meditation* is referred to as an instrument, precisely as the lyre and harp are, the latter being joined with it as a mere accompaniment.—*J. A. Alexander.*

Verse 3.—" *With a solemn sound.*" Let Christians abound as much as they will in the holy, heavenly exercise of singing in God's house and in their own houses ; but let it be performed as a holy act, wherein they have immediately and visibly to do with God. When any social open act of devotion or solemn worship of God is performed, God should be reverenced as present. As we would not have the ark of God depart from us, nor provoke God to make a breach upon us, we should take heed that we handle the ark with reverence.—*Jonathan Edwards, in " Errors connected with singing praises to God."*

Verse 4.—" *Thou Lord hast made me glad through thy work.*" One of the parts of the well-spending of the Sabbath, is the looking upon, and consideration of the works of creation. The consideration of the Lord's works will afford us much sweet refreshment and joy when God blesses the meditation ; and when it is so we ought to acknowledge our gladness most thankfully and lift up our heart in his ways.—*David Dickson.*

Verse 4.—" *Thy work.*" The " work of God " here is one no less marvellous than that of creation, which was the original ground of hallowing the Sabbath (see *title* of this Psalm)—namely, the final redemption of his people.—*A. R. Fausset.*

Verse 4.—" *Made me glad through thy work,*" etc. Surely there is nothing in the world, short of the most undivided reciprocal attachment, that has such power over the workings of the human heart as the mild sweetness of Nature. The most ruffled temper, when emerging from the town, will subside into a calm at the sight of an extended landscape reposing in the twilight of a fine evening. It is then that the spirit of peace settles upon the heart, unfetters the thoughts, and elevates the soul to the Creator. It is then that we behold the Parent of the universe in his works ; we see his grandeur in earth, sea, sky ; we feel his affection in the emotions which they raise, and half-mortal, half-etherealized, forget where we are in the anticipation of what that world must be, of which this lovely earth is merely the shadow.—*Miss Porter.*

Verse 4.—" *I will triumph in the works of thy hands.*" Here it will be most fitting to remind the reader of those three great bursts of adoring song, which in different centuries have gushed forth from souls enraptured with the sight of nature. They are each of them clear instances of triumphing in the works of God's hands. How majestically Milton sang when he said of our unfallen parents,—

> "Nor holy rapture wanted they to praise
> Their Maker, in fit strains pronounc'd or sung
> Unmeditated ; such prompt eloquence
> Flow'd from their lips, in prose or numerous verse,
> More tunable than needed lute or harp
> To add more sweetness."

Then he gives us that noble hymn, too well-known for us to quote, the reader will find it in the fifth book of the Paradise Lost, commencing—

> " These are thy glorious works, Parent of good, Almighty ! "

Thomson also, in his Seasons, rises to a wonderful height, as he closes his poem with a hymn—

> " These, as they change, Almighty Father, these
> Are but the varied God."

Coleridge in his " Hymn before Sun-rise. in the Vale of Chamouni," equally well treads the high places of triumphant devotion, as he cries—

> "Awake my soul ! not only passive praise
> Thou owest ! not alone these swelling tears,
> Mute thanks and secret ecstacy ! Awake,
> Voice of sweet song ! Awake, my heart, awake !
> Green vales and icy cliffs, all join my hymn."

Verse 5.—" *Thy thoughts.*" The plural of מַחֲשָׁבָה, from the verb חָשַׁב, to meditate, to count, to *weave* ; and this last word gives a good idea of what is here made the subject of admiration and praise, the wonderful intricacy and contrivance with which the Divine Mind designs and executes his plans, till at length the result is seen in a beautifully woven tissue of many delicately mingled and coloured threads.— *Christopher Wordsworth.*

Verse 5.—" *Thy thoughts are very deep.*" Verily, my brethren, there is no sea so deep as these thoughts of God, who maketh the wicked flourish, and the good suffer : nothing so profound, nothing so deep : therein every unbelieving soul is wrecked, in that depth, in that profundity. Dost thou wish to cross this depth ? Remove not from the wood of Christ's cross ; and thou shalt not sink : hold thyself fast to Christ.—*Augustine.*

Verse 6.—Expressively he wrote : " The *man-brute* will not know ; the fool will not understand this," viz., that when the wicked spring up with rapid and apparently vigorous growth as the summer flowers in Palestine, it is that they may ripen soon for a swift destruction. The *man-brute* precisely translates the Hebrew words ; one whom God has endowed with manhood, but who has debased himself to brute-hood ; a man as being of God's creation in his own image, but a brute as being self-moulded (shall we say self-made ?) into the image of the baser animals !—*Henry Cowles.*

Verse 6.—" *A brutish man knoweth not,*" etc. A sottish sensualist who hath his *soul for salt* only, to keep his body from putrefying (as we say of swine) he takes no knowledge of God's great works, but grunts and goes his ways, contenting himself with a natural use of the creatures, as beasts do.—*John Trapp.*

Verse 6.—" *A brutish man knoweth not,*" etc. That is, he being a beast, and having no sanctified principle of wisdom in him, looks no further than a beast into all the works of God and occurrences of things ; looks on all blessings as things provided for man's delight by God ; but he extracts seldom holy, spiritual, and useful thoughts out of all, he wants the art of doing it.—*Thomas Goodwin.*

Verse 6.—" *A brutish man knoweth not.*" How universally do men strive, by the putrid joys of sense and passion, to destroy the fineness of the sensibilities which God has given them ! This mind, which might behold a world of glory in created things, and look through them as through a transparent veil to things infinitely *more* glorious, signified or contained within the covering, is as dull and heavy as a piece of anthracite coal. Who made it so ? Alas, habits of sense and sin have done this. If from childhood the soul had been educated for God, in habits accordant with its spiritual nature, it would be full of life, love, and sensibility, in harmony with all lovely things in the natural world, beholding the spiritual world through the natural, alive to all excitement from natural and intellectual beauty, and as ready to its duty as a child to its play. What a dreadful destruction of the mind's inner sensibilities results from a sensual life ! What a decline, decay, and paralysis of its intuitive powers, so that the very existence of such a thing as spiritual intuition, in reference to a spiritual world, may be questioned, if not denied !

A man may be frightfully successful in such a process of destruction if long enough continued, upon his own nature. " Who can read without indignation of Kant," remarks De Quincey, " that at his own table, in social sincerity and con-fidential talk, let him say what he would in his books, he exulted in the prospect of absolute and ultimate annihilation ; that he planted his glory in the grave, and was ambitious of rotting for ever ! The King of Prussia, though a personal friend of Kant's, found himself obliged to level his State thunders at some of his doctrines, and terrified him in his advance ; else I am persuaded that Kant would have formally delivered Atheism from the Professor's chair, and would have enthroned the horrid ghoulish creed, which privately he professed, in the University of Königsberg. It required the artillery of a great king to make him pause. The fact is, that as the stomach has been known by means of its natural secretion, to attack not only what-soever alien body is introduced within it, but also (as John Hunter first showed), sometimes to attack itself and its own organic structure ; so, and with the same preternatural extension of instinct, did Kant carry forward his destroying functions, until he turned them upon his own hopes, and the pledges of his own superiority to the dog, the ape, the worm."—*George B. Cheever, in " Voices of Nature,"* 1852.

Verse 6.—*" A fool."* The simpleton is an automaton, he is a machine, he is worked by a spring ; mere gravity carries him forward, makes him move, makes him turn, and that unceasingly and in the same way, and exactly with the same equable pace : he is uniform, he is never inconsistent with himself ; whoever has seen him once, has seen him at all moments, and in all periods of his life ; he is like the ox who bellows, or the blackbird which whistles : that which is least visible in him is his soul ; it does not act, it is not exercised, it takes its rest.—*Jean de la Bruyère* (1639—1696), *quoted by Ramage.*

Verse 6.—*" Neither doth a fool understand this."*

> He roved among the vales and streams,
>   In the green wood and hollow dell ;
> They were his dwellings night and day,
> But nature ne'er could find the way
>   Into the heart of Peter Bell.
>
> In vain, through every changeful year,
>   Did Nature lead him as before ;
> A primrose by a river's brim
> A yellow primrose was to him,
>   And it was nothing more.
>
> In vain, through water, earth, and air,
>   The soul of happy sound was spread,
> When Peter on some April morn,
> Beneath the broom or budding thorn,
>   Made the warm earth his lazy bed.
>
> At noon, when by the forest's edge
>   He lay beneath the branches high,
> The soft blue sky did never melt
> Into his heart ; he never felt
>   The witchery of the soft blue sky !
>
> There was a hardness in his cheek,
>   There was a hardness in his eye.
> As if the man had fixed his face,
> In many a solitary place,
>   Against the wind and open sky.
>   —*W. Wordsworth,* 1770—1850.

Verse 7.—*" When the wicked spring as the grass,"* etc.   Their felicity is the greatest infelicity.—*Adam Clarke.*

Verse 7.—Little do they think that they are suffered to prosper that like *beasts* they may be fitter for slaughter.   The fatter they are, the fitter for slaughter, and the sooner slain : " He slew the fattest of them," Ps. lxxviii., 31.—*Zachary Bogan.*

Verse 8.—Here is the central pivot of the Psalm. *" But thou, Lord, art most high for evermore,"* lit., " art *height,"* &c., the abstract used for the concrete, to imply that the essence of all that is *high* is concentrated in Jehovah.   When God and the cause of holiness *seem low,* God *is really* never higher than then ; for out of seeming weakness he perfects the greatest strength.   When the wicked seem *high,* they are then on the verge of being cast down for ever.   The believer who can realize this will not despair at the time of his own depression, and of the seeming exaltation of the wicked.   If we can feel *" Jehovah most high for evermore,"* we can well be unruffled, however low we lie.—*A. R. Fausset.*

Verse 9.—*" Lo thine enemies ; " " lo thine enemies."*   He represents their destruc-tion as present, and as certain, which the repetition of the words implies.—*Matthew Pool.*

Verse 9.—" *Thine enemies shall perish."* This is the only Psalm in the Psalter which is designated a Sabbath-song. The older Sabbath was a type of our rest in Christ from sin ; and therefore the final extirpation of sin forms one of the leading subjects of the Psalm.—*Joseph Francis Thrupp.*

Verse 9.—" *All the workers of iniquity shall be scattered."* The wicked may unite and confederate together, but the bands of their society are feeble. It is seldom that they long agree together ; at least as to the particular object of their pursuit. Though they certainly harmonize in the general one, that of working iniquity. But God will soon by his power, and in his wrath, confound and scatter them even to destruction.—*Samuel Burder.*

Verse 10.—" *Thou shalt lift up, as a rĕĕym, my horn,"* seems to point to the mode in which the *bovidæ* use their horns, lowering the head and then tossing it up.—*William Houghton, in Smith's Bible Dictionary.*

Verse 10.—" *The horn of an unicorn."*—After discussing the various accounts which are given of this animal by ancient and modern writers, Winer says, I do not hesitate to say, it is the *Antelope Leucoryx,* a species of goat with long and sharp horns.—*William Walford.*

Verse 10.—" *I shall be anointed with fresh oil."* Montanus has, instead of " *fresh oil,"* given the literal meaning of the original *virido oleo,* " *with green oil."* Ainsworth also renders it : " *fresh or green oil."* The remark of Calmet is : " The plants imparted somewhat of their colour, as well as of their fragrance, hence the expression, " *green oil."* Harmer says, " I shall be anointed with green oil." Some of these writers think the term *green,* as it is in the original, signifies " precious fragrant oil ;" others, literally " green " in colour ; and others, " fresh " or newly-made oil. But I think it will appear to mean " cold-drawn oil," that which has been expressed or squeezed from the nut or fruit without the process of boiling. The Orientals prefer this kind to all others for anointing themselves ; it is considered the most precious, the most pure and efficacious. Nearly all their medicinal oils are thus extracted ; and because they cannot gain so much by this method as by the boiling process, oils so drawn are very dear. Hence their name for the article thus prepared is also *patche,* that is, " *green oil."* But this term, in Eastern phraseology, is applied to other things which are unboiled or raw ; thus unboiled water is called *patche-tameer,* " *green* water : " *patche-pal,* likewise, " *green milk,"* means that which has not been boiled, and the butter made from it is called " *green* butter ; " and uncooked meat or yams are known by the same name. I think, therefore, the Psalmist alludes to that valuable article which is called " *green* oil," on account of its being expressed from the nut or fruit, without the process of boiling.—*Joseph Roberts's Oriental Illustrations.*

Verse 10.—" *Anointed with fresh oil."* Every kind of benediction and refreshment I have received, do receive, and shall receive, like one at a feast, who is welcomed as a friend, and whose *head* is copiously anointed with oil or fragrant balm. In this way, the spirits are gently refreshed, an inner joyousness excited, the beauty of the face and limbs, according to the custom of the country, brought to perfection. Or, there is an allusion to the custom of *anointing* persons at their solemn installation in some splendid office. Compare Ps. xxiii. 5, " *Thou anointest my head with oil,"* and Ps. xlv. 7, " *God, thy God, hath anointed thee with the oil of gladness."*—*Martin Geier.*

Verse 10 (last clause).—The phrase is not " I am anointed," מָשַׁה ; but בַּלֹּתִי, *imbutus sum—perfusus sum ;* apparently in reference to the abundance of perfume employed on the occasion, viz., his being elected King over all the tribes, as indicative of the greater popularity of the act, or the higher measure of Jehovah's blessing on his people. The difference, indeed, between the first anointing of David and that of Saul, as performed by Samuel, is well worthy of notice on the present occasion. When Samuel was commanded to anoint Saul, he " took a *vial* of oil, and poured it upon his head," in private, 1 Sam. xvi. 13. Here we find the horn again made use of, and apparently full to the brim—*David was soaked or imbued with it.*—*John Mason Good.*

Verse 11.—" *Mine enemies."*—The word here used שׁוּר *shur*—occurs nowhere else. It means, properly, a lier-in-wait, one who *watches* ; one who is in ambush ; and refers to persons who *watched* his conduct ; who *watched* for his ruin.—*A. Barnes.*

Verse 12.—"*Like the palm tree.*" Look now at those stately palm-trees, which stand here and there on the plain, like military sentinels, with feathery plumes nodding gracefully on their proud heads. The stem, tall, slender, and erect as Rectitude herself, suggests to the Arab poets many a symbol for their lady-love; and Solomon, long before them, has sung, "How fair and how pleasant art thou, O love, for delights! This thy stature is like a palm-tree," (S. Song vii. 6, 7). Yes; and Solomon's father says, "*The righteous shall flourish like the palm-tree,*" etc. The royal poet has derived more than one figure from the customs of men, and the habits of this noble tree, with which to adorn his sacred ode. The palm grows slowly, but steadily, from century to century uninfluenced by those alternations of the seasons which affect other trees. It does not rejoice over much in winter's copious rain, nor does it droop under the drought and the burning sun of summer. Neither heavy weights which men place upon its head, nor the importunate urgency of the wind, can sway it aside from perfect uprightness. There it stands, looking calmly down upon the world below, and patiently yielding its large clusters of golden fruit from generation to generation. They "*bring forth fruit in old age.*"

The allusion to being "*planted in the house of the Lord*" is probably drawn from the custom of planting beautiful and long-lived trees in the courts of temples and palaces, and in all "high places" used for worship. This is still common; nearly every palace, and mosque, and convent in the country has such trees in the courts, and being well protected there, they flourish exceedingly.

Solomon covered all the walls of the "Holy of Holies" round about with palm-trees. They were thus planted, as it were, within the very house of the Lord; and their presence there was not only ornamental, but appropriate and highly suggestive. The very best emblem, not only of patience in well-doing, but of the rewards of the righteous—a fat and flourishing old age—a peaceful end—a glorious immortality.— *W. M. Thomson.*

Verse 12.—"*The palm tree.*" The palms were entitled by Linnæus, "the princes of the vegetable world;" and Von Martius enthusiastically says, "The common-world atmosphere does not become these vegetable monarchs: but in those genial climes where nature seems to have fixed her court, and summons around her of flowers, and fruits, and trees, and animated beings, a galaxy of beauty,—there they tower up into the balmy air, rearing their majestic stems highest and proudest of all. Many of them, at a distance, by reason of their long perpendicular shafts, have the appearance of columns, erected by the Divine architect, bearing up the broad arch of heaven above them, crowned with a capital of gorgeous green foliage." And Humboldt speaks of them as "the loftiest and stateliest of all vegetable forms." To these, above all other trees, the prize of beauty has always been awarded by every nation, and it was from the Asiatic palm world, or the adjacent countries, that human civilization sent forth the first rays of its early dawn.

On the northern borders of the Great Desert, at the foot of the Atlas mountains, the groves of date palms form the great feature of that parched region, and few trees besides can maintain an existence. The excessive dryness of this arid tract, where rain seldom falls, is such that wheat refuses to grow, and even barley, maize, and Caffre corn, (Holcus sorghum,) afford the husbandman only a scanty and uncertain crop. The hot blasts from the south are scarcely supportable even by the native himself, and yet here forests of date palms flourish, and form a screen impervious to the rays of the sun, beneath the shade of which the lemon, the orange, and the pomegranate, are cherished, and the vine climbs up by means of its twisted tendrils; and although reared in constant shade, all these fruits acquire a more delicious flavour than in what would seem a more favourable climate. How beautiful a comment do these facts supply to the words of Holy Writ, "*The righteous shall flourish like the palm tree!*" Unmoved by the scorching and withering blasts of temptations or persecutions, the Christian sustained by the secret springs of Divine grace, lives and grows in likeness to his Divine Master, when all others are overcome, and their professions wither. How striking is the contrast in the Psalm. The wicked and worldlings are compared to grass, which is at best but of short duration, and which is easily withered; but the emblem of the Christian is the palm tree, which stands for centuries. Like the grateful shade of the palm groves, the Christian extends around him a genial, sanctified, and heavenly influence; and just as the great value of the date palm lies in its abundant, wholesome, and delicious fruit, so do those who are the true disciples of Christ abound in "fruits of righteousness," for, said our Saviour, "Herein is my Father glorified, that ye bear much fruit; so shall ye be my disciples."—" *The Palm Tribes and their Varieties.*" *R. T. Society's Monthly Volume.*

Verse 12.—" *The righteous shall flourish.*" David here tells us *how* he shall flourish. " He shall flourish *like the palm tree :* he shall grow like a cedar in Lebanon." Of the wicked he had said just before, " When the wicked spring as the grass, and when all the workers of iniquity do flourish; it is that they shall be destroyed for ever." They flourish as the *grass*, which to-day is, and to-morrow is cast into the oven. What a contrast with the worthlessness, the weakness, transitoriness, and destiny, of grass—in a warm country too—are the palm tree and cedar of Lebanon ! They are evergreens. How beautifully, how firmly, how largely, they grow ! How strong and lofty is the cedar ! How upright, and majestic, and tall, the palm tree. The palm also bears fruit, called dates, like bunches of grapes. It sometimes yields a hundredweight at once.

He tells us *where* he shall flourish. " Those that be planted in the house of the Lord shall flourish in the courts of our God." The allusion is striking. It compares the house of God to a garden, or fine well-watered soil, favourable to the life, and verdure, and fertility, of the trees fixed there. The reason is, that in the sanctuary we have the communion of saints. *There* our fellowship is with the Father, and with his Son Jesus Christ. *There* are dispensed the ordinances of religion, and the word of truth. *There* God commandeth the blessing, even life for evermore.

He also tells us *when* he shall flourish. " They shall still bring forth fruit in old age." This is to show the permanency of their principles, and to distinguish them from natural productions.

> " The plants of grace shall ever live ;
> Nature decays, but grace must thrive ;
> Time, that doth all things else impair,
> Still makes them flourish strong and fair."

The young Christian is lovely, like a tree in the blossoms of spring : the aged Christian is valuable, like a tree in autumn, bending with ripe fruit. We therefore look for something superior in old disciples. More deadness to the world, the vanity of which they have had more opportunities to see ; more meekness of wisdom ; more disposition to make sacrifices for the sake of peace ; more maturity of judgment in divine things ; more confidence in God ; more richness of experience.

He also tells us *why* he shall flourish. " They shall be fat and flourishing ; to shew that the Lord is upright." We might rather have supposed that it was necessary to shew that *they* were upright. But by the grace of God they are what they are— not they, but the grace of God which is in them. From *him* is their fruit found. Their preservation and fertility, therefore, are to the praise and glory of God ; and as what he does for them he had *engaged* to do, it displays his truth as well as his mercy, and proves that he is upright.—*William Jay.*

Verse 12.—" *The righteous shall flourish like the palm tree.*"

1. *The palm tree grows in the desert.* Earth is a desert to the Christian ; true believers are ever refreshed in it as a palm is in the Arabian desert. So *Lot* amid Sodom's wickedness, and *Enoch* who walked with God amongst the antediluvians.

2. *The palm tree grows from the sand, but the sand is not its food ;* water from below feeds its tap roots, though the heavens above be brass. Some Christians grow, not as the lily, Hos. xiv. 5, by green pastures, or the willow by water-courses, Isai. xliv. 4, but as the palm of the desert ; so *Joseph* among the Cat-worshippers of Egypt, *Daniel* in voluptuous Babylon. Faith's penetrating root reaches the fountains of living waters.

3. *The palm tree is beautiful,* with its tall and verdant canopy, and the silvery flashes of its waving plumes ; so the Christian virtues are not like the creeper or bramble, tending downwards, their palm branches shoot upwards, and seek the things above where Christ dwells, Col. iii. 1 : some trees are crooked and gnarled, but the Christian is a tall palm as a son of the light, Matt. iii. 12 ; Phil. ii. 15. The Jews were called a crooked generation, Deut. xxxii. 5, and Satan a crooked serpent, Isai. xxvii., but the Christian is upright like the palm. Its beautiful, unfading leaves make it an emblem of victory ; it was twisted into verdant booths at the feast of Tabernacles ; and the multitude, when escorting Christ to his coronation in Jerusalem, spread leaves on the way, Matt. xxi. 8 ; so victors in heaven are represented as having palms in their hands, Rev. vii. 9. No dust adheres to the leaf as it does with the *battree* ; the Christian is in the world, not of it ; the dust of earth's desert adheres

not to his palm leaf. The leaf of the palm is the same—it does not fall in winter, and even in the summer it has no holiday-clothing, it is an evergreen ; the palm trees' rustling is the desert orison.

4. *The palm tree is very useful.* The Hindus reckon it has 360 uses. Its shadow shelters, its fruit refreshes the weary traveller, it points out the place of water : such was *Barnabas*, a son of consolation, Acts iv. 36 ; such Lydia, Dorcas, and others, who on the King's highway showed the way to heaven, as Philip did to the Ethiopian eunuch, Acts ix. 34. Jericho was called the City of Palms, Deut. xxxiv. 3.

5. *The palm tree produces even to old age.* The best dates are produced when the tree is from thirty to one hundred years old ; 300lbs. of dates are annually yielded : so the Christian grows happier and more useful as he becomes older. Knowing his own faults more, he is more mellow to others : he is like the sun setting, beautiful, mild, and large, looking like Elim, where the wearied Jews found twelve wells and seventy palm trees.—*J. Long, in " Scripture Truth in Oriental Dress," 1871.*

Verse 12.—" *Palm-tree.*" The open country moreover wears a sad aspect now : the soil is rent and dissolves into dust at every breath of wind; the green of the meadows is almost entirely gone,—the *palm-tree* alone preserves in the drought and heat its verdant roof of leaves.—*Gotthelf H. von Schubert, 1780—1860.*

Verse 12.—" *A cedar in Lebanon.*" Laying aside entirely any enquiry as to the palm-tree, and laying aside the difficulty contained in the 13th verse, I have only to compare this description of the cedar in Lebanon with the accounts of those who have visited them in modern days. Without believing (as the Maronites or Christian inhabitants of the mountains do), that the seven very ancient cedars which yet remain in the neighbourhood of the village of Eden in Lebanon are the remains of the identical forest which furnished Solomon with timber for the Temple, full three thousand years ago, they can yet be proved to be of very great antiquity. These very cedars were visited by Belonius in 1550, nearly three hundred years ago, who found them twenty-eight in number. Rawolf, in 1575, makes them twenty-four. Dandini, in 1600, and Thevenot about fifty years after, make them twenty-three. Maundrell, in 1696, found them reduced to sixteen. Pococke, in 1738, found fifteen standing, and a sixteenth recently blown down, or (may we not conjecture ?) shivered by the voice of God. In 1810, Burckhardt counted eleven or twelve ; and Dr. Richardson, in 1818, states them to be no more than seven. There cannot be a doubt, then, that these cedars which were esteemed ancient nearly three hundred years ago, must be of a very great antiquity ; and yet they are described by the last of these travellers as " large, and tall, and beautiful, the most picturesque productions of the vegetable world that we had seen." The oldest are large and massy, rearing their heads to an enormous height, and spreading their branches afar. Pococke also remarks, that " the young cedars are not easily known from pines. I observed, they bear a *greater quantity* of fruit than the large ones." This shows that the old ones still bear fruit, though not so abundantly as the young cedars, which, according to Richardson, are very productive, and cast many seeds annually. How appropriate, then, and full of meaning, is the imagery of the Psalmist : " The righteous shall flourish like the palm tree : he shall grow like a cedar in Lebanon. They shall still bring forth fruit in old age ; they shall be fat and flourishing."—*R. M. M'Cheyne.*

Verses 12—15.—The life and greenness of the branches is an honour to the root by which they live. Spiritual greenness and fruitfulness is in a believer an honour to Jesus Christ who is his life. The fulness of Christ is manifested by the fruitfulness of a Christian.—*Ralph Robinson.*

Verse 13.—" *Those that be planted in the house of the Lord shall flourish in the courts of our God,*" are not distinctive of some from others, as though some only of the flourishing righteous were so planted ; but they are descriptive of them all, with an addition of the way and means whereby they are caused so to grow and flourish. And this is their implantation in the house of the Lord,—that is, in the church, which is the seat of all the means of spiritual life, both as unto growth and flourishing, which God is pleased to grant unto believers. To be planted in the house of the Lord, is to be fixed and rooted in the grace communicated by the ordinances of divine worship. Unless we are planted in the house of the Lord, we cannot flourish in his courts. See Ps. i. 3. Unless we are partakers of the grace administered in the ordinances, we cannot flourish in a fruitful profession.—*John Owen.*

Verse 13.—" *Those that be planted in the house of the Lord,*" etc. Saints are planted in the house of God ; they have a kind of rooting there : but though the tabernacle be a good rooting-place, yet we cannot root firmly there, unless we are rooted in Jesus Christ. To root in tabernacle work, or in the bare use of ordinances, as if that would carry it, and commend us to God, when there is no heart work, when there is no looking to the power of godliness, and to communion with Christ, what is this but building upon the sand ? Many come often to the tabernacle, who are mere strangers to Christ ; they use pure ordinances, but are themselves impure. These may have a great name in the tabernacle for a while, but God blots their names, and roots their hopes out of the tabernacle, yea, he puts them from the horns of the altar, or slays them there, as Solomon gave commandment concerning Joab.—*Abraham Wright.*

Verse 13.—" *In the house of the Lord.*" As if in a most select viridarium, or as if in a park, abounding in trees dedicated to God. And as in v. 12 he had made mention of Lebanon, where the cedars attain their highest perfection, so now he tacitly opposes to Lebanon the *house of God,* or church, wherein we bloom, grow, and bring forth fruit pleasing to God.—*Martin Geier.*

Verse 14.—" *They shall still bring forth fruit in old age.*" The point on which the Psalmist in this passage fixes, as he contemplates the blessedness of God's own children, is the beauty and happiness of their old age. The court or open area in the centre of an eastern dwelling, and especially the court of any great and stately dwelling, was often adorned with a tree, or sometimes with more than one, for beauty, for shade, and, as it might be, for fruit. There sometimes the palm tree, planted by the cool fountain, shot up its tall trunk toward the sky, and waved its green top, far above the roof, in the sun-light and the breeze. There sometimes the olive, transplanted from the rocky hillside, may have flourished under the protection and culture of the household, and may have rewarded their care with the rich abundance of its nutritious berries. With such images in his mind, the Psalmist, having spoken of the brief prosperity of the wicked, and having compared it with the springing and flourishing of the grass, which grows to its little height only to be immediately cut down, naturally and beautifully compares the righteous, not with the deciduous herbage, but with the hardy tree that lives on through the summer's drought and the winter's storms, and from season to season still renews its growth. These trees of righteousness, as the poet conceives of them, are " planted in the house of the Lord ;" they stand fair and "flowering in the courts of our God"— even " in old age they bring forth fruit "—they are " full of sap and flourishing "— they are living memorials " to show that the Lord is faithful," and that those who trust in him shall never be confounded.—*Leonard Bacon,* 1845.

Verse 14.—There be three things which constitute a spiritual state, or belong to the life of God. 1. That believers be fat ; that is, by the heavenly juice, sap, or fatness of the true olive, of Christ himself, as Rom. xi. 17. This is the principle of spiritual life and grace derived from him. When this abounds in them, so as to give them strength and vigour in the exercise of grace, to keep them from decays and withering, they are said to be fat ; which, in the Scripture phrase, is strong and healthy. 2. That they flourish in the greenness (as the word is) and verdure of profession ; for vigorous grace will produce a flourishing profession. 3. That they still bring forth fruit in all duties of holy obedience. All these are promised unto them even in old age.

Even trees, when they grow old (the palm and the cedar), are apt to lose a part of their juice and verdure : and men in old age are subject unto all sorts of decays, both outward and inward. It is a rare thing to see a man in old age naturally vigorous, healthy, and strong ; and would it were not more rare to see any spiritually so at the same season ! But this is here promised unto believers as an especial grace and privilege, beyond what can be represented in the growth or fruit-bearing of plants and trees. The grace intended is, that when believers are under all sorts of bodily and natural decays, and, it may be, have been overtaken with spiritual decays also, there is provision made in the covenant to render them fat, flourishing, and fruitful,—vigorous in the power of internal grace, and flourishing in the expression of it in all duties of obedience ; which is that which we now inquire after. Blessed be God for this good word of his grace, that he hath given us such encouragement against all the decays and temptations of old age which we have to conflict withal !

And the Psalmist, in the next words, declares the greatness of the privilege: "*To shew that the Lord is upright : he is my rock, and there is no unrighteousness in him.*" Consider the oppositions that lie against the flourishing of believers in old age, the difficulties of it, the temptations that must be conquered, the actings of the mind above its natural abilities which are decayed, the weariness that is apt to befall us in a long spiritual conflict, the cries of the flesh to be spared, and we shall see it to be an evidence of the faithfulness, power, and righteousness of God in covenant; nothing else could produce this mighty effect. So the prophet, treating of the same promise, Hosea xiv. 4—8, closeth his discourse with that blessed remark, ver. 9, " Who is wise, and he shall understand these things ? prudent, and he shall know them ? for the ways of the Lord are right, and the just shall walk in them." Spiritual wisdom will make us to see that the faithfulness and power of God are exerted in this work of preserving believers flourishing and fruitful unto the end.— *John Owen.*

Verse 14.—Constancy is an ingredient in the obedience Christ requires. His trees bring forth fruit in old age. Age makes other things decay, but makes a Christian flourish. Some are like hot horses, mettlesome at the beginning of a journey, and tired a long time before they come to their journey's end. A good disciple, as he would not have from God a temporary happiness, so he would not give to God a temporary obedience ; as he would have his glory last as long as God lives, so he would have his obedience last as long as he lives. Judas had a fair beginning, but destroyed all in the end by betraying his Master.—*Stephen Charnock.*

Verse 14.—" *Flourishing.*" Here is not only mention of growing but of *flourishing*, and here's flourishing three times mentioned, and 'tis growing and flourishing not only like a tree, but like a " *palm tree,*" (which flourisheth under oppression), and like a " *cedar* " (not growing in ordinary places, but) " in *Lebanon,*" where were the goodliest cedars. Nor doth the Spirit promise here a flourishing in boughs and leaves only (as some trees do, and do no more), but in fruit ; and this not only fruit for once in a year, or one year, but they " *still bring forth fruit,*" and that not only in the years of their youth, or beginnings in grace, but " *in old age,*" and that not only in the entrance of that state which is called *old age,* threescore years, but that which the Scripture calls the perfection of *old age,* threescore years and ten, as the learned Hebrews observe upon the word used in the Psalm. What a *divine climax* doth the Spirit of God make in this Scripture, to show that the godly man as to his state, is so far from declining, that he is still climbing higher and higher !— *Joseph Caryl.*

Verse 15.—" *He is my rock, and there is no unrighteousness in him.*" Implying that God can no more be moved or removed from doing righteously, than a rock can be removed out of its place.—*Joseph Caryl.*

HINTS TO PREACHERS.

Verse 1.—I. It is a good thing to have cause for gratitude. Every one has this. II. It is a good thing to have the principle of gratitude. This is the gift of God. III. It is a good thing to give expression to gratitude. This may excite gratitude in others.—*G. R.*

Verses 1—3.—The blessedness of praise, verse 1. The theme of praise, verse 2. The ingenuity of praise, verse 3—inanimate nature enlisted in the holy work.—*C. A. Davis.*

Verse 2.—I. Our praises of God should be *intelligent,* declaring his varied attributes. II. *Seasonable,* declaring each attribute in appropriate time. III. *Continual,* every night, and every day.

Verse 3.—I. All the powers of the soul should be praise. " Upon an instrument of ten strings," all the chords of the mind, affections, will, etc. II. All the utterances of the lips should be praise. III. All the actions of the life should be praise.

Verse 3.—In our praise of God there should be, I. *Preparation*—for instruments should be tuned. II. *Breadth of thought*—" upon an instrument of ten strings." III. *Absorption of the whole nature*—" ten strings." IV. *Variety*—psaltery, harp, etc. V. *Deep reverence*—" solemn sound."

Verse 4 (first sentence).—I. My state—" glad." II. How I arrived at it—" thou hast made me glad." III. What is the ground of it ?—" through thy work." IV. What, then, shall I do ?—ascribe it all to God, and bless him for it.

Verse 4.—I. The divinest gladness—of God's creation, having God's work for its argument. II. The divinest triumph—caused by the varied works of God in creation, providence, redemption, &c. The first is for our own hearts, the second is for the convincing of those around us.

Verse 5.—The unscalable mountains and the fathomless sea : or the divine works and the divine thoughts (God-revealed and hidden) equally beyond human apprehension.—*C. A. Davis.*

Verse 7.—Great prosperity the frequent forerunner of destruction to wicked men, for it leads them to provoke divine wrath—I. By hardness of heart, as Pharaoh. II. By pride, as Nebuchadnezzar. III. By haughty hatred of the saints, as Haman. IV. By carnal security, as the rich fool. V. By self-exaltation, as Herod.

Verses 7—10.—Contrasts. Between the wicked and God, verses 7, 8. Between God's enemies and his friends, verses 9, 10.—*C. A. Davis.*

Verses 7, 12—14.—The wicked and the righteous pourtrayed.—*C. A. Davis.*

Verse 10 (last clause).—Christian illumination, consecration, gladness, and graces, are all of them the anointing of the Spirit.—*William Garrett Lewis*, 1872.

Verse 10 (last clause).—The subject of David's confidence was—I. Very comprehensive, including renewed strength, fresh tokens of favour, confirmation in office, qualification for it, and new joys. II. Well grounded, since it rested in God and his promises. III. Calming all fears. IV. Exciting hopes. V. Causing pity for those who have no such confidence.

Verse 12.—I. The righteous flourish in all places. Palm in the valley, cedar on the mountain. II. In all seasons. Both trees are evergreen. III. Under all circumstances. Palm in drought, cedar in storm and frost.—*G. R.*

Verses 14—16.—I. Regeneration—" planted." II. Growth in grace—" flourish." III. Usefulness—" fruit." IV. Perseverance—" old age." V. The reason of it all—" to shew that the Lord," etc.

Verses 15, 16.—The reason and the pledge of final perseverance.—*C. A. Davis.*

PSALM XCIII.

This brief Psalm is without title or name of author, but its subject is obvious enough, being stated in the very first line. It is the Psalm of Omnipotent Sovereignty: Jehovah, despite all opposition, reigns supreme. Possibly at the time this sacred ode was written, the nation was in danger from its enemies, and the hopes of the people of God were encouraged by remembering that the Lord was still King. What sweeter and surer consolation could they desire?

EXPOSITION.

THE LORD reigneth, he is clothed with majesty; the LORD is clothed with strength, *wherewith* he hath girded himself: the world also is stablished, that it cannot be moved.

2 Thy throne *is* established of old: thou *art* from everlasting.

3 The floods have lifted up, O LORD, the floods have lifted up their voice; the floods lift up their waves.

4 The LORD on high *is* mightier than the noise of many waters, *yea, than* the mighty waves of the sea.

5 Thy testimonies are very sure: holiness becometh thine house, O LORD, for ever.

1. "*The Lord reigneth,*" or Jehovah reigns. Whatever opposition may arise, his throne is unmoved; he has reigned, does reign, and will reign for ever and ever. Whatever turmoil and rebellion there may be beneath the clouds, the eternal King sits above all in supreme serenity; and everywhere he is really Master, let his foes rage as they may. All things are ordered according to his eternal purposes, and his will is done. In the verse before us it would seem as if the Lord had for a while appeared to vacate the throne, but on a sudden he puts on his regal apparel and ascends his lofty seat, while his happy people proclaim him with new joy, shouting "The Lord reigneth." What can give greater joy to a loyal subject than a sight of the king in his beauty? Let us repeat the proclamation, "the Lord reigneth," whispering it in the ears of the desponding, and publishing it in the face of the foe. "*He is clothed with majesty.*" Not with emblems of majesty, but with majesty itself: everything which surrounds him is majestic. His is not the semblance but the reality of sovereignty. In nature, providence, and salvation the Lord is infinite in majesty. Happy are the people among whom the Lord appears in all the glory of his grace, conquering their enemies, and subduing all things unto himself; then indeed is he seen to be clothed with majesty.

"*The Lord is clothed with strength.*" His garments of glory are not his only array, he wears strength also as his girdle. He is always strong, but sometimes he displays his power in a special manner, and may therefore be said to be clothed with it; just as he is always majestic essentially, but yet there are seasons when he reveals his glory, and so wears his majesty, or shows himself in it. May the Lord appear in his church, in our day, in manifest majesty and might, saving sinners, slaying errors, and honouring his own name. O for a day of the Son of man, in which the King Immortal and Almighty shall stand upon his glorious high throne, to be feared in the great congregation, and admired by all them that believe. "*Wherewith he hath girded himself.*" As men gird up their loins for running or working, so the Lord appears in the eyes of his people to be preparing for action, girt with his omnipotence. Strength always dwells in the Lord Jehovah, but he hides his power full often, until, in answer to his children's cries, he puts on strength, assumes the throne, and defends his own. It should be a constant theme for prayer, that in our day the reign of the Lord may be conspicuous, and his power displayed in his church and on her behalf. "Thy kingdom come" should be our daily prayer: that the Lord Jesus does actually reign should be our daily praise.

"*The world also is stablished, that it cannot be moved.*" Because Jehovah reigns terrestrial things for a while are stable. We could not be sure of anything if we were not sure that he has dominion. When he withdraws his manifest presence from among men all things are out of order ; blasphemers rave, persecutors rage, the profane grow bold, and the licentious increase in wantonness ; but when the divine power and glory are again manifested order is restored, and the poor distracted world is at peace again. Society would be the football of the basest of mankind if God did not establish it, and even the globe itself would fly through space, like thistle-down across the common, if the Lord did not hold it in its appointed orbit. That there is any stability, either in the world or in the church, is the Lord's doings, and he is to be adored for it. Atheism is the mother of anarchy ; the reigning power of God exhibited in true religion is the only security for the human common-wealth. A belief in God is the foundation and corner-stone of a well-ordered state.

2. " *Thy throne is established of old.*" Though thou mayest just now appear in more conspicuous sovereignty, yet thine is no upstart sovereignty : in the most ancient times thy dominion was secure, yea, before time was, thy throne was set up. We often hear of ancient dynasties, but what are they when compared with the Lord ? Are they not as the bubble on the breaker, born an instant ago and gone as soon as seen ? " *Thou art from everlasting.*" The Lord himself is eternal. Let the believer rejoice that the government under which he dwells has an immortal ruler at its head, has existed from all eternity and will flourish when all created things shall have for ever passed away. Vain are the rebellions of mortals, the kingdom of God is not shaken.

3. " *The floods have lifted up, O Lord.*" Men have raged like angry waves of the sea, but vain has been their tumult. Observe that the Psalmist turns to the Lord when he sees the billows foam, and hears the breakers roar ; he does not waste his breath by talking to the waves, or to violent men ; but like Hezekiah he spreads the blasphemies of the wicked before the Lord. " *The floods have lifted up their voice ; the floods lift up their waves.*" These repetitions are needed for the sake both of the poetry and the music, but they also suggest the frequency and the violence of wicked assaults upon the government of God, and the repeated defeats which they sustain. Sometimes men are furious in words—they lift up their voice, and at other times they rise to acts of violence—they lift up their waves ; but the Lord has control over them in either case. The ungodly are all foam and fury, noise and bluster, during their little hour, and then the tide turns or the storm is hushed, and we hear no more of them ; while the kingdom of the Eternal abides in the grandeur of its power.

4. " *The Lord on high is mightier than the noise of many waters.*" The utmost of their power is to him but a sound and he can readily master it, therefore he calls it a noise by way of contempt. When men combine to overthrow the kingdom of Jesus, plot secretly, and by-and-by rage openly, the Lord thinks no more of it than of so much noise upon the sea-beach. Jehovah, the self-existent and omnipotent, cares not for the opposition of dying men, however many or mighty they may be.

> "Loud the stormy billows spoke,
> Loud the billows raised their cry ;
> Fierce the stormy billows broke,
> Sounding to the echoing sky.
> Strong the breakers tossing high,
> Stronger is Jehovah's might,
> True thy words ; and sanctity
> Well becomes thy temple bright."

" *Yea, than the mighty waves of the sea.*" When the storm raises Atlantic billows, and drives them on with terrific force, the Lord is still able to restrain them, and so also when impious men are haughty and full of rage the Lord is able to subdue them and overrule their malice. Kings or mobs, emperors or savages, all are in the Lord's hands, and he can forbid their touching a hair of the heads of his saints.

5. " *Thy testimonies are very sure.*" As in providence the throne of God is fixed beyond all risk, so in revelation his truth is beyond all question. Other teachings are uncertain, but the revelations of heaven are infallible. As the rocks remain unmoved amid the tumult of the sea, so does divine truth resist all the currents of man's opinion and the storms of human controversy ; they are not only sure, but *very sure*. Glory be to God, we have not been deluded by a cunningly-devised fable : our faith is grounded upon the eternal truth of the Most High. " *Holiness becometh thine house, O Lord, for ever.*" Truth changes not in its doctrines, which are very sure, nor holiness in its precepts, which are incorruptible. The teaching

and the character of God are both unaltered. God has not admitted evil to dwell with him, he will not tolerate it in his house, he is eternally its enemy, and is for ever the sworn friend of holiness. The church must remain unchanged, and for ever be holiness unto the Lord ; yea, her King will preserve her undefiled by the intruder's foot. Sacred unto the Lord is the church of Jesus Christ, and so shall she be kept evermore. " Jehovah reigns," is the first word and the main doctrine of the Psalm, and holiness is the final result : a due esteem for the great King will lead us to adopt a behaviour becoming his royal presence. Divine sovereignty both confirms the promises as sure testimonies, and enforces the precepts as seemly and becoming in the presence of so great a Lord.

The whole Psalm is most impressive, and is calculated to comfort the distressed, confirm the timorous, and assist the devout. O thou who art so great and gracious a King, reign over us for ever ! We do not desire to question or restrain thy power, such is thy character that we rejoice to see thee exercise the rights of an absolute monarch. All power is in thine hands, and we rejoice to have it so. Hosanna ! Hosanna !

EXPLANATORY NOTES AND QUAINT SAYINGS.

Whole Psalm.—This is one of those magnificent Psalms which describe Jehovah's reign. Even Jewish interpreters say of them : " These all treat of the things which will take place in the times of Messiah." Throughout it reads like a commentary and application of the great fundamental truth, " Jehovah reigneth." Already he hath laid the foundations of his kingdom in his Church, and anon shall he in his faithfulness and power establish it. Those elements which have hitherto resisted shall not be allowed to continue. Right royally he manifests himself. " *He is clothed with majesty ; clothed is Jehovah, might hath he girt about him.*" The present state of things is connected with Christ's humiliation. But when he puts on his royal mantle of majesty, and girds about him the sword of his might : " *thus the world shall be established ; it cannot be moved.*" And yet, though seemingly the enemy has long prevailed, " *Thy throne is established of old : thou art from everlasting.*" The establishment of his throne is the ground and the pledge of the establishment of the world and of his kingdom. " Jesus Christ, the same yesterday, and to-day, and for ever." In view of all this the Church stands a wondering spectator, first struck with awe, and then filled with adoring gratitude. " *The floods have lifted up, O Jehovah, they have lifted up their roaring ; the floods are lifting up their dashing noise.*" The latter term refers to the sound of the waves *as they break*, and in connexion with it the change of tense is very marked. The enemies of God and his kingdom have risen like the floods or waves of the sea, lashed by the storm ; with roaring noise have they advanced ; but as they near the vessel which bears the King, their noise is that of waves dashing into foam. Their utmost nearness is— to their destruction ; their utmost noise is—in breaking. And even now, and in the height of the storm also, far overtopping not only all danger, but even its threatening noise is Jehovah. " *Jehovah on high* " (even there) " *is mightier than the roaring of many waters and mighty, than the breaking waves of the sea* " (the word here rendered " *breaking waves* " being literally a *derivative* from the verb to break). What a picture this of our safety ; what an epitome of the history of God's government and of his church ! Thus the calming of the storm on the lake of Galilee was not only a parabolic representation of the history of the Kingdom of God, but also typical of the final consummation of all things ; a summary of the past, a prophecy of the future, a type of the end. And what applies to the Church as a whole, holds equally true of individual believers. Let us ever remember that the noise is that of the *breaking* wave. Our greatest dangers are only breaking waves ; waves which break at his feet. The same expression is also sometimes applied to the waves of God's wrath or judgments threatening to engulf the believer, as in Ps. xlii. 7 ; lxxxviii. 7. These also, blessed be his name, are only breaking waves. Meanwhile, while waiting for the manifestation of his majesty and might, " we have the more sure word of prophecy." " *Thy testimonies are very sure* " (very reliable, literally very Amen-ed) : and, so far as we are concerned, our faith and patience are tried and proved : " *Holiness becometh thine house, O Lord, for ever.*"

Thus we have here the history of the Church of God deduced from the text,
" *Jehovah reigneth.*" These words are to us as " a light that shineth in a dark place,
until the day dawn and the day-star arise in our hearts." So long as they are left
us, all that threatens us from without is only like the noise of the breaking wave.
The unspeakable comfort conveyed in this assurance is ever tested in the experience
of God's people. There is no truth more precious to the heart of the Christian than
that " *the Lord reigneth.*" The conviction of this must carry us far above all cares
and fears. A personal God, a living God, a reigning God—alike in the armies of
heaven and among the inhabitants of the earth—and this God the Father of our Lord
and Saviour Jesus Christ,—such are the steps by which we reach a height, where,
far removed from the turmoil of men, we gain a comprehensive and clear view of
earth and its concerns. I would not exchange the assurance which these two words,
" *Jehovah reigneth,*" convey, for all the wisdom, combined with all the power, of
this world. Received into my heart, they are the solution of every difficulty, the
end of all perplexity. It seems to me as if, after puzzling over the cross-writing and
hieroglyphics of men, I turned a fresh leaf, on the top of which stood these words,
as the text to be preached out in all history, whether of the individual, the family,
or the nation, the Church or the world. It seems as if, after revolving sorrowfully
and helplessly all the difficulties and wants which distress my heart, I were at once
rising above those floating clouds into clear atmosphere : as if all at once I were
unburdened ; as if I had reached a haven of rest ; as if I had found a firm foundation,
an ultimate principle. After all, in every real trial there is but this one final and
full comfort. What matters the opinion of men,—who may be for and who against
me ; who may be with me, or who may leave me ? Who would speak of prospects
or probabilities, of the support to be derived from wealth or power, or of the defections
of friends on whose sympathy and help we had counted ? " *Jehovah reigneth !* "
There is light here across my every path, provided I follow Christ, walking in the
narrow way. Only let me be sure that, in any and every respect, I am on the Lord's
side and in the Lord's way, and I ask no more. My God has all the silver and all
the gold in his own hand. He holdeth the hearts of all men at his disposal ; he
directeth all events, from the least to the greatest. If I want power with God or
with men, let me pray ; for, Jehovah reigneth. Nor let me think that special interpositions are either impossible or rare. They are constant. The course of God's
providence is one of constant interposition ; for " all things work together for good
to them that love God." Only these interpositions are not violent, and therefore
not noticed by the superficial observer ; they are the interpositions of all-wise and
almighty God, not of poor, weak man ; they are the *interpositions*, not *interferences* ;
they are the working of the machinery by the Master-mind which designed, and the
Master-hand which framed it. They are not the stoppage, but the working of the
machinery, whereby its real object is wrought out.

Lastly, let me note in the Psalm these three things.

In *creation and nature :* pre-established law *along with* continuous, personal
government,—not as opposed to, but as pre-supposing one another (vers. 1, 2).
In *Providence :* " The LORD on *high* is mightier than the noise of many waters "—
which would otherwise strike terror, even as their swelling would threaten constant
danger. And in *grace :* " His testimonies are *very* sure." I can rest on them.
Not one tittle or iota shall fall to the ground. Wherever I have a word of promise,
I can safely plant my steps. The conclusion and inference from the whole matter
is that " *holiness* "—not fear nor man-serving, but separation unto the Lord—
" *becometh,*" or is the right, wise, and proper attitude of his house and people.—
*Alfred Edersheim, in " The Golden Diary of Heart Converse with Jesus in the Book
of Psalms,"* 1866.

Whole Psalm.—It is mentioned in the Babylonian Talmud that it was the custom
of the Jews to sing this Psalm on the sixth day of the week, to which it is well suited
as celebrating the re-establishing and founding again of the world in the new creation
(ver. 1) : which is confirmed by a title given to it in the Septuagint—" *On the day
before the Sabbath, when the earth was founded : A Psalm of thanksgiving to* (or *for*)
David "—adopted by the Vulgate and the Oriental Versions in general. And thus
is this Psalm identified in subject with the preceding : as also Hengstenberg observes—" The reference, which it is impossible not to notice, in which ' The Lord
on high is mightier,' here (ver. 4) stands to ' But Thou, Lord, art most high for
evermore ' (Ps. xcii. 8)—the kernel and middle point of the whole Psalm—has
already led commentators to notice a near connexion between these two Psalms . . . .

which is decidedly favoured by the contents ; both Psalms minister consolation to the Church, exposed to danger by the might of the world." He might have added —in the promise they give of " the *rest* [the Sabbatism] that remains to the people of God," when both shall be fulfilled.—*W. De Burgh.*

Verse 1.—" *The Lord reigneth.*" It is a kind of proclamation in which God's people are invited to declare before men and angels that the Lord is King, he and he only. It is the response of the Church to the preaching of the gospel—so rapturously hailed in Isaiah—the preaching of the messenger " that bringeth good tidings, that publisheth peace ; that bringeth good tidings of good, that publisheth salvation ; that saith unto Zion, Thy God reigneth ! "—*William Binnie.*

Verse 1.—" *The Lord.*" He describes God by the name *Jehovah*, partly, to lead us to think of the God of Israel, accustomed by this name to be distinguished from the gods of the nations ; partly, to call to mind the virtues of veracity, grace and justice, comprehended by this name, and now clearly made known. . . . When he says, Jehovah *reigns*, without adding any restriction, or mentioning any people, it would seem that the *Kingdom of Jehovah is* to be taken absolutely and generally, with equal reference to the government of *the world* and *the church.* In the *former* sense Jehovah may be said *to reign*, not as if he then at last begun to reign, but because he proved himself to be the King of the world in an extraordinary way, by giving public and manifest signs ; by which it was clearly established that Jehovah is the true God, the Creator of heaven and earth, the Lord and Ruler of the whole universe, and a just and equitable judge, in inflicting notable judgments upon sinners, in casting down the idols, and vindicating the cause of true religion and virtue. This meaning I regard as contained in the general proposition : yet directly in its primary signification I understand the Kingdom of God in his Church, partly, because God is here said to vindicate the cause of religion, and of his people ; partly, he is said, in Ps. xcix. to show himself *exalted in Zion*, and *there to undertake the Kingdom*, Is. xxiv. 23, and often elsewhere in the Prophetic word ; and lastly, because *Jehovah*, the King of his people, he himself *who reigns*, is set forth as the *ruler* of the universe. He is the King therefore of his people, he has his *Kingdom* in their midst, but to him all things in heaven and earth are subject as well.

In this latter sense, therefore, the phrase, *Jehovah has reigned*, will stand for, *He has undertaken the Kingdom, he is become King*, as it is often used in the histories of the Kings of Judah and Israel ; so also in Is. xxiii. 23, and elsewhere. . . . When he is said to *have taken* the Kingdom in the midst of his people, it must not be understood absolutely, but in a restricted sense, in reference partly to the *manner* and form of rule, being more or less *theocratic* ; partly, to the displays of the Divine Majesty, being more or less conspicuous ; and partly, to the servile or afflicted state of his people, as extending from the Babylonish exile up to the time of the Maccabees. In which times God is said *to have taken the Kingdom*, in many other prophecies beside this, Is. xxiv., Obad. ult., Mic. iv. 8, &c.—*Venema.*

Verse 1.—" *The Lord reigneth.*" These are the initial words of Pss. xcvii. and xcix. also. Perhaps a threefold manner of reigning is suggested, namely, over things subjected to God by a natural necessity, over those that resist his will and as far as in them lies withdraw themselves from his dominion, and over those who spontaneously and freely obey. For in this place the Kingdom is declared to be co-extensive with the foundation of the world : in Ps. xcvii. it is hinted at for the exultation of the earth, and for the gladness of the isles ; in Ps. xcix. God is said to reign, although the people are angry, and the earth is filled with commotion.—*Lorinus.*

Verse 1.—" *The Lord reigneth.*" Having considered in all quarters the worldly rule of idols, and earthly deities or kings, the Psalmist at last bursts forth into the words which attribute supreme government to none other, but to Jehovah the true God. Let it be granted that the monarchs of Assyria, the kings of Egypt, and the masters of other nations, extend their empire far and wide ; let it be allowed that royal majesty is ascribed to the idols by their worshippers ; yet all these are as nothing to the kingdom and majesty of Jehovah.—*Martin Geier.*

Verse 1.—" *The Lord reigneth*," *i.e.*, the Lord has become King (Ps. xcvi. 10 ; xcvii. 1 ; xcix. 1). The formula proclaimed at *the accession* of earthly sovereigns (2 Sam. xv. 10 ; 1 Kings i. 11, 13 ; *margin*, 2 Kings ix. 13, " Jehu *reigneth* "). The reference is not to the *ordinary and constant* government of God, but to his *assuming* a *new* and glorious kingdom. The arrogant proclamation of the world-power was virtually "the Assyrian reigneth"; the overthrow of him was God's counter-proclamation: "The Lord (Jehovah) reigneth." The antitypical sense is, the world-powers under Antichrist, energized by Satan (Rev. xvi. 14; xvii. 12—14, 17), shall make one last desperate stroke, seemingly for the moment successful, for the dominion of the earth, in defiance of the Lord, (2 Thess. ii.) But Christ will take his great power and reign as King of kings and Lords of lords, having overthrown utterly the antichristian enemy. (Isai. xxiv. 23; Obad. 21; Zech. xiv. 9; Rev. xi. 15, 17; xix. 6.)—*A. R. Fausset.*

Verse 1.—"*The Lord reigneth.*" The very first words of this Psalm seem to indicate a morning of calm repose after a night of storm, a day of stillness after the tumult of battle. "The LORD reigneth." "He hath put all enemies under his feet."—*Barton Bouchier.*

Verse 1.—"*The world also is established.*" The word *world* is properly taken for the habitable globe, and metonymically for the inhabitants of the earth. This is clear from Ps. xxiv. 1; l, 2; lxxxix. 12; ix. 9; xcvi. 1, 3; xcviii. 9. In this passage the former signification seems to obtain, because this majestic King has fortified no tower or palace strongly, but the whole *world*, by the word of his power, that therein there might be a constant habitation for the men who worship him, even to the destined day of the last judgment.—*Martin Geier.*

Verse 2.—"*Thy throne is established.*" The invariable perpetuity of the divine kingdom is celebrated in these words. No vicissitudes are apprehended there, as in earthly monarchies and kingdoms, where thrones are not infrequently shaken, either on account of the death of their kings or principal men, or by reason of the unfaithfulness of subjects or ministers, or because of the schemes or attacks of enemies: none of which can disturb the divine rule.—*Martin Geier.*

Verse 2.—"*Thy throne is established of old.*" Lest any one should suspect that the royal dignity depicted and demonstrated in the previous verse by the creation of the world, which was the effect of kingly power and majesty, was a new thing or came into existence yesterday or the day before, or that God had recently obtained the office of ruling and governing, or that by long use and experience he had acquired skill, or held a somewhat foreign throne as other kings are wont, he says that this dignity is as ancient as creation itself, so that the throne of this kingdom was founded at the very time when the foundations of the earth were laid; and as the earth was established by him as his *footstool, so the heaven was his throne,* (Isai. lxvi. 1), which endures for ever. Especially does he teach that from eternity, before the formation of the world, God always remained the same in himself, not needing creation or any creature, thereby to obtain any new perfection.—*Lorinus.*

Verse 2.—"*Of old.*" The Italian, *from all eternity:* Hebrew, *from then,* an Hebrew phrase to signify an eternity without any beginning, Prov. viii. 22; as eternity without end is signified by another term, which is as much as, *until then.*— *Diodati.*

Verse 3.—"*The floods have lifted up,*" etc. Advisedly in this place does he make mention of floods, in order better to depict the effects of war. For when rivers are raised and swollen with inundations, they burst the restraining banks, and sweep far and wide over the neighbouring plains, carrying everything in their course. Such is the manner of war; when armies are despatched into countries, they lay waste and fill all places with slaughter. Whence Virgil employs this simile (Æneid II.) in describing the violence of the Grecian army breaking into the Citadel of Priam,— [rendered by Dryden thus]—

> "In rush the Greeks, and all the apartments fill;
> Those few defendents whom they find, they kill.
> Not with so fierce a rage the foaming flood
> Roars, when he finds his rapid course withstood;
> Bears down the dams with unresisted sway,
> And sweeps the cattle and the cots away."

—*Mollerus.*

Verse 3.—"*Their waves.*" The word ־, signifies a wave; because the water being dashed against a rock, or the shore, or another wave, is broken into spray. For the central idea of the word is breaking. And this aptly serves to picture the issue of those commotions and wars which are undertaken for the overthrow of empires and the church. For as mighty waves fill the beholders with horror, so great and powerful armies fill all things with fear and terror. But as the waves striking, in a moment are broken, and disappear, so the mighty power of kings and princes is often dissolved at one glance of God. The Church dwells in this life, like as a rock in the waves, beaten by the waves of every tempest ; but yet remains immutable, because the Son of God confirms and sustains her.—*Mollerus.*

Verse 4.—" *The Lord on high.*" " *On high* " is not to be regarded in the sense of locality, as none compete with God in that, but in reference to dominion and glory.—*Martin Geier.*

Verse 4.—" *The Lord on high is mightier,*" etc. Therefore consider not so much thy distress, as thy Deliverer ; and when men's malicious combination may affright thee, let Divine association support thee. The danger may exceed thy resistance, but not God's assistance ; the enemies' power may surpass thy strength, their subtlety outwit thy prudence, but neither can excel the wisdom and might of God that is with thee. O learn therefore to try God in his strength, to trust him in difficulties ; and when the merciless waves are ready to swallow thee, commit thyself to his custody. The mariner in straits looks up to heaven, do thou so ; and remember that when the waters of affliction are never so high, yet " *the Lord on high is mightier than they.*"—*Abraham Wright.*

Verse 5.—" *Thy testimonies,*" *i.e.,* thy words ; either, 1, Thy precepts, which are commonly called God's *testimonies.* And so having spoken of God's kingdom, he now showeth that the laws of that kingdom are just, and true, and holy ; which is a singular commendation of it. Or, 2, Thy promises, as may be gathered from the following words, " *are sure,*" or *true,* or *faithful* ; which attribute properly belongs, and everywhere in Scripture is ascribed, to promises rather than to precepts. And the promises no less than the precepts are God's *testimonies,* or the witnesses or declarations of his mind and will to mankind. And he seems here to speak of those great and precious promises concerning the erection and establishment of his kingdom in the world by the Messias ; which, saith he, are infallibly true, and shall certainly be accomplished in thy time.—*Matthew Pool.*

Verse 5.—" *Holiness becometh thine house, O Lord.*" Singular things are expected of all that draw nigh to God in any duty, but especially in the office of the ministry ; they must sanctify themselves with a singular care above that of the rest of the people. Those that stand in the presence of princes must be exact in their carriage. God appointed both the weights and measures of the sanctuary to be twice as large as those of the commonwealth, to shew that he expects much more of those that serve him there, than he doth of others. Holiness becomes every house well, but best God's ; and every man, but most of all the minister, who is the mirror in which the people behold heaven, and the convoy to direct them thither. Now if the glass be spotted, instead of an angel they look upon a fury ; and if the conduct be false, there is more danger in the guide than the way. None, therefore, are to walk so strictly as the ministry.—*Abraham Wright.*

Verse 5.—" *Holiness becometh thine house, O Lord, for ever.*" No hangings, no tapestry become God's house so well as holiness ; and no place is so proper as the house of God for this costly, comely furniture. . . . . The blind heathen were choice and devout in the service of dumb idols ; they served them in white, an emblem of purity ; they thought nothing too good for those false gods, for whom the worst was not bad enough. Solon, the Athenian lawgiver, enacted, that none should serve the gods *obiter,* or by the by, that their sacrificers should purify themselves some days beforehand.—*George Swinnock.*

HINTS TO PREACHERS.

Whole Psalm.—Revivals of religion described. I. God reigns. II. His power is felt. III. His kingdom is established. IV. Opposition is overcome. V. The word is valued. VI. Holiness is cultivated.

Verses 1, 2.—The prophet in the first verse describes our King ; I. From his office. 1. He " reigns." He is the great and chief Monarch ; he is no idle spectator of things below ; but wisely, and justly, and powerfully administers all things. 2. He is a glorious King : " He is clothed with majesty." 3. He is a potent King : " The Lord is clothed with strength." 4. He is a warlike King : " He hath girded himself," buckled his sword upon his armour ; for offence towards his enemies, for defence of his kingdom. II. From his kingdom. 1. It is universal : " The world." 2. It is fixed, firm, and stable : " The world also is stablished, and cannot be moved." 3. It is an everlasting kingdom : " From everlasting to everlasting ; thy throne is established of old : thou art from everlasting."—*Adam Clarke.*

Verses 1, 2.—Shew, I. The royal proclamation. II. The imperial robe. III. The stable kingdom. IV. The ancient throne. V. The Eternal King.—*C. A. D.*

Verses 1, 2.—I. Make the great proclamation. The right, stability, antiquity, extent, perpetuity of the Lord's dominion. II. Note the different emotions it inspires. In the rebellious, condemned, loyal, &c. III. Negotiate for submission to the King.—*C. A. D.*

Verse 3.—The voice of the floods. I. The voice of Nature is the voice *of* God. II. It is a voice *from* God. III. It is a voice *for* God.

> " God hath a voice that ever is heard,
> In the peal of thunder, the chirp of the bird :
> It comes in the torrent, all rapid and strong,
> In the streamlet's soft gush, as it ripples along ;
> In the waves of the ocean, the furrows of land,
> In the mountains of granite, the atom of sand ;
> Turn where ye may, from the sky to the sod,
> Where can ye gaze that ye see not a God ? "

—G. R. Poetry by Eliza Cook.

Verse 4.—I. God is mighty in creation. II. He is mightier in providence. III. He is mightiest in redemption.—*G. R.*

Verse 5.—I. Faithfulness becometh the word of God. II. Holiness becometh the house of God.—*G. R.*

Verse 5 (*last clause*).—I. Holiness becometh God's typical house, the temple. II. His greater spiritual house, the church. III. His smaller spiritual house, the believer. IV. His eternal house, heaven.—*C. A. D.*

PSALM XCIV.

SUBJECT.—*The writer sees evil-doers in power, and smarts under their oppressions. His sense of the divine sovereignty, of which he had been singing,in the previous Psalm, leads him to appeal to God as the great Judge of the earth ; this he does with much vehemence and importunity, evidently tingling under the lash of the oppressor. Confident in God's existence, and assured of his personal observation of the doings of men, the Psalmist rebukes his atheistic adversaries, and proclaims his triumph in his God : he also interprets the severe dispensation of Providence to be in very deed most instructive chastisements, and so he counts those happy who endure them. The Psalm is another pathetic form of the old enigma—" Wherefore do the wicked prosper ? " It is another instance of a good man, perplexed by the prosperity of the ungodly, cheering his heart by remembering that there is, after all, a King in heaven, by whom all things are overruled for good.*

DIVISIONS.—*In the first seven verses the Psalmist utters his complaint against wicked oppressors. From 8 to 11 he reasons against their sceptical notion that God did not notice the actions of men. He then shews that the Lord does bless his people and will deliver them, though for a while they may be chastened, 12—15. He again pleads for help in verse 16, and declares his entire dependence upon God for preservation, 17—19 ; yet a third time urges his plaint, 20, 21 ; and then concludes with the confident assurance that his enemies, and all other wicked men, would certainly be made to reap the due reward of their deeds,—" yea, the Lord our God shall cut them off."*

EXPOSITION.

O LORD God, to whom vengeance belongeth ; O God, to whom vengeance belongeth, shew thyself.

2 Lift up thyself, thou judge of the earth : render a reward to the proud.

3 LORD, how long shall the wicked, how long shall the wicked triumph ?

4 *How long* shall they utter *and* speak hard things ? *and* all the workers of iniquity boast themselves ?

5 They break in pieces thy people, O LORD, and afflict thine heritage.

6 They slay the widow and the stranger, and murder the fatherless.

7 Yet they say, The LORD shall not see, neither shall the God of Jacob regard *it*.

1. " *O Lord God, to whom vengeance belongeth ; O God, to whom vengeance belongeth, shew thyself :* " or, *God of retributions, Jehovah, God of retributions, shine forth !* A very natural prayer when innocence is trampled down, and wickedness exalted on high. If the execution of justice be a right thing,—and who can deny the fact ? —then it must be a very proper thing to desire it ; not out of private revenge, in which case a man would hardly dare to appeal to God, but out of sympathy with right, and pity for those who are made wrongfully to suffer. Who can see a nation enslaved, or even an individual downtrodden, without crying to the Lord to arise and vindicate the righteous cause ? The toleration of injustice is here attributed to the Lord's being hidden, and it is implied that the bare sight of him will suffice to alarm the tyrants into ceasing their oppressions. God has but to shew himself, and the good cause wins the day. *He* comes, he sees, he conquers ! Truly in these evil days we need a manifest display of his power, for the ancient enemies of God and man are again struggling for the mastery, and if they gain it, woe unto the saints of God.

2. " *Lift up thyself, thou judge of the earth.*" Ascend thy judgment-seat and be acknowledged as the ruler of men : and, moreover, raise thyself as men do who are about to strike with all their might ; for the abounding sin of mankind requires a heavy blow from thy hand. " *Render a reward to the proud,*" give them measure for measure, a fair retaliation, blow for blow. The proud look down upon the

gracious poor and strike them from above, as a giant might hurl down blows upon his adversary ; after the same manner, O Lord, lift up thyself, and " return a recompense upon the proud," and let them know that thou art far more above them than they can be above the meanest of their fellow men. The Psalmist thus invokes the retributions of justice in plain speech, and his request is precisely that which patient innocence puts up in silence, when her looks of anguish appeal to heaven.

3. " *Lord, how long shall the wicked, how long shall the wicked triumph ?* " Shall wrong for ever rule ? Are slavery, robbery, tyranny, never to cease ? Since there is certainly a just God in heaven, armed with almighty power, surely there must be sooner or later an end to the ascendancy of evil, innocence must one day find a defender. This " *how long ?* " of the text is the bitter plaint of all the righteous in all ages, and expresses wonder caused by that great enigma of providence, the existence and predominance of evil. The sound " how long ? " is very akin to howling, as if it were one of the saddest of all the utterances in which misery bemoans itself. Many a time has this bitter complaint been heard in the dungeons of the Inquisition, at the whipping-posts of slavery, and in the prisons of oppression. In due time God will publish his reply, but the full end is not yet.

4. " *How long shall they utter and speak hard things ?* " The ungodly are not content with deeds of injustice, but they add hard speeches, boasting, threatening, and insulting over the saints. Will the Lord for ever endure this ? Will he leave his own children much longer to be the prey of their enemies ? Will not the insolent speeches of his adversaries and theirs at last provoke his justice to interfere ? Words often wound more than swords, they are as hard to the heart as stones to the flesh ; and these are poured forth by the ungodly in redundance, for such is the force of the word translated *utter ;* and they use them so commonly that they become their common speech (they utter and speak them)—will this always be endured ? " *And all the workers of iniquity boast themselves ?* "—they even soliloquise and talk to themselves, and of themselves, in arrogance of spirit, as if they were doing some good deed when they crush the poor and needy, and spit their spite on gracious men. It is the nature of workers of iniquity to boast, just as it is a characteristic of good men to be humble—will their boasts always be suffered by the great Judge, whose ear hears all that they say ? Long, very long, have they had the platform to themselves, and loud, very loud, have been their blasphemies of God, and their railings at his saints—will not the day soon come when the threatened heritage of shame and everlasting contempt shall be meted out to them ?

Thus the oppressed plead with their Lord, and shall not God avenge his own elect ? Will he not speak out of heaven to the enemy, and say, " Why persecutest thou me ? "

5. " *They break in pieces thy people, O Lord,*" grinding them with oppression, crushing them with contempt. Yet the men they break in pieces are God's own people, and they are persecuted because they are so ; this is a strong plea for the divine interposition. " *And afflict thine heritage,*" causing them sorrowful humiliation and deep depression of heart. The term, " thine heritage," marks out the election of the saints, God's peculiar interest and delight in them, his covenant relation, of long standing, to them and their fathers ; this also is a storehouse of arguments with their faithful God. Will he not defend his own ? Will a man lose his inheritance, or permit it to be contemptuously despoiled ? Those who are ground down, and trampled on, are not strangers, but the choice and chosen ones of the Lord ; how long will he leave them to be a prey to cruel foes ?

6. " *They slay the widow and the stranger, and murder the fatherless.*" They deal most arrogantly with those who are the most evident objects of compassion. The law of God especially commends these poor ones to the kindness of good men, and it is peculiar wickedness which singles them out to be the victims not only of fraud but of murder. Must not such inhuman conduct as this provoke the Lord ? Shall the tears of widows, the groans of strangers, and the blood of orphans be poured forth in vain ? As surely as there is a God in heaven, he will visit those who perpetrate such crimes ; though he bear long with them, he will yet take vengeance, and that speedily.

7. " *Yet they say, the Lord shall not see.*" This was the reason of their arrogance, and the climax of their wickedness : they were blindly wicked because they dreamed of a blind God. When men believe that the eyes of God are dim, there is no reason to wonder that they give full license to their brutal passions. The persons mentioned above not only cherished an infidel unbelief, but dared to avow it, uttering the

monstrous doctrine that God is too far away to take notice of the actions of men. " *Neither shall the God of Jacob regard it.*" Abominable blasphemy and transparent falsehood ! If God has actually become his people's God, and proved his care for them by a thousand acts of grace, how dare the ungodly assert that he will not notice the wrongs done to them ? There is no limit to the proud man's profanity, reason itself cannot restrain him ; he has broken through the bounds of common sense. Jacob's God heard him at the brook Jabbok ; Jacob's God led him and kept him all his life long, and said concerning him and his family, " Touch not mine anointed, and do my prophets no harm ; " and yet these brutish ones profess to believe that he neither sees nor regards the injuries wrought upon the elect people ! Surely in such unbelievers is fulfilled the saying of the wise, that those whom the Lord means to destroy he leaves to the madness of their corrupt hearts.

8 Understand, ye brutish among the people : and *ye* fools, when will ye be wise ?

9 He that planted the ear, shall he not hear ? he that formed the eye, shall he not see ?

10 He that chastiseth the heathen, shall not he correct ? he that teacheth man knowledge, *shall not he know ?*

11 The LORD knoweth the thoughts of man, that they *are* vanity.

8. " *Understand, ye brutish among the people.*" They said that God did not *note*, and now, using the same word in the original, the Psalmist calls on the wicked to *note*, and have regard to the truth. He designates them as boors, boarish, swinish men, and well was the term deserved ; and he bids them understand or consider, if they can. They thought themselves to be wise, and indeed the only men of wit in the world, but he calls them " boars among the people " : wicked men are fools, and the more they know, the more foolish they become. " No fool like a learned fool " is a true proverb. When a man has done with God, he has done with his manhood, and has fallen to the level of the ox and the ass, yea, beneath them, for " the ox knoweth his owner, and the ass his master's crib." Instead of being humbled in the presence of scientific infidels, we ought to pity them ; they affect to look down upon us, but we have far more cause to look down upon them. " *And ye fools, when will ye be wise ?*" Is it not high time ? Ye know the ways of folly, what profit have ye in them ? Have ye no relics of reason left ? no shreds of sense ? If as yet there lingers in your minds a gleam of intelligence, hearken to argument, and consider the questions now about to be proposed to you.

9. " *He that planted the ear, shall he not hear ?*" He fashioned that marvellous organ, and fixed it in the most convenient place near to the brain, and is he deaf himself ? Is he capable of such design and invention, and yet can he not discern what is done in the world which he made ? He made you hear, can he not himself hear ? Unanswerable question ! It overwhelms the sceptic, and covers him with confusion. " *He that formed the eye, shall he not see ?*" He gives us vision ; is it conceivable that he has no sight himself ? With skilful hand he fashioned the optic nerve, and the eyeball, and all its curious mechanism, and it surpasses all conception that he can himself be unable to observe the doings of his creatures. If there be a God, he must be a personal intelligent being, and no limit can be set to his knowledge.

10. " *He that chastiseth the heathen, shall not he correct ?*" He reproves whole nations, can he not reprove individuals ? All history shows that he visits national sin with national judgment, and can he not deal with single persons ? The question which follows is equally full of force, and is asked with a degree of warmth which checks the speaker, and causes the inquiry to remain incomplete. It begins, " *He that teacheth man knowledge,*" and then it comes to a pause, which the translators have supplied with the words, " *shall not he know ?*" but no such words are in the original, where the sentence comes to an abrupt end, as if the inference were too natural to need to be stated, and the writer had lost patience with the brutish men with whom he had argued. The earnest believer often feels as if he could say, " Go to, you are not worth arguing with ! If you were reasonable men, these things would be too obvious to need to be stated in your hearing. I forbear." Man's knowledge comes from God. Science in its first principles was taught to our progenitor Adam,

and all after advances have been due to divine aid ; does not the author and revealer of all knowledge himself know ?

11. Whether men admit or deny that God knows, one thing is here declared, namely, that " *The Lord knoweth the thoughts of man, that they are vanity.*" Not their words alone are heard, and their works seen, but he reads the secret motions of their minds, for men themselves are not hard to be discerned of him, before his glance they themselves are but vanity. It is in the Lord's esteem no great matter to know the thoughts of such transparent pieces of vanity as mankind are, he sums them up in a moment as poor vain things. This is the sense of the original, but that given in the authorised version is also true—the thoughts, the best part, the most spiritual portion of man's nature, even these are vanity itself, and nothing better. Poor man ! And yet such a creature as this boasts, plays at monarch, tyrannises over his fellow worms, and defies his God ! Madness is mingled with human vanity, like smoke with the fog, to make it fouler but not more substantial than it would have been alone.

How foolish are those who think that God does not know their actions, when the truth is that their vain thoughts are all perceived by him ! How absurd to make nothing of God when in fact we ourselves are as nothing in his sight.

12 Blessed *is* the man whom thou chastenest, O LORD, and teachest him out of thy law ;

13 That thou mayest give him rest from the days of adversity, until the pit be digged for the wicked.

14 For the LORD will not cast off his people, neither will be forsake his inheritance.

15 But judgment shall return unto righteousness : and all the upright in heart shall follow it.

12. " *Blessed is the man whom thou chastenest, O Lord.*" The Psalmist's mind is growing quiet. He no longer complains to God or argues with men, but tunes his harp to softer melodies, for his faith perceives that with the most afflicted believer all is well. Though he may not feel blessed while smarting under the rod of chastisement, yet blessed he is ; he is precious in God's sight, or the Lord would not take the trouble to correct him, and right happy will the results of his correction be. The Psalmist calls the chastened one a " *man* " in the best sense, using the Hebrew word which implies strength. He is a man, indeed, who is under the teaching and training of the Lord. " *And teachest him out of thy law.*" The book and the rod, the law and the chastening, go together, and are made doubly useful by being found in connection. Affliction without the word is a furnace for the metal, but there is no flux to aid the purifying : the word of God supplies that need, and makes the fiery trial effectual. After all, the blessing of God belongs far rather to those who suffer under the divine hand than to those who make others suffer : better far to lie and cry out as a " man " under the hand of our heavenly Father, than to roar and rave as a brute, and to bring down upon one's self a death blow from the destroyer of evil. The afflicted believer is under tuition, he is in training for something higher and better, and all that he meets with is working out his highest good, therefore is he a blessed man, however much his outward circumstances may argue the reverse.

13. " *That thou mayest give him rest from the days of adversity, until the pit be digged for the wicked.*" The chastening hand and instructive book are sanctified to us, so that we learn to rest in the Lord. We see that his end is our everlasting benefit, and therefore abide quiet under all trying providences and bitter persecutions, waiting our time. The Mighty Hunter is preparing the pit for the brutish ones ; they are prowling about at this time, and tearing the sheep, but they will soon be captured and destroyed, therefore the people of the Lord learn to rest in days of adversity, and tarry the leisure of their God. Wicked men may not yet be ripe for punishment, nor punishment ready for them : hell is a prepared place for a prepared people ; as days of grace ripen saints for glory, so days of wantonness help sinners to rot into the corruption of eternal destruction.

14. " *For the Lord will not cast off his people.*" He may cast them down, but he never can cast them off. During fierce persecutions the saints have been apt to think that the Lord had left his own sheep, and given them over to the wolf ; but

it has never been so, nor shall it ever be, for the Lord will not withdraw his love, "*neither will he forsake his inheritance.*" For a time he may leave his own with the design of benefiting them thereby, yet never can he utterly desert them.

> "He may chasten and correct,
> But he never can neglect ;
> May in faithfulness reprove,
> But he ne'er can cease to love."

15. "*But judgment shall return unto righteousness.*" The great Judge will come, the reign of righteousness will commence, the course of affairs will yet be turned into the right channel, and then all the godly will rejoice. The chariot of right will be drawn in triumph through our streets, "*and all the upright in heart shall follow it,*" as in gladsome procession. A delightful hope is here expressed in poetic imagery of much beauty. The government of the world has been for a while in the hands of those who have used it for the basest and most vicious ends ; but the cry of prayer will bring back righteousness to the throne, and then every upright heart will have its portion of joy.

16 Who will rise up for me against the evildoers ? *or* who will stand up for me against the workers of iniquity ?

Notwithstanding the Psalmist's persuasion that all would be well eventually, he could not at the time perceive any one who would stand side by side with him in opposing evil ; no champion of the right was forthcoming, the faithful failed from among men. This also is a bitter trial, and a sore evil under the sun ; yet it has its purpose, for it drives the heart still more completely to the Lord, compelling it to rest alone in him. If we could find friends elsewhere, it may be our God would not be so dear to us ; but when, after calling upon heaven and earth to help, we meet with no succour but such as comes from the eternal arm, we are led to prize our God, and rest upon him with undivided trust. Never is the soul safer or more at rest than when, all other helpers failing, she leans upon the Lord alone. The verse before us is an appropriate cry, now that the church sees error invading her on all sides, while faithful ministers are few, and fewer still are bold enough to " stand up " and defy the enemies of truth. Where are our Luthers and our Calvins ? A false charity has enfeebled the most of the valiant men of Israel. One John Knox would be worth a mint at this hour, but where is he ? Our grand consolation is that the God of Knox and Luther is yet with us, and in due time will call out his chosen champions.

17 Unless the LORD *had been* my help, my soul had almost dwelt in silence.
18 When I said, My foot slippeth ; thy mercy, O LORD, held me up.
19 In the multitude of my thoughts within me thy comforts delight my soul.

17. "*Unless the Lord had been my help, my soul had almost dwelt in silence.*" Without Jehovah's help the Psalmist declares that he should have died outright, and gone into the silent land, where no more testimonies can be borne for the living God. Or he may mean that he would not have had a word to speak against his enemies, but would have been wrapped in speechless shame. Blessed be God, we are not left to that condition yet, for the Almighty Lord is still the helper of all those who look to him. Our inmost soul is bowed down when we see the victories of the Lord's enemies—we cannot brook it, we cover our mouths in confusion ; but he will yet arise and avenge his own cause, therefore have we hope.

18. "*When I said, My foot slippeth*"—is slipping even now : I perceived my danger, and cried out in horror, and then, at the very moment of my extremity, came the needed help, "*thy mercy, O Lord, held me up.*" Often enough is this the case, we feel our weakness, and see our danger, and in fear and trembling we cry out. At such times nothing can help us but *mercy* ; we can make no appeal to any fancied merit, for we feel that it is our inbred sin which makes our feet so ready to fail us ; our joy is that mercy endureth for ever, and is always at hand to pluck us out of the danger, and hold us up, where else we should fall to our destruction. Ten thousand times has this verse been true in relation to some of us, and especially to the writer of this comment. The danger was imminent, it was upon us, we were

going ; the peril was apparent, we saw it, and were aghast at the sight ; our own heart was failing, and we concluded that it was all over with us ; but then came the almighty interposition : we did not fall, we were held up by an unseen hand, the devices of the enemy were frustrated, and we sang for joy. O faithful Keeper of our souls, be thou extolled for ever and ever ! We will bless the Lord at all times, his praise shall continually be in our mouths.

19. *" In the multitude of my thoughts within me."* When I am tossed to and fro with various reasonings, distractions, questionings, and forebodings, I will fly to my true rest, for *" thy comforts delight my soul."* From my sinful thoughts, my vain thoughts, my sorrowful thoughts, my griefs, my cares, my conflicts, I will hasten to the Lord ; he has divine *comforts*, and these will not only console but actually *delight* me. How sweet are the comforts of the Spirit ! Who can muse upon eternal love, immutable purposes, covenant promises, finished redemption, the risen Saviour, his union with his people, the coming glory, and such like themes, without feeling his heart leaping with joy ? The little world within is, like the great world without, full of confusion and strife ; but when Jesus enters it, and whispers " Peace be unto you," there is a calm, yea, a rapture of bliss. Let us turn away from the mournful contemplation of the oppression of man and the present predominance of the wicked, to that sanctuary of pure rest which is found in the God of all comfort.

20 Shall the throne of iniquity have fellowship with thee, which frameth mischief by a law ?

21 They gather themselves together against the soul of the righteous, and condemn the innocent blood.

20. *" Shall the throne of iniquity have fellowship with thee ? "* Such thrones there are, and they plead a right divine, but their claim is groundless, a fraud upon mankind and a blasphemy of heaven. God enters into no alliance with unjust authority, he gives no sanction to unrighteous legislation. *" Which frameth mischief by a law ? "* They legalise robbery and violence, and then plead that it is the law of the land ; and so indeed it may be, but it is a wickedness for all that. With great care men prepare enactments intended to put down all protests, so as to render wrong-doing a permanent institution, but one element is necessary to true conservatism, viz., righteousness ; and lacking that, all their arrangements of the holders of power must come to an end, and all their decrees must in process of time be wiped out of the statute-book. Nothing can last for ever but impartial right. No injustice can be permanent, for God will not set his seal upon it, nor have any fellowship with it, and therefore down it must come, and happy shall be the day which sees it fall.

21. *" They gather themselves together against the soul of the righteous,"* so many are there of them that they crowd their assemblies, and carry their hard measures with enthusiasm ; they are the popular party, and are eager to put down the saints. In counsel, and in action, they are unanimous ; their one resolve is to hold their own tyrannical position, and put down the godly party. *" And condemn the innocent blood."* They are great at slander and false accusation, nor do they stick at murder ; no crime is too great for them, if only they can trample on the servants of the Lord. This description is historically true in reference to persecuting times ; it has been fulfilled in England, and may be again if Popery is to advance in future time at the same rate as in the past few years. The dominant sect has the law on its side, and boasts that it is the national church ; but the law which establishes and endows one religion rather than another is radically an injustice, God has no fellowship with it, and therefore the synagogue of Ritualism will yet be a stench in the nostrils of all sane men. What evil times are in store for us it is not for us to prophesy ; it is ours to leave the matter in the hands of him who cannot be in fellowship with an oppressive system, and will not always endure to be insulted to his face by Popish idols, and their priests.

22 But the LORD is my defence ; and my God *is* the rock of my refuge.

23 And he shall bring upon them their own iniquity, and shall cut them off in their own wickedness ; *yea,* the LORD our God shall cut them off.

22. Let the wicked gather as they may, the Psalmist is not afraid, but sweetly sings, *" The Lord is my defence; and my God is the rock of my refuge."* Firm as a rock is Jehovah's love, and there do we betake ourselves for shelter. In him, even

in him alone, we find safety, let the world rage as it may ; we ask not aid from man, but are content to flee into the bosom of omnipotence.

23. The natural result of oppression is the destruction of the despot ; his own iniquities crush him ere long. Providence arranges retaliations as remarkable as they are just. High crimes in the end bring on heavy judgments, to sweep away evil men from off the face of the earth ; yea, God himself interposes in a special manner, and cuts short the career of tyrants while they are in the very midst of their crimes. Wicked men are often arrested by the pursuivants of divine justice redhanded, with the evidences of their guilt upon them. " *He shall bring upon them their own iniquity, and shall cut them off in their own wickedness.*" While the stolen bread is in their mouths wrath slays them, while the illgotten wedge of gold is yet in their tent judgment overtakes them. God himself conspicuously visits them, and reveals his own power in their overthrow, " *yea, the Lord our God shall cut them off.*"

Here, then, the matter ends ; faith reads the present in the light of the future, and ends her song without a trembling note.

EXPLANATORY NOTES AND QUAINT SAYINGS.

Verse 1.—" *O Lord God, to whom vengeance belongeth.*" It may perhaps seem to accord too little with a lover of piety, so strenuously to urge upon God to show himself an avenger against the wicked, and to rouse him as if he were lingering and procrastinating. But this supplication must be regarded in its proper bearing : for David does not pray, neither should we pray, that God would take vengeance on the wicked in the same way that men, inflamed with anger and hatred, are wont often to avenge themselves of their enemies, but that he would punish them after his own divine manner and measure. The vengeance of God is for the most part a medicine for the evil ; but ours is at times destruction even to the good. Therefore truly the Lord is alone the God of revenges. For we, when we think we have inflicted a penalty upon our enemy, are often much mistaken. What injury to us was the body of our enemy ? in depriving him of which we nevertheless express all our bitterness. What wounded thee and wrought thee harm and shame, was the spirit of thine enemy, and that thou art not able to seize and hold, but God is able ; and he alone has such power that in no way can the spirit escape his strength and force. Leave vengeance with him, and he will repay. He admonishes us, that if we ourselves wish to be avengers of our own pains and injuries we may hurt ourselves more deeply than our enemy : for when we take vengeance on him, we indeed wound and do violence to his body, which in itself is vile and of little regard ; but in our own best and most precious part, that is, in our spirit ; we ourselves, by losing patience, receive a deep stain, because when virtue and humanity have been expelled thence, we meanwhile incur faults to be atoned for therein. Wherefore God is entreated to become himself the avenger of our injuries, for he alone knows aright and is able to avenge ; and to become such an avenger that only the very thing which injured us may be punished. Some greedy man has cheated thee in money, may he punish avarice in him. A proud man has treated thee with scorn, may he destroy his pride, etc. . . . This is vengeance most worthy to be inflicted of God, and by us to be sought.—*Jacopo Sadoleto,* 1477—1547.

Verse 1.—I do not think that we sufficiently attend to the distinction that exists between revenge and vengeance. " Revenge," says Dr. Johnson, " is an act of passion, vengeance of justice ; injuries are revenged, crimes avenged." And it is from not attending to this essential distinction that the scorner has been led into such profane remarks, as if there were a vindictive spirit in the Almighty, and as if he found delight in wreaking vengeance on an adversary. The call which the Psalmist here makes on God as a God to whom vengeance belongeth, is no other than if he had said, " O God, to whom justice belongeth ! " Vengeance indeed is not for man, because with man's feelings and propensities it would ever degenerate into revenge. " I will be even with him," says nature ; " I will be above him," says grace.—*Barton Bouchier.*

Verse 1.—The two divine names (*El* and *Jehovah,*—*God* and *Lord*) recognize

God as almighty, eternal, self-existent, bound by covenant to his people, and alone entitled to take vengeance.—*J. A. Alexander.*

Verses 1—6.—

> "Avenge, O Lord, thy slaughter'd saints, whose bones
> Lie scatter'd on the Alpine mountains cold ;
> Even them who kept thy truth so pure of old,
> When all our fathers worshipt stocks and stones,
> Forget not : in thy book record their groans
> Who were thy sheep, and in their ancient fold
> Slain by the bloody Piemontese that roll'd
> Mother with infant down the rocks.   Their moans
> The vales redoubled to the hills, and they
> To heaven.   Their martyr'd blood and ashes sow
> O'er all the Italian fields, where still doth sway
> The triple Tyrant ; that from these may grow
> A hundredfold, who, having learn'd the way,
> Early may fly the Babylonian woe."
>
> *John Milton.*

Verse 3.—" How long shall the wicked, how long," etc.   Twice he saith it, because the wicked boast day after day, with such insolency and outrage, as if they were above control.—*John Trapp.*

Verse 3.—" How long shall the wicked triumph ? "   For " *triumph*," the Hebrew word is עלז which signifies *to exalt.*   That is, they give themselves vain applause on account of their prosperity, and declare their success both with words and with the gestures of their body, like peacocks spreading their feathers.   " *How long shall they utter ? "* etc.   For " *utter* " the Hebrew is יביע, *they shall flow, they shall cast forth.*   The metaphor is taken from fountains springing out of the rock with a rush and abundance of water.   Where the abundance of words is noted, their rashness, their waste and profusion, their sound and eagerness, their continuance and the difficulty of obstructing them.—*Le Blanc.*

Verse 3.—" How long shall the wicked triumph ? "   What answer shall we give, what date shall we put to this, " *How long ? "*   The answer is given in verse 23, " *He shall bring upon them their own iniquity, and shall cut them off in their own wickedness,"* etc.   As if he had said, Except the Lord cut them off in their wickedness, they will never leave off doing wickedly.   They are men of such a kind that there is no curing of them, they will never have done doing mischief until they be cut off by death, therefore God threatens death to deter men from sin.   A godly man saith, " If God kill me, yet will I trust in him ; " and some wicked men say (in effect, if not in the letter), Till God kills us we will sin against him.—*Joseph Caryl.*

Verses 3, 4.—" Triumph," " utter and speak," " boast."   In the very terms wherein the Psalmist complains of the continued prevalence of the wicked, there is matter of comfort, for we have three (rather four, as in the authorised version) words to denote speaking, and only one, *workers,* to denote action, showing us that they are far more powerful with their tongues than with their hands.—*Hugo Cardinalis, quoted by Neale.*

Verse 5.—" They break in pieces thy people."   They tread down ; they grind ; they crush.   The Hebrew word is often used as meaning to crush under foot ; to trample on ; and hence it means to oppress.   Lam. iii. 34, Isai. iii. 15.—*Albert Barnes.*

Verse 6.—" Widow " ; " fatherless."   An old Jewish writer * has pointed out how aptly the titles of *widow* and *orphan* befitted the Hebrew nation, because it had no helper save God only, and was cut off from all other people by its peculiar rites and usages, whereas the Gentiles, by their mutual alliances and intercourse, had, as it were, a multitude of kindred to help them in any strait.—*J. M. Neale.*

Verse 7.—" They say, The Lord shall not see."   As if they had said, Though God should set himself to search us out, and would greatly wish to see what we are doing, yet he shall not.   We will carry it so closely and cunningly, that the eye of God shall not reach us.   Their works were so foul and bloody, that the sun might be

---

* Philo Judæus.

ashamed to look upon them, and they were so secret that they believed God could not look upon them, or bring them to shame for them.—*Joseph Caryl.*

Verse 7.—" *The Lord . . . the God of Jacob.*" The divine names are, as usual, significant. That the self-existent and eternal God should not see, is a palpable absurdity ; and scarcely less so, that the God of Israel should suffer his own people to be slaughtered without even observing it. The last verb means to mark, note, notice.—*J. A. Alexander.*

Verses 8—11.—In these words the following particulars are to be observed. (1.) A certain spiritual *disease* charged on *some* persons, *viz.* darkness, and *blindness* of mind, appearing in their ignorance and folly. (2.) The great *degree* of this disease ; so as to render the subjects of it *fools.* " *Ye fools, when will ye be wise ?*" And so as to reduce them to a degree of *brutishness.* " *Ye brutish among the people.*" This ignorance and folly were to such a degree as to render men like beasts. (3.) The *obstinacy* of this disease ; expressed in that interrogation, " *When will ye be wise ?*" Their blindness and folly were not only very great, but deeply rooted and established, resisting all manner of cure. (4.) Of what *nature* this blindness is. It is especially in things pertaining to God. They were strangely *ignorant* of his perfections, like beasts ; and had *foolish* notions of him, as though he did not see, nor know : and as though he would not execute justice, by chastising and punishing wicked men. (5.) The *unreasonableness* and *sottishness* of the notion they had of God, that he did not *hear*, did not *observe* their reproaches of him and his people, is shown by observing that he *planted* the ear. It is very *unreasonable* to suppose that he who gave power of perceiving words to *others*, should not perceive them himself. And the sottishness of their being insensible of God's all-seeing eye, and particularly of his seeing their wicked actions, appears, in that God is the being who *formed* the eye, and gave others a *power* of seeing. The sottishness of their apprehension of God, as though he did not know what they did, is argued from his being the *fountain* and original of all knowledge. The unreasonableness of their expecting to escape God's just chastisements and judgments for sin, is set forth by his chastising even the *heathen*, who did not sin against that light, or against so great mercies, as the wicked in Israel did ; nor had ever made such a profession as they. (6.) We may observe, that this dreadful disease is ascribed to *mankind in general.* " *The Lord knoweth the thoughts of* MAN, *that they are vanity.*" The Psalmist had been setting forth the vanity and unreasonableness of the thoughts of *some* of the children of men ; and immediately upon it he observes, that this vanity and foolishness of thought is *common* and *natural* to mankind. From these particulars we may fairly deduce the following doctrinal observation : *That there is an extreme and brutish blindness in things of religion, which naturally possesses* the *hearts of mankind.*—*Jonathan Edwards.*

Verses 8—15.—God hath ability, bowels, verity. Ability, *He that made the eye, cannot he see ? He that planted the ear, cannot he hear ?* verses 8, 9, 10, 11. Bowels, *He doth but chasten his, not cast them off*, verses 12, 13, 14. Verity, *this is but until a pit be made for the wicked*, verse 13. *Mordecai* is frowned upon, but till a gallows be made for Haman, and then *judgment returns unto righteousness.*—*Nicholas Lockyer.*

Verse 9.—" *He that planted the ear, shall he not hear ?* " etc. The Psalmist does not say, He that planteth the ear, *hath he not an ear ?* He that formed the eye, *hath he not eyes ?* No ; but, Shall he not *hear ?* Shall he not *see ?* And why does he say so ? To prevent the error of humanizing God, of attributing members or corporeal parts to the infinite Spirit.—*Adam Clarke.*

Verse 9.—" *Planted the ear.*" The mechanism of the ear, like a root *planted* in the earth, is sunk deep into the head, and concealed from view.—*Bagster's Comprehensive Bible.*

Verse 9.—The *planting* or deep seated position of the ear, as well as its wonderful construction, are illustrated by the following extract :—" The organ or instrument of hearing is in all its most important parts so hidden within the head, that we cannot perceive its construction by a mere external inspection. What in ordinary language we call the ear, is only the outer porch or entrance-vestibule of a curious series of intricate, winding passages, which, like the lobbies of a great building, lead from the outer air into the inner chambers. Certain of these passages are full of air ; others are full of liquid ; and their membranes are stretched like parchment curtains across the corridors at different places, and can be thrown into vibration, or made to tremble, as the head of a drum or the surface of a tambourine does when struck with a stick or the fingers. Between two of these parchment-like curtains, a chain of very small bones extends, which serves to tighten or relax these membranes, and to communicate vibrations to them. In the innermost place of all, rows of fine threads, called nerves, stretch like the strings of a piano from the last points to which the tremblings or thrillings reach, and pass inwards to the brain. If these threads or nerves are destroyed, the power of hearing as infallibly departs as the power to give out sound is lost by a piano or violin when its strings are broken. We know far less, however, of the ear than of the eye. The eye is a single chamber open to the light, and we can see into it, and observe what happens there. But the ear is many-chambered, and its winding tunnels traversing the rock-like bones of the skull are narrow, and hidden from us as the dungeons of a castle are, like which, also, they are totally dark. Thus much, however, we know, that it is in the innermost recesses of these unilluminated ivory vaults, that the mind is made conscious of sound. Into these gloomy cells, as into the bright chamber of the eye, the soul is ever passing and asking for news from the world without ; and ever and anon, as of old in hidden subterranean caverns where men listened in silence and darkness to the utterance of oracles, reverberations echo along the surrounding walls, and responses come to the waiting spirit, whilst the world lifts up its voice and speaks to the soul. The sound is that of a hushed voice, a low but clear whisper ; for as it is but a dim shadow of the outer world we see ; so it is but a faint echo of the outer world we hear."—*George Wilson, in " The Five Gateways of Knowledge,"* 1861.

Verse 9.—*" He that planted the ear, &c."* Shall the Author of these senses be senseless ? Our God is not as that Jupiter of Crete, who was pictured without ears, and could not be at leisure to attend upon small matters. He is οὖς καὶ νοῦ ; he is also ὁλοφθαλμὸς, all eye, all ear. We read of a people called *Panotii* ; God only is so, to speak properly.—*John Trapp.*

Verse 9.—*" Formed the eye."* The term used of the creation of the eye, is not merely *" made,"* as the Prayer Book version reads, but *" formed,"* πλάσας, *finxit,* directing our attention to the wonderful mechanism of the organs of sight, and thence to the marvellous skill of the Artificer.—*J. M. Neale.*

Verse 9.—*" He that formed the eye."* The word here used is frequently employed in reference to a *potter* ; and the idea is that God has moulded or formed the eye as the potter fashions the clay. The more the eye is studied in its structure, the more deeply shall we be impressed with the wonderful skill and wisdom of God.— *Albert Barnes.*

Verse 9.—*" The eye."* As illustrating the wisdom displayed in the eye we have selected the following. " Our physical good demands that we should have the power of comprehending the world in all the respects in which it is possible for matter or its forces to affect our bodies. The senses completely meet this want. . . . . We are too apt to confine ourselves to the mere mechanism of the eye or ear, without considering how the senses supplement each other, and without considering the provision made in the world that it may be a fit place for the exercise of the senses. The eye would be useless without all the properties of light ; the ear would have no power in a world without an atmosphere. Sight enables us to avoid danger, and seek distant needful objects. What a vast length of time and wearisome labour would it require for a blind man to learn what one glance of the eye may give to one blessed with sight. A race of blind men could not exist on this globe.

The sense of sight alone, as a means of adapting us to the world, would strike us as wonderful in its results, and worthy of the conception of the highest intelligence in adapting means to ends, if we knew nothing of the adjustments by which sight is secured. We can conceive of the power of sight as direct perception, without the aid of light, or of a special organ corresponding to the eye. But constituted as we are, we see only through the agency of light ; and we perceive light only by a special organ ; and objects only in consequence of a peculiar structure of that organ. Of all these relationships of light to objects, and of light to the eye, and of the parts of the eye to each other, not one of them is a necessary condition of matter. The arrangement of so many things by which this wonderful power of perceiving distant objects is secured, is the only one that will secure the end desired, out of an endless number of arrangements that can be conceived of. . . . . Whoever contrived the organ through which we are to perceive, understood perfectly all the properties of light, and the wants of the being that was to use it. The eye of man, though limited in its power to a certain range, gives all that the common wants of life demand. And if man needs greater range of vision, he has but to study the eye itself, and fashion instruments to increase its power; as he is able when the proper time has come in his civilization, to increase by science and art the efficacy of nearly all his physical powers. For the ordinary purposes of life, neither telescopic nor microscopic adjustment of the eye is needful.

But the eye has not only the power of vision so necessary to man, but it is an instrument of power, an instrument made up of distinct parts, of solids and liquids, of transparent and opaque tissues, of curtains, and lenses, and screens. Its mechanism can be accurately examined and the use of each part as perfectly understood as any of the works of man. We examine every part of it as we would a microscope. We have first the solid case which is to hold all the machinery, and upon which are to be fastened the cords and pulleys of its skilful mounting. This covering, opaque, white, and glistening, like silver on the back and sides of the eye, in front, where the light must enter, suddenly becomes transparent as the clearest crystal. Within this is a second coating that coming to the front changes just as suddenly into an opaque screen, through the tissues of which no ray of light can pass. That screen is self-adjusting, with a net-work that no art of man ever equalled. Whether expanding or contracting, its opening in the centre always remains a perfect circle, adapted in size to the intensity of the light. How much light shall enter the eye it determines without aid from us. Next there must be connection with the brain, the seat of the being for whom the provision is made. These two coatings are pierced upon the back part of the eye, and a thread drawn out from the brain is passed through this opening and spread out within the eye as a delicate screen upon which all impressions are to be made. To fill the larger portion of the cavity, there is packed into it a clear jelly, and imbedded in this a lens, fashioned with a skill that no artist can equal, to refract the light and throw the image on the perceptive screen. In front of this lens is another humor, not like jelly as the other, because in this, that delicate fringe the iris, is to float, and nothing but a watery fluid will answer its purpose. Here then we have a great variety of materials all brought together, of the exact quality and in the quantity needed, placed in the exact position which they ought to occupy, so perfectly adjusted that the most that man can do is to imitate the eye without ever hoping to equal it.

Nor is the curious structure of the eye itself all that is worthy of our attention. The instrument when finished must be mounted for use. A cavity is formed in solid bone, with grooves and perforations for all the required machinery. The eye, when placed, is packed with soft elastic cushions and fastened by strings and pulleys to give it variety and rapidity of motion. Its outer case is to cover it when not in use, and protect it when in danger. The delicate fringe upon its border never needs clipping ; and set like a well-arranged defence, its points all gracefully turned back, that no ray of light may be obstructed. Above the protecting brow is another defence to turn aside the acrid fluids from the forehead, while near the eye is placed a gland that bathes the whole organ with a clear soothing fluid, to prevent all friction and keep its outward lens free from dust, and polished for constant use. When we consider all this, the perfect adaptation of the eye to our wants, the arrangement of every part of its structure on strict mechanical and optical principles, and all the provisions for its protection, we pronounce the instrument perfect, the work of a Being like man, but raised immeasurably above the most skilful human workman. What shall we say when we learn that this instrument was prepared in long anticipation of its use ; that there is a machinery within it to keep it in constant repair ; that the Maker not only adjusted the materials, but that he was the chemist who formed all these substances from the dust of the earth ? We may be told that the architect found this dust ready at hand, existing from all eternity. We may not be able to prove the contrary, nor do we need to do so for this argument. It is enough for our present purpose to know that the eyes with which we now see, these wonderfully complex and perfect instruments, were not long since common earth, dust upon which we perchance have trod.

We can understand the mechanism of the eye, we can comprehend the wisdom that devised it ; but the preparation of materials, and the adjustment of parts, speak of a power and skill to which man can never hope to attain. When he sees his most cunning workmanship surpassed both in plan and execution, shall he fail to recognise design ? Shall we fail to recognise a builder when we contemplate such a work ? "—*P. A. Chadbourne, in " Lectures on Natural Theology ; or, Nature and the Bible from the same Author. New York, 1867."*

Verse 9.—" *Shall he not see ?*" A god or a saint that should really cast the glance of a pure eye into the conscience of the worshipper would not long be held in repute. The grass would grow again around that idol's shrine. A seeing god would not do : the idolater wants a blind god. The first cause of idolatry is a desire in an impure heart to escape from the look of the living God, and none but a dead image would serve the turn.—*William Arnot.*

Verse 9.—He who made the sun itself, and causes it to revolve, being a small portion of his works, if compared with the whole, is he unable to perceive all things ? —*Epictetus.*

Verse 9.—That is wise counsel of the Rabbins, that the three best safeguards against falling into sin are to remember, first, that there is an ear which hears everything ; secondly, that there is an eye which sees everything ; thirdly, that there is a hand which writes everything in the Book of Knowledge, which shall be opened at the Judgment.—*J. M. Neale.*

Verses 9, 10.—It was no limited power that could make this eye to see, this ear to hear, this heart to understand ; and, if that eye which he hath given us, can see all things that are within our prospect, and that ear, that he hath planted, can hear all sounds that are within our compass, and that heart, that he hath given us, can know all matters within the reach of our comprehension ; how much more shall the sight, and hearing, and knowledge of that Infinite Spirit, which can admit of no bounds, extend to all the actions and events of all the creatures, that lie open before him that made them !—*Joseph Hall.*

Verse 10.—" *He that teacheth man knowledge——.*" The question posts midway (for the words in Italics are not Scripture), the point of application being too obvious to need mention. " He that teacheth man all his knowledge." [Fill out the rest yourselves : think, What then ?]—*Henry Cowles.*

Verse 10.—" *He that teacheth man knowledge.*" What knowledge have we but that which is derived from himself, or from the external world ?—and what is that world, but his Creation ?—and what is creation, but the composition, structure, and arrangement of all things according to his previous designs, plans, intentions, will, and mandate ? In studying creation in any of its departments, we therefore study his mind : and all that we can learn from it must be his ideas, his purposes, and his performances. No author, in his compositions—no artificer, in his mechanisms, can more truly display their talents and ideas to others, than the unseen Creator manifests his thoughts and intelligence to us in the systems and substances which he has formed, and presents to our continual contemplation. In this sense, Nature is an unceasing revelation of them to us.—*Sharon Turner.*

Verse 11.—" *The Lord knoweth the thoughts.*" The thoughts of man's heart— what millions are there of them in a day ! The twinkling of the eye is not so sudden a thing as the twinkling of a thought ; yet those thousands and thousands of thoughts which pass from thee, that thou canst not reckon, they are all known to God.— *Anthony Burgess.*

Verse 11.—" *The Lord knoweth the thoughts of man, that they are vanity.*" What a humbling thought is here suggested to us ! Let us examine it.

1. If vanity had been ascribed to the meaner parts of the creation—if all inanimate and irrational beings, whose days are as a shadow, and who know not whence they came nor whither they go, had thus been characterized—it had little more than accorded with our own ideas. But the humiliating truth belongs to man, the *lord* of the lower creation—to man, that distinguished link in the chain of being which unites in his person mortality and immortality, heaven and earth. " The LORD knoweth the thoughts of *man*, that they are vanity."

2. Had vanity been ascribed only to the exercise of our sensual or mortal part, or of that which we possess in common with other animals, it had been less humiliating. But the charge is pointed at that which is the peculiar glory of man, the intellectual part, his *thoughts*. It is here, if anywhere, that we excel the creatures which are placed around us. We can contemplate our own existence, dive into the past and the future, and understand whence we came and whither we go. Yet in this tender part we are touched. Even the " *thoughts* " of man are vanity.

3. If vanity had been ascribed merely to those loose and trifling excursions of

the imagination which fall not under the influence of choice, a kind of comers and goers, which are ever floating in the mind, like insects in the air on a summer's evening, it had been less affecting. The soul of man seems to be necessarily active. Everything we see, hear, taste, feel, or perceive, has some influence upon thought, which is moved by it as leaves on the trees are moved by every breeze of wind. But "thoughts" here include those exercises of the mind in which it is voluntarily or intensely engaged, and in which we are in earnest ; even all our schemes, contrivances, and purposes. One would think, if there were anything in man to be accounted of, it should be those exercises in which his intellectual faculty is seriously and intensely employed. Yet the Lord knoweth that even these are vanity.

4. If during our state of childhood and youth only vanity had been ascribed to our thoughts, it would have been less surprising. This is a truth of which number-less parents have painful proof ; yea, and of which children themselves, as they grow up to maturity, are generally conscious. Vanity at this period, however, admits of some apology. The obstinacy and folly of some young people, while they provoke disgust, often excite a tear of pity. But the charge is exhibited against man. "Man *at his best estate* is altogether vanity."

5. The decision proceeds from a quarter from which there can be no appeal. "*The Lord knoweth*" it. Opinions dishonourable to our species may sometimes arise from ignorance, sometimes from spleen and disappointment, and sometimes from a gloomy turn of mind, which views mankind through a distorted medium. But the judgment given in this passage is the decision of him who cannot err ; a decision therefore to which, if we had no other proof, it becomes us to accede.— *Andrew Fuller.*

Verse 11.—"*They are vanity.*" The Syriac version is, *for they are a vapour.* Compare James iv. 14.—*John Gill.*

Verse 12.—"*Blessed is the man,*" &c. I shall show the various benefits of afflic-tion, when it is sanctified by the Spirit of God to those persons who are exercised by it. I. The Great God has made affliction the occasion of converting sinners, and bringing them into a spiritual acquaintance with Christ his Son. See Isa. xlviii. 10. II. God not only makes affliction the occasion of converting sinners at first, but after conversion he sanctifies an afflicted state to the saints, to weaken the remains of indwelling sin in them, and make them afraid of sinning against him in future time. III. God, in afflicting the saints, increases that good work of grace, which his Spirit has implanted in them. God causes his saints to grow in grace, when he corrects them with the rod of sorrow ; God assimilates and makes the saints like unto himself, in a greater degree, by temporal troubles and distresses. Heb. xii. 10, 11. IV. God afflicts the saints for the improvement of their knowledge in divine things. The Psalmist says, in the words of the text, "*Blessed is the man whom thou chastenest, O Lord, and teachest him out of thy law.*" See also Ps. cxix. 71. V. The great God, by afflicting the saints, brings them unto him with greater nearness and frequency, by prayer and supplication. VI. God afflicts the saints, to make them better acquainted with the perfections of his nature. VII. To make them more conformed to Christ his Son. VIII. To subdue the pride of their hearts, and make them more humble. IX. God oftentimes discovers to the saints, in the season of their affliction, in a clearer manner, that grace which he has implanted in them, and refreshes their souls with the consolations of his Spirit. X. God afflicts the saints, to divide their hearts more from the love of the world, and to make them more meet for heaven.—*Outline of a Sermon by John Farmer,* 1744.

Verse 12.—Here observe generally, what it is which afflictions, or God by afflic-tions, teacheth his children ; even the self-same thing which he teacheth in his word ; as the schoolmaster teacheth his scholars the same thing by the rod, which he teacheth by words. The word, then, is the storehouse of all instruction. Look not for any new diverse doctrine to be taught thee by affliction, which is not in the word. For, in truth, herein stands our teaching by affliction, that it fits and pre-pares us for the word, by breaking and sub-dividing the stubbornness of our hearts, and making them pliable, and capable of the impression of the word. Wherefore, as the Apostle saith, that the law is our schoolmaster to Christ, Gal. iii. Because the law, by showing unto us our disease, forceth us to the physician. So likewise it may be said that afflictions are schoolmasters to the law. For whilst we are at ease and in prosperity, though the sons of thunder terrify never so much with the fearful cracks of legal menaces, yet are we as deaf men, nothing moved therewith.

But when we are humbled and meekened by affliction, then is there way made for the terrors of the law ; then do we begin with some reverence of attention to listen and give ear unto them. When therefore God sends us any affliction, we must know that then he sends us to the law and to the testimony. For he teaches us indeed in our affliction, but it is in his law. And therefore if in our affliction we will learn anything, we must take God's book into our hands, and carefully and seriously peruse it. And hereby shall it appear that our afflictions have been our teachers, if by them we have felt ourselves stirred up to greater diligence, zeal, and reverence in reading and hearing the word. . . . . After that the prophet had preferred his complaint to the Lord against the adversaries of the church, from the first verse to the eighth, he leaveth God, and in a sudden conversion of speech, turns himself from the party complained unto, to the parties complained of, the cruel oppressors of the church, terrifying them by those just judgments of God, which in fine must overtake them, and so consequently cheering and comforting the distressed church. But because the distress of the church's enemies of itself could be no sufficient matter of comfort unto her, therefore a second argument of further and that far more effectual consolation is added in this twelfth verse, drawn from the happy condition of the church, even whilst she is thus overborne with those tigerly and tyrannical persecutors. And the argument is propounded by the prophet, not directing his speech to the church, but rather in his own person bringing in the church suddenly turning her speech from her enemies, with whom she was expostulating, to God himself, and breaking forth into this pathetical expostulation, " *Blessed is the man whom thou chastenest, O Lord, and teachest him out of thy law.*" From the coherence of which words with the former, we may observe, that the outward miseries of our enemies is but cold comfort, unless withal we have a persuasion of our own inward happiness. . . . It would do the child little good to see the rod cast into the fire, if he himself should be cast in after it. Therefore the church having in this place meditated of the just judgments of God, which should in due time befall her adversaries, and not finding sufficiency of comfort therein, here in this verse proceedeth to a further meditation of her own case and condition. Wherein she seemeth thus to reason to herself. What though these mine enemies be brought to their deserved ends ? what though I know they be reserved for shame and confusion ? What ease can this bring to my mind now dejected, and happy thinking itself as miserable as these my foes ? Now these doubtful thoughts something disquieting her, further comfort is ministered unto her by the Spirit of God in this verse, whereby she is enabled to answer that objection she made against herself, namely, that she is assured, that as her adversaries' case is wretched, so is her own most happy and blessed.— *Daniel Dyke, in " The Schoole of Affliction," 1633.*

Verse 12.—" *Blessed is the man whom thou chastenest,*" etc. If by outward afflictions thy soul be brought more under the inward teachings of God, doubtless thy afflictions are in love. All the chastening in the world, without divine teaching, will never make a man blessed ; that man that finds correction attended with instruction, and lashing with lessoning, is a happy man. If God, by the affliction that is upon thee, shall teach thee how to loathe sin more, how to trample upon the world more, and how to walk with God more, thy afflictions are in love. If God shall teach thee by afflictions how to die to sin more, and how to die to thy relations more, and how to die to thy self-interest more, thy afflictions are in love. If God shall teach thee by afflictions how to live to Christ more, how to lift up Christ more, and how to long for Christ more, thy afflictions are in love. If God shall teach thee by afflictions to get assurance of a better life, and to be still in a gracious readiness and preparedness for the day of thy death, thy afflictions are in love. If God shall teach thee by afflictions how to mind heaven more, and how to fit for heaven more, thy afflictions are in love. If God by afflictions shall teach thy proud heart how to lie more low, and thy hard heart how to grow more humble, and thy censorious heart how to grow more charitable, and thy carnal heart how to grow more spiritual, and thy froward heart how to grow more quiet, &c., thy afflictions are in love. Pambo, an illiterate dunce, as the historian terms him, was a-learning that one lesson, " I said I will take heed to my ways, that I sin not with my tongue," nineteen years, and yet had not learned it. Ah ! it is to be feared that there are many who have been in this school of affliction above this nineteen years, and yet have not learned any saving lesson all this while. Surely their afflictions are not in love, but in wrath. Where God loves, he afflicts in love, and wherever God afflicts in love, there he will first and last teach such souls such lessons as shall do them good to all eternity.

If you enjoy the special presence of God with your spirits in your affliction, then your affliction is in love. Hast thou a special presence of God with thy spirit, strengthening of that, stilling of that, satisfying of that, cheering and comforting of that ? " *In the multitude of my thoughts*,"—that is, of my troubled, intricate, ensnared, intertwined, and perplexed thoughts, as the branches of a tree by some strong wind are twisted one within another, as the Hebrew word properly signifies,— " *Thy comforts delight my soul*." Here is a presence of God with his soul, here are comforts and delights that reach the soul, here is a cordial to strengthen the spirit.— *Thomas Brooks*.

Verse 12.—You may and ought to get especial rejoicing faith out of sanctified afflictions. Thus : " Whom God doth correct and teach, *him* he loves, *he* is blessed : (Ps. xciv. 12 : Heb. xii. 6 :) but God doth so to me : *ergo*." Here are bills and prayers for mercies ; but who looks after the issue, the teaching, the holy use ? Sanctified afflictions are very good evidences, and so very comfortable. There are those who would not have lost their sufferings, temptations, afflictions, for any good. The blessed Spirit hath taught them that way many a divine truth by heart out of the word ; they are sensible of it, and from it conclude the love of God in Christ to them ; and thence they have joy and comfort,—*that* joy that angels cannot give, and devils cannot take. Sanctified troubles are tokens of special love.—*Christopher Fowler* (1610—1678,) *in* " *The Morning Exercises*."

Verse 12.—If we have nothing but the rod, we profit not by the rod ; yea, if we have nothing but the word, we shall never profit by the word. It is the Spirit given with the word, and the Spirit given with the rod, by which we profit under both, or either. Chastening and divine teaching must go together, else there will be no profit by chastening.—*Joseph Caryl*.

Verse 12.—God sees that the sorrows of life are very good for us ; for, as seeds that are deepest covered with snow in winter flourish most in spring ; or as the wind by beating down the flame raiseth it higher and hotter ; and as when we would have fires flame the more, we sprinkle water upon them ; even so, when the Lord would increase our joy and thankfulness, he allays it with the tears of affliction.— *H. G. Salter*.

Verse 12.—" *And teachest*." *Teaching* implies both a schoolmaster, *a teacher*, instructing and *lessons taught*. In this *teaching* both these points are here noted out. And for the first, namely, the *schoolmaster*, it is twofold : 1. The outward affliction and chastisement, " *Whom thou chastisest, teachest*," that is, whom by chastising thou teachest. 2. God himself, who is the chief and principal head schoolmaster, the other being but an inferior and subordinate one : " *Whom thou teachest*." And for the second point, *the lessons taught*, they are included generally in those words, " *in thy law*." To begin then with the schoolmasters, and first with the first.

The first schoolmaster is affliction. A sharp and severe and swingeing schoolmaster indeed, and so much the fitter for such stout and stubborn scholars as we are ; who because we will not be overcome by fair means, must needs therefore be dealt withal by foul. For God doth not willingly afflict us, but being necessarily thereunto enforced, by that strength of corruption in us, which otherwise will not be subdued. So physicians and surgeons are constrained to come to cutting, lancing, and burning, when milder remedies will not prevail. Let us therefore hereby take notice of the hardness of our hearts, the fallow ground whereof cannot be broken up but by this sharp plough of affliction. See what dullards and blockheads we are, how slow to understand spiritual things, not able to conceive of them by the instruction of words, unless they be even beaten and driven into our brains by blows. So thick and brawny is that foreskin which is drawn over our uncircumcised ears and hearts, that no doctrine can enter, unless it be pegged, and hammered, and knocked into us by the fists of this sour and crabbed *schoolmaster*.

The second schoolmaster is God himself. Afflictions of themselves, though severe schoolmasters, yet can do us no good, unless God come by his Spirit, and teach our hearts inwardly. Let us therefore pray, that as in the ministry of God's word, so also of his works and judgments, we may be *all taught of God*. For it is his Spirit that quickeneth and animateth the outward means, which otherwise are a dead letter. And this is the reason that many men have rather grown worse by their afflictions, than anything better ; because God's Spirit hath not gone with the affliction, to put life and spirit into it, as Moses observed in the Israelites, Deut. **xxix.** 2—4.—*Daniel Dyke*.

Verse 13.—" *That thou mayest give him rest.*" Here usually, but hereafter certainly. *Mors ærumnarum requies,* was Chaucer's motto : those that die in the Lord *shall rest from their labours.* Meanwhile they are chastened of the Lord, that they may not be condemned with the world. 1 Cor. xi. 32.—*John Trapp.*

Verse 13.—" *To give him rest.*" This is the end of God's teaching, that his servant may wait in patience, unmoved by, safe *from, the days of evil* (comp. xlix. 5) seeing the evil all round lifting itself up, but seeing also the secret, mysterious retribution, slowly but surely accomplishing itself. In this sense the " rest " is the rest of a calm, self-possessed spirit, as Isai. vii. 4 ; **xxx. 15 ; xxxii. 17 ; lvii. 20 ;** and " *to give him*" signifies " that thou mayest give him."—*J. J. S. Perowne.*

Verse 13.—" *Rest.*" Let there be a revival of the passive virtues. Mr. Hume calls them the " monkish virtues." Many speak of them slightingly, especially as compared with the dashing qualities so highly esteemed in the world. But quietness of mind and of spirit, like a broken heart, is of great price in the sight of God. Some seem to have forgotten that silence and meekness are graces.—*William S. Plumer.*

Verse 13.—" *Rest from the days of adversity.*" *To rest from the days of adversity* is not to be disturbed by them to such an extent as to murmur, or despond in spirit, but to trust in God, and in silence of the mind and affections expect from God deliverance. See Isai. vii. 4 ; xxvi. 20, &c. Moreover he says not יְמֵי *in,* but מִימֵי *from the days* of adversity, an expression of greater elegancy and wider range of meaning. For there is a reference to the primary form of the verb שָׁקַט *to sink, to settle down,* as when the dregs of disturbed liquor fall to the bottom ; when it is applied to the mind when shaken with a great agitation of cares, and full of bitterness. The dregs, therefore, sprung *from the days of adversity,* are pointed out as settling down. Besides, not only is rest of mind while the evils continue indicated, but also while they are ceasing, since מ, *from,* has here, as not infrequently elsewhere, a *negativf orce.*—*Venema.*

Verse 13.—" *Until the pit be digged for the wicked.*" Behold, thou hast the counsel of God, and the reason why he spareth the wicked : the pit is being digged for the sinner. Thou wishest to bury him at once : the pit is as yet being dug for him : do not be in haste to bury him.—*Augustine.*

Verse 15.—My text contains two parts ; the providence of God to his people, and the prosperity of the providence among them. The providence of God to his people lies much in after-games : God seems to go away from his, and then the wicked have the better : anon he returns, and then his people carry the day. "*Judgment shall return unto righteousness ;*" or *justice shall return unto judgment ;* a phrase of speech frequent in the Old Testament to note retaliation, *quid* for *quo,* like for like. The term is distinct as well as the phrase, and helps to give the sense of the Spirit of God here ; צֶדֶק, from צָדַק, *se asseruit,* justice shall assert itself ; Christ shall assert his people, his promises, his threatenings. " Shall *return,*" *retro-agi :* what evil men do to good shall be re-done to them, done back again upon them by God. Or this root, here rendered " *return,*" may be rendered to abide and rest. In Psalm xxiii. 6, it is so rendered : " I shall dwell in the house of the Lord for ever." Justice doth, as it were, go from home sometimes, when it visits the saints ; but it returns to its home and dwelling, *i.e.,* the wicked. Justice is, as it were, from home, till it returns to the wicked, there it abides and dwells. " *Justice shall dwell and rest in judgment,*" *i.e.,* in the execution of punishments upon wicked men. מִשְׁפָּט, from שָׁפַט, *judicium exercuit,* notes the exercise and execution of justice : a thing rests in its end ; justice dwells and rests in judgment, *i.e.,* in its execution, in its end for which, and unto which and whom it is appointed.—*Nicholas Lockyer,* 1612—1684-5.

Verse 15.—" *Shall follow it.*" The right reading is in the margin,—*shall be after it,* or *after that;* that is, (1) *shall observe it.* " He poureth contempt upon princes ; he setteth the poor on high from affliction ; whoso is wise *shall observe these things,*" etc., Ps. cvii. 43 : this Scripture, I think, in part explains the text. (2) " *Shall be after it ;* " that is, shall confess and acknowledge it. 'Tis not a small thing to bring men to confess the justice of God in his dealings. (3) " *Shall be after it ;* " that is, shall triumph in it, and so to be compared with and opened by Ps. lviii. 10, 11. (4) " *Shall be after it ;* " that is, the works of God shall be of effectual operation, to bring such as are upright in heart more to love and obey God, and so it is to be compared with Ps. xxxi. 23.—*Nicholas Lockyer.*

Verse 16.—" *Who will rise up,*" etc.   I think we ought to look upon David here
in a public capacity, as a prince or magistrate ; and then as such he deplores the
increase and confidence of the wicked ; and having fortified himself in God by
prayer, he resolves, in the words of the text, to do the duty of his station, to employ
all the power God had given him for the extirpation of wickedness, and the reformation of an impious people ; and earnestly invites and calls in to his assistance all
that had either heart or ability for such a work, as being well aware of the great
difficulty of it.   This is the sense I prefer, because it best becomes the zeal and faith
of David, best suits the spirit and genius of several other parallel Psalms, and seems
plainly to me to have the countenance of the Targum and the Septuagint.

In the words thus explained we have these three things : 1. *The deplorable state
of Israel.*   This is easily to be collected from the form and manner of David's expressing himself here, " *Who will stand up for me ?*" or *who will take my part ?*   As
if he should have said, Such is the number and power of the wicked, that how much
soever my heart is set upon a reformation, I can hardly hope to effect it, without the
concurrence and joint endeavours of good men.   And yet, alas ! how little is the
assistance I can reasonably expect of this kind ?   How few are the sincere friends
of goodness ?   How great and how general is the coldness and indifference which
possesses men in the things of God ?   2. *The duty of the magistrate.*   This is plainly
implied here, and is, to curb and restrain wickedness, and to promote a general
reformation.   3. *The duty of all good people.*   Which is, as far as in them lies, to
assist and encourage the magistrate in this good work.—*Richard Lucas,* 1697.

Verse 16.—" *Who will rise up for me against the wicked ?*"   In all ages, men who
neither feared God nor regarded man have combined together and formed confederacies, to carry on the works of darkness.   And herein they have shown themselves wise in their generation, for by this means they more effectually promoted the
kingdom of their father the devil, than otherwise they could have done.   On the
other hand, men who did fear God, and desire the happiness of their fellow-creatures,
have in every age found it needful to join together in order to oppose the works of
darkness, to spread the knowledge of God their Saviour, and to promote his kingdom
upon earth.   Indeed he himself has instructed them so to do.   From the time that
men were upon the earth, he hath taught them to join together in his service, and
has united them in one body by one Spirit.   And for this very end he has joined
them together, " that he might destroy the works of the devil ; " first in them that
are already united, and by them that are round about them.—*John Wesley, in a
Sermon on these words, preached before the Society for Reformation of Manners, Jan.* 30,
1763.

Verse 17.—" *Had been my help.*"   The word signifieth not only *help,* but *summum
et plenum auxilium,* an *helpfulness,* or *full help :* the Hebrew hath a letter more
than ordinary, to increase the signification, as learned Mr. Leigh observeth : there
is the sufficiency of help.—*Nathaniel Whiting, in " The Saints' Dangers, Deliverances,
and Duties,"* 1659.

Verse 19.—" *In the multitude of my thoughts,*" etc.   That is, just when they
were come to their height and extremity in me.   The comforts of God are seasonable,
and observe the proper time for their coming, neither too soon, nor too late, but
" *in,*" that is, just in the very point and nick of time.   There is another thing here
spoken of.   In the " *thoughts* " and in the " *multitude* " of the " thoughts ; " not
in the indifferency of thoughts, but in the perplexity ; not in the paucity of thoughts,
but in the plurality : our extremity is God's opportunity.   " In the mount will
the Lord be seen," when we have thought and thought and thought all we could,
and know not what to think more, then does God delight to tender and exhibit his
comforts to us. . . .

In the words " *within me* " we have, next, the intimacy or closeness of this grief.
The Hebrew word is בְּקִרְבִּי, *in medio mei.*   The Arabic *be-kalbi, in corde meo.*   And
so likewise the Septuagint, ἐν τῇ καρδίᾳ μου, *in my very heart.*   This is added by
way of further intention and aggravation of the present evil and distress.   *First,*
To show the *secrecy* of this grief.   Those evils which are external, and in the body,
every one is ready to bemoan them, and to bewail them, and to take notice of them,
and to shew a great deal of bowels towards those which are afflicted with them ;
but these griefs which are inward, and in the mind, they are such as are known but

to God himself. "The heart knoweth his own bitterness," saith Solomon, Proverbs xiv. 10.

Secondly, Here is hereby denoted the *settledness* and *radication* of this evil: it was within him and it was within his heart, that is, it was deeply rooted and fastened, and such as had a strong ground-work and foundation in him; such were these troublesome "*thoughts*," they were got into his very inwards and bowels, and so were not easily got out again. *Thirdly*, Here is hereby also signified the *impression* which they had upon him, and the *sense* which he himself had of them. They were such as did grievously afflict him, and pierce him, and went near unto him, they went to his very heart, and touched him, as it were, to the quick, through the grievousness of them, as he speaks in another place concerning the reproaches of his enemies, Psalm xlii. 10: "As with a sword (or killing) in my bones, mine enemies reproach me; while they say daily unto me, Where is thy God?"

Now what are these "*comforts*" of God which the Psalmist does more especially intend here in this place? In a word, they are the comforts which do flow from our *communion* with him. The comforts of his attributes, and the comforts of his promises, and the comforts of his gracious presence drawing near unto our souls, when it pleases him to shine upon us, and to express his good will to us, and to give us some evidence and assurance of his love and favour towards us; these are his comforts.

"*Delight*." This is a transcendent expression, which the Holy Ghost in the pen of the prophet David comes up unto. It had been a great matter to have said, they satisfy my soul, or, they quiet me, no more but so; that is the highest pitch which a perplexed spirit can wish to itself. Those which are in great pain, they would be glad if they might have but ease, they cannot aspire so high as *pleasure and delight*, this is more than can be expected by them; but see here now the notable efficacy of these Divine comforts; they do not only *pacify* the mind, but they *joy* it; they do not only *satisfy* it, but *ravish* it; they not only *quiet*, but *delight* it. "*Thy comforts delight my soul.*" That is, not only take away the present grief, but likewise put in the room and place of it most unspeakable comfort and consolation; as the *sun* does not only dispel darkness, but likewise brings in a glorious light in the stead of it.

"*My soul.*" We showed before how the grief was in the mind, and therefore the comfort must be so also, that the remedy may answer the malady. Bodily pleasure will not satisfy for mind distraction: nothing will ease the soul but such comforts as are agreeable to itself, and such are these present comforts of God, they delight the soul.—*Thomas Horton.*

Verse 19.—*Thoughts* considered simply in themselves do not contain any matter of grief or evil; they are the proper and natural issue and emanations of the soul which come from it with a great deal of easiness, and with a great deal of delight; but it is the *exorbitancy* and *irregularity* of them which is here intended, when they do not proceed *evenly and fairly* as they ought to do, but with some kind of *interruption*; and so the word which is here used in the text seems to import; the Hebrew *sagnaphim* carrying an affinity with *segnaphim*, which is derived from a root which signifies properly a bough. Now we know that in a bough there are two things especially considerable, as pertinent to our present purpose. First, there's the *perplexity* of it. And, secondly, there's the *agitation*. Boughs usually catch, and intangle one in another, and boughs they are easily shaken, and moved up and down by the wind. If there be never so little *air* or *breath* stirring abroad, the boughs presently discover it, and are made sensible of it. So that this expression does serve very well to intimate and set forth unto us the perplexity and inconstancy of thoughts, which David was now troubled withal, and whereof he now complains, as grievous and offensive to him. They were not thoughts *in any consideration*, but *thoughts of distraction*, such thoughts as did bring some grief and trouble with them. This the Septuagint translators were so fully apprehensive of, that they quite leave out *thoughts*, and render it only by *griefs*, κατὰ τὸ πλῆθος τῶν ὀδυνῶν μου: *according to the multitude of my sorrows.* But it is more full and agreeable to the word to put them both together,—*my grievous and sorrowful thoughts*—such thoughts as in regard of the carriage and ordering of them, do bring grief and sorrow with them.

And here we may by the way observe thus much, that God need not go far to punish and afflict men when he pleases; he can do it even with *their own thoughts*, no more but so. He can gather a rod of these boughs, and make a scourge of these twistings, wherewith to lash them, and that to purpose. If he does but raise a tempest in the mind, and cause these thoughts to bluster and bustle one with another, there will be trouble and affliction enough, though there were nothing else. It is no matter whether there be any *ground* or *occasion* for it in the things themselves; it is enough that there be so but in the *conceit and apprehension*. God can so use a *fancy*, a mere toy and imagination itself, and so set it on upon the soul, that there shall be no quiet nor rest for it.—*Thomas Horton.*

Verse 19.—Observe the greatness of this man's distress. This is forcibly expressed in the text, though in our translation it is scarcely obvious. The word in it rendered "*thoughts*," scholars tell us, signifies originally the small branches of trees. The idea in the Psalmist's mind appears to be this: 'Look at a tree, with its branches shooting in every direction, entangling and entwining themselves one with another; let the wind take them—see how they feel it, how restless they become and confused, beating against and striving one with another. Now my mind is like that tree. I have a great many thoughts in it; and thoughts which are continually shifting and changing; they are perplexed and agitated thoughts, battling one with another. There is no keeping the mind quiet under them; they bring disorder into it as well as sorrow. And mark the word "*multitude*" in the text; there is exactly the same idea in that. It signifies more than number; confusion. Think of a crowd collected and hurrying about: 'so,' says the Psalmist, 'are my thoughts. I have a crowd of them in my mind, and a restless confused crowd. One painful thought is bad enough, but I have many; a multitude of them; and almost countless, a disturbed throng.' We now, then, understand the case we have before us. The man's sorrow arose, at this time, from disquieting thoughts within his own breast; and his sorrow was great, because these thoughts were many, and at the same time tumultuous. When the Psalmist says, "*Thy comforts*," he means more than comforts of which God is the author or giver. God is the author and giver of all our comforts—of all the earthly comforts that surround us; they are all the work and gift of his gracious hand. . . . We are to understand *here* such comforts as are peculiarly and altogether God's, such as flow at once from God; not from him through creatures to us, but from him immediately to us without the intervention of creatures. The comforts that we get from his attributes—from meditating on, and what we call realising them; the comforts we get from his promises —believing and hoping in him; and the comforts of his presence, he drawing near to our souls and shining into them—we knowing he is near us, conscious of it by the light and happiness and renewed strength within us. "*Thy* comforts"—the comforts we get from the Lord Jesus Christ; from looking at him, considering him; thinking of his person, and offices, and blood, and righteousness, and intercession, and exaltation, and glory, and his second coming; our meeting him, seeing him, being like him. "*Thy* comforts"—the comforts which come from the Holy Spirit, "the Comforter": when he opens the Scriptures to us, or speaks through ceremonies and ordinances, or witnesses within us of our adoption of God; shining in on his own work of grace in our hearts; enabling us to see that work, and to see in it God's peculiar, eternal love to us; not opening to us the book of life, and showing us our names there, but doing something that makes us almost as joyful as though that book were opened to us; showing us the hand of God in our own souls—his converting, saving hand—his hand apprehending us as his own; making us feel, as it were, his grasp of love, and feel, too, that it is a grasp which he will never loosen.—*Charles Bradley.*

Verse 19.—"*Thy comforts delight my soul.*" Xerxes offered great rewards to him that could find out a new pleasure; but the comforts of the Spirit are satisfactory, they recruit the heart. There is as much difference between heavenly comforts and earthly, as between a banquet that is eaten and one that is painted on the wall.—*Thomas Watson.*

Verse 19.—"*Thy comforts.*" Troubles may be of our own begetting; but true comforts come only from that infinite fountain, the God of consolation; for so he hath styled himself.—*Thomas Adams.*

Verse 19.—"*Delight my soul.*" The original word, יְשַׁעַשְׁעוּ, signifies "*to cause to leap or dance for joy*"; but the English language will not bear an application of this image to the soul; though we say "to make the *heart* leap for joy."—*Samuel Horsley.*

Verse 19.—Because the malignant host is first entered into the ground of my text, consider with me: 1. The rebels, or mutineers, "*thoughts.*" 2. The number of them, no less than a "*multitude.*" 3. The captain whose colours they bear; a disquieted mind ; " *my* thoughts." 4. The field where the battle is fought ; in the heart ; *apud me,* " within me." In the other army we find, 1. *Quanta,* how puissant they are ; " *comforts.*" 2. *Quota,* how many they are ; indefinitely set down ; abundant comfort. 3. *Cujus,* whose they are ; the Lord's, he is their general ; " *thy* comforts." 4. *Quid operantur,* what they do ; they delight the soul. In the nature of them, being comforts, there is tranquillity ; in the number of them, being many comforts, there is sufficiency ; in the owner of them, being " *thy* " comforts, there is omnipotency ; and in the effect of them, delighting the soul, there is security. —*From Thomas Adams' Sermon entitled " Man's Comfort."*

Verse 19.—A text of this kind shows us forcibly the power of Divine grace in the human heart : how much it can do to sustain and cheer the heart. The world may afflict a believer, and pain him ; but if the grace which God has given him is in active exercise in his soul, the world cannot make him unhappy. It rather adds by its ill treatment to his happiness ; for it brings God and his soul nearer together—God the fountain of all happiness, the rest and satisfaction of his soul.

This Psalm was evidently written by a deeply afflicted man. The wicked, he says, were triumphing over him ; and had been so for a long while. He could find no one on earth to take his part against them. " *Who will rise up for me against the evildoers ?* " he asks in the 16th verse ; " *or who will stand up for me against the workers of iniquity ?* " And it seemed, too, as though God had abandoned him. His enemies thought so, and he seems to have been almost ready to think so himself. But what was the fact ? All this time the Lord was secretly pouring consolation into his soul, and in the end made that consolation abundant. In appearance a wretched, he was in reality a happy man ; suffering, yet comforted ; yea, the text says *delighted*—" *Thy comforts delight my soul.*"—*Charles Bradley,* 1845.

Verse 20.—" *The throne of iniquity . . . . which frameth mischief by a law.*" The first pretext of wicked men to colour their proceedings against innocent men is their *throne* ; the second is the *law* ; and the third is their *council.* What tyrant could ask more ? But God has prepared an awful hell for impenitent tyrants, and they will be in it long before they now expect to leave the world.—*William Nicholson.*

Verse 20.—" *The throne of iniquity . . . . which frameth mischief by a law.*" If there never had been such thrones in the world, there would not have been that mention made of them in the Scripture. But such there have been. That of Jeroboam was one, who would not suffer the people, according to the divine command, to go up to Jerusalem to worship God, who had there placed his name ; but spread, for them that went, nets upon Mizpah, and set snares upon Mount Tabor. (Hosea v. 1.) And such thrones there have been since, too many of them. Well saith the Psalmist, " *Shall they have fellowship with thee ?* " No, no ; God keeps his distance from them. Those that we call " stinking dunghills " are not so offensive to God as thrones of iniquity are, which shall neither be approved by him nor secured. Stay a while, Christians, and " in patience possess your souls ; " for the world shall see that in due time he will overturn them all.—*Samuel Slater, in " The Morning Exercises."*

Verse 20.—" *Which frameth mischief by a law,*" *i.e.,* frame wicked laws, or under the colour of law and justice, oppress the innocent. *Summum jus, summa injuri,* the higher the law, the greater the injustice, and injuries may and are too often done *ex pravâ interpretatione legis,* from a wicked interpretation of the law. With those who do injustice with the sword of justice, God will have no fellowship.—*William Nicholson.*

Verse 23.—" *He shall bring upon them their own iniquity,*" etc. It is an ill work wicked ones are about, they make fetters for their own feet, and build houses for to fall upon their own heads ; so mischievous is the nature of sin that it damnifies and destroys the parents of it.—*William Greenhill.*

HINTS TO PREACHERS.

Verse 1.—I. Retribution the prerogative of God alone. II. Under what aspects may we desire his rendering it. III. How, and when he will surely fulfil this righteous wish.

Verse 1.—I. Vengeance belongs to God and not to man. II. Vengeance is better in the hands of God than of man. " Let us fall into the hands of God," etc.—*G. R.*

Verse 2.—The peculiar provocation of the sin of pride and its kindred vices. Its influence on the proud, on their fellow men, and upon God himself.

Verse 3.—The duration of the reign of evil. I. Till it has filled up its measure of guilt. II. Till it has proved its own folly. III. Till it has developed the graces and prayers of saints. IV. Till it has emptied man of all human trust and driven us to look to the Lord alone, his Spirit, and his advent.

Verse 3.—I. The sweet potion of the wicked—present triumph. II. The gall which embitters it—it is but temporary, and is prayed against.—*C. A. Davis.*

Verses 5—10.—I. High-handed oppression by the wicked (verses 5, 6). II. Hard-hearted indifference to Divine supervision (verse 7). III. Clear-headed demonstration of the Divine cognisance and vengeance (verses 8—10).—*C. A. D.*

Verses 6—9.—I. Conspicuous sin. II. Absurd supposition. III. Overwhelming argument.

Verse 8.—Practical Atheists. I. Truly described. II. Wisely counselled.—*C. A. D.*

Verses 8—11.—I. The Exhortation (verse 8). II. The Expostulation (verses 9, 10). III. The Affirmation (verse 11).—*G. R.*

Verses 9, 10.—True Rationalism ; or, Reason's Revelation of God.—*C. A. D.*

Verse 11.—I. With respect to the present world, consider what multitudes of thoughts are employed in vain. 1. In seeking satisfaction where it is not to be found. 2. In poring on events which cannot be recalled. 3. In anticipating evils which never befall us. 4. To these may be added the valuing ourselves on things of little or no account. 5. In laying plans which must be disconcerted. II. Let us see what are man's thoughts with regard to religion, and the concerns of a future life. 1. What are the thoughts of the heathen world about religion ? 2. What are all the thoughts of the Christian world, where God's thoughts are neglected ? 3. What is all that practical atheism which induces multitudes to act as if there were no God ? 4. What are all the unbelieving, self-flattering imaginations of wicked men, as though God were not in earnest in his declarations and threatenings ? 5. What are the conceits of the self-righteous, by which they buoy up their minds with vain hopes, and refuse to submit to the righteousness of God ?—*Andrew Fuller.*

Verse 11.—God's intimate knowledge of man. A startling truth. A humiliating truth.

Verses 12, 13.—Christ's College. The Master, the Book, the Rod, the blessed Scholar, and the result of his education.

Verses 12, 13.—I. The Blessed. 1. Divinely taught. 2. Divinely chastised. II. The Blessing. 1. Rest in Affliction. 2. Rest from Affliction.—*G. R.*

Verse 14.—I. Fear implied. That God will cast off, forsake, etc. II. Fear denied. God will not cast off—will not forsake.—*G. R.*

Verse 14.—I. Display this bright doctrine on a dark background. What if the converse were true ? Considerations that might lead us to apprehend it true. II. Joyfully regard the glowing truth itself. The doctrine declared. The reasons hinted (His people. His inheritance). The confidence expressed.—*C. A. D.*

Verse 15.—I. Judgment suspended. II. Judgment returned. III. Judgment acknowledged.—*G. R.*

Verse 16.—I. The question asked by the church of her champions. II. The answer of every true-hearted man. III. The yet more encouraging answer of her Lord.

Verses 16, 17.—The sole source of succour. I. A loud cry for help. As from a champion, or advocate. II. Earth's answer. A dead silence, disturbed only by echo (verse 17). III. The succouring voice that breaks the silence—the Lord's (verse 17).—*C. A. D.*

Verse 18.—The blessedness of the confession of weakness. I. The confession. II. The succour. III. The time. IV. The acknowledgment.—*C. A. D.*

Verse 19.—I. In the multitude of my *unbelieving* thoughts thy comforts delight my soul. II. In the multitude of my *penitential* thoughts thy comforts, etc. III. In the multitude of my *worldly* thoughts, etc. IV. In the multitude of my *family* or *social* thoughts, etc. V. Of my *desponding* thoughts, etc. VI. Of my *prospective* thoughts, etc. Or, I. There is no consolation for man in himself. II. There is no consolation for him in other creatures. III. His only consolation is in God.—*G. R.*

Verse 19.—I. The soul jostled in the thoroughfare of anxious thoughts.   II. The delectable company nevertheless enjoyed.—*C. A. D.*

Verse 20.—" It is the law of the land, you know,"—the limit of this authority both in temporal and spiritual matters.

Verse 20.—I. God can have no fellowship with the wicked.   II. The wicked can have no fellowship with God.—*G. R.*

Verse 20.—Divine politics.   I. There are thrones erected in opposition to the throne of God, " thrones of iniquity," *e.g.* which trespass on civil liberty, which infringe religious equality, which derive revenue from evil commerce, etc.   II. Such thrones, whatever their pretensions, are excluded from divine fellowship ; between them and God a great gulf is fixed.—*C. A. D.*

Verses 21, 22.—I. The Danger of the righteous (verse 21).   II. Their Defence (verse 22).—*G. R.*

Verses 21—23.—I. Sentence passed in the court of injustice (verse 21).   II. An element in the case not considered by the court (verse 22).   III. The sentence consequently alighting on the right heads (verse 23).   (This passage, under a very thin veil, exhibits Christ.   Matt. xxvii. 1.)—*C. A. D.*

Verse 23.—I. None may punish God's enemies but himself.   " He shall bring," etc.   II. None need punish them but himself.   1. It will be complete,—" shall cut them off."   2. Certain.   " Yea," etc.—*G. R.*

PSALM XCV.

This Psalm has no title, and all we know of its authorship is that Paul quotes it as " in David." (Heb. iv. 7.) It is true that this may merely signify that it is to be found in the collection known as David's Psalms ; but if such were the Apostle's meaning it would have been more natural for him to have written, " saying in the Psalms ; " we therefore incline to the belief that David was the actual author of this poem. It is in it: original a truly Hebrew song, directed both in its exhortation and warning to the Jewish people, but we have the warrant of the Holy Spirit in the epistle to the Hebrews for using its appeals and entreaties when pleading with Gentile believers. It is a Psalm of invitation to worship. It has about it a ring like that of the church bells, and like the bells it sounds both merrily and solemnly, at first ringing out a lively peal, and then dropping into a funeral knell as if tolling at the funeral of the generation which perished in the wilderness. We will call it THE PSALM OF THE PROVOCATION.

DIVISION.—*It would be correct as to the sense to divide this Psalm into an invitation and a warning, so as to commence the second part with the last clause of verse 7 : but upon the whole it may be more convenient to regard verse 6 as " the beating heart of the Psalm," as Hengstenberg calls it, and make the division at the end of verse 5. Thus it will form (1) an invitation with reasons, and (2) an invitation with warnings.*

EXPOSITION.

O COME, let us sing unto the LORD, let us make a joyful noise to the rock of our salvation.

2 Let us come before his presence with thanksgiving, and make a joyful noise unto him with psalms.

3 For the LORD *is* a great God, and a great King above all gods.

4 In his hand *are* the deep places of the earth : the strength of the hills *is* his also.

5 The sea *is* his, and he made it : and his hands formed the dry *land*.

1. " *O come, let us sing unto the Lord.*" Other nations sing unto their gods, let us sing unto Jehovah. We love him, we admire him, we reverence him, let us express our feelings with the choicest sounds, using our noblest faculty for its noblest end. It is well thus to urge others to magnify the Lord, but we must be careful to set a worthy example ourselves, so that we may be able not only to cry " Come," but also to add " *let us* sing," because we are singing ourselves. It is to be feared that very much even of religious singing is not unto the Lord, but unto the ear of the congregation : above all things we must in our service of song take care that all we offer is with the heart's sincerest and most fervent intent directed towards the Lord himself. " *Let us make a joyful noise to the rock of our salvation.*" With holy enthusiasm let us sing, making a sound which shall indicate our earnestness ; with abounding joy let us lift up our voices, actuated by that happy and peaceful spirit which trustful love is sure to foster. As the children of Israel sang for joy when the smitten rock poured forth its cooling streams, so let us make a joyful noise to the rock of our salvation. The author of this song had in his mind's eye the rock, the tabernacle, the Red Sea, and the mountains of Sinai, and he alludes to them all in this first part of his hymn. God is our abiding, immutable, and mighty rock, and in him we find deliverance and safety, therefore it becomes us to praise him with heart and with voice from day to day ; and especially should we delight to do this when we assemble as his people for public worship.

> "Come let us to the Lord sing out
> With trumpet voice and choral shout."

2. " *Let us come before his presence with thanksgiving.*" Here is probably a reference to the peculiar presence of God in the Holy of Holies above the mercy-seat, and also to the glory which shone forth out of the cloud which rested above

164

the tabernacle. Everywhere God is present, but there is a peculiar presence of grace and glory into which men should never come without the profoundest reverence. We may make bold to come before the immediate presence of the Lord—for the voice of the Holy Ghost in this Psalm invites us, and when we do draw near to him we should remember his great goodness to us and cheerfully confess it. Our worship should have reference to the past as well as to the future ; if we do not bless the Lord for what we have already received, how can we reasonably look for more. We are permitted to bring our petitions, and therefore we are in honour bound to bring our thanksgivings. " *And make a joyful noise unto him with Psalms.*" We should shout as exultingly as those do who triumph in war, and as solemnly as those whose utterance is a Psalm. It is not always easy to unite enthusiasm with reverence, and it is a frequent fault to destroy one of these qualities while straining after the other. The perfection of singing is that which unites joy with gravity, exultation with humility, fervency with sobriety. The invitation given in the first verse is thus repeated in the second with the addition of directions, which indicate more fully the intent of the writer. One can imagine David in earnest tones persuading his people to go up with him to the worship of Jehovah with sound of harp and hymn, and holy delight. The gladsomeness of his exhortation is noteworthy, the noise is to be *joyful* ; this quality he insists upon twice. It is to be feared that this is too much overlooked in ordinary services, people are so impressed with the idea that they ought to be serious that they put on the aspect of misery, and quite forget that joy is as much a characteristic of true worship as solemnity itself.

3. " *For the Lord is a great God, and a great King above all gods.*" No doubt the surrounding nations imagined Jehovah to be a merely local deity, the god of a small nation, and therefore one of the inferior deities ; the Psalmist utterly repudiates such an idea. Idolaters tolerated gods many and lords many, giving to each a certain measure of respect ; the monotheism of the Jews was not content with this concession, it rightly claimed for Jehovah the chief place, and the supreme power. He is great, for he is all in all ; he is a great King above all other powers and dignitaries, whether angels or princes, for they owe their existence to him ; as for the idol gods, they are not worthy to be mentioned. This verse and the following supply some of the reasons for worship, drawn from the being, greatness, and sovereign dominion of the Lord.

4. " *In his hand are the deep places of the earth.*" He is the God of the valleys and the hills, the caverns, and the peaks. Far down where miners sink their shafts, deeper yet where lie the secret oceans by which springs are fed, and deepest of all in the unknown abyss where rage and flame the huge central fires of earth, there Jehovah's power is felt, and all things are under the dominion of his hand. As princes hold the mimic globe in their hands, so does the Lord in very deed hold the earth. When Israel drank of the crystal fount which welled up from the great deep, below the smitten rock, the people knew that in the Lord's hands were the deep places of the earth. " *The strength of the hills is his also.*" When Sinai was altogether on a smoke the tribes learned that Jehovah was God of the hills as well as of the valleys. Everywhere and at all times is this true ; the Lord rules upon the high places of the earth in lonely majesty. The vast foundations, the gigantic spurs, the incalculable masses, the untrodden heights of the mountains are all the Lord's. These are his fastnesses and treasure-houses, where he stores the tempest and the rain ; whence also he pours the ice-torrents and looses the avalanches. The granite peaks and adamantine aiguilles are his, and his the precipices and the beetling crags. Strength is the main thought which strikes the mind when gazing on those vast ramparts of cliff which front the raging sea, or peer into the azure sky, piercing the clouds, but it is to the devout mind the strength of God ; hints of Omnipotence are given by those stern rocks which brave the fury of the elements, and like walls of brass defy the assaults of nature in her wildest rage.

5. " *The sea is his.*" This was seen to be true at the Red Sea when the waters saw their God, and obediently stood aside to open a pathway for his people. It was not Edom's sea though it was red, nor Egypt's sea though it washed her shores. The Lord on high reigned supreme over the flood, as King for ever and ever. So is it with the broad ocean, whether known as Atlantic or Pacific, Mediterranean or Arctic ; no man can map it out and say " 'Tis mine " ; the illimitable acreage of waters knows no other lord but God alone. Jehovah rules the waves. Far down in vast abysses, where no eye of man has gazed, or foot of diver has descended, he is sole proprietor ; every rolling billow and foaming wave owns him for monarch ;

Neptune is but a phantom, the Lord is God of ocean. " *And he made it.*" Hence his right and sovereignty. He scooped the unfathomed channel and poured forth the overflowing flood ; seas were not fashioned by chance, nor their shores marked out by the imaginary finger of fate ; God made the main, and every creek, and bay, and current, and far-sounding tide owns the great Maker's hand. All hail, Creator and Controller of the sea, let those who fly in the swift ships across the wonder-realm of waters worship thee alone !

" *And his hands formed the dry land.*" Whether fertile field or sandy waste, he made all that men call *terra firma*, lifting it from the floods and fencing it from the overflowing waters. " The earth is the Lord's, and the fulness thereof." He bade the isles upraise their heads, he levelled the vast plains, upreared the table-lands, cast up the undulating hills, and piled the massive Alps. As the potter moulds his clay, so did Jehovah with his hands fashion the habitable parts of the earth. Come ye, then, who dwell on this fair world, and worship him who is conspicuous where'er ye tread ! Count it all as the floor of a temple where the footprints of the present Deity are visible before your eyes if ye do but care to see. The argument is overpowering if the heart be right ; the command to adore is alike the inference of reason and the impulse of faith.

6 O come, let us worship and bow down : let us kneel before the LORD our maker.

7 For he *is* our God ; and we *are* the people of his pasture, and the sheep of his hand. To-day if ye will hear his voice,

8 Harden not your heart, as in the provocation, *and* as *in* the day of temptation in the wilderness :

9 When your fathers tempted me, proved me, and saw my work.

10 Forty years long was I grieved with *this* generation, and said, It *is* a people that do err in their heart, and they have not known my ways :

11 Unto whom I sware in my wrath that they should not enter into my rest.

6. Here the exhortation to worship is renewed and backed with a motive which, to Israel of old, and to Christians now, is especially powerful ; for both the Israel after the flesh and the Israel of faith may be described as the people of his pasture, and by both he is called " our God." " *O come, let us worship and bow down.*" The adoration is to be humble. The " joyful noise " is to be accompanied with lowliest reverence. We are to worship in such style that the bowing down shall indicate that we count ourselves to be as nothing in the presence of the all-glorious Lord. " *Let us kneel before the Lord our maker.*" As suppliants must we come ; joyful, but not presumptuous ; familiar as children before a father, yet reverential as creatures before their maker. Posture is not everything, yet is it something ; prayer is heard when knees cannot bend, but it is seemly that an adoring heart should show its awe by prostrating the body, and bending the knee.

7. " *For he is our God.*" Here is the master reason for worship. Jehovah has entered into covenant with *us*, and from all the world beside has chosen us to be his own elect. If others refuse him homage, we at least will render it cheerfully. He is ours, and our God ; ours, therefore will we love him ; our God, therefore will we worship him. Happy is that man who can sincerely believe that this sentence is true in reference to himself. " *And we are the people of his pasture, and the sheep of his hand.*" As he belongs to us, so do we belong to him. " My Beloved is mine, and I am his." And we are his as the people whom he daily feeds and protects. Our pastures are not ours, but his ; we draw all our supplies from his stores. We are his, even as sheep belong to the shepherd, and his hand is our rule, our guidance, our government, our succour, our source of supply. Israel was led through the desert, and we are led through this life by " that great Shepherd of the sheep." The hand which cleft the sea and brought water from the rock is still with us, working equal wonders. Can we refuse to " worship and bow down " when we clearly see that " this God is our God for ever and ever, and will be our guide, even unto death " ?

But what is this warning which follows ? Alas, it was sorrowfully needed by the Lord's ancient people, and is not one whit the less required by ourselves. The favoured nation grew deaf to their Lord's command, and proved not to be truly his sheep, of whom it is written, " My sheep hear my voice " : will this turn out to be our character also ? God forbid. " *To day if ye will hear his voice.*" Dreadful " *if.*" Many would not hear, they put off the claims of love, and provoked their God. " To-day," in the hour of grace, in the day of mercy, we are tried as to whether we have an ear for the voice of our Creator. Nothing is said of to-morrow, " he limiteth a certain day," he presses for immediate attention, for our own sakes he asks instantaneous obedience. Shall we yield it ? The Holy Ghost saith " To-day," will we grieve him by delay ?

8. " *Harden not your heart.*" If ye will hear, learn to fear also. The sea and the land obey him, do not prove more obstinate than they !

> " Yield to his love who round you now
> The bands of a man would cast."

We cannot soften our hearts, but we can harden them, and the consequences will be fatal. To-day is too good a day to be profaned by the hardening of our hearts against our own mercies. While mercy reigns let not obduracy rebel. " *As in the provocation, and as in the day of temptation in the wilderness* " (or, " like Meribah, like the day of Massah in the wilderness "). Be not wilfully, wantonly, repeatedly, obstinately rebellious. Let the example of that unhappy generation serve as a beacon to you ; do not repeat the offences which have already more than enough provoked the Lord. God remembers men's sins, and the more memorably so when they are committed by a favoured people, against frequent warnings, in defiance of terrible judgments, and in the midst of superlative mercies ; such sins write their record in marble. Reader, this verse is for you, for you even if you can say, " He is our God, and we are the people of his pasture." Do not seek to turn aside the edge of the warning ; thou hast good need of it, give good heed to it.

9. " *When your fathers tempted me.*" As far as they could do so they tempted God to change his usual way, and to do their sinful bidding, and though he cannot be tempted of evil, and will never yield to wicked requests, yet their intent was the same, and their guilt was none the less. God's way is perfect, and when we would have him alter it to please us, we are guilty of tempting him ; and the fact that we do so in vain, while it magnifies the Lord's holiness, by no means excuses our guilt. We are in most danger of this sin in times of need, for then it is that we are apt to fall into unbelief, and to demand a change in those arrangements of providence which are the transcript of perfect holiness and infinite wisdom. Not to acquiesce in the will of God is virtually to tempt him to alter his plans to suit our imperfect views of how the universe should be governed. " *Proved me.*" They put the Lord to needless tests, demanding new miracles, fresh interpositions, and renewed tokens of his presence. Do not we also peevishly require frequent signs of the Lord's love other than those which every hour supplies ? Are we not prone to demand specialities, with the alternative secretly offered in our hearts, that if they do not come at our bidding we will disbelieve ? True, the Lord is very condescending, and frequently grants us marvellous evidences of his power, but we ought not to require them. Steady faith is due to one who is so constantly kind. After so many proofs of his love, we are ungrateful to wish to prove him again, unless it be in those ways of his own appointing, in which he has said, " Prove me now." If we were for ever testing the love of our wife or husband, and remained unconvinced after years of faithfulness, we should wear out the utmost human patience. Friendship only flourishes in the atmosphere of confidence, suspicion is deadly to it : shall the Lord God, true and immutable, be day after day suspected by his own people ? Will not this provoke him to anger ? " *And saw my work.*" They tested him again and again, throughout forty years, though each time his work was conclusive evidence of his faithfulness. Nothing could convince them for long.

> " They saw his wonders wrought,
> And then his praise they sung ;
> But soon his works of pow'r forgot,
> And murmur'd with their tongue.

> " Now they believe his word,
> While rocks with rivers flow ;
> Now with their lusts provoke the Lord,
> And he reduc'd them low."

Fickleness is bound up in the heart of man, unbelief is our besetting sin ; we must

for ever be seeing, or we waver in our believing. This is no mean offence, and will bring with it no small punishment.

10. "*Forty years long was I grieved with this generation.*" The impression upon the divine mind is most vivid ; he sees them before him now, and calls them "*this* generation." He does not leave his prophets to upbraid the sin, but himself utters the complaint and declares that he was grieved, nauseated, and disgusted. It is no small thing which can grieve our long-suffering God to the extent which the Hebrew word here indicates, and if we reflect a moment we shall see the abundant provocation given ; for no one who values his veracity can endure to be suspected, mistrusted, and belied, when there is no ground for it, but on the contrary the most overwhelming reason for confidence. To such base treatment was the tender Shepherd of Israel exposed, not for a day or a month, but for forty years at a stretch, and that not by here and there an unbeliever, but by a whole nation, in which only two men were found so thoroughly believing as to be exempted from the doom which at last was pronounced upon all the rest. Which shall we most wonder at, the cruel insolence of man, or the tender patience of the Lord ? Which shall leave the deepest impression on our minds, the sin or the punishment ? unbelief, or the barring of the gates of Jehovah's rest against the unbelievers ? "*And said, It is a people that do err in their heart, and they have not known my ways.*" Their heart was obstinately and constantly at fault ; it was not their head which erred, but their very heart was perverse : love, which appealed to their affections, could not convert them. The heart is the mainspring of the man, and if it be not in order, the entire nature is thrown out of gear. If sin were only skin-deep, it might be a slight matter ; but since it has defiled the soul, the case is bad indeed. Taught as they were by Jehovah himself in lessons illustrated by miracles, which came to them daily in the manna from heaven, and the water from the flinty rock, they ought to have learned something, and it was a foul shame that they remained obstinately ignorant, and would not know the ways of God. Wanderers in body, they were also wanderers in heart, and the plain providential goodness of their God remained to their blinded minds as great a maze as those twisting paths by which he led them through the wilderness. Are we better than they ? Are we not quite as apt to misinterpret the dealings of the Lord ? Have we suffered and enjoyed so many things in vain ? With many it is even so. Forty years of providential wisdom, yea, and even a longer period of experience, have failed to teach them serenity of assurance, and firmness of reliance. There is ground for much searching of heart concerning this. Many treat unbelief as a minor fault, they even regard it rather as an infirmity than a crime, but the Lord thinketh not so. Faith is Jehovah's due, especially from those who claim to be the people of his pasture, and yet more emphatically from those whose long life has been crowded with evidences of his goodness : unbelief insults one of the dearest attributes of Deity, it does so needlessly and without the slightest ground, and in defiance of all-sufficient arguments, weighty with the eloquence of love. Let us in reading this Psalm examine ourselves, and lay these things to heart.

11. "*Unto whom I sware in my wrath that they should not enter into my rest.*" There can be no rest to an unbelieving heart. If manna and miracles could not satisfy Israel, neither would they have been content with the land which flowed with milk and honey. Canaan was to be the typical resting-place of God, where his ark should abide, and the ordinances of religion should be established ; the Lord had for forty years borne with the ill manners of the generation which came out of Egypt, and it was but right that he should resolve to have no more of them. Was it not enough that they had revolted all along that marvellous wilderness march ? Should they be allowed to make new Massahs and Meribahs in the Promised Land itself ? Jehovah would not have it so. He not only said but swore that into his rest they should not come, and that oath excluded every one of them ; their carcases fell in the wilderness. Solemn warning this to all who leave the way of faith for paths of petulant murmuring and mistrust. The rebels of old could not enter in because of unbelief, "let us therefore fear, lest, a promise being left us of entering into his rest, any of us should even seem to come short of it."

One blessed inference from this Psalm must not be forgotten. It is clear that there is a rest of God, and that some must enter into it : but "they to whom it was first preached entered not in because of unbelief, there remaineth therefore a rest to the people of God." The unbelievers could not enter, but "we which have believed do enter into rest." Let us enjoy it, and praise the Lord for it for ever. Ours is the true Sabbatic rest, it is ours to rest from our own works as God did from his. While we do so, let us " come into his presence with thanksgiving, and make a joyful noise unto him with Psalms."

EXPLANATORY NOTES AND QUAINT SAYINGS.

Whole Psalm.—These six Psalms, xcv. to c., form, if I mistake not, one entire prophetic poem, cited by St. Paul in the Epistle to the Hebrews, under the title of the Introduction of the First Born into the world. Each Psalm has its proper subject, which is some particular branch of the general argument, the establishment of the Messiah's Kingdom. The 95th Psalm asserts Jehovah's Godhead, and his power over all nature, and exhorts his people to serve him. In Psalm 96th all nations are exhorted to join in his service, because he cometh to judge all mankind, Jew and Gentile. In the 97th Psalm, Jehovah reigns over all the world, the idols are deserted, the Just One is glorified. In the 98th Psalm, Jehovah hath done wonders, and wrought deliverance for himself : he hath remembered his mercy towards the house of Israel; he comes to judge the whole world. In the 99th, Jehovah, seated between the cherubim in Zion, the visible Church, reigns over all the world, to be praised for the justice of his government. In the 100th Psalm, all the world is called upon to praise Jehovah the Creator, whose mercy and truth are everlasting.—*Samuel Horsley.*

Whole Psalm.—This Psalm is twice quoted in the Epistle to the Hebrews, as a warning to the Jewish Christians at Jerusalem, in the writer's day, that they should not falter in the faith, and despise God's promises, as their forefathers had done in the wilderness, lest they should fail of entering into his rest ; see Heb. iii. 7, where verse 7 of this Psalm is introduced with the words, " As the Holy Ghost saith, To-day if ye will hear his voice," and see Heb. iv. 7, where it is said, " Again, he limiteth a certain day, saying *in David*, To-day." It has by some been inferred from these words, that the writer of the Epistle to the Hebrews ascribes this Psalm to *David*. It may be so. But it seems not improbable that the words " in David " mean simply " the Book of Psalms," the whole being named from the greater part ; and that if he had meant that David wrote the Psalm, he would have written, " David spake," or, " the Holy Ghost spake by David," and not as it is written, " as it is said *in David*."—*Christopher Wordsworth.*

Verse 1.—" *O come, let us sing unto the Lord,*" etc. The first verse of the Psalm begins the invitation unto praise and exultation. It is a song of three parts, and every part (like Jacob's part of the sheep) brings forth twins ; each a double string, as it were, in the music of this praise, finely twisted of two parts into a kind of *discordant concord*, falling into a musical close through a differing yet reconciled diapason. The first couple in this song of praise are *multitude* and *unity*, *concourse* and *concord* : " *O come*," there's *multitude* and *concourse* ; " *let us*," there's *unity* and *concord*. The second twisted pair, are *tongue* and *heart*, " *let us sing*," there's the voice and sound ; and " *heartily rejoice*," there's the heart and soul. The third and last intertwisted string, or part of the musick, is *might* and *mercy*, (rock or) *strength* and *salvation* ; *God's strength* and *our salvation* : " to the strength (or rock) of our salvation."—*Charles Herle* (1598—1659) *in a " Sermon before the House of Lords," entitled " David's Song of Three Parts."*

Verse 1.—" *Come.*" The word " *come* " contains an exhortation, exciting them to join heart and lips in praising God ; just as the word is used in Genesis where the people, exciting and encouraging each other, say, " Come, let us make bricks ; " and " Come, let us make a city and a town ; " and, in the same chapter, the Lord says, " Come, let us go down, and there confound their tongue."—*Bellarmine.*

Verse 1.—If it be so that one " *come, let us* " goes further than twenty times *go and do*, how careful should such be whom God hath raised to eminence of place that their examples be Jacob's ladders to help men to heaven, not Jeroboam's stumbling-blocks to lie in their way, and make Israel to sin.—*Charles Herle.*

Verse 1.—There is a silent hint here at that human listlessness and distraction of cares whereby we are more prompt to run after other things than to devote ourselves seriously to the becoming praises and service of God. Our foot has a greater proclivity to *depart* to the field, the oxen, and the new wife, than to *come* to the sacred courts, Luke xiv. 18, *seq*. See Is. ii. 3, " Come ye, and let us go up to the mountain of the Lord."—*Martin Geier*.

Verse 1.—" *Joyful noise.*" The verb הָרִיע, signifies to make a loud sound of any sort, either with the voice or with instruments. In the Psalms, it generally refers to the mingled din of voices and various instruments, in the Temple service. This wide sense of the word cannot be expressed otherwise in the English language than by a periphrasis.—*Samuel Horsley*.

Verse 1.—" *The rock of our salvation.*" Jesus is the Rock of ages, in which is opened a fountain for sin and uncleanness ; the Rock which attends the church in the wilderness, pouring forth the water of life, for her use and comfort ; the Rock which is our fortress against every enemy, shadowing and refreshing a weary land.—*George Horne*.

Verse 2.—" *Let us come before his presence.*" Hebrew, *prevent his face*, be there with the first. " *Let us go speedily. . . . I will go also,*" Zech. viii. 21. Let praise wait for God in Sion, Ps. lxv. 1.—*John Trapp*.

Verse 2 (second clause).—" *Let us chaunt aloud to him the measured lay.*" נְמִרוֹת, I take to be songs, in measured verse, adjusted to the bars of a chaunt.—*S. Horsley*.

Verse 3.—He that hath a mind to praise God, shall not want matter of praise, as they who come before princes do, who for want of true grounds of praise in them, do give them flattering words ; " *for the Lord is a great God,*" for power and pre-eminency, for strength and continuance.—*David Dickson*.

Verse 3.—The Supreme Being has *three* names here : אֵל *El*, יְהוָֹה *Jehovah*, אֱלֹהִים *Elohim*, and we should apply none of them to *false gods*. The *first* implies his *strength* ; the *second*, his *being* and *essence* ; the *third*, his *covenant relation* to mankind. In public worship these are the views we should entertain of the Divine Being.—*Adam Clarke*.

Verse 3.—" *Above all gods.*" When he is called a great *God* and *King* above *all gods*, we may justly imagine that the reference is to the angels who are wont to be introduced absolutely under this name, and to the supreme *Judges* in the land, who also wear this title, as we have it in Ps. lxxxii.—*Venema*.

Verse 4.—" *In his hand.*" The dominion of God is founded upon his preservation of things. " The Lord is a great King above all gods." Why ? " *In his hand are the deep places of the earth.*" While his hand holds, his hand hath a dominion over them. He that holds a stone in the air exerciseth a dominion over its natural inclination in hindering it from falling. The creature depends wholly upon God in its preservation ; as soon as that divine hand which sustains everything were withdrawn, a languishment and swooning would be the next turn in the creature. He is called Lord, *Adonai*, in regard of his sustentation of all things by his continual influx, the word coming of אֵן, which signifies a basis or pillar that supports a building. God is the Lord of all, as he is the sustainer of all by his power, as well as the Creator of all by his word.—*Stephen Charnock*.

Verse 4.—

> " In whose hand are the recesses of the earth
> And the treasures of the mountains are his."
>
> —*Thomas J. Conant's Translation*.

Verse 4.—" *In his hand are the deep places of the earth.*" This affords consolation to those, who for the glory of the divine name are cast into prisons and subterraneous caves ; because they know, that even there it is not possible to be the least separated from the presence of Christ. Wherefore he preserved Joseph when hurled by his brethren into the old pit, and when thrust by his shameless mistress into prison ; Jeremiah also when sent down into the dungeon ; Daniel among the lions, and his companions in the furnace. So all who cleave to him with a firm faith, he wonderfully keeps and delivers to this day.—*Solomon Gesner*, 1559—1605.

Verse 4.—" *In his hand are the deep places of the earth.*" As an illustration of the working and presence of the Lord in the mines amid the bowels of the earth we have selected the following :—" The natural disposition of coal in detached portions," says the author of an excellent article in the Edinburgh Review, " is not simply a phenomenon of geology, but it also bears upon natural considerations.

It is remarkable that this natural disposition is that which renders the fuel most accessible and most easily mined. Were the coal situated at its normal geological depth, that is, supposing the strata to be all horizontal and undisturbed or upheaved, it would be far below human reach. Were it deposited continuously in one even superficial layer, it would have been too readily, and therefore too quickly, mined, and therefore all the superior qualities would be wrought out, and only the inferior left; but as it now lies it is broken up by geological disturbances into separate portions, each defined and limited in area, each sufficiently accessible to bring it within man's reach and labour, each manageable by mechanical arrangements, and each capable of gradual excavation without being subject to sudden exhaustion. Selfish plundering is partly prevented by natural barriers, and we are warned against reckless waste by the comparative thinness of coal-seams, as well as by the ever augmenting difficulty of working them at increased depths. By the separation of seams one from another, and by varied intervals of waste sandstones and shales, such a measured rate of winning is necessitated as precludes us from entirely robbing posterity of the most valuable mineral fuel, while the fuel itself is preserved from those extended fractures and crumblings and falls, which would certainly be the consequence of largely mining the best bituminous coal, were it aggregated into one vast mass. In fact, by an evident exercise of forethought and benevolence in the Great Author of all our blessings, our invaluable fuel has been stored up for us in deposits the most compendious, the most accessible, yet the least exhaustible, and has been locally distributed into the most convenient situations. Our coalfields are so many *Bituminous Banks*, in which there is abundance for an adequate currency, but against any sudden run upon them nature has interposed numerous checks; whole reserves of the precious fuel are always locked up in the bank-cellar under the invincible protection of ponderous stone-beds. It is a striking fact, that in this nineteenth century, after so long an inhabitation of the earth by man, if we take the quantities in the broad view of the whole known coal-fields, so little coal has been excavated, and that there remains an abundance for a very remote posterity, even though our own best coal-fields may be then worked out."

But it is not only in these inexhaustible supplies of mineral fuel that we find proofs of divine foresight, all the other treasures of the earth-rind equally convince us of the intimate harmony between its structure and the wants of man. Composed of a wonderful variety of earths and ores, it contains an inexhaustible abundance of all the substances he requires for the attainment of a higher grade of civilisation. It is for his use that iron, copper, lead, silver, tin, marble, gypsum, sulphur, rock-salt, and a variety of other minerals and metals, have been deposited in the veins and crevices, or in the mines and quarries, of the subterranean world. It is for his benefit that, from the decomposition of the solid rocks results that mixture of earths and alkalis, of marl, lime, sand, or chalk, which is most favourable to agriculture.

It is for him, finally, that, filtering through the entrails of the earth, and dissolving salutary substances on their way, the thermal springs gush forth laden with treasures more inestimable than those the miner toils for. Supposing man had never been destined to live, we well may ask why all those gifts of nature—useless to all living beings but to him—why those vast coal-fields, those beds of iron ore, those deposits of sulphur, those hygeian fountains, should ever have been created? *Without* him there is no design, no purpose, in their existence; *with* him they are wonderful sources of health or necessary instruments of civilisation and improvement. Thus the geological revolutions of the earth-rind harmoniously point to man as to its future lord; thus, in the life of our planet and that of its inhabitants, we everywhere find proofs of a gigantic unity of plan, embracing unnumbered ages in its development and progress.—*G. Hartwig, in " The Harmonies of Nature,"* 1866.

Verse 4.—*" The deep places of the earth,"* penetralia terræ, which are opposed to the heights of the hills, and plainly mean the deepest and most retired parts of the terraqueous globe, which are explorable by the eye of God, and by his only.—*Richard Mant.*

Verse 4.—*" The strength of the hills."* The word translated *" strength "* is plural in Hebrew, and seems properly to mean fatiguing exertions, from which some derive the idea of strength, others that of extreme height, which can only be reached by exhausting effort.—*J. A. Alexander.*

Verse 4.—*" The strength of the hills is his also."* The reference may be to *the wealth of the hills*, obtained only by *labour* [Gesenius], corresponding to the former—*" the deep places of the earth,"* explained as referring to *the mines* [Mendelssohn].

Go where man may, with all his toil and searching in the heights or in the depths of the earth, he cannot find a place beyond the range of God's dominion.—*A. R. Fausset.*

Verses 4, 5.—" *Hills,*" " *The Sea,*" " *the dry land.*" The relation of areas of land to areas of water exercises a great and essential influence on the distribution of heat, variations of atmospheric pressure, directions of the winds, and that condition of the air with respect to moisture, which is so necessary for the health of vegetation. Nearly three-fourths of the earth's surface is covered with water, but neither the exact height of the atmosphere nor the depth of the ocean are fully determined. Still we know that with every addition to or subtraction from the present bulk of the waters of the ocean, the consequent variation in the form and magnitude of the land would be such, that if the change was considerable, many of the existing harmonies of things would cease. Hence, the inference is, that the magnitude of the sea is one of the conditions to which the structure of all organised creatures is adapted, and on which indeed they depend for well-being. The proportions between land and water are exactly what the world as constituted requires ; and the whole mass of earth, sea, and air, must have been balanced with the greatest nicety before even a crocus could stand erect, or a snowdrop or a daffodil bend their heads to the ground. The proportions of land and sea are adjusted to their reciprocal functions. Nothing deduced from modern science is more certain than this. —*Edwin Sidney, in " Conversations on the Bible and Science."*

Verse 5.—" *The sea is his.*" When God himself makes an oration in defence of his sovereignty, Job xxxviii., his chief arguments are drawn from creation : " The Lord is a great King above all gods. The sea is his, and he made it." And so the apostle in his sermon to the Athenians. As he " made the world, and all things therein," he is styled " Lord of heaven and earth," Acts xvii. 24. His dominion also of property stands upon this basis : Ps. lxxxix. 11, " The heavens are thine, the earth also is thine : as for the world and the fulness thereof, thou hast founded them." Upon this title of forming Israel as a creature, or rather as a church, he demands their services to him as their Sovereign. " O Jacob and Israel, thou art my servant : I have formed thee ; thou art my servant, O Israel," Isa. xliv. 21. The sovereignty of God naturally ariseth from the relation of all things to himself as their entire creator, and their natural and inseparable dependence upon him in regard of their being and well-being.—*Stephen Charnock.*

Verse 5.—" *He made it.*"

> The Earth was form'd, but in the womb as yet
> Of waters, embryon immature involv'd,
> Appear'd not : over all the face of Earth
> Main ocean flow'd, not idle ; but, with warm
> Prolifick humour softening all her globe,
> Fermented the great mother to conceive,
> Satiate with genial moisture ; when God said,
> Be gather'd now, ye waters under Heaven
> Into one place, and let dry land appear.
> Immediately the mountains huge appear
> Emergent, and their broad bare backs upheave
> Into the clouds ; their tops ascend the sky :
> So high as heav'd the tumid hills, so low
> Down sunk a hollow bottom broad and deep,
> Capacious bed of waters.
>
> —*John Milton.*

Verse 6.—You hold it a good rule in worldly business, not to say to your servants, " O come," " arise ye, go ye ; " but, *Let us* come, let us go, let us arise. Now shall the children of this world be wiser in their generation than the children of light ? Do we commend this course in mundane affairs, and neglect it in religious offices ? Assuredly, if our zeal were as great to religion, as our love is towards the world, masters would not come to church (as many do) without their servants, and servants without their masters ; parents without their children, and children without their parents ; husbands without their wives, and wives without their husbands ; but all of us would call one to another, as Esay prophesied (ch. ii. 3) : " Come ye, and let us go up to the mountain of the LORD, to the house of the God of Jacob ; and he will teach us of his ways, and we will walk in his paths," and as David here practised.—*John Boys.*

Verse 6.—" *Let us worship and bow down.*" To fall upon the ground is a gesture of worship, not only when the worshipper mourns, but when the worshipper rejoiceth. It is said (Matthew ii. 10, 11) that the wise men when they found Christ, " *rejoiced with exceeding great joy,*" and presently, " *they fell down, and worshipped him.*" Neither is this posture peculiar to worship in times or upon occasions of extraordinary joy and sorrow ; for the ordinary invitation was, " *O come, let us worship and bow down : let us kneel before the Lord our maker.*"—*Joseph Caryl.*

Verse 6.—" *Let us worship and bow down : let us kneel before the Lord our maker.*" Not before a crucifix, not before a rotten image, not before a fair picture of a foul saint : these are not *our makers ;* we made them, they made not us. Our God, unto whom we must sing, in whom we must rejoice, before whom we must worship, " *is a great King above all gods* " : he is no god of lead, no god of bread, no brazen god, no wooden god ; we must not fall down and worship our *Lady,* but our *Lord ;* not any *martyr,* but our *Maker* ; not any *saint,* but our *Saviour :* " *O come, let us sing unto the Lord : let us make a joyful noise to the rock of our salvation.*" *Wherewith :* with voice, " *Let us sing* " ; with soul, " *Let us heartily rejoice* " ; with hands and knees, " *Let us worship and bow down : let us kneel* " ; with all that is within us, with all that is without us : he that made all, must be worshipped with all, especially when we " come before his presence."—*John Boys.*

Verse 6.—" *Bow down.*" That is, so as to touch the floor with the forehead, while the worshipper is prostrate on his hands and knees. See 2 Chron. vii. 3.—*John Fry,* 1842.

Verse 6.—" *Worship,*" " *bow down,*" " *kneel.*" Kimchi distinguishes the several gestures expressed by the different words here used. The first we render " worship," signifies, according to him, the prostration of the whole body on the ground, with the hands and legs stretched out. The second a bowing of the head, with part of the body ; and the third a bending of the knees on the ground.—*Samuel Burder.*

Verse 7.—" *We are the people of his pasture, and the sheep of his hand.*" See how elegantly he hath transposed the order of the words, and as it were not given its own attribute to each word ; that we may understand these very same to be " *the sheep,*" who are also " *the people.*" He said not, the sheep of his pasture, and the people of his hand ; which might be thought more congruous, since the sheep belong to the pasture ; but he said, " *the people of his pasture* " : the people themselves are sheep. But again, since we have sheep which we buy, not which we create ; and he had said above, " *Let us fall down before our Maker* " ; it is rightly said, " *the sheep of his hand.*" No man maketh for himself sheep, he may buy them, they may be given, he may find them, he may collect them, lastly he may steal them ; make them he cannot. But our Lord made us ; therefore " *the people of his pasture, and the sheep of his hand,*" are the very sheep which he hath deigned by his grace to create unto himself.—*Augustine.*

Verse 7.—" *The sheep of his hand,*" is a fit though figurative expression, the shepherd that feeds, and rules, and leads the *sheep,* doing it by his *hand,* which manageth the rod and staff (Ps. xxiii. 4), by which they are administered. The Jewish Arab reads, *the people of his feeding,* or *flock, and the sheep of his guidance.*—*H. Hammond.*

Verse 7.—" *For we are his people whom he feeds in his pastures, and his sheep whom he leads as by his hand.*" [French Version.] Here is a reason to constrain us to praise God ; it is this,—that not only has he created us, but that he also directs us by special providence, as a shepherd governs his flock. Jesus Christ, Divine Shepherd of our souls, who not only feeds us in his pastures, but himself *leads* us *with his hand,* as intelligent sheep. Loving Shepherd, who *feeds* us not only from the pastures of Holy Writ, but even with his own flesh. What subjects of ceaseless adoration for a soul penetrated by these great verities ! What a fountain of tears of joy at the sight of such prodigious mercy !—*Quesnel.*

Verse 7.—" *To-day if ye will hear his voice.*" If we put off repentance another day, we have a day more to repent of, and a day less to repent in.—*W. Mason.*

Verse 7.—He that hath promised pardon on our repentance hath not promised to preserve our lives till we repent.—*Francis Quarles.*

Verse 7.—You cannot repent too soon, because you do not know how soon it may be too late.—*Thomas Fuller.*

Verse 7.—" *If ye will hear his voice."* Oh ! what an *if* is here ! what a reproach is here to those that hear him not ! " My sheep hear my voice, and I know them, and they follow me " ; " but ye will not come to me that ye might have life." And yet there is mercy, there is still salvation, if ye will hear that voice. Israel heard it among the thunders of Sinai, " which voice they that heard it entreated that the word should not be spoken to them any more " ; so terrible was the sight and sound that even Moses said, " I exceedingly quake and fear " : and yet they heard too the Lord's still voice of love in the noiseless manna that fell around their tents, and in the gushing waters of the rock that followed them through every march for forty years. Yet the record of Israel's ingratitude runs side by side with the record of God's mercies—" My people would not hearken to my voice, and Israel would none of me."—*Barton Bouchier.*

Verse 7.—" *If ye will hear his voice."* And yet, as S. Bernard tells us, there is no difficulty at all in hearing it ; on the contrary, the difficulty is to stop our ears effectually against it, so clear is it in enunciation, so constant in appeal. Yet there are many who do not hear, from divers causes ; because they are far off ; because they are deaf ; because they sleep ; because they turn their heads aside ; because they stop their ears ; because they hurry away to avoid hearing ; because they are dead ; all of them types of various forms and degrees of unbelief.—*Bernard and Hugo Cardinalis, in Neale and Littledale.*

Verse 7.—" *If ye will hear his voice."* These words seem to allude to the preceding words, in which we are represented as the *sheep of God's pasture,* and are to be considered as an affectionate call of our heavenly Shepherd to follow and obey him.— *From " Lectures on the Liturgy, from the Commentary of Peter Waldo,"* 1821.

Verses 7, 8.—It will be as difficult, nay, more difficult, to come to Christ to-morrow, than it is to-day : therefore " *to-day hear his voice, and harden not your heart."* Break the ice now, and by faith venture upon your present duty, wherever it lies : do what you are now called to. You will never know how easy the yoke of Christ is, till it is bound about your necks, nor how light his burden is, till you have taken it up. While you judge of holiness at a distance, as a thing without you and contrary to you, you will never like it. Come a little nearer to it ; do but take it in, actually engage in it, and you will find religion carries meat in its mouth ; it is of a reviving, nourishing, strengthening nature. It brings that along with it, that enables the soul cheerfully to go through with it.—*Thomas Cole* (1627—1697) *in the " Morning Exercises."*

Verse 8.—" *Harden not your hearts."* An old man, one day taking a child on his knee, entreated him to seek God *now*—to pray to him, and to love him ; when the child, looking up at him, asked, " But why do not *you* seek God ? " The old man, deeply affected, answered, " I would, child ; but my heart is *hard*—my heart is *hard."*—*Arvine's Anecdotes.*

Verse 8.—" *Harden not your heart."*—*Heart* is ascribed to reasonable creatures, to signify sometimes the whole soul, and sometimes the several faculties appertaining to the soul.

1. It is frequently put for the whole soul, and that for the most part when it is set alone ; as where it is said, " Serve the Lord with all your heart," 1 Sam. xii. 20.

2. For that principal part of the soul which is called the mind or understanding. " I gave my heart to know wisdom," Eccles. i. 17. In this respect darkness and blindness are attributed to the heart, Eph. iv. 18, Rom. i. 21.

3. For the will : as when heart and soul are joined together, the two essential faculties of the soul are meant, namely, the mind and will : *soul* put for the mind, heart for the will. " Serve the Lord with all your heart and with all your soul," Deut. xi. 13.

4. For the memory. " I have hid thy word in my heart," saith the prophet, Psalm cxix. 11. The memory is that faculty wherein matters are laid up and hid.

5. For the conscience. It is said that " David's heart smote him," that is, his conscience, 1 Sam. xxiv. 5, 2 Sam. xxiv. 10. Thus is heart taken, 1 John iii. 20, 21.

6. For the affections : as where it is said, " Thou shalt love the Lord thy God with all thy heart, and with all thy soul, and with all thy mind," Matt. xxii. 37. By the *mind* is meant the understanding faculty ; by the *soul,* the will ; by the *heart,* the affections.

Here in this text the heart is put for the whole soul, even for mind, will, and affections. For blindness of mind, stubbornness of will, and stupidity of affections go together.—*William Gouge.*

Verse 8.—In " Massah—in Meribah." Our translators say, *" in the provocation, in the day of temptation."* But the places were denominated by names taken from the transactions that occurred in them ; and the introduction of those names gives more liveliness to the allusion. See to the same effect Ps. lxxxi. 7 ; where the Bible translation retains the proper name.—*Richard Mant.*

Verse 8.—Let us not fail to notice, that while it is *the flock* who speak in verses 1—7, it is *the Shepherd* who takes up their expostulating words, and urges them home himself at verse 8 to the end, using the argument which by the Holy Ghost is addressed to us also in Hebrews iii. There is something very powerful in this expostulation, when connected with the circumstances that give rise to it. In themselves, the burst of adoring love, and the full outpouring of affection in verses 1—7 are irresistibly persuasive ; but when (verse 8) the voice of the Lord himself is heard (such a voice, using terms of vehement entreaty !) we cannot imagine expostulation carried further. Unbelief alone could resist this voice ; blind, malignant unbelief alone could repel *The flock, and then the Shepherd, inviting men now to enter the fold.*— *Andrew A. Bonar.*

Verse 9.—" Your fathers tempted me." Though God cannot be tempted with evil he may justly be said to be tempted whenever men, by being dissatisfied with his dealings, virtually ask that he will alter those dealings, and proceed in a way more congenial to their feelings. If you reflect a little, you will hardly fail to perceive, that in a very strict sense, this and the like may be called tempting God. Suppose a man to be discontented with the appointments of providence, suppose him to murmur and to repine at what the Almighty allots him to do or to bear ; is he not to be charged with the asking God to change his purposes ? And what is this if it is not tempting God, and striving to induce him to swerve from his plans, though every one of those plans has been settled by Infinite Wisdom ?

Or again, if any one of us, notwithstanding the multiplied proofs of Divine loving-kindness, doubt or question whether or not God do indeed love him, of what is he guilty, if not of tempting the Lord, seeing that he solicits God to the giving additional evidence, as though there was a deficiency, and challenges him to a fresh demonstration of what he has already abundantly displayed ? This would be called tempting amongst men. If a child were to show by his actions that he doubted or disbelieved the affection of his parents, he would be considered as striving to extract from them new proofs, by asking them to evince their love more, though they may already have done as much as in wisdom and in justice they ought to do. And this is clearly tempting them, and that too in the ordinary sense of the term. In short, unbelief of every kind and every degree may be said to tempt God. For not to believe upon the evidence which he has seen fit to give, is to provoke him to give more, offering our possible assent if proof were increased as an inducement to him to go beyond what his wisdom has prescribed. And if in this, and the like sense, God may be tempted, what can be more truly said of the Israelites, than that they tempted God in Massah ? . . . . We are perhaps not accustomed to think of unbelief or murmuring as nothing less than a tempting God, and therefore, we do not attach to what is so common, its just degree of heinousness. It is so natural to us to be discontented whenever God's dealings are not just what we like, to forget what has been done for us as soon as our wishes seem thwarted, to be impatient and fretful under every new cross, that we are scarcely conscious of committing a sin, and much less one more than usually aggravated. Yet we cannot be dissatisfied with God's dealings, and not be virtually guilty of tempting God. It may seem a harsh definition of a slight and scarcely avoidable fault, but nevertheless it is a true definition. You cannot mistrust God, and not accuse him of want either of power or of goodness. You cannot repine, no, not even in thought, without virtually telling him that his plans are not the best, nor his dispensations the wisest which he might have appointed in respect of yourselves. So that your fear, or your despondency, or your anxiety in circumstances of perplexity, or peril, are nothing less than the calling upon God to depart from his fixed course—a suspicion, or rather an assertion that he might proceed in a manner more worthy of himself, and, therefore, a challenge to him to alter his dealings if he would prove that he possesses the attributes which he claims. You may not intend thus to accuse or to provoke God whenever you murmur, but your murmuring does all this, and cannot fail to do it. You cannot be dissatisfied without virtually saying that God might order things better ; you cannot say that he might order things better without virtually demanding that he change his course of acting, and give other proofs of his Infinite perfections.—*Henry Melvill.*

Verse 9.—" *Your fathers tempted me.*" There are two ways of interpreting the words which follow. As *tempting God* is nothing else than yielding to a diseased and unwarrantable craving after proof of his power, we may consider the verse as connected throughout, and read, *They tempted me and proved me, although they had already seen my work.* God very justly complains, that they should insist upon new proof, after his power had been already amply testified by undeniable evidences. There is another meaning, however, that may be given to the term " *proved,*"—according to which, the meaning of the passage would run as follows :—Your fathers tempted me in asking where God was, notwithstanding all the benefits I had done them ; and they proved me, that is, they had actual experience of what I am, inasmuch as I did not cease to give them open proofs of my presence, and consequently they saw my work.—*John Calvin.*

Verse 9.—" *Proved me,*" put me to the proof of my existence, presence, and power, by requiring me to work, *i.e.* to act in an extraordinary manner. And this desire, unreasonable as it was, I gratified. They not only demanded, but they גַּם־רָאוּ likewise saw " *my work,*" *i.e.* what I could do.—*J. A. Alexander.*

Verse 9.—" *Forty years.*" To understand this passage we must bear in mind the event referred to. The same year in which the people of Israel came forth from Egypt, they were distressed for water at Rephidim, (Ex. xvii. 1 ;) and the place had two names given to it, Massah and Meribah, because the people tempted God and chided with Moses. The Lord did not swear *then* that they should not enter into the land of Canaan ; but this was in the following year, after the return of the spies. (Num. xiv. 20—38.) And God said then that they had tempted him " ten times " ; that is, during the short time since their deliverance from Egypt. It was after *ten* temptations that God deprived them of the promised land.

Bearing in mind these facts, we shall be able to see the full force of the passage. The " provocation " or contention, and " temptation " refer clearly to the latter instance, as recorded in Numb. xiv., because it was then that God sware that the people should not enter into his rest. The people's conduct was alike in both instances.

To connect " forty years " with grieved, was the work of the Punctuists, and this mistake the Apostle corrected ; and it is to be observed that he did not follow in this instance the *Septuagint*, in which the words are arranged as divided by the Masorites. Such a rendering as would correspond with the Hebrew is as follows,—

> " To-day when ye hear his voice,
> 8. Harden not your hearts as in the provocation,
>   In the day of temptation in the wilderness.
> 9. When your fathers tempted me, they proved me
>   And saw my works forty years :
> 10. I was therefore offended with that generation and said.
>   Always do they go astray in heart,
>   And they have not known my ways ;
> 11. So that I sware in my wrath,
>   ' They shall by no means enter into my rest.' "

The meaning of the ninth verse is, that when the children of Israel tempted God, they proved him, *i.e.*, found out by bitter experience how great his displeasure was, and saw his works or his dealings with them forty years. He retained them in the wilderness during that period until the death of all who disbelieved his word at the return of the spies ; he gave them this proof of his displeasure.—*John Owen, of Thrussington*, 1853.

Verse 10.—O the desperate presumption of man, that he should offend his Maker " *forty years* " ! O the patience and longsuffering of his Maker, that he should allow him forty years to offend in ! Sin begins in the " *heart,*" by its desires *wandering* and going astray after forbidden objects ; whence follows inattention to the " *ways* " of God, to his dispensations, and our own duty. Lust in the heart, like vapour in the stomach, soon affects the head, and clouds the understanding.—*George Horne.*

Verse 10.—" *Forty Years.*" It is curious to know that the ancient Jews believed that " the days of the Messiah were to be forty years." Thus Tanchuma, F. 79, 4.

" Quamdiu durant anni Messiæ ?   R. Akiba dixit, xl. annos, quemadmodum Israelitæ
per tot annos in deserto fuerunt."   It is remarkable, that in forty years after the
ascension, the whole Jewish nation were cut off equally as they who fell in the wilderness.—*John Brown, in " An Exposition of the Epistle to the Hebrews."* 1862.

Verse 10.—*" Was I grieved."* The word is a strong word, expressive of *loathing*
and *disgust.—J. J. S. Perowne.*

Verse 10.—*" This generation."* The word דור, *dor*, signifies an age, or the allotted
term of human life ; and it is here applied to the men of an age, as if the Psalmist
had said, that the Israelites whom God had delivered were incorrigible, during the
whole period of their lives.—*John Calvin.*

Verse 10.—*" It is a people that do err in their heart."* We may observe here,
that he does not simply say, This people errs. What mortal is there that does not
err ? Or, where is there a multitude of mortals, exposed to no errors ? But he adds,
" In their heart." Every error therefore is not blamed here, but the error of their
heart is fastened upon. It is to be noted, therefore, that there is a twofold kind of
error :

1. One is of the intellect, by which we go astray through ignorance. In this
kind of erring Paul erred when he persecuted the Church of Christ ; the Sadducees
erred, not knowing the Scriptures, Matt. xxii. ; and to this day many in the Church
go astray, endowed with zeal for God, but destitute of a true knowledge of Him.

2. The other kind of erring is of the heart and affections, by which men go astray,
not through ignorance, but through corruption and perversity of heart. This error
of heart is a mind averse to God, and alienated from the will and way of God, which
is elsewhere thus described in the case of this very people : " And their heart was
not right with him."—*Musculus.*

Verse 10.—*" It is a people that do err in their heart."* To err in *heart* may mean
either to err in judgment, or in disposition, intention : for the Hebrew לֵבָב, and after
it the Greek καρδία, means either *animus, judicium,* or, *mens, cogitatio, desiderium.*
I understand καρδία here, as used according to the Hebrew idiom (in which it is often
pleonastic, at least it seems so to us,) so that the phrase imports simply, *They always
err,* i.e. they are continually departing from the right way.—*Moses Stuart.*

Verse 10.—*" Err in their heart."* He had called them sheep, and now he notes
their wandering propensity, and their incapacity for being led ; for the footsteps
of their Shepherd they did not know, much less follow.—*C. H. S.*

Verse 10.—*" They have not known my ways "* ; that is, they have not regarded
my ways, have not allowed of them, or loved them ; for otherwise they were not
ignorant of them ; they heard his words, and *saw his works.—David Dickson.*

Verse 10.—*" They have not known my ways."* This ungrateful people did not
approve of God's ways—they did not enter into his designs—they did not conform
to his commands—they paid no attention to his miracles—and did not acknowledge
the benefits which they received from his hands.—*Adam Clarke.*

Verse 10.—*" A people that do err in their heart,"* &c. These words are not to
be found in Numb. xiv. ; but the inspired Psalmist expresses the sense of what
Jehovah said on that occasion. *" They do always err in their heart,"* [Heb. iii. 10].
They are radically and habitually evil. *" They have not known my ways."* God's
" ways " may mean either his dispensations or his precepts. The Israelites did not
rightly understand the former, and they obstinately refused to acquire a practical
knowledge—the only truly valuable species of knowledge—of the latter. The
reference is probably to God's mode of dealing: Rom. xi. 33 ; Deut. iv. 32, viii. 2,
xxix. 2—4. Such a people deserved severe punishment, and they received it. *" So
I sware in my wrath, They shall not enter into my rest."* The original words in the
Hebrew are, *" If they shall enter into my rest."* This elliptical mode of expressing
oaths is common in the Old Testament : Deut. i. 35 ; 1 Sam. iii. 14 ; Ps. lxxxix. 35 ;
Isai. lxii. 8. This awful oath is recorded in the 14th chapter of Numbers : " But
as truly as I live, all the earth shall be filled with the glory of the LORD. Because
all those men which have seen my glory, and my miracles, which I did in Egypt
and in the wilderness, and have tempted me now these ten times, and have not
hearkened to my voice ; surely they shall not see the land which I sware unto their
fathers, neither shall any of them that provoked me see it : but my servant Caleb,
because he had another spirit with him, and hath followed me fully, him will I bring
into the land whereinto he went ; and his seed shall possess it. (Now the Amalekites
and the Canaanites dwelt in the valley.) To morrow turn you, and get you into
the wilderness by the way of the Red Sea. And the LORD spake unto Moses and

unto Aaron, saying, How long shall I bear with this evil congregation, which murmur against me ? I have heard the murmurings of the children of Israel, which they murmur against me. Say unto them, As truly as I live, saith the LORD, as ye have spoken in mine ears, so will I do to you : your carcases shall fall in this wilderness ; and all that were numbered of you, according to your whole number, from twenty years old and upward, which have murmured against me." The words of the oath seem here borrowed from the account in Deut. i. 35. There are many threatenings of God which have a tacit condition implied in them ; but when God interposes his oath, the sentence is irreversible.

The curse was not causeless, and it did come. We have an account of its actual fulfilment, Numb. xxvi. 64, 65. The " rest " from which they were excluded was the land of Canaan. Their lives were spent in wandering. It is termed " God's rest," as there he was to finish his work of bringing Israel into the land promised to their fathers, and fix the symbol of his presence in the midst of them,—dwelling in that land in which his people were to rest from their wanderings, and to dwell in safety under his protection. It is *his* rest, as of his preparing, Deut. xii. 9. It is *his* rest—rest like his, rest along with him. We are by no means warranted to conclude that all who died in the wilderness came short of everlasting happiness. It is to be feared many of them, most of them, did ; but the curse denounced on them went only to their exclusion from the earthly Canaan.—*John Brown.*

Verses 10, 11.—" *And said.*" Mark the gradation, first grief or *disgust* with those who *erred* made him *say* ; then *anger* felt more heavily against those who did not *believe* made him *swear.* The people had been called sheep in verse 7, to sheep the highest good is rest, but into this rest they were never to come, for they had not known or delighted in the ways in which the good Shepherd desired to lead them. —*John Albert Bengel.*

Verse 11.—The word *swearing* is very significant, and seems to import these two things. 1st. The certainty of the sentence here pronounced. Every word of God both is, and must be truth ; but ratified by an oath, it is truth with an advantage. It is signed irrevocable. This fixes it like the laws of the Medes and Persians, beyond all possibility of alteration ; and makes God's word, like his very nature, unchangeable. 2ndly. It imports the terror of the sentence. If the children of Israel could say, " Let not God speak to us, lest we die," what would they have said had God then sworn against them ? It is terrible to hear an oath from the mouth but of a poor mortal, but from the mouth of an omnipotent God, it does not only terrify, but confound. An oath from God is truth delivered in anger ; truth, as I may so speak, with a vengeance. When God speaks, it is the creature's duty to hear ; but when he swears, to tremble.—*Robert South.*

Verse 11.—" *That they should not enter into my rest.*" There is something unusual and abrupt in the conclusion of this Psalm, without any cheering prospect to relieve the threatening. This may be best explained by assuming, that it was not meant to stand alone, but to form one of a series.—*J. A. Alexander.*

HINTS TO PREACHERS.

Verse 1.—An invitation to praise the Lord. I. A favourite method of worship —" let us sing." II. A fitting state of mind for singing—joyful gratitude. III. A fitting subject to excite both gladness and thankfulness—the rock of our salvation.

Verse 1.—" *The rock of our salvation.*" Expressive imagery. Rock of shelter, support, indwelling, and supply—illustrate this last by the water flowing from the rock in the wilderness.

Verse 2.—I. What is meant by coming before his presence ? Certainly not the holiness of places, etc. II. What offering is most appropriate when we come into his presence ?

Verse 3.—I. The greatness of God as god. He is to be conceived of as great in goodness, power, glory, etc. II. His dominion over all other powers in heaven or earth. III. The worship which is consequently due to him.

Verses 4, 5.—The universality of the divine government. I. In all parts of the globe. II. In all providences. III. In every phase of moral condition. Or, Things deep, or high, dark or perilous are in his hand ; circumstances shifting, terrible, overwhelming as the sea, are under his control as much as the comfortable terra firma of peace and prosperity.

Verse 6.—A true conception of God begets—I. A disposition to worship. II. Mutual incitement to worship. III. Profound reverence in worship. IV. Overwhelming sense of God's presence in worship.—*C. A. Davis*.

Verses 6, 7.—God is to be worshipped—I. As our Creator—" our maker." II. As our Redeemer, " the people," etc. III. As our Preserver, " the sheep, etc."—*George Rogers*.

Verse 7.—The entreaty of the Holy Ghost. I. The special voice—" the Holy Ghost saith "—1. In Scripture. 2. In the hearts of his people. 3. In the awakened. 4. By his deeds of grace. II. A special duty, " hear his voice," instructing, commanding, inviting, promising, threatening. III. A special time—" to-day." While God speaks, after so long a time, in the day of grace, now, in your present state. IV. The special danger—" harden not your hearts," by indifference, unbelief, asking for signs, presumption, worldly pleasures, etc.

Verse 7.—Sinners entreated to hear God's voice. " Hear his voice," because— I. Life is short and uncertain ; II. You cannot properly or lawfully promise to give what is not your own ; III. If you defer, though but till to-morrow, you must harden your hearts ; IV. There is great reason to fear that, if you defer it to-day, you will never commence ; V. After a time God ceases to strive with sinners ; VI. There is nothing irksome or disagreeable in a religious life, that you should wish to defer its commencement.—*Edward Payson*.

Verse 7.—The Difference of Times with respect to Religion.—Upon a spiritual account there is great difference of time. To make this out, I will shew you, I. That *sooner* and *later* are not alike, in respect of eternity. II. That *times of ignorance* and of *knowledge* are not alike. III. That *before* and *after voluntary commission of known iniquity*, are not alike. IV. That *before* and *after contracted naughty habits*, are not alike. V. That the time of *God's gracious and particular visitation* and the time when God *withdraws* his gracious presence and assistance, are not alike. VI. The flourishing time of our *health and strength*, and the hour of *sickness, weakness*, and approach of *death*, are not alike. VII. Now and hereafter, present and future, *this world* and *the world to come*, are not alike.—*Benjamin Whichcot*.

Verse 7.—This supposition, " *If ye will hear*," and the consequence inferred thereupon, " *harden not your hearts*," doth evidently demonstrate that a right hearing will prevent hardness of heart ; especially hearing of Christ's voice, that is, the gospel. It is the gospel that maketh and keepeth a soft heart.—*William Gouge*.

Verses 8—11.—I. Israel's fearful experiment in tempting God. II. The awful result. III. Let it not be tried again.—*C. A. Davis*.

Verse 10.—The error and the ignorance which are fatal.

Verse 11.—The fatal moment of the giving up of a soul, how it may be hastened, what are the signs of it, and what are the terrible results.

Verses 10, 11.—The kindling, increasing, and full force of divine anger, and its dreadful results.

PSALM XCVI.

SUBJECT.—*This Psalm is evidently taken from that sacred song which was composed by David at the time when " the ark of God was set in the midst of the tent which David had prepared for it, and they offered burnt sacrifices and peace offerings before God." See the sixteenth chapter of the first book of the Chronicles. The former part of that sacred song was probably omitted in this place because it referred to Israel, and the design of the Holy Ghost in this Psalm was to give forth a song for the Gentiles, a triumphant hymn wherewith to celebrate the conversion of the nations to Jehovah in gospel times. It follows fitly upon the last Psalm, which describes the obstinacy of Israel, and the consequent taking of the gospel from them that it might be preached among the nations who would receive it, and in due time be fully won to Christ by its power. It thus makes a pair with the Ninety-fifth Psalm. It is a grand* MISSIONARY HYMN, *and it is a wonder that Jews can read it and yet remain exclusive. If blindness in part had not happened unto Israel, they might have seen long ago, and would now see, that their God always had designs of love for all the families of men, and never intended that his grace and his covenant should relate only to the seed of Abraham after the flesh. We do not wonder that the large-hearted David rejoiced and danced before the ark, while he saw in vision all the earth turning from idols to the one living and true God. Had Michal, Saul's daughter, only been able to enter into his delight, she would not have reproached him, and if the Jews at this day could only be enlarged in heart to feel sympathy with all mankind, they also would sing for joy at the great prophecy that all the earth shall be filled with the glory of the Lord.*

DIVISIONS.—*We will make none, for the song is one and indivisible, a garment of praise without seam, woven from the top throughout.*

EXPOSITION.

O SING unto the LORD a new song : sing unto the LORD, all the earth.

2 Sing unto the LORD, bless his name ; shew forth his salvation from day to day.

3 Declare his glory among the heathen, his wonders among all people.

4 For the LORD *is* great, and greatly to be praised : he *is* to be feared above all gods.

5 For all the gods of the nations *are* idols : but the LORD made the heavens.

6 Honour and majesty *are* before him : strength and beauty *are* in his sanctuary.

7 Give unto the LORD, O ye kindreds of the people, give unto the LORD glory and strength.

8 Give unto the LORD the glory *due unto* his name : bring an offering, and come into his courts.

9 O worship the LORD in the beauty of holiness : fear before him, all the earth.

10 Say among the heathen *that* the LORD reigneth : the world also shall be established that it shall not be moved : he shall judge the people righteously :

11 Let the heavens rejoice, and let the earth be glad ; let the sea roar, and the fulness thereof.

12 Let the field be joyful, and all that *is* therein : then shall all the trees of the wood rejoice

13 Before the LORD : for he cometh, for he cometh to judge the earth : he shall judge the world with righteousness, and the people with his truth.

1. *" O sing unto the Lord a new song."* New joys are filling the hearts of men, for the glad tidings of blessing to all people are proclaimed, therefore let them sing

a new song. Angels inaugurated the new dispensation with new songs, and shall not we take up the strain ? The song is for Jehovah alone, the hymns which chanted the praises of Jupiter and Neptune, Vishnoo and Siva are hushed for ever ; Bacchanalian shouts are silenced, lascivious sonnets are no more. Unto the one only God all music is to be dedicated. Mourning is over, and the time of the singing of hearts has come. No dismal rites are celebrated, no bloody sacrifices of human beings are presented, no cutting with knives, and outcries of lamentation are presented by deluded votaries. Joy is in the ascendant, and singing has become the universal expression of love, the fitting voice of reverent adoration. Men are made new creatures, and their song is new also. The names of Baalim are no more on their lips, the wanton music of Ashtaroth ceaseth ; the foolish ditty and the cruel warsong are alike forgotten ; the song is holy, heavenly, pure, and pleasant. The Psalmist speaks as if he would lead the strain and be the chief musician, he invites, he incites, he persuades to sacred worship, and cries with all his heart, " O sing unto Jehovah a new song."

" *Sing unto the Lord, all the earth.*"—National jealousies are dead ; a Jew invites the Gentiles to adore, and joins with them, so that all the earth may lift up one common Psalm as with one heart and voice unto Jehovah, who hath visited it with his salvation. No corner of the world is to be discordant, no race of heathen to be dumb. All the earth Jehovah made, and all the earth must sing to him. As the sun shines on all lands, so are all lands to delight in the light of the Sun of Righteousness. *E Pluribus Unum*, out of many one song shall come forth. The multitudinous languages of the sons of Adam, who were scattered at Babel, will blend in the same song when the people are gathered at Zion. Nor men alone, but the earth itself is to praise its Maker. Made subject to vanity for a while by a sad necessity, the creation itself also is to be delivered from the bondage of corruption, and brought into the glorious liberty of the children of God, so that sea and forest, field and flood, are to be joyful before the Lord. Is this a dream ? then let us dream again. Blessed are the eyes which shall see the kingdom, and the ears which shall hear its songs. Hasten thine advent, good Lord ! Yea, send forth speedily the rod of thy strength out of Zion, that the nations may bow before the Lord and his Anointed.

2. " *Sing unto the Lord, bless his name.*" Thrice is the name of the Lord repeated, and not without meaning. Is it not unto the Three-One Lord that the enlightened nations will sing ? Unitarianism is the religion of units ; it is too cold to warm the world to worship ; the sacred fire of adoration only burns with vehement flame where the Trinity is believed in and beloved. In other ways beside singing, the blessed Lord is to be blessed. His name, his fame, his character, his revealed word and will are to be delighted in, and remembered with perpetual thanksgiving. We may well bless him who so divinely blesses us. At the very mention of his name it is meet to say, " Let him be blessed for ever." " *Shew forth his salvation from day to day.*" The gospel is the clearest revelation of himself, salvation outshines creation and providence ; therefore let our praises overflow in that direction. Let us proclaim the glad tidings, and do so continually, never ceasing the blissful testimony. It is ever new, ever suitable, ever sure, ever perfect ; therefore let us show it forth continually until he come, both by words and deeds, by songs and sermons, by sacred Baptism and by the Holy Supper, by books and by speech, by Sabbath services and week-day worship. Each day brings us deeper experience of our saving God, each day shows us anew how deeply men need his salvation, each day reveals the power of the gospel, each day the Spirit strives with the sons of men ; therefore, never pausing, be it ours to tell out the glorious message of free grace. Let those do this who know for themselves what *his* salvation means ; they can bear witness that there is salvation in none other, and that in him salvation to the uttermost is to be found. Let them show it forth till the echo flies around the spacious earth, and all the armies of the sky unite to magnify the God who hath displayed his saving health among all people.

3. " *Declare his glory among the heathen.*" His salvation is his glory, the word of the gospel glorifies him ; and this should be published far and wide, till the remotest nations of the earth have known it. England has spent much blood and treasure to keep up her own prestige among barbarians ; when will she be equally anxious to maintain the honour of her religion, the glory of her Lord ? It is to be feared that too often the name of the Lord Jesus has been dishonoured among the heathen by the vices and cruelties of those who call themselves Christians ; may this fact excite true believers to greater diligence in causing the gospel to be proclaimed

as with a trumpet in all quarters of the habitable globe. "*His wonders among all people.*" The gospel is a mass of wonders, its history is full of wonders, and it is in itself far more marvellous than miracles themselves. In the person of his Son the Lord has displayed wonders of love, wisdom, grace, and power. All glory be unto his name ; who can refuse to tell out the story of redeeming grace and dying love ? All the nations need to hear of God's marvellous works ; and a really living, self-denying church would solemnly resolve that right speedily they all shall hear thereof. The tribes which are dying out are not to be excluded from gospel teaching any more than the great growing families which, like the fat kine of Pharaoh, are eating up other races : Red Indians as well as Anglo-Saxons are to hear of the wonders of redeeming love. None are too degraded, none too cultured, none too savage, and none too refined.

4. "*For the Lord is great and greatly to be praised.*" He is no petty deity, pre-siding, as the heathen imagined their gods to do, over some one nation, or one depart-ment of nature. Jehovah is great in power and dominion, great in mind and act ; nothing mean or narrow can be found in him or his acts, in all things he is infinite. Praise should be proportionate to its object, therefore let it be infinite when rendered unto the Lord. We cannot praise him too much, too often, too zealously, too care-fully, too joyfully. He deserves that nothing in his worship should be little, but all the honour rendered unto him should be given in largeness of heart, with the utmost zeal for his glory. "*He is to be feared above all gods.*" Other gods have been worshipped at great cost, and with much fervour, by their blinded votaries, but Jehovah should be adored with far greater reverence. Even if the graven images had been gods they could not have borne comparison for an instant with the God of Israel, and therefore his worship should be far more zealous than any which has been rendered to them. He is to be feared, for there is cause to fear. Dread of other gods is mere superstition, awe of the Lord is pure religion. Holy fear is the beginning of the graces, and yet it is the accompaniment of their highest range. Fear of God is the blush upon the face of holiness enhancing its beauty.

5. "*For all the gods of the nations are idols.*" Mere images of wood and stone, vanities, nothings. "*But the Lord made the heavens.*" The reality of his God-head is proved by his works, and foremost among these the Psalmist mentions that matchless piece of architecture which casts its arch over every man's head, whose lamps are the light of all mankind, whose rains and dew fall upon the fields of every people, and whence the Lord in voice of thunder is heard speaking to every creature. The idol gods have no existence, but our God is the author of all existences ; they are mere earthly vanities, while he is not only heavenly, but made the heavens. This is mentioned as an argument for Jehovah's universal praise. Who can be worshipped but he ? Since none can rival him, let him be adored alone.

6. "*Honour and majesty are before him.*" Men can but mimic these things ; their pompous pageants are but the pretence of greatness. Honour and majesty are with him and with him alone. In the presence of Jehovah real glory and sovereignty abide, as constant attendants. "*Strength and beauty are in his sanctuary.*" In him are combined all that is mighty and lovely, powerful and resplendent. We have seen rugged strength devoid of beauty, we have also seen elegance without strength ; the union of the two is greatly to be admired. Do we desire to see the " sublime and beautiful " at one glance ? Then we must look to the eternal throne. In the Chronicles we read strength and *gladness* ; and the two renderings do not disagree in sense, for in the highest degree in this instance it is true that " a thing of beauty is a joy for ever." Not in outward show or parade of costly robes does the glory of God consist ; such things are tricks of state with which the ignorant are dazzled ; holiness, justice, wisdom, grace, these are the splendours of Jehovah's courts, these the jewels and the gold, the regalia, and the pomp of the courts of heaven.

7. The first six verses commenced with an exhortation to sing, three times repeated, with the name of the Lord thrice mentioned ; here we meet with the expression "*Give unto the Lord,*" used in the same triple manner. This is after the manner of those poets whose flaming sonnets have best won the ear of the people, they reiterate choice words till they penetrate the soul and fire the heart. The invocation of the sweet singer is still addressed to all mankind, to whom he speaks as " *Ye kindreds of the people.*" Divided into tribes and families, we are called in our courses and order to appear before him and ascribe to him all honour. " All worship be to God only," is the motto of one of our City companies, and it may

well be the motto of all the families upon earth. Family worship is peculiarly pleasing unto him who is the God of all the families of Israel. " *Give unto the Lord glory and strength,*" that is to say, recognise the glory and power of Jehovah, and ascribe them unto him in your solemn hymns. Who is glorious but the Lord? Who is strong, save our God? Ye great nations, who count yourselves both famous and mighty, cease your boastings! Ye monarchs, who are styled imperial and puissant, humble yourselves in the dust before the only Potentate. Glory and strength are nowhere to be found, save with the Lord, all others possess but the semblance thereof. Well did Massillon declare, " God alone is great."

8. " *Give unto the Lord the glory due unto his name.*" But who can do that to the full? Can all the nations of the earth put together discharge the mighty debt? All conceivable honour is due to our Creator, Preserver, Benefactor, and Redeemer, and however much of zealous homage we may offer to him, we cannot give him more than his due. If we cannot bring in the full revenue which he justly claims, at least let us not fail from want of honest endeavour. " *Bring an offering, and come into his courts.*" Come with an unbloody sacrifice ; atonement for sin having been made, it only remains to bring thank-offerings, and let not these be forgotten. To him who gives us all, we ought gladly to give our grateful tithe. When assembling for public worship we should make a point of bringing with us a contribution to his cause, according to that ancient word, " None of you shall appear before me empty." The time will come when from all ranks and all nations the Lord will receive gifts when they gather together for his worship. O long expected day begin !

9. " *O worship the Lord in the beauty of holiness.*" This is the only beauty which he cares for in our public services, and it is one for which no other can compensate. Beauty of architecture and apparel he does not regard ; moral and spiritual beauty is that in which his soul delighteth. Worship must not be rendered to God in a slovenly, sinful, superficial manner ; we must be reverent, sincere, earnest, and pure in heart both in our prayers and praises. Purity is the white linen of the Lord's choristers, righteousness is the comely garment of his priests, holiness is the royal apparel of his servitors. " *Fear before him, all the earth.*" " Tremble " is the word in the original, and it expresses the profoundest awe, just as the word " worship " does, which would be more accurately translated by " bow down." Even the bodily frame would be moved to trembling and prostration if men were thoroughly conscious of the power and glory of Jehovah. Men of the world ridiculed " the Quakers " for trembling when under the power of the Holy Spirit ; had they been able to discern the majesty of the Eternal they would have quaked also. There is a sacred trembling which is quite consistent with joy, the heart may even quiver with an awful excess of delight. The sight of the King in his beauty caused no alarm to John in Patmos, and yet it made him fall at his feet as dead. Oh, to behold him and worship him with prostrate awe and sacred fear !

10. " *Say among the heathen that the Lord reigneth.*" This is the gladdest news which can be carried to them,—the Lord Jehovah, in the person of his Son has assumed the throne, and taken to himself his great power. Tell this out among the heathen, and let the heathen themselves, being converted, repeat the same rejoicingly. The dominion of Jehovah Jesus is not irksome, his rule is fraught with untold blessings, his yoke is easy, and his burden is light. " *The world also shall be established that it shall not be moved.*" Society is safe where God is king, no revolutions shall convulse his empire, no invasions shall disturb his kingdom. A settled government is essential to national prosperity, the reign of the God of truth and righteousness will promote this to the highest degree. Sin has shaken the world, the reign of Jesus will set it fast again upon sure foundations. " *He shall judge the people righteously.*" This is the best method for establishing society on a secure basis, and this is the greatest source of joy to oppressed nations. Iniquity makes the dynasties of tyrants fall, equity causes the throne of Jesus to stand. He will impartially rule over Jew and Gentile, prince and peasant, and this will bring happiness to those who are now the victims of the despot's arbitrary will.

11. " *Let the heavens rejoice, and let the earth be glad.*" Above and below let the joy be manifested. Let the angels who have stood in amaze at the wickedness of men, now rejoice over their repentance and restoration to favour, and let men themselves express their pleasure in seeing their true prince set upon his throne. The book of creation has two covers, and on each of these let the glory of the Lord be emblazoned in letters of joy. " *Let the sea roar, and the fulness thereof.*" Let it be no more a troubled sea, wailing over ship-wrecked mariners, and rehearsing the

griefs of widows and orphans, but let it adopt a cheerful note, and rejoice in the kingdom of the Lord. Let it thunder out the name of the Lord when its tides are at its full, and let all its teeming life express the utmost joy because the Lord reigneth even in the depth of the sea. In common with the rest of the creation, the sea has groaned and travailed until now : is not the time close at hand in which its hollow murmur shall be exchanged for an outburst of joy ? Will not every billow soon flash forth the praises of him who once trod the sea ?

> " Waft, waft, ye winds, his story !
>   And you, ye waters, roll,
> Till, like a sea of glory,
>   It spreads from pole to pole."

12. " *Let the field be joyful, and all that is therein.*" Let the cultivated plains praise the Lord. Peace enables their owners to plough and sow and reap, without fear of the rapine of invaders, and therefore in glad notes they applaud him whose empire is peace. Both men, and creatures that graze the plain, and the crops themselves are represented as swelling the praises of Jehovah, and the figure is both bold and warranted, for the day shall come when every inhabited rood of ground shall yield its song, and every farmstead shall contain a church. " *Then shall all the trees of the wood rejoice.*" He does not say let them rejoice, but they shall do so. The faith of the Psalmist turns itself from the expression of desire to the fully assured prediction of the event. Groves have in old times stood shuddering at the horrid orgies which have been performed within their shade, the time shall come when they shall sing for joy because of the holy worship, the sounds of which they shall hear. The bush is the stronghold of savage men and robbers, but it shall be sanctified to retirement and devotion. Perhaps the Psalmist was thinking of the birds ; so Keble must have supposed, for he versifies the passage thus—

> " Field exults and meadow fair,
> With each bud and blossom there,
> In the lonely woodlands now
> Chants aloud each rustling bough."

13. " *Before the Lord : for he cometh.*" Even now he is near, his advent should, therefore, be the cause of immediate rejoicing : already are we in his presence, let us worship him with delight. " *For he cometh to judge the earth,*" to rule it with discretion ; not to tax it, and control it by force, as kings often do, but to preside as magistrates do whose business it is to see justice carried out between man and man. All the world will be under the jurisdiction of this great Judge, and before his bar all will be summoned to appear. At this moment he is on the road, and the hour of his coming draweth nigh. His great assize is proclaimed. Hear ye not the trumpets ? His foot is on the threshold. " *He shall judge the world with righteousness.*" His essential rectitude will determine all causes and cases, there will be no bribery and corruption there, neither can error or failure be found in his decisions. " *And the people with his truth,*" or rather " the nations in faithfulness." Honesty, veracity, integrity, will rule upon his judgment-seat. No nation shall be favoured there, and none be made to suffer through prejudice. The black man shall be tried by the same law as his white master, the aboriginal shall have justice executed for him against his civilised exterminator, the crushed and hunted Bushman shall have space to appeal against the Boer who slaughtered his tribe, and the South Sea Islander shall gain attention to his piteous plaint against the treacherous wretch who kidnapped him from his home. There shall be true judgment given without fear or favour. In all this let the nations be glad, and the universe rejoice.

In closing, let us ourselves join in the song. Since the whole universe is to be clothed with smiles, shall not we be glad ? As John Howe observes, " Shall we not partake in this common dutiful joy, and fall into concert with the adoring loyal chorus ? Will we cut ourselves off from this gladsome obsequious throng ? And what should put a pleasant face and aspect upon the whole world, shall it only leave our faces covered with clouds and a mournful sadness ? "

EXPLANATORY NOTES AND QUAINT SAYINGS.

Whole Psalm.—What has been said of Psalm lxvii. may be fitly applied to the present Psalm. We need not hesitate to add that it is a *millennial* anthem. It accords with the condition of the world when Christ shall sit enthroned in the willing loyalty of our race. The nations join in an acclaim of praise to him as their rightful Judge and King. There is a unanimity in the song, as if it ascended from a world purged into a temple of holiness, and whose inhabitants were indeed a royal priesthood, with one heart to make Jesus king, with one voice to sound forth one peal of melody in praise of the name above every name.

Fix the eye for a moment on the precious vision of which we thus catch a glimpse. It holds true to the deepest principles of our nature, that what we contemplate as possible, much more what we anticipate as certain, lends us the very hope and energy conducive to its realisation. On the contrary, despair paralyses effort. Is it on this account that everywhere in prophecy, old and new, there floats before us the ideal of a recovered and rejoicing world, at times transfigured into a loftier scene, the new heavens and new earth wherein dwelleth righteousness ? So largely did this thought imbue the prophetic mind, that the language of Paul warms into the animation of poetry, when even " the creature itself," according to his own vivid personification, like some noble bird, drooping under the weight of its chain, with neck outstretched and eyeball distended, is described as looking down into the vista of coming time for its deliverance from the bondage of corruption into the glorious liberty of the sons of God (Rom. viii. 19). He hastens to add, that " we are saved by hope." It is true of the soul individually, we are saved by hope. It is true of our race collectively, if ever a millennium is to dawn upon it, we are saved by such a hope. Our earth may be in ruins meanwhile, blackness on the sky, barrenness on the soil, because sin is everywhere ; but a change is promised. What we hope for, we labour for all the more that our hope is no dream of fancy, but has its basis in the science and certainty of absolute truth. " For as the earth bringeth forth her bud, and as the garden causeth the things that are sown in it to spring forth ; so the Lord God will cause righteousness and praise to spring forth before all the nations." (Isai. lxi. 11.) The tuning of the instrument is sometimes heard before the music comes. The mother teaches her child to lisp a hymn before he comprehends its full scope and meaning. And so here, in this holy Psalm, the Jerusalem from above, the mother of us all, trains us to the utterance of a song suitable to seasons of millennial glory, when the Moloch of oppression, the Mammon of our avarice, the Ashtaroth of fiery lust, every erring creed, every false religion, shall have given place to the worship of the one true and living God—to the faith and love of Christ. " Let the peoples praise thee, O God ; let all the peoples praise thee."—*W. H. Goold, in " The Mission Hymn of the Hebrew Church : a Sermon."* 1865.

Whole Psalm.—This Psalm is entitled in the *Septuagint,* " *A Hymn of David ; when the Temple was rebuilt after the Captivity,*" and this appears to be a true description of it ; for the substance of it is found in 1 Chron. xvi. 23—33, where it is described as having been delivered by David into the hand of Asaph and his brethren, to thank the Lord when the Ark was brought up to Zion. David's Psalm here receives a new name, and is called *a new song (sir chadash),* because new mercies of God were now to be celebrated ; mercies greater than David had ever received, even when he brought the Ark to Zion. They who now sang the old song, which had thus become a new song, identified themselves with David, and identified him with themselves.—*Chr. Wordsworth.*

Whole Psalm.—Subject.—Call to praise, in view of Christ's second advent and glorious reign.—*To apply it.*—Look forward to the glorious day of the Lord's coming ; and realise its approach that you may prepare for it.—*A. R. C. Dallas.*

Verse 1.—" *O sing unto the Lord a new song,*" etc. ' A new song," unknown to you before. Come, all ye nations of the wide earth, who, up to this hour, have been giving your worship to dead gods that were no gods at all ; come and give your hearts to the true and only God in this *new* song !—*Henry Cowles.*

Verse 1.—" *A new song.*" It must be " *a new canticle,*" a beautiful canticle, and elegantly composed ; also a canticle for fresh favours ; in like manner, a canticle befitting men who have been regenerated, in whom avarice has been supplanted by charity ; and finally, a canticle not like that of Moses, or Deborah, or any of the old canticles that could not be sung outside the land of promise, according to Psalm cxxxvii., "How shall we sing the LORD's song in a strange land?" but a new canticle that may be sung all over the world; and he, therefore, adds, "Sing unto the Lord, all the earth," not only Judea, but the whole world.—*Bellarmine.*

Verse 1.—"*New.*" The word is used to describe that which is delightful, exquisite, precious, etc.—*Martin Geier.*

Verse 1.—"*New.*" New things are generally most approved, and especially in songs; for Pindar praises old wine and new songs.—*John Cocceius, 1603—1669.*

Verse 1.—"*A new song.*" Our old songs were those of pride, of gluttony, of luxury, in hope of gain, prosperity, or harm to others; our "*new song*" is of praise, reverence, and obedience, and love to God, in newness of life, in the Spirit that quickeneth, no longer in the letter that killeth, but keepeth that new commandment, that we love one another, not with the narrow patriotism and fellow-feeling of a small tribe, or a mere national church, but with a citizenship which embraces *all the whole earth.*—*Neale and Littledale.*

Verse 1.—"*Sing unto the Lord.*" We find it thrice said, *sing unto the Lord*, that we may understand that we are to sing unto him with mind, and tongue, and deed. For all these things must be joined together, and the life ought to correspond with the mouth and mind. As Abbot Absolom says, *When the speech does not jar with the life, there is a sweet harmony.*—*Le Blanc.*

Verse 1.—"*All the earth.*" It is a *missionary-hymn* for all ages of the church; and it becomes more and more appropriate to our times in proportion as the heathen begin to respond to the call, "Sing unto the Lord a new song," and in proportion as we find in the melancholy condition of the church at home occasion to look with a hopeful eye towards the heathen world.—*E. W. Hengstenberg.*

Verse 2.—"*From day to day.*" Continually; always. It is a fit subject for unceasing praise. Every man should praise God every day—on each returning morning, and on every evening—for the assurance that there is a way of salvation provided for him, and that he may be happy for ever. If we had right feelings, this would be the first thought which would burst upon the mind each morning, irradiating, as with sunbeams, all around us; and it would be the last thought which would linger in the soul as we lie down at night, and close our eyes in slumber—making us grateful, calm, happy, as we sink to rest, for whether we wake or not in this world, we may be for ever happy.—*Albert Barnes.*

Verse 2.—"*From day to day.*" Other news delights us only at first hearing; but the good news of our redemption is sweet from day to day, *ac si in eodem die redemptio fuisset operata,* saith Kimchi here, as if it were done but to-day. *Tam recens mihi nunc Christus est,* saith Luther, *ac si hac hora fudisset sanguinem,* Christ is now as fresh unto me as if he had shed his blood but this very hour.—*John Trapp.*

Verse 3.—"*Declare.*" The corresponding word is *a book*; and the participle is often rendered a *scribe*, a *writer*, Ps. xlv. 1. The verb is rendered, *tell, shew forth, declare.* The variety of verbs used in verses 1—3, proves that we are to employ all proper means for making known the Saviour. One of these methods is by writing.—*W. S. Plumer.*

Verse 3.—"*Declare his glory*"—what a glorious person the Messiah is; the brightness of his Father's glory; having all the perfections of Deity in him; how the glory of God appears in him, and in all that he has done; and especially in the work of redemption, in which the glory of divine wisdom, power, justice, truth, and faithfulness, love, grace, and mercy, is richly displayed; say what glory he is advanced unto, having done his work, being highly exalted, set at the right hand of God, and crowned with glory and honour, and what a fulness of grace there is in him, for the supply of his people; and what a glory is on him, which they shall behold to all eternity.—*John Gill.*

Verse 3.—*His glory* shines from every ray of light that reaches us from a thousand stars; it sparkles from the mountain tops that reflect the earliest and retain the last rays of the rising and the setting sun; it spreads over the expanse of the sea, and speaks in the murmur of its restless waves; it girdles the earth with a zone of light, and flings over it an aureole of beauty. In the varied forms of animal tribes; in the relations of our world to other worlds, in the revolutions of planets, in the springing of flowers, in the fall of waters, and in the flight of birds; in the sea, the rivers, and the air; in heights and depths, in wonders and mysteries,—Christ wears the crown, sways the sceptre, and receives from all a tribute to his sovereignty. We cannot augment it ; we cannot add one ray of light to the faintness of a distant star, nor give wings to an apterous insect, nor change a white hair into black. We can unfold, but not create ; we can adore, but not increase ; we can recognise the footprints of Deity, but not add to them.—*John Cumming in " From Patmos to Paradise, 1873."*

Verse 3.—" *Declare his glory among the heathen,"* etc. It is a part of the commission given to the ministers of the gospel, not only to teach their congregations concerning Christ, but also to have a care that they who never did hear of him, may know what he is, what he hath done and suffered, and what good may be had by his mediation. Nothing so glorious to God, nothing so wonderful in itself, as is the salvation of man by Christ ; to behold God saving his enemies by the incarnation, sufferings, and obedience of Christ the eternal Son of God : " *Declare his glory among the heathen, his wonders among all people."*—*David Dickson.*

Verse 3.—" *Declare his glory."* It is *his* glory which should be proclaimed, not the learning, ability, and eloquence of the orator who professes to speak for him ; it is his *glory,* the loving beauty, the attractiveness of his gospel, the lavish promises to repentant sinners, the blessedness of heaven, which should be the chief themes of discourse ; not threats, menaces, sermons on hell or torment to affright men, and at best make them God's trembling slaves, not his loving friends. The preaching is to be " *unto all people,"* in obscure country districts, amongst unpolished and illiterate congregations, and not to be confined, as fashionable preachers like to confine it, to the cultivated and critical audiences of the capital.—*Hugo, quoted by Neale and Littledale.*

Verse 3.—" *His glory."* What he had before called *salvation,* he now names *glory,* and afterwards *wonders.* And since this salvation, whereby the human race is redeemed from eternal death and damnation, is glorious and full of wonders, it is therefore worthy of admiration and praise.—*Mollerus.*

Verse 3.—" *His wonders."* What a wonderful person he is, for he is God manifest in the flesh ; what wonderful love he has shown in his incarnation, obedience, sufferings, and death ; what amazing miracles he wrought, and what a wonderful work he performed ; the work of our redemption, the wonder of men and angels ; declare his wonderful resurrection from the dead, his ascension to heaven, sitting at the right hand of God, and intercession for his people ; the wonderful effusion of his Spirit, and the conquests of his grace, and the enlargement of his kingdom in the world ; as also what wonders will be wrought by him when he appears a second time ; how the dead will be raised, and all will be judged.—*John Gill.*

Verse 5.—" *For all the gods of the nations are idols."* Nothings, nonentities, a favourite description of idols in Isaiah's later prophecies. See e.g. Isaiah xli. 24, and compare Lev. xix. 4, xxvi. 1, 1 Cor. viii. 4—6, x. 19. A less probable etymology of the Hebrew word makes it a diminutive of (אֵל) *El,* analogous to *godlings* as an expression of contempt.—*J. A. Alexander.*

Verse 5.—" *The gods of the nations are idols."* Their Elohim are *elilim.* See 1 Chron. xvi. 26. The word *elilim* occurs in two places in the Psalms, here and xcvii. 7. It is used most frequently by Isaiah, and properly signifies *nothings,* as St. Paul says, " an *idol* is *nothing."* (1 Cor. viii. 4.)—*Chr. Wordsworth.*

Verse 5.—" *The Lord made the heavens."* Verse 5 is a notandum. What a tribute to astronomy is it that the Lord is so often done homage to as having made the heavens ! Let the theology of nature be blended with the theology of conscience —a full recognition of the strength and the glory which shine palpably forth in the wonders of creation, with the spiritual offerings of holy worship and holy service.—*Thomas Chalmers.*

Verse 6.—" *Beauty . . . in his sanctuary."*

> Oh, if so much of beauty doth reveal
> Itself in every vein of life and nature,
> How beautiful must be the Source itself,
> The Ever-Bright One !

—Esaias Tegner, 1782—1847.

Verse 6.—" *In his sanctuary."* That is to say (1) his ark, tabernacle, or temple, as many writers consider. Kimchi, as quoted by Muis, suggests that where joy or beauty is mentioned as being in his temple, it is set in opposition to the perpetual grief of the Philistines when the ark was in their cities. They saw the Lord's strength, but not his beauty. (2) Others refer the word sanctuary to the church of Christ, which, as Munster remarks, is adorned with heavenly ornaments, and was typified by the magnificence of Solomon's temple. Certainly it is in the church that the spiritual power and beauty of the Lord are to be most clearly seen. (3) The passage may refer to heaven, where the divine presence is more peculiarly manifest.—*C. H. S.*

Verse 7.—" *Ye kindreds of the people.*" There is a peculiar force, observes an early commentator [Cassiodorus], in this phrase, " *kindreds of the people,*" much more than if we had the word " *peoples* " alone ; for in every nation there are at all times strangers, aliens, sojourners abiding permanently or for a time, but not reckoned among the natives ; while the phrase here includes all such, and provides that none shall be shut out because of his origin.—*Neale and Littledale.*

Verse 7.—" *Ye kindreds of the people.*" He calls upon them to come in kindreds or families, in allusion to the Jewish custom of families coming by themselves on the several festival days to worship in Jerusalem ; and the Holy Ghost gives us here to understand that such custom was to serve as a model for Christians, whose families should unite in coming to the church to give glory and honour to God for all the wonderful things he accomplished in the redemption of man ; for it was not by our own industry, or by our merits, that we have come to grace, and to be the adopted children of God, but through God's mercy, to whom, therefore, is due all honour and glory.—*Bellarmine.*

Verse 8.—" *Give unto the Lord the glory due unto his name.*" It is a debt ; and a debt, in equity, must be paid. The honour due to his name is to acknowledge him to be holy, just, true, powerful : " The Lord, the faithful God," " good, merciful, long-suffering," etc. Defraud not his name of the least honour.—*Adam Clarke.*

Verse 8.—" *Give unto the Lord the glory due unto his name.*" Is all the glory due unto God's name, and ought it, in strict justice, to have been ascribed unto him by men, ever since man began to exist ? How immeasurably great then is the debt which our world has contracted, and under the burden of which it now groans ! During every day and every hour which has elapsed since the apostasy of man, this debt has been increasing ; for every day and every hour all men ought to have given unto Jehovah the glory which is due to his name. But no man has ever done this fully. And a vast proportion of our race have never done it at all. Now the difference between the tribute which men ought to have paid to God and that which they actually have paid constitutes the debt of which we are speaking. How vast, then, how incalculable is it !—*Edward Payson.*

Verse 8.—" *Give unto the Lord the glory due unto his name.*" Every glory will not serve the turn, but such glory as is proper and peculiar for that God we serve. It is a stated rule in Scripture that, *respects to God must be proportioned to the nature of God.* God is a *spirit,* therefore will be worshipped in *spirit and truth.* God is a God of *peace,* therefore lift up pure hands, without *wrath and doubting.* God is a *holy* God, therefore will be *sanctified.* They which worship the sun, among the heathens, they used a flying horse, as a thing most suitable to the swift motion of the sun. Well, then, they that will glorify and honour God with a glory due to his name, must sanctify him as well as honour him. Why ? For " God is glorious in holiness," Exod. xv. 11. This is that which God counteth to be his chief excellency, and the glory which he will manifest among the sons of men.—*Thomas Manton.*

Verse 8.—" *Bring an offering.*" This is language taken from the temple-worship, and means that God is to be worshipped, in the manner which he has prescribed, as a suitable expression of his majesty. The word here rendered " *offering* "—מִנְחָה, *minkhah*—is that which is commonly used to denote a *bloodless* offering, a thank-offering.—*Albert Barnes.*

Verse 9.—" *In the beauty of holiness,*" or, in the ornament of holiness, alluding to the splendid robes of eastern worshippers.—*W. Wilson.*

Verse 9.—" *The beauty of holiness.*" Shall I call *holiness* an attribute ? Is it not rather the glorious combination of all his attributes into one perfect whole ? As all his attributes proceed from the absolute, so all again converge and meet in holiness. As from the insufferable white light of the Absolute they all seem to diverge and separate into prismatic hues, so they all seem again to converge and meet and combine in the dazzling white radiance of his holiness. This, therefore, is rather the intense whiteness, purity, clearness, the infinite lustre and splendour of his perfect nature—like a gem without flaw, without stain, and without colour. All of his attributes are glorious, but in this we have a combination of all into a still more glorious whole. It is for this reason that it is so frequently in Scripture associated with the Divine beauty. The poetic nature of the Psalmist is exalted to ecstasy in contemplation of the " *beauty of holiness,*" the " *beauty of the Lord.*" Beauty is a combination of elements according to the laws of harmony ; the more beautiful the parts or elements, and the more perfect the harmonious combination, the higher the beauty. How high and glorious, therefore, must be the beauty of this attribute which is the perfect combination of all his infinite perfections !

You see, then, why this attribute is awful to us. In the ideal man all the faculties and powers, mental, moral, and bodily, work together in perfect harmony, making sweet music—the image of God is clear and pure in the human heart. But, alas ! how far are we from the ideal ! In the actual man the purity is stained, the beauty is defaced, the harmony is changed into jarring discord, "like sweet bells jangled out of tune." How it came so, we are not now inquiring. We all feel that it *is* so. Therefore is this attribute so awful to us. It is the awfulness of absolute purity in the presence of impurity ; it is the awfulness of perfect beauty in the presence of deformity ; it is the awfulness of honour in the presence of dishonour and shame ; in one word, it is the awfulness of holiness in the presence of sinfulness. How, then, shall we approach him before whom angels bow and archangels veil their faces— him in whose sight the white radiance of heaven itself is stained with impurity ?— *Joseph Le Coute, in " Religion and Science,"* 1874.

Verse 9.—" *The beauty of holiness.*" The religion of the gospel of Christ is " *the beauty of holiness,*" as it concerns its Author, its plan, its fruits. 1st, As it concerns its *Author.* Whatever we can understand as meant by beauty or holiness, we see in the attributes of God, whether we consider them in all their harmony, or contemplate any one of them in particular. . . . 2ndly, As to its plan. Survey the gospel where we will, or regard whatever we can that is revealed concerning it, we find it to be all " *beauty* " ; and we cannot call it by a more appropriate name than " *the beauty of holiness.*" 3rdly, As to its *fruits.* There is a holy separation, a beautiful character of holiness, a separation as to character, feelings, and conduct ; these are all the various fruits of grace ; and so the man becomes beautiful in holiness. —*Legh Richmond,* 1772—1827.

Verse 10.—" *Say among the heathen that the Lord reigneth.*" This clause reads in the old Latin version, " Tell it out among the heathen, that the Lord reigneth *from the tree.*" Justin Martyr accuses the Jews, that they have erased the words " a ligno," ἀπὸ ξύλου, which are wanting in the original and in the Septuagint. Mrs. Charles renders the verse thus :—

> " The truth that David learned to sing,
> Its deep fulfilment here attains ;
> ' Tell all the earth the Lord is King ! '
> Lo, from the cross, a King he reigns ! "

—*From " Christ in Song. Hymns of Immanuel, with Notes by P. Schaff,"* 1870.

Verse 10.—" *Say among the heathen that the Lord reigneth.*" It is not enough to feel *desire* ; we must " *say* among the heathen, the Lord reigneth." There is a commandment given us of the LORD to " go into all the world, and preach the gospel to every creature "—to tell them what Christ hath taught us—to say to them, in fact, " The LORD reigneth." . . . .

We go among the heathen, and say, " the LORD reigneth "—point them to all the various objects in *creation*—to the stars of heaven, to the beauties of vegetation, to the daily occurrences of *providence,* to the body fearfully and wonderfully made, to its continual preservation and supply. We may easily take our text from every thing by which we are surrounded, and say, " The LORD reigneth." But we must not stop here. It is well to have right views of God as the Creator ; but it is only as we view him as the God of *Redemption,* that we can praise him " in the beauty of holiness."—*Legh Richmond.*

Verse 10.—" *Say among the heathen that the Lord reigneth* " must be the Christian's as it was the Israelite's motto. The earliest preaching of our Saviour and his disciples was the preaching of the gospel of the *kingdom.* It was because *all power was given unto him in heaven and in earth,* that, after his resurrection from the dead, Jesus sent forth his apostles to go and teach all nations. The substance of the apostles' subsequent preaching was, confessedly, the *kingdom* of God.—*J. F. Thrupp.*

Verse 10.—" *Say among the heathen.*" Go, ye that are already become proselytes unto him, and publish everywhere, in all countries, that the Lord [Christ] is the sovereign of the world, who alone can make it happy: for he shall settle those in peace that submit unto his government: and they shall not be so disturbed as they were wont with wars and tumults: he shall administer equal justice unto all; and neither suffer the good to be unrewarded, nor the evil to escape unpunished.—*Symon Patrick.*

Verse 10.—" *The world also,*" etc. The natural world shall be established; the standing of the world, and its stability, is owing to the mediation of Christ. Sin had given it a shock, and still threatens it; but Christ, as redeemer, upholds all things, and preserves the course of nature. The world of mankind shall be established, shall be preserved, till all that belong to the election of grace are called in, though a guilty, provoking world. The Christian religion, as far as it is embraced, shall establish states and kingdoms, and preserve good order among men. The church in the world shall be established, that it cannot be moved, for it is built upon a rock, and the gates of hell shall never prevail against it; it is a " kingdom that cannot be shaken."—*Matthew Henry.*

Verse 10.—" *It shall not be moved.*" When we learn from the records of geology, as they are inscribed upon the rocks, how numerous and thorough have been the revolutions of the surface and the crust of the globe in past ages; how often and how long the present dry land has been alternately above and beneath the ocean; how frequently the crust of the globe has been fractured, bent, and dislocated; now lifted upward, and now thrown downward, and now folded by lateral pressure; how frequently melted matter has been forced through its strata and through its fissures to the surface; in short, how every particle of the accessible portions of the globe has undergone entire metamorphoses; and especially when we recollect what strong evidence there is that oceans of liquid matter exist beneath the solid crust, and that probably the whole interior of the earth is in that condition, with expansive energy sufficient to rend the globe into fragments; when we review all these facts, we cannot but feel that the condition of the surface of the globe must be one of great insecurity and liability to change. But it is not so. On the contrary, the present state of the globe is one of permanent uniformity and entire security, except those comparatively slight catastrophes which result from earthquakes, volcanoes, and local deluges. Even the climate has experienced no general change within historic times, and the profound mathematical researches of Baron Fourier have demonstrated that, even though the internal parts of the globe are in an incandescent state, beneath a crust thirty or forty miles, the temperature of the surface has long since ceased to be affected by the melted central mass; that it is not now more than one seventeenth of a degree higher than it would be if the interior were ice; and that hundreds of thousands of years will not see it lowered, from this cause, more than the seventeenth part of a degree. And as to the apprehension that the entire crust of the globe may be broken through, and fall into the melted matter beneath, just reflect what solidity and strength there must be in a mass of hard rock from fifty to one hundred miles in thickness, and your fears of such a catastrophe will probably vanish.

Now, such a uniformity of climate and security from general ruin are essential to the comfort and existence of animal nature. But it must have required infinite wisdom and benevolence so to arrange and balance the mighty elements of change and ruin which exist in the earth, that they should hold one another in check, and make the world a quiet, unchanged, and secure dwelling-place for so many thousands of years. Surely that wisdom must have been guided by infinite benevolence.— *Edward Hitchcock, in " The Religion of Geology,*" 1851.

Verse 11.—" *Let the heavens rejoice.*" As the whole creation, both animate and inanimate, has groaned beneath the weight of the curse, so shall the whole creation partake of the great deliverance.—" *The Speaker's Commentary,*" 1873.

Verse 11.—" *Let the sea roar.*"—

> Thou paragon of elemental powers,
> Mystery of waters—never-slumbering sea !
> Impassioned orator with lips sublime,
> Whose waves are arguments which prove a God !

Robert Montgomery, 1807—1855.

Verses 11, 12.—God will graciously accept the holy joys and praises of all the hearty well-wishers to the kingdom of Christ, be their capacity never so mean. " *The sea* " can but " *roar,*" and how " *the trees of the wood* " can shew that they " *rejoice,*" I know not ; but " he that searcheth the heart, knows what is the mind of the Spirit," and understands the language, the broken language of the weakest.— *Matthew Henry.*

Verses 11—13.—These verses are full of comprehensive beauty and power. They present the gathering together of everything under the confessed dominion of the reigning Christ. Things in heaven, as well as things on earth, rejoice together in the acknowledged blessing of the Lord of peace. The Psalm is throughout a very sweet strain of millennial prophecy.—*Arthur Pridham.*

Verses 11—13.—Nothing can excel that noble exultation of universal nature in the 96th Psalm, which has been so often commended, where the whole animate and inanimate creation unite in the praises of their Maker. Poetry here seems to assume the highest tone of triumph and exultation, and to revel, if I may so express myself, in all the extravagance of joy.—*Robert Lowth.*

Verses 11—13.—Although there are some who by *heaven* understand *angels ;* by the *earth, men ;* by the *sea,* troublesome *spirits ;* by *trees* and *fields*, the *Gentiles* who were to believe, yet this need not be thought strange, because such *prosopopœias* are frequent in Scripture.—*Adam Clarke.*

Verse 12.—" *Let the field be joyful,*" etc. Let the husbandmen, and the shepherds, and all that dwell in the fields, leap for joy ; and the woodmen and foresters shout for joy, to see the happy day approaching ; when all the idols that are worshipped there shall be thrown down together with their groves.—*Symon Patrick.*

Verse 12.—" *Rejoice.*" The verb רֵנֵן expresses the vibratory motion, either of a dancer's feet, or of a singer's lip.—*Samuel Horsley.*

Verse 12.—" *The trees of the wood.*"

> His praise, ye winds, that from four quarters blow,
> Breathe soft or loud ; and wave your tops, ye Pines,
> With every plant, in sign of worship wave.
>
> > *John Milton.*

Verses 12, 13.—" *He cometh,*" etc.

> It chanced upon the merry, merry Christmas eve,
> I went sighing past the church across the moorland dreary—
> " Oh ! never sin and want and woe this earth will leave,
> And the bells but mock the wailing round, they sing so cheery
> How long, O Lord ! how long before thou come again ?
> Still in cellar, and in garret, and on moorland dreary
> The orphans moan, and widows weep, and poor men toil in vain,
> Till earth is sick of hope deferred, though Christmas bells be cheery."
>
> Then arose a joyous clamour from the wild fowl on the mere,
> Beneath the stars, across the snow, like clear bells ringing,
> And a voice within cried, " Listen ! Christmas carols even here !
> Though thou be dumb, yet o'er their work the stars and snows are singing.
> Blind ! I live, I love, I reign ; and all the nations through
> With the thunder of my judgments even now are ringing ;
> Do thou fulfil thy work but as yon wild fowl do,
> Thou wilt heed no less the wailing, yet hear through it angels singing."
>
> > *Charles Kingsley,* 1858.

Verse 13.—" *For he cometh, for he cometh.*" Because the thing was hard to be believed, the Prophet asserts twice that God should come, that he should be Judge and King, and Governor of all.—*Martinus Bucerus* in *Expos. Ecclesiast.*

Verse 13.—" *He cometh.*" Not יבוא, " *He shall come ;* " but בָּא לִשְׁפֹּט, " *He cometh ;* " to show how near the time is. It is almost day-break, and the court is ready to sit: " The Judge standeth at the door," James v. 9.—*Thomas Watson.*

Verse 13.—" *To judge.*" Vatablus remarks that *to judge* is the word used instead of *to reign, judicare pro regere,* because judges in the early days of the Holy Land exercised the power both of kings and magistrates. The Lord comes to be to all nations a wiser judge than Samuel, a greater champion than Samson, a mightier deliverer than Gideon.—*C. H. S.*

Verse 13.—" *He cometh to judge the earth.*" That is, to put earth in order, to be its Gideon and Samson, to be its *ruler*, to fulfil all that the Book of Judges delineates of a judge's office. It is, as Hengstenberg says, " a gracious judging," not a time of mere adjudication of causes or pronouncing sentences—it is a day of jubilee. It is the happiest day our world has ever seen. Who would not long for it ? Who is there that does not pray for it ? It is the day of the Judge's glory, as well as of our world's freedom—the day when " *the judgment of this world* " (John xii. 31, and xvi. 11), which his cross began and made sure, is completed by the total suppression of Satan's reign, and the removal of the curse. All this is anticipated here ; and so we entitle this Psalm, *The glory due to him who cometh to judge the earth.*—*Andrew A. Bonar.*

Verse 13.—" *He cometh to judge the earth,*" etc. In this new song they take up the words of Enoch, the seventh from Adam (Jude xiv.), who preached of the Coming of the Lord to judge the world.—*Chr. Wordsworth.*

HINTS TO PREACHERS.

Verse 1.—The novelties of grace. I. A new salvation. II. Creates a new heart. III. Suggests a new song. IV. Secures new testimonies, and these, V. Produce new converts.

Verses 1—3.—I. The end desired—to see the earth singing unto the Lord, and blessing his name. II. The means suggested—the showing forth his salvation from day to day ; declaring his glory, etc. III. The certainty of its accomplishment. The Lord hath said it. " O sing," etc. When he commands earth must obey.—*G. R.*

Verses 1—3.—The progress of zeal. I. The spring of expansive desire, ver. 1. II. The streamlet of practical daily effort, ver. 2. III. The broad river of foreign missions, ver. 3.—*C. D.*

Verses 1—9.—We are to honour God. I. With songs, verses 1, 2. II. With sermons, verse 3. III. With religious services, verses 7, 8, 9.—*Matthew Henry.*

Verse 3 (first clause).—I. Declare among the heathen the glory of God's perfections, that they may acknowledge him as the true God. II. Declare the glory of his salvation, that they may accept him as their only Redeemer. III. Declare the glory of his providence, that they may confide in him as their faithful guardian. IV. Declare the glory of his word, that they may prize it as their chief treasure. V. Declare the glory of his service, that they may choose it as their noblest occupation. VI. Declare the glory of his residence, that they may seek it as their best home.—*William Jackson.*

Verse 3.—I. What the gospel is, " God's glory," " his wonders." II. What shall we do with it—declare it. III. To whom. " Among the heathen," all people.

Verse 3 (last clause).—" *His wonders among the people.*" I. The wonders of his Being, to inspire them with awe. II. The wonders of his creation, to fill them with amazement. III. The wonders of his judgments, to restrain them with fear. IV. The wonders of his grace, to allure them with love.—*W. Jackson.*

Verses 4—6.—Missionary sermon. I. Contrast Jehovah of the Bible with gods of human device. II. Decide between divine worship and idolatry. III. Appeal for effort on behalf of idolaters.—*C. D.*

Verse 6.—" *Honour and majesty are before him.*" I. As emanations from him. II. As excellencies ascribed to him. III. As characteristics of what is done by him. IV. As marks of all that dwell near him.—*W. Jackson.*

Verse 6 (latter clause).—What we may see in God's sanctuary (strength and beauty). What we may obtain there, Ps. xc. 17 (strength and beauty).—*C. D.*

Verse 8.—Jehovah possesses a nature and character peculiar to himself ; he sustains various offices and relations, and he has performed many works which he alone could perform. On all these accounts something is due to him from his creatures. And when we regard him with such affections, and yield him such services, as his nature, character, offices, and works deserve, then we give unto him the glory which is due to his name. I. Let us inquire what is due to Jehovah on account of his nature. II. What is due to Jehovah on account of the character he possesses. III. What is due to God on account of the relations and offices which he sustains—

that of a creator, preserver.   IV. What is due to Jehovah on account of the works which he has performed, in nature, providence and redemption.—*E. Payson.*

Verse 8.—The object of worship.   The nature of worship.   The accompaniment of worship (an offering).   The place of worship.—*C. D.*

Verse 9 (first clause).—An examination of true and false worship.   I. False worship, in the obscurity of ignorance, in the dulness of formalism, in the offensiveness of indulged sin, in the hideousness of hypocrisy.   II. True worship, in the beauty of holiness.—*C. D.*

Verse 9.—Holy fear an essential ingredient in true religion.

Verses 10—13.—The reign of righteousness.   I. The announcement of a righteous king and judge.   II. The joyful reception prepared for him.   III. His glorious coming. —*C. D.*

Verses 11, 12.—The sympathy of nature with the work of grace ; especially dwelling upon its fuller display in the millennial period.

PSALM XCVII.

SUBJECT.—*As the last Psalm sang the praises of the Lord in connection with the proclamation of the gospel among the Gentiles, so this appears to foreshadow the mighty working of the Holy Ghost in subduing the colossal systems of error, and casting down the idol gods. Across the sea to maritime regions a voice cries for rejoicing at the reign of Jesus (verse 1), the sacred fire descends (verse 3), like lightning the gospel flames forth (verse 4), difficulties vanish (verse 5), and all the nations see the glory of God (verse 6). The idols are confounded (verse 7), the church rejoices (verse 8), the Lord is exalted (verse 9). The Psalm closes with an exhortation to holy steadfastness under the persecution which would follow, and bids the saints rejoice that their path is bright, and their reward glorious and certain. Modern critics, always intent upon ascribing the Psalms to anybody rather than to David, count themselves successful in dating this song further on than the captivity, because it contains passages similar to those which occur in the later prophets; but we venture to assert that it is quite as probable that the prophets adopted the language of David as that some unknown writer borrowed from them. One Psalm in this series is said to be " in David," and we believe that the rest are in the same place, and by the same author. The matter is not important, and we only mention it because it seems to be the pride of certain critics to set up new theories; and there are readers who imagine this to be a sure proof of prodigious learning. We do not believe that their theories are worth the paper they are written upon.*

DIVISION.—*The Psalm divides itself into four portions, each containing three verses. The coming of the Lord is described (1—3); its effect upon the earth is declared (4—6); and then its influence upon the heathen and the people of God. The last part contains both exhortation and encouragement, urging to holiness and inculcating happiness.*

EXPOSITION.

THE LORD reigneth; let the earth rejoice; let the multitude of isles be glad *thereof*.

2 Clouds and darkness *are* round about him : righteousness and judgment *are* the habitation of his throne.

3 A fire goeth before him, and burneth up his enemies round about.

1. " *The Lord reigneth.*" This is the watchword of the Psalm—Jehovah reigns. It is also the essence of the gospel proclamation, and the foundation of the gospel kingdom. Jesus has come, and all power is given unto him in heaven and in earth, therefore men are bidden to yield him their obedient faith. Saints draw comfort from these words, and only rebels cavil at them. " *Let the earth rejoice,*" for there is cause for joy. Other reigns have produced injustice, oppression, bloodshed, terror; the reign of the infinitely gracious Jehovah is the hope of mankind, and when they all yield to it the race will have its paradise restored. The very globe itself may well be glad that its Maker and liege Lord has come to his own, and the whole race of man may also be glad, since to every willing subject Jesus brings untold blessings. " *Let the multitude of isles be glad thereof.*" To the ancient Israelites all places beyond the seas were isles, and the phrase is equivalent to all lands which are reached by ships. It is remarkable, however, that upon actual islands some of the greatest victories of the Cross have been achieved. Our own favoured land is a case in point, and not less so the islands of Polynesia and the kingdom of Madagascar. Islands are very numerous; may they all become Holy Islands, and Isles of Saints, then will they all be Fortunate Islands, and true Formosas. Many a land owes its peace to the sea; if it had not been isolated it would have been desolated, and therefore the inhabitants should praise the Lord who has moated them about, and given them a defence more available than bars of brass. Jesus deserves to be Lord of the Isles, and to have his praises sounded along every sea-beaten shore. Amen, so let it be.

2. " *Clouds and darkness are round about him.*" So the Lord revealed himself at Sinai, so must he ever surround his essential Deity when he shows himself to the

sons of men, or his excessive glory would destroy them. Every revelation of God must also be an obvelation ; there must be a veiling of his infinite splendour if anything is to be seen by finite beings. It is often thus with the Lord in providence ; when working out designs of unmingled love he conceals the purpose of his grace that it may be the more clearly discovered at the end. " It is the glory of God to conceal a thing." Around the history of his church dark clouds of persecution hover, and an awful gloom at times settles down, still the Lord is there ; and though men for a while see not the bright light in the clouds, it bursts forth in due season to the confusion of the adversaries of the gospel. This passage should teach us the impertinence of attempting to pry into the essence of the Godhead, the vanity of all endeavours to understand the mystery of the Trinity in Unity, the arrogance of arraigning the Most High before the bar of human reason, the folly of dictating to the Eternal One the manner in which he should proceed. Wisdom veils her face and adores the mercy which conceals the divine purpose ; folly rushes in and perishes, blinded first, and by-and-by consumed by the blaze of glory.

" *Righteousness and judgment are the habitation of his throne.*' There he abides, he never departs from strict justice and right, his throne is fixed upon the rock of eternal holiness. Righteousness is his immutable attribute, and judgment marks his every act. What though we cannot see or understand what he doeth, yet we are sure that he will do no wrong to us or any of his creatures. Is not this enough to make us rejoice in him and adore him ? Divine sovereignty is never tyrannical. Jehovah is an autocrat, but not a despot. Absolute power is safe in the hands of him who cannot err, or act unrighteously. When the roll of the decrees, and the books of the divine providence shall be opened, no eye shall there discern one word that should be blotted out, one syllable of error, one line of injustice, one letter of unholiness. Of none but the Lord of all can this be said.

3. " *A fire goeth before him.*" Like an advance guard clearing the way. So was it at Sinai, so must it be : the very Being of God is power, consuming all opposition ; omnipotence is a devouring flame which " *burneth up his enemies round about.*" God is longsuffering, but when he comes forth to judgment he will make short work with the unrighteous, they will be as chaff before the flame. Reading this verse in reference to the coming of Jesus, and the descent of the Spirit, we are reminded of the tongues of fire, and of the power which attended the gospel, so that all opposition was speedily overcome. Even now where the gospel is preached in faith, and in the power of the Spirit, it burns its own way, irresistibly destroying falsehood, superstition, unbelief, sin, indifference, and hardness of heart. In it the Lord reigneth, and because of it let the earth rejoice.

4 His lightnings enlightened the world : the earth saw, and trembled.

5 The hills melted like wax at the presence of the Lord, at the presence of the Lord of the whole earth.

6 The heavens declare his righteousness, and all the people see his glory.

4. " *His lightnings enlightened the world.*" In times of tempest the whole of nature is lighted up with a lurid glare, even the light of the sun itself seems dim compared with the blaze of lightning. If such are the common lights of nature what must be the glories of the Godhead itself ? When God draws aside the curtain for a moment how astonished are the nations, the light compels them to cover their eyes and bow their heads in solemn awe. Jesus in the gospel lights up the earth with such a blaze of truth and grace as was never seen or even imagined before. In apostolic times the word flashed from one end of the heavens to the other, no part of the civilised globe was left unilluminated. " *The earth saw, and trembled.*" In God's presence the solid earth quakes, astonished by his glory it is convulsed with fear. To the advent of our Lord and the setting up of his kingdom among men these words are also most applicable ; nothing ever caused such a shaking and commotion as the proclamation of the gospel, nothing was more majestic than its course, it turned the world upside down, levelled the mountains, and filled up the valleys. Jesus came, he saw, he conquered. When the Holy Ghost rested upon his servants their course was like that of a mighty storm, the truth flashed with the force and speed of a thunderbolt, and philosophers and priests, princes and people were utterly confounded, and altogether powerless to withstand it. It shall be so again. Faith even now sets the world on fire, and rocks the nations to and fro.

5. " *The hills melted like wax at the presence of the Lord.*" Inanimate nature

knows its Creator, and worships him in its own fashion. States and kingdoms which stand out upon the world like mountains are utterly dissolved when he decrees their end. Systems as ancient and firmly-rooted as the hills pass away when he does but look upon them. In the Pentecostal era, and its subsequent age, this was seen on all hands, heathenism yielded at the glance of Jehovah Jesus, and the tyrannies based upon it dissolved like melted wax. " *At the presence of the Lord of the whole earth.*" His dominion is universal, and his power is everywhere felt. Men cannot move the hills, with difficulty do they climb them, with incredible toil do they pierce their way through their fastnesses, but it is not so with the Lord, his presence makes a clear pathway, obstacles disappear, a highway is made, and that not by his hand as though it cost him pains, but by his mere presence, for power goes forth from him with a word or a glance. O for the presence of the Lord after this sort with his church at this hour! It is our one and only need. With it the mountains of difficulty would flee away, and all obstacles would disappear. O that thou wouldest rend the heavens and come down, that the mountains might flow down at thy presence, O Lord.

In the little world of our nature the presence of Jesus in reigning power is as a fire to consume our lusts and melt our souls to obedience. Sometimes we doubt the presence of the Lord within, for he is concealed with clouds, but we are again assured that he is within us when his light shines in and fills us with holy fear, while at the same time the warmth of grace softens us to penitence, resignation and obedience, even as wax becomes soft in the presence of fire.

6. " *The heavens declare his righteousness.*" It is as conspicuous as if written across the skies, both the celestial and the terrestrial globes shine in its light. It is the manner of the inspired poets to picture the whole creation as in sympathy with the glory of God, and indeed it is not *mere* poetry, for a great truth underlies it, the whole creation has been made to groan through man's sin, and it is yet to share in the joy of his restoration. " *And all the people see his glory.*" The glorious gospel became so well known and widely promulgated, that it seemed to be proclaimed by every star, and published by the very skies themselves, therefore all races of men became acquainted with it, and were made to see the exceeding glory of the grace of God which is resplendent therein. May it come to pass ere long that, by a revival of the old missionary ardour, the glad tidings may yet be carried to every tribe of Adam's race, and once again all flesh may see the glory of Jehovah. It must be so, therefore let us rejoice before the Lord.

7 Confounded be all they that serve graven images, that boast themselves of idols : worship him, all *ye* gods.

8 Zion heard, and was glad ; and the daughters of Judah rejoiced because of thy judgments, O Lord.

9 For thou, Lord, *art* high above all the earth : thou art exalted far above all gods.

7. " *Confounded be all they that serve graven images, that boast themselves of idols.*" They shall be so ; shame shall cover their faces, they shall blush to think of their former besotted boastings. When a man gravely worships what has been engraved by a man's hand, and puts his trust in a mere nothing and nonentity, he is indeed brutish, and when he is converted from such absurdity he may well be ashamed. A man who worships an image is but the image of a man, his senses must have left him. He who boasts of an idol makes an idle boast. " *Worship him, all ye gods.*" Bow down yourselves, ye fancied gods. Let Jove do homage to Jehovah, let Thor lay down his hammer at the foot of the cross, and Juggernaut remove his blood-stained car out of the road of Immanuel. If the false gods are thus bidden to worship the coming Lord, how much more shall they adore him who are godlike creatures in heaven, even the angelic spirits ? Paul quotes this passage as the voice of God to angels when he sent his Son into the world. All powers are bound to recognise the chief power ; since they derive their only rightful authority from the Lord, they should be careful to acknowledge his superiority at all times by the most reverent adoration.

8. " *Zion heard, and was glad.*" While the heathen are confounded the people of God are made to triumph, for they love to see their God exalted. The day shall come when the literal Zion, so long forsaken, shall joy in the common salvation. It

did so at the first when the apostles dwelt at Jerusalem, and the good days will come back again. "*And the daughters of Judah rejoiced.*" Each individual believer is glad when he sees false systems broken up and idol gods broken down ; the judgments of the Lord afford unalloyed delight to those who worship the true God in spirit and in truth. In the first ages of Christianity the believing Israel rejoiced to see Christ's kingdom victorious among the heathen, and even yet, though for a while turning aside, the daughters of Judah will sympathise in the wide-spread reign of Jehovah their God, through the gospel of his dear Son. As the women of Judah went forth to meet David in the dance, singing his victory over the Philistine, so shall they chant the triumphs of David's son and Lord.

9. "*For thou, Lord, art high above all the earth.*" And therefore do we rejoice to see the idols abolished and to see all mankind bending at thy throne. There is but one God, there cannot be another, and he is and ever must be over all. "*Thou art exalted far above all gods.*" As much as ALL is exalted above nothing, and perfection above folly. Jehovah is not alone high over Judea, but over all the earth, nor is he exalted over men only, but over everything that can be called god : the days are on their way when all men shall discern this truth, and shall render unto the Lord the glory which is due alone to him.

10 Ye that love the LORD, hate evil : he preserveth the souls of his saints ; he delivereth them out of the hand of the wicked.

11 Light is sown for the righteous, and gladness for the upright in heart.

12 Rejoice in the LORD, ye righteous ; and give thanks at the remembrance of his holiness.

10. "*Ye that love the Lord, hate evil.*" For he hates it, his fire consumes it, his lightnings blast it, his presence shakes it out of its place, and his glory confounds all the lovers of it. We cannot love God without hating that which he hates. We are not only to avoid evil, and to refuse to countenance it, but we must be in arms against it, and bear towards it a hearty indignation. "*He preserveth the souls of his saints.*" Therefore they need not be afraid of proclaiming war with the party which favours sin. The saints are the safe ones : they have been saved and shall be saved. God keeps those who keep his law. Those who love the Lord shall see his love manifested to them in their preservation from their enemies, and as they keep far from evil so shall evil be kept far from them. "*He delivereth them out of the hand of the wicked.*" It is not consistent with the glory of his name to give over to the power of his foes those whom his grace has made his friends. He may leave the bodies of his persecuted saints in the hand of the wicked, but not their souls, these are very dear to him, and he preserves them safe in his bosom. This foretells for the church a season of battling with the powers of darkness, but the Lord will preserve it and bring it forth to the light.

11. "*Light is sown for the righteous.*" All along their pathway it is strewn. Their night is almost over, their day is coming, the morning already advancing with rosy steps is sowing the earth with orient pearls. The full harvest of delight is not yet ours, but it is sown for us ; it is springing, it will yet appear in fulness. This is only for those who are right before the Lord in his own righteousness, for all others the blackness of darkness is reserved. "*And gladness for the upright in heart.*" Gladness is not only for one righteous man in the singular, but for the whole company of the upright, even as the apostle, after speaking of the crown of life laid up for himself, immediately amended his speech by adding, " and not for me only, but also for all them that love his appearing." The upright ought to be glad, they have cause to be glad, yea and they shall be glad. Those who are right-hearted shall also be glad-hearted. Right leads to light. In the furrows of integrity lie the seeds of happiness, which shall develop into a harvest of bliss. God has lightning for sinners and light for saints. The gospel of Jesus, wherever it goes, sows the whole earth with joy for believers, for these are the men who are righteous before the Lord.

12. "*Rejoice in the Lord, ye righteous.*" The Psalmist had bidden the earth rejoice, and here he turns to the excellent of the earth and bids them lead the song. If all others fail to praise the Lord, the godly must not. To them God is peculiarly revealed, by them he should be specially adored. "*And give thanks at the remembrance of his holiness*"—which is the harmony of all his attributes, the superlative wholeness of his character. This is a terror to the wicked, and a cause of thankfulness

to the gracious. To remember that Jehovah is holy is becoming in those who dwell in his courts, to give thanks in consequence of that remembrance is the sure index of their fitness to abide in his presence. In reference to the triumphs of the gospel, this text teaches us to rejoice greatly in its purifying effect ; it is the death of sin and the life of virtue. An unholy gospel is no gospel. The holiness of the religion of Jesus is its glory, it is that which makes it glad tidings, since while man is left in his sins no bliss can be his portion. Salvation from sin is the priceless gift of our thrice holy God, therefore let us magnify him for ever and ever. He will fill the world with holiness, and so with happiness, therefore let us glory in his holy name, world without end. Amen.

EXPLANATORY NOTES AND QUAINT SAYINGS.

Whole Psalm.—The two preceding Psalms are songs of joy and thanksgiving, in which the gladness of Christ's people is poured forth as they go to meet their triumphant Lord at his second advent, and to bring him back in glory to assume his kingdom. The present Psalm, in language sufficiently explicit, describes the completion of this great event, " the Lord reigneth ; " Messiah is on his throne, and now the words of the second Psalm, verse 6, are fulfilled, " I have set my king upon my holy hill of Sion." Messiah's first act of sovereignty is judgment. Scriptures bearing upon that event are 2 Thess. i. 7 ; Jude 14 ; Isa. lxvi. 15. The character of these judgments is given in the Psalm : clouds and darkness encircling his throne, where, however, righteousness and mercy dwell ; a fire which burns up his enemies round about ; lightnings flashing upon the world, the earth trembling, and the hills melting like wax at the presence of the Lord, at the presence of the Lord of the whole earth. Peter, in his second Epistle, and third chapter, evidently refers to these events as yet future in his day.—*R. H. Ryland.*

Verse 1.—" *The Lord reigneth.*" Here's good news, glad tidings : " *The Lord reigneth.*" It cannot be published without *praise*, without *rejoicing*, without *singing*, without *blessing.* We should dishonour this truth if we did not publish it ; if we should with silence suppress it ; if we should not speak well of it. It is so sweet and comfortable, that it fills the whole world with joy ; and calls in every ear, and every tongue, and every heart, to be glad to rejoice, and to praise God. " *Let the earth rejoice ; let the multitude of isles be glad.*" As though he should say, Let nothing fear but hell : let nothing be disquieted but devils. Let the *lowest*, the *poorest* of the people of God, though but *earth*, yet let them rejoice in this, " *The Lord reigneth.*" . . .
Here are two things of very sweet consideration, 1. The *reign* of the Lord ; and, 2. The *reign* of the Lord *in the saints.* First, This *kingdom* that God is now setting up is his everlasting kingdom. It will not be administered by the weakness of man, but by the power of God ; not by the folly of man, but by the judgment of God. God will, in this kingdom, nakedly manifest his own righteousness, his own compassion and pity ; his own love, his own peace : he will do all things immediately by his own self. And therefore all the pride and ambition, all the oppression and tyranny, and miscarriages that have been in the government of men, shall be wholly taken away. Pure righteousness and judgment and equity shall be infallibly dispensed ; and infinite power, strength, holiness, goodness, and authority shall shine forth nakedly in the face of God ; and that shall be the judge of all men. We shall no longer be abused and oppressed by the will of men, by the lusts of men. The poor people shall no longer groan under the burden of men's lusts, nor sweat for the pleasure and contents of men ; nor their faces any longer be ground by the hardness of the spirit of men ; but they shall be under the protection of God. The great cry now of the people is, " Let's have a King ! " Ye shall have one, one that will " reign in righteousness," the Lord himself.
Secondly, And this *reign* of the Lord shall be *in his saints ;* according to that in Dan. vii. 27. " And the kingdom and dominion, and the greatness of the kingdom under the whole heaven, shall be given to the people of the saints of the Most High, whose kingdom is an everlasting kingdom, and all dominions shall serve and obey

him." As this kingdom shall be administered in the glory of God; so also in the sweetness and gentleness of man, by brethren, by friends, by the saints of the Most High. God lifting up himself in the saints will administer this reign; and as he will do it by the saints, so he will do it by the softness and tenderness of the saints; "The kingdom and dominion under the whole earth shall be given to the people of the saints of the Most High." It's now doing; that ye shall obey none but the Lord; ye shall know no other laws but the law of God; ye shall know no other master but Jehovah. He hath made us priests and kings, and we shall reign with him on the earth. This nature of ours, this body of ours, shall reign with Christ, with God, and that upon earth.

"*The Lord reigns.*" The Lord hath served, hath been hitherto much, yea, mostly, "in the form of a servant." It hath been, as it were, the business of the Lord, whilst this world stood, to give supplies to men; to serve men; to give men strength, and wisdom, and riches, and authority, and power, that men might be great and happy, with the goodness of God: and (in this) God hath been *King* too, but in an under way; as saith the Lord, "I have served with your sins" and lusts: now he will no longer *serve*, but *reign;* God will take all the power and authority into his own hands. He will not be any longer under men, but above all men. It's time he should be so; it's reason he should be so; it's just he should be so. Everything now must bow, stoop, and submit to the law, and rule, and will of God. No man shall any longer say, it shall be so, because it is my will to have it so: there shall not be found an heart, or tongue, that shall move against the dominion of the Lord.

Satan hath been a prince; he hath made laws of your captivity and misery; he hath kept you to his task, to do him service. He hath said, *Be angry,* and then you have been full of rage. He hath said, *Be covetous,* and then you have been full of covetousness. He hath said, *Be dark,* and then you have been full of blindness. He hath said, *Be proud,* and then ye have been full of haughtiness. And so he hath, as a monstrous tyrant, tormented the world. The sting of Satan's whips is in your consciences, I know. Your errors and mistakes have been through the kingdom of darkness in you, that you do not know God, or his holy will. You would come into the enjoyment of God; Satan will not let you: you would know God; he will not suffer you: you would be wise unto salvation; he will not permit you. He hath fettered you with his chains of darkness; he hath captivated your judgments; he hath made you to grind at his mill and to drudge in his service; and hath made you to cry out, "O when will the Lord come!" But now his wicked reign is at an end: what ye had, ye shall want, and what ye want, ye shall have; what hath been shall not be; that which shall be, must be, and cannot choose but be: ye shall have love, because the law of God is love; and ye shall have peace, because the kingdom of God is peace; and ye shall have light, because the inheritance is marvellous light; ye shall have righteousness, because this state is true holiness; ye shall have liberty, settledness, stability, and every good thing in this kingdom of God. It's always ill with us while Satan reigns. It's always well with us while God reigns; when our Husband is King we shall have preferment, and honour, and riches, and greatness, and power, and authority, because our God reigns. "*The Lord reigns,*" for us; the Lord takes his kingdom, and it is for us: the Lord hath reigned in himself all this while; now he reigns by us: the Lord counts himself not to have a kingdom, till we have it with him: the Lord thinks himself mean and despised, till we are exalted. He is poor without us. He is weak, while absent from us. He is not himself unless he enjoys us. "Thou art my excellency, my first-born." The power of God is in weakness, till we become mighty. The kingdom of God is in darkness, till we shine forth. The treasures of God were of no worth to him, if we were not his richest jewels.

"*The Lord* doth *reign.*" This is not to be passed by; it's in the present tense. This is the song that we hear and see angels sing. The elders and saints in heaven sing it perpetually; we daily hear it. *Hallelujah, Hallelujah, the Lord reigneth!* There is administered into our hearts and ears *an hallelujah; the Lord reigneth;* indeed every creature speaks it, all in heaven and earth.

"*The Lord doth reign,*" and saith, "I am upon my throne. I am great; none is great but myself. I am King; I have the sceptre in my hand. I am powerful; none is powerful but I." All the power of men is broken. All the thrones of men are shattered into dust. All the wisdom of men is turned into folly. All the strength of men is melted into weakness and water. The meltings and moulderings away of the powers and dignities of the world, speak it aloud, *The Lord reigns.*—*William Sedgwick, in " Some Flashes of Lightnings of the Son of Man,"* 1648.

Verse 1.—*" The Lord reigneth."* He who stood before the judge, he who received the blows, he who was scourged, he who was spit upon, he who was crowned with thorns, he who was struck with fists, he who hung upon the cross, he who as he hung upon the wood was mocked, he who died upon the cross, he who was pierced with the spear, he who was buried, himself arose from the dead. *" The Lord reigneth."* Let kingdoms rage as much as they can ; what can they do to the King of kingdoms, the Lord of all kings, the Creator of all worlds ?—*Augustine.*

Verse 1.—*" The Lord reigneth."* I am glad that Christ is Lord of all, for otherwise I should utterly have been out of hope, saith *Miconius* in an epistle to *Calvin,* upon a view of the church's enemies.—*John Trapp.*

Verse 1.—*" The Lord reigneth ; let the earth rejoice."* Consider the divine government in various views, as legislative, providential, mediatorial, and judicial, and in each of these views the divine government is matter of universal joy.

I. "The Lord reigneth" *upon a throne of legislation,* " let the earth rejoice." He is the one supreme law-giver and is perfectly qualified for that important trust. Nothing tends more to the advantage of civil society than to have good laws established, according to which mankind are to conduct themselves, and according to which their rulers will deal with them. Now the supreme and universal King has enacted and published the best laws for the government of the moral world, and of the human race in particular. Let the earth then rejoice that God has clearly revealed his will to us and not left us in inextricable perplexities about our duty to him and mankind. . . . . Again, " Let the earth rejoice " that these laws are suitably enforced with proper sanctions. The sanctions are such as become a God of infinite wisdom, almighty power, inexorable justice, untainted holiness, and unbounded goodness and grace, and such as are agreeable to the nature of reasonable creatures formed for an immortal duration. Let the earth rejoice that the divine laws reach the inner man, and have power upon the hearts and consciences of men. Human laws can only smooth our external conduct at best, but the heart in the meantime may be disloyal and wicked. Now this defect is supplied by the laws of the King of Heaven, which are spiritual. They require a complete uniformity and self-consistency in us that heart and life may agree, and therefore they are wisely framed to make us entirely good.

II. " The Lord reigneth " *by his providence,* " let the earth rejoice." The providence of God is well described in our shorter catechism, " It is his most holy, wise, and powerful preserving and governing all his creatures and all their actions." " The Lord reigneth " over the kingdoms of the earth, and manages all their affairs according to his sovereign and wise pleasure, and he doth the same for his church. He can reduce confusion into order, make the wrath of man to praise him, and restrain the remainder of it.

III. " The Lord reigneth " *upon a throne of grace !* " let the earth rejoice." It is the mediatorial government of the Messiah which the Psalmist had more immediately in view, and this is the principal cause of joy to the earth and its guilty inhabitants.

IV. And, lastly, the Lord will reign ere long upon *a throne of universal judgment* conspicuous to the assembled universe, " let the earth therefore rejoice, and the multitude of the isles be glad."—*Condensed from a Sermon by Samuel Davies,* 1724—1761.

Verse 1.—*" Let the earth rejoice."* The earth is called upon to rejoice because the Lord reigneth ; and well it may, on the day of its enlargement and final emancipation from evil, which seems to be here set forth—a day of judgment, and so also a day of terror and destruction to the enemies of God and goodness—a day when at his presence " the elements shall melt with fervent heat ; " but his own righteousness and glory shall be manifested in the sight of all people. Then will the worldly, who serve idols in loving the creature more than the Creator, be confounded and overthrown ; but then, too, will the righteous lift up their heads and rejoice because of God's judgments.—*Thomas Chalmers.*

Verse 1.—*" The multitude of the isles."* In Poole's Synopsis we find from the various interpretations of different authors that the word may mean maritime regions, places beyond sea usually reached in ships, and all countries bordering on the ocean.—*C. H. S.*

Verse 1.—*" The isles."* Figuratively the isles may be taken for all the churches.

Why isles ? Because the waves of all temptations roar around them. But as an isle may be beaten by the waves which on every side dash around it, yet cannot be broken, and rather itself doth break the advancing waves, than by them is broken : so also the churches of God, springing up throughout the world, have suffered the persecutions of the ungodly, who roar around them on every side ; and behold the isles stand fixed, and at last the sea is calmed.—*Augustine.*

Verse 1.—When Bulstrode Whitelock was embarked as Cromwell's envoy to Sweden, in 1653, he was much disturbed in mind, as he rested at Harwich the preceding night, which was very stormy, as he thought upon the distracted state of the nation. It happened that a confidential servant slept in an adjacent bed, who, finding that his master could not sleep, at length said :—

" Pray, sir, will you give me leave to ask you a question ? "

" Certainly."

" Pray, sir, do you think God governed the world very well before you came into it ? "

" Undoubtedly."

" And pray, sir, do you think that he will govern it quite as well when you are gone out of it ? "

" Certainly."

" Then pray, sir, excuse me, but do not you think you may trust him to govern it quite as well as long as you live ? "

To this question Whitelock had nothing to reply ; but turning about, soon fell fast asleep, till he was summoned to embark.—*G. S. Bowes, in " Illustrative Gatherings,"* 1862.

Verse 2.—" *Clouds and darkness are round about him."* The figurative language in the poetical parts of the Old Testament is frequently taken from the historical books, and refers to the facts therein recorded ; thus the appearances of God to the saints and patriarchs in old times is the origin of the figure in our text. If you look at the history of these appearances, you will find they were all accompanied with clouds and darkness. The cloud of the Lord went before the children of Israel when they departed from the land of bondage. This cloud had a dark and bright side, and was a symbol of the divine presence. Thus it preceded the people in all their marches, as a pillar of fire by night, and of a cloud by day. When Solomon dedicated the temple, the glory of the Lord filled the house, and the priest could not enter into the house of the Lord, because the glory of the Lord filled the house. When God descended upon Mount Sinai, " there were thunders and lightnings, and a thick cloud upon the mount, and the voice of the trumpet exceeding loud. And Mount Sinai was altogether on a smoke, because the Lord descended upon it in fire ; and the smoke thereof ascended as the smoke of a furnace, and the whole mount quaked greatly. And the Lord came down upon Mount Sinai, upon the top of the mount " (Exod. xix. 16, 18, 20). When our Saviour was transfigured before three of his disciples, " a bright cloud overshadowed them," from which proceeded the voice of the Father, saying, " This is my beloved Son, in whom I am well pleased ; hear ye him." And Peter, who was present there, afterwards referring to the fact, says that the voice proceeded " from the excellent glory." Thus, in all the symbols of the divine presence, there was a mixture of splendour with darkness and obscurity. So it is in the operations of Providence : in a moral and figurative sense, we may say that clouds and darkness surround all the operations of divine power and wisdom. Clouds are emblems of obscurity ; darkness, of distress. The works of God's providence are often obscure and productive of distress to mankind, though righteousness and judgment are the habitation of his throne.—*Robert Hall.*

Verse 2.—" *Clouds and darkness are round about him."* God doth govern the world *mysteriously.* As there are mysteries in the word, so in the works of God ; δυσνόητά, " things hard to be understood," (2 Pet. iii. 16,) many riddles which nonplus and puzzle men of the largest and most piercing intellectuals : " Behold, I go forward, but he is not there ; and backward, but I cannot perceive him : on the left hand, where he doth work, but I cannot behold him : he hideth himself on the right hand, that I cannot see him : but he knoweth the way that I take." Job xxiii. 8—10. God knoweth our ways, and counteth our steps ; but the wisest of men do not know all God's ways. His way is frequently in the sea, and his chariot in the clouds ; so that he is invisible, not only in his essence, but also in the design and tendence of his operations. Those that behold him with an eye of faith, do not yet see him

with an eye of understanding, so as to discern his way, and whither he is going. Paul
assures us, " His judgments are unsearchable, and his ways past finding out." Rom.
xi. 33. Some of them, indeed, are obvious, plain, and easy ; we may upon the first
view give a satisfactory account of them ; we may read righteousness, equity, mercy,
goodness, love, in them, because written in capital letters, and with such beams of
light as he that runs may read them. But others of God's ways are dark and obscure,
so that they are out of our reach and above our sight. He that goes about in them
to trace God, may quickly lose himself. They are like that hand-writing upon the
wall, which none of Belshazzar's wise men could read or give the interpretation of
(Dan. v. 8). There are *arcana imperii*, " secrets of state and government," which
are not fit to be made common. But this may be our comfort :—though God doth
not now give any account of his matters, nor is he obliged thereunto, yet he can
give a very good and satisfactory account ; and one day his people shall be led into
the mystery ; and, though many things which God doeth they know not now, yet
they shall know them afterward ; and when they know, they shall approve and
admire both the things, and the reason, and the end. They shall then be perfectly
reconciled to all providences, and see that all were worthy of God, and that in all
he acted θεοπρεπῶς, " as did highly become himself."—*Samuel Slater* (1704) *in* " *The
Morning Exercises.*"

Verse 2.—How despicable soever Christ's kingdom may seem to the world, yet
it is full of heavenly majesty : " *clouds and darkness are round about him.*" The
glory of Christ's kingdom is unsearchable, and hid from the eyes of the world, who
cannot take up the things of God, except he reveal himself to them, and do open
the eyes of the understanding : " *clouds and darkness are round about him.*"—*David
Dickson.*

Verse 2.—" *Darkness.*" This and the four following verses have a striking
resemblance to the awful pomp of the march of God, as described Ps. xviii. 8, 9,
and lxviii. 8. All the dread phenomena and meteoric array of nature are in attendance ; thunder and lightning, and earthquakes and volcanoes, with streams of
melting lava, like streams of melting wax. Yet all is justice and equity, joy, exultation, and glory ; and the wicked alone—the adversaries of Jehovah—feel his judgments—the host of idols and their brutish worshippers.—*John Mason Good.*

Verse 2.—" *Righteousness and judgment.*" *Righteousness* is the essential perfection
of the Divine Being. It is his nature : if there had been no creatures for him to
govern, he would have had an unchangeable and invincible love of rectitude. *Judgment* is the application of the principle of righteousness in his government of his
creatures and their actions ; it is a development of his rectitude in the management
of the affairs of his great empire ; it is that superintendence over all, whereby the
operations of all things are directed, to some vast and important end. Judgment
implies measure and equity, in opposition to what is done without rule and consideration. All the divine conduct is equitable, regulated by rectitude, and everything is directed by a judgment that cannot err.—*Robert Hall.*

Verse 2.—" *Righteousness and judgment,*" etc. When the mercy and grace of
our heavenly King are to be described, he is likened to the sun shining in a clear
firmament, and gladdening universal nature with his beneficent ray. But when
we are to conceive an idea of him, as going forth, in justice and judgment, to dis-
comfit and punish his adversaries, the imagery is then borrowed from a troubled
sky ; he is pictured as surrounded by clouds and darkness ; from whence issue
lightnings and thunders, storms and tempests, affrighting and confounding the
wicked and the impenitent.—*Samuel Burder.*

Verse 2.—The Lord manageth his kingdom and government with perfect equity.
" *Righteousness and judgment are the habitation of his throne.*" *Righteousness*, whereby
he preserves, saves, and rewards the good ; *judgment*, whereby he punishes, confounds, and destroys the wicked : these are " *the habitation of his throne,*" his tribunal,
his seat of judicature. These are the basis or foundation, which give unto his throne
rectitudinem et stabilitatem, " rectitude and establishment." His throne is established
in righteousness, and " the sceptre of his kingdom is a right sceptre : " though there
be clouds, yet no blemishes ; though darkness, yet no deformities : Ps. xcii. 15.
Ever since the creation, all things have been done with that unreprovable exactness,
that if the world were to begin again, and the affairs of it to be acted over again,
there should not be an alteration in a tittle. All hath been so well, that nothing
can be mended. Those dark and obscure passages of Providence, at which good
men are startled, and by which all men are posed, are most excellent and curious

strokes, and as so many well-placed shades, which commend the work and admirably set off the beauty of Providence.—*Samuel Slater.*

Verse 2.—

> Jove's firm decree, tho' wrapt in night,
> Beams midst the gloom a constant light ;
> Man's fate obscure in darkness lies,
> Not to be pierc'd by mortal eyes :
> The just resolves of his high mind
> A glorious consummation find ;
> Tho' in majestic state enthron'd
> Thick clouds and dark enclose him round,
> As from the tower of heav'n his eye
> Surveys man's bold impiety ;
> Till his ripe wrath on vengeance bent,
> He arms each god for punishment,
> And from his high and holy throne
> Sends all his awful judgments down.

—*Æschylus* [*R. Potter's translation,* 1808.]

Verse 3.—" *A fire goeth before him.*" Like a marshal or advance guard before a royal presence, or as the javelin men who precede a judge. Fire is the sign both of grace and wrath (Ex. iii. 2 ; Ps. xviii. 9). Majesty marches forth in both displays of Deity.—*C. H. S.* from *Poli Synopsis.*

Verse 3.—" *A fire goeth before him.*" That fire which Christ came to send upon the earth, the kindling blaze of the Holy Ghost, which came down in tongues of fire at Pentecost, to burn freely throughout the world, for the destruction of obstinate unbelievers and the purifying of those who gladly received the Word. And of this the prophet spake, saying, " I will send a fire on Magog, and among them that dwell carelessly in the isles : and they shall know that I am the LORD." (Ezek. xxxix. 6.) This divine flame goes still before the face of the Lord in his coming to every faithful soul, as it kindles with longing for him, and burns up all its sins therewith, as he heaps his coals of fire upon its head, to soften and purify it. " It must needs be," teaches a great saint,* " that the fervour of holy desire must go before his face to every soul to which he means to come, a flame which will burn up all the mildew of sin, and make ready a place for the Lord. And then the soul knows that the Lord is at hand, when it feels itself kindled with that fire, and it saith with the prophet, ' My heart was hot within me ; then spake I with my tongue.' "—Psalm xxxix. 3.—*Augustine, and others, quoted by Neale and Littledale.*

Verse 3.—" *A fire goeth before him.*" There is no less, but rather more wrath attending the despisers of the Gospel, than did attend the giving out of the law. Heb. xii. 29.—*David Dickson.*

Verse 4.—" *His lightnings enlightened the world.*" This passage is applied by Munster to the rapid increase of the kingdom of Christ : for the sound of the Gospel sped through all the world like lightning. There is a prediction almost to this effect in Zech. ix. 14 : " His arrow shall go forth as the lightning, and the Lord God shall blow the trumpet."—*Martin Geier.*

Verse 4.—" *The earth saw and trembled.*" The bare *sight* of thee caused the earth to tremble (Ps. lxxvii. 16).—*A. R. Faussett.*

Verse 5.—" *The hills melted like wax at the presence of the Lord.*" For a parallel passage see Mic. i. 4. There the words are applied to the judgment of God about to fall on the *people of the covenant :* here they are applied to the judgment on the *God-opposing world.* The fact that ' judgment has begun at the house of God ' is a token that judgments of a far more destructive kind will overtake ' the (openly) ungodly and sinners ' (1 Pet. iv. 7). " *The hills* " symbolize the heights of man's self-exalting pride of intellect, wealth, and power.—*A. R. Faussett.*

Verse 5.—" *The Lord of the whole earth.*" In this title lies concealed the reason for the liquefaction of the hills, for the God who here manifests himself is he who created the earth, and is able therefore to reduce it to nothing.—*Martin Geier.*

Verse 6.—" *The heavens declare,*" etc. He does not say, the heavens exercise,

* S. Bernard.

but they declare his righteousness. To the eyes of the wicked the righteousness of God is hidden, until it is made manifest by an astonishing miracle.

" *The heavens.*" This phrase is not, *God* declares, but *the heavens* declare his righteousness. The creature is the servant and revealer of the righteousness of God.

" *His righteousness.*" He says not, the heavens declare *our* righteousness, but *his* righteousness. They testify that God is the righteous judge, rather than that the saints themselves are righteous.

" *All the people.*" Not only do the wicked, those oppressive monsters, see, but " all the people." God so reveals his glory that not only the wicked who are punished may see it, but also other mortals to their edification.

" *And shall see.*" They shall not simply hear or know, but they shall see. This at last is a powerful and convincing demonstration of the righteousness of God, which is put before their eyes.

" *His glory.*" Not merely the destruction of the wicked and vengeance on the enemies of God, but his glory ; for in the destruction of the wicked, and the deliverance of the innocent, the glory of God is declared. Thus the prophet rejoices not so much concerning the destruction of the wicked as concerning the glory of God.—*Musculus.*

Verse 7.—" *Confounded be all they that serve graven images,*" etc. Albeit such as are lovers of imagery not only do serve images, but also will defend the use of images in the exercise of religion, and glory in them ; yet shall they at length be ashamed of their boasting.—*David Dickson.*

Verse 7.—" *Worship him, all ye gods,*" or " *Let all the angels of God worship him.*" The matter of the Psalm itself makes it manifest that the Holy Ghost treateth in it about God's bringing in the firstborn into the world, and the setting up of his kingdom in him. A kingdom is described wherein God would reign, which should destroy idolatry and false worship ; a kingdom wherein the isles of the Gentiles should rejoice, being called to an interest therein ; a kingdom that was to be preached, proclaimed, declared, unto the increase of light and holiness in the world, with the manifestation of the glory of God unto the ends of all the earth : every part whereof declareth the kingdom of Christ to be intended in the Psalm, and consequently that it is a prophecy of the bringing in of the first-begotten into the world. Our inquiry is, whether the angels be intended in these words. They are כָּל־אֱלֹהִים *omnes dii ;* and are so rendered by Jerome, *Adorate eum, omnes dii ;* and by our authorised version, " *Worship him, all ye gods.*" The preceding words are, " *Confounded be all they that serve graven images,*" הַמִּתְהַלְלִים בָּאֱלִילִים, *that boast themselves in* or *of* " *idols,*" " *vanities, nothings,*" as the word signifies, wherein ensues this apostrophe, " *Worship him,* כָּל־אֱלֹהִים, *all ye gods.*" And who they are is our present inquiry. Some, as all the modern Jews, say that it is the gods of the Gentiles, those whom they worship, that are intended ; so making אֱלֹהִים and אֱלִילִים, " *gods,*" and " *vain idols,*" to be the same in this place.

But (1) It cannot be that the Psalmist should exhort the *idols of the heathen,* some whereof were *devils,* some *dead men,* some *inanimate parts of the creation,* unto a reverential worshipping of God reigning over all. Hence the Targumist, seeing the vanity of that interpretation, perverts the words, and renders them, " Worship before him, all ye nations which serve idols."

(2) אֱלֹהִים, " Elohim," is so far in this place from being exegetical of אֱלִילִים " gods," or " vain idols " ; that it is put in direct opposition to it, as is evident from the words themselves.

(3) The word Elohim, which most frequently denoteth the true God, doth never alone, and absolutely taken, signify *false gods* or idols, but only when it is joined with some other word discovering its application, as *his god,* or *their gods,* or *the gods of this or that people,* in which case it is rendered by the LXX., sometimes εἴδωλον, an " idol ; " sometimes χειροποίητον, an " idol made with hands ; " sometimes βδέλυγμα an " abomination." But here it hath no such limitation or restriction.

Whereas, therefore, there are some creatures who, by reason of some peculiar excellency and likeness unto God, or subordination unto him in their work, are called gods, it must be those, or some of them, that are intended in the expression. Now these are either *magistrates* or *angels.*

(1) *Magistrates* are somewhere called elohim, because of the representation they make of God in his power, and their peculiar subordination unto him in their working.

The Jews, indeed, contend that no other magistrates but those only of the great Sanhedrim are anywhere called gods; but that concerns not our present inquiry. Some magistrates are so called, but none of them are intended by the Psalmist, there being no occasion administered unto him of any such apostrophe unto them.

(2) Angels are called elohim: Λεγόμενοι θεοί, 1 Cor. viii. 5. They have the name of God attributed unto them, and these are they whom the Psalmist speaks unto. Having called on the whole creation to rejoice in the bringing forth of the kingdom of God, and pressed his exhortation upon things on the earth, he turns unto the ministering angels, and calls on them to the discharge of their duty unto the King of that kingdom. Hence the Targumist, in the beginning of Psalm xcvi. expressly mentioned "his high angels," joining in his praise and worship, using the Greek word ἄγγελος, for distinction's sake, as on the same account it often occurs in the Targum.

We have thus evinced that the Psalm treats about the bringing in of the firstborn into the world; as also that they are the ministering angels who are here commanded to worship him.—*John Owen.*

Verse 8.—" *Zion heard*," etc. But why, it may be asked, does he speak of those things being *heard*, rather than *seen*? Two reasons may be given for this. First, he would have God's believing people anticipate the blessing by hope, ere the consummation of it arrived; and, again, the language intimates, that the glory of the Gospel would be spread to such distant quarters, that the Jews would rather hear of it by report, than witness it with their own eyes.—*John Calvin.*

Verse 8.—" *The daughters of Judah rejoiced.*" David alludes to a custom familiar in Judea, of forming choral bands of maidens after a victory or some happy circumstance. Thus after the passage of the Red Sea, when the Egyptians were drowned and the people of God brought in safety to the farther shore, Miriam the prophetess, the sister of Aaron, took a timbrel in her hand, and all the women followed her with timbrels and dancing, saying, Let us sing unto the Lord, for he hath triumphed gloriously; the horse and his rider hath he thrown into the sea. When Goliath was slain by David, it is said 1 Sam. xviii. 6, 7, " When David returned from the slaughter of the Philistine, the women came out of all cities of Israel, singing and dancing, to meet king Saul, with tabrets, with joy, and with instruments of music. And the women sang as they played, and said, Saul hath slain his thousands, and David his ten thousands."—*Le Blanc.*

Verse 10.—" *Ye that love the Lord, hate evil.*" It is evident that our conversion is sound when we loathe and hate sin from the heart: a man may know his hatred of evil to be true, first, if it be universal: he that hates sin truly, hates all sin. Secondly, true hatred is fixed; there is no appeasing it but by abolishing the thing hated. Thirdly, hatred is a more rooted affection than anger: anger may be appeased, but hatred remains and sets itself against the whole kind. Fourthly, if our hatred be true, we hate all evil, in ourselves first, and then in others; he that hates a toad, would hate it most in his own bosom. Many, like Judah, are severe in censuring others (Gen. xxxviii. 24), but partial to themselves. Fifthly, he that hates sin truly, hates the greatest sin in the greatest measure; he hates all evil in a just proportion. Sixthly, our hatred is right if we can endure admonition and reproof for sin, and not be enraged; therefore, those that swell against reproof do not appear to hate sin.—*Richard Sibbes.*

Verse 10.—" *Hate evil.*" Sin seemeth to have its name of *sana*, שנא (the word here used) because it is most of all to be hated, as the greatest evil; as that which setteth us furthest from God the greatest good.—*John Trapp.*

Verse 10.—Get mortifying graces, especially love to God, for *those that love the Lord, will hate evil.* And the more they love him, the more they will hate it.—*David Clarkson.*

Verse 10.—God is a Spirit, and he looks to our very spirits; and what we are in our spirits, in our hearts and affections, that we are to him. Therefore, what ill we shun, let us do it from the heart, by hating it first. A man may avoid an evil action from fear, or out of other respects, but that is not sincerity. Therefore look to thy heart, see that thou hate evil, and let it come from sincere looking to God. " *Ye that love the Lord, hate evil,*" saith David: not only avoid it, but hate it; and not only hate it, but hate it out of love to God.—*Richard Sibbes.*

Verse 10.—" *Hate evil.*"

LUCIAN. I am the declared enemy of all false pretence, all quackery, all lies, and all puffing. I am a lover of truth, of beauty, of undisguised nature ; in short, of everything that is lovely.

PHILOSOPHY. To love and to hate, they say, spring from one and the same source.

LUCIAN. That, O philosophy, must be best known to you. My business is to hate the bad, and to love and commend the good ; and that I stick to.—*Lucian. Piscat. c. 8.*

Verse 10.—" *He preserveth the souls of his saints.*" Let us observe that there are two parts of divine protection—preservation and deliverance. Preservation is keeping lest we should be imperilled : deliverance has reference to those already involved in perils. The shepherd keeps his sheep lest they should fall among wolves ; but if perchance they should fall into the clutches of the wolf he pursues and delivers. Both parts the Prophet exhibits, persuading us that it is the Lord who keeps the souls of his saints lest they fall into the hands of the wicked ; and if they should fall, he will deliver them.—*Musculus.*

Verse 11.—" *Light is sown.*" זרע does not here signify sown = strewn into the earth, but strewn along his life's way, so that he, the righteous one, advances step by step in the light. Hitzig rightly compares κίδναται, σκίδναται, used of the dawn and of the sun. Of the former Virgil also says, *Et jam prima novo spargebat lumine terras.*—*Franz Delitzsch.*

Verse 11.—" *Light is sown.*"

> And now Aurora, from the saffron bed
> Of her Tithonus rising, sow'd the earth
> With dewy light.
>
> —*C. R. Kennedy's Translation of Virgil.*

Verse 11.—" *Light is sown.*"

> Now Morn, her rosy steps in the eastern clime
> Advancing, sow'd the earth with orient pearl.
>
> —*John Milton.*

Verse 11.—" *Light is sown for the righteous.*" Most thoughtful men increase in faith and spiritual discernment by often doubting, and by having their doubts cleared up. Religious thought in this way grows into a personal feeling ; and the solid rock of truer conviction and deeper trust as a firm foundation for the soul to build upon for eternity, remains behind after all the abrasion of loose and more perishable materials through speculation. A different if not a truer revelation of heavenly realities is given to us through the dark distressing process of doubting, than through the bright joyful exercise of unhesitating faith ; just as our knowledge of the chemistry of the sun and stars, of the physical constitution of distant worlds, is derived not from the bright bands of their spectrum, which reveal only their size and shape, but from Fraunhofer's wonderful lines—those black blank spaces breaking up the spectrum bands—which tell us of rays arrested in their path and prevented from bearing their message to us by particular metallic vapours. Unto the upright, just because of the purity and singleness of their motives and the earnestness of their quest after truth, there ariseth light in the darkness. We must remember that " light is *sown* for the righteous " ; that its more or less rapid germination and development depend upon the nature of the soil on which it falls and the circumstances that influence it ; that, like seed, it at first lies concealed in the dark furrow, under the cheerless clod, in the cold ungenial winter ; but that even then, while shining in the darkness, while struggling with doubts and difficulties of the mind and heart, it is nevertheless the source of much comfort, and in its slow, quickening, and hidden growth the cause of lively hope, and of bright anticipation of that time when it shall blossom and ripen in the summer-time of heaven—shine more and more unto the perfect day.—*Hugh Macmillan, in " The Ministry of Nature,*" 1871.

Verse 11.—" *Light is sown for the righteous :*" sown in these two fields, 1. *Of God's eternal decree*, in his power, promise, grace and love. These are the " upper springs." 2. In the field of their *graces*, and holy *duties* ; these are the " nether springs ; " both which fall into one river, and " make glad the city of God ; " both these fields yield a plentiful harvest of comfort to the godly.—*John Sheffield, in " The Rising Sun,*" 1654.

Verse 11.—" *Sown.*" The righteous man's harvest is secret and hidden. It lieth, like the corn covered in the ground ; " their life is hid ; " and " it is not manifest what they shall be ; " " no eye hath seen, or ear heard, neither hath it entered into the heart of man, what the Lord hath laid up for them that love him " (Col. iii. 3 ; 1 John iii. 2 ; 1 Cor. ii. 9). Name what you can, and it will be a mystery, a secret thing, that belongs to the upright in heart. First, is not the decree of God a hidden thing ? a depth unsearchable ? and able to make a man astonied ? Did not Paul cry out, " O the depth of the riches both of the wisdom and knowledge of God ! how unsearchable are his judgments, and his ways past finding out ! " (Rom. xii. 33). And is not the incarnation of Christ a secret too ? what more to be admired than that God should become man, and be manifested in the flesh ? The very angels desired to peep into this mystery. 1 Tim. iii. 16 ; 1 Pet. i. 12 ; Isai. vii. 14. Again, the conversion and regeneration of a sinner is admirable ; it's a noble, yet a secret work : Nicodemus a great doctor could not see it. And if natural births be so strange, what shall we judge of this ? Moreover, peace of conscience and joy in the Holy Ghost is no open matter ; none knoweth it, but he that hath it. So is the earnest of the Spirit, and true seal of salvation ; the power, life and sweetness of the word ; the remission and pardon of sin, with certainty of salvation. And in the fifth place, the harvest is secret, if we consider where it is growing. One close is, *the secret purpose of God ;* and who can understand it ? A second is, *his word ;* and how hardly is that to be searched into ? A third is, *a man's own heart ;* and is not that both secret and deceitful ? And last of all, the very principal part of the harvest is hid *with Christ in heaven ;* and when he appears, it will appear what it shall be.—*John Barlow.*

Verses 11 *and* 12 are both most savoury and precious notanda.—Give me to experience, O Lord, those revelations which follow in the train of obedience ; and O that I felt the charm and enjoyment of holiness, so as to give thanks, in the reflection that with a holy God holiness is an indispensable requisite for our appearing in his presence. We should further be grateful because of this essential attribute in the Godhead ; for it is in virtue of his holiness that evil cannot dwell with him, and that the world will at length be delivered, and this conclusively, from the wickedness and malice and vile sensualities by which it is now so disquieted and deformed. Hasten this consummation, O Lord.—*Thomas Chalmers.*

Verse 12.—" *Rejoice in the Lord.*" We must " rejoice evermore ; " for even holy mourning hath the seed of joy in it, which the soul finds by that time it is over, if not in it.—*William Cooper, in the " Morning Exercises."*

Verse 12.—" *Rejoice in the Lord.*" I. Our rejoicing in the Lord denotes our taking a very sincere and cordial pleasure in whatever relates to the ever-blessed God, particularly his existence, perfections, and providence ; the discoveries of his will to us, especially in his word ; the interest we have in him, and the relations wherein we stand to him ; his continual protection, guidance and influence ; his gracious intercourse with us in the duties of religious worship ; and, finally, the hope he has given us of fulness of joy, in his beatific and most glorious presence above. II. Rejoicing in the Lord signifies that our joy in God is superior to all our other joys, otherwise it is a joy unworthy of him, and no way, or not savingly, profitable to us. III. Whatever else we rejoice in, we are to rejoice in such a manner, that we may be properly said to rejoice in the Lord, even when other things are the immediate occasions of our joy. The God we serve is not an envious and a malevolent Being, but exceeding liberal and kind ; he has created us with an inextinguishable desire after happiness, as a secret intimation that he intends to make us happy, if we do not make ourselves miserable ; and while our principal happiness is lodged in himself, and to be found nowhere else, (in which he has shown the singular regard he has to our nature), he feeds our hearts with a thousand little rivulets of joy and satisfaction from created objects : our bodies are endowed with a variety of senses and appetites, and our souls with powers and faculties of their own ; nor was any one sense or faculty made in vain, or to lie always idle and useless ; but every sense, and much more every mental faculty, has not one, but a great number of things provided to entertain it. But then the soul is not to lose itself in this maze and labyrinth of delight ; it is not by this variety to be diverted from that one infinite good, who eminently contains in himself all the various kinds and degrees of true joy.—*Henry Grove,* 1683—1737-8.

Verse 12.—" *Rejoice . . . and give thanks.*" Two things are to be observed : One, that he unites joy in the Lord and praise of God. Rightly : for it is not possible for a man to praise the Lord truly and from the soul, unless he rejoices in him. Another, that he connects the praise of God with the remembrance of his holiness. And with good reason : for it is the chief use of divine praise, that by the exercise thereof, we should keep fresh in our souls the remembrance of God and of all the blessings received from him. Thus this verse contains the root and fruit of divine praise. The root is joy in God ; the fruit is the remembrance of God and his good-ness.—*Musculus*.

Verse 12.—" *Ye righteous . . . all ye that are upright in heart.*" Some may say the *just* or the *righteous* man may thus rejoice ; but where are any such ? " Who can say," saith Solomon, " I have made my heart clean, I am pure from my sin " ? No ; " There is not a just man upon earth, that doeth good, and sinneth not." A vain thing may it seem then to exhort men to rejoice, when the condition annexed is such as excludeth all from rejoicing. To what end is it to incite the *just* to rejoice when there are none such that may rejoice ? The answer is ready at hand in the latter part of the verse. By *just* are meant all such as are " *upright in heart,*" which clause is added partly to exclude the hypocrite, and partly to temper and qualify the rigour of the term before used, if it were strictly and exactly taken. So that it is a note as well of *extent*, as of *restraint*.

1. Of *restraint*, to exclude from this joy, and all right therein, all dissemblers, all counterfeit Christians, all hollow-hearted hypocrites, that repent in the face but not in the heart ; that make a sour face that they may seem to fast, saith our Saviour, that justify themselves in the sight of men, but God seeth their hearts what they are, and seeth them to be far other than either they should be, or they pretend themselves to be.

2. Of *extent*, to extend and enlarge this joy, the ground of it and the right to it, to all that are single and sincere-hearted ; and so to give and afford a share and a portion in it as well to those that are sincerely righteous on earth, as to those that are perfectly righteous in heaven. It is as a *key* to let in the one. It is as a *bolt* to bar out the other.—*Thomas Gataker*.

HINTS TO PREACHERS.

Verse 1.—The sovereignty of God a theme for joy in many respects and to many persons, especially when exhibited in the reign of grace.

Verses 3—6.—The accompaniments of Christ's gospel advent. I. The fire of his Spirit. II. The light of the word. III. The commotion in the world. IV. The removal of obstacles. V. The display of the divine glory.

Verses 4, 5.—I. The terrors which accompanied the giving of the law : " his lightnings," etc. II. The reasons for those terrors. I. To show the guilt of man. 2. His inability to keep the law. 3. To show his need of a law-fulfiller on his behalf. —*G. R.*

Verses 4—6.—A description of the giving of the law. I. The lawgiver's heralds, or, *conviction*, ver. 4. II. The effect of his presence, or, *contrition*, ver. 5. III. The proclamation of the law, or, *instruction* (as by a voice from heaven, ver. 6). IV. The effect of the lawgiving, or, divine *manifestation* (ver. 6, latter clause).—*C. D.*

Verse 5.—The presence of God in the church her invincible power.

Verse 6.—The confusion of heart which will ensue from idolatrous worship, even if it be only spiritual. Breaking of the idol, disappointment in it, injury by it, removal from it, etc.

Verse 8.—I. The world is terrified at the divine judgments. II. The church rejoices in them, " Zion heard," etc. ; or, I. When the world is glad the church is sad. II. When the world is sad the church is glad.—*G. R.*

Verse 10.—I. What you do now :—" Love the Lord." Reciprocally, personally, who, supremely, habitually, progressively. II. What you must do :—" Hate evil." Evil working, evil writing, evil speaking, evil thinking ; renounce evil, master it, supplant it.—*W. J.*

Verse 10.—I. The distinguishing peculiarity of the people of God : " Ye that love the Lord." II. Its manifestation : " Hate evil." III. Its reward : " The Lord preserveth," etc. ; " He delivereth," etc.—*G. R.*

Verses 10, 11.—David notes in God three characteristics of a true friend : First, with fidelity and good will he keepeth the souls of the pious.   Secondly, with his power and majesty he delivereth them from their enemies.   Thirdly, with his wisdom and holiness he enlightens and refreshes them.—*Le Blanc.*

Verse 11.—I. *Where is it sown ?* The answer to this will come under the following heads, viz. In the purpose of God, In the purchase of Christ, In the office of the Spirit, In the promises of the Word, In the work of Grace wrought in the heart, and, In the preparations made above in glory. II. *When is the season of reaping ?* And to this, the answer is, The season of reaping the first fruits, of reaping in part, is at certain times in the present life ; the season of reaping more fully is at death ; and of reaping most fully and perfectly commenceth at the day of judgment and is continued throughout eternity. 1. The season of reaping in part falls out at some times within the course of this present life. Particularly (1) Times of affliction have been to the upright, seasons of reaping the joy sown. By this they have been prepared for sufferings, supported under them, and made afterwards to forget their sorrows, by reason of the gladness breaking in from the affecting discovery of what God has done for them, and wrought in them. Thus God causeth light to arise in darkness, and in a rainy day refresheth them with a beam from heaven, brightening the drops that fall ; brings his people into the wilderness, and there speaks com·fortably unto them. (2.) Seasons of suffering for the sake of Christ and the gospel, have been seasons wherein the upright have begun to reap the joy sown. When called to resist unto blood, striving against sin, they have need of more than ordinary comfort, to enable them to meet, and hold firm through the fiery trial : and they have found that then encouragement hath been yielded them in a degree they never before experienced (John xvi. 33). (3.) Seasons wherein God has called the righteous to great and difficult service, have been seasons of reaping the beginnings of joys sown. When their heavenly Father has lifted up the light of his countenance upon them, and shed abroad the sense of his love within them, they are prepared to go whither he sends them, and to do whatever he bids them. (4.) After sore conflicts with Satan, the upright have been revived by the springing of the joy sown. After Christ was tempted came an angel to comfort him. And for the encouragement of his followers, he declares, Rev. ii. 17, " To him that overcometh will I give to eat of the hidden manna, and I will give him a white stone, and in the stone a new name written, which no man knoweth saving he that receiveth it." (5.) In waiting upon God in the sanctuary the upright have met with him, and so have had the beginnings of joy sown. 2. A fuller reaping time will be at death ; with some as the soul is going ; but with all immediately after its release from the body. 3. The season in which the righteous shall reap their joy sown, to the full, and in perfection, shall be at the last day. Then Christ shall come to be glorified in his saints, and admired in all them that believe, and lead them all in a body, and all of them perfected, into that presence of God, where there is fulness of joy, and where there are pleasures for evermore.—*Daniel Wilcox.*

Verse 12.—" *Give thanks at the remembrance of his holiness.*"   Be thankful for—1. Its unsullied perfection. 2. Its wondrous forbearance. 3. Its place in our salvation. 4. Its approachableness through Christ. 5. Its predicted triumphs.—*W. J.*

Verse 12.—I. A remembrance at which the world does not give thanks. II. Reasons which make it a matter of thanksgiving with the righteous. Its bearing on the way of salvation ; on the doctrines of the gospel ; on the law of the Christian life.—*C. D.*

PSALM XCVIII.

TITLE AND SUBJECT.—*This sacred ode, which bears simply the title of " A Psalm,"
follows fitly upon the last, and is evidently an integral part of the series of royal Psalms.
If xcvii. described the publication of the gospel, and so the setting up of the kingdom
of heaven, the present Psalm is a kind of* CORONATION HYMN, *officially proclaiming
the conquering Messiah as Monarch over the nations, with blast of trumpets, clapping
of hands, and celebration of triumphs. It is a singularly bold and lively song. The
critics have fully established the fact that similar expressions occur in Isaiah, but we
see no force in the inference that therefore it was written by him; on this principle half
the books in the English language might be attributed to Shakespeare. The fact is that
these associated Psalms make up a mosaic, in which each one of them has an appropriate
place, and is necessary to the completeness of the whole; and therefore we believe them
to be each and all the work of one and the same mind. Paul, if we understand him
aright, ascribes Psalm ninety-five to David, and as we believe that the same writer must
have written the whole group, we ascribe this also to the son of Jesse. However that may
be, the song is worthy to rank among the most devout and soul-stirring of sacred lyrics.*

DIVISION.—*We have here three stanzas of three verses each. In the first, 1—3,
the subject of praise is announced; in the second, 4—6, the manner of that praise is
prescribed; and in the third, 7—9, the universal extent of it is proclaimed.*

EXPOSITION.

O SING unto the LORD a new song; for he hath done marvellous things:
his right hand, and his holy arm, hath gotten him the victory.

2 The LORD hath made known his salvation: his righteousness
hath he openly shewed in the sight of the heathen.

3 He hath remembered his mercy and his truth toward the house of Israel:
all the ends of the earth have seen the salvation of our God.

1. "*O sing unto the Lord a new song; for he hath done marvellous things.*" We
had a new song before (Ps. xcvi.) because the Lord was coming, but now we have
another new song because he has come, and seen and conquered. Jesus, our King,
has lived a marvellous life, died a marvellous death, risen by a marvellous resurrection, and ascended marvellously into heaven. By his divine power he has sent forth
the Holy Spirit doing marvels, and by that sacred energy his disciples have also
wrought marvellous things and astonished all the earth. Idols have fallen, superstitions have withered, systems of error have fled, and empires of cruelty have perished.
For all this he deserves the highest praise. His acts have proved his Deity, Jesus
is Jehovah, and therefore we sing unto him as the LORD. "*His right hand, and
his holy arm, hath gotten him the victory*"; not by the aid of others, but by his own
unweaponed hand his marvellous conquests have been achieved. Sin, death, and
hell fell beneath his solitary prowess, and the idols and the errors of mankind have
been overthrown and smitten by his hand alone. The victories of Jesus among
men are all the more wonderful because they are accomplished by means to all
appearance most inadequate; they are due not to physical but to moral power—
the energy of goodness, justice, truth; in a word, to the power of his *holy* arm. His
holy influence has been the sole cause of success. Jesus never stoops to use policy,
or brute force; his unsullied perfections secure to him a real and lasting victory
over all the powers of evil, and that victory will be gained as dexterously and easily
as when a warrior strikes his adversary with his *right hand* and stretches him prone
upon the earth. Glory be unto the Conqueror, let new songs be chanted to his
praise. Stirred by contemplating his triumphs, our pen could not forbear to praise
him in the following hymn:—

Forth to the battle rides our King;
He climbs his conquering car;
He fits his arrows to the string,
And smites his foes afar.

Convictions pierce the stoutest hearts,
 They bleed, they faint, they die ;
Slain by Immanuel's well-aimed darts,
 In helpless heaps they lie.

Behold, he bares his two-edged sword,
 And deals almighty blows,
His all-revealing, killing word
 'Twixt joints and marrow goes.

Anon arrayed in robes of grace
 He rides the trampled plain,
With pity beaming from his face,
 And mercy in his train.

Mighty to save he now appears,
 Mighty to raise the dead,
Mighty to stanch the bleeding wound,
 And lift the fallen head.

Victor alike in love and arms,
 Myriads before him bend ;
Such are the Conqueror's matchless charms,
 Each foe becomes his friend.

They crown him on the battle-field
 Of all the nations King ;
With trumpets and with cornets loud
 They make the welkin ring.

The salvation which Jesus has accomplished is wrought out with wonderful wisdom, hence it is ascribed to his right hand ; it meets the requirements of justice, hence we read of his holy arm ; it is his own unaided work, hence all the glory is ascribed to him ; and it is marvellous beyond degree, hence it deserves a new song.

2. " *The Lord hath made known his salvation*,"—by the coming of Jesus and by the outpouring of the Holy Ghost, by whose power the gospel was preached among the Gentiles. The Lord is to be praised not only for effecting human salvation, but also for making it known, for man would never have discovered it for himself ; nay, not so much as one single soul would ever have found out for himself the way of mercy through a Mediator ; in every case it is a divine revelation to the mind and heart. In God's own light his light is seen. He must reveal his Son in us, or we shall be unable to discern him. " *His righteousness hath he openly shewed in the sight of the heathen.*" This word " righteousness " is the favourite word of the apostle of the Gentiles ; he loves to dwell on the Lord's method of making man righteous, and vindicating divine justice by the atoning blood. What songs ought we to render who belong to a once heathen race, for that blessed gospel which is the power of God unto salvation, " for therein is the righteousness of God revealed from faith to faith." This is no close secret ; it is clearly taught in Scripture, and has been plainly preached among the nations. What was hidden in the types is " openly shewed " in the gospel.

3. " *He hath remembered his mercy and his truth toward the house of Israel.*" To them Jesus came in the flesh, and to them was the gospel first preached ; and though they counted themselves unworthy of eternal life, yet the covenant was not broken, for the true Israel were called into fellowship and still remain so. The mercy which endureth for ever, and the fidelity which cannot forget a promise, secure to the chosen seed the salvation long ago guaranteed by the covenant of grace. " *All the ends of the earth have seen the salvation of our God.*" Not to Abraham's seed alone after the flesh, but to the elect among all nations, has grace been given ; therefore, let the whole church of God sing unto him a new song. It was no small blessing, or little miracle, that throughout all lands the gospel should be published in so short a time, with such singular success and such abiding results. Pentecost deserves a new song as well as the Passion and the Resurrection ; let our hearts exult as we remember it. *Our* God, our own for ever blessed God, has been honoured by those who once bowed down before dumb idols ; his salvation has not only been heard of but seen among all people, it has been experienced as well as explained ; his Son is the actual Redeemer of a multitude out of all nations.

4 Make a joyful noise unto the LORD, all the earth : make a loud noise, and rejoice, and sing praise.

5 Sing unto the LORD with the harp ; with the harp, and the voice of a Psalm.

6 With trumpets and sound of cornet make a joyful noise before the LORD, the King.

In these three verses we are taught how to praise the Lord.

4. " *Make a joyful noise unto the Lord, all the earth.*" Every tongue must applaud, and that with the vigour which joy of heart alone can arouse to action. As men shout when they welcome a king, so must we. Loud hosannas, full of happiness, must be lifted up. If ever men shout for joy it should be when the Lord comes among them in the proclamation of his gospel reign. John Wesley said to his people, " Sing lustily, and with a good courage. Beware of singing as if you were half dead or half asleep ; but lift up your voice with strength. Be no more afraid of your voice now, nor more ashamed of its being heard, than when you sung the songs of Satan." " *Make a loud noise, and rejoice, and sing praise ;*" or " *Burst forth, and sing, and play.*" Let every form of exultation be used, every kind of music pressed into the service till the accumulated praise causes the skies to echo the joyful tumult. There is no fear of our being too hearty in magnifying the God of our salvation, only we must take care that the song comes from the heart, otherwise the music is nothing but a noise in his ears, whether it be caused by human throats, or organ pipes, or far-resounding trumpets. Loud let our hearts ring out the honours of our conquering Saviour ; with all our might let us extol the Lord who has vanquished all our enemies, and led our captivity captive. He will do this best who is most in love with Jesus :—

> " I've found the pearl of greatest price,
> My heart doth sing for joy ;
> And sing I must, a Christ I have,
> Oh, what a Christ have I ! "

5. " *Sing unto the Lord with the harp.*" Skill in music should not be desecrated to the world's evil mirth, it should aid the private devotions of the saint, and then, like George Herbert, he will sing,—

> " My God, my God,
> My music shall find thee,
> And every string
> Shall have his attribute to sing."

Martin Luther was thus wont to praise the Lord, whom he loved so well. God's praises should be performed in the best possible manner, but their sweetness mainly lies in spiritual qualities. The concords of faith and repentance, the harmonies of obedience and love are true music in the ear of the Most High, and better please him than " heaving bellows taught to blow," though managed by the noblest master of human minstrelsy. " *With the harp.*" A very sweet instrument of music, and capable of great expression. The repetition of the word is highly poetical, and shows that the daintiest expressions of poetry are none too rich for the praise of God. His worship should be plain, but not uncouth, if we can compass elegancies of expression there are occasions upon which they will be most appropriate ; God, who accepts the unlettered ditty of a ploughman, does not reject the smooth verse of a Cowper, or the sublime strains of a Milton. All repetitions are not vain repetitions, in sacred song there should be graceful repeats, they render the sense emphatic, and help to fire the soul ; even preachers do not amiss when they dwell on a word and sound it out again and again, till dull ears feel its emphasis. " *And the voice of a Psalm,*" or with *a musical voice*, as distinguished from common speech. Our voice has in it many modulations ; there is the voice of conversation, the voice of complaint, the voice of pleading, the voice of command, and there ought to be with each of us the voice of a Psalm. Man's voice is at its best when it sings the best words in the best spirit to the best of Beings. Love and war must not monopolise the lyric muse ; the love of God and the conquests of Immanuel should win to themselves man's sweetest strains. Do we sing enough unto the Lord ? May not the birds of the air rebuke our sullen and ungrateful silence ?

6. "*With trumpets and sound of cornet make a joyful noise.*" God's worship should be heartily loud. The far resounding trump and horn well symbolise the power which should be put forth in praise. "*Before the Lord, the King.*" On coronation days, and when beloved monarchs ride abroad, the people shout and the trumpets sound till the walls ring again. Shall men be more enthusiastic for their earthly princes than for the divine King? Is there no loyalty left among the subjects of the blessed and only Potentate? *King Jehovah* is his name; and there is none like it, have we no joyful noise for him? Let but the reigning power of Jesus be felt in the soul and we shall cast aside that chill mutter, drowned by the pealing organ, which is now so commonly the substitute for earnest congregational singing.

> Say, if your hearts are tuned to sing,
> Is there a subject greater?
> Harmony all its strains may bring,
> But Jesus' name is sweeter.
>
> Who of his love doth once partake,
> He evermore rejoices;
> Melody in our hearts we make,
> Melody with our voices.

7 Let the sea roar, and the fulness thereof; the world, and they that dwell therein.

8 Let the floods clap *their* hands: let the hills be joyful together

9 Before the LORD; for he cometh to judge the earth: with righteousness shall he judge the world, and the people with equity.

7. "*Let the sea roar, and the fulness thereof.*" Even its thunders will not be too grand for such a theme. Handel, in some of his sublime choruses, would have been glad of its aid to express his lofty conceptions, and assuredly the inspired Psalmist did well to call in such infinite uproar. The sea is his, let it praise its Maker. Within and upon its bosom it bears a wealth of goodness, why should it be denied a place in the orchestra of nature? Its deep bass will excellently suit the mystery of the divine glory. "*The world, and they that dwell therein.*" The land should be in harmony with the ocean. Its mountains and plains, cities and villages, should prolong the voice of jubilee which welcomes the Lord of all. Nothing can be more sublime than this verse; the muses of Parnassus cannot rival the muse of Zion, the Castalian fount never sparkled like that "fount of every blessing" to which sacred bards are wont to ascribe their inspiration. Yet no song is equal to the majesty of the theme when Jehovah, the King, is to be extolled.

8. "*Let the floods clap their hands.*" The rolling rivers, the tidal estuaries, the roaring cataracts, are here summoned to pay their homage, and to clap their hands, as men do when they greet their sovereigns with acclamation. "*Let the hills be joyful together*," or in concert with the floods. Silent as are the mighty mountains, let them forget themselves, and burst forth into a sublime uproariousness of mirth, such as the poet described when he wrote those vivid lines—

> "Far along,
> From peak to peak, the rattling crags among,
> Leaps the live thunder! Not from one lone cloud,
> But every mountain now hath found a tongue,
> And Jura answers, through her misty shroud,
> Back to the joyous Alps, who call to her aloud."

9. "*Before the Lord; for he cometh to judge the earth.*" Stiller music such as made the stars twinkle with their soft kind eyes suited his first coming at Bethlehem, but his second advent calls for trumpets, for he is a judge; and for all earth's acclamations, for he has put on his royal splendour. The rule of Christ is the joy of nature. All things bless his throne, yea, and the very coming of it. As the dawn sets the earth weeping for joy at the rising of the sun, till the dewdrops stand in her eyes, so should the approach of Jesu's universal reign make all creation glad. "*With righteousness shall he judge the world, and the people with equity.*" This is the joy of it. No tyrant and no weakling is he, to oppress the good or to indulge the vain, his law is good, his action right, his government the embodiment of justice. If ever there was a thing to rejoice in upon this poor, travailing earth, it is the coming

of such a deliverer, the ascension to the universal throne of such a governor. All
hail, Jesus! all hail! Our soul faints with delight at the sound of thine approaching
chariots, and can only cry, " Come quickly. Even so, come quickly, Lord Jesus!"

Keble's version of the last four verses is so truly beautiful that we cannot deny
our readers the luxury of perusing it :—

> " Ring out, with horn and trumpet ring,
>   In shouts before the Lord the King :
>   Let ocean with his fulness swing
>   In restless unison :
>
> " Earth's round and all the dwellers there,
>   The mighty floods the burden bear,
>   And clap the hand : in choral air
>   Join every mountain lone.
>
> " Tell out before the Lord, that he
>   Is come, the Judge of earth to be,
>   To judge the world in equity,
>   Do right to realm and throne."

EXPLANATORY NOTES AND QUAINT SAYINGS.

Title.—The inscription of the Psalm in Hebrew is only the single word מִזְמוֹר
Mizmor, " Psalm " (whence probably the title " orphan Mizmor " in the Talmudic
treatise Avodah Zara).—*J. J. S. Perowne.*

Title.—Hengstenberg remarks, " This is the only Psalm which is entitled simply
a Psalm.' This common name of all the Psalms cannot be employed here in its
general sense, but must have a peculiar meaning." He considers that it indicates
that this is the lyric accompaniment of the more decidedly prophetical Psalm which
precedes it,—in fact, the Psalm of that prophecy. He also notes that in the original
we have in verses 5 and 6 words akin to the title brought into great prominence,
and perhaps this may have suggested it.

Title.—It is at least interesting to notice that a song of Zion which so exults
in the king's arrival should be called pre-eminently מִזְמוֹר *Mizmor* ; as if the Psalm
of Psalms were that which celebrates *Israel, and the earth at large, blessed in Messiah's
Advent.*—*Andrew A. Bonar.*

Whole Psalm.—A noble, spirit-stirring Psalm. It may have been written on
the occasion of a great national triumph at the time ; but may, perhaps, afterwards
be taken up at the period of the great millennial restoration of all things. The
victory here celebrated may be in prophetic vision, and that at Armageddon. Then
will salvation and righteousness be openly manifested in the sight of the hostile
nations. Israel will be exalted ; and the blessed conjunction of mercy and truth
will gladden and assure the hearts of all who at that time are Israelites indeed.
Godliness will form the reigning characteristic of the whole earth.—*Thomas Chalmers.*

Whole Psalm.—The subject of the Psalm is the praise of Jehovah. It consists
of three strophes of three verses each. The first strophe shows *why,* the second
how Jehovah is to be praised ; and the third *who* are to praise him.—*Frederick Fysh.*

Whole Psalm.—This Psalm is an evident prophecy of Christ's coming to save
the world ; and what is here *foretold* by David is, in the Blessed Virgin's Song, chanted
forth as being *accomplished.* David is the *Voice,* and Mary is the *Echo.*

1. DAVID. " O sing unto the Lord a new song." (The *Voice.*)
    MARY. " My soul doth magnify the Lord." (The *Echo.*)
2. DAVID. " He hath done marvellous things." (The *Voice.*)
    MARY. " He that is mighty hath done great things." (The *Echo.*)
3. DAVID. " With his own right hand and holy arm hath he gotten himself the
        victory." (The *Voice.*)
    MARY. " He hath showed strength with his arm, and scattered the proud in
        the imagination of their hearts." (The *Echo.*)

4. DAVID. "The Lord hath made known his salvation; his righteousness hath he openly showed," &c. (The *Voice*.)

MARY. "His mercy is on them that fear him, from generation to generation." (The *Echo*.)

5. DAVID. "He hath remembered his mercy and his truth toward the house of Israel." (The *Voice*.)

MARY. "He hath holpen his servant Israel, in remembrance of his mercy." (The *Echo*.)

These parallels are very striking; and it seems as if Mary had this Psalm in her eye when she composed her song of triumph. And this is a farther argument that the whole Psalm, whether it record the deliverance of Israel from Egypt, or the Jews from the Babylonish captivity, is yet to be ultimately understood of the redemption of the world by Jesus Christ, and the proclamation of his gospel through all the nations of the earth: and taken in this view, no language can be too strong, nor poetic imagery too high, to point out the unsearchable riches of Christ.—*Adam Clarke.*

Verse 1.—"*O sing unto the Lord a new song.*" This is man's end, to seek God in this life, to see God in the next; to be a subject in the kingdom of grace, and a saint in the kingdom of glory. Whatsoever in this world befalleth us, we must sing: be thankful for weal, for woe: songs ought always to be in our mouth, and sometimes a new song: for so David here, "*sing a new song:*" that is, let us put off the old man, and become new men, new creatures in Christ: for the old man sings old songs: only the new man sings a new song: he speaketh with a new tongue, and walks in new ways, and therefore doth new things, and sings new songs; his language is not of Babylon or Egypt, but of Canaan; his communication doth edify men, his song glorify God. Or a *new* song, that is, a fresh song, *nova res, novum canticum,* new for a new benefit, Eph. v. 20: "*Give thanks always for all things.*" It is very gross to thank God only in gross, and not in parcel. Hast thou been sick and now made whole? praise God with the *leper*, Luke xvii.: sing a new song for this new salve. Dost thou hunger and thirst after righteousness, whereas heretofore thou couldst not endure the words of exhortation and doctrine? sing a new song for this new grace. Doth Almighty God give thee a true sense of thy sin, whereas heretofore thou didst draw iniquity with cords of vanity, and sin as it were with cart ropes, and wast given over to work all uncleanness with greediness? *O sing, sing, sing,* a new song for this new mercy.

Or *new*, that is, no common or ordinary song; but as God's mercy toward us is exceeding marvellous and extraordinary, so our thanks ought to be most exquisite, and more than ordinary: not new in regard of the matter, for we may not pray to God or praise God otherwise than he hath prescribed in his word, which is the old way, but new in respect of the manner and making, that as occasion is offered, we may bear our wits after the best fashion to be thankful.

Or, because this Psalm is prophetical, a *new* song, that is, the song of the glorious angels at Christ's birth, "Glory to God in the highest, and on earth peace, good will toward men," (Luke ii. 14); a song which the world never heard before: that the seed of the woman should bruise the serpent's head is an old song, the first that ever was sung; but this was no *plain song*, till Christ did manifest himself in the flesh. In the Old Testament there were many old songs, but in the New Testament a new song. That "unto us is born a Saviour, which is Christ the Lord," is in many respects *a new song*; for whereas Christ was but shadowed in the Law, he is showed in the Gospel; and *new*, because sung of new men, of all men. For the sound of the Gospel is gone through all the earth, unto the ends of the world (Rom. x. 18); whereas in old time God's old songs were sung in Jewry: "His name is great in Israel. In Salem also is his tabernacle, and his dwelling place in Zion," Psalm lxxvi. 1, 2.—*John Boys.*

Verse 1.—"*A new song.*" O ye who are new in Christ, though formerly old in the Old Adam, sing ye to the Lord.—*Psalter of Peter Lombard*, 1474.

Verse 1.—"*He hath done marvellous things.*" He has opened his greatness and goodness in the work of redemption. What *marvels* has not Christ done? 1. He was conceived by the Holy Ghost. 2. Born of a virgin. 3. Healed all manner of diseases. 4. Fed thousands with a few loaves and fishes. 5. Raised the dead. 6. And what was more *marvellous*, died himself. 7. Rose again by his own power. 8. Ascended to heaven. 9. Sent down the Holy Ghost. 10. And made his apostles and their testimony the instruments of enlightening, and ultimately converting, the world.—*Adam Clarke.*

Verse 1.—"*His right hand.*" Since the Psalmist says, that Christ hath gotten him the victory by his right hand and his arm, it is not only a demonstration of his divine and infinite power, but also excludes all other means, as the merits of saints and their meretricious works.—*Martin Luther.*

Verse 1.—"*Holy arm.*" The creation was the work of God's *fingers :* "When I consider thy heavens, the work of thy fingers," Ps. viii. 3 ; redemption a work of his *arm ;* "*His holy arm* hath gotten him the victory" : yea, it was a work of his heart, even that bled to death to accomplish it.—*Thomas Adams.*

Verse 1.—A clergyman in the county of Tyrone had, for some weeks, observed a little ragged boy come every Sunday, and place himself in the centre of the aisle, directly opposite the pulpit, where he seemed exceedingly attentive to the services. He was desirous of knowing who the child was, and for this purpose hastened out, after the sermon, several times, but never could see him, as he vanished the moment service was over, and no one knew whence he came, or anything about him. At length the boy was missed from his usual situation in the church for some weeks. At this time a man called on the minister, and told him a person very ill was desirous of seeing him ; but added, " I am really ashamed to ask you to go so far ; but it is a child of mine, and he refuses to have any one but you ; he is altogether an extraordinary boy, and talks a great deal about things that I do not understand." The clergyman promised to go, and went, though the rain poured down in torrents, and he had six miles of rugged mountain country to pass. On arriving where he was directed, he saw a most wretched cabin indeed, and the man he had seen in the morning was waiting at the door. He was shown in, and found the inside of the hovel as miserable as the outside. In a corner, on a little straw, he beheld a person stretched out, whom he recognised as the little boy who had so regularly attended his church. As he approached the wretched bed the child raised himself up, and, stretching forth his arms, said, "*His own right hand and his holy arm hath gotten him the victory,*" and immediately he expired.—*K. Arvine.*

Verse 2.—"*The Lord hath made known his salvation.*" By the appearance of his Son in the flesh, and the wonders which he did. "*His righteousness hath he openly shewed,*" etc., in the gospel, to all men ; that righteousness which is called the "righteousness of God," and which is enjoyed by faith of Jesus Christ, unto all and upon all them that believe : for there is no difference. Rom. iii. 22.—*B. Boothroyd.*

Verse 2.—"*The Lord hath made known,*" etc. The word חדיע denotes not only a *publication* and promulgation, but also a clear and certain demonstration which produces conviction and causes the matter to be *laid up* in the mind and memory and preserved : for the proper signification of the root ירע is *to lay up what is to be preserved.* The word גלה is added, which properly means to *uncover, to be uncovered,* hence *he revealed* or *uncovered,* that it might be both naked and clear, for the purpose of more fully illustrating the character of the manifestation of the Gospel, opposed to what is obscure, involved in shadows and types, and veiled in legal ceremonies. Of which the apostle treats expressly in 2 Cor. iii. Lastly, when it is added, that *in the sight of the nations* this uncovering is done, it signifies that this salvation pertains to them also, that it comes to them without distinction, since the Gospel is nakedly and clearly announced. From which it also clearly appears, that the matter and reason of the *new song* are found in such a singular event, since God who formerly permitted the nations to walk in their own ways, now under Messiah calls all without distinction to salvation through faith and newness of life.—*Venema.*

Verse 2.—"*Made known :*" He says not, He shewed, but He *made known.* Adam knew him, and predicted concerning him, " A man shall leave father and mother, and shall cleave to his wife, and they twain shall be one flesh." Abel knew him, who offered the lamb ; Seth knew him, and called upon him ; Noah knew him, and saved all the race in the ark ; Abraham knew him, and offered up his son to him. But because the world had forgotten him and worshipped idols, the Lord made his Jesus *known,* when he sent the Word in flesh to the Jews, and *revealed his righteousness* to the nations, when he justified them through faith. Wherefore did he reveal him to the nations ? Because of his mercy. Wherefore did he make him known to the Jews ? Because of his truth, that is, his promise.—*Honorius, the Continuator of Gerhohus.*

Verse 3.—"*He hath remembered his mercy and his truth.*" The Psalmist very properly observes, that God in redeeming the world "*remembered his truth,*" which

to us by the apostle is far more pleasing to him.   Paul allows us to bless God in the public assembly of the saints only in a known tongue, 1 Cor. xiv. 16.   The voice of man, although not understood by the generality, assuredly excels all inanimate instruments of music ; and yet we see what Paul determines concerning speaking in an unknown tongue.   What shall we then say of chanting, which fills the ears with nothing but an empty sound ?   Does any one object that music is very useful for awakening the minds of men and moving their hearts ?   I own it ; but we should always take care that no corruption creep in, which might both defile the pure worship of God and involve men in superstition.   Moreover, since the Holy Spirit expressly warns us of this danger by the mouth of Paul, to proceed beyond what we are there warranted by him, is not only, I must say, unadvised zeal, but wicked and perverse obstinacy.—*John Calvin.*

Verses 5, 6.—The song and the stringed instruments belonged to the Levites, and the trumpets to the priests alone.   Kitto says the trumpets did not join in the concert, but were sounded during certain regulated pauses in the vocal and instrumental music.   The harps and voices made the sweetness, while the trumpets and horns added the strength ; melody and energy should combine in the worship of God.—*C. H. S.*

Verse 6.—" *Trumpets.*" חֲצֹצְרוֹת, *Chatsotseroth* : here only in the Psalter.   These were the straight trumpets (such as are seen on the Arch of Titus) used by the priests for giving signals.   Numb. x. 2—10 ; 1 Chron. xv. 24, 28, etc.   The *shofar,* שׁוֹפָר (*cornet*), was the ordinary curved trumpet, cornet, or horn.—*William Kay.*

Verse 6.—" *Trumpets.*"   The word here used is uniformly rendered *trumpets* in the Scriptures, Num. x. 2, 8—10 ; xxxi. 6 ; *et al.*   The trumpet was mainly employed for convening a public assembly for worship, or for assembling the hosts for battle.   The original word, חֲצֹצְרָה *chatsotserah,* is supposed to have been designed to imitate " the broken pulse-like sound of the trumpet, like the Latin, *taratantara.*" So the German *trarara,* and the Arabic, *hadâdera.*   The word here used was given to the long, straight trumpet.—*Albert Barnes.*

Verse 6.—" *Trumpets.*"   The trumpet served the same purpose, in a religious and civil sense, as bells among Christians, and the voice among Mohammedans. Indeed, it is understood that Mohammed directed the voice to be employed, in order to mark a distinction between his own sect and the Jews with their trumpets and the Christians with their bells.—*Kitto's Pictorial Bible.*

Verse 6.—" *With trumpets.*"   Origen calls the writings of the evangelists and the apostles *trumpets,* at whose blast all the structures of idolatry and the dogmas of the philosophers were utterly overthrown.   He teaches likewise that by the sound of the *trumpets* is prefigured the trumpet of the universal judgment, at which the world shall fall in ruin, and whose sound shall be joy to the just, and lamentation to the unjust.—*Lorinus.*

Verse 6.—" *Before the Lord, the King.*"   Since it is distinctly added *before Jehovah the King,* and the words, *with trumpets and sound of cornet make a joyful noise,* are used, there seems to be a reference to that public rejoicing commonly manifested at the coronation of kings, or the celebration of undertakings for the public safety. This idea is not foreign to the present passage, since Jehovah is represented as King and Saviour of the people.—*Venema.*

Verses 7, 8.—" *Let the sea roar, and the fulness thereof ; the world, and they that dwell therein.   Let the floods clap their hands.*"

And thou, majestic main !
A secret world of wonders in thyself,
Sound his stupendous praise, whose greater voice
Or bids you roar, or bids your roarings fall.

—*James Thomson.*

Verses 7, 8.—These appeals to nature in her great departments—of the sea in its mighty amplitude, and the earth with its floods and hills—form, not a warrant, but a call on Christian ministers to recognise God more in their prayers and sermons as the God of Creation, instead of restricting themselves so exclusively to the peculiar doctrines of Christianity.   Do the one, and not leave the other undone.—*Thomas Chalmers.*

Verses 7, 8.—The setting forth the praise of Christ for the redemption of sinners, may not only furnish work to all reasonable creatures ; but also if every drop of water in the sea, and in every river and flood, every fish in the sea, every fowl of the air, every living creature on the earth, and whatsoever else is in the world : if they all had reason and ability to express themselves ; yea, and if all the hills were able by motion and gesticulation to communicate their joy one to another ; there is work for them all to set out the praise of Christ.—*David Dickson.*

Verses 7—9.—Matthew Henry on these verses quotes from Virgil's 4th Eclogue the verses (of which we subjoin Dryden's translation) in which the poet, he says, " either ignorantly or basely applies to Asinius Pollio the ancient prophecies which at that time were expected to be fulfilled ; " adding that Ludovicus Vives thinks that these and many other things which Virgil says of this long looked-for child " are applicable to Christ."

> O of celestial seed ! O foster son of Jove !
> See, lab'ring Nature calls thee to sustain
> The nodding frame of heav'n, and earth, and main !
> See to their base restor'd, earth, seas, and air ;
> And joyful ages, from behind, in crowding ranks appear.

Verse 8.—" *Let the floods clap their hands.*" The clapping of the hands being a token of delight and approbation, and the striking or dashing of the water in a river being, for the noise of it, a resemblance of that, *the rivers* are here said to *clap their hands.*—*Henry Hammond.*

Verse 8.—Though the language be figurative, so far as it gives a voice to the inanimate creation in its various departments, yet, like all the figurative language of Scripture, it expresses a truth—that which the Apostle has stated without a metaphor in the express revelation that the " creation shall be delivered from the bondage of corruption into the glorious liberty of the children of God." And this because the reason of that bondage will no more exist. It is the consequence of sin : but when the world shall be subjected to the righteous rule of its coming King (as predicted in the last verse of this Psalm), then earth and all creation shall own its present Lord, and join its tribute of praise to that of Israel and the nations, and the redeemed and glorified church.—*William De Burgh.*

Verse 9.—The Psalter is much occupied in celebrating *the benign fruits which Christ's reign is to yield* in all the earth. It will be a reign of HOLINESS. This is its proper and distinctive nature. Under it, the ends of the earth will fear God, and rejoice in his salvation. It will be a reign of JUSTICE. Under it, the wars and oppressions and cruelties, the unequal laws and iniquitous institutions that have so long vexed and cursed the world, shall find a place no more. This happy reformation is usually foretold in the form of a proclamation that the Lord is coming " *to judge the earth.*" It is important, therefore, to keep in mind the true sense and intention of that oft-repeated proclamation. It does not refer, as an unwary reader might suppose, to the Judgment of the Great Day. There is no terror in it. The Psalms that have it for their principal burden are jubilant in the highest degree. The design of the proclamation is to announce Christ in the character of a Peaceful Prince coming to administer equal laws with an impartial hand, and so to cause wrong and contention to cease in the earth. This is Christ's manner of judging the earth. What he has already done in this direction enables us to form a clear conception of what he will yet set himself to do. When he designs to accomplish great and salutary reforms in the political and social institutions of a people, he begins by dislodging bad principles from men's minds and planting Scriptural principles in their stead ; by purging evil passions from men's hearts, and baptizing them with the Spirit of truth and justice, godliness and lovingkindness. A sure foundation having been thus laid for a better order of things, he will by some storm of controversy, or of revolution sweep away the institutions in which injustice has entrenched itself, and will thus make it possible for righteousness to have free course. Oh what a store of comfort for the down-trodden, the enslaved, the needy, is laid up in the announcement that the Lord is coming to be the avenger of all such ! Well may all the creatures be invited to clap their hands for joy at the thought that he has taken this work in hand ; that he sitteth upon the floods ; and that the storms that agitate the nations are the chariot in which he rides to take possession of the earth, and make it an abode of righteousness and peace.—*William Binnie.*

HINTS TO PREACHERS.

Verse 1.—" *A new song.*" The duty, beauty, and benefit of maintaining freshness in piety, service, and worship.

Verse 1.—" *He hath done marvellous things.*" I. He hath created a marvellous universe. II. He has established a marvellous government. III. He hath bestowed a marvellous gift. IV. He hath provided a marvellous redemption. V. He hath inspired a marvellous book. VI. He hath opened a marvellous fulness. VII. He hath effected a marvellous transformation.—*W. Jackson.*

Verse 1.—" *The victory.*" The victories of God in judgment, and in mercy : especially the triumphs of Christ on the cross, and by his Spirit in the heart, and in and by the church at large.

Verse 2.—" *The Lord hath made known his salvation.*" I. The contents of which it is composed. II. The reasons for which it has been provided. III. The price at which it has been procured. IV. The terms on which it shall be imparted. V. The way in which it must be propagated. VI. The manner in which its neglect will be punished.—*W. J.*

Verse 2 (*first clause*).—I. What is salvation ? II. Why it is called the Lord's :— " Salvation is of the Lord." III. How he has made it known. IV. For what purpose. V. With what results.—*E. G. Gange.*

Verse 2.—The great privilege of knowing the gospel. I. *In what it consists.* 1. Revelation by the Bible. 2. Declaration by the minister. 3. Illumination by the Spirit. 4. Illustration in daily providence. II. *To what it has led.* 1. We have believed it. 2. We have so far understood it as to growingly rejoice in it. 3. We are able to tell it to others. 4. We abhor those who mystify it.

Verse 2.—Salvation's glory. I. It is divine—" his salvation." II. It is consistent with justice—" his righteousness." III. It is plain and simple—" openly showed." IV. It is meant for all sorts of men—" heathen."

Verse 3 (*first clause*).—The Lord's memory of his covenant. Times in which he seems to forget it ; ways in which even in those times he proves his faithfulness ; great deeds of grace by which at other times he shows his memory of his promises ; and reasons why he must ever be mindful of his covenant.

Verse 3 (*last clause*).—" *All the ends of the earth.*" I. Literally. Missionaries have visited every land. II. Spiritually. Men ready to despair, to perish. III. Prophetically. Dwell on the grand promises concerning the future, and the triumphs of the church.—*E. G. G.*

Verse 3.—" *All the ends of the earth have seen,*" &c. I. The greatest foreigners have seen it ; many have " come from the east and the west ; " Greeks, Peter's hearers, the Eunuch, Greenlanders, South Sea Islanders, Negroes, Red Indians, &c., &c. II. The ripest saints have seen it ; they are at the right end of the earth, stepping out of the wilderness into Canaan, &c. III. The vilest sinners have seen it ; those who have wandered so far that they could get no farther without stepping into hell. The dying thief. The woman who was a sinner. Those whom Whitfield called " the devil's castaways."—*W. J.*

Verse 4.—The right use of noise. I. " Make a noise." Awake, O sleeper. Speak, O dumb. II. " Make a joyful noise." The shout of deliverance, of gratitude, of gladness. III. " Make a loud noise, all the earth." Nature with her ten thousand voices. The church with myriad saints. IV. " Make a joyful noise unto God." Praise him alone. Praise him for ever.—*E. G. G.*

Verse 6.—Joy a needful ingredient of praise. The Lord as King, an essential idea in adoration. Expression in various ways incumbent upon us, when praising joyfully such a King.

Verses 7, 8.—Nature at worship. The congregation is—I. Vast. Sea, earth, rivers, hills. II. Varied. Diverse in character, word, aspect, each from the other, constant and alike in this alone, that *all*, *always* worship God. III. Gladsome. In this like the worshippers in heaven, and for the same reason—sin is absent.— *E. G. G.*

Verse 8.—The song of the sea, and the hallelujah of the hills.

Verse 9.—The last judgment as a theme for thankfulness.

Verse 9.—" *Before the Lord.*" Where we are, where our joy should be, where all our actions should be felt to be, where we shall be—" *before the Lord.*" Enquire— What are we before the Lord ? What shall we be when he cometh ?

PSALM XCIX.

This may be called THE SANCTUS, *or,* THE HOLY, HOLY, HOLY PSALM, *for the word " holy " is the conclusion and the refrain of its three main divisions. Its subject is the holiness of the divine government, the sanctity of the mediatorial reign. It seems to us to declare the holiness of Jehovah himself in verses 1, 2, 3 ; it mentions the equity of the king whom the Lord had appointed, as an illustration of the Lord's love of holiness, or more probably it describes the Lord as himself the king, in verses 4 and 5, and it then sets forth the severely righteous character of God's dealings with those favoured persons whom in former times he had selected to approach him on behalf of the people, 6—9. It is a hymn fitted for the cherubim who surround the throne, who are mentioned in verse 1 ; it is a Psalm most fitting for saints who dwell in Zion, the holy city, and especially worthy to be reverently sung by all who, like David the king, Moses the lawgiver, Aaron the priest, or Samuel the seer, are honoured to lead the church of God, and plead for her with her Lord.*

EXPOSITION.

THE LORD reigneth ; let the people tremble : he sitteth *between* the cherubims ; let the earth be moved.

2 The LORD *is* great in Zion ; and he *is* high above all the people.

3 Let them praise thy great and terrible name ; *for it is* holy.

1. *" The Lord reigneth."* One of the most joyous utterances which ever leaped from mortal lip. The overthrow of the reign of evil and the setting up of Jehovah's kingdom of goodness, justice, and truth, is worthy to be hymned again and again, as we have it here for the third time in the Psalms. *" Let the people tremble."* Let the chosen people feel a solemn yet joyful awe, which shall thrill their whole manhood. Saints quiver with devout emotion, and sinners quiver with terror when the rule of Jehovah is fully perceived and felt. It is not a light or trifling matter, it is a truth which, above all others, should stir the depths of our nature. *" He sitteth between the cherubims."* In grandeur of sublime glory, yet in nearness of mediatorial condescension, Jehovah revealed himself above the mercy-seat, whereon stood the likeness of those flaming ones who gaze upon his glory, and for ever cry, " Holy, Holy, Holy, Lord God of hosts." The Lord reigning on that throne of grace which is sprinkled with atoning blood, and veiled with the covering wings of mediatorial love, is above all other revelations wonderful, and fitted to excite emotion among all mankind, hence it is added, *" Let the earth be moved."* Not merely " the people," but the whole earth should feel a movement of adoring awe when it is known that on the mercy seat God sits as universal monarch. The pomp of heaven surrounds him, and is symbolised by the outstretched wings of waiting cherubs ; let not the earth be less moved to adoration, rather let all her tribes bow before his infinite majesty, yea, let the solid earth itself with reverent tremor acknowledge his presence.

2. *" The Lord is great in Zion."* Of old the temple's sacred hill was the centre of the worship of the great King, and the place where his grandeur was most clearly beheld : his church is now his favoured palace, where his greatness is displayed, acknowledged, and adored. He there unveils his attributes and commands the lowliest homage ; the ignorant forget him, the wicked despise him, the atheistical oppose him, but among his own chosen he is great beyond comparison. He is great in the esteem of the gracious, great in his acts of mercy, and really great in himself : great in mercy, power, wisdom, justice, and glory. *" And he is high above all the people ;"* towering above their highest thoughts and loftiest conceptions. The highest are not high to him, yet, blessed be his name, the lowliest are not despised by him. In such a God we rejoice, his greatness and loftiness are exceedingly delightful in our esteem ; the more he is honoured and exalted in the hearts of men, the more exultant are his people. If Israel delighted in Saul because he was head and shoulders above the people, how much more should we exult in our God and King, who is as high above us as the heavens are above the earth.

3. "*Let them praise thy great and terrible name :*" let all the dwellers in Zion and all the nations upon the earth praise the Lord, or "acknowledge thankfully" the goodness of his divine nature, albeit that there is so much in it which must inspire their awe. Under the most terrible aspect the Lord is still to be praised. Many profess to admire the milder beams of the sun of righteousness, but burn with rebellion against its more flaming radiance : so it ought not to be : we are bound to praise a terrible God and worship him who casts the wicked down to hell. Did not Israel praise him "who overthrew Pharaoh and his hosts in the Red Sea, for his mercy endureth for ever." The terrible Avenger is to be praised, as well as the loving Redeemer. Against this the sympathy of man's evil heart with sin rebels ; it cries out for an effeminate God in whom pity has strangled justice. The well-instructed servants of Jehovah praise him in all the aspects of his character, whether terrible or tender. Grace streaming from the mercy-seat can alone work in us this admirable frame of mind. "*For it is holy,*" or "*He is holy.*" In him is no flaw or fault, excess or deficiency, error or iniquity. He is wholly excellent, and is therefore called holy. In his words, thoughts, acts, and revelations as well as in himself, he is perfection itself. O come let us worship and bow down before him.

4 The king's strength also loveth judgment ; thou dost establish equity, thou executest judgment and righteousness in Jacob.

5 Exalt ye the LORD our God, and worship at his footstool ; *for* he *is* holy.

4. "*The king's strength also loveth judgment.*" God is the king, the mercy-seat is his throne, and the sceptre which he sways is holy like himself. His power never exerts itself tyranically ; he is a sovereign, and he is absolute in his government, but his might delights in right, his force is used for just purposes only. Men in these days are continually arraigning the Lord's government, and setting up to judge whether he does right or not ; but saintly men in the olden time were of another mind, they were sure that what the Lord did was just, and instead of calling him to account they humbly submitted themselves to his will, rejoicing in the firm persuasion that with his whole omnipotence God was pledged to promote righteousness, and work justice among all his creatures. "*Thou dost establish equity.*" Not a court of equity merely, but equity itself thou dost set up, and that not for a time or upon an occasion, but as an established institution, stable as thy throne. Not even for the sake of mercy does the Lord remove or injure the equity of his moral government ; both in providence and in grace he is careful to conserve the immaculate purity of his justice. Most kingdoms have an establishment of some kind, and generally it is inequitable ; here we have an establishment which is equity itself. The Lord our God demolishes every system of injustice, and right alone is made to stand. "*Thou executest judgment and righteousness in Jacob.*" Justice is not merely established, but executed in God's kingdom ; the laws are carried out, the executive is as righteous as the legislative. Herein let all the oppressed, yea, and all who love that which is right, find large occasion for praise. Other nations under their despots were the victims and the perpetrators of grievous wrong, but when the tribes were faithful to the Lord they enjoyed an upright government within their own borders, and acted with integrity towards their neighbours. That king-craft which delights in cunning, favouritism, and brute force is as opposite to the divine kingship as darkness to light. The palace of Jehovah is no robber's fortress nor despot's castle, built on dungeons, with stones carved by slaves, and cemented with the blood of toiling serfs. The annals of most human governments have been written in the tears of the downtrodden, and the curses of the oppressed : the chronicles of the Lord's kingdom are of another sort, truth shines in each line, goodness in every syllable, and justice in every letter. Glory be to the name of the King, whose gentle glory beams from between the cherubic wings.

5. "*Exalt ye the Lord our God.*" If no others adore him, let his own people render to him the most ardent worship. Infinite condescension makes him stoop to be called *our* God, and truth and faithfulness bind him to maintain that covenant relationship ; and surely we, to whom by grace he so lovingly gives himself, should exalt him with all our hearts. He shines upon us from under the veiling wings of cherubim, and above the seat of mercy, therefore let us come *and worship at his footstool.* When he reveals himself in Christ Jesus, as our reconciled God, who allows

us to approach even to his throne, it becomes us to unite earnestness and humility, joy and adoration, and, while we exalt him, prostrate ourselves in the dust before him. Do we need to be thus excited to worship ? How much ought we to blush for such backwardness ! It ought to be our daily delight to magnify so good and great a God. " *For he is holy.*" A second time the note rings out, and as the ark, which was the divine footstool, has just been mentioned, the voice seems to sound forth from the cherubim where the Lord sitteth, who continually do cry, " Holy, Holy, Holy, Lord God of Sabaoth ! " Holiness is the harmony of all the virtues. The Lord has not one glorious attribute alone, or in excess, but all glories are in him as a whole ; this is the crown of his honour and the honour of his crown. His power is not his choicest jewel, nor his sovereignty, but his holiness. In this all comprehensive moral excellence he would have his creatures take delight, and when they do so their delight is evidence that their hearts have been renewed, and they themselves have been partakers of his holiness. The gods of the heathen were, according to their own votaries, lustful, cruel, and brutish ; their only claim to reverence lay in their supposed potency over human destinies : who would not far rather adore Jehovah, whose character is unsullied purity, unswerving justice, unbending truth, unbounded love, in a word, perfect holiness ?

6 Moses and Aaron among his priests, and Samuel among them that call upon his name ; they called upon the LORD, and he answered them.

7 He spake unto them in the cloudy pillar : they kept his testimonies, and the ordinance *that* he gave them.

8 Thou answeredst them, O LORD our God : thou wast a God that forgavest them, though thou tookest vengeance of their inventions.

9 Exalt the LORD our God, and worship at his holy hill ; for the LORD our God *is* holy.

6. " *Moses and Aaron among his priests, and Samuel among them that call upon his name.*" Though not ordained to the typical priesthood, Moses was a true priest, even as Melchizedek had been before him. God has ever had a priesthood beside and above that of the law. The three holy men here mentioned all stood in his courts, and saw his holiness, each one after his own order. Moses saw the Lord in flaming fire revealing his perfect law, Aaron full often watched the sacred fire devour the sin-offering, and Samuel witnessed the judgment of the Lord on Eli's house, because of the error of his way. These each one stood in the gap when the wrath of God broke forth, because his holiness had been insulted ; and acting as intercessors, they screened the nation from the great and terrible God, who otherwise would in a dreadful manner have executed judgment in Jacob. Let these men, or such as these, lead us in our worship, and let us approach the Lord at the mercy-seat as they did, for he is as accessible to us as to them. They made it their life's business to call upon him in prayer, and by so doing brought down innumerable blessings upon themselves and others. Does not the Lord call us also to come up into the mount with Moses, and to enter the most holy place with Aaron ? Do we not hear him call us by our name as he did Samuel ? And do we not answer, " Speak, Lord, for thy servant heareth " ? " *They called upon the Lord, and he answered them.*" Not in vain were their prayers ; but being a holy God he was true to his promises, and hearkened to them from off the mercy-seat. Here is reason for praise, for answers to the petitions of some are proofs of God's readiness to hear others. These three men asked large things, they pleaded for a whole nation, and they stayed great plagues and turned away fiery wrath ; who would not exercise himself in adoring so great and merciful a God ? If he were unholy he would be false to his word and refuse his people's cries ; this, then, is recorded for our joy and for his glory, that holy men of old were not suffered to pray in vain.

7. " *He spake unto them in the cloudy pillar.*" We have had mention of the ark and the shekinah, and now of the fiery cloudy pillar, which was another visible token of the presence of God in the midst of Israel. Responses came to Moses and Aaron out of that glorious overshadowing cloud, and though Samuel saw it not, yet to him also came the mystic voice which was wont to thunder forth from that divine canopy. Men have had converse with God, let men therefore speak to God in return. He has told us things to come, let us in return confess the sins which are past ; he has revealed his mind to us, let us then pour out our hearts before him.

"*They kept his testimonies.*" When others turned aside they were faithful; in their hearts they laid up his word, and in their lives they obeyed it. When he spake to them they observed his will, and therefore when they spake to him he yielded to their desires. This keeping of the divine testimonies is a virtue all too rare in these our days; men run after their own views and opinions, and make light of the truth of God; hence it is that they fail in prayer, and scoffers have even dared to say that prayer avails not at all. May the good Lord bring back his people to reverence his word, and then will he also have respect unto the voice of their cry. "*And the ordinance that he gave them.*" His practical precept they observed as well as his doctrinal instruction. Ordinances are not to be trifled with, or testimonies will also be despised; and the converse is also true, a light estimate of inspired dogma is sure to end in neglect of moral virtues. To Moses, Aaron, and Samuel special and personal charges were committed, and they were all true to their trust, for they stood in awe of the Lord their God, and worshipped him with their whole souls. They were very different men, and had each one a work to do peculiar to himself, yet because each was a man of prayer they were all preserved in their integrity, fulfilled their office, and blessed their generation. Lord, teach us like Moses to hold up our hands in prayer and conquer Amalek, like Aaron to wave the censer between the living and the dead till the plague is stayed, and like Samuel to say to a guilty people, "God forbid that I should sin against the Lord in ceasing to pray for you;" if thou wilt make us mighty with thee in prayer, we shall also be kept faithful before thee in the service which thou hast laid upon us.

8. "*Thou answeredst them, O Lord our God.*" A sweet title and a cheering fact. Our covenant God in a very special manner heard his three servants when they pleaded for the people. "*Thou wast a God that forgavest them, though thou tookest vengeance of their inventions.*" He forgave the sinners, but he slew their sins. Some apply this verse to Moses, Aaron, and Samuel, and remind us that each of these fell into a fault and received chastisement. Of Samuel they assert that, for having set up his sons as his successors, he was compelled to submit to the anointing of Saul as king, which was a great grief to him; this is to our mind a very doubtful statement, and leads us to abandon the interpretation altogether. We believe that the passage refers to the nation which was spared through the intercession of these three holy men, but yet was severely chastened for its transgressions. In answer to the cry of Moses the tribes lived on, but the then existing generation could not enter Canaan: Aaron's golden calf was broken, though the fire of the Lord did not consume the people; and Israel smarted under the harsh government of Saul, though at Samuel's request its murmurings against the theocratic rule of their fathers' God was not visited with pestilence or famine. So to forgive sin as at the same time to express abhorrence of it, is the peculiar glory of God, and is best seen in the atonement of our Lord Jesus. Reader, are you a believer? Then your sin is forgiven you; but so surely as you are a child of God the rod of paternal discipline will be laid upon you if your walk be not close with God. "You only have I known of all the nations of the earth, therefore I will punish you for your iniquities."

9. "*Exalt the Lord our God.*" A second time the delightful title of Jehovah our God is used, and it is quickly followed by a third. The Psalm is Trinitarian in its whole structure. In each of his sacred persons the Lord is the God of his people; the Father is ours, the Son is ours, and the Holy Spirit is ours: let us exalt him with all our ransomed powers. "*And worship at his holy hill.*" Where he appoints his temple let us resort. No spot of ground is now fenced about as peculiarly holy, or to be regarded as more sacred than another; yet his visible church is his chosen hill, and there would we be found, numbered with his people, and unite with them in worship. "*For the Lord our God is holy.*" Again this devout description is repeated, and made the climax of the song. Oh for hearts made pure within, so that we may rightly perceive and worthily praise the infinite perfection of the Triune Lord.

EXPLANATORY NOTES AND QUAINT SAYINGS.

Whole Psalm.—This Psalm has three parts, in which the Lord is celebrated as he who is to come, as he who is, and as he who was.—*John Albert Bengel*, 1687—1752.

Whole Psalm.—In each of the three strophes Jehovah is acknowledged in his peculiar covenant relation to his people. In the first he is " great in *Zion* " (ver. 2) ; in the second, he has " executed righteousness in *Jacob* " (ver. 4) ; and he is " Jehovah *our* God " (ver. 5) ; in the third, the great examples of this covenant relationship are cited from Israel's ancient history ; and again God is twice claimed as " Jehovah *our* God " (ver. 8 and 9).—*J. J. S. Perowne.*

Whole Psalm.—There are *three* Psalms which begin with the words, " The LORD (JEHOVAH) reigneth." (Pss. xciii., xcvii., xcix.) This is the third and last of these Psalms ; and it is remarkable that in this Psalm the words " *He is holy* " are repeated *three* times (verses 3, 5, 9). Thus this Psalm is one of the links in the chain which connects the first revelation of God in Genesis with the full manifestation of the doctrine of the blessed Trinity, which is revealed in the commission of the risen Saviour to his apostles : " Go ye, and make disciples of all nations, baptizing them into the name of the Father, and of the Son, and of the Holy Ghost," and which prepares the faithful to join in the heavenly Hallelujah of the church glorified, " Holy, holy, holy, Lord God Almighty, which was, and is, and is to come." The other links in this chain in the Old Testament are, the Aaronic benediction, in Num. vi. 24—27 ; and the Seraphic Trisagion, in Isa. vi. 1—3.—*Christopher Wordsworth.*

Whole Psalm.—Many of the preceding Psalms, in extolling the Dominion and Supremacy of the Messiah, have spoken of him solely as the object of triumph and rejoicing. He has been represented in all the bounteousness of his mercy, and the excess of his lovingkindness ; and the ideas of might and majesty, with which he has been accompanied, seem chiefly to have been regarded as the means by which these gracious designs will be carried into a sure effect. There is always a great danger in such a feeling, lest our *reciprocal* covenant should be too much forgotten ; and we should rest on our privileges to the exclusion of our practice. This was a constant error to the Jews. " We have Abraham to our Father," was continually on their lips ; as if the given promise to their nation had been inalienable for ever. Subsequent ages have shown the existence of the same false principle amongst the Gentiles. It is a part of the weakness of human nature ; and hence was the prophet inspired to warn the world of the evil, and draw their minds to a just sense of the *awfulness* of the Redeemer's majesty. In this view, joined as it is throughout with assertions of his readiness at all times to listen to the believer and to grant his supplication, the Psalm is at once of great power and of an exceeding consolation.—*William Hill Tucker.*

Verse 1.—" *Let the people tremble . . . let the earth be moved.*" That fear which proceeds from simple reverence as well as that which arises from apprehension of evil, produces bodily shaking. Thus this exhortation may concern believing as well as unbelieving nations.—*Amyraldus.*

Verse 1.—" *Let the people tremble.*" He bids a defiance, as it were, to all his enemies, ὀργιζέσθωσαν, *irascantur, commoveantur, fremant populi ;* let the people be angry, fret, and be unquiet, as Psal. ii. 1. " *Let the earth,*" that is, the tyrants of the earth, be moved at it ; yet let them know that all their endeavours are but vain.—*William Nicholson.*

Verse 1.—" *Let the people tremble.*" Jarchi refers this to the war of Gog and Magog.—*John Gill.*

Verse 1.—" *Let the people tremble.*" Albeit the church be compassed about with enemies, as the lily among the thorns, yet because her Lord reigneth in the midst of her, she hath reason not only to comfort herself in him, but also hath ground of defying her enemies, and boasting against them : " *The Lord reigneth ; let the people tremble.*" The Lord's people do not worship an unknown God, they know who he is, and where to find him ; to wit, in his ordinances, on the throne of grace, reconciling himself to the world in Christ : " *He sitteth between the cherubims.*"—*David Dickson.*

Verse 1.—" *The cherubims.*" These were figures, or representations of angels, inclining their faces one towards the other, and touching one another with their wings. Ex. xxv. 18. The use of these was to cover or overshadow the *mercy-seat* with their wings, ver. 20, and from this *seat* God used to speak unto Moses, ver. 22 ; Num. vii. 8, 9. Which may be applied unto Christ, whose mediation was signified by the *mercy-seat ;* whence it is said, that *he is a propitiation* or covering mercy-seat, Rom. iii. 25 ; 1 John ii. 2 ; iv. 10, because by his obedience all our unrighteousness is covered.—*Thomas Wilson* (—1621), *in " A Complete Christian Dictionary,"* 1678

Verse 1.—" *He sitteth between the cherubims.*" Our friend Mr. Charles Stanford, in his delicious work, " Symbols of Christ," has beautifully brought out the connection between the 37th and 38th verses of Matt. xxiii. The house was left desolate because Christ, who was set forth by the symbol of shelter, was rejected by them, and was not permitted to cover them with his wings. It was customary for the Jews to say of a proselyte, " He has taken refuge under the wings of the Shekinah." We now see that to take shelter under the wings of the Shekinah is to hide beneath the wings of Christ. Beneath that living shield which beats back the destroying stroke, and is broad enough to canopy a fugitive world, we take shelter, and there the promise is fulfilled, " He shall cover thee with his feathers, and under his wings shalt thou trust."

Verse 1.—" He sitteth between the cherubims." The cherubim is the seat of God, as the scripture sheweth us, a certain exalted heavenly throne, which we see not ; but the word of God knoweth it, knoweth it as his own seat : and the word of God and the Spirit of God hath itself revealed to the servants of God where God sitteth. Not that God doth sit, as doth man, but thou, if thou dost wish that God sit in thee, if thou wilt be good, shalt be the seat of God ; for thus is it written, " The soul of the righteous is the seat of wisdom " [Septuagint translation]. For a throne is in our language called a seat. For some, conversant with the Hebrew tongue, have interpreted cherubim in the Latin language (for it is a Hebrew term) by the words fulness of knowledge. Therefore, because God surpasseth all knowledge, he is said to sit above the fulness of knowledge. Let there be therefore in thee fulness of knowledge, and even thou shalt be the throne of God.—Augustine.

Verse 1.—" Let the earth be moved." Those that submit to him shall be established, and not " moved," Psal. xcvi. 10 ; but they that oppose him will be moved. Heaven and earth shall be shaken, and all nations; but the kingdom of Christ cannot be moved. The " things which cannot be shaken shall remain," Heb. xii. 27.—Matthew Henry.

Verse 2.—" He is high above all the people." The metaphor is taken from such great objects as trees, animals, palaces, towers, which are the more valued, and are regarded as possessing the greater strength, the higher they rise above others. So Deut. i. 28 ; ii. 10, 21 ; ix. 2, Concerning the Canaanites and the giants.—Martin Geier.

Verse 3.—" Let them praise thy great and terrible name," etc. Although the enemies of the Church of God are in a tumult, and the whole earth is moved, do you nevertheless with joyful spirit entrust your salvation to him, and acknowledge and diligently celebrate his power displayed in the defence of his people and the overthrow of his foes.—Mollerus.

Verse 3.—" Thy great and terrible name ; for it is holy." The FATHER'S name is " great," for he is the source, the Creator, the Lord of all ; the SON'S name is " terrible," for he is to be our judge ; the name of the HOLY GHOST is " holy," for he it is who bestows hallowing and sanctification. The Hebrew commentators see here the mystic Tetragrammaton יהוה, whose true pronunciation was kept a profound secret by the Rabbins, owing to a feeling of awful reverence ; while the Greeks are precise in bidding us take it of that name, which is " terrible " to God's enemies, " holy " to his friends, and " great " to both, the name of JESUS.—Hugo Cardinalis, Genebrardus, and Balthazar Corderius, in Neale's Commentary.

Verse 3.—" Let them praise thy terrible name." What force the experience of a burdened conscience attaches to the expression, " Thy great and terrible name ; for it is holy ! " The misery of sin consists not merely in its consequences, but in its very nature, which is to separate between God and our souls, and to shut us out from God, and God from us. Yet the Spirit of God indicates, in the covenant of grace, a threefold practical influence of his holiness upon us, of which the issue is the opposite of despair. The various steps are marked as praise, exaltation, and worship (verses 3, 5, 9). Of these the last seems by far the most difficult to realise. For it is in the nature of conscious sin to prevent even our approaches to God, to keep us from all comfortable fellowship with God, and to fill us with a heavy sense of our infinite and almost hopeless distance from him. Yet we will " praise thy great and terrible name ; for it is holy." Great it is ; most glorious and high ; far above all human conceptions. Viewed in this light, even the fact otherwise so consoling, " The Lord reigneth," leads only to the inference, " Let the people tremble ; " and " He sitteth between the cherubim " (or manifesteth himself as the covenant God) to the conclusion, " Let the earth be moved," or *stagger*. But his name is not only great and terrible in its manifestations, " it is holy," and *therefore* we " praise " it. His greatness is all arrayed on the side of goodness, his power on that of righteousness and truth.—*Alfred Edersheim, in " The Golden Diary of Heart Converse with Jesus in the Book of Psalms,"* 1873.

Verse 3.—" *Thy terrible name . . . . holy."* In acts of man's vindictive justice, there is something of impurity, perturbation, passion, some mixture of cruelty ; but none of these fall upon God in the several acts of wrath. When God appears to Ezekiel in the resemblance of fire, to signify his anger against the house of Judah for their idolatry, " from his loins downward there was the appearance of fire, but from the loins upward the appearance of brightness, as the colour of amber." Ezek. viii. 2. His heart is clean in his most terrible acts of vengeance ; it is a pure flame wherewith he scorcheth and burns his enemies. He is holy in the most fiery appearance.—*Stephen Charnock.*

Verse 3.—" *It is holy."* No attribute is sounded out so loftily, with such solemnity, and so frequently by angels that stand before his throne, as this. Where do you find any other attribute trebled in the praises of it as this ? Isaiah vi. 3 : " Holy, holy, holy, is the LORD of hosts : the whole earth is full of his glory ; " and Rev. iv. 8 : " The four living creatures rest not day and night saying, Holy, holy, holy, Lord God Almighty," &c. His power of sovereignty as Lord of hosts is but once mentioned, but with a ternal repetition of his holiness. Do you hear in any evangelical song any other perfection of the divine nature thrice repeated ? Where do we read of the crying out, Eternal, eternal, eternal ; or Faithful, faithful, faithful, Lord God of hosts ! Whatsoever other attribute is left out, this God would have to fill the mouths of angels and blessed spirits for ever in heaven. . . . . As it seems to challenge an excellency above all his other perfections, so it is the glory of all the rest ; as it is the glory of the Godhead, so it is the glory of every perfection in the Godhead ; as his power is the strength of them, so his holiness is the beauty of them ; as all would be weak without almightiness to back them, so all would be uncomely without holiness to adorn them : should this be sullied all the rest would lose their honour and their comfortable efficacy ; as at the same instant that the sun should lose its light, it would lose its heat, its strength, its generative and quickening virtue. As sincerity is the lustre of every grace in a Christian, so is purity the splendour of every attribute in the Godhead. His justice is a holy justice, his wisdom a holy wisdom, his arm of power a " holy arm," Psalm xcviii. 1 ; his truth or promise a " holy promise," Psalm cv. 42. *Holy* and *true* go hand and hand, Rev. vi. 10. " His *name,"* which signifies all his attributes in conjunction, " *is holy."*—*Stephen Charnock.*

Verse 4.—" *The king's strength."* They will remember his strength with joy, because he " *loveth judgment,"* and there is no reason, therefore, to be afraid of him in consequence of his great strength, so long as they continue to walk in the good way.—*George Phillips.*

Verses 4, 5.—Our King *loveth righteousness :* he will execute perfect justice, tempered with perfect mercy. He will judge every man according to his works, summing up and completing the unnoticed righteousness of his providence by an open manifestation to the universe of his holiness and equity. " We believe that he will come to be our judge," therefore let us magnify and exalt him with our lips and hearts ; and let us fall down and worship the man Christ Jesus, who took our nature, even his manhood, from the earth, which is his footstool, into the eternity of the Godhead, in which he is equal to the Father. As heaven, which is the throne of God, and earth, which is his footstool, form one universe, so is God and man one Christ, the everlasting Lord, " holy and true," in whom we sinners may appeal from the throne of eternal justice to the footstool of eternal mercy.—" *Plain Commentary."*

Verse 5 (second clause). Mark the peculiar expression, " *Worship at his footstool."* What humility and subjection does it imply ! It is the worship of one whose heart has been subdued by divine grace.—*W. Wilson.*

Verse 5.—Bishop Horsley thus renders this verse :—

> " Exalt ye Jehovah our God,
> And make prostration before his footstool ;
> *It is holy."*

Thus he connects " holy " with Jehovah's footstool, mentioned in the preceding clause. There appears to me great propriety and beauty in this construction, which divides the poem into three members. Of these the first terminates with ascribing " holiness " to the *name* of Jehovah : the second, with ascribing the same property to his *abode* : and then, at the conclusion of the hymn, " holiness," essential holiness, is ascribed to Jehovah himself. Our Bible marginal translation recognises this construction of the 5th verse.—*Richard Mant.*

Verse 6.—" *Moses and Aaron among his priests,*" or chief *officers,* as in 1 Chron. xviii. 17. Moses was, if not a priest, yet a continual intercessor for the people, and a type of Christ the great Mediator of his church. *Aben-Ezra* called him *Cohen haccohanim,* the priest of priests ; and *Philo,* writing his life, concludeth, This was the life and death of Moses the king, the lawgiver, the prophet, and the chief priest.— *John Trapp.*

Verse 6.—*Moses* twice performed acts essentially priestly (Ex. xxiv. and xl. 22, compared with Leviticus viii.), at the ratification of the covenant, and at the consecration of the priests. For this reason he could the more readily be placed here among the priestly mediators.—*C. B. Moll.*

Verse 6.—" *Priests.*" The word *cohen* is not confined as a title to the priests of the Levitical order, it is applied to Melchizedek and others. Moses is included among God's priests in accordance with the true idea of a priest, as being the official exponent of the divine love and mercy—one who represented God though acting in the interests of man.—*Robert Baker Girdlestone, in " Synonyms of the Old Testament."*

Verse 6.—" *His priests.*" At the foundation of this there is another spiritual idiom, that, namely, according to which all are called priests who possess what constitutes the essence of the ordinary priestly office (although not the externals), inward connection with God, free access to the throne of grace, and the gift and power of intercessory prayer. This figurative idiom occurs even in the law itself, compare Exodus xix. 6, where it is said to all Israel, " Ye shall be unto me a kingdom of *priests,* and an holy nation."—*F. W. Hengstenberg.*

Verse 6.—*Priests.* The word *cohen,* Priest, is from *cahan, to plead a cause,* as an intercessor, mediator, or advocate ; hence the strict propriety of its use here in reference to Moses.—*C. H. S.*

Verse 6.—" *Them that call upon his name.*" The Hebrew word which we translate to *call* upon God, notes a sort of men whose chief business or trade was to call upon or invocate the name of God, and in this instance it implies that it was the special calling of these men to call upon God.—*Joseph Caryl.*

Verses 6—9.—This third strophe is in reality a prophetical picture of the future holy worship of God, in which Moses, Aaron, and Samuel appear as the living representatives of the redeemed church, like the four and twenty elders in the more fully developed Apocalyptic scene of St. John. Rev. v.—*Joseph Francis Thrupp.*

Verse 7.—" *They kept his testimonies.*" For this reason they were so promptly heard, even as the Lord himself says, " If a man love me he will keep my words," and again, " If ye abide in me and my words abide in you, ye shall ask what ye will and it shall be done unto you." " *And the ordinance that he gave them.*" They not only observed the precepts which bind men in general, but the peculiar obligation of governing, directing, and teaching the people committed to them.—*Bellarmine.*

Verse 8.—The construction of the verse seems to be this :—" O Lord our God, thou didst hear or answer them," that is, the aforementioned typical mediators, Moses, Aaron, and Samuel ; " thou becamest a forbearing God for them," or, at their intercession ; and that " even when punishing," or, when thou hadst begun to punish " the wicked deeds of them," that is, not of Moses, Aaron, and Samuel, but of the people, who had transgressed, and for whom they interceded. This was the case when Moses interceded for the idolaters, Exod. xxii. 32, Aaron for the schismatics, Numb. xvi. 47, and Samuel for the whole nation, 1 Sam. vii. 9.—*George Horne.*

Verse 8.—" *Thou answeredst them . . . . forgavest them.*" Oh, the blessed assurance that nothing can disturb our standing in the covenant. Answer and forgiveness are certain, though vengeance is taken of our inventions. How every word and expression here seems to go right to our hearts ! The very designation of our sins and punishments is so true. Yet, withal, we are not shut out from God. We are able to speak to, and to hear him; we receive what we need, and much more; and, above all, we have the sweet, abiding sense of forgiveness, notwithstanding " our inventions." When we smart under chastisements or disappointments, we know that it is the fire which burns up the hay, wood, and stubble—a Father's dealings in compassion and mercy. We willingly, we gladly take these chastisements, which now are to us fresh pledges of our safety. For safe, eternally safe, remains the foundation, and unclosed the way of access. O surely with all our heart do we accord: *"Exalt Jehovah our God, and worship at his holy hill; for Jehovah our God is holy."—Alfred Edersheim.*

Verse 8.—The words of this verse have in them three remarkable particulars. I. The behaviour of the men it speaks of, which is partly good, and partly evil. The former verse saith, " *They kept God's testimonies, and the ordinance that he gave them;* " this insinuates (what was also expressed, ver. 6) that they used to *call upon God;* all this was very good. But withal they did sometimes some things amiss, they had some inventions, by-paths, and steps awry, which, as they needed pardon, so they occasionally incensed him so much against them that he would not let them escape altogether, without taking some vengeance for such untowardness. II. God's graciousness in a double respect: 1, in *answering them,* granting their suits and supplications ordinarily. 2. In *forgiving them,* pardoning their failings and faults evermore; never dealing with them altogether according to their sins, but in the midst of any offence of theirs, or judgment of his, remembering mercy. III. His holy justice, notwithstanding, *taking vengeance on their inventions;* chastening them for some faults sometimes, and not letting them always go unpunished, how faithful soever they were generally, or how gracious soever he was eternally.— *Herbert Palmer (1601—1647), in a Sermon entitled " The Glass of God's Providence."* 1644.

Verse 8.—" *Thou wast a God that forgavest them,"* literally " *for* them; " on account of their intercessions. God did not destroy those for whom his devoted servants pleaded, in the day of threatened vengeance. Their sins, indeed, he visited with the rod of divine chastisement; but their forfeited lives he spared in answer to prayer.—*John Morison.*

Verse 8.—" *Thou . . . . forgavest them, though thou tookest vengeance of their inventions."* Because he loves the person, and hates only the sin; therefore he preserves the one, destroys only the other. This is all the fruit, to take away his sin. The covenant that is made with us in Christ is not a covenant made with works, but with persons; and therefore, though the works be often hateful, yet he goes on to love the persons; and that he may continue to love them, destroys out of them what he hates, but cutteth not them off. A member that is leprous or ulcerous, a man loves it as it is " his own flesh," Eph. v. 29, though he loathes the corruption and putrefaction that is in it; and therefore he doth not presently cut it off, but purgeth it daily, lays plasters to it to eat the corruption out: whereas a wart or even a wen that grows to a man's body, a man gets it cut off, for he doth not reckon it as his flesh.—*Thomas Goodwin.*

Verse 8.—" *Thou tookest vengeance of their inventions."* It is not a light punishment, but a " *vengeance,"* " he takes on their inventions; " to manifest that he hates sin as sin, and not because the worst persons commit it. Perhaps, had a profane man touched the ark, the hand of God had not so suddenly reached him. But when Uzzah, a man zealous for him, as may be supposed by his care for the support of the tottering ark, would step out of his place, he strikes him down for his disobedient action, by the side of the ark, which he would indirectly (as not being a Levite) sustain, 2 Sam. vi. 7. Nor did our Saviour so sharply reprove the Pharisees, and turn so short from them as he did from Peter, when he gave a carnal advice, and contrary to that wherein was to be the greatest manifestation of God's holiness, viz., the death of Christ, Mat. xvi. 23. He calls him Satan, a name sharper than the title of the devil's children, wherewith he marked the Pharisees, and given (besides him) to none but Judas, who made a profession of love to him, and was outwardly ranked in the number of his disciples. A gardener hates a weed the more for being in the bed with the most precious flowers.—*Stephen Charnock.*

Verse 8.—" *Thou tookest vengeance."* Sometimes the sins of a people may be such, that God will not pardon them as to temporal punishments; nay, not the godly themselves. Even they may have been partakers with others in their sins, or may have so provoked God themselves, and sinned in such a way as to cause his name to be blasphemed ; so that he is concerned in honour to bring some exemplary punishment upon them. So it was with David (2 Sam. xii.) : though he pardoned him as to the guilt of eternal death, saved his soul, and spared his life, which was forfeited to divine justice for the murder of Uriah ; yet the prophet announced that sharp afflictions must come on him, the sword must never " depart from his house," and the child begotten in adultery must die, and his wives must be given to his neighbours. So, in Psalm xcix. 8, it seems to be spoken of Moses himself, and other godly among the Israelites who died in the wilderness, and were not permitted to come into the land of promise, that *" God forgave them,"* yet *" took vengeance of their inventions."—John Collins* (—1687) *in the Morning Exercises.*

Verse 8.—" Vengeance of their inventions." It is remarkable, that in the preceding verses mention is made of Moses, and Aaron, and Samuel in a way which seems to imply that they were upon the Psalmist's mind when he uttered the declaration of the text. These three persons, all eminent for their piety, were also conspicuous for having suffered the Divine displeasure on account of their failings. Moses angered the Lord at the waters of strife, and he is not suffered to enter the promised land ; Aaron provoked the Divine anger by making the golden calf, and would have been destroyed, had not Moses by fervent intercession turned away the anger of the Lord lest he should destroy him ; so Samuel placed his sons over Israel, who walked not in his ways, and therefore God gave Israel a king, whose crimes caused the prophet to go down with sorrow to the grave.—*Stephen Bridge*, 1852.

HINTS TO PREACHERS.

Verse 1.—I. The doctrine of divine sovereignty enunciated. II. The apprehension of divine sovereignty demanded. It ought to be *spiritually* apprehended. God wants to be King in the *hearts* of men. All mortals must tremble before the Immortal; especially the wicked. III. The accessories of divine sovereignty hinted at. Sovereignty never forsakes the mercy-seat. Angels are represented on the mercy-seat, the ministers of sovereignty. IV. The effect of divine sovereignty described. Men should be " moved " to fear and obey the King before whom angels bow. Men should be moved to seek the mercy which angels study.—*William Durban.*

Verse 1.—" He sitteth between the cherubims," etc. I. Statement made ; where God dwells, on the mercy seat. To hear prayer, and confession, and to grant salvation. II. Effect produced—" Earth moved ; " to admiration, to prayer, to sorrowful contrition, to draw near, etc.—*E. G. Gange.*

Verse 2.—I. God is great in Zion *in himself*, all his perfections are here, which cannot be said of creation, or of his Law, or of the heaven of angels. II. Great in his works of *saving* sinners which he cannot do elsewhere. III. Great in his glory as displayed in *redemption* through his Son. IV. Great in his *love* to his redeemed.—*G. R.*

Verse 2.—" The Lord is great in Zion." I. In the condescension he displays —Zion is his " habitation," his " rest." II. In the glory he manifests—power and glory are in the sanctuary, Ps. lxiii. 2. III. In the assemblage he draws. " Every one in Zion appeareth before God," Ps. lxxxiv. 7. IV. In the blessings he imparts. V. In the authority he exerts.—*W. Jackson.*

Verse 3.—The terrors of the Lord, connected with holiness, and worthy of praise.

Verse 4.—I. Trace the process of the working of right principles through three stages—Love, Establishment, Execution. II. Illustrate from God's character and action. III. Apply to national, and to daily, life.—*C. D.*

Verse 5.—" Exalt the Lord your God." I. Why ? For what he is to you. For what he has done for you. For what he has told you. II. How ? In your affection. In your meditation. In your supplication. In your conversation. In your profession. In your consecration. In your co-operation. In your expectation.—*W. J.*

Verse 5.—I. The loyal enthusiasm of worship, it exalts the Lord. II. The humble diffidence of worship not aspiring to his exaltation, it kneels at his footstool. III. The good reason for worship.—" He is holy."—*C. D.*

Verses 6, 7.—I. Prayer offered. Moses the prophet, Aaron the priest, Samuel the ruler, "They called," &c. II. Prayer answered. "He answered them," "he spake," &c. III. Prayer vindicated. They kept the other testimonies, &c.—*G. R.*

Verse 7 (first clause).—The revelation of the cloud, or what God foreshadowed to Israel in the cloudy pillar. I. That God was willing to commune with man. 2. That sinful man could not see God and live. 3. That God should become incarnate, veiled in flesh as in the cloud. 4. That he should be their shelter, protector, guide. 5. That God manifest in the flesh should lead them to the Promised Land—Heaven. —*C. D.*

Verse 8.—Mercy and judgment, or the sea of glass mingled with fire.—*C. D.*

Verse 8.—Observe, I. That God's vengeance for sin does not prevent his forgiveness of sin ; and, II. That God's forgiveness of sin does not prevent his taking vengeance. —*Stephen Bridge.*

Verse 9.—"*The Lord our God.*" A very sweet topic will be found in the consideration of the questions, "In what respect is Jehovah ours ? and in what relations does he stand to his people ? "

PSALM C.

TITLE.—A Psalm of Praise ; *or rather* of thanksgiving. *This is the only Psalm bearing this precise inscription. It is all ablaze with grateful adoration, and has for this reason been a great favourite with the people of God ever since it was written. " Let us sing the Old Hundredth " is one of the everyday expressions of the Christian church, and will be so while men exist whose hearts are loyal to the Great King. Nothing can be more sublime this side heaven than the singing of this noble Psalm by a vast congregation. Watts' paraphrase, beginning " Before Jehovah's awful throne," and the Scotch " All people that on earth do dwell," are both noble versions ; and even Tate and Brady rise beyond themselves when they sing—*

> " With one consent let all the earth
> To God their cheerful voices raise."

In this divine lyric we sing with gladness the creating power and goodness of the Lord, even as before with trembling we adored his holiness.

EXPOSITION.

MAKE a joyful noise unto the LORD, all ye lands.

2 Serve the LORD with gladness : come before his presence with singing.

3 Know ye that the LORD he *is* God : *it is* he *that* hath made us and not we ourselves ; *we are* his people, and the sheep of his pasture.

4 Enter into his gates with thanksgiving, *and* into his courts with praise : be thankful unto him, *and* bless his name.

5 For the LORD *is* good ; his mercy *is* everlasting ; and his truth *endureth* to all generations.

1. " *Make a joyful noise unto the Lord, all ye lands.*" This is a repetition of the fourth verse of Psalm xcviii. The original word signifies a glad shout, such as loyal subjects give when their king appears among them. Our happy God should be worshipped by a happy people ; a cheerful spirit is in keeping with his nature, his acts, and the gratitude which we should cherish for his mercies. In every land Jehovah's goodness is seen, therefore in every land should he be praised. Never will the world be in its proper condition till with one unanimous shout it adores the only God. O ye nations, how long will ye blindly reject him ? Your golden age will never arrive till ye with all your hearts revere him.

2. " *Serve the Lord with gladness.*" " Glad homage pay with awful mirth." He is our Lord, and therefore he is to be served ; he is our gracious Lord, and therefore to be served with joy. The invitation to worship here given is not a melancholy one, as though adoration were a funeral solemnity, but a cheery, gladsome exhortation, as though we were bidden to a marriage feast. " *Come before his presence with singing.*" We ought in worship to realise the presence of God, and by an effort of the mind to approach him. This is an act which must to every rightly instructed heart be one of great solemnity, but at the same time it must not be performed in the servility of fear, and therefore we come before him, not with weepings and wailings, but with Psalms and hymns. Singing, as it is a joyful, and at the same time a devout, exercise, should be a constant form of approach to God. The measured, harmonious, hearty utterance of praise by a congregation of really devout persons is not merely decorous but delightful, and is a fit anticipation of the worship of heaven, where praise has absorbed prayer, and become the sole mode of adoration. How a certain society of brethren can find it in their hearts to forbid singing in public worship is a riddle which we cannot solve. We feel inclined to say with Dr. Watts—

> " Let those refuse to sing
> Who never knew our God ;
> But favourites of the heavenly king
> Must speak his praise abroad "

3. "*Know that the Lord he is God.*" Our ,worship must be intelligent. We ought to know whom we worship and why. "Man, know thyself," is a wise aphorism, yet to know our God is truer wisdom ; and it is very questionable whether a man can know himself until he knows his God. Jehovah is God in the fullest, most absolute, and most exclusive sense, he is God alone ; to know him in that character and prove our knowledge by obedience, trust, submission, zeal, and love is an attainment which only grace can bestow. Only those who practically recognise his Godhead are at all likely to offer acceptable praise. "*It is he that hath made us, and not we ourselves.*" Shall not the creature reverence its Maker ? Some men live as if they made themselves ; they call themselves " self-made men," and they adore their supposed creators ; but Christians recognise the origin of their being and their well-being, and take no honour to themselves either for being, or for being what they are. Neither in our first or second creation dare we put so much as a finger upon the glory, for it is the sole right and property of the Almighty. To disclaim honour for ourselves is as necessary a part of true reverence as to ascribe glory to the Lord. " Non nobis, domine ! " will for ever remain the true believer's confession. Of late philosophy has laboured hard to prove that all things have been developed from atoms, or have, in other words, made themselves : if this theory shall ever find believers, there will certainly remain no reason for accusing the superstitious of credulity, for the amount of credence necessary to accept this dogma of scepticism is a thousandfold greater than that which is required even by an absurd belief in winking Madonnas, and smiling Bambinos. For our part, we find it far more easy to believe that the Lord made us than that we were developed by a long chain of natural selections from floating atoms which fashioned themselves. "*We are his people, and the sheep of his pasture.*" It is our honour to have been chosen from all the world besides to be *his* own people, and our privilege to be therefore guided by his wisdom, tended by his care, and fed by his bounty. Sheep gather around their shepherd and look up to him ; in the same manner let us gather around the great Shepherd of mankind. The avowal of our relation to God is in itself praise ; when we recount his goodness we are rendering to him the best adoration ; our songs require none of the inventions of fictions, the bare facts are enough ; the simple narration of the mercies of the Lord is more astonishing than the productions of imagination. That we are the sheep of his pasture is a plain truth, and at the same time the very essence of poetry.

4. "*Enter into his gates with thanksgiving.*" To the occurrence of the word *thanksgiving* in this place the Psalm probably owes its title. In all our public service the rendering of thanks must abound ; it is like the incense of the temple, which filled the whole house with smoke. Expiatory sacrifices are ended, but those of gratitude will never be out of date. So long as we are receivers of mercy we must be givers of thanks. Mercy permits us to enter his gates ; let us praise that mercy. What better subject for our thoughts in God's own house than the Lord of the house. "*And into his courts with praise.*" Into whatever court of the Lord you may enter, let your admission be the subject of praise : thanks be to God, the innermost court is now open to believers, and we enter into that which is within the veil ; it is incumbent upon us that we acknowledge the high privilege by our songs. "*Be thankful unto him.*" Let the praise be in your heart as well as on your tongue, and let it all be for him to whom it all belongs. "*And bless his name.*" He blessed you, bless him in return ; bless his name, his character, his person. Whatever he does, be sure that you bless him for it : bless him when he takes away as well as when he gives ; bless him as long as you live, under all circumstances ; bless him in all his attributes, from whatever point of view you consider him.

5. "*For the Lord is good.*" This sums up his character and contains a mass of reasons for praise. He is good, gracious, kind, bountiful, loving ; yea, God is love. He who does not praise the good is not good himself. The kind of praise inculcated in the Psalm, viz. that of joy and gladness, is most fitly urged upon us by an argument from the goodness of God. "*His mercy is everlasting.*" God is not mere justice, stern and cold : he has bowels of compassion, and wills not the sinner's death. Towards his own people mercy is still more conspicuously displayed ; it has been theirs from all eternity, and shall be theirs world without end. Everlasting mercy is a glorious theme for sacred song. "*And his truth endureth to all generations.*" No fickle being is he, promising and forgetting. He has entered into covenant with his people, and he will never revoke it, nor alter the thing that has gone out of his lips. As our fathers found him faithful, so will our sons, and

their seed for ever.   A changeable God would be a terror to the righteous, they would have no sure anchorage, and amid a changing world they would be driven to and fro in perpetual fear of shipwreck.   It were well if the truth of divine faithfulness were more fully remembered by some theologians ; it would overturn their belief in the final fall of believers, and teach them a more consolatory system.   Our heart leaps for joy as we bow before One who has never broken his word or changed his purpose.

> " As well might he his being quit
> As break his promise or forget."

Resting on his sure word, we feel that joy which is here commanded, and in the strength of it we come into his presence even now, and speak good of his name.

EXPLANATORY NOTES AND QUAINT SAYINGS.

Title.—This is the only Psalm in the whole collection entitled " *A Psalm of Praise.*"   It is supposed to have received this appellation because peculiarly adapted, if not designed to be sung, when the *sacrifices of thanksgiving* were offered.   See Lev. vii. 12.   The Greeks think it was written by David, who here invites all the world to join with the Israelites in the service of God, whose divine sovereignty he here recognises.—*Samuel Burder.*

Whole Psalm.—If we are right in regarding Psalms xciii.—xcix. as forming one continuous series, one great prophetic oratorio, whose title is " Jehovah is King," and through which there runs the same great idea, this Psalm may be regarded as the doxology which closes the strain.   We find lingering in it notes of the same great harmony.   It breathes the same gladness ; it is filled with the same hope, that all nations shall bow down before Jehovah, and confess that he is God.— *J. J. S. Perowne.*

Whole Psalm.—This Psalm contains a promise of Christianity, as winter at its close contains the promise of spring.   The trees are ready to bud, the flowers are just hidden by the light soil, the clouds are heavy with rain, the sun shines in his strength ;   only a genial wind from the south is wanted to give a new life to all things.—" *The Speaker's Commentary,*" 1873.

Whole Psalm.—Luther would have immortalized his name had he done no more than written the majestic air and harmony to which we are accustomed to sing this Psalm, and which, when the mind is in a truly worshipping frame, seems to bring heaven down to earth, and to raise earth to heaven, giving us anticipations of the pure and sublime delights of that noble and general assembly in which saints and angels shall for ever celebrate the praises of God.—*Ingram Cobbin.*

Verse 2.—The first half of this verse is from Psalm ii. 11, only that instead of " *with fear,*" there, where the Psalmist has to do with fierce rebels, there is substituted here " *gladness* " or joy.—*F. W. Hengstenberg.*

Verse 2.—" *Serve the Lord with gladness.*"   It is a sign the oil of grace hath been poured into the heart " when the oil of gladness " shines on the countenance. Cheerfulness credits religion.—*Thomas Watson.*

Verse 2.—" *Serve the Lord.*"   It is our privilege to serve the Lord in all things. It is ours to please the Lord in loosing the latchet of a shoe ;   and to enjoy the ex- pression of his favour therein.   The servant of God is not serving at the same time another master ;   he has not been hired for occasional service ;   he abides in the service of his God, and cannot be about anything but his Master's business ;   he eats, he drinks, he sleeps, he walks, he discourses, he findeth recreation, all by the way of serving God.   " *Serve the Lord with gladness.*"   Can you bear to be waited upon by a servant who goes moping and dejected to his every task ?   You would rather have no servant at all, than one who evidently finds your service cheerless and irksome.—*George Bowen.*

Verse 3.—" *Know ye that the Lord he is God,*" &c.   From the reasons of this exhortation, learn, that such is our natural atheism, that we have need again and again to be instructed, *that the Lord is God ;* of whom, and through whom, and for whom are all things.—*David Dickson.*

Verse 3.—" *It is he that made us . . . we are his."* Now, the ground of God's property in all things is his creating of all. . . . Accordingly, you may observe in many scriptures, where the Lord's propriety is asserted, this, as the ground of it, is annexed : Ps. lxxxix. 11, 12, the heavens, the earth, the whole world, and all therein is thine. Why so ? " Thou hast founded them." And so are all the regions and quarters of the world, northern and southern, western and eastern ; for Tabor was on the west and Hermon on the east ; all are thine, for thou hast created them. So sea and land, Ps. xcv. 5. As all things measured by time, so time itself, the measure of all, Ps. lxxiv. 16, 17. " Thou hast made the light," *i.e.* the moon for the night and the sun for the day. He lays claim to all the climes of the earth, and all the seasons of the year, on this account ; he made them. This will be more evident and unquestionable, if we take notice of these particulars :—

1. He made all for himself. He was not employed by any to make it for another, for in that case sometimes the maker is not the owner ; but the Lord did employ himself in that great work, and for himself did he undertake and finish it. Prov. xvi. 4, Col. i. 15, 16.

2. He made all things of nothing, either without any matter at all, or without any but what himself had before made of nothing. A potter when he makes an earthenware vessel, if the clay be not his own which he makes it of, he is not the full owner of the vessel, though he formed it : " the form is his, the matter is another's ; " but since the Lord made all of nothing, or of such matter as himself had made, all is wholly his, matter and form, all entirely.

3. He made all without the help or concurrence of any other. There was none that assisted him, or did in the least co-operate with him in the work of creation. . . . Those that assist and concur with another in the making of a thing may claim a share in it ; but here lies no such claim in this case, where the Lord alone did all, alone made all. All is his only.

4. He upholds all things in the same manner as he created, continues the being of all things in the same way as he gave it. He does it of himself, without other support, without any assistant. All would fall into nothing in a moment, if he did not every moment bear them up. So that all things on this account have still their being from him every moment, and their well-being too, and all the means which conduce to it ; and therefore all are his own.—*David Clarkson.*

Verse 3.—" *It is he that made us."* The emperor Henry, while out hunting on the Lord's day called Quinquagesima, his companions being scattered, came unattended to the entrance of a certain wood ; and seeing a church hard by, he made for it, and feigning himself to be a soldier, simply requested a mass of the priest. Now that priest was a man of notable piety, but so deformed in person that he seemed a monster rather than a man. When he had attentively considered him, the emperor began to wonder exceedingly why God, from whom all beauty proceeds, should permit so deformed a man to administer his sacraments. But presently, when mass commenced, and they came to the passage, " *Know ye that the Lord he is God,"* which was chanted by a boy, the priest rebuked the boy for singing negligently, and said with a loud voice, " *It is he that hath made us, and not we ourselves."* Struck by these words, and believing the priest to be a prophet, the emperor raised him, much against his will, to the archbishopric of Cologne, which see he adorned by his devotion and excellent virtues.—*From " Roger of Wendover's (—1237) Flowers of History."*

Verse 3.—" *It is he that hath made us . . . we are his."* Many a one has drawn balsamic consolation from these words ; as for instance Melancthon when disconsolately sorrowful over the body of his son in Dresden on the 12th July, 1559. But in " *He made us and we are his,"* there is also a rich mine of comfort and of admonition, for the Creator is also the Owner, his heart clings to his creature, and the creature owes itself entirely to him, without whom it would not have had a being, and would not continue in being.—*F. Delitzsch.*

Verse 3.—" *He that made us,"* i.e. made us what we are, a people to himself ; as in Ps. xcv. 5, 1 Sam. xii. 6, and Deut. xxxii. 6. It was not we that made ourselves his (compare Ezek. xxix. 3). " *He* (and not we ourselves) *made us his people, and the flock whom he feeds."*—*Andrew A. Bonar.*

Verse 3.—" *Not we"* is added, because any share, on the part of the church, in effecting the salvation bestowed upon her, would weaken the testimony which this bears to the exclusive Godhead of the Lord.—*F. W. Hengstenberg.*

Verses 3, 5.—" *Know ye* " what God is in himself, and what he is to you. Knowledge is the mother of devotion, and of all obedience ; blind sacrifices will never please a seeing God. " Know " it, *i.e.* consider and apply it, and then you will be more close and constant, more inward and serious, in the worship of him. Let us know, then, these seven things concerning the Lord Jehovah, with whom we have to do in all the acts of religious worship.

1. " *That the Lord he is God,*" the only living and true God ; that he is a being infinitely perfect, self-existent, and self-sufficient, and the fountain of all being. 2. That he is our *Creator :* " *it is he that hath made us, and not we ourselves.*" We do not, we could not make ourselves ; it is God's prerogative to be his own cause ; our being is derived and depending. 3. That therefore *he is our rightful owner.* The Masorites, by altering one letter in the Hebrew, read it, " He made us, and his we are," or, " to him we belong." Put both the readings together, and we learn, that because God " made us, and not we ourselves," therefore we are not our own, but his. 4. That *he is our sovereign Ruler.* " *We are his people,*" or subjects, and he is our prince, our rector or governor, that gives laws to us as moral agents, and will call us to an account for what we do. 5. That *he is our bountiful Benefactor ;* we are not only his sheep whom he is entitled to, but " *the sheep of his pasture,*" whom he takes care of. 6. That he is a God of infinite mercy and good (verse 5) ; " *The Lord is good,*" and therefore doth good ; " his mercy is everlasting." 7. That he is a God of inviolable truth and faithfulness ; " *His truth endureth to all generations,*" and no word of his shall fall to the ground as antiquated or revoked.—*Matthew Henry.*

Verse 4.—" *Enter into his gates ;* " for to the most guilty are the gates of his church open.—*Francis Hill Tucker.*

Verse 4.—" *With thanksgiving.*" On the word תודה [the word used in Levit. vii. 12 for sacrifices of thanksgivings], Rabbi Menachen remarks : All sacrifices will be abolished ; but the sacrifice of thanksgiving will remain.—*George Phillips.*

Verse 4.—The former part of this Psalm may have been chanted by the precentor when the peace-offering was brought to the altar ; and this last verse may have been the response, sung by the whole company of singers, at the moment when fire was applied to the offering.—*Daniel Cresswell.*

Verse 5.—" *His mercy is everlasting.*" The everlasting unchangeable mercy of God, is the first motive of our turning to him, and of our continuing stedfast in his covenant, and it shall be the subject of unceasing praise in eternity. As the Lord is good, and his mercy everlasting, so the full perfection of these attributes in a perfect state will call forth praise unwearied from hearts that never faint.—*W. Wilson.*

HINTS TO PREACHERS.

Whole Psalm.—This is a bunch of the grapes of Eshcol. It is a taste of what is still the promised land. The Jewish church came to its perfection in the reign of Solomon, but a greater than Solomon is here. The perfection of the New Testament church is here anticipated. This Psalm teaches, I. *That there will be a joyful state of the whole world* (verse 1). 1. To whom the address is given—to " all lands," and all in those lands. 2. The subject of the address—" Make a joyful noise." What a doleful noise it *has* made ! 3. By whom the address is given, by him who secures what he commands. II. *That this joyful state of the whole world will arise from the enjoyment of the Divine Being* (verse 2). 1. Men have long tried to be happy without God. 2. They will find at last that their happiness is in God. The conversion of an individual in this respect is a type of the conversion of the world. III. *That this enjoyment of God will arise from a new relation to him* (verse 3). 1. Of knowledge on our part : he will be known as the Triune God, as a covenant God, as the God of salvation—as God. 2. Of rightful claim on his part ; (1) by right of creation—" He hath made us ; " (2) By right of redemption—" Ye were not a people.

but are now the people of God," &c.; " I have redeemed thee; thou art mine " (3) by right of preservation—" We are the sheep," &c. IV. *That this new relation to God will endear to us the ordinances of his house* (verse 4). 1. Of what the service will consist—" thanksgiving " and praise. 2. To whom it will be rendered. Enter into *his gates—his courts—be thankful unto him—bless his name. V. *That this service will be perpetual;* begun on earth, continued in heaven. This fact is founded— 1. Upon essential goodness. " For the Lord is good." 2. Upon everlasting mercy. " His mercy," etc. 3. Upon immutable truth. " His truth," etc.—*G. R.*

Verse 2.—" *Serve the Lord with gladness,*" 1. For he is the best of beings. 2. For his commandments are not grievous. 3. For he is your Saviour, as well as Creator; your friend, as well as Lord. 4. The angels, so much greater than yourself, know no reason why they should not serve him with gladness. 5. In serving him you serve yourself. 6. You make religion attractive. 7. You get fitness for heaven. —*George Bowen.*

Verse 2 (first clause).—A true heart, I. Is humble—*serves.* II. Is pious—" serve the Lord." III. Is active—*serves.* IV. Is consequently joyful—" with gladness."

Verse 2 (first clause).—" Serving the Lord with gladness." See " Spurgeon's Sermons," No. 769.

Verse 3.—" *Know ye that the Lord he is God.*" That you may be true amid superstition, hopeful in contrition, persistent in supplication, unwearied in exertion, calm in affliction, firm in temptation, bold in persecution, and happy in dissolution.—*W. J.*

Verse 3.—" *We are his people.*" We have been twice born, as all his people are. We love the society of his people. We are looking unto Jesus like his people. We are separated from the world as his people. We experience the trials of his people. We prefer the employment of his people. We enjoy the privileges of his people.—*W. J.*

Verse 4.—A Discourse of Thankfulness which is due to God for his benefits and blessings.—*A Sermon by Thomas Goodwin. Works, vol. ix., pp. 499—514. Nichol's edition.*

Verse 4.—I. The privileges of access. II. The duty of thankfulness. III. The reasons for enjoying both.

Verse 5.—I. The inexhaustible fount—the goodness of God. II. The everflowing stream—the mercy of God. III. The fathomless ocean—the truth of God. " O the depths ! "—*W. Durban.*

PSALM CI.

TITLE.—*A Psalm of David. This is just such a Psalm as the man after God's own heart would compose when he was about to become king in Israel. It is David all over, straightforward, resolute, devout; there is no trace of policy or vacillation,— the Lord has appointed him to be king, and he knows it, therefore he purposes in all things to behave as becomes a monarch whom the Lord himself has chosen. If we call this* THE PSALM OF PIOUS RESOLUTIONS, *we shall perhaps remember it all the more readily. After songs of praise a Psalm of practice not only makes variety, but comes in most fittingly. We never praise the Lord better than when we do those things which are pleasing in his sight.*

EXPOSITION.

I WILL sing of mercy and judgment : unto thee, O LORD, will I sing.

2 I will behave myself wisely in a perfect way. O when wilt thou come unto me ? I will walk within my house with a perfect heart.

3 I will set no wicked thing before mine eyes : I hate the work of them that turn aside ; *it* shall not cleave to me.

4 A froward heart shall depart from me : I will not know a wicked *person.*

5 Whoso privily slandereth his neighbour, him will I cut off : him that hath an high look and a proud heart will not I suffer.

6 Mine eyes *shall be* upon the faithful of the land, that they may dwell with me : he that walketh in a perfect way, he shall serve me.

7 He that worketh deceit shall not dwell within my house : he that telleth lies shall not tarry in my sight.

8 I will early destroy all the wicked of the land ; that I may cut off all wicked doers from the city of the LORD.

1. "*I will sing of mercy and judgment.*" He would extol both the love and the severity, the sweets and the bitters, which the Lord had mingled in his experience ; he would admire the justice and the goodness of the Lord. Such a song would fitly lead up to godly resolutions as to his own conduct, for that which we admire in our superiors we naturally endeavour to imitate. Mercy and judgment would temper the administration of David, because he had adoringly perceived them in the dispensations of his God. Everything in God's dealings with us may fittingly become the theme of song, and we have not viewed it aright until we feel we can sing about it. We ought as much to bless the Lord for the judgment with which he chastens our sin, as for the mercy with which he forgives it ; there is as much love in the blows of his hand as in the kisses of his mouth. Upon a retrospect of their lives instructed saints scarcely know which to be most grateful for—the comforts which have cheered them, or the afflictions which have purged them. "*Unto thee, O Lord, will I sing.*" Jehovah shall have all our praise. The secondary agents of either the mercy or the judgment must hold a very subordinate place in our memory, and the Lord alone must be hymned by our heart. Our soul's sole worship must be the lauding of the Lord. The Psalmist forsakes the minor key, which was soon to rule him in the one hundred and second Psalm, and resolves that, come what may, he will sing, and sing to the Lord too, whatever others might do.

2. "*I will behave myself wisely in a perfect way.*" To be holy is to be wise ; a perfect way is a wise way. David's resolve was excellent, but his practice did not fully tally with it. Alas ! he was not always wise or perfect, but it was well that it was in his heart. A king had need be both sage and pure, and, if he be not so in intent, when he comes to the throne, his after conduct will be a sad example to his people. He who does not even resolve to do well is likely to do very ill. House-holders, employers, and especially ministers, should pray for both wisdom and holiness, for they will need them both. "*O when wilt thou come unto me ?*"—an ejaculation, but not an interruption. He feels the need not merely of divine help,

but also of the divine presence, that so he may be instructed, and sanctified, and made fit for the discharge of his high vocation. David longed for a more special and effectual visitation from the Lord before he began his reign. If God be with us we shall neither err in judgment nor transgress in character ; his presence brings us both wisdom and holiness : away from God we are away from safety. Good men are so sensible of infirmity that they cry for help from God, so full of prayer that they cry at all seasons, so intense in their desires that they cry with sighs and groanings which cannot be uttered, saying, " O when wilt thou come unto me ? " " *I will walk within my house with a perfect heart.*" Piety must begin at home. Our first duties are those within our own abode. We must have a perfect heart at home, or we cannot keep a perfect way abroad. Notice that these words are a part of a song, and that there is no music like the harmony of a gracious life, no Psalm so sweet as the daily practice of holiness. Reader, how fares it with your family ? Do you sing in the choir and sin in the chamber ? Are you a saint abroad and a devil at home ? For shame ! What we are at home, that we are indeed. He cannot be a good king whose palace is the haunt of vice, nor he a true saint whose habitation is a scene of strife, nor he a faithful minister whose household dreads his appearance at the fireside.

3. " *I will set no wicked thing before mine eyes.*" I will neither delight in it, aim at it, nor endure it. If I have wickedness brought before me by others I will turn away from it, I will not gaze upon it with pleasure. The Psalmist is very sweeping in his resolve, he declines the least, the most reputable, the most customary form of evil—*no* wicked thing : not only shall it not dwell in his heart, but not even before his eyes, for what fascinates the eye is very apt to gain admission into the heart, even as Eve's apple first pleased her sight, and then prevailed over her mind and hand. " *I hate the work of them that turn aside.*" He was warmly against it ; he did not view it with indifference, but with utter scorn and abhorrence. Hatred of sin is a good sentinel for the door of virtue. There are persons in courts who walk in a very crooked way, leaving the high road of integrity ; and these, by short cuts, and twists, and turns, are often supposed to accomplish work for their masters which simple honest hearts are not competent to undertake; but David would not employ such, he would pay no secret service money, he loathed the practices of men who deviate from righteousness. He was of the same mind as the dying statesman who said, " Corruption wins not more than honesty." It is greatly to be deplored that in after years he did not keep himself clear in this matter in every case, though, in the main he did ; but what would he have been if he had not commenced with this resolve, but had followed the usual crooked policy of Oriental princes ? How much do we all need divine keeping ! We are no more perfect than David, nay, we fall far short of him in many things ; and, like him, we shall find need to write a Psalm of penitence very soon after our Psalm of good resolution. " *It shall not cleave to me.*" I will disown their ways, I will not imitate their policy : like dirt it may fall upon me, but I will wash it off, and never rest till I am rid of it. Sin, like pitch, is very apt to stick. In the course of our family history crooked things will turn up, for we are all imperfect, and some of those around us are far from being what they should be ; it must, therefore, be one great object of our care to disentangle ourselves, to keep clear of transgression, and of all that comes of it : this cannot be done unless the Lord both comes to us, and abides with us evermore.

4. " *A froward heart shall depart from me.*" He refers both to himself and to those round about him ; he would neither be crooked in heart himself, nor employ persons of evil character in his house ; if he found such in his court he would chase them away. He who begins with his own heart begins at the fountain head, and is not likely to tolerate evil companions. We cannot turn out of our family all whose hearts are evil, but we can keep them out of our confidence, and let them see that we do not approve of their ways. " *I will not know a wicked person.*" He shall not be my intimate, my bosom friend. I must know him as a man, or I could not discern his character ; but if I know him to be wicked, I will not know him any further, and with his evil I will have no communion. " To know " in Scripture means more than mere perception, it includes fellowship, and in that sense it is here used. Princes must disown those who disown righteousness ; if they know the wicked they will soon be known as wicked themselves.

5. " *Whoso privily slandereth his neighbour, him will I cut off.*" He had known so bitterly the miseries caused by slanderers that he intended to deal severely with such vipers when he came into power, not to revenge his own ills, but to prevent

others from suffering as he had done. To give one's neighbour a stab in the dark is one of the most atrocious of crimes, and cannot be too heartily reprobated, yet such as are guilty of it often find patronage in high places, and are considered to be men of penetration, trusty ones who have a keen eye, and take care to keep their lords well posted up. King David would lop the goodly tree of his state of all such superfluous boughs, " *Him that hath an high look and a proud heart will not I suffer.*" Proud, domineering, supercilious gentlemen, who look down upon the poor as though they were so many worms crawling in the earth beneath their feet, the Psalmist could not bear. The sight of them made him suffer, and therefore he would not suffer them. Great men often affect aristocratic airs and haughty manners, David therefore resolved that none should be great in his palace but those who had more grace and more sense than to indulge in such abominable vanity. Proud men are generally hard, and therefore very unfit for office ; persons of high looks provoke enmity and discontent, and the fewer of such people about a court the better for the stability of a throne. If all slanderers were now cut off, and all the proud banished, it is to be feared that the next census would declare a very sensible diminution of the population.

6. " *Mine eyes shall be upon the faithful of the land, that they may dwell with me.*" He would seek them out, engage their services, take care of them, and promote them to honour : this is a noble occupation for a king, and one which will repay him infinitely better than listening to the soft nothings of flatterers. It would be greatly for the profit of us all if we chose our servants rather by their piety than by their cleverness ; he who gets a faithful servant gets a treasure, and he ought to do anything sooner than part with him. Those who are not faithful to God will not be likely to be faithful to men ; if we are faithful ourselves, we shall not care to have those about us who cannot speak the truth or fulfil their promises ; we shall not be satisfied until all the members of our family are upright in character. " *He that walketh in a perfect way, he shall serve me.*" What I wish myself to be, that I desire my servant to be. Employers are to a great degree responsible for their servants, and it is customary to blame a master if he retains in his service persons of notorious character ; therefore, lest we become partakers of other men's sins, we shall do well to decline the services of bad characters. A good master does well to choose a good servant ; he may take a prodigal into his house for the sinner's good, but if he consults his own he will look in another quarter. Wicked nurses have great influence for evil over the minds of little children, and ungodly servants often injure the morals of the older members of the family, and therefore great care should be exercised that godly servants should be employed as far as possible. Even irreligious men have the sense to perceive the value of Christian servants, and surely their own Christian brethren ought not to have a lower appreciation of them.

7. " *He that worketh deceit shall not dwell within my house.*" He had power to choose his courtiers, and he meant to exercise it. Deceit among most Orientals is reckoned to be a virtue, and is only censured when it is not sufficiently cunning, and therefore comes to be found out ; it was therefore all the more remarkable that David should have so determinedly set his face against it. He could not tell what a deceitful man might be doing, what plots he might be contriving, what mischief he might be brewing, and therefore he resolved that he would at any rate keep him out of his house, that his palace might not become a den of villainy. Cheats in the market are bad enough, but deceivers at our own table we cannot bear. " *He that telleth lies shall not tarry in my sight.*" He would not have a liar within sight or hearing ; he loathed the mention of him. Grace makes men truthful, and creates in them an utter horror of everything approaching to falsehood. If David would not have a liar in his sight, much less will the Lord ; neither he that loves nor he who makes a lie shall be admitted into heaven. Liars are obnoxious enough on earth ; the saints shall not be worried with them in another world.

8. " *I will early destroy all the wicked of the land.*" At the very outset of his government he would promptly deal out justice to the worthless, he would leave them no rest, but make them leave their wickedness or feel the lash of the law. The righteous magistrate " beareth not the sword in vain." To favour sin is to discourage virtue ; undue leniency to the bad is unkindness to the good. When our Lord comes in judgment, this verse will be fulfilled on a large scale ; till then he sinks the judge in the Saviour, and bids men leave their sins and find pardon. Under the gospel we also are bidden to suffer long, and to be kind, even to the unthankful and the evil ; but the office of the magistrate is of another kind, and he

must have a sterner eye to justice than would be proper in private persons. Is he not to be a terror to evil doers? " *That I may cut off all wicked doers from the city of the Lord.*" Jerusalem was to be a holy city, and the Psalmist meant to be doubly careful in purging it from ungodly men. Judgment must begin at the house of God. Jesus reserves his scourge of small cords for sinners inside the temple. How pure ought the church to be, and how diligently should all those who hold office therein labour to keep out and chase out men of unclean lives. Honourable offices involve serious responsibilities; to trifle with them will bring our own souls into guilt, and injure beyond calculation the souls of others. Lord, come to us, that we, in our several positions in life, may walk before thee with perfect hearts.

EXPLANATORY NOTES AND QUAINT SAYINGS.

Whole Psalm.—The contents of this Psalm show that it was written at some remarkable period of David's life. Three different times have been fixed upon as respectively giving occasion for the solemn resolutions which are announced in it. The first is supposed to be when David, immediately after the death of Saul, succeeded to the government of a part of the kingdom; the second, when the whole kingdom was united under the dominion of David; and the third, when he removed the ark from the house of Obededom to Zion, and placed it in the vicinity of his own abode. It is certainly of little importance which of these periods we select, but the second verse of the Psalm has some appearance of relating to the last mentioned. The Psalmist here says, " *When will thou come to me?*" which seems to intimate that when he was to have the symbols of God's presence so near to him, he experienced a solemn sentiment respecting the holiness that was now more than ever incumbent upon him—a sentiment which induced him to form the sacred purposes and resolutions which he has specified. These purposes relate to the character of the persons whom he would select for his household, and those whom he would employ in carrying on his government, which appeared to be more firmly established by the divine condescension that was manifested to him, in having the earthly residence of God placed so near to himself. It was quite in agreement with David's character to form purposes of more fervent and steadfast obedience, in proportion to the advantages and favours which the divine goodness bestowed upon him.—*William Walford.*

Whole Psalm.—This Psalm has been appropriately called " The Householder's Psalm;" and assuredly if every master of a family would regulate his household by these rules of the conscientious Psalmist, there would be a far greater amount, not merely of domestic happiness and comfort, but of fulfilment of the serious and responsible duties which devolve on the respective members of a household. David in some measure may be supposed to speak of the regulation of a royal court and household; and of course with such we in our humbler sphere can have but little in common; yet though there may not be the same duties and the same requirements, yet the same principles should actuate all alike, and the same virtues that adorn the lowlier station may shed a radiance even on the highest.—*Barton Bouchier.*

Whole Psalm.—This is the Psalm which the old expositors used to designate " The Mirror for Magistrates;" and an excellent mirror it is. It would mightily accelerate the coming of the time when every nation shall be Christ's possession, and every capital a " City of the Lord," if all magistrates could be persuaded to dress themselves by it every time they go forth to perform the functions of their godlike office. When Sir George Villiers became the favourite and prime minister of King James, Lord Bacon, in a beautiful Letter of Advice, counselled him to take this Psalm for his rule in the promotion of courtiers. " In those the choice had need be of honest and faithful servants, as well as of comely outsides who can bow the knee and kiss the hand. King David (Psalm ci. 6, 7) propounded a rule to himself for the choice of his courtiers. He was a wise and a good king; and a wise and a good king shall do well to follow such a good example; and if he find any to be faulty, which perhaps cannot suddenly be discovered, let him take on him this resolution as King David did, ' *There shall no deceitful person dwell in my house.*' "

It would have been well both for the Philosopher and the Favourite if they had been careful to walk by this rule.—*William Binnie.*

Whole Psalm.—Eyring, in his " Life of Ernest the Pious " (Duke of Saxe-Gotha), relates that he sent an unfaithful minister a copy of the 101st Psalm, and that it became a proverb in the country when an official had done anything wrong : He will certainly soon receive the prince's Psalm to read.—*F. Delitzsch.*

Whole Psalm.—The 101st Psalm was one beloved by the noblest of Russian princes, Vladimir Monomachos ; and by the gentlest of English reformers, Nicholas Ridley. But it was its first leap into life that has carried it so far into the future. It is full of a stern exclusiveness, of a noble intolerance, not against theological error, not against uncourtly manners, not against political insubordination, but against the proud heart, the high look, the secret slanderer, the deceitful worker, the teller of lies. These are the outlaws from king David's court ; these are the rebels and heretics whom he would not suffer to dwell in his house or tarry in his sight.—*Arthur Penrhyn Stanley, in " Lectures on the History of the Jewish Church,"* 1870.

Whole Psalm.—Such a hymn of praise as the grand doxology of Psalm xcix. could not die away without an echo. Accordingly Psalm c. may be regarded as forming the chorus of the church, and this as taking up and applying that part of the doxology which celebrated the *present* manifestation of the " King in his beauty." —*Alfred Edersheim.*

Whole Psalm.—Mr. Fox reports that Bishop Ridley often read and expounded this Psalm to his household, hiring them with money to get it by heart.—*Thomas Lye, in " The Morning Exercises."*

Verse 1.—" *I will sing.*" If thou bestowest mercies upon me ; or if thou bringest any judgment upon me ; before thee, O Lord, will I sing my hymn for all.—*Chaldee Paraphrase.*

Verse 1.—" *I will sing.*" The manner of expression imports a *cordial* resolution ; heart and will are engaged in it ; there is twice *I will* in the text. The manner of expression imports a *humble* resolution ; I cannot sing of merit ; but I will sing of mercy, and through mercy I will sing of mercy. To sing of mercy must be a humble song, for mercy towards a miserable sinner is a melting word ; and to sing of judgment must be a humble song, for judgment in every sense is an awful word. The manner of the expression imports a *skilful* harper, a dexterous musician, even in a spiritual sense ; he knew what should be the subject of the song, and he says, " I will sing of mercy and judgment ; " and he knew what should be the object of the song, or to whom it should be sung, and therefore says, " To thee, O Lord, I will sing " ; he knew who should be the singer, and therefore says, " I will " do it ; he knew what should be the manner ; and therefore says, " I will sing of mercy and judgment ; to thee, O Lord, will I *sing.*" It is before the Lord he resolves to sing, as he did before the ark, which was a type of Christ ; and so is it a song to the praise of God in Christ. The manner of the expression imports *a firm, fixed, and constant* resolution ; so the redoubling of it seems to import ; " I will sing, I will sing." He had a mind this exercise of singing should not go down, but be his continual trade, " I will sing, I will sing ; " I will sing on earth and I will sing in heaven ; I will sing in time and I will sing in eternity. And, indeed, all on whom the spirit of praise and gratitude is poured out resolve never to give over singing. . . . David had heard once, yea, twice, that mercy as well as power belongs to the Lord ; and therefore not only once, but twice in a breath he resolves to sing unto the Lord. The word hath a great deal of elegancy and emphasis in it ; I will sing of mercy, I will sing of judgment ; O, I will sing, O Lord, I will sing ; and I will sing unto thee.—*Ralph Erskine.*

Verse 1.— This song of the sweet singer of Israel is peculiar to earth ; they do not sing of " *judgment*" in heaven, for there is no sin there ; they do not sing of " *mercy* " in hell, for there is no propitiation for sin there. Time was when the song was not heard even on earth ; for in Paradise man walked in innocence, and walking in innocence he walked in the light of his Father's face.—*Hugh Stowell*, 1856.

Verse 1.— " *I will sing of mercy and judgment.*" It comes all to this, as if the Psalmist should say, " I will sing of *merciful judgments* ; " for judgment is mercy, as it is the matter of the song : or, to take them separately, " I will sing of mercy *in* mercies, and, I will sing of mercy *in* judgment : " and so I will sing of my blinks and of my showers ; I will sing both of my cloudy and my clear day ; both of my ups and downs.—*Ralph Erskine.*

Verse 1.—" *Mercy and judgment.*" As the badge of the ship S. Paul sailed in was *Castor and Pollux*, twin brothers, so the badge of this Psalm is *Mercy and Judgment*, inseparable companions ; of whom it may be said, as our prophet sometimes spake of Saul and Jonathan, " They were lovely and pleasant in their lives, and in their deaths they were not divided." These are the two brightest stars in the firmament of majesty ; the two fairest flowers, and choicest jewels in the imperial crown ; like the carnation and the lily, the ruby and the sapphire, or the carbuncle and the diamond, yielding a mutual and interchangeable lustre each to other. They resemble not unfitly the two supporters of the king's arms, or the two seraphim stretching out their golden wings over the propitiatory, or the white and red rose in the same escutcheon.

We read that Solomon set up two goodly pillars in the porch of the temple, the one called *Jachin*, the other *Boaz*, which signify stability and strength : such pillars of the state are *mercy and judgment*. The throne of the King is borne up by them, as Solomon's was with lions of ivory on each side. Therefore, as in one place it is said that " *the throne is established by justice* " (Prov. xvi. 12) ; so in another that it is " *upheld by mercy* " (Prov. xx. 28) ; justice being as the bones and sinews in the body politic, and mercy as the veins and arteries. They are the two hands of action, the two eyes of virtue, and the two wings of honour. And as the eyes, if they be rightly set, do both look one way ; so do *mercy and judgment*, however in the apprehension of the vulgar they seem to look contrary ways. And as the treble and the bass accord best in music ; so do they in managing the commonwealth. Wherefore David promiseth to make them both sound tunable in his song without jar or discord : " *I will sing of mercy and judgment.*" . . . .

As *mercy* is here set in the first place ; so shall the sentence of mercy and absolution be first pronounced at the last day. And it is a laudable custom of princes, at their first entrance to their kingdoms, to shew mercy, by hearing the mourning of the prisoner, and delivering the children of death, by loosing the bands of wickedness, by taking off the heavy burdens, by letting the oppressed go free, and by breaking every yoke of former extortions. Thus, our prophet himself, as soon as the crown was settled on his head, made inquiry if there remained yet alive any of the house of Saul, on whom he might shew mercy (2 Sam. ix.). O how fair a thing is this mercy in the time of anguish and trouble ! It is like a cloud of rain that cometh in the time of drought. But this *mercy*, here spoken of in the first part of our prophet's song, stretcheth further ; unfolding itself in *clemency*, in *courtesy*, and in *compassion*. In *clemency*, by pardoning malefactors ; in *compassion*, by relieving the afflicted ; in *courtesy*, towards all.—*George Hakewill*, or *Hakewell*, 1579–1649.

Verse 1.—" *Mercy and judgment.*" What is the history of every poor sinner, plucked as a brand from the fire, and brought to heaven in peace at last, but a history of " mercy and judgment ? " Judgment first awakes to terror and to fear ; mercy meets the poor, trembling, returning prodigal, and falls on his neck, and kisses, and forgives. Then, through all his chequered course, God hems up his way with judgment, that he may not wander, and yet brightens his path with mercy, that he may not faint. Is there a child of God that can look into the varied record of his heart or of his outward history, and not see goodness and severity, severity and goodness, tracking him all his journey through ? Has he ever had a cup so bitter that he could say, " There is no mercy here " ? Has he ever had a lot so bright that he could say, " There is no chastisement or correction here " ? Has he ever had any bad tidings, and there have been no good tidings set over against them to relieve them ? Has he ever had a sky so dark that he could see in it no star, or a cloud so unchequered that he could trace no rainbow of promise there ? . . .

What a beautifully woven web of judgment and mercy does every man's secret history, in his way through the wilderness of life to the land of promise, present ! and how good, and how wholesome, and how kindly, and how gracious is this blessed intermingling of both ! How do we need the judgment, to keep us humble and watchful and pure ! and how do we need the mercy, to keep us hopeful, and to nerve our efforts, and to stir our hearts, and to sustain us in patience, amid life's battle and struggle, and disappointment and vexation ! Oh, how good it is for us, that we should thus, therefore, have the rod and staff together—the rod to chasten, and the staff to solace and sustain ! How good it is for us, that we should have to " *sing of mercy and judgment* " ! And yet, what is judgment itself, but mercy with a sterner aspect ? And what are the chidings of judgment, but the sterner tones of the voice of a Father's love ? For even judgment is one of the " all things " that " work together for good to them that love God, to them that are the called according to his purpose."—*Hugh Stowell.*

Verse 1.—" *Mercy and judgment.*" God intermixeth mercy with affliction: he steeps his sword of justice in the oil of mercy; there was no night so dark, but Israel had a pillar of fire in it; there is no condition so dismal, but we may see a pillar of fire to give light. If the body be in pain, conscience is in peace,—there is mercy: affliction is for the prevention of sin,—there is mercy. In the ark there was a rod and a pot of manna, the emblem of a Christian's condition, mercy interlined with judgment.—*Thomas Watson.*

Verse 2.—" *I will behave myself wisely.*" The first thing he vows touching himself, is wise behaviour; prudence, not sapience; not wise contemplation, but wise action. It is not wise thoughts, or wise speaking, or wise writing, or wise gesture and countenance, will serve the turn, but wise behaviour; the former are graceful, but the other needful. For as the apostle saith of godliness, "Having a show of godliness, but denying the power thereof;" so certainly there are those who in point of wisdom and sufficiency that do little or nothing thoroughly, but *magno conatu nugas*, they make much ado about small matters; using all the perspectives of shifting they can devise to make an empty *superficies* seem a body that hath depth and bulk.—*George Hakewill.*

Verse 2.—" *I will walk.*" Walking is a word often used in Holy Scripture, and especially by our prophet in this book of the Psalms; yet more often figuratively than properly. It shall not be amiss, then, out of the property and nature of it, to consider the duties included and implied in it. The natural acts of it, then, are three; *motion, progress,* and *moderation.* As it includes *motion,* so is it opposed to lying, or standing, or sitting; as it includes *progress in motion,* so is it opposed to jumping or capering up and down in the same place; as it includes *moderation* in a *progressive motion,* so is it opposed to violent running.—*George Hakewill.*

Verse 2.—" *I will walk within my house.*" Much, though not all of the power of godliness, lies within doors. It is in vain to talk of holiness if we can bring no letters testimonial from our holy walking with our relations. Oh, it is sad when they that have reason to know us best, by their daily converse with us, do speak least for our godliness! Few so impudent as to come naked into the streets: if men have anything to cover their naughtiness they will put it on when they come abroad. But what art thou within doors? What care and conscience to discharge thy duty to thy near relations? He is a bad husband that hath money to spend among company abroad, but none to lay in provisions to keep his family at home. And can he be a good Christian that spends all his religion abroad, and leaves none for his nearest relations at home? that is, a great zealot among strangers and little or nothing of God comes from him in his family? Yea, it were well if some that gain the reputation of Christians abroad, did not fall short of others that pretend not to profession in those moral duties which they should perform to their relations. There are some who are great strangers to profession, who yet are loving and kind in their way to their wives. What kind of professors then are they who are dogged and currish to the wife of their bosom? who by their tyrannical lording it over them embitter their spirit, and make them cover the Lord's altar with tears and weeping? There are wives to be found that are not clamorous, peevish and froward to their husbands, who yet are far from a true work of grace in their hearts; do they then walk as becomes holiness who trouble the whole house with their violent passions? There are servants who from the authority of a natural conscience, are kept from railing and reviling language, when reproved by their masters, and shall not grace keep pace with nature? Holy David knew very well how near this part of a saint's duty lies to the very heart of godliness; and therefore, when he makes his solemn vow to walk holily before God, he instanceth this, as one stage wherein he might eminently discover the graciousness of his spirit; " *I will walk within my house with a perfect heart.*"—*William Gurnall.*

Verse 2.— " *Within my house.*" It is easier for most men to walk with a perfect heart in the *church,* or even in the *world,* than in their *own families.* How many are as meek as lambs among *others,* when at *home* they are *wasps* or *tigers.*—*Adam Clarke.*

Verse 2.— " *Within my house with a perfect heart.*" Even in our best directed establishments, as well as in private families, cultivation is still in a great measure confined to intellect alone; and the *direct* exercise and training of the moral and religious sentiments and affections are rarely thought of as essential to their full and vigorous development. Moral precepts are, no doubt, offered in abundance; but these address themselves chiefly to the intellect. We must not be satisfied with merely exclaiming, " Be kind, just, and affectionate," when perhaps at the very moment we are counteracting the effect of the advice by our own opposite conduct. "She told me not to lie," said Guy Rivers in speaking of his mother, " and she set me the example herself by frequently deceiving my father, and teaching me to disobey and deceive him." Conduct like this is more common in real life than is supposed, although generally less flagrant in degree. Parents and teachers indeed too often forget that the sentiments *feel* and *do not reason*, and that, consequently, even a stupid child may, by the instinctive operation of its moral nature at once detect and revolt at the immorality of practices, the true character of which its *reason* is unable to penetrate or expose. It is one of the most effectual methods of cultivating and exciting the moral sentiments in children, to set before them the manifestations of these in our habitual conduct. . . .

What kind of moral duties does the parent encourage, who, recommending kindness, openness, and justice, *tricks* the child into the confession of a fault, and then basely punishes it, having previously promised forgiveness ? And how is openness best encouraged—by practising it in conduct, or by neglecting it in practice, and prescribing it in words ? Is it to be cultivated by thrusting suspicions in the face of honest intentions ? And how is justice to be cultivated by a guardian who *speaks* about it, recommends it, and *in practice* charges each of four pupils the whole fare of a hackney-coach ? Or what kind of moral education is that which says, " Do as I bid you, and I will give you sweetmeats or money, or I will tell your mama how good you were," holding out the lowest and most selfish propensities as the motives to moral conduct ? Did space permit, I might indeed pursue the whole round of moral and religious duties, and ask similar questions at each. But it is needless. These examples will suffice ; and I give them, not as applicable generally either to parents or teachers, but simply as individual instances from among both, which have come within the sphere of my own knowledge, and which bear directly upon the principle under discussion.—*Andrew Combe, in " The Principles of Physiology,"* 1836.

Verse 3.—" *Wicked thing.*" The original hath it, if we will render it word for word, " *I will set no word of Belial before mine eyes.*" But *word* is figuratively there put for *thing ;* as likewise Ps. xli. 8 ; and so is it rendered both by *Montanus* in the margin, and in the text by *Junius ;* howbeit, in his comment upon this Psalm, he precisely follows the original, applying it against sycophants and flatterers, the mice and moths of court.—*George Hakewill.*

Verse 3.—" *I hate the work of them that turn aside.*" Mr. Schultens hath shown in his commentary on Prov. vii. 25 that שׂטֵה hath a much stronger and more significant meaning than that of mere *turning aside ;* and that it is used of an unruly horse, that champs upon the bit through his fiery impatience ; and when applied to a bad man, denotes one impatient of all restraint, of unbridled passions, and that is headstrong and ungovernable in the gratification of them, trampling on all the obligations of religion and virtue. Such as these are the deserved objects of the hatred of all good men, whose criminal deviations and presumptuous crimes they detest ; none of which " *shall cleave to them ;* " they will not harbour the love of, or inclination to, them, nor habitually commit them, nor encourage the practice of them. Persons of this character are too frequently about the courts of princes, but it is their honour and interest, as far as ever they can, to discountenance them.—*Samuel Chandler.*

Verse 3.—" *It shall not cleave to me.*" A bird may light upon a man's house, but he may choose whether she shall nestle or breed there, or no : and the devil or his instruments may represent a wicked object to a man's sight ; but he may choose whether he will entertain or embrace it or no. For a man to set wicked things before his eyes is nothing else but to sin of set purpose, to set himself to sin, or to sell himself to sin, as Ahab did, 1 Kings xxi.—*George Hakewill.*

Verse 3.—" *It shall not cleave to me.*" A wicked plan or purpose is thus represented as having a tendency to fasten itself on a man, or to " *stick to him* "—as pitch or wax, or a *burr* does.—*Albert Barnes.*

Verse 4.—" *A froward heart.*" The original sense of עִקֵּשׁ is *torsit, contorsit*, to twist together, and denotes, when applied to men, persons of a perverse, subtle disposition, that can twist and twine themselves into all manner of shapes, and who have no truth and honour to be depended on.—*Samuel Chandler.*

Verse 4.—" *A froward heart.*" By which I understand " *from-wardness* "—giving way to sudden impulses of anger, or quick conception, and casting it forth in words or deeds of impetuous violence.—*Thomas Chalmers.*

Verse 5.—" *Privily slandereth* "—literally, he that *tongueth* his neighbour secretly. " *Will I not suffer,*" is properly, " him I *cannot,*" *i.e.,* cannot live with, cannot bear about me, as the same verb is used in Isai. i. 13.—*Henry Cowles.*

Verse 5.—" *Him that hath an high look.*" Pride will sit and show itself in the eyes as soon as anywhere. A man is seen what he is *in oculis, in poculis, in loculis* (in his eyes, his cups, and his resorts) say the Rabbins. See Proverbs vi. 17.—*John Trapp.*

Verse 5.—" *Proud heart.*" From רָחַב *latus* or *dilatatus est,* is the noun רְחַב here, *broad,* or *wide,* or *large ;* and being applied to the *heart* or *soul,* it notes *largeness of desires.*—*Henry Hammond.*

Verse 5.—Detraction, ambition, and avarice are three weeds which spring and flourish in the rich soil of a court. The Psalmist declareth his resolution to undertake the difficult task of eradicating them for the benefit of his people, that Israelites might not be harassed by informers, or repressed by insolent and rapacious ministers. Shall we imagine these vices less odious in the eyes of that King whose character was composed of humility and charity ; or will Christ admit those tempers into the court of heaven, which David determined to exclude from his court upon earth ? —*George Horne.*

Verses 5—10.—Perfect, as prophetic of Christ, is the delineation of his associates and disciples. The perverse ; the evil-doers ; the slanderers, and the proud found no fellowship with him. There were no common principles ; no bond of union between them. There was " a gulph" interposed, as in the parable, which they could not pass ; and what they saw of Christ, they beheld only from a distance. Nor even now, as then, can " the deceitful " dwell in Christ's " house "—his holy temple ; nor the man of " lies be established " by his love and favour. They must renounce their vices before they can be admitted to his covenant ; or, however they may claim communion with *him,* he in return can have no sympathy with them.—*William Hill Tucker.*

Verse 6.—" *Mine eyes shall be upon the faithful.*" There is an eye of *search,* and an eye of *favour :* the one is for the seeking and finding them out, that they may serve ; the other for countenancing of their persons, and rewarding of their service.—*George Hakewill.*

Verse 6.—" *Mine eyes shall be upon the faithful of the land,*" etc. Christ's eyes are upon faithful persons, or faithful ministers of the word, who preach the Gospel faithfully, administer the ordinances truly, are faithful to the souls of men in watching over them, reproving and exhorting them ; his eyes are upon them to keep and preserve them, and to honour and reward them with a crown of life that fadeth not away. His eyes are also on faithful members of churches, such who truly believe in him, who hold fast the faithful word, and keep close to his worship and ordinances ; his eyes are upon them, to show favour to them, to bestow blessings upon them, and to protect and defend them, and to preserve them from perishing : " *That they may dwell with me ;* " or, *sit with me ;* at his table, or at the council-board, or in judgment, and assist him in the affairs of government ; so such as are faithful shall dwell with Christ both here and hereafter ; they dwell in him and with him by faith, and have communion with him ; they dwell in his house below, and shall dwell with him above for evermore.—*John Gill.*

Verse 6.—" *He that walketh in a perfect way, he shall serve me.*" Art thou a godly master ? When thou takest a servant into thy house, choose for God as well as thyself. Remember there is a work for God to be done by thy servant as well as by thyself : and shall he be fit for thy turn that is not for God's ? Thou desirest the work should prosper thy servant takes in hand, dost thou not ? And what ground hast thou, from the promise, to hope that the work should prosper in his hand that sins all the while he is doing of it ? " The ploughing of the wicked is sin," Prov. xxi. 4. A godly servant is a greater blessing than we think on. He can work, and set God on work also, for his master's good : Gen. xxiv. 12, " O Lord God of my master Abraham, I pray thee, send me good speed this day, and shew kindness unto my master." And sure he did his master as much service by his prayer as by his prudence in that journey. If you were but to plant an orchard, you would get the best fruit trees, and not cumber your ground with crabs. There is more loss in a graceless servant in the house than a fruitless tree in the orchard. Holy David observed, while he was at Saul's court, the mischief of having wicked and ungodly servants, for with such was that unhappy king compassed, that David compares his court to the profane and barbarous heathens', among whom there was scarce more wickedness to be found : Ps. cxx. 5. " Woe is me, that I sojourn in Mesech, that I dwell in the tents of Kedar ; " that is, among those who were as prodigiously wicked as any there. And no doubt but this made this gracious man in his banishment, before he came to the crown, having seen the evil of a disordered house, to resolve what he would do when God should make him the head of such a royal family. " *He that worketh deceit shall not dwell within my house : he that telleth lies shall not tarry in my sight.*" He instanceth those sins, not as if he would spend all his zeal against these, but because he had observed them principally to abound in Saul's court, by which he had suffered so much, as you may perceive by Psalm cxx.— *William Gurnall.*

Verse 8.—" *That I may cut off all wicked doers from the city of the Lord.*" As the kingdom of David was only a faint image of the kingdom of Christ, we ought to set Christ before our view ; who, although he may bear with many hypocrites, yet as he will be the judge of the world, will at length call them all to an account, and separate the sheep from the goats. And if it seems to us that he tarries too long, we should think of that morning which will suddenly dawn, that all filthiness being purged away, true purity may shine forth.—*John Calvin.*

Verse 8.—" *Early.*" From some incidental notices of Scripture (2 Sam. xv. 2 ; Ps. ci. 8 ; Jer. xxi. 12), it has been inferred that judges ordinarily held their sessions in the morning. In a climate like that of Palestine, such a custom would be natural and convenient. It is doubtful, however, whether this passage expresses anything more than the promptness and zeal which a righteous judge exercises in the discharge of his duty.—*E. P. Barrows, in " Biblical Geography and Antiquities."*

Verse 8.—The holy vow " *to destroy all the wicked of the land,*" and to " *cut off all wicked doers from the city of the Lord,*" must begin at our own hearts as his sanctuary, the temple of the Holy Ghost.—*Alfred Edersheim.*

HINTS TO PREACHERS.

Whole Psalm.—This is a Psalm of wills and shalls. There are nine wills and five shalls. Resolutions should be made, 1. With deliberation ; not, therefore, upon trifling matters. 2. With reservation. " If the Lord will," etc. 3. With dependence upon divine strength for their fulfilment.—*G. R.*

Verse 1.—I. The sweet work that is resolved upon is to " *sing.*" II. The sweet singer that thus resolves, namely, David, " *I* will sing." III. The sweet subject of the song, " *mercy and judgment.*" IV. The sweet object of this praise, and the manner in which he would sing it—" *Unto thee, O Lord, will I sing.*"—*Ralph Erskine.*

Verse 1.—What there is in mercy that affords ground of singing. I. The freeness and undeservedness of mercy. II. The unexpectedness of mercy. When I was expecting a frown I got a smile ; when I was expecting nothing but wrath, I got a glance of love ; instead of a stroke of vengeance, I got a view of glory. III. The seasonableness of mercy is a ground of singing—grace to help in time of need. IV. The greatness and riches of mercy make the recipients thereof sing. V. The sweetness of mercy makes them sing. VI. The sureness and firmness of mercy make them sing—" The sure mercies of David."—*From Ralph Erskine's Sermon, entitled " The Militant's Song."*

Verse 1.—I. The different conditions of the righteous man in this life. Not all mercy, nor all judgment, but mercy and judgment. II. His one duty and privilege in reference to them : " I will sing," etc. 1. Because they are both from God. 2. Because they are both from love. 3. Because they are both for present good. 4. Because they are both preparative for the heavenly rest.—*G. R.*

Verses 1, 2.—The blending of song with holy living. The bell of praise and the pomegranate of holy fruitfulness should both adorn the Lord's priests.

Verse 2.—I. The end desired: "To behave wisely," etc.; consistency of conduct. II. The means employed: "When wilt thou come," etc.; only when God is with us we walk in a perfect way. III. The test proposed: "Within my house," where I am most myself and am best known.—*G. R.*

Verse 2.—The wisdom of holiness. 1. In selecting our sphere of duty. 2. In timing, arranging, and balancing duties. 3. In managing others according to their tempers. 4. In avoiding disputes with adversaries. 5. In administering rebuke, giving alms, rendering advice, etc.; the blending of the serpent with the dove.

Verse 2.—"*O when wilt thou come unto me?*" A devout ejaculation. I. Revealing the Psalmist's need of the divine presence in order to holiness. II. His intense longing. III. His full expectation. IV. His thorough appreciation of the condescending visit.

Verse 2 (*last clause*).—Home piety. Its duty, excellence, influence, sphere, and reward. Note also the change of heart and firmness of purpose necessary to it.

Verse 3.—I. The sight of wickedness is to be avoided: "I will set no wicked thing," etc. II. When seen it is to be loathed: "I hate," etc. III. When felt it is to be repudiated. It may touch me, but "it shall not cleave to me."

Verse 4.—The need of extreme care in the choice of our intimates.

Verse 5.—The detestable nature of slander, hurting three persons at once—the speaker, hearer, and person slandered.

Verse 6.—The duty of believers who are wealthy to encourage and employ persons of pious character.

Verse 8.—The work of the great King when he comes in judgment.

PSALM CII.

SUBJECT.—*This is a patriot's lament over his country's distress. He arrays himself in the griefs of his nation as in a garment of sackcloth, and casts her dust and ashes upon his head as the ensigns and causes of his sorrow. He has his own private woes and personal enemies, he is moreover sore afflicted in body by sickness, but the miseries of his people cause him a far more bitter anguish, and this he pours out in an earnest, pathetic lamentation. Not, however, without hope does the patriot mourn; he has faith in God, and looks for the resurrection of the nation through the omnipotent favour of the Lord; this causes him to walk among the ruins of Jerusalem, and to say with hopeful spirit, " No, Zion, thou shalt never perish. Thy sun is not set for ever; brighter days are in store for thee." It is in vain to enquire into the precise point of Israel's history which thus stirred a patriot's soul, for many a time was the land oppressed, and at any of her sad seasons this song and prayer would have been a most natural and appropriate utterance.*

TITLE.—*A prayer of the afflicted, when he is overwhelmed, and poureth out his complaint before the* LORD. *This Psalm is a prayer far more in spirit than in words. The formal petitions are few, but a strong stream of supplication runs from beginning to end, and like an under-current, finds its way heavenward through the moanings of grief and confessions of faith which make up the major part of the Psalm. It is a prayer of the afflicted, or of " a sufferer," and it bears the marks of its parentage; as it is recorded of Jabez, that " his mother bore him with sorrow," so may we say of this Psalm; yet as Rachel's Benoni, or child of sorrow, was also her Benjamin, or son of her right hand, so is this Psalm as eminently expressive of consolation as of desolation. It is scarcely correct to call it a penitential Psalm, for the sorrow of it is rather of one suffering than sinning. It has its own bitterness, and it is not the same as that of the Fifty-first. The sufferer is afflicted more for others than for himself, more for Zion and the house of the Lord, than for his own house. When he is overwhelmed, or sorely troubled, and depressed. The best of men are not always able to stem the torrent of sorrow. Even when Jesus is on board, the vessel may fill with water and begin to sink. And poureth out his complaint before the* LORD. *When a cup is overwhelmed or turned bottom over, all that is in it is naturally poured out; great trouble removes the heart from all reserve, and causes the soul to flow out without restraint; it is well when that which is in the soul is such as may be poured out in the presence of God, and this is only the case where the heart has been renewed by divine grace. The word rendered " complaint " has in it none of the idea of fault-finding or repining, but should rather be rendered " moaning," —the expression of pain, not of rebellion.*

To help the memory we will call this Psalm THE PATRIOT'S PLAINT.

DIVISION.—*In the first part of the Psalm, from 1—11, the moaning monopolizes every verse, the lamentation is unceasing, sorrow rules the hour. The second portion, from 12—28, has a vision of better things, a view of the gracious Lord, and his eternal existence and care for his people, and therefore it is interspersed with sunlight as well as shaded by the cloud, and it ends up right gloriously with calm confidence for the future, and sweet restfulness in the Lord. The whole composition may be compared to a day which, opening with wind and rain, clears up at noon and is warm with the sun, continues fine, with intervening showers, and finally closes with a brilliant sunset.*

EXPOSITION.

HEAR my prayer, O LORD, and let my cry come unto thee.

2 Hide not thy face from me in the day *when* I am in trouble; incline thine ear unto me: in the day *when* I call answer me speedily.

3 For my days are consumed like smoke, and my bones are burned as an hearth.

4 My heart is smitten, and withered like grass; so that I forget to eat my bread.

5 By reason of the voice of my groaning my bones cleave to my skin.

6 I am like a pelican of the wilderness : I am like an owl of the desert.

7 I watch, and am as a sparrow alone upon the house top.

8 Mine enemies reproach me all the day : *and* they that are mad against me are sworn against me.

9 For I have eaten ashes like bread, and mingled my drink with weeping.

10 Because of thine indignation and thy wrath : for thou hast lifted me up, and cast me down.

11 My days *are* like a shadow that declineth ; and I am withered like grass.

1. *" Hear my prayer, O Lord."* Or O JEHOVAH. Sincere suppliants are not content with praying for praying's sake, they desire really to reach the ear and heart of the great God. It is a great relief in time of distress to acquaint others with our trouble, we are eased by their hearing our lamentations, but it is the sweetest solace of all to have God himself as a sympathizing listener to our plaint. That he is such is no dream or fiction, but an assured fact. It would be the direst of all our woes if we could be indisputably convinced that with God there is neither hearing nor answering ; he who could argue us into so dreary a belief would do us no better service than if he had read us our death-warrants. Better die than be denied the mercy-seat. As well be atheists at once as believe in an unhearing, unfeeling God. *" And let my cry come unto thee."* When sorrow rises to such a height that words become too weak a medium of expression, and prayer is intensified into a cry, then the heart is even more urgent to have audience with the Lord. If our cries do not enter within the veil, and reach to the living God, we may as well cease from prayer at once, for it is idle to cry to the winds ; but, blessed be God, the philosophy which suggests such a hideous idea is disproved by the facts of everyday experience, since thousands of the saints can declare, " Verily, God hath heard us."

2. *" Hide not thy face from me in the day when I am in trouble."* Do not seem as if thou didst not see me, or wouldst not own me. Smile now at any rate. Reserve thy frowns for other times when I can bear them better, if, indeed, I can ever bear them ; but now in my heavy distress, favour me with looks of compassion. *" Incline thine ear unto me."* Bow thy greatness to my weakness. If because of sin thy face is turned away, at least let me have a side view of thee, lend me thine ear if I may not see thine eye. Turn thyself to me again if my sin has turned thee away, give to thine ear an inclination to my prayers. *" In the day when I call answer me speedily."* Because the case is urgent, and my soul little able to wait. We may ask to have answers to prayer as soon as possible, but we may not complain of the Lord if he should think it more wise to delay. We have permission to request and to use importunity, but no right to dictate or to be petulant. If it be important that the deliverance should arrive at once, we are quite right in making an early time a point of our entreaty, for God is as willing to grant us a favour now as to-morrow, and he is not slack concerning his promise. It is a proverb concerning favours from human hands, that " he gives twice who gives quickly," because a gift is enhanced in value by arriving in a time of urgent necessity ; and we may be sure that our heavenly Patron will grant us the best gifts in the best manner, granting us grace to help in time of need. When answers come upon the heels of our prayers they are all the more striking, more consoling, and more encouraging.

In these two verses the Psalmist has gathered up a variety of expressions all to the same effect ; in them all he entreats an audience and answer of the Lord, and the whole may be regarded as a sort of preface to the prayer which follows.

3. *" For my days are consumed like smoke."* My grief has made life unsubstantial to me, I seem to be but a puff of vapour which has nothing in it, and is soon dissipated. The metaphor is very admirably chosen, for, to the unhappy, life seems not merely to be frail, but to be surrounded by so much that is darkening, defiling, blinding, and depressing, that, sitting down in despair, they compare themselves to men wandering in a dense fog, and themselves so dried up thereby that they are little better than pillars of smoke. When our days have neither light of joy nor fire of energy in them, but become as a smoking flax which dies out ignobly in darkness, then have we cause enough to appeal to the Lord that he would not utterly quench us. *" And my bones are burned as an hearth."* He became as dry as the hearth on which a wood fire has burned out, or as spent ashes in which scarcely a trace of fire can be found. His soul was ready to be blown away as smoke, and his body seemed likely to remain as the bare hearth when the last comforting ember is

quenched. How often has our piety appeared to us to be in this condition ! We have had to question its reality, and fear that it never was anything more than a smoke ; we have had the most convincing evidence of its weakness, for we could not derive even the smallest comfort from it, any more than a chilled traveller can derive from the cold hearth on which a fire had burned long ago. Soul-trouble experienced in our own heart will help us to interpret the language here employed ; and church-troubles may help us also, if unhappily we have been called to endure them. The Psalmist was moved to grief by a view of national calamities, and these so wrought upon his patriotic soul that he was wasted with anxiety, his spirits were dried up, and his very life was ready to expire. There is hope for any country which owns such a son ; no nation can die while true hearts are ready to die for it.

4. " *My heart is smitten,*" like a plant parched by the fierce heat of a tropical sun, " *and withered like grass,*" which dries up when once the scythe has laid it low. The Psalmist's heart was as a wilted, withered flower, a burned up mass of what once was verdure. His energy, beauty, freshness, and joy, were utterly gone, through the wasting influence of his anguish. " *So that I forget to eat my bread,*" or " because I forget to eat my bread." Grief often destroys the appetite, and the neglect of food tends further to injure the constitution and create a yet deeper sinking of spirit. As the smitten flower no longer drinks in the dew, or draws up nutriment from the soil, so a heart parched with intense grief often refuses consolation for itself and nourishment for the bodily frame, and descends at a doubly rapid rate into weakness, despondency, and dismay. The case here described is by no means rare, we have frequently met with individuals so disordered by sorrow that their memory has failed them even upon such pressing matters as their meals, and we must confess that we have passed through the same condition ourselves. One sharp pang has filled the soul, monopolized the mind, and driven everything else into the background, so that such common matters as eating and drinking have been utterly despised, and the appointed hours of refreshment have gone by unheeded, leaving no manifest faintness of body, but an increased weariness of heart.

5. " *By reason of the voice of my groaning my bones cleave to my skin.*" He became emaciated with sorrow. He had groaned himself down to a living skeleton, and so in his bodily appearance was the more like the smoke-dried, withered, burnt-up things to which he had previously compared himself. It will be a very long time before the distresses of the church of God make some Christians shrivel into anatomies, but this good man was so moved with sympathy for Zion's ills that he was wasted down to skin and bone.

6. " *I am like a pelican of the wilderness,*" a mournful and even hideous object, the very image of desolation. " *I am like an owl of the desert ;* " loving solitude, moping among ruins, hooting discordantly. The Psalmist likens himself to two birds which were commonly used as emblems of gloom and wretchedness ; on other occasions he had been as the eagle, but the griefs of his people had pulled him down, the brightness was gone from his eye, and the beauty from his person ; he seemed to himself to be as a melancholy bird sitting among the fallen palaces and prostrate temples of his native land. Should not we also lament when the ways of Zion mourn and her strength languishes ? Were there more of this holy sorrow we should soon see the Lord returning to build up his church. It is ill for men to be playing the peacock with worldly pride when the ills of the times should make them as mournful as the pelican ; and it is a terrible thing to see men flocking like vultures to devour the prey of a decaying church, when they ought rather to be lamenting among her ruins like the owl.

7. " *I watch, and am like a sparrow alone upon the house top :* " I keep a solitary vigil as the lone sentry of my nation ; my fellows are too selfish, too careless to care for the beloved land, and so like a bird which sits alone on the house top, I keep up a sad watch over my country. The Psalmist compared himself to a bird,—a bird when it has lost its mate or its young, or is for some other reason made to mope alone in a solitary place. Probably he did not refer to the cheerful sparrow of our own land, but if he did, the illustration would not be out of place, for the sparrow is happy in company, and if it were alone, the sole one of its species in the neighbourhood, there can be little doubt that it would become very miserable, and sit and pine away. He who has felt himself to be so weak and inconsiderable as to have no more power over his times than a sparrow over a city, has also, when bowed down with despondency concerning the evils of the age, sat himself down in utter wretchedness to lament the ills which he could not heal. Christians of an earnest. watchful kind often find

themselves among those who have no sympathy with them ; even in the church they look in vain for kindred spirits ; then do they persevere in their prayers and labours, but feel themselves to be as lonely as the poor bird which looks from the ridge of the roof, and meets with no friendly greeting from any of its kind.

8. *" Mine enemies reproach me all the day."* Their rage was unrelenting and unceasing, and vented itself in taunts and insults, the Psalmist's patriotism and his griefs were both made the subjects of their sport. Pointing to the sad estate of his people they would ask him, " Where is your God ? " and exult over him because their false gods were in the ascendant. Reproach cuts like a razor, and when it is continued from hour to hour, and repeated all the day and every day, it makes life itself undesirable. *" And they that are mad against me are sworn against me."* They were so furious that they bound themselves by oath to destroy him, and used his name as their usual execration, a word to curse by, the synonym of abhorrence and contempt. What with inward sorrows and outward persecutions he was in as ill a plight as may well be conceived.

9. *" For I have eaten ashes like bread."* He had so frequently cast ashes upon his head in token of mourning, that they had mixed with his ordinary food, and grated between his teeth when he ate his daily bread. One while he forgot to eat, and then the fit changed, and he ate with such a hunger that even ashes were devoured. Grief has strange moods and tenses. *" And mingled my drink with weeping."* His drink became as nauseous as his meat, for copious showers of tears had made it brackish. This is a telling description of all-saturating, all-embittering sadness,— and this was the portion of one of the best of men, and that for no fault of his own, but because of his love to the Lord's people. If we, too, are called to mourn, let us not be amazed by the fiery trial as though some strange thing had happened unto us. Both in meat and drink we have sinned ; it is not therefore wonderful if in both we are made to mourn.

10. *" Because of thine indignation and thy wrath : for thou hast lifted me up and cast me down."* A sense of the divine wrath which had been manifested in the overthrow of the chosen nation and their sad captivity led the Psalmist into the greatest distress. He felt like a sere leaf caught up by a hurricane and carried right away, or the spray of the sea which is dashed upwards that it may be scattered and dissolved. Our translation gives the idea of a vessel uplifted in order that it may be dashed to the earth with all the greater violence and the more completely broken in pieces ; or to change the figure, it reminds us of a wrestler whom his opponent catches up that he may give him a more desperate fall. The first interpretation which we have given is, however, more fully in accordance with the original, and sets forth the utter helplessness which the writer felt, and the sense of overpowering terror which bore him along in a rush of tumultuous grief which he could not withstand.

11. *" My days are like a shadow that declineth."* His days were but a shadow at best, but now they seem to be like a shadow which was passing away. A shadow is unsubstantial enough, how feeble a thing must a declining shadow be ? No expression could more forcibly set forth his extreme feebleness. *" And I am withered like grass."* He was like grass, blasted by a parching wind, or cut down with a scythe, and then left to be dried up by the burning heat of the sun. There are times when through depression of spirit a man feels as if all life were gone from him, and existence had become merely a breathing death. Heart-break has a marvellously withering influence over our entire system ; our flesh at its best is but as grass, and when it is wounded with sharp sorrows, its beauty fades, and it becomes a shrivelled, dried, uncomely thing.

12 But thou, O LORD, shalt endure for ever ; and thy remembrance unto all generations.

13 Thou shalt arise, *and* have mercy upon Zion : for the time to favour her, yea, the set time, is come.

14 For thy servants take pleasure in her stones, and favour the dust thereof.

15 So the heathen shall fear the name of the LORD, and all the kings of the earth thy glory.

16 When the LORD shall build up Zion, he shall appear in his glory.

17 He will regard the prayer of the destitute, and not despise their prayer.

18 This shall be written for the generation to come : and the people which shall be created shall praise the LORD.

19 For he hath looked down from the height of his sanctuary ; from heaven did the LORD behold the earth ;

20 To hear the groaning of the prisoner ; to loose those that are appointed to death ;

21 To declare the name of the LORD in Zion, and his praise in Jerusalem ;

22 When the people are gathered together, and the kingdoms, to serve the LORD.

23 He weakened my strength in the way ; he shortened my days.

24 I said, O my God, take me not away in the midst of my days : thy years *are* throughout all generations.

25 Of old hast thou laid the foundation of the earth : and the heavens *are* the work of thy hands.

26 They shall perish, but thou shalt endure : yea, all of them shall wax old like a garment ; as a vesture shalt thou change them, and they shall be changed :

27 But thou *art* the same, and thy years shall have no end.

28 The children of thy servants shall continue, and their seed shall be established before thee.

12.   Now the writer's mind is turned away from his personal and relative troubles to the true source of all consolation, namely, the Lord himself, and his gracious purposes towards his own people. " *But thou, O Lord, shalt endure for ever.*"   I perish, but thou wilt not, my nation has become almost extinct, but thou art altogether unchanged.   The original has the word " sit,"—" thou, Jehovah, to eternity shalt sit : " that is to say, thou reignest on, thy throne is still secure even when thy chosen city lies in ruins, and thy peculiar people are carried into captivity.   The sovereignty of God in all things is an unfailing ground for consolation ; he rules and reigns whatever happens, and therefore all is well.

> Firm as his throne his promise stands,
>   And he can well secure,
> What I've committed to his hands,
>   Till the decisive hour.

" *And thy remembrance unto all generations.*"   Men will forget me, but as for thee, O God, the constant tokens of thy presence will keep the race of man in mind of thee from age to age.   What God is now he always will be, that which our forefathers told us of the Lord we find to be true at this present time, and what our experience enables us to record will be confirmed by our children and their children's children. All things else are vanishing like smoke, and withering like grass, but over all the one eternal, immutable light shines on, and will shine on when all these shadows have declined into nothingness.

13. " *Thou shalt arise, and have mercy upon Zion.*"   He firmly believed and boldly prophesied that apparent inaction on God's part would turn to effective working.   Others might remain sluggish in the matter, but the Lord would most surely bestir himself.   Zion had been chosen of old, highly favoured, gloriously inhabited, and wondrously preserved, and therefore by the memory of her past mercies it was certain that mercy would again be showed to her.   God will not always leave his church in a low condition ; he may for a while hide himself from her in chastisement, to make her see her nakedness and poverty apart from himself, but in love he must return to her, and stand up in her defence, to work her welfare.   " *For the time to favour her, yea, the set time, is come.*"   Divine decree has appointed a season for blessing the church, and when that period has arrived, blessed she shall be.   There was an appointed time for the Jews in Babylon, and when the weeks were fulfilled, no bolts nor bars could longer imprison the ransomed of the Lord.   When the time came for the walls to rise stone by stone, no Tobiah or Sanballat could stay the

work, for the Lord himself had arisen, and who can restrain the hand of the Almighty ? When God's own time is come, neither Rome, nor the devil, nor persecutors, nor atheists, can prevent the kingdom of Christ from extending its bounds. It is God's work to do it,— he must " *arise* " ; he will do it, but he has his own appointed season ; and meanwhile we must, with holy anxiety and believing expectation, wait upon him.

14. " *For thy servants take pleasure in her stones, and favour the dust thereof.*" They delight in her so greatly that even her rubbish is dear to them. It was a good omen for Jerusalem when the captives began to feel a home-sickness, and began to sigh after her. We may expect the modern Jews to be restored to their own land when the love of their country begins to sway them, and casts out the love of gain. To the church of God no token can be more full of hope than to see the members there-of deeply interested in all that concerns her ; no prosperity is likely to rest upon a church when carelessness about ordinances, enterprises, and services is manifest ; but when even the least and lowest matter connected with the Lord's work is carefully attended to, we may be sure that the set time to favour Zion is come. The poorest church member, the most grievous backslider, the most ignorant convert, should be precious in our sight, because forming a part, although possibly a very feeble part, of the new Jerusalem. If we do not care about the prosperity of the church to which we belong, need we wonder if the blessing of the Lord is withheld ?

15. " *So the heathen shall fear the name of the Lord.*" Mercy within the church is soon perceived by those without. When a candle is lit in the house, it shines through the window. When Zion rejoices in her God, the heathen begin to reverence his name, for they hear of the wonders of his power, and are impressed thereby. " *And all the kings of the earth thy glory.*" The restoration of Jerusalem was a marvel among the princes who heard of it, and its ultimate resurrection in days yet to come will be one of the prodigies of history. A church quickened by divine power is so striking an object in current history that it cannot escape notice, rulers cannot ignore it, it affects the Legislature, and forces from the great ones of the earth a recognition of the divine working. Oh that we might see in our day such a revival of religion that our senators and princes might be compelled to pay homage to the Lord, and own his glorious grace. This cannot be till the saints are better edified, and more fully builded together for an habitation of God through the Spirit. Internal pros-perity is the true source of the church's external influence.

16. " *When the Lord shall build up Zion, he shall appear in his glory.*" As kings display their skill and power and wealth in the erection of their capitals, so would the Lord reveal the splendour of his attributes in the restoration of Zion, and so will he now glorify himself in the edification of his church. Never is the Lord more honourable in the eyes of his saints than when he prospers the church. To add con-verts to her, to train these for holy service, to instruct, illuminate, and sanctify the brotherhood, to bind all together in the bonds of Christian love, and to fill the whole body with the energy of the Holy Spirit—this is to build up Zion. Other builders do but puff her up, and their wood, hay, and stubble come to an end almost as rapidly as it was heaped together ; but what the Lord builds is surely and well done, and redounds to his glory. Truly, when we see the church in a low state, and mark the folly, helplessness, and indifference of those who profess to be her builders ; and, on the other hand, the energy, craft, and influence of those opposed to her, we are fully prepared to own that it will be a glorious work of omnipotent grace should she ever rise to her pristine grandeur and purity.

17. " *He will regard the prayer of the destitute.*" Only the poorest of the people were left to sigh and cry among the ruins of the beloved city ; as for the rest, they were strangers in a strange land, and far away from the holy place, yet the prayers of the captives and the forlorn offscourings of the land would be heard of the Lord, who does not hear men because of the amount of money they possess, or the breadth of the acres which they call their own, but in mercy listens most readily to the cry of the greatest need. " *And not despise their prayer.*" When great kings are building their palaces it is not reasonable to expect them to turn aside and listen to every beggar who pleads with them, yet when the Lord builds up Zion, and appears in his robes of glory, he makes a point of listening to every petition of the poor and needy. He will not treat their pleas with contempt ; he will incline his ear to hear, his heart to consider, and his hand to help. What comfort is here for those who account themselves to be utterly destitute ; their abject want is here met with a most condescending promise. It is worth while to be destitute to be thus assured of the divine regard.

18. " *This shall be written for the generation to come.*" A note shall be made of it,

for there will be destitute ones in future generations,—" the poor shall never cease out of the land,"—and it will make glad their eyes to read the story of the Lord's mercy to the needy in former times. Registers of divine kindness ought to be made and preserved : we write down in history the calamities of nations,—wars, famines, pestilences, and earthquakes are recorded ; how much rather then should we set up memorials of the Lord's lovingkindnesses ! Those who have in their own souls endured spiritual destitution, and have been delivered out of it, cannot forget it ; they are bound to tell others of it, and especially to instruct their children in the goodness of the Lord. *" And the people which shall be created shall praise the Lord."* The Psalmist here intends to say that the rebuilding of Jerusalem would be a fact in history for which the Lord would be praised from age to age. Revivals of religion not only cause great joy to those who are immediately concerned in them, but they give encouragement and delight to the people of God long after, and are indeed perpetual incentives to adoration throughout the church of God. This verse teaches us that we ought to have an eye to posterity, and especially should we endeavour to perpetuate the memory of God's love to his church and to his poor people, so that young people as they grow up may know that the Lord God of their fathers is good and full of compassion. Sad as the Psalmist was when he wrote the dreary portions of this complaint, he was not so absorbed in his own sorrow, or so distracted by the national calamity, as to forget the claims of coming generations ; this, indeed, is a clear proof that he was not without hope for his people, for he who is making arrangements for the good of a future generation has not yet despaired of his nation. The praise of God should be the great object of all that we do, and to secure him a revenue of glory both from the present and the future is the noblest aim of intelligent beings.

19, 20. *" For he hath looked down from the height of his sanctuary,"* or " leaned from the high place of his holiness," *" from heaven did the Lord behold the earth,"* looking out like a watcher from his tower. What was the object of this leaning from the battlements of heaven ? Why this intent gaze upon the race of men ? The answer is full of astounding mercy : the Lord does not look upon mankind to note their grandees, and observe the doings of their nobles, but *" to hear the groaning of the prisoner ; to loose those that are appointed to death."* Now the groans of those in prison so far from being musical are very horrible to hear, yet God bends to hear them : those who are bound for death are usually ill company, yet Jehovah deigns to stoop from his greatness to relieve their extreme distress and break their chains. This he does by providential rescues, by restoring health to the dying, and by finding food for the famishing ; and spiritually this need of grace is accomplished by sovereign grace, which delivers us by pardon from the sentence of sin, and by the sweetness of the promise from the deadly despair which a sense of sin had created within us. Well may those of us praise the Lord who were once the children of death, but are now brought into the glorious liberty of the children of God. The Jews in captivity were in Haman's time appointed to death, but their God found a way of escape for them, and they joyfully kept the feast of Purim in memorial thereof ; let all souls that have been set free from the crafty malice of the old dragon with even greater gratitude magnify the Lord of infinite compassion.

21. *" To declare the name of the Lord in Zion, and his praise in Jerusalem."* Great mercy displayed to those greatly in need of it, is the plainest method of revealing the attributes of the Most High. Actions speak more loudly than words ; deeds of grace are a revelation even more impressive than the most tender promises. Jerusalem restored, the church re-edified, desponding souls encouraged, and all other manifestations of Jehovah's power to bless, are so many manifestoes and proclamations put up upon the walls of Zion to publish the character and glory of the great God. Every day's experience should be to us a new gazette of love, a court circular from heaven, a daily despatch from the headquarters of grace. We are bound to inform our fellow Christians of all this, making them helpers in our praise, as they hear of the goodness which we have experienced. While God's mercies speak so eloquently, we ought not to be dumb. To communicate to others what God has done for us personally and for the church at large is so evidently our duty, that we ought not to need urging to fulfil it. God has ever an eye to the glory of his grace in all that he does, and we ought not wilfully to defraud him of the revenue of his praise.

22. *" When the people are gathered together, and the kingdoms, to serve the Lord."* The great work of restoring ruined Zion is to be spoken of in those golden ages when the heathen nations shall be converted unto God ; even those glorious times will not be able to despise that grand event, which, like the passage of Israel through the

Red Sea, will never be eclipsed and never cease to awaken the enthusiasm of the chosen people. Happy will the day be when all nations shall unite in the sole worship of Jehovah, then shall the histories of the olden times be read with adoring wonder, and the hand of the Lord shall be seen as having ever rested upon the sacra mental host of his elect : then shall shouts of exulting praise ascend to heaven in honour of him who loosed the captives, delivered the condemned, raised up the desolations of ages, and made out of stones and rubbish a temple for his worship.

23. " *He weakened my strength in the way.*" Here the Psalmist comes down again to the mournful string, and pours forth his personal complaint. His sorrow had cast down his spirit, and even caused weakness in his bodily frame, so that he was like a pilgrim who limped along the road, and was ready to lie down and die. " *He shortened my days.*" Though he had bright hopes for Jerusalem, he feared that he should have departed this life long before those visions had become realities ; he felt that he was pining away and would be a shortlived man. Perhaps this may be our lot, and it will materially help us to be content with it, if we are persuaded that the grandest of all interests is safe, and the good old cause secure in the hands of the Lord.

24. " *I said, O my God, take me not away in the midst of my days.*" He betook himself to prayer. What better remedy is there for heart-sickness and depression ? We may lawfully ask for recovery from sickness and may hope to be heard. Good men should not dread death, but they are not forbidden to love life : for many reasons the man who has the best hope of heaven, may nevertheless think it desirable to continue here a little longer, for the sake of his family, his work, the church of God, and even the glory of God itself. Some read the passage, " Take me not up," let me not ascend like disappearing smoke, do not whirl me away like Elijah in a chariot of fire, for as yet I have only seen half my days, and that a sorrowful half ; give me to live till the blustering morning shall have softened into a bright afternoon of happier existence. " *Thy years are throughout all generations.*" Thou livest, Lord ; let me live also. A fulness of existence is with thee, let me partake therein. Note the contrast between himself pining and ready to expire, and his God living on in the ful ness of strength for ever and ever ; this contrast is full of consolatory power to the man whose heart is stayed upon the Lord. Blessed be his name, he faileth not, and, therefore, our hope shall not fail us, neither will we despair for ourselves or for his church.

25. " *Of old hast thou laid the foundation of the earth.*" Creation is no new work with God, and therefore to " create Jerusalem a praise in the earth " will not be difficult to him. Long ere the holy city was laid in ruins the Lord made a world out of nothing, and it will be no labour to him to raise the walls from their heaps and replace the stones in their courses. We can neither continue our own existence nor give being to others ; but the Lord not only is, but he is the Maker of all things that are ; hence, when our affairs are at the very lowest ebb we are not all despairing, because the Almighty and Eternal Lord can yet restore us. " *And the heavens are the work of thine hands.*" Thou canst therefore not merely lay the foundations of Zion, but complete its roof, even as thou hast arched in the world with its ceiling of blue ; the loftiest stories of thine earthly palace shall be piled on high without difficulty when thou dost undertake the building thereof, since thou art architect of the stars, and the spheres in which they move. When a great labour is to be performed it is eminently reassur ing to contemplate the power of him who has undertaken to accomplish it ; and when our own strength is exhausted it is supremely cheering to see the unfailing energy which is still engaged on our behalf.

26. " *They shall perish, but thou shalt endure.*" The power which made them shall dissolve them, even as the city of thy love was destroyed at thy command ; yet neither the ruined city nor the ruined earth can make a change in thee, reverse thy purpose, or diminish thy glory. Thou standest when all things fall. " *Yea, all of them shall wax old like a garment ; as a vesture shalt thou change them, and they shall be changed.*" Time impairs all things, the fashion becomes obsolete and passes away. The visible creation, which is like the garment of the invisible God, is waxing old and wearing out, and our great King is not so poor that he must always wear the same robes ; he will ere long fold up the worlds and put them aside as worn out vestures, and he will array himself in new attire, making a new heaven and a new earth wherein dwelleth righteousness. How readily will all this be done. " Thou shalt change them and they shall be changed ; " as in the creation so in the restoration, omnipotence shall work its way without hindrance.

27. "*But thou art the same*," or, "thou art he." As a man remains the same when he has changed his clothing, so is the Lord evermore the unchanging One, though his works in creation may be changed, and the operations of his providence may vary. When heaven and earth shall flee away from the dread presence of the great Judge, he will be unaltered by the terrible confusion, and the world in conflagration will effect no change in him ; even so, the Psalmist remembered that when Israel was vanquished, her capital destroyed, and her temple levelled with the ground, her God remained the same self-existent, all-sufficient being, and would restore his people, even as he will restore the heavens and the earth, bestowing at the same time a new glory never known before. The doctrine of the immutability of God should be more considered than it is, for the neglect of it tinges the theology of many religious teachers, and makes them utter many things of which they would have seen the absurdity long ago if they had remembered the divine declaration, "I am God, I change not, therefore ye sons of Jacob are not consumed." "*And thy years shall have no end.*" God lives on, no decay can happen to him, or destruction overtake him. What a joy is this ! We may lose our dearest earthly friends, but not our heavenly Friend. Men's days are often suddenly cut short, and at the longest they are but few, but the years of the right hand of the Most High cannot be counted, for they have neither first nor last, beginning nor end. O my soul, rejoice thou in the Lord always, since he is always the same.

28. "*The children of thy servants shall continue.*" The Psalmist had early in the Psalm looked forward to a future generation, and here he speaks with confidence that such a race would arise and be preserved and blessed of God. Some read it as a prayer, "let the sons of thy servants abide." Any way, it is full of good cheer to us ; we may plead for the Lord's favour to our seed, and we may expect that the cause of God and truth will revive in future generations. Let us hope that those who are to succeed us will not be so stubborn, unbelieving and erring as we have been. If the church has been minished and brought low by the lukewarmness of the present race, let us entreat the Lord to raise up a better order of men, whose zeal and obedience shall win and hold a long prosperity. May our own dear ones be among the better generation who shall continue in the Lord's ways, obedient to the end. "*And their seed shall be established before thee.*" God does not neglect the children of his servants. It is the rule that Abraham's Isaac should be the Lord's, that Isaac's Jacob should be beloved of the Most High, and that Jacob's Joseph should find favour in the sight of God. Grace is not hereditary, yet God loves to be served by the same family time out of mind, even as many great landowners feel a pleasure in having the same families as tenants upon their estates from generation to generation. Here is Zion's hope, her sons will build her up, her offspring will restore her former glories. We may, therefore, not only for our own sakes, but also out of love to the church of God, daily pray that our sons and daughters may be saved, and kept by divine grace even unto the end,—established before the Lord.

We have thus passed through the cloud, and in the next Psalm we shall bask in the sunshine. Such is the chequered experience of the believer. Paul in the seventh of Romans cries and groans, and then in the eighth rejoices and leaps for joy ; and so, from the moaning of the hundred and second Psalm, we now advance to the songs and dancing of the hundred and third, blessing the Lord that, "though weeping may endure for a night, joy cometh in the morning."

EXPLANATORY NOTES AND QUAINT SAYINGS.

Title.—"*A prayer,*" etc. The prayer following is longer than others. When Satan, the Law-Adversary, doth extend his pleas against us, it is meet that we should enlarge our counter pleas for our own souls ; as the powers of darkness do lengthen and multiply their wrestlings, so must we our counter wrestlings of prayer. Eph. vi. 12, 18.—*Thomas Cobbet, 1657.*

Title.—"*When he . . . poureth out,*" etc. Here we have the manner of the church's prayer suitable to her extremity illustrated by a simile taken from a vessel overcharged with new wine or strong liquor, that bursts for vent. Oh the heart-bursting cries she sends out all the day ! Here is no lazy, slothful, lip labour, stinted form of prayer, no empty sounds of verbal expressions, which can never procure her a comfortable answer from her God, or the least ease to her burthened soul ; but poured-out prayers as *Hannah*, 1 Sam. i. 15, and *Jeremy*, Lam. ii. 12, pressed forth with vehemence of spirit and heart pangs of inward grief : thus the Lord deals with his church and people ; ere he pours out cups of consolation they must pour out tears in great measure.—*Finiens Canus Vove.*

Title.—

> This is the mourner's prayer when he is faint,
> And to the Eternal Father breathes his plaint.
> —*John Keble.*

Whole Psalm.—The Psalm has been attributed to *Daniel*, to *Jeremiah*, to *Nehemiah*, or to some of the other *prophets* who flourished during the time of the captivity. The author of the Epistle to the Hebrews has applied the *twenty-fifth, twenty-sixth,* and *twenty-seventh* verses to our Lord, and the perpetuity of his kingdom.—*Adam Clarke.*

Whole Psalm.—I doubt whether, without apostolic teaching, any of us would have had the boldness to understand it ; for in many respects it is the most remarkable of all the Psalms—the Psalm of " THE AFFLICTED ONE "—while his soul is overwhelmed within him in great affliction, and sorrow, and anxious fear.—*Adolph Saphir, in " Expository Lectures on the Epistle to the Hebrews."*

Verse 1.— *" Hear my prayer, O Lord, and let my cry come unto thee."* When, at any time, we see the beggars, or poor folks, that are pained and grieved with hunger and cold, lying in the streets of cities and towns, full of sores, we are somewhat moved inwardly with pity and mercy ; but if we our own selves attend and give ear to their wailings, cryings, and lamentable noises that they make, we should be much more stirred to show our pity and mercy on them ; for no man else can show the grief of the sick and sore persons, so well and in so pathetic a manner as he himself. Therefore, since the miserable crying and wailing of those that suffer bodily pain and misery can prevail so much upon the hearts of mortal creatures ; I doubt not, Good Lord, but thou, who art all merciful, must needs be inclined to exercise thy mercy, if *my* sorrowful cry and petition may *come unto* thine ears, or into thy presence.—*John Fisher* (1459–1535) *in " A Treatise concerning the fruitful Sayings of David,"* 1714.

Verse 1.—*" My prayer."* His own, and not another's ; not what was composed for him, but composed by him ; which came out of his own heart, and out of unfeigned lips, and expressed under a feeling sense of his own wants and troubles ; and though dictated and inwrought in his heart by the Spirit of God, yet, being put up by him in faith and fervency, it is called his own, and which he desires might be heard. —*John Gill.*

Verse 1.—*" My cry."* Lest my praying should not prevail, behold, O God, I raise it to a cry ; and crying, I may say, is the greatest bell in all the ring of praying : for louder than crying I cannot pray. O, then, if not my prayer, at least *" let my cry come unto thee."* If I be not heard when I cry, I shall cry for not being heard ; and if heard when I cry, I shall cry to be heard yet more ; and so whether heard or not heard, I shall cry still, and God grant I may cry still ; so thou be pleased, O God, to " hear my prayer," and to " let my cry come unto thee."—*Sir R. Baker.*

Verses 1, 2.—This language is the language of godly sorrow, of faith, of tribulation, and of anxious hope : of *faith*, for the devout suppliant lifts up his heart and voice to heaven, " as seeing him who is invisible," (Heb. xi. 27) and entreats him to hear his prayer and listen to his crying : *of tribulation*, for he describes himself as enduring affliction, and unwilling to lose the countenance of the Lord *in the time of his trouble :* *of anxious hope*, for he seems to expect, in the midst of his groaning, that his prayers, like those of Cornelius, will " go up for a memorial before God " who will hear him, " and that right soon."—*Charles Oxenden, in " Sermons on the Seven Penitential Psalms,"* 1838.

Verses 1, 2.—The Lord suffereth his babbling children to speak to him in their own form of speech, (albeit the terms which they use be not fitted for his spiritual, invisible, and incomprehensible majesty) ; such as are, " *Hear me*," " *hide not thy face*," " *incline thine ear to me*," and such like other speeches.—*David Dickson.*

Verses 1, 2.—Note, David sent his prayer as a sacred ambassador to God. Now there are four things requisite to make an embassy prosperous. The ambassador must be regarded with favourable eye : he must be heard with a ready ear : he must speedily return when his demands are conceded.   These four things David as a suppliant asks from God his King.—*Le Blanc.*

Verse 2.—" *Incline thine ear unto me.*"   The great exhaustion of the afflicted one is hinted at : so worn out is he, that he is hardly able to cry any more, but with a faint voice only feebly mutters, like a weak, sick man, whose voice if we would catch, we must *incline the ear.*—*Martin Geier.*

Verse 3.—" *Consumed like smoke,*" would be better read, " pass away as *in smoke,*" as if they disappeared into smoke and ashes.   " *Burned as an hearth,*" is not a felicitous translation, for a " hearth " should be incombustible.   Better " burned as a faggot," as any fuel.   The sentiment, My days waste away to nothing, turn to no good account, are lost.—*Henry Cowles.*

Verse 3.—" *My days are consumed like smoke ;* " or, as Hebrew, literally, " *in (into) smoke.*"   The very same expression which David, in Ps. xxxvii. 20, had used of " the enemies of the Lord : " " They shall consume into smoke " (compare Ps. lxviii. 2).   Hereby the ideal sufferer virtually complains that the lot of the wicked befalls him, though being righteous (Ps. ci.).—*A. R. Fausset.*

Verse 3.—" *My days are consumed like smoke.*"   As the smoke is a vapour proceeding from the fire, yet hath no heat in it ; so my days are come from the torrid zone of youth into the region of cold and age ; and as the smoke seems a thick substance for the present, but presently vanisheth into air ; so my days made as great shew at first as if they would never have been spent ; but now, alas, are wasted and leave me scarce a being.   As the smoke is fuliginous and dark, and affords no pleasure to look upon it ; so my days are all black and in mourning ; no joy nor pleasure to be taken in them.   And as the smoke ascends indeed, but by ascending wastes itself and comes to nothing : so my days are wasted in growing, are diminished in increasing ; their plenty hath made a scarcity, and the more they have been the fewer they are.   And how, indeed, can my days choose but be consumed as smoke, when " *my bones are burned as an hearth* " ? for as when the hearth is burned there can be made no more fire upon it ; so, when my bones, which are as the hearth upon which my fire of life is made, come once to be burned ; how can any more fire of life be made upon them ? and when no fire can be made, what will remain but only smoke ?—*Sir R. Baker.*

Verse 3.—" *As an hearth.*"   Or, as a *trivet,* or, *gridiron ;* so the Targum : or, as a *frying-pan :* so the Arabic version.—*John Gill.*

Verse 4.—" *My heart is smitten, and withered like grass.*"   The metaphor here is taken from grass, cut down in the meadow.   Is is first " *smitten* " with the *scythe,* and then " *withered* " by the *sun.*   Thus the Jews were smitten with the judgments of God ; and they are now withered under the fire of the *Chaldeans.*—*Adam Clarke.*

Verse 4.—" *I forget to eat my bread.*"   I have heard of some that have forgotten their own names, but I never heard of any that forgot to eat his meat ; for there is a certain prompter called hunger that will make a man to remember his meat in spite of his teeth.   And yet it is true, when the heart is blasted and withered like grass, such a forgetfulness of necessity will follow.   Is it that the withering of the heart is the prime cause of sorrow ; at least cause of the prime sorrow ; and immoderate sorrow is the mother of stupidity, stupefying and benumbing the animal faculties, that neither the understanding nor the memory can execute their functions ?   Or is it, that sorrow is so intentive to that it sorrows for, that it cannot intend to think anything else ?   Or is it, that nature makes account, that to feed in sorrow were to feed sorrow, and therefore thinks best to forbear all eating ?   Or is it, that as sorrow draws moisture from the brain and fills the eyes with water ; so it draws a like juice from other parts, which fills the stomach instead of meat ?   However it be, it shews a wonderful operation that is in sorrow ; to make not only the stomach to refuse its meat, but to make the brain forget the stomach, between whom there is so natural a sympathy and so near a correspondence.   But as the vigour of the heart breeds plenty of spirits, which conveyed to all the parts, gives every one a natural appetite ; so when the heart is blasted and withered like grass, and that there is no more any vigour in it, the spirits are presently at a stand, and then no marvel if the stomach lose its appetite, and forget to eat bread.—*Sir R. Baker.*

Verse 4.—" *I forget to eat my bread.*"   When grief hath thus dejected the spirits, the man has no appetite for that food which is to recruit and elevate them. Ahab, smitten with one kind of grief, David with another, and Daniel with a third, all forgot, or refused, to eat their bread. 1 Kings xxi. 4 ; 2 Sam. xii. 16 ; Dan. x. 3. Such natural companions are mourning and fasting.—*Samuel Burder.*

Verse 5.—" *My bones cleave to my skin.*" When the bones cleave to the skin, both are near cleaving to the dust.—*Joseph Caryl.*

Verse 5.—That grief readily causes the body to pine away is very well known. It is related of Cardinal Wolsey, by an eye-witness, that when he heard that his master's favour was turned from him, he was wrung with such an agony of grief, which continued a whole night, that in the morning his face was dwindled away into half its usual dimensions.

Verse 6.—" *I am like a pelican of the wilderness.*" The Kaath was a bird of solitude that was to be found in the " *wilderness,*" *i.e.*, far from the habitations of man. This is one of the characteristics of the *pelican*, which loves not the neighbourhood of human beings, and is fond of resorting to broad, uncultivated lands, where it will not be disturbed. In them it makes its nest and hatches its young, and to them it retires after feeding, in order to digest in quiet the ample meal which it has made. Mr. Tristram well suggests that the metaphor of the Psalmist may allude to the habit common to the pelican and its kin, of sitting motionless for hours after it has gorged itself with food, its head sunk on its shoulders, and its bill resting on its breast.— *J. G. Wood.*

Verse 6.—" *A pelican of the wilderness.*" Here only [at Hulet] have I seen the pelican of the wilderness, as David calls it. I once had one of them shot just below this place, and, as it was merely wounded in the wing, I had a good opportunity to study its character. It was certainly the most sombre, austere bird I ever saw. It gave one the blues merely to look at it. David could find no more expressive type of solitude and melancholy by which to illustrate his own sad state. It seemed as large as a half-grown donkey, and when fairly settled on its stout legs, it looked like one. The pelican is never seen but in these unfrequented solitudes.—*W. M. Thomson.*

Verse 6.—Consider that thou needest not complain, like Elijah, that thou art left *alone*, seeing the best of God's *saints* in all ages have smarted in the same kind—instance in *David :* indeed sometimes he boasts how he 'lay in green pastures, and was led by still waters ;' but after he bemoans that he ' sinks in deep mire, where there was no standing.' What is become of those green pastures ? parched up with the drought. Where are those still waters ? troubled with the tempest of affliction. The same David compares himself to an " *owl,*" and in the next Psalm resembles himself to an " *eagle.*" Do two fowls fly of more different kind ? The one the *scorn,* the other the *sovereign ;* the one the *slowest,* the other the *swiftest ;* the one the most *sharp-sighted,* the other the most *dim-eyed* of all birds. Wonder not, then, to find in thyself sudden and strange alterations. It fared thus with all God's servants in their agonies of temptation ; and be confident thereof, though now run aground with grief, in due time thou shalt be all afloat with comfort.—*Thomas Fuller.*

Verse 6.—" *Owl.*" Some kind of owl, it is thought, is intended by the Hebrew word *côs*, translated " *little owl,*" in Lev. xi. 17 ; Deut. xiv. 16, where it is mentioned amongst the unclean birds. It occurs also in Ps. cii. 6. " *I am like a pelican of the wilderness : I am like an owl of ruined places* " (A. V., " desert "). The Hebrew word *côs* means a " cup " in some passages of Scripture, from a root meaning to " receive," to " hide," or " bring together " ; hence the pelican, " the cup," or " pouch-bird," has been suggested as the bird intended. In this case the verse in the Psalm would be rendered thus :—" I am become like a pelican in the wilderness, even as the pouch-bird in the desert places." But the fact that both the pelican and the *côs* are enumerated in the list of birds to be avoided as food is against this theory, unless the word changed its meaning in the Psalmist's time, which is improbable. The expression *côs* " of ruined places " looks very much as if some owl were denoted. The Arabic definitely applies a kindred expression as one of the names of an owl, viz., *um elcharab, i.e.,* " mother of ruins." The Septuagint gives νυκτικόραξ as the meaning of *côs ;* and we know from Aristotle that the Greek word was a synonym of ὦτος, evidently, from his description of the bird, one of the eared owls. Dr. Tristram is disposed to refer the *côs* to the little *Athene Persica,* the most common of all the owls in Palestine, the representative of the *A. noctua* of Southern Europe. The Arabs call this bird " *boomah,*" from his note ; he is described " as a grotesque and comical-looking little bird, familiar and yet cautious ; never moving unnecessarily, but remaining glued to his perch, unless he has good reason for believing he has been detected, and twisting and turning his head instead of his eyes to watch what is going on." He is to be found amongst rocks in the wadys or trees by the water-side, in olive yards, in the tombs and on the ruins, on the sandy mounds of Beersheba, and on " the spray-beaten fragments of Tyre, where his low wailing note is sure to be heard at sunset, and himself seen bowing and keeping time to his own music." *W. Houghton, in " Cassell's Biblical Educator," 1874.*

Verse 6.—" Owl of the desert."

> Save that from yonder ivy-mantled tower,
> The moping owl does to the moon complain
> Of such as, wand'ring near her secret bow'r,
> Molest her ancient solitary reign.
> —*Thomas Gray* (1716–1771).

Verse 7.—" I watch." During the hours allotted to sleep " *I wake*," like a little bird which sits solitary on the house top, while all beneath enjoy the sleep which he giveth to his beloved.—*Alfred Edersheim.*

Verse 7.—" A sparrow alone upon the house top." When one of them has lost its mate—a matter of every-day occurrence—he will sit on the house top alone, and lament by the hour his sad bereavement.—*W. M. Thomson.*

Verse 7.—" I am as a sparrow alone," etc. It is evident that the " sparrow alone and melancholy upon the house tops" cannot be the lively, gregarious sparrow which assembles in such numbers on these favourite feeding-places [the house tops of the East]. We must therefore look for some other bird, and naturalists are now agreed that we may accept the *Blue Thrush (Petrocossyphus cyaneus)* as the particular tzippor, or small bird, which sits alone on the house tops. The colour of this bird is a dark blue, whence it derives its popular name. Its habits exactly correspond with the idea of solitude and melancholy. The Blue Thrushes never assemble in flocks, and it is very rare to see more than a pair together. It is fond of sitting on the tops of houses, uttering its note, which, however agreeable to itself, is monotonous and melancholy to a human ear.—*J. G. Wood, in " Bible Animals."*

Verse 7.—" A sparrow." Most readers are struck with the incongruity of the image, as it appears in our version, intended by the Psalmist to express a condition of distress and desolation. The sparrow is found, indeed, all over the East, in connection with houses, as it is with ourselves ; but it is everywhere one of the most social of birds, cheerful to impertinence ; and mischievously disposed, instead of being retiring in its habits, and melancholy in its demeanour. The word, in the original, is a general term for all the small birds, insectivorous and frugivirous, denominated clean, and that might be eaten according to the law, the thrushes, larks, wagtails, finches, as well as sparrows. It seems to be, indeed, a mere imitation of their common note, like the one which we have in the word " chirrup." Most critics are, therefore, content with the rendering " solitary bird," or " solitary little bird." But this is very unsatisfactory. It does not identify the species ; and there is every probability that there must have been a particular bird which the Psalmist, writing at the close of the Babylonish captivity, had in his eye, corresponding to his representation of it, and illustrative of his isolated condition.

Such there is at the present day, of common occurrence in Southern Europe and Western Asia. Its history is very little known to the world, and its existence has hitherto escaped the notice of all biblical commentators. Remarkably enough, the bird is commonly, but erroneously, called a sparrow, for it is a real thrush in size, in shape, in habits, and in song. It differs singularly from the rest of the tribe, throughout all the East, by a marked preference for sitting solitary upon the habitation of man. It never associates with any other, and only at one season with its own mate ; and even then it is often seen quite alone upon the house top, where it warbles its sweet and plaintive strains, and continues its song, moving from roof to roof. America has its solitary thrush, of another species, and of somewhat different habits. The dark solitary cane and myrtle swamps of the southern states are there the favourite haunts of the recluse bird ; and the more dense and gloomy these are the more certainly is it to be found flitting in them.—*" The Biblical Treasury."*

Verse 7.—" Alone." But little do men perceive what solitude is, and how far it extendeth ; for a crowd is not company, and faces are but a gallery of pictures, and talk but a tinkling cymbal where there is no love. The Latin adage meeteth it a little : " *magna civitas, magno solitudo ;* " because in a great town friends are scattered, so that there is not that fellowship, for the most part, which is in less neighbourhoods ; but we may go further, and affirm most truly, that it is a mere and miserable solitude to want true friends, without which the world is but a wilderness ; and even in this sense also of solitude, whosoever in the frame of his nature and affections is unfit for friendship, he taketh it of the beast, and not from humanity.— *Francis Bacon.*

Verse 7.—" *Alone.*" See the reason why people in trouble love solitariness. They are full of sorrow ; and sorrow, if it have taken deep root, is naturally reserved, and flies all conversation. Grief is a thing that is very silent and private. Those people that are very talkative and clamorous in their sorrows, are never very sorrowful. Some are apt to wonder, *why melancholy people delight to be so much alone,* and I will tell you the reason of it. 1. Because the disordered humours of their bodies alter their temper, their humours, and their inclinations, that *they are no more the same that they used to be ;* their very distemper is averse to what is joyous and diverting ; and they that wonder at them may as wisely wonder why they will be diseased, which they would not be if they knew how to help it ; but the *Disease of Melancholy* is so obstinate, and so unknown to all but those who have it, that nothing but the power of God can totally overthrow it, and I know no other cure for it. 2. *Another reason why they choose to be alone is,* because *people do not generally mind what they say,* nor believe them, but rather deride them, which they do not use so cruelly to do with those that are in other distempers ; and no man is to be blamed for avoiding society, when it does not afford the common credit to his words that is due to the rest of men. But, 3, Another, and the principal reason why people in trouble and sadness choose to be alone, is, because *they generally apprehend themselves singled out to be the marks of God's peculiar displeasure,* and they are often by their sharp afflictions a terror to themselves, and a wonder to others. It even breaks their hearts to see how low they are fallen, how oppressed, that were once as easy, as pleasant, as full of hope as others are, Job vi. 21 : " Ye see my casting down, and are afraid." Ps. lxxi. 7. " I am as a wonder unto many." And it is usually unpleasant to others to be with them. Ps. lxxxviii. 18 : " Lover and friend hast thou put far from me, and mine acquaintance into darkness." And though it was not so with the friends of Job, to see a man whom they had once known happy, to be so miserable ; one whom they had seen so very prosperous, to be so very poor, in such sorry, forlorn circumstances, did greatly affect them ; he, poor man, was changed, they knew him not, Job. ii. 12, 13, " And when they lifted up their eyes afar off, and knew him not, they lifted up their voice, and wept ; and they rent every one his mantle, and sprinkled dust upon their heads toward heaven. So they sat down with him upon the ground seven days and seven nights, and none spake a word unto him : for they saw that his grief was very great." As the prophet represents one under spiritual and great afflictions, " that *he sitteth alone,* and keepeth silence," Lam. iii. 28.—*Timothy Rogers* (1660–1729), *in* " *A Discourse on Trouble of Mind, and the Disease of Melancholy.*"

Verse 8.—" *Mine enemies reproach me.*" It is true what Plutarch writes, that men are more touched with reproaches than with other injuries ; affliction, too, gives a keener edge to calumny, for the afflicted are more fitting objects of pity than of mockery.—*Mollerus.*

Verse 8.—" *Mine enemies reproach me,*" etc. If I be where they are they rail at me to my face ; and if I be not amongst them they revile me behind my back ; and they do it not by starts and fits, that might give me some breathing time ; but they are spitting their poison *all the day long ;* and not single and one by one, that might leave hope of resisting ; but they make combinations, and enter leagues against me ; and to make their leagues the stronger, and less subject to dissolving, they bind themselves by oath, and take the sacrament upon it. And now sum up all these miseries and afflictions ; begin with my fasting ; then take my groaning ; then add my watching ; then the shame of being wondered at in company ; then the discomfort of sitting disconsolate alone ; and, lastly, add to these the spite and malice of my enemies ; and what marvel, then, if these miseries joined all together make me altogether miserable ; what marvel if I be nothing but skin and bone, when no flesh that were wise would ever stay upon a body to endure such misery.— *Sir R. Baker.*

Verse 8 (last clause). Swearing by one, means, to make his name a by-word

of execration, or an example of cursing.   (Isai. lxv. 15 ; Jer. xxix. 22 ; xlii. 18).—
Carl Bernard Moll, in Lange's Commentary.

Verse 9.—" *I have eaten ashes like bread.*"   Though the bread indeed be strange,
yet not so strange as this,—that having complained before of forgetting to eat his
bread, he should now on a sudden fall to *eating of ashes like bread.*   For had he not
been better to have forgotten it still, unless it had been more worth remembering ?
For there is not in nature so unfit a thing to eat as *ashes* ; it is worse than Nebuchadnezzar's grass.—*Sir R. Baker.*

Verse 9.—" *I have mingled my drink with weeping.*"   If you think his bread to
be bad, you will find his drink to be worse ; for *he mingles his drink with tears :* and
what are tears, but brinish and salt humours ? and is brine a fit liquor to quench
one's thirst ?   May we not say here, the remedy is worse than the disease ? for were
it not better to endure any thirst, than to seek to quench it with such drink ? Is it
not a pitiful thing to have no drink to put in the stomach, but that which is drawn
out of the eyes ? and yet whose case is any better ?   No man certainly commits sin,
but with a design of pleasure ; but sin will not be so committed ; for whosoever commit sin, let them be sure at some time or other to find a thousand times more trouble
about it than ever they found pleasure in it.   For all sin is a kind of surfeit, and
there is no way to keep it from being mortal but by this strict diet of eating ashes
like bread and mingling his drink with tears.   O my soul, if these be works of repentance in David, where shall we find a penitent in the world besides himself ?   To
talk of repentance is obvious in everyone's mouth ; but where is any that eats ashes
like bread, and mingles his drink with tears ?—*Sir R. Baker.*

Verse 10.—" *For thou hast lifted me up, and cast me down.*"   Thou hast lifted
me up of a great height, in that thou madest me like unto thine image, touching
my reasonable soul, and hast given me power, by thy grace, to inherit the everlasting joys of heaven, both body and soul, if I did live here after thy commandments.   What greater gift canst thou give me, Lord, than to have the fruition of
thee that art all in all things ?   How canst thou lift me higher than to eternal
beatitude ?   But then, alas, thou hast letten me fall down again, for thou hast
joined my noble soul with an earthly, heavy, and a frail body ; the weight and
burden thereof draweth down my mind and heart from the consideration of thy
goodness, and from well doing, unto all kinds of vices, and to the regarding of temporal things according to his nature.   The earthly mansion keepeth down the understanding.   Thus setting me up, as it were, above the wind, thou hast given me a
very great fall (Job xxx. 22).   I am in creation above all other kind of earthly creatures, and almost equal with angels ; but being in this estate thou hast knit a knot
thereto, that for breaking the least of thy commandments I shall suffer damnation.
So that without thy continual mercy and help I am in worse case herein than any
brute beast, whose life or soul dieth with the body.—*Sir Anthony Cope* (1551).

Verse 10.—" *For thou hast lifted me up and cast me down.*"   That is that I might
fall with greater poise.   *Significatur gravissima collisio.*   Here the prophet accuseth
not God of cruelty, but bewaileth his own misery.   *Miserum est fuisse felicem,* it
is no small unhappiness to have been happy.—*John Trapp.*

Verse 11 (*first clause*).—My days (my term of life) are as the lengthened shade,
the lengthening shade of evening, that shows the near approach of night.   The
comparison, though not strictly expressed, is beautifully suggestive of the thought
intended.—*Thomas J. Conant.*

Verse 11 (*last clause*).—The " *and I,*" in the Hebrew, stands in designed contrast to " But *thou,*" ver. 12.—*A. R. Fausset.*

Verse 13.—" *Thou shalt arise, and have mercy,*" etc.   *Tu miserebere,* " Thou
shalt," as the Shunamite to the prophet, catching hold on his feet, though Gehazi
thrust her away, *Vivit Dominus,* " As the Lord liveth, and as thy soul liveth, I will
not let thee go ; " and, as Jacob to the angel, when he had wrestled the whole night
with him, *Non dimittam,* I will not let thee loose till I have a blessing from thee.—
From " *A Sermon at Paules Crosse on behalfe of Paules Church, March* 26, 1620.   *By
the B. of London* " [*John King*].

Verse 13.—" *The set time.*"   There is a certain set time for God's great actions.
He lets the powers of darkness have their hour, and God will take his hour.   He

hath a set time for the discovery of his mercy, and he will not stay a jot beyond it. What is this time? verse 9, etc. When they "eat ashes like bread, and mingle their drink with weeping;" when they are most humble, and when the servants of God have moral affection to the church; when their humble and ardent affections are strong, even to the ruin and rubbish of it; when they have a mighty desire and longing for the reparation of it, as the Jews in captivity had for the very dust of the temple: verse 14: "For thy servants take pleasure in her stones, and favour the dust thereof." "For" there notes it to be a reason why the set time was judged by them to be come. That is God's set time when the church is most believing, most humble, most affectionate to God's interest in it, and most sincere. Without faith we are not fit to desire mercy, without humility we are not fit to receive it, without affection we are not fit to value it, without sincerity we are not fit to improve it. Times of extremity contribute to the growth and exercise of these qualifications. —*Stephen Charnock.*

Verse 14.—"*For thy servants take pleasure in her stones.*" That is, they are still attached to her, and regard her with extreme affection, although in ruins. Jerusalem itself affords at this day a touching illustration of this passage. There is reason to believe that a considerable portion of the *lower part* of the walls which enclose the present mosque of Omar, which occupies the site of the ancient Jewish temple, are the same, or at least the southern, western, and eastern sides are the same as those of Solomon's temple. At one part where the remains of this old wall are the most considerable and of the most massive character—where two courses of masonry, composed of massive blocks of stone, rising to the height of thirty feet —is what is called the Wailing Place of the Jews. "Here," says Dr. Olin, "at the foot of the wall, is an open place paved with flags, where the Jews assemble every Friday, and in small numbers on other days, for the purpose of praying and bewailing the desolations of their holy places. Neither the Jews nor Christians are allowed to enter the Haram, which is consecrated to Mohammedan worship, and this part of the wall is the nearest approach they can make to what they regard as the precise spot within the forbidden enclosure upon which the ancient temple stood. They keep the pavement swept with great care, and take off their shoes, as on holy ground. Standing or kneeling with their faces towards the ancient wall, they gaze in silence upon its venerable stones, or pour forth their complaints in half-suppressed, though audible tones. This, to me, was always a most affecting sight, and I repeated my visit to this interesting spot to enjoy and sympathise with the melancholy yet pleasing spectacle. The poor people sometimes sobbed aloud, and still found tears to pour out for the desolations of their ' beautiful house.' ' If I forget thee, O Jerusalem, let my right hand forget her cunning. If I do not remember thee, let my tongue cleave to the roof of my mouth; if I prefer not Jerusalem above my chief joy.' "— *Kitto's Pictorial Bible.*

Verse 16.—"*When the Lord shall build up Zion, he shall appear in his glory.*" So sincere is God to his people, that he gives his own glory in hostage to them for their security; his own robes of glory are locked up in their prosperity and salvation: he will not, indeed he cannot, present himself in all his magnificence and royalty, till he hath made up his intended thoughts of mercy to his people; he is pleased to prorogue the time of his appearing in all his glory to the world till he hath actually accomplished their deliverance, that he and they may come forth together in their glory on the same day: "*When the Lord shall build up Zion, he shall appear in his glory.*" The sun is ever glorious in the most cloudy day, but appears not so till it hath scattered the clouds that muffle it up from the sight of the lower world: God is glorious when the world sees him not; but his declarative glory then appears, when the glory of his mercy, truth and faithfulness break forth in his people's salvation. Now, what shame must this cover thy face with, O Christian, if thou shouldst not sincerely aim at thy God's glory, who loves thee, yea, all his children so dearly, as to ship his own glory and your happiness in one bottom, that he cannot now lose the one, and save the other!—*William Gurnall.*

Verse 16.—"*When the Lord shall build up Zion, he shall appear in his glory.*" There are two reasons why the Lord appears thus glorious in this work rather than in any other. First, because it is a work that infinitely pleaseth him. Men choose to appear in their clothes and behaviour suitable to the work that they are to be employed in: the woman of Tekoah must feign herself to be a mourner when she goes on a mournful message ; and David, when he goes on a doleful journey, covers his face, and puts on mourning apparel ; but when Solomon is to be crowned, he goes in all his royalty ; and a bride adorns herself gloriously when she is to be married : verily so doth the Lord, when he goes about a work he takes no pleasure in, he puts on his mourning apparel, he covers himself with a cloud and the heavens with blackness ; when he is to do a strange work of judgment, then he mourns, " How shall I give thee up, Ephraim ? how shall I deliver thee, Israel ? how shall I make thee as Admah ? how shall I set thee as Zeboim ? mine heart is turned within me, my repentings are kindled together." Hosea xi. 8. But the building of Zion doth infinitely please him, because Zion is as the apple of his eye to him ; he bought Zion at a dear rate, with his own blood ; he lays Zion in his bosom, he is ravished with Zion, Zion is his love, his dove, his fair one ; he hath chosen Zion, and loves the gates of it, better than all the palaces of Jacob ; and being so pleasing to him, no marvel if he put on all his glorious apparel when he is to adorn and build up Zion. And, secondly, it is because all the glory that he looks for to eternity must arise out of this one work of building Zion ; this one work shall be the only monument of his glory to eternity : this goodly world, this heaven and earth, that you see and enjoy the use of, is set up only as a shop, as a workshop, to stand only for a week, for six or seven thousand years, (" a thousand years is with the Lord but as a day ") ; and when his work is done he will throw this piece of clay down again, and out of this he looks for no other glory than from a *cabul*, a land of dirt, or a shepherd's cottage, or a gourd which springs up in a night and withers in a day ; but this piece he sets up for a higher end, to be the eternal mansion of his holiness and honour ; this is his *metropolis*, his temple, his house where his fire and furnace is, his court, his glorious high throne, and therefore his glory is much concerned in this work. When Nebuchadnezzar would have a city for the honour of his kingdom, and the glory of his majesty, he will make it a stately piece. Solomon made all his kingdom very rich and glorious, but he made his court, and especially his throne, another manner of thing, so stately that the like was not to be seen in any other kingdom ; and therefore no wonder though he appear in his glory in building up of that, which we may boldly say must be one day made as glorious as his wisdom can contrive, and his power bring to pass.—*Stephen Marshall, in a Sermon preached to the Right Honourable the House of Peers, entitled " God's Master-Piece," 1645.*

Verses 16, 17.—" *Shall build—shall appear—will regard—and will not despise.*" These futures, in the original, are all present ; " *buildeth—appeareth—regardeth— and despiseth not.*" The Psalmist, in his confidence of the event, speaks of it as doing. —*Samuel Horsley.*

Verse 17.—" *He will regard the prayer of the destitute,*" etc. The persons are here called " *the destitute.*" The Hebrew word which is here translated " *destitute*" doth properly signify *myrica*, a low shrub, *humiles myricæ,* low shrubs that grow in wildernesses, some think they were *juniper shrubs,* some a kind of wild *tamaris,* but a base wild shrub that grew nowhere but in a desolate forlorn place ; and sometimes the word in the text is used to signify the deserts of Arabia, the sandy desert place of Arabia, which was a miserable wilderness. Now when this word is applied to men, it always means such as were *forsaken* men, *despised* men; such men as are stripped of all that is comfortable to them : either they never had children, or else their children are taken away from them, and all comforts banished, and themselves left utterly forlorn, like the barren heath in a desolate howling wilderness. These are the people of whom my text speaks, that the Lord will regard the prayer of " *the destitute ;* " and this was now the state of the Church of God when they offered up this prayer, and yet by faith did foretell that God would grant such a glorious answer. . . .

This is also a lesson of singular comfort to every afflicted soul, to assure them their prayers and supplications are tenderly regarded before God. I have often observed such poor forsaken ones, who in their own eyes are brought very low, that of all other people they are most desirous to beg and obtain the prayers of their friends, when they see any that hath gifts, and peace, and cheerfulness of spirit, and liberty, and abilities to perform duties, O how glad they are to get such a man's prayers ! " I beseech you, will you pray for me, will you please to remember me at the throne of grace," whereas, in truth, if we could give a right judgment, all such would rather desire the *poor,* and the *desolate,* to be *mediators* for them ; for, certainly, whomsoever God neglects, he will listen to the cry of those that are forsaken and

destitute. And therefore, O thou afflicted and tossed with tempests, who thinkest
thou art wholly rejected by the Lord, continue to pour out thy soul to him ; thou
hast a faithful promise from him to be rewarded : " *he will regard the prayer of the
destitute.*"—*Stephen Marshall, in a Sermon entitled " The Strong Helper,"* 1645.

Verse 17.—" *He will regard the prayer of the destitute.*" It is worthy of observation that he ascribes the redemption and restoration of the people to the prayers
of the faithful. That is truly a free gift, and dependent wholly upon the divine
mercy, and yet God himself often attributes it to our prayers, to stir us up and render
us the more active in the pursuit of prayer.—*Mollerus.*

Verse 17.—" *The prayer of the destitute.*" A man that is destitute knows how
to pray. He needs not any instructor. His miseries indoctrinate him wonderfully
in the art of offering prayer. Let us know ourselves destitute, that we may know
how to pray ; destitute of strength, of wisdom, of due influence, of true happiness,
of proper faith, of thorough consecration, of the knowledge of the Scriptures, of
righteousness.

These words introduce and stand in immediate connection with a prophecy of
glorious things to be witnessed in the latter times. We profess to be eager for the
accomplishment of those marvellous things ; but are we offering the prayer of the
destitute ? On the contrary, is not the Church at large too much like the church
at Laodicea ? Will not a just interpretation of many of its acts and ways bring
forth the words, " I am rich and increased in goods, and have need of nothing " ?
And do not its prayers meet with this reproachful answer, " Thou art wretched, and
miserable, and poor, and blind, and naked, and knowest it not. Thy temporal
affluence implies not spiritual affluence. Thy spiritual condition is inversely as
the worldly prosperity that has turned thy head. I counsel thee to buy of me gold
tried in the fire. Give all thy trashy gold—trashy while it is with thee—give it to my
poor ; and I will give thee true gold—namely, a sense of thy misery and meanness ;
a longing for grace, purity, usefulness ; a love of thy fellow-men ; and my love
shed abroad in thy heart."—*George Bowen.*

Verse 17.—" *Not despise their prayer.*" How many in every place (who have
served the Lord in this great work) hath prayer helped at a dead lift ? Prayer hath
hitherto saved the kingdom. I remember a proud boast of our enemies, when we
had lost *Bristol* and the *Vies,* they then sent abroad even into other kingdoms a
triumphant paper, wherein they concluded all was now subdued to them, and among
many other confident expressions, there was one to this purpose, *Nil restat superare
Regem,* etc., which might be construed two ways ; either thus,—*There remains nothing
for the King to conquer, but only the prayers of a few fanatic people ;* or thus,—*There
is nothing left to conquer the King, but the prayers of a few fanatic people :* everything.
else was lost, all was now their own. And indeed we were then in a very low condition. Our strongholds taken, our armies melted away, our hearts generally failing
us for fear, multitudes flying out of the kingdom, and many deserting the cause as
desperate, making their peace at *Oxford ;* nothing almost left us but *preces et lachrymæ ;*
but blessed be God, *prayer was not conquered ;* they have found it the hardest wall
to climb, the strongest brigade to overthrow ; it hath hitherto preserved us, it hath
raised up unexpected helps, and brought many unhoped for successes and deliverances. Let us therefore, under God, set the crown upon the head of prayer. Ye
nobles and worthies, be ye all content to have it so ; it will wrong none of you in your
deserved praise ; God and man will give you your due. *Many of you have done
worthily, but prayer surpasses you all :* and this is no new thing, prayer hath always
had the pre-eminence in the building of Zion. God hath reserved several works
for several men and several ages ; but in all ages and among all men, prayer
hath been the chiefest instrument, especially in the building up of Zion.—*Stephen
Marshall.*

Verse 17.—" *Not despise their prayer.*" He will, then, give ear to the suits of
the poor, and not reject their supplications. But who will believe this ? Is it likely,
that when God is in his glory, he will attend to such mean things as hearkening to
the poor ? Can it stand with the honour of his glory to stand reading petitions, and
specially of men that come *in forma pauperis ?* scarce credible indeed with men, who,
raised in honour, keep a distance from the poor and count it a degree of falling to
look downwards : but credible enough with God, who counts it his glory to regard
the inglorious ; and being the Most High, yet looks as low as to the lowest, and favours
them most who are most despised. And this did Christ after his transfiguration, when
he had appeared in his glory ; he then shewed acts of greatest humility ; he then

washed the disciples' feet ; and made Peter as much wonder to see his humbleness, as he had done before to see his glory.—*Sir R. Baker.*

Verse 18.—*" Shall praise the Lord."* The people whom God in mercy brings from a low and mean condition, are the people from whom God promises to receive praise and glory. Indeed, such is the selfishness of our corrupt nature, that if we are anything, or do anything, we are prone to forget God, and sacrifice to our own nets, and burn incense to our own yarn ; inasmuch, that whenever God finds a people who shall either trust in him, or praise him, it must be " an afflicted and poor people," (Zeph. iii. 11—13 ; Ps. xxii. 22—25), or a people brought from such an estate : free grace is even most valued by such a people. And if you look all the Scripture over, you will find that all the praises and songs of deliverance that have been made to God have proceeded from a people that have thus judged of themselves, as those that were brought to nothing ; but God in mercy had brought them back again from the gates of death, and usually until they had such apprehensions of themselves they never gave unto God the glory due unto his name.—*Stephen Marshall.*

Verse 18.—Expositors observe upon this text, that this redeemed Church takes no thought *concerning themselves*, about their own *ease, pleasure, wealth, gain,* or anything else which might accrue unto themselves by this deliverance, to make their own life easy or sweet ; but their thoughts and studies are wholly laid out, how the present and succeeding generations should give all glory to God for it. . . .

There are three special reasons why this should be the great work of the Lord's saved and rescued people, and why indeed they can do no other than study thus to exalt him. I. One is, because they well know that the Lord hath reserved nothing to himself but only his glory ; the benefits he gives to them ; all the sweetness and honey that can be found in them he gives them leave to suck out ; but his glory and his praise is his own, and that which he hath wholly reserved ; of that he is jealous, lest it should either be denied, eclipsed, diminished, or any the least violation offered to it in any kind. All God's people know this of him, and therefore they cannot but endeavour to preserve it for him. II. Secondly, besides, they know, as God is jealous in that point, so it is all the work that he hath appointed them to do ; he hath therefore separated them to himself out of all nations of the world, to be his peculiar ones for this very end, that they might give him all the glory and praise of his mercy. " I have (said God) *created* him, *formed,* and *made* him *for my glory."* Isai. xliii. 7. This is the law of his *new creation*, which is as powerful in them as the law of *nature*, or the *first creation*, is in the rest of his works. And therefore with a holy and spiritual naturalness (if I may so call it) the hearts of all the saints are carried to give God the glory, as really as the stones are carried to the centre, or the fire to fly upwards : this is fixed in their hearts, the work of grace hath moulded them to it, that they can do no other but endeavour to exalt God, it being the very end why their spiritual life and all their other privileges are conferred upon them.

III. Yea, thirdly, they know their own interests are much concerned in God's glory, they never are losers by it : if in any work of God he want his praise, they will want their comfort ; but if God be a gainer, they shall certainly be no losers. Whatever is poured upon the head of Christ—what ointment soever of praise or glory, it will in a due proportion fall down to the skirts of his garments ; nor is there any other way to have any sweetness, comfort, praise, or glory to be derived unto themselves, but by giving all unto him, to whom alone it belongeth, and then although he will never give away his glory—the glory of being the *fountain*, the *first, supreme, original giver* of all good ; yet they shall have the glory of instruments, and of fellow workers with him, which is a glory and praise sufficient.—*Stephen Marshall.*

Verse 18 *(first clause).*—Calvin translates thus,—*" This shall be registered for the generations to come ; "* and observes,—" The Psalmist intimates, that this will be a memorable work of God, the praise of which shall be handed down to succeeding ages. Many things are worthy of praise, which are soon forgotten ; but the prophet distinguishes between the salvation of the Church, for which he makes supplication, and common benefits. By the word *register* he means that the history of this would be worthy of having a place in the public records, that the remembrance of it might be transmitted to future generations."

Verse 18.—*" This shall be written."* Nothing is more tenacious than man's memory when he suffers an injury ; nothing more lax if a benefit is conferred. For this reason God desires lest his gifts should fall out of mind, to have them committed to writing.—*Le Blanc.*

Verse 20.—" *To hear the groaning of the prisoner.*" God takes notice not only of the prayers of his afflicted people, which are the language of grace ; but even of their groans, which are the language of nature.—*Matthew Henry.*

Verse 20.—" *Appointed unto death.*" Who, in their captivity, are experiencing so much affliction, that it is manifest their cruel enemies are desirous of destroying them utterly ; or, at least, of bringing them into such a low and pitiable state, as to blot out their name from among the nations of the earth.—*William Keatinge Clay.*

Verse 24.—" *O my God.*" The leaving out one word in a will may mar the estate and disappoint all a man's hopes ; the want of this one word, *my* (God,) is the wicked man's loss of heaven, and the dagger which will pierce his heart in hell to all eternity. The degree of satisfaction in any good is according to the degree of our union to it, (hence our delight is greater in food than in clothes, and the saint's joy is greater in God in the other world than in this, because the union is nearer ;) but where there is no property there is no union, therefore no complacency. The pronoun *my* is as much worth to the soul as the boundless portion. All our comfort is locked up in that private cabinet. Wine in the glass doth not cheer the heart, but taken down into the body. The property of the Psalmist's in God was the mouth whereby he fed on those dainties which did so exceedingly delight him. No love potion was ever so effectual as this pronoun. When God saith to the soul, as Ahab to Benhadad " Behold, I am thine, and all that I have," who can tell how the heart leaps for joy in, and expires almost in desires after him upon such news ! Others, like strangers, may behold his honour and excellencies, but this saint only, like the wife, enjoyeth him. Luther saith, Much religion lieth in pronouns. All our consolation, indeed, consisteth in this pronoun. It is the cup which holdeth all our cordial waters. I will undertake as bad as the devil is, he shall give the whole world, were it in his power, more freely than ever he offered it to Christ for his worship, for leave from God to pronounce those two words, MY GOD. All the joys of the believer are hung upon this one string ; break that asunder, and all is lost. I have sometimes thought how David rolls it as a lump of sugar under his tongue, as one loth to lose its sweetness too soon : " I will love thee, O LORD, my strength, my buckler, and the horn of my salvation, and my high tower," Ps. xviii. 1, 2. This pronoun is the door at which the King of saints entereth into our hearts, with his whole train of delights and comforts.—*George Swinnock.*

Verse 24.—" *Take me not away,*" is more exactly, Take me not *up,* with possible reference to the case of Elijah, " taken up."—*Henry Cowles.*

Verse 24.—" *Take me not away in the midst of my days.*" The word is, " *Let me not ascend in the midst of my days,*" that is, before I have measured the usual course of life. Thus, *to ascend* is the same as to be *cut off ;* death cuts off the best from this world, and then they ascend to a better. The word *ascend* is conceived to have in it a double allusion ; first, to corn which is taken up by the hand of the reaper, and then laid down on the stubble. Secondly, unto the light of a candle, which as the candle spends, or as that which is the food of the fire is spending, ascends, and at last goes out and vanisheth.—*Joseph Caryl.*

Verse 24.—" *Thy years are throughout all generations.*" The Psalmist says of Christ, " *Thy years are throughout all generations,*" Ps. cii. 24 ; which Psalm the apostle quoteth of him, Heb. i. 10. Let us trace his existence punctually through all times. Let us go from point to point, and see how in particulars the Scriptures accord with it. The first joint of time we will begin that chronology of his existence withal is that instant afore he was to come into the world.

First, We find him to have existed just afore he came into the world, the instance of his conception, Heb. x. 5, in these words, " Wherefore when he comes into the world, says he, A body hast thou prepared me." Ver. 7, " Lo, I come to do thy will, O God." Here is a person distinct from God the Father, a *me,* an *I,* distinct also from that human nature he was to assume, which he terms a " body prepared." . . . Therefore besides and afore that human nature there was a divine person that existed, that was not of this world, but that came into it, " when he cometh into the world, he says," etc., to become a part of it, and be manifested in it.

Secondly, We find him to have existed afore John the Baptist, though John was conceived and born some months afore him. I note these several joints of time because the Scripture notes them, and hath set a special mark upon them : John i. 15. " John bare witness of him, and cried, saying, This was he of whom I spake, He that cometh after me is preferred before me : for he was before me." This priority of existence is that which John doth specially give witness to. And it is priority in existence, for he allegeth it as a reason why he was preferred afore him; "for he was before me."

Thirdly, We find him existing when all the prophets wrote and spake, 1 Pet. i. 11. The Spirit of Christ is said to have been in all the prophets, even as Paul, who came after Christ, also speaks, " You seek a proof of Christ speaking in me," 2 Cor. xiii. 3. And therefore he himself, whose Spirit it was, or whom he sent, must needs exist as a person sending him.

Fourthly, We find him existing in Moses' time, both because it was he that was tempted in the wilderness, " Neither let us tempt Christ as some of them also tempted, and were destroyed of serpents," 1 Cor. x. 9 ; and it was Christ that was the person said to be tempted by them, as well as now by us, as the word καὶ " as they also," evidently shows. And it points to that angel that was sent with them, Exod. xxiii. 20, 21, in whom the name of God was, and who as God had the power of pardoning sins, ver. 21. See also Acts. vii. 35, Heb. xii. 26.

Fifthly, We find him existing in and afore Abraham's time: "Verily, verily, I say unto you, Before Abraham was, I am," John viii. 58.

Sixthly, We find him existing in the days of Noah, 1 Pet. iii. 19. He says of Christ, that he was " put to death in the flesh, but quickened in the Spirit." He evidently distinguisheth of two natures, his divine and human, even as Rom. i. 3, 4 and elsewhere ; and then declares how by that divine nature, which he terms " Spirit," in which he was existent in Noah's times, he went and preached to those of the old world, whose souls are now in prison in hell. These words, " in Spirit," are not put to signify the subject of vivification ; for such neither his soul nor Godhead could be said to be, for that is not quickened which was not dead ; but for the principal and cause of his vivification, which his soul was not, but his Godhead was. And besides by his Spirit is not meant his soul, for that then must be supposed to have preached to souls in hell (where these are affirmed to be). Now, there is no preaching where there is no capacity of faith. But his meaning is, that those persons that lived in Noah's time, and were preached unto, their souls and spirits were now, when this was written, spirits in prison, that is, in hell. And therefore he also adds this word " sometimes" : " who were sometimes disobedient in Noah's days." These words give us to understand that this preaching was performed by Noah ministerially, yet by Christ in Noah ; who according to his divine person was extant, and went with him, as with Moses, and the church in the wilderness, and preached unto them.

Seventhly, He was extant at the beginning of the world, " In the beginning was the Word." In which words, there being no predicate or attribute affirmed of this word, the sentence or affirmation is terminated or ended merely with his existence : " he was," and he was then, " in the beginning." He says not that he was made in the beginning, but that " he was in the beginning." And it is in the beginning absolutely, without any limitation. And therefore Moses's beginning, Gen. i. 1, is meant, as also the words after show, " All was made by him that was made ; " and, ver. 10, the world he came into was made by him. And as from the beginning is usually taken from the first times or infancy of the world ; so then, when God began to create, then was our Christ. And this here is set in opposition (John i. 14) unto the time of his being made flesh, lest that should have been thought his beginning. And unto this accords that of Heb. i. 10, where, speaking of Christ, out of Psalm cii., " *Thou, Lord, in the beginning hast laid the foundations of the earth ;* " so as to be sure he existed then. But further, in Psalm cii. 24, it runs thus, " *Thy years are throughout all generations.*" We have run, you see, through all generations since the creation, and have found his years throughout them all. And yet lest that should be taken only of the generations of this world, he adds (as Rivet expounds it), " *Before thou laidst the foundation of the earth.*"

Eighthly, So then we come to this, that he hath been before the creation, yea, from everlasting.

But, *Ninthly*, If you would have his eternity yet more express, see Heb. vii. 3, where mentioning Melchisedec, Christ's type, he renders him to have been his type in this—" Without father, without mother, without descent, having neither beginning of days, nor end of life ; but made like unto the Son of God ; abideth a priest continually." Where his meaning is to declare that, look what Melchisedec was *typicè*, or *umbraiter*, in a shadow, that our Christ was really and substantially.

Lastly, Add to this that in Micah v. 2, " But thou, Bethlehem Ephratah, though thou be little among the thousands of Judah, yet out of thee shall he come forth unto me that is to be ruler in Israel ; whose goings forth have been from of old, from everlasting ; " where he evidently speaks of two births Christ had, under the metaphor of going forth : one as man at Bethlehem in the fulness of time, the other as Son of God from everlasting. As Son of God, his goings forth (that is, his birth) are from everlasting. And it is termed, " goings forth," in the plural ; because it is *actus continuus*, and hath been every moment continued from everlasting. As the sun begets light and beams every moment, so God doth his Son. So then we have *two everlastings* attributed to Christ's person ; one to come, Heb. i. 10, and another past, here in Micah v. 2. And so as of God himself it is said, Ps. xc. 2, " From everlasting to everlasting thou art God," so also of Christ.—*Condensed from T. Goodwin's Treatise on " The Knowledge of God the Father, and his Son Jesus Christ."*

Verse 25.—" *Earth.*" " *Heavens.*" He names here the most stable parts of the world, and the most beautiful parts of the creation, those that are freest from corruptibility and change, to illustrate thereby the immutability of God, that though the heavens and earth have a prerogative of fixedness above other parts of the world, and the creatures that reside below, the heavens remain the same as they were created, and the centre of the earth retains its fixedness, and are as beautiful and fresh in their age as they were in their youth many years ago, notwithstanding the change of the elements, fire and water being often turned into air, so that there may remain but little of that air which was first created, by reason of the continual transmutation ; yet this firmness of the earth and heavens is not to be regarded in comparison of the unmoveableness and fixedness of the being of God. As their beauty comes short of the glory of his being, so doth their firmness come short of his stability.—*Stephen Charnock.*

Verse 26.—" *They shall perish.*" The greater the corruption, the vaster the destruction. Some think that the fiery deluge shall ascend no higher than did the watery. It may be the *earth* shall be burned, that is the worst guest at the table, the common sewer of all other creatures, but shall the heavens pass away ? It may be the airy heaven ; but shall the starry heaven where God hath printed such figures of his glory ? Yes, *cælum, elementum, terra*, when *ignis ubique ferox ruptis regnabit habenis*. The former deluge is called the world's winter, the next the world's summer. The one was with a cold and moist element, the other shall be with an element hot and dry. But what then shall become of the saints ? They shall be delivered out of all ; walking like those three servants in the midst of that great furnace, the burning world, and not be scorched, because there is one among them to deliver them, " the Son of God," Dan. iii. 25, their Redeemer. But shall all quite perish ? No, there is rather a mutation than an abolition of their substance. " *Thou shalt change them, and they shall be changed,*" not abolished. The concupiscence shall pass, not the essence ; the form, not the nature. In the altering of an old garment, we destroy it not, but trim it, refresh it, and make it seem new. They pass, they do not perish ; the dross is purged, the metal stays. The corrupt quality shall be renewed, and all things restored to that original beauty wherein they were created. " The end of all things is at hand," 1 Pet. iv. 7 : an end of us, an end of our days, an end of our ways, an end of our thoughts. If a man could say as Job's messenger, I alone am escaped, it were somewhat ; or might find an ark with Noah. But there is no ark to defend them from that heat, but only the bosom of Jesus Christ.—*Thomas Adams.*

Verse 26.—" *Like a garment.*" The whole creation is as a garment, wherein the Lord shows his power clothed unto men ; whence in particular he is said to clothe himself with light as with a garment. And in it is the hiding of his power. Hid it is, as a man is hid with a garment ; not that he should not be seen at all, but that he should not be seen perfectly and as he is. It shows the man, and he is known by it ; but also it hides him, that he is not perfectly or fully seen. So are the works of creation unto God, he so far makes them his garment or clothing as in them to give out some instances of his power and wisdom ; but he is also hid in them, in that by them no creature can come to the full and perfect knowledge of him. Now, when this work shall cease, and God shall unclothe or unveil all his glory to his saints, and they shall know him perfectly, see him as he is, so far as a created nature is capable of that comprehension, then will he lay them aside and fold them up, at least as to that use, as easily as a man lays aside a garment that he will wear or use no more. This lies in the metaphor.—*John Owen.*

Verse 27.—" *Thou art the same.*" The essence of God, with all the perfections of his nature, are pronounced the same, without any variation from eternity to eternity. So that the text doth not only assert the eternal duration of God, but his immutability in that duration ; his eternity is signified in that expression, " thou shalt endure ; " his immutability in this, " thou art the same." To endure, argues indeed this immutability as well as eternity ; for what endures is not changed, and what is changed doth not endure. " *But thou art the same,*" אַתָּה חוּא, doth more fully signify it. He could not be the same if he could be changed into any other thing than what he is. The Psalmist therefore puts, not thou *hast been* or *shall be*, but *thou art* the same, without any alteration ; thou art the same, that is, the same God, the same in essence and nature, the same in will and purpose, thou dost change all other things as thou pleaseth ; but thou art immutable in every respect, and receivest no shadow of change, though never so light and small. The Psalmist here alludes to the name *Jehovah, I am,* and doth not only ascribe immutability to God, but exclude everything else from partaking in that perfection.—*Stephen Charnock.*

Verse 28.—" *The children of thy servants shall continue.*" In what sense is " *children* " taken ? Either the children of their flesh, or of their faith. Some say the children of the same faith with the godly teachers and servants of the Lord, begotten by them to God, as noting the perpetuity of the church, who shall in every age bring forth children to God. 'Tis the comfort of God's people to see a young brood growing up to continue his remembrance in the world, that when they die religion shall not die with them, nor the succession of the church be interrupted. This sense is not altogether incongruous ; but rather I think the children of their body are here intended ; it being a blessing often promised : see the next Psalm, verse 17. " The mercy of the LORD is from everlasting to everlasting upon them that fear him, and his righteousness unto children's children," " *Shall continue ; *" " *shall be established.*" In what sense is it spoken ? Some think only *pro more fœderis,* according to the fashion of that covenant which the people of God were then under, when eternity was but more darkly revealed and shadowed out, either by long life, or the continuance of their name in their posterity, which was a kind of literal immortality. Clearly such a kind of regard is had, as appeareth by that which you find in Ps. xxxvii. 28. " *The Lord loveth judgment, and forsaketh not his saints ; they are preserved for ever.*" How ? since they die as others do : mark the antithesis, and that will explain it. " *They are preserved for ever : but the seed of the wicked shall be cut off.*" They are preserved in their posterity. Children are but the parents multiplied, and the parent continued ; 'tis *nodosa æternitas ;* when the father's life is run out to the last, there is a knot tied, and the line is still continued by the child. I confess, temporal blessings, such as long life, and the promise of a happy posterity, are more visible in the eye of that dispensation of the covenant ; but yet God still taketh care for the children of his people, and many promises run that way that belong to the gospel-administration, and still God's service is the surest way to establish a family, as sin is the ready way to root it out. And if it doth not always fall out accordingly, yet for the most part it doth ; and we are no competent judges of God's dispensations in this kind, because we see Providence by pieces, and have not the skill to set them together ; but at the day of judgment, when the whole contexture of God's dealings is laid before us, we shall clearly understand how *the children of his servants continue, and their seed is established.*—*Thomas Manton.*

Verse 28.—O the folly of the world, that seeks to make perpetuities to their houses by devises in the law, which may perhaps reach to continue their estates, but can it reach to continue their seed ? It may entail lands to their heirs, but can it entail heirs to their lands ? No, God knows ! This is a perpetuity of only God's making, a privilege of only God's servants : for " *The children of his servants shall continue, and their seed shall be established before him ; *" but that any others shall continue is no part of David's warrant.—*Sir R. Baker.*

HINTS TO PREACHERS.

Title.—I. Afflicted men may pray. II. Afflicted men should pray even when overwhelmed. III. Afflicted men can pray—for what is wanted is a pouring out of their complaint, not an oratorical display. IV. Afflicted men are accepted in prayer —for this prayer is placed on record.

Verses 1, 2.—Five steps to the mercy-seat. The Psalmist prays for, I. Audience : " Hear my prayer." II. Access : " Let my cry come before thee." III. Unveiling : " Hide not thy face." IV. An intent ear : " Incline thine ear." V. Answer.— *C. Davis.*

Verses 1, 17, 19, 20.—An interesting discourse may be founded upon these passages. I. The Lord entreated to hear—verse 1. II. The Promise given that he will hear— verse 17. III. The Record that the Lord has heard—verses 19 and 20.

Verse 2.—I. Prayer in trouble is most needed. II. Prayer in trouble is most heeded. III. Prayer in trouble is most speeded : " Answer me speedily." Or, I. Prayer in trouble : " In the day," etc. II. The prayer of trouble : " Hide not thy face ; " not remove the trial, but be with me in it. A fiery furnace is a paradise when God is with us there.—*G. R.*

Verse 2 (first clause)'—He deprecates the loss of the divine countenance when under trouble. I. That would intensify it a thousandfold. II. That would deprive him of strength to bear the trouble. III. That would prevent his acting so as to glorify God in the trouble. IV. That might injure the result of the trouble.

Verse 2 (last clause).—I. We often need to be answered speedily. II. God can so answer. III. God has so answered. IV. God has promised so to answer.

Verses 3—11.—I. The causes of grief. 1. The brevity of life. *v.* 3. 2. Bodily pain. *v.* 3. 3. Dejection of spirit. *v.* 4, 5. 4. Solitariness. *v.* 6, 7. 5. Reproach. *v.* 8. 6. Humiliation. *v.* 9. 7. The hidings of God's countenance. *v.* 10. 8. Wasting away. *v.* 11. II. The eloquence of grief. 1. The brevity of life is as vanishing " smoke." 2. Bodily pain is fire in the bones. 3. Dejection of spirit is " withered grass." Who can eat when the heart is sad ? 4. Solitariness is like " The pelican in the wilderness, the owl in the desert, and the sparrow upon the house top." 5. Reproach is being surrounded by madmen—" they that are mad." 6. Humiliation is " eating ashes like bread," and " drinking tears." 7. The hidings of God's countenance is lifting up in order to be cast down. 8. Wasting away is a shadow declining and grass withering.—*G. R.*

Verse 4.—Unbelieving sorrow makes us forget to use proper means for our support. I. We forget the promises. II. Forget the past and its experiences. III. Forget the Lord Jesus, our life. IV. Forget the everlasting love of God. This leads to weakness, faintness, etc., and is to be avoided.

Verse 6.—This as a text, together with ciii. 5, makes an interesting contrast, and gives scope for much experimental teaching.

Verse 7.—The evils and benefits of solitude ; when it may be sought, and when it becomes a folly. Or, the mournful watcher—alone, outside the pale of communion, insignificant, wishful for fellowship, set apart to watch.

Verse 9.—The sorrows of the saints—their number, bitterness, sources, correctives, influences, and consolations.

Verse 10.—I. The trial of trials—*thine* indignation and *thy* wrath. II. The aggravation of that trial—former favour, " thou hast lifted me up," etc. III. The best behaviour under it : see former verse, and verses 12 and 13.

Verse 10 (last clause.)—The prosperity of a church or an individual often followed by declension ; worldly aggrandisement frequently succeeded by affliction ; great joy in the Lord very generally succeeded by trial.

Verses 11, 12.—*I* and *Thou*, or the notable contrast. I. *I :* my days are like a shadow, 1. Because it is unsubstantial ; because it partakes of the nature of the darkness which is to absorb it ; because the longer it becomes the briefer its continuance. 2. I am like grass cut down by the scythe ; scorched by drought. II. *Thou.* Lord. Ever enduring. Ever memorable. Ever the study of passing generations of men.—*C. D.*

Verse 13.—I. Zion often needs restoration. It needs " mercy." II. Its restoration is certain : " Thou shalt arise," etc. III. The seasons of its restoration are determined. There is a " time " to favour her ; a " set " time. IV. Intimations of those coming seasons are often given : " The time, the set time, is come."—*G. R.*

Verses 13, 14.—I. Visitation expected. II. Predestination relied upon. III.

Evidence observed.   IV. Enquiry suggested—Do we take pleasure in her stones ? etc.

Verses 13, 14.—The interest of the Lord's people in the concerns of Zion one of the surest signs of her returning prosperity.

Verse 15.—The inward prosperity of the church essential to her power in the world.

Verse 16.—God is Zion's purchaser, architect, builder, inhabitant, Lord.   I. Zion built up.   Conversions frequent ; confessions numerous ; union firm ; edification solid ;   missions extended.   II. God glorified.   In its very foundation ; by its ministry ;   by difficulties and enemies ;   by poor workers, and poor materials ;   and even by our failures.   III. Hope excited.   Because we may expect the Lord to glorify himself.   IV. Inquiry suggested.   Am I concerned, as built, or building ? not merely doctrinally, but experimentally ?

Verse 17.—I. The destitute pray.   II. They pray most.   III. They pray best. IV. They pray most effectually.   Or the surest way to succeed in prayer is to pray as the destitute ; show the reason of this.

Verse 18.—I. A memorial.   II. A magnificat.—*W. Durban.*

Verses 18—21.—I. Misery in extremis.   II. Divinity observant.   III. Deity actively assisting.   IV. Glory consequently published.

Verses 19—22.—I. The notice which God takes of the world, *v.* 19.   1. The place from which he beholds it :   " from heaven," not from an earthly point of view. 2. The character in which he beholds it ;   " from the height of his sanctuary," from the mercy-seat.   II. What attracts his notice most in the world.   The groaning of the prisoner and of those appointed to death.   III. The purpose for which he notices them.   " To loose," etc. ;   " to declare," etc.   1. For human comfort. 2. For his own glory.   IV. When his notice is thus fixed upon the earth.   " When," etc., *v.* 22.—*G. R.*

Verse 23.—For the sick.   I. Submission—The Lord sent the trial—" *He* weakeneth," etc.   II. Service—exonerated from some work, he now requires of me patience, earnestness, etc.   III. Preparation—for going home.   IV. Prayer—for others to occupy my place.   V. Expectation—I shall soon be in heaven, now that my days are shortened.

Verse 24.—I. *The prayer.*   " Take me not away," etc.   1. Not in the midst of life, is the prayer of some.   2. Not in the midst of worldly prosperity, is the prayer of many, for the sake of those dependent upon them.   3. Not in the midst of spiritual growth, is the prayer of not a few :   " Oh spare me, that I may recover strength," etc.   4. Not in the midst of Christian work and usefulness, is the prayer of others. II. *The plea.*   " Thy years," etc. ;   years are plentiful with thee, therefore to give me longer days will be an easy gift—and thine own are throughout all generations. —*G. R.*

Verses 25—27.—I. The unchangeableness of God amidst past changes : " of old," etc.   1. He was the same before as after he had laid the foundations of the earth.   2. He was the same after as before.   II. The unchangeableness of God amidst future changes.   " They shall perish," etc.   1. The same before they perish as after.   2. After as before.   III. The unchangeableness of God in the past and the future.   " Thou art the same," etc.—*G. R.*

Verses 26, 27.—I. How far God may change—only in his garments, or outward manifestations of creation and providence.   II. Wherein he cannot change—his nature, attributes, covenant, love, etc.   III. The comfortable truths which may be safely inferred, or which gather support from this fact.

Verses 26, 27.—I. The material universe of God.   1. No more to him than a garment to the wearer.   2. Ever waxing old, but he the same.   3. Soon to be changed, and left to perish, but of his years no end.   II. Our relation to each—1. Let us never love the dress more than the wearer.   2. Nor trust more in the changeful than in the abiding.   3. Nor live for that which will die out.

Verse 28.—The true apostolical succession.   I. There always will be saints. II. They will frequently be the seed of the saints after the flesh.   III. They will always be the spiritual seed of the godly, for God converts one by means of another. **IV.**   We should order our efforts with an eye to the church's future.

PSALM CIII.

TITLE.— A Psalm of David.—*Doubtless by David ; it is in his own style when at its best, and we should attribute it to his later years when he had a higher sense of the preciousness of pardon, because a keener sense of sin, than in his younger days. His clear sense of the frailty of life indicates his weaker years, as also does the very fulness of his praiseful gratitude. As in the lofty Alps some peaks rise above all others, so among even the inspired Psalms there are heights of song which overtop the rest. This one hundred and third Psalm has ever seemed to us to be the Monte Rosa of the divine chain of mountains of praise, glowing with a ruddier light than any of the rest. It is as the apple tree among the trees of the wood, and its golden fruit has a flavour such as no fruit ever bears unless it has been ripened in the full sunshine of mercy. It is man's reply to the benedictions of his God, his Song on the Mount answering to his Redeemer's Sermon on the Mount. Nebuchadnezzar adored his idol with flute, harp, sacbut, psaltery, dulcimer and all kinds of music ; and David, in far nobler style, awakens all the melodies of heaven and earth in honour of the one only living and true God. Our attempt at exposition is commenced under an impressive sense of the utter impossibility of doing justice to so sublime a composition ; we call upon our soul and all that is within us to aid in the pleasurable task ; but, alas, our soul is finite, and our all of mental faculty far too little for the enterprise. There is too much in the Psalm for a thousand pens to write, it is one of those all-comprehending Scriptures which is a Bible in itself, and it might alone almost suffice for the hymn-book of the church.*

DIVISION.—*First the Psalmist sings of personal mercies which he had himself received,* 1—5 ; *then he magnifies the attributes of Jehovah as displayed in his dealings with his people,* 6—19 ; *and he closes by calling upon all the creatures in the universe to adore the Lord and join with himself in blessing Jehovah, the ever gracious.*

EXPOSITION.

BLESS the LORD, O my soul: and all that is within me, *bless* his holy name.

2 Bless the LORD, O my soul, and forget not all his benefits :

3 Who forgiveth all thine iniquities ; who healeth all thy diseases ;

4 Who redeemeth thy life from destruction ; who crowneth thee with lovingkindness and tender mercies ;

5 Who satisfieth thy mouth with good *things ; so that* thy youth is renewed like the eagle's.

1. " *Bless the Lord, O my soul.*" Soul music is the very soul of music. The Psalmist strikes the best key-note when he begins with stirring up his inmost self to magnify the Lord. He soliloquizes, holds self-communion and exhorts himself, as though he felt that dulness would all too soon steal over his faculties, as, indeed, it will over us all, unless we are diligently on the watch. Jehovah is worthy to be praised by us in that highest style of adoration which is intended by the term *bless*— " All thy works praise thee, O God, but thy saints shall bless thee." Our very life and essential self should be engrossed with this delightful service, and each one of us should arouse his own heart to the engagement. Let others forbear if they can : " Bless the Lord, O MY soul." Let others murmur, but do thou *bless*. Let others bless themselves and their idols, but do thou bless *the Lord*. Let others use only their tongues, but as for me I will cry, " Bless the Lord, O my *soul*." " *And all that is within me, bless his holy name.*" Many are our faculties, emotions, and capacities, but God has given them all to us, and they ought all to join in chorus to his praise. Half-hearted, ill-conceived, unintelligent praises are not such as we should render to our loving Lord. If the law of justice demanded all our heart and soul and mind for the Creator, much more may the law of gratitude put in a comprehensive claim for the homage of our whole being to the God of grace. It is

instructive to note how the Psalmist dwells upon the *holy* name of God, as if his holiness were dearest to him ; or, perhaps, because the holiness or wholeness of God was to his mind the grandest motive for rendering to him the homage of his nature in its wholeness. Babes may praise the divine goodness, but fathers in grace magnify his holiness. By *the name* we understand the revealed character of God, and assuredly those songs which are suggested, not by our fallible reasoning and imperfect observation, but by unerring inspiration, should more than any others arouse all our consecrated powers.

2. " *Bless the Lord, O my soul.*" He is in real earnest, and again calls upon himself to arise. Had he been very sleepy before ? Or was he now doubly sensible of the importance, the imperative necessity of adoration ? Certainly, he uses no vain repetitions, for the Holy Spirit guides his pen ; and thus he shews us that we have need, again and again, to bestir ourselves when we are about to worship God, for it would be shameful to offer him anything less than the utmost our souls can render. These first verses are a tuning of the harp, a screwing up of the loosened strings that not a note may fail in the sacred harmony. " *And forget not all his benefits.*" Not so much as one of the divine dealings should be forgotten, they are all really beneficial to us, all worthy of himself, and all subjects for praise. Memory is very treacherous about the best things ; by a strange perversity, engendered by the fall, it treasures up the refuse of the past and permits priceless treasures to lie neglected, it is tenacious of grievances and holds benefits all too loosely. It needs spurring to its duty, though that duty ought to be its delight. Observe that he calls *all* that is within him to remember *all* the Lord's benefits. For our task our energies should be suitably called out. God's all cannot be praised with less than our all.

Reader, have we not cause enough at this time to bless him who blesses us ? Come, let us read our diaries and see if there be not choice favours recorded there for which we have rendered no grateful return. Remember how the Persian king, when he could not sleep, read the chronicles of the empire, and discovered that one who had saved his life had never been rewarded. How quickly did he do him honour ! The Lord has saved us with a great salvation, shall we render no recompense ? The name of *ingrate* is one of the most shameful that a man can wear ; surely we cannot be content to run the risk of such a brand. Let us awake then, and with intense enthusiasm bless Jehovah.

3. " *Who forgiveth all thine iniquities.*" Here David begins his list of blessings received, which he rehearses as themes and arguments for praise. He selects a few of the choicest pearls from the casket of divine love, threads them on the string of memory, and hangs them about the neck of gratitude. Pardoned sin is, in our experience, one of the choicest boons of grace, one of the earliest gifts of mercy,— in fact, the needful preparation for enjoying all that follows it. Till iniquity is forgiven, healing, redemption, and satisfaction are unknown blessings. Forgiveness is first in the order of our spiritual experience, and in some respects first in value. The pardon granted is a present one—*forgiveth* ; it is continual, for he still *forgiveth* ; it is divine, for God gives it ; it is far reaching, for it removes *all* our sins ; it takes in omissions as well as commissions, for both of these are *in-equities* ; and it is most effectual, for it is as real as the healing, and the rest of the mercies with which it is placed. " *Who healeth all thy diseases.*" When the cause is gone, namely, iniquity, the effect ceases. Sicknesses of body and soul came into the world by sin, and as sin is eradicated, diseases bodily, mental, and spiritual will vanish, till " the inhabitant shall no more say, I am sick." Many-sided is the character of our heavenly Father, for, having forgiven as a judge, he then cures as a physician. He is all things to us, as our needs call for him, and our infirmities do but reveal him in new characters.

> " In him is only good,
> In me is only ill,
> My ill but draws his goodness forth,
> And me he loveth still."

God gives efficacy to medicine for the body, and his grace sanctifies the soul. Spiritually we are daily under his care, and he visits us, as the surgeon does his patient ; *healing* still (for that is the exact word) each malady as it arises. No disease of our soul baffles his skill, he goes on healing *all*, and he will do so till the last trace of taint has gone from our nature. The two *alls* of this verse are further reasons for *all* that is within us praising the Lord.

The two blessings of this verse the Psalmist was personally enjoying, he sang not of others but of himself, or rather of his Lord, who was daily forgiving and healing him. He must have known that it was so, or he could not have sung of it. He had no doubt about it, he felt in his soul that it was so, and, therefore, he bade his pardoned and restored soul bless the Lord with all its might.

4. *" Who redeemeth thy life from destruction."* By purchase and by power the Lord redeems us from the spiritual death into which we had fallen, and from the eternal death which would have been its consequence. Had not the death penalty of sin been removed, our forgiveness and healing would have been incomplete portions of salvation, fragments only, and but of small value, but the removal of the guilt and power of sin is fitly attended by the reversal of the sentence of death which had been passed upon us. Glory be to our great Substitute, who delivered us from going down into the pit, by giving himself to be our ransom. Redemption will ever constitute one of the sweetest notes in the believer's grateful song. *" Who crowneth thee with lovingkindness and tender mercies."* Our Lord does nothing by halves, he will not stay his hand till he has gone to the uttermost with his people. Cleansing, healing, redemption, are not enough, he must needs make them kings and crown them, and the crown must be far more precious than if it were made of corruptible things, such as silver and gold; it is studded with gems of grace and lined with the velvet of lovingkindness; it is decked with the jewels of mercy, but made soft for the head to wear by a lining of tenderness. Who is like unto thee, O Lord ! God himself crowns the princes of his family, for their best things come from him directly and distinctly; they do not earn the crown, for it is of *mercy* not of merit; they feel their own unworthiness of it, therefore he deals with *tenderness ;* but he is resolved to bless them, and, therefore, he is ever *crowning* them, always surrounding their brows with coronets of mercy and compassion. He always crowns the edifice which he commences, and where he gives pardon he gives acceptance too. " Since thou wast precious in my sight thou hast been honourable, and I have loved thee." Our sin deprived us of all our honours, a bill of attainder was issued against us as traitors; but he who removed the sentence of death by redeeming us from destruction, restores to us more than all our former honours by crowning us anew. Shall God crown us and shall not we crown him ? Up, my soul, and cast thy crown at his feet, and in lowliest reverence worship him, who has so greatly exalted thee, as to lift thee from the dunghill and set thee among princes.

5. *" Who satisfieth thy mouth with good things,"* or rather " filling with good thy soul." No man is ever filled to satisfaction but a believer, and only God himself can satisfy even him. Many a worldling is satiated, but not one is satisfied. God satisfies the very soul of man, his noblest part, his ornament and glory; and of consequence he satisfies his mouth, however hungry and craving it might otherwise be. Soul-satisfaction loudly calls for soul-praise, and when the mouth is filled with good it is bound to speak good of him who filled it. Our good Lord bestows really *good things*, not vain toys and idle pleasures; and these he is always giving, so that from moment to moment he is *satisfying* our soul with good : shall we not be still praising him ? If we never cease to bless him till he ceases to bless us, our employment will be eternal. *" So that thy youth is renewed like the eagle's."* Renewal of strength, amounting to a grant of a new lease of life, was granted to the Psalmist; he was so restored to his former self that he grew young again, and looked as vigorous as an eagle, whose eye can gaze upon the sun, and whose wing can mount above the storm. Our version refers to the annual moulting of the eagle, after which it looks fresh and young; but the original does not appear to allude to any such fact of natural history, but simply to describe the diseased one as so healed and strengthened, that he became as full of energy as the bird which is strongest of the feathered race, most fearless, most majestic, and most soaring. He who sat moping with the owl in the last Psalm, here flies on high with the eagle : the Lord works marvellous changes in us, and we learn by such experiences to bless his holy name. To grow from a sparrow to an eagle, and leave the wilderness of the pelican to mount among the stars, is enough to make any man cry, " Bless the Lord, O my soul."

Thus is the endless chain of grace complete. Sin is forgiven, its power subdued, and its penalty averted, then we are honoured, supplied, and our very nature renovated, till we are as new-born children in the household of God. O Lord, we must bless thee, and we will; as thou dost withhold nothing from us so we would not keep back from thy praise one solitary power of our nature, but with all our heart, and soul, and strength praise thy holy name.

6 The Lord executeth righteousness and judgment for all that are oppressed.

7 He made known his ways unto Moses, his acts unto the children of Israel.

8 The Lord *is* merciful and gracious, slow to anger, and plenteous in mercy.

9 He will not always chide: neither will he keep *his anger* for ever.

10 He hath not dealt with us after our sins; nor rewarded us according to our iniquities.

11 For as the heaven is high above the earth, *so* great is his mercy toward them that fear him.

12 As far as the east is from the west, *so* far hath he removed our transgressions from us.

13 Like as a father pitieth *his* children, *so* the Lord pitieth them that fear him.

14 For he knoweth our frame; he remembereth that we *are* dust.

15 *As for* man, his days *are* as grass: as a flower of the field, so he flourisheth.

16 For the wind passeth over it, and it is gone; and the place thereof shall know it no more.

17 But the mercy of the Lord *is* from everlasting to everlasting upon them that fear him, and his righteousness unto children's children;

18 To such as keep his covenant, and to those that remember his commandments to do them.

19 The Lord hath prepared his throne in the heavens; and his kingdom ruleth over all.

6. "*The Lord executeth righteousness and judgment for all that are oppressed.*" Our own personal obligations must not absorb our song; we must also magnify the Lord for his goodness to others. He does not leave the poor and needy to perish at the hands of their enemies, but interposes on their behalf, for he is the executor of the poor and the executioner of the cruel. When his people were in Egypt he heard their groanings and brought them forth, but he overthrew Pharaoh in the Red Sea. Man's injustice shall receive retribution at the hand of God. Mercy to his saints demands vengeance on their persecutors, and he will repay it. No blood of martyrs shall be shed in vain; no groans of confessors in prison shall be left without inquisition being made concerning them. *All* wrongs shall be righted, *all* the oppressed shall be avenged. Justice may at times leave the courts of man, but it abides upon the tribunal of God. For this every right-minded person will bless God. Were he careless of his creature's good, did he neglect the administration of justice, did he suffer high-handed oppressors finally to escape, we should have greater reason for trembling than rejoicing: it is not so, however, for our God is a God of justice, and by him actions are weighed; he will mete out his portion to the proud and make the tyrant bite the dust,—yea, often he visits the haughty persecutor even in this life, so that "the Lord is known by the judgments which he executeth."

7. "*He made known his ways unto Moses.*" Moses was made to see the manner in which the Lord deals with men; he saw this in each of the three periods of his life, in the court, in retirement, and at the head of the tribes of Israel. To him the Lord gave specially clear manifestations of his dispensations and modes of ruling among mankind, granting to him to see more of God than had before been seen by mortal man, while he communed with him upon the mount. "*His acts unto the children of Israel.*" They saw less than Moses, for they beheld the deeds of God without understanding his method therein, yet this was much, very much, and might have been more if they had not been so perverse; the stint was not in the revelation, but in the hardness of their hearts. It is a great act of sovereign grace and condescending love when the Lord reveals himself to any people, and they ought to appreciate the distinguished favour shown to them. We, as believers in Jesus, know the Lord's *ways* of covenant grace, and we have by experience been made to see his *acts* of mercy towards us; how heartily ought we to praise our divine teacher, the Holy Spirit, who has made these things known to us, for had it not been for him

we should have continued in darkness unto this day. "Lord, how is it that thou wilt manifest thyself unto us and not unto the world?" Why hast thou made us "of the election who have obtained it" while the rest are blinded?

Observe how prominent is the personality of God in all this gracious teaching— "*He* made known." He did not leave Moses to discover truth for himself, but became his instructor. What should we ever know if he did not make it known? God alone can reveal himself. If Moses needed the Lord to make him known, how much more do we who are so much inferior to the great law-giver?

8. "*The Lord is merciful and gracious.*" Those with whom he deals are sinners. However much he favours them they are guilty and need mercy at his hands, nor is he slow to compassionate their lost estate, or reluctant by his grace to lift them out of it. Mercy pardons sin, grace bestows favour; in both the Lord abounds. This is that way of his which he made known to Moses (Ex. xxxiv. 6), and in that way he will abide as long as the age of grace shall last, and men are yet in this life. He who "executeth righteousness and judgment," yet delighteth in mercy. "*Slow to anger.*" He can be angry, and can deal out righteous indignation upon the guilty, but it is his strange work; he lingers long, with loving pauses, tarrying by the way to give space for repentance and opportunity for accepting his mercy. Thus deals he with the greatest sinners, and with his own children much more so : towards them his anger is shortlived and never reaches into eternity, and when it is shown in fatherly chastisements he does not afflict willingly, and soon pities their sorrows. From this we should learn to be ourselves slow to anger ; if the Lord is longsuffering under our great provocations how much more ought we to endure the errors of our brethren ! "*And plenteous in mercy.*" Rich in it, quick in it, overflowing with it ; and so had he need to be or we should soon be consumed. He is God, and not man, or our sins would soon drown his love ; yet above the mountains of our sins the floods of his mercy rise.

> "Plenteous grace with thee is found,
>   Grace to cover all my sin ;
> Let the healing streams abound ;
>   Make and keep me pure within."

All the world tastes of his sparing mercy, those who hear the gospel partake of his inviting mercy, the saints live by his saving mercy, are preserved by his upholding mercy, are cheered by his consoling mercy, and will enter heaven through his infinite and everlasting mercy. Let grace abounding be our hourly song in the house of our pilgrimage. Let those who feel that they live upon it glorify the plenteous fountain from which it so spontaneously flows.

9. "*He will not always chide.*" He will sometimes, for he cannot endure that his people should harbour sin in their hearts, but not for ever will he chasten them; as soon as they turn to him and forsake their evil ways he will end the quarrel. He might find constant cause for striving with us, for we have always something in us which is contrary to his holy mind, but he refrains himself lest our spirits should fail before him. It will be profitable for any one of us who may be at this time out of conscious fellowship with the Lord, to inquire at his hands the reason for his anger, saying, "Shew me wherefore thou contendest with me?" For he is easily entreated of, and soon ceaseth from his wrath. When his children turn from their sins he soon turns from his chidings. "*Neither will he keep his anger for ever.*" He bears no grudges. The Lord would not have his people harbour resentments, and in his own course of action he sets them a grand example. When the Lord has chastened his child he has done with his anger : he is not punishing as a judge, else might his wrath burn on, but he is acting as a father, and, therefore, after a few blows he ends the matter, and presses his beloved one to his bosom as if nothing had happened ; or if the offence lies too deep in the offender's nature to be thus overcome, he continues to correct, but he never ceases to love, and he does not suffer his anger with his people to pass into the next world, but receives his erring child into his glory.

10. "*He hath not dealt with us after our sins ; nor rewarded us according to our iniquities.*" Else had Israel perished outright, and we also had long ago been consigned to the lowest hell. We ought to praise the Lord for what he has not done as well as for what he has wrought for us ; even the negative side deserves our adoring gratitude. Up to this moment, at our very worst estate, we have never suffered as we deserved to suffer ; our daily lot has not been apportioned upon the rule of what we merited, but on the far different measure of undeserved kindness.

Shall we not bless the Lord ? Every power of our being might have been rent with anguish, instead of which we are all in the enjoyment of comparative happiness, and many of us are exceedingly favoured with inward joy ; let then every faculty, yea, all that is within us, bless his holy name.

11. " *For as the heaven is high above the earth, so great is his mercy toward them that fear him.*" Boundless in extent towards his chosen is the mercy of the Lord ; it is no more to be measured than the height of heaven or the heaven of heavens. " *Like the height of the heaven* " is the original language, which implies other points of comparison besides extent, and suggests sublimity, grandeur, and glory. As the lofty heavens canopy the earth, water it with dews and rains, enlighten it with sun, moon, and stars, and look down upon it with unceasing watchfulness, even so the Lord's mercy from above covers all his chosen, enriches them, embraces them, and stands for ever as their dwelling-place. The idea of our version is a very noble one, for who shall tell how exceeding great is the height of heaven ? Who can reach the first of the fixed stars, and who can measure the utmost bounds of the starry universe ? Yet so great is his mercy ! Oh, that great little word so ! All this mercy is for " *them that fear him ;* " there must be a humble, hearty reverence of his authority, or we cannot taste of his grace. Godly fear is one of the first products of the divine life in us, it is the beginning of wisdom, yet it fully ensures to its possessor all the benefits of divine mercy, and is, indeed, here and elsewhere, employed to set forth the whole of true religion. Many a true child of God is full of filial fear, and yet at the same time stands trembling as to his acceptance with God ; this trembling is groundless, but it is infinitely to be preferred to that baseborn presumption, which incites men to boast of their adoption and consequent security, when all the while they are in the gall of bitterness. Those who are presuming upon the infinite extent of divine mercy, should here be led to consider that although it is wide as the horizon and high as the stars, yet it is only meant for them that fear the Lord, and as for obstinate rebels, they shall have justice without mercy measured out to them.

12. " *As far as the east is from the west, so far hath he removed our transgressions from us.*" O glorious verse, no word even upon the inspired page can excel it ! Sin is removed from us by a miracle of love ! What a load to move, and yet is it removed so far that the distance is incalculable. Fly as far as the wing of imagination can bear you, and if you journey through space eastward, you are further from the west at every beat of your wing. If sin be removed so far, then we may be sure that the scent, the trace, the very memory of it must be entirely gone. If this be the distance of its removal, there is no shade of fear of its ever being brought back again ; even Satan himself could not achieve such a task. Our sins are gone, Jesus has borne them away. Far as the place of sunrise is removed from yonder west, where the sun sinks when his day's journey is done, so far were our sins carried by our scapegoat nineteen centuries ago, and now if they be sought for, they shall not be found, yea, they shall not be, saith the Lord. Come, my soul, awaken thyself thoroughly and glorify the Lord for this richest of blessings. Hallelujah. The Lord alone could remove sin at all, and he has done it in a godlike fashion, making a final sweep of all our transgressions.

13. " *Like as a father pitieth his children, so the Lord pitieth them that fear him.*" To those who truly reverence his holy name, the Lord is a father and acts as such. These he pities, for in the very best of men the Lord sees much to pity, and when they are at their best state they still need his compassion. This should check every propensity to pride, though at the same time it should yield us the richest comfort. Fathers feel for their children, especially when they are in pain, they would like to suffer in their stead, their sighs and groans cut them to the quick : thus sensitive towards us is our heavenly Father. We do not adore a god of stone, but the living God, who is tenderness itself. He is at this moment compassionating us, for the word is in the present tense ; his pity never fails to flow, and we never cease to need it.

14. " *For he knoweth our frame.*" He knows how we are made, for he made us. Our make and build, our constitution and temperament, our prevailing infirmity and most besetting temptation he well perceives, for he searches our inmost nature. " *He remembereth that we are dust.*" Made of dust, dust still, and ready to return to dust. We have sometimes heard of " the Iron Duke," and of iron constitutions, but the words are soon belied, for the Iron Duke is dissolved, and other men of like vigour are following to the grave, where " dust to dust " is an appropriate requiem. We too often forget that we are dust, and try our minds and bodies unduly by ex-

cessive mental and bodily exertion, we are also too little mindful of the infirmities of others, and impose upon them burdens grievous to be borne ; but our heavenly Father never overloads us, and never fails to give us strength equal to our day, because he always takes our frailty into account when he is apportioning to us our lot. Blessed be his holy name for this gentleness towards his frail creatures.

15. " *As for man, his days are as grass.*" He lives on the grass and lives like the grass. Corn is but educated grass, and man, who feeds on it, partakes of its nature. The grass lives, grows, flowers, falls beneath the scythe, dries up, and is removed from the field : read this sentence over again, and you will find it the history of man. If he lives out his little day, he is cut down at last, and it is far more likely that he will wither before he comes to maturity, or be plucked away on a sudden, long before he has fulfilled his time. " *As a flower of the field, so he flourisheth.*" He has a beauty and a comeliness even as the meadows have when they are yellow with the king-cups, but, alas, how shortlived ! No sooner come than gone, a flash of love-liness and no more ! Man is not even like a flower in the conservatory or in the sheltered garden border, he grows best according to nature, as the field-flower does, and like the unprotected beautifier of the pasture, he runs a thousand risks of coming to a speedy end. A large congregation, in many-coloured attire, always reminds us of a meadow bright with many hues ; and the comparison becomes sadly true when we reflect, that as the grass and its goodliness soon pass away, even so will those we gaze upon, and all their visible beauty. Thus, too, must it be with all that comes of the flesh, even its greatest excellencies and natural virtues, for " that which is born of the flesh is flesh," and therefore is but as grass which withers if but a breath of wind assails it. Happy are they who, born from above, have in them an incorruptible seed which liveth and abideth for ever.

16. " *For the wind passeth over it, and it is gone.*" Only a little wind is needed, not even a scythe is demanded, a breath can do it, for the flower is so frail.

> " If one sharp wind sweep o'er the field,
> It withers in an hour."

How small a portion of deleterious gas suffices to create a deadly fever, which no art of man can stay. No need of sword or bullet, a puff of foul air is deadlier far, and fails not to lay low the healthiest and most stalwart son of man. " *And the place thereof shall know it no more.*" The flower blooms no more. It may have a successor, but as for itself its leaves are scattered, and its perfume will never again sweeten the evening air. Man also dies and is gone, gone from his old haunts, his dear home, and his daily labours, never to return. As far as this world is concerned, he is as though he ne'er had been ; the sun rises, the moon increases or wanes, summer and winter run their round, the rivers flow, and all things continue in their courses as though they missed him not, so little a figure does he make in the affairs of nature. Perhaps a friend will note that he is gone, and say,

> " One morn, I miss'd him on the accustom'd hill.
> Along the heath, and near his favourite tree ;
> Another came, nor yet beside the rill,
> Nor up the lawn, nor at the wood was he."

But when the " dirges due " are silent, beyond a mound of earth, and perhaps a crumbling stone, how small will be the memorial of our existence upon this busy scene ! True there are more enduring memories, and an existence of another kind coeval with eternity, but these belong, not to our flesh, which is but grass, but to a higher life, in which we rise to close fellowship with the Eternal.

17. " *But the mercy of the Lord is from everlasting to everlasting upon them that fear him.*" Blessed *but !* How vast the contrast between the fading flower and the everlasting God ! How wonderful that his mercy should link our frailty with his eternity, and make us everlasting too ! From old eternity the Lord viewed his people as objects of mercy, and as such chose them to become partakers of his grace ; the doctrine of eternal election is most delightful to those who have light to see it and love wherewith to accept it. It is a theme for deepest thought and highest joy. The " *to everlasting* " is equally precious. Jehovah changes not, he has mercy without end as well as without beginning. Never will those who fear him find that either their sins or their needs have exhausted the great deep of his grace. The main question is, " Do we *fear him ?* " If we are lifting up to heaven the eye of filial fear, the gaze of

paternal love is never removed from us, and it never will be, world without end. *" And his righteousness unto children's children."* Mercy to those with whom the Lord makes a covenant is guaranteed by *righteousness ;* it is because he is just that he never revokes a promise, or fails to fulfil it. Our believing sons and their seed for ever will find the word of the Lord the same ; to them will he display his grace and bless them even as he has blessed us. Let us sing, then, for posterity. The past commands our praise and the future invites it. For our descendants let us sing as well as pray. If Abraham rejoiced concerning his seed, so also may the godly, for " instead of the fathers shall be the children," and as the last Psalm told us in its concluding verse, " the children of thy servants shall continue, and their seed shall be established before thee."

18. Children of the righteous are not, however, promised the Lord's mercy without stipulation, and this verse completes the statement of the last by adding : *" To such as keep his covenant, and to those that remember his commandments to do them."* The parents must be obedient and the children too. We are here bidden to abide by the covenant, and those who run off to any other confidence than the finished work of Jesus are not among those who obey this precept ; those with whom the covenant is really made stand firm to it, and having begun in the Spirit, they do not seek to be made perfect in the flesh. The truly godly keep the Lord's commands carefully—they *" remember " ;* they observe them practically—*" to do them " :* moreover they do not pick and choose, but remember *" his commandments "* as such, without exalting one above another as their own pleasure or convenience may dictate. May our offspring be a thoughtful, careful, observant race, eager to know the will of the Lord, and prompt to follow it fully, then will his mercy enrich and honour them from generation to generation.

This verse also suggests praise, for who would wish the Lord to smile on those who will not regard his ways ? That were to encourage vice. From the manner in which some men unguardedly preach the covenant, one might infer that God would bless a certain set of men however they might live, and however they might neglect his laws. But the word teaches not so. The covenant is not legal, but it is holy. It is all of grace from first to last, yet it is no panderer to sin ; on the contrary, one of its greatest promises is, " I will put my laws in their hearts and in their minds will I write them " ; its general aim is the sanctifying of a people unto God, zealous for good works, and all its gifts and operations work in that direction. Faith keeps the covenant by looking alone to Jesus, while at the same time by earnest obedience it remembers the Lord's commandments to do them.

19. *" The Lord hath prepared his throne in the heavens."* Here is a grand burst of song produced by a view of the boundless power, and glorious sovereignty of Jehovah. His throne is *fixed,* for that is the word ; it is established, settled, immovable.

> " He sits on no precarious throne,
> Nor borrows leave to be."

About his government there is no alarm, no disorder, no perturbation, no hurrying to and fro in expedients, no surprises to be met or unexpected catastrophes to be warded off ; —all is prepared and fixed, and he himself has prepared and fixed it. He is no delegated sovereign for whom a throne is set up by another ; he is an autocrat, and his dominion arises from himself and is sustained by his own innate power. This matchless sovereignty is the pledge of our security, the pillar upon which our confidence may safely lean.

" And his kingdom ruleth over all." Over the whole universe he stretches his sceptre. He now reigns universally, he always has done so, and he always will. To us the world may seem rent with anarchy, but he brings order out of confusion. The warring elements are marching beneath his banner when they most wildly rush onward in furious tempest. Great and small, intelligent and material, willing and unwilling, fierce or gentle,—all, all are under his sway. His is the only universal monarchy, he is the blessed and only Potentate, King of kings and Lord of lords. A clear view of his ever active, and everywhere supreme providence, is one of the most delightful of spiritual gifts ; he who has it cannot do otherwise than bless the Lord with all his soul.

Thus has the sweet singer hymned the varied attributes of the Lord as seen in nature, grace, and providence, and now he gathers up all his energies for one final outburst of adoration, in which he would have all unite, since all are subjects of the Great King.

20 Bless the LORD, ye his angels, that excel in strength, that do his commandments, hearkening unto the voice of his word.

21 Bless ye the LORD, all *ye* his hosts; *ye* ministers of his, that do his pleasure.

22 Bless the LORD, all his works in all places of his dominion: bless the LORD, O my soul.

20. " *Bless the Lord, ye his angels, that excel in strength.*" Finding his work of praise growing upon his hands, he calls upon " the firstborn sons of light " to speak the praises of the Lord, as well they may, for as Milton says, they best can tell. Dwelling nearer to that prepared throne than we as yet have leave to climb, they see in nearer vision the glory which we would adore. To them is given an exceeding might of intellect, and voice, and force which they delight to use in sacred services for him ; let them now turn all their strength into that solemn song which we would send up to the third heaven. To him who gave angelic strength let all angelic strength be given. They are *his* angels, and therefore they are not loth to ring out his praises. " *That do his commandments, hearkening unto the voice of his word.*" We are bidden to do these commandments, and alas we fail ; let those unfallen spirits, whose bliss it is never to have transgressed, give to the Lord the glory of their holiness. They hearken for yet more commands, obeying as much by reverent listening as by energetic action, and in this they teach us how the heavenly will should evermore be done ; yet even for this surpassing excellence let them take no praise, but render all to him who has made and kept them what they are. O that we could hear them chant the high praises of God, as did the shepherds on that greatest of all birth nights—

" When such music sweet
Their hearts and ears did greet
    As never was by mortal finger struck ;
Divinely-warbled voice
Answering the stringèd noise,
    As well their souls in blissful rapture took:
The air, such pleasure loth to lose,
With thousand echoes still prolongs each heavenly close."

Our glad heart anticipates the hour when we shall hear them " harping in loud and solemn guise," and all to the sole praise of God.

21. " *Bless ye the Lord, all ye his hosts ;* " to whatever race of creatures ye may belong, for ye are all his troops, and he is the Generallissimo of all your armies. The fowl of the air and the fish of the sea, and whatsoever passeth through the paths of the sea, should all unite in praising their Creator, after the best of their ability. " *Ye ministers of his, that do his pleasure* " ; in whatever way ye serve him, bless him as ye serve. The Psalmist would have every servant in the Lord's palace unite with him, and all at once sing out the praises of the Lord. We have attached a new sense to the word " ministers " in these latter days, and so narrowed it down to those who serve in word and doctrine. Yet no true minister would wish to alter it, for we are above all men bound to be the Lord's servants, and we would, beyond all other ministering intelligences or forces, desire to bless the glorious Lord.

22. " *Bless the Lord, all his works in all places of his dominion.*" Here is a trinity of blessing for the thrice blessed God, and each one of the three blessings is an enlargement upon that which went before. This is the most comprehensive of all, for what can be a wider call than to all in all places ? See how finite man can awaken unbounded praise ! Man is but little, yet, placing his hands upon the keys of the great organ of the universe, he wakes it to thunders of adoration ! Redeemed man is the voice of nature, the priest in the temple of creation, the precentor in the worship of the universe. O that all the Lord's works on earth were delivered from the vanity to which they were made subject, and brought into the glorious liberty of the children of God : the time is hastening on and will most surely come ; then will all the Lord's works bless him indeed. The immutable promise is ripening, the sure mercy is on its way. Hasten ye winged hours !

" *Bless the Lord, O my soul.*" He closes on his key-note. He cannot be content to call on others without taking his own part ; nor because others sing more loudly and perfectly, will he be content to be set aside. O my soul, come home to thyself and to thy God, and let the little world within thee keep time and tune to the spheres which are ringing out Jehovah's praise. O infinitely blessed Lord, favour us with this highest blessing of being for ever and ever wholly engrossed in blessing thee.

EXPLANATORY NOTES AND QUAINT SAYINGS.

Title.—*A Psalm of David,* which he wrote when carried out of himself as far as heaven, saith Beza.—*John Trapp.*

Whole Psalm.—How often have saints in Scotland sung this Psalm in days when they celebrated the *Lord's Supper !* It is thereby specially known in our land. It is connected also with a remarkable case in the days of John Knox. Elizabeth Adamson, a woman who attended on his preaching, " because he more fully opened the fountain of God's mercies than others did," was led to Christ and to rest, on hearing this Psalm, after enduring such agony of soul that she said, concerning racking pains of body, " A thousand years of this torment, and ten times more joined, are not to be compared to a quarter of an hour of my soul's trouble." She asked for this Psalm again before departing : " It was in receiving it that my troubled soul first tasted God's mercy, which is now sweeter to me than if all the kingdoms of the earth were given me to possess."—*Andrew A. Bonar.*

Whole Psalm.—The number of verses in this Psalm is that of the letters of the Hebrew alphabet ; and the completeness of the whole is further testified by its return at the close to the words with which it started, " Bless the LORD, O my soul."— *J. F. Thrupp.*

Whole Psalm.—The Psalm, in regard to number, is an alphabetical one, harmonised in such a way as that the concluding turns back into the introductory verse, the whole being in this manner finished and rounded off. In like manner, the name Jehovah occurs eleven times. The Psalm is divided into two strophes, the first of ten and the second of twelve verses. The ten is divided by the five, and the twelve falls into three divisions, each of four verses. Jehovah occurs in the first strophe four, and in the second seven times.

The Psalm bears the character of quiet tenderness. It is a still clear brook of the praise of God. In accordance with this, we find that the verses are of equal length as to structure, and consist regularly of two members. It is only at the conclusion, where the tone rises, that the verses become longer : the vessel is too small for the feeling.

The testimony which the *title* bears on behalf of the composition of the Psalm by David, is confirmed by the fact that the Psalm in passages, the independence of which cannot be mistaken, bears a striking resemblance to the other Psalms of David, and by the connection with Psalm cii. David here teaches his posterity to *render thanks,* as in the previous Psalm he had taught them to *pray :* the deliverance from deep distress which formed there the subject of prayer, forms here the subject of thanks.— *E. W. Hengstenberg.*

Whole Psalm.—It is observable that no petition occurs throughout the entire compass of these twenty-two verses. Not a single word of supplication is in the whole Psalm addressed to the Most High. Prayer, fervent, heartfelt prayer, had doubtless been previously offered on the part of the Psalmist, and answered by his God. Innumerable blessings had been showered down from above in acknowledgment of David's supplications ; and, therefore, an overflowing gratitude now bursts forth from their joyful recipient. He touches every chord of his harp and of his heart together, and pours forth a spontaneous melody of sweetest sound and purest praise. —*John Stevenson, in " Gratitude : an Exposition of the Hundred and Third Psalm,"* 1856.

Verse 1.—" *Bless the Lord, O my soul.*" O how well they are fitted ! for what work so fit for my soul as this ? Who so fit for this work as my soul ? My body, God knows, is gross and heavy, and very unfit for so sublime a work. No, my soul, it is thou must do it ; and indeed what hast thou else to do ? it is the very work for which thou wert made, and O that thou wert as fit to do the work as the work is fit for thee to do ! But, alas, thou art become in a manner earthy, at least hast lost a great part of thy abilities, and will never be able to go through with this great work thyself alone. If to bless the Lord were no more but to say, Lord, Lord, like to them that cried, " The temple of the Lord, the temple of the Lord ; " then my tongue alone would be sufficient for it, and I should not need to trouble any other about it ; but to bless the Lord is an eminent work, and requires not only many but very able agents to perform it ; and therefore, my soul, when thou goest about it, go not alone ; but, take with thee " *all that is within thee* ; " all the forces in my whole magazine, whether it be my heart, or my spirits ; whether my will, or my affections ; whether my understanding, or my memory ; take them all with thee, and bless the Lord.— *Sir R. Baker.*

Verse 1.—" *All that is within me.*" The literal translation of the form here used is *my insides* or *inner parts*, the strong and comprehensive meaning of the plural being further enhanced by the addition of *all*, as if to preclude exception and reserve, and comprehend within the scope of the address all the powers and affections.—*J. A. Alexander.*

Verse 1.—" *All that is within me,*" etc. Let your *conscience* " bless the Lord " by unvarying fidelity. Let your *judgment* bless him, by decisions in accordance with his word. Let your *imagination* bless him, by pure and holy musings. Let your *affections* praise him, by loving whatsoever he loves. Let your *desires* bless him, by seeking only his glory. Let your *memory* bless him, by not forgetting any of his benefits. Let your *thoughts* bless him, by meditating on his excellencies. Let your *hope* praise him, by longing and looking for the glory that is to be revealed. Let your every *sense* bless him by its fealty, your every *word* by its truth, and your every *act* by its integrity.—*John Stevenson.*

Verse 1.—" *Bless the Lord, O my soul.*" You have often heard, that when God is said to bless men, and they on the other hand are excited to bless him, the word is taken in two very different senses. God is the only fountain of being and happiness, from which all good ever flows ; and hence he is said to bless his creatures when he bestows mercies and favours upon them, gives them any endowments of body and mind, delivers them from evils, and is the source of their present comforts and future hopes. But in this sense, you'll see there is no possibility of any creature's blessing God ; for as his infinite and unblemished perfection renders him incapable of receiving any higher excellency, or improvement in happiness ; so, could we put the supposition that this immense ocean of good might be increased, it is plain that we, who receive our very being and everything that we have or are from him, could in no case contribute thereto. To *bless* God, then, is, with an ardent affection humbly to acknowledge those divine excellencies, which render him the best and greatest of beings, the only object worthy of the highest adoration ; it is to give him the praise of all those glorious attributes which adorn his nature, and are so conspicuously manifested in his works and ways. To bless God, is to embrace every proper opportunity of owning our veneration and esteem of his excellent greatness, and to declare to all about us, as loudly as we can, the goodness and grace of his conduct towards men, and our infinite obligations for all our enjoyments to him, *in whom we live, move, and have our being.* And a right *blessing of God* must take its rise from a heart that is full of esteem and gratitude, which puts life into the songs of praise.

And then, of all others, the most lively and acceptable method of blessing God, is a holy conversation and earnest endeavour to be purified from all iniquity ; for blessing of God consists, as I told you, in adoring his excellencies, and expressing our esteem and veneration of them : but what can be so effectual a way of doing this, as the influence that the views of them have upon our lives ? That person best exalts the glory of the divine power, who fears God above all, and trembles at the apprehensions of his wrath ; and of his justice, who flees from sin, which exposes him to the inexorable severity thereof ; and of his love, who is softened thereby into grateful returns of obedience ; and then we celebrate his holiness, when we endeavour to imitate it in our lives, and abandon everything that is an abomination to the eyes of his purity. —*William Dunlop*, 1692—1720.

Verse 1.—" *O my soul.*" God's eye is chiefly upon the soul : bring a hundred dishes to table, he will carve of none but this ; this is the savoury meat he loves. He who is best, will be served with the best ; when we give him the soul in a duty, then we give him the flower and the cream ; by a holy chemistry we still out the spirits. A soul inflamed in service is the cup of " spiced wine of the juice of the pomegranate " (Cant. viii. 2) which the spouse makes Christ to drink of.—*Thomas Watson.*

Verse 1.—" *Bless his holy name.*" The *name* of God frequently signifies his nature and attributes, in Scripture. Now, *holiness* is the glory of this name ; the purity of God is that which beautifies all his perfections, and renders them worthy to be praised. His eternity, and knowledge, and power, without justice, and goodness, and truth, might indeed frighten and confound us ; but could not inflame our love, or engage us to hearty blessing. But when infinite mightiness, and unerring wisdom, and eternal dominion, are mixed with unchangeable love, and inviolable veracity and goodness, which exalts itself above all his works ; when thus it becomes a *holy name*, then the divine perfections are rendered truly amiable, and suitable objects of our hope and confidence and loudest songs ; so that you see how elegantly the Psalmist upon this occasion mentions the purity of God : " *Bless his holy name.*"

And besides this, there is indeed nothing that more exalts the glory of divine grace and of redeeming love towards a soul, than the consideration of *God's holiness ;* for if your Maker were not *of purer eyes than man is*, yea, if his hatred to sin, and love to righteousness, were not greater than that of the noblest angel, his pardoning of sin, and patience towards transgressors would not be such a wonderful condescension ; but is his name infinitely holy so that " *the heavens are not clean in his sight ?* " Is the smallest iniquity the abhorrence of his soul, and what he hates with a perfect hatred ? Surely, then, his grace and love must be incomparably greater than our thoughts.—*William Dunlop.*

Verses 1, 2.—The well is seldom so full that water will at first pumping flow forth ; neither is the heart commonly so spiritual, after our best care in our worldly converse (much less when we somewhat overdo therein) as to pour itself into God's bosom freely, without something to raise and elevate it ; yea, often, the springs of grace lie so low, that pumping only will not fetch the heart up to a praying frame, but arguments must be poured into the soul before the affections rise. Hence are those soliloquies and discourses which we find holy men use with their own hearts to bring them into a gracious temper, suitable for communion with God in ordinances. It seems [by these verses] David either found or feared his heart would not be in so good a frame as he desired ; consequently he redoubles his charge : he found his heart somewhat drowsy, which made him thus rouse himself.—*William Gurnall.*

Verses 1—3.—The Psalmist's gratitude here has four attributes. The first is *personal.* " *Bless the Lord, my soul.*" He has the self-same application in the close of the Psalm, after he has called on others to do this work. Our religion must be social as well as personal : but while it must not end at home, it must begin at home ; and relative religion, without personal, will always be found wanting in excitement, in energy, in extent, in continuance, and very commonly in success. Secondly, it is *fervent.* " *And all that is within me, bless his holy name*"—all my thoughts, my feelings, my understanding, my will, my memory, my conscience, my affections, my passions.

> " If there be passions in my soul,
> (And passions, Lord, there be) ;
> Let them be all at thy control,
> My gracious Lord, for thee."

Thirdly, it is *rational*, and demanded by the facts of his past life. Therefore " forget not all his benefits." Nothing can properly affect or influence us when it is out of our recollection. " Out of sight out of mind " ; and out of mind, out of motive. Whence arose the ingratitude of the Jews of old ? Bad memories. " Of the rock that begat thee thou art unmindful, and hast forgotten the God that formed thee." " The ox knoweth his owner, and the ass his master's crib : but Israel doth not know, my people doth not consider." It should therefore be your concern, not only to recall your mercies, but to reckon them. Lastly, it is *specific :* " *Who forgiveth all thine iniquities ; who healeth all thy diseases.*" When all the words in a discourse are emphatic, nothing is emphatic, when we dwell on everything, we dwell on nothing effectively. We are more struck, in a landscape, with a selected point of vision for inspection, than by the general prospect. David was a poet, and understood poetry well ; and poetry differs from philosophy. The one seeks to rise from particular facts and instances, to establish general principles and rules : the other is always for descending from generalization to particularization ; and much of its beauty and force arises from individualities.—*William Jay*, 1849.

Verse 2.—"*Bless the Lord, O my soul.*" David found some dulness and drowsiness ; hence he so often puts the thorn to his breast ; hence he so impetuously instigateth his soul, as one here phraseth it.—*John Trapp.*

Verse 2.—"*Forget not.*" This touches the secret spring of so much ingratitude —forgetfulness, the want of re-collection, or gathering together again of all the varied threads of mercy. Compare Deut. vi. 12 ; viii. 11, 14. "*Si oblivisceris, tacebis*" (If thou forgettest, thou wilt be silent).—*J. J. S. Perowne.*

Verse 2.—"*Forget not all his benefits.*" That is, forget not any of his benefits, as the form of speech in the original doth import.—*David Dickson.*

Verse 2.—"*Benefits.*" The word rendered "benefits"—גמול, *gemul*, means properly an act, work, doing, whether good or evil, Ps. cxxxvii. 8 ; and then, *desert,* or what a man deserves *for* his act ; *recompense.* It is rendered *deserving* in Judges ix. 16 ; *benefit,* as here, in 2 Chron. xxxii. 25 ; *desert,* Ps. xxviii. 4 ; *reward,* Ps. xciv. 2 ; Isai. iii. 11 ; Obad. 15 ; *recompense,* Prov. xii. 14 ; Isai. xxxv. 4 ; lix. 18 ; lxvi. 6 ; Jer. li. 6 ; Lam. iii. 64 ; Joel. iii. 4, 7. The proper reference here is to the Divine *dealings,* to what God had *done,* as a reason for blessing his name. His *dealings* with the Psalmist had been such as to call for praise and gratitude. What those *dealings* particularly were he specifies in the following verses.—*Albert Barnes.*

Verse 3.—"*Who forgiveth all thine iniquities.*" Thine iniquities are more than can be numbered ; and they are an intolerable burden, so that thy soul under them "can in no wise lift up herself." He forgiveth them *all.* He relieveth thee of *all.* He taketh the dreadful burden from thy back, the galling yoke from thy neck, and makes thee free. . . . Thine iniquities are in-equities. There is nothing just or right in thee. Thy very nature is an in-equity, bringing forth nothing but in-equities. In-equities towards thy God, in-equities towards thy neighbour, and in-equities towards thyself, make up the whole of thy life. Thou art a bad tree, and a bad tree cannot bring forth good fruit.—*John Pulsford, in "Quiet Hours,"* 1857.

Verse 3.—"*All thine iniquities.*" In this lovely and well-known Psalm, we have great fulness of expression, in reference to the vital subject of redemption.

"Who forgiveth *all* thine iniquities." It is not "*some*" or "*many*" of thine iniquities." This would never do. If so much as the very smallest iniquity, in thought, word, or act, were left unforgiven, we should be just as badly off, just as far from God, just as unfit for heaven, just as exposed to hell, as though the whole weight of our sins were yet upon us. Let the reader ponder this deeply. It does not say, "Who forgiveth thine iniquities previous to conversion." There is no such notion as this in Scripture. When God forgives, he forgives like himself. The source, the channel, the power, and the standard of forgiveness are all divine. When God cancels a man's sins, he does so according to the measure in which Christ bore those sins. Now, Christ not only bore *some* or *many* of the believer's sins, he bore them "*all,*" and, therefore, God forgives "*all.*" God's forgiveness stretches to the length of Christ's atonement ; and Christ's atonement stretches to the length of every one of the believer's sins, past, present, and future. "The blood of Jesus Christ his Son cleanseth us from *all* sin." 1 John i.—"*Things New and Old,*" 1858.

Verse 3.—"*Who healeth all thy diseases.*" In one of the prisons of a certain country, was a man who had committed high treason : for this crime he was in due time tried, and, being found guilty, was condemned to die. But more than this ; he was afflicted with an inward disease, which generally proves mortal. Now we may truly say, that this man is *doubly* dead ; that his life is forfeited twice over : the laws of his country have pronounced him guilty of death, and therefore his life is forfeited *once* to the laws of his country, and, if he had not died in *this* way, he must die of his disease ; he is, therefore, "twice dead." Now suppose that the sovereign of that country had made up his mind to wish to save that prisoner's life, *could* he save it ? He could indeed take off the penalty of the law ; he could give him a free pardon, and so restore the life, as sure as it is forfeited by the just sentence of the law ; but, unless he could also send a physician, who could cure the man of his disease, he would die by *that,* and his pardon would only lengthen out for a few weeks or months, a miserable existence. And if this disease were not only a mortal disease, but an *infectious* one, likely to spread itself by the *breath* of the patient, and a *contagious* one, likely to spread by the *touch* of the patient's body or clothes, then it would be dangerous to others to come near that man ; and unless he were cured, and thoroughly and entirely cured, the man, though pardoned, would still be a fit inmate only for the pest-house, and could not be received into the houses of the healthy. You have *seen* such a case as this, brethren ; you are at this very moment, perhaps, sitting close by a person in this case ; yes, and perhaps you are in this very case yourself ! *Perhaps,* do I say ? I should say, you ARE in this very case, unless you are really and truly a Christian, a believer in Christ Jesus.—*W. Weldon Champneys,* 1842.

Verse 3.—" *All thy diseases.*" The body experienceth the melancholy consequences of Adam's offence, and is subject to many infirmities ; but the soul is subject to as many. What is pride, but lunacy ; what is anger, but a fever ; what is avarice, but a dropsy ; what is lust, but a leprosy ; what is sloth, but a dead palsy ? Perhaps, there are spiritual maladies similar to all corporeal ones.—*George Horne.*

Verse 3.—" *All thy diseases.*" O my soul, consider the multitude of infirmities, to which thou art subject ; thou hast many suggestions of the flesh ; and thou art apt to yield unto them, and strivest not against them by earnest prayer and holy meditations ; this is an infirmity. In thy prayers to God, thy thoughts are often wandering, and thou thinkest of other matters, far unworthy of that great Majesty to whom thou prayest : or if not so, yet thou art quickly weary, thy spirits are drowsy in it, and thou hadst rather be doing of something else ; this is an infirmity. And indeed thou hast infirmities in all thy senses. In thy seeing, thou canst see a mote in thy brother's eye, and canst not see a beam in thine own eye. In thy smelling, thou thinkest *suavis odor lucri ex re qualibet,* that the savour of gain is sweet, from whence soever it rise. In thy hearing, thou art gladder to hear the profane and idle discourses, than such as be serious and holy ; these are thy infirmities : and, O my soul, if I should cut thee up into as many parts as an anatomist, and examine the infirmities of every part, should I not have cause, just cause, to cry out with Saint Paul, O wretch that I am, who shall deliver me from this body of sin ? Who shall heal me of all these infirmities ? for whether we call them sins, and then God forgives them ; or call them infirmities, and then he heals them ; they are to us, all one benefit ; in God, all one kindness ; that as either of them is well worth remembering ; so for both of them, we have just cause to bless him and to praise his name.—*Sir Richard Baker.*

Verse 3.—" *All thy diseases.*" Our *understandings* are so bad that they understand not their own badness ; our *wills,* which are the queens of our souls, become the vassals of sin ; our *memory,* like jet, good only to draw straws and treasure up trifles of no moment ; our *consciences,* through errors in our own understanding, sometimes accusing us when we are innocent, sometimes acquitting us when we are guilty ; our *affections* all disaffected and out of order. Must not that needs be a monstrous face, wherein the blueness which should be in the veins is in the lips, the redness which should be in the cheeks, in the nose ; the hair that should grow on the head, on the face ? and must not our souls needs seem ugly in the sight of God, who have grief growing there where joy should, and joy where grief should ? We love what we should hate and hate where we should love ; we fear where no fear is, and fear not where we ought to fear ; and all our affections either mistake their object, or exceed their due measure.—*Thomas Fuller.*

Verse 4.—" *Who redeemeth thy life from destruction.*" From his earliest days the Psalmist was the child of Providence. Many were the hairbreadth escapes, and the wonderful deliverances, which he experienced. Dangers of various kinds presented themselves as his years advanced. The jaw of the lion, and the paw of the bear, at various times threatened to terminate his existence, and at others the ruthless hand of man. The same God who delivered him from the sword of Goliath, rescued his life from the javelin of Saul. The Almighty Friend who had covered his head in the day of battle, delivered him, at one moment, from the lords of the Philistines, saved him at another out of the hands of the men of Keilah ; and again preserved to him his life and throne from the unnatural rebellion of his own son. Well, therefore, might the Psalmist stir up his soul, and all that was within him, to bless the Lord with most fervent gratitude, who, by so many signal deliverances, had " *redeemed his life from destruction.*"—*John Stevenson.*

Verse 4.—" *Who redeemeth.*" Preservation from destruction, גואל *haggoel,* properly, *redemption of life by the kinsman ;* possibly looking forward, in the spirit of prophecy, to him who became partaker of our flesh and blood, that he might have the right to redeem our souls from death by dying in our stead.—*Adam Clarke.*

Verse 4.—" *From the pit,*" including death, the grave, Hades. The Targum renders " from Gehenna."—*J. J. S. Perowne.*

Verse 4.—" *Tender mercies.*" I do not know that I can do better than tell you a little incident that took place in my native town of Stirling. Workmen were blasting the castle rock, near where it abuts upon a walk that lies open to the street. The train was laid and lit, and an explosion was momentarily expected. Suddenly trotting round the great wall of the cliff, came a little child going straight to where the match burned. The men shouted—(it was *mercy*)—and by their very terror in shouting, alarmed and bewildered the poor little thing. By this time the mother also had come round : in a moment saw the danger ; opened wide her arms, and cried from her very heart, " *Come to me, my darling,*"—(that was *tender* mercy)— and instantly, with eager pattering feet, and little arms opened to her arms, and tear-filled eyes answering to her eyes—the little thing ran back and away, and stopped not until she was clasped in her mother's bosom—wealth of sunny hair loosened on it, and lips coral red pressed to mother's pallid lip of fear—as the motherly heart gave way to tears, in the thought of so imperilled an escape : for it was barely by a second, as the roar of the shattered rock told.—*Alexander B. Grosart, in " The Pastor an Helper of Joy,*" 1865.

Verse 5.—" *Who satisfieth thy mouth.*" The word rendered " *mouth* " is עֶדְיֵךְ, which is rendered *ornaments* in our version in all other passages—eleven in number —where it occurs, except here and in xxxii. 9, where it is rendered " *mouth ;* " and even there it ought properly to be translated *ornament*, and here the sense seems to be *thy ornament*, that which is thy glory, thy spirit, xvi. 9 ; lxii. 8. It is true that the soul (נֶפֶשׁ) is here addressed (see v. 1) ; but the spirit may be called the *ornament* or *glory* of the *soul*.—*Christopher Wordsworth.*

Verse 5.—" *Satisfieth thy mouth.*" Kimchi understands the phrase as expressing David's recovery from sickness. In sickness the soul abhorreth bread, and even dainty meat, Job xxxiii. 20. The physician, too, limits the diet of the patient, and prescribes things which are nauseous to the palate. The commentator, therefore, supposes that David here describes the blessing of health, by *his mouth being filled with good things.*—*Editorial Note to Calvin in loc.*

Verse 5.—" *Satisfieth.*" God can so satisfy the soul, that each chink and cranny therein shall be filled with spiritual joy.—*Thomas Fuller.*

Verse 5.—" *With good things.*" Mark, what does the Lord satisfy with ?— " *good* things." Not *rich* things, not *many* things, not *everything* I ask for, but " *good* things." All my *need* fully supplied, and everything " *good.*" Goodness is God expressed. All his blessings partake of his own nature. They are holy blessings, holy mercies. Everything that *satisfies* must have the nature of God in it. Nothing else will ever " satisfy." The heart was made for God, and only God can meet it.— *Frederick Whitfield,* 1874.

Verse 5.—" *Thy youth is renewed like the eagle's.*" It is an ancient fable that the eagle is able to renew his youth when very old, and poetical allusion is made to it in this Psalm ; but this idea is doubtless founded in reality on the great longevity of the bird, and its power, in common with other birds, of moulting its plumage periodically, and so increasing its strength and activity.—*Hugh Macmillan.**

Verse 5.—" *Thy youth is renewed like the eagle's.*"—The Scripture knows nothing of the idea that the eagle when old renews its youth. That there is nothing of this kind contained in Is. xl. 31, which is commonly appealed to, but that it is rather the powerful flight of the eagle that is there referred to, " they mount up on wings like the eagle, they run and are not weary," is evident from the parallel, to *fly, run, march.*— *E. W. Hengstenberg.*

Verse 5.—" *Thy youth is renewed like the eagle's.*" Thy activity will renew itself *like the eagle.* That is to say, From day to day he will receive and increase his strength and vigour, so that he may thrive and flourish like the eagle. The comparison with the eagle is not drawn in point of *renovation*, but in point of vigour and *activity* con-

---

* We might have filled much of our space with fables from the rabbis and the fathers in reference to eagles ; but they are too absurd, and ought never to be repeated We hope, therefore, that the reader will excuse if not commend the omission.

tinually renewing itself; as Is. xl. 31, says, " *They that wait upon the Lord shall renew their strength, they shall mount up with wings as eagles.*"—*Venema*.

Verse 5.—" *Thy youth is renewed like the eagle's.*"—This renovation of his youth may be understood three ways. First, as to his natural state, or bodily strength. Secondly, as to his civil state, or worldly successes, as to his honour and kingly renown. Thirdly, as to his spiritual state, or the heightening of his gifts, graces, and comforts. 'Tis probable David had found a declension in all these, and at last, through the goodness of God and his blessing upon him, the renewing of them all from that oldness to a youthfulness again, like that of eagles.—*Joseph Caryl*.

Verse 5.—" *Thy youth is renewed like the eagle's.*"—However bold it may sound, we say not too much when we speak of an *eternal youth*, as the glorious privilege of the devout servant of the Lord, but of him alone. All that with reason charms and captivates in the appearance of youth, is seen in heightened measure where the spiritual life develops itself undisturbed in fellowship with God. Does the *innocence* of youth attract you ? In the natural life it is but too frequently a misleading appearance ; but in the life of the soul it returns to a certain extent when the heart is purified through the power of the Holy Ghost, and the life is renewed in conformity with that of Christ the Lord. Does the *enjoyment* of youth surpass in your estimation that of any other here below ? Be it so ; yet all too speedily it is driven away by the cares of later years, whilst enjoyment free from care even in the dark days may dwell in the heart whereon has descended the peace of God through faith. The *strength* of youth, seems it to you desirable ? Ah ! day by day stamps truth upon the words : " Youth shall faint and be weary ; " but even when the natural strength has already long attained its zenith, the Christian often feels himself elevated through a power from on high, which lifts him above physical weakness ; and what no strength of sinew or muscle could accomplish is attained through the power of implicit faith. Yea, even the beautiful *development* which the period of youth shows you, ye would not seek in vain in that man who, leaning on God's hand, forgetting the things that are behind, stretches forward from light to light, from strength to strength, from bliss to bliss. How, finally, can *hope*, that makes the youthful heart beat high with throbs of joy, be lacking to him ? The fairest part of life the sensual man sees soon behind him, the spiritual man always in prospect ; and like the eagle, this last can often from the low atmosphere around him soar to the pure, clear ether, whence already from afar the image, nay, the ineffable reality, shows him a more than earthly joy.

Eternal youth : it may, yet much more than for David, now be the portion of every Christian, but for these alone. Without faith and hope in the heart, even the bravest determination to remain young always, or at least as long as possible, must give way before the first great storm of life. Yet even when faith and hope are not strangers to us, whence is it that in our spiritual life there is frequently so little of the " *eagle* " spoken of here, and so much of the " sparrow alone upon the house top," referred to in Psalm cii. 7 ? Can it be that we allow ourselves too little to be satisfied with the good things of which David had spoken immediately before ; that is to say, that we *live* so little on the best things which God has to bestow,— his word, his Spirit, his grace ? Only through these do we attain that lasting second birth, of which the eagle is the emblem, and an unfading youth of heart the inestimable fruit. Ye who are young in years, seek this undying youth above all the joys of early life ! Recover it, ye middle-aged, in living fellowship with him who maketh all things new within ! Preserve it, old friends of God and of his Christ, as your fairest crown here on earth, and the earnest of your bliss in heaven. And thou, Christian, who sittest down disconsolate, bethink thyself ; the eagle lets his wings hang down, only thereafter to soar with stronger flight !—*J. J. Van Oosterzee, in* " *The Year of Salvation,*" 1874.

Verse 6.—" *The Lord executeth righteousness,*" &c. Rising from personal blessings to general, the comprehensive fact, evermore to the glory of God, is his sympathy with the suffering and oppressed, and his ready and effective interposition in their case. Who will not praise him that he careth so kindly and so gloriously for those who suffer cruel wrongs from wicked oppressors ?—*Henry Cowles*.

Verse 7.—" *He made known his ways unto Moses.*" When Moses went up to Mount Sinai and tarried there with God the space of forty days, we may well think that God in that time, revealed many secrets to him ; and particularly " *made known his ways;"* (Ex. xxxiii. 19); not only his ways in which he would have us to walk, but his ways in which he walks himself, and the course he holds in the government of worldly affairs; why he suffers the wicked to prosper, and why the godly to be oppressed. These *"ways"* of his he made known to Moses; to the children of Israel, only *"* his acts." He showed them his wonders upon Pharaoh, and that was his judgment; and he showed them his wonderful favours to themselves in the wilderness, and that was his righteousness; but he showed them not his ways, and the course he held in them: they saw only the events of things, they saw not the reasons of them, as Moses did.—*Sir Richard Baker.*

Verse 8.—*" Merciful and gracious, slow to anger and plenteous in mercy."* O my soul, here are four properties spoken of to be in God, and are all so necessary, that we could not miss one of them. If he were not *" merciful "* we could hope for no pardon; and if he were no more but merciful we could hope for no more but pardon; but when besides his being merciful he is also *" gracious,"* this gives us a further hope, a hope of a donative; and then it will not be what we are worthy to receive, but what it is fit for him to give. If he were not *" slow to anger "* we could expect no patience; but when besides his slowness to anger he is also *" full of compassion ; "* this makes us expect he will be the good Samaritan, and not only bind up our wounds, but take care also for our further curing. What though he chide and be angry for a time; it is but our being patient a while with him, as he a long time hath been patient with us.—*Sir R. Baker.*

Verse 8.—*" Slow to anger."* In Scripture we find that slowness to anger, and hastiness to be angry, are expressed by the different frame of the nostrils; as, namely, when the Lord is said to be *" slow to anger,"* the Hebrew is, *long of nostrils.*—*Joseph Caryl.*

Verse 8.—*" Plenteous in mercy."* וְרַב־חָסֶד *"* great, mighty in mercy," placing his chief glory in this attribute, and hereby teaching us how to estimate true greatness.—*George Horne.*

Verse 8.—*" Plenteous in mercy."* It is a thing marvellously satisfactory and pleasing to the heart of a man to be still taking from a great heap; and upon this ground are those proverbial sayings, There is no fishing like to fishing in the sea, no service like the service of a king: because in one there is the greatest plenty and abundance of that kind of pleasure that fishers look after; and for them that serve, and must live by their service, there is none like that of princes, because they have abundance of reward and of opportunity whereby to recompense the services of those that do wait and attend upon them. . . . . And upon the same ground it is that the Scriptures, in several places, do not only assert and testify that God is *" merciful "* and *" gracious,"* but abundant in mercy and full of grace; and not simply that there is redemption in him, but plenteousness of redemption, Ps. lxxxvi. 5; and cxxx. 7; Isai. lv. 7, " Let the wicked forsake his way," etc.; " Let him return unto the Lord and he will have mercy upon him; and to our God, for he will abundantly pardon." The commodity which we stand in need of is mercy and the pardon of our sins, because we have been unholy and ungodly creatures; this commodity is abundantly in God. There it is treasured up as waters are in the store-house of the sea; there is no end of the treasures of his grace, mercy, pardon, and compassion. There is no man, being in want, but had rather go to a rich man's door to be relieved, than to the door of a poor man, if he knoweth the rich man to be as liberal and as bountifully disposed as the poor man can be.—*John Goodwin, on " Being filled with the Spirit."*

Verse 9.—*" He will not always chide."*—Certainly it is as unpleasing to God to chide, as it is to us to be chidden; and so little he likes of anger, that he rids his hands of it as fast as he can: he is not so slow in coming to it, but he is as quick in getting from it; for chiding is a bar to mercy, and anger an impediment to compassion; nothing is so distasteful to God as that any block should lie in the way of his mercy, or that the liberty of his compassion should have any cause of restraint: and then we may be sure he will not himself lay a block in the way with chiding, nor be a cause to restrain his compassion by keeping his anger.—*Sir R. Baker.*

Verse 9 (Second clause).—*To keep anger for ever,* corresponds with the French phrase, *Je lui garde, Il me l'a gardé,** which we use when the man, who cannot forgive

* " I am watching him, as he has watched to do a bad turn to me "

the injuries he has received, cherishes secret revenge in his heart, and waits for an opportunity of retaliation. Now David denies that God, after the manner of men, keeps anger on account of injuries done to him, since he condescends to be reconciled.—*Calvin.*

Verse 10.—" *He hath not dealt with us after our sins.*" Might we not have expected, with such conduct, that God would have withdrawn from us the blessing of his providence, withheld from us the communication of his Spirit, permitted us to find the means of grace profitless, left our temptations to multiply, and suffered us to sink into a state of fixed backsliding ?—and then, with our hearts at last sinking into too natural depression, might we not have seemed to hear him saying to us this day, " Thine own wickedness shall correct thee, and thy backslidings shall reprove thee ; know, therefore, and see that it is an evil thing and bitter, that thou hast forsaken the Lord thy God, and that my fear is not in thee, saith the Lord God of Hosts."—*Baptist W. Noel,* 1798—1873.

Verse 10.—" *He hath not dealt with us after our sins.*" Why is it that God hath not dealt with us after our sins ? Is it not because he hath dealt with another after our sins ? Another who took our sins upon him ; of whom it is said, that " God chastened him in his fierce wrath " ? and why did he chasten him, but for our sins ? O gracious God, thou art too just to take revenge twice for the same faults ; and therefore, having turned thy fierce wrath upon him, thou wilt not turn it upon us too ; but having rewarded him according to our iniquities, thou wilt now reward us according to his merits.—*Sir R. Baker.*

Verse 11.—Our mind cannot find a comparison too large for expressing the superabundant mercy of the Lord toward his people.—*David Dickson.*

Verse 12.—" *As far as the east is from the west.*" The expression taken from the distance of the *east from west* is pitched upon, saith Kimchi, because those two quarters of the world are of greatest extent, being all known and inhabited. From whence it is that geographers reckon that way their longitudes, as from north to south their latitudes.—*Henry Hammond.*

Verse 12.—When sin is pardoned, it is never charged again ; the guilt of it can no more return than east can become west, or west become east.—*Stephen Charnock.*

Verse 13.—" *Like as a father pitieth his children,*" etc. A chaplain to seamen, at an American port, visited a sailor who appeared to be near death. He spoke kindly to the man upon the state of his soul, and directed him to cast himself on Jesus. With an oath, the sick man bade him begone. The chaplain then told him that he must be faithful to him, for if he died impenitent he would be lost for ever. The man was sullen and silent, and pretended to fall asleep. The visit was repeated more than once, with similar ill success. At length the chaplain, suspecting that the sailor was a Scotchman, repeated a verse of the old version of the Psalms :

> " Such pity as a father hath
> Unto his children dear,
> Like pity shows the Lord to such
> As worship him in fear."

Tears started into the sailor's eyes as he listened to these words. The chaplain asked him if he had not had a pious mother. The man broke into tears. Yes, his mother had, in years gone by, taught him these words, and had also prayed to God for him. Since then he had been a wanderer by sea and land ; but the memory of her faith and love moved his heart. The appeals made to him were blessed by the Spirit of God. His life was spared, and proved the reality of his conversion.

Verse 13.—" *Like as a father.*" It is to be observed in this verse, what kind of mercy the prophet attributes to God. He says not, As man pities man, as the rich the poor man, as the strong the feeble, as the freeman the captive, but he makes mention of that pity which a father shews to his son, which is the greatest of all. The word םֶחֶר itself supports this view, as it properly signifies *viscarum commotis.* An example of this we have in 1 Kings iii. in the case of the woman who could not bear the slaughter of her child. . . . And afterwards in the case of the father of the prodigal. Luke xv.—*Musculus.*

Verse 13.—" *As a father pitieth his children.*" The father pitieth his children that are weak in knowledge, and instructs them ; pities them when they are froward, and bears with them ; pities them when they are sick, and comforts them ; when they are fallen, and helps them up again ; when they have offended, and upon their submission, forgives them ; when they are wronged, and rights them. Thus " the Lord pitieth them that fear him."—*Matthew Henry.*

Verse 13.—" *So the Lord pitieth,*" &c. So and ten thousand times more than so. For he is the " Father of all mercies," and the Father of all the fatherhoods in heaven and earth. Eph. iii. 15.—*John Trapp.*

Verse 13.—" *The Lord pitieth.*" Though it be commonly said, " It is better to be envied, than pitied ; " yet here it is not so ; but it is a far happier thing to be pitied of God, than to be envied of men.—*Sir R. Baker.*

Verse 13.—" *Them that fear him.*" The fear of God is that deference to God which leads you to subordinate your will to his ; makes you intent on pleasing him ; penitent in view of past wilfulness ; happy in his present smile ; transported by his love ; hopeful of his glory.—*George Bowen.*

Verse 13.—" *Them that fear him.*" It may be understood of those who have not yet " received the spirit of adoption," but are yet " trembling at his word," those he " pities."—*Matthew Henry.*

Verses 13, 14.—The good father doth not turn off the child for being weak and sickly ; but is so much the more indulgent, as his necessity requires succour. If his stomach refuse meat, or cannot answer it with digestion, will he put him out of doors ? No ; when the Shunamite's son complains of his head, she lays him in her bosom. A mother is good to all the fruit of her womb, most kind to the sick infant : when it lies with its eyes fixed on her, not able to declare its grief, or to call for what it desires, this doubles her compassion : " So the Lord doth pity us, remembering our frame, considering that we are but dust " ; that our soul works by a lame instrument ; and therefore he requires not that of an elemental composition, which he doth of angelical spirits. The son is commanded to write out such a copy fairly ; he doth his best, far short of the original ; yet the father doth not chide, but encourage him. Or he gives him a bow and arrows, bids him shoot to such a mark ; he draws his utmost strength, lets go cheerfully ; the arrow drops far short, yet the son is praised, the father pleased. Temptation assaults us, lust buffets us, secular business diverts us, manifold is our weakness, but not beyond our Father's forgiveness : " He will spare us, as a man spareth his own son that serveth him," Mal. iii. 17.—*Thomas Adams.*

Verse 14.—" *He knoweth our frame.*" " Our formation ; " the *manner* in which we are constructed, and the *materials* of which we are made.—*Adam Clarke.*

Verse 14.—" *He knoweth our frame ; he remembereth that we are dust.*" Not like some unskilled empiric, who hath but one receipt for all, strong or weak, young or old ; but as a wise physician considers his patient, and then writes his bill. Men and devils are but God's apothecaries, they make not our physic, but give what God prescribes. Balaam loved Balak's fee well enough, but could not go a hair's breadth beyond God's commission.—*William Gurnall.*

Verse 14.—" *He remembereth that we are dust.*" As if the very matter out of which man was first made, though without sin, were a disadvantage to him in the resisting of sin. It was a disadvantage before man had any sin in him, how much more is it now when most men have nothing at all in them but sin, and the best have very much. " *That which is born of the flesh,*" saith Christ " *is flesh.*" Corrupt nature can produce none but corrupt acts.—*Joseph Caryl.*

Verse 14.—" *We are dust.*"

> O how in this thy quire of souls I stand,
> —Propt by thy hand—
> A heap of sand !
> Which busie thoughts—like winds—would scatter quite,
> And put to flight,
> But for thy might ;
> Thy hand alone doth tame
> Those blasts, and knit my frame.
>
> —*Henry Vaughan.*

Verses 14, 16.—" *We are dust.*" I never see one of those spiral pillars of dust which, like a mimic simoom, rush along the road upon a windy day, without thinking, " There is an image of life." Dust and a breath ! Observe how the apparent "pillar" is but a condition, an active condition, of the particles of dust, and those particles continually changing. The form depends upon the incessant movement. The heavy sand floats on the impalpable air while it partakes its motion ; let that cease and it falls. So the dull clods of the field, smitten by force, take wings and soar in life, partake for a time its rapid course, and then, the force exhausted, fall back into their former state. A whirl, a flux, maintained by forces without, and ceasing when they are withdrawn ; that is our life.—*James Hinton, in " Thoughts on Health and some of its Conditions,"* 1871.

Verse 15.—*" As for man."* The insignificance of man is especially brought out by the use of ENOSH here.—*Robert Baker Girdlestone.*

Verse 15.—Man comes forth, says Job, like *a flower,* and is cut down ; he is sent into the world the fairest and noblest part of God's works, fashioned after the image of his Creator, with respect to reason and the great faculties of the mind ; he cometh forth glorious as the flower of the field ; as it surpasses the vegetable world in beauty, so does he the animal world in the glory and excellence of his nature. The one, if no untimely accident oppress it, soon arrives at the full period of its perfection,—is suffered to triumph for a few moments, and is plucked up by the roots in the very pride and gayest stage of its being ; —or if it happens to escape the hands of violence, in a few days it necessarily sickens of itself, and dies away. Man likewise, though his progress is slower, and his duration somewhat longer, yet the periods of his growth and declension are nearly the same, both in the nature and manner of them. If he escapes the dangers which threaten his tenderer years, he is soon got into the full maturity and strength of life ; and if he is so fortunate as not to be hurried out of it then by accidents, by his own folly and intemperance—if he escapes these, he naturally decays of himself,—a period comes fast upon him, beyond which he was not made to last. Like flowers or fruits which may be plucked up by force before the time of their maturity, yet cannot be made to outgrow the period when they are to fade and drop of themselves ; when that comes, the hand of nature then plucks them both off, and no art of the botanist can uphold the one, or skill of the physician preserve the other, beyond the periods to which their original frames and constitutions were made to extend. As God has appointed and determined the several growths and decays of the vegetable race, so he seems as evidently to have prescribed the same laws to man, as well as all living creatures, in the first rudiments of which there are contained the specific powers of their growth, duration and extinction ; and when the evolutions of those animal powers are exhausted and run down, the creature expires and dies of itself, as ripe fruit falls from the tree, or a flower preserved beyond its bloom, drops and perishes upon the stalk.—*Lawrence Sterne,* 1713—1768.

Verse 15.—The Psalmist saith of man, " *as a flower of the field, so he flourisheth.*" It is not a flower of the *garden,* but of the " *field.*" This latter is more subject to decay than the former, because it lies more open to the nipping air and violent winds, and to the browsing mouth of the beast, and is more liable to be trampled upon : by all these ways it decayeth as well as by the scorching sun, and its own fading temper.—*John Edwards, in " Theologia Reformata."*

Verse 15.—*" As a flower of the field."*

> What is life ! like a flower, with the bane in its bosom,
> To-day full of promise—to-morrow it dies !—
> And health—like the dew-drop that hangs in its blossom,
> Survives but a night, and exhales to the skies !
> How oft 'neath the bud that is brightest and fairest,
> The seeds of the canker in embryo lurk !
> How oft at the root of the flower that is rarest—
> Secure in its ambush the worm is at work ?
> —*James Beattie,* 1735—1803.

Verse 16.—*" The wind passeth over it, and it is gone,"* etc. A breath of air, a gentle wind (רוּחַ) passes over him and he is gone. It would not be so strange if a tempest, a whirlwind, passing over should sweep him away. The Psalmist means much more than this. The gentlest touch, the whispering breeze, bears him off. He soon becomes a stranger, no more known in the little space he once filled, going out and coming in.—*Henry Cowles.*

Verse 16.—*" The wind passeth over it, and it is gone."* It is well known that a hot wind in the east destroys at once every green thing. Nor is this to be wondered at, if as Dr. Russell says, the winds sometimes " bring with them a degree and kind of heat, which one would imagine came out of an oven, and which, when it blows hard, will affect metals within the houses, such as locks of room doors, nearly as much as if they had been exposed to the rays of the sun." The blasting effect which seems to be here alluded to, of certain pestilential winds upon the animal frame, is by no means exaggerated by the comparison to the sudden fading of a flower. Maillet describes hundreds of persons in a caravan as stifled on the spot by the fire and dust, of which the deadly wind, that sometimes prevails in the eastern deserts, seems to be composed. And Sir John Chardin describes this wind " as making a great hissing noise," and says that " it appears red and fiery, and kills those whom it strikes by a kind of stifling them, especially when it happens in the day time."— *Richard Mant.*

Verse 16.—" *The place thereof shall know him no more,*" &c. Man, once turned to dust, is blown about by every wind, from place to place ; and what knows the place, when dust falls upon it ; whether it be the dust of a prince, or of a peasant ; whether of a man, or of a beast ? And must not man then needs be very miserable, when time and place, the two best helps of life, do both forsake him ? for what help can we have of time, when his days are but as grass ? What help of place, when his place denies him, and will not know him ?—*Sir R. Baker.*

Verse 17.—" *But the mercy of the Lord is from everlasting to everlasting.*" No human benevolence is perpetually the same ; but by experience we see that those who are kind to-day, may be changed into tyrants to-morrow. Examples of this we have in the life of Nero, and many other rulers. Therefore lest we should suspect the goodness of God to bear any similar character, it is said with inconceivable consolation, that it shall never cease, but is prepared for ever for all those who fear and serve God.—*Musculus.*

Verse 17.—" *From everlasting to everlasting.*" From everlasting, by predestination ; to everlasting, by glorification : the one without beginning, the other without end.—*Bernard.*

Verse 18.—" *To do them.*" Commands are to be remembered in order to practice ; a vain speculation is not the intent of the publication of them.—*Stephen Charnock.*

Verse 19.—" *The Lord hath prepared his throne.*" The word signifies *established* as well as prepared, and might be so rendered. Due preparation is the natural way to the establishment of a thing ; hasty resolves break and moulder. This notes,

1. The peculiarity of his authority. He prepares it, and none else for him. It is a dominion that originally resides in his nature, not derived from any by birth or commission ; he alone prepared it. He is the sole cause of his own kingdom ; his authority therefore is unbounded, as infinite as his nature. None can set laws to him, because none but himself prepared his throne for him. As he will not impair his own happiness, so he will not abridge himself of his own authority.

2. Readiness to exercise it upon due occasions. He hath prepared his throne, he is not at a loss, he needs not stay for a commission or instructions from any how to act. He hath all things ready for the assistance of his people, he hath rewards and punishments ; his treasures and axes, the great mark of authority lying by him, the one for the good, the other for the wicked. His mercy he keeps by him for thousands, Exod. xxxiv. 7 ; his arrows he hath prepared by him for rebels, Ps. vii. 13.

3. Wise management of it. It is prepared : preparations imply prudence ; the government of God is not a rash and heady authority. A prince upon his throne, a judge upon the bench, manages things with the greatest discretion, or should be supposed so to do.

4. Successfulness and duration of it. He hath prepared or established it. It is fixed, not tottering ; it is an unmovable dominion ; all the strugglings of men and devils cannot overturn it, not so much as shake it. It is established above the reach of obstinate rebels ; he cannot be deposed from it, he cannot be mated in it. His dominion, as himself, abides for ever. And as his counsel, so his authority, shall stand ; and " he will do all his pleasure," Isai. xlvi. 10.—*Stephen Charnock.*

Verse 19.—" *His throne in the heavens,*" denotes : 1. The glory of his dominion. The heavens are the most stately and comely pieces of the creation ; his majesty is there most visible, his glory most splendid, Ps. xix. 1. In heaven his dominion is more acknowledged by the angels : his dominion is not disputed there by the angels

that attend him, as it is on earth by the rebels that arm themselves against him.
2. The supremacy of his empire. The heavens are the loftiest part of the creation,
and the only fit palace for him. 3. Peculiarity of this dominion. He rules in the
heavens alone. His authority is not delegated to any creature, he rules the blessed
spirits by himself; but he rules men that are on his footstool by others of the same
kind, men of their own nature. 4. The vastness of his empire. The earth is but
a spot to the heavens. What is England in a map to the whole earth, but a spot
you may cover with your finger; much less must the whole earth be to the extended
heavens. You cannot conceive the many millions of little particles that are in the
earth; and if all put together be but one point to that place where the throne of
God is seated, how vast must his empire be! He rules there over the angels, which
excel in strength, those hosts of his which do his pleasure, in comparison of whom
all the men in the world, and the power of the greatest potentates, is no more than
the strength of an ant or fly. And since his throne is in the heavens, it will follow
that all things under the heaven are part of his dominion; the inferior things of earth
cannot but be subject to him; and it necessarily includes his influence on all things
below, because the heavens are the cause of all the motion in the world. See Hosea ii.
21, 22. 5. The easiness of managing this government. His throne being placed on
high, he cannot but behold all things that are done below; the height of a place gives
advantage to a clear eye to behold things below it. "*The Lord looked down from
heaven upon the children of men, to see if there were any that did understand,*" Ps. xiv. 2.
He looks not down from heaven as if his presence were confined there, but he looks
down majestically, and by way of authority. 6. Duration of it. The heavens are
incorruptible, his throne is placed there in an incorruptible state. The throne of God
outlives the dissolution of the world.—*Condensed from Charnock.*

Verse 19.—"*His kingdom ruleth over all.*" His Lordship is universal. First,
over all *time :* other lords die, but he is eternal. Eternity is properly the duration
of an uncreated Ens. It is improperly taken, either for things that have both beginning and end, as everlasting mountains; divers such phrases in Scripture; or
for things that have a beginning but shall have no end; so are angels and men's
souls eternal; so, eternal life, eternal fire. But God calls himself, "I AM," Exod. iii.
14: I am what I have been, I have been what I am, what I am and have been I
shall be. This attribute is incommunicable: all other things had a *non esse* preceding their *esse*; and they have a mutation tending to nothing. "They that war against
thee shall be as nothing," Isa. xli. 12: all come to nothing unless they be upheld
by the manutency of God: but "Thou art the same, and thy years shall have no
end," Ps. cii. 27. Thou turnest man to destruction, and again sayest, Return:
"even from everlasting to everlasting thou art God," Ps. xc. 2; the sole umpire
and measurer of beginning and ending. Secondly, over all *places*, heaven, earth,
hell, Ps. cxxxv. 6. Kings are limited, and cannot do many things they desire: they
cannot command the sun to stand still, nor the wind to blow which way they would:
in the lofty air, in the depths of the sea no king reigns. They fondly flatter the
pope with his long arms that they reach to purgatory; (but indeed both power
and place are alike imaginary;) it is Christ alone that hath the keys of all places.
Thirdly, over all *creatures*; binding the influences of Pleiades, and loosing the bands
of Orion, Job xxxviii. 31; commanding the fire against the nature of it, to descend,
2 Kings i. 12; creating and ruling the stars, Amos v. 8; overruling the lions, Dan. vi.
22, sending the meteors, Psal. cxlviii. 8, hedging in the sea, lapping it up like a child
in swaddling-clothes, Job xxxviii. 8, dividing, diverting, filling it. In both fire and
water, those two raging elements that have no mercy, he shows mercy; delivers us
from both in both. He calls the fowls, and they come; the beasts, and they hear;
the trees, and they spring to obey him. He hath a raven for Elijah, a gourd for
Jonah, a dog for Lazarus. Makes the leviathan, the hugest living creature, preserve
his prophet. That a terrible lion should be killed, as was by Samson; or not kill, as
they forbore Daniel; or kill and not eat, as that prophet, 1 Kings xiii.: here was the
Lord. Over metals; he makes iron to swim, stones to cleave asunder. Over the
devils; they must obey him though unwillingly. But they continually rebel against
him, and break his will! They do indeed against his complacency, not against his
permission. There is then no time, not the hour of death; no place, not the sorest
torment; no creature, not the devil; but the Lord can deliver us from them. Therefore at all times, in all places, and against all creatures, let us trust in him for
deliverance.—*Thomas Adams.*

Verse 19.—"*His kingdom ruleth over all.*" When Melancthon was extremely solicitous about the affairs of the church in his days, Luther would have him admonished in these terms, *Monendus est Philippus ut desinat esse rector mundi :* Let not Philip make himself any longer governor of the world.—*David Clarkson.*

Verse 20.—" *Bless the Lord, ye his angels,*" etc. The weight of offering praise unto God is too heavy for men to lift ; and as for angels, it will take up all their strength and their best abilities to go about it.—*David Dickson.*

Verse 20.—" *Angels, that excel in strength, that do his commandments.*" The chief excellence of the angels, the main cause of their strength and power, and of their immense superiority to mankind, is that which is set forth in the following words of the text. After the Psalmist has described the angels as excelling in strength, he adds that they *do God's commandments, hearkening to the voice of his word.* For this is the only living source of lasting strength and power. They who do the will of God faithfully and obediently, have God for them ; and then what can be against them ? Then work itself strengthens them, and is like a tide bearing them onward ; because it is *his* work. They on the other hand who run counter to the will of God, have God against them ; and then what can be for them ? Can a man push back the sea ? can he lay hold on the sun, and drag him out of his course ? Then may he hope to be strong, when he is fighting against the will of God. . . .
Hence we see the falsehood of that maxim, so common on the lips of those who plume themselves upon their mastery in the wisdom of this world,—that Might is Right,—a maxim which exactly inverts the truth, and whereby the Prince of darkness is ever setting himself up against the Lord of heaven. The true principle, which is inverted and perverted in this falsehood,—the principle which ought to be written up in the council-chambers of princes and on the walls of senate-houses,—the principle which explains the secret of the strength of the angels, and indeed of all true strength, that is in accordance with the will of God,—may be stated in the selfsame words, if we only invert their order, Right is Might.—*Julius Charles Hare,* 1849.

Verse 20.—" *His angels that do his commandments,*" etc. They hearken to the voice of his word, they look upon God as the great General, and if he give out the word, they give out their strength, and go about the work willingly. They are very attentive to his commands ; if he says, Go smite Herod for his pride, Balaam for his covetousness, David for his vainglory, Sennacherib for his blasphemy, and Sodom for its uncleanness, presently they go.—*William Greenhill.*

Verse 20.—" *Commandments.*" *Davar* (דָּבָר), to speak, is rendered, " *command* " twenty times . . . direct personal communion between the Lord and his messengers seems to be implied.—*R. B. Girdlestone.*

Verse 20.—" *Hearkening unto the voice of his word.*" Not only, mightily executing the word when heard ; but, ever intently listening, *ready to catch the intimation of his will.*—*William Kay.*

Verse 20.—" *Hearkening unto the voice of his word.*" Angels are vigilant creatures, and wait for opportunities, and when they come they will not lose them. They neither slumber nor sleep, but hearken constantly what the Lord will say, what opportunity there will be for action ; so, in Ezekiel i. 11, they are described with their wings stretched upward, manifesting their watchfulness and readiness for service. When Christ was born, a multitude of them appeared and celebrated his nativity, Luke ii. 13 ; when Christ was taken by Judas and his train, Peter drew his sword in his Master's defence ; but what saith Christ ? " Put up thy sword, it is not a time now to fight, but to suffer : thinkest thou that I cannot pray to my Father, and he shall presently give me more than twelve legions of angels ? It is not a time now to pray for help, I must die, and the Scripture must be fulfilled ; but if I would, my Father would bid the angels to aid me, and they presently would come, whole legions of them, yea, all the angels in heaven." Let us learn of angels to watch for opportunities, and take them. There are nicks of time wherein to do the work of Christ.—*William Greenhill.*

Verse 21.—" *Bless ye the Lord, all ye his hosts . . . that do his pleasure.*" The sun, moon, stars, and planets do " *his pleasure* " (Ps. xix. 1) unconsciously ; the " *angels* " consciously, and with instinctive love, " hearken unto the voice of his word " (v. 20). Both together constitute the Lord's hosts.—*A. R. Fausset.*

Verse 22.—" *Bless the Lord, O my soul.*" That is to say, " Let thy vocation be that of the seraphim, O my soul, and enter on the life of heaven ! " Why should

I praise him ? Can my praise be of any advantage to him ? No ; nor that of all the heavenly hosts. It is infinite condescension in him to hearken unto the praises of his most exalted creatures.

Let me bless the Lord, because no function will be more rich in blessings to my soul than this. The admiring contemplation of his excellence is in reality the appropriation thereof ; the heart cannot delight in God, without becoming like God. Let me do it, because it is the peculiar privilege of man on this earth to bless the Lord. When he would find any to join him in this, he has to ascend the skies. Let me do it, because the earth is fully furnished with the materials of praise. The sands, the seas, the flowers, the insects ; animals, birds, fields, mountains, rivers, trees, clouds, sun, moon, stars,—all wait for me to translate their attributes and distinctions into praise. But, above all, the new creation.

Let me do it, because of him, through him, and to him, are all the things that pertain to my existence, health, comfort, knowledge, dignity, safety, progress, power, and usefulness. A thousand of his ministers in earth, sea, and sky, are concerned in the production and preparation of every mouthful that I eat. The breath that I am commanded and enabled to modulate in praise, neither comes nor goes without a most surprising exhibition of the condescension, kindness, wisdom, power, and presence of him whom I am to praise. Is it not dastardly to be receiving benefits, without even mentioning the name, or describing the goodness of the giver ? Let candidates for heaven bless the Lord. There is no place there for such as have not learned this art. How shall I praise him ? Not with fine words. No poetic talent is here necessary. Any language that expresses heart-felt admiration will be accepted. Praise him so far as you know him ; and he will make known to you more of his glory.—*George Bowen*, 1873.

Verse 22.—The last specification is completely comprehensive ; " *all his works in all places of his wide dominions* "—all that he has made, whether intelligent or not intelligent ; " *in all places* "—above, beneath, around : in heaven, earth, or hell : let them all fall into this universal chorus of praise and blessing, extolling Jehovah, the One supremely great, supremely good ! Nor will he exempt himself ; for his personal responsibilities as to his own heart, are his highest. Therefore he closes as he begun, " *Bless the Lord, O my soul.*"—*Henry Cowles.*

Verse 22.—" *Bless the Lord, O my soul.*" Inasmuch as the poet thus comes back to his own soul, his Psalm also turns back into itself and assumes the form of a converging circle.—*Franz Delitzsch.*

Verse 22.—" *Bless the Lord, all his works in all places of his dominion : bless the Lord, O my soul.*" We are very much struck by this sudden transition from " all God's works, in all places of his dominion," to himself, a solitary individual. Of course he had already included himself ; himself had been summoned when he summoned all God's works in all places of his dominion ; but it seems as if a sudden fear had seized the Psalmist, the fear of by any possibility omitting himself ; or, if not a fear, yet a consciousness that his very activity in summoning others to praise, might make him forgetful that he was bound to praise God himself, or sluggish in the duty, or ready to take for granted that he could not himself be neglecting what he was so strenuous in pressing on all orders of being. We have a great subject of discourse here. Solomon has said, " They made me keeper of the vineyards, but mine own vineyard have I not kept." Alas ! how possible, how easy, to take pains for others, and to be neglectful of one's self : nay, to make the pains we take for others the reason by which we persuade ourselves that we cannot be neglecting ourselves. How important, then, that, if with the Psalmist we call on all God's works in all places of his dominions to bless the Lord ; how important, I say, that we add, like persons bent on self-examination, and fearful of self-deceit, " *Bless the Lord, O my soul.*"—*Henry Melvill.*

Verses 1, 2, 22.—" *Bless the Lord, O my soul* . . . . *Bless the Lord, O my soul,*" with the " *Bless the Lord all his works in all places of his dominion : bless the Lord, O my soul,*" verse 22 ; these two form the thrice-repeated blessing from the Lord to the soul in the Mosaic formula, Num. vi. 24—26.—*A. R. Fausset.*

HINTS TO PREACHERS.

Verse 1.—" The Saints blessing the Lord." See " Spurgeon's Sermons," No. 1,078.

Verse 1.—I. We should bless the Most High himself. It is possible to fail to bless *him*, while we praise his gifts, his word, his works, his ways. II. We should bless him individually : " *My* soul." Not merely the family through the father, nor the people through the pastor ; nor the congregation through the choir ; but personally. III. We should bless him spiritually : " soul." Not only with organ, voice, offering, works, &c. IV. We should bless him unreservedly : " All that is within me." V. We should bless him resolutely, David preached self-communion, self-encouragement, and self-command.—*W. Jackson.*

Verse 1.—Here is, I. Self-converse : " Oh my soul." Many talk freely enough to others, but never talk to themselves. They are strangers to themselves—not on speaking terms with themselves—take no interest in their own souls—are dull and melancholy when alone. II. Self-exhortation : " Bless the Lord, O my soul." Thy Creator, thy Benefactor, thy Redeemer. III. Self-encouragement : " All that is within me "—every faculty of my mental, moral and spiritual being : with ten strings—every chord in motion. No need for one faculty of the soul to say to another, " know the Lord, for all shall know him from the least even unto the greatest."— G. R.

Verse 1 (First clause, and v. 22, last clause).—Personal worship the Alpha and Omega of religion.—*C. Davis.*

Verse 2.—Inquire into the causes of our frequent forgetfulness of the Lord's mercies, show the evil of it, and advise remedies.

Verse 3.—I. Forgiveness is *in* God : " There is forgiveness with thee." It is his nature to forgive as well as to punish sin. II. It is *from* God. None can forgive sin but God. None can reveal forgiveness but God. III. It is *like* God, full, free, and everlasting—" all thine iniquities."—*G. R.*

Verse 3.—" *Who healeth all thy diseases.*" I. Why is sin called a disease ? 1. As it destroys the moral beauty of the creature. 2. As it excites pain. 3. As it disables from duty. 4. As it leads to death. II. The variety of sinful diseases to which we are subject. Mark vii. 21—23 ; Gal. v. 19, &c. III. The remedy by which God heals these diseases. 1. His pardoning mercy through the redemption of Christ. 2. The sanctifying influences of grace. 3. The means of grace. 4. The resurrection of the body.—*From " The Study,"* 1873.

Verse 3 (last clause).—Our diseases by nature, our great Physician, the perfect soundness which he works in us, results of that soundness.

Verses 3, 4, 5.—Mercy's Hexapla. I. Three curses removed. 1. Guilt put away. 2. Corruption cured. 3. Destruction averted. II. Three blessings bestowed. 1. Favours that can gratify. 2. Pleasures that can satisfy. 3. Life that can never die. Or (*Verse 3*) I. Pardon. II. Purification. (*Verse 4*) III. Redemption. IV. Coronation. (*Verse 5*) V. Plenty bestowed. VI. Power renewed.—*W. Durban.*

Verse 4 (first clause).—The Redemption of David's life from destruction. 1. His shepherd life. 2. His military life. 3. His persecuted life. 4. His regal life. 5. His spiritual life.—*W. J.*

Verse 4.—What is redeemed, and from what ? Who are redeemed, and by whom ?

Verse 5.—I. A singular condition—satisfaction. II. A singular provision— good things. III. A singular result—youth renewed.

Verse 5.—" Rejuvenescence." See Macmillan's " Ministry of Nature," pp. 321—347.

Verse 7.—I. God would have men know him. II. He is his own revealer. III. There are degrees in the revelation. IV. We may pray for increased knowledge of him.

Verse 8.—I. Mercy specified : " Merciful and gracious." II. Mercy qualified : " Slow to anger." Mercy itself may be angered, and then how terrible is the anger. III. Mercy amplified : " Plenteous in mercy." " He will abundantly pardon ; " and he only knows what abundant pardon means.—*G. R.*

Verse 9.—I. What God will do to his people. He will sometimes chide—contend with them. 1. Providentially, by outward trials. 2. Experimentally, by inward conflicts. II. What he will not do to them. 1. Not chide continually in this life. 2. Not chide in the least hereafter. " The days of their mourning shall be ended."— G. R.

Verse 10.—Work out the terrible supposition, show the reasons why it has not yet been actually so ; then suggest that it may yet become a terrible fact, and exhort the guilty to seek mercy.

Verses 11, 12, 13.—The height, length and depth of divine love.

Verse 12.—" Plenary Absolution." See " Spurgeon's Sermons," No. 1,108.

Verse 12.—I. The union implied. Between man and his transgressions. 1. Legally. 2. Actually. 3. Experimentally. 4. Eternally, in themselves considered. II. The separation effected. 1. By whom ? " He hath," etc. 2. How ? By his own Son coming between the sinner and his sins. III. The Re-union prevented. " As far," etc. When east and west meet, then, and not till then, will the re-union take place. As the two extremities of a straight line can never meet, and cannot be lengthened without receding further from each other, so it will ever be with a pardoned sinner and his sins.—*G. R.*

Verses 13, 14.—" The Tender Pity of the Lord." See " Spurgeon's Sermons." No. 941.

Verses 13, 14.—I. Whom God pities ; " them that fear him." II. How he pities " as a father pitieth his children." III. Why he pities ; " for he knoweth our frame." He hath reason to know our frame, for he framed us, and having himself made man of the dust, " he remembers that we are dust."—*Matthew Henry.*

Verse 14.—I. Man's Constitution. II. God's Consideration.—*W. D.*

Verse 15.—Man's earthly career. His rise, progress, glory, fall, and oblivion.

Verses 15—18.—I. What man is when left to himself. " As for man," etc. 1. What here ? His days are as grass, his glory as the flower of grass. 2. What hereafter ? swept away by a blighting wind, by a blast of divine anger—known no more on the earth, known only in perdition. II. What the mercy of God does for him. 1. Makes a covenant of grace on his behalf from everlasting. 2. Makes a covenant of peace with him in this life. 3. Makes a covenant of promise to him for an eternity to come. III. Who are the objects of this mercy ? 1. Those who fear God. 2. Who walk in the footsteps of pious ancestors. 3. Who rely upon covenant mercy. 4. Who are faithful to their covenant engagements.—*G. R.*

Verse 18.—The covenant, in what respects we can keep it, in what frame of mind it must be kept, and what is the practical proof of so doing.

Verse 19.—" A Discourse upon God's Dominion." See Charnock's Works [Nicol's Edition, Vol. II., pp. 400—499].

Verse 19.—I. The nature of the throne. II. The extent of the dominion. III. The character of the monarch. IV. The consequent joy of the subjects : " Bless the Lord."

Verse 20.—The angels' service instructive to us. I. Their personal strength is excellent. As servants of God we also should see to our own spiritual health and vigour. II. They are practical in their obedience, not theorists. III. They are attentive while at work, ready to learn more, and holding fellowship with God, who speaks personally to them. IV. They do all in the spirit of joyful praise, blessing the Lord.

Verses 20, 21.—I. The centre of praise : " Bless the Lord." All praise centres in him. II. The concert of praise. 1. Angels. 2. The hosts of the redeemed. 3. Ministers in particular. 4. The surrounding creation. III. The climax of praise : " Bless the Lord, O my soul." This has the highest claim upon me for gratitude and praise. Vast as the chorus may be, it will not be perfect without my note of praise. This is the culminating note : " Bless the Lord, O my soul."—*G. R.*

Verse 21.—Who are God's ministers ? What is their business ? To do his pleasure. What is their delight ? To bless the Lord.

Verses 21, 22.—Henry Melvill has a notable sermon upon " The Peril of the Spiritual Guide." The drift of it may be gathered from the extract which we have placed as a note upon the passage.

Verse 22.—I. The Chorus. II. The Echo.—*W. D.*

PSALM CIV.

GENERAL REMARKS.—*Here we have one of the loftiest and longest sustained flights of the inspired muse. The Psalm gives an interpretation to the many voices of nature, and sings sweetly both of creation and providence. The poem contains a complete cosmos : sea and land, cloud and sunlight, plant and animal, light and darkness, life and death, are all proved to be expressive of the presence of the Lord. Traces of the six days' of creation are very evident, and though the creation of man, which was the crowning work of the sixth day, is not mentioned, this is accounted for from the fact that man is himself the singer : some have even discerned marks of the divine rest upon the seventh day in verse 31. It is a poet's version of Genesis. Nor is it alone the present condition of the earth which is here the subject of song ; but a hint is given of those holier times when we shall see " a new earth wherein dwelleth righteousness," out of which the sinner shall be consumed, verse 35. The spirit of ardent praise to God runs through the whole, and with it a distinct realization of the divine Being as a personal existence, loved and trusted as well as adored.*

We have no information as to the author, but the Septuagint assigns it to David, and we see no reason for ascribing it to any one else. His spirit, style, and manner of writing are very manifest therein, and if the Psalm must be ascribed to another, it must be to a mind remarkably similar, and we could only suggest the wise son of David —Solomon, the poet preacher, to whose notes upon natural history in the Proverbs some of the verses bear a striking likeness. Whoever the human penman may have been, the exceeding glory and perfection of the Holy Spirit's own divine authorship are plain to every spiritual mind.

DIVISION.—*After ascribing blessedness to the Lord the devout Psalmist sings of the light and the firmament, which were the work of the first and second days (verses 1—6). By an easy transition he describes the separation of the waters from the dry land, the formation of rain, brooks, and rivers, and the uprising of green herbs, which were the produce of the third day (7—18). Then the appointment of the sun and moon to be the guardians of day and night commands the poet's admiration (19—23), and so he sings the work of the fourth day. Having already alluded to many varieties of living creatures, the Psalmist proceeds from verse 24 to verse 30 to sing of the life with which the Lord was pleased to fill the air, the sea, and the land ; these forms of existence were the peculiar produce of the fifth and sixth days. We may regard the closing verses (31—35) as a Sabbath meditation, hymn, and prayer. The whole lies before us as a panorama of the universe viewed by the eye of devotion. O for grace to render due praise unto the Lord while reading it.*

EXPOSITION.

BLESS the LORD, O my soul. O LORD my God, thou art very great ; thou art clothed with honour and majesty.

2 Who coverest *thyself* with light as *with* a garment : who stretchest out the heavens like a curtain :

3 Who layeth the beams of his chambers in the waters : who maketh the clouds his chariot : who walketh upon the wings of the wind :

4 Who maketh his angels spirits ; his ministers a flaming fire.

5 *Who* laid the foundations of the earth, *that* it should not be removed for ever.

6 Thou coveredst it with the deep as *with* a garment : the waters stood above the mountains.

1.—*" Bless the Lord, O my soul."* This Psalm begins and ends like the Hundred and Third, and it could not do better : when the model is perfect it deserves to exist in duplicate. True praise begins at home. It is idle to stir up others to praise if we are ungratefully silent ourselves. We should call upon our inmost hearts to awake and bestir themselves, for we are apt to be sluggish, and if we are so when called upon to bless God, we shall have great cause to be ashamed. When we magnify the Lord, let us do it heartily : our best is far beneath his worthiness, let us not dishonour him by rendering to him half-hearted worship. *" O Lord my God, thou art very great."* This ascription has in it a remarkable blending of the boldness of faith, and the awe of holy fear : for the Psalmist calls the infinite Jehovah *" my God,"* and at the same time, prostrate in amazement at the divine greatness, he cries out in utter astonishment, *" Thou art very great."* God was great on Sinai, yet the opening words of his law were, " I am the Lord thy God ; " his greatness is no reason why faith should not put in her claim, and call him all her own. The declaration of Jehovah's greatness here given would have been very much in place at the end of the Psalm, for it is a natural inference and deduction from a survey of the universe : its position at the very commencement of the poem is an indication that the whole Psalm was well considered and digested in the mind before it was actually put into words ; only on this supposition can we account for the emotion preceding the contemplation. Observe also, that the wonder expressed does not refer to the creation and its greatness, but to Jehovah himself. It is not " the universe is very great ! " but " Thou art very great." Many stay at the creature, and so become idolatrous in spirit ; to pass onward to the Creator himself is true wisdom. *" Thou art clothed with honour and majesty."* Thou thyself art not to be seen, but thy works, which may be called thy garments, are full of beauties and marvels which redound to thine honour. Garments both conceal and reveal a man, and so do the creatures of God. The Lord is seen in his works as worthy of *honour* for his skill, his goodness, and his power, and as claiming *majesty*, for he has fashioned all things in sovereignty, doing as he wills, and asking no man's permit. He must be blind indeed who does not see that nature is the work of a king. These are solemn strokes of God's severer mind, terrible touches of his sterner attributes, broad lines of inscrutable mystery, and deep shadings of overwhelming power, and these make creation's picture a problem never to be solved, except by admitting that he who drew it giveth no account of his matters, but ruleth all things according to the good pleasure of his will. His *majesty* is, however, always so displayed as to reflect *honour* upon his whole character ; he does as he wills, but he wills only that which is thrice holy, like himself. The very robes of the unseen Spirit teach us this, and it is ours to recognise it with humble adoration.

2. *" Who coverest thyself with light as with a garment : "* wrapping the light about him as a monarch puts on his robe. The conception is sublime : but it makes us feel how altogether inconceivable the personal glory of the Lord must be ; if light itself is but his garment and veil, what must be the blazing splendour of his own essential being ! We are lost in astonishment, and dare not pry into the mystery lest we be blinded by its insufferable glory. *" Who stretchest out the heavens like a curtain "*—within which he might dwell. Light was created on the first day and the firmament upon the second, so that they fitly follow each other in this verse. Oriental princes put on their glorious apparel and then sit in state within curtains, and the Lord is spoken of under that image : but how far above all comprehension the figure must be lifted, since the robe is essential light, to which suns and moons owe their brightness, and the curtain is the azure sky studded with stars for gems. This is a substantial argument for the truth with which the Psalmist commenced his song, " O Lord my God, thou art very great."

3. *" Who layeth the beams of his chambers in the waters."* His lofty halls are framed with the waters which are above the firmament. The upper rooms of God's great house, the secret stories far above our ken, the palatial chambers wherein he resides, are based upon the floods which form the upper ocean. To the unsubstantial he lends stability ; he needs no joists and rafters, for his palace is sustained by his own power. We are not to interpret literally where the language is poetical, it would be simple absurdity to do so. *" Who maketh the clouds his chariot."* When he comes forth from his secret pavilion 'tis thus he makes his royal progress. " His chariot of wrath deep thunder-clouds form," and his chariot of mercy drops plenty as it traverses the celestial road. *" Who walketh* [or rather *goes*] *upon the wings of the wind."* With the clouds for a car, and the winds for winged steeds, the Great King hastens on his movements whether for mercy or for judgment. Thus we have the idea of a king still further elaborated—his lofty palace, his chariot, and his coursers are before us ; but what a palace must we imagine, whose beams are of crystal, and whose base is consolidated vapour ! What a stately car is that which

is fashioned out of the flying clouds, whose gorgeous colours Solomon in all his glory could not rival ; and what a Godlike progress is that in which spirit wings and breath of winds bear up the moving throne. " O Lord, my God, thou art very great ! "

4. " *Who maketh his angels spirits ; * " or *winds,* for the word means either. Angels are pure spirits, though they are permitted to assume a visible form when God desires us to see them. God is a spirit, and he is waited upon by spirits in his royal courts. Angels are like winds for mystery, force, and invisibility, and no doubt the winds themselves are often the angels or messengers of God. God who makes his angels to be as winds, can also make winds to be his angels, and they are constantly so in the economy of nature. " *His ministers a flaming fire.* " Here, too, we may choose which we will of two meanings : God's ministers or servants he makes to be as swift, potent, and terrible as fire, and on the other hand he makes fire, that devouring element, to be his minister flaming forth upon his errands. That the passage refers to angels is clear from Heb. i. 7 ; and it was most proper to mention them here in connection with light and the heavens, and immediately after the robes and palace of the Great King. Should not the retinue of the Lord of Hosts be mentioned as well as his chariot ? It would have been a flaw in the description of the universe had the angels not been alluded to, and this is the most appropriate place for their introduction. When we think of the extraordinary powers entrusted to angelic beings, and the mysterious glory of the seraphim and the four living creatures, we are led to reflect upon the glory of the Master whom they serve, and again we cry out with the Psalmist, " O Lord, my God, thou art very great."

5. " *Who laid the foundations of the earth.* " Thus the commencement of creation is described, in almost the very words employed by the Lord himself in Job xxxviii. 4. " Where wast thou when I laid the foundations of the earth ? Whereupon are the foundations thereof fastened, and who laid the corner stone thereof ? " And the words are found in the same connection too, for the Lord proceeds to say, " When the morning stars sang together and all the sons of God shouted for joy." " *That it should not be removed for ever.* " The language is, of course, poetical, but the fact is none the less wonderful : the earth is so placed in space that it remains as stable as if it were a fixture. The several motions of our planet are carried on so noiselessly and evenly that, as far as we are concerned, all things are as permanent and peaceful as if the old notion of its resting upon pillars were literally true. With what delicacy has the great Artificer poised our globe ! What power must there be in that hand which has caused so vast a body to know its orbit, and to move so smoothly in it ! What engineer can save every part of his machinery from an occasional jar, jerk, or friction ? yet to our great world in its complicated motions no such thing has ever occurred. " O Lord, my God, thou art very great."

6. " *Thou coveredst it with the deep as with a garment.* " The new-born earth was wrapt in aqueous swaddling bands. In the first ages, ere man appeared, the proud waters ruled the whole earth, " *the waters stood above the mountains,* " no dry land was visible, vapour as from a steaming cauldron covered all. Geologists inform us of this as a discovery, but the Holy Spirit had revealed the fact long before. The passage before us shows us the Creator commencing his work, and laying the foundation for future order and beauty : to think of this reverently will fill us with adoration ; to conceive of it grossly and carnally would be highly blasphemous.

7 At thy rebuke they fled ; at the voice of thy thunder they hasted away.

8 They go up by the mountains ; they go down by the valleys unto the place which thou hast founded for them.

9 Thou hast set a bound that they may not pass over ; that they turn not again to cover the earth.

10 He sendeth the springs into the valleys, *which* run among the hills.

11 They give drink to every beast of the field : the wild asses quench their thirst.

12 By them shall the fowls of the heaven have their habitation, *which* sing among the branches.

13 He watereth the hills from his chambers : the earth is satisfied with the fruit of thy works.

14 He causeth the grass to grow for the cattle, and herb for the service of man : that he may bring forth food out of the earth ;

15 And wine *that* maketh glad the heart of man, *and* oil to make *his* face to shine, and bread *which* strengtheneth man's heart.

16 The trees of the LORD are full *of sap ;* the cedars of Lebanon, which he hath planted ;

17 Where the birds make their nests : *as for* the stork, the fir trees *are* her house.

18 The high hills *are* a refuge for the wild goats ; *and* the rocks for the conies.

7. " *At thy rebuke they fled ; at the voice of thy thunder they hasted away.*" When the waters and vapours covered all, the Lord had but to speak and they disappeared at once. As though they had been intelligent agents the waves hurried to their appointed deeps and left the land to itself ; then the mountains lifted their heads, the high lands rose from the main, and at length continents and islands, slopes and plains were left to form the habitable earth. The voice of the Lord effected this great marvel. Is not his word equal to every emergency ? potent enough to work the greatest miracle ? By that same word shall the waterfloods of trouble be restrained, and the raging billows of sin be rebuked : the day cometh when at the thunder of Jehovah's voice all the proud waters of evil shall utterly haste away. " O Lord, my God, thou art very great."

8. The vanquished waters are henceforth obedient. " *They go up by the moun-tains,*" climbing in the form of clouds even to the summits of the Alps. " *They go down by the valleys unto the place which thou hast founded for them :* " they are as willing to descend in rain, and brooks, and torrents as they were eager to ascend in mists. The loyalty of the mighty waters to the laws of their God is most notable ; the fierce flood, the boisterous rapid, the tremendous torrent, are only forms of that gentle dew which trembles on the tiny blade of grass, and in those ruder shapes they are equally obedient to the laws which their Maker has impressed upon them. Not so much as a solitary particle of spray ever breaks rank, or violates the command of the Lord of sea and land, neither do the awful cataracts and terrific floods revolt from his sway. It is very beautiful among the mountains to see the divine system of water supply—the rising of the fleecy vapours, the distillation of the pure fluid, the glee with which the new-born element leaps adown the crags to reach the rivers, and the strong eagerness with which the rivers seek the ocean, their appointed place.

9. " *Thou hast set a bound that they may not pass over ; that they turn not again to cover the earth.*" That bound has once been passed, but it shall never be so again. The deluge was caused by the suspension of the divine mandate which held the floods in check : they knew their old supremacy, and hastened to reassert it, but now the covenant promise for ever prevents a return of that carnival of waters, that revolt of the waves : ought we not rather to call it that impetuous rush of the indignant floods to avenge the injured honour of their King, whom men had offended? Jehovah's word bounds the ocean, using only a narrow belt of sand to confine it to its own limits : that apparently feeble restraint answers every purpose, for the sea is obedient as a little child to the bidding of its Maker. Destruction lies asleep in the bed of the ocean, and though our sins might well arouse it, yet are its bands made strong by covenant mercy, so that it cannot break loose again upon the guilty sons of men.

10. " *He sendeth the springs into the valleys, which run among the hills.*" This is a beautiful part of the Lord's arrangement of the subject waters : they find vents through which they leap into liberty where their presence will be beneficial in the highest degree. Depressions exist in the sides of the mountains, and adown these the waterbrooks are made to flow, often taking their rise at bubbling fountains which issue from the bowels of the earth. It is God who sends these springs even as a gardener makes the water courses, and turns the current with his foot. When the waters are confined in the abyss *the Lord* sets their bound, and when they sport at liberty *he* sends them forth.

11. " *They give drink to every beast of the field.*" Who else would water them if the Lord did not ? They are *his* cattle, and therefore he leads them forth to watering. Not one of them is forgotten of him. " *The wild asses quench their thirst.*" The good Lord gives them enough and to spare. They know their Master's crib. Though bit or bridle of man they will not brook, and man denounces them as un-teachable, they learn of the Lord, and know better far than man where flows the

cooling crystal of which they must drink or die. They are only asses, and wild, yet our heavenly Father careth for them. Will he not also care for us ? We see here, also, that nothing is made in vain ; though no human lip is moistened by the brooklet in the lone valley, yet are there other creatures which need refreshment, and these slake their thirst at the stream. Is this nothing ? Must everything exist for man, or else be wasted ? What but our pride and selfishness could have suggested such a notion ? It is not true that flowers which blush unseen by human eye are wasting their sweetness, for the bee finds them out, and other winged wanderers live on their luscious juices. Man is but one creature of the many whom the heavenly Father feedeth and watereth.

12. "*By them shall the fowls of the heaven have their habitation, which sing among the branches.*" How refreshing are these words ! What happy memories they arouse of plashing waterfalls and entangled boughs, where the merry din of the falling and rushing water forms a sort of solid background of music, and the sweet tuneful notes of the birds are the brighter and more flashing lights in the harmony. Pretty birdies, sing on ! What better can ye do, and who can do it better ? When we too drink of the river of God, and eat of the fruit of the tree of life, it well becomes us to " sing among the branches." Where ye dwell ye sing ; and shall not we rejoice in the Lord, who has been our dwelling-place in all generations. As ye fly from bough to bough, ye warble forth your notes, and so will we as we flit through time into eternity. It is not meet that birds of Paradise should be outdone by birds of earth.

13. "*He watereth the hills from his chambers.*" As the mountains are too high to be watered by rivers and brooks, the Lord himself refreshes them from those waters above the firmament which the poet had in a former verse described as the upper chambers of heaven. Clouds are detained among the mountain crags, and deluge the hill sides with fertilizing rain. Where man cannot reach the Lord can, whom none else can water with grace he can, and where all stores of refreshment fail he can supply all that is needed from his own halls. " *The earth is satisfied with the fruit of thy works.*" The result of the divine working is fulness everywhere, the soil is saturated with rain, the seed germinates, the beasts drink, and the birds sing —nothing is left unsupplied. So, too, is it in the new creation, he giveth more grace, he fills his people with good, and makes them all confess, " of his fulness have all we received and grace for grace."

14. "*He causeth the grass to grow for the cattle, and herb for the service of man.*" Grass grows as well as herbs, for cattle must be fed as well as men. God appoints to the lowliest creature its portion and takes care that it has it. Divine power is as truly and as worthily put forth in the feeding of beasts as in the nurturing of man ; watch but a blade of grass with a devout eye and you may see God at work within it. The herb is for man, and he must till the soil, or it will not be produced, yet it is God that causeth it to grow in the garden, even the same God who made the grass to grow in the unenclosed pastures of the wilderness. Man forgets this and talks of his produce, but in very truth without God he would plough and sow in vain. The Lord causeth each green blade to spring and each ear to ripen : do but watch with opened eye and you shall see the Lord walking through the cornfields. " *That he may bring forth food out of the earth.*" Both grass for cattle and corn for man are food brought forth out of the earth, and they are signs that it was God's design that the very dust beneath our feet, which seems better adapted to bury us than to sustain us, should actually be transformed into the staff of life. The more we think of this the more wonderful it will appear. How great is that God who from among the sepulchres finds the support of life, and out of the ground which was cursed brings forth the blessings of corn and wine and oil.

15. "*And wine that maketh glad the heart of man.*" By the aid of genial showers the earth produces not merely necessaries but luxuries, that which furnishes a feast as well as that which makes a meal. O that man were wise enough to know how to use this gladdening product of the vine ; but, alas, he full often turns it to ill account, and debases himself therewith. Of this he must himself bear the blame ; he deserves to be miserable who turns even blessings into curses. " *And oil to make his face to shine.*" The easterns use oil more than we do, and probably are wiser in this respect than we are : they delight in anointings with perfumed oils, and regard the shining of the face as a choice emblem of joy. God is to be praised for all the products of the soil, not one of which could come to us were it not that he causeth it to grow. " *And bread which strengtheneth man's heart.*" Men have more

courage after they are fed : many a depressed spirit has been comforted by a good substantial meal. We ought to bless God for strength of heart as well as force of limb, since if we possess them they are both the bounties of his kindness.

16. The watering of the hills not only produces the grass and the cultivated herbs, but also the nobler species of vegetation, which come not within the range of human culture :—

> " Their veins with genial moisture fed,
> Jehovah's forests lift the head :
> Nor other than his tostering hand
> Thy cedars, Lebanon, demand.''

" *The trees of the Lord* ''—the greatest, noblest, and most royal of trees, those too which are unowned of man, and untouched by his hand. " *Are full of sap,*'' or are full, well supplied, richly watered, so that they become, as the cedars, full of resin, flowing with life, and verdant all the year round. " *The cedars of Lebanon, which he hath planted.*'' They grow where none ever thought of planting them, where for ages they were unobserved, and where at this moment they are too gigantic for man to prune them. What would our Psalmist have said to some of the trees in the Yosemite valley ? Truly these are worthy to be called the trees of the Lord, for towering stature and enormous girth. Thus is the care of God seen to be effectual and all-sufficient. If trees uncared for by man are yet so full of sap, we may rest assured that the people of God who by faith live upon the Lord alone shall be equally well sustained. Planted by grace, and owing all to our heavenly Father's care, we may defy the hurricane, and laugh at the fear of drought, for none that trust in him shall ever be left unwatered.

17. " *Where the birds make their nests : as for the stork, the fir trees are her house.*'' So far from being in need, these trees of God afford shelter to others, birds small and great make their nests in the branches. Thus what they receive from the great Lord they endeavour to return to his weaker creatures. How one thing fits into another in this fair creation, each link drawing on its fellow : the rains water the fir trees, and the fir trees become the happy home of birds ; thus do the thunder clouds build the sparrow's house, and the descending rain sustains the basis of the stork's nest. Observe, also, how everything has its use—the boughs furnish a home for the birds ; and every living thing has its accommodation—the stork finds a house in the pines. Her nest is called a house, because this bird exhibits domestic virtues and maternal love which make her young to be comparable to a family. No doubt this ancient writer has seen storks' nests in fir trees ; they appear usually to build on houses and ruins, but there is also evidence that where there are forests they are content with pine trees. Has the reader ever walked through a forest of great trees and felt the awe which strikes the heart in nature's sublime cathedral ? Then he will remember to have felt that each bird was holy, since it dwelt amid such sacred solitude. Those who cannot see or hear of God except in Gothic edifices, amid the swell of organs, and the voices of a surpliced choir, will not be able to enter into the feeling which makes the simple, unsophisticated soul hear " the voice of the Lord God walking among the trees.''

18. " *The high hills are a refuge for the wild goats ; and the rocks for the conies.*'' All places teem with life. We call our cities populous, but are not the forests and the high hills more densely peopled with life ? We speak of uninhabitable places, but where are they ? The chamois leaps from crag to crag, and the rabbit burrows beneath the soil. For one creature the loftiness of the hills, and for another the hollowness of the rocks, serves as a protection : —

> " Far o'er the crags the wild goats roam,
> The rocks supply the coney's home.''

Thus all the earth is full of happy life, every place has its appropriate inhabitant, nothing is empty and void and waste. See how goats, and storks, and conies, and sparrows, each contribute a verse to the Psalm of nature ; have we not also our canticles to sing unto the Lord ? Little though we may be in the scale of importance, yet let us fill our sphere, and so honour the Lord who made us with a purpose.

19 He appointed the moon for seasons : the sun knoweth his going down.

20 Thou makest darkness, and it is night: wherein all the beasts of the forest do creep *forth*.

21 The young lions roar after their prey, and seek their meat from God.

22 The sun ariseth, they gather themselves together, and lay them down in their dens.

23 Man goeth forth unto his work and to his labour until the evening.

19. The appointed rule of the great lights is now the theme for praise. The moon is mentioned first, because in the Jewish day the night leads the way. "*He appointed the moon for seasons.*" By the waxing and waning of the moon the year is divided into months, and weeks, and by this means the exact dates of the holy days are arranged. Thus the lamp of night is made to be of service to man, and in fixing the period of religious assemblies (as it did among the Jews) it enters into connection with his noblest being. Never let us regard the moon's motions as the inevitable result of inanimate impersonal law, but as the appointment of our God. "*The sun knoweth his going down.*" In finely poetic imagery the sun is represented as knowing when to retire from sight, and sink below the horizon. He never loiters on his way, or pauses as if undecided when to descend; his appointed hour for going down, although it is constantly varying, he always keeps to a second. We need to be aroused in the morning, but he arises punctually, and though some require to watch the clock to know the hour of rest, he, without a timepiece to consult, hides himself in the western sky the instant the set time has come. For all this man should praise the Lord of the sun and moon, who has made these great lights to be our chronometers, and thus keeps our world in order, and suffers no confusion to distract us.

20. "*Thou makest darkness, and it is night.*" Drawing down the blinds for us, he prepares our bedchamber that we may sleep. Were there no darkness we should sigh for it, since we should find repose so much more difficult if the weary day were never calmed into night. Let us see God's hand in the veiling of the sun, and never fear either natural or providential darkness, since both are of the Lord's own making. "*Wherein all the beasts of the forest do creep forth.*" Then is the lion's day, his time to hunt his food. Why should not the wild beast have his hour as well as man? He has a service to perform, should he not also have his food? Darkness is fitter for beasts than man; and those men are most brutish who love darkness rather than light. When the darkness of ignorance broods over a nation, then all sorts of superstitions, cruelties, and vices abound; the gospel, like the sunrising, soon clears the world of the open ravages of these monsters, and they seek more congenial abodes. We see here the value of true light, for we may depend upon it where there is night there will also be wild beasts to kill and to devour.

21. "*The young lions roar after their prey, and seek their meat from God.*" This is the poetic interpretation of a roar. To whom do the lions roar? Certainly not to their prey, for the terrible sound tends to alarm their victims, and drive them away. They after their own fashion express their desires for food, and the expression of desire is a kind of prayer. Out of this fact comes the devout thought of the wild beast's appealing to its Maker for food. But neither with lions nor men will the seeking of prayer suffice, there must be practical seeking too, and the lions are well aware of it. What they have in their own language asked for they go forth to seek; being in this thing far wiser than many men who offer formal prayers not half so earnest as those of the young lions, and then neglect the means in the use of which the object of their petitions might be gained. The lions roar and seek; too many are liars before God, and roar but never seek.

How comforting is the thought that the Spirit translates the voice of a lion, and finds it to be a seeking of meat from God! May we not hope that our poor broken cries and groans, which in our sorrow we have called "the voice of our roaring" (Ps. xxii. 10), will be understood by him, and interpreted in our favour. Evidently he considers the meaning rather than the music of the utterance, and puts the best construction upon it.

22. "*The sun ariseth.*" Every evening has its morning to make the day. Were it not that we have seen the sun rise so often we should think it the greatest of miracles, and the most amazing of blessings. "*They gather themselves together, and lay them down in their dens.*" Thus they are out of man's way, and he seldom encounters them unless he desires to do so. The forest's warriors retire to their quarters when the

morning's drum is heard, finding in the recesses of their dens a darkness suitable for their slumbers; there they lay them down and digest their food, for God has allotted even to them their portion of rest and enjoyment. There was one who in this respect was poorer than lions and foxes, for he had not where to lay his head: all were provided for except their incarnate Provider. Blessed Lord, thou hast stooped beneath the conditions of the brutes to lift up worse than brutish men!

It is very striking how the Lord controls the fiercest of animals far more readily than the shepherd manages his sheep. At nightfall they separate and go forth each one upon the merciful errand of ending the miseries of the sickly and decrepit among grass-eating animals. The younger of these animals being swift of foot easily escape them and are benefited by the exercise, and for the most part only those are overtaken and killed to whom life would have been protracted agony. So far lions are messengers of mercy, and are as much sent of God as the sporting dog is sent by man on his errands. But these mighty hunters must not always be abroad, they must be sent back to their lairs when man comes upon the scene. Who shall gather these ferocious creatures and shut them in? Who shall chain them down and make them harmless? The sun suffices to do it. He is the true lion-tamer. They gather themselves together as though they were so many sheep, and in their own retreats they keep themselves prisoners till returning darkness gives them another leave to range. By simply majestic means the divine purposes are accomplished. In like manner even the devils are subject unto our Lord Jesus, and by the simple spread of the light of the gospel these roaring demons are chased out of the world. No need for miracles or displays of physical power, the Sun of Righteousness arises, and the devil and the false gods, and superstitions and errors of men, all seek their hiding places in the dark places of the earth among the moles and the bats.

23. "*Man goeth forth.*" It is his turn now, and the sunrise has made things ready for him. His warm couch he forsakes and the comforts of home, to find his daily food; this work is good for him, both keeping him out of mischief, and exercising his faculties. "*Unto his work and to his labour until the evening.*" He goes not forth to sport but to work, not to loiter but to labour; at least, this is the lot of the best part of mankind. We are made for work and ought to work, and should never grumble that so it is appointed. The hours of labour, however, ought not to be too long. If labour lasts out the average daylight it is certainly all that any man ought to expect of another, and yet there are poor creatures so badly paid that in twelve hours they cannot earn bread enough to keep them from hunger. Shame on those who dare so impose upon helpless women and children. Night work should also be avoided as much as possible. There are twelve hours in which a man ought to work: the night is meant for rest and sleep.

Night, then, as well as day has its voice of praise. It is more soft and hushed, but it is none the less true. The moon lights up a solemn silence of worship among the fir trees, through which the night wind softly breathes its "songs without words." Every now and then a sound is heard, which, however simple by day, sounds among the shadows startling and weird-like, as if the presence of the unknown had filled the heart with trembling, and made the influence of the Infinite to be realized. Imagination awakens herself; unbelief finds the silence and the solemnity uncongenial, faith looks up to the skies above her and sees heavenly things all the more clearly in the absence of the sunlight, and adoration bows itself before the Great Invisible! There are spirits that keep the night watches, and the spell of their presence has been felt by many a wanderer in the solitudes of nature: God also himself is abroad all night long, and the glory which concealeth is often felt to be even greater than that which reveals. Bless the Lord, O my soul.

24 O LORD, how manifold are thy works! in wisdom hast thou made them all: the earth is full of thy riches.

25 *So is* this great and wide sea, wherein *are* things creeping innumerable, both small and great beasts.

26 There go the ships: *there is* that leviathan, *whom* thou hast made to play therein.

27 These wait all upon thee; that thou mayest give *them* their meat in due season.

28 *That* thou givest them they gather : thou openest thine hand, they are filled with good.

29 Thou hidest thy face, they are troubled : thou takest away their breath, they die, and return to their dust.

30 Thou sendest forth thy spirit, they are created : and thou renewest the face of the earth.

24. " *O Lord, how manifold are thy works !* "   They are not only many for number but manifold for variety.   Mineral, vegetable, animal—what a range of works is suggested by these three names !   No two even of the same class are exactly alike, and the classes are more numerous than science can number.   Works in the heavens above and in the earth beneath, and in the waters under the earth, works which abide the ages, works which come to perfection and pass away in a year, works which with all their beauty do not outlive a day, works within works, and works within these— who can number one of a thousand ?   God is the great worker, and ordainer of variety.   It is ours to study his works, for they are great, and sought out of all them that have pleasure therein.   The kingdom of grace contains as manifold and as great works as that of nature, but the chosen of the Lord alone discern them.   " *In wisdom hast thou made them all,*" or *wrought* them all.   They are all his works, wrought by his own power, and they all display his wisdom.   It was wise to make them—none could be spared ; every link is essential to the chain of nature—wild beasts as much as men, poisons as truly as odoriferous herbs.   They are wisely made—each one fits its place, fills it, and is happy in so doing.   As a whole, the " all " of creation is a wise achievement, and however it may be chequered with mysteries, and clouded with terrors, it all works together for good, and as one complete harmonious piece of workmanship it answers the great Worker's end.   " *The earth is full of thy riches.*" It is not a poor-house, but a palace ; not a hungry ruin, but a well-filled store-house. The Creator has not set his creatures down in a dwelling-place where the table is bare, and the buttery empty, he has filled the earth with food ; and not with bare necessaries only, but with *riches*—dainties, luxuries, beauties, treasures.   In the bowels of the earth are hidden mines of wealth, and on her surface are teeming harvests of plenty. All these riches are the Lord's ; we ought to call them not " the wealth of nations," but " thy riches " O Lord !   Not in one clime alone are these riches of God to be found, but in all lands—even the Arctic ocean has its precious things which men endure much hardness to win, and the burning sun of the equator ripens a produce which flavours the food of all mankind.   If his house below is so full of riches what must his house above be, where

> " The very streets are paved with gold
> Exceeding clear and fine " ?

25. " *So is this great and wide sea.*"   He gives an instance of the immense number and variety of Jehovah's works by pointing to the sea.   " Look," saith he, " at yonder ocean, stretching itself on both hands and embracing so many lands, it too swarms with animal life, and in its deeps lie treasures beyond all counting."   The heathen made the sea a different province from the land, and gave the command thereof to Neptune, but we know of a surety that Jehovah rules the waves.   " *Wherein are things creeping innumerable, both small and great beasts ;* " read *moving things and animals small and great,* and you have the true sense.   The number of minute forms of animal life is indeed beyond all reckoning : when a single phosphorescent wave may bear millions of infusoria, and around a fragment of rock armies of microscopic beings may gather, we renounce all idea of applying arithmetic to such a case. The sea in many regions appears to be all alive, as if every drop were a world.   Nor are these tiny creatures the only tenants of the sea, for it contains gigantic mammals which exceed in bulk those which range the land, and a vast host of huge fishes which wander among the waves, and hide in the caverns of the sea as the tiger lurks in the jungle, or the lion roams the plain.   Truly, O Lord, thou makest the sea to be as rich in the works of thy hands as the land itself.

26. " *There go the ships.*"   So that ocean is not altogether deserted of mankind. It is the highway of nations, and unites, rather than divides, distant lands.   " *There is that leviathan, whom thou hast made to play therein.*"   The huge whale turns the sea into his recreation ground, and disports himself as God designed that he should do.

The thought of this amazing creature caused the Psalmist to adore the mighty Creator who created him, formed him for his place and made him happy in it. Our ancient maps generally depict a ship and whale upon the sea, and so show that it is most natural, as well as poetical, to connect them both with the mention of the ocean.

27. *" These wait all upon thee."* They come around thee as fowls around the farmer's door at the time for feeding, and look up with expectation. Men or marmots, eagles or emmets, whales or minnows, they alike rely upon thy care. *" That thou mayest give them their meat in due season ; "* that is to say, when they need it and when it is ready for them. God has a time for all things, and does not feed his creatures by fits and starts ; he gives them daily bread, and a quantity proportioned to their needs. This is all that any of us should expect ; if even the brute creatures are content with a sufficiency we ought not to be more greedy than they.

28. *" That thou givest them they gather."* God gives it, but they must gather it, and they are glad that he does so, for otherwise their gathering would be in vain. We often forget that animals and birds in their free life have to work to obtain food even as we do ; and yet it is true with them as with us that our heavenly Father feeds all. When we see the chickens picking up the corn which the housewife scatters from her lap we have an apt illustration of the manner in which the Lord supplies the needs of all living things—he gives and they gather. *" Thou openest thine hand, they are filled with good."* Here is divine liberality with its open hand filling needy creatures till they want no more : and here is divine omnipotence feeding a world by simply opening its hand. What should we do if that hand were closed ? there would be no need to strike a blow, the mere closing of it would produce death by famine. Let us praise the open-handed Lord, whose providence and grace satisfy our mouths with good things.

29. *" Thou hidest thy face, they are troubled."* So dependent are all living things upon God's smile, that a frown fills them with terror, as though convulsed with anguish. This is so in the natural world, and certainly not less so in the spiritual : saints when the Lord hides his face are in terrible perplexity. *" Thou takest away their breath, they die, and return to their dust."* The breath appears to be a trifling matter, and the air an impalpable substance of but small importance, yet, once withdrawn, the body loses all vitality, and crumbles back to the earth from which it was originally taken. All animals come under this law, and even the dwellers in the sea are not exempt from it. Thus dependent is all nature upon the will of the Eternal. Note here that death is caused by the act of God, *" thou takest* away their breath " ; we are immortal till he bids us die, and so are even the little sparrows, who fall not to the ground without our Father.

30. *" Thou sendest forth thy spirit, they are created : and thou renewest the face of the earth."* The loss of their breath destroys them, and by Jehovah's breath a new race is created. The works of the Lord are majestically simple, and are performed with royal ease—a breath creates, and its withdrawal destroys. If we read the word *spirit* as we have it in our version, it is also instructive, for we see the Divine Spirit going forth to create life in nature even as we see him in the realms of grace. At the flood the world was stripped of almost all life, yet how soon the power of God refilled the desolate places ! In winter the earth falls into a sleep which makes her appear worn and old, but how readily does the Lord awaken her with the voice of spring, and make her put on anew the beauty of her youth. Thou, Lord, doest all things, and let glory be unto thy name.

31 The glory of the LORD shall endure for ever : the LORD shall rejoice in his works.

32 He looketh on the earth, and it trembleth : he toucheth the hills, and they smoke.

33 I will sing unto the LORD as long as I live : I will sing praise to my God while I have my being.

34 My meditation of him shall be sweet : I will be glad in the LORD.

35 Let the sinners be consumed out of the earth, and let the wicked be no more. Bless thou the LORD, O my soul. Praise ye the LORD.

31. *" The glory of the Lord shall endure for ever."* His works may pass away, but not his glory. Were it only for what he has already done, the Lord deserves

to be praised without ceasing. His personal being and character ensure that he would be glorious even were all the creatures dead. " *The Lord shall rejoice in his works.*" He did so at the first, when he rested on the seventh day, and saw that everything was very good ; he does so still in a measure where beauty and purity in nature still survive the Fall, and he will do so yet more fully when the earth is renovated, and the trail of the serpent is cleansed from the globe. This verse is written in the most glowing manner. The poet finds his heart gladdened by beholding the works of the Lord, and he feels that the Creator himself must have felt unspeakable delight in exercising so much wisdom, goodness, and power.

32. " *He looketh on the earth, and it trembleth.*" The Lord who has graciously displayed his power in acts and works of goodness might, if he had seen fit, have overwhelmed us with the terrors of destruction, for even at a glance of his eye the solid earth rocks with fear. " *He toucheth the hills, and they smoke.*" Sinai was altogether on a smoke when the Lord descended upon it. It was but a touch, but it sufficed to make the mountain dissolve in flame. Even our God is a consuming fire. Woe unto those who shall provoke him to frown upon them, they shall perish at the touch of his hand. If sinners were not altogether insensible a glance of the Lord's eye would make them tremble, and the touches of his hand in affliction would set their hearts on fire with repentance. "Of reason all things show some sign," except man's unfeeling heart.

33. " *I will sing unto the Lord as long as I live,*" or, literally, *in my lives.* Here and hereafter the Psalmist would continue to praise the Lord, for the theme is an endless one, and remains for ever fresh and new. The birds sang God's praises before men were created, but redeemed men will sing his glories when the birds are no more. Jehovah, who ever lives and makes us to live shall be for ever exalted, and extolled in the songs of redeemed men. " *I will sing praise to my God while I have my being.*" A resolve both happy for himself and glorifying to the Lord. Note the sweet title—*my God.* We never sing so well as when we know that we have an interest in the good things of which we sing, and a relationship to the God whom we praise.

34. " *My meditation of him shall be sweet.*" Sweet both to him and to me. I shall be delighted thus to survey his works and think of his person, and he will graciously accept my notes of praise. Meditation is the soul of religion. It is the tree of life in the midst of the garden of piety, and very refreshing is its fruit to the soul which feeds thereon. And as it is good towards man, so is it towards God. As the fat of the sacrifice was the Lord's portion, so are our best meditations due to the Most High and are most acceptable to him. We ought, therefore, both for our own good and for the Lord's honour to be much occupied with meditation, and that meditation should chiefly dwell upon the Lord himself : it should be " meditation *of him.*" For want of it much communion is lost and much happiness is missed. " *I will be glad in the Lord.*" To the meditative mind every thought of God is full of joy. Each one of the divine attributes is a well-spring of delight now that in Christ Jesus we are reconciled unto God.

35. " *Let the sinners be consumed out of the earth, and let the wicked be no more.*" They are the only blot upon creation.

> " Every prospect pleases,
> And only man is vile."

In holy indignation the Psalmist would fain rid the world of beings so base as not to love their gracious Creator, so blind as to rebel against their Benefactor. He does but ask for that which just men look forward to as the end of history : for the day is eminently to be desired when in all God's kingdom there shall not remain a single traitor or rebel. The Christian way of putting it will be to ask that grace may turn sinners into saints, and win the wicked to the ways of truth. " *Bless thou the Lord, O my soul.*" Here is the end of the matter—whatever sinners may do, do thou, my soul, stand to thy colours, and be true to thy calling. Their silence must not silence thee, but rather provoke thee to redoubled praise to make up for their failures. Nor canst thou alone accomplish the work ; others must come to thy help. O ye saints, " *Praise ye the Lord.*" Let your hearts cry HALLELUJAH,— for that is the word in the Hebrew. Heavenly word ! Let it close the Psalm : for what more remains to be said or written ? HALLELUJAH. *Praise ye the Lord.*

EXPLANATORY NOTES AND QUAINT SAYINGS.

Whole Psalm.—This Psalm is an inspired "Oratorio of Creation."—*Christopher Wordsworth.*

Whole Psalm.—The Psalm is delightful, sweet, and instructive, as teaching us the soundest views of nature (la mas sana fisica), and the best method of pursuing the study of it, viz., by admiring with one eye the works of God, and with the other God himself, their Creator and Preserver.—*Sanchez, quoted by Perowne.*

Whole Psalm.—It might almost be said that this one Psalm represents the image of the whole Cosmos. We are astonished to find in a lyrical poem of such a limited compass, the whole universe—the heavens and the earth—sketched with a few bold touches. The calm and toilsome labour of man, from the rising of the sun to the setting of the same, when his daily work is done, is here contrasted with the moving life of the elements of nature. This contrast and generalisation in the conception of the mutual action of natural phenomena, and this retrospection of an omnipresent invisible power, which can renew the earth or crumble it to dust, constitute a solemn and exalted rather than a glowing and gentle form of poetic creation. —*A. Von Humboldt's Cosmos.*

Whole Psalm.—Its touches are indeed few, rapid—but how comprehensive and sublime! Is it God?—" He is clothed with light as with a garment," and when he walks abroad, it is on "the wings of the wind." The winds or lightnings?—They are his messengers or angels: " Stop us not," they seem to say; " the King's business requireth haste." The waters?—The poet shows them in flood, covering the face of the earth, and then as they now lie, enclosed within their embankments, to break forth no more for ever. The springs?—He traces them, by one inspired glance, as they run among the hills, as they give drink to the wild and lonely creatures of the wilderness, as they nourish the boughs, on which sing the birds, the grass, on which feed the cattle, the herb, the corn, the olive-tree, the vine, which fill man's mouth, cheer his heart, and make his face to shine. Then he skims with bold wing all lofty objects—the trees of the Lord on Lebanon, " full of sap,"—the fir-trees, and the storks which are upon them—the high hills, with their wild goats—and the rocks with their conies. Then he soars up to the heavenly bodies—the sun and the moon. Then he spreads abroad his wings in the darkness of the night, which " hideth not from him," and hears the beasts of the forest creeping abroad to seek their prey, and the roar of the lions to God for meat, coming up upon the winds of midnight. Then as he sees the shades and the wild beasts fleeing together, in emulous haste, from the presence of the morning sun, and man, strong and calm in its light as in the smile of God, hieing to his labour, he exclaims, " O Lord, how manifold are thy works! in wisdom hast thou made them all!" He casts, next, one look at the ocean—a look glancing at the ships which go there, at the leviathan which plays there; and then piercing down to the innumerable creatures, small and great, which are found below its unlifted veil of waters. He sees, then, all the beings, peopling alike earth and sea, waiting for life and food around the table of their Divine Master —nor waiting in vain—till, lo! he hides his face, and they are troubled, die, and disappear in chaos and night. A gleam, next, of the great resurrection of nature and of man comes across his eye. " Thou sendest forth thy Spirit, they are created, and thou renewest the face of the earth." But a greater truth still succeeds, and forms the climax of the Psalm—(a truth Humboldt, with all his admiration of it, notices not, and which gives a Christian tone to the whole)—" *The Lord shall rejoice in his works.*" He contemplates a yet more perfect Cosmos He is " to consume sinners " and sin " out of " this fair universe: and then, when man is wholly worthy of his dwelling, shall God say of both it and him, with a yet deeper emphasis than when he said it at first, and smiling at the same time a yet warmer and softer smile, " It is very good." And with an ascription of blessing to the Lord does the poet close this almost angelic descant upon the works of nature, the glory of God, and the prospects of man. It is not merely the unity of the Cosmos that he had displayed in it, but its progression, as connected with the parallel progress of man—its thorough dependence on one Infinite Mind—the " increasing purpose " which runs along it— and its final purification, when it shall blossom into " the bright consummate flower " of the new heavens and the new earth, " wherein dwelleth righteousness; "—this is the real burden and the peculiar glory of the 104th Psalm.—*George Gilfillan, in " The Bards of the Bible."*

Whole Psalm.—It is a singular circumstance in the composition of this Psalm, that each of the parts of the First Semichorus, after the first, begins with a participle. And these participles are accusatives, agreeing with יְהוָֹה, the object of the verb בָּרְכִי, at the beginning of the whole Psalm. Bless the Jehovah—putting on—extending—laying—constituting—travelling—making—setting—sending—watering—making—making. Thus, this transitive verb, in the opening of the Psalm, extending its government through the successive parts of the same semichorus, except the last, unites them all in one long period.—*Samuel Horsley.*

Whole Psalm.—As to the details,—the sections intervening between verses 2 and 31,—they may be read as a meditation upon creation and the first " ordering of the world," as itself the counterpart and foreshadowing of the new and restored order in the great Sabbath or Millenary period, or, it may be, they are actually descriptive of this—beginning with the coming of the Lord in the clouds of heaven (verse 3 with Ps. xviii. 9—11), attended with " the angels of his power" (verse 4 with 2 Thess. i. 7, *Gr.*); followed by the " establishing" of the earth, no more to be " moved " or " agitated " by the convulsions and disturbances which sin has caused : after which Nature is exhibited in the perfection of her beauty—all things answering the end of their creation : all the orders of the animal world in harmony with each other, and all at peace with man ; all provided for by the varied produce of the earth, no longer cursed, but blessed, and again made fruitful by God, " on whom all wait . . . who openeth his hand and fills them with good " ; and all his goodness meeting with its due acknowledgment from his creatures, who join in chorus to praise him, and say—" O Lord, how manifold are thy works ! In wisdom hast thou made them all : the earth is full of thy riches. Hallelujah."—*William De Burgh.*

Verse 1.—" *Bless the Lord, O my soul.*" A good man's work lieth most within doors, he is more taken up with his own soul, than with all the world besides ; neither can he ever be alone so long as he hath God and his own heart to converse with.—*John Trapp.*

Verse 1.—With what reverence and holy awe doth the Psalmist begin his meditation with that acknowledgment ! " *O Lord, my God, thou art very great ;* " and it is the joy of the saints that he who is their God is a great God : the grandeur of the prince is the pride and pleasure of all his good subjects.—*Matthew Henry.*

Verse 1.—" *Thou art clothed with honour and majesty.*" That is, as Jerome says, Thou art arrayed and adorned with magnificence and splendour ; Thou art acknowledged to be glorious and illustrious by thy works, as a man by his garment. Whence it is clear that the greatness celebrated here is not the intrinsic but the exterior or revealed greatness of God.—*Lorinus.*

Verses 1—4.—Each created, redeemed, regenerated soul is bound to praise the Lord, the Creator, Redeemer, Sanctifier; for that God the Son, who in the beginning made the worlds, and whose grace is ever carrying on his work to its perfect end by the operation of the Holy Ghost, has been revealed before us in his exceeding glory. He, as the eternal High-priest, hath put on the Urim and Thummim of majesty and honour, and hath clothed himself with light, as a priest clothes himself with his holy vestments : his brightness on the mount of transfiguration was but a passing glimpse of what he is now, ever hath been, and ever shall be. He is the true Light, therefore his angels are the angels of light, his children the children of light, his doctrine the doctrine of light. The universe is his tabernacle ; the heavens visible and invisible are the curtains which shroud his holy place. He hath laid the beams and foundations of his holy of holies very high, even above the waters which are above the firmament. The clouds and the winds of the lower heaven are his chariot, upon which he stood when he ascended from Olivet, upon which he will sit when he cometh again.—" *Plain Commentary.*"

Verse 2.—" *Who coverest thyself with light as with a garment.*" In comparing *the light* with which he represents God as *arrayed* to " *a garment,*" he intimates, that although God is invisible, yet his glory is conspicuous enough. In respect of his essence, God undoubtedly dwells in light that is inaccessible ; but as he irradiates the whole world by his splendour, this is the garment in which he, who is hidden in himself, appears in a manner visible to us. The knowledge of this truth is of the greatest importance. If men attempt to reach the infinite height to which God is exalted, although they fly above the clouds, they must fail in the midst of their course. Those who seek to see him in his naked majesty are certainly very foolish. That we may enjoy the sight of him, he must come forth to view with his clothing; that is to say, we must cast our eyes upon the very beautiful fabric of the world in which he wishes to be seen by us, and not be too curious and rash in searching into his secret essence. Now, since God presents himself to us clothed with light, those who are seeking pretexts for their living without the knowledge of him, cannot allege in excuse of their slothfulness, that he is hidden in profound darkness. When it is said that *the heavens are a curtain,* it is not meant that under them God hides himself, but that by them his majesty and glory are displayed, being, as it were, his royal pavilion.—*John Calvin.*

Verse 2.—" *With light.*" The first creation of God in the works of the days was the light of sense; the last was the light of reason; and his Sabbath work ever since is the illumination of the spirit.—*Francis Bacon.*

Verse 2.—" *Who stretchest out the heavens like a curtain.*" It is usual in the East, in the summer season, and upon all occasions when a large company is to be received, to have the court of the house sheltered from the heat of the weather by an umbrella or veil, which being expanded upon ropes from one side of the parapet wall to another may be folded or unfolded at pleasure. The Psalmist seems to allude to some covering of this kind in that beautiful expression of *stretching out the heavens like a curtain.*—*Kitto's Pictorial Bible.*

Verse 2.—" *Like a curtain.*" With the same ease, by his mere word, with which a man spreads out a tent-curtain, Isai. liv. 2. Is. xl. 22 is parallel, " that stretcheth out the heavens as a curtain, and spreadeth them out as a tent to dwell in." Ver. 3 continues the description of the work of the second day. There lie at bottom, in the first clause, the words of Gen. i. 7: " God made the vaulted sky and divided between the waters which are under the vault and the waters which are above the vault." The waters above are the materials with which, or out of which, the structure is reared. To construct out of the movable waters a firm palace, the cloudy heaven, " firm as a molten glass " (Job xxxvii. 18), is a magnificent work of divine omnipotence.—*E. W. Hengstenberg.*

Verse 2.—" *Like a curtain.*" Because the Hebrews conceived of heaven as a temple and palace of God, that sacred azure was at once the floor of his, the roof of our, abode. Yet methinks the dwellers in tents ever loved best the figure of the heavenly tent. They represent God as daily spreading it out, and fastening it at the extremity of the horizon to the pillars of heaven, the mountains: it is to them a tent of safety, of rest, of a fatherly hospitality in which God lives with his creatures.—*Herder, quoted by Perowne.*

Verse 3.—The metaphorical representation of God, as *laying the beams of his chambers in the waters,* seems somewhat difficult to understand; but it was the design of the prophet, from a thing incomprehensible to us, to ravish us with the greater admiration. Unless *beams* be substantial and strong, they will not be able to sustain even the weight of an ordinary house. When, therefore, God makes the waters the foundation of his heavenly palace, who can fail to be astonished at a miracle so wonderful? When we take into account our slowness of apprehension, such hyperbolical expressions are by no means superfluous; for it is with difficulty that they awaken and enable us to attain even a slight knowledge of God.—*John Calvin.*

Verse 3.—" *Who layeth the beams of his chambers in the waters;* " or, " *who layeth his upper chambers above the waters.*" His upper chamber (people in the East used to retire to the upper chamber when they wished for solitude) is reared up in bright æther on the slender foundation of rainy clouds.—*A. F. Tholuck.*

Verse 3.—" *Who layeth the beams,*" etc. " He flooreth his chambers with waters," i.e., the clouds make the flooring of his heavens.—*Zachary Mudge.*

Verse 3.—" *Who walketh upon the wings of the wind;* " see Ps. xviii. 10; which is expressive of his swiftness in coming to help and assist his people in time of need; who helps, and that right early; and may very well be applied both to the first and second coming of Christ, who came leaping upon the mountains, and skipping upon the hills, when he first came; and, when he comes a second time will be as a roe or a young hart upon the mountains of spices, Cant. ii. 8, and viii. 14. The Targum is, " upon the swift clouds, like the wings of an eagle "; hence, perhaps, it is the heathens have a notion that Jupiter is being carried in a chariot through the air when it thunders and lightens.—*John Gill.*

Verse 3.—" *Who walketh upon the wings of the wind.*" In these words there is an unequalled elegance; not, he *fleeth*—he *runneth*, but—he *walketh;* and that *on the very wings of the wind*; on the most impetuous element raised into the utmost rage, and sweeping along with incredible rapidity. We cannot have a more sublime idea of the Deity; serenely walking on an element of inconceivable swiftness, and, as it seems to us, uncontrollable impetuosity!—*James Hervey*, 1713-14—1758.

Verse 4.—" *Who maketh his angels spirits.*" Some render it, *Who maketh his angels* as *the winds*, to which they may be compared for their invisibility, they being not to be seen, no more than the wind, unless when they assume an external form; and for their penetration through bodies in a very surprising manner; see Acts xii. 6—10; and for their great force and power, being mighty angels, and said to excel in strength, Ps. ciii. 20; and for their swiftness in obeying the divine commands; so the Targum, " He maketh his messengers, or angels, swift as the wind."—*John Gill.*

Verse 4.—" *Who maketh his angels spirits.*" The words, " *creating his angels spirits*," may either mean ' creating them spiritual beings, not material beings,' or ' creating them winds '—*i.e.*, like the winds, invisible, rapid in their movements, and capable of producing great effects. The last mode of interpretation seems pointed out by the parallelism—" *and his ministers*"—or, ' servants '—who are plainly the same as his angels,—" *a flame of fire*," *i.e.*, like the lightning. The statement here made about the angels seems to be this: ' They are created beings, who in their qualities bear a resemblance to the winds and the lightning.'

The argument deduced by Paul, in Heb. ii. 7, from this statement for the inferiority of the angels is direct and powerful:—He is the Son; they are the creatures of God. " *Only begotten*" is the description of his mode of existence; *made* is the description of theirs. *All* their powers are communicated powers; and however high they may stand in the scale of creation, it is in that scale they stand, which places them infinitely below him, who is so the Son of God as to be " God over all, blessed for ever "—*John Brown, in " An Exposition of the Epistle to the Hebrews."*

Verse 4.—" *A flaming fire.*" Fire is expressive of irresistible power, immaculate holiness, and ardent emotion. It is remarkable that the seraphim, one class at least of these ministers, have their name from a root signifying to burn; and the altar, from which one of them took the live coal, Isai. vi. 6, is the symbol of the highest form of holy love.—*James G. Murphy, in " A Commentary on the Book of Psalms,"* 1875.

Verse 5.—" *Not be removed for ever.*" The stability of the earth is of God, as much as the being and existence of it. There have been many earthquakes or movings of the earth in several parts of it, but the whole body of the earth was never removed so much as one hair's breadth out of its place, since the foundations thereof were laid. *Archimedes*, the great mathematician, said, " If you will give me a place to set my engine on, I will remove the earth." It was a great brag; but the Lord hath laid it too fast for man's removing. Himself can make it quake and shake, he can move it when he pleaseth; but he never hath nor will remove it. He hath laid the foundations of the earth that it shall not be removed, nor can it be at all moved, but at his pleasure; and when it moves at any time, it is to mind the sons of men that they by their sins have moved him to displeasure.—*Joseph Caryl.*

Verse 5.—The philosophical mode of stating this truth may be seen in *Amédée Guillemin's* work entitled " THE HEAVENS." " How is it that though we are carried along with a vast rapidity by the motion of the earth, we do not ourselves perceive our movement? It is because the entire bulk of the earth, atmosphere, and clouds, participate in the movement. This constant velocity, with which all bodies situated on the surface of the earth are animated, would be the cause of the most terrible and general catastrophe that could be imagined, if, by any possibility, the rotation of the earth were abruptly to cease. Such an event would be the precursor of a most sweeping destruction of all organized beings. But the constancy of the laws of nature permits us to contemplate such a catastrophe without fear. It is demonstrated that the position of the poles of rotation on the surface of the earth is invariable. It has also been asked whether the velocity of the earth's rotation has changed, or, which comes to the same thing, if the length of the sidereal day and that of the solar day deduced from it have varied within the historical period? Laplace has replied to this question, and his demonstration shows that it has not varied the one hundredth of a second during the last two thousand years."

Verses 5—9.—

God of the earth and sea, Thou hast laid earth's foundations :
　　Because thy hand sustaineth,
　　It ever firm remaineth.
Once didst thou open its deep, hidden fountains,
And soon the rising waters stood above the mountains.

At thy rebuke they fled, at the voice of thy thunder,
　　The flood thy mandate heeded,
　　And hastily receded :
The waters keep the place Thou hast assigned them,
And in the hills and vales a channel Thou dost find them.

A limit Thou hast set, which they may not pass over ;
　　The deep within bound inclosing,
　　Strong barriers interposing,
That its proud waves no more bring desolation,
And sweep away from earth each human habitation.

*—John Barton, in " The Book of Psalms in English Verse : a
New Testament Paraphrase," 1871.*

Verses 6—8.—" Stood," " fled," " hasted away." The words of the Psalm put
the original wondrous process graphically before the eye. The change of tense,
too, from past to present, in verses 6, 7, 8, is expressive, and paints the scene in its
progress. In ver. 6 " *stood* " should be STAND : in ver. 7 " *fled* " should be FLEE :
and " *hasted away* " should be HASTE AWAY, as in the P. B. V.—" *The Speaker's
Commentary.*"

Verse 7.—" At thy rebuke they fled." The famous description of Virgil comes
to mind, who introduces Neptune as sternly rebuking the winds for daring without
his consent to embroil earth and heaven, and raise such huge mountain-waves :
then swifter than the word is spoken, he calms the swollen seas, scatters the gathered
clouds, and brings back the sun.—*Lorinus.*

Verse 7.—" At the voice of thy thunder they hasted away ; " ran off with great
precipitance : just as a servant, when his master puts on a stern countenance, and
speaks to him in a thundering, menacing manner, hastes away from him to do his
will and work. This is an instance of the mighty power of Christ ; and by the same
power he removed the waters of the deluge, when they covered the earth, and the
tops of the highest hills ; and rebuked the Red Sea, and it became dry land ; and
drove back the waters of Jordan for the Israelites to pass through ; and who also
rebuked the Sea of Galilee when his disciples were in distress ; and with equal ease can
he and does he remove the depth of sin and darkness from his people at conversion ;
rebukes Satan, and delivers out of his temptations, when he comes in like a flood ;
and commands off the waters of affliction when they threaten to overwhelm ; who
are his servants, and come when he bids them come, and go when he bids them
go.—*John Gill.*

Verse 7.—" At the voice of thy thunder." It is very likely God employed the
electric fluid as an agent in this separation.—*Ingram Cobbin.*

Verse 7.—" They hasted away."

　　　　　　　　　　　　　　　　God said,
　　Be gather'd now, ye waters under heaven
　　Into one place, and let dry land appear.
　　Immediately the mountains huge appear
　　Emergent, and their broad bare backs upheave
　　Into the clouds ; their tops ascend the sky :
　　So high as heav'd the tumid hills, so low
　　Down sunk a hollow bottom broad and deep,
　　Capacious bed of waters : Thither they
　　Hasted with glad precipitance, uproll'd
　　As drops on dust conglobing from the dry :
　　Part rise in crystal wall, or ridge direct,
　　For haste : such flight the great command impress'd
　　On the swift floods : As armies at the call
　　Of trumpet (for of armies thou hast heard)

> Troop to their standard ; so the watery throng,
> Wave rolling after wave, where way they found,
> If steep, with torrent rapture, if through plain,
> Soft-ebbing ; nor withstood them rock or hill ;
> But they, or under ground, or circuit wide
> With serpent errour wandering, found their way,
> And on the washy ooze deep channels wore ;
> Easy, ere God had bid the ground be dry,
> All but within those banks, where rivers now
> Stream, and perpetual draw their tumid train.
> The dry land, Earth ; and the great receptacle
> Of congregated waters, he called Seas :
> And saw that it was good.
>
> —*John Milton.*

Verse 8.—" *They go up by the mountains,*" etc. The Targum is, " They ascend out of the deep to the mountains " ; that is, the waters, when they went off the earth at the divine orders, steered their course up the mountains, and then went down by the valleys to the place appointed for them ; they went over hills and dales, nothing could stop them or retard their course till they came to their proper place ; which is another instance of the almighty power of the Son of God.—*John Gill.*

Verse 9.—" *Thou hast set a bound,*" etc. The Baltic Sea, in our own time, inundated large tracts of land, and did great damage to the Flemish people and other neighbouring nations. By an instance of this kind we are warned what would be the consequence, were the restraint imposed upon the sea, by the hand of God, removed. How is it that we have not thereby been swallowed up together, but because God has held in that outrageous element by his word ? In short, although the natural tendency of the waters is to cover the earth, yet this will not happen, because God has established, by his word, a counteracting law, and as his truth is eternal, this law must remain stedfast.—*John Calvin.*

Verse 9.—" *Thou hast set a bound,*" etc. In these words the Psalmist gives us three things clearly concerning the waters. First, that once (he means it not of the deluge, but of the chaos), the waters did cover the whole earth, till God by a word of command sent them into their proper channels, that the dry land might appear. Secondly, that the waters have a natural propension to return back and cover the earth again. Thirdly, that the only reason why they do not return back and cover the whole earth is, because God hath " *set a bound, that they cannot pass.*" They would be boundless and know no limits, did not God bound and limit them. Wisdom giveth us the like eulogium of the power of God in this, Prov. viii. 29, " He gave to the sea his decree, that the waters should not pass his commandment." What cannot he command, who sendeth his commandment to the sea and is obeyed ? Some great princes, heated with rage and drunken with pride, have cast shackles into the sea, as threatening it with imprisonment and bondage if it would not be quiet ; but the sea would not be bound by them ; they have also awarded so many strokes to be given the sea as a punishment of its contumacy and rebellion against either their commands or their designs. How ridiculously ambitious have they been, who would needs pretend to such a dominion ! Many princes have had great power at and upon the sea, but there was never any prince had any power over the sea ; that's a flower belonging to no crown but the crown of heaven.—*Joseph Caryl.*

Verse 9.—" *Thou hast set a bound,*" etc. A few feet of increase in the ocean wave that pursues its tidal circuit round the globe, would desolate cities and provinces innumerable. . . . But with what immutable and safe control God has marked its limits ! You shall observe a shrub or a flower on a bank of verdure that covers a sea cliff, or hangs down in some hollow ; nay, you shall mark a pebble on the beach, you shall lay a shred of gossamer upon it ; and this vast, ungovernable, unwieldy, tempestuous element shall know how to draw a line of moisture by its beating spray at the very edge, or on the very point of your demarcation, and then draw off its forces, not having passed one inch or hand's breadth across the appointed margin. And all this exact restraint and measurement in the motion of the sea, by that mysterious power shot beyond unfathomable depths of space, from orbs rolling in ether ! a power itself how prodigious, how irresistible, yet how invisible, how gentle, how with minutest exactness measured and exerted.—*George B. Cheever, in " Voices of Nature to her Foster Child, the Soul of Man,"* 1852.

Verse 9.—" A bound that they may not pass over."

> Now stretch your eye off shore, o'er waters made
> To cleanse the air, and bear the world's great trade,
> To rise and wet the mountains near the sun,
> Then back into themselves in rivers run,
> Fulfilling mighty uses, far and wide,
> Through earth, in air, or here, as ocean-tide.
> Ho ! how the giant heaves himself, and strains
> And flings to break his strong and viewless chains ;
> Foams in his wrath ; and at his prison doors,
> Hark ! hear him ! how he beats, and tugs, and roars,
> As if he would break forth again, and sweep
> Each living thing within his lowest deep.
>
> *—Richard Henry Dana (1787—   ).*

Verse 10.—" He sendeth the springs into the valleys," etc. Having spoken of the salt waters, he treats afterwards of the sweet and potable, commending the wisdom and providence of God, that from the lower places of the earth and the hidden veins of the mountains, he should cause the fountains of water to gush forth.—*Lorinus.*

Verse 10.—" He sendeth the springs into the valleys." The more of humility the more of grace ; if in valleys some hollows are deeper than others the waters collect in them.—*Martin Luther.*

Verse 10.—" He sendeth the springs into the valleys." Men cut places for rivers to run in, but none but God can cut a channel to bring spiritual streams into the soul. The Psalmist speaks of the sending forth of springs as one great act of the providence of God. It is a secret mystery which those that have searched deepest into nature cannot resolve us in, how those springs are fed, how they are maintained and nourished, so as to run without ceasing in such great streams as many of them make. Philosophy cannot show the reason of it. The Psalmist doth it well : *God sends them into the valleys,* his providence and power keeps them continually running : he that would have his soul watered must go to God in prayer.—*Ralph Robinson.*

Verse 10.—" Which run among the hills." That is, the *streams* or *springs* run. In many a part of the world can be found a Sault, a *dancing water,* and a Minne-ha-ha, a *laughing water.* The mountain streams *walk,* and *run,* and leap, and praise the Lord.—*William S. Plumer.*

Verse 10, 13, 14.—" He." " He." " He."

> All things are here of *Him* ; from the black pines,
> Which are his shade on high, and the loud roar
> Of torrents, where he listeneth, to the vines
> Which slope his green path downward to the shore,
> Where the bow'd waters meet him, and adore,
> Kissing his feet with murmurs.
>
> *—Byron.*

Verse 11.—" The wild asses quench their thirst." It is particularly remarked of the *asses,* that though they are dull and stupid creatures, yet by Providence they are taught the way to the waters, in the dry and sandy deserts, and that there is no better guide for the thirsty travellers to follow, than to observe the herds of them descending to the streams.—*Thomas Fenton.*

Verse 11.—" The wild asses quench their thirst." As evening approached we saw congregated, near a small stream, what appeared to be a large company of dismounted Arabs, their horses standing by them. As we were already near them, and could not have escaped the watchful eye of the Bedouins, we prepared for an encounter. We approached cautiously, and were surprised to see that the horses still remained without their riders ; we drew still nearer, when they galloped off towards the desert. They were *wild asses.—Henry Austen Layard.*

Verse 12.—" By them shall the fowls of the heaven have their habitation." Never shall I forget my first ride from Riha to Ain Sultân ; our way lay right across the oasis evoked by the waters. It may be that the contrast with the arid desert of the previous day heightened the feelings of present enjoyment, but certainly they echoed the words of Josephus,—a " Divine region." At one time I was reminded of Epping Forest, and then of a neglected orchard with an undergrowth of luxuriant vegetation.

Large thorn bushes and forest shrubs dotted the plain on every side.   In some places the ground was carpeted with flowers, and every bush seemed vocal with the cheerful twittering of birds.   I use the word " twittering," because I do not think that I ever heard a decided warble during the whole time I was in Syria.   Coleridge speaks of the " merry nightingale,"

> " That crowds, and hurries, and precipitates
> With fast, quick warble, his delicious notes."

The song of my little Syrian friends seemed to consist of a series of cheerful chirps. Other travellers have been more fortunate.   Bonar speaks of the note of the cuckoo ; Dr. Robinson of the nightingale.   Lord Lindsay tells us of the delight of an evening spent by the Jordan, " the river murmuring along, and the nightingale singing from the trees."   Canon Tristram, describing the scenery near Tell-el-Kady, says that " the bulbul and nightingale vied in rival song in the branches above, audible over the noise of the torrent below."   In the face of these statements it seems to me remarkable, considering the innumerable references to nature in the Bible, that the singing of birds is only mentioned three times.   In the well-known passage which so exquisitely depicts a Syrian spring, we read " the time of the singing of birds is come " (Song of Solomon ii. 12).   The Psalmist in speaking of the mighty power and wondrous Providence of God, mentions the springs in " the valleys, which run among the hills.   They give drink to every beast of the field : the wild asses quench their thirst.   By them shall the fowls of the heaven have their habitation, which sing among the branches."   Canon Tristram commenting on this passage, says, that it may refer especially to the " bulbul and the nightingale, both of which throng the trees that fringe the Jordan and abound in all the wooded valleys, filling the air in early spring with the rich cadence of their notes."—*James Wareing Bardsley, in " Illustrative Texts,"* 1876.

Verse 12.—" *By them shall the fowls of the heaven have their habitation,*"etc.   To such birds may saints be compared ; being, like them, weak, defenceless, and timorous ; liable to be taken in snares, and sometimes wonderfully delivered ; as well as given to wanderings and strayings ; and to fowls *of the heaven,* being heaven-born souls, and partakers of the heavenly calling.   These have their habitation by the fountain of Jacob, by the river of divine love, beside the still waters of the sanctuary, where they sing the songs of Zion, the songs of electing, redeeming, and calling grace.—*John Gill.*

Verse 12.—" *The fowls . . . which sing among the branches.*"   The music of birds was the first song of thanksgiving which was offered from the earth, before man was formed.—*John Wesley.*

Verse 12.—" *The fowls of the heaven which sing among the branches.*"   How do the blackbird and thrassel [thrush], with their melodious voices, bid welcome to the cheerful spring, and in their fixed months warble forth such ditties as no art or instrument can reach to ? . . . .   But the nightingale, another of my airy creatures, breathes such sweet loud music out of her little instrumental throat, that it makes mankind to think miracles are not ceased.   He that at midnight, when the very labourer sleeps securely, should hear, as I have very often, the clear airs, the sweet descants, the natural rising and falling, the doubling and redoubling of her voice, might well be lifted above earth, and say, " Lord, what music hast thou provided for the saints in heaven, when thou affordest bad man such music on earth ? "—*Izaak Walton.*

Verse 12.—

> While o'er their heads the hazels hing,
> The little birdies blithely sing,
> Or lightly flit on wanton wing
> In the birks of Aberfeldy.
> The braes ascend like lofty wa's,
> The foaming stream deep-roaring fa's,
> O'erhung wi' fragrant spreading shaws,
> The birks of Aberfeldy.
>
> —*Robert Burns,* 1759—1796.

Verse 13.—" *The earth is satisfied with the fruit of thy works ;* " that is, with the rain, which is thy work, causing it to be showered down when thou pleasest upon the earth ; or, with the rain, which proceeds from the clouds ; or, with the fruits, which thou causeth the earth by this means to bring forth.—*Arthur Jackson.*

Verse 14.—" He causeth the grass to grow." Surely it should humble men to know that all human power united cannot make anything, not even the grass to grow.—*William S. Plumer.*

Verse 14.—" For the cattle," etc. To make us thankful, let us consider, 1. That God not only provides for us, but for our servants ; the cattle that are of use to man, are particularly taken care of ; grass is made to grow in great abundance for them, when " the young lions," that are not for the service of man, often " lack, and suffer hunger." 2. That our food is nigh us, and ready to us : having our habitation on the earth, there we have our storehouse, and depend not on " the merchant ships that bring food from afar," Prov. xxxi. 14. 3. That we have even from the products of the earth, not only for necessity, but for ornament and delight, so good a master do we serve. Doth nature call for something to support it, and repair its daily decays ? Here is *" bread which strengtheneth man's heart,"* and is therefore called the staff of life ; let none that have that complain of want. Doth nature go further, and covet something pleasant ? Here is " *wine that maketh glad the heart,"* refresheth the spirits, and exhilarates them, when it is soberly and moderately used ; that we may not only go through our business, but go through it cheerfully ; it is a pity that that should be abused to overcharge the heart, and disfit men for their duty, which was given to revive their heart, and quicken them in their duty. Is nature yet more humoursome, and doth it crave something for ornament too ? Here is that also out of the earth ; *" oil to make the face to shine,"* that the countenance may not only be cheerful, but beautiful, and we may be the more acceptable to one another.—*Matthew Henry.*

Verse 14.—" For the service of man." The common version of these words can only mean for his benefit or use, a sense not belonging to the Hebrew word, which, as well as its verbal root, is applied to man's servitude or bondage as a tiller of the ground (Gen. iii. 17—19), and has here the sense of husbandry or cultivation, as in Exod. i. 14, Lev. xxv. 39, it has that of compulsory or servile labour, the infinitive in the last clause indicates the object for which labour is imposed on man.—*J. A. Alexander.*

Verse 14.—" That he may bring forth food out of the earth." The Israelites at the feast of the Passover and before the breaking of bread, were accustomed to say, " Praise be to the Lord our God, thou King of the world, who hath brought forth our bread from the earth " : and at each returning harvest we ought to be filled with gratitude, as often as we again receive the valuable gift of bread. It is the most indispensable and necessary means of nourishment of which we never tire, whilst other food, the sweeter it is, the more easily it surfeits : everybody, the child and the old man, the beggar and the king, like bread. We remember the unfortunate man, who was cast on the desert isle, famishing with hunger, and who cried at the sight of a handful of gold, " Ah, it is only gold ! " He would willingly have exchanged for a handful of bread, this to him, useless material, which in the mind of most men is above all price. O let us never sin against God, by lightly esteeming bread ! Let us gratefully accept the sheaves we gather, and thankfully visit the barns which preserve them ; that we may break bread to the hungry, and give to the thirsty from the supplies God has given us. Let us never sit down to table without asking God to bless the gifts we receive from his gracious hand, and never eat bread without thinking of Christ our Lord, who calls himself the living bread, who came down from heaven to give life unto the world. And above all, may we never go to the table of the Lord without enjoying, through the symbols of bread and wine, his body and blood, whereby we receive strength to nourish our spiritual life ! Yes, Lord, thou satisfiest both body and soul, with bread from earth and bread from heaven. Praise be to thy holy name, our hearts and mouths shall be full of thy praises for time and eternity !—*Frederick Arndt, in " Lights of the Morning,"* 1861.

Verse 15.—When thou wert taken out of the womb, what a stately palace did he bring thee into, the world, which thou foundest prepared and ready furnished with all things for thy maintenance, as Canaan was to the children of Israel ; a stately house thou buildedst not, trees thou plantedst not, a rich canopy spangled, spread as a curtain over thy head ; he sets up a taper for thee to work by, the sun, till thou art weary (v. 23), and then it goes down without thy bidding, for it *knows its going down* " (v. 19) ; then he draws a curtain over half the world, that men may go to rest : " *Thou causest darkness, and it is night* " (v. 20). As an house this world is, so curiously contrived that to every room of it, even to every poor village, springs do come as pipes to find thee water (v. 10, 11). The pavement of which house thou treadest on, and it brings forth thy food (v. 14), " *Bread for strength, wine to cheer thy heart, oil to make thy face to shine* " (v. 15). Which three are there synecdochically put for all things needful to strength, ornament, and delight.—*Thomas Goodwin.*

Verse 15.—" *Wine that maketh glad the heart of man.*" The wine mentioned had the quality of fermented liquors ; it gladdened the heart. Thus, if taken to excess, it would have led to intoxication. The Hebrew term is *yayin,* answering to the Greek *oinos,* and including every form which the juice of the grape might be made to assume as a beverage. It was this of which Noah partook when he became drunken (Gen. ix. 21, 24). Melchizedek brought it forth to Abraham (Gen. xiv. 18). Lot's daughters gave it to their father and made him drunk (Gen. xix. 35). From this the Nazarite was to separate himself (Num. vi. 3—20). This is the highly intoxicating drink so often mentioned by Isaiah (v. 11—22, xxii. 13, xxviii. 1—7, etc.); but just because of this, it might become to man one of those mercies in connection with the use of which he was to exercise constant self-control. Taken to excess it was a curse ; enjoyed as from God, it was something for which man was called to be thankful.—*John Duns.*

Verse 15.—" *And oil to make his face to shine.*" Observe, after the mention of wine, he speaks of oil or ointment, because at the banquets among the Jews and other Eastern people, as afterwards among the Greeks and Romans, there was a frequent use of ointments. The reasons why ointment was poured upon the head were : To avoid intoxication : To improve the health : To contribute to pleasure and delight. Homer often refers to this custom, and there is an allusion to it by Solomon, Eccles. ix. 8, " *Let thy garments be always white ; and let thy head lack no ointment.*" See also Ps. xxiii. 5.—*Le Blanc.*

Verse 15.—The ancients made much use of oil to beautify their persons. We read of " *oil to make man's face to shine.*" Ruth anointed herself for decoration (Ruth iii. 3), and the woman of Tekoah and the prophet Daniel omitted the use of oil for the contrary reason (2 Sam. xiv. 3 ; Dan. x. 3). The custom is also mentioned in Matt. vi. 17 ; Luke vii. 46.—*Ambrose Serle in* " *Horæ Solitariæ,*" 1815.

Verse 15.—" *Bread which strengtheneth man's heart.*" In hunger not only the *strength* is prostrated, but the *natural courage* is also abated. *Hunger* has no enterprise, emulation, nor courage. But when, in such circumstances, a little bread is received into the stomach, even before concoction can have time to prepare it for nutriment, the *strength* is restored, and the *spirits* revived. This is a surprising effect ; and it has not yet been satisfactorily accounted for.—*Adam Clarke.*

Verse 15.—" *Bread which strengtheneth man's heart.*" In Homer's Odyssey we meet with the expression " Bread, the marrow of men."

Verse 15.—" *Man's heart.*" It is not without reason that instead of the word האדם *of Adam,* which was used in v. 14, there is here employed the word אנוש, an *infirm* and *feeble* man, because he mentions those nourishments of which there was no need before the fall, and which are specially suitable to nourish and exhilarate feeble man.—*Venema.*

Verse 15.—If the transitory earth is so full of the good things of God, what will we have when we come to the land of the living ?—*Starke, in Lange's Commentary.*

Verse 16.—" *The trees of the Lord.*" The transition which the prophet makes from men to trees is as if he had said, It is not to be wondered at, if God so bountifully nourishes men who are created after his own image, since he does not grudge to extend his care even to trees. By " *the trees of the Lord,*" is meant those which are high and of surpassing beauty ; for God's blessing is more conspicuous in them. It seems scarcely possible for any juice of the earth to reach so great a height, and yet they renew their foliage every year.—*John Calvin.*

Verse 16.—" *The trees of the Lord* " may be so named from their size and stature —this name being used as a superlative in the Hebrew, or to denote aught which is great and extraordinary.—*Thomas Chalmers.*

Verse 16.—" *The trees of the Lord,*" etc. The cedars are indeed the trees of the Lord. They are especially his planting. There is a sense in which, above all other trees, they belong to him, and shadow forth in a higher degree his glory. The peculiar expression of the text, however, must not be limited to one particular species of cedar. . . . Encouraged by this Scripture usage, I shall use the word in a somewhat wider sense than the conventional one, to denote three remarkable examples which may be selected from the *coniferæ* to show the power and wisdom of God as displayed in the trees of the forest.   These are, the cedar of Lebanon, the cedar of the Himalayas, and the cedar of the Sierra Nevada.   The epithet which the Psalmist applies to one, may most appropriately be applied to all of them ;   and there are various reasons why the Lord may be said to have a special interest and property in each of them, to a few of which our attention may now be profitably directed.

1. They are " trees of the Lord " on account of the *peculiarities of their structure.* In common with all the pine tribe, they are exceptional in their organization.   They reveal a new idea of the creative mind.   2. The cedars are " the trees of the Lord " on account of the *antiquity of their type.*   It was of this class of trees that the pre-Adamite forests were principally composed.   3. The cedars are the " trees of the Lord," on account of the *majesty of their appearance.*   It is the tree, *par excellence,* of the Bible—the type of all forest vegetation.—*Condensed from Hugh Macmillan's " Bible Teachings in Nature,"* 1868.

Verse 16.—" *Full of sap.*"   The cedar has a store of resin.   It flows from wounds made in the bark, and from the scales of the cones, and is abundant in the seeds. Both the resin and the wood were much valued by the ancients.   The Romans believed that the gum which exuded from the cedar had the power of rendering whatever was steeped in it incorruptible ;   and we are told that the books of Numa, the early king of Rome, which were found uninjured in his tomb, five hundred years after his death, had been steeped in oil of cedar.   The Egyptians also used the oil in embalming their dead.—*Mary and Elizabeth Kirby, in " Chapters on Trees,"* 1873.

Verse 17.—" *Birds.*"   The word rendered " *birds* " here is the word which in Ps. lxxxiv. 3 is translated *sparrow,* and which is commonly used to denote *small* birds.   Comp. Lev. xiv. 4 (*margin*), and 5—7, 49—53.   It is used, however, to denote birds of any kind.   See Gen. vii. 14 ; Ps. viii. 8 ; xi. 1 ; cxlviii. 10.—*Albert Barnes.*

Verse 17.—" *The stork* " is instanced as one of the largest of nest-building birds, as the cedars of Lebanon were introduced in verse 16 as being the largest of uncultivated trees.—*A. C. Jennings and W. H. Lowe, in " The Psalms, with Introductions and Critical Notes,"* 1875.

Verse 17.—" *The stork, the fir trees are her house.*"   In many cases the stork breeds among old ruins, and under such circumstances it is fond of building its nest on the tops of pillars or towers, the summits of arches, and similar localities.   When it takes up its abode among mankind, it generally selects the breeding-places which have been built for it by those who know its taste, but it frequently chooses the top of a chimney, or some such locality.   When it is obliged to build in spots where it can find neither rocks nor buildings, it builds on trees, and, like the heron, is sociable in its nesting, a whole community residing in a clump of trees.   It is not very particular about the kind of tree, provided that it be tolerably tall, and strong enough to bear the weight of its enormous nest ;   and the reader will at once see that the *fir trees* are peculiarly fitted to be the houses for the stork.

The particular species of *fir tree* to which the Psalmist alludes is probably the Aleppo pine (*Pinus halepensis*), which comes next to the great cedars of Lebanon in point of size.   It was this tree that furnished the timber and planks for Solomon's temple and palace, a timber which was evidently held in the greatest estimation. This tree fulfils all the conditions which a stork would require in nest-building.   It is lofty, and its boughs are sufficiently horizontal to form a platform for the nest, and strong enough to sustain it.   On account of its value and the reckless manner in which it has been cut down without new plantations being formed, the Aleppo pine has vanished from many parts of Palestine wherein it was formerly common, and would afford a dwelling-place for the stork.   There are, however, several other species of fir which are common in various parts of the country, each species flourishing in the soil best suited to it so that the stork would never be at a loss to find a nesting-place in a country which furnished so many trees suitable to its purposes.— *J. G. Wood, in " Bible Animals."*

Verse 17.—" *The stork, the fir trees are her house.*"   Well-wooded districts are for the most part the favourite resorts of the storks, as they constantly select trees both for breeding purposes and as resting-places for the night ;   some few species, however, prove exceptions to this rule, and make their nests on roofs, chimneys, or other elevated situations in the immediate vicinity of men.—*From " Cassell's Book of Birds." From the Text of Dr. Brehm. By T. R. Jones, F.R.S.*

Verse 17.—" The fir trees." The doors of the temple were made of the fir tree ; even of that tree which was a type of the humanity of Jesus Christ. Consider Heb. ii. 14. The fir tree is also the house of the stork, that unclean bird, even as Christ is a harbour and shelter for sinners. " As for the stork," saith the text, " the fir trees are her house ; " and Christ saith to the sinners that see their want of shelter, " Come unto me, and I will give you rest." He is a refuge for the oppressed, a refuge in time of trouble. He is, as the doors of fir of the temple, the inlet of God's house, to God's presence, and to a partaking of his glory. Thus God did of old, by similitudes, teach his people his way.—*John Bunyan, in " Solomon's Temple Spiritualized."*

Verse 17.—

The eagle and the stork
On cliffs and cedar-tops their eyries build.

—*John Milton.*

Verse 18.—" The high hills are a refuge for the wild goats." There is scarcely any doubt that the *Azel* of the Old Testament is the *Arabian Ibex* or *Beden* (*Capra Nubiana*). This animal is very closely allied to the well-known Ibex of the Alps, or Steinbock, but may be distinguished from it by one or two slight differences, such as the black beard and the slighter make of the horns, which moreover have three angles instead of four, as is the case with the Alpine Ibex. . . . . The colour of its coat resembles so nearly that of the rocks, that an inexperienced eye would see nothing but bare stones and sticks where a practised hunter would see numbers of *Beden*, conspicuous by their beautifully curved horns.

The agility of the *Beden* is extraordinary. Living in the highest and most craggy parts of the mountain ridge, it flings itself from spot to spot with a recklessness that startles one who has not been accustomed to the animal, and the wonderful certainty of its foot. It will, for example, dash at the face of a perpendicular precipice that looks as smooth as a brick wall, for the purpose of reaching a tiny ledge which is hardly perceptible, and which is some fifteen feet or so above the spot whence the animal sprang. Its eye, however, has marked certain little cracks and projections on the face of the rock, and as the animal makes its leap, it takes these little points of vantage in rapid succession, just touching them as it passes upwards, and by the slight stroke of its foot keeping up the original impulse of its leap. Similarly the Ibex comes sliding and leaping down precipitous sides of the mountains, sometimes halting with all the four feet drawn together, on a little projection scarcely larger than a penny, and sometimes springing boldly over a wild crevasse, and alighting with exact precision upon a projecting piece of rock that seems scarcely large enough to sustain a rat comfortably.—*J. G. Wood.*

Verse 18.—" Conies." When we were exploring the rocks in the neighbourhood of the convent, I was delighted to point attention to a family or two of the *Wubar*, engaged in their gambols on the heights above us. Mr. Smith and I watched them narrowly, and were much amused with the liveliness of their motions, and the quickness of their retreat within the clefts of the rock when they apprehended danger. We were, we believe, the first European travellers who actually noticed this animal, now universally admitted to be the shaphan, or coney of Scripture, within the proper bounds of the Holy Land ; and we were not a little gratified by its discovery. . . . . The preparer of the skin mistook it for a rabbit, though it is of a stronger build, and of a duskier colour, being of a dark brown. It is destitute of a tail, and has some bristles at its mouth, over its head, and down its back, along the course of which there are traces of light and dark shade. In its short ears, small, black, and naked feet, and pointed snout, it resembles the hedgehog. It does not, however, belong to the insectivora, but, though somewhat anomalous, it is allied to the pachydermata, among which it is now classed by naturalists.—*John Wilson, in " The Lands of the Bible,"* 1847.

Verse 18.—" Conies." People used to think the conies of Solomon the same as our rabbits, which are indeed " a feeble folk," but which do not " make their houses in the rock." Now that the *coney* is ascertained to be the Damon or Hyrax,— a shy defenceless creature, which lurks among the cliffs of the mountains, and darts into its den at the least approach of danger, the words of Agar acquire their full significance.—*James Hamilton.*

Verse 19.—" *He appointed the moon for seasons.*" When it is said, that the *moon was appointed to distinguish seasons*, interpreters agree that this is to be understood of the ordinary and appointed feasts. The Hebrews having been accustomed to compute their months by the moon, this served for regulating their festival days and assemblies, both sacred and political. The prophet, I have no doubt, by the figure synecdoche, puts a part for the whole, intimating that the moon not only distinguishes the days from the nights, but likewise marks out the festival days, measures years and months, and, in fine, answers many useful purposes, inasmuch as the distinction of times is taken from her course.—*John Calvin.*

Verse 19.—" *He appointed the moon for seasons.*" "He made the moon to serve in her season, for a declaration of times, and a sign to the world. From the moon is the sign of feasts, a light that decreaseth in her perfection. The month is called after her name, increasing wonderfully in her changing, being an instrument of the armies above, shining in the firmament of heaven; the beauty of heaven, the glory of the stars, an ornament giving light in the highest places of the Lord."—*Ecclesiasticus x.* 7.

Verse 19.—" *The sun knoweth his going down.*" The second clause is not to be rendered in the common way, "*The sun knoweth his going down,*" but according to the usual idiom, *He,* i.e., *God knoweth the going down of the sun.* Not to mention the unwonted and harsh form of the phrase, by which *the knowledge of his setting* is attributed to the sun, there appears no reason why it should be here used, since it is destitute of force,* or why he should turn from God as a cause, to the moving sun, when both before and afterwards he speaks of God, saying, "*He appointed the moon,*" "*Thou makest darkness.*" Far more fitly, therefore, is he to be understood as speaking of God, as before and after, so in the middle, of the directing cause of the appearances of the moon, the setting of the sun, and the spread of darkness. God also is said more correctly to *know* the going down of the sun, than the sun himself, since to *know* has in effect the force of to *care for,* as is often the case in other passages.—*Venema.*

Verse 20.—" *Thou makest darkness.*" Some observe with Augustine that in Genesis it is said that *light was made,* but not that *darkness was made,* because darkness is nothing, it is mere non-existence. But in this passage it is also said that *night was made;* and the Lord calls himself the *Maker of light and the Creator of darkness.—Lorinus.*

Verse 20.—" *Thou makest darkness,*" etc. It would be interesting to consider the wonderful adaptation of the length of the day to the health of man, and to the vigour and perhaps existence of the animal and vegetable tribes. The rejoicing of life depends so much upon the grateful alternation of day and night. For a full consideration of this subject I must refer the reader to Dr. Whewell's Bridgewater Treatise. The subjoined extracts may, however, aid reflection. "The terrestrial day, and consequently the length of the cycle of light and darkness, being what it is, we find various parts of the constitution both of animals and vegetables, which have a periodical character in their functions, corresponding to the diurnal succession of external conditions; and we find that the length of the period, as it exists in their constitution, coincides with the length of the natural day. The alternation of processes which takes place in plants by day and by night is less obvious, and less obviously essential to their well-being, than the annual series of changes. But there are abundance of facts which serve to show that such an alternation is part of the vegetable economy. . . .

"Animals also have a period in their functions and habits; as in the habits of waking, sleeping, etc., and their well-being appears to depend on the coincidence of this period with the length of the natural day. We see that in the day, as it now is, all animals find seasons for taking food and repose, which agree perfectly with their health and comfort. Some animals feed during the day, as nearly all the ruminating animals and land birds; others feed only in the twilight, as bats and owls, and are called *crepuscular;* while many beasts of prey, aquatic birds, and others, take their food during the night. These animals, which are nocturnal feeders, are diurnal sleepers, while those which are crepuscular sleep partly in the night and partly in the day; but in all, the complete period of these functions is twenty-

* This excellent expounder cannot see the beauty of the poetic expression, and so proses in this fashion.

four hours.   Man in like manner, in all nations and ages, takes his principal rest once in twenty-four hours ; and the regularity of this practice seems most suitable to his health, though the duration of time allotted to repose is extremely different in different cases.   So far as we can judge, this period is of a length beneficial to the human frame, independently of the effect of external agents.   In the voyages recently made into high northern latitudes, where the sun did not rise for three months, the crews of the ships were made to adhere, with the utmost punctuality, to the habit of retiring to rest at nine, and rising a quarter before six ; and they enjoyed, under circumstances apparently the most trying, a state of salubrity quite remarkable. This shows, that according to the common constitution of such men, the cycle of twenty-four hours is very commodious, though not imposed on them by external circumstances."—*William Whewell* (1795—1866).

Verse 21.—" *The young lions . . . . seek their meat from God.*"   God feeds not only sheep and lambs, but wolves and lions.   It is a strange expression that young lions when they roar after their prey, should be said to *seek their meat of God ;* implying that neither their own strength nor craft could feed them without help from God. The strongest creatures left to themselves cannot help themselves.   As they who fear God are fed by a special providence of God, so all creatures are fed and nourished by a general providence.   The lion, though he be strong and subtle, yet cannot get his own prey ; we think a lion might shift for himself ; no, 'tis the Lord that provides for him ; the young lions seek their meat of God.   Surely, then, the mightiest of men cannot live upon themselves : as it is of God that we receive life and breath, so all things needful for the maintenance of this life.—*Joseph Caryl.*

Verse 21.—" *The young lions roar.*"   The roar of a lion, according to Burchell, sometimes resembles the sound which is heard at the moment of an earthquake ; and is produced by his laying his head on the ground, and uttering a half-stifled growl, by which means the noise is conveyed along the earth.   The instant it is heard by the animals reposing in the plains, they start up in alarm, fly in all directions, and even rush into the danger which they seek to avoid.—*From Cassell's Popular Natural History.*

Verse 21.—The roaring of the young lions, like the crying of the ravens, is interpreted, *asking their meat of God.*   Doth God put this construction upon the language of mere nature, even in venomous creatures, and shall he not much more interpret favourably the language of grace in his own people, though it be weak and broken groanings which cannot be uttered ?—*Matthew Henry.*

Verse 22.—" *The sun ariseth . . . . they lay them down in their dens.*"   As wild beasts since the fall of man may seem to be born to do us hurt, and to rend and tear in pieces all whom they meet with, this savage cruelty must be kept under check by the providence of God.   And in order to keep them shut up within their dens, the only means which he employs is to inspire them with terror, simply by the light of the sun.   This instance of divine goodness, the prophet commends the more on account of its necessity ; for were it otherwise, men would have no liberty to go forth to engage in the labours and business of life.—*John Calvin.*

Verse 23.—" *Man goeth forth unto his work,*" etc.   Man alone, among all creatures, in distinction from the involuntary instruments of the Almighty, has a real daily work.   He has a definite part to play in life ; and can recognise it.—*Carl Bernhard Moll, in Lange's Commentary.*

Verse 23.—When the light of truth and righteousness shineth, error and iniquity fly away before it, and the " roaring lion " himself departeth for a time.   Then the Christian *goeth forth to the work* of his salvation, and to his *labour* of love, until *the evening* of old age warns him to prepare for his last repose, in faith of a joyful resurrection.—*George Horne.*

Verse 24.—" *O Lord, how manifold are thy works !* " etc.   If the number of the creatures be so exceeding great, how great, nay, immense, must needs be the power and wisdom of him who formed them all !   For (that I may borrow the words of a noble and excellent author) as it argues and manifests more skill by far in an artificer, to be able to frame both *clocks* and *watches,* and *pumps* and *mills,* and *granadoes* and *rockets,* than he could display in making but one of those sorts of engines; so the Almighty discovers more of his wisdom in forming such a vast multitude of different sorts of creatures, and all with admirable and irreprovable art, than if he had created but a few; for this declares the greatness and unbounded capacity of his understanding. Again, the same superiority of knowledge would be displayed by contriving engines of the same kind, or for the same purposes, after different fashions, as the moving of clocks by springs instead of weights: so the infinitely wise Creator hath shown in many instances that he is not confined to one only instrument for the working one effect, but can perform the same thing by divers means. So, though feathers seem necessary for flying, yet hath he enabled several creatures to fly without them, as two sorts of fishes, one sort of lizard, and the bat, not to mention the numerous tribes of flying insects. In like manner, though the air-bladder in fishes seems necessary for swimming, yet some are so formed as to swim without it, *viz.*, First, the *cartilaginous* kind, which by what artifice they poise themselves, ascend and descend at pleasure, and continue in what depth of water they list, is as yet unknown to us. Secondly, the *cetaceous* kind, or sea-beasts, differing in nothing almost but the want of feet. The air which in respiration these receive into their lungs, may serve to render their bodies equiponderant to the water; and the construction or dilatation of it, by the help of the diaphragm and muscles of respiration, may probably assist them to ascend or descend in the water, by a light impulse thereof with their fins. . . .

Again, the great use and convenience, the beauty and variety of so many springs and fountains, so many brooks and rivers, so many lakes and standing pools of water, and these so scattered and dispersed all the earth over, that no great part of it is destitute of them, without which it must, without a supply other ways, be desolate and void of inhabitants, afford abundant arguments of wisdom and counsel: that springs should break forth on the sides of mountains most remote from the sea: that there should way be made for rivers through straits and rocks, and subterraneous vaults, so that one would think that nature had cut a way on purpose to derive the water, which else would overthrow and drown whole countries.—*John Ray* (1678–1705), *in " The Wisdom of God manifested in the Works of the Creation."*

Verse 24.—" *How manifold are thy works!* " When we contemplate the wonderful works of Nature, and walking about at leisure, gaze upon this ample theatre of the world, considering the stately beauty, constant order, and sumptuous furniture thereof; the glorious splendour and uniform motion of the heavens; the pleasant fertility of the earth; the curious figure and fragrant sweetness of plants; the exquisite frame of animals; and all other amazing miracles of nature, wherein the glorious attributes of God, especially his transcendant goodness, are more conspicuously displayed: so that by them, not only large acknowledgments, but even gratulatory hymns, as it were, of praise have been extorted from the mouths of Aristotle, Pliny, Galen, and such like men, never suspected guilty of an excessive devotion; then should our hearts be affected with thankful sense, and our lips break forth in praise.—*William Barrow*, 1754—1836.

Verse 24.—He does not undertake to answer his own question, " *How manifold?* " for he confesses God's works to be greater than his own power of expression; whether these " *works* " belong to the creation of nature or to that of grace. And observe how the concurrent operation of the Blessed Trinity is set forth: " *O Lord, how manifold are thy works,*" teaches of the Father, the Source of all things; " *in wisdom hast thou made them all,*" tells of the Son, the Eternal Word, " Christ the power of God and the Wisdom of God, by whom were all things made, and without him was not anything made that was made" (1 Cor. i. 24; John i. 3); " *the earth is full of thy riches,*" is spoken of the Holy Ghost, who filleth the world.—*Augustine, Hugo, and Cassiodorus, in Neale and Littledale.*

Verse 24.—" *In wisdom hast thou made them all.*" Not only one thing, as the heavens, Ps. cxxxvi. 5; but everything is wisely contrived and made; there is a most glorious display of the wisdom of God in the most minute thing his hands have made; he has made everything beautiful in its season. A skilful artificer, when he has finished his work and looks it over again, often finds some fault or another in it: but when the Lord had finished his works of creation, and looked over them, he saw that all was good; infinite wisdom itself could find no blemish in them: what weak, foolish, stupid creatures must they be that pretend to charge any of the works of God with folly or want of wisdom?—*John Gill.*

Verse 24.—" *The earth is full of thy riches,*" literally, *thy possessions;* these thou keepest not to thyself, but blessest thy creatures with.—*A. R. Fausset.*

Verse 25.—*" Things innumerable."* The waters teem with more life than the land. Beneath a surface less varied than that of the continents, the sea enfolds in its bosom an exuberance of life, of which no other region of the globe can afford the faintest idea. Its life extends from the poles to the equator, from east to west. Everywhere the sea is peopled ; everywhere, down to its unfathomable depths, live and sport creatures suited to the locality. In every spot of its vast expanse the naturalist finds instruction, and the philosopher meditation, while the very varieties of life tend to impress upon our souls a feeling of gratitude to the Creator of the universe. Yes, the shores of the ocean and its depths, its plains and its mountains, its valleys and its precipices, even its *débris*, are enlivened and beautified by thousands of living beings. There are the solitary or sociable plants, upright or pendant, stretching in prairies, grouped in oases, or growing in immense forests. These plants give a cover to and feed millions of animals which creep, run, swim, fly, burrow in the soil, attach themselves to roots, lodge in the crevices, or build for themselves shelters, which seek or fly from one another, which pursue or fight each other, which caress each other with affection or devour each other without pity. Charles Darwin truly says that the terrestrial forests do not contain anything like the number of animals as those of the sea. The ocean, which is for man the element of death, is for myriads of animals a home of life and health. There is joy in its waves, there is happiness upon its shores, and heavenly blue everywhere.—*Moquin Tandon, in " The World of the Sea," Translated and enlarged by H. Martin Hart, 1869.*

Verses 25, 26.—*" Both small and great beasts."*

> The sounds and seas, each creek and bay,
> With fry innumerable swarm, and shoals
> Of fish that with their fins and shining scales
> Glide under the green wave, in shoals that oft
> Bank the mid sea ; part single, or with mate,
> Graze the sea-weed their pasture, and through groves
> Of coral stray ; or, sporting with quick glance,
> Show to the sun their wav'd coats drop't with gold ;
> Or, in their pearly shells at ease, attend
> Moist nutriment ; or under rocks their food
> In jointed armour watch : on smooth the seal
> And bended dolphins play : part huge of bulk
> Wallowing unwieldy, enormous in their gait,
> Tempest the ocean : there leviathan,
> Hugest of living creatures, on the deep
> Stretch'd like a promontory sleeps or swims,
> And seems a moving land ; and at his gills
> Draws in, and at his trunk spouts out, a sea.
>
> —*John Milton.*

Verse 26.—*" Ships."* The original of ships was doubtless Noah's ark, so that they owe their first draught to God himself.—*John Gill.*

Verse 26.—*" There go the ships."* Far from separating from each other the nations of the earth (as the ancients, still inexperienced in navigation, supposed), the sea is the great highway of the human race, and unites all its various tribes into one common family by the beneficial bonds of commerce. Countless fleets are constantly furrowing its bosom, to enrich, by perpetual exchanges, all the countries of the globe with the products of every zone, to convey the fruits of the tropical world to the children of the chilly north, or to transport the manufactures of colder climes to the inhabitants of the equatorial regions. With the growth of commerce civilization also spreads athwart the wide causeway of the ocean from shore to shore ; it first dawned on the borders of the sea, and its chief seats are still to be found along its confines.—*G. Hartwig, in " The Harmonies of Nature," 1866.*

Verse 26.—*" Leviathan."* There is ground for thinking (though this is denied by some) that in several passages the term *leviathan* is used generically, much as we employ *dragon ;* and that it denotes a great sea-monster.—*E. P. Barrows, in " Biblical Geography and Antiquities."*

Verse 26.—*" To play therein."* Dreadful and tempestuous as the sea may appear, and uncontrollable in its billows and surges, it is only the field of *sport*, the *play-ground*, the *bowling green*, to those huge marine monsters.—*Adam Clarke.*

Verse 26.—*" Leviathan . . . made to play therein."* With such wonderful strength is the tail of the whale endowed, that the largest of these animals, measuring some eighty feet in length, are able by its aid to leap clear out of the water, as if they were little fish leaping after flies. This movement is technically termed " breaching," and the sound which is produced by the huge carcase as it falls upon the water is so powerful as to be heard for a distance of several miles.—*J. G. Wood, in " The Illustrated Natural History,"* 1861.

Verse 26.—" *Leviathan . . . made to play therein.*" Though these immense mammiferous fish have no legs, they swim with great swiftness, and they gambol in the mountains of water lashed up by the storms.—*Moquin Tandon.*

Verse 26.—" *Leviathan . . . made to play.*" He is made to " *play in the sea* " ; he hath nothing to do as man hath, that " goes forth to his work " ; he hath nothing to fear as the beasts have, that lie down in their dens ; and therefore he plays with the waters : it is a pity any of the children of men, that have nobler powers, and were made for nobler purposes, should live as if they were sent into the world like the leviathan into the waters, to play therein, spending all their time in pastime.— *Matthew Henry.*

Verse 26.—" *Therein.*" Fish, great and small, sport and play in the element, but as soon as they are brought out of it, they languish and die. Mark, O soul ! what thy element is, if thou wouldest live joyful and blessed.—*Starke, in Lange's Commentary.*

Verse 27.—There are five things to be observed in God's sustaining all animals. His power, which alone suffices for all : " *These wait all upon thee.*" Wisdom, which selects a fitting time : " *That thou mayest give them their meat in due season.*" His majesty rising above all : " *That thou givest them they gather,*" like the crumbs falling from the table of their supreme Lord. His liberality, which retains nothing in his open hand that it does not give : " *Thou openest thine hand.*" His original goodness that flows down to all : " *They are filled with good,*" that is, with the good things that spring from thy goodness.—*Le Blanc.*

Verse 27.—" *That thou mayest give them their meat in due season ;* " or, *in his time ;* every one in its own time which is natural to them, and they have been used to, at which time the Lord gives it to them, and they take it ; it would be well if men would do so likewise, eat and drink in proper and due time, Eccles. x. 17. Christ speaks a word in season to weary souls ; his ministers give to every one his portion of meat in due season ; and a word spoken in due season, how good and sweet is it ? Is. vii. 4 ; Luke xii. 12 ; Prov. xv. 23.—*John Gill.*

Verses 27—32.—

> These, Lord, all wait on thee, that thou their food may'st give them ;
> Thou to their wants attendest ;
> They gather what thou sendest;
> Thine hand thou openest, all their need supplying,
> O'erlookest not the least, the greatest satisfying.
>
> When thou dost hide thy face a sudden change comes o'er them
> Their breath in myriads taken,
> They die, no more t' awaken ;
> But myriads more thy Spirit soon createth,
> And the whole face of nature quickly renovateth.
>
> The glory of the Lord, changeless, endures for ever ;
> In all his works delighting,
> Nor e'en the smallest slighting ;
> Yet, if he frown, earth shrinks with fear before him,
> And, at his touch, the hills with kindling flames adore him.
>
> —*John Burton.*

Verse 28.—" *That thou givest them they gather.*" This sentence describes *The Commissariat of Creation.* The problem is the feeding of " the creeping things innumerable, both small and great beasts," which swarm the sea ; the armies of birds which fill the air, and the vast hordes of animals which people the dry land ; and in this sentence we have the problem solved, " *That thou givest them they gather.*" The work is stupendous, but it is done with ease because the Worker is infinite : if he were not at the head of it the task would never be accomplished. Blessed be God for the great Thou of the text. It is every way our sweetest consolation that the personal God is still at work in the world : leviathan in the ocean, and the sparrow on the bough, may be alike glad of this ; and we, the children of the great Father, much more.

The general principle of the text is, God gives to his creatures, and his creatures gather. That general principle we shall apply to our own case as men and women; for it is as true of us as it is of the fish of the sea, and the cattle on the hills : " *That thou givest them they gather.*" I. *We have only to gather, for God gives.* In *temporal* things : God gives us day by day our daily bread, and our business is simply to gather it. As to *spirituals*, the principle is true, most emphatically, we have, in the matter of grace, only to gather what God gives. The natural man thinks that he has to earn divine favour ; that he has to purchase the blessing of heaven ; but he is in grave error : the soul has only to receive that which Jesus freely gives. II. *We can only gather what God gives ;* however eager we may be, there is the end of the matter. The diligent bird shall not be able to gather more than the Lord has given it ; neither shall the most avaricious and covetous man. " It is vain for you to rise up early and to sit up late, to eat the bread of carefulness ; for so he giveth his beloved sleep." III. *We must gather what God gives*, or else we shall get no good by his bountiful giving. God feeds the creeping things innumerable, but each creature collects the provender for itself. The huge leviathan receives his vast provision, but he must go ploughing through the boundless meadows and gather up the myriads of minute objects which supply his need. The fish must leap up to catch the fly, the swallow must hawk for its food, the young lions must hunt for their prey. IV. The fourth turn of the text gives us the sweet thought that, *we may gather what he gives.* We have divine permission to enjoy freely what the Lord bestows. V. The last thing is, *God will always give us something to gather.* It is written, " The Lord will provide." Thus is it also in spiritual things. If you are willing to gather, God will always give.—*C. H. S.*

Verse 28.—" *Gather.*" The verb rendered " *gather* " means to pick up or collect from the ground. It is used in the history of the manna (Ex. xvi. 1, 5, 16), to which there is obvious allusion. The act of gathering from the ground seems to presuppose a previous throwing down from heaven.—*J. A. Alexander.*

Verse 28.—" *Thou openest thine hand.*" The Greek expositors take *the opening of the hand* to indicate facility. I am of opinion that it refers also to abundance and liberality, as in Ps. cxlv. 16 :—" *Thou openest thine hand, and satisfiest the desire of every living thing.*" Using this same formula, God commands us *not to close the hand, but to open it to the poor.*—*Lorinus.*

Verse 29.—" *They are troubled.*" They are confounded ; they are overwhelmed with terror and amazement. The word " *troubled* " by no means conveys the sense of the original word—בהל, *bahal*—which means properly to tremble ; to be in trepidation ; to be filled with terror ; to be amazed ; to be confounded. It is that kind of consternation which one has when all support and protection are withdrawn, and when inevitable ruin stares one in the face. So when God turns away, all their support is gone, all their resources fail, *and they must die.* They are represented as conscious of this ; or this is what would occur if they *were* conscious.—*Albert Barnes.*

Verse 30.—" *Thou sendest forth thy spirit, they are created.*" The Spirit of God creates every day : what is it that continueth things in their created being, but providence ? That is a true axiom in divinity, *Providence is creation continued.* Now the Spirit of God who created at first, creates to this day : " *Thou sendest forth thy spirit, they are created.*" The work of creation was finished in the first six days of the world, but the work of creation is renewed every day, and so continued to the end of the world. Successive providential creation as well as original creation is ascribed to the Spirit. " *And thou renewest the face of the earth.*" Thou makest a new world ; and thus God makes a new world every year, sending forth his Spirit, or quickening power, in the rain and sun to renew the face of the earth. And as the Lord sends forth his power in providential mercies, so in providential judgments. —*Joseph Caryl.*

Verse 31.—" *The Lord shall rejoice in his works.*" Man alone amongst the creatures grieves God, and brought tears from the eyes of Christ, who rejoiced in Spirit, because the Father had deigned to reveal the mysteries to the little ones. It repented God that he had made man, because as a wise son maketh a glad father, so a foolish one is a vexation to him.—*Lorinus.*

Verse 31 (*last clause*),—What the Psalmist adds, *Let Jehovah rejoice in his works,* is not superfluous, for he desires that the order which God has established from the beginning may be continued in the lawful use of his gifts. As we read in Gen. vi. 6, that " it repented the Lord that he had made man on the earth ; " so when he sees that the good things which he bestows are polluted by our corruptions, he ceases to take delight in bestowing them. And certainly the confusion and disorder which take place, when the elements cease to perform their office, testify that God, displeased and wearied out, is provoked to discontinue, and put a stop to the regular course of his beneficence ; although anger and impatience have strictly speaking no place in his mind. What is here taught is, that he bears the character of the best of fathers, who takes pleasure in tenderly cherishing his children, and in bountifully nourishing them.—*John Calvin.*

Verse 32.—" *He looketh on the earth and it trembleth.*" As man can soon give a cast with his eye, so soon can God shake the earth, that is, either the whole mass of the earth, or the inferior sort of men on the earth when he " *looketh,*" or casteth an angry eye " *upon the earth, it trembleth.*" " *He toucheth the hills*" (that is, the powers and principalities of the world), " *and they smoke ;* " if he do but touch them they smoke, that is, the dreadful effects of the power and judgment of God are visible upon them.—*Joseph Caryl.*

Verse 32.—No one save a photographer can sketch the desert around Sinai. Roberts' views are noble, and to a certain extent true ; but they do not represent these desert cliffs and ravines. No artist can rightly do it. Only the photographer can pourtray the million of minute details that go to make up the bleakness, the wildness, the awfulness, and the dismal loneliness of these unearthly wastes.

About noon I went out and walked upon the convent roof. The star-light over the mountain-peaks was splendid, while the gloom that hung round these enormous precipices and impenetrable ravines was quite oppressive to the spirit. This is the scene of which David spoke. " *He looketh on the earth, and it trembleth : he toucheth the hills, and they smoke.*" This is the mountain " that was touched, and that burned with fire " (Heb. xii. 18). Not the mount that " might be touched," as our translators have rendered it, but the mount " that was touched," ψηλα φωμενω,—the mount on which the finger of God rested.

We could imagine the black girdle of the thick darkness with which the mountain was surrounded, and the lightnings giving forth their quick fire through this covering, making its blackness blacker. We could imagine, too, the supernatural blaze, kindled by no earthly hand, that shot up out of the midst of this, like a living column of fire, ascending, amid the sound of angelic trumpets and superangelic thunders, to the very heart of heaven.—*Horatius Bonar, in " The Desert of Sinai,"* 1858.

Verse 32.—The philosopher labours to investigate the natural cause of earthquakes and volcanoes. Well, let him account as he will, still the immediate power of Jehovah is the true and ultimate cause. God works in these tremendous operations. " *He looketh on the earth, and it trembleth ; he toucheth the hills, and they smoke.*" This is the philosophy of Scripture : this, then, shall be my philosophy. Never was a sentence uttered by uninspired man so sublime as this sentence. The thought is grand beyond conception ; and the expression clothes the thought with suitable external majesty. God needs no means by which to give effect to his purpose by his power, yet, in general, he has established means through which he acts. In conformity with this Divine plan, he created by means, and he governs by means. But the means which he has employed in creation, and the means which he employs in providence, are effectual only by his almighty power. The sublimity of the expression in this passage arises from the infinite disproportion between the means and the end. An earthly sovereign looks with anger, and his courtiers tremble. God looks on the earth, and it trembles to its foundation. He touches the mountains, and the volcano smokes, vomiting forth torrents of lava. Hills are said to melt at the presence of the Lord, " Tremble, thou earth, at the presence of the Lord, at the presence of the God of Jacob." How chill and withering is the breath of that noxious philosophy, that would detach our minds from viewing God in his works of Providence ! The Christian who lives in this atmosphere, or on the borders of it, will be unhealthy and unfruitful in true works of righteousness. This malaria destroys all spiritual life.—*Alexander Carson.*

Verse 32.—" *He toucheth the hills, and they smoke.*" It's therefore ill falling into his hands, who can do such terrible things with his looks and touches.—*John Trapp.*

Verse 33.—" *I will sing unto the Lord.*" The Psalmist, exulting in the glorious prospect of the renovation of all things, breaks out in triumphant anticipation of the great event, and says, " I will sing unto the Lord," בְּחַיַּי *bechaiyai,* " with my lives," the life that I *now* have, and the *life* that I *shall have* hereafter.

" *I will sing praise to my God,*" בְּעוֹדִי *beodi,* " *in my eternity ;* " my going on, my endless progression. What astonishing ideas ! But then, how shall this great work be brought about ? and how shall the new earth be inhabited with righteous spirits only ? The answer is (verse 35), " *Let the sinners be consumed out of the earth, and let the wicked be no more.*"—*Adam Clarke.*

Verses 33—35.—All having been admonished to glorify God, he discloses what he himself is about to do : with his voice he will declare his praises, " *I will sing unto the Lord as long as I live :* " with his hand he will write Psalms, and set them to music, " *I will sing Psalms to my God while I have my being :* " with his mind he will make sweet meditations, " *My meditation of him shall be sweet :* " with will and affection he will seek after God alone, " *I will be glad in the Lord :* " he predicts and desires the destruction of all sinners who think not of praising God, but dishonour him in their words and works, " *Let the sinners be consumed out of the earth, and let the wicked be no more :* " lastly, with his whole soul and all his powers he will bless God, " *Bless thou the Lord, O my soul.*"—*Le Blanc.*

Verse 34.—" *My meditation of him shall be sweet.*" A Christian needs to study nothing but *Christ,* there is enough in Christ to take up his study and contemplation all his days ; and the more we study Christ, the more we may study him ; there will be new wonders still appearing in him.—*John Row,* 1680.

Verse 34.—" *My meditation of him shall be sweet.*" The last words ever written by Henry Martyn, dying among Mohammedans in Persia, was : I sat in the orchard and thought with sweet comfort and peace of my God, in solitude my company, my Friend and Comforter.

Verse 34.—" *My meditation of him shall be sweet.*" I must meditate on Christ. Let philosophers soar in their contemplations, and walk among the stars ; what are the stars to Christ, the Sun of righteousness, the brightness of the Father's glory, and the express image of his person ? God manifest in the flesh is a theme which angels rejoice to contemplate.—*Samuel Lavington.*

Verse 34.—" *My meditation of him shall be sweet.*" First. Take this as *an assertion.* The meditation on God is sweet. And the sweetness of it should stir us up to the putting of it in practice. Secondly. Take it as *a resolution*—that he would make it for his own practice ; that is, that he would comfort himself in such perform-ances as these are ; whilst others took pleasure in other things, he would please himself in communion with God, this should be his solace and delight upon all occa-sions. David promises himself a great deal of contentment in this exercise of divine meditation which he undertook with much delight : and so likewise do others of God's servants of the same nature and disposition with him in the like undertakings. Thirdly. Take it as *a prayer and petition.* It " *shall be,*" that is, *let it be,* the future put for the imperative, as it frequently uses to be ; and so the word *gnatam* is to be trans-lated, not, *of God,* but *to God.* Let my meditation, cr prayer, or converse, be sweet unto him. *Placeat illi meditatio mea,* so some good authors interpret it. The English translation, " Let my words be acceptable," and the other before that, " Oh that my words might please him," which comes to one and the same effect, all taking it in the notion of *a prayer :* this is that which the servants of God have still thought to be most necessary for them (as indeed it is) ; God's acceptance of the performances which have been presented by them.—*Condensed from Thomas Horton.*

Verse 34 (first clause).—All the ancients join in understanding it thus, " *My meditation shall be sweet to him,*" or, as the Jewish Arab, עמדה *with him,* according to that of the Psalmist, Psalm xix. 14 : " Let the meditation of my heart be always acceptable in thy sight." Thus the Chaldee here, קדמוי, *before him ;* the LXXII. ἡδυνθείη αὐτῷ, " *Let it be sweet to him* " ; the Syriac ܥܠ *to him,* and so the others also. And so עַל signifies *to* as well as *on.*—*Henry Hammond.*

Verse 34.—" *I will be glad in the Lord.*" Compare this with verse 31, and observe the mutual and reciprocal pleasure and delight between God who is praised and the soul that praises him. God, *who rejoices in his works,* takes the highest delight in man, the compendium of his other works, and in that work, than which none more excellent can be pursued by man, the work of praising God in which the blessed are employed. Thus in this very praise of God which is so pleasing to him, David professes to be evermore willing to take delight. *My beloved is mine*, sings the Spouse, *and I am his.—Lorinus.*

Verse 35.—" Let the sinners be consumed out of the earth," etc.—It fell to my lot some years ago, to undertake a walk of some miles, on a summer morning, along a sea-shore of surpassing beauty. It was the Lord's day, and the language of the Hundred and fourth Psalm rose spontaneously in my mind as one scene after another unfolded itself before the eye. About half way to my destination the road lay through a dirty hamlet, and my meditations were rudely interrupted by the brawling of some people, who looked as if they had been spending the night in a drunken debauch. Well, I thought, the Psalmist must have had some such unpleasant experience. He must have fallen in with people, located in some scene of natural beauty, who, instead of being a holy priesthood to give voice to nature in praise of her Creator, instead of being, in the pure and holy tenor of their lives, the heavenliest note of the general song,—filled it with a harsh discord. His prayer is the vehement expression of a desire that the earth may no longer be marred by the presence of wicked men, —that they may be utterly consumed, and may give place to men animated with the fear of God, just and holy men, men that shall be a crown of beauty on the head of this fair creation. If this be the right explanation of the Psalmist's prayer, it is not only justifiable, but there is something wrong in our meditations on nature, if we are not disposed to join in it.—*William Binnie.*

Verse 35.—" Let the sinners be consumed out of the earth." This imprecation depends on the last clause of the 31st verse, *" Let Jehovah rejoice in his works."* As the wicked infect the world with their pollutions, the consequence is, that God has less delight in his own workmanship, and is even almost displeased with it. It is impossible, but that this uncleanness, which, being extended and diffused through every part of the world, vitiates and corrupts such a noble product of his hands, must be offensive to him. Since then the wicked, by their perverse abuse of God's gifts, cause the world in a manner to degenerate and fall away from its first original, the prophet justly desires that they may be exterminated, until the race of them entirely fails. Let us, then, take care so to weigh the providence of God, as that being wholly devoted to obeying him, we may rightly and purely use the benefits which he sanctifies for our enjoying them. Further, let us be grieved, that such precious treasures are wickedly squandered away, and let us regard it as monstrous and detestable, that men not only forget their Maker, but also, as it were, purposely turn to a perverse and an unworthy end, whatever good things he has bestowed upon them.—*John Calvin.*

Verse 35.—" The sinners."

> All true, all faultless, all in tune,
>   Creation's wondrous choir,
> Opened in mystic unison,
>   To last till time expire.
>
> And still it lasts : by day and night,
>   With one consenting voice,
> All hymn thy glory, Lord, aright,
>   All worship and rejoice.
>
> Man only mars the sweet accord,
>   O'erpowering with harsh din
> The music of thy works and word,
>   Ill matched with grief and sin.
>   —*John Keble, in " The Christian Year."*

Verse 35.—" Bless thou the Lord, O my soul." Rehearse the first words of the Psalm which are the same as these. They are here repeated as if to hint that the end of good men is like their beginning, and that he is not of the number who begin in the spirit and seek to be made perfect in the flesh. A worthy beginning of the Psalm, says Cassiodorus, and a worthy end, ever to bless him who never at any time fails to be with the faithful. The soul which blesses shall be made fat. . . . Reined in by this rein of divine praise, he shall never perish.—*Lorinus.*

*Verse 35.—*This is the first place where HALLELUJAH *(" Praise ye the Lord ")* occurs in the Book of Psalms. It is produced by a retrospect of *Creation*, and by the contemplation of God's goodness in the preservation of all the creatures of his hand, and also by a prospective view of that future Sabbath, when, by the removal of evil men from communion with the good, God will be enabled to look on his works, as he did on the first Sabbath, before the Tempter had marred them, and see " everything very good." See Gen. i. 31 ; ii. 2, 3.—*Christopher Wordsworth.*

Verse 35.—" *Praise ye the Lord.*" This is the first time that we meet with *Hallelujah ;* and it comes in here upon occasion of the destruction of the wicked ; and the last time we meet with it, it is upon the like occasion, when the New Testament Babylon is consumed, this is the burthen of the song, " *Hallelujah,*" Rev. xix. 1, 3, 4, 6.—*Matthew Henry.*

HINTS TO PREACHERS.

Verse 1 (first clause).—An exhortation to one's own heart. I. To remember the Lord as the first cause of all good. Bless not man, or fate, but *the Lord.* II. To do this in a loving, grateful, hearty, praiseful manner. *Bless* the Lord. III. To do it truly and intensely. *O my soul.* IV. To do it *now*—for various reasons and in all possible ways.

Verse 1 (second clause).—He is all this essentially, and in nature, providence, grace, and judgment.

Verse 2 (first clause).—The clearest revelation of God is still a concealment ; even light is but a covering to him. God is clothed with light as we see him in his omniscience, his revelation, his glory in heaven, and his grace on earth.

Verse 3 (last clause).—I. God is leisurely in his haste : " he *walketh,*" etc. II. God is swift even in his slackness : " he walketh *on the wings of the wind.*" III. The practical conclusions are that there is time enough for the divine purposes, but none for our trifling ; and that we should both wait with patience for the victory of his cause and hasten it by holy activity.

Verse 4.—I. The Nature of Angels. Spirits. II. The Lord of Angels. " Who maketh," etc. What must his own spirituality be who maketh spirits ? III. The ministry of Angels. 1. Their office : " ministers." 2. Their activity or zeal : " a flaming fire." 3. Their dependence : *made* ministers.—*G. Rogers.*

Verse 7.—The power of the divine word in nature shows its power in other spheres.

Verse 9.—I. All things have their appointed bounds. II. To pass those bounds without special permission by God is transgression. " Thou hast set a bound that they *may not* pass." III. Extraordinary cases should be followed by a return to ordinary duties. " That they turn not again," etc.—*G. R.*

Verse 10.—The thoughtfulness of God for those who, like the valleys, are lowly, hidden, and needy : the abiding character of his supplies : and the joyous results of his care.

Verses 10, 11.—God's care for wild creatures, reflections from it. (1.) Shall he not much more care for his people ? (2.) Will he not look after wild, wandering men ? (3.) Ought we not also to care for all that live ?

Verses 10—12.—From the fertility, life and music which mark the course of a stream, illustrate the beneficial influences of the Gospel.—*C. A. Davis.*

Verse 14.—" In the Hayfield." (See " Spurgeon's Sermons," No. 757.) " *He causeth the grass to grow for the cattle.*" I. Grass is in itself instructive. 1. As the symbol of our mortality : " All flesh is grass." 2. As an emblem of the wicked. 3. As a picture of the elect of God. Isai. xxxv. 7 ; xliv. 4 ; Ps. lxxii. 6, 16. 4. Grass is comparable to the food wherewith the Lord supplies the necessities of his chosen ones. Ps. xxiii. 2 ; S. of Sol. i. 7. II. God is seen in the growing of the grass. 1. As a worker : " He causeth," etc. See God in common things—in solitary things. 2. See God as a care-taker : " He causeth the grass to grow for the cattle." God cares for the beasts—the helpless—dumb and speechless things—providing suitable food for them : " grass." Let us, then, see his hand in providence at all times. III. God's working in the grass for the cattle gives us illustrations concerning grace. 1. God " cares for oxen " and satisfies their wants : there must then be something somewhere to satisfy the needs of the nobler creature man, and his immortal soul. 2. Though God provides the grass for the cattle, the cattle must eat it themselves.

The Lord Jesus Christ is provided as the food of the soul. We must, by faith, receive and feed upon Christ. 3. Preventing grace may here be seen in a symbol : before the cattle were made, in this world there was grass. There were covenant supplies for God's people before they were in the world. 4. Here is an illustration of free grace : the cattle bring nothing to purchase the food. Why is this ? (1) Because they belong to him, Ps. l. 10. (2) Because he has entered into a covenant with them to feed them, Gen. ix. 9, 10.

In the text there is a mighty blow to free-will : " *He causeth* the grass to grow." Grace does not grow in the heart without a divine cause. If God cares to make grass grow he will also make us grow in grace. Again ; the grass does not grow without an object ; it is " for the cattle " : but the cattle grow for man. What, then, does man grow for ? Observe, further, that the existence of the grass is necessary to complete the chain of nature. So the meanest child of God is necessary to the family.

Verse 16.—" The Cedars of Lebanon." (See " Spurgeon's Sermons," No. 529.) I. The absence of all human culture. These trees are peculiarly the Lord's trees, because, 1. They owe their planting entirely to him : " He hath planted." 2. They are not dependent upon man for their watering. 3. No mortal might protects them. 4. As to their inspection—they preserve a sublime indifference to human gaze. 5. Their exultation is all for God. 6. There is not a cedar upon Lebanon which is not independent of man in its expectations. II. The glorious display of divine care. 1. In the abundance of their supply. 2. They are always green. 3. Observe the grandeur and size of these trees. 4. Their fragrance. 5. Their perpetuity. 6. They are very venerable. III. The fulness of living principle : " The trees of the Lord are full of sap." 1. This is vitally necessary. 2. It is essentially mysterious. 3. It is radically secret. 4. It is permanently active. 5. It is externally operative. 6. It is abundantly to be desired.

Verses 17, 18.—"Lessons from Nature." (See " Spurgeon's Sermons," No. 1,005.) I. For each place God has prepared a suitable form of life : for " the fir trees," " the stork " ; for " the high hills," " the wild goat," etc. So, for all parts of the spiritual universe God has provided suitable forms of divine life. 1. Each age has its saints. 2. In every rank they are to be found. The Christian religion is equally well adapted for all conditions. 3. In every church spiritual life is to be found. 4. God's people are to be found in every city. II. Each creature has its appropriate place. 1. Each man has by God a providential position appointed to him. 2. This is also true of our spiritual experience. 3. The same holds good as to individuality of character. III. Every creature that God has made is provided with shelter. IV. For each creature the shelter is appropriate. V. Each creature uses its shelter.

Verse 19.—I. The wisdom of God as displayed in the material heavens. In the changes of the moon and the variety of the seasons. II. The goodness of God as there displayed. In the adaptation of these changes to the wants and enjoyments of men. III. The faithfulness of God as there displayed. Inspiring confidence in his creatures by their regularity.

> " So like the sun may I fulfil
> The appointed duties of the day ;
> With ready mind and active will
> March on and keep my heavenly way."

Verse 20.—Darkness and the beasts that creep forth therein. 1. Ignorance of God, and unrestrained lusts. Rom. i. 2. Sins discovered. Beasts there before, but not noticed, now terrify man. 3. Spiritual despondency, dismay, despair, etc. 4. Church lethargy. All sorts of heresies, etc., begin to creep forth. 5. Papal influence. Monks, friars, priests, etc., creep about in this dark age.—*A. G. Brown.*

Verses 20—23.—I. Night work is for wild beasts : " Thou makest darkness," etc. II. Day work is for men : " Man goeth forth," etc. Good men do their work by day ; bad men by night : their work is in the dark. Ministers who creep into their studies by night, and " roar after their prey," and " seek their meat from God," are more like wild beasts than rational men.—*G. R.*

Verse 21.—Inarticulate prayers, or how faulty the expression may be and yet how real the prayer in the esteem of God.

Verse 22.—From the effect of sunrise on the beasts of prey, exhibit the influence of Divine Grace on our evil passions.—*C. A. D.*

Verse 23.—" *Early Closing.*" A sermon preached on behalf of the " Early Closing Association," by *James Hamilton,* D.D., 1850. In the " Pulpit," Vol. 57.

Verse 24.—I. The language of wonder: " O Lord, how manifold," etc.   Their number, variety, co-operation, harmony.   II. Of admiration : " In wisdom," etc. Everywhere the same wisdom displayed.   God, says Dr. Chalmers, is as great in minutiæ as in magnitude.   III. Of gratitude : " The earth is full," etc.—*G. R.*

Verse 24.—I. The works of the Lord are multitudinous and varied.   II. They are so constructed as to show the most consummate wisdom in their *design*, and in the *end* for which they are formed.   III. They are all God's *property*, and should be used only in reference to the end for which they were created.   All *abuse* and *waste* of God's creatures are spoil and robbery on the property of the Creator.—*Adam Clarke.*

Verse 26.—" *There go the ships.*"   (See " Spurgeon's Sermons," No. 1,259.)   I. We see that the ships go.   1. The ships are intended for going.   2. The ships in going at last disappear from view.   3. The ships as they go are going upon business. 4. The ships sail upon a changeful sea.   II. How go the ships ?   1. They must go according to the wind.   2. But still the mariner does not go by the wind without exertion on his own part.   3. They have to be guided and steered by the helm.   4. He who manages the helm seeks direction from charts and lights.   5. They go according to their build.   III. Let us signal them.   1. Who is your owner ?   2. What is your cargo ?   3. Where are you going ?

Verses 27—30.—Trace the analogy in the spiritual world.   The saints waiting, v. 27 ; their sustenance from the opened hand, v. 28 ; their trouble under the hidden face ; their death if the Spirit were gone, v. 29 ; their revival when the Spirit returns, v. 30.

Verses 29, 30.—I. The commencement of life is from God : " Thou sendest forth thy Spirit," etc.   II. The continuance of life is from God : " Thou renewest," etc. III. The decline of life is from God : " Thou hidest thy face," etc.   IV. The cessation of life is from God : " Thou takest away their breath," etc.   V. The resurrection of life is from God : " Thou renewest," etc.—*G. R.*

Verse 30.—The season of Spring and its mortal analogies.   See John Foster's " Lectures," 1844.

Verse 32.—I. What there is in a look of God.   " He looketh," etc.   1. What in a look of anger.   2. What in a look of love.   He looked out of the fiery pillar upon the Egyptians.   " The Lord hath looked out from his pillar of glory," etc.   He gave another look from the same pillar to Israel.   II. What there is in a Touch of God : " He toucheth," etc.   A touch of his may raise a soul to heaven, or sink a soul to hell.—*G. R.*

Verse 33.—I. The singer—" I."   II. The song—" praises."   III. The audience —" The Lord," " My God."   IV. The length of the song—" long as I live ; while I have my being."—*A. G. B.*

Verse 33.—Two " I wills."   I. Because he made me live.   II. Because he has made me to live in him.   III. Because he is JEHOVAH and " my God."   IV. Because I shall live for ever, in the best sense.

Verse 34.—I. David's contemplation.   II. David's exultation.—*Thomas Horton.*

Verse 35.—I. They who praise not God are not fit to be on the earth : " Let the sinners be consumed," etc.   II. Much less are they fit to be in heaven.   III. They who praise God are fit for both earth and heaven.   Though others do not praise him here, the saints will.   " Bless thou the Lord," etc.   1. In opposition to others, they praise him on earth.   2. In harmony with others, they praise him in heaven, etc.   Everywhere it is with them, " Praise ye the Lord."—*G. R.*

PSALM CV.

This historical Psalm was evidently composed by King David, for the first fifteen verses of it were used as a hymn at the carrying up of the ark from the house of Obed-edom, and we read in 1 Chron. xvi. 7. " Then on that day David delivered first this Psalm, to thank the Lord, into the hand of Asaph and his brethren." Such a song was suitable for the occasion, for it describes the movements of the Lord's people and his guardian care over them in every place, and all this on account of the covenant of which the ark, then removing, was a symbol. Our last Psalm sang the opening chapters of Genesis, and this takes up its closing chapters and conducts us into Exodus and Numbers.

The first verses are full of joyful praise, and call upon the people to extol Jehovah, 1—7; then the earliest days of the infant nation are described, 8—15; the going into Egypt, 16—23, the coming forth from it with the Lord's outstretched arm, 24—38, the journeying through the wilderness and the entrance into Canaan.

We are now among the long Psalms, as at other times we have been among the short ones. These varying lengths of the sacred poems should teach us not to lay down any law either of brevity or prolixity in either prayer or praise. Short petitions and single verses of hymns are often the best for public occasions, but there are seasons when a whole night of wrestling or an entire day of Psalm singing will be none too long. The Spirit is ever free in his operations, and is not to be confined within the rules of conventional propriety. The wind bloweth as it listeth, and at one time rushes in short and rapid sweep, while at another it continues to refresh the earth hour after hour with its reviving breath.

EXPOSITION.

O GIVE thanks unto the LORD; call upon his name: make known his deeds among the people.

2 Sing unto him, sing Psalms unto him: talk ye of all his wondrous works.

3 Glory ye in his holy name: let the heart of them rejoice that seek the LORD.

4 Seek the LORD, and his strength: seek his face evermore.

5 Remember his marvellous works that he hath done; his wonders, and the judgments of his mouth;

6 O ye seed of Abraham his servant, ye children of Jacob his chosen.

7 He *is* the LORD our God: his judgments *are* in all the earth.

1. " *O give thanks unto the Lord.*" Jehovah is the author of all our benefits, therefore let him have all our gratitude. " *Call upon his name,*" or call him by his name; proclaim his titles and fill the world with his renown. " *Make known his deeds among the people,*" or among the nations. Let the heathen hear of our God, that they may forsake their idols and learn to worship him. The removal of the ark was a fit occasion for proclaiming aloud the glories of the Great King, and for publishing to all mankind the greatness of his doings, for it had a history in connection with the nations which it was well for them to remember with reverence. The rest of the Psalm is a sermon, of which these first verses constitute the text.

2. " *Sing unto him.*" Bring your best thoughts and express them in the best language to the sweetest sounds. Take care that your singing is " unto him," and not merely for the sake of the music or to delight the ears of others. Singing is so delightful an exercise that it is a pity so much of it should be wasted upon trifles or worse than trifles. O ye who can emulate the nightingale, and almost rival the angels, we do most earnestly pray that your hearts may be renewed that so your floods of melody may be poured out at your Maker's and Redeemer's feet. " *Talk ye of all his wondrous works.*" Men love to speak of marvels, and others are generally glad to hear of surprising things; surely the believer in the living God has before him the most amazing series of wonders ever heard of or imagined, his themes are inex-

haustible and they are such as should hold men spellbound. We ought to have more of this " talk " : no one would be blamed as a Mr. Talkative if this were his constant theme. Talk ye, all of you : you all know something by experience of the marvellous loving-kindness of the Lord—" talk ye." In this way, by all dwelling on this blessed subject, " all " his wondrous works will be published. One cannot do it, nor ten thousand times ten thousand, but if all speak to the Lord's honour, they will at least come nearer to accomplishing the deed. We ought to have a wide range when conversing upon the Lord's doings, and should not shut our eyes to any part of them. Talk ye of his wondrous works in creation and in grace, in judgment and in mercy, in providential interpositions and in spiritual comfortings ; leave out none, or it will be to your damage. Obedience to this verse will give every sanctified tongue some work to do : the trained musicians can sing, and the commoner voices can talk, and in both ways the Lord will receive a measure of the thanks due to him, and his deeds will be made known among the people.

3. " *Glory ye in his holy name.*" Make it a matter of joy that you have such a God. His character and attributes are such as will never make you blush to call him your God. Idolaters may well be ashamed of the actions attributed to their fancied deities, their names are foul with lust and red with blood, but Jehovah is wholly glorious ; every deed of his will bear the strictest scrutiny ; his name is holy, his character is holy, his law is holy, his government is holy, his influence is holy. In all this we may make our boast, nor can any deny our right to do so. " *Let the heart of them rejoice that seek the Lord.*" If they have not yet found him so fully as they desire, yet even to be allowed and enabled to seek after such a God is cause for gladness. To worship the Lord and seek his kingdom and righteousness is the sure way to happiness, and indeed there is no other. True seekers throw their hearts into the engagement, hence their hearts receive joy ; according to the text they have a permit to rejoice and they have the promise that they shall do so. How gladsome all these sentences are ! Where can men's ears be when they talk of the gloom of Psalm-singing ? What worldly songs are fuller of real mirth ? One hears the sound of the timbrel and the harp in every verse. Even seekers find bliss in the name of the Lord Jesus, but as for the finders, we may say with the poet,

" And those who find thee find a bliss,
Nor tongue nor pen can show :
The love of Jesus what it is,
None but his loved ones know."

4. " *Seek the Lord and his strength.*" Put yourselves under his protection. Regard him not as a puny God, but look unto his omnipotence, and seek to know the power of his grace. We all need strength ; let us look to the strong One for it. We need infinite power to bear us safely to our eternal resting-place, let us look to the Almighty Jehovah for it. " *Seek his face evermore.*" Seek, seek, seek, we have the word three times, and though the words differ in the Hebrew, the sense is the same. It must be a blessed thing to *seek*, or we should not be thus stirred up to do so. To seek his face is to desire his presence, his smile, his favour consciously enjoyed. First we seek *him*, then his *strength*, and then his *face ;* from the personal reverence, we pass on to the imparted power, and then to the conscious favour. This seeking must never cease—the more we know the more we must seek to know. Finding him, we must " our minds inflame to seek him more and more." He seeks spiritual worshippers, and spiritual worshippers seek him ; they are therefore sure to meet face to face ere long.

5. " *Remember his marvellous works that he hath done.*" Memory is never better employed than upon such topics. Alas, we are far more ready to recollect foolish and evil things than to retain in our minds the glorious deeds of Jehovah. If we would keep these in remembrance our faith would be stronger, our gratitude warmer, our devotion more fervent, and our love more intense. Shame upon us that we should let slip what it would seem impossible to forget. We ought to need no exhortation to remember such wonders, especially as he has wrought them all on the behalf of his people. " *His wonders, and the judgments of his mouth* "—these also should be had in memory. The judgments of his mouth are as memorable as the marvels of his hand. God had but to speak and the enemies of his people were sorely afflicted ; his threats were not mere words, but smote his adversaries terribly. As the Word of God is the salvation of his saints, so is it the destruction of the ungodly : out of his mouth goeth a two-edged sword with which he will slay the wicked.

6. "*O ye seed of Abraham his servant, ye children of Jacob his chosen.*" Should all the world forget, ye are bound to remember. Your father Abraham saw his wonders and judgments upon Sodom, and upon the kings who came from far, and Jacob also saw the Lord's marvellous works in visiting the nations with famine, yet providing for his chosen a choice inheritance in a goodly land ; therefore let the children praise their father's God. The Israelites were the Lord's elect nation, and they were bound to imitate their progenitor, who was the Lord's faithful servant and walked before him in holy faith : the seed of Abraham should not be unbelieving, nor should the children of so true a servant become rebels. As we read this pointed appeal to the chosen seed we should recognise the special claims which the Lord has upon ourselves, since we too have been favoured above all others. Election is not a couch for ease, but an argument for seven-fold diligence. If God has set his choice upon us, let us aim to be choice men.

7. "*He is the Lord our God.*" Blessed be his name. Jehovah condescends to be *our* God. This sentence contains a greater wealth of meaning than all the eloquence of orators can compass, and there is more joy in it than in all the sonnets of them that make merry. "*His judgments are in all the earth,*" or *in all the land,* for the whole of the country was instructed by his law, ruled by his statutes, and protected by his authority. What a joy it is that our God is never absent from us, he is never non-resident, never an absentee ruler, his judgments are in all the places in which we dwell. If the second clause of this verse refers to the whole world, it is very beautiful to see the speciality of Israel's election united with the universality of Jehovah's reign. Not alone to the one nation did the Lord reveal himself, but his glory flashed around the globe. It is wonderful that the Jewish people should have become so exclusive, and have so utterly lost the missionary spirit, for their sacred literature is full of the broad and generous sympathies which are so consistent with the worship of "the God of the whole earth." Nor is it less painful to observe that among a certain class of believers in God's election of grace there lingers a hard exclusive spirit, fatal to compassion and zeal. It would be well for these also to remember that their Redeemer is "the Saviour of all men, specially of them that believe."

8 He hath remembered his covenant for ever, the word *which* he commanded to a thousand generations.

9 Which *covenant* he made with Abraham, and his oath unto Isaac ;

10 And confirmed the same unto Jacob for a law, *and* to Israel *for* an everlasting covenant :

11 Saying, Unto thee will I give the land of Canaan, the lot of your inheritance :

12 When they were *but* a few men in number ; yea, very few, and strangers in it.

13 When they went from one nation to another, from *one* kingdom to another people ;

14 He suffered no man to do them wrong : yea, he reproved kings for their sakes ;

15 *Saying*, Touch not mine anointed, and do my prophets no harm.

8. "*He hath remembered his covenant for ever.*" Here is the basis of all his dealings with his people : he had entered into covenant with them in their father Abraham, and to this covenant he remained faithful. The exhortation to *remember* (in verse 5) receives great force from the fact that God has remembered. If the Lord has his promise in memory, surely we ought not to forget the wonderful manner in which he keeps it. To us it should be matter for deepest joy that never in any instance has the Lord been unmindful of his covenant engagements, nor will he be so world without end. O that we were as mindful of them as he is. "*The word which he commanded to a thousand generations.*" This is only an amplification of the former statement, and serves to set before us the immutable fidelity of the Lord during the changing generations of men. His judgments are threatened upon the third and fourth generations of them that hate him, but his love runs on for ever, even to "a thousand generations." His promise is here said to be *commanded*, or vested

with all the authority of a law. It is proclamation from a sovereign, the *firman* of an Emperor, whose laws shall stand fast in every jot and tittle though heaven and earth shall pass away. Therefore let us give thanks unto the Lord and talk of all his wondrous works, so wonderful for their faithfulness and truth.

9. " *Which covenant he made with Abraham.*" When the victims were divided and the burning lamp passed between the pieces (Gen. xv.) then the Lord made, or ratified, the covenant with the patriarch. This was a solemn deed, performed not without blood, and the cutting in pieces of the sacrifice : it points us to the greater covenant which in Christ Jesus is signed, sealed, and ratified, that it may stand fast for ever and ever. " *And his oath unto Isaac.*" Isaac did not in vision see the solemn making of the covenant, but the Lord renewed unto him his oath (Gen. xxvi. 2—5). This was enough for him, and must have established his faith in the Most High. We have the privilege of seeing in our Lord Jesus both the sacrificial seal, and the eternal oath of God, by which every promise of the covenant is made yea and amen to all the chosen seed.

10. " *And confirmed the same unto Jacob for a law.*" Jacob in his wondrous dream (Gen. xxviii. 10—15) received a pledge that the Lord's mode of procedure with him would be in accordance with covenant relations : for said Jehovah, " I will not leave thee till I have done that which I have spoken to thee of." Thus, if we may so speak with all reverence, the covenant became a law unto the Lord himself by which he bound himself to act. O matchless condescension, that the most free and sovereign Lord should put himself under covenant bonds to his chosen, and make a law for himself, though he is above all law. " *And to Israel for an everlasting covenant.*" When he changed Jacob's name he did not change his covenant, but it is written, " he blessed him there " (Gen. xxxii. 29), and it was with the old blessing, according to the unchangeable word of abiding grace.

11, 12. " *Saying, Unto thee will I give the land of Canaan, the lot of your inheritance.*" This repetition of the great covenant promise is recorded in Gen. xxxv. 9—12 in connection with the change of Jacob's name, and very soon after that slaughter of the Shechemites, which had put the patriarch into such great alarm and caused him to use language almost identical with that of the next verse. " *When they were but a few men in number ; yea, very few, and strangers in it.*" Jacob said to Simeon and Levi, " Ye have troubled me to make me to stink among the inhabitants of the land, among the Canaanites and the Perizzites : and I being few in number, they shall gather themselves together against me, and slay me, and I shall be destroyed, and my house." Thus the fears of the man of God declared themselves, and they were reasonable if we look only at the circumstances in which he was placed, but they are soon seen to be groundless when we remember that the covenant promise, which guaranteed the possession of the land, necessarily implied the preservation of the race to whom the promise was made. We often fear where no fear is.

The blessings promised to the seed of Abraham were not dependent upon the number of his descendants, or their position in this world. The covenant was made with one man, and consequently the number could never be less, and that one man was not the owner of a foot of soil in all the land, save only a cave in which to bury his dead, and therefore his seed could not have less inheritance than he. The smallness of a church, and the poverty of its members, are no barriers to the divine blessing, if it be sought earnestly by pleading the promise. Were not the apostles few, and the disciples feeble, when the good work began ? Neither because we are strangers and foreigners here below, as our fathers were, are we in any the more danger : we are like sheep in the midst of wolves, but the wolves cannot hurt us, for our shepherd is near.

13. " *When they went from one nation to another, from one kingdom to another people.*" Migrating as the patriarchs did from the region of one tribe to the country of another they were singularly preserved. The little wandering family might have been cut off root and branch had not a special mandate been issued from the throne for their protection. It was not the gentleness of their neighbours which screened them ; they were hedged about by the mysterious guardianship of heaven. Whether in Egypt, or in Philistia, or in Canaan, the heirs of the promises, dwelling in their tents, were always secure.

14. " *He suffered no man to do them wrong.*" Men cannot wrong us unless he suffers them to do so; the greatest of them must wait his permission before they can place a finger upon us. The wicked would devour us if they could, but they cannot even cheat us of a farthing without divine sufferance. " *Yea, he reproved kings for*

their sakes." Pharaoh and Abimelech must both be made to respect the singular strangers who had come to sojourn in their land, the greatest kings are very second-rate persons with God in comparison with his chosen servants.

15. *" Saying, touch not mine anointed, and do my prophets no harm."* Abraham and his seed were in the midst of the world a generation of priests anointed to present sacrifice unto the Most High God ; since to them the oracles were committed, they were also the prophets of mankind ; and they were kings too—a royal priesthood ; hence they had received a threefold anointing. Their holy offices surrounded them with a sacredness which rendered it sacrilege to molest them. The Lord was pleased to impress the wild tribes of Canaan with a respectful awe of the pious strangers who had come to abide with them, so that they came not near them to do them ill. The words here mentioned may not have been actually spoken, but the impression of awe which fell upon the nations is thus poetically described. God will not have those touched who have been set apart unto himself. He calls them his own, saying, *" Mine* anointed ; "* he declares that he has *" anointed "* them to be prophets, priests, and kings unto himself, and yet again he claims them as *his* prophets—" Do *my prophets* no harm." All through the many years in which the three great fathers dwelt in Canaan no man was able to injure them : they were not able to defend themselves by force of arms, but the eternal God was their refuge. Even so at this present time the remnant according to the election of grace cannot be destroyed, nay, nor so much as touched, without the divine consent. Against the church of Christ the gates of hell cannot prevail. In all this we see reasons for giving thanks unto the Lord, and proclaiming his name according to the exhortation of the first verse of the Psalm. Here ends the portion which was sung at the moving of the ark : its fitness to be used for such a purpose is very manifest, for the ark was the symbol both of the covenant and of that mystic dwelling of God with Israel which was at once her glory and her defence. None could touch the Lord's peculiar ones, for the Lord was among them, flaming forth in majesty between the cherubims.

16 Moreover he called for a famine upon the land : he brake the whole staff of bread.

17 He sent a man before them, *even* Joseph, *who* was sold for a servant :

18 Whose feet they hurt with fetters : he was laid in iron :

19 Until the time that his word came : the word of the LORD tried him.

20 The king sent and loosed him ; *even* the ruler of the people, and let him go free.

21 He made him lord of his house, and ruler of all his substance :

22 To bind his princes at his pleasure ; and teach his senators wisdom.

23 Israel also came into Egypt ; and Jacob sojourned in the land of Ham.

The presence of God having remained with his chosen ones while they sojourned in Canaan, it did not desert them when they were called to go down into Egypt. They did not go there of their own choice, but under divine direction, and hence the Lord prepared their way and prospered them until he saw fit to conduct them again to the land of promise.

16. *" Moreover he called for a famine upon the land."* He had only to call for it as a man calls for his servant, and it came at once. How grateful ought we to be that he does not often call in that terrible servant of his, so meagre and gaunt, and grim, so pitiless to the women and the children, so bitter to the strong men, who utterly fail before it. *" He brake the whole staff of bread."* Man's feeble life cannot stand without its staff—if bread fail him he fails. As a cripple with a broken staff falls to the ground, so does man when bread no longer sustains him. To God it is as easy to make a famine as to break a staff. He could make that famine universal, too, so that all countries should be in like case : then would the race of man fall indeed, and its staff would be broken for ever. There is this sweet comfort in the matter, that the Lord has wise ends to serve even by famine : he meant his people to go down into Egypt, and the scarcity of food was his method of leading them there, for " they heard that there was corn in Egypt."

17. *" He sent a man before them, even Joseph."* He was the advance guard and pioneer for the whole clan. His brethren sold him, but God sent him. Where the hand of the wicked is visible God's hand may be invisibly at work, overruling

their malice. No one was more of *a man*, or more fit to lead the van than Joseph :
an interpreter of dreams was wanted, and his brethren had said of him, " Behold,
this dreamer cometh." " *Who was sold for a servant*," or rather for a slave. Joseph's
journey into Egypt was not so costly as Jonah's voyage when he paid his own fare :
his free passage was provided by the Midianites, who also secured his introduction
to a great officer of state by handing him over as a slave. His way to a position
in which he could feed his family lay through the pit, the slaver's caravan, the slave
market and the prison, and who shall deny but what it was the right way, the surest
way, the wisest way, and perhaps the shortest way. Yet assuredly it seemed not so. Were
we to send a man on such an errand we should furnish him with money—Joseph goes as
a pauper ; we should clothe him with authority—Joseph goes as a slave ; we should
leave him at full liberty—Joseph is a bondman : yet money would have been of little
use when corn was so dear, authority would have been irritating rather than influential with Pharaoh, and freedom might not have thrown Joseph into connection
with Pharaoh's captain and his other servants, and so the knowledge of his skill
in interpretation might not have reached the monarch's ear. God's way is *the* way.
Our Lord's path to his mediatorial throne ran by the cross of Calvary ; our road to
glory runs by the rivers of grief.

18. " *Whose feet they hurt with fetters.*"   From this we learn a little more of
Joseph's sufferings than we find in the book of Genesis : inspiration had not ceased,
and David was as accurate an historian as Moses, for the same Spirit guided his pen.
" *He was laid in iron*," or " into iron came his soul." The prayer book version,
" the iron entered into his soul," is ungrammatical, but probably expresses much the
same truth. His fetters hurt his mind as well as his body, and well did Jacob say,
" The archers shot at him, and sorely grieved him." Under the cruelly false accusation, which he could not disprove, his mind was, as it were, belted and bolted around
with iron, and had not the Lord been with him he might have sunk under his sufferings. In all this, and a thousand things besides, he was an admirable type of him
who in the highest sense is " the Shepherd, the stone of Israel." The iron fetters
were preparing him to wear chains of gold, and making his feet ready to stand on
high places. It is even so with all the Lord's afflicted ones, they too shall one day
step from their prisons to their thrones.

19. " *Until the time that his word came.*" God has his times, and his children must
wait till his " until " is fulfilled. Joseph was tried as in a furnace, until the Lord's
assaying work was fully accomplished. The word of the chief butler was nothing,
he had to wait until God's word came, and meanwhile " *the word of the Lord tried
him.*" He believed the promise, but his faith was sorely exercised. A delayed
blessing tests men, and proves their metal, whether their faith is of that precious
kind which can endure the fire. Of many a choice promise we may say with Daniel
" the thing was true, but the time appointed was long." If the vision tarry it is
good to wait for it with patience. There is a trying word and a delivering word,
and we must bear the one till the other comes to us. How meekly Joseph endured
his afflictions, and with what fortitude he looked forward to the clearing of his
slandered character we may readily imagine : it will be better still if under similar
trials we are able to imitate him, and come forth from the furnace as thoroughly
purified as he was, and as well prepared to bear the yet harder ordeal of honour
and power.

20. " *The king sent and loosed him.*" He was thrust into the roundhouse by
an officer, but he was released by the monarch himself. " *Even the ruler of the people,
and let him go free.*" The tide had turned, so that Egypt's haughty potentate gave
him a call from the prison to the palace. He had interpreted the dreams of captives,
himself a captive ; he must now interpret for a ruler and become a ruler himself.
When God means to enlarge his prisoners, kings become his turnkeys.

21. " *He made him lord of his house.*" Reserving no power, but saying " only
in the throne will I be greater than thou." The servitor of slaves becomes lord
over nobles. How soon the Lord lifteth his chosen from the dunghill to set them
among princes. " *And ruler of all his substance.*" He empowered him to manage
the storing of the seven plenteous harvests, and to dispense the provisions in the
coming days of scarcity. All the treasures of Egypt were under his lock and key,
yea, the granaries of the world were sealed or opened at his bidding. Thus was he
in the best conceivable position for preserving alive the house of Israel with whom
the covenant was made. As our Lord was himself secured in Egypt from Herod's
enmity, so, ages before, the redeemed race found an equally available shelter in the

hour of need. God has always a refuge for his saints, and if the whole earth could not afford them sanctuary, the Lord himself would be their dwelling-place, and take them up to lie in his own bosom. We are always sure to be fed if all the world should starve. It is delightful to think of our greater Joseph ruling the nations for the good of his own household, and it becomes us to abide in quiet confidence in every political disaster, since Jesus is on the throne of providence, King of kings and Lord of lords, and will be so till this dispensation ends.

22. " *To bind his princes at his pleasure.*" He who was bound obtains authority to bind. He is no longer kept in prison, but keeps all the prisons, and casts into them the greatest nobles when justice demands it. " *And teach his senators wisdom.*" The heads of the various peoples, the elders of the nations, learned from him the science of government, the art of providing for the people. Joseph was a great instructor in political economy, and we doubt not that he mingled with it the purest morals, the most upright jurisprudence, and something of that divine wisdom without which the most able senators remain in darkness. The king's authority made him absolute both in the executive and in the legislative courts, and the Lord instructed him to use his power and discretion. What responsibilities and honours loaded the man who had been rejected by his brothers, and sold for twenty pieces of silver ! What glories crown the head of that greater one who was " separated from his brethren."

23. " *Israel also came into Egypt.*" The aged patriarch came, and with him that increasing company which bore his name. He was hard to bring there. Perhaps nothing short of the hope of seeing Joseph could have drawn him to take so long a journey from the tombs of his forefathers ; but the divine will was accomplished and the church of God was removed into an enemy's country, where for a while it was nourished. " *And Jacob sojourned in the land of Ham.*" Shem the blessed came to lodge awhile with Ham the accursed : the dove was in the vulture's nest. God so willed it for a time, and therefore it was safe and right : still it was only a sojourn, not a settlement. The fairest Goshen in Egypt was not the covenant blessing, neither did the Lord mean his people to think it so ; even so to us " earth is our lodge," but only our lodge, for heaven is our home. When we are best housed we ought still to remember that here we have no continuing city. It were ill news for us if we were doomed to reside in Egypt for ever, for all its riches are not worthy to be compared with the reproach of Christ.

Thus the song rehearsed the removals of the Lord's people, and was a most fit accompaniment to the upbearing of the ark, as the priests carried it into the city of David, where the Lord had appointed it a resting-place.

24 And he increased his people greatly ; and made them stronger than their enemies.

25 He turned their heart to hate his people, to deal subtilly with his servants.

26 He sent Moses his servant ; *and* Aaron whom he had chosen.

27 They shewed his signs among them, and wonders in the land of Ham.

28 He sent darkness, and made it dark ; and they rebelled not against his word.

29 He turned their waters into blood, and slew their fish.

30 Their land brought forth frogs in abundance, in the chambers of their kings.

31 He spake, and there came divers sorts of flies, *and* lice in all their coasts.

32 He gave them hail for rain, *and* flaming fire in their land.

33 He smote their vines also and their fig-trees ; and brake the trees of their coasts.

34 He spake, and the locusts came, and caterpillars, and that without number,

35 And did eat up all the herbs in their land, and devoured the fruit of their ground.

36 He smote also all the firstborn in their land, the chief of all their strength.

37 He brought them forth also with silver and gold : and *there was* not one feeble *person* among their tribes.

38 Egypt was glad when they departed : for the fear of them fell upon them.

24. " *And he increased his people greatly.*" In Goshen they seem to have increased rapidly from the first, and this excited the fears of the Egyptians, so that they tried to retard their increase by oppression, but the Lord continued to bless them, " *And make them stronger than their enemies.*" Both in physical strength and in numbers they threatened to become the more powerful race. Nor was this growth of the nation impeded by tyrannical measures, but the very reverse took place, thus giving an early instance of what has since become a proverb in the church —" the more they oppressed them the more they multiplied." It is idle to contend either with God or his people.

25. " *He turned their heart to hate his people.*" It was his goodness to Israel which called forth the ill-will of the Egyptian court, and so far the Lord caused it, and moreover he made use of this feeling to lead on to the discomfort of his people, and so to their readiness to leave the land to which they had evidently become greatly attached. Thus far but no further did the Lord turn the hearts of the Egyptians. God cannot in any sense be the author of sin so far as to be morally responsible for its existence, but it often happens through the evil which is inherent in human nature that the acts of the Lord arouse the ill-feelings of ungodly men. Is the sun to be blamed because while it softens wax it hardens clay ? Is the orb of day to be accused of creating the foul exhalations which are drawn by its warmth from the pestilential marsh ? The sun causes the reek of the dunghill only in a certain sense, had it been a bed of flowers his beams would have called forth fragrance. The evil is in men, and the honour of turning it to good and useful purposes is with the Lord. Hatred is often allied with cunning, and so in the case of the Egyptians, they began " *to deal subtilly with his servants.*" They treated them in a fraudulent manner, they reduced them to bondage by their exactions, they secretly concerted the destruction of their male children, and at length openly ordained that cruel measure, and all with the view of checking their increase, lest in time of war they should side with invaders in order to obtain their liberty. Surely the depths of Satanic policy were here reached, but vain was the cunning of man against the chosen seed.

26. " *He sent Moses his servant ; and Aaron whom he had chosen.*" When the oppression was at the worst, Moses came. For the second time we have here the expression, " he sent"; he who sent Joseph sent also Moses and his eloquent brother. The Lord had the men in readiness and all he had to do was to commission them and thrust them forward. They were two, for mutual comfort and strength, even as the apostles and the seventy in our Lord's day were sent forth two and two. The men differed, and so the one became the supplement of the other, and together they were able to accomplish far more than if they had been exactly alike : the main point was that they were both *sent*, and hence both clothed with divine might.

27. " *They shewed his signs among them, and wonders in the land of Ham.*" The miracles which were wrought by Moses were the Lord's, not his own ; hence they are here called " *his* signs," as being the marks of Jehovah's presence and power. The plagues were " words of his signs " (see margin), that is to say, they were speaking marvels, which testified more plainly than words to the omnipotence of Jehovah, to his determination to be obeyed, to his anger at the obstinacy of Pharaoh. Never were discourses more plain, pointed, personal, or powerful, and yet it took ten of them to accomplish the end designed. In the preaching of the gospel there are words, and signs, and wonders, and these leave men without excuse for their impenitence ; to have the kingdom of God come nigh unto them, and yet to remain rebellious is the unhappy sin of obstinate spirits. Those are wonders of sin who see wonders of grace, and yet are unaffected by them : bad as he was, Pharaoh had not this guilt, for the prodigies which he beheld were marvels of judgment and not of mercy.

28. " *He sent darkness, and made it dark.*" It was no natural or common darkness to be accounted for by the blinding dust of the simoon, it was beyond all precedent and out of the range of ordinary events. It was a horrible palpable obscurity which men felt clinging about them as though it were a robe of death. It was a thick darkness, a total darkness, a darkness which lasted three days, a darkness in which no

one dared to stir. What a condition to be in ! This plague is first mentioned, though it is not first in order, because it fitly describes all the period of the plagues : the land was in the darkness of sorrow, and in the darkness of sin all the time. If we shudder as we think of that long and terrible gloom, let us reflect upon the gross darkness which still covers heathen lands as the result of sin, for it is one of the chief plagues which iniquity creates for itself. May the day soon come when the people which sit in darkness shall see a great light. *" And they rebelled not against his word."* Moses and Aaron did as they were bidden, and during the darkness the Egyptians were so cowed that even when it cleared away they were anxious for Israel to be gone, and had it not been for the pride of Pharaoh they would have rejoiced to speed them on their journey there and then. God can force men to obey, and even make the stoutest heart eager to pay respect to his will, for fear his plagues should be multiplied. Possibly, however, the sentence before us neither refers to Moses nor the Egyptians, but to the plagues which came at the Lord's bidding. The darkness, the hail, the frogs, the murrain, were all so many obedient servants of the great Lord of all.

29. *" He turned their waters into blood, and slew their fish."* So that the plague was not a mere colouring of the water with red earth, as some suppose, but the river was offensive and fatal to the fish. The beloved Nile and other streams were all equally tainted and ensanguined. Their commonest mercy became their greatest curse. Water is one of the greatest blessings, and the more plentiful it is the better, but blood is a hideous sight to look upon, and to see rivers and pools of it is frightful indeed. Fish in Egypt furnished a large part of the food supply, and it was no small affliction to see them floating dead and white upon a stream of crimson. The hand of the Lord thus smote them where all classes of the people would become aware of it and suffer from it.

30. *" Their land brought forth frogs in abundance."* If fish could not live frogs might, yea, they multiplied both on land and in the water till they swarmed beyond all count. *" In the chambers of their kings."* They penetrated the choicest rooms of the palace, and were found upon the couches of state. The Lord called for them and they marched forth. Obnoxious and even loathsome their multitudes became, but there was no resisting them ; they seemed to spring out of the ground, the very land brought them forth. Their universal presence must have inspired horror and disgust which would cause sickness and make life a burden ; their swarming even in the king's own chambers was a rebuke to his pride, which his pride must have felt. Kings are no more than other men with God, nay less than others when they are first in rebellion ; if the frogs had abounded elsewhere, but had been kept out of his select apartments, the monarch would have cared little, for he was a heartless being, but God took care that there should be a special horde of the invaders for the palace ; they were more than ordinarily abundant in the chambers of their kings.

31. *" He spake."* See the power of the divine word. He had only to say it and it was done : *" and there came divers sorts of flies."* Insects of various annoying kinds came up in infinite hordes, a mixture of biting, stinging, buzzing gnats, mosquitos, flies, beetles, and other vermin such as make men's flesh their prey, the place of deposit for their eggs, and the seat of peculiar torments. *" And lice in all their coasts."* These unutterably loathsome forms of life were as the dust of the ground, and covered their persons, their garments, and all they ate. Nothing is too small to master man when God commands it to assail him. The sons of Ham had despised the Israelites and now they were made to loathe themselves. The meanest beggars were more approachable than the proud Egyptians ; they were reduced to the meanest condition of filthiness, and the most painful state of irritation. What armies the Lord can send forth when once his right arm is bared for war ! And what scorn he pours on proud nations when he fights them, not with angels, but with lice ! Pharaoh had little left to be proud of when his own person was invaded by filthy parasites. It was a slap in the face which ought to have humbled his heart, but, alas, man, when he is altogether polluted, still maintains his self-conceit, and when he is the most disgusting object in the universe he still vaunts himself. Surely pride is moral madness.

32. *" He gave them hail for rain."* They seldom had rain, but now the showers assumed the form of heavy, destructive hail-storms, and being accompanied with a hurricane and thunderstorm, they were overwhelming, terrible, and destructive. *" And flaming fire in their land."* The lightning was peculiarly vivid, and seemed to run along upon the ground, or fall in fiery flakes. Thus all the fruit of the trees and the harvests of the fields were either broken to pieces or burned on the spot,

and universal fear bowed the hearts of men to the dust. No phenomena are more appalling to the most of mankind than those which attend a thunderstorm; even the most audacious blasphemers quail when the dread artillery of heaven opens fire upon the earth.

33. " *He smote their vines also and their fig trees.*" So that all hope of gathering their best fruits was gone, and the trees were injured for future bearing. All the crops were destroyed, and these are mentioned as being the more prominent forms of their produce, used by them both at festivals and in common meals. " *And brake the trees of their coasts.*" From end to end of Egypt the trees were battered and broken by the terrible hailstorm. God is in earnest when he deals with proud spirits, he will either end them or mend them.

34, 35. " *He spake, and the locusts came, and caterpillars, and that without number.*" One word from the Captain and the armies leaped forward. The expression is very striking, and sets forth the immediate result of the divine word. The caterpillar is called *the licker*, because it seems to lick up every green thing as in a moment. Perhaps the caterpillar here meant is still the locust in another form. That locusts swarm in countless armies is a fact of ordinary observation, and the case would be worse on this occasion. We have ourselves ridden for miles through armies of locusts, and we have seen with our own eyes how completely they devour every green thing. The description is not strained when we read, " *And did eat up all the herbs in their land, and devoured the fruit of their ground.*" Nothing escapes these ravenous creatures, they even climb the trees to reach any remnant of foliage which may survive. Commissioned as these were by God, we may be sure they would do their work thoroughly, and leave behind them nothing but a desolate wilderness.

36. " *He smote also all the firstborn in their land, the chief of all their strength.*" Now came the master blow. The Lord spoke before, but now he smites; before he only smote vines, but now he strikes men themselves. The glory of the household dies in a single night, the prime and pick of the nation are cut off, the flower of the troops, the heirs of the rich, and the hopes of the poor all die at midnight. Now the target was struck in the centre, there was no confronting this plague. Pharaoh feels it as much as the woman-slave at the mill; he had smitten Israel, the Lord's firstborn, and the Lord repaid him to his face. What a cry went up throughout the land of Egypt when every house wailed its firstborn at the dead of night! O Jehovah, thou didst triumph in that hour, and with an outstretched arm didst thou deliver thy people.

37. " *He brought them forth also with silver and gold.*" This they asked of the Egyptians, perhaps even demanded, and well they might, for they had been robbed and spoiled for many a day, and it was not meet that they should go forth empty handed. Glad were the Egyptians to hand over their jewels to propitiate a people who had such a terrible friend above; they needed no undue pressure, they feared them too much to deny them their requests. The Israelites were compelled to leave their houses and lands behind them, and it was but justice that they should be able to turn these into portable property. " *And there was not one feeble person among their tribes* "—a great marvel indeed. The number of their army was very great and yet there was not one in hospital, not one carried in an ambulance, or limping in the rear. Poverty and oppression had not enfeebled them. Jehovah Rophi had healed them; they carried none of the diseases of Egypt with them, and felt none of the exhaustion which sore bondage produces. When God calls his people to a long journey he fits them for it; in the pilgrimage of life our strength shall be equal to our day. See the contrast between Egypt and Israel—in Egypt one dead in every house, and among the Israelites not one so much as limping.

38. " *Egypt was glad when they departed,*" which would not have been the case had the gold and silver been borrowed by the Israelites, for men do not like to see borrowers carry their goods into a far country. The awe of God was on Egypt, and they feared his people and were glad to pay them to be gone. What a change from the time when the sons of Jacob were the drudges of the land, the offscouring of all things, the brickmakers whose toil was only requited by the lash or the stick. Now they were reverenced as prophets and priests; " *for the fear of them fell upon them,*" the people proceeded even to a superstitious terror of them. Thus with cheers and good wishes their former taskmasters sent them on their way: Pharaoh was foiled and the chosen people were once more on the move, journeying to the place which the Lord had given to them by a covenant of salt. " O give thanks unto Jehovah; call upon his name, make known his deeds among the people."

39 He spread a cloud for a covering ; and fire to give light in the night.

40 *The people* asked, and he brought quails, and satisfied them with the bread of heaven.

41 He opened the rock, and the waters gushed out ; they ran in the dry places *like* a river.

42 For he remembered his holy promise, *and* Abraham his servant.

43 And he brought forth his people with joy, *and* his chosen with gladness :

44 And gave them the lands of the heathen : and they inherited the labour of the people ;

45 That they might observe his statutes, and keep his laws. Praise ye the LORD.

39. "*He spread a cloud for a covering.*" Never people were so favoured. What would not travellers in the desert now give for such a canopy ? The sun could not scorch them with its burning ray ; their whole camp was screened like a king in his pavilion. Nothing seemed to be too good for God to give his chosen nation, their comfort was studied in every way. "*And fire to give light in the night.*" While cities were swathed in darkness, their town of tents enjoyed a light which modern art with all its appliances cannot equal. God himself was their sun and shield, their glory and their defence. Could they be unbelieving while so graciously shaded, or rebellious while they walked at midnight in such a light ? Alas, the tale of *their* sin is as extraordinary as this story of *his* love ; but this Psalm selects the happier theme and dwells only upon covenant love and faithfulness. O give thanks unto the Lord for he is good. We, too, have found the Lord all this to us, for he has been our sun and shield, and has preserved us alike from the perils of joys and the evils of grief ;

> "He hath been my joy in woe,
> Cheered my heart when it was low ;
> And with warnings softly sad
> Calm'd my heart when it was glad."

So has the promise been fulfilled to us, "the sun shall not hurt thee by day, nor the moon by night."

40. "*The people asked.*" But how badly, how wickedly ! And yet his grace forgave the sin of their murmuring and heard its meaning : or perhaps we may consider that while the multitude murmured there were a few, who were really gracious people, who prayed, and therefore the blessing came. "*He brought quails, and satisfied them with the bread of heaven.*" He gave them what they asked amiss as well as what was good for them, mingling judgment with goodness, for their discipline. The quails were more a curse than a blessing in the end, because of their greed and lust, but in themselves they were a peculiar indulgence, and favour : it was their own fault that the dainty meat brought death with it. As for the manna it was unmingled good to them, and really satisfied them, which the quails never did. It was bread *from* heaven, and the bread *of* heaven, sent *by* heaven ; it was a pity that they were not led to look up to heaven whence it came, and fear and love the God who out of heaven rained it upon them. Thus they were housed beneath the Lord's canopy and fed with food from his own table ; never people were so lodged and boarded. O house of Israel, praise ye the Lord.

41. "*He opened the rock, and the waters gushed out.*" With Moses' rod and his own word he cleft the rock in the desert, and forth leaped abundant floods for their drinking where they had feared to die of thirst. From most unlikely sources the all-sufficient God can supply his people's needs ; hard rocks become springing fountains at the Lord's command. "*They ran in the dry places like a river*" : so that those at a distance from the rock could stoop down and refresh themselves, and the stream flowed on, so that in future journeyings they were supplied. The desert sand would naturally swallow up the streams, and yet it did not so, the refreshing river ran " in the dry places." We know that the rock set forth our Lord Jesus Christ, from whom there flows a fountain of living waters which shall never be exhausted till the last pilgrim has crossed the Jordan and entered Canaan.

42. "*For he remembered his holy promise, and Abraham his servant.*" Here is the secret reason for all this grace. The covenant and he for whose sake it was made are ever on the heart of the Most High. He remembered his people because he remembered his covenant. He could not violate that gracious compact for it was sacred to him,—" his holy promise." A holy God must keep his promise holy. In our case the Lord's eye is upon his beloved Son, and his engagements with him on our behalf, and this is the source and well-head of those innumerable favours which enrich us in all our wanderings through this life's wilderness.

43. " And he brought forth his people with joy, and his chosen with gladness." Up from the wilderness he led them, rejoicing over them himself and making them rejoice too. They were his people, his chosen, and hence in them he rejoiced, and upon them he showered his favours, that they might rejoice in him as their God, and their portion.

44. " And gave them the lands of the heathen." He drove out the Canaanites and allotted the lands to the tribes. They were called on to fight, but the Lord wrought so wonderfully that the conquest was not effected by their bow or spear—the Lord gave them the land. " And they inherited the labour of the people," they dwelt in houses which they had not built, and gathered fruit from vines and olives which they had not planted. They were not settled in a desert which needed to be reclaimed, but in a land fertile to a proverb, and cultivated carefully by its inhabitants. Like Adam, they were placed in a garden. This entrance into the goodly land was fitly celebrated when the ark was being moved to Zion.

45. " That they might observe his statutes, and keep his laws." This was the practical design of it all. The chosen nation was to be the conservator of truth, the exemplar of morality, the pattern of devotion : everything was so ordered as to place them in advantageous circumstances for fulfilling this trust. Theirs was a high calling and a glorious election. It involved great responsibilities, but it was in itself a distinguished blessing, and one for which the nation was bound to give thanks. Most justly then did the music close with the jubilant but solemn shout of HALLELUJAH. " Praise ye the Lord." If this history did not make Israel praise God, what would ?

EXPLANATORY NOTES AND QUAINT SAYINGS.

Whole Psalm.—This is the first of a series of " Confitemini Domino " Psalms, " O give thanks unto the Lord " (cv. 1 ; cvi. 1 ; cvii. 1 ; cxviii. 1 ; and cxxxvi. 1). —Christopher Wordsworth.

Whole Psalm.—The 105th Psalm is a meditation on the covenant as performed on the part of God, the 106th on the covenant as kept by Israel. They both dwell on the predestinating will of God, electing men to holiness and obedience, and the mode in which human sin opposes itself to that will, and yet cannot make it void.— Plain Commentary.

Verses 1—15.—The first fifteen verses were written at the bringing up of the Ark, 1 Chron. xvi. They tell that it is sovereign grace that ruleth over all—it is a sovereign God. Out of a fallen world he takes whom he pleases—individuals, families, nations. He chose Israel long ago, that they might be the objects of grace, and their land the theatre of its display. He will yet again return to Israel, when the days of his Kingdom of Glory draw near ; and Israel shall have a full share—the very fullest and richest—in his blessings, temporal and spiritual.—Andrew A. Bonar.

Verse 1.—" Call upon his name." The original meaning of this phrase is call (him) by his name, i.e., give him the descriptive title most expressive of his divine perfections ; or more specifically, call him by his name Jehovah, i.e., ascribe to him the attributes which it denotes, to wit, eternity and self-existence, together with that covenant relation to his people, which though not denoted by the name was constantly associated with it, and therefore necessarily suggested by it. The meaning of the next phrase is obscured, if not entirely concealed in the common version, " among the people." The plural form and sense of the original expression are essential to the writer's purpose, which is to glorify the God of Israel among the nations.—Joseph Addison Alexander.

Verse 1.—" Make known his deeds among the people." The people of God were not shut up in that narrow corner of the earth for the purpose of confining within their straitened territories the true knowledge and worship of God : but God wished that to be the fixed seat of the church, from which the sound of heavenly doctrine should go forth into all nations. Therefore he chose Canaan, which is interjected among the most powerful nations of the world, that from it as from a fountain might more easily issue the doctrine of God to the rest of the nations: as Isaiah says, " Out of Zion shall go forth the law."—*Mollerus.*

Verse 2.—" *Talk ye of all his wondrous works*," נִפְלְאֹתָיו *niphleothaiv,* " of his miracles." Who have so many of these to boast of as Christians ! Christianity is a tissue of miracles ; and every part of the work of grace on the soul is a miracle. Genuine Christian converts may talk of miracles from morning to night ; and they *should talk of them,* and recommend to others their miracle-working God and Saviour. —*Adam Clarke.*

Verse 2.—" *Sing*" . . . . " *talk,*" etc. Music and conversation are two things by which the mind of man receiveth much good, or a great deal of harm. They who make " Jehovah " and his " wondrous works " the subjects of both, enjoy a heaven upon earth. And they who do in reality love the Saviour, will always find themselves inclined to " *sing to him,*" and to " *talk of him.*"—*George Horne.*

Verse 2.—" *Sing Psalms.*" It is not sufficient to offer the empty vessel of our joy unto God, or our singing voice in musical tune only ; but also it is required that we fill our joyful voice with holy matter and good purpose, whereby God only may be reasonably praised : " Sing *Psalms* unto him."—*David Dickson.*

Verse 2.—" *Sing Psalms.*" Psalmody is the calm of the soul, the repose of the spirit, the arbiter of peace. It silences the wave, and conciliates the whirlwind of our passions, soothing the impetuous, tempering the unchaste. It is an engenderer of friendship, a healer of dissension, a reconciler of enemies. For who can longer count him his enemy, with whom to the throne of God he hath raised the strain ? Psalmody repels the demons, and lures the ministry of angels. It is a weapon of defence in nightly terrors and a respite from daily toil. To the infant it is a presiding genius ; to manhood a crown of glory ; a balm of comfort to the aged ; a congenial ornament to women.—*Basil.*

Verse 4.—" *Seek the Lord, and be strengthened* " ; so divers ancient versions read it. They that would be " strengthened in the inward man," must fetch in strength from God by faith and prayer. " *Seek his strength,*" and then seek his face ; for by his strength we hope to prevail with him for his favour, as Jacob did, Hosea xii. 3. " *Seek his face evermore,*" *i.e.,* seek to have his favour to eternity, and therefore continue seeking it to the end of the time of your probation. Seek it while you live in this world, and you shall have it while you live in the other world, and even there shall be for ever seeking it, in an infinite progression, and yet be for ever satisfied in it.—*Matthew Henry.*

Verse 4.—" *His strength.*" In classical language, his ægis, or protection, his ark, the symbol of the divine presence.—*John Mason Good.*

Verse 4.—" *Seek his face evermore.*" It is added " *evermore,*" lest they should imagine that they had performed their duty, if they assembled twice or three times in the year at the tabernacle, and observed the external rites according to the law. —*Mollerus.*

Verse 4.—" *Seek* . . . . *seek.*" None do seek the Lord so earnestly, but they have need of stirring up to seek him more earnestly ; neither have any attained to such a measure of communion with God, but they have need to seek for a further measure : therefore it is said, " *Seek the Lord, seek his strength, seek his face evermore.*" —*David Dickson.*

Verse 5.—" *Remember.*" How others may be affected I do not ask. For myself, I confess, that there is no care or sorrow, by which I am so severely harassed, as when I feel myself guilty of ingratitude to my most kind Lord. It not seldom appears to be a fault so inexplicable, that I am alarmed when I read these words, inasmuch as I consider them addressed to myself, and others like me. Remember, O ye forgetful, thoughtless, and ungrateful, the works of God, which he hath done to us, with so many signs and proofs of his goodness. What more could he have done, which he hath not done ?—*Folengius.*

Verse 6.—" *O ye seed of Abraham his servant.*" Consider the relation ye stand in to him. Ye are " *the seed of Abraham his servant* " ; you are born in his house, and being thereby entitled to the privilege of his servants, protection and provision, you are also bound to do the duty of servants, to attend your master, consult his honour, obey his commands, and do what you can to advance his interests.—*Matthew Henry.*

Verse 8.—" *He hath remembered his covenant.*" As a long series of years had elapsed between the promise and the performance, the prophet uses the word " *remember,*" intimating that the Divine promise does not become obsolete by length of time, but that even when the world imagines that they are extinguished and wholly forgotten, God retains as distinct a remembrance of them as ever, that he may accomplish them in due season.—*John Calvin.*

Verse 8.—" *The word which he commanded.*" All that God says must of necessity be said with authority, so that even his promises partake of the nature of commands. —*Joseph Addison Alexander.*

Verse 11.—" *The lot of your inheritance :* " literally חֶבֶל, *the cord of your inheritance,* an expression taken from the ancient method of measuring land by the cord or line ; whence the measuring cord is *metonymically* put for the part measured, and divided by the cord. Thus, " *the lines,* חֲבָלִים, the cords, *are fallen unto me in pleasant places,*" i.e., as the Psalmist explains it : " I have a goodly heritage." Ps. xvi. 6.—*Samuel Chandler.*

Verse 11.—" YOUR *inheritance.*" The change of the number (from " thee " to " your ") points out that God made a covenant with all the people in general, though he spake the words only to a few individuals ; even as we have seen a little before, that it was a decree or an everlasting law. The holy patriarchs were the first and principal persons into whose hands the promise was committed ; but they did not embrace the grace which was offered to them as belonging only to themselves, but as a blessing which their posterity in common with them were to become sharers of.— *John Calvin.*

Verse 12.—" *When they were but a few men in number.*" מְתֵי מִסְפָּר. Literally, *homines numeri,* men of number ; so few as easily to be numbered : in opposition to what their posterity afterwards were, as the sand of the sea, without number.— *Samuel Chandler.*

Verses 12—14.—One would think that all the world would have been upon them ; but here was the protection, God has a negative voice, " *He suffered no man to do them wrong.*" Many had (as we say) an aching tooth at the people of God, their finger itched to be dealing with them, and the text shews four advantages the world had against them. First, " *They were few.*" Secondly, " *very few.*" Thirdly, " *strangers.*" Fourthly, " *unsettled.*" What hindered their enemies ? It was the Lord's negative voice. " *He reproved kings for their sakes ; saying, Touch not mine anointed, and do my prophets no harm.*" We see an instance of this (Gen. xxxv. 5). When Jacob and his family journeyed, " the terror of God was upon the cities that were round about them, and they did not pursue after the sons of Jacob." They had a mind to pursue after them, to revenge the slaughter of the Shechemites ; but God said, *Pursue not,* and then they could not pursue, they must stay at home. And when his people the Jews were safe in Canaan he encourages them to come up freely to worship at Jerusalem, by this assurance, " No man shall desire the land, when thou shalt go up to appear before the Lord thy God, thrice in the year " (Exod. xxxiv. 24). God can stop not only hands from spoiling, but hearts from desiring.—*Joseph Caryl.*

Verse 13.—" *From one kingdom to another people.*" Where we might have expected *from kingdom to kingdom,* the ear is somewhat disappointed by the phrase, " *from one kingdom to another people,*" which may have been intended to distinguish the Egyptian and other monarchies from the more democratical or patriarchal institutions of the Arabians and other nations.—*Joseph Addison Alexander.*

Verse 13.—Though frequent flitting is neither desirable nor commendable, yet sometimes there is a just and necessary occasion for it, and it may be the lot of some of the best men.—*Matthew Henry.*

Verse 14.—" *He suffered no man to do them wrong.*" As many rose up, one after another, in troops against them, the Psalmist says indefinitely, that men were withheld from hurting them ; for אָדָם, *Adam,* is the word here used, which is the one most generally employed to signify *man.*—*John Calvin.*

Verses 14, 15.—I resolve the words into these three parts. 1. Here is the nearness and the dearness of the saints unto God. They are dearer to him than kings and states, simply considered ; that is, otherwise than as they in their persons are also saints ; for you see that for their sakes he reproved kings, and so sheweth that he preferreth them to kings.

2. Here is the great danger to kings and states, to deal with his saints otherwise than well. Which appeareth many ways ; for he doth not only in words give a charge not to touch them, but he carries it in a high way (for so God will do when he pleads their cause). Touch them not ; as if he had said, Let me see if you dare so much as touch them ; and it is with an intimation of the highest threatening if they should ; upon your peril if you do so ; for that is the scope of such a speech. And accordingly in deeds he made this good ; for the text saith he suffered no man to do them wrong ; not that he did altogether prevent all wrong and injuries, for they received many as they went through those lands ; but at no time did he let it go unpunished. In that sense he suffered them not. You know how he plagued Pharaoh, king of Egypt, with great plagues, and all his household, for Abraham's wife's sake, Gen. xii. And so Abimelech, king of Gerar, the Lord cometh upon him with a greatness, and his first word is in Gen. xx. 3, " Behold, thou art but a dead man," afore he had first told him why or wherefore, though then he adds the reason ; he brings him upon his knees, verse 4, bids him look to it, that he give satisfaction to Abraham, and restore his wife to him again, verse 7 ; and well he escaped so ; and tells him also that he must be beholden to Abraham's prayers for his life. " He is a prophet," saith he, " and he shall pray for thee, and thou shalt live."

3. The third is the care and protection which God had over them, set and amplified, 1, by the number and condition of the persons whom he defended ; though " *few men in number,*" that is, soon reckoned, for their power and strength a few, or very small, εἰς μικρούς, so the Septuagint in the parallel place, 1 Chron. xvi. 19 ; as also, 2, by what he did for them : He suffered no man, how great soever, to do them any wrong, how small soever ; not without recompense and satisfaction ; not to do it, though they had a mind to it. Though the people had an ill eye at them, Gen. xxvi. 11, God causeth Abimelech to make a law on purpose ; Abimelech charged all his people in Isaac's behalf, and spake in the very words of the text, " He that toucheth this man or his wife shall be put to death."—*Thomas Goodwin.*

Verse 15.—" *Mine anointed.*" Abraham, Isaac and Jacob had no external anointing. They were, however, called " *anointed,*" because they were separated by God from the multitude of wicked men, and endowed with the Spirit and his gifts, of which the oil was an emblem.—*Mollerus.*

Verse 15.—" *Touch not mine anointed, and do my prophets no harm.*" We see here a vivid description of the people of God. They are " his anointed ones," " having the residue of his Spirit " ; they are his prophets, to whom is intrusted the word of life, that they may be witnesses in the world. To these he gives as it were a safe passport through the world. Though they have ever been but men of number, accounted as a vile thing, they are precious in his sight. They are not distinguished by external dignity, numbers and power, as Rome sets forth the marks of her communion. They are in the midst of kingdoms, but not of them. They form usually the humblest portions of most communities, and yet they receive honour from God. Despised by the world, but unto God kings and priests, ordained and anointed to reign with Christ for ever.—*W. Wilson.*

Verse 15.—" *Prophets.*" The נָבִיא is the prophet, or forth-speaker ; the term laying stress on the utterance, and not upon the vision. The Hebrew word comes from a root which means to bubble up and overflow as from a full fountain. But the fulness of the true prophets of Jehovah was not that of their own thoughts and emotions. It was of the Divine Spirit within them. " The prophecy came not in old time by the will of man : but holy men of God spake as they were moved by the Holy Ghost," 2 Peter i. 21. The first application of the word is to Abraham (Gen. xx. 7) ; although, long before Abraham, " Enoch the seventh from Adam, prophesied," Jude 14.—*Donald Fraser, in " Synoptical Lectures on the Books of Holy Scripture."* 1873.

Verse 16.—"*He called for a famine.*" As a master *calls for* a servant ready to do his bidding. On the contrary, God says (Ezek. xxxvi. 29), "I will call for the corn, and will increase it, and lay no famine upon you." Compare the centurion's words as to sickness being Christ's servant, ready to come or go at his call, Matt. viii. 8, 9. — *A. R. Fausset.*

Verses 17—22.—Joseph may be a fit type to us of our spiritual deliverance. Consider him sold into Egypt, not without the determinate counsel of God, who preordained this to good; "God did send me before you to preserve life," Gen. xlv. 5. Here is the difference, the brethren sold Joseph, we sold ourselves. Consider us thus sold unto sin and death; God had a purpose to redeem us; there is election. Joseph was delivered out of prison, and we ransomed out of the house of bondage; there was redemption. Joseph's cause was made known, and himself acquitted; we could not be found innocent ourselves, but were acquitted in Christ; wherein consists our justification. Lastly, Joseph was clothed in glorious apparel, and adorned with golden chains, and made to ride in the second chariot of Egypt; so our last step is to be advanced to high honour, even the glory of the celestial court; "This honour have all the saints," Psalm cxlix. 9.—*Thomas Adams.*

Verses 17—22.—In many circumstances concerning Joseph—in his being beloved of his father—in his being hated of his brethren—in his sufferings and deep abasement—in his being brought out of prison—in his advancement and exaltation —in his wisdom and prudence—in his providing for his father's family—in his free forgiveness of the injuries he had sustained from his brethren—it may be truly said, we have Christ delineated therein, and set forth thereby, in type, figure, and representatively. But I have nothing to do with this here; I only give this hint to the reader.—*Samuel Eyles Pierce,* 1817.

Verse 18.—"*His soul came into iron*" (margin). The whole person is denoted by the *soul,* because the soul of the captive suffers still more than the body. Imprisonment is one of the most severe trials to the soul. Even to spiritual heroes, such as a Savonarola and St. Cyran, the waters often go over the soul.—*E. W. Hengstenberg.*

Verse 18.—"*His soul came into iron.*" Till we have felt it, we cannot conceive that sickness of heart, which at times will steal upon the patient sufferer; that sense of loneliness, that faintness of soul, which comes from hopes deferred and wishes unshared, from the selfishness of brethren and the heartlessness of the world. We ask ourselves, If the Lord were with me, should I suffer thus, not only the scorn of the learned and the contempt of the great, but even the indifference and neglect of those whom I have served, who yet forget me? So Joseph might have asked; and so till now may the elect ask, as they stand alone without man's encouragement or sympathy, not turned aside by falsehood or scorn, with their face set as a flint, yet deeply feeling what it costs them.—*Andrew Jukes, in " The Types of Genesis,"* 1858.

Verse 19.—"*Until the time that his word came : the word of the Lord tried him.*" This verse forms the key to the whole meaning of Joseph's mysterious trial, and at the same time illustrates a deep mystery in the spiritual life of man. By " *the word of the Lord* " that " *tried him,*" the Psalmist evidently refers to the dreams of his future destiny which were sent to Joseph from God; and in saying that they tried him " *until his word came,*" he evidently means that his faith in those promises was tested by his long imprisonment, until the day of his deliverance dawned. Consider for a moment his position, and you will see the purpose of that trial. A youth educated amidst all the quiet simplicity of the early patriarchal life, he was haunted by dream-visions of a mighty destiny. Those visions were mysteriously foretelling his government in Egypt, and the blessings which his wise and just rule would confer on the land; but while unable to comprehend them, he yet believed that they were voices of the future, and promises of God. But the quietude of that shepherd life was not the preparation for the fulfilment of his promised destiny. The education that would form the man who could withstand, firmly, the temptations of Egyptian life with its cities and civilization; the education that would form the ruler whose clear eye should judge between the good and the evil, and discern the course of safety in the hour of a nation's peril—all this was not to be gained under the shadow of his father's tent; it must come through trial, and through trial arising from the very promise of God in which he believed. Hence, a great and startling change crossed his life, that seemed to forbid the fulfilment of that dream-promise, and tempted him to doubt its truth.   Sold into Egypt as a slave, cast into prison through his fidelity to God, the word of the Lord most powerfully tried his soul.   In the gloom of that imprisonment it was most hard to believe in God's faithfulness, when his affliction had risen from his obedience ; and most hard to keep the promise clearly before him, when his mighty trouble would perpetually tempt him to regard it as an idle dream.   But through the temptation, he gained the strong trust which the pomp and glory of the Egyptian court would have no power to destroy ; and when the word of deliverance came, the man came forth, strong through trial, to fulfil his glorious destiny of ruling Egypt in the name of God, and securing for it the blessings of heaven.   Thus his trial by the word of the Lord—his temptation to doubt its truth—was a divine discipline preparing him for the fulfilment of the promise.

And looking at it in this aspect, this verse presents to us a deep spiritual truth : The promises of God try man, that through the trial he may be prepared for their fulfilment.   Our subject then is this : The trial of man by the promises of God. This verse suggests three great facts which exhibit the three aspects of that trial.

I. God's promises must try man.   Every promise of the Lord is *of necessity* a trial.   Now, this necessity arises from two sources ; from man's secret unbelief, and from God's purposes of discipline.

1. *God's word must try man by revealing his secret unbelief.*   We never know our want of faith till some glorious promise rouses the soul into the attitude of belief ; then the coldness and unfaithfulness of the heart are lighted up by that flash of belief, and the promise is a trial.   Thus Paul with his profound insight into the facts of spiritual experience, says, " The word of the Lord is sharper than a two-edged sword, piercing even to the dividing asunder of soul and spirit, and of the joints and marrow, and is a *discerner of the thoughts and intents of the heart.*"   In illustration of this we may observe that many promises of the Lord come to us, as they came to Joseph, like dream-visions of the future.   Visions come to the Christian soul, as grand and wonderful as those which came to the Hebrew youth of old ; and they, too, are prophecies of what we are destined to be.   There comes a time when the voice of God is more clearly heard, and the great inheritance revealed.   No dream of the night— no spirit of the dead—has visited us ; but like a spirit some truth of God has entered the soul's presence-chamber, and summoned it to noble aspiration and Christ-like endeavour.   Then the earnest of the future gleams on life's horizon.   The Sabbath of eternity, with all its balm and music, seems near, and rapt with its glory, we are roused to all-surrendering zeal.   But I appeal to your experience whether it is not true that such revelations of the promise rapidly become times of trial.   Then the mocking voice of unbelief tells us that aspiration is vain.   The cold cross-currents of indifference chill the fiery impulses of the heart.   We are prisoned like Joseph, by no material bars indeed, but by the invisible bonds of unbelief ; and we find it most hard to keep the promise clear and bright, while tempted to believe that our aspirations were merely idle dreams.   And *there* is that arousing, by the promise, of the soul's hidden unbelief, which makes every promise an inevitable trial.

2. Again : *God causes his promises to try us, that he may accomplish his own purposes of discipline.*   It is a law of our nature that no belief in any unseen thing can ever pass into the active form of strong endeavour to attain it, until we are tempted to disbelieve it.   Thus the great idea of an undiscovered land across the wastes of the Atlantic smote the soul of Columbus ; but it remained a dreamy faith until by opposition and ridicule he was tempted to regard it as a dream, and then it became heroic endeavour, and the land was found.   Thus with all men of genius.   They stand in the front of their age, with thoughts which the world cannot understand ; but those thoughts are dreams until suffering and scorn try the men, and then they are awakened into effort to realise them.   Hence God leads us into circumstances in which we are tempted to doubt his promises, that by temptation he may discipline faith into power.   There is a wilderness of temptation in every life, and like Christ, we are often led into it, from the solemn hour when we heard the voice, " Thou art my son ; " but like Christ, we come forth strong, through the long, silent wrestling with temptation, to do our Father's will.

II. God sends the Hour of Deliverance : " *until the time that his word came.*" When the discipline was *perfected*, Joseph came forth ready for his mission.   But our deliverance does not always come in *this* way.   Take from the Bible histories the four great methods by which God sends deliverance.   *Sometimes by death.*   Thus with Elijah.   Weariness, loneliness, failure, had wrung from the strong man the cry, " Take away my life for I am not better than my fathers." The temptation was becoming too strong, and God sent deliverance in the chariot of fire. *Sometimes by transforming the height of trial into the height of blessing.* The three youths in Babylon had clenched their nerves for the climax of agony, when the fire became a Paradise. So, now, God makes the climax of trial the herald of spiritual blessedness. By suffering we are loosened from the bonds of time and sense ; there is one near us like the Son of God ; and deliverance has come. *Sometimes by the glance of love on the falling soul.* Thus with Peter. The temptation was mastering him : one glance of *that* eye, and he went out weeping and delivered. *Sometimes by continuing the trial, but increasing the power to endure it.* Thus with Paul. After the vision of the third heaven came " the thorn in the flesh." The temptation made him cry thrice to God ; the trial remained, but here was the deliverance—" my grace is sufficient for thee." The suffering lost none of its pressure, but he learned to glory in infirmity ; and *then* came his delivering hour.

III. God makes the Trial by Promise fulfil the Promise itself. In Joseph the temptation to doubt the word of God silently meetened him for its fulfilment. So with us all. We hope not for an Egyptian kingdom, our dream-vision is of a heavenly inheritance, and the palace of a heavenly King. But every temptation resisted, every mocking voice of doubt overcome, is an aid upwards and onwards. Trials, sufferings, struggles, are angels arraying the soul, in the white robes of the heavenly world, and crowning it with the crown that fadeth not away. And when the end comes, then it will be seen that the long dreary endeavour to hold fast the dream-promise—the firm resolute " no " to the temptation to disbelieve, are all more than recompensed with " the exceeding and eternal weight of glory."—*Edward Luscombe Hull, in " Sermons preached at King's Lynn,"* 1867.

Verse 19.—" *The word of the Lord tried him.*" As we try God's word, so God's word tries us ; and happy if, when we are tried, we come forth as gold ; and the trial of our faith proves more precious than that of gold which perisheth, though it be tried with fire.—*William Jay.*

Verse 19.—" *Tried him.*" I doubt not that Joseph's brethren were humbled, yet Joseph may be more, he must be cast into the ditch, and into the prison, and the iron must enter not only into his legs, but into his soul. He must be more affected in spirit, because he was to do greater work for God, and was to be raised up higher than the rest, and therefore did need the more ballast.—*Thomas Shepard, in " The Sound Believer,"* 1649.

Verse 19.—" *Tried.*" צָרַף, " assayed ; " Ps. xii. 6 ; xvii. 3 ; xviii. 30. He came out of the ordeal, as gold from the fining-pot, more pure and lustrous.—*William Kay.*

Verses 19—21.—" *Tried him.*" " *Made him lord of his house.*" Joseph's feet were hurt in irons, to fit him to tread more delicately in the King's Palace at Zoan ; and when the Lord's time was come, by the same stairs which winded him into the dungeon he climbs up into the next chariot to Pharaoh's. Few can bear great and sudden mercies without pride and wantonness, till they are hampered and humbled to carry it moderately.—*Samuel Lee, in " The Triumph of Mercy in the Chariot of Praise,"* 1677.

Verse 20.—" *The king sent and loosed him.*" And that by his own master, Potiphar, who had clapt him up there by his wanton wife's wicked instigation. He had been bound ignominiously, but now comes he to be loosed honourably.—*Christopher Ness.*

Verse 21.—" *Ruler of all his substance,*" or " *possession.*" Herein also he was a type of Jesus Christ, who, as God, is possessor of heaven and earth, being the creator of them.—*John Gill.*

Verses 21—22.—He was received into the Royal Society of the right honourable the king's privy councillors, and was constituted as Chairman of the council-table, which, though Moses doth not express, yet David intimateth in Ps. cv. 21, 22. All the privy-councillors, as well as the private people were bound (possibly by oath) to obey him in all things, and, as out of the chair, he magisterially *taught these senators wisdom.* Thus the Hebrew reading runs : *He bound the princes to his soul* (or according to his will) and *made wise his elders ;* teaching them not only civil and moral, but also divine wisdom, for which cause God sent Joseph (saith he) into Egypt, that some sound of the redemption of fallen mankind might be heard in that kingdom, at that time the most flourishing in the world : neither is Moses altogether silent herein, for he calls him a *master of wisdom*, or *father to* Pharaoh (Gen. xlv. 8). Much more to his councillors, and he says that no hand or foot shall move (to wit, in affairs of state, at home, or, in foreign embassies, abroad) without Joseph's order ; he was the king's plenipotentiary, Gen. xli. 44.—*Christopher Ness.*

Verse 22.—" *To bind his princes.*" The meaning of לֶאְסֹר שָׂרָיו signifies to exercise control over the greatest men in the kingdom, which power was conferred on Joseph by Pharaoh : see Gen. xli. 40 ; also verses 43, 44. The capability of binding is to be regarded as an evidence of authority ; a power of compelling obedience ; or, in default thereof, of inflicting punishment.—*George Phillips.* 1846.

Verse 22.—" *At his pleasure.*" Literally, *with his soul*, which some explain as a bold metaphor, describing Joseph's mind or soul as the cord or chain with which he bound the Egyptians, *i.e.*, forced them to perform his will. But see Ps. xvii. 9 ; xxvii. 12 ; xli. 2.—*Joseph Addison Alexander.*

Verse 22.—" *And teach his senators wisdom.*" That is that wisdom wherein he had been instructed of God he might also instruct the princes, and teach prudence to those who were much his seniors. Herein some sparks of divine wisdom shine, that he should order even the princes and old men to learn wisdom from one who was a slave and a foreigner, although the Egyptians are always wont to boast that Egypt is the native place of wisdom.—*Jansenius.*

Verse 23.—" *Egypt*" . . . " *the land of Ham.*" The Egyptians were a branch of the race of Ham. They came from Asia through the desert of Syria to settle in the valley of the Nile. This is a fact clearly established by science, and entirely confirms the statements of the book of Genesis.—*F. Lenormant and E. Chevalier, in " A Manual of Ancient History,*" 1869.

Verse 24.—" *He increased his people greatly.*" Behold here the concealed blessing in the secret of the cross. Under it the people of God are in the most fruitful state. —*Berleb. Bible.*

Verse 25.—" *He turned their heart to hate his people.*" Not by putting this wicked hatred into them, which is not consistent either with the holiness of God's nature, or with the truth of his word, and which was altogether unnecessary, because they had that and all other wickedness in them by nature ; but partly, by withdrawing the common gifts and operations of his Spirit, and all the restraints and hindrances to it, and wholly leaving them to their own mistakes, and passions, and corrupt affections, which of their own accord were ready to take that course ; and partly, by directing and governing that hatred, which was wholly in and from themselves, so as it should fall upon the Israelites rather than upon other people.—*Matthew Pool.*

Verses 25—26.—When by the malice of enemies God's people are brought to greatest straits, there is deliverance near to be sent from God unto them. " *They dealt subtilly with his servants. He sent Moses his servant.*"—*David Dickson.*

Verse 26.—" *Moses and Aaron.*"—God usually sendeth his servants by two and two for mutual helps and comfort.—*John Trapp.*

Verse 28.—" *He sent darkness.*" The darkness here stands at the beginning (not in the historical order that the particular plague of darkness stood), to mark how *God's wrath* hung over Egypt as a *dark cloud* during all the plagues.—*A. R. Fausset.*

Verse 28.—" *Darkness.*" There is an awful significance in this plague of darkness. The sun was a leading object of devotion among the Egyptians under the name of Osiris. The very name Pharaoh means not only the king but also the sun, and characterises the king himself as the representative of the sun and entitled in some sort of divine honours. But now the very light of the sun has disappeared and primeval chaos seems to have returned. Thus all the forms of Egyptian will-worship were covered with shame and confusion by the plagues.—*James G. Murphy, in " A Commentary on Exodus,*" 1866.

Verse 28.—" *Made it dark.*" God is often described as manifesting his displeasure in a cloud. Joel speaks of the day of God's vengeance as " a day of darkness and of gloominess, a day of clouds and of thick darkness " (Joel ii. 2) ; and Zephaniah employs nearly the same language (i. 15). The pillar that went before the Israelites, and gave them light, was to the Egyptians " a cloud and darkness " (Exod. xiv. 20). The darkness which was upon the face of the earth " in the beginning," is described by Jehovah in the book of Job as a cloud : " When I made the cloud the garment thereof, and thick darkness a swaddling-band for it " (Job. xxxviii. 9). So now the land of Egypt may have been wrapped about by a thick palpable cloud, cold, damp, impenetrable : the people would feel it upon their limbs, as swaddling-bands ; the sun would be blotted out by it, and all things reduced almost to a state of death—of which this ninth plague was in a certain sense the shadow cast before. Such a cloud would be even more terrible in Egypt, sunny Egypt, than in other countries ; for there the sky is almost always clear, and heavy rains unknown. But in any place, and under any conditions, it must have been full of horror and misery. Nothing could represent this more forcibly than the short sentence, " Neither rose any from his place for three days." It was an horror of great darkness ; it rested on them like a pall ; they knew not what dangers might be around them, what judgment was next to happen : they had not been forewarned of this plague, and they could not tell but it might be only a prelude to some more awful visitation : their soul melted in them, for fear of those things that might come upon them : they dared not move from chamber to chamber, nor even from seat to seat : wherever they chanced to be at the moment when the darkness fell upon them, there they must remain. Pharaoh might call in vain for his guards ; they could not come to him. Moses and Aaron were no longer within reach, for none could go to seek them. Masters could not command their slaves, nor slaves hasten to obey their master's call ; the wife could not flee to her husband, nor the child cling to its parents : the same fear was upon all, both high and low ; the same paralysing terror and dismay possessed them every one. As says the patriarch Job, they " laid hold on horror " (Job xviii. 20). And this continued for three days and nights : they had no lamps nor torches ; either they could not kindle them, or they dared not move to procure them : they were silent in darkness, like men already dead. Hope and expectation of returning light might at first support them ; but hope delayed through seventy-two weary hours would presently die out, and leave them to despair. The darkness would become more oppressive and intolerable the longer it continued ; " felt " upon their bodies as a physical infliction, and " felt " even more in their souls in agonies of fear and apprehension ; such a darkness as that which, in the book of Revelation, the fifth angel pours out upon the seat of the beast—" Whose kingdom was full of darkness ; and they gnawed their tongues for pain, and blasphemed the God of heaven because of their pains and their sores, and repented not of their deeds " (Rev. xvi. 10, 11). If there be any truth in the traditions of the Jews on this subject, there were yet greater alarms under this canopy of darkness, this palpable obscurity, than any which would arise out of the physical infliction. Darkness is a type of Satan's kingdom ; and Satan had some liberty in Egypt to walk up and down upon the land, and to go to and fro in it. The Jewish Rabbis tell us that the devil and his angels were let loose during these three dreadful days ; that they had a wider range and greater liberty than usual for working mischief. They describe these evil spirits going among the wretched people, glued to their seats as they were, with terror ; frightening them with fearful apparitions ; piercing their ears with hideous shrieks and groans ; driving them almost to madness with the intensity of their fears ; making their flesh creep, and the hair of their head to stand on end. Such a climax seems to be referred to by the Psalmist, " He cast upon them the fierceness of his anger, wrath, and indignation, and trouble, by sending evil angels among them " (Ps. lxxviii. 49).—*Thomas S. Millington, in " Signs and Wonders in the Land of Ham," 1873.*

Verse 28.—" *And they rebelled not against his word.*" The plague of darkness and the rest of the plagues which God commanded ; these as they were his servants, were not disobedient to him, they came at his word. See verses 31, 34.—*John Gill.*

Verse 28.—" *They rebelled not against his word* " ; as Jonah did, who, when he was sent to denounce God's judgments against Nineveh, went to Tarshish. Moses and Aaron were not moved, either with a foolish fear of Pharaoh's wrath, or a foolish pity of Egypt's misery, to relax or retard any of the plagues which God ordered them to inflict on the Egyptians ; but stretched forth their hand to inflict them as God appointed. They that are instructed to execute judgment, will find their remissness construed a rebellion against God's word.—*Matthew Henry.*

Verse 29.—" *He turned their waters into blood,*" etc. The Nile begins to rise about the end of June, and attains its highest point at the end of September. About the commencement of the rise it assumes a greenish hue, is disagreeable to the taste, unwholesome, and often totally unfit for drinking. It soon, however, becomes red and turbid, and continues in this state for three or more weeks. In this condition it is again healthy and fit for use. The miracle now performed was totally different from this annual change. For, 1, it occurred after the winter, not the summer, solstice; 2, the water was turned into blood, and not merely reddened by an admixture of red clay or animalcula; 3, the fish died, a result which did not follow from the periodical change of colour; 4, the river stank, and became offensive, which it ceased to be when the ordinary redness made its appearance; 5, the stroke was arrested at the end of seven days, whereas the natural redness continued for at least three weeks; and 6, the change was brought on instantly at the word of command before the eyes of Pharaoh. The calamity was appalling. The sweet waters of the Nile were the common beverage of Egypt. It abounded in all kinds of fish, which formed a principal article of diet for the inhabitants. It was revered as a god by Egypt. And now it was a putrid flood, from which they turned away with loathing.—*James G. Murphy.*

Verse 29.—" *He turned their waters into blood.*" By the miraculous change of the waters into blood, a practical rebuke was given to their superstitions. This sacred and beautiful river, the benefactor and preserver of the country, this birthplace of their chief gods, this abode of their lesser deities, this source of all their prosperity, this centre of all their devotion, is turned to blood: the waters stink; the canals and pools, the vessels of wood and vessels of stone, which were replenished from the river, all are alike polluted. The Nile, according to Pliny, was the " only source from whence the Egyptians obtained water for drinking " (Hist. Nat. 76, c. 33). This water was considered particularly sweet and refreshing; so much so that the people were in the habit of provoking thirst in order that they might partake more freely of its soft and pleasant draughts. Now it was become abominable to them, and they loathed to drink it.—*Thomas S. Millington.*

Verse 29.—" *And slew their fish.*" Besides the fish cured, or sent to market for the table, a very great quantity was set apart expressly for feeding the sacred animals and birds,—as the cats, crocodiles, ibises, and others; and some of the large reservoirs, attached to the temples, were used as well for keeping fish as for the necessary ablutions of the devout, and for various purposes connected with religion. The quantity of fish in Egypt was a very great boon to the poor classes, and when the Nile overflowed the country inhabitants of the inland villages benefited by this annual gift of the river, as the land did by the fertilizing mud deposited upon it. The canals, ponds, and pools, on the low lands, continued to abound in fish, even after the inundation had ceased; and it was then that their return to the Nile was intercepted by closing the mouths of the canals.—*Sir J. Gardner Wilkinson, in " A Popular Account of the Ancient Egyptians,"* 1854.

Verse 30.—" *Their land brought forth frogs in abundance.*" This is the natural appearance next in the order of occurrence to the Red Nile, and of it also the God of nature availed himself to vindicate his power before Pharaoh, and before Egypt. The Nile, its branches, and the great canals of irrigation are all bank-full, and the exuberant moisture has aroused from their summer torpor, into life and activity, the frogs of the Nile, in numbers inconceivable to those who have not been in hot countries. Even in ordinary years the annoyance of these loathsome creatures night and day, gives some idea of what this plague must have been, and renders abundantly reasonable the creation of a goddess, *Ranipula,** at the very commencement of the mythology of ancient Egypt. In the whole of this fearful succession of judgments there is not one more personally revolting than the plague of frogs.—*William Osburn.*

Verse 30.—" *Their land brought forth frogs in abundance.*" It is not difficult for an Englishman, in an Eastern wet monsoon, to form a tolerable idea of that plague of Egypt, in which frogs were in the " houses, bed-chambers, beds and kneading-troughs," of the Egyptians. In the rainy season, myriads of them send forth their

* " Driver away of frogs." Her name was Heki; *Birch* ap. Bunsen. She was the *Buto* of the Greek authors.

constant croak in every direction ; and a man not possessed of over-much patience, becomes as petulant as was the licentious god, and is ready to exclaim,

> " Croak, croak ! Indeed I shall choke,
> If you pester and bore my ears any more
> With your croak, croak, croak ! "

A new-comer, on seeing them leap about the rooms, becomes disgusted, and forth-with begins an attack upon them ; but the next evening will bring a return of his active visitors. It may appear almost incredible, but in one evening we killed upwards of forty of these guests in the Jaffna Mission-house. They had principally concealed themselves in a small tunnel connected with the bathing room, where their noise had become almost insupportable.—*Joseph Roberts, in "Oriental Illustrations," 1844.*

Verse 30.—" *Chambers of their kings.*" God plagued Pharaoh in his *bed-chamber :* it may be because he would show that his judgments can penetrate the greatest privacy ; for the field, and the hall, and the *bed-chamber*, and the closet are all one to God.

It is like enough that it would not move Pharaoh much that his borders were filled with frogs ; but they must come into his *house, and into his bed-chamber.* My observation is—the greatest princes in the world if they offend God are not exempted from judgments. Princes and great persons, are usually exempted from the reproof of men. As for the laws, ofttimes they are as cobwebs, the great flies break through them. Who dare say to a prince, " Thou art wicked " ? Nay, one saith concerning the Pope, it is not lawful to say, " What doth he so ? " Now when they are not within the compass of human reproof, God strikes them.—*Josias Shute, in " Judgment and Mercy : or, the Plague of Frogs,"* 1645.

Verse 31.—" *Flies.*" This term serves to denote a kind of insect that alights on the skin or leaves of plants, by its bite inflicting pain in the one case, and causing destruction in the other. The swarms of flies in Egypt are usually numerous and excessively annoying. They alight on the moist part of the eyelids and nostrils, and inflict wounds that produce great pain, swelling and inflammation. They are also ruinous to the plants in which they lay their eggs. Philo (vit. Mos. ii. p. 110) describes the dog-fly or gad-fly as a grievous pest of Egypt. Gnats and mosquitoes are also abundant and virulent. A plague of such creatures would cause immense suffering and desolation.—*James G. Murphy.*

Verse 31.—As an illustration of the power of flies we give an extract from Charles Marshall's " Canadian Dominion." " I have been told by men of unquestioned veracity, that at mid-day the clouds of mosquitoes on the plains would sometimes hide the leaders in a team of four horses from the sight of the driver. Cattle could only be recognised by their shape ; all alike becoming black with an impenetrable crust of mosquitoes. The line of the route over the Red River plains would be marked by the carcases of oxen stung to death by this insignificant foe."

Verse 31.—" *Lice in all their coasts.*" The priests, being polluted by this horrible infection, could not stand to minister before their deities. The people could not, in their uncleanness, be admitted within the precincts of their temples. If they would offer sacrifice, there were no victims fit for the purpose. Even the gods, the oxen, and goats, and cats, were defiled with the vermin. The Egyptians not only writhed under the loathsome scourge, but felt themselves humbled and disgraced by it. Josephus notices this :—" Pharaoh," he says, " was so confounded at this new plague, that, what with the danger, the *scandal*, and the nastiness of it, he was half sorry for what he had done " (b. ii. c. 14). The plague assumed the form of a disease, being " in the people." Exod. viii. 17. As Josephus says again, " The bodies of the people bred them, and they were all covered over with them, gnawing and tearing intolerably, and no remedy, for baths and ointments did no good." But, however distressing to their bodies, the foul and disgraceful character of the plague, and the offence brought upon their religion by the defilement of their deities and the interruption of all their religious ceremonies, was its most offensive feature. —*Thomas S. Millington.*

Verse 31.—" *Lice.*" Vermin of the kind is one of the common annoyances of Egypt. Herodotus tells us (ii. 37) that the priests shave their whole body every other day, that no lice or other impure thing may adhere to them when they are engaged in the service of the gods. It is manifest that this species of vermin was particularly disgusting to the Egyptians.—*James G. Murphy.*

Verse 32.—" *He gave them hail for rain.*" I had ridden out to the excavations [at Gizeh], when seeing a large black cloud approaching, I sent a servant to the tents to take care of them, but as it began to rain slightly, I soon rode after him myself. Shortly after my arrival a storm of wind began ; I therefore ordered the cords of the tents to be secured, but soon a violent shower of rain came in addition, which alarmed all our Arabs, and drove them into the rock-tomb, in which is our kitchen. . . . Suddenly the storm became a regular hurricane, such as I had never witnessed in Europe, and a hailstorm came down on us, which almost turned the day into night. . . . It was not long before first our common tent fell down, and when I had hastened from that into my own, in order to hold it from the inside, this also broke down above me.—*Carl Richard Lepsius, in " Letters from Egypt, Ethiopia, and the Peninsula of Sinai."* 1853.

Verse 32.—" *Hail.*" Extraordinary reports of the magnitude of hailstones, which have fallen during storms so memorable as to find a place in general history, have come down from periods of antiquity more or less remote. According to the " Chronicles," a hailstorm occurred in the reign of Charlemagne, in which hailstones fell which measured fifteen feet in length by six feet in breadth, and eleven feet in thickness ; and under the reign of Tippoo Sahib, hailstones equal in magnitude to elephants are said to have fallen. Setting aside these and like recitals, as partaking rather of the character of fable than of history, we shall find sufficient to create astonishment in well authenticated observations on this subject.

In a hailstorm which took place in Flintshire on the 9th April, 1672, Halley saw hailstones which weighed five ounces.

On the 4th May, 1697, Robert Taylor saw fall hailstones measuring fourteen inches in circumference.

In the storm which ravaged Como on 20th August, 1787, Volta saw hailstones which weighed nine ounces.

On 22nd May, 1822, Dr. Noggerath saw fall at Bonn hailstones which weighed from twelve to thirteen ounces.

It appears, therefore, certain that in different countries hailstones have occurred in which stones weighing from half to three-quarters of a pound have fallen.—*Dionysius Lardner, in " The Museum of Science and Art,"* 1854.

Verse 34.—" *Locusts came, and caterpillars, and that without number.*" In this country, and in all the dominions of Prete Janni, is a very great and horrible plague, which is an innumerable company of locusts, which eat and consume all the corn and trees ; and the number of them is so great, as it is incredible ; and with their multitude they cover the earth, and fill the air in such wise, that it is a hard matter to be able to see the sun. . . . We travelled five days' journey through places wholly waste and destroyed, wherein millet had been sown, which had stalks as great as those we set in our vineyards, and we saw them all broken and beaten down as if a tempest had been there ; and this the locusts did. The trees were without leaves, and the bark of them was all devoured ; and no grass was there to be seen, for they had eaten up all things ; and if we had not been warned and advised to carry victual with us, we and our cattle had perished. This country was all covered with locusts without wings ; and they told us these were the seed of them which had eaten up all, and that as soon as their wings were grown they would seek after the old ones. The number of them was so great, that I shall not speak of it, because I shall not be believed : but this I will say, that I saw men, women, and children sit as forlorn and dead among the locusts.—*Samuel Purchas, 1577—1628.*

Verse 34.—" *Locusts and caterpillars.*" God did not bring the same plague twice ; but when there was occasion for another, it was still a new one ; for he has many arrows in his quiver.—*Matthew Henry.*

Verse 34.—" *Without number.*" A swarm [of locusts], which was observed in India in 1825, occupied a space of forty English square miles, contained at least forty millions of locusts in one line, and cast a long shadow on the earth. And Major Moore thus describes an immense army of these animals which ravaged the Mahratta country : " The column they composed extended five hundred miles ; and so compact was it when on the wing, that like an eclipse, it completely hid the sun, so that no shadow was cast by any object." Brown, in his travels in Africa, states that an area of nearly two thousand square miles was literally covered by them ; and Kirby and Spence mention that a column of them was so immense, that they took four hours to fly over the spot where the observer stood.—*M. Kalisch.*

Verse 34.—" Came . . . and that without number."

> Onward they came, a dark continuous cloud
> Of congregated myriads numberless ;
> The rushing of whose wings was as the sound
> Of some broad river, headlong in its course,
> Plunged from a mountain summit ; or the roar
> Of a wild ocean in the autumnal storm,
> Shattering its billows on a shore of rocks,
> Onward they came, the winds impelled them on.
>   *Robert Southey,* 1774—1843.

Verse 35.—" Did eat up all the herbs." The locusts had devoured every green herb and every blade of grass ; and had it not been for the reeds, on which our cattle entirely subsisted while we skirted the banks of the river, the journey must have been discontinued, at least in the line that had been proposed. The larvæ, as generally is the case in this class of nature, are much more voracious than the perfect insect ; nothing that is green seems to come amiss to them. . . . The traces of their route over the country are very obvious for many weeks after they have passed it, the surface appearing as if swept by a broom, or as if a harrow had been drawn over it.—*John Barrow,* 1764—1849.

Verse 36.—" He smote also all the firstborn." Did you hear that cry ? 'Tis the moment of midnight, and some tragedy is enacted in that Egyptian dwelling, for such an unearthly shriek ! and it is repeated and re-echoed, as doors burst open and frantic women rush into the street, and, as the houses of priests and physicians are beset, they only shake their heads in speechless agony, and point to the death-sealed features of their own first-born. Lights are flashing at the palace gates, and flitting through the royal chambers ; and as king's messengers hasten through the town enquiring where the two venerable Hebrew brothers dwell, the whisper flies, " The prince-royal is dead ! " Be off, ye sons of Jacob ! speed from your house of bondage, ye oppressed and injured Israelites ! And in their eagerness to " thrust forth " the terrible because Heaven-protected race, they press upon them gold and jewels, and bribe them to be gone.—*James Hamilton.*

Verse 37.—" There was not one feeble person among their tribes," when Israel came out of Egypt ; there was while dwelling there : so there shall be no *feeble saint* go to heaven, but they shall be perfect when carried hence by the angels of God, though they complain of feebleness here. " There shall be no more thence an infant of days, nor an old man that hath not filled his days : for the child shall die an hundred years old ; " Isa. lxv. 20. As there is in all *dying* or departed persons a great *shooting* in their stature observed ; so is there in the *soul* much more. The least infant shoots in the *instant of dissolution* to such a perfect knowledge of God, and such a measure of grace as is not attainable here, that he is " as David ; " and the tallest Christian comes to such a height, that he is " as an angel of God," Zech. xii. 8.—*John Sheffield, in " The Rising Sun,"* 1654.

Verse 37.—" There was not one feeble person among their tribes." They came out all in good health, and brought not with them any of the diseases of Egypt. Surely never was the like ; that among so many thousands there was not one sick ! so false was the representation which the Jews' enemies in after ages gave to the matter, that they were all sick of a leprosy, or some loathsome disease, and therefore the Egyptians thrust them out of their land.—*Matthew Henry.*

Verse 37.—" Feeble person." A *totterer* or *stumbler.* The word denotes a person unfit for military service.—*Joseph Addison Alexander.*

Verse 39.—In the army of Alexander the Great, the march was begun by a great beacon being set upon a pole as a signal from head-quarters, so that " the fire was seen at night, the smoke in the day-time ; " and the plan is still found in use amongst the caravans of Arabia. It is probable enough, in that unchanging land, that such may have been the custom at the time of the Exodus, and that God taught the people by parable in this wise, as well as by fact, that he was their true leader, and heaven the general pavilion, whence the order of march was enjoined.—*Neale and Littledale.*

Verse 39.—

> When Israel, of the Lord beloved,
> Out of the land of bondage came,
> Her father's God before her moved,
> An awful guide in smoke and flame.
>
> By day, along the astonished lands,
> The cloudy pillar glided slow ;
> By night, Arabia's crimson sands
> Returned the fiery column's glow.
>
> There rose the choral hymn of praise,
> And trump and timbrel answered keen,
> And Zion's daughters poured their lays,
> With priest's and warrior's voice between.
>
> But present still, though now unseen,
> When brightly shines the prosperous day,
> Be thoughts of Thee a cloudy screen,
> To temper the deceitful ray !
>
> And oh, when stoops on Judah's path,
> In shade and storm, the frequent night,
> Be Thou—long-suffering, slow to wrath—
> A burning and a shining light.
>
> —*Sir Walter Scott*, 1771—1832.

Verse 40.—" *Quails.*" The quail is met with abundantly in Syria and Judæa, and there seems to be little doubt of its identity with the quails so frequently mentioned in the Holy Scriptures. " We have," says Tristram, " a clear proof of the identity of the common quail with the Hebrew *selav*, in its Arabic name, *salwa*, from a root signifying ' to be fat '—very descriptive of the round, plump form and fat flesh of the quail. . . . It migrates in vast flocks, and regularly crosses the Arabian desert, flying for the most part at night, and when the birds settle they are so utterly exhausted that they may be captured in any numbers by the hand. Notwithstanding their migratory habits, they instinctively select the shortest sea passages, and avail themselves of any island as a halting-place. Thus in Spring and Autumn they are slaughtered in numbers on Malta and many of the Greek islands, very few being seen till the period of migration comes round. They also fly with the wind, never facing it like many other birds." " The Israelites ' spread them out ' when they had taken them before they were sufficiently refreshed to escape ; exactly as Herodotus tells us that the Egyptians were in the habit of doing with quails—drying them in the sun." Brehm mentions having been a witness to the arrival of a huge flock of quails upon the coast of North Africa, and tells us that the weary birds fell at once to the ground completely exhausted by their toilsome journey, and remained therefore some minutes as though stupefied.—*Cassell's " Book of Birds."*

Verses 40—42.—

> Brought from his store, at sute of Israell,
> Quailes, in whose beavies each remove pursue ;
> Himself from skies their hunger to repell,
> Candies the grasse with swete congealed dew.
> He woundes the rock, the rock doth wounded, swell :
> Swelling affoordes new streames to channells new,
> All for God's mindfull will can not be dryven,
> From sacred word once to his Abraham given.
>
> —*Sir Philip Sidney*, 1554—1586.

Verse 44.—" *They inherited the labour of the people.*" In like manner the heavenly Canaan is enjoyed by the saints without any labour of theirs ; this inheritance is not of the law, nor of the works of it ; it is the gift of God. Rom. iv. 14 and vi. 23. —*John Gill.*

HINTS TO PREACHERS.

Verse 1.—I. Praise God for former mercies. II. Pray for further mercies. III. Publish his famous mercies.

Verses 1—5.—A series of holy exercises. "Give thanks"—"call upon his name"—"make known"—"sing"—"talk"—"glory"—"rejoice"—"seek"—"remember."

Verse 2.—I. The pleasure of talking *to* God—"Sing," etc. ; making melody in the heart. II. The duty of talking *of* God.—"Talk ye," etc.—*G. R.*

Verse 2.—The Christian's table-talk.

Verse 3.—I. Those who find : or—"glory ye," etc. II. Those who seek : or—"rejoice."

Verse 3 (*second clause*).—Let the seeker rejoice that there is such a God to seek, that he invites us to seek, that he moves us to seek, enables us to seek, and promises to be found of us. The tendency of the seeker is to despond, but there are many grounds of comfort.

Verse 4.—How can we seek the Lord's strength ? 1. By desiring to be subject to it. 2. By being supported by it. 3. By being equipped with it for service. 4. By seeing its results upon others.

Verse 4.—Threefold seeking. I. The Lord for mercy. II. His strength for service. III. His face for happiness.—*A. G. Brown.*

Verse 4 (*last clause*).—Seeking the Lord the perpetual occupation of a believer.

Verse 5.—Themes for memory. I. What God has done. II. What he has said.

Verses 5 and 8.—Our memory and God's memory. "Remember." "He hath remembered."

Verse 7.—God's relation to his elect and to all mankind.

Verses 9, 10.—The making, swearing, and confirming of the covenant. See our comment on these verses with the passages referred to.

Verse 12.—Comfort to the few. The typical and spiritual Israel few at first. A few in the ark peopled the world. Small companies have done wonders. Christ's presence is promised to two or three. God saveth not by many or by few, etc.

Verses 13, 14.—I. God's people may be often removed. II. They can never be injured. III. God's property in them will not be renounced.

Verses 14, 15. *Dr. T. Goodwin* has an excellent sermon on these verses, entitled "The Interest of England," in which he condenses the history of the world, to show, that those nations which have persecuted and afflicted the people of God have invariably been broken in pieces.—(*Goodwin's Works*, vol. xii. pp. 34—60, Nichol's edition).

Verse 15.—In what respect Abraham was a prophet, and how far believers are the same.

Verse 16.—I. All things come at the call of God. He called for plenty, and it came ; for famine, and it came ; for captivity, and it came ; for deliverance, and it came. II. The most unlikely means of accomplishing an end with man is often the direct way with God. He fulfilled the promise of Canaan to Abraham by banishing him from it ; of plenty, by sending a famine ; of freedom, by bringing into captivity.—*G. R.*

Verse 19.—The duration of our troubles, the testing power of the promise, the comfortable issue which is secured to us.

Verse 24.—Church prosperity *desirable*. Increase of numbers, increase of vigour. *Attainable* under great persecution and opposition. *Divine in its origin*—"he increased." *Satisfactory as a test*—it is only true of "his people."

Verse 24 (*second clause*).—In what respects grace can make believers stronger than their enemies.

Verse 25.—I. The natural hatred of the world to the church. II. God's permitting it to be shown. When ? Why ? III. The subtle manner in which this enmity seeks its object.

Verse 32.—"*He gave them hail for rain.*" Judgment substituted for mercy.

Verse 37 (*first clause*).—Wealth found upon us after affliction.

Verse 37 (*second clause*).—A consummation to be desired. This was the direct result of the divine presence. The circumstances out of which it grew were hard labour and persecution. It enabled them to leave Egypt, to journey far, to carry burdens, to fight enemies, etc.

Verse 39.—I. A dark cloud of providence is the guide of the people of God by day.   II. A bright cloud of promises is their guide by night.—*G. R.*

Verse 39.—The Lord's goodness exemplified in our varying conditions.   I. For prosperity—a cloud.   II. For adversity—a light.   A good text would be found in " light in the night."

Verse 40.—I. God often gives in love what is not asked.   So the bread from heaven which was beyond all they could ask or think.   II. He sometimes gives in anger what is asked.   They asked for flesh to eat—" and he brought quails." *G. R.*

Verse 41.—We have, I.   A type of the person of Christ, in the rock   1. Unsightly as Horeb—" When we shall see him, there is no beauty," etc. (Isai. liii. 2). 2. Firm and immovable—" Who is a rock, save our God ? " (2 Sam. xxi. 32).   II. A type of the sufferings of Christ, in the smitten rock.   1. Smitten by the rod of the Law.   2. Smitten to the heart.   III. A type of the benefits of Christ, in the water flowing from the rock—pure, refreshing, perpetual, abundant.—*James Bennett*, 1828.

Verse 41.—I. The miraculous energy of God's grace in the conversion of a sinner : " He opened the rock, and the waters gushed out."   II. The effect in relation to others, which demonstrates at once the excellence and the reality of the miracle in ourselves : " They ran in the dry places like a river."—*Thomas Dale*, 1836.

Verse 41.—I. The grand source—the rock opened.   II. The liberal stream— " gushed out."   III. The continued flow—" in dry places."

Verse 42.—I. The Lord mindful of *his* promise.   II. The Lord mindful of *our* persons.   III. The Lord working wonders as the result of both.

Verse 45.—Obedience to God the design of his mercies to us.

PSALM CVI.

GENERAL REMARKS.—*This Psalm begins and ends with Hallelujah—" Praise ye the Lord." The space between these two descriptions of praise is filled up with the mournful details of Israel's sin, and the extraordinary patience of God ; and truly we do well to bless the Lord both at the beginning and the end of our meditations when sin and grace are the themes. This sacred song is occupied with the historical part of the Old Testament, and is one of many which are thus composed : surely this should be a sufficient rebuke to those who speak slightingly of the historical Scriptures ; it ill becomes a child of God to think lightly of that which the Holy Spirit so frequently uses for our instruction. What other Scriptures had David beside those very histories which are so depreciated, and yet he esteemed them beyond his necessary food, and made them his songs in the house of his pilgrimage ?*

Israel's history is here written with the view of showing human sin, even as the preceding Psalm was composed to magnify divine goodness. It is, in fact, A NATIONAL CONFESSION, and includes an acknowledgment of the transgressions of Israel in Egypt, in the wilderness, and in Canaan, with devout petitions for forgiveness such as rendered the Psalm suitable for use in all succeeding generations, and especially in times of national captivity. It was probably written by David,—at any rate its first and last two verses are to be found in that sacred song which David delivered to Asaph when he brought up the ark of the Lord (1 Chron. xvi. 34, 35, 36).

While we are studying this holy Psalm, let us all along see ourselves in the Lord's ancient people, and bemoan our own provocations of the Most High, at the same time admiring his infinite patience, and adoring him because of it. May the Holy Spirit sanctify it to the promotion of humility and gratitude.

DIVISION.—*Praise and prayer are blended in the introduction (verses 1—5). Then comes the story of the nation's sins, which continues till the closing prayer and praise of the last two verses. While making confession the Psalmist acknowledges the sins committed in Egypt and at the Red Sea (verses 6—12), the lusting in the wilderness (13—15), the envying of Moses and Aaron (16—18), the worship of the golden calf (19—23), the despising of the promised land (24—27), the iniquity of Baal-Peor (28—30), and the waters of Meribah (32—33). Then he owns the failure of Israel when settled in Canaan, and mentions their consequent chastisements (34—44), together with the quick compassion which came to their relief when they were brought low (44—46). The closing prayer and doxology fill up the remaining verses.*

EXPOSITION.

PRAISE ye the LORD. O give thanks unto the LORD ; for *he is* good : for his mercy *endureth* for ever.

2 Who can utter the mighty acts of the LORD? *who* can shew forth all his praise ?

3 Blessed *are* they that keep judgment, *and* he that doeth righteousness at all times.

4 Remember me, O LORD, with the favour *that thou bearest unto* thy people ; O visit me with thy salvation ;

5 That I may see the good of thy chosen, that I may rejoice in the gladness of thy nation, that I may glory with thine inheritance.

1. *" Praise ye the Lord."* Hallelujah. Praise ye Jah. This song is for the assembled people, and they are all exhorted to join in praise to Jehovah. It is not meet for a few to praise and the rest to be silent ; but all should join. If David were present in churches where quartettes and choirs carry on all the singing, he would turn to the congregation and say, " Praise ye the Lord." Our meditation dwells upon human sin ; but on all occasions and in all occupations it is seasonable and profitable to praise the Lord. *" O give thanks unto the Lord ; for he is good."* To us needy creatures the goodness of God is the first attribute which excites praise.

and that praise takes the form of gratitude.   We praise the Lord truly when we give him thanks for what we have received from his goodness.   Let us never be slow to return unto the Lord our praise ; to thank him is the least we can do—let us not neglect it.   " *For his mercy endureth for ever.*"   Goodness towards sinners assumes the form of mercy, mercy should therefore be a leading note in our song.   Since man ceases not to be sinful, it is a great blessing that Jehovah ceases not to be merciful. From age to age the Lord deals graciously with his church, and to every individual in it he is constant and faithful in his grace, even for evermore.   In a short space we here have two arguments for praise, " for he is good : for his mercy endureth for ever ; " and these two arguments are themselves praises.   The very best language of adoration is that which adoringly in the plainest words sets forth the simple truth with regard to our great Lord.   No rhetorical flourishes or poetical hyperboles are needed, the bare facts are sublime poetry, and the narration of them with reverence is the essence of adoration.   This first verse is the text of all that which follows ; we are now to see how from generation to generation the mercy of God endured to his chosen people.

2. " *Who can utter the mighty acts of the Lord ?*"   What tongue of men or angels can duly describe the great displays of divine power ?   They are unutterable. Even those who saw them could not fully tell them.   " *Who can shew forth all his praise ?*"   To declare his works is the same thing as to praise him, for his own doings are his best commendation.   We cannot say one tenth so much for him as his own character and acts have already done ?   Those who praise the Lord have an infinite subject, a subject which will not be exhausted throughout eternity by the most enlarged intellects, nay, nor by the whole multitude of the redeemed, though no man can number them.   The questions of this verse never can be answered ; their challenge can never be accepted, except in that humble measure which can be reached by a holy life and a grateful heart.

3. Since the Lord is so good and so worthy to be praised, it must be for our happiness to obey him.   " *Blessed are they that keep judgment, and he that doeth righteousness at all times.*"   Multiplied are the blessednesses which must descend upon the whole company of the keepers of the way of justice, and especially upon that one rare man who at all times follows that which is right.   Holiness is happiness.   The way of right is the way of peace.   Yet men leave this road, and prefer the paths of the destroyer.   Hence the story which follows is in sad contrast with the happiness here depicted, because the way of Israel was not that of judgment and righteousness, but that of folly and iniquity.   The Psalmist, while contemplating the perfections of God, was impressed with the feeling that the servants of such a being must be happy, and when he looked around and saw how the tribes of old prospered when they obeyed, and suffered when they sinned, he was still more fully assured of the truth of his conclusion.   O could we but be free of sin we should be rid of sorrow ! We would not only be just, but " keep judgment " ; we would not be content with occasionally acting rightly, but would " do justice at all times."

4. " *Remember me, O Lord, with the favour which thou bearest unto thy people.*" Insignificant as I am, do not forget me.   Think of me with kindness, even as thou thinkest of thine own elect.   I cannot ask more, nor would I seek less.   Treat me as the least of thy saints are treated and I am content.   It should be enough for us if we fare as the rest of the family.   If even Balaam desired no more than to die the death of the righteous, we may be well content both to live as they live, and die as they die.   This feeling would prevent our wishing to escape trial, persecution, and chastisement ; these have fallen to the lot of saints, and why should we escape them ?

> " Must I be carried to the skies
>   On flowery beds of ease ?
> While others fought to win the prize,
>   And sailed through bloody seas."

At the same time we pray to have their sweets as well as their bitters.   If the Lord smiled upon their souls we cannot rest unless he smile upon us also.   We would dwell where they dwell, rejoice as they rejoice, sorrow as they sorrow, and in all things be for ever one with them in the favour of the Lord.   The sentence before us is a sweet prayer, at once humble and aspiring, submissive and expansive ; it might be used by a dying thief or a living apostle ; let us use it now.

" *O visit me with thy salvation.*"   Bring it home to me.   Come to my house and to my heart, and give me the salvation which thou hast prepared, and art alone able to bestow. We sometimes hear of a man's dying by the visitation of God, but here is one who knows that he can only *live* by the visitation of God. Jesus said of Zaccheus, " This day is salvation come to this house," and that was the case, because he himself had come there. There is no salvation apart from the Lord, and he must visit us with it or we shall never obtain it. We are too sick to visit our Great Physician, and therefore he visits us. O that our great Bishop would hold a visitation of all the churches, and bestow his benediction upon all his flock. Sometimes the second prayer of this verse seems to be too great for us, for we feel that we are not worthy that the Lord should come under our roof. Visit me, Lord ! Can it be ? Dare I ask for it ? And yet I must, for thou alone canst bring me salvation : therefore, Lord, I entreat thee come unto me, and abide with me for ever.

5. " *That I may see the good of thy chosen.*" His desire for the divine favour was excited by the hope that he might participate in all the good things which flow to the people of God through their election. The Father has blessed us with all spiritual blessings in Christ Jesus, according as he has chosen us in him, and in these precious gifts we desire to share through the saving visitation of the Lord. No other good do we wish to see, perceive, and apprehend, but that which is the peculiar treasure of the saints. " *That I may rejoice in the gladness of thy nation.*" The Psalmist, having sought his portion in the good of the chosen, now also begs to be a partaker in their joy : for of all the nations under heaven the Lord's true people are the happiest. " *That I may glory with thine inheritance.*" He would have a part and lot in their honour as well as their joy. He was willing to find glory where saints find it, namely, in being reproached for truth's sake. To serve the Lord and endure shame for his sake is the glory of the saints below : Lord, let me rejoice to bear my part therein. To be with God above, for ever blessed in Christ Jesus, is the glory of saints above : O Lord, be pleased to allot me a place there also.

These introductory thanksgivings and supplications, though they occur first in the Psalm, are doubtless the result of the contemplations which succeed them, and may be viewed not only as the preface, but also as the moral of the whole sacred song.

6 We have sinned with our fathers, we have committed iniquity, we have done wickedly.

7 Our fathers understood not thy wonders in Egypt ; they remembered not the multitude of thy mercies ; but provoked *him* at the sea, *even* at the Red sea.

8 Nevertheless he saved them for his name's sake, that he might make his mighty power to be known.

9 He rebuked the Red Sea also, and it was dried up : so he led them through the depths, as through the wilderness.

10 And he saved them from the hand of him that hated *them*, and redeemed them from the hand of the enemy.

11 And the waters covered their enemies : there was not one of them left.

12 Then believed they his words ; they sang his praise.

6. " *We have sinned with our fathers.*" Here begins a long and particular confession. Confession of sin is the readiest way to secure an answer to the prayer of verse 4 ; God visits with his salvation the soul which acknowledges its need of a Saviour. Men may be said to have sinned with their fathers when they imitate them, when they follow the same objects, and make their own lives to be mere continuations of the follies of their sires. Moreover, Israel was but one nation in all time, and the confession which follows sets forth the national rather than the personal sin of the Lord's people. They enjoyed national privileges, and therefore they shared in national guilt. " *We have committed iniquity, we have done wickedly.*" Thus is the confession repeated three times, in token of the sincerity and heartiness of it. Sins of omission, commission, and rebellion we ought to acknowledge under distinct heads, that we may show a due sense of the number and heinousness of our offences.

7. " *Our fathers understood not thy wonders in Egypt.*" The Israelites saw the miraculous plagues and ignorantly wondered at them : their design of love, their

deep moral and spiritual lessons, and their revelation of the divine power and justice they were unable to perceive. A long sojourn among idolaters had blunted the perceptions of the chosen family, and cruel slavery had ground them down into mental sluggishness. Alas, how many of God's wonders are not understood, or misunderstood by us still. We fear the sons are no great improvement upon the sires. We inherit from our fathers much sin and little wisdom ; they could only leave us what they themselves possessed. We see from this verse that a want of understanding is no excuse for sin, but is itself one count in the indictment against Israel. "*They remembered not the multitude of thy mercies.*" The sin of the understanding leads on to the sin of the memory. What is not understood will soon be forgotten. Men feel little interest in preserving husks ; if they know nothing of the inner kernel they will take no care of the shells. It was an aggravation of Israel's sin that when God's mercies were so numerous they yet were able to forget them all. Surely some out of such a multitude of benefits ought to have remained engraven upon their hearts ; but if grace does not give us understanding, nature will soon cast out the memory of God's great goodness. "*But provoked him at the sea, even at the Red sea.*" To fall out at starting was a bad sign. Those who did not begin well can hardly be expected to end well. Israel is not quite out of Egypt, and yet she begins to provoke the Lord by doubting his power to deliver, and questioning his faithfulness to his promise. The sea was only *called* Red, but their sins were scarlet in reality ; it was known as the " sea of weeds," but far worse weeds grew in their hearts.

8. "*Nevertheless he saved them for his name's sake, that he might make his mighty power to be known.*" When he could find no other reason for his mercy he found it in his own glory, and seized the opportunity to display his power. If Israel does not deserve to be saved, yet Pharaoh's pride needs to be crushed, and therefore Israel shall be delivered. The Lord very jealously guards his own name and honour. It shall never be said of him that he cannot or will not save his people, or that he cannot abate the haughtiness of his defiant foes. This respect unto his own honour ever leads him to deeds of mercy, and hence we may well rejoice that he is a jealous God.

9. "*He rebuked the Red sea also, and it was dried up.*" A word did it. The sea heard his voice and obeyed. How many rebukes of God are lost upon *us !* Are *we* not more unmanageable than the ocean ? God did, as it were, chide the sea, and say, "Wherefore dost thou stop the way of my people ? Their path to Canaan lies through thy channel, how darest thou hinder them ? " The sea perceived its Master and his seed royal, and made way at once. "*So he led them through the depths, as through the wilderness.*" As if it had been the dry floor of the desert the tribes passed over the bottom of the gulf ; nor was their passage venturesome, for HE bade them go ; nor dangerous, for HE led them. We also have under divine protection passed through many trials and afflictions, and with the Lord as our guide we have experienced no fear and endured no perils. We have been led through the deeps as through the wilderness.

10. "*And he saved them from the hand of him that hated them.*" Pharaoh was drowned, and the power of Egypt so crippled that throughout the forty years' wanderings of Israel they were never threatened by their old masters. "*And redeemed them from the hand of the enemy.*" This was a redemption by power, and one of the most instructive types of the redemption of the Lord's people from sin and hell by the power which worketh in them.

11. "*And the waters covered their enemies : there was not one of them left.*" The Lord does nothing by halves. What he begins he carries through to the end. This, again, made Israel's sin the greater, because they saw the thoroughness of the divine justice, and the perfection of the divine faithfulness. In the covering of their enemies we have a type of the pardon of our sins ; they are sunk as in the sea, never to rise again ; and, blessed be the Lord, there is " not one of them left."—Not one sin of thought, or word, or deed, the blood of Jesus has covered all. " I will cast their iniquities into the depths of the sea."

12. "*Then believed they his words.*" That is to say, they believed the promise when they saw it fulfilled, but not till then. This is mentioned, not to their credit, but to their shame. Those who do not believe the Lord's word till they see it performed are not believers at all. Who would not believe when the fact stares him in the face ? The Egyptians would have done as much as this. "*They sang his praise.*" How could they do otherwise ? Their song was very excellent, and is the type of the song of heaven : but sweet as it was, it was quite as short, and when it was ended

they fell to murmuring. " They sang his praise," but " they soon forgat his works."
Between Israel singing and Israel sinning there was scarce a step. Their song was
good while it lasted, but it was no sooner begun than over.

13 They soon forgat his works ; they waited not for his counsel ;
14 But lusted exceedingly in the wilderness, and tempted God in the
desert.
15 And he gave them their request ; but sent leanness into their soul.

13. " *They soon forgat his works.*" They seemed in a hurry to get the Lord's
mercies out of their memories ; they hasted to be ungrateful. " *They waited not
for his counsel,*" neither waiting for the word of command or promise ; eager to have
their own way, and prone to trust in themselves. This is a common fault in the Lord's
family to this day ; we are long in learning to wait *for* the Lord, and *upon* the Lord.
With him is counsel and strength, but we are vain enough to look for these to ourselves,
and therefore we grievously err.

14. " *But lusted exceedingly in the wilderness.*" Though they would not wait
God's will, they are hot to have their own. When the most suitable and pleasant
food was found them in abundance, it did not please them long, but they grew dainty
and sniffed at angel's food, and must needs have flesh to eat, which was unhealthy
diet for that warm climate, and for their easy life. This desire of theirs they dwelt
upon till it became a mania with them, and, like a wild horse, carried away its rider.
For a meal of meat they were ready to curse their God and renounce the land which
floweth with milk and honey. What a wonder that the Lord did not take them
at their word ! It is plain that they vexed him greatly, " *And tempted God in the
desert.*" In the place where they were absolutely dependent upon him and were
every day fed by his direct provision, they had the presumption to provoke their
God. They would have him change the plans of his wisdom, supply their sensual
appetites, and work miracles to meet their wicked unbelief : these things the Lord
would not do, but they went as far as they could in trying to induce him to do so.
They failed not in their wicked attempt because of any goodness in themselves, but
because God " cannot be tempted,"—temptation has no power over him, he yields
not to man's threats or promises.

15. " *And he gave them their request.*" Prayer may be answered in anger and
denied in love. That God gives a man his desire is no proof that he is the object
of divine favour, everything depends upon what that desire is. " *But sent leanness
into their soul.*" Ah, that " but " ! It embittered all. The meat was poison to
them when it came without a blessing ; whatever it might do in fattening the body,
it was poor stuff when it made the soul lean. If we must know scantiness, may God
grant it may not be scantiness of soul : yet this is a common attendant upon worldly
prosperity. When wealth grows with many a man his worldly estate is fatter, but
his soul's state is leaner. To gain silver and lose gold is a poor increase ; but to win
for the body and lose for the soul is far worse. How earnestly might Israel have
unprayed her prayers had she known what would come with their answer ! The
prayers of lust will have to be wept over. We fret and fume till we have our
desire, and then we have to fret still more because the attainment of it ends in
bitter disappointment.

16 They envied Moses also in the camp, *and* Aaron the saint of the LORD.
17 The earth opened and swallowed up Dathan, and covered the company
of Abiram.
18 And a fire was kindled in their company ; the flame burned up the
wicked.

16. " *They envied Moses also in the camp.*" Though to him as the Lord's chosen
instrument they owed everything they grudged him the authority which it was
needful that he should exercise for their good. Some were more openly rebellious
than others, and became leaders of the mutiny, but a spirit of dissatisfaction was
general, and therefore the whole nation is charged with it. Who can hope to escape
envy when the meekest of men was subject to it ? How unreasonable was this envy,
for Moses was the one man in all the camp who laboured hardest and had most to

bear. They should have sympathised with him ; to envy him was ridiculous. " *And Aaron the saint of the Lord.*" By divine choice Aaron was set apart to be holiness unto the Lord, and instead of thanking God that he had favoured them with a high priest by whose intercession their prayers would be presented, they cavilled at the divine election, and quarrelled with the man who was to offer sacrifice for them. Thus neither church nor state was ordered aright for them ; they would snatch from Moses his sceptre, and from Aaron his mitre. It is the mark of bad men that they are envious of the good, and spiteful against their best benefactors.

17. " *The earth opened and swallowed up Dathan, and covered the company of Abiram.*" Korah is not mentioned, for mercy was extended to his household, though he himself perished. The earth could no longer bear up under the weight of these rebels and ingrates : God's patience was exhausted when they began to assail his servants, for his children are very dear to him, and he that toucheth them touches the apple of his eye. Moses had opened the sea for their deliverance, and now that they provoke him, the earth opens for their destruction. It was time that the nakedness of their sin was covered, and that the earth should open her mouth to devour those who opened their mouths against the Lord and his servants.

18. " *And a fire was kindled in their company ; the flame burned up the wicked.*" The Levites who were with Korah perished by fire, which was a most fitting death for those who intruded into the priesthood, and so offered strange fire. God has more than one arrow in his quiver, the fire can consume those whom the earthquake spares. These terrible things in righteousness are mentioned here to show the obstinacy of the people in continuing to rebel against the Lord. Terrors were as much lost upon them as mercies had been ; they could neither be drawn nor driven.

19 They made a calf in Horeb, and worshipped the molten image.

20 Thus they changed their glory into the similitude of an ox that eateth grass.

21 They forgat God their saviour, which had done great things in Egypt ;

22 Wondrous works in the land of Ham, *and* terrible things by the Red sea.

23 Therefore he said that he would destroy them, had not Moses his chosen stood before him in the breach, to turn away his wrath, lest he should destroy *them*.

19. " *They made a calf in Horeb.*" In the very place where they had solemnly pledged themselves to obey the Lord they broke the second, if not the first, of his commandments, and set up the Egyptian symbol of the ox, and bowed before it. The ox image is here sarcastically called " a calf " ; idols are worthy of no respect, scorn is never more legitimately used than when it is poured upon all attempts to set forth the Invisible God. The Israelites were foolish indeed when they thought they saw the slightest divine glory in a bull, nay, in the mere image of a bull. To believe that the image of a bull could be the image of God must need great credulity. " *And worshipped the molten image.*" Before it they paid divine honours, and said, " These be thy gods, O Israel." This was sheer madness. After the same fashion the Ritualists must needs set up their symbols and multiply them exceedingly. Spiritual worship they seem unable to apprehend ; their worship is sensuous to the highest degree, and appeals to eye, and ear, and nose. O the folly of men to block up their own way to acceptable worship, and to make the path of spiritual religion, which is hard to our nature, harder still through the stumbling-blocks which they cast into it. We have heard the richness of Popish paraphernalia much extolled, but an idolatrous image when made of gold is not one jot the less abominable than it would have been had it been made of dross and dung : the beauty of art cannot conceal the deformity of sin. We are told also of the suggestiveness of their symbols, but what of that, when God forbids the use of them ? Vain also is it to plead that such worship is *hearty*. So much the worse. Heartiness in forbidden actions is only an increase of transgression.

20. " *Thus they changed their glory into the similitude of an ox that eateth grass.*" They said that they only meant to worship the one God under a fitting and suggestive similitude by which his great power would be set forth to the multitude ; they pleaded the great Catholic revival which followed upon this return to a more ornate ceremonial, for the people thronged around Aaron, and danced before the calf with all their

might. But in very deed they had given up the true God, whom it had been their glory to adore, and had set up a rival to him, not a representation of him ; for how should he be likened to a bullock ? The Psalmist is very contemptuous, and justly so : irreverence towards idols is an indirect reverence to God. False gods, attempts to represent the true God, and indeed, all material things which are worshipped are so much filth upon the face of the earth, whether they be crosses, crucifixes, virgins, wafers, relics, or even the Pope himself. We are by far too mealy-mouthed about these infamous abominations : God abhors them, and so should we. To renounce the glory of spiritual worship for outward pomp and show is the height of folly, and deserves to be treated as such.

21, 22. *" They forgat God their Saviour."* Remembering the calf involved forgetting God. He had commanded them to make no image, and in daring to disobey they forgot his commands. Moreover, it is clear that they must altogether have forgotten the nature and character of Jehovah, or they could never have likened him to a grass-eating animal. Some men hope to keep their sins and their God too— the fact being that he who sins is already so far departed from the Lord that he has actually forgotten him. *" Which had done great things in Egypt."* God in Egypt had overcome all the idols, and yet they so far forgot him as to liken him to them. Could an ox work miracles ? Could a golden calf cast plagues upon Israel's enemies ? They were brutish to set up such a wretched mockery of deity, after having seen what the true God could really achieve. *" Wondrous works in the land of Ham, and terrible things by the Red sea."* They saw several ranges of miracles, the Lord did not stint them as to the evidences of his eternal power and godhead, and yet they could not rest content with worshipping him in his own appointed way, but must needs have a *Directory* of their own invention, an elaborate ritual after the old Egyptian fashion, and a manifest object of worship to assist them in adoring Jehovah. This was enough to provoke the Lord, and it did so ; how much he is angered every day in our own land no tongue can tell.

23. *" Therefore he said that he would destroy them."* The threatening of destruction came at last. For the first wilderness sin he chastened them, sending leanness into their soul ; for the second he weeded out the offenders, the flame burned up the wicked ; for the third he threatened to destroy them ; for the fourth he lifted up his hand and almost came to blows (verse 26) ; for the fifth he actually smote them, " and the plague brake in among them " ; and so the punishment increased with their perseverance in sin. This is worth noting, and it should serve as a warning to the man who goeth on his iniquities. God tries words before he comes to blows, " he *said* that he would destroy them " ; but his words are not to be trifled with, for he means them, and has power to make them good. *" Had not Moses his chosen stood before him in the breach."* Like a bold warrior who defends the wall when there is an opening for the adversary and destruction is rushing in upon the city, Moses stopped the way of avenging justice with his prayers. Moses had great power with God. He was an eminent type of our Lord, who is called, as Moses here is styled, " mine *elect*, in whom my soul delighteth." As the Elect Redeemer interposed between the Lord and a sinful world, so did Moses stand between the Lord and his offending people. The story as told by Moses himself is full of interest and instruction, and tends greatly to magnify the goodness of the Lord, who thus suffered himself to be turned from the fierceness of his anger.

With disinterested affection, and generous renunciation of privileges offered to himself and his family, the great Lawgiver interceded with the Lord *" to turn away his wrath, lest he should destroy them."* Behold the power of a righteous man's intercession. Mighty as was the sin of Israel to provoke vengeance, prayer was mightier in turning it away. How diligently ought we to plead with the Lord for this guilty world, and especially for his own backsliding people ! Who would not employ an agency so powerful for an end so gracious ! The Lord still hearkens to the voice of a man, shall not our voices be often exercised in supplicating for a guilty people ?

24 Yea, they despised the pleasant land, they believed not his word :

25 But murmured in their tents, *and* hearkened not unto the voice of the Lord.

26 Therefore he lifted up his hand against them, to overthrow them in the wilderness :

27 To overthrow their seed also among the nations, and to scatter them in the lands.

24. "*Yea, they despised the pleasant land.*" They spoke lightly of it, though it was the joy of all lands : they did not think it worth the trouble of seeking and conquering ; they even spoke of Egypt, the land of their iron bondage, as though they preferred it to Canaan, the land which floweth with milk and honey. It is an ill sign with a Christian when he begins to think lightly of heaven and heavenly things ; it indicates a perverted mind, and it is moreover, a high offence to the Lord to despise that which he esteems so highly that he in infinite love reserves it for his own chosen. To prefer earthly things to heavenly blessings is to prefer Egypt to Canaan, the house of bondage to the land of promise. "*They believed not his word.*" This is the root sin. If we do not believe the Lord's word, we shall think lightly of his promised gifts. "They could not enter in because of unbelief"—this was the key which turned the lock against them. When pilgrims to the Celestial City begin to doubt the Lord of the way, they soon come to think little of the rest at the journey's end, and this is the surest way to make them bad travellers. Israel's unbelief demanded spies to see the land ; the report of those spies was of a mingled character, and so a fresh crop of unbelief sprang up, with consequences most deplorable.

25. "*But murmured in their tents.*" From unbelief to murmuring is a short and natural step ; they even fell to weeping when they had the best ground for rejoicing. Murmuring is a great sin and not a mere weakness ; it contains within itself unbelief, pride, rebellion, and a whole host of sins. It is a home sin, and is generally practised by complainers " in their tents," but it is just as evil there as in the streets, and will be quite as grievous to the Lord. "*And hearkened not unto the voice of the Lord.*" Making a din with their own voices, they refused attention to their best Friend. Murmurers are bad hearers.

26, 27. "*Therefore he lifted up his hand against them, to overthrow them in the wilderness.*" He swore in his wrath that they should not enter into his rest; he commenced his work of judgment upon them, and they began to die. Only let God lift his hand against a man and his day has come ; he falls terribly whom Jehovah overthrows. "*To overthrow their seed also among the nations, and to scatter them in the lands.*" Foreseeing that their descendants would reproduce their sins, he solemnly declared that he would give them over to captivity and the sword. Those whose carcases fell in the wilderness were, in a sense, exiles from the land of promise, and, being surrounded by many hostile tribes, they were virtually in a foreign land : to die far off from their father's inheritance was a just and weighty doom, which their rebellions had richly deserved. Our own loss of fellowship with God, and the divisions in our churches, doubtless often come to us as punishments for the sins out of which they grow. If we will not honour the Lord we cannot expect him to honour us. Our captains shall soon become captives, and our princes shall be prisoners if we forget the Lord and despise his mercies. Our singing shall be turned into sighing, and our mirth into misery if we walk contrary to the mind of the Lord.

28 They joined themselves also unto Baal-peor, and ate the sacrifices of the dead.

29 Thus they provoked *him* to anger with their inventions : and the plague brake in upon them.

30 Then stood up Phinehas, and executed judgment : and *so* the plague was stayed.

31 And that was counted unto him for righteousness unto all generations for evermore.

28. "*They joined themselves also unto Baal-peor.*" Ritualism led on to the adoration of false gods. If we choose a false way of worship we shall, ere long, choose to worship a false god. This abomination of the Moabites was an idol in whose worship women gave up their bodies to the most shameless lust. Think of the people of a holy God coming down to this. "*And ate the sacrifices of the dead.*" In the orgies with which the Baalites celebrated their detestable worship Israel joined, partaking even in their sacrifices as earnest inner-court worshippers, though

the gods were but dead idols. Perhaps they assisted in necromantic rites which were intended to open a correspondence with departed spirits, thus endeavouring to break the seal of God's providence, and burst into the secret chambers which God has shut up. Those who are weary of seeking the living God have often shown a hankering after dark sciences, and have sought after fellowship with demons and spirits. To what strong delusions those are often given up who cast off the fear of God! This remark is as much needed now as in days gone by.

29. " *Thus they provoked him to anger with their inventions : and the plague brake in upon them.*" Open licentiousness and avowed idolatry were too gross to be winked at. This time the offences clamoured for judgment, and the judgment came at once. Twenty-four thousand persons fell before a sudden and deadly disease which threatened to run through the whole camp. Their new sins brought on them a disease new to their tribes. When men invent sins God will not be slow to invent punishments. Their vices were a moral pest, and they were visited with a bodily pest : so the Lord meets like with its like.

30. " *Then stood up Phinehas, and executed judgment : and so the plague was stayed.*" God has his champions left in the worst times, and they will stand up when the time comes for them to come forth to battle. His righteous indignation moved him to a quick execution of two open offenders. His honest spirit could not endure that lewdness should be publicly practised at a time when a fast had been proclaimed. Such daring defiance of God and of all law he could not brook, and so with his sharp javelin he transfixed the two guilty ones in the very act. It was a holy passion which inflamed him, and no enmity to either of the persons whom he slew. The circumstances were so remarkable and the sin so flagrant that it would have involved great sin in a public man to have stood still and seen God thus defied, and Israel thus polluted. Phinehas was not of this mind, he was no trimmer, or palliator of sin, his heart was sound in God's statutes, and his whole nature was ablaze with zeal for God's glory, and therefore, though a priest, and therefore not obliged to be an executioner, he undertook the unwelcome task, and though both transgressors were of princely stock he had no respect of persons, but dealt justice upon them as if they had been the lowest of the people. This brave and decided deed was so acceptable to God as a proof that there were some sincere souls in Israel that the deadly visitation went no further. Two deaths had sufficed to save the lives of the multitude.

31. " *And that was counted unto him for righteousness unto all generations for evermore.*" Down to the moment when this Psalm was penned the house of Phinehas was honoured in Israel. His faith had performed a valorous deed, and his righteousness was testified of the Lord, and honoured by the continuance of his family in the priesthood. He was impelled by motives so pure that what would otherwise have been a deed of blood was justified in the sight of God ; nay, more, was made *the* evidence that Phinehas was righteous. No personal ambition, or private revenge, or selfish passion, or even fanatical bigotry, inspired the man of God ; but zeal for God, indignation at open filthiness, and true patriotism urged him on.

Once again we have cause to note the mercy of God that even when his warrant was out, and actual execution was proceeding, he stayed his hand at the suit of one man : finding, as it were, an apology for his grace when justice seemed to demand immediate vengeance.

32 They angered *him* also at the waters of strife, so that it went ill with Moses for their sakes :

33 Because they provoked his spirit, so that he spake unadvisedly with his lips.

32. " *They angered him also at the waters of strife.*" Will they never have done ? The scene changes, but the sin continues. Aforetime they had mutinied about water when prayer would soon have turned the desert into a standing pool, but now they do it again after their former experience of the divine goodness. This made the sin a double, yea a sevenfold offence, and caused the anger of the Lord to be the more intense. " *So that it went ill with Moses for their sakes.*" Moses was at last wearied out, and began to grow angry with them, and utterly hopeless of their ever improving ; can we wonder at it, for he was man and not God ? After forty years bearing with them the meek man's temper gave way, and he called them rebels, and

showed unhallowed anger ; and therefore he was not permitted to enter the land which he desired to inherit. Truly, he had a sight of the goodly country from the top of Pisgah, but entrance was denied him, and thus it went ill with him. It was *their* sin which angered him, but *he* had to bear the consequences ; however clear it may be that others are more guilty than ourselves, we should always remember that this will not screen *us*, but every man must bear his own burden.

33. " *Because they provoked his spirit, so that he spake unadvisedly with his lips.*" Which seems a small sin compared with that of others, but then it was the sin of Moses, the Lord's chosen servant, who had seen and known so much of the Lord, and therefore it could not be passed by. He did not speak blasphemously, or falsely, but only hastily and without care ; but this is a serious fault in a law-giver, and especially in one who speaks for God. This passage is to our mind one of the most terrible in the Bible. Truly we serve a jealous God. Yet he is not a hard master, or austere ; we must not think so, but we must the rather be jealous of ourselves, and watch that we live the more carefully, and speak the more advisedly, because we serve such a Lord. We ought also to be very careful how we treat the ministers of the gospel, lest by provoking their spirit we should drive them into any unseemly behaviour which should bring upon them the chastisement of the Lord. Little do a murmuring, quarrelsome people dream of the perils in which they involve their pastors by their untoward behaviour.

34 They did not destroy the nations, concerning whom the LORD commanded them :

35 But were mingled among the heathen, and learned their works.

36 And they served their idols : which were a snare unto them.

37 Yea, they sacrificed their sons and their daughters unto devils,

38 And shed innocent blood, *even* the blood of their sons and of their daughters, whom they sacrificed unto the idols of Canaan : and the land was polluted with blood.

39 Thus were they defiled with their own works, and went a whoring with their own inventions.

40 Therefore was the wrath of the LORD kindled against his people, insomuch that he abhorred his own inheritance.

41 And he gave them into the hands of the heathen ; and they that hated them ruled over them.

42 Their enemies also oppressed them, and they were brought into subjection under their hand.

43 Many times did he deliver them ; but they provoked *him* with their counsel, and were brought low for their iniquity.

34. " *They did not destroy the nations, concerning whom the Lord commanded them.*" They were commissioned to act as executioners upon races condemned for their unnatural crimes, and through sloth, cowardice, or sinful complacency they sheathed the sword too soon, very much to their own danger and disquietude. It is a great evil with professors that they are not zealous for the total destruction of all sin within and without. We make alliances of peace where we ought to proclaim war to the knife ; we plead our constitutional temperament, our previous habits, the necessity of our circumstances, or some other evil excuse as an apology for being content with a very partial sanctification, if indeed it be sanctification at all. We are slow also to rebuke sin in others, and are ready to spare respectable sins, which like Agag walk with mincing steps. The measure of our destruction of sin is not to be our inclination, or the habit of others, but the Lord's command. We have no warrant for dealing leniently with any sin, be it what it may.

35. " *But were mingled among the heathen, and learned their works.*" It was not the wilderness which caused Israel's sins ; they were just as disobedient when settled in the land of promise. They found evil company, and delighted in it. Those whom they should have destroyed they made their friends. Having enough faults of their own, they were yet ready to go to school to the filthy Canaanites, and educate themselves still more in the arts of iniquity. It was certain that they could learn

no good from men whom the Lord had condemned to utter destruction. Few would wish to go to the condemned cell for learning, yet Israel sat at the feet of accursed Canaan, and rose up proficient in every abomination. This, too, is a grievous but common error among professors: they court worldly company and copy worldly fashions, and yet it is their calling to bear witness against these things. None can tell what evil has come of the folly of worldly conformity.

36. "*And they served their idols: which were a snare unto them.*" They were fascinated by the charms of idolatry, though it brings misery upon its votaries. A man cannot serve sin without being ensnared by it. It is like birdlime, and to touch it is to be taken by it. Samson laid his head in the Philistine woman's lap, but ere long he woke up shorn of his strength. Dalliance with sin is fatal to spiritual liberty.

37 and 38. "*Yea, they sacrificed their sons and their daughters unto devils.*" This was being snared indeed; they were spell-bound by the cruel superstition, and were carried so far as even to become murderers of their own children, in honour of the most detestable deities, which were rather devils than gods. "*And shed innocent blood.*" The poor little ones whom they put to death in sacrifice had not been partakers of their sin, and God looked with the utmost indignation upon the murder of the innocent. "*Even the blood of their sons and of their daughters, whom they sacrificed unto the idols of Canaan.*" Who knows how far evil will go? It drove men to be unnatural as well as ungodly. Had they but thought for a moment, they must have seen that a deity who could be pleased with the blood of babes spilt by their own sires could not be a deity at all, but must be a demon, worthy to be detested and not adored. How could they prefer such service to that of Jehovah? Did *he* tear their babes from their bosoms and smile at their death throes? Men will sooner wear the iron yoke of Satan than carry the pleasant burden of the Lord; does not this prove to a demonstration the deep depravity of their hearts? If man be not totally depraved, what worse would he do if he were? Does not this verse describe the *ne plus ultra* of iniquity? "*And the land was polluted with blood.*" The promised land, the holy land, which was the glory of all lands, for God was there, was defiled with the reeking gore of innocent babes, and by the bloodred hands of their parents, who slew them in order to pay homage to devils. Alas! alas! What vexation was this to the spirit of the Lord.

39. "*Thus were they defiled with their own works, and went a whoring with their own inventions.*" Not only the land but the inhabitants of it were polluted. They broke the marriage bond between them and the Lord, and fell into spiritual adultery. The language is strong, but the offence could not be fitly described in less forcible words. As a husband is deeply dishonoured and sorely wounded should his wife become unchaste and run riot with many paramours in his own house, so was the Lord incensed at his people for setting up gods many and lords many in his own land. They made and invented new gods, and then worshipped what they had made. What a folly! Their novel deities were loathsome monsters and cruel demons, and yet they paid them homage. What wickedness! And to commit this folly and wickedness they cast off the true God, whose miracles they had seen, and whose people they were. This was provocation of the severest sort.

40, 41. "*Therefore was the wrath of the Lord kindled against his people, insomuch that he abhorred his own inheritance.*" Not that even then he broke his covenant or utterly cast off his offending people, but he felt the deepest indignation, and even looked upon them with abhorrence. The feeling described is like to that of a husband who still loves his guilty wife, and yet when he thinks of her lewdness feels his whole nature rising in righteous anger at her, so that the very sight of her afflicts his soul. How far the divine wrath can burn against those whom he yet loves in his heart it were hard to say, but certainly Israel pushed the experiment to the extreme. "*And he gave them into the hand of the heathen.*" This was the manifestation of his abhorrence. He gave them a taste of the result of sin; they spared the heathen, mixed with them and imitated them, and soon they had to smart from them, for hordes of invaders were let loose upon them to spoil them at their pleasure. Men make rods for their own backs. Their own inventions become their punishments. "*And they that hated them ruled over them.*" And who could wonder? Sin never creates true love. They joined the heathen in their wickedness, and they did not win their hearts, but rather provoked their contempt. If we mix with men of the world they will soon become our masters and our tyrants, and we cannot want worse.

42. "*Their enemies also oppressed them.*" This was according to their nature;

an Israelite always fares ill at the hands of the heathen. Leniency to Canaan turned out to be cruelty to themselves. "*And they were brought into subjection under their hand.*" They were bowed down by laborious bondage, and made to lie low under tyranny. In their God they had found a kind master, but in those with whom they had perversely sought fellowship they found despots of the most barbarous sort. He who leaves his God leaves happiness for misery. God can make our enemies to be rods in his hands to flog us back to our best Friend.

43. "*Many times did he deliver them.*" By reading the book of Judges we shall see how truthful is this sentence: again and again their foes were routed, and they were set free again, only to return with vigour to their former evil ways. "*But they provoked him with their counsel.*" With deliberation they agreed to transgress anew; self-will was their counsellor, and they followed it to their own destruction. "*And were brought low for their iniquity.*" Worse and worse were the evils brought upon them, lower and lower they fell in sin, and consequently in sorrow. In dens and caves of the earth they hid themselves; they were deprived of all warlike weapons, and were utterly despised by their conquerors; they were rather a race of serfs than of free men until the Lord in mercy raised them up again. Could we but fully know the horrors of the wars which desolated Palestine, and the ravages which caused famine and starvation, we should shudder at the sins which were thus rebuked. Deeply engrained in their nature must the sin of idolatry have been, or they would not have returned to it with such persistence in the teeth of such penalties; we need not marvel at this, there is a still greater wonder, man prefers sin and hell to heaven and God.

The lesson to ourselves, as God's people, is to walk humbly and carefully before the Lord, and above all to keep ourselves from idols. Woe unto those who become partakers of Rome's idolatries, for they will be joined with her in her plagues. May grace be given to *us* to keep the separated path, and remain undefiled with the fornication of the scarlet harlot of Babylon.

44 Nevertheless he regarded their affliction, when he heard their cry:

45 And he remembered for them his covenant, and repented according to the multitude of his mercies.

46 He made them also to be pitied of all those that carried them captives.

47 Save us, O Lord our God, and gather us from among the heathen, to give thanks unto thy holy name, *and* to triumph in thy praise.

44. "*Nevertheless he regarded their affliction, when he heard their cry.*" Notwithstanding all these provoking rebellions and detestable enormities the Lord still heard their prayer and pitied them. This is very wonderful, very godlike. One would have thought that the Lord would have shut out their prayer, seeing they had shut their ears against his admonitions; but no, he had a father's heart, and a sight of their sorrows touched his soul, the sound of their cries overcame his heart, and he looked upon them with compassion. His fiercest wrath towards his own people is only a temporary flame, but his love burns on for ever like the light of his own immortality.

45. "*And he remembered for them his covenant.*" The covenant is the sure foundation of mercy, and when the whole fabric of outward grace manifested in the saints lies in ruins this is the fundamental basis of love which is never moved, and upon it the Lord proceeds to build again a new structure of grace. Covenant mercy is sure as the throne of God. "*And repented according to the multitude of his mercies.*" He did not carry out the destruction which he had commenced. Speaking after the manner of men he changed his mind, and did not leave them to their enemies to be utterly cut off, because he saw that his covenant would in such a case have been broken. The Lord is so full of grace that he has not only mercy but mercies, yea a multitude of them, and these hive in the covenant and treasure up good for the erring sons of men.

46. "*He made them also to be pitied of all those that carried them captives.*" Having the hearts of all men in his hands he produced compassion even in heathen bosoms. Even as he found Joseph friends in Egypt, so did he raise up sympathisers for his captive servants. In our very worst condition our God has ways and means for allaying the severity of our sorrows: he can find us helpers among those who have been our oppressors, and he will do so if we be indeed his people.

47. This is the closing prayer, arranged by prophecy for those who would in future time be captives, and suitable for all who before David's days had been driven from home by the tyranny of Saul, or who had remained in exile after the various scatterings by famine and distress which had happened in the iron age of the judges. *" Save us, O Lord our God."* The mention of the covenant encouraged the afflicted to call the Lord their God, and this enabled them with greater boldness to entreat him to interpose on their behalf and rescue them. *" And gather us from among the heathen."* Weary now of the ungodly and their ways, they long to be brought into their own separated country, where they might again enjoy the means of grace, enter into holy fellowship with their brethren, escape from contaminating examples, and be free to wait upon the Lord. How often do true believers now-a-days long to be removed from ungodly households, where their souls are vexed with the conversation of the wicked. *" To give thanks unto thy holy name, and to triumph in thy praise."* Weaned from idols, they desire to make mention of Jehovah's name alone, and to ascribe their mercies to his ever abiding faithfulness and love. The Lord had often saved them for his holy name's sake, and therefore they feel that when again restored they would render all their gratitude to that saving name, yea, it should be their glory to praise Jehovah and none else.

48 Blessed *be* the LORD God of Israel from everlasting to everlasting : and let all the people say, Amen. Praise ye the LORD.

48. *" Blessed be the Lord God of Israel from everlasting to everlasting."* Has not his mercy endured for ever, and should not his praise be of like duration ? Jehovah, the God of Israel, has blessed his people, should they not also bless him ? *" And let all the people say, Amen."* They have all been spared by his grace, let them all join in the adoration with loud unanimous voice. What a thunder of praise would thus be caused ! Yet should a nation thus magnify him, yea, should all the nations past and present unite in the solemn acclaim, it would fall far short of his deserts. O for the happy day when all flesh shall see the glory of God, and all shall aloud proclaim his praise. *" Praise ye the Lord,"* or *" Hallelujah."*

Reader, praise thou the Lord, as he who writes this feeble exposition now does with his whole heart.

> " Now blest, for ever blest, be He,
> The same throughout eternity,
> Our Israel's God adored !
> Let all the people join the lay,
> And loudly, ' Hallelujah,' say,
> ' Praise ye the living Lord ! ' "

EXPLANATORY NOTES AND QUAINT SAYINGS.

Verse 1.—*" For he is good ; "* essentially, solely and originally ; is communicative and diffusive of his goodness ; is the author of all good and no evil ; and is gracious and merciful and ready to forgive.—*John Gill.*

Verse 1.—*" For he is good : for his goodness endureth for ever."* Observe here what is a true and perfect confession of the divine goodness. Whenever God so blesses his own people that his goodness is perceived by carnal sense, in bestowing riches, honours, peace, health and things of that kind, then it is easy to acknowledge that God is good, and that acknowledgment can be made by the most carnal men. The case stands otherwise when he visits offenders with the rod of correction and scourges them with the grace of chastisement. Then the flesh hardly bears to confess what by its own sense it does not perceive. It fails to discern the goodness of God unto salvation in the severity of the rod and the scourging, and therefore refuses to acknowledge that goodness in strokes and sufferings. The prophet, however, throughout this Psalm celebrates in many instances the way wherein the sinning people were arrested and smitten. And when he proposed that this Psalm should be sung in the church of God, Israel was under the cross and afflictions. Yet he demands that Israel should acknowledge that the Lord is good, that his mercy endureth for ever, even in the act of smiting the offender. That therefore alone is a true and full confession of the divine goodness which is made not only in prosperity but also in adversity.—*Musculus.*

Verses 1—3.—There is, (1.) The doxology; (2.) Invitation; (3.) The reason that we should, and why we should, give thanks always; (4.) The greatness of the work. But "who can utter the mighty acts of the LORD? who can shew forth all his praise?" That is, it is impossible for any man in the world to do this great duty aright, as he should. (5.) The best mode and method of giving thanks. "Blessed are they that keep judgment, and he that doeth righteousness at all times." As if he had said, "This is indeed a vast duty; but yet *he* makes the best essay towards it that sets himself constantly to serve God and keep his commandments."—*William Cooper, in the " Morning Exercises."*

Verses 1, 47, 48.—The first and two last verses of this Psalm form a part of that Psalm which David delivered into the hand of Asaph and his brethren, to be sung before the ark of the covenant, after it was brought from the house of Obed-edom to Mount Zion. See 1 Chron. xvi. 34—36. Hence it has been ascribed to the pen of David. Many of the ancients thought, and they are followed by Horsley and Mudge, that it was written during the captivity; resting their opinion chiefly on verse 47; but as that verse occurs in the Psalm of David recorded in 1 Chron. xvi., at the 35th verse, this argument is clearly without force.—*James Anderson's Note to Calvin in loc.*

Verse 2.—" *Who can utter?* " etc. This verse is susceptible of two interpretations; for if you read it in connection with the one immediately following, the sense will be, that all men are not alike equal to the task of praising God, because the ungodly and the wicked do nothing else than profane his holy name with their unclean lips; as it is said in the fiftieth Psalm: " But unto the wicked God saith, What hast thou to do to declare my statutes, or that thou shouldest take my covenant in thy mouth? " And hence to this sentence the following clause should have been annexed, in the form of a reply, " Blessed are they that keep judgment." I am of opinion, however, that the prophet had another design, namely, that there is no man who has ever endeavoured to concentrate all his energies, both physical and mental, in the praising of God, but will find himself inadequate for so lofty a subject, the transcendant grandeur of which overpowers all our senses. Not that he exalts the power of God designedly to deter us from celebrating its praises, but rather as the means of stirring us up to do so to the utmost of our power. Is it any reason for ceasing our exertions, that with whatever alacrity we pursue our course, we yet come far short of perfection? But the thing which ought to inspire us with the greatest encouragement is the knowledge that, though ability may fail us, the praises which from the heart we offer to God are pleasing to him; only let us beware of callousness; for it would certainly be very absurd for those who cannot attain to a tithe of perfection, to make that the occasion of their not reaching to the hundredth part of it. —*John Calvin.*

Verse 2.—" *Who can utter the mighty acts of the Lord?* " etc. Our sight fails us when we look upon the sun, overpowered by the splendour of his rays; and the mind's eye suffers the like in every meditation on God, and the more attention is bestowed in thinking of God, the more is the mental vision blinded by the very light of its own thoughts. For what canst thou say of him, what, I repeat, canst thou adequately say of him, who is sublimer than all loftiness, and more exalted than all height, and deeper than all depth, and clearer than all light, and brighter than all brightness, and more splendid than all splendour, stronger than all strength, more vigorous than all vigour, fairer than all beauty, truer than all truth, and more puissant than puissance, and greater than all majesty, and mightier than all might, richer than all riches, wiser than all wisdom, gentler than all gentleness, juster than all justice, more merciful than all mercy?—*Tertullian, quoted by Neale and Littledale.*

Verse 2.—" *Who can utter the mighty acts of the Lord?* " etc. This may be resolved either into a negation or restriction. Few or none can " utter the mighty acts of the LORD," can " show forth all his praise "; few can do it in an acceptable manner, and none can do it in a perfect manner. And indeed it is not unusual in Scripture for such kind of interrogations to amount unto either a negation, or at least an expression of the rareness and difficulty of the thing spoken of: 1 Cor. ii.

16 ; Ps. xcii. ; Isai. liii. 1.   Without a full confession of mercies it is not possible to make either a due valuation of them, or a just requital of them.   And how impossible a thing it is fully to recount mercies, you may see by Psal. xl. 5 : " Many, O Lord my God, are thy wonderful works which thou hast done, and thy thoughts which are to us-ward : they cannot be reckoned up in order unto thee : if I would declare and speak of them, they are more than can be numbered."—*Henry Jeanes, in " The Works of Heaven upon Earth,"* 1649.

Verse 2.—*" Mighty acts of the Lord."*   Or *powers,* to which answers the Greek word for the miracles of Christ (Matt. xi. 20, 21), and Kimchi here restrains them to the wonders wrought in Egypt and at the Red Sea ; but they may as well be extended to the mighty acts of God, and the effects of his power, in the creation of all things out of nothing ; in the sustentation and government of the world ; in the redemption of his people by Christ ; in the conversion of sinners, and in the final perseverance of the saints ; in all which there are such displays of the power of God as cannot be uttered and declared by mortal tongues.—*John Gill.*

Verse 3.—*" Blessed are they that keep judgment,"* etc.   That are of right principles and upright practices ; this is real and substantial praising of God.   Thanks-doing is the proof of thanksgiving ; and the good life of the thankful is the life of thankfulness.   Those that say, God-a-thank only, and no more, are not only contumelious, but injurious.—*John Trapp.*

Verse 3.—*" Keep judgment " ; " doeth righteousness."*   I doubt not that there is some difference ; viz. that he is said to keep judgment who judgeth rightly, but he to do righteousness who acts righteously.—*Augustine.*

Verse 3.—I have read of Louis, king of France, that when he had through inadvertency granted an unjust suit, as soon as ever he had read those words of the Psalmist, " *Blessed is he that doeth righteousness at all times,"* he presently recollected himself, and upon better thoughts gave his judgment quite contrary.—*Thomas Brooks.*

Verse 4.—*" O visit me."*   This is a beautiful figure.   The prayer is not, " Give me a more intense desire, increased energy of action, that I may please thee, that I may serve thee, that I may go step by step up to thee, every step bringing with it a fresh sense of meritorious claim upon thee."   No such thing.   It is " *Visit me ; "* " descend down upon me " daily from thine own lofty throne, for the fulfilment of thine own purposes.   " *Visit me."*—*George Fisk,* 1851.

Verse 4.—*" O visit me with thy salvation."*   Hugo takes the *visit* of God as that of a physician of whom healing of the eyes is sought, because it is immediately added, " *That I may see,"* etc.—*Lorinus.*

Verse 4.—There is an ancient Jewish gloss which is noteworthy, that the petition is for a share in the resurrection in the days of Messiah, in order to see his wonderful restoration of his suffering people.—*Neale and Littledale.*

Verse 5.—We may note that the threefold nature of man prompts the union of the three petitions of this verse in one.   " *That I may see,"* is the prayer of the body, desiring the open vision of God ; " *and rejoice,"* is the wish of the soul or mind, that the affections may likewise be gratified ; *and give thanks,* as the spirit needs to pour itself out in worship.   Further, there are three names here given to the saints, each for a reason of its own.   They are God's " *chosen,"* because of his predestinating grace, " according as he hath chosen us in him before the foundation of the world, that we should be holy and without blame before him in love " (Eph. i. 4) ; they are his " *nation,"* having one law and one worship under him as sole king, " And what nation is there so great, that hath statutes and judgments so righteous as all this law ? " (Deut. iv. 8) ; they are his " *inheritance,"* for it is written, " I shall give the heathen for thine inheritance " (Ps. ii. 8).—*Hugo Cardinalis and Albertus Magnus, in Neale and Littledale.*

Verse 5.—*" That I may see the good of thy chosen."*   That, having been predestined, and justified, we may come to see the good of thy chosen, which means that the very face of the Lord may be made conspicuous to us.   " For we shall be then like him when we shall see him as he is " (1 John iii. 2).   By the " *good of thy chosen "* we are not to understand their own probity or goodness, but the supreme happiness that is their lot.   " *That I may rejoice in the gladness of thy nation."*   That we may partake in that unspeakable joy which arises from the beatific vision, which is the peculiar property of the chosen people, of which strangers cannot taste, of which the gospel says, " Enter into the joy of thy Lord."—*Robert Bellarmine*, 1542—1621.

Verse 6.—" *We have sinned with our fathers.*" Let us look a little further back, to find the age of sin ; even as far as the original, from whence comes all the copy of imitation. Be they never so new in act, they are old in example : " *We have sinned with our fathers.*" God tells them they had rebelled of old ; " As your fathers did, so do ye " (Acts viii. 51). Antiquity is no infallible argument of goodness : though Tertullian says the first things were the best things ; and the less they distanced from the beginning, the poorer they were ; but he must be understood only of holy customs. For iniquity can plead antiquity : he that commits a new act of murder finds it old in the example of Cain ; drunkenness may be fetched from Noah ; contempt of parents from Ham ; women's lightness from the daughters of Lot. There is no sin but hath white hairs upon it, and is exceeding old. But let us look further back yet, even to Adam ; there is the age of sin. This is that St. Paul calls the old man ; it is almost as old as the root, but older than all the branches. Therefore our restitution by Christ to grace is called the new man.—*Thomas Adams*.

Verse 6.—" *We have sinned with our fathers.*" It enhances the sin considerably by adding " *with our fathers.*" He would have seemed to extenuate, not exaggerate, if he had said, We have sinned with other mortals. But by saying, *We have sinned with our fathers*, he by no means lessens but aggravates their offences, while he hereby extols the goodness of God who blessed not only those who acted sinfully and impiously, but also the children and descendants of the sinful and impious, even those whom he could with the highest justice have cut off as doubly detestable.—*Musculus*.

Verse 6.—" *Sinned ; committed iniquity ; done wickedly.*" The Rabbins tell us that there are three kinds and degrees of sin here set down in an ascending scale ; against one's self, against one's neighbour, against God ; sins of ignorance, sins of conscious deliberation, sins of pride and wickedness.—*R. Levi and Genebrardus, in Neale and Littledale.*

Verses 6, 12, 13, 14, 21, 24.—Though the writers of the Scriptures were by divine inspiration infallibly preserved from extravagance, yet they use every appropriate variety of strong and condemnatory language against sin (ver. 6). Surely moral evil cannot be a trifle. Yet it breaks forth on all occasions and on all hands. Sometimes it is in the form of forgetfulness of God (ver. 13, 21), sometimes of rash impetuosity towards evil (ver. 13), sometimes of strong, imperious lusts (ver. 14), sometimes of vile unbelief (ver. 12, 24), and so of the whole catalogue of offences against God and man. O how vile we are !—*William S. Plumer*.

Verse 7.—" *Our fathers understood not thy wonders in Egypt.*" Though the elders went along with Moses, and heard him shew his commission to Pharaoh, and make his demands in the name of the Lord to let Israel go (Exod. iii. 16) ; yea, and they saw the judgments of God on Egypt ; yet " *they did not understand* " that these wonders would do the work of their deliverance. At first they thought it was worse with them. Much less did they understand, that their deliverance should be a type of eternal deliverance, that God would be their God, as after is explained in the preface to the ten commandments. And because they " *understood not his wonders,*" therefore they " *remembered not his mercies.*" A shallow understanding causeth a short memory.—*Nathaniel Homes*, 1652.

Verse 7.—" *Our fathers understood not thy wonders in Egypt.*" It is more than probable, that many of the Israelites ascribed most of these wonders to the skill of Moses transcending that of the Egyptian magicians, or to his working by the assistance of a higher and more potent spirit than that which assisted them. Or, in case they did believe them to have been the effects of a Divine Power, yet they did not inure their minds seriously to consider it, so as to have a standing awe of that power imprinted upon their hearts by such a consideration : and he that considers great and important matters superficially, in the language of the Scripture, does not *understand them.*—*Robert South*.

Verse 7.—" *Understood not* " . . . " *remembered not.*" He reproveth both their understanding and memory. Understanding there was need of, that they might meditate unto what eternal blessings God was calling them through these temporal ones ; and of memory, that at least they might not forget the temporal wonders which had been wrought, and might faithfully believe, that by the same power which they had already experienced, God would free them from the persecution of their enemies ; whereas they forgot the aid which he had given them in Egypt, by means of such wonders, to crush their enemies.—*Augustine.*

Verse 7.—One sin is a step to another more heinous ; for *not observing*, is followed with *not remembering*, and *forgetfulness* of duty draweth on *disobedience* and rebellion. —*David Dickson.*

Verse 7.—" *They provoked him.*" To *provoke*, is an expression setting forth a peculiar and more than ordinary degree of misbehaviour, and seems to import an insolent daring resolution to offend. A resolution not contented with one single stroke of disobedience, but such a one as multiplies and repeats the action, till the offence greatens, and rises into an affront ; and as it relates to God, so I conceive it as aimed at him in a threefold respect. 1st, Of his power. 2ndly, Of his goodness. 3rdly, Of his patience.

1st. And first it rises up against *the power and prerogative of God.* It is, as it were, an assault upon God sitting upon his throne, a snatching at his sceptre, and a defiance of his very royalty and supremacy. He that provokes God does in a manner dare him to strike, and to revenge the injury and invasion upon his honour. He considers not the weight of God's almighty arm, and the edge of his sword, the swiftness and poison of his arrows, but puffs at all, and looks the terrors of sin-revenging justice in the face. The Israelites could not sin against God, after those miracles in Egypt, without a signal provocation of that power that they had so late, and so convincing an experience of : a power that could have crushed an Israelite as easily as an Egyptian ; and given as terrible an instance of its consuming force upon false friends, as upon professed enemies ; in the sight of God, perhaps, the less sort of offenders of the two.

2ndly. Provoking God imports an abuse of *his goodness.* God, as he is clothed with power, is the proper object of our fear ; but as he displays his goodness, of our love. By one he would command, by the other he would win and (as it were) court our obedience. And an affront to his goodness, his tenderness, and his mercy, as much exceeds an affront of his power as a wound at the heart transcends a blow on the hand. For when God shall show miracles of mercy, step out of the common road of providence, commanding the host of heaven, the globe of the earth, and the whole system of nature out of its course, to serve a design of goodness upon a people, as he did upon the Israelites ; was not a provocation, after such obliging passages, infinitely base and insufferable, and a degree of ingratitude, higher than the heavens struck at, and deeper than the sea that they passed through ?

3rdly. Provoking God imports an affront upon *his longsuffering, and his patience.* The movings of nature in the breasts of mankind, tell us how keenly, how regretfully, every man resents the abuse of his love ; how hardly any prince, but one, can put up an offence against his acts of mercy ; and how much more affrontive it is to despise majesty ruling by the golden sceptre of pardon, than by the iron rod of penal law. But now patience is a further and an higher advance of mercy ; it is mercy drawn out at length ; mercy wrestling with baseness, and striving, if possible, even to weary and outdo ingratitude ; and therefore a sin against this is the highest pitch, the utmost improvement, and, as I may so speak, the *ne plus ultra* of provocation. For when patience shall come to be tired, and even out of breath with pardoning, let all the invention of mankind find something further, either upon which an offender may cast his hope, or against which he can commit a sin. But it was God's patience the ungrateful Israelites sinned against ; for they even plied and pursued him with sin upon sin, one offence following and thronging upon the neck of another, the last account still rising highest, and swelling bigger, till the treasures of grace and pardon were so far drained and exhausted, that they provoked God to *swear*, and what is more, *to swear in his wrath*, and with a full purpose of revenge, *that they should never enter into his rest.*—*Robert South.*

Verse 7.—" *They provoked him.*" Wherein lay their provocation ? " *They remembered not the multitude of his mercies :* " the former mercies of the Lord did not strengthen their trust in present troubles ; that was one provocation. And as former mercies did not strengthen their trust, so the present troubles drew out their distrust, as another Scripture assures, reporting their behaviour in it (Exod. xiv. 11) : " And they said unto Moses, Because there were no graves in Egypt, hast thou taken us away to die in the wilderness ? wherefore hast thou dealt thus with us, to carry us forth out of Egypt ? " What were these fearful forecasts, these amazing bodements of an unavoidable (as they apprehended) ruin, but the over-flowings of unbelief, or distrust in God ; and this was another provocation. Former mercies are forgotten, yea, eaten up by unbelief, as the seven lean kine in Pharaoh's dream eat up the fat ones, and present difficulties are aggravated by unbelief, as if all the power of God could not remove and overcome them. And will not the Lord (think you) visit in anger such a sin as this ?—*Joseph Caryl.*

Verse 7.—" *At the Red Sea.*" That is to say, *at the Arabian Gulph :* literally, *at the Sea of Suph,* which, if *Suph* be not here a proper name, (as it seems to be in Deut. i. 1, and, with a slight variation, in Numb. xxxi. 14,) means *the sea of weeds,* and that sea is still called by a similar name, in modern Egypt. Its designation, throughout the books of the Old Testament, is in the Syriac version, and the Chaldee Paraphrase, likewise rendered *the sea of weeds ;* which name may have been derived from the reeds growing near its shore ; or from the weeds, or coralline productions, with which, according to Diodorus Siculus, and Kircher, it abounded ; and which were seen through its translucent waters. Finati, quoted by Laborde, speaks of the transparency of its waters, and the corals seen at its bottom. . . . Pliny states, that it is called the Red Sea from King Erythras, or from the reflection of a red colour by the sun, or from its sand and its ground, or from the nature of its water. —*Daniel Cresswell.*

Verses 7, 8.—This Psalm is a Psalm of thanksgiving, as the first and last verses declare. Now because a man is most fit to praise God when he is most sensible of his own sin and unworthiness ; the Psalmist doth throughout this Psalm lay Israel's sin and God's mercy together. Ver. 7, " *Our Fathers* (says he) *understood not thy wonders in Egypt.*" They saw them with their eyes, but they did not understand them with their heart ; they did not apprehend the design and scope and end of God in those wonders : and therefore, " *they remembered not* (says the text) *thy mercies ;* " for a man remembers no more than he understands.

But it may be these mercies were very few, and so their sin in forgetfulness the less ? Nay, not so, for verse 7, " *They remembered not the multitude of thy mercies.*"

But it may be this was their infirmity or weakness, and so they were rather to be borne withal ? Not so, " *but they rebelled against him ;* " so Montanus reads it better.

But it may be this sin was committed whilst they were in Egypt, or among the Egyptians, being put on by them ? Not so neither, but when they were come out of Egypt, and only had to deal with God, and saw his glorious power at the Red Sea, then they rebelled against him, " *at the sea, even at the Red Sea.*"

What then, did not the Lord destroy them ? No says the text, " *Notwithstanding* " all their grievance, unthankfulness, and their rebellion, " *he saved them for his name's sake.*"—*William Bridge, in a Sermon preached before the House of Commons, Nov. 5, 1647.*

Verse 8.—" *Nevertheless he saved them.*"—If God should not shew mercy to his people with a *nevertheless,* how should the glory of his mercy appear ? If a physician should only cure a man that hath the head-ache or the tooth-ache ; one that hath taken cold, or some small disease ; it would not argue any great skill and excellency in the physician. But when a man is nigh unto death, hath one foot in the grave, or is, in the eye of reason, past all recovery ; if then the physician cure him, it argues much the skill and excellency of that physician. So now, if God should only cure, and save a people that were less evil and wicked ; or that were good indeed, where should the excellence of mercy appear ? But when a people shall be drawing near to death, lying bed-rid, as it were, and the Lord out of his free love, for his own name's sake, shall rise, and cure such an unworthy people, this sets out the glory of his mercy. It is said in the verse precedent, " They rebelled at the sea, even at the Red Sea," or, as in the Hebrew, " even *in* the Red Sea " ; when the waters stood like walls on both sides of them ; when they saw those walls of waters that never people saw before, and saw the power, the infinite power of God leading them through on dry land ; *then* did they rebel, at the sea, *even in* the sea ; and yet for all this the Lord saved them with a *notwithstanding* all this. And I say, shall the Lord put forth so much of grace upon a people, that were under the law ; and not put forth much more of his grace upon those that are under the gospel ?—*William Bridge.*

Verse 8.—" *For his name's sake.*" Improve his name in every case ; for he hath a name suiting every want, every need. Do you need wonders to be wrought for you ? His name is Wonderful ; look to him so to do, for his name's sake. Do you need counsel and direction ? His name is the Counsellor : cast yourself on him and his name for this. Have you mighty enemies to debate with ? His name is the Mighty God ; seek that he may exert his power for his name's sake. Do you need his fatherly pity ? His name is the everlasting Father ; " As a father pitieth his children, so the Lord pitieth them that fear him." Plead his pity, for his name's sake. Do you need peace external, internal, or eternal ? His name is the Prince of Peace ; seek for his name's sake, that he may create peace. O sirs, his name is JEHOVAH-ROPHI, the Lord, the healer and physician ; seek, for his name's sake, that he may heal all your diseases. Do you need pardon ? His name is JEHOVAH-TSID-KENU, the Lord our righteousness : seek, for his name's sake, that he may be merciful to your unrighteousness. Do you need defence and protection ? His name is JEHOVAH-NISSI, the Lord your banner ; seek, for his name's sake, that his banner of love and grace may be spread over you. Do you need provision in extreme want ? His name is JEHOVAH-JIREH, in the mount of the Lord it shall be seen, the Lord will provide. Do you need his presence ? His name is JEHOVAH-SHAMMAH, the Lord is there : IMMANUEL, God with us : look to him to be with you, for his name's sake. Do you need audience of prayer ? His name is the Hearer of prayer. Do you need strength ? His name is the Strength of Israel. Do you need comfort ? His name is the Consolation of Israel. Do you need shelter ? His name is the City of Refuge. Have you nothing and need all ? His name is All in all. Sit down and devise names to your wants and needs, and you will find he hath a name suitable thereunto ; for your supply, he hath wisdom to guide you ; and power to keep you ; mercy to pity you ; truth to shield you ; holiness to sanctify you ; righteousness to justify you ; grace to adorn you ; and glory to crown you. Trust in his name, who saves for his name's sake.—*Ralph Erskine*, 1685—1752.

Verse 9.—" *He rebuked the Red Sea also, and it was dried up.*" A poetical expression, signifying that the Red Sea retired at God's command, just as a slave would fly from his master's presence on being severely rebuked.—*Robert Bellarmine.*

Verse 9.—" *He rebuked.*" We do not read that any voice was sent forth from heaven to rebuke the sea ; but he hath called the Divine Power by which this was effected, a rebuke, unless indeed any one may choose to say, that the sea was secretly rebuked, so that the waters might hear, and yet men could not. The power by which God acteth is very abstruse and mysterious, a power by which he causeth that even things devoid of sense instantly obey at his will.—*Augustine.*

Verse 9.—" *Wilderness.*" *Midbar ;* a broad expanse of poor dry land, suited for sheep-walks (like our South-Downs, or Salisbury Plain). Compare Isa. lxiii. 13. —*William Kay.*

Verse 11.—" *There was not one of them left.*" An emblem this of the utter destruction of all our spiritual enemies by Christ, who has not only saved us from them, but has entirely destroyed them ; he has made an end of sin, even of all the sins of his people ; he has spoiled Satan, and his principalities and powers ; he has abolished death, the last enemy, and made his saints more than conquerors over all. Likewise it may be a representation of the destruction of the wicked at the last day, who will all be burnt up at the general conflagration, root and branch, not one will be left. See Mal. iv. 1.—*John Gill.*

Verse 12.—" *Then believed they his words.*" There is a temporary faith, as Mark calls it (iv. 17), which is not so much a fruit of the Spirit of regeneration, as of a certain mutable affection, and so it soon passeth away. It is not a voluntary faith which is here extolled by the prophet, but rather that which is the result of compulsion, namely, because men, whether they will or not, by a sense which they have of the power of God, are constrained to show some reverence for him. This passage ought to be well considered, that men, when once they have yielded submission to God, may not deceive themselves, but may know that the touchstone of faith is when they spontaneously receive the word of God, and constantly continue firm in their obedience to it.—*John Calvin.*

Verse 12.—Natural affections raised high in a profession of religion will withstand temptations for a fit, but wait till the stream runs lower, and you will see. What a fit of affection had the Israelites when their eyes had seen that miraculous deliverance at the Red Sea ! What songs of rejoicing had they ! what resolves never to distrust him again ! " *Then believed they his words ; they sang his praise.*" Satan doth not presently urge them to murmuring and unbelief, though that was his design, but he staid till the fit was over, and then he could soon tempt them to " *forget his works.*" —*Richard Gilpin in " A Treatise of Satan's Temptations,*" 1677.

Verse 12.—In the very brevity of this verse, the only one of its kind in the narrative portion of the Psalm, we may well see how short-lived were their gratitude, belief, and worship of God ; as it follows at once, " *They soon forgat,*" etc.—*Neale and Littledale.*

Verses 12, 13.—" *They sang his praise. They soon forgat his works.*" This was said of that generation of the Israelites, which came out of Egypt. The chapter which contains the portion of their history here alluded to, begins with rapturous expressions of gratitude, and ends with the murmurs of discontent ; both uttered by the same lips, within the short space of three days. Their expressions of gratitude were called forth by that wonderful display of the divine perfections, which delivered them from the host of Pharaoh, and destroyed their enemies. Their murmurs were excited by a comparatively trifling inconvenience, which in a few hours was removed. Of persons whose thanksgivings were so quickly, and so easily changed to murmurings, it might well be said,—though they *sang God's praises,* " *they soon forgat his works.*"

Unhappily, the Israelites are by no means the only persons of whom this may, in truth, be said. Their conduct, as here described, affords a striking exemplification of that spurious gratitude, which often bursts forth in a sudden flash, when dreaded evils are averted, or unexpected favours bestowed ; but expires with the occasion that gave it birth ; a gratitude resembling the joy excited in an infant's breast by the gift of some glittering toy, which is received with rapture, and pleases for an hour ; but when the charm of novelty vanishes, is thrown aside with indifference ; and the hand that bestowed it is forgotten. Springing from no higher principle than gratified self-love, it is neither acceptable to God, nor productive of obedience to his laws ; nor does it in any respect really resemble that holy, heaven-born affection, whose language it often borrows, and whose name it assumes. It may be called, distinctively, the gratitude of sinners ; who, as they love those that love them, will of course be grateful to those that are kind to them ; grateful even to God when they view him as kind.

Of these instances, the first which I shall notice is furnished by the works of *creation* ; or, as they are often, though not very properly, called, the works of nature. In so impressive a manner do these works present themselves to our senses ; so much of variety, and beauty, and sublimity do they exhibit ; such power, and wisdom, and goodness do they display ; that perhaps no man, certainly no man who possesses the smallest share of sensibility, taste, or mental cultivation, can, at all times, view them without emotion ; without feelings of awe, or wonder, or admiration, or delight.

But, alas, how transient, how unproductive of salutary effects, have all these emotions proved ? Appetite and passion, though hushed for a moment, soon renewed their importunities ; the glitter of wealth and distinction, and power, eclipsed, in our view, the glories of Jehovah ; we sunk from that heaven toward which we seemed rising, to plunge afresh into the vortex of earthly pleasures and pursuits ; we neglected and disobeyed him, whom we had been ready to adore ; and continued to live without God, in a world which we had just seen to be full of his glory.

A second instance of a similar nature is afforded by the manner in which men are often affected by God's works of *providence.* In these works his perfections are so constantly, and often so clearly displayed ; our dependence on them is at all times so real, and sometimes so apparent ; and they bear, in many cases, so directly and evidently upon our dearest temporal interests, that even the most insensible cannot, always, regard them with indifference.

But the feeling is usually transient ; and the acknowledgment is forgotten almost as soon as it is made.

In a similar manner are men often affected by God's works of *grace ;* or those works whose design and tendency it is, to promote the spiritual and eternal interests of man. These works most clearly display, not only the natural, but the moral perfections of Jehovah. Here his character shines, full-orbed and complete.

That an exhibition of these wonders should make, at least, a temporary impression upon our minds, is no more than might naturally be expected. For a moment our hearts seem to be melted. We feel, and are ready to acknowledge, that God is good ; that the Saviour is kind ; that his love ought to be returned ; that heaven is desirable ! Like a class of hearers described by one great Teacher, we receive the word with joy ; a joy not unmingled with something which resembles gratitude ; and we sing, or feel as if we could with pleasure sing, God's praises. But we leave his house ; the emotions there excited subside ; like the earth, when partially softened by a wintry sun, our hearts soon regain their icy hardness ; the wonders of divine grace are forgotten ; and God has reason to say in sorrow and displeasure,—Your goodness is as the morning cloud ; and as the early dew it goeth away.—*Condensed from a Sermon by Edward Payson, 1783—1827.*

Verse 13.—" *They soon forgat his works.*" They forgat, yea, " *soon* " ; they made haste to forget, so the original is : " They made haste, they forgat." Like men that in sleep shake Death by the hand, but when they are awake they will not know him.—*Thomas Adams.*

Verse 13.—How may we know that we are rightly thankful ? When we are careful to register God's mercy, 1 Chron. xvi. 4 : " David appointed certain of the Levites, to record, and to thank and praise the Lord God of Israel." Physicians say the memory is the first thing that decays ; it is true in spirituals : " *They soon forgat his works.*"—*Thomas Watson.*

Verse 13.—" *They soon forgat.*" As it is with a sieve or boulter, the good corn and fine flour goes through, but the light chaff and coarse bran remains behind ; or as a strainer, that the sweet liquor is strained out, but the dregs are left behind : or as a grate, that lets the pure water run away, but if there be any straws, sticks, mud, or filth, that it holds. Thus it is with most men's memories ; by nature they are but, as it were, *pertusa dolia*, mere river tubs, especially in good things very treacherous, so that the vain conceits of men are apt to be held in, when divine instructions and gracious promises run through ; trifles and toys, and worldly things, they are apt to remember, tenacious enough ; but for spiritual things they leak out ; like Israel, *they soon forget them.*—*William Gouge.*

Verse 13.—" *They soon forgat his works.*" Three days afterwards, at the waters of Marah (Exod. xv. 24).—*Adam Clarke.*

Verse 13.—" *They waited not.*" The insatiable nature of our desires is astonishing, in that scarcely a single day is allowed to God to gratify them. For should he not immediately satisfy them, we at once become impatient, and are in danger of eventually falling into despair. This, then, was the fault of the people, that they did not cast all their cares upon God, did not calmly call upon him, nor wait patiently until he was pleased to answer their requests, but rushed forward with reckless precipitation, as if they would dictate to God what he was to do. And, therefore, to heighten the criminality of their rash course, he employs the term " *counsel* " ; because men will neither allow God to be possessed of wisdom, nor do they deem it proper to depend upon his counsel, but are more provident than becomes them, and would rather rule God than allow themselves to be ruled by him according to his pleasure. That we may be preserved from provoking God, let us ever retain this principle, That it is our duty to let him provide for us such things as he knows will be for our advantage. And verily, faith divesting us of our own wisdom, enables us hopefully and quietly to wait until God accomplishes his own work ; whereas, on the contrary, our carnal desire always goes before the counsel of God, by its too great haste.—*John Calvin.*

Verse 13.—" *They waited not.*" They ought to have thought, that so great works of God towards themselves were not without a purpose, but that they invited them to some endless happiness, which was to be waited for with patience ; but they hastened to make themselves happy with temporal things, which give no man true happiness, because they do not quench insatiable longing : " for whosoever," saith our Lord, " shall drink of this water, shall thirst again." John iv. 13.— *Augustine.*

Verse 13.—" *They waited not for his counsel.*"—Which neglect of theirs may be understood two ways. First, that they waited not for his open or declared counsel, to direct them what to do, but without asking his advice would needs venture and run on upon their own heads, to do what seemed good in their own eyes. Secondly, that they waited not for the accomplishment of his hidden and secret counsel concerning them ; they would not tarry God's time for the bringing forth and bringing about his counsels. Not to wait upon God either way is very sinful. Not to wait for his counsel to direct us what to do, and not to wait for his doing or fulfilling his own counsel, argues at once a proud and an impatient spirit ; in the one, men do even slight the wisdom of God, and in the other vainly presume and attempt to prevent his providence.—*Joseph Caryl.*

Verse 13.—" *They waited not for his counsel.*" A believer acting his faith, hath great advantage of an unbeliever. An unbeliever is froward and passionate, and heady and hasty, when he is put to plunge ; *he waits not for the counsel of God.* **He** leaps before he looks, before he hath eyes to see his way ; but a believer is quiet and confident, and silent and patient, and prayerful, and standing upon his watch-tower, to see what God will answer at such a time.—*Matthew Lawrence, in " The Use and Practice of Faith,"* 1657.

Verse 14.—" *In the wilderness.*"   When God by circumstances of time and place doth call for moderation of carnal appetite, the transgression is more heinous and offensive unto God : " They lusted exceedingly in the wilderness," where they should have contented themselves with any sort of provision.—*David Dickson.*

Verse 14.—" *In the wilderness.*"   There, *where they had bread enough and to spare,* yet nothing would serve them but they must have flesh to eat. They were now *purely at God's finding ;* so that this was a reflection upon the wisdom and goodness of their Creator. They were now, in all probability, *within a step of Canaan,* yet had not patience to stay for dainties till they came thither. *They had flocks and herds of their own,* but they will not kill them ; God must give them flesh as he gave them bread, or they will never give him credit or their good word :   they did not only wish for flesh, " but " they " lusted exceedingly " after it. A desire even of lawful things, when it is inordinate and violent, becomes sinful ; and therefore this is called "lusting after evil things " (1 Cor. x. 6), though the quails as God's gift, were good things, and were so spoken of, Ps. cv. 40.   Yet this was not all, " they tempted God in the desert," *where they had had such experience of his goodness and power,* and questioned whether he could and would gratify them therein. See Psalm lxxviii. 19, 20.—*Matthew Henry.*

Verse 15.—" *And he gave them their request,*" etc. The throat's pleasure did shut up paradise, sold the birthright, beheaded the Baptist, and it was the chief of the cooks, Nebuzaradan, that first set fire to the temple, and razed the city. These effects are, 1. Grossness ; which takes away agility to any good work ; which makes a man more like a tun upon two pottle pots.   Cæsar said he mistrusted not Antony and Dolabella for any practices, because they were fat ; but Casca and Cassius, lean, hollow fellows, who did think too much. The other are the devil's crammed fowls, too fat to lay.   Indeed, what need they travel far, whose felicity is at home ; placing paradise in their throats, and heaven in their food ?   2. Macilency of grace ; for as it puts fatness into their bodies, so leanness into their souls. God fatted the Israelites with quails, but withal " *sent leanness into their soul.*" The flesh is blown up, the spirit doth languish.   They are worse than man-eaters, for they are self-eaters : they put a pleurisy into their bloods, and an apoplexy into their souls.— *Thomas Adams.*

Verse 15.—" *Sent leanness into their soul.*"   God affords us as great means for our increase in these Gospel times as ever he did ; he puts us into fat pastures, and well watered, Ps. xxiii. ; therefore it is a shame for God's people not to grow, not " to bring forth twins," as Cant. vi. 6.   They should grow twice as fast, bring forth twice as fast, bring forth twice as many lambs, twice as much wool, twice as much milk, as those that go upon bare commons.   All the world may cry shame on such a man that is high fed, and often fed with fat and sweet ordinances, if he be still like Pharaoh's lean kine, as lean and ill-favoured as ever he was before.   Certainly, fat ordinances and lean souls do not well agree.   We are to look upon it as the greatest of judgments to have *leanness sent into our souls* while we are fed with *manna.* We look on it as an affliction to have an over-lean body ; but it's a far sadder condition to have a lean soul. Of the two, it were far better to have a well-thriving soul and a lean body: it is a great mercy when both prosper, 3 John 2 : " I wish above all things that thou mayest prosper and be in health, even as thy soul prospereth." Oh it is a sweet thing, especially to have a prospering soul, and still upon the growing hand : and God expects it should be so, where he affords good diet, great means of grace ; as Dan. i. 10 : " The prince of the eunuchs said unto Daniel, I fear my lord the king, who hath appointed your meat and your drink."   If you should look ill, who fare so well, I should be sure to bear the blame ; it were so much as my head is worth.   So certainly, where God affords precious food for precious souls, if these souls be lean under fat ordinances, either those that are fed, or those that feed them ; either the stewards or the household ; either minister, or people, or both, are sure to bear the blame.   It is but equal and just that such should grow.   We do not wonder to see lean sheep upon bare commons, but when we see sheep continue lean in fat pastures, we think their meat is ill bestowed on them ; and therefore let us strive to be on the growing land.—*Matthew Lawrence.*

Verse 15.—" *Leanness* " is rendered " loathing " by Bishop Horsley, which accords with the literal state of the case ; but I think *leanness,* as applied to the soul, is exceedingly descriptive of its spiritual barrenness and emptiness of aught like Divine tastes or enjoyments.—*Thomas Chalmers.*

Verse 17.—" *The earth opened,*" etc. This element was not used to such morsels. It devours the carcases of men ; but bodies informed with living souls, never before. To have seen them struck dead upon the earth had been fearful ; but to see the earth at once their executioner and grave, was more horrible. Neither the sea nor the earth are fit to give passage ; the sea is moist and flowing, and will not be divided, for the continuity of it ; the earth is dry and massy, and will neither yield naturally, nor meet again when it hath yielded : yet the waters did cleave to give way unto Israel for their preservation ; the earth did cleave to give way to the conspirators in judgment ; both sea and earth did shut their jaws again upon the adversaries of God. There was more wonder in this latter. It was a marvel that the waters opened ; it was no wonder that they shut again ; for the retiring and flowing was natural. It was no less marvel that the earth opened ; but more marvel that it shut again ; because it had no natural disposition to meet when it was divided. Now might Israel see they had to do with a God that could revenge with ease.

There are two sorts of traitors : the earth swallowed up the one, the fire the other. All the elements agree to serve the vengeance of their Maker. Nadab and Abihu brought fit persons, but unfit fire, to God ; these Levites bring the right fire, but unwarranted persons, before him : fire from God consumes both. It is a dangerous thing to usurp sacred functions. The ministry will not grace the man ; the man may disgrace the ministry.—*Joseph Hall.*

Verse 17.—Dathan and Abiram only are mentioned, and this in strict agreement with Numb. xxvi. 11, where it is said, " *the children of Korah died not.*" And the same thing is at least *implied* in Numb. xvi. 27, where it is said, that, just before the catastrophe took place, " Dathan and Abiram " (there is no mention of Korah) " came out and stood in the door of their tents." See this noticed and accounted for in Blunt's *Veracity of the Books of Moses,* Part I. § 20, p. 86.—*J. J. Stewart Perowne.*

Verse 19.—" *They made a calf.*" And why a calf ? Could they find no fitter resemblance of God amongst all the creatures ? Why not rather the lordly lion, to show the sovereignty ; vast elephant, the immensity ; subtle serpent, the wisdom ; long-lived hart, the eternity ; swift eagle, the ubiquity of God, rather than the silly senseless calf, that eateth hay ? But the shape mattereth not much, for if God be made like anything, he may be made like anything, it being as unlawful to fashion him an angel as a worm, seeing the commandment forbids as well the likeness of things in heaven above as in earth beneath (Exod. xx. 4). But probably a calf was preferred before other forms because they had learned it from the Egyptians' worshipping their ox Apis. Thus the Israelites borrowed (Exod. xii. 35) not all gold and silver, but some dross from the Egyptians, whence they fetch the idolatrous forms of their worship.

Verse 19.—The modern Jews are of opinion that all the afflictions which ever since have, do, or shall befall their nation, are still the just punishments on them for this their first act of idolatry. And the rabbins have a saying that God never inflicts any judgment upon them, but there is an ounce of his anger on them for their ancestors' making the golden calf. A reverend friend of mine, conversing at Amsterdam with a Jewish youth (very capable and ingenious for one of that nation) endeavoured to make him sensible of God's anger upon them for rejecting and crucifying of Christ, for which foul act he showed how the Jews have lived many hundred years in miserable banishment. But the youth would in no wise acknowledge in their sufferings any effect or punishment of their murdering of Christ, but taking his Bible turned to God's threatening immediately after their making of the calf (Exod. xxxiii. 34) : " Nevertheless in the day when I visit, I will visit their sin upon them," so interpreting and applying all the numerous calamities which since have befallen them to relate to no other cause than that their first idolatry. Whereas, indeed, the arrears of their idolatry long ago were satisfied, and this is a new debt of later date contracted on themselves by their infidelity.—*Thomas Fuller,* 1608—1661, *in* " *A Pisgah Sight of Palestine.*"

Verse 19.—" *They made a calf*," etc. This people had seen this idolatrous service in Egypt ; and now they did not more long after Egyptian food, than after this Egyptian god. . . . It is an easy matter for men to be drawn to the practice of that idolatry that they have been accustomed to see practised in those places that they have a long time lived in. He that would take heed of idolatry, let him take heed of Egypt : the very air of Egypt (as I may so say) is infectious in this kind. See here, they had seen the worship of a young bullock in Egypt, and they must have a bullock. . . .

The local seat of Antichrist (and what seat can that be but *Rome ?*) is called in the Revelation by three names : it is called *Egypt*, Rev. ii. 8. It is called *Sodom* in the same verse. It is called *Babylon* in many places of the Revelation. It is called *Babylon*, in regard to her cruelty. It is called *Sodom*, in regard to her filthiness ; and *Egypt*, in regard to her *idolatry*.

It is a hard matter for a man to live in Egypt, and not to taste and savour somewhat of the idolatry of Egypt. We had sometime, in England, a proverb about going to Rome. They said, a man that went the first time to Rome, he went to see a wicked man there ; he that went the second time to Rome, went to be acquainted with that wicked man there ; he that went the third time, brought him home with him. How many have we seen (and it is pity to see so many) of our nobility and gentry to go to those *Egyptian* parts, and return home again : but few of them bring home the same manners, the same religion, nor the same souls they carried out with them.—*Thomas Westfield, Bishop of Bristow, in " England's Face in Israel's Glasse*," 1658.

Verse 19.—" *In Horeb*." There is a peculiar stress on the words " *in Horeb*," as denoting the very place where the great manifestation of God's power and presence has been made, and where the law had been given, whose very first words were a prohibition of the sin of idolatry.—*Agellius, in Neale and Littledale.*

Verses 19, 20.—Apis, or Serapis, was a true living black bull, with a white list or streak along the back, a white mark in fashion of an half-moon on his right shoulder, only two hairs growing on his tail (why just so many and no more, the devil knows), with a fair square blaze on his forehead, and a great bunch called cantharus under his tongue. What art their priests did use to keep up the breed and preserve succession of cattle with such γωρίσματα, or privy marks, I list not to inquire. . . . Besides this natural and living bull, kept in one place, they also worshipped βοῦν διάχρυσον, a golden or gilded ox, the image or portraiture of the former. Some conceive this Apis to have been the symbol and emblem of Joseph the patriarch, so called from אב, *ab*, a father, seeing he is said to be made by God a father to Pharaoh (Gen. xlv. 8), that is, preserver of him and his country ; and therefore the Egyptians, in after ages, gratified his memory with statues of an ox, a creature so useful in ploughing, sowing, bringing home, and treading out of corn, to perpetuate that gift of grain he had conferred upon them. They strengthen their conjecture because Serapis (which one will have to be nothing else but Apis with addition of שר, *sar*, that is, a prince, whence perchance our English Sir) was pictured with a bushel over his head, and Joseph (we know) was corn-meter-general in Egypt. Though others, on good ground, conceive ox-worship in Egypt of far greater antiquity.

However, hence Aaron (Exod. xxxii. 4), and hence afterwards Jeroboam (who flying from Solomon, lived some years with Shishak, king of Egypt, 1 Kings xi. 40) had the pattern of their calves, which they made for the children of Israel to worship. If any object the Egyptians' idols were bulls or oxen, the Israelites' but calves, the difference is not considerable ; for (besides the objector never looked into the mouths of the latter to know their age) *gradus non variat speciem*, a less character is not another letter. Yea, Herodotus calls Apis himself χόσμος, a calf, and Vitulus is of as large acceptation among the Latins. Such an old calf the poet describes—

> *Ego hanc vitalam (ne forte recuses,*
> *Bis venit ad mulctram binos alit ubere fœtus)*
> *Depono.*

> My calf I lay (lest you mistake't both tides
> She comes to th' pail and suckles twain besides).

But to put all out of doubt, what in Exodus is termed a calf, the Psalmist calleth an ox (Ps. cvi. 20).—*Thomas Fuller.*

Verses 19—22.—It is to be hoped, we shall never live to see a time, when the miracles of *our* redemption shall be forgotten; when the return of Jesus Christ from heaven shall be despaired of; and when the people shall solicit their teachers to fabricate a new philosophical deity, for them to worship, instead of the God of their ancestors, to whom glory hath been ascribed from generation to generation.—*George Horne.*

Verse 20.—" *An ox that eateth grass.*" The Egyptians, when they consulted Apis, presented a bottle of hay or of grass, and if the ox received it, they expected good success.—*Daniel Cresswell.*

Verse 20.—Although some of the Rabbins would excuse this gross idolatry of their forefathers, yet others more wise bewail them, and say that there is an ounce of this golden calf in all their present sufferings.—*John Trapp.*

Verse 21.—" *They forgat God.*" To devise images and pictures to put us in the mind of God, is a very forgetting both of God's nature, and of his authority, which prohibits such devices, for so doth the Lord expound it : " *They forgat God their Saviour.*"—*David Dickson.*

Verse 21.—Let us observe in this place that Israel is now for the third time accused of forgetting God; above in ver. 7, afterwards in ver. 13, and now in ver. 21. And that he might shew the greatness of this forgetfulness he does not simply say they forgat God, but adds, *their Saviour :* not the Saviour of their fathers in former times, but *their own Saviour.*—*Musculus.*

Verse 22.—" *Land of Ham.*" Egypt is called the land of *Ham,* or rather *Cham,* םח, because it was peopled by Mizraim, the son of Ham, and grandson of Noah. Plutarch (De Iside and Osiride) informs us, that the Egyptians called their country Xημια, *Chemia ;* and the Copts give it the name of Xημι, *Chemi,* to the present day. —*Comprehensive Bible.*

Verse 23.—" *Moses his chosen stood before him in the breach.*" Moses stood in the gap, and diverted the wrath of God; the hedge of religion and worship was broken down by a golden calf, and he made it up : Numb. xvi. 41, 42, the people murmured, rose up against Moses and Aaron, trod down the hedge of authority, whereupon the plague brake in upon them; presently Aaron steps into the gap, makes up the hedge, and stops the plague, ver. 47, 48. That which they did was honourable; and they were repairers of breaches. We, through infinite mercy, have had some like Moses and Aaron, to make up our hedges, raise up our foundations, and stop some gaps; but all our gaps are not yet stopped. Are there not gaps in the hedge of doctrine? If it were not so, how came in such erroneous, blasphemous, and wild opinions amongst us? Are there not gaps in the hedges of civil and ecclesiastical authority? Do not multitudes trample upon magistracy and ministry, all powers, both human and divine? Are there not gaps in the worship of God? Do not too many tread down all churches, all ordinances, yea, the very Scriptures? Are there not gaps in the hedge of justice, through which the bulls of Bashan enter, which oppress the poor, and crush the needy? Amos iv. 1 : are there not gaps in the hedge of love; is not that bond of perfection broken? Are there not bitter envyings and strife among us; do we not bite and devour one another? are there not gaps in the hedge of conscience? is not the peace broken between God and your souls? doth not Satan come in oft at the gap, and disturb you? are there not gaps also in your several relations, whereby he gets advantage? Surely, if our eyes be in our heads, we may see gaps enough.—*William Greenhill.*

Verse 23.—" *The breach.*" This is a metaphor taken from a city which is besieged, and in the walls of which the enemy having made a " *breach,*" is just entering in, to destroy it, unless he be driven back by some valiant warrior. Thus *Moses* stood, as it were " *in the breach,*" and averted the wrath of God, when he was just going to destroy the Israelites. See Exod. xxxii.—*Thomas Fenton.*

Verse 23.—If Christians could be brought to entertain a just sense of the value and power of intercessory prayer, surely it would abound. It is a terrible reproof against the lying prophets of Ezekiel's time : " Ye have not gone up into the gaps, neither made up the hedge for the house of Israel to stand in the battle in the day of the Lord " (Ezek. xiii. 5). Compare Ex. xxxii. 9—14.—*William S. Plumer.*

Verse 24.—" *Yea, they despised.*" When the promised inheritance of heaven (which was figured by the pleasant *land of promise*), is not counted worthy of all the pains and difficulties which can be sustained and met with in the way of going toward it, the promised inheritance is but little esteemed of, as appeareth in the Israelites, who for love of ease, and fear of the Canaanites, were ready to turn back to Egypt : " *They despised the pleasant land.*"—*David Dickson.*

Verse 24.—" *They despised the pleasant land.*" This was a type of heaven, the good land afar off ; the better country, the land of promise and rest ; in which is fulness of provisions, and where there will be no hunger and thirst ; where flows the river of the water of life, and stands the tree of life, bearing all manner of fruits ; where there is fulness of joy and pleasures for evermore ; the most delightful company of Father, Son, and Spirit, angels and glorified saints, and nothing to disturb their peace and pleasure neither from within nor from without. And yet this pleasant land may be said to be despised by such who do not care to go through any difficulty to it ; to perform the duties of religion ; to bear reproach for God's sake ; to go through tribulation ; to walk in the narrow and afflicted way which leads unto it ; and by all such who do not care to part with their sinful lusts and pleasures ; but prefer them and the things of this world to the heavenly state.—*John Gill.*

Verse 24.—One great bar to salvation is spiritual sloth. It is said of Israel, " *They despised the pleasant land.*" What should be the reason ? Canaan was a paradise of delight, a type of heaven ; aye, but they thought it would cost them a great deal of trouble and hazard in the getting, and they would rather go without it, they despised the pleasant land. Are there not millions of us who would rather go sleeping to hell, than sweating to heaven ? I have read of certain Spaniards that live near where there is great store of fish, yet are so lazy that they will not be at the pains to catch them, but buy of their neighbours : such a sinful stupidity and sloth is upon the most, that though Christ be near them, though salvation is offered in the Gospel, yet they will not work out salvation.—*Thomas Watson.*

Verses 24, 25.—Murmuring hath in it much unbelief and distrust of God. " *They believed not his word ; but murmured in their tents.*" They could not believe that the wilderness was the way to Canaan, that God would provide and furnish a table for them there, and relieve them in all their straits. So it is with us in trouble. We quarrel with God's providence, because we do not believe his promises ; we do not believe that this can be consistent with love, or can work for good in the end.—*John Willison*, 1680—1750.

Verse 25.—" *But murmured.*" Murmuring ! It must have been a malady characteristic of the Hebrew people, or a disease peculiar to that desert. As we proceed with this narrative we are constantly meeting it, creaking along in discord harsh and chronic, or amazing earth and heaven by its shrill, ear-piercing paroxysms. They lift up their eyes, and as the Egyptians pursue, the people murmur. They come to a fountain, the water is bitter, and once more they murmur. Then no bread ; murmurings redoubled. Moses is no longer in the Mount ; murmurs. He takes too much upon him ; more murmurs. When shall we reach that promised land ?—murmurs extraordinary, loud murmurs. We are close to the land, but its inhabitants are giants, and their towns walled up to heaven. Oh, what a take-in ! and the last breath of the last survivors of that querulous race goes forth in a hurricane of reproach and remonstrance—a perfect storm of murmurs.—*James Hamilton* (1814—1867) *in* " *Moses the man of God.*"

Verse 25.—The murmuring on this occasion seems to have been a social evil, they *murmured in their tents.* So do men in social life promote among each other prejudice and aversion to true religion.—*W. Wilson.*

Verse 28.—" *They joined themselves also unto Baal-peor,*"—rather " bound themselves with his badge " : for it was the custom in ancient times, as it is now, in all Pagan countries, for every idol to have some specific badge, or ensign, by which his votaries are known.—*John Kitto, in* " *Daily Bible Illustrations.*"

Verse 28.—" *They joined themselves also unto Baal-peor.*" The narrative (Num. xxv.) seems clearly to show that this form of Baal-worship was connected with licentious rites. Without laying too much stress on the Rabbinical derivation of the word ‏ופעור‎ *hiatus, i.e.,* " *aperire hymenem virgineum,*" we seem to have reason to conclude that this was the nature of the worship. Baal-Peor was identified by the Rabbins and early fathers with Priapus (see the authorities quoted by Selden, *De Diis Syris,* i. 4, p. 302, sq., who, however, dissents from this view). This is, moreover, the view of

Creuzer (ii. 411), Winer, Gesenius, Fürst, and almost all critics.   The reader is referred for more detailed information particularly to Creuzer's *Symbolik* and Movers' *Phönizier.—William Gotch, in " Smith's Dictionary of the Bible."*

Verse 28.—*" Ate the sacrifices."*   It was usual for the officers to eat the chief part of the sacrifice.   Hence the remarks of Paul on this subject, 1 Cor. viii., 1—13.— *Benjamin Boothroyd.*

Verse 28.—*" The dead."*   The word מֵתִים, *maithim,* signifies *dead men ;* for the idols of the heathen were generally *men,*—warriors, kings, or lawgivers,—who had been deified after their death ; though many of them had been execrated during their life.—*Comprehensive Bible.*

Verse 28.—*" And they ate the sacrifices of the dead."*

> His obsequies to Polydorus paying
> A tomb we raise, and altars to the dead
> With dark blue fillets and black cypress bind
> Our dames with hair dishevell'd stand to mourn ;
> Warm frothy blows of milk and sacred blood
> We offer, in his grave the spirit lay,
> Call him aloud, and bid our last farewell.   *—Virgil.*

Verse 29.—*" They provoked him to anger with their inventions."*   Note, that it is not said, *with their deeds,* but with their pursuits (*studies*).   It is one thing simply to do a thing ; it is quite another to pursue it earnestly night and day.   The first may take place by chance, or through ignorance, or on account of some temptation, or violence, and that without the consent and against the inclination of the mind. But the latter is brought about in pursuance of a fixed purpose and design and by effort and forethought.   We see, therefore, in this passage that the patience of God was at length provoked to anger and fury when the people sinned not merely once and again, but when the pursuit of sin grew and strengthened.—*Musculus.*

Verse 29.—*" Their inventions."*   Their sins are here called by the name of *" their inventions."*   And so, sure, they are ; as no ways taught us by God, but of our own imagining or finding out.   For, indeed, our inventions are the cause of all sins. And if we look well into it we shall find our inventions are so.   By God's injunction we should all live, and his injunction is, " You shall not do every man what seems good in his own eyes " (or finds out in his own brains), " but whatsoever I command you, that shall you do."   Deut. xii. 8.   But we, setting light by that charge of his, out of the old disease of our father Adam (" ye shall be as gods, knowing good and evil "), think it a goodly matter to be witty, and to find out things ourselves to make to ourselves, to be authors, and inventors of somewhat, that so we may seem to be as wise as *God,* if not wiser ; and to know what is for our turns, as well as he, if not better.   It was Saul's fault.   God bade him destroy Amalek altogether, and he would invent a better way, to save some (forsooth) for sacrifice, which God could not think of.   And it was St. Peter's fault, when he persuaded Christ from his passion, and found out a better way (as he thought) than Christ could devise.—*Lancelot Andrewes.*

Verse 29.—*" Brake in upon them."*   The image is that of a river which had burst its barriers ; see Exod. xix. 24.   The plague is the slaughter inflicted upon the people by command of Moses ; Numb. xxv. 4, 5, 8, 9, 18.—*" The Speaker's Commentary."*

Verse 30.—*" Then stood up Phinehas."*   All Israel saw the bold lewdness of Zimri, but their hearts and eyes were so full of grief, that they had not room enough for indignation.   Phinehas looked on with the rest, but with other affections.   When he saw this defiance bidden to God, and this insultation upon the sorrow of his people (that while they were wringing their hands, a proud miscreant durst outface their humiliation with his wicked dalliance), his heart boils with a desire of a holy revenge ; and now that hand, which was used to a censer and sacrificing knife, takes up his javelin, and, with one stroke, joins these two bodies in their death, which were joined in their sin, and in the very flagrance of their lust, makes a new way for their souls to their own place.   O noble and heroical courage of Phinehas ! which, as it was rewarded of God, so is worthy to be admired of men.   He doth not stand casting of scruples : Who am I to do this ?   The son of the high priest.   My place is all for peace and mercy : it is for me to sacrifice, and pray for the sin of the people, not to sacrifice any of the people for their sin.   My duty calls me to appease the anger of God what I may, not to revenge the sins of men ; to pray for their conversion, not to work the confusion of any sinner. And who are these ? Is not the one a great prince in Israel, the other a princess of Midian ? Can the death of two so famous personages go unrevenged ? Or, if it be safe and fit, why doth my uncle Moses rather shed his own tears than their blood ? I will mourn with the rest ; let them revenge whom it concerneth. But the zeal of God hath barred out all weak deliberations ; and he holds it now both his duty and his glory, to be an executioner of so shameless a pair of offenders. . . .

Now the sin is punished, the plague ceaseth. The revenge of God sets out ever after the sin ; but if the revenge of men (which commonly comes later) can overtake it, God gives over the chase. How oft hath the infliction of a less punishment avoided a greater ! There are none so good friends to the state, as courageous and impartial ministers of justice : these are the reconcilers of God and the people, more than the prayers of them that sit still and do nothing.—*Joseph Hall.*

Verse 30.—" *Then stood up Phinehas,*" etc. Mark the mighty principle, which rolled like a torrent in the heart of Phinehas. The Spirit leaves it not obscure. The praise is this, " He was zealous for his God," Numb. xxv. 13. He could not fold his arms, and see God's law insulted, his rule defied, his majesty and empire scorned. The servant's heart blazed in one blaze of godly indignation. He must be up to vindicate his Lord. His fervent love, his bold resolve, fear nothing in a righteous cause. The offending Zimra was a potent prince : nevertheless he spared him not.

Believer, can you read this and feel no shame ? Do your bold efforts testify your zeal ? Sinners blaspheme God's name. Do you rebuke ? His Sabbaths are profaned. Do you protest ? False principles are current ? Do you expose the counterfeits ? Vice stalks in virtue's garb. Do you tear down the mask ? Satan enthrals the world. Do you resist ? Nay, rather are you not dozing unconcerned ? Whether Christ's cause succeeds, or be cast down, you little care. If righteous zeal girded your loins, and braced your nerves, and moved the rudder of your heart, and swelled your sails of action, would God be so unknown, and blasphemy so daring ?

Mark, next, the zeal of Phinehas is sound-minded. It is not as a courser without rein, a torrent unembanked, a hurricane let loose. Its steps are set in order's path. It executes God's own will in God's own way. The mandate says, let the offenders die. He aims a death-blow, then, with obedient hand. The zeal, which heaven kindles, is always a submissive grace.—*Henry Law, in " Christ is All,"* 1858.

Verse 30.—" *Stood up,*" as valiantly to do his work of zeal, as Moses had done to discharge the office of intercessor, and because he alone rose to set the example of resistance to the foul rites of Baal-Peor.—*Cassiodorus, quoted by Neale and Littledale.*

Verse 30.—" *So the plague was stayed.*" God himself puts this peculiar honour of staying the plague (when he was about to destroy the whole camp) upon this fact of Phinehas, saying, " He hath turned away my wrath," Num. xxv. 10, 11, because he was acted with the same zeal for God's glory and Israel's good, as God himself is acted with for them, and feared not to lose his life in God's cause, by putting to death a prince and a princess in the very flagrancy of their lust at one blow. There is such an accent and such an emphasis put by the Lord on this act (as the Jewish Rabbis observe), that here they begin the forty-first section or lecture of the Law, or (as Vatablus saith) the seventh section of the book, which they call Phinehas. Moreover, it teacheth us, that zeal of justice in the cause of God is an hopeful means to remove God's wrath from, and to procure his mercy to, man. Thus David also made an atonement by doing justice on Saul's house, 2 Sam. xxi. 3, etc. . . .

Phinehas by virtue of this promise of the priesthood (Num. xxv. 12, 13) lived himself to a great old age, even (as some say) to three hundred years, as appeareth by Judg. xx. 28, where he then is found alive, for his zeal at this time. He lived so long that some of the Rabbis are of opinion that he died not at all, but is still alive, whom they suppose to be the Elias that is to come before the coming of Christ ; but this notion is confuted by others of their Rabbis, and by the mention of his seed succeeding him in sacred Scripture. However, though few after the Flood did near attain to any such age, yet must Phinehas be very old in that time of Israel's warring with Benjamin. . . . Phinehas's priesthood is called " everlasting," not in his person, but in his posterity, whose sons were successively high priests till the captivity of Babylon, 1 Chron. vi. 4—16 ; and at the return out of captivity, Ezra, the great priest and scribe, was of his line, Ezra vii. 1—6 ; and so it continued in that line until, or very near, the approach of our evangelical High Priest (as Christ is called, Heb. v. 6), who was of the order of Melchizedek.—*Christopher Ness.*

Verse 30.—Why is the pacifying of God's wrath, and the staying of the plague ascribed to Phinehas, having a blush of irregularity in it, rather than to the acts of Moses and the judges, which were by express command from God and very regular ? For answer, the acts of Moses and the judges *slaked the fire* of God's wrath, that of Phinehas *quenched* it ; again the acts of Moses and the judges had a rise from a *spark*, that of Phinehas from a *flame of zeal* and holy indignation in him ; hence the Lord, who is exceedingly taken with the springs and roots of actions, sets the crown upon the head of Phinehas.—*Edmund Staunton, in a Sermon preached before the House of Lords,* 1644.

Verse 30.—" *So the plague was stayed.*"   A man doth not so live by his own faith, but in *temporal respects* the faith of another man may do him good.   Masters by their faith obtained healing for their servants, parents for their children, Matt. xv. 28. " Oh, man, great is thy faith ! " " Jesus seeing their faith," healed the sick of the palsy.   God's people for the town or place where they live : " The innocent " (*i.e.*, the faithful doer) " shall deliver the island," Job xxii. 30. Gen. xviii. 32, " If ten righteous persons shall be found there, I will not destroy it for ten's sake." Especially in Magistrates, *Moses,* Numb. xiv. ; *Hezekiah,* Isai. xxxvii., put up prayers, and God saved the people and places they prayed for : " *Then Phinehas executed judgment* (appeased God by faith) *and so the plague was stayed.*"—*Matthew Lawrence.*

Verse 32.—" *It went ill with Moses.*"   This judgment of God on that sin did not imply that he had blotted Moses out of the book of life, or the number of the saints, or otherwise than forgive his sin.   For he continued still to talk with him, and advise with him of the governing of his people, and spake to Joshua that he should be faithful to him as his servant Moses.   That was not the true Canaan from which he was shut out, but only the figure and shadow ; and that he was allowed to see ; a vision well worthy of all his labours, for the more excellent things signified by it. —*Isaac Williams, in " The Characters of the Old Testament,"* 1873.

Verse 33.—" *They provoked his spirit.*"   As Abraham was distinguished for his faith, so was Moses for his meekness ; for Scripture has declared that he was " very meek, above all the men which were on the face of the earth," Numb. xii. 3.   Yet judging from facts recorded of him, we should be inclined to suppose that he was by nature remarkable for sensitiveness and hastiness of temper—that was his one besetting infirmity.   Such appears to have been evinced when he slew the Egyptian ; when he twice smote the rock in the wilderness ; and on that occasion when he was " punished," as the Psalmist says, " *because they provoked his spirit, so that he spake unadvisedly with his lips,*" and when he broke the two tables of stone.   Something of the same kind appears to have been the case with our own Hooker, whose biographer attributes to him such singular meekness, while his private writings indicate a temper keenly alive and sensitive to the sense of wrong.—*Isaac Williams.*

Verse 33.—" *They provoked his spirit.*"—In a dispensation itself mainly gracious, and foreshadowing one which would be grace altogether, it was of prime importance that the mediating men should be merciful and gracious, long-suffering, and slow to anger.   And such they were in marvellous manner. ...

Brimming over with instruction as is this passage, we must leave it with a few remarks.

1. How careful preachers of the gospel and expounders of Scripture should be not to give an erroneous impression of God's mind or message.   The mental acumen is rare, but the right spirit is rarer.   But what is the right spirit ?—A loving spirit, a gentle spirit, a faithful spirit, a meek and weaned spirit, a spirit which says, " Speak, Lord, for thy servant heareth," and a spirit which adds, " All that the Lord giveth me, that will I speak," that excellent spirit which is only imparted by the good Spirit of God.   For if he withdraw, even a Moses ceases to be meek, and ceasing to be meek, even a Moses becomes a bad divine and an erroneous teacher, striking the rock that has been already stricken once for all, and preaching glad tidings gruffly.   He who gives the living water does not grudge it ; but sometimes, instead of " Ho ! every one that thirsteth," the preacher says, " Hear now, ye rebels ; must we fetch you water out of this rock ? " and makes the very invitation repulsive.

2. When any one has run long and run well, how sad it is to stumble within a few steps of the goal ! If Moses had an earthly wish, it was to see Israel safe in their inheritance, and his wish was all but consummated.   Faith and patience had held out well nigh forty years, and in a few months more the Jordan would be crossed

and the work would be finished. And who can tell but this very nearness of the prize helped to create something of a presumptuous confidence ? The blood of Moses was hot to begin with, and he was not the meekest of men when he smote the Egyptian and hid him in the sand. But he had got a good lesson in ruling his spirit, and betwixt the long sojourn with Jethro and the self-discipline needful in the charge of this multitude, he might fancy that he had now his foot on the neck of this enemy : when lo ! the sin revives and Moses dies.

Blessed is the man that feareth alway ! Blessed is the man who, although years have passed without an attempt at burglary, still bars his doors and sees his windows fastened ! Blessed is the man who, although a generation has gone since the last eruption, forbears to build on the volcanic soil, and dreads fires which have smouldered for fourscore years ! Blessed is the man who, even when the high seas are crossed and the land is made, still keeps an outlook ! Blessed is the man who, even on the confines of Canaan, takes heed of the evil heart, lest, with a promise of entering in, he should come short through unbelief !

3. Elevation of mind and sweetness of spirit are pearls of great price, and if we wish to preserve them we had better intrust them to God's own keeping. If Moses lost his faith, it was by first losing self-command : and if a man lose this, it is hard to say what next he may lose : like the mad warrior who makes a missile of his shield and hurls it at the head of an enemy, he is henceforward open to every fiery dart, to the cut and thrust of every assailant. But, as John Newton remarks, " The grace of God is as necessary to create a right temper in a Christian on the breaking of a china plate as on the death of an only son ; " and as no man can tell on any dawning day but what that may be the most trying day in all his life, how wise to pray without ceasing, " uphold me according unto thy word. Hold thou me up, and I shall be safe." " Set a watch, O Lord, before my mouth : keep the door of my lips." " Who can understand his errors ? Cleanse thou me from secret faults. Keep back thy servant also from presumptuous sins ; let them not have dominion over me : then shall I be upright, and I shall be innocent from the great transgression."—*James Hamilton.*

Verse 33.—" *They provoked his spirit,*" etc. Angry he certainly was ; and when, reverting to a former miracle, the Most High directed him to take the wonder-staff— his rod of many miracles—and at the head of the congregation " speak to the rock," and it would " give forth its water," in the heat and agitation of his spirit he failed to implement implicitly the Divine command. Instead of speaking to the rock he spoke to the people, and his harangue was no longer in the language calm and dignified of the lawgiver, but had a certain tone of petulance and egotism. " Hear now, ye rebels ; must we—must I and Aaron, not must Jehovah—fetch you water out of this rock ?" And instead of simply *speaking* to it, he raised the rod and dealt it two successive strokes, just as if the rock were sharing the general perversity, and would no more than the people obey its Creator's bidding. He was angry, and he sinned. He sinned and was severely punished. Water flowed sufficient for the whole camp and the cattle, clear, cool, and eagerly gushing, enough for all the million ; but at the same moment that its unmerited bounty burst on you, ye rebels, " a cup of wrath was put into the hand of Moses." * To you, ye murmurers, there came forth living water ; to your venerable leaders the cup of God's anger.

" The Lord spake unto Moses and Aaron, Because ye believed me not, to sanctify me in the eyes of the children of Israel, therefore ye shall not bring this congregation into the land which I have given them." Numb. xx. 12.—*James Hamilton.*

Verse 33.—" *He spake unadvisedly with his lips.*" The Lord desires him to address the rock, but Moses speaks to Israel. God wishes him to speak a word to the inanimate stone, and Moses strikes it twice. God still is willing that the people shall remain as his inheritance, but Moses evidently treats them with ill-will and much offensiveness. God wishes to relieve, and give refreshing to the people in their thirst, and Moses is selected to co-operate with him in all such joy ; but mark how, on this very day, a deep discord between God's inclination and the mind of Moses shows itself. God is inclined to grant forgiveness,—Moses inclines to punishment : before, the very opposite seemed to prevail. God is forbearing,—Moses, filled with bitterness ; God seeks to glorify his grace,—with Moses, self, not God, comes into prominence. " Must we,"—not, " must the Lord,"—but " must we fetch you water out of this rock ? " We see now, in this prophet, strong at other times, the first plain indications of decay and weariness. He has grown tired (and truly it should

* Van Oosterzee.

not seem strange, for which of us could have sustained a struggle such as his for half the time ?) of carrying these stubborn children any longer now. This man, so truly great, has never for an instant hitherto forgotten his own dignity in presence of all Israel ; but now, he is no longer master of himself.—*J. J. Van Oosterzee.*

Verse 33.—" *He spake unadvisedly.*" A gracious person may be surprised and fall suddenly among thieves that lurk behind the bushes. Nay, very holy men, unless wonderful wary, may be quickly tript up by sudden questions and unexpected emergencies. Who knows the subtilty of sin, and the deceitfulness of his own heart ? Take heed of answering quickly, and send up sudden ejaculations to heaven before you reply to a weighty and doubtful motion.—*Samuel Lee.*

Verses 34—38.—The miracles and mercies which settled them in Canaan made no more deep and durable impressions upon them than those that fetched them out of Egypt ; for by that time they were well warm in Canaan ; they corrupted themselves, and forsook God. Observe the steps of their apostasy.

1. They spared the nations which God had doomed to destruction (ver. 34). When they had got the good land God had promised them, they had no zeal against the wicked inhabitants, whom the Lord commanded them to extirpate, pretending pity ; but so merciful is God, that no man needs to be in any case more compassionate than he.

2. When they spared them, they promised themselves, that for all this, they would not join in any dangerous affinity with them ; but the way of sin is downhill ; omissions make way for commissions ; when they neglect to destroy the heathen, the next news we hear is, they " *were mingled among the heathen,*" made leagues with them, and contracted an intimacy with them, so that they " *learned their works* " (ver. 35). That which is rotten will sooner corrupt that which is sound, than be cured or made sound by it.

3. When they mingled with them, and learned some of their works that seemed innocent diversions and entertainments, yet they thought they would never join with them in their worship ; but by degrees they learned that too (ver. 36). " *They served their idols* " in the same manner, and with the same rites that they served them ; and they became a snare unto them, that sin drew on many more, and brought the judgments of God upon them, which they themselves could not but be sensible of, and yet knew not how to recover themselves.

4. When they joined with them in some of their idolatrous services, which they thought had least harm in them, they little thought that ever they should be guilty of that barbarous and inhuman piece of idolatry, the sacrificing of their living children to their dead gods : but they came to that at last (verses 37, 38) in which Satan triumphed over his worshippers, and regaled himself in blood and slaughter. " *They sacrificed their sons and daughters,*" pieces of themselves " *to devils ;* " and added murder, the most unnatural murder, to their idolatry ; one cannot think of it without horror ; they " *shed innocent blood,*" the most innocent, for it was infant blood, nay, it was the " *blood of their sons and their daughters.*" See the power of the spirit that works in the children of disobedience, and see his malice. The beginning of idolatry and superstition, like that of strife, is as the letting forth of water, and there is no villainy which they that venture upon it can be sure they shall stop short of, for God justly " gives them up to a reprobate mind " (Rom. i. 28).—*Matthew Henry.*

Verse 37.—" *Yea, they sacrificed their sons and their daughters unto devils.*" We need no better argument to discover the nature of these gods than this very service in my text accepted of them : for both by the record of sacred writ, and relation of heathen authors and other writers, we know that nothing was so usually commanded nor gratefully accepted by these heathenish gods, as was the shedding of man's blood, and the sacrificing of men, maids, and children unto them, as appears by the usual practice of men in former times. From the testimonies of Scripture, I give only the example of the king of Moab, mentioned in 2 Kings iii. 27, where it is said, that, being in some straits, " He took his eldest son that should have reigned in his stead, and offered him for a burnt offering upon the wall."

The stories likewise of the heathen are full of like examples. When the oracle of Apollo was asked by the Athenians how they might make amends for their killing of Androgeus, it willed them to send yearly to king Minos seven bodies of each sex to appease the wrath of the god. Now this kind of yearly sacrifice continued still in Athens in the time of Socrates. Thus the Carthaginians, being vanquished by Agathocles, king of Sicily, and supposing their god to be displeased, to appease him did sacrifice two hundred noble men's children. This custom was ancient even before the Trojan war, for then was Iphigenia sacrificed. Thus we read that the Latins sacrificed the tenth of their children to Jupiter; that men and children were usually sacrificed to Saturn in many places in Candia, Rhodomene, Phœnice, Africa, and those commonly the choice and dearest of their children and most nobly descended. The manner of sacrificing their children to Saturn, Diodorus relates to be this: bringing their children to the statue or image of Saturn, which was of huge greatness, they gave them into his hands, which were made so hollow and winding that the children offered slipped and fell down through into a cave and furnace of fire. These sacrifices continued in use till the birth and death of our Saviour Christ, who came to destroy the work of the devil; for such sacrifices were first forbidden by Augustus Cæsar; after more generally by Tiberius (in whose reign our Saviour suffered) who, as Tertullian writes, so straitly forbade them, that he crucified the priests who offered them; howbeit, even in Tertullian's time, and after in Eusebius' and Lactantius' times, such sacrifices were offered (but closely) to Jupiter Latialis.

Who can now doubt, seeing such exceeding superstitious cruelty, but that the gods commanding such sacrifices were very devils and enemies to mankind? God commands no such thing, but forbids it, and threatens plagues to his people, because they had forsaken him and " built also the high places of Baal, to burn their sons with fire for burnt offerings unto Baal, which I commanded not, nor spake it, neither came it into my mind " (Jer. xix. 5). Most infallibly then we may conclude that none but Satan, that arch-devil, with his angels, were the commanders of such service, for this agrees right well with his nature, who hath been a murderer from the beginning.—*Robert Jenison in " The Height of Israel's Heathenish Idolatrie, in Sacrificing their Children to the Devill,"* 1621.

Verse 37.—" *Yea, they sacrificed their sons,*" etc. From this we learn that inconsiderate zeal is a flimsy pretext in favour of any act of devotion. For by how much the Jews were under the influence of burning zeal, by so much does the prophet convict them of being guilty of greater wickedness; because their madness carried them away to such a pitch of enthusiasm, that they did not spare even their own offspring. Were good intentions meritorious, as idolaters suppose, then indeed the laying aside of all natural affection in sacrificing their own children was a deed deserving the highest praise. But when men act under the impulse of their own capricious humour, the more they occupy themselves with acts of external worship, the more do they increase their guilt. For what difference was there between Abraham and those persons of whom the prophet makes mention, but that the former, under the influence of faith, was ready to offer up his son, while the latter, carried away by the impulse of intemperate zeal, cast off all natural affection, and imbrued their hands in the blood of their own offspring.—*John Calvin.*

Verse 37.—" *Devils,*" שדים, *Shedim.* It appears that children were sacrificed to the deities thus named; that they were considered to be of an angry nature, and inimical to the human race, and thus the object of the homage rendered to them was to avert calamities. The name שדים may signify either *lord* or *master*, or anything that is *black*, it being derived from an Arabic verb meaning, *to be black*, or *to be master.*—*John Jahn, in " Biblical Antiquities."*

Verses 37, 38.—We stand astonished doubtless, at this horrid, barbarous, and unnatural impiety, of offering children by fire to a Moloch: but how little is it considered, that children, brought up in the ways of ignorance, error, vanity, folly, and vice, are more effectually sacrificed to the great adversary of mankind!—*George Horne.*

Verse 39.—" *And went a whoring with their own inventions.*"—As harlotry is one of the most abominable of sins that can be committed by a daughter or a wife; so often in the Scriptures turning from God and especially the practice of idolatry is called whoredom and fornication, Ps. lxxiii. 27; Ex. xxxiv. 15, 16.—*William S. Plumer.*

Verse 40.—" *He abhorred his own inheritance.*" Whenever great love sinks into great hate it is termed *abhorrence.*—*Lorinus.*

Verse 43.—" *They were brought low for their iniquity.*" Sin is of a weakening and impoverishing nature; it has weakened all mankind, and taken from them their moral strength to do good ; and has brought them to poverty and want ; to be beggars on the dunghill ; to a pit wherein is no water ; and left them in a hopeless and helpless condition ; yea, it brings the people of God often times after conversion into a low estate, when God hides his face because of it, temptations are strong, grace is weak, and they become lukewarm and indifferent to spiritual things.—*John Gill.*

Verse 46.—" *He made them also to be pitied of all those that carried them captives.*" This improved feeling towards the Jews through God's influence appears in Dan. i. 9 ; as Joseph similarly had his captivity improved by God's favour (Gen. xxxix. 21). So Evil-merodach, King of Babylon, treated kindly Jehoiachin, king of Judah (2 Kings xxv. 27).—*A. R. Fausset.*

Verse 47.—" *Gather us.*"   Bishop Patrick says that, in his opinion, this verse refers to those, who, in the days of Saul, or before, were taken prisoners by the Philistines, or other nations ; whom David prays God to gather to their own land again ; that they might worship him in that place which he had prepared for the ark of his presence.—*Thomas Fenton.*

Verse 48.—" *Amen.*"   Martin Luther said once of the Lord's Prayer that " it was the greatest martyr on earth, because it was used so frequently without thought and feeling, without reverence and faith."   This quaint remark, as true as it is sad, applies perhaps with still greater force to the word " Amen."

Familiar to us from our infancy is the sound of this word, which has found a home wherever the natives have learnt to adore Israel's God and Saviour.   It has been adopted, and without translation retained, in all languages in which the gospel of Jesus the Son of David is preached.   The literal signification, " So be it," is known to all ;   yet few consider the deep meaning, the great solemnity, and the abundant consolation treasured up in this word, which has formed for centuries the conclusion of the prayers and praises of God's people.   A word which is frequently used without due thoughtfulness, and unaccompanied with the feeling which it is intended to call forth, loses its power from this very familiarity, and though constantly on our lips, lies bedridden in the dormitory of our soul.   But it is a great word this word " *Amen* " ; and Luther has truly said, " As your Amen is, so has been your prayer."

It is a word of venerable history in Israel and in the church.   The word dates as far back as the law of Moses.   When a solemn oath was pronounced by the priest, the response of the person who was adjured consisted simply of the word " Amen." In like manner the people responded " Amen " when, from the heights of Ebal and Gerizim, the blessings and the curses of the divine law were pronounced.   Again, at the great festival which David made when the ark of God was brought from Obed-Edom, the Psalm of praise which Asaph and his brethren sang concluded with the words, " Blessed be the Lord God of Israel for ever and ever.   And all the people said, Amen " (1 Chron. xvi. 36).   Thus we find in the Psalms, not merely that David concludes his Psalm of praise with the word *Amen,* but he says, " *And let all the people say, Amen.*"—*Adolph Saphir, in* " *The Lord's Prayer,*" 1870.

HINTS TO PREACHERS.

Verse 1.—Take this verse as the theme of the Psalm, and we shall then see that its exhortation to praise, I. Is directed to a special people : chosen, redeemed, but sinful, borne with, and forgiven.   II. Is supported by abundant arguments.   Man not to be praised, for he sins.   God gives in his goodness, and forgives in his mercy, and is therefore to be thanked.   III. Is as applicable now as ever : for our story is a transcript of Israel's.

Verse 2.—I. A challenge.   II. A suggestion :   at least let us do what we can. III. An ambition :   in the ages to come we will make known with the church to angels, and all intelligent beings, the mighty acts of divine grace.   IV. A question—shall I be there ?

Verse 3.—The blessedness of a godly life.

Verse 4.—I. The language of Humility :   " Remember me, O Lord."   Let me not escape thy notice amongst the many millions of creatures under thy care.   II.

The language of Faith. 1. That God has a people to whom he shows special favour. 2. That he himself has provided salvation for them. III. The language of prayer. 1. For the free gift of salvation. 2. For the common salvation—not wishing to be peculiar, but to be as " Thy people," taking them for all in all, both here and hereafter. Walking in the footsteps of the flock.

> " Be this my glory, Lord, to be
> Joined to thy saints, and near to thee."

—*G. R.*

Verses 4, 7, 45.—In verse 4, a remembrance desired. In verse 7, a failure of remembrance deplored. In verse 45, a divine remembrance extolled.

Verse 5.—The Persons: " Thy chosen "; " Thy nation "; " Thine inheritance." II. The Privileges: " The good of thy chosen "; " The gladness of thy nation "; " The glory of thine inheritance." III. The Pleas: " That I may see," etc. They were once as I am: make me what they are now. 2. My salvation is everything to me. " That I may see," etc. " That I may rejoice," etc. They are many, I am but one. " That I may glory," etc.—*G. R.*

Verse 6.—In what respects men may be partakers in the sins of their ancestors.

Verses 7, 8.—I. On man's part a darkened understanding, ungrateful forgetfulness, and provocation. II. On God's part: understanding discovering a reason for mercy; memory mindful of the covenant; patience revealing its power.

Verses 7, 8.—I. A special provocation: they murmured at the Red Sea. II. A special deliverance; " Nevertheless," etc. III. A special Design: " For his own sake "; " That he might make his power known."—*G. R.*

Verse 8.—Salvation by grace a grand display of power.

Verse 8.—" Why are men saved ? " See " Spurgeon's Sermons," No. 115. I. The glorious Saviour, " He." II. The favoured persons, who are they ? 1. They were a stupid people : " Our fathers understood not," etc., ver. 7. 2. An ungrateful people : " They remembered not," etc., verses 7, 13, 24, etc. 3. A provoking people. III. The reason of salvation : " He saved them for his name's sake." The name of God is his person, his attributes, and his nature. We might, perhaps, include this also : " My name is in him "—that is, in Christ ; he saves us for the sake of Christ, who is the name of God. He saved them that he might manifest his nature : " God is love." He saved them to vindicate his name. IV. The obstacles removed : " Nevertheless."

Verse 9.—" Israel at the Red Sea." See " Spurgeon's Sermons," No. 72. I. Israel's three difficulties. 1. The Red Sea in front of them. This was not put there by an enemy ; but by God himself. The Red Sea represents some great and trying providence placed in the path of every new-born child of God, to try his faith, and the sincerity of his trust in God. 2. The Egyptians behind them,—the representatives of the sins which we thought were dead and gone. 3. The third difficulty was faint hearts within them. II. Israel's three helps. 1. Providence. 2. Their knowledge that they were the covenant people of God. 3. The man,—Moses. So the believer's hope and help is in the God-man Christ Jesus. III. God's grand design in it. To give them a thorough baptism into his service, consecrating them for ever to himself (1 Cor. x. 1, 2).

Verse 9 (second clause).—Dangerous and difficult paths rendered safe and easy by God's leadership.

Verse 11 (second clause).—Song over sins forgiven.

Verses 12—14.—The faith of nature, based on sight, causes transient joy, soon evaporates, dies in utter unbelief, and conducts to greater sin.

Verses 13—15.—I. Mercies are sooner forgotten than trials : " They soon forgat," etc. We write our afflictions on marble, our mercies upon sand. II. We should wait *for* God, as well as *upon* God : " They waited not," etc. III. Immoderate desire for what we have not of worldly goods, tempts God to deprive us of what we have : ver. 14. IV. Prayer may be answered for evil as well as for good : " He gave them their request," then smote them with a plague. V. Carnal indulgence is inimical to spiritual-mindedness : ver. 15. Better have a lean body and healthy soul, than a healthy body and leanness of soul. " Poor in this world, rich in faith." There are few of whom it can be said, " I wish thou mayest prosper and be in health," etc. (3 John 2).—*G. R.*

Verse 14.—The wickedness of inordinate desires. I. They are out of place—

" in the wilderness." II. They are assaults upon God—" and tempted God." III. They are despisers of former mercies—see preceding verses. IV. They involve solemn danger—see following verse.

Verse 16.—The sin of envy. Its base nature, its cruel actions, its unscrupulous ingratitude, its daring assaults, its abomination before God.

Verse 19.—The sinner as an inventor.

Verses 19—22.—I. The Sin remembered. 1. Idolatry: not forgetting God merely, or disowning him, but setting up an idol in his place. 2. Idolatry of the worst kind: changing the glory of God into the similitude of an ox, etc. 3. The idolatry of Egypt under which they had suffered, and from which they had been delivered. 4. Idolatry after many wonderful interpositions of the true God in their behalf. II. The Remembrance of Sin. 1. For Humiliation. It was the sin of their fathers. 2. For self-condemnation. "We have sinned with our fathers." It was our nature in them, and it is their nature in us that has committed this great sin.

Verse 23.—Moses, the intercessor, a type of our Lord. Carefully study his pleading as recorded in Exod. xxxii.

Verse 23.—Mediation required: "He said that he would destroy them," etc. II. Mediation offered: "Moses stood before him in the breach." III. Mediation accepted: "To turn away his wrath," etc. Exod. xxxii.—*G. R.*

Verses 24—26.—Murmuring. I. Arises from despising our mercies. II. Is fostered by unbelief. III. Is indulged in all sorts of places. IV. Makes men deaf to the Lord's voice. V. Provokes great judgments from the Lord.

Verses 24—27.—I. The Rest promised: "The pleasant land." II. The Refusal of the Rest: "They despised," etc. III. The Reason of the Refusal: unbelief. "They could not enter in because of unbelief."—*G. R.*

Verses 30, 31.—The effects of one decisive act for God; immediate, personal, and for posterity.

Verses 32, 33.—I. The afflictions of God's people are for the trial of their faith. II. The trial of their faith is to bring them from dependence upon circumstances to depend upon God himself. III. The forbearance of God with his people is greater than that of the best of men.—*G. R.*

Verse 33.—I. What it is so to speak unadvisedly. II. What is the great cause of it—" they provoked his spirit." III. What the results may be.

Verses 34—42.—I. What Israel did not do. They began well, but did not complete the conquest of their foes: ver. 34. II. What they did do: ver. 35—39. 1. They became friendly with them. 2. They adopted their habits: "learned their works." 3. They embraced their religion: "served their idols." 4. They imitated their cruelties; ver. 37, 38. 5. They did worse than the heathen (ver. 39), they added wicked inventions of their own. III. What God did to them: ver. 40—42. He gave them into the hands of their enemies, and suffered them to be severely oppressed by them. We must either conquer all our foes or be conquered by them. Bring your shield from the battle or be brought home upon it.—*G. R.*

Verse 37.—Moloch-worship in modern times. Children sacrificed to fashion, wealth, and loveless marriage among the higher classes. Bad example, drinking customs, etc., among the poorer sort. A needful subject.

Verses 44, 45.—Sin in God's people. I. Is very provoking to God. II. Ensures chastisement. III. Is to be sincerely mourned—" their cry." IV. Will be graciously forgiven, and its effect removed. So the covenant promises.

Verse 47.—I. An earnest Prayer: "Save us, O Lord," etc. II. A Believing Prayer: "O Lord *our* God." III. A humble Prayer: "Gather us from among the heathen." IV. A sincere Prayer: "To give thanks unto thy holy name"; to own thy justice and holiness in all thy ways. V. A confident Prayer: "To triumph in thy praise." None but bruised spices give forth such odours.—*G. R.*

Verse 48.—I. God is to be praised as the "God of Israel." 1. Of typical Israel. 2. Of the true Israel. II. He is to be praised as the God of Israel under all circumstances: for his judgments as well as for his mercies. III. At all times: "From everlasting to everlasting." IV. By all people. "Let all the people say, Amen." V. As the beginning and end of every song: "Praise ye the Lord."—*G. R.*

Verse 48.—" *Let all the people say, Amen.*"—The exhortation to universal praise. All men are indebted to the Lord, all have sinned, all hear the gospel, all his people are saved. Unanimity in praise is pleasant, and promotes unity in other matters.

HERE ENDETH THE FOURTH BOOK OF THE PSALMS.

PSALM CVII.

SUBJECT, ETC.—*This is a choice song for the redeemed of the Lord (verse 2). Although it celebrates providential deliverances, and therefore may be sung by any man whose life has been preserved in time of danger; yet, under cover of this, it mainly magnifies the Lord for spiritual blessings, of which temporal favours are but types and shadows. The theme is thanksgiving, and the motives for it. The construction of the Psalm is highly poetical, and merely as a composition it would be hard to find its compeer among human productions. The bards of the Bible hold no second place among the sons of song.*

DIVISION.—*The Psalmist commences by dedicating his poem to the redeemed who have been gathered from captivity,* 1—3; *he then likens their history to that of travellers lost in the desert,* 4—9; *to that of prisoners in iron bondage,* 10—16; *to that of sick men,* 17—22; *and to that of mariners tossed with tempest,* 23—32. *In the closing verses the judgment of God on the rebellious, and the mercies of God to his own afflicted people are made the burden of the song,* 33—42; *and then the Psalm closes with a sort of summing up, in verse* 43, *which declares that those who study the works and ways of the Lord shall be sure to see and praise his goodness.*

EXPOSITION.

O GIVE thanks unto the LORD, for *he is* good: for his mercy *endureth* for ever.

2 Let the redeemed of the LORD say *so*, whom he hath redeemed from the hand of the enemy;

3 And gathered them out of the lands, from the east, and from the west, from the north, and from the south.

1. "*O give thanks unto the Lord, for he is good.*" It is all we can give him, and the least we can give; therefore let us diligently render to him our thanksgiving. The Psalmist is in earnest in the exhortation, hence the use of the interjection "O," to intensify his words: let us be at all times thoroughly fervent in the praises of the Lord, both with our lips and with our lives, by thanksgiving and thanks-living. JEHOVAH, for that is the name here used, is not to be worshipped with groans and cries, but with thanks, for he is good; and these thanks should be heartily rendered, for his is no common goodness: he is good by nature, and essence, and proven to be good in all the acts of his eternity. Compared with him there is none good, no, not one: but he is essentially, perpetually, superlatively, infinitely good. We are the perpetual partakers of his goodness, and therefore ought above all his creatures to magnify his name. Our praise should be increased by the fact that the divine goodness is not a transient thing, but in the attribute of mercy abides for ever the same, "*for his mercy endureth for ever.*" The word *endureth* has been properly supplied by the translators, but yet it somewhat restricts the sense, which will be better seen if we read it, "*for his mercy for ever.*" That mercy had no beginning, and shall never know an end. Our sin required that goodness should display itself to us in the form of mercy, and it has done so, and will do so evermore; let us not be slack in praising the goodness which thus adapts itself to our fallen nature.

2. "*Let the redeemed of the Lord say so.*" Whatever others may think or say, the redeemed have overwhelming reasons for declaring the goodness of the Lord. Theirs is a peculiar redemption, and for it they ought to render peculiar praise. The Redeemer is so glorious, the ransom price so immense, and the redemption so complete, that they are under sevenfold obligations to give thanks unto the Lord, and to exhort others to do so. Let them not only feel so but *say* so; let them both sing and bid their fellows sing. "*Whom he hath redeemed from the hand of the enemy.*" Snatched by superior power away from fierce oppressions, they are bound above all men to adore the Lord, their Liberator. Theirs is a divine redemption, "he hath redeemed" them, and no one else has done it. His own unaided arm has wrought

398

out their deliverance. Should not emancipated slaves be grateful to the hand which set them free ? What gratitude can suffice for a deliverance from the power of sin, death, and hell ? In heaven itself there is no sweeter hymn than that whose burden is, " Thou hast redeemed us unto God by thy blood."

3. " *And gathered them out of the lands, from the east, and from the west, from the north, and from the south.*" Gathering follows upon redeeming. The captives of old were restored to their own land from every quarter of the earth, and even from beyond the sea ; for the word translated *south* is really *the sea*. No matter what divides, the Lord will gather his own into one body, and first on earth by " one Lord, one faith, and one baptism," and then in heaven by one common bliss they shall be known to be the one people of the One God. What a glorious Shepherd must he be who thus collects the blood-bought flock from the remotest regions, guides them through countless perils, and at last makes them to lie down in the green pastures of Paradise. Some have wandered one way and some another, they have all left Immanuel's land and strayed as far as they could, and great are the grace and power by which they are all collected into one flock by the Lord Jesus. With one heart and voice let the redeemed praise the Lord who gathers them into one.

4 They wandered in the wilderness in a solitary way ; they found no city to dwell in.

5 Hungry and thirsty, their soul fainted in them.

6 Then they cried unto the LORD in their trouble, *and* he delivered them out of their distresses.

7 And he led them forth by the right way, that they might go to a city of habitation.

8 Oh that *men* would praise the LORD *for* his goodness, and *for* his wonderful works to the children of men !

9 For he satisfieth the longing soul, and filleth the hungry soul with goodness.

4. " *They wandered in the wilderness.*" They *wandered*, for the track was lost, no vestige of a road remained ; worse still, they wandered *in a wilderness*, where all around was burning sand. They were lost in the worst possible place, even as the sinner is who is lost in sin ; they wandered up and down in vain searches and researches as a sinner does when he is awakened and sees his lost estate ; but it ended in nothing, for they still continued in the wilderness, though they had hoped to escape from it. " *In a solitary way.*" No dwelling of man was near, and no other company of travellers passed within hail. Solitude is a great intensifier of misery. The loneliness of a desert has a most depressing influence upon the man who is lost in the boundless waste. The traveller's way in the wilderness is a *waste* way, and when he leaves even that poor, barren trail, to get utterly beyond the path of man, he is in a wretched plight indeed. A soul without sympathy is on the borders of hell : a solitary way is the way of despair. " *They found no city to dwell in.*" How could they ? There was none. Israel in the wilderness abode under canvas, and enjoyed none of the comforts of settled life ; wanderers in the Sahara find no town or village. Men when under distress of soul find nothing to rest upon, no comfort and no peace ; their efforts after salvation are many, weary, and disappointing, and the dread solitude of their hearts fills them with dire distress.

5. " *Hungry and thirsty, their soul fainted in them.*" The spirits sink when the bodily frame becomes exhausted by long privations. Who can keep his courage up when he is ready to fall to the ground at every step through utter exhaustion ? The supply of food is all eaten, the water is spent in the bottles, and there are neither fields nor streams in the desert, the heart therefore sinks in dire despair. Such is the condition of an awakened conscience before it knows the Lord Jesus ; it is full of unsatisfied cravings, painful needs, and heavy fears. It is utterly spent and without strength, and there is nothing in the whole creation which can minister to its refreshment.

6. " *Then they cried unto the Lord in their trouble.*" Not till they were in extremities did they pray, but the mercy is that they prayed *then*, and prayed in the right manner, with a *cry*, and to the right person, even *to the Lord*. Nothing else

remained for them to do ; they could not help themselves, or find help in others, and therefore they cried to God. Supplications which are forced out of us by stern necessity are none the less acceptable with God ; but, indeed, they have all the more prevalence, since they are evidently sincere, and make a powerful appeal to the divine pity. Some men will never pray till they are half-starved, and for their best interests it is far better for them to be empty and faint than to be full and stouthearted. If hunger brings us to our knees it is more useful to us than feasting ; if thirst drives us to the fountain it is better than the deepest draughts of worldly joy ; and if fainting leads to crying it is better than the strength of the mighty. " *And he delivered them out of their distresses.*" Deliverance follows prayer most surely. The cry must have been very feeble, for they were faint, and their faith was as weak as their cry ; but yet they were heard, and heard at once. A little delay would have been their death ; but there was none, for the Lord was ready to save them. The Lord delights to come in when no one else can be of the slightest avail. The case was hopeless till Jehovah interposed, and then all was changed immediately ; the people were shut up, straitened, and almost pressed to death, but enlargement came to them at once when they began to remember their God, and look to him in prayer. Those deserve to die of hunger who will not so much as ask for bread, and he who being lost in a desert will not beg the aid of a guide cannot be pitied even if he perish in the wilds and feed the vultures with his flesh.

7. " *And he led them forth by the right way.*" There are many wrong ways, but only one right one, and into this none can lead us but God himself. When the Lord is leader the way is sure to be right ; we never need question that. Forth from the pathless mazes of the desert he conducted the lost ones ; he found the way, made the way, and enabled them to walk along it, faint and hungry as they were. " *That they might go to a city of habitation.*" The end was worthy of the way : he did not lead them from one desert to another, but he gave the wanderers an abode, the weary ones a place of rest. *They* found no city to dwell in, but *he* found one readily enough. What *we* can do and what *God* can do are two very different things. What a difference it made to them to leave their solitude for a city, their trackless path for well-frequented streets, and their faintness of heart for the refreshment of a home ! Far greater are the changes which divine love works in the condition of sinners when God answers their prayers and brings them to Jesus. Shall not the Lord be magnified for such special mercies ? Can we who have enjoyed them sit down in ungrateful silence ?

8. " *Oh that men would praise the Lord for his goodness.*" Men are not mentioned here in the original, but the word is fitly supplied by the translators ; the Psalmist would have all things in existence magnify Jehovah's name. Surely *men* will do this without being exhorted to it when the deliverance is fresh in their memories. They must be horrible ingrates who will not honour such a deliverer for o happy a rescue from the most cruel death. It is well that the redeemed should be stirred up to bless the Lord again and again, for preserved life deserves life-long thankfulness. Even those who have not encountered the like peril, and obtained the like deliverance, should bless the Lord in sympathy with their fellows, sharing their joy. " *And for his wonderful works to the children of men.*" These favours are bestowed upon *our* race, upon children of the family to which we belong, and therefore we ought to join in the praise. The children of men are so insignificant, so feeble, and so undeserving, that it is a great wonder that the Lord should do anything for them ; but he is not content with doing little works, he puts forth his wisdom, power, and love to perform marvels on the behalf of those who seek him. In the life of each one of the redeemed there is a world of wonders, and therefore from each there should resound a world of praises. As to the marvels of grace which the Lord has wrought for his church as a whole there is no estimating them, they are as high above our thoughts as the heavens are high above the earth. When shall the day dawn when the favoured race of man shall be as devoted to the praise of God as they are distinguished by the favour of God ?

9. " *For he satisfieth the longing soul.*" This is the summary of the lost traveller's experience. He who in a natural sense has been rescued from perishing in a howling wilderness ought to bless the Lord who brings him again to eat bread among men. The spiritual sense is, however, the more rich in instruction. The Lord sets us longing and then completely satisfies us. That longing leads us into solitude, separation, thirst, faintness, and self-despair, and all these conduct us to prayer, faith, divine guidance, satisfying of the soul's thirst, and rest : the good hand of the Lord

is to be seen in the whole process and in the divine result. " *And filleth the hungry soul with goodness.*" As for thirst he gives satisfaction, so for hunger he supplies filling. In both cases the need is more than met, there is an abundance in the supply which is well worthy of notice : the Lord does nothing in a niggardly fashion ; satisfying and filling are his peculiar modes of treating his guests ; none who come under the Lord's providing ever complain of short commons. Nor does he fill the hungry with common fare, but with *goodness* itself. It is not so much good, as the essence of goodness which he bestows on needy suppliants. Shall man be thus royally supplied and return no praise for the largesses of love ? It must not be so. We will even now give thanks with all the redeemed church, and pray for the time when the whole earth shall be filled with his glory.

10 Such as sit in darkness and in the shadow of death, *being* bound in affliction and iron ;

11 Because they rebelled against the words of God, and contemned the counsel of the most High :

12 Therefore he brought down their heart with labour ; they fell down, and *there was* none to help.

13 Then they cried unto the LORD in their trouble, *and* he saved them out of their distresses.

14 He brought them out of darkness and the shadow of death, and brake their bands in sunder.

15 Oh that *men* would praise the LORD *for* his goodness, and *for* his wonderful works to the children of men !

16 For he hath broken the gates of brass, and cut the bars of iron in sunder.

10. " *Such as sit in darkness and in the shadow of death.*" The cell is dark of itself, and the fear of execution casts a still denser gloom over the prison. Such is the cruelty of man to man that tens of thousands have been made to linger in places only fit to be tombs ; unhealthy, suffocating, filthy sepulchres, where they have sickened and died of broken hearts. Meanwhile the dread of sudden death has been the most hideous part of the punishment ; the prisoners have felt as if the chill shade of death himself froze them to the very marrow. The state of a soul under conviction of sin is forcibly symbolized by such a condition ; persons in that state cannot see the promises which would yield them comfort, they sit still in the inactivity of despair, they fear the approach of judgment, and are thereby as much distressed as if they were at death's door. " *Being bound in affliction and iron.*" Many prisoners have been thus doubly fettered in heart and hand ; or the text may mean that affliction becomes as an iron band to them, or that the iron chains caused them great affliction. None know these things but those who have felt them ; we should prize our liberty more if we knew by actual experience what manacles and fetters mean. In a spiritual sense affliction frequently attends conviction of sin, and then the double grief causes a double bondage. In such cases the iron enters into the soul, the poor captives cannot stir because of their bonds, cannot rise to hope because of their grief, and have no power because of their despair. Misery is the companion of all those who are shut up and cannot come forth. O ye who are made free by Christ Jesus, remember those who are in bonds.

11. " *Because they rebelled against the words of God.*" This was the general cause of bondage among the ancient people of God, they were given over to their adversaries because they were not loyal to the Lord. God's words are not to be trifled with, and those who venture on such rebellion will bring themselves into bondage. " *And contemned the counsel of the Most High.*" They thought that they knew better than the Judge of all the earth, and therefore they left his ways and walked in their own. When men do not follow the divine counsel they give the most practical proof of their contempt for it. Those who will not be bound by God's law will, ere long, be bound by the fetters of judgment. There is too much contemning of the divine counsel, even among Christians, and hence so few of them know the liberty wherewith Christ makes us free.

12. " *Therefore he brought down their heart with labour.*" In eastern prisons men are frequently made to labour like beasts of the field. As they have no liberty,

so they have no rest. This soon subdues the stoutest heart, and makes the proud boaster sing another tune. Trouble and hard toil are enough to tame a lion. God has methods of abating the loftiness of rebellious looks : the cell and the mill make even giants tremble. " *They fell down, and there was none to help.*" Stumbling on in the dark beneath their weary task, they at last fell prone upon the ground, but no one came to pity them or to lift them up. Their fall might be fatal for aught that any man cared about them ; their misery was unseen, or, if observed, no one could interfere between them and their tyrant masters. In such a wretched plight the rebellious Israelite became more lowly in mind, and thought more tenderly of his God and of his offences against him. When a soul finds all its efforts at self-salvation prove abortive, and feels that it is now utterly without strength, then the Lord is at work hiding pride from man and preparing the afflicted one to receive his mercy. The spiritual case which is here figuratively described is desperate, and therefore affords the finer field for the divine interposition ; some of us remember well how brightly mercy shone in our prison, and what music the fetters made when they fell off from our hands. Nothing but the Lord's love could have delivered us ; without it we must have utterly perished.

13. " *Then they cried unto the Lord in their trouble.*" Not a prayer till then. While there was any to help below they would not look above. No cries till their hearts were brought down and their hopes were all dead—*then* they cried, but not before. So many a man offers what he calls prayer when he is in good ease and thinks well of himself, but in very deed the only real cry to God is that which is forced out of him by a sense of utter helplessness and misery. We pray best when we are fallen on our faces in painful helplessness. " *And he saved them out of their distresses.*" Speedily and willingly he sent relief. They were long before they cried, but he was not long before he saved. They had applied everywhere else before they came to him, but when they did address themselves to him, they were welcome at once. He who saved men in the open wilderness can also save in the close prison : bolts and bars cannot shut him out, nor long shut in his redeemed ones.

14. " *He brought them out of darkness and the shadow of death.*" The Lord in providence fetches out prisoners from their cells and bids them breathe the sweet fresh air again, and then he takes off their fetters and gives liberty to their aching limbs. So also he frees men from care and trouble, and especially from the misery and slavery of sin. This he does with his own hand, for in the experience of all the saints it is certified that there is no jail-delivery unless by the Judge himself. " *And brake their bands in sunder.*" Set them free by force, so liberating them that they could not be chained again, for he had broken the manacles to pieces. The Lord's deliverances are of the most complete and triumphant kind, he neither leaves the soul in darkness nor in bonds, nor does he permit the powers of evil again to enthral the liberated captive. What he does is done for ever. Glory be to his name.

15. " *Oh that men would praise the Lord for his goodness, and for his wonderful works to the children of men.*" The sight of such goodness makes a right-minded man long to see the Lord duly honoured for his amazing mercy. When dungeon doors fly open, and chains are snapped, who can refuse to adore the glorious goodness of the Lord ? It makes the heart sick to think of such gracious mercies remaining unsung : we cannot but plead with men to remember their obligations and extol the Lord their God.

16. " *For he hath broken the gates of brass, and cut the bars of iron in sunder.*" This verse belongs to that which precedes it, and sums up the mercy experienced by captives. The Lord breaks the strongest gates and bars when the time comes to set free his prisoners : and spiritually the Lord Jesus has broken the most powerful of spiritual bonds and made us free indeed. Brass and iron are as tow before the flame of Jesus' love. The gates of hell shall not prevail against us, neither shall the bars of the grave detain us. Those of us who have experienced his redeeming power must and will praise the Lord for the wonders of his grace displayed on our behalf.

17 Fools because of their transgression, and because of their iniquities, are afflicted.

18 Their soul abhorreth all manner of meat ; and they draw near unto the gates of death.

19 Then they cry unto the LORD in their trouble, *and* he saveth them out of their distresses.

20 He sent his word, and healed them, and delivered *them* from their destructions.

21 Oh that *men* would praise the LORD *for* his goodness, and *for* his wonderful works to the children of men!

22 And let them sacrifice the sacrifices of thanksgiving, and declare his works with rejoicing.

17. " *Fools because of their transgression, and because of their iniquities, are afflicted.*" Many sicknesses are the direct result of foolish acts. Thoughtless and lustful men by drunkenness, gluttony, and the indulgence of their passions fill their bodies with diseases of the worst kind. Sin is at the bottom of all sorrow, but some sorrows are the immediate results of wickedness : men by a course of transgression afflict themselves and are fools for their pains. Worse still, even when they are in affliction they are fools still ; and if they were brayed in a mortar among wheat with a pestle, yet would not their folly depart from them. From one transgression they go on to many iniquities, and while under the rod they add sin to sin. Alas, even the Lord's own people sometimes play the fool in this sad manner.

18. " *Their soul abhorreth all manner of meat.*" Appetite departs from men when they are sick : the best of food is nauseous to them, their stomach turns against it. " *And they draw near unto the gates of death.*" From want of food, and from the destructive power of their malady, they slide gradually down till they lie at the door of the grave ; neither does the skill of the physician suffice to stay their downward progress. As they cannot eat there is no support given to the system, and as the disease rages their little strength is spent in pain and misery. Thus it is with souls afflicted with a sense of sin, they cannot find comfort in the choicest promises, but turn away with loathing even from the gospel, so that they gradually decay into the grave of despair. The mercy is that though near the gates of death they are not yet inside the sepulchre.

19. " *Then they cry unto the Lord in their trouble.*" They join the praying legion at last. Saul also is among the prophets. The fool lays aside his motley in prospect of the shroud, and betakes himself to his knees. What a cure for the soul sickness of body is often made to be by the Lord's grace ! " *And he saveth them out of their distresses.*" Prayer is as effectual on a sick bed as in the wilderness or in prison ; it may be tried in all places and circumstance with certain result. We may pray about our bodily pains and weaknesses, and we may look for answers too. When we have no appetite for meat we may have an appetite for prayer. He who cannot feed on the word of God may yet turn to God himself and find mercy.

20. " *He sent his word and healed them.*" Man is not healed by medicine alone, but by the word which proceedeth out of the mouth of God is man restored from going down to the grave. A word will do it, a word has done it thousands of times. " *And delivered them from their destructions.*" They escape though dangers had surrounded them, dangers many and deadly. The word of the Lord has a great delivering power ; he has but to speak and the armies of death flee in an instant. Sin-sick souls should remember the power of *the Word*, and be much in hearing it and meditating upon it.

Spiritually considered, these verses describe a sin-sick soul : foolish but yet aroused to a sense of guilt, it refuses comfort from any and every quarter, and a lethargy of despair utterly paralyses it. To its own apprehension nothing remains but utter destruction in many forms : the gates of death stand open before it, and it is, in its own apprehension, hurried in that direction. Then is the soul driven to cry in the bitterness of its grief unto the Lord, and Christ, the eternal Word, comes with healing power in the direst extremity, saving to the uttermost.

21. " *Oh that men would praise the Lord for his goodness, and for his wonderful works to the children of men.*" It is marvellous that men can be restored from sickness and yet refuse to bless the Lord. It would seem impossible that they should forget such great mercy, for we should expect to see both themselves and the friends to whom they are restored uniting in a lifelong act of thanksgiving. Yet when ten are healed it is seldom that more than one returns to give glory to God. Alas, where are the nine ? When a spiritual cure is wrought by the great Physician, praise is one of the surest signs of renewed health. A mind rescued from the disease of sin and the weary pains of conviction, must and will adore Jehovah Rophi, the healing God : yet it were well if there were a thousand times as much even of this.

22. "*And let them sacrifice the sacrifices of thanksgiving.*" In such a case let there be gifts and oblations as well as words. Let the good Physician have his fee of gratitude. Let life become a sacrifice to him who has prolonged it, let the deed of self-denying gratitude be repeated again and again : there must be many cheerful sacrifices to celebrate the marvellous boon. "*And declare his works with rejoicing.*" Such things are worth telling, for the personal declaration honours God, relieves ourselves, comforts others, and puts all men in possession of facts concerning the divine goodness which they will not be able to ignore.

23 They that go down to the sea in ships, that do business in great waters ;

24 These see the works of the LORD, and his wonders in the deep.

25 For he commandeth, and raiseth the stormy wind, which lifteth up the waves thereof.

26 They mount up to the heaven, they go down again to the depths : their soul is melted because of trouble.

27 They reel to and fro, and stagger like a drunken man, and are at their wit's end.

28 Then they cry unto the LORD in their trouble, and he bringeth them out of their distresses.

29 He maketh the storm a calm, so that the waves thereof are still.

30 Then are they glad because they be quiet ; so he bringeth them unto their desired haven.

31 Oh that *men* would praise the LORD *for* his goodness, and *for* his wonderful works to the children of men !

32 Let them exalt him also in the congregation of the people, and praise him in the assembly of the elders.

23. "*They that go down to the sea in ships.*" Navigation was so little practised among the Israelites that mariners were invested with a high degree of mystery, and their craft was looked upon as one of singular daring and peril. Tales of the sea thrilled all hearts with awe, and he who had been to Ophir or to Tarshish and had returned alive was looked upon as a man of renown, an ancient mariner to be listened to with reverent attention. Voyages were looked on as descending to an abyss, " going down to the sea in ships ; " whereas now our bolder and more accustomed sailors talk of the " high seas." "*That do business in great waters.*" If they had not had business to do, they would never have ventured on the ocean, for we never read in the Scriptures of any man taking his pleasure on the sea : so averse was the Israelitish mind to seafaring, that we do not hear of even Solomon himself keeping a pleasure boat. The Mediterranean was " the great sea " to David and his countrymen, and they viewed those who had business upon it with no small degree of admiration.

24. "*These see the works of the Lord.*" Beyond the dwellers on the land they see the Lord's greatest works, or at least such as stayers at home judge to be so when they hear the report thereof. Instead of the ocean proving to be a watery wilderness, it is full of God's creatures, and if we were to attempt to escape from his presence by flying to the uttermost parts of it, we should only rush into Jehovah's arms, and find ourselves in the very centre of his workshop. "*And his wonders in the deep.*" They see wonders in it and on it. It is in itself a wonder and it swarms with wonders. Seamen, because they have fewer objects around them, are more observant of those they have than landsmen are, and hence they are said to *see* the wonders in the deep. At the same time, the ocean really does contain many of the more striking of God's creatures, and it is the scene of many of the more tremendous of the physical phenomena by which the power and majesty of the Lord are revealed among men. The chief wonders alluded to by the Psalmist are a sudden storm and the calm which follows it.

All believers have not the same deep experience ; but for wise ends, that they may do business for him, the Lord sends some of his saints to the sea of soul-trouble, and there they see, as others do not, the wonders of divine grace. Sailing over the deeps of inward depravity, the waste waters of poverty, the billows of persecution, and the rough waves of temptation, they need God above all others, and they find him.

25. " *For he commandeth :* " his word is enough for anything, he has but to will it and a tempest rages. " *And raiseth the stormy wind.*" It seemed to lie asleep before, but it knows its Master's bidding, and is up at once in all its fury. " *Which lifteth up the waves thereof.*" The glassy surface of the sea is broken, and myriads of white heads appear and rage and toss themselves to and fro as the wind blows upon them. Whereas they were lying down in quiet before, the waves rise in their might and leap towards the sky as soon as the howling of the wind awakens them.

Thus it needs but a word from God and the soul is in troubled waters, tossed to and fro with a thousand afflictions. Doubts, fears, terrors, anxieties lift their heads like so many angry waves, when once the Lord allows the storm-winds to beat upon us.

26. " *They mount up to the heaven.*" Borne aloft on the crest of the wave, the sailors and their vessels appear to climb the skies, but it is only for a moment, for very soon in the trough of the sea " *they go down again to the depths.*" As if their vessel were but a sea bird, the mariners are tossed " up and down, up and down, from the base of the wave to the billows' crown." " *Their soul is melted because of trouble.*" Weary, wet, dispirited, hopeless of escape, their heart is turned to water, and they seem to have no manhood left.

Those who have been on the spiritual deep in one of the great storms which occasionally agitate the soul know what this verse means. In these spiritual cyclones presumption alternates with despair, indifference with agony ! No heart is left for anything, courage is gone, hope is almost dead. Such an experience is as real as the tossing of a literal tempest and far more painful. Some of us have weathered many such an internal hurricane, and have indeed seen the Lord's wondrous works.

27. " *They reel to and fro, and stagger like a drunken man.*" The violent motion of the vessel prevents their keeping their legs, and their fears drive them out of all power to use their brains, and therefore they look like intoxicated men. " *And are at their wit's end.*" What more can they do ? They have used every expedient known to navigation, but the ship is so strained and beaten about that they know not how to keep her afloat.

Here too the spiritual mariner's log agrees with that of the sailor on the sea. We have staggered frightfully ! We could stand to nothing and hold by nothing. We knew not what to do, and could have done nothing if we had known it. We were as men distracted, and felt as if destruction itself would be better than our horrible state of suspense. As for wit and wisdom, they were clean washed out of us ; we felt ourselves to be at a nonplus altogether.

28. " *Then they cry unto the Lord in their trouble.*" Though at their wit's end, they had wit enough to pray ; their heart was melted, and it ran out in cries for help. This was well and ended well, for it is written, " *And he brought them out of their distresses.*" Prayer is good in a storm. We may pray staggering and reeling, and pray when we are at our wit's end. God will hear us amid the thunder and answer us out of the storm. He brought their distresses upon the mariners, and therefore they did well to turn to him for the removal of them ; nor did they look in vain.

29. " *He maketh the storm a calm.*" He reveals his power in the sudden and marvellous transformations which occur at his bidding. He commanded the storm and now he ordains a calm : God is in all natural phenomena, and we do well to recognise his working. " *So that the waves thereof are still.*" They bow in silence at his feet. Where huge billows leaped aloft there is scarce a ripple to be seen. When God makes peace it is peace indeed, the peace of God which passeth all understanding. He can in an instant change the condition of a man's mind, so that it shall seem an absolute miracle to him that he has passed so suddenly from hurricane to calm. O that the Lord would thus work in the reader, should his heart be storm-beaten with outward troubles or inward fears. Lord, say the word and peace will come at once.

30. " *Then are they glad because they be quiet.*" No one can appreciate this verse unless he has been in a storm at sea. No music can be sweeter than the rattling of the chain as the shipmen let down the anchor ; and no place seems more desirable than the little cove, or the wide bay, in which the ship rests in peace. " *So he bringeth them unto their desired haven.*" The rougher the voyage the more the mariners long

for port, and heaven becomes more and more " a desired haven," as our trials multiply. By storms and by favourable breezes, through tempest and fair weather, the great Pilot and Ruler of the sea brings mariners to port, and his people to heaven. He must have the glory of the successful voyage of time, and when we are moored in the river of life above we shall take care that his praises are not forgotten. We should long ago have been wrecked if it had not been for his preserving hand, and our only hope of outliving the storms of the future is based upon his wisdom, faithfulness and power. Our heavenly haven shall ring with shouts of grateful joy when once we reach its blessed shore.

31. " *Oh that men would praise the Lord for his goodness, and for his wonderful works to the children of men!*" Let the sea sound forth Jehovah's praises because of his delivering grace. As the sailor touches the shore let him lift the solemn hymn to heaven, and let others who see him rescued from the jaws of death unite in his thanksgiving.

32. " *Let them exalt him also in the congregation of the people.*" Thanks for such mercies should be given in public in the place where men congregate for worship. " *And praise him in the assembly of the elders.*" The praise should be presented with great solemnity in the presence of men of years, experience, and influence. High and weighty service should be rendered for great and distinguished favours, and therefore let the sacrifice be presented with due decorum and with grave seriousness. Often when men hear of a narrow escape from shipwreck they pass over the matter with a careless remark about good luck, but it should never be thus jested with.

When a heart has been in great spiritual storms and has at last found peace, there will follow as a duty and a privilege the acknowledgment of the Lord's mercy before his people, and it is well that this should be done in the presence of those who hold office in the church, and who from their riper years are better able to appreciate the testimony.

33 He turneth rivers into a wilderness, and the watersprings into dry ground ;

34 A fruitful land into barrenness, for the wickedness of them that dwell therein.

35 He turneth the wilderness into a standing water, and dry ground into watersprings.

36 And there he maketh the hungry to dwell, that they may prepare a city for habitation ;

37 And sow the fields, and plant vineyards, which may yield fruits of increase.

38 He blesseth them also, so that they are multiplied greatly ; and suffereth not their cattle to decrease.

39 Again, they are minished and brought low through oppression, affliction, and sorrow.

40 He poureth contempt upon princes, and causeth them to wander in the wilderness, *where there is* no way.

41 Yet setteth he the poor on high from affliction, and maketh *him* families like a flock.

42 The righteous shall see *it*, and rejoice : and all iniquity shall stop her mouth.

33. " *He turneth rivers into a wilderness, and the watersprings into dry ground.*" When the Lord deals with rebellious men he can soon deprive them of those blessings of which they feel most assured : their rivers and perennial springs they look upon as certain never to be taken from them, but the Lord at a word can deprive them even of these. In hot climates after long droughts streams of water utterly fail, and even springs cease to flow, and this also has happened in other parts of the world when great convulsions of the earth's surface have occurred. In providence this physical catastrophe finds its counterpart when business ceases to yield profit and sources of wealth are made to fail ; as also when health and strength are taken

away, when friendly aids are withdrawn, and comfortable associations are broken up. So, too, in soul matters, the most prosperous ministries may become dry, the most delightful meditations cease to benefit us, and the most fruitful religious exercises grow void of the refreshment of grace which they formerly yielded. Since

> " 'Tis God who lifts our comforts high,
> Or sinks them in the grave,"

it behoves us to walk before him with reverential gratitude, and so to live that it may not become imperative upon him to afflict us.

34. "*A fruitful land into barrenness.*" This has been done in many instances, and notably in the case of the Psalmist's own country, which was once the glory of all lands and is now almost a desert. "*For the wickedness of them that dwell therein.*" Sin is at the bottom of sorrow. It first made the ground sterile in father Adam's day, and it continues to have a blighting effect upon all that it touches. If we have not the salt of holiness we shall soon receive the salt of barrenness, for the text in the Hebrew is—" a fruitful land into saltness." If we will not yield the Lord a harvest of obedience he may forbid the soil to yield us a harvest of bread, and what then ? If we turn good into evil can we wonder if the Lord pays us in kind, and returns our baseness into our own bosoms ? Many a barren church owes its present sad estate to its inconsistent behaviour, and many a barren Christian has come into this mournful condition by a careless, unsanctified walk before the Lord. Let not saints who are now useful run the risk of enduring the loss of their mercies, but let them be watchful that all things may go well with them.

35. "*He turneth the wilderness into a standing water.*" With another turn of his hand he more than restores that which in judgment he took away. He does his work of mercy on a royal scale, for a deep lake is seen where before there was only a sandy waste. It is not by natural laws, working by some innate force, that this wonder is wrought, but by himself—HE TURNETH. "*And dry ground into water-springs.*" Continuance, abundance, and perpetual freshness are all implied in water-springs, and these are created where all was dry. This wonder of mercy is the precise reversal of the deed of judgment, and wrought by the selfsame hand. Even thus in the church, and in each individual saint, the mercy of the Lord soon works wonderful changes where restoring and renewing grace begin their benign work. O that we might see this verse fulfilled in all around us, and within our own hearts : then would these words serve us for an exclamation of grateful astonishment, and a song of well deserved praise.

36. "*And there he maketh the hungry to dwell,*" where none could dwell before. They will appreciate the change and prize his grace ; as the barrenness of the land caused their hunger so will its fertility banish it for ever, and they will settle down a happy and thankful people to bless God for every handful of corn which the land yields to them. None are so ready to return a revenue of praise to God for great mercies as those who have known the lack of them. Hungry souls make sweet music when the Lord fills them with his gracious gifts. Are we hungry ? Or are we satisfied with the husks of this poor, swinish world ? "*That they may prepare a city for habitation.*" When the earth is watered and men cultivate it, cities spring up and teem with inhabitants ; when grace abounds where sin formerly reigned, hearts find peace and dwell in God's love as in a strong city. The church is built up where once all was a waste when the Lord causes the broad rivers and streams of gospel grace to flow forth.

37. "*And sow the fields, and plant vineyards, which may yield fruits of increase.*" Men work when God works. His blessing encourages the sower, cheers the planter, and rewards the labourer. Not only necessaries but luxuries are enjoyed, wine as well as corn, when the heavens are caused to yield the needed rain to fill the watercourses. Divine visitations bring great spiritual riches, foster varied works of faith and labours of love, and cause every good fruit to abound to our comfort and to God's praise. When God sends the blessing it does not supersede, but encourages and develops human exertion. Paul plants, Apollos waters, and God gives the increase.

38. "*He blesseth them also, so that they are multiplied greatly ; and suffereth not their cattle to decrease.*" God's blessing is everything. It not only makes men happy, but it makes men themselves, by causing men to be multiplied upon the earth. When the Lord made the first pair he blessed them and said, " be fruitful

and multiply," and here he restores the primeval blessing. Observe that beasts as well as men fare well when God favours his people : they share with men in the goodness or severity of divine providence. Plagues and pests are warded off from the flock and the herd when the Lord means well towards a people ; but when chastisement is intended, the flocks and herds rot from off the face of the earth. O that nations in the day of their prosperity would but own the gracious hand of God, for it is to his blessing that they owe their all.

39. " *Again they are minished and brought low through oppression, affliction, and sorrow.*" As they change in character, so do their circumstances alter. Under the old dispensation, this was very clearly to be observed ; Israel's ups and downs were the direct consequences of her sins and repentances. Trials are of various kinds ; here we have three words for affliction, and there are numbers more : God has many rods and we have many smarts, and all because we have many sins. Nations and churches soon diminish in number when they are diminished in grace. If we are low in love to God, it is small wonder that he brings us low in other respects. God can reverse the order of our prosperity, and give us a *diminuendo* where we had a *crescendo ;* therefore let us walk before him with great tenderness of spirit, conscious of our dependence upon his smile.

40, 41. In these two verses we see how the Lord at will turns the wheel of providence. Paying no respect to man's imaginary grandeur, he puts princes down and makes them wander in banishment as they had made their captives wander when they drove them from land to land : at the same time, having ever a tender regard for the poor and needy, the Lord delivers the distressed and sets them in a position of comfort and happiness. This is to be seen upon the roll of history again and again, and in spiritual experience we remark its counterpart : the selfsufficient are made to despise themselves and search in vain for help in the wilderness of their nature, while poor convicted souls are added to the Lord's family and dwell in safety as the sheep of his fold.

42. " *The righteous shall see it, and rejoice.*" Divine providence causes joy to God's true people ; they see the hand of the Lord in all things, and delight to study the ways of his justice and of his grace. " *And all iniquity shall stop her mouth.*" What can she say ? God's providence is often so conclusive in its arguments of fact, that there is no replying or questioning. It is not long that the impudence of ungodliness can be quiet, but when God's judgments are abroad it is driven to hold its tongue.

43 Whoso *is* wise, and will observe these *things*, even they shall understand the lovingkindness of the LORD.

Those who notice providences shall never be long without a providence to notice. It is wise to observe what the Lord doth, for he is wonderful in counsel ; has given us eyes to see with, and it is foolish to close them when there is most to observe ; but we must observe wisely, otherwise we may soon confuse ourselves and others with hasty reflections upon the dealings of the Lord. In a thousand ways the lovingkindness of the Lord is shown, and if we will but prudently watch, we shall come to a better understanding of it. To understand the delightful attribute of lovingkindness is an attainment as pleasant as it is profitable : those who are proficient scholars in this art will be among the sweetest singers to the glory of Jehovah.

EXPLANATORY NOTES AND QUAINT SAYINGS.

Whole Psalm.—Dr. Lowth, in his 20th prelection, remarks of this Psalm :— " No doubt the composition of this Psalm is admirable throughout ; and the descriptive part of it adds at least its share of beauty to the whole ; but what is most to be admired is its *conciseness*, and withal the expressiveness of the diction, which strikes the imagination with inimitable elegance. The *weary* and *bewildered traveller*, the miserable *captive* in the hideous dungeon, the sick and dying man, the *seaman foundering* in a storm, are described in so affecting a manner, that they far exceed anything of the kind, though never so much laboured." I may add that had such an Idyle appeared in Theocritus or Virgil, or had it been found as a scene in any of the Greek tragedians, even in Æschylus himself, it would probably have been produced as their master-piece.—*Adam Clarke.*

Whole Psalm.—I do not believe that the special care of God over his own people is here rather *indirectly* than *directly* touched upon, and that therefore this Psalm is composed to illustrate the general care of God : 1, Because the subjects of the various deliverances are called *the redeemed of Jehovah*, verse 2, which is the customary title of the people of God. 2, Because among the instances given, there are those which are peculiar to the people of God, as in verse 3 the return of the dispersed out of every part of the globe, a singular blessing, promised in the prophecies to the people of God, see Ps. cvi. 47. 3, The sick of verse 17 are those who are spiritually sick even unto death, as is clear from the fact of their being healed by the *word* of God ; which is not in the order of common providence. The *imprisoned* of verse 2 are those who on account of the worship of God fall into the power of their enemies, which you cannot well apply to any other than the people of God. If you understand the *wicked*, for others among the heathen cannot be said to be thrust into prison on account of the violation of the laws, then the *liberation* belongs not to them. 4, *Calling* upon God, especially upon *Jehovah*, under which name he was known only to his people, you cannot apply unless in a diluted and partial sense to those who are afflicted in the general course of providence. . . . 5, He commands those who are delivered to celebrate the divine goodness in *the congregation of the people and the assembly of the elders*, verse 32, which is the mark of the true Church and her usual description. 6, Lastly, instances of general providences are not wont to come under the name of חסד, *grace*, by which these deliverances are described, nor do they require such great and such careful attention in their consideration, as here the sacred poet enjoins upon the pious and the wise.: such things are easily observed, and are of every day occurrence.—*Venema.*

Whole Psalm.—The Psalm divides itself into five parts ; the four first, as it should seem, describing four divisions of the returning Israelites, and recounting the particular accidents that had befallen each party on their journey, and the particular mercies for which they ought to be thankful. The fifth part describes what befalls the collected nations, or a part of them, when they arrive at the land which was the object of their journey—I think the first restoration or colonization before the general gathering. Whether the four divisions of travellers are supposed to come exactly from the four distinct quarters of the earth, perhaps is not quite certain. The first divisions are plainly described (verses 4, 5), as coming across the desert, and meeting with all the disasters usual on that route.—*John Fry.*

Whole Psalm.—Without insisting on an exclusive application of this Psalm to Israel, there may be traced, I think, not indistinctly, the leading incidents of the nation's changeful experience in the descriptive language of the narrative part.

In verses 4—7 the story of the wilderness is briefly told, to the praise of the glory of his grace who satisfieth the longing soul and filleth the hungry soul with goodness. The strong discipline of national affliction which visited the rebellious house, until the turning again of their captivity, when the appointed term of Babylonish exile was accomplished, appears to form the historical groundwork of verses 10—16 ; but in its prophetic intention this passage would demand a far wider interpretation. The resuscitation of Israel, both spiritually and politically, would alone adequately fulfil these words.

The sufferings of the " foolish nation " when, filled with Jehovah's indignation, they find a snare in that which should have fed them, and pine beneath the pressure of a more grievous famine than that of bread, until, in answer to their cry of sorrow, the word of saving health is sent them from above, seem to be indicated in the next division (verses 17—20). The language of verse 22 is in agreement with this. They who had daily gone about to establish their own righteousness are called on now to offer the sacrifice of thanksgiving, and to declare his works with singing.

Besides the obvious force and beauty of the following verses (23—30) in their simple meaning and their general application, we have, I believe, a figure of Jacob's restless trouble when, like a vexed and frightened mariner, he wandered up and down the wide sea of nations without ease, a friendless pilgrim of the Lord's displeasure, until the long-desired rest was gained at last, under the faithful guidance of him who seeks his people in the dark and cloudy day. Accordingly we find in the hortatory remembrancer of praise which follows (verse 32), a mention of the gathered people and their elders, who are now called on to celebrate, in the quiet resting-places of Immanuel's land, his faithful goodness and his might, who had turned their long-endured tempest of affliction to the calm sunshine of perpetual peace.—*Arthur Pridham, in " Notes and Reflections on the Psalms,"* 1869.

Verse 1.—*" O give thanks unto the Lord."* Unto no duty are we more dull and untoward, than to the praise of God, and thanksgiving unto him ; neither is there any duty whereunto there is more need that we should be stirred up, as this earnest exhortation doth import.—*David Dickson.*

Verse 1.—*" For he is good,"* etc. The first words of the Psalm are abundant in thought concerning Jehovah. *" For he is good."* Is not this the Old Testament version of *" God is love "* ? 1 John iv. 8. And then, *" For his mercy endureth for ever."* Is not this the gushing stream from the fountain of Love ?—the never-failing stream, on whose banks *" the redeemed of the Lord "* walk, *" those whom he has redeemed from the hand of the enemy "* (Hengstenberg, *" hand of trouble,"* צָר). Nor is the rich significance of these clauses diminished by our knowing that they were, from time to time, the burden of the *altar-song.* When the ark came to its resting-place (1 Chron. xvi. 34), they sang to the Lord—*" For he is good : for his mercy endureth for ever !"* In Solomon's temple, the singers and players on instruments were making the resplendent walls of the newly-risen temple resound with these very words, when the glory descended (2 Chron. v. 13) ; and these were the words that burst from the lips of the awe-struck and delighted worshippers, who saw the fire descend on the altar (2 Chron. vii. 3). And in Ezra's days (iii. 11), again, as soon as the altar rose, they sang to the Lord—*" Because he is good ; for his mercy endureth for ever."* Our God is known to be *" Love,"* by the side of the atoning sacrifice. Jeremiah (xxxiii. 11) too, shows how restored Israel shall exult in this name.—*Andrew A. Bonar.*

Verse 1.—*" His mercy endureth for ever."* St. Paul assures us, that the covenant of grace, which is the fountain of all mercy, was made before the foundation of the world, and this he repeats in several of his epistles. The Psalmist teaches the same doctrine, and frequently calls upon us to thank God, because his mercy is for ever and ever—because his mercy is everlasting—and in the text, because *" his mercy endureth for ever ; "* the word *" endureth "* is inserted by the translators, for there is no verb in the original, neither could in strictness of speech there be any ; because there was no time when this mercy was not exercised, neither will there be any time when the exercise of it will fail. It was begun before all worlds, when the covenant of grace was made, and it will continue to the ages of eternity, after this world is destroyed. So that *mercy* was, and is, and will be, *" for ever,"* and sinful miserable man may always find relief in this eternal mercy, whenever the sense of his misery disposes him to seek for it. And does not this motive loudly call upon us to *" give thanks "* ? because there is mercy with God—mercy to pity the miserable—and even to relieve them—although they do not deserve it : for mercy is all free grace and unmerited love. Oh ! how adorable, then, and gracious is this attribute ! how sweet is it and full of consolation to the guilty.—*William Romaine (1714—1795), in " A Practical Comment on the Hundred and Seventh Psalm."*

Verse 2.—*" Redeemed."* Moses has given us in the law a clear and full idea of what we are to understand by the word *goel,* here rendered *" redeemed."* If any person was either sold for a slave, or carried away for a captive, then his kinsman, who was nearest to him in blood, had the right and equity of redemption. But no other person was suffered to redeem. And such a kinsman was called *"* the redeemer," when he paid down the price for which his relation was sold to be a slave, or paid the ransom for which he was led captive. And there is another remarkable instance in the law, wherein it was provided, that in case any person was found murdered, then the nearest to him in blood was to prosecute the murderer, and to bring him to justice, and this nearest relation thus avenging the murder is called by the same name, a *redeemer.* And how beautifully is the office of our great Redeemer represented under these three instances ! he was to us such a Redeemer in spirituals, as these were in temporals : for sin had brought all mankind into slavery and captivity, and had murdered us. . . . This most high God, who was also man, united in one Christ, came into the world to redeem us, and the same person being both God and man, must merit for us as God in what he did for us as man. Accordingly, by the merits of his obedience and sufferings, he paid the price of our redemption, and we were no longer the servants of sin ; and by his most precious blood shed upon the cross, by his death and resurrection, he overcame both death, and him who had the power of death, and by delivering us in this manner from slavery and captivity, he fulfilled the third part of the Redeemer's office : for Satan was the murderer from the beginning, who had given both body and soul a mortal wound of sin, which was certain death and eternal misery, and the Redeemer came to avenge the murder. He took our cause in hand, as being our nearest kinsman, and it cost him his own life to avenge ours.—*William Romaine.*

Verse 2.—" *From the hand of the enemy.*" From all their sins which war against their souls ; from Satan their implacable adversary, who is stronger than they ; from the law, which threatens and curses them with damnation and death ; from death itself, the last enemy, and indeed from the hand of all their enemies, be they who they may.—*John Gill.*

Verse 3.—" *And gathered.*" If anything can inspire us with gratitude, this motive should prevail, because we cannot but feel the force of it, as it reminds us of that misery from which we in particular were redeemed. The *Gentiles* had wandered from God, and were so lost and bewildered in the mazes of error and superstition, that nothing but the almighty love of our Lord Jesus could have gathered them together into one church.—*William Romaine.*

Verse 3.—" *Gathered them.*" The Syriac gives as the title of this Psalm : God collects the Jews out of captivity, and brings them back out of Babylon ; the only begotten Son of God also, Jesus Christ, collects the nations from the four corners of the world, by calling upon man to be baptized.—*E. W. Hengstenberg.*

Verse 3.—" *From the west.*" The mention of the *west* leads the Psalmist's thoughts to Egypt ; and the remembrance of the bondage and labours of the ancestors of the Israelites in Egypt, coupled with the description in a previous Psalm (cv. 17) of the imprisonment of Joseph.—*Joseph Francis Thrupp.*

Verse 4.—" *They wandered,*" etc. In these words it is not easy to ascertain the persons immediately intended. But this is a circumstance not to be lamented. It is even an advantage ; it constrains us to a more spiritual and evangelical interpretation of the subject. And thus the whole representation is fully and easily embodied. For the people of God are " *redeemed* "—redeemed from the curse of the law, the powers of darkness, and the bondage of corruption. They are " *gathered* " —gathered by his grace out of all the diversities of the human race ; " out of all nations and kindreds and peoples and tongues." Whatever this world is to others, they find it to be " a wilderness " ; where they are often tried, but their trials urge them to prayer, and prayer brings them relief. And being divinely *conducted*, they at length reach their destination : and this is the conclusion of the whole, and it applies to each of them : " *And he led them forth by the right way, that they might go to a city of habitation.*"—*William Jay.*

Verse 4.—" *Wandered.*" Their passage through the wilderness was not a journeying, such as when men pass on in a road to some inhabited place ; but a *wandering* up and down away from all path and road, and so in an endless maze of desolation. —*Henry Hammond.*

Verse 4.—" *Wandered in the wilderness,*" etc. He has *lost his way.* When he was in the world, he had no difficulties ; the path was so broad that he could not mistake it. But when the work of divine grace begins in a sinner's heart, he loses his way. He cannot find his way into the world ; God has driven him out of it, as he drove Lot out of Sodom. He cannot find his way to heaven ; because he at present lacks those clear testimonies, those bright manifestations whereby alone he can see his path. This is his experience then, that he has lost his way ; having turned his back upon the world ; and yet unable to realise those enjoyments in his soul that would make heaven his home. He has so lost his way, that whether he turns to the right hand or the left, he has no plain land-marks to show him the path in which his soul longs to go.

We need not stray from the text to find where the wanderer is. " They wandered *in the wilderness.*" The wilderness is a type and figure of what this life is to the Lord's people. There is nothing that grows in it fit for their food or nourishment. In it the fiery flying serpents—sin and Satan—are perpetually biting and stinging them : and there is nothing in it that can give them any sweet and solid rest. The barren sands of carnality below, and the burning sun of temptation above, alike deny them food and shelter.

But there is a word added which throws a further light upon the character of the wilderness. "They wandered in the wilderness, *in a solitary way;*" a way not tracked ; a path in which each has to walk alone ; a road where no company cheers him, and without landmarks to direct his course. This is a mark peculiar to the child of God—that the path by which he travels is, in his own feelings, " *a solitary way.*" This much increases his exercises, that they appear peculiar to himself. His perplexities are such as he cannot believe any living soul is exercised with ; the fiery darts which are cast into his mind by the Wicked One are such as he thinks no child of God has ever experienced ; the darkness of his soul, the unbelief and infidelity of his heart, and the workings of his powerful corruptions, are such as he supposes none ever knew but himself. It is this walking " *in a solitary way,*" that makes the path of trial and temptation so painful to God's family.—*J. C. Philpot* (1802—1869), *in a Sermon entitled " The Houseless Wanderer."*

Verse 4.—" *In a solitary way.*"—The greater part of the desert being totally destitute of water is seldom visited by any human being ; unless where the trading caravans trace out their toilsome and dangerous route across it. In some parts of this extensive waste the ground is covered with low, stunted shrubs, which serve as landmarks for the caravans, and furnish the camels with a scanty forage. In other parts, the disconsolate wanderer, wherever he turns, sees nothing around him but a vast interminable expanse of sand and sky ; a gloomy and barren void, where the eye finds no particular object to rest upon, and the mind is filled with painful apprehensions of perishing with thirst. Surrounded by this dreary solitude, the traveller sees the dead bodies of birds, that the violence of the wind has brought from happier regions ; and, as he ruminates on the fearful length of his remaining passage, listens with horror to the driving blast, the only sound that interrupts the awful repose of the desert.*—*Mungo Park*, 1771—1806 (?).

Verse 4.—" *In a solitary way.*" See the reason why people in trouble love solitariness. They are full of sorrow ; and sorrow, if it have taken deep root, is naturally reserved, and flies all conversation. Grief is a thing that is very silent and private. Those people that are very talkative and clamorous in their sorrows, are never very sorrowful. Some are apt to wonder *why melancholy people delight to be so much alone*, and I will tell you the reason of it. 1. Because the disordered humours of their bodies alter their temper, their humours, and their inclinations, *that they are no more the same that they used to be ;* their very distemper is averse to what is joyous and diverting ; and they that wonder at them, may as wisely wonder why they will be diseased, which they would not be, if they knew how to help it ; but the *disease of melancholy* is so obstinate, and so unknown to all but those who have it, that nothing but the power of God can totally overthrow it, and I know no other cure for it. 2. *Another reason why they choose to be alone*, is, because *people do not generally mind what they say*, nor believe them, but deride them, which they do not use so cruelly to do with those that are in other distempers ; and no man is to be blamed for avoiding society, when it does not afford the common credit to his words, that is due to the rest of men. But, 3. Another, and the principal reason why people in trouble and sadness choose to be alone, is, because *they generally apprehend themselves singled out to be the marks of God's peculiar displeasure*, and they are often by their sharp afflictions a terror to themselves, and a wonder to others. It even breaks their hearts to see how low they are fallen, how oppressed, that were once as easy, as pleasant, as full of hope as others are, Job vi. 21 ; " Ye see my casting down, and are afraid." Ps. lxxi. 7 ; "I am as a wonder unto many." And it is usually unpleasant to others to be with them. Ps. lxxxviii. 18 ; " Lover and friend hast thou put far from me, and mine acquaintance into darkness." And though it was not so with the friends of Job ; to see a man whom they had once known happy, to be so miserable, one whom they had seen so very prosperous, to be so very poor, in such sorry, forlorn circumstances, did greatly affect them ; he, poor man, was changed, they knew him not, Job ii. 12, 13 : " And when they lifted up their eyes afar off, and knew him not, they lifted up their voice and wept ; and they rent every one his mantle, and sprinkled dust upon their heads toward heaven. So they sat down with him upon the ground seven days and seven nights, and none spake a word unto him : for they saw that his grief was very great." As the prophet represents one under spiritual and great afflictions, that " he sitteth alone, and keepeth silence," Lam. iii. 28. *Timothy Rogers* (1660—1729) *in " Trouble of Mind, and the Disease of Melancholy."*

Verse 4.—" *They found no city to dwell in* " ; nor even to call at or lodge in, for

* " Proceedings of the African Association "

miles together ; which is the case of travellers in some parts, particularly in the desert of Arabia. Spiritual travellers find no settlement, rest, peace, joy, and comfort, but in Christ ; nor any indeed in this world, and the things of it ; here they have no continuing city, Hebrews xiii. 14.—*John Gill.*

Verse 5.—" *Their soul fainted in them.*" The word here used, עָטַף, *ataph*, means properly to cover, to clothe, as with a garment, Ps. lxxiii. 6 ; or a field with grain, Ps. lxv. 13 ; then, to hide oneself, Job xxiii. 9 ; then, to cover with darkness, Ps. lxxvii. 3 ; cii. *title ;* thus it denotes the state of mind when darkness seems to be in the way—a way of calamity, trouble, sorrow ; of weakness, faintness, feebleness. Here it would seem from the connection to refer to the exhaustion produced by the want of food and drink.—*Albert Barnes.*

Verse 6.—" *Then they cried,*" etc. In these words we find three things remarkable ; first, the condition of God's church and people, *trouble and distress :* Secondly, the practice and the exercise of God's people in this state : " *Then they cried unto the Lord* " *:* Thirdly, their success, and the good issue of this practice : " *And he delivered them,*" etc.—*Peter Smith, in a Sermon preached before the House of Commons,* 1644.

Verse 6.—" *Then they cried.*" The root צָעַק has here a peculiar force : it denotes a cry of that kind into which any one, when shaken with a violent tempest of emotion, in the extremity of his grief and anxiety, breaks with a *crash* and with *complainings,* as the heavens send forth thunder and lightning. The original idea of the word being a *crash,* it indicates such complaints and cries as they send forth, who are oppressed by others, or are held fast in straits, in imploring public protection and help. See Deut. xxii. 24, 1 Kings xx. 39, Is. xix. 20.—*Venema.*

Verse 6.—" *In their trouble.*" Observe the words, " Then they cried unto the Lord *in* their trouble." Not *before,* not *after,* but *in* it. When they were in the midst of it ; when trouble was wrapped round their head, as the weeds were wrapped round the head of Jonah ; when they were surrounded by it, and could see no way out of it ; when, like a person in a mist, they saw no way of escape before or behind ; when nothing but a dark cloud of trouble surrounded their souls, and they did not know that ever that cloud would be dispersed ;—then it was that they cried.— *J. C. Philpot.*

Verse 6.—" *Trouble.*" " *Distresses.*" The condition of the Church, or its most usual lot, is to be under sorrows and afflictions. I say, most usual : " For I will not contend for ever, neither will I be always wroth : for the spirit should fail before me, and the souls which I have made," Isai. lvii. 16. But as we say of the several callings and trades of life, this man professeth such a calling, and that man another ; and as the poet said of Hermogenes, Though he hold his peace (peradventure being asleep) yet he's a good singer, and a musician by profession : so say I of the people of God, their trade of life is suffering and as Julian told the Christians, when they complained of his cruelty, '*Tis your profession to endure tribulation.*—*Peter Smith.*

Verse 7.—" *He led them forth.*" Forth out of the world—forth out of a profession— forth out of a name to live—forth out of every thing hateful in his holy and pure eyes.—*J. C. Philpot.*

Verse 7.—" *And he led them forth by the right way,*" etc. Alexander translates this verse—" *And he led them in a strait course, to go to a city of habitation* " *;* and adds, " No exact version can preserve or imitate the paronomasia arising from the etymological affinity of the first verb and noun, analogous to that between the English *walk* and *to walk,* though the Hebrew forms are only similar and not identical. The idea of physical rectitude or straightness necessarily suggests that of moral rectitude or honesty, commonly denoted by the Hebrew word."

Verse 7.—" *A city of habitation.*" Not a city of *inspection !* Many—(Eternal God, will it be any of this company ?)—will look in ; and " there shall be weeping and wailing and gnashing of teeth, when they shall see Abraham, Isaac, and Jacob in the kingdom of God, and they themselves shut out." Not a city of *visitation.* Christians shall not only enter, but abide. They shall go no more out—it is " a city of *habitation.*" This conveys the idea of *repose.* The Christian is now a traveller ; then he will be a resident : he is now on the road ; he will then be at home : " there remaineth a *rest* for the people of God." It reminds us of a *social state.* It is not a solitary condition ; we shall partake of it with an innumerable company of angels, with all the saved from among men, with patriarchs, prophets, apostles. martyrs, our kindred in Christ. "These are fellow-citizens of the saints, and of the household of God." It suggests *magnificence*. It is not a village, or a town, but a *city* of habitation. A city is the highest representation of civil community. There have been famous cities; but what are they all to this!—*William Jay.*

Verse 8.—*He does wonders for the children of men;* and therefore, men should *praise the Lord.* And he is the more to be praised because these wonders, נִפְלָאוֹת, *niphlaoth*, miracles of mercy and grace, are done for the *undeserving*. There are done לִבְנֵי אָדָם, *libney Adam*, for the children of *Adam*, the corrupt descendants of a rebel father.—*Adam Clarke.*

Verse 8.—"*Oh that men would praise the Lord,*" etc. Hebrew, That they would confess it to the Lord, both in secret, and in society. This is all the rent that God requireth; he is content that we have the comfort of his blessings, so he may have the honour of them. This was all the fee Christ looked for for his cures: go and tell what God hath done for thee. Words seem to be a poor and slight recompense; but Christ, saith Nazienzen, called himself the Word.—*John Trapp.*

Verse 8.—"*To the children of men!*" We must acknowledge God's goodness to the children of men, as well as to the children of God: to others as well as to ourselves.—*Matthew Henry.*

Verse 9.—"*For he satisfieth the longing soul.*" This is the reason which the Psalmist gives for the *duty* of thankfulness which he prescribes. "*The longing soul,*" נֶפֶשׁ שֹׁקֵקָה, *nephesh shokekah, the soul that pushes forward in eager desire* after salvation.—*Adam Clarke.*

Verse 10.—"*Such as sit in darkness and in the shadow of death, being bound in affliction and iron.*" Every son of Adam in his natural state before he is redeemed is in "*darkness*" and "*the shadow of death,*" and is fast "*bound*" with the chains of *sin* and *misery*, and there is no help for him upon earth—the Almighty God and Saviour alone is able to deliver him.—*William Romaine.*

Verse 11.—"*Because they rebelled against the words of God.*" There is in the Hebrew a play upon similar sounds—*Himru Imree.* God's *words* are those spoken in the *Law* and by *the prophets*. "*And contemned the counsel of the Most High*"— another play upon like sounds in the Hebrew—*Hatzath Naatzu.—A. R. Fausset.*

Verse 12.—"*He brought down their heart.*" O believer, God may see you have many and strong lusts to be subdued, and that you need many and sore afflictions to bring them down. Your pride and obstinacy of heart may be strong, your distempers deeply rooted, and therefore the physic must be proportioned to them.— *John Willison.*

Verse 12.—"*He brought down their heart with labour.*" Those towering passions by which they vainly vaunted themselves above the law and the worship of God, he weakened and curbed, so that they began to submit themselves to God. The root עָנָה taken from the Arabic, describes a process of *weakening* by *compressing the wings* or shrinking the fingers, and is properly applied to *birds*, which when their wings are compressed are obliged to fall to the ground, or to men, who by the shrivelling up of their fingers lose the power of working; whence it is transferred to *oppressions* or *depressions* of any kind.—*Venema.*

Verse 12.—"*They fell down, and there was none to help.*" Affliction is then come to the height and its complete measure, when the sinner is made sensible of his own weakness, and doth see there is no help for him, save in God alone.—*David Dickson.*

Verse 12.—"*They fell down.*" They threw themselves prostrate at his feet for mercy; their heart and strength failed them, as the word signifies, and is used in Ps. xxxi. 10; terrified with a sense of divine wrath, they could not stand before the Lord, nor brave it out against him. "*And there was none to help.*" They could not help themselves, nor was there any creature that could. There is salvation in no other than in Christ; when he saw there was none to help him in that work his own arm brought salvation to him; and when sinners see there is help in no other, they apply to him.—*John Gill.*

Verse 17.—"*Fools.*" There is nothing more foolish than an act of wickedness; there is no wisdom equal to that of obeying God.—*Albert Barnes.*

Verse 17—20.—" *Fools because of their transgression, and because of their iniquities, are afflicted. Their soul abhorreth all manner of meat*" (they are so sick that they can relish, take down nothing,) and " *they draw near unto the gates of death*," they are almost in, they were on the brink of hell ; what course must be used for their cure ? Truly this, " *He sent his word, and healed them, and delivered them from their destructions.*" No herb in the garden of the whole world can do these distressed creatures the least good. Friends may speak, and ministers may speak, yea, angels may speak, and all in vain ; the wounds are incurable for all their words ; but if God please to speak, the dying soul reviveth. This word is the only balm that can cure the wounded conscience : " he sendeth his word and healeth them." Conscience is God's prisoner, he claps it in hold, he layeth it in fetters, that the iron enters the very soul ; this he doth by his word, and truly he only who shuts up can let out ; all the world cannot open the iron gate, knock off the shackles, and set the poor prisoner at liberty, till God speak the word.—*George Swinnock*, 1627—1673.

Verse 18.—" *Their soul abhorreth all manner of meat.*" Nor is it without emphasis that it is not the sick man who is said to spurn food, but *his soul.* . . . The Hebrew word שֶׁפֶנ which properly means a breath, hence a panting appetite, is applied to a *very vehement appetite* for food. When, therefore the *soul* is said *to abhor food*, it is equivalent to saying *for the vehement appetite for food abhors food :* that is, in the place of an appetite for food, they are oppressed with a loathing : when they ought to be moved with a sharp desire of food, that their exhausted powers might be refreshed, appetite itself becomes a *loathing of food*, which is a most vivid description of the utmost loathing, and utter prostration of all desire.—*Venema.*

Verse 18.—" *Their soul abhorreth all manner of meat.*" The best of creature-comforts are but vain comforts. What can dainty meat do a man good, when he is sick and ready to die ? Then gold and silver, lands and houses, which are the dainty meat of a covetous man, are loathsome to him. When a man is sick to death, his very riches are sapless and tasteless to him ; wife and children, friends and acquaintance, can yield but little comfort in that dark hour, yea, they often prove miserable comforters : when we have most need of comfort, these things administer least or no comfort at all to us. Is it not our wisdom, then, to get a stock of such comforts, as will hold and abide fresh with us, when all worldly comforts either leave us, or become tasteless to us ? Is it not good to get a store of that food, which how sick soever we are, our stomachs will never loathe ? yea, the sicker we are, our stomachs will the more like, hunger after, and feed the more heartily upon. *The flesh of Christ is meat indeed* (John vi. 55). Feed upon him by faith, in health and sickness, ye will never loathe him. His flesh is the true meat of desires, such meat as will fill and fatten us, but never cloy us. A hungry craving appetite after Christ, and sweet satisfaction in him, are inseparable, and still the stronger is our appetite, the greater is our satisfaction. And (which is yet a greater happiness) our souls will have the strongest appetite, the most sharp-set stomach after Christ, when, through bodily sickness, our stomachs cannot take down, but loathe the very scent and sight of the most pleasant perishing meat, and delicious earthly dainties. Look, that ye provide somewhat to eat, that will go down upon a sick-bed ; your sick-bed meat is Christ ; all other dainty food may be an abhorring to you.—*Joseph Caryl.*

Verse 18.—" *Their soul abhorreth all manner of meat.*" The case is then growing desperate, and there seems to be no hope left, when it comes to the last stage here described, *viz.*, to *loathe and " abhor all manner of meat.*" The stomach turns at the sight of it, and the man has this loathing and abhorrence of " *all manner of meat.*" What he most loved, and had the best appetite for, is now become so very offensive, that at the smell of it he grows sick and faints away. Nature cannot support itself long under this disorder. If this loss of appetite, and loathing even the smell of the most simple food continue, it must wear the patient out. Indeed, it is not always a mortal distemper ; there may be an entire loathing of food, and even fainting away at the smell of it, and the patient may sometimes recover ; but in the present case the distemper had continued so long, and was grown so inveterate that there were no hopes, for " *they draw nigh*," the Psalmist says, " *to the gates of death.*" Those gates of brass and bars of iron with which death locks up his prisoners in the grave ; and you may judge how great must be the strength of these gates and bars, since only one person was ever able to break through them, and if he had not been more than man, he could never have broken these gates of brass, nor cut these bars of iron in sunder.—*William Romaine.*

Verse 18.—"*They draw near unto the gates of death.*" Death is a great commander, a great tyrant, and hath gates to sit in, as judges and magistrates used to ' sit in the gates.' There are three things implied in this phrase. 1. First, "*They draw near unto the gates of death,*" that is, they were "*near to death*"; as he that draws near the gates of a city is near the city, because the gates enter into the city. 2. Secondly, gates are applied to death *for authority.* They were almost in death's jurisdiction. Death is a great tyrant. He rules over all the men in the world, over kings and potentates, and over mean men; and the greatest men fear death most. He is "the king of fears," as Job calls him, Job xviii. 14; ay, and the fear of kings. . . . Therefore it is called "the gate of death." It rules and overrules all mankind. Therefore it is said "to reign," Rom. v. 21. Death and sin came in together. Sin was the gate that let in death, and ever since death reigned, and will, till Christ perfectly triumph over it, who is the King of that lord and commander, and hath " the key of hell and death," Rev. i. 18. To wicked men, I say, he is a tyrant, and hath a gate; and when they go through the "*gate of death,*" they go to a worse, to a lower place, to hell. It is the trap-door to hell. 3. Thirdly. By the "*gate of death,*" is meant not only the authority, but *the power of death ;* as in the gospel, " The gates of hell shall not prevail against it," Matt. xvi. 18 : that is, the power and strength of hell. So here it implies the strength of death, which is very great, for it subdues all. It is the executioner of God's justice.—*Richard Sibbes.*

Verse 20.—When George Wishart arrived at Dundee, where the plague was raging [1545], he caused intimation to be made that he would preach ; and for that purpose chose his station upon the head of the East-gate, the infected persons standing without, and those that were whole within. His text was Psalm cvii. 20, " *He sent his word, and healed them,*" etc., wherein he treated of the profit and comfort of God's word, the punishment that comes by contempt of it, the readiness of God's mercy to such as truly turn to him, and the happiness of those whom God takes from this misery, etc. By which sermon he so raised up the hearts of those that heard him, that they regarded not death, but judged them more happy that should then depart, rather than such as should remain behind, considering that they knew not whether they should have such a comforter with them.—*Samuel Clarke* (1599— 1682), *in " A General Martyrologie."*

Verse 20.—"*He sent his word.*" The same expression occurs in cxlvii. 15, 18 ; comp. Is. lv. 11. We detect in such passages the first glimmering of St. John's doctrine of the agency of the personal Word. The Word by which the heavens were made, xxxiii. 6, is seen to be not merely the expression of God's will, but his messenger mediating between himself and his creatures. It is interesting to compare with this the language of Elihu in the parallel passage of Job xxxiii. 23, where what is here ascribed to the agency of the Word is ascribed to that of the " mediating angel, or messenger."—*J. J. Stewart Perowne.*

Verse 20.—"*His word*" who "*healed them*" was his essential Word, even the second person in the Godhead, our Lord Jesus Christ, the word who was made flesh and dwelt among us : of this divine Word it was foretold in the Old Testament, that he should arise with the glory of the morning sun, bringing healing in his wings for all our maladies ; and accordingly the New Testament relates, that Jesus went about all Galilee, preaching the gospel of the kingdom, and healing ALL manner of sickness, and ALL manner of disease among the people. He healed the bodily disease miraculously, to prove that he was the Almighty Physician of the soul. And it is remarkable that he never rejected any person who applied to him for an outward cure, to demonstrate to us, that he would never cast out any person who should apply to him for a spiritual cure.—*William Romaine.*

Verse 20.—"*And delivered them from their destructions.*" From their pits : or, From their sepulchres. That is, from the deaths to which they were near. Others render, From their nets or snares. Others, *their destructions,* the diseases in which they were miserable prisoners.—*Franciscus Vatablus.*

Verse 20.—"*And delivered them from their destructions.*" From the destruction of the body, of the beauty and strength of it by diseases ; restoring to health is a redeeming of the life from destruction ; from the grave, the pit of corruption and destruction, so called because in it bodies corrupt, putrefy, and are destroyed by worms ; and such who are savingly convinced of sin, and blessed with pardoning grace and mercy, are delivered from the everlasting destruction of body and soul in hell.—*John Gill.*

Verse 22.—"*And let them sacrifice.*" For their *healing* they should bring a *sacrifice ;* and they should offer the *life* of the innocent animal unto God, as he has offered their *lives ;* and let them thus *confess* that God has spared *them* when they deserved to die ; and let them "*declare*" also "his works with rejoicing" ; for who will not rejoice when he is delivered from death ?—*Adam Clarke.*

As a specimen of mediæval spiritualizing we give the following from the Hermit of Hampole :—

Verse 23.—"*They that go down to the sea in ships,*" etc. *They that* (are true prelates and preachers,) *go down* from the sublimity of contemplation, *to the sea,* that is, suiting themselves to the lowly, that they also may be saved, *in ships,* that is, in the faith, hope, and charity of the church, without which they would be drowned in the waters of pleasure, *that do business,* that is, continue preaching, *in great waters,* that is, among many people in order that they may become fishers of men.—*Richardus Hampolitanus.*

Verses 23—27.

> While thus our keels still onward boldly strayed—
> Now tossed by tempests, now by calms delayed ;
> To tell the terrors of the deep untried,
> What toils we suffered, and what storms defied ;
> What rattling deluges the black clouds poured,
> What dreary weeks of solid darkness low'red ;
> What mountain surges mountain surges lashed,
> What sudden hurricanes the canvas dashed ;
> What bursting lightnings, with incessant flare,
> Kindled in one wide flame the burning air ;
> What roaring thunders bellowed o'er our head,
> And seemed to shake the reeling ocean's bed :
> To tell each horror in the deep revealed,
> Would ask an iron throat with tenfold vigour steeled
> Those dreadful wonders of the deep I saw,
> Which fill the sailor's breasts with sacred awe ;
> And what the sages, of their learning vain,
> Esteem the phantoms of a dreamful brain.
>
> *Luiz de Camoens* (1524—1579), *in "the Lusiad."*

Verses 23—31.—No language can be more sublime than the description of a storm at sea in this Psalm. It is the very soul of poetry. The utmost simplicity of diction is employed to convey the grandest thoughts. The picture is not crowded ; none but the most striking circumstances are selected ; and everything is natural, simple, and beyond measure interesting. The whole is an august representation of the Providence of God, ruling in what appears the most ungovernable province of nature. It is God who raises the storm ; it is God who stilleth it. The wise men of this world may look no farther than the physical laws by which God acts ; but the Holy Spirit, by the Psalmist, views the awful conflict of the elements as the work of God.—*Alexander Carson.*

Verses 23—32.—This last picture springs naturally from the mention in verse 3 of the sea ; and here the Psalmist may have directed his imagination to the usual tempestuousness of the season at which the Psalm was sung.—*Joseph Francis Thrupp.*

Verse 24.—"*These see the works of the Lord.*" There are sinners who, like Jonah, fleeing from the face of God, go down to the sea, to the cares and pleasures of the world, away from the solid land of humility, quiet, and grace. They occupy themselves in many waters, in needless toils and excessive pleasures, and yet even there God does not leave them, but causes them to see his works and wonders even in the deep of their sins, by giving them timely and sufficient warnings, and alarming them with fear of the abyss.—*Le Blanc in Neale and Littledale.*

Verses 25—31.

Think, O my soul, devoutly think,
    How, with affrighted eyes
Thou saw'st the wide extended deep
    In all its horrors rise !

Confusion dwelt in every face,
    And fear in every heart ;
When waves on waves, and gulfs on gulfs,
    O'ercame the pilot's art.

Yet then from all my griefs, O Lord,
    Thy mercy set me free,
Whilst in the confidence of prayer
    My soul took hold on thee.

For though in dreadful whirls we hung
    High on the broken wave,
I knew thou wert not slow to hear,
    Nor impotent to save.

The storm was laid, the winds retired,
    Obedient to thy will ;
The sea that roared at thy command,
    At thy command was still.

In midst of dangers, fears, and death,
    Thy goodness I'll adore,
And praise thee for thy mercies past ;
    And humbly hope for more.

My life, if thou preserv'st my life,
    Thy sacrifice shall be ;
And death, if death must be my doom
    Shall join my soul to thee.

                              Joseph Addison.

Verse 26.—" *They mount up to the heaven.*" There be three heavens. 1. *Cœlum aërium*. 2. *Cœlum astriferum*. 3. *Cœlum beatorum*. It is not the latter now they go to in storms, but the two former.—*Daniel Pell, in " An Improvement of the Sea,"* 1659.

Verse 26.—" *They mount up to the heaven, they go down again to the depths.*"

To larboard all their oars and canvas bend ;
We on a ridge of waters to the sky
Are lifted, down to Erebus again
Sink with the falling wave ; thrice howl'd the rocks
Within their stony caverns, thrice we saw
The splash'd-up foam upon the lights of heaven
                              Virgil.

Verse 28.—" *They cry unto the Lord.*" His attributes are much honoured in calling upon him, especially in times of dangers and distresses. 1. When you call upon God at sea, you honour his *sovereignty*. God says to these proud waves, " So far and no farther ! " So, " the storm and hail," they fulfil his will, and when he pleases he commands a calm. 2. Prayer in time of danger honours God's *wisdom*, when we see no way open for mercies and deliverance to come in at, then to look up to him, believing. " He knows how to deliver out of temptation." O how much of the wisdom of God appears in preservation in time of danger ! and is it not a good token of mercy coming in when persons pray, though all visible ways are blocked up ? This honours God's *wisdom*, which we acknowledge is never at a loss as to ways of bringing in mercy and deliverance. 3. The *faithfulness* of God is much honoured in times of danger, when he is called upon. The faithfulness of a friend doth most appear in a strait : now if you can rely upon his promise, God's faithfulness is the best line men sinking at sea can lay hold on. So I might add, calling upon God honours all his other attributes. *John Ryther (1632—1681) in " A Plea for Mariners : or, The Seaman's Preacher,"* 1675.

Verse 28.—" *Then they cry.*" Tempestuous storms and deadly dangers have brought those upon their knees, that would never have bended in a calm : " *Then they cry.*" If any one would know at what time the sailors take up the duty of prayer, let me say it is when death stares them in the face. If ever you see the heavens veiled in sable blackness, the clouds flying, and the winds roaring under them ; you may conclude that some of them (though God knows but few) are at prayer, yea, hard at it with their God. But never believe it that there is any prayer amongst them when the skies are calm, the winds down, and the seas smooth. David tells you not of their praying in good and comfortable weather, but that it is in time of storms, for I believe that neither he nor I ever saw many of them on that strain. . . .

God hears oftener from an afflicted people, than he either does or can from a people that are at ease, quiet, and out of danger. " *Then they cry.*" The prodigal son was very high, and resolved never to return till brought low by pinching and nipping afflictions, then his father had some tidings of him. Hagar was proud in Abraham's house, but humbled in the wilderness. Jonah was asleep in the ship, but awake and at prayer in the whale's belly, Jonah ii. 1. Manasses lived in Jerusalem like a libertine, but when bound in chains at Babel, his heart was turned to the Lord, 2 Chron. xxxiii. 11, 12. Corporal diseases forced many under the gospel to come to Christ, whereas others that enjoyed bodily health would not acknowledge him. One would think that the Lord would abhor to hear those prayers that are made only out of the fear of danger, and not out of the love, reality, and sincerity of the heart. If there had not been so many miseries of blindness, lameness, palsies, fevers, etc., in the days of Christ, there would not have been that flocking after him. —*Daniel Pell.*

Verse 28.—" *Then they cry unto the Lord.*" " *Then,*" if ever : hence that speech of one, *Qui nescit orare, discat navigare,* He that cannot pray, let him go to sea, and there he will learn.—*John Trapp.*

Verse 28.—" *Then they cry,*" etc. Gods of the sea and skies (for what resource have I but prayer ?) abstain from rending asunder the joints of our shattered bar. —*Ovid.*

Verse 29.—" *He maketh the storm a calm,*" etc. The image is this. Mankind before they are redeemed are like a ship in a stormy sea, agitated with passions, tossed up and down with cares, and so blown about with various temptations, that they are never at rest. This is their calmest state in the smiling day of smooth prosperity : but afflictions will come, and afflictions of sin and Satan, and the world will raise a violent storm, which all the wit and strength of man cannot escape. He will soon be swallowed up of the devouring waves ; unless that same God who created the sea speak to it, " Peace, be still." We are all in the same situation the apostles were, when they were alone in the evening in the midst of the sea, and the wind and the waves were contrary ; against which they toiled rowing in vain, until Christ came to them walking upon the sea, and commanded the winds to cease and the waves to be still. Upon which there was a great calm ; for they knew his voice, who had spoken them into being, and they obeyed. His word is almighty to compose and still the raging war of the most furious elements. And he is as almighty in the spiritual world, as he is in the natural. Into whatever soul he enters, he commands all the jarring passions to be still, and there is indeed a blessed calm. O may the Almighty Saviour speak thus unto you all, that you may sail on a smooth unruffled sea, until you arrive safe at the desired haven of eternal rest !—*William Romaine.*

Verse 29.—If the sailor can do nothing so wise and oftentimes indeed can do nothing else than trust in the Lord, so is it with us in the storms of life. Like the mariner, we must use lawful means for our protection ; but what are means without the divine blessing ?—*William S. Plumer.*

Verse 30.—" *Desired haven.*" At such a time as this sweet April morning, indeed, a breakwater like this [of Portland] may seem of little value, when the waves of the ocean only just suffice to break its face into gems of changing brilliance, and to make whispering music ; while vessels of all sizes, like those whose clustering masts we see yonder under the promontory, ride with perfect security in the open road. But in the fierce gales of November or March, when the shrieking blasts drive furiously up the Channel, and the huge mountain billows, green and white, open threatening graves on every side, how welcome would be a safe harbour, easy of access, and placed at a part of the coast which else would be unsheltered for many leagues on either side ! Blessed be God for the gift of his beloved Son, the only Harbour of Refuge for poor tempest-tossed sinners ! We may think lightly of it now, but in the coming day of gloom and wrath, when " the rain descends, and the floods come, and the winds blow," they only will escape who are sheltered there !—*Philip Henry Gosse, in " The Aquarium,"* 1856.

Verse 31.—" *Oh.*" This verse seems to include the ardent earnestness of the Psalmist's spirit, that seamen would be much in thankfulness, and much and frequent in praising of the Lord their deliverer out of all their distresses. " *Oh,*" seems he to say, that I could put men upon this duty, it would be more comfortable to me, seems the Psalmist to say, to find such a principle in the hearts of those that are employed in the great waters, than any one thing in the world again whatsoever. " *Oh* " is but a little word consisting of two letters, but no word that ever man utters with his tongue comes with that force and affection from the heart as this doth. " *Oh* " is a word of the highest expression, a word when a man can say no more. This inter-jection oftentimes starts out of the heart upon a sudden from some unexpected conception, or admiration, or other.—*Daniel Pell.*

Verse 33.—" *He turneth rivers into a wilderness,*" etc. God is *the father of the rain.* If he withholds that refreshment for a long time, all nature droops, and every green thing dies. The imagery is drawn from Palestine where there were but two annual rainy seasons, and if either of them was long deferred, the effect was frightful. The channels of considerable rivers were dried up.—*William S. Plumer.*

Verse 33.—" *Rivers* " . . . " *Watersprings.*" A church enriched with the graces of heaven is compared by the prophets to a well-watered garden (Isai. lviii. 11 ; Jer. xxxi. 12), to the paradise of God, watered with its four fruitful rivers : for as everything useful and ornamental in the vegetable world is raised up by water, so is everything in the spiritual world raised up by the Holy Spirit.—*William Romaine.*

Verse 34.—" *A fruitful land unto barrenness.*" Hereof Judæa is at this day a notable instance (besides many parts of Asia, and Africa, once very fruitful, now, since they become Mahometan, dry and desert). Judæa, saith one, hath now only some few parcels of rich ground found in it ; that men may guess the goodness of the cloth by the fineness of the shreds.—*John Trapp.*

Verse 34.—" *For the wickedness of them that dwell therein.*" When I meet with a querulous husbandman, he tells me of a churlish soil, of a wet seed-time, of a green winter, of an unkindly spring, of a lukewarm summer, of a blustering autumn ; but I tell him of a displeased God, who will be sure to contrive and fetch all seasons and elements, to his own most wise drifts and purposes.—*Joseph Hall.*

Verse 34.—" *For the wickedness.*" God locketh up the clouds, because we have shut up our mouths. The earth is grown hard as iron to us, because we have hard-ened our hearts against our miserable neighbours. The cries of the poor for bread are loud, because our cries against sin have been so low. Sicknesses run apace from house to house, and sweep away the poor unprepared inhabitants, because we sweep not out the sin that breedeth them.—*Richard Baxter,* 1615—1691.

Verse 35.—" *Dry ground into watersprings.*" If God afflict, his justice findeth the cause of it in man ; but if he do good to any man, it is of his own good pleasure, without any cause in man : therefore no reason is given here of this change, as was of the former, but simply, " *He turneth dry ground into watersprings.*"—*David Dickson.*

Verse 40.—" *He poureth contempt upon princes.*" Mighty potentates, who have been the terror and dread of the whole world, when once denuded of their dignity and power, have become the sport even of their own dependents.—*John Calvin.*

Verse 40.—" *Princes.*" Persons of high rank are the most exempt, in ordinary times, from destitution and want, and misery must reach a great height when it invades them. No part of the world probably has witnessed so many and great reverses of this kind as the regions and countries of the East.—*William Walford.*

Verse 41.—" *He setteth the poor on high from affliction.*" How high ? Above the reach of the curse, which shall never touch him ; above the power of Satan, which shall never ruin him ; above the reigning influence of sin, which " shall not have dominion over him " ; above the possibility of being banished from his presence, for " Israel shall be saved in the Lord with an everlasting salvation." This is the way God sets his people on high, instructing them in the mysteries of his word, and giving them to partake the joys that are contained therein.—*Joseph Irons, 1786—1852.*

Verse 42.—" *The righteous shall see it."* The word here rendered " *righteous* " is not what the Scripture commonly uses to signify righteous or justified persons ; but it is another word, and conveys another idea. It signifies to *direct*, to *set right ;* and the " *righteous* " here mentioned are they, who are directed in the right way, and walk, as Enoch did, with God in his way, and not in the way of the world. And these " *shall see* " the goodness and mercy of God's dealings with the fallen race of man. They shall have eyes to see the ways of his providence. The same grace which set them right, will manifest to them the reasonableness of the plan of redemption. They shall see and admire, and be thankful for the wonders of his redeeming love, which are recorded in this divine hymn.—*William Romaine.*

Verse 42.—" *All iniquity shall stop her mouth."* " *Iniquity* " is here personified, and denotes the *iniquitous ;* but the abstract is more poetical. " *Stop her mouth."* Tongue-tied, literally, *mouth-shut ;* which, perhaps, might be not improperly vernaculized.—*Alexander Geddes.*

Verse 43.—" *Whoso is wise,"* etc. Or as it may be read interrogatively, " *Who is wise ?* " as in Jer. ix. 12 ; Hosea xiv. 9 ; that is, spiritually wise, wise unto salvation ; who is made to know wisdom in the hidden part ; for not such as are possessed of natural wisdom, or worldly-wise men, much less who are wise to do evil, are here meant, " *And will observe these things ;* " the remarkable appearances of divine Providence to persons in distress ; the various changes and vicissitudes in the world ; the several afflictions of God's people, and their deliverances out of them ; the wonderful works of God in nature, providence, and grace ; these will be observed, taken notice of, laid up in the mind, and kept by such who are truly wise, who know how to make a right use and proper improvement of them. " *Even they shall understand the lovingkindness of the Lord* " ; every one of the wise men ; they will perceive the kindness of God unto men, in the several dispensations of his providence towards them, and his special love and kindness towards his own people, even in all their afflictions they will perceive this to be at the bottom of every mercy and blessing ; they will understand more of the nature and excellency of it, and know more of the love of God and Christ, which passeth knowledge. Or, *the kindnesses of the Lord shall be understood ;* that is, by wise men ; so R. Moses in Aben Ezra renders the words.—*John Gill.*

Verse 43.—" *Will observe these things,"* etc. Will carefully note and remark what is here said of the fall and recovery of mankind, of our state by nature and by grace. True wisdom consists in observing these two things, what we are in ourselves, and what we are in Christ ; in a deep sense of our misery by sin, stirring us up to seek our remedy in the Redeemer. This is wisdom. And whosoever is thus wise unto salvation " *shall understand the lovingkindness of the Lord ;* " shall be able to apply what he understands of it to his own private use and benefit. The verb in the original rendered " *shall understand,"* is in the conjugation called *Hithpael,* which signifies to act upon itself. Whosoever observes those things properly finds his own interest in them. He makes the understanding of them useful to himself. He does not study them as a science or theory, but as interesting points in which he is nearly concerned, and which he therefore tries to bring home for his own private advantage. When he hears of the mercies of the Lord Jesus recorded in this Psalm he desires to partake of them. When he hears of the great deliverances vouchsafed to sinful ruined man, he studies to have his own share in them. What is said of these persons who wandered out of the way in the wilderness, and fell into the bondage of sin, and were afflicted with its diseases, and troubled like a stormy sea, with its continual tempests ; all this he knows was his own case, and therefore what follows of their flourishing state after Christ delivered them may be his also if he cry unto the Lord, as they did, for help. And he never ceases praying and seeking, until the blessed Jesus brings him to the haven of the church, where he would be. And if he find the church diminished and brought low, he is not discouraged ; but relies on the promises of his God, who will set him on high out of the reach of public calamity, when he comes to destroy an infidel church. He observes what is said on this Psalm concerning those things ; and he knows it to be true, by his own experience. And therefore the lovingkindness of the Lord here recorded is to him a subject of exceeding great joy, because he has tasted of it. Whoso is wise will bring his knowledge of this Psalm home to his own heart, and he shall understand the lovingkindness of the Lord, he shall be able to apply what he understands to his own benefit, and shall therefore be continually praising the Lord for his goodness, and declaring the wonders which he hath done for the salvation of men.—*William Romaine.*

Verse 43.—" *Observe these things.*" " *To observe,* signifieth not only with our eyes to behold it ; but so to stir up our minds to the consideration of a thing, that one may grow the better by it," saith a grave author. Now in this notion of it, how few are they that observe " *these things* " ? . . . .

If you would by observing the providence of God understand his lovingkindness, and gain a spiritual wisdom, *let your eye affect your heart.* Mollerus telleth us, such an observation is here intended *unde ad pietatem exuscitemur, ut inde meliores evadamus,* " as will quicken us to piety, and help to make us better." There are many careless observers of providence, who indeed see *events* rather than providences ; they see much that comes to pass in the world, but consider nothing of God in them. . . . They do by the book of providence, as Augustine complained of himself, that in his unregenerate state he did by the book of Scripture ; he rather brought to it *discutiendi acumen,* than *discendi pietatem.* So men bring to the great works of God rather an acute eye and wit to find out the immediate causes, and reasons natural and political, than a *trembling, humble heart,* that they might learn by them more to acknowledge, *love, fear, adore,* and revere the great and mighty God whose works these are. Let not yours be such an observation ; but let your eye, beholding God in his providential dispensations, affect your hearts with that adoration and veneration, that love and fear of the great and mighty God, which such works of God do call to you for.—*John Collinges* (1623—1690), *in " Several Discourses concerning the actual Providence of God."*

Verse 43.—" *Observe these things.*" These mighty doings of our Saviour and our God in delivering his feeble creatures from the trackless wilderness of error,—from the noisome chain of carnal lust,—from the deadly sickness of a corrupt nature, —and from the wild tempest of earthly passion, deserve the thoughtful joy of all who would be faithful servants of their Lord. The mouth of unbelief and the excuses of iniquity are stopped by the sight of the marvels of that mercy which endureth for ever. " The accuser of the brethren " is silenced and cast down. The truly wise will ponder these things, for in the knowledge of them is true wisdom ; and so pondering, there shall open before them, ever plainer, fuller, clearer, brighter, the revelation of that mighty love of their eternal Father which surpasses all understanding, and is vaster than all thought.—" *Plain Commentary.*"

Verse 43.—How great a volume might be wrote, *de observandis Providentiæ,* concerning the observable things of Divine Providence. I have seen a picture (one of those you call kitchen-pieces) concerning which it hath been proposed to me, that for so many hours I should view it as curiously as I could ; yet the proposer would for any wager undertake to show me something in it which I did not observe. Truly Providence is such a thing, I can never look upon it, I can never take the motions of it into my thoughts, but some new observation tendereth itself into my thoughts. I must turn my eyes from this wonderful work, for I see they will not be satisfied with seeing, my mind will never be filled with observation.—*John Collinges.*

Verse 43.—When we speak of the love and favour of God to his people, we are prone to understand by it nothing but pleasing providences, grateful to our senses : now the " *lovingkindness* " of God is not only seen in pleasing dispensations, but in adverse providences also : " Whom he loveth he chasteneth, and scourgeth every child whom he receiveth " : " all things are yours," saith the apostle. This knowledge must be gained by *observation.*—*John Collinges.*

HINTS TO PREACHERS.

Whole Psalm.—This Psalm is like the Interpreter's house in Bunyan's " Pilgrim's Progress." Pilgrim is told that he will there see excellent and profitable things. The same promise is given in the introduction to this Psalm, where we have, I. The source of these excellent things—the goodness and all-enduring mercy of God ;

mercy not exhausted by the unworthiness of its objects. II. Their acknowledgment, " Let the redeemed of the Lord say so." Men will not own it, but the redeemed of the Lord will. It is the experience of such that is pictorially represented in this Psalm. Let every one speak of God as he finds. Is he good when he takes away as well as when he gives ? " The redeemed of the Lord will say so." Is he merciful when he frowns as well as when he smiles ? " The redeemed of the Lord say so." Does he make all things work together for good to them that love him ? " Let the redeemed of the Lord say so." III. Their end. Praise and thanksgiving : " Oh give," etc. 1, For general mercies ; 2, for redemption ; 3, for special deliverances.—*G. R.*

Verses 1, 2.—The duty of praise is universal, the real presentation of it remains with the redeemed. Particular redemption should lead to special praise, special testimony to truth and special faith in God : " Let the redeemed of the Lord say so."

Verse 3.—The ingathering of the chosen. I. All wandered. II. Their ways different. III. All observed of the Lord. IV. All brought to Jesus as to one centre. Note ways, and times of gathering.

Verse 4.—Wandering Jews. Illustrate the roaming of a mind in search of truth, peace, love, purity, etc.

Verses 4—10.—The words contain a brief history of man's fall and misery and of his restoration by Jesus Christ ; which are described under these particulars. I. The lost state of men by nature. II. They are brought to a right sense of it, and cry to the Lord Jesus for deliverance. III. He hears them and delivers them out of all their distresses. IV. The tribute of thanks due to him for this great deliverance.—*W. Romaine.*

Verse 5.—Spiritual hunger the cause of faintness. Necessity of feeding the soul.

Verse 7.—Divine grace stimulating our exertions. " He led them forth . . . that they might go."

Verse 8.—He who has enjoyed God's help should mark, 1, in what distress he has been ; 2, how he has called to God ; 3, how God has helped him ; 4, what thanks he has returned ; and, 5, what thanks he is yet bound to render.—*Lange's Commentary.*

Verse 9.—A great general fact. The condition, the benefactor, the blessing— " goodness," the result—" satisfieth." Then the further result of praise as seen in verse 8.

Verses 12, 13.—I. The convicted soul's abject condition—humbled, exhausted, prostrate, deserted. II. His speedy deliverance. Cried, cried while in trouble, unto the Lord, he saved, out of their distresses.

Verse 13.—Man's work and God's work. *They* cried and *he* saved.

Verse 14.—God gives light, life, liberty.

Verse 17, etc.—A Rescue from Death, with a Return of Praise.—*R. Sibbes' Works*, Vol. VI. ; Nichol's edition.

Verses 17—21.—I. The distress of the sick. II. Their cure by the Great Physician. III. Their grateful behaviour to him.—*W. Romaine.*

Verses 17—22.—A Visit to Christ's Hospital. I. The names and characters of the patients—" fools " ; all sinners are fools. II. The cause of their pains and afflictions—" because of their transgressions," etc. III. The progress of the disease —" their soul abhorreth all manner of meat " ; and, " they draw near unto the gates of death." IV. The interposition of the physician—" then they cry," etc., ver. 19, 20. 1, Note, when the physician comes in—when " they cry," etc. 2, The kind of prayer—a cry. 3, What the physician did—" saved," " healed," " delivered." 4. How this was effected—" He sent his word," etc. V. The consequent conduct of those who were healed ; they praised God for his goodness. They added sacrifice to this praise, verse 22. In addition to sacrifice the healed ones began to offer songs —" sacrifice of thanksgiving." They added a declaration of joy—" Let them declare his works with rejoicing."

Verse 18.—The sin-sick soul without appetite for invitations, encouragements, or promises, however presented. Milk too simple, strong meat too heavy, wine too heating, manna too light, etc.

Verse 18.—Teacheth us, that even appetite to our meat is a good gift of the Lord ; also that when men are in greatest extremity, then is God most commonly nigh unto them.—*T. Wilcocks.*

Verse 20.—Recovery from sickness must be ascribed to the Lord, and gratitude should flow forth because of it. But the text describes spiritual and mental sickness.

Notice, I. The Patient in his extremity. 1. He is a fool : by nature inclined to evil. 2. He has played the fool (see verse 17), " transgression," " iniquities." 3. He now has lost all appetite and is past all cure. 4. He is at death's door. 5. But he has begun to pray. II. The Cure in its simplicity. 1. Christ the Word is the essential cure. He heals the guilt, habit, depression, and evil results of sin. For every form of malady Christ has healing ; hence preachers should preach him much, and all meditate much upon him. 2. The word in the Book is the instrumental cure : its teachings, doctrines, precepts, promises, encouragements, invitations, examples. 3. The word of the Lord by the Holy Spirit is the applying cure. He leads us to believe. He is to be sought by the sick soul. He is to be relied upon by those who would bring others to the Great Physician.

Verse 26.—The ups and downs of a convicted sinner's experience.

Verse 27.—The awakened sinner staggered and nonplussed.

Verses 33, 34.—The scene which here opens with a landscape of beauty and fertility is suddenly changed into a dry and barren wilderness. The rivers are dried up, the springs cease to flow among the hills, and the verdant fields are scorched and bare. The reason assigned for this is " the wickedness of them that dwell therein." This picture needs no interpretation to the people of God. It is precisely what happens within them when they have fallen into sin.—*G. R.*

Verse 34.—The curse, cause, and cure of barrenness in a church.

Verse 35.—Hope for decayed churches lies in God ; he can work a marvellous change, he does do it—" turneth " : he will do it when the cause of barrenness is removed by repentance.

Verses 35—38. Here the scene again changes. The springs again gush forth, calm lakes again repose in the midst of foliage and flowers, the hills are clothed with luxuriant vines, and the fields are covered with corn ; plenty abounds both in town and country, and men and cattle increase. This picture, too, has its counterpart in experimental godliness. " Instead of the thorn shall come up," etc., " The wilderness and the solitary place shall be glad for them," etc. The one scene precedes prayer, the other follows it. A desolate wilderness before, the garden of Eden behind. —*G. R.*

Verses 39—41.—The scene again is reversed. There is a change again from freedom to oppression ; from plenty to want ; from honour to contempt. Then a revival again as suddenly appears. The poor and afflicted are lifted up, and the bereaved have " families like a flock." Such are the changeful scenes through which the people of God are led ; and such the experience by which they are made meet for the pure, perfect, and perpetual joys of heaven.—*G. R.*

Verses 42, 43.—Such surprising turns are of use, 1, For the solacing of saints ; they observe these dispensations with pleasure : " The righteous shall see it, and rejoice," in the glorifying of God's attributes, and the manifestation of his dominion over the children of men. 2. For the silencing of sinners : " all iniquity shall stop her mouth " ; *i.e.* it shall be a full conviction of the folly of those that deny the divine presence. 3. For the satisfying of all concerning the divine goodness : " Whoso is wise, and will observe these things "—these various dispensations of divine providence, " even they shall understand the lovingkindness of the Lord."—*M. Henry.*

Verse 43.—The best observation and the noblest understanding.

PSALM CVIII.

TITLE AND SUBJECT.—A Song or Psalm of David,—*To be sung jubilantly as a national hymn, or solemnly as a sacred Psalm.* We cannot find it in our heart to dismiss this Psalm by merely referring the reader first to Psalm lvii. 7—11 and then to Psalm lx. 5—12, though it will be at once seen that those two portions of Scripture are almost identical with the verses before us. It is true that most of the commentators have done so, and we are not so presumptuous as to dispute their wisdom ; but we hold for ourselves that the words would not have been repeated if there had not been an object for so doing, and that this object could not have been answered if every hearer of it had said, " Ah, we had that before, and therefore we need not meditate upon it again." The Holy Spirit is not so short of expressions that he needs to repeat himself, and the repetition cannot be meant merely to fill the book : there must be some intention in the arrangement of two former divine utterances in a new connection ; whether we can discover that intent is another matter. It is at least ours to endeavour to do so, and we may expect divine assistance therein.

We have before us THE WARRIOR'S MORNING SONG, with which he adores his God and strengthens his heart before entering upon the conflicts of the day. As an old Prussian officer was wont in prayer to invoke the aid of " his Majesty's August Ally," so does David appeal to his God and set up his banner in Jehovah's name.

DIVISION.—*First we have an utterance dictated by the spirit of praise, verses 1—5 ; then a second deliverance evoked by the spirit of believing prayer, verses 6—12 ; and then a final word of resolve (verse 13), as the warrior hears the war-trumpet summoning him to join battle immediately, and therefore marches with his fellow soldiers at once to the fray.*

EXPOSITION.

O GOD, my heart is fixed ; I will sing and give praise, even with my glory.

2 Awake, psaltery and harp ; I *myself* will awake early.

3 I will praise thee, O LORD, among the people : and I will sing praises unto thee among the nations.

4 For thy mercy *is* great above the heavens : and thy truth *reacheth* unto the clouds.

5 Be thou exalted, O God, above the heavens : and thy glory above all the earth ;

These five verses are found in Psalm lvii. 7—11 almost verbatim : the only important alteration being the use of the great name of JEHOVAH in verse 3 instead of Adonai in lvii. 9. This the English reader will only be able to perceive by the use of capitals in the present Psalm and not in Psalm lvii. There are other inconsiderable alterations, but the chief point of difference probably lies in *the position* of the verses. In lvii. these notes of praise follow prayer and grow out of it ; but in this case the Psalmist begins at once to sing and give praise, and afterwards prays to God in a remarkably confident manner, so that he seems rather to seize the blessing than to entreat for it. Sometimes we must climb to praise by the ladder of prayer, and at other times we must bless God for the past in order to be able in faith to plead for the present and the future. By the aid of God's Spirit we can both pray ourselves up to praise, or praise the Lord till we get into a fit frame for prayer. In Psalm lvii. these words are a song in the cave of Adullam, and are the result of faith which is beginning its battles amid domestic enemies of the most malicious kind : but here they express the continued resolve and praise of a man who has already weathered many a campaign, has overcome all home conflicts, and is looking forward to conquests far and wide. The passage served as a fine close for one Psalm, and it makes an equally noteworthy opening for another. We cannot too often with fixed heart resolve to magnify the Lord ; nor need we ever hesitate to use the same words in drawing near to God, for the Lord who cannot endure vain repetitions is equally weary of vain variations. Some expressions are so admirable that they ought to be used again : who would throw away a cup because he drank from it before ? God should be served with the best words, and when we have them they are surely good enough to be used twice. To use the same words continually and never utter a new song would show great slothfulness, and would lead to dead formalism, but we need not regard novelty of language as at all essential to devotion, nor strain after it as an urgent necessity. It may be that our heavenly Father would here teach us that if we are unable to find a great variety of suitable expressions in devotion, we need not in the slightest degree distress ourselves, but may either pray or praise, " using the same words."

1. " *O God, my heart is fixed.*" Though I have many wars to disturb me, and many cares to toss me to and fro, yet I am settled in one mind and cannot be driven from it. My heart has taken hold and abides in one resolve. Thy grace has overcome the fickleness of nature, and I am now in a resolute and determined frame of mind. " *I will sing and give praise.*" Both with voice and music will I extol thee— " I will sing and play," as some read it. Even though I have to shout in the battle I will also sing in my soul, and if my fingers must needs be engaged with the bow, yet shall they also touch the ten-stringed instrument and show forth thy praise. " *Even with my glory* "—with my intellect, my tongue, my poetic faculty, my musical skill, or whatever else causes me to be renowned, and confers honour upon me. It is my glory to be able to speak and not to be a dumb animal, therefore my voice shall show forth thy praise ; it is my glory to know God and not to be a heathen, and therefore my instructed intellect shall adore thee ; it is my glory to be a saint and no more a rebel, therefore the grace I have received shall bless thee ; it is my glory to be immortal and not a mere brute which perisheth, therefore my inmost life shall celebrate thy majesty. When he says *I will*, he supposes that there might be some temptation to refrain, but this he puts on one side, and with fixed heart prepares himself for the joyful engagement. He who sings with a fixed heart is likely to sing on, and all the while to sing well.

2. " *Awake, psaltery and harp.*" As if he could not be content with voice alone, but must use the well-tuned strings, and communicate to them something of his own liveliness. Strings are wonderful things when some men play upon them, they seem to become sympathetic and incorporated with the minstrel, as if his very soul were imparted to them and thrilled through them. Only when a thoroughly enraptured soul speaks in the instrument can music be acceptable with God : as mere musical sound the Lord can have no pleasure therein, he is only pleased with the thought and feeling which are thus expressed. When a man has musical gift, he should regard it as too lovely a power to be enlisted in the cause of sin. Well did Charles Wesley say :—

> " If well I know the tuneful art
> To captivate a human heart,
> The glory, Lord, be thine.
> A servant of thy blessed will,
> I here devote my utmost skill
> To sound the praise divine.
>
> " Thine own musician, Lord, inspire,
> And let my consecrated lyre
> Repeat the Psalmist's part.
> His Son and Thine reveal in me,
> And fill with sacred melody
> The fibres of my heart."

" *I myself will awake early.*" I will call up the dawn. The best and brightest hours of the day shall find me heartily aroused to bless my God. Some singers had need to awake, for they sing in drawling tones, as if they were half asleep ; the tune drags wearily along, there is no feeling or sentiment in the singing, but the listener hears only a dull mechanical sound, as if the choir ground out the notes from a worn-out barrel-organ. Oh, choristers, wake up, for this is not a work for dreamers, but such as requires your best powers in their liveliest condition. In all worship this should be the personal resolve of each worshipper : " I myself will awake."

3. " *I will praise thee, O Lord, among the people.*" Whoever may come to hear me, devout or profane, believer or heathen, civilized or barbarian, I shall not cease

my music. David seemed inspired to foresee that his Psalms would be sung in every land, from Greenland's icy mountains to India's coral strand. His heart was large, he would have the whole race of man listen to his joy in God, and lo, he has his desire, for his psalmody is cosmopolitan ; no poet is so universally known as he. He had but one theme, he sang Jehovah and none beside, and his work being thus made of gold, silver, and precious stones, has endured the fiery ordeal of time, and was never more prized than at this day. Happy man, to have thus made his choice to be the Lord's musician, he retains his office as the Poet Laureate of the kingdom of heaven, and shall retain it till the crack of doom. " *And I will sing praises unto thee among the nations.*" This is written, not only to complete the parallelism of the verse, but to reaffirm his fixed resolve. He would march to battle praising Jehovah, and when he had conquered he would make the captured cities ring with Jehovah's praises. He would carry his religion with him wherever he pushed his conquests, and the vanquished should not hear the praises of David, but the glories of the Lord of Hosts. Would to God that wherever professing Christians travel they would carry the praises of the Lord with them ! It is to be feared that some leave their religion when they leave their homes. Nations and peoples would soon know the gospel of Jesus if every Christian traveller were as intensely devout as the Psalmist. Alas, it is to be feared that the Lord's name is profaned rather than honoured among the heathen by many who are named by the name of Christ.

4. " *For thy mercy is great above the heavens,*" and therefore there must be no limit of time, or place, or people, when that mercy is to be extolled. As the heavens over-arch the whole earth, and from above mercy pours down upon men, so shalt thou be praised everywhere beneath the sky. Mercy is greater than the mountains, though they pierce the clouds ; earth cannot hold it all, it is so vast, so boundless, so exceeding high that the heavens themselves are over-topped thereby. " *And thy truth reacheth unto the clouds.*" As far as we can see we behold thy truth and faithfulness, and there is much beyond which lies shrouded in cloud, but we are sure that it is all mercy, though it be far above and out of our sight. Therefore shall the song be lifted high and the Psalm shall peal forth without stint of far-resounding music. Here is ample space for the loudest chorus, and a subject which deserves thunders of praise.

5. " *Be thou exalted, O God, above the heavens : and thy glory above all the earth.*" Let thy praise be according to the greatness of thy mercy. Ah, if we were to measure our devotion thus, with what ardour should we sing ! The whole earth with its over-hanging dome would seem too scant an orchestra, and all the faculties of all mankind too little for the hallelujah. Angels would be called in to aid us, and surely they would come. They will come in that day when the whole earth shall be filled with the praises of Jehovah. We long for the time when God shall be universally worshipped, and his glory in the gospel shall be everywhere made known. This is a truly missionary prayer. David had none of the exclusiveness of the modern Jew or the narrow-heartedness of some nominal Christians. For God's sake, that his glory might be everywhere revealed, he longed to see heaven and earth full of the divine praise. Amen, so let it be.

6 That thy beloved may be delivered : save *with* thy right hand, and answer me.

7 God hath spoken in his holiness ; I will rejoice, I will divide Shechem, and mete out the valley of Succoth.

8 Gilead *is* mine ; Manasseh *is* mine ; Ephraim also *is* the strength of mine head ; Judah *is* my lawgiver ;

9 Moab *is* my washpot ; over Edom will I cast out my shoe ; over Philistia will I triumph.

10 Who will bring me into the strong city ? who will lead me into Edom ?

11 *Wilt* not *thou*, O God, *who* hast cast us off ? and wilt not thou, O God, go forth with our hosts ?

12 Give us help from trouble : for vain *is* the help of man.

Now prayer follows upon praise, and derives strength of faith and holy boldness therefrom. It is frequently best to begin worship with a hymn, and then to bring forth our vials full of odours after the harps have commenced their sweeter sounds.

6. "*That thy beloved may be delivered : save with thy right hand, and answer me.*" Let my prayer avail for all the beloved ones. Sometimes a nation seems to hang upon the petitions of one man. With what ardour should such an one pour out his soul! David does so here. It is easy praying for the Lord's beloved, for we feel sure of a favourable answer, since the Lord's heart is already set upon doing them good : yet it is solemn work to plead when we feel that the condition of a whole beloved nation depends upon what the Lord means to do with us whom he has placed in a representative position. "Answer *me*, that thy many beloved ones may be delivered" : it is an urgent prayer. David felt that the case demanded the *right hand* of God,—his wisest, speediest, and most efficient interposition, and he feels sure of obtaining it for himself, since his cause involved the safety of the chosen people. Will the Lord fail to use his right hand of power on behalf of those whom he has set at his right hand of favour? Shall not the beloved be delivered by him who loves them? When our suit is not a selfish one, but is bound up with the cause of God, we may be very bold about it.

7. "*God has spoken in his holiness.*" Aforetime the Lord had made large promises to David, and these his holiness had guaranteed. The divine attributes were pledged to give the son of Jesse great blessings ; there was no fear that the covenant God would run back from his plighted word. "*I will rejoice.*" If God has spoken we may well be glad : the very fact of a divine revelation is a joy. If the Lord had meant to destroy us he would not have spoken to us as he has done. But what God has spoken is a still further reason for gladness, for he has declared "the sure mercies of David," and promised to establish his seed upon his throne, and to subdue all his enemies. David greatly rejoiced after the Lord had spoken to him by the mouth of Nathan. He sat before the Lord in a wonder of joy. See 1 Chronicles xvii., and note that in the next chapter David began to act vigorously against his enemies, even as in this Psalm he vows to do. "*I will divide Shechem.*" Home conquests come first. Foes must be dislodged from Israel's territory, and lands properly settled and managed. "*And mete out the valley of Succoth.*" On the other side Jordan as well as on this the land must be put in order, and secured against all wandering marauders. Some rejoicing leads to inaction, but not that which is grounded upon a lively faith in the promise of God. See how David prays, as if he had the blessing already, and could share it among his men : this comes of having sung so heartily unto the Lord his helper. See how he resolves on action, like a man whose prayers are only a part of his life, and vital portions of his action.

8. "*Gilead is mine.*" Thankful hearts dwell upon the gifts which the Lord has given them, and think it no task to mention them one by one. "*Manasseh is mine.*" I have it already, and it is to me the token and assurance that the rest of the promised heritage will also come into my possession in due time. If we gratefully acknowledge what we have we shall be in better heart for obtaining that which as yet we have not received. He who gives us Gilead and Manasseh will not fail to put the rest of the promised territory into our hands. "*Ephraim also is the strength of mine head.*" This tribe furnished David with more than twenty thousand "mighty men of valour, famous throughout the house of their fathers" : the faithful loyalty of this band was, no doubt, a proof that the rest of the tribe were with him, and so he regarded them as the helmet of the state, the guard of his royal crown. "*Judah is my lawgiver.*" There had he seated the government and chief courts of justice. No other tribe could lawfully govern but Judah : till Shiloh came the divine decree fixed the legal power in that state. To us also there is no lawgiver but our Lord who sprang out of Judah ; and whenever Rome, or Canterbury, or any other power shall attempt to set up laws and ordinances for the church, we have but one reply— "Judah is my lawgiver." Thus the royal Psalmist rejoiced because his own land had been cleansed of intruders, and a regular government had been set up, and guarded by an ample force, and in all this he found encouragement to plead for victory over his foreign foes. Even thus do we plead with the Lord that as in one land and another Christ's holy gospel has been set up and maintained, so also in other lands the power of his sceptre of grace may be owned till the whole earth shall bow before him, and the Edom of Antichrist shall be crushed beneath his feet.

9. "*Moab is my washpot.*" This nation had shown no friendly spirit to the Israelites, but had continually viewed them as a detested rival, therefore they were to be subdued and made subject to David's throne. He claims by faith the victory, and regards his powerful enemy with contempt. Nor was he disappointed, for "the Moabites became David's servants and brought him gifts" (2 Sam. viii. 2).

As men wash their feet after a long journey, and so are revived, so vanquished difficulties serve to refresh us : we use Moab for a washpot. " *Over Edom will I cast out
my shoe.*" It shall be as the floor upon which the bather throws his sandals, it shall
lie beneath his foot, subject to his will and altogether his own. Edom was proud,
but David throws his slipper at it ; its capital was high, but he casts his sandal over
it ; it was strong, but he hurls his shoe at it as the gage of battle. He had not
entered yet into its rock-built fortresses, but since the Lord was with him he felt
sure that he would do so. Under the leadership of the Almighty, he felt so secure
of conquering even fierce Edom itself that he looks upon it as a mere slave, over
which he could exult with impunity. We ought never to fear those who are defending
the wrong side, for since God is not with them their wisdom is folly, their strength
is weakness, and their glory is their shame. We think too much of God's foes and
talk of them with too much respect. Who is this Pope of Rome ? His Holiness ?
Call him not so, but call him His Blasphemy ! His Profanity ! His Impudence !
What are he and his cardinals, and his legates, but the image and incarnation of
Antichrist, to be in due time cast with the beast and the false prophet into the lake
of fire ? " *Over Philistia will I triumph.*" David had done so in his youth, and he
is all the more sure of doing it again. We read that " David smote the Philistines
and subdued them " (2 Sam. viii. 1), even as he had smitten Edom and filled it with
his garrisons. The enemies with whom we battled in our youth are yet alive, and
we shall have more brushes with them before we die, but, blessed be God, we are by
no means dismayed at the prospect, for we expect to triumph over them even more
easily than aforetime.

> Thy right hand shall thy people aid ;
> Thy faithful promise makes us strong ;
> We will Philistia's land invade,
> And over Edom chant the song.
>
> Through thee we shall most valiant prove,
> And tread the foe beneath our feet ;
> Through thee our faith shall hills remove,
> And small as chaff the mountains beat.

10. Faith leads on to strong desire for the realisation of the promise, and hence
the practical question, " *Who will bring me into the strong city ? who will lead me into
Edom ?* " The difficulty is plainly perceived. Petra is strong and hard to enter :
the Psalmist warrior knows that he cannot enter the city by his own power, and he
therefore asks who is to help him. He asks of the right person, even of his Lord,
who has all men at his beck, and can say to this man, " show my servant the road,"
and he will show it, or to this band, " cut your way into the rock city," and they will
assuredly do it. Of Edom it is written by Obadiah, " The pride of thine heart hath
deceived thee, thou that dwellest in the clefts of the rock, whose habitation is high ;
that saith in his heart, who shall bring me down to the ground ? Though thou exalt
thyself as the eagle, and though thou set thy nest among the stars, thence will I bring
thee down, saith the Lord." David looked for his conquest to Jehovah's infinite
power, and he looked not in vain.

11. " *Wilt not thou, O God, who hast cast us off ?* " This is grand faith which can
trust the Lord even when he seems to have cast us off. Some can barely trust him
when he pampers them, and yet David relied upon him when Israel seemed under
a cloud and the Lord had hidden his face. O for more of this real and living faith.
The casting off will not last long when faith so gloriously keeps her hold. None but
the elect of God who have obtained " like precious faith " can sing—

> " Now thou array'st thine awful face
> In angry frowns, without a smile ;
> We, through the cloud, believe thy grace,
> Secure of thy compassion still."

" *And wilt not thou, O God, go forth with our hosts ?* " Canst thou for ever forsake
thine own and leave thy people to be overthrown by thine enemies ? The sweet
singer is sure that Edom shall be captured, because he cannot and will not believe
that God will refrain from going forth with the armies of his chosen people. When
we ask ourselves, " Who will be the means of our obtaining a promised blessing ? "
we need not be discouraged if we perceive no secondary agent, for we may then

fall back upon the great Promiser himself, and believe that he himself will perform his word unto us. If no one else will lead us into Edom, the Lord himself will do it, if he has promised it. Or if there must be visible instruments he will use *our hosts*, feeble as they are. We need not that any new agency should be created, God can strengthen our present hosts and enable them to do all that is needed ; all that is wanted even for the conquest of a world is that the Lord go forth with such forces as we already have. He can bring us into the strong city even by such weak weapons as we wield to-day.

12. "*Give us help from trouble : for vain is the help of man.*" This prayer has often fallen from the lips of men who have been bitterly disappointed by their fellows, and it has also been poured out unto the Lord in the presence of some gigantic labour in which mortal power is evidently of no avail. Edom cannot be entered by any human power, yet from its fastnesses the robber bands come rushing down ; therefore, O Lord, do thou interpose and give thy people deliverance. Help divine is expected because help human is of no avail. We ought to pray with all the more confidence in God when our confidence in man is altogether gone. When the help of man is vain, we shall not find it vain to seek the help of God.

13 Through God we shall do valiantly : for he *it is that* shall tread down our enemies.

13. God's help shall inspire us to help ourselves. Faith is neither a coward nor a sluggard : she knows that God is with her, and therefore she does valiantly ; she knows that he will tread down her enemies, and therefore she arises to tread them down in his name. Where praise and prayer have preceded the battle, we may expect to see heroic deeds and decisive victories. "*Through God*" is our secret support ; from that source we draw all our courage, wisdom, and strength. "*We shall do valiantly.*" This is the public outflow from that secret source : our inward and spiritual faith proves itself by outward and valorous deeds. "*He shall tread down our enemies.*" They shall fall before him, and as they lie prostrate he shall march over them, and all the hosts of his people with him. This is a prophecy. It was fulfilled to David, but it remains true to the Son of David and all who are on his side. The church shall yet arouse herself to praise her God with all her heart, and then with songs and hosannas she will advance to the great battle ; her foes shall be overthrown and utterly crushed by the power of her God, and the Lord's glory shall be above all the earth. Send it in our time, we beseech thee, O Lord.

EXPLANATORY NOTES AND QUAINT SAYINGS.

Whole Psalm.—Note the different application of the words as they are used in Psalms lvii. and lx., and as they are employed in Psalm cviii. In the former they were prophetic of prosperity yet to come, and consolatory in the expectation of approaching troubles. In the latter, they are eucharistic for mercies already received, and descriptive of the glorious things which God has prepared for his Son and for Israel his people. The Psalm, thus interpreted, announces that Messiah's travail is ended, when the troubles of Israel are brought to a close. David's Son and David's Lord has taken to himself his great power and begun to reign, and sitting upon the throne of glory, he sings this hymn, verses 1 to 6. But with the glory of the Redeemer is associated also the restoration, to favour and happiness, of Israel, his long cast off, but not forgotten people. The setting up of King Messiah upon the holy hill of Zion is graphically described, and all Jehovah's promises are realised in the amplest measure. Messiah is described as a conqueror when the battle is won, and kings and nations, prostrate at his feet, await his sentence and judgment upon them. " I will rejoice. I will divide and portion out Shechem and the valley of Succoth. Gilead it mine, and I give it to the children of Gad and Reuben. And Manasseh also is mine. Ephraim is my strength in war : my horn of defence. Judah is my king." Thus in gracious and flattering words, the victor addresses his confederates and subjects. In a different strain, a strain of sarcasm and contempt, he announces his pleasure respecting his vanquished enemies. " Moab I will use as a vessel to wash my feet in. Over proud Edom I will cast my shoe, as an angry master to a slave

ministering to him. Philistia follow my chariot, and shout forth my triumph."
But what is to be understood of the next passage, verse 10, " Who will bring me into
Edom ? " Edom is already treated as a vassal state, verse 9. When all the nations
become the kingdoms of Messiah, what is this Edom that is to be amongst his latest
triumphs ? One passage only seems to bear upon it, Isaiah lxiii. 1, and from this we
learn that it is from Edom as the last scene of his vengeance, the conquering Messiah
will come forth, " clothed with a vesture dipped in blood." This Edom is therefore
named with anxiety, because after its overthrow, Messiah will shine out " King of
kings, and Lord of lords," Rev. xix. 13—16.—*R. H. Ryland.*

Whole Psalm.—This Psalm hath two parts : in the former is the thanksgiving
of faith, and promise of praise, in hope of obtaining all which the church is here to
pray for (ver. 1—5). In the latter part is the prayer for preservation of the church,
ver. 6, with confidence to be heard and helped, whatsoever impediment appear,
against all who stand out against Christ's kingdom, whether within the visible church
(ver. 7, 8), or whether without, such as are professed enemies unto it (ver. 9, 10, 11),
which prayer is followed forth (ver. 12), and comfortably closed with assurance of
the Church's victory by the assistance of God, ver. 13.—*David Dickson.*

Verse 1.—" *O God, my heart is fixed.*" The wheels of a chariot revolve, but the
axletree turns not ; the sails of a mill move with the wind, but the mill itself moves
not ; the earth is carried round its orbit, but its centre is fixed. So should a Christian
be able, amidst changing scenes and changing fortunes, to say, " *O God, my heart
is fixed, my heart is fixed.*"—*G. S. Bowes, in " Illustrative Gatherings,"* 1862.

Verse 1.—" *My heart is fixed.*" The prophet saith *his heart was ready*, so the old
translation hath it ; the new translation, " *My heart is fixed.*" The word in the
Hebrew signifies, first, *ready*, or *prepared.* Then, secondly, it signifies *fixed.* We first
fit, prepare a thing, sharpen it, before we drive it into the ground, and then drive it in
and fix it. So ask seriously and often, that thy heart may be ready, and may also
be fixed, and this by a *habit* which brings readiness and fixedness, as in other holy
duties, so in that of meditation.—*Nathanael Ranew, in " Solitude improved by Divine
Meditation,"* 1670.

Verse 1.—Meditation is a fixed duty. It is not a cursory work. Man's thoughts
naturally labour with a great inconsistency ; but meditation chains them, and fastens
them upon some spiritual object. The soul when it meditates lays a command on
itself, that the thoughts which are otherwise flitting and feathery should fix upon
its object ; and so this duty is very advantageous. As we know a garden which is
watered with sudden showers is more uncertain in its fruit than when it is refreshed
with a constant stream ; so when our thoughts are sometimes on good things, and then
run off ; when they only take a glance of a holy object, and then flit away, there is
not so much fruit brought into the soul. In meditation, then, there must be a fixing
of the heart upon the object, a steeping the thoughts, as holy David : " *O God, my
heart is fixed.*" We must view the holy object presented by meditation, as a limner
who views some curious piece, and carefully heeds every shade, every line and colour ;
as the Virgin Mary kept all these things, and pondered them in her heart. Indeed,
meditation is not only the busying the thoughts, but the centering of them ; not only
the employing of them, but the staking them down upon some spiritual affair. When
the soul, meditating upon something divine, saith as the disciples in the transfiguration
(Matt. xvii. 4), " It is good to be here."—*John Wells, in the " Practical Sabbatarian,"*
1668.

Verse 1.—" *With my glory.*" The parallel passage in the Prayer-book version
is, " with the best member I have." The tongue, being considered the best member,
is here described as the *glory* of man—as that which tends to elevate him in the scale
of creation ; and therefore the pious man resolves to employ his speech in giving
utterance to the goodness of God. God is glorified by the praise of his redeemed,
and the instrument whereby it is effected is man's *glory.*—*The Quiver.*

Verses 1, 2.—As a man first tuneth his instrument, and then playeth on it :
so should the holy servant of God first labour to bring his spirit, heart, and
affections into a solid and settled frame for worship, and then go to work ; " *My
heart is fixed,*" or prepared firmly, " *I will sing and give praise.*" As the glory of man
above the brute creatures, is that from a reasonable mind he can express what is
his will by his tongue : so the glory of saints above other men, is to have a tongue
directed by the heart, for expressing of God's praise : " *I will sing and give praise,
even with my glory.*" Under typical terms we are taught to make use of all sanctified

means for stirring of us up into God's service : for this the Psalmist intendeth, when he saith, " *Awake psaltery and harp.*" We ourselves must first be stirred up to make right use of the means, before the means can be fit to stir us up : therefore saith he, " *I myself will awake right early.*"—*David Dickson.*

Verses 1—5.—After David has professed a purpose of praising God (verses 1, 2, 3) he tells you, next, the proportion that is between the attributes which he praiseth in God, and his praise of him. The greatness of the attributes " *mercy and truth* " we have in verse 4, " *Thy truth reaches unto the clouds* " ; and there is an answerable greatness in his praises of God for them, verse 5 : " *Be thou exalted, O God, above the heavens : and thy glory above all the earth.*" He wisheth and endeavoureth to exalt him as high in his praises as he is in himself ; to exalt him above the earth, above the heaven, and the clouds.—*Henry Jeanes.*

Verse 2.—With reference to this passage the Talmud says, " A cithern used to hang above David's bed ; and when midnight came the north wind blew among the strings, so that they sounded of themselves ; and forthwith he arose and busied himself with the Tôra until the pillar of the dawn ascended." Rashi observes, " The dawn awakes the other kings ; but I, said David, will awake the dawn."— *Franz Delitzsch.*

Verse 2.—When the Hebrew captives were sitting in sorrow " by the waters of Babylon," they wept, and hung their harps on the willows, and could not be prevailed upon by the conquerors to sing " the songs of Zion in that land " (Ps. cxxxvii. 1, 4). But when " the Lord turned again the captivity of Zion, then was their mouth filled with laughter and their tongue with singing " (cxxvi. 1, 2). Then the " *psaltery and harp* " of former generations " *awoke* " (v. 2). The old songs revived on their lips, and the melodies of David acquired new charms for them.—*Christopher Wordsworth.*

Verse 2.—" *Awake early.*"

> " Yet never sleep the sun up ; prayer should
> Dawn with the day, there are set awful hours
> 'Twixt heaven and us ; the manna was not good
> After sun-rising, for day sullies flowers."
> *Henry Vaughan,* 1621—1695.

Verse 4.—" *For thy mercy is great,*" etc. His mercy is great—that mercy sung of lately (Ps. cvii. 1 and 43). It is " *from* above the heavens " (מֵעַל־שָׁמָיִם) ; *i.e.*, coming down to us as do drops of a fertilizing shower ; even as the " *Peace on earth,*" of Luke ii. 14, was first " peace in heaven " (Luke xix. 38).—*Andrew A. Bonar.*

Verse 4.—The mercy of God was then great *above* the heavens, when the God-man, Christ Jesus, was raised to the highest heavens, and the truth of our salvation established on the very throne of God.—*W. Wilson.*

Verses 4, 5.—There is more stuff and substance of good in the Lord's promises than the sharpest-sighted saint did or can perceive ; for when we have followed the promise, to find out all the truth which is in it, we meet with a cloud of unsearchable riches, and are forced to leave it there ; for so much is included in this, " *Thy truth reacheth unto the clouds.*" The height of our praising of God is to put the work of praising God upon himself, and to point him out unto others as going about the magnifying of his own name, and to be glad for it, as here ; " *Be thou exalted, O God, above the heavens ; and thy glory above all the earth.*"—*David Dickson.*

Verses 4, 5, 6.—There is great confidence here, and, as ever, mercy to the soul which knows itself and comes before truth. But, then, for its own deliverance and blessing, it looks to the exalting of God. This shows it must be a holy, righteous exalting. " Be *thou* exalted, O God, above the heavens : and thy glory above all the earth ; that thy beloved may be delivered." It is a blessed thought, and this is what faith has to lay hold of now, even in the time of trial, that our blessing and God's glory are one, only we must put his glory first.—*J. N. Darby.*

Verse 6.—" *That thy beloved may be delivered,*" etc. The church is the Lord's " beloved," or the incorporation, more loved than anything else in the world, therefore here called, " *Thy beloved.*" Because the church is God's beloved, the care of it should be most in our mind, and the love of the preservation of it should draw forth our prayer most in favour of it. " *That thy beloved may be delivered : save.*"— *David Dickson.*

Verse 6.—God being thus exalted according to the majesty of his truth, the special plea of the Spirit of Jesus, founded on the mercy which has throned itself above the heavens, is next urged (verse 6) on behalf of the nation of his ancient love. " *That thy beloved [ones] may be delivered, save with thy right hand and answer me.*" It is the Spirit of Immanuel that thus makes intercession for his well-remembered people according to God. His land should be rid in due time of those who had burdened it with wickedness. For *God* had spoken in his holiness concerning the portion of his anointed.—*Arthur Pridham.*

Verse 7.—" *God hath spoken* " the word of assurance. This refers to all the words in which the land of their inheritance was defined, especially Gen. xv. 18, Ex. xxiii. 31, Deut. xi. 24, and that remarkable prediction concerning the perpetuity of David's line, 2 Sam. vii., which must have made a deep impression on his mind. From these passages it is evident that Aram as well as Edom was included in the full compass of the territory designed for Israel, and that David felt himself to be in the path of destiny when he was endeavouring to extend his sway from the river of Egypt to the great river, even the Euphrates. " *In his holiness,*" in the immutable integrity of his heart, which was an infallible guarantee for the fulfilment of his promise. " *I will exult.*" This is the exclamation of the representative head of the people, when he ponders upon the divine utterance.—*James G. Murphy.*

Verse 7.—Faith closing with a promise, will furnish joy to the believer before he enjoys the performance of it : " *God hath spoken,*" saith he, " *I will rejoice.*"— —*David Dickson.*

Verse 7.—He, the second David, had accomplished his warfare, and had crowned himself with victory. Henceforth he would apportion the kingdoms of the world and subdue them unto himself at his own holy will. Ephraim and Judah, Moab and Philistia, the Jew first and then the Gentile, were to be brought to confess him as their Lord.—*Plain Commentary.*

Verse 8.—" *Ephraim also is the strength of mine head.*" As *Ephraim* was the most populous of all the tribes, he appropriately terms it *the strength of his head,* that is, of his dominions.—*John Calvin.*

Verse 9.—*Moab,* who had enticed Israel to impurity, is made a vessel for its purifying. *Edom,* descendant of him who despised his birthright, is deprived of his independence ;—for " flinging a shoe " was a sign of the transference of a prior claim on land. Ruth iv. 7.—*William Kay.*

Verse 9.—" *Moab is my washpot.*" The office of washing the feet was in the East commonly performed by slaves, and the meanest of the family, as appears from what Abigail said to David when he took her to wife, " Behold, let thine hand-maid be a servant to wash the feet of the servants of my lord," 1 Sam. xxv. 41 ; and from the fact of our Saviour washing his disciples' feet, to give them an example of humility, John xiii. 5. The word νιπτήρ, used in this last passage, signifies in general *a washing-pot,* and is put for the word ποδόνιπτρον, the term which the Greeks, in strict propriety of speech, applied to a vessel for washing the feet. As this office was servile, so the vessels employed for this purpose were a mean part of household stuff. Gataker and Le Clerc illustrate this text from an anecdote related by Herodotus, concerning Amasis, king of Egypt, who expressed the meanness of his own origin by comparing himself to a pot for washing the feet in (Herod, Lib. ii. c. 172). When, therefore, it is said, " *Moab is my washing-pot,*" the complete and servile subjection of Moab to David is strongly marked. This is expressed, not by comparing Moab to a slave who performs the lowest offices, as presenting to his master the basin for washing his feet, but by comparing him to the mean utensil itself. See 2 Sam. viii. 2 ; 1 Chron. xviii. 1, 2, 12, 13.—*James Anderson's Note to Calvin on Ps. lx.*

Verse 9.—" *Moab is my washpot ; over Edom will I cast my shoe.*" This somewhat difficult expression may be thus explained. Moab and Edom were to be reduced to a state of lowest vassalage to the people of God. The one was to be like a pot or tub fit only for washing the feet in, while the other was to be like the domestic slave standing by to receive the sandals thrown to him by the person about to perform his ablutions, that he might first put them by in a safe place, and then come and wash his master's feet.—" *Rays from the East.*"

Verse 9.—" *Over Edom will I cast my shoe.*" David overthrew their army in the " Valley of Salt," and his general, Joab, following up the victory, destroyed nearly the whole male population (1 Kings xi. 15, 16), and placed Jewish garrisons in all the strongholds of Edom (2 Sam. viii. 13, 14). In honour of that victory the Psalmist-warrior may have penned the words in Ps. lx. 8, " *Over Edom will I cast my shoe.*"—*J. L. Porter, in " Smith's Dictionary of the Bible."*

Verse 10.—The strong city built on the rock, even man's hardened heart, stronger and more stony than the tomb, he had conquered and overcome ; and in him and his might are his people to carry on his warfare, and to cast down all the strongholds of human pride, and human stubbornness, and human unrepentance.—*Plain Commentary.*

Verses 10, 11.—It is not conclusive evidence that we are not called to undertake a given work or perform a certain duty, because it is very difficult, or even impossible for us to succeed without special help from God. If God calls David to take Petra, he shall take Petra.—*William S. Plumer.*

Verse 11.—" *Wilt not thou, O God ?* " His hand shall lead him even to Petra, which seems unapproachable by human strength. That marvellous rock-city of the Edomites is surrounded by rocks some of which are three hundred feet high, and a single path twelve in width leads to it. The city itself is partly hewn out of the cloven rocks, and its ruins, which however belong to a later period, fill travellers with amazement.—*Augustus F. Tholuck.*

Verse 11.—He who came victorious from Edom, and with garments dyed in the blood of his passion from Bozrah, will henceforth now go forth with the armies of the true Israel,—for what are hosts without the Lord of hosts ?—to subdue their enemy.—*Plain Commentary.*

Verse 12.—" *Give us help from trouble,*" etc. He who would have God's help in any business, must quit confidence in man's help ; and the seeing of the vanity of man's help must make the believer to trust the more unto, and expect the more confidently God's help, as here is done. " *Give us help from trouble : for vain is the help of man.*"—*David Dickson.*

HINTS TO PREACHERS.

Whole Psalm.—Parts of two former Psalms are here united in one. I. Repetition is here sanctioned by inspiration. 1. Of what ? Of hymns, of prayers, of sermons. 2. For what ? For impression. " As we said before so say I now again, if any man preach," etc. For confirmation : " Rejoice in the Lord, and again I say rejoice " : they went through Syria and Cilicia again confirming the churches. For preservation : quotations authenticate originals, a writing in two copies is safer than in one. II. Rearrangement is here sanctioned by inspiration. 1. Different experiences may require it. Sometimes the heart is most fixed at the commencement of a spiritual exercise : sometimes at its close. Hence the commencement of one Psalm is the close of another. 2. Different occasions may require it. As of sorrow and joy. Two parts of two different hymns may better harmonise with a particular occasion than either one separately considered.—*G. R.*

Verse 1.—I. The best occupation : praise. Worthy—1. Of the heart in its best condition. 2. Of the best faculties of the best educated man. II. The best resolution. 1. Arising from a fixed heart. 2. Deliberately formed. 3. Solemnly expressed. 4. Joyfully executed. III. The best results. To praise God makes a man both happier and holier, stronger and bolder—as the succeeding verses show.

Verse 2.—The benefit of early rising. The sweetness of the Sabbath morning early prayer-meeting.

Verse 3.—We must not restrain praise because we are overheard by strangers, nor because the listeners are heathen, or ungodly, or are numerous, or are likely to oppose. There may be all the more reason for our outspoken praise of God when we are in such circumstances.

Verses 4, 5.—The greatness of mercy, the height of truth, and the immensity of the Divine praise.

Verse 6.—The prayer of a representative man. There are times when to answer *me* is to deliver the church—at such times I have a powerful plea.

Verse 7.—God's voice the cause of joy, the reason for action, the guarantee of success.

Verse 8.—" *Judah is my lawgiver.*" Jesus the sole and only lawmaker in the church.

Verse 11 (*first clause*).—Confidence in a frowning God.

Verse 11 (*second clause*).—Whether God will go forth with our hosts depends upon—Who they are ? What is their object ? What is their motive and spirit ? What weapons do they use ? etc.

Verse 12.—The failure of human help is often—1. The direct cause of our prayer. 2. The source of urgency in pleading. 3. A powerful argument for the pleader. 4. A distinct reason for hope to light upon.

Verse 13.—How, when, and why a believer should do valiantly.

PSALM CIX.

To the Chief Musician.—*Intended therefore to be sung, and sung in the temple service ! Yet is it by no means easy to imagine the whole nation singing such dreadful imprecations. We ourselves, at any rate, under the gospel dispensation, find it very difficult to infuse into the Psalm a gospel sense, or a sense at all compatible with the Christian spirit ; and therefore one would think the Jews must have found it hard to chant such strong language without feeling the spirit of revenge excited ; and the arousal of that spirit could never have been the object of divine worship in any period of time— under law or under gospel. At the very outset this title shows that the Psalm has a meaning with which it is fitting for men of God to have fellowship before the throne of the Most High : but what is that meaning? This is a question of no small difficulty, and only a very childlike spirit will ever be able to answer it.*

A Psalm of David. *Not therefore the ravings of a malicious misanthrope, or the execrations of a hot, revengeful spirit. David would not smite the man who sought his blood, he frequently forgave those who treated him shamefully ; and therefore these words cannot be read in a bitter, revengeful sense, for that would be foreign to the character of the son of Jesse. The imprecatory sentences before us were penned by one who with all his courage in battle was a man of music and of tender heart, and they were meant to be addressed to God in the form of a Psalm, and therefore they cannot possibly have been meant to be mere angry cursing.*

Unless it can be proved that the religion of the old dispensation was altogether hard, morose, and Draconian, and that David was of a malicious, vindictive spirit, it cannot be conceived that this Psalm contains what one author has ventured to call " a pitiless hate, a refined and insatiable malignity." To such a suggestion we cannot give place, no, not for an hour. But what else can we make of such strong language ? Truly this is one of the hard places of Scripture, a passage which the soul trembles to read ; yet as it is a Psalm unto God, and given by inspiration, it is not ours to sit in judgment upon it, but to bow our ear to what God the Lord would speak to us therein.

This Psalm refers to Judas, for so Peter quoted it ; but to ascribe its bitter denunciations to our Lord in the hour of his sufferings is more than we dare to do. These are not consistent with the silent Lamb of God, who opened not his mouth when led to the slaughter. It may seem very pious to put such words into his mouth ; we hope it is our piety which prevents our doing so. See our first note from Perowne on page 445.

Division.—*In the first five verses David humbly pleads with God that he may be delivered from his remorseless and false-hearted enemies. From 6—20, filled with a prophetic furor, which carries him entirely beyond himself, he denounces judgment upon his foes, and then from 21—31 he returns to his communion with God in prayer and praise. The central portion of the Psalm in which the difficulty lies must be regarded not as the personal wish of the Psalmist in cool blood, but as his prophetic denunciation of such persons as he describes, and emphatically of one special " son of perdition" whom he sees with prescient eye. We would all pray for the conversion of our worst enemy, and David would have done the same ; but viewing the adversaries of the Lord, and doers of iniquity, as such, and as incorrigible, we cannot wish them well ; on the contrary, we desire their overthrow and destruction. The gentlest hearts burn with indignation when they hear of barbarities to women and children, of crafty plots for ruining the innocent, of cruel oppression of helpless orphans, and gratuitous ingratitude to the good and gentle. A curse upon the perpetrators of the atrocities in Turkey may not be less virtuous than a blessing upon the righteous. We wish well to all mankind, and for that very reason we sometimes blaze with indignation against the inhuman wretches by whom every law which protects our fellow creatures is trampled down, and every dictate of humanity is set at nought.*

EXPOSITION.

HOLD not thy peace, O God of my praise ;

2 For the mouth of the wicked and the mouth of the deceitful are opened against me : they have spoken against me with a lying tongue.

3 They compassed me about also with words of hatred ; and fought against me without a cause.

4 For my love they are my adversaries : but I *give myself unto* prayer.

5 And they have rewarded me evil for good, and hatred for my love.

1. "*Hold not thy peace.*" Mine enemies speak, be thou pleased to speak too. Break thy solemn silence, and silence those who slander me. It is the cry of a man whose confidence in God is deep, and whose communion with him is very close and bold. Note, that he only asks the Lord to speak : a word from God is all a believer needs. "*O God of my praise.*" Thou whom my whole soul praises, be pleased to protect my honour and guard my praise. "My heart is fixed," said he in the former Psalm, " I will sing and give praise," and now he appeals to the God whom he had praised. If we take care of God's honour he will take care of ours. We may look to him as the guardian of our character if we truly seek his glory. If we live to God's praise, he will in the long run give us praise among men.

2. "*For the mouth of the wicked and the mouth of the deceitful are opened against me.*" Wicked men must needs say wicked things, and these we have reason to dread ; but in addition they utter false and deceitful things, and these are worst of all. There is no knowing what may come out of mouths which are at once lewd and lying. The misery caused to a good man by slanderous reports no heart can imagine but that which is wounded by them : in all Satan's armoury there are no worse weapons than deceitful tongues. To have a reputation, over which we have watched with daily care, suddenly bespattered with the foulest aspersions, is painful beyond description ; but when wicked and deceitful men get their mouths fully opened we can hardly expect to escape any more than others. "*They have spoken against me with a lying tongue.*" Lying tongues cannot lie still. Bad tongues are not content to vilify bad men, but choose the most gracious of saints to be the objects of their attacks. Here is reason enough for prayer. The heart sinks when assailed with slander, for we know not what may be said next, what friend may be alienated, what evil may be threatened, or what misery may be caused to us and others. The air is full of rumours, and shadows impalpable flit around ; the mind is confused with dread of unseen foes and invisible arrows. What ill can be worse than to be assailed with slander,

"Whose edge is sharper than the sword, whose tongue
Outvenoms all the worms of Nile " ?

3. "*They compassed me about also with words of hatred.*" Turn which way he would they hedged him in with falsehood, misrepresentation, accusation, and scorn. Whispers, sneers, insinuations, satires, and open charges filled his ear with a perpetual buzz, and all for no reason, but sheer hate. Each word was as full of venom as an egg is full of meat : they could not speak without showing their teeth. "*And fought against me without a cause.*" He had not provoked the quarrel or contributed to it, yet in a thousand ways they laboured to " corrode his comfort, and destroy his ease." All this tended to make the suppliant feel the more acutely the wrongs which were done to him.

4. "*For my love they are my adversaries.*" They hate me because I love them. One of our poets says of the Lord Jesus—" Found guilty of excess of love." Surely it was his only fault. Our Lord might have used all the language of this complaint most emphatically—they hated him without a cause and returned him hatred for love. What a smart this is to the soul, to be hated in proportion to the gratitude which it deserved, hated by those it loved, and hated because of its love. This was a cruel case, and the sensitive mind of the Psalmist writhed under it. "*But I give myself unto prayer.*" He did nothing else but pray. He became prayer as they became malice. This was his answer to his enemies, he appealed from men and their injustice to the Judge of all the earth, who must do right. True bravery alone can teach a man to leave his traducers unanswered, and carry the case unto the Lord.

" Men cannot help but reverence the courage that walketh amid calumnies unanswering."

" He standeth as a gallant chief unheeding shot or shell."

5. " *And they have rewarded me evil for good, and hatred for my love.*" Evil for good is devil-like. This is Satan's line of action, and his children upon earth follow it greedily : it is cruel, and wounds to the quick. The revenge which pays a man back in his own coin has a kind of natural justice in it ; but what shall be said of that baseness which returns to goodness the very opposite of what it has a right to expect ? Our Lord endured such base treatment all his days, and, alas, in his members, endures it still.

Thus we see the harmless and innocent man upon his knees pouring out his lamentation : we are now to observe him rising from the mercy-seat, inspired with prophetic energy, and pouring forth upon his foes the forewarnings of their doom. We shall hear him speak like a judge clothed with stern severity, or like the angel of doom robed in vengeance, or as the naked sword of justice when she bares her arm for execution. It is not for himself that he speaks so much as for all the slandered and the down-trodden, of whom he feels himself to be the representative and mouth-piece. He asks for justice, and as his soul is stung with cruel wrongs he asks with solemn deliberation, making no stint in his demands. To pity malice would be malice to mankind ; to screen the crafty seekers of human blood would be cruelty to the oppressed. Nay, love, and truth, and pity lift their wounds to heaven, and implore vengeance on the enemies of the innocent and oppressed ; those who render goodness itself a crime, and make innocence a motive for hate, deserve to find no mercy from the great Preserver of men. Vengeance is the prerogative of God, and as it would be a boundless calamity if evil were for ever to go unpunished, so it is an unspeakable blessing that the Lord will recompense the wicked and cruel man, and there are times and seasons when a good man ought to pray for that blessing. When the Judge of all threatens to punish tyrannical cruelty and falsehearted treachery, virtue gives her assent and consent. Amen, so let it be, saith every just man in his inmost soul.

6 Set thou a wicked man over him : and let Satan stand at his right hand.

7 When he shall be judged, let him be condemned : and let his prayer become sin.

8 Let his days be few ; *and* let another take his office.

9 Let his children be fatherless, and his wife a widow.

10 Let his children be continually vagabonds, and beg : let them seek *their bread* also out of their desolate places.

11 Let the extortioner catch all that he hath ; and let the strangers spoil his labour.

12 Let there be none to extend mercy unto him : neither let there be any to favour his fatherless children.

13 Let his posterity be cut off ; *and* in the generation following let their name be blotted out.

14 Let the iniquity of his fathers be remembered with the LORD ; and let not the sin of his mother be blotted out.

15 Let them be before the LORD continually, that he may cut off the memory of them from the earth.

16 Because that he remembered not to shew mercy, but persecuted the poor and needy man, that he might even slay the broken in heart.

17 As he loved cursing, so let it come unto him : as he delighted not in blessing, so let it be far from him.

18 As he clothed himself with cursing like as with his garment, so let it come into his bowels like water, and like oil into his bones.

19 Let it be unto him as the garment *which* covereth him, and for a girdle wherewith he is girded continually.

20 *Let* this *be* the reward of mine adversaries from the LORD, and of them that speak evil against my soul.

6. *"Set thou a wicked man over him."* What worse punishment could a man have ? The proud man cannot endure the proud, nor the oppressor brook the rule of another like himself. The righteous in their patience find the rule of the wicked a sore bondage ; but those who are full of resentful passions, and haughty aspirations, are slaves indeed when men of their own class have the whip hand of them. For Herod to be ruled by another Herod would be wretchedness enough, and yet what retribution could be more just ? What unrighteous man can complain if he finds himself governed by one of like character ? What can the wicked expect but that their rulers should be like themselves ? Who does not admire the justice of God when he sees fierce Romans ruled by Tiberius and Nero, and Red Republicans governed by Marat and Robespierre ? *" And let Satan stand at his right hand."* Should not like come to like ? Should not the father of lies stand near his children ? Who is a better right-hand friend for an adversary of the righteous than the great adversary himself ? The curse is an awful one, but it is most natural that it should come to pass : those who serve Satan may expect to have his company, his assistance, his temptations, and at last his doom.

7. *" When he shall be judged, let him be condemned."* He judged and condemned others in the vilest manner, he suffered not the innocent to escape ; and it would be a great shame if in his time of trial, being really guilty, he should be allowed to go free. Who would wish Judge Jeffries to be acquitted if he were tried for perverting justice ? Who would desire Nero or Caligula to be cleared if set at the bar for cruelty ? When Shylock goes into court, who wishes him to win his suit ? *" And let his prayer become sin."* It is sin already, let it be so treated. To the injured it must seem terrible that the black-hearted villain should nevertheless pretend to pray, and very naturally do they beg that he may not be heard, but that his pleadings may be regarded as an addition to his guilt. He has devoured the widow's house, and yet he prays. He has put Naboth to death by false accusation and taken possession of his vineyard, and then he presents prayers to the Almighty. He has given up villages to slaughter, and his hands are red with the blood of babes and maidens, and then he pays his vows unto Allah ! He must surely be accursed himself who does not wish that such abominable prayers may be loathed of heaven and written down as new sins. He who makes it a sin for others to pray will find his own praying become sin. When he at last sees his need of mercy, mercy herself shall resent his appeal as an insult. *" Because that he remembered not to show mercy,"* he shall himself be forgotten by the God of grace, and his bitter cries for deliverance shall be regarded as mockeries of heaven.

8. *" Let his days be few."* Who would desire a persecuting tyrant to live long ? As well might we wish length of days to a mad dog. If he will do nothing but mischief the shortening of his life will be the lengthening of the world's tranquillity. *" Bloody and deceitful men shall not live out half their days,"*—this is bare justice to them, and great mercy to the poor and needy. *" And let another take his office."* Perhaps a better man may come, at any rate it is time a change were tried. So used were the Jews to look upon these verses as the doom of traitors, of cruel and deceitful mind, that Peter saw at once in the speedy death of Judas a fulfilment of this sentence, and a reason for the appointment of a successor who should take his place of oversight. A bad man does not make an office bad : another may use with benefit that which he perverted to ill uses.

9. *" Let his children be fatherless, and his wife a widow."* This would inevitably be the case when the man died, but the Psalmist uses the words in an emphatic sense, he would have his widow " a widow indeed," and his children so friendless as to be orphaned in the bitterest sense. He sees the result of the bad man's decease, and includes it in the punishment. The tyrant's sword makes many children fatherless, and who can lament when his barbarities come home to his own family, and they, too, weep and lament. Pity is due to all orphans and widows as such, but a father's atrocious actions may dry up the springs of pity. Who mourns that Pharaoh's children lost their father, or that Sennacherib's wife became a widow ? As Agag's sword had made women childless none wept when Samuel's weapon made his mother childless among women. If Herod had been slain when he had just murdered the innocents at Bethlehem no man would have lamented it even though Herod's wife would have become a widow. These awful maledictions are not for common men to use, but for judges, such as David was, to pronounce over the enemies of God and man. A judge may sentence a man to death whatever the consequences may be to the criminal's family, and in this there will be no feeling of private revenge, but

simply the doing of justice because evil must be punished. We are aware that this may not appear to justify the full force of these expressions, but it should never be forgotten that the case supposed is a very execrable one, and the character of the culprit is beyond measure loathsome and not to be met by any common abhorrence. Those who regard a sort of effeminate benevolence to all creatures alike as the acme of virtue are very much in favour with this degenerate age ; these look for the salvation of the damned, and even pray for the restoration of the devil. It is very possible that if they were less in sympathy with evil, and more in harmony with the thoughts of God, they would be of a far sterner and also of a far better mind. To us it seems better to agree with God's curses than with the devil's blessings ; and when at any time our heart kicks against the terrors of the Lord we take it as a proof of our need of greater humbling, and confess our sin before our God.

10. " *Let his children be continually vagabonds, and beg.*" May they have neither house nor home, settlement nor substance ; and while they thus wander and beg may it ever be on their memory that their father's house lies in ruins,—" *let them seek their bread also out of their desolate places.*" It has often been so : a race of tyrants has become a generation of beggars. Misused power and abused wealth have earned the family name universal detestation, and secured to the family character an entail of baseness. Justice herself would award no such doom except upon the supposition that the sin descended with the blood ; but supreme providence which in the end is pure justice has written many a page of history in which the imprecation of this verse has been literally verified.

We confess that as we read some of these verses we have need of all our faith and reverence to accept them as the voice of inspiration ; but the exercise is good for the soul, for it educates our sense of ignorance, and tests our teachableness. Yes, Divine Spirit, we can and do believe that even these dread words from which we shrink have a meaning consistent with the attributes of the Judge of all the earth, though his name is LOVE. How this may be we shall know hereafter.

11. " *Let the extortioner catch all that he hath.*" A doom indeed. Those who have once fallen into the hands of the usurer can tell you what this means : it were better to be a fly in the web of a spider. In the most subtle, worrying, and sweeping manner the extortioner takes away, piece by piece, his victim's estate, till not a fraction remains to form a pittance for old age. Baiting his trap, watching it carefully, and dexterously driving his victim into it, the extortioner by legal means performs unlawful deeds, *catches* his bird, strips him of every feather, and cares not if he die of starvation. He robs with law to protect him, and steals with the magistrate at his back : to fall into his clutches is worse than to be beset by professed thieves. " *And let the strangers spoil his labour,*"—so that his kindred may have none of it. What with hard creditors and pilfering strangers the estate must soon vanish ! Extortion drawing one way, and spoliation the other, a known moneylender and an unknown robber both at work, the man's substance would soon disappear, and rightly so, for it was gathered by shameless means. This too has been frequently seen. Wealth amassed by oppression has seldom lasted to the third generation : it was gathered by wrong and by wrong it is scattered, and who would decree that it should be otherwise ? Certainly those who suffer beneath high-handed fraud will not wish to stay the retributions of the Almighty, nor would those who see the poor robbed and trampled on desire to alter the divine arrangements by which such evils are recompensed even in this life.

12. " *Let there be none to extend mercy unto him.*" He had no mercy, but on the contrary, he crushed down all who appealed to him. Loath to smite him with his own weapon, stern justice can do no otherwise, she lifts her scales and sees that this, too, must be in the sentence. " *Neither let there be any to favour his fatherless children.*" We are staggered to find the children included in the father's sentence, and yet as a matter of fact children do suffer for their father's sins, and, as long as the affairs of this life are ordered as they are, it must be so. So involved are the interests of the race, that it is quite impossible in all respects to view the father and the child apart. No man among us could desire to see the fatherless suffer for their deceased father's fault, yet so it happens, and there is no injustice in the fact. They share the parent's ill-gotten gain or rank, and their aggrandizement is a part of the object at which he aimed in the perpetration of his crimes ; to allow them to prosper would be an encouragement and reward of his iniquity ; therefore, for these and other reasons, a man perishes not alone in his iniquity. The ban is on his race. If the man were innocent this would be a crime ; if he were but commonly guilty it

would be excessive retribution; but when the offence reeks before high heaven in unutterable abomination, it is little marvel that men devote the man's whole house to perpetual infamy, and that so it happeneth.

13. "*Let his posterity be cut off; and in the generation following let their name be blotted out.*" Both from existence and from memory let them pass away till none shall know that such a vile brood existed. Who wishes to see the family of Domitian or Julian continued upon earth? Who would mourn if the race of Tom Paine or of Voltaire should come to an utter end? It would be undesirable that the sons of the utterly villainous and bloodthirsty should rise to honour, and if they did they would only revive the memory of their father's sins.

14. This verse is, perhaps, the most terrible of all, but yet as a matter of fact children do procure punishment upon their parents' sins, and are often themselves the means of such punishment. A bad son brings to mind his father's bad points of character; people say, "Ah, he is like the old man. He takes after his father." A mother's sins also will be sure to be called to mind if her daughter becomes grossly wicked. "Ah," they will say, "there is little wonder, when you consider what her mother was." These are matters of everyday occurrence. We cannot, however, pretend to explain the righteousness of this malediction, though we fully believe in it. We leave it till our heavenly Father is pleased to give us further instruction. Yet, as a man's faults are often learned from his parents, it is not unjust that his consequent crimes should recoil upon him.

15. Again, he wishes that his father's sins may follow up the transgressor and assist to fill the measure of his own iniquities, so that for the whole accumulated load the family may be smitten with utter extinction. A king might justly wish for such an end to fall upon an incorrigible brood of rebels; and of persecutors, continuing in the same mind, the saints might well pray for their extinction; but the passage is dark; and we must leave it so. It must be right or it would not be here, but how we cannot see. Why should we expect to understand all things? Perhaps it is more for our benefit to exercise humility, and reverently worship God over a hard text, than it would be to comprehend all mysteries.

16. "*Because that he remembered not to shew mercy.*" Because he had no memory to show mercy the Judge of all will have a strong memory of his sins. So little mercy had he ever shown that he had forgotten how to do it, he was without common humanity, devoid of compassion, and therefore only worthy to be dealt with after the bare rule of justice. "*But persecuted the poor and needy man.*" He looked on poor men as a nuisance upon the earth, he ground their faces, oppressed them in their wages, and treated them as the mire of the streets. Should he not be punished, and in his turn laid low? All who know him are indignant at his brutalities, and will glory to see him overthrown. "*That he might even slay the broken in heart.*" He had malice in his heart towards one who was already sufficiently sorrowful, whom it was a superfluity of malignity to attack. Yet no grief excited sympathy in him, no poverty ever moved him to relent. No, he would kill the heart-broken and rob their orphans of their patrimony. To him groans were music, and tears were wine, and drops of blood precious rubies. Would any man spare such a monster? Will it not be serving the ends of humanity if we wish him gone, gone to the throne of God to receive his reward? If he will turn and repent, well: but if not, such a upas tree ought to be felled and cast into the fire. As men kill mad dogs if they can, and justly too, so may we lawfully wish that cruel oppressors of the poor were removed from their place and office, and, as an example to others, made to smart for their barbarities.

17. "*As he loved cursing, so let it come unto him.*" Deep down in every man's soul the justice of the *lex talionis* is established. Retaliation, not for private revenge, but as a measure of public justice, is demanded by the Psalmist and deserved by the crime. Surely the malicious man cannot complain if he is judged by his own rule, and has his corn measured with his own bushel. Let him have what he loved. They are his own chickens, and they ought to come home to roost. He made the bed, let him lie on it himself. As he brewed, so let him drink. So all men say as a matter of justice, and though the higher law of love overrides all personal anger, yet as against the base characters here described even Christian love would not wish to see the sentence mitigated. "*As he delighted not in blessing, so let it be far from him.*" He felt no joy in any man's good, nor would he lift a hand to do another a service, rather did he frown and fret when another prospered or mirth was heard under his window; what, then, can we wish him? Blessing was wasted on him, he hated

those who gently sought to lead him to a better mind ; even the blessings of providence he received with murmurs and repinings, he wished for famine to raise the
price of his corn, and for war to increase his trade. Evil was good to him, and good
he counted evil. If he could have blasted every field of corn in the world he would
have done so if he could have turned a penny by it, or if he could thereby have
injured the good man whom he hated from his very soul. What can we wish for him ?
He hunts after evil, he hates good ; he lays himself out to ruin the godly whom God
has blessed, he is the devil's friend, and as fiendish as his patron ; should things go
well with such a being ? Shall we " wish him good luck in the name of the Lord " ?
To invoke blessings on such a man would be to participate in his wickedness, therefore
let blessing be far from him, so long as he continues what he now is.

18, 19. He was so openly in the habit of wishing ill to others that he seemed
to wear robes of cursing, therefore let it be as his raiment girded and belted about
him, yea, let it enter as water into his bowels, and search the very marrow of his bones
like a penetrating oil. It is but common justice that he should receive a return for
his malice, and receive it in kind, too.

20. This is the summing up of the entire imprecation, and fixes it upon the persons
who had so maliciously assailed the inoffensive man of God. David was a man of
gentle mould, and remarkably free from the spirit of revenge, and therefore we may
here conceive him to be speaking as a judge or as a representative man, in whose
person great principles needed to be vindicated and great injuries redressed.

Thousands of God's people are perplexed with this Psalm, and we fear we have
contributed very little towards their enlightenment, and perhaps the notes we have
gathered from others, since they display such a variety of view, may only increase
the difficulty. What then ? Is it not good for us sometimes to be made to feel that
we are not yet able to understand all the word and mind of God ? A thorough
bewilderment, so long as it does not stagger our faith, may be useful to us by confounding our pride, arousing our faculties, and leading us to cry, " What I know
not teach thou me."

21 But do thou for me, O God the Lord, for thy name's sake : because
thy mercy *is* good, deliver thou me.

22 For I *am* poor and needy, and my heart is wounded within me.

23 I am gone like the shadow when it declineth : I am tossed up and
down as the locust.

24 My knees are weak through fasting ; and my flesh faileth of fatness.

25 I became also a reproach unto them : *when* they looked upon me they
shaked their heads.

26 Help me, O Lord my God : O save me according to thy mercy :

27 That they may know that this *is* thy hand ; *that* thou, Lord, hast
done it.

28 Let them curse, but bless thou : when they arise, let them be ashamed ;
but let thy servant rejoice.

29 Let mine adversaries be clothed with shame, and let them cover themselves with their own confusion, as with a mantle.

30 I will greatly praise the Lord with my mouth ; yea, I will praise him
among the multitude.

31 For he shall stand at the right hand of the poor, to save *him* from
those that condemn his soul.

21. " *But do thou for me, O God the Lord, for thy name's sake.*" How eagerly
he turns from his enemies to his God ! He sets the great Thou in opposition to
all his adversaries, and you see at once that his heart is at rest. The words are
very indistinct, and though our version may not precisely translate them, yet it
in a remarkable manner hits upon the sense and upon the obscurity which hang
over it. " Do thou for me "—what shall he do ? Why, do whatever he thinks
fit. He leaves himself in the Lord's hands, dictating nothing, but quite content
so long as his God will but undertake for him. His plea is not his own merit, but
the name. The saints have always felt this to be their most mighty plea. God

himself has performed his grandest deeds of grace for the honour of his name, and his people know that this is the most potent argument with him. What the Lord himself has guarded with sacred jealousy we should reverence with our whole hearts and rely upon without distrust. *"Because thy mercy is good, deliver thou me."* Not because I am good, but because thy mercy is good : see how the saints fetch their pleadings in prayer from the Lord himself. God's mercy is the star to which the Lord's people turn their eye when they are tossed with tempest and not comforted, for the peculiar bounty and goodness of that mercy have a charm for weary hearts. When man has no mercy we shall still find it in God. When man would devour we may look to God to deliver. His name and his mercy are two firm grounds for hope, and happy are those who know how to rest upon them.

22. *"For I am poor and needy."* When he does plead anything about himself he urges not his riches or his merits, but his poverty and his necessities : this is gospel supplication, such as only the Spirit of God can indite upon the heart. This lowliness does not comport with the supposed vengeful spirit of the preceding verses : there must therefore be some interpretation of them which would make them suitable in the lips of a lowly-minded man of God. *"And my heart is wounded within me."* The Lord has always a tender regard to broken-hearted ones, and such the Psalmist had become : the undeserved cruelty, the baseness, the slander of his remorseless enemies had pierced him to the soul, and this sad condition he pleads as a reason for speedy help. It is time for a friend to step in when the adversary cuts so deep. The case has become desperate without divine aid ; now, therefore, is the Lord's time.

23. *"I am gone like the shadow when it declineth."* I am a mere shadow, a shadow at the vanishing point, when it stretches far, but is almost lost in the universal gloom of evening which settles over all, and so obliterates the shadows cast by the setting sun. Lord, there is next to nothing left of me, wilt thou not come in before I am quite gone ? *"I am tossed up and down as the locust,"* which is the sport of the winds, and must go up or down as the breeze carries it. The Psalmist felt as powerless in his distress as a poor insect, which a child may toss up and down at its pleasure. He entreats the divine pity, because he had been brought to this forlorn and feeble condition by the long persecution which his tender heart had endured. Slander and malice are apt to produce nervous disorders and to lead on to pining diseases. Those who use these poisoned arrows are not always aware of the consequences ; they scatter firebrands and death and say it is sport.

24. *"My knees are weak through fasting ; "* either religious fasting, to which he resorted in the dire extremity of his grief, or else through loss of appetite occasioned by distress of mind. Who can eat when every morsel is soured by envy ? This is the advantage of the slanderer, that he feels nothing himself, while his sensitive victim can scarcely eat a morsel of bread because of his sensitiveness. However, the good God knoweth all this, and will succour his afflicted. The Lord who bids us confirm the feeble knees will assuredly do it himself. *"And my flesh faileth of fatness."* He was wasted to a skeleton, and as his body was emaciated, so was his soul bereft of comfort : he was pining away, and all the while his enemies saw it and laughed at his distress. How pathetically he states his case ; this is one of the truest forms of prayer, the setting forth of our sorrow before the Lord. Weak knees are strong with God, and failing flesh has great power in pleading.

25. *"I became also a reproach unto them."* They made him the theme of ridicule, the butt of their ribald jests : his emaciation by fasting made him a tempting subject for their caricatures and lampoons. *"When they looked upon me they shaked their heads."* Words were not a sufficient expression of their scorn, they resorted to gestures which were meant both to show their derision and to irritate his mind. Though these things break no bones, yet they do worse, for they break and bruise far tenderer parts of us. Many a man who could have answered a malicious speech, and so have relieved his mind, has felt keenly a sneer, a putting out of the tongue, or some other sign of contempt. Those, too, who are exhausted by such fasting and wasting as the last verse describes are generally in a state of morbid sensibility, and therefore feel more acutely the unkindness of others. What they would smile at during happier seasons becomes intolerable when they are in a highly nervous condition.

26. *"Help me, O Lord my God."* Laying hold of Jehovah by the appropriating word *my*, he implores his aid both to help him to bear his heavy load and to enable him to rise superior to it. He has described his own weakness, and the strength and fury of his foes, and by these two arguments he urges his appeal with double force.

This is a very rich, short, and suitable prayer for believers in any situation of peril, difficulty, or sorrow. " *O save me according to thy mercy.*" As thy mercy is, so let thy salvation be. The measure is a great one, for the mercy of God is without bound. When man has no mercy it is comforting to fall back upon God's mercy. Justice to the wicked is often mercy to the righteous, and because God is merciful he will save his people by overthrowing their adversaries.

27. " *That they may know that this is thy hand.*" Dolts as they are, let the mercy shown to me be so conspicuous that they shall be forced to see the Lord's agency in it. Ungodly men will not see God's hand in anything if they can help it, and when they see good men delivered into their power they become more confirmed than ever in their atheism ; but all in good time God will arise and so effectually punish their malice and rescue the object of their spite that they will be compelled to say like the Egyptian magicians, " this is the finger of God." " *That thou, Lord, hast done it.*" There will be no mistaking the author of so thorough a vindication, so complete a turning of the tables.

28. " *Let them curse, but bless thou,*" or, " *they will curse and thou wilt bless.*" Their cursing will then be of such little consequence that it will not matter a straw. One blessing from the Lord will take the poison out of ten thousand curses of men. " *When they arise, let them be ashamed.*" They lift up themselves to deal out another blow, to utter another falsehood, and to watch for its injurious effects upon their victim, but they see their own defeat and are filled with shame. " *But let thy servant rejoice.*" Not merely as a man protected and rescued, but as God's servant in whom his master's goodness and glory are displayed when he is saved from his foes. It ought to be our greatest joy that the Lord is honoured in our experience ; the mercy itself ought not so much to rejoice us as the glory which is thereby brought to him who so graciously bestows it.

29. " *Let mine adversaries be clothed with shame.*" It is a prophecy as well as a wish, and may we read both in the indicative and the imperative. Where sin is the underclothing, shame will soon be the outer vesture. He who would clothe good men with contempt shall himself be clothed with dishonour. " *And let them cover themselves with their own confusion, as with a mantle.*" Let their confusion be broad enough to wrap them all over from head to foot, let them bind it about them and hide themselves in it, as being utterly afraid to be seen. Now they walk abroad unblushingly and reveal their own wickedness, acting as if they either had nothing to conceal or did not care whether it was seen or no ; but they will be of another mind when the great Judge deals with them, then will they entreat mountains to hide them and hills to fall upon them, that they may not be seen : but all in vain, they must be dragged to the bar with no other covering but their own confusion.

30. " *I will greatly praise the Lord with my mouth.*" Enthusiastically, abundantly, and loudly will he extol the righteous Lord, who redeemed him from all evil ; and that not only in his own chamber or among his own family, but in the most public manner. " *Yea, I will praise him among the multitude.*" Remarkable and public providences demand public recognition, for otherwise men of the world will judge us to be ungrateful. We do not praise God to be heard of men, but as a natural sense of justice leads every one to expect to hear a befriended person speak well of his benefactor, we therefore have regard to such natural and just expectations, and endeavour to make our praises as public as the benefit we have received. The singer in the present case is the man whose heart was wounded within him because he was the laughing-stock of remorseless enemies ; yet now he praises, praises greatly, praises aloud, praises in the teeth of all gainsayers, and praises with a right joyous spirit. Never let us despair, yea, never let us cease to praise.

31. " *For he shall stand at the right hand of the poor.*" God will not be absent when his people are on their trial ; he will hold a brief for them and stand in court as their advocate, prepared to plead on their behalf. How different is this from the doom of the ungodly who has Satan at his right hand (verse 6). " *To save him from those that condemn his soul.*" The court only met as a matter of form, the malicious had made up their minds to the verdict, they judged him guilty, for their hate condemned him, yea, they pronounced sentence of damnation upon the very soul of their victim : but what mattered it ? The great King was in court, and their sentence was turned against themselves. Nothing can more sweetly sustain the heart of a slandered believer than the firm conviction that God is near to all who are wronged, and is sure to work out their salvation.

O Lord, save us from the severe trial of slander : deal in thy righteousness with all those who spitefully assail the characters of holy men, and cause all who are smarting under calumny and reproach to come forth unsullied from the affliction, even as did thine only-begotten Son. Amen.

EXPLANATORY NOTES AND QUAINT SAYINGS.

Whole Psalm.—" *Mysterious* " was the one word written opposite this Psalm in the pocket Bible of a late devout and popular writer. It represents the utter perplexity with which it is very generally regarded.—*Joseph Hammond.*

Whole Psalm.—In this Psalm David is supposed to refer to Doeg the Edomite, or to Ahithophel. It is the most imprecatory of the Psalms, and may well be termed *the Iscariot Psalm.* What David here refers to his mortal enemy, finds its accomplishment in the betrayer of the Son of David. It is from the 8th verse that Peter infers the necessity of filling up the vacancy occasioned by the death of Judas : it was, says he, predicted that another should take his office.—*Paton J. Gloag, in " A Commentary on the Acts,"* 1870.

Whole Psalm.—We may consider Judas, at the same time, as the virtual head of the Jewish nation in their daring attempt to dethrone the Son of God. The doom pronounced, and the reasons for it, apply to the Jews as a nation, as well as to the leader of the band who took Jesus.—*Andrew A. Bonar.*

Whole Psalm.—Is it possible that this perplexing and distressing Psalm presents us after all, not with David's maledictions upon his enemies, but with their maledictions upon him ? Not only do I hold this interpretation to be quite legitimate, I hold it to be by far the more natural and reasonable interpretation.—*Joseph Hammond.*

[In Dr. Cox's *Expositor,* Vol. II. p. 225, this theory is well elaborated by Mr. Hammond, but we cannot for an instant accept it.—*C. H. S.*]

The Imprecations of the Psalm.—The language has been justified, not as the language of David, but as the language of Christ, exercising his office of Judge, or, in so far as he had laid aside that office during his earthly life, calling upon his Father to accomplish the curse. It has been alleged that this is the prophetic foreshadowing of the solemn words, " Woe unto that man by whom the Son of Man is betrayed ! it had been good for that man if he had not been born " (Matt. xxvi. 24). The curse in the words of Chrysostom is, " a prophecy in the form of a curse" (προφητεία ἐν εἴδει ἀρᾶς).

The strain which such a view compels us to put on much of the language ought to have led long since to its abandonment. Not even the words denounced by our Lord against the Pharisees can really be compared to the anathemas which are here strung together. Much less is there any pretence for saying that those words so full of deep and holy sorrow, addressed to the traitor in the gospels, are merely another expression of the appalling denunciations of the Psalm. But terrible as these undoubtedly are, to be accounted for by the spirit of the Old Dispensation, not to be defended by that of the New, still let us learn to estimate them aright.— *J. J. Stewart Perowne.*

The Imprecations.—These imprecations are not appropriate in the mouth of the suffering Saviour. It is not the spirit of Zion but of Sinai which here speaks out of the mouth of David ; the spirit of Elias, which, according to Luke ix. 58, is not the spirit of the New Testament. This wrathful spirit is overpowered by the spirit of love. But these anathemas are still not on this account so many beatings of the air. There is in them a divine energy, as in the blessing and cursing of every man who is united to God, and more especially of a man whose temper of mind is such as David's. They possess the same power as the prophetical threatenings, and in this sense they are regarded in the New Testament as fulfilled in the son of perdition (John xvii. 12). To the generation of the time of Jesus they were a deterrent warning not to offend against the Holy One of God, and this *Psalmus Ischarioticus* (Acts i. 20) will ever be such a mirror of warning to the enemies and persecutors of Christ and his church.—*Franz Delitzsch.*

The Imprecations.—Respecting the imprecations contained in this Psalm, it will be proper to keep in mind what I have said elsewhere, that when David forms such maledictions, or expresses his desire for them, he is not instigated by any immoderate carnal propensity, nor is he actuated by zeal without knowledge, nor is he influenced by any private personal considerations. These three matters must be carefully weighed, for in proportion to the amount of self-esteem which a man possesses, is he so enamoured with his own interests as to rush headlong upon revenge. Hence it comes to pass that the more a person is devoted to selfishness, he will be the more immoderately addicted to the advancement of his own individual interests. This desire for the promotion of personal interest gives birth to another species of vice : for no one wishes to be avenged upon his enemies because such a thing would be right and equitable, but because it is the means of gratifying his own spiteful propensity. Some, indeed, make a pretext of righteousness and equity in the matter ; but the spirit of malignity, by which they are inflamed, effaces every trace of justice, and blinds their minds.

When the two vices, selfishness and carnality, are corrected, there is still another thing demanding correction : we must repress the ardour of foolish zeal, in order that we may follow the Spirit of God as our guide. Should any one, under the influence of perverse zeal, produce David as an example of it, that would not be an example in point ; for to such a person may be very aptly applied the answer which Christ returned to his disciples, " Ye know not what spirit ye are of," Luke ix. 55. How detestable a piece of sacrilege is it on the part of the monks, and especially the Franciscan friars, to pervert this Psalm by employing it to countenance the most nefarious purposes ! If a man harbour malice against a neighbour, it is quite a common thing for him to engage one of those wicked wretches to curse him, which he would do by daily repeating this Psalm. I know a lady in France who hired a parcel of these friars to curse her own and only son in these words. But I return to David, who, free from all inordinate passion, breathed forth his prayers under the influence of the Holy Spirit.—*John Calvin.*

The Imprecations.—It is possible, as Tholuck thinks, that in some of the utterances in what are called the *vindictive Psalms*, especially the imprecations in Psalm cix., unholy personal zeal may have been mingled with holy zeal, as was the case seemingly with the two disciples James and John, when the Lord chided their desire for vengeance (Luke ix. 54—56). But, in reality, the feeling expressed in these Psalms may well be considered as virtuous anger, such as Bishop Butler explains and justifies in his sermons on " Resentment and the Forgiveness of Injuries," and such as Paul teaches in Ephesians iv. 26, " Be ye angry, and sin not." Anger against sin and a desire that evildoers may be punished, are not opposed to the spirit of the gospel, or to that love of enemies which our Lord both enjoined and exemplified. If the emotion or its utterance were essentially sinful, how could Paul wish the enemy of Christ and the perverter of the gospel to be accursed (ἀνάθεμα, 1 Cor. xvi. 22 ; Gal. i. 8) ; and especially, how could the spirit of the martyred saints in heaven call on God for vengeance (Rev. vi. 10), and join to celebrate its final execution (Rev. xix. 1—6) ; Yea, resentment against the wicked is so far from being necessarily sinful that we find it manifested by the Holy and Just One himself, when in the days of his flesh he looked around on his hearers " with anger, being grieved for the hardness of their hearts " (Mark iii. 5) ; and when in " the great day of his wrath " (Rev. vi. 17), he shall say to " all workers of iniquity " (Luke xiii. 27), " Depart from me, ye cursed " (Matt. xxv. 41).—*Benjamin Davies* (1814—1875), *in Kitto's Cyclopædia.*

Imprecations.—It is true that this vengeance is invoked on the head of the betrayer of Christ : and we may profit by reading even the severest of the passages when we regard them as dictated by a burning zeal for the honour of Jehovah, a righteous indignation and a jealousy of love, and generally, if not universally, as denunciations of just judgment against the obstinate enemies of Christ, and all who obey not the Gospel of God. At the same time, these passages cannot be fully accounted for without a frank recognition of the fact that the Psalter was conceived and written under the Old Covenant. That dispensation was more stern than ours. God's people had with all other peoples a conflict with sword and spear. They wanted to tread down their enemies, to crush the heathen ; and thought it a grand religious triumph for a righteous man to wash his feet in the blood of the wicked, Ps. lviii. 10 ; lxviii. 23. Now the struggle is without carnal weapons, and the tone of the dispensation is changed.—*Donald Fraser,* 1873.

Imprecations.—Imprecations of judgment on the wicked *on the hypothesis of their continued impenitence* are not inconsistent with simultaneous efforts to bring them to repentance ; and Christian charity itself can do no more than labour for the sinners' conversion. The law of holiness requires us to pray for the fires of divine retribution : the law of love to seek meanwhile to rescue the brand from the burning. The last prayer of the martyr Stephen was answered not by any general averting of doom from a guilty nation, but by the conversion of an individual persecutor to the service of God.—*Joseph Francis Thrupp.*

Imprecations.—That explanation which regards the "enemies" as spiritual foes has a large measure of truth. It commended itself to a mind so far removed from mysticism as Arnold's. It is most valuable for devout private use of the Psalter. For, though we are come to Mount Sion, crested with the eternal calm, the opened ear can hear the thunder rolling along the peaks of Sinai. In the Gospel, the wrath of God is revealed from heaven against all ungodliness and unrighteousness. Sin is utterly hateful to God. The broad gates are flung wide open to the city that lies foursquare towards all the winds of heaven ; for its ruler is divinely tolerant. But there shall in no wise enter it anything that defileth, neither whatever worketh abomination ; for he is divinely intolerant too. And thus when, in public or private, we read these Psalms of imprecation, there is a lesson that comes home to us. We must read them, or dishonour God's word. Reading them, we must depart from sin, or pronounce judgment upon ourselves. Drunkenness, impurity, hatred, every known sin of flesh or spirit—these, and not mistaken men, are the worst enemies of God and of his Christ. Against these we pray in our Collects for Peace at Morning and Evening Prayer—"Defend us in all assaults of our enemies, that by thee we being defended from the fear of our enemies, may pass our time in rest and quietness." These were the dark hosts which swept through the Psalmist's vision when he cried, "Let all mine enemies be ashamed and sore vexed," Ps. vi. 10.—*William Alexander, in " The Witness of the Psalms to Christ and Christianity,"* 1877.

Imprecations.—I cannot forbear the following little incident that occurred the other morning at family worship. I happened to be reading one of the imprecatory Psalms, and as I paused to remark, my little boy, a lad of ten years, asked with some earnestness : "Father, do you think it right for a good man to pray for the destruction of his enemies like that ? " and at the same time referred me to Christ as praying for his enemies. I paused a moment to know how to shape the reply so as to fully meet and satisfy his enquiry, and then said, " My son, if an assassin should enter the house by night, and murder your mother, and then escape, and the sheriff and citizens were all out in pursuit, trying to catch him, would you not pray to God that they might succeed and arrest him, and that he might be brought to justice ? " " Oh, yes ! " said he, " but I never saw it so before. I did not know that that was the meaning of these Psalms." " Yes," said I, " my son, the men against whom David prays were bloody men, men of falsehood and crime, enemies to the peace of society, seeking his own life, and unless they were arrested and their wicked devices defeated, many innocent persons must suffer." The explanation perfectly satisfied his mind.—*F. G. Hibbard, in " The Psalms chronologically arranged,"* 1856.

Title.—It is worth noting, that the superscription, " *to the chief Musician,*" to the precentor (לַמְנַצֵּחַ), proves it to have been designed, such as it is, for the Tabernacle or Temple service of song.—*Joseph Hammond, in " The Expositor,"* 1875.

Title.—*Syriac inscription.*—The verbs of the Hebrew text through nearly the whole of the imprecatory part of this Psalm are read in the singular number, as if some particular subject were signified by the divine prophet. But our translators always change the verbs into the plural number ; which is not done by the Seventy and the other translators, who adhere more closely to the Hebrew text. But without doubt this has arisen, because the Syriac Christians explain this Psalm of the sufferings of Christ, which may be understood from the Syriac inscription of this Psalm, and which in Polyglottis Angl. reads thus :—" *Of David : when they made Absolom king, he not knowing : and on account of this he was killed. But to us it sets forth the sufferings of Christ.*" For this reason all these imprecations are transferred to the enemies or murderers of Jesus Christ.—*John Augustus Dathe,* 1731—1791.

Verse 1.—" *Hold not thy peace, O God of my praise.*" All commendation or manifestation of our innocence is to be sought from God when we are assailed with calumnies on all sides. When God is silent, we should cry all the more strongly ; nor should we because of such delay despair of help, nor impatiently cease from praying.—*Martin Geier.*

Verse 1.—" *Hold not thy peace.*" How appropriately this phrase is applied to God, with whom *to speak* is the same as *to do* ; for by his word he made all things. Rightly, therefore, is he said to be silent when he seems not to notice the things which are done by the wicked, and patiently bears with their malice. The Psalmist begs him to rise up and speak with the wicked in his wrath, and thus take deserved vengeance on them; which is as easy for him to do as for an angry man to break forth in words of rebuke and blame. This should be to us a great solace against the wickedness of this last age, which God, our praise, can restrain with one little word.—*Wolfgang Musculus.*

Verse 1.—" *O God.*" As the most innocent and holy servants of God are subject to heavy slanders and false calumnies raised against them, so the best remedy and relief in this case is to go to God, as here the Psalmist doth.—*David Dickson.*

Verse 1.—" *God of my praise.*" Thou, who art the constant object of my praise and thanksgiving, Jer. xvii. 14.—*William Keatinge Clay.*

Verse 1.—" *O God of my praise.*" In denominating him *the God of his praise*, he intrusts to him the vindication of his innocence, in the face of the calumnies by which he was all but universally assailed.—*John Calvin.*

Verse 1.—" *The God of* MY *praise.*" Give me leave, in order to expound it the better, to expostulate. What, David, were there no saints but thyself that gave praise to God? Why dost thou then seem to appropriate and engross God unto thyself, as the God of thy praise, as if none praised him else but thee? It is because his soul had devoted all the praise he was able to bestow on any, unto the Lord alone; as whom he had set himself to praise, and praise alone. As of a beloved son we use to say, " the son of my love." And further, it is as if he had said, If I had all the ability of all the spirits of men and angels wherewith to celebrate him, I would bestow them all on him, he is the God of my praise. And as he was David's, so he should be ours.—*Thomas Goodwin.*

Verse 2.—" *For the mouth of the wicked and the mouth of the deceitful are opened against me.*" Speak, says Arnobius, to thine own conscience, O man of God, thou who art following Christ; and when the mouth of the wicked and deceitful man is opened concerning thee, rejoice and be secure; because while the mouth of the wicked is opened for thy slander in the earth, the mouth of God is opened for thy praise in heaven.—*Lorinus.*

Verses 2, 3.—Note, first, the detractor opens his mouth, that he may pour forth his poison, and that he may devour his victim. Hence, David says, " the mouth of the wicked is opened against me." Note, secondly, the detractor is talkative— " They have spoken," etc. The mouth of the detractor is a broken pitcher leaking all over. Note, thirdly, detraction springs from hatred, " they compassed me about also *with words of hatred.*" In Greek, ἐκύκλωσάν με, *i.e.*, as in a circle they have enclosed me. St. Climacus says, " Detraction is *odii partus*, a subtle disease, a fat but hidden leech which sucks the blood of charity and after destroys it.—*Lorinus.*

Verses 2—5.—" *The mouth of the wicked*," etc.

Vice—deformed
Itself, and ugly, and of flavour rank—
To rob fair Virtue of so sweet an incense,
And with it to anoint and salve its own
Rotten ulcers, and perfume the path that led
To death, strove daily by a thousand means:
And oft succeeded to make Virtue sour
In the world's nostrils, and its loathly self
Smell sweetly. Rumour was the messenger
Of defamation, and so swift that none
Could be the first to tell an evil tale.

'Twas Slander filled her mouth with lying words
Slander, the foulest whelp of Sin. The man
In whom this spirit entered was undone.
His tongue was set on fire of hell; his heart
Was black as death; his legs were faint with haste
To propagate the lie his tongue had framed
His pillow was the peace of families
Destroyed, the sigh of innocence reproached,
Broken friendships, and the strife of brotherhoods.
Yet did he spare his sleep, and hear the clock
Number the midnight watches, on his bed
Devising mischief more; and early rose,
And made most hellish meals of good men's names.

Peace fled the neighbourhood in which he made
His haunts ; and, like a moral pestilence,
Before his breath the healthy shoots and blooms
Of social joy and happiness decayed.
Fools only in his company were seen,
And those forsaken of God, and to themselves
Given up. The prudent man shunned him and his house
As one who had a deadly moral plague.
                                        —*Robert Pollok.*

Verse 3.—Although an individual may be absent, so that he cannot corporeally be encompassed and fought with ; nevertheless, so great is the force and malice of an envenomed tongue, that an absent man may be none the less dangerously surrounded and warred against. Thus David, though absent and driven into exile, was nevertheless surrounded and assailed by the calumnies of Doeg and the other flatterers of Saul, so that at length he was also corporeally surrounded ; in which contest he would clearly have perished unless he had been divinely delivered : see 1 Sam. xxiii. And this kind of surrounding and assault is so much the more deadly as it is so much the less possible to be avoided. For who can be so innocent as to escape the snares of a back-biting and calumnious tongue ? What place can be so remote and obscure as that this evil will not intrude when David could not be safe in the mountains and caves of the rocks ?—*Wolfgang Musculus.*

Verse 4 (first clause).—None prove worse enemies than those that have received the greatest kindnesses, when once they turn unkind. As the sharpest vinegar is made of the purest wine, and pleasant meats turn to the bitterest humours in the stomach ; so the highest love bestowed upon friends, being ill digested or corrupt, turns to the most unfriendly hatred, *proximorum odia sunt acerrima.*—*Abraham Wright.*

Verse 4.—" *For my love they are my adversaries* " ; that's an ill requital ; but how did David requite them ? We may take his own word for it ; he tells us how, " *But I give myself unto prayer* " ; yea, he seemed a man wholly given unto prayer. The elegant conciseness of the Hebrew is, " *But I prayer* " ; we supply it thus, " *But I give myself unto prayer.*" They are sinning against me, requiting my love with hatred, " *But I give myself unto prayer.*" But for whom did he pray ? Doubtless he prayed and prayed much for himself ; he prayed also for them. We may understand these words, " *I give myself unto prayer,*" two ways. First, I pray against their plots and evil dealings with me (prayer was David's best strength always against his enemies), yet that was not all. But, secondly, " *I give myself unto prayer,*" that the Lord would pardon their sin, and turn their hearts, when they are doing me mischief ; or, though they have done me mischief, I am wishing them the best good. David (in another place) showed what a spirit of charity he was clothed with, when no reproof could hinder him from praying for others, Ps. cxli. 5.—*Joseph Caryl.*

Verse 4.—The translator of the Syriac version has inserted in the 4th verse ܘܐ ܡܨ݁ܠܐ ܗܘܝܬ ܚܠܦܝܗܘܢ " *and I have prayed for them,*" as if he had copied them from the words of our Lord in Matt. v. 44, where in the Syriac version of the New Testament we have exactly the same construction. It is in keeping with the inscription of the Psalm, which applies it directly to Christ. It would seem as if the Translator understood this verse of the crucifixion and of the Redeemer's prayer for his murderers, or as if the only way to understand the elliptical language of the Psalmist was from the teaching and example of our Lord.—*E. T. Gibson, of Crayford.*

Verse 4.—" *I prayer.*" The Messiah says in this prophetic Psalm, " *I am prayer.*" During his pilgrimage on earth, his whole life was communion with God ; and now in his glory he is constantly making intercession for us. But this does not exhaust the idea, " *I am prayer.*" He not merely prayed and is now praying, he not merely teaches and influences us to pray, but he *is* prayer, the fountain and source of all prayer, as well as the foundation and basis of all answers to our petitions. He is the Word in this sense also. From all eternity his Father heard him, heard him as interceding for that world which, created through him, he represented, and in which, through him, divine glory was to be revealed. In the same sense, therefore, in which he is light and gives light, in which he is life and resurrection, and therefore quickens, Jesus *is* prayer.—*Adolph Saphir, in Lectures on the Lord's Prayer,* 1870.

Verse 4.—Persecuted saints are men of prayer, yea, they are as it were made up all of prayer. David prayed before ; but, oh, when his enemies fell a persecuting of him, then he gave himself up wholly to prayer. Oh, then he was more earnest, more fervent, more frequent, more diligent, more constant, and more abundant in the work of prayer ! When Numa, king of the Romans, was told that his enemies were in arms against him, he did but laugh at it, and answered, " And I do sacrifice " ; so when persecutors arm themselves against the people of God, they do but divinely smile and laugh at it, and give themselves the more up to prayer. When men arm against them, then they arm themselves with all their might to the work of prayer ; and woe, woe to them that have armies of prayers marching against them.—*Thomas Brooks.*

Verse 4.—" *I give myself unto prayer.*" The instruction to ourselves from these words is most comforting and precious. Are we bowed down with sorrow and distress ? " *I give myself unto prayer.*" Are we persecuted, and reviled, and compassed about with words of hatred ? " *I give myself unto prayer.*" Has death entered our dwellings ? and as we gaze in heart-broken anguish on the no longer answering look of one who was our earthly stay, and we feel as if all hope as well as all help were gone, still there remains the same blessed refuge for all the Lord's sorrowing ones, " *I give myself unto prayer.*" In the allegory of the ancients, Hope was left at the bottom of the casket, as the sweetener of human life ; but God, in far richer mercy, gives prayer as the balm of human trial.—*Barton Bouchier.*

Verse 4.—A Christian is all over prayer : he prays at rising, at lying down, and as he walks : like a prime favourite at court, who has the key to the privy stairs, and can wake his prince by night.—*Augustus Montague Toplady,* 1740—1778.

Verse 6.—" *Set thou a wicked man over him,*" etc. Here commences that terrible series of maledictions, unparalleled in Holy Writ, as directed against an individual sinner, albeit 't is little more than a special reduplication of the national woes denounced in Leviticus xxvi. and Deuteronomy xxviii.—*Neale and Littledale.*

Verse 6.—" *Set thou a wicked man over him.*" The first thing that the Psalmist asks is, that his foe might be subjected to the evil of having a man placed over him like himself :—a man regardless of justice, truth, and right ; a man who would respect character and propriety no more than he had himself done. It is, in fact, a prayer that he might be punished *in the line of his offences.* It cannot be wrong that a man should be treated as he treats others ; and it cannot be in itself wrong to desire that a man should be treated according to his character and deserts, for this is the object of all law, and this is what all magistrates and legislators are endeavouring to secure.—*Albert Barnes.*

Verse 6.—" *Over* HIM." Consider what would have been the effect if these denunciations had been against the *sins* of men and not, as they are in these passages, against the *sinners.* Men would have said, " My sin is denounced, not *me.*" What a license would have been given to sin ! The depraved nature would have said, " if *I* am not condemned, but only my *sin,* I can do as I like ; I shall not be called to account for it. I *love* sin and can go on in it." This is what men would have said. There would have been no effort to get rid of it. Why should there be, if only *sin* is condemned and not the *sinner* ? But man's *sin* is identified with *himself,* and this makes him tremble. God's wrath rests on *him* because of his sin. Condemnation is awaiting *him* because of his sin. This makes him anxious to get rid of it.—*Frederick Whitfield.*

Verse 6.—" *Let Satan stand at his right hand.*" It appears to have been the custom at trials before the Jewish tribunals for a pleader to stand at the right hand of the accused : See Zech. iii. 1, where are described Joshua the High Priest, standing before the Angel of Jehovah, and the adversary (שָׂטָן, *Satan,* as here) standing at his right hand to oppose him. See also verse 31.—*John Le Clerc,* 1657—1736.

Verse 6.—" *Let Satan stand at his right hand.*" Hugo observes that the Devil is on the left hand of those whom he persecutes in temporal things : on the right of those whom he rules in spiritual things : before the face of those who are on their guard against his wiles : behind those who are not foreseeing and prudent : above those whom he treads down : below, and beneath the feet of those who tread him down. A recent Spanish author,* writing in that language, thinks that there cannot be anything worse than that man who diligently and of set purpose injures others by speaking deceitfully, by surrounding with speeches of hatred, by attacking without

---

* *Peter Vega* On the Penitential Psalms.

cause, by slandering, by returning evil for good, and hatred for love : therefore, in this place it is desired that a wicked man may be set over such a one, and the devil at his right hand ; as if he should be doomed to take the lowest place because he is the worst.—*Lorinus.*

Verse 6.—" *At his right hand.*" The strength or force of the body shows itself principally in the right hand. Therefore, he who wishes to obstruct another, and to hinder his endeavour, stands at his right hand ; and thus easily parries his stroke or attempt. This I consider to be the most simple meaning of this passage which shows that God represses and restrains the ragings of the enemies of the Church, who withstand each other by their opposing efforts, either from envy or from other causes. Thus, 2 Sam. xvii., the counsels of Ahithophel are broken by Hushai ; and in one day we see that the counsels and attempts of our enemies have been frequently and wonderfully restrained by the hindrances they have given one to the other : in which matter the goodness of God is to be discerned.—*Mollerus.*

Verse 6.—He beginneth to prophesy what they should receive for their great impiety, detailing their lot in such a manner as if he wished its realisation from a desire of revenge ; while he declareth what was to happen with the most absolute certainty, and what of God's justice would worthily come upon such. Some not understanding this mode of predicting the future under the appearance of wishing evil, suppose hatred to be returned for hatred, and an evil will for an evil will : since in truth it belongeth to few to distinguish in what way the punishment of the wicked pleaseth the accuser, who longeth to satiate his enmity ; and in how widely different a way it pleaseth the judge, who with a righteous mind punisheth sins. For the former returneth evil for evil, but the judge when he punisheth doth not return evil for evil, since he returneth justice to the unjust ; and what is just is surely good. He therefore punisheth not from delight in another's misery, which is evil for evil, but from love of justice, which is good for evil. Let not then the blind pervert the light of the Scriptures, imagining that God doth not punish sins : nor let the wicked flatter themselves, as if he rendered evil for evil. Let us therefore hear the sequel of this divine composition ; and in the words of one who seemeth to wish ill, let us recognise the predictions of a prophet ; and let us see God making a just retribution, raising our mind up to his eternal laws.—*Augustine.*

Verses 6—19.—These terrible curses are repeated with many words and sentences, that we may know that David has not let these words fall rashly or from any precipitate impulse of mind ; but, the Holy Spirit having dictated, he employs this form of execration that it may be a perpetual prophecy or prediction of the bitter pains and destruction of the enemies of the Church of God. Nor does David imprecate these punishments so much on his own enemies and Judas the betrayer of Christ ; but that similar punishments await all who fight against the kingdom of Christ.—*Mollerus.*

Verse 6—20.—I had also this consideration, that if I should now venture all for God, I engaged God to take care of my concernments ; but if I forsook him and his ways for fear of any trouble that should come to me or mine, then I should not only falsify my profession, but should count also that my concernments were not so sure, if left at God's feet, while I stood to and for his name, as they would be if they were under my own tuition [or care] though with the denial of the way of God. This was a smarting consideration, and was as spurs unto my flesh. This Scripture [Ps. cix. 6—20] also greatly helped it to fasten the more upon me, where Christ prays against Judas, that God would disappoint him in all his selfish thoughts, which moved him to sell his master : pray read it soberly. I had also another consideration, and that was, the dread of the torments of hell, which I was sure they must partake of, that for fear of the cross do shrink from their profession of Christ, his words, and laws, before the sons of men. I thought also of the glory that he had prepared for those that, in faith, and love, and patience, stood to his ways before them. These things, I say, have helped me, when the thoughts of the misery that both myself and mine might for the sake of my profession be exposed to, hath lain pinching on my mind.—*John Bunyan.*

Verse 7.—" *Let his prayer become sin.*" As the clamours of a condemned malefactor not only find no acceptance, but are looked upon as an affront to the court. The prayers of the wicked now become sin, because soured with the leaven of hypocrisy and malice ; and so they will in the great day, because then it will be too late to cry, " Lord, Lord, open unto us."—*Matthew Henry.*

Verse 7.—" *Let his prayer become sin.*" Evidently his prayer in reference to his *trial* for crime; his prayer that he might be acquitted and discharged. Let it be seen in the result that such a prayer was *wrong*; that it was, in fact, a prayer for the discharge of a bad man—a man who *ought* to be punished. Let it be seen to be what a prayer *would* be if offered for a murderer, or violator of the law,—a prayer that he might escape or not be punished. All must see that *such* a prayer would be wrong, or would be a " sin "; and so, in his own case, it would be equally true that a prayer *for his own escape* would be " sin." The Psalmist asks that, by the result of the trial, such a prayer might be *seen* to be in fact a prayer for the protection and escape of a *bad man*. A just sentence in the case would demonstrate this; and this is what the Psalmist prays for.—*Albert Barnes.*

Verse 7.—" *Let his prayer become sin.*" Kimchi in his annotations thus explains these words: *i.e.,* " let it be without effect, so that he does not get what he asks for; let him not hit the mark at which he aims: for חָטָא sometimes has the meaning ' to miss.' "—*Wolfgang Musculus.*

Verse 7.—" *Let his prayer become sin.*" St. Jerome says that Judas's prayer was turned into sin, by reason of his want of hope when he prayed: and thus it was that in despair he hanged himself.—*Robert Bellarmine.*

Verse 7.—" *Let his prayer become sin.*" The prayer of the hypocrite is sin formally, and it is sin in the effect, that is, instead of getting any good by it, he gets hurt, and the Lord instead of helping him because he prayeth, punisheth him because of the sinfulness of his prayers. Thus his prayer becomes sin to him, because he receives no more respect from God when he prays than when he sins. And sin doth not only mingle with his prayer (as it doth with the prayers of the holiest), but his prayer is nothing else but a mixture or mingle-mangle (as we speak) of many sins.—*Joseph Caryl.*

Verse 7.—" *Let his prayer become sin.*" We should be watchful in prayer lest the most holy worship of God should become an abomination: Isaiah i. 15; lxvi. 3; James iv. 3; Hosea vii. 14; Amos v. 23. If the remedy be poisoned, how shall the diseased be cured?—*Martin Geier.*

Verses 7—19.—These and the following verses, although they contain terrible imprecations, will become less dreadful if we understand them as spoken concerning men pertinaciously cleaving to their vices, against whom only has God threatened punishments; not against those who repent with all their heart, and become thoroughly changed in life.—*John Le Clerc.*

Verse 8.—" *Let his days be few.*" By " *his days,*" he meant the days of his apostleship, which were few; since before the passion of our Lord, they were ended by his crime and death. And as if it were asked, What then shall become of that most sacred number twelve, within which our Lord willed, not without a meaning, to limit his twelve first apostles? he at once addeth, " *and let another take his office.*" As much as to say, let both himself be punished according to his desert, and let his number be filled up. And if any one desire to know how this was done, let him read the Acts of the Apostles.—*Augustine.*

Verse 8.—" *Let another take his office.*" So every man acts, and practically prays, who seeks to remove a bad and corrupt man from office. As such an office must be filled by some one, all the efforts which he puts forth to remove a wicked man tend to bring it about that " another should take his office," and for this it is *right* to labour and pray. The act does not of itself imply malignity or bad feeling, but is consistent with the purest benevolence, the kindest feelings, the strictest integrity, the sternest patriotism, and the highest form of piety.—*Albert Barnes.*

Verse 9.—" *Let his children be fatherless.*" Helpless and shiftless. A sore vexation to many on their death-beds, and just enough upon graceless persecutors. But happy are they who, when they lie a-dying, can say as Luther did, " *Domine Deus gratias ago tibi quod velueris me esse pauperem, et mendicum,* &c. Lord God, I thank thee for my present poverty, but future hopes. I have not an house, lands, possessions, or monies to leave behind me. Thou hast given me wife and children; behold, I return them back to thee, and beseech thee to nourish them, teach them, keep them safe, as hitherto thou hast done, O thou father of the fatherless, and judge of widows.—*John Trapp.*

Verses 9, 10, 12, 13.—" *His children;* " " *his posterity.*" Though in matters of a civil or judicial character, we have it upon the highest authority that the children are not to be made accountable for the fathers, nor the fathers for the children, but every transgressor is to bear the penalty of his own sin ; yet, in a moral, and in a social and spiritual sense, it is impossible that the fathers should eat sour grapes, and yet that the children's teeth should not be set on edge. The offspring of the profligate and the prodigal may, and often do, avoid the specific vices of the parent ; but rarely, if ever, do they escape the evil consequences of those vices. And this re-action cannot be prevented, until it shall please God first to unmake and then to remodel his whole intelligent creation.—*T. Dale, in a Sermon to Heads of Families,* 1839.

Verses 9—13.—Under the Old Covenant, calamity, extending from father to son, was the meed of transgression ; prosperity, *vice versa,* of obedience : (see Solomon's prayer, 2 Chron. vi. 23) : and these prayers of the Psalmist (cf. Pss. x. 13, xii. 1, lviii. 10, etc.) may express the wish that God's providential government of his people should be asserted in the chastisement of the enemy of God and man.—*Speaker's Commentary.*

Verse 10.—" *Let his children be continually vagabonds.*" The word used in the sentence pronounced upon *Cain,* Gen. iv. 12. Compare Ps. lix. 11, 15.—*William Kay.*

Verse 10.—" *Let them seek,*" etc. Horsley renders this clause, " *Let them be driven out from the-very-ruins-of their dwellings,*" and remarks that the image is that of " vagabonds seeking a miserable shelter among the ruins of decayed or demolished buildings, and not suffered to remain even in such places undisturbed."

Verses 9, 10.—When we consider of whom this Psalm is used there will be no difficulty about it. No language could be more awful than that of verses 6 to 19. It embraces almost every misery we can think of. But could any man be in a more wretched condition than Judas was ? Could any words be too severe to express the depth of his misery—of him, who, for three whole years, had been the constant attendant of the Saviour of mankind ; who had witnessed his miracles, and had shared his miraculous powers ; who had enjoyed all the warnings, all the reproofs of his love, and then had betrayed him for thirty pieces of silver ? Can we conceive a condition more miserable than that of Judas ? And this Psalm is *a prophecy of the punishment* that should overtake him for his sin. S. Peter, in the Acts of the Apostles, quotes part of this Psalm, and applies it to Judas : he applies it as a prophecy of the punishment he should suffer on the betrayal of the Son of God.

It is probable that in this Psalm, when it uses the word children, it does not mean those who are his offspring by natural descent, but those *who resemble him,* and *who partake with him in his wickedness.* This is a common meaning of the word sons, or children, in Holy Scripture. As where our blessed Lord tells the Jews, " *Ye are of your father the devil,*" he could not mean that the Jews were the natural descendants of the devil, but that they were his children because they did his works. Again, when they are called Abraham's children, it means those who do the works of Abraham. So in this Psalm, where it is foretold that fearful punishment should happen to Judas for the betrayal of his Lord, and should be extended to his children, it means *his associates, his companions, and imitators in wickedness.*—*F. H. Dunwell, in " A Tract on the Commination Service,"* 1853.

Verses 10, 12, 13.—It is for public ends that the Psalmist prayed that the families of the wicked might be involved in their ruin. These are very terrible petitions ; but it is God, not man, who has appointed these calamities as the ordinary conse-quences of persistence in wickedness. It is God, not man, who visits the iniquity of the fathers upon the children, to the third and fourth generations. It is because this is the ordinary portion of the transgressors, and *that thus in God's wonted way his abhorrence of the transgressions* of his enemies might be marked, that the Psalmist prays for these calamities. He asks God to do what he had declared he would do, and this for public ends, for he says : " I will greatly praise the Lord with my mouth ; yea, I will praise him *among the multitude.* For he shall stand at the right hand of the poor, to save him from those that condemn his soul," verses 30, 31.—*R. A. Bertram, in " The Imprecatory Psalms,"* 1867.

Verses 10—13.—Many penurious fathers are so scraping for their children, that they ravish the poor children of God ; but the hand of the Lord shall be against their young lions. Nah. ii. 13. They join house to house, and field to field, but their children shall be " *vagabonds and beg,*" " *seeking their bread out of their desolate places.*" How many a covetous mole is now digging a house in the earth for his posterity, and never dreams of this sequel, that God should make those children beggars, for whose sake their fathers had made so many beggars! This is a quittance which the sire will not believe, but as sure as God is just the son shall feel. Now if he had but leave to come out of hell for an hour, and see this, how should he curse his folly! Sure, if possible, it would double the pain of his infernal torture. Be moderate, then, ye that so insatiately devour, as if you had an infinite capacity: you overload your stomachs, it is fit they should be disburdened in shameful spewing. How quickly doth a worldly-minded man grow a defrauder, from a defrauder to a usurer, from a usurer to an oppressor, from an oppressor to an extortioner! if his eyes do but tell his heart of a booty, his heart will charge his hand, and he must have it, Micah ii. 2. They do but see it, like it, and take it. Observe their due payment. " *Let the extortioner catch all that he hath* ": they got all by extortion, they shall lose all by extortion. They spoiled their neighbours, strangers shall spoil them. How often hath the poor widow and orphan cried, wept, groaned to them for mercy, and found none! They have taught God how to deal with themselves; " *let there be none to extend mercy to them.*" They have advanced houses for a memorial, and dedicated lands to their own names, Ps. xlix. 11 ; all to get them a name; and even in this they shall be crossed : " *In the next generation their name shall be quite put out.*"—*Thomas Adams.*

Verse 11.—" *Let the extortioner catch all that he hath.*" Note : he is most miserable who falls into the hands of usurers ; for they will flay him alive and drain his blood. The Romans, that they might deter the citizens from usury, placed a statue of Marsyas in the Forum or law-court, by which they signified that those who came into the hands of usurers would be skinned alive ; and to show that usurers, as the most unjust litigants, deserved hanging, they placed a rope in the hand of the figure. —*Le Blanc.*

Verse 11.—" *Catch.*" This refers to the obligations between creditors and debtors, and he calls these snares, by which, as it were, the insolvent debtors are caught, and at last come to servitude.—*Mollerus.*

Verse 12.—" *Let there be none to extend mercy to him.*" He does not say, None who shall shew, but none who shall " *extend* " kindness to him. The extending of kindness is, when after a friend's death it is shown to his children, and true friendship is of this sort, that the kindness which friends shewed to each other while alive is maintained, not extinguished with the death of the friend.—*Wolfgang Musculus.*

Verse 12.—" *Let there be none to extend mercy to him.*" Let God in his justice set off all hearts from him that had been so unreasonably merciless. Thus no man opened his mouth to intercede for Haman ; Judas was shaken off by the priests, and bid *see to himself*, etc.—*John Trapp.*

Verse 15.—" *Let them be before the Lord continually.*" The fearful punishment of sinners is, to be always under the eye of an angry God : then the soul of the sinner is dismayed at its own deformity.—*Le Blanc.*

Verse 15.—" *Let them be before the Lord continually.*" Lafayette, the friend and ally of Washington, was in his youth confined in a French dungeon. In the door of his cell there was cut a small hole, just big enough for a man's eye ; at that hole a sentinel was placed, whose duty it was to watch, moment by moment, till he was relieved by a change of guard. All Lafayette saw was the winking eye, but the eye was always there ; look when he would, it met his gaze. In his dreams, he was conscious it was staring at him. " Oh," he says, " it was horrible ; there was no escape ; when he lay down and when he rose up, when he ate and when he read, that eye searched him."—" *New Cyclopædia of Illustrative Anecdote,*" 1875.

Verses 15—19, 29.—Strict justice, and nothing more, breathes in every petition. Cannot you say, Amen! to all these petitions? Are you not glad when the wicked man falls into the ditch he has made for another's destruction, and when his mischief returns upon his own head? But you say, " These petitions are unquestionably just, but why did not the Psalmist ask, not for justice, but for *mercy* ? " The answer is, that in his public capacity, he was bound to think first about justice.

No government could stand upon the basis of forgiveness, justice must always go before mercy. Suppose that in the course of the next session Parliament should decree that henceforth, instead of justice being shown to thieves, by sending them to prison, they should be treated charitably, and compelled to restore *one-half* of what they stole, what would honest men say about the government? The thieves would doubtless be very complimentary, but what would honest men say? Why, they would say the government had altogether failed of its function, and it would not live to be a week older. And just so, the Psalmists were bound first of all to seek for the vindication and establishment of justice and truth. Like the magistrates of to-day, they considered first the well-being of the community. This they had in view in all the calamities they sought to bring upon wrong-doers.—*R. A. Bertram.*

Verse 16.—"*Because.*" Why, what is the crime? "*Because that he remembered not to shew mercy,*" etc. See what a long vial full of the plagues of God is poured out upon the unmerciful man!—*Thomas Watson.*

Verse 16.—"*But persecuted the poor.*" If any man will practice subtraction against the poor, God will use it against him, and take his name out of the book of life. If he be damned that gives not his own, what shall become of him that takes away another man's? (*Augustine.*) If judgment without mercy shall be to him that shows no mercy (Jam. ii. 13) where shall subtraction and rapine appear? "*Let the extortioner catch all that he hath; and let strangers spoil his labour,*" ver. 11: there is one subtraction, his estate. "*Let his posterity be cut off; and in the generation following let their name be blotted out,*" ver. 13: there is another subtraction, his memory. "*Let there be none to extend mercy unto him: neither let there be any to favour the fatherless children,*" ver. 12: there is another subtraction, a denial of all pity to him and his. "*Let him be condemned: and let his prayer become sin,*" ver. 7: there is another subtraction, no audience from heaven. "*Let another take his office;*" there is a subtraction of his place: "*let his days be few,*" ver. 8: there is a subtraction of his life. "*Let him be blotted out of the book of the living, and not be written with the righteous,*" Ps. lxix. 28; there is the last, the subtraction of his soul. This is a fearful arithmetic: if the wicked add sins, God will add plagues. If they subtract from others their rights, God shall subtract from them his mercies.—*Thomas Adams.*

Verse 17.—*Cursing* is both good and bad. For we read in the Scriptures that holy men have often cursed. Indeed none can offer the Lord's Prayer rightly without cursing. For when he prays, "Hallowed be thy name, thy kingdom come, thy will be done," etc., he must include in the same outpouring of his desires all that is opposed to these, and say, cursed and execrated and dishonoured must all other names be, and all kingdoms which are opposed to thee must be destroyed and rent in pieces, and all devices and purposes formed against thee fall to the ground.—*Martin Luther.*

Verse 17.—"*As he delighted not in blessing, so let it be far from him.*"

> He was a wolf in clothing of the lamb,
> That stole into the fold of God, and on
> The blood of souls, which he did sell to death,
> Grew fat; and yet, when any would have turned
> Him out, he cried, "Touch not the priest of God."
> And that he was anointed, fools believed;
> But knew, that day, he was the devil's priest,
> Anointed by the hands of Sin and Death,
> And set peculiarly apart to ill—
> While on him smoked the vials of perdition,
> Poured measureless. Ah, me! What cursing then
> Was heaped upon his head by ruined souls,
> That charged him with their murder, as he stood
> With eye, of all the unredeemed, most sad,
> Waiting the coming of the Son of Man!
> *Robert Pollok.*

Verses 17—19.—Possibly verses 17 and 18 describe as fact what verse 19 amplifies in a wish, or prayer. "He loved cursing, and it loved him in return, and came to him: he delighted not in blessing, and it was far from him. He clothed himself with cursing as with a garment, and it permeated his inmost parts as water, as the refreshing oil with which the body is anointed finds a way into marrow and bones." The images are familiar; the daily dress, the water that permeates daily every part of the body, the oil used daily for nourishment (Ps. civ. 15) and gladness (Ps. xxiii. 5). In the wish that follows (verse 19), the mantle, or *garment*, which is always worn, and the girdle or belt with which the accursed one is always girded, are substituted, apparently, for more general terms.—*Speaker's Commentary.*

Verses 17—19.—As the loss of the soul is a loss peculiar to itself, and a loss double, so it is a loss most fearful, because it is attended with the most heavy curse of God. This curse lieth in a deprivation of all good, and in a being swallowed up of all the most fearful miseries that a holy and just and eternal God can righteously inflict, or lay upon the soul of a sinful man. Now let reason here come in and exercise itself in the most exquisite manner ; yea, let him now count up all, and all manner of curses and torments that a reasonable and an immortal soul is, or can be made capable of, and able to suffer, and when he has done, he shall come infinitely short of this great anathema, this master curse which God has reserved amongst his treasuries, and intends to bring out in that day of battle and war, which he proposeth to make upon damned souls in that day. And this God will do, partly as a retaliation, as the former, and partly by way of revenge. 1. By way of retaliation : " *As he loved cursing, so let it come unto him : as he delighted not in blessing, so let it be far from him.*" Again, " *As he clothed himself with cursing like as with his garment, so let it come into his bowels like water, and like oil into his bones. Let it be unto him as the garment which covereth him, and for a girdle wherewith he is girded continually.*" " *Let this,*" saith Christ, " *be the reward of mine adversaries from the Lord,*" etc. 2. As this curse comes by way of retaliation, so it cometh by way of revenge. God will right the wrongs that sinners have done him, will repay vengeance for the despite and reproach wherewith they have affronted him, and will revenge the quarrel of his covenant. As the beginnings of revenges are terrible (Deut. xxxii. 41, 42) ; what, then, will the whole execution be, when he shall come in flaming fire, taking vengeance on them that know not God, and that obey not the gospel of Jesus Christ ? And, therefore, this curse is executed in wrath, in jealousy, in anger, in fury ; yea, the heavens and the earth shall be burned up with the fire of that jealousy in which the great God will come when he cometh to curse the souls of sinners, and when he cometh to defy the ungodly, 2 Thess. i. 7—9.—*John Bunyan.*

Verse 18.—The three figures in this verse are climatic : he has clothed himself in cursing, he has drunk it in like water (Job xv. 16, xxxiv. 7), it has penetrated to the marrow of his bones, like the oily preparations which are rubbed in and penetrate to the bones.—*Franz Delitzsch.*

Verse 18.—We must not pass this verse without remarking that there is an allusion in its tone to Num. v. 21, 22, 24—the unfaithful wife. Her curse was to penetrate into her bowels ; " the water that causeth the curse shall enter into her " ; and such a curse comes on unfaithful Judas, who violates his engagement to the Lord, and upon Israel at large also, who have departed from him " as a wife treacherously departeth from her husband," and have committed adultery against the Bridegroom. —*Andrew A. Bonar.*

Verses 18, 19.—Peter, in Acts i. 20, applies this Psalm to Christ when the Jews cried, " His blood be upon us and upon our children " ; then did they put on the envenomed garment which has tormented them ever since. It is girded about their loins ; the curse has penetrated like water, and entered the very bones like oil. How awful will be the state of those who crucify him afresh, and again put him to open shame.—*Samuel Horsley.*

Verse 21.—" *For thy name's sake.*" My enemies would soon become my friends and my protectors, if I would but renounce my allegiance to thee ; my refusal to disobey thee constitutes all my crime in their eyes. My cause, therefore, becomes thine, it will be to thy glory to declare thyself on my side, lest the impious should take occasion from my sufferings to blaspheme thy holy name, as if thou hadst not the power to deliver, or wert utterly indifferent to those who, renouncing all human help, have put their confidence in thee.—*Jean Baptiste Massillon.*

Verse 21.—" *For thy name's sake.*" He does not say, For *my* name, that it may be vindicated from reproach and shame : but for *Thy* name ; as if he would say, whatever I may be, O Lord, and whatever may befall me, have respect to Thy name, have regard to it only. I am not worthy, that I should seek Thy help, but Thy name is worthy which thou mayest vindicate from contempt. We learn here with what passion for the glory of the divine name they ought to be animated who are peculiarly consecrated to the name of God.

He does not say, " Because my case is good," but " *because thy mercy is good.*" Note this also, he does not simply say, Because thou art good, or because thou art merciful ; but because thy mercy is good. He had experienced a certain special goodness in the Divine mercy ; *i.e.*, such timeliness, kind readiness in all afflictions, and help for every kind of affliction prepared and provided.   On this he rests hope and confidence, in this takes refuge.   All those are truly happy who have had experience of this mercy, and can depend on it with firm hope and confidence.—*Wolfgang Musculus.*

Verse 21.—Unto a truly broken, humbled sinner, the mercies that are in God, out of which he pardons, should have infinitely more of goodness and sweetness in them than the pardon itself, or all things else that are in the promises.   This a soul that hath tasted how good the Lord is will instantly acknowledge.   A promise of life to a condemned man is sweet, for life is sweet, as we say ; but " thy lovingkindness," said David, who had tasted how good the Lord is, " is better than life," and infinitely sweeter, Ps. lxiii. 3.   And again says David, " *Because thy mercy is good, deliver thou me.*"   Deliverance was good ; yea, but the mercy of God apprehended therewith was infinitely more good to him, which was the greatest inducement to him to seek deliverance.   And indeed God's mercy doth eminently bear the style of goodness.—*Thomas Goodwin.*

Verses 21—25.—The thunder and lightning are now as it were followed by a shower of tears of deep sorrowful complaint.—*Franz Delitzsch.*

Verse 22.—" *For I am poor and needy, and my heart is wounded within me.*"   Note here, how beautifully he unites these arguments.   He had said, " *Because Thy mercy is good* ; and he adds, " *Because I am poor and needy.*"   He could not have added anything more appropriate : for this is the nature of goodness and mercy, even in the human heart, much more in God, the best and most merciful of all beings, that nothing more easily moves it to give succour, than the affliction, calamity, and misery of those by whom it is invoked.—*Wolfgang Musculus.*

Verse 22.—" *My heart is wounded within me.*"   The hearts of the saints and pious men are not as brass or stone, that the apathy of the Stoics should have lodging in them, but are susceptible to griefs and passions.—*Musculus.*

Verse 23.—" *I am gone like the shadow when it declineth.*"—Bishop Horsley renders, " *I am just gone, like the shadow stretched to its utmost length*" ; and remarks :— " The state of the shadows of terrestrial objects at sunset, lengthening every instant, and growing faint as they lengthen ; and in the instant that they shoot to an immeasurable length disappearing."

Verse 23.—" *I am tossed up and down as the locust.*"   Although the locusts have sufficient strength of flight to remain on the wing for a considerable period, and to pass over great distances, they have little or no command over the direction of their flight, always travel with the wind, in the same way as the quail.   So entirely are they at the mercy of the wind, that if a sudden gust arises the locusts are tossed about in the most helpless manner ; and if they should happen to come across one of the circular air-currents that are so frequently found in the countries which they inhabit, they are whirled round and round without the least power of extricating themselves.—*J. G. Wood.*

Verse 23.—" *I am tossed up and down as the locust.*"   This reference is to the flying locust.   I have had frequent opportunities to notice how these squadrons are tossed up and down, and whirled round and round by the ever-varying currents of the mountain winds.—*W. M. Thomson.*

Verse 28.—" *Let them curse, but bless thou.*"   Fear not thou, who art a saint, their imprecations ; this is but like false fire in the pan of an uncharged gun, it gives a crack, but hurts not ; God's blessings will cover thee from their curse.—*William Gurnall.*

Verse 28 (*first clause*).—Men's curses are impotent, God's blessings are omnipotent. —*Matthew Henry.*

Verse 30.—" *I will greatly praise the Lord with my mouth.*"   In the celebration of God's praises, there can be no question that these must issue from the heart ere they can be uttered by the lips ; at the same time, it would be an indication of great coldness, and of want of fervour, did not the tongue unite with the heart in this exercise.   The reason why David makes mention of the tongue only is, that he takes it for granted that, unless there be a pouring out of the heart before God, those praises which reach no farther than the ear are vain and frivolous ; and, therefore, from the very bottom of his soul, he pours forth his heart-felt gratitude in fervent strains of praise ; and this he does from the same motives which ought to influence all the faithful—the desire of mutual edification ; for to act otherwise would be to rob God of the honour which belongs to him.—*John Calvin.*

Verse 31.—" *He shall stand at the right hand of the poor.*" This expression implies, first, that he appears there as a *friend.* How cheering, how comforting it is to have a friend to stand by us when we are in trouble ! Such a friend is Jesus. In the hour of necessity he comes as a friend to stand by the right hand of the poor creature whose soul is condemned by guilt and accusation. But he stands in a far higher relation than that of a friend ; he stands, too, as *surety and a deliverer.* He goes, as it were, into the court ; and when the prisoner stands at the bar, he comes forward and stands at his right hand as his surety and bondsman ; he brings out of his bosom the acquittance of the debt, signed and sealed with his own blood, he produces it to the eyes of the court, and claims and demands the acquittal and absolution of the prisoner at whose right hand he stands. He stands there, then, that the prisoner may be freely pardoned, and completely justified from those accusations that " *condemn his soul.*" O sweet standing ! O blessed appearance !—*Joseph C. Philpot* (1802—1869).

Verse 31.—" *He shall stand at the right hand of the poor.*" One of the oldest Rabbinical commentaries has a very beautiful gloss on this passage. " Whenever a poor man stands at thy door, the Holy One, blessed be his Name, stands at his right hand. If thou givest him alms, know that thou shalt receive a reward from him who standeth at his right hand."—*Alfred Edersheim, in* " *Sketches of the Jewish Social Life in the Days of Christ,*" 1876.

HINTS TO PREACHERS.

Verse 1.—The silence of God. What it may mean : what it involves : how we may endeavour to break it.

Verse 1.—" *God of my praise.*" A text which may be expounded in its double meaning.

Verse 2.—Slander. Its cause—wickedness and malice. Its instruments—deceit and lies. Its frequency—Jesus and the saints slandered. Its punishment. Our resort when tried by it—prayer to God.

Verses 1—3.—I. God is for his people when the wicked are against them (verse 1) ; 1. for his people's sake ; 2. for his own sake. II. The wicked are against his people when he is for them (verses 2, 3) ; 1. from hatred to God ; 2. from hatred to his people.—*G. R.*

Verse 4.—On the excellency of prayer. See Expository Notes.

Verse 4.—Our Lord's adversaries, and his resort.

Verses 4, 5.—I. David's spirit and conduct towards his enemies. 1. His spirit is love—love for hatred ; hence his denunciations are against their sins, rather than against them. 2. His conduct. He returned good for evil : he interceded for them. II. Their spirit and conduct towards him. 1. Hatred for love. 2. Evil for good.—*G. R.*

Verse 5.—" *Evil for good.*" This is devil-like. Have not men been guilty of this to parents, to those who have warned them, to saints and ministers, and especially to the Lord himself ?

Verse 5.—How has the Redeemer been recompensed ? Show what he deserves and what he receives from various individuals. He feels the unkindness of those who are ungrateful.

Verse 6.—It is the law of retribution to punish the wicked by means of the wicked. —*Starke.*

Verse 7.—When may prayer become sin ? From what is sought, how sought, by whom sought, and wherefore sought.

Verse 8.—" *Let his days be few.*" Sin the great shortener of human life. After the flood the whole race lived a shorter time ; passion and avaricious care shorten life, and some sins have a peculiar power to do this, lust, drunkenness, &c.

Verses 20, 21.—I. David leaves his enemies in the hand of God (verse 20). II. He puts himself into the same hands (verse 21).—*G. R.*

Verse 21.—The plea of a believer must be drawn from his God,—his " name " and " mercy." The opposite habit of searching for arguments in self very common and very disappointing.

Verse 21.—The peculiar goodness of divine mercy.

Verse 22.—The inward sorrows of a saint. Their cause, effects, consolations, and cure.

Verses 26, 27.—I. The Prayer. II. The Believing Title : " *O Lord my God.*" III. The attribute relied upon. IV. The motive for the petition.

Verse 28.—The divine cure for human ill-will ; and the saint's temper when he trusts therein—" let thy servant rejoice."

Verse 29.—I. A prayer for the repentance of David's adversaries. II. A prophecy for their confusion if they remain impenitent.—*G. R.*

Verse 29.—The sinner's last mantle.

Verse 30.—Vocal praise. Should be personal, resolute, intelligent, abundant, hearty. It should attract others, join with others, stimulate others, but never lose its personality.

Verses 30, 31.—I. David's *will* with respect to himself : " I will . . . yea, I will," etc. (verse 30). II. His *shall* with respect to God : " he shall," etc. (verse 31).— *G. R.*

Verses 30, 31.—He promiseth God that he will praise him, verse 30. He promiseth himself that he shall have cause to praise God, ver. 31.—*Matthew Henry.*

Verse 31.—I. The character to whom the promise is made—the poor. II. The danger to which he is exposed—those that condemn his soul. III. The deliverance which is promised to him—divine, opportune, efficient, complete, everlasting.

PSALM CX.

TITLE.—*A Psalm of David. Of the correctness of this title there can be no doubt, since our Lord in Matthew xxii. says, " How then doth David in spirit call him Lord."* Yet some critics are so fond of finding new authors for the Psalms that they dare to fly in the face of the Lord Jesus himself. To escape from finding Jesus here, they read the title, " Psalm of (or concerning) David," as though it was not so much written by him as of him ; but he that reads with understanding will see little enough of David here except as the writer. He is not the subject of it even in the smallest degree, but Christ is all. How much was revealed to the patriarch David ! How blind are some modern wise men, even amid the present blaze of light, as compared with this poet-prophet of the darker dispensation. May the Spirit who spoke by the man after God's own heart give us eyes to see the hidden mysteries of this marvellous Psalm, in which every word has an infinity of meaning.

SUBJECT AND DIVISION.—*The subject is* THE PRIEST-KING. *None of the kings of Israel united these two offices, though some endeavoured to do so. Although David performed some acts which appeared to verge upon the priestly, yet he was no priest, but of the tribe of Judah, " of which tribe Moses spake nothing concerning the priesthood "; and he was far too devout a man to thrust himself into that office uncalled. The Priest-King here spoken of is David's Lord, a mysterious personage typified by Melchizedek, and looked for by the Jews as the Messiah. He is none other than the apostle and high-priest of our profession, Jesus of Nazareth, the King of the Jews. The Psalm describes the appointment of the kingly priest, his followers, his battles, and his victory. Its centre is verse 4, and so it may be divided, as Alexander suggests, into the introduction, verses 1—3 ; the central thought, verse 4 ; and the supplementary verses, 5—7.*

EXPOSITION.

THE LORD said unto my Lord, Sit thou at my right hand, until I make thine enemies thy footstool.

2 The LORD shall send the rod of thy strength out of Zion : rule thou in the midst of thine enemies.

3 Thy people *shall be* willing in the day of thy power, in the beauties of holiness from the womb of the morning : thou hast the dew of thy youth.

1. *" The Lord said unto my Lord "*—Jehovah said unto my Adonai : David in spirit heard the solemn voice of Jehovah speaking to the Messiah from of old. What wonderful intercourse there has been between the Father and the Son ! From this secret and intimate communion spring the covenant of grace and all its marvellous arrangements. All the great acts of grace are brought into actual being by the word of God ; had he not spoken, there had been no manifestation of Deity to us ; but in the beginning was the Word, and from of old there was mysterious fellowship between the Father and his Son Jesus Christ concerning his people and the great contest on their behalf between himself and the powers of evil. How condescending on Jehovah's part to permit a mortal ear to hear, and a human pen to record his secret converse with his co-equal Son ! How greatly should we prize the revelation of his private and solemn discourse with the Son, herein made public for the refreshing of his people ! Lord, what is man that thou shouldst thus impart thy secrets unto him !

Though David was a firm believer in the Unity of the Godhead, he yet spiritually discerns the two persons, distinguishes between them, and perceives that in the second he has a peculiar interest, for he calls him " *my Lord*." This was an anticipation of the exclamation of Thomas, " My Lord and my God," and it expresses the Psalmist's reverence, his obedience, his believing appropriation, and his joy in Christ. It is well to have clear views of the mutual relations of the persons of the blessed Trinity ; indeed, the knowledge of these truths is essential for our comfort and growth in grace. There is a manifest distinction in the divine persons, since one speaks to another ; yet the Godhead is one.

" *Sit thou at my right hand, until I make thine enemies thy footstool.*" Away from the shame and suffering of his earthly life, Jehovah calls the Adonai, our Lord, to the repose and honours of his celestial seat. His work is done, and he may sit ; it is well done, and he may sit at his right hand ; it will have grand results, and he may therefore quietly wait to see the complete victory which is certain to follow. The glorious Jehovah thus addresses the Christ as our Saviour ; for, says David, he said "unto my Lord." Jesus is placed in the seat of power, dominion, and dignity, and is to sit there by divine appointment while Jehovah fights for him, and lays every rebel beneath his feet. He sits there by the Father's ordinance and call, and will sit there despite all the raging of his adversaries, till they are all brought to utter shame by his putting his foot upon their necks. In this sitting he is our representative. The mediatorial kingdom will last until the last enemy shall be destroyed, and then, according to the inspired word, "cometh the end, when he shall have delivered up the kingdom to God even the Father." The work of subduing the nations is now in the hand of the great God, who by his Providence will accomplish it to the glory of his Son ; his word is pledged to it, and the session of his Son at his right hand is the guarantee thereof ; therefore let us never fear as to the future. While we see our Lord and representative sitting in quiet expectancy, we, too, may sit in the attitude of peaceful assurance, and with confidence await the grand outcome of all events. As surely as Jehovah liveth Jesus must reign, yea, even now he is reigning, though all his enemies are not yet subdued. During the present interval, through which we wait for his glorious appearing and visible millennial kingdom, he is in the place of power, and his dominion is in no jeopardy, or otherwise he would not remain quiescent. He sits because all is safe, and he sits at Jehovah's right hand because omnipotence waits to accomplish his will. Therefore there is no cause for alarm whatever may happen in this lower world ; the sight of Jesus enthroned in divine glory is the sure guarantee that all things are moving onward towards ultimate victory. Those rebels who now stand high in power shall soon be in the place of contempt, they shall be his footstool. He shall with ease rule them, he shall sit and put his foot on them ; not rising to tread them down as when a man puts forth force to subdue powerful foes, but retaining the attitude of rest, and still ruling them as abject vassals who have no longer spirit to rebel, but have become thoroughly tamed and subdued.

2. "*The Lord shall send the rod of thy strength out of Zion.*" It is in and through the church that for the present the power of the Messiah is known. Jehovah has given to Jesus all authority in the midst of his people, whom he rules with his royal sceptre, and this power goes forth with divine energy from the church for the ingathering of the elect, and the subduing of all evil. We have need to pray for the sending out of the rod of divine strength. It was by his rod that Moses smote the Egyptians, and wrought wonders for Israel, and even so whenever the Lord Jesus sends forth the rod of his strength, our spiritual enemies are overcome. There may be an allusion here to Aaron's rod which budded and so proved his power ; this was laid up in the ark, but our Lord's rod is sent forth to subdue his foes. This promise began to be fulfilled at Pentecost, and it continues even to this day, and shall yet have a grander fulfilment. O God of eternal might, let the strength of our Lord Jesus be more clearly seen, and let the nations see it as coming forth out of the midst of thy feeble people, even from Zion, the place of thine abode. "*Rule thou in the midst of thine enemies ;*" as he does whenever his mighty sceptre of grace is stretched forth to renew and save them. Moses' rod brought water out of the flinty rock, and the gospel of Jesus soon causes repentance to flow in rivers from the once hardened heart of man. Or the text may mean that though the church is situated in the midst of a hostile world, yet it exerts a great influence, it continues to manifest an inward majesty, and is after all the ruling power among the nations because the shout of a king is in her midst. Jesus, however hated by men, is still the King of kings. His rule is over even the most unwilling, so as to overrule their fiercest opposition to the advancement of his cause. Jesus, it appears from this text, is not inactive during his session at Jehovah's right hand, but in his own way proves the abiding nature of his kingdom both *in* Zion and *from* Zion, both among his friends and his foes. We look for the clearer manifestation of his almighty power in the latter days ; but even in these waiting times we rejoice that to the Lord all power is given in heaven and in earth.

3. "*Thy people shall be willing in the day of thy power, in the beauties of holiness from the womb of the morning : thou hast the dew of thy youth.*" In consequence of the sending forth of the rod of strength, namely, the power of the gospel, out of

Zion, converts will come forward in great numbers to enlist under the banner of the Priest-King. Given to him of old, they are his people, and when his power is revealed, these hasten with cheerfulness to own his sway, appearing at the gospel call as it were spontaneously, even as the dew comes forth in the morning. This metaphor is further enlarged upon, for as the dew has a sparkling beauty, so these willing armies of converts have a holy excellence and charm about them ; and as the dew is the lively emblem of freshness, so are these converts full of vivacity and youthful vigour, and the church is refreshed by them and made to flourish exceedingly. Let but the gospel be preached with divine unction, and the chosen of the Lord respond to it like troops in the day of the mustering of armies ; they come arrayed by grace in shining uniforms of holiness, and for number, freshness, beauty, and purity, they are as the dewdrops which come mysteriously from the morning's womb. Some refer this passage to the resurrection, but even if it be so, the work of grace in regeneration is equally well described by it, for it is a spiritual resurrection. Even as the holy dead rise gladly into the lovely image of their Lord, so do quickened souls put on the glorious righteousness of Christ, and stand forth to behold their Lord and serve him. How truly beautiful is holiness ! God himself admires it. How wonderful also is the eternal youth of the mystical body of Christ ! As the dew is new every morning, so is there a constant succession of converts to give to the church perpetual juvenility. Her young men have a dew from the Lord upon them, and arouse in her armies an undying enthusiasm for him whose " locks are bushy and black as a raven " with unfailing youth. Since Jesus ever lives, so shall his church ever flourish. As his strength never faileth, so shall the vigour of his true people be renewed day by day. As he is a Priest-King, so are his people all priests and kings, and the beauties of holiness are their priestly dress, their garments for glory and for beauty : of these priests unto God there shall be an unbroken succession. The realisation of this day of power during the time of the Lord's tarrying is that which we should constantly pray for ; and we may legitimately expect it since he ever sits in the seat of honour and power, and puts forth his strength, according to his own word, " My Father worketh hitherto, and I work."

4 The LORD hath sworn, and will not repent, Thou *art* a priest for ever after the order of Melchizedek.

We have now reached the heart of the Psalm, which is also the very centre and soul of our faith. Our Lord Jesus is a Priest-King by the ancient oath of Jehovah : " he glorified not himself to be made a high priest," but was ordained thereunto from of old, and was called of God a high priest after the order of Melchizedek. It must be a solemn and a sure matter which leads the Eternal to swear, and with him an oath fixes and settles the decree for ever ; but in this case, as if to make assurance a thousand times sure, it is added, " *and will not repent.*" It is done, and done for ever and ever ; Jesus is sworn in to be the priest of his people, and he must abide so even to the end, because his commission is sealed by the unchanging oath of the immutable Jehovah. If his priesthood could be revoked, and his authority removed, it would be the end of all hope and life for the people whom he loves ; but this sure rock is the basis of our security—the oath of God establishes our glorious Lord both in his priesthood and in his throne. It is the Lord who has constituted him a priest for ever, he has done it by oath, that oath is without repentance, is taking effect now, and will stand throughout all ages : hence our security in him is placed beyond all question.

The declaration runs in the present tense as being the only time with the Lord, and comprehending all other times. " *Thou art,*" i.e., thou wast and art, and art to come, in all ages a priestly King. The order of Melchizedek's priesthood was the most ancient and primitive, the most free from ritual and ceremony, the most natural and simple, and at the same time the most honourable. That ancient patriarch was the father of his people, and at the same time ruled and taught them ; he swayed both the sceptre and the censer, reigned in righteousness, and offered sacrifice before the Lord. There has never arisen another like to him since his days, for whenever the kings of Judah attempted to seize the sacerdotal office they were driven back to their confusion : God would have no king-priest save his son. Melchizedek's office was exceptional : none preceded or succeeded him ; he comes upon the page of history mysteriously ; no pedigree is given, no date of birth, or mention of death ; he blesses Abraham, receives tithe, and vanishes from the scene amid honours which show that he was greater than the founder of the chosen nation.   He is seen but once, and that once suffices.   Aaron and his seed came and went ; their imperfect sacrifice continued for many generations, because it had no finality in it, and could never make the comers thereunto perfect.   Our Lord Jesus, like Melchizedek, stands forth before us as a priest of divine ordaining ; not made a priest by fleshly birth, as the sons of Aaron ; he mentions neither father, mother, nor descent, as his right to the sacred office ; he stands upon his personal merits, by himself alone ; as no man came before him in his work, so none can follow after ; his order begins and ends in his own person, and in himself it is eternal, " having neither beginning of days nor end of years."   The King-priest has been here and left his blessing upon the believing seed, and now he sits in glory in his complete character, atoning for us by the merit of his blood, and exercising all power on our behalf.

> " O may we ever hear thy voice
> In mercy to us speak,
> And in our Priest we will rejoice,
> Thou great Melchizedek."

5 The Lord at thy right hand shall strike through kings in the day of his wrath.

6 He shall judge among the heathen, he shall fill *the places* with the dead bodies : he shall wound the heads over many countries.

7 He shall drink of the brook in the way : therefore shall he lift up the head.

The last verses of this Psalm we understand to refer to the future victories of the Priest-King.   He shall not for ever sit in waiting posture, but shall come into the fight to end the weary war by his own victorious presence.   He will lead the final charge in person ; his own right hand and his holy arm shall get unto him the victory.

5. " *The Lord at thy right hand shall strike through kings in the day of his wrath.*" Now that he has come into the field of action, the infinite Jehovah comes with him as the strength of his right hand.   Eternal power attends the coming of the Lord, and earthly power dies before it as though smitten through with a sword.   In the last days all the kingdoms of the earth shall be overcome by the kingdom of heaven, and those who dare oppose shall meet with swift and overwhelming ruin.   What are kings when they dare oppose the Son of God ?   A single stroke shall suffice for their destruction.   When the angel of the Lord smote Herod there was no need of a second blow ; he was eaten of worms and gave up the ghost.   Concerning the last days, we read of the Faithful and True, who shall ride upon a white horse, and in righteousness judge and make war : " Out of his mouth goeth a sharp sword, that with it he should smite the nations : and he shall rule them with a rod of iron : and he treadeth the winepress of the fierceness and wrath of Almighty God."

6. " *He shall judge among the heathen,*" or, among the nations.   All nations shall feel his power, and either yield to it joyfully or be crushed before it.   " *He shall fill the places with the dead bodies.*"   In the terrible battles of his gospel all opponents shall fall till the field of fight is heaped high with the slain.   This need not be understood literally, but as a poetical description of the overthrow of all rebellious powers and the defeat of all unholy principles.   Yet should kings oppose the Lord with weapons of war, the result would be their overwhelming defeat and the entire destruction of their forces.   Read in connection with this prophecy the passage which begins at the seventeenth verse of Rev. xix. and runs on to the end of the chapter.   Terrible things in righteousness will be seen ere the history of this world comes to an end.   " *He shall wound the heads over many countries.*"   He will strike at the greatest powers which resist him, and wound not merely common men, but those who rule and reign.   If the nations will not have Christ for their Head, they shall find their political heads to be powerless to protect them.   Or the passage may be read, " he has smitten the head over the wide earth."   The monarch of the greatest nation shall not be able to escape the sword of the Lord ; nor shall that dread spiritual prince who rules over the children of disobedience be able to escape without a deadly wound. Pope and priest must fall, with Mahomet and other deceivers who are now heads of the people.   Jesus must reign and they must perish.

7. " *He shall drink of the brook in the way.*" So swiftly shall he march to conquest that he shall not stay for refreshment, but drink as he hastens on. Like Gideon's men that lapped, he shall throw his heart into the fray and cut it short in righteousness, because a short work will the Lord make in the earth. " *Therefore shall he lift up the head.*" His own head shall be lifted high in victory, and his people, in him, shall be upraised also. When he passed this way before, he was burdened and had stern work laid upon him ; but in his second advent he will win an easy victory ; aforetime he was the man of sorrows, but when he comes a second time his head will be lifted in triumph. Let his saints rejoice with him. " Lift up your heads, for your redemption draweth nigh." In the latter days we look for terrible conflicts and for a final victory. Long has Jesus borne with our rebellious race, but at length he will rise to end the warfare of long-suffering, by the blows of justice. God has fought with men's sins for their good, but he will not always by his Spirit strive with men ; he will cease from that struggle of long-suffering love, and begin another which shall soon end in the final destruction of his adversaries. O King-priest, we who are, in a minor degree, king-priests too, are full of gladness because thou reignest even now, and wilt come ere long to vindicate thy cause and establish thine empire for ever. Even so, come quickly. Amen.

EXPLANATORY NOTES AND QUAINT SAYINGS.

Whole Psalm.—The preceding Psalm is a Passion-Psalm, and it is now followed by a Psalm of Christ's Resurrection, Ascension, and Session in glory. We have seen the same connection in Ps. xxii.—xxiv., and in Ps. xlv.—xlvii. The present Psalm grows up from the former Psalm, as the Hill of Olivet, the Hill of Ascension, rises up from the Vale of Gethsemane below it.—*Christopher Wordsworth.*

Whole Psalm.—This Psalm has been well designated the crown of all the Psalms, of which Luther saith that it is worthy to be overlaid with precious jewels. More especially does the Reformer call verse 5 a well-spring,—nay, a treasury of all Christian doctrines, understanding, wisdom, and comfort, richer and fuller than any other passage of Holy Writ. In his own peculiar manner, he styles Christ the *Sheblimini* (' Sit on my right hand '). ' Full sure, the devil must let alone my *Sheblimini*, and cannot bring him down either by his scorn or by his wrath.' Christ still liveth and reigneth, and his title is *Sheblimini*. On his stirrup is engraven, " I will make thine enemies thy footstool," and upon his diadem, " Thou art a priest for ever."— *Alfred Edersheim,* 1873.

Whole Psalm.—The ancients (by Cassiodorus' collection) term this Psalm *the sun of our faith, the treasure of holy writ* : *verbis brevis, sensu infinitus* (saith Augustine), short in words, but in sense infinite. Theodoret notes how it is connected with the Psalm going before : " there (saith he) we have his cross and sufferings, here his conquest and trophies." For he cometh forth as the *heir apparent* of the Almighty, the brightness of his glory, and the express image of his person, graced with, 1. *Title,* " My Lord." 2. *Place,* " *Sit thou on my right hand.*" 3. *Power,* " *Until I make thine enemies thy footstool.*"—*John Prideaux,* in a Sermon entitled, " The Draught of the Brooke," 1636.

Whole Psalm.—This Psalm is one of the fullest and most compendious prophecies of the person and offices of Christ in the whole Old Testament, and so full of fundamental truth, that I shall not shun to call it *Symbolum Davidicum,* the prophet David's creed. And indeed there are very few, if any, of the articles of that creed which we all generally profess, which are not either plainly expressed, or by most evident implication couched in this little model. First, the *Doctrine of the Trinity* is in the first words ; " *The Lord said unto my Lord.*" There is *Jehovah the Father,* and *my Lord,* the Son, and the consecrating of him to be David's Lord, which was by the *Holy Ghost,* by whose fulness he was anointed unto the offices of king and priest ; for so our Saviour himself expounds this word " *said,*" by the sealing and sanctification of him to his office, John x. 34, 35, 36. Then we have the *Incarnation of Christ,* in the words, " *my Lord,*" together with his dignity and honour above David (as our Saviour himself expounds it, Matt. xxii. 42, 45). *Mine,* that is, my Son by descent and genealogy after the flesh, and yet my Lord too, in regard of his higher sonship. We have also the *Sufferings of Christ,* in that he was consecrated a priest (ver. 4) to offer up himself once for all, and so *to drink of the brook in the way.*

We have his *Completed Work* and conquest over all his enemies and sufferings ; *his Resurrection,* " *he shall lift up his head* " ; his *Ascension* and *Intercession,* " *Sit thou on my right hand.*" We have here also a *Holy Catholic Church* gathered together by the sceptre of his kingdom, and holding in the parts thereof a blessed and beautiful *Communion of Saints ;* " *The Lord shall send the rod of thy strength out of Zion : rule thou in the midst of thine enemies. Thy people shall be willing in the day of thy power, in the beauties of holiness from the womb of the morning : thou hast the dew of thy youth.*" We have the *Last Judgment,* for *all his enemies must be put under his feet* (which is the Apostle's argument to prove the end of all things, 1 Cor. xv. 25) ; and there is the *day of his wrath,* wherein he shall accomplish that judgment over the heathen, and that victory over the kings of the earth (*who take counsel and band themselves together against him*), which he doth here in his word begin. We have the *Remission of sins,* comprised in his priesthood, for he was to offer sacrifices for the remission of sins, and " to put away sin by the sacrifice of himself," Eph. i. 7 ; Heb. ix. 26. We have the *Resurrection of the body,* because he must " subdue all enemies under his feet, and the last enemy to be destroyed is death," as the Apostle argues out of this Psalm, 1 Cor. xv. 25, 26. And lastly, we have *life everlasting,* in the ever-lasting merit and virtue of his priesthood, " *Thou art a priest for ever after the order of Melchizedek,*" and in his sitting at the right hand of God, whither he is gone as our forerunner, and to prepare a place for us, Heb. vi. 20 ; John xiv. 2 ; and therefore the apostle from his sitting there, and living ever, inferreth the perfection and certainty of our salvation, Rom. vi. 8, 11 ; viii. 17 ; Eph. ii. 16 ; Col. iii. 1—4 ; 1 Cor. xv. 49 ; Phil. iii. 20, 21 ; 1 Thess. iv. 14 ; Heb. vii. 25 ; 1 John iii. 2.—*Edward Reynolds,* 1599—1676.

Whole Psalm.—Although the Jews of later times have gone about to wrest it to another meaning, yet this Psalm is so approved and undoubted a prophecy of Christ, that the Pharisees durst not deny it, when being questioned by our Saviour (Matt. xxii. 42, 43) how it should be, seeing Christ is the son of David, that David notwithstanding should call him Lord, saying, " *The Lord said unto my Lord,*" they could not answer him a word, whereas the answer had been very easy and ready if they could have denied this Psalm to be meant of Christ. But they knew it could not be otherwise understood, and it was commonly taken amongst them to be a prophecy of their Messias, according to the very evidence of the text itself, which cannot be fitted to any other, but only to Christ our Saviour, the Son of God. For whereas some of them since then have construed all these things as spoken in the name of the people of Judah concerning David their king, the text itself refuseth that construction, when in those words, " *Sit thou at my right hand,*" it mentioneth an honour done to him of whom it speaketh, greater than can be fitted to the angels, and therefore much less to be applied unto David. Again, that which is spoken in the fourth verse of the priesthood, cannot be understood of David, who was indeed a king, but never had anything spoken as touching the priesthood to appertain unto him, and of whom it cannot be conceived how it should be said, " *Thou art a priest for ever,*" etc. Yea, there is nothing here spoken whereof we may see in David any more but some little shadow in comparison of that which hath come to pass in Jesus Christ.—*Robert Abbot* (1560—1617) *in* " *The Exaltation of the Kingdom and Priesthood of Christ.*"

Whole Psalm.—The sixty-eighth Psalm hails the ascent of the Messiah, pre-figured by the translation of the ark, and gives a rapid and obscure view of the glories and the blessings consequent upon that event. The twenty-fourth exhibits to us the Messiah ascending to his redemption throne upborne by the wings of angels and archangels, and hosannahed by the whole intelligent creation ; it marks in the most glowing colours the triumphant entry of Messiah into the heavenly regions, and the tone of authority and power with which he commands that entrance—it sends him attended by the angelic host to his Father's throne, there to claim that pre-eminence which was his by inheritance and by conquest. At this point the Psalm before us " takes up the wondrous tale " : it exhibits to us the awful solemnities of his recep-tion, it represents the Father bestowing on his well-beloved Son the kingdom which he had earned, exalting him to the throne, and putting all things under his feet ; receiving him in his office of prophet, and promising universality and permanence to " the rod of his strength " ; receiving him in the office of priesthood, his own peculiar priesthood, and confirming its efficacy and duration by an oath ; thus perfecting the redemption scheme, and completing the conquest over sin and death, and him who had the power of death. Man united with God was raised to the throne of being : man united with God perfected the sacrifice which was demanded, and the angelic host is represented by the Psalmist as taking up the strain, and hymning the future triumphs of the King of Glory—triumphs over his foes, whom he will visit in the day of his wrath, and triumphs with his willing people, whom he will assist with his Spirit, refine by his grace, and exalt into his glory.　Such do I conceive to be the occasion, the object, and the tendency of this sacred song : to me it appears to be eminently an *epinicion*, or song of victory : it celebrates the triumph of the conqueror, it presents him with the rewards of victory, and it predicts future conquests as crowning his glory ; while elsewhere we see the Captain of our salvation militant, here we see him triumphant ; while elsewhere we see his offices inchoate, here they are perfected by the approval of the Godhead, and the promise of eternity : here we have instruction consolidating empire, and the atonement completed by the everlasting priesthood.—*J. H. Singer, in " The Irish Pulpit," 1839.*

Verse 1.—In this one verse we have a description of Christ's person, his wars and his victory ; so that we may say of it (and so indeed of the whole Psalm, which is an epitome of the Gospel), as Tully did of Brutus in his laconical epistle, *Quam multa, quam paucis !* How much in a little.—*John Trapp.*

Verse 1.—" *The Lord said unto my Lord, sit thou at my right hand.*"　An oftquoted passage—because it contains a memorable truth.　We find it quoted by Messiah himself to lead Israel to own him as greater than David, Matt. xxii. 44. It is quoted in Heb. i. 13, to prove him higher far than angels.　It is brought forward by Peter, Acts ii. 34, to show him Lord as well as Christ.　It is referred to in Heb. x. 12, 13, as declaring that Jesus has satisfactorily finished what he undertook to accomplish on earth, " the one sacrifice for ever," and is henceforth on that seat of divine honour " expecting till his enemies be made his footstool " in the day of his Second Coming.—*Andrew A. Bonar.*

Verse 1.—" *The Lord said.*"　Albeit the understanding of Christ's person and office be necessary unto the church, yet none know the Son save the Father, and they to whom he will reveal him : for David knew Christ only by the Father's teaching : " *The Lord said,*" said he.—*David Dickson.*

Verse 1.—" *My Lord.*"　From hence we learn that though Christ was man, yet he was more than a bare man, since he is Lord to his father David.　For *jure naturæ* no son is lord to his father ; domination doth never ascend.　There must be something above nature in him to make him his father's sovereign, as our Saviour himself argueth from these words, Matt. xxii. 42, 45.—*Edward Reynolds.*

Verse 1.—" *My Lord.*"　It was a higher honour to have Christ for his son, than to be a king ; yet David does not say that Christ is his son, but rejoices that Christ is his Lord, yea Christ's servant.　But this joy has also been procured *for it :* see Luke i. 43 ; John xx. 28 ; Phil. iii. 3, 8.　They who regard the Messiah only as the son of David, regard the lesser part of the conception of him.　A dominion to which David himself is subject, shows the heavenly majesty of the King, and the heavenly character of his kingdom.—*John Albert Bengel.*

Verse 1.—" *Until I make thine enemies thy footstool.*"　Every word is full of weight.　For though ordinarily subdivisions of holy Scripture and crumbling of the bread of life be rather a loosing than an expounding of it ; yet in such parts of it as were of purpose intended for models and summaries of fundamental doctrines (of which sort this Psalm is one of the fullest and briefest in the whole Scriptures), as in little maps of large countries, there is no word whereupon some point of weighty consequence may not depend.　Here then is to be considered the *term of duration* or *measure of Christ's kingdom :* " *until.*"　The *author* of subduing Christ's enemies under him : " *I, the Lord.*"　The *manner* thereof ; *ponam,* and *ponam scabellum,* put thy foes as a stool under thy feet.　Victory is a relative word, and presupposeth enemies, and they are expressed in the text.　.　.　.　Enmity shows itself against Christ in all the offices of his mediation.　There is enmity against him as a *prophet.*　Enmity against his *truth,*—in opinion by adulterating it with human mixtures and superinducements, teaching for doctrines the traditions of men ; in affection, by wishing many divine truths were razed out of the Scriptures, as being manifestly contrary to those pleasures which they love rather than God ; in conversation, by keeping down the truth in unrighteousness, and in those things which they know, as brute beasts, corrupting themselves.　Enmity against his *teaching,* by quenching the motions, and resisting the evidence of his Spirit in the Word, refusing to hear his voice, and rejecting the counsel of God against themselves.　There is enmity against him as a *priest*, by undervaluing his person, sufferings, righteousness, or merits. And as a *king*; enmity to his worship, by profaneness neglecting it, by idolatry misappropriating it, by superstition corrupting it. Enmity to his ways and service, by ungrounded prejudices, misjudging them as grievous, unprofitable, or unequal ways; and by wilful disobedience forsaking them to walk in the ways of our own heart.—*Edward Reynolds.*

Verse 1.—" *Make thine enemies thy footstool."* This expression, that the conquest of Christ's enemies shall be but as the removing of a stool into its place, noteth unto us two things : first, *the easiness of God's victory* over the enemies of Christ. They are before him as nothing, less than nothing, the drop of a bucket, the dust of the balance, a very little thing. . . . Secondly, as this putting of Christ's enemies like a stool under the feet noteth easiness, so also it noteth *order* or *beauty* too. When Christ's enemies shall be under his foot, then there shall be a right order in things ; then it shall indeed appear that God is a *God of order,* and therefore the day wherein that shall be done, is called " *the times of the restitution of all things,"* Acts iii. 21. The putting of Christ's enemies under his feet is an *act of justice ;* and of all others, justice is the most orderly virtue, that which keepeth beauty upon the face of a people, as consisting itself in symmetry and proportion.

This putting of Christ's enemies as a stool under his feet, also denotes unto us two things in reference to Christ : first, his *rest,* and secondly, his *triumph. To stand,* in the Scripture phrase, denoteth *ministry,* and *to sit, rest ;* and there is no posture so easy as to sit with a stool under one's feet. Till Christ's enemies then be all under his feet, he is not fully in his rest.

Furthermore, this " *footstool "* under Christ's feet, in reference to his enemies, denoteth unto us four things. First, *the extreme shame and confusion* which they shall everlastingly suffer, the utter abasing and bringing down of all that exalteth itself against Christ. Secondly, hereby is noted *the burden which wicked men must bear* : the footstool beareth the weight of the body, so must the enemies of Christ bear the weight of his heavy and everlasting wrath upon their souls. Thirdly, herein is noted *the relation which the just recompense* of God bears unto the sins of ungodly men. Thus will Christ deal with his enemies at the last day. Here they trample upon Christ in his word, in his ways, in his members ; they make the saints bow down for them to go over, and make them as the pavements on the ground ; they tread under foot the blood of the covenant, and the sanctuary of the Lord, and put Christ to shame ; but there their own measure shall be returned into their bosoms, they shall be constrained to confess as Adonibezek, " As I have done, so God hath requited me."   Lastly, herein we may note *the great power and wisdom of Christ* in turning the malice and mischief of his enemies unto his own use and advantage, and so ordering wicked men that though they intend nothing but extirpation and ruin to his kingdom, yet they shall be useful unto him, and, against their own wills, serviceable to those glorious ends, in the accomplishing whereof he shall be admired by all those that believe. As in a great house there is necessary use of vessels of dishonour, destined unto sordid and mean, but yet daily, services : so in the great house of God, wicked men are his utensils and household instruments, as footstools and staves, and vessels wherein there is no pleasure, though of them there may be good use.—*Condensed from Reynolds.*

Verse 1.—" *Thy footstool."* As this our king has a glorious throne, so has he also a wonderful footstool ; and as his royal throne imparts to us comfort in the highest degree, so his footstool also imparts to us joy. How joyful shall his poor subjects be when they hear that their prince and king has slain their enemies and delivered them out of their hands ! How did their poor subjects go forward to meet Saul and Jonathan when those kings had slain the Philistines ! . . . Moreover, because our King has *his* enemies under his feet, thus shall he also bring all *our* enemies under our feet, for his victory is ours, God be thanked, who has given us the victory through Christ our Lord.—*Joshua Arnd,* 1626—1685.

Verse 2.—" *The rod of thy strength,"* or rather, " *The sceptre of thy might,"* i.e., of " Thy kingly majesty," as in Jer. xlviii. 17 ; Ezek. xix. 14. Chrysostom plays upon the word ῥάβδος (LXX) as a rod of strength and consolation, as in Ps. xxiii. 4 ; a rod of chastisement, as in Ps. ii. 9, 1. Cor. iv. 21 ; a symbol of kingly rule, as in Is. xi. 1, Ps. xlv. 6. It was by this rod, he says, that the disciples wrought when they subdued the world, in obedience to the command, " Go and make disciples of all nations " ; a rod far more powerful than that of Moses, " for that divided rivers, this brake in pieces the ungodliness of the world." And then with profound truth he adds, " Nor would one err who should call the Cross the rod of power ; for this rod converted sea and land, and filled them with a vast power. Armed with this rod, the Apostles went forth throughout the world, and accomplished all that they did, beginning at Jerusalem." The Cross, which to men seemed the very emblem of shame and weakness, was, in truth, the power of God.—*J. J. Stewart Perowne.*

Verse 2.—" *The rod of thy strength.*" The power of this sceptre and word of Christ appeareth greatly in the saving of his elect. . . . So mightily hath it prevailed and overruled the minds of men against nature, and reason, and learning, and wisdom, and custom, and whatsoever else is strong to hold men in the liking of those things which they have once received and followed, as that they have been content to renounce the devotions which their forefathers had so long embraced ; to cast away the gods which themselves had devoutly served ; to stop their ears against the contrary motives and persuasions of father and mother ; to harden their hearts against the kneelings and weepings and embracings of wife and children ; to forego their honours, and inheritances, yea, and their lives also, rather than lose that peace and joy of heart which the same word of Christ had ministered unto them. Yea, how strange is it, and how greatly doth it commend the power of this word, to see weakness hereby prevailing against strength, simplicity against policy ; to see the lamb standing without fear before the lion, the gentle turtle before the devouring kite ; women and children and weaklings before the great monarchs and potentates of the world, not fearing their threatening words, nor dreading their tormenting hands, but boldly uttering the word of their testimony (Rev. xii. 11), in despite of all their fury, and never yielding to shrink from it, by anything that could be devised against them. The word of God in their hearts gave them courage and resolution and strength to go through fire and water, to bear all adventures of wind and weather, and howsoever they seemed to be beaten against the rocks, yet they escaped shipwreck, and arrived safe at the haven of their desire.—*Robert Abbot.*

Verse 2.—" *Out of Zion.*" We need not say much about how the omniscience of God is displayed in the wonderful fact, that in the very land of the covenant— in the very midst of that people who rejected and crucified the Saviour, the first church of Christ on earth was established. What would cavillers and blasphemers have said, had it been otherwise ? had the Christian community been formed in any of the heathen countries ? Would it not have been considered as a fiction of the idolatrous priests ? Israel scattered among the nations, and the Church of Christ having begun in Zion at Jerusalem, are the most wonderful and enduring monuments, and incontestable witnesses of the truth of Christianity.—*Benjamin Weiss.*

Verse 2.—From his ruling *in the midst of enemies* we learn that the kingdom of Christ in this life is the kingdom of the Cross, of persecutions, and of dangers. Enemies are never wanting, not only external adversaries, but also spiritual and eternal ; and therefore great sorrow is always awaiting the godly. In this most terrible conflict, however, their minds are lifted up by this consolation, *viz.*, that the rod of the kingdom is strong, and cannot be overcome by any force or power ; yea, more, albeit assailed with contendings and all kinds of storms, it will continue stable, firm, and perpetual : and there will always be a Church among men, which will fear and worship this King ; because the experience of all the ages teaches, that this kingdom has the more grown and increased the more it has been opposed, according to that saying of Basil, ἐν ταῖς θλίψεσι μᾶλλον θάλλει ἡ ἐκκλησία, the Church flourishes more by tribulation.—*Rivetus.*

Verse 2.—" *Rule thou in the midst of thine enemies.*" Set up thy power over them and reign in them. This is a commission to set up a kingdom *in the very midst* of those who were his enemies ; in the hearts of those who had been and were rebellious. His kingdom is set up not by destroying them, but by *subduing* them, so that they become his willing servants. They yield to him, and he rules over them. It is not here a commission to cut them off, but one much more difficult of execution,— to make them his friends, and to dispose them to submit to his authority. Mere *power* may crush men ; it requires more than that to make rebels willingly submissive, and to dispose them voluntarily to obey.—*Albert Barnes.*

Verse 3.—" *Thy people.*" That is, those whom thou dost receive from thy Father, and, by setting up the standard and ensign of the Gospel, gather to thyself " *Shall be willing.*" The word is *willingnesses*, that is, a people of *great willingness and devotion,* or (as the original word is elsewhere used, Psalm cxix. 108), shall be *freewill offerings* unto thee. The abstract being put for the concrete, and the plural for the singular, notes how exceeding forward and free they should be ; as the Lord, to signify that his people were most rebellious, saith, that they were *rebellion itself,* Ezek. ii. 8. So then the meaning is, thy people shall, with most ready and forward cheerfulness, devote, consecrate, and render up themselves to thy government as a reasonable sacrifice, shall be of a most liberal, free, noble, and unconstrained spirit in thy service, and shall be *voluntaries* in the wars of thy kingdom.—*Edward Reynolds.*

Verse 3.—" *Thy people,*" O Jesus Christ, which were given thee by the Father, purchased and redeemed by thee, who acknowledge thee for their Lord, and are bound to thee by a military oath, are *extremely willing,* being devoted to thy service with the greatest readiness of soul, alacrity, inclination, and voluntary obedience. Nor are they willing only, but *willingness* itself in the abstract ; nay, *willingnesses* in the plural number, the highest and most excellent willingnesses, all which add an emphasis. This is seen to be so בְּיוֹם חֵילֶךְ " *in the day of thy* [*valour*] *power,*" in which thy generous spirit laying hold of them, animates them to grand and bold enterprises. Then they go forth in the beauties of holiness, by which they are a terror to the devil, a delight to God and angels, and a mutual edification to one another.—*Hermann Witsius,* 1636—1708.

Verse 3.—" *Thy people shall be willing.*" Willing to do what ? They shall be willing while others are unwilling. The simple term " *willing,*" is very expressive. It denotes the beautiful condition of creatures who suffer themselves to be wrought upon, and moved, according to the will of God. They suffer God to work in them to will and to do. They are *willing* to die unto all sin, they are willing to crucify the old man, or self, in order that the new man, or Christ, may be formed in them. They are *willing* to be weaned from their own thoughts and purposes, that the thoughts and purposes of God may be fulfilled in them. They are *willing* to be transferred from nature's steps of human descent to God's steps of human ascent. Or, to abide by the simplicity of our text, God is Will, and they are " *willing.*" God will beautify them with salvation, because there is nothing in them to hinder his working. They will be wise, they will be good, they will be lovely, they will be *like God,* for they are " *willing*" ; and there proceeds from God a mighty spirit, the whole tendency of which is to make his creatures like himself.—*John Pulsford, in " Quiet Hours,*" 1857.

Verse 3.—" *Thy people shall be willing.*" They are willing in believing, loving, obeying, adhering, living piously and justly in this world ; so that they do not need the constraints of laws or threats, because they are led by the Spirit of God, and where the Spirit of the Lord is, there, also, is liberty.—*Wolfgang Musculus.*

Verse 3.—" *Thy people shall be willing.*" Am I one of the " willing people "— not only my obedience and allegiance secured from a conviction of the truth, but my heart inclined, and my will renewed ? To *do* the will of God, to *bear* the will of God, to *coincide* with the will of God—and that with calm if not cheerful consent of the heart, as seeing him who is invisible, and holding fast my living apprehension of his person and character ? All unwillingness, whether practical or lurking in the heart, springs from unbelief—from a failure to realise him or his purposes. Were Jesus, as God become incarnate, and as giving himself for me, and his counsel of grace towards me, ever or even in any measure before my heart, how could I hesitate to yield myself, absolutely and implicitly, to him and his guidance ? Again, this " willingness " is the essence of holiness; it constitutes " the beauties of holiness " —the beauty of Christ cast over the soul. The cure, therefore, for all my misery and sin is more faith, more of Christ, and nearer to him. This let me seek and ask with ever increasing earnestness.—*Alfred Edersheim.*

Verse 3.—" *Thy people shall be willing in the day of thy power,*" etc. The prophet here notes three things respecting the subjects of the kingdom of the Messiah : 1. Their prompt obedience. 2. Their attire or vesture. 3. Their abundance, or multitude. This representation admirably agrees with what precedes. He had said that the Messiah should reign in the midst of his enemies, but lest any one should think that he would reign only over enemies, unwilling and opposing, as the devils are made subject to Christ, now he lets us know that he will have a loyal people, and obedient subjects, for else there would be wanting that same glory of which Solomon speaks in Prov. xiv. 28, " In the multitude of people is the king's honour." He affirms also, that he would have his own people, who would recognise, receive, and serve him as King, with true obedience, nor would it be a small company, but like the dew, which waters the face of the whole earth.—*Rivetus.*

Verse 3.—" *Thy people shall be willing in the day of thy power.*" It is power acted and executed *with all sweetness, mildness, and gentleness.* Here is " leading, but no force ; conduct, but no compulsion," *vehemens inclinatio, non coactio :* * the will is determined, but not the least violence is done to it, to the infringing of its liberty. How spontaneously does the person led follow him that leads him ! So it is here. This and all other workings of the Spirit are admirably suited to the nature of reasonable and free agents. Efficacious grace does not at all destroy natural liberty. Where the Spirit does not find sinners willing, by his sweet method he makes them willing : " *Thy people shall be willing in the day of thy power.*" A " *day of power,*" yet " *willing.*" Even the Spirit's drawing is managed with all consistency to the freedom of the will. Ελκυει ὁ Θεος, αλλα βουλομενον ελκυει.† " He draws ; but it is one that he makes willing to follow." " Behold, I will allure her " (Hosea ii. 14) : ay, there is the Spirit's leading ! this being the constant and avowed doctrine of the Protestants, and particularly their explication of the Spirit's leading in the text [Rom. viii. 14] ; how injurious and invidious are the Popish writers in their traducing and calumniating of them, as if they asserted the Spirit, in this or any other act, to work with compulsion, or in a way destructive to man's essential liberty ! It is a vile scandal !— *Thomas Jacomb, in " The Morning Exercises.*"

Verse 3.—" *In the day of thy power.*" In the day of thy *strength,* saith the *Vulgate :* of thy force and *valour,* say Tremellius and Junius : of the *assemblies,* say they of Geneva : of the *armies,* saith Munster ; " at such times as thou shalt bring thy bands and join battle," so Vatablus, Castalio, and the Chaldee Paraphrase have it. All which the original בְּיוֹם חֵילֶךָ may bear without straining.—*John Prideaux,* 1578— 1650.

Verse 3.—The subjects of the Priest-King are willing soldiers. In accordance with the warlike tone of the whole Psalm, our text describes the subjects as an army. That military metaphor comes out more closely when we attach the true meaning of the words, " *in the day of thy power.*" The word rendered, and rightly rendered, " *power,*" has the same ambiguity which that word has in the English of the date of our translation, and for a century later, as you may find in Shakspeare and Milton, who both used it in the sense of " army." Singularly enough we do not employ " powers " in that meaning, but we do another word which means the same thing— and talk of " forces," meaning thereby " troops." . . . " *The day of thy power* " is not a mere synonym for " *the time of thy might,*" but means specifically " *the day of thine army,*" that is " the day when thou dost muster thy forces and set them in array for the war." The King is going forth to conquest. But he goes not alone. Behind him come his faithful followers, all pressing on with willing hearts and high courage.—*Alexander McLaren,* 1871.

Verse 3.—" *In the day of thy power.*" This refers in a general way to the gospel dispensation, and in particular to the period of conversion. To the perishing sinner the gospel comes, " not in word only, but also in *power,* and in the Holy Ghost, and in much assurance." It is an *arresting* power ; it meets the sinner, and stays his mad career, as in the case of Saul of Tarsus. It is a *convincing* power, it teaches the sinner that he is ruined in every respect, and leads him to cry out, " What shall I do to be saved ? " . . . It is a *life-giving* power ; it quickens dead souls, and will eventually bring the dead bodies from their graves ; " all that are in the graves *shall hear* the voice of the Son of God and *shall live.*" This is the style of Jehovah, " *I will, they shall* " ; none other dare speak thus. It is also *liberating* power ; " if the Son shall make you free, ye shall be free indeed."—*Theophilus Jones, in a Sermon preached at Surrey Chapel,* 1823.

Verse 3.—" *Thy people,*" etc. In *homage,* they shall be like a company of priests in sacred vestments, for they shall appear " *in the beauties of holiness.*" In *number,* they shall be like the countless dewdrops " *from the womb of the morning,*" sparkling in the rays of the rising sun, and reflecting his radiance. In *glory* they shall bear the likeness of Christ's resurrection in all its vernal freshness : " *Thou hast the dew of thy youth.*"—*Benjamin Wildon Carr.*

Verse 3.—" *In the beauties of holiness.*" In holy vestments as priests. They are at once warriors and priests ; meet for the service of him who was King and Priest. Neander (*Mem. of Chr. Life,* ch. iv.) remarks on the connection between

* Gorranus   † Chrysostom.

these two sides of the Christian character. God's soldiers can only *maintain their war* by priestly self-consecration. Conversely: God's priests can only *preserve their purity* by unintermitted conflict.—*William Kay.*

Verse 3.—" *In the beauties of holiness.*" This expression is usually read as if it belonged either to the words immediately preceding, or to those immediately following. But in either case the connection is somewhat difficult and obscure. It seems better regarded as a distinct and separate clause, adding a fresh trait to the description of the army. And what that is we need not find any difficulty in ascertaining. " *The beauties of holiness* " is a frequent phrase for the sacerdotal garments, the holy festal attire of the priests of the Lord. So considered, how beautifully it comes in here. The conquering King whom the Psalm hymns is a Priest for ever ; and he is followed by an army of priests. The soldiers are gathered in the day of the muster, with high courage and willing devotion, ready to fling away their lives ; but they are clad not in mail, but in priestly robes ; like those who wait before the altar rather than like those who plunge into the fight, like those who compassed Jericho with the ark for their standard and the trumpets for all their weapons. We can scarcely fail to remember the words which echo these and interpret them. " The armies which were in heaven followed him on white horses, clothed in fine linen, white and clean "—a strange armour against sword-cut and spear-thrust.—*Alexander McLaren.*

Verse 3.—" *The beauties of holiness.*" Godliness is our spiritual beauty. Godliness is to the soul as the light to the world, to illustrate and adorn it. It is not greatness that sets us off in God's eye, but goodness : what is the beauty of the angels but their sanctity ? Godliness is the curious embroidery and workmanship of the Holy Ghost : a soul furnished with godliness is damasked with beauty, and enamelled with purity : this is the " clothing of wrought gold " which makes the King of heaven fall in love with us. Were there not an excellency in holiness, the hypocrite would never go about to paint it. Godliness sheds a glory and lustre upon the saints : what are the graces but the golden feathers in which Christ's dove shines ? Ps. lxviii. 13.—*Thomas Watson.*

Verse 3.—" *Thou hast the dew of thy youth.*" These words are often misunderstood, and taken to be a description of the fresh, youthful energy attributed by the Psalm to the Priest-King of this nation of soldier-priests. The misunderstanding, I suppose, has led to the common phrase, " the dew of one's youth." But the reference of the expression is to the army, not to its leader. " *Youth* " here is a collective noun, equivalent to " *young men.*" The host of his soldier-subjects is described as a band of young warriors, whom he leads, in their fresh strength and countless numbers and gleaming beauty like the dew of the morning. . . . It is as a symbol of the refreshing which a weary world will receive from the conquests and presence of the King and his host, that they are likened to the glittering morning dew. Another prophetic Scripture gives us the same emblem when it speaks of Israel being " in the midst of many people as a dew from the Lord." Such ought to be the effect of our presence. We are meant to gladden, to adorn, to refresh this parched, prosaic world, with a freshness brought from the chambers of the sunrise.

The dew, formed in the silence of the darkness while men sleep, falling as willingly on a bit of dead wood as anywhere, hanging its pearls on every poor spike of grass, and dressing everything on which it lies with strange beauty, each separate globule tiny and evanescent, but each flashing back the light, and each a perfect sphere : feeble one by one, but united mighty to make the pastures of the wilderness rejoice— so, created in silence by an unseen influence, feeble when taken in detail, but strong in their myriads, glad to occupy the lowliest place, and each " bright with something of celestial light," Christian men and women are to be in the midst of many people as a dew from the Lord.—*Alexander McLaren.*

Verse 3.—" *The dew of thy youth.*" There does not, indeed, appear to me any reason to doubt that, in this place, David extols the divine favour displayed in increasing the number of Christ's people ; and hence, in consequence of their extraordinary increase, he compares the youth or race which would be born to him to the *dew.* As men are struck with astonishment at seeing the earth moistened and refreshed with dew, though its descent be imperceptible, even so, David declares that an innumerable offspring shall be born to Christ, who shall be spread over the whole earth. The youth, therefore, which, like the dew-drops, are innumerable, are here designated *the dew of childhood,* or *of youth.*—*John Calvin.*

Verse 3.—" *From the womb of the morning* " is, with the utmost pertinency, applied to the conception and production of dews ; agreeably to a delicate line in that great master of just description and lively painting, Mr. Thomson :

>   "The meek ey'd morn appears, mother of dews."

We meet with a fine expression in the book of Job, which may serve to confirm this remark ; and may illustrate the propriety of the phrase used in this connection: " Hath the rain a father, or who hath begotten the drops of dew ? "   It seems, the oriental writers delighted to represent the dew as a kind of birth, as the offspring of the morning.   And if so, surely there could be no image in the whole compass of the universe better adapted to the Psalmist's purpose, or more strongly significant of those multitudes of proselytes, which were born, not of blood, nor of the will of the flesh, nor of the will of man, but of God ; by the powerful energy of his word and Spirit.   Upon this supposition, the whole verse describes the willing subjection, the gracious accomplishments, and the vast number of Christ's converts.—*James Hervey* (1713-14—1758), in " *Meditations and Contemplations.*"

Verse 3.—" *The dew of thy youth.*"   The most apparent reference is to multitude. Compare Ps. lxxii., 16, and the proverbial use of the dew together with the sand of the sea shore to express a vast number.   The people of the Messiah are a great number that no man can number : Rev. vii. 9.   But this is only the common enwrapping veil of a further sense.   We must further note, *First*, THE ORIGIN OF THE DEW.   *From what comes it ?*   From earthly matter, vapour and mist, as the new born soldier of Christ comes from the confused, dark substance of the old nature.   *By what is it produced ?*   Through the influence of the heavenly warmth of the beams of the morning sun : so the people of God owe themselves to the light from above.   In the vivifying light of heaven, the dewdrops are begotten, and from it they come more properly than from the earth-water.   *How are they produced ?* Invisibly, wonderfully, by the secret, incomprehensible influence of the divine power.   We have by no means exhausted the figure, for we notice, *Secondly*, THE DESIGN OF THE DEW.   It is for the *fertilizing and refreshing* of the earth.   The spiritual Israel are a fructifying, quickening dew among men.   It is also for the *ornament* of the earth, which the dew bestrews as with precious stones ; and this beauty is caused because each little drop of dew reflects the morning sun and is an earthly reflection of the heavenly light.—*Condensed from Rudolph Stier.*

Verse 3 (*last clause*).—With singular beauty and propriety does the Psalmist compare the first preachers of the gospel to dew.   In the first place, they may be compared to the drops of dew on account of their multitude.   But, in order to judge of the correctness of the comparison in this respect, we must consider, that, in the Holy Land, the dews are remarkably abundant.   A French traveller * has observed of Judea, that in the morning the ground is as much moistened by dew, as if it had rained.   We are informed in the sacred history, that, when the Dayspring from on high visited the earth, many were the followers of Christ ; and that very soon after his ascension into heaven, "multitudes both of men and women were added to the Lord."   Justly then may those who hastened to the blessed Jesus, when the glorious light of his gospel first dawned upon the world, or immediately on the commencement of his mediatorial kingdom, be compared in number to the drops of dew, which at the dawn of day fall to the earth.

It is mentioned also in this verse, that the first subjects of the Messiah were to present themselves adorned " with the beauties of holiness " ; בהדרי קדש in the splendours of holiness.   In brightness, then, as well as in multitude, did they resemble the glittering drops of the morning dew.   Our great poet has combined these two ideas in his beautiful comparison of an host innumerable to the

>   " Stars of morning, dew-drops which the sun impearls." †

The formation of the dew is represented in Scripture as the work of God, and not of man ; and its descending to refresh and fertilize the earth is mentioned as his peculiar gift, and in opposition to human means of rendering the earth more fruitful. " Who," saith Job, " hath begotten the drops of dew ? " (ch. xxxviii. 28).   And the prophet Micah declares, that " the remnant of Jacob shall be in the midst of many people as a dew from the LORD, as the showers upon the grass, that tarrieth not for

---

* Eugene Rogers.
† Milton's " Paradise Lost," Book v., line 745.

man, nor waiteth for the sons of men " (ch. v. 7). Well, then, might the term be applied by the Psalmist to those whom " God of his own will begat with the word of truth " ; and who were his appointed instruments, by their preaching, to cause " the desert to rejoice and to blossom abundantly " ; and " the wilderness to become a fruitful field."

Let it also be remembered, that those whom the Psalmist compares to dew are described under the image of young soldiers, going forth to fight the battles of a victorious prince.   Now this comparison is used in 2 Sam. xvii. 11, 12 : " I counsel," said Hushai to Ahitophel, " that all Israel be generally gathered unto thee, from Dan even to Beer-sheba, as the sand that is by the sea for multitude ; and that thou go to battle in thine own person.   So shall we come upon him in some place where he shall be found, and we will light upon him as the dew falleth upon the ground."   It is perhaps not undeserving of notice, that amongst the Romans those troops who first attacked the enemy, and who were composed of young men, were, from a supposed resemblance to dew, called Rorarii.   It is not incumbent upon me to investigate the reason of their receiving that name ; it is sufficient to point out its similarity with the expression of the Psalmist, which is applied to those who were first to engage in the conflict with the enemies of the Gospel of Christ.—*Richard Dixon*, 1811.

Verse 3.—

> Thee, in thy power's triumphant day,
>   The willing nations shall obey ;
> And, when thy rising beams they view,
>   Shall all (redeem'd from error's night)
> Appear as numberless and bright
>   As crystal drops of morning dew.
>   *N. Brady and N. Tate.*

Verse 3.—

> Lord, let thy day of power be known,
>   Thy people be confessed ;
> Eager and valiant—priests each one,
>   In holy garments dressed.

> Countless they shine, as dews from heaven
>   When eastern skies grow bright—
> More glorious than those dews are given,
>   Sparkling in morning light.
>   *George Rawson, in " Hymns, Verses, and Chants,"* 1876.

Verse 4.—" The Lord hath sworn, and will not repent," etc.   It should be diligently considered, that God has consecrated Christ priest by an oath, and that this was done for our sakes : First, That we might know how exceedingly momentous was this transaction, and the more reverently and with the stronger faith believe it.   Secondly, That we might acknowledge the goodness of God, who, being most truthful in himself, and concerning whose faithfulness it is the greatest crime to doubt, nevertheless has been pleased to speak to us not only with a bare word, but also, after the manner of men, to confirm his decree by an oath.—*Rivetus.*

Verse 4.—" Sworn, and will not repent, Thou art a priest for ever."   God might have made the levitical priest by oath, and yet he might have been changed ; but if he had made him by oath to be a priest for ever, then he could not have repented, that is, changed ; but he must of necessity have been a priest for ever.   Therefore you must take special notice, that God did not only swear that Christ should be a priest, or that he should be a priest for a long time, but a priest " *for ever ;* " so that there should never be any priest joined with him, or come after him.   So that if we consider the oath, and the thing confirmed by this oath, two things will be manifest : 1. That Christ's priesthood is personal, and settled in one single person for ever ; so that he can have no fellow nor co-partner, nor any successor in his priesthood. 2. That, by this oath, God did limit his own supreme and absolute power in this particular ; and took away the use and exercise of it, and that for ever.   For now he hath no power to make Christ no priest, or take away his priesthood at will and pleasure : and in this God discovered his unspeakable love unto Christ, in that he did so much honour him, and so highly reward him.   By this he also displayed his abundant mercy to man ; for by this oath known unto man, he signifies that man shall never be destitute of a powerful and effectual priest, able for ever to save ; and this doth minister unto sinful man most sweet and heavenly comfort.—*George Lawson,* 1662.

Verse 4.—The form and manner of our Saviour's investiture or consecration was most honourable and glorious, God the Father performing the rites ; which were not imposition of hands, and breathing on him the Holy Ghost, but a solemn *testimony,* with a protestation, *" Thou art a priest" :* ceremonies never used by any but God, nor in the investiture of any but Christ, nor in his investiture into any office but the priesthood. At his coronation we hear nothing, but the Lord said, *" Sit thou on my right hand " :* the rule of the whole world is imposed upon our Saviour by command ; and even in this did Christ show his obedience to his Father, that he took upon him the government of his church. But at the consecration of Christ we have a great deal more of ceremony and solemnity, God his Father taketh an oath, and particularly expresseth the nature and condition of his office, a *priesthood for ever after the order of Melchizedek :* and he confirmeth it unto him for ever, saying, " Thou art a priest for ever."—*Daniel Featley, in " Clavis Mystica."* 1636.

Verse 4.—What doctrine doth the Scripture afford more comfortable to a drooping soul than this, that *God hath sworn his Son a priest for ever,* to sanctify our persons, and purge our sins, and tender all our petitions to his Father ? What sin is so heinous, for which such a priest cannot satisfy by the oblation of himself ? what cause so desperate, in which such an advocate, if he will plead, may not prevail ? We may be sure God will not be hard to be intreated of us, who himself hath appointed us such an intercessor, to whom he can deny nothing ; and to that end hath appointed him to sit at his right hand to make intercession for us.—*Abraham Wright.*

Verse 4.—" *And will not repent.*" The meaning of this phrase is, that the priesthood of Christ is not like that of Aaron, which was after a time to expire, and is now actually with all the ceremonial law abolished, but a priesthood never to be altered or changed.—*Daniel Featley.*

Verse 4.—" *Thou art a priest.*" The reasons which moved our Lord to take upon him the office of priest are conceived to be these. 1. Because the salvation and redemption of mankind, wrought by the sacrifice of his priesthood, being a most noble work, and not inferior to the creation, it was not fit that any should have the honour of it, but the Son of God. 2. Neither was it agreeable that any should offer him, who was the only sacrifice that could expiate the sins of the whole world, but himself : therefore by offering himself he added infinite worth to the sacrifice, and great honour to the priesthood of the Gospel. For, as the gold sanctifieth not the altar, but the altar the gold ; so it may be truly said without impeachment to the dignity of that calling, that Christ was rather an honour to the priesthood, than the priesthood an addition to him. For what got he by the priesthood which cost him his life ? What preferment could it be to him, to take upon him an office, whereby he was to abase himself below himself, and be put to an ignominious and accursed death ? What were we vile miscreants, conceived and born in original sin, and soiled with the filth of numberless actual transgressions, that to purge and cleanse our polluted souls and defiled consciences, the second person in the Trinity should be made a Priest ? It was wonderful humility in him to wash his disciples' feet ; but in his divine person to wash our unclean souls, is as far above human conceit, as it seemeth below divine majesty. There is nothing so impure as a foul conscience ; no matter so filthy, no corruption so rotten and unsavoury as is found in the sores of an exulcerated mind ; yet the Son of God vouchsafed to wash and bathe them in his own blood. O bottomless depth of humility and mercy ! Other priests were appointed by men for the service of God, but he was appointed by God for the service and salvation of men : other priests spilt the blood of beasts to save men, but he shed his own blood to save us, more like beasts than men : other priests offered sacrifice for themselves, he offered himself for a sacrifice : other priests were fed by the sacrifices which the people brought, but he feeds us with the sacrifice of his own body and blood : lastly, others were appointed priests but for a time, he was ordained a priest " *for ever.*"—*Daniel Featley.*

Verse 4.—" *Thou art a priest.*" This word, " *Thou art,*" is *verbum constitutivum,* a " constituting word," whereon the priesthood of Christ was founded. And it may be considered,—1. As *declarative* of God's eternal decree, with the covenant between the Father and the Son, whereby he was designed unto this office. 2. As *demonstrative* of his mission, or his actual sending to the discharge of his office. These words are the symbol and solemn sign of God's conferring that honour upon him, which gave him his instalment. 3. As *predictive,* for there is included in them a supposition that God would prepare a body for him, wherein he might exercise his priesthood, and which he might offer up unto him.—*John Owen.*

Verse 4.—" *Melchizedek.*" Some heretics of old affirmed that he was the *Holy Ghost.* Others, that he was an *angel.* Others that he was *Shem,* the son of Noah. Others that he was a *Canaanite,* extraordinarily raised up by God to be a priest of the Gentiles. Others that he was *Christ himself,* manifested by a special dispensation and privilege unto Abraham in the flesh, who is said to have seen his day, and rejoiced, John viii. 56. Difference there is also about *Salem,* the place of which he was king. Some take it for *Jerusalem,* as Josephus and most of the ancients. Others for a city in the half tribe of Manasseh, within the river Jordan, where Hierom reports that some ruins of the palace of Melchizedek were in his days conceived to remain. Tedious I might be in insisting on this point who Melchizedek was. But when I find the Holy Ghost purposely concealing his name, genealogy, beginning, ending, and descent, and that to special purpose, I cannot but wonder that men should toil themselves in the dark to find out that of which they have not the least ground of solid conjecture, and the inevidence whereof is expressly recorded, to make Melchizedek thereby the fitter type of Christ's everlasting priesthood.— *Edward Reynolds.*

Verse 4.—" *Melchizedek.*" These things concerning are certain : *First, That he was a mere man, and no more ;* for, 1. " Every high priest " was to be " taken from among men," Heb. v. 1 ;—so that the Son of God himself could not have been a priest had he not assumed our nature : 2. That if he were more than a man, there would be no mystery in his being introduced in Scripture as, " without father, without mother, without pedigree," for none but men have such : 3. Without this conception of him there is no force in the apostle's argument against the Jews. *Secondly, That he came not to his office by the right of primogeniture* (which includes a genealogy) or by any way of succession, but was raised up and immediately called of God thereunto ; for in that respect Christ is said to be a priest after his order. *Thirdly, That he had no successor on the earth,* nor could have ; for there was no law to constitute an order of succession, and he was a priest only after an extraordinary call. These things belong unto faith in this matter, and no more. . . . The first personal instituted type of Christ was a priest ; this was Melchizedek. There were before *real* instituted types of his work, as sacrifices ; and there were *moral* types of his person, as Adam, Abel, and Noah, which represented him in sundry things ; but the first person who was solemnly designed to teach and represent him, by what he was and did, was a priest. And that which God taught herein was, that the foundation of all that the Lord Christ had to do in and for the church was laid in his priestly office, whereby he made atonement and reconciliation for sin. Everything else that he doth is built on the supposition of his priesthood. And we must begin in the application where God begins in the exhibition. An interest in the effects of the priestly office of Christ is that which in the first place we ought to look after. This being attained, we shall be willing to be taught and ruled by him. It may not be amiss to observe the likeness between Melchizedec and Christ. As for our Lord ;

1. He was said to be, and he really was, and he only, first *the king of righteousness, and then the king of peace ;* seeing he alone brought in everlasting righteousness and made peace with God for sinners. In his kingdom alone are these things to be found.

2. He was really and truly the *priest of the most high God ;* and properly he was so alone. He offered that sacrifice, and made that atonement, which was signified by all the sacrifices offered by holy men from the foundation of the world.

3. He *blesseth all the faithful, as Abraham, the father of the faithful, was blessed by Melchizedec.* In him were they to be blessed, by him are they blessed,—through him delivered from the curse, and all the fruits of it ; nor are they partakers of any blessing but from him.

4. He *receiveth all the homage of his people,* all their grateful acknowledgments of the love and favour of God, in the conquest of their spiritual adversaries, and deliverance from them, as Melchizedec received the tenth of the spoils from Abraham.

5. He was really *without progenitors or predecessors* in his office ; nor would I exclude that mystical sense from the intention of the place, that he was without father as to his human nature, and without mother as to his divine.

6. He was a *priest without genealogy,* or derivation of his pedigree from the loins of Aaron, or any other that ever was a priest in the world, and moreover, mysteriously, was of a generation which none can declare.

7. He had, *in his divine person,* as the high priest of the church, *neither beginning*

of days nor end of life, as no such thing is reported of Melchizedec; for the death which he underwent, in the discharge of his office, being not the death of his whole person, but of his human nature only, no interruption of his endless office did ensue thereon. For although the person of the Son of God died, whence God is said to "redeem his church with his own blood," Acts xx. 28; yet he died not in his whole person: but in his divine nature was still alive. Absolutely, therefore, and in respect of his office, he had neither beginning of days nor end of life.

8. He was *really the Son of God,* as Melchizedec in many circumstances was made like to the Son of God.

9. He *alone abideth a priest for ever*; whereof we must particularly treat afterwards.—*Condensed from John Owen.*

Verse 5.—" *The Lord . . . . shall strike through kings,"* etc. He really threatens such great heads in an awful manner, that if they will not hear, and cannot obey, they shall be terrified to death. And assuredly he would willingly, by these means, allure them to repentance, and persuade them to turn, and to cease from raging against the Lord. But if they will not, they shall know against whom it is that they go on. . . . . This is our consolation which upholds us, and makes our heart joyful and glad against the persecution and rage of the world, that we have such a Lord, who not only delivers us from sin and eternal death, but also protects us, and delivers us in sufferings and temptations, so that we do not sink under them. And though men rage in a most savage manner against Christians, yet neither the gospel nor Christianity shall perish; but their heads shall be destroyed against it. If their persecutions were to go on unceasingly Christianity could not remain, wherefore he gives them a time, and says he will connive at them for a while, but not longer than till the hour comes which he here calls the " *day of his wrath."* And if they will not now cease in the name of God, they must then cease in the name of the devil.—*Martin Luther.*

Verse 5.—" *Shall strike through kings."* To *strike through* notes a complete victory and full confusion of the enemy, an incurable wound, that they may stagger, and fall, and rise up no more, and that affliction may not arise a second time, Nahum i. 9; 1 Sam. xxvi. 8. The only difficulty is what is meant by " kings." For which we must note that the kingdom of Christ is spiritual, and his war spiritual, and therefore his enemies for the most part spiritual.—*Edward Reynolds.*

Verse 5.—" *In the day of his wrath."* Note that it is not simply said, he will strike through kings in his wrath, but in the *day* of his wrath. Therefore as there is a time of grace and patience, so there is also an appointed time of wrath and vengeance of God. Frequent mention is made of this in the sacred Scriptures, that we may be admonished that the wicked will not be left always unpunished, because they contemn the patience of God, aye, provoke his anger; but that there will be a time when they will experience the wrath of God. Thus, armed with patience, we should persevere in the practice of piety, nor be turned aside from it, either by the example of the wicked, or from fear of them.—*Wolfgang Musculus.*

Verses 5, 6, 7.

> The sentenc'd heathen he shall slay,
> And fill with carcases his way,
> Till he hath struck earth's tyrants dead;
> But in the high-way brooks shall first,
> Like a poor pilgrim, slake his thirst,
> And then in triumph raise his head.
>
> *N. Brady and N. Tate.*

Verse 6.—" *He shall fill the places with the dead bodies."* This notes *the greatness* of the victory, that none should be left to bury the dead. There shall be an universal destruction of wicked men *together* in the day of God's wrath, they shall be bound up in bundles, and heaped for damnation, Matt. xiii. 30; Psal. xxxvii. 38; Isai. i. 28; lxvi. 17. And it notes the *shame* and dishonour of the enemy, they shall be like dung upon the face of the earth, and shall be beholden to their victors for a base and dishonourable burial, as we see in the great battle with Gog and Magog, Ezekiel xxxix. 11—16.—*Edward Reynolds.*

Verse 6.—" *Dead bodies."* Either the corpses of the vanquished enemy; or (possibly) the living bodies of men in a state of *servitude,* as in Gen. xlvii. 18; Neh. ix. 37. (The construction as in Exod. xv. 9.) In the latter case, the meaning may be : that the bodies of those who had been enslaved by the Usurper, Death, were now claimed back by their rightful Lord. The full number is claimed back. The " last enemy " being destroyed, " *all* things " are brought beneath Christ's sway.— *William Kay.*

Verse 6.—" *The heads.*" Rather, *the head ;* doubtless, the head of the Old Serpent (according to the prophecy in Gen. iii. 15), who acts in all who resist Christ. The verb *machats*, which is used here, is employed to describe the prophetical and typical act of Jael, smiting the *head* of God's enemy, Sisera (Jud. v. 26 and iv. 22) ; and it is used in Ps. lxviii. 21, which describes Christ's victory, " God shall *wound* the *head* of his enemies " ; and also by Hab. iii. 13, " Thou *woundest* the *head* out of the house of the wicked."—*Christopher Wordsworth.*

Verse 7.—" *He shall drink of the brook,*" etc. He describeth the passion of Christ and his glory. " *In the way,*" saith he, that is, in his life while he is in this misery, " *he shall drink out of the brook,*" that is, he shall suffer and be overcome. For to drink out of the cup is to suffer : but to drink out of the brook, is to be altogether full of trouble, to be vexed and tormented and utterly to be overwhelmed with a strong stream of troubles. Thus was it in David's mind to declare the passion of Christ. Afterward he saith, " *therefore shall he lift up the head.*" After the passion followeth the glory, with the resurrection and ascension. Paul (Philip ii.) speaketh of both, and saith : " Christ humbled himself, and became obedient unto death, even the death of the cross. Wherefore God hath exalted him, and given him a name which is above every name," etc.—*Myles Coverdale, 1487—1568.*

Verse 7.—I conceive that the " *brook* " here spoken of was not intended to give us the idea of a clear brook of refreshing water, which was to afford the Redeemer strength to endure the amazing conflict ; as the drinking of the water enabled Gideon's chosen band of men to go forth to battle against the Midianites. No ; in our Lord's case it was a polluted and turbid stream. Like the water of *Marah*, which the Israelites could not drink, it was bitter ; for sin had made it so. It bore along with it, as it flowed, the curse of the broken law, and the vengeance of offended justice, and the wrath of the eternal God. It was pain, sorrow, suffering, death. *This* was the " *brook* " of which he drank. The " cup " which his Father gave him to drink was filled with the bitter water of this " *brook* " ; and he may be said to have first put his lips to it, when he declared to his disciples, in his way to Gethsemane, " My soul is exceedingly sorrowful, even unto death."

But it is stated in the text that this " *brook* " was " *in the way.*" It is described here as running by the path in which the Redeemer was going in order to the accomplishment of his great work of man's salvation ; that work which he had engaged in the everlasting covenant to perform ; and by the performance of which, man could alone be accepted of God. The sin of man was the *source* from whence this water issued ; and it flowed along in the Saviour's " *way,*" through the wilderness of this world to his kingdom of glory in the next ; as the brook *Kidron*, red with the blood of the typical sacrifices, flowed in his way to *Calvary.*—*Fountain Elwin, 1842.*

Verse 7.—In the expositions of most of the ancients and moderns, we are told that he drank of the brook, 1, of *mortality* by his incarnation ; 2, of strictness and *hardness* in all his passage, by his voluntary wants and poverty ; 3, of the *strong potion of the law*, by his exact obedience and subjection ; 4, of the *Jews' malice*, by their continual indignities ; 5, of the *floods of Belial*, by apparent and unknown temptations ; 6, of the *heaviest wrath* of his Father, by his unspeakable agony and bloody sweat in the garden. And last of all, *of death itself* on the cross, by his sad and extreme passion.—*John Prideaux.*

Verse 7.—" *He shall drink of the brook in the way.*" These words were understood by Junius and Tremellius long ago as meaning, " He shall steadily press on to victory, as generals of energy act, who in pursuing routed foes, stay not to indulge themselves in meat or drink." Hengstenberg and others substantially approve of this view. While a few hold that allusion may be made to Samson at Ramath-Lehi (as if the words spoke of Christ having a secret spring of refreshment when needful). Most seem inclined to take *Gideon* as the type that best expresses the idea. Pressing on to victory, Messiah, like Gideon, " faint yet pursuing " as he passed over Jordan, shall not desist till all is won. " He shall not fail nor be discouraged till he hath set judgment in the earth." Perhaps the full idea is this :—His career was irresistibly successful like that of Gideon ; for he allowed nothing to detain him, nor did he shrink in the enterprise from any fatigue, nor did he stop to indulge the flesh. If we take it thus, there is both the Humiliation and the Exaltation of the Son of Man contained in the words ; and Phil. ii. 8, 9 supplies a commentary.—*Andrew A. Bonar.*

Verse 7.—" Schnurrer," says Rosenmüller, " seems to have perceived the meaning of the verse, which he gives in the following words :—' Though fatigued with the slaughter of his enemies, yet he will not desist : but, having refreshed himself with water from the nearest stream, will exert his renovated strength in the pursuit of the routed foe.' "—*Messianic Psalms.*

Verse 7.—Christ shall *" lift up the head "* by way of triumphing and rejoicing, when he shall have taken full vengeance of his adversaries, and freed, not himself only, but the whole body of his church from the assaults and dangers of all enemies. We see now that oftentimes, though not in himself, yet in his members, he is fain to hang down the head, and to wear the badges of reproach and shame, whilst the ungodly vaunt themselves (Job xxxi. 26) and in their hearts despise the righteous, accounting more vilely of them than of the dust of their feet.—*Robert Abbot.*

HINTS TO PREACHERS.

Verse 1.—Here the Holy Ghost begins with the *kingdom of Christ,* which he describeth and magnifieth,—1. By his *unction* and *ordination* thereunto, by the word or decree of his Father : " *The Lord said.*" 2. By the *greatness of his person* in himself, while yet he is nearly allied in blood and nature unto us ; " *My Lord.*" 3. By the *glory,* power, and heavenliness of his kingdom, for in the administration thereof he sitteth at the right hand of his Father : " *Sit thou at my right hand.*" 4. By the *continuance* and victories thereof : " *Until I make thy foes thy footstool.*"—*Edward Reynolds.*

Verse 1.—" *My Lord.*" I. Christ's condescending nearness to us does not destroy our reverence : he was David's son, and yet he calls him Lord ; he is our brother, bridegroom, and so on, and yet our *Lord.* II. Christ's glory does not diminish his nearness to us, or familiarity with us. Sitting on the throne as Lord, he is yet " *my* Lord." III. It is under the double aspect as Lord, and yet ours, that Jehovah regards him, and speaks with him, and ordains him to the priesthood. Ever in these two lights let us regard him.

Verse 1.—" *Sit,*" etc. I. Our Lord's quiet amid passing events. II. The abundance of his present power. III. The working of all history towards the ultimate end, which will be—IV. His easy victory : putting his foot on his foes as readily as we tread on a footstool.

Verse 2.—I. What is that rod ? The gospel (Illustrated by Moses' rod). II. Who sends it ? " The Lord." III. Whence it comes ? Out of the church of God. IV. What is the result ? Jesus reigns.

Verse 3.—A willing people and an immutable Leader. I. The promise made to Christ concerning his people : " Thy people shall be willing," etc. 1. A promise of time : " In the day," etc. 2. Of persons : " Thy people." 3. Of disposition : " Shall be willing." 4. Of character : " In the beauties of holiness." 5. The majestic figure employed : " From the womb of the morning : thou hast the dew of thy youth." II. The promise made to Christ concerning himself : " Thou hast the dew of thy youth." Jesus Christ has the dew of his youth personally, doctrinally, and mystically, being surrounded by new converts, who are as the early dew.— *Spurgeon's Sermons, No.* 74.

Verse 3.—This is a prophecy of the subjects of Christ's kingdom. I. Who they are ; " Thy people." 1. A people. This denotes distinction, separation, similarity, organization. They are not a confused rabble, but a united community. 2. *His* people. By gift, by purchase, by effectual calling. II. What they are. 1. A loyal people : " willing." 2. A conquered people : " in the day of thy power." 3. A holy people : " in the beauties of holiness." 4. A numerous people : " from the womb of the morning," etc. The number of converts at the first proclamation of Christ's gospel was but the dew of his youth.—*G. R.*

Verse 3.—First, *the internal evidence of Christ's kingdom is in his people's willingness :* " Thy people shall be willingness—thy people shall be a people all willing "— all volunteers, not pressed men. Secondly, *the external evidence of it lies in his people's holiness ;* " the beauties of holiness ; " or as it may be rendered—" in the magnificence of his sanctuary," for the ornaments of the sanctuary and the dress of the priests were very splendid. When you once give yourselves to God, you become temples of God ; and sanctity must adorn that heart which is a living temple of the Holy Ghost.—*J. Bennett, in a Sermon*, 1829.

Verse 3.—All true followers of Jesus are (1) priests—beauties of holiness are their sacerdotal robes ; (2) soldiers—" in the day of thine armies ; " (3) volunteers ; (4) benefactors—as the dew.—*Suggested by a paper in The Baptist Magazine.*

Verse 3.—Here we have a cluster of subjects :—the willingness of the Lord's people, the beauty of holiness, young converts the life and glory of the church, the mystery of conversion, and so on.

Verse 4.—The eternal priesthood of Christ. On what its perpetuity is founded and the blessed results flowing therefrom.

Verse 4.—These words offer three points of special observation. 1. The ceremony used at the consecration of our Lord : " *The Lord sware.*" 2. The office conferred upon him by this rite or ceremony : " *Thou art a priest.*" 3. The prerogatives of his office ; which office is here declared to be, (1), Perpetual " *for ever.*" (2), Regular, " *after the order.*" (3), Royal, " *of Melchizedek.*"—*Daniel Featley.*

Verse 4.—Melchizedek : a fruitful subject. See notes.

Verse 5.—The certain overthrow of every power which opposes the gospel.

Verse 6.—The fearful calamities which have happened to nations through their sinful rejection of the Lord Jesus.

Verse 7.—Christ's alacrity, self-denial, and simplicity, the causes of his success. Example to be imitated.

Verse 7.—Christ's humiliation and exaltation.

THE
TREASURY OF DAVID

PREFACE.

At length I am able to present to the Christian public another part of " The Treasury of David." It has demanded longer labour than its predecessors, but that labour has been freely given to it ; and to the utmost of my ability I have kept the volume up to the level of those which have gone before. In the production of this exposition I had far rather be long than lax ; for I know by experience the disappointment which comes to readers when, after a promising beginning, they see a serious declension towards the end. The general acceptance given to this Commentary has placed me under a heavy obligation to do my best even to the end. Towards that end I am still proceeding with all possible diligence, and it is with great pleasure that I look forward to the speedy issue of the last volume of the work. Many labours distract me from this favourite employment, but I hope to press on with more speed than of late, if my life be spared. It would be imprudent to make too sure of *that ;* for the most fragile Venice glass is not more brittle than human life :

> " The spider's most attenuated thread
> Is cord, is cable, to the tender film
> Which holds our soul in life."

I have been all the longer over this portion of my task because I have been bewildered in the expanse of the One Hundred and Nineteenth Psalm, which makes up the bulk of this volume. Its dimensions and its depth alike overcame me. It spread itself out before me like a vast, rolling prairie, to which I could see no bound, and this alone created a feeling of dismay. Its expanse was unbroken by a bluff or headland, and hence it threatened a monotonous task, although the fear has not been realized. This marvellous poem seemed to me a great sea of holy teaching, moving, in its many verses, wave upon wave ; altogether without an island of special and remarkable statement to break it up. I confess I hesitated to launch upon it. Other Psalms have been mere lakes, but this is the main ocean. It is a continent of sacred thought, every inch of which is fertile as the garden of the Lord : it is an amazing level of abundance, a mighty stretch of harvest-fields. I have now crossed the great plain for myself, but not without persevering, and, I will add, pleasurable, toil. Several great authors have traversed this region and left their tracks behind them, and so far the journey has been all the easier for me ; but yet to me and to my helpers it has been no mean feat of patient authorship and research. This great Psalm is a book in itself : instead of being one among many Psalms, it is worthy to be set forth by itself as a poem of surpassing excellence. Those who have never studied it may pronounce it commonplace, and complain of its repetitions ; but to the thoughtful student it is like the great deep, full, so as never to be measured ; and varied, so as never to weary the eye. Its depth is as great as its length ; it is mystery, not set forth as mystery, but concealed beneath the simplest statements ; may I say that it is experience allowed to prattle, to preach, to praise, and to pray like a child-prophet in his own father's house ?

My venerable friend, Mr. Rogers, has been spared to help me with his admirable suggestions ; but Mr. Gibson, who so industriously translated from the Latin authors, has fallen asleep, leaving behind him copious notes upon the rest of the Psalms. Aid in the homiletical department has been given me by several of the ministers who were educated at the Pastor's College, and their names are duly appended to the hints and skeletons which they have supplied. In this department the present volume is believed to be superior to the former ones. May it prove to be really useful to my brethren, and my desire is fulfilled. I know so well the use of a homiletic hint when the mind is in search for a subject, that I have felt peculiar pleasure in supplying my readers with a full measure of such helps.

In hunting up rare authors, and making extracts from them, Mr. Keys has rendered me great assistance, and I am also a debtor to others who have cheerfully rendered me service when I have sought it. Burdened with the care of many institutions, and the oversight of a singularly large church, I cannot do such justice to my theme as I could wish. Learned leisure would be far more accurate than my busy pen can ever hope to be. If I had nothing else to think of, I would have thought of nothing else, and undivided energies could have accomplished what spare strength can never perform. Hence, I am glad of help ; so glad, that I am happy to acknowledge it. Not in this thing only, but in all other labours, I owe in the first place all to God, and secondarily, very, very much to those generous friends who find a delight in making my efforts successful.

Above all, I trust that the Holy Spirit has been with me in writing and compiling these volumes, and therefore I expect that he will bless them both to the conversion of the unrenewed and to the edification of believers. The writing of this book has been a means of grace to my own heart ; I have enjoyed for myself what I have prepared for my readers. The Book of Psalms has been a royal banquet to me, and in feasting upon its contents I have seemed to eat angels' food. It is no wonder that old writers should call it,— the school of patience, the soul's soliloquies, the little Bible, the anatomy of conscience, the rose garden, the pearl island, and the like. It is the Paradise of devotion, the Holy Land of poesy, the heart of Scripture, the map of experience, and the tongue of saints. It is the spokesman of feelings which else had found no utterance. Does it not say just what we wished to say ? Are not its prayers and praises exactly such as our hearts delight in ? No man needs better company than the Psalms ; therein he may read and commune with friends human and divine ; friends who know the heart of man towards God and the heart of God towards man ; friends who perfectly sympathize with us and our sorrows, friends who never betray or forsake. Oh, to be shut up in a cave with David, with no other occupation but to hear him sing, and to sing with him ! Well might a Christian monarch lay aside his crown for such enjoyment, and a believing pauper find a crown in such felicity.

It is to be feared that the Psalms are by no means so prized as in earlier ages of the Church. Time was when the Psalms were not only rehearsed in all the churches from day to day, but they were so universally sung that the common people knew them, even if they did not know the letters in which they were written. Time was when bishops would ordain no man to the ministry unless he knew "David" from end to end, and could repeat each Psalm correctly ; even Councils of the Church have decreed that none should hold ecclesiastical office unless they knew the whole Psalter by heart. Other practices of those ages had better be forgotten, but to *this* memory accords an honourable record. Then, as Jerome tells us, the labourer, while he held the plough, sang Hallelujah; the tired reaper refreshed himself with the Psalms, and the vinedresser, while trimming the vines with his curved hook, sang something of David. He tells us that in his part of the world, Psalms were the Christian's ballads; could they have had better? They were the love-songs of the people of God; could any others be so pure and heavenly? These sacred hymns express all modes of holy feeling; they are fit both for childhood and old age; they furnish maxims for the entrance of life, and serve as watchwords at the gates of death. The battle of life, the repose of the Sabbath, the ward of the hospital, the guest-chamber of the mansion the church, the oratory, yea, even heaven itself may be entered with Psalms,

Finally, when I reach the last Psalm, it is my firm conviction that I shall find no truer closing words for myself than those of Bishop Horne, which I take liberty here to quote, using them as if they were my own, since they admirably express my present feelings and past experiences :—

" And now, could the author flatter himself that anyone would take half the pleasure in reading the following exposition which he hath taken in writing it, he would not fear the loss of his labour. The employment detached him from the bustle and hurry of life, the din of politics, and the noise of folly. Vanity and vexation flew for a season, care and disquietude came not near his dwelling. He arose fresh as the morning to his task; the silence of the night invited him to pursue it; and he can truly say, that food and rest were not preferred before it. Every Psalm improved infinitely upon his acquaintance with it, and no one gave him uneasiness but the last; for then he grieved that his work was done. Happier hours than those which have been spent on these meditations on the songs of Zion he never expects to see in this world. Very pleasantly did they pass, and they moved smoothly and swiftly along; for when thus engaged, he counted no time. The meditations are gone, but have left a relish and a fragrance upon the mind, and the remembrance of them is sweet."

Reader,

I am,

Thine to serve

For Christ's sake,

C. H. Spurgeon

INDEX

OF AUTHORS QUOTED OR REFERRED TO

"WESTWOOD." C. H. SPURGEON'S HOME ON BEULAH HILL.

Specially drawn for "The Treasury of David" by E. H. Fitchew.

PSALM· CXI.

There is no title to this Psalm, but it is an alphabetical hymn of praise, having for its subject the works of the Lord in creation, providence, and grace. The sweet singer dwells upon the one idea that God should be known by his people, and that this knowledge when turned into practical piety is man's true wisdom, and the certain cause of lasting adoration. Many are ignorant of what their Creator has done, and hence they are foolish in heart, and silent as to the praises of God : this evil can only be removed by a remembrance of God's works, and a diligent study of them ; to this, therefore, the Psalm is meant to arouse us. It may be called THE PSALM OF GOD'S WORKS *intended to excite us to the work of praise.*

DIVISION.—*The Psalmist begins with an invitation to praise, verse* 1 ; *and then proceeds to furnish us with matter for adoration in God's works and his dealings with his people,* 2—9. *He closes his song with a commendation of the worship of the Lord and of the men who practise it.*

EXPOSITION.

PRAISE ye the LORD. I will praise the LORD with *my* whole heart, in the assembly of the upright, and *in* the congregation.

1. *"Praise ye the* LORD," or, *Hallelujah!* All ye his saints unite in adoring Jehovah, who worketh so gloriously. Do it now, do it always : do it heartily, do it unanimously, do it eternally. Even if others refuse, take care that ye have always a song for your God. Put away all doubt, question, murmuring, and rebellion, and give yourselves up to the praising of Jehovah, both with your lips and in your lives. *"I will praise the* LORD *with my whole heart."* The sweet singer commences the song, for his heart is all on flame : whether others will follow him or not, he will at once begin and long continue. What we preach we should practise. The best way to enforce an exhortation is to set an example ; but we must let that example be of the best kind, or we may lead others to do the work in a limping manner. David brought nothing less than his whole heart to the duty ; all his love went out towards God, and all his zeal, his skill, and his ardour went with it. Jehovah the one and undivided God cannot be acceptably praised with a divided heart, neither should we attempt so to dishonour him ; for our whole heart is little enough for his glory, and there can be no reason why it should not all be lifted up in his praise. All his works are praiseworthy, and therefore all our nature should adore him. *"In the assembly of the upright, and in the congregation"* ;—whether with few or with many he would pour forth his whole heart and soul in praise, and whether the company was made up of select spirits or of the general mass of the people he would continue in the same exercise. For the choicest society there can be no better engagement than praise, and for the general assembly nothing can be more fitting. For the church and for the congregation, for the family or the community, for the private chamber of pious friendship, or the great hall of popular meeting, the praise of the Lord is suitable ; and at the very least the true heart should sing hallelujah in any and every place. Why should we fear the presence of men ? The best of men will join us in our song, and if the common sort, will not do so, our example will be a needed rebuke to them. In any case let us praise God, whether the hearers be a little band of saints or a mixed multitude. Come, dear reader, he who pens this comment is in his heart magnifying the Lord : will you not pause for a moment and join in the delightful exercise ?

2 The works of the LORD *are* great, sought out of all them that have pleasure therein.

3 His work *is* honourable and glorious : and his righteousness endureth for ever.

4 He hath made his wonderful works to be remembered : the LORD *is* gracious and full of compassion.

5 He hath given meat unto them that fear him : he will ever be mindful of his covenant.

6 He hath shewed his people the power of his works, that he may give them the heritage of the heathen.

7 The works of his hands *are* verity and judgment ; all his commandments *are* sure.

8 They stand fast for ever and ever, *and are* done in truth and uprightness.

9 He sent redemption unto his people : he hath commanded his covenant for ever : holy and reverend *is* his name.

2. "*The works of the Lord are great.*" In design, in size, in number, in excellence, all the works of the Lord are great. Even the little things of God are great. In some point of view or other each one of the productions of his power, or the deeds of his wisdom, will appear to be great to the wise in heart. "*Sought out of all them that have pleasure therein.*" Those who love their Maker delight in his handiworks, they perceive that there is more in them than appears upon the surface, and therefore they bend their minds to study and understand them. The devout naturalist ransacks nature, the earnest student of history pries into hidden facts and dark stories, and the man of God digs into the mines of Scripture, and hoards up each grain of its golden truth. God's works are worthy of our researches, they yield us instruction and pleasure wonderfully blended, and they grow upon, appearing to be far greater, after investigation than before. Men's works are noble from a distance ; God's works are great when sought out. Delitzsch reads the passage, " Worthy of being sought after in all their purposes," and this also is a grand truth, for the end and design which God hath in all that he makes or does is equally admirable with the work itself. The hidden wisdom of God is the most marvellous part of his works, and hence those who do not look below the surface miss the best part of what he would teach us. Because the works are great they cannot be seen all at once, but must be looked into with care, and this seeking out is of essential service to us by educating our faculties, and strengthening our spiritual eye gradually to bear the light of the divine glory. It is well for us that all things cannot be seen at a glance, for the search into their mysteries is as useful to us as the knowledge which we thereby attain. The history of the Lord's dealings with his people is especially a fit subject for the meditation of reverent minds who find therein a sweet solace, and a never failing source of delight.

3. "*His work is honourable and glorious.*" His one special work, the salvation of his people, is here mentioned as distinguished from his many other *works*. This reflects honour and glory upon him. It is deservedly the theme of the highest praise, and compels those who understand it and experience it to ascribe all honour and glory unto the Lord. Its conception, its sure foundations, its gracious purpose, its wise arrangements, its gift of Jesus as Redeemer, its application of redemption by the Holy Ghost in regeneration and sanctification, and all else which make up the one glorious whole, all redound to the infinite honour of Him who contrived and carried out so astounding a method of salvation. No other work can be compared with it : it honours both the Saviour and the saved, and while it brings glory to God it also brings us to glory. There is none like the God of Jeshurun, and there is no salvation like that which he has wrought for his people. "*And his righteouesnss endureth for ever.*" In the work of grace righteousness is not forgotten, nor deprived of its glory ; rather, it is honoured in the eyes of the intelligent universe. The bearing of guilt by our great Substitute proved that not even to effect the purposes of his grace would the Lord forget his righteousness ; no future strain upon his justice can ever be equal to that which it has already sustained in the bruising of his dear Son ; it must henceforth assuredly endure for ever. Moreover, the righteousness of God in the whole plan can never now be suspected of failure, for all that it requires is already performed, its demands are satisfied by the double deed of our Lord in enduring the vengeance due, and in rendering perfect obedience to the law. Caprice does not enter into the government of the Lord, the rectitude of it is and must for ever be beyond all question. In no single deed of God can unrighteousness be found, nor shall there ever be : this is the very glory of his work, and even its adversaries cannot gainsay it. Let believers, therefore, praise him

evermore, and never blush to speak of that work which is so honourable and glorious.

4. *"He hath made his wonderful works to be remembered."* He meant them to remain in the recollection of his people, and they do so : partly because they are in themselves memorable, and because also he has taken care to record them by the pen of inspiration, and has written them upon the hearts of his people by his Holy Spirit. By the ordinances of the Mosaic law, the coming out of Egypt, the sojourn in the wilderness, and other memorabilia of Israel's history were constantly brought before the minds of the people, and their children were by such means instructed in the wonders which God had wrought in old time. Deeds such as God has wrought are not to be admired for an hour and then forgotten, they are meant to be perpetual signs and instructive tokens to all coming generations ; and especially are they designed to confirm the faith of his people in the divine love, and to make them know that *"the Lord is gracious and full of compassion."* They need not fear to trust his grace for the future, for they remember it in the past. Grace is as conspicuous as righteousness in the great work of God, yea, a fulness of tender love is seen in all that he has done. He treats his people with great consideration for their weakness and infirmity ; having the same pity for them as a father hath towards his children. Should we not praise him for this ? A silver thread of lovingkindness runs through the entire fabric of God's work of salvation and providence, and never once is it left out in the whole piece. Let the memories of his saints bear witness to this fact with grateful joy.

5. *"He hath given meat unto them that fear him."* Or *spoil*, as some read it, for the Lord's people both in coming out of Egypt and at other times have been enriched from their enemies. Not only in the wilderness with manna, but everywhere else by his providence he has supplied the necessities of his believing people. Somewhere or other they have had food convenient for them, and that in times of great scarcity. As for spiritual meat, that has been plentifully furnished them in Christ Jesus ; they have been fed with the finest of the wheat, and made to feast on royal dainties. His word is as nourishing to the soul as bread to the body, and there is such an abundance of it that no heir of heaven shall ever be famished. Truly the fear of the Lord is wisdom, since it secures to a man the supply of all that he needs for soul and body. *"He will ever be mindful of his covenant."* He could not let his people lack meat, because he was in covenant with them, and they can never want in the future, for he will continue to act upon the terms of that covenant. No promise of the Lord shall fall to the ground, nor will any part of the great compact of eternal love be revoked or allowed to sink into oblivion. The covenant of grace is the plan of the great work which the Lord works out for his people, and it will never be departed from : the Lord has set his hand and seal to it, his glory and honour are involved in it, yea, his very name hangs upon it, and he will not even in the least jot or tittle cease to be mindful of it. Of this the feeding of his people is the pledge : he would not so continually supply their needs if he meant after all to destroy them. Upon this most blessed earnest let us settle our minds ; let us rest in the faithfulness of the Lord, and praise him with all our hearts every time that we eat bread or feed upon his word.

6. *"He hath shewed his people the power of his works."* They have seen what he is able to do and what force he is prepared to put forth on their behalf. This power Israel saw in physical works, and we in spiritual wonders, for we behold the matchless energy of the Holy Ghost and feel it in our own souls. In times of dire distress the Lord has put forth such energy of grace that we have been astonished at his power ; and this was part of his intent in bringing us into such conditions that he might reveal to us the arm of his strength. Could we ever have known it so well if we had not been in pressing need of his help ? We may well turn this verse into a prayer and ask to see more and more the power of the Lord at work among us in these latter days. O Lord, let us now see how mightily thou canst work in the saving of sinners and in preserving and delivering thine own people. *"That he may give them the heritage of the heathen."* He put forth all his power to drive out the Canaanites and bring in his people. Even thus may it please his infinite wisdom to give to his church the heathen for her inheritance in the name of Jesus. Nothing but great power can effect this, but it will surely be accomplished in due season.

7. *"The works of his hands are verity and judgment."* Truth and justice are conspicuous in all that Jehovah does. Nothing like artifice or crooked policy can ever be seen in his proceedings ; he acts faithfully and righteously towards his people,

and with justice and impartiality to all mankind. This also should lead us to praise him, since it is of the utmost advantage to us to live under a sovereign whose laws, decrees, acts, and deeds are the essence of truth and justice. *"All his commandments are sure."* All that he has appointed or decreed shall surely stand, and his precepts which he has proclaimed shall be found worthy of our obedience, for surely they are founded in justice and are meant for our lasting good. He is no fickle despot, commanding one thing one day and another another, but his commands remain absolutely unaltered, their necessity equally unquestionable, their excellence permanently proven, and their reward eternally secure. Take the word *commandments* to relate either to his decrees or his precepts, and we have in each case an important sense ; but it seems more in accordance with the connection to take the first sense and consider the words to refer to the ordinances, appointments, or decrees of the great King.

> " Whate'er the mighty Lord decrees,
>   Shall stand for ever sure,
> The settled purpose of his heart
>   To ages shall endure."

8. *"They stand fast for ever and ever."* That is to say, his purposes, commands, and courses of action. The Lord is not swayed by transient motives, or moved by the circumstances of the hour ; immutable principles rule in the courts of Jehovah, and he pursues his eternal purposes without the shadow of a turning. Our works are too often as wood, hay, and stubble, but his doings are as gold, silver, and precious stones. We take up a purpose for a while and then exchange it for another, but he is of one mind, and none can turn him : he acts in eternity and for eternity, and hence what he works abides for ever. Much of this lasting character arises out of the fact which is next mentioned, namely, that they *"are done in truth and uprightness."* Nothing stands but that which is upright. Falsehood soon vanishes, for it is a mere show, but truth has salt in it which preserves it from decay. God always acts according to the glorious principles of truth and integrity, and hence there is no need of alteration or revocation ; his works will endure to the end of time.

9. *"He sent redemption unto his people."* When they were in Egypt he sent not only a deliverer, but an actual deliverance ; not only a redeemer, but complete redemption. He has done the like spiritually for all his people, having first by blood purchased them out of the hand of the enemy, and then by power rescued them from the bondage of their sins. Redemption we can sing of as an accomplished act : it has been wrought for us, sent to us, and enjoyed by us, and we are in very deed the Lord's redeemed. *"He hath commanded his covenant for ever."* His divine decree has made the covenant of his grace a settled and eternal institution : redemption by blood proves that the covenant cannot be altered, for it ratifies and establishes it beyond all recall. This, too, is reason for the loudest praise. Redemption is a fit theme for the heartiest music, and when it is seen to be connected with gracious engagements from which the Lord's truth cannot swerve, it becomes a subject fitted to arouse the soul to an ecstacy of gratitude. Redemption and the covenant are enough to make the tongue of the dumb sing. *"Holy and reverend is his name."* Well may he say this. The whole name or character of God is worthy of profoundest awe, for it is perfect and complete, whole or holy. It ought not to be spoken without solemn thought, and never heard without profound homage. His name is to be trembled at, it is something terrible ; even those who know him best rejoice with trembling before him. How good men can endure to be called " reverend " we know not. Being unable to discover any reason why our fellow-men should reverence *us*, we half suspect that in other men there is not very much which can entitle them to be called reverend, very reverend, right reverend, and so on. It may seem a trifling matter, but for that very reason we would urge that the foolish custom should be allowed to fall into disuse.

10 The fear of the LORD *is* the beginning of wisdom : a good understanding have all they that do *his commandments : his praise endureth for ever.

10. *"The fear of the LORD is the beginning of wisdom."* It is its first principle, but it is also its head and chief attainment. The word " beginning " in Scripture sometimes means the chief ; and true religion is at once the first element of wisdom, and its chief fruit. To know God so as to walk aright before him is the greatest of

all the applied sciences. Holy reverence of God leads us to praise him, and this is the point which the psalm drives at, for it is a wise act on the part of a creature towards his Creator. "*A good understanding have all they that do his commandments.*" Obedience to God proves that our judgment is sound. Why should he not be obeyed? Does not reason itself claim obedience for the Lord of all? Only a man void of understanding will ever justify rebellion against the holy God. Practical godliness is the test of wisdom. Men may know and be very orthodox, they may talk and be very eloquent, they may speculate and be very profound; but the best proof of their intelligence must be found in their actually doing the will of the Lord. The former part of the Psalm taught us the doctrine of God's nature and character, by describing his works: the second part supplies the practical lesson by drawing the inference that to worship and obey him is the dictate of true wisdom. We joyfully own that it is so. "*His praise endureth for ever.*" The praises of God will never cease, because his works will always excite adoration, and it will always be the wisdom of men to extol their glorious Lord. Some regard this sentence as referring to those who fear the Lord—their praise shall endure for ever: and, indeed, it is true that those who lead obedient lives shall obtain honour of the Lord, and commendations which will abide for ever. A word of approbation from the mouth of God will be a mede of honour which will outshine all the decorations which kings and emperors can bestow.

Lord, help us to study thy works, and henceforth to breathe out hallelujahs as long as we live.

EXPLANATORY NOTES AND QUAINT SAYINGS.

Whole Psalm.—This is the first alphabetical Psalm which is regular throughout. The four former alphabetical Psalms, namely, ix. and x., xxxiv. and xxxvii., are irregular and defective in many particulars, for the rectification of which neither Hebrew MS. editions nor ancient versions afford sanction and authority. It is singular that not only are Psalms cxi. and cxii. perfectly regular, but, furthermore, that not one various reading of note or importance occurs in either of these Psalms.—*John Noble Coleman.*

Whole Psalm.—The following translation is given to enable the reader to realize the alphabetical character of the Psalm. It is taken from "The Psalms Chronologically Arranged. By Four Friends."

All my heart shall praise Jehovah,   1
    Before the congregation of the righteous;
Deeds of goodness are the deeds of Jehovah,   2
    Earnestly desired of all them that have pleasure therein;
For his righteousness endureth for ever,   3
    Glorious and honourable is his work;
He hath made his wonderful works to be remembered,   4
    In Jehovah is compassion and goodness;
Jehovah hath given meat to them that fear him,   5
    Keeping his covenant for ever,
Learning his people the power of his works,   6
    Making them to possess the heritage of the heathen;
Nought save truth and equity are the works of his hands,   7
    Ordered and sure are his commands,
Planted fast for ever and ever,   8
    Righteous and true are his testimonies;
Salvation hath he sent unto his people,   9
    Their covenant hath he made fast for ever;
Upright and holy is his name,   10
    Verily, the fear of the Lord is the beginning of wisdom,
Yea, a good understanding have all they that do thereafter;
Zealously shall he be praised for ever.

Whole Psalm.—The general opinion of interpreters is, that this and some of the following Psalms were usually sung at the eating of the Paschal lamb, of which custom mention is also made, Matt. xxvi., that Christ and the disciples sang a hymn before they went out into the garden.—*Solomon Gesner.*

Whole Psalm.—The two Psalms, cxi. and cxii., resemble one another in construction, alphabetical arrangement, and general tone and manner. They are connected in this way : Ps. cxi. sets forth the greatness, mercy, and righteousness of God : Ps. cxii. the reflection of these attributes in the greatness, ver. 2, mercy, ver. 5, and righteousness, ver. 4, 9, of his chosen. The correspondence of purpose in the two Psalms is important to the right appreciation of some difficulties connected with the latter Psalm.—*Speaker's Commentary.*

Whole Psalm.—The scope of this Psalm is to stir up all to praise God, and that for so many reasons as there are verses in the Psalm. The exhortation is in the first words, *"Praise ye the Lord."* The reasons follow in order. The Psalm is composed so after the order of the Hebrew alphabet, as every sentence or half verse beginneth with a several letter of the A B C in order, and all the Psalm is of praise only. Whence we learn in general, 1. Sometimes it is expedient to set all other things apart, and employ ourselves expressly to proclaim the praises of the Lord only ; for so is done in this Psalm. 2. The praises of the Lord are able to fill all the letters and words composed of letters, in all their possible junctures of composition ; for so much doth the going through all the letters of the A B C point out unto us, he is Alpha and Omega, and all the middle letters of the A B C of praise. 3. The praises of the Lord are worthy to be kept in memory : for that this Psalm may be the better remembered, it is composed after the manner of the A B C, and so it insinuateth thus much to us.—*David Dickson.*

Verse 1.—*"Praise ye the* LORD*,"* etc. The exhortation is immediately succeeded by the expression of a firm resolve ; the Psalmist having commenced by urging the duty of gratitude upon others—*"Praise ye the Lord,"* forthwith announces his determination to act upon his own advice—*"I will praise the Lord with my whole heart."* Such a conjunction of ideas is fraught with several most important lessons. 1. It teaches us, very emphatically, that our preaching, if it is to carry weight and conviction, must be backed and exemplified by our conduct ; that we need never expect to persuade others by arguments which are too weak to influence ourselves. 2. Another inference is similarly suggested—that our own decision should be given without reference to the result of our appeal. The Psalmist did not wait to ascertain whether those whom he addressed would attend to his exhortation, but, before he could receive a reply, declared unhesitatingly the course he would himself adopt.— *W. T. Maudson, in a Sermon on Thanksgiving,* 1855.

Verse 1.—*"With my whole heart."* That is, earnestly, and with a sincere affection ; meaning also, that he would do it privately, and, as it were, within himself, as by the next words he noteth that he will do it openly.—*Thomas Wilcocks.*

Verse 1.—*"With my whole heart."* We see the stress here laid upon a whole heart, and the want of which is the great canker of all vital godliness. Men are ever attempting to unite what the word of God has declared to be incapable of union—the love of the world and of God—to give half their heart to the world, and the other half to God. Just see the energy, the entireness of every thought and feeling and effort which a man throws into a work in which he is deeply interested ; the very phrase we use to describe such an one is, that " he gives his whole mind to it." Attempt to persuade him to divert his energies and divide his time with some other pursuit, and he would wonder at the folly and the ignorance that could suggest such a method of success. " Just take a hint from Satan," says some one; " see how he plies his powers on the individual, as if there were but that one, and as if he had nothing else to do but to ruin that one soul." It was a holy resolution of the Psalmist that he would praise God ; and a wise one to add, *"with my whole heart."* And we have the result of this determination in the following verses of the Psalm.—*Barton Bouchier.*

Verse 1.—Two words are used, *"assembly"* and *"congregation."* The former implies a more private meeting of worshippers, the latter the more public. The former may apply to the family circle of those who were celebrating the passover, the latter to the public worship connected with the feast.—*W. Wilson.*

Verse 2.—*"The works of the* LORD *are great."* Their greatness is known from comparison with the works and powers of men, which, verily, die and perish quickly. We should, therefore, admire, fear, confide, obey.—*Martin Geier.*

Verse 2.—*"The works of the* Lord *are great,"* etc. Their greatness is equally manifest when we turn from the *immensity* to the *variety* of his works. . . . . How great are the works of him who gives to every plant its leaf and flower and fruit; to every animal its faculties and functions; to every man his understanding, affections, and will. What an accumulative idea of the magnitude of his works do we gather from the innumerable multitudes and endless diversities of being called into existence by his powers.—*Samuel Summers,* 1837.

Verse 2.—*"The works of the* Lord *are great."* The workman who never makes a small article, an inferior article, but makes all his articles both great and valuable, deserves much praise; and any one that will study God's works, which we think so little of by reason of their being so constantly before us, cannot fail to behold God's infinite power and wisdom in every one of them, even though he cannot comprehend them.—*Robert Bellarmine.*

Verse 2.—*"Great."* The word גדול (gadol) *"great,"* has in the Hebrew so extensive a range of meaning, that in the English there is no single substitute expressive enough to take its place. It denotes greatness and augmentation of various kinds. In this passage " the works of Jehovah " are described as greatly *"magnified or augmented"* in their influences and effects on the minds of men who behold them. The *greatness* ascribed to these works, is a greatness in number, in character, in dignity, in beauty, in variety, in riches.—*Benjamin Weiss.*

Verses 2, 4.—*"Great . . . sought out." "Remembered."* The works of Jehovah surpass the reach of human discovery, but are yet searched and explored with delight by all the members of his church; for if they are too great to be understood, they are also too great to be forgotten.—*Edward Garrard Marsh.*

Verse 2.—*"Sought out."* To see God in his creatures, and to love him and converse with him, was the employment of man in his upright state. This is so far from ceasing to be our duty, that it is the work of Christ, by faith, to bring us back to it; and therefore the most holy men are the most excellent students of God's works; and none but the holy can rightly study or know them. Your studies of physics and other sciences are not worth a rush, if it be not God by them that you seek after. To see and admire, to reverence and adore, to love and delight in God appearing to us in his works, and purposely to peruse them for the knowledge of God; this is the true and only philosophy, and the contrary is mere foolery, and so called again and again by God himself.—*Richard Baxter,* 1615—1691.

Verse 2.—It does not follow, that because the study of nature is now of itself an insufficient guide to the knowledge of the Creator and the enjoyment of eternal felicity, such studies are either to be thrown aside, or considered as of no importance in a religious point of view. To overlook the astonishing scene of the universe, or to view it with indifference, is virtually to " disregard the works of Jehovah, and to refuse to consider the operations of his hands." It is a violation of Christian duty, and implies a reflection on the character of the Deity, for any one to imagine that he has nothing to do with God considered as manifested in the immensity of his works; for his word is pointed and explicit in directing the mind to such contemplations. " Hearken unto this, stand still, and consider the wonderful works of God." " Lift up thine eye on high, and behold who hath created these orbs." " Remember that thou magnify his works which men behold." " Great and marvellous are thy works, Lord God Almighty! Thy saints shall speak of the glory of thy kingdom and talk of thy power, to make known to the sons of men thy mighty operations and the glorious majesty of thy kingdom."—*Thomas Dick* (1772—) *in* "*The Sidereal Heavens.*"

Verse 2.—*"Sought out of all them that have pleasure therein."* This is a true characteristic of the upright and pious. The works of God are said to be *"sought out of them,"* when they regard them, call them to mind, and carefully, taking them one by one, investigate them; and at the same time explain them to others, and recount them: all which is included in the verb דרש; for that verb, properly is *"trivit"* [to rub, beat, or bray] hence by thrashing and grinding he has *investigated* perfectly, and has *rubbed* out the *kernel of it* for the use and profit of another: whence it is used for *concionari,* etc.—*Hermann Venema.*

Verse 2.—*"Sought out,"* . . . . *" have pleasure therein."* Philosophy seeks truth, Theology finds it, but Religion possesses it. Human things must be known to be loved, but divine things must be loved to be known.—*Blaise Pascal,* 1623—1662.

Verses 2—4.—*"Sought out."* . . . *"The* Lord *is gracious and full of compassion."* This is the grand discovery of all the searching, and therein lies the glory that is the conclusion of all. As in searching into any experiments in nature, there is an infinite pleasure that accompanies such a study to them that are addicted thereunto ; so to him that hath pleasure in the works of God, and is addicted to spy out his kindness in them, there is nothing so pleasant as the discovery of new circumstances of mercy that render his work *"glorious and honourable."* Get, therefore, skill in his dealings with thee, and study thy friend's carriage to thee. It is the end why he raised thee up, and admitted thee into friendship with him, to show his art of love and friendship to thee ; to show, in a word, how well he could love thee.—*Thomas Goodwin.*

Verse 3.—*"His work is honourable and glorious."* The first thing that we notice is, that whereas the preceding verse spoke of the Lord's *"works"* in the *plural* number, this speaks of his *"work"* in the singular number ; it would seem as if the Psalmist, from the contemplation of the works of the Lord in general, was, as it were, irresistibly drawn away to the study of one work in particular ; his mind and whole attention, so to speak, absorbed in that one work : a work so pre-eminently glorious and divine, that it eclipses, at least in his eyes, all the other works, although he has just said of them that they are great, and sought out of all them that have pleasure therein. " The works of the Lord are great. His work is honourable and glorious." My next remark is, that the words used in the original are different, and as the former more strictly signifies *makings*, or *things made*, so the word in this verse more properly imports a *doing* or a *thing done*, and this, perhaps, is not without its significance. It leads me to the inference, that from the contemplation of the great works of creation, God's makings, wonderful, and interesting, and useful as they are, the spiritual mind of God's servant rapidly passes to some greater deed which the Lord hath done, some more marvellous act which he has accomplished, and which he designates as an honourable and a glorious deed. Now, since I consider that he spoke before of Christ, as the visible and immediate agent in creation, without whom was not anything made that was made, can we hesitate long as to this greater work, the rather as to it is immediately subjoined the suggestive sentence, " And his righteousness endureth for ever." Is not this doing, the making an end of sin, and the bringing in of an everlasting righteousness ? Is it not the great mystery, in which, as in creation, though the Eternal Father is the Fountain source, the Original Contriver, He, the co-eternal Son, is the Doer the Worker ? Is it not, in short, *salvation*, the all-absorbing subject of God's people's wonder, love, and praise ?—*James H. Vidal, in "Jesus, God and Man,"* 1863.

Verse 4.—*"He hath made his wonderful works to be remembered."* The *memorials* of the Divine benefits are always valued greatly by a grateful heart, as making present with us the things which transpired ages before : such under the Old Testament was the sacrament of the paschal Lamb ; but now the sacred Supper under the New Testament. Therefore, whatever recalls the Divine works to the *memory*, e.g. the *ministry of the church*, also the *Sacred Scriptures*, are worthy of the highest reverence.—*Martin Geier.*

Verse 4.—The sweet spices of divine works must be beaten to powder by meditation, and then laid up in the cabinet of our memories. Therefore, says the Psalmist here, *"God hath made his wonderful works to be remembered"* ; he gives us the jewels of deliverance, not (because of the commonness of them) to wear them on our shoes, as the Romans did their pearls ; much less to tread them under our feet ; but rather to tie them as a chain about our necks. The impression of God's marvellous acts upon us must not be like that which the stone makes in the water, raising circles, beating one wave on another, and for a time making a noise, but soon after it sinks down, and the water returneth to its former smoothness ; and so we, while judgment is fresh, are apt to publish it from man to man, but soon after we let it sink into the depth of oblivion, and we return to our old sins.—*Abraham Wright.*

Verse 4.—*"Made his wonderful works to be remembered."* The most amazing perverseness in man is proven by the fact that he does not remember what God has so arranged that it would seem impossible that it should be forgotten.—*William S. Plumer.*

Verse 4.—

> For wonderful indeed are all his works,
> Pleasant to know and worthiest to be all
> Had in remembrance always with delight.

—*John Milton.*

Verse 5.—The first hemistich is the consequence of what is stated in the second, *i.e., because* God remembered his covenant, *therefore* he gave food to them who fear him.—*George Phillips.*

Verse 5.—*"He hath given meat,"* etc. The *"meat"* here mentioned is supposed to respect the paschal lamb, when they were to remember the works of God.— *Thomas Manton.*

Verse 5.—*"Meat."* Literally, *booty* or *spoil :* the *spoil* (Exod. xii. 36) brought by Israel out of Egypt, as God had engaged by " covenant " to Abraham, Gen. xv. 14, " They shall come out with great *substance* " (Kimchi). Rather the *manna* and *quails,* which to the hungry people were like a booty thrown in their way. The word is used for *"meat"* in general, in Prov. xxxi. 15 ; Mal. iii. 10.—*A. R. Fausset.*

Verse 5.—*"He hath given meat."* I rather choose to render it *portion,* in which sense it is taken in Prov. xxx. 8, and xxxi. 15 ; as if he should say, that God has given his people all that was needful, and that, considered as a portion, it was large and liberal ; for we know that the people of Israel were enriched, not in consequence of their own industry, but by the blessing of God, who, like the father of a family, bestows upon his household everything necessary for their subsistence. In the following clause of the verse, he assigns as the reason for his care and kindness his desire of effectually demonstrating that his covenant was not null and void.—*John Calvin.*

Verse 5.—*"He will ever be mindful of his covenant."* This clause would seem to be introduced parenthetically—a passing thought, a happy thought, presenting itself spontaneously to the Psalmist's mind, and immediately expressed with his lips. It will be observed it is in the future tense, while all the other clauses are in the past— " He *hath made* his wonderful works to be remembered " ; " He *hath given* meat unto them that fear him " ; " He *will ever be* mindful of his covenant " ; not *he hath ever been.* Dwelling on these past favours of God to Israel, it is his joy to think that they were but partial fulfilments of a covenant promise, which still remained, and in its highest sense should remain for ever ; and that covenant itself the memorial or type of the better, the spiritual covenant, the gospel. So out of the abundance of the heart his mouth speaketh, and he celebrates God's promised truth to Israel as the memorial and pledge of his eternal faithfulness to the New Testament Israel, his blood-ransomed church.—*James H. Vidal.*

Verse 6.—*"He hath shewed his people,"* etc. The Prophet indicates the unbelief of the Jews, who murmured against God in the desert, as if he could not enable them to enter into the promised land, and possess it, because the cities were walled, and the inhabitants strong, and giants dwelt in it. *"He shewed,"* he says, *i.e.,* he placed before their eyes, *"the power of His works,"* when he gave the lands of the heathen to be inhabited by his own people.—*Wolfgang Musculus.*

Verse 6.—*"He hath shewed his people the power of his works."* So he hath showed his works of power to his people in Gospel times, as the miracles of Christ, his resurrection from the dead, redemption by him, and the work of grace on the hearts of men in all ages.—*John Gill.*

Verse 6.—*"He hath shewed his people,"* etc. To them it is given to see, but not to others who are delivered up to a judicial blindness. " Call unto me, and I will answer thee, and show thee great and mighty things, which thou knowest not." Jer. xxxiii. 3.—*John Trapp.*

Verse 6.—*"To give them the heritage of the heathen."* The heathen themselves are bequeathed to God's people, and they must take possession of this inheritance to draw them to themselves.—*Richter, in Lange's Commentary.*

Verse 7.—The works of God expound his word, in his works his word is often made visible. That is an excellent expression, *"The works of his hands are verity and judgment."* *The acts of God are verity,* that is, God acts his own truths. As the works of our hands ought to be the verity and judgments of God, (every action of a Christian ought to be one of Christ's truths), so it is with God himself ; the works of his hands are his own verity and judgments. When we cannot find the meaning of God in his word, we may find it in his works : his works are a comment an infallible comment upon his word.—*Joseph Caryl.*

Verses 7, 8.—God is known to be faithful and just both in his works and in his word, insomuch that the most beautiful harmony is apparent between the things he has spoken and those he has done. This wonderfully confirms the hope and faith of the godly.—*Mollerus.*

Verse 8.—*"They stand fast for ever and ever."* סמוכים, *semuchim,* they are *propped up, buttressed for ever.* They can never fail; for God's power supports his works, and his providence preserves the record of what he has done.—*Adam Clarke.*

Verse 8.—*"They stand fast,"* are established, *"for ever and ever,"* etc. This verse seems to have reference to the works of God mentioned in the former. His doings were not the demand of an occasion, they were in unison with a great and extensive purpose, with respect to the people of Israel and the Messiah. Not one jot or tittle shall pass from the law of his mouth, till all be fulfilled.—*W. Wilson.*

Verse 8.—*"They are done in truth."* It is impossible that any better way should be directed, than that which the Lord useth in the disposal of all things here below, for all the works of the Lord are done in truth. As the word of God is a word of truth, so all his works are works of truth; for his works are nothing else but the making good of his word, and they are answerable to a threefold word of his. First, to his word of *prophecy.* Whatsoever changes God makes in the world, they hit some word of prophecy. Secondly, the works of God are answerable to his word for *threatening.* God threatens before he smites, and he never smote any man with a rod or sword, but according to his threatening. Thirdly, the works of God are answerable to his word of *promise.* All mercies are promised, and every work of mercy is the fulfilling of some promise. Now seeing all the works of God are reducible, either to prophecies, threatenings, or promises; they *"are done in truth"*; and what can be better done than that which is done in truth? The Jewish doctors observe, that the word *emeth* here used for truth, consists of *aleph,* the first letter of the alphabet, *mem,* the middle letter thereof, and *tau,* the last; to shew, that as God is *alpha* and *omega,* so the truth of God is the all in all of our comfort. Grace and truth by Christ is the sum of all the good news in the world.—*Abraham Wright.*

Verse 8.—*"Are done."* Verses 7 and 8 contain a precious meaning for the soul whose rest is the finished work of Christ. Jehovah has commanded, giving it in trust to Jesus to make sure, in perfect obedience, the word of truth and holiness. The commandment therefore has been *"done."* It has been done *"in truth and uprightness"* by him whose meat it was to do it; who willingly received it with a knowledge of its end, and in whose accomplishment of it the believing sinner finds his assurance and eternal peace. John xii. 50. Jesus held the law within his heart, to keep it there for ever. As the fulfiller in truth of the commandment, he has become its end for righteousness to every believer in his name.—*Arthur Pridham.*

Verse 9.—*"He sent redemption to his people."* Once out of Egypt, ever out of Satan's thraldom.—*John Trapp.*

Verse 9.—*"Sent redemption"* . . . . *"commanded his covenant."* The deliverance was the more thankworthy, as being upon a covenant account; for thus every mercy is a token of the Lord's favour to his favourite: it is this which makes common mercies to become special mercies. Carnal men, so that they enjoy mercies, they mind not which way they come in, so as they can but have them; but a child of God knows that everything that comes through the Redeemer's hands and by his covenant is the better for it, and tastes the sweeter by far.—*William Cooper, in the Morning Exercises.*

Verse 9.—*"Redemption."* Praise our Triune Jehovah for his redemption. Write it down where you may read it. Affix it where you may see it. Engrave it on your heart that you may understand it. It is a word big with importance. In it is enfolded *your* destinies and those of the Church, to all future ages. There are heights in it you never can have scaled, and depths you never can have fathomed. You have never taken the wings of the morning, and gained the utmost parts of earth, to measure the length and breadth of it. Wear it as a seal on your arm, as a signet on your right hand, for Jesus is the author of it. O! prize it as a precious stone, more precious than rubies. . . . Let it express your best hopes while living, and dwell on your trembling lips in the moment of dissolution; for it shall form the chorus of the song of the redeemed throughout eternity.—*Isaac Saunders,* 1818.

Verse 9.—*"He hath commanded his covenant for ever."* As he covenanted, so he looketh that his covenants should be respected, which are as binding to us, as his covenant is to him; and, through grace, his covenant is as binding to him, as those are to us.—*John Trapp.*

Verse 9.—*"Holy and reverend, or, terrible, is his name."* "Holy is his name," and therefore *"terrible"* to those who, under all the means of grace, continue unholy. —*George Horne.*

Verse 9.—*"Holy and reverend is his name."* Which therefore we should not presume on a sudden to blurt out. The Jews would not pronounce it. The Grecians (as Suidas observeth), when they would swear by their Jupiter, forbare to mention him. This should act as a check to the profaneness common amongst us. Let those that would have their *name reverend*, labour to be *holy* as God is holy.—*John Trapp.*

Verse 10 (*first clause*).—In this passage *"fear"* is not to be understood as referring to the first or elementary principles of piety, as in 1 John iv. 18, but is comprehensive of all true godliness, or the worship of God.—*John Calvin.*

Verse 10.—*"The fear of the LORD is the beginning of wisdom,"* etc. The text shows us the first step to true wisdom, and the test of common sense. It is so frequently repeated, that it may pass for a Scripture maxim, and we may be sure it is of singular importance. Job starts the question, "Where shall wisdom be found? and where is the place of understanding?" He searches nature through in quest of it, but cannot find it: he cannot purchase it with the gold of Ophir, and its price is above rubies. At length he recollects the primitive instruction of God to man, and there he finds it: "To man he said, Behold, the fear of the Lord, that is wisdom; and to depart from evil is understanding."—Job xxviii. 28. Solomon, the wisest of men, begins his Proverbs with this maxim, "The fear of the LORD is the beginning of knowledge," Prov. i. 7. And he repeats it again: "The fear of the LORD is the beginning of wisdom; and the knowledge of the holy," (the knowledge of those that may be called *saints* with a sneer), "is understanding," Prov. ix. 10. *"The fear of the LORD"* in Scripture signifies not only that pious passion or filial reverence of our adorable Father who is in heaven, but it is frequently put for the whole of practical religion; hence it is explained in the last part of the verse by *"doing his commandments."* The fear of the Lord, in this latitude, implies all the graces and all the virtues of Christianity; in short, all that holiness of heart and life which is necessary to the enjoyment of everlasting happiness. So that the sense of the text is this: To practise religion and virtue, to take that way which leads to everlasting happiness, is *wisdom*, true wisdom, the *beginning* of wisdom, the first step towards it: unless you begin here you can never attain it; all your wisdom without this does not deserve the name; it is madness and nonsense. *"To do his commandments"* is the best test of a *"good understanding"*: a *"good"* sound *"understanding"* have *"all they"* that do this, *"all"* of them without exception: however weak some of them may be in other things, they are wise in the most important respect; but without this, however cunning they are in other things, they have lost their understandings; they contradict common sense; they are beside themselves. In short, to pursue everlasting happiness as the end, in the way of holiness as the mean, this is *"wisdom,"* this is common sense, and there can be none without this.—*Samuel Davies, A.M. (1724—1761) President of Princeton College, New Jersey.*

Verse 10.—*"The fear of the LORD is the beginning of wisdom."* Now, then, I demand of the worldling what is the most high and deep point of wisdom? Is it to get an opulent fortune, to be *so wise as fifty thousand pounds?* Behold, "godliness is great gain," saith Paul, and the Christian only rich, quoth the renowned catechist [Clement] of Alexandria. Is it to live joyfully, (or to use the gallant's phrase) jovially? Behold, there is joyful gladness for such as are true hearted, Ps. xcvii. 11. A wicked man in his mad-merry humour for a while may be *Pomponius Lætus*, but a good man only is *Hilarius;* only he which is faithful in heart is joyful in heart. Is it to get honour? *the praise of God's fear* (saith our text) *endures for ever.* Many worthies of the world are most unhappy, because they be commended where they be not, and tormented where they be; hell rings of their pains, earth of their praise; but "blessed is the man that feareth the Lord" (Ps. cxii. 1), for his commendation is both here lasting, and hereafter everlasting; in this world he is renowned among men, in the next he shall be rewarded amongst saints and angels in the kingdom of glory.—*John Boys.*

Verse 10.—*"The fear of the LORD is the beginning of wisdom."* It is not only the beginning of wisdom, but the middle and the end. It is indeed the Alpha and Omega, the essence, the body and the soul, the sum and substance. He that hath the fear of God is truly wise. . . . It is surely wisdom to love that which is most lovable, and to occupy our hearts with that which is most worthy of our attachment, and the most capable of satisfying us.—*From the French of Daniel de Superville,* 1700.

Verse 10 (*first clause*).—Fear is not all then ; no, for it is but the beginning. God will have us begin, but not end there. We have begun with *qui timet Eum,* "who fears him ; " we must end with *et operatur juslitiam,* "and does justice," and then comes *acceptus est Illi,* and not before. For neither fear, if it be fear alone ; nor faith, if it be faith alone, is accepted of Him. If it be true fear, if such as God will accept, it is not *timor piger,* " a dull lazy fear " ; his fear that feared his lord and " went and digged his talent into the ground," and did nothing with it. Away with his fear and him " into outer darkness."—*Lancelot Andrewes.*

Verse 10.—Can it then be said that the non-religious world is without wisdom ? Has it no Aristotle, no Socrates, no Tacitus, no Goethe, no Gibbon ? Let us understand what wisdom is. It is not any mere amount of knowledge that constitutes wisdom. Appropriate knowledge is essential to wisdom. A man who has not the knowledge appropriate to his position, who does not know himself in his relation to God and to his fellow-men, who is misinformed as to his duties, his dangers, his necessities, though he may have written innumerable works of a most exalted character, yet is he to be set down as a man without wisdom. What is it to you that your servant is acquainted with mathematics, if he is ignorant of your will, and of the way to do it ? The genius of a Voltaire, a Spinoza, a Byron, only makes their folly the more striking. As though a man floating rapidly onwards to the falls of Niagara, should occupy himself in drawing a very admirable picture of the scenery. Men who are exceedingly great in the world's estimation have made the most signal blunders with regard to the most important things ; and it is only because these things are not considered important by the world, that the reputation of these men remains.

If you have learned to estimate things in some measure as God estimates them, to desire what he offers, to relinquish what he forbids, and to recognise the duties that he has appointed you, you are in the path of wisdom, and the great men we have been speaking about are far behind you—far from the narrow gate which you have entered. He only is wise, who can call Christ the wisdom of God.—*George Bowen.*

Verse 10.—"*The beginning of wisdom.*" That is, the principle whence it springs, and the fountain from which it flows.—*William Walford.*

Verse 10.—As there are degrees of wisdom, so of the fear of the Lord ; but there is no degree of this fear so inferior or low, but it is a beginning, at least, of wisdom ; and there is no degree of wisdom so high or perfect, but it hath its root in, or beginning, from this fear.—*Joseph Caryl.*

Verse 10.—"*Beginning of wisdom.*" The word translated *beginning* is of uncertain sense. It may signify the *first* in *time* only, and so the rudiments, first foundation, or groundwork, and so though the most necessary, yet the most imperfect part of the work. And if it should thus be understood here and in other places, the sense would be no more but this, that there were no true *wisdom,* which had not its foundation in piety and fear of God. But the word signifies the *first* in *dignity* as well as in order of time, and is frequently used for the chief or principal of any kind. . . . And thus it is to be understood here, that "*the fear of the Lord*" (which signifies all piety) *is the principal or chief of wisdom,* as *sapientia prima* in Horace is the *principal* or most excellent wisdom ; according to that of Job xxviii. 28 : " Unto man he said, Behold, the fear of the Lord, that is wisdom ; and to depart from evil is understanding," *that,* by way of eminence, the most excellent *wisdom* and understanding.—*Henry Hammond.*

Verse 10.—"*A good understanding have all they that do his commandments.*" They which *do* the commandments have a good understanding ; not they which speak of the commandments, nor they which write of the commandments, nor they which preach of the commandments, but they which do the commandments, have a good understanding. The rest have a false understanding, a vain understanding, an understanding like that of the scribes and pharisees, which was enough to condemn them, but not to save them.—*Henry Smith.*

Verse 10.—"*A good understanding have all they that do,*" etc. So much a man knoweth in true account, as he doth ; hence understanding is here ascribed to the will ; so Job xxviii. 28. Some render it *good success.—John Trapp.*

Verse 10 *(last clause).—"The praise of it endures for ever"* ; or as other translations, *"his praise"* ; referring it either to God, or else to the man who fears God. Some divines ascribe this praise to God alone, because *tehilla* properly signifieth only that kind of praise which is due to God ; and so they make this clause to contain both a precept and a promise. *Precept*, exhorting us to praise God with all our heart, both in the secret assemblies of the faithful and in the public congregation. And lest any man in executing this office should be discouraged, the prophet addeth a promise, " God's praise doth endure for ever " ; as if he should have said, " The Lord is King, be the people never so impatient ; the Lord is God, albeit the Gentiles furiously rage together, and the Jews imagine a vain thing ; the kings of the earth stand up, and the rulers combine themselves against him," Ps. xcix. 1 ; xviii. 31 ; ii. 1. He that dwelleth in heaven hath all his enemies in derision, and makes them all his footstool ; his power is for ever, and so consequently his praise shall endure for ever ; in the militant church, unto the world's end ; in the triumphant, world without end.

Most interpreters have referred this unto the good man who fears the Lord, yet diversely. S. Augustine expoundeth it thus, *"his praise,"* that is, his praising of the Lord, *"shall endure for ever,"* because he shall be one of them of whom it is said (Ps. lxxxiv. 4) " Blessed are they that dwell in thy house : they will be still praising thee." Others understand by *"his praise"* the commendation of the good man, both in the life present and in that which is to come, for his righteousness shall be had in an everlasting remembrance. Ps. cxii. 6.—*John Boys.*

Verse 10 *(second clause).*—Where the fear of the Lord rules in the heart, there will be a constant conscientious care to keep his commandments : not to talk them, but to do them ; and such *"have a good understanding,"* *i.e.*, First, They are well understood, their obedience is graciously accepted as a plain indication of their mind, that they do indeed fear God. Secondly, They understand well. 1. It is a sign they do understand well : the most obedient are accepted as the most intelligent. They are wise that make God's law their rule, and are in everything ruled by it. 2. It is the way to understand better. " A good understanding are they to all that do them " ; *i.e.*, the fear of the Lord, and the laws of God give men a good understanding, and are able to make them wise unto salvation.—*Condensed from Matthew Henry.*

HINTS TO PREACHERS.

Verse 1.—*"Praise ye the Lord"* ; there is an exhortation. *"I will praise the Lord ;"* there is a vow. It shall be *"with my whole heart"* ; there is experimental godliness. It shall be *"in the assembly of the upright"* ; there is a relative position occupied along with the family of God.—*Joseph Irons.*

Verse 1.—*"With my whole heart."* This includes spirituality, simplicity, and earnestness.—*Joseph Irons.*

Verse 1.—I. Who are the upright ? II. What are they doing ? Praising God. III. What shall I do if I am favoured to stand among them ? " I will praise the Lord."

Verse 1.—Where I love to be, and what I love to do.

Verse 2.—The Christian philosopher. I. His sphere : " The works of the Lord." II. His work : " Sought out." III. His qualification : " Pleasure therein." IV. His conclusion : " Praise," as in verse 1.

Verses 2—9.—The Psalmist furnishes us with matter for praise from the works of God. 1. The greatness of his works and the glory of them. 2. The righteousness of them. 3. The goodness of them. 4. The power of them. 5. The conformity of them to his word of promise. 6. The perpetuity of them.—*Matthew Henry.*

Verse 3 *(last clause).*—As an essential attribute, as revealed in providence, as vindicated in redemption, as demonstrated in punishment, as appropriated by believers.

Verse 4.—The compassion of the Lord as seen in aiding the memories of his people.

Verses 4, 5.—God's marvels ought not to be nine-day wonders. I. *It is God's design that his wonders should be remembered*, therefore, 1. He made them great. 2. He wrought them for an undeserving people. 3. He wrought them at memorable times. 4. He put them on record. 5. He instituted memorials. 6. He bade them tell their children. 7. He so dealt with them as to refresh their memories. II. *It is our wisdom to remember the Lord's wonders.* 1. To assure us of his compassion : " The Lord is gracious." 2. To make us consider his bounty : " he hath given meat." 3. To certify us of his faithfulness : " he will ever be mindful of his covenant." 4. To arouse our praise : " Praise ye the Lord."

Verse 5.—There is, I. Encouragement from the past : " He hath given meat," etc. II. Confidence for the future : " He will ever be mindful," etc.—*G. R.*

Verse 6.—The power of God an encouragement for the evangelization of the heathen.

Verse 9.—*Redemption.* Conceived, arranged, executed, and applied by God. By price and by power. From sin and death. That we may be free, the Lord's own, the Lord's glory.

Verse 9.—Redemption. I. Its author : " He sent." II. Its objects : " Unto his people." III. The pledge it gives us : " He hath commanded his covenant," etc. IV. The praise it creates in us.

Verse 9.—"*Holy and reverend.*" I. The holiness of God the object of our reverence. II. Such reverence has much useful influence over us. III. It should always accompany our faith in redemption and covenant. See preceding clauses of verse.

Verse 10.—I. The beginner in Christ's school. II. The man who has taken a degree : " a good understanding," etc. III. The Master who receives the praise.

Verse 10.—I. The beginning of wisdom : " the fear of the Lord "—God is feared. II. Its continuance : " a good understanding have all they that do his commandments "—when the fear of the Lord in the heart is developed in the life. III. Its end, praising God for ever : " his praise," etc.—*G. R.*

PSALM CXII.

TITLE AND SUBJECT.—*There is no title to this Psalm, but it is evidently a companion to the hundred and eleventh, and, like it, it is an alphabetical Psalm. Even in the number of verses, and clauses of each verse, it coincides with its predecessor, as also in many of its words and phrases. The reader should carefully compare the two Psalms line by line. The subject of the poem before us is*—the blessedness of the righteous man, and so it bears the same relation to the preceding which the moon does to the sun ; for, while the first declares the glory of God, the second speaks of the reflection of the divine brightness in men born from above. God is here praised for the manifestation of his glory which is seen in his people, just as in the preceding Psalm he was magnified for his own personal acts. The hundred and eleventh speaks of the great Father, and this describes his children renewed after his image. The Psalm cannot be viewed as the extolling of man, for it commences with "Praise ye the Lord ; " and it is intended to give to God all the honour of his grace which is manifested in the sons of God.*

DIVISION.—*The subject is stated in the first verse, and enlarged upon under several heads from 2 to 9. The blessedness of the righteous is set forth by contrast with the fate of the ungodly in verse 10.*

EXPOSITION.

PRAISE ye the LORD. Blessed *is* the man *that* feareth the LORD, *that* delighteth greatly in his commandments.

1. *"Praise ye the LORD."* This exhortation is never given too often ; the Lord always deserves praise, we ought always to render it, we are frequently forgetful of it, and it is always well to be stirred up to it. The exhortation is addressed to all thoughtful persons who observe the way and manner of life of men that fear the Lord. If there be any virtue, if there be any praise, the Lord should have all the glory of it, for we are his workmanship. *"Blessed is the man that feareth the Lord."* According to the last verse of Psalm cxi., " the fear of the Lord is the beginning of wisdom " ; this man, therefore, has begun to be wise, and wisdom has brought him present happiness, and secured him eternal felicity. Jehovah is so great that he is to be feared and had in reverence of all them that are round about him, and he is at the same time so infinitely good that the fear is sweetened into filial love, and becomes a delightful emotion, by no means engendering bondage. There is a slavish fear which is accursed ; but that godly fear which leads to delight in the service of God is infinitely blessed. Jehovah is to be praised both for inspiring men with godly fear and for the blessedness which they enjoy in consequence thereof. We ought to bless God for blessing any man, and especially for setting the seal of his approbation upon the godly. His favour towards the God-fearing displays his character and encourages gracious feelings in others, therefore let him be praised. *"That delighteth greatly in his commandments."* The man not only studies the divine precepts and endeavours to observe them, but rejoices to do so : holiness is his happiness, devotion is his delight, truth is his treasure. He rejoices in the precepts of godliness, yea, and delights *greatly* in them. We have known hypocrites rejoice in the doctrines, but never in the commandments. Ungodly men may in some measure obey the commandments out of fear, but only a gracious man will observe them with delight. Cheerful obedience is the only acceptable obedience ; he who obeys reluctantly is disobedient at heart, but he who takes pleasure in the command is truly loyal. If through divine grace we find ourselves described in these two sentences, let us give all the praise to God, for he hath wrought all our works in us, and the dispositions out of which they spring. Let self-righteous men praise themselves, but he who has been made righteous by grace renders all the praise to the Lord.

2 His seed shall be mighty upon earth : the generation of the upright shall be blessed

3 Wealth and riches *shall be* in his house : and his righteousness endureth for ever.

4 Unto the upright there ariseth light in the darkness : *he is* gracious and full of compassion, and righteous.

5 A good man sheweth favour, and lendeth : he will guide his affairs with discretion.

6 Surely he shall not be moved for ever : the righteous shall be in everlasting remembrance.

7 He shall not be afraid of evil tidings : his heart is fixed, trusting in the LORD.

8 His heart *is* established, he shall not be afraid, until he see *his desire* upon his enemies.

9 He hath dispersed, he hath given to the poor ; his righteousness endureth for ever ; his horn shall be exalted with honour.

2. *"His seed shall be mighty upon earth,"* that is to say, successive generations of God-fearing men shall be strong and influential in society, and in the latter days they shall have dominion. The true seed of the righteous are those who follow them in their virtues, even as believers are the seed of Abraham, because they imitate his faith ; and these are the real heroes of their era, the truly great men among the sons of Adam ; their lives are sublime, and their power upon their age is far greater than at first sight appears. If the promise must be regarded as alluding to natural seed, it must be understood as a general statement rather than a promise made to every individual, for the children of the godly are not all prosperous, nor all famous. Nevertheless, he who fears God, and leads a holy life, is, as a rule, doing the best he can for the future advancement of his house ; no inheritance is equal to that of an unblemished name, no legacy can excel the benediction of a saint ; and, taking matters for all in all, the children of the righteous man commence life with greater advantages than others, and are more likely to succeed in it, in the best and highest sense. *"The generation of the upright shall be blessed."* The race of sincere, devout, righteous men, is kept up from age to age, and ever abides under the blessing of God. The godly may be persecuted, but they shall not be forsaken ; the curses of men cannot deprive them of the blessing of God, for the words of Balaam are true, "He hath blessed, and I cannot reverse it." Their children also are under the special care of heaven, and as a rule it shall be found that they inherit the divine blessing. Honesty and integrity are better corner-stones for an honourable house than mere cunning and avarice, or even talent and push. To fear God and to walk uprightly is a higher nobility than blood or birth can bestow.

3. *"Wealth and riches shall be in his house."* Understood literally this is rather a promise of the old covenant than of the new, for many of the best of the people of God are very poor ; yet it has been found true that uprightness is the road to success, and, all other things being equal, the honest man is the rising man. Many are kept poor through knavery and profligacy ; but godliness hath the promise of the life that now is. If we understand the passage spiritually it is abundantly true. What wealth can equal that of the love of God ? What riches can rival a contented heart ? It matters nothing that the roof is thatched, and the floor is of cold stone : the heart which is cheered with the favour of heaven is "rich to all the intents of bliss." *"And his righteousness endureth for ever."* Often when gold comes in the gospel goes out ; but it is not so with the blessed man. Prosperity does not destroy the holiness of his life, or the humility of his heart. His character stands the test of examination, overcomes the temptations of wealth, survives the assaults of slander, outlives the afflictions of time, and endures the trial of the last great day. The righteousness of a true saint endureth for ever, because it springs from the same root as the righteousness of God, and is, indeed, the reflection of it. So long as the Lord abideth righteous he will maintain by his grace the righteousness of his people. They shall hold on their way, and wax stronger and stronger. There is also another righteousness which belongs to the Lord's chosen, which is sure to endure for ever, namely, the imputed righteousness of the Lord Jesus, which is called "everlasting righteousness," belonging as it does to the Son of God himself, who is "the Lord our righteousness."

4. *"Unto the upright there ariseth light in the darkness."* He does not lean to injustice in order to ease himself, but like a pillar stands erect, and he shall be found so standing when the ungodly, who are as a bowing wall and a tottering fence, shall lie in ruins. He will have his days of darkness, he may be sick and sorry, poor and pining, as well as others; his former riches may take to themselves wings and fly away, while even his righteousness may be cruelly suspected; thus the clouds may lower around him, but his gloom shall not last for ever, the Lord will bring him light in due season, for as surely as a good man's sun goes down it shall rise again. If the darkness be caused by depression of spirit, the Holy Ghost will comfort him; if by pecuniary loss or personal bereavement, the presence of Christ shall be his solace; and if by the cruelty and malignity of men, the sympathy of his Lord shall be his support. It is as ordinary for the righteous to be comforted as for the day to dawn. Wait for the light and it will surely come; for even if our heavenly Father should in our last hours put us to bed in the dark, we shall find it morning when we awake. *"He is gracious, and full of compassion, and righteous."* This is spoken of God in the fourth verse of the hundred and eleventh Psalm, and now the same words are used of his servant: thus we are taught that when God makes a man upright, he makes him like himself. We are at best but humble copies of the great original; still we are copies, and because we are so we praise the Lord, who hath created us anew in Christ Jesus. The upright man is " gracious," that is, full of kindness to all around him; he is not sour and churlish, but he is courteous to friends, kind to the needy, forgiving to the erring, and earnest for the good of all. He is also " full of compassion "; that is to say, he tenderly feels for others, pities them, and as far as he can assists them in their time of trouble. He does not need to be driven to benevolence, he is brimful of humanity; it is his joy to sympathize with the sorrowing. He is also said to be " righteous ": in all his transactions with his fellow men he obeys the dictates of right, and none can say that he goes beyond or defrauds his neighbour. His justice is, however, tempered with compassion, and seasoned with graciousness. Such men are to be found in our churches, and they are by no means so rare as the censorious imagine; but at the same time they are far scarcer than the breadth of profession might lead us to hope. Lord, make us all to possess these admirable qualities.

5. *"A good man sheweth favour, and lendeth."* Having passed beyond stern integrity into open-handed benevolence he looks kindly upon all around him, and finding himself in circumstances which enable him to spare a little of his wealth he lends judiciously where a loan will be of permanent service. Providence has made him able to lend, and grace makes him willing to lend. He is not a borrower, for God has lifted him above that necessity; neither is he a hoarder, for his new nature saves him from that temptation; but he wisely uses the talents committed to him. *"He will guide his affairs with discretion."* Those who neglect their worldly business must not plead religion as an excuse, for when a man is truly upright he exercises great care in managing his accounts, in order that he may remain so. It is sometimes hard to distinguish between indiscretion and dishonesty; carelessness in business may become almost as great an evil to others as actual knavery; a good man should not only *be* upright, but he should be so discreet that no one may have the slightest reason to suspect him of being otherwise. When the righteous man lends he exercises prudence, not risking his all, for fear he should not be able to lend again, and not lending so very little that the loan is of no service. He drives his affairs, and does not allow them to drive him; his accounts are straight and clear, his plans are wisely laid, and his modes of operation carefully selected. He is prudent, thrifty, economical, sensible, judicious, discreet. Men call him a fool for his religion, but they do not find him so when they come to deal with him. " The beginning of wisdom " has made him wise, the guidance of heaven has taught him to guide his affairs, and with half an eye one can see that he is a man of sound sense. Such persons greatly commend godliness. Alas, some professedly good men act as if they had taken leave of their senses; this is not religion, but stupidity. True religion is sanctified common sense. Attention to the things of heaven does not necessitate the neglect of the affairs of earth; on the contrary, he who has learned how to transact business with God ought to be best able to do business with men. The children of this world often are in their generation wiser than the children of light, but there is no reason why this proverb should continue to be true.

6. *"Surely he shall not be moved for ever."* God has rooted and established

him so that neither men nor devils shall sweep him from his place. His prosperity shall be permanent, and not like that of the gambler and the cheat, whose gains are evanescent : his reputation shall be bright and lustrous from year to year, for it is not a mere pretence ; his home shall be permanent, and he shall not need to wander from place to place as a bird that wanders from her nest ; and even his memory shall be abiding, for a good man is not soon forgotten, and *"the righteous shall be in everlasting remembrance."* They are of a most ancient family, and not mushrooms of an hour, and their grand old stock shall be found flourishing when all the proud houses of ungodly men shall have faded into nothing. The righteous are worth remembering, their actions are of the kind which record themselves, and God himself takes charge of their memorials. None of us likes the idea of being forgotten, and yet the only way to avoid it is to be righteous before God.

7. *"He shall not be afraid of evil tidings."* He shall have no dread that evil tidings will come, and he shall not be alarmed when they do come. Rumours and reports he despises ; prophecies of evil, vented by fanatical mouths, he ridicules ; actual and verified information of loss and distress he bears with equanimity, resigning everything into the hands of God. *"His heart is fixed, trusting in the Lord."* He is neither fickle nor cowardly ; when he is undecided as to his course he is still fixed in heart : he may change his plan, but not the purpose of his soul. His heart being fixed in solid reliance upon God, a change in his circumstances but slightly affects him ; faith has made him firm and steadfast, and therefore if the worst should come to the worst, he would remain quiet and patient, waiting for the salvation of God.

8. *"His heart is established."* His love to God is deep and true, his confidence in God is firm and unmoved ; his courage has a firm foundation, and is supported by omnipotence. He has become settled by experience, and confirmed by years. He is not a rolling stone, but a pillar in the house of the Lord. *"He shall not be afraid."* He is ready to face any adversary—a holy heart gives a brave face. *"Until he see his desire upon his enemies."* All through the conflict, even till he seizes the victory, he is devoid of fear. When the battle wavers, and the result seems doubtful, he nevertheless believes in God, and is a stranger to dismay. Grace makes him desire his enemies' good : though nature leads him to wish to see justice done to his cause, he does not desire for those who injure him anything by way of private revenge.

9. *"He hath dispersed, he hath given to the poor."* What he received, he distributed ; and distributed to those who most needed it. He was God's reservoir, and forth from his abundance flowed streams of liberality to supply the needy. If this be one of the marks of a man who feareth the Lord, there are some who are strangely destitute of it. They are great at gathering, but very slow at dispersing ; they enjoy the blessedness of receiving, but seldom taste the greater joy of giving. " It is more blessed to give than to receive "—perhaps they think that the blessing of receiving is enough for them. *"His righteousness endureth for ever."* His liberality has salted his righteousness, proved its reality, and secured its perpetuity. This is the second time that we have this remarkable sentence applied to the godly man, and it must be understood as resulting from the enduring mercy of the Lord. The character of a righteous man is not spasmodic, he is not generous by fits and starts, nor upright in a few points only ; his life is the result of principle, his actions flow from settled, sure, and fixed convictions, and therefore his integrity is maintained when others fail. He is not turned about by companions, nor affected by the customs of society ; he is resolute, determined, and immovable. *"His horn shall be exalted with honour."* God shall honour him, the universe of holy beings shalll honour him, and even the wicked shall feel an unconscious reverence of him. Let it be observed, in summing up the qualities of the God-fearing man, that he is described not merely as righteous, but as one bearing the character to which Paul refers in the memorable verse, " For scarcely for a righteous man will one die : yet peradventure for *a good man* some would even dare to die." Kindness, benevolence, and generosity, are essential to the perfect character ; to be strictly just is not enough, for God is love, and we must love our neighbour as ourselves : to give every one his due is not sufficient, we must act upon those same principles of grace which reign in the heart of God. The promises of establishment and prosperity are not to churlish Nabals, nor to niggard Labans, but to bountiful souls who have proved their fitness to be stewards of the Lord by the right way in which they use their substance.

10 The wicked shall see *it*, and be grieved ; he shall gnash with his teeth, and melt away : the desire of the wicked shall perish.

The tenth and last verse sets forth very forcibly the contrast between the righteous and the ungodly, thus making the blessedness of the godly appear all the more remarkable. Usally we see Ebal and Gerizim, the blessing and the curse, set the one over against the other, to invest both with the greater solemnity. " *The wicked shall see it, and be grieved.*" The ungodly shall first see the example of the saints to their own condemnation, and shall at last behold the happiness of the godly and to the increase of their eternal misery. The child of wrath shall be obliged to witness the blessedness of the righteous, though the sight shall make him gnaw his own heart. He shall fret and fume, lament and wax angry, but he shall not be able to prevent it, for God's blessing is sure and effectual. " *He shall gnash with his teeth.*" Being very wrathful, and exceedingly envious, he would fain grind the righteous between his teeth ; but as he cannot do that, he grinds his teeth against each other. " *And melt away.*" The heat of his passion shall melt him like wax, and the sun of God's providence shall dissolve him like snow, and at the last the fire of divine vengeance shall consume him as the fat of rams. How horrible must that life be which like the snail melts as it proceeds, leaving a slimy trail behind. Those who are grieved at goodness deserve to be worn away by such an abominable sorrow. " *The desire of the wicked shall perish.*" He shall not achieve his purpose, he shall die a disappointed man. By wickedness he hoped to accomplish his purpose— that very wickedness shall be his defeat. While the righteous shall endure for ever, and their memory shall be always green ; the ungodly man and his name shall rot from off the face of the earth. He desired to be the founder of a family, and to be remembered as some great one : he shall pass away and his name shall die with him. How wide is the gulf which separates the righteous from the wicked, and how different are the portions which the Lord deals out to them. O for grace to be blessed of the Lord ! This will make us praise him with our whole heart.

EXPLANATORY NOTES AND QUAINT SAYINGS.

Whole Psalm.—The hundred and eleventh and the hundred and twelfth Psalms, two very short poems, dating apparently from the latest age of inspired psalmody, present such features of resemblance as to leave no doubt that they came from the same pen. In structure they are identical ; and this superficial resemblance is designed to call attention to something deeper and more important. The subject of the one is the exact counterpart of the subject of the other. The first celebrates the character and works of *God ;* the second, the character and felicity of *the godly man.*—*William Binnie.*

Whole Psalm.—Here are rehearsed the blessings which God is wont to bestow on the godly. And as in the previous Psalm the praises of God were directly celebrated, so in this Psalm they are indirectly declared by those gifts which are conspicuous in those who fear him.—*Solomon Gesner.*

Whole Psalm.—This Psalm is a banquet of heavenly wisdom ; and as Basil speaketh of another part of Scripture, likening it to an apothecary's shop ; so may this book of Psalms fitly be compared ; in which are so many sundry sorts of medicines, that every man may have that which is convenient for his disease.— *T. S.*, 1621.

Whole Psalm.—The righteousness of the Mediator, I make no doubt, is celebrated in this Psalm ; for surely that alone is worthy to be extolled in songs of praise: especially since we are taught by the Holy Ghost to say, " I will make mention of thy righteousness, even of thine only." I conclude, therefore, that in this alphabetical Psalm, for such is its construction, Christ is " the Alpha and the Omega." —*John Fry.*

Verse 1.—This Psalm is a praising of God for blessing the believer, and the whole Psalm doth prove that the believer is blessed : which proposition is set down in verse 1, and confirmed with as many reasons as there are verses following. Whence learn, 1. Albeit, in singing of certain Psalms, or parts thereof, there be nothing directly spoken of the Lord, or to the Lord, yet he is praised when his truth is our song, or when his works and doctrine are our song ; as here it is said, "*Praise ye the Lord*," and then in the following verses the blessedness of the believer taketh up all the Psalm.   2. It is the Lord's praise that his servants are the only blessed people in the world.   "*Praise ye the Lord.*"   Why ? because "*Blessed is the man that feareth the Lord.*"   3. He is not the blessed man who is most observant to catch opportunities to have pleasure, profit, and worldly preferment, and careth not how he cometh by them : but he is the blessed man who is most observant of God's will, and careful to follow it.—*David Dickson.*

Verse 1.—"*Blessed is the man that feareth the Lord.*"   It is not said simply, *Blessed is the man who fears :* for there is a fear which of itself produces misery and wretchedness rather than happiness.   It has to do, therefore, chiefly with what is feared.   To fear when it is not becoming, and not to fear when fear is proper, these are not blessedness for a man, but misery and wretchedness.   The prophet, therefore, says rightly, "Blessed is the man that feareth *the Lord* " : and in the 7th and 8th verses he says of this blessed one that he shall not be afraid of evil tidings. Therefore, he who fears God and, according to the exhortation of Christ, does not fear those who can kill the body, he truly may be numbered among the blessed.— *Wolfgang Musculus.*

Verse 1.—"*Feareth the Lord.*"   Filial fear is here intended.   Whereby we are both restrained from evil, Prov. iii. 7 ; and incited unto well doing, Eccles. xii. 13 ; and whereof God alone is the author, Jer. xxxii. 39, 40 ; A duty required of every one, Ps. xxxiii. 8 ; Early, 1 Kings xviii. 12 ; Only, Luke xii. 5 ; Continually, Prov. xxiii. 17 ; With confidence, Ps. cxv. 11 ; With joyfulness, Ps. cxix. 74 ; With thankfulness, Rev. xix. 5.—*Thomas Wilson, in "A Complete Christian Dictionary,"* 1661.

Verse 1.—"*That delighteth greatly in his commandments.*"   The Hebrew word חפץ, *chaphets*, is rather emphatical, which is, as it were, to *take his pleasure*, and I have rendered it *to delight himself*.   For the prophet makes a distinction between a willing and prompt endeavour to keep the law, and that which consists in mere servile and constrained obedience.—*John Calvin.*

Verse 1.—" *That delighteth greatly in his commandments* "—defining what constitutes the true " fear of the Lord," which was termed " the beginning of wisdom," Ps. cxi. 10.   He who hath this true " fear " *delights* (Ps. cxi. 2) not merely in the theory, but in the practice of all " the Lord's commandments."   Such fear, so far from being a " hard " service, is the only " blessed " one (Jer. xxxii. 39). Compare the Gospel commandments, 1 John iii., 23, 24 : v. 3.   True obedience is not task-work, as formalists regard religion, but a " delight " (Ps. i. 2).   Worldly delights, which made piety irksome, are supplanted by the new-born delight in and taste for the will and ways of God (Ps. xix. 7—10).—*A. R. Fausset.*

Verse 1.—" *In his commandments.*"   When we cheerfully practise all that the Lord requireth of us, love sweeteneth all things, and it becomes our meat and drink to do his will.   The thing commanded is excellent, but it is sweeter because commanded *by him*—" *his* commandments."   A man is never thoroughly converted till he delighteth in God and his service, and his heart is overpowered by the sweetness of divine love.   A slavish kind of religiousness, when we had rather not do than do our work, is no fruit of grace, and cannot evidence a sincere love.—*Thomas Manton.*

Verse 2.—" *His seed.*"   If any one should desire to leave behind him a flourishing posterity, let him not think to accomplish it by accumulating heaps of gold and silver, and leaving them behind him ; but by rightly recognising God and serving Him ; and commending his children to the guardianship and protection of God.— *Mollerus.*

Verse 2.—" *The generation of the upright* "—the family ; the children—" *shall be blessed.*"   Such promises are expected to be fulfilled *in general ;* it is not required by any proper rules of interpreting language that this should be universally and always true.—*Albert Barnes.*

Verse 2.—" *The generation of the upright shall be blessed.*"   Albeit, few do believe it, yet is it true, that upright dealing hath better fruits than witty projecting and cunning catching.—*David Dickson.*

Verses 2, 3.—It is probable that Lot thought of enriching his family when he chose the fertile plains of wicked Sodom, yet the event was very different; but Abraham "feared the Lord, and delighted greatly in his commandments," and his descendants were "*mighty upon earth.*" And thus it will generally be, in every age, with the posterity of those who imitate the father of the faithful; and their disinterested and liberal conduct shall prove, in the event, a far preferable inheritance laid up for their children, than gold and silver, houses and lands, would have been.— *Thomas Scott.*

Verse 3.—"*Wealth and riches shall be in his house, and his righteousness endureth for ever.*" He is not the worse for his wealth, nor drawn aside by the deceitfulness of riches, which yet is hard and happy.—*John Trapp.*

Verse 3.—In the lower sense, we may read these words literally of abundant wealth bestowed on the righteous by God, and used, not for pride and luxury, but for continual works of mercy, whence it is said of the person so enriched, that "*his righteousness endureth for ever.*" But the higher meaning bids us see here those true spiritual riches which are stored up for the poor in spirit, often most needy in the prosperity of the world; and we may come at the truest sense by comparing the words wherein the great apostle describes his own condition, "As poor, yet making many rich; as having nothing, and yet possessing all things." 2 Cor. vi. 10. For who can be richer than he who is heir of God and joint heir with Jesus Christ ?—*Agellius, Chrysostom, and Didymus, in Neale and Littledale.*

Verse 3.—"*His righteousness endureth for ever.*" It seems a bold thing to say this of anything human, and yet it is true; for all human righteousness has its root in the righteousness of God. It is not merely man striving to copy God. It is God's gift and God's work. There is a living connexion between the righteousness of God and the righteousness of man, and therefore the imperishableness of the one appertains to the other also. Hence the same thing is affirmed here of the human righteousness which in cxi. 3 is affirmed of the Divine.—*J. J. S. Perowne.*

Verse 3.—"*His righteousness endureth for ever.*" We are justified before God by faith only: Rom. iii. 4: but they are righteous before men, who live honestly, piously, humbly, as the law of God requires. Concerning this righteousness the Psalmist says that *it endureth for ever*, while the feigned and simulated uprightness of hypocrites is abominable before God, and with men speedily passes away.— *Solomon Gesner.*

Verse 4.—"*Unto the upright there ariseth light in the darkness.*" The arising of light out of darkness, although one of the most common, is one of the most beautiful, as it is one of the most beneficent natural phenomena. The sunrise is a daily victory of light over darkness. Every morning the darkness flees away. Heavy sleepers in the city are not apt to be very well acquainted with the rising sun. They know the tender beauties of the dawning, and the glories of sunrise by poetical description, or by the word of others. The light has fully come, and the day has long begun its work, especially if it be summer time, before ordinary citizens are awake; and, unless on some rare occasions, the millions of men who, every day, see more or less the fading of the light into the dark, never see the rising of the light out of the dark again; and, perhaps, seldom or never think with what thankfulness and joy it is hailed by those who need it—by the sailor, tempest-tossed all night, and driven too near the sand-bank or the shore; by the benighted traveller lost in the wood, or in the wild, who knows not south from north until the sun shall rise; but the night watcher in the sick room, who hears, and weeps to hear, through the weary night, the moaning of that old refrain of sorrow, "Would God it were morning!" What intensity of sorrow, fear, hope, there may be in that expression, "more than they that watch for the morning; I say, more than they that watch for the morning"! Now I make no doubt that there is at least some-what of that intenser meaning carried up into the higher region of spiritual experience, and expressed by the text, "Unto the upright there ariseth light in the darkness." . . . Sincerity: an honest desire to know the truth: readiness to make any sacrifice in order to the knowledge: obedience to the truth so far as it is known already— these will bring the light *when nothing else will bring it.*—*Alexander Raleigh, in* "*The Little Sanctuary and other Meditations,*" 1872.

Verse 4.—"*Unto the upright there ariseth light in the darkness.*" The great lesson taught by this simile is the connection which obtains between integrity of purpose and clearness of perception, insomuch that a duteous conformity to what is right, is generally followed up by a ready and luminous discernment of what is true. It tells us that if we have but grace to *do* as we ought, we shall be made to *see* as we ought. It is a lesson repeatedly affirmed in Scripture, and that in various places both of the Old and New Testament : " The path of the just is as the shining light, that shineth more and more unto the perfect day " ; " The righteousness of the upright shall deliver them " ; " Light is sown for the righteous, and gladness for the upright in heart " ; or still more specifically, " To him that ordereth his conversation aright will I shew the salvation of God."—*Thomas Chalmers,* 1780—1847.

Verse 4.—*"Unto the upright there ariseth light in the darkness " :* that is, comfort in affliction. He hath comforted others in affliction, and been light to them in their darkness, as is showed in the latter end of the fourth verse, and in the fifth, and therefore by way of gracious retaliation, the Lord will comfort him in his affliction, and command the light to rise upon him in his darkness.—*Joseph Caryl.*

Verse 4.—*"Light." "Darkness."* While we are on earth, we are subject to a threefold *"darkness"* ; the darkness of error, the darkness of sorrow, and the darkness of death. To dispel these, God visiteth us, by his Word, with a threefold " light " ; the light of truth, the light of comfort, and the light of life.—*George Horne.*

Verse 4.—*"Gracious, and full of compassion, and righteous "*—attributes usually applied to *God,* but here said of *"the upright."* The children of God, knowing in their own experience that God our Father is " gracious, full of compassion, and righteous," seek themselves to be the same towards their fellow men from instinctive imitation of him (Matt. v. 45, 48 ; Eph. v. 8 ; Luke vi. 36).—*A. R. Fausset.*

Verse 5.—*"A good man sheweth favour,"* etc. Consider that power to do good is a dangerous ability, unless we use it. Remember that it is God who giveth wealth, and that he expecteth some answerable return of it. Live not in such an inhuman manner as if Nabal and Judas were come again into the world. Think frequently and warmly of the love of God and Jesus to you. You will not deny your crumbs to the miserable, when you thankfully call to mind that Christ gave for you his very flesh and blood. Consider as one great end of poverty is patience, so one great end of wealth is charity. Think how honourable it is to make a present to the great King of the world ; and what a condescension it is in his all-sufficiency to do that good by us, which he could so abundantly do without us.—*Thomas Tenison,* 1636—1715.

Verse 5.—*"Lendeth."* The original word here, לוה, *lavah,* means to join oneself to any one ; to cleave to him ; then to form the union which is constituted between debtor and creditor, borrower and lender. Here it is used in the latter sense, and it means that a good man will accommodate another—a neighbour—with money, or with articles to be used temporarily and returned again. A man who always *borrows* is not a desirable neighbour ; but a man who never lends—who never is willing to accommodate—is a neighbour that no one would wish to live near—a crooked, perverse, bad man. True religion will always dispose a man to do acts of kindness in any and every way possible.—*Albert Barnes.*

Verse 5.—Charity though it springs in the heart should be guided by the head, that it may spread itself abroad to the best advantage. *"He will guide his affairs with discretion,"* and no affairs are so properly the good man's own as the dispensation and stewardship of those blessings which God has entrusted him with, for *"it is required in stewards that a man be found faithful."*—*Michael Cox,* 1748.

Verse 5.—*"He will guide his affairs with discretion."* Just as a steward, servant, or agent in any secular concern has to feel that his *mind* is his master's, as well as his hands, and that his attention, thought, tact, and talent, should be vigorously and faithfully given to the interests of his employer ; so the Christian stewardship of money, demands on the part of God's servant, in respect to every form of its use and disposal, the exercise of reflexion ; a reference to conscience ; the recollection of responsibility to God ; attention to the appeals of humanity is addressed to the ear of justice and love. Everything is to be weighed as in the balance of the sanctuary ; a decision formed ; and then energy, skill schemes, and plans wisely constructed, prudential limitations or beneficent liberality as may seem best. Spending, saving, giving, or lending, all being done so as best to meet what may be felt to be the Master's will, and what may best evince at once the wisdom and the fidelity of his servant.—*Thomas Binney, in "Money : a Popular Exposition in Rough Notes,"* 1865.

Verse 5.—*"Discretion."* There is a story, concerning divers ancient Fathers, that they came to St. Anthony, enquiring of him, what virtue did by a direct line lead to perfection, that so a man might shun the snares of Satan. He bade every one of them speak his opinion ; one said, watching and sobriety ; another said, fasting and discipline ; a third said, humble prayer ; a fourth said, poverty and obedience ; and another, piety and works of mercy ; but when every one has spoken his mind, his answer was, That all these were excellent graces indeed, but discretion was the chief of them all. And so beyond doubt it is ; being the very *Auriga virtutum*, the guide of all virtuous and religious actions, the moderator and orderer of all the affections ; for whatsoever is done with it is virtue, and what without it is vice. An ounce of discretion is said to be worth a pound of learning. .As zeal without knowledge is blind, so knowledge without discretion is lame, like a sword in a madman's hand, able to do much, apt to do nothing. *Tolle hanc et virtus vitium erit.* He that will fast must fast with discretion, he must so mortify that he does not kill his flesh ; he that gives alms to the poor, must do it with discretion, *Omni petenti non omnia petenti*—to every one that doth ask, but not everything that he doth ask ; so likewise pray with discretion, observing place and time ; place, lest he be reputed a hypocrite ; time, lest he be accounted a heretic. Thus it is that discretion is to be made the guide of all religious performances.—*Quoted by John Spencer,* 1658.

Verse 6.—What doth the text say ? *"The righteous* (that is the bountiful) *shall be in everlasting remembrance."* God remembers our good deeds, when he rewards them (as he does our prayers, when he hears them). If to remember, then, be to reward, an everlasting reward is our everlasting remembrance. . . . Now in those who are to be partakers of mercy, the divine wisdom requires this congruity, that they be such as have been ready to show mercy to others.—*Joseph Mede,* 1586—1638.

Verse 6.—*"The righteous shall be in everlasting remembrance."* The stately and durable pyramids of Egypt have not transmitted to posterity even the names of those buried in them. And what has even embalming done, but tossed them about, and exposed them to all the world as spectacles to the curious, of meanness, or horror ? But the piety of Abraham, of Jacob, of David and Samuel, of Hezekiah, Josiah and others, is celebrated to this very day. So when pyramids shall sink, and seas cease to roll, when sun and moon and stars shall be no more, *"the righteous shall be in everlasting remembrance."*—*John Dun,* 1790

Verse 7.—*"He shall not be afraid of evil tidings."* How can you affright him ? Bring him word his estate is ruined ; " yet my inheritance is safe," says he. Your wife, or child, or dear friend is dead ; " yet my Father lives." You yourself must die ; " well, then, I go home to my Father, and to my inheritance."

For the public troubles of the Church, doubtless it is both a most pious and generous temper, to be more deeply affected for these than for all our private ones ; and to sympathise in the common calamities of any people, but especially of God's own people, hath been the character of men near unto him. Observe the pathetical strains of the prophet's bewailing, when he foretells the desolation even of foreign kingdoms, much more of the Lord's chosen people, still mindful of Sion, and mournful of her distresses. (Jer. ix. 1, and the whole Book of Lamentations.) Yet even in this, with much compassion, there is a calm in a believer's mind ; he finds amidst all hard news, yet still a fixed heart, trusting, satisfied in this, that deliverance shall come in due time, Ps. cii. 13, and that in those judgments that are inflicted, men shall be humbled and God exalted, Isaiah ii. 11, and v. 15, 16 ; and that in all tumults and changes, and subversion of states, still the throne of God is fixed, and with that the believer's heart likewise, Ps. xciii. 2. So Ps. xxix. 10.—*Robert Leighton.*

Verse 7.—*"He shall not be afraid,"* etc. If a man would lead a happy life, let him but seek a sure object for his trust, and he shall be safe : *"He shall not be afraid of evil tidings : his heart is fixed, trusting in the Lord."* A man that puts his confidence in God, if he hears bad news of mischief coming towards him, as suppose a bad debt, a loss at sea, accidents by fire, tempests, or earthquakes, as Job had his messengers of evil tidings, which came thick and threefold upon him, yet he is not afraid, for his heart is fixed on God : he hath laid up his confidence in God, therefore his heart is kept in an equal poise ; he can say, as Job, " The Lord gave, and the Lord hath taken away ; blessed be the name of the Lord," Job i. 21. His comforts did not ebb and flow with the creature, but his heart was fixed, trusting in the Lord.—*Thomas Manton.*

Verse 7 (first clause).—The good man will not be alarmed by any report of danger, whilst the dishonest man, conscious of his wickedness, is always in a state of fear.— *George Phillips.*

Verse 7.—"*His heart is fixed,*" or prepared, ready, and in arms for all services ; resolved not to give back, able to meet all adventures, and stand its ground. God is unchangeable ; and therefore faith is invincible, for it sets the heart on him ; fastens it there on the rock of eternity ; then let winds blow and storms arise, it cares not.—*Robert Leighton.*

Verse 7.—"*His heart is fixed*"—established fearlessly. So Moses, with the Red Sea before and the Egyptian foes behind (Exod. xiv. 13) ; Jehoshaphat before the Ammonite horde of invaders (2 Chron. xx. 12, 15, 17) ; Asa before Zerah, the Ethiopian's " thousand thousand, and three hundred chariots " (2 Chron. xiv. 9—12). Contrast with the persecuted David's fearless trust, Saul's panic-stricken feeling at the Philistine invasion, inasmuch as he repaired for help to a witch. How bold were the three youths in prospect of Nebuchadnezzar's fiery furnace ! How fearless Stephen before the council ! Basilius could say, in answer to the threats of Cæsar Valens, " such bug-bears should be set before children." Athanasius said of Julian, his persecutor, " He is a mist that will soon disappear."—*A. R. Fausset.*

Verse 7.—"*Trusting in the Lord,*" I need not prove that a man can have no other sure comfort and support. For what can he confide in ? His *treasure ?* This may soon be exhausted, or it may awaken the avarice or ambition of a powerful enemy, as Hezekiah's did the king of Babylon, and so instead of being a defence, prove the occasion of his ruin. Can he confide in *power ?* Alas, he knows that when this is grown too big to fall by any other hands, it generally falls by its own. Can he finally confide in worldly *wisdom ?* Alas, a thousand unexpected accidents, and unobserved latent circumstances, cross and frustrate this, and render the Ahithophels not only unfortunate, but often contemptible too.—*Richard Lucas,* 1648—1715.

Verse 8.—"*His heart is established.*" Happy, surely, is the man whose heart is thus established. Others may be politic, he only is wise ; others may be fortunate, he only is great ; others may drink deeper draughts of sensual pleasure, he only can eat of the tree of life, which is in the midst of the paradise of God. He is an image of that great Being whom he trusts . . . . and in the midst of storms, and thunders, and earthquakes sits himself serene and undisturbed, bidding the prostrate world adore the Lord of the universe.—*George Gleig,* 1803.

Verse 8.—"*Until he see his desire upon his enemies.*" His faith will not fail, nor shrink, nor change, while one by one his enemies are brought to the knowledge of the truth and the love of Christ, and he shall see his heart's desire fulfilled upon them, even that they may be saved.—*Plain Commentary.*

Verse 8.—"*Until he see his desire upon his enemies.*" Or, according to the original, *Until he looks upon his oppressors ;* that is, till he behold them securely, and, as we say, confidently *looks in their faces ;* as being now no longer under their power, but being freed from their tyranny and oppression.—*Thomas Fenton.*

Verse 9.—When all the flashes of sensual pleasure are quite extinct, when all the flowers of secular glory are withered away ; when all earthly treasures are buried in darkness ; when this world, and all the fashion of it, are utterly vanished and gone, the bountiful man's state will be still firm and flourishing, and "*his righteousness shall endure for ever.*" "*His horn shall be exalted with honour.*" A horn is an emblem of *power ;* for it is the beast's strength, offensive and defensive : and of *plenty,* for it hath within it a capacity apt to contain what is put into it ; and of *sanctity,* for in it was put the holy oil, with which kings were consecrated ; and of *dignity,* both in consequence upon the reasons mentioned (as denoting might, and influence, and sacredness accompanying sovereign dignity) and because also it is an especial beauty and ornament to the creature which hath it ; so that this expression, "*his horn shall be exalted with honour,*" may be supposed to import that an abundance of high, and holy, of firm and solid honour shall attend upon the bountiful person. . . . God will thus exalt the bountiful man's horn even here in this world, and to an infinitely higher pitch he will advance it in a future state.—*Isaac Barrow,* 1630—1677.

Verse 9.—"*For ever.*" The Hebrew phrase in this text is not לְעוֹלָם, *in seculum,* which is sometimes used of a limited eternity, but עַד, *in eternum*, which seems more expressive of an endless duration, and is the very same phrase whereby the duration of God's righteousness is expressed in the foregoing Psalm at the third verse.— *William Berriman*, 1688—1749.

Verses 9, 10.—These words are an enlargement of the character, begun at the first verse, of the blessed man that feareth the Lord, that delighteth greatly in his commandments. The author closes that character with an amiable description of his charity, and so leaves on our minds a strong impression, that benevolence of heart when displayed in the benefaction of the hand is the surest mark and fairest accomplishment of a moral and religious mind ; which, whether it rewards the worthy, or relieves the unworthy object, is the noblest imitation of the dealings of God with mankind. For he rewardeth the good if any can be called so but himself, (though the name *good* is but *God* spread out). He beareth even with the wicked and stretcheth out his hand to save even them.—*Michael Cox.*

Verse 10.—"*The wicked.*" The word רָשָׁע, *the wicked*, is used emphatically, by the Jews, to denote him who neither gives to the poor himself, nor can endure to see other people give ; while he who deserves but one part of this character is only said to have an *evil eye in regard of other people's substance, or in regard of his own.*— *Mishna.*

Verse 10.—"*The wicked shall see it and be grieved*," etc.—The sight of Christ in glory with his saints, will, in an inexpressible manner torment the crucifiers of the one, and the persecutors of the other ; as it will show them the hopes and wishes of their adversaries all granted to the full, and all their own " desires " and designs for ever at an end ; it will excite envy which must prey upon itself, produce a grief which can admit of no comfort, give birth to a worm which can never die, and blow up those fires which nothing can quench.—*George Horne.*

Verse 10.—"*The wicked shall see it, and be grieved*," etc. It is the property of the Devil, not to mistake the nature of virtue, and esteem it criminal, but to hate it for this reason, because it is good, and therefore most opposite to his designs. The wicked, as his proper emissaries, resemble him in this, and grieve to have the foulness of their vices made conspicuous by being placed near the light of virtuous example. . . . They may, like the giants of ancient fable, attempt a romantic war with heaven ; but all their preparations for that purpose must recoil with double force upon themselves, and cover them with shame and confusion. . . . If such be the effect of their malice in the present life, that, instead of injuring those they rage against, it usually turns to their own vexation, how much more, when the scene shall open in the life to come. . . . They shall continue then to gnash their teeth (the wretched amusement of that cursed state) as well in grief and anguish for their own torments, as in rage and envy at the abundant honour which is done the saints.—*William Berriman.*

Verse 10.—"*The wicked shall see it, and be grieved* " ; that is, he shall have secret indignation in himself to see matters go so ; "*he shall gnash with his teeth, and melt away.*" Gnashing of teeth is caused by vexing the heart ; and therefore it follows, " *he melts away* " ; which notes (melting is from the heart) an extreme heat within. The sense is very suitable to that of Eliphaz (Job v. 2) " wrath slayeth the foolish," or wrath makes him melt away, it melts his grease with chafing, as we say of a man furiously vexed. Hence that deplorable condition of the damned, who are cast out of the presence of God for ever, is described by " weeping, and wailing, and gnashing of teeth " ; which imports not only pain, but extreme vexing at, or in themselves. These finally impenitent ones shall be slain for ever with their own wrath, as well as with the wrath of God.—*Joseph Caryl.*

Verse 10.—"*The wicked shall see it.*" The Psalm which speaks of the blessedness of the saints also bears solemn testimony to the doom of the wicked. Cowper sings as if this verse was before his eyes.

> . . . The same word, that like the polished share
> Ploughs up the roots of a believer's care,
> Kills, too, the flow'ry weeds where'er they grow,
> That bind the sinner's Bacchanalian brow.
> Oh that unwelcome voice of heavenly love,
> Sad messenger of mercy from above,
> How does it grate upon his thankless ear,
> Crippling his pleasures with the cramp of fear ;

His will and judgment at continual strife,
That civil war embitters all his life ;
In vain he points his pow'rs against the skies,
In vain he closes or averts his eyes ;
Truth will intrude.

Verse 10.—"*He shall gnash with his teeth.*" An enraged man snaps his teeth together, as if about to bite the object of his anger. Thus in the book *Rāmyanum*, the giant Rāvanan is described as in his fury gnashing together his " thirty-two teeth ! " Of angry men it is frequently said, " Look at the beast, how he gnashes his teeth ! " "*Go near that fellow !* not I, indeed ! he will only gnash his teeth."— *Joseph Roberts.*

Verse 10.—"*He shall gnash with his teeth, and melt away.*" The effect of envy, which consumes the envious. Thus the poet : " Envy is most hateful, but has some good in it, for it makes the eyes and the heart of the envious to pine away."— *John Le Clerc, 1657—1736.*

HINTS TO PREACHERS.

Verse 1.—"*Praise ye the* LORD." I. Who should be praised ? Not man, self, wealth, etc., but God only. II. Who should praise him ? All men, but specially his people, the blessed ones described in this Psalm. III. Why should they do it ? For all the reasons mentioned in succeeding verses. IV. How should they do it ? Chiefly by leading such a life as is here described.

Verse 1 (second clause).—I. Fear of the Lord ; what it is. II. Its connection with the delight mentioned. III. The qualities in the commandments which excite delight in godfearing minds.

Verse 2.—The real might of the holy seed and their true blessedness.

Verse 3.—The riches of a Christian : content, peace, security, power in prayer, promises, providence, yea, God himself.

Verse 3.—The enduring character of true righteousness. 1. Based on eternal principles. 2. Growing out of an incorruptible seed. 3. Sustained by a faithful God. 4. United to the everliving Christ.

Verse 3.—Connection of the two clauses—How to be wealthy and righteous. Note the following verses, and show how liberality is needful if rich men would be righteous men.

Verse 4 (whole verse)—I. The upright have their dark times. II. They shall receive comfort. III. Their own character will secure this.

Verse 4 (first clause).—I. The character of the righteous : " upright," " gracious," etc. II. His privilege. 1. Light as well as darkness. 2. More light than darkness. 3. Light in darkness : inward light in the midst of surrounding darkness. Light seen above, when all is dark below. Even darkness itself becomes the harbinger of day.—*G. R.*

Verse 4 (last clause).—A Trinity of excellencies found in true Christians, in Christ, and in God : their union forms a perfect character when they are well balanced. Show how they are exemplified in daily life.

Verse 5.—I. A good man is benevolent, but a benevolent man is not always good. II. A good man is prudent, but a prudent man is not always a good man. There must first be goodness and then its fruits. " Make the tree good," etc.— *G. R.*

Verse 5.—"*Lending.*" I. It is to be done. II. It is to be done as a favour ; borrowing is seeking alms. III. It should be done very discreetly. Add to this a homily on borrowing and repaying.

Verse 6.—I. In this life the Christian is, 1, Steadfast ; 2, Calm ; 3, Unconquerable : and II. When this life is over his memory is, 1, Beloved ; 2, Influential ; 3, Perpetual.

Verse 6.—I. The character of the righteous is eternal : " surely," etc. II. His influence upon others is eternal : " shall be had," etc.—*G. R.*

Verse 7.—1. "*He shall not be afraid,*" etc. : peaceful. 2. "*His heart is fixed*" : restful. 3. "*Trusting in the Lord*" : trustful ; the cause of the former.

Verse 7.—I. The waves: "evil tidings." II. The steady ship: "he shall not be afraid." III. The anchor: "his heart is fixed, trusting." IV. The anchorage: "in the Lord."

Verse 8.—Heart establishment, the confidence which flows from it, the sight which shall be seen by him who possesses it.

Verse 8.—I. The security of the righteous: "his heart is established." II. His tranquillity: "he shall not be afraid;" and, III. His expectancy: "until," etc. —*G. R.*

Verse 9.—Benevolence: its exercise in almsgiving, its preserving influence upon character, and the honour which it wins.

Verse 10.—I. What the wicked must see, and its effect upon them. II. What they shall never see (their desire), and the result of their disappointment.

PSALM CXIII.

TITLE AND SUBJECT.—*This Psalm is one of pure praise, and contains but little which requires exposition; a warm heart full of admiring adoration of the Most High will best of all comprehend this sacred hymn. Its subject is the greatness and condescending goodness of the God of Israel, as exhibited in lifting up the needy from their low estate. It may fitly be sung by the church during a period of revival after it has long been minished and brought low. With this Psalm begins the Hallel, or Hallelujah of the Jews, which was sung at their solemn feasts: we will therefore call it* THE COMMENCEMENT OF THE HALLEL. *Dr. Edersheim tells us that the Talmud dwells upon the peculiar suitableness of the Hallel to the Passover, "since it not only recorded the goodness of God towards Israel, but especially their deliverance from Egypt, and therefore appropriately opened with 'Praise ye Jehovah, ye servants of Jehovah,'—and no longer servants of Pharaoh." Its allusions to the poor in the dust and the needy upon the dunghill are all in keeping with Israel in Egypt, and so also is the reference to the birth of numerous children where they were least expected.*

DIVISION.—*No division need be made in the exposition of this Psalm, except it be that which is suggested by the always instructive headings supplied by the excellent authors of our common version: an exhortation to praise God, for his excellency, 1—5; for his mercy, 6—9.*

EXPOSITION.

PRAISE ye the LORD. Praise, O ye servants of the LORD, praise the name of the LORD.

2 Blessed be the name of the LORD from this time forth and for evermore.

3 From the rising of the sun unto the going down of the same the LORD's name *is* to be praised.

4 The LORD *is* high above all nations, *and* his glory above the heavens.

5 Who *is* like unto the LORD our God, who dwelleth on high,

6 Who humbleth *himself* to behold *the things that are* in heaven, and in the earth!

7 He raiseth up the poor out of the dust, *and* lifteth the needy out of the dunghill;

8 That he may set *him* with princes, *even* with the princes of his people.

9 He maketh the barren woman to keep house, *and to be* a joyful mother of children. Praise ye the LORD.

1. "*Praise ye the LORD*," or Hallelujah, praise to JAH Jehovah. Praise is an essential offering at all the solemn feasts of the people of God. Prayer is the myrrh, and praise is the frankincense, and both of these must be presented unto the Lord. How can we pray for mercy for the future if we do not bless God for his love in the past? The Lord hath wrought all good things for us, let us therefore adore him. All other praise is to be excluded, the entire devotion of the soul must be poured out unto Jehovah only. "*Praise, O ye servants of the LORD.*" Ye above all men, for ye are bound to do so by your calling and profession. If God's own servants do not praise him, who will? Ye are a people near unto him, and should be heartiest in your loving gratitude. While they were slaves of Pharaoh, the Israelites uttered groans and sighs by reason of their hard bondage; but now that they had become servants of the Lord, they were to express themselves in songs of joy. His service is perfect freedom, and those who fully enter into it discover in that service a thousand reasons for adoration. They are sure to praise God best who serve him best; indeed, service is praise. "*Praise the name of the Lord*": extol his revealed character, magnify every sacred attribute, exult in all his doings, and reverence the very name

by which he is called. The name of Jehovah is thrice used in this verse, and may by us who understand the doctrine of the Trinity in Unity be regarded as a thinly-veiled allusion to that holy mystery. Let Father, Son and Holy Spirit, all be praised as the one, only, living, and true God. The close following of the words, "Hallelu-jah, Hallelu, Hallelu," must have had a fine effect in the public services. Dr. Edersheim describes the temple service as responsive, and says " Every first line of a Psalm was repeated by the people, while to each of the others they responded by a 'Hallelu-Jah ' or ' Praise ye the Lord ' thus—

The Levites began : *'Hallelujah '* (Praise ye the Lord).
The people repeated : *'Hallelu Jah.'*
The Levites : ' Praise (*Hallelu*), O ye servants of Jehovah.'
The people responded : *'Hallelu Jah.'*
The Levites : ' Praise (*Hallelu*) the name of Jehovah.'
The people responded : *'Hallelu Jah.'* "

These were not vain repetitions, for the theme is one which we ought to dwell upon ; it should be deeply impressed upon the soul, and perseveringly kept prominent in the life.

2. *"Blessed be the name of the LORD."* While praising him aloud, the people were also to *bless* him in the silence of their hearts, wishing glory to his name, success to his cause, and triumph to his truth. By mentioning *the name*, the Psalmist would teach us to bless each of the attributes of the Most High, which are as it were the letters of his name ; not quarrelling with his justice or his severity, nor servilely dreading his power, but accepting him as we find him revealed in the inspired word and by his own acts, and loving him and praising him as such. We must not give the Lord a new name nor invent a new nature, for that would be the setting up of a false god. Every time we think of the God of Scripture we should bless him, and his august name should never be pronounced without joyful reverence. *"From this time forth."* If we have never praised him before, let us begin now. As the Passover stood at the beginning of the year it was well to commence the new year with blessing him who wrought deliverance for his people. Every solemn feast had its own happy associations, and might be regarded as a fresh starting-place for adoration. Are there not reasons why the reader should make the present day the opening of a year of praise ? When the Lord says, " From this time will I bless you," we ought to reply, " Blessed be the name of the Lord from this time forth."

"And for evermore" : eternally. The Psalmist could not have intended that the divine praise should cease at a future date however remote. " For evermore " in reference to the praise of God must signify endless duration : are we wrong in believing that it bears the same meaning when it refers to gloomier themes ? Can our hearts ever cease to praise the name of the Lord ? Can we imagine a period in which the praises of Israel shall no more surround the throne of the Divine Majesty ? Impossible. For ever, and more than " for ever," if more can be, let him be magnified.

3. *"From the rising of the sun unto the going down of the same the LORD'S name is to be praised."* From early morn till eve the ceaseless hymn should rise unto Jehovah's throne, and from east to west over the whole round earth pure worship should be rendered unto his glory. So ought it to be ; and blessed be God, we are not without faith that so it shall be. We trust that ere the world's dread evening comes, the glorious name of the Lord will be proclaimed among all nations, and all people shall call him blessed. At the first proclamation of the gospel the name of the Lord was glorious throughout the whole earth ; shall it not be much more so ere the end shall be ? At any rate, this is the desire of our souls. Meanwhile, let us endeavour to sanctify every day with praise to God. At early dawn let us emulate the opening flowers and the singing birds,

> " Chanting every day their lauds,
> While the grove their song applauds ;
> Wake for shame my sluggish heart,
> Wake and gladly sing thy part."

It is a marvel of mercy that the sun should rise on the rebellious sons of men, and prepare for the undeserving fruitful seasons and days of pleasantness ; let us for this prodigy of goodness praise the Lord of all. From hour to hour let us renew the strain, for each moment brings its mercy ; and when the sun sinks to his rest, let us not cease our music, but lift up the vesper hymn—

> " Father of heaven and earth !
> I bless thee for the night,
>   The soft still night !
> The holy pause of care and mirth,
>   Of sound and light.
> Now far in glade and dell,
>   Flower-cup, and bud, and bell
> Have shut around the sleeping woodlark's nest,
> The bee's long-murmuring toils are done,
>   And I, the o'erwearied one,
> Bless thee, O God, O Father of the oppressed !
> With my last waking thought."

4. *"The* LORD *is high above all nations."* Though the Gentiles knew him not, yet was Jehovah their ruler : their false gods were no gods, and their kings were puppets in his hands. The Lord is high above all the learning, judgment, and imagination of heathen sages, and far beyond the pomp and might of the monarchs of the nations. Like the great arch of the firmament, the presence of the Lord spans all the lands where dwell the varied tribes of men, for his providence is universal : this may well excite our confidence and praise. *"And his glory above the heavens : "* higher than the loftiest part of creation ; the clouds are the dust of his feet, and sun, moon, and stars twinkle far below his throne. Even the heaven of heavens cannot contain him. His glory cannot be set forth by the whole visible universe, nor even by the solemn pomp of angelic armies ; it is above all conception and imagination, for he is God—infinite. Let us above all adore him who is above all.

5. *"Who is like unto the* LORD *our God ?"* The challenge will never be answered. None can be compared with him for an instant ; Israel's God is without parallel ; our own God in covenant stands alone, and none can be likened unto him. Even those whom he has made like himself in some respects are not like him in godhead, for his divine attributes are many of them incommunicable and inimitable. None of the metaphors and figures by which the Lord is set forth in the Scriptures can give us a complete idea of him : his full resemblance is borne by nothing in earth or in heaven. Only in Jesus is the Godhead seen, but he unhesitatingly declared " he that hath seen me hath seen the Father." *"Who dwelleth on high."* In the height of his abode none can be like him. His throne, his whole character, his person, his being, everything about him, is lofty, and infinitely majestic, so that none can be likened unto him. His serene mind abides in the most elevated condition, he is never dishonoured, nor does he stoop from the pure holiness and absolute perfection of his character. His saints are said to dwell on high, and in this they are the reflection of his glory ; but as for himself, the height of his dwelling-place surpasses thought, and he rises far above the most exalted of his glorified people.

> " Eternal Power ! whose high abode
> Becomes the grandeur of a God :
> Infinite lengths beyond the bounds
> Where stars revolve their little rounds.

> " The lowest step around thy seat
> Rises too high for Gabriel's feet ;
> In vain the tall archangel tries
> To reach thine height with wond'ring eyes.

> " Lord, what shall earth and ashes do ?
> We would adore our Maker too ;
> From sin and dust to thee we cry,
> The Great, the Holy, and the High ! "

6. *"Who humbleth himself to behold the things that are in heaven, and in the earth ! "* He dwells so far on high that even to observe heavenly things he must humble himself. He must stoop to view the skies, and bow to see what angels do. What, then, must be his condescension, seeing that he observes the humblest of his servants upon earth, and makes them sing for joy like Mary when she said, " Thou hast regarded the low estate of thine handmaiden." How wonderful are those words of Isaiah, " For thus saith the high and lofty One that inhabiteth eternity, whose name is Holy ; I dwell in the high and holy place, with him also that is of a contrite and humble spirit, to revive the spirit of the humble, and to revive the heart of the

contrite ones." Heathen philosophers could not believe that the great God was observant of the small events of human history; they pictured him as abiding in serene indifference to all the wants and woes of his creatures. " Our Rock is not as their rock"; we have a God who is high above all gods, and yet who is our Father, knowing what we have need of before we ask him; our Shepherd, who supplies our needs; our Guardian, who counts the hairs of our heads; our tender and considerate Friend, who sympathizes in all our griefs. Truly the name of our condescending God should be praised wherever it is known.

7. *"He raiseth up the poor out of the dust."* This is an instance of his gracious stoop of love: he frequently lifts the lowest of mankind out of their poverty and degradation, and places them in positions of power and honour. His good Spirit is continually visiting the down-trodden, giving beauty for ashes to those who are cast down, and elevating the hearts of his mourners till they shout for joy. These upliftings of grace are here ascribed directly to the divine hand, and truly those who have experienced them will not doubt the fact that it is the Lord alone who brings his people up from the dust of sorrow and death. When no hand but his can help he interposes, and the work is done. It is worth while to be cast down to be so divinely raised from the dust. *"And lifteth the needy out of the dunghill,"* whereon they lay like worthless refuse, cast off and cast out, left as they thought to rot into destruction and to be everlastingly forgotten. How great a stoop from the height of his throne to a dunghill! How wonderful that power which occupies itself in lifting up beggars, all befouled with the filthiness in which they lay! For he lifts them *out of* the dunghill, not disdaining to search them out from amidst the base things of the earth that he may by their means bring to nought the great ones, and pour contempt upon all human glorying. What a dunghill was that upon which we lay by nature! What a mass of corruption is our original estate! What a heap of loathsomeness we have accumulated by our sinful lives! What reeking abominations surround us in the society of our fellow men! We could never have risen out of all this by our own efforts, it was a sepulchre in which we saw corruption, and were as dead men. Almighty were the arms which lifted us, which are still lifting us, and will lift us into the perfection of heaven itself. Praise ye the Lord.

8. *"That he may set him with princes."* The Lord does nothing by halves: when he raises men from the dust he is not content till he places them among the peers of his kingdom. We are made kings and priests unto God, and we shall reign for ever and ever. Instead of poverty, he gives us the wealth of princes; and instead of dishonour, he gives us a more exalted rank than that of the great ones of the earth. *"Even with the princes of his people."* All his people are princes, and so the text teaches us that God places needy souls whom he favours among the princes of princes. He often enables those who have been most despairing to rise to the greatest heights of spirituality and gracious attainment, for those who once were last shall be first. Paul, though less than the least of all saints was, nevertheless, made to be not a whit behind the very chief of the apostles; and in our own times, Bunyan, the blaspheming tinker, was raised into another John, whose dream almost rivals the visions of the Apocalypse.

> " Wonders of grace to God belong,
> Repeat his mercies in your song."

Such verses as these should give great encouragement to those who are lowest in their own esteem. The Lord poureth contempt upon princes; but as for those who are in the dust and on the dunghill, he looks upon them with compassion, acts towards them in grace, and in their case displays the riches of his glory by Christ Jesus. Those who have experienced such amazing favour should sing continual hallelujahs to the God of their salvation.

9. *"He maketh the barren woman to keep house, and to be a joyful mother of children."* The strong desire of the easterns to have children caused the birth of offspring to be hailed as the choicest of favours, while barrenness was regarded as a curse; hence this verse is placed last as if to crown the whole, and to serve as a climax to the story of God's mercy. The glorious Lord displays his condescending grace in regarding those who are despised on account of their barrenness, whether it be of body or of soul. Sarah, Rachel, the wife of Manoah, Hannah, Elizabeth, and others were all instances of the miraculous power of God in literally fulfilling the statement of the Psalmist. Women were not supposed to have a house till they had children; but in certain cases where childless women pined in secret the Lord visited them in

mercy, and made them not only to have a house, but to keep it.   The Gentile church is a spiritual example upon a large scale of the gift of fruitfulness after long years of hopeless barrenness ; and the Jewish church in the latter days will be another amazing display of the same quickening power : long forsaken for her spiritual adultery, Israel shall be forgiven, and restored, and joyously shall she keep that house which now is left unto her desolate.   Nor is this all, each believer in the Lord Jesus must at times have mourned his lamentable barrenness ; he has appeared to be a dry tree yielding no fruit to the Lord, and yet when visited by the Holy Ghost, he has found himself suddenly to be like Aaron's rod, which budded, and blossomed, and brought forth almonds.   Or ever we have been aware, our barren heart has kept house, and entertained the Saviour, our graces have been multiplied as if many children had come to us at a single birth, and we have exceedingly rejoiced before the Lord.   Then have we marvelled greatly at the Lord who dwelleth on high, that he has deigned to visit such poor worthless things.   Like Mary, we have lifted up our Magnificat, and like Hannah, we have said "There is none holy as the Lord ; for there is none beside thee : neither is there any rock like our God."

"Praise ye the Lord."   The music concludes upon its key-note.   The Psalm is a circle, ending where it began, praising the Lord from its first syllable to its last. May our life-psalm partake of the same character, and never know a break or a conclusion.   In an endless circle let us bless the Lord, whose mercies never cease. Let us praise him in youth, and all along our years of strength ; and when we bow in the ripeness of abundant age, let us still praise the Lord, who doth not cast off his old servants.   Let us not only praise God ourselves, but exhort others to do it ; and if we meet with any of the needy who have been enriched, and with the barren who have been made fruitful, let us join with them in extolling the name of him whose mercy endureth for ever.   Having been ourselves lifted from spiritual beggary and barrenness, let us never forget our former estate or the grace which has visited us, but world without end let us praise the Lord.   Hallelujah.

EXPLANATORY NOTES AND QUAINT SAYINGS.

Whole Psalm.—With this Psalm begins the *Hallel*, which is recited at the three great feasts, at the feast of the Dedication (*Chanucca*) and at the new moons, and not on New Year's day and the day of Atonement, because a cheerful song of praise does not harmonise with the mournful solemnity of these days.   And they are recited only in fragments during the last days of the Passover, for " my creatures, saith the Holy One, blessed be He, were drowned in the sea, and ought ye to break out into songs of rejoicing ? "   In the family celebration of the Passover night it is divided into two parts, the one half, Ps. cxiii. cxiv, being sung before the repast, before the emptying of the second festal cup, and the other half, Ps. cxv.—cxviii., after the repast, after the filling of the fourth cup, to which the ὑμνήσαντες (Matt. xxvi. 30, Mark xiv. 26), or singing a hymn, after the institution of the Lord's Supper, which was connected with the fourth festal cup, may refer.   Paulus Burgensis styles Ps. cxiii.—cxviii.   *Alleluja Judæorum magnum.*   (The great Alleluiah of the Jews). This designation is also frequently found elsewhere.   But according to the prevailing custom, Ps. cxiii.—cxviii., and more particularly Ps. cxv.—cxviii., are called only *Hallel* and Ps. cxxxvi., with its "for his mercy endureth for ever" repeated twenty-six times, bears the name of "The Great Hallel" (הַלֵּל הַגָּדוֹל).—*Frank Delitzsch.*

Whole Psalm.—The Jews have handed down the tradition, that this Psalm, and those that follow on to the cxviiith, were all sung at the Passover ; and they are denominated "The Great Hallel."   This tradition shows, at all events, that the ancient Jews perceived in these six Psalms some link of close connection.   They all sing of God the Redeemer, in some aspect of his redeeming character ; and this being so, while they suited the paschal feast, we can see how appropriate they would be in the lips of the Redeemer, in his Upper Room.   Thus—

In Psalm cxiii., he sang praise to him who redeems from the lowest depth.

In Psalm cxiv., he sang praise to him who once redeemed Israel, and shall redeem Israel again.

In Psalm cxv., he uttered a song—over earth's fallen idols—to him who blesses Israel and the world.

In Psalm cxvi., he sang his resurrection-song of thanksgiving by anticipation.

In Psalm cxvii., he led the song of praise for the great congregation.

In Psalm cxviii. (just before leaving the Upper Room to go to Gethsemane), he poured forth the story of his suffering, conflict, triumph and glorification.—A. A. Bonar.

Whole Psalm.—An attentive reader of the Book of Psalms will observe, that almost every one of them has a view to Christianity. Many, if not most of the Psalms, were without doubt occasioned originally by accidents of the life that befell their royal author ; they were therefore at the same time both descriptive of the situation and life, the actions and sufferings, of King David, and predictive also of our Saviour, who was all along represented by King David, from whose loins he was descended according to the flesh. But *this* Psalm appears to be *wholly* written with a view to Christianity. It begins with an exhortation to all true servants and zealous worshippers of God, to *"praise his name,"* at all times, and in all places ; *"from this time forth and for evermore,"* and *"from the rising of the sun unto the going down thereof."* And the ground of this praise and adoration is set forth in the following verses to be,—first, the glorious majesty of his Divine nature ; and next, the singular goodness of it as displayed to us in his works of providence, particularly by exalting those who are abased, and his making the barren to become fruitful. His lifting the poor out of the mire, and making the barren woman to become fruitful, may, at first sight, seem an odd mixture of ideas. But a right notion of the prophetic language will solve the difficulty ; and teach us, that both the expressions are in fact very nearly related, and signify much the same thing. For by the *" poor "* are here meant those who are destitute of all heavenly knowledge (the only true and real riches) and who are sunk in the mire and filth of sin. So, again, his making *" the barren woman to keep house, and to be a joyful mother of children,"* is a prophetic metaphor, or allusion to the fruitfulness of the Church in bringing forth sons or professors of the true religion. My interpretation of both these expressions is warrantable from so many parallel passages of Scripture. I shall only observe that here the profession of the Christian faith throughout the whole earth is foretold ; as also the particular direction or point of the compass, toward which Christianity should by the course of God's providence be steered and directed, *viz.,* from East to West, or *" from the rising of the sun unto the going down of the same."*—*James Bate,* 1703—1775.

Verse 1.—*"Praise ye the* LORD." *"Praise."* The הללו is repeated. This repetition is not without significance. It is for the purpose of waking us up out of our torpor. We are all too dull and slow in considering and praising the blessings of God. There is, therefore, necessity for these stimuli. Then this repetition signifies assiduity and perseverance in sounding forth the praises of God. It is not sufficient once and again to praise God, but his praises ought to be always sung in the Church.—*Mollerus.*

Verse 1.—*"Praise ye the* LORD." This praising God rests not in the mere speculation or idle contemplation of the Divine excellence, floating only in the brain, or gliding upon the tongue, but in such quick and lively apprehensions of them as to sink down into the heart, and there beget affections suitable to them ; for it will make us love him for his goodness, respect him for his greatness, fear him for his justice, dread him for his power, adore him for his wisdom, and for all his attributes make us live in constant awe and obedience to him. This is to praise God, without which all other courting and complimenting of him is but mere flattery and hypocrisy. . . . God Almighty endowed us with higher and nobler faculties than other creatures, for this end, that we should set forth his praise ; for though other things were made to administer the matter and occasion, yet man alone was designed and qualified to exercise the act of glorifying God. . . . In short, God Almighty hath so closely twisted his own glory and our happiness together, that at the same time we advance the one we promote the other.—*Matthew Hole,* 1730.

Verse 1.—*"Praise, O ye servants of the* LORD." From the exhortation to praise God, and the declaration of his deserving to be praised ; learn, that as it is all men's duty to praise the Lord, so in special it is the duty of his ministers, and officers of his house. First, because their office doth call for the discharge of it publicly. Next, because as they should be best acquainted with the reasons of his praise, so also should they be the fittest instruments to declare it. And lastly, because the ungodly are deaf unto the exhortation, and dumb in the obedience of it ; therefore when he hath said, *"Praise ye the Lord,"* he sub-joineth, *"Praise, O ye servants of the l ord."*—*David Dickson.*

Verse 1.—*"Ye servants of the* LORD*."*—All men owe this duty to God, as being the workmanship of his hands ; Christians above other men, as being the sheep of his pasture ; preachers of the word above other Christians, as being pastors of his sheep, and so consequently patterns in word, in conversation, in love, in spirit, in faith, in pureness. 1 Tim. iv. 12.—*John Boys.*

Verses 1—3,

> Hallelujah, praise the Lord
> Praise, ye servants, praise his name !
> Be Jehovah's praise ador'd,
> Now and evermore the same !
> Where the orient sun-beams gleam,
> Where they sink in ocean's stream,
> Through the circuit of his rays
> Be your theme Jehovah's praise.

Richard Mant.

Verse 2.—*"Blessed be the name of the* LORD*."* Let then, O man, thy labouring soul strive to conceive (for 'tis impossible to express) what an immense debt of gratitude thou owest to him, who, by his creating goodness called thee out of nothing to make thee a partaker of reason, and even a sharer of immortality with himself ; who, by his preserving goodness, designs to conduct thee safe through the various stages of thy eternal existence ; and who, by his redeeming goodness, hath prepared for thee a happiness too big for the comprehension of a human understanding. Canst thou receive such endearments of love to thee and all mankind with insensibility and coldness ? . . . In the whole compass of language what word is expressive enough to paint the black ingratitude of that man, who is unaffected by, and entirely re-gardless of, the goodness of God his Creator, and the mercies of Christ ?—*Jeremiah Seed*, 1747.

Verse 2.—*"Blessed be the name of the* LORD*,"* etc. No doubt the disciples that sat at that paschal table, would repeat with mingled feelings of thanksgiving and sadness that ascription of praise. *"Blessed be the name of the* LORD *from this time forth and for evermore."* But what Israelite, in all the paschal chambers at Jerusalem on that night, as he sang the Hallel or hymn, or which of the disciples at the sorrowing board of Jesus, could have understood or entered into the full meaning of the ex-pression, *"from this time forth?"* From what time ? I think St. John gives us a clue to the very hour and moment of which the Psalmist, perhaps unconsciously, spake. He tells us, that when the traitor Judas had received the sop, he immediately went out ; and that when he was gone out to clench as it were and ratify his treacherous purpose, Jesus said, *"Now* is the Son of man glorified, and God is glorified in Him." From that time forth, when by the determinate counsel and foreknowledge of God, the Son of man was about to be delivered into the hands of wicked men, and crucified and slain, as Jesus looked at those around him, as sorrow had indeed filled their hearts, and as with all-seeing, prescient eye he looked onwards and beheld all those that should hereafter believe on him through their word, with what signi-ficance and emphasis of meaning may we imagine the blessed Jesus on that night of anguish to have uttered these words of the hymn, *"Blessed be the name of the* LORD *from this time forth and for evermore"* ! "A few more hours and the covenant will be sealed in my own blood ; the compact ratified, when I hang upon the cross." And with what calm and confident assurance of triumph does he look upon that cross of shame ; with what overflowing love does he point to it and say, " And I, if I be lifted up, will draw all men unto me " ! It is the very same here in this Paschal Psalm ; and how must the Saviour's heart have rejoiced even in the con-templation of those sufferings that awaited him, as he uttered this prediction, *"From the rising of the sun unto the going down of the same the* LORD'S *name is to be praised"* ! "That which thou sewest is not quickened except it die : " and thus from that hour to the present the Lord hath added daily to the church those whom in every age and in every clime he hath chosen unto salvation, till, in his own appointed fulness of time, from the east and from the west, from the north and from the south, all nations shall do him service, and the earth be filled with the knowledge of the Lord as the waters cover the sea."—*Barton Bouchier.*

Verse 2.—*"From this time forth and for evermore."* The servants of the Lord are to sing his praises in this life to the world's end ; and in the next life, world without end.—*John Boys.*

Verse 3.—*"From the rising of the sun unto the going down of the same."* That is everywhere, from east to west. These western parts of the world are particularly prophesied of to enjoy the worship of God after the Jews which were in the east ; and these islands of ours that lie in the sea, into which the sun is said to go down, which is an expression of the old Greek poets ; and the prophet here useth such a word in the Hebrew, where the west is called, according to the vulgar conceit, the sunset, or the sun's going down, or going in.—*Samuel Torshell*, 1641.

Verses 4, 5.—*"The LORD is high."* . . . *"The LORD our God dwelleth on high."* But how *high* is he ? *Answer* I. So high, that all creatures bow before him and do homage to him according to their several aptitudes and abilities. John brings them all in, attributing to him the crown of glory, putting it from themselves, but setting it upon his head, as a royalty due only to him. (Rev. v. 13). 1. Some by way of *subjection*, stooping to him : angels and saints worship him, acknowledging his highness, by denying their own, but setting up his will as their supreme law and excellency. 2. Others acknowledge his eminency by their *consternation* upon the least shining forth of his glory ; when he discovers but the emblems of his greatness, devils tremble, men quake, James ii. 19 ; Isai. xxxiii. 14. Thirdly, even inanimate creatures, by *compliance* with, and ready subjection to, the impressions of his power, Hab. iii. 9—11 ; Isai. xlviii. 13 ; Dan. iv. 35. . . . II. He is so high that he surmounts all created capacity to comprehend him, Job. xi. 7—9. So that indeed, in David's phrase, his greatness is *"unsearchable,"* Ps. cxlv. 3. In a word, he is so high, 1. That no bodily eye hath ever, or can possibly see him. 2. Neither can the eye of the understanding perfectly reach him. He dwells in inaccessible light that no mortal eye can attain to.—*Condensed from a sermon by Thomas Hodges, entitled,* "A Glimpse of God's Glory," 1642.

Verse 5.—*" Who is like unto the LORD our God ? "* It is the nature of love, that the one whom we love we prefer to all others, and we ask, *Who is like my beloved ?* The world has not his like. Thus love thinks ever of one, who in many things is inferior to many others ; for in human affairs the judgment of love is blind. But those who love the Lord their God, though they should glow with more ardent love for him, and should ask, Who is as the Lord our God ? in this matter would not be mistaken, but would think altogether most correctly. For there is no being, either in heaven or in earth, who can be in any way likened unto the Lord God. Even love itself cannot conceive, think, speak concerning God whom we love as he really is.—*Wolfgang Musculus.*

Verse 5.—*" Who is like unto the Lord our God,"* etc. Among the gods of the nations as Kimchi ; or among the angels of heaven, or among any of the mighty monarchs on earth ; there is none like him for the perfections of his nature, for his wisdom, power, truth, and faithfulness ; for his holiness, justice, goodness, grace, and mercy. Who is eternal, unchangeable, omnipotent, omniscient, and omnipresent ? Nor for the works of his hands, his works of creation, providence, and grace ; none ever did the like. What makes this reflection the more delightful to truly good men is, that this God is their God ; and all this is true of our Immanuel, God with us, who is God over all, and the only Saviour and Redeemer ; and there is none in heaven and earth like him, or to be desired beside him.—*John Gill.*

Verse 5.—*"The Lord our God who dwelleth on high."* God is on high in respect of place or dwelling. It is true he is in the aërial and starry heaven by his essence and power ; but the heaven of the blessed is his throne : not as if he were so confined to that place as to be excluded from others, for " the heaven of heavens cannot contain him " ; but in respect of manifestation he is said to be there, because in that place he chiefly manifests his glory and goodness. In respect of his essence he is *high* indeed, inexpressibly high in excellency above all beings, not only in Abraham's phrase, *"The High God,"* but in David's, *"The Lord most High."* Alas ! what are all created beings in respect of him, with all their excellences, but nothing and vanity ? . . . For these excellences are divers things in the creatures, but one in God ; they are accidents in the creatures, but essence in God ; they are in the creature with some alloy or other, they are like the moon when they shine brightest, yet are spots of imperfection to be found in them. In respect to measure, he is infinitely above them all. Alas, they possess some small drops in respect to the fountain, some poor glimmering rays in respect to this glorious sun ; in a word, he is an infinite ocean of perfection, without either brink or bottom.—*Thomas Hodges*, in a *Sermon preached before the House of Commons*, 1642.

Verse 5.—God is said not only to be on high, but to "*dwell*" on high ; this intimates *calm and composed operation*, and it is proper for us to take this view of the character of God's administration. You recollect that in all ages unbelief has been in some respect rendered plausible by the delays of God in the accomplishment of his designs. So, in St. Peter's time, it would seem that because the apostles and preachers of Christianity had dwelt much on Christ's coming to judgment, they cried out, " Where is the promise of his coming, for since the fathers fell asleep, all things continue as they were from the beginning of the creation ? " What is the apostle's answer to this ? His first answer, I grant, is, that all things have not continued as they were from the creation, for there was a flood of waters, and those who said, Where is the promise of his coming ? in the days of Noah were at last answered by the bursting earth and the breaking heavens. . . . That was his first answer ; but his second answer contains the principle that, " One day is with the Lord as a thousand years, and a thousand years as one day." The Being who is from everlasting to everlasting is under no necessity to hurry his plans ; therefore he hath fixed the times and the seasons—they are all with him, and *he dwelleth on high.*—*Richard Watson*, 1831.

Verses 5, 6.—The philosophy of the world, even in the present day, has its elevated and magnificent views of the Divine Being ; yet it would seem uniform, whether among the sages of the heathen world or among the philosophers of the present day, that the loftier their views are even of the Divine nature, the more they tend to distrust and unbelief ; and that, just in proportion as they have thought nobly of God, so the impression has deepened—that, with respect to individuals at least, they were not the subjects of his immediate care. The doctrine of a particular providence, and the doctrine of direct divine influence upon the heart of man, have by them always been considered absurd and fanatical. Now, when I turn to the sages of inspiration—to the holy men of old, who thought and spoke as they were moved by the Holy Ghost, I find quite a different result—that in proportion to the views they had of the glory of God, so was their confidence and hope.

That two such opposite results should spring from the same order of thoughts with respect to the Divine Being, is a singular fact, which demands and deserves some enquiry. How is it that, among the men of the world, wise as they are, in proportion as they have had high and exalted views of God, those lofty ideas tend to distrust ; while just in proportion as we are enlightened on the very same subjects by the Scriptures of truth, rightly and spiritually understood, that we as well as the authors of these sacred books, in proportion as we see the glory and the grandeur of God, are excited to a filial and comforting trust ? There are two propositions in the text which human reason could never unite. "*Who dwelleth on high* "—but yet he " *humbleth himself to behold the things that are in heaven, and in the earth.*" And the reason why the mere unassisted human faculties could never unite these two ideas is, that they could not, in the nature of things, be united, but by a third discovery, which must have come from God himself, and show the two in perfect harmony—the discovery that " God so loved the world that he gave his only begotten Son, that whosoever believeth in him should not perish, but have everlasting life."— *Richard Watson*, 1831.

Verses 5, 6.—The structure of this passage in the original is singular, and is thus stated and commented on by Bp. Lowth, in his 19th Prælection :—

Who is like Jehovah our God ?
Who dwelleth on high.
Who looketh below.
In heaven and in earth.

The latter member is to be divided, and assigned in its two divisions to the two former members ; so that the sense may be, " who dwelleth on high in heaven, and looketh below on the things which are in earth."—*Richard Mant.*

Verse 6.—"*Who humbleth himself.*" Whatever may be affirmed of God, may be affirmed of him infinitely, and whatever he is, he is infinitely. So the Psalmist, in this place, does not speak of God as humble, but as infinitely and superlatively so, humble beyond all conception and comparison ; he challenges the whole universe of created nature, from the highest immortal spirit in heaven to the lowest mortal on earth, to show a being endued with so much humility, as the adorable majesty of the great God of Heaven and earth. . . . If some instances of the Divine humility surprise, the following may amaze us :—To see the great King of heaven stooping from his height, and condescending himself to offer terms of reconciliation to his rebellious creatures ! To see offended majesty courting the offenders to accept of pardon ! To see God persuading, entreating and beseeching men to return to him with such earnestness and importunity, as if his very life were bound up in them, and his own happiness depended upon theirs ! To see the adorable Spirit of God, with infinite long-suffering and gentleness, submitting to the contempt and insults of such miserable, despicable wretches as sinful mortals are ! Is not this amazing ?— *Valentine Nalson*, 1641—1724.

Verse 6.—"*Who humbleth himself to behold.*"—If it be such condescension for God to behold things in heaven and earth, what an amazing condescension was it for the Son of God to come from heaven to earth and take our nature upon him, that he might seek and save them that were lost ! Here indeed he humbled himself.— *Matthew Henry.*

Verse 7.—"*He raiseth up the poor,*" etc. There is no doubt a reference in this to the respect which God pays even to the lower ranks of the race, seeing that " he raiseth up the poor, and lifteth up the needy." I have no doubt there is reference throughout the whole of this Psalm to evangelical times ; that, in this respect, it is a prophetic psalm, including a reference especially to Christianity, as it may be called by eminence and distinction the religion of the poor—its greatest glory. For when John the Baptist sent two disciples to Jesus, to know whether he was the Messiah or not, the answer of our Lord was, " The blind see, the lepers are cleansed, the dead are raised "—all extraordinary events—miracles, in short, which proved his divine commission. And he summed up the whole by saying, " The poor have the gospel preached unto them ; " as great a miracle as any—as great a distinction as any. There never was a religion but the true religion, in all its various dispensations, that had equal respect to all classes of society. In all others there was a privileged class, but here there is none. Perhaps one of the most interesting views of Christianity we can take is its wonderful adaptation to the character and circumstances of the poor. What an opportunity does it furnish for the manifestation of the bright and mild graces of the Holy Spirit ! What sources of comfort does it open to mollify the troubles of life ! and how often, in choosing the poor, rich in faith, to make them heirs of the kingdom, does God exalt the poor out of the dust, and the needy from the dunghill !—*Richard Watson.*

Verse 7.—"*He raiseth up the poor,*" etc. Gideon is fetched from threshing, Saul from seeking the asses, and David from keeping the sheep ; the apostles from fishing are sent to be " fishers of men." The treasure of the gospel is put into earthen vessels, and the weak and the foolish ones of the world pitched upon to be preachers of it, to confound the " wise and mighty " (1 Cor. i. 27, 28,) that the excellency of the power may be of God, and all may see that promotion comes from him.—*Matthew Henry.*

Verse 7.—"*He raiseth up the poor.*" The highest honour, which was ever done to any mere creature, was done out of regard to the lowest humility ; the Son of God had such regard to the lowliness of the blessed virgin, that he did her the honour to choose her for the mother of his holy humanity. It is an observation of S. Chrysostom, that that very hand which the humble John Baptist thought not worthy to unloose the shoe on our blessed Saviour's feet, that hand our Lord thought worthy to baptize his sacred head.—*Valentine Nalson.*

Verse 7.—"*And lifteth the needy out of the dunghill*" ; which denotes a mean condition ; so one born in a mean place, and brought up in a mean manner, is sometimes represented as taken out of a dunghill ; and also it is expressive of a filthy one ; men by sin are not only brought into a low estate, but into a loathsome one, and are justly abominable in the sight of God, and yet he lifts them out of it : the phrases of *raising up* and *lifting out* suppose them to be fallen, as men are in Adam, fallen from a state of honour and glory, in and out of which they cannot deliver themselves ; it is Christ's work, and his only, to raise up the tribes of Jacob, and to help or lift up his servant Israel. Isa. xlix. 6 ; Luke i. 54 ; see 1 Sam. ii. 8.— *John Gill.*

Verse 7.—"The poor . . the needy." Rejoice, then, in the favourable notice God taketh of you. The highest and greatest of beings vouchsafes to regard *you.* Though you are poor and mean, and men overlook you ; though your brethren hate you, and your friends go far from you, yet hear ! God looketh down from his majestic throne upon you. Amidst the infinite variety of his works, you are not overlooked. Amidst the nobler services of ten thousand times ten thousand saints and angels, not *one* of your fervent prayers or humble groans escapes his ear.—*Job Orton*, 1717— 1783.

Verse 7.—Almighty God cannot look above himself, as having no superiors ; nor about himself, as having no equals ; he beholds such as are below him ; and therefore the lower a man is, the nearer unto God ; he resists the proud, and gives grace to the humble, 1 Pet. v. 5. He pulls down the mighty from their seat, and exalteth them of low degree. The Most High hath special eye to such as are most humble ; for, as it followeth in our text, *"he taketh up the simple out of the dust, and lifteth the poor out of the dirt."—John Boys.*

Verse 7.—"Dunghill." An emblem of the deepest poverty and desertion ; for in Syria and Palestine the man who is shut out from society lies upon the *mezbele* (the dunghill or heap of ashes), by day calling upon the passers-by for alms, and by night hiding himself in the ashes that have been warmed by the sun.—*Franz Delitzsch.*

Verse 7.—"Dunghill." The passages of the Bible, in which the word occurs, all seem to refer, as Parkhurst remarks, to the stocks of cow-dung and other offal stuff, which the easterns for want of wood were obliged to lay up for fuel.—*Richard Mant.*

Verses 7, 8.—These verses are taken almost word for word from the prayer of Hannah, 1 Sam. ii. 8. The transition to the *"people"* is all the more natural, as Hannah, considering herself at the conclusion as the type of the church, with which every individual among the Israelites felt himself much more closely entwined than can easily be the case among ourselves, draws out of the salvation imparted to herself joyful prospects for the future.—*E. W. Hengstenberg.*

Verse 8.—"Even with the princes of his people." It is the honour that cometh from God that alone exalts. Whatever account the world may take of a poor man, he may be more precious in the eyes of God than the highest among men. The humble poor are here ranked, not with the princes of the earth, but with *"the princes of his people."* The distinctions in this world, even among those who serve the same God, are as nothing in his sight when contrasted with that honour which is grounded on the free grace of God to his own. But here, also, the fulness of this statement will only be seen in the world to come, when all the faithful will be owned as kings and priests unto God.—*W. Wilson.*

Verse 9.—"He maketh the barren woman to keep house," etc. Should a married woman, who has long been considered sterile, become a mother, her joy, and that of her husband and friends, will be most extravagant. " They called her *Malady,*" that is, " Barren," " but she has given us good fruit." " My neighbours pointed at me, and said, *Malady* : but what will they say now ? " A man who on any occasion manifests great delight, is represented to be like the barren woman who has at length borne a child. Anything which is exceedingly valuable is thus described : " This is as precious as the son of the barren woman " ; that is, of her who had long been reputed barren.—*Joseph Roberts.*

Verse 9.—"He maketh the barren woman to keep house," etc. As baseness in men, so barrenness in women is accounted a great unhappiness. But as God lifteth up the beggar out of the mire, to set him with princes, even so doth he *"make the barren woman a joyful mother of children."* He governs all things in the private family, as well as in the public weal. Children and the fruit of the womb are a gift and heritage that cometh of the Lord, Ps. cxxvii. 3 ; and therefore the Papists in praying to S. Anne for children, and the Gentiles in calling upon Diana, Juno, Latona, are both in error. It is God only who makes the barren women *"a mother,"* and that *"a joyful mother."* Every mother is joyful at the first, according to that of Christ, " a woman when she travaileth hath sorrow, because her hour is come : but as soon as she is delivered of the child, she remembereth no more the anguish, for joy that a man is born into the world."

Divines apply this also mystically to Christ, affirming that he made the church of the Gentiles, heretofore *"barren," "a joyful mother of children,"* according to that of the prophet : " Rejoice, O barren, that didst not bear ; break forth into joy and rejoice, thou that didst not travail with child : for the desolate hath more children than the married wife, saith the Lord," Isai. liv. 1. Or it may be construed of true Christians : all of us are by nature barren of goodness, conceived and born in sin not able to think a good thought (2 Cor. iii. 5) ; but the Father of lights and mercies makes us fruitful and abundant always in the work of the Lord (1 Cor. xv. 58) ; he giveth us grace to be fathers and mothers of many good deeds, which are our children and best heirs, eternizing our name for ever.—*John Boys.*

Verse 9.—"*The barren woman* " is the poor, forsaken, distressed Christian church, whom the false church oppresses, defies, and persecutes, and regards as useless, miserable, barren, because she herself is greater and more populous, the greatest part of the world.—*Joshua Arndt,* 1626—1685.

Verse 9.—"*Praise ye the* LORD." We may look abroad, and see abundant occasion for praising God,—in his condescension to human affairs,—in his lifting up the poor from the humblest condition,—in his exalting those of lowly rank to places of honour, trust, wealth, and power ; but, after all, if we wish to find occasions of praise that will most tenderly affect the heart, and be connected with the warmest affections of the soul, they will be most likely to be found in the domestic circle—in the mutual love—the common joy—the tender feelings—which bind together the members of a family.—*Albert Barnes.*

Verse 9.—"*Praise ye the* LORD." The very hearing of the comfortable changes which the Lord can make and doth make the afflicted to find, is a matter of refreshment to all, and of praise to God from all.—*David Dickson.*

HINTS TO PREACHERS.

Whole Psalm.—The Psalm contains three parts :—I. An exhortation to God's servants to praise him.   II. A form set down how and where to praise him, ver. 2, 3. III. The reasons to persuade us to it. 1. By his infinite power, ver. 4, 5. 2. His providence, as displayed in heaven and earth, ver. 6.—*Adam Clarke.*

Verse 1.—The repetitions show, 1. The importance of praise. 2. Our many obligations to render it. 3. Our backwardness in the duty. 4. The heartiness and frequency with which it should be rendered. 5. The need of calling upon others to join with us.

Verse 1.—I. To whom praise is due : " the Lord." II. From whom it is due : " ye servants of the Lord." III. For what is it due : his " name." 1. For all names descriptive of what he is in himself. 2. For all names descriptive of what he is to his servants.—*G. R.*

Verses 1, 9.—" Praise ye the Lord." I. Begin and end life with it, and do the same with holy service, patient suffering, and everything else. II. Fill up the interval with praise. Run over the intervening verses.

Verse 2.—I. The work of heaven begun on earth : to praise the name of the Lord. II. The work of earth continued in heaven : " and for evermore." If the praise begun on earth be continued in heaven, we must be in heaven to continue the praise.—*G. R.*

Verse 2.—1. It is time to begin to praise : " from this time." Is there not special reason, from long arrears, from present duty, etc. ? 2. There is no time for leaving off praise : " and for evermore." None supposable or excusable.

Verse 3.—God is to be praised. 1. All the day. 2. All the world over. 3. Publicly in the light. 4. Amidst daily duties. 5. Always—because it is always day somewhere.

Verse 3.—1. Canonical hours abolished. 2. Holy places abolished—since we cannot be always in them. 3. Every time and place consecrated.

Verses 5, 6.—The greatness of God as viewed from below, ver. 5. II. The condescension of God as viewed from above, ver. 6. 1. In creation. 2. In the Incarnation. 3. In redemption.—*G. R.*

Verses 5, 6.—The unparalleled condescension of God. 1. None are so great, and therefore able to stoop so low. 2. None are so good, and therefore so willing to stoop. 3. None are so wise, and therefore so able to " behold " or know the needs of little things. 4. None are infinite, and therefore able to enter into minutiæ and sympathize with the smallest grief : Infinity is seen in the minute as truly as in the immense.

Verse 6.—I. The same God rules in heaven and earth. II. Both spheres are dependent for happiness upon his beholding them. III. They both enjoy his consideration. IV.—All things done in them are equally under his inspection.

Verse 7.—The gospel and its special eye to the poor.

Verses 7, 8.—I. Where men are ? In the dust of sorrow and on the dunghill of sin. II. Who interferes to help them ? He who dwelleth on high. III. What does he effect for them ? " Raiseth, lifteth, setteth among princes, among princes of his people."

Verse 8.—Elevation to the peerage of heaven ; or, the Royal Family increased.

Verse 9.—For mothers' meetings. " A joyful mother of children." I. It is a joy to be a mother. II. It is specially so to have living, healthy, obedient children. III. But best of all to have Christian children. Praise is due to the Lord who gives such blessings.

Verse 9.—I. A household God, or, God in the Household : " He maketh," etc. Have you children ? It is of God. Have you lost children ? It is of God. Have you been without children ? It is of God. II. Household worship, or, the God of the Household : " Praise ye the Lord." 1. In the family. 2. For family mercies.— *G. R.*

PSALM CXIV.

SUBJECT AND DIVISION.—*This sublime* SONG OF THE EXODUS *is one and indivisible. True poetry has here reached its climax : no human mind has ever been able to equal, much less to excel, the grandeur of this Psalm. God is spoken of as leading forth his people from Egypt to Canaan, and causing the whole earth to be moved at his coming. Things inanimate are represented as imitating the actions of living creatures when the Lord passes by. They are apostrophised and questioned with marvellous force of language, till one seems to look upon the actual scene. The God of Jacob is exalted as having command over river, sea, and mountain, and causing all nature to pay homage and tribute before his glorious majesty.*

EXPOSITION.

WHEN Israel went out of Egypt, the house of Jacob from a people of strange language ;

2 Judah was his sanctuary, *and* Israel his dominion.

3 The sea saw *it*, and fled : Jordan was driven back.

4 The mountains skipped like rams, *and* the little hills like lambs.

5 What *ailed* thee, O thou sea, that thou fleddest ? thou Jordan, *that* thou wast driven back ?

6 Ye mountains, *that* ye skipped like rams ; *and* ye little hills, like lambs ?

7 Tremble, thou earth, at the presence of the Lord, at the presence of the God of Jacob ;

8 Which turned the rock *into* a standing water, the flint into a fountain of waters.

1. "*When Israel went out of Egypt.*" The song begins with a burst, as if the poetic fury could not be restrained, but overleaped all bounds. The soul elevated and filled with a sense of divine glory cannot wait to fashion a preface, but springs at once into the middle of its theme. Israel emphatically came out of Egypt, out of the population among whom they had been scattered, from under the yoke of bondage, and from under the personal grasp of the king who had made the people into national slaves. Israel came out with a high hand and a stretched-out arm, defying all the power of the empire, and making the whole of Egypt to travail with sore anguish, as the chosen nation was as it were born out of its midst. "*The house of Jacob from a people of strange language.*" They had gone down into Egypt as a single family—" the house of Jacob " ; and, though they had multiplied greatly, they were still so united, and were so fully regarded by God as a single unit, that they are rightly spoken of as the house of Jacob. They were as one man in their willingness to leave Goshen ; numerous as they were, not a single individual stayed behind. Unanimity is a pleasing token of the divine presence, and one of its sweetest fruits. One of their inconveniences in Egypt was the difference of languages, which was very great. The Israelites appear to have regarded the Egyptians as stammerers and babblers, since they could not understand them, and they very naturally considered the Egyptians to be barbarians, as they would no doubt often beat them because they did not comprehend their orders. The language of foreign taskmasters is never musical in an exile's ear. How sweet it is to a Christian who has been compelled to hear the filthy conversation of the wicked, when at last he is brought out from their midst to dwell among his own people !

2. "*Judah was his sanctuary, and Israel his dominion.*" The pronoun " his " comes in where we should have looked for the name of God ; but the poet is so full of thought concerning the Lord that he forgets to mention his name, like the spouse in the Song, who begins, " Let *him* kiss me," or Magdalene when she cried, " Tell me where thou hast laid *him*." From the mention of Judah and Israel certain critics have inferred that this Psalm must have been written after the division

of the two kingdoms ; but this is only another instance of the extremely slender basis upon which an hypothesis is often built up. Before the formation of the two kingdoms David had said, "Go, number Israel and Judah," and this was common parlance, for Uriah the Hittite said, "The ark and Israel, and Judah abide in tents " ; so that nothing can be inferred from the use of the two names. No division into two kingdoms can have been intended here, for the poet is speaking of the coming out of Egypt when the people were so united that he has just before called them " the house of Judah." It would be quite as fair to prove from the first verse that the Psalm was written when the people were in union as to prove from the second that its authorship dates from their separation. Judah was the tribe which led the way in the wilderness march, and it was forseen in prophecy to be the royal tribe, hence its poetical mention in this place. The meaning of the passage is that the whole people at the coming out of Egypt were separated unto the Lord to be a peculiar people, a nation of priests whose motto should be, "Holiness unto the Lord." Judah was the Lord's "holy thing," set apart for his special use. The nation was peculiarly Jehovah's dominion, for it was governed by a theocracy in which God alone was King. It was his domain in a sense in which the rest of the world was outside his kingdom. These were the young days of Israel, the time of her espousals, when she went after the Lord into the wilderness, her God leading the way with signs and miracles. The whole people were the shrine of Deity, and their camp was one great temple. What a change there must have been for the godly amongst them from the idolatries and blasphemies of the Egyptians to the holy worship and righteous rule of the great King in Jeshurun. They lived in a world of wonders, where God was seen in the wondrous bread they ate and in the water they drank, as well as in the solemn worship of his holy place. When the Lord is manifestly present in a church, and his gracious rule obediently owned, what a golden age has come, and what honourable privileges his people enjoy ! May it be so among us.

3. *"The sea saw it, and fled"* ; or rather, " The sea saw and fled"—it saw God and all his people following his lead, and it was struck with awe and fled away. A bold figure ! The Red Sea mirrored the hosts which had come down to its shore, and reflected the cloud which towered high over all, as the symbol of the presence of the Lord : never had such a scene been imagined upon the surface of the Red Sea, or any other sea, before. It could not endure the unusual and astounding sight, and fleeing to the right and to the left, opened a passage for the elect people. A like miracle happened at the end of the great march of Israel, for *"Jordan was driven back."* This was a swiftly-flowing river, pouring itself down a steep decline, and it was not merely divided, but its current was driven back so that the rapid torrent, contrary to nature, flowed up-hill. This was God's work : the poet does not sing of the suspension of natural laws, or of a singular phenomenon not readily to be explained ; but to him the presence of God with his people is everything, and in his lofty song he tells how the river was driven back because the Lord was there. In this case poetry is nothing but the literal fact, and the fiction lies on the side of the atheistic critics who will suggest any explanation of the miracle rather than admit that the Lord made bare his holy arm in the eyes of all his people. The division of the sea and the drying up of the river are placed together though forty years intervened, because they were the opening and closing scenes of one great event. We may thus unite by faith our new birth and our departure out of the world into the promised inheritance, for the God who led us out of the Egypt of our bondage under sin will also conduct us through the Jordan of death out of our wilderness wanderings in the desert of this tried and changeful life. It is all one and the same deliverance, and the beginning ensures the end.

4. *"The mountains skipped like rams, and the little hills like lambs."* At the coming of the Lord to Mount Sinai, the hills moved ; either leaping for joy in the presence of their Creator like young lambs ; or, if you will, springing from their places in affright at the terrible majesty of Jehovah, and flying like a flock of sheep when alarmed. Men fear the mountains, but the mountains tremble before the Lord. Sheep and lambs move lightly in the meadows ; but the hills, which we are wont to call eternal, were as readily made to move as the most active creatures. Rams in their strength, and lambs in their play, are not more stirred than were the solid hills when Jehovah marched by. Nothing is immovable but God himself : the mountains shall depart, and the hills be removed, but the covenant of his grace abideth fast for ever and ever. Even thus do mountains of sin and hills of trouble

move when the Lord comes forth to lead his people to their eternal Canaan. Let us never fear, but rather let our faith say unto this mountain, "Be thou removed hence and cast into the sea," and it shall be done.

5. "*What ailed thee, O thou sea?*" Wert thou terribly afraid? Did thy strength fail thee? Did thy very heart dry up? "What ailed thee, O thou sea, *that thou fleddest?*" Thou wert neighbour to the power of Pharaoh, but thou didst never fear his hosts; stormy wind could never prevail against thee so as to divide thee in twain; but when the way of the Lord was in thy great waters thou wast seized with affright, and thou becamest a fugitive from before him. "*Thou Jordan, that thou wast driven back?*" What ailed thee, O quick descending river? Thy fountains had not dried up, neither had a chasm opened to engulph thee! The near approach of Israel and her God sufficed to make thee retrace thy steps. What aileth all our enemies that they fly when the Lord is on our side? What aileth hell itself that it is utterly routed when Jesus lifts up a standard against it? "Fear took hold upon them there," for fear of HIM the stoutest hearted did quake, and became as dead men.

6. "*Ye mountains, that ye skipped like rams; and ye little hills, like lambs?*" What ailed ye that ye were thus moved? There is but one reply: the majesty of God made you to leap. A gracious mind will chide human nature for its strange insensibility, when the sea and the river, the mountains and the hills, are all sensitive to the presence of God. Man is endowed with reason and intelligence, and yet he sees unmoved that which the material creation beholds with fear. God has come nearer to us than ever he did to Sinai, or to Jordan, for he has assumed our nature, and yet the mass of mankind are neither driven back from their sins, nor moved in the paths of obedience.

7. "*Tremble, thou earth, at the presence of the Lord, at the presence of the God of Jacob.*" Or "from before the Lord, the Adonai, the Master and King." Very fitly does the Psalm call upon all nature again to feel a holy awe because its Ruler is still in its midst.

> "Quake when Jehovah walks abroad,
> Quake, earth, at sight of Israel's God."

Let the believer feel that God is near, and he will serve the Lord with fear and rejoice with trembling. Awe is not cast out by faith, but the rather it becomes deeper and more profound. The Lord is most reverenced where he is most loved.

8. "*Which turned the rock into a standing water,*" causing a mere or lake to stand at its foot, making the wilderness a pool: so abundant was the supply of water from the rock that it remained like water in a reservoir. "*The flint into a fountain of waters,*" which flowed freely in streams, following the tribes in their devious marches. Behold what God can do! It seemed impossible that the flinty rock should become a fountain; but he speaks, and it is done. Not only do mountains move, but rocks yield rivers when the God of Israel wills that it should be so.

> "From stone and solid rock he brings
> The spreading lake, the gushing springs."

"O magnify the Lord with me, and let us exalt his name together," for he it is and he alone who doeth such wonders as these. He supplies our temporal needs from sources of the most unlikely kind, and never suffers the stream of his liberality to fail. As for our spiritual necessities they are all met by the water and the blood which gushed of old from the riven rock, Christ Jesus: therefore let us extol the Lord our God.

Our deliverance from under the yoke of sin is strikingly typified in the going up of Israel from Egypt, and so also was the victory of our Lord over the powers of death and hell. The Exodus should therefore be earnestly remembered by Christian hearts. Did not Moses on the mount of transfiguration speak to our Lord of "the exodus" which he should shortly accomplish at Jerusalem; and is it not written of the hosts above that they sing the song of Moses the servant of God, and of the Lamb? Do we not ourselves expect another coming of the Lord, when before his face heaven and earth shall flee away and there shall be no more sea? We join then with the singers around the Passover table and make their Hallel ours, for we too have been led out of bondage and guided like a flock through a desert land, wherein the Lord supplies our wants with heavenly manna and water from the Rock of ages. Praise ye the Lord.

EXPLANATORY NOTES AND QUAINT SAYINGS.

Whole Psalm.—The cxivth Psalm appears to me to be an admirable ode, and I began to turn it into our own language. As I was describing the journey of Israel from Egypt, and added the Divine Presence amongst them, I perceived a beauty in this Psalm, which was entirely new to me, and which I was going to lose; and that is, that the poet utterly conceals the presence of God in the beginning of it, and rather lets a possessive pronoun go without a substantive, than he will so much as mention anything of divinity there. " Judah was his sanctuary, and Israel his dominion " or kingdom. The reason now seems evident, and this conduct necessary; for, if God had appeared before, there could be no wonder why the mountains should leap and the sea retire; therefore, that this convulsion of nature may be brought in with due surprise, his name is not mentioned till afterwards; and then with a very agreeable turn of thought, God is introduced at once in all his majesty. This is what I have attempted to imitate in a translation without paraphrase, and to preserve what I could of the spirit of the sacred author.

When Israel, freed from Pharaoh's hand,
Left the proud tyrant and his land,
The tribes with cheerful homage own
Their King, and Judah was his throne.

Across the deep their journey lay,
The deep divides to make them way;
The streams of Jordan saw, and fled
With backward current to their head.

The mountains shook like frightened sheep,
Like lambs the little hillocks leap;
Not Sinai on her base could stand,
Conscious of sovereign power at hand.

What power could make the deep divide?
Make Jordan backward roll his tide?
Why did ye leap, ye little hills?
And whence the fright that Sinai feels?

Let ev'ry mountain, ev'ry flood,
Retire, and know th' approaching God,
The King of Israel! see him here:
Tremble, thou earth, adore and fear.

He thunders—and all nature mourns;
The rock to standing pools he turns;
Flints spring with fountains at his word,
And fires and seas confess their Lord.

Isaac Watts, in "The Spectator," 1712.

Verse 1.—*"When Israel went out of Egypt."* Out of the midst of that nation, that is, out of the bowels of the Egyptians, who had, as it were, devoured them; thus the Jew-doctors gloss upon this text.—*John Trapp.*

Verse 1.—*"Israel went out of Egypt."* This was an emblem of the Lord's people in effectual vocation, coming out of bondage into liberty, out of darkness into light, out of superstition, and idolatry, and profaneness, to the service of the true God in righteousness and true holiness; and *from a people of strange language* to those that speak the language of Canaan, a pure language, in which they can understand one another when they converse together, either about experience or doctrine; and the manner of their coming out is much the same, by strength of hand, by the power of divine grace, yet willingly and cheerfully, with great riches, the riches of grace, and a title to the riches of glory, and with much spiritual strength; for though weak in themselves, yet they are strong in Christ.—*John Gill.*

Verse 1.—*"The house of Jacob."* The Israelites though they were a great number when they went forth from Egypt, nevertheless formed one house or family; thus the church at the present time dispersed throughout the whole world is called one house : 1 Tim. iii. 15 ; Heb. iii. 6 ; 1 Pet. ii. 5 : and that because of one faith, one God, one Father, one baptism, Ephes. iv. 5.—*Marloratus*.

Verse 1.—"*A people of strange language*." When we find in verse 1, as in Psalm lxxxi. 5, Egypt spoken of as a land where the people were of a "*strange tongue*," it seems likely that the reference is to their being a people who could not *speak of God*, as Israel could ; even as Zeph. iii. 9 tells of the "*pure lip*," viz. the lip that calls on the name of the Lord.—*Andrew A. Bonar*.

Verse 1.—"*A people of strange language*." Mant translates this "*tyrant land*," and has the following note :—" The Hebrew word here rendered " tyrant," has been supposed to signify " barbarous " ; that is, " using a barbarous or foreign language or pronunciation." But, says Parkhurst, the word seems rather to refer to the " violence " of the Egyptians towards the Israelites, or " the barbarity of their behaviour," which was more to the Psalmist's purpose than " the barbarity of their language " ; even supposing the reality of the latter in the time of Moses. The epithet " barbarous " would leave the same ambiguity as Parkhurst supposes to belong to the text. Bishop Horsley renders " a tyrannical people."

Verse 1.—"*A people of strange language*." The strange language is evidently an annoyance. Israel could not feel at home in Egypt.—*Justus Olshausen*.

Verse 2.—"*Judah was his sanctuary, and Israel his dominion*." These people were God's *sanctification and dominion*, that is, witnesses of his holy majesty in adopting them, and of his mighty power in delivering them : or, his *sanctification*, as having his holy priests to govern them in the points of piety ; and *dominion*, as having godly magistrates ordained from above to rule them in matters of policy : or, his *sanctuary*, both actually, because sanctifying him ; and passively, because sanctified of him. . . . This one verse expounds and exemplifies two prime petitions of the Lord's Prayer. " Hallowed be thy name, thy kingdom come " : for *Judah* was God's sanctuary, because *hallowing his name ;* and *Israel* his dominion, as desiring his *kingdom to come*. Let every man examine himself by this pattern, whether he be truly the servant of Jesus his Saviour, or the vassal of Satan the destroyer. If any man submit himself willingly to the domineering of the devil, and suffer sin to reign in his mortal members, obeying the lusts thereof, and working all uncleanness even with greediness ; assuredly that man is yet a chapel of Satan, and a slave to sin. On the contrary, whosoever unfeignedly desires that God's kingdom may come, being ever ready to be ruled according to his holy word, acknowledging it a lantern to his feet, and a guide to his paths; admitting obediently his laws, and submitting himself alway to the same ; what is he, but a citizen of heaven, a subject of God, a saint, a *sanctuary ?—John Boys*.

Verse 2.—"*Judah was his sanctuary*," etc. Reader, do not fail to remark when Israel was brought out of Egypt the Lord set up his tabernacle among them, and manifested his presence to them. And what is it now, when the Lord Jesus brings out his people from the Egypt of the world ? Doth he not fulfil that sweet promise, " Lo, I am with you alway, even unto the end of the world " ? Is it not the privilege of his people, to live *to* him, to live *with* him, and to live *upon* him ? Doth he not in every act declare, " I will say, it is my people ; and they shall say, the Lord is my God " ? Matt. xxviii. 20 ; Zech. xiii. 9.—*Robert Hawker*.

Verse 2.—"*Judah was his sanctuary*." Meaning not the tribe of Judah only, though they in many things had the pre-eminence ; the kingdom belonged to it, the chief ruler being out of it, especially the Messiah ; its standard was pitched and moved first ; it offered first to the service of the Lord ; and the Jews have a tradition, mentioned by Jarchi and Kimchi, that this tribe with its prince at the head of it, went into the Red Sea first ; the others fearing, but afterwards followed, encouraged by their example. In this place all the tribes are meant, the whole body of the people.—*John Gill*.

Verse 2.—One peculiarity of the second verse requires attention. It twice uses the word "*his*," without naming any one. There are two theories to account for this circumstance. One is that Psalm cxiv. was always sung in immediate connection with cxiii., in which the name of God occurs no less than six times, so that the continuance of the train of thought made a fresh repetition of it here unnecessary. But this view, to be fully consistent with itself, must assume that the two Psalms are really one, with a merely arbitrary division, which does not, on the face of the matter, seem by any means probable, as the scope of thought in the two is perfectly distinct. The other, which is more satisfactory, regards the omission of the Holy

Name in this part of the Psalm as a practical artifice to heighten the effect of the answer to the sudden apostrophe in verses five and six. There would be nothing marvellous in the agitation of the sea, and river, and mountains in the presence of God, but it may well appear wonderful till that potent cause is revealed, as it is most forcibly in the dignified words of the seventh verse.—*Ewald and Perowne, in Neale and Littledale.*

Verse 3.—*"The sea saw it"* : to wit this glorious work of God in bringing his people out of Egypt.—*Matthew Pool.*

Verse 3.—*"The sea saw it."* Saw there that " Judah " was " God's sanctuary," " and Israel his dominion," and therefore *"fled"* ; for nothing could be more awful. It was this that *drove Jordan back*, and was an invincible dam to his streams ; God was at the head of that people, and therefore they must give way to them, must make room for them, they must retire, contrary to their nature, when God speaks the word.—*Matthew Henry.*

Verse 3.—*"The sea saw it, and fled."*

> The waves on either side
> Unloose their close embraces, and divide,
> And backwards press, as in some solemn show
> The crowding people do,
> (Though just before no space was seen,)
> To let the admirèd triumph pass between.
> The wondering army saw, on either hand,
> The no less wondering waves like rocks of crystal stand.
> They marched betwixt, and boldly trod
> The secret paths of God.
> *Abraham Cowley,* 1618—1667.

Verse 3.—*"Jordan was driven back."* And now the glorious day was come when, by a stupendous miracle, Jehovah had determined to show how able he was to remove every obstacle in the way of his people, and to subdue every enemy before their face. By his appointment the host, amounting probably to two millions-and-a-half of persons (about the same number as had crossed the Red Sea on foot), had removed to the banks of the river three days before, and now in marching array awaited the signal to cross the stream. At any time the passage of the river by such a multitude, with their women and children, their flocks and herds, and all their baggage, would have presented formidable difficulties ; but now the channel was filled with a deep and impetuous torrent, which overflowed its banks and spread widely on each side, probably extending nearly a mile in width ; while in the very sight of the scene were the Canaanitish hosts, who might be expected to pour out from their gates, and exterminate the invading multitude before they could reach the shore. Yet these difficulties were nothing to Almighty power, and only served to heighten the effect of the stupendous miracle about to be wrought.

By the command of Jehovah, the priests, bearing the ark of the covenant, the sacred symbol of the Divine presence, marched more than half-a-mile in front of the people, who were forbidden to come any nearer to it. Thus it was manifest that Jehovah needed not protection from Israel, but was their guard and guide, since the unarmed priests feared not to separate themselves from the host, and to venture with the ark into the river in the face of their enemies. And thus the army, standing aloof, had a better opportunity of seeing the wondrous results, and of admiring the mighty power of God exerted on their behalf ; for no sooner had the feet of the priests touched the brim of the overflowing river, than the swelling waters receded from them ; and not only the broad lower valley, but even the deep bed of the stream was presently emptied of water, and its pebbly bottom became dry. The waters which had been in the channel speedily ran off, and were lost in the Dead Sea ; whilst those which would naturally have replaced them from above, were miraculuosly suspended, and accumulated in a glassy heap far above the city Adam, that is beside Zaretan. These places are supposed to have been at least forty miles above the Dead Sea, and may possibly have been much more ; so that nearly the whole channel of the Lower Jordan, from a little below the Lake of Tiberias to the Dead Sea, was dry. . . . . . What a glorious termination of the long pilgrimage of Israel was this ! and how worthy of the power, wisdom, and goodness of their Divine Protector ! " The passage of this deep and

rapid river," remarks Dr. Hales, " at the most unfavourable season, was more
manifestly miraculous, if possible, than that of the Red Sea ; because here was
no natural agency whatever employed ; no mighty wind to sweep a passage, as
in the former case ; no reflux of the tide, on which minute philosophers might
fasten to depreciate the miracle.   It seems, therefore, to have been providentially
designed to silence cavils respecting the former ; and it was done at noon-day,
in the face of the sun, and in the presence, we may be sure, of the neighbouring
inhabitants, and struck terror into the kings of the Canaanites and Amorites westward of the river."—*Philip Henry Gosse, in "Sacred Streams,"* 1877.

Verse 3.—*"Jordan was driven back."* The waters know their Maker : that
Jordan which flowed with full streams when Christ went into it to be baptized,
now gives way when the same God must pass through it in state : then there was
use of his water, now of his sand.   I hear no more news of any rod to strike the
waters ; the presence of the ark of the Lord God, Lord of all the world, is sign
enough to these waves, which now, as if a sinew were broken, run back to their
issues, and dare not so much as wet the feet of the priests that bare it.   How subservient are all the creatures to the God that made them !   How glorious a God
do we serve ; whom all the powers of the heavens and elements are willingly subject
unto, and gladly take that nature which he pleaseth to give them.—*Abraham Wright.*

Verse 3.—*"Jordan was driven back."* It was probably at the point near the
present southern fords, crossed at the time of the Christian era by a bridge.   The
river was at its usual state of flood at the spring of the year, so as to fill the whole
of the bed, up to the margin of the jungle with which the river banks are lined.
On the broken edge of the swollen stream, the band of priests stood with the ark
on their shoulders.   At the distance of nearly a mile in the rear was the mass of
the army.   Suddenly the full bed of the Jordan was dried before them.   High
up the river, " far, far away," " in Adam, the city which is beside Zaretan," " as
far as the parts of Kirjath-jearim " (Josh. iii. 16), that is, at a distance of thirty
miles from the place of the Israelite encampment, the waters there stood which
" descended " " from the heights above,"—stood and rose up, as if gathered into
a waterskin ; as if in a barrier or heap, as if congealed ; and those that " descended "
towards the sea of " the desert," the salt Sea, " failed and were cut off."   Thus
the scene presented is of the " descending stream " (the words employed seem
to have a special reference to that peculiar and most significant name of the
" Jordan "), not parted asunder, as we generally fancy, but, as the Psalm expresses
it, " turned backwards " ; the whole bed of the river left dry from north to south,
through its long windings ; the huge stones lying bare here and there, imbedded
in the soft bottom ; or the shingly pebbles drifted along the course of the channel.—
Arthur Penrhyn Stanley, in "The History of the Jewish Church," 1870.

Verse 4.—*"The mountains skipped like rams,"* etc.   The figure drawn from
the *lambs* and *rams* would appear to be inferior to the magnitude of the subject.
But it was the prophet's intention to express in the homeliest way the incredible
manner in which God, on these occasions, displayed his power.   The stability of
the earth being, as it were, founded on the mountains, what connection can they
have with rams and lambs, that they should be agitated, skipping hither and thither ?
In speaking in this homely style, he does not mean to detract from the greatness
of the miracle, but more forcibly to engrave these extraordinary tokens of God's
power on the illiterate.—*John Calvin.*

Verse 4.—*"Skipped."* A poetic description of the concussion caused by the
thunder and lightning that accompanied the divine presence.—*James G. Murphy.*

Verse 4.—At the giving of the law at Sinai, Horeb and the mountains around,
both great and small, shook with a sudden and mighty earthquake, like rams leaping
in a grassy plain, with the young sheep frisking round them.—*Plain Commentary.*

Verses 4—6.—When Christ descends upon the soul in the work of conversion,
what strength doth he put forth !   The strongholds of sin are battered down, every
high thing that exalts itself against the knowledge of Christ is brought into captivity
to the obedience of his sceptre, 2 Cor. x. 4, 5.   Devils are cast out of the possession
which they have kept for many years without the least disturbance.   Strong lusts
are mortified and the very constitution of the soul is changed.   *"What ailed thee,
O thou sea, that thou fleddest ? thou Jordan, that thou wast driven back ? ye mountains,
that ye skipped like rams ?"* etc.   The prophet speaks those words of the powerful
entrance of the children of Israel into Canaan.   The like is done by Christ in the

conversion of a sinner. Jordan is driven back, the whole course of the soul is altered, the mountains skip like rams. There are many mountains in the soul of a sinner, as pride, unbelief, self-conceitedness, atheism, profaneness, etc. These mountains are plucked up by the roots in a moment when Christ begins the work of conversion. —*Ralph Robinson.*

Verse 5.—

> Fly where thou wilt, O sea !
> And Jordan's current cease !
> Jordan, there is no need of thee,
> For at God's word, whene'er he please,
> The rocks shall weep new waters forth instead of these.
>
> *Abraham Cowley.*

Verses 5, 6.—A singular animation and an almost dramatic force are given to the poem by the beautiful apostrophe in verses 5, 6, and the effect of this is heightened in a remarkable degree by the use of the present tenses. The awe and the trembling of nature are a spectacle on which the poet is looking. The parted sea through which Israel walks as on dry land, the rushing Jordan arrested in its course, the granite cliffs of Sinai shaken to their base—he sees it all, and asks in wonder what it means ?—*J. J. Stewart Perowne.*

Verses 5, 6.—This questioning teaches us that we should ourselves consider and inquire concerning the reason of those things, which we see to have been done in a wondrous way, out of the course of nature. There are signs in the sun, moon, stars, heaven, etc., concerning which Christ has spoken. Let us inquire the reason why they are, that we be not stupid and inaccurate spectators. The things which are done miraculously do speak : and they can give answer why they are done. Nay, rather, portents, signs, earthquakes, extraordinary appearances are loud-speaking, and they declare from themselves what they are : namely, that they are prophetic of the anger and future vengeance of God. Such inquiry as this is not prying curiosity, but is pious and useful, working to this end, that we become observant of the judgments of God, with which he visits this world, and yield ourselves to his grace, and so we escape the coming vengeance.—*Wolfgang Musculus.*

Verses 5, 6.—

> What ails thee, sea, to part,
> Thee, Jordan, back to start ?
> Ye mountains, like the rams to leap,
> Ye little hills, like sheep ?
>
> *John Keble.*

Verse 7.—"*Tremble, thou earth.*" Hebrew, *Be in pain*, as a travailing woman ; for if the giving of the law had such dreadful effects, what should the breaking thereof have ?—*John Trapp.*

Verse 7.—

> " At the presence of the Lord be in pangs, O earth.'

"*Lord,*" *Adon,* the Sovereign Ruler. " Pangs," *Chuli* : Mic. iv. 10. The convulsions of nature, which accompanied the Exodus, were as the birth-throes of the Israelite people. " A nation was born in a day." But the deliverance out of Babylon saw the prelude to a far more wondrous truth ;—that of him, in whom nature was to be regenerated.—*William Kay.*

Verses 7, 8.—"*Tremble,*" etc. This is an answer to the preceding question : as if he had said, It is no wonder that Sinai, and Horeb, and a few adjoining hills should tremble at the majestic presence of God ; for the whole earth must do so, whenever he pleases.—*Thomas Fenton.*

Verse 8.—"*Which turned the rock into a standing water.*" *Into a pool.* The divine poet represents the very substance of the rock as being converted into water, not literally, but poetically ; thus ornamenting his sketch of the wondrous power displayed on this occasion.—*William Walford.*

Verse 8.—The remarkable rock in Sinai which tradition regards as the one which Moses smote, is at least well chosen in regard to its situation, whatever opinion we may form of the truth of that tradition, which it seems to be the disposition of late travellers to regard with more respect than was formerly entertained. It is an isolated mass of granite, nearly twenty feet square and high, with its base concealed in the earth—we are left to conjecture to what depth. In the face of the rock are a number of horizontal fissures, at unequal distances from each other ; some near the top, and others at a little distance from the surface of the ground. An American traveller* says : " The colour and whole appearance of the rock are such that, if seen elsewhere, and disconnected from all traditions, no one would hesitate to believe that they had been produced by water flowing from these fissures. I think it would be extremely difficult to form these fissures or produce these appearances by art. It is not less difficult to believe that a natural fountain should flow at the height of a dozen feet out of the face of an isolated rock. Believing, as I do, that the water was brought out of a rock belonging to this mountain, I can see nothing incredible in the opinion that this is the identical rock, and that these fissures, and the other appearances, should be regarded as evidences of the fact."—*John Kitto.*

Verse 8.—Shall *the hard rock be turned into a standing water, and the flint-stone into a springing well ?* and shall not our hard and flinty hearts, in consideration of our own miseries, and God's unspeakable mercies in delivering us from evil, (if not gush forth into fountains of tears) express so much as a little *standing water* in our eyes ? It is our hard heart indeed, *quod nec compunctione scinditur, nec pietate mollitur, nec movetur precibus, minis non cedit, flagellis duratur,†* etc. O Lord, touch thou the mountains and they shall smoke, touch our lips with a coal from thine altar, and our mouth shall show forth thy praise. Smite, Lord, our flinty hearts as hard as the nether millstone, with the hammer of thy word, and mollify them also with the drops of thy mercies and dew of thy Spirit ; make them humble, fleshy, flexible, circumcised, soft, obedient, new, clean, broken, and then " a broken and a contrite heart, O God, shalt thou not despise." Ps. li. 17. " O Lord my God, give me grace from the very bottom of my heart to desire thee ; in desiring, to seek thee ; in seeking, to find ; in finding, to love thee ; in loving, utterly to loathe my former wickedness ; " that living in thy fear, and dying in thy favour, when I have passed through this Egypt and wilderness of this world, I may possess the heavenly Canaan and happy land of promise, prepared for all such as love thy coming, even for every Christian one, which is thy *"dominion"* and *"sanctuary."‡*—*John Boys.*

Verse 8.—The same almighty power that turned waters into a rock to be a wall to Israel (Exod. xiv. 22), turned the rock into waters to be a well to Israel. As they were protected, so they were provided for, by miracles, standing miracles ; for such was the standing water, that fountain of waters, into which the rock, the flinty rock, was turned, " and that rock was Christ," 1 Cor. x. 4. For he is a fountain of living waters to his Israel, from whom they receive grace for grace.—*Matthew Henry.*

Verse 8.—*"The flint into a fountain of waters."* The causing of water to gush forth out of the flinty rock is a practical proof of unlimited omnipotence and of the grace which converts death into life. Let the earth then tremble before the Lord, the God of Jacob. It has always trembled before him, and before him let it tremble. For that which he has been he still ever is ; and as he came once he will come again. —*Franz Delitzsch*

HINTS TO PREACHERS.

Verses 1, 2.—The time of first delivery from sin a season notable for the peculiar presence of God.

Verses 1, 2.—The Lord was to his people—I. A deliverer. II. A priest—" his sanctuary." III. A king—" his dominion."

Verses 1, 7.—" The house of Jacob " and " the God of Jacob," the relation between the two.

Verse 2.—The church the temple of sanctity and the domain of obedience.

---

* Dr. Olin. † Bernard. ‡ Augustine.

Verse 3.—The impenitence of sinners rebuked by the inanimate creation.

Verse 3.—" Jordan was driven back," or death overcome.

Verse 4.—The movableness of things which appear to be fixed and settled. God's power of creating a stir in lethargic minds, among ancient systems, and prejudiced persons of the highest rank.

Verses 7, 8.—Holy awe. I. Should be caused by the fact of the divine presence. Should be increased by his covenant character—" the God of Jacob." III. Should culminate when we see displays of his grace towards his people—" which turned," etc. IV. Should become universal.

Verse 8.—Wonders akin to the miracle at the rock. I. Christ's death the source of life. II. Adversity a means of prosperity. III. Hard hearts made penitent. IV. Barrenness of soul turned into abundance.

Verse 8.—Divine supplies. 1. Sure—for he will fetch them even from a rock 2. Plentiful—" a mere or standing water." 3. Continual " fountain of waters.'. 4. Instructive. Should create in us holy awe at the power, etc., of the Lord.

PSALM CXV.

SUBJECT.—*In the former Psalm the past wonders which God had wrought were recounted to his honour, and in the present Psalm he is entreated to glorify himself again, because the heathen were presuming upon the absence of miracles, were altogether denying the miracles of former ages, and insulting the people of God with the question, "Where is now their God?" It grieved the heart of the godly that Jehovah should be thus dishonoured, and treating their own condition of reproach as unworthy of notice, they beseech the Lord at least to vindicate his own name. The Psalmist is evidently indignant that the worshippers of foolish idols should be able to put such a taunting question to the people who worshipped the only living and true God; and having spent his indignation in sarcasm upon the images and their makers, he proceeds to exhort the house of Israel to trust in God and bless his name. As those who were dead and gone could no longer sing Psalms unto the Lord among the sons of men, he exhorts the faithful who were then living to take care that God is not robbed of his praise, and then he closes with an exulting Hallelujah. Should not living men extol the living God?*

DIVISION.—*For the better expounding of it, the Psalm may be divided into an entreaty of God to vindicate his own honour, verses 1, 2; a contemptuous description of the false gods and their worshippers, 3—8; an exhortation to the faithful to trust in God and to expect great blessings from him, 9—15; an explanation of God's relationship to their present condition of things, verse 16; and a reminder that, not the dead, but the living, must continually praise God here below, 17, 18.*

EXPOSITION.

NOT unto us, O LORD, not unto us, but unto thy name give glory, for thy mercy, *and* for thy truth's sake.

2 Wherefore should the heathen say, Where *is* now their God?

1. It will be well to remember that this Psalm was sung at the Passover, and therefore it bears relationship to the deliverance from Egypt. The burden of it seems to be a prayer that the living God, who had been so glorious at the Red Sea and at the Jordan, should again for his name's sake display the wonders of his power. "*Not unto us, O LORD, not unto us, but unto thy name give glory.*" The people undoubtedly wished for relief from the contemptuous insults of idolaters, but their main desire was that Jehovah himself should no longer be the object of heathen insults. The saddest part of all their trouble was that their God was no longer feared and dreaded by their adversaries. When Israel marched into Canaan, a terror was upon all the people round about, because of Jehovah, the mighty God; but this dread the nations had shaken off since there had been of late no remarkable display of miraculous power. Therefore Israel cried unto her God that he would again make bare his arm as in the day when he cut Rahab and wounded the dragon. The prayer is evidently tinctured with a consciousness of unworthiness; because of their past unfaithfulness they hardly dared to appeal to the covenant, and to ask blessings for themselves, but they fell back upon the honour of the Lord their God—an old style of argument which their great lawgiver, Moses, had used with such effect when he pleaded, "Wherefore should the Egyptians speak and say, For mischief did he bring them out, to slay them in the mountains, and to consume them from the face of the earth? Turn from thy fierce wrath, and repent of this evil against thy people." Joshua also used the like argument when he said, "What wilt thou do unto thy great name?" In such manner also let us pray when no other plea is available because of our sense of sin; for the Lord is always jealous of his honour, and will work for his name's sake when no other motive will move him.

The repetition of the words, "Not unto us," would seem to indicate a very serious desire to renounce any glory which they might at any time have proudly appropriated to themselves, and it also sets forth the vehemence of their wish that God would at any cost to them magnify his own name. They loathed the idea of seeking their own glory, and rejected the thought with the utmost detestation; again and again disclaiming any self-glorifying motive in their supplication. *"For thy mercy, and for thy truth's sake."* These attributes seemed most in jeopardy. How could the heathen think Jehovah to be a merciful God if he gave his people over to the hands of their enemies? How could they believe him to be faithful and true if, after all his solemn covenant engagements, he utterly rejected his chosen nation? God is very jealous of the two glorious attributes of grace and truth, and the plea that these may not be dishonoured has great weight with him. In these times, when the first victories of the gospel are only remembered as histories of a dim and distant past, sceptics are apt to boast that the gospel has lost its youthful strength and they even presume to cast a slur upon the name of God himself. We may therefore rightly entreat the divine interposition that the apparent blot may be removed from his escutcheon, and that his own word may shine forth gloriously as in the days of old. We may not desire the triumph of our opinions, for our own sakes, or for the honour of a sect, but we may confidently pray for the triumph of truth, that God himself may be honoured.

2. *"Wherefore should the heathen say, Where is now their God?"* Or, more literally, "Where, pray, is their God?" Why should the nations be allowed with a sneer of contempt to question the existence, and mercy, and faithfulness of Jehovah? They are always ready to blaspheme; we may well pray that they may not derive a reason for so doing from the course of providence, or the decline of the church. When they see the godly down-trodden while they themselves live at ease, and act the part of persecutors, they are very apt to speak as if they had triumphed over God himself, or as if he had altogether left the field of action and deserted his saints. When the prayers and tears of the godly seem to be unregarded, and their miseries are rather increased than assuaged, then do the wicked multiply their taunts and jeers, and even argue that their own wretched irreligion is better than the faith of Christians, because for the present their condition is so much preferable to that of the afflicted saints. And, truly, this is the very sting of the trials of God's chosen when they see the veracity of the Lord questioned, and the name of God profaned because of their sufferings. If they could hope that some good result would come out of all this they would endure it with patience; but as they are unable to perceive any desirable result consequent thereon, they enquire with holy anxiety, "Wherefore should the heathen be permitted to speak thus?" It is a question to which it would be hard to reply, and yet no doubt there is an answer. Sometimes the nations are permitted thus to blaspheme, in order that they may fill up the measure of their iniquity, and in order that the subsequent interposition of God may be rendered the more illustrious in contrast with their profane boastings. Do they say, "Where is now their God?" They shall know by-and-by, for it is written, "Ah, I will ease me of mine adversaries"; they shall know it also when the righteous shall "shine forth as the sun in the kingdom of their Father." Do they say, "Where is the promise of his coming?" That coming shall be speedy and terrible to them. In our own case, by our own lukewarmness and the neglect of faithful gospel preaching, we have permitted the uprise and spread of modern doubt, and we are bound to confess it with deep sorrow of soul; yet we may not therefore lose heart, but may still plead with God to save his own truth and grace from the contempt of men of the world. Our honour and the honour of the church are small matters, but the glory of God is the jewel of the universe, of which all else is but the setting; and we may come to the Lord and plead his jealousy for his name, being well assured that he will not suffer that name to be dishonoured. Wherefore should the pretended wise men of the period be permitted to say that they doubt the personality of God? Wherefore should they say that answers to prayer are pious delusions, and that the resurrection and the deity of our Lord Jesus are moot points? Wherefore should they be permitted to speak disparagingly of atonement by blood and by price, and reject utterly the doctrine of the wrath of God against sin, even that wrath which burneth for ever and ever? They speak exceeding proudly, and only God can stop their arrogant blusterings: let us by extraordinary intercession prevail upon him to interpose, by giving to his gospel such a triumphant vindication as shall utterly silence the perverse opposition of ungodly men.

3 But our God *is* in the heavens: he hath done whatsoever he hath pleased.

4 Their idols *are* silver and gold, the work of men's hands.

5 They have mouths, but they speak not : eyes have they, but they see not :

6 They have ears, but they hear not : noses have they, but they smell not :

7 They have hands, but they handle not : feet have they, but they walk not : neither speak they through their throat.

8 They that make them are like unto them ; *so is* every one that trusteth in them.

3. *"But our God is in the heavens"*—where he should be ; above the reach of mortal sneers, over-hearing all the vain janglings of men, but looking down with silent scorn upon the makers of the babel. Supreme above all opposing powers, the Lord reigneth upon a throne high and lifted up. Incomprehensible in essence, he rises above the loftiest thought of the wise ; absolute in will and infinite in power, he is superior to the limitations which belong to earth and time. This God is *our* God, and we are not ashamed to own him, albeit he may not work miracles at the beck and call of every vain-glorious boaster who may choose to challenge him. Once they bade his Son come down from the cross and they would believe in him, now they would have God overstep the ordinary bounds of his providence and come down from heaven to convince them : but other matters occupy his august mind besides the convincement of those who wilfully shut their eyes to the super-abundant evidences of his divine power and Godhead, which are all around them. If our God be neither seen nor heard, and is not to be worshipped under any outward symbol, yet is he none the less real and true, for he is where his adversaries can never be—in the heavens, whence he stretches forth his sceptre, and rules with boundless power.

"He hath done whatsoever he hath pleased." Up till this moment his decrees have been fulfilled, and his eternal purposes accomplished ; he has not been asleep, nor oblivious of the affairs of men ; he has worked, and he has worked effectually, none have been able to thwart, nor even so much as to hinder him. " Whatsoever he hath pleased " : however distasteful to his enemies, the Lord has accomplished all his good pleasure without difficulty ; even when his adversaries raved and raged against him they have been compelled to carry out his designs against their will. Even proud Pharoah, when most defiant of the Lord was but as clay upon the potter's wheel, and the Lord's end and design in him were fully answered. We may well endure the jeering question, " Where is now their God ? " while we are perfectly sure that his providence is undisturbed, his throne unshaken, and his purposes unchanged. What he hath done he will yet do, his counsel shall stand, and he will do all his pleasure, and at the end of the great drama of human history, the omnipotence of God and his immutability and faithfulness will be more than vindicated to the eternal confusion of his adversaries.

4. *"Their idols are silver and gold."* mere dead inert matter ; at the best only made of precious metal, but that metal quite as powerless as the commonest wood or clay. The value of the idol shows the folly of the maker in wasting his substance, but certainly does not increase the power of the image, since there is no more life in silver and gold than in brass or iron. *"The work of men's hands."* Inasmuch as the maker is always greater than the thing that he has made, these idols are less to be honoured than the artificers, who fashioned them. How irrational that men should adore that which is less than themselves ! How strange that a man should think that he can make a god ! Can madness go further ? Our God is a spirit, and his hands made the heavens and the earth : well may we worship him, and we need not be disturbed at the sneering question of those who are so insane as to refuse to adore the living God, and yet bow their knees before images of their own carving. We may make an application of all this to the times in which we are now living. The god of modern thought is the creation of the thinker himself, evolved out of his own consciousness, or fashioned according to his own notion of what a god should be. Now, it is evident that such a being is no God. It is impossible that there should be a God at all except the God of revelation. A god who can be fashioned by our own thoughts is no more a god than the image manu-factured or produced by our own hands. The true God must of necessity be his own

revealer. It is clearly impossible that a being who can be excogitated and comprehended by the reason of man should be the infinite and incomprehensible God. Their idols are blinded reason and diseased thought, the product of men's muddled brains, and they will come to nought.

5. "*They have mouths, but they speak not.*" The idols cannot utter even the faintest sound, they cannot communicate with their worshippers, they can neither promise nor threaten, command nor console, explain the past nor prophesy the future. If they had no mouths they might not be expected to speak, but having mouths and speaking not, they are mere dumb idols, and not worthy to be compared with the Lord God who thundered at Sinai, who in old time spake by his servants the prophets, and whose voice even now breaketh the cedars of Lebanon. "*Eyes have they, but they see not.*" They cannot tell who their worshippers may be or what they offer. Certain idols have had jewels in their eyes more precious than a king's ransom, but they were as blind as the rest of the fraternity. A god who has eyes, and cannot see, is a blind deity ; and blindness is a calamity, and not an attribute of godhead. He must be very blind who worships a blind god : we *pity* a blind man, it is strange to *worship* a blind image.

6. "*They have ears, but they hear not.*" The Psalmist might have pointed to the monstrous ears with which some heathen deities are disfigured,—truly they *have* ears ; but no prayer of their votaries, though shouted by a million voices, can ever be heard by them. How can gold and silver hear, and how can a rational being address petitions to one who cannot even hear his words ? "*Noses have they, but they smell not.*" The Psalmist seems to heap together these sentences with something of the grim sardonic spirit of Elijah when he said, " Cry aloud : for he is a god ; either he is talking, or he is pursuing, or he is on a journey, or peradventure he sleepeth, and must be awaked." In sacred scorn he mocks at those who burn sweet spices, and fill their temples with clouds of smoke, all offered to an image whose nose cannot perceive the perfume. He seems to point his finger to every part of the countenance of the image, and thus pours contempt upon the noblest part of the idol, if any part of such a thing can be noble even in the least degree.

7. "*They have hands, but they handle not.*" Looking lower down upon the images, the Psalmist says, " They have hands, but they handle not," they cannot receive that which is handed to them, they cannot grasp the sceptre of power or the sword of vengeance, they can neither distribute benefits nor dispense judgments, and the most trifling act they are utterly unable to perform. An infant's hand excels them in power. "*Feet have they, but they walk not.*" They must be lifted into their places or they would never reach their shrines ; they must be fastened in their shrines or they would fall ; they must be carried or they could never move ; they cannot come to the rescue of their friends, nor escape the iconoclasm of their foes. The meanest insect has more power of locomotion than the greatest heathen god. "*Neither speak they through their throat.*" They cannot even reach so far as the guttural noise of the lowest order of beasts ; neither a grunt, nor a growl, nor a groan, nor so much as a mutter, can come from them. Their priests asserted that the images of the gods upon special occasions uttered hollow sounds, but it was a mere pretence, or a crafty artifice: images of gold or silver are incapable of living sounds. Thus has the Psalmist surveyed the idol from head to foot, looked in its face, and sounded its throat, and he writes it down as utterly contemptible.

8. "*They that make them are like unto them.*" Those who make such things for worship are as stupid, senseless, and irrational as the figures they construct. So far as any spiritual life, thought, and judgment are concerned, they are rather the images of men than rational beings. The censure is by no means too severe. Who has not found the words leaping to his lips when he has seen the idols of the Romanists ? "*So is every one that trusteth in them.*" Those who have sunk so low as to be capable of confiding in idols have reached the extreme of folly, and are worthy of as much contempt as their detestable deities. Luther's hard speeches were well deserved by the Papists ; they must be mere dolts to worship the rotten relics which are the objects of their veneration.

The god of modern thought exceedingly resembles the deities described in this Psalm. Pantheism is wondrously akin to Polytheism, and yet differs very little from Atheism. The god manufactured by our great thinkers is a mere abstraction : he has no eternal purposes, he does not interpose on the behalf of his people, he cares but very little as to how much man sins, for he has given to the initiated " a larger hope " by which the most incorrigible are to be restored. He is what the last set of critics chooses to make him, he has said what they choose to say, and he will do what they please to prescribe. Let this creed and its devotees alone, and they will work out their own refutation, for as now their god is fashioned like themselves, they will by degrees fashion themselves like their god ; and when the principles of justice, law, and order shall have all been effectually sapped we may possibly witness in some form of socialism, similar to that which is so sadly spreading in Germany, a repetition of the evils which have in former ages befallen nations which have refused the living God, and set up gods of their own.

9 O Israel, trust thou in the LORD : he *is* their help and their shield.

10 O house of Aaron, trust in the LORD : he *is* their help and their shield.

11 Ye that fear the LORD, trust in the LORD : he *is* their help and their shield,

12 The LORD hath been mindful of us : he will bless *us ;* he will bless the house of Israel ; he will bless the house of Aaron.

13 He will bless them that fear the LORD, *both* small and great.

14 The LORD shall increase you more and more, you and your children.

15 Ye *are* blessed of the LORD which made heaven and earth.

9. *"O Israel, trust thou in the LORD."* Whatever others do, let the elect of heaven keep fast to the God who chose them. Jehovah is the God of Jacob, let his children prove their loyalty to their God by their confidence in him. Whatever our trouble may be, and however fierce the blasphemous language of our enemies, let us not fear nor falter, but confidently rest in him who is able to vindicate his own honour, and protect his own servants. *"He is their help and their shield."* He is the friend of his servants, both actively and passively, giving them both aid in labour and defence in danger. In the use of the pronoun " their," the Psalmist may have spoken to himself, in a sort of soliloquy : he had given the exhortation, " trust in Jehovah," and then he whispers to himself, " They may well do so, for he is at all times the strength and security of his servants."

10. *"O house of Aaron, trust in the LORD."* You who are nearest to him, trust him most ; your very calling is connected with his truth and is meant to declare his glory, therefore never entertain a doubt concerning him, but lead the way in holy confidence. The priests were the leaders, teachers, and exemplars of the people, and therefore above all others they should place an unreserved reliance upon Israel's God. The Psalmist is glad to add that they did so, for he says, *"He is their help and their shield."* It is good to exhort those to faith who have faith : " These things have I written unto you that believe on the name of the Son of God; . . . that ye may believe on the name of the Son of God." We may stir up pure minds by way of remembrance, and exhort men to trust in the Lord because we know that they are trusting already.

11. The next verse is of the same tenor—"*Ye that fear the LORD, trust in the LORD,*" whether belonging to Israel, or to the house of Aaron, or not, all those who reverence Jehovah are permitted and commanded to confide in him. *"He is their help and their shield."* He does aid and protect all those who worship him in filial fear, to whatever nation they may belong. No doubt these repeated exhortations were rendered necessary by the trying condition in which the children of Israel were found : the sneers of the adversary would assail all the people, they would most bitterly be felt by the priests and ministers, and those who were secret proselytes would groan in secret under the contempt forced upon their religion and their God. All this would be very staggering to faith, and therefore they were bidden again and again and again to trust in Jehovah.

This must have been a very pleasant song to households in Babylon, or far away in Persia, when they met together in the night to eat the Paschal supper in a land which knew them not, where they wept as they remembered Zion. We seem to hear them repeating the three-fold word, " Trust in Jehovah," men and women and little children singing out their scorn of the dominant idolatry, and declaring their adhesion to the one God of Israel. In the same manner in this day of blasphemy and rebuke it becomes us all to abound in testimonies to the truth of God. The sceptic is loud in his unbelief, let us be equally open in the avowal of our faith.

12. *"The* LORD *hath been mindful of us,"* or " Jehovah hath remembered us." His past mercies prove that we are on his heart, and though for the present he may afflict us, yet he does not forget us. We have not to put him in remembrance as though he found it hard to recollect his children, but he hath remembered us and therefore he will in future deal well with us. *"He will bless us."* The word *"us"* is supplied by the translators, and is superfluous, the passage should run, *"He will bless ; he will bless the house of Israel ; he will bless the house of Aaron."* The repetition of the word " bless " adds great effect to the passage. The Lord has many blessings, each one worthy to be remembered, he blesses and blesses and blesses again. Where he has once bestowed his favour he continues it ; his blessing delights to visit the same house very often and to abide where it has once lodged. Blessing does not impoverish the Lord : he has multiplied his mercies in the past, and he will pour them forth thick and threefold in the future. He will have a general blessing for all who fear him, a peculiar blessing for the whole house of Israel, and a double blessing for the sons of Aaron. It is his nature to bless, it is his prerogative to bless, it is his glory to bless, it is his delight to bless ; he has promised to bless, and therefore be sure of this, that he will bless and bless and bless without ceasing.

13. *"He will bless them that fear the* LORD, *both small and great."* So long as a man fears the Lord it matters nothing whether he be prince or peasant, patriarch or pauper, God will assuredly bless him. He supplies the want of every living thing, from the leviathan of the sea to the insect upon a leaf, and he will suffer none of the godly to be forgotten, however small their abilities, or mean their position. This is a sweet cordial for those who are little in faith, and own themselves to be mere babes in the family of grace. There is the same blessing for the least saint as for the greatest ; yea, if anything, the " small " shall be first ; for as the necessity is the more pressing, the supply shall be the more speedy.

14. *"The* LORD *shall increase you more and more, you and your children."* Just as in Egypt he multiplied the people exceedingly, so will he increase the number of his saints upon the earth ; not only shall the faithful be blessed with converts, and so with a spiritual seed ; but those who are their spiritual children shall become fruitful also, and thus the multitude of the elect shall be accomplished ; God shall increase the people, and shall increase the joy. Even to the end of the ages the race of true believers shall be continued, and shall growingly multiply in number and in power. The first blessing upon mankind was, " Be fruitful, and multiply, and replenish the earth " ; and it is this blessing which God now pronounces upon them that fear him. Despite the idols of philosophy and sacramentarianism, the truth shall gather its disciples, and fill the land with its defenders.

15. *"Ye are blessed of the* LORD *which made heaven and earth."* This is another form of the blessing of Melchizedek : " Blessed be Abram of the Most High God, possessor of heaven and earth " ; and upon us through our great Melchizedek this same benediction rests. It is an omnipotent blessing, conveying to us all that an Almighty God can do, whether in heaven or on earth. This fulness is infinite, and the consolation which it brings is unfailing ; he that made heaven and earth can give us all things while we dwell below, and bring us safely to his palace above. Happy are the people upon whom such a blessing rests ; their portion is infinitely above that of those whose only hope lies in a piece of gilded wood, or an image of sculptured stone.

16 The heaven, *even* the heavens, *are* the LORD'S : but the earth hath he given to the children of men.

16. *"The heaven, even the heavens, are the* LORD'S." There he specially reigns, and manifests his greatness and his glory : *"but the earth hath he given to the children of men."* He hath left the world during the present dispensation in a great measure under the power and will of men, so that things are not here below in the same perfect order as the things which are above. It is true the Lord rules over all things by his providence, but yet he allows and permits men to break his laws and persecute his people for the time being, and to set up their dumb idols in opposition to him. The free agency which he gave to his creatures necessitated that in some degree he should restrain his power and suffer the children of men to follow their own devices ; yet nevertheless, since he has not vacated heaven, he is still master of earth, and can at any time gather up all the reins into his own hands. Perhaps,

however, the passage is meant to have another meaning, viz., that God will increase his people, because he has given the earth to them, and intends that they shall fill it. Man was constituted originally God's vicegerent over the world, and though so yet we see not all things put under him, we see Jesus exalted on high, and in him the children of men shall receive a loftier dominion even on earth than as yet they have known. "The meek shall inherit the earth ; and shall delight themselves in the abundance of peace " : and our Lord Jesus shall reign amongst his ancients gloriously. All this will reflect the exceeding glory of him who reveals himself personally in heaven, and in the mystical body of Christ below. The earth belongs to the sons of God, and we are bound to subdue it for our Lord Jesus, for he must reign. The Lord hath given him the heathen for his inheritance, and the uttermost parts of the earth for his possession.

17 The dead praise not the LORD, neither any that go down into silence.

18 But we will bless the LORD from this time forth and for evermore. Praise the LORD.

17. *"The dead praise not the LORD "*—so far as this world is concerned. They cannot unite in the Psalms and hymns and spiritual songs with which the church delights to adore her Lord. The preacher cannot magnify the Lord from his coffin, nor the Christian worker further manifest the power of divine grace by daily activity while he lies in the grave. *"Neither any that go down into silence."* The tomb sends forth no voice ; from mouldering bones and flesh-consuming worms there arises no sound of gospel ministry nor of gracious song. One by one the singers in the consecrated choir of saints steal away from us, and we miss their music. Thank God, they have gone above to swell the harmonies of the skies, but as far as we are concerned, we have need to sing all the more earnestly because so many songsters have left our choirs.

18. *"But we will bless the LORD from this time forth and for evermore."* We who are still living will take care that the praises of God shall not fail among the sons of men. Our afflictions and depressions of spirit shall not cause us to suspend our praises ; neither shall old age, and increasing infirmities damp the celestial fires, nay, nor shall even death itself cause us to cease from the delightful occupation. The spiritually dead cannot praise God, but the life within us constrains us to do so. The ungodly may abide in silence, but we will lift up our voices to the praise of Jehovah. Even though for a time he may work no miracle, and we may see no peculiar interposition of his power, yet on the strength of what he has done in ages past we will continue to laud his name " until the day break, and the shadows flee away," when he shall once more shine forth as the sun to gladden the faces of his children. The present time is auspicious for commencing a life of praise, since to-day he bids us hear his voice of mercy. " From this time forth " is the suggestion of wisdom, for this duty ought not to be delayed ; and it is the dictate of gratitude, for there are pressing reasons for prompt thankfulness. Once begin praising God and we have entered upon an endless service. Even eternity cannot exhaust the reasons why God should be glorified. *"Praise the LORD,"* or Hallelujah. Though the dead cannot, and the wicked will not, and the careless do not praise God, yet we will shout " Hallelujah " for ever and ever. Amen.

EXPLANATORY NOTES AND QUAINT SAYINGS.

Whole Psalm.—Several manuscripts and editions, also the Septuagint, the Syriac, and many of the old translators join this Psalm to the preceding, and make one of them. But the argument and the arrangement of the two Psalms do not allow of the least doubt as to their original independence of each other.—*Justus Olshausen.*

Verse 1.—*"Not unto us, O LORD, not unto us, but unto thy name give glory."* The Psalmist, by this repetition, implies our natural tendency to self-idolatry, and to magnifying of ourselves, and the difficulty of cleansing our hearts from these self-reflections. If it be angelical to refuse an undue glory stolen from God's throne,

Rev. xxii. 8, 9 ; it is diabolical to accept and cherish it. " To seek our own glory is not glory," Prov. xxv. 27. It is vile, and the dishonour of a creature, who, by the law of his creation, is referred to another end. So much as we sacrifice to our own credit, to the dexterity of our hands, or the sagacity of our wit, we detract from God.—*Stephen Charnock.*

Verse 1.—*"Not unto us, but unto thy name give glory,"* etc. This is not a doxology, or form of thanksgiving, but a prayer. Not for our safety or welfare, so much as for thy glory, be pleased to deliver us. Not to satisfy our revenge upon our adversaries ; not for the establishment of our own interest ; but for the glory of thy grace and truth do we seek thine aid, that thou mayest be known to be a God keeping covenant ; for mercy and truth are the two pillars of that covenant. It is a great dishonouring of God when anything is sought from him more than himself, or not for himself. Saith Austin, it is but a carnal affection in prayer when men seek self more than God. Self and God are the two things that come in competition. Now there are several sorts of self ; there is carnal self, natural self, and glorified self ; above all these God must have the pre-eminence.—*Thomas Manton.*

Verse 1.—There are many sweet and precious texts of Scripture which are so endeared, and have become so habituated to us, and we to them, that one cannot but think we must carry them with us to heaven, and that they will form not only the theme of our song, but a portion of our blessedness and joy even in that happy home. . . . But if there be one text which more especially belongs to all, and which must, I think, break forth from *every* redeemed one as he enters heaven, and form the unwearying theme of eternity, it is the first verse of this Psalm. I am sure that not one of the Lord's chosen ones on earth, as he reviews the way by which he has been led, as he sees enemy after enemy prostrate before his utter feebleness, and has such thorough evidence and conviction that his weakness is made perfect in the Lord's strength, but must, from the very ground of his heart, say, *"Not unto us, O LORD, not unto us, but unto thy name "* be the praise and the glory ascribed. And could we see heaven opened—could we hear its glad and glorious hallelujahs —could we see its innumerable company of angels, and its band of glorified saints, as they cast their crowns before the throne, we should hear as the universal chorus from every lip, *"Not unto us, O LORD, not unto us, but unto thy name give glory, for thy mercy, and for thy truth's sake."* I know not why this should not be as gladly and as gratefully the angel's song as the song of the redeemed : they stand not in their own might nor power,—they kept not their first estate through any inherent strength of their own, but, like their feebler brethren of the human race, are equally " kept by the power of God " ; and from their ranks, I doubt not, is re-echoed the same glorious strain, *"Not unto us, O LORD, not unto us, but unto thy name give glory."* Even our blessed Lord, as on that night of sorrow he sung this hymn of praise, could truly say, in that nature which had sinned, and which was to suffer, " Not unto us,"—not unto man, be ascribed the glory of this great salvation, which I am now with my own blood to purchase, but unto thy name and thy love be the praise given.—*Barton Bouchier.*

Verse 1.—*"Non nobis, Domine, sed tibi sit gloria."* A part of the Latin version of this Psalm is frequently sung after grace at public dinners, but why we can hardly imagine, except it be for fear that donors should be proud of the guineas they have promised, or gourmands should be vainglorious under the influence of their mighty feeding.—*C. H. S.*

Verses 1, 2.—He, in a very short space, assigns three reasons why God should seek the glory of his name in preserving his people. First, because he is merciful ; secondly, because he is true and faithful in observing his promise ; thirdly, that the Gentiles may not see God's people in a state of destitution, and find cause for blaspheming him or them. He therefore says, *"for thy mercy, and for thy truth's sake,"* show thy glory, or give glory to thy name, for it is then thy glory will be exhibited when thou showest mercy to thy people ; and then thou wilt have carried out the truth of the promise which thou hast made to our fathers. *"Lest the Gentiles should say, Where is their God ? "* lest the incredulous Gentiles should get an occasion of detracting from thy power, and, perhaps, of ignoring thy very existence.—*Robert Bellarmine.*

Verses 2, 3.—If God be everywhere, why doth Christ teach us to pray, " Our Father which art in heaven " ? And when the heathen made that scoffing demand, *"Where is now their God ? "* why did David answer, *"Our God is in the heavens " ?*

To these and all other texts of like import we may answer ; *heaven* is not there spoken of as bounding the presence of God, but as guiding the faith and hope of man. " In the morning " (saith David, Ps. v. 3) " will I direct my prayer unto thee, amd will look up." When the eye hath no sight of any help on earth, then faith may have the clearest vision of it in heaven. And while God appears so little in any gracious dispensation for his people on earth, that the enemy begins to scoff, *"Where is now their God ? "* then his people have recourse by faith to heaven, where the Lord not only is, but is glorious in his appearings. From whence as he the better seeth how it is with us, so he seems to have a position of advantage for relieving us.—*Joseph Caryl.*

Verses 2—8.—Contrast Jehovah with any other God. Why should the heathen say, "Where, pray, (אּ) *is your God ? "* Take up Moses' brief description in Deut. iv. 28, and expand it as is done here. Idols of gold and silver have a *mouth*, but give no counsel to their worshippers ; *eyes*, but see not the devotions nor the wants of those who serve them ; *ears*, but hear not their cries of distress or songs of praise ; *nostrils*, but smell not the fragrant incense presented to their images ; *hands*, but the thunderbolt which they seem to hold (as Jupiter Tonans in after days), is a *brutum fulmen*, they cannot launch it ; *feet*, but they cannot move to help the fallen. Ah ! they cannot so much as whisper one syllable of response, or even mutter in their throat ! And as man becomes like his God, (witness Hindoo idolaters whose cruelty is just the reflection of the cruelty of their gods,) so these gods of the heathen being " soul-less, the worshippers become soul-less themselves " (Tholuck).— *Andrew A. Bonar.*

Verse 3.—*"And our God (is) in heaven ; all that he pleased he has done."* The word *"and,"* though foreign from our idiom, adds sensibly to the force of the expression. They ask thus, as if our God were absent or had no existence ; and yet all the while our God is in heaven, in his exalted and glorious dwelling-place.—*Joseph Addison Alexander.*

Verse 3 *(first clause).*—It would be folly to assert the like concerning idols; therefore, if the heathen say, *Where is your God ?* we reply, *He is in heaven,* etc. : but where are your idols ? In the earth, not making the earth, but made from the earth, etc.—*Martin Geier.*

Verse 3.—*"But our God is in the heavens."* When they place God in heaven, they do not confine him to a certain locality, nor set limits to his infinite essence ; but on the contrary they deny the limitation of his power, its being shut up to human instrumentality only, or its being subject to fate or fortune. In short, they put the universe under his control ; and teach us that, being superior to every obstruction, he does freely everything that may seem good to him. This truth is still more plainly asserted in the subsequent clause, *"he hath done whatsoever he hath pleased."* God then may be said to dwell in heaven, as the world is subject to his will, and nothing can prevent his accomplishing his purposes.—*John Calvin.*

Verse 4.—*"Their idols are silver and gold."* Can there be anything more absurd than to expect assistance from them, since neither the materials of which they are formed, nor the forms which are given them by the hand of men possess the smallest porton of divinity so as to command respect for them. At the same time, the prophet tacitly indicates that the value of the material does not invest the idols with more excellence, so that they deserve to be more highly esteemed. Hence the passage may be translated adversatively, thus, Though they are of gold and silver, yet they are not gods, because they are the work of men's hands.—*John Calvin.*

Verse 4.—*"Their idols are silver,"* etc. They are metal, stone, and wood. They are genererally made in the form of man, but can neither see, hear, smell, feel, walk, nor speak. How brutish to trust in such ! and next to them, in stupidity and inanity, must they be who form them, with the expectation of deriving any good from them. So obviously vain was the whole system of idolatry that the more serious heathens ridiculed it, and it was a butt for the jests of their freethinkers and buffoons. How keen are these words of Juvenal !

> Audis,
> Jupiter, hæc ? nec labra moves, cum mittere vocem
> Debueras, vel marmoreus vel aheneus ? aut cur
> In carbone tuo charta pia thura soluta
> Ponimus, et sectum vituli jecur, albaque porci
> Omenta ? ut video, nullum discrimen habendum est
> Effigies inter vestras, statuamque Bathylli.   Sat. xiii., ver. 113.

" Dost thou hear, O Jupiter, these things ? nor move thy lips when thou oughtest to speak out, whether thou art of marble or of bronze ? Or, why do we put the sacred incense on thy altar from the opened paper, and the extracted liver of a calf, and the white caul of a hog ? As far as I can discern, there is no difference between thy statue and that of Bathyllus."

This irony will appear the keener, when it is known that Bathyllus was a fiddler and player, whose image, by the order of Polycrates, was erected in the temple of Juno at Samos.—*Adam Clarke.*

Verse 4.—"*Idols.*" Idolators plead in behalf of their idols, that they are only intended to represent their gods, and to maintain a more abiding sense of their presence. The Spirit, however, does not allow this plea, and treats their images as the very gods they worship. The gods they profess to represent do not really exist, and therefore their worship is altogether vain and foolish. Must not the same be said of the pretended worship of many in the present day, who would encumber their worship with representative rites and ceremonies, or expressive symbols, or frame to themselves in their imaginations a god other than the God of revelation ?—*W. Wilson.*

Verse 4.—"*Silver and gold* "—proper things to make money of, but not to make gods of.—*Matthew Henry,*

Verse 4.—"*The work of men's hands.*" The following advertisement is copied from a Chinese newspaper :—" Archen Tea Chinchin, sculptor, respectfully acquaints masters of ships, trading from Canton to India, that they may be furnished with figure-heads of any size, according to order, at one-fourth of the price charged in Europe. He also recommends for private venture, the following idols, brass, gold, and silver : the hawk of Vishnoo, which has reliefs of his incarnation in a fish, boar, lion, and turtle. An Egyptian apis, a golden calf and bull, as worshipped by the pious followers of Zoroaster. Two silver mammosits, with golden ear-rings ; an aprimanes, for Persian worship ; a ram, an alligator, a crab, a laughing hyena, with a variety of household gods on a small scale, calculated for family worship. Eighteen months' credit will be given, or a discount of fifteen per cent. for prompt payment of the sum affixed to each article. Direct, China-street, Canton, under the marble Rhinoceros and Gilt Hydra."—*Arvine's Anecdotes.*

Verse 4.—"*The work of men's hands.*" Works, and not the makers of works.—*Adam Clarke.*

Verse 4.—"*The work of men's hands.*" And therefore they must needs be goodly gods, when made by bunglers especially, as was the rood of *Cockram,* which if it were not good enough to make a god would make an excellent devil, as the Mayor of Doncaster merrily told the complainants.—*John Trapp.*

Verses 4—7.—A beautiful contrast is formed between the God of Israel and the heathen idols. He made everything, they are themselves made by men ; he is in heaven, they are upon earth ; he doeth whatsoever he pleaseth, they can do nothing ; he seeth the distresses, heareth and answereth the prayers, accepteth the offerings, cometh to the assistance, and effecteth the salvation of his servants ; they are blind, deaf, and dumb, senseless, motionless, and impotent. Equally slow to hear, equally impotent to save, in time of greatest need, will every worldly idol prove, on which men have set their affections, and to which they have, in effect, said, " Thou art my God."—*George Horne.*

Verses 4—7.—In Alexandria there was a most famous building called the *Serapion,* a temple of *Serapis,* who presided over the inundations of the Nile, and the fertility of Egypt. It was a vast structure of masonry, crowning a hill in the centre of the city, and was ascended by a hundred steps. It was well fortified and very handsome. The statue of the god was a colossal image, which touched with outstretched hands, both sides of the building, while the head reached the lofty roof. It was adorned with rich metals and jewels.

The Emperor Theodosius, having commanded the demolition of the heathen temple, Theophilus, the bishop, attended by the soldiers, hastened to ascend the steps and enter the fane. The sight of the image, for a moment, made even the Christian destructives pause. The bishop ordered a soldier to strike without delay. With a hatchet he smote the statue on the knee. All waited in some emotion, but there was neither sound nor sign of divine anger. The soldiers next climbed to the head and struck it off. It rolled on the ground. A large family of rats, disturbed in their tranquil abode within the sacred image, poured out from the trembling statue and raced over the temple floor. The people now began to laugh, and to destroy with increased zeal. They dragged the fragments of the statue through the streets. Even the Pagans were disgusted with gods who did not defend themselves. The huge edifice was slowly destroyed, and a Christian church was built in its place. There was still some fear among the people that the Nile would show displeasure by refusing its usual inundation. But as the river rose with more than usual fulness and bounty, every anxiety was dispelled.—*Andrew Reed, in "The Story of Christianity," 1877.*

Verses 4—8.—Theodoret tells us of S. Publia, the aged abbess of a company of nuns at Antioch, who used to chant, as Julian went by in idolatrous procession, the Psalm, " Their idols are silver and gold, the work of men's hands. . . . They that make them are like unto them ; so is every one that trusteth in them " ; and he narrates how the angry Emperor caused his soldiers to buffet her till she bled, unable as he was to endure the sting of the old Hebrew song.—*Neale and Littledale.*

Verse 5.—"*Mouths, but they speak not.*" The noblest function of the mouth is to speak. Eyes, ears, and nose are the organs of certain senses. The mouth contains the organ of taste, and the hands and feet belong to the organ of touch, but speech is the glory of the mouth.—*James G. Murphy.*

Verse 6.—"*They have ears, but they hear not.*" But are as deaf as door-nails to the prayers of their suppliants. The Cretians pictured their Jupiter without ears, so little hearing or help they hoped for from him. Socrates, in contempt of heathen gods, swore by an oak, a goat, a dog ; as holding these better gods than those.— *John Trapp.*

Verse 7.—"*They have hands, but they handle not.*" Even their artist therefore surpasseth them, since he had the faculty of moulding them by the motion and functions of his limbs ; though thou wouldest be ashamed to worship that artist. Even thou surpassest them, though thou hast not made these things, since thou doest what they cannot do.—*Augustine.*

Verse 7.—"*Neither speak they through their throat.*" *Yehgu ;* not so much as the low faint moaning of a dove. Isaiah xxxviii. 14.—*William Kay.*

Verse 7.—"*Speak,*" or, as the Hebrew word likewise signifies, *breathe.* They are not only irrational, but also inanimate.—*Thomas Fenton.*

Verse 8.—"*They that make them are like unto them.*" They that make them *images* show their ingenuity, and doubtless are sensible men ; but they that make them *gods* show their stupidity, and are as senseless, blockish things as the idols themselves.—*Matthew Henry.*

Verse 8.—"*They that make them are like unto them.*" They are like idols, because, though they hear and see, it is more in appearance than in reality ; for they neither see nor hear the things that pertain to salvation, the things that only are worth seeing, so that they may be said more to dream than to see or hear ; as St. Mark has it, " Having eyes ye see not, having ears ye hear not."—*Robert Bellarmine.*

Verse 8.—"*Like unto them,*" etc. Every one is just what his God is ; whoever serves the Omnipotent is omnipotent with him : whoever exalts feebleness, in stupid delusion, to be his god, is feeble along with that god. This is an important preservative against fear for those who are sure that they worship the true God. —*E. W. Hengstenberg.*

Verse 8.—"*Like unto them.*" Namely, " hollowness," vanity, unprofitableness : (*tohu*). Isaiah xliv. 9, 10.—*William Kay.*

Verse 8.—They that serve a base god cannot but be of a base spirit, and so can do nothing worthily and generously. Every man's temper is as his god is.—*Thomas Manton.*

Verse 9.—"*He is their help.*" We should rather have expected, " Our help and our shield," etc. But the burden thrice introduced, appears to be a well-known formula of praise. "*Their,*" i.e., " of all who trust in him." The verses contain a climax : (1) Israel in general is addressed ; (2) the priests or ministers of God's service ; (3) the true Israelites ; not only chosen out of all people, or out of the chosen people for outward service ; but serving God in sincerity of heart.—*Speaker's Commentary.*

Verse 10.—*"He is the help"* of his people ; they are helpless in themselves, and vain is the help of man, for there is none in him ; there is no help but in the Lord, and he is a present, seasonable, and sufficient help. Jehovah the Father has promised them help, and he is both able and faithful to make it good ; he has laid help upon his Son for them ; and has set up a throne of grace, where they may come for grace to help them in time of need. Christ has helped them out of the miserable estate they were fallen into by sin ; he helps them on in their way to heaven, by his power and grace, and at last brings them thither. The Spirit of God helps them to the things of Christ ; to many exceeding great and precious promises ; and out of many difficulties, snares and temptations ; and he helps them in prayer under all their infirmities, and makes intercession for them, according to the will of God ; and therefore they should trust in the Lord, Father, Son, and Spirit.—*John Gill.*

Verse 12.—*"The LORD hath been mindful of us : he will bless us."* God hath, and therefore God will, is an ordinary Scripture argument.—*John Trapp.*

Verse 13.—*"He will bless . . . . both small and great."* Mercy, according to the covenant of grace, giveth the same grounds of faith and hope to everyone within the church ; so that whatever of favour is shown to one of God's people, it is of a general use and profit to others. This Scripture sheweth that as the duty of trusting in the Lord is common to all sorts of persons, so the blessing of trust is common, and doth belong to all sorts of believers, small and great. God's Israel consists of several degrees of men. There are magistrates who have their peculiar service ; there are ministers who intercede between God and man in things belonging to God, and there are the common sort of them that fear God, and are admitted to the honour of being his people. Now these have all the same privileges. If God be the help and shield of the one, he will be the help and shield of the other ; if he bless the one he will bless the other. Every one that feareth God, and is in the number of the true Israelites, may expect his blessing as well as public persons ; the meanest peasant as well as the greatest prince, as they have leave to trust in God, so they may expect his blessing. The reason is that they have all an equal interest in the same God, who is a God of goodness and power, able and willing to relieve all those that trust in him. He is alike affected to all his children, and beareth them the same love.—*Thomas Manton.*

Verse 13.—He says, " *both small and great*," by which circumstance he magnifies God's paternal regard the more, showing that he does not overlook even the meanest and the most despised, provided they cordially seek his aid. Now as there is no acceptance of persons before God, our low and abject condition ought to be no obstruction to our drawing near to him, since he so kindly invites to approach him those who appear to be held in no reputation. The repetition of the word *"bless"* is intended to mark the uninterrupted stream of his loving-kindness.—*John Calvin.*

Verse 14.—*"The LORD shall increase you,"* etc. This is expressive of the further and increasing blessing of Jehovah on his Israel, upon his ministers, and upon the whole church. They are to be increased in light and knowledge, in gifts and graces, in faith and utterance, in numbers and multitude.—*Samuel Eyles Pierce.*

Verse 14.—
> The Lord will heap his blessings upon you,
> Upon you and your children.
> —*William Green, in "A New Translation of the Psalms,"* 1762.

Verse 15.—*"Blessed are ye,"* etc. Ye are the people blessed of old in the person of your father Abraham, by Melchizedek, priest of the Most High God, Creator of heaven and earth," Gen. xiv. 19. *"Of Jehovah,"* literally, *to Jehovah,* as an object of benediction to him. Or the Hebrew preposition, as in many other cases, may be simply equivalent to our *by.* The creative character of God is mentioned, as ensuring his ability, no less than his willingness, to bless his people.—*Joseph Addison Alexander.*

Verse 16.—*"The heaven, even the heavens, are the LORD'S."* He demonstrates, that, as God has his dwelling-place in the heavens, he must be independent of all worldly riches ; for, assuredly, neither wine, nor corn, nor anything requisite for the support of the present life, is produced there. Consequently, God has every resource in himself. To this circumstance the repetition of the term *"heavens"* refers. The *heavens, the heavens are enough for God ;* and as he is superior to all aid, he is to himself instead of a hundred more.—*John Calvin.*

Verse 16.- -"The earth hath he given," etc.—This verse is full of beauty, when read in connection with what follows, as a descriptive declaration of the effect of " the regeneration " on this lower scene. For until then, man has rather been given to the earth than the earth to the sons of men. It is but a place of graves, and the day of death seems better than the day of birth, so long as men walk in no brighter light than that of the sun.—*Arthur Pridham.*

Verse 17.—"The dead praise not the LORD*,"* etc. David considers not here what men do, or do not, in the next world ; but he considers only that in this world he was bound to propagate God's truth, and that he could not do so if God took him away by death. Now there is a double reason given of David's and other holy men's deprecation of death in the Old Testament ; one in relation to themselves, *qui promissiones obscuræ,* because Moses had conveyed to those men all God's future blessings, all the joy and glory of heaven, only in the types of earthly things, and said little of the state of the soul after this life. And therefore the promises belonging to the godly after this life, were not so clear that in the contemplation of them they could deliver themselves confidently into the jaws of death : he that is not fully satisfied of the next world, makes shift to be content with this. The other reason was *quia operarii pauci,* because God had a great harvest in hand, and few labourers in it, they were loth to be taken from the work ; and this reason was not in relation to themselves, but to God's church, since they would not be able to do God's cause any more good here. This was the other reason that made those good men so lothe to die. *Quid facies nomini tuo ?* says Joshua in his prayer to God. If the Canaanites come in to destroy us, and blaspheme thee, what wilt thou do unto thy mighty name ? What wilt thou do unto thy glorious church, said the saints of God under the Old Testament, if thou take those men out of the world, whom thou hast chosen, enabled, and qualified, for the edification, sustentation, and propagation of that church ? Upon this account David desired to live, not for his own sake, but for God's glory, and his church's good ; neither of which could be advanced by him when he was dead.—*Abraham Wright.*

Verse 17.—"The dead praise not the LORD*,"* etc. Who are here meant by *"the dead " ?* I cannot rest in the view taken by those who consider this verse simply as a plea by those who use it, that they may be saved from death. They are words provided for the church at large, as the subsequent verse proves. By *"the dead,"* then, I understand those who descend to the silence of eternal death, who have not praised God, and never can. For them the earth might seem never to have been given.—*W. Wilson.*

Verse 17.—"Into silence." Into the grave—the land of silence. Ps. xciv. 17. Nothing is more impressive in regard to the grave than its utter *silence.* Not a voice, not a sound, is heard there,—of birds or men—of song or conversation—of the roaring of the sea, the sighing of the breeze, the fury of the storm, the tumult of battle. Perfect stillness reigns there ; and the first sound that shall be heard there will be the archangel's trump.—*Albert Barnes.*

Verses 17, 18.—The *people* of God cannot die, because the *praise* of God would die with them, which would be impossible.—*E. W. Hengstenberg.*

Verses 17, 18.—It is not to be overlooked that there do occur, in certain Psalms, words which have the appearance of excluding the hope of eternal life.* . . . Yet it is a very significant fact, that in all the Psalms in question, there is an earnest solicitude expressed for the glory of God. If death is deprecated, it is in order that the Lord may not lose the glory, nor his church the services which a life prolonged might furnish. This is well exemplified in the hundred and fifteenth, which I the rather cite because, being the sole exception to the rule, that the dark views of death are found in Psalms of contrition and deep sorrow ; it is the only Psalm to which the preceding observations are inapplicable. It is a tranquil hymn of praise.

> 17. It is not the dead who praise Jah :
>   Neither any that go down into silence.
> 18. But WE will bless Jah,
>   From this time forth and for evermore.
>   Hallelujah !

The Psalm thus closed, was one of the Songs of the Second Temple.

---

* Psalm vi. 5, xxx. 9, lxxxviii. 10, 12, lxxxix. 47, cxv. 17.

What we hear in it is the voice of the church, rather than of an individual soul. And this may assist us in perceiving its entire harmony with faith in the heavenly glory. It much concerns the honour of God that there be continued, on the earth, a visible church, in which his name may be recorded from generation to generation. That is a work which cannot be performed by the dead. Since, therefore, the uppermost desire of the church ought ever to be that God's name may be hallowed, his kingdom advanced, and his will done in the earth ; it is her duty to pray for continued subsistence here, on the earth, to witness for God. And it is to be carefully observed, that not only in this passage, but in all the parallel texts in which the Psalmists seem to speak doubtfully or disparagingly of the state of the departed, it is in connection with the interest of God's cause on the earth. The thought that is uppermost in their hearts is, that " in death there is no commemoration " of God—no recording of his name for the salvation of men. This single circumstance might, I think, suffice to put the reader on his guard against a precipitate fastening on them of a meaning which would exclude the hope of eternal life. It goes far to show that what the Psalmist deprecates, is not death simply considered, but premature death. Their prayer is, " O my God, take me not away in the midst of my days." Ps. cii. 24. And I do not hesitate to say that there are men so placed in stations of eminent usefulness, that it is their duty to make the prayer their own.—*William Binnie*.

HINTS TO PREACHERS.

Verse 1.—The passage may be used as, I. A powerful plea in prayer. II. An expression of the true spirit of piety. III. A safe guide in theology. IV. A practical direction in choosing our way of life. V. An acceptable spirit when surveying past or present success.

Verse 1.—I. No praise is due to man. Have we a being ? Not unto us, etc. Have we health ? Not unto us, etc. Have we outward comforts ? Not unto us, etc. Friends ? Not unto us, etc. The means of grace ? Not unto us, etc. Saving faith in Christ ? Not unto us, etc. Gifts and graces ? Not unto us, etc. The hope of glory ? Not unto us, etc. Usefulness to others ? Not unto us, etc. II. All praise is due to God. 1. Because all we have is from mercy. 2. Because all we expect is from faithfulness.—*G. R.*

Verse 2.—A taunting question, to which we can give many satisfactory replies.

Verse 2.—Why do they say so ? Why doth God permit them to say so ?—*Matthew Henry*.

Verses 2, 3.—I. The inquiry of heathens : ver. 2. 1. Of ignorance. They see a temple but no god. 2. Of reproach to the people of God when their God has forsaken them for a time : " While they say daily unto me, where," etc. II. The reply to their inquiry : ver. 3. Do you ask where is our God ? Ask rather where he is not ? Do you ask what he has done ? " He has done whatsoever he hath pleased."—*G. R.*

Verse 3.—I. His position betokens absolute dominion. II. His actions prove it. III. Yet he condescends to be " our God."

Verse 3 (*second clause*).—The sovereignty of God. Establish and improve the great scriptural doctrine, that the glorious God has a right to exercise dominion over all his creatures ; and to do, in all respects, as he pleases. This right naturally results from his being the *Former* and the *Possessor* of heaven and earth. Consider (1) He is infinitely wise ; he perfectly knows all his creatures, all their actions, and all their tendencies. (2) He is infinitely righteous. (3) He is infinitely good.—*George Burder*.

Verses 4—8.—I. The character of idol gods. Whether our gods are natural objects or riches or worldly pleasures, they have no eye to pity, no ear to hear petitions, no tongue to counsel, no hand to help. II. The character of the true God. He is all eye, all ear, all tongue, all hand, all feet, all mind, all heart. III. The character of the idol worshippers. All become naturally assimilated to the objects of their worship.

Verse 8.—The likeness between idolators and their idols. Work it out in the particulars mentioned.

Verse 9.—The living God claims spiritual worship ; the life of such worship is faith ; faith proves God to be a living reality—" He is their help," etc. Only elect Israel will ever render this living worship.

Verses 9—11.—I. The reproof. " O Israel ! " " O house of Aaron ! " " Ye who fear the Lord." Have you been unbelieving towards your God ? II. The correction or admonition. " Trust in the Lord." Have you trusted in the true God as others have in their false gods ? III. The instruction. " He is their help," etc. Let churches, ministers, and all who fear God know that at all times and under all circumstances he is their help and their shield.—*G. R.*

Verse 10.—I. Those who publicly serve should specially trust. " O house of Aaron, trust." II. Those who are specially called shall be specially helped. " He is their help." III. Those who are specially helped in service may be sure of special protection in danger—" and their shield."

Verse 11.—Filial fear the foundation of fuller faith.

Verse 12.—What we have experienced. What we may expect.—*Matthew Henry.*

Verses 12, 13.—I. What God *has done* for his people : " He hath been mindful of us." 1. Our preservation proves this. 2. Our mercies. 3. Our trials. 4. Our guidance. 5. Our consolations. Everything, even the minutest blessing, represents a thought in the mind of God respecting us. " How precious are thy thoughts concerning me, O God, how great," etc., and those thoughts go back to an eternity before we came into being. " The Lord hath been mindful of us " ; then should we not be more mindful of him ? II. What he *will do* for his people—" He will bless us." 1. Greatly. His blessings are like himself, great. They are blessed whom he blesses. 2. Suitably. The house of Israel, the house of Aaron, all who fear him, according to their need, both small and great. 3. Assuredly. " He will," " he will," " he will," " he will." With one " will " he curses, with four " wills " he blesses.—*G. R.*

Verse 13.—I. The general character—" fear the Lord." II. The degrees of development—" small and great." III. The common blessing.

Verse 14.—I. Gracious increase—in knowledge, love, power, holiness, usefulness, etc. II. Growing increase—we grow faster, and advance not only more, but more and more. III. Relative increase—our children grow in grace through our examples, etc.

Verse 14.—The blessings of God are, I. *Ever-flowing*—" more and more." II. *Over-flowing*—" you and your children." Let parents seek more grace for themselves for the sake of their children. 1. That they may be more influenced by their example. 2. That their prayers may be more prevalent on their behalf. 3. That their children may be more blessed for their sakes.—*G. R.*

Verse 15.—A blessing. I. Belonging to a peculiar people—" ye." II. Coming from a peculiar quarter—" of the Lord," etc. III. Bearing a peculiar date—" are." IV. Stamped with peculiar certainty—" Ye are blessed." V. Involving a peculiar duty—" Bless the Lord now and evermore."

Verse 15.—The Creator's blessing—its greatness, fulness, variety, etc.

Verse 16.—Man's lordship over the world, its limit, its abuse, its legitimate bound, its grand design.

Verses 17, 18.—I. Missing voices—" The dead praise not." II. Their stimulus upon ourselves—" But we." III. Their cry to others—" Praise ye the Lord." Let us make up for the silent voices.

Verses 17, 18.—I. They who do not praise God here will not praise him hereafter. No reprieve therefore from punishment. II. They who praise God in this life will praise him for evermore. Hallelujah for this. " Praise the Lord."—*G. R.*

Verses 17, 18.—A new year's sermon. I. A mournful memory—" the dead." II. A happy resolve—" but we will bless the Lord." III. An appropriate commencement—" from this time forth." IV. An everlasting continuance—" and for evermore."

PSALM CXVI.

SUBJECT.—*This is a continuation of the Paschal Hallel, and therefore must in some measure be interpreted in connection with the coming out of Egypt. It has all the appearance of being a personal song in which the believing soul, reminded by the Passover of its own bondage and deliverance, speaks thereof with gratitude, and praises the Lord accordingly. We can conceive the Israelite with a staff in his hand singing, "Return unto thy rest, O my soul," as he remembered the going back of the house of Jacob to the land of their fathers ; and then drinking the cup at the feast using the words of the thirteenth verse, "I will take the cup of salvation." The pious man evidently remembers both his own deliverance and that of his people as he sings in the language of the sixteenth verse, "Thou hast loosed my bonds" ; but he rises into sympathy with his nation as he thinks of the courts of the Lord's house and of the glorious city, and pledges himself to sing "in the midst of thee, O Jerusalem." Personal love fostered by a personal experience of redemption is the theme of this Psalm, and in it we see the redeemed answered when they pray, preserved in time of trouble, resting in their God, walking at large, sensible of their obligations, conscious that they are not their own but bought with a price, and joining with all the ransomed company to sing hallelujahs unto God.*

Since our divine Master sang this hymn, we can hardly err in seeing here words to which he could set his seal,—words in a measure descriptive of his own experience ; but upon this we will not enlarge, as in the notes we have indicated how the Psalm has been understood by those who love to find their Lord in every line.

DIVISION.—*David Dickson has a somewhat singular division of this Psalm, which strikes us as being exceedingly suggestive. He says, "This Psalm is a threefold engagement of the Psalmist unto thanksgiving unto God, for his mercy unto him, and in particular for some notable delivery of him from death, both bodily and spiritual. The first engagement is, that he shall out of love have recourse unto God by prayer, verses 1 and 2 ; the reasons and motives whereof are set down, because of his former deliverances, 3—8 ; the second engagement is to a holy conversation, verse 9 ; and the motives and reasons are given in verses 10 to 13 ; the third engagement is to continual praise and service, and specially to pay those vows before the church, which he had made in days of sorrow, the reasons whereof are given in verses 14—19."*

EXPOSITION.

I LOVE the LORD, because he hath heard my voice *and* my supplications.

2 Because he hath inclined his ear unto me, therefore will I call upon *him* as long as I live.

3 The sorrows of death compassed me, and the pains of hell gat hold upon me : I found trouble and sorrow.

4 Then called I upon the name of the LORD ; O LORD, I beseech thee, deliver my soul.

5 Gracious *is* the LORD, and righteous ; yea, our God *is* merciful.

6 The LORD preserveth the simple : I was brought low, and he helped me.

7 Return unto thy rest, O my soul ; for the LORD hath dealt bountifully with thee.

8 For thou hast delivered my soul from death, mine eyes from tears, *and* my feet from falling.

1. *"I love the LORD."* A blessed declaration : every believer ought to be able to declare without the slightest hesitation, " I love the Lord." It was required under the law, but was never produced in the heart of man except by the grace of God, and upon gospel principles. It is a great thing to say " I love the Lord " ; for the sweetest of all graces and the surest of all evidences of salvation is love. It is great goodness on the part of God that he condescends to be loved by such poor

creatures as we are, and it is a sure proof that he has been at work in our heart when we can say, " Thou knowest all things, thou knowest that I love thee." *"Because he hath heard my voice and my supplications."* The Psalmist not only knows that he loves God, but he knows why he does so. When love can justify itself with a reason, it is deep, strong, and abiding. They say that love is blind ; but when we love God our affection has its eyes open and can sustain itself with the most rigid logic. We have reason, superabundant reason, for loving the Lord ; and so because in this case principle and passion, reason and emotion go together, they make up an admirable state of mind. David's reason for his love was the love of God in hearing his prayers. The Psalmist had used his *"voice"* in prayer, and the habit of doing so is exceedingly helpful to devotion. If we can pray aloud without being overheard it is well to do so. Sometimes, however, when the Psalmist had lifted up his voice, his utterance had been so broken and painful that he scarcely dared to call it prayer ; words failed him, he could only produce a groaning sound, but the Lord heard his moaning voice. At other times his prayers were more regular and better formed : these he calls *"supplications."* David had praised as best he could, and when one form of devotion failed him he tried another. He had gone to the Lord again and again, hence he uses the plural and says " my supplications," but as often as he had gone, so often had he been welcome. Jehovah had heard, that is to say, accepted, and answered both his broken cries and his more composed and orderly supplications ; hence he loved God with all his heart. Answered prayers are silken bonds which bind our hearts to God. When a man's prayers are answered, love is the natural result. According to Alexander, both verbs may be translated in the present, and the text may run thus, " I love because Jehovah hears my voice, my supplications." This also is true in the case of every pleading believer. Continual love flows out of daily answers to prayer.

2. *"Because he hath inclined his ear unto me "* :—bowing down from his grandeur to attend to my prayer ; the figure seems to be that of a tender physician or loving friend leaning over a sick man whose voice is faint and scarcely audible, so as to catch every accent and whisper. When our prayer is very feeble, so that we ourselves can scarcely hear it, and question whether we do pray or not, yet God bows a listening ear, and regards our supplications. *"Therefore will I call upon him as long as I live,"* or, " in my days." Throughout all the days of my life I will address my prayer to God alone, and to him I will unceasingly pray. It is always wise to go where we are welcome and are well treated. The word " call " may imply praise as well as prayer : calling upon the name of the Lord is an expressive name for adoration of all kinds. When prayer is heard in our feebleness, and answered in the strength and greatness of God, we are strengthened in the habit of prayer, and confirmed in the resolve to make ceaseless intercession. We should not thank a beggar who informed us that because we had granted his request he would never cease to beg of us, and yet doubtless it is acceptable to God that his petitioners should form the resolution to continue in prayer : this shows the greatness of his goodness, and the abundance of his patience. In all days let us pray and praise the Ancient of days. He promises that as our days our strength shall be ; let us resolve that as our days our devotion shall be.

3. The Psalmist now goes on to describe his condition at the time when he prayed unto God. *"The sorrows of death compassed me."* As hunters surround a stag with dogs and men, so that no way of escape is left, so was David enclosed in a ring of deadly griefs. The bands of sorrow, weakness, and terror with which death is accustomed to bind men ere he drags them away to their long captivity were all around him. Nor were these things around him in a distant circle, they had come close home, for he adds, *"and the pains of hell gat hold upon me."* Horrors such as those which torment the lost seized me, grasped me, found me out, searched me through and through, and held me a prisoner. He means by the pains of hell those pangs which belong to death, those terrors which are connected with the grave ; these were so closely upon him that they fixed their teeth in him as hounds seize their prey. *"I found trouble and sorrow,"* trouble was around me, and sorrow within me. His griefs were double, and as he searched into them they increased. A man rejoices when he finds a hid treasure ; but what must be the anguish of a man who finds, where he least expected it, a vein of trouble and sorrow ? The Psalmist was sought for by trouble and it found him out, and when he himself became a seeker he found no relief, but double distress.

4. *"Then called I upon the name of the LORD."* Prayer is never out of season, he

prayed *then*, when things were at their worst. When the good man could not run to God, he *called* to him. In his extremity his faith came to the front : it was useless to call on man, and it may have seemed almost as useless to appeal to the Lord ; but yet he did with his whole soul invoke all the attributes which make up the sacred name of Jehovah, and thus he proved the truth of his confidence. We can some of us remember certain very special times of trial of which we can now say, "*then* called I upon the name of the Lord." The Psalmist appealed to the Lord's mercy, truth, power, and faithfulness, and this was his prayer,—"*O Lord, I beseech thee, deliver my soul.*" This form of petition is short, comprehensive, to the point, humble, and earnest. It were well if all our prayers were moulded upon this model ; perhaps they would be if we were in similar circumstances to those of the Psalmist, for real trouble produces real prayer. Here we have no multiplicity of words, and no fine arrangement of sentences ; everything is simple and natural ; there is not a redundant syllable, and yet there is not one lacking.

5. "*Gracious is the* LORD, *and righteous.*" In hearing prayer the grace and righteousness of Jehovah are both conspicuous. It is a great favour to hear a sinner's prayer, and yet since the Lord has promised to do so, he is not unrighteous to forget his promise and disregard the cries of his people. The combination of grace and righteousness in the dealings of God with his servants can only be explained by remembering the atoning sacrifice of our Lord Jesus Christ. At the cross we see how gracious is the Lord and righteous. "*Yea, our God is merciful,*" or compassionate, tender, pitiful, full of mercy. We who have accepted him as ours have no doubt as to his mercy, for he would never have been our God if he had not been merciful. See how the attribute of righteousness seems to stand between two guards of love :— gracious, *righteous*, merciful. The sword of justice is scabbarded in a jewelled sheath of grace.

6. "*The* LORD *preserveth the simple.*" Those who have a great deal of wit may take care of themselves. Those who have no worldly craft and subtlety and guile, but simply trust in God, and do the right, may depend upon it that God's care shall be over them. The worldly-wise with all their prudence shall be taken in their own craftiness, but those who walk in their integrity with single-minded truthfulness before God shall be protected against the wiles of their enemies, and enabled to outlive their foes. Though the saints are like sheep in the midst of wolves, and comparatively defenceless, yet there are more sheep in the world than wolves, and it is highly probable that the sheep will feed in safety when not a single wolf is left upon the face of the earth : even so the meek shall inherit the earth, when the wicked shall be no more. "*I was brought low, and he helped me,*"—simple though I was, the Lord did not pass me by. Though reduced in circumstances, slandered in character, depressed in spirit, and sick in body, the Lord helped me. There are many ways in which the child of God may be brought low, but the help of God is as various as the need of his people : he supplies our necessities when impoverished, restores our character when maligned, raises up friends for us when deserted, comforts us when desponding, and heals our diseases when we are sick. There are thousands in the church of God at this time who can each one of them say for himself, "*I* was brought low, and he helped *me.*" Whenever this can be said it should be said to the praise of the glory of his grace, and for the comforting of others who may pass through the like ordeal. Note how David after stating the general doctrine that the Lord preserveth the simple, proves and illustrates it from his own personal experience. The habit of taking home a general truth and testing the power of it in our own case is an exceedingly blessed one ; it is the way in which the testimony of Christ is confirmed in us, and so we become witnesses unto the Lord our God.

7. "*Return unto thy rest, O my soul.*" He calls the rest still his own, and feels full liberty to return to it. What a mercy it is that even if our soul has left its rest for a while we can tell it—" it is thy rest still." The Psalmist had evidently been somewhat disturbed in mind, his troubles had ruffled his spirit ; but now with a sense of answered prayer upon him he quiets his soul. He had rested before, for he knew the blessed repose of faith, and therefore he returns to the God who had been the refuge of his soul in former days. Even as a bird flies to its nest, so does his soul fly to his God. Whenever a child of God even for a moment loses his peace of mind, he should be concerned to find it again, not by seeking it in the world or in his own experience, but in the Lord alone. When the believer prays, and the Lord inclines his ear, the road to the old rest is before him, let him not be slow to follow it. "*For the* LORD *hath dealt bountifully with thee.*" Thou hast served a good

God, and built upon a sure foundation ; go not about to find any other rest, but come back to him who in former days hath condescended to enrich thee by his love. What a text is this ! and what an exposition of it is furnished by the biography of every believing man and woman ! The Lord hath dealt bountifully with us, for he hath given us his Son, and in him he hath given us all things : he hath sent us his Spirit, and by him he conveys to us all spiritual blessings. God dealeth with us like a God ; he lays his fulness open to us, and of that fulness have all we received, and grace for grace. We have sat at no niggard's table, we have been clothed by no penurious hand, we have been equipped by no grudging provider ; let us come back to him who has treated us with such exceeding kindness. More arguments follow.

8. *"For thou hast delivered my soul from death, mine eyes from tears, and my feet from falling."* The triune God has given us a trinity of deliverances : our life has been spared from the grave, our heart has been uplifted from its griefs, and our course in life has been preserved from dishonour. We ought not to be satisfied unless we are conscious of all three of these deliverances. If our soul has been saved from death, why do we weep ? What cause for sorrow remains ? Whence those tears ? And if our tears have been wiped away, can we endure to fall again into sin ? Let us not rest unless with steady feet we pursue the path of the upright, escaping every snare and shunning every stumblingblock. Salvation, joy, and holiness must go together, and they are all provided for us in the covenant of grace. Death is vanquished, tears are dried, and fears are banished when the Lord is near.

Thus has the Psalmist explained the reasons of his resolution to call upon God as long as he lived, and none can question but that he had come to a most justifiable resolve. When from so great a depth he had been uplifted by so special an interposition of God, he was undoubtedly bound to be for ever the hearty worshipper of Jehovah, to whom he owed so much. Do we not all feel the force of the reasoning, and will we not carry out the conclusion ? May God the Holy Spirit help us so to pray without ceasing and in everything to give thanks, for this is the will of God in Christ Jesus concerning us.

9 I will walk before the LORD in the land of the living.
10 I believed, therefore have I spoken : I was greatly afflicted :
11 I said in my haste, All men *are* liars.
12 What shall I render unto the LORD *for* all his benefits toward me ?
13 I will take the cup of salvation, and call upon the name of the LORD.

9. *"I will walk before the LORD in the land of the living."* This is the Psalmist's second resolution, to live as in the sight of God in the midst of the sons of men. By a man's walk is understood his way of life : some men live only as in the sight of their fellow men, having regard to human judgment and opinion ; but the truly gracious man considers the presence of God, and acts under the influence of his all-observing eye. " Thou God seest me " is a far better influence than " My master sees me." The life of faith, hope, holy fear, and true holiness is produced by a sense of living and walking before the Lord, and he who has been favoured with divine deliverances in answer to prayer finds his own experience the best reason for a holy life, and the best assistance to his endeavours. We know that God in a special manner is nigh unto his people : what manner of persons ought we to be in all holy conversation and godliness ?

10. *"I believed, therefore have I spoken."* I could not have spoken thus if it had not been for my faith : I should never have spoken unto God in prayer, nor have been able now to speak to my fellow men in testimony if it had not been that faith kept me alive, and brought me a deliverance, whereof I have good reason to boast. Concerning the things of God no man should speak unless he believes ; the speech of the waverer is mischievous, but the tongue of the believer is profitable ; the most powerful speech which has ever been uttered by the lip of man has emanated from a heart fully persuaded of the truth of God. Not only the Psalmist, but such men as Luther, and Calvin, and other great witnesses for the faith, could each one most heartily say, " I believed, therefore have I spoken." *"I was greatly afflicted."* There was no mistake about that ; the affliction was as bitter and as terrible as it well could be, and since I have been delivered from it, I am sure that the deliverance is no fanatical delusion, but a self-evident fact ; therefore am I the more resolved

to speak to the honour of God. Though greatly afflicted, the Psalmist had not ceased to believe : his faith was tried but not destroyed.

11. *"I said in my haste, All men are liars."* In a modified sense the expression will bear justification, even though hastily uttered, for all men will prove to be liars if we unduly trust in them ; some from want of truthfulness, and others from want of power. But from the expression, " I said in my haste," it is clear that the Psalmist did not justify his own language, but considered it as the ebullition of a hasty temper. In the sense in which he spoke his language was unjustifiable. He had no right to distrust all men, for many of them are honest, truthful, and conscientious ; there are faithful friends and loyal adherents yet alive ; and if sometimes they disappoint us, we ought not to call them liars for failing when the failure arises entirely from want of power, and not from lack of will. Under great affliction our temptation will be to form hasty judgments of our fellow men, and knowing this to be the case we ought carefully to watch our spirit, and to keep the door of our lips. The Psalmist had believed, and therefore he spoke ; he had doubted, and therefore he spoke in haste. He believed, and therefore he rightly prayed to God ; he disbelieved, and therefore he wrongfully accused mankind. Speaking is as ill in some cases as it is good in others. Speaking in haste is generally followed by bitter repentance. It is much better to be quiet when our spirit is disturbed and hasty, for it is so much easier to say than to unsay ; we may repent of our words, but we cannot so recall them as to undo the mischief they have done. If even David had to eat his own words, when he spoke in a hurry, none of us can trust our tongue without a bridle.

12. *"What shall I render unto the Lord for all his benefits toward me ?"* He wisely leaves off fretting about man's falsehood and his own ill humour, and directs himself to his God. It is of little use to be harping on the string of man's imperfection and deceitfulness ; it is infinitely better to praise the perfection and faithfulness of God. The question of the verse is a very proper one : the Lord has rendered so much mercy to us that we ought to look about us, and look within us, and see what can be done by us to manifest our gratitude. We ought not only to do what is plainly before us, but also with holy ingenuity to search out various ways by which we may render fresh praises unto our God. His benefits are so many that we cannot number them, and our ways of acknowledging his bestowments ought to be varied and numerous in proportion. Each person should have his own peculiar mode of expressing gratitude. The Lord sends each one a special benefit, let each one enquire, " What shall *I* render ? What form of service would be most becoming in me ? "

13. *"I will take the cup of salvation."* " I will take " is a strange answer to the question, " What shall I render ? " and yet it is the wisest reply that could possibly be given.

> " The best return for one like me,
> So wretched and so poor,
> Is from his gifts to draw a plea
> And ask him still for more."

To take the cup of salvation was in itself an act of worship, and it was accompanied with other forms of adoration, hence the Psalmist says, *"and call upon the name of the Lord."* He means that he will utter blessings and thanksgivings and prayers, and then drink of the cup which the Lord had filled with his saving grace. What a cup this is ! Upon the table of infinite love stands the cup full of blessing ; it is ours by faith to take it in our hand, make it our own, and partake of it, and then with joyful hearts to laud and magnify the gracious One who has filled it for our sakes that we may drink and be refreshed. We can do this figuratively at the sacramental table, we can do it spiritually every time we grasp the golden chalice of the covenant, realizing the fulness of blessing which it contains, and by faith receiving its divine contents into our inmost soul. Beloved reader, let us pause here and take a long and deep draught from the cup which Jesus filled, and then with devout hearts let us worship God.

14 I will pay my vows unto the Lord now in the presence of all his people.

15 Precious in the sight of the Lord *is* the death of his saints.

16 O Lord, truly I *am* thy servant : I *am* thy servant, *and* the son of thine handmaid : thou hast loosed my bonds.

17 I will offer to thee the sacrifice of thanksgiving, and will call upon the name of the LORD.

18 I will pay my vows unto the LORD now in the presence of all his people,

19 In the courts of the LORD's house, in the midst of thee, O Jerusalem. Praise ye the LORD.

14. *"I will pay my vows unto the LORD now in the presence of all his people."* The Psalmist has already stated his third resolution, to devote himself to the worship of God evermore, and here he commences the performance of that resolve. The vows which he had made in anguish, he now determines to fulfil : " I will pay my vows unto the Lord." He does so at once, *"now,"* and that publicly, " in the presence of all his people." Good resolutions cannot be carried out too speedily ; vows become debts, and debts should be paid. It is well to have witnesses to the payment of just debts, and we need not be ashamed to have witnesses to the fulfilling of holy vows, for this will show that we are not ashamed of our Lord, and it may be a great benefit to those who look on and hear us publicly sounding forth the praises of our prayer-hearing God. How can those do this who have never with their mouth confessed their Saviour ? O secret disciples, what say you to this verse ! Be encouraged to come into the light and own your Redeemer. If, indeed, you have been saved, come forward and declare it in his own appointed way.

15. *"Precious in the sight of the LORD is the death of his saints,"* and therefore he did not suffer the Psalmist to die, but delivered his soul from death. This seems to indicate that the song was meant to remind Jewish families of the mercies received by any one of the household, supposing him to have been sore sick and to have been restored to health, for the Lord values the lives of his saints, and often spares them where others perish. They shall not die prematurely ; they shall be immortal till their work is done ; and when their time shall come to die, then their deaths shall be precious. The Lord watches over their dying beds, smooths their pillows, sustains their hearts, and receives their souls. Those who are redeemed with precious blood are so dear to God that even their deaths are precious to him. The death-beds of saints are very precious to the church, she often learns much from them ; they are very precious to all believers, who delight to treasure up the last words of the departed ; but they are most of all precious to the Lord Jehovah himself, who view the triumphant deaths of his gracious ones with sacred delight. If we have walked before him in the land of the living, we need not fear to die before him when the hour of our departure is at hand.

16. The man of God in paying his vows re-dedicates himself unto God ; the offering which he brings is himself, as he cries, *"O LORD, truly I am thy servant,"* rightfully, really, heartily, constantly, I own that I am thine, for thou hast delivered and redeemed me." *"I am thy servant, and the son of thine handmaid,"* a servant born in thy house, born of a servant and so born a servant, and therefore doubly thine. My mother was thine handmaid, and I, her son, confess that I am altogether thine by claims arising out of my birth. O that children of godly parents would thus judge ; but, alas, there are many who are the sons of the Lord's handmaids, but they are not themselves his servants. They give sad proof that grace does not run in the blood. David's mother was evidently a gracious woman, and he is glad to remember that fact, and to see in it a fresh obligation to devote himself to God. *"Thou hast loosed my bonds,"*—freedom from bondage binds me to thy service. He who is loosed from the bonds of sin, death, and hell should rejoice to wear the easy yoke of the great Deliverer. Note how the sweet singer delights to dwell upon his belonging to the Lord ; it is evidently his glory, a thing of which he is proud, a matter which causes him intense satisfaction. Verily, it ought to create rapture in our souls if we are able to call Jesus Master, and are acknowledged by him as his servants.

17. *"I will offer to thee the sacrifice of thanksgiving."* Being thy servant, I am bound to sacrifice to thee, and having received spiritual blessings at thy hands I will not bring bullock or goat, but I will bring that which is more suitable, namely, the thanksgiving of my heart. My inmost soul shall adore thee in gratitude. *"And will call upon the name of the LORD,"* that is to say, I will bow before thee reverently, lift up my heart in love to thee, think upon thy character, and adore thee as thou dost reveal thyself. He is fond of this occupation, and several times in this Psalm

declares that " he will call upon the name of the Lord," while at the same time he rejoices that he had done so many a time before. Good feelings and actions bear repeating : the more of hearty callings upon God the better.

18. *"I will pay my vows unto the LORD now in the presence of all his people."* He repeats the declaration. A good thing is worth saying twice. He thus stirs himself up to greater heartiness, earnestness, and diligence in keeping his vow,—really paying it at the very moment that he is declaring his resolution to do so. The mercy came in secret, but the praise is rendered in public ; the company was, however, select ; he did not cast his pearls before swine, but delivered his testimony before those who could understand and appreciate it.

19. *"In the courts of the LORD'S house "* : in the proper place, where God had ordained that he should be worshipped. See how he is stirred up at the remembrance of the house of the Lord, and must needs speak of the holy city with a note of joyful exclamation—*"In the midst of thee, O Jerusalem."* The very thought of the beloved Zion touched his heart, and he writes as if he were actually addressing Jerusalem, whose name was dear to him. There would he pay his vows, in the abode of fellowship, in the very heart of Judea, in the place to which the tribes went up, the tribes of the Lord. There is nothing like witnessing for Jesus, where the report thereof will be carried into a thousand homes. God's praise is not to be confined to a closet, nor his name to be whispered in holes and corners, as if we were afraid that men should hear us ; but in the thick of the throng, and in the very centre of assemblies, we should lift up heart and voice unto the Lord, and invite others to join with us in adoring him, saying, *"Praise ye the LORD,"* or Hallelujah. This was a very fit conclusion of a song to be sung when all the people were gathered together at Jerusalem to keep the feast. God's Spirit moved the writers of these Psalms to give them a fitness and suitability which was more evident in their own day than now ; but enough is perceptible to convince us that every line and word had a peculiar adaptation to the occasions for which the sacred sonnets were composed. When we worship the Lord we ought with great care to select the words of prayer and praise, and not to trust to the opening of a hymn-book, or to the unconsidered extemporizing of the moment. Let all things be done decently and in order, and let all things begin and end with Hallelujah, Praise ye the Lord.

EXPLANATORY NOTES AND QUAINT SAYINGS.

Whole Psalm.—A Psalm of Thanksgiving in the Person of Christ. He is imagined by the prophet to have passed through the sorrows and afflictions of life. The atonement is passed. He has risen from the dead. He is on the right hand of the Majesty on High ; and he proclaims to the whole world the mercies he experienced from God in the day of his incarnation, and the glories which he has received in the kingdom of his Heavenly Father. Yet, although the Psalm possesses this power, and, by its own internal evidence, proves the soundness of the interpretation, it is yet highly mystic in its mode of disclosure, and requires careful meditation in bringing out its real results. Its language, too, is not so exclusively appropriate to the Messiah, that it shall not be repeated and applied by the believer to his own trials in the world ; so that while there is much that finds a ready parallel in the exaltation of Christ in heaven, there is much that would seem to be restrained to his condition upon earth. It therefore depends much on *the mind* of the individual, whether he will receive it in the higher sense of the Redeemer's glory ; or restrict it *solely* to a thanksgiving for blessings amidst those sufferings in life to which all men have been subject in the same manner, though not to the same extent as Jesus. The most perfect and the most profitable reading would combine the two, taking Christ as *the exemplar* of God's mercies towards ourselves.

1. Enthroned in eternity, and triumphant over sin and death—I—Christ—am well pleased that my Heavenly Father listened to the anxious prayers that I made to him in the day of my sorrows ; when I had neither strength in my own mind, nor assistance from men ; therefore *"through my days "*—through the endless ages

of my eternal existence—will I call upon him in my gratitude, and praise him with my whole heart.

3. In the troublous times of my incarnation I was encircled with snares, and urged onwards towards my death. The priest and ruler ; the Pharisee and the scribe ; the rich and the poor, clamoured fiercely for my destruction. The whole nation conspired against me. *"The bands of the grave"* laid hold of me, and I was hurried to the cross.

4. Then, *truly* did Christ find heaviness and affliction. " His soul was exceeding sorrowful, even unto death." He prayed anxiously to his Heavenly Father, that " the cup might pass from him." The fate of the whole world was in the balance ; and he supplicated with agony, that his *soul* might be delivered.

5. The abrupt breaking off in this verse from the direct narrative of his own sorrows is wonderfully grand and beautiful. Nor less so, is the expression *"our God "* as applied by Christ to his own disciples and believers. *" I called,"* he states, *"on the name of the* Lord." But he does not yet state the answer. He leaves that to be inferred from the assurance that God is *ever* gracious to the faithful ; yea, *"our God"*—the protector of the Christian church, as well as of myself—*"our God is merciful."*

6. Instantly, however, he resumes. Mark the energy of the language, " I was afflicted ; and he delivered me." And how delivered ? The soul of Christ has returned freely to its tranquillity ; for though the body and the frame perished on the tree, yet the soul burst through the bands of death. Again in the full stature of a perfect man Christ rose resplendent in glory to the mansions of eternity. The tears ceased ; the sorrows were hushed ; and henceforward, through the boundless day of immortality, doth he " walk before Jehovah, in the land of *the living."* This last is one of those expressions in the Psalm which might, without reflection, seem adapted to the rescued believer's state on earth, rather than Christ's in heaven. But applying the language of earthly things to heavenly—which is usual, even in the most mystic writings of Scripture—nothing can be finer than the appellation of *"the land of the living,"* when assigned to the future residence of the soul. It is the noblest application of the metaphor, and is singularly appropriate to those eternal mansions where death and sorrow are alike unknown.

10. This stanza will bear an emendation.

> I felt confidence, although I said,—
> " I am sore afflicted."
> I said in my sudden terror,—
> " All mankind are false."—*French.*

It alludes to the eve of his crucifixion, when worn down with long watchfulness and fasting, his spirit almost fainted in the agony of Gethsemane. Still, oppressed and stricken as he was in soul, he yet trusted in Jehovah, for he felt assured that he would not forsake him. But, sustained by God, he was deserted by men, the disciples with whom he had lived ; the multitudes whom he had taught ; the afflicted whom he had healed, *"all* forsook him and fled." Not one—not even the " disciples whom he loved "—remained ; and in the anguish of that desertion he could not refrain from the bitter thought, that all mankind were alike false and treacherous.

12. But that dread hour has passed. He has risen from the dead ; and stands girt with truth and holiness and glory. What then is his earliest thought ? Hear it, O man, and blush for thine oft ingratitude ! I will lift up *"the cup of deliverance "* —the drink-offering made to God with sacrifice after any signal mercies received— and bless the Lord who has been thus gracious to me. In the sight of the whole world will I pay my past vows unto Jehovah, and bring nations from every portion of the earth, reconciled and holy through the blood of my atonement.

The language in these verses, as in the concluding part of the Psalm, is wholly drawn from earthly objects and modes of religious service, well recognized by the Jews. It is in these things that the *spiritual* sense is required to be separated from the external emblem. For instance, the sacramental cup was without a doubt drawn and instituted from the cup used in commemoration of deliverances by the Jews. It is used figuratively by Christ in heaven ; but the reflective mind can scarcely fail to see the beauty of imagining it in his hand in thankfulness for his triumph, *because* " he has burst his bonds in sunder " : the bonds which held him fast in death, and confined him to the tomb : the assertion that " precious in the sight of Jehovah is the death of his saints " *specially includes* the sacrifice of Christ within its more general allusion to the blood shed, in such abundance, by prophets and martyrs to the truth. In the same manner the worship of Jehovah in the courts of his temple at Jerusalem is used in figure for the open promulgation of Christianity to the whole world. The temple services were the most solemn and most public which were offered by the Jews ; and when Christ is said to " offer his sacrifices of thanksgiving " to God *in the sight of all his people*, the figure is easily separated from the grosser element ; and *the conversion* of all people intimated under the form of Christ *seen* by all.—*William Hill Tucker*.

Verse 1.—"*I love.*" The expression of the prophet's affection is in this short abrupt phrase, "*I love*," which is but one word in the original, and expressed as a full and entire sentence in itself, thus—"*I love because the Lord hath heard*," etc. Most translators so turn it, as if, by a trajection, or passing of a word from one sentence to another, this title Lord were to be joined with the first clause, thus— (אֲהַבְתִּי פִּי־יִשְׁמַע יְהֹוָה), "*I love the Lord, because he hath heard*," etc. I deny not but that thus the sense is made somewhat the more perspicuous, and the words run the more roundly ; yet are they not altogether so emphatical. For when a man's heart is inflamed, and his soul ravished with a deep apprehension of some great and extraordinary favour, his affection will cause interruption in the expression thereof, and make stops in his speech ; and therefore this concise and abrupt clause, "*I love*," declareth a more entire and ardent affection than a more full and round phrase would do. Great is the force of true love, so that it cannot be sufficiently expressed.—*William Gouge*, 1575—1653.

Verse 1.—"*I love the Lord.*" Oh that there were such hearts in us that we could every one say, as David, with David's spirit, upon his evidence, "*I love the Lord*" ; that were more worth than all these, viz. ; First, to know all scerets. Secondly, to prophesy. Thirdly, to move mountains, etc., 1 Cor. xiii. 1, 2, etc. "*I love the Lord*" ; it is more than I know the Lord ; for even castaways are enlightened, (Heb. vi. 4) ; more than I fear the Lord, for devils fear him unto trembling (James ii. 19) ; more than I pray to God (Isai. i. 15). What should I say ? More than all services, than all virtues separate from charity : truly say the schools, charity is the form of all virtues, because it forms them all to acceptability, for nothing is accepted but what issues from charity, or, in other words, from the love of God.—*William Slater*, 1638.

Verse 1.—"*I love the Lord, because*," etc. How vain and foolish is the *talk*, " To love God for his benefits towards us is mercenary, and cannot be pure love ! " Whether pure or impure, there is no other love that can flow from the heart of the creature to its Creator. " We love him," said the holiest of Christ's disciples, " because he first loved us ; " and the increase of our love and filial evidence is in proportion to the increased sense we have of our obligation to him. We love him for the benefits bestowed on us.—*Love begets love.—Adam Clarke*.

Verse 1.—"*He hath heard my voice.*" But is this such a benefit to us, that God hears us ? Is his hearing our voice such an argument of his love ? Alas ! he may hear us, and we be never the better : he may hear our voice, and yet his love to us may be but little, for he will not give a man the hearing, though he love him not at all ? With men perhaps it may be so, but not with God ; for his hearing is not only voluntary, but reserved ; *non omnibus dormit :* his ears are not open to every one's cry ; indeed, to hear us, is in God so great a favour, that he may well be counted his favourite whom he vouchsafes to hear : and the rather, for that his hearing is always operative, and with a purpose of helping ; so that if he hear my voice, I may be sure he means to grant my supplication ; or rather perhaps in David's manner of expressing, and in God's manner of proceeding, to hear my voice is no less in effect than to grant my supplication.—*Sir Richard Baker*.

Verse 1.—"*Hath heard.*" By hearing prayer God giveth evidence of the notice which he taketh of our estates, of the respect he beareth to our persons, of the pity he hath of our miseries, of his purpose to supply our wants, and of his mind to do us good according to our needs.—*William Gouge*.

Verses 1 and 2.—The first יִשְׁמַע is more of an aorist. The Lord hears always ; and then, making a distinction חִנָּה אָזְנוֹ. He has done it hitherto ; אֶקְרָא Therefore will I call upon him as long as I live, cleaving to Him in love and faith ! It should be noticed, in addition, that קְרָא here is not simply the prayer for help, but includes also the praising and thanksgiving, according to the twofold signification of קְרָא בְשֵׁם יְהֹוָה, in verses 4, 13, and 17: therefore, Jarchi very excellently says: *In the time of my distress I will call upon Him, and in the time of my deliverance I will praise Him.—Rudolph Stier.*

Verses 1, 2.—*"I love." "Therefore will I call upon him."* It is love that doth open our mouths, that we may praise God with joyful lips; " I will love the Lord because he hath heard the voice of my supplications "; and then, ver. 2, " I will call upon him as long as I live." The proper intent of mercies is to draw us to God. When the heart is full of a sense of the goodness of the Lord, the tongue cannot hold its peace. Self-love may lead us to prayers, but love to God excites us to praises: therefore to seek and not to praise, is to be lovers of ourselves rather than of God.—*Thomas Manton.*

Verses 1, 12.—*"I love." "What shall I render?"* Love and thankfulness are like the symbolical qualities of the elements, easily resolved into each other. David begins with, *"I love the LORD, because he hath heard my voice"*; and to enkindle this grace into a greater flame, he records the mercies of God in some following verses; which done, then he is in the right mood for praise; and cries, *"What shall I render unto the LORD for all his benefits?"* The spouse, when thoroughly awake, pondering with herself what a friend had been at her door, and how his sweet company was lost through her unkindness, shakes off her sloth, riseth, and away she goes after him; now, when by running after her beloved, she hath put her soul into a heat of love, she breaks out in praising him from top to toe. Cant. v. 10. That is the acceptable praising which comes from a warm heart; and the saint must use some holy exercise to stir up his habit of love, which like natural heat in the body, is preserved and increased by motion.—*William Gurnall.*

Verse 2.—*"He hath inclined his ear unto me."* How great a blessing, is the inclining of the Divine ear, may be judged from the conduct of great men, who do not admit a wretched petitioner to audience: but, if they do anything, receive the main part of the complaint through the officer appointed for such matters, or through a servant. But God himself hears immediately, and *inclines his ear,* hearing readily, graciously, constantly, etc. Who would not pray?—*Wolfgang Musculus.*

Verse 2.—And now *because he hath inclined his ear unto me,* I will therefore *call upon him as long as I live:* that if it be expected I should call upon any other, it must be when I am dead; for as long as I live, I have vowed to call upon God. But will this be well done? May I not, in so doing, do more than I shall have thanks for? Is this the requital that God shall have for his kindness in hearing me, that now he shall have a customer of me, and never be quiet because of my continual running to him, and calling upon him? Doth God get anything by my calling upon him, that I should make it a vow, as though in calling upon him I did him a pleasure? O my soul, I would that God might indeed have a customer of me in praying: although I confess I should not be so bold to call upon him so continually, if his own commanding me did not make it a duty: for hath not God bid me call upon him when I am in trouble? and is there any time that I am not in trouble, as long as I live in this vale of misery? and then can there be any time as long as I live, that I must not call upon him? For shall God bid me, and shall I not do it? Shall God incline his ear, and stand listening to hear, and shall I hold my peace that he may have nothing to hear?—*Sir Richard Baker.*

Verse 2.—*"Therefore will I call upon him."* If the hypocrite speed in prayer, and get what he asks, then also he throws up prayer, and will ask no more. If from a sick bed he be raised to health, he leaves prayer behind him, as it were, sick-abed; he grows weak in calling upon God, when at his call God hath given him strength. And thus it is in other instances. When he hath got what he hath a mind to in prayer, he hath no more mind to pray. Whereas a godly man prays after he hath sped, as he did before, and though he fall not into those troubles again, and so is not occasioned to urge those petitions again which he did in trouble, yet he cannot live without prayer, because he cannot live out of communion with God. The creature is as the white of an egg, tasteless to him, unless he enjoy God. David saith, *"I love the LORD, because he hath heard my voice and my supplications,"* that is, because he hath granted me that which I supplicated to him for. But did this grant of what he had asked take him off from asking more? The next words show us what his resolution was upon that grant. *"Because he hath inclined his ear unto me, therefore will I call upon him as long as I live";* as if he had said, I will never give over praying, forasmuch as I have been heard in prayer.—*Joseph Caryl.*

Verse 2.—"As long as I live." Not on some few days, but every day of my life; for to pray on certain days, and not on all, is the mark of one who loathes and not of one who loves.—*Ambrose.*

Verse 3.—Here beginneth the exemplification of God's kindness to his servant; the first branch whereof is a description of the danger wherein he was and out of which he was delivered. Now, to magnify the kindness of God the more in delivering him out of the same, he setteth it out with much variety of words and phrases.

The first word חֶבְלֵי, "*sorrows*," is diversely translated. Some expound it snares, some cords, some sorrows. The reason of this difference is because the word itself is metaphorical. It is taken from cruel creditors, who will be sure to tie their debtors fast, as with cords, so that they shall not easily get loose and free again. The pledge which the debtor leaveth with his creditor as a pawn, hath this name in Hebrew; so also a cord wherewith things are tied fast; and the mast of a ship fast fixed, and tied on every side with cords; and bands or troops of men combined together; and the pain of a woman in travail, which is very great; and destruction with pain and anguish. Thus we see that such a word is used here as setteth out a most lamentable and inextricable case.

The next word, "*of death*" מָוֶת, sheweth that his case was deadly; death was before his eyes; death was as it were threatened. He is said to be "*compassed*" herewith in two respects: (1) To show that these sorrows were not far off, but even upon him, as waters that compass a man when he is in the midst of them, or as enemies that begird a place. (2) To show that they were not few, but many sorrows, as bees that swarm together.

The word translated "*pains*," מְצָרֵי, in the original is put for sacks fast bound together, and flint stones, and fierce enemies, and hard straits; so that this word also aggravateth his misery.

The word translated "*hell*," שְׁאוֹל, is usually taken in the Old Testament for the grave; it is derived from שָׁאַל, a verb that signifieth to crave, because the grave is ever craving, and never satisfied.

The words translated "*gat hold on me*," מְצָאוּנִי, and "*I found*," אֶמְצָא, are both the same verb; they differ only in circumstances of tense, number, and person. The former showeth that these miseries found him, and as a serjeant they seized on him; he did not seek them, he would wittingly and willingly have escaped them, if he could. The latter sheweth that indeed he found them; he felt the tartness and bitterness, the smart and pain of them.

The word translated *trouble*, צָרָה of צוּר, hath a near affinity with the former word translated pain, מֵצַר of צוּר, and is used to set out as great misery as that; and yet further to aggravate the same, another word is added thereto, "*sorrow*."

The last word, "*sorrow*," יָגוֹן of יָגָה, importeth such a kind of calamity as maketh them that lie under it much to grieve, and also moveth others that behold it much to pity them. It is often used in the Lamentations of Jeremiah. Either of these two last words, trouble and sorrow, do declare a very perplexed and distressed estate; what then both of them joined together? For the Holy Ghost doth not multiply words in vain.—*William Gouge.*

Verse 3.—"Gat hold upon me." The original word is, *found me,* as we put in the margin. They found him, as an officer or serjeant finds a person that he is sent to arrest; who no sooner finds him, but he takes hold of him, or takes him into custody. When warrants are sent out to take a man who keeps out of the way, the return is, *Non est inventus,* the man is not found, he cannot be met with, or taken hold of. David's pains quickly found him, and having found him they gat hold of him. Such finding is so certainly and suddenly followed with taking hold, and holding what is taken, that one word in the Hebrew serves to express both acts. When God sends out troubles and afflictions as officers to attack any man, they will find him, and finding him, they will take hold of him. The days of affliction will take hold; there's no striving, no struggling with them, no getting out of their hands. These divine pursuivants will neither be persuaded nor bribed to let you go, till God speak the word, till God say, Deliver him, release him. "*I found trouble and sorrow.*" I found trouble which I looked not for. I was not searching after sorrow, but I found it. There's an elegancy in the original. The Hebrew is, "*The pains of hell found me.*" They found me, I did not find them;

but no sooner had the pains of hell found me, than I found trouble and sorrow, enough, and soon enough.—*Joseph Caryl.*

Verse 3.—See how the saints instead of lessening the dangers and tribulations, with which they are exercised by God, magnify them in figurative phraseology: neither do they conceal their distress of soul, but clearly and willingly set it forth. Far otherwise are the minds of those who regard their own glory and not the glory of God. The saints, that they may make more illustrious the glory of the help of God, declare things concerning themselves which make but little for their own glory.—*Wolfgang Musculus.*

Verses 3—7.—Those usually have most of heaven upon earth, that formerly have met with most of hell upon earth. *"The sorrows of death compassed me, and the pains of hell gat hold upon me: I found trouble and sorrow:* (as Jonas crying in the belly of hell). But look upon him within two or three verses after, and you may see him in an ecstasy, as if he were in heaven; verse 7: *"Return unto thy rest, O my soul; for the LORD hath dealt bountifully with thee."*—*Matthew Lawrence.*

Verse 4.—*"The name of the LORD."* God's name, as it is set out in the word, is both a glorious name, full of majesty; and also a gracious name, full of mercy. His majesty worketh fear and reverence, his mercy faith and confidence. By these graces man's heart is kept within such a compass, that he will neither presume above that which is meet, nor despond more than there is cause. But where God's name is not rightly known, it cannot be avoided but that they who come before him must needs rush upon the rock of presumption, or sink into the gulf of desperation. Necessary, therefore, it is that God be known of them that pray to him, that in truth they may say, *"We have called upon the name of the LORD."* Be persuaded hereby so to offer up your spiritual sacrifice of supplication to God, that he may have respect to your persons and prayers, as he had respect to Abel and his offering. Learn to know the name of God, as in his word it is made known; and then, especially when you draw near to him, meditate on his name. Assuredly God will take good notice of them that take due notice of him, and will open his ears to them by name who rightly call upon his name.—*William Gouge.*

Verse 4.—*"O LORD, I beseech thee, deliver my soul."* A short prayer for so great a suit, and yet as short as it was, it prevailed. If we wondered before at the power of God, we may wonder now at the power of prayer, that can prevail with God, for obtaining of that which in nature is impossible, and to reason is incredible.—*Sir Richard Baker.*

Verse 4.—We learn here that there is nothing better and more effectual in distressing agonies than assiduous prayer—*"Then called I upon the name of the LORD;"* but in such prayers the first care ought to be for the salvation of the soul—*"I beseech thee, deliver my soul";* for, this being done, God also either removes or mitigates the bodily disease.—*Solomon Gesner.*

Verse 5.—*"Gracious is the LORD,"* etc. He is *gracious* in hearing, he is *"righteous"* in judging, he is *"merciful"* in pardoning, and how, then, can I doubt of his will to help me? He is righteous to reward according to deserts; he is gracious to reward above deserts; yea, he is merciful to reward without deserts; and how, then, can I doubt of his will to help me? He is gracious, and this shews his bounty; he is righteous, and this shews his justice; yea, he is merciful, and this shews his love; and how, then, can I doubt of his will to help me? If he were not gracious I could not hope he would hear me; if he were not righteous, I could not depend upon his promise; if he were not merciful, I could not expect his pardon; but now that he is gracious and righteous and merciful too, how can I doubt of his will to help me?—*Sir Richard Baker.*

Verse 5.—The first attribute, *"gracious,"* (חַנּוּן) hath especial respect to that goodness which is in God himself. The root (חָנַן) whence it cometh signifieth to do a thing gratis, freely, of one's own mind and goodwill. This is that word which is used to set out the free grace and mere goodwill of God, thus (וְחַנֹּתִי אֶת־אֲשֶׁר אָחֹן), " I will be gracious to whom I will be gracious," Exod. xxxiii. 19. There is also an adverb (חִנָּם) derived thence, which signifieth gratis, freely, as where Laban thus speaketh to Jacob, " Shouldst thou serve me for nought?" Thus is the word opposed to merit. And hereby the prophet acknowledged that the deliverance which God gave was for the Lord's own sake, upon no desert of him that was delivered.

The second attribute, *"righteous"* or just, (צַדִּיק), hath particular relation to the promise of God. God's righteousness largely taken is the integrity or equity of all his counsels, words, and actions. . . . Particularly is God's righteousness manifested in giving reward and taking vengeance. Thus it is said to be " a righteous thing with God to recompense tribulation to them that trouble you ; and to you who are troubled rest," 2 Thess. i. 6, 7. . . . But the occasion of mentioning God's righteousness here in this place being to show the ground of his calling on God, and of God's delivering him, it must needs have respect to God's word and promise, and to God's truth in performing what he hath promised.—*William Gouge.*

Verse 5.—"*The* LORD " ; "*our God.*" The first title, "*Lord,*" sets out the excellency of God. Fit mention is here made thereof, to shew the blessed concurrence of greatness and goodness in God. Though he be Jehovah the Lord, yet is he gracious, and righteous, and merciful. The second title, "*our God,*" manifesteth a peculiar relation betwixt him and the faithful that believe in him, and depend on him, as this prophet did. And to them in an especial manner the Lord is gracious, which moved him thus to change the person ; for where he had said in the third person " the Lord is gracious," here, in the first person, he says, "*our God,*" yet so that he appropriateth not this privilege to himself, but acknowledgeth it to be common to all of like character by using the plural number, "*our.*"—*William Gouge.*

Verse 5.—The " Berlenburger Bibelwerk " says, " The righteousness is very significantly placed between the grace and the mercy : for it is still necessary, that the evil should be mortified and driven out. Grace lays, as it were, the foundation for salvation, and mercy perfects the work ; but not till righteousness has finished its intermediary work."—*Rudolph Stier.*

Verse 5.—"*Our God is merciful.*" Mercy is God's darling attribute ; and by his infinite wisdom he has enabled mercy to triumph over justice without in any degree violating his honour or his truth. The character of merciful is that by which our God seems to delight in being known. When he proclaimed himself amid terrific grandeur to the children of Israel, it was as " the Lord, the Lord God merciful and gracious, pardoning iniquity, transgression, and sin." And such was the impression of this his character on the mind of Jonah that he says to him, " I knew that thou wert a merciful God." These, however, are not mere assertions—claims made to the character by God on the one hand, and extorted without evidence from man on the other ; for in whatever way we look upon God, and examine into his conduct towards his creatures, we perceive it to bear the impression of mercy. Nor can we more exalt the Lord our God than by speaking of his mercy and confiding in it ; for our " Lord's delight is in them that fear him, and put their trust in his mercy."— *John Gwyther,* 1833.

Verse 6.—"*The* LORD *preserveth the simple.*" God taketh most care of them that, being otherwise least cared for, wholly depend on him. These are in a good sense simple ones ; simple in the world's account, and simple in their own eyes. Such as he that said, " I am a worm, and no man ; a reproach of men, and despised of the people." Ps. xxii. 6. And again, " I am poor and needy, yet the Lord thinketh on me." Ps. xl. 17. These are those poor ones of a contrite spirit on whom the Lord looketh. Isai. lxvi. 2. Of such fatherless is God a father ; and of such widows a judge. Read Ps. lxviii. 5, and cxlvi. 7, 8, 9. Yea, read observantly the histories of the Gospel, and well weigh who they were to whom Christ in the days of his flesh afforded succour, and you shall find them to be such simple ones as are here intended.

By such objects the free grace and merciful mind of the Lord is best manifested. Their case being most miserable, in reference to human helps, the greater doth God's mercy appear to be ; and since there is nothing in them to procure favour or succour from God, for in their own and others' eyes they are nothing, what God doth for them evidently appeareth to be freely done.

Behold here how of all others they who seem to have least cause to trust on God have most cause to trust on him. Simple persons, silly wretches, despicable fools in the world's account, who have not subtle brains, or crafty wits to search after indirect means, have, notwithstanding, enough to support them, in the grand fact that they are such as the Lord preserveth. Now, who knoweth not that " It is better to trust in the Lord, than to put confidence in man ; it is better to trust in the Lord, than to put confidence in princes " ? Ps. cxviii. 8, 9.—*William Gouge.*

Verse 6.—"*The* LORD *preserveth the simple.*" How delightful it is to be able to reflect on the character of God as *preserving* the soul. The word properly signifies to defend us at any season of danger.   The Hebrew word which is translated "simple," signifies one who has no control over himself, one that cannot resist the power and influence of those around, and one, therefore, subject to the greatest peril from which he has naturally no deliverance. " The Lord preserveth ": his eye is upon them, his hand is over them, and they cannot fall. The word "simple" signifies likewise those that are ignorant of their condition, and not watching over their foes. Delightful thought, that though we may be thus ignorant, yet we are blessed with the means of escape! We may be simple to the last extent, and our simplicity may be such as to involve our mind in the greatest doubt : the Lord preserveth us, and let us rest in him. It is delightful to reflect, that it is the simple in whom the Lord delights, whom he loves to bless. We are sometimes especially in the condition in which we may be inclined to make the inquiry, how we may be saved. We suppose there are many truths to be apprehended, many principles to be realized before we can be saved. No ; " the Lord preserveth the simple." We may be able to reconcile scarcely any of the doctrines of Christianity with each other ; we may find ourselves in the greatest perplexity when we examine the evidences on which they rest ; we may be exposed to great difficulty when we seek to apply them to practical usefulness ; but still we may adopt the language before us : "The LORD preserveth the simple : I was brought low, and he helped me. Return unto thy rest, O my soul."— R. S. M'All, 1834.

Verse 6.—"The LORD preserveth the simple."   The term simple equals the " simplicity " of the New Testament, namely, that pure mind towards God, which, without looking out for help from any other quarter, and free from all dissimulation, expects salvation from him alone.—Augustus F. Tholuck.

Verse 6.—"The simple."   They are such as honestly keep the plain way of God's commandments, without those slights, or creeks of carnal policy, for which men are in the world esteemed wise ; see Gen. xxv. 27, where Jacob is called a plain man. Simple or foolish he calls them, because they are generally so esteemed amongst the wise of the world ; not that they are so silly as they are esteemed ; for if the Lord can judge of wisdom or folly, the only fool is the Atheist and profane person (Ps. xiv. 1) ; the only wise man in the world is the plain, downright Christian (Deut. iv. 6), who keeps himself precisely in all states to that plain, honest course the Lord hath prescribed him. To such simple ones, God's fools, who in their misery and affliction keep them only to the means of deliverance and comfort which the Lord hath prescribed them, belongs this blessing of preservation from mischief, or destruction : so Solomon (Prov. xvi. 17), " The highway of the upright is to depart from evil." " He that keepeth his way preserveth his soul " ; see also Prov. xix. 16, 23 ; for exemplification see in Asa, 2 Chron. xiv. 9—12, and xvi. 7, 8, 9, read the excellent speech of Hanani the seer.—William Slater, 1638.

Verse 6.—"I was brought low." By affliction and trial. The Hebrew literally means to hang down, to be pendulous, to swing, to waive—as a bucket in a well, or as the slender branches of the palm, the willow, etc. Then it means to be slack, feeble, weak, as in sickness, etc. It probably refers to the prostration of strength by disease. "And he helped me." He gave me strength ; he restored me.—Albert Barnes.

Verse 6.—"I was brought low, and he helped me." The word translated "brought low," דַּלֹּתִי à דָּלָה , properly signifieth to be drawn dry. The metaphor is taken from ponds, or brooks, or rivers that are clean exhausted and dried up, where water utterly faileth. Thus doth Isaiah use this word, " The brooks shall be emptied and dried up," Isai. xix. 6, דָּלְלוּ וְחָרְבוּ יְאֹרֵי. Being applied to man, it setteth out such an one as is spent, utterly wasted, or, as we use to speak, clean gone, who hath no ability to help himself, no means of help, no hope of help from others.

The other word whereby the succour which God afforded is expressed, and translated "helped" יְהוֹשִׁיעַ ab יָשַׁע, signifieth such help as freeth out of danger. It is usually translated " to save."—William Gouge.

Verse 6.—"I was brought low, and he helped me." Then is the time of help, when men are brought low : and therefore God who does all things in due time when I was brought low, then helped me. Wherefore, O my soul, let it never trouble thee how low soever thou be brought, for when thy state is at the lowest, then is God's assistance at the nearest. We may truly say, God's ways are not as the ways of the world, for in the world when a man is once brought low, he is commonly trampled upon, and nothing is heard then but, " down with him, down to the ground": but with God it is otherwise ; for his delight is to raise up them that fall, and when they are brought low, then to help them. Hence it is no such hard case for a man to be brought low, may I not rather say his case is happy ? For is it not better to be brought low, and have God to help him, than to be set aloft and left to help himself ? At least, O my body, this may be a comfort to thee : for thou art sure to be brought low, as low as the grave, which is low indeed : yet there thou mayest rest in hope ; for even there the Lord will not fail to help thee.—*Sir Richard Baker.*

Verse 6.—*"He helped me."* Helped me both to bear the worst and to hope the best ; helped me to pray, else desire had failed ; helped me to wait, else faith had failed.—*Matthew Henry.*

Verse 7.—*"Return unto thy rest, O my soul."* The Psalmist had been at a great deal of unrest, and much *off the hooks,* as we say ; now, having prayed (for prayer hath *vim pacativam,* a pacifying property), he calleth his soul to rest ; and rocketh it asleep in a spiritual security. Oh, learn this holy art ; acquaint thyself with God, acquiesce in him, and be at peace ; so shall good be done unto thee. Job xxii. 21. *Sis Sabbathum Christi.* Luther.—*John Trapp.*

Verse 7.—Gracious souls rest in God ; they and none else. Whatever others may speak of a rest in God, only holy souls know what it means. *"Return unto thy rest, O my soul,"* to thy rest in calm and cheerful submission to God's will, delight in his service, satisfaction in his presence, and joy in communion begun with him here below, which is to be perfected above in its full fruition. Holy souls rest in God, and in his will ; in his will of precept as their sovereign Lord, whose commands concerning all things are right, and in the keeping of which there is great reward ; in his will of providence as their absolute owner, and who does all things well ; in himself as their God, their portion, and their chief good, in whom they shall have all that they can need, or are capable of enjoying to complete their blessedness for ever.—*Daniel Wilcox.*

Verse 7.—*"Return unto thy rest."* Return to that rest which Christ gives to the weary and heavy laden, Matt. xi. 28. Return to thy Noah, his name signifies *rest,* as the dove when she found no rest returned to the ark. I know no word more proper to close our eyes when at night when we go to sleep, nor to close them with at death, that long sleep, than this, *"Return unto thy rest, O my soul."*—*Matthew Henry.*

Verse 7.—*"Return unto thy rest."* Consider the variety of aspects of that rest which a good man seeks, and the ground upon which he will endeavour to realize it. It consists in, 1. Rest from the perplexities of ignorance, and the wanderings of error. 2. Rest from the vain efforts of self-righteousness, and the disquietude of a proud and legal spirit. 3. Rest from the alarms of conscience, and the apprehensions of punishment hereafter. 4. Rest from the fruitless struggles of our degenerate nature, and unaided conflicts with indwelling sin. 5. Rest from the fear of temporal suffering and solicitude arising from the prospect of danger and trial. 6. Rest from the distraction of uncertainty and indecision of mind, and from the fluctuations of undetermined choice.—*R. S. M'All.*

Verse 7.—*"Return,"* שׁוּבִי. This is the very word which the angel used to Hagar when she fled from her mistress, " Return," Gen. xvi. 9. As Hagar through her mistress' rough dealing with her fled from her, so the soul of this prophet by reason of affliction fell from its former quiet confidence in God. As the angel therefore biddeth Hagar " return to her mistress," so the understanding of this prophet biddeth his soul return to its rest.—*William Gouge.*

Verse 7.—*"Rest."* The word *"rest "* is put in the plural, as indicating complete and entire rest, at all times, and under all circumstances.—*A. Edersheim.*

Verses 7, 8.—*"For the* LORD *hath dealt bountifully with thee."* He hath dealt indeed most bountifully with thee, for where thou didst make suit but for one thing, he hath granted thee three. Thou didst ask but to have my soul delivered, and he hath delivered mine eyes and my feet besides ; and with a deliverance in each of them the greatest that could be : for what greater deliverance to my soul than to be delivered from death ? What greater deliverance to my eyes than to be delivered from tears ? What to my feet than to be delivered from falling ? That if now, O my soul, thou return not to thy rest, thou wilt show thyself to be most insatiable ; seeing thou hast not only more than thou didst ask, but as much indeed as was possible to be asked.

But can my soul die ? and if not, what bounty is it to deliver my soul from that to which it is not subject ? The soul indeed, though immortal, hath yet her ways of dying. It is one kind of death to the soul to be parted from the body, but the truest kind is to be parted from God ; and from both these kinds of death he hath delivered my soul. From the first, by delivering me from a dangerous sickness that threatened a dissolution of my soul and body ; from the other, by delivering me from the guilt of sin, which threatened a separation from the favour of God ; and are not these bounties so great as to give my soul just cause of returning to her rest ?—*Sir Richard Baker.*

Verses 7, 9.—"*Return unto thy rest, O my soul.*" . . . "*I will walk.*" How can these two stand together ? *Motus et quies private opponuntur*, saith the philosopher, motion and rest are opposite ; now *walking* is a *motion*, as being an act of the loco- motive faculty. How then could David *return to his rest* and yet *walk ?* You must know that *walking* and *rest* here mentioned, being of a *divine* nature, do not oppose each other ; *spiritual rest* maketh no man *idle*, and therefore it is no enemy to walking ; *spiritual walking* maketh no man *weary*, and therefore it is no enemy to rest. Indeed, they are so far from being opposite that they are subservient to each other, and it is hard to say whether that *rest* be the *cause* of this *walking*, or this *walking* a *cause* of that *rest*. Indeed, both are true, since he that *rests in God* cannot but *walk before him*, and by *walking before*, we come to *rest in God*. *Returning to rest* is an act of *confidence*, since there is no rest to be had but in God, nor in God but by believing affiance in, and reliance on him. *Walking before God* is an act of *obedience* ; when we disobey we wander and go astray, only by obedience we walk. Now these two are so far from being enemies, that they are companions and ever go together ; confidence being a means to quicken obedience, and obedience to strengthen con- fidence.—*Nathanael Hardy.*

Verse 8.—"*Thou hast delivered my soul from death, mine eyes from tears, and my feet from falling.*" Lo, here a deliverance, not from one, but many dangers, to wit, "*death*," "*tears*," "*falling*." Single deliverances are as threads ; but when multiplied, they become a cord twisted of many threads, more potent to draw us to God. Any one mercy is as a link, but many favours are as a chain consisting of several links, to bind us the closer to our duty ; *vis unita fortior.* Frequent droppings of the rain cannot but make an impression even on the stone, and renewed mercies may well prevail with the stony heart. Parisiensis relateth a story of a man whom (notwithstanding his notorious and vicious courses) God was pleased to accumulate favours upon, so that at last he cried out, "*Vicisti, benignissime Deus, indefatigabili sua bonitate*, Most gracious God, thy unwearied goodness hath overcome my obstinate wickedness " ; and from that time devoted himself to God's service. No wonder, then, if David upon deliverance from such numerous and grievous afflictions, maketh this his resolve, to "*walk before the Lord in the land of the living.*"—*Nathanael Hardy.*

Verse 8.—As an humble and sensible soul will pack up many troubles in one, so a thankful soul will divide one mercy into sundry particular branches, as here the Psalmist distinguisheth, the delivery of his soul from death, of his eyes from tears, and of his feet from falling.—*David Dickson.*

Verse 8.—Some distinguish the three particulars thus : "*He hath delivered my soul from death*," by giving me a good conscience ; "*mine eyes from tears*," by giving a quiet conscience ; "*my feet from falling*," by giving an enlightened and assured conscience.—*William Gouge.*

Verse 8.—"*My feet from falling.*" Whether means he, into penal misery and mischief, or into sin ? There is a *lapsus moralis*, as 1 Cor. x. 12. Err I ? or would David here be understood of sinning ? So Ps. lxxiii. 2 : " My feet were almost gone ; my steps had well nigh slipped." And if I be not deceived, the text leans to that meaning, rising still from the less to the greater. First. It is more bounty to be kept from grief than from death, for there is a greater enlargement from misery. It is not more bounty to be kept from the sense of affliction than to be kept from death, which is the greatest of temporal evils ; but it is more bounty in a gracious eye to be kept from sin than from death. Secondly. *How his eyes from tears ?* If not kept from sin ? That had surely cost him many a tear, as Peter (Matt. xxvi. 75). But understand it *de lapsu morali*, so the gradation still riseth to enlarge God's bounty ; yea, which I count the greatest blessing, in these afflictions he kept me steady in my course of piety, and suffered not afflictions to sway my heart from him. Still, in a gracious eye, the benefit seems greater to be delivered from sinning than from the greatest outward affliction. That is the reason Paul (Rom. viii. 37) triumphs over all afflictions. 2 Cor. xi. and xii. He counts them his glory, his crown ; but speaking of the prevailing of corruption in particular, he bemoans himself as the miserablest man alive. Rom. vii. 24.—*William Slater.*

Verse 9.—"*I will walk*," etc. It is a holy resolution which this verse records. The previous verse had mentioned among the mercies vouchsafed, " Thou hast delivered my feet from falling"; and the first use of the restored limb is, "*I will walk before the* LORD." It reminds one of the crippled beggar at the Beautiful Gate of the temple, to whom Peter had said, " In the name of Jesus Christ rise up and walk "; and " immediately his ancle-bones received strength, and he leaping up stood and walked, and entered with them into the temple, walking, and leaping, and praising God." It is a very sure mark of a grateful heart to employ the gift to the praise of the giver, in such a manner as he would most wish it to be employed.— *Barton Bourchier.*

Verse 9.—When thou, my soul, returnest to this rest, thou shalt walk in order that thou mayest have some exercise in thy rest, that thy resting may not make thee restive. "*I will walk before the* LORD *in the land of the living.*" For now that my feet are delivered from falling, how can I better employ them than in walking ? Were they delivered from falling that they should stand still and be idle ? No, my soul, but to encourage me to walk : and where is so good walking as in the land of the living ? Alas ! what walking is it in the winter, when all things are dead, when the very grass lies buried under ground, and scarce anything that has life in it is to be seen ? But then is the pleasant walking, when nature spreads her green carpet to walk upon, and then it is the land of the living, when the trees shew they live, by bringing forth, if not fruits, at least leaves ; when the valleys shew they live, by bringing forth sweet flowers to delight the smell, at least fresh grass to please the eyes. But is this the walking in the land of the living that David means ? O my soul, to walk in the land of the living is to walk in the paths of righteousness : for there is no such death to the soul as sin, no such cause of tears to the eyes as guiltiness of conscience, no such falling of the feet as to fall from God : and therefore, to say the truth, the soul can never return to its rest if we walk not withal in the paths of righteousness ; and we cannot well say whether this rest be a cause of the walk, or the walking be a cause of the resting : but this we may say, they are certainly companions the one to the other, which is in effect but this—that justification can never be without sanctification. Peace of conscience, and godliness of life, can never be one without the other. Or is it perhaps that David means that land of the living where Enoch and Elias are living, with the living God ? But if he mean so, how can he speak so confidently, and say, "*I will walk in the land of the living*" ? as though he could come to walk there by his own strength, or at his own pleasure ? He therefore gives his reason : "*I believed, and therefore I spake,*" for the voice of faith is strong, and speaks with confidence ; and because in faith he believes that he should come to walk in the land of the living, therefore with confidence he speaks it, "*I will walk in the land of the living.*"—*Sir Richard Baker.*

Verse 9.—"*I will walk before the* LORD *in the land of the living,*" *i.e.*, I shall pass the whole of my life under his fatherly care and protection. The prophet has regard to the custom of men, and chiefly of parents : for those who ardently love their children have them always in their thoughts and carry them there, never ceasing from care and anxiety about them, but being always attentive to their safety. *Omnis enim in natis chari stat cura parentis.* Children are, therefore, said to walk before and in the sight of their parents, because they have them as constant guardians of their health and safety. Thus also the godly in this life walk before God, that is to say, are defended by his care and protection.—*Mollerus.*

Verse 9.—"*I will walk before the* LORD." According to a different reading of the first word, "*I shall,*" and, "*I will,*" the clause puts on several senses ; if read "*I shall walk,*" they are words of *confident expectation ;* if "*I will,*" they are words of *obedient resolution.* According to the former, the Psalmist promiseth somewhat to himself from God ; according to the latter, he promiseth somewhat of himself to God. Both these constructions are probable and profitable. "*Before God*"; that is, in his service ; or, "*before God,*" that is, under his care. Let us consider both senses. 1. "*I shall walk before the* LORD *in the land of the living*" ; that is, by continuing in this world, I shall have opportunity of doing God service. It was not because those holy men had less assurance of God's love than we, but because they had greater affections to God's service than we, that this life was so amiable in their eyes. To this purpose the reasonings of David and Hezekiah concerning death and the grave are very observable. " Shall the dust praise thee ? shall it declare thy truth"? so David, Ps. xxx. 9. " The grave cannot praise thee, death cannot celebrate thee"; so Hezekiah, Isai. xxxviii. 18. They saw death would render them useless for God's honour, and therefore they prayed for life.

It lets us see why a religious man may desire life, that he may *"walk before the LORD,"* and minister to him in the place wherein he hath set him. Indeed, that joy, hope, and desire of life which is founded upon this consideration is not only lawful, but commendable : and truly herein is a vast difference between the wicked and the godly. To walk in the land of the living is the wicked man's desire, yea, were it possible he would walk here for ever ; but for what end ? only to enjoy his lusts, have his fill of pleasure, and increase his wealth : whereas the godly man's aim in desiring to live is that he may *"walk before God,"* advance his glory, and perform his service. Upon this account it is that one hath fitly taken notice how David doth not say, I shall now satiate myself with delights in my royal city, but, *"I shall walk before the Lord in the land of the living."*

2. And most suitably to this interpretation, this *"before the* LORD," means *under the Lord's careful eye.* The words according to the Hebrew may be read, *before the face of the* LORD, by which is meant his presence, and that not general, before which all men walk, but special, before which only good men walk. Indeed, in this sense *God's face* is as much as his favour ; and as to be cast out of his sight is to be under his anger, so to walk before his face is to be in favour with him : so that the meaning is, as the Psalmist had said, I shall live securely and safely in this world under the careful protection of the Almighty ; and this is the confidence which he here seemeth to utter with so much joy, that God's gracious providence should watch over him the remainder of his days.—*Nathanael Hardy, in a Sermon entitled "Thankfulness in Grain,"* 1654.

Verse 9.—"In the land of the living." These words admit of a threefold interpretation, being understood by some, especially for *the land of Judea.* By others, erroneously for *the Jerusalem which is above.* By the most, and most probably, for this *habitable earth,* the *present world.*

1. That exposition which Cajetan, Lorinus, with others, give of the words, would not be rejected, who conceive that by *"the land of the living"* David here meaneth Judea, in which, or rather over which being constituted king, he resolveth to walk before God, and do him service. This is not improbably that *"land of the living"* in which the Psalmist when an exile " believed to see the goodness of the Lord"; this is certainly that *"land of the living"* wherein God promiseth to " set his glory"; nor was this title without just reason appropriated to that country. (1.) *Partly,* because it was a " *land*" which afforded the most plentiful supports and comforts of natural life, in regard of the wholesomeness of the climate, the goodness of the soil, the overflowing of milk and honey, with other conveniences both for food and delight. (2.) *Chiefly,* because it was the "*land*" in which the living God was worshipped, and where he vouchsafed to place his name ; whereas the other parts of the world worshipped lifeless things, of which the Psalmist saith, " They have mouths, and speak not ; eyes, and see not ; ears, and hear not."

2. *"The land of the living"* is construed by the ancients to be that *heavenly country,* the place of the blessed. Indeed, this appellation does most fitly agree with heaven : this world is *desertum mortuorum,* a desert of dead, at least, dying men ; that only is *regio vivorum,* a region of living saints. " He who is our life " is in heaven, yea, " our life is hid with him in God," and therefore we cannot be said to live till we come thither. . . . In this sense no doubt that devout bishop and martyr, Babilas, used the words, who being condemned by Numerianus, the emperor, to an unjust death, a little before his execution repeated this and the two preceding verses, with a loud voice. Nor is it unfit for any dying saint to comfort himself with the like application of these words, and say in a confident hope of that blessed sight, *"I shall walk before the* LORD *in the land of the living."*

3. But doubtless the literal and proper meaning of these words is of *David's abode in the world ;* during which time, wheresoever he should be, he would *"walk before God" ;* for that seems to be the emphasis of the plural number, *lands,* according to the original. The world consists of many countries, several lands, and it is possible for men either by force, or unwillingly, to remove from one country to another : but a good man when he changeth his country, yet altereth not his religion, yea, wherever he is he resolveth to serve his God.—*Nathanael Hardy.*

Verse 9.—"Land of the living." How unmeet, how shameful, how odious a thing it is that dead men should be here on the face of the earth, which is *"the land of the living."* That there are such is too true. "She that liveth in pleasure is dead while she liveth," 1 Tim. v. 6 ; Sardis had a name that she lived, but was dead, Rev. iii. 1 ; "The dead bury their dead," Matt. viii. 22 ; all natural men are "dead in sins," Eph. ii. 1, 2 Cor. v. 14.—*William Gouge.*

Verses 9, 12, etc.—The Hebrew word that is rendered *walk*, signifies a continued action, or the reiteration of an action. David resolves that he will not only take a turn or two with God, or walk a pretty way with God, as Orpah did with Ruth, and then take his leave of God, as Orpah did of her mother, Ruth i. 10—15 ; but he resolves, whatever comes on it, that he will walk constantly, resolutely, and perpetually before God ; or before the face of the Lord. Now, walking before the face of the Lord doth imply a very exact, circumspect, accurate, and precise walking before God ; and indeed, no other walking is either suitable or pleasing to the eye of God. But is this all that he will do upon the receipt of such signal mercies ? Oh, no ! for he resolves to take the cup of salvation, and to call upon the name of the Lord, and to offer the sacrifice of thanksgiving, vers. 13, 17. But is this all that he will do ? Oh, no ! for he resolves that he will presently pay his vows unto the Lord in the presence of all his people, vers. 14, 18. But is this all that he will do ? Oh, no ! for he resolves that he will love the Lord better than ever and more than ever, vers. 1, 2. He loved God before with a real love, but having now received such rare mercies from God, he is resolved to love God with a more raised love, and with a more inflamed love, and with a more active and stirring love, and with a more growing and increasing love than ever.—*Thomas Brooks.*

Verse 10.—*"I believed, therefore have I spoken."* It is not sufficient to believe, unless thou also openly confessest before unbelievers, tyrants, and all others. Next to believing follows confession ; and therefore, those who do not make a confession ought to fear ; as, on the contrary, those should hope who speak out what they have believed.—*Paulus Palanterius.*

Verse 10.—*"I believed, therefore have I spoken."* That is to say, I firmly believe what I say, therefore I make no scruple of saying it. This should be connected with the preceding verse, and the full stop should be placed at "spoken."—*Samuel Horsley.*

Verse 10.—*"I believed,"* etc. Some translate the words thus : *I believed when I said, I am greatly afflicted :* I believed when I said in my haste, *"all men are liars" ; q.d.,* Though I have had my *offs* and my *ons,* though I have passed several frames of heart and tempers of soul in my trials, yet I believed still, I never let go my hold, my grip of God, in my perturbation.—*John Trapp.*

Verse 10.—The heart and tongue should go together. The tongue should always be the heart's interpreter, and the heart should always be the tongue's suggester ; what is spoken with the tongue should be first stamped upon the heart and wrought off from it. Thus it should be in all our communications and exhortations, especially when we speak or exhort about the things of God, and dispense the mysteries of heaven. David spake from his heart when he spake from his faith. *"I believed, therefore have I spoken."* Believing is an act of the heart, "with the heart man believeth" ; so that to say, *"I believed, therefore have I spoken,"* is as if he had said, I would never have spoken these things, if my heart had not been clear and upright in them. The apostle takes up that very protestation from David (2 Cor. iv. 13) : "According as it is written, I believed, and therefore have I spoken ; we also believe, and therefore speak" ; that is, we move others to believe nothing but what we believe, and are fully assured of ourselves.—*Joseph Caryl.*

Verse 10.—*"I was greatly afflicted."* After that our minstrel hath made mention of faith and of speaking the word of God, whereby are to be understood all good works that proceed and come forth out of faith, he now singeth of the cross, and sheweth that he was very sore troubled, grievously threatened, uncharitably blasphemed, evil reported, maliciously persecuted, cruelly troubled, and made to suffer all kinds of torments for uttering and declaring the word of God. *"I believed,"* saith he, *"therefore have I spoken ; but I was very sore troubled."* Christ's word and the cross are companions inseparable. As the shadow followeth the body, so doth the cross follow the word of Christ : and as fire and heat cannot be separated, so cannot the gospel of Christ and the cross be plucked asunder.—*Thomas Becon* (1511—1567 or 1570).

Verses 10, 11.—The meaning seems to be this—I spake as I have declared (ver. 4) because I trusted in God. I was greatly afflicted, I was in extreme distress, I was in great astonishment and trembling (as the word rendered *"haste"* signifies trembling as well as haste, as it is rendered in Deut. xx. 3;) and in these circumstances I did not trust in man ; I said, *"all men are liars"*—*i.e.*, not fit to be trusted in ; those that will fail and deceive the hopes of those who trust in them, agreeable to Psalm lxii. 8, 9.—*Jonathan Edwards.*

Verse 11.—*"I said in my haste, All men are liars,"* Rather, in an ecstacy of despair, I said, the whole race of man is a delusion.—*Samuel Horsley.*

Verse 11.—*"All men are liars."* That is to say, every man who speaks in the ordinary manner of men concerning happiness, and sets great value on the frail and perishable things of this world, is a liar ; for true and solid happiness is not to be found in the country of the living. This explanation solves the sophism proposed by St. Basil. If every man be a liar, then David was a liar ; therefore he lies when he says, every man is a liar—thus contradicting himself, and destroying his own position. This is answered easily ; for when David spoke he did so not as man, but from an inspiration of the Holy Ghost.—*Robert Bellarmine.*

Verse 11.—*"All men are liars."* Juvenal said, " Dare to do something worthy of transportation and imprisonment, if you mean to be of consequence. Honesty is praised, but starves." A pamphlet was published some time ago with the title, *"Whom shall we hang ?"* A very appropriate one might *now* be written with a slight change in the title—*"Whom shall we trust ?"*—*From " A New Dictionary of Quotations,"* 1872.

Verses 11—15.—It seems that to give the lie was not so heinous an offence in David's time as it is in these days ; for else how durst he have spoken such words, *"That all men are liars,"* which is no less than to give the lie to the whole world ? and yet no man, I think, will challenge him for saying so ; no more than challenge St. John for saying that all men are sinners, and indeed how should any man avoid being a liar, seeing the very being of man is itself a lie ? not only is it a vanity, and put in the balance less than vanity ; but a very lie, promising great matters, and able to do just nothing, as Christ saith, " without me ye can do nothing " : and so Christ seems to come in, to be David's second, and to make his word good, that *all men are liars.* And now let the world do its worst, and take the lie how it will, for David having Christ on his side, will always be able to make his part good against all the world, for Christ hath overcome the world.

But though all men may be said to be liars, yet not all men in all things ; for then David himself should be a liar in this : but all men perhaps in something or other, at sometime or other, in some kind or other. Absolute truth is not found in any man, but in that man only who was not man only ; for if he had been so, it had not perhaps been found in him neither, seeing absolute truth and deity are as relatives, never found to be asunder.

But in what thing is it that all men should be liars ? Indeed, in this for one ; to think that God regards not, and loves not them whom he suffers to be afflicted ; for we may rather think he loves them most whom he suffers to be most afflicted ; and we may truly say he would never have suffered his servant Job to be afflicted so exceeding cruelly, if he had not loved him exceeding tenderly ; for there is nothing lost by suffering afflictions. No, my soul, they do but serve to make up the greater weight of glory, when it shall be revealed.

But let God's afflictions be what they can be, yet I will always acknowledge they can never be in any degree so great as his benefits : and oh, that *I could think of something that I might render to him for all his benefits :* for shall I receive such great, such infinite benefits from him, and shall I render nothing to him by way of gratefulness ? But, alas, what have I to render ? All my rendering to him will be but taking more from him : for all I can do is but to *"take the cup of salvation, and call upon his name,"* and what rendering is there in this taking ? If I could take the cup of tribulation, and drink it off for his sake, this might be a rendering of some value ; but this, God knows, is no work for me to do. It was his work, who said, " Can ye drink of the cup, of which I shall drink ? " Indeed, he drank of the cup of tribulation, to the end that we might take the cup of salvation ; but then in taking it we must call upon his name ; upon his name and upon no other ; for else we shall make it a cup of condemnation, seeing there is no name under heaven, in which we may be saved, but only the name of Jesus.

Yet it may be some rendering to the Lord if I pay my vows, and do, as it were, my penance openly; *"I will therefore pay my vows to the* LORD, *in the presence of all his people."* But might he not pay his vows as well in his closet, between God and himself, as to do it publicly? No, my soul, it serves not his turn, but he must pay them in the presence of all his people; yet not to the end he should be applauded for a just prayer; for though he pay them, yet he can never pay them to the full; but to the end, that men seeing his good works, may glorify God by his example. And the rather perhaps, for that David was a king, and the king's example prevails much with the people, to make them pay their vows to God: but most of all, that by this means David's piety may not be barren, but may make a breed of piety in the people also: which may be one mystical reason why it was counted a curse in Israel to be barren; for he that pays not his vows to God in the presence of his people may well be said to be barren in Israel seeing he begets no children to God by his example. And perhaps, also, the vows which David means here was the doing of some mean things, unfit in show for the dignity of a king; as when it was thought a base thing in him to dance before the ark; he then vowed he would be baser yet: and in this case, to pay his vows before the people becomes a matter of necessity: for as there is no honour to a man whilst he is by himself alone, so there is no shame to a man but before the people: and therefore to shew that he is not ashamed to do any thing how mean soever, so it may tend to the glorifying of God; *"he will pay his vows in the presence of all his people."* And he will do it though it cost him his life, for if he die for it he knows that *"Precious in the sight of the* LORD *is the death of his saints."* But that which is precious is commonly desired: and doth God then desire the death of his saints? He desires, no doubt, that death of his saints which is to die to sin: but for any other death of his saints, it is therefore said to be precious in his sight, because he lays it up with the greater carefulness. And for this it is there are such several mansions in God's house, that to them whose death is precious in his sight he may assign the most glorious mansions. This indeed is the reward of martyrdom, and the encouragement of martyrs, though their sufferings be most insufferable, their troubles most intolerable; yet this makes amends for all; that *"Precious in the sight of the* LORD *is the death of his saints."* For if it be so great a happiness to be acceptable in his sight, how great a happiness must it be to be precious in his sight? When God, at the creation looked upon all his works, it is said he saw them to be all exceeding good: but it is not said that any of them were precious in his sight. How then comes death to be precious in his sight, that was none of his works, but is a destroyer of his works? Is it possible that a thing which destroys his creatures should have a title of more value in his sight, than his creatures themselves? O, my soul, this is one of the miracles of his saints, and perhaps one of those which Christ meant, when he said to his apostles, that greater miracles than he did they should do themselves: for what greater miracle than this, that death, which of itself is a thing most vile in the sight of God, yet once embraced by his saints, as it were by their touch only, becomes precious in his sight? To alter a thing from being vile to be precious, is it not a greater miracle than to turn water into wine? Indeed so it is; death doth not damnify his saints, but his saints do dignify death. Death takes nothing away from his saints' happiness, but his saints add lustre to death's vileness. It is happy for death that ever it met with any of God's saints; for there was no way for it else in the world, to be ever had in any account: but why say I, in the world? For it is of no account in the world for all this: it is but only in the sight of God; but indeed this only is all in all; for to be precious in God's sight is more to be prized than the world itself. For when the world shall pass away, and all the glory of it be laid in the dust; then shall trophies be erected for the death of his saints: and when all monuments of the world shall be utterly defaced, and all records quite rased out; yet the death of his saints shall stand registered still, in fair red letters in the calendar of heaven. If there be glory laid up for them that die in the Lord; much more shall they be glorified that die for the Lord.

I have wondered oftentimes, why God will suffer his saints to die; I mean not the death natural, for I know *statutum est omnibus semel mori;* but the death that is by violence, and with torture: for who could endure to see them he loves so cruelly handled? But now I see the reason of it; for, *"Precious in the sight of the* LORD *is the death of his saints."* And what marvel then if he suffer his saints to die; when by dying they are wrought, and made fit jewels to be set in his cabinet: for as God has a bottle which he fills up with the tears of his saints, so I may say he hath a cabinet which he decks up with the deaths of his saints: and, O my soul, if thou couldst but comprehend what a glory it is to serve for a jewel in the decking up of God's cabinet, thou wouldest never wonder why he suffers his saints to be put to death, though with never so great torments, for it is but the same which Saint Paul saith : " The afflictions of this life are not worthy to be compared with the glory that shall be revealed."—*Sir Richard Baker.*

Verse 12.—"*What shall I render unto the* LORD *?* " Rendering to the true God, in a true and right manner, is the sum of true religion. This notion is consonant to the scriptures : thus : " Render unto God the things that are God's." Matt. xxii. 21. As true loyalty is a giving to Cæsar the things that are Cæsar's, so true piety is the giving to God the things that are God's. And so, in that parable of the vineyard let out to husbandmen, all we owe to God is expressed by the *rendering the fruit of the vineyard ;* Matt. xxi. 41. Particular acts of religion are so expressed in the Scriptures Psalm lvi. 12 ; Hosea xiv. 2 ; 2 Chron. xxxiv. 31. Let this, then, be the import of David's מָה־אָשִׁיב לַיהוָה, "*What shall I render unto the* LORD *?*" " In what things, and by what means, shall I promote religion in the exercise thereof ? How shall I show myself duly religious towards him who hath been constantly and abundantly munificent in his benefits towards me ? "—*Henry Hurst.*

Verse 12.—"*All his benefits toward me.*" What reward shall we give unto the Lord, for all the benefits he hath bestowed ? From the cheerless gloom of non-existence he waked us into being ; he ennobled us with understanding ; he taught us arts to promote the means of life ; he commanded the prolific earth to yield its nurture ; he bade the animals to own us as their lords. For us the rains descend ; for us the sun sheddeth abroad its creative beams ; the mountains rise, the valleys bloom, affording us grateful habitation and a sheltering retreat. For us the rivers flow ; for us the fountains murmur ; the sea opens its bosom to admit our commerce ; the earth exhausts its stores ; each new object presents a new enjoyment ; all nature pouring her treasures at our feet, through the bounteous grace of him who wills that all be ours.—*Basil,* 326—379.

Verse 12.—"*All his benefits.*" As partial obedience is not good, so partial thanks is worthless : not that any saint is able to keep all the commands, or reckon up all the mercies of God, much less return particular acknowledgment for every single mercy ; but as he " hath respect unto all the commandments " (Ps. cxix. 6), so he desires to value highly every mercy, and to his utmost power give God the praise of all. An honest soul would not conceal any debt he owes to God, but calls upon itself to give an account for all his benefits. The skipping over one note in a lesson may spoil the grace of the music ; unthankfulness for one mercy disparageth our thanks for the rest.—*William Gurnall.*

Verse 13.—"*I will take the cup of salvation.*" It may probably allude to the libation offering, Numb. xxviii. 7 ; for the three last verses seem to intimate that the Psalmist was now at the temple, offering the meat-offering, drink-offering, and sacrifices to the Lord. "*Cup*" is often used by the Hebrews to denote plenty or abundance. So, " the cup of trembling," an abundance of *misery ;* " the cup of salvation," an abundance of *happiness.*—*Adam Clarke.*

Verse 13.—"*Cup of salvation.*" In holy Scripture there is mention made of drink-offerings, Gen. xxv. 14 ; Levit. xxiii. 13 ; Num. xv. 5 ; which were a certain quantity of wine that used to be poured out before the Lord ; as the very notation of the word importeth, coming from a root נָסַךְ, *effudit,* that signifieth to pour out. As the meat-offerings, so the drink-offerings, were brought to the Lord in way of gratulation and thanksgiving. Some therefore in allusion hereunto so expound the text, as a promise and vow of the Psalmist, to testify his public gratitude by such an external and solemn rite as in the law was prescribed. This he termeth *a cup,* because that drink-offering was contained in a cup and poured out thereof ; and he adds this epithet, " salvation," because that rite was an acknowledgment of salvation, preservation and deliverance from the Lord.

After their solemn gratulatory sacrifices they were wont to have a feast. When David had brought the ark of God into the tabernacle, they offered burnt offerings and peace offerings, which being finished, " he dealt to every one of Israel, both man and woman, to every one a loaf of bread, and a good piece of flesh, and a flagon of wine." 1 Chron. xvi. 3. Hereby is implied that he made so bountiful a feast, as he had to give thereof to all the people there assembled. In this feast the master thereof was wont to take a great cup, and in lifting it up to declare the occasion of that feast, and then in testimony of thankfulness to drink thereof to the guests, that they in order might pledge him. This was called a cup of salvation, or deliverance, because they acknowledged by the use thereof that God had saved and delivered them. Almost in a like sense the apostle styleth the sacramental cup, the cup of blessing. Here the prophet useth the plural number, thus, "cup of *salvations*," whereby, after the Hebrew elegancy, he meaneth many deliverances, one after another ; or some great and extraordinary deliverance which was instead of many, or which comprised many under it. The word translated *take* (אשׂא *a* נשׂא) properly signifieth to lift up, and in that respect may the more fitly be applied to the forementioned taking of the festival cup and lifting it up before the guests. Most of our later expositors of this Psalm apply this phrase, "I will take the cup of salvation," to the forenamed gratulatory drink-offering, or to the taking and lifting up of the cup of blessing in the feast, after the solemn sacrifice. Both of these import one and the same thing, which is, that saints of old were wont to testify their gratefulness for great deliverances with some outward solemn rite.—*William Gouge.*

Verse 13.—"*Cup of salvation.*" *Yeshuoth :* Ps. xviii. 50, xxviii. 8, liii. 6. The *cup* of salvation, symbolized by the eucharistic cup of the Passover Supper.—Zion that had drunk of the "cup of trembling" (Isai. li. 17, 22) might now rise and drink of the cup of salvation.

To the church these words have had a yet deeper significancy added to them by St. Matt. xxvi. 27. Jesus, on that Passover night, drank of the bitter wine of God's wrath, that he might refill the cup with joy and health for his people.—*William Kay.*

Verses 13, 14, 17—19.—A fit mode of expressing our thanks to God is by solemn acts of worship, secret, social, and public. "The closet will be the first place where the heart will delight in pouring forth its lively joys ; thence the feeling will extend to the family altar ; and thence again it will proceed to the sanctuary of the Most High." (*J. Morison*). To every man God has sent a large supply of benefits, and nothing but perverseness can deny to him the praise of our lips.—*William S. Plumer.*

Verse 14.—A man that would have his credit as to the truth of his word kept up, would choose those to be witnesses of his performing who were witnesses of his promising. I think David took this heed in his rendering and paying his vows : "*I will do it*," saith he, "*now in the presence of all his people.*" The people were witnesses to his straits, prayers, and vows ; and he will honour religion by performing in their sight what he sealed, signed, and delivered as his vow to the Lord. Seek not more witnesses than providence makes conscious of thy vows, lest this be interpreted ostentation and vain self-glorying : take so many, lest the good example be lost, or thou suspected of falsifying thy vow. Brifley and plainly : Didst thou on a sick bed make thy vow before thy family, and before the neighbourhood ? Be careful to perform it before them ; let them see thou art what thou vowedst to be. This care in thy vow will be a means to make it most to the advantage of religion, whilst all that heard or knew thy vow bear thee testimony that thou art thankful, and thus thou givest others occasion to glorify thy Father who is in heaven.—*Henry Hurst* (1690) *in "The Morning Exercises."*

Verse 14.—"*I will pay my vows*," etc. Foxe, in his Acts and Monuments, relates the following concerning the martyr, John Philpot :—"He went with the sheriffs to the place of execution ; and when he was entering into Smithfield the way was foul, and two officers took him up to bear him to the stake. Then he said merrily, What, will ye make me a pope ? I am content to go to my journey's end on foot. But first coming into Smithfield, he kneeled down there, saying these words, "I will pay my vows in thee, O Smithfield.""

Verse 15.—"*Precious in the sight of the LORD is the death of his saints.*" It is of value or importance in such respects as the following :—(1) As it is the removal of another of the redeemed to glory—the addition of one more to the happy hosts above ; (2) as it is a new triumph of the work of redemption,— showing the power and the value of that work ; (3) as it often furnishes a more direct proof of the reality of religion than any abstract argument could do. How much has the cause of religion been promoted by the patient deaths of Ignatius, Polycarp, and Latimer, and Ridley, and Huss, and Jerome of Prague, and the hosts of martyrs ! What does not the world owe, and the cause of religion owe, to such scenes as occurred on the death-beds of Baxter, and Thomas Scott, and Halyburton, and Payson ! What an argument for the truth of religion,—what an illustration of its sustaining power —

what a source of comfort to those who are about to die,—to reflect that religion does not leave the believer when he most needs its support and consolation ; that it can sustain us in the severest trial of our condition here ; that it can illuminate what seems to us of all places *most* dark, cheerless, dismal, repulsive—" the valley of the shadow of death."—*Albert Barnes.*

Verse 15.—*"Precious in the sight of the* LORD *is the death of his saints."* The death of the saints is precious in the Lord's sight. First, because he *"seeth not as man seeth."* He judgeth not according to the appearance ; he sees all things as they really are, not partially : he traces the duration of his people, not upon the map of time, but upon the infinite scale of eternity ; he weighs their happiness, not in the little balance of earthly enjoyment, but in the even and equipoised balance of the sanctuary. In the next place, I think the death of the saints is precious in the Lord's sight, because *they are taken from the evil to come ;* they are delivered from the burden of the flesh ; ransomed by the blood of the Redeemer, they are his purchased possession, and now he receives them to himself. Sin and sorrow for ever cease ; there is no more death, the death of Christ is their redemption ; by death he overcame him that had the power of death ; therefore, they in him are enabled to say, " O death, where is thy sting ? O grave, where is thy victory ? " Again, the death of the saints is precious in the Lord's sight, for in it *he often sees the very finest evidences of the work of his own Spirit upon the soul ;* he sees faith in opposition to sense, leaning upon the promises of God. Reposing upon him who is mighty to save, he sees hope even against hope, anchoring the soul secure and steadfast on him who is passed within the veil ; he sees patience acquiescing in a Father's will— humility bending beneath his sovereign hand—love issuing from a grateful heart. Again, the death of the saints is precious in the Lord's sight, *as it draws out the tendernesses of surviving Christian friends,* and is abundant in the thanksgivings of many an anxious heart ; it elicits the sympathies of Christian charity, and realises that communion of saints, of which the Apostle speaks, when he says, " if one member suffer, all the members suffer with it ; if one rejoice they all joy." . . . The death of saints is precious, because the sympathy of prayer is poured forth from many a kindly Christian heart. . . . Nor is this all—the death of saints is precious, for *that is their day of seeing Jesus face to face.—Patrick Pounden's Sermon in "The Irish Pulpit,"* 1831.

Verse 15.—*"Precious."* Their death is precious (*jakar*) ; the word of the text is, *in pretio fuit, magni estimatum est.* See how the word is translated in other texts. 1. Honourable, Isai. xliii. 4 (*jakarta*) ; " thou wast precious in my sight, thou hast been honourable." 2. Much set by, 1 Sam. xviii. 30 ; " His name was much set by." 3. Dear, Jer. xxxi. 20. *An filius* (*jakkir*) *pretiosus mihi Ephraim :* " Is Ephraim my dear son ? " 4. Splendid, clear, or glorious, Job xxxi. 16. *Si vidi lunam* (*jaker*) *pretiosam et abeuntem :* " the moon walking in brightness."

Put all these expressions together, and then we have the strength of David's word, *"The death of the saints is precious" ;* that is, 1. honourable ; 2. much set by ; 3. dear ; 4. splendid and glorious in the sight of the Lord.—*Samuel Torshell, in "The House of Mourning,"* 1660.

Verse 15.—*"Precious."* It is proper to advert, in the first place, to the apparent primary import of the phrase, namely, *Almighty God watches over, and sets a high value upon the holy and useful lives of his people,* and will not lightly allow those lives to be abbreviated or destroyed. In the second place, the words lead us to advert to *the control which he exercises over the circumstances of their death.* These are under his special arrangement. They are too important in his estimation to be left to accident. In fact, chance has no existence. In the intervention of second causes, he takes care always to overrule and control them for good. Let the weakest believer among you be quite sure, be " confident of this very thing," that he will never suffer your great enemy to take advantage of anything in the manner of your death, to do you spiritual harm. No, on the contrary, he takes all its circumstances under his immediate and especial disposal. The sentiment will admit, perhaps, of a third illustration ; *when the saints are dying, the Lord looks upon them, and is merciful unto them.* Who can say how often he answers prayer, even in the cases of dying believers ? Never does he fail to support, even where he does not see good to spare. By the whispers of his love, by the witness of his Spirit, by the assurance of his presence, by the preparatory revelation of heavenly glory, he strengthens his afflicted ones, he makes all their bed in their sickness. Ah ! and when, perhaps, they scarcely possess a bed to languish upon, when poverty or other calamitous circumstances leave them, in the sorrow of sickness, no place of repose but the bare ground for their restless bodies, and his bosom for their spirits, do they ever find God fail them ? No ; many a holy man has slept the sleep of death with the missionary Martyn, in a strange and inhospitable land, or with the missionary Smith, upon the floor of a dungeon, and yet

> " Jesus has made their dying bed
> As soft as downy pillows are."

When no other eye saw, when no other heart felt, for these two never-to-be-forgotten martyrs, murdered men of God, and apostles of Jesus, then were they precious in God's sight, and he was present with them. And so it is with all his saints, who are faithful unto death. Fourthly, we are warranted by the text and the tenor of Scripture, in affirming that *the Lord attaches great importance to the death-bed itself.* This is in his estimate—whatever it may be in ours—too precious, too important, to be overlooked ; and hence it is often with emphasis, though always with a practical bearing, recorded in Scripture. It is possible, certainly, to make too much of it, by substituting, as a criterion of character, that which may be professed under the excitement of dying sufferings, for the testimony of a uniform, conspicuous career of holy living. But it is equally indefensible, and even ungrateful to God, to make too little of it, to make too little account of a good end, when connected with a good beginning and with a patient continuance in well-doing.

> " The chamber where the good man meets his fate
> Is privileged beyond the common walk of virtuous life."

Its transactions are sometimes as fraught with permanent utility as with present good. The close of a Christian's career on earth, his defiance, in the strength of his Saviour, of his direst enemy, the good confession which he acknowledges when he is enabled to witness before those around his dying bed, all these are precious and important in the sight of the Lord, and ought to be so in our view, and redound, not only to his own advantage, but to the benefit of survivors, " to the praise of the glory of his grace."—*W. M. Bunting, in a Sermon at the City Road Chapel,* 1836.

Verse 15.—Why need they beforehand be afraid of death, who have the Lord to take such care about it as he doth ? We may safely, without presuming, we ought securely without wavering, to rest upon this, that our blood being precious in God's eyes, either it shall not be split, or it is seasonable, and shall be profitable to us to have it spilt. On this ground " the righteous are bold as a lion," Prov. xxviii. 1. " Neither do they fear what man can do unto them." Heb. xiii. 6. Martyrs were, without question, well instructed herein, and much supported hereby. When fear of death hindereth from any duty, or draweth to any evil, then call to mind this saying, *"Precious in the sight of the* LORD *is the death of his favourites."* For who would not valiantly, without fainting, take such a death as is precious in God's sight.—*William Gouge.*

Verse 15.—"*His saints* " imports *appropriation.* Elsewhere Jehovah asserts, " All souls are mine." But he has an especial property in—and therefore claim upon—all saints. It is he that made them such. Separate from God there could be no sanctity. And as his right, his original right, in all men, is connected with the facts of their having been created and endowed by his hand, and thence subjected to his moral government, so, and much more, do all holy beings, all holy men, who owe to his grace their very existence as such, who must cease to be saints, if they could cease to be *his* saints, whom he has created anew in Christ Jesus by the communication of his own love, his own purity, his own nature, whom he continually upholds in this exalted state, so, and much more, do such persons belong to God. They are " *his* saints " through him and in him, saints of his making, and modelling, and establishing, and therefore *his* exclusively. Let this reference to the mighty working of God by his Spirit in you, your connection, your spiritual connection, with him, and your experience of his saving power,—let this reference convert the *mystery* into the *mercy* of sanctification in your hearts.

"*His* saints " denotes, in the second place, *devotedness.* They are saints not only *through* him, but *to* him ; holy unto the Lord, sanctified or set apart to his service, self-surrendered to the adorable Redeemer.

"*His* saints " may import *resemblance*—close resemblance. Such characters are emphatically *God-like,* holy and pure ; children of their Father which is in heaven ;

certifying to all around their filial relationship to him, by their manifest participation of his nature, by their reflection of his image and likeness.

"*His* saints" suggests associations of *endearment*, of complacency. "The Lord taketh pleasure in them that fear him, in all them that hope in his mercy"; "a people near unto him"; "the Lord's portion is his people"; and "Happy is that people that is in such a case, yea, happy is that people whose God is the Lord."—*Condensed from a Sermon by W. M. Bunting,* 1836.

Verse 15.—"*Saints.*" The persons among whom implicitly he reckons himself, styled *saints,* are in the original set out by a word (חֲסִידִים) that importeth an especial respect of God towards them. The root whence that word issueth signifieth *mercy* (חָסַד *consecravit, benefecit*). Whereupon the Hebrews have given such a name to a stork, which kind among fowls is the most merciful; and that not only the old to their young ones, as most are, but also the young ones to the old, which they use to feed and carry when through age they are not able to help themselves.

This title is attributed to men in a double respect; 1. Passively, in regard of God's mind and affection to them; 2. Actively, in regard of their mind and affection to others. God's merciful kindness is great towards them; and their mercy and kindness are great towards their brethren. They are, therefore, by a kind of excellency and property styled "men of mercy." Isai. lvii. 1. In regard of his double acceptation of the word, some translate it, "merciful, tender, or courteous," Ps. xviii. 25. Others with a paraphrase with many words, because they have not one fit word to express the full sense, thus, "Those whom God followeth with bounty, or to whom God extendeth his bounty." This latter I take to be the most proper to this place; for the word being passively taken for such as are made partakers of God's kindness, it sheweth the reason of that high account wherein God hath them, even his own grace and favor. We have a word in English that in this passive signification fitly answereth the Hebrew, which is this, *favourite.—William Gouge.*

Verse 15.—*Death* now, as he hath done also to mine, has paid full many a visit to your house; and in very deed, he has made fell havoc among our comforts. We shall yet be avenged on this enemy—this King of Terrors. I cannot help at times clenching my fist in his face, and roaring out in my agony and anguish, "Thou shalt be swallowed up in victory!" There is even, too, in the meantime, this consolation; "O Death, where is thy sting?" "Precious in the sight of the Lord is the death *for* his saints," in the first place; in the second place, and resting on the propitiatory death, "Precious in the sight of the Lord is the death *of* his saints." The Holy Ghost, Psalm cxvi. 15, states the first; our translators, honest men, have very fairly and truly inferred the second. We are obliged to them. The death of your lovely child, loveliest in the beauties of holiness, with all that was most afflictive and full of sore trial in it, is nevertheless, among the things in your little family which are right precious in the sight of the Lord; and this in it, is that which pleases you most; precious, because of the infinite, the abiding, and the unchanging worth of the death of God's own holy child Jesus. The calm so wonderful, the consolation so felt, yea, the joy in tribulation so great, have set before your eyes a new testimony, heart-touching indeed, that, after eighteen hundred years have passed, "*the death of his saints*" is still precious as ever in the sight of the Lord. Take your book of life, sprinkled with the blood of the covenant, and in your family record, put the death of Rosanna down among the precious things in your sight also—I should rather have said likewise.

Present my kindest regards to Miss S—. Tell her to wipe that tear away—Rosanna needs it not. I hope they are all well at L—, and that your young men take the way of the Lord in good part. My dear Brother, "Go thy way, thy child liveth," is still as fresh as ever it was, from the lips of Him that liveth for ever and ever, and rings with a loftier and sweeter sound, even than when it was first heard in the ears and heart of the parent who had brought and laid his sick and dying at the feet of Him who hath the keys of hell and of death.—*John Jameson, in "Letters; True Fame,"* etc., 1838.

Verse 16.—"*O* Lord, *truly I am thy servant.*" Thou hast made me free, and I am impatient to be bound again. Thou hast broken the bonds of sin; now, Lord, bind me with the cords of love. Thou hast delivered me from the tyranny of Satan, make me as one of thy hired servants. I owe my liberty, my life, and all that I have, or hope, to thy generous rescue: and now, O my gracious, my Divine Friend and Redeemer, I lay myself and my all at thy feet.—*Samuel Lavington,* 1728—1807.

Verse 16.—*"I am thy servant."* The saints have ever had a holy pride in being God's servants ; there cannot be a greater honour than to serve such a Master as commands heaven, earth, and hell. Do not think thou dost honour God in serving him ; but this is how God honours thee, in vouchsafing thee to be his servant. David could not study to give himself a greater style than—" O Lord, or, truly I am thy servant, and the son of thy handmaid," and this he spake, not in the phrase of a human compliment, but in the humble confession of a believer. Yea, so doth the apostle commend this excellency, that he sets the title of servant before that of an apostle ; first servant, then apostle. Great was his office in being an apostle, greater his blessing in being a servant of Jesus Christ : the one is an outward calling, the other an inward grace. There was an apostle condemned, never any servant of God.—*Thomas Adams.*

Verse 16.—*"I am thy servant."* This expression of the king of Israel implies (1). *A humble sense of his distance from God and his dependence upon him.* This is the first view which a penitent hath of himself when he returns to God. It is the first view which a good man hath of himself in his approaches to, or communion with God. And, indeed, it is what ought to be inseparable from the exercise of every other pious affection. To have, as it were, high and honourable thoughts of the majesty and greatness of the living God, and a deep and awful impression of the immediate and continual presence of the heart-searching God, this naturally produces the greatest self-abasement, and the most unfeigned subjection of spirit before our Maker. It leads to a confession of him as Lord over all, and having the most absolute right, not only to the obedience, but to the disposal of all his creatures. I cannot help thinking this is conveyed to us in the language of the Psalmist, when he says, *"O Lord, truly I am thy servant."* He was a prince among his subjects, and had many other honourable distinctions, both natural and acquired, among men ; but he was sensible of his being a servant and subject of the King of kings ; and the force of his expression, *"Truly, I am thy servant,"* not only signifies the certainty of the thing, but how deeply and strongly he felt a conviction of its truth.

This declaration of the Psalmist implies (2) *a confession of his being bound by particular covenant and consent unto God,* and a repetition of the same by a new adherence. This, as it was certainly true with regard to him, having often dedicated himself to God, so I take it to be confirmed by the reiteration of the expression here, *"O Lord, truly I am thy servant; I am thy servant."* As if he had said, " O Lord, it is undeniable ; it is impossible to recede from it. I am thine by many ties. I am by nature thy subject and thy creature ; and I have many times confessed thy right and promised my own duty." I need not mention to you, either the example in the Psalmist's writings, or the occasions in his history, on which he solemnly surrendered himself to God. It is sufficient to say, that it was very proper that he should frequently call this to mind, and confess it before God, for though it could not make his Creator's right any stronger, it would certainly make the guilt of his own violation of it so much the greater.

This declaration of the Psalmist is (3) *an expression of his peculiar and special relation to God. "I am thy servant, and the son of thine handmaid."* There is another passage of his writings where the same expression occurs : Ps. lxxxvi. 16. " O turn unto me, and have mercy upon me ; give thy strength unto thy servant, and save the son of thine handmaid." There is some variation among interpreters in the way of illustrating this phrase. Some take it for a figurative way of affirming, that he was bound in the strongest manner to God, as those children who were born of a maid-servant, and born in his own house, were in the most absolute manner their master's property. Others take it to signify his being not only brought up in the visible church of God, but in a pious family, and educated in his fear ; and others would have it to signify still more especially that the Psalmist's mother was an eminently pious woman. And indeed I do not think that was a circumstance, if true, either unworthy of him to remember, or of the Spirit of God to put upon record. —*John Witherspoon,* 1722—1797.

Verse 16.—O Lord, *I am thy servant* by a double right ; (and, oh, that I could do thee double service ;) as thou art the Lord of my life, and I am the son of thy handmaid : not of Hagar, but of Sarah ; not of the bondwoman, but of the free ; and therefore I serve thee not in fear, but in love ; or therefore in fear, because in love : and then is service best done when it is done in love. In love indeed I am bound to serve thee, for, *"Thou hast loosed my bonds" ;* the bonds of death which compassed me about, by delivering me from a dangerous sickness, and restoring me to health : or in a higher kind ; thou hast loosed my bonds by freeing me from being a captive to be a servant ; and which is more, from being a servant to be a son : and more than this from being a son of thy handmaid, to be a son of thyself.—*Sir Richard Baker.*

Verse 16.—Bless God for the privilege of being the children of godly parents. Better be the child of a godly than of a wealthy parent. I hope none of you are of so vile a spirit as to contemn your parents because of their piety. Certainly it is a great privilege when you can go to God, and plead your Father's covenant : *"Lord, truly I am thy servant; I am thy servant, and the son of thy handmaid."* So did Solomon, 1 Kings viii. 25, 26, " Lord, make good thy word to thy servant David, my father." That you are not born of infidels, nor of papists, nor of upholders of superstition and formality, but in a strict, serious, godly family, it is a great advantage that you have. It is better to be the sons of faithful ministers than of nobles.—*Thomas Manton, in a Sermon preached before the Sons of the Clergy.*

Verse 16.—*"Thou hast loosed my bonds."* Mercies are given to encourage us in God's service, and should be remembered to that end. Rain descends upon the earth, not that it might be more barren, but more fertile. We are but stewards ; the mercies we enjoy are not our own, but to be improved for our Master's service. Great mercies should engage to great obedience. God begins the Decalogue with a memorial of his mercy in bringing the Israelites out of Egypt,—" I am the Lord thy God, which brought thee out of the land of Egypt." How affectionately doth the Psalmist own his relation to God as his servant, when he considers how God had loosed his bonds: *"O Lord, truly I am thy servant; thou hast loosed my bonds !"* the remembrance of thy mercy shall make me know no relation but that of a servant to thee. When we remember what wages we have from God, we must withal remember that we owe more service, and more liveliness in service, to him. Duty is but the ingenuous consequent of mercy. It is irrational to encourage ourselves in our way to hell by a remembrance of heaven, to foster a liberty in sin by a consideration of God's bounty. When we remember that all we have or are is the gift of God's liberality, we should think ourselves obliged to honour him with all that we have, for he is to have honour from all his gifts. It is a sign we aimed at God's glory in begging mercy, when we also aim at God's glory in enjoying it. It is a sign that love breathed the remembrance of mercy into our hearts, when at the same time it breathes a resolution into us to improve it. It is not our tongues, but our lives must praise him. Mercies are not given to one member, but to the whole man.—*Stephen Charnock.*

Verse 17.—*"The sacrifice of thanksgiving."*

" When all the heart is pure, each warm desire
Sublimed by holy love's ethereal fire,
On winged words our breathing thoughts may rise,
And soar to heaven, a grateful sacrifice."

James Scott.

Verse 18.—*"Vows."* Are well-composed vows such promoters of religion ? and are they to be made so warily ? and do they bind so strictly ? Then be sure to wait until God give you just and fit seasons for vowing. Be not over-hasty to vow : it is an inconsiderate and foolish haste of Christians to make more occasions of vowing than God doth make for them. Make your vows, and spare not, so often as God bids you ; but do not do it oftener. You would wonder I should dissuade you from vowing often, when you have such constant mercies ; and wonder well you might, if God did expect your extraordinary bond and security for every ordinary mercy : but he requires it not ; he is content with ordinary security of gratitude for ordinary mercies ; when he calls for extraordinary security and acknowledgment, by giving extraordinary mercies, then give it and do it.—*Henry Hurst.*

Verse 18.—*"Now."*—God gave an order that no part of the thankoffering should be kept till the third day, to teach us to present our praises when benefits are newly received, which else would soon wax stale and putrefy as fish doth. *"I will pay my vows now,"* saith David.—*Samuel Clarke* (1599—1682) *in "A Mirrour or Looking-glasse, both for Saints and Sinners."*

Verse 18.—*"In the presence of all his people."* For good example's sake. This also was prince-like, Ezek. xlvi. 10. The king's seat in the sanctuary was open, that all might see him there, 2 Kings xi. 14, and xxiii. 3.—*John Trapp.*

Verse 18.—*"In the presence of all his people."* Be bold, be bold, ye servants of the Lord, in sounding forth the praises of your God. Go into presses of people ; and in the midst of them praise the Lord. Wicked men are over-bold in pouring forth their blasphemies to the dishonour of God ; they care not who hear them. They stick not to do it in the midst of cities. Shall they be more audacious to dishonour God, than ye zealous to honour him ? Assuredly Christ will shew himself as forward to confess you, as you are, or can be to confess him. Matt. x. 32. This holy boldness is the ready way to glory.—*William Gouge.*

Verse 19 (*second clause*).—He does not simply say in the midst of Jerusalem : but, *"in the midst of thee, O Jerusalem."* He speaks to the city as one who loved it and delighted in it. We see here, how the saints were affected towards the city in which was the house of God. Thus we should be moved in spirit towards that church in which God dwells, the temple he inhabits, which is built up, not of stones, but of the souls of the faithful.—*Wolfgang Musculus.*

HINTS TO PREACHERS.

Verses 1, 2.—I. Present—" I love." II. Past—" He hath." III. Future—" I will."

Verses 1, 2.—Personal experience in reference to prayer. I. We have prayed, often, constantly, in different ways, etc. II. We have been heard. A grateful retrospect of usual answers and of special answers. III. Love to God has thus been promoted. IV. Our sense of the value of prayer has become so intense that we cannot cease praying.

Verses 1, 2, 9.—If you cast your eyes on the first verse of the Psalm, you find a *profession of love*—*"I love the* LORD*" ;* if on the second, a *promise of prayer*—*"I will call on the* LORD*" ;* if on the ninth, a *resolve of walking*—*"I will walk before the* LORD*."* There are three things should be the object of a saint's care, the devotion of the soul, profession of the mouth, and conversation of the life : that is the sweetest melody in God's ears, when not only the voice sings, but the heartstrings keep tune, and the hand keepeth time.—*Nathanael Hardy.*

Verse 2.—" He hath," and therefore " I will." Grace moving to action.

Verses 2, 4, 13, 17.—Calling upon God mentioned four times very suggestively—I will do it (verse 2), I have tried it (4), I will do it when I take (13), and when I offer (17).

Verses 2, 9, 13, 14, 17.—The " I wills " of the Psalm. I will call (verse 2), I will walk (9), I will take (13), I will pay (14), I will offer (17).

Verses 3, 4, 8.—See Spurgeon's Sermon, " To Souls in Agony," Metropolitan Tabernacle Pulpit, No. 1216.

Verses 3—5.—The story of a tried soul. I. Where I was. Verse 3. II. What I did. Verse 4. III. What I learned. Verse 5.

Verses 3—6.—I. *The occasion.* 1. Bodily affliction. 2. Terrors of conscience. 3. Sorrow of heart. 4. Self-accusation : " I found," etc. II. *The petition.* 1. Direct : " I called," etc. 2. Immediate : " then," when the trouble came ; prayer was the first remedy sought, not the last, as with many. 3. Brief—limited to the one thing needed : " deliver my soul." 4. Importunate : " O Lord, I beseech thee." III. *The restoration.* 1. Implied : " gracious," etc., v. 5. 2. Expressed, v. 6, generally : " The Lord preserveth," etc. ; particularly : " I was brought low," etc. : helped me to pray, helped me out of trouble in answer to prayer, and helped me to praise him for the mercy, the faithfulness, the grace, shown in my deliverance. God is glorified through the afflictions of his people : the submissive are preserved in them, and the lowly are exalted by them.—*G. R.*

Verse 5.—I. Eternal grace, or the purpose of love. II. Infinite justice, or the difficulty of holiness. III. Boundless mercy, or the outcome of atonement.

Verse 6.—I. A singular class—" simple." II. A singular fact—" the Lord preserveth the simple." III. A singular proof of the fact—" I was," etc.

Verse 7.—*"Return unto thy rest, O my soul."* Rest in God may be said to belong to the people of God on a fourfold account. I. By designation. The rest which the people of God have in him is the result of his own purpose, and design, taken up from his mere good pleasure and love. II. By purchase. The rest which they wanted as *creatures* they had forfeited as *sinners*. This, therefore, Christ laid down his life to procure. III. By promise. This is God's kind engagement. He has said, " My presence shall go with thee, and I will give thee rest," Exod. xxxiii. 14. IV. By their own choice gracious souls have a rest in God.—*D. Wilcox.*

Verse 7.—"*Return unto thy rest, O my soul.*" When, or upon what occasion a child of God should use the Psalmist's language. I. After converse with the world in the business of his calling every day. II. When going to the sanctuary on the Lord's-day. III. In and under any trouble he may meet with. IV. When departing from this world at death.—*D. Wilcox.*

Verse 7.—I. The rest of the soul : " My rest," this is in God. 1. The soul was created to find its rest in God. 2. On that account it cannot find rest elsewhere. II. Its departure from that rest. This is implied in the word " Return." III. Its return. 1. By repentance. 2. By faith, in the way provided for its return. 3. By prayer. IV. Its encouragement to return. 1. Not in itself, but in God. 2. Not in the justice, but in the goodness of God : " for the Lord," etc. " The goodness of God leadeth thee to repentance."—*G. R.*

Verse 8.—The trinity of experimental godliness. I. It is a unity—" Thou hast delivered " ; all the mercies come from one source. II. It is a trinity of deliverance, *of* soul, eyes, feet ; *from* punishment, sorrow, and sinning ; *to* life, joy, and stability. III. It is a trinity in unity : all this was done for me and in me—" my soul, mine eyes, my feet."

Verse 9.—The effect of deliverance upon ourselves. " I will walk," etc. I. Walk by faith in him. II. Walk in love with him. III. Walk by obedience to him.—*G. R.*

Verses 10, 11.—I. The rule : " I believed," etc. In general the Psalmist spoke what he had well considered and tested by his own experience, as when he said, " I was brought low and he helped me." " The Lord hath dealt bountifully with me." II. The exception : " I was greatly afflicted, I said," etc. 1. He spoke wrongfully : he said " All men are liars," which had some truth in it, but was not the whole truth. 2. Hastily : " I said in my haste," without due reflection. 3. Angrily, under the influence of affliction, probably from the unfaithfulness of others. Nature acts before grace—the one by instinct, the other from consideration. —*G. R.*

Verse 11.—A hasty speech. I. There was much truth in it. II. It erred on the right side, for it showed faith in God rather than in the creature. III. It did err in being too sweeping, too severe, too suspicious. IV. It was soon cured. The remedy for all such hasty speeches is—Get to work in the spirit of verse 12.

Verse 12.—Overwhelming obligations. I. A sum in arithmetic—" all his benefits." II. A calculation of indebtedness—" What shall I render ? " III. A problem for personal solution—" What shall *I* ? " See Spurgeon's Sermon, No. 910.

Verses 12, 14.—Whether well-composed religious vows do not exceedingly promote religion. Sermon by Henry Hurst, A.M., in " The Morning Exercises."

Verse 13.—Sermon on the Lord's supper. We take the cup of the Lord—I. In memory of him who is our salvation. II. In token of our trust in him. III. In evidence of our obedience to him. IV. In type of communion with him. V. In hope of drinking it new with him ere long.

Verse 13.—The various cups mentioned in Scripture would make an interesting subject.

Verse 14.—"*Now.*" Or the excellence of time present.

Verse 15.—I. *The declaration.* Not the death of the wicked, nor even the death of the righteous is in itself precious ; but, 1, because their persons are precious to him. 2. Because their experience in death is precious to him. 3. Because of their conformity in death to their Covenant-Head ; and 4. Because it puts an end to their sorrows, and translates them to their rest. II. *Its manifestation.* 1. In preserving them from death. 2. In supporting them in death. 3. In giving them victory over death. 4. In glorifying them after death.

Verse 15.—See Spurgeon's Sermon, " Precious Deaths," No. 1036.

Verse 16.—*Holy Service.* I. Emphatically avowed. II. Honestly rendered— " truly." III. Logically defended—" son of thine handmaid." IV. Consistent with conscious liberty.

Verse 17.—This is due to our God, good for ourselves, and encouraging to others.

Verse 17.—"*The sacrifice of thanksgiving.*" I. How it may be rendered. In secret love, in conversation, in sacred song, in public testimony, in special gifts and works. II. Why we should render it. For answered prayers (verses 1, 2), memorable deliverances (3), choice preservation (6) ; remarkable restoration (7, 8), and for the fact of our being his servants (16). III. When should we render it. *Now*, while the mercy is on the memory, and as often as fresh mercies come to us.

Verse 18.—I. How vows may be paid in public. By going to public worship as the first thing we do when health is restored. By uniting heartily in the song. By coming to the communion. By special thankoffering. By using fit opportunities for open testimony to the Lord's goodness. II. The special difficulty in the matter. To pay them *to the Lord*, and not in ostentation or as an empty form. III. The peculiar usefulness of the public act. It interests others, touches their hearts, reproves, encourages, etc.

Verse 19.—The Christian at home. I. In God's house. II. Among the saints. III. At his favourite work, " Praise."

PSALM CXVII.

SUBJECT.—*This Psalm, which is very little in its letter, is exceedingly large in its spirit ; for, bursting beyond all bounds of race or nationality, it calls upon all mankind to praise the name of the Lord. In all probability it was frequently used as a brief hymn suitable for almost every occasion, and especially when the time for worship was short. Perhaps it was also sung at the commencement or at the close of other Psalms, just as we now use the doxology. It would have served either to open a service or to conclude it. It is both short and sweet. The same divine Spirit which expatiates in the 119th, here condenses his utterances into two short verses, but yet the same infinite fulness is present and perceptible. It may be worth noting that this is at once the shortest chapter of the Scriptures and the central portion of the whole Bible.*

EXPOSITION.

O PRAISE the LORD, all ye nations : praise him, all ye people.

2 For his merciful kindness is great toward us : and the truth of the LORD endureth for ever. Praise ye the LORD.

1. *"O praise the LORD, all ye nations."* This is an exhortation to the Gentiles to glorify Jehovah, and a clear proof that the Old Testament spirit differed widely from that narrow and contracted national bigotry with which the Jews of our Lord's day became so inveterately diseased. The nations could not be expected to join in the praise of Jehovah unless they were also to be partakers of the benefits which Israel enjoyed ; and hence the Psalm was an intimation to Israel that the grace and mercy of their God were not to be confined to one nation, but would in happier days be extended to all the race of man, even as Moses had prophesied when he said, " Rejoice, O ye nations, his people." (Deut. xxxii. 43), for so the Hebrew has it. The nations were to be his people. He would call them a people that were not a people, and her beloved that was not beloved. We know and believe that no one tribe of men shall be unrepresented in the universal song which shall ascend unto the Lord of all. Individuals have already been gathered out of every kindred and people and tongue by the preaching of the gospel, and these have right heartily joined in magnifying the grace which sought them out, and brought them to know the Saviour. These are but the advance-guard of a number which no man can number who will come ere long to worship the all-glorious One. *"Praise him, all ye people."* Having done it once, do it again, and do it still more fervently, daily increasing in the reverence and zeal with which you extol the Most High. Not only praise him nationally by your rulers, but popularly in your masses. The multitude of the common folk shall bless the Lord. Inasmuch as the matter is spoken of twice, its certainty is confirmed, and the Gentiles must and shall extol Jehovah—all of them, without exception. Under the gospel dispensation we worship no new god, but the God of Abraham is our God for ever and ever ; the God of the whole earth shall he be called.

2. *"For his merciful kindness is great toward us."* By which is meant not only his great love toward the Jewish people, but towards the whole family of man. The Lord is kind to us as his creatures, and merciful to us as sinners, hence his merciful kindness to us as sinful creatures. This mercy has been very great, or powerful. The mighty grace of God has prevailed even as the waters of the flood prevailed over the earth : breaking over all bounds, it has flowed towards all portions of the multiplied race of man. In Christ Jesus, God has shown mercy mixed with kindness, and that to the very highest degree. We can all join in this grateful acknowledgment, and in the praise which is therefore due. *"And the truth of the LORD endureth for ever."* He has kept his covenant promise that in the seed of Abraham should all nations of the earth be blessed, and he will eternally keep every single promise of that covenant to all those who put their trust in him. This should be a cause of constant and grateful praise, wherefore the Psalm concludes as it began, with another Hallelujah, *"Praise ye the LORD."*

EXPLANATORY NOTES AND QUAINT SAYINGS.

Whole Psalm.—A very short Psalm if you regard the words, but of very great compass and most excellent if you thoughtfully consider the meaning. There are here five principal points of doctrine.

First, *the calling of the Gentiles*, the Apostle being the interpreter, Rom. xv. 11 ; but in vain might the Prophet invite the Gentiles to praise Jehovah, unless they were to be gathered into the unity of the faith together with the children of Abraham.

Second, *The summary of the Gospel*, namely, the manifestation of grace and truth, the Holy Spirit being the interpreter, John i. 17.

Third, *The end of so great a blessing*, namely, the worship of God in spirit and in truth, as we know that the kingdom of the Messiah is spiritual.

Fourth, *the employment of the subjects of the great King* is to praise and glorify Jehovah.

Lastly, *the privilege of these servants :* that, as to the Jews, so also to the Gentiles, who know and serve God the Saviour, eternal life and blessedness are brought, assured in this life, and prepared in heaven.—*Mollerus.*

Whole Psalm.—This Psalm, the shortest portion of the Book of God, is quoted, and given much value to, in Rom. xv. And upon this it has been profitably observed, " It is a small portion of Scripture, and as such we might easily overlook it. But not so the Holy Ghost. He gleans up this precious little testimony which speaks of grace to the Gentiles, and presses it on our attention."—*From Bellett's Short Meditations on the Psalms, chiefly in their Prophetic character,* 1871.

Whole Psalm.—The occasion and the author of this Psalm are alike unknown. De Wette regards it as *a Temple-Psalm*, and agrees with Rosenmüller in the supposition that it was sung either at the beginning or the end of the service in the temple. Knapp supposes that it was used as an intermediate service, sung during the progress of the general service to vary the devotion, and to awaken a new interest in the service, either sung by the choir or by the whole people.—*Albert Barnes.*

Whole Psalm.—In God's worship it is not always necessary to be long ; few words sometimes say what is sufficient, as this short Psalm giveth us to understand. —*David Dickson.*

Whole Psalm.—This is the shortest, and the next but one is the longest, of the Psalms. There are times for short hymns and long hymns, for short prayers and long prayers, for short sermons and long sermons, for short speeches and long speeches. It is better to be too short than too long, as it can more easily be mended. Short addresses need no formal divisions : long addresses require them, as in the next Psalm but one.—*G. Rogers.*

Verse 1.—*"O praise the* LORD," etc. The praise of God is here made both the beginning and the end of the Psalm ; to show, that in praising God the saints are never satisfied with their own efforts, and would infinitely magnify him, even as his perfections are infinite. Here they make a circle, the beginning, middle, and end whereof is *hallelujah*. In the last Psalm, when David had said, " Let everything that hath breath praise the Lord," and so in all likelihood had made an end, yet he repeats the *hallelujah* again, and cries, " Praise ye the Lord." The Psalmist had made an end and yet he had not done ; to signify, that when we have said our utmost for God's praise, we must not be content, but begin anew. There is hardly any duty more pressed in the Old Testament upon us, though less practised, than this of praising God. To quicken us therefore to a duty so necessary, but so much neglected, this and many other Psalms were penned by David, purposely to excite us, that are the *nations* here meant, to consecrate our whole lives to the singing and setting forth of God's worthy praises.—*Abraham Wright.*

Verse 1.—*"All ye nations."* Note : each nation of the world has some special gift bestowed on it by God, which is not given to the others, whether you have regard to nature or grace, for which it ought to praise God.—*Le Blanc.*

Verse 1.—*"Praise him."* A different word is here used for *"praise"* than in the former clause : a word which is more frequently used in the Chaldee, Syriac, Arabic, and Ethiopic languages ; and signifies the celebration of the praises of God with a high voice.—*John Gill.*

Verse 2.—*"For his merciful kindness is great toward us."* We cannot part from this Psalm without remarking that even in the Old Testament we have more than one instance of a recognition on the part of those that were without the pale of the church that God's favour to Israel was a source of blessing to themselves. Such were probably to some extent the sentiments of Hiram and the Queen of Sheba, the contemporaries of Solomon ; such the experience of Naaman ; such the virtual acknowledgments of Nebuchadnezzar and Darius the Mede. They beheld " his merciful *kindness* " toward his servants of the house of Israel, and they praised him accordingly.—*John Francis Thrupp.*

Verse 2.—*"For his merciful kindness is great toward us."* Albeit there be matter of praise unto God in himself, though we should not be partakers of any benefit from him, yet the Lord doth give his people cause to praise him for favours to them in their own particular cases.—*David Dickson.*

Verse 2.—*"For his merciful kindness is great."* גָּבַר, *gabar*, is *strong :* it is not only *great* in *bulk* or *number ;* but it is *powerful ;* it prevails over sin, Satan, death and hell.—*Adam Clarke.*

Verse 2.—*"Merciful kindness . . . . and the truth of the Lord."* Here, and so in divers other Psalms, God's mercy and truth are joined together ; to show that all passages and proceedings, both in ordinances and in providences, whereby he cometh and communicateth himself to his people are not only mercy, though that is very sweet, but truth also. Their blessings come to them in the way of promise from God, as bound to them by the truth of his covenant. This is soul-satisfying indeed ; this turns all that a man hath to cream, when every mercy is a present sent from heaven by virtue of a promise. Upon this account, God's mercy is ordinarily in the Psalms bounded by his truth ; that none may either presume him more merciful than he hath declared himself in his word ; nor despair of finding mercy *gratis*, according to the truth of his promise. Therefore, though thy sins be great, believe the text, and know that God's mercy is greater than thy sins. The high heaven covereth as well tall mountains as small molehills, and mercy can cover all. The more desperate thy disease, the greater is the glory of thy physician, who hath perfectly cured thee.—*Abraham Wright.*

HINTS TO PREACHERS.

Whole Psalm.—The universal kingdom. I. The same God. II. The same worship. III. The same reason for it.

Verse 2.—*"Merciful kindness."* In God's kindness there is mercy, because, I. Our sin deserves the reverse of kindness. II. Our weakness requires great tenderness. III. Our fears can only be so removed.

Verse 2 (last clause).—I. In his attribute—he is always faithful. II. In his revelation—always infallible. III. In his action—always according to promise.

PSALM CXVIII.

AUTHOR AND SUBJECT.—*In the book of Ezra, iii. 10, 11, we read that "when the builders laid the foundation of the temple of the Lord, they set the priests in their apparel with trumpets, and the Levites the sons of Asaph with cymbals, to praise the Lord, after the ordinance of David king of Israel. And they sang together by course in praising and giving thanks unto the Lord ; because he is good, for his mercy endureth for ever toward Israel. And all the people shouted with a great shout, when they praised the Lord, because the foundation of the house of the Lord was laid." Now the words mentioned in Ezra are the first and last sentences of this Psalm, and we therefore conclude that the people chanted the whole of this sublime song ; and, moreover, that the use of this composition on such occasions was ordained by David, whom we conceive to be its author. The next step leads us to believe that he is its subject, at least in some degree ; for it is clear that the writer is speaking concerning himself in the first place, though he may not have strictly confined himself to all the details of his own personal experience. That the Psalmist had a prophetic view of our Lord Jesus is very manifest ; the frequent quotations from this song in the New Testament prove this beyond all question ; but at the same time it could not have been intended that every particular line and sentence should be read in reference to the Messiah, for this requires very great ingenuity, and ingenious interpretations are seldom true. Certain devout expositors have managed to twist the expression of the seventeenth verse, "I shall not die, but live," so as to make it applicable to our Lord, who did actually die, and whose glory it is that he died ; but we cannot bring our minds to do such violence to the words of holy writ.*

The Psalm seems to us to describe either David or some other man of God who was appointed by the divine choice to a high and honourable office in Israel. This elect champion found himself rejected by his friends and fellow-countrymen, and at the same time violently opposed by his enemies. In faith in God he battles for his appointed place, and in due time he obtains it in such a way as greatly to display the power and goodness of the Lord. He then goes up to the house of the Lord to offer sacrifice, and to express his gratitude for the divine interposition, all the people blessing him, and wishing him abundant prosperity. This heroic personage, whom we cannot help thinking to be David himself, broadly typified our Lord, but not in such a manner that in all the minutiæ of his struggles and prayers we are to hunt for parallels. The suggestion of Alexander that the speaker is a typical individual representing the nation, is exceedingly well worthy of attention ; but it is not inconsistent with the idea that a personal leader may be intended, since that which describes the leader will be in a great measure true of his followers. The experience of the Head is that of the members, and both may be spoken of in much the same terms. Alexander thinks that the deliverance celebrated cannot be identified with any one so exactly as with that from the Babylonian exile ; but we judge it best to refer it to no one incident in particular, but to regard it as a national song, adapted alike for the rise of a chosen hero, and the building of a temple. Whether a nation is re-founded by a conquering prince, or a temple founded by the laying of its corner-stone in joyful state, the Psalm is equally applicable.

DIVISION.—*We propose to divide the Psalm thus, from verses 1 to 4 the faithful are called upon to magnify the everlasting mercy of the Lord ; from 5 to 18 the Psalmist gives forth a narrative of his experience, and an expression of his faith ; in verses 19 to 21 he asks admittance into the house of the Lord, and begins the acknowledgment of the divine salvation. In verses 22 to 27 the priests and people recognize their ruler, magnify the Lord for him, declare him blessed, and bid him approach the altar with his sacrifice. In the two closing verses the grateful hero himself exalts God the ever-merciful.*

EXPOSITION.

O GIVE thanks unto the LORD ; for *he is* good : because his mercy *endureth* for ever.

2 Let Israel now say, that his mercy *endureth* for ever.

3 Let the house of Aaron now say, that his mercy *endureth* for ever.
4 Let them now that fear the LORD say, that his mercy *endureth* for ever.

1. *"O give thanks unto the LORD."* The grateful hero feels that he cannot himself alone sufficiently express his thankfulness, and therefore he calls in the aid of others. Grateful hearts are greedy of men's tongues, and would monopolize them all for God's glory. The whole nation was concerned in David's triumphant accession, and therefore it was right that they should unite in his adoring song of praise. The thanks were to be rendered unto Jehovah alone, and not to the patience or valour of the hero himself. It is always well to trace our mercies to him who bestows them, and if we cannot give him anything else, let us at any rate give him our thanks. We must not stop short at the second agent, but rise at once to the first cause, and render all our praises *unto the Lord* himself. Have we been of a forgetful or murmuring spirit ? Let us hear the lively language of the text, and allow it to speak to our hearts : " Cease your complainings, cease from all self-glorification, and give thanks unto the Lord." *"For he is good."* This is reason enough for giving him thanks ; goodness is his essence and nature, and therefore he is always to be praised whether we are receiving anything from him or not. Those who only praise God because he *does* them good should rise to a higher note and give thanks to him because he *is* good. In the truest sense he alone is good, " There is none good but one, that is God " ; therefore in all gratitude the Lord should have the royal portion. If others seem to be good, he *is* good. If others are good in a measure, he is good beyond measure. When others behave badly to us, it should only stir us up the more heartily to give thanks unto the Lord, because he is good ; and when we ourselves are conscious that we are far from being good, we should only the more reverently bless him that " he is good." We must never tolerate an instant's unbelief as to the goodness of the Lord ; whatever else may be questionable, this is absolutely certain, that Jehovah is good ; his dispensations may vary, but his nature is always the same, and always good. It is not only that he was good, and will be good, but he *is* good, let his providence be what it may. Therefore let us even at this present moment, though the skies be dark with clouds, yet give thanks unto his name.

"Because his mercy endureth for ever." Mercy is a great part of his goodness, and one which more concerns us than any other, for we are sinners and have need of his mercy. Angels may say that he is good, but they need not his mercy and cannot therefore take an equal delight in it ; inanimate creation declares that *he is good,* but it cannot feel his *mercy,* for it has never transgressed ; but man, deeply guilty and graciously forgiven, beholds mercy as the very focus and centre of the goodness of the Lord. The endurance of the divine mercy is a special subject for song : notwithstanding our sins, our trials, our fears, his mercy *endureth for ever.* The best of earthly joys pass away, and even the world itself grows old and hastens to decay, but there is no change in the mercy of God ; he was faithful to our forefathers, he is merciful to us, and will be gracious to our children and our children's children. It is to be hoped that the philosophical interpreters who endeavour to clip the word " for ever " into a mere period of time will have the goodness to let this passage alone. However, whether they do or not, we shall believe in endless mercy—mercy to eternity. The Lord Jesus Christ, who is the grand incarnation of the mercy of God, calls upon us at every remembrance of him to give thanks unto the Lord, for " he is good."

2. *"Let Israel now say, that his mercy endureth for ever."* God had made a covenant with their forefathers, a covenant of mercy and love, and to that covenant he was faithful evermore. Israel sinned in Egypt, provoked the Lord in the wilderness, went astray again and again under the judges, and trangressed at all times ; and yet the Lord continued to regard them as his people, to favour them with his oracles, and to forgive their sins. He speedily ceased from the chastisements which they so richly deserved, because he had a favour towards them. He put his rod away the moment they repented, because his heart was full of compassion. " His mercy endureth for ever " was Israel's national hymn, which, as a people, they had been called upon to sing upon many former occasions ; and now their leader, who had at last gained the place for which Jehovah had destined him, calls upon the whole nation to join with him in extolling, in this particular instance of the divine goodness, the eternal mercy of the Lord. David's success was mercy to Israel, as well as mercy to himself. If Israel does not sing, who will ? If Israel

does not sing of mercy, who can? If Israel does not sing when the Son of David ascends the throne, the very stones will cry out.

3. *"Let the house of Aaron now say, that his mercy endureth for ever."* The sons of Aaron were specially set apart to come nearest to God, and it was only because of his mercy that they were enabled to live in the presence of the thrice holy Jehovah, who is a consuming fire. Every time the morning and evening lamb was sacrificed, the priests saw the continual mercy of the Lord, and in all the holy vessels of the sanctuary, and all its services from hour to hour, they had renewed witness of the goodness of the Most High. When the high priest went in unto the holy place and came forth accepted, he might, above all men, sing of the eternal mercy. If this Psalm refers to David, the priests had special reason for thankfulness on his coming to the throne, for Saul had made a great slaughter among them, and had at various times interfered with their sacred office. A man had now come to the throne who for their Master's sake would esteem them, give them their dues, and preserve them safe from all harm. Our Lord Jesus, having made all his people priests unto God, may well call upon them in that capacity to magnify the everlasting mercy of the Most High. Can any one of the royal priesthood be silent?

4. *"Let them now that fear the Lord say, that his mercy endureth for ever."* If there were any throughout the world who did not belong to Israel after the flesh, but nevertheless had a holy fear and lowly reverence of God, the Psalmist calls upon them to unite with him in his thanksgiving, and to do it especially on the occasion of his exaltation to the throne; and this is no more than they would cheerfully agree to do, since every good man in the world is benefited when a true servant of God is placed in a position of honour and influence. The prosperity of Israel through the reign of David was a blessing to all who feared Jehovah. A truly God-fearing man will have his eye much upon God's mercy, because he is deeply conscious of his need of it, and because that attribute excites in him a deep feeling of reverential awe. "There is forgiveness with thee that thou mayest be feared."

In the three exhortations, to Israel, to the house of Aaron, and to them that fear the Lord, there is a repetition of the exhortation to *say*, "that his mercy endureth for ever." We are not only to believe, but to declare the goodness of God; truth is not to be hushed up, but proclaimed. God would have his people act as witnesses, and not stand silent in the day when his honour is impugned. Specially is it our joy to speak out to the honour and glory of God when we think upon the exaltation of his dear Son. We should shout "Hosannah," and sing loud "Hallelujahs" when we behold the stone which the builders rejected lifted into its proper place.

In each of the three exhortations notice carefully the word *"now."* There is no time like time present for telling out the praises of God. The present exaltation of the Son of David now demands from all who are the subjects of his kingdom continual songs of thanksgiving to him who hath set him on high in the midst of Zion. *Now* with us should mean always. When would it be right to cease from praising God, whose mercy never ceases?

The fourfold testimonies to the everlasting mercy of God which are now before us speak like four evangelists, each one declaring the very pith and marrow of the gospel; and they stand like four angels at the four corners of the earth holding the winds in their hands, restraining the plagues of the latter days that the mercy and long-suffering of God may endure towards the sons of men. Here are four cords to bind the sacrifice to the four horns of the altar, and four trumpets with which to proclaim the year of jubilee to every quarter of the world. Let not the reader pass on to the consideration of the rest of the Psalm until he has with all his might lifted up both heart and voice to praise the Lord, " for his mercy endureth for ever."

> " Let us with a gladsome mind
> Praise the Lord, for he is kind;
> For his mercies shall endure
> Ever faithful, ever sure."

5 I called upon the Lord in distress: the Lord answered me, *and set me* in a large place.

6 The Lord *is* on my side; I will not fear: what can man do unto me?

7 The Lord taketh my part with them that help me: therefore shall I see *my desire* upon them that hate me.

8 *It is* better to trust in the LORD than to put confidence in man.

9 *It is* better to trust in the LORD than to put confidence in princes.

10 All nations compassed me about : but in the name of the LORD will I destroy them.

11 They compassed me about ; yea, they compassed me about : but in the name of the LORD I will destroy them.

12 They compassed me about like bees ; they are quenched as the fire of thorns : for in the name of the LORD I will destroy them.

13 Thou hast thrust sore at me that I might fall : but the LORD helped me.

14 The LORD *is* my strength and song, and is become my salvation.

15 The voice of rejoicing and salvation *is* in the tabernacles of the righteous : the right hand of the LORD doeth valiantly.

16 The right hand of the LORD is exalted : the right hand of the LORD doeth valiantly.

17 I shall not die, but live, and declare the works of the LORD.

18 The LORD hath chastened me sore : but he hath not given me over unto death.

5. *"I called upon the* LORD *in distress,"* or, " out of anguish I invoked Jah." Nothing was left him but prayer, his agony was too great for aught beside ; but having the heart and the privilege to pray he possessed all things. Prayers which come out of distress generally come out of the heart, and therefore they go to the heart of God. It is sweet to recollect our prayers, and often profitable to tell others of them after they are heard. Prayer may be bitter in the offering, but it will be sweet in the answering. The man of God had called upon the Lord when he was not in distress, and therefore he found it natural and easy to call upon him when he was in distress. He worshipped, he praised, he prayed : for all this is included in calling upon God, even when he was in a straitened condition. Some read the original " a narrow gorge "; and therefore it was the more joy to him when he could say " The Lord answered me, and set me in a large place." He passed out of the defile of distress into the well-watered plain of delight. He says, " Jah heard me in a wide place," for God is never shut up, or straitened. In God's case hearing means answering, hence the translators rightly put, " The Lord answered me," though the original word is *"heard."* The answer was appropriate to the prayer, for he brought him out of his narrow and confined condition into a place of liberty where he could walk at large, free from obstruction and oppression. Many of us can join with the Psalmist in the declarations of this verse : deep was our distress on account of sin, and we were shut up as in a prison under the law, but in answer to the prayer of faith we obtained the liberty of full justification wherewith Christ makes men free, and we are free indeed. It was the Lord who did it, and unto his name we ascribe all the glory ; we had no merits, no strength, no wisdom, all we could do was to call upon him, and even that was his gift ; but the mercy which is to eternity came to our rescue, we were brought out of bondage, and we were made to delight ourselves in the length and breadth of a boundless inheritance. What a large place is that in which the great God has placed us ! All things are ours, all times are ours, all places are ours, for God himself is ours ; we have earth to lodge in and heaven to dwell in,—what larger place can be imagined ? We need all Israel, the whole house of Aaron, and all them that fear the Lord, to assist us in the expression of our gratitude ; and when they have aided us to the utmost, and we ourselves have done our best, all will fall short of the praises that are due to our gracious Lord.

6. *"The* LORD *is on my side,"* or, he is " for me." Once his justice was against me, but now he is my reconciled God, and engaged on my behalf. The Psalmist naturally rejoiced in the divine help ; all men turned against him, but God was his defender and advocate, accomplishing the divine purposes of his grace. The expression may also be translated " to me," that is to say, Jehovah belongs to me, and is mine. What infinite wealth is here ! If we do not magnify the Lord we are of all men most brutish. *"I will not fear."* He does not say that he should

not suffer, but that he would not fear : the favour of God infinitely outweighed the hatred of men, therefore setting the one against the other he felt that he had no reason to be afraid. He was calm and confident, though surrounded with enemies, and so let all believers be, for thus they honour God. *"What can man do unto me ? "* He can do nothing more than God permits ; at the very uttermost he can only kill the body, but he hath no more that he can do. God having purposed to set his servant upon the throne, the whole race of mankind could do nothing to thwart the divine decree : the settled purpose of Jehovah's heart could not be turned aside, nor its accomplishment delayed, much less prevented, by the most rancorous hostility of the most powerful of men. Saul sought to slay David, but David outlived Saul, and sat upon his throne. Scribe and Pharisee, priest and Herodian, united in opposing the Christ of God, but he is exalted on high none the less because of their enmity. The mightiest man is a puny thing when he stands in opposition to God, yea, he shrinks into utter nothingness. It were a pity to be afraid of such a pitiful, miserable, despicable object as a man opposed to the almighty God. The Psalmist here speaks like a champion throwing down the gauntlet to all comers, defying the universe in arms ; a true Bayard, without fear and without reproach, he enjoys God's favour, and he defies every foe.

7. *"The Lord taketh my part with them that help me."* Jehovah condescended to be in alliance with the good man and his comrades ; his God was not content to look on, but he took part in the struggle. What a consolatory fact it is that the Lord takes our part, and that when he raises up friends for us he does not leave them to fight for us alone, but he himself as our chief defender deigns to come into the battle and wage war on our behalf. David mentioned those that helped him, he was not unmindful of his followers ; there is a long record of David's mighty men in the book of Chronicles, and this teaches us that we are not to disdain or think little of the generous friends who rally around us ; but still our great dependence and our grand confidence must be fixed upon the Lord alone. Without him the strong helpers fail ; indeed, apart from him in the sons of men there is no help ; but when our gracious Jehovah is pleased to support and strengthen those who aid us, they become substantial helpers to us.

"Therefore shall I see my desire upon them that hate me." The words, " my desire," are added by the translators ; the Psalmist said, " I shall look upon my haters : I shall look them in the face, I shall make them cease from their contempt, I shall myself look down upon them instead of their looking down upon me. I shall see their defeat, I shall see the end of them." Our Lord Jesus does at this moment look down upon his adversaries, his enemies are his footstool ; he shall look upon them at his second coming, and at the glance of his eyes they shall flee before him, not being able to endure that look with which he shall read them through and through.

8. *"It is better to trust in the Lord than to put confidence in man."* It is better in all ways, for first of all it is wiser : God is infinitely more able to help, and more likely to help, than man, and therefore prudence suggests that we put our confidence in him above all others. It is also morally better to do so, for it is the duty of the creature to trust in the Creator. God has a claim upon his creatures' faith, he deserves to be trusted ; and to place our reliance upon another rather than upon himself, is a direct insult to his faithfulness. It is better in the sense of safer, since we can never be sure of our ground if we rely upon mortal man, but we are always secure in the hands of our God. It is better in its effect upon ourselves : to trust in man tends to make us mean, crouching, dependent ; but confidence in God elevates, produces a sacred quiet of spirit, and sanctifies the soul. It is, moreover, much better to trust in God, as far as the result is concerned ; for in many cases the human object of our trust fails from want of ability, from want of generosity, from want of affection, or from want of memory ; but the Lord, so far from failing, does for us exceeding abundantly above all that we ask or even think. This verse is written out of the experience of many who have first of all found the broken reeds of the creature break under them, and have afterwards joyfully found the Lord to be a solid pillar sustaining all their weight.

9. *"It is better to trust in the Lord than to put confidence in princes."* These should be the noblest of men, chivalrous in character, and true to the core. The royal word should be unquestionable. They are noblest in rank and mightiest in power, and yet as a rule princes are not one whit more reliable than the rest of mankind. A gilded vane turns with the wind as readily as a meaner weathercock. Princes are

but men, and the best of men are poor creatures. In many troubles they cannot help us in the least degree ; for instance, in sickness, bereavement, or death ; neither can they assist us one jot in reference to our eternal state. In eternity a prince's smile goes for nothing ; heaven and hell pay no homage to royal authority. The favour of princes is proverbially fickle, the testimonies of worldlings to this effect are abundant. All of us remember the words put by the world's great poet into the lips of the dying Wolsey ; their power lies in their truth :—

> " O how wretched
> Is that poor man that hangs on princes' favours !
> There is betwixt that smile we would aspire to,
> That sweet aspect of princes, and their ruin,
> More pangs and fears than wars or women have ;
> And when he falls, he falls like Lucifer,
> Never to hope again.'

Yet a prince's smile has a strange witchery to many hearts, few are proof against that tuft-hunting which is the index of a weak mind. Principle has been forgotten and character has been sacrificed to maintain position at court ; yea, the manliness which the meanest slave retains has been basely bartered for the stars and garters of a profligate monarch. He who puts his confidence in God, the great King, is thereby made mentally and spiritually stronger, and rises to the highest dignity of manhood ; in fact, the more he trusts the more is he free, but the fawning sycophant of greatness is meaner than the dirt he treads upon. For this reason and a thousand others it is infinitely better to trust in the Lord than to put confidence in princes.

10. *"All nations compassed me about."* The hero of the Psalm, while he had no earthly friend upon whom he could thoroughly rely, was surrounded by innumerable enemies, who heartily hated him. He was hemmed in by his adversaries, and scarce could find a loophole of escape from the bands which made a ring around him. As if by common consent all sorts of people set themselves against him, and yet he was more than a match for them all, because he was trusting in the name of the Lord. Therefore does he joyfully accept the battle, and grasp the victory, crying, *"but in the name of the* Lord *will I destroy them,"* or " cut them in pieces." They thought to destroy *him,* but he was sure of destroying *them ;* they meant to blot out his name, but he expected to render not only his own name but the name of the Lord his God more illustrious in the hearts of men. It takes grand faith to be calm in the day of actual battle, and especially when that battle waxes hot ; but our hero was as calm as if no fight was raging. Napoleon said that God was always on the side of the biggest battalions, but the Psalmist-warrior found that the Lord of hosts was with the solitary champion, and that in his name the battalions were cut to pieces. There is a grand touch of the *ego* in the last sentence, but it is so evershadowed with the name of the Lord that there is none too much of it. He recognized his own individuality, and asserted it : he did not sit still supinely and leave the work to be done by God by some mysterious means ; but he resolved with his own trusty sword to set about the enterprise, and so become in God's hand the instrument of his own deliverance. He did all in the name of the Lord, but he did not ignore his own responsibility, nor screen himself from personal conflict, for he cried, *"I* will destroy them." Observe that he does not speak of merely escaping from them like a bird out of the snare of the fowler, but he vows that he will carry the war into his enemies' ranks, and overthrow them so thoroughly that there should be no fear of their rising up a second time.

11. *"They compassed me about ; yea, they compassed me about."* He had such a vivid recollection of his danger that his enemies seem to live again in his verses. We see their fierce array, and their cruel combination of forces. They made a double ring, they surrounded him in a circle of many ranks, they not only talked of doing so, but they actually shut him up and enclosed him as within a wall. His heart had vividly realized his position of peril at the time, and now he delights to call it again to mind in order that he may the more ardently adore the mercy which made him strong in the hour of conflict, so that he broke through a troop, yea, swept a host to destruction. *"But in the name of the* Lord *will I destroy them."* I will subdue them, get them under my feet, and break their power in pieces. He is as certain about the destruction of his enemies as he was assured of their having compassed him about. They made the circle three and four times deep, but for all that he felt confident of victory. It is grand to hear a man speak in this fashion when it is not boasting, but the calm declaration of his heartfelt trust in God.

12. *"They compassed me about like bees."* They seemed to be everywhere, like a swarm of bees, attacking him at every point ; nimbly flying from place to place, stinging him meanwhile, and inflicting grievous pain. They threatened at first to baffle him : what weapon could he use against them ? They were so numerous, so inveterate ; so contemptible, yet so audacious ; so insignificant and yet so capable of inflicting agony, that to the eye of reason there appeared no possibility of doing anything with them. Like the swarm of flies in Egypt, there was no standing against them ; they threatened to sting a man to death with their incessant malice, their base insinuations, their dastardly falsehoods. He was in an evil case, but even there faith availed. All-powerful faith adapts itself to all circumstances, it can cast out devils, and it can drive out bees. Surely, if it outlives the sting of death, it will not die from the sting of a bee. *"They are quenched as the fire of thorns."* Their fierce attack soon came to an end, the bees lost their stings and the buzz of the swarm subsided : like thorns which blaze with fierce crackling and abundant flame, but die out in a handful of ashes very speedily, so did the nations which surrounded our hero soon cease their clamour and come to an inglorious end. They were soon hot and soon cold, their attack was as short as it was sharp. He had no need to crush the bees, for like crackling thorns they died out of themselves. For a third time he adds, *"for in the name of the* LORD *will I destroy them,"* or ' 'cut them down," as men cut down thorns with a scythe or reaping-hook.

What wonders have been wrought in the name of the Lord ! It is the battle-cry of faith before which his adversaries fly apace. " The sword of the Lord and of Gideon " brings instant terror into the midst of the foe. The name of the Lord is the one weapon which never fails in the day of battle : he who knows how to use it may chase a thousand with his single arm. Alas ! we too often go to work and to conflict in our own name, and the enemy knows it not, but scornfully enquires, " Who are ye ? " Let us take care never to venture into the presence of the foe without first of all arming ourselves with this impenetrable mail. If we knew this name better, and trusted it more, our life would be more fruitful and sublime.

> "Jesus, the name high over all,
> In hell, or earth, or sky,
> Angels and men before it fall ;
> And devils fear and fly."

13. *"Thou hast thrust sore at me,"* " Thrusting, thou hast thrust at me." It is a vigorous apostrophe, in which the enemy is described as concentrating all his thrusting power into the thrusts which he gave to the man of God. He thrust again and again with the keenest point, even as bees thrust their stings into their victim. The foe had exhibited intense exasperation, and fearful determination, nor had he been without a measure of success ; wounds had been given and received, and these smarted much, and were exceeding sore. Now, this is true of many a tried child of God who has been wounded by Satan, by the world, by temptation, by affliction ; the sword has entered into his bones, and left its mark. *"That I might fall."* This was the object of the thrusting : to throw him down, to wound him in such a way that he would no longer be able to keep his place, to make him depart from his integrity, and lose his confidence in God. If our adversaries can do this they will have succeeded to their heart's content : if we fall into grievous sin they will be better pleased than even if they had sent the bullet of the assassin into our heart, for a moral death is worse than a physical one. If they can dishonour us, and God in us, their victory will be complete. " Better death than false of faith " is the motto of one of our noble houses, and it may well be ours. It is to compass our fall that they compass *us ;* they fill us with their venom that they may fill us with their sin. *"But the* LORD *helped me"*; a blessed " but." This is the saving clause. Other helpers were unable to chase away the angry nations, much less to destroy all the noxious swarms ; but when the Lord came to the rescue the hero's single arm was strong enough to vanquish all his adversaries. How sweetly can many of us repeat in the retrospect of our past tribulations this delightful sentence, " But the Lord helped *me.*" I was assailed by innumerable doubts and fears, but the Lord helped me ; my natural unbelief was terribly inflamed by the insinuations of Satan, but the Lord helped me ; multiplied trials were rendered more intense by the cruel assaults of men, and I knew not what to do, but the Lord helped me. Doubtless, when we land on the hither shore of Jordan, this will be one of our songs, " Flesh and heart were failing me, and the adversaries of my soul surrounded me in the swellings of Jordan, but the Lord helped me. Glory be unto his name."

14. *"The Lord is my strength and song,"* my strength while I was in the conflict, my song now that it is ended ; my strength against the strong, and my song over their defeat. He is far from boasting of his own valour ; he ascribes his victory to its real source, he has no song concerning his own exploits, but all his peans are unto *Jehovah Victor,* the Lord whose right hand and holy arm had given him the victory. *"And is become my salvation."* The poet warrior knew that he was saved, and he not only ascribed that salvation unto God, but he declared God himself to be his salvation. It is an all-comprehending expression, signifying that from beginning to end, in the whole and in the details of it, he owed his deliverance entirely to the Lord. Thus can all the Lord's redeemed say, " Salvation is of the Lord." We cannot endure any doctrine which puts the crown upon the wrong head and defrauds the glorious King of his revenue of praise. Jehovah has done it all ; yea, in Christ Jesus he *is* all, and therefore in our praises let him alone be extolled. It is a happy circumstance for us when we can praise God as alike our strength, song, and salvation ; for God sometimes gives a secret strength to his people, and yet they question their own salvation, and cannot, therefore, sing of it. Many are, no doubt, truly saved, but at times they have so little strength, that they are ready to faint, and therefore they cannot sing : when strength is imparted and salvation is realised then the song is clear and full.

15. *"The voice of rejoicing and salvation is in the tabernacles of the righteous."* They sympathised in the delight of their leader and they abode in their tents in peace, rejoicing that one had been raised up who, in the name of the Lord, would protect them from their adversaries. The families of believers are happy, and they should take pains to give their happiness a voice by their family devotion. The dwelling-place of saved men should be the temple of praise ; it is but righteous that the righteous should praise the righteous God, who is their righteousness. The struggling hero knew that the voice of woe and lamentation was heard in the tents of his adversaries, for they had suffered severe defeat at his hands ; but he was delighted by the remembrance that the nation for whom he had struggled would rejoice from one end of the land to the other at the deliverance which God had wrought by his means. That hero of heroes, the conquering Saviour, gives to all the families of his people abundant reasons for incessant song now that he has led captivity captive and ascended up on high. Let none of us be silent in our households : if we have salvation let us have joy, and if we have joy let us give it a tongue wherewith it may magnify the Lord. If we hearken carefully to the music which comes from Israel's tents, we shall catch a stanza to this effect, *"the right hand of the Lord doeth valiantly"* : Jehovah has manifested his strength, given victory to his chosen champion, and overthrown all the armies of the foe. " The Lord is a man of war, the Lord is his name." When he comes to blows, woe to his mightiest opponent.

16. *"The right hand of the Lord is exalted,"* lifted up to smite the foeman, or extolled and magnified in the eyes of his people. It is the Lord's *right* hand, the hand of his skill, the hand of his greatest power, the hand which is accustomed to defend his saints. When that is lifted up, it lifts up all who trust in him, and it casts down all who resist him. *"The right hand of the Lord doeth valiantly."* The Psalmist speaks in triplets, for he is praising the triune God, his heart is warm and he loves to dwell upon the note ; he is not content with the praise he has rendered, he endeavours to utter it each time more fervently and more jubilantly than before. He had dwelt upon the sentence, " they compassed me about," for his peril from encircling armies was fully realised ; and now he dwells upon the valour of Jehovah's right hand, for he has as vivid a sense of the presence and majesty of the Lord. How seldom is this the case ; the Lord's mercy is forgotten and only the trial is remembered.

17. *"I shall not die, but live."* His enemies hoped that he would die, and perhaps he himself feared he should perish at their hand : the news of his death may have been spread among his people, for the tongue of rumour is ever ready with ill news, the false intelligence would naturally cause great sorrow and despondency, but he proclaims himself as yet alive and as confident that he shall not fall by the hand of the destroyer. He is cheerfully assured that no arrow could carry death between the joints of his harness, and no weapon of any sort could end his career. His time had not yet come, he felt immortality beating within his bosom. Perhaps he had been sick, and brought to death's door, but he had a presentiment that the sickness was not unto death, but to the glory of God. At any rate, he knew that he should

not so die as to give victory to the enemies of God ; for the honour of God and the good of his people were both wrapped up in his continued success. Feeling that he would live he devoted himself to the noblest of purposes : he resolved to bear witness to the divine faithfulness, *"and declare the works of the Lord."* He determined to recount the works of Jah ; and he does so in this Psalm, wherein he dwells with love and admiration upon the splendour of Jehovah's prowess in the midst of the fight. While there is a testimony for God to be borne by us to any one, it is certain that we shall not be hurried from the land of the living. The Lord's prophets shall live on in the midst of famine, and war, and plague, and persecution, till they have uttered all the words of their prophecy ; his priests shall stand at the altar unharmed till their last sacrifice has been presented before him. No bullet will find its billet in our hearts till we have finished our allotted period of activity.

> " Plagues and deaths around me fly,
> Till he please I cannot die :
> Not a single shaft can hit,
> Till the God of love sees fit."

18. *"The Lord hath chastened me sore."* This is faith's version of the former passage, " Thou hast thrust sore at me ; " for the attacks of the enemy are chastisements from the hand of God. The devil tormented Job for his own purposes, but in reality the sorrows of the patriarch were chastisements from the Lord. " Chastening, Jah hath chastened me," says our poet : as much as to say that the Lord had smitten him very severely, and made him sorrowfully to know the full weight of his rod. The Lord frequently appears to save his heaviest blows for his best-beloved ones ; if any one affliction be more painful than another it falls to the lot of those whom he most distinguishes in his service. The gardener prunes his best roses with most care. Chastisement is sent to keep successful saints humble, to make them tender towards others, and to enable them to bear the high honours which their heavenly Friend puts upon them. *"But he hath not given me over unto death."* This verse, like the thirteenth, concludes with a blessed " but," which constitutes a saving clause. The Psalmist felt as if he had been beaten within an inch of his life, but yet death did not actually ensue. There is always a merciful limit to the scourging of the sons of God. Forty stripes save one were all that an Israelite might receive, and the Lord will never allow that one, that killing stroke, to fall upon his children. They are " chastened, but not killed " ; their pains are for their instruction, not for their destruction. By these things the ungodly die, but gracious Hezekiah could say, " By these things men live, and in all these things is the life of my spirit." No, blessed be the name of God, he may chastise us, but he will not condemn us ; we must feel the smarting rod, but we shall not feel the killing sword. He does not give us over unto death at any time, and we may be quite sure that he has not done so while he condescends to chasten us, for if he intended our final rejection he would not take the pains to place us under his fatherly discipline. It may seem hard to be under the afflicting rod, but it would be a far more dreadful thing if the Lord were to say, " He is given unto idols, let him alone." Even from our griefs we may distil consolation, and gather sweet flowers from the garden in which the Lord has planted salutary rue and wormwood. It is a cheering fact that if we endure chastening God dealeth with us as with sons, and we may well be satisfied with the common lot of his beloved family.

The hero, restored to health, and rescued from the dangers of battle, now lifts up his own song unto the Lord, and asks all Israel, led on by the goodly fellowship of the priests, to assist him in chanting a joyful Te Deum.

19 Open to me the gates of righteousness : I will go into them, *and* I will praise the Lord :

20 This gate of the Lord, into which the righteous shall enter.

21 I will praise thee : for thou hast heard me, and art become my salvation.

19. *"Open to me the gates of righteousness."* The grateful champion having reached the entrance of the temple, asks for admission in set form, as if he felt that he could only approach the hallowed shrine by divine permission, and wished only to enter in the appointed manner. The temple of God was meant for the righteous to enter and offer the sacrifices of righteousness, hence the gates are called the gates

of righteousness. Righteous deeds were done within its walls, and righteous teachings sounded forth from its courts. The phrase "the gate" is sometimes used to signify power or empire; as, for instance, "the Sublime Porte" signifies the seat of empire of Turkey; the entrance to the temple was the true Sublime Porte, and what is better, it was the *porta justitiæ*, the gate of righteousness, the palace of the great King, who is in all things just. *"I will go into them, and I will praise the LORD."* Only let the gate be opened, and the willing worshipper will enter; and he will enter in the right spirit, and for the best of purposes, that he may render homage unto the Most High. Alas, there are multitudes who do not care whether the gates of God's house are opened or not; and although they know that they are opened wide they never care to enter, neither does the thought of praising God so much as cross their minds. The time will come for them when they shall find the gates of heaven shut against them, for those gates are peculiarly the gates of righteousness through which there shall by no means enter anything that defileth. Our champion might have praised the Lord in secret, and doubtless he did so; but he was not content without going up to the assembly, there to register his thanksgivings. Those who neglect public worship generally neglect all worship; those who praise God within their own gates are among the readiest to praise him within his temple gates. Our hero had also in all probability been sore sick, and therefore like Hezekiah he says, "The Lord was ready to save me: therefore we will sing my songs to the stringed instruments all the days of my life in the house of the Lord." Public praise for public mercies is every way most appropriate, most acceptable to God, and most profitable to others.

20. *"This gate of the LORD, into which the righteous shall enter."* The Psalmist loves the house of God so well that he admires the very gate thereof, and pauses beneath its arch to express his affection for it. He loved it because it was the gate of the Lord, he loved it because it was the gate of righteousness, because so many godly people had already entered it, and because in all future ages such persons will continue to pass through its portals. If the gate of the Lord's house on earth is so pleasant to us, how greatly shall we rejoice when we pass that gate of pearl, to which none, but the righteous shall ever approach, but through which all the just shall in due time enter to eternal felicity. The Lord Jesus has passed that way, and not only set the gate wide open, but secured an entrance for all those who are made righteous in his righteousness: all the righteous must and shall enter there, whoever may oppose them. Under another aspect our Lord is himself that gate, and through him, as the new and living Way, all the righteous delight to approach unto the Lord. Whenever we draw near to praise the Lord we must come by this gate; acceptable praise never climbs over the wall, or enters by any other way, but comes to God in Christ Jesus; as it is written, "no man cometh unto the Father but by me." Blessed, for ever blessed, be this wondrous gate of the person of our Lord.

21. Having entered, the champion exclaims, *"I will praise thee,"* not "I will praise the Lord," for now he vividly realizes the divine presence, and addresses himself directly to Jehovah, whom his faith sensibly discerns. How well it is in all our songs of praise to let the heart have direct and distinct communion with God himself! The Psalmist's song was personal praise too :—*"I will* praise thee "; resolute praise, for he firmly resolved to offer it; spontaneous praise, for he voluntarily and cheerfully rendered it, and continuous praise, for he did not intend soon to have done with it. It was a life-long vow to which there would never come a close, "I will praise thee." *"For thou hast heard me, and art become my salvation."* He praises God by mentioning his favours, weaving his song out of the divine goodness which he had experienced. In these words he gives the reason for his praise,—his answered prayer, and the deliverance which he had received in consequence. How fondly he dwells upon the personal interposition of God! *"Thou* hast heard me." How heartily he ascribes the whole of his victory over his enemies to God; nay, he sees God himself to be the whole of it: *"Thou* art become my salvation." It is well to go directly to God himself, and not to stay even in his mercy, or in the acts of his grace. Answered prayers bring God very near to us; realised salvation enables us to realise the immediate presence of God. Considering the extreme distress through which the worshipper had passed, it is not at all wonderful that he should feel his heart full of gratitude at the great salvation which God had wrought for him, and should at his first entrance into the temple lift up his voice in thankful praise for personal favours so great, so needful, so perfect.

22 The stone *which* the builders refused is become the head *stone* of the corner.

23 This is the LORD's doing; it *is* marvellous in our eyes.

24 This *is* the day *which* the LORD hath made; we will rejoice and be glad in it.

25 Save now, I beseech thee, O LORD : O LORD, I beseech thee, send now prosperity.

26 Blessed *be* he that cometh in the name of the LORD : we have blessed you out of the house of the LORD.

27 God *is* the LORD, which hath showed us light : bind the sacrifice with cords, *even* unto the horns of the altar.

This passage will appear to be a mixture of the expressions of the people and of the hero himself.

22. *"The stone which the builders refused is become the head stone of the corner."* Here the people magnify God for bringing his chosen servant into the honourable office, which had been allotted to him by divine decree. A wise king and valiant leader is a stone by which the national fabric is built up. David had been rejected by those in authority, but God had placed him in a position of the highest honour and the greatest usefulness, making him the chief corner-stone of the state. In the case of many others whose early life has been spent in conflict, the Lord has been pleased to accomplish his divine purposes in like manner; but to none is this text so applicable as to the Lord Jesus himself : he is the living stone, the tried stone, elect, precious, which God himself appointed from of old. The Jewish builders, scribe, priest, Pharisee, and Herodian, rejected him with disdain. They could see no excellence in him that they should build upon him; he could not be made to fit in with their ideal of a national church, he was a stone of another quarry from themselves, and not after their mind nor according to their taste; therefore they cast him away and poured contempt upon him, even as Peter said, " This is the stone which was set at nought of you builders " : they reckoned him to be as nothing, though he is Lord of all. In raising him from the dead the Lord God exalted him to be the head of his church, the very pinnacle of her glory and beauty. Since then he has become the confidence of the Gentiles, even of them that are afar off upon the sea, and thus he has joined the two walls of Jew and Gentile into one stately temple, and is seen to be the binding corner-stone, making both one. This is a delightful subject for contemplation.

Jesus in all things hath the pre-eminence, he is the principal stone of the whole house of God. We are accustomed to lay some one stone of a public building with solemn ceremony, and to deposit in it any precious things which may have been selected as a memorial of the occasion : henceforth that corner-stone is looked upon as peculiarly honourable, and joyful memories are associated with it. All this is in a very emphatic sense true of our blessed Lord, " The Shepherd, the Stone of Israel." God himself laid him where he is, and hid within him all the precious things of the eternal covenant; and there he shall for ever remain, the foundation of all our hopes, the glory of all our joys, the uniting bond of all our fellowship. He is " the head over all things to the church," and by him the church is fitly framed together, and groweth unto a holy temple in the Lord. Still do the builders refuse him : even to this day the professional teachers of the gospel are far too apt to fly to any and every new philosophy sooner than maintain the simple gospel, which is the essence of Christ : nevertheless, he holds his true position amongst his people, and the foolish builders shall see to their utter confusion that his truth shall be exalted over all. Those who reject the chosen stone will stumble against him to their own hurt, and ere long will come his second advent, when he will fall upon them from the heights of heaven, and grind them to powder.

23. *"This is the LORD's doing."* The exalted position of Christ in his church is not the work of man, and does not depend for its continuation upon any builders or ministers; God himself has wrought the exaltation of our Lord Jesus. Considering the opposition which comes from the wisdom, the power, and the authority of this world, it is manifest that if the kingdom of Christ be indeed set up and maintained in the world it must be by supernatural power. Indeed, it is so even in the smallest detail. Every grain of true faith in this world is a divine creation, and every hour

in which the true church subsists is a prolonged miracle. It is not the goodness of human nature, nor the force of reasoning, which exalts Christ, and builds up the church, but a power from above. This staggers the adversary, for he cannot understand what it is which baffles him : of the Holy Ghost he knows nothing. *"It is marvellous in our eyes."* We actually see it ; it is not in our thoughts and hopes and prayers alone, but the astonishing work is actually before our eyes. Jesus reigns, his power is felt, and we perceive that it is so. Faith sees our great Master, far above all principality, and power, and might, and dominion, and every name that is named, not only in this world, but also in that which is to come ; she sees and marvels. It never ceases to astonish us, as we see, even here below, God by means of weakness defeating power, by the simplicity of his word baffling the craft of men, and by the invisible influence of his Spirit exalting his Son in human hearts in the teeth of open and determined opposition. It is indeed "marvellous in our eyes," as all God's works must be if men care to study them. In the Hebrew the passage reads, *"It is wonderfully done "* : not only is the exaltation of Jesus of Nazareth itself wonderful, but the way in which it is brought about is marvellous : it is wonderfully done. The more we study the history of Christ and his church the more fully shall we agree with this declaration.

24. *"This is the day which the* LORD *hath made."* A new era has commenced. The day of David's enthronement was the beginning of better times for Israel ; and in a far higher sense the day of our Lord's resurrection is a new day of God's own making, for it is the dawn of a blessed dispensation. No doubt the Israelitish nation celebrated the victory of its champion with a day of feasting, music and song ; and surely it is but meet that we should reverently keep the feast of the triumph of the Son of David. We observe the Lord's-day as henceforth our true Sabbath, a day made and ordained of God, for the perpetual remembrance of the achievements of our Redeemer. Whenever the soft Sabbath light of the first day of the week breaks upon the earth, let us sing,

> ' This is the day the Lord hath made,
> He calls the hours his own ;
> Let heaven rejoice, let earth be glad,
> And praise surround the throne."

We by no means wish to confine the reference of the passage to the Sabbath, for the whole gospel day is the day of God's making, and its blessings come to us through our Lord's being placed as the head of the corner. *"We will rejoice and be glad in it."* What else can we do ? Having obtained so great a deliverance through our illustrious leader, and having seen the eternal mercy of God so brilliantly displayed, it would ill become us to mourn and murmur. Rather will we exhibit a double joy, rejoice in heart and be glad in face, rejoice in secret and be glad in public, for we have more than a double reason for being glad in the Lord. We ought to be specially joyous on the Sabbath : it is the queen of days, and its hours should be clad in royal apparel of delight. George Herbert says of it :—

> " Thou art a day of mirth,
> And where the week-days trail on ground,
> Thy flight is higher as thy birth."

Entering into the midst of the church of God, and beholding the Lord Jesus as all in all in the assemblies of his people, we are bound to overflow with joy. Is it not written, " then were the disciples glad when they saw the Lord " ? When the King makes the house of prayer to be a banqueting house, and we have grace to enjoy fellowship with him, both in his sufferings and in his triumphs, we feel an intense delight, and we are glad to express it with the rest of his people.

25. *"Save now, I beseech thee, O* LORD*."* Hosanna ! God save our king ! Let David reign ! Or as we who live in these latter days interpret it,—Let the Son of David live for ever, let his saving help go forth throughout all nations. This was the peculiar shout of the feast of tabernacles ; and so long as we dwell here below in these tabernacles of clay we cannot do better than use the same cry. Perpetually let us pray that our glorious King may work salvation in the midst of the earth. We plead also for ourselves that the Lord would save us, deliver us, and continue to sanctify us. This we ask with great earnestness, beseeching it of Jehovah. Prayer should always be an entreating and beseeching. *"O* LORD*, I beseech thee, send now prosperity."* Let the church be built up : through the salvation of sinners may

the number of the saints be increased ; through the preservation of saints may the church be strengthened, continued, beautified, perfected. Our Lord Jesus himself pleads for the salvation and the prosperity of his chosen ; as our Intercessor before the throne he asks that the heavenly Father would save and keep those who were of old committed to his charge, and cause them to be one through the indwelling Spirit. Salvation had been given, and therefore it is asked for. Strange though it may seem, he who cries for salvation is already in a measure saved. None can so truly cry, " Save, I beseech thee," as those who have already participated in salvation ; and the most prosperous church is that which most imploringly seeks prosperity. It may seem strange that, returning from victory, flushed with triumph, the hero should still ask for salvation ; but so it is, and it could not be otherwise. When all our Saviour's work and warfare were ended, his intercession became even more prominently a feature of his life ; after he had conquered all his foes he made intercession for the transgressors. What is true of him is true of his church also, for whenever she obtains the largest measure of spiritual blessing she is then most inclined to plead for more. She never pants so eagerly for prosperity as when she sees the Lord's doings in her midst, and marvels at them. Then, encouraged by the gracious visitation, she sets apart her solemn days of prayer, and cries with passionate desire, " Save now," and " Send now prosperity." She would fain take the tide at the flood, and make the most of the day of which the Lord has already made so much.

26. *"Blessed is he that cometh in the name of the LORD."* The champion had done everything "in the name of the Lord": in that name he had routed all his adversaries, and had risen to the throne, and in that name he had now entered the temple to pay his vows. We know who it is that cometh in the name of the Lord beyond all others. In the Psalmist's days he was The Coming One, and he is still The Coming One, though he hath already come. We are ready with our hosannas both for his first and second advent ; our inmost souls thankfully adore and bless him and invoke upon his head unspeakable joys. " Prayer also shall be made for him continually ; and daily shall he be praised." For his sake everybody is blessed to us who comes in the name of the Lord, we welcome all such to our hearts and our homes ; but chiefly, and beyond all others, we welcome *himself* when he deigns to enter in and sup with us and we with him. O sacred bliss, fit antepast of heaven !. Perhaps this sentence is intended to be the benediction of the priests upon the valiant servant of the Lord, and if so, it is appropriately added, *"We have blessed you out of the house of the LORD."* The priests whose business it was to bless the people, in a sevenfold degree blessed the people's deliverer, the one chosen out of the people whom the Lord had exalted. All those whose high privilege it is to dwell in the house of the Lord for ever, because they are made priests unto God in Christ Jesus, can truly say that they bless the Christ who has made them what they are, and placed them where they are. Whenever we feel ourselves at home with God, and feel the spirit of adoption, whereby we cry, " Abba Father," the first thought of our hearts should be to bless the elder Brother, through whom the privilege of sonship has descended to such unworthy ones. In looking back upon our past lives we can remember many delightful occasions in which with joy unutterable we have in the fulness of our heart blessed our Saviour and our King ; and all these memorable seasons are so many foretastes and pledges of the time when in the house of our great Father above we shall for ever sing, " Worthy is the Lamb that was slain," and with rapture bless the Redeemer's name.

27. *"God is the LORD, which hath shewed us light,"* or " God is Jehovah," the only living and true God. There is none other God but he. The words may also be rendered, " Mighty is Jehovah." Only the power of God could have brought us such light and joy as spring from the work of our Champion and King. We have received light, by which we have known the rejected stone to be the head of the corner, and this light has led us to enlist beneath the banner of the once despised Nazarene, who is now the Prince of the kings of the earth. With the light of knowledge has come the light of joy ; for we are delivered from the powers of darkness and translated into the kingdom of God's dear Son. Our knowledge of the glory of God in the face of Jesus Christ came not by the light of nature, nor by reason, nor did it arise from the sparks which we ourselves had kindled, nor did we receive it of men ; but the mighty God alone hath showed it to us. He made a day on purpose that he might shine upon us like the sun, and he made our faces to shine in the light of that day, according to the declaration of the twenty-fourth verse. Therefore,

unto him be all the honour of our enlightenment. Let us do our best to magnify the great Father of lights from whom our present blessedness has descended. "*Bind the sacrifice with cords, even unto the horns of the altar.*" Some think that by this we are taught that the king offered so many sacrifices that the whole area of the court was filled, and the sacrifices were bound even up to the altar ; but we are inclined to keep to our own version, and to believe that sometimes restive bullocks were bound to the altar before they were slain, in which case Mant's verse is correct :—

> " He, Jehovah, is our Lord :
> He, our God, on us hath shined :
> Bind the sacrifice with cord,
> To the hornèd altar bind."

The word rendered " cords " carries with it the idea of wreaths and boughs, so that it was not a cord of hard, rough rope, but a decorated band ; even as in our case, though we are bound to the altar of God, it is with the cords of love and the bands of a man, and not by a compulsion which destroys the freedom of the will. The sacrifice which we would present in honour of the victories of our Lord Jesus Christ is the living sacrifice of our spirit, soul, and body. We bring ourselves to his altar, and desire to offer him all that we have and are. There remains a tendency in our nature to start aside from this ; it is not fond of the sacrificial knife. In the warmth of our love we come willingly to the altar, but we need constraining power to keep us there in the entirety of our being throughout the whole of life. Happily there is a cord which, twisted around the atonement, or, better still, around the person of our Lord Jesus Christ, who is our only Altar, can hold us, and does hold us : " For the love of Christ constraineth us ; because we thus judge, that if one died for all, then all died ; and that he died for all, that they that live should not henceforth live unto themselves, but unto him which died for them, and rose again." We are bound to the doctrine of atonement ; we are bound to Christ himself, who is both altar and sacrifice ; we desire to be more bound to him than ever, our soul finds her liberty in being tethered fast to the altar of the Lord. The American Board of Missions has for its seal an ox, with an altar on one side and a plough on the other, and the motto " Ready for either,"—ready to live and labour, or ready to suffer and die. We would gladly spend ourselves for the Lord actively, or be spent by him passively, whichever may be his will ; but since we know the rebellion of our corrupt nature we earnestly pray that we may be kept in this consecrated mind, and that we may never, under discouragements, or through the temptations of the world, be permitted to leave the altar, to which it is our intense desire to be for ever fastened. Such consecration as this, and such desires for its perpetuity, well beseem that day of gladness which the Lord hath made so bright by the glorious triumph of his Son, our covenant head, our well-beloved.

28 Thou *art* my God, and I will praise thee : *thou art* my God, I will exalt thee.

29 O give thanks unto the LORD ; for *he is* good : for his mercy *endureth* for ever.

Now comes the closing song of the champion, and of each one of his admirers. 28. " *Thou art my God, and I will praise thee,*" my mighty God who hath done this mighty and marvellous thing. Thou shalt be mine, and all the praise my soul is capable of shall be poured forth at thy feet. " *Thou art my God, I will exalt thee.*" Thou hast exalted me, and as far as my praises can do it, I will exalt thy name. Jesus is magnified, and he magnifies the Father according to his prayer, " Father, the hour is come ; glorify thy Son, that thy Son also may glorify thee." God hath given us grace and promised us glory, and we are constrained to ascribe all grace to him, and all the glory of it also. The repetition indicates a double determination, and sets forth the firmness of the resolution, the heartiness of the affection, the intensity of the gratitude. Our Lord Jesus himself saith, " I will praise thee " ; and well may each one of us, humbly and with confidence in divine grace add, on his own account, the same declaration, " *I* will praise thee." However others may blaspheme thee, I will exalt thee : however dull and cold I may sometimes feel myself, yet will I rouse up my nature, and determine that as long as I have any being that being shall be spent to thy praise. For ever thou art my God, and for ever I will give thee thanks.

29. "*O give thanks unto the* LORD *; for he is good : for his mercy endureth for ever."* The Psalm concludes as it began, making a complete circle of joyful adoration. We can well suppose that the notes at the close of the loud hallelujah were more swift, more sweet, more loud than at the beginning. To the sound of trumpet and harp, Israel, the house of Aaron, and all that feared the Lord, forgetting their distinctions, joined in one common hymn, testifying again to their deep gratitude to the Lord's goodness, and to the mercy which is unto eternity. What better close could there be to this right royal song ? The Psalmist would have risen to something higher, so as to end with the climax, but nothing loftier remained. He had reached the height of his grandest argument, and there he paused. The music ceased, the song was suspended, the great *hallel* was all chanted, and the people went every one to his own home, quietly and happily musing upon the goodness of the Lord, whose mercy fills eternity.

EXPLANATORY NOTES AND QUAINT SAYINGS.

Whole Psalm.—This is the last of those Psalms which form the great *Hallel*, which the Jews sang at the end of the passover.—*Adam Clarke.*

Whole Psalm.—The whole Psalm has a peculiar formation. It resembles the *Maschal* Psalms, for each verse has of itself its completed sense, its own scent and hue ; one thought is joined to another as branch to branch and flower to flower.— *Franz Delitzch.*

Whole Psalm.—Nothing can surpass the force and majesty, as well as the richly varied beauty, of this Psalm. Its general burden is quite manifest. It is the prophetic expression, by the Spirit of Christ, of that exultant strain of anticipative triumph, wherein the virgin daughter of Zion will laugh to scorn, in the immediate prospect of her Deliverer's advent, the congregated armies of the Man of Sin (verses 10—13).—*Arthur Pridham.*

Whole Psalm.—The two Psalms, 117th and 118th, are placed together because, though each is a distinct portion in itself, the 117th is an exordium to that which follows it, an address and an invitation to the Gentile and heathen world to acknowledge and praise Jehovah.

We are now arrived at the concluding portion of the hymn, which Christ and his disciples sung preparatory to their going forth to the Mount of Olives. Nothing could be more appropriate or better fitted to comfort and encourage, at that awful period, than a prophecy which, overleaping the suffering to be endured, showed forth the glory that was afterwards to follow, and a song of triumph, then only recited, but in due time to be literally acted, when the cross was to be succeeded by a crown. This Psalm is not only frequently quoted in the New Testament, but it was also partially applied at one period of our Saviour's sojourn on earth, and thus we are afforded decisive testimony to the purpose for which it is originally and prophetically destined. It was partially used at the time when Messiah, in the days of his humiliation, was received with triumph and acclamation into Jerusalem ; and we may conclude it will be fully enacted, when our glorified and triumphant Lord, coming with ten thousand of his saints, will again stand upon the earth and receive the promised salutation, " Blessed be the King that cometh in the name of Jehovah." This dramatic representation of Messiah coming in glory, to take his great power and reign among us, is apportioned to the chief character, " the King of kings and Lord of lords," to his saints following him in procession, and to priests and Levites, representing the Jewish nation.

The Conqueror and his attendants sing the 117th Psalm, an introductory hymn, inviting all, Jews and Gentiles, to share in the merciful kindness of God, and to sing his praises. It is a gathering together of all the Lord's people, to be witnesses and partakers of his glory. The first, second, and third verses of the 118th Psalm are sung by single voices. As the procession moves along, the theme of rejoicing is announced. The first voice repeats, " *O give thanks unto the* LORD *; for he is good, because his mercy endureth for ever."* Another single voice calls on Israel to acknowledge this great truth ; and a third invites the house of Aaron, the priesthood.

to acknowledge their share in Jehovah's love.   The fourth verse is a chorus ; the whole procession, the living, and the dead who are raised to meet Christ (1 Thess. iv. 16), shout aloud the burden of the song, verse 1.   Arrived at the temple gate, or rather, the gate of Jerusalem, the Conqueror alone sings, verses 5, 6, 7.   He begins by recounting the circumstances of his distress.   Next, he tells of his refuge : I betook me to God, I told him my sorrows, and he heard me.   The procession, in chorus, sings verses 8 and 9, taking up the substance of Messiah's chaunt, and fully echoing the sentiment, "*It is better to trust in the LORD than to put confidence in princes.*" The Conqueror alone again sings verses 10, 11, 12, 13, 14.   He enlarges on the magnitude of his dangers, and the hopelessness of his situation.   It was not a common difficulty, or a single enemy, whole nations compassed him about.   The procession in chorus, verses. 15, 16, attributes their Lord's great deliverance to his righteous person, and to his righteous cause.   Justice and equity and truth, all demanded that Messiah should not be trodden down.   "Was it not thine arm, O Jehovah, which has gotten thee the victory ? "   Messiah now takes up the language of a conqueror, verses 17, 18, 19.   My sufferings were sore, but they were only for a season.   I laid down my life, and I now take it up again : and then, with a loud voice, as when he roused Lazarus out of the grave, he cries to those within the walls, "*Open to me the gates of righteousness : I will go into them, and I will praise the LORD.*"   The priests and Levites within instantly obey his command, and while they throw open the gates, they sing, "*This is the gate of the LORD, into which the righteous shall enter.*"   As he enters, the Conqueror alone repeats verse 21. His sorrows are ended, his victory is complete.   The objects for which he lived and died, and for which his prayers were offered, are now fulfilled, and thus, in a few short words, he expresses his joy and gratitude to God.   The priests and Levites sing in chorus verses 22, 23, 24.   Depositaries and expounders of the prophecies as they had long been, they now for the first time, quote and apply one, Isai. xxviii. 16, which held a conspicuous place, but never before was intelligible to Jewish ears.   "The man of sorrows," the stone which the builders refused, is become the headstone of the corner.   The Conqueror is now within the gates, and proceeds to accomplish his good purpose, Luke i. 68.   "*Hosannah, save thy people, O LORD, and send them now prosperity,*" verse 25.   The priests and Levites are led by the Spirit to use the words foretold by our Lord, Matt. xxiii. 39.   Now at length the veil is removed, and his people say, "*Blessed be he that cometh in the name of the LORD,*" verse 26.   The Conqueror and his train (verse 27) now praise God, who has given light and deliverance and salvation, and they offer to him the sacrifice of thanksgiving for all that they enjoy.   The Conqueror alone (verse 28) next makes a solemn acknowledgment of gratitude and praise to Jehovah. and then, all being within the gates, the united body, triumphant procession, priests and Levites, end, as they commenced, "*O give thanks unto the LORD ; for he is good : for his mercy endureth for ever.*"—*R. H. Ryland, in " The Psalms restored to Messiah,"* 1853.

Whole Psalm.—It was Luther's favourite Psalm, his beauteous *Confitemini,* which " had helped him out of what neither emperor nor king, nor any other man on earth, could have helped him."   With the exposition of this his noblest jewel, his defence and his treasure, he occupied himself in the solitude of his Patmos (Coburg).—*Franz Delitzsch.*

Whole Psalm.—This is my Psalm, my chosen Psalm.   I love them all ; I love all holy Scripture, which is my consolation and my life.   But this Psalm is nearest my heart, and I have a peculiar right to call it mine.   It has saved me from many a pressing danger, from which nor emperor, nor kings, nor sages, nor saints, could have saved me.   It is my friend ; dearer to me than all the honours and power of the earth. . . .   But it may be objected, that this Psalm is common to all ; no one has a right to call it his own.   Yes ; but Christ is also common to all, and yet Christ is mine.   I am not jealous of my property ; I would divide it with the whole world. . . .   And would to God that all men would claim the Psalm as especially theirs !   It would be the most touching quarrel, the most agreeable to God—a quarrel of union and perfect charity.—*Luther.   From his Dedication of his Translation of Psalm CXVIII. to the Abbot Frederick of Nuremberg.*

Verse 1.—" *For he is good.*"   The praise of God could not be expressed in fewer words than these, " *For he is good.*"   I see not what can be more solemn than this brevity, since goodness is so peculiarly the quality of God, that the Son of God himself when addressed by some one as " Good Master," by one, namely, who beholding his flesh, and comprehending not the fulness of his divine nature, considered him as man only, replied, " Why callest thou me good ? There is none good but one, that is God." And what is this but to say, If thou wishest to call me good, recognize me as God ?—*Augustine.*

Verse 1.—*" His mercy endureth for ever."* What the close of Ps. cxvii. says of God's truth, viz., that it endureth for ever, the beginning of Ps. cxviii. says of its sister, his mercy or loving-kindness.—*Franz Delitzsch.*

Verses 1—4.—As the salvation of the elect is one, and the love of God to them one, so should their song be one, as here four several times it is said, " *His mercy endureth for ever."*—*David Dickson.*

Verses 1—4.—Because we hear the sentence so frequently repeated that, " *the mercy of the LORD endureth for ever,"* we are not to think that the Holy Spirit has employed empty tautology, but our great necessity demands it : for in temptations and dangers the flesh begins to doubt of the mercy of God : therefore nothing should be so frequently impressed on the mind as this, that the mercy of God does not fail, that the Eternal Father wearies not in remitting our sins.—*Solomon Gesner.*

Verse 2.—*" Let Israel now say."* Albeit all the elect have interest in God's praise for mercies purchased by Christ unto them, yet the elect of Israel have the first room in the song ; for Christ is first promised to them, and came of them according to the flesh, and will be most marvellous about them.—*David Dickson.*

Verse 2.—*" Let Israel now say, that his mercy endureth for ever."* Let such who have had an experience of it, acknowledge and declare it to others ; not only believe it with their hearts, and privately give thanks for it, but with the mouth make confession of it to the glory of divine grace.—*John Gill.*

Verses 2, 3, 4.—*" Now."* Beware of delaying. Delays be dangerous, our hearts will cool, and our affections will fall down. It is good then to be doing while it is called *to-day,* while it is called *now. Now, now, now,* saith David ; there be three nows, and all to teach us that for aught we know, it is *now* or never, to-day or not at all ; we must praise God while the heart is hot, else our iron will cool. Satan hath little hope to prevail unless he can persuade us to omit our duties when the clock strikes, and therefore his skill is to urge us to put it off till another time as fitter or better. Do it anon, next hour, next day, next week (saith he) ; and why not next year ? Hereafter (saith he) it will be as well as now. This he saith indeed, but his meaning (by hereafter) is never : and he that is not fit to-day, hath no promise but he shall be more unapt to-morrow. We have neither God nor our own hearts at command ; and when we have lost the opportunity, God to correct us perhaps will not give us affections. The cock within shall not crow to awaken us, the sun shall not shine, and then we are in danger to give over quite ; and if we come once to a total omission of one duty, why not of another, and of another, and so of all ? and then farewell to us.—*Richard Capel (1586–1656) in " Tentations, their Nature, Danger, Cure."*

Verse 4.—*" Them that fear the LORD."* Who were neither of " the house of Aaron," that is, of the priests or Levites ; nor of " the house of Israel," that is, native Jews ; yet might be of the Jewish religion, and *" fear the LORD."* These were called *proselytes,* and are here invited to praise the Lord.—*Joseph Caryl.*

Verse 4.—*" God's mercy endureth for ever."* That is, his covenant mercy, that precious church privilege : this is perpetual to his people, and should perpetually remain as a memorial in our hearts. And therefore it is that this is the foot or burthen of these first four verses. Neither is there any idle repetition, but a notable expression of the saints' insatiableness of praising God for his never failing mercy. These heavenly birds having got a note, sing it over and over. In the last Psalm there are but six verses, yet twelve Hallelujahs.—*Abraham Wright.*

Verse 5.—Perhaps verse 5, which says, *"I called upon the LORD in distress"* literally, out of the narrow gorge), *"and the LORD answered me on the open plain"* —which describes the deliverance of Israel from their captivity,—may have been sung as they defiled from a narrow ravine into the plain ; and when they arrived at the gate of the temple, then they broke forth in full chorus into the words, " Open to me the gates of righteousness " (ver. 19).—*Christopher Wordsworth.*

Verse 5.—It is said, *"I called upon the LORD."* Thou must learn to call, and not to sit there by thyself, and lie on the bench, hang and shake thy head, and bite and devour thyself with thy thoughts; but come on, thou indolent knave, down upon thy knees, up with thy hands and eyes to heaven, take a Psalm or a prayer, and set forth thy distress with tears before God.—*Martin Luther.*

Verse 5.—"*The* LORD *answered me, and set me in a large place.*" It may be rendered, *The* LORD *answered me largely;* as he did Solomon, when he gave him more than he asked for; and as he does his people, when he gives then a sufficiency and an abundance of his grace; not only above their deserts, but above their thoughts and expectations. See Eph. iii. 20.—*John Gill.*

Verse 6.—"*The* LORD *is on my side.*" The reason which the Psalmist gives here for his trusting, or for his not fearing, is the great fact, that the Lord is on his side; and the prominent idea which this brings before us is *Alliance; the making common cause,* which the great God undoubtedly does, with imperfect, yet with earnest, trusting man.

We know very well the great anxiety shown by men, in all their worldly conflicts, to secure the aid of a powerful ally; in their lawsuits, to retain the services of a powerful advocate; or, in their attempts at worldly advancement, to win the friendship and interest of those who can further the aims they have in view. When Herod was highly displeased with the armies of Tyre and Sidon, they did not venture to approach him until they had made Blastus, the king's chamberlain, their friend. If such and such a person be on their side, men think that all must go well. Who so well off as he who is able to say, "*The* LORD *is on my side*"?—*Philip Bennet Power, in "The I Will's of the Psalms,"* 1861.

Verse 6.—God is with those he calls and employs in public service. Joshua was exhorted to be strong and of good courage, "For the Lord thy God is with thee" (Josh. i. 9). So also was Jeremiah, "Be not afraid of their faces; for I am with thee to deliver thee" (Jer. i. 8). God's presence should put life into us. When inferior natures are backed with a superior, they are full of courage: when the master is by, the dog will venture upon creatures greater than himself and fear not; at another time he will not do it when his master is absent. When God is with us, who is the supreme, it should make us fearless. It did David; "*The* LORD *is on my side; I will not fear what man can do unto me.*" Let him do his worst, frown, threat, plot, arm, strike; the Lord is on my side, he hath a special care for me, he is a shield unto me, I will not fear, but hope; as it is in the next verse, "I shall see my desire on them that hate me," I shall see them changed or ruined. Our help is in the name of the Lord, but our fears are in the name of man.—*William Greenhill.*

Verse 6.—"*I will not fear.*" David, (or God's people, if you will,) being taught by experience, exults in great confidence, but does not say, the Lord is my helper, and I shall suffer no more, knowing that while he is a pilgrim here below he will have much to suffer from his daily enemies; but he says, "*The* LORD *is my helper, I will not fear what man can do unto me.*"—*Robert Bellarmine.*

Verse 6.—"*Man*" does not here mean *a man,* but *mankind,* or man as opposed to God.—*Joseph Addison Alexander.*

Verse 8.—It may perhaps be considered beneath the dignity and solemnity of our subject to remark, that this 8th verse of this Psalm is the middle verse of the Bible. There are, I believe, 31,174 verses in all, and this is the 15,587th. I do not wish, nor would I advise you to occupy your time in counting for yourselves, nor should I indeed have noticed the subject at all, but that I wish to suggest one remark upon it, and that is, that though we may generally look upon such calculations as only laborious idleness,—and they certainly have been carried to the most minute dissection of every part of Scripture, such as to how many times the word "Lord," the word "God," and even the word "and," occurs,—yet I believe that the integrity of the holy volume owes a vast deal to this scruple-weighing of these calculators. I do not say, nor do I think, that they had such motives in their minds; but whatever their reasons were, I cannot but think that there was an overruling Providence in thus converting these trifling and apparently useless investigations into additional guards and fences around the sacred text.—*Barton Bouchier.*

Verse 8.—"*It is better to trust in the* LORD," etc. Luther on this text calleth it, *artem artium, et mirificam, ac suam artem, non fidere hominibus,* that is, the art of arts, and that which he had well studied, not to put confidence in man : as for trust in God, he calleth it *sacrificium omnium gratissimum et suavissimum, et cultum omnium pulcherrimum,* the most pleasant and sweetest of all sacrifices, the best of all services we perform to God.—*John Trapp.*

Verse 8.—*"It is better to trust in the LORD."* All make this acknowledgment, and yet there is scarcely one among a hundred who is fully persuaded that God alone can afford him sufficient help. That man has attained a high rank among the faithful, who resting satisfied in God, never ceases to entertain a lively hope, even when he finds no help upon earth.—*John Calvin.*

Verse 8.—It is a great cause oftentimes why God blesseth not means, because we are so apt to trust in them, and rob God of his glory, not waiting for a blessing at his hands. This causeth the Lord to cross us, and to curse his own benefits, because we seek not him, but sacrifice to our own nets, putting confidence in outward means. Therefore when we hope for help from them, God bloweth upon them, and turneth them to our hurt and destruction.—*Abraham Wright.*

Verse 8.—When my enemies have been brought to contempt, let not my friend present himself unto me as a good man, and bid me repose my hope in himself ; for still must I trust in the Lord alone.—*Augustine.*

Verses 8, 9.—Nothing is more profitable than dwelling on familiar truths. Was there ever a good man who did not believe that it was better to trust in Jehovah than rely on any created arm ? Yet David here repeats this truth, that if possible it may sink deep into every mind.—*William S. Plumer.*

Verse 9.—*"It is better to trust in the LORD than to put confidence in princes."* David knew that by experience, for he confided in Saul his king, at another time in Achish, the Philistine, at another time in Ahithophel his own most prudent minister, besides some others ; and they all failed him ; but he never confided in God without feeling the benefit of it.—*Robert Bellarmine.*

Verse 9.—*"It is better,"* etc. Literally, " Good is it to trust in Jehovah more than to confide in man." This is the Hebrew form of comparison, and is equivalent to what is stated in our version. " It is *better,*" etc. It is better, (1) because man is weak,—but God is Almighty ; (2) because man is selfish,—but God is benevolent ; (3) because man is often faithless and deceitful,—God never ; (4) because there are emergencies, as death, in which man cannot aid us, however faithful, kind, and friendly he may be,—but there are no circumstances in this life, and none in death, where God cannot assist us ; and (5) because the ability of man to help us pertains at best only to the present life,—the power of God will be commensurate with eternity.—*Albert Barnes.*

Verse 9.—*"Than to put confidence in princes."* Great men's words, saith one, are like dead men's shoes ; he may go barefoot that waiteth for them.—*John Trapp.*

Verse 9.—They who constantly attend upon God, and depend upon him, have a much sweeter life, than those that wait upon princes with great observance and expectation. A servant of the Lord is better provided for than the greatest favourites and minions of princes.—*Thomas Manton.*

Verse 10.—*"All nations compassed me about."* A multitude of enemies everywhere cannot hinder the presence of God with us. Acts xvii. 28. They are without ; He is within, in our hearts ; they are flesh ; He is Spirit : they are frail ; He is immortal and invincible.—*Martin Geier.*

Verse 11.—Whether Tertullus persecute the church with his tongue, or Elymas with his hand, God hath the command of both. Indeed the wicked are the mediate causes of our troubles : the righteous are as the centre, the other the circumference ; which way soever they turn, they find themselves environed ; yet still the centre is fixed and immovable, being founded upon Christ. It is good for some men to have adversaries ; for often they more fear to sin, lest they should despise them, than dislike it for conscience, lest God should condemn them. They speak evil of us : if true, let us amend it ; if false, contemn it ; whether false or true, observe it. Thus we shall learn good out of their evil ; make them our tutors, and give them our pupilage. In all things let us watch them, in nothing fear them : " which is to them an evident token of perdition, but to us of salvation," Phil. i. 28. The church is that tower of David ; if there be a thousand weapons to wound us, there are a thousand shields to guard us, Cant. iv. 4.—*Thomas Adams.*

Verse 12.—*"They compassed me about like bees."* **Christ's enemies are so spiteful,** that in fighting against his kingdom, they regard not what become of themselves, so they may hurt his people ; but as the bee undoeth herself in stinging, and loseth her life or her power with her sting, so do they. All that the enemies of Christ's church can do against his people is but to trouble them externally ; their wounds are like the sting of a bee, that is, unto pain and swelling, and a short trouble only, but are not deadly.—*David Dickson.*

Verse 12.—*"They compassed me about like bees."* Now, as the north-east wind of course was adverse to any north-east progress, it was necessary that the boat should be towed by the crew. As the rope was being drawn along through the grass on the banks it happened that it disturbed a swarm of bees. In a moment, like a great cloud, they burst upon the men who were dragging ; everyone of them threw himself headlong into the water and hurried to regain the boat. The swarm followed at their heels, and in a few seconds filled every nook and cranny of the deck. What a scene of confusion ensued may readily be imagined.

Without any foreboding of ill, I was arranging my plants in my cabin, when I heard all around me a scampering which I took at first to be merely the frolics of my people, as that was the order of the day. I called out to enquire the meaning of the noise, but only got excited gestures and reproachful looks in answer. The cry of " Bees ! bees ! " soon broke upon my ear, and I proceeded to light a pipe. My attempt was entirely in vain ; in an instant bees in thousands are about me, and I am mercilessly stung all over my face and hands. To no purpose do I try to protect my face with a handkerchief, and the more violently I fling my hands about, so much the more violent becomes the impetuosity of the irritated insects. The maddening pain is now on my cheek, now in my eye, now in my hair. The dogs from under my bed burst out frantically, overturning everything in their way. Losing well nigh all control over myself, I fling myself into the river ; I dive down, but all in vain, for the stings rain down still upon my head. Not heeding the warnings of my people, I creep through the reedy grass to the swampy bank. The grass lacerates my hands, and I try to gain the mainland, hoping to find shelter in the woods. All at once four powerful arms seize me and drag me back with such force that I think I must be choked in the mud. I am compelled to go back on board, and flight is not to be thought of. . . . I felt ready, in the evening, for an encounter with half a score of buffaloes or a brace of lions rather than have anything more to do with bees ; and this was a sentiment in which all the ship's company heartily concurred.—*George Schweinfurth, in "The Heart of Africa,"* 1873.

Verse 12.—David said of his enemies, that they came about him like *"bees"* ; he doth not say like *wasps.* For though they used their stings, yet he found honey in them too.—*Peter Smith,* 1644.

Verse 12.—*"They compassed me about like bees."*

> As wasps, provoked by children in their play,
> Pour from their mansions by the broad highway,
> In swarms the guiltless traveller engage,
> Whet all their stings, and call forth all their rage,
> All rise in arms, and with a general cry,
> Assert their waxen domes, and buzzing progeny ;
> Thus from the tents the fervent legion swarms,
> So loud their clamours, and so keen their arms.
>
>   —*Homer.*

Verse 12.—*"They are quenched as the fire of thorns."* The illustration from the *"fire of thorns "* is derived from the fact that they quickly kindle into a blaze, and then the flame soon dies away. In Eastern countries it was common to burn over their fields in the dry time of the year, and thus to clear them of thorns and briers and weeds. Of course, at such a time they would kindle quickly, and burn rapidly, and would soon be consumed. So the Psalmist says it was with his enemies. He came upon them, numerous as they were, as the fire runs over a field in a dry time, burning everything before it.—*Albert Barnes.*

Verse 12.—*"In the name of the LORD."* This has been understood as the *tessera,* the sentence of attack, or signal to engage, like those of Cyrus—Jupiter is our leader and ally—Jupiter our captain and preserver. Cyropæd. l. 3 and 7 ; and Gideon, Judges vii. 18. This interpretation being only founded on the repetition, may it not more probably be designed as suited to the musical performance ?—*Samuel Burder.*

Verse 13.—*"Thou hast thrust sore at me that I might fall."* The apostrophe is strong, and probably directed to some particular person in the battle, who had put David in great danger.—*Samuel Burder.*

Verse 13.—*"Thou hast thrust sore at me that I might fall."* Thou hast indeed. Thou hast done thy part, O Satan, and it has been well done. Thou hast known all my weakest parts, thou hast seen where my armour was not buckled on tightly, and thou hast attacked me at the right time and in the right way. The great Spanish poet, Calderon, tells of one who wore a heavy suit of armour for a whole year, and laid it by for one hour, and in that hour the enemy came, and the man paid for his negligence with his life. "Blessed is the man that endureth temptation ; for when he is tried he shall receive the crown of life, which the Lord hath promised to them that love him."—*John Mason Neale.*

Verse 14.—*"The* Lord *is my strength and song, and is become my salvation."* *"My strength,"* that I am able to resist my enemies ; *" my salvation,"* that I am delivered from my enemies ; *"my song,"* that I may joyfully praise him and sing of him after I am delivered.—*William Nicholson,* 1662.

Verse 14.—Good songs, good promises, good proverbs, good doctrines are none the worse for age. What was sung just after the passage of the Red Sea, is here sung by the prophet, and shall be sung to the end of the world by the saints of the Most High.—*William S. Plumer.*

Verse 14.—*"And is become my salvation."* Not that he hath become anything which he was not before, but because his people, when they believed on him, became what they were not before, and then he began to be salvation unto them when turned towards him, which he was not to them when turned away from himself.—*Augustine.*

Verse 15.—*"The voice of rejoicing and salvation is in the tabernacles of the righteous."* Every one should be careful that his dwelling is one of the *tabernacles of the righteous,* and that he himself together with his household should walk in righteousness (Luke i. 75). And he should be so diligent in hymns and sacred songs, that his rooms should resound with them.—*Martin Geier.*

Verse 16.—*"The right hand of the* Lord *doeth valiantly."* Thrice he celebrateth God's right hand, to set forth his earnest desire to say the utmost ; or, in reference to the Sacred Trinity, as some will have it.—*John Trapp.*

Verse 17.—*"I shall not die, but live."* As Christ is risen, " we shall not die, but live"; we shall not die eternally, but we shall live in this world, the life of grace, and in the world to come, the life of glory ; that we may in both declare the " works " and chant the praises of God our Saviour. We are " chastened " for our sins, but " not given over to death" and destruction everlasting ; nay, our being " chastened " is now a proof that we are not so given over ; " for what son is he whom the father chasteneth not ? " Heb. xii. 7.—*George Horne.*

Verse 17.—*"I shall not die, but live."* To live, signifies, not barely to live, but to live comfortably, to have content with our life ; to live is to prosper. Thus the word is often used in Scripture. *"I shall not die, but live."* David did not look upon himself as immortal, or that he should never die ; he knew he was subject to the statute of death : but the meaning is, I shall not die now, I shall not die by the hands of these men, I shall not die the death which they have designed me to ; or when he saith, *"I shall not die, but live,"* his meaning is, I shall live comfortably and prosperously, I shall live as a king. That which we translate (1 Sam. x. 24) "God save the king," is, " Let the king *live,*" that is, let him prosper, and have good days ; let him have peace with all, or victory over his enemies.—*Joseph Caryl.*

Verse 17.—*"I shall not die,"* etc. The following incident is worth recording : " Wicliffe was now getting old, but the Reformer was worn out rather by the harassing attacks of his foes, and his incessant and ever-growing labours, than with the weight of years, for he was not yet sixty. He fell sick. With unbounded joy the friars heard that their great enemy was dying. Of course he was over-whelmed with horror and remorse for the evil he had done them, and they would hasten to his bedside and receive the expression of his penitence and sorrow. In a trice a little crowd of shaven crowns assembled round the couch of the sick man —delegates from the four orders of friars. ' They began fair,' wishing him ' health and restoration from his distemper"; but speedily changing their tone, they exhorted him, as one on the brink of the grave, to make full confession, and express his unfeigned grief for the injuries he had inflicted on their order. Wicliffe lay silent till they should have made an end, then, making his servant raise him a little on his pillow, and fixing his keen eyes upon them, he said with a loud voice, ' I shall not die, but live, and declare the evil deeds of the friars.' The monks rushed in astonishment and confusion from the chamber.—*J. A. Wylie, in "The History of Protestantism."*

Verse 17.—*"I shall not die,"* not absolutely, for see Psalm lxxxix. 48 ; Heb. ix. 27 ; but not in the midst of my days, Psalm cii. 24 ; nor according to the will of mine enemies, who *"thrust at me that I might fall,"* verse 13. *But,* on the contrary, *I shall live,* not simply as he had hitherto lived, in the greatest distress, which would be a wretched life, a living death : but lively, joyous, happy. Of this, he says he is secure ; this the word asserts. On what foundation does he rest ? Verses 14, 15, *"Because God had become his salvation,"* and *"the right hand of the Lord doeth valiantly."* —*Jacob Alting.*

Verse 17.—*"And declare the works of the Lord."* Matter of praise abounds in all the divine works, both of the general creation and preservation and of the redemption of our souls : chiefly, that God, besides the life of nature, has given to us the life of grace, without which we could not properly praise God and declare his works.—*Rivetus.*

Verse 17.—*"And declare the works of the Lord."* In the second member of the verse, he points out the proper use of life, God does not prolong the lives of his people, that they may pamper themselves with meat and drink, sleep as much as they please, and enjoy every temporal blessing ; but to magnify him for his benefits which he is daily heaping upon them.—*John Calvin.*

Verse 17.—According to Matthesius, Luther had this verse written against his study wall.

Verse 18.—*"The Lord hath chastened me sore."* Strong humours require strong physic to purge them out. Where corruption is deeply rooted in the heart, a light or small matter will not serve the turn to work it out. No ; but a great deal of stir and ado must be made with it.—*Thomas Horton.*

Verse 18.—*"But he hath not given me over unto death."* It might have been worse, may the afflicted saint say, and it will be better ; it is in mercy and in measure that God chastiseth his children. It is his care that " the spirit fail not before him, nor the souls which he hath made," Isai. lvii. 16. If his child swoons in the whipping, God lets fall the rod, and falls a kissing it, to fetch life into it again.—*John Trapp.*

Verse 19.—*"Open to me the gates of righteousness."* The gates won by his righteousness, to whom we daily say, " Thou only art holy"; the gates which needed the " Via Dolorosa " and the cross, before they could roll back on their hinges. On a certain stormy afternoon, after the sun had been for three hours darkened, the world again heard of that Eden from which, four thousand years before, Adam had been banished. " Verily I say unto thee, this day shalt thou be with me in paradise." O blessed malefactor, who thus entered into the heavenly gardens ! O happy thief, that thus stole the kingdom of heaven ! And see how valiantly he now enters it. *"Open to me the gates of righteousness."* Not " God be merciful to me a sinner " ; not " Lord, if thou wilt, thou canst make me clean." But this is what is called the suppliant omnipotency of prayer. " Blessed are they that do his commandments, that they may have right to the tree of life, and may enter in through the gates into the city.—*John Mason Neale.*

Verse 21.—*"I will praise thee : for thou hast heard me."* There is a point which we would especially notice, and that is, praise for *hearing* prayer. In this point, almost above all others, God is frequently robbed of his praise. Men pray ; they receive an answer to their prayers ; and then forget to praise. This happens especially in small things ; we should ever remember that whatever is worth praying for, is worth praising for also. The fact is, we do not recognize God in these small things as much as we should ; if we do praise, it is for the receipt of the blessing, with which we are pleased, leaving out of account the One from whom the blessing has come. This is not acceptable to God ; we must see him in the blessing, if we would really praise. The Psalmist says, *"I will praise thee : for thou hast heard me"* ; he praised not only because he had *received*, but also because he had *heard*— because the living God, as a hearing God, was manifested in his mercies. And when we know that God has heard us, let us not delay our praise ; if we put off our thanksgiving until perhaps only the evening, we may forget to praise at all ; and if we do praise, it will in all probability be with only half the warmth which would animate our song at first. God loves a quick return for his blessings ; one sentence of heartfelt thanksgiving is worth all the formalism of a more laboured service. There is a freshness about immediate praise which is like the bloom upon the fruit ; its being spontaneous adds ineffably to its price.

Trace, then, dear reader, a connection between your God and your blessing. Recognize his hearing ear as well as his bounteous hand, and be yours the Psalmist's words, *"I will praise thee: for thou hast heard me."—Philip Bennet Power.*

Verse 22.—"The stone." "The head stone of the corner." Christ Jesus is a stone : no firmness, but in him. A fundamental stone : no building, but on him. A corner stone : no piecing nor reconciliation, but in him.—*James Ford*, 1856.

Verse 22.—"The Stone which the builders rejected," etc. To apply it to Christ *"The Stone"* is the ground of all. Two things befall it ; two things as contrary as may be,—1. *Refused*, cast away ; then, called for again, and *made head of the building.* So, two parts there are to the eye. 1. The *refusing* ; 2. the *raising* ; which are his two estates, his *humiliation*, and his *exaltation*. In either of these you may observe two degrees, *a quibus*, and *quosque*, by whom and how far. *By whom refused ?* We weigh the word, *ædificantes :* not by men unskilful, but by workmen, professed *builders* ; it is so much the worse. *How far ?* We weigh the word,—*reprobaverunt ; usque ad reprobari*, even to a reprobation. It is not *improbaverunt, disliked*, as not fit for some eminent place ; but *reprobaverunt, utterly reprobate*, for any place at all.

Again, *exalted*, by whom ? The next words are *a Domino*, by *God*, as good a *builder*, nay, better than the best of them ; which makes amends for the former. And *How far ?* Placed by him, not in any part of the *building* ; but in the part most in the eye (*the corner*), and in the highest place of it, *the very head.*

So *rejected*, and that by the *builders*, and to the *lowest estate :* and from the *lowest estate exalted, in caput anguli*, to the chiefest place of all ; and that by God himself.—*Lancelot Andrewes.*

Verse 22.—"The stone which the builders refused," etc. We need not wonder, that not only the powers of the world are usually enemies to Christ, and that the contrivers of policies, those builders, leave out Christ in their building, but that the pretended builders of the church of God, though they use the name of Christ, and serve their turn with that, yet reject himself, and oppose the power of his spiritual kingdom. There may be wit and learning, and much knowledge of the Scriptures, amongst those that are haters of the Lord Jesus Christ, and of the power of godliness, and corrupters of the worship of God. It is the spirit of humility and obedience, and saving faith, that teach men to esteem Christ, and build upon him. The vanity and folly of these builders' opinion appears in this, that they are overpowered by the great Architect of the church : his purpose stands. Notwithstanding their rejection of Christ, he is still made the head corner stone. They cast him away by their reproaches, and by giving him up to be crucified and then cast into the grave, causing a stone to be rolled upon this *stone* which they had so rejected, that it might appear no more, and so thought themselves sure. But even from thence did he arise, and *"became the head of the corner."—Robert Leighton.*

Verse 22.—"The stone which the builders refused," etc. That is to say, God sent a living, precious, chosen stone on earth ; but the Jews, who then had the building of the church, rejected that stone, and said of it, " This man, who observeth not the Sabbath, is not of God " ; and, " We have no king but Cæsar," and, " That seducer said, I will arise after three days " ; and many similiar things beside. But this stone, so rejected by the builders as unfit for raising the spiritual edifice, *"is become the head of the corner"* ; has been made by God, the principal architect, the bond to connect the two walls and keep them together ; that is to say, has been made the head of the whole church, composed of Jews and Gentiles ; and such a head, that whoever is not under him cannot be saved ; and whoever is built under him, the living stone, will certainly be saved. Now all this *"is the Lord's doing,"* done by his election and design, without any intervention on the part of man, and therefore, *"it is wonderful in our eyes."* For who is there that must not look upon it as a wonderful thing, to find a man crucified, dead and buried, rising, after three days, from the dead, immortal, with unbounded power, and declared Prince of men and angels, and a way opened through him for mortal man, to the kingdom of heaven, to the society of the angels, to a happy immortality ?—*Robert Bellarmine.*

Verse 22.—*"The stone which the builders refused."* Here we behold with how strong and impregnable a shield the Holy Ghost furnishes us against the empty vauntings of the Papal clergy. Be it so, that they possess the name, " chief-builders "; but if they disown Christ, does it necessarily follow that we must disown him also ? Let us rather contemn and trample under our feet all their decrees, and let us reverence this precious stone upon which our salvation rests. By the expression, *"is become the head of the corner,"* we are to understand the real foundation of the church, which sustains the whole weight of the edifice ; it being requisite that the corners should form the main strength of buildings.—*John Calvin.*

Verse 22.—*"The stone,"* etc. That is I, whom the great men and rulers of the people rejected (1 Sam. xxvi. 19), as the builders of a house reject a stone unfit to be employed in it, am now become king over Israel and Judah ; and a type of that glorious King who shall hereafter be in like manner refused (Luke xix. 14, and xx. 17), and then be by God exalted to be Lord of all the world, and the foundation of all men's happiness.—*Thomas Fenton.*

Verse 22.—*"The stone."* The author of *Historia Scholastica* mentions it as a tradition that at the building of the second temple there was a particular *stone* of which that was literally true, which is here parabolically rehearsed, viz., that it had the hap to be often taken up by the builders, and as oft rejected, and at last was found to be perfectly fit for the most honourable place, that of the *chief corner-stone,* which coupled the sides of the walls together, the extraordinariness whereof occasioned the speech here following : *"This is the LORD'S doing ; it is marvellous in our eyes."*—*Henry Hammond.*

Verse 22.—*"The head stone of the corner."* How of the *"corner" ?* The *corner* is the place where two walls meet : and there be many twos in this *building :* the two walls of nations, *Jews* and *Gentiles ;* the two of conditions, *bond* and *free ;* the two of sex, *male* and *female :* the great two (which this [Easter] day we celebrate) of the *quick* and the *dead ;* above all, the greatest two of all, *heaven* and *earth.*—*Lancelot Andrewes.*

Verse 22.—*"Is become the head stone of the corner."*

Higher yet and ever higher, passeth he those ranks above,
Where the seraphs are enkindled, with the flame of endless love
Passeth them, for not e'en seraphs ever loved so well as he
Who hath borne for his beloved, stripes, and thorns, and shameful tree ;
Ever further, ever onward, where no angel's foot may tread,
Where the four-and-twenty elders prostrate fall in mystic dread :
Where the four strange living creatures sing their hymn before the throne,
The Despised One and rejected passeth, in his might alone ;
Passeth through the dazzling rainbow, till upon the Father's right
He is seated, his Co-equal, God of God, and Light of Light.

R. F. Littledale.

Verse 22.—*"Head stone of the corner."* It is now clear to all by divine grace whom Holy Scripture calls the corner-stone. Him in truth who, taking unto himself from one side the Jewish, and from the other the Gentile people, unites, as it were, two walls in the one fabric of the Church ; them of whom it is written " He hath made both one " ; who exhibited himself as the Corner-stone, not only in things below, but in things above, because he united on earth the nations of the Gentiles to the people of Israel, and both together to angels. For at his birth the angels exclaimed, " On earth peace, good will toward men."—*Gregory, quoted by Henry Newland, 1860.*

Verse 22.—*"The corner."* By Bede it is rendered as a reason why the Jewish builders refused our Saviour Christ for the *head*-place, *Quia in uno pariete, stare amabant.* They could endure no *corner ;* they must stand alone upon their own single wall ; be of themselves, not join with Gentiles or Samaritans. And Christ they endured not, because they thought if he had been *head* he would have inclined that way. *Alias oves oportet me adducere* (John x. 16). *Alias* they could not abide. But sure, a purpose there must be, *alias oves adducendi,* of bringing in others, of joining *a corner,* or else we do not *facere secundum exemplar,* build not according to Christ's pattern ; our fashion of fabric is not like his.—*Lancelot Andrewes.*

Verses 22—27.—By the consent of all expositors, in this Psalm is typed the coming of Christ, and his kingdom of the gospel. This is manifested by an *exaltation,* by an *exultaton,* by a *petition,* by a *benediction.* The *exaltation :* ver. 22, "*The stone which the builders refused is become the head stone of the corner.*" The Jews refused this stone, but God hath built his church upon it.

The *exaltation :* ver. 24, "*This is the day which the* LORD *hath made ; we will rejoice and be glad in it.*" A more blessed day than that was wherein he made man, when he had done making the world ; "*Rejoice we, and be glad in it.*"

The *petition :* ver. 25, "*Save now, I beseech thee, O* LORD *: O* LORD, *I beseech thee, send now prosperity.*" Thy justice would not suffer thee to save without the Messiah ; he is come, "*Save now, O* LORD, *I beseech thee.*" Our Saviour is come, let mercy and salvation come along with him.

The *benediction* makes all clear : ver. 26, "*Blessed be he that cometh in the name of the* LORD." For what David here prophesied, the people after accomplished Matt. xxi. 9, "Blessed is he that cometh in the name of the LORD." The corollary or sum is in my text : ver. 27, "*God is the* LORD, *which hath shewed us light : bind the sacrifice with cords, even unto the horns of the altar.*"—*Thomas Adams.*

Verse 24.—"*This is the day which the* LORD *hath made.*" 1. Here is the doctrine of the Christian sabbath : "*it is the day which the* LORD *hath made,*" has made remarkable, made holy, has distinguished it from other days ; he has made it for man ; it is therefore called the Lord's day, for it bears his image and superscription. 2. The duty of the Sabbath, "*we will rejoice and be glad in it*" ; not only in the institution of the day, that there is such a day appointed, but in the occasion of it, Christ's becoming "*the head of the corner.*" This we ought to rejoice in, both as his honour and our advantage. Sabbath days must be rejoicing days, and then they are to us as the days of heaven. See what a good Master we serve, who having instituted a day for his service, appoints it to be spent in holy joy.—*Matthew Henry.*

Verse 24.—"*This is the day,*" etc. The " queen of days," as the Jews call the Sabbath. Arnobius interpreteth this text of the Christian Sabbath ; others, of the day of salvation by Christ exalted to be the head corner-stone ; in opposition to that dismal day of man's fall.—*John Trapp.*

Verse 24.—Because believers have ever cause for comfort, therefore they are commanded always to rejoice, Phil. iii. Whether their sins or sufferings come into their hearts, they must not sorrow as they that have no hope. In their saddest conditions, they have the Spirit of consolation. There is seed of joy sown within them when it is turned under the clods, and appears not above ground. But there are special times when God calls for this grain to spring up. They have some red letters, some holy days in the calendar of their lives, wherein this joy, as wine at a wedding, is most seasonable ; but among all those days it never relisheth so well, it never tasteth so pleasantly, as on a Lord's-day. Joy suits no person so much as a saint, and it becomes no season so well as a Sabbath.

Joy in God on other days is like the birds chirping in winter, which is pleasing ; but joy on the Lord's-day is like their warbling times and pretty notes in spring, when all other things look with a suitable delightful aspect. "*This is the day which the* LORD *hath made,*" (he that made all days, so especially this day, but what follows ?) "*we will rejoice and be glad in it.*" In which words we have the church's solace, or joy, and the season, or day of it. Her solace was great : "*We will rejoice and be glad.*" Those expressions are not needless repetitions, but shew the exuberancy or high degree of their joy. The season of it : "*This is the day which the* LORD *hath made.*" Compare this place with Matt. xxi. 22, 23, and Acts iv. 11, and you will find that the precedent verses are a prophetical prediction of Christ's resurrection, and so this verse foretells the church's joy upon that memorable and glorious day. And, indeed, if " a feast be made for laughter," Eccles. x. 19, then that day wherein Christ feasteth his saints with the choicest mercies may well command their greatest spiritual mirth. A thanksgiving-day hath a double precedency of a fast-day. On a fast-day we eye God's anger ; on a thanksgiving-day we look to God's favour, In the former we specially mind our corruptions ; in the latter, God's compassions ; —therefore a fast-day calls for sorrow, a thanksgiving-day for joy. But the Lord's-day is the highest thanksgiving-day, and deserveth much more than the Jewish Purim, to be a day of feasting and gladness, and a good day.—*George Swinnock.*

Verse 24.—*"Day which the LORD hath made."* As the sun in heaven makes the natural day by his light, so does Christ the Sun of Righteousness make ours a spiritual day.—*Starke.*

Verse 24.—*"Day which the LORD hath made."* Adam introduced a day of sadness, but another day is made by Christ : Abraham saw his day from afar, and was glad ; we will walk even now in his light.—*Johann David Friesch*, 1731.

Verse 25.—*"Save."* With the Hebrews *salvation* is a wide word, comprising all the favours of God that may lead to preservation ; and therefore the Psalmist elsewhere extends this act both to man and beast, and, as if he would comment upon himself, expounds σῶσον *save*, by εὐόδωσον *prosper*. It is so dear a title of God, that the prophet cannot have enough of it.—*Joseph Hall.*

Verse 25.—*"Save now, I beseech thee, O LORD."* Let him have the acclamations of the people as is usual at the inauguration of a prince ; let every one of his loyal subjects shout for joy, *"Save now, I beseech thee, O LORD."* This is like *vivat rex*, and speaks both a hearty joy for his accession to the crown, an entire satisfaction in his government, and a zealous affection to the interests and honour of it. Hosanna signifies, *"Save now, I beseech thee."* Lord, save me, I beseech thee ; let this Saviour be my Saviour ; and in order to that my Ruler ; let me be taken under his protection, and owned as one of his willing subjects. His enemies are my enemies ; Lord, I beseech thee, save me from them. Send me an interest in that prosperity which his kingdom brings with it to all those that entertain it. Let my soul prosper and be in health, in that peace and righteousness which his government brings. Ps. lxxii. 3. Let me have victory over those lusts that war against my soul, and let divine grace go on in my heart, conquering and to conquer.—*Matthew Henry.*

Verse 25.—*"Save now,"* or, *hosanna.* Our thanksgivings on earth must always be accompanied with prayers for further mercies, and the continuance of our prosperity ; our hallelujahs with hosannas.—*Ingram Cobbin.*

Verse 25.—*"Save now, I beseech thee, O LORD,"* etc. Hosanna. The cry of the multitudes as they thronged in our Lord's triumphal procession into Jerusalem (Matt. xxi. 9, 18 ; Mar. xi. 9, 15, John xii. 13) was taken from this Psalm, from which they were accustomed to recite the 25th and 26th verses at the Feast of Tabernacles. On that occasion the great *Hallel*, consisting of Psalms cxiii.—cxviii. was chanted by one of the priests and at certain intervals the multitudes joined in the responses, waving their branches of willow and palm, and shouting as they waved them, Hallelujah, or *Hosannah*, or *"O LORD, I beseech thee, send now prosperity."* This was done at the recitation of the first and last verses of Ps. cxviii. ; but according to the school of Hillel, at the words *"Save now, we beseech thee."* The school of Shammai, on the contrary, say it was at the words, *"Send now prosperity."* Rabban Gamaliel and R. Joshua were observed by R. Akiba to wave their branches only at the words, *"Save now, we beseech thee"* (Mishna, *Succah*, iii. 9). On each of the seven days during which the feast lasted the people thronged the court of the temple, and went in procession about the altar, setting their boughs bending towards it ; the trumpets sounding as they shouted *Hosanna.* But on the seventh day they marched seven times round the altar, shouting meanwhile the great Hosannah to the sound of the trumpets of the Levites (Lightfoot, *Temple Service*, xvi. 2). The very children who could wave the palm branches were expected to take part in the solemnity (Mishna, *Succah*, iii. 15 ; Matt iii. 15). From the custom of waving the boughs of myrtle and willow during the service the name Hosannah was ultimately transferred to the boughs themselves, so that according to Elias Levita (*Thisbi.* s. v.), "the bundles of the willows of the brook which they carry at the Feast of Tabernacles are called Hosannahs."—*William Aldis Wright, in "Smith's Dictionary of the Bible,"* 1863.

Verse 25.—*" Send now prosperity."* God will send it, but his people must pray for it. " I came for thy prayers," Dan. x. 12.—*John Trapp.*

Verse 26.—*"Blessed is he that cometh in the name of the LORD."* The difference between Christ and Antichrist is to be noticed, because Christ did not come in his own name, but in the name of the Father ; of which he himself testified, John v., *"I am come in my Father's name, and ye receive me not ; if another shall come in his own name, him ye will receive."* Thus all faithful ministers of the Church must not come in their own name, or the name of Baal, or of Mammon and their own

belly, but in the name of God, with a lawful call ; concerning which see Heb. v.,
Rom. x. and xv.—*Solomon Gesner.*

Verse 27.—"*God is the* LORD, *which hath shewed us light.*" The Psalmist was
clearly possessed of light, for he says, "*God is the* LORD, *which hath shewed us light.*"
He was evidently, then, possessed of light ; and this light was in him as " the light
of life." This light had shone into his heart ; the rays and beams of divine truth
had penetrated into his conscience. He carried about with him a light which had
come from God ; in this light he saw light, and in this light he discerned everything
which the light manifested. Thus by this internal light he knew what was good
and what was evil, what was sweet and what was bitter, what was true and what
was false, what was spiritual and what was natural. He did not say, This light
came from creature exertion, this light was the produce of my own wisdom, this
light was nature transmuted by some action of my own will, and thus gradually
rose into existence from long and assiduous cultivation. But he ascribes the whole
of that light which he possessed unto God the Lord, as the sole author and the only
giver of it. Now, if God the Lord has ever showed you and me the same light which
he showed his servant of old, we carry about with us more or less of a solemn conviction that we have received this light from him. There will indeed, be many
clouds of darkness to cover it ; there will often be doubts and fears, hovering like
mists and fogs over our souls, whether the light which we have received be from
God or not. But in solemn moments when the Lord is pleased a little to revive
his work ; at times and seasons when he condescends to draw forth the affections
of our hearts unto himself, to bring us into his presence, to hide us in some measure in
the hollow of his hand, and give us access unto himself, at such moments and seasons
we carry about with us, in spite of all our unbelief, in spite of all the suggestions
of the enemy, in spite of all doubts and fears and suspicions that rise from the depths
of the carnal mind, in spite of all these counter-workings and underminings, we
carry about with us at these times a solemn conviction that we have light, and that
this light we have received from God. And why so ? Because we can look back
to a time when we walked in no such light, when we felt no such light, when everything spiritual and heavenly was dark to us, and we were dark to them.
    Those things which the Spirit of God enables a man to do, are in Scripture some-
times called *sacrifices.* " That we may offer," we read, " spiritual *sacrifices* acceptable
to God by Jesus Christ." The apostle speaks of " receiving of Epaphroditus
the things which were sent from the brethen at Philippi ; an odour of a sweet
smell ; a *sacrifice* acceptable and well-pleasing to God." Phil. iv. 18. So he says
to the Hebrew church : " But to do good and to communicate (that is, to the wants
of God's people), forget not ; for with such *sacrifices* God is well pleased." Heb.
xiii. 16. Well, then, these spiritual sacrifices which a man offers unto God are
bound also *to the horns of the altar.* They are not well-pleasing in the sight of God,
except they are bound to the horns of the altar, so as to derive all their acceptance
from the altar. Our prayers are only acceptable to God as they are offered through
the cross of Jesus. Our praises and thanksgivings are only acceptable to God
as they are connected with the cross of Christ, and ascend to the Father through
the propitiation of his dear Son. The ordinances of God's house are only
acceptable to God as spiritual sacrifices, when they are bound to the horns of the
altar. Both the ordinances of the New Testament—baptism and the Lord's supper
—have been bound by the hands of God himself to the horns of the altar ; and
no one either rightly went through the one, or rightly received the other, who had
not been first spiritually bound by the same hand to the horns of the altar. Every
act of liberality, every cup of cold water given in the name of a disciple, every
feeling of sympathy and affection, every kind word, every compassionate action
shown to a brother ; all and each are only acceptable to God as they ascend to him
through the mediation of his dear Son. And, therefore, every sacrifice of our
own comfort, or of our own advantage, of our own time, or of our own money, for
the profit of God's children, is only a spiritual and acceptable sacrifice so far as
it is bound to the horns of the altar, linked on to the cross of Jesus, and deriving
all its fragrance and odour from its connection with the incense there offered by
the Lord of life and glory.—*J. C. Philpot.*
    Verse 27.—How comfortable is the light ! 'Tis so comfortable that light
and comfort are often put for the same thing : " *God is the* LORD, *which hath shewed
us light,*" that is, the light of counsel what to do, and the light of comfort in what

we do, or after all our sufferings. Light is not only a candle held to us to do our work by, but it comforts and cheereth us in our work. Eccl. xi. 7.—*Joseph Caryl.*

Verse 27.—" *Shewed us light* : " " *bind the sacrifice.*" Here is somewhat received ; somewhat to be returned. God hath blessed us, and we must bless God. His grace and our gratitude, are the two lines my discourse must run upon. They are met in my text ; let them as happily meet in your hearts, and they shall not leave you till they bring you to heaven.—*Thomas Adams.*

Verse 27.—"*Bind the sacrifice with cords,*" etc. The sacrifice we are to offer to God, in gratitude for redeeming love, is ourselves, not to be slain upon the altar, but " living sacrifices " (Rom. xii. 1) to be bound to the altar ; spiritual sacrifices of prayer and praise, in which our hearts must be fixed and engaged, as the sacrifice was bound " with cords to the horns of the altar."—*Matthew Henry.*

Verse 27.—"*Bind the sacrifice,*" etc. 'Tis a saying among the Hebrews, that the beasts that were offered in sacrifice, they were the most struggling beasts of all the rest ; such is the nature of us unthankful beasts, when we should love God again, we are readier to run away from him ; we must be tied to the altar with cords, to draw from us love or fear.—*Abraham Wright.*

Verse 27.—"*With cords.*" This word is sometimes used for thick *twisted cords*, Judges xv. 13 ; sometimes for *thick branches* of trees, used at some feasts, Ezek. xix. 11, Levit. xxiii. 40. Hereupon this sentence may two ways be read ; *bind the feast with thick branches*, or *bind the sacrifice with cords ;* both mean one thing that men should keep the festivity with joy and thanks to God, as Israel did at their solemnities.—*Henry Ainsworth.*

Verse 27.—"*Even unto the horns of the altar.*" Before these words must be understood, *lead it* : for the victims were bound to rings fixed in the floor. "*The horns*" were architectural ornaments, a kind of capitals, made of iron or of brass, somewhat in the form of the curved horns of an animal, projecting from the four angles of the altar. The officiating priest, when he prayed, placed his hands on them, and sometimes sprinkled them with the blood of the sacrifice : compare Exod. xxx. 3 ; Lev. iv. 7, 18. At the end of this verse the word *saying* must be supplied.—*Daniel Cresswell.*

Verse 27.—"*Unto the horns.*" That is, all the court over, until you come even to the horns of the altar, intending hereby many sacrifices or boughs.—*Henry Ainsworth.*

Verse 28.—"*God.*" The original for "*God*" gives force to this passage : Thou art my "*El*"—the Mighty One ; therefore will I praise thee : my "*Eloah*"—a varied form with substantially the same sense, " and I will extol thee "—lift thee high in glory and honour.—*Henry Cowles.*

Verse 28.—This " extolling the Lord " will accomplish one of the great ends of praise, viz., his exaltation. It is true that God both can and will exalt himself but it is at once the duty and the privilege of his people to exalt him. His name should be upborne and magnified by them ; the glory of that name is now, as it were, committed to them : what use are we making of the opportunity and the privilege ?—*Philip Bennet Power.*

HINTS TO PREACHERS.

Verses 1—4.—I. The subject of song—" O give thanks unto the Lord, for he is good." II. The chorus—" His mercy endureth for ever." III. The choir—" Let Israel now say," etc. ; " Let the house of Aaron," etc. ; " Let them that fear the Lord," etc. IV. The rehearsal—" Let them *now* say," that they may be better prepared for universal praise hereafter.

Verse 5.—I. The season for prayer—" in distress." II. The answer in season —" The Lord answered me." III. The answer beyond the request—" And set me," etc.

Verse 6.—I. When may a man know that God is on his side ? II. What confidence may that man enjoy who is assured of divine aid ?

Verse 7.—I. The value of true friends. II. The greater value of help from above.

Verses 8, 9.—*"Better."* It is wiser, surer, morally more right, more ennobling, more happy in result.

Verse 10.—Take a wide range and consider what has been done, should be done, and may be done " in the name of the Lord."

Verse 12.—I. Faith's innumerable annoyances. II. Their speedy end. III. Faith's complete victory.

Verse 13.—I. Our great antagonist. II. His fierce attacks. III. His evident object: " that I might fall." IV. His failure: " but the Lord helped me."

Verse 14.—I. Strength under affliction. II. Song in hope of deliverance. III. Salvation, or actual escape out of trial.

Verse 15.—The joy of Christian households. It is joy in salvation : it is expressed,—" The voice " : it abides: " the voice *is* " : it is joy in the protection and honour given by the Lord's right hand.

Verses 15, 16.—I. True joy is peculiar *to* the righteous. II. *In* their tabernacles : in their pilgrimage state. III. *For* salvation : rejoicing and salvation go together. IV. *From* God: " the right hand," etc.: three right hands ; both the salvation and the joy are from the hand of the Father and the Son and the Holy Ghost ; the right hand of each doeth valiantly.—*G. R.*

Verse 17.—I. Good men are often in special danger : Joseph in the pit ; Moses in the ark of bulrushes ; Job on the dunghill ; David's narrow escapes from the hand of Saul ; Paul let down in a basket ; what a fruit basket was that ! How much was suspended upon that cord ! The salvation of how many ! II. Good men have often a presentiment of their recovery from special danger : " I shall not die, but live." III. Good men have a special desire for the preservation of their lives : " live and declare the works of the Lord."—*G. R.*

Verses 17, 19, 22.—The victory of the risen Saviour and its far-reaching consequences : (1) Death is vanquished ; (2) the gates of righteousness are opened ; (3) the corner-stone of the church is laid.—*Deichert, in Lange's Commentary.*

Verse 18.—I. The afflictions of the people of God are chastisements. " The Lord hath chastened me." II. Those chastisements are often severe : " hath chastened me *sore.*" III. The severity is limited : " it is not unto death."—*G. R.*

Verse 19.—I. Access to God desired. II. Humbly requested : " Open to me." III. Boldly accepted : " I will go into them." IV. Gratefully enjoyed : " And praise the Lord."

Verse 22.—In these words we may notice the following particulars. I. The metaphorical view in which the church is here represented, namely, that of a *house* or *building.* II. The character that our Immanuel bears with respect to this building ; he is *the stone* in a way of eminence, without whom there can be no building, no house for God to dwell in among the children of men. III. The character of the workmen employed in this spiritual structure ; they are called *builders.* IV. A fatal error they are charged with in building the house of God ; they *refuse* the stone of God's choosing ; they do not allow him a place in his own house. V. Notice the place that Christ should and shall have in this building, let the builders do their worst ; he *is made the head stone of the corner.* The words immediately following declare how this effected, and how the saints are affected with the views of his exaltation, notwithstanding the malice of hell and earth : " This is the Lord's doing, and it is wonderful in our eyes."—*Ebenezer Erskine.*

Verses 22, 23.—I. The mystery stated. 1. That which is least esteemed by men as a means of salvation is most esteemed by God. 2. That which is most esteemed by God when made known is least esteemed by man. II. The mystery explained. The way of salvation is the Lord's doing, therefore marvellous in our eyes.—*G. R.*

Verses 22—25.—I. Christ rejected. II. Christ exalted. III. His exaltation is due to God alone. IV. His exaltation commences a new era. V. His exaltation suggests a new prayer. See Spurgeon's Sermon, No. 1,420.

Verse 24.—I. What is spoken of. 1. The gospel day. 2. The sabbath day. II. What is said of it. 1. It is given by God. 2. To be joyfully received by man.—*G. R.*

Verse 25.—What is church prosperity ? Whence must it come ? How can we obtain it ?

Verse 25.—I. The object of the prayer. 1. Salvation from sin. 2. Prosperity in righteousness. II. The earnestness of the prayer: "I beseech thee, I beseech thee." III. The urgency of the prayer, "now—now"—now that the gates of righteousness are open, now that the foundation stone is laid, now that the gospel day has come—now, Lord! now!—*G. R.*

Verse 27.—*"Bind the sacrifice,"* etc. Devotion is the mother, and she hath four daughters. 1. Constancy: "Bind the sacrifice." 2. Fervency: Bind it "with cords." 3. Wisdom. Bind it "to the altar." 4. Confidence. Even to the "horns" of the altar.—*Thomas Adams.*

Verse 27.—*"Bind the sacrifice with cords,"* etc. I. What is the sacrifice? Our whole selves, every talent, all our time, property, position, mind, heart, temper, life to the last. II. Why does it need binding? It is naturally restive. Long delay, temptations, wealth, rank, discouragement, scepticism, all tend to drive it from the altar. III. To what is it bound? To the doctrine of atonement. To Jesus and his work. To Jesus and our work. IV. What are the cords? Our own vows. The need of souls. Our joy in the work. The great reward. The love of Christ working upon us by the Holy Spirit.

Verse 28.—I. The gladdest fact in all the world: "Thou art my God." II. The fittest spirit in which to enjoy it: "Praise thee."

Verse 28.—I. The effect of Christ being sacrificed for us: "Thou art my God." II. The effect of our being offered as an acceptable sacrifice to him. "I will praise thee, I will exalt thee." Or, I. The covenant blessing: "Thou art my God." II. The covenant obligation: "I will praise thee."—*G. R.*

Verse 29.—I. The beginning and the end of salvation is mercy. II. The beginning and end of its requirements is thanksgiving.—*G. R.*

PSALM CXIX.

TITLE.—*There is no title to this Psalm, neither is any author's name mentioned. It is* THE LONGEST PSALM, *and this is a sufficiently distinctive name for it. It equals in bulk twenty-two Psalms of the average length of the Songs of Degrees. Nor is it long only ; for it equally excels in breadth of thought, depth of meaning, and height of fervour. It is like the celestial city which lieth four-square, and the height and the breadth of it are equal. Many superficial readers have imagined that it harps upon one string, and abounds in pious repetitions and redundancies ; but this arises from the shallowness of the reader's own mind : those who have studied this divine hymn, and carefully noted each line of it, are amazed at the variety and profundity of the thought. Using only a few words, the writer has produced permutations and combinations of meaning which display his holy familiarity with his subject, and the sanctified ingenuity of his mind. He never repeats himself ; for if the same sentiment recurs it is placed in a fresh connection, and so exhibits another interesting shade of meaning. The more one studies it the fresher it becomes. As those who drink the Nile water like it better every time they take a draught, so does this Psalm become the more full and fascinating the oftener you turn to it. It contains no idle word ; the grapes of this cluster are almost to bursting full with the new wine of the kingdom. The more you look into this mirror of a gracious heart the more you will see in it. Placid on the surface as the sea of glass before the eternal throne, it yet contains within its depths an ocean of fire, and those who devoutly gaze into it shall not only see the brightness, but feel the glow of the sacred flame. It is loaded with holy sense, and is as weighty as it is bulky. Again and again have we cried while studying it, " Oh the depths ! " Yet these depths are hidden beneath an apparent simplicity, as Augustine has well and wisely said, and this makes the exposition all the more difficult. Its obscurity is hidden beneath a veil of light, and hence only those discover it who are in thorough earnest, not only to look on the word, but, like the angels, to look into it.*

The Psalm is alphabetical. Eight stanzas commence with one letter, and then another eight with the next letter, and so the whole Psalm proceeds by octonaries quite through the twenty-two letters of the Hebrew alphabet. Besides which, there are multitudes of appositions of sense, and others of those structural formalities with which the oriental mind is pleased,—formalities very similar to those in which our older poets indulged. The Holy Spirit thus deigned to speak to men in forms which were attractive to the attention and helpful to the memory. He is often plain or elegant in his manner, but he does not disdain to be quaint or formal if thereby his design of instruction can be the more surely reached. He does not despise even contracted and artificial modes of speech, if by their use he can fix his teaching upon the mind. Isaac Taylor has worthily set forth the lesson of this fact :—" In the strictest sense this composition is conditioned ; nevertheless in the highest sense is it an utterance of spiritual life ; and in thus finding these seemingly opposed elements, intimately commingled as they are throughout this Psalm, a lesson full of meaning is silently conveyed to those who shall receive it—that the conveyance of the things of God to the human spirit is in no way damaged or impeded, much less is it deflected or vitiated by its subjugation to those modes of utterance which most of all bespeak their adaptation to the infancy and the childlike capacity of the recipient."

AUTHOR.—*The fashion among modern writers is, as far as possible, to take every Psalm from David. As the critics of this school are usually unsound in doctrine and unspiritual in tone, we gravitate in the opposite direction, from a natural suspicion of everything which comes from so unsatisfactory a quarter. We believe that David wrote this Psalm. It is Davidic in tone and expression, and it tallies with David's experience in many interesting points. In our youth our teacher called it " David's pocket book," and we incline to the opinion then expressed that here we have the royal diary written at various times throughout a long life. No, we cannot give up this Psalm to the enemy. " This is David's spoil." After long reading an author one gets to know his style, and a measure of discernment is acquired by which his composition is detected even if his name be concealed ; we feel a kind of critical certainty that the hand of David is in this thing, yea, that it is altogether his own.*

SUBJECT.—*The one theme is the word of the Lord. The Psalmist sets his subject* in many lights, and treats of it in divers ways, but he seldom omits to mention the word of the Lord in each verse under some one or other of the many names by which he knows it ; and even if the name be not there, the subject is still heartily pursued in every stanza. He who wrote this wonderful song was saturated with those books of Scripture which he possessed.   Andrew Bonar tells of a simple Christian in a farmhouse who had meditated the Bible through three times.   This is precisely what this Psalmist had done,—he had gone past reading into meditation.   Like Luther, David had shaken every fruit-tree in God's garden, and gathered golden fruit therefrom.   " The most," says Martin Boos, " read their Bibles like cows that stand in the thick grass, and trample under their feet the finest flowers and herbs."   It is to be feared that we too often do the like.   This is a miserable way of treating the pages of inspiration.   May the Lord prevent us from repeating that sin while reading this precious Psalm.

There is an evident growth in the subject matter.   The earlier verses are of such a character as to lend themselves to the hypothesis that the author was a young man, while many of the later passages could only have suggested themselves to age and wisdom.   In every portion, however, it is the fruit of deep experience, careful observation, and earnest meditation.   If David did not write it, there must have lived another believer of exactly the same order of mind as David, and he must have addicted himself to psalmody with equal ardour, and have been an equally hearty lover of Holy Writ.

Our best improvement of this sacred composition will come through getting our minds into intense sympathy with its subject.   In order to this, we might do well to commit it to memory.   Philip Henry's daughter wrote in her diary, " I have of late taken some pains to learn by heart Psalm CXIX., and have made some progress therein."   She was a sensible, godly woman.   Having done this, we should consider the fulness, certainty, clearness, and sweetness of the word of God, since by such reflections we are likely to be stirred up to a warm affection for it.   What favoured beings are those to whom the Eternal God has written a letter in his own hand and style.   What ardour of devotion, what diligence of composition can produce a worthy eulogium for the divine testimonies ! If ever one such has fallen from the pen of man it is this CXIX. Psalm, which might well be called the holy soul's soliloquy before an open Bible.

This sacred ode is a little Bible, the Scriptures condensed, a mass of Bibline, Holy Writ rewritten in holy emotions and actions.   Blessed are they who can read and understand these saintly aphorisms ; they shall find golden apples in this true Hesperides, and come to reckon that this Psalm, like the whole Scripture which it praises, is a pearl island, or, better still, a garden of sweet flowers.

NOTES RELATING TO THE PSALM AS A WHOLE.

Eulogium upon the whole Psalm.—This psalm shines and shows itself among the rest.

> *Velut inter ignes*
> *Luna minores.**

a star in the firmament of the Psalms, of the first and greatest magnitude. This will readily appear if you consider either the manner it is composed in, or the matter it is composed of. The manner it is composed in is very elegant. The matter it is composed of is very excellent. 1. The manner it is composed in is very elegant; full of art, rule, method; theological matter in a logical manner, a spiritual alphabet framed and formed according to the Hebrew alphabet. 2. The matter it is composed of is very excellent; full of rare sublimities, deep mysteries, gracious activities, yea, glorious ecstacies. The Psalm is made up of three things,—1. prayers, 2. praises, 3. protestations. Payers to God; praises of God; protestations unto God.—*Rev. W. Simmons, in a sermon in the " Morning Exercises,"* 1661.

Eulogium.—This Psalm is called the Alphabet of Divine Love, the Paradise of all the Doctrines, the Storehouse of the Holy Spirit, the School of Truth, also the deep mystery of the Scriptures, where the whole moral discipline of all the virtues shines brightly. And as all moral instruction is delightsome, therefore this Psalm because excelling in this kind of instruction, should be called delightsome, inasmuch as it surpasses the rest. The other Psalms, truly, as lesser stars shine somewhat; but this burns with the meridian heat of its full brightness, and is wholly resplendent with moral loveliness.—*Johannes Paulus Palanterius,* 1600.

Eulogium.—In our German version it has the appropriate inscription, " The Christian's golden A B C of the praise, love, power, and use of the Word of God."—*Franz Delitzsch,* 1871.

Eulogium.—It is recorded of the celebrated St. Augustine, who among his voluminous works left a Comment on the Book of Psalms, that he delayed to comment on this one till he had finished the whole Psalter; and then yielded only to the long and vehement urgency of his friends, " because," he says, " as often as I essayed to think thereon, it always exceeded the powers of my intent thought and the utmost grasp of my faculties." While one ancient father † entitles this Psalm " the perfection of teaching and instruction "; another ‡ says that " it applies an all-containing medicine to the varied spiritual diseases of men—sufficing to perfect those who long for perfect virtue, to rouse the slothful, to refresh the dispirited, and to set in order the relaxed ; " to which might be added many like testimonies of ancient and modern commentators on it.—*William De Burgh,* 1860.

Eulogium.—In proportion as this Psalm seemeth more open, so much the more deep doth it appear to me ; so that I cannot show how deep it is. For in others, which are understood with difficulty, although the sense lies hid in obscurity, yet the obscurity itself appeareth ; but in this, not even this is the case ; since it is superficially such, that it seemeth not to need an expositor, but only a reader and listener.—*Augustine,* 354—430.

Eulogium.—In Matthew Henry's " Account of the Life and Death of his father, Philip Henry," he says : " Once, pressing the study of the Scriptures, he advised us to take a verse of this Psalm every morning to meditate upon, and so go over the Psalm twice in the year ; and that, saith he, will bring you to be in love with all the rest of the Scriptures. He often said, " All grace grows as love to the word of God grows."

Eulogium.—It is strange that of all the pieces of the Bible which my mother taught me, that which cost me most to learn, and which was to my child's mind most repulsive—the 119th Psalm—has now become of all the most precious to me in its overflowing and glorious passion of love for the law of God.—*John Ruskin, in " Fors Clavigera."*

Eulogium.—This Psalm is a prolonged meditation upon the excellence of the word of God, upon its effects, and the strength and happiness which it gives to a

---

* And like the moon, the feebler fires among,
Conspicuous shines." —*Horace.*

† St. Hilary.   ‡ Theodoret.

man in every position. These reflections are interspersed with petitions, in which the Psalmist, deeply feeling his natural infirmity, implores the help of God for assistance to walk in the way mapped out for him in the divine oracles. In order to be able to understand and to enjoy this remarkable Psalm, and that we may not be repelled by its length and by its repetitions, we must have had, in some measure at least, the same experiences as its author, and, like him, have learned to love and practise the sacred word. Moreover, this Psalm is in some sort a touch-stone for the spiritual life of those who read it. The sentiments expressed in it perfectly harmonise with what the historical books and other Psalms teach concerning David's obedience and his zeal for God's glory. There are, however, within it words which breathe so elevated a piety, that they can have their full sense and perfect truthfulness only in the mouth of Him of whom the prophet-king was the type.—*From the French of Armand de Mestral*, 1856.

Eulogium.—The 119th Psalm has been spoken of by a most distinguished living rationalistic critic (Professor Reuss) as " not poetry at all, but simply a litany—a species of chaplet." Such does not seem to be the opinion of the angels of God, and of the redeemed spirits, when that very poem supplies with the language of praise—the pæan of victory, " Just and true are thy ways " (Rev. xv. 3) ; the cry of the angel of the waters, " Thou art righteous, O Lord ! " (Rev. xvi. 5) ; the voice of much people in heaven, " True and righteous are his judgments " (Rev. xix. 2) ; what is this but the exclamation of him, whoever he may have been, who wrote the Psalm—" Righteous art thou, O Lord, and upright are thy judgments " (Psalm cxix. 137).—*William Alexander, in " The Quiver,"* 1880.

Incident.—In the midst of a London season ; in the stir and turmoil of a political crisis, 1819 ; William Wilberforce writes in his Diary—" Walked from Hyde Park Corner repeating the 119th Psalm in great comfort."—*William Alexander, in " The Witness of the Psalms."* 1877.

Incident.—George Wishart, the chaplain and biographer of " the great Marquis of Montrose," as he was called, would have shared the fate of his illustrious patron but for the following singular expedient. When upon the scaffold, he availed himself of the custom of the times, which permitted the condemned to choose a Psalm to be sung. He selected the 119th Psalm, and before two-thirds of the Psalm had been sung, a pardon arrived, and his life was preserved. It may not be out of place to add that the George Wishart, Bishop of Edinburgh, above referred to, has been too often confounded with the godly martyr of the same name who lived and died a century previously. We only mention the incident because it has often been quoted as a singular instance of the providential escape of a saintly personage ; whereas it was the very ingenious device of a person who, according to Woodrow, was more renowned for shrewdness than for sanctity. The length of this Psalm was sagaciously employed as the means of gaining time, and, happily, the expedient succeeded.—*C. H. S.*

Alphabetical Arrangement.—It is observed that the 119th Psalm is disposed according to the letters of the Hebrew alphabet, perhaps to intimate that children, when they begin to learn their alphabet, should learn that Psalm.—*Nathanael Hardy,* 1618—1670.

Alphabetical Arrangement.—True it is that the verses indeed begin not either with the English or yet the Latin letters, but with the Hebrew, wherein David made and wrote this Psalm. The will and purpose of the Holy Ghost is to make us to feel and understand that the doctrine herein contained is not only set down for great clerks which have gone to school for ten or twenty years ; but also for the most simple ; to the end none should pretend any excuse of ignorance.—*From Calvin's Two-and-Twenty Sermons upon the cxixth Psalm,* 1580.

Alphabetical Arrangement.—There may be something more than fancy in the remark, that Christ's name, " *the Alpha and Omega* "—equivalent to declaring him all that which every letter of the alphabet could express—may have had a reference to the peculiarity of this Psalm,—a Psalm in which (with the exception of ver. 84 and 122, exceptions that make the rule more marked) every verse speaks of God's revelation of himself to man.—*Andrew A. Bonar,* 1859.

Alphabetical Arrangement.—Origen says it is alphabetical because it contains the elements or principles of all knowledge and wisdom ; and that it repeats each letter eight times, because eight is the number of perfection.

Alphabetical Arrangement.—That the unlearned reader may understand what is meant by the Psalm being alphabetical, we append the following specimen upon the section *Aleph :*—

A blessing is on them that are undefiled in the way
    and walk in the law of Jehovah ;
A blessing is on them that keep his testimonies,
    and seek him with their whole heart ;
Also on them that do no wickedness,
    but walk in his ways.
A law hast thou given unto us,
    that we should diligently keep thy commandments.
Ah ! Lord, that my ways were made so direct
    that I might keep thy statutes !
And then shall I not be confounded,
    while I have respect unto all thy commandments.
As for me, I will thank thee with an unfeigne heart,
    when I shall have learned thy righteous judgments.
An eye will I have unto thy ceremonies,
    O forsake me not utterly.

From " The Psalms Chronologically Arranged. By Four Friends." 1867.

Author and Subject.—This is a Psalm by itself, it excels them all, and shines brightest in this constellation. It is much longer than any of them ; more than twice as long as any of them. It is not making long prayers that Christ censures ; but making them for a pretence ; which intimates that they are in themselves good and commendable. It seems to me to be a collection of David's pious and devout ejaculations, the short and sudden breathings of his soul to God, which he wrote down as they occurred, and towards the latter end of his time gathered them out of his day-book where they lay scattered, added to them many like words, and digested them into this Psalm, in which there is seldom any coherence between the verses ; but, like Solomon's proverbs, it is a chest of gold rings, not a chain of gold links. And we may not only learn by the Psalmist's example to accustom ourselves to such pious ejaculations, which are an excellent means of maintaining constant communion with God, and keeping the heart in frame for the more solemn exercises of religion ; but we must make use of the Psalmist's words, both for the exciting and the expressing of our devout affections. Some have said of this Psalm, He that shall read it considerately, it will either warm him or shame him ; and this is true.—*Matthew Henry,* 1662—1714.

Author and Subject.—This very singular poem has descended to us without name or title ; and with some difficulty in fixing its date. It is by many critics supposed to have been written by King David ; and there is in it so much of the peculiar language and strain of feeling that distinguish his compositions, with so perpetually shifting a complication of every condition of life through the whole scale of adversity and prosperity, that seems to distinguish his own history from that of every other individual, as to afford much reason for adopting this opinion, and for inducing us to regard it as a series of poems composed originally by David, at different times under different circumstances, or collected by him, and arranged in their present form, from floating passages of antecedent bards, that were in danger of being lost or forgotten. If this view of the subject approaches to correctness, it may constitute one of the poems which Josephus tells us David gave to the public on the re-establishment of tranquillity after the discomfiture of the traitor Sheba, and the return of the ten refractory tribes to a state of loyalty.

This poem, or rather collection of poems, is designed for private devotion, alone ; and we have, here, no distinct reference to any historical or national event, to any public festival, or any place, of congregational worship ; though a few general hints are occasionally scattered upon one or two of these points. We have nothing of David or Solomon, of Moses or Aaron, of Egypt or the journey through the wilderness ; nothing of Jerusalem, or Mount Zion, or Ephrata ; of the temple, or the altar, of the priests or the people. It consists of the holy effusions of a devout soul, in a state of closet retirement, unbosoming itself in blessed communion with its God, and descanting on the holy cycle of his attributes, and the consolations of his revealed will under every trial to which man can be exposed.

The form of this Psalm is singular ; and, though alphabetical, it is without an exact parallel in any of the others. It is, in truth, a set or collection of canticles,

or smaller poems, each forming a literal octrain or
octrain taking the first letter of the Hebrew alphabe
line ; the second, the second letter, and in the same n.
whole extent of the twenty-two letters that constitute 135
tongue ; and consequently extending the entire poem
discourses of eight lines each. Poetical collections of this first
the East, and especially among the Persian poets, who d very
poems, or canticles, by the name of gazels, and the entire set the
diwan. By the Arabian poet Temoa they are happily denomina or
an idea which the Persian poets have caught hold of, and play in
various ways.

From this peculiarity of construction the couplets of Psalm cx
Hebrew tongue, be committed to memory with far more ease than in
language : for, as each versicle under every octrain commences with the
and the progressive octrains follow up the order of the alphabet, the lett
a powerful help to the memory of the learner, and enables him to go thr
whole without hesitation.—*John Mason Good*, 1764—1827.

Author and Subject.—It is at least possible that the plaited work of so lo
Psalm, which, in connection with all that is artificial about it from beginning to e
gives us a glimpse of the subdued, afflicted mien of a confessor, is the work of one n
prison, who whiled away his time with this plaiting together of his complaints and
his consolatory thoughts.—*Franz Delitzsch*, 1871.

Subject.—The 119th Psalm is the appropriate sermon, after the Hallel, on the
text which is its epitome (Ps. i. 1, 2), " Blessed is the man that walketh not in the
counsel of the ungodly . . . . . but his delight is in the law of the Lord." Except
in two verses (122, 132), the law is expressly extolled in every verse.—*Andrew Robert
Fausset, in " Studies in the CL. Psalms,"* 1876.

Subject.—Every verse contains in it either a praise of God's word, from some
excellent quality of it ; or a protestation of David his unfeigned affection towards
it ; or else a prayer for grace, to conform himself unto it ; for unto one of these three,
—*praises, prayers,* or *protestations,* may all the verses of this Psalm be reduced.—
William Cowper.

Subject.—I know of no part of the Holy Scriptures where the nature and evidences
of true and sincere godliness are so fully and largely insisted on and delineated as in
the 119th Psalm. The Psalmist declares his design in the first verses of the Psalm,
keeps his eye on it all along, and pursues it to the end. The excellency of holiness
is represented as the immediate object of a spiritual taste and delight. God's law
—that grand expression and emanation of the holiness of God's nature, and prescription of holiness to the creature—is all along represented as the great object of the
love, the complacence, and the rejoicing of the gracious nature, which prizes God's
commandments " above gold, yea, the finest gold ; " and to which they are " sweeter
than honey and the honey-comb."—*Jonathan Edwards*, 1703—1758.

Subject and Connection of its parts.—This Psalm, no less excellent in virtue than
large in bulk, containeth manifold reflections on the nature, the properties, the
adjuncts, and effects of God's law ; many sprightly ejaculations about it, conceived
in different forms of speech ; some in way of petition, some of thanksgiving, some of
resolution, some of assertion or aphorism ; many useful directions, many zealous
exhortations to the observance of it ; the which are not ranged in any strict order,
but, like a variety of wholesome herbs in a fair field, do with a grateful confusion lie
dispersed, as they freely did spring in the heart, or were suggested by the devout
spirit of him who indited this Psalm, where no coherence of sentences being designed,
we may consider any one of them absolutely, or by itself.—*Isaac Barrow*, 1630—1677.

Subject and Connection.—Upon considering the matter of this Psalm, it will be
found that the stanzas beginning with the same letter have very little, and sometimes
not the least connection with each other ; and the praises of Jehovah, the excellencies
of his law, and supplications, are mingled together without order or coherence.
Hence I have been led to think, that the Psalm was never intended for an ode to be
performed at one time, *tout de suite,* but was a collection of stanzas of prayer and
praise arranged in alphabetical order, from which the pious worshipper might select
such as suited his situation and circumstances, using, as he saw fit, either one line
or two lines of each stanza, and uniting them together so as to make a connected

...position proper for the occasion and the circumstances in which he
...reet, 1790.

...Connection.—In view of the alphabetic or acrostic arrangement of
...: . Adam Clarke ventures the following remark :—" All connection, as
...lly be expected, is sacrificed to this artificial and methodical arrange-
...s is hardly probable, as Dr. Clarke himself felt when he endeavoured in
..." to show the connection which the eight verses of each part have among
...." Each group of eight verses seems to have a theme or subject common
...nd while the peculiar structure of the Psalm has obscured this arrangement,
...t is sometimes difficult to trace, it must not be said that the connection is
...ed.—F. G. Marchant, of Hitchin, 1879.

...ject and Connection.—In stanza Aleph the blessedness of walking in the way
...'s word is declared ; in Beth, that word is pronounced to be the only safeguard
...e young against sin ; in Gimel, is a pious resolve to cleave to the word, in spite
...ne sneers of the world. Daleth expresses a longing for the consolation of God's
...d to fortify good resolutions ; He declares an earnest desire for grace to obey
...e word ; Vau expresses firm trust and intense delight in God's word, and an earnest
...esire to see its full accomplishment ; Zain describes the blessed comfort derived
from God's word in evil days ; Cheth utters the joy which is inspired by the consciousness that God is his portion, and by communion with those that love his word,
and by a persuasion that all things work for good to all who love him ; Teth describes
the blessed effects of affliction, as described in God's word, in weaning the soul from
the world and drawing it nearer to him ; Jod represents the example of the resignation and piety of the faithful, especially in affliction, as gently drawing others to
God ; Caph is an expression of intense desire for the coming of God's kingdom, and
the subjection of all things to him, according to the promises of his word. Lamed
declares that the word of God is everlasting, immutable, and infinite in perfection :
and, therefore, in Mem it is asserted that God's word is the only treasure-house of
true wisdom ; and in Nun, that it is the only beacon-light in the darkness and storms
of this world ; and in Samech, that all sceptical attempts to undermine men's faith
in that word are hateful and deadly, and will recoil with confusion on those that
make them ; and in Ain, is a prayer for steadfastness and soundness of heart and
mind, amid all the impiety and unbelief of a godless world ; which is followed by an
assurance in Pe, that the word of God brings its own light and comfort with it to
those who earnestly pray for them, and fills the heart with compassion for those who
despise it. In Tzaddi is a declaration that even the youthful soul may stand strong
and steadfast, if it has faith in the purity, and truth, and righteousness of God's
law ; and therefore in Koph, is an earnest prayer for the grace of faith, especially, as
is expressed in Resh, in times of affliction, desolation, and persecution, as Schin adds,
from the powerful of this world ; but even then there is peace, joy, and exultation
for those who love God's word. And therefore the Psalm concludes, in Tau, with
an earnest prayer for the bestowal of the gifts of understanding, assistance, and grace
from God, to the soul which owns its weakness, and rests on him alone for support.—
Christopher Wordsworth, 1872.

Subject and Connection.—This Psalm has been called Psalmus literatus, or alpha-
betites ; and the Masora calls it alpa betha rabba. The name Jehovah occurs twenty-
two times in the Psalm. Its theme is the word of God, which it mentions under one
of the ten terms, תּוֹרָה, law ; דֶּרֶךְ, way ; עֵדָה, testimony ; פִּקּוּד, precept ; חֹק, statute ;
מִצְוָה, commandments ; מִשְׁפָּט, judgment ; דָּבָר, word ; אִמְרָה, saying ; אֱמוּנָה, truth ; in
every verse except verse 122. The last of these terms is scarcely admissible as a
term for the word ; but it has to suffice only in verse 90. According to this alphabetical series of eight stanzas, the word is the source of happiness to those who walk
by it (aleph), of holiness to those who give heed to it (beth), of truth to those whose
eyes the Lord opens by his Spirit (gimel), of law to those whose heart he renews
(daleth), begets perseverance by its promises (he), reveals the mercy and salvation of
the Lord (vau), awakens the comfort of hope in God (zayin), presents the Lord as the
portion of the trusting soul (cheth), makes affliction instructive and chastening (teth),
begets a fellowship in the fear of God (jod), and a longing for the full peace of salvation (kaph), is faithful and immutable (lamed), commands the approval of the heart
(mem), is a light to the path (nun), from which to swerve is hateful (samek), warrants
the plea of innocence (ayin), is a testimony to God's character and will (pe), is a law
of rectitude (tsade), warrants the cry for salvation (qoph), and payer for deliverance
from affliction (resh), and from persecution without a cause (shin), and assures of an

answer in due time (*tau*).   There is here as much order as could be expected in a long alphabetical acrostic.—*James G. Murphy, in a " Commentary on the Book of Psalms,"* 1875.

Whole Psalm.—Dr. Luther and Hilary, and other excellent men, think that here a compendium of the whole of theology is briefly set forth : for the things which are said, generally, about the Scripture, and the word of God, and theology, are helpful to the examination of doctrinal questions.   In the first place, it speaks of the author of that doctrine.   Secondly, of its authority and certainty.   Thirdly, it is declared that the doctrine, contained in the Apostolic and Prophetic books, is perfect, and contains all things which are able to give us instruction unto everlasting salvation. Fourthly, it affirms the perspicuity of the Scripture.   Fifthly, its usefulness.   Sixthly, its true and saving knowledge and interpretation.   Lastly, it treats of practice; how, for instance, the things which we are taught in the word of God are to be manifested and reduced to practice, in piety, moderation, obedience, faith, and hope, in temptations and adversities.—*Solomon Gesner*, 1559—1605.

Names given to the Law of God.—The things contained in Scripture, and drawn from it, are here called, 1. God's *law*, because they are enacted by him as our Sovereign.   2. His *way*, because they are the rule both of his providence and of our obedience.   3. His *testimonies*, because they are solemnly declared to the world, and attested beyond contradiction.   4. His *commandments*, because given with authority, and (as the word signifies) lodged with us as a trust.   5. His *precepts*, because prescribed to us, and not left indifferent.   6. His *word*, or saying, because it is the declaration of his mind, and Christ the essential, eternal Word is all in all in it.   7. His *judgments*, because framed in infinite wisdom, and because by them we must both judge and be judged.   8. His *righteousness*, because it is all holy, just, and good, and the rule and standard of righteousness.   9. His *statutes*, because they are fixed and determined, and of perpetual obligation.   10. His *truth* or *faithfulness*, because the principles upon which divine law is built are eternal truths.—*Matthew Henry.*

Names given to the Law of God.—The next peculiarity to be observed in this Psalm is, the regular recurrence of nine characteristic words, at least one or other of which is found in each distich, with one solitary exception, the second distich of the 12th division.   These words—*law, testimonies, precepts, statutes, commandments, judgments, word, saying,* and a word which only twice occurs as a characteristic—*way.*

These are, doubtless, all designations of the Divine Law ; but it were doing a deep injury to the cause of revealed truth to affirm that they are mere synonyms ; in other words, that the sentiments of this compendium of heavenly wisdom are little better than a string of tautologies.   The fact is, as some critics, both Jewish and Christian, have observed, that each of these terms designates the same law of God, but each under a different aspect, signifying the different modes of its promulgation, and of its reception.

Each of these words will now be examined in order, and an attempt will be made to discriminate them.

1. *" Law."*   This word is formed from a verb which means to direct, to guide, to aim, to shoot forwards.   Its etymological meaning, then, would be a rule of conduct, a κανών σαφής.   It means God's law in general, whether it be that universal rule called the law of nature, or that which was revealed to his Church by Moses, and perfected by Christ.   In strictness, the law means a plain rule of conduct, rather placed clearly in man's sight, than enforced by any command ; that is to say, this word does not necessarily include its sanctions.

2. *" Testimonies "* are derived from a word which signifies to bear witness, to testify.   The ark of the tabernacle is so called, as are the two tables of stone, and the tabernacle ;   the earnests and witnesses of God's inhabitation among his people. Testimonies are more particularly God's revealed law ;   the witnesses and confirmation of his promises made to his people, and earnests of his future salvation.

3. *" Precepts,"* from a word which means *to place in trust*, mean something entrusted to man, " that is committed to thee " ;   appointments of God, which consequently have to do with the conscience, for which man is responsible, as an intelligent being.

4. *" Statutes."*   The verb from which this word is formed means to engrave or

inscribe.   The word means a definite, prescribed, written law.   The term is applied
to Joseph's law about the portion of the priests in Egypt, to the law about the passover, etc.   But in this Psalm it has a more internal meaning ;—that moral law of
God which is engraven on the fleshy tables of the heart ; the inmost and spiritual
apprehension of his will : not so obvious as the law and testimonies, and a matter of
more direct spiritual communication than his precepts ; the latter being more
elaborated by the efforts of the mind itself, divinely guided indeed, but perhaps more
instrumentally, and less passively employed.

5. " *Commandments*," derived from a verb signifying to command or ordain.
Such was God's command to Adam about the tree ; to Noah about constructing
the ark.

6. " *Judgments*," derived from a word signifying to govern, to judge or determine,
mean judicial ordinances and decisions ; legal sanctions.

7. " *Word*."   There are two terms, quite distinct Hebrew, but both rendered
" word " in each of our authorised versions.   The latter of these is rendered "*saying*"
in the former volume of this work.   They are closely connected : since out of twenty-
two passages in which " *word* " occurs, in fourteen it is parallel to it, or in connection
with, " *saying*."   From this very circumstance it is evident they are not synonymous.

The term here rendered " *word* " seems the Λογος, or Word of God, in its most
divine sense ; the announcement of God's revealed will ; his command ; his oracle ;
at times, the special communication to the prophets.   The ten commandments are
called by this term in Exodus ; and דְּבִיר is the oracle in the temple.   In this Psalm
it may be considered as,—(1) God's revealed commandments in general.   (2) As
a revealed promise of certain blessings to the righteous.   (3) As a thing committed
to him as the minister of God.   (4) As a rule of conduct ; a channel of illumination.

8. As to the remaining word " *way*," that occurs but twice as a characteristic
word, and the place in which it occurs must rather be considered as exceptions to
the general rule ; so that I am not disposed to consider it as intended to be a cognate
expression with the above.   At all events, its meaning is so direct and simple as to
require no explanation ; a plain rule of conduct ; in its higher sense, the assisting
grace of God through Christ our Lord, who is the Way, the Truth, and the Life.
John Jebb, 1846.

EXPOSITION OF VERSES 1 TO 8.

BLESSED *are* the undefiled in the way, who walk in the law of the LORD.

2 Blessed *are* they that keep his testimonies, *and that* seek him with the whole heart.

3 They also do no iniquity : they walk in his ways.

4 Thou hast commanded *us* to keep thy precepts diligently.

5 O that my ways were directed to keep thy statutes !

6 Then shall I not be ashamed, when I have respect unto all thy commandments.

7 I will praise thee with uprightness of heart, when I shall have learned thy righteous judgments.

8 I will keep thy statutes : O forsake me not utterly.

These first eight verses are taken up with a contemplation of the blessedness which comes through keeping the statutes of the Lord. The subject is treated in a devout manner rather than in a didactic style. Heart-fellowship with God is enjoyed through a love of that word which is God's way of communing with the soul by his Holy Spirit. Prayer and praise and all sorts of devotional acts and feelings gleam through the verses like beams of sunlight through an olive grove. You are not only instructed, but influenced to holy emotion, and helped to express the same.

Lovers of God's holy words are blessed, because they are preserved from defilement (verse 1), because they are made practically holy (verses 2 and 3), and are led to follow after God sincerely and intensely (verse 2). It is seen that this holy walking must be desirable because God commands it (verse 4) ; therefore the pious soul prays for it (verse 5), and feels that its comfort and courage must depend upon obtaining it (verse 6). In the prospect of answered prayer, yea, while the prayer is being answered the heart is full of thankfulness (verse 7), and is fixed in solemn resolve not to miss the blessing if the Lord will give enabling grace (verse 8).

The changes are rung upon the words " *way* "—" undefiled in the way," " walk in his ways," " O that my ways were directed " ; " *keep* "—" keep his testimonies," " keep thy precepts diligently," " directed to keep," " I will keep " ; and " *walk* "— " walk in the law," " walk in his ways." Yet there is no tautology, nor is the same thought repeated, though to the careless reader it may seem so.

The change from statements about others and about the Lord to more personal dealing with God begins in the third verse, and becomes more clear as we advance, till in the later verses the communion becomes most intense and soul moving. O that every reader may feel the glow.

1. " *Blessed.*" The Psalmist is so enraptured with the word of God that he regards it as his highest ideal of blessedness to be conformed to it. He has gazed on the beauties of the perfect law, and, as if this verse were the sum and outcome of all his emotions, he exclaims, " Blessed is the man whose life is the practical transcript of the will of God." True religion is not cold and dry ; it has its exclamations and raptures. We not only judge the keeping of God's law to be a wise and proper thing, but we are warmly enamoured of its holiness, and cry out in adoring wonder, " Blessed are the undefiled ! " meaning thereby, that we eagerly desire to become such ourselves, and wish for no greater happiness than to be perfectly holy. It may be that the writer laboured under a sense of his own faultiness, and therefore envied the blessedness of those whose walk had been more pure and clean ; indeed, the very contemplation of the perfect law of the Lord upon which he now entered was quite enough to make him bemoan his own imperfections, and sigh for the blessedness of an undefiled walk.

True religion is always practical, for it does not permit us to delight ourselves in a perfect rule without exciting in us a longing to be conformed to it in our daily lives. A blessing belongs to those who hear and read and understand the word of the Lord ; yet is it a far greater blessing to be actually obedient to it, and to carry out in our walk and conversation what we learn in our searching of the Scriptures. Purity in our way and walk is the truest blessedness.

This first verse is not only a preface to the whole Psalm, but it may also be regarded as the text upon which the rest is a discourse.   It is similar to the benediction of the first Psalm, which is set in the forefront of the entire book : there is a likeness between this 119th Psalm and the Psalter, and this is one point of it, that it begins with a benediction.   In this, too, we see some foreshadowing of the Son of David, who began his great sermon as David began his great Psalm.   It is well to open our mouth with blessings.   When we cannot bestow them, we can show the way of obtaining them, and even if we do not yet possess them ourselves, it may be profitable to contemplate them, that our desires may be excited, and our souls moved to seek after them.   Lord, if I am not yet so blessed to be among the undefiled in thy way, yet I will think much of the happiness which these enjoy, and set it before me as my life's ambition.

As David thus begins his Psalm, so should young men begin their lives, so should new converts commence their profession, so should all Christians begin every day. Settle it in your hearts as a first postulate and sure rule of practical science that holiness is happiness, and that it is our wisdom first to seek the Kingdom of God and his righteousness.   Well begun is half done.   To start with a true idea of blessedness is beyond measure important.   Man began with being blessed in his innocence, and if our fallen race is ever to be blessed again, it must find it where it lost it at the beginning, namely, in conformity to the command of the Lord.

" *The undefiled in the way.*"   They are in the way, the right way, the way of the Lord, and they keep that way, walking with holy carefulness and washing their feet daily, lest they be found spotted by the flesh.   They enjoy great blessedness in their own souls ; indeed, they have a foretaste of heaven where the blessedness lieth much in being absolutely undefiled ; and could they continue utterly and altogether without defilement, doubtless they would have the days of heaven upon the earth. Outward evil would little hurt us if we were entirely rid of the evil of sin, an attainment which with the best of us lies still in the region of desire, and is not yet fully reached, though we have so clear a view of it that we see it to be blessedness itself ; and therefore we eagerly press towards it.

He whose life is in a gospel sense undefiled, is blessed, because he could never have reached this point if a thousand blessings had not already been bestowed on him.   By nature we are defiled and out of the way, and we must therefore have been washed in the atoning blood to remove defilement, and we must have been converted by the power of the Holy Ghost, or we should not have been turned into the way of peace, nor be undefiled in it.   Nor is this all, for the continual power of grace is needed to keep a believer in the right way, and to preserve him from pollution.   All the blessings of the covenant must have been in a measure poured upon those who from day to day have been enabled to perfect holiness in the fear of the Lord.   Their way is the evidence of their being the blessed of the Lord.

David speaks of a high degree of blessedness ; for some are in the way, and are true servants of God, but they are as yet faulty in many ways and bring defilement upon themselves.   Others who walk in the light more fully, and maintain closer communion with God, are enabled to keep themselves unspotted from the world, and these enjoy far more peace and joy than their less watchful brethren.   Doubtless, the more complete our sanctification the more intense our blessedness.   Christ is our way, and we are not only alive in Christ, but we are to live in Christ ; the sorrow is that we bespatter his holy way with our selfishness, self-exaltation, wilfulness, and carnality, and so we miss a great measure of the blessedness which is in him as our way.   A believer who errs is still saved, but the joy of his salvation is not experienced by him ; he is rescued but not enriched, greatly borne with, but not greatly blessed.

How easily may defilement come upon us even in our holy things, yea, even *in the way.*   We may even come from public or private worship with defilement upon the conscience gathered when we were on our knees.   There was no floor to the tabernacle but the desert sand, and hence the priests at the altar were under frequent necessity to wash their feet, and by the kind foresight of their God, the laver stood ready for their cleansing, even as for us our Lord Jesus still stands ready to wash our feet, that we may be clean every whit.   Thus our text sets forth the blessedness of the apostles in the upper room when Jesus had said of them, " Ye are clean."

What blessedness awaits those who follow the Lamb whithersoever he goeth, and are preserved from the evil which is in the world through lust.   These shall be the envy of all mankind " in that day."   Though now they despise them as precise fanatics and Puritans, the most prosperous of sinners shall then wish that they could change places with them.   O my soul, seek thou thy blessedness in following hard after thy Lord, who was holy, harmless, undefiled ; for there hast thou found peace hitherto, and there wilt thou find it for ever.

" *Who walk in the law of the Lord.*" In them is found habitual holiness.   Their walk, their common everyday life is obedience unto the Lord.   They live by rule, that rule the command of the Lord God.   Whether they eat or drink, or whatsoever they do, they do all in the name of their great Master and Exemplar.   To them religion is nothing out of the way, it is their everyday walk : it moulds their common actions as well as their special devotions.   This ensures blessedness.   He who walks in God's law walks in God's company, and he must be blessed ; he has God's smile, God's strength, God's secret with him, and how can he be otherwise than blessed ?

The holy life is a walk, a steady progress, a quiet advance, a lasting continuance. Enoch walked with God.   Good men always long to be better, and hence they go forward.   Good men are never idle, and hence they do not lie down or loiter, but they are still walking onward to their desired end.   They are not hurried, and worried, and flurried, and so they keep the even tenor of their way, walking steadily towards heaven ; and they are not in perplexity as to how to conduct themselves, for they have a perfect rule, which they are happy to walk by.   The law of the Lord is not irksome to them ; its commandments are not grievous, and its restrictions are not slavish in their esteem.   It does not appear to them to be an impossible law, theoretically admirable but practically absurd, but they walk by it and in it.   They do not consult it now and then as a sort of rectifier of their wanderings, but they use it as a chart for their daily sailing, a map of the road for their life-journey.   Nor do they ever regret that they have entered upon the path of obedience, else they w uld leave it, and that without difficulty, for a thousand temptations offer them opportunity to return ; their continued walk in the law of the Lord is their best testimony to the blessedness of such a condition of life.   Yes, they are blessed even now.   The Psalmist himself bore witness to the fact : he had tried and proved it, and wrote it down, as a fact which defied all denial.   Here it stands in the forefront of David's *magnum opus,* written on the topmost line of his greatest Psalm—" BLESSED ARE THEY WHO WALK IN THE LAW OF THE LORD."   Rough may be the way, stern the rule, hard the discipline,—all these we know and more,—but a thousand heaped-up blessednesses are still found in godly living, for which we bless the Lord.

We have in this verse blessed persons who enjoy five blessed things, A blessed way, blessed purity, a blessed law, given by a blessed Lord, and a blessed walk therein ; to which we may add the blessed testimony of the Holy Ghost given in this very passage that they are in very deed the blessed of the Lord.

The blessedness which is thus set before us we must aim at, but we must not think to obtain it without earnest effort.   David has a great deal to say about it ; his discourse in this Psalm is long and solemn, and it is a hint to us that the way of perfect obedience is not learned in a day ; there must be precept upon precept, line upon line, and after efforts long enough to be compared with the 176 verses of this Psalm we may still have to cry, " I have gone astray like a lost sheep ; seek thy servant ; for I do not forget thy commandments."

It must, however, be our plan to keep the word of the Lord much upon our minds ; for this discourse upon blessedness has for its pole-star the testimony of the Lord, and only by daily communion with the Lord by his word can we hope to learn his way, to be purged from defilement, and to be made to walk in his statutes. We set out upon this exposition with blessedness before us ; we see the way to it, and we know where the law of it is to be found : let us pray that as we pursue our meditation we may grow into the habit and walk of obedience, and so feel the blessedness of which we read.

2. " *Blessed are they that keep his testimonies.*"   What !   A second blessing ? Yes, they are doubly blessed whose outward life is supported by an inward zeal for God's glory.   In the first verse we had an undefiled way, and it was taken for granted that the purity in the way was not mere surface work, but was attended by the inward truth and life which comes of divine grace.   Here that which was implied is expressed.   Blessedness is ascribed to those who treasure up the testimonies of the Lord : in which is implied that they search the Scriptures, that they come to an understanding of them, that they love them, and then that they continue in the practice of them.   We must first get a thing before we can keep it.   In order to keep it well we must get a firm grip of it : we cannot keep in the heart that which we have not heartily embraced by the affections.   God's word is his witness or testimony to

grand and important truths which concern himself and our relation to him : this we should desire to know ; knowing it, we should believe it ; believing it, we should love it ; and loving it, we should hold it fast against all comers. There is a doctrinal keeping of the word when we are ready to die for its defence, and a practical keeping of it when we actually live under its power. Revealed truth is precious as diamonds, and should be kept or treasured up in the memory and in the heart as jewels in a casket, or as the law was kept in the ark ; this however is not enough, for it is meant for practical use, and therefore it must be kept or followed, as men keep to a path, or to a line of business. If we keep God's testimonies they will keep us ; they will keep us right in opinion, comfortable in spirit, holy in conversation, and hopeful in expectation. If they were ever worth having—and no thoughtful person will question that—then they are worth keeping ; their designed effect does not come through a temporary seizure of them, but by a persevering keeping of them : " in keeping of them there is great reward."

We are bound to keep with all care the word of God, because it is *his* testimonies. He gave them to us, but they are still his own. We are to keep them as a watchman guards his master's house, as a steward husbands his lord's goods, as a shepherd keeps his employer's flock. We shall have to give an account, for we are put in trust with the gospel, and woe to us if we be found unfaithful. We cannot fight a good fight, nor finish our course, unless we keep the faith. To this end the Lord must keep us : only those who are kept by the power of God unto salvation will ever be able to keep his testimonies. What a blessedness is therefore evidenced and testified by a careful belief in God's word, and a continual obedience thereunto. God has blessed them, in blessing them, and will bless them for ever. That blessedness which David saw in others he realized for himself, for in verse 168 he says, " I have kept thy precepts and thy testimonies," and in verses 54 to 56 he traces his joyful songs and happy memories to this same keeping of the law, and he confesses, " This I had because I kept thy precepts." Doctrines which we teach to others we should experience for ourselves.

"And that seek him with the whole heart." Those who keep the Lord's testimonies are sure to seek after himself. If his word is precious we may be sure that he himself is still more so. Personal dealing with a personal God is the longing of all those who have allowed the word of the Lord to have its full effect upon them. If we once really know the power of the gospel we must seek the God of the gospel. " O that I knew where I might find HIM," will be our whole-hearted cry. See the growth which these sentences indicate : first, in the way, then walking in it, then finding and keeping the treasure of truth, and to crown all, seeking after the Lord of the way himself. Note also that the further a soul advances in grace the more spiritual and divine are its longings ; an outward walk does not content the gracious soul, nor even the treasured testimonies ; it reaches out in due time after God himself, and when it in a measure finds him, still yearns for more of him, and seeks him still.

Seeking after God signifies a desire to commune with him more closely, to follow him more fully, to enter into more perfect union with his mind and will, to promote his glory, and to realize completely all that he is to holy hearts. The blessed man has God already, and for this reason he seeks him. This may seem a contradiction : it is only a paradox.

God is not truly sought by the cold researches of the brain : we must seek him with the heart. Love reveals itself to love : God manifests his heart to the heart of his people. It is in vain that we endeavour to comprehend him by reason ; we must apprehend him by affection. But the heart must not be divided with many objects if the Lord is to be sought by us. God is one, and we shall not know him till our heart is one. A broken heart need not be distressed at this, for no heart is so whole in its seekings after God as a heart which is broken, whereof every fragment sighs and cries after the great Father's face. It is the divided heart which the doctrine of the text censures, and strange to say, in scriptural phraseology, a heart may be divided and not broken, and it may be broken but not divided ; and yet again it may be broken and be whole, and it never can be whole until it is broken. When our whole heart seeks the holy God in Christ Jesus it has come to him of whom it is written, " as many as touched him were made perfectly whole."

That which the Psalmist admires in this verse he claims in the tenth, where he says, " With my whole heart have I sought thee." It is well when admiration of a virtue leads to the attainment of it. Those who do not believe in the blessedness of seeking the Lord will not be likely to arouse their hearts to the pursuit, but he who calls another blessed because of the grace which he sees in him is on the way to gaining the same grace for himself.

If those who *seek* the Lord are blessed, what shall be said of those who actually dwell with him and know that he is theirs ?

> " To those who fall, how kind thou art !
> How good to those who seek
> But what to those who find ? Ah ! this
> Nor tongue nor pen can show !
> The love of Jesus—what it is,
> None but his loved ones know."

3. " *They also do no iniquity.*" Blessed indeed would those men be of whom this could be asserted without reserve and without explanation : we shall have reached the region of pure blessedness when we altogether cease from sin. Those who follow the word of God do no iniquity, the rule is perfect, and if it be constantly followed no fault will arise. Life, to the outward observer, at any rate, lies much in doing, and he who in his doings never swerves from equity, both towards God and man, has hit upon the way of perfection, and we may be sure that his heart is right. See how a whole heart leads to the avoidance of evil, for the Psalmist says, " That seek him with the whole heart. They also do no iniquity." We fear that no man can claim to be absolutely without sin, and yet we trust there are many who do not designedly, wilfully, knowingly, and continuously do anything that is wicked, ungodly, or unjust. Grace keeps the life righteous as to act even when the Christian has to bemoan the transgressions of the heart. Judged as men should be judged by their fellows, according to such just rules as men make for men, the true people of God do no iniquity : they are honest, upright, and chaste, and touching justice and morality they are blameless. Therefore are they happy.

" *They walk in his ways.*" They attend not only to the great main highway of the law, but to the smaller paths of the particular precepts. As they will perpetrate no sin of commission, so do they labour to be free from every sin of omission. It is not enough to them to be blameless, they wish also to be actively righteous. A hermit may escape into solitude that he may do no iniquity, but a saint lives in society that he may serve his God by walking in his ways. We must be positively as well as negatively right : we shall not long keep the second unless we attend to the first, for men will be walking one way or another, and if they do not follow the path of God's law they will soon do iniquity. The surest way to abstain from evil is to be fully occupied in doing good. This verse describes believers as they exist among us : although they have their faults and infirmities, yet they hate evil, and will not permit themselves to do it ; they love the ways of truth, right and true godliness, and habitually they walk therein. They do not claim to be absolutely perfect except in their desires, and there they are pure indeed, for they pant to be kept from all sin, and to be led into all holiness.

4. " *Thou hast commanded us to keep thy precepts diligently.*" So that when we have done all we are unprofitable servants, we have done only that which it was our duty to have done, seeing we have our Lord's command for it. God's precepts require *careful* obedience : there is no keeping them by accident. Some give to God a careless service, a sort of hit or miss obedience, but the Lord has not commanded such service, nor will he accept it. His law demands the love of all our heart, soul, mind, and strength ; and a careless religion has none of these. We are also called to *zealous* obedience. We are to keep the precepts abundantly : the vessels of obedience should be filled to the brim, and the command carried out to the full of its meaning. As a man diligent in business arouses himself to do as much trade as he can, so must we be eager to serve the Lord as much as possible. Nor must we spare pains to do so, for a diligent obedience will also be *laborious and self-denying.* Those who are diligent in business rise up early and sit up late, and deny themselves much of comfort and repose. They are not soon tired, or if they are they persevere even with aching brow and weary eyes. So should we serve the Lord. Such a Master deserves diligent servants ; such service he demands, and will be content with nothing less. How seldom do men render it, and hence many through their negligence miss the double blessing spoken of in this Psalm.

Some are diligent in superstition and will worship ; be it ours to be diligent in keeping God's precepts. It is no use travelling fast if we are not in the right road. Men have been diligent in a losing business, and the more they have traded the more they have lost : this is bad enough in commerce, we cannot afford to have it so in our religion.

God has not commanded us to be diligent in *making* precepts, but in *keeping* them.   Some bind yokes upon their own necks, and make bonds and rules for others : but the wise course is to be satisfied with the rules of holy Scripture, and to strive to keep them all, in all places, towards all men, and in all respects.   If we do not this, we may become eminent in our own religion, but we shall not have kept the command of God, nor shall we be accepted of him.

The Psalmist began with the third person : he is now coming near home, and has already reached the first person plural, according to our version ; we shall soon hear him crying out personally and for himself.   As the heart glows with love to holiness, we long to have a personal interest in it.   The word of God is a heart-affecting book, and when we begin to sing its praises it soon comes home to us, and sets us praying to be ourselves conformed to its teachings.

5. "*O that my ways were directed to keep thy statutes !*" Divine commands should direct us in the subject of our prayers.   We cannot of ourselves keep God's statutes as he would have them kept, and yet we long to do so : what resort have we but prayer ? We must ask the Lord to work our works in us, or we shall never work out his commandments.   This verse is a sigh of regret because the Psalmist feels that he has not kept the precepts diligently, it is a cry of weakness appealing for help to one who can aid, it is a request of bewilderment from one who has lost his way and would fain be directed in it, and it is a petition of faith from one who loves God and trusts in him for grace.

Our ways are by nature opposed to the way of God, and must be turned by the Lord's direction in another direction from that which they originally take or they will lead us down to destruction.   God can direct the mind and will without violating our free agency, and he will do so in answer to prayer ; in fact, he has begun the work already in those who are heartily praying after the fashion of this verse.   It is for present holiness that the desire arises in the heart.   O that it were so now with me: but future persevering holiness is also meant, for he longs for grace to keep henceforth and for ever the statutes of the Lord.

The sigh of the text is really a prayer, though it does not exactly take that form. Desires and longings are of the essence of supplication, and it little matters what shape they take.   "O that" is as acceptable a prayer as "Our Father."

One would hardly have expected a prayer for direction ; rather should we have looked for a petition for enabling.   Can we not direct ourselves ? What if we cannot row, we can steer.   The Psalmist herein confesses that even for the smallest part of his duty he felt unable without grace.   He longed for the Lord to influence his will, as well as to strengthen his hands.   We want a rod to point out the way as much as a staff to support us in it.

The longing of the text is prompted by admiration of the blessedness of holiness, by a contemplation of the righteous man's beauty of character, and by a reverent awe of the command of God.   It is a personal application to the writer's own case of the truths which he had been considering.   "O that *my* ways," etc.   It were well if all who hear and read the word would copy this example and turn all that they hear into prayer.   We should have more keepers of the statutes if we had more who sighed and cried after the grace to do so.

6. "*Then shall I not be ashamed.*" He had known shame, and here he rejoices in the prospect of being freed from it.   Sin brings shame, and when sin is gone, the reason for being ashamed is banished.   What a deliverance this is, for to some men death is preferable to shame ! "*When I have respect unto all thy command-ments.*" When he respects God he shall respect himself and be respected.   When-ever we err we prepare ourselves for confusion of face and sinking of heart : if no one else is ashamed of me I shall be ashamed of myself if I do iniquity.   Our first parents never knew shame till they made the acquaintance of the old serpent, and it never left them till their gracious God had covered them with sacrificial skins. Disobedience made them naked and ashamed.   We, ourselves, will always have cause for shame till every sin is vanquished, and every duty is observed.   When we pay a continual and universal respect to the will of the Lord, then we shall be able to look ourselves in the face in the looking-glass of the law, and we shall not blush at the sight of men or devils, however eager their malice may be to lay somewhat to our charge.

Many suffer from excessive diffidence, and this verse suggests a cure.   An abiding sense of duty will make us bold, we shall be afraid to be afraid. No shame in the presence of man will hinder us when the fear of God has taken full possession of our minds. When we are on the king's highway by daylight, and are engaged upon royal business, we need ask no man's leave. It would be a dishonour to a king to be ashamed of his livery and his service ; no such shame should ever crimson the cheek of a Christian, nor will it if he has due reverence for the Lord his God. There is nothing to be ashamed of in a holy life ; a man may be ashamed of his pride, ashamed of his wealth, ashamed of his own children, but he will never be ashamed of having in all things regarded the will of the Lord his God.

It is worthy of remark that David promises himself no immunity from shame till he has carefully paid homage to all the precepts. Mind that word " *all*," and leave not one command out of your respect. Partial obedience still leaves us liable to be called to account for those commands which we have neglected. A man may have a thousand virtues, and yet a single failing may cover him with shame.

To a poor sinner who is buried in despair, it may seem a very unlikely thing that he should ever be delivered from shame. He blushes, and is confounded, and feels that he can never lift up his face again. Let him read these words : " Then shall I not be ashamed." David is not dreaming, nor picturing an impossible case. Be assured, dear friend, that the Holy Spirit can renew in you the image of God, so that you shall yet look up without fear. O for sanctification to direct us in God's way, for then shall we have boldness both towards God and his people, and shall no more crimson with confusion.

7. "*I will praise thee.*" From prayer to praise is never a long or a difficult journey. Be sure that he who prays for holiness will one day praise for happiness. Shame having vanished, silence is broken, and the formerly silent man declares, " I will praise thee." He cannot but promise praise while he seeks sanctification. Mark how well he knows upon what head to set the crown. " I will praise *thee*." He would himself be praiseworthy, but he counts God alone worthy of praise. By the sorrow and shame of sin he measures his obligations to the Lord who would teach him the art of living as that he should clean escape from his former misery.

" *With uprightness of heart*," His heart would be upright if the Lord would teach him, and then it should praise its teacher. There is such a thing as false and feigned praise, and this the Lord abhors ; but there is no music like that which comes from a pure soul which standeth in its integrity. Heart praise is required, upright-ness in that heart, and teaching to make the heart upright. An upright heart is sure to bless the Lord, for grateful adoration is a part of its uprightness ; no man can be right unless he is upright towards God, and this involves the rendering to him the praise which is his due.

" *When I shall have learned thy righteous judgments.*" We must learn to praise, learn that we may praise, and praise when we have learned. If we are ever to learn, the Lord must teach us, and especially upon such a subject as his judgments, for they are a great deep. While these are passing before our eyes, and we are learning from them, we ought to praise God, for the original is not, " when I have learned," but, " in my learning." While yet I am a scholar I will be a chorister : my upright heart shall praise thine uprightness, my purified judgment shall admire thy judg-ments. God's providence is a book full of teaching, and to those whose hearts are right it is a music book, out of which they chant to Jehovah's praise. God's word is full of the record of his righteous providences, and as we read it we feel compelled to burst forth into expressions of holy delight and ardent praise. When we both read of God's judgments and become joyful partakers in them, we are doubly moved to song—song in which there is neither formality, nor hypocrisy, nor lukewarmness, for the heart is upright in the presentation of its praise.

8. " *I will keep thy statutes.*" A calm resolve. When praise calms down into solid resolution it is well with the soul. Zeal which spends itself in singing, and leaves no practical residuum of holy living, is little worth : " I will praise " should be coupled with " I will keep." This firm resolve is by no means boastful, like Peter's " though I should die with thee, yet will I not forsake thee," for it is followed by a humble prayer for divine help, " *O forsake me not utterly.*" Feeling his own incapacity he trembles lest he should be left to himself, and this fear is increased by the horror which he has of falling into sin. The " I will keep " sounds rightly enough now that the humble cry is heard with it. This is a happy amalgam : resolution and depen-dence. We meet with those who to all appearance humbly pray, but there is no force of character, no decision in them, and consequently the pleading of the closet is not

embodied in the life: on the other hand, we meet with abundance of resolve attended with an entire absence of dependence upon God, and this makes as poor a character as the former. The Lord grant us to have such a blending of excellences that we may be "perfect and entire, wanting nothing."

This prayer is one which is certain to be heard, for assuredly it must be highly pleasing to God to see a man set upon obeying his will, and therefore it must be most agreeable to him to be present with such a person, and to help him in his endeavours. How can he forsake one who does not forsake his law?

The peculiar dread which tinges this prayer with a sombre hue is the fear of utter forsaking. Well may the soul cry out against such a calamity. To be left, that we may discover our weakness, is a sufficient trial: to be altogether forsaken would be ruin and death. Hiding the face in a little wrath for a moment brings us very low: an absolute desertion would land us ultimately in the lowest hell. But the Lord never has utterly forsaken his servants, and he never will, blessed be his name. If we long to keep his statutes he will keep us; yea, his grace will keep us keeping his law.

There is rather a descent from the mount of benediction with which the first verse began to the almost wail of this eighth verse, yet this is spiritually a growth, for from admiration of goodness we have come to a burning longing after God and communion with him, and an intense horror lest it should not be enjoyed. The sigh of verse 5 is now supplanted by an actual prayer from the depths of a heart conscious of its undesert, and its entire dependence upon divine love. The two "I wills" needed to be seasoned with some such lowly petition, or it might have been thought that the good man's dependence was in some degree fixed upon his own determination. He presents his resolutions like a sacrifice, but he cries to heaven for the fire.

NOTES ON THE VERSES.

The first eight verses commence with Aleph, and may be alphabetically rendered thus :—

1. **A**ll they that are undefiled in the way, walking in the law of the Lord, are blessed.
2. **A**ll they that keep his testimonies, and that seek him with the whole heart, are blessed.
3. **A**lso they do no iniquity : they walk in his ways.
4. **A**ll thy precepts diligently to keep thou hast commanded us.
5. **A**h, Lord ! that my ways were directed to keep thy statutes !
6. **A**shamed I shall never be, when I have respect unto all thy commandments.
7. **A**lways will I praise thee, with uprightness of heart, when I shall have learned thy righteous judgments.
8. **A**ll thy statutes will I keep : O forsake me not utterly.

Pastor Theodore Kübler, of Islington, 1880.

Whole eight verses, 1—8.—Every line begins with Aleph, to which the Jews ascribe the meaning of *an ox*, that is, the beast of useful service, and thus of many blessings. Key of the section : " O the blessings."—*F. G. Marchant.*

Whole eight verses, 1—8.—These eight verses teach that true piety is sincere, consistent, practical, hearty, intelligent, earnest, active, stirring, diligent, humble, distrustful of itself, systematical, guileless, unspotted from the world, self-renouncing, confident in God, delighting in thankfulness, fully purposed to keep the law, and as ready to confess that without divine grace it can do nothing.

They also teach us how great is the sin of not believing God's word. As it is a law, the faithless refuse to walk by it ; as it is a testimony, they refuse to believe their Maker ; as it demands righteousness, they refuse to seek it ; as it gives precepts, they will not obey them ; as it ordains statutes, they rebel against them ; as it has excellent commandments, they stand out in opposition to them ; as it abounds with righteous judgments, they refuse to stand by them. They will not pray for grace ; they will not praise God for mercies received ; they do not feel their dependence or impotence, and they never look to the Father of lights from whom cometh down every good and perfect gift.—*William S. Plumer*,—1880.

Verse 1.—" *Blessed.*" The Psalmist beginneth with a description of the way to true blessedness, as Christ began his Sermon on the Mount, and as the whole Book of Psalms is elsewhere begun. Blessedness is that which we all aim at, only we are either ignorant or reckless of the way that leadeth to it, therefore the holy Psalmist would first set us right as to the true notion of a blessed man : " *Blessed are the undefiled in the way, who walk in the law of the* LORD."—*Thomas Manton*, 1620—1677.

Verse 1.—" *Blessed.*" Here the Lord, who in the last day will pronounce some to be blessed and some to be cursed, doth now tell us who they are. What can comfort them to whom the Lord shall say, Depart from me, ye cursed ? Where away shall they go when the Lord shall command them to depart from him ? And what greater joy can come to a man, than to hear the Judge of all saying unto him, Come to me, ye blessed ? Oh that we were wise in time, to think of this, that so we might endeavour to become such men as God in his word hath blessed !—*William Cowper*, 1566—1619.

Verse 1.—The Scripture speaketh of blessedness two ways ; *casually*, in reference to that which is the cause whereby we get a right to this blessed estate ; and in this sense it is attributed to faith in Christ, to forgiveness of sin, and to justification of life which we obtain in Christ. Sometimes the Scripture speaketh *formally* of blessedness, in order to the actual execution of it ; and thus it pronounceth them blessed who are perfect in their course ; for this is a blessedness actually executed, and doth fit us to have the full execution and consummation of blessedness begun in us ; thus they are blessed who endure patiently, who are poor in spirit, who are merciful, who are peacemakers, etc. If I speak of a sick man, and say he is happy, for he hath met with a good physician ; here I pronounce him blessed because he hath found one who will restore him to health. If I say of the same man, he is a happy man, he can now digest very well what he eateth, he can sleep, and walk abroad ; I speak of him now as actually blessed with health of body.

The end of everything being the good of that thing, and the prosperity of everything being the end of it,—to attain in some latitude this perfection of action must needs make a man actually blessed. Hence blessedness is ascribed to *walking* in God's way. If we have not the habit of doing anything, we do it with difficulty, we are ready to cease from doing it ; as a horse will continually break out of the pace to which he is not perfectly broken. Thence it is that the saints find their estate miserable till they form the habit which maketh them with facility and constancy *walk* with God ; there being no greater misery than to see themselves doing good duties uncheerfully, no sooner entering them than out again, and desisting from them. On the contrary, they count it of all things most blessed to have attained some degree of permanent habit in godliness. The blessedness which is here spoken of is the actual execution of that blessedness which comes to us by faith in Christ.—*Paul Bayne,* —1617.

Verse 1.—" *The undefiled.*" You ask, Why does God will that we be undefiled ? I reply, because he has chosen us for himself, for servants, for spouses, for temples. These three privileges or names mean that all defilement must be shunned by us.— *Thomas Le Blanc.*

Verse 1.—" *Undefiled in the way.*" In the 1st Psalm it was " Blessed is the man that walketh not in the counsel of the ungodly " ; but who could think to walk in that way, and not have his feet soiled ? " Who could go upon hot coals and his feet be not burned ? " Here, however, the caution is, to take heed not to get any soil or defilement " *in the way,*"—in the Lord's way. Oh ! what an insight does this give us of the pit-falls and snares that beset us in the road, and of the plague and evil of our own hearts, that even in the midst of holy things, somewhat of stain, or spot, or wrinkle will stick to us !—*Barton Bouchier,* 1856.

Verse 1.—" *The undefiled in the way.*" How can our feet be undefiled ? How can our garments be unsoiled ? We cannot guide ourselves. Unaided, we stumble into sloughs of defilement. But all help is near. Jesus is at hand to keep us by his mighty power. Let us lean on his supporting arm at every step, and when we fall let us rise and wash our robes in his all-cleansing blood. So may we ever be among " *the undefiled in the way*" ; and let the law of the Lord, lovely in purity, glorious in holiness, perfect in love, be the path in which our feet advance. Jesus is our model and our all. God's law was in his heart.—*Henry Law, in " Family Devotion,*" 1878.

Verse 1.—" *In the way.*" They are blessed who are in *the* way, not *a* way, any chance or uncertain road, but " the King's Highway"; that path which the Lord himself has declared to us, saying, " I am the way."—*Hilary and Theodoret, quoted by Neale and Littledale.*

Verse 1.—" *The way.*" There is much ado now about the way : many say, " Which is the way?" Some say, " This "; some, " That." Would you not mistake, inquire for "the old way, the way of holiness," and follow it, and thou shalt not perish. Some would go a new way ; some a shorter, some an easier way. Do you go the holy way.—*John Sheffield (about 1660), in " The Morning Exercises.*"

Verse 1.—" *Who walk.*" In this way there must be no standing, sitting, or reclining, but *walking,* so that all our movements may be regular, going on unto perfection : Matt. v. 48 ; 1 Cor. xiv. 20 ; James i. 4 ; Heb. vi. 1.—*Martin Geier,* 1614—1681.

Verse 1.—" *Who walk in the law of the LORD.*" To go on with liberty in good duties is a point of blessed perfection. He is not truly able to *walk* who can only go twice or thrice about his chamber, or stir himself on some plain ground for a quarter of an hour ; but he which can go strongly and freely up a hill in ways craggy and uneven : so Christians who can go while God maketh their way inoffensive, putting everything away which might hinder, but presently give over if ought disturbeth, they are not come to this free walking in which standeth a traveller's perfection. Look at those who are fat at heart, pursey (as we say), or have inward lameness, and ache of joints, or have caught a thorn from without, so that they are forced to lie by, and cannot walk ; or those whose limbs are so feeble, that they cannot trip upon anything, but down they come ;—all these lame folk do esteem other travellers to be happy who are able to exercise themselves in walking at will. Thus, when Christians find themselves hindered, and wearied, and stumbling, they deem others blessed who can go on constantly in their holy course, through good report and evil report, in want, in abundance, in every estate and condition. Wherefore, let us strive after this blessed walking.—*Paul Bayne.*

Verse 1.—" *Who walk in the law of the LORD.*" Who walk towards heaven in heaven's way, avoiding the corruptions that are in the world through lust.—*John Trapp,* 1611—1662.

Verse 2.—The doubling of the sentence, *"Blessed," "Blessed,"* in the first verse and second, is to let us see the certainty of the blessing belonging to the godly. The word of God is as true in itself when it is once spoken, as when it is many times repeated : the repetition of it is for confirmation of our weak faith. That which Isaac spake of Jacob,—" I have blessed him, and he shall be blessed," is the most sure decree of God upon all his children. Satan would fain curse Israel, by the mouth of such as Balaam was ; but he shall not be able to curse, because God hath blessed.— *William Cowper.*

Verse 2.—*" Blessed are they that keep his testimonies, and that seek him with the whole heart."* In the former verse a blessed man is described by the course of his actions, " Blessed are the undefiled in the way : " in this verse he is described by the frame of his heart.—*Thomas Manton.*

Verse 2.—*" Keep his testimonies."* The careful keeping in mind of God's testimonies is blessedness ; for though there is a keeping of them in conversation mentioned in the former verse, here another thing is intimated diverse from the former ; he that keepeth this plant or holy seed so that the devil cannot take it out of his heart, he is happy. The word here used signifieth such a careful custody as that is wherewith we use to keep tender plants.—*Paul Bayne.*

Verse 2.—*" Testimonies."* The notion by which the word of God is expressed is *" testimonies "* ; whereby is intended the whole declaration of God's will, in doctrines, commands, examples, threatenings, promises. The whole word is the testimony which God hath deposed for the satisfaction of the world about the way of their salvation. Now because the word of God brancheth itself into two parts, the law and the gospel, this notion may be applied to both. First, *to the law*, in regard whereof the ark was called " the ark of testimony " (Exod. xxv. 16), because the two tables were laid up in it. *The gospel* is also called the testimony, " the testimony of God concerning his Son." " To the law, and to the testimony " (Isa. viii. 20) ; where testimony seems to be distinguished from the law. The gospel is so called, because therein God hath testified how a man shall be pardoned, reconciled to God, and obtain a right to eternal life. We need a testimony in this case, because it is more unknown to us. The law was written upon the heart, but the gospel is a stranger. Natural light will discern something of the law, and pry into matters which are of a moral strain and concernment ; but evangelical truths are a mystery, and depend upon the mere testimony of God concerning his Son.—*Thomas Manton.*

Verse 2.—*" Testimonies."* The word of God is called his testimony, not only because it testifies his will concerning his service, but also his favour and goodwill concerning his own in Christ Jesus. If God's word were no more than a law, yet were we bound to obey it, because we are his creatures ; but since it is also a testimony of his love, wherein as a father he witnesseth his favour towards his children, we are doubly inexcusable if we do not most joyfully embrace it.—*William Cowper.*

Verse 2.—*" Blessed are they . . . . that seek him with the whole heart."* He pronounces *" blessed "* not such as are wise in their own conceit, or assume a sort of fantastical holiness, but those who dedicate themselves to the covenant of God, and yield obedience to the dictates of his law. Farther, by these words, he tells us that God is by no means satisfied with mere external service, for he demands the sincere and honest affection of the heart. And assuredly, if God be the sole Judge and Disposer of our life, the truth must occupy the principal place in our heart, because it is not sufficient to have our hands and feet only enlisted in his service.—*John Calvin,* 1509—1564.

Verse 2.—*" The whole heart."* Whosoever would have sound happiness must have a sound heart. So much sincerity as there is, so much blessedness there will be ; and according to the degree of our hypocrisy, will be the measure of our misery.— *Richard Greenham*, 1531—1591.

Verses 2, 3.—Observe the verbs *seek, do, walk*, all making up the subject to whom the blessedness belongs.—*Henry Hammond*, 1605—1660.

Verse 3.—*" They also do no iniquity."* If it be demanded here, How is it that they who walk in God's ways work no iniquity ? Is there any man who lives, and sins not ? And if they be not without sin, how then are they to be blessed ? The answer is, as the apostle says of our knowledge, " We know but in part : " so is it true of our felicity on earth, we are blessed but in a part. It is the happiness of angels that they never sinned ; it is the happiness of triumphant saints, that albeit they have been sinners, yet now they sin no more ; but the happiness of saints militant is, that our sins are forgiven us ; and that albeit sin remains in us, yet it reigns not over us ; it is done in us, but not by our allowance : " I do the evil which I would not." " Not I, but sin that dwells in me," Rom. vii. 17.

To the *doing of iniquity*, these three things must concur ; first, a purpose to do it ; next, a delight in doing it ; thirdly, a continuance in it ; which three in God's children never concur ; for in sins done in them by the old man, the new man makes his exceptions and protestations against them.   It is not I, says he ; and so far as he from delighting in them, that rather his soul is grieved with them ; even as Lot, dwelling among the Sodomites, was vexed by hearing and seeing their unrighteous deeds.   In a word, the children of God are rather sufferers of sin against their wills than actors of it with their wills ; like men spiritually oppressed by the power of their enemy ; for which they sigh and cry unto God.   " Miserable man that I am ! who shall deliver me from the body of this death ? " And in this sense it is that the apostle saith, " He who is born of God sinneth not " (1 John iii. 9).—*William Cowper.*

Verse 3.—*" They also do no iniquity."*   The blessedness of those who walk in the law : they do—or have done—no wickedness : but walk—or have always walked —in his ways.   Throughout the Psalm it may be noticed that sometimes the present tense is employed indicating present action : sometimes the perfect to indicate past and present time verses 10, 11, 13, 14, 21, 51—61, 101, 102, 131, 145, 147.—*The Speaker's Commentary,* 1873.

Verse 3.—*" They also do no iniquity."*   That is, they make not a trade and common practice thereof.   Slip they do, through the infirmity of the flesh, and subtlety of Satan, and the allurements of the world : but they do not ordinarily and customably go forward in unlawful and sinful courses.   In that the Psalmist setteth down this as a part (and not the least part neither) of blessedness, *that they work none iniquity, which walk in his ways :*   the doctrine to be learned here is this, that it is a marvellous great prerogative to be freed from the bondage of sin.—*Richard Greenham.*

Verse 3.—*" They do no iniquity."*   All such as are renewed by grace, and reconciled to God by Christ Jesus ; to these God imputeth no sin to condemnation, and in his account *they do no iniquity.*   Notable is that which is said of David. " He kept my commandments, and followed me with all his heart, and did that only which was right in mine eyes " (1 Kings xiv. 8).   How can that be ?   We may trace David by his failings, they are upon record everywhere in the word ; yet here a veil is drawn upon them ; God laid them not to his charge.   There is a double reason why their failings are not laid to their charge.   *Partly, because of their general state,* they are in Christ, taken into favour through him, and " there is no condemnation to them that are in Christ " (Rom. viii. 1), therefore particular errors and escapes do not alter their condition ; which is not to be understood as if a man should not be humbled, and ask God pardon for his infirmities ; no, for then they prove iniquities and they will lie upon record against him.   It was a gross fancy of the Valentinians, who held that they were not defiled with sin, whatsoever they committed ; though base and obscene persons, yet still they were as gold in the dirt.   No, no, we are to recover ourselves by repentance, to sue out the favour of God.   When David humbled himself, and had repented, then, saith Nathan, " The Lord hath put away thy sin " (2 Sam. xii. 13).   *Partly, too, because their bent and habitual inclination is to do otherwise.*   They set themselves to comply with God's will, to seek and serve the Lord, though they are clogged with many infirmities.   A wicked man sinneth with deliberation and delight, his bent is to do evil, he makes " provision for lusts " (Rom. xiii. 14), and " serves " them by a voluntary subjection (Titus iii. 3).   But those that are renewed by grace are not " debtors " to the flesh, they have taken another debt and obligation, which is to serve the Lord (Rom. viii. 12).

Partly, too, because their general course and way is to do otherwise.   Everything works according to its form ;   the constant actions of nature are according to the kind.   So the new creature, his constant operations are according to grace.   A man is known by his custom, and the course of his endeavours shows what is his business. If a man be constantly, easily, frequently carried away to sin, it discovers the habit of his soul, and the temper of his heart.   Meadows may be overflowed, but marsh ground is drowned with every return of the tide.   A child of God may be occasionally carried away, and act contrary to the inclination of the new nature ; but when men are drowned and overcome by the return of every temptation, it argues a habit of sin.

And partly, because sin never carries sway completely, but it is opposed by dislikes and resistances of the new nature.   The children of God make it their business to avoid all sin, by watching, praying, mortifying : " I said I will take heed to my ways, that I sin not with my tongue " (Ps. xxxix. 1), and thus there is a resistance of the sin. God hath planted graces in their hearts, the fear of his Majesty, that works a resistance ; and therefore there is not a full allowance of what they do. This resistance sometimes is more strong, then the temptation is overcome : " How can I do this wickedness, and sin against God ? " (Gen. xxxix. 9). Sometimes it is more weak, and then sin carries it, though against the will of the holy man : " The evil which I hate, that do I " (Rom. vii. 15, 18). It is the evil which they hate; they protest against it ; they are like men which are oppressed by the power of the enemy. And then there is a remorse after the sin : David's heart smote him. It grieves and shames them that they do evil. Tenderness goes with the new nature : Peter sinned foully, but he went out and wept bitterly.—*Thomas Manton.*

Verse 3.—They that have mortified their sins live in the contrary graces. Hence it is that the Psalmist said, that " *they work no iniquity, but walk in thy paths.*" First they crucify all their sins, " *they do no iniquity:*" secondly, as they do no iniquity, so they follow all the ways of God, contrary to that iniquity : as they *give up all* the ways of sin, so they *take up all* the ways of grace. It is a rule in divinity, that *grace takes not away nature ;* that is, grace comes not to take away a man's affections, but to take them up.—*William Fenner, 1600—1640.*

Verse 3.—" *They walk in his ways.*" It reproves those that rest in negatives. As it was said of a certain emperor, he was rather *not vicious* than virtuous. Many men, all their religion runs upon *nots : *" I am *not* as this publican " (Luke xviii. 11). That ground is naught, though it brings not forth briars and thorns, if it yields not good increase. Not only the unruly servant is cast into hell, that beat his fellow-servant, that ate and drank with the drunken ; but the idle servant that wrapped up his talent in a napkin. Meroz is cursed, not for opposing and fighting, but for not helping (Judges v. 23). Dives did not take away food from Lazarus, but he did not give him of his crumbs. Many will say, I set up no other gods ; ay, but dost thou love, reverence, and obey the true God ? For if not, thou dost fail in the first commandment. As to the second, thou sayest, I abhor idols ; but dost thou delight in ordinances ? I do not swear and rend the name of God by cursed oaths ; ay, but dost thou glorify God, and honour him ? I do not profane the Sabbath ; but dost thou sanctify it ? Thou dost not plough and dance ; but thou art idle, and toyest away the Sabbath. Thou dost not wrong thy parents ; but dost thou reverence them ? Thou dost not murder ; but dost thou do good to thy neighbour ? Thou art no adulterer ; but dost thou study temperance and a holy sobriety in all things ? Thou art no slanderer ; but art thou tender of thy neighbour's honour and credit, as of thy own ? Usually men cut off half their bill, as the unjust steward bade his lord's debtor set down fifty when he owed a hundred. We do not think of sins of omission. If we are not drunkards, adulterers, and profane persons, we do not think what it is to omit respect to God, and reverence for his holy Majesty.—*Thomas Manton.*

Verse 3.—" *They walk in his ways.*" Not in those of his enemies, nor even in their own.—*Joseph Addison Alexander,*—1860.

Verse 3.—" *They walk in his ways.*" Habitually, constantly, characteristically. They are not *merely* honest, upright, and just in their dealings with men ; but they walk in the ways of God ; they are *religious.—Albert Barnes, 1798—1870.*

Verse 4.—" *Thou hast commanded us to keep thy precepts diligently.*" It is not a matter ἀδιάφορος, and left to the discretion of men, either to hear, or to neglect sacred discourses, theological readings, and expositions of the Sacred Book ; but God has commanded, and not commanded cursorily when speaking of another matter, but צִוִּיתָה, earnestly and greatly he has commanded us to keep his precepts. There should be infixed in our mind the words found in Deut. vi. 6, " *My words shall be in thy heart ;* " in Matt. xvii., " *Hear ye him :* " in John v., " *Search the Scriptures.*" Above all things, students of theology should remember the Pauline rule in 1 Tim. iii., " *Give attention to reading.*"—*Solomon Gesner.*

Verse 4.—" *Thou hast commanded us,*" etc. Hath God enjoined us to observe his precepts so exceeding carefully and diligently ? Then let nothing draw us therefrom, no, not in the least circumstance ; let us esteem nothing needless, frivolous, or superfluous, that we have a warrant for out of his word ; nor count those too wise or precise that will stand resolutely upon the same : if the Lord require anything, though the world should gainsay it, and we be derided and abused for the doing of it, yet let us proceed still in the course of our obedience.—*Richard Greenham.*

Verse 4.—"*Diligently.*" For three causes should we keep the commandments of the Lord with diligence : first, because our adversary that seeks to snare us by the transgression of them is diligent in tempting, for he goes about, night and day, seeking to devour us ; next, because we ourselves are weak and infirm, by the greater diligence have we need to take heed to ourselves ; thirdly, because of the great loss we sustain by every vantage Satan gets over us ; for we find by experience, that as a wound is sooner made than it is healed, so guiltiness of conscience is easily contracted, but not so easily done away.—*William Cowper.*

Verse 4.—"*Diligently.*" In this verse he reminds the reader how well he knew that this study of the divine law must necessarily be severe (earnest), since God has commanded that it should be observed diligently ; that is, with the profoundest study ; as that which alone is good, and as everything is good which it commands.—*Antonio Brucioli*, 1534.

Verse 4.—The word translated "*diligently*," doth signify in the original tongue *wonderful much*, so that the words go thus : "*Thou hast commanded to keep thy precepts wonderful much.*"—*Richard Greenham.*

Verses 4, 5.—"*Thou hast commanded us to keep thy precepts diligently*," verse 4 ; this is God's imperative. "*O that my ways were directed to keep thy statutes !*" verse 5 ; this should be our optative.—*Thomas Adams*, 1614.

Verses 4, 5.—It is very observable concerning David, that when he prayeth so earnestly, "*O that my ways were directed to keep thy statutes*," he premiseth this as the reason, "*Thou hast commanded us to keep thy statutes diligently*," thereby intimating that the ground of his obedience to God's precepts was the stamp of divine authority enjoining him. To this purpose it is that he saith in this same Psalm, ver. 94, "*I have sought thy precepts*," thereby implying that what he sought in his obedience was the fulfilling of God's will. Indeed, that only and properly is obedience which is done *intuitu voluntatis divinæ*, with a respect to and eye upon the divine will. As that is only a divine faith which believeth a truth, not because of human reason, but divine revelation, so that only is a true obedience which conformeth to the command, not because that it may consist with any selfish ends, but because it carrieth in it an impression of Christ's authority.—*Nathanael Hardy.*

Verse 5.—In tracing the connection of this verse with the preceding, we cannot forbear to remark how accurately the middle path is preserved, as keeping us at an equal distance from the idea of self-sufficiency to "*keep the Lord's statutes*," and self-justification in neglecting them. The first attempt to render spiritual obedience will quickly convince us of our utter helplessness. We might as soon create a world as create in our hearts one pulse of spiritual life. And yet our inability does not cancel our obligation. It is the weakness of a heart that "cannot be subject to the law of God," for no other reason than because it is "carnal," and therefore "enmity against God." Our inability is our sin, our guilt, our condemnation, and instead of excusing our condition, stops our mouth, and leaves us destitute of any plea of defence before God. Thus our obligation remains in full force. We are bound to obey the commands of God, whether we can or not. What, then, remains for us, but to return the mandate to heaven, accompanied with an earnest prayer, that the Lord would write upon our hearts those statutes to which he requires obedience in his word ? "*Thou hast commanded us to keep thy statutes diligently.*" We acknowledge, Lord, our obligation, but we feel our impotency. Lord, help us ; we look unto thee. "*O that my ways were directed to keep thy statutes.*"—*Charles Bridges*, 1849.

Verse 5.—"*O that*," etc. In the former verse the prophet David observes the charge which God gives, and that is, that his commandments be diligently kept : here, then, he observes his own weakness and insufficiency to discharge that great duty, and therefore, as one by the spirit desirous to discharge it, and yet by the flesh not able to discharge it, he breaketh out into these words, "*O that my ways were directed*," etc. Much like unto a child that being commanded to take up some great weight from the ground, is willing to do it, though not able to do it : or a sick patient advised to walk many turns in his chamber, finds a desire in his heart, though inability in his body to do that which he is directed unto.—*Richard Greenham.*

Verse 5.—"*O that my ways*," etc. It is the use and duty of the people of God to turn precepts into prayers.   That this is the practice of God's children appeareth : " Turn thou me, and I shall be turned ; for thou art the Lord my God " (Jer. xxxi. 18).   God had said, " Turn you, and you shall live," and they ask it of God, " Turn us," as he required it of them.   It was Austin's prayer, *Da quod jubes, et jube quod vis*, " Give what thou requirest, and require what thou wilt."   It is the duty of the saints ; for, 1st, *It suiteth with the Gospel-covenant*, where precepts and promises go hand in hand ; where God giveth what he commandeth, and worketh all our works in us and for us.   They are not conditions of the covenant only, but a part of it. What God hath required at our hands, that we may desire at his hands.   God is no Pharaoh, to require brick where he giveth no straw.   *Lex jubet, gracia juvat*.   The articles of the new covenant are not only put into the form of precepts, but promises. The law giveth no strength to perform anything, but the Gospel offereth grace. 2ndly, Because, *by this means, the ends of God are fulfilled*.   Why doth God require what we cannot perform by our own strength ?   He doth it, (1.) To keep up his right.   (2.) To convince us of our impotency, and that, upon a trial, without his grace we cannot do his work.   (3.) That the creature may express his readiness to obey.   (4.) To bring us to lie at his feet for grace.—*Thomas Manton*.

Verse 5.—" *O that*," etc.   The whole life of a good Christian is *an holy desire*, saith Augustine ; and this is always seconded with endeavour without the which, affection is like Rachel, beautiful, but barren.—*John Trapp*.

Verse 5.—" *O that my ways were directed*," etc.   The original word נכ, *kun*, is sometimes rendered to *establish*, and, accordingly, it may seem as if the prophet were soliciting for himself the virtue of perseverence.   I am rather inclined to understand it as signifying *to direct ;* for, although God is plainly instructing us in his law, the obtuseness of our understanding and the perversity of our hearts constantly need the direction of his Spirit.—*John Calvin*.

Verse 6.—" *Then shall I not be ashamed*."   No one likes *to be ashamed* or *to blush :* therefore all things which bring shame after them must be avoided : Ezra ix. 6 ; Jer. iii. 25 ; Dan. ix. 7, 9.   As the workman keeps his eye fixed on his pattern, and the scholar on the copy of his writing-master ; so the godly man ever and anon turns his eyes to the word of his God.—*Martin Geier*.

Verse 6.—There is a twofold shame ;   the shame of a guilty conscience ;   and the shame of a tender conscience.   The one is the merit and fruit of sin ;   the other is an act of grace.   This which is here spoken of is to be understood not of a holy self-loathing, but a confounding shame.—*Thomas Manton*.

Verse 6.—" *Then shall I not be ashamed*," etc.   Then shall I have confidence both towards God and man, and mine own soul, when I can pronounce of myself that my obedience is impartial, and uniform, and universal, no secret sin reserved for my favour, no least commandment knowingly or willingly neglected by me.— *Henry Hammond*.

Verse 6.—" *Then shall I not be ashamed*," etc.   You ask, Why is he not ashamed who has " *respect unto all the commandments of God ?* "   I answer, the sense is, as if he had said, The commandments of God are so pure and excellent, that though thou shouldest regard the whole and each one of them most attentively, thou wouldest not find anything that would cause thee to blush.   The laws of Lycurgus are praised ; but they permitted theft.   The statutes of Plato are praised ; but they commended the community of wives.   " *The law of the Lord is perfect, converting the soul :* Ps. xix. 7.   It is a mirror, reflecting the beautiful light of the stars on him who looks into it.—*Thomas Le Blanc*.

Verse 6.—The blessing here spoken of is freedom from shame in looking unto *all* the commandments.   If God hear prayer, and establish the soul in this habit of keeping the commandments, there will be yet this further blessing of being able to look unto every precept without shame.   Many men can look at *some* commandments without shame.   Turning to the ten commandments, the honest man feels no shame as he gazes on the eighth, the pure man is free from reproach as he reads the seventh, he who is reverent and hates blasphemy is not rebuked by the thought that he has violated the third, while the filial spirit rather delights in than shuns the fifth.   So on with the remainder.   Most men perhaps can look at some of the precepts with comparative freedom from reproof.   But who can so look unto them all ?   Yet this, also, the godly heart aspires to.   In this verse we find the Psalmist consciously anticipating the truth of a word in the New Testament : " He that offendeth in one point is guilty of all."—*Frederick G. Marchant*.

Verse 6.—" Ashamed."

> I can bear scorpion's stings, tread fields of fire,
> In frozen gulfs of cold eternal lie ;
> Be toss'd aloft through tracts of endless void.
> But cannot live in shame.

Joanna Baillie, 1762—1851.

Verse 6.—" When I have respect unto all thy commandments." Literally, " In my looking at all thy commandments." That is, in his regarding them ; in his feeling that all were equally binding on him ; and in his having the consciousness that he had not intentionally neglected, violated, or disregarded any of them.   There can be no true piety except where a man *intends* to keep ALL the commands of God. If he makes a selection among them, keeping this one or that one, as may be most convenient for him, or as may be most for his interest, or as may be most popular, it is full proof that he knows nothing of the nature of true religion.   A child has no proper respect for a parent if he obeys him only as shall suit his whim or his convenience ; and no man *can* be a pious man who does not purpose, in all honesty, to keep ALL the commandments of God ; to submit to his will *in everything.—Albert Barnes.*

Verse 6.—" All thy commandments."   There is the same reason for obedience to one command as another,—God's authority, who is the Lawgiver (James ii. 11) ; and therefore when men choose one duty and overlook others, they do not so much obey the will of God, as gratify their own humours and fancies, pleasing him only so far as they can please themselves too ; and this is not reasonable ; we never yield him a " reasonable service," but when it is universal.—*Edward Veal* (1632— 1708), *in " The Morning Exercises."*

Verse 6.—" All thy commandments."   A partial obedience will never satisfy a child of God.   The exclusion of any commandment from its supreme regard in the heart is the brand of hypocrisy.   Even Herod could " do many things," and yet one evil way cherished, and therefore unforsaken, was sufficient to show the sovereign power of sin undisturbed within.   Saul slew all the Amalekites but one ; and that single exception in the path of universal obedience marked the unsoundness of his profession, cost him the loss of his throne, and brought him under the awful displeasure of his God.   And thus the foot, or the hand, or the right eye, the corrupt unmortified members, bring the whole body to hell.   Reserves are the canker of Christian sincerity.—*Charles Bridges.*

Verse 6.—" Unto all thy commandments."   Allow that *any* of God's commandments *may* be transgressed, and we shall soon have the whole decalogue set aside.— *Adam Clarke, 1760—1832.*

*Verse 6.—*Many will do some good, but are defective in other things and usually in those which are most necessary.   They cull out the easiest and cheapest parts of religion, such as do not contradict their lusts and interests.   We can never have sound peace till we regard all.   " *Then shall I not be ashamed when I have respect unto all thy commandments."*   Shame is fear of a just reproof.   This reproof is either from the supreme or the deputy judge.   The supreme judge of all our actions is God. This should be our principal care, that we may not be ashamed before him at his coming, nor disapproved in the judgment.   But there is a deputy judge which every man has in his own bosom.   Our consciences do acquit or condemn us as we are partial or sincere in our duty to God, and much dependeth on that.   1 John iii. 20, 21, " For if our heart condemn us, God is greater than our heart, and knoweth all things. Beloved, if our heart condemn us not, then have we confidence towards God."   Well, then, that our hearts may not reprove or reproach us, we should be complete in all the will of God.   Alas, otherwise you will never have evidence of your sincerity.— *Thomas Manton.*

*Verse 6.—*Such is the mercy of God in Christ to his children, that he accepts their weak endeavours, joined with sincerity and perseverance in his service, as if they were a full obedience. . . .   O, who would not serve such a Lord ?   You hear servants sometimes complain of their masters as so rigid and strict, that they can never please them ; no, not when they do their utmost ; but this cannot be charged upon God.   Be but so faithful as to do thy best, and God is so gracious that he will pardon thy worst.   David knew this gospel indulgence when he said, " *Then shall I not be ashamed, when I have respect unto all thy commandments,"* when my eye is to all thy commandments.   The traveller hath his eye on or towards the place he is going to, though he be as yet short of it ; there he would be, and he is putting on all he can to reach it ; so stands the saint's heart to all the commands of God ; he presseth on to come nearer and nearer to full obedience ; such a soul shall never be put to shame.—*William Gurnall*, 1617—1679.

Verse 7.—" *I will praise thee . . . . when I shall have learned,*" etc. There is no way to please God entirely and sincerely until we have learned both to know and do his will. Practical praise is the praise God looks after.—*Thomas Manton*.

Verse 7.—" *I will praise thee.*" What is the matter for which he praises God ? It is that he has been taught something of him and by him amongst men. To have learned any tongue, or science, from some school of philosophy, bindeth us to our alma mater. We praise those who can teach a dog, a horse, this or that ; but for us ass-colts to learn the will of God, how to walk pleasing before him, this should be acknowledged of us as a great mercy from God.—*Paul Bayne*.

Verse 7.—" *Praise thee . . . when I shall have learned,*" etc. But when doth David say that he will be thankful ? Even when God shall teach him. Both the matter and the grace of thankfulness are from God. As he did with Abraham, he commanded him to worship by sacrifice, and at the same time gave him the sacrifice : so doth he with all his children ; for he gives not only good things, for which they should thank him, but in like manner grace by which they are able to thank him.— *William Cowper*.

Verse 7.—" *When I shall have learned.*" By learning he means his attaining not only to the knowledge of the word, but the practice of it. It is not a speculative light, or a bare notion of things : " Every man therefore that hath heard, and hath learned of the Father, cometh unto me " (John vi. 45). It is such a learning as the effect will necessarily follow, such a light and illumination as doth convert the soul, and frame our hearts and ways according to the will of God. For otherwise, if we get understanding of the word, nay, if we get it imprinted in our memories, it will do us no good without practice. The best of God's servants are but scholars and students in the knowledge and obedience of his word. For saith David, " *When I shall have learned.*" The professors of the Christian religion were primitively called disciples or learners : Τὸ πλῆθος τῶν μαθητῶν, " the multitude of the disciples " (Acts vi. 2.)—*Thomas Manton*.

Verse 7.—" *Learned thy righteous judgments.*" We see here what David especially desired to learn, namely, the word and will of God : he would ever be a scholar in this school, and sought daily to ascend to the highest form ; that learning to know, he might remember ; remembering, might believe ; believing, might delight ; delighting, might admire ; admiring, might adore ; adoring, might practise ; and practising, might continue in the way of God's statutes. This learning is the old and true learning indeed, and he is best learned in this art, who turneth God's word into good works.—*Richard Greenham*.

Verse 7.—" *Judgments of thy righteousness* " are the decisions concerning right and wrong which give expression to and put in execution the righteousness of God.— *Franz Delitzsch*.

Verse 8.—This verse, being the last of this portion, is the result of his meditation concerning the utility and necessity of the keeping the law of God. Here take notice :—1. Of his resolution, " *I will keep thy statutes.*" II. Of his prayer, " *O forsake me not utterly.*" It is his purpose to keep the law ; yet because he is conscious to himself of many infirmities, he prays against desertion. In the prayer more is intended than is expressed. " *O forsake me not ;* " he means, strengthen me in this work ; and if thou shouldst desert me, yet but for a while, Lord, not for ever ; if in part, not in whole, Four points we may observe hence :—1. That it is a great advantage to come to a resolution as to a course of godliness. 2. Those that resolve upon a course of obedience have need to fly to God's help. 3. Though we fly to God's help, yet sometimes God may withdraw, and seem to forsake us. 4. Though God seem to forsake us, and really doth so in part ; yet we should pray that it may not be a total and utter desertion.—*Thomas Manton*.

Verse 8 with 7.—" *I will keep thy statutes,*" etc. The resolution to " *keep the Lord's statutes* " is the natural result of having " *learned his righteous judgments.*" And on this point David illustrates the inseparable and happy union of " simplicity " of dependence, and " godly sincerity " of obedience. Instantly upon forming his resolution, he recollects that the performance of it is beyond the power of human strength, and therefore the next moment he follows it with prayer : " *I will keep thy statutes ; O forsake me not utterly.*"—*Charles Bridges.*

Verse 8.—" *I will.*" David setteth a personal example of holiness. If the king of Israel keep God's statutes, the people of Israel will be ashamed to neglect them. Cæsar was wont to say, Princes must not say, *Ite,* go ye, without me ; but, *Venite,* come ye, along with me. So said Gideon (Jud. v. 17): " As ye see me do, so do ye."—*R. Greenham.*

Verse 8.—" *Forsake me not utterly.*" There is a total and a partial desertion. Those who are bent to obey God may for a while, and in some degree, be left to themselves. We cannot promise ourselves an utter immunity from desertion ; but it is not total. We shall find for his great name's sake, " The Lord will not forsake his people " (1 Sam. xii. 22), and, " I will never leave thee nor forsake thee " (Heb. xiii. 5). Not utterly, yet in part they may be forsaken. Elijah was forsaken, but not as Ahab : Peter was forsaken in part, but not as Judas, who was utterly forsaken, and made a prey to the Devil. David was forsaken to be humbled and bettered ; but Saul was forsaken utterly to be destroyed. Saith Theophylact, God may forsake his people so as to shut out their prayers (Ps. lxxx. 4), so as to interrupt the peace and joy of their heart, and abate their strength, so that their spiritual life may be much at a stand, and sin may break out, and they may fall foully ; but they are not *utterly* forsaken. One way or other, God is still present ; present in light sometimes when he is not present in strength, when he manifests the evil of their present condition, so as to make them mourn under it ; and present in awakening their desires, though not in giving them enjoyment. As long as there is any esteem of God, he is not yet gone ; there is some light and love yet left, manifested by our desires of communion with him.—*Thomas Manton.*

Verse 8.—" *Forsake me not utterly.*" The desertions of God's elect are first of all *partial,* that is, such as wherein God doth not wholly forsake them, but in some part. Secondly, *temporary,* that is, for some space of time, and never beyond the compass of this present life. " For a moment (saith the Lord in Esay) in mine anger I hid my face from thee for a little season, but with everlasting kindness will I have mercy on thee, saith the Lord thy Redeemer." And to this purpose David, well acquainted with this matter, prayeth, " *Forsake me not overlong.*" This sort of desertions, though it be but for a time, yet no part of a Christian man's life is free from them ; and very often taking deep place in the heart of man, they are of long continuance. David continued in his dangerous fall about the space of a whole year before he was recovered. Luther confesseth of himself, that, after his conversion, he lay three years in desperation. Common observation in such like cases hath made record of even longer times of spiritual forsakings.—*Richard Greenham.*

Verse 8.—"*O forsake me not utterly.*" This prayer reads like the startled cry of one who was half afraid that he had been presumptuous in expressing the foregoing resolve. He desired to keep the divine statutes, and like Peter he vowed that he would do so ; but remembering his own weakness, he recoils from his own venturesomeness, and feels that he must pray. I have made a solemn vow, but what if I have uttered it in my own strength ? What if God should leave me to myself ? He is filled with terror at the thought. He breaks out with an " O." He implores and beseeches the Lord not to test him by leaving him even for an instant entirely to himself. To be forsaken of God is the worst ill that the most melancholy saint ever dreams of. Thank God, it will never fall to our lot ; for no promise can be more express than that which saith, " I will never leave thee, nor forsake thee." This promise does not prevent our praying, but excites us to it. Because God will not forsake his own, therefore do we cry to him in the agony of our feebleness, " O forsake me not utterly."—*C. H. S.*

EXPOSITION OF VERSES 9 TO 16.

WHEREWITHAL shall a young man cleanse his way? by taking heed *thereto* according to thy word.

10 With my whole heart have I sought thee : O let me not wander from thy commandments.

11 Thy word have I hid in mine heart, that I might not sin against thee.

12 Blessed *art* thou, O LORD : teach me thy statutes.

13 With my lips have I declared all the judgments of thy mouth.

14 I have rejoiced in the way of thy testimonies, as *much as* in all riches.

15 I will meditate in thy precepts, and have respect unto thy ways.

16 I will delight myself in thy statutes : I will not forget thy word.

9. *" Wherewithal shall a young man cleanse his way ? "* How shall he become and remain practically holy ? He is but a young man, full of hot passions, and poor in knowledge and experience ; how shall he get right, and keep right ? Never was there a more important question for any man ; never was there a fitter time for asking it than at the commencement of life. It is by no means an easy task which the prudent man sets before him. He wishes to choose a clean way, to be himself clean in it, to cleanse it of any foulness which may arise in the future, and to end by showing a clear course from the first step to the last ; but, alas, his way is already unclean by actual sin which he has already committed, and he himself has within his nature a tendency towards that which defileth. Here, then, is the difficulty, first of beginning aright, next of being always able to know and choose the right, and of continuing in the right till perfection is ultimately reached : this is hard for any man, how shall a youth accomplish it ? The way, or life, of the man has to be cleansed from the sins of his youth behind him, and kept clear of the sins which temptation will place before him : this is the work, this is the difficulty.

No nobler ambition can lie before a youth, none to which he is called by so sure a calling ; but none in which greater difficulties can be found. Let him not, however, shrink from the glorious enterprise of living a pure and gracious life ; rather let him enquire the way by which all obstacles may be overcome. Let him not think that he knows the road to easy victory, nor dream that he can keep himself by his own wisdom ; he will do well to follow the Psalmist, and become an earnest enquirer asking how he may cleanse his way. Let him become a practical disciple of the holy God, who alone can teach him how to overcome the world, the flesh, and the devil, that trinity of defilers by whom many a hopeful life has been spoiled. He is young and unaccustomed to the road, let him not be ashamed often to enquire his way of him who is so ready and so able to instruct him in it.

Our *" way "* is a subject which concerns us deeply, and it is far better to enquire about it than to speculate upon mysterious themes which rather puzzle than enlighten the mind. Among all the questions which a young man asks, and they are many, let this be the first and chief : " Wherewithal shall I cleanse my way ? " This is a question suggested by common sense, and pressed home by daily occurrences ; but it is not to be answered by unaided reason, nor, when answered, can the directions be carried out by unsupported human power. It is ours to ask the question, it is God's to give the answer and enable us to carry it out.

" By taking heed thereto according to thy word." Young man, the Bible must be your chart, and you must exercise great watchfulness that your way may be according to its directions. You must take heed to your daily life, as well as study your Bible, and you must study your Bible that you may take heed to your daily life. With the greatest care a man will go astray if his map misleads him ; but with the most accurate map he will still lose his road if he does not take heed to it. The narrow way was never hit upon by chance, neither did any heedless man ever lead a holy life. We can sin without thought, we have only to neglect the great salvation and ruin our souls ; but to obey the Lord and walk uprightly will need all our heart and soul and mind. Let the careless remember this.

Yet the *" word "* is absolutely necessary ; for, otherwise, care will darken into morbid anxiety, and conscientiousness may become superstition. A captain may watch from his deck all night ; but if he knows nothing of the coast, and has no pilot on board, he may be carefully hastening on to shipwreck.   It is not enough to desire to be right ; for ignorance may make us think that we are doing God service when we are provoking him, and the fact of our ignorance will not reverse the character of our action, however much it may mitigate its criminality.   Should a man carefully measure out what he believes to be a dose of useful medicine, he will die if it should turn out that he has taken up the wrong vial, and has poured out a deadly poison : the fact that he did it ignorantly will not alter the result.   Even so, a young man may surround himself with ten thousand ills, by carefully using an unenlightened judgment, and refusing to receive instruction from the word of God.   Wilful ignorance is in itself wilful sin, and the evil which comes of it is without excuse.   Let each man, whether young or old, who desires to be holy have a holy watchfulness in his heart, and keep his Holy Bible before his open eye.   There he will find every turn of the road marked down, every slough and miry place pointed out, with the way to go through unsoiled ; and there, too, he will find light for his darkness, comfort for his weariness, and company for his loneliness, so that by its help he shall reach the benediction of the first verse of the Psalm, which suggested the Psalmist's enquiry, and awakened his desires.

Note how the first section of eight verses has for its first verse, " Blessed are the undefiled in the way," and the second section runs parallel to it, with the question " Wherewithal shall a young man cleanse his way ? "   The blessedness which is set before us in a conditional promise should be practically sought for in the way appointed. The Lord saith, " For this will I be enquired of by the house of Israel to do it for them."

10. " *With my whole heart have I sought thee.*"   His heart had gone after God himself : he had not only desired to obey his laws, but to commune with his person. This is a right royal search and pursuit, and well may it be followed with the whole heart.   The surest mode of cleansing the way of our life is to seek after God himself, and to endeavour to abide in fellowship with him.   Up to the good hour in which he was speaking to his Lord, the Psalmist had been an eager seeker after the Lord, and if faint, he was still pursuing.   Had he not sought the Lord he would never have been so anxious to cleanse his way.

It is pleasant to see how the writer's heart turns distinctly and directly to God. He had been considering an important truth in the preceding verse, but here he so powerfully feels the presence of his God that he speaks to him, and prays to him as to one who is near.   A true heart cannot long live without fellowship with God.

His petition is founded on his life's purpose : he is seeking the Lord, and he prays the Lord to prevent his going astray in or from his search.   It is by obedience that we follow after God, hence the prayer, " *O let me not wander from thy commandments ; *" for if we leave the ways of God's appointment we certainly shall not find the God who appointed them.   The more a man's whole heart is set upon holiness the more does he dread falling into sin ; he is not so much fearful of deliberate transgression as of inadvertent wandering : he cannot endure a wandering look, or a rambling thought, which might stray beyond the pale of the precept.   We are to be such whole-hearted seekers that we have neither time nor will to be wanderers, and yet with all our whole-heartedness we are to cultivate a jealous fear lest even then we should wander from the path of holiness.

Two things may be very like and yet altogether different : saints are " strangers " —" I am a stranger in the earth " (verse 19), but they are not wanderers : they are passing through an enemy's country, but their route is direct ; they are seeking their Lord while they traverse this foreign land.   Their way is hidden from men ; but yet they have not lost their way.

The man of God exerts himself, but does not trust himself : his heart is in his walking with God ; but he knows that even his whole strength is not enough to keep him right unless his King shall be his keeper, and he who made the commands shall make him constant in obeying them : hence the prayer, " *O let me not wander.*" Still, this sense of need, was never turned into an argument for idleness ; for while he prayed to be kept in the right road he took care to run in it, with his whole heart seeking the Lord.

It is curious again to note how the second part of the Psalm keeps step with the first ; for where verse 2 pronounces that man to be blessed who seeks the Lord with his whole heart, the present verse claims the blessing by pleading the character : " *With my whole heart have I sought thee.*"

11. When a godly man sues for a favour from God he should carefully use every

means for obtaining it, and accordingly, as the Psalmist had asked to be preserved from wandering, he here shows us the holy precaution which he had taken to prevent his falling into sin. *" Thy word have I hid in mine heart."* His heart would be kept by the word because he kept the word in his heart. All that he had of the word written, and all that had been revealed to him by the voice of God,—all, without exception, he had stored away in his affections, as a treasure to be preserved in a casket, or as a choice seed to be buried in a fruitful soil : what soil more fruitful than a renewed heart, wholly seeking the Lord ? The word was God's own, and therefore precious to God's servant. He did not wear a text *on* his heart as a charm, but he hid it *in* his heart as a rule. He laid it up in the place of love and life, and it filled the chamber with sweetness and light. We must in this imitate David, copying his heart-work as well as his outward character. First, we must mind that what we believe is truly God's word ; that being done, we must hide or treasure it each man for himself ; and we must see that this is done, not as a mere feat of the memory, but as the joyful act of the affections.

" That I might not sin against thee." Here was the object aimed at. As one has well said,—Here is the best thing,—" thy word ; " hidden in the best place,—" in my heart ; " for the best of purposes,—" that I might not sin against thee." This was done by the Psalmist with personal care, as a man carefully hides away his money when he fears thieves,—in this case the thief dreaded was sin. Sinning " against God " is the believer's view of moral evil ; other men care only when they offend against men. God's word is the best preventive against offending God, for it tells us his mind and will, and tends to bring our spirit into conformity with the divine Spirit. No cure for sin in the life is equal to the word in the seat of life, which is the heart. There is no hiding from sin unless we hide the truth in our souls.

A very pleasant variety of meaning is obtained by laying stress upon the words " thy " and " thee." He speaks to *God*, he loves the word because it is *God's* word, and he hates sin because it is sin against *God* himself. If he vexed others, he minded not so long as he did not offend his God. If we would not cause God displeasure we must treasure up his own word.

The personal way in which the man of God did this is also noteworthy : " With my whole heart have *I* sought thee." Whatever others might choose to do he had already made his choice and placed the Word in his innermost soul as his dearest delight, and however others might transgress, his aim was after holiness : " That *I* might not sin against thee." This was not what he purposed to do, but what he had already done ; many are great at promising, but the Psalmist had been true in performing : hence he hoped to see a sure result. When the word is hidden in the heart the life shall be hidden from sin.

The parallelism between the second octave and the first is still continued. Verse 3 speaks of doing no iniquity, while this verse treats of the method of not sinning. When we form an idea of a blessedly holy man (verse 3) it becomes us to make an earnest effort to attain unto the same sacred innocence and divine happiness, and this can only be through heart-piety founded on the Scriptures.

12. *" Blessed art thou, O Lord."* These are words of adoration arising out of an intense admiration of the divine character, which the writer is humbly aiming to imitate. He blesses God for all that he has revealed to him, and wrought in him ; he praises him with warmth of reverent love, and depth of holy wonder. These are also words of perception uttered from a remembrance of the great Jehovah's infinite happiness within himself. The Lord is and must be blessed, for he is the perfection of holiness ; and this is probably the reason why this is used as a plea in this place. It is as if David had said—I see that in conformity to thyself my way to happiness must lie, for thou art supremely blessed ; and if I am made in my measure like to thee in holiness, I shall also partake in thy blessedness.

No sooner is the word in the heart than a desire arises to mark and learn it. When food is eaten, the next thing is to digest it ; and when the word is received into the soul the first prayer is—Lord, teach me its meaning. *"Teach me thy statutes" ;* for thus only can I learn the way to be blessed. Thou art so blessed that I am sure thou wilt delight in blessing others, and this boon I crave of thee that I may be instructed in thy commands. Happy men usually rejoice to make others happy, and surely the happy God will willingly impart the holiness which is the fountain of happiness. Faith prompted this prayer and based it, not upon anything in the praying man, but solely upon the perfection of the God to whom he made supplication. Lord, thou art blessed, therefore bless me by teaching me.

We need to be disciples or learners—" *teach me;* " but what an honour to have God himself for a teacher : how bold is David to beg the blessed God to teach him! Yet the Lord put the desire into his heart when the sacred word was hidden there, and so we may be sure that he was not too bold in expressing it. Who would not wish to enter the school of such a Master to learn of him the art of holy living ? To this Instructor we must submit ourselves if we would practically keep the statutes of righteousness. The King who ordained the statutes knows best their meaning, and as they are the outcome of his own nature he can best inspire us with their spirit. The petition commends itself to all who wish to cleanse their way, since it is most practical, and asks for teaching, not upon recondite lore, but upon statute-law. If we know the Lord's statutes we have the most essential education.

Let us each one say, " *Teach me thy statutes.*" This is a sweet prayer for everyday use. It is a step above that of verse 10, " O let me not wander," as that was a rise beyond that of 8, " O forsake me not utterly." It finds its answer in verses 98—100 : " Thou through thy commandments hast made me wiser than mine enemies," etc. ; but not till it had been repeated even to the third time in the " Teach me " of verses 33 and 66, all of which I beg my reader to peruse. Even after this third pleading the prayer occurs again in so many words in verses 124 and 139, and the same longing comes out near the close of the Psalm in verse 171—" My lips shall utter praise when thou hast taught me thy statutes."

13. " *With my lips have I declared all the judgments of thy mouth.*" The taught one of verse 12 is here a teacher himself. What we learn in secret we are to proclaim upon the housetops. So had the Psalmist done. As much as he had known he had spoken. God has revealed many of his judgments by his mouth, that is to say, by a plain and open revelation ; these it is our duty to repeat, becoming, as it were, so many exact echoes of his one infallible voice. There are judgments of God which are a great deep, which he does not reveal, and with these it will be wise for us not to intermeddle. What the Lord has veiled it would be presumption for us to uncover, but, on the other hand, what the Lord has revealed it would be shameful for us to conceal. It is a great comfort to a Christian in time of trouble when in looking back upon his past life he can claim to have done his duty by the word of God. To have been, like Noah, a preacher of righteousness, is a great joy when the floods are rising, and the ungodly world is about to be destroyed. Lips which have been used in proclaiming God's statutes are sure to be acceptable when pleading God's promises. If we have had such regard to that which cometh out of God's mouth that we have published it far and wide, we may rest quite assured that God will have respect unto the prayers which come out of our mouths.

It will be an effectual method of cleansing a young man's way if he addicts himself continually to preaching the gospel. He cannot go far wrong in judgment whose whole soul is occupied in setting forth the judgments of the Lord. By teaching we learn ; by training the tongue to holy speech we master the whole body ; by familiarity with the divine procedure we are made to delight in righteousness ; and thus in a threefold manner our way is cleansed by our proclaiming the way of the Lord.

14. " *I have rejoiced in the way of thy testimonies.*" Delight in the word of God is a sure proof that it has taken effect upon the heart, and so is cleansing the life. The Psalmist not only says that he does rejoice, but that he has rejoiced. For years it had been his joy and bliss to give his soul to the teaching of the word. His rejoicing had not only arisen out of the word of God, but out of the practical characteristics of it. The Way was as dear to him as the Truth and the Life. There was no picking and choosing with David, or if indeed he did make a selection, he chose the most practical first. " *As much as in all riches.*" He compared his intense satisfaction with God's will with that of a man who possesses large and varied estates, and the heart to enjoy them. David knew the riches that come of sovereignty, and which grow out of conquest ; he valued the wealth which proceeds from labour, or is gotten by inheritance : he knew " all riches." The gracious king had been glad to see the gold and silver poured into his treasury that he might devote vast masses of it to the building of the Temple of Jehovah upon Mount Zion. He rejoiced in all sorts of riches consecrated and laid up for the noblest uses, and yet the way of God's word had given him more pleasure than even these. Observe that his joy was personal, distinct, remembered, and abundant. Wonder not that in the previous verse he glories in having spoken much of that which he had so much enjoyed : a man may well talk of that which is his delight.

15. "*I will meditate in thy precepts.*"   **He** who has an inward delight in anything will not long withdraw his mind from it.   As the miser often returns to look upon his treaure, so does the devout believer by frequent meditation turn over the priceless wealth which he has discovered in the book of the Lord.   To some men meditation is a task ;   to the man of cleansed way it is a joy.   He who has meditated will meditate ;   he who saith, " I have rejoiced," is the same who adds, " I will meditate." No spiritual exercise is more profitable to the soul than that of devout meditation ; why are many of us so exceeding slack in it ?   It is worthy of observation that the preceptory part of God's word was David's special subject of meditation, and this was the more natural because the question was still upon his mind as to how a young man should cleanse his way.   Practical godliness is vital godliness.

" *And have respect unto thy ways,*" that is to say, I will think much about them so as to know what thy ways are ;   and next, I will think much of them so as to have thy ways in great reverence and high esteem.   I will see what thy ways are towards me that I may be filled with reverence, gratitude, and love ;   and then, I will observe what are those ways which thou hast prescribed for me, thy ways in which thou wouldest have me follow thee ;   these I would watch carefully that I may become obedient, and prove myself to be a true servant of such a Master.

Note how the verses grow more *inward* as they proceed ;   from the speech of verse 13 we advanced to the manifested joy of verse 14, and now we come to the secret meditation of the happy spirit.   The richest graces are those which dwell deepest.

16. " *I will delight myself in thy statutes.*"   In this verse delight follows meditation, of which it is the true flower and outgrowth.   When we have no other solace, but are quite alone, it will be a glad thing for the heart to turn upon itself, and sweetly whisper, " I will delight myself.   What if no minstrel sings in the hall, I will delight myself.   If the time of the singing of birds has not yet arrived, and the voice of the turtle is not heard in our land, yet I will delight myself."   This is the choicest and noblest of all rejoicing ;   in fact, it is the good part which can never be taken from us ; but there is no delighting ourselves with anything below that which God intended to be the soul's eternal satisfaction.   The statute-book is intended to be the joy of every loyal subject.   When the believer once peruses the sacred pages his soul burns within him as he turns first to one and then to another of the royal words of the great King, words full and firm, immutable and divine.

" *I will not forget thy word.*"   Men do not readily forget that which they have treasured up, that which they have meditated on (verse 15), and that which they have often spoken of (verse 13).   Yet since we have treacherous memories it is well to bind them well with the knotted cord of " I will not forget."

Note how two " I wills " follow upon two " I haves."   We may not promise for the future if we have altogether failed in the past ;   but where grace has enabled us to accomplish something, we may hopefully expect that it will enable us to do more.

It is curious to observe how this verse is moulded upon verse 8 :   the changes are rung on the same words, but the meaning is quite different, and there is no suspicion of a vain repetition.   The same thought is never given over again in this Psalm ;   they are dullards who think so.   Something in the position of each verse affects its meaning, so that even where its words are almost identical with those of another the sense is delightfully varied.   If we do not see an infinite variety of fine shades of thought in this Psalm we may conclude that we are colour-blind ;   if we do not hear many sweet harmonies, we may judge our ears to be dull of hearing, but we may not suspect the Spirit of God of monotony.

NOTES ON VERSES 9 TO 16.

The eight verses alphabetically arranged :—

9. **B**y what means shall a young man cleanse his way ? By taking heed thereto according to thy word.
10. **B**y day and by night have I sought thee with my whole heart : O let me not wander from thy commandments.
11. **B**y thy grace I have hid thy word in my heart, that I might not sin against thee.
12. **B**lessed art thou, O Lord : teach me thy statutes.
13. **B**y the words of my lips will I declare all the judgments of thy mouth.
14. **B**y far more than in all riches I have rejoiced in the way of thy testimonies.
15. **B**y thy help I will meditate in thy precepts, and have respect unto thy ways.
16. **B**y thy grace I will delight myself in thy statutes : I will not forget thy word.

Theodore Kübler.

Whole eight verses, 9—16. Every verse in the section begins with ב, *a house.* The subject of the section is, The Law of Jehovah purifying the Life. Key-word, וכח (*zacah*), *to be pure,* to make pure, to cleanse.—*F. G. Marchant.*

Verse 9.—*Whole verse.* In this passage there is, (1) A question. (2) An answer given. In the question, there is the person spoken of, "*a young man,*" and his work, "*Wherewithal shall he cleanse his way ?*" In this question there are several things supposed. 1. That we are from the birth, polluted with sin ; for we must be cleansed. It is not *direct* "his way," but "cleanse his way." 2. That we should be very early and betimes sensible of this evil ; for the question is propounded concerning the young man. 3. That we should earnestly seek for a remedy, how to dry up the issue of sin that runneth upon us. All this is to be supposed.

That which is enquired after is, What remedy there is against it ? What course is to be taken ? So that the sum of the question is this : How shall a man that is impure, and naturally defiled with sin, be made able, as soon as he cometh to the use of reason, to purge out that natural corruption, and live a holy and pure life to God ? The answer is given : "*By taking heed thereto according to thy word.*" Where two things are to be observed. 1. The remedy. 2. The manner how it is applied and made use of.

1. The remedy is the word ; by way of address to God, called "*Thy word ;*" because, if God had not given direction about it, we should have been at an utter loss. 2. The manner how it is applied and made use of, "*by taking heed thereto,*" etc. ; by studying and endeavouring a holy conformity to God's will.—*Thomas Manton.*

Verse 9.—'*Wherewithal shall a young man cleanse his way ?*" etc. Aristotle, that great dictator in philosophy, despaired of achieving so great an enterprise as the rendering a young man capable of his ηθικα ακροαματα, "his grave and severe lectures of morality ;" for that age is light and foolish, yet headstrong and untractable. Now, take a young man all in the heat and boiling of his blood, in the highest fermentation of his youthful lusts ; and, at all these disadvantages, let him enter that great school of the Holy Spirit, the divine Scriptures, and commit himself to the conduct of those blessed oracles ; and he shall effectually be convinced, by his own experience, of the incredible virtue, the vast and mighty power, of God's word, in the success it hath upon him, and in his daily progressions and advances in heavenly wisdom.—*John Gibbon (about 1660) in "The Morning Exercises."*

Verse 9.—"*A young man.*" A prominent place—one of the twenty-two parts— is assigned to young men in the 119th Psalm. It is meet that it should be so. Youth is the season of impression and improvement, young men are the future props of society, and the fear of the Lord, which is the beginning of wisdom, must begin in youth. The strength, the aspirations, the unmarred expectations of youth, are in requisition for the world ; O that they may be consecrated to God.—*John Stephen, in "The Utterances of the cxix. Psalm,"* 1861.

Verse 9.—For "*young man,*" in the Hebrew the word is נער, *naar,* i.e., "shaken off ;" that is to say, from the milder and more tender care of his parents. Thus Mercerus and Savallerius. Secondly, *naar* may be rendered "*shaking off ;*" that is to say, the yoke, for a young man begins to cast off the material, and frequently the paternal, yoke.—*Thomas Le Blanc.*

Verse 9.—"*Cleanse his way.*" The expression does not absolutely convey the

impression that the given young man is in a corrupt and discr[...]
requires cleansing, though this be true of all men originally : [...]ble way which
which follows makes known that such could not be the case wit[...] liii. 6. That
The very inquiry shows that his heart is not in a corrupt state. [...] young man.
direction is required.   The inquiry is—How shall a young man m[...] is present,
a pure line of conduct—through this defiling world ?   It is a ques[...]an way—
of great anxiety to every convert whose mind is awakened to a sen[...]ubt not,
shall keep clear of the sin, avoid the loose company, and rid hims[...]how he
pleasures and practices of this enslaving world.   And as he moves[...] wicked
integrity—many temptations coming in his way, and much inward [...]ine of
up to control him—how often will the same anxious inquiry arise : [...]sing
It is only in a false estimate of one's own strength that any can t[...]sing
and the spirit of such false estimate will be brought low.   How felt 24.
friends, who have been brought to Christ, in the day of your resolve[...]
But for all such anxiety there seems to be an answer in the text.   [...]

" *By taking heed thereto according to thy word.*"   It is not that you[...]
day require information : they require the inclination.   In the g[...]
man there are both, and the word that began feeds the proper motive[...]
threatenings and the sweet encouragements both move him in the ri[...]
The answer furnished to this anxious inquiry is sufficiently plain and p[...]
is directed to the word of God for all direction, and we might say, for[...]
assistance.   Still the matter presented in this light does not appear to[...]
out the full import of the passage.   The inquiry to me would seem to [...]
the whole verse.*   There is required the cleansing that his way be acco[...]
Divine Word.   The enquiry is of the most enlarged comprehension, [...]
made only by one who can say that he has been honestly putting himself [...]
as the young man in the 10th and 11th verses ; and it can be answered [...]
heart that takes in all the strength provided by the blessed God, as is [...]
here in the 12th verse.   The Psalmist makes the inquiry, he shows how earn[...]
had sought to be in the right way, and immediately he finds all his strength i[...]
Thus he declares how he has been enabled to do rightly, and how he will do ri[...]
in the future.—*John Stephen.*

Verse 9.—Instead of question and answer both in this one verse, the Hebre[...]
demands the construction with question only, leaving the answer to be inferred
from the drift of the entire Psalm—thus : " *Wherewithal shall a young man cleanse
his way to keep it according to thy word ?*"   This translation gives precisely the force
of the last clause.   Hebrew punctuation lacks the interrogation point, so that we
have no other clue but the form of the sentence and the sense by which to decide
where the question ends.—*Henry Cowles,* 1872.

Verse 9.—"*His way.*"   ארח, *orach*, which we translate *way* here, signifies a *track*,
a *rut*, such as is made by the wheel of a cart or chariot.   A *young sinner* has no *broad
beaten* path ; he has his *private ways* of offence, his *secret pollutions ;* and how shall
he be cleansed from these ?   how can he be saved from what will destroy mind, body,
and soul ?   Let him hear what follows ; the description is from God.

1. He is to *consider* that his way is *impure ;* and how abominable this must
make him appear in the sight of God.   2. He must examine it *according to God's
word,* and carefully hear what God has said concerning *him* and *it.*   3. He must
take heed to it, לשמר, *lishmor,* to *keep, guard,* and *preserve his way*—his general course
of life, from all defilement.—*Adam Clarke.*

Verse 9.—"*By taking heed,*" etc.   I think the words may be better rendered
and supplied thus, *by observing* what is *according to thy word ;* which show how a
sinner is to be cleansed from his sins by the blood of Christ, and justified by his
righteousness, and be clean through his word ; and also how and by whom the work
of sanctification is wrought in the heart, even by the Spirit of God, by means of the
word, and what is the rule of a man's walk and conversation : he will find the word
of God to be profitable, to inform in the doctrines of justification and pardon, to
acquaint him with the nature of regeneration and sanctification ; and for the correction and amendment of his life and manners, and for his instruction in every branch
of manners : 2 Tim. iii. 16.—*John Gill,* 1697—1771.

Verse 9.—"*By taking heed.*"   There is an especial necessity for this " *Take
heed,*" because of the proneness of a young man to thoughtlessness, carelessness,

---

* This opinion is confirmed by the quotation which follows from Cowles.

-confidence. There is an especial necessity for "*taking heed*," *presumption* difficulty of the way. "Look well to thy goings;" it is a narrow *because of* well to thy goings," it is a new path. "Look well to thy goings;" *path.* path. "Look well to thy goings;" it is an eventful path.—*James* *it is a ...ins*, 1785—1849. *Harr... 'According to thy word.*" God's word is the glass which discovereth all *... Bayne.* ...rmity, and also the water and soap which washeth and scoureth it —"*According to thy word.*" I do not say that there are no other guides, ...nces. I do not say that conscience is worth nothing, and conscience in ...specially sensitive and tender; I do not say that prayer is not a most ...ence, but prayer without taking heed is only another name for presumption; ...d carelessness can never walk hand in hand together; and I therefore say ...re is no fence nor guard that can so effectually keep out every enemy as ...l reading of the word of God, bringing every solicitation from the world or ...ompanions, every suggestion from our own hearts and passions, to the test ...'s word:—What says the Bible? The answer of the Bible, with the teaching ...nlightenment of the Holy Spirit, will in all the intricacies of our road be a lamp ...our feet and a light unto our path.—*Barton Bouchier.*

Verse 9.—"*Thy word.*" The word is the only weapon (like Goliath's sword, none ...equal this), for the hewing down and cutting off of this stubborn enemy, our lusts. ...e word of God can master our lusts when they are in their greatest pride: if ever ...st rageth at one time more than another, it is when youthful blood boils in our ...eins. Youth is giddy, and his lust is hot and impetuous: his sun is climbing higher ...still, and he thinks it is a great while to night; so that it must be a strong arm that brings a young man off his lusts, who hath his palate at best advantage to taste sensual pleasure. The vigour of his strength affords him more of the delights of the flesh than crippled age can expect, and he is farther from the fear of death's gun-shot, as he thinks, than old men who are upon the very brink of the grave, and carry the scent of the earth about them, into which they are suddenly to be resolved. Well, let the word of God meet this young gallant in all his bravery, with his feast of sensual delights before him, and but whisper a few syllables in his ear, give his conscience but a prick with the point of its sword, and it shall make him fly in as great haste from them all, as Absalom's brethren did from the feast when they saw Amnon their brother murdered at the table. When David would give the young man a receipt to cure him of his lusts, how he may cleanse his whole course and way, he bids him only wash in the waters of the word of God.—*William Gurnall.*

Verse 9.—The Scriptures teach us the best way of living, the noblest way of suffering, and the most comfortable way of dying.—*John Flavel*, 1627—1691.

Verse 10.—"*With my whole heart have I sought thee.*" There are very few of us that are able to say with the prophet David that we have sought God with our whole heart; to wit, with such integrity and pureness that we have not turned away from that mark as from the most principal thing of our salvation.—*John Calvin.*

Verse 10.—"*With my whole heart have I sought thee.*" Sincerity is in every expression; the heart is open before God. The young man can so speak to the Searcher of hearts. . . . . Let us consider the directness of this kind of converse with God. We use round-about expressions in drawing nigh to God. We say, With my whole heart would I seek thee. We are afraid to be direct. . . . . See how decided in his conscious actings is the young man before you, how open and confiding he is, and such you will find to be the characteristic of his pious mind throughout the varied expressions unfolded in this Psalm. Here he declares to the Omniscient One that he had sought him with all his heart. He desired to realize God in everything.—*John Stephen.*

Verse 10 (first clause).—God alone sees the heart; the heart alone sees God.— *John Donne*, 1573—1631.

Verse 10.—"*O let me not wander from thy commandments.*" David after he had protested that he sought God with his whole heart, besought God that he would not suffer him to decline from his commandments. Hereby let us see what great need we have to call upon God, to the end he may hold us with a mighty strong hand. Yea, and though he hath already mightily put to his helping hand, and we also know that he hath bestowed upon us great and manifest graces; yet this is not all: for there are so many vices and imperfections in our nature, and we are so feeble and weak that we have very great need daily to pray unto him, yea, and that more and more, that he will not suffer us to decline from his commandments.—*John Calvin.*

Verse 10.—The more experience a man hath in the ways of God, the more sensible is he of his own readiness to wander insensibly, by ignorance and inadvertency, from the ways of God ; but the young soldier dares run hazards, ride into his adversary's camp, and talk with temptation, being confident he cannot go wrong ; he is not so much in fear as David who here cries, " *O let me not wander.*"—*David Dickson,* 1583—1662.

Verse 11.—" *Thy word have I hid in mine heart, that I might not sin against thee.*" There laid up in the heart the word has effect. When young men only read the letter of the Book, the word of promise and instruction is deprived of much of its power. Neither will the laying of it up in the mere memory avail. The word must be known and prized, and laid up in the heart ; it must occupy the affection as well as the understanding; the whole mind requires to be impregnated with the word of God. Revealed things require to be seen. Then the word of God in the heart—the threatenings, the promises, the excellencies of God's word—and God himself realized, the young man would be inwardly fortified ; the understanding enlightened, conscience quickened—he would not sin against his God.—*John Stephen.*

Verse 11.—" *Thy word have I hid in mine heart, that I might not sin against thee.*" In proportion as the word of the King is present in the heart, " *there* is power " against sin (Eccles. viii. 4). Let us use this means of absolute power more, and more life and more holiness will be ours.—*Frances Ridley Havergal,* 1836—1879.

Verse 11.—" *Thy word have I hid in mine heart.*" It is fit that the word, being " more precious than gold, yea, than much fine gold," a peerless pearl, should not be laid up in the porter's lodge only—the outward ear ; but even in the cabinet of the mind.—*Dean Boys, quoted by James Ford.*

Verse 11.—" *Thy word have I hid in mine heart.*" There is great difference between Christians and worldlings. The worldling hath his treasure in jewels without him ; the Christian hath them within. Neither indeed is there any receptacle wherein to receive and keep the word of consolation but the heart only. If thou have it in thy mouth only, it shall be taken from thee ; if thou have it in thy book only, thou shalt miss it when thou hast most to do with it ; but if thou lay it up in thy heart, as Mary did the words of the angel, no enemy shall ever be able to take it from thee, and thou shalt find it a comfortable treasure in the time of thy need.—*William Cowper.*

Verse 11.—" *Thy word have I hid in mine heart.*" This saying, *to hide,* importeth that David studied not to be ambitious to set forth himself and to make a glorious show before men ; but that he had God for a witness of that secret desire which was within him. He never looked to worldly creatures ; but being content that he had so great a treasure, he knew full well that God who had given it him would so surely and safely guard it, as that it should not be laid open to Satan to be taken away. Saint Paul also declareth unto us (1 Tim. i. 19) that the chest wherein this treasure must be hid is a good conscience. For it is said, that many being void of this good conscience, have lost also their faith, and have been robbed thereof. As if a man should forsake his goods and put them in hazard, without shutting a door, it were an easy matter for thieves to come in and rob and spoil him of all ; even so, if we leave at random to Satan the treasures which God hath given us in his word, without it be hidden in this good conscience, and in the very bottom of our heart as David here speaketh, we shall be spoiled thereof.—*John Calvin.*

Verse 11.—" *Thy word have I hid in mine heart.*"—Remembered, approved, delighted in it.—*William Nicholson* (—1671), *in " David's Harp Strung and Tuned.*"

Verse 11.—" *Thy word.*" Thy saying, thy oracle ; any communication from God to the soul, whether promise, or command, or answer. It means a direct and distinct message, while " word " is more general, and applies to the whole revelation. This is the ninth of the ten words referring to the revelation of God in this Psalm.—*James G. Murphy,* 1875.

Verse 11.—" *In my heart.*" Bernard observes, bodily bread in the cupboard may be eaten of mice, or moulder and waste : but when it is taken down into the body, it is free from such danger. If God enable thee to take thy soul-food into thine heart, it is free from all hazards.—*George Swinnock,* 1627—1673.

Verse 11.—" *That I might not sin against thee.*" Among many excellent virtues of the word of God, this is one ; that if we keep it in our heart, it keeps us from sin, which is against God and against ourselves. We may mark it by experience, that the word is first stolen either out of the mind of man, and the remembrance of it is away ; or at least out of the affection of man ; so that the reverence of it is gone, before that a man can be drawn to the committing of a sin. So long as Eve kept by faith the word of the Lord, she resisted Satan ; but from the time she doubted of that, which God made most certain by his word, at once she was snared.—*William Cowper.*

Verse 12.—*" Blessed art thou, O Lord : teach me thy statutes."* This verse contains a prayer, with the reason of the prayer. The prayer is. *" Teach me thy statutes ;"* the reason, moving him to seek this, ariseth of a consideration of that infinite good which is in God. He is a blessed God, the fountain of all felicity, without whom no welfare or happiness can be to the creature. And for this cause David earnestly desiring to be in fellowship and communion with God, which he knows none can attain unto unless he be taught of God to know God's way and walk in it ; therefore, I say, he prayeth the more earnestly that the Lord would teach him his statutes. Oh that we also could wisely consider this, that our felicity stands in fellowship with God.—*William Cowper.*

Verse 12.—In this verse we have two things, 1. An acknowledgment of God's blessedness, *" Blessed art thou, O Lord ; "* i.e., being possessed of all fulness, thou hast an infinite complacency in the enjoyment of thyself ; and thou art he alone in the enjoyment of whom I can be blessed and happy ; and thou art willing and ready to give out of thy fulness, so that thou art the fountain of blessedness to thy creatures. 2. A request or petition, *" Teach me thy statutes ;"* q.d., seeing thou hast all fulness in thyself, and art sufficient to thy own blessedness ; surely thou hast enough for me. There is enough to content thyself, therefore enough to satisfy me. This encourages me in my address.

Again,—Teach me that I may know wherein to seek my blessedness and happiness, even in thy blessed self ; and that I may know how to come by the enjoyment of thee, so that I may be blessed in thee. Further,—Thou art blessed originally, the Fountain of all blessing ; thy blessedness is an everlasting fountain, a full fountain ; always pouring out blessedness : O, let me have this blessing from thee, this drop from the fountain.—*William Wisheart, in " Theologia, or, Discourses of God,"* 1716.

Verse 12.—Since God is blessed, we cannot but desire to learn his ways. If we see any earthly being happy, we have a great desire to learn out his course, as thinking by it we might be happy also. Every one would sail with that man's wind who prospereth ; though in earthly things it holdeth not alway : yet a blessed God cannot by any way of his bring to other than blessedness. Thus, he who is blessedness itself, he will be ready to communicate his ways to other : the excellentest things are most communicative.—*Paul Bayne.*

Verse 12.—*" Teach me."* He had Nathan, he had priests to instruct him, himself was a prophet ; but all their teaching was nothing without God's blessing, and therefore he prays, *" Teach me."*—*William Nicholson.*

Verse 12.—*" Teach me."* These words convey more than the simple imparting of knowledge, for he said before he had such, when he said he hid God's words in his heart ; and in verse 7 he said he *" had learned the judgments of his justice : "* it includes grace to observe his law.—*Robert Bellarmine,* 1542—1621.

Verse 12.—*"Teach me."* If this were practised now, to join prayer with hearing, that when we offer ourselves to be taught of men, we would therewith send up prayer to God, before preaching, in time of preaching and after preaching, we would soon prove more learned and religious than we are.—*William Cowper.*

Verse 12.—*" Teach me thy statutes."* Whoever reads the Psalm with attention must observe in it one great characteristic, and that is, how decisive are its statements that in keeping the commandments of God nothing can be done by human strength ; but that it is he who must create the will for the performance of such duty. The Psalmist entreats the Lord to open his eyes that he may behold the wondrous things of the law, to teach him his statutes, to remove from him the way of lying, to incline his heart unto his testimonies, and not to covetousness, to turn away his eyes from beholding vanity, and not to take the word of truth utterly out of his mouth. Each of these petitions shows how deeply impressed he was of his entire helplessness as regarded himself, and how completely dependent upon God he felt himself for any

advancement he could hope to make in the knowledge of the tr_h._ All his studies
in the divine law, all his aspirations after holiness of life, he wi_,_ well assured could
never meet with any measure of success, except by the grace of_d_ preventing and
co-operating, implanting in him a right desire, and acting as _infallible guide,_
whereby alone he would be enabled to arrive at the proper sens_Holy Scripture,_
as well as to correct principles of action in his daily walk befor _and man._—
George Phillips, 1846.

Verse 12.—" _Teach me thy statutes._"—If it be asked why the P _entreats to_
be taught, when he has just before been declaring his knowledge, _ver is that_
he seeks instruction as to the practical working of those principles w _as learnt_
theoretically.—_Michael Ayguan_ (1416), _in Neale and Littledale._

Verse 13.—" _With my lips have I declared,_" etc. Above all, be
of that to others which you do daily learn yourself, and out of the _talk_
your heart speak of good things unto men.—_Richard Greenham._ _of_

Verse 13.—Having hid the purifying word in his heart, the Psalm
it with his lips ; and as it is so pure throughout, he will declare all
exception. When the fountain of the heart is purified, the streams
will be pure also. The declaring lips of the Psalmist are here placed
to the mouth of Jehovah, by which the judgments were originally pr
F. G. Marchant.

Verse 13.—As the consciousness of having communicated our knowle
spiritual gifts is a means of encouragement to seek a greater measure,
evidence of the sincerity and fruitfulness of what knowledge we have : "
thy statutes. _With my lips have I declared all the judgments of thy mouth_
Dickson.

Verse 13.—" _With my lips,_" etc. The tongue is a most excellent meml
body, being well used to the glory of God and the edification of others ;
cannot pronounce without help of the lips. The Lord hath made the body
with such marvellous wisdom, that no member of it can say to another, I h
need of thee ; but such is man's dulness, that he observes not how useful unto
is the smallest member in the body, till it be taken from him. If our lips we
clasped for a time, and our tongue thus shut up, we would esteem it a great mercy
to have it loosed again ; as that cripple, when he found the use of his feet, leaped for
joy and glorified God.—_William Cowper._

Verse 13.—" _Declared all the judgments._" He says in another place (Ps. xxxvi.
6), " _Thy judgments are like a great deep._" As the apostle says (Rom. xi. 33, 34),
" _O the depth of the wisdom and knowledge of God ! how unsearchable are his judgments,_
and his ways past finding out. For who hath known the mind of the Lord ?" If the
judgments are unsearchable, how then says the prophet, " _I have declared all the judg-_
ments of thy mouth ?" We answer,—peradventure there are judgments of God which
are not the judgments of his mouth, but of his heart and hand only.

We make a distinction, for we have no fear that the sacred Scripture weakens
itself by contradictions. It has not said, The judgments of his mouth are a great
deep ; but " _Thy judgments._" Neither has the apostle said, The unsearchable
judgments of his mouth ; but " _His unsearchable judgments._" We may regard the
judgments of God, then, as those hidden ones which he has not revealed to us ; but
the judgments of his mouth, those which he has made known, and has spoken by
the mouth of the prophets.—_Ambrose,_ 340—397.

Verse 14.—" _I have rejoiced in the way of thy testimonies,_" etc. The Psalmist
saith not only, " I have rejoiced in thy testimonies," but, " in the _way_ of thy testimonies." Way is one of the words by which the law is expressed. God's laws are
ways that lead us to God ; and so it may be taken here, " the way which thy testimonies point out, and call me unto ; or else his own practice, as a man's course is
called his way ; his delight was not in speculation or talk, but in obedience and
practice : " _in the way of thy testimonies._" He tells us the degree of his joy, " _as_
much as in all riches :" " as much," not to show the equality of these things, as if
we should have the same affection for the world as for the word of God ; but " as
much," because we have no higher comparison. This is that which worldlings doat
upon, and delight in ; now as much as they rejoice in worldly possessions, so much
do I rejoice in the way of thy testimonies. For I suppose David doth not compare

his own delight in ...ealth; but his own choice and delight, with the delight and choice
of others. ...d spoken of himself both in the one respect and in the other, the
expression was ...f h... high. David, who was called to a crown, and in a capacity of
enjoying mu...the world, gold, silver, land, goods, largeness of territory, and a
compound ...that which all men jointly, and all men severally do possess; yet
was more ...d in the holiness of God's ways, than in all the world: "For what
shall it ... man, if he shall gain the whole world, and lose his own soul?"
(Mark ...—Thomas Manton.

..."The way of thy testimonies." The testimony of God is his word,
...his will; the "way" of his testimony is the practice of his word, and
...Vt which he hath declared to be his will, and wherein he hath promised
for his love. David found not this sweetness in hearing, reading, and pro-
d...word only; but in practising of it; and in very deed, the only cause why
...t the comfort that is in the word of God is that we practise it not by walking
...y thereof. It is true, at the first it is bitter to nature, which loves carnal
...to render itself as captive to the word: laboriosa virtutis via, and much
...ust be taken before the heart be subdued; but when it is once begun, it
...s such joy as abundantly recompenses all the former labour and grief.—
...am Cowper.

...erse 14.—Riches are acquired with difficulty, enjoyed with trembling, and lost
...a bitterness.—Bernard, 1091—1157.

...Verse 14.—A poor, good woman said, in time of persecution, when they took
...vay the Christian's Bibles, "I cannot part with my Bible; I know not how to live
...ithout it." When a gracious soul has heard a profitable sermon, he says, "Methinks it does me good at heart; it is the greatest nourishment I have:" "I have
rejoiced in the way of thy testimonies, as much as in all riches."—Oliver Heywood,
1629—1702.

Verse 15.—"I will meditate in thy precepts," etc. All along David had shown
what he had done; now, what he will do. Verse 10, "I have sought;" verse 11,
"I have hid;" verse 12, "I have declared;" verse 14, "I have rejoiced." Now
in the two following verses he doth engage himself to set his mark towards God for
time to come. "I will meditate in thy precepts," etc. We do not rest upon anything
already done and past, but continue the same diligence unto the end. Here is
David's hearty resolution and purpose, to go on for time to come. Many will say,
Thus I have done when I was young, or had more leisure and rest; in that I have
meditated and conferred. You must continue still in a holy course. To begin to
build, and leave unfinished, is an argument of folly.—Thomas Manton.

Verse 15.—"I will meditate in thy precepts." Not only of thy precepts or concerning them, but in them, while engaged in doing them.—Joseph Addison Alexander.

Verse 15.—"I will." See this "I will" repeated again and again (verses 48,
78). In meditation it is hard (sometimes at least) to take off our thoughts from
the pre-engagements of other subjects, and apply them to the duty. But it is
harder to become duly serious in acting in it, harder yet to dive and ponder; and
hardest of all to continue in an abode of thoughts, and dwell long enough, and after
views to make reviews, to react the same thinkings, to taste things over and over,
when the freshness and newness is past, when by long thinking the things before us
seem old. We are ready to grow dead and flat in a performance except we stir up
ourselves often in it. It is hard to hold on and hold up, unless we hold up a wakeful
eye, a warm affection, a strong and quick repeated resolution; yea, and without
often lifting up the soul to Christ for fresh recruits of strength to hold on. David,
that so excellent artist in this way, saith he will meditate, he often saith he will.
Doubtless, he not only said "I will" when he was to make his entrance into this
hard work; but likewise for continuance in it, to keep up his heart from flagging,
till he well ended his work. It is not the digging into the golden mine, but the
digging long, that finds and fetches up the treasure. It is not the diving into the sea,
but staying longer, that gets the greater quantity of pearls. To draw out the golden
thread of meditation to its due length till the spiritual ends be attained, this is a
rare and happy attainment.—Nathanael Ranew, 1670.

Verse 15.—"I will meditate." How much our "rejoicing in the testimonies"
of God would be increased by a more habitual meditation upon them! This is, however, a resolution which the carnal mind can never be brought to make, and to
which the renewed mind through remaining depravity is often sadly reluctant. But

it is a blessed employment, and will repay a thousandfold th~~~ ~~~
the too backward heart in the duty.—*Charles Bridges.*

Verse 15.—Meditation is of that happy influence, it mak~~~
affections warm, the soul fat and flourishing, and the conversa~~~
Nathanael Ranew.

Verse 15.—" *Meditate in thy precepts.*"   Study the Scripture~~~
do but write an excellent book, O how we do long to see it ! ~~~
tell you that there is in France or Germany a book that God h~~~
confident men may draw all the money out of your purses to ge~~~
have it by you : O that you would study it ! When the eunuch~~~
chariot, he was studying the prophet Isaiah.   He was not an~~~
came and, as we would have thought, asked him a bold question : ~~~
thou what thou readest ? " (Acts viii. 27—30) ; he was glad of it. ~~~
of the year of release was, that the law might be read (Deut. xxxi~~~
the wisdom of God that speaks in the Scripture (Luke xi. 49) ; there~~~
else you mind, really and carefully study the Bible.—*Samuel Jacomb*~~~
in " *The Morning Exercises.*"

Verse 15.—" *I will have respect.*"   The one is the fruit of the oth~~~
meditate ; " and then, " *I will have respect.*"   Meditation is in order~~~
and if it be right, it will beget a respect to the ways of God.   We do n~~~
that we may rest in contemplation, but in order to obedience : " Thou sha~~~
in the book of the law day and night, that thou mayest observe to do ac~~~
all that is written therein " (Joshua i. 8).—*Thomas Manton.*

Verse 15.—" *And have respect unto thy ways.*"—As an archer hath to his~~~
John Trapp.

Verse 15.—" *Respect unto thy ways.*"   It is not without a peculiar pleasur~~~
travelling, that we *contemplate* the splendid buildings, the gardens, the fortific~~~
or the fine-art galleries.   But what are all these sights to the *contemplation*~~~
ways of God, which he himself has traversed, or has maked out for man ?   And ~~~
practical need there is that we consider the way, for else we shall be as a slee~~~
coachman, not carefully observant of the road, who may soon upset himself and his~~~
passengers.—*Martin Geier.*

Verse 15.—" *Thy ways.*"   David's second internal action concerning the word~~~
is consideration ;   where mark well, how by a most proper speech he calls the word of
God the *ways* of God ;   partly, because by it God comes near unto men, revealing
himself to them, who otherways could not be known of them ;   for he dwells in light
inaccessible ;   and partly, because the word is the *way* which leads men to God.   So
then, because by it God cometh down to men, and by it men go up unto God, and
know how to get access to him, therefore is his word called his *way.*—*William Cowper.*

Verses 15, 16.—The two last verses of this section present to us a threefold internal
action of David's soul toward the word of God ;   first, meditation ;   secondly, consideration ;   thirdly, delectation ;   every one of those proceeds from another, and
they mutually strengthen one another.   Meditation brings the word to the mind ;
consideration views it and looks at length into it, whereof is bred delectation.   That
which comes into the mind, were it never so good, if it be not considered, goes as it
came, leaving neither instruction nor joy ;   but being once presented by meditation,
if it be pondered by consideration, then it breeds delectation, which is the perfection
of godliness, in regard of the internal action.—*William Cowper.*

Verse 16.—" *I will delight myself,*" etc.   He protested before that he had great
delight in the testimonies of God : now he saith he will still delight in them.   A man
truly godly, the more good he doth, the more he desireth, delighteth and resolveth
to do.   Temporisers, on the contrary, who have but a show of godliness, and the
love of it is not rooted in their heart, how soon are they weary of well-doing !   If
they have done any small external duty of religion, they rest as if they were fully
satisfied, and there needed no more good to be done by them.   True religion is
known by hungering and thirsting after righteousness, by perseverance in well-doing
and an earnest desire to do more.

But to this he adds that *he will not forget the word.*   The graces of the Spirit do
every one fortify and strengthen another ;   for ye see meditation helps consideration.
Who can consider of that whereof he thinks not ?   Consideration again breeds delectation ;   and as here ye see, delectation strengthens memory : because he delights in
the word he will not forget the word ;   and memory again renews meditation.   Thus

...rit helps another ; and by the contrary, one of them neglected, ...ecay of the remnant.—*William Cowper.*

Verse 16.—*"I will delight myself."* When righteousness, from a matter of constraint, is a matter of choice, it instantly changes its whole nature, and rises to a higher moral rank than before. The same God whom it is impossible to move by law, moves of his own proper and original inclination in the very path of that righteousness. And so, we, in proportion as we are like unto God, are alive to the virtues of that same law, to the terror of whose severities we are altogether [before]. We are no longer under a schoolmaster ; but obedience is changed from [a thing] of force into a thing of freeness. It is moulded to a higher state and [character] than before. We are not driven to it by the God of authority. We are [won] by the regards of a now willing heart to all moral and all spiritual excel[lence].—*Thomas Chalmers, 1780—1847.*

Verse 16.—Meditation must not be a dull, sad, and dispirited thing : not a[s] like the chariots of the Egyptians when their wheels were taken off, but like [cha]riots of Amminadib (Cant. vi. 12) that ran swiftly. So let us pray,—Lord, [med]itation make me like the chariots of Amminadib, that my swift running may [advan]ce my delight in meditating. Holy David makes delight such an ingredient [con]sistant here, that sometimes he calls the exercise of meditation by the name of [de]*light,"* speaking in the foregoing verse of this meditation, " *I will meditate of thy [pre]cepts,"* and in the 16th verse, " *I will delight myself in thy statutes ; "* which is the [sa]me with meditation, only with superadding the excellent qualification due medi[t]ation should have ; the name of delight is givn to meditation because of its noble concomitant—holy joy and satisfaction.—*Nathanael Ranew.*

Verse 16.—" *Delight myself."* The word is very emphatical : אשתעשע, *eshtaasha,* I will skip about and jump for joy.—*Adam Clarke.*

Verse 16.—" *I will not forget."* Delight preventeth forgetfulness : the mind will run upon that which the heart delighteth in ; and the heart is where the treasure is (Matt. vi. 21). Worldly men that are intent upon carnal interests, forget the word, because it is not their delight. If anything displeases us, we are glad if we can forget it ; it is some release from an inconvenience, to take off our thoughts from it ; but it doubleth the contentment of a thing that we are delighted in, to remember it, and call it to mind. In the outward school, if a scholar by his own averseness from learning, or by the severity and imprudence of his master, hath no delight in his book, all that he learneth is lost and forgotten, it goeth in at one ear, and out at the other : but this is the true art of memory, to cause them to delight in what they learn. Such instructions as we take in with sweetness, they stick with us, and run in our minds night and day. So saith David here, *"I will delight myself in thy statutes ; I will not forget thy word."*—*Thomas Manton.*

Verse 16.—" *Forget."* I never yet heard of a covetous old man, who had forgotten where he had buried his treasure.—*Cicero de Senectute.*

EXPOSITION OF VERSES 17 TO 24.

DEAL bountifully with thy servant, *that* I may live, and keep thy word.

18 Open thou mine eyes, that I may behold wondrous things out of thy law.

19 I *am* a stranger in the earth : hide not thy commandments from me.

20 My soul breaketh for the longing *that it hath* unto thy judgments at all times.

21 Thou hast rebuked the proud *that are* cursed, which do err from thy commandments.

22 Remove from me reproach and contempt ; for I have kept thy testimonies.

23 Princes also did sit *and* speak against me : *but* thy servant did meditate in thy statutes.

24 Thy testimonies also *are* my delight *and* my counsellors.

In this section the trials of the way appear to be manifest to the Psalmist's mind, and he prays accordingly for the help which will meet his case. As in the last eight verses he prayed as a youth newly come into the world, so here he pleads as a servant and a pilgrim, who growingly finds himself to be a stranger in an enemy's country. His appeal is to God alone, and his prayer is specially direct and personal. He speaks with the Lord as a man speaketh with his friend.

17. " *Deal bountifully with thy servant.*" He takes pleasure in owning his duty to God, and counts it the joy of his heart to be in the service of his God. Out of his condition he makes a plea, for a servant has some hold upon a master ; but in this case the wording of the plea shuts out the idea of legal claim, since he seeks bounty rather than reward. Let my wages be according to thy goodness, and not according to my merit. Reward me according to the largeness of thy liberality, and not according to the scantiness of my service. The hired servants of our Father have all of them bread enough and to spare, and he will not leave one of his household to perish with hunger. If the Lord will only treat us as he treats the least of his servants we may be well content, for all his true servants are sons, princes of the blood, heirs of life eternal. David felt that his great needs required a bountiful provision, and that his little desert would never earn such a supply ; hence he must throw himself upon God's grace, and look for the great things he needed from the great goodness of the Lord. He begs for a liberality of grace, after the fashion of one who prayed. " O Lord, thou must give me great mercy or no mercy, for little mercy will not serve my turn."

" *That I may live.*" Without abundant mercy he could not live. It takes great grace to keep a saint alive. Even life is a gift of divine bounty to such undeserving ones as we are. Only the Lord can keep us in being, and it is mighty grace which preserves to us the life which we have forfeited by our sin. It is right to desire to live, it is meet to pray to live, it is just to ascribe prolonged life to the favour of God. Spiritual life, without which this natural life is mere existence, is also to be sought of the Lord's bounty, for it is the noblest work of divine grace, and in it the bounty of God is gloriously displayed. The Lord's servants cannot serve him in their own strength, for they cannot even live unless his grace abounds towards them.

" *And keep thy word.*" This should be the rule, the object, and the joy of our life. We may not wish to live and sin ; but we may pray to live and keep God's word. Being is a poor thing if it be not well-being. Life is only worth keeping while we can keep God's word ; indeed, there is no life in the highest sense apart from holiness : life while we break the law is but a name to live.

The prayer of this verse shows that it is only through divine bounty or grace that we can live as faithful servants of God, and manifest obedience to his commands. If we give God service it must be because he gives us grace. We work *for* him because he works *in* us. Thus we may make a chain out of the opening verses of the three first octaves of this Psalm : verse 1 blesses the holy man, verse 9 asks how we can attain to such holiness, and verse 17 traces such holiness to its secret source, and shows us how to seek the blessing. The more a man prizes holiness and the more earnestly he strives after it, the more will he be driven towards God for help therein, for he will plainly perceive that his own strength is insufficient, and that he cannot even so much as live without the bounteous assistance of the Lord his God.

18. *" Open thou mine eyes."*   This is a part of the bountiful dealing which he has asked for ; no bounty is greater than that which benefits our person, our soul, our mind, and benefits it in so important an organ as the eye.   It is far better to have the eyes opened than to be placed in the midst of the noblest prospects and remain blind to their beauty.   *" That I may behold wondrous things out of thy law."* Some men can perceive no wonders in the gospel, but David felt sure that there were glorious things in the law : he had not half the Bible, but he prized it more than some men prize the whole.   He felt that God had laid up great bounties in his word, and he begs for power to perceive, appreciate, and enjoy the same.   We need not so much that God should give us more benefits, as the ability to see what he has given.

The prayer implies a conscious darkness, a dimness of spiritual vision, a power-lessness to remove that defect, and a full assurance that God can remove it.   It shows also that the writer knew that there were vast treasures in the word which he had not yet fully seen, marvels which he had not yet beheld, mysteries which he had scarcely believed.   The Scriptures teem with marvels ; the Bible is wonder-land ; it not only relates miracles, but it is itself a world of wonders.   Yet what are these to closed eyes ?   And what man can open his own eyes, since he is born blind ? God himself must reveal revelation to each heart.   Scripture needs opening, but not one half so much as our eyes do : the veil is not on the book, but on our hearts. What perfect precepts, what precious promises, what priceless privileges are neglected by us because we wander among them like blind men amongst the beauties of nature, and they are to us as a landscape shrouded in darkness !

The Psalmist had a measure of spiritual perception, or he would never have known that there were wondrous things to be seen, nor would he have prayed, " open thou mine eyes ; " but what he had seen made him long for a clearer and wider sight.   This longing proved the genuineness of what he possessed, for it is a test mark of the true knowledge of God that it causes its possessor to thirst for deeper knowledge.

David's prayer in this verse is a good sequel to verse 10, which corresponds to it in position in its octave : there he said, " O let me not wander," and who so apt to wander as a blind man ? and there, too, he declared, " with my whole heart have I sought thee," and hence the desire to see the object of his search.   Very singular are the interlacings of the boughs of the huge tree of this Psalm, which has many wonders even within itself if we have opened eyes to mark them.

19. *" I am a stranger in the earth."*   This is meant for a plea.   By divine com-mand men are bound to be kind to strangers, and what God commands in others he will exemplify in himself.   The Psalmist was a stranger for God's sake, else had he been as much at home as worldlings are ; he was not a stranger to God, but a stranger to the world, a banished man so long as he was out of heaven.   Therefore he pleads, *"Hide not thy commandments from me."*   If these are gone, what have I else ?   Since nothing around me is mine, what can I do if I lose thy word ?   Since none around me know or care to know the way to thyself, what shall I do if I fail to see thy com-mands, by which alone I can guide my steps to the land where thou dwellest ?   David implies that God's commands were his solace in his exile : they reminded him of home, and they showed him the way thither, and therefore he begged that they might never be hidden from him, by his being unable either to understand them or to obey them.   If spiritual light be withdrawn the command is hidden, and this a gracious heart greatly deprecates.   What would be the use of opened eyes if the best object of sight were hidden from their view?   While we wander here we can endure all the ills of this foreign land with patience if the word of God is applied to our hearts by the Spirit of God ; but if the heavenly things which make for our peace were hid from our eyes we should be in an evil case,—in fact, we should be at sea without a compass, in a desert without a guide, in an enemy's country without a friend.

This prayer is a supplement to " open thou mine eyes," and, as the one prays to see, the other deprecates the negative of seeing, namely, the command being hidden, and so out of sight.   We do well to look at both sides of the blessing we are seeking, and plead for it from every point of view.   The prayers are appropriate to the characters mentioned : as he is a servant he asks for opened eyes that his eyes may ever be towards his Lord, as the eyes of a servant should be ; as a stranger he begs that he may not be strange to the way in which he is to walk towards his home.   In each case his entire dependence is upon God alone.

Note how the third of the second octave (11) has the same keyword as this third of the third octave : " Thy word have I hid," " Hide not thy commandments from me." This invites a meditation upon the different senses of hiding *in* and hiding *from.*

20. " *My soul breaketh for the longing that it hath unto thy judgments at all times.*" True godliness lies very much in desires.   As we are not what we shall be, so also we are not what we would be.   The desires of gracious men after holiness are intense,— they cause a wear of heart, a straining of the mind, till it feels ready to snap with the heavenly pull.   A high value of the Lord's commandment leads to a pressing desire to know and to do it, and this so weighs upon the soul that it is ready to break in pieces under the crush of its own longings.   What a blessing it is when all our desires are after the things of God.   We may well long for such longings.

God's judgments are his decisions upon points which else had been in dispute. Every precept is a judgment of the highest court upon a point of action, an infallible and immutable decision upon a moral or spiritual question.   The word of God is a code of justice from which there is no appeal.

> " This is the Judge which ends the strife
> Where wit and reason fail ;
> Our guide through devious paths of life,
> Our shield when doubts assail."

David had such reverence for the word, and such a desire to know it, and to be conformed to it, that his longings caused him a sort of heart-break, which he here pleads before God.   Longing is the soul of praying, and when the soul longs till it breaks, it cannot be long before the blessing will be granted.   The most intimate communion between the soul and its God is carried on by the process described in the text.   God reveals his will, and our heart longs to be conformed thereto.   God judges, and our heart rejoices in the verdict.   This is fellowship of heart most real and thorough.

Note well that our desire after the mind of God should be constant ; we should feel holy longings " *at all times.*"   Desires which can be put off and on like our garments are at best but mere wishes, and possibly they are hardly true enough to be called by that name,—they are temporary emotions born of excitement, and doomed to die when the heat which created them has cooled down.   He who always longs to know and do the right is the truly right man.   His judgment is sound, for he loves all God's judgments, and follows them with constancy.   His times shall be good, since he longs to be good and to do good at all times.

Remark how this fourth of the third eight chimes with the fourth of the fourth eight.   " My soul breaketh ; "   " my soul melteth."   There is surely some recondite poetic art about all this, and it is well for us to be careful in studying what the Psalmist was so careful in composing.

21. " *Thou hast rebuked the proud that are cursed.*"   This is one of God's judgments :   he is sure to deal out a terrible portion to men of lofty looks.   God rebuked Pharaoh with sore plagues, and at the Red Sea " the foundations of the world were discovered at thy rebuke, O Lord."   In the person of the haughty Egyptian he taught all the proud that he will certainly abase them.   Proud men are cursed men : nobody blesses them, and they soon become a burden to themselves.   In itself, pride is a plague and torment.   Even if no curse came from the law of God, there seems to be a law of nature that proud men should be unhappy men.   This led David to abhor pride ; he dreaded the rebuke of God and the curse of the law.   The proud sinners of his day were his enemies, and he felt happy that God was in the quarrel as well as he.

" *Which do err from thy commandments.*"   Only humble hearts are obedient, for they alone will yield to rule and government.   Proud men's looks are high, too high to mark their own feet and keep the Lord's way.   Pride lies at the root of all sin : if men were not arrogant they would not be disobedient.

God rebukes pride even when the multitudes pay homage to it, for he sees in it rebellion against his own majesty, and the seeds of yet further rebellions.   It is the sum of sin.   Men talk of an honest pride ; but if they were candid they would see that it is of all sins the least honest, and the least becoming in a creature, and especially in a fallen creature : yet so little do proud men know their own true condition under the curse of God, that they set up to censure the godly, and express contempt for them, as may be seen in the next verse. They are themselves contemptible, and yet they are contemptuous towards their betters. We may well love the judgments of God when we see them so decisively levelled against the haughty upstarts who would fain lord it over righteous men ; and we may well be of good comfort under the rebukes of the ungodly since their power to hurt us is destroyed by the Lord himself. "The Lord rebuke thee" is answer enough for all the accusations of men or devils.

In the fifth of the former octave the Psalmist wrote, " I have declared all the judgments of thy mouth, and here he continues in the same strain, giving a particular instance of the Lord's judgments against haughty rebels. In the next two portions the fifth verses deal with lying and vanity, and pride is one of the most common forms of those evils.

22. "*Remove from me reproach and contempt.*" These are painful things to tender minds. David could bear them for righteousness' sake, but they were a heavy yoke, and he longed to be free from them. To be slandered, and then to be despised in consequence of the vile accusation, is a grievous affliction. No one likes to be traduced, or even to be despised. He who says, " I care nothing for my reputation," is not a wise man, for in Solomon's esteem " a good name is better than precious ointment." The best way to deal with slander is to pray about it : God will either remove it, or remove the sting from it. Our own attempts at clearing ourselves are usually failures ; we are like the boy who wished to remove the blot from his copy, and by his bungling made it ten times worse. When we suffer from a libel it is better to pray about it than go to law over it, or even to demand an apology from the inventor. O ye who are reproached, take your matters before the highest court, and leave them with the Judge of all the earth. God will rebuke your proud accuser ; be ye quiet and let your advocate plead your cause.

"*For I have kept thy testimonies.*" Innocence may justly ask to be cleared from reproach. If there be truth in the charges alleged against us what can we urge with God ? If, however, we are wrongfully accused our appeal has a *locus standi* in the court and cannot be refused. If through fear of reproach we forsake the divine testimony we shall deserve the coward's doom ; our safety lies in sticking close to the true and to the right. God will keep those who keep his testimonies. A good conscience is the best security for a good name ; reproach will not abide with those who abide with Christ, neither will contempt remain upon those who remain faithful to the ways of the Lord.

This verse stands as a parallel both in sense and position to verse 6, and it has the catchword of " testimonies," by which it chimes with 14.

23. "*Princes also did sit and speak against me.*" David was high game, and the great ones of the earth went a hawking after him. Princes saw in him a greatness which they envied, and therefore they abused him. On their thrones they might have found something better to consider and speak about, but they turned the seat of judgment into the seat of the scorner. Most men covet a prince's good word, and to be spoken ill of by a great man is a great discouragement to them, but the Psalmist bore his trial with holy calmness. Many of the lordly ones were his enemies, and made it their business to speak ill of him : they held sittings for scandal, sessions for slander, parliaments of falsehood, and yet he survived all their attempts upon him.

"*But thy servant did meditate in thy statutes.*" This was brave indeed. He was God's servant, and therefore he attended to his Master's business ; he was God's servant, and therefore felt sure that his Lord would defend him. He gave no heed to his princely slanderers, he did not even allow his thoughts to be disturbed by a knowledge of their plotting in conclave. Who were these malignants that they should rob God of his servant's attention, or deprive the Lord's chosen of a moment's devout communion. The rabble of princes were not worth five minutes' thought, if those five minutes had to be taken from holy meditation. It is very beautiful to see the two sittings : the princes sitting to reproach David, and David sitting with his God and his Bible, answering his traducers by never answering them at all. Those who feed upon the word grow strong and peaceful, and are by God's grace hidden from the strife of tongues.

Note that in the close of the former octave he had said, " I will meditate," and here he shows how he had redeemed his promise, even under great provocation to forget it. It is a praiseworthy thing when the resolve of our happy hours is duly carried out in our seasons of affliction.

Verse 24. " *Thy testimonies also are my delight and my counsellors.*" They were not only themes for meditation, but " also " sources of delight and means of guidance. While his enemies took counsel with each other the holy man took counsel with the testimonies of God. The fowlers could not drive the bird from its nest with all their noise. It was *their* delight to slander and *his* delight to meditate. The words of the Lord serve us for many purposes ; in our sorrows they are our delight, and in our difficulties they are our guide ; we derive joy from them and discover wisdom in them. If we desire to find comfort in the Scriptures we must submit ourselves to their counsel, and when we follow their counsel it must not be with reluctance but with delight. This is the safest way of dealing with those who plot for our ruin ; let us give more heed to the true testimonies of the Lord than to the false witness of our foes. The best answer to accusing princes is the word of the justifying King.

In verse 16 David said, " I will delight in thy statutes," and here he says " they are my delight : " thus resolutions formed in God's strength come to fruit, and spiritual desires ripen into actual attainments. O that it might be so with all the readers of these lines.

NOTES ON VERSES 17 TO 24.

Verse 17.—" *Deal bountifully with thy servant,*" etc. These words might be— Render unto thy servant, or upon thy servant. A deep signification seems to be here involved. The holy man will take the responsibility of being dealt with, not certainly as a mere sinful man, but as a man placing himself in the way appointed for reconciliation. Such we find to be the actual case, as you read in the 16th verse, in the Part immediately preceding —" I will delight myself in thy statutes ; I will not forget thy word." Now, the statutes of the Lord referred pre-eminently to the sacrifice for sin, and the cleansings for purifications that were prescribed in the Law. You have to conceive of the man of God as being in the midst of the Levitical ritual, for which you find him making all preparations : 1 Chron. xxii., xxiii., xxiv. Placing himself, therefore, upon these, he woud pray the Lord to deal with him according to them ; or, as we, in New Testament language, would say,—placing himself on the great atonement, the believer would pray the Lord to deal with him acco ding to his standing in Christ, which would be in graciousness or bounty. For if the Lord be just to condemn without the atonement, he is also just to pardon through the atonement ; yea, he is just, and the justifier of him that believeth in Jesus.—*John Stephen.*

Verse 17.—" *Deal bountifully,*" etc. O Lord, ı am constantly resolved to obey and adhere to thy known will all the days of my life : O make me those gracious returns which thou hast promised to all such.—*Henry Hammond.*

Verse 17.—" *Deal bountifully . . . that I may keep thy word,*" etc. A faithful servant should count his by-past service richly rewarded by being employed yet more in further service, as this prayer teacheth : for David entreats that he may live and keep God's word.—*David Dickson.*

Verse 17.—" *Bountifully.*" And indeed, remembering what a poor, weak, empty, and helpless creature the most experienced believer is in himself, it is not to be conceived that anything short of a *bountiful* supply of grace can answer the emergency.—*Charles Bridges.*

Verse 17.—" *Thy servant.*" That he styles himself so frequently the servant of God notes the reverent estimation he had of his God, in that he accounts it more honourable to be called the servant of God who was above him than the king of a mighty, ancient, and most famous people that were under him. And indeed, since the angels are styled his ministers, shall men think it a shame to serve him ? and especially since he of his goodness hath made them our servants, " ministering spirits " to us ? Should we not joyfully serve him who hath made all his creatures to serve us, and exempted us from the service of all other, and hath only bound us to serve himself ?—*William Cowper.*

Verse 17.—" *That I may live.*" As a man must " *live* " in order to work, the first petition is, that God would " *deal with his servant,*" according to the measure of grace and mercy, enabling him to " *live* " the life of faith, and strengthening him by the Spirit of might in the inner man.—*George Horne, 1730—1792.*

Verse 17.—" *That I may live, and keep thy word.*" David joins here two together, which whosoever disjoins cannot be blessed. He desires to live ; but so to live that he may keep God's word. To a reprobate man, who lives a rebel to his Maker, it had been good (as our Saviour said of Judas) that he had never been born. The shorter his life is, the fewer are his sins and the smaller his judgments. But to an elect man, life is a great benefit ; for by it he goes from election to glorification, by the way of sanctification. The longer he lives, the more good he doth, to the glory of God, the edification of others, and confirmation of his own salvation ; making it sure to himself by wrestling and victory in temptations, and perseverance in well doing.—*William Cowper.*

Verse 18.—" *Open thou mine eyes.*" Who is able to know the secret and hidden things of the Scriptures unless Christ opens his eyes ? Certainly, no one ; for " No man knoweth the Son but the Father ; neither knoweth any man the Father save the Son, and he to whom the Son will reveal him." Wherefore, as suppliants, we draw near to him, saying, " *Open thou mine eyes,*" etc. The words of God cannot be kept except they be known; neither can they be known unless the eyes shall be opened,—hence it is written, " *That I may live and keep thy word ;* " and then, " *Open thou mine eyes.*"—*Paulus Palanterius.*

Verse 18.—*" Open thou mine eyes."* " What wilt thou that I shall do unto thee ? " was the gracious inquiry of the loving Jesus to a poor longing one on earth. " Lord ! that I may receive my sight," was the instant answer. So here, in the same spirit, and to the same compassionate and loving Lord, does the Psalmist pray, " *Open thou mine eyes;"* and both in this and the preceding petition, "Deal bountifully with thy servant, " we see at once who prompted the prayer.—*Barton Bouchier.*

Verse 18.—*" Open thou mine eyes."* If it be asked, seeing David was a regenerate man, and so illumined already, how is it that he prays for the opening of his eyes ? The answer is easy : that our regeneration is wrought by degrees. The beginnings of light in his mind made him long for more ; for no man can account of sense, but he who hath it. The light which he had caused him to see his own darkness ; and therefore, feeling his wants, he sought to have them supplied by the Lord.—*William Cowper.*

Verse 18.—*" Open thou mine eyes."* The saints do not complain of the obscurity of the law, but of their own blindness. The Psalmist doth not say, Lord make a plainer law, but, Lord, *open mine eyes :* blind men might as well complain of God, that he doth not make a sun whereby they might see. The word is " a light that shineth in a dark place " (2 Pet. i. 19). There is no want of light in the Scripture, but there is a veil of darkness upon our hearts ; so that if in this clear light we cannot see, the defect is not in the word, but in ourselves.

The light which they beg is not anything besides the word. When God is said to enlighten us, it is not that we should expect new revelations, but that we may see the wonders in his word, or get a clear sight of what is already revealed. Those that vent their own dreams under the name of the Spirit, and divine light, they do not give you *mysteria,* but *monstra,* portentous opinions ; they do not show you the wondrous things of God's law, but the prodigies of their own brain ; unhappy abortives, that die as soon as they come to light. " To the law and to the testimony : if they speak not according to this word, it is because there is no light in them " (Isaiah viii. 20). The light which we have is not without the word, but by the word.

The Hebrew phrase signifieth *" unveil mine eyes."* There is a double work, negative and positive. There is a taking away of the veil, and an infusion of light. Paul's cure of his natural blindness is a fit emblem of our cure of spiritual blindness : " Immediately there fell from his eyes as it had been scales : and he received sight forthwith " (Acts ix. 18). First, the scales fall from our eyes, and then we receive sight.—*Thomas Manton.*

Verse 18.—The Psalmist asks for no new revelation. It was in God's hand to give this, and he did it in his own time to those ancient believers ; but to all of them at every time there was enough given for the purposes of life. The request is not for more, but that he may employ well that which he possesses. Still better does such a form of request suit us, to whom life and immortality have been brought to light in Christ. If we do not find sufficient to exercise our thoughts with constant freshness, and our soul with the grandest and most attractive subjects, it is because we want the eyesight. It is of great importance for us to be persuaded of this truth, that there are many things in the Bible still to be found out, and that, if we come in the right spirit, we may be made discoverers of some of them. These things disclose themselves, not so much to learning, though that is not to be despised, as to spiritual sight, to a humble, loving heart.

And this at least is certain, that we shall always find things that are new to *ourselves.* However frequently we traverse the field, we shall perceive some fresh golden vein turning up its glance to us, and we shall wonder how our eyes were formerly holden that we did not see it. It was all there waiting for us, and we feel that more is waiting, if we had the vision. There is a great Spirit in it that holds deeper and even deeper converse with our souls.

This further may be observed, that the Psalmist asks for no new faculty. The eyes are there already, and they need only to be opened. It is not the bestowal of a new and supernatural power which enables a man to read the Bible to profit, but the quickening of a power he already possesses. In one view it is supernatural, as God is the Author of the illumination by a direct act of his Spirit ; in another it is natural, as it operates through the faculties existing in a man's soul. God gives " the spirit of wisdom and revelation in the knowledge of Christ, that the eyes of man's understanding may be enlightened." (Eph. i. 17.) It is important to re-remember this also, for here lies our responsibility, that we have the faculty, and here also is the point at which we must begin action with the help of God. A man will never grow into the knowledge of God's word by idly waiting for some new gift of discernment, but by diligently using that which God has already bestowed upon him, and using at the same time all other helps that lie within his reach.   There are men and books that seem, beyond others, to have the power of aiding insight.   All of us have felt it in the contact of some affinity of nature which makes them our best helpers ; the kindred clay upon the eyes by which the great Enlightener removes our blindness (John ix. 6).   Let us seek for such, and if we find them let us employ them without leaning on them.   Above all, let us give our whole mind in patient, loving study to the book itself, and where we fail, at any essential part, God will either send his evangelist Philip to our aid (Acts. viii) or instruct us himself.   But it is only to patient, loving study that help is given.   God could have poured all knowledge into us by easy inspiration, but it is by earnest search alone that it can become the treasure of the soul.

But if so, it may still be asked what is the meaning of this prayer, and why does the Bible itself insist so often on the indispensable need of the Spirit of God to teach ? Now there is a side here as true as the other, and in no way inconsistent with it. If prayer without effort would be presumptuous, effort without prayer would be vain.   The great reason why men do not feel the power and beauty of the Bible is a spiritual one.   They do not realize the grand evil which the Bible has come to cure, and they have not a heart to the blessings which it offers to bestow.   The film of a fallen nature, self-maintained, is upon their eyes while they read : " The eyes of their understanding are darkened, being alienated from the life of God " (Eph. iv. 18).   All the natural powers will never find the true key to the Bible, till the thoughts of sin and redemption enter the heart, and are put in the centre of the Book.   It is the part of the Father of lights, by the teaching of his Spirit, to give this to the soul, and he will, if it humbly approaches him with this request.   Thus we shall study as one might a book with the author at hand, to set forth the height of its argument, or as one might look on a noble composition, when the artist breathes into us a portion of his soul, to let us feel the centre of its harmonies of form and colour.   Those who have given to the Bible thought and prayer will own that these are not empty promises.—*John Kerr, in a Sermon entitled, " God's Word Suited to Man's Sense of Wonder,"* 1877.

Verse 18.—O let us never forget, that the wonderful things contained in the divine law can neither be discovered nor relished by the " natural man," whose powers of perception and enjoyment are limited in their range to the objects of time and sense.   It is the divine Spirit alone who can lighten the darkness of our sinful state, and who can enable us to perceive the glory, the harmony, and moral loveliness which everywhere shine forth in the pages of revealed truth.—*John Morison,* 1829.

Verse 18.—" *Uncover my eyes and I will look—wonders out of thy law.*"   The last clause is a kind of exclamation after his eyes have been uncovered.   This figure is often used to denote inspiration or a special divine communication.   " *Out of thy law,*" *i.e.,* brought out to view, as if from a place of concealment.—*Joseph Addison Alexander.*

Verse 18.—" *Wondrous things.*"   Many were the signs and miracles which God wrought in the midst of the people of Israel, which they did not understand.   What was the reason ?   Moses tells us expressly what it was : " Yet the Lord hath not given you an heart to perceive, and eyes to see, and ears to hear, unto this day " (Deut. xxix. 4).   They had sensitive eyes and ears, yea, they had a rational heart or mind ; but they wanted a spiritual ear to hear, a spiritual heart or mind to apprehend and improve those wonderful works of God ; and these they had not, because God had not given them such eyes, ears, and hearts.   Wonders without grace cannot open the eyes fully ; but grace without wonders can.   And as man hath not an eye to see the wonderful works of God spiritually, until it is given ; so, much less hath he an eye to see the wonders of the word of God till it be given him from above ; and therefore David prays, " *Open thou mine eyes, that I may behold wondrous things out of thy law.*"   And if the wondrous things of the law are not much seen till God give an eye then much less are the wondrous things of the Gospel.   The light of nature shows us somewhat of the Law ; but nothing of the Gospel was ever seen by the light of nature.   Many who have seen and admired, some excellencies in the Law could never see, and therefore have derided, that which is the excellency of the Gospel, till God had opened their heart to understand.—*Joseph Caryl,* 1602—1673.

Verse 18.—" The word is very nigh " unto us ; and, holding in our hand a document that teems with what is wonderful, the sole question is, " Have we an eye to its marvels, a heart for its mercies ? " Here is the precise use of the Holy Spirit. The Spirit puts nothing new into the Bible ; he only so enlightens and strengthens our faculties, that we can discern and admire what is there already.   It is not the telescope which draws out that rich sparkling of stars on the blue space, which to the naked eye seem points of light, and untenanted : it is not the microscope which condenses the business of a stirring population into the circumference of a drop of water, and clothes with a thousand tints the scarcely discernible wing of the ephemeral insect.   The stars are shining in their glory, whether or no we have the instruments to penetrate the azure ; and the tiny tenantry are carrying on their usual concerns, and a rich garniture still forms the covering of the insect, whether or no the powerful lens has turned for us the atom into a world, and transformed the almost imperceptible down into the sparkling plumage of the bird of paradise.   Thus the wonderful things are already in the Bible.   The Spirit who indited them at first brings them not as new revelations to the individual ; but, by removing the mists of carnal prejudice, by taking away the scales of pride and self-sufficiency, and by rectifying the will, which causes the judgment to look at truth through a distorted medium,—by influencing the heart, so that the affections shall no longer blind the understanding,— by these and other modes, which might be easily enumerated, the Holy Ghost enables men to recognize what is hid, to perceive beauty and to discover splendour where all before had appeared without form and comeliness ; and thus brings round the result of the Bible, in putting on the lip the wonderful prayer which he had himself inspired : " *Open thou mine eyes, that I may behold wondrous things out of thy law,*"—*Henry Melvill*, 1798—1871.

Verse 18.—The " *wondrous things* " seem to be the great things of an eternal world—he had turned his enquiring eyes upon the wonders of nature, sun, moon, and stars, mountains, trees, and rivers.   He had seen many of the wonders of art ; but now, he wanted to see the spiritual wonders contained in the Bible.   He wanted to know about God himself in all his majesty, purity, and grace.   He wanted to learn the way of salvation by a crucified Redeemer, and the glory that is to follow. " *Open mine eyes.*"—David was not blind—his eye was not dim.   He could read the Bible from end to end, and yet he felt that he needed more light.   He felt that he needed to see deeper, to have the eyes of his understanding opened.   He felt that if he had nothing but his own eyes and natural understanding, he would not discover the wonders which he panted to see.   He wanted divine teaching—the eye-salve of the Spirit ; and therefore he would not open the Bible without this prayer, " *Open thou mine eyes.*"—*Robert Murray M'Cheyne*, 1813—1843.

Verse 18.—" *Wondrous things.*"   Wherefore useth he this word " *wondrous ?* " It is as if he would have said, Although the world taketh the law of God to be but a light thing, and it seemeth to be given but as it were for simple souls and young children ; yet for all that there seemeth such a wisdom to be in it, as that it surmounteth all the wisdom of the world, and that therein lie hid wonderful secrets.— *John Calvin.*

Verse 18.—" *Thy law.*"   That which is the *object* of the understanding prayed for, that in the knowledge whereof the Psalmist would be illuminated, is תּוֹרָה.   The word signifies instruction ; and being referred unto God, it is his teaching or instruction of us by the revelation of himself, the same which we intend by the Scripture. When the books of the Old Testament were completed they were, for distinction's sake, distributed into תּוֹרָה, כְּתוּבִים and נְבִיאִים, or the " Law," the "Psalms," and the " Prophets," Luke xxiv. 44.   Under that distribution *Torah* signifies the five books of Moses.   But whereas these books of Moses were, as it were, the foundation of all future revelations under the Old Testament, which were given in the explication thereof, all the writings of it were usually called " the Law," Isaiah viii. 20.   By the *law*, therefore, in this place, the Psalmist understands all the books that were then given unto the church by revelation for the rule of its faith and obedience. And that by the *law*, in the Psalms, the written law is intended, is evident from the first of them, wherein he is declared blessed who " meditateth therein day and night," Ps. i. 2 ; which hath respect unto the command of reading and meditating on the *books thereof* in that manner, Josh. i. 8.   That, therefore, which is intended by this word is the entire revelation of the will of God, given unto the church for the rule of its faith and obedience—that is, the holy Scrpiture.

In this law there are נִפְלָאוֹת " *wonderful things,*" פָּלָא signifies to be " wonderful," to be " hidden," to be " great " and " high ; " that which men by the use of reason cannot attain unto or understand (hence נִפְלָאוֹת are things that have such an impression of divine wisdom and power upon them as that they are justly the object of our admiration) ; that which is too hard for us ; as Deut. xvii. 8, כִּי יִפָּלֵא מִמְּךָ דָבָר "If a matter be too hard for thee," hid from thee. And it is the name whereby the miraculous works of God are expressed, Ps. lxxvii. 11, lxxviii. 11. Wherefore, these "wonderful things of the law" are those expressions and effects of divine wisdom in the Scripture which are above the natural reason and understanding of men to find out and comprehend. Such are the mysteries of divine truth in the Scripture, especially because Christ is in them, whose name is "Wonderful," Isa. ix. 6 ; for all the great and marvellous effects of infinite wisdom meet in him.—*John Owen*, 1616—1683.

Verse 18.—"*Wondrous things.*" There are promises in God's word that no man has ever tried to find. There are treasures of gold and silver in it that no man has taken the pains to dig for. There are medicines in it for the want of knowledge of which hundreds have died. It seems to me like some old baronial estate that has descended to a man who lives in a modern house, and thinks it scarcely worth while to go and look into the venerable mansion. Year after year passes away and he pays no attention to it, since he has no suspicion of the valuable treasures it contains, till, at last, some man says to him, "Have you been up in the country to look at that estate ? " He makes up his mind that he will take a look at it. As he goes through the porch he is surprised to see the skill that has been displayed in its construction : he is more and more surprised as he goes through the halls. He enters a large room and is astonished as he beholds the wealth of pictures on the walls, among which are portraits of many of his revered ancestors. He stands in amazement before them. There is a Titians, there a Raphael, there is a Correggio, and there is a Giorgione. He says, " I never had any idea of these before." " Ah," says the steward, " there is many another thing that you know nothing about in the castle," and he takes him from room to room and shows carved plate, and wonderful statues, and the man exclaims, " Here I have been for a score of years the owner of this estate, and have never before known what things were in it." But no architect ever conceived of such an estate as God's word, and no artist, or carver, or sculptor, ever conceived of such pictures, and carved dishes, and statues as adorn its apartments. It contains treasures that silver, and gold, and precious stones are not to be mentioned with.— *Henry Ward Beecher*, 1872.

Verse 18.—"*That I may behold wondrous things.*" The great end of the Word of God in the Psalmist's time, as now, was practical ; but there is a secondary use here referred to, which is worthy of consideration,—its power of meeting man's faculty of wonder. God knows our frame, for he made it, and he must have adapted the Bible to all its parts. If we can show this, it may be another token that the book comes from Him who made man . . . . That God has bestowed upon man the faculty of wonder we all know. It is one of the first and most constant emotions in our nature. We can see this in children, and in all whose feelings are still fresh and natural. It is the parent of the desire to know, and all through life it is urging men to enquire.—*John Ker*.

Verse 18.—"*Wondrous things out of thy law.*" In cxviii. we had the "wondrous" character of redemption ; in cxix. we have the "wonders" (verses 18, 27, 129), of God's revelation.—*William Kay*, 1871.

Verses 18, 19.—When I cannot have Moses to tell me the meaning, saith Saint Augustine, give me that Spirit that thou gavest to Moses. And this is that which every man that will understand must pray for : this David prayed for ;—"*Open thou mine eyes that I may see the wonders of the Law ;* " and (verse 19) " *hide not thy commandments from me.*" And Christ saith, "If you, being evil, can give good gifts to your children ; how much more shall your heavenly Father give his Holy Spirit to them that ask him ? " so that then we shall see the secrets of God.—*Richard Stock* (—1626).

Verse 19.—"*I am a stranger in the earth.*" David had experience of peace and war, of riches and poverty, of pleasure and woe. He had been a private and public person ; a shepherd, a painful calling ; a soldier, a bloody trade ; a courtier, an honourable slavery, which joineth together in one the lord and the parasite, the gentleman and the drudge ; and he was a king,—a glorious name, filled up with fears and cares. All these he had passed through, and found least rest when he was at the highest, less content on the throne than in the sheepfolds. All this he had observed and laid up in his memory, and this his confession is an epitome and brief of all ; and in effect he telleth us, that whatsoever he had seen in this his passage, whatsoever he had enjoyed, yet he found nothing so certain as this,—that he had found nothing certain, nothing that he could abide with or would abide with him, but that he was still as a passenger and " *stranger in the earth.*"—*Anthony Farindon,* 1596—1658.

Verse 19.—" *I am a stranger in the earth,*" etc.   As a sojourner, he hath renounced the world, which is therefore become his enemy ; as " *a stranger* " he is fearful of losing his way ; on these accounts he requesteth that God would compensate the loss of earthly comforts by affording the light of heaven ; that he would not " *hide his commandments,*" but show and teach him those steps, by which he may ascend toward heaven, rejoicing in hope of future glory.—*George Horne,* 1730—1792.

Verse 19.—" *I am a stranger in the earth.*"   This confession from a solitary wanderer would have had little comparative meaning ; but in the mouth of one who was probably surrounded with every source of worldly enjoyment, it shows at once the vanity of " earth's best joys," and the heavenly tendency of the religion of the Bible.—*Charles Bridges.*

Verse 19.—" *I am a stranger in the earth,*" etc.   1. Every man here upon earth (especially a godly man) is but a stranger and a passenger.   2. It concerns him that is a stranger to look after a better and a more durable state.   Every man should do so.   A man's greatest care should be for that place where he lives longest ; therefore eternity should be his scope.   A godly man will do so.   Those whose hearts are not set upon earthly things, they must have heaven.   The more their affections are estranged from the one, the more they are taken up about the other (Col. iii. 2) ; heaven and earth are like two scales in a balance, that which is taken from the one is put into the other.   3. There is no sufficient direction how to obtain this durable estate, but in the word of God.   Without this we are but like poor pilgrims and way-faring men in a strange country, not able to discern the way home.   A blessed state is only sufficiently revealed in the word : " Life and immortality is brought to light through the gospel " (2 Tim. i. 10).   The heathens did but guess at it, and had some obscure sense of an estate after this life; but as it is brought to light with most clear-ness in the word, so the way thither is only pointed out by the word.   It is the word of God makes us wise to salvation, and which is our line and rule to heavenly Canaan ; and therefore it concerns those that look after this durable state to consult with the word.   4. There is no understanding God's word but by the light of the Spirit. " There is a spirit in man : and the inspiration of the Almighty giveth them under-standing " (Job xxxii. 8).   Though the word have light in it, yet the spirit of man cannot move till God enlightens us with that lively light that makes way for the dominion of the truth in our hearts, and conveyeth influence into our hearts.   This is the light David begs when he says, " *Hide not thy commandments from me.*"   David was not ignorant of the Ten Commandments, of their sound ; but he begs their spiritual sense and use.   5. If we would have the Spirit we must ask it of God in prayer ; for God gives the " Spirit to them that ask him " (Luke xi. 13) ; and there-fore we must say, as David, " O send out thy light and thy truth : let them lead me : let them bring me unto thy holy hill, and to thy tabernacles " (Ps. xliii. 33).—*Thomas Manton.*

Verse 19.—" *I am a stranger in the earth,*" etc.   When a child is born, it is spoken of sometimes under the designation of " a little stranger ! "   Friends calling will ask if, as a privilege, they may " see the little stranger."   A stranger, indeed ! come from far.   From the immensities.   From the presence, and touch, and being of God !   And going—into the immensities again—into, and through all the unreckon-able ages of duration.

But the little stranger grows, and in a while begins to take vigorous root.   He works, and wins, and builds, and plants, and buys, and holds, and, in his own feeling, becomes so " settled " that he would be almost amused with anyone who should describe him as a stranger now.

And still life goes on, deepening and widening in its flow, and holding in itself manifold and still multiplying elements of interest.   Increasingly the man is caught by these—like a ship, from which many anchors are cast into the sea.   He strives among the struggling, rejoices with the gay, feels the spur of honour, enters the race of acquisition, does some hard and many kindly things by turns ; multiplies his engagements, his relationships, his friends, and then—just when after such prepara-tions, life ought to be fully beginning, and opening itself out into a great, restful, sunny plain—lo ! the shadows begin to fall, which tell, too surely, that it is drawing fast to a close.   The voice, which, soon or late, everyone must hear, is calling for " the little stranger," who was born not long ago, whose first lesson is over, and who is wanted now to enter by the door called death, into another school. And the stranger is not ready. He has thrown out so many anchors, and they have taken such a fast hold of the ground that it will be no slight matter to raise them. He is *settled*. He has no pilgrim's staff at hand ; and his eye, familiar enough with surrouding things, is not accustomed to the onward and ascending way, cannot so well measure the mountain altitude, or reckon the far distance. The progress of time has been much swifter than the progress of his thought. Alas ! he has made one long mistake. He has " looked at the things which are seen," and forgotten the things which are not seen. And " the things which are seen " are temporal, and go with time into extinction ; while " those which are not seen, are eternal." And so there is hurry, and confusion, and distress in the last hours, and in the going away. Now, all this may be obviated and escaped, thoroughly, if a man will but say—" *I am a stranger in the earth : hide not thy commandments from me.*"—*Alexander Raleigh, in " The Little Sanctuary, and other Meditations."* 1872.

Verse 19.—" *I am a stranger in the earth,*" etc. In the law, God recommends strangers to the care and compassion of his people ; now David returns the arguments to him, to persuade him to deal kindly with him.—*Robert Leighton,* 1611—1684.

Verse 19.—" *In the earth.*" He makes no exception here ; the whole earth he acknowledged a place of his pilgrimage. Not only when he was banished among the Moabites and Philistines was he a stranger ; but even when he lived peaceably at home in Canaan, still he thinks himself a stranger. This consideration moved godly Basil to despise the threatening of Modestus, the deputy of Valens the emperor, when he braved him with banishment. *Ab exilii metu liber sum, unam hominum cognoscens esse patriam, paradisum omnem autem terram commune naturæ exilium.* And it shall move us to keep spiritual sobriety in the midst of pleasures, if we remember that in our houses, at our own fireside, and in our own beds, we are but strangers from which we must shortly remove, to give place to others.—*William Cowper.*

Verse 19.—" *Hide not thy commandments from me.*" The manner of David's reasoning is this. I am here a stranger and I know not the way, therefore, Lord, direct me. The similitude is taken from passengers, who coming to an uncouth country where they are ignorant of the way, seek the benefit of a guide. But the dissimilitude is here : in any country people can guide a stranger to the place where he would be ; but the dwellers of the earth cannot show the way to heaven ; and therefore David seeks no guide among them, but prays the Lord to direct him.— *William Cowper.*

Verse 19.—" *Hide not thy commandments from me.*" There is a hiding of the word of God when means to hear it explained by preachers are wanting ; and there is a hiding of the comfortable and lively light of the Spirit, who must quicken the word unto us. From both those evils we may, and we should, pray to be saved.— *David Dickson.*

Verse 20.—" *My soul breaketh,*" etc. Here is a protestation of that earnest desire he had to the obedience of the word of God ; he amplifies it two ways : first, it was no light motion, but such as being deeply rooted made his heart to *break* when he saw that he could not do in the obedience thereof what he would. Next, it was no vanishing motion, like the morning dew ; but it was permanent, *omni tempore,* he had it *at all times.*—*William Cowper.*

Verse 20.—" *My soul breaketh for the longing,*" as one that with straining breaks a vein.—*William Gurnall.*

Verse 20.—" *My soul breaketh,*" etc. This breaking is by rubbing, chafing, or crushing. The spirit was so *fretted* with its yearning desire after the things which Jehovah had spoken, that it was broken as by heavy friction. The " *longing* " to find out and follow the hidden wonders was almost unbearable. This *longing* continued with the Psalmist " *at all times,*" or " in every season." Prosperity could not make him forget it ; adversity could not quench it. In sickness or health, in happiness or sadness, in company or alone, nothing overcame that *longing.* "*The wondrous things*" were so wonderful, and still so hidden. To see a little of " the beauty of the Lord " is to get to know how much there is which we fail to see, and thus to *long* more than ever. He who pursues ardently the wonders of the word of the Lord, will never set that *longing* at rest as long as he remains " in the earth." It is only when we shall " be like him," and " shall see him as he is," that we shall cry " Enough, Lord ! " " I shall be satisfied when I awake in thy likeness."—*F. G. Marchant.*

Verse 20.—" *My soul breaketh for the longing.*" For the earnest desire. " That it hath *unto thy judgments at all times.*" Thy law ; thy commands. This was a constant feeling. It was not fitful, or spasmodic. It was the steady, habitual state of the soul on the subject. He had never seen enough of the beauty and glory of the law of God to feel that all the wants of his nature were satisfied, or that he could see and know no more ; he had seen and felt enough to excite in him an ardent desire to be made fully acquainted with *all* that there is in the law of God.—*Albert Barnes.*

Verse 20.—" *My soul breaketh for the longing,*" etc. The desire after God's appointments becomes painfully intense. A longing—an intense longing—for the judgments of the Lord at all times. These are the particulars of his breaking soul. His whole mind is toward the things of God. He prays that he may behold the wondrous things of Jehovah's law, and that he may not hide his commandments from him ; and here his soul breaks for longing towards his judgments at all times. The state of the Psalmist's mind would not lead us here to suppose that he was awaiting the manifestation of the Lord's judgments in vindicating his cause against ungodly men, or that he was longing for opportunity of fulfilling all the deeds of righteousnes towards his fellow-men ; for this he was doing to the utmost. Evidently he is intent upon the ordinances of religion, which were called " *judgments* " in reference to the solemn sanctions with which they were enjoined. The man of God so longed to join with the Lord's people in these, that his heart was ready to break with desire, as he was forced from place to place in the wilderness. The renewed heart is here. Another might long to be delivered from persecution, to be at rest, to be restored to home, relations, and comfort. The man of God could not but desire those natural enjoyments ; but, over all, his holy mind longed with ardour for the celebration of Jehovah's worship.—*John Stephen.*

Verse 20.—" *Thy judgments.*" God's judgments are of two sorts : first, his commands ; so called because by them right is judged and discerned from wrong. Next, his plagues executed upon transgressors according to his word. David here refers to the first. Let men who have not the like of David's desire, remember, that they whose heart cannot break for transgressing God's word because they love it, shall find the plagues of God to bruise their body and break their heart also. Let us delight in the first sort of these judgments, and the second shall never come upon us.—*William Cowper.*

Verse 20.—Mark that word, "*at all times.*" Bad men have their good moods, as good men have their bad moods. A bad man may, under gripes of conscience, a smarting rod, the approaches of death, or the fears of hell, or when he is sermon sick, cry out to the Lord for grace, for righteousness, for holiness ; but he is the only blessed man that hungers and thirsts after righteousness at all times.—*Thomas Brooks,* 1608—1680.

Verse 20.—" *At all times.*" Some prize the word in adversity, when they have no other comfort to live upon ; then they can be content to study the word to comfort them in their distresses ; but when they are well at ease, they despise it. But David made use of it " *at all times ;* " in prosperity, to humble him ; in adversity, to comfort him ; in the one, to keep him from pride ; in the other, to keep him from despair in affliction, the word was his cordial ; in worldly increase, it was his antidote ; and so at all times his heart was carried out to the word either for one necessity or another.—*Thomas Manton.*

Verse 20.—" *At all times.*" How few are there even among the servants of God who know anything of the intense feeling of devotion here expressed ! O that our cold and stubborn hearts were warmed and subdued by divine grace, that we might be ready to faint by reason of the longing which he had " *at all times* " for the judgments of our God. How fitful are our best feelings ! If to-day we ascend the mount of communion with God, to-morrow we are in danger of being again entangled with the things of earth. How happy are they whose hearts are " *at all times* " filled with longings after fellowship with the great and glorious object of their love !—*John Morison,* 1829.

Verse 20.—If you read the lives of good men, who have been, also, intellectually great, you will be struck, I think, even to surprise, a surprise, however, which will not be unpleasant, to find them, at the close of life, in their own estimation so ignorant, so utterly imperfect, so little the better of the long life-lesson. Dr. Chalmers, after kindling churches and arousing nations to their duties, summed up his own attainments in the word " desirousness," and took as the text that best described his inner

state, that passionate, almost painful cry of David, " *My soul breaketh for the longing
that it hath unto thy judgments.*" But how grand was the attainment! To be in old
age as simple as a little child before God! To be still learning at threescore years
and ten! How beautiful seem the great men in their simplicity!—*Alexander Raleigh,
in " The Little Sanctuary,"* 1872.

Verse 21.—" *Thou hast rebuked the proud that are cursed.*" If the proud escape
here, as sometimes they do, hereafter they shall not ; for, " *the proud man is an
abomination to the Lord ;*" Prov. xvi. 5. *God cannot endure him ;* Ps. ci. 5. And
what of that ? *Tu perdes superbos,* Thou shalt destroy the proud. The very heathens
devised the proud giants struck with thunder from heaven. And *if God spared not
the angels,* whom he placed in the highest heavens, *but* for their pride *threw them down
headlong to the nethermost hell,* how much less shall he spare the proud dust and ashes
of the sons of men, but shall cast them from the height of their earthly altitude to
the bottom of that infernal dungeon! " Humility makes men angels ; pride makes
angels devils ;" as that father said : I may well add, makes devils of men. Αλαζονείας
ούτις εκφεύγει δικήν, says the heathen poet, Menander ; " Never soul escaped the
revenge of pride," never shall escape it. So sure as God is just, pride shall not go
unpunished. I know now we are all ready to call for a bason, with Pilate, and to
wash our hands from this foul sin. Honourable and beloved, this vice is a close
one ; it will cleave fast to you ; yea, so close that ye can hardly discern it from a
piece of yourselves : this is it that aggravates the danger of it. For, as Aquinas
notes well, some sins are more dangerous, *propter vehementiam impugnationis,* " for
the fury of their assault ;" as the sin of anger : others for their correspondence
to nature ; as the sins of lust : other, *propter latentiam sui,* " for their close skulking "
in our bosom ; as the sin of pride. Oh, let us look seriously into the corners of our
false hearts, even with the lanthorn of God's law, and find out this subtle devil ;
and never give peace to our souls till we have dispossessed him. Down with your
proud plumes, O ye glorious peacocks of the world : look upon your black legs, and
your snake-like head : be ashamed of your miserable infirmities : else, God will
down with them and yourselves in a fearful vengeance. There is not the holiest of
us but is this way faulty : oh, let us be humbled by our repentance, that we may not
be brought down to everlasting confusion : let us be cast down upon our knees,
that we may not be cast down upon our faces. For God will make good his own
word, one way ; " A man's pride shall bring him low."—*Joseph Hall,* 1574—1656.

Verse 21.—" *Thou hast rebuked the proud.*" Let the histories of Cain, Pharaoh,
Haman, Nebuchadnezzar, and Herod, exhibit the proud under the rebuke and curse
of God. He abhors their persons and their offerings : he "knows them afar off :"
he "resisteth them :" he scattereth them in the imaginations of their hearts."
Yet more especially hateful are they in his sight, when cloaking themselves under a
spiritual garb,—" which say, Stand by thyself, come not near to me : for I am holier
than thou. These are a smoke in my nose, a fire that burneth all the day." David
and Hezekiah are instructive beacons in the church, that God's people, whenever
they give place to the workings of a proud heart, must not hope to escape his rebuke.
" Thou wast a God that forgavest them, though thou tookest vengeance on their
inventions :" Ps. xcix. 8.—*Charles Bridges.*

Verse 21.—" *Thou hast rebuked the proud.*" David addeth another reason whereby
he is more enflamed to pray unto God and to address himself unto him to be taught
in his word ; to wit, when he seeth that he hath so " *rebuked the proud.*" For the
chastisements and punishments which God layeth upon the faithless and rebellious
should be a good instruction for us ; as it is said that God hath executed judgment,
and that the inhabitants of the land should learn his righteousness. It is not without
cause that the prophet Isaiah also hath so said ; for he signifieth unto us that God
hath by divers and sundry means drawn us unto him, and that chiefly when he
teacheth us to fear his majesty. For without it, alas, we shall soon become like
unto brute beasts : if God lay the bridle on our necks, what license we will give
unto ourselves experience very well teacheth us. Now God seeing that we are so
easily brought to run at random, sendeth us examples, because he would bring us to
walk in fear and carefully.—*John Calvin.*

Verse 21.—" *The proud.*" This is a style commonly given to the wicked ; because
as it is our oldest evil, so is it the strongest and first that strives in our corrupt nature
to carry men to transgress the bounds appointed by the Lord. From the time that
pride entered into Adam's heart, that he would be higher than God had made him,

he spared not to eat of the forbidden tree.   And what else is the cause of all trans-gression, but that man's ignorant pride will have his will preferred to the will of God.—*William Cowper.*

Verse 21.—" *The proud.*"   Peter speaks of the proud, as if they did challenge God like champions, and provoke him like rebels, so that unless he did resist them, they would go about to deprive him of his rule, as Korah, Dathan, and Abiram under-mined Moses.   *Num.* xvi.

For so the proud man saith, I will be like the highest, Isa. xiv., and, if he could, above the highest too.   This is the creature that was taken out of the dust, Gen. ii. 7, and so soon as he was made, he opposed himself against that majesty which the angels adore, the thrones worship, the devils fear, and the heavens obey.   How many sins are in this sinful world ! and yet, as Solomon saith of the good wife, Prov. xxxi. 29, " Many daughters have done virtuously, but thou surmountest them all ; " so may I say of pride, many sins have done wickedly, but thou surmountest them all ; for the wrathful man, the prodigal man, the lascivious man, the surfeiting man, the slothful man, is rather an enemy to himself than to God ; but the proud man sets himself against God, because he doth against his laws ; he maketh himself equal with God, because he doth all without God, and craves no help of him ; he exalteth himself above God, because he will have his own will though it be contrary to God's will. As the humble man saith, Not unto us, Lord, not unto us, but to thy name give the glory, Ps. cxv. i. ; so the proud man saith, Not unto Him, not unto Him, but unto us give the glory.   Like unto Herod which took the name of God, and was honoured of all but the worms, and they showed that he was not a god, but a man, Acts xii. 21.   Therefore proud men may be called God's enemies, because as the covetous pull riches from men, so the proud pull honour from God.   Beside, the proud man hath no cause to be proud, as other sinners have ; the covetous for riches, the ambitious for honour, the voluptuous for pleasure, the envious for wrong, the slothful for ease ; but the proud man hath no cause to be proud, but pride itself, which saith, like Pharaoh, " I will not obey," Exod. v. 2.—*Henry Smith,* 1560—1591.

Verse 21.—" *Proud that are cursed.*"—Proud men endure the curse of never having friends ; not in prosperity, because they know nobody ; not in adversity, because then nobody knows them.—*John Whitecross, in " Anecdotes illustrative of the Old Testament."*

Verse 21.—This use of God's judgments upon others must we make to ourselves ; first, that we may be brought to acknowledge our deserts, and so may fear ; and, next, that we may so behold his justice upon the proud that we may have assurance of his mercy to the humble.   This is hard to flesh and blood ; for some can be brought to rejoice at the destructon of others, and cannot fear ; and others, when they are made to fear, cannot receive comfort.   But those which God hath joined together let us not separate : therefore let us make these uses of God's judgments.—*Richard Greenham.*

Verse 22.—" *Remove from me reproach and contempt.*"   Here David prays against the reproach and contempt of men ; that they might be *removed,* or, as the word is, *rolled from off him.*   This intimates that they lay upon him, and neither his greatness nor his goodness could secure him from being libelled and lampooned : some despise him and endeavoured to make him mean, others reproached him and endeavoured to make him odious.   It has often been the lot of those that do well to be ill spoken of.   It intimates, that this burden lay heavy upon him.   Hard words indeed and foul words break no bones, and yet they are very grievous to a tender and ingenuous spirit : therefore David prays, Lord, " *remove* " them from me, that I may not be thereby either driven from any duty, or discouraged in it.—*Matthew Henry.*

Verse 22.—" *Remove from me reproach and contempt,*" etc.   In the words (as in most of the other verses) you have,—1. A request : " *Remove from me reproach and contempt.*" 2. A reason and argument to enforce the request : " *For I have kept thy testimonies.*"

First, for the request, " *Remove from me reproach and contempt ;* " the word signifies, Roll from upon me, let it not come at me, or let it not stay with me.   And then the argument : " *for I have kept thy testimonies.*"   The reason may be either thus : (1) He pleads that he was innocent of what was charged upon him, and had not deserved those aspersions.   (2) He intimates that it was for his obedience, for this very cause, that he had kept the word, therefore was reproach rolled upon him.   (3) It may be conceived thus, that his respect to God's word was not abated by this reproach, he still kept God's testimonies, how wicked soever he did appear in the eyes of the world. It is either an assertion of his innocency, or he shows the ground why this reproach came upon him, or he pleads that his respect to God and his service was not lessened, whatever reproach he met with in the performance of it. The points from hence are many. 1. It is no strange thing that they which keep God's testimonies should be slandered and reproached. 2. As it is the usual lot of God's people to be reproached ; so it is very grievous to them, and heavy to bear. 3. It being grievous, we may lawfully seek the removal of it. So doth David, and so may we, with submission to God's will. 4. In removal of it, it is best to deal with God about it ; for God is the great witness of our sincerity, as knowing all things, and so to be appealed to in the case. Again, God is the most powerful asserter of our innocency ; he hath the hearts and tongues of men in his own hands, and can either prevent the slanderer from uttering reproach, or the hearer from the entertainment of the reproach. He that hath such power over the consciences of men can clear up our innocency ; therefore it is best to deal with God about it ; and prayer many times proves a better vindication than an apology. 5. In seeking relief with God from this evil, it is a great comfort and ground of confidence when we are innocent of what is charged. In some cases we must humble ourselves, and then God will take care for our credit ; we must plead guilty when, by our own fault, we have given occasion to the slanders of the wicked : so, " Turn away my reproach which I fear ; for thy judgments are good " (Ps. cxix. 39). " My reproach," for it was in part deserved by himself, and therefore he feared the sad consequences of it, and humbled himself before God. But at other times we may stand upon our integrity, as David saith here : " *Turn away my reproach which I fear : for thy judgments are good.*"—*Thomas Manton.*

Verse 23.—" *Princes also did sit,*" under the shadow of justice, "*and speak against me.*" Now this was a great temptation to David, that he was not only mocked and scorned at the taverns and inns, being there blazoned by dissolute jesters and scoffers, and talked of in the streets and market-place ; but even in the place of justice (which ought to be holy) ; it could not therefore be chosen but that they also would utterly defame and slander him, and condemn him to be, as it were, a most wicked and cursed man. When David then did see that he was thus unjustly entreated and handled, he maketh his complaint unto God and sayeth, " O Lord, the princes and governors themselves do sit and speak evil against me ; *and yet for all that I have kept thy testimonies.*" Here in sum we are to gather out of this place, that if it so fall out, when we have walked uprightly and in a good conscience, that we are falsely slandered, and accused of this and that whereof we never once thought ; yet ought we to bear all things patiently ; for let us be sure of that, that we are not better than David, whatever great protestation of our integrity and purity we may dare to make. —*John Calvin.*

Verse 23.—" *But thy servant did meditate in thy statutes.*" As husbandmen, when their ground is overflowed by waters, make ditches and water-furrows to carry it away ; so, when our minds and thoughts are overwhelmed with trouble, it is good to divert them to some other matter. But every diversion will not become saints, it must be a holy diversion : " In the multitude of my thoughts within me thy comforts delight my soul " (Psalm xciv. 19). The case was the same with that of the text, when the throne of iniquity frameth mischief by a law ; as you shall see here, when he had many perplexed thoughts about the abuse of power against himself. But now where lay his ease in diversion ? Would every diversion suit his purpose ? No ; " *Thy* comforts,"—comforts of God's allowance, of God's providing, comforts proper to saints. Wicked men in trouble run to their pot and pipe, and games and sports, and merry company, and so defeat the providence rather than improve it : but David, who was God's servant, must have God's comforts. So, elsewhere, when his thoughts were troubled about the power of the wicked : " I went into the sanctuary of God ; then understood I their end " (Psalm lxxiii. 17). He goeth to divert his mind by the use of God's ordinances, and so cometh to be settled against the temptation.—*Thomas Manton.*

Verse 23.—" *But thy servant did meditate in thy statutes.*"—Perceive here the armour by which David fights against his enemy. *Arma justi quibus omnes adversariorum repellit impetus,* his weapons are the word and prayer. He renders not injury for injury, reproach for reproach. It is dangerous to fight against Satan or his instruments with their own weapons ; for so they shall easily overcome us. Let us fight with the armour of God—the exercises of the word and prayer : for a man may peaceably rest in his secret chamber, and in these two see the miserable end of all those who are enemies to God's children for God's sake.—*William Cowper.*

Verse 23.—*" Thy statutes."* It is impossible to live either *Christianly* or *comfortable* without the daily use of Scripture. It is absolutely necessary for our direction in all our ways before we begin them, and when we have ended them, for the warrant of our approbation of them, for resolving of our doubts, and comforting us in our griefs. Without it our conscience is a blind guide, and leadeth us in a mist of ignorance, error, and confusion. Therein we hear God speaking to us, declaring his good will to us concerning our salvation, and the way of our obedience to meet him in his good will. What book can we read with such profit and comfort ? For matter, it is wisdom : for authority, it is divine and absolute : for majesty, God himself under common words and letters expressing an unspeakable power to stamp our heart. Where shall we find our minds so enlightened, our hearts so deeply affected, our conscience so moved, both for casting us down and raising us up ? I cannot find in all the books of the world, such an one speak to me, as in Scripture, with so absolute a conquest of all the powers of my soul.

Contemners of Scripture lack food for their souls, light for their life, and weapons for their spiritual warfare ; but the lovers of Scripture have all that furniture. Therein we hear the voice of our Beloved, we smell the savour of his ointments, and have daily access unto the art of propitiation. If in our knowledge we desire divinity, excellency, antiquity, and efficiency, we cannot find it, but in God's word alone. It is the extract of heavenly wisdom, which Christ the eternal Word brought out of the bosom of his Father.—*William Struther,* 1633.

Verses 23, 24.—The two last verses of this section contain two protestations of David's honest affection to the word. The first is, that albeit he was persecuted and evil spoken of, and that by great and honourable men of the world, such as Saul, and Abner, and Ahithophel ; yet did he still meditate in the statutes of God. It is a hard temptation when the godly are troubled by any wicked men ; but much harder when they are troubled by men of honour and authority. And that, first, by reason of their *place :* the greater *power* they have, the greater *peril* is to encounter with their displeasure ; therefore said Solomon, " The wrath of a king is as messengers of death." Next, because authorities and powers are ordained by God, not for the terror of the good, but of the evil : Rom. xiii. 3. And therefore it is no small grief to the godly, when they find them abused to a contrary end : that where a ruler should be to good men like rain to the fields new mown, he becomes a favourer of evil men and a persecutor of the good. Then justice is turned into wormwood ; that which should bring comfort to such as fear God, is abused to oppress them. And therefore it should be accounted a great benefit of God, when he gives a people good and religious rulers.—*William Cowper.*

Verses 23, 51.—If the 119th Psalm came from the pen of David, as multitudes believe, then I do not wonder that many have connected its composition with his residence in the school of the prophets of Naioth. The calm in which he then found himself, and the studies which he then prosecuted, might well have led his musings in the direction of that alphabetic code, while there are in it not a few expressions which, to say the least, may have particular reference to the dangers out of which he had so recently escaped, and by which he was still threatened. Such, for example, are the following : *"Princes also did sit and speak against me : but thy servant did meditate in thy statutes." " The proud have had me greatly in derision : yet have I not declined from thy law."*—*William M. Taylor, in " David King of Israel ; his Life and its Lessons."* 1880.

Verse 24.—*Thy testimonies also are my delight and my counsellors."* His delight and his counsellors, that is, his delight *because* his counsellors ; his counsellors, and therefore his delight. We know how delightful it is to any to have the advantage of good counsel, according to the perplexities and distractions in which they may be. " Ointment and perfume rejoice the heart : so doth the sweetness of a man's friend by hearty counsel," says Solomon, Prov. xxvii. 9. Now this is the sweetness of Divine communion, and of meditation on God and his word ; it employs a man with *seasonable counsel,* which is a very great refreshment to us.—*T. Horton,* 1673.

Verse 24.—*" Thy testimonies also are my delight,"* etc. Those that would have God's testimonies to be their delight, must take them for their counsellors and be advised by them ; and let those that take them for their counsellors in close walking, take them for their delight in comfortable walking.—*Matthew Henry.*

Verse 24.—" *Thy testimonies also are my delight and my counsellors.*" What could we want more in a time of difficulty than comfort and direction ? David hath both these blessings. As the fruit of his " meditation in the Lord's statutes," in his distress they were his " *delight ;* " in his seasons of perplexity they were his " *counsellors,*" directing his behaviour in the perfect way.—*Charles Bridges.*

Verse 24.—" *My counsellors.*" In the Hebrew it is, " the men of my counsel," which is fitly mentioned, for he had spoken of princes sitting in council against him. Princes do nothing without the advice of their Privy-Council ; a child of God hath also his Privy-Council, God's testimonies. On the one side there was Saul and his nobles and counsellors ; on the other side there was David and God's testimonies. Now who was better furnished, think you, they to persecute and trouble him, or David how to carry himself under this trouble ? Alphonsus, king of Arragon, being asked who were the best counsellors ? answered, " The dead (meaning books), which cannot flatter, but do without partiality declare the truth." How of all such dead counsellors, God's testimonies have the pre-eminence. A poor, godly man, even then when he is deserted of all, and hath nobody to plead for him, he hath his senate and his council of state about him, the prophets and apostles, and " other holy men of God, that spake as they were moved by the Holy Ghost." A man so furnished, is never less alone than when alone ; for he hath counsellors about him that tell him what is to be believd or done ; and they are such counsellors as cannot err, as will not flatter him, nor applaud him in any sin, nor discourage or dissuade him from that which is good, whatever hazard it expose him to. And truly, if we be wise, we should choose such counsellors as these : " *Thy testimonies are the men of my counsel.*"—*Thomas Manton.*

Verse 24.—" *My counsellors.*" See here a sentence worthy to be weighed of us, when David calleth the commandments of God his " *counsellors.*" For, in the first place, he meaneth that he might scorn all the wisdom of the most able and most expert men in the world, since he was conducted by the word of God, and governed thereby. In the second place, he meaneth that when he shall be so governed by the word of God, he would not only be truly wise, but that it would be as if he had all the wisdom of all the men in the world, yea, and a great deal more.—*John Calvin.*

EXPOSITION OF VERSES 25 TO 32.

MY soul cleaveth unto the dust : quicken thou me according to thy word.
26 I have declared my ways, and thou heardest me : teach me thy statutes.

27 Make me to understand the way of thy precepts : so shall I talk of thy wondrous works.

28 My soul melteth for heaviness : strengthen thou me according unto thy word.

29 Remove from me the way of lying : and grant me thy law graciously.

30 I have chosen the way of truth : thy judgments have I laid before me.

31 I have stuck unto thy testimonies : O LORD, put me not to shame.

32 I will run the way of thy commandments, when thou shalt enlarge my heart.

Here, it seems to me, we have the Psalmist in trouble bewailing the bondage to earthly things in which he finds his mind to be held. His soul cleaves to the dust, melts for heaviness, and cries for enlargement from its spiritual prison. In these verses we shall see the influence of the divine word upon a heart which laments its downward tendencies, and is filled with mourning because of its deadening surroundings. The word of the Lord evidently arouses prayer (25—29), confirms choice (30), and inspires renewed resolve (32) : it is in all tribulation whether of body or mind the surest source of help.

This portion has D for its alphabetical letter : it sings of Depression, in the spirit of Devotion, Determination, and Dependence.

25. " *My soul cleaveth unto the dust.*" He means in part that he was full of sorrow ; for mourners in the east cast dust on their heads, and sat in ashes, and the Psalmist felt as if these ensigns of woe were glued to him, and his very soul was made to cleave to them because of his powerlessness to rise above his grief. Does he not also mean that he felt ready to die ? Did he not feel his life absorbed and fast held by the grave's mould, half choked by the death-dust ? It may not be straining the language if we conceive that he also felt and bemoaned his earthly-mindedness and spiritual deadness. There was a tendency in his soul to cling to earth which he greatly bewailed. Whatever was the cause of his complaint, it was no surface evil, but an affair of his inmost spirit ; his *soul* cleaved to the dust ; and it was not a casual and accidental falling into the dust, but a continuous and powerful tendency, or *cleaving* to the earth. But what a mercy that the good man could feel and deplore whatever there was of evil in the cleaving ! The serpent's seed can find their meat in the dust, but never shall the seed of the woman be thus degraded. Many are of the earth earthy, and never lament it ; only the heaven-born and heaven-soaring spirit pines at the thought of being fastened to this world, and bird-limed by its sorrows or its pleasures.

" *Quicken thou me according to thy word.*" More life is the cure for all our ailments. Only the Lord can give it. He can bestow it, bestow it at once, and do it according to his word, without departing from the usual course of his grace, as we see it mapped out in the Scriptures. It is well to know what to pray for,—David seeks quickening : one would have thought that he would have asked for comfort or upraising, but he knew that these would come out of increased life, and therefore he sought that blessing which is the root of the rest. When a person is depressed in spirit, weak, and bent towards the ground, the main thing is to increase his stamina and put more life into him ; then his spirit revives, and his body becomes erect. In reviving the life, the whole man is renewed. Shaking off the dust is a little thing by itself, but when it follows upon quickening, it is a blessing of the greatest value ; just as good spirits which flow from established health are among the choicest of our mercies. The phrase, " according to thy word," means.—according to thy revealed way of quickening thy saints. The word of God shows us that he who first made us must keep us alive, and it tells us of the Spirit of God who through the ordinances pours fresh life into our souls ; we beg the Lord to act towards us in this his own regular method of grace. Perhaps David remembered the word of the Lord in Deut. xxxii. 39, where Jehovah claims both to kill and to make alive, and he beseeches the Lord to exercise that life-giving power upon his almost expiring servant. Certainly, the man of God had not so many rich promises to rest upon as we have, but even a single word was enough for him, and he right earnestly urges " according to thy word." It is a grand thing to see a believer in the dust and yet pleading the promise, a man at the grave's mouth crying, " quicken me," and hoping that it shall be done.

Note how his first verse of the 4th octonary tallies with the first of the third (17). —" That I may live : " . . . " Quicken me." While in a happy state he begs for bountiful dealing, and when in a forlorn condition he prays for quickening. Life is in both cases the object of pursuit : that he may have life, and have it more abundantly.

26. " *I have declared my ways.*" Open confession is good for the soul. Nothing brings more ease and more life to a man than a frank acknowledgment of the evil which has caused the sorrow and the lethargy. Such a declaration proves that the man knows his own condition, and is no longer blinded by pride. Our confessions are not meant to make God know our sins, but to make us know them. " *And thou heardest me.*" His confession had been accepted ; it was not lost labour ; God had drawn near to him in it. We ought never to go from a duty till we have been accepted in it. Pardon follows upon penitent confession, and David felt that he had obtained it. It is God's way to forgive our sinful way when we from our hearts confess the wrong.

" *Teach me thy statutes.*" Being truly sorry for his fault, and having obtained full forgiveness, he is anxious to avoid offending again, and hence he begs to be taught obedience. He was not willing to sin through ignorance, he wished to know all the mind of God by being taught it by the best of teachers. He pined after holiness. Justified men always long to be sanctified. When God forgives our sins we are all the more fearful of sinning again. Mercy, which pardons transgression, sets us longing for grace which prevents transgression. We may boldly ask for more when God has given us much ; he who has washed out the past stain will not refuse that which will preserve us from present and future defilement. This cry for teaching is frequent in the Psalm ; in verse 12 it followed a sight of God, here follows from a sight of self. Every experience should lead us thus to plead it with God.

27. " *Make me to understand the way of thy precepts.*" Give me a deep insight into the practical meaning of thy word ; let me get a clear idea of the tone and tenor of thy law. Blind obedience has but small beauty ; God would have us follow him with our eyes open. To obey the letter of the word is all that the ignorant can hope for ; if we wish to keep God's precepts in their spirit we must come to an understanding of them, and that can be gained nowhere but at the Lord's hands. Our understanding needs enlightenment and direction : he who made our understanding must also make us understand. The last sentence was, " teach me thy statutes," and the words, " make me to understand," are an instructive enlargement and exposition of that sentence : we need to be so taught that we understand what we learn. It is to be noted that the Psalmist is not anxious to understand the prophecies, but the precepts, and he is not concerned about the subtleties of the law, but the commonplaces and everyday rules of it, which are described as " the way of thy precepts."

" *So shall I talk of thy wondrous works.*" It is ill talking of what we do not understand. We must be taught of God till we understand, and then we may hope to communicate our knowledge to others with a hope of profiting them. Talk without intelligence is mere talk, and idle talk ; but the words of the instructed are as pearls which adorn the ears of them that hear. When our heart has been opened to understand, our lips should be opened to impart knowledge ; and we may hope to be taught ourselves when we feel in our hearts a willingness to teach the way of the Lord to those among whom we dwell.

" *Thy wondrous works.*" Remark that the clearest understanding does not cause us to cease from wondering at the ways and works of God. The fact is that the more we know of God's doings the more we admire them, and the more ready we are to speak upon them. Half the wonder in the world is born of ignorance, but holy wonder is the child of understanding. When a man understands the way of the divine precepts he never talks of his own works, and as the tongue must have some theme to speak upon, he begins to extol the works of the all-perfect Lord.

Some in this place read " meditate " or " muse " instead of " talk ; " it is singular that the words should be so near of kin, and yet it is right that they should be, for none but foolish people will talk without thinking. If we read the passage in this sense, we take it to mean that in proportion as David understood the word of God he would meditate upon it more and more. It is usually so ; the thoughtless care not to know the inner meaning of the Scriptures, while those who know them best are the very men who strive after a greater familiarity with them, and therefore give themselves up to musing upon them.

Observe the third verse of the last eight (19), and see how the sense is akin to this. There he was a stranger in the earth, and here he prays to know his way ; there, too, he prayed that the word might not be hid from himself, and here he promises that he will not hide it from others.

28. " *My soul melteth for heaviness.*" He was dissolving away in tears. The solid strength of his constitution was turning to liquid as if molten by the furnace-heat of his afflictions. Heaviness of heart is a killing thing, and when it abounds it threatens to turn life into a long death, in which a man seems to drop away in a perpetual drip of grief. Tears are the distillation of the heart ; when a man weeps he wastes away his soul. Some of us know what great heaviness means, for we have been brought under its power again and again, and often have we felt ourselves to be poured out like water, and near to being like water spilt upon the ground, never again to be gathered up. There is one good point in this downcast state, for it is better to be melted with grief than to be hardened by impenitence.

" *Strengthen thou me according unto thy word.*" He had found out an ancient promise that the saints shall be strengthened, and here he pleads it. His hope in his state of depression lies not in himself, but in his God ; if he may be strengthened from on high he will yet shake off his heaviness and rise to joy again. Observe how he pleads the promise of the word, and asks for nothing more than to be dealt with after the recorded manner of the Lord of mercy. Had not Hannah sung, " He shall give strength unto his King, and exalt the horn of his anointed ? " God strengthens us by infusing grace through his word : the word which creates can certainly sustain. Grace can enable us to bear the constant fret of an abiding sorrow, it can repair the decay caused by the perpetual tear-drip, and give to the believer the garment of praise for the spirit of heaviness. Let us always resort to prayer in our desponding times, for it is the surest and shortest way out of the depths. In that prayer let us plead nothing but the word of God ; for there is no plea like a promise, no argument like a word from our covenant God.

Note how David records his inner soul-life. In verse 20 he says, " My soul breaketh ; " in verse 25, " My soul cleaveth to the dust ; " and here, " My soul melteth." Further on, in verse 81, he cries, " My soul fainteth ; " in 109, " My soul is continually in my hand ; " in 167, " My soul hath kept thy testimonies ; " and lastly, in 175, " Let my soul live." Some people do not even know that they have a soul, and here is David all soul. What a difference there is between the spiritually living and the spiritually dead.

29. " *Remove from me the way of lying.*" This is the way of sin, error, idolatry, folly, self-righteousness, formalism, hypocrisy. David would not only be kept from that way, but have it kept from him ; he cannot endure to have it near him, he would have it swept away from his sight. He desired to be right and upright, true and in the truth ; but he feared that a measure of falsehood would cling to him unless the Lord took it away, and therefore he earnestly cried for its removal. False motives may at times sway us, and we may fall into mistaken notions of our own spiritual condition before God, which erroneous conceits may be kept up by a natural prejudice in our own favour, and so we may be confirmed in a delusion, and abide under error unless grace comes to the rescue. No true heart can rest in a false view of itself ; it finds no anchorage, but is tossed to and fro till it gets into the truth and the truth into it. The true-born child of heaven sighs out and cries against a lie, desiring to have it taken away as much as a man desires to be set at a distance from a venomous serpent or a raging lion.

" *And grant me thy law graciously.*" He is in a gracious state who looks upon the law itself as a gift of grace. David wishes to have the law opened up to his understanding, engraved upon his heart, and carried out in his life ; for this he seeks the Lord, and pleads for it as a gracious grant. No doubt he viewed this as the only mode of deliverance from the power of falsehood : if the law be not in our hearts the lie will enter. David would seem to have remembered those times when, according to the eastern fashion, he had practised deceit for his own preservation, and he saw that he had been weak and erring on that point ; therefore he was bowed down in spirit and begged to be quickened and delivered from transgressing in that manner any more. Holy men cannot review their sins without tears, nor weep over them without entreating to be saved from further offending.

There is an evident opposition between falsehood and the gracious power of God's law. The only way to expel the lie is to accept the truth. Grace also has a clear affinity to truth : no sooner do we meet with the sound of the word " graciously " than we hear the footfall of truth : " I have chosen the way of truth." Grace and truth are ever linked together, and a belief of the doctrines of grace is a grand preservative from deadly error.

In the fifth of the preceding octave (21) David cries out against pride, and here against lying—these are much the same thing. Is not pride the greatest of all lies ?

30. " *I have chosen the way of truth.*" As he abhorred the way of lying, so he chose the way of truth : a man must choose one or the other, for there cannot be any neutrality in the case. Men do not drop into the right way by chance ; they must choose it, and continue to choose it, or they will soon wander from it. Those whom God has chosen in due time choose his way. There is a doctrinal way of truth which we ought to choose, rejecting every dogma of man's devising ; there is a ceremonial way of truth which we should follow, detesting all the forms which apostate churches have invented ; and then there is a practical way of truth, the way of holiness, to which we must adhere whatever may be our temptation to forsake it. Let our election be made, and made irrevocably. Let us answer to all seducers, " I have chosen, and what I have chosen I have chosen." O Lord, by thy grace lead us with a hearty free-will to choose to do thy will ; thus shall thine eternal choice of us bring forth the end which it designs.

" *Thy judgments have I laid before me.*" What he had chosen he kept in mind, laying it out before his mind's eye. Men do not become holy by a careless wish : there must be study, consideration, deliberation, and earnest enquiry, or the way of truth will be missed. The commands of God must be set before us as the mark to aim at, the model to work by, the road to walk in. If we put God's judgments into the background we shall soon find ourselves departing from them.

Here again the sixth stanzas of the third and fourth octaves ring out a similar note. " I have kept thy testimonies " (22), and " Thy judgments have I laid before me." This is a happy confession, and there is no wonder that is is repeated.

31. " *I have stuck unto thy testimonies,*"—or I have cleaved, for the word is the same as in verse 25. Though cleaving to the dust of sorrow and of death, yet he kept fast hold of the divine word. This was his comfort, and his faith stuck to it, his love and his obedience held on to it, his heart and his mind abode in meditation upon it. His choice was so heartily and deliberately made that he stuck to it for life, and could not be removed from it by the reproaches of those who despised the way of the Lord. What could he have gained by quitting the sacred testimony ? Say rather, what would he not have lost if he had ceased to cleave to the divine word ? It is pleasant to look back upon past perseverance and to expect grace to continue equally steadfast in the future. He who has enabled us to stick to him will surely stick to us.

" *O Lord, put me not to shame.*" This would happen if God's promises were unfulfilled, and if the heart of God's servant were suffered to fail. This we have no reason to fear, since the Lord is faithful to his word. But it might also happen through the believer's acting in an inconsistent manner, as David had himself once done, when he fell into the way of lying, and pretended to be a madman. If we are not true to our profession we may be left to reap the fruit of our folly, and that will be the bitter thing called " shame." It is evident from this that a believer ought never to be ashamed, but act the part of a brave man who has done nothing to be ashamed of in believing his God, and does not mean to adopt a craven tone in the presence of the Lord's enemies. If we beseech the Lord not to put us to shame, surely we ought not ourselves to be ashamed without cause.

The prayer of this verse is found in the parallel verse of the next section (39) : " Turn away my reproach which I fear." It is evidently a petition which was often on the Psalmist's heart. A brave heart is more wounded by shame than by any weapon which a soldier's hand can wield.

32. " *I will run the way of thy commandments.*" With energy, promptitude, and zeal he would perform the will of God, but he needed more life and liberty from the

hand of God. *"When thou shalt enlarge my heart."* Yes, the heart is the master ; the feet soon run when the heart is free and energetic. Let the affections be aroused and eagerly set on divine things, and our actions will be full of force, swiftness, and delight. God must work in us first, and then we shall will and do according to his good pleasure. He must change the heart, unite the heart, encourage the heart, strengthen the heart, and enlarge the heart, and then the course of the life will be gracious, sincere, happy, and earnest ; so that from our lowest up to our highest state in grace we must attribute all to the free favour of our God. We must run ; for grace is not an overwhelming force which compels unwilling minds to move contrary to their will : our running is the spontaneous leaping forward of a mind which has been set free by the hand of God, and delights to show its freedom by its bounding speed.

What a change from verse 25 to the present, from cleaving to the dust to running in the way. It is the excellence of holy sorrow that it works in us the quickening for which we seek, and then we show the sincerity of our grief and the reality of our revival by being zealous in the ways of the Lord.

For the third time an octave closes with, " I will." These " I wills " of the Psalms are right worthy of being each one the subject of study and discourse.

Note how the heart has been spoken of up to this point : " whole heart " (2), " uprightness of heart " (7), " hid in mine heart " (11), " enlarge my heart." There are many more allusions further on, and these all go to show what heart-work David's religion was. It is one of the great lacks of our age that heads count for more than hearts, and men are far more ready to learn than to love, though they are by no means eager in either direction.

NOTES ON VERSES 25 TO 32.

The eight verses alphabetically arranged :—

25. **Depressed** to the dust is my soul : quicken thou me according to thy word.
26. **Declared** have I (to thee) my ways, and thou heardest me : teach me thy statutes.
27. **Declare** thou to me the way of thy precepts : so shall I talk of thy wondrous works.
28. **Dropping** (*marg.*) is my soul for heaviness : strengthen thou me according unto thy word.
29. **Deceitful** ways remove from me ; and grant me thy law graciously.
30. **Determined** have I upon the way of truth ; thy judgments have I laid before me.
31. **Deliberately** I have stuck unto thy testimonies : O Lord, put me not to shame.
32. **Day** by day I will run the way of thy commandments, when thou shalt enlarge my heart.

Theodore Kübler.

Verse 25.—" *My soul cleaveth unto the dust."* The Hebrew word for " cleaveth " signifies " *is joined,"* " *has adhered,"* " *has overtaken,"* " *has taken hold,"* "*has joined itself."* Our soul is a polypus : as the polypus readily adheres to the rocks, so does the soul cleave to the earth ; and hardly can it be torn from the place to which it has once strongly attached itself. Though thy soul be now more perfect, and escaping from the waters of sin has become a bird of heaven, be not careless ; earthly things are birdlime and glue ; if thou rubbest thy wings against these thou wilt be held, and joined to the earth.—*Thomas Le Blanc.*

Verse 25.—" *My soul cleaveth unto the dust,"* etc. The word rendered " cleaveth " means to be glued to ; to stick fast. It has the sense of adhering firmly to anything, so that it cannot easily be separated from it. The word " *dust "* here may mean either the earth, and earthly things, considered as low, base, unworthy, worldly ; or it may mean the grave, as if he were near to that, and in danger of dying. De Wette understands it in the latter sense. Yet the word *cleave* would hardly suggest this idea ; and the force of that word would be better represented by the idea that his soul, as it were, *adhered* to the things of earth ; that it seemed to be so fastened to them—*so glued* to them that it could not be detached from them ; that his affections were low, earthly, grovelling, so as to give him deep distress, and lead him to cry to God for life and strength that he might break away from them.—*Albert Barnes.*

Verse 25.—" *My soul cleaveth unto the dust,"* etc. The first clause seems intended to suggest two consistent but distinct ideas, that of deep degradation, as in Ps. xliv. 25, and that of death, as in Ps. xxii. 29. The first would be more obvious in itself, and in connection with the parallel referred to ; but the other seems to be indicated as the prominent idea by the correlative petition for quickening in the last clause. " *Quicken,"* i.e., save me alive, or restore me to life, the Hebrew word being a causative of the verb *to live.*—*Joseph Addison Alexander.*

Verse 25.—" *My soul cleaveth to the dust,"* etc. In this verse, David hath a complaint ; " *My soul cleaveth to the dust ; "* and a prayer ; " *Quicken thou me according to thy word."* The prayer, being well considered, shall teach us the meaning of the complaint ; that it was not, as some think, any hard bodily estate which grieved him, but a very sore spiritual oppression (as I may call it), bearing down his soul ; that where he should have mounted up toward heaven, he was pressed down to the earth, and was so clogged with earthly cogitations, or affections, or perturbations, that he could not mount up. His particular temptation he expresseth not : for the children of God many times are in that estate that they cannot tell their own griefs ; and sometimes so troubled ; that it is not expedient, albeit they might, to express them to others.

And hereof we learn, how that which the worldling counts wisdom, to the Christian is folly ; what is joy to the one, is grief to the other. The joy of a worldling is to cleave unto the earth ; when he gripes it surest, he thinks himself happiest, for it is his portion : to take heed to his worldly affairs, and have his mind upon them (in his estimation) is only wisdom. For the serpent's curse is upon him, he creeps on the earth, and licks the dust all the days of his life. This is the miserable condition of the wicked, that even their heavenly soul is become earthly. *Qui secundum corporis appetentiam vivit caro est, etiam anima eorum caro est ;* as the Lord spake of those who perished in the Deluge, that they were but flesh, no spirit in them ; that is, no spiritual or heavenly motion.

But the Christian, considering that his soul is from above, sets his affection also on those things which are above : he delights to have his conversation in heaven and it is a grief to him when he finds his motions and affections drawn down and entangled with the earth. His life is to cleave to the Lord ; but it is death to him when the neck of his soul is bowed down to the yoke of the world.—*William Cowper.*

Verse 25.—" *My soul cleaveth to the dust.*" " Look up now to the heavens." So once spake the Lord to Abraham his friend, and he speaketh thus to us also. Alas ! why must it be so always that, when we come to know ourselves even but a little, we are constantly answering with the mournful sigh, " *My soul cleaveth to the dust?*" Ah ! that is indeed the *deepest pain* of a soul which has already tasted that the Lord is merciful, when, although desiring to soar on high, it sadly feels how impossible it is to rise. There is much hidden pain in every heart of man even in the spiritual life ; but what can deeper grieve us than the perception that we are chained as with leaden weights to things concerning which we know that they may weary but cannot satisfy us ? Nay, we could never have supposed, when we first heard the Psalm of the Good Shepherd, that it could issue from a heart that panteth after God, so often and so bitterly ; we could never have imagined that it could become so cold, so dry, so dark within a heart which at an earlier period had tasted so much of the power of that which is to come. Have we not formerly, with this same Psalm, been able to vaunt, " I have rejoiced in the way of thy testimonies, as much as in all riches ? " But afterwards, or now perhaps. . . . Oh sad hours, when the beams of the sun within seem quenched, and nothing but a blood-red disc remains ! The fervency of the first love is cooled ; earthly cares and sins have, as it were, attached a leaden plummet to the wings of a soul which, God knows, would fain soar upwards. We would render thanks, and scarce can pray ; we would pray, and scarce can sigh, Our treasure is in heaven, but our soul cleaves to the earth ; at least earth cleaves on all sides so to it, and weighs it down, that the eye merely sees the clouds, the tongue can but breathe forth complaints. Ah, so completely can the earth fetter us, that the heavens appear to be only a problem, and our old man is like the Giant of Mythology, who, cast to the ground in the exhausting combat, receives by contact with his mother earth fresh strength. Oh, were it otherwise ! Shall it not at last, at last be altered ?

Dost thou really desire it, thou who out of the depths of thy soul so complainest, and canst scarcely find more tears to bewail the sorrow of thy heart ? Well is it for thee if the pain thou sufferest teach thee to cry to God : " Quicken thou me, according to thy word." Yea, this is the *best comfort* for him who too well knows what it is to be bowed together with pain ; this is the only hope for a heart which almost sinks in still despair. There is an *atmosphere* of life, high above this dust, which streams to us from every side, and penetrates even the darkest dungeon. There is a *spring* of life by which the weary soul may be refeshed ; and the entrance to this spring stands open, in spite of all the clouds of dust which obscure this valley of shadows here. There is a *power* of life which can even so completely make an end of our dead state, that we shall walk again before the face of the Lord in the land of the living, and, instead, of uttering lamentation, we shall bear a song of praise upon our lips. Does not the Prince of life yet live in order also to repeat to us, " Awake and rejoice, thou that dwellest in the dust ; " and the Spirit, that bloweth whither he listeth, can, will, shall he not in his own good time, with his living breath, blow from our wings the dust that cleaveth to them ? But, indeed, even the gnawing pain of the soul over so much want of spirituality and dulness is ever an encouraging sign that the good work is begun in our hearts : that which is really dead shivers no more at its own cold. " *My soul cleaveth to the dust,*" sayest thou, with tears ? thus wouldest thou not speak except that already a higher hand between the soul and this dust had cleft a hollow which was unknown to it before. No one has less cause for despair than he who has lost hope in himself, and really learns to seek in God that, which he deeply feels, he least of all can give himself.

Yes, this is the *way* from the deepest pain to procure the best consolation ; the humble, earnest, persevering prayer, that he who lives would also give life to our souls, and continue to increase it, till freed from all dryness and deadness of spirit, and unrooted from the earth, we ascend to the eternal mount of light, where at last we behold all earthly clouds beneath us. This the God of life alone can work ; but he is willing—nay, we have his own word as pledge, that he promises and bestows on us true life. Only, let us not forget that he who will quicken us " *according* " to his word, also performs this *through* his word. Let us then draw from out the eternally-flowing fountain, and henceforth leave it unconditionally to him, how he will listen to our cry, even though he lead us through dark paths! Even through means of death God can quicken us and keep us alive. . . . Lo, we are here; Lord, do with us as seemeth good to thee! Only, let our souls live, that they may praise thee, here and eternally!—*J. J. Van Oosterzee, in "The Year of Salvation,"* 1874.

Verse 25.—*"Cleaveth to the dust."* Is weighed down by the flesh, which itself is dust.—*James G. Murphy.*

Verse 25.—*"The dust"* is the place of the afflicted, the wounded, and the dead. *"Quicken me,"* viz., to life, peace, and joy.—*A. R. Fausset.*

Verse 25.—*"Quicken thou me,"* etc. Seeing he was alive, how prays he that God would quicken him? I answer,—The godly esteem of life, not according to that they have in their body, but in their soul. If the soul lacks the sense of mercy, and a heavenly disposition to spiritual things, they lament over it, as a dead soul: for sure it is, temporal desertions are more heavy to the godly than temporal death. *"According to thy word."* This is a great faith, that where in respect of his present feeling he found himself dead, yet he hopes for life from God, according to his promise. Such was the faith of Abraham, who under hope, believed above hope. And truly, many times are God's children brought to this estate, that they have nothing to uphold them but the word of God; no sense of mercy, no spiritual disposition; but on the contrary, great darkness, horrible fears and terrors. Only they are sustained by looking to the promise of God, and kept in some hope that he will restore them to life again, because it is his praise to finish the work which he begins.—*William Cowper.*

Verse 25.—*"Quicken thou me."* This phrase occurs nine times, and only in this Psalm. It is of great importance, as it expresses the spiritual change by which a child of Adam becomes a child of God. Its source is God; the instrument by which it is effected is the word, verse 50.—*James G. Murphy.*

Verse 25.—*"Quicken thou me according to thy word."* Where there is life there will be the endeavour to rise—the believer will not lie prone in his aspirations after God. From the lowest depths the language of faith is heard ascending to God most high, who performeth all things for the believer. The true child cannot but look towards the loving Father, who is the Almighty, All-sufficient One. Have you not found it so? But will you mark the intelligence that shines around the believer's prayer? He prays that the Lord may quicken him *according to his word.* The *word* may be regarded in the light of the standard after which he is to be fashioned; or the Psalmist may have in view the requirements contained in the word regarding the believer's progress; or he may be thinking of the promises found therein in behalf of the poor and needy when they apply. Indeed, all these significations may be wrapt up in the one expression—*"according to thy word"*—the standard of perfection, the requirements of the word, and the promises concerning it. The great exemplar of the believer is Christ,—of old it was the Christ of prophecy. Then the requirements of the Lord's will were scattered through the word. The Psalmist, however, may be dwelling upon the large promises which the Lord hath given towards the perfecting of his people. You see after what the spiritual nature aspires. It is quite enough to the natural man or the formalist that he be as the generally well-behaved and esteemed among professors—the spiritual man aspires beyond—he aspires after being quickened according to God's word. Judge of yourselves.—*John Stephen.*

Verse 25.—*"Quicken thou me according to thy word."* By thy providence put life into my affairs, by thy grace put life into my affections; cure me of my spiritual deadness, and make me lively in my devotion.—*Matthew Henry.*

Verse 25.—*"Quicken thou me according to thy word."* Albeit the Lord suffer his own to lie so long low in their heavy condition of spirit, that they may seem dead; yet by faith in his word he keepeth in them so much life as doth furnish unto them prayer to God for comfort: *"Quicken thou me according to thy word."*—*David Dickson.*

Verse 25.—*"Quicken thou me."* To whom shall the godly fly when life faileth but to that Well-spring of all life? Even as to remove cold the next way is to draw near the fire, so to dispel any death, the next way is to look to him who is our root, by whom we live this natural life. All preservatives and restoratives are nothing, all colleges of physicians are vanity, if compared with him. Other things which have not life, give life as the instruments of him who is life, as fire burneth being the instrument of heat. *"When heart and flesh fail, God is the strength of my heart."* As a man can let a fire almost go out which had been kindled, and then blow it up, and by application of new fuel make it blaze as much as ever : so can God deal with this flame of life which he hath kindled.—*Paul Bayne.*

Verse 25.—" *According to thy word.*"   The word removes deadness of conscience and hardness.   Is not this word a hammer to soften the heart, and is not this the immortal seed by which we are begotten again ?   Therefore David, finding his conscience in a dead frame, prayeth, " My soul cleaveth to the dust ; quicken thou me according to thy word."   The *word* is the first thing by which conscience is purified and set right.—*John Sheffield, in " A Good Conscience the Strongest Hold,"* 1650.

Verse 25.—" *According to thy word.*"   What word doth David mean ?   Either the general promises in the books of Moses or Job ;   which intimate deliverance to the faithful observers of God's law, or help to the miserable and distressed ;   or some particular promise given to him by Nathan, or others.   Chrysostom saith, " Quicken me according to thy word : but it is not a word of command, but a word of promise." Mark here,—he doth not say *secundum meritum meum,* but, *secundum verbum tuum;* the hope, or that help which we expect from God, is founded upon his word; there is our security, in his promises, not in our deservings: *Promittendo se fecit debitorem, etc.*

When there was so little Scripture written, yet David could find out a word for his support.   Alas ! in our troubles and afflictions, no promise occurreth to mind. As in outward things, many that have less live better than those that have abundance ;   so here, now Scripture is so large, we are less diligent, and therefore, though we have so many promises, we are apt to faint, we have not a word to bear us up. This word did not help David, till he had lain so long under this heavy condition, that he seemed dead.   Many, when they have a promise, think presently to enjoy the comfort of it.   No, waiting and striving are first necessary.   We never relish the comfort of the promises till the creatures have spent their allowance, and we have been exercised.   God will keep his word, and yet we must expect to be tried.

In this his dead condition, faith in God's word kept him alive.   When we have least feeling, and there is nothing left us, the word will support us : " And being not weak in faith, he considered not his own body now dead, when he was about an hundred years old, neither yet the deadness of Sarah's womb : he staggered not at the promise of God through unbelief ; but was strong in faith, giving glory to God " (Rom. iv. 19, 20).   One way to get comfort is to plead the promise of God in prayer, *Chirographa tua injiciebat tibi Domine,* show him his handwriting ;   God is tender of his word.   These arguings in prayer, are not to work upon God, but ourselves.— *Thomas Manton.*

Verses 25—32.—One does not wonder at the fluctuations which occur in the feelings and experience of a child of God—at one time high on the mountain, near to God and communing with God, at another in the deep and dark valley.   All, more or less, know these changes, and have their sorrowing as well as their rejoicing seasons.   When we parted with David last, what was he telling us of his experience ? that God's testimonies were *his delight and his counsellors ;* but now what a different strain ! all joy is darkened, and *his soul cleaveth to the dust.*   And there must have been seasons of deep depression and despondency in the heart of David—driven as a fugitive and wanderer from his home, hunted as a partridge upon the mountains, and holding, as he himself says, his life continually in his hands.   Yet I think in this portion of the Psalm there is evidence of a deeper abasement and sorrow of heart than any mere worldly suffering could produce.   He had indeed said, " I shall one day perish by the hand of Saul ; " but, even in that moment of weak and murmuring faith, he knew that he was God's anointed one to sit on the throne of Israel.   But here there is indication of sin, of grievous sin which had laid his soul low in the dust ; and I think the petition in the 29th verse gives us some clue to what that sin had been : " *Remove me from the way of lying.*"   Had David—you may well ask in wonder—had David ever lied ?   had he ever deviated from the strait and honourable path of truth ?   I am afraid we must own that he had at one time gone so near the confines of a falsehood, that he would be but a poor casuist and a worse moralist who should attempt to defend the Psalmist from the imputation.   We cannot read the 27th chapter of the 1st of Samuel without owning into what a sad tissue of equivocation and deceit David was unhappily seduced.   Well might his soul cleave to the dust as he reviewed that period of his career ; and though grace did for him what it afterwards did for Peter, and he was plucked as a brand out of the burning, yet one can well imagine that, like the Apostle afterwards, when he thought thereon he wept, and that bitterly.—*Barton Bouchier.*

Verse 26.—" *I have declared my ways,*" etc. This verse contains a prayer, with a reason after this form :—O Lord, I have oft before declared unto thee the whole state and course of my life, my wanderings, my wants, my doubts, my griefs ; I hid nothing from thee, and thou, according to my necessity, didst always hear me : therefore now, Lord, I pray thee to teach me ; by thy light illuminate me that I may know thy statutes and receive grace to walk in them. This is a good argument in dealing with the Lord,—I have gotten many mercies and favourable answers from thee ; therefore, Lord, I pray thee to give me more ; for whom he loves he loves to the end ; and where he begins to show mercy he ceaseth not till he crown his children with mercy. And so gracious is the Lord, that he esteems himself to be honoured as oft as we give him the praise that we have found comfort in him, and therefore come to seek more.

Next, it is to be marked how he saith, " *I have declared my ways, and thou heardest me :* " these two go well together, Mercy and Truth : truth in the heart of man confessing ; mercy in God, hearing and forgiving : happy is the soul wherein these two meet together. Many there are who are destitute of this comfort ; they cannot say, God hath heard me, and all because they deal not plainly and truly with the Lord in *declaring their ways* unto him.—*William Cowper.*

Verse 26.—" *I have declared my ways.*" In verse 59 he *thinketh upon his ways,* that is, his inward imperfections and outward aberrations from the strait and straight ways of God ; and here he is not ashamed to *declare them,* that is, to acknowledge and confess that all this came upon him because he was forgetful to do God's will. Note the connection between this and the previous verse : My soul clave unto the dust, because I clave not to thee.—*Richard Greenham.*

Verse 26.—" *I have declared my ways.*" ‏ספרתי‎, *sipparti,* " I have remembered my ways ; " I have searched them out ; I have investigated them. And that he had earnestly *prayed* for pardon of what was wrong in them, is evident ; for he adds, " *Thou heardest me.*"—*Adam Clarke.*

Verse 26.—" *I have declared my ways,*" etc. Him whom thou hast heard in humble confessing of his sins, him thou must teach thy statutes. The saints lay open to God what they find, both good and evil, seeking deliverance, supply, strengthening, directing : even as sick patients tell to their doctor both what good and what otherwise they perceive or as clients lay bare their case to their counsel.

" *Declared.*" As if he had read them out of a book. The saints know their ways. A man that hath light with him seeth the way, and can tell you all about it ; another is in darkness and knoweth nothing : the one taketh observation of his course, the other doth not.

" *Thou hast heard me.*" God's goodness is seen in his hearing what we lay open before him. If great ones let a poor man tell his tale at large we count it honourable patience ; but it is God's glory to hear our wants, our weakness through sin, the invincibleness of our evils, our utter impotency in ourselves even to seek redress. That mode of procedure would lose the favour of man, but it winneth favour with God. The more humbly we confess all our wants, the more confident we may be that God will hear us. *He teacheth the humble,* for the humble scholar will give to his master the honour of that he learneth.

I have rehearsed (said with myself) my ways ; and " thou hast heard my private confession." " *I have declared* " to others what my way is, and " thou hast heard me " so discoursing ; wherefore " *teach me,*" seeing I communicate what I receive. It is a plea derived from his carefulness to learn, and from the use he had made of that he had learned. The godly, like candles, light each other.—*Paul Bayne.*

Verse 26.—" *I have declared my ways.*" They that would speed with God, should learn this point of Christian ingenuity, unfeignedly to lay open their whole case to him. That is, to declare what they are about, the nature of their affairs, the state of their hearts, what of good or evil they find in themselves, their conflicts, supplies, distresses, hopes ; this is declaring our ways—the good and evil we are conscious of. As a sick patient will tell the physician how it is with him, so should we deal with God, if we would find mercy. This declaring his ways may be looked upon, 1. As an act of faith and dependence. 2. As an act of holy friendship. 3. As an act of spiritual contrition, and brokenness of heart : for this declaring must be explained according to what David meant by the expression, " *My ways.*"

First, By his " *ways* " may be meant his businesses or undertakings : I have still made them known to thee, committing them to the direction of thy providence ;

and so it is an act of faith and dependence, consulting with God, and acquainting him with all our desires.

Secondly, By his " *ways* " may be meant, all his straits, sorrows, and dangers ; and so this declaration is an act of holy friendship, when a man comes as one friend to another, and acquaints God with his whole state, lays his condition before the Lord, in hope of pity and relief.

Thirdly, By " *ways* " is meant temptations and sins ; and so this declaring is an act of spiritual contrition or brokenness of heart. Sins are properly our ways, as Ezek. xviii. 25.—*Thomas Manton.*

Verses 26, 27, 29, 30.—" *The way of thy precepts." " My ways." " The way of lying." " The way of truth."* Here should be noticed the two contrasts by which the Prophet teaches what must be shunned both in life and in doctrine, and what embraced. The first respects *the life* of Christians, as the Prophet sets the way of God's commandments over against his own ways, verses 26, 27 ; and respecting these he confesses that they have pressed him down to the dust and have greatly distressed him ; but respecting those he declares that they have again raised him up. He means by his own ways a depraved nature, carnal desire, and the carnal mind which is enmity against God, Rom. viii. ; but by the ways of the Lord he denotes the will of God expressed in the Word. Therefore the boastings of the papists of the perfect obedience of the renewed are empty ; for David, assured by having been renewed, complains bitterly and with many tears that his soul, under the intolerable weight of sins, had been brought down to the dust of death and almost suffocated ; but that God had heard his prayers and brought him back to the way of his commandments. We here, also, gather that in this life all the saints experience the wrestling and contest of the flesh and the spirit, so that they are continually compelled to mourn that their flesh turns them aside from the way of the Lord into the by-paths of sin : just as Paul cries out, " I see another law in my members, warring against the law of my mind, etc. O wretched man that I am ! who shall deliver me from the body of this death ? " Rom. vii. 23, 24.

The second contrast concerneth the *doctrine ;* for David opposes the way of lying to the way of truth. We are taught by this contrast that we should eschew false doctrine, and steadfastly adhere to divine truth. To this applies the precept of Paul, Eph. iv. 25, " Wherefore, having put away the lie, speak truth each one with his neighbour." Further, we learn, if we hate our own ways, *i.e.*, confess our sins to the Lord, and, trusting in the Mediator, pray for forgiveness, that God is wont to hear and mercifully to forgive our sins ; as it is written, 1 John i. 9, " If we confess our sins, he is faithful and just to forgive us our sins, and to cleanse us from all unrighteousness."—*Solomon Gesner.*

Verse 26.—" *Thou heardest me."* Past answers to prayer should encourage us to come the more boldly to the throne of grace.—Jacob never forgot the night he spent at Bethel.—*William S. Plumer.*

Verse 26.—" *Teach me thy statutes."* The often repetition of this one thing in this Psalm argueth, 1. The necessity of this knowledge. 2. The desire he had to obtain it. 3. That such repetitions are not frivolous when they proceed from a sound heart, a zealous affection, and a consideration of the necessity of the thing prayed for. 4. That such as have most light have little in respect of what they should have. 5. As covetous men think they have never gold enough, so Christian men should think they have never knowledge enough.—*Richard Greenham.*

Verse 26.—" *Teach me."* We can never do without *teaching*, even in old age. Unless the Spirit of God teaches us we learn in vain.—*Martin Geier.*

Verses 26, 27.—Here is David's earnest desire for the continuance of that intimacy that had been between him and his God ; not by visions and voices from heaven, but by the Word and Spirit in an ordinary way : " *Teach me thy statutes,"* that is, " *make me to understand the way of thy precepts."* When he knew God had heard his declaration of his ways, he doth not say, Now, Lord, tell me my lot, and let me know what the event will be ; but, Now, Lord, tell me my duty, let me know what thou wouldest have me to do as the case stands. Note, Those that in all their ways acknowledge God, may pray in faith that he will direct their steps in the right way. And the surest way of keeping up our communion with God is, by learning his statutes, and walking diligently in the *way of his precepts.*—*Matthew Henry.*

Verse 27.—" *Make me to understand."* Natural blindness is an obstinate disease, and hardly cured : therefore again and again we had need to pray, " Open mine

eyes ; " " Teach me thy statutes ; " " *Make me to understand the way of thy precepts.*"
Our ignorance is great even when it is cured in part. The clouds of temptation and
carnal affection cause it to return upon us, so that we know not what we know.
Therefore he cries, " open my eyes ; cause me to understand." Yea, the more we
know the more is our ignorance discovered to us : " Surely I am more brutish than
any man, and have not the understanding of a man. I neither learned wisdom, nor
have the knowledge of the holy " (Prov. xxx. 2, 3). " I have heard of thee by the
hearing of the ear, but now mine eye seeth thee ; wherefore I abhor myself, and
repent in dust and ashes " (Job xlii. 5, 6). Alas, a poor, little, hearsay knowledge
availeth not ; they abhor themselves when they have more intimate acquaintance.
None so confident as a young professor that knoweth a few truths, but in a weak
and imperfect manner : the more we know indeed, the more sensible we are of our
ignorance, and how liable to this mistake and that, so that we dare not trust
ourselves for an hour.—*Thomas Manton.*

Verse 27.—" *Understand the way . . . so shall I talk.*" We can talk with a
better grace of God's " *wondrous works,*" the wonders of providence, and especially
the wonders of redeeming love, when we understand *the way* of God's precepts, and
walk in that way.—*Matthew Henry.*

Verse 27.—" *The way of thy precepts.*" He desireth that God would, partly by
his Spirit, partly by his ministers, partly by affliction, partly by study and labour,
make him to have a right and sound understanding, not only of his *statutes,* but of
the *way* of his statutes, that is, after what sort and order he may live and direct his
life, according to those things which God hath commanded him in his law. Learn
here how hard a thing it is for man, overweening himself in his own wisdom, to know
God's will till God *make* him to know.—*Richard Greenham.*

Verse 27.—" *So shall I talk of thy wondrous works.*" He that is sensible of the
wondrous things that are in God's word, will be talking of them. 1. It will be so.
2. It should be so.

1. *It will be so.* When the heart is deeply affected, the tongue cannot hold, but
will run out in expressions of it ; " for out of the abundance of the heart the mouth
speaketh." When cheered and revived in their afflictions saints are transported
with the thought of the excellency of God. " Come, and I will tell you what God
hath done for my soul " (Ps. lxvi. 15). The woman, when she had found the lost
groat, calleth her neighbours to rejoice with her. He that hath but a cold knowledge,
will not be so full of good discourse.

2. *It should be so* in a threefold respect : for the honour of God ; the edification
of others ; and for our own profit.

(1). For the honour of God, to whom we are so much indebted, to bring him
into request with those about us. Experience deserveth praise ; when you have
found the Messiah, call another to him : " Andrew calleth Peter, and saith unto
him, We have found the Messias : and Philip called Nathanael and saith unto him,
We have found him, of whom Moses in the law, and the prophets, did write, Jesus of
Nazareth, the son of Joseph " (John i. 41—45).

(2). For the edification of others : " And thou, being converted, strengthen thy
brethren " (Luke xxii. 32). True grace is communicative as fire, etc.

(3). For our own profit. He that useth his knowledge, shall have more. Whereas
on the contrary, full breasts, if not sucked, become dry. In the dividing, the loaves
increased. All gifts, but much more spiritual, which are the best, are improved by
exercise.—*Thomas Manton.*

Verse 27.—" *So shall I talk,*" etc. Desire of knowledge should not be for satisfying of curiosity, or for ostentation, or for worldly gain, but to edify ourselves and
others in wisdom. . . . " *Thy wondrous works.*" The works of creation, redemption
and providence, either set down in Scripture, or observed in our own experience,
transcend our capacity, and cannot but draw admiration from them that see them
well.—*David Dickson.*

Verse 27.—" *So shall I talk.*" It is a frequent complaint with Christians, that
they are straitened in religious conversation, and often feel unable to speak " to
the use of edifying, that they may minister grace to the hearers," Eph. iv. 29. Here,
then, is the secret disclosed, by which we shall be kept from the danger of dealing in
unfelt truths, for " out of the abundance of the heart our mouths shall speak,"
Matt. xii. 34. Seek to have the heart searched, cleansed, filled with the graces of
the Spirit. Humility, teachableness, simplicity, will bring light unto the under-

standing, influence the heart, "open the lips," and unite every member that we have in the service and praise of God.—*Charles Bridges.*

Verse 27.—" *I shall talk of.*"   There is a close affinity between all the duties of religion.   The same word is rendered *pray, meditate,* and *talk of.*   We think of God's excellent majesty ; we cry to him in humble prayer ; we study his word until our souls are filled with gladness and admiration ; and then how can we but *talk of his wondrous works ?*—*William S. Plumer.*

Verse 28.—" *My soul melteth for heaviness.*"   In the original the word signifies, " droppeth away."   The Septuagint hath it thus : " My soul fell asleep through weariness."   Probably by a fault of the transcribers, putting one word for another.   My soul droppeth.   It may relate (1) to the plenty of his tears, as the word is used in Scripture : " My friends scorn me : but mine eye poureth out tears unto God " (Job xvi. 20), or droppeth to God, the same word ; so it notes his deep sorrow and sense of his condition.   The like allusion is in Joshua vii. 5 : " The heart of the people melted, and became as water."   Or (2) it relates to his languishing under the extremity of his sorrow ; as an unctuous thing wasteth by dropping, so was his soul even dropping away.   Such a like expression is used in Psalm cvii. 26 : " Their soul is melted because of trouble ; " and of Jesus Christ, whose strength was exhausted by the greatness of his sorrows, it is said, Psalm xxii. 14, " I am poured out like water and all my bones are out of joint : my heart is like wax ; it is melted in the midst of my bowels."   Be the allusion either to the one or to the other ; either to the dropping of tears, or to the melting and wasting away of what is fat or unctuous, it notes a vehement sorrow, and brokenness of heart.   So much is clear, his soul was even melting away, and unless God did help, he could hold out no longer.—*Thomas Manton.*

Verse 28.—" *My soul melteth.*"   The oldest versions make it mean *to slumber* (LXX. ἐνύσταθεν, Vulg. *dormitavit*), which would make the clause remarkably coincident with Luke xxii. 45.—*Joseph Addison Alexander.*

Verse 28.—" *Heaviness.*"   There is nothing may comfort a natural man but David had it ; yet cannot all these keep him from that heaviness whereunto, as witnesseth S. Peter, the children of God are subject in this life, through their manifold temptations.   The men of the world are so far from this disposition, that if they have health and wealth, they marvel what it is should make a man heavy : they are not acquainted with the exercise of a feeling conscience ; they know not the defects of the spiritual life, and are not grieved at them : being dead in sin they feel not that they want life ; all their care is to eat and drink and make merry.   But miserable are they ; for in their best estate they are as oxen fed for the slaughter.   Woe be to them who laugh now, they shall mourn ; but blessed are they who mourn now, for they shall be comforted.—*William Cowper.*

Verse 28.—" *Strengthen thou me according unto thy word.*"   Strengthen me to do the duties, resist the temptations, and bear up under the burdens of an afflicted state, that the spirit may not fail.—*Matthew Henry.*

Verse 28.—" *Strengthen thou me according unto thy word.*"   What is that word which David pleaded ?   " As thy days, so shall thy strength be," Deut. xxxiii. 25. " Will he plead against me," said Job, " with his great power ?   No ; but he will put strength in me," Job xxiii. 6.—*Charles Bridges.*

Verse 28.—" *Strengthen thou me.*"   Gesenius translates this, " *Keep me alive,*" Thus, קיּמני, in this verse, answers to חיּני, in the first verse.   This prayer for new strength, or life, is an entreaty that the waste of life through tears might be restored by the life-giving word.—*Frederick G. Marchant.*

Verse 29.—It says, " *Remove from me the way,*" and not me from the way ; because that way of iniquity is within us, for we are born children of wrath, and the passions innate in us run to the lie, and make the wretched way of crimes in our souls.— *Thomas Le Blanc.*

Verse 29.—" *Remove from me the way of lying.*"   Here he acknowledgeth that although he were already exercised in the law of God and in his knowledge, and that although he were a prophet to teach others, nevertheless he was subject to a number of wicked thoughts and imaginations which might always wickedly lead him from the right way, except God had held him with his mighty and strong hand.   And this is a point which we ought here rightly to note ; for we see how men greatly abuse themselves.   When any of us shall have had a good beginning, we straightway think that we are at the highest ; we never bethink us to pray any more to God, when once he hath showed us favour enough to serve our turns ; but if we have done any small deed, we by-and-by lift up ourselves and wonder at our great virtues, thinking straightway that the Devil can win no more of us. This foolish arrogancy causeth God to let us go astray, so that we fall mightily, yea, that we break both arms and legs, and are in great hazard of breaking our necks. I speak not now of our natural body, but of our soul. Let us look upon David himself ; for he it is that hath made proof hereof. It came to pass that he villainously and wickedly erred when he took Bathsheba the wife of his subject, Uriah, to play the whoremonger with her, that he was the cause of so execrable a murder, yea, and that of many; for he did as much as in him lay, to cause the whole army of the Lord and all the people of Israel to be utterly overthrown. See, then, the great negligence and security into which David fell ; and see also wherefore he saith, " Alas, my good God, I beseech thee so to guide me, that I may forsake the way of lying."—*John Calvin.*

Verse 29.—" *Lying.*" A sin that David, through diffidence, fell into frequently. See 1 Sam. xxi. 2, 8, where he roundly telleth three or four lies ; and the like he did, 1 Sam. xxvii. 8, 10 : this evil he saw by himself, and here prayeth against it.—*John Trapp*

Verse 29.—" *The way of lying,*" etc. Lying ways are all ways, except the ways of God's commandments : reason, sense, example, custom, event, deceivable lusts, these tell a man he is safe, or that he shall repent of them, and take no hurt in the end, and they promise ease and blessedness, but perform it not. Such as desire to obey God must be kept from evil ways : we are not so sanctified but that temptation will injure our graces. As a fire in kindling, not throughly alight, may be quenched by a little water, so may our holiness be damped by temptation. We find within us a proneness to false ways, as candles new blown out are soon blown in again. Therefore as burnt children dread the fire, so do we fear the way of lying. God doth not suffer temptations to come into the presence of some ; and in others God maketh the heart averse from sin when temptation is present. We must come out of the ways of sin, ere we can walk in the ways of God.—*Paul Bayne.*

Verse 29.—" *The way of lying.*" The whole life of sin is a *lie* from beginning to end. The word " *lying* " occurs *eight* times in this Psalm.—*William S. Plumer.*

Verse 29.—" *The way of lying.*" By *the way of lying* is to be understood all that is in man's nature, not agreeable to the word, whether it be counsels, or conclusions of the heart, or external actions ; and it is called a lying way, because nature promises a good to be gotten by sin which man shall not find in it.—*William Cowper.*

Verse 29.—" *The way of lying.*" The prophet here desireth to be confirmed by God against all corruptions in doctrine, and disorder of conversation, which Satan by his witty and wily instruments doth seek to set abroach in the world. These are called " *the way of lying.*" 1. Because they are invented by Satan, the father of lies. 2. They are countenanced by man's wit, the storehouse of lies. 3. They seem to be that which they are not, which is of the nature of lies. 4. They are contrary to God and his truth, the discoverers of lies.—*Richard Greenham.*

Verse 29.—" *Grant me thy law graciously.*" He opposes the law of God to the way of lying. First, because it is the only rule of all truth, both in religion and manners : that which is not agreeable to it is but a lie which shall deceive man. Secondly, it destroys and shall at length utterly destroy all contrary errors. As the rod of Aaron devoured the rods of the enchanters ; so the word, which is the rod of the mouth of God, shall, in the end, eat up and consume all untruths whatsoever. Thirdly, according to the sentence of this word, so shall it be unto every man ; it deceives none. Men shall find by experience it is true : he who walks in a way condemned by the word, shall come to a miserable end. And on the contrary, it cannot but be well with them who live according to this rule.—*William Cowper.*

Verse 29.—" *Grant me thy law graciously.*" David had ever the book of the law ; for every king of Israel was to have it always by him, and the Rabbis say, written with his own hand. But, " *Grant me thy law graciously ;* " that is, he desires he might have it not only written by him, but upon him, to have it imprinted upon his heart, that he might have a heart to observe and keep it. That is the blessing he begs for, " *the law ;* " and this is begged " *graciously,*" or upon terms of grace, merely according to thine own favour, and good pleasure. Here is,—I. The sin deprecated, " *Remove from me the way of lying.*" II. The good supplicated and asked, " *Grant me thy law graciously.*" In the first clause you have his malady, David had been enticed to a course of lying. In the second we have his remedy, and that is the law of God.—*Thomas Manton.*

Verse 30.—" I have chosen the way of truth." Here you have the working of a gracious soul. This is more than sitting and hearing the word—having no objection to what you hear. Such hearing is all that can be affirmed of the generality of gospel hearers, except we add, that none are more ready to be caught by false and easy ways of salvation, for they assent to all they hear. The man of God strikes a higher and more spiritual note—he goes into the *choice* of the thing ; he chooses the way of truth ; and he cannot but choose it ; it is the bent of his renewed nature, the effect indeed of all he has been pleading. How act we ? The way of truth is all that God has revealed concerning his Son Jesus. The willing heart chooses this way, and all of it ; the bitterness of it, the self-denial of it, as well as the comfort of it ; a Saviour from sin as well as a Saviour from hell ; a Saviour whose Spirit can lead from prayerfulness to godliness, from idleness upon the Sabbath-day to a holy keeping of that day, from self-seeking to the seeking of Christ, from slack, inconsistent conduct to a careful observance of all the Lord's will. Where God's people meet, there such will delight to be. O for such to abound among us !—*John Stephen.*

Verse 30.—" I have chosen the way of truth." Religion is not a matter of chance, but of choice. Have we weighed things in the balance, and, upon mature deliberation, made an election,—" We will have God upon any terms ? " Have we sat down and reckoned the cost,—or what religion *must* cost us,—the parting with our lusts ; and what it *may* cost us,—the parting with our lives ? Have we resolved, through the assistance of grace, to own Christ when the swords and staves are up ? and to sail with him, not only in a pleasure-boat, but in a man-of-war ? This choosing God speaks him to be ours : hypocrites profess God out of worldly design, not religious choice.—*Thomas Watson, in " The Morning Exercises."*

Verse 30.—" I have chosen the way of truth." The choice which David makes here of God's truth proceeds from that choice and election whereby the Lord before all time made choice of David, in Christ, to be one of his elect. For as it is true of love " Herein is love, not that we loved God, but that he loved us "—we could never have loved him, if first he had not loved us ; so is it true of election ; if he before time had not chosen us to be his people, we could never in time have chosen him to be our God. And this I mark in them who love the word of God, and delight in it, who can say out of a good heart, that the Lord is their portion and the joy of their soul : this is a sure seal of their election, imprinted by the finger of God in their heart.—*William Cowper.*

*Verse 30.—*In all our religious exercises, let deliberation precede our resolution, and consideration usher in determination. David did so ; and therefore he says here, " *I have chosen the way of truth : thy judgments have I laid before me.*" Indeed, he cannot but resolve upon, and make choice of, the way of piety, who layeth before him the goodness, the rectitude and pleasantness of the way. When the prodigal considereth with himself how well his father's servants fared, he thinketh of, yea, determineth to go home ; " I will arise and go to my father."—*Abraham Wright,* 1661.

Verse 30.—" I have chosen." No man ever served the Lord but he first made choice of him to be his Master. Every man when he comes to years of discretion so as to be master of himself, adviseth with himself what course he shall take, whether he will serve God or the world. Now all the saints of God have made this distinct choice ; we will serve the Lord, and no other. Moses when both stood before him, the pleasures of Egypt on the one hand, and God and his people with their afflictions on the other, he chose the latter before the former, Heb. xi. 25. So David saith he did, " *I have chosen the way of truth : thy judgments have I laid before me ;*" for to choose is, when a thing lies before a man, and he considers and takes it. So Joshua, " I and my house will serve the Lord."—*John Preston* (1587—1628) *in " The Golden Sceptre held forth to the Humble."* 1638.

Verse 30.—" Truth." There are three kinds of truth ; truth in heart, truth in word, truth in deed (2 Kings xx. 3 ; Zech. viii. 16 ; Heb. x. 22).—*Ayguan. From " The Preacher's Storehouse," by J. E. Vaux.*

Verse 30.—" Thy judgments." God's word is called his judgment, because it discerns good from evil ; and is not a naked sentence ; but, as it points out evil, so it pronounceth plagues against it, which shall be executed according to the sentence thereof.—*William Cowper.*

Verses 30, 31.—" I have chosen ; " " I have stuck." The choosing Christian is likely to be the sticking Christian ; when those that are Christians by chance tack about if the wind turn.—*Matthew Henry.*

Verse 30.—"Thy judgments have I laid before me." The solid consideration that God's word is God's decree or judgment may guard a believer against men terrors and allurements, and fix him in his right choice, as here.—*David Dickson.*

Verse 30.—*"Thy judgments have I laid before me."* Men that mean to travel the right way will lay before them a map : so David, as his will had resolved upon the ways of truth, so he setteth before his eyes the map of the law, which did manifest this unto him, as the ship-man hath his card with the compass.—*Paul Bayne.*

Verse 31.—*"I have stuck unto thy testimonies."* It is not a little remarkable, that while the Psalmist says (verse 25), " My soul *cleaveth* to the dust," he should say here, *"I have cleaved unto thy testimonies";* for it is the same original word in both verses. The thing is altogether compatible with the experience of the believer. Without there is the body of indwelling sin, and within there is the undying principle of divine grace. There is the contest between them—" the flesh lusteth against the spirit and the spirit against the flesh " (Gal. v. 17), and the believer is constrained to cry out, " O wretched man that I am " (Rom. vii. 24). It is the case ; and all believers find it so. While the soul is many times felt cleaving to the dust, the spirit strives to cleave unto God's testimonies. So the believer prays, Cause that I be not put to shame. And keeping close to Christ, brethren, you shall not be put to shame, world without end.—*John Stephen.*

Verse 31.—*"I have stuck unto thy testimonies."* He adhered to them when momentary interests might have dictated a different line of conduct, when unbelief would have been ready to shrink from the path of duty, when outward appearances were greatly discouraging to fidelity, when all were ready to deride his preposterous determination.—*John Morison.*

Verse 31.—*"I have stuck."* True godliness evermore wears upon her head the garland of perseverance.—*William Cowper.*

Verse 31.—*"Put me not to shame."* Forasmuch as David, in a good conscience, endeavoured to serve God, he craves that the Lord would not confound him. This is two ways done ; either when the Lord forsakes his children, so that in their trouble they feel not his promised comforts, and great confusion of mind and perturbation is upon them ; or otherwise when he leaves them as a prey to their enemies, who scorn them for their godly and sincere life, and exult over them in their time of trouble ; when they see that all their prayer and other exercises of religion cannot keep them out of their enemies' hands. " He trusted in God : let him deliver him." From this shame and contempt he desires the Lord would keep him, and that he should never be like unto them, who, being disappointed of that wherein they trusted, are ashamed.—*William Cowper.*

Verse 32.—*"I will run in the way of thy commandments when,"* etc. You must remember that the speaker, the Psalmist, is not an unconverted man, but one who had long before been brought under the dominion of religion. He is not, therefore, soliciting the first entrance, but the after and multiplied workings of a principle of grace ; and he states his desire in an expression which is singularly descriptive of the outgoing of an influence from the heart over the rest of the man. His wish is that his heart might be enlarged ; and this wish amounted to a longing that the whole of himself might act in unison with the heart, so that he might become, as it were, all heart, and thus the heart in the strictest sense be enlarged, through the spreading of itself over the body and soul, expanding itself till it embraced all the powers of both. If there be the love of God in the heart, then gradually the heart, possessed and actuated by so noble and stirring a principle, will bring over to a lofty consecration all the energies, whether mental or corporeal, and will be practically the same as though the other departments of man were thus the result turned into heart, and he became, according to the phrase which we are accustomed to employ when describing a character of unwonted generosity and warmth, " all heart." So that the desire after an enlarged heart you may fairly consider tantamount to a desire that every faculty might be brought into thorough subjection to God, and that just as God himself is love—love being rather the Divine essence than a Divine attribute, and therefore love mingling itself with all the properties of Godhead, so the man having love in the heart might become all heart, the heart throwing itself into all his capacities, pervading but not obliterating the characteristics of his nature. And exactly in accordance with this view of the enlargement of heart which the Psalmist desired is the practical result which was to follow on its attainment. He was already walking in the way of God's commandments ; but what he proposed to himself was the *running* that way : *"I will run the way of thy commandments, when thou shalt enlarge my heart."*   A quickened pace, a more rapid progress, a greater alacrity, a firmer constancy, a more resolute and unflinching obedience, these were the results which the Psalmist looked for from the enlargement of his heart.   And truly if all the faculties of mind and body be dedicated to God, with a constant and vigorous step will man press on in the way that leadeth to heaven.   So long as the dedication is at best only partial, the world retaining some fraction of its empire, notwithstanding the setting up of the kingdom of God, there can be nothing but a slow and impeded progress, a walking interrupted by repeated haltings, if not backslidings, by much of loitering, if not of actual retreat ; but if the man be all heart, then he will be all life, all warmth, all zeal, all energy, and the consequence of this complete surrender to God will be exactly that which is prophetically announced by Isaiah : " They that wait upon the Lord shall renew their strength ; they shall mount up with wings as eagles ; they shall run, and not be weary ; and they shall walk, and not faint."—*Henry Melvill*, 1798—1871.

Verse 32.—*"I will run."*   By running is meant cheerful, ready, and zealous observance of God's precepts : it is not go, or walk, but *run*.   They that would come to their journey's end, must run in the way of God's commandments.   It noteth a speedy or a ready obedience, without delay.   We must begin with God betimes.   Alas ! when we should be at the goal, we have many of us scarce set forth.   And it noteth earnestness ; when a man's heart is set upon a thing, he thinks he can never do it soon enough.   And this is running, when we are vehement and earnest upon the enjoyment of God and Christ in the way of obedience.   And it notes again, that the heart freely offereth itself to God.

This running is the fruit of effectual calling.   When the Lord speaks of effectual calling, the issue of it is running ; when he speaks of the conversion of the Gentiles, " Nations that know not thee shall run unto thee " ; and, " Draw me, and we will run after thee."   When God draws there is a speedy, earnest motion of the soul.

This running, as it is the fruit of effectual calling, so it is very needful ; for cold and faint motions are soon overborne by difficulty and temptation : " Let us run with patience the race that is set before us " (Heb. xii. 1).   When a man hath a mind to do a thing, though he be hindered and jostled, he takes it patiently, he goes on and cannot stay to debate the business.   A slow motion is easily stopped, whereas a swift one bears down that which opposeth it ; so is it when men run and are not tired in the service of God.   Last of all, the prize calls for running : " So run that ye may obtain " (1 Cor. ix. 24).—*Thomas Manton.*

Verse 32.—*"I will run."*   It was not the *walking* " the way of God's commandments," but the *running* " the way of God's commandments," to which David aspired.   The text has no connection with the case of one who habitually pursues the opposite path ; it has exclusive reference to the pace at which the line of duty is to be traversed. . . . . It may not unnaturally excite surprise, that " the sweet singer of Israel "—he who was emphatically declared to be " a man after God's own heart "—should, nevertheless, in the words of the text, seem to imply that *he* was not yet " running the way of God's commandments."   But, dear brethren, the greater an individual's comparative holiness, the more intense will be his longing for absolute holiness.   To others, David might appear to be speeding marvellously along the path of life ; and yet he himself deemed his movements to be far less rapid.   His humility was one of the evidences of his holiness.—*Hugh B. Moffat*, 1871.

Verse 32.—*"I will run the way."*   His intended course in this way he expresses by running.   It is good to be in this way even in the slowest motions ; love will creep where it cannot walk.   But if thou art so indeed, then thou wilt long for a swifter motion ; if thou do but creep, creep on, desire to be enabled to go.   If thou goest, but yet haltingly and lamely, yet desire to be strengthened to walk straight ; and if thou walkest, let not that satisfy thee, desire to run.   So here, David did walk in this way ; but he earnestly wishes to mend his pace ; he would willingly run, and for that end he desires an enlarged heart.

Some dispute and descant too much whether they go or no, and childishly tell their steps, and would know at every step whether they advance or no, and how much they advance, and thus amuse themselves, and spend the time of doing and going in questioning and doubting.   Thus it is with many Christians ; but it were a more wise and comfortable way to be endeavouring onwards, and if thou make little progress, at least to be desiring to make more ; to be praying and walking, and praying that thou mayest walk faster, and that in the end thou mayest run, not satisfied with anything attained. Yet by that unsatisfiedness we must not be so dejected as to sit down, or to stand still, but rather we must be excited to go on.—*Robert Leighton.*

Verse 32.—*"Enlarged my heart,"* or dilated it, namely, with joy. It is obvious to remark the philosophical propriety with which this expression is applied : since the heart is dilated, and the pulse by consequence becomes strong and full, from the exultation of joy as well as of pride. (See Parkhurst on רחב.)—*Richard Mant.*

Verse 32.—*"Thou wilt enlarge my heart."* God would enlarge the very seat of life, and thus give his weak servant more strength ; such strength that he need no longer lie prone on the dust struggling to arise ; but strength to enable him to run in the way of truth. Thus, he who prays, *"O Lord, put me not to shame,"* finds for himself the truth of an earlier song : " They looked unto him, and were lightened, and their faces were not ashamed."—*Frederick G. Marchant.*

Verse 32.—*"Enlarge my heart."* It is said of Solomon, that he had " a large heart (the same word that is used here), as the sand of the sea shore : " that is a vast, comprehensive spirit, that could fathom much of nature, both its greater and lesser things. Thus, I conceive, the enlargement of the heart compriseth the enlightening of the understanding. There arises a clearer light there to discern spiritual things in a more spiritual manner ; to see the vast difference betwixt the vain things the world goes after, and the true, solid delight that is in the way of God's commandments ; to know the false blush of the pleasures of sin, and what deformity is under that painted mask, and not be allured by it ; to have enlarged apprehensions of God, his excellency, and greatness and goodness ; how worthy he is to be obeyed and served ; this is the great dignity and happiness of the soul ; all other pretensions are low and poor in respect of this. Here then is enlargement to see the purity and beauty of his law, how just and reasonable, yea, how pleasant and amiable it is ; that his commandments are not grievous, that they are beds of spices ; the more we walk in them, still the more of their fragrant smell and sweetness we find.—*Robert Leighton.*

Verse 32.—Narrow is the way unto life, but no man can run in it save with widened heart.—*Prosper, of Aquitaine* (403—463), *quoted by Neale and Littledale.*

Verse 32.—*"Enlarged."* Surely a temple for the great God (such as our hearts should be) should be fair and ample. If we would have God dwell in our hearts, and shed abroad his influences, we should make room for God in our souls, by a greater largeness of faith and expectation. The rich man thought of enlarging his barns, when his store was increased upon him (Luke xii.), so should we stretch out the curtains of Christ's tent and habitation, have larger expectations of God, if we would receive more from him. The vessels failed before the oil failed. We are not straitened in God, but in ourselves ; by the scantiness of our thoughts, we do not make room for him, nor greaten God : " My soul doth magnify the Lord " (Luke i. 46). Faith doth greaten God. How can we make God greater than he is ? As to the declarative being, we can have greater and larger apprehensions of his greatness, goodness, and truth.

1. There needs a large heart, because the command is exceedingly broad : " I have seen an end of all perfection ; but thy commandment is exceeding broad " (Ps. cxix. 96). A broad law and a narrow heart will never suit : we need love, faith, knowledge, and all to carry us through this work, which is of such a vast extent and latitude.

2. We need enlarged heart, because of the lets and hindrances within ourselves. There is lust drawing off from God to sensual objects : " Every man is tempted, when he is drawn away of his own lust, and enticed " (James i. 14). Therefore there needs something to draw us on, to carry us out with strength and life another way, to urge us in the service of God. Lust sits as a clog upon us, it is a weight of corruption (Heb. xii. 1), retarding us in all our flights and motions, thwarting, opposing, breaking the force of spiritual impulsions, if not hindering them altogether (Gal. v. 17). Well then, lust drawing so strongly one way, God needs to draw us more strongly the other way. When there is a weight to poise us to worldly and sensual objects, we need a strength to carry us on with vigorous and lively motions of soul towards God, an earnest bent upon our souls, which is this enlargement of heart.—*Thomas Manton.*

Verse 32.—*"My heart."* The great Physician knows at once where to look for the cause, when he sees anything amiss in the outward life of his people. He well knows that all spiritual disease is heart disease, and it is the heart remedies that he must apply.   At one time, our Physician sees symptoms which are violent in their nature ; at another, he sees symptoms of languor and debility ; but he knows that both come from the heart ; and so, it is upon the heart that he operates, when he is about to perform a cure.

The strong action of the heart in all holy things comes from the blessed operation of the Spirit upon it ; then only can we " *run* " the way of God's commandments, when he has enlarged our heart.

Heartiness in action is the subject to which the reader's attention is here directed, and it is one of considerable importance.

There are many believers, who for want of enlargement of heart are occupying a poor position in the church of God.   They are trusting to Jesus for life eternal, and he will doubtless not disappoint them ; he will be true to his word, that " he that believeth shall be saved ; " but they are still, alas ! to a deplorable degree, shut up in self ; they have contracted hearts ; still do they take narrow views of God's claim, and their own privileges, and the position in which they are set in the world ; and however much they might be said to stand, or sit, or walk in the way of God's commandments, they cannot be said to "*run*" in it.   Running is a strong and healthy action of the body ; it requires energy, it is an exercise that needs a sound heart ; none can run in the way of God's commandments, except in strength and vigour imparted by him.   The *running* Christians are comparatively few ; walking and sitting Chrsitians are comparatively common ; but the running Christian is so uncommon as often to be thought almost mad.

Let us, for the sake of order, classify our observations on this subject under the following heads :—

i. *What heartiness is.*   The heartiness spoken of here under the term, " enlargement of the heart," is cheerfulness in doing God's will—love for that will—a drawing out of the affections towards it—an interest in it ; all this it is, and a great deal more, which it is not easy to describe or define.

ii. *What heartiness does.*   Where there is enlargement of the heart by God, there is an outgoing beyond all the limits which fallen selfishness assigns.   The heart contracted at the fall ; it shrank when sin entered into it ; it became unequal to containing great and generous thoughts ; it became a bondaged heart.   True ! the responsibilities of duty could not be escaped, not could the directions of conscience ; but the affections are voluntary, and the fallen heart drew in its affections from God ; it felt that it had the power of withholding them from him and his commandments, and it rejoiced to shew its enmity in withholding its sympathy, where it could not withhold its obedience. . . . .

iii. *Whence heartiness comes.*   Now, as we have already said, where the heart is operated on by the Spirit, and all its natural evil overruled, it has outgoings which are entirely beyond the limits that fallen selfishness assigns.   Love is inwrought with it : the union of sentiment, the identity of interest which love inspires, pervade it, in all belonging to God, for it has received these from God ; the heart becomes unbondaged from mere rules, or perhaps to speak more correctly, it rises above them, and it feels—not merely it *knows*, but it *feels*—so much of the beauty of God's commandments, that it delights to "*run*" in them ; it loves to be hearty in them ; its interests, its affections are in them.—*Philip Bennet Power, in "The 'I Wills' of the Psalms,"* 1862.

Verse 32.—Disquiets of heart unfit us for duty, by hindering our activity in the prosecution of duty.   The whole heart, soul, and strength should be engaged in all religious services ; but these troubles are as clogs and weights to hinder motion.   Joy is the dilatation of the soul, and widens it for anything which it undertakes ; but grief contracts the heart, and narrows all the faculties.   Hence doth David beg an " enlarged heart," as the principle of activity : "*I will run the way of thy commandments, when thou shalt enlarge my heart*" ; for what else can be expected when the mind is so distracted with fear and sorrow, but that it should be uneven, tottering, weak, and confused ? so that if it do set itself to anything, it acts troublesomely, drives on heavily, and doth a very little with a great deal ado ; and yet, the unfitness were less, if that little which it can do were well done ; but the mind is so interrupted in its endeavours that sometimes in prayer the man begins, and then is presently at a stand, and dares not proceed, his words are swallowed up, " he is so troubled that he cannot speak," Ps. lxxvii. 4.—*Richard Gilpin,* (1625—1699), *in "Dæmonologia Sacra."*

EXPOSITION OF VERSES 33 TO 40.

TEACH me, O LORD, the way of thy statutes ; and I shall keep it *unto* the end.

34 Give me understanding, and I shall keep thy law ; yea, I shall observe it with *my* whole heart.

35 Make me to go in the path of thy commandments ; for therein do I delight.

36 Incline my heart unto thy testimonies, and not to covetousness.

37 Turn away mine eyes from beholding vanity ; *and* quicken thou me in thy way.

38 Stablish thy word unto thy servant, who *is devoted* to thy fear.

39 Turn away my reproach which I fear : for thy judgments *are* good.

40 Behold, I have longed after thy precepts : quicken me in thy righteousness.

A sense of dependence and a consciousness of extreme need pervade this section, which is all made up of prayer and plea. The former eight verses trembled with a sense of sin, quivering with a childlike sense of weakness and folly, which caused the man of God to cry out for the help by which alone his soul could be preserved from falling back into sin.

33. *"Teach me, O LORD, the way of thy statutes."* Child-like, blessed words, from the lips of an old, experienced believer, and he a king, and a man inspired of God. Alas, for those who will never be taught. They dote upon their own wisdom ; but their folly is apparent to all who rightly judge. The Psalmist will have the Lord for his teacher ; for he feels that his heart will not learn of any less effectual instructor. A sense of great slowness to learn drives us to seek a great teacher. What condescension it is on our great Jehovah's part that he deigns to teach those who seek him. The lesson which is desired is thoroughly practical ; the holy man would not only learn the *statutes*, but the *way* of them, the daily use of them, their tenor, spirit, direction, habit, tendency. He would know that path of holiness which is hedged in by divine law, along which the commands of the Lord stand as sign-posts of direction and mile-stones of information, guiding and marking our progress. The very desire to learn this way is in itself an assurance that we shall be taught therein, for he who made us long to learn will be sure to gratify the desire.

"And I shall keep it unto the end." Those who are taught of God never forget their lessons. When divine grace sets a man in the true way he will be true to it. Mere human wit and will have no such enduring influence : there is an end to all perfection of the flesh, but there is no end to heavenly grace except its own end, which is the perfecting of holiness in the fear of the Lord. Perseverance to the end is most certainly to be predicted of those whose beginning is in God, and with God, and by God ; but those who commence without the Lord's teaching soon forget what they learn, and start aside from the way upon which they professed to have entered. No one may boast that he will hold on his way in his own strength, for that must depend upon the continual teaching of the Lord : we shall fall like Peter, if we presume on our own firmness as he did. If God keeps us we shall keep his way ; and it is a great comfort to know that it is the way with God to keep the feet of his saints. Yet we are to watch as if our keeping of the way depended wholly on ourselves ; for, according to this verse, our perseverance rests not on any force or compulsion, but on the teaching of the Lord, and assuredly teaching, whoever be the teacher, requires learning on the part of the taught one : no one can teach a man who refuses to learn. Earnestly, then, let us drink in divine instruction, that so we may hold fast our integrity, and to life's latest hour follow on in the path of uprightness ! If we receive the living and incorruptible seed of the word of God we must live : apart from this we have no life eternal, but only a name to live.

The " *end* " of which David speaks is the end of life, or the fulness of obedience. He trusted in grace to make him faithful to the utmost, never drawing a line and saying to obedience, "Hitherto shalt thou go, but no further." The end of our keeping the law will come only when we cease to breathe ; no good man will think of marking a date and saying, " It is enough, I may now relax my watch, and live after the manner of men." As Christ loves us to the end, so must we serve him to the end. The end of divine teaching is that we may persevere to the end.

The portions of eight show a relationship still. GIMEL begins with prayer for life, that he may keep the word (17) ; DALETH cries for more life, according to that word (25) ; and now HE opens with a prayer for teaching, that he may keep the way of God's statutes. If a keen eye is turned upon these verses a closer affinity will be discerned.

34. "*Give me understanding, and I shall keep thy law.*" This is the same prayer enlarged, or rather it is a supplement which intensifies it. He not only needs teaching, but the power to learn : he requires not only to understand, but to obtain *an understanding.* How low has sin brought us ; for we even lack the faculty to understand spiritual things, and are quite unable to know them till we are endowed with spiritual discernment. Will God in very deed give us understanding ? This is a miracle of grace. It will, however, never be wrought upon us till we know our need of it ; and we shall not even discover that need till God gives us a measure of understanding to perceive it. We are in a state of complicated ruin, from which nothing but manifold grace can deliver us. Those who feel their folly are by the example of the Psalmist encouraged to pray for understanding : let each man by faith cry, " Give *me* understanding." Others have had it, why may it not come to *me ?* It was a gift to them ; will not the Lord also freely bestow it upon *me ?*

We are not to seek this blessing that we may be famous for wisdom, but that we may be abundant in our love to the law of God. He who has understanding will learn, remember, treasure up, and obey the commandment of the Lord. The gospel gives us grace to keep the law ; the free gift leads us to holy service ; there is no way of reaching to holiness but by accepting the gift of God. If God gives, we keep ; but we never keep the law in order to obtaining grace. The sure result of regeneration, or the bestowal of understanding, is a devout reverence for the law and a resolute keeping of it in the heart. The spirit of God makes us to know the Lord and to understand somewhat of his love, wisdom, holiness, and majesty ; and the result is that we honour the law and yield our hearts to the obedience of the faith.

"*Yea, I shall observe it with my whole heart.*" The understanding operates upon the affections ; it convinces the heart of the beauty of the law, so that the soul loves it with all its powers ; and then it reveals the majesty of the lawgiver, and the whole nature bows before his supreme will. An enlightened judgment heals the divisions of the heart, and bends the united affections to a strict and watchful observance of the one rule of life. He alone obeys God who can say, " My Lord, I would serve thee, and do it with all my heart" ; and none can truly say this till they have received as a free grant the inward illumination of the Holy Ghost. To observe God's law with all our heart at all times is a great grace, and few there be that find it ; yet it is to be had if we will consent to be taught of the Lord.

Observe the parallel of verses 2 and 10 where the *whole* heart is spoken of in reference to seeking, and in 58 in pleading for mercy ; these are all second verses in their octonaries. The frequent repetition of the phrase shows the importance of undivided love : the heart is never whole or holy till it is whole or united. The heart is never one with God till it is one within itself.

35. "*Make me to go in the path of thy commandments ; for therein do I delight.*" " To will is present with me ; but how to perform that which is good I find not." Thou hast made me to love the way, now make me to move in it. It is a plain path, which others are treading through thy grace ; I see it and admire it ; cause me to travel in it. This is the cry of a child that longs to walk, but is too feeble ; of a pilgrim who is exhausted, yet pants to be on the march ; of a lame man who pines to be able to run. It is a blessed thing to delight in holiness, and surely he who gave us this delight will work in us the yet higher joy of possessing and practising it. Here is our only hope ; for we shall not go in the narrow path till we are made to do so by the Maker's own power. O thou who didst once make me, I pray thee make me again : thou hast made me to know ; now make me to go. Certainly I shall never be happy till I do, for my sole delight lies in walking according to thy bidding.

The Psalmist does not ask the Lord to do for him what he ought to do for himself: he wishes himself to "go" or tread in the path of the command. He asks not to be carried while he lies passive ; but to be made "to go." Grace does not treat us as stocks and stones, to be dragged by horses or engines, but as creatures endowed with life, reason, will, and active powers, who are willing and able to go of themselves if once made to do so. God worketh in us, but it is that we may both will and do according to his good pleasure. The holiness we seek after is not a forced compliance with command, but the indulgence of a whole-hearted passion for goodness, such as shall conform our life to the will of the Lord. Can the reader say, " therein do I delight"? Is practical godliness the very jewel of your soul, the coveted prize of your mind ? If so, the outward path of life, however rough will be clean, and lead the soul upward to delight ineffable. He who delights in the law should not doubt but what he will be enabled to run in its ways, for where the heart already finds its joy the feet are sure to follow.

Note that the corresponding verse in the former eight (35) was " Make me to understand," and here we have " Make me to go." Remark the order, first understanding and then going ; for a clear understanding is a great assistance towards practical action.

During the last few octaves the fourth has been the heart verse : see 20, 28, and now 36. Indeed in all the preceeding fourths great heartiness is observable. This also marks the care with which this sacred song was composed.

36. "Incline my heart unto thy testimonies." Does not this prayer appear to be superfluous, since it is evident that the Psalmist's heart was set upon obedience ? We are sure that there is never a word to spare in Scripture. After asking for active virtue it was meet that the man of God should beg that his heart might be in all that he did. What would his goings be if his heart did not go ? It may be that David felt a wandering desire, an inordinate leaning of his soul to wordly gain,— possibly it even intruded into his most devout meditations, and at once he cried out for more grace. The only way to cure a wrong leaning is to have the soul bent in the opposite direction. Holiness of heart is the cure for covetousness. What a blessing it is that we may ask the Lord even for an inclination. Our wills are free, and yet without violating their liberty, grace can incline us in the right direction. This can be done by enlightening the understanding as to the excellence of obedience, by strengthening our habits of virtue, by giving us an experience of the sweetness of piety, and by many other ways. If any one duty is irksome to us it behoves us to offer this prayer with special reference thereto : we are to love all the Lord's testimonies, and if we fail in any one point we must pay double attention to it. The leaning of the heart is the way in which the life will lean : hence the force of the petition, "Incline my heart." Happy shall we be when we feel habitually inclined to all that is good. This is not the way in which a carnal heart ever leans ; all its inclinations are in opposition to the divine testimonies.

" And not to covetousness." This is the inclination of nature, and grace must put a negative upon it. This vice is as injurious as it is common ; it is as mean as it is miserable. It is idolatry, and so it dethrones God ; it is selfishness, and so it is cruel to all in its power ; it is sordid greed, and so it would sell the Lord himself for pieces of silver. It is a degrading, grovelling, hardening, deadening sin, which withers every-thing around it that is lovely and Christlike. He who is covetous is of the race of Judas, and will in all probability turn out to be himself a son of perdition. The crime of covetousness is common, but very few will confess it ; for when a man heaps up gold in his heart the dust of it blows into his eyes, and he cannot see his own fault. Our hearts must have some object of desire, and the only way to keep out worldly gain is to put in its place the testimonies of the Lord. If we are inclined or bent one way, we shall be turned from the other ; the negative virtue is most surely attained by making sure of the positive grace which inevitably produces it.

37. " Turn away mine eyes from beholding vanity." He had prayed about his heart, and one would have thought that the eyes would so surely have been influenced by the heart that there was no need to make them the objects of a special petition ; but our author is resolved to make assurance doubly sure. If the eyes do not see, perhaps the heart may not desire ; at any rate, one door of temptation is closed when we do not even look at the painted bauble. Sin first entered man's mind by the eye, and it is still a favourite gate for the incoming of Satan's allurements ; hence the need of a double watch upon that portal. The prayer is not so much that the eyes may be shut as " turned away ; " for we need to have them open, but directed to right objects. Perhaps we are now gazing upon folly, we need to have our eyes

turned away ; and if we are beholding heavenly things we shall be wise to beg that our eyes may be kept away from vanity.   Why should we look on vanity ?—it melts away as a vapour.   Why not look upon things eternal ?   Sin is vanity, unjust gain is vanity, self-conceit is vanity, and, indeed, all that is not of God comes under the same head.   From all this we must turn away.   It is a proof of the sense of weakness felt by the Psalmist and of his entire dependence upon God that he even asks to have his eyes turned for him ;   he meant not to make himself passive, but he intended to set forth his own utter helplessness apart from the grace of God.   For fear he should forget himself and gaze with a lingering longing upon forbidden objects, he entreats the Lord speedily to make him turn away his eyes, hurrying him off from so dangerous a parley with iniquity.   If we are kept from looking on vanity we shall be preserved from loving iniquity.

" *And quicken thou me in thy way.*"   Give me so much life that dead vanity may have no power over me.   Enable me to travel so swiftly in the road to heaven that I may not stop long enough within sight of vanity to be fascinated thereby.   The prayer indicates our greatest need—more life in our obedience.   It shows the preserving power of increased life to keep us from the evils which are around us, and it, also, tells us where that increased life must come from, namely, from the Lord alone. Vitality is the cure of vanity.   When the heart is full of grace the eyes will be cleansed from impurity.   On the other hand, if we would be full of life as to the things of God we must keep ourselves apart from sin and folly, or the eyes will soon captivate the mind, and, like Samson, who could slay his thousands, we may ourselves be overcome through the lusts which enter by the eye.   This verse is parallel to verses 21 and 29 in the previous eights :   " rebuke," " remove," " turn away ; "   or " proud," " lying," " vanity."

38. " *Stablish thy word unto thy servant.*"   Make me sure of thy sure word : make it sure to me and make me sure of it.   If we possess the spirit of service, and yet are troubled with sceptical thoughts we cannot do better than pray to be established in the truth.   Times will arise when every doctrine and promise seems to be shaken, and our mind gets no rest :   then we must appeal to God for establishment in the faith, for he would have all his servants to be well instructed and confirmed in his word.   But we must mind that we are the Lord's servants, for else we shall not long be sound in his truth.   Practical holiness is a great help towards doctrinal certainty :   if we are God's servants he will confirm his word in our experience.   " If any man will do his will, he shall know of the doctrine ; " and so know it as to be fully assured of it.   Atheism in the heart is a horrible plague to a God-fearing man, it brings more torment with it than can well be described and nothing but a visitation of grace can settle the soul after it has been violently assailed thereby.   Vanity or falsehood is bad for the eyes, but it is even worse when it defiles the understanding and casts a doubt upon the word of the living God.

" *Who is devoted to thy fear,*" or simply—" *to thy fear.*"   That is, make good thy word to godly fear wherever it exists ; strengthen the whole body of reverent men. Stablish thy word, not only to me, but to all the godly ones under the sun.   Or, again, it may mean—" Stablish thy word to thy fear," namely, that men may be led to fear thee ; since a sure faith in the divine promise is the fountain and foundation of godly fear.   Men will never worship a God in whom they do not believe.   More faith will lead to more godly fear.   We cannot look for the fulfilment of promises in our experience unless we live under the influence of the fear of the Lord : establishment in grace is the result of holy watchfulness and prayerful energy.   We shall never be rooted and grounded in our belief unless we daily practise what we profess to believe.   Full assurance is the reward of obedience.   Answers to prayer are given to those whose hearts answer to the Lord's command.   If we are devoted to God's fear we shall be delivered from all other fear.   He has no fear as to the truth of the word who is filled with fear of the Author of the word.   Scepticism is both the parent and the child of impiety ; but strong faith both begets piety and is begotten of it. We commend this whole verse to any devout man whose tendency is to scepticism : it will be an admirable prayer for use in seasons of unusually strong misgivings.

39. " *Turn away my reproach which I fear.*"   He feared just reproach, trembling lest he should cause the enemy to blaspheme through any glaring inconsistency. We ought to fear this, and watch that we may avoid it.   Persecution in the form of calumny may also be prayed against, for it is a sore trial, perhaps the sorest of trials to men of sensitive minds.   Many would sooner bear burning at the stake than the trial of cruel mockings.   David was quick tempered, and he probably had all the

greater dread of slander because it raised his anger, and he could hardly tell what he might not do under great provocation. If God turns away our eyes from falsehood, we may also expect that he will turn away falsehood from injuring our good name. We shall be kept from lies if we keep from lies.

"*For thy judgments are good.*" Therefore he is anxious that none may speak evil of the ways of God through hearing an ill report about himself. We mourn when we are slandered ; because the shame is cast rather upon our religion than ourselves. If men would be content to attribute evil *to us*, and go no further, we might bear it, for we are evil ; but our sorrow is that they cast a slur upon the word and character of God, who is so good, that there is none good in comparison with him. When men rail at God's government of the world it is our duty and privilege to stand up for him, and openly to declare before him, " thy judgments are good ; " and we should do the same when they assail the Bible, the gospel, the law, or the name of our Lord Jesus Christ. But we must take heed that they can bring no truthful accusation against us, or our testimony will be so much wasted breath.

This prayer against reproach is parallel to verse 31, and in general to many other of the seventh verses in the octaves, which usually imply opposition from without and a sacred satisfaction within. Observe the things which are good : " *thy judgments are good ; * " " thou art good and doest good " (68) ; " good for me to have been afflicted " (71) ; " teach me good judgment " (66).

40. "*Behold, I have longed after thy precepts.*" He can at least claim sincerity. He is deeply bowed down by a sense of his weakness and need of grace ; but he does desire to be in all things conformed to the divine will. Where our longings are, there are we in the sight of God. If we have not attained perfection, it is something to have hungered after it. He who has given us to desire, will also grant us to obtain. The precepts are grievous to the ungodly, and therefore when we are so changed as to long for them we have clear evidence of conversion, and we may safely conclude that he who has begun the good work will carry it on. "*Quicken me in thy righteousness.*" Give me more life wherewith to follow thy righteous law ; or give me more life because thou hast promised to hear prayer, and it is according to thy righteousness to keep thy word. How often does David plead for quickening ! But never once too often. We need quickening every hour of the day for we are so sadly apt to become slow and languid in the ways of God. It is the Holy Spirit who can pour new life into us ; let us not cease crying to him. Let the life we already possess show itself by longing for more.

The last verses of the octaves have generally exhibited an onward look of resolve, hope, and prayer. Here past fruits of grace are made the plea for further blessing. Onward in the heavenly life is the cry of this verse.

SPECIAL NOTES ON VERSES 33 TO 40.

Upon this Octonary the Notes furnished by Mr. Marchant, one of the Tutors of the Pastors' College, are so excellent that we give them entire.

SECTION ה, HE.

SUBJECT: THE LAW OF JEHOVAH TO BE SET BEFORE THE EYES, THE MIND, THE FEET, AND THE HEART.

Key phrase : הֵם לְעַבְדְּךָ אִמְרָתֶךָ. " *Set up before thy servant thy word* " (ver. 38).

Verse 33.—THE WORD SET UP BEFORE THE EYES. "*Teach me ;*" literally, "*point out,*" "*indicate to me.*" יָרָה, as used here, means "*to send out the hand,*" especially in the sense of pointing out. Hence "*to show,*" "*to indicate,*" "*to teach.*" The Psalmist here prays for direction in its more superficial form. Many paths were before his eyes, leading down to death : one path was before him, leading unto life. He here asks to be shown *which* is Jehovah's way. If the Lord will ever show his eyes which way is the right way, then he will keep it unto the end. Here is light wanted for the eyes. As the Indian pursues his trail with unerring eye and unfaltering step, so, watching for every deviation which might take us astray, we should pursue the way which leadeth unto life.

Verse 34.—THE WORD SET BEFORE THE MIND. "*Give me understanding.*" The word used here refers to mental comprehension, as distinguished from the mere direction, or pointing out, asked for in the previous verse. Here the prayer is, "*Make me to discern,*" "*Cause me to perceive,*" *i.e.,* with the understanding. "Faith cometh by hearing, and hearing by the word of God." The outer senses must first see the way, then the mind must understand it, then, with faith and love, the heart should follow it. Thus, too, the Psalmist, if God will cause him to understand the law, will keep it with all his heart. Still, the heart is prone to lean to things earthly and sinful, and divine help has presently to be invoked for that also.

Verse 35.—THE WORD SET BEFORE THE FEET. The word תַּדְרִיכֵנִי is from דָּרַךְ "*to tread with the feet,*" "*to trample.*" Hence, "*Make me to go,*" alludes here to the very act of walking in the divine way, in distinction from mere perception of the way with the eyes and with the understanding. It is in this matter of practical walking that the actual difficulties of the way seem to come more forcibly into sight ; hence we no longer have דֶּרֶךְ used (as in verse 33) which may mean a broad open way, but נָתִיב, which (says Gesenius) " never denotes a public and royal road, such as was raised up and formed by art, but always a footpath." So the younger Buxtorf renders the word by *Semita.* When the feet really come to tread it, the way of truth is ever found to be " the narrow way."

Verse 36.—THE WORD SET BEFORE THE HEART. " *Incline my heart unto thy testimonies.*" It is nothing for the eyes to see, for the mind to understand, nor even for the feet to be made to go in the way of truth, if the heart be not inclined thereunto also. It is with the heart that man believeth unto righteousness. To be without love is, according to 1 Cor. xiii., to be without everything.

Thus the sense of these four methodical petitions in this section is as follows : Make me to see, make me to understand, make me to go in, and make me to love to go in, the beaten and narrow path of thy testimonies. So far as I gather, Luther gives almost the exact sense of the foregoing exposition ; for he translates the opening words of verses 33, 34, 35, and 36 by terms signifying respectively, " Point out to me," " Explain to me," " Lead me," and " Incline (bend, slope) my heart," etc.

Verse 37.—" *Turn away mine eyes,*" etc. Literally, " *Make mine eyes to pass from seeing vanity ;* " as though he would pray, Whatever is of vanity, make me to pass without seeing it. The sentiment is strikingly like that in our Lord's prayer : " Lead us not into temptation." Having prayed for what he wanted to see, the Psalmist here prays for the hiding of what he would not see.

Verse 38.—" *Stablish thy word unto thy servant.*"   In view of the exposition of the previous verses of the section this would be more correctly rendered, " *Hold up thy word before thy servant ;* " *i.e.,* hold it up to my eyes, to my mind, to my steps, and to my heart.   Make all that is vain to pass, so that I see it not ; but let thy word be so set up before my whole being that I shall always see it, and thus, by it, see my way to thee.

Verse 39.—" *Turn away my reproach which I fear.*"   " Cause to pass my reproach which *I feared.*"   This also, like the vanity spoken of in verse 37, the Psalmist prays that he may not see.   He would have the gaze of his whole manhood bent only on the word.   The reproach which he feared is that to which he had already referred in verses 21, 22, and perhaps again in verse 31.   The proud had erred from the commandments, and had inherited rebuke ; it was the reproach and shame which were theirs that the Psalmist would have to be turned aside, so that they should not be seen.   " *For thy judgments are good.*"   This is given as a reason why the reproach should be thus turned aside.   The proud had thought lightly and contemptuously on the divine judgments, hence their reproach ; the Psalmist held those judgments to be good, and thus hoped that he might not see reproach.

Verse 40.—" *Behold, I have longed after,*" etc.   This is given as an intenser form of the statement which he had just made, that he esteemed the judgments to be good.   They were so good that he longed after them.   Not only so, but he desired to long after them even more.   Thus he prays for even more life and vigour in pursuing the path which they pointed out—" *Quicken me in thy righteousness.*"   He who really longs after divine truth, mourns that he does not long more.   When the heart has no love, the mind has no light, and can only judge the precepts erroneously.   " The pure in heart " see better with the mind than can the impure.   " Unto the upright there ariseth light in the darkness."   Love so enlarges discernment that he who really loves often finds that his judgment of the blessedness of truth has outstripped even his longing for it.   Hence it is the quick who cry, " *Quicken me ;* " it is those who have living desires who pray for yet more life in the way of righteousness

NOTES ON VERSES 33 TO 40.

Verses 33—40.—In this Octonarius, now and again, the same prayer is repeated, of which several times mention has before been made.   For he prays that he may be divinely taught, governed, strengthened, and defended against the calumnies, reproaches, and threatenings of his enemies.   And the prayer is full of the most ardent longings, which is manifest from the same resolve being so frequently repeated. For the more he knows the ignorance, obscurity, doubts, and the imbecility of the human mind, and sees how men are impelled by a slight momentum, so that they fall away from the truth and embrace errors repugnant to the divine word, or fall into great sins, the more ardently and strongly does he ask in prayer that he may be divinely taught, governed, and strengthened, lest he should cast away acknowledged truth, or plunge himself into wickedness.   And by his example he teaches that we, also, against blindness born with us, and the imbecility of our flesh, and also against the snares and madnesses of devils should fortify ourselves with those weapons ; namely, with the right study and knowledge of the divine Word, and with constant prayer.   For if so great a man, who had made such pre-eminent attainments, prayed for this, how much more ought they to do so, who are but novices and ignorant beginners.   This is the sum of this Octonarius.—*D. H. Mollerus.*

Verses 33—40.—In this part, nine times does the Psalmist send up his petition to his God, and six of these he accompanies with a reason for being heard. . . .   These petitions are the utterances of a renewed heart ; the man of God could not but give utterance to them—such was the new refining process that had taken place upon him. . . . .   The outline runs thus :—Petitions are offered for Instruction (33) and Understanding (34), and likewise for Spiritual Ability (35) and Inclination (36). These are followed by petitions for Exemption from the Spirit of Vanity (37), and for Divine Quickening (37).   The Lord is besought to make good his Word of Promise to his servant (38), and to deliver him from Feared Reproach.   Last of all, the man of God places his prayer for quickening upon the ground of the Divine Righteousness (40).   May the Divine Spirit teach us to compare ourselves with what we find here, as we would see the salvation of our God !—*John Stephen.*

Verses 33—40.—I observe that in this one octonary which is not to be found in any of the rest, namely, that in every several verse there is a several prayer.   In the first whereof he prayeth to be taught, and then promiseth to take in that which God shall teach him.   He had before resolved to run in this way ; but he felt forthwith his own natural aberrations, and therefore he cometh to this guide to be taught. —*Richard Greenham.*

Verse 33.—" *Teach me, O Lord, the way of thy statutes,*" etc.   Instruction from above is necessary for the children of God, while they continue in this world.   The more we know, the more we shall desire to know ; we shall beg a daily supply of grace, as well as of bread ; and a taste of " the cluster of Eshcol " will make us long after the vintage of Canaan (Numb. xiii. 23).   Religion is the art of holy living, and then only known when it is practised ; as he is not a master of music who can read the notes which compose it, but he who has learnt to take a lesson readily from the book, and play it on his instrument ; after which the pleasure it affords will be sufficient motive for continuing so to do.—*George Horne.*

Verse 33.—" *Teach me, O Lord, the way of thy statutes,*" etc.   In the sincerity of your hearts go to God for his teaching.   God is pleased with the request.   " Give therefore thy servant an understanding heart to judge thy people, that I may discern between good and bad : for who is able to judge this thy so great a people ?   And the speech pleased the Lord, that Solomon had asked this thing " (1 Kings iii. 9, 10). Oh, beg it of God, for these three reasons—1. The way of God's statutes is worthy to be found by all. 2. It is hard to be found and kept by any. 3. It is so dangerous to miss it, that this should quicken us to be earnest with God.—*Thomas Manton.*

Verse 33.—" *Teach me, O Lord,*" etc.   " He who is his own pupil," remarks S. Bernard, " has a fool for his master."   A soldier who enters on a march does not settle for himself the order of his going, nor begin the journey at his own will, nor yet choose pleasant short-cuts, lest he should fall out of rank, away from the standards, but gets the route from his general, and keeps to it ; advances in a prescribed order, walks armed, and goes straight on to the end of his march, to find there the supplies provided by the commissariat.   If he goes by any other road, he gets no rations, and finds no quarters ready, because the general's orders are that all things of this kind shall be prepared for those who follow him, and turn not aside to the right hand or the left. And thus he who follows his general does not break down, and that for good reasons ; for the general consults not for his own convenience, but for the capability of his whole army. And this, too, is Christ's order of march, as he leads his great host out of the spiritual Egypt to the eternal Land of Paradise.—*Ambrose, quoted by Neale and Littledale.*

Verse 33.—" *Teach me, O* LORD, *the way,*" etc. It should never be forgotten, as this fifth section teaches us, that there is a way marked out by God's own appointment for all his people to walk in, and in which to persevere. Others lay down a path each for himself, and keeping to it think they are safe. David did not trust to anything of this kind ; he was only desirous of being found in the way of God's ordinance, and to be so taught of God as to keep it to the end ; or as the original reads, keep it the end, the end of his profession, the salvation of his soul.—*W. Wilson.*

Verse 33.—" *Teach me, O* LORD, *the way of thy statutes ; and I shall keep it,*" etc. If thou continue a teacher of me, saith David, I shall continue a servant to thee. Perseverance cannot be, unless continual light and grace be furnished to us from the Lord. As the tree which hath not sap at the root may flourish for a while, but cannot continue ; a man, whose heart is not watered with the dew of God's grace continually, may for a time make a fair show of godliness, but in the end he will fall away. We bear not the root, but the root bears us : let us tremble and fear. If we abide not in our Lord, we become withered branches, good for nothing but the fire. Let us alway pray that he would ever abide with us, to inform us by his light, and lead us by his power, in that way which may bring us to himself.—*William Cowper.*

Verse 33.—" *Statutes,*" from a word signifying to *mark, trace out, describe* and *ordain ;* because they *mark out* our way, *describe* the line of conduct we are to pursue, and *order* or *ordain* what we are to observe.—*Adam Clarke.*

Verse 33.—God's " *statutes* " declare his authority and power of giving us laws.— *Matthew Pool,* 1624—1679.

Verse 33.—" *Unto the end,*" or, *by way of return,* or *reward,* or *gratitude* to thee ; God's mercy in *teaching* being in all reason to be *rewarded* or answered by our *observing* and taking exact care of what he teaches. Or else by analogy with Psalm xix. 11, where the *keeping* his *commandments* brings *great reward* with it : it may here be rendered עקב (understanding the preposition ל) *for the reward,* meaning the present joy of it, verse 32, not excluding the future crown.—*H. Hammond.*

Verse 33.—" *Unto the end.*" *Quite through ;* the Hebrew is, *to the heel.* The force of the words seems to be " Quite through, from head to foot."—*Zachary Mudge,* 1744.

Verses 33, 34.—" *Unto the end.*" He will be no *temporizer ;* he will keep it " *to the end.*" He will be no *hypocrite ;* he will keep it " *with his whole heart.*"—*Adam Clarke.*

Verse 34.—" *Give me understanding.*" The Psalmist goes to the root of the matter ; he is taught to do so by the Spirit of all teaching. He would not merely be taught, as a master would teach, but he would have his mind remoulded and informed as only the Creator could do. The words imply as much. " *Give me understanding* "—make me to understand. Not merely did he want to know a thing— the general nature of it ; but he wished to understand the beginning, the outgoing and the end of it. He wanted to attain the power of distinction between right and wrong—spiritual discernment that so he might discern the right, and, at the same time, all that was contrary to it ; he wanted understanding, that so he might know, and discern, and prize the truth, the true way of God, carefully avoiding all that would be aside from it.—*John Stephen.*

Verse 34.—" *Give me understanding.*" This is that which we are indebted to Christ for ; for " the Son of God is come, and hath given us an understanding (1 John v. 20).—*Matthew Henry.*

Verse 34.—" *Understanding.*" The understanding is the pilot and guide of the whole man ; that faculty which sits at the stern of the soul : but as the most expert guide may mistake in the dark, so may the understanding, when it wants the light of knowledge. " Without knowledge the mind cannot be good " (Prov. xix. 2) ; nor the life good ; nor the external condition safe (Eph. iv. 18). " My people are destroyed for the lack of knowledge " (Hosea iv. 6).

It is ordinary in Scripture to set profaneness, and all kinds of miscarriages, upon the score of ignorance. Diseases in the body have many times their rise from distempers in the *head ;* and exorbitances in practice, from errors in the judgment. And, indeed. in every sin, there is something both of ignorance and error at the bottom : for did sinners truly know what they do in sinning, we might say of every sin what the Apostle speaks concerning that great sin, " Had they known him, they would not have crucified the Lord of glory " (1 Cor. ii. 8).   Did they truly know that every sin is a provoking the Lord to jealousy, a proclaiming war against heaven, a crucifying the Lord Jesus afresh, a treasuring up wrath afresh unto themselves against the day of wrath ; and that if ever they be pardoned, it must be at no lower a rate than the price of his blood—*it were scarce possible* but sin, instead of alluring, should affright, and instead of tempting, scare.—*From the " Recommendatory Epistle prefixed to the Westminster Confession and Catechisms."*

Verse 34.—*" My whole heart."*   The whole man is God's by every kind of right and title ; and therefore, when he requireth the whole heart, he doth but require that which is his own.   God gave us the whole by creation, preserveth the whole, redeemeth the whole, and promiseth to glorify the whole.   If we had been mangled in creation we would have been troubled ; if born without hands or feet.   If God should turn us off to ourselves to keep that part to ourselves which we reserved from him, or if he should make such a division at death, take a part to heaven, or if Christ had bought part :   " Ye are bought with a price : therefore glorify God in your body, and in your spirit, which are God's."   (1 Cor. vi. 20).   If you have had any good work upon you, God sanctified the whole in a gospel-sense, that is every part :   " And the very God of peace sanctify you wholly ;   and I pray God your whole spirit and soul and body be preserved blameless unto the coming of our Lord Jesus Christ."   (1 Thess. v. 23).   Not only conscience, but will and affections, appetite and body.   And you have given all to him for his use :   " I am my beloved's ! " not a part, but the whole.   He could not endure Ananias that kept back part of the price ; all is his due.   When the world, pleasure, ambition, pride, desire of riches. unchaste love, desire a part in us, we may remember we have no affections to dispose of without God's leave.   It is all his, and it is sacrilege to rob or detain any part from God.   Shall I alienate that which is God's to satisfy the world, the flesh, and the Devil ?—*Thomas Manton.*

Verses 34, 35.—*"Give me understanding." "Make me to go."*   The understanding which he seeks leads to going, and is sought to that end.   God's teaching begets obedience ;   he showeth us the path of life, and he maketh us to go in it.   It is such instruction as giveth strength, that exciteth the sluggish will, and breaketh the force of corrupt inclinations ;   it removeth the darkness which corruption and sin have brought upon the mind, and maketh us pliable and ready to obey ;   yea, it giveth not only the will, but the deed ;   in short, it engageth us in a watchful, careful, uniform, and constant obedience.—*Thomas Manton.*

Verse 35.—*"Make me to go in the path of thy commandments."*   David, in the former verses, had begged for light, now for strength to walk according to this light.   We need not only light to know our way, but a heart to walk in it.   Direction is necessary because of the blindness of our minds ;   and the effectual impulsions of grace are necessary because of the weakness of our hearts.   It will not answer our duty to have a naked notion of truths, unless we embrace and pursue them. So, accordingly, we need a double assistance from God ;   the mind must be enlightened, the will moved and inclined.   The work of a Christian lies not in depth of speculation, but in the height of practice.   The excellency of Divine grace consisteth in this,—That God doth first teach what is to be done, and then make us to do what is taught :   *"Make me to go in the path of thy commandments."*—*Thomas Manton.*

Verse 35.—*"The path of thy commandments."*   They are termed *"the paths,"* because paths are narrow, short, straight, clean passages for people on foot only, and not for horses and carriages ;   and such is the way of the Lord, as compared with that of the flesh and of the world, all the ways of which are broad, filthy, and crooked, trodden by the brute beasts, the type of carnal, animal man.   He assigns a reason for being heard when he says, *"For this same I have desired" ;*   because, through God's grace, I have chosen this path, and desired to walk in it, and it is only meet that he who gives the will should give the grace to accomplish, as St. Paul says, " Who worketh in you both to will and to do."—*Robert Bellarmine.*

Verse 35.—*"The path "* is *"the path of thy commandments."*   Not any new way, but the old and pathed way wherein all the servants of God have walked before him, and for which the Grecians (as Euthymius noteth) called it τριβον, *quasi viam tritam.* But howsoever this way be pathed, by the walking and treading of many in it, yet he acknowledgeth it is but one, yea, and a narrow and difficult path to keep, and therefore seeks he to be guided into it.—*William Cowper.*

Verse 35.—"*The path.*" It is a "*path,*" not a public road; a path where no *beast* goes, and *men* seldom.—*Adam Clarke,*

Verses 35, 37.—"*The path.*" "*Thy way.*" The Hindus call *panth* or *way* the line of doctrine of any sect followed, in order to attain to *mukti,* or deliverance from sin. *Way* signifies the chief means to an end, and is applied to the Scriptures, Ps. cxix. 27, to God's counsels, to God's works. This spiritual way is—(1) *easy* to find, Isa. xxxv. 8; (2) *clean,* no mud of sin; (3) never out of *repair*—Christ the same as 6,000 years ago; (4) no *lion* or wild beasts on; (5) *costly,* the blood of Christ made it; (6) not *lonely,* many believers on it, Heb. xii. 1; (7) no *toll,* all may come; (8) *wide.* The way to the cities of refuge was forty-eight feet wide. The map of the Bible shows this path; (9) the *end* pleasant—Heaven.—*J. Long, in " Eastern Proverbs and Maxims illustrating old Truths,"* 1881.

Verses 35, 36.—"*Therein do I delight. Incline my heart unto thy testimonies.*" A child of God hath not the bent of his heart so perfectly fixed towards God but it is ever and anon returning to its old bent and bias again. The best may find that they cannot keep their affections as loose from the world when they have houses, and lands, and all things at their will, as they could when they are kept low and bare. The best may find that their love to heavenly things is on the wane as worldly things are on the increase. It is reported of Pius Quintus that he should say of himself that, when he first entered into orders, he had some hopes of his salvation; when he came to be a cardinal, he doubted of it; but since he came to be pope, he did even almost despair. Many may find a very great change in themselves, much decay of zeal for God's glory, and love to and relish of God's word, and mindfulness of heavenly things, as it fares better with them in the world. Now it is good to observe this before the mischief increaseth. Look, as jealousy and caution are necessary to prevent the entrance and beginning of this mischief, so observation is necessary to prevent the increase of it. When the world doth get too deep an interest in our hearts, when it begins to insinuate and entice us from God, and weaken our delight in the ways of God and zeal for his glory, then we need often to tell you how hard it is for a rich man to enter into the kingdom of heaven.—*Thomas Manton.*

Verse 36.—"*Incline my heart unto thy testimonies, and not to covetousness.*" We must be convinced that covetousness, I mean that our covetousness, is a vice; for it holds something of a virtue, of frugality, which is not to waste that which one hath: and this makes us entertain thoughts that it is no vice; and we often say that it is good to be a little worldly; a little covetousness we like well; which shows that we do not indeed and in heart, hold it to be a sin. For if sin be naught, a little of sin cannot be good. As good say, a little poison were good, so it be not too much. And so we find, that men will rate at their children for spending, and are ready to turn them out of doors, if they be given unto waste; but if they be near and pinching then we like that too much; and I scarce know a man who doth use to call upon his children that they spare not, save not. I know youth is rather addicted the other way, and is more subject to waste and consume, by reason that the natural heat is quick and active in them; and therefore indeed there is more fear and danger that they prove prodigal and turn wasters, and therefore the more may be said and done that way to youth. But the thing I press is, that in case we see our children in their youth to begin to be covetous and worldly, we call them good husbands, and are but too glad to see it so, and are too much pleased with them for it. Little do they think that worldliness is a most guiltful sin in respect of God, and most hurtful in respect of men. Hark what the word of God saith of it, Ephesians v. 5: *It is idolatry,* and idolatry is the first sin of the first table. *It is the root of all evils,* 1 Tim. vi. 10. There is no evil but a worldly man will do it to save his purse. Thus David: "*Incline my heart unto thy testimonies, and not to covetousness*": he saith not, this or that testimony, but (as including all the laws of God) he saith "*testimonies*"; to show us that covetousness draws us away, not from some only, but from all God's commandments. So St. Paul: where covetousness is, there are " many lusts," 1 Tim. vi. 9, and " many sorrows," 1 Tim. vi. 10. " It drowns men in perdition and destruction," 1 Tim. vi. 9. And the Greek word signifies such a drowning as is almost past all hope and recovery. It is the bane of all society : men cry out of it, because they would have none covetous, none rich but themselves. A hater he is of mankind ; he hates all poor, because they would beg something of him ; and all rich, because they have riches which he would have. A covetous man would have all that all have. Thus speaks a noble father.* Such believe not the word, they trust neither God nor man. For he that trusts not God, cannot trust man. It robs God of that confidence we should have in him, and dependence we owe unto him ; it turns a man from all the commandments. Hence the prophet David prays God to turn his heart to his commandments, *"and not to covetousness."* For not only we *ought* not, but as the phrase is, " we *cannot* serve God and mammon," Luke xvi. 13.—*Richard Capel, in "Tentations : their Nature, Danger, Cure."* 1655.

Verse 36.—*"Incline my heart unto thy testimonies, and not to covetousness."* Without a restraining hand the heart is prone to turn aside into the byeways of petty love of pelf. The remedy must be from above. Heavenly aid is therefore sought.—*Henry Law.*

Verse 36.—*"Incline my heart."* Were we naturally and spontaneously inclined to the righteousness of the law, there would be no occasion for the petition of the Psalmist, *"Incline my heart."* It remains, therefore, that our hearts are full of sinful thoughts, and wholly rebellious until God by his grace change them.—*John Calvin.*

Verse 36.—*"Incline my heart."* In the former verses David had asked understanding and direction to know the Lord's will ; now he asketh an inclination of heart to do the Lord's will. The understanding needs not only to be enlightened, but the will to be moved and changed. Man's heart is of its own accord averse from God and holiness, even then when the wit is most refined, and the understanding is stocked and stored with high notions about it : therefore David doth not only say, " Give me understanding," but, *"Incline my heart."* We can be worldly of ourselves, but we cannot be holy and heavenly of ourselves ; that must be asked of him who is the Father of lights, from whom cometh down every good and perfect gift. They that plead for the power of nature, shut out the use of prayer. But Austin hath said well, *Natura vera confessione non falsa defensione opus habet :* we need rather to confess our weakness, than defend our strength. Thus doth David, and so will every broken-hearted Christian that hath had an experience of the inclinations of his own soul, he will come to God, and say, *"Incline my heart unto thy testimonies, and not to covetousness."*—*Thomas Manton.*

Verse 36.—*"Incline."* Then shall I not decline.—*James G. Murphy.*

Verse 36.—*"Unto thy testimonies."* The contrast is most striking. There are the *divine testimonies* on the one hand, and there is *"covetousness"* on the other. God stands on one side, the world on the other. The renewed man chooses between the two ; he does not require long to think, and God is his choice.—*John Stephen.*

Verse 36.—*"Not to covetousness."* He prays in particular that his heart may be diverted from covetousness, which is not only an evil, but as saith the Apostle, " the root of all evil." David here opposes it as an adversary to all the righteousness of God's testimonies : it inverts the order of nature, and makes the heavenly soul earthly. It is a handmaid of all sins ; for there is no sin which a covetous man will not serve for his gain. We should beware of all sins, but specially of mother-sins.—*William Cowper.*

Verse 36.—*"Covetousness,"* or rather, " gain unjustly acquired." . . . . The Hebrew word בצע can only mean *plunder, rapine, unjust gain.*—*J. J. Stewart Perowne.*

Verse 36.—*"Covetousness."*—S. Bonaventura, on our Psalm, says *Covetousness* must be hated, shunned, put away : must be hated, because it attacks the life of nature : must be shunned, because it hinders the life of grace : must be put away, because it obstructs the life of glory. Clemens Alexandrinus says that covetousness is the citadel of the vices, and Ambrose says that it is the loss of the soul.—*Thomas Le Blanc.*

Verse 36.—*"Covetousness."* I would observe to the reader, and desire him duly and seriously to consider, that although this commandment, " Thou shalt not covet," is placed the last in number, yet it is too often the first that is broken, man's covetous heart leading the van in transgression.—*William Crouch, in "The Enormous Sin of Covetousness detected,"* 1708.

---

* Chrysostom.

Verse 36.—"*Covetousness*" is an immoderate desire of riches, in which these vices concur. *First*, An excessive love of riches, and the fixing of our hearts upon them. *Secondly*, A resolution to become rich, either by lawful or unlawful means, 1 Tim. vi. 9. *Thirdly*, Too much haste in gathering riches, joined with impatience of any delay, Prov. xxviii. 20, 22, and xx. 21. *Fourthly*, An insatiable appetite, which can never be satisfied ; but when they have too much, they still desire more, and have never enough, Eccles. iv. 8. Like the horseleech, Prov. xxx. 15 ; the dropsy, and hell itself, Prov. xxvii. 20. *Fifthly*, Miser-like tenacity, whereby they refuse to communicate their goods, either for the use of others, or themselves. *Sixthly*, Cruelty. Prov. i. 18, 19, exercised both in their unmercifulness and oppression of the poor. Covetousness is a most heinous vice ; for it is idolatry, and the root of all evil, Col. iii. 5 ; 1 Tim. vi. 10 ; a pernicious thorn, that stifles all grace and choketh the seed of the word, Matt. xiii. 22, and pierceth men through with many sorrows, 1 Tim. vi. 10, and drowneth them in destruction and perdition.— *James Usher*, 1580—1655.

Verse 37.—"*Turn away mine eyes,*" etc. Having prayed for his heart, he now prayeth for his eyes also. *Omnia à Deo petit, docens illum omnia efficere.* By the eyes oftentimes, as by windows, death enters into the heart ; therefore to keep the heart in a good estate three things are requisite, First, a careful study of the senses, specially of the eyes ; for it is a righteous working of the Lord, *ut qui exteriori oculo negligenter utitur, interiori non injusté cæcetur ;* that he who negligently useth the external eye of his body, should be punished with blindness in the internal eye of his mind. And for this cause Nazianzen, deploring the calamities of his soul, wished that a door might be set before his eyes and ears, to close them when they opened to anything that is not good ; *malis autem sua sponte utrumque clauderetur.* The second thing is, a subduing of the body by discipline. And the third is, continuance in prayer.—*William Cowper.*

Verse 37.—"*Turn away mine eyes from beholding vanity.*" Notice this, that he does not say, I will turn away mine eyes ; but, "*Turn away mine eyes.*" This shows that it is not possible for us sufficiently to keep our eyes by our own caution and diligence ; but there must be divine keeping. For, first, wheresoever in this world you turn yourself provocations to evil are met with. Secondly, with the unwary, and with far different persons, the eyes, the servants of a corrupt heart, wander after the things which are vanities. Thirdly, before you are aware, the evil contracted through the eyes creeps in to the inmost recesses of the heart, and casts in the seeds of perdition. This the Psalmist himself had experienced, not without the greatest trouble both of heart and condition.—*Wolfgang Musculus*, 1497—1563.

Verse 37.—"*Turn away mine eyes from beholding vanity.*" It may seem a strange prayer of David, to say, "*Turn away mine eyes from seeing vanity ;*" as though God meddled with our looking ; or that we had not power in ourselves to cast our eyes upon what objects we list. But is it not, that what we delight in, we delight to look upon ? and what we love, we love to be seeing ? and so to pray to God, that our eyes may not see vanity, is as much as to pray for grace, that we be not in love with vanity. For, indeed, vanity hath of itself so graceful an aspect, that it is not for a natural man to leave looking upon it ; unless the fairer aspect of God's grace draw our eyes from vanity, to look upon itself ; which will always naturally be looking upon the fairest. And as David here makes his prayer in the particular, against temptations of prosperity, so Christ teacheth us to make our prayer in the general, against the temptations, both of prosperity and adversity, and very justly. For many can bear the temptations of one kind, who are quickly overcome by temptations of the other kind. So David could bear persecution without murmuring, but when he came to prosperity he could not turn away his eyes from vanity.— *Sir Richard Baker.*

Verse 37.—"*Turn away mine eyes from beholding vanity.*" An ugly object loses much of its deformity when we look often upon it. Sin follows this general law, and is to be avoided altogether, even in its contemplation, if we would be safe. A man should be thankful in this world that he has eyelids ; and as he can close his eyes, so he should often do it.—*Albert Barnes.*

Verse 37.—"*Turn away,*" then "*quicken,*" etc. The first request is for the removing the impediments of obedience, the other for the addition of new degrees of grace. These two are fitly joined, for they have a natural influence upon one another ; unless we turn away our eyes from vanity, we shall soon contract deadness of heart.   Nothing causeth it so much as an inordinate liberty in carnal vanities ; when our affections are alive to other things, they are dead to God, therefore the less we let loose our hearts to these things, the more lively and cheerful in the work of obedience.   On the other side, the more the vigour of grace is renewed, and the habits of it quickened into actual exercise, the more is sin mortified and subdued. Sin dieth, and our senses are restored to their proper use.—*Thomas Manton.*

Verse 37.—*"Turn away mine eyes from beholding vanity."*   That sin may be avoided we must avoid whatsoever leads to or occasions it.   As this caused Job (ch. xxxi. 1) to covenant strongly with his eyes, so it caused David to pray earnestly about his eyes.   *"Turn away mine eyes* (or as the Hebrew may be rendered, *make them to pass,) from beholding vanity."*   The eye is apt to make a stand, or fix itself, when we come in view of an ensnaring object ; therefore it is our duty to hasten it away, or to pray that God would make it pass off from it. . . He that feareth burning must take heed of playing with fire : he that feareth drowning must keep out of deep waters.   He that feareth the plague must not go into an infected house. Would they avoid sin who present themselves to the opportunities of it ?—*Joseph Caryl.*

Verse 37.—*"Turn away mine eyes."*   Lest looking cause liking and lusting : 1 John ii. 16.   In Hebrew the same word signifieth both an *eye* and a *fountain ;* to show that from the eye, as from a fountain, floweth much mischief ; and by that window Satan often winds himself into the soul.   This David found by experience, and therefore prays here, *"Turn away,"* transfer, make to pass *"mine eyes,"* etc. He knew the danger of irregular glancing and inordinate gazing.—*John Trapp.*

Verse 37.—*"Turn away mine eyes from beholding vanity."*   It is a most dangerous experiment for a child of God to place himself within the sphere of seductive temptations.   Every feeling of duty, every recollection of his own weakness, every remembrance of the failure of others, should induce him to hasten to the greatest possible distance from the scene of unnecessary conflict and danger.— *John Morison.*

Verse 37.—*"Turn away mine eyes from beholding vanity."*   From gazing at the delusive *mirages* which tempt the pilgrim to leave the safe highway.— *William Kay.*

Verse 37.—Is it asked—" What will most effectually turn my eyes from vanity ? " Not the seclusion of contemplative retirement—not the relinquishment of our lawful connexion with the world—but the transcendent beauty of Jesus unveiled to our eyes, and fixing our hearts.—*Charles Bridges.*

Verse 37.—*"Turn away mine eyes,"* etc.   The fort-royal of your souls is in danger of a surprise while the outworks of your senses are unguarded.   Your eyes, which may be floodgates to pour out tears, should not be casements to let in lusts. A careless eye is an index to a graceless heart.   Remember, the whole world died by a wound in the eye.   The eyes of a Christian should be like sunflowers, which are opened to no blaze but that of the sun.—*William Secker,* 1660.

Verse 37.—*"Vanity,"* in Hebrew usage, has often special reference to idols and the accompaniments of idol worship.   The Psalmist prays that he may never be permitted even to see such tempting objects.—*Henry Cowles.*

Verse 37.—*"Quicken thou me."*   Every saint is very apt to be a sluggard in the way and work of God.   *"Quicken me,"* says one of the chiefest and choicest of saints, *"in thy way";* and it is as much as if he should say in plain terms, "Ah, Lord ! I am a dull jade, and have often need of thy spur, thy Spirit."   This prayer of David seems proof enough to this point ; but if you desire farther confirmation, I shall produce an argument *instar omnium,* " that none shall dare to deny, nor be able to disapprove " ; and that is drawn from the topic of your own experience ; and this is *argumentum lugubre,* like a funeral anthem, " very sad and sorrowful." Do you not feel and find, to the grief of your own souls, that, whereas you should weep as if you wept not, rejoice as if you rejoiced not, and buy as if you were possessed not ; *inverso ordine,* [" inverting this order,"] you weep for losses as if you would weep out your eyes ; you rejoice in temporal comforts as if you were in heaven ; and you buy as if it were for ever a day (Ps. xlix. 11).   But *e contrario,* [" on the contrary,"] you pray as if you prayed not ; hear as if you heard not ; work for God as if you worked not.   Now, we know, *experto credas,** a man that sticks fast in a ditch needs no reason to prove he is in, but remedies to pull him out.   Your best course will be to propose the case how you may get rid of this unwelcome guest,

---

* " You may yield credence to that of which you have made trial."

spiritual sloth : it is a case we are all concerned in. *Asini aures quis non habet ?* [*]
Every man and mortal hath some of the ass's dulness and sloth in him.—*Mr. Simmons
in "The Morning Exercises," 1661.*

Verse 37.—*"Quicken thou me."* Another quickening ordinance is *prayer.* How
often doth David pray for quickening grace ? five or six times in one Psalm. He
begins many a prayer with a heavy heart, and before he hath done he is full of life.
Therefore, pray much, because all life is from God, and he quickens whom he will.
Only let me add this caution, before I let this pass,—Be sure thy understanding
and affection go along together in every ordinance, and in every part of the ordinance,
as thou wouldst have it a quickening ordinance.—*Matthew Lawrence, in "The Use
and Practice of Faith," 1657.*

Verse 37.—*"Thy way,"* by way of emphasis, in opposition to and exaltation of,
above, all other ways. There is a fourfold way :—1. *Via mundi,* the way of the
world ; and that is *spinosa,* thorny. 2. *Via carnis,* the way of the flesh ; and
that is *insidiosa,* treacherous. 3. *Via Satana,* the way of the devil ; and that is
tenebricosa, darksome. 4. *Via Domini,* the way of God ; and that is *gratiosa,*
gracious.—*Simmons.*

Verses 37, 38.—Prayer is nothing but the promise reversed, or God's word formed
into an argument, and retorted by faith upon God again. Know, Christian, thou
hast law on thy side. Bills and bonds must be paid. David prays against the
sins of a wanton eye and a dead heart : *"Turn away mine eyes from beholding vanity ;
and quicken thou me in thy way";* and see how he urgeth his argument in the next
words,—*"Stablish thy word unto thy servant."* A good man is as good as his word,
and will not a good God be so ? But where finds David such a word for help against
these sins ? Surely in the covenant. It is in the magna charta. The first promise
held forth thus much,—" The seed of the woman shall bruise the serpent's head."
—*William Gurnall.*

Verse 38.—*"Stablish thy word unto thy servant,"* etc.—Well, but here is a strange
thing—a man who is a true *"servant of God," "devoted to his fear,"* praying for what
he surely must already have, else how could he be a servant ? or be living in Jehovah's
fear ? He seems to assume, clearly and without any doubt, his own personal consecration, and then he prays for that which must surely be, at least in considerable
measure, assumed and comprehended in the very idea of a true personal consecration.
Unless God's word is made sure to a man he will never become his servant. If he
is his servant, why should he pray, *"Stablish thy word" ?* Why, too, should he say
in the thirty-fifth verse, *"Make me to go in the path of thy commandments ; for therein
do I delight" ?* "Therein do I delight. It is the way of my choice, of my joy ! "
And yet, " Make me to go in it," as if I were unwilling. This apparent contradiction
or discrepancy is easily solved in a true experience, and can be, in fact, solved in no
other way. Is not this the very condition of many and many a one ? "Stablished,"
yet moved ; *"devoted,"* yet uncertain ; *"serving"* God truly, yet looking and longing
for clear warrant, and higher sanction, and more inward grace, to make the service
better ; " believing," yet crying, sometimes, " with tears, Help thou mine unbelief ! "
—*Alexander Raleigh.*

Verse 38.—*"Stablish thy word unto thy servant."* Why doth David pray thus,
"Stablish thy word to me ;" since God's word is most certain and so stable in itself
that it cannot be more so ? (2 Pet. i. 19). " We have a more sure," or a more
stable, " word of prophecy," as the word signifies. How can the word be more
stable than it is ? I answer, it is sure in regard of God from whom it comes, and
in itself. In regard of the things propounded it cannot be more or less stable, it
cannot be fast and loose : but in regard of us, it may be more or less established.
And that two ways,—1. By the inward assurance of the Spirit increasing our faith.
2. By the outward performance of what is promised.

1st, By the inward assurance of the Spirit, by which our faith is increased. Great
is the weakness of our faith, as appears by our fears, doubts, distrusts, so that we
need to be assured more and more. We need say with tears as he doth in the gospel :
" Lord, I believe ; help thou mine unbelief " (Mark ix. 24) ; and to cry out with
the apostles, " Lord, increase our faith " (Luke xvii. 5). There is none believeth so,
but he may yet believe more. And in this sense the word is more established,
when we are confirmed in the belief of it, and look upon it as sure ground for faith

---

[*] " Where is the man who hath not the ears of an ass ? "

to rest upon. 2ndly, By actual performance, when the promise is made good for us. Every event which falls out according to the word is a notable testimony of the truth of it, and a seal to confirm and strengthen our faith. Three ways may this be made good.

1. The making good of some promises at one time strengthens our faith in expecting the like favour at another. Christ was angry with his disciples for not remembering the miracle of the loaves, when they fell into a like strait again. " Do ye not yet understand, neither remember the five loaves ? " (Matt. xvi. 9). We are to seek upon every difficulty ; whereas former experience in the same kind should be a means of establishment to us : " He hath delivered, and doth deliver : in whom we trust that he will yet deliver us " (2 Cor. i. 10). In teaching a child to spell we are angry, if, when we have showed him a letter once, twice, and a third time, yet when he meets with it again still he misseth : so, God is angry with us when we have had experience of his word in this, that, and the other providence, yet still our doubts return upon us.

2. The accomplishment of one promise confirms another ; for God, that keepeth touch at one time, will do so at another : " I was delivered out of the mouth of the lion. And the Lord shall deliver me from every evil work, and will preserve me unto his heavenly kingdom " (2 Tim. iv. 17, 18). In such a strait God failed not, and surely he that hath been true hitherto will not fail at last.

3. When the word is performed in part, it assureth us of the performance of the whole. It is an earnest given us of all the rest : " For all the promises of God in him are yea, and in him amen " (2 Cor. i. 20). A Christian hath a great many promises, and they are being performed daily ; God is delivering, comforting, protecting him, speaking peace to his conscience ; but the greater part are yet to be performed. Present experiences do assure us of what is to come. Thus, *"Stablish thy word,"* that is, make it good by the event, that I may learn to trust another time either for the same, or other promises or accomplishments of thy whole word.— *Thomas Manton.*

Verse 38.—*"Stablish thy word unto thy servant."* Confirm it ; make it *seem* firm and true ; let not my mind be vacillating or sceptical in regard to thy truth. This seems to be a prayer against the influence of doubt and scepticism ; a prayer that doubts might not be suffered to spring up in his mind, and that the objections and difficulties of scepticism might have no place there. There is a class of men whose minds are naturally sceptical and unbelieving, and for such men such a prayer is peculiarly appropriate. For none can it be improper to pray that the word of God may always seem to them to be true ; that their minds may never be left to the influence of doubt and unbelief.—*Albert Barnes.*

Verse 38.—*"Who is devoted to thy fear."* The word may be rendered either which or who ; as relating either to thy word or to thy servant. 1. Thy word ; for in the original Hebrew the posture of the verse is thus, " Stablish to thy servant thy word, which is to the fearing of thee," or, " which is given that thou mayest be feared ; " there being in the word of God the greatest arguments and inducements to fear, to reverence, and to obey him. The word of God was appointed to plant the fear of God in our hearts, and to increase our reverence of God ; not that we may play the wantons with promises, and feed our lusts with them. 2. I rather take our own translation, and it hath such a sense as that passage, " But I give myself unto prayer " (Psalm cxix. 4). In the original it is, " But I prayer." So in this place it may be read, Stablish thy word to thy servant, " Who is to thy fear." Our translators add, to make the sense more full, addicted, or " devoted to thy fear," that is, who makes it his business, care, and desire to stand in the fear of God.

Now this is added as a true note and description of God's servants, as being a main thing in religion, " The fear of the Lord is the beginning of wisdom " (Psalm cxi. 10), it is the first in point of order, and it is the first thing when we begin to be wise, to think of God, to have awful thoughts of God, it is a chief point of wisdom, the great thing that makes us wise to salvation. And it is added as an argument of prayer, " O Lord, let thine ear be attentive to the prayer of thy servants, who desire to fear thy name " (Neh. i. 11). The more any are given to the fear of God, the more assurance they have of God's love, and of his readiness to hear them at the throne of grace.—*Thomas Manton.*

Verse 38.—*"Who is devoted to thy fear."* He who hath received from the Lord grace to fear him may be bold to seek any necessary good thing from him ; because the fear of God hath annexed the promises of all other blessings with it.—*William Cowper.*

Verse 38.—He that chooses God, devotes himself to God as the vessels of the sanctuary were consecrated and set apart from the common to holy uses, so he that has chosen God to be his God, has dedicated himself to God, and will no more be devoted to profane uses.—*Thomas Watson.*

Verse 39.—"*Turn away my reproach*," etc. In these words you have,—1. A request, "*Turn away my reproach.*" 2. A reason to enforce it. "*For thy judgments are good.*"

First, for the request. "*Turn away*," roll from upon me, so it signifies. He was clothed with reproach ; now roll from me "*my reproach.*" Some think he means God's condemnatory sentence, which would turn to his reproach, or some remarkable rebuke from God, because of his sin. Rather, I think, the calumnies of his enemies ; and he calls it "*my reproach,*" either as deserved by himself, or as having personally lighted upon him, the reproach which was like to be his lot and portion in the world, through the malice of his enemies : "*the reproach which I fear,*" that is, which I have cause to expect, and am sensible of the sad consequences of it.

Secondly, for the reason by which this is enforced: "*for thy judgments are good.*" There are different opinions about the form of this argument. Some take the reason thus : Let me not suffer reproach for adhering to thy word, thy word which is so good. But David doth not speak here of suffering reproach for righteousness, sake, but such reproach as was likely to befall him because of his own infirmities and failings. Reproaches for righteousness' sake are to be "rejoiced in ;" but he saith, this I "*fear,*" and therefore I suppose this doth not hit the reason. Neither do I accept the other sense,—Why should I be looked upon as an evil-doer as long as I keep thy law, and observe thy statutes ? Others judge badly of me, but I appeal to thy good judgment.

By "*judgments*" we may understand God's dealings. Thou dost not deal with men according to their desert. Thy dispensations are kind and gracious. Better still : by "*judgments*" are meant the ways, statutes, and ordinances of God called judgments, because all our words, works, thoughts are to be judged according to the sentence of the word : now these, it is a pity they should suffer in my reproach and ignominy. This is that I fear more than anything else that can happen to me. I think the reason will better run thus : Lord, there is in thy law, word, covenant, many promises to encourage thy people, and therefore rules to provide for the due honour and credit of thy people.—*Thomas Manton.*

Verse 39.—"*Turn away my reproach.*" In the Hebrew it is, "*Take away my rebuke*" ; as if he should have said, O Lord, I may commit some such evil against thy good law, yea, some such notorious transgression, as may tend to my shame ; I beseech thee, take it away. Or else he meaneth, I have already, O Lord, by divers sins, and by name through adultery and murder brought shame and rebuke upon myself among men ; I entreat thee to remove this shame and rebuke.

Out of the first exposition we learn, First, that the godly are subject unto notorious sins. Secondly, that those sins will cause shame in them, though the wicked will not be ashamed. Thirdly, that God only can take away this shame. Fourthly, that we may pray for the removing of shame even amongst men, especially that which may bring with it some dishonour to God. Fifthly, that the godly are most jealous over themselves. Sixthly, the way to avoid sin is ever to be afraid lest we should sin.

Out of the second exposition note, that the remembrance of our former sins must draw out of us prayers unto God, that for them we may not be rebuked in displeasure in this life, nor confounded and abashed in the life to come.—*Richard Greenham.*

Verse 39.—"*My reproach*" is the reproach which the world casts on the God-fearing. This is dreaded as a great temptation to apostasy.—*James G. Murphy.*

Verse 39.—"*For thy judgments are good.*" One would have expected him to say—For thou art merciful—Cause my reproach which I fear to pass over from me, for thou art merciful. No, he does not add this as his present reason, but "*Thy judgments are good.*" We should catch the meaning at once, were the words these —For thy judgments are *awful*—" Turn away my reproach which I fear," for thy judgments are awful. But as the words are—" For thy judgments are *good,*" we find he verily takes refuge in the " judgments "—viz., that the Lord would vindicate him against all the unjust judgments of men ; and as to judgment with God, since he took refuge in the atonement which the Lord had appointed, the Lord would vindicate him there also.—*John Stephen.*

Verse 39.—*"For thy judgments are good."* The judgments of the wicked are bad judgments, but the judgments of God are good ; I pray against those, I appeal to these : I fear the one, I approve the other. Now the judgments which God pronounceth in his word, be they threatenings in the law, or consolations in the Gospel, yea, and those also which he executeth in the world, whether upon the godly or godless, they must needs be good. 1. Because God is goodness itself. 2. He cannot be deceived. 3. He will not be bribed. 4. He alone is no respecter of persons, but judgeth according to every man's work.—*Richard Greenham.*

Verse 39.—The " reproach " which the poet fears in this verse is not the reproach of confessing, but of denying God.—*Franz Delitzsch.*

Verse 39.—*"For thy judgments are good."* This reason shows he feared God's rebuke. Man's " reproach " comes from a corrupt judgment, he condemns where God will absolve, I pass not for it ; but I know thy rebuke is always deserved, " *for thy judgments are good.*"—*William Nicholson.*

Verse 40.—*"I have longed after thy precepts."* We are sometimes unconsciously led to " long " after the promises, more than " *after the precepts*" of God ; forgetting that it is our privilege and safety to have an equal regard to both—to obey his precepts in dependence on his promises, and to expect the accomplishment of the promises in the way of obedience to the precepts.—*Charles Bridges.*

Verse 40.—*"Precepts,"* from a word which means to *place in trust*, mean something entrusted to man, " that which is committed to thee " ; appointments of God, which consequently have to do with the conscience, for which man is responsible as an intelligent being. The precepts are not so obviously apprehended as the law and the testimonies. They must be sought out. "*Behold, my desire is for thy precepts* " (ver. 40). "*Thy precepts I seek* " (ver. 45). "*Thy precepts I have sought* " (ver. 94). . . . They are a law of liberty : "*And I will walk at liberty : for I seek thy precepts* " (ver. 45).—*John Jebb.*

Verse 40.—*"Quicken me in thy righteousness."* He said before, " Quicken me in thy word," here, " in thy righteousness " ; all is one ; for the word of God is the righteousness of God, in which is set down the will of righteousness. In this the prophet desires to be quickened, that is, to be confirmed, that in cheerfulness and gladness of spirit he might rely upon the word of God.—*Richard Greenham.*

Verse 40.—*"Quicken me in thy righteousness."* The petition is for liveliness in the knowledge and practice of holiness, according to the tenor of God's word and by its operation on the heart. If any prefer by " *righeousness* " to understand the faithfulness or justice of God, whereby he has bound himself to give grace to those who trust in him, there is no objection to such an interpretation. It is in fact implied in the others. Whoever can truly use the language of this verse is regenerate. Before renewing grace the law was a dead letter. It was more ; it was a hated letter. The carnal mind is not subject to the law of God, neither indeed can be. A sinner desires no restraint from the divine precepts.—*William S. Plumer.*

EXPOSITION OF VERSES 41 TO 48.

L ET thy mercies come also unto me, O Lord, *even* thy salvation, according to thy word.

42 So shall I have wherewith to answer him that reproacheth me : for I trust in thy word.

43 And take not the word of truth utterly out of my mouth ; for I have hoped in thy judgments.

44 So shall I keep thy law continually for ever and ever.

45 And I will walk at liberty : for I seek thy precepts.

46 I will speak of thy testimonies also before kings, and will not be ashamed.

47 And I will delight myself in thy commandments, which I have loved.

48 My hands also will I lift up unto thy commandments, which I have loved ; and I will meditate in thy statutes.

In these verses holy fear is apparent and prominent. The man of God trembles lest in any way or degree the Lord should remove his favour from him. The eight verses are one continued pleading for the abiding of grace in his soul, and it is supported by such holy arguments as would only suggest themselves to a spirit burning with love to God.

41. "*Let thy mercies come also unto me, O Lord.*" He desires *mercy* as well as teaching, for he was guilty as well as ignorant. He needed much mercy and varied mercy, hence the request is in the plural. He needed mercy from God rather than from man, and so he asks for "thy mercies." The way sometimes seemed blocked, and therefore he begs that the mercies may have their way cleared by God, and may "come" to him. He who said, "Let there be light," can say, "Let there be mercy." It may be that under a sense of unworthiness the writer feared lest mercy should be given to others, and not to himself ; he therefore cries, "Bless me, even me also, O my Father." Viewed in this light the words are tantamount to our well-known verse—

> "Lord, I hear of showers of blessing
> Thou art scattering, full and free ;
> Showers, the thirsty land refreshing ;
> Let some droppings fall on me,
> Even me."

Lord, thine enemies come to me to reproach me, let thy mercies come to defend me ; trials and troubles abound, and labours and sufferings not a few approach me ; Lord, let thy mercies in great number enter by the same gate, and at the same hour ; for art thou not the God of my mercy ?

"*Even thy salvation.*" This is the sum and crown of all mercies—deliverance from all evil, both now and for ever. Here is the first mention of salvation in the Psalm, and it is joined with mercy : "By grace are ye saved." Salvation is styled "thy salvation," thus ascribing it wholly to the Lord : "He that is our God is the God of salvation." What a mass of mercies are heaped together in the one salvation of our Lord Jesus ! It includes the mercies which spare us before our conversion, and lead up to it. Then comes calling mercy, regenerating mercy, converting mercy, justifying mercy, pardoning mercy. Nor can we exclude from complete salvation any of those many mercies which are needed to conduct the believer safe to glory. Salvation is an aggregate of mercies incalculable in number, priceless in value, incessant in application, eternal in endurance. To the God of our mercies be glory, world without end.

"*According to thy word.*" The way of salvation is described in the word, salvation itself is promised in the word, and its inward manifestation is wrought by the word ; so that in all respects the salvation which is in Christ Jesus is in accordance with the word. David loved the Scriptures, but he longed experimentally to know the salvation contained in them : he was not satisfied to read the word, he longed to experience its inner sense. He valued the field of Scripture for the sake of the treasure which he had discovered in it.   He was not to be contented with chapter and verse, he wanted mercies and salvation.

Note that in the first verse of HE (33) the Psalmist prayed to be taught to keep God's word, and here in VAU he begs the Lord to keep his word.   In the first case he longed to come to the God of mercies, and here he would have the Lord's mercies come to him : there he sought grace to persevere in faith, and here he seeks the end of his faith, even the salvation of his soul.

42. " *So shall I have wherewith to answer him that reproacheth me.*"   This is an unanswerable answer.   When God, by granting us salvation, gives to our prayers an answer of peace, we are ready at once to answer the objections of the infidel, the quibbles of the sceptical, and the sneers of the contemptuous.   It is most desirable that revilers should be answered, and hence we may expect the Lord to save his people in order that a weapon may be put into their hands with which to rout his adversaries.   When those who reproach *us* are also reproaching God, we may ask him to help us to silence them by sure proofs of his mercy and faithfulness.

" *For I trust in thy word.*"   His faith was seen by his being trustful while under trial, and he pleads it as a reason why he should be helped to beat back reproaches by a happy experience.   Faith is our argument when we seek mercies and salvation ; faith in the Lord who has spoken to us in his word.   " I trust in thy word " is a declaration more worth the making than any other ; for he who can truly make it has received power to become a child of God, and so to be the heir of unnumbered mercies.   God hath more respect to a man's trust than to all else that is in him ; for the Lord hath chosen faith to be the hand into which he will place his mercies and his salvation.   If any reproach us for trusting in God, we reply to them with arguments the most conclusive when we show that God has kept his promises, heard our prayers, and supplied our needs.   Even the most sceptical are forced to bow before the logic of facts.

In this second verse of this eight the Psalmist makes a confession of faith, and a declaration of his belief and experience.   Note that he does the same in the corresponding verses of the sections which follow.   See 50, " Thy word hath quickened me"; 58, " I entreated thy favour"; 66, " I have believed thy commandments"; 74, " I have hoped in thy word."   A wise preacher might find in these a series of experimental discourses.

43. " *And take not the word of truth utterly out of my mouth.*"   Do not prevent my pleading for thee by leaving me without deliverance ; for how could I continue to proclaim thy word if I found it fail me ? such would seem to be the run of the meaning.   The word of truth cannot be a joy to our mouths unless we have an experience of it in our lives, and it may be wise for us to be silent if we cannot support our testimonies by the verdict of our consciousness.   This prayer may also refer to other modes by which we may be disabled from speaking in the name of the Lord : as, for instance, by our falling into open sin, by our becoming depressed and despairing, by our labouring under sickness or mental aberration, by our finding no door of utterance, or meeting with no willing audience.   He who has once preached the gospel from his heart is filled with horror at the idea of being put out of the ministry ; he will crave to be allowed a little share in the holy testimony, and will reckon his dumb Sabbaths to be days of banishment and punishment.

" *For I have hoped in thy judgments.*"   He had expected God to appear and vindicate his cause, that so he might speak with confidence concerning his faithfulness. God is the author of our hopes, and we may most fittingly entreat him to fulfil them.   The judgments of his providence are the outcome of his word ; what he says in the Scriptures he actually performs in his government ; we may therefore look for him to show himself strong on the behalf of his own threatenings and promises, and we shall not look in vain.

God's ministers are sometimes silenced through the sins of their people, and it becomes them to plead against such a judgment ; better far that they should suffer sickness or poverty than that the candle of the gospel should be put out among them, and that thus they should be left to perish without remedy.   The Lord save us, who are his ministers, from being made the instruments of inflicting such a penalty.   Let us exhibit a cheerful hopefulness in God, that we may plead it in prayer with him when he threatens to close our lips.

In the close of this verse there is a declaration of what the Psalmist had done in reference to the word of the Lord, and in this the thirds of the octaves are often alike. See 35, "therein do I delight"; 43, "I have hoped in thy judgments"; 51, "yet have I not declined from thy law"; 59, "I turned my feet to thy testimonies"; and verses 67, 83, 99, etc. These verses would furnish an admirable series of meditations.

44. "*So shall I keep thy law continually for ever and ever.*" Nothing more effectually binds a man to the way of the Lord than an experience of the truth of his word, embodied in the form of mercies and deliverances. Not only does the Lord's faithfulness open our mouths against his adversaries, but it also knits our hearts to his fear, and makes our union with him more and more intense. Great mercies lead us to feel an inexpressible gratitude which, failing to utter itself in time, promises to engross eternity with praises. To a heart on flame with thankfulness, the "always, unto eternity and perpetuity" of the text will not seem to be redundant; yea, the hyperbole of Addison in his famous verse will only appear to be solid sense :—

> "Through all eternity to thee
> A joyful song I'll raise ;
> But oh ! eternity's too short
> To utter all thy praise."

God's grace alone can enable us to keep his commandments without break and without end; eternal love must grant us eternal life, and out of this will come everlasting obedience. There is no other way to ensure our perseverance in holiness but by the word of truth abiding in us, as David prayed it might abide with him.

The verse begins with "So," as did verse 42. When God grants his salvation we are *so* favoured that we silence our worst enemy and glorify our best friend. Mercy answereth all things. If God doth but give us salvation we can conquer hell and commune with heaven, answering reproaches and keeping the law, and that to the end, world without end.

We may not overlook another sense which suggests itself here. David prayed that the word of truth might not be taken out of his mouth, and so would he keep God's law : that is to say, by public testimony as well as by personal life he would fulfil the divine will, and confirm the bonds which bound him to his Lord for ever. Undoubtedly the grace which enables us to bear witness with the mouth is a great help to ourselves as well as to others : we feel that the vows of the Lord are upon us, and that we cannot run back.

45. "*And I will walk at liberty : for I seek thy precepts.*" Saints find no bondage in sanctity. The Spirit of holiness is a free spirit ; he sets men at liberty and enables them to resist every effort to bring them under subjection. The way of holiness is not a track for slaves, but the King's highway for freemen, who are joyfully journeying from the Egypt of bondage to the Canaan of rest. God's mercies and his salvation, by teaching us to love the precepts of the word, set us at a happy rest ; and the more we seek after the perfection of our obedience the more shall we enjoy complete emancipation from every form of spiritual slavery. David at one time of his life was in great bondage through having followed a crooked policy. He deceived Achish so persistently that he was driven to acts of ferocity to conceal it, and must have felt very unhappy in his unnatural position as an ally of Philistines, and captain of the body guard of their king. He must have feared lest through his falling into the crooked ways of falsehood the truth would no longer be on his tongue, and he therefore prayed God in some way to work his deliverance, and set him at liberty from such slavery. By terrible things in righteousness did the Lord answer him at Ziklag : the snare was broken, and he escaped.

The verse is united to that which goes before, for it begins with the word "And," which acts as a hook to attach it to the preceding verses. It mentions another of the benefits expected from the coming of mercies from God. The man of God had mentioned the silencing of his enemies (42), power to proceed in testimony (43), and perseverance in holiness ; now he dwells upon liberty, which next to life is dearest to all brave men. He says, "I shall walk," indicating his daily progress through life ; "at liberty," as one who is out of prison, unimpeded by adversaries, unencumbered by burdens, unshackled, allowed a wide range, and roaming without fear. Such liberty would be dangerous if a man were seeking himself or his own lusts ; but when the one object sought after is the will of God, there can be no need to restrain the searcher. We need not circumscribe the man who can say, "I seek thy precepts." Observe, in the preceding verse he said he would keep the law ;

but here he speaks of seeking it. Does he not mean that he will obey what he knows, and endeavour to know more ? Is not this the way to the highest form of liberty,—to be always labouring to know the mind of God and to be conformed to it ? Those who *keep* the law are sure to *seek* it, and bestir themselves to keep it more and more.

46. *"I will speak of thy testimonies also before kings, and will not be ashamed."* This is part of his liberty ; he is free from fear of the greatest, proudest, and most tyrannical of men. David was called to stand before kings when he was an exile ; and afterwards, when he was himself a monarch, he knew the tendency of men to sacrifice their religion to pomp and statecraft ; but it was his resolve to do nothing of the kind. He would sanctify politics, and make cabinets know that the Lord alone is governor among the nations. As a king he would speak to kings concerning the King of kings. He says, *" I will speak "* : prudence might have suggested that his life and conduct would be enough, and that it would be better not to touch upon religion in the presence of royal personages who worshipped other gods, and claimed to be right in so doing. He had already most fittingly preceded this resolve by the declaration, " I will walk," but he does not make his personal conduct an excuse for sinful silence, for he adds, " I will speak." David claimed religious liberty, and took care to use it, for he spoke out what he believed, even when he was in the highest company. In what he said he took care to keep to God's own word, for he says, " I will speak of *thy testimonies.*" No theme is like this, and there is no way of handling that theme like keeping close to the book, and using its thought and language. The great hindrance to our speaking upon holy topics in all companies is shame, but the Psalmist will *"not be ashamed";* there is nothing to be ashamed of, and there is no excuse for being ashamed, and yet many are as quiet as the dead for fear some creature like themselves should be offended. When God gives grace, cowardice soon vanishes. He who speaks for God in God's power, will not be ashamed when beginning to speak, nor while speaking, nor after speaking ; for his theme is one which is fit for kings, needful to kings, and beneficial to kings. If kings object, we may well be ashamed of *them,* but never of our Master who sent us, or of his message, or of his design in sending it.

47. *" And I will delight myself in thy commandments, which I have loved."* Next to liberty and courage comes delight. When we have done our duty, we find a great reward in it. If David had not spoken for his Master before kings, he would have been afraid to think of the law which he had neglected ; but after speaking up for his Lord he feels a sweet serenity of heart when musing upon the word. Obey the command, and you will love it ; carry the yoke, and it will be easy, and rest will come by it. After speaking of the law the Psalmist was not wearied of his theme, but he retired to meditate upon it ; he discoursed and then he delighted, he preached and then he repaired to his study to renew his strength by feeding yet again upon the precious truth. Whether he delighted others or not when he was speaking, he never failed to delight himself when he was musing on the word of the Lord. He declares that he loved the Lord's commands, and by this avowal he unveils the reason for his delight in them : where our love is, there is our delight. David did not delight in the courts of kings, for there he found places of temptation to shame, but in the Scriptures he found himself at home ; his heart was in them, and they yielded him supreme pleasure. No wonder that he spoke of keeping the law, which he loved ; Jesus says, " If a man love me, he will keep my words." No wonder that he spoke of walking at liberty, and speaking boldly, for true love is ever free and fearless. Love is the fulfilling of the law ; where love to the law of God reigns in the heart the life must be full of blessedness. Lord, let thy mercies come to us that we may love thy word and way, and find our whole delight therein.

The verse is in the future, and hence it sets forth, not only what David had done, but what he would do ; he would in time to come delight in his Lord's commands. He knew that they would neither alter, nor fail to yield him joy. He knew also that grace would keep him in the same condition of heart towards the precepts of the Lord, so that he should throughout his whole life take a supreme delight in holiness. His heart was so fixed in love to God's will that he was sure that grace would always hold him under its delightful influence.

All the Psalm is fragrant with love to the word, but here for the first time love is expressly spoken of. It is here coupled with delight, and in verse 165 with " great peace." All the verses in which love declares itself in so many words are worthy of note. See verses 47, 97, 113, 119, 127, 140, 159, 163, 165, 167.

48. *"My hands also will I lift up unto thy commandments, which I have loved."* He will stretch out towards perfection as far as he can, hoping to reach it one day ; when his hands hang down he will cheer himself out of languor by the prospect of glorifying God by obedience ; and he will give solemn sign of his hearty assent and consent to all that his God commands. The phrase " lift up my hands " is very full of meaning, and doubtless the sweet singer meant all that we can see in it, and a great deal more. Again he declares his love ; for a true heart loves to express itself ; it is a kind of fire which must send forth its flames. It was natural that he should reach out towards a law which he delighted in, even as a child holds out its hands to receive a gift which it longs for. When such a lovely object as holiness is set before us, we are bound to rise towards it with our whole nature, and till that is fully accomplished we should at least lift up our hands in prayer towards it. Where holy hands and holy hearts go, the whole man will one day follow.

"And I will meditate in thy statutes." He can never have enough of meditation upon the mind of God. Loving subjects wish to be familiar with their sovereign's statutes, for they are anxious that they may not offend through ignorance. Prayer with lifted hands, and meditation with upward-glancing eyes will in happy union work out the best inward results. The prayer of verse 41 is already fulfilled in the man who is thus struggling upward and studying deeply. The whole of this verse is in the future, and may be viewed not only as a determination of David's mind, but as a result which he knew would follow from the Lord's sending him his mercies and his salvation. When mercy comes down, our hands will be lifted up ; when God in favour thinks upon us, we are sure to think of him. Happy is he who stands with hands uplifted both to receive the blessing and to obey the precept ; he shall not wait upon the Lord in vain.

NOTES ON VERSES 41 TO 48.

Verses 41—48.—This commences a new portion of the Psalm, in which each verse begins with the letter *Vau*, or *v.* There are almost no words in Hebrew that begin with this letter, which is properly a conjunction, and hence in each of the verses in this section the beginning of the verse is in the original a conjunction,—*vau.*— *Albert Barnes.*

Verses 41—48.—This whole section consists of petitions and promises. The petitions are two ; verses 41, 43. The promises are six. This, among many, is a difference between godly men and others : all men seek good things from God, but the wicked so seek that they give him nothing back again, nor yet will promise any sort of return. Their prayers must be unprofitable, because they proceed from love of themselves, and not of the Lord. If so be they obtain that which is for their necessity, they care not to give to the Lord that which is for his glory : but the godly, as they seek good things, so they give praise to God when they have gotten them, and return the use of things received, to the glory of God who gave them. They love not themselves for themselves, but for the Lord ; what they seek from him they seek it for this end, that they may be the more able to serve him.   Let us take heed unto this ; because it is a clear token whereby such as are truly religious are distinguished from counterfeit dissemblers.—*William Cowper.*

Verse 41.—*"Let thy mercies come also unto me."* The way was blocked up with sins and difficulties, yet mercy could clear all, and find access to him, or make its own way : *"Let it come,"* that is, let it be performed or come to pass, as it is rendered : " Now let thy words come to pass " (Judg. xiii. 12)—Hebrew, " Let it come." Here we read, let it come home *to me*, for my comfort and deliverance. David elsewhere saith, " Goodness and mercy shall follow me all the days of my life " (Psalm xxiii. 6) ; go after him, find him out in his wanderings. So, " What shall I render to the Lord for all his benefits *toward me ?* " (Psalm cxvi. 12). They found their way to him though shut up with sins and dangers.—*Thomas Manton.*

Verse 41.—*"Let thy mercies come also unto me, O Lord."* The mercies of God everywhere meet the man whom God *quickens* (verse 40). David understood that God blesses the soul, the body, the household, the ordinances, and all things else that belong to his servants ; the whole of which blessing is from mercy, without merit, bestowed largely, wonderfully, etc.—*Martin Geier.*

Verse 41.—*"Let thy mercies come also unto me, O Lord,"* etc. Ministers of the Word and students of Theology are reminded by this prayer that they ought not only to preach to others the true way of attaining everlasting salvation, but that they should also with earnest prayers cry unto God that they might themselves be made partakers of the Divine mercies, and receive " the end of their faith, the salvation of their souls." Paul, indeed, was greatly anxious respecting this matter, and was constrained to write, that he kept his body under, and brought it into subjection, lest after preaching to others he should himself be a castaway.—*Solomon Gesner.*

Verse 41.—*"Thy mercies."* " *Thy word.*" We should consider here the way in which the Prophet seeks salvation from God. In this prayer he conjoins two things, as those which uphold his confidence, viz., the mercy of God and his Word. These are to the man of faith the two strongest pillars of his hope.—*Wolfgang Musculus.*

Verse 41.—*"Even thy salvation,"* etc. It is not any sort of delivery by any means, which the servant of God being in straits doth call for, or desire, but such a deliverance as God will allow, and be pleased to give in a holy way. *"Let thy salvation come."* As the word of promise is the rule of our petition, so is it a pawn of the thing promised, and must be held fast till the performance come : *"Let thy mercies come also unto me, O Lord, even thy salvation, according to thy word ";* and this is one reason of the petition.—*David Dickson.*

Verse 42.—*"So shall I have,"* etc. I shall have something by which I may reply to those who calumniate me. So the Saviour replied to the suggestions of the tempter almost wholly by passages of Scripture (Matthew iv. 4, 7, 10) ; and so, in many cases, the best answer that can be given to reproaches on the subject of religion will be found in the very words of Scripture. A man of little learning, except that which he has derived from the Bible, may often thus silence the cavils and reproaches of the learned sceptic ; a man of simple-hearted, pure piety, with no weapon but the word of God, may often thus be better armed than if he had all the arguments of the schools at his command. Comp. Eph. vi. 17.—*Albert Barnes.*

Verse 42.—*"So shall I have wherewith to answer,"* etc. When the heart realizes assured salvation, it is supplied with abundant answers to those who sneer at the delights of faith.—*Henry Law.*

Verse 42.—*"So shall I have wherewith to answer,"* etc. Hugo Cardinalis observeth that there are three sorts of blasphemers of the godly,—the devils, heretics, and slanderers. The devil must be answered by the internal word of humility ; heretics by the external word of wisdom ; slanderers by the active word of a good life.— *Richard Greenham.*

Verse 42.—*"So shall I have,"* etc. For I should give them a short answer, and a true one,—*that I trust in thy word ;* I put my confidence in thee, who canst make good thy promises, because thou art omnipotent ; and wilt, because thou art merciful.—*William Nicholson.*

Verse 42.—*"So shall I have wherewith to answer,"* etc. This follows the phrase, *"according to thy word."* Christians should learn from the example of David what to oppose to the reproaches and false accusations of the enemies of the truth. Nothing is done by railing ; but weapons should be taken from the word of God ; and these are strong through faith in God for the overturning of both the Devil himself and his instruments. For truly with weapons of this kind the Saviour himself discomfited Satan in the wilderness (Matt. iv.) ; and Paul (Ephes. vi.) puts on himself, and commends to the Christian soldier, the girdle of Divine truth, the breast-plate of righteousness, the shoes of the Gospel, the shield of faith, and the sword of the Spirit, which is the Word of God.—*Solomon Gesner.*

Verse 42.—*"Wherewith to answer,"* etc. It is not forbidden to believers, modestly and fully, *to answer* those that reproach them, and to rebut the lie. See Prov. xxvi. 5, xxvii. 11. But to be able to answer them is received as a blessing from God.— *Martin Geier.*

Verses 42, 43.—In verse 42 there is a play upon the two senses of the term *"word,"* thus : " and I will answer my revilers a word, for I have trusted in thy word." Having trusted in thy word of promise, I shall have a word of reply to make to them when thou shalt graciously hear this prayer. *"Take not thy word of truth"* (*i.e.,* of promise) *"out of my mouth"*; let me have it still to speak of before my enemies and to rest upon for my own soul. If God were to fail in fulfilling his word of promise, it would, in the sense here contemplated, be quite taken out of his mouth.—*Henry Cowles.*

Verse 43.—*"Take not the word of truth,"* etc. It is well known that men do, when persecution threatens, either altogether deny the truth, or weakly and luke-warmly confess it ; but lest this should happen to him, David therefore prays here, *"O Lord, take not the word of truth utterly out of my mouth,"* i.e., make me, with an intrepid spirit, always to confess the avowed truth boldly and manfully. In the Hebrew text it is עַד מְאֹד, *"veru." "very much,"* or, as Augustine renders it, *"wholly and altogether "*; and he thinks that David prayed for this, that, if through human weakness it should happen to him to fall, and at some time or other not steadfastly to confess the word, yet that God would not allow him to continue in that sin, but again restore and establish him ; and he illustrates this by the example of Peter. Further, David adds the reason which has impelled him thus to pray : *"Because I hope for,"* and even with great desire, as the Hebrew verb יָחַל signifies, *"thy judgments,"* with which in the last day thou wilt openly pass sentence on heretics, fanatics, and all tyrants.—*Solomon Gesner.*

Verse 43.—*"Take not the word of truth utterly out of my mouth."* The word is taken out of the mouth, when it is said to the sinner, *"Wherefore dost thou declare my statutes ? "* And eloquence itself becomes dumb if the conscience be evil. The birds of heaven come and take the word out of thy mouth, even as they took the seed of the word from off the rock lest it should bring forth fruit.—*Ambrose.*

Verse 43.—*The word is also taken out of our mouth* when in strong temptations all things, as it were, fail, neither can we discover where we may make a stand : Psalm lxix. 2.—*Martin Geier.*

Verse 43.—*"Take not the word of truth utterly out of my mouth."* Sometimes we are afraid to speak for the Saviour, lest we should incur the charge of hypocrisy. At other times we are ashamed to speak, from the absence of that only constraining principle—" the love of Christ." And thus *the word of truth is taken out of our mouths."* Often have we wanted a word to speak for the relief of the Lord's tempted people, and have not been able to find it ; so that the recollection of precious lost opportunities may well give utterance to the prayer—*"Take not the word of truth utterly out of my mouth."* Not only do not take it out of my heart ; but let it be ready in my mouth for a confession of my Master. Some of us know the painful trial of the indulgence of worldly habits and conversation, when a want of liberty of spirit has hindered us from standing up boldly for our God. We may perhaps allege the plea of bashfulness or judicious caution in excuse for silence ; which however, in many instances, we must regard as a self-deceptive covering for the real cause of restraint—the want of apprehension of the mercy of God to the soul.—*Charles Bridges.*

Verse 43.—*"Take not the word of truth utterly out of my mouth."* Oh, what service can a dumb body do in Christ's house ! Oh, I think the word of God is imprisoned also ! Oh, I am a dry tree ! Alas, I can neither plant nor water ! Oh, if my Lord would make but dung of me, to fatten and make fertile his own corn-ridges in Mount Zion! Oh, if I might but speak to three or four herd-boys of my worthy Master, I would be satisfied to be the meanest and most obscure of all the pastors in this land, and to live in any place, in any of Christ's basest outhouses ! But he saith, " Sirrah, I will not send you ; I have no errands for you there away." My desire to serve him is sick of jealousy, lest he be unwilling to employ me. . . . I am very well every way, all praise to him in whose books I must stand for ever as his debtor ! Only my silence paineth me. I had one joy out of heaven, next to Christ my Lord, and that was to preach him to this faithless generation ; and they have taken that from me. It was to me as the poor man's one eye, and they have put out that eye.—*Samuel Rutherford.*

Verse 43.—*"For I have hoped in thy judgments,"* the word םיטפשמ, *judgment,* signifieth either the law, or the execution of the sentence thereof.

1. The law or whole word of God ; so that, *"I have hoped in thy judgments,"* is no more, but in thy word do I hope ; as it is, " I wait for the Lord, my soul doth wait, and in his word do I hope " (Ps. cxxx. 5).

2. Answerable execution of the law, when the promise or threatening is fulfilled. (1) When the promise is fulfilled : that is judgment in a sense when God accomplisheth what he hath promised for our salvation and deliverance. Thus God is said to judge his people, when he righteth and saveth them according to his word : " O Lord, thou hast seen my wrong : judge thou my cause " (Lam. iii. 59). (2) But the more usual notion of judgment is the execution of the threatening on wicked men ; which being a benefit to God's faithful servants, and done in their favour, David might well be said to hope for it. Their " judgment " is our obtaining the promise.—*Thomas Manton.*

Verses 43, 44.—Lord, let me have the word of truth in *"my mouth"* that I may commit that sacred *depositum* to the rising generation (2 Tim. ii. 22), and by them it may be transmitted to succeeding ages ; so shall *"thy law"* be kept *"for ever and ever,"* i.e., from one generation to another, according to that promise (Isa. lix. 21) : " My words in thy mouth shall not depart out of the mouth of thy seed, nor out of the mouth of thy seed's seed."—*Matthew Henry.*

Verse 44.—*"So shall I keep thy law continually,"* etc. The Lord's keeping our heart in faith, and our mouth and outward man in the course of confession and obedience, is the cause of our perseverance.—*David Dickson.*

Verse 44.—*"So shall I keep."* Mark, the promise of obedience is brought in by way of argument ; *"So shall I keep," "so,"* that is, this will encourage me, this will enable me.

1st. The granting of his requests would give him encouragement : when God answers our hope and expectation, gratitude should excite and quicken us to give all manner of obedience. If he will give us a heart, and a little liberty to confess his name, and serve him, we should not be backward or uncertain, but walk closely with him.

2ndly. This would give him assistance and strength. If God do daily give assistance, we shall stand ; if not, we fall and falter ; this will be a means of his perseverance, not only to engage and oblige him, but to help him to hold on to the end.

Then mark the constancy of this obedience, *"Continually, and for ever and ever."* David would not keep it for a fit, or for a few days, or a year, but always, even to the end of his life. Here are three words to the same sense: *"continually," "for ever," "and ever."* And the Septuagint expresses it thus: " I shall keep thy law always, and for ever, and for ever, and ever ; " four words there. This heaping of words is not in vain.

1. It shows the difficulty of perseverance : unless believers do strongly persist in the resistance of temptation, they will soon be turned out of the way ; therefore David binds his heart firmly : we must do it now, yea, always, unto the end.

2. He expresseth his vehemence of affection : those that are deeply affected with anything are wont to express themselves as largely as they can. As Paul, who had a deep sense of God's power : " Exceeding greatness of his power, according to the working of his mighty power " (Eph. i. 19). He heaps up several words, because his sense of them was so great : so David here doth heap up words—*"continually, and for ever, and ever, and ever."*

3. Some think the words are so many, that they may express not only this life, but that which is to come. I will keep them continually, and for ever, and ever ; that is, all the days of my life, and in the other world. So Chrysostom, " I will keep them continually," etc., points out the other life, where there will be pure and exact keeping of the law of God. Here we are every hour in danger, but then we shall be put out of all danger, and without fear of sinning, we shall remain in a full and perfect righteousness ; we hope for that which we have not attained unto, and this doth encourage us for the present : so would he make David express himself.

4. If we must distinguish these words, I suppose they imply the continuity and perpetuity of obedience ; the continuity of obedience, that he would serve God continually, without intermission ; and the perpetuity of obedience, that he would serve God for ever and ever, without defection or revolt, at all times, and to the end. Constancy and perseverance in obedience is the commendation of it.—*Thomas Manton.*

Verse 44.—*"So shall I keep thy law continually."* That is, if thou wilt not take the word of thy truth out of my mouth, *"I will alway keep thy law."* *"Yea, unto age, and age of age : "* he showeth what is meant by *alway.* For sometimes by *"alway"* is meant, as long as we live here ; but this is not, *"unto age, and age of age."* For it is better thus translated than as some copies have, *"to eternity, and to age of age,"* since they could not say, and to eternity of eternity. That law therefore should be understood, of which the apostle saith, " Love is the fulfilling of the law." For this will be kept by the saints, from whose mouth the word of truth is not taken, that is, by the church of Christ herself, not only during this world, that is, until this world is ended ; but for another world which is styled *world without end.* For we shall not there receive the commandments of the law, as here, to keep them, but we shall keep the fulness of the law itself without any fear of sinning ; for we shall love God the more fully when we shall have seen him ; and our neighbour too ; for " God will be all in all " ; nor will there be room for any false suspicion concerning our neighbour, where no man will be hidden to any.—*Augustine.*

Verse 44.—*"Continually, for ever and ever."* The language of this verse is very emphatic. Perfect obedience will constitute a large proportion of heavenly happiness to all eternity ; and the nearer we approach to it on earth, the more we anticipate the felicity of heaven.—*Note in Bagster's Comprehensive Bible.*

Verse 45.—*"I will walk at liberty."* Wherever God pardons sin, he subdues it (Micah vii. 19). Then is the condemning power of sin taken away, when the commanding power of it is taken away. If a malefactor be in prison, how shall he know that his prince hath pardoned him ? If a jailer come and knock off his chains and fetters, and lets him out of prison, then he may know he is pardoned : so, how shall we know God hath pardoned us ? If the fetters of sin be broken off, and we walk at liberty in the ways of God, this is a blessed sign we are pardoned.—*Thomas Watson.*

Verse 45.—*"I will walk at liberty : for I seek thy precepts."* As he who departs from confessing of God's truth doth cast himself in straits, in danger and bonds ; so he that beareth out the confession of the truth doth walk as a free man ; the truth doth set him free.—*David Dickson.*

Verse 45.—*"I will walk at liberty : for I seek thy precepts."* When the Bible says that a man led by the Spirit is not under the law, it does not mean that he is free because he may sin without being punished for it ; but it means that he is free because being taught by God's Spirit to love what his law commands he is no longer conscious of acting from restraint. The law does not drive him, because the Spirit leads him. . . . There is a state, brethren, when we recognize God, but do not love God in Christ. It is that state when we admire what is excellent, but are not able to perform it. It is a state when the love of good comes to nothing, dying away in a mere desire. That is a state of nature, when we are under the law, and not converted to the love of Christ. And then there is another state, when God writes his law upon our hearts by love instead of fear. The one state is this, " I cannot do the things that I would ; " the other state is this, " I will walk at liberty, for I seek thy commandments."—*Frederick William Robertson, 1816—1853.*

Verse 45.—"I will walk at liberty." The Psalmist's mind takes in the enlargement of his position. A little while ago, and he felt like a man straitened—hemmed in by rocks, in a narrow dangerous pass—who could not make his way out. You know the characteristics of Canaan, and you can easily conceive of the position of a traveller exploring his dreaded way through one of the mountain passes. The traveller before us has attained to tread upon secure ground. Now, all at once, favoured of the Most High, and conscious of being in his way, he finds himself in a spacious place, and he walks at large : *"And I will walk at liberty ; for I seek thy precepts."* He had made diligent enquiry into all that the Lord had enjoined, and seeking conformity thereto, he felt that he could walk with comfort. He recreates himself in his spiritual emancipation. The secret evil-doer of fair profession cannot know this spiritual liberty at all. As long as a man finds himself to be wrong, and especially a man of a tender conscience, he feels hampered on all sides, depressed in mind, and evilly circumstanced. To what expansion of mind does a man awake when he becomes conscious of being in the appointed way of God ! And he is actually at liberty ; for the good providence of God is around him, and his grace supports him.—*John Stephen.*

Verse 45.—He who goes the beaten and right path will have no brambles hit him across the eyes.—*Saxon proverb.*

Verses 45—48.—Five things David promiseth himself here in the strength of God's grace. 1. That he should be free and easy in his duty : *"I will walk at liberty :"* freed from that which is evil, not hampered with the fetters of my own corruptions, and free to that which is good. 2. That he should be bold and courageous in his duty : *"I will speak of thy testimonies before kings."* 3. That he should be cheerful and pleasant in his duty : *"I will delight myself in thy commandments,"* in conversing with them, in conforming to them. 4. That he should be diligent and vigorous in his duty : *"I will lift up my hands unto thy commandments ;"* which notes not only a vehement desire towards them, but a close application of mind to the observance of them. 5. That he should be thoughtful and considerate in his duty : *"I will meditate in thy statutes."*—*Matthew Henry.*

Verses 45—48.—In these four verses he explains, *seriatim*, in what the observance of the law consists ; a thing he promised, when he said in the fourth verse of this division, that he would observe God's law in his heart, in his words, in his mind, and in his acts ; and the prophet seems all at once, as having been heard, to have changed his mode of speaking, for he says, *"And I walked at large."* When God's mercy visited me, I did not walk in the narrow ways of fear, but in the wide one of love ; that is to say, I observed the law willingly, joyfully, with all the affections of my heart, *"because I have sought after thy commandments"* as a thing of great value, and most important to come at ; *"and I spoke"* openly and fearlessly on the justice of his most holy law, even *"before kings, and I was not ashamed";* and I constantly turned the law in my mind, and made its mysteries the subject of my meditation, *"and I lifted up my hands,"* to carry out his high and sublime commands ; that is, his extremely perfect and arduous commands. Finally, in all manner of ways, in heart, mind, word, and deed, *"I was exercised in thy justifications."*—*Robert Bellarmine.*

Verse 46.—"I will speak of thy testimonies also before kings." In these words he seems to believe that he is in possession of that which he formerly prayed for. He had said, " Take not the word of truth out of my mouth," and now, as if he had obtained what he requested, he rises up, and maintains that he would not be dumb, even were he called upon to speak in the presence of kings. He affirms that he would willingly stand forward in vindication of the glory of God in the face of the whole world.—*John Calvin.*

Verse 46.—"I will speak of thy testimonies also before kings." The terror of kings and of men in power is an ordinary hindrance of free confession of God's truth in time of persecution ; but faith in the truth sustained in the heart by God is able to bring forth a confession at all hazards.—*David Dickson.*

Verse 46.—"I will speak of thy testimonies also before kings." Before David came to the crown kings were sometimes his *judges,* as Saul and Achish ; but if he were called before them to give a reason of the hope that was in him, he would speak of God's testimonies, and profess to build his hope upon them, and make them his council, his guard, his crown, his all. We must never be afraid to own our religion, though it should expose us to the wrath of kings, but speak of it as that which we will live and die by, like the three children before Nebuchadnezzar, Dan. iii. 16, Acts iv. 20. After David came to the crown kings were sometimes his *companions,* they visited him, and he returned their visits ; but he did not, in complaisance to them, talk of everything but religion for fear of affronting them, and making his converse uneasy to them : no, God's testimonies shall be the principal subject of his discourse with the kings, not only to show that he was not ashamed of his religion, but to instruct them in it, and bring them over to it. It is good for kings to hear of *God's testimonies,* and it will adorn the conversation of princes themselves to speak of them.—*Matthew Henry.*

Verse 46.—"I will speak of thy testimonies also before kings." Men of greatest holiness have been men of greatest boldness ; witness Nehemiah, the three children, Daniel, and all the holy prophets and apostles : Prov. xxviii. 1, " The wicked flee when no man pursueth : but the righteous are bold as a lion," yea, as a young lion, as the Hebrew has it, one that is in his hot blood and fears no colours, and that is more bold than any others. Holiness made Daniel not only as bold as a lion, but also to daunt the lions with his boldness. Luther was a man of great holiness, and a man of great boldness : witness his standing out against all the world ; and when the emperor sent for him to Worms, and his friends dissuaded him from going, as sometimes Paul's did him, " Go," said he, " I will surely go, since I am sent for, in the name of our Lord Jesus Christ ; yea, though I knew that there were as many devils in Worms to resist me as there be tiles to cover the houses, yet I would go." And when the same author and his associates were threatened with many dangers from opposers on all hands, he lets fall this heroic and magnanimous speech : " Come, let us sing the 46th Psalm, and then let them do their worst." Latimer was a man of much holiness, counting the darkness and profaneness of those times wherein he lived, and a man of much courage and boldness ; witness his presenting to King Henry the Eighth, for a New Year's gift, a New Testament, wrapped up in a napkin, with this posie or motto about it, " Whoremongers and adulterers God will judge."— *Thomas Brooks.*

Verse 46.—Note that in this verse we are taught to shun four vices. First, overmuch silence : hence he says, *"I will speak."* Secondly, useless talkativeness : *"of thy testimonies."* The Hebrew doctors say that ten measures of speaking had descended to the earth,—that nine had been carried off by the women, but one left for all the rest of the world. Hieronymus rightly exhorts all Christians : " Consecrate thy mouth to the Gospel : be unwilling to open it with trifles or fables." Thirdly, we are taught to shun cowardice : *"before kings."* For, as it is said (Prov. xxix. 25), *"The fear of man bringeth a snare."* Fourthly, and lastly, we are taught to shun cowardly bashfulness : *"and will not be ashamed."*—*Thomas Le Blanc.*

Verse 46.—"I will not be ashamed." That is, I shall not be cast down from my position or my hope ; I shall not be afraid ; nor will I, from fear of danger or reproach, shun or renounce the confession ; nor shall I be overcome by terrors or threats.— *D. H. Mollerus.*

Verses 46, 47, 48. In these three last verses David promiseth a threefold duty of thankfulness. First, the service of his tongue. Next, the service of his affections. Thirdly, the service of his actions. A good conscience renders always great consolation ; and an honest life makes great boldness to speak without fear or shame, as ye see in David towards Saul, in Elias to Ahab, in Paul to Agrippa, to Festus, and to Felix.—*William Cowper.*

Verse 47.—"I will delight myself in thy commandments." It is but poor comfort to the believer to be able to talk well to others upon the ways of God, and even to " bear the reproach " of his people, when his own heart is cold, insensible, and dull. He longs for *"delight"* in these ways ; and he shall delight in them. —*Charles Bridges.*

Verse 47.—He who would preach boldly to others must himself *"delight"* in the practice of what he preacheth. If there be in us a new nature, it will *"love the commandments of God"* as being congenial to it ; on that which we love we shall continually be *"meditating,"* and our meditation will end in action ; we shall " lift up the hands which hang down " (Heb. xii. 12), that they may " work the works of God whilst it is day, because the night cometh when no man can work." (John ix. 4).—*George Horne.*

Verse 47.—*"Thy commandments, which I have loved."* On the word *"loved,"* the Carmelite quotes two sayings of ancient philosophers, which he commends to the acceptance of those who have learnt the truer philosophy of the Gospel. The first is Aristotle's answer to the question of what profit he had derived from philosophy : " I have learnt to do without constraint that which others do from fear of the law." The second is a very similar saying of Aristippus : " If the laws were lost, all of us would live as we do now that they are in force." And for us the whole verse is summed up in the words of a greater Teacher than they : " If a man love me, he will keep my words " : John xiv. 23.—*Neale and Littledale.*

Verses 47, 48.—What is in the word a law of precept, is in the heart a law of love ; what is in the one a law of command, is in the other a law of liberty. " Love is the fulfilling of the law," Gal. v. 14. The law of love in the heart, is the fulfilling the law of God in the Spirit. It may well be said to be written in the heart, when a man doth love it. As we say, a beloved thing is in our hearts, not physically, but morally, as Calais was said to be in Queen Mary's heart. They might have looked long enough before they could have found there the map of the town ; but grief for the loss of it killed her. It is a love that is inexpressible. David delights to mention it in two verses together : *"I will delight myself in thy commandments, which I have loved. My hands also will I lift up unto thy commandments, which I have loved,"* and often in the Psalm resumes the assertion. Before the new creation, there was no affection to the law : it was not only a dead letter, but a devilish letter in the esteem of a man : he wished it razed out of the world, and another more pleasing to the flesh enacted. He would be a law unto himself ; but when this is written within him, he is so pleased with the inscription, that he would not for all the world be without that law, and the love of it ; whereas what obedience he paid to it before was out of fear, now out of affection ; not only because of the authority of the lawgiver, but of the purity of the law itself. He would maintain it with all his might against the power of sin within, and the powers of darkness without him. He loves to view this law ; regards every lineament of it, and dwells upon every feature with delightful ravishments. If his eye be off, or his foot go away, how doth he dissolve in tears, mourn and groan, till his former affection hath recovered breath, and stands upon its feet !—*Stephen Charnock.*

Verse 48.—*"My hands also will I lift up unto thy commandments,"* etc. The duty that David promiseth God here, is the service of his actions, that he will lift up his hands to the practice of God's commandments. The kingdom of God is not in word, but in power ; we are the disciples of that Master, who first began to do and then to teach. But now the world is full of mutilated Christians ; either they want an ear and cannot hear God's word, or a tongue and cannot speak of it ; or if they have both, they want hands and cannot practise it.—*William Cowper.*

Verse 48.—*"My hands also will I lift up."* To lift up the hands is taken variously and it signifies :—1. *To pray :* as in Psalm xxviii. 2 ; Lam. ii. 19 ; Hab. iii. 10.— 2. *To bless* others : as Levit. ix. 22 ; Ps. cxxxiv. 2.—3. *To swear :* as Gen. xiv. 22 ; Exod. vi. 8.—4. *To set about some important matter :* as Gen. xli. 44 ; " without thee shall no man lift up his hand ; " *i.e.* shall attempt anything, or shall accomplish ; Psalm x. 12, " lift up thine hand," viz., effectively, to bring help : Heb. xii. 12, " lift up the hands," etc. ; *i.e.* strongly stimulate Christians. Perhaps all these may be accommodated to the present passage ; for it is possible to be either, 1. Prayer for Divine grace for the doing of the precepts : or, 2. Blessing, *i.e.* praise of God because of them, and the advantages which have thence accrued to us : which the Syriac translator approves, who adds, " and I will glory in thy faithfulness : "— or, 3. Vow, or oath of constant obedience, etc. :—or, 4. Active and earnest undertaking of them ; which, also, appears to be here chiefly meant.—*Henry Hammond in Synopsis Poli.*

Verse 48.—*"My hands also will I lift up unto thy commandments ; "* vowing obedience to them : Genesis xiv. 22.—*William Kay.*

Verse 48.—*"My hands also will I lift up."* I will present every victim and sacrifice which the law requires.   I will make prayer and supplication before thee, lifting up holy hands without wrath and doubting.—*Adam Clarke.*

Verse 48.—*"My hands also will I lift up."*   Aben Ezra explains, (and perhaps rightly,) that the metaphor, in this place, is taken from the action of those who receive any one whom they are glad or proud to see.—*Daniel Cresswell,* 1776—1844.

Verse 48.—" I will lift up my hands *in admiration of* thy precepts, And meditate on thy statutes."—*W. Green, in "A New Translation of the Psalms,"* 1762.

Verse 48.—To lift up the hand is a gesture importing readiness, and special intention in doing a thing.   *"My hands* (saith David) *also will I lift up unto thy commandments "* ; as a man that is willing to do a thing and addresseth himself to the doing of it, lifts up his hand ; so a godly man is described as lifting up his hand to fulfil the commands of God.—*Joseph Caryl.*

Verse 48.—*"Thy commandments."*   By *commandments* he understandeth the word of God, yet it is more powerful than so ; it is not, I have loved thy *word ;* but, I have loved that part of thy word that is thy *"commandments,"* the *mandatory* part.   There are some parts of the will and word of God that even ungodly men will be content to love.   There is the *promissory* part ; all men gather and catch at the promises, and show love to these.   The reason is clear ; there is pleasure, and profit, and gain, and advantage in the promises ; but a pious soul doth not only look to the promises, but to the *commands.*   Piety looks on Christ as a *Lawgiver,* as well as a *Saviour,* and not only on him as a *Mediator,* but as a *Lord* and *Master ;* it doth not only live by *faith,* but it liveth by *rule ;* it makes indeed the *promises* the stay and *staff* of a Christian's life, but it makes the commandments of God the *level.* A pious heart knows that some command is implied in the qualification and condition of every promise ; it knows that as for the fulfilling of the promises, it belongs to God ; but the fulfilling of the commands belongs to us.   Therefore it looks so, upon the enjoying of that which is promised that it will first do that which is commanded. There is no hope of attaining comfort in the promise but in keeping of the precept ; therefore he pitcheth the emphasis, " I have loved thy *word,"* that is true, and *all* thy word, and this part, the *mandatory* part :   " I have loved thy *commandments."*

Observe the number, " thy commandments " ; it is plural, that is, *all* thy commandments without exception ;   otherwise even ungodly men will be content to love *some* commandments, if they may choose them for themselves.—*Richard Holdsworth* (1590—1649), *in "The Valley of Vision."*

Verse 48.—*"Which I love,"* or *"have loved,"* as in verse 47, the terms of which are studiously repeated with a fine rhetorical effect, which is further heightened by the *and* at the beginning, throwing both verses, as it were, into one sentence.   As if he had said :   I will derive my happiness from thy commandments, which I love and have loved, and to these commandments, which I love and have loved, I will lift up my hands and heart together.—*Joseph Addison Alexander.*

Verse 48.—*"I will meditate."*   It is in holy meditation on the word of God that all the graces of the Spirit are manifested.   What is the principle of faith but the reliance of the soul upon the promises of the word ?   What is the sensation of godly fear but the soul trembling before the threatenings of God ?   What is the object of hope but the apprehended glory of God ?   What is the excitement of desire or love but longing, endearing contemplations of the Saviour, and of his unspeakable blessings ?   So that we can scarcely conceive of the influences of grace separated from spiritual meditation in the word.—*Charles Bridges.*

Verse 48.—The Syriac has an addition to verse 48, which I am surprised has not been noticed.   The addition is, *"and I will glory in thy faithfulness."*   Dathe in a note says, THE SEVENTY seem to have read some such addition, although not exactly the same.—*Edward Thomas Gibson,* 1819—1880.

EXPOSITION OF VERSES 49 TO 56.

REMEMBER the word unto thy servant, upon which thou hast caused me to hope.

50 This *is* my comfort in my affliction : for thy word hath quickened me.

51 The proud have had me greatly in derision : *yet* have I not declined from thy law.

52 I remembered thy judgments of old, O LORD, and have comforted myself.

53 Horror hath taken hold upon me because of the wicked that forsake thy law.

54 Thy statutes have been my songs in the house of my pilgrimage.

55 I have remembered thy name, O LORD, in the night, and have kept thy law.

56 This I had, because I kept thy precepts.

This octrain deals with the comfort of the word. It begins by seeking the main consolation, namely, the Lord's fulfilment of his promise, and then it shows how the word sustains us under affliction, and makes us so impervious to ridicule that we are moved by the harsh conduct of the wicked rather to horror of their sin than to any submission to their temptations. We are then shown how the Scripture furnishes songs for pilgrims, and memories for night-watchers ; and the Psalm concludes by the general statement that the whole of this happiness and comfort arises out of keeping the statutes of the Lord.

49. "*Remember the word unto thy servant.*" He asks for no new promise, but to have the old word fulfilled. He is grateful that he has received so good a word, he embraces it with all his heart, and now entreats the Lord to deal with him according to it. He does not say, " remember my service to thee," but " thy word to me." The words of masters to servants are not always such that servants wish their lords to remember them ; for they usually observe the faults and failings of the work done, inasmuch as it does not tally with the word of command. But we who serve the best of masters are not anxious to have one of his words fall to the ground, since the Lord will so kindly remember his word of command as to give us grace wherewith we may obey, and he will couple with it a remembrance of his word of promise, so that our hearts shall be comforted. If God's word to us as his servants is so precious, what shall we say of his word to us as his sons ?

The Psalmist does not fear a failure in the Lord's memory, but he makes use of the promise as a plea, and this is the form in which he speaks, after the manner of men when they plead with one another. When the Lord remembers the sins of his servant, and brings them before his conscience, the penitent cries, Lord, remember thy word of pardon, and therefore remember my sins and iniquities no more. There is a world of meaning in that word "*remember*," as it is addressed to God ; it is used in Scripture in the tenderest sense, and suits the sorrowing and the depressed. The Psalmist cried, " Lord, remember David, and all his afflictions " : Job also prayed that the Lord would appoint him a set time, and remember him. In the present instance the prayer is as personal as the " Remember me " of the thief, for its essence lies in the words—" unto thy servant." It would be all in vain for us if the promise were remembered to all others if it did not come true to ourselves ; but there is no fear, for the Lord has never forgotten a single promise to a single believer.

"*Upon which thou hast caused me to hope.*" The argument is that God, having given grace to hope in the promise, would surely never disappoint that hope. He cannot have caused us to hope without cause. If we hope upon his word we have a sure basis : our gracious Lord would never mock us by exciting false hopes. Hope deferred maketh the heart sick, hence the petition for immediate remembrance of the cheering word. Moreover, it is the hope of a servant, and it is not possible that a great and good master would disappoint his dependent ; if such a master's word were not kept it could only be through an oversight, hence the anxious cry, " Remember." Our great Master will not forget his own servants, nor disappoint the expectation which he himself has raised : because we are the Lord's, and endeavour to remember his word by obeying it, we may be sure that he will think upon his own servants, and remember his own promise by making it good.

This verse is the prayer of love fearing to be forgotten, of humility conscious of insignificance and anxious not to be overlooked, of penitence trembling lest the evil of its sin should overshadow the promise, of eager desire longing for the blessing, and of holy confidence which feels that all that is wanted is comprehended in the word. Let but the Lord remember his promise, and the promised act is as good as done.

50. *"This my comfort in my affliction : for thy word hath quickened me."* He means,—Thy word is my comfort, or the fact that thy word has brought quickening to me is my comfort. Or he means that the hope which God had given him was his comfort, for God had quickened him thereby. Whatever may be the exact sense, it is clear that the Psalmist had affliction,—affliction peculiar to himself which he calls *"my* affliction"; that he had comfort in it,—comfort specially his own, for he styles it *"my* comfort"; and that he knew what the comfort was, and where it came from, for he exclaims—*"this is* my comfort." The worldling clutches his money-bag, and says, " this is my comfort "; the spendthrift points to his gaiety and shouts, " this is my comfort"; the drunkard lifts his glass and sings, " this is my comfort"; but the man whose hope comes from God feels the life-giving power of the word of the Lord, and he testifies, " this is my comfort." Paul said, " I know whom I have believed." Comfort is desirable at all times ; but comfort in affliction is like a lamp in a dark place. Some are unable to find comfort at such times ; but it is not so with believers, for their Saviour has said to them, " I will not leave you comfortless." Some have comfort and no affliction, others have affliction and no comfort ; but the saints have comfort in their affliction.

The word frequently comforts us by increasing the force of our inner life ; " this is my comfort ; thy word hath quickened me." To quicken the heart is to cheer the whole man. Often the near way to consolation is sanctification and invigoration. If we cannot clear away the fog, it may be better to rise to a higher level, and so to get above it. Troubles which weigh us down while we are half dead become mere trifles when we are full of life. Thus have we often been raised in spirit by quickening grace, and the same thing will happen again, for the comforter is still with us, the Consolation of Israel ever liveth, and the very God of peace is evermore our Father. On looking back upon our past life there is one ground of comfort as to our state—the word of God has made us alive, and kept us so. We were dead, but we are dead no longer. From this we gladly infer that if the Lord had meant to destroy he would not have quickened us. If we were only hypocrites worthy of derision, as the proud ones say, he would not have revived us by his grace An experience of quickening is a fountain of good cheer.

See how this verse is turned into a prayer in verse 107. " Quicken me, O Lord, according unto thy word." Experience teaches us how to pray, and furnishes arguments in prayer.

51. *"The proud have had me greatly in derision."* Proud men never love gracious men, and as they fear them they veil their fear under a pretended contempt. In this case their hatred revealed itself in ridicule, and that ridicule was loud and long. When they wanted sport they made sport of David because he was God's servant. Men must have strange eyes to be able to see farce in faith, and a comedy in holiness ; yet it is sadly the case that men who are short of wit can generally provoke a broad grin by jesting at a saint. Conceited sinners make footballs of godly men. They call it roaring fun to caricature a faithful member of " The Holy Club"; his methods of careful living are the material for their jokes about " the Methodist"; and his hatred of sin sets their tongues a-wagging at long-faced Puritanism, and strait-laced hypocrisy. If David was greatly derided, we may not expect to escape the scorn of the ungodly. There are hosts of proud men still upon the face of the earth, and if they find a believer in affliction they will be mean enough and cruel enough to make jests at his expense. It is the nature of the son of the bondwoman to mock the child of the promise.

"Yet have I not declined from thy law." Thus the deriders missed their aim : they laughed, but they did not win. The godly man, so far from turning aside from the right way, did not even slacken his pace, or in any sense fall off from his holy habits. Many would have declined, many have declined, but David did not do so. It is paying too much honour to fools to yield half a point to them. Their

unhallowed mirth will not harm us if we pay no attention to it, even as the moon suffers nothing from the dogs that bay at her. God's law is our highway of peace and safety, and those who would laugh us out of it wish us no good.

From verse 61 we note that David was not overcome by the spoiling of his goods any more than by these cruel mockings. See also verse 157, where the multitude of persecutors and enemies were baffled in their attempts to make him decline from God's ways.

52. *"I remembered thy judgments of old, O Lord ; and have comforted myself."* He had asked the Lord to remember, and here he remembers God and his judgments. When we see no present display of the divine power it is wise to fall back upon the records of former ages, since they are just as available as if the transactions were of yesterday, seeing the Lord is always the same. Our true comfort must be found in what our God works on behalf of truth and right, and as the histories of the olden times are full of divine interpositions it is well to be thoroughly acquainted with them. Moreover, if we are advanced in years we have the providences of our early days to review, and these should by no means be forgotten or left out of our thoughts. The argument is good and solid : he who has shown himself strong on behalf of his believing people is the immutable God, and therefore we may expect deliverance at his hands. The grinning of the proud will not trouble us when we remember how the Lord dealt with their predecessors in bygone periods ; he destroyed them at the deluge, he confounded them at Babel, he drowned them at the Red Sea, he drove them out of Canaan : he has in all ages bared his arm against the haughty, and broken them as potters' vessels. While in our own hearts we humbly drink of the mercy of God in quietude, we are not without comfort in seasons of turmoil and derision ; for then we resort to God's justice, and remember how he scoffs at the scoffers : "He that sitteth in the heavens doth laugh, the Lord doth have them in derision."

When he was greatly derided the Psalmist did not sit down in despair, but rallied his spirits. He knew that comfort is needful for strength in service, and for the endurance of persecution, and therefore he comforted himself. In doing this he resorted not so much to the sweet as to the stern side of the Lord's dealings, and dwelt upon his judgments. If we can find sweetness in the divine justice, how much more shall we perceive it in divine love and grace. How thoroughly must that man be at peace with God who can find comfort, not only in his promises, but in his judgments. Even the terrible things of God are cheering to believers. They know that nothing is more to the advantage of all God's creatures than to be ruled by a strong hand which will deal out justice. The righteous man has no fear of the ruler's sword, which is only a terror to evil doers. When the godly man is unjustly treated he finds comfort in the fact that there is a Judge of all the earth who will avenge his own elect, and redress the ills of these disordered times.

53. *"Horror hath taken hold upon me because of the wicked that forsake thy law."* He was horrified at their action, at the pride which led them to it, and at the punishment which would be sure to fall upon them for it. When he thought upon the ancient judgments of God he was filled with terror at the fate of the godless ; as well he might be. Their laughter had not distressed him, but he was distressed by a foresight of their overthrow. Truths which were amusement to them caused amazement to him. He saw them utterly turning away from the law of God, and leaving it as a path forsaken and overgrown from want of traffic, and this forsaking of the law filled him with the most painful emotions : he was astonished at their wickedness, stunned by their presumption, alarmed by the expectation of their sudden overthrow, amazed by the terror of their certain doom.

See verses 106 and 158, and note the tenderness which combined with all this. Those who are the firmest believers in the eternal punishment of the wicked are the most grieved at their doom. It is no proof of tenderness to shut one's eyes to the awful doom of the ungodly. Compassion is far better shown in trying to save sinners than in trying to make things pleasant all round. Oh that we were all more distressed as we think of the portion of the ungodly in the lake of fire ! The popular plan is to shut your eyes and forget all about it, or pretend to doubt it ; but this is not the way of the faithful servant of God.

54. *"Thy statutes have been my songs in the house of my pilgrimage."* Like others of God's servants, David knew that he was not at home in this world, but a pilgrim through it, seeking a better country. He did not, however, sigh over this fact, but he sang about it. He tells us nothing about his pilgrim sighs, but

speaks of his pilgrim songs. Even the palace in which he dwelt was but *"the house of his pilgrimage,"* the inn at which he rested, the station at which he halted for a little while. Men are wont to sing when they come to their inn, and so did this godly sojourner; he sang the songs of Zion, the statutes of the great King. The commands of God were as well known to him as the ballads of his country, and they were pleasant to his taste and musical to his ear. Happy is the heart which finds its joy in the commands of God, and makes obedience its recreation. When religion is set to music it goes well. When we sing in the ways of the Lord it shows that our hearts are in them. Ours are pilgrim Psalms, songs of degrees; but they are such as we may sing throughout eternity; for the statutes of the Lord are the psalmody of heaven itself.

Saints find horror in sin, and harmony in holiness. The wicked shun the law, and the righteous sing of it. In past days we have sung the Lord's statutes, and in this fact we may find comfort in present affliction. Since our songs are so very different from those of the proud, we may expect to join a very different choir at the last, and sing in a place far removed from their abode.

Note how in the sixth verses of their respective octaves we often find resolves to bless God, or records of testimony. In verse 46 it is, " I will speak," and in 62, " I will give thanks," while here he speaks of songs.

55. *"I have remembered thy name, O* LORD, *in the night."* When others slept I woke to think of thee, thy person, thy actions, thy covenant, thy *name*, under which last term he comprehends the divine character as far as it is revealed. He was so earnest after the living God that he woke up at dead of night to think upon him. These were David's Night Thoughts. If they were not Sunny Memories they were memories of the Sun of Righteousness. It is well when our memory furnishes us with consolation, so that we can say with the Psalmist,—Having early been taught to know thee, I had only to remember the lessons of thy grace, and my heart was comforted. This verse shows not only that the man of God had remembered, but that he still remembered the Lord his God. We are to hallow the name of God, and we cannot do so if it slips from our memory.

"And have kept thy law." He found sanctification through meditation; by the thoughts of the night he ruled the actions of the day. As the actions of the day often create the dreams of the night, so do the thoughts of the night produce the deeds of the day. If we do not keep the name of God in our memory we shall not keep the law of God in our conduct. Forgetfulness of minds leads up to forgetfulness of life.

When we hear the night songs of revellers we have in them sure evidence that they do not keep God's law; but the quiet musings of gracious men are proof positive that the name of the Lord is dear to them. We may judge of nations by their songs, and so we may of men; and in the case of the righteous, their singing and their thinking are both indications of their love to God: whether they lift up their voices, or sit in silence, they are still the Lord's. Blessed are the men whose " night-thoughts " are memories of the eternal light; they shall be remembered of their Lord when the night of death comes on. Reader, are your thoughts in the dark full of light, because full of God? Is his name the natural subject of your evening reflections? Then it will give a tone to your morning and noonday hours. Or do you give your whole mind to the fleeting cares and pleasures of this world? If so, it is little wonder that you do not live as you ought to do. No man is holy by chance. If we have no memory for the name of Jehovah we are not likely to remember his commandments: if we do not think of him secretly we shall not obey him openly.

56. *"This I had, because I kept thy precepts."* He had this comfort, this remembrance of God, this power to sing, this courage to face the enemy, this hope in the promise, because he had earnestly observed the commands of God, and striven to walk in them. We are not rewarded for our works, but there is a reward *in* them. Many a comfort is obtainable only by careful living: we can surely say of such consolations, " This I had because I kept thy precepts." How can we defy ridicule if we are living inconsistently? how can we comfortably remember the name of the Lord if we live carelessly? It may be that David means that he had been enabled to keep the law because he had attended to the separate precepts: he had taken the commands in detail, and so had reached to holiness of life. Or, by keeping certain of the precepts he had gained spiritual strength to keep others: for God gives more grace to those who have some measure of it, and those who improve

their talents shall find themselves improving. It may be best to leave the passage open just as our version does ; so that we may say of a thousand priceless blessings, " these came to us in the way of obedience." All our possessions are the gifts of grace, and yet some of them come in the shape of reward ; yet even then the reward is not of debt, but of grace. God first works in us good works, and then rewards us for them.

Here we have an apt conclusion to this section of the Psalm, for this verse is a strong argument for the prayer with which the section commenced. The sweet singer had evidence of having kept God's precepts, and therefore he could the more properly beg the Lord to keep his promises. All through the passage we may find pleas, especially in the two *remembers*. " I have remembered thy judgments," and " I have remembered thy name" ; " Remember thy word unto thy servant."

NOTES ON VERSES 49 TO 56.

Verse 49.—"*Remember the word unto thy servant,*" etc. Those that make God's promises their portion, may with humble boldness make them their plea. God gave the promise in which the Psalmist hoped, and the hope by which he embraced the promise.—*Matthew Henry.*

Verse 49.—"*Remember the word unto thy servant,*" etc. When we hear any promise in the word of God, let us turn it into a prayer. God's promises are his bonds. Sue him on his bond. He loves that we should wrestle with him by his promises. Why, Lord, thou hast made this and that promise, thou canst not deny thyself, thou canst not deny thine own truth ; thou canst not cease to be God, and thou canst as well cease to be God, as deny thy promise, that is thyself. " '*Lord, remember thy word.*' I put thee in mind of thy promise, '*whereon thou hast caused me to hope.*' If I be deceived, thou hast deceived me. Thou hast made these promises, and caused me to trust in thee, and ' thou never failest those that trust in thee, therefore keep thy word to me.' "—*Richard Sibbes.*

Verse 49.—"*Remember the word unto thy servant,*" etc. God promiseth salvation before he giveth it, to excite our desire of it, to exercise our faith, to prove our sincerity, to perfect our patience. For these purposes he seemeth sometimes to have forgotten his word, and to have deserted those whom he had engaged to succour and relieve ; in which case he would have us, as it were, to remind him of his promise, and solicit his performance of it. The Psalmist here instructeth us to prefer our petition upon these grounds : first that God cannot prove false to his own word : "*Remember thy word ;* " secondly, that he will never disappoint an expectation which himself hath raised : "*upon which thou hast caused me to hope.*" —*George Horne.*

Verses 49, 52, 55.—"*Remember.*" "*I remembered.*" As David beseecheth the Lord to remember his promise, so he protests, in verse 52, that he remembered the judgments of God, and was comforted ; and in verse 55, that he remembered the name of the Lord in the night. It is but a mockery of God, to desire him to remember his promise made to us, when we make no conscience of the promise we have made to him. But alas, how often we fail in this duty, and by our own default diminish that comfort we might have of God's promises in the day of our trouble.—*William Cowper.*

Verse 49.—"*Thy servant.*" Be sure of your qualification ; for David pleadeth here, partly as a servant of God, and partly as a believer. First, " Remember the word unto thy servant ;" and then, " upon which thou hast caused me to hope." There is a double qualification : with respect to the precept of subjection, and the promise of dependence. The precept is before the promise. They have right to the promises, and may justly lay hold upon them, who are God's servants ; they who apply themselves to obey his precepts, these only can rightly apply his promises to themselves. None can lay claim to rewarding grace but those who are partakers of sanctifying grace. Make it clear that you are God's servants, and then these promises which are generally offered are your own, no less than if your name were inserted in the promise, and written in the Bible.—*Thomas Manton.*

Verse 49.—"*Thou hast caused me to hope.*" Let us remember, first, that the promises made to us are of God's free mercy ; that the grace to believe, which is the condition of the promise, is also of himself ; for " faith is the gift of God " ; thirdly, that the arguments by which he confirms our faith in the certainty of our salvation are drawn from himself, not from us.—*William Cowper.*

Verse 50.—"*This is my comfort,*" etc. The word of promise was David's comfort because the word had quickened him to receive comfort. The original is capable of another modification of thought—"*This is my consolation that thy word hath quickened me.*" He had the happy experience within him ; he felt the reviving, restoring, life-giving power of the word, as he read, as he dwelt upon it, as he meditated therein, and as he gave himself up to the way of the word. The believer has all God's unfailing promises to depend upon, and as he depends he gains strength by his own happy experiences of the faithfulness of the word.—*John Stephen.*

Verse 50.—"*My comfort.*" "*Thy word.*" God hath given us his Scriptures, his word ; and the comforts that are fetched from thence are strong ones, because they are his comforts, since they come from his word. The word of a prince comforts, though he be not there to speak it. Though it be by a letter, or by a messenger, yet he whose word it is, is one that is able to make his word good. He is Lord and Master of his word. The word of God is comfortable, and all the reasons that are in it, and that are deduced from it, upon good ground and consequence, are comfortable, because it is God's word. Those comforts in God's word, and reasons from thence, are wonderful in variety. There is comfort from the liberty of a Christian, that he hath free access to the throne of grace ; comfort from the prerogatives of a Christian, that he is the child of God, that he is justified, that he is the heir of heaven, and such like ; comforts from the promises of grace, of the presence of God, of assistance by his presence.—*Richard Sibbes.*

Verse 50.—"*Comfort.*"   *Nechamah,* consolation ; whence the name of Nehemiah was derived. The word occurs only in Job vi. 9.

Verse 50.—"*Comfort.*"   The Hebrew verb rendered *to comfort* signifies, first, to repent, and then to comfort. And certainly the sweetest joy is from the surest tears. Tears are the breeders of spiritual joy. When Hannah had wept, she went away, and was no more sad. The bee gathers the best honey from the bitterest herbs. Christ made the best wine of water. . . .

Gospel comforts are, first, unutterable comforts, 1 Pet. i. 8 ; Philip. iv. 4. Secondly, they are real, John xiv. 27 ; all others are but seeming comforts, but painted comforts. Thirdly, they are holy comforts, Isa. lxiv. 5 ; Ps. cxxxviii. 5 ; they flow from a Holy Spirit, and nothing can come from the Holy Spirit but that which is holy. Fourthly, they are the greatest and strongest comforts, Eph. vi. 17. Few heads and hearts are able to bear them, as few heads are able to bear strong wines. Fifthly, they reach to the inward man, to the soul, 2 Thess. ii. 17, the noble part of man. " My soul rejoiceth in God my Saviour." Our other comforts only reach the face ; they sink not so deep as the heart. Sixthly, they are the most soul-filling and soul-satisfying comforts, Ps. xvi. 11, Cant. ii. 3. Other comforts cannot reach the soul, and therefore they cannot fill nor satisfy the soul. Seventhly, they comfort in saddest distresses, in the darkest night, and in the most stormy day, Ps. xciv. 19, Hab. iii. 7, 8. Eighthly, they are everlasting, 2 Thess. ii. 16. The joy of the wicked is but as a glass, bright and brittle, and evermore in danger of breaking ; but the joy of the saints is lasting.—*Thomas Brooks.*

Verse 50.—"*Thy word hath quickened me.*"   It is a reviving comfort which quickeneth the soul. Many times we seem to be dead to all spiritual operations, our affections are damped and discouraged ; but the word of God puts life into the dead, and relieveth us in our greatest distresses. Sorrow worketh death, but joy is the life of the soul. Now, when dead in all sense and feeling, " the just shall live by faith " (Hab. ii. 4), and the hope wrought in us by the Scriptures is " a lively hope " (1 Pet. i. 3). Other things skin the wound, but our sore breaketh out again, and runneth ; faith penetrateth into the inwards of a man, doth good to the heart ; and the soul reviveth by waiting upon God, and gets life and strength.—*Thomas Manton.*

Verse 50.—"*Thy word hath quickened me.*"   Here, as is evident from the mention of " affliction "—and indeed throughout the Psalm—the verb "*quicken*" is used not merely in an external sense of " preservation from death " (Hupfeld), but of " reviving the heart," " imparting fresh courage," etc.—*J. J. Stewart Perowne.*

Verse 50.—"*Thy word hath quickened me.*"   It made me alive when I was dead in sin ; it has many a time made me lively when I was dead in duty ; it has quickened me to that which is good, when I was backward and averse to it ; and it has quickened me in that which is good, when I was cold and indifferent.—*Matthew Henry.*

Verse 50.—(*Second Clause*).   Adore God's distinguishing grace, if you have felt the power and authority of the word upon your conscience ; if you can say as David, "*Thy word hath quickened me.*" Christian, bless God that he has not only given thee his word to be a rule of holiness, but his grace to be a principle of holiness. Bless God that he has not only written his word, but sealed it upon thy heart, and made it effectual. Canst thou say it is of divine inspiration, because thou hast felt it to be of lively operation ? Oh free grace ! That God should send out his word, and heal thee ; that he should heal thee and not others !   That the same Scripture which to them is a dead letter, should be to thee a savour of life.—*Thomas Watson.*

Verse 51.—"*The proud have had me greatly in derision.*"   The saints of God have complained of this in all ages : David of his busy mockers ; the abjects jeered him.

Job was disdained of those children whose fathers he would have scorned to set with the dogs of his flock, Job xxx. 1.   Joseph was nicknamed a dreamer, Paul a babbler, Christ himself a Samaritan, and with intent of disgrace a carpenter. . . . Michal was barren, yet she hath too many children, that scorn the habit and exercises of holiness.   There cannot be a greater argument of a foul soul, than the deriding of religious services.   Worldly hearts can see nothing in those actions, but folly and madness ; piety hath no relish, but is distasteful to their palates.—*Thomas Adams.*

Verse 51.—"*The proud,*" etc.   Scoffing proceedeth from pride.   Prov. iii. 34, with 1 Peter v. 5.—*John Trapp.*

Verse 51.   "*Greatly.*"   The word noteth " continually," the Septuagint translates it by αφόδρα, the vulgar Latin by *usque valde,* and *usque longe.*   They derided him with all possible bitterness ;   and day by day they had their scoffs for him, so that it was both a grievous and a perpetual temptation.—*Thomas Manton.*

Verse 51.—"*Derision.*"   David tells that he had been jeered for his religion, but yet he had not been jeered out of his religion.   They laughed at him for his praying and called it cant, for his seriousness and called it mopishness, for his strictness and called it needless preciseness.—*Matthew Henry.*

Verse 51.—It is a great thing in a soldier to behave well under fire ; but it is a greater thing for a soldier of the cross to be unflinching in the day of his trial.   It does not hurt the Christian to have the dogs bark at him.—*William S. Plumer.*

Verses 50, 51.—The life and vigour infused into me by the promise which "*quickened me,*" caused me "*not to decline from thy law,*" even though "*the proud did iniquitously altogether*"; doing all in their power, through their jeerings at me, to deter me from its observance.—*Robert Bellarmine.*

Verse 52.—"*I remembered thy judgments of old.*"   It is good to have a number of examples of God's dealings with his servants laid up in the storehouse of a sanctified memory, that thereby faith may be strengthened in the day of affliction ; for so are we here taught.—*David Dickson.*

Verse 52.—"*I remembered thy judgments.*"   He remembered that at the beginning Adam, because of transgression of the divine command, was cast out from dwelling in Paradise ; and that Cain, condemned by the authority of the divine sentence, paid the price of his parricidal crime ; that Enoch, caught up to heaven because of his devotion, escaped the poison of earthly wickedness ; that Noah, because of righteousness the victor of the deluge, became the survivor of the human race ; that Abraham, because of faith, diffused the seed of his posterity through the whole earth ; that Israel, because of the patient bearing of troubles, consecrated a believing people by the sign of his own name ; that David himself, because of gentleness, having had regal honour conferred, was preferred to his elder brothers.—*Ambrose.*

Verse 52.—"*I remembered,*" etc.   Jerome writes of that religious lady Paula, that she had got most of the Scriptures by heart.   We are bid to have the " word dwell in " us : Col. iii. 16.   The word is a jewel that adorns the hidden man ; and shall we not remember it ?   " Can a maid forget her ornaments ? " Jer. ii. 32. Such as have a disease they call *lienteria,* in which the meat comes up as fast as they eat it, and stays not in the stomach, are not nourished by it.   If the word stays not in the memory, it cannot profit.   Some can better remember a piece of news than a line of Scripture : their memories are like those ponds, where frogs live, but fish die.—*Thomas Watson, in "The Morning Exercises."*

Verse 52.—"*I remembered thy judgments, and have comforted myself.*"   A case of conscience may be propounded : how could David be comforted by God's judgments, for it seemeth a barbarous thing to delight in the destruction of any ? it is said, " He that is glad at calamities shall not be unpunished " (Prov. xvii. 5).

1. It must be remembered that judgment implies both parts of God's righteous dispensation, the deliverance of the godly, and the punishment of the wicked.   Now, in the first sense there is no ground of scruple, for it is said, " Judgment shall return unto righteousness " (Ps. xciv. 15) ; the sufferings of good men shall be turned into the greatest advantages, as the context showeth that God will not cast off his people, but judgment shall return unto righteousness.   2. Judgment, as it signifieth punishment of the wicked, may yet be a comfort, not as it importeth the calamity of any, but either,—

(1) When the wicked is punished, the snare and allurement to sin is taken away, which is the hope of impunity ; for by their punishment men see that it is dangerous to sin against God : " When thy judgments are in the earth, the inhabitants

of the world will learn righteousness " (Isai. xxvi. 9) ; the snare is removed from many a soul.

(2) Their derision and mockage of godliness ceaseth, they do no longer vex and pierce the souls of the godly, saying, " Aha, aha " (Ps. xl. 15) ; it is as a wound to their heart when they say, " Where is thy God ? " (Ps. xlii. 10). Judgment slayeth this evil.

(3) The impediments and hindrances of worshipping and serving God are taken away : when the nettles are rooted up, the corn hath the more room to grow.

(4) Opportunity of molesting God's servants is taken away, and they are prevented from afflicting the church by their oppressions ; and so way is made for the enlarging of Christ's kingdom.

(5) Thereby also God's justice is manifested : When it goeth well with the righteous, the city rejoiceth : and when the wicked perish, there is shouting " (Prov. xi. 10) ; " The righteous also shall see, and fear, and shall laugh at him : lo this is the man that made not God his strength " (Ps. lii. 6, 7) ; rejoice over Babylon, " ye holy apostles and prophets, for God hath avenged you on her " (Rev. xviii. 20). When the word of God is fulfilled, surely then we may rejoice that his justice and truth are cleared.—*Thomas Manton.*

Verse 52.—The word *mishphatim,* *"judgments,"* is used in Scripture either for laws enacted, or judgments executed according to those laws. The one may be called the judgments of his mouth, as, " Remember his marvellous works that he hath done ; his wonders, and the judgments of his mouth " (Ps. cv. 5), the other, the judgments of his hand. As both will bear the name of judgments, so both may be said to be *"of old."* His decrees and statutes which have an eternal equity in them, and were graven upon the heart of man in innocency, may well be said to be of old : and because from the beginning of the world God hath been punishing the wicked, and delivering the godly in due time, his judiciary dispensations may be said to be so also. The matter is not much, whether we interpret it of either his statutes or decrees, for they both contain matter of comfort, and we may see the ruin of the wicked in the word, if we see it not in providence. Yet I rather interpret it of those righteous acts recorded in Scripture, which God as a just judge hath executed in all ages, according to the promises and threatenings annexed to his laws. Only in that sense I must note to you, judgments imply his mercies in the deliverance of his righteous servants, as well as his punishments on the wicked : the seasonable interpositions of his relief for the one in their greatest distresses, as well as his just vengeance on the other notwithstanding their highest prosperities.—*Thomas Manton.*

Verses 52, 55.—*"I remembered thy judgments,"* *"thy name in the night."* Thomas Fuller thus writes in his " David's Heartie Repentance " :—

" For sundry duties he did dayes devide,
Making exchange of worke his recreation ;
For prayer he set the precious morne aside,
The mid-day he bequeathed to meditation :
Sweete sacred stories he reserved for night,
To reade of Moses' meeknes, Sampson's might :
These were his joy, these onely his delight."

Verse 53.—*"Horror hath taken hold upon me because of the wicked."* I have had clear views of *eternity ;* have seen the blessedness of the *godly,* in some measure ; and have longed to share their happy state ; as well as been comfortably satisfied that through grace I shall do so ; but, oh, what anguish is raised in my mind, to think of an *eternity* for those who are *Christless,* for those who are mistaken, and who bring their false hopes to the grave with them ! The sight was so dreadful I could by no means bear it : my thoughts recoiled, and I said, (under a more affecting sense than ever before,) " Who can dwell with everlasting burnings ? "—*David Brainerd,* 1718—1747.

Verse 53.—*"Horror hath taken hold upon me,"* etc. Oh who can express what the state of a soul in such circumstances is ! All that we can possibly say about it gives but a very feeble, faint representation of it ; it is inexpressible and inconceivable ; for who knows the power of God's anger ?

How dreadful is the state of those that are daily and hourly in danger of this great wrath and infinite misery ! But this is the dismal case of every soul in this congregation that has not been born again, however moral and strict, sober and religious, they may otherwise be. Oh that you would consider it, whether you be young or old ! There is reason to think, that there are many in this congregation now hearing this discourse, that will actually be the subjects of this very misery to all eternity. We know not who they are, or in what seats they sit, or what thoughts they now have. It may be they are now at ease, and hear all these things without much disturbance, and are now flattering themselves that they are not the persons, promising themselves that they shall escape. If we knew that there was one person, and but one, in the whole congregation, that was to be the subject of this misery, what an awful thing would it be to think of ! If we knew who it was, what an awful sight would it be to see such a person ! How might all the rest of the congregation lift up a lamentable and bitter cry over him ! But, alas ! instead of one, how many is it likely will remember this discourse in hell !—*Jonathan Edwards, in a Sermon entitled, "Sinners in the Hands of an angry God."*

Verse 53.—*"Horror."* ולעפה, *zilâphah,* properly signifies the pestilential burning wind called by the Arabs simoon (see Ps. xi. 6) ; and is here used in a figurative sense for the *most horrid mental distress ;* and strongly marks the idea the Psalmist had of the corrupting, pestilential, and destructive nature of sin.—*Note in Bagster's Comprehensive Bible.*

Verse 53.—*"Horror."* The word for *"horror "* signifieth also a tempest or storm. Translations vary ; some read it, as Junius, " a storm overtaking one " ; Ainsworth, " a burning horror hath seized me," and expoundeth it a storm of terror and dismay. The Septuagint, ἀθυμία κατέχε μὲ, " faintness and dejection of mind hath possessed me " ; our own translation, " I am horribly afraid " ; all translations, as well as the original word, imply a great trouble of mind, and a vehement commotion ; like a storm, it was matter of disquiet and trembling to David.—*Thomas Manton.*

Verse 53.—*"Because of the wicked that forsake thy law."* David grieved, not because he was himself attacked ; but because the law of God was forsaken ; and he bewailed the condemnation of those who so did, because they are lost to God. Just as a good father in the madness of his son, when he is ill-used by him, mourns not his own but the misery of the diseased ; and he grieves at the contumely, not because it is cast on himself, but because the diseased person knows not what he does in his madness : so a good man, when he sees a sinner neither reverence nor honour the grey hairs of a parent, that to his face he can insult him, that he does not know in the madness of sinning what unbecoming and shameful things he does, grieves for him as one on the point of death, laments him as one despaired of by the physicians. As a good physician in the first place advises, then, even if he receive hard words, though he be beaten, nevertheless as the man is ill he bears with him ; and if he be cursed he does not leave ; and any medicine that may be applied he does not refuse ; nor does he go away as from a stubborn fellow, but strives with all diligence to heal him as one that has deserved well from him, exercising not only the skill of science but also benignity of disposition. Even so, a righteous man, when he is treated with contempt, does not turn away, but when he is calumniated he regards it as madness, not as depravity ; and desires rather to apply his own remedy to the wound, and sympathises, and grieves not for himself, but for him who labours under an incurable disease.—*Ambrose.*

Verse 53.—*"The wicked that forsake thy law" ;* not only transgress the law of the Lord, as every man does, more or less ; but wilfully and obstinately despise it, and cast it behind their backs, and live in a continued course of disobedience to it ; or who apostatize from the doctrine of the word of God ; wilfully deny the truth, after they have had a speculative knowledge of it, whose punishment is very grievous (Heb. x. 26—29) ; and now partly because of the daring impiety of wicked men, who stretch out their hands against God, and strengthen themselves against the Almighty, and run upon him, even on the thick bosses of his bucklers : because of the shocking nature of their sin, the sad examples thereby set to others, the detriment they are to themselves, and the dishonour they bring to God ; and partly because of the dreadful punishment that shall be inflicted on them here, and especially hereafter, when a horrible tempest of wrath will come upon them. Hence such trembling seized the Psalmist : and often so it is, that good men tremble more for the wicked than they do for themselves : see verse 120.—*John Gill.*

Verse 54.—*" Thy statutes have been my songs."* The Psalmist rejoiced, doubtless, as the good do now, 1. In law itself ; law, as a rule of order ; law as a guide of conduct ; law, as a security for safety. 2. In *such* a law as that of God—so pure, so holy, so fitted to promote the happiness of man. 3. In the stability of that law, as constituting his own personal security, the ground of his hope.   4. In law in its influence on the universe, preserving order and securing harmony.—*Albert Barnes.*

Verse 54.—"Thy statutes have been my songs."   In the early ages it was customary to versify the laws, that the people might learn them by heart, and sing them.— *Williams.*

Verse 54.—"Thy statutes have been my songs."   God's statutes are here his *"songs,"* which give him spiritual refreshing, sweeten the hardships of the pilgrimage, and measure and hasten his steps.—*Franz Delitzsch.*

Verse 54.—"Songs."   Travellers sing to deceive the tediousness of the way; so did David; and hereby he solaced himself under that horror which he speaks of in verse 53.   Great is the comfort that cometh in by singing of Psalms with grace in our hearts.—*John Trapp.*

Verse 54.—"Songs."

"Such songs have power to quiet
The restless pulse of care,
And come like the benediction
That follows after prayer.

"And the night shall be filled with music,
And the cares that infest the day
Shall fold their tents like the Arabs,
And as silently steal away."

Henry Wadsworth Longfellow.

Verse 54.—"Songs in the house of my pilgrimage."   Wherefore is everything like warmth in religion branded with the name of enthusiasm ?   Warmth is expected in the poet, in the musician, in the scholar, in the lover—and even in the tradesman it is allowed, if not commended—why then is it condemned in the concerns of the soul—a subject which, infinitely above all others, demands and deserves all the energy of the mind ?   Would a prisoner exult at the proclamation of deliverance, and is the redeemed sinner to walk forth from his bondage, unmoved, unaffected, without gratitude or joy ?   No, " Ye shall go out with joy, and be led forth with peace : the mountains and the hills shall break forth before you into singing, and all the trees of the field shall clap their hands."   Shall the condemned criminal feel I know not what emotions, when instead of the execution of the sentence he receives a pardon ? and is the absolved transgressor to be senseless and silent ?   No.   " Being justified by faith, we have peace with God through our Lord Jesus Christ : by whom also we have access by faith into this grace wherein we stand, and rejoice in hope of the glory of God.   And not only so, but we glory in tribulations also : and not only so, but we also joy in God through our Lord Jesus Christ, by whom we have now received the atonement."

Other travellers are accustomed to relieve the tediousness of their journey with a song.   The Israelites, when they repaired from the extremities of the country three times a year to Jerusalem to worship, had songs appointed for the purpose, and travelled singing as they went.   And of the righteous it is said, " They shall sing in the ways of the Lord.   The redeemed of the Lord shall return, and come to Zion with songs ; and everlasting joy shall be upon their heads."—*William Jay.*

Verse 54.—"Songs in the house of my pilgrimage."   See how the Lord in his wise dispensation attempers himself to our infirmities.   Our life is subject to many changes, and God by his word hath provided for us also many instructions and remedies.   Every cross hath its own remedy, and every state of life its own instruction. Sometimes our grief is so great that we cannot sing ; then let us pray : sometimes our deliverance so joyful that we must break out in thanksgiving ; then let us sing. " If any man among you be afflicted, let him pray ; if he be merry, let him sing." Prayers for every cross, and psalms for every deliverance, hath God by his own Spirit penned for us ; so that now we are more than inexcusable if we fail in this duty.— *William Cowper.*

Verse 54.—"In the house of my pilgrimage."   According to the original, *"the house of my pilgrimages";* that is, whatever places I have wandered to during Saul's persecution of me.—*Samuel Burder.*

Verse 54.—"In the house of my pilgrimage."   Vatablus expounds this of his banishment amongst the Philistines ; that when he was put from his native country and kindred, and all other comforts failed him, the word of the Lord furnished matter of joy to him. And indeed, the banishment of God's servants may cast them far from their kindred and acquaintance ; but it chaseth them nearer to the Lord, and the Lord nearer to them. Proof of this in Jacob, when he was banished and lay without, all night in the fields, he found a more familiar presence of God than he did when he slept in the tent with father and mother.

But we may rather, with Basil, refer it to the whole time of David's mortal life : *omnem vitam suam peregrinationem vocare arbitror.* So Jacob acknowledgeth to Pharaoh, that his life was a pilgrimage ; and Abraham and Isaac dwelt in the world as strangers.

S. Peter therefore teacheth us as pilgrims to abstain from the lusts of the flesh ; and S. Paul, to use this world as if we used it not ; for the fashion thereof goeth away. Many ways are we taught this lesson ; but slow are we to learn it. Alas, what folly is this, that a man should desire to dwell in the earth, when God calleth him to be a citizen of heaven ! Yet great is the comfort we have of this, that the houses wherein we lodge upon earth are but *houses of our pilgrimage.* The faithful Israelites endured their bondage in Egypt the more patiently, because they knew they were to be delivered from it. If the houses of our servitude were eternal mansions, how lamentable were our condition ! But God be thanked, they are but wayfaring cottages, and houses of our pilgrimage. Such a house was the womb of our mother : if we had been enclosed there for ever, what burden had it been to her, what bondage to ourselves ! Such a house will be the grave ; of the which we must all say with Job, " The grave shall be my house, and I shall make my bed in the dark." If we were there to abide for ever, how comfortless were our estate. But, God be praised, our mansion house is above ; and the houses we exchange here on earth are but the houses of our pilgrimage ; and happy is he who can so live in the world as esteeming himself in his own house, in his own bed, yea, in his own body, to be but a stranger, in respect of his absence from the Lord.—*William Cowper.*

Verse. 54.—"*My pilgrimage.*" If men have been termed pilgrims, and life a journey, then we may add that the Christian pilgrimage far surpasses all others in the following important particulars :—in the goodness of the road, in the beauty of the prospects, in the excellence of the company, and in the vast superiority of the accommodation provided for the Christian traveller when he has finished his course.— *H. G. Salter, in "The Book of Illustrations," 1840.*

Verse 55.—"*I have remembered thy name, O LORD, in the night,*" etc. As the second clause of the verse depends on the first, I consider the whole verse as setting forth one and the same truth ; and, therefore, the prophet means that he was induced, by the remembrance he had of God, to keep the law. Contempt of the law originates in this, that few have any regard for God : and hence, the Scripture, in condemning the impiety of men, declares that they *have forgotten* God (Psalm l. 22 ; lxxviii. 11 ; cvi. 21) . . . .

The word "*night*" is not intended by him to mean the remembering of God merely for a short time, but a perpetual remembrance of him ; he, however, refers to that season in particular, because then almost all our senses are overpowered with sleep. " When other men are sleeping, God occurs to my thoughts during my sleep." He has another reason for alluding to the night-season,—that we may be apprised, that though there was none to observe him, and none to put him in remembrance of it ; yea, though he was shrouded in darkness, yet he was as solicitous to cherish the remembrance of God as if he occupied the most public and conspicuous place.—*John Calvin.*

Verse 55.—"*I have remembered thy name in the night,*" and therefore I "*have kept thy law*" all day.—*Matthew Henry.*

Verse 55.—"*I have remembered thy name, O LORD, in the night.*" This verse contains a new protestation of his honest affection toward the word of God. Wherein, first, let us mark his *sincerity ;* he was religious not only in public, but in private ; for private exercises are the surest trials of true religion. In public, oftentimes hypocrisy carries men to simulate that which they are not ; it is not so in the private devotion ; for then, either doth a man, if he make no conscience of God's worship, utterly neglect it, because there is no eye of man to see him ; or otherwise, if he be indeed religious, even in private he presents his heart to God, seeking it to be approved by him ; for his " praise is not of man, but of God."

Again, this argueth his *fervency* in religion : for as elsewhere he protests that he loved the word more than his appointed food ; so here he protests that he gave up his night's rest that he might meditate in the word.   But now, so far is zeal decayed in professors, that they will not forego their superfluities, far less their needful refreshment, for love of the word of God.—*William Cowper.*

Verse 55. *"Thy name, O Lord."*   The *"name"* of the Lord is his character, his nature, his attributes, the manifestations he hath made of his holiness, his wisdom, goodness and truth.—*John Stephen.*

Verse 55.—*"In the night."*   First, that is, *continually,* because he remembered God in the day also.   Secondly, *sincerely,* because he avoided the applause of men. Thirdly, *cheerfully,* because he avoided the heaviness of natural sleep could not overcome him. All these show that he was *intensely* given to the word ; as we see men of the world will take some part of the night for their delights.   And in that he did keep God's testimonies in the night, he showeth that he was the same in secret that he was in the light ; whereby he condemned all those that will cover their wickedness with the dark.   Let us examine ourselves whether we have broken our sleeps to call upon God, as we have to fulfil our pleasures.—*Richard Greenham.*

Verse 55.—*"In the night."*   Pastor Harms of Hermansburg used to preach and pray and instruct his people for nine hours on the Sabbath.   And then when his mind was utterly exhausted, and his whole body was thrilling with pain, and he seemed almost dying for the want of rest, he could get no sleep.   But he used to say that he loved to lie awake all night in the silence and darkness and think of Jesus.   The night put away everything else from his thoughts, and left his heart free to commune with the One whom his soul most devoutly loved, and who visited and comforted his weary disciple in the night watches.   And so God's children have often enjoyed rare seasons of communion with him in the solitude of exile, in the deep gloom of the dungeon, in the perpetual night of blindness, and at times when all voices and instructions from the world have been most completely cut off, and the soul has been left alone with God.—*Daniel March, in "Night unto Night."*   1880.

Verse 55.—*"In the night."*   There is never a time in which it is not proper to turn to God and think on his name.   In the darkness of midnight, in the darkness of mental depression, in the darkness of outward providences, God is still a fitting theme.—*William S. Plumer.*

Verse 55.—*"The night."*—

> " Dear night ! this world's defeat ;
> The stop to busy fools ; Care's check and curb ;
> The day of spirits ; my soul's calm retreat
>   Which none disturb !
> Christ's progress, and his prayer time ;
> The hours to which high heaven doth chime.
>
> " God's silent, searching flight ;
> When my Lord's head is filled with dew, and all
> His locks are wet with the clear drops of night ;
>   His still, soft call ;
> His knocking time ; the soul's dumb watch,
> When spirits their fair kindred catch."
>
>   *Henry Vaughan, 1621—1695.*

Verse 55.—*"And have kept thy law" ;* though imperfectly, yet spiritually, sincerely, heartily, and from a principle of love and gratitude, and with a view to the glory of God, and without mercenary, sinister ends.—*John Gill.*

Verse 55.—*"And have kept thy law."*   Hours of secret fellowship with God must issue in the desire of increased conformity to his holy will.   It is the remembrance of God that leads to the keeping of his laws, as it is forgetfulness of God that fosters every species of transgression.—*John Morison.*

Verse 55.—*"And have kept."*   The verb is in the future, and perhaps is better so rendered, thus making it the expression of a solemn, deliberate purpose to continue, his obedience.—*William S. Plumer.*

Verses 55, 56.—He that delights to keep God's law, God will give him more grace to keep it, according to that remarkable text, *"I have remembered thy name, O* LORD, *in the night, and have kept thy law.   This I had, because I kept thy precepts."*   What had David for keeping God's precepts ?   He had power to keep his law ; that is, to grow and increase in keeping of it.   As the prophet (Hosea vi. 3) speaks of the

knowledge of God : "Then shall we know, if we follow on to know the Lord";
that is, if we industriously labour to know God, we shall have this reward, to be
made able to know him more. So may I say of the grace of God : he that delights
to keep God's law shall have his reward,—to be enabled to keep it more perfectly.
A true delight in God's word is grace increasing. Grace is the mother of all true
joy (Isai. xxxii. 17), and joy is as the daughter, and the mother and daughter live
and die together.—*Edmund Calamy* (1600—1666), *in "The Godly Man's Ark."*

Verse 56.—*"This I had, because I kept thy precepts."* As sin is a punishment of
sin, and the wicked waxeth ever worse and worse ; so godliness is the recompense
of godliness. The right use of one talent increaseth more, and the beginnings of
godliness are blessed with a growth of godliness. David's good exercises here held
him in memory of his God, and the memory of God made him more godly and
religious.—*William Cowper.*

Verse 56.—*"This I had,"* etc. The Rabbins have an analogous saying,—*The
reward of a precept is a precept ;* or, *A precept draws a precept.* The meaning of
which is, that he who keeps one precept, to him God grants, as if by way of reward,
the ability to keep another and more difficult precept. The contrary to this is that
other saying of the Rabbins, that *the reward of a sin is a sin ;* or, *Transgression
draws transgression.*—*Simon de Muis*, 1587—1644.

Verse 56.—*"This I had,"* that is, this happened to me, etc. I experienced many
evils and adversities ; but, on the other hand, I drew sweetest consolations from
the word, and I was crowned with many blessings from God.
Others thus render it, This is my business, This I care for and desire, to keep
thy commandments ; *i.e.*, to hold fast the doctrine incorrupt with faith and a good
conscience.—*D. H. Mollerus.*

Verse 56.—*"This I had,"* etc. I had the comfort of keeping thy law *because I
kept it.* God's work is its own wages.—*Matthew Henry.*

Verse 56.—*"This I had,"* etc. What is that ? This comfort I had, this
supportation I had in all my afflictions, this consolation I had, this sweet communion
with God I had. Why ? *"Because I kept thy precepts,"* I obeyed thy will. Look,
how much obedience is yielded to the commands of God, so much comfort doth flow
into the soul : God usually gives in comforts proportionably to our obedience.
O the sweet, soul-satisfying consolation a child of God finds in the ways of God, and
in doing the will of God, especially when he lies on his death-bed ; then it will be
sweeter to him than honey and the honeycomb ; then will he say with good king
Hezekiah, when he lay upon his death-bed, " Lord, remember how I have walked
before thee in truth, and with a perfect heart, and have done that which was good
in thy sight." O the sweet satisfaction that a soul shall find in God, when he comes
to appear before God !—*James Nalton*, 1664.

Verse 56.—*"This I had,"* etc. Or, " This was my *consolation*, that I kept thy
precepts ; " which is nearly the reading of the Syriac, and renders the sense more
complete.—*Note in Bagster's Comprehensive Bible.*

Verse 56.—*"This I had,"* etc. When I hear the faithful people of God telling
of his love, and saying—*"This I had,"* must I not, if unable to join their cheerful
acknowledgment, trace it to my unfaithful walk, and say—" This I had not "—
because I have failed in obedience to thy precepts ; because I have been careless
and self-indulgent ; because I have slighted thy love ; because I have " grieved
thy Holy Spirit," and forgotten to " ask for the old paths, that I might walk therein,
and find rest to my soul " ? Jer. vi. 16.—*Charles Bridges.*

Verse 56.—David saith indefinitely, *" This I had";* not telling us what good or
privilege it was ; only in the general, it was some benefit that accrued to him in this
life. He doth not say, This I hope for ; but, *"This I had ; "* and therefore he doth
not speak of the full reward in the life to come. In heaven we come to receive the
full reward of obedience ; but a close walker, that waiteth upon God in an humble
and constant obedience, shall have sufficient encouragement even in this life. Not
only he shall be blessed, but he is blessed ; he hath something on hand as well as
in hope : as David saith in this the 119th Psalm, not only he shall be blessed, but
he is blessed ; as they that travelled towards Zion, they met with a well by the
way : " Who passing through the valley of Baca make it a well ; the rain also filleth
the pools " (Ps. lxxxiv. 6). In a dry and barren wilderness, through which they
were to pass, they were not left wholly comfortless, but met with a well or a cistern ;
that is, they had some comfort vouchsafed to them before they came to enjoy God's

presence in Zion; some refreshments they had by the way. As servants, that, besides their wages, have their veils; so, besides the recompense of reward hereafter, we have our present comforts and supports during our course of service, which are enough to counterbalance all worldly joys, and outweigh the greatest pleasures that men can expect in the way of sin. In the benefits that believers find by walking with God in a course of obedience every one can say, *"This I had, because I kept thy precepts."—Thomas Manton.*

EXPOSITION OF VERSES 57 TO 64.

*T*HOU *art* my portion, O LORD : I have said that I would keep thy words.

58 I intreated thy favour with *my* whole heart : be merciful unto me according to thy word.

59 I thought on my ways, and turned my feet unto thy testimonies.

60 I made haste, and delayed not to keep thy commandments.

61 The bands of the wicked have robbed me : *but* I have not forgotten thy law.

62 At midnight I will rise to give thanks unto thee because of thy righteous judgments.

63 I *am* a companion of all *them* that fear thee, and of them that keep thy precepts.

64 The earth, O LORD, is full of thy mercy : teach me thy statutes.

In this section the Psalmist seems to take firm hold upon God himself ; appropriating him (57), crying out for him (58), returning to him (59), solacing himself in him (61, 62), associating with his people (63), and sighing for personal experience of his goodness (64). Note how the first verse of this octave is linked to the last of the former one, of which indeed it is an expanded repetition. " This I had because I kept thy precepts. Thou art my portion, O Lord : I have said that I would keep thy words."

57. "*Thou art my portion, O LORD.*" A broken sentence. The translators have mended it by insertions, but perhaps it had been better to have left it alone, and then it would have appeared as an exclamation,—" My portion, O Lord ! " The poet is lost in wonder while he sees that the great and glorious God is all his own ! Well might he be so, for there is no possession like Jehovah himself. The form of the sentence expresses joyous recognition and appropriation,—" My portion, O Jehovah ! " David had often seen the prey divided, and heard the victors shouting over it ; here he rejoices as one who seizes his share of the spoil ; he chooses the Lord to be his part of the treasure. Like the Levites, he took God to be his portion, and left other matters to those who coveted them. This is a large and lasting heritage, for it includes all, and more than all, and it outlasts all ; and yet no man chooses it for himself until God has chosen and renewed him. Who that is truly wise could hesitate for a moment when the infinitely blessed God is set before him to be the object of his choice ? David leaped at the opportunity, and grasped the priceless boon. Our author here dares exhibit the title-deeds of his portion before the eye of the Lord himself, for he addresses his joyful utterance directly to God whom he boldly calls his own. With much else to choose from, for he was a king, and a man of great resources, he deliberately turns from all the treasures of the world, and declares that the Lord, even Jehovah, is his portion.

"*I have said that I would keep thy words.*" We cannot always look back with comfort upon what we have said, but in this instance David had spoken wisely and well. He had declared his choice : he preferred the word of God to the wealth of worldlings. It was his firm resolve to keep—that is, treasure up and observe—the words of his God, and as he had aforetime solemnly expressed it in the presence of the Lord himself, so here he confesses the binding obligation of his former vow. Jesus said, " If a man love me, he will keep my words," and this is a case which he might have quoted as an illustration ; for the Psalmist's love to God as his portion led to his keeping the words of God. David took God to be his Prince as well as his Portion. He was confident as to his interest in God, and therefore he was resolute in his obedience to him. Full assurance is a powerful source of holiness. The very words of God are to be stored up ; for whether they relate to doctrine, promise, or precept, they are most precious. When the heart is determined to keep these words, and has registered its purpose in the court of heaven, it is prepared for all the temptations and trials that may befall it ; for, with God as its heritage, it is always in good case.

58. "*I intreated thy favour with my whole heart.*" A fully assured possession of God does not set aside prayer, but rather urges us to it ; he who knows God to

be his God will seek his face, longing for his presence. Seeking God's presence is the idea conveyed by the marginal reading, "thy face," and this is true to the Hebrew. The presence of God is the highest form of his favour, and therefore it is the most urgent desire of gracious souls : the light of his countenance gives us an antepast of heaven. O that we always enjoyed it ! The good man entreated God's smile as one who begged for his life, and the entire strength of his desire went with the entreaty. Such eager pleadings are sure of success ; that which comes from our heart will certainly go to God's heart. The whole of God's favours are ready for those who seek them with their whole hearts.

"*Be merciful unto me according to thy word.*" He has entreated favour, and the form in which he most needs it is that of mercy, for he is more a sinner than anything else. He asks nothing beyond the promise, he only begs for such mercy as the word reveals. And what more could he want or wish for ? God has revealed such an infinity of mercy in his word that it would be impossible to conceive of more. See how the Psalmist dwells upon favour and mercy, he never dreams of merit. He does not demand, but entreat ; for he feels his own unworthiness. Note how he remains a suppliant, though he knows that he has all things in his God. God is his portion, and yet he begs for a look at his face. The idea of any other standing before God than that of an undeserving but favoured one never entered his head. Here we have his " Be merciful unto me " rising with as much intensity of humble pleading as if he still remained among the most trembling of penitents. The confidence of faith makes us bold in prayer, but it never teaches us to live without prayer, or justifies us in being other than humble beggars at mercy's gate.

59. "*I thought on my ways, and turned my feet unto thy testimonies.*" While studying the word he was led to study his own life, and this caused a mighty revolution. He came to the word, and then he came to himself, and this made him arise and go to his father. Consideration is the commencement of conversion : first we think and then we turn. When the mind repents of ill ways the feet are soon led into good ways ; but there will be no repenting until there is deep, earnest thought. Many men are averse to thought of any kind, and as to thought upon their ways, they cannot endure it, for their ways will not bear thinking of. David's ways had not been all that he could have wished them to be, and so his thoughts were sobered o'er with the pale cast of regret ; but he did not end with idle lamentations, he set about a practical amendment ; he turned and returned, he sought the testimonies of the Lord, and hastened to enjoy once more the conscious favour of his heavenly friend. Action without thought is folly, and thought without action is sloth : to think carefully and then to act promptly is a happy combination. He had entreated for renewed fellowship, and now he proved the genuineness of his desire by renewed obedience. If we are in the dark, and mourn an absent God, our wisest method will be not so much to think upon our sorrows as upon our ways : though we cannot turn the course of providence, we can turn the way of our walking, and this will soon mend matters. If we can get our feet right as to holy walking, we shall soon get our hearts right as to happy living. God will turn to his saints when they turn to him ; yea, he has already favoured them with the light of his face when they begin to think and turn.

60. "*I made haste, and delayed not to keep thy commandments.*" He made all speed to get back into the royal road from which he had wandered, and to run in that road upon the King's errands. Speed in repentance and speed in obedience are two excellent things. We are too often in haste to sin ; O that we may be in a greater hurry to obey. Delay in sin is increase of sin. To be slow to keep the commands is really to break them. There is much evil in a lagging pace when God's command is to be followed. A holy alacrity in service is much to be cultivated. It is wrought in us by the Spirit of God, and the preceding verses describe the method of it : we are made to perceive and mourn our errors, we are led to return to the right path, and then we are eager to make up for lost time by dashing forward to fulfil the precept.

Whatever may be the slips and wanderings of an honest heart, there remains enough of true life in it to produce ardent piety when once it is quickened by the visitations of God. The Psalmist entreated for mercy, and when he received it he became eager and vehement in the Lord's ways. He had always loved them, and hence when he was enriched with grace he displayed great vivacity and delight in them. He made double speed ; for positively he " made haste," and negatively he refused to yield to any motive which suggested procrastination,—he " delayed not." Thus he made rapid advances and accomplished much service, fulfilling thereby the vow which is recorded in the 57th verse : " I said that I would keep thy words." The commands which he was so eager to obey were not ordinances of man, but precepts of the Most High. Many are zealous to obey custom and society, and yet they are slack in serving God. It is a crying shame that men should be served post-haste, and that God's work should have the go-by, or be performed with dreamy negligence.

61. *"The bands of the wicked have robbed me."* Aforetime they derided him, and now they have defrauded him. Ungodly men grow worse, and become more and more daring, so that they go from ridicule to robbery. Much of this bold opposition arose from their being banded together : men will dare to do in company what they durst not have thought of alone. When firebrands are laid together there is no telling what a flame they will create. It seems that whole bands of men assailed this one child of God, they are cowardly enough for anything ; though they could not kill him, they robbed him ; the dogs of Satan will worry saints if they cannot devour them. David's enemies did their utmost : first the serpents hissed, and then they stung. Since words availed not, the wicked fell to blows. How much the ungodly have plundered the saints in all ages, and how often have the righteous borne gladly the spoiling of their goods !

"But I have not forgotten thy law." This was well. Neither his sense of injustice, nor his sorrow at his losses, nor his attempts at defence diverted him from the ways of God. He would not do wrong to prevent the suffering of wrong, nor do ill to avenge ill. He carried the law in his heart, and therefore no disturbance of mind could take him off from following it. He might have forgotten himself if he had forgotten the law : as it was, he was ready to forgive and forget the injuries done him, for his heart was taken up with the word of God. The bands of the wicked had not robbed him of his choicest treasure, since they had left him his holiness and his happiness.

Some read this passage, " The bands of the wicked environ me." They hemmed him in, they cut him off from succour, they shut up every avenue of escape, but the man of God had his protector with him ; a clear conscience relied upon the promise, and a brave resolve stuck to the precept. He could not be either bribed or bullied into sin. The cordon of the ungodly could not keep God from him, nor him from God : this was because God was his portion, and none could deprive him of it either by force or fraud. That is true grace which can endure the test : some are barely gracious among the circle of their friends, but this man was holy amid a ring of foes.

62. *"At midnight I will rise to give thanks unto thee because of thy righteous judgments."* He was not afraid of the robbers ; he rose, not to watch his house, but to praise his God. Midnight is the hour for burglars, and there were bands of them around David, but they did not occupy his thoughts ; these were all up and away with the Lord his God. He thought not of thieves, but of thanks ; not of what *they* would steal, but of what *he* would give to his God. A thankful heart is such a blessing that it drives out fear and makes room for praise. Thanksgiving turns night into day, and consecrates all hours to the worship of God. Every hour is canonical to a saint.

The Psalmist observed posture ; he did not lie in bed and praise. There is not much in the position of the body, but there is something, and that something is to be observed whenever it is helpful to devotion and expressive of our diligence or humility. Many kneel without praying, some pray without kneeling ; but the best is to kneel and pray : so here. it would have been no virtue to rise without giving thanks, and it would have been no sin to give thanks without rising ; but to rise and give thanks is a happy combination. As for the season, it was quiet, lonely, and such as proved his zeal. At midnight he would be unobserved and undisturbed ; it was his own time which he saved from his sleep, and so he would be free from the charge of sacrificing public duties to private devotions. Midnight ends one day and begins another, it was therefore meet to give the solemn moments to communion with the Lord. At the turn of the night he turned to his God. He had thanks to give for mercies which God had given : he had on his mind the truth of verse fifty-seven, " Thou art my portion," and if anything can make a man sing in the middle of the night that is it.

The *righteous* doings of the great Judge gladdened the heart of this godly man.

His *judgments* are the terrible side of God, but they have no terror to the righteous; they admire them, and adore the Lord for them : they rise at night to bless God that he will avenge his own elect. Some hate the very notion of divine justice, and in this they are wide as the poles asunder from this man of God, who was filled with joyful gratitude at the memory of the sentences of the Judge of all the earth. Doubtless in the expression, " thy righteous judgments," David refers also to the written judgments of God upon various points of moral conduct ; indeed, all the divine precepts may be viewed in that light ; they are all of them the legal decisions of the Supreme Arbiter of right and wrong. David was charmed with these judgments. Like Paul, he could say, " I delight in the law of God after the inward man." He could not find time enough by day to study the words of divine wisdom, or to bless God for them, and so he gave up his sleep that he might tell out his gratitude for such a law and such a Law-giver.

This verse is an advance upon the sense of verse fifty-two, and contains in addition the essence of fifty-five. Our author never repeats himself : though he runs up and down the same scale, his music has an infinite variety. The permutations and combinations which may be formed in connection with a few vital truths are innumerable.

63. *"I am a companion of all them that fear thee."* The last verse said, " I will," and this says, " I am." We can hardly hope to be right in the future unless we are right now. The holy man spent his nights with God and his days with God's people. Those who fear God love those who fear him, and they make small choice in their company so long as the men are truly God-fearing. David was a king, and yet he consorted with *"all"* who feared the Lord, whether they were obscure or famous, poor or rich. He was a fellow-commoner of the College of All-saints.

He did not select a few specially eminent saints and leave ordinary believers alone. No, he was glad of the society of those who had only the beginning of wisdom in the shape of " the fear of the Lord": he was pleased to sit with them on the lower forms of the school of faith. He looked for inward godly fear, but he also expected to see outward piety in those whom he admitted to his society ; hence he adds, *"and of them that keep thy precepts."* If they would keep the Lord's commands the Lord's servant would keep their company. David was known to be on the godly side, he was ever of the Puritanic party : the men of Belial hated him for this, and no doubt despised him for keeping such unfashionable company as that of humble men and women who were strait-laced and religious ; but the man of God is by no means ashamed of his associates ; so far from this, he even glories to avow his union with them, let his enemies make what they can of it. He found both pleasure and profit in saintly society ; he grew better by consorting with the good, and derived honour from keeping right honourable company. What says the reader ? Does he relish holy society ? Is he at home among gracious people ? If so, he may derive comfort from the fact. Birds of a feather flock together. A man is known by his company. Those who have no fear of God before their eyes seldom desire the society of saints ; it is too slow, too dull for them. Be this our comfort, that when we are let go by death we shall go to our own company, and those who loved the saints on earth shall be numbered with them in heaven.

There is a measure of parellelism between this seventh of its octave and the seventh of Teth (71) and of Jod (79) ; but, as a rule, the similarities which were so manifest in earlier verses are now becoming dim. As the sense deepens, the artificial form of expression is less regarded.

64. *"The earth, O LORD, is full of thy mercy."* David had been exiled, but he had never been driven beyond the range of mercy, for he found the world to be everywhere filled with it. He had wandered in deserts and hidden in caves, and there he had seen and felt the lovingkindness of the Lord. He had learned that far beyond the bounds of the land of promise and the race of Israel the love of Jehovah extended, and in this verse he expressed that large-hearted idea of God which is so seldom seen in the modern Jew. How sweet it is to us to know that not only is there mercy all over the world, but there is such an abundance of it that the earth is " full " of it. It is little wonder that the Psalmist, since he knew the Lord to be his portion, hoped to obtain a measure of this mercy for himself, and so was encouraged to pray, *"teach me thy statutes."* It was to him the *beau-ideal* of mercy to be taught of God, and taught in God's own law. He could not think of a greater mercy than this. Surely he who fills the universe with his grace will

grant such a request as this to his own child. Let us breathe the desire to the All-merciful Jehovah, and we may be assured of its fulfilment.

The first verse of this eight is fragrant with full assurance and strong resolve, and this last verse overflows with a sense of the divine fulness, and of the Psalmist's personal dependence. This is an illustration of the fact that full assurance neither damps prayer nor hinders humility. It would be no error if we said that it creates lowliness and suggests supplication. "Thou art my portion, O Lord," is well followed by " teach me "; for the heir of a great estate should be thoroughly educated, that his behaviour may comport with his fortune. What manner of disciples ought we to be whose inheritance is the Lord of hosts ? Those who have God for their Portion long to have him for their Teacher. Moreover, those who have resolved to obey are the most eager to be taught. " I have said that I would keep thy words " is beautifully succeeded by " teach me thy statutes." Those who wish to keep a law are anxious to know all its clauses and provisions lest they should offend through inadvertence. He who dares not care to be instructed of the Lord has never honestly resolved to be holy.

NOTES ON VERSES 57 TO 64.

This begins a new division of the Psalm, indicated by the Hebrew letter *Cheth*, which may be represented in English by *hh*.—*Albert Barnes*.

Verses 57—64.—In this section David laboureth to confirm his faith, and to comfort himself in the certainty of his regeneration, by eight properties of a sound believer, or eight marks of a new creature. The first whereof is his choosing of God for his portion. Whence learn, 1. Such as God hath chosen and effectually called, they get grace to make God their choice, their delight, and their portion ; and such as have chosen God for their portion have an evidence of their regeneration and election also ; for here David maketh this a mark of his regeneration : *"Thou art my portion."* 2. It is another mark of regeneration, after believing in God, and choosing him for our portion, to resolve to bring forth the fruits of faith in new obedience, as David did : *"I have said that I would keep thy words."* 3. As it is usual for God's children, now and then because of sin falling out, to be exercised with a sense of God's displeasure, so it is a mark of a new creature not to lie stupid and senseless under this exercise, but to deal with God earnestly, for restoring the sense of reconciliation, and giving new experience of his mercy, as the Psalmist did ; *"I intreated thy favour with my whole heart;"* and this is the evidence of a new creature. 4. The penitent believer hath the word of grace and the covenant of God for his assurance to be heard when he seeketh mercy : *"Be merciful unto me according to thy word."* 5. The searching in what condition we are in, and examination of our ways according to the word, and renewing of repentance, with an endeavour of amendment, is a fourth mark of a new creature : *"I thought on my ways, and turned my feet unto thy testimonies."* 6. When we do see our sin we are naturally slow to amend our doings ; but the sooner we turn us to the way of God's obedience, we speed the better, and the more speedy the reforming of our life be, the more sound mark is it of a new creature : *"I made haste, and delayed not to keep thy commandments."* 7. Enduring of persecution and spoiling of our goods, for adhering to God's word, without forsaking of his cause, is a fifth mark of a new creature : *"The bands of the wicked have robbed me : but I have not forgotten thy law."* 8. As it is the lot of God's children who resolve to be godly, to suffer persecution, and to be forced either to lose their temporal goods or else to lose a good cause and a good conscience ; so it is the wisdom of the godly to remember what the Lord's word requireth of us and speaketh unto us, and this shall comfort our conscience more than the loss of things temporal can trouble our minds : *"The bands of the wicked have robbed me : but I have not forgotten thy law."* 9. A sixth mark of a new creature is, to be so far from fretting under hard exercise as to thank God in secret cheerfully for his gracious word, and for all the passages of his providence, where none seeth us, and where there is no hazard of ostentation : *"At midnight I will rise to give thanks unto thee because of thy righteous judgments."* 10. A seventh mark of a renewed creature is, to associate ourselves and keep communion with such as are truly gracious, and do fear God indeed, as we are able to discern them : *"I am a companion of all them that fear thee."* 11. The fear of God is evidenced by believing and obeying the doctrine and direction of the Scripture, and no other ways : *"I am a companion of all them that fear thee, and of them that keep thy precepts."* 12. The eighth mark of a new creature is, not to rest in any measure of renovation, but earnestly to deal with God for the increase of saving knowledge, and fruitful obedience of it ; for, *"Teach me thy statutes,"* is the prayer of the man of God, in whom all the former marks are found. 13. As the whole of the creatures are witnesses of God's bounty to man, and partakers of that bounty themselves, so are they pawns of God's pleasure to bestow upon his servants greater gifts than these, even the increase of sanctification, in further illumination of mind and reformation of life : for this the Psalmist useth for an argument to be more and more sanctified : *"The earth, O LORD, is full of thy mercy : teach me thy statutes."*—*David Dickson*.

Verse 57.—*"Thou art my portion, O LORD."* The sincerity of this claim may be gathered, because he speaks by way of address to God. He doth not say barely, " He is my portion " ; but challengeth God to his face : *"Thou art my portion, O LORD."* Elsewhere it is said, " The Lord is my portion, saith my soul " (Lam. iii. 24). There he doth not speak it by way of address to God, but he adds, " saith my soul "; but here to God himself, who knows the secrets of the heart. To speak thus of God to God, argues our sincerity, when to God's face we avow our trust and choice; as Peter, " Lord, thou knowest all things; thou knowest that I love thee " (John xxi. 17).—*Thomas Manton.*

Verse 57.—*"Thou art my portion, O Lord."* Luther counsels every Christian to answer all temptations with this short saying, *"Christianus sum,"* I am a Christian; and I would counsel every Christian to answer all temptations with this short saying, " The Lord is my portion." O Christian, when Satan or the world shall tempt thee with honours, answer, " The Lord is my portion"; when they shall tempt thee with riches, answer, " The Lord is my portion"; when they shall tempt thee with preferments, answer, "The Lord is my portion "; and when they shall tempt thee with the favours of great ones, answer, " The Lord is my portion "; yea, and when this persecuting world shall threaten thee with the loss of thy estate, answer, " The Lord is my portion"; and when they shall threaten thee with the loss of thy liberty, answer, " The Lord is my portion "; and when they shall threaten thee with the loss of friends, answer, " The Lord is my portion; " and when they shall threaten thee with the loss of life, answer, " The Lord is my portion." O sir, if Satan should come to thee with an apple, as once he did to Eve, tell him that " the Lord is your portion"; or with a grape, as once he did to Noah, tell him that " the Lord is your portion"; or with a change of raiment, as once he did to Gehazi, tell him that " the Lord is your portion"; or with a wedge of gold, as once he did to Achan, tell him that " the Lord is your portion"; or with a bag of money, as once he did to Judas, tell him that " the Lord is your portion"; or with a crown, a kingdom, as once he did to Moses, tell him that " the Lord is your portion."—*Thomas Brooks.*

Verse 57.—*"Thou art my portion, O Lord."* God is all sufficient; get him for your *"portion,"* and you have all; then you have infinite wisdom to direct you, infinite knowledge to teach you, infinite mercy to pity and save you, infinite love to care and comfort you, and infinite power to protect and keep you. If God be yours; all his creatures, all his works of providence, shall do you good, as you have need of them. He is an eternal, full, satisfactory portion. He is an ever-living, ever-loving, ever-present friend; and without him you are a cursed creature in every condition, and all things will work against you.—*John Mason*—1694.

Verse 57.—*"Thou art my portion, O Lord."* If there was a moment in the life of David in which one might feel inclined to envy him, it would not be in that flush of youthful victory, when Goliath lay prostrate at his feet, nor in that hour of even greater triumph, when the damsels of Israel sang his praise in the dance, saying, " Saul hath slain his thousands, and David his ten thousands"; it would not be on that royal day, when his undisputed claim to the throne of Israel was acknowledged on every side and by every tribe; but it would be in that moment when, with a loving and trustful heart, he looked up to God and said, *"Thou art my portion."* In a later Psalm (cxlii.), which bears with it as its title. " A prayer of David, when he was in the cave," we have the very same expression: " I said, Thou art my refuge and my portion in the land of the living." It adds immeasurably to such an expression, if we believe it to have been uttered at a time when every other possession and inheritance was taken from him, and the Lord alone was his portion.—*Barton Bouchier.*

Verse 57.—He is an exceedingly covetous fellow to whom God is not sufficient; and he is an exceeding fool to whom the world is sufficient. For God is an inexhaustible treasury of all riches, sufficing innumerable men; while the world has mere trifles and fascinations to offer, and leads the soul into deep and sorrowful poverty. —*Thomas Le Blanc.*

Verse 57.—They who are without an ample patrimony in this life, may make to themselves a portion in heavenly blessedness.—*Solomon Gesner.*

Verse 57.—*"I have said that I would keep thy words."* This he brings in by way of proving that which he said in the former words. Many will say with David, that God is their portion; but here is the point; how do they prove it? If God were their portion they would love him; if they loved him they would love his word; if they loved his word they would live by it and make it the rule of their life.—*William Cowper.*

Verse 57.—*"I have said that I would keep thy words."* He was resolved to keep his commandments, lay up his promises, observe his ordinances, profess and retain a belief in his doctrines.—*John Gill.*

Verse 58.—"*I intreated thy favour*," or ; I seek thy face. To seek the face is to come into the presence. Thus the Hebrews speak when desirous of expressing that familiar intercourse to which God admits his people when he bids them make known their requests. It is truly the same as speaking face to face with God.— *Franciscus Vatablus*, 1545.

Verse 58.—"*I intreated thy favour with my whole heart.*" I have often remarked how graciously and lovingly the Lord delights to return an answer to prayer in the very words that have gone up before him, as if to assure us that they have reached his ear, and been speeded back again from him laden with increase. "*I intreated thy favour with my whole heart.*" Hear the Lord's answer to his praying people : " I will rejoice over them to do them good, assuredly *with my whole heart and with my whole soul.*"—*Barton Bouchier.*

Verse 58.—"*With my whole heart.*" The Hebrew expresses great earnestness and humility in supplication.—*A. R. Fausset.*

Verse 58.—"*With my whole heart.*" Prayer is chiefly a heart-work. God heareth the heart without the mouth, but never heareth the mouth acceptably without the heart.—*Walter Marshall.*

Verse 58.—"*Be merciful unto me,*" etc. He protested before that he sought the Lord with his whole heart, and now he prayeth that he may find mercy. So indeed it shall be ; boldly may that man look for mercy at God's hand who seeks him truly. Mercy and truth are wont to meet together, and embrace one another : where truth is in the soul to seek, there cannot but be mercy in God to embrace. If truth be in us to confess our sins and forsake them, we shall find mercy in God to pardon and forgive them.—*William Cowper.*

Verse 58.—"*According to thy word.*" He prayeth not for what he lusteth after, but for that which the Lord promised ; for St. James saith, " You pray and have not," etc., and this is the cause, that we have not the thing we pray for, because we pray not according to the word. His word must be the rule of our prayers, and then we shall receive ; as Solomon prayed and obtained. God hath promised forgiveness of sins, the knowledge of his word, and many other blessings. If we have these, let not our hearts be set on other things.—*Richard Greenham.*

Verse 58.—"*According to thy word.*" The Word of God may be divided into three parts ; into commandments, threatenings, and promises ; and though a Christian must not neglect the commanding and threatening word, yet if ever he would make the Word a channel for Divine comfort, he must study the promising word ; for the promises are a Christian's magna charta for heaven. All comfort must be built upon a Scripture promise, else it is presumption, not true comfort. The promises are *pabulum fidei, et anima fidei*, the food of faith, and the soul of faith. As faith is the life of a Christian, so the promises are the life of faith : faith is a dead faith if it hath no promise to quicken it. As the promises are of no use without faith to apply them, so faith is of no use without a promise to lay hold on.—*Edward Calamy.*

Verse 58.—The rule and ground of confidence is, "*according to thy word.*" God's word is the rule of our confidence ; for therein is God's stated course. If we would have favour and mercy from God, it must be upon his own terms. God will accept of us in Christ, if we repent, believe, and obey, and seek his favour diligently : he will not deny those who seek, ask, knock. Many would have mercy, but will not observe God's direction. We must ask according to God's will, not without a promise, nor against a command. God is made a voluntary debtor by his promise. These are notable props of faith, when we are encouraged to seek by the offer, and urged to apply by the promise. We thrive no more in a comfortable sense of God's love, because we take not this course.—*Thomas Manton.*

Verse 59.—"*I thought on my ways, and turned my feet unto thy testimonies.*" The transition which is made in the text from the occasion of this alteration, "*I thought on my ways,*" to the change itself, is very lofty and elegant. He does not tell us that, after a review of them, he saw the folly and danger of sin, the debasedness of its pleasures, and the poison of its delights ; or that, upon a search into God's law, he was convinced that what he imagined so severe, rigid, and frightful before, was now all amiable and lovely ; no, but immediately adds, "*I turned my feet unto thy testimonies*"; than which I can conceive nothing more noble or strong ; for it emphatically says, that there was no need to express the appearance his ways had when once he thought upon them.   What must be the consequence of his deliberation was so plain, namely, that sin never prevails but where it is masked over with some false beauties, and the inconsiderate, foolish sinner credulously gives ear to its enchantments, and is not at pains and care to enquire into them ; for a deep, thorough search would soon discover that its fairest appearances are but lying vanities, and that he who is captivated with that empty show is in the same circumstances with a person in a dream, who can please himself with his fancy only while asleep, and that his awakening out of it no sooner or more certainly discovers the cheat, than a serious thinking upon the ways of iniquity and rebellion against God will manifest the fatal madness of men in ever pursuing them.—*William Dunlop*, 1692—1720.

Verse 59.—"*I thought on my ways, and turned my feet unto thy testimonies.*"   Some translate the original, I looked on both sides upon my ways, I considered them every way, " and turned my feet unto thy testimonies."   I considered that I was wandering like a lost sheep, and then I returned.—*George Swinnock.*

Verse 59.—"*I thought on my ways,*" etc.   The Hebrew word חשב that is here used for thinking, signifies to think on a man's ways accurately, advisedly, seriously, studiously, curiously.   This holy man of God thought exactly and curiously on all his purposes and practices, on all his doings and sayings, on all his words and works, and finding too many of them to be short of the rule, yea, to be against the rule, he turned his feet to God's testimonies ; having found out his errors, upon a diligent search, a strict scrutiny, he turned over a new leaf, and framed his course more exactly by rule.   O Christians ! you must look as well to your spiritual wants as to your spiritual enjoyments ; you must look as well to your layings out as to your layings up ; you must look as well forward to what you should be, as backward to what you are.   Certainly that Christian will never be eminent in holiness that hath many eyes to behold a little holiness, and never an eye to see his further want of holiness.—*Thomas Brooks.*

Verse 59.—"*I thought on my ways.*"   The word signifies a fixed, abiding thought. Some make it an allusion to those that work embroidery ; that are very exact and careful to cover the least flaw ; or to those that cast accounts.   Reckon with yourselves, What do I owe ?   what am I worth ?   "*I thought*" not only on my wealth, as the covetous man, Ps. xlix. 11 ; but "*on my ways*" ; not what I have, but what I do ; because what we do will follow us into another world, when what we have must be left behind.   Many are critical enough in their remarks upon other people's ways that never think of their own, but " let every man prove his own work."

This account which David here gives of himself may refer either to his constant practice every day ; he reflected on his ways at night, directed his feet to God's testimonies in the morning, and what his hand found to do that was good he did it without delay : or it may refer to his first acquaintance with God and religion, when he began to throw off the vanity of childhood and youth, and to remember his Creator ; that blessed change was by the grace of God thus wrought.   Note, 1. Conversion begins in serious consideration ; Ezek. xviii. 28 ; Luke xv. 17. 2. Consideration must end in a sound conversion.   To what purpose have we thought on our ways, if we do not turn our feet with all speed to God's testimonies ?—*Matthew Henry.*

Verse 59.—"*I thought on my ways.*"   Be frequent in this work of serious consideration.   If daily you called yourselves to an account, all acts of grace would thrive the better.   Seneca asked of Sextius, *Quod hodie malum sanasti ? cui vitio obstitisti ?* You have God's example in reviewing every day's work, and in dealing with Adam before he slept.   The man that was unclean was to wash his clothes at eventide.—*Thomas Manton.*

Verse 59.—"*I thought on my ways,*" etc.   Poisons may be made medicinable. Let the thoughts of old sins stir up a commotion of anger and hatred.   We feel shiverings in our spirits, and a motion in our blood, at the very thought of a bitter potion we have formerly taken.   Why may we not do that spiritually, which the very frame and constitution of our bodies doth naturally, upon the calling a loathsome thing to mind ?   The Romans' sins were transient, but the shame was renewed every time they reflected on them : Rom. vi. 21, " Whereof ye are now ashamed."   They reacted the detestation instead of the pleasure : so should the revivings of old sins in our memories be entertained with our sighs, rather than with joy.   We should also manage the opportunity, so as to promote some further degrees of our conversion : "*I thought on my ways, and turned my feet unto thy testimonies.*" There is not the most hellish motion, but we may strike some sparks from it, to kindle our love to God, renew our repentance, raise our thankfulness, or quicken our obedience.—*Stephen Charnock.*

Verse 59.—*"And turned my feet unto thy testimonies."* Mentioning this passage, Philip Henry observed, that the great turn to be made in heart and life is, from all other things to the word of God. Conversion turns us to the word of God, as our touch-stone, to examine ourselves, our state, our ways, spirits, doctrines, worships, customs ; as our glass, to dress by, James i. ; as our rule to walk and work by, Galatians vi. 16 ; as our water, to wash us, Psalm cxix. 9 ; as our fire to warm us, Luke xxiv. ; as our food to nourish us, Job xxiii. 12 ; as our sword to fight with, Ephesians vi. ; as our counsellor, in all our doubts, Ps. cxix. 24 ; as our cordial, to comfort us ; as our heritage, to enrich us.

Verse 59.—*"And turned my feet unto thy testimonies."* No itinerary to the heavenly city is simpler or fuller than the ready answer made by an English prelate to a scoffer who asked him the way to heaven ; " First turn to the right, and keep straight on."—*Neale and Littledale.*

Verse 59.—*"And turned."* Turn to God, and he will turn to you ; then you are happy, though all the world turn against you.—*John Mason.*

Verse 60.—*"I made haste, and delayed not,"* etc. Duty discovered should instantly be discharged. There is peril attending every step which is taken in the indulgence of any known sin, or in the neglect of any acknowledged obligation. A tender conscience will not trifle with its convictions, lest the heart should be hardened through the deceitfulness of sin. It is unsafe, it is unreasonable, it is highly criminal to hesitate to carry that reformation into effect which conscience dictates. He who delays when duty calls may never have it in his power to evince the sincerity of his contrition for past folly and neglect. *"I made haste,"* said the Psalmist, *"and delayed not to keep thy commandments"* ; that is, being fully convinced of the necessity and excellency of obedience, I instantly resolved upon it, and immediately put it into execution.—*John Morison.*

Verse 60.—*"I made haste, and delayed not to keep thy commandments."* We often hear the saying, " Second thoughts are best." This does not hold in the religious life. In the context the Psalmist says, " I thought on my ways, and turned my feet unto thy testimonies," that is, I did not wait to think again. In religion it may be a deadly habit to take time to reflect. Make haste.—*Henry Melvill.*

Verse 60.—*"I made haste, and delayed not."* When anyone is lawfully called either to the study of theology, or to the teaching it in the church, he ought not to hesitate, as Moses, or turn away, as Jonah ; but, leaving all things, he should obey God who calls him ; as David says, *"I made haste, and delayed not."* Matt. iv. 20 ; Luke ix. 62.—*Solomon Gesner.*

Verse 60.—*"I made haste, and delayed not."* Sound faith is neither suspicious, nor curious ; it believes what God says, without sight, without examining. For since it is impossible for God to lie (for how should truth lie ?) it is fit his word be credited for itself's sake. It must not be examined with hows and whys. That which the Psalmist says of observing the law, that must the Christian say of receiving the gospel. לֹא הִתְמַהְמָהְתִּי, *"I disputed not,"* saith David ; I argued not *with God.* The word is very elegant in the original tongue, derived in the Hebrew from the pronoun מָה, which signifieth *quid.* Faith reasons not with God, asketh no *quids,* no *quares,* no *quomodos,* no whats, no hows, no wherefores : it moveth no questions. It meekly yields assent, and humbly says *Amen* to every word of God. This is the faith at which our Saviour wondered in the centurion's story.—*Richard Clerke,*—1634.

Verse 60.—*"I made haste, and delayed not."* The original word, which we translate *"delayed not,"* is amazingly emphatical. וְלֹא הִתְמַהְמָהְתִּי, *velo hithmahmahti,* I did not stand *what-what-whating ;* or, as we used to express the same sentiment, *shilly-shallying* with myself : I was *determined,* and so set out. The Hebrew word as well as the English, strongly marks indecision of mind, positive action being suspended, because the mind is so unfixed as not to be able to make a choice.—*Adam Clarke.*

Verse 60.—Take heed of delays and procrastination, of putting it off from day to day, by saying there will be time enough hereafter ; it will be time enough for me to look after heaven when I have got enough of the world ; if I do it in the last year of my life, in the last month of the last year, in the last week of the last month, it will serve. O take heed of delays ; this putting off repentance hath ruined thousands of souls ; shun that pit into which many have fallen, shun that rock upon which many have suffered shipwreck ; say with David, *"I made haste, and delayed not to keep thy commandments."—James Nalton, 1664.*

Verse 60.—"I made haste, and delayed not," etc. In the verse immediately preceding, the man of God speaks of repentance as the fruit of consideration and self-examining : " I thought on my ways, and turned my feet unto thy testimonies." But when did he turn ? for, though we see the evil of our ways, we are naturally slow to get it redressed. Therefore David did not only turn to God, but he did it speedily : we have an account of that in this verse, *"I made haste,"* etc. This readiness in the work of obedience is doubly expressed ; affirmatively and negatively. Affirmatively, *"I made haste"*; negatively, *"I delayed not."* This double expression increaseth the sense according to the manner of the Hebrews ; as, " I shall not die, but live " (Ps. cxviii. 17) ; that is, surely live ; so here, *"I made haste, and delayed not ;"* that is, I verily delayed not a moment ; as soon as he had thought of his ways, and taken up the resolution to walk closely with God, he did put it into practice. The Septuagint read the words thus, " I was ready, and was not troubled or diverted by fear of danger." Indeed, besides our natural slowness to good, this is one usual ground of delays ; we distract ourselves with fears ; and, when God hath made known his will to us in many duties, we think of tarrying till the times are more quiet, and favourable to our practice, or till our affairs are in a better posture. A good improvement may be made of that translation ; but the words run better, as they run more generally, with us, *"I made haste, and delayed not,"* etc.

David *delayed not.* When we dare not flatly deny, then we delay. *Non vacat,* that is the sinner's plea, " I am not at leisure "; but, *Non placet,* there is the reality. They which were invited to the wedding varnished their denial over with an excuse (Matt. xxii. 5). Delay is a denial ; for, if they were willing, there would be no excuse. To be rid of importunate and troublesome creditors, we promise them payment another time : though we know our estate will be more wasted by that time, it is but to put them off : so this delay and putting off of God is but a shift. Here is the misery, God always comes unseasonably to a carnal heart. It was the devils that said, "Art thou come hither to torment us before the time ? " (Matt. viii. 29). Good things are a torment to a carnal heart ; and they always come out of time. Certainly, that is the best time when the word is pressed upon thy heart with evidence, light, and power, and when God treats with thee about thine eternal peace.—*Thomas Manton.*

Verse 60.—"Delayed." *Hithmahmah ;* the word used of Lot's lingering, in Genesis xix. 16.—*William Kay.*

Verse 60.—Delay in the Lord's errands is next to disobedience, and generally springs out of it, or issues in it. " God commanded me to make haste " (2 Chron. xxxv. 21). Let us see to it that we can say, *"I made haste, and delayed not to keep thy commandments."—Frances Ridley Havergal.*

Verse 60.—Avoid all delay in the performance of this great work of believing in Christ. Until we have performed it we continue under the power of sin and Satan, and under the wrath of God ; and there is nothing between hell and us besides the breath of our nostrils. It is dangerous for Lot to linger in Sodom, lest fire and brimstone come down from heaven upon him. The manslayer must fly with all haste to the city of refuge, lest the avenger of blood pursue him, while his heart is hot, and slay him. We should make haste, and not delay to keep God's commandments.—*Walter Marshall.*

Verse 60.—If convictions begin to work, instantly yield to their influence. If any worldly or sinful desire is touched, let this be the moment for its crucifixion. If any affection is kindled towards the Saviour, give immediate expression to its voice. If any grace is reviving, let it be called forth into instant duty. This is the best, the only, expedient to fix and detain the motion of the Spirit now striving in the heart ; and who knoweth but the improvement of the present advantage may be the moment of victory over difficulties hitherto found insuperable, and may open our path to heaven with less interruption and more steady progress ?—*Charles Bridges.*

Verse 61.—"The bands of the wicked have robbed me." Two readings remain, either of which may be admitted : *The cords of the wicked have caught hold of me,* or, *The companies of the wicked have robbed me.* Whether we adopt the one or the other of these readings, what the prophet intends to declare is, that when Satan assailed the principles of piety in his soul, by grievous temptations, he continued with undeviating steadfastness in the love and practice of Go law. Cords may, however, be understood in two ways ; either, first, as denoting deceptive allure-ments by which the wicked endeavoured to get him entang in their society ; or, secondly, the frauds which they practised to effect his rui John Calvin.

Verse 61.—"The bands of the wicked have robbed me."—Som ve it, "Cords of wicked men have entwined me." Others, "Snares of wicked surround me." The meaning is that wicked men by their plots and contrivanc beset him, as men would ensnare a wild beast in their toils. They might, inc im him round about in the wilderness, but they could not enthral the free m would still feel at liberty in spirit, he would not forget God's law.—John Se

Verse 61.—"The bands of the wicked have robbed me." They his goods, and spoiled him of them, either by plunder in the time of wai fines and confiscations under colour of law. Saul (it is likely) seized his Absalom his palace ; the Amalekites rifled Ziklag.—Matthew Henry.

Verse 61.—The friendship of the wicked must be shunned. ause it binds us, as they are bound together—"bands of the wicked." er is a gladiator with net and sword, going down into the arena, and ng to enmesh any one who comes near him. A second reason for shunn ship of the wicked, which may be taken from the Hebrew word, is and barbarity ; for not only do the wicked bind their friends, but t oil and a prey of them : "have robbed me." They are decoying thieves th an unwary traveller, until they have led him into thick and dark w strip him of heavenly riches.—Thomas Le Blanc.

Verses 61.—"The bands of the wicked have robbed me." Then y his fellow, Now I call to remembrance that which was told me of a thin to a good man hereabout. The name of the man was Little-Faith, l and he dwelt in the town of Sincere. The thing was this ; at the en passage there comes down from Broadway-gate a lane called Dead-called because of the murders that are commonly done there. And going on pilgrimage, as we do now, chanced to sit down there and sle happened, at that time, to come down that lane from Broad-way-ga rogues, and their names were Faint-heart, Mistrust, and Guilt, (three they espying Little-Faith where he was came galloping up with spe good man was just awaked from his sleep, and was getting up to go o So they came all up to him, and with threatening language bid him st Little-Faith looked as white as a clout, and had neither power to fight n said Faint-heart, Deliver thy purse ; but he making no haste to do it loth to lose his money,) Mistrust ran up to him, and thrusting his h pocket, pulled out thence a bag of silver. Then he cried out, Thiev With that Guilt, with a great club that was in his hand, struck Little-head, and with that blow felled him flat to the ground, where he lay blee that would bleed to death. . . . The place where his jewels were they never r so those he kept still ; but, as I was told, the good man was much afflicte loss. For the thieves got most of his spending money. That which they (as I said) were jewels, also he had a little odd money left, but scarce enou bring him to his journey's end ; nay, (if I was not misinformed,) he was forc beg as he went, to keep himself alive (for his jewels he might not sell). But and do what he could he went (as we say) with many a hungry belly, the most pa of the rest of the way.—John Bunyan.

Verse 61.—"Bands." Howsoever, to strengthen themselves in an evil course, the wicked go together by bands and companies, yet shall it not avail them, nor hurt us. Babel's builders ; Moab, Ammon, Edom, conspiring in one, may tell us, "Though hand join in hand, the wicked shall not escape unpunished." The wicked are like thorns before the fire ; their multitude may well embolden the flame, but cannot resist it.—William Cowper.

Verse 61.—It is a salutary reflection to bear in mind, that thousands of spiritual adversaries are ever watching to make us their prey.—John Morison.

Verse 62.—"At midnight I will rise to give thanks." Though we cannot enforce the particular observance upon you, yet there are many notable lessons to be drawn from David's practice.

1. The ardency of his devotion, or his earnest desire to praise God : "at midnight," when sleep doth most invade men's eyes, then he would rise up. His heart was so

set upon the praise of God, and the sense of his righteous providence did so affect him, and urge and excite him to this duty, that he would not only employ himself in this work in the daytime, and so show his love to God, but he would rise out of his bed to worship God and celebrate his praise. That which hindereth the sleep of ordinary men either the cares of this world, the impatient resentment of injuries, or the sting of an evil conscience : these keep others waking, but David was awaked by a desire of affection to God when others take their rest. Thus we read of our expressing to praise God. No hour is unseasonable to a gracious heart : he is Lord Christ that he spent whole nights in prayer (Luke vi. 12). It is said of the glorified in heaven, that they praise God continually : "Therefore are they before the of God, and serve him day and night in his temple : and he that sitteth on the throne shall dwell among them" (Rev. vii. 15). Now, holy men, though hindered by their bodily necessities, will come as near to continual prayer and praise as present frailty will permit. Alas, we oftentimes begin the day with some prayer and praise, but we faint ere the evening comes.

sincerity, seen in his secrecy. David would profess his faith in God and no witness by him ; "at midnight," when there was no hazard of It was a secret cheerfulness and delighting in God : when alone he had no respect to the applause of men, but only to approve himself to God in secret. See Christ's direction : "But thou, when thou prayest, enter closet, and when thou hast shut thy door, pray to thy Father which is in and thy Father which seeth in secret shall reward thee openly" (Matt. vi. 6). Christ's own practice : "Rising up a great while before day, he went out, parted into a solitary place, and there prayed" (Mark i. 35) : before day he to a desert to pray ; both time and place implied secrecy.

We learn hence the preciousness of time : it was so to David ; see how he with the time of his life. We read of David, when he lay down at night, he had his couch with his tears, after the examination of his heart (Psalm vi. 6) ; midnight he rose to give thanks ; in the morning he prevented the morning times ; and seven times a-day he praised God : morning, noon, and night he consecrated. These are all acts of eminent piety. We should not content ourselves so much grace as will merely serve to save us. Alas ! we have much idle time hanging upon our hands : if we would give that to God, it were well.

4. The value of godly exercises above our natural refreshings. The word is sweeter than appointed food : "I have esteemed the words of his mouth more than my necessary food" (Job xxiii. 12). David preferreth the praises of God before his sleep and rest in the night. Surely, this should shame us for our sensuality. We can dispense with other things for our vain pleasures : we have done as much for sin, for vain sports, etc. ; and shall we not deny ourselves for God ?

5. The great reverence to be used in secret adoration. David did not only raise up his spirits to praise God, but rise up out of his bed, to bow the knee to him. Secret duties should be performed with solemnity, not slubbered over. Praise, a special act of adoration, requireth the worship of body and soul.—*Thomas Manton.*

Verse 62.—"*At midnight I will rise to give thanks.*" He had praised God in the courts of the Lord's house, and yet he will do it in his bed-chamber. Public worship will not excuse us from secret worship.—*Matthew Henry.*

Verse 62.—"*At midnight I will rise to give thanks unto thee.*" Was he not ready also to praise God at midday? Certainly ; but he says, "*at midnight,*" that he may express the ardour and longing of his soul. We are wont to assure our friends of our good will by saying that we will rise at midnight to consult about their affairs.—*Wolfgang Musculus.*

Verse 62.—"*At midnight I will rise to give thanks,*" etc. In these words observe three things :—1. David's holy employment, or the duty promised, giving thanks to God. 2. His earnestness and fervency implied in the time mentioned, "At midnight I will rise"; he would rather interrupt his sleep and rest, than God should want his praise. 3. The cause or matter of his thanksgiving, "because of thy righteous judgments": whereby he meaneth the dispensations of God's providence in delivering the godly and punishing the wicked, according to his word.—*Thomas Manton.*

Verse 62.—"*At midnight I will rise to give thanks.*" Cares of this world, impatience of wrongs, a bad conscience, keep awake the ungodly and disturb their sleep (*Rivetus*) ; but what I awake for is to give thanks to thee.—*A. R. Faussett.*

Verse 63.—*"I am a companion,"* etc. He said in the first verse of this section that God was his portion ; now he saith, that all the saints of God are his companions. These two go together—the love of God and the love of his saints. He that loveth not his brother, made in God's image, whom he seeth, how shall he love God whom he hath not seen ? Seeing our goodness extends not to the Lord ; if it be showed to his saints and excellent ones upon earth, for his sake, it shall be no small argument of our loving affection towards himself.

Godly David, when Jonathan was dead, made diligent inquisition, Is there none of Jonathan's posterity to whom I may show kindness for Jonathan's sake ? and at length he found a silly, lame Mephibosheth. So if we enquire diligently, Is there none upon earth to whom I may show kindness for Christ's sake who is in heaven ? we shall ever find some, to whom whatsoever we do shall be accepted as done to himself.

His great modesty is to be marked. He saith not, I am companion of all that follow thee, but of all that fear thee. The fear of God is the beginning of wisdom. He places himself among novices in humility, though he excelled ancients in piety.— *William Cowper.*

Verse 63.—*"I am a companion of all them that fear thee."* How weak is human nature ! Verily there are times when the presence of one so great as the Almighty becomes oppressive, and we feel our need of one like ourselves to sympathize with us. . . . And there have been provided for us by the way many kind, sympathizing friends, like Jesus. As we pass on, we get the human supports which the Lord hath provided. We get them for fellowship too.—*John Stephen.*

Verse 63.—*"I am a companion of all them that fear thee."* Birds of a feather will flock together. Servants of the same Lord, if faithful, will join with their fellows, and not with the servants of his enemy. When a man comes to an inn you may give a notable guess for what place he is bound by the company he enquires after. His question,—" Do you know of any travelling towards London ? I should be heartily glad of their company," will speak his mind and his course. If he hear of any bound for another coast he regards them not ; but if he know of any honest passengers that are to ride in the same road, and set out for the same city with himself, he sends to them, and begs the favour of their good company. This world is an inn, all men are in some sense pilgrims and strangers, they have no abiding-place here. Now the company they enquire after, and delight in, whether those that walk in the " broad way " of the flesh, or those who walk in the " narrow way " of the Spirit, will declare whether they are going towards heaven or towards hell. A wicked man will not desire the company of them who walk in a contrary way, nor a saint delight in their society who go cross to his journey. " Can two walk together except they be agreed ? " The young partridges hatched under a hen go for a time along with her chickens, and keep them company, scraping in the earth together ; but when they are grown up, and their wings fit for the purpose, they mount up into the air, and seek for birds of their own nature. A Christian, before his conversion, is brought up under the prince of darkness, and walks in company with his cursed crew, according to the course of this world ; but when the Spirit changes his disposition, he quickly changes his companions, and delights only in the saints that are on earth.—*George Swinnock.*

Verse 63.—*"I am a companion of all them that fear thee."* 1. The person speaking. The disparity of the persons is to be observed. David, who was a great prophet, yea, a king, yet saith, *"I am a companion of all them that fear thee."* Christ himself called them his " fellows": " Thy God hath anointed thee with the oil of gladness above thy fellows " (Ps. xlv. 7) ; and therefore David might well say, *"I am a companion."*

2. The persons spoken of. David saith of *"all them that fear thee."* The universal particle is to be observed ; not only some, but *"all":* when any lighted upon him, or he upon any of them, they were welcome to him. How well would it be for the world, if the great potentates of the earth would thus think, speak, and do, *"I am a companion of all that fear thee."* Self-love reigneth in most men : we love the rich and despise the poor, and so have the faith of our Lord Jesus Christ with respect of persons (James ii. 1) : therefore this universality is to be regarded. Hearing of your faith and love to all the saints (Eph. i. 15), to the mean as well as the greatest. Meanness doth not take away church relations (1 Cor. xi. 20). There are many differences in worldly respects between one Christian and another ; yea, in spiritual gifts, some weaker, some stronger ; but we must love all ; for all are children

of one Father, all owned by Christ : " He is not ashamed to call them brethren " (Heb. ii. 11).

This, I say, is observable, the disparity of the persons : on the one side, David, on the other, all the people of God.—*Thomas Manton.*

Verse 63.—"*I am a companion,*" etc. : as if he would say, This is a sign to me that I belong to thy family ; because "*I am the companion of all those fearing thee*" with a filial fear, and keeping "*thy precepts.*"—*Paulus Palanterius.*

Verse 63.—"*A companion,*" properly is such an one as I do choose to walk and converse with ordinarily in a way of friendship ; so that company keeping doth imply three things ; first, it is a matter of choice, and therefore relations, as such, are not properly said to be our companions ; secondly, it implies a constant walking and converse with another, and so it is expressed, Job xxxiv. 8 ; Prov. xiii. 20. And, thirdly, this ordinary converse or walking with another, must be in a way of friendship.—*William Bridge,* 1600—1670.

Verse 63.—Shun the company that shuns God, and keep the company that God keeps. Look on the society of the carnal or profane as infectious, but reckon serious, praying persons the excellent ones of the earth. Such will serve to quicken you when dead, and warm you when cold. Make the liveliest of God's people your greatest intimates, and see that their love and likeness to Christ be the great motive of your love to them, more than their love or likeness to you.—*John Willison,* 1680—1750.

Verse 64.—"*The earth, O* LORD, *is full of thy mercy.*" The humble and devoted servant of God does not look with a jaundiced eye upon that scene through which he is passing to his eternal home. Amidst many sorrows and privations, the necessary fruits of sin, he beholds all nature and providence shining forth in the rich expression of God's paternal benignity and mercy to the children of men.— *John Morison.*

Verse 64.—"*The earth, O* LORD, *is full of thy mercy.*" The molten sea, the shew-bread, the sweet incense, the smoke of the sacrifices, Aaron's breastplate, the preaching of the cross, the keys of the kingdom of heaven : do not all these proclaim mercy ? Who could enter a sanctuary, search conscience, look up to heaven, pray or sacrifice, call upon God, or think of the tree of life in the midst of the paradise of God, if there were no mercy ? Do not all visions, covenants, promises, messages, mysteries, legal purifications, evangelical pacifications, confirm this ? Yes, mercy is in the air which we breathe, the daily light which shines upon us, the gracious rain of God's inheritance ; it is the public spring for all the thirsty, the common hospital for all the needy ; all the streets of the church are paved with these stones. What would become of the children if there were not these breasts of consolation ? How should the bride, the Lamb's wife, be trimmed, if her bridegroom did not deck her with these habiliments ? How should Eden appear like the Garden of God, if it were not watered by these rivers ? It is mercy that takes us out of the womb, feeds us in the days of our pilgrimage, furnishes us with spiritual provisions, closes our eyes in peace, and translates us to a secure resting-place. It is the first petitioner's suit, and the first believer's article, the contemplation of Enoch, the confidence of Abraham, the burden of the Prophetic Songs, the glory of all the apostles, the plea of the penitent, the ecstacies of the reconciled, the believer's hosannah, the angel's hallelujah. Ordinances, oracles, altars, pulpits, the gates of the grave, and the gates of heaven, do all depend upon mercy. It is the load-star of the wandering, the ransom of the captive, the antidote of the tempted, the prophet of the living, and the effectual comfort of the dying :—there would not be one regenerate saint upon earth, nor one glorified saint in heaven, if it were not for mercy.—*From G. S. Bowes's "Illustrative Gatherings,*" 1869.

Verse 64.—"*The earth, O* LORD, *is full of thy mercy.*"

" Why bursts such melody from tree and bush,
The overflowing of each songster's heart,
So filling mine that it can scarcely hush
Awhile to listen, but would take its part ?
'Tis but one song I hear where'er I rove,
Though countless be the notes, that God is Love.

" Why leaps the streamlet down the mountain-side ?
 Hasting so swiftly to the vale beneath,
To cheer the shepherd's thirsty flock, or glide
 Where the hot sun has left a faded wreath,
Or, rippling, aid the music of a grove ?
Its own glad voice replies, that God is Love

" Is it a fallen world on which I gaze ?
 Am I as deeply fallen as the rest,
Yet joys partaking, past my utmost praise,
 Instead of wandering forlorn, unblest ?
It is as if an unseen spirit strove
To grave upon my heart, that God is Love ! "

Thomas Davis, 1864.

EXPOSITION OF VERSES 65 TO 72.

THOU hast dealt well with thy servant, O LORD, according unto thy
　　word.

66 Teach me good judgment and knowledge : for I have believed thy
commandments.

67 Before I was afflicted I went astray : but now have I kept thy word.

68 Thou *art* good, and doest good ; teach me thy statutes.

69 The proud have forged a lie against me : *but* I will keep thy precepts
with *my* whole heart.

70 Their heart is as fat as grease ; *but* I delight in thy law.

71 *It is* good for me that I have been afflicted ; that I might learn thy
statutes.

72 The law of thy mouth *is* better unto me than thousands of gold and
silver.

In this ninth section the verses all begin with the letter Teth. They are the
witness of experience, testifying to the goodness of God, the graciousness of his
dealings, and the preciousness of his word. Especially the Psalmist proclaims the
excellent uses of adversity, and the goodness of God in afflicting him. The sixty-fifth
verse is the text of the entire octave.

65. *"Thou hast dealt well with thy servant, O LORD, according unto thy word."*
This is the summary of his life, and assuredly it is the sum of ours. The Psalmist
tells the Lord the verdict of his heart ; he cannot be silent, he must speak his gratitude
in the presence of Jehovah, his God. From the universal goodness of God in nature,
in verse 64, it is an easy and pleasant step to a confession of the Lord's uniform
goodness to ourselves personally. It is something that God has *dealt* at all with
such insignificant and undeserving beings as we are, and it is far more that he has
dealt *well* with us, and so well, so wondrously well. He hath done all things well :
the rule has no exception. In providence and in grace, in giving prosperity and
sending adversity, in everything Jehovah hath dealt well with us. It is dealing
well on our part to tell the Lord that we feel that he hath dealt well with us ; for
praise of this kind is specially fitting and comely. This kindness of the Lord is,
however, no chance matter : he promised to do so, and he has done it according to
his word. It is very precious to see the word of the Lord fulfilled in our happy
experience ; it endears the Scripture to us, and makes us love the Lord of the Scripture. The book of providence tallies with the book of promise : what we read in
the page of inspiration we meet with again in the leaves of our life-story. We may
not have thought that it would be so, but our unbelief is repented of now that we
see the mercy of the Lord to us, and his faithfulness to his word ; henceforth we are
bound to display a firmer faith both in God and in his promise. He has spoken
well, and he has dealt well. He is the best of Masters ; for it is to a very unworthy
and incapable *servant* that he has acted thus blessedly : does not this cause us to
delight in his service more and more ? We cannot say that we have dealt well with
our Master ; for when we have done all, we are unprofitable servants ; but as for
our Lord, he has given us light work, large maintenance, loving encouragement, and
liberal wages. It is a wonder that he has not long ago discharged us, or at least
reduced our allowances, or handled us roughly ; yet we have had no hard dealings,
all has been ordered with as much consideration as if we had rendered perfect

obedience. We have had bread enough and to spare, our livery has been duly supplied, and his service has ennobled us and made us happy as kings. Complaints we have none. We lose ourselves in adoring thanksgiving, and find ourselves again in careful thanks-living.

66. *"Teach me good judgment and knowledge."* Again he begs for teaching, as in verse 64, and again he uses God's mercy as an argument. Since God had dealt well with him, he is encouraged to pray for judgment to appreciate the Lord's goodness. Good judgment is the form of goodness which the godly man most needs and most desires, and it is one which the Lord is most ready to bestow. David felt that he had frequently failed in judgment in the matter of the Lord's dealings with him : from want of knowledge he had misjudged the chastening hand of the heavenly Father, and therefore he now asks to be better instructed, since he perceives the injustice which he had done to the Lord by his hasty conclusions. He means to say—Lord, thou didst deal well with me when I thought thee hard and stern, be pleased to give me more wit, that I may not a second time think so ill of my Lord. A sight of our errors and a sense of our ignorance should make us teachable. We are not able to judge, for our knowledge is so sadly inaccurate and imperfect ; if the Lord teaches us knowledge we shall attain to good judgment, but not otherwise. The Holy Ghost alone can fill us with light, and set the understanding upon a proper balance : let us ardently long for his teachings, since it is most desirable that we should be no longer mere children in knowledge and understanding.

"For I have believed thy commandments." His heart was right, and therefore he hoped his head would be made right. He had faith, and therefore he hoped to receive wisdom. His mind had been settled in the conviction that the precepts of the word were from the Lord, and were therefore just, wise, kind, and profitable ; he believed in holiness, and as that belief is no mean work of grace upon the soul, he looked for yet further operations of divine grace. He who believes the commands is the man to know and understand the doctrines and the promises. If in looking back upon our mistakes and ignorances we can yet see that we heartily loved the precepts of the divine will, we have good reason to hope that we are Christ's disciples, and that he will teach us and make us men of good judgment and sound knowledge. A man who has learned discernment by experience, and has thus become a man of sound judgment, is a valuable member of a church, and the means of much edification to others. Let all who would be greatly useful offer the prayer of this verse : " Teach me good judgment and knowledge."

67. *"Before I was afflicted I went astray."* Partly, perhaps, through the absence of trial. Often our trials act as a thorn hedge to keep us in the good pasture, but our prosperity is a gap through which we go astray. If any of us remember a time in which we had no trouble, we also probably recollect that then grace was low, and temptation was strong. It may be that some believer cries, " O that it were with me as in those summer days before I was afflicted." Such a sigh is most unwise, and arises from a carnal love of ease : the spiritual man who prizes growth in grace will bless God that those dangerous days are over, and that if the weather be more stormy it is also more healthy. It is well when the mind is open and candid, as in this instance : perhaps David would never have known and confessed his own strayings if he had not smarted under the rod. Let us join in his humble acknowledgments, for doubtless we have imitated him in his strayings. Why is it that a little ease works in us so much disease ? Can we never rest without rusting ? Never be filled without waxing fat ? Never rise as to one world without going down as to another ? What weak creatures we are to be unable to bear a little pleasure ! What base hearts are those which turn the abundance of God's goodness into an occasion for sin.

"But now have I kept thy word." Grace is in that heart which profits by its chastening. It is of no use to plough barren soil. When there is no spiritual life affliction works no spiritual benefit ; but where the heart is sound trouble awakens conscience, wandering is confessed, the soul becomes again obedient to the command, and continues to be so. Whipping will not turn a rebel into a child ; but to the true child a touch of the rod is a sure corrective. In the Psalmist's case the medicine of affliction worked a change—*"but"* ; an immediate change—*"now" ;* a lasting change—*"have I" ;* an inward change—*"have I kept" ;* a change Godward—*"thy word."* Before his trouble he wandered, but after it he kept within the hedge of the word, and found good pasture for his soul : the trial tethered him to his proper place ; it kept him, and then he kept God's word. Sweet are the uses of adversity,

and this is one of them, it puts a bridle upon transgression and furnishes a spur for holiness.

68. *"Thou art good, and doest good."* Even in affliction God is good, and does good. This is the confession of experience. God is essential goodness in himself, and in every attribute of his nature he is good in the fullest sense of the term ; indeed, he has a monopoly of goodness, for there is none good but one, that is God. His acts are according to his nature : from a pure source flow pure streams. God is not latent and inactive goodness ; he displays himself by his doings, he is actively beneficent, he does good. How much good he does no tongue can tell ! How good he is no heart can conceive ! It is well to worship the Lord as the poet here does by describing him. Facts about God are the best praise of God. All the glory we can give to God is to reflect his own glory upon himself. We can say no more good of God than God is and does. We believe in his goodness, and so honour him by our faith ; we admire that goodness, and so glorify him by our love ; we declare that goodness, and so magnify him by our testimony.

"Teach me thy statutes." The same prayer as before, backed with the same argument. He prays, " Lord be good, and do good to me that I may both be good and do good through thy teaching." The man of God was a learner, and delighted to learn : he ascribed this to the goodness of the Lord, and hoped that for the same reason he would be allowed to remain in the school and learn on till he could perfectly practise every lesson. His chosen class-book was the royal statutes, he wanted no other. He knew the sad result of breaking those statutes, and by a painful experience he had been led back to the way of righteousness ; and therefore he begged as the greatest possible instance of the divine goodness that he might be taught a perfect knowledge of the law, and a complete conformity to it. He who mourns that he has not kept the word longs to be taught it, and he who rejoices that by grace he has been taught to keep it is not less anxious for the like instruction to be continued to him.

In verse 12, which is the fourth verse of Beth, we have much the same sense as in this fourth verse of Teth.

69. *"The proud have forged a lie against me."* They first derided him (51), then defrauded him (61), and now they have defamed him. To injure his character they resorted to falsehood, for they could find nothing against him if they spoke the truth. They forged a lie as a blacksmith beats out a weapon of iron, or they counterfeited the truth as men forge false coin. The original may suggest a common expression—" They have patched up a lie against me." They were not too proud to lie. Pride is a lie, and when a proud man utters lies " he speaketh of his own." Proud men are usually the bitterest opponents of the righteous : they are envious of their good fame and are eager to ruin it. Slander is a cheap and handy weapon if the object is the destruction of a gracious reputation ; and when many proud ones conspire to concoct, exaggerate, and spread abroad a malicious falsehood, they generally succeed in wounding their victim, and it is no fault of theirs if they do not kill him outright. O the venom which lies under the tongue of a liar ! Many a happy life has been embittered by it, and many a good repute has been poisoned as with the deadliest drug. It is painful to the last degree to hear unscrupulous men hammering away at the devil's anvil forging a new calumny ; the only help against it is the sweet promise, " No weapon that is formed against thee shall prosper, and every tongue that riseth against thee in judgment thou shalt condemn."

"But I will keep thy precepts with my whole heart." My one anxiety shall be to mind my own business and stick to the commandments of the Lord. If the mud which is thrown at us does not blind our eyes or bruise our integrity it will do us little harm. If we keep the precepts, the precepts will keep us in the day of contumely and slander. David renews his resolve—*"I will keep"* ; he takes a new look at the commands, and sees them to be really the Lord's—*"thy precepts"* ; and he arouses his entire nature to the work—*"with my whole heart."* When slanders drive us to more resolute and careful obedience they work our lasting good ; falsehood hurled against us may be made to promote our fidelity to the truth, and the malice of men may increase our love to God. If we try to answer lies by our words we may be beaten in the battle ; but a holy life is an unanswerable refutation of all calumnies. Spite is balked if we persevere in holiness despite all opposition.

70. *"Their heart is as fat as grease."* They delight in fatness, but I delight in thee. Their hearts, through sensual indulgence, have grown insensible, coarse, and grovelling ; but thou hast saved me from such a fate through thy chastening hand.

Proud men grow fat through carnal luxuries, and this makes them prouder still. They riot in their prosperity, and fill their hearts therewith till they become insensible, effeminate, and self-indulgent. A greasy heart is something horrible ; it is a fatness which makes a man fatuous, a fatty degeneration of the heart which leads to feebleness and death. The fat in such men is killing the life in them. Dryden wrote—

> " O souls ! In whom no heavenly fire is found,
> Fat minds and ever grovelling on the ground."

In this condition men have no heart except for luxury, their very being seems to swim and stew in the fat of cookery and banqueting. Living on the fat of the land, their nature is subdued to that which they have fed upon ; the muscle of their nature has gone to softness and grease.

"But I delight in thy law." How much better is it to joy in the law of the Lord than to joy in sensual indulgences ! This makes the heart healthy, and keeps the mind lowly. No one who loves holiness has the slightest cause to envy the prosperity of the worldling. Delight in the law elevates and ennobles, while carnal pleasure clogs the intellect and degrades the affections. There is and always ought to be a vivid contrast between the believer and the sensualist, and that contrast is as much seen in the affections of the heart as in the actions of the life : *their* heart is as fat as grease, and our heart is delighted with the law of the Lord. Our delights are a better test of our character than anything else : as a man's heart is, so is the man. David oiled the wheels of life with his delight in God's law, and not with the fat of sensuality. He had his relishes and dainties, his festivals and delights, and all these he found in doing the will of the Lord his God. When law becomes delight, obedience is bliss. Holiness in the heart causes the soul to eat the fat of the land. To have the law for our delight will breed in our hearts the very opposite of the effects of pride ; deadness, sensuality, and obstinacy will be cured, and we shall become teachable, sensitive, and spiritual. How careful should we be to live under the influence of the divine law that we fall not under the law of sin and death.

71. *"It is good for me that I have been afflicted."* Even though the affliction came from bad men, it was overruled for good ends ; though it was bad as it came from them it was good for David. It benefited him in many ways, and he knew it. Whatever he may have thought while under the trial, he perceived himself to be the better for it when it was over. It was not good to the proud to be prosperous, for their hearts grew sensual and insensible ; but affliction was good for the Psalmist. Our worst is better for us than the sinner's best. It is bad for sinners to rejoice, and good for saints to sorrow. A thousand benefits have come to us through our pains and griefs, and among the rest is this—that we have thus been schooled in the law. *"That I might learn thy statutes."* These we have come to know and to keep by feeling the smart of the rod. We prayed the Lord to teach us (66), and now we see how he has already been doing it. Truly he has dealt well with us, for he has dealt wisely with us. We have been kept from the ignorance of the greasy-hearted by our trials, and this, if there were nothing else, is just cause for constant gratitude. To be larded by prosperity is not good for the proud ; but for the truth to be learned by adversity is good for the humble. Very little is to be learned without affliction. If we would be scholars we must be sufferers. As the Latins say, *Experientia docet,* experience teaches. There is no royal road to learning the royal statutes ; God's commands are best read by eyes wet with tears.

72. *"The law of thy mouth."* A sweetly expressive name for the word of God. It comes from God's own mouth with freshness and power to our souls. Things written are as dried herbs ; but speech has a liveliness and dew about it. We do well to look upon the word of the Lord as though it were newly spoken into our ear ; for in very truth it is not decayed by years, but is as forcible and sure as though newly uttered. Precepts are prized when it is seen that they come forth from the lips of our Father who is in heaven. The same lips which spoke us into existence have spoken the law by which we are to govern that existence. Whence could a law so sweetly proceed as from the mouth of our covenant God ? Well may we prize beyond all price that which comes from such a source.

"Is better unto me than thousands of gold and silver." If a poor man had said this, the world's witlings would have hinted that the grapes are sour, and that men who have no wealth are the first to despise it ; but this is the verdict of a man who owned his thousands, and could judge by actual experience of the value of

money and the value of truth. He speaks of great riches, he heaps it up by thousands, he mentions the varieties of its forms,—"gold and silver"; and then he sets the word of God before it all, as better *to him*, even if others did not think it better to them. Wealth is good in some respects, but obedience is better in all respects. It is well to keep the treasures of this life; but far more commendable to keep the law of the Lord. The law is better than gold and silver, for these may be stolen from us, but not the word; these take to themselves wings, but the word of God remains; these are useless in the hour of death, but then it is that the promise is most dear. Instructed Christians recognize the value of the Lord's word, and warmly express it, not only in their testimony to their fellow-men, but in their devotions to God. It is a sure sign of a heart which has learned God's statutes when it prizes them above all earthly possessions; and it is an equally certain mark of grace when the precepts of Scripture are as precious as its promises. The Lord cause us thus to prize the law of his mouth.

See how this portion of the Psalm is flavoured with goodness. God's dealings are good (65), holy judgment is good (66), affliction is good (67), God is good (68), and here the law is not only good, but better than the best of treasure. Lord, make us good through thy good word. Amen.

NOTES ON VERSES 65 TO 72.

TETH.—In the original each stanza begins with T, and in our own version it is so in all but verses 67 and 70, which can easily be made to do so by reading, " Till I was afflicted," and " 'Tis good for me that I have been afflicted."—*C. H. S.*

Verse 65.—"Thou hast dealt well with thy servant, O LORD."

1. The party dealing is God himself : all good is to be referred to God as the author of it.

2. The benefit received is generally expressed, *"Thou hast dealt well."* Some translate it out of the Hebrew, *Bonum fecisti,* thou hast done good with thy servant ; the Septuagint, Χρηστότητα ἐποίησας μετα του δουλου σου, thou hast made goodness to or with thy servant ; out of them, the Vulgate, *Bonitatem fecisti.* Some take this cause generally, " Whatever thou dost for thy servants is good " : they count it so, though it be never so contrary to the interest of the flesh : sickness is good, loss of friends is good ; and so are poverty and loss of goods, to an humble and thankful mind. But surely David speaketh here of some supply and deliverance wherein God had made good some promise to him. The Jewish rabbies understand it of his return to the kingdom ; but most Christian writers understand it of some spiritual benefit ; that good which God had done to him. If anything may be collected from the subsequent verses, it was certainly some spiritual good. The Septuagint repeat χρηστότητα twice in this and the following verse, as if he acknowledged the benefit of that good judgment and knowledge of which there he beggeth an increase. It was in part given him already, and that learned by afflictions, as we see, in the third verse of this portion : " Before I was afflicted, I went astray, but now have I kept thy word." His prayer is—Now, then, go on to increase this work, this goodness which thou hast shown to thy servant.

3. The object, *"thy servant" :* it is an honourable, comfortable style ; David delighted in it. God is a bountiful and a gracious master, ready to do good to his servants, rewarding them with grace here, and crowning that grace with glory hereafter : " He that cometh to God, must believe that he is, and that he is a rewarder of them that diligently seek him " (Heb. xi. 6).—*Thomas Manton.*

Verse 65.—"Thou hast dealt well." If the children of God did but know what was best for them, they would perceive that God did that which was best for them. —*John Mason.*

Verse 65.—"Thou hast dealt well with thy servant." He knew that God's gifts are without repentance, and that he is not weary of well-doing, but will finish the thing he hath begun ; and therefore he pleads past favours. Nothing is more forcible to obtain mercy than to lay God's former mercies before him. Here are two grounds, First. If he dealt well with him when he was not regenerate, how much more will he now ? and Secondly, all the gifts of God shall be perfectly finished, therefore he will go on to deal well with his servant. Here is a difference between faith and an accusing conscience : the accusing conscience is afraid to ask more, because it hath abused the former mercies : but faith, assuring us that all God's benefits are tokens of his love bestowed on us according to his word, is bold to ask for more.—*Richard Greenham.*

Verse 65.—"Thou hast dealt well with thy servant." " No doubt," said the late Rev. J. Brown, of Haddington, Scotland, " I have met with trials as well as others ; yet so kind has God been to me, that I think if he were to give me as many years as I have already lived in the world, I should not desire one single circumstance in my lot changed, except that I wish I had less sin. It might be written on my coffin, ' Here lies one of the cares of Providence, who early wanted both father and mother, and yet never missed them.' "—*Arvine's Anecdotes.*

Verse 65.—"Thou hast dealt well with thy servant, O LORD, according unto thy word." The expression, *"according to thy word,"* is so often repeated in this Psalm, that we are apt to overlook it, or to give it only the general meaning of " because of thy promise." But in reality it implies much more. Had God dealt *"well"* with David according to man's idea ? If so, what mean such expressions as these —" O forsake me not utterly " (ver. 8)—" I am a stranger in the earth " (ver. 19)— " My soul cleaveth unto the dust " (ver. 25)—" My soul melteth for heaviness " (ver. 28)—" Turn away my reproach which I fear " (ver. 39)—" The proud have had me greatly in derision " (ver. 51)—" Horror hath taken hold upon me " (ver. 53) ?

In view of such passages as these, can it be said that God " dealt *well* " with David, according to man's idea ?   David's experience was one of very great and very varied trial.   There is not a phase of our feelings in sorrow which does not find ample expression in his Psalms.   And yet he says, " Thou hast dealt well with thy servant, *according to thy word*."

How, then, are we to interpret the expression, so often repeated here, in accordance with the facts of David's spiritual life ?

God dealt well with him " according to his word," in the sense of dealing with him *according to what his word explained was the true good*—not delivering him from all trial, but sending him such trial as he specially required.   He felt truly that God had dealt *well* with him when he could say (ver. 67), " Before I was afflicted I went astray, but now have I kept thy word."   Again (ver. 71), " It is good for me that I have been afflicted, that I might learn thy statutes."   Such dealing was hard for flesh and blood to bear, but it was indeed "*well*," in the sense of accomplishing most blessed results.

It was " according to his word " too, in the sense of being *in accordance with his revealed manner of dealing with his people*, who are chastened for their profit.

Again, God had " dealt well " with David *according to his word or covenant;* the present fulfilment (even if in itself bitter) being a sure earnest of his final perfecting of his work, and glorifying himself in the entire fulfilment of his word, in the completed salvation of his servant.

According to thy word, O Lord, thou hast dealt well with thy servant.   Thy word is the light and lamp that shows things in their true aspect, and teaches us to know that all things work together for good to thy people ; that thou doest all things well.   " Open thou mine eyes, O Lord, that I may see wondrous things out of thy law."   What can be more wonderful than such views to our eyes ?

" According to thy word ": not only " because of thy promise," but in such a manner and measure as thy word declares.   See how such an understanding of the expression opens out the idea of " Be merciful to me according to thy word " (ver. 58). All the sweet promises and declarations of God's infinite mercy rise before us, and make it a vast request.   Again, " Quicken thou me," and " strengthen thou me according to thy word "—*up to the full measure of what thou hast promised and provided for thy people.*   See the fulness in this view, of ver. 76, " Let, I pray thee, thy merciful kindness be for my comfort, *according to thy word*."   Again, ver. 169, " Give me understanding *according to thy word*";   ver. 170, " Deliver me *according to thy word*."   In each of these we are to feel that the request includes the thought of all that the word teaches on the subject.

Let our prayer then for mercy, and strength, and comfort, and understanding, and deliverance, ever be a prayer for these, in the full measure in which they are revealed and promised in the word of God.—*Mary B. M. Duncan* (1835—1865) *in "Under the Shadow."*

Verse 66.—*"Teach me good judgment,"* etc.   David, who discovered a holy taste (Ps. xix. 10 ; civ. 34 ; cxix. 103) ; and recommended it to others (xxxiv. 8), requests in our text to have it increased.   For the word rendered "*judgment*," properly signifies *taste*, and denotes that relish for divine truth, and for the divine goodness and holiness, which is peculiar to true saints.   I propose therefore to consider the nature and objects of that spiritual taste which is possessed by every gracious soul, and which all true saints desire to possess in a still greater degree.

The original word, which is often applied to those objects of sense which are distinguished by the palate, is here used in a metaphorical sense, as the corresponding term frequently is in our own language.   " Doth not the ear try words, and the mouth taste meat ? " (Job xii. 11).   Our translators in this place render it, "*judgment*," which is nearly the same thing ; yet as the terms are applied among us, there is a difference between them.   Taste is that which enables a man to form a more compendious judgment.   Judgment is slower in its operations than taste ; it forms its decisions in a more circuitous way.   So we apply the term *taste* to many objects of mental decision, to the beauty of a poem, to excellence of style, to elegance of dress or of deportment, to painting, to music, etc., in which a good taste will lead those who possess it, to decide speedily, and yet accurately, on the beauty, excellence, and propriety of the objects with which it has long been conversant without laborious examination.

Just so, true saints have a power of receiving pleasure from the beauty of holiness, which shines forth resplendently in the word of God, in the divine character, in the law, in the gospel, in the cross of Christ, in the example of Christ, and in the conduct of all his true followers, so far as they are conformed to his lovely image. I do not mean by this that they are influenced by a blind instinct, for which they can assign no sufficient reason : the genuine feelings of a true Christian can all of them be justified by the soundest reason : but those feelings which were first produced by renewing grace, are so strengthened by daily communion with God, and by frequent contemplation of spiritual things, that they acquire a delicacy and readiness of perception, which no one can possess who has never tasted how gracious the Lord is. You cannot touch, as it were, a certain string, but the renewed heart must needs answer to it.   Whatever truly tends to exalt God, to bring the soul near to him, and to insure his being glorified and enjoyed, will naturally attract the notice, excite the affections and influence the conduct of one who is born of God.   "Sweeter also than honey, and the honeycomb."   "My meditation of thee shall be sweet." "How sweet are thy words to my taste ! sweeter than honey to my mouth." "O taste and see that the Lord is good."—*John Ryland*, 1753—1825.

Verse 66.—*"Teach me good judgment and knowledge,"* etc. Literally it may be rendered thus,—Teach me goodness, discernment and knowledge ; for I have believed or confided in thy commandments.   In our system of divine things, we might be inclined to place knowledge and discernment first, as begetting the " goodness."   But it is a well ascertained fact, that the intellectual and moral powers are reciprocal—that the moral also give strength to the intellectual.   Moreover, it is only the spiritual man that discerns the things of God.   The state of being spiritually minded, and also conversant with divine things, gives a vigour and breadth to the intellect itself, that remarkably appears in the lives of eminent men.   And if you remark that some have been eminent who were devoid of spiritual qualities, the reply might be—How much more eminent would they have been had they possessed these qualities.   The petition is, *"Teach me goodness, discernment and knowledge."*   The principle of pleasing God may be within, and yet the mind may require to be enlightened in all duty ; and again, though all duty be known, we may require spiritual discernment to see and feel it aright.—*John Stephen.*

Verse 66.—*"Teach me good judgment."*   In a lecture of Sir John Lubbock's [on the fertilization of flowers by the agency of insects], a striking distinction is noted in regard to this operation between beautiful and hideous plants.   Bees, it would appear, delight in pleasant odours and bright colours, and invariably choose those plants which give pleasure to man.   If we watch the course of these insects on their visit to a garden, we shall observe them settling upon the rose, the lavender, and all other similar agreeable flowers of brilliant hues or sweet scent.   In marked contrast with this is the conduct of flies, which always show a preference for livid yellow or dingy red plants, and those which possess an unpleasant smell.   The bee is a creature of fine and sensitive tastes.   The fly is " a species of insectoid vulture," naturally turning to such vegetable food as resembles carrion.   Let two plates be placed on a lawn, at a little distance apart, the one containing that ill-scented under-ground fungus, the Stink-horn, and the other a handful of moss roses, and this difference will be immediately discerned.   The foul-odoured and unsightly fungus will soon be covered with flies, while the bees will resort to the plate of roses.   To this love of bees for fine colours and fragrant perfumes we are indebted for our choicest flowers.   For by taking the pollen dust of some conspicuous flower to the stigma of another, they have by this union produced the seed of a still richer variety.   Thus, age after age, many blossoms have been growing increasingly beautiful.   On the other hand, strange to say, through a similar process, a progress in the opposite direction has taken place in those plants which are frequented by flies, and their unwholesome and repulsive qualities have become intensified.

So is it with the two great classes into which mankind may be divided—the men of this world, and the men of the next.   While the purified affections of the one centre continually on " whatsoever things are honest, whatsoever things are just, whatsoever things are pure, whatsoever things are lovely, whatsoever things are of good report," so the earthward and vile affections of the other fasten on corruption. Not more surely does the laborious bee fly from one beautiful flower to another, than does the Christian seek of set purpose all that is fairest, sweetest, and best on earth.   His prayer is that of David, in Psalm cxix. 66, *"Teach me good taste "* (which is the literal translation) ; and " if there be any virtue, and if there be any praise," he thinks on these things.—*James Neil, in "Rays from the Realms of Nature,"* 1879.

Verse 66.—*"Good judgment and knowledge."* No blessings are more suitable than *"good judgment and knowledge"*—*"knowledge"* of ourselves, of our Saviour, of the way of obedience—and *"good judgment"* to direct and apply this knowledge to some valuable end. These two parts of our intellectual furniture have a most important connexion and dependence upon each other. *"Knowledge"* is the speculative perception of general truth. *"Judgment"* is the practical application of it to the heart and conduct.—*Charles Bridges.*

Verse 66.—*"For I have believed thy commandments."* These words deserve a little consideration, because believing is here joined to an unusual object. Had it been, "for I have believed thy promises," or, "obeyed thy commandments," the sense of the clause had been more obvious to every vulgar apprehension. To believe commandments, sounds as harsh to a common ear, as to see with the ear, and hear with the eye ; but, for all this, the commandments are the object ; and of them he saith, not, "I have obeyed"; but, *"I have believed."*

To take off the seeming asperity of the phrase, some interpreters conceive that *"commandments"* is put for the word in general ; and so promises are included, yea, they think, principally intended, especially those promises which encouraged him to look to God for necessary things, such as good judgment and knowledge are. But this interpretation would divert us from the weight and force of these significant words. Therefore let us note,—

1. Certainly there is a faith in the commandments, as well as in the promises. We must believe that God is their author, and that they are the expressions of his commanding and legislative will, which we are bound to obey. Faith must discern the sovereignty and goodness of the law-maker and believe that his commands are holy, just and good ; it must also teach us that God loves those who keep his law and is angry with those who transgress, and that he will see to it that his law is vindicated at the last great day.

2. Faith in the commandments is as necessary as faith in the promises ; for, as the promises are not esteemed, embraced, and improved, unless they are believed to be of God, so neither are the precepts ; they do not sway the conscience, nor incline the affections, except as they are believed to be divine.

3. Faith in the commands must be as lively as faith in the promises. As the promises are not believed with a lively faith, unless they draw off the heart from carnal vanities to seek that happiness which they offer to us ; so the precepts are not believed rightly, unless we be fully resolved to acquiesce in them as the only rule to guide us in obtaining that happiness, and unless we are determined to adhere to them, and obey them. As the king's laws are not kept as soon as they are believed to be the king's laws, unless also, upon the consideration of his authority and power, we subject ourselves to them ; so this believing noteth a ready alacrity to hear God's voice and obey it, and to govern our hearts and actions according to his counsel and direction in the word.—*Thomas Manton.*

Verse 66.—*"For I have believed thy commandments."* The commandments of God are not alone ; but they have promises of grace on the right hand, and threatenings of wrath on the left : upon both of these faith exercises itself, and without such faith no one will be able to render obedience to God's commands.— *Wolfgang Musculus.*

Verse 67.—*"Before I was afflicted I went astray,"* etc. Not that he wilfully, wickedly, maliciously, and through contempt, departed from his God ; this he denies (Ps. xviii. 21) ; but through the weakness of the flesh, the prevalence of corruption, and the force of temptation, and very much through a careless, heedless, and negligent frame of spirit, he got out of the right way, and wandered from it before he was well aware. The word is used of erring through ignorance (Lev. v. 18). This was in his time of prosperity, when, though he might not, like Jeshurun, wax fat and kick, and forsake and lightly esteem the Rock of his salvation ; or fall into temptations and hurtful lusts, and err from the faith, and be pierced with many sorrows ; yet he might become inattentive to the duties of religion, and be negligent of them, which is a common case.—*John Gill.*

Verse 67.—*"Before I was afflicted."* The Septuagint and Latin Vulgate, "Before I was humbled." The Hebrew word has the general sense of being afflicted, and may refer to any kind of trial.—*Albert Barnes.*

Verse 67.—*"Before I was afflicted."* Prosperity is a more refined and severe test of character than adversity, as one hour of summer sunshine produces geater corruption than the longest winter day.—*Eliza Cook.*

Verse 67.—*"I was afflicted."* God in wisdom deals with us as some great person would do with a disobedient son, that forsakes his house, and riots among his tenants. His father gives orders that they should treat him ill, affront, and chase him from them, and all, that he might bring him back. The same doth God : man is his wild and debauched son ; he flies from the commands of his father, and cannot endure to live under his strict and severe government. He resorts to the pleasures of the world, and revels and riots among the creatures. But God resolves to recover him, and therefore commands every creature to handle him roughly. " Burn him, fire ; toss him, tempests, and shipwreck his estate ; forsake him, friends ; designs, fail him ; children, be rebellious to him, as he is to me ; let his supports and dependencies sink under him, his riches melt away, leave him poor, and despised, and destitute." These are all God's servants, and must obey his will. And to what end is all this, but that, seeing himself forsaken of all, he may at length, like the beggared prodigal, return to his father ?—*Ezekiel Hopkins,* 1633—1690.

Verse 67.—*"I was afflicted."* As men clip the feathers of fowls, when they begin to fly too high or too far ; even so doth God diminish our riches, etc., that we should not pass our bounds, and glory too much of such gifts.—*Otho Wermullerus.*

Verse 67.—*"But now have I kept thy word."*

Affliction brings Man Home.

" Man like a silly sheep doth often stray,
   Not knowing of his way,
Blind deserts and the wilderness of sin
   He daily travels in ;
There's nothing will reduce him sooner than
   Afflictions to his pen.
He wanders in the sunshine, but in rain
   And stormy weather hastens home again.

" Thou, the great Shepherd of my soul, O keep
   Me, thy unworthy sheep
From gadding : or if fair means will not do it,
   Let foul, then, bring me to it.
Rather then I should perish in my error,
   Lord bring me back with terror ;
Better I be chastizèd with thy rod
   And Shepherd's staff, than stray from thee, my God.

" Though for the present stripes do grieve me sore,
   At last they profit more,
And make me to observe thy word, which I
   Neglected formerly ;
Let me come home rather by weeping cross
   Then still be at a loss.
For health I'd rather take a bitter pill,
   Then eating sweet-meats to be always ill."

Thomas Washbourne, 1606—1687.

Verse 67.—From the countless throng before the throne of God and the Lamb, we may yet hear the words of the Psalmist, *"Before I was afflicted I went astray : but now I have kept thy word."* There is many an one who will say, " Behold, happy is the man whom God correcteth " (Job v. 17). One would tell you that his worldly undoing was the making of his heavenly prospects ; and another that the loss of all things was the gain of All in All. There are multitudes whom God has afflicted with natural blindness that they might gain spiritual sight ; and those who under bodily infirmities and diseases of divers sorts have pined and wasted away this earthly life, gladly laying hold on glory, honour, and immortality instead.—*William Garrett Lewis, in "Westbourne Grove Sermons,"* 1872.

Verse 67.—By affliction God separates the sin which he hates from the soul which he loves.—*John Mason.*

Verse 68.—*"Thou art good, and doest good."* There is a good God set before us, that we may not take up with any low pattern of goodness. He is represented to us as all goodness. He is good in his nature ; and his work is agreeable to his nature; nothing is wanting to it, or defective in it. Nothing can be added to it to make it better. Philo saith, "'Ο ὄντως ὤν το πρῶτον ἀγαθόν": the first being must needs be the first good. As soon as we conceive that there is a God, we presently conceive that he is good, He is good of himself, good in himself, goodness itself, and both the fountain and the pattern of all the good that is in the creatures.

1. As to his NATURE, he is originally "*good*," good in himself, and good to others; as the sun hath light in himself, and giveth light to all other things. Essentially good; not only good, but goodness itself. Goodness in us is an accessory quality or superadded gift; but in God it is not a quality, but his essence. In a vessel that is gilded with gold the gilding or lustre is a superadded quality; but in a vessel all of gold, the lustre and the substance is the same. God is infinitely good; the creatures' good is limited, but there is nothing to limit the perfection of God, or give it any measure. He is an ocean of goodness without banks or bottom. Alas! what is our drop to this ocean! God is immutably good; his goodness can never be more or less than it is; as there can be no addition to it, so no subtraction from it. Man in his innocency was *peccabilis*, or liable to sin, afterwards *peccator*, or an actual sinner; but God ever was and is good. Now this is the pattern propounded to us, but his nature is a great deep. Therefore—

2. As to his WORK, "*he doeth good.*" What hath God been acting upon the great theatre of the world but goodness for these six thousand years? Acts xiv. 17, " Nevertheless he left not himself without witness, in that he did good, and gave us rain from heaven, and fruitful seasons, filling our hearts with food and gladness." He left not himself without a witness, ἀγαθοποιῶν, not by taking vengeance of their idolatries, but by distributing benefits. This is propounded to our imitation, that our whole life may be nothing else but doing good: Matt. v. 48, " Be ye therefore perfect, even as your Father which is in heaven is perfect." Well, therefore, doth the Psalmist say, "*Teach me thy statutes.*"—*Thomas Manton.*

Verse 68.—"*Thou art good, and doest good.*" We should bless the Lord at all times, and keep up good thoughts of God on every occasion, especially in the time of affliction. Hence we are commanded to glorify God in the fires (Isai. xxiv. 15); and this the three children did in the hottest furnace. . . . . I grant, indeed, we cannot give thanks for affliction as affliction, but either as it is the means of some good to us, or as the gracious hand of God is some way remarkable therein toward us. In this respect there is no condition on this side of hell but we have reason to praise God in it, though it be the greatest of calamities. Hence it was that David, when he speaks of his affliction, adds presently, "*Thou art good, and doest good*"; and he declares (ver. 65), "*Thou hast dealt well with thy servant, O LORD, according unto thy word.*" Hence Paul and Silas praised God when they were scourged and imprisoned. —*John Willison, 1680—1750.*

Verse 68.—"*Thou art good.*" The blessed effects of chastisement, as a special instance of the Lord's goodness, might naturally lead to an acknowledgment of his general goodness, in his own character, and in his unwearied dispensations of love. Judging in unbelieving haste of his providential and gracious dealings, feeble sense imagines a frown, when the eye of faith discerns a smile upon his face; and therefore in proportion as faith is exercised in the review of the past, and the experience of the present, we shall be prepared with the ascription of praise—"*Thou art good.*"—*Charles Bridges.*

Verse 69.—"*The proud have forged a lie against me.*" If in the present day the enemies of the truth in their lying writings rail against the orthodox teachers in the Church, that is a very old artifice of the Devil, since David complains that in his day it happened unto him.—*Solomon Gesner.*

Verse 69.—"*The proud have forged a lie.*" They trim up lies with shadows of truth and neat language; they have mints to frame their lies curiously in, and presses to print their lies withal.—*William Greenhill, 1591—1677.*

Verse 69.—"*The proud.*" Faith humbleth, and infidelity maketh proud. Faith humbleth, because it letteth us see our sins, and the punishments thereof, and that we have no dealing with God but through the mediation of Christ; and that we can do no good, nor avoid evil, but by grace. But when men know not this, then they think much of themselves, and therefore are proud. Therefore all ignorant men, all heretics, and worldlings are proud. They that are humbled under God's hands, are humble to men; but they that despise God do also persecute his servants. —*Richard Greenham.*

Verse 69.—"Forged a lie." Vatablus translates it, *concinnarunt mendacia.* So Tremellius : *they have trimmed up lies.* As Satan can transform himself into an angel of light, so he can trim up his lies under coverings of truth, to make them the more plausible unto men. And indeed this is no small temptation, when lies made against the godly are trimmed up with the shadows of truth, and wicked men cover their unrighteous dealings with appearances of righteousness. Thus, not only are the godly unjustly persecuted, but simple ones are made to believe that they have most justly deserved it. In this case the godly are to sustain themselves by the testimony of a good conscience.—*William Cowper.*

Verse 69.—"Forged" expresses the essential meaning of the Hebrew word, but not its figurative form, which seems to be that of sewing, analogous to that of weaving, as applied to the same thing, both in Hebrew and in other languages. We may also compare our figurative phrase, *to patch up,* which, however, is not so much suggestive of artifice or skill as of the want of it. The connection of the clauses is, that all the craft and malice of his enemies should only lead him to obey God with a more undivided heart than ever.—*Joseph Addison Alexander.*

Verse 69.—"Forged." The metaphor may be like the Greek (ράπτειν δόλους), from sewing or patching up : or, from *smearing,* or *daubing* (Delitzsch, Moll, etc.), a wall, so as to hide the real substance. The Psalmist remains true to God despite the faslehoods with which the proud smear and hide his true fidelity.—*The Speaker's Commentary.*

Verse 69.—"A lie."—Satan's two arms by which he wrestles against the godly are violence and lies : where he cannot or dare not, use violence, there be sure he will not fail to fight with lies. And herein doth the Lord greatly show his careful providence, in fencing his children against Satan's malice and the proud brags of his instruments, in such sort, that their proudest hearts are forced to forge lies ; their malice being so great that they must do evil ; and yet their power so bridled that they cannot do what they would.—*William Cowper.*

Verse 69.—"I will keep thy precepts with my whole heart." Let the word of the Lord come, let it come ; and if we had six hundred necks, we would submit them all to its dictates.—*Augustine.*

Verse 70.—"Their heart is as fat as grease." The word שׁפּט occurs nowhere else in Scripture, but with the Chaldees שׁפּט signifies *to fatten, to make fat;* also *to make stupid and doltish,* because such the fat ofttimes are . . . . For this reason the proud, who are mentioned in the preceding verse, are described by their fixed resolve in evil, because they are almost insensible ; as is to be seen in pigs, who pricked through the skin with a bodkin, and that slowly, as long as the bodkin only touches the fat, do not feel the prick until it reaches to the flesh. Thus the proud, whose great prosperity is elsewhere likened to fatness, have a heart totally insusceptible, which is insensible to the severe reproofs of the Divine word, and also to its holy delights and pleasures, by reason of the affluence of carnal things ; aye, more, is altogether unfitted for good impulses ; just as elsewhere is to be seen with fat animals, how slow they are and unfit for work, when, on the contrary, those are agile and quick which are not hindered by this same fatness.—*Martin Geier.*

Verse 70.—"Their heart is as fat as grease." This makes them—1. *Senseless* and secure ; they are past feeling : thus the phrase is used (Isa. vi. 10) : " Make the heart of the people fat." They are not sensible of the teaching of the word of God, or his rod. 2. *Sensual* and voluptuous : " Their eyes stand out with fatness " (Psa. lxxiii. 7) : they roll themselves in the pleasures of sense, and take up with them as their chief good ; and much good may it do them : I would not change conditions with them ; *"I delight in thy law."*—*Matthew Henry.*

Verse 70.—"Their heart is as fat as grease ; but I delight in thy law ; " as if he should say, My heart is a lean heart, a hungry heart, my soul loveth and rejoiceth in thy word. I have nothing else to fill it but thy word, and the comforts I have from it ; but their hearts are fat hearts ; fat with the world, fat with lust ; they hate the word. As a full stomach loatheth meat and cannot digest it ; so wicked men hate the word, it will not go down with them, it will not gratify their lusts.—*William Fenner.*

Being anxious to know the medical significance of fatty heart, I applied to an eminent gentleman who is well known as having been President of the College of Physicians. His reply shows that the language is rather figurative than literal. He kindly replied to me as follows :—

There are two forms of so-called " fatty heart."   In the one there is an excessive amount of fatty tissue covering the exterior of the organ, especially about the base. This may be observed in all cases where the body of the animal is throughout over fat, as in animals fattened for slaughter.   It does not necessarily interfere with the action of the heart, and may not be of much importance in a medical point of view.   The second form is, however, a much more serious condition.   In this, the muscular structure of the heart, on which its all-important function, as the central propelling power, depends, undergoes a degenerative change, by which the contractile fibres of the muscles are converted into a structure having none of the properties of the natural fibres, and in which are found a number of fatty, oily globules, which can be readily seen by means of the microscope.   This condition, if at all extensive, renders the action of the heart feeble and irregular, and is very perilous, not infre- quently causing sudden death.   It is found in connection with a general unhealthy condition of system, and is evidence of general mal-nutrition.   It is brought about by an indolent, luxurious mode of living, or, at all events, by neglect of bodily exercise and those hygienic rules which are essential for healthy nutrition.   It cannot, however, be said to be incompatible with mental vigour, and certainly is not necessarily associated with stupidity.   But the heart, in this form of disease, is literally " greasy," and may be truly described as " fat as grease."   So much for physiology and pathology.   May I venture on the sacred territory of biblical exegesis without risking the charge of fatuousness ?   Is not the Psalmist contrasting those who lead an animal, self-indulgent, vicious life, by which body and mind are incapacitated for their proper uses, and those who can *run* in the way of God's commandments, *delight* to do his will, and *meditate* on his precepts ?   Sloth, fatness, and stupidity, *versus* activity, firm muscles, and mental vigour.   Body *versus* mind.   Man become as a beast *versus* man retaining the image of God.—*Sir James Risdon Bennett*, 1881.

Verse 71.—"*It is good for me,*" etc.   I am mended by my sickness, enriched by my poverty, and strengthened by my weakness, and with S. Bernard desire, *Irascaris mihi Domine,* O Lord, be angry with me.   For if thou chidest me not, thou considerest me not ; if I taste no bitterness, I have no physic ; if thou correct me not, I am not thy son.   Thus was it with the great-grandchild of David, Manasseh, when he was in affliction, " He besought the Lord his God " : even that king's iron was more precious to him than his gold, his jail a more happy lodging than his palace, Babylon a better school than Jerusalem.   What fools are we, then, to frown upon our afflictions !   These, how crabbed soever, are our best friends.   They are not indeed for our pleasure, they are for our profit ; their issue makes them worthy of a welcome.   What do we care how bitter that potion be that brings health.— *Abraham Wright.*

Verse 71.—"*It is good for me that I have been afflicted.*" Saints are great gainers by affliction, because " godliness," which is " great gain," which is " profitable for all things," is more powerful than before.   The rod of correction, by a miracle of grace, like that of Aaron's, buds and blossoms, and brings forth the fruits of righteousness, which are most excellent.   A rare sight it is indeed to see a man coming out of a bed of languishing, or any other furnace of affliction, more like to angels in purity, more like to Christ who was holy, harmless, undefiled, and separate from sinners ; more like unto God himself, being more exactly righteous in all his ways, and more exemplarily holy in all manner of conversation.—*Nathanael Vincent,*—1697.

Verse 71.—"*It is good for me that I have been afflicted.*" If I have no cross to bear to-day, I shall not advance heavenwards.   A cross (that is anything that disturbs our peace), is the spur which stimulates, and without which we should most likely remain stationary, blinded with empty vanities, and sinking deeper into sin.   A cross helps us onwards, in spite of our apathy and resistance.   To lie quietly on a bed of down, may seem a very sweet existence ; but pleasant ease and rest are not the lot of a Christian : if he would mount higher and higher, it must be by a rough road.   Alas ! for those who have no daily cross !   Alas ! for those who repine and fret against it !—*From* "*Gold Dust,*" 1880.

Verse 71.—"*It is good for me,*" etc.   There are some things good but not pleasant, as *sorrow* and *affliction.*   Sin is pleasant, but unprofitable ; and sorrow is profitable, but unpleasant.   As waters are purest when they are in motion, so saints are generally holiest when in affliction. Some Christians resemble those children who will learn their books no longer than while the rod is on their backs. It is well known that by the greatest affliction the Lord has sealed the sweetest instruction. Many are not bettered by the judgments they see, when they are by the judgments they have felt. The purest gold is the most pliable. That is the best blade which bends well without retaining its crooked figure.—*William Secker*, 1660.

Verse 71.—*"It is good for me,"* etc. Piety hath a wondrous virtue to change all things into matter of consolation and joy. No condition in effect can be evil or sad to a pious man : his very sorrows are pleasant, his infirmities are wholesome, his wants enrich him, his disgraces adorn him, his burdens ease him ; his duties are privileges, his falls are the grounds of advancement, his very sins (as breeding contrition, humility, circumspection, and vigilance), do better and profit him : whereas impiety doth spoil every condition, doth corrupt and embase all good things, doth embitter all the conveniences and comforts of life.—*Isaac Barrow*, 1630—1677.

Verse 71.—*"It is good for me that I have been afflicted."* In Miss E. J. Whately's very interesting Life of her Father, the celebrated Archbishop of Dublin, a fact is recorded, as told by Dr. Whately, with reference to the introduction of the larch-tree into England. When the plants were first brought, the gardener, hearing that they came from the south of Europe, and taking it for granted that they would require warmth,—forgetting that they might grow near the snow-line,—put them into a hot-house. Day by day they withered, until the gardener in disgust threw them on a dung-heap outside; there they began to revive and bud, and at last grew into trees. They needed the cold.

The great Husbandman often saves his plants by throwing them out into the cold. The nipping frosts of trial and affliction are ofttimes needed, if God's larches are to grow. It is under such discipline that new thoughts and feelings appear. The heart becomes more dead to the world and self. From the night of sorrow rises the morning of joy. Winter is the harbinger of spring. From the crucifixion of the old man comes the resurrection of the new, as in nature life is the child of death

> " The night is the mother of the day,
>   And winter of the spring ;
> And ever upon old decay,
>   The greenest mosses spring."

James Wareing Bardsley in "Illustrated Texts and Texts Illustrated," 1876.

Verse 71.—*"It is good for me that I have been afflicted."* It is a remarkable circumstance that the most brilliant colours of plants are to be seen on the highest mountains, in spots that are most exposed to the wildest weather. The brightest lichens and mosses, the loveliest gems of wild flowers, abound far up on the bleak, storm-scalped peak. One of the richest displays of organic colouring I ever beheld was near the summit of Mount Chenebettaz, a hill about 10,000 feet high, immediately above the great St. Bernard Hospice. The whole face of an extensive rock was covered with a most vivid yellow lichen, which shone in the sunshine like the golden battlement of an enchanted castle. There, in that lofty region, amid the most frowning desolation, exposed to the fiercest tempest of the sky, this lichen exhibited a glory of colour such as it never showed in the sheltered valley. I have two specimens of the same lichen before me while I write these lines, one from the great St. Bernard, and the other from the wall of a Scottish castle, deeply embosomed among sycamore trees ; and the difference in point of form and colouring between them is most striking. The specimen nurtured amid the wild storms of the mountain peak is a lovely primrose hue, and is smooth in texture and complete in outline ; while the specimen nurtured amid the soft airs and the delicate showers of the lowland valley is of a dim rusty hue, and is scurfy in texture, and broken in outline. And is it not so with the Christian who is afflicted, tempest-tossed, and not comforted ? Till the storms and vicissitudes of God's providence beat upon him again and again, his character appears marred and clouded by selfish and worldly influences. But trials clear away the obscurity, perfect the outlines of his disposition, and give brightness and blessings to his piety.

> " Amidst my list of blessings infinite
> Stands this the foremost, that my heart has bled ;
> For *all* I bless thee, *most* for the *severe*."

—*Hugh Macmillan.*

Verse 71.—*"That I might learn thy statutes."* He speaks not of that learning which is gotten by hearing or reading of God's word ; but of the learning which he had gotten by experience ; that he had felt the truth and comfort of God's word more effectual and lively in trouble than he could do without trouble ; which also made him more godly, wise, and religious when the trouble was gone.—*William Cowper.*

Verse 71.—*"That I might learn."* " I had never known," said Martin Luther's wife, " what such and such things meant, in such and such Psalms, such complaints and workings of spirit ; I had never understood the practice of Christian duties, had not God brought me under some affliction." It is very true that God's rod is as the schoolmaster's pointer to the child, pointing out the letter, that he may the better take notice of it ; thus he pointeth out to us many good lessons which we should never otherwise have learned.—*From John Spencer's "Things New and Old,"* 1658.

Verse 71.—*"That I might learn."* As prosperity blindeth the eyes of men, even so doth adversity open them. Like as the salve that remedieth the disease of the eyes doth first bite and grieve the eyes, and maketh them to water, but yet afterward the eyesight is clearer than it was ; even so trouble doth vex men wonderfully at the first, but afterwards it lighteneth the eyes of the mind, that it is afterward more reasonable, wise and circumspect. For trouble bringeth experience, and experience bringeth wisdom.—*Otho Wermullerus,* 1551.

Verse 71.—*"Learn thy statutes."* The Christian has reason to thank God that things have not been accommodated to his wishes. When the mist of tears was in his eyes, he looked into the word of God and saw magnificent things. When Jonah came up from the depths of ocean, he showed that he had learned the statutes of God. One could not go too deep to get such knowledge as he obtained. Nothing now could hinder him from going to Nineveh. It is just the same as though he had brought up from the deep an army of twelve legions of the most formidable troops. The word of God, grasped by faith, was all this to him, and more. He still, however, needed further affliction ; for there were some statutes not yet learned. Some gourds were to wither. He was to descend into a further vale of humiliation. Even the profoundest affliction does not, perhaps, teach us everything ; a mistake we sometimes make. But why should we compel God to use harsh measures with us ? Why not sit at the feet of Jesus and learn quietly what we need to learn ?—*George Bowen, in "Daily Meditations,"* 1873.

Verse 71.—*"Statutes."* The verb from which this word is formed means to engrave or inscribe. The word means a definite, prescribed, written law. The term is applied to Joseph's law about the portion of the priests in Egypt, to the law about the passover, etc. But in this Psalm it has a more internal meaning ; that moral law of God which is engraven on the fleshy tables of the heart ; the inmost and spiritual apprehension of his will ; not so obvious as the law and the testimonies, and a matter of more direct spiritual communication than his precepts ; the latter being more elaborated by the efforts of the mind itself, divinely guided indeed, but perhaps more instrumentally, and less passively, employed. They are continually spoken of as things yet to be learned, either wholly or in part, not objectively apprehended already, like God's law . . . . They are learned, not suddenly, but by experience, and through the means of trials mercifully ordained by God ; lessons therefore which are deeply engraven on the heart. " Good is it for me that I have been in trouble, that I might learn thy statutes." " I have more understanding than my teachers, because thy statutes I have observed."—*John Jebb.*

Verse 72.—*"The law of thy mouth is better unto me,"* etc. Highly prize the Scriptures. Can he make a proficiency in any art, who doth slight and deprecate it ? Prize this book above all other books. St. Gregory calls the Bible " the heart and soul of God." The rabbins say, that a mountain of sense hangs upon every apex and tittle of Scripture. " The law of the Lord is perfect " : Ps. xix. 7. The Scripture is the library of the Holy Ghost ; it is a pandect of divine knowledge, an exact model and platform of religion. The Scripture contains in it the *credenda,* " the things which we are to believe," and the *agenda,* " the things which we are to practise." It is " able to make us wise unto salvation " : 2 Tim. iii. 15. The Scripture is the standard of truth, the judge of controversies ; it is the pole-star to direct us to heaven : Isai. viii. 20. " The commandment is a lamp ": Prov. vi. 23. The Scripture is the compass by which the rudder of our will is to be steered ; it is the field in which Christ, the Pearl of price, is hid ; it is a rock of diamonds ; it is a sacred collyrium, or eye-salve ; it mends their eyes that look upon it ; it is a spiritual optic-glass in which the glory of God is resplendent ; it is the panacy, or universal medicine for the soul. The leaves of Scripture are like the " leaves of the tree of life, for the healing of the nations " : Rev. xxii. 2. The Scripture is both the breeder and feeder of grace. How is the convert born, but by " the word of truth " ? James i. 18. How doth he grow, but by " the sincere milk of the word " ? 1 Pet. ii. 2. The word written is the book out of which our evidences for heaven are fetched ; it is the sea-mark which shows us the rocks of sin to avoid ; it is the antidote against error and apostasy, the two-edged sword which wounds the old serpent. It is our bulwark to withstand the force of lust ; like the Capitol of Rome, which was a place of strength and ammunition. The Scripture is the " tower of David," wherein the shields of our faith hang : Cant. iv. 4. " Take away the word and you deprive us of the sun," said Luther. The word written is above an angelic embassy, or voice from heaven. " This voice which came from heaven we heard. . . . We have also a more sure word " : 2 Pet. i. 18, 19. O, prize the word written ; prizing is the way to profiting. If Cæsar so valued his commentaries, that for preserving them he lost his purple robe, how should we estimate the sacred oracles of God ? " I have esteemed the words of his mouth more than my necessary food."—*Thomas Watson, in "The Morning Exercises."*

Verse 72.—"*The law of thy mouth is better unto me.*" The sacred Scriptures are the treasures and pleasures of a gracious soul : to David they were better than thousands of gold and silver. A mountain of transparent pearls, heaped as high as heaven, is not so rich in treasure as these ; hence that good man chose these as his heritage for ever, and rejoiced in them as in all riches. A covetous miser could not take such delight in his bags, nor a young heir in a large inheritance, as holy David did in God's word.

The word *law* comes from a root that signifies to try as merchants that search and prove the wares that they buy and lay up ; hence also comes the word for gems and jewels that are tried, and found right. The sound Christian is the wise merchant, seeking goodly pearls ; he tries what he reads or hears by the standard or touchstone of Scripture, and having found genuine truths he lays them up to the great enriching of this supreme and sovereign faculty of the understanding.— *Oliver Heywood.*

Verse 72.—The word of God must be nearer to us than our friends, dearer to us than our lives, sweeter to us than our liberty, and pleasanter to us than all earthly comforts.—*John Mason.*

Verse 72.—One lesson, taught by sanctified affliction, is, the love of *God's word.* " This is my *comfort,* in my affliction : thy word hath quickened me." In reading a part of the one hundred and nineteenth Psalm to Miss Westbrook, who died, she said, " Stop, sir, I never said so much to you before—I never could ; but now I *can* say, ' The word of thy mouth is dearer to me, than *thousands* of gold and silver.' What can gold and silver do for me *now* ? "—*George Redford, in "Memoirs of the late Rev. John Cooke,* 1828."

Verse 72.—"*Thousands of gold and silver.*" Worldly riches are gotten with labour, kept with care, lost with grief. They are false friends, farthest from us when we have most need of comfort ; as all worldlings shall find to be true in the hour of death. For then, as Jonah's gourd was taken from him in a morning, when he had most need of it against the sun ; so is it with the comfort of worldlings. It is far otherwise with the word of God ; for if we will lay it up in our hearts, as Mary did, the comfort thereof shall sustain us, when all other comfort shall fail us.

This it is that makes us rich unto God, when our souls are storehouses, filled with the treasures of his word. Shall we think it poverty to be scant of gold and silver ? *An ideo angelus pauper est, quia non habet jumenta,* etc.* Shall we esteem the angels poor, because they have not flocks of cattle ? or that S. Peter was poor, because he had not gold nor silver to give unto the cripple ? No, he had store of grace, by infinite degrees more excellent than it.

Let the riches of gold be left unto worldlings : these are not current in Canaan, not accounted of in our heavenly country. If we would be in any estimation

---

*Chrysostom.

there, let us enrich our souls with spiritual graces, which we have in abundance in the mines and treasures of the word of God.—*William Cowper.*

Verse 72.—The Scripture is an ever-overflowing fountain that cannot be drawn dry, and an inexhausted treasure that cannot be emptied. To this purpose tend those resemblances of the law made use of by David in this Psalm, and no less justly applicable to the gospel ; it is not only better than *"gold and silver,"* which are things of value, but *"thousands,"* which implieth abundance. In another verse he compares it to all riches and great spoil, both which contain in them *multiplex genus,* all sorts of valuable commodities, sheep, oxen, lands, houses, garments, goods, moneys, and the like : thus are all sorts of spiritual riches, yea, abundance of each sort, to be had in the gospel. And therefore the Greek fathers compare Scripture verities to precious stones, and our Saviour to a pearl of great price. A minister, in this respect, is called a merchant of invaluable jewels ; for, indeed, gospel truths are choice and excellent, as much worth as our souls, as heaven, as salvation is. Nay, should I go higher, look what worth there is in the riches of God's grace, the precious blood of Christ, that may secondarily be applied to the gospel, which discovereth and offereth both to us.—*Abraham Wright.*

Verses 72, 127.—When David saw how some make void the law of God, he saith, *"Therefore I love thy commandments above gold : yea, above fine gold."* As if he had said, I love thy law all the more because I see some men esteem and reckon it as if it were dross, and throw it up as void and antiquated, or taking the boldness, as it were, to repeal and make it void, that they may set up their own lusts and vain imaginations. Because I see both profane and superstitious men thus out of love with thy law, therefore my love is more enflamed to it, *"I love it above gold,"* which leads the most of men away captives in the love of it ; and I esteem it more than that which is most esteemed by men, and gains men most esteem in this world, *"fine gold" ;* yea, as he said (Ps. xix. 10) *"more than much fine gold."*—*Joseph Caryl.*

Verse 72.—You that are gentlemen, remember what Hierom reports of Nepotianus, a young gentleman of Rome, *qui longa et assidua meditatione Scripturarum pectus suum fecerat bibliothecam Christi,* who by long and assiduous meditation of the Scriptures, made his breast the library of Christ. Remember what is said of King Alfonsus, that he read over the Bible fourteen times, together with such commentaries as those times afforded.

You that are scholars, remember Cranmer and Ridley ; the former learned the New Testament by heart in his journey to Rome, the latter in Pembroke-hall walks in Cambridge. Remember what is said of Thomas-à-Kempis,—that he found rest nowhere *nisi in angulo, cum libello,* but in a corner with this Book in his hand. And what is said of Beza,—that when he was above fourscore years old he could say perfectly by heart any Greek chapter in Paul's Epistles.

You that are women, consider what Hierom saith of Paula, Eustochiam, and other ladies, who were singularly versed in the Holy Scriptures.

Let all men consider that hyperbolical speech of Luther, that he would not live in Paradise without the Word ; and with it he could live well enough in hell. This speech of Luther must be understood *cum grano salis.*—*Edmund Calamy.*

EXPOSITION OF VERSES 73 TO 80.

THY hands have made me and fashioned me : give me understanding, that I may learn thy commandments.

74 They that fear thee will be glad when they see me ; because I have hoped in thy word.

75 I know, O LORD, that thy judgments *are* right, and *that* thou in faithfulness hast afflicted me.

76 Let, I pray thee, thy merciful kindness be for my comfort, according to thy word unto thy servant.

77 Let thy tender mercies come unto me, that I may live : for thy law *is* my delight.

78 Let the proud be ashamed ; for they dealt perversely with me without a cause : *but* I will meditate in thy precepts.

79 Let those that fear thee turn unto me, and those that have known thy testimonies.

80 Let my heart be sound in thy statutes ; that I be not ashamed.

We have now come to the tenth portion, which in each stanza begins with Jod, but it certainly does not treat of jots and titles and other trifles. Its subject would seem to be personal experience and its attractive influence upon others. The prophet is in deep sorrow, but looks to be delivered and made a blessing. Endeavouring to teach, the Psalmist first seeks to be taught (verse 73), persuades himself that he will be well received (74), and rehearses the testimony which he intends to bear (75). He prays for more experience (76, 77), for the baffling of the proud (78), for the gathering together of the godly to him (79), and for himself again that he may be fully equipped for his witness-bearing and may be sustained in it (80). This is the anxious yet hopeful cry of one who is heavily afflicted by cruel adversaries, and therefore makes his appeal to God as his only friend.

73. *"Thy hands have made me and fashioned me."* It is profitable to remember our creation, it is pleasant to see that the divine hand has had much to do with us, for it never moves apart from the divine thought. It excites reverence, gratitude, and affection towards God when we view him as our Maker, putting forth the careful skill and power of his hands in our forming and fashioning. He took a personal interest in us, making us with his own hands ; he was doubly thoughtful, for he is represented both as making and moulding us. In both giving existence and arranging existence he manifested love and wisdom ; and therefore we find reasons for praise, confidence, and expectation in our being and well-being. *"Give me understanding, that I may learn thy commandments."* As thou hast made me, teach me. Here is the vessel which thou hast fashioned ; Lord, fill it. Thou hast given me both soul and body ; grant me now thy grace that my soul may know thy will, and my body may join in the performance of it. The plea is very forcible ; it is an enlargement of the cry, " Forsake not the work of thine own hands." Without understanding the divine law and rendering obedience to it we are imperfect and useless ; but we may reasonably hope that the great Potter will complete his work and give the finishing touch to it by imparting to it sacred knowledge and holy practice. If God had roughly made us, and had not also elaborately fashioned us, this argument would lose much of its force ; but surely from the delicate art and marvellous skill which the Lord has shown in the formation of the human body, we may infer that he is prepared to take equal pains with the soul till it shall perfectly bear his image.

A man without a mind is an idiot, the mere mockery of a man ; and a mind without grace is wicked, the sad perversion of a mind. We pray that we may not be left without a spiritual judgment : for this the Psalmist prayed in verse 66, and he here pleads for it again ; there is no true knowing and keeping of the commandments without it. Fools can sin ; but only those who are taught of God can be holy. We often speak of gifted men ; but he has the best gifts to whom God has given a sanctified understanding wherewith to know and prize the ways of the Lord. Note well that David's prayer for understanding is not for the sake of speculative knowledge, and the gratification of his curiosity : he desires an enlightened judgment that he may learn God's commandments, and so become obedient and holy. This is the best of learning. A man may abide in the College where this science is taught all his days, and yet cry out for ability to learn more. The commandment of God is exceeding broad, and so it affords scope for the most vigorous and instructed mind : in fact, no man has by nature an understanding capable of compassing so wide a field, and hence the prayer, " give me understanding " ;—as much as to say—I can learn other things with the mind I have, but thy law is so pure, so perfect, spiritual and sublime, that I need to have my mind enlarged before I can become proficient in it. He appeals to his maker to do this, as if he felt that no power short of that which made him could make him wise unto holiness. We need a new creation, and who can grant us that but the Creator himself ? He who made us to live must make us to learn ; he who gave us power to stand must give us grace to understand. Let us each one breathe to heaven the prayer of this verse ere we advance a step further, for we shall be lost even in these petitions unless we pray our way through them, and cry to God for understanding.

74. "*They that fear thee will be glad when they see me : because I have hoped in thy word.*" When a man of God obtains grace for himself he becomes a blessing to others, especially if that grace has made him a man of sound understanding and holy knowledge. God-fearing men are encouraged when they meet with experienced believers. A hopeful man is a God-send when things are declining or in danger. When the hopes of one believer are fulfilled his companions are cheered and established, and led to hope also. It is good for the eyes to see a man whose witness is that the Lord is true ; it is one of the joys of saints to hold converse with their more advanced brethren. The fear of God is not a left-handed grace, as some have called it ; it is quite consistent with gladness ; for if even the sight of a comrade gladdens the God-fearing, how glad must they be in the presence of the Lord himself ! We do not only meet to share each others' burdens, but to partake in each others' joys, and some men contribute largely to the stock of mutual gladness. Hopeful men bring gladness with them. Despondent spirits spread the infection of depression, and hence few are glad to see them, while those whose hopes are grounded upon God's word carry sunshine in their faces, and are welcomed by their fellows. There are professors whose presence scatters sadness, and the godly quietly steal out of their company : may this never be the case with us.

75. "*I know, O Lord, that thy judgments are right.*" He who would learn most must be thankful for what he already knows, and be willing to confess it to the glory of God. The Psalmist had been sorely tried, but he had continued to hope in God under his trial, and now he avows his conviction that he had been justly and wisely chastened. This he not only thought but knew, so that he was positive about it, and spoke without a moment's hesitation. Saints are sure about the rightness of their troubles, even when they cannot see the intent of them. It made the godly glad to hear David say this, "*And that thou in faithfulness hast afflicted me.*" Because love required severity, therefore the Lord exercised it. It was not because God was unfaithful that the believer found himself in a sore strait, but for just the opposite reason : it was the faithfulness of God to his covenant which brought the chosen one under the rod. It might not be needful that others should be tried just then ; but it was necessary to the Psalmist, and therefore the Lord did not withhold the blessing. Our heavenly Father is no Eli : he will not suffer his children to sin without rebuke, his love is too intense for that. The man who makes the confession of this verse is already progressing in the school of grace, and is learning the commandments. This third verse of the section corresponds to the third of Teth (67), and in a degree to several other verses which make the thirds in their octaves.

76. "*Let, I pray thee, thy merciful kindness be for my comfort, according to thy word unto thy servant.*" Having confessed the righteousness of the Lord, he now appeals to his mercy, and while he does not ask that the rod may be removed, he earnestly begs for comfort under it. Righteousness and faithfulness afford us no consolation if we cannot also taste of mercy, and, blessed be God, this is promised us in the word, and therefore we may expect it. The words " merciful kindness," are a happy combination, and express exactly what we need in affliction : mercy to forgive the sin, and kindness to sustain under the sorrow. With these we can

be comfortable in the cloudy and dark day, and without them we are wretched indeed ; for these, therefore, let us pray unto the Lord, whom we have grieved by our sin, and let us plead the word of his grace as our sole reason for expecting his favour. Blessed be his name, notwithstanding our faults we are still his servants, and we serve a compassionate Master. Some read the last clause, " according to thy saying unto thy servant " ; some special saying of the Lord was remembered and pleaded : can we not remember some such " faithful saying," and make it the groundwork of our petitioning ? That phrase, " according to thy word," is a very favourite one ; it shows the motive for mercy and the manner of mercy. Our prayers are according to the mind of God when they are according to the word of God.

77. *"Let thy tender mercies come unto me, that I may live."* He was so hard pressed that he was at death's door if God did not succour him. He needed not only mercy, but " mercies," and these must be of a very gracious and considerate kind, even " tender mercies," for he was sore with his wounds. These gentle favours must be of the Lord's giving, for nothing less would suffice ; and they must " come " all the way to the sufferer's heart, for he was not able to journey after them ; all he could do was to sigh out, " Oh that they would come." If deliverance did not soon come, he felt ready to expire, and yet he told us but a verse or so ago that he hoped in God's word : how true it is that hope lives on when death seems written on all besides. A heathen said, " dum spiro spero," while I breathe I hope ; but the Christian can say, " dum expiro spero," even when I expire I still expect the blessing. Yet no true child of God can live without the tender mercy of the Lord ; it is death to him to be under God's displeasure. Notice, again, the happy combination of the words of our English version. Was there ever a sweeter sound than this— " tender mercies " ? He who has been grievously afflicted, and yet tenderly succoured is the only man who knows the meaning of such choice language.

How truly we live when tender mercy comes to us. Then we do not merely exist, but live ; we are lively, full of life, vivacious, and vigorous. We know not what life is till we know God. Some are said to die by the visitation of God, but we live by it.

"For thy law is my delight." O blessed faith ! He is no mean believer who rejoices in the law even when its broken precepts cause him to suffer. To delight in the word when it rebukes us, is proof that we are profiting under it. Surely this is a plea which will prevail with God, however bitter our griefs may be ; if we still delight in the law of the Lord he cannot let us die, he must and will cast a tender look upon us and comfort our hearts.

78. *"Let the proud be ashamed."* He begged that the judgments of God might no longer fall upon himself, but upon his cruel adversaries. God will not suffer those who hope in his word to be put to shame, for he reserves that reward for haughty spirits : they shall yet be overtaken with confusion, and become the subjects of contempt, while God's afflicted ones shall again lift up their heads. Shame is for the proud, for it is a shameful thing to be proud. Shame is not for the holy, for there is nothing in holiness to be ashamed of.

"For they dealt perversely with me without a cause." Their malice was wanton, he had not provoked them. Falsehood was employed to forge an accusation against him ; they had to bend his actions out of their true shape before they could assail his character. Evidently the Psalmist keenly felt the malice of his foes. His consciousness of innocence with regard to them created a burning sense of injustice, and he appealed to the righteous Lord to take his part and clothe his false accusers with shame. Probably he mentioned them as " the proud," because he knew that the Lord always takes vengeance on proud men, and vindicates the cause of those whom they oppress. Sometimes he mentions the proud, and sometimes the wicked, but he always means the same persons ; the words are interchangeable : he who is proud is sure to be wicked, and proud persecutors are the worst of wicked men.

"But I will meditate in thy precepts." He would leave the proud in God's hands, and give himself up to holy studies and contemplations. To obey the divine precepts we have need to know them, and think much of them, hence this persecuted saint felt that meditation must be his chief employment. He would study the law of God and not the law of retaliation. The proud are not worth a thought. The worst injury they can do us is to take us away from our devotions ; let us baffle them by keeping all the closer to our God when they are most malicious in their onslaughts.

In a similar position to this we have met with the proud in other octaves, and shall meet them yet again. They are evidently a great plague to the Psalmist but he rises above them.

79. "*Let those that fear thee turn unto me, and those that have known thy testimonies.*" Perhaps the tongue of slander had alienated some of the godly, and probably the actual faults of David had grieved many more. He begs God to turn to him, and then to turn his people towards him. Those who are right with God are also anxious to be right with his children. David craved the love and sympathy of gracious men of all grades,—of those who were beginners in grace, and of those who were mature in piety—"those that fear thee," and "those that have known thy testimonies." We cannot afford to lose the love of the least of the saints, and if we have lost their esteem we may most properly pray to have it restored. David was the leader of the godly party in the nation, and it wounded him to the heart when he perceived that those who feared God were not as glad to see him as aforetime they had been. He did not bluster and say that if they could do without *him* he could very well do without *them ;* but he so deeply felt the value of their sympathy, that he made it a matter of prayer that the Lord would turn their hearts to him again. Those who are dear to God, and are instructed in his word, should be very precious in our eyes, and we should do our utmost to be upon good terms with them.

David has two descriptions for the saints, they are God-fearing and God-knowing. They possess both devotion and instruction ; they have both the spirit and the science of true religion. We know some believers who are gracious, but not intelligent ; and, on the other hand, we also know certain professors who have all head and no heart : he is the man who combines devotion with intelligence. We neither care for devout dunces nor for intellectual icebergs. When fearing and knowing walk hand in hand they cause men to be thoroughly furnished unto every good work. If these are my choice companions I may hope that I am one of their order. Let such persons ever turn to me because they find in me congenial company.

80. "*Let my heart be sound in thy statutes ; that I be not ashamed.*" This is even more important than to be held in esteem by good men. This is the root of the matter. If the heart be sound in obedience to God, all is well, or will be well. If right at heart we are right in the main. If we be not sound before God, our name for piety is an empty sound. Mere profession will fail, and undeserved esteem will disappear like a bubble when it bursts ; only sincerity and truth will endure in the evil day. He who is right at heart has no reason for shame, and he never shall have any ; hypocrites ought to be ashamed now, and they shall one day be put to shame without end ; their hearts are rotten, and their names shall rot. This eightieth verse is a variation of the prayer of the seventy-third verse ; there he sought sound understanding, here he goes deeper, and begs for a sound heart. Those who have learned their own frailty by sad experience, are led to dive beneath the surface, and cry to the Lord for truth in the inward parts. In closing the consideration of these eight verses, let us join with the writer in the prayer, "Let my heart be sound in thy statutes."

NOTES ON VERSES 73 TO 80.

In this section each verse begins with the Hebrew letter *Jod*, or *i*, the smallest letter in the Hebrew alphabet, called in Matthew v. 18, *jot*; one jot or tittle shall in no wise pass from the law.—*Albert Barnes.*

Verses 73—80.—The usual account of this section, as given by the mediæval theologians, is that it is the prayer of man to be restored to his state of original innocence and wisdom by being conformed to the image of Christ. And this squares with the obvious meaning, which is partly a petition for divine grace and partly an assertion that the example of piety and resignation in trouble is attractive enough to draw men's hearts on towards God, a truth set forth at once by the Passion, and by the lives of all those saints who have tried to follow it.—*Neale and Littledale.*

Verse 73.—"*Thy hands have made me and fashioned me,*" etc. This verse hath a petition for understanding and a reason with it : I am the workmanship of thine hands, therefore give me understanding. There is no man but favours the works of his hands. And shall not the Lord much more love his creatures, especially man, his most excellent creature ? whom, if ye consider according to the fashion of his body, ye shall find nothing on earth more precious than he ; but in that which is not seen, namely, his soul, he is much more beautiful. So you see, David's reasoning is very effectual ; all one as if he should say as he doth elsewhere, " Forsake not, O Lord, the work of thine hands "; thou art my author and maker ; thine help I seek, and the help of none other.

No man can rightly seek good things from God, if he consider not what good the Lord hath already done to him. But many are in this point so ignorant, that they know not how wonderfully God did make them ; and therefore can neither bless him, nor seek from him, as from their Creator and Conserver. But this argument, drawn from our first creation, no man can rightly use, but he who is through grace partaker of the second creation ; for all the privileges of our first creation we have lost by our fall. So that now by nature it is no comfort to us, nor matter of our hope, that God did make us ; but rather matter of our fear and distrust, that we have mismade ourselves, have lost his image, and are not now like unto that which God created us in the beginning.—*William Cowper.*

Verse 73.—"*Thy hands have made me and fashioned me,*" etc. Mark here two things : first, that in making his prayer for holy understanding, he justly accuseth himself and all others of blindness, which proceeded not from the Creator, but from man corrupted. Secondly, that even from his creation he conceived hope that God would continue his work begun in him, because God leaveth not his work, and therefore he beggeth God to bestow new grace upon him, and to finish that which he had begun in him.—*Thomas Wilcocks*, 1586.

Verse 73.—Hugo ingeniously notices in the different verbs of this verse the particular vices to be shunned : ingratitude, when it is said, "*Thy hands have made me*"; pride, "*and fashioned me*"; confidence in his own judgment, "*give me understanding*"; prying inquisitiveness, "*that I may learn thy commandments.*"

Verse 73.—"*Thy hands.*" Hilary and Ambrose think that by the plural "*hands*" is intimated that there is a more exact and perfect workmanship in man, and as if it were with greater labour and skill he had been formed by God, because *after the image and likeness of God :* and that it is not written that any other thing but man was made by God with both hands, for he saith in Isaiah, " Mine hand also hath laid the foundation of the earth ": Isa. xlviii. 13.*—*John Lorinus*, 1569—1634.

Verse 73.—"*Thy hands.*" Oh, look upon the *wounds* of thine hands, and forget not the *work* of thine hands : so Queen Elizabeth prayed.—*John Trapp.*

Verse 73.—Some refer the verb עשה, "*made*," to the soul, כונן, "*fashioned*," to the body.—*D. H. Mollerus.*

Verse 73.—"*Made me and fashioned me : give me understanding.*" The greatness of God is no hindrance to his intercourse with us, for one special part of the divine greatness is to be able to condescend to the littleness of created beings, seeing that

---

* This, however, is an error, as Augustine notes ; for it is written, " The heavens are the work of thine hands." Ps. cii. 25.—C. H. S.

creaturehood must, from its very nature, have this littleness ; inasmuch as God must ever be God, and man must ever be man : the ocean must ever be the ocean, the drop must ever be the drop. The greatness of God compassing our littlenesses about, as the heavens the earth, and fitting into it on every side, as the air into all parts of the earth, is that which makes the intercourse so complete and blessed : " In his hand is the soul of every living thing, and the breath of all mankind " (Job xii. 10). Such is his nearness to, such is his intimacy with, the works of his hands.

It is nearness, not distance, that the name Creator implies ; and the simple fact of his having *made* us is the assurance of his desire to bless us and to hold intercourse with us. Communication between the thing made and its maker is involved in the very idea of creation. *"Thy hands have made me and fashioned me : give me understanding, that I may learn thy commandments."* " Faithful Creator " is his name (1 Pet. iv. 19), and as such we appeal to him, " Forsake not the work of thine own hands " (Ps. cxxxviii. 8).—*Horatius Bonar, in "The Rent Veil,"* 1875.

Verse 73. — *" Give me understanding,"* etc. The book of God is like the apothecary's shop, there is no wound but therein is a remedy ; but if a stranger come unto the apothecary's shop, though all these things be there, yet he cannot tell where they are, but the apothecary himself knoweth ; so in the Scriptures, there are cures for any infirmities ; there is comfort against any sorrows, and by conferring chapter with chapter, we shall understand them. The Scriptures are not wanting to us, but we to ourselves ; let us be conversant in them, and we shall understand them, when great clerks who are negligent remain in darkness.—*Richard Stock.*

Verse 73.—*"Give me understanding."* Let us pray unto God that he would open our understandings ; that as he hath given us consciences to guide us, so also he would give eyes to these guides that they may be able to direct us aright. The truth is, it is God only that can soundly enlighten our consciences ; and therefore let us pray unto him to do it. All our studying, and hearing, and reading, and conferring will never be able to do it ; it is only in the power of him who made us to do it. He who made our consciences, he only can give them this heavenly light of true knowledge and right understanding ; and therefore let us seek earnestly to him for it.—*William Fenner,* 1600—1640.

Verse 73.—*"That I may learn thy commandments."* That he might *learn* them so as to know the sense and meaning of them, their purity and spirituality ; and so as to do them from a principle of love, in faith, and to the glory of God : for it is not a bare learning of them by heart or committing them to memory, nor a mere theory of them, but the practice of them in faith and love, which is here meant.—*John Gill.*

Verses 73, 74.—From these verses, learn, 1. Albeit nothing can satisfy unbelief, yet true faith will make use of the most common benefit of creation to strengthen itself : *"Thine hands have made me and fashioned me."* 2. It is a good way of reasoning with God, to ask another gift, because we have received one ; and because he hath given common benefits, to ask that he would give us also saving graces : *"Thy hands have made me and fashioned me : give me understanding, that I may learn thy commandments."* 3. Seeing that God is our Creator, and that the end of our creation is to serve God, we may confidently ask whatsoever grace may enable us to serve him, as the Psalmist's example doth teach us. . . . 4. It should be the joy of all believers to see one of their number sustained and borne up in his sufferings ; for in the proof and example of one sufferer a pawn is given to all the rest, that God will help them in like case : *"They that fear thee will be glad when they see me."*—*David Dickson.*

Vese 74.—*"They that fear thee will be glad,"* etc. They who *"fear God "* are naturally *"glad when they see "* and converse with one like themselves ; but more especially so, when it is one whose faith and patience have carried him through troubles, and rendered him victorious over temptations; one who hath " *hoped in God's word,"* and hath not been disappointed. Every such instance affordeth fresh encouragement to all those, who, in the course of their welfare, are to undergo like troubles, and to encounter like temptations. In all our trials let us, therefore, remember, that our brethren, as well as ourselves, are deeply interested in the event, which may either strengthen or weaken the hands of the multitudes.—*George Horne.*

Verse 74.—*"They that fear thee will be glad when they see me,"* etc. How comfortable it is for the heirs of promise to see one another, or meet together : *aspectus boni viri delectat*, the very look of a good man is delightful : it is a pleasure to converse with those that are careful to please God, and fearful to offend him. How much affected they are with one another's mercies : *" they will be glad when they see me,"* since I have obtained an event answerable to my hope. They shall come and look upon me as a monument and spectacle of the mercy and truth of God. But what mercy had he received ? The context seemeth to carry it for grace to obey God's commandments ; that was the prayer immediately preceding, to be instructed and taught in God's law (ver. 73). Now they will rejoice to see my holy behaviour, how I have profited and glorified God in that behalf. The Hebrew writers render the reason, " Because then I shall be able to instruct them in those statutes, when they shall see me, their king, study the law of God." It may be expounded of any other blessing or benefit God had given according to his hope ; and I rather understand it thus, they will be glad to see him sustained, supported, and borne out in his troubles and sufferings. " They will be glad when they shall see in me a notable example of the fruit of hoping in thy grace."—*Thomas Manton.*

Verse 74.—*"Because I have hoped in thy word."* And have not been disappointed. The Vulgate rendereth it *supersperavi*, I have over-hoped ; and then Aben-Ezra glosseth, *"I have hoped in all thy decree" ;* even that of afflicting me, as in the next verse.—*John Trapp.*

Verse 75.—*"I know, O LORD, that thy judgments are right."* In very early life the tree of knowledge seemed a very fine, a glorious tree in my sight ; but how many mistakes have I made upon that subject ! And how many are the mistakes which yet abound upon that which we are pleased to call knowledge, in common speech. He that hath read the classics ; he that hath dipped into mathematical science ; he that is versed in history, and grammar, and common elocution ; he that is apt and ready to solve some knotty question, and versed in the ancient lore of learning, is thought to be a man of knowledge ; and so he is, compared with the ignorant mass of mankind. But what is all this compared with the knowledge in my text ? Knowledge of which few of the learned, as they are called, have the least acquaintance with at all.

"I know "—What, David ? what do you know ?—" I know, O Lord, that thy judgments are right, and that thou in faithfulness hast afflicted me."

Fond as I may yet be of other speculations, I would rather, much rather, possess the knowledge of this man in this text, than have the largest acquaintance with the whole circle of the sciences, as it is proudly called. . . . I am apprehensive that, in the first clause, the Psalmist speaks, in general, of the ordinances, appointments, providences, and judgments of God ; and the assertion is, he doth know that they are right, that they are equitable, that they are wise, that they are fair, and that they are not to be found fault with ; and that though men, through folly, bring themselves into distress, and then their hearts fret against God. He was blessed with superior understanding. He excepts nothing : " I know that *all* thy judgments are right." Then, in the latter part of the text, he makes the matter personal. It might be said, it is an easy thing for you so to think when you see the revolutions of kingdoms, the tottering of thrones, the distresses of some mortals, and the pains of others, that they are all right. " Yes," saith he, " but I have the same persuasion about all my own sorrows ; I do know that in faithfulness thou hast afflicted *me*."— *From a Sermon by John Martin*, 1817.

Verse 75.—*"I know, O LORD, that thy judgments are right,"* etc. The text is in the form of an address to God. We often find this in David, that, when he would express some deep feeling, or some point of spiritual experience, he does so in this way—addressing himself to God. Those who love God delight to hold communion with him ; and there are some feelings which the spiritual mind finds peculiar comfort and pleasure in telling to God himself. *"I know, O LORD, that thy judgments are right."* God orders all things, and his *"judgments"* here mean his general orderings, decisions, dealings—not afflictions only, though including them. And when the Psalmist says, *"thy judgments,"* he means especially God's judgments towards *him*, God's dealings with him, and thus all that had happened to him, or should happen to him. For in the Psalmist's creed there was no such thing as chance. God ordered all that befell him, and he loved to think so He expresses a sure and happy confidence in all that God did, and would do, with regard to him. He trusted fully in God's wisdom, God's power, God's love. *"I know thy judgments are right"*—quite right, right in every way, without one single point that might have been better, perfectly wise and good. He shows the firmest persuasion of this. "*I know,*" he says, not merely, "I think." But these very words, "I *know,*" clearly show that this was a matter of faith, not of sight. For he does not say, "I can *see* that thy judgments are right," but "I *know.*" The meaning plainly is, "Though I cannot see all—though there are some things in thy dealings which I cannot fully understand—yet I believe, I am persuaded, and thus I *know,* O Lord, that thy judgments are right."

"Thy judgments." Not some of them, but all. He takes into view all God's dealings with him, and says of them without exception, "*I know, O Lord, that thy judgments are right.*" When the things that happen to us are plainly for our comfort and good, as many of them are, then we thankfully receive what God thus sends to us, and own him as the Giver of all, and bless him for his gracious dealing ; and this is right. But all the faith required for this (and some faith there is in it) is to own God as dealing with us, instead of thanklessly receiving the gifts with no thought of the Giver. It is a far higher degree of faith, that says of *all* God's dealings, even when seemingly not for our happiness, "*I know that thy judgments are right.*"

Yet this is the meaning here, or certainly the chief meaning. For though the word "*judgments*" does mean God's dealings of every kind, yet *here* the words that follow make it apply especially to God's afflictive dealings, that is, to those dealings of his that do not seem to be for our happiness ; "*I know, O Lord, that thy judgments are right, and that thou in faithfulness hast afflicted me.*" The judgments which the Psalmist chiefly had in view, and which he felt so sure were right, were not joys, but sorrows ; not things bestowed, but things taken away ; those blessings in disguise, those veiled mercies, those gifts clad in the garb of mourning, which God so often sends to his children. The Psalmist knew, and knew against all appearance to the contrary, that these judgments were "*right.*" Whatever they might be—losses, bereavements, disappointments, pain, sickness—they were right ; as right as the more manifest blessings which went before them ; quite right, perfectly right ; so right that they could not have been better ; just what were best ; and all because they were God's judgments. That one thing satisfied the Psalmist's mind, and set every doubt at rest. The dealings in themselves he might have doubted, but not him whose dealings they were. "*Thy* judgments." That settled all. "*And that thou in faithfulness hast afflicted me.*" This means that, in appointing trouble as his lot, God had dealt with him in faithfulness to his word, faithfulness to his purposes of mercy, with a faithful, not a weak love. He had sent him just what was most for his good, though not always what was most pleasing ; and in this he had shown himself faithful. Gently and lovingly does the Lord deal with his children. He gives no unnecessary pain ; but that which is needful he will not withhold.—*Francis Bourdillon,* 1881.

Verse 75.—*"Thy judgments."* There are *judicia oris,* and there are *judicia operis ;* the judgments of God's mouth, and the judgments of God's hands. Of the former there is mention at verse 13 : "With my lips have I declared all the judgments of thy mouth." And by these "*judgments*" are meant nothing else but the holy law of God, and his whole written word ; which everywhere in this Psalm are indifferently called his "statutes," his "commandments," his "precepts," his "testimonies," his "judgments." And the laws of God are therefore, amongst other reasons, called by the name of "*judgments,*" because by them we come to have a right judgment whereby to discern between good and evil. We could not otherwise with any certainty judge what was meet for us to do, and what was needful for us to shun. *A lege tua intellexi,* at verse 104 : "By the law have I gotten understanding." St. Paul confesseth (Rom. vii.), that he had never rightly known what sin was if it had not been for the law ; and he instanceth in that of lust, *which he had not known to be a sin if the law* had not said, "thou shalt not covet." And no question but these "*judgments,*" these *judicia oris,* are all "*right*" too ; for it were unreasonable to think that God should make that a rule of right to us, which were itself not right. We have both the name (that of "*judgments ;*") and the thing too, (that they are "*right*") in the 19th Psalm ; where having highly commended the law of God, under the several appellations of the "law," testimonies, statutes and commandments, verses 7 and 8, the prophet then concludeth under this name of " judgments," verse 9 : " The judgments of the Lord are true and righteous altogether."

Besides these *judicia oris*, which are God's judgments of *direction*, there are also *judicia operis*, which are his judgments for *correction*. And these do ever include *aliquid pænale*, something inflicted upon us by Almighty God, as it were by way of punishment ; something that breedeth in us trouble or grief. The apostle saith (Heb. xii.) that every chastening is grievous ; and so it is, more or less ; or else it could be to us no punishment. And these, again, are of two sorts ; yet not distinguished so much by the things themselves that are inflicted, as by the condition of the persons on whom they are inflicted, and especially by the affection and intention of God that inflicteth them. For all, whether public calamities that light upon whole nations, cities, or other greater or lesser societies of men (such as are pestilences, famine, war, inundations, unseasonable weather, and the like ;) or private afflictions, that light upon particular families or persons, (as sickness, poverty disgrace, injuries, death of friends, and the like ;) all these, and whatsoever other of either kind, may undergo a twofold consideration ; in either of which they may not unfitly be termed the judgments of God, though in different respects.

Now we see the several sorts of God's judgments : which of all these may we think is here meant ? If we should take them all in, the conclusion would hold them, and hold true too. *Judicia oris*, and *judicia operis ;* public and private judgments ; those plagues wherewith in fury he punisheth his enemies, and those rods wherewith in mercy he correcteth his children : most certain it is they are all " *right*." But yet I conceive those *judicia oris* not to be so properly meant in this place ; for the exegesis in the latter part of the verse (wherein what are here called *judgments* are there expounded by *troubles*) seemeth to exclude them, and to confine to the text in the proper intent thereof to these *judicia operis* only ; but yet to all them of what sort soever ; public or private, plagues or corrections. Of all which he pronounceth that they are " *right ;* " which is the predicate of the conclusion : "*I know, O Lord, that thy judgments are right*."—*Robert Sanderson.*

Verse 75.—"*Thou in faithfulness hast afflicted me.*" Mark the emphasis : he doth not barely acknowledge that God was faithful, though notwithstanding he had afflicted him, but faithful in sending the afflictions. Affliction and trouble are not only consistent with God's love plighted in the covenant of grace ; but they are parts and branches of the new-covenant administration. God is not only faithful notwithstanding afflictions, but faithful in sending them. There is a difference between these two : the one is like an exception to the rule, *quæ firmat regulam in non exceptis :* the other makes it a part of the rule, God cannot be faithful without doing all things that tend to our good and eternal welfare. The conduct of his providence is one part of the covenant engagement ; as to pardon our sins, and sanctify us, and give us glory at the last, so to suit his providence as our need and profit require in the way to heaven. It is an act of his sovereign mercy which he hath promised to his people, to use such discipline as conduceth to their safety. In short, the cross is not an exception to the grace of the covenant, but a part of the grace of the covenant.

The cause of all afflictions is sin, therefore justice must be acknowledged : their end is repentance, and therefore faithfulness must be acknowledged. The end is not destruction and ruin, so afflictions would be acts of justice, as upon the wicked ; but that we may be fit to receive the promises, and so they are acts of faithfulness. —*Thomas Manton.*

Verse 75.—"*Thou in faithfulness hast afflicted me.*" That is with a sincere intention of doing me good. God thoroughly knows our constitution, what is noxious to our health, and what may remedy our distempers ; and therefore accordingly disposeth to us

Pro jucundis aptissima quæque *

instead of pleasant honey, he sometimes prescribes wholesome wormwood for us. We are ourselves greatly ignorant of what is conducible to our real good, and, were the choice of our condition wholly permitted to us, should make very foolish, very disadvantageous elections.

We should (be sure) all of us embrace a rich and plentiful estate ; when, as God knows, that would make us slothful and luxurious, swell us with pride and

---

* Juv. Sat. x. 349.

haughty thoughts, encumber us with anxious cares and expose us to dangerous temptations; would render us forgetful of ourselves and neglectful of him. Therefore he wisely disposeth poverty unto us; poverty, the mother of sobriety, the nurse of industry, the mistress of wisdom; which will make us understand ourselves and our dependence on him, and force us to have recourse unto his help. And is there not reason we should be thankful for the means by which we are delivered from those desperate mischiefs, and obtain these excellent advantages?

We should all (certainly) choose the favour and applause of man: but this. God also knows, would corrupt our minds with vain conceit, would intoxicate our fancies with spurious pleasure, would tempt us to ascribe immoderately to ourselves, and sacrilegiously to deprive God of his due honour. Therefore he advisedly suffers us to incur the disgrace and displeasure, the hatred and contempt of men; that so we may place our glory only in the hopes of his favour, and may pursue more earnestly the purer delights of a good conscience. And doth not this part of divine providence highly merit our thanks?

We would all climb into high places, not considering the precipices on which they stand, nor the vertiginousness of our own brains: but God keeps us safe in the humble valleys, allotting to us employments which we are more capable to manage.

We should perhaps insolently abuse power, were it committed to us: we should employ great parts on unwieldy projects, as many do, to the disturbance of others, and their own ruin: vast knowledge would cause us to overvalue ourselves and contemn others: enjoying continual health, we should not perceive the benefit thereof, nor be mindful of him that gave it. A suitable mediocrity therefore of these things the divine goodness allotteth unto us, that we may neither starve for want, nor surfeit with plenty.

In fine, the advantages arising from afflictions are so many, and so great, that it were easy to demonstrate that we have great reason, not only to be contented with, but to rejoice in, and to be very thankful for, all the crosses and vexations we meet with; to receive them cheerfully at God's hand, as the medicines of our soul, and the condiments of our fortune; as the arguments of his goodwill, and the instruments of virtue; as solid grounds of hope, and comfortable presages of future joy unto us.—*Isaac Barrow.*

Verse 75.—"*Thou in faithfulness hast afflicted me.*" When a father disowns and banishes a child, he corrects him no more. So God may let one whom he intends to destroy go unchastened; but never one with whom he is in covenant.—*William S. Plumer.*

Verse 75.—"*I know, O Lord,*" etc.

> Yet, Lord, in memory's fondest place
> I shrine those seasons sad,
> When, looking up, I saw thy face
> In kind austereness clad.
>
> I would not miss one sigh or tear,
> Heart-pang, or throbbing brow;
> Sweet was the chastisement severe,
> And sweet its memory now.
>
> Yes! let the fragrant scars abide,
> Love-tokens in thy stead,
> Faint shadows of the spear-pierced side,
> And thorn-encompassed head.
>
> And such thy tender force be still,
> When self would swerve or stray,
> Shaping to truth the froward will
> Along thy narrow way.
> —*John Henry Newman,* 1829.

Verse 76.—"*Let, I pray thee, thy merciful kindness be for my comfort.*" In the former verse he acknowledged that the Lord had afflicted him; now in this he prayeth the Lord to comfort him. This is strange that a man should seek comfort at the same hand that strikes him: it is the work of faith; nature will never teach us to do it. "Come, and let us return unto the Lord; for he hath spoiled, and he will heal us: he hath wounded, and he will bind us up." Again, we see that the crosses which God lays on his children, are not to confound, not to consume them ; only to prepare them for greater consolations. With this David sustained himself against Shimei's cursing ; " The Lord will look on my affliction, and do me good for this evil " : with this our Saviour comforts his disciples ; " Your mourning shall be turned into joy." As the last estate of Job was better than his first ; so shall the Lord render more to his children at the last than now at the first he takes from them : let us therefore bear his cross, as a preparative to comfort.—*William Cowper.*

Verse 76.—*"Let thy merciful kindness be for my comfort."* Several of the preceding verses have spoken of affliction (verses 67, 71, 75). The Psalmist now presents his petition for alleviation under it. But of what kind ? He does not ask to have it removed. He does not " beseech the Lord, that it might depart from him " : 2 Cor. xii. 8. No. His repeated acknowledgments of the supports vouchsafed under it, and the benefits he had derived from it, had reconciled him to commit its measure and continuance to the Lord. All that he needs, and all that he asks for, is a sense of his *" merciful kindness "* upon his soul. Thus he submits to his justice in his accumulated trials, and expects consolation under them solely upon the ground of his free favour.—*Charles Bridges.*

Verse 76.—*"Let thy merciful kindness,"* etc. Let me derive my comfort and happiness from a diffusion of thy love and mercy, חסדך, *chasdecha,* thy exuberant goodness through my soul.—*Adam Clarke.*

Verse 76.—*"According to thy word unto thy servant."* If his promise did not please him, why did he make it ? If our reliance on the promise did not please him, why did his goodness work it ? It would be inconsistent with his goodness to mock his creature, and it would be the highest mockery to publish his word, and create a temper in the heart of his supplicant suited to his promise, which he never intended to satisfy. He can as little wrong his creature as wrong himself, and therefore he can never disappoint that faith which after his own methods casts itself into the arms of his kindness, and is his own workmanship, and calls him author. That goodness which imparted itself so freely to the irrational creation will not neglect those nobler creatures that put their trust in him. This renders God a fit object for trust and confidence.—*Stephen Charnock.*

Verse 76.—*"According to thy word."* David had a particular promise of a particular benefit ; to wit, the kingdom of Israel. And this promise God performed unto him ; but his comfort stood not in it ; for Saul before him had the kingdom, but the promises of mercy belonged not to him, and therefore, when God forsook him, his kingdom could not sustain him. But David here depends upon the general promises of God's mercy made to his children ; wherein he acknowledgeth a particular promise of mercy made to him. For the general promises of mercy and grace made in the gospel are by faith made particular to every believer.—*William Cowper.*

Verse 76.—*"Thy word unto thy servant."* Here we may use the eunuch's question : " Of whom speaketh the prophet this, of himself or of some other man ? " Of himself questionless, under the denomination of God's servant. But then the question returneth,—Is it a word of promise made to himself in particular, or to God's servants in the general ? Some say the former, the promises brought to him by Nathan. I incline to the latter, and it teacheth us these three truths :—

1st. That God's servants only are capable of the sweet effects of his mercy and the comforts of his promises. Who are God's servants ? (1) Such as own his right and are sensible of his interest in them : " God, whose I am, and whom I serve " (Acts xxviii. 23). (2) Such as give up themselves to him, renouncing all other masters. Renounce we must, for we were once under another master (Rom. vi. 17 ; Matt. vi. 24 ; Rom. vi. 13 ; 1 Chron. xxx. 8). (3) Such as accordingly frame themselves to do his work sincerely : " serve with my spirit " (Rom. i. 9) ; and, " in newness of spirit " (Rom. vii. 6), even as becomes those who are renewed by the Spirit : diligently (Acts xxvi. 7), and universally (Luke i. 74, 75), and wait upon him for grace to do so (Heb. xii. 28). These are capable of comfort. The book of God speaketh no comfort to persons that live in sin, but to God's servants, such as do not live as if they were at their own disposal, but at God's beck. If he say go, they go. They give up themselves to be and do what God will have them to be and do.

2ndly. If we have the benefit of the promise, we must thrust in ourselves under one title or other among those to whom the promise is made ; if not as God's children, yet as God's servants. Then the promise is as sure to us as if our name were in it.

3rdly. All God's servants have common grounds of comfort : every one of God's servants may plead with God as David doth. The comforts of the word are the common portion of God's people.—*Thomas Manton.*

Verse 76.—*"Thy word unto thy servant."* Our Master has passed his word to all his servants that he will be kind to them, and they may plead it with him.—*Matthew Henry.*

Verse 77.—*"Let thy tender mercies come unto me, that I may live."* If we mark narrowly we shall find that David here seeks another sort of mercy than he sought before. For first he sought mercy to forgive his sins ; then he sought mercy to comfort him in his troubles ; now he seeks mercy to live, and sin no more. Alas, many seek the first mercy, of remission ; and the second mercy of consolation in trouble, who are altogether careless of the third mercy, to live well. It is a great mercy of God to amend thy life : where this is not, let no man think he hath received either of the former. It is a great mercy of God, which not only pardons evil that is done, but strengthens us also to further good that we have not done ; and this is the mercy which here David seeks.—*William Cowper.*

Verse 77.—*"Let thy tender mercies come unto me,"* etc. The mercies of God are *" tender mercies,"* they are the mercies of a father to his children, nay, tender as the compassion of a mother over the son of her womb. They *"come unto"* us, when we are not able to go to them. By them alone we *" live "* the life of faith, of love, of joy and gladness. And to such as *" delight "* in his law, God will grant these mercies, and this life ; he will give them pardon, and, by so doing, he will give them life from the dead.—*George Horne.*

Verse 77.—*"Let thy tender mercies,"* etc. Taking the more literal rendering, the words express high confidence—" Thy tender mercies *shall* come unto me, and I shall live ; for thy law is my delight." Had the believer nothing but his own deserts to support his plea at the throne of grace, he could never rise into this high confidence. He goes upon the foundation of the divine goodness, manifested through the anointed One, and he goes surely.—*John Stephen.*

Verse 77.—*"Come."* Coming to him noteth a personal and effectual application. 1st. A personal application, as in the 41st verse of this Psalm : " Let thy mercies come also unto me, O Lord, even thy salvation, according to thy word." David would not be forgotten, or left out or lost in the throng of mankind, when mercy was distributing the blessing to them. 2ndly. Effectual application : which signifieth, 1. The removal of obstacles and hindrances ; 2. The obtaining the fruits and effects of this mercy.

First. The removing of obstacles. Till there be a way made, the mercy of God cannot come at us ; for the way is barricaded and shut up by our sins : as the Lord maketh a way for his anger (Ps. lxxviii. 50), by removing the hindrances, so the Lord maketh way for his mercy, or mercy maketh way for itself, when it removeth the obstruction. Sin is the great hindrance of mercy. We ourselves raise the mists and the clouds which intercept the light of God's countenance ; we build up the partition wall which separates between God and us ; yet mercy finds the way.

Secondly. The obtaining the fruits of mercy . . . . It is not enough to hear somewhat of God's saving mercies ; but we should beg that they may come unto us, be effectually and sensibly communicated unto us, that we may have experience of them in our own souls. A man that hath read of honey, or heard of honey, may know the sweetness of it by guess and imagination ; but a man that hath tasted of honey knoweth the sweetness of it in truth : so, by reading and hearing of the grace and mercy of God in Christ, we may guess that it is a sweet thing ; but he that hath had an experimental proof of the sweet effects and fruits of it in his own heart perceives that all which is spoken of God's pardoning and comforting of sinners is verified in himself.—*Thomas Manton.*

Verse 77.—*"Thy law is my delight."* A child of God, though he cannot serve the Lord perfectly, yet he serves him willingly ; his will is in the law of the Lord ; he is not a pressed soldier, but a volunteer. By the beating of this pulse we may judge whether there be spiritual life in us or no. David professeth that God's law was his delight ; he had his crown to delight in, he had his music to delight in ; but the love he had to God's law did drown all other delights ; as the joy of harvest and vintage exceeds the joy of gleaning.—*Thomas Watson.*

Verse 78.—*"Let the proud be ashamed,"* etc. Here is the just recompense of his pride. He would fain have honour and pre-eminence, but God will not give them unto him : he flies shame and contempt, but God shall pour them upon him. *"For they dealt perversely with me without a cause."* David complains of the wicked and false dealing of his enemies against him ; and his prayer is written to uphold us in the like temptation. For Satan is alway like himself, hating them whom the Lord loveth. He can scarce be worse, he can never be better ; and therefore with restless malice stirs he up all his cursed instruments in whom he reigns, to persecute those who are loved and protected of the Lord. *"But I will meditate in thy precepts."* David's enemies fought against him with the weapons of the flesh, wickedness and falsehood : he withstands them by the armour of the Spirit ; not meeting wickedness with wickedness, and falsehood with falsehood. For if we fight against Satan with Satan's weapons he will soon overcome us ; but if we put upon us the complete armour of God to resist him, he shall flee from us.—*William Cowper.*

Verse 78.—*"Let the proud be ashamed."* That is, that they may not prosper or succeed in their attempts ; for men are ashamed when they are disappointed. All their endeavours for the extirpation of God's people are vain and fruitless, and those things which they have subtilely devised have not that effect which they propounded unto themselves. *"For they dealt perversely with me without a cause."* The Septuagint have it ἀδίκως, unjustly. Ainsworth readeth, " With falsehood they have depraved me." It implieth two things : first, that they pretended a cause ; but, secondly, David avoucheth his innocency to God ; and so, without any guilt of his, they accused, defamed, condemned his actions, as is usual in such cases. When the proud are troublesome and injurious to God's people the saints may boldly commend their cause to God. . . . The Lord may be appealed unto upon a double account ; partly, as he is an enemy to the proud, and as a friend to the humble (James iv. 6 ; Ps. cxxxviii. 6) ; partly, as he is the portion of the afflicted and oppressed (Ps. cxl. 12). When Satan stirreth up his instruments to hate those whom the Lord loveth, the Lord will stir up his power to help and defend them. Is not this a revengeful prayer ?

Answer, No. 1st. Because those who pray it are seeking their own deliverance, that they may more freely serve God by consequence. Indeed, by God's showing mercy to his people, the pride of wicked ones is suppressed (verse 134) ; but mercy is the main object of the prayer.

2ndly. As it concerneth his enemies, he expresseth it in mild terms—that they may " be ashamed"; that is, disappointed, in their counsels, hopes, machinations, and endeavours. And therefore it is not against the persons of his enemies, but their plots and enterprises. In such cases shame and disappointment may even do them good. They think to bring in the total suppression of God's people, but that would harden them in their sins ; therefore God's people desire that he would not let their innocency be trampled upon, but disappoint their adversaries, that the proud may be ashamed in the failing of their attempts.

3rdly. The prayers of the righteous for the overthrow of the wicked, are a kind of prophecies ; so that, in praying, David doth in effect foretell, that such as dealt perversely should soon be ashamed, since a good cause will not always be oppressed : " But he shall appear to your joy, and they shall be ashamed " (Isa. lxvi. 5).

4thly. Saints have a liberty to imprecate vengeance, but such as must be used sparingly and with great caution : " Let them be confounded and consumed that are adversaries to my soul " (Ps. lxxi. 13). Malicious enemies may be expressly prayed against.—*Thomas Manton.*

Verse 78.—*"Let the proud be ashamed."* This suggests a word to the wicked. Take heed that by your implacable hatred to the truth and church of God you do not engage her prayers against you. These imprecatory prayers of the saints, when shot at the right mark, and duly put up, are murdering pieces, and strike dead where they light. " Shall not God avenge his own elect, which cry day and night unto him, though he bear long with them ? I tell you that he will avenge them speedily." Luke xviii. 7, 8. They are not empty words—as the imprecations of the wicked poured into the air, and there vanishing with their breath—but are received into heaven, and shall be sent back with thunder and lightning upon the pates of the wicked. David's prayer unravelled Ahithophel's fine-spun policy, and twisted his halter for him. The prayers of the saints are more to be feared—as once a great person said and felt—than an army of twenty thousand men in the field. Esther's fast hastened Haman's ruin, and Hezekiah's against Sennacherib brought his huge host to the slaughter, and fetched an angel from heaven to do the execution in one night upon them.—*William Gurnall.*

Verse 78.—*"The proud."* The wicked, especially the persecutors of God's people, are usually characterized by this term in this Psalm, *" the proud "* (verses 51, 69, 122). Pride puts wicked men upon being troublesome and injurious to the people of God. But why are the persecutors and the injurious called *"the proud"?* 1. Because wicked men shake off the yoke of God, and will not be subject to their Maker, and therefore desist not from troubling his people : "Who is the Lord, that I should obey his voice to let Israel go"? (Exod. v. 2). What was in his tongue, is in all men's hearts ; they contemn God and his laws. Every sin hath a degree of pride, and a depreciation of God included in it, (2 Sam xii. 9). 2. Because they are drunk with worldly felicity, and never think of changes. " Our soul is exceedingly filled with the scorning of those that are at ease, and with the contempt of the proud " (Ps. cxxiii. 4). When men go on prosperously, they are apt wrongfully to trouble others, and then to flout at them in their misery, and to despise the person and cause of God's people, which is a sure effect of great arrogancy and pride. They think they may do what they please : " They have no changes ; therefore they fear not God," and put forth their hands against such as be at peace with them (Ps. lv. 19, 20) : whilst they go on prosperously and undisturbedly, they cannot abstain from violence and oppression. 3. Because they effect a life of pomp, and ease, and carnal greatness, and so despise the affliction, and meanness, and simplicity of God's people. The false church hath usually the advantage of worldly power and external glory ; and the true church is known by the Divine power, gifts and graces, and the lustre of holiness. 4. They are called " proud," because of their insolent carriage towards the Lord's people ; partly in their laws and injunctions, requiring them to give them more honour, respect, and obedience, than in conscience can be afforded them ; as Haman would have Mordecai to devote himself to him after the manner of the Persians (Esther iii. 5).—*Condensed from Manton.*

Verse 78.—" When any of you," says Cæsarius, " is singing the verse of the Psalm wherein it is said, 'Let the proud be put to shame,' let him be earnest to avoid pride, that he may escape everlasting shame."—*William Kay.*

Verse 78.—*"But I will meditate in thy precepts."* He repeateth the same thing often, and surely if the world could not contain the books that might be written of Christ, and yet for our infirmity the Lord hath comprised them in such a few books, and yet one thing in them is often repeated, it showeth that the matter is weighty, and of us duly and often to be considered. And again we are taught that this is a thing that none do so carefully look unto as they ought. And he showeth that as his enemies sought by evil means to hurt him ; so he sought to keep a good conscience, that so they might not hurt him. Then we must not set policy against policy nor *cretizare cum Cretensibus ;* but let us always tend to the word, and keep within the bounds of that, and fight with the weapons that it lendeth us. . . . . If we would give over ourselves to God and his word, and admit nothing but that which agreeth to the word, then should we be made wiser than our enemies. —*Richard Greenham.*

Verse 78.—*"I will meditate in thy precepts."* The verb אשׂיח, *asiach,* in the second clause of the verse, may be rendered, *"I will speak of,"* as well as, *"I will meditate upon"*; implying that, when he had obtained the victory, he would proclaim the goodness of God, which he had experienced. *To speak of God's statutes,* is equivalent to declaring out of the law how faithfully he guards his saints, how securely he delivers them, and how righteously he avenges their wrongs.—*John Calvin.*

Verse 78.—*"Meditate."* Truths lie hid in the heart without efficacy or power, till improved by deep, serious, and pressing thoughts . . . . A sudden carrying a candle through a room, giveth us not so full a survey of the object, as when you stand a while beholding it. A steady contemplation is a great advantage.—*Thomas Manton.*

Verse 79.—*"Let those that fear thee turn unto me."* Some think it intimates that when David had been guilty of that foul sin in the murder of Uriah, though he was a king, they that feared God grew strange to him, and turned from him, for they were ashamed of him ; this troubled him, and therefore he prays, Lord, let them *"turn to me"* again.   He desires especially the company of those that were not only honest but intelligent, *"that have known thy testimonies,"* have good heads as well as good hearts, and whose conversation will be edifying.   It is desirable to have an intimacy with such.—*Matthew Henry.*

Verse 79.—*"Let those that fear thee turn unto me,"* etc.   As he had not his own flesh to fight against only, but the world also, so he did not only himself fight, but he seeketh the help of others.   When many see that religion cannot be truly professed but danger will come of it, because many set themselves against it, they flee from it, and go to the greater part, which is the wicked.   If we will avoid this, let us join ourselves to God's children, and they will help us with counsel and advice; for one may be strong when we are weak, another may have counsel when we shall not know what to do; therefore by them we shall be kept from many evil things.   So Paul (2 Tim. i. 16), after he had complained of the wrong that many had done unto him, he straightway giveth thanks for the family of Onesiphorus, which refreshed him more than all his enemies could discourage him ; so that he durst oppose this one household to the whole rabble of the wicked.—*Richard Greenham.*

Verse 79.—*"Let those that fear thee,"* etc.   You must go to God and beseech him to choose your company for you.   Mark what David said and did ; in verse 63 he saith, *"I am a companion of all them that fear the Lord";* yet in this verse he goes to God, and prayeth, saying, *Let those that fear thee, O Lord, turn unto me, and those that have known thy testimonies."*   As if he should say, "Of a truth, Lord, I am a companion of all that do fear thee ; but it is not in my power to bend their hearts unto me ; the hearts of all men are in thy hands, now therefore *"let those that fear thee turn unto me."*   So do you go to God, and say likewise : Lord, do thou choose my company for me ; oh, do thou bow and incline their hearts to be my companions. —*William Bridge.*

Verse 79.—*"Those that fear." "Those that have known."*   Fear and knowledge do make up a godly man.   Knowledge without fear breedeth presumption ; and fear without knowledge breedeth superstition ; and blind zeal, as a blind horse, may be full of mettle, but is ever and anon stumbling.   Knowledge must direct fear, and fear must season knowledge ; then it is a happy mixture and composition.— *Thomas Manton.*

Verse 79.—One great means to restore a good understanding among God's people is prayer.   David goeth to God about it : *"Lord, let them turn to me."*   The Lord governeth hearts and interests, both are in his hands, and he useth their alienation or reconciliation, either for judgment or mercy.   God, when he pleaseth, can divert from us the comfort of godly friends ; and when he pleaseth, he can bring them back again to us.   The feet of God's children are directed by God himself ; if they come to us, it is a blessing of God ; if not, it is for a correction.   He made Jacob and Laban meet peaceably (Gen. xxx.), and in the next chapter, Jacob and Esau.— *Thomas Manton.*

Verse 80.—*"Let my heart be sound."*   What is a sound heart ?   It noteth reality and solidity in grace.   The Septuagint hath it, *Let my heart be without spot and blemish.*   It implieth the reality of grace, opposed to the bare form of godliness, or the fair shows of hypocrites, and the sudden and vanishing motions of temporaries. If you would have me unfold what this sound heart is, there is required these four things :—

1. An enlightened understanding ; that is, the directive part of the soul ; and it is sound when it is kept free from the leaven and contagion of error : " A man of understanding walketh uprightly," Prov. xv. 21.   A sound mind is a good help to a sound heart.

2. There is required an awakened conscience, that warneth us of our duty, and riseth up in dislike of sin upon all occasions : " When thou goest, it shall lead thee ; when thou sleepest, it shall keep thee ; and when thou awakest, it shall talk with thee " (Prov. vi. 22): to have a constant monitor in our bosoms to put us in mind of God, when our reins preach to us in the night season (Ps. xvi. 7) : there is a secret spy in our bosoms that observes all that we do, and think, and speak ; a domestic chaplain, that is always preaching to us.   His heart is his Bible.

3. There is required a rightly disposed will, or a steadfast purpose to walk with God in all conditions, and to do what is good and acceptable in his sight : " He exhorted them all that with purpose of heart they would cleave unto the Lord," Acts xi. 23.   Many have light inclinations, or wavering resolutions ; but their

hearts are not fixedly, habitually bent to please God ; therein chiefly lieth this sound heart, that it doth inseparably cleave to God in all things.

4. There is required that the affections be purged and quickened : these are the vigorous motions of the will, and therefore this must be heedfully regarded ; purged they must be from that carnality and fleshliness that cleaveth to them. This is called in Scripture the circumcision of the heart (Deut. xxx. 6).—*Condensed from Manton.*

Verse 80.—*"Let my heart be sound."* " A sound mind in a sound body," was the prayer of a heathen, and his desire was according to the extent of his knowledge ; but a heart sound in God's statutes, sound to the very core, with no speck, nor spot, nor wrinkle, nor any such thing, and like the king's daughter, " all glorious within," this is what the Psalmist prays for, this is what every child of God aims at, and prays for too,—" Even as He is pure."—*Barton Bouchier.*

Verse 80.—*"Let my heart be sound."*

True-hearted, whole-hearted, faithful and loyal,
King of our lives, by thy grace will we be !
Under thy standard, exalted and royal,
Strong in thy strength, we will battle for thee !

True-hearted, whole-hearted ! Fullest allegiance
Yielding henceforth to our glorious King ;
Valiant endeavour and loving obedience
Freely and joyously now would we bring.

True-hearted, Saviour, thou knowest our story ;
Weak are the hearts that we lay at thy feet,
Sinful and treacherous ! yet for thy glory,
Heal them, and cleanse them from sin and deceit

Whole-hearted ! Saviour, belovèd and glorious,
Take thy great power, and reign thou alone,
Over our wills and affections victorious,
Freely surrendered, and wholly thine own.

Half-hearted ! false-hearted ! Heed we the warning !
Only the whole can be perfectly true ;
Bring the whole offering, all timid thought scorning,
True-hearted only if whole-hearted too.

Half-hearted ! Saviour, shall aught be withholden,
Giving thee part who hast given us all ?
Blessings outpouring, and promises golden
Pledging, with never reserve or recall.

Half-hearted ! Master, shall any who know thee
Grudge thee their lives, who hast laid down thine own ?
Nay ; we would offer the hearts that we owe thee,—
Live for thy love and thy glory alone.

Sisters, dear sisters, the call is resounding,
Will ye not echo the silver refrain,
Mighty and sweet, and in gladness abounding,—
" True-hearted, whole-hearted ! " ringing again ?

Jesus is with us, his rest is before us,
Brightly his standard is waving above.
Brothers, dear brothers, in gathering chorus,
Peal out the watchword of courage and love !

Peal out the watchword, and silence it never,
Song of our spirits rejoicing and free !
" True-hearted, whole-hearted, now and for ever,
King of our lives, by thy grace we will be ! "

Frances Ridley Havergal (1836—1879) *in "Loyal Responses."*

Verse 80.—*"Let my heart be sound,"* etc. This is a plain difference between a sound heart and a false heart ; in the receiving of Christ the sound heart receives him as a favourite receives a prince, he gives up all to him, and lets him have the command of all.   A mere innkeeper entertains him that comes next to him ; he will take any man's money, and will give welcome to any man ; if it be the worst man that comes he cares not, for he loves gain above all things.   Not so the good heart ; he welcomes Christ alone, and resigns up all to Christ.   Whatsoever is pleasing to Christ he will do it, and whatsoever comes from Christ he will welcome.— *Thomas Hooker* (1586—1647) *in "The Soules Implantation."*

Verse 80.—*"Be sound."*   Heb.   *Be perfect ;* as the word from the same root is rendered in Job i. 1.   Dr. R. Young gives as the meaning of the word as used by the Psalmist, *whole, complete, plain.*

Verse 80.—*"Sound in thy statutes,"* etc.   Though an *orthodox creed* does not constitute true religion, yet it is the basis of it, and it is a great blessing to have it.— *Nicolson, quoted by W. S. Plumer.*

Verse 80.—If you would be faithful to Christ, be sincere in your profession of him, make David's prayer and desire to be yours : *"Let my heart be sound in thy statutes ; that I be not ashamed."*   Religion which is begun in hypocrisy will certainly end in apostasy, and this always carries with it reproach and ignominy.—*William Spurstow* (—1666).

Verse 80.—*"Ashamed."*   We may be ashamed either before God or men, ourselves or others.

1. Before God : either in our addresses to him at the throne of grace or when summoned to appear at the last day before the tribunal of his justice.   (1) If you understand it of our approach to him, we cannot come into his presence with confidence if we have not a sound heart.   " If our heart condemn us not, then have we confidence toward God " : 1 John iii. 21.   We lose that holy familiarity and cheerfulness, when we are unbosoming ourselves to our heavenly Father, when our hearts are not sound.   (2) When we are summoned to appear before the tribunal of his justice.   Many, now, with a bold impudence, will obtrude themselves upon the worship of God, because they see him not, and have not a due sense of his majesty ; but the time will come, when the most impudent and outbraving sinners will be astonished, even then when the secrets of all hearts shall be laid open and made manifest, and hidden things brought to light (1 Cor. iv. 5) ; and every **one** is to receive his judgment from God according to what he hath done, either **good** or evil.

2. Before men a man may be ashamed, and so before ourselves and others. (1) Ourselves.   It was a saying of Pythagoras, Reverence thyself ; be not ashamed of thyself.   God hath a spy and deputy within us, and taketh notice of our conformity and unconformity to his will, and, after sin committed, lasheth the soul with the sense of its own guilt and folly, as the body is lashed with stripes : " What fruit had ye then in those things whereof ye are now ashamed ? " Rom. vi. 21.   (2) Before others.   And so our shame may be occasioned by our scandals, or our punishments ; it is hard to say which is intended here.—*Condensed from Manton.*

EXPOSITION OF VERSES 81 TO 88.

MY soul fainteth for thy salvation : *but* I hope in thy word.

82 Mine eyes fail for thy word, saying, When wilt thou comfort me ?

83 For I am become like a bottle in the smoke ; *yet* do I not forget thy statutes.

84 How many *are* the days of thy servant ? when wilt thou execute judgment on them that persecute me ?

85 The proud have digged pits for me, which *are* not after thy law.

86 All thy commandments *are* faithful : they persecute me wrongfully : help thou me.

87 They had almost consumed me upon earth ; but I forsook not thy precepts.

88 Quicken me after thy lovingkindness ; so shall I keep the testimony of thy mouth.

This portion of the gigantic Psalm sees the Psalmist *in extremis.* His enemies have brought him to the lowest condition of anguish and depression ; yet he is faithful to the law and trustful in his God. This octave is the midnight of the Psalm, and very dark and black it is. Stars, however, shine out, and the last verse gives promise of the dawn. The strain will after this become more cheerful ; but meanwhile it should minister comfort to us to see so eminent a servant of God so hardly used by the ungodly : evidently in our own persecutions, no strange thing has happened unto us.

81. "*My soul fainteth for thy salvation.*" He wished for no deliverance but that which came from God : his one desire was for " thy salvation." But for that divine deliverance he was eager to the last degree,—up to the full measure of his strength, yea, and beyond it till he fainted. So strong was his desire that it produced prostration of spirit. He grew weary with waiting, faint with watching, sick with urgent need. Thus the sincerity and the eagerness of his desires were proved. Nothing else could satisfy him but deliverance wrought out by the hand of God, his inmost nature yearned and pined for salvation from the God of all grace, and he must have it or utterly fail. "*But I hope in thy word.*" Therefore he felt that salvation would come, for God cannot break his promise, nor disappoint the hope which his own word has excited : yea, the fulfilment of his word is near at hand when our hope is firm and our desire fervent. Hope alone can keep the soul from fainting by using the smelling-bottle of the promise. Yet hope does not quench desire for a speedy answer to prayer ; it increases our importunity, for it both stimulates ardour and sustains the heart under delays. To faint for salvation, and to be kept from utterly failing by the hope of it, is the frequent experience of the Christian man. We are " faint yet pursuing." Hope sustains when desire exhausts. While the grace of desire throws us down, the grace of hope lifts us up again.

82. "*Mine eyes fail for thy word, saying, When wilt thou comfort me ?*" His eyes gave out with eagerly gazing for the kind appearance of the Lord, while his heart in weariness cried out for speedy comfort. To read the word till the eyes can no longer see is but a small thing compared with watching for the fulfilment of the promise till the inner eyes of expectancy begin to grow dim with hope deferred. We may not set times to God, for this is to limit the Holy One of Israel ; yet we may urge our suit with importunity, and make fervent enquiry as to why the promise tarries. David sought no comfort except that which comes from God ; his question is, " When wilt *thou* comfort me ? " If help does not come from heaven it will never come at all : all the good man's hopes look that way, he has not a glance to

dart in any other direction. This experience of waiting and fainting is well-known by full-grown saints, and it teaches them many precious lessons which they would never learn by any other means. Among the choice results is this one—that the body rises into sympathy with the soul, both heart and flesh cry out for the living God, and even the eyes find a tongue, " saying, When wilt thou comfort me ? " It must be an intense longing which is not satisfied to express itself by the lips, but speaks with the eyes, by those eyes failing through intense watching. Eyes can speak right eloquently ; they use both mutes and liquids, and can sometimes say more than tongues. David says in another place, " The Lord hath heard the voice of my weeping " (Ps. vi. 8). Specially are our eyes eloquent when they begin to fail with weariness and woe. A humble eye lifted up to heaven in silent prayer may flash such flame as shall melt the bolts which bar the entrance of vocal prayer, and so heaven shall be taken by storm with the artillery of tears. Blessed are the eyes that are strained in looking after God. The eyes of the Lord will see to it that such eyes do not actually fail. How much better to watch for the Lord with aching eyes than to have them sparkling at the glitter of vanity.

83. *"For I am become like a bottle in the smoke."* The skins used for containing wine, when emptied, were hung up in the tent, and when the place reeked with smoke the skins grew black and sooty, and in the heat they became wrinkled and worn. The Psalmist's face through sorrow had become dark and dismal, furrowed and lined ; indeed, his whole body had so sympathized with his sorrowing mind as to have lost its natural moisture, and to have become like a skin dried and tanned. His character had been smoked with slander, and his mind parched with persecution ; he was half afraid that he would become useless and incapable through so much mental suffering, and that men would look upon him as an old worn-out skin bottle, which could hold nothing and answer no purpose. What a metaphor for a man to use who was certainly a poet, a divine, and a master in Israel, if not a king, and a man after God's own heart ! It is little wonder if we, commoner folk, are made to think very little of ourselves, and are filled with distress of mind. Some of us know the inner meaning of this simile, for we, too, have felt dingy, mean, and worthless, only fit to be cast away. Very black and hot has been the smoke which has enveloped us ; it seemed to come not alone from the Egyptian furnace, but from the bottomless pit ; and it had a clinging power which made the soot of it fasten upon us and blacken us with miserable thoughts.

"Yet do I not forget thy statutes." Here is the patience of the saints and the victory of faith. Blackened the man of God might be by falsehood, but the truth was in him, and he never gave it up. He was faithful to his King when he seemed deserted and left to the vilest uses. The promises came to his mind, and, what was a still better evidence of his loyalty, the statutes were there too : he stuck to his duties as well as to his comforts. The worst circumstances cannot destroy the true believer's hold upon his God. Grace is a living power which survives that which would suffocate all other forms of existence. Fire cannot consume it, and smoke cannot smother it. A man may be reduced to skin and bone, and all his comfort may be dried out of him, and yet he may hold fast his integrity and glorify his God. It is, however, no marvel that in such a case the eyes which are tormented with the smoke cry out for the Lord's delivering hand, and the heart heated and faint longs for the divine salvation.

84. *"How many are the days of thy servant?"* I cannot hope to live long in such a condition, thou must come speedily to my rescue or I shall die. Shall all my short life be consumed in such destroying sorrows ? The brevity of life is a good argument against the length of an affliction. Perhaps the Psalmist means that his days seemed too many when they were spent in such distress. He half wished that they were ended, and therefore he asked in trouble, " How many are the days of thy servant ? " Like a hired servant, he had a certain term to serve, and he would not complain ; but still the time seemed long because his griefs were so heavy. No one knows the appointed number of our days except the Lord, and therefore to him the appeal is made that he would not prolong them beyond his servant's strength. It cannot be the Lord's mind that his own servant should always be treated so unjustly ; there must be an end to it ; when would it be ?

"When wilt thou execute judgment on them that persecute me?" He had placed his case in the Lord's hands, and he prayed that sentence might be given and put into execution. He desired nothing but justice, that his character might be cleared and his persecutors silenced. He knew that God would certainly avenge his own

elect, but the day of rescue tarried, the hours dragged heavily along, and the persecuted one cried day and night for deliverance.

85. "*The proud have digged pits for me, which are not after thy law.*" As men
who hunt wild beasts are wont to make pitfalls and snares, so did David's foes
endeavour to entrap him. They went laboriously and cunningly to work to ruin
him, "they digged *pits*"; not one, but many. If one would not take him, perhaps
another would, and so they digged again and again. One would think that such
haughty people would not have soiled their fingers with digging; but they swallowed
their pride in hopes of swallowing their victim. Whereas they ought to have been
ashamed of such meanness, they were conscious of no shame, but, on the contrary,
were proud of their cleverness; proud of setting a trap for a godly man. "*Which
are not after thy law.*" Neither the men nor their pits were according to the divine
law: they were cruel and crafty deceivers, and their pits were contrary to the
Levitical law, and contrary to the command which bids us love our neighbour.
If men would keep to the statutes of the Lord, they would lift the fallen out of the
pit, or fill up the pit so that none might stumble into it; but they would never
spend a moment in working injury to others. When, however, they become proud,
they are sure to despise others; and for this reason they seek to circumvent them,
that they may afterwards hold them up to ridicule.

It was well for David that his enemies were God's enemies, and that their attacks
upon him had no sanction from the Lord. It was also much to his gain that he
was not ignorant of their devices, for he was thus put upon his guard, and led to
watch his ways lest he should fall into their pits. While he kept to the law of the
Lord he was safe, though even then it was an uncomfortable thing to have his path
made dangerous by the craft of wanton malice.

86. "*All thy commandments are faithful.*" He had no fault to find with God's
law, even though he had fallen into sad trouble through obedience to it. Whatever
the command might cost him it was worth it; he felt that God's way might be
rough, but it was right; it might make him enemies, but still it was his best friend.
He believed that in the end God's command would turn out to his own profit, and
that he should be no loser by obeying it.

"*They persecute me wrongfully.*" The fault lay with his persecutors, and neither
with his God nor with himself. He had done no injury to anyone, nor acted otherwise than according to truth and justice; therefore he confidently appeals to his
God, and cries, "*Help thou me.*" This is a golden prayer, as precious as it is short.
The words are few, but the meaning is full. Help was needed that the persecuted
one might avoid the snare, might bear up under reproach, and might act so prudently
as to baffle his foes. God's help is our hope. Whoever may hurt us, it matters
not so long as the Lord helps us; for if indeed the Lord help us, none can really
hurt us. Many a time have these words been groaned out by troubled saints, for
they are such as suit a thousand conditions of need, pain, distress, weakness, and
sin. "Help, Lord," will be a fitting prayer for youth and age, for labour and
suffering, for life and death. No other help is sufficient, but God's help is all-sufficient
and we cast ourselves upon it without fear.

87. "*They had almost consumed me upon earth.*" His foes had almost destroyed
him so as to make him altogether fail. If they could they would have eaten him,
or burned him alive; anything so that they could have made a full end of the good
man. Evidently he had fallen under their power to a large extent, and they had
so used that power that he was well nigh consumed. He was almost gone from off
the earth; but almost is not altogether, and so he escaped by the skin of his teeth.
The lions are chained: they can rage no further than our God permits. The Psalmist
perceives the limit of their power: they could only touch his earthly life and earthly
goods. Upon earth they almost ate him up, but he had an eternal portion which they
could not even nibble at. "*But I forsook not thy precepts.*" Nothing could drive
him from obeying the Lord. If we stick to the precepts we shall be rescued by the
promises. If ill-usage could have driven the oppressed saint from the way of right
the purpose of the wicked would have been answered, and we should have heard
no more of David. If we are resolved to die sooner than forsake the Lord, we may
depend upon it that we shall not die, but shall live to see the overthrow of them that
hate us.

88. "*Quicken me after thy lovingkindness.*" Most wise, most blessed prayer!
If we are revived in our own personal piety we shall be out of reach of our assailants.
Our best protection from tempters and persecutors is more life. Lovingkindness

itself cannot do us greater service than by making us to have life more abundantly. When we are quickened we are able to bear affliction, to baffle cunning, and to conquer sin.   We look to the lovingkindness of God as the source of spiritual revival, and we entreat the Lord to quicken us, not according to our deserts, but after the boundless energy of his grace.   What a blessed word is this "lovingkindness."   Take it to pieces, and admire its double force of love.   *"So shall I keep the testimony of thy mouth."*   If quickened by the Holy Ghost we shall be sure to exhibit a holy character. We shall be faithful to sound doctrine when the Spirit visits us and makes us faithful. None keep the word of the Lord's mouth unless the word of the Lord's mouth quickens them.   We ought greatly to admire the spiritual prudence of the Psalmist, who does not so much pray for freedom from trial as for renewed life that he may he supported under it.   When the inner life is vigorous all is well.   David prayed for a sound heart in the closing verse of the last octave, and here he seeks a revived heart ; this is going to the root of the matter, by seeking that which is the most needful of all things.   Lord let it be heart-work with us, and let our hearts be right with thee.

NOTES ON VERSES 81 TO 88.

The whole eight verses, 81—89.—The eleventh letter, *Caph*, signifies the *hollowed hand*. The expositors, however, looking only to the meaning *curved*, which is but half of its import, explain the section as signifying the act of bowing down in penitence or as noting that the fathers of the Old Testament were like veteran soldiers, stooping with years and toil, and bowed down yet further by the heavy weight of the law, only removable by that coming of Christ for which they prayed. Others extend the notion to the saints of the church, weighed down by the sorrows and cares of this life and therefore desiring to be dissolved and to be with Christ. The true meaning is to be sought in the full interpretation of the word; for the hand is hollowed either in order to retain something which actually lies in it, or to receive something about to be placed in it by another. Thus the hand may be God's, as the giver of bounty, or man's, as the receiver of it; and the whole scope of the section, as a prayer for speedy help, is that man holds out his hand as a beggar, supplicating the mercy of God.—*Jerome, Ambrose, and others, in Neale and Littledale.*

Verse 81.—"*My soul fainteth for thy salvation.*" The word here rendered "*fainteth*" is the same that in Ps. lxxiii. 26 is translated "*faileth*": "My flesh and my heart *faileth.*" The idea is, that his strength gave way; he had such an intense *desire* for salvation that he became weak and powerless. Any strong emotion *may* thus prostrate us; and the love of God, the desire of his favour, the longing for heaven may be so intense as to produce this result.—*Albert Barnes.*

Verse 81.—"*My soul fainteth.*" Fainting is proper to the body, but here it is ascribed to the soul; as also in many other places. The Apostle saith, "Lest ye be wearied and faint in your minds" (Heb. xii. 3); where two words are used, weariness and fainting, both taken from the body. Weariness is a lesser, fainting is a higher degree of deficiency: in weariness, the body requireth some rest or refreshment, when the active power is weakened, and the vital spirits and principles of motion are dulled; but, in fainting, the vital power is contracted, and retireth, and leaveth the outward parts lifeless and senseless. When a man is wearied, his strength is abated; when he fainteth, he is quite spent. These things, by a metaphor, are applied to the soul, or mind. A man is weary, when the fortitude of his mind, his moral or spiritual strength, is broken, or begins to abate, when his soul sits uneasy under sufferings; but when he sinketh under the burden of grievous, tedious, or long affliction, then he is said to faint, when all the reasons and grounds of his comfort are quite spent and he can hold out no longer.—*Thomas Manton.*

Verse 81.—"*My soul fainteth.*" What is this fainting but the lofty state of raptured contemplation in which the strength of heavenly affections weakens those of earth. Just as the ascent into the highest mountains causes a new respiration, as when Daniel had a great vision from God, he tells us " he fainted and was sick certain days."—*E. Paxton Hood, 1871.*

Verse 81.—"*My soul fainteth for thy salvation; but I hope.*" Believe under a cloud, and wait for him when there is no moonlight nor starlight. Let faith live and breathe, and lay hold of the sure salvation of God, when clouds and darkness are about you, and appearance of rotting in the prison before you. Take heed of unbelieving hearts, which can father lies upon Christ. Beware of " Doth his promise fail for evermore?" for it was a man, and not God said it. Who dreameth that a promise of God can fail, fall aswoon, or die? Who can make God sick, or his promises weak? When we are pleased to seek a plea with Christ, let us plead that we hope in him. O stout word of faith, " Though he slay me, yet will I trust in him!" O sweet epitaph, written upon the grave-stone of a departed believer, namely, " I died hoping, and my dust and ashes believe in life!" Faith's eyes, that can see through a mill-stone, can see through a gloom* of God, and under it read God's thoughts of love and peace. Hold fast Christ in the dark; surely ye shall see the salvation of God. Your adversaries are ripe and dry for the fire. Yet a little while, and they shall go up in a flame; the breath of the Lord, like a river of brimstone, shall kindle about them.—*Samuel Rutherford, 1600—1661.*

Verse 81.—"*For thy salvation.*" Understood in a higher sense, the holy man longs for the coming of the Saviour in the flesh.—*Cornelius Jansen.*

---

* Frown.

Verse 81.—*"Thy salvation."* A believer in God, how afflicted so ever he be, seeketh not to be delivered but in a way allowed by God ; *"My soul fainteth for thy salvation"*; or, till thou deliver me in thy good way.—*David Dickson.*

Verse 81.—*"I hope in thy word."* David knew where he moored his ship. Hope without a promise is like an anchor without ground to hold by ; but David's hope fixed itself upon the divine word.—*William Gurnall.*

Verse 81.—*"I hope in thy word:"* *i.e.* I hope beyond anything I understand, and beyond anything I can possibly do, and beyond anything I deserve, and beyond all carnal and spiritual consolations, for I desire and look for Thee only. I seek Thee, not Thine : I long to hear *"Thy word,"* that I may obey it in patience and meekness.—*Le Blanc.*

Verses 81, 83.—It is good in all times of persecution or affliction to have an eye both on the promises and on the precepts ; for the looking to the promise doth encourage to hope, and the eyeing of the precepts doth prove the hope to be sound. The Psalmist *hoped in the word* (verse 81), and (verse 83), *he forgot not the statutes.* —*David Dickson.*

Verse 82.—*"Mine eyes fail for thy word."* Has a mother promised to visit her son or daughter ? should she not be able to go, the remark of the son or daughter will be : " Alas ! my mother promised to come to me : how long have I been looking for her ? But a speck has grown on my eye." " I cannot see, my eyes have failed me " ; that is, by looking so intensely for her coming.—*Joseph Roberts.*

Verse 82.—*"Mine eyes fail for thy word."* He was continuously lifting the eyes to heaven, looking for help from God. He was so perpetually doing this, that at length the eyes themselves became dim.

"When wilt thou comfort me ?" He was saying this in his heart ; he was saying this with his mouth ; he was saying the same thing with his eyes perpetually looking up to heaven.—*Wolfgang Musculus.*

Verse 82.—*"For thy word."* The children of God make more of a promise than others do ; and that upon a double account : partly, because they value the blessing promised ; partly, because they are satisfied with the assurance given by God's word ; so that, whereas others pass by these things with a careless eye, their souls are lifted up to the constant and earnest expectation of the blessing promised. It is said of the hireling, that he must have his wages before the sun go down, because he is poor and hath set his heart upon it (Deut. xxiv. 15) ; or, as it is in the Hebrew, lifted up his soul to it, meaning thereby both his desire and hope. He esteemeth his wages ; for it is the solace of his labours, and the maintenance of his life ; and he assuredly expecteth it, upon the promise and covenant of him who setteth him awork. So it is with the children of God ; they esteem the blessings promised, and God's word giveth them good assurance that they do not wait upon him in vain.—*Thomas Manton.*

Verse 82.—*"Saying, When."* The same spirit of faith which teaches a man to cry earnestly, teaches him to wait patiently ; for as it assures him that mercy is in the Lord's hand, so it assures him, it will come forth in the Lord's time.—*John Mason,* 1688.

Verse 82.—*"When wilt thou comfort me ?"* It is a customable manner of God's working with his children, to delay the answer to their prayers, and to suspend the performance of his promises : not because he is unwilling to give, but because he will have them better prepared to receive. *Tardius dando quod pettimus instantia nobis orationis indicit :* [*] he is slow to give that which we seek, that we should not seek slowly, but may be awakened to instancy and fervency in prayer, which he knows to be the service most acceptable unto him, and most profitable unto ourselves. —*William Cowper.*

Verse 82.—*"When wilt* thou *comfort me?"* Let us complain not *of* God, but *to* God. Complaints of God give a vent to murmuring ; but complaints to God, to faith, hope, and patience.—*Thomas Manton.*

Verse 82.—The prophet, to prevent it from being supposed that he was too effeminate and faint-hearted, intimates that his fainting was not without cause. In asking God, *"When wilt thou comfort me ?"* he shows, with sufficient plainness, that he was for a long time, as it were, cast off and forsaken.—*John Calvin.*

Verse 82.—*"When wilt thou comfort me ?"* The people of God are sometimes

---

† *Chrysostom.*

very disconsolate, and need comforting, through the prevalence of sin, the power of Satan's temptations, the hidings of God's face, and a variety of afflictions, when they apply to God for comfort, who only can comfort them, and who has set them to do it ; but they are apt to think it long, and enquire, as David here, when it will be.—*John Gill.*

Verse 82.—*"When wilt thou comfort me ? "* A poor woman had been long time questioning herself, and doubting of her salvation ; when at last the Lord made it good unto her soul that Christ was her own, then her minister said unto her, The Lord will not always give his children a cordial, but he hath it ready for them when they are fainting.—*Thomas Hooker.*

Verse 82.—*"When wilt thou comfort me ? "* Comfort is necessary because a great part of our temptations lies in troubles, as well as allurements. Sense of pain may discompose us as well as pleasure entice us. The world is a persecuting as well as a tempting world. The flesh troubleth as well as enticeth. The Devil is a disquieting as well as an ensnaring Devil. But yet comfort, though necessary, is not so necessary as holiness : therefore, though comfort is not to be despised, yet sincere love to God is to be preferred, and, though it be not dispensed so certainly, so constantly, and in so high a degree in this world, we must be contented. The Spirit's comforting work is oftener interrupted than the work of holiness ; yet so much as is necessary to enable us to serve God in this world we shall assuredly receive.— *Thomas Manton.*

Verse 83.—*"A bottle in the smoke."* Sleep was out of the question, for I was . . . almost smothered with the smoke from a wood fire, for there was no chimney. I was indeed *"like a bottle in the smoke,"* turned black and dried almost to cracking ; for this was something of what the Psalmist had in view. The bottles being of leather, and being hung up in rooms with large fires of wood, and without chimneys, they became smoke-dried, shrivelled, and unfit for use.—*From "My Wanderings," by John Gadsby,* 1860.

Verse 83.—*"Like a bottle in the smoke."* The tent of a common Arab is so smoky a habitation, that I consider the expression of *a bottle in the smoke,* to be equivalent to that of *a bottle in the tent of an Arab.* There was a fire, we find, in that Arab tent to which Bishop Pococke was conducted when he was going to Jerusalem. How smoky must such an habitation be, and how black all its utensils ! Le Bruyn in going from Aleppo to Scanderoon was made sufficiently sensible of this : for being obliged to pass a whole night in a hut of reeds, in the middle of which there was a fire, to boil a kettle of meat that hung over it, and to bake some bread among the ashes, he found the smoke intolerable, the door being the only place by which it could get out of the hut.

To the *blackness* of a goat-skin bottle. in a tent. but to the *meanness* also of such a drinking-vessel, the Psalmist seems to refer, and it was a most natural image for him to make use of, driven from among the vessels of silver and gold in the palace of Saul, to live as the Arabs do and did, and consequently often obliged to drink out of a smoked leather-bottle.—*Thomas Harmer,* 1719—1788.

Verse 83.—*"For I am become like a bottle in the smoke."* A bottle in the smoke has very little inflation, fatness, moisture, beauty. Thus God wastes away, debases, and empties his people, while he exercises them with tribulations and the disquiet of hoping and waiting. The glory and eagerness of the flesh must be emptied, that the Divine gifts may find room, and the remembrance of the commandments of God may be restrained, which cannot be well kept in bottles which are swollen, inflated, and filled.—*Wolfgang Musculus.*

Verse 83.—*"A bottle in the smoke."* One object amongst the ancients of such exposure was to mellow the wine by the gradual ascent of the heat and smoke from the fire over which the skin was suspended ; and thus the words teach us the uses of affliction in ripening and improving the soul.—*Rosenmüller, quoted in Neale and Littledale.*

Verse 83.—*"For I am become like a bottle in the smoke,"* etc. Satan can afflict the *body* by the *mind.* For these two are so closely bound together that their good and bad estate is shared between them. If the heart be merry the countenance is cheerful, the strength is renewed, the bones do flourish like an herb. If the heart be troubled, the health is impaired, the strength is dried up, the marrow of the bones wasted, etc. Grief in the heart is like a moth in the garment, it insensibly consumeth the body and disordereth it. This advantage of weakening the body falls into Satan's hands by necessary consequence, as the prophet's ripe figs, that fell into the mouth of the eater. And surely he is well pleased with it, as he is an enemy both to body and soul. But 'tis a greater satisfaction to him, in that as he can make the sorrows of the mind produce the weakness and sickness of the body ; so can he make the distemper of the body (by a reciprocal requital) to augment the trouble of the mind. How little can a sickly body do ? it disables a man for all services ; he cannot oft pray, nor read, nor hear. Sickness takes away the sweetness and comfort of religious exercises ; this gives occasion for them to think the worse of themselves ; they think the soul is weary of the ways of God when the body cannot hold out.—*Richard Gilpin, in "A Treatise of Satan's Temptations," 1677.*

Verse 83.—*"Like a bottle in the smoke."* In this did the afflicted Psalmist find a striking emblem of his own spiritual state. He waited for the Lord to come. In spirit he was dried up by pressure upon him ; and he still waited for the Lord to come, declaring his shrivelled condition. Perhaps his outward man partook of the same sad qualities at this time. . . . The outward appearance of the man of God, to which he may be alluding, was, however, but the semblance of his spiritual nature at this period, whatever may have been the visible effects. David was exposed to the calumnious reports of evil-minded men, and to the hot persecution of relentless enemies, till the effect upon his mind was such that his whole spiritual nature resembled, in his own mind, a skin hung up in the smoke for a length of time. Not only was he shrivelled in public estimation, but also in his own mind ; not indeed because at this time, and on the ground of the charges made against him, he felt that he deserved it ; but because so incessant and multifarious was the bitter invasion of his spirit, that even with all his faith in God, he well-nigh literally sunk under it. The term given in our translation to the original would imply, that he bore himself well notwithstanding—*"For I am become like a bottle in the smoke ; yet do I not forget thy statutes."* Whereas the words rendered more literally would convey the import that all this happened to him even while he was in the very way of duty : *"I am become like a bottle in the smoke—I do not forget thy statutes."* He was directly in the way of the Lord's appointments for all salvation ; yet trouble came. It is sad when our spiritual man becomes shrivelled and dried up because of our falling into sin, or because of guilty omissions ; but here seems to be a falling off of the spiritual man, and of the physical man, while the believer is conscious that he is not forgetting the statutes of his gracious God.—*John Stephen.*

Verse 83.—Observe here the difference between the beauty and strength of the body and of the soul : the beauty of the soul groweth fairer by afflictions, whereas that of the body is blasted. David was a bottle shrivelled and shrunk up ; yet the holy frame of his soul was not altered : his beauty was gone, but not his grace.—*Thomas Manton.*

Verse 83.—*"I am become like a bottle in the frost"* (so the Seventy translate it). When spiritual desires burn, carnal desires without doubt cool : on this account followeth, *"Since I am become like a bottle in the frost I do not forget thy righteousness."* Truly he desireth this mortal flesh to be understood by the bottle, the heavenly blessing by the frost, whereby the lusts of the flesh as it were by the binding of the frost become sluggish : and hence it ariseth that the righteousnesses of God do not slip from the memory so long as we do not meditate apart from them ; since what the apostle saith (Rom. xiii. 14) is brought to pass : " Make not provision for the flesh, to fulfil the lusts thereof." Therefore when he had said, *"For I have become like a bottle in the frost,"* he added, *"and I do not forget thy righteousnesses,"* that is, I forget them not, because I have become such. For the fervour of lust had cooled, that the memory of love might glow.—*Augustine.*

Verse 84.—*"How many are the days of thy servant ? "* etc. Some read the two clauses apart, as if the first were a general complaint of the brevity of human life, such as is to be met with in other Psalms, and more frequently in the book of Job ; and next in their opinion, there follows a special prayer of the Psalmist that God would take vengeance upon his enemies. But I rather prefer joining the two clauses together, and limit both to David's afflictions ; as it it had been said, Lord, how long hast thou determined to abandon thy servant to the will of the ungodly ? when wilt thou set thyself in opposition to their cruelty and outrage, in order to take vengeance upon them ? The Scriptures often use the word *"days"* in this sense. . . . By the use of the plural number is denoted a determinate portion of time, which, in other places, is compared to the " days of an hireling " : Job xiv. 6 ;

Isaiah xvi. 14. The Psalmist does not, then, bewail in general the transitory life of man, but he complains that the time of his state of warfare in this world had been too long protracted; and, therefore, he naturally desires that it might be brought to a termination. In expostulating with God about his troubles, he does not do so obstinately, or with a murmuring spirit; but still, in asking how long it will be necessary for him to suffer, he humbly prays that God would not delay to succour him.—*John Calvin.*

Verse 84.—*"When wilt thou execute judgment on them that persecute me?"* He declares that he does not doubt but that there will be at some period an end to his afflictions, and that there will be a time in which his haters and enemies will be judged and punished. He assumes the fact and therefore enquires the date. Thus in the saints their very impatience of delay does itself prove their confidence of future salvation and deliverance.—*Wolfgang Musculus.*

Verse 84.—*"When wilt thou execute judgment,"* etc. This is an ordinary prayer, not against any certain persons, but rather generally against God's enemies, and their evil courses. For the Lord executeth judgment upon his children for their conversion, as Paul (Acts ix.), and upon the wicked for their confusion. He prayeth against them that belonged not to God, and yet not so much against their persons as their evil causes; and no otherwise against their persons than as they are joined with the evil causes. Thus we may pray for the confusion of God's enemies; otherwise we cannot.—*R. Greenham.*

Verse 84.—In this verse there is none of the ten words used in reference to God's law.—*Adam Clarke.* [Is not judgment one of them?—C. H. S.]

Verse 85.—*"Pits."* Hajji said he would tell me a tale or two about crocodiles, and he would begin by telling me how they catch them sometimes. A deep pit, he said, is dug by the side of the river, and then covered with doura straw. The crocodiles fall into these pits, and cannot get out again. . . . . There can be no doubt that formerly pits were dug for the crocodiles, as Hajji described, as is the case still in some parts of the world for other animals. To this custom allusion is made in Ps. vii. 15; ix. 15; x. 2; xxxv. 8; cxli. 10; Prov. xxvi. 27; Eccles. x. 8: etc. "He made a pit and digged it, and is fallen into the ditch which he made." Probably also this was the kind of pit referred to in Exod. xxi. 33: "If a man shall dig a pit, and not cover it"; *i.e.,* not cover it effectually; "and an ass or an ox fall therein," etc.

Prisoners were sometimes shut up in pits, and left without water, literally to die of thirst. What a dreadful death! It is said that nothing can be more terrible. How dreadful must be their groans!—*John Gadsby.*

Verse 85.—*"The proud have digged pits."* It seems strange that a proud man should be a digger of pits; but so it is; for pride for a time can submit itself to gain a greater vantage over him whom it would tread under foot. "The wicked is so proud that he seeks not God, yet he croucheth and boweth, to cause heaps of the poor to fall by his might," Ps. x. 4, 10. So proud Absalom abased himself to meanest subjects that so he might prepare a way to usurpation over his king and father. But mark, he saith not that he had fallen into the pits which his enemies had digged. No, no: in God's righteous judgments, the wicked are snared in the work of their own hands, while the good escape free. "He made a pit, and digged it, and is fallen into the ditch which he made. His mischief shall return upon his own head, and his violent dealing shall come down upon his own pate." Ps. viii. 15, 16. Thus Haman hanselled the gallows which he raised for Mordecai; and Saul when he thought by subtlety to slay David with the Philistine's sword (when he sent him out to seek two hundred of their foreskins in a dowry) was disappointed of his purpose; but he himself at length was slain by the sword.—*William Cowper.*

Verse 85.—Let men beware how they *dig pits* for others. All God's word testifies against such wickedness. How many tests are invented simply for the purpose of entangling men's consciences and furnishing ground for persecution.—*William S. Plumer.*

Verse 85.—*"Which are not after thy law."* Hebrew, Not after thy law. It may refer to the men or to the practice. The men walk not according to thy law, and their fraudulent practices are not agreeable to thy law. The law of God condemned pits for tame beasts: Exodus xxi. 33, 34. Though it was lawful for hunters to take wild beasts, yet they were to take heed that a tame beast fell not therein, at their peril.—*Thomas Manton.*

Verse 85.—*"Which are not after thy law."* After God's law they could not be while they were doing such things. Perhaps he refers to the deed more than to the men : " The proud have digged pits for me, which is not after thy law "—which is against thy law ; and they would seem to do it because it is against thy law— delighting in wickedness as they do. Such men would seem to imbibe the foul spirit which Milton ascribes to the fallen archangel : " Evil, be thou my good." Obviously, however, the words contain this sentiment,—The proud have sought to overthrow me, because they are not obedient to thy law. Hereupon he sets their conduct in the light of God's holy commandments, that the comparison may be made : *"All thy commandments are faithful : they persecute me wrongfully."* Whatever the Lord did was done in truth ; these men acted against his servant without cause, and in so doing they also acted in defiance of his known will.—*John Stephen.*

Verse 85.—*"The wicked have told me fables, but not as thy law"* (So the Septuagint). The special reason why he desires to be freed from the company of the wicked is, because they always tempt the pious by relating the pleasures of the world, which are nothing but fables, filthy, fleeting pleasures, more fallacious than real—nothing like the grand and solid pleasure that always flows from a pious observance of the law of the Lord.—*Robert Bellarmine.*

Verse 86.—*"All thy commandments are faithful."* David setteth down here three points. The one is that God is true ; and after that he addeth a protestation of his good conduct and guidance, and of the malice of his adversaries : thirdly, he calleth upon God in his afflictions. Now as concerning the first, he showeth us that although Satan to shake us, and in the end utterly to carry us away, subtilly and cunningly goeth about to deceive us, we must, to the contrary, learn how to know his ambushes, and to keep us from out of them. So often then as we are grieved with adversity and affliction, where must we begin ? See Satan how he pitcheth his nets and layeth his ambushes to induce and persuade us to come into them, what sayeth he ? Dost thou not see thyself forsaken of thy God ? Where are the promises whereunto thou didst trust ? Now here thou seest thyself to be a wretched, forlorn creature. So then thou right well seest that God hath deceived thee, and that the promises whereunto thou trustedst appertain nothing at all unto thee. See here the subtlety of Satan. What is now to be done ? We are to conclude with David and say, yet God is true and faithful. Let us, I say, keep in mind the truth of God as a shield to beat back whatsoever Satan is able to lay unto our charge. When he shall go about to cause us to deny our faith, when he shall lie about us to make us believe that God thinketh no more of us, or else that it is in vain for us to trust unto his promises ; let us know the clean contrary and believe that it is very plain and sound truth which God saith unto us. Although Satan casteth at us never so many darts, although he have never so exceeding many devices against us, although now and then by violence, sometimes with subtilty and cunning, it seemeth in very deed to us that he should overcome us ; nevertheless he shall never bring it to pass, for the truth of God shall be made sure and certain in our hearts.—*John Calvin.*

Verse 86.—*"All thy commandments are faithful."* The Hebrew is *Faithfulness ;* that is to say, they are true, sure, equal, infallible. *"They have persecuted me wrongfully :"* no doubt for asserting God's truths and commands, and adhering thereto.—*John Trapp.*

Verse 86.—*"They persecute me wrongfully."* There is a stress on the word *falsely* (or *wrongfully*) ; for that is a true saying of a martyr saint,* " The cause, not the pain, makes the martyr." Wherefore the apostle teaches us, " Let none of you suffer as a murderer or as a thief, or as an evil-doer, or as a busybody in other men's matters. Yet if any man suffer as a Christian, let him not be ashamed ; but let him glorify God on this behalf."—*Neale and Littledale.*

Verse 86.—*"Help thou me,"* " God help me " is an excellent, comprehensive prayer ; it is a pity it should ever be used lightly and as a bye-word.—*Matthew Henry.*

Verse 87.—*"Almost consumed."* The lives of good men are full of narrow escapes. The righteous are scarcely saved. Many a time their feet do almost

* Cyprian.

slip. Yet he, who has redeemed them, will not let them so fall that they can rise no more. One of their greatest perils is, a temptation to use unlawful means for terminating their trials.—*William S. Plumer.*

Verse 87.—It should be noticed that he says *"upon the earth:"* for it shows, that even if his enemies had taken away his life on earth, he nevertheless confidently looked for another life in heaven, and that already he had by faith entered into heaven, and was living a heavenly life; so that if the life of the body should be taken away, it was not to be regarded as an evil. They who live such a life speedily recover from despair.—*D. H. Mollerus.*

Verse 88.—*"Quicken me after thy lovingkindness."* Finally, the man of God appears entreating to be quickened, that so he may be enabled to keep the divine testimony. . . . Here is a last resort, but it is a sure one. Let the living principles of divine grace be imparted to the soul, and the believer will be raised above dismay at the face of men. How does the spiritual mind triumph over even the infirmities of the body! We may behold this from the death-bed of the believer, and we may recall this in the lives and deaths of many eminent ones. The man of pure mind goes right to the fountain of life. He goes, with understanding, for he takes in the character in which the Lord hath spoken of himself: *"Quicken me after thy lovingkindness."* All at once he lays aside thought of his enemies; he is present with his God. His desire is to rise into higher spiritual existence, that he may hold closer communion with the Father of lights with whom there is no variableness. —*John Stephen.*

Verse 88.—*"Quicken me,"* etc. He had prayed before, "Quicken me in thy righteousness" (verse 40); but here "Quicken me after thy lovingkindness." The surest token of God's good-will towards us is his good work in us.—*Matthew Henry.*

Verse 88.—*"Quicken me."* Many a time in this Psalm doth David make this petition; and it seems strange that so often he should acknowledge himself a dead man, and desire God to quicken him. But so it is unto the child of God: every desertion and decay of strength is a death. So desirous are they to live unto God, that when they fail in it, and find any inability in their souls to serve God as they would, they account themselves but dead, and pray the Lord to quicken them.— *William Cowper.*

Verse 88.—*"The testimony of thy mouth."* The title here given to the directory of our duty—*"The testimony of God's mouth,"* gives increasing strength to our obligations. Thus let every word we read or hear be regarded as coming directly from the "mouth of God" (John vi. 63). What reverence! what implicit submission does it demand! May it ever find us in the posture of attention, humility, and faith! each one of us ready to say, "Speak Lord, for thy servant heareth."—*Charles Bridges.*

EXPOSITION OF VERSES 89 TO 96.

FOR ever, O LORD, thy word is settled in heaven.

90 Thy faithfulness *is* unto all generations : thou hast established the earth, and it abideth.

91 They continue this day according to thine ordinances : for all *are* thy servants.

92 Unless thy law *had been* my delights, I should then have perished in mine affliction.

93 I will never forget thy precepts : for with them thou hast quickened me.

94 I *am* thine, save me ; for I have sought thy precepts.

95 The wicked have waited for me to destroy me : *but* I will consider thy testimonies.

96 I have seen an end of all perfection : *but* thy commandment *is* exceeding broad.

89. *"For ever, O Lord, thy word is settled in heaven."* The strain is more joyful, for experience has given the sweet singer a comfortable knowledge of the word of the Lord, and this makes a glad theme. After tossing about on a sea of trouble the Psalmist here leaps to shore and stands upon a rock. Jehovah's word is not fickle nor uncertain ; it is settled, determined, fixed, sure, immovable. Man's teachings change so often that there is never time for them to be settled ; but the Lord's word is from of old the same, and will remain unchanged eternally. Some men are never happier than when they are unsettling everything and everybody ; but God's mind is not with them. The power and glory of heaven have confirmed each sentence which the mouth of the Lord has spoken, and so confirmed it that to all eternity it must stand the same,—settled in heaven, where nothing can reach it. In the former section David's soul fainted, but here the good man looks out of self and perceives that the Lord fainteth not, neither is weary, neither is there any failure in his word.

The verse takes the form of an ascription of praise : the faithfulness and immutability of God are fit themes for holy song, and when we are tired with gazing upon the shifting scene of this life, the thought of the immutable promise fills our mouth with singing. God's purposes, promises, and precepts are all settled in his own mind, and none of them shall be disturbed. Covenant settlements will not be removed, however unsettled the thoughts of men may become ; let us therefore settle it in our minds that we abide in the faith of our Jehovah as long as we have any being.

90. *"Thy faithfulness is unto all generations."* This is an additional glory : God is not affected by the lapse of ages ; he is not only faithful to one man throughout his lifetime, but to his children's children after him, yea, and to all generations so long as they keep his covenant and remember his commandments to do them. The promises are ancient things, yet they are not worn out by centuries of use, for the divine faithfulness endureth for ever. He who succoured his servants thousands of years ago still shows himself strong on the behalf of all them that trust in him. *"Thou hast established the earth, and it abideth."* Nature is governed by fixed laws ; the globe keeps its course by the divine command, and displays no erratic movements : the seasons observe their predestined order, the sea obeys the rule of ebb and flow, and all things else are marshalled in their appointed order. There is an analogy between the word of God and the works of God, and specially

in this, that they are both of them constant, fixed, and unchangeable. God's word which established the world is the same as that which he has embodied in the Scriptures ; by the word of the Lord were the heavens made, and specially by him who is emphatically THE WORD. When we see the world keeping its place and all its laws abiding the same, we have herein assurance that the Lord will be faithful to his covenant, and will not allow the faith of his people to be put to shame. If the earth abideth the spiritual creation will abide ; if God's word suffices to establish the world surely it is enough for the establishment of the individual believer.

91. "*They continue this day according to thine ordinances.*" Because the Lord has bid the universe abide, therefore it stands, and all its laws continue to operate with precision and power. Because the might of God is ever present to maintain them, therefore do all things continue. The word which spake all things into existence has supported them till now, and still supports them both in being and in well-being. God's ordinance is the reason for the continued existence of creation. What important forces these ordinances are ! "*For all are thy servants.*" Created by thy word they obey that word, thus answering the purpose of their existence, and working out the design of their Creator. Both great things and small pay homage to the Lord. No atom escapes his rule, no world avoids his government. Shall we wish to be free of the Lord's sway and become lords unto ourselves ? If we were so, we should be dreadful exceptions to a law which secures the well-being of the universe. Rather while we read concerning all things else—they continue and they serve, let us continue to serve, and to serve more perfectly as our lives are continued. By that word which is settled may we be settled ; by that voice which establishes the earth may we be established ; and by that command which all created things obey may we be made the servants of the Lord God Almighty.

92. "*Unless thy law had been my delights, I should then have perished in mine affliction.*" That word which has preserved the heavens and the earth also preserves the people of God in their time of trial. With that word we are charmed ; it is a mine of delight to us. We take a double and treble delight in it, and derive a multiplied delight from it, and this stands us in good stead when all other delights are taken from us. We should have felt ready to lie down and die of our griefs if the spiritual comforts of God's word had not uplifted us ; but by their sustaining influence we have been borne above all the depressions and despairs which naturally grow out of severe affliction. Some of us can set our seal to this statement. Our affliction, if it had not been for divine grace, would have crushed us out of existence, so that we should have perished. In our darkest seasons nothing has kept us from desperation but the promise of the Lord : yea, at times nothing has stood between us and self-destruction save faith in the eternal word of God. When worn with pain until the brain has become dazed and the reason well-nigh extinguished, a sweet text has whispered to us its heart-cheering assurance, and our poor struggling mind has reposed upon the bosom of God. That which was our delight in prosperity has been our light in adversity ; that which in the day kept us from presuming has in the night kept us from perishing. This verse contains a mournful supposition —"*unless*"; describes a horrible condition—"*perished in mine affliction*"; and implies a glorious deliverance, for he did not die, but lived to proclaim the honours of the word of God.

93.—"*I will never forget thy precepts : for with them thou hast quickened me.*" When we have felt the quickening power of a precept we never can forget it. We may read it, learn it, repeat it, and think we have it, and yet it may slip out of our minds ; but if it has once given us life or renewed that life, there is no fear of its falling from our recollection. Experience teaches, and teaches effectually. How blessed a thing it is to have the precepts written on the heart with the golden pen of experience, and graven on the memory with the divine stylus of grace. Forgetfulness is a great evil in holy things ; we see here the man of God fighting against it, and feeling sure of victory because he knew the life-giving energy of the word in his own soul. That which quickens the heart is sure to quicken the memory.

It seems singular that he should ascribe quickening to the precepts, and yet it lies in them and in all the words of the Lord alike. It is to be noted that when the Lord raised the dead he addressed to them the word of command. He said, " Lazarus, come forth," or, " Maid, arise." We need not fear to address gospel precepts to dead sinners, since by them the Spirit gives them life. Remark that the Psalmist does not say that the precepts quickened him, but that the Lord quickened him by their means : thus he traces the life from the channel to the source, and places the glory where it is due. Yet at the same time he prized the instruments of the blessing, and resolved never to forget them. He had already remembered them when he likened himself to a bottle in the smoke, and now he feels that whether in the smoke or in the fire the memory of the Lord's precepts shall never depart from him.

94. *"I am thine, save me."* A comprehensive prayer with a prevailing argument. Consecration is a good plea for preservation. If we are conscious that we are the Lord's we may be confident that he will save us. We are the Lord's by creation, election, redemption, surrender, and acceptance; and hence our firm hope and assured belief that he will save us. A man will surely save his own child : Lord, save *me*. The need of salvation is better seen by the Lord's people than by any others, and hence their prayer—" save me "; they know that only God can save them, and hence they cry to him alone; and they know that no merit can be found in themselves, and hence they urge a reason fetched from the grace of God,—" I am thine." *"For I have sought thy precepts."* Thus had he proved that he was the Lord's. He might not have attained to all the holiness which he desired, but he had studiously aimed at being obedient to the Lord, and hence he begged to be saved even to the end. A man may be seeking the doctrines and the promises, and yet be unrenewed in heart; but to seek the precepts is a sure sign of grace; no one ever heard of a rebel or a hypocrite seeking the precepts. The Lord had evidently wrought a great work upon the Psalmist, and he besought him to carry it on to completion. Saving is linked with seeking, " save me, for I have sought "; and when the Lord sets us seeking he will not refuse us the saving. He who seeks holiness is already saved; if we have sought the Lord we may be sure that the Lord has sought us, and will certainly save us.

95.—*"The wicked have waited for me to destroy me : but I will consider thy testimonies."* They were like wild beasts crouching by the way, or highwaymen waylaying a defenceless traveller; but the Psalmist went on his way without considering them, for he was considering something better, namely, the witness or testimony which God has borne to the sons of men. He did not allow the malice of the wicked to take him off from his holy study of the divine word. He was so calm that he could " consider "; so holy that he loved to consider the Lord's "testimonies"; so victorious over all their plots that he did not allow them to drive him from his pious contemplations. If the enemy cannot cause us to withdraw our thoughts from holy study, or our feet from holy walking, or our hearts from holy aspirations, he has met with poor success in his assaults. The wicked are the natural enemies of holy men and holy thoughts; if they could, they would not only damage us but destroy us, and if they cannot do this to-day they will wait for further opportunities, ever hoping that their evil designs may be compassed. They have waited hitherto in vain, and they will have to wait much longer yet; for if we are so unmoved that we do not even give them a thought their hope of destroying us must be a very poor one.

Note the double waiting,—the patience of the wicked who watch long and carefully for an opportunity to destroy the godly, and then the patience of the saint who will not quit his meditations, even to quiet his foes. See how the serpent seed lie in wait as an adder that biteth at the horse's heels; but see how the chosen of the Lord live above their venom, and take no more notice of them than if they had no existence.

96.—*"I have seen an end of all perfection."* He had seen its limit, for it went but a little way; he had seen its evaporation under the trials of life, its detection under the searching glance of truth, its exposure by the confession of the penitent. There is no perfection beneath the moon. Perfect men, in the absolute sense of the word, live only in a perfect world. Some men see no end to their own perfection, but this is because they are perfectly blind. The experienced believer has seen an end of all perfection in himself, in his brethren, in the best man's best works. It would be well if some who profess to be perfect could even see the beginning of perfection, for we fear they cannot have begun aright, or they would not talk so exceeding proudly. Is it not the beginning of perfection to lament your imperfection ? There is no such thing as perfection in anything which is the work of man. *"But thy commandment is exceeding broad."* When the breadth of the law is known the notion of perfection in the flesh vanishes : that law touches every act, word, and thought, and is of such a spiritual nature that it judges the motives, desires, and emotions of the soul. It reveals a perfection which convicts us for shortcomings as well as for transgressions, and does not allow us to make up for deficiencies in one direction by special carefulness in others. The divine ideal of holiness is far too broad for us to hope to cover all its wide arena, and yet it is no broader than it ought to be. Who would wish to have an imperfect law? Nay, its perfection is its glory; but it is the death of all glorying in our own perfection. There is a breadth about the commandment which has never been met to the full by a corresponding breadth of holiness in any mere man while here below; only in Jesus do we see it fully embodied. The law is in all respects a perfect code; each separate precept of it is far-reaching in its hallowed meaning, and the whole ten cover all, and leave no space wherein to please our passions. We may well adore the infinity of divine holiness, and then measure ourselves by its standard, and bow before the Lord in all lowliness, acknowledging how far we fall short of it.

NOTES ON VERSES 89 TO 96.

LAMED.—*Verse 89.*—Here the climax of the delineation of the suppliant's pilgrimage is reached. We have arrived at the centre of the Psalm, and the thread of the connexion is purposely broken off. The substance of the first eleven strophes has evidently been: " Hitherto hath the Lord brought me: shall it be that I now perish ? " To this the eleven succeeding strophes make answer, " The Lord's word changeth not ; and in spite of all evil forebodings, the Lord will perfect concerning me the work that he hath already begun."—*Joseph Francis Thrupp*, 1860.

Verse 89.—*"For ever, O LORD, thy word is settled in heaven."* These words are usually rendered as making but one proposition ; but the accent *athnab* showeth there are two branches ; the one asserting the eternity of God ; the other, the constancy and permanency of his word. Thus, 1. *"For ever [art thou] O LORD."* 2. *"Thy word is settled in heaven."* So the Syriac readeth it ; and Geierus, and, after him, others prove and approve this reading. And so this verse and the following do the better correspond one with the other, if we observe beginning and ending : As thou art " for ever, O Lord," and " thy faithfulness is unto all generations," which are exactly parallel. And so also will the last clauses agree : " Thy word is settled in heaven," and, " thou hast established the earth, and it abideth."

It implieth that as God is eternal, so is his word, and that it hath a fit representation both in heaven and in earth : in heaven, in the constant motion of the heavenly bodies ; in earth, in the consistency and permanency thereof ; that as his word doth stand fast in heaven, so doth his faithfulness on earth, where the afflictions of the godly seem to contradict it.—*Thomas Manton.*

Verse 89.—*"For ever, O LORD, thy word is settled in heaven."* When Job considers his body turned to dust and worms (Job xix. 19, 25), yet by faith he says, " My Redeemer lives," etc. Even when patience failed in Job, yet *faith* failed not. Though God kill all other graces and comforts, and my soul too, yet he shall not kill my faith, says he. If he separate my soul from my body, yet not faith from my soul. And therefore the just lives by faith, rather than by other graces, because when all is gone, yet faith remains, and faith remains because the *promise* remains : *"For ever, O LORD, thy word is settled in heaven."* And this is the proper and principal meaning of this place.—*Matthew Lawrence.*

Verse 89.—*"For ever, O LORD, thy word is settled in heaven."* If we look at God's word of promise, as it is in our unsettled hearts, we dream that it's as ready to waver as our hearts are ; as the shadow of the sun and moon in the water seems to shake as much as the water doth which it shines upon. Yet for all this seeming shaking here below, the sun and moon go on in a steadfast course in heaven. So the Psalmist tells us that however our hearts stagger at a promise through unbelief ; nay, and our unbelief makes us believe that the promise often is shaken ; yet *God's word is settled*, though not *in our hearts*, yet *"in heaven"* ; yea, and there *"for ever,"* as settled as heaven itself is ; yea, more than so ; for " heaven and earth may pass," but " not one jot or tittle of the law (and therefore of the gospel) shall fail " : Luke xvi. 17.—*Anthony Tuckney*, 1599—1670.

Verse 89.—*"Settled."* J. M. Good translates the verse as follows—" For ever, O Jehovah, hath thy word given array to the heavens," and observes that the Hebrew word נצב is a military term, and applies to arraying and marshalling the divisions of an army in their proper stations when taking the field. The hosts of heaven are here supposed to be arrayed or marshalled with a like exact order ; and to maintain for ever the relative duties imposed on them : while the earth, like the heavens, has as established a march prescribed to it, which it equally fulfils ; for all are the servants of the great Creator ; and hence, as they change, produce the beautiful regularity of the seasons, the rich returns of harvest, and daily declare the glory of the Lord.

Verse 89.—*"In heaven."* Whenever you look to heaven, remember that within you have a God, who hath fixed his residence and shown his glory there, and made it the seat both of his mercy and justice. You have also there a Saviour, who, after he had died for our sins, sat down at the right hand of Majesty, to see his promises accomplished, and by his word to subdue the whole world. There are angels that "do his commandment, hearkening to the voice of his word": Ps. ciii. 20. There are glorified saints, who see God face to face, and dwell with him for evermore, and came thither by the same covenant which is propounded to us, as the charter of our peace and hope. In the outer region of heaven we see the sun and moon, and all the heavenly bodies, move in that fixed course and order wherein God hath set them; and will God show his constancy in the course of nature, and be fickle and changeable in the covenant of grace, wherein he hath disposed the order and method of his mercies?—*Thomas Manton.*

Verses 89, 91.—In these verses there is affirmed to be an analogy between the word of God and the works of God. It is said of his *"word,"* that it is *"settled in heaven,"* and that it sustains its faithfulness from one generation to another. It is said of his *"works,"* and more especially of those that are immediately around us, even of the earth which we inhabit, that as it was established at the first so it abideth afterwards. And then, as if to perfect the assimilation between them, it is said of both in the 91st verse, "*They continue this day according to thine ordinances: for all are thy servants"*; thereby identifying the sureness of that word which proceeded from his lips, with the unfailing constancy of that Nature which was formed and is upholden by his hands.

The constancy of Nature is taught by universal experience, and even strikes the popular eye as the most characteristic of those features which have been impressed upon her. It may need the aid of philosophy to learn how unvarying Nature is in all her processes—how even the seeming anomalies can be traced to a law that is inflexible —how what appears at first to be the caprices of her waywardness, are, in fact, the evolutions of a mechanism that never changes—and that the more thoroughly she is sifted and put to the test by the interrogations of the curious, the more certainly will they find that she walks by a rule which knows no abatement, and perseveres with obedient footstep in that even course from which the eye of strictest scrutiny has never yet detected one hair-breadth of deviation. It is no longer doubted by men of science, that every remaining semblance of irregularity in the universe is due, not to the fickleness of Nature, but to the ignorance of man—that her most hidden movements are conducted with a uniformity as rigorous as *Fate*—that even the fitful agitations of the weather have their law and their principle—that the intensity of every breeze, and the number of drops in every shower, and the formation of every cloud, and all the occurring alternations of storm and sunshine, and the endless shiftings of temperature, and those tremulous varieties of the air which our instruments have enabled us to discover but have not enabled us to explain—that still, they follow each other by a method of succession, which, though greatly more intricate, is yet as absolute in itself as the order of the seasons, or the mathematical courses of astronomy. This is the impression of every philosophical mind with regard to Nature, and it is strengthened by each new accession that is made to science. . . . . But there is enough of patent and palpable regularity in Nature to give also to the popular mind the same impression of her constancy. There is a gross and general experience that teaches the same lesson, and that has lodged in every bosom a kind of secure and steadfast confidence in the uniformity of her processes. The very child knows and proceeds upon it. He is aware of an abiding character and property in the elements around him, and has already learned as much of the fire, and the water, and the food that he eats, and the firm ground that he treads upon, and even of the gravitation by which he must regulate his postures and his movements, as to prove that, infant though he be, he is fully initiated in the doctrine, that Nature has her laws and her ordinances, and that she continueth therein, and the proofs of this are ever multiplying along the journey of human observation; insomuch that when we come to manhood, we read of Nature's constancy throughout every department of the visible world. It meets us wherever we turn our eyes. . . . . God has so framed the machinery of my perceptions, as that I am led irresistibly to expect that everywhere events will follow each other in the very train in which I have ever been accustomed to observe them; and when God so sustains the uniformity of Nature, that in every instance it is rigidly so, he is just manifesting the faithfulness of his character. Were it otherwise, he would be practising a mockery on the expectation which he himself had inspired. God may be said to have promised to every human being that Nature will be constant—if not by the whisper of an inward voice to every heart, at least by the force of an uncontrollable bias which he has impressed on every constitution. So that, when we behold Nature keeping up its constancy, we behold the God of Nature keeping up his faithfulness ; and the system of visible things with its general laws, and its successions which are invariable, instead of an opaque materialism to intercept from the view of mortals the face of the Divinity, becomes the mirror which reflects upon the truth that is unchangeable, the ordination that never fails. . . . . And so it is, that in our text there are represented together, as if there was a tie of likeness between them—that the same God who is fixed as to the ordinances of Nature, is faithful as to the declarations of his word ; and as all experience proves how firmly he may be trusted for the one, so is there an argument as strong as experience, to prove how firmly he may be trusted for the other. By his work in us he hath awakened the expectation of a constancy in Nature, which he never disappoints. By his word to us, should he awaken the expectation of a certainty in his declarations, this he will never disappoint. It is because Nature is so fixed, that we apprehend the God of Nature to be so faithful. He who never falsifies the hope that hath arisen in every bosom, from the instinct which he himself hath communicated, will never falsify the hope that shall arise in any bosom from the express utterance of his voice. Were he a God in whose hand the processes of nature were ever shifting, then might we conceive him a God from whose mouth the proclamations of grace had the like characters of variance and vacillation. But it is just because of our reliance on the one that we feel so much of repose in our dependence upon the other ; and the same God who is so unfailing in the ordinances of his creation, we hold to be equally unfailing in the ordinances of his word.— *Thomas Chalmers.*

Verse 90.—*"Thy faithfulness is unto all generations."* As he gathered the certainty of God's word from the endurance of heaven, so now he confirms it by considering the foundation of the earth. Since the foundation of the earth, made by the word of God, abides sure, shall we not think that the foundation of our salvation, laid in Jesus Christ, is much more sure ? Though the creatures cannot teach us the way of our salvation (for that we must learn by the word), yet do they confirm that which the word saith, " Thus saith the LORD, which giveth the sun for a light by day, and the ordinances of the moon and of the stars for a light by night, which divideth the sea when the waves thereof roar ; the LORD of hosts is his name : if those ordinances depart from before me, saith the LORD, then the seed of Israel also shall cease from being a nation before me for ever : " Jerem. xxxi. 35, 36. As there Jeremy gathers the stability of the church from the stability of the creatures ; so here David confirms the certainty of our salvation by the most certain and unchangeable course of creation ; and both of them are amplified by Christ Jesus : " Heaven and earth may pass away, but one jot of God's word shall not fall to the ground." Let us therefore be strengthened in faith and give glory to God.—*William Cowper.*

Verse 90.—*"Thou hast established the earth, and it abideth."* Every time we set foot on the ground, we may remember the stability of God's promises, and it is also a confirmation of faith. Thus,—

1. The stability of the earth is the effect of God's word ; this is the true pillar upon which the earth standeth ; for he upholdeth all things by the word of his power ; " For he spake, and it was done ; he commanded, and it stood fast " : Ps. xxxiii. 9. Now, his word of power helpeth us to depend upon his word of promise.

2. Nothing appeareth whereon the globe of the earth should lean and rest : " He stretcheth out the north over the empty place, and hangeth the earth upon nothing : " Job xxvi. 7. Now, that this vast and ponderous body should lean upon the fluid air as upon a firm foundation, is matter of wonder ; the question is put in the book of Job : " Whereupon are the foundations thereof fastened ? or who laid the corner-stone thereof ? " ch. xxxviii. 6. Yet firm it is, though it hang as a ball in the air. . . . Now, since his word beareth up such a weight, and all the church's weight, and our own burden leaneth on the promise of God, he can, by the power of his word, bear up all without visible means. Therefore his people may trust his providence ; he is able to support them in any distresses, when no way of help appeareth.

3. The firmness and stability offereth itself to our thoughts. The earth abideth in the same seat and condition wherein God left it, as long as the present course

and order of nature is to continue : Ps. civ. 5.   God's truth is as immovable as the earth : Ps. cxvii. 2.   Surely if the foundation of the earth abideth sure, the foundation of our salvation, laid by Jesus Christ, is much more sure.

4. The stability remains in the midst of changes : Eccles. i. 4.   All things in the world are subject to many revolutions, but God's truth is one and the same.

5. In upholding the frame of the world, all those attributes are seen, which are a firm stay to a believer's heart, such as wisdom, power, and goodness.   The covenant of grace is as sure as the covenant made after the deluge.   We cannot look upon this earth without seeing therein a display of those same attributes which confirm our faith, in waiting upon God till his promises be fulfilled to us.—*Condensed from T. Manton.*

Verse 90.—"*It abideth.*"   Creation is as the mother, and Providence the nurse which preserveth all the works of God.   God is not like man ; for man, when he hath made a work, cannot maintain it : he buildeth a ship, and cannot save it from shipwreck ; he edifies a house, but cannot keep it from decay.   It is otherwise with God ; we daily see his conserving power, upholding his creatures ; which should confirm us that he will not cast us off, nor suffer us to perish (since we are the works of his hands) if we so depend upon him, and give him glory as our Creator, Conserver, and Redeemer.—*William Cowper.*

Verse 91.—"*They continue this day according to thine ordinances,*" etc.   Which of the works of God are not pervaded by a beautiful *order ?*   Think of the succession of day and night.   Think of the revolution of the seasons.   Think of the stars as they walk in their majestic courses,—one great law of harmony " binding the sweet influence of the Pleiades, ... and guiding Arcturus with his sons " : Job xxxviii. 31, 32.   Look upwards, amid the magnificence of night, to that crowded concave,—worlds piled on worlds—and yet see the calm grandeur of that stately march ;—not a discordant note there to mar the harmony, though wheeling at an inconceivable velocity in their intricate and devious orbits !   These heavenly sentinels all keep their appointed watch-towers.   These Levites in the upper firmament, light their altar fires " at the time of the evening incense," and quench them again, when the sun, who is appointed to rule the day, walks forth from his chamber.   " These wait all upon thee" : Ps. civ. 27.   "*They continue this day according to thine ordinances : for all are thy servants.*"—*J. R. Macduff, in "Sunsets on the Hebrew Mountains,"* 1862.

Verse 91.—"*They continue this day according to thine ordinances.*"   Man may destroy a plant, but he is powerless to force it into disobedience to the laws given it by the common Creator.   " If," says one, " man would employ it for his use, he must carefully pay attention to its wants and ways, and bow his own proud will to the humblest grass at his feet.   Man may forcibly obstruct the path of a growing twig, but it turns quietly aside, and moves patiently and irresistibly on its appointed way."   Do what he may, turf will not grow in the tropics, nor the palm bear its fruit in a cold climate.   Rice refuses to thrive out of watery swamps, or cotton to form its fleece of snowy fibres where the rain can reach them.   Some of the handsomest flowers in the world, and stranger still, some of the most juicy and succulent plants with which we are acquainted, adorn the arid and desolate sands of the Cape of Good Hope, and will not flourish elsewhere.   If you twist the branch of a tree so as to turn the under surface of its leaves towards the sky, in a very little while all those leaves will turn down and assume their appointed position.   This process will be performed sooner or later, according to the heat of the sun and the flexibility of the leaves, but none the less it will surely take place.   You cannot induce the Sorrowful tree of India to bloom by day, or cause it to cease all the year round from loading the night air with the rich perfume of its orange-like flowers.   The philosopher need not go far to find the secret of this.   The Psalmist declares it when, speaking of universal nature, he traces the true cause of its immutable order.   God he says, " hath established them for ever and ever : He hath made a decree which shall not pass ; " or, as it is in the Prayer-book version, " hath given them a law which shall not be broken " : Psalm cxlviii. 6.   Truly is it said in another Psalm (cxix. 91), "*They continue this day according to thine ordinances : for all are thy servants.*"   Wilful man may dare to defy his Maker, and set at nought his wise and merciful commands ; but not so all nature besides. Well, indeed, is it for us that his other works have not erred after the pattern of our rebellion ; that seed-time and harvest, cold and heat, summer and winter, day and night, with all their accompanying provision, have not ceased! To the precepts imposed upon vegetation when first called into being on creation's third day, it still yields implicit submission, and the tenderest plant will die rather than transgress. What an awful contrast to this is the conduct of man, God's noblest work, endowed with reason and a never-dying soul, yet too often ruining his health, wasting and destroying his mental power, defiling his immortal spirit, and, in a word, madly endeavouring to frustrate every purpose for which he was framed.— *James Neil, in "Rays from the Realms of Nature,"* 1879.

Verse 91.—All creatures punctually observe the law he hath implanted on their nature, and in their several capacities acknowledge him their sovereign; they move according to the inclinations he imprinted on them. The sea contains itself in its bounds, and the sun steps not out of his sphere; the stars march in their order: *"They continue this day according to thine ordinances : for all are thy servants."* If he orders things contrary to their primitive nature they obey him. When he speaks the word, the devouring fire becomes gentle, and toucheth not the hair of the children he will preserve; the hunger-starved lions suspend their ravenous nature when so good a morsel as Daniel is set before them; and the sun, which had been in perpetual motion since its creation, obeys the writ of ease God sent in Joshua's time, and stands still.—*Stephen Charnock.*

Verse 91.—*"All are thy servants."* We should consider how great is that perversity by which man only, formed in the image of God, together with reprobate angels, has fallen away from obedience to God; so that what is said of all other creatures cannot be said of him, unless renewed by singular grace.—*Wolfgang Musculus.*

Verse 91.—*"For all are thy servants."* Since all creatures must serve God, therefore we ought neither to use them for any other purpose, nor turn them to the service of sin. The creature by the sin of our first parents has been made subject to vanity, and groans and longs to be delivered, Rom. viii. : Christians, therefore, who use the creature and the world, should use as not abusing, 1 Cor. vii. ; but enjoy them with praise of the divine majesty and goodness, 1 Tim. iv.—*Solomon Gesner.*

Verse 91.—*"All are thy servants."*

> Say not, my soul, " From whence
> Can God relieve my care ? "
> Remember that Omnipotence
> Has servants everywhere.
>
> *Thomas T. Lynch*, 1855.

Verse 92.—*"Unless thy law had been my delights,"* etc. This text sets out the great benefit and comfort which David found in the law of God in the time of his affliction. It kept him from perishing : *"Had not thy law been my delights, I had perished in my affliction"* . . . . David speaks this (saith Musculus) of the distressful condition he was in when persecuted by Saul, forced to fly to the Philistines, and sometimes to hide himself in the rocks and caves of the earth. It is very likely (saith he) that he had the book of God's law with him, by the reading of which he mitigated and allayed his sorrows, and kept himself pure from communicating with the heathen in their superstitions. The Greek scholiasts say that David uttered these words when driven from Saul, and compelled to live among the Philistines, etc. For he would have been allured to have communicated with them in their impieties had he not carried about him the meditation of the word of God. The word of God delighted in is the afflicted saint's antidote against ruin and destruction. The word of God is the sick saint's salve, the dying saint's cordial, a precious medicine to keep God's people from perishing in time of affliction. This upheld Jacob from sinking, when his brother Esau came furiously marching to destroy him (Gen. xxxii. 12). He pleaded, " And thou saidst, I will surely do thee good," etc. Thus the promise of God supported him. This also upheld Joshua and enabled him courageously to fight the Lord's battles, because God had said, " He would never leave him nor forsake him " (Josh. i. 5). Melancthon saith that the Landgrave of Hesse told him at Dresden that it had been impossible for him to have borne up under the manifold miseries of so long an imprisonment, *Nisi habuisset consolationem verbo divino in suo corde,* but for the comfort of the Scriptures in his heart.—*Edmund Calamy* (1600—1666), *in "The Godly Man's Ark."*

Verse 92.—Certainly the reading of most part of the Scriptures must needs be a very comfortable thing ; and I think a godly heart (disposed as it ought to be) can hardly tell how to be sad while it does it. For what a comfort is it for a man to read an earthly father's letters sent to him, though they were written long ago ? With what care do we keep such letters in our chests ? With how much delight do we ever and anon take them out and look upon them ? and with how much sorrow do we lose them ? Is my love to my *earthly* father so great, and shall my love to my *heavenly* Father be less ? Can my heart choose but rejoice and my bones flourish like an herb, as oft as I look upon my Redeemer's last will and testament, whereby I know that he gave me so much, and that he doth so much for me continually, and that I shall be ever with him ?

How is David ever and anon talking of his *delight in the law of God*, and in his statutes and testimonies. It was to him instead of all other delights ; standing by him when all delights else left him ; "*Unless thy law had been my delight* (or, *my very great delight*), *I should then have perished in mine affliction*," ver. 92. Let *princes sit and speak* against him never so much ; yet will he meditate in God's statutes, ver. 23. Let him have never so many *persecutors and enemies ;* yet will he not decline from God's testimonies, ver. 157. Let him be in a strange place, there shall God's statutes be his song, ver. 54. Let him be a *stranger in the earth* all his life ; so that he be not a stranger to God's commandments he cares not, ver. 19. Although he should have never so much *contempt* cast upon him, yet will he not forget God's precepts, ver. 141. Although his *soul* should be *continually in his hand*, yet that should not make him forget God's law. Yea, although he became like *a bottle in the smoke*, yet will he not forget God's precepts, ver. 83. And therefore was it that he rejoiced, because he had been *afflicted* upon this account, that it made him learn God's statutes. He cared for no other *wealth*. "*Thy testimonies have I taken as an heritage for ever : for they are the rejoicing of my heart*," ver. 111. Neither cared he much for *life*, but only to keep God's word, ver. 17. Whatever he had said before, or meant to say next, he still cries, "*Teach me thy statutes*," and, "*I have longed for thy precepts*," etc. ; or some such expression or other. He could not forbear to speak of them, for they were still before him, ver. 30. No wonder, then, that he meditated upon them so often, as he saith he did. "*O how I love thy law ! it is my meditation all the day*," ver. 97. And "*Thy testimonies are my meditation*," ver. 99. God's commandments were to David sweeter in his mouth than honey, to talk and discourse of them, ver. 103.—*Zachary Bogan*, 1653.

Verse 92.—The persons to whose *delight* the word of God actually conduces are the children of God, and none else. None but they are prepared to take in the consolation of the word.

1. As they only are spiritually enlightened to discern the great and comfortable things contained in it, enlightened in a manner in which no others are : "The natural man receiveth not the things of the Spirit of God, for they are foolishness unto him : neither can he know them, because they are spiritually discerned" (1 Cor. ii. 14).

2. As they have the highest value for the word of God, this prepares them for receiving consolation from it.

3. As they have their hearts and ways suited to the word of God, this is another reason of the delight they fetch from it. "For they that are after the flesh do mind the things of the flesh," and take pleasure in them ; "but they that are after the Spirit the things of the Spirit " (Rom. viii. 5). The comforts of the word are spiritual ; and only the spiritual heart, as it is renewed by grace, can taste and relish them. The delight which the people of God have from the word, is a privilege peculiar to themselves : and this word hath enough to give delight to all of their number.—*Daniel Wilcox*, 1676—1733.

Verse 92.—"*My delights*." The word signifieth delights in the plural number. Many were the sorrows of David's life ; but against them all he found as many comforts and delectations in God's word. With such variety of holy wisdom hath God penned his word, that it hath convenient comfort for every state of life, and therefore the children of God account nothing so dear as it ; they prefer it to their appointed food.—*William Cowper.*

Verse 92.—"*Thy law . . . my delights . . . in mine affliction*." I happened to be standing in a grocer's shop one day in a large manufacturing town in the west of Scotland, when a poor, old, frail widow came in to make a few purchases. There never was, perhaps, in that town a more severe time of distress. Nearly every loom was stopped. Decent and respectable tradesmen who had seen better days, were obliged to subsist on public charity. So much money per day (but a trifle at most) was allowed to the really poor and deserving. The poor widow had received her daily pittance, and she had now come into the shop of the grocer to lay it out to the best advantage. She had but a few coppers in her withered hands. Carefully did she expend her little stock—a pennyworth of this and the other necessary of life nearly exhausted all she had. She came to the last penny, and with a singular expression of heroic contentment and cheerful resignation on her wrinkled face, she said, " Now I must buy oil with this, that I may see to read my Bible during these long dark nights, for it is my only comfort now when every other comfort has gone away."—*Alexander Wallace, in "The Bible and the Working Classes,"* 1853.

Verse 92.—This verse I may call a Perfume against the Plague ; The Sick Man's Salve ; The Afflicted Man's Consolation ; and a blessed Triumph, in and over all troubles.—*Richard Greenham.*

Verse 93.—"*I will never forget thy precepts,*" etc. *Forgetfulness* must be striven against in every possible way, lest it should gradually creep in, through ingratitude, old age, weakness of mind, or other overwelming cares. See verses 16, 61, 83.—*Martin Geier.*

Verse 93.—"*I will never forget thy precepts,*" etc. This afflicted good man is now comforted ; his comfort came from his delight in God's law ; he thinks of it, he feels the force of it, and therefore to the end that he might ever receive the like comforts, he will bind himself by a promise to the Lord that he will never forget his precepts ; adding a reason, namely, that they were to him spirit and life. "*With them hast thou quickened me.*" Quickened he was, as he saith, by God, but yet also by the word, soundly preached, savingly understood, and particularly applied to the conscience. Thus then doth the power of Christ's death make us to walk on in newness of life. No *aqua vitæ,* or *celestis,* like unto this, by which we have inward peace of conscience, and an outward obedience to God's commandments. David rejoiced in this blessing, so ought we : we desire to be ever quick, and cheerful to all good duties ; it is only God, by his Spirit, in the word, that can give it.—*Richard Greenham.*

Verse 93.—"*With them thou hast quickened me.*" The quickening Spirit delights to work by means of the word ; but though the word be the means, yet the benefit comes from God : " For with them *thou* hast quickened me." Life comes from the fountain of life. The gospel is a sovereign plaster ; but it is God's hand that must apply it, and make it stick ; make it to be peace, comfort, and quickening to our souls. There is a double quickening, when, from dead, we are made living ; or when, from cold, and sad, and heavy, we are made lively . . . . and so not only have life, but enjoy it more abundantly, according to Christ's gracious promise (John x. 10) ; that they may be living, lively, kept still in vigour. Now, this second quickening may be taken, either more largely, for the vitality of grace ; or, strictly, for actual comfort. Largely taken ; so God quickens by increasing the life of grace ; either internally, by promising the life of grace ; or morally and externally, by promising the life of glory. More strictly, his quickening may be taken for comfort and support in his affliction ; so it is likely to be taken here : he had said immediately before, " Unless thy law had been my delights, I should then have perished in my affliction" ; and now, " I will never forget thy precepts, for with them thou hast quickened me." It was great comfort and support to him ; and therefore he should prize the word as long as he lived.—*Thomas Manton.*

Verse 93.—"*Thou hast quickened me.*" Leave not off reading the Bible till you find your hearts warmed. Read the word, not only as a history, but labour to be affected with it. Let it not only inform you, but inflame you. " Is not my word like a fire ? saith the Lord " : Jer. xxiii. 29. Go not from the word till you can say as those disciples, " Did not our hearts burn within us ? " Luke xxiv. 32.—*Thomas Watson.*

Verse 94.—"*I am thine, save me.*" David, a man after God's own heart, would be saved, but not after the manner of the men of this world, that would be saved to be their own and to enjoy themselves at their own will ; but he in being saved would be God's, and at his disposing : "*I am thine, save me.*"

There is a threefold strength in this argument.

1. The *law of nature,* which obligeth a father to be good to his child, the husband to his wife, etc., and God hath subjected himself more unto the law of nature, he

lies more under it, than any of these ; and doth more perfectly, fully, and gloriously fulfil this law of nature than any ; there is no father like him, no friend, no husband like him. " Can a woman forget her sucking child ? yet will I not forget thee : " Isai. xlix. 15. A mother can hardly do it ; nature teacheth her to have bowels, and a merciful remembrance towards her child ; much more will I, saith God.

2. When we can say to God, *"I am thine,"* we plead *the covenant which God hath made with us,* wherein he is become our father and friend : and this is that which was pleaded in Isai. lxiii. 16 : " Doubtless thou art our father, though Abraham be ignorant of us, and Israel acknowledge us not (because they are gone, and so have no cognizance of us now) ; yet thou, O Lord, art our Father, our Redeemer ; thy name is from everlasting." See what a conclusion here is made ; doubtless thou art our Father, and therefore we call to thee for help.

3. There is this encouragement and strength that the spirit of a man receives in thus arguing with God, *that if he can say in truth, "I am thine," God much more will say to the creature, "I am thine."* If we have so much love to offer ourselves to God, to become his ; much more will the love of God make him to become ours ; for God loves first, and most, and surest. If mine heart rise toward God, much more is the heart of God toward me ; because there love is in the fountain. Never did a spouse speak to her husband, whom her soul loved to the highest, more willingly, and say, *"I am thine,"* than the spirit of an upright man saith to God, *"Lord, I am thine."* And he loves him with a *love of thankfulness.* Hast thou given thyself to me, saith he, and shall I then withhold myself from thee ? Hast thou, who art so great, done all this for me, and shall I stand out against thee ? The gracious man will willingly acknowledge himself to be the Lord's. The saints often do this : David above twenty times comes with this acknowledgment in this Psalm, and in Psalm cxvi. 16 : *"I am thy servant ; I am thy servant."* To say it once was not enough ; he saith it again, to show the sincerity of his spirit, and to witness that his heart was fully pleased with this, that he was not his own, but the Lord's. The knowledge of our interest in God doth much further our approaches to God. When a man is once assured, and can say with a clear spirit, *"I am thine,"* he will naturally cry, *"Save me."* Such a man is a man of prayer, he is much in addresses to God, and conversing with him.—*Joseph Symonds,* 1653.

Verse 94.—"I am thine." This is an excellent motive to draw from the Lord help in trouble,—*"I am thine."* Thine by *creation,* I was made by thee ; thine by *adoption,* I was assigned over to thee ; thine by *donation,* I was given to thee ; thine by *marriage,* I was espoused to thee ; thine by *redemption,* I was purchased by thee ; thine by *stipulation,* I have vowed myself unto thee.—*Richard Greenham.*

Verse 94.—"For I have sought thy precepts." See here how David qualifies his protestation : from his earnest affection to the word of God, he proves that he was God's man and not his own servant. It is not words, but affections and actions which must prove us to be the Lord's. *Tuus sum, quia id solum quod tuum est quæsivi :* I am thine because I sought nothing but that which is thine, and how I might please thee. *Mihi in tuis justificationibus est omne patrimonium :* in the observance of thy precepts is all my patrimony.—*William Cowper.*

Verse 95.—"The wicked have waited for me to destroy me." Two things again he notes in his enemies ; diligence, in waiting all occasions whereby to do him evil ; and cruelty without mercy, for their purpose was to destroy him : wherein, still we see how restless and insatiable is the malice of the wicked against the godly. Daniel's preservation in the lions' den was a great miracle ; but it is no less a marvellous work of God, that the godly who are the flock of Christ, are daily preserved in the midst of the wicked, who are but ravening wolves, and thirst for the blood of the saints of God, having a cruel purpose in their heart if they might perform it, utterly to destroy them.—*William Cowper.*

Verse 95.—"But I will consider thy testimonies." It was a grievous temptation to be sought for to be given up to slaughter, but a greater mercy to consider God's testimonies, even then when his life was sought for. Had it not been for the consideration of God's testimonies, a thousand to one he had fallen away.—*Richard Greenham.*

Verse 96.—"I have seen an end of all perfection," etc. These words are variously rendered and understood by interpreters, who in this variety do very much conspire and agree in the same sense. The *Chaldee* Paraphrase renders the words thus, *"I have seen an end of all things about which I have employed my care; but thy commandment is very large."* The *Syriac* version thus, *"I have seen an end of all regions and countries"* (that is, I have found the compass of the habitable world to be finite and limited) *" but thy commandment is of a vast extent."* Others explain it thus, *"I have seen an end of all perfection,"* that is, of all the things of this world which men value and esteem at so high a rate; of all worldly wisdom and knowledge, of wealth, and honour, and greatness, which do all perish and pass away; *" but thy law is eternal, and still abideth the same";* or, as the Scripture elsewhere expresses it, " The word of the Lord endureth for ever."—*John Tillotson,* 1630—1694.

Verse 96.—*"I have seen an end of all perfection."* Poor perfection which one sees an end of ! Yet such are all those things in this world which pass for perfections. David in his time had seen Goliath, the strongest, overcome; Asahel, the swiftest, overtaken; Ahithophel, the wisest, befooled; Absalom, the fairest, deformed.—*Matthew Henry.*

Verse 96.—*"I have seen an end of all perfection,"* etc. The Psalmist's words offer us a double comfort and encouragement. We may read them in two ways: (1) " I have seen an end of all perfection; *for* thy commandment is exceeding broad "; and (2) " I have seen an end of all perfection, *but* thy commandment is exceeding broad."

Read in the first way, they suggest the animating thought, that our haunting consciousness of imperfection springs from the bright and awful perfection of the Law we are bent on obeying, of the ideal we have set before us. It is not because we are worse than those who are without law, or who are a law unto themselves, that we are restless and dissatisfied with ourselves; but because we measure both ourselves and our fellows by the lofty standard of God's commandment. It is because that commandment is so broad, that we cannot embrace it; it is because it is so high, that we cannot attain to it; it is because it is so perfect, that we cannot perfectly obey it.

But we may read the verse in another way, and still derive comfort and encouragement from it. We may say: " I have seen an end of all perfection in myself, and in the world; *but* thy commandment is exceeding broad: *that* is perfect, though *I* am imperfect, and in its perfection I find the promise of my own." For shall God give a law for human life, and that law remain for ever unfulfilled ! Impossible ! " The gifts of God are without repentance "—irreversible, never to be lessened or withdrawn. His purpose is not to be made of none effect by our weaknesses and sins. In the Law he has shown us what he would have us to be. And shall we never become what he would have us to be? Can the Law remain for ever without any life that corresponds to it and fulfils it ? Nay, God will never take back the fair and perfect ideal of human life depicted in his Law, never retract his purpose to raise the life of man till it touches and fulfils its ideal. And so the very Law which is our despair is our comfort also; for if *that* be perfect *we* must become perfect; its perfection is the pledge of ours.—*From "The Expositor,"* 1876.

Verse 96.—*"I have seen an end of all perfection."* David's natural eye had seen the end of many human perfections, and the eye of his understanding saw the end of them all. He had seen some actually end, and he saw that all must end. Adam did not continue in that perfection which had no imperfection in it; how then shall any of his children continue in what is at best an imperfect perfection ?—*Abraham Wright.*

Verse 96.—*"I have seen an end,"* etc. The laws of Lycurgus among the Grecians, and of Numa among the Romans, had somewhat of good in them, but not all; prohibited somewhat that was evil, but not all that was evil. But the Christian religion is of a larger extent, both in its precepts and prohibitions: *"I have seen an end of all perfection: but thy commandment is exceeding broad."* A man with the eye of his body may behold an end of many worldly perfections, of many fair estates, great beauties, large parts, hopeful families; but a man with the eye of his soul (or by faith) may see an end of all earthly perfections. He may see the world in a flame, and all its pomp and pride, and glory, and gallantry, and crowns and sceptres, and riches, and treasures, turned into ashes. He may see the heavens passing away like a scroll, and the elements melting with fervent heat, and the earth, with the things thereon, consumed; and all its perfections, which men doated so much on, vanished into smoke and nothing. It is easy to see to the end of all terrene perfections, but it is difficult, yea, impossible, to see to the end of divine precepts: *"But thy commandments are exceeding broad,"* of a vast latitude, beyond our apprehension. They are so deep that none can fathom them, Ps. xxxvi. 6, so high that they are established in heaven, Ps. cxix. 48; so long that they endure for ever. 2 Pet. i.; and so broad, that none can measure them. They are not only *"broad,"* but *"exceeding* broad": " higher than heaven, longer than the earth, broader than the sea." The commands of God reach the inward parts, the most secret motions and retired recesses of the soul. They reach all the privy thoughts, they pierce even to the dividing asunder of soul and spirit, and of the joints and marrow, and discern the thoughts and intents of the heart, Heb. iv. 12. They reach to all our actions; to those that seem smallest and of less concernment, as well as to those that are greater and of more concernment.—*George Swinnock.*

Verse 96.—*"Thy commandment is exceeding broad."* As there is more mercy in the gospel than we are able to comprehend, so there is more holiness in the law than we are able to comprehend. No man ever saw into the depths of that righteousness. There is an infinite holiness in the law. *"I have seen an end of all perfection: but thy commandment is exceeding broad."* He speaks not in the concrete, I have seen an end of *perfect things,* but in the abstract, " an end of *perfection,"* I have come to the outside or to the very bottom of all (a man may soon travel through all the perfections that are in the world, and either see their end, or see that they end); *"but thy commandment is exceeding broad,"* that is, it is exceedingly broader than any of these perfections; I cannot see the end of it, and I know it shall never have an end. There is a vastness of purity and spiritualness in the law.—*Joseph Caryl.*

Verse 96.—*"Thy commandment is exceeding broad."* It is so by the comprehensive applicableness of its grand, simple rules. " Thou shalt love the Lord thy God with all thy heart, and soul, and strength, and thy neighbour as thyself." It is so by the ample order of its special injunctions. Where is there a spot without a signal of the divine will? It is so by laying an authoritative hand on the first principles and origin from which any thing can proceed, in human spirit and action; then it reaches to all things that do or can proceed thence. It asserts a jurisdiction over all thought and inward affection. All language is uttered under this same jurisdiction. All that the world and each man is in action about. And even over what is not done it maintains its authority, and pronounces its dictates and judgments. It is a positive thing with respect to what is negative, omission, non-existence. Like the divine government in the material world, over the wastes, deserts, and barren sands. And from these spaces of nothing (as it were) it can raise up substantial forms of evil, of sin, in evidence against men. As at the resurrection men will rise from empty wastes, where it would not have been suspected that any were concealed. Let a man look back on all his omissions, and think what the divine law can raise from them against him. Thus the law in its exceeding breadth, is vacant nowhere; it is not stretched to this wide extent by chasms and void spaces. If a man could find one such, he might there take his position for sin with impunity, if not with innocence.—*John Foster,* 1768—1843.

Verse 96.—*"Thy commandment is exceeding broad."* In the popular religious literature of the present times, the terms " broad " and " free " are of frequent occurrence. The fascination that surrounds them is enhanced by the use, at the same time, of their opposites, " narrow " and " bigoted." By an adroit manipulation of these terms and their equivalents, the heterodoxy of the day is labouring to stamp out the doctrine and spirit of the evangelical faith, and to allure the Christian multitude within the influence of the spreading rationalistic drift. Going to the market where the heterodox wares are exhibited with labels so attractive, the unsuspecting purchaser soon discovers that " their vine is of the vine of Sodom, and of the fields of Gomorrah: their grapes are grapes of gall, their clusters are bitter." Is the time not come when the adherents of the true faith should make an effort to wrest from their opponents the monopoly in the use of these terms, which they seem desirous of establishing for themselves? Those who, in the spirit of their Master, abide most closely by, and contend most tenaciously for, the whole faith that has been delivered to the saints, must be the most liberal-minded and catholic; and those who forsake the " old paths " must, in proportion to the extent of their departures, become contracted in their mental grasp, and narrow in their soul. Is not the Bible—the whole Bible—the only manual of Broad-churchism in its truest and highest sense? Is not the revelation of God's Son in us, the great soul-expanding power? " If the Son shall make you free, ye shall be free indeed."

Must we not infer, from the words of Christ, " Ye shall know the truth, and the truth shall make you free," that the mind which apprehends the truth is a home of mental liberty ?   Does not strict conformity of the life to God's law produce real breadth of character ?   For *"Thy commandment is exceeding broad."*   Is not the gospel system the only true Broad-churchism—" the perfect law of liberty " ?   Is not the believer—and the more so in proportion to the strength of his faith—the only true Broad-churchman, "increasing with the increase of God," "filled with all the fulness of God " ?—*James Kerr, in "The Modern Scottish Pulpit," 1880.*

Verse 96.—*"Exceeding broad."*   Notwithstanding many things do show the way of life to be narrow, yet unto the godly man it is a way of great breadth ; though not for sin, yet for duty and delight.   He makes haste and progress in it.—*Robert Trail, 1642—1716.*

Verse 96.—Take notice that the law, which is your mark, is *exceeding broad*. And yet not the more easy to be hit ; because you must aim to hit it, in every duty of it, with a performance of equal breadth, or else you cannot hit it at all.—*Stephen Marshall.*

EXPOSITION OF VERSES 97 TO 104.

O HOW love I thy law ! it *is* my meditation all the day.

98 Thou through thy commandments hast made me wiser than mine enemies : for they *are* ever with me.

99 I have more understanding than all my teachers : for they testimonies *are* my meditation.

100 I understand more than the ancients, because I keep thy precepts.

101 I have refrained my feet from every evil way, that I might keep thy word.

102 I have not departed from thy judgments : for thou hast taught me.

103 How sweet are thy words unto my taste ! *yea, sweeter* than honey to my mouth !

104 Through thy precepts I get understanding : therefore I hate every false way.

97. "*O how love I thy law !*" It is a note of exclamation. He loves so much that he must express his love, and in making the attempt he perceives that it is inexpressible—and therefore cries, " O how I love ! " We not only reverence but love the law, we obey it out of love, and even when it chides us for disobedience we love it none the less. The law is God's law, and therefore it is our love. We love it for its holiness, and pine to be holy ; we love it for its wisdom, and study to be wise ; we love it for its perfection, and long to be perfect. Those who know the power of the gospel perceive an infinite loveliness in the law as they see it fulfilled and embodied in Christ Jesus. "*It is my meditation all the day.*" This was both the effect of his love and the cause of it. He meditated in God's word because he loved it, and then loved it the more because he meditated in it. He could not have enough of it, so ardently did he love it : all the day was not too long for his converse with it. His matin prayer, his noonday thought, his evensong were all out of Holy Writ ; yea, in his worldly business he still kept his mind saturated with the law of the Lord. It is said of some men that the more you know them the less you admire them ; but the reverse is true of God's word. Familiarity with the word of God breeds affection, and affection seeks yet greater familiarity. When " thy law," and " my meditation " are together all the day, the day grows holy, devout, and happy, and the heart lives with God. David turned away from all else ; for in the preceding verse he tells us that he had seen an end of all perfection ; but he turned in unto the law and tarried there the whole day of his life on earth, growing henceforth wiser and holier.

98. "*Thou through thy commandments hast made me wiser than mine enemies.*" The commands were his book, but God was his teacher. The letter can make us knowing, but only the divine Spirit can make us wise. Wisdom is knowledge put to practical use. Wisdom comes to us through obedience : " If any man will do his will he shall know of the doctrine." We learn not only from promise, and doctrine, and sacred history, but also from precept and command ; in fact, from the commandments we gather the most practical wisdom, and that which enables us best to cope with our adversaries. A holy life is the highest wisdom and the surest defence. Our enemies are renowned for subtlety, from the first father of them, the old serpent, down to the last cockatrice that has been hatched from the egg ; and it would be vain for us to try to be a match with them in the craft and mystery of cunning, for the children of this world are in their generation wiser than the children of light. We must go to another school and learn of a different instructor, and then by uprightness we shall baffle fraud, by simple truth we shall vanquish deep-laid scheming, and by open candour we shall defeat slander. A thoroughly straightforword man, devoid of all policy, is a terrible puzzle to diplomatists ; they suspect him of a subtle duplicity through which they cannot see, while he, indifferent to their suspicions, holds on the even tenor of his way, and baffles all their arts. Yes, " honesty is the best policy." He who is taught of God has a practical wisdom such as malice cannot supply to the crafty ; while harmless as a dove he also exhibits more than the serpent's wisdom.

"For they are ever with me."   He was always studying or obeying the commandments ; they were his choice and constant companions.   If we wish to become proficient we must be indefatigable.   If we keep the wise law ever near us we shall become wise, and when our adversaries assail us we shall be prepared for them with that ready wit which lies in having the word of God at our fingers' ends.   As a soldier in battle must never lay aside his shield, so must we never have the word of God out of our minds ; it must be ever with us.

99. *"I have more understanding than all my teachers."*   That which the Lord had taught him had been useful in the camp, and now he finds it equally valuable in the schools.   Our teachers are not always to be trusted ; in fact, we may not follow any of them implicitly, for God holds us to account for our personal judgments. It behoves us then to follow closely the chart of the Word of God, that we may be able to save the vessel when even the pilot errs.   If our teachers should be in all things sound and safe, they will be right glad for us to excel them, and they will ever be ready to own that the teaching of the Lord is better than any teaching which they can give us.   Disciples of Christ who sit at his feet are often better skilled in divine things than doctors of divinity.   *"For thy testimonies are my meditation."* This is the best mode of acquiring understanding.   We may hear the wisest teachers and remain fools, but if we meditate upon the sacred word we must become wise. There is more wisdom in the testimonies of the Lord than in all the teachings of men if they were all gathered into one vast library.   The one book outweighs all the rest.

David does not hesitate to speak the truth in this place concerning himself, for he is quite innocent of self-consciousness.   In speaking of his understanding he means to extol the law and the Lord, and not himself.   There is not a grain of boasting in these bold expressions, but only a sincere childlike desire to set forth the excellence of the Lord's word.   He who knows the truths taught in the Bible will be guilty of no egotism if he believes himself to be possessed of more important truth than all the agnostic professors buried and unburied.

100. *"I understand more than the ancients, because I keep thy precepts."*   The men of old age, and the men of old time, were outdone by the holier and more youthful learner.   He had been taught to observe in heart and life the precepts of the Lord, and this was more than the most venerable sinner had ever learned, more than the philosopher of antiquity had so much as aspired to know.   He had the word with him, and so outstripped his foes ; he meditated on it, and so outran his friends ; he practised it, and so outshone his elders.   The instruction derived from Holy Scripture is useful in many directions, superior from many points of view, unrivalled everywhere and in every way.   As our soul may make her boast in the Lord, so may we boast in his word.   " There is none like it : give it me," said David as to Goliath's sword, and we may say the same as to the word of the Lord.   If men prize antiquity they have it here.   The ancients are had in high repute, but what did they all know compared with that which we perceive in the divine precepts ?   " The old is better " says one : but the oldest of all is the best of all, and what is that but the word of the Ancient of days.

101. *"I have refrained my feet from every evil way, that I might keep thy word."* There is no treasuring up the holy word unless there is a casting out of all unholiness : if we keep the good word we must let go the evil.   David had zealously watched his steps and put a check upon his conduct,—he had refrained his feet.   No one evil way could entice him, for he knew that if he went astray but in one road he had practically left the way of righteousness, therefore he avoided every false way. The by-paths were smooth and flowery, but he knew right well that they were evil, and so he turned his feet away, and held on along the straight and thorny pathway which leads to God.   It is a pleasure to look back upon self-conquests,—" I have refrained," and a greater delight still to know that we did this out of no mere desire to stand well with our fellows, but with the one motive of keeping the law of the Lord.   Sin avoided that obedience may be perfected is the essence of this verse ; or it may be that the Psalmist would teach us that there is no real reverence for the book where there is not carefulness to avoid every transgression of its precepts. How can we keep God's word if we do not keep our own works from becoming vile ?

102. *"I have not departed from thy judgments : for thou hast taught me."*   They are well taught whom God teaches.   What we learn from the Lord we never forget. God's instruction has a practical effect,—we follow his way when he teaches us ;

and it has an abiding effect,—we do not depart from holiness. Read this verse in connection with the preceding and you get the believer's "I have," and his "I have not": he is good both positively and negatively. What he did, namely, "refrained his feet," preserved him from doing that which otherwise he might have done, namely, "departed from thy judgments." He who is careful not to go an inch aside will not leave the road. He who never touches the intoxicating cup will never be drunk. He who never utters an idle word will never be profane. If we begin to depart a little we can never tell where we shall end. The Lord brings us to persevere in holiness by abstinence from the beginning of sin; but whatever be the method he is the worker of our perseverance, and to him be all the glory.

103. "*How sweet are thy words unto my taste!*" He had not only heard the words of God, but fed upon them: they affected his palate as well as his ear. God's words are many and varied, and the whole of them make up what we call "the word": David loved them each one, individually, and the whole of them as a whole; he tasted an indescribable sweetness in them. He expresses the fact of their sweetness, but as he cannot express the degree of their sweetness he cries, "How sweet!" Being God's words they were divinely sweet to God's servant; he who put the sweetness into them had prepared the taste of his servant to discern and enjoy it. David makes no distinction between promises and precepts, doctrines and threatenings; they are all included in God's words, and all are precious in his esteem. Oh for a deep love to all that the Lord has revealed, whatever form it may take.

"*Yea, sweeter than honey to my mouth.*" When he did not only eat but also speak the word, by instructing others, he felt an increased delight in it. The sweetest of all temporal things fall short of the infinite deliciousness of the eternal word: honey itself is outstripped in sweetness by the word of the Lord. When the Psalmist fed on it he found it sweet; but when he bore witness of it it became sweeter still. How wise it will be on our part to keep the word on our palate by meditation and on our tongue by confession. It must be sweet to our taste when we think of it, or it will not be sweet to our mouth when we talk of it.

104. "*Through thy precepts I get understanding.*" God's direction is our instruction. Obedience to the divine will begets wisdom of mind and action. As God's way is always best, those who follow it are sure to be justified by the result. If the Lawgiver were foolish his law would be the same, and obedience to such a law would involve us in a thousand mistakes; but as the reverse is the case, we may count ourselves happy to have such a wise, prudent, and beneficial law to be the rule of our lives. We are wise if we obey and we grow wise by obeying!

"*Therefore I hate every false way,*" Because he had understanding, and because of the divine precepts, he detested sin and falsehood. Every sin is a falsehood; we commit sin because we believe a lie, and in the end the flattering evil turns a liar to us and we find ourselves betrayed. True hearts are not indifferent about falsehood, they grow warm in indignation; as they love the truth, so they hate the lie. Saints have a universal horror of all that is untrue, they tolerate no falsehood or folly, they set their faces against all error of doctrine or wickedness of life. He who is a lover of one sin is in league with the whole army of sins; we must have neither truce nor parley with even one of these Amalekites, for the Lord hath war with them from generation to generation, and so must we. It is well to be a good hater. And what is that? A hater of no living being, but a hater of "every false way." The way of self-will, of self-righteousness, of worldliness, of pride, of unbelief, of hypocrisy,—these are all false ways, and therefore not only to be shunned, but to be abhorred.

This final verse of the strophe marks a great advance in character, and shows that the man of God is growing stronger, bolder, and happier than aforetime. He has been taught of the Lord, so that he discerns between the precious and the vile, and while he loves the truth fervently he hates falsehood intensely. May all of us reach this state of discrimination and determination, so that we may greatly glorify God.

NOTES ON VERSES 97 TO 104.

Verse 97.—"O how love I thy law ! " He speaketh not of his knowing, reading, hearing, speaking, or outward practising of the law, but of *love* to the law : this is more than all the former : all the former may be without this, but this cannot be without the former. We may know, read, hear, speak, yea, preach the law, and all God's word, as also outwardly perform outward works prescribed and commanded by the law, and yet not love it ; but where this love is there cannot but be all the former. Love is the principal affection of all other ; like a queen commanding and overruling all the rest : all the rest depend upon it ; yea, sometimes also the judgment itself. As the love is set, whether rightly or wrongly, towards good or evil, so are all the affections swayed ; yea, judgment itself sometimes blinded by love, erreth, as the love itself erreth ; and so words and all actions are accordingly. Doth not daily experience daily teach the truth hereof ? Moreover, besides this observation of this word, in respect of other, and in a kind of opposition unto other ; let us observe two other things therein : 1. The first person ; 2. The present tense. He saith not, O how is thy word to be loved, namely, by others ; but O, how do *I myself* love thy law or thy word ! Neither doth he say, O, how have I loved thy law in times past, or, how will I love it hereafter, how unfeignedly do I purpose to love it, when I shall be advanced unto and settled in my kingdom ; or, how would I love it if I were so advanced and settled, or were I in this or that estate, or had this or that which I yet have not, or that others have ; the prophet, I say, speaketh not in such manner ; but he speaketh, as in the first person, so also in the present tense, saying, O how do I (now, such as I am) love thy law ! Both these things are very worthy of our observation, and they be in the greater in respect of the person of the prophet ; for albeit the name of the writer of this Psalm be not expressed in the title thereof (as in many other Psalms), yet the stream of most interpreters carrieth it to David. The matter also and style of the Psalm, compared with the matter and style of other Psalms which are David's, do both savour of David, and argue it was written by David. . . . . Whether David were now in full and quiet possession of his kingdom (though not without many adversaries), or whether he was only known to be the heir-apparent, appointed to succeed Saul (as most do think), or whether he were for a time in flight from the cruel and rebellious insurrection of his unnatural son Absalom, yet is it a great matter that here he speaketh of his great love towards the law of God. If he were in full and quiet possession of his kingdom, then had he many other things that he might have loved, and wherewith the hearts of such princes are commonly taken up, yea, also stolen away from those things that are much more worthy of love. What need I speak of the daily experience, whereby the truth hereof is manifest in far more mean persons than princes are ? If David were in exile or flight, a man would think that his wife, and children, and other friends, as also his country, would have so occupied and fully possessed his heart, that there should have been little place for other things therein ; but that rather he should have said, Oh, how love I those things ! Oh, how is my heart troubled with thoughts of them, and care for them in my great love towards them ! Moreover, that neither any troubles on the one side, wherewith David was continually exercised ; nor his honours, riches, or pleasures either in possession or in hope on the other side, did extinguish, or cool, or abate his love, is it not a thing of great note ?

The next word to be observed is that word *"how"* : " Oh *how* love I thy law ! " This noteth the manner or measure of his love. It is a word of admiration, or a note of comparison ; so is it taken in divers other places . . . . . it noteth a kind of excess or excellency, even such as cannot be well expressed. The prophet seemeth to speak with a kind of sighing, as being so ravished with love towards the law of God, that he was even sick of love, as the church saith (Cant. ii. 5 ; v. 8), she was sick of love towards Christ : so seemeth the prophet to be sick of love towards the word of God. This word *"how,"* also importeth a comparison, and noteth a greater love in David towards the word than towards riches or any other thing ; in which respect he saith afterward in this very Psalm (ver. 127), that he loveth the Lord's commandments " above gold, yea, above fine gold " ; yea, as whosoever so loveth not Christ, that in respect of Christ, and for Christ's sake, he forsaketh father, and mother, and brethren, and sisters, wife and children, and his own life also (much more riches and other things not to be compared to life) is not worthy of him ; so he that doth not love the word above all other things ; yea, he that hateth not all other things below here, in respect of the word, is not worthy of the word.   Christ himself loved the word of God more than he loved any riches ; for did he not for the performance of the word submit himself to such want, that the foxes had holes, and the birds had nests, but he had not whereon to lay his head ? and that, although he were the heir of all things, yet he was ministered unto by certain women ?   He loved the word of God more than he loved his mother, brethren, and sisters . . . . . Yea, Christ loved the word of God more than he loved his own life ; for did he not lay down his life to fulfil the word of God ? . . . . If Christ Jesus himself loved the word more than all other things, yea, more than his life, which was more than the life of all angels, was there not great reason why David should love it in like manner ? had not David as much need of it as Christ ? . . . .

"*It is my meditation.*"   The noun "*meditation*" seemeth to be more than if he had said only that he meditated. For he seemeth to mean that though he did often think upon other matters, yet he made nothing his " meditation " but that which he here speaketh of, and that this was his only, or his chief and principal meditation and set study.

The object of David's meditation is not only to be understood of the bare letter of the word, as if he did always meditate of some text or other of the word before written ; but also of the matters contained in the word ; as of the justice, power, wisdom, mercy and goodness of God ; of the frailty, corruption, and wickedness that is in man naturally, of the sins that God forbiddeth, and of the virtues that God commandeth in the word, and other the like. For he that meditateth of these things, though he meditate not of any one text of the word, yet he may be truly said to meditate of the word.

"*All the day.*"   We are not to imagine that the prophet did nothing else but meditate on the word ; but this, first of all ; that no day passed over his head wherein he did not meditate on the word ; yea, that he took every occasion of meditating on the word. He was never weary of meditating. Though he had many other things wherein to employ himself, yet he forgot not the meditation of the word. His mind was not by any other employment alienated from the meditation of the word, but the more thereby provoked thereunto. As a man that hath laboured never so much one day in his calling, is not to be wearied thereby, but that he laboureth afresh the next day, and so day after day : so was it with the prophet touching this act of meditation. Secondly, when he saith he meditated on the word continually, or all the day, he meaneth that he did nothing at any time of the day without meditation on the word for doing thereof. Therefore we may safely say that continual meditation is more necessary than continual praying, as being necessary before the doing of everything, and in the very doing of everything ; yea, even before the said duty of prayer, and in the very act thereof, this work of meditation of the word is always necessary ; as without which, we know not either for what to pray, or in what sort and manner to pray : it is God's word only that can and must teach us both to pray for and also how to pray.—*Thomas Stoughton, in "Two Profitable Treatises,"* 1616.

Verse 97.—"*O how love I thy law !*"   Who without love attempts anything in the law of God, does it coldly, and quickly gives it up. For the mind cannot give itself earnestly and perseveringly to things which are not loved. Only he who loves the law makes it his meditation all the day.—*Wolfgang Musculus.*

Verse 97.—"*O how love I thy law !*"   Were I to enjoy Hezekiah's grant, and to have fifteen years added to my life, I would be much more frequent in my applications to the throne of grace. Were I to renew my studies, I would take my leave of those accomplished trifles—the historians, the orators, the poets of antiquity —and devote my attention to the Scriptures of truth. I would sit with much greater assiduity at my Divine Master's feet, and desire to know nothing but " Jesus Christ, and him crucified." This wisdom, whose fruits are peace in life, consolation in death, and everlasting salvation after death—this I would trace—this I would seek—this I would explore through the spacious and delightful fields of the Old and New Testament.—*James Hervey,* 1713-14—1758.

Verse 97.—This most precious jewel is to be preferred above all treasures. If thou be hungry, it is meat to satisfy thee ; if thou be thirsty, it is drink to refresh thee ; if thou be sick, it is a present remedy ; if thou be weak, it is a staff to lean unto ; if thine enemy assault thee, it is a sword to fight withal ; if thou be in darkness, it is a lanthorn to guide thy feet ; if thou be doubtful of the way, it is a bright shining

star to direct thee ; if thou be in displeasure with God, it is the message of reconciliation ; if thou study to save thy soul, receive the word engrafted, for that is able
to do it : it is the word of life. Whoso loveth salvation will love this word, love
to read it, love to hear it ; and such as will neither read nor hear it, Christ saith
plainly, they are not of God. For the spouse gladly heareth the voice of the bridegroom ; and " my sheep hear my voice," saith the Prince of pastors (John x. 27).—
Edwin Sandys, 1519—1587.

Verse 97.—*"O how love I thy law !"* As faith worketh by love unto God, so
it worketh by love unto his word. Love me, love my word : love a king, love
his laws. So it did on David ; so it should do on us : " O how love I thy law ! "
saith David. *"O how love I thy law ! "* should every one of us say ; not only because
it is a good law, but chiefly because it is God's law.—*Richard Capel, 1586—1656.*

Verse 97.—*"O how love I thy law ! "* He calls God himself to be judge of his
love to the word ; witnessing thereby that it was no counterfeit love, but complete
and sincere love which he bore unto it. The like protestation was used by S. Peter :
" Thou knowest, O Lord, that I love thee ! "—*William Cowper.*

Verse 97.—*"Thy law."* In every one of these eight verses the Bible is spoken
of as the Lord's, as, indeed, all through the Psalm. Who is the author of Scripture ?
God. What is the matter of Scripture ? God ; it was not fit that any should write
of God, but God himself. What is the end of Scripture ? God. Why was the
Scripture written, but that we might everlastingly enjoy the blessed God ? As
Cæsar wrote his own commentaries ; so God, when there was none above him of
whom he could write, he wrote of himself ; by histories, laws, prophecies, and
promises, and many other doctrines, hath he set himself forth to be the Creator,
Preserver, Deliverer, and Glorifier of mankind ; and all this is done in a perfect
manner.—*Thomas Manton.*

Verse 97.—*"It is my meditation."* Holy Scripture is not a book for the slothful ;
it is not a book which can be interpreted without, and apart from, and by the deniers
of, that Holy Spirit by whom it came. Rather is it a field, upon the surface of
which, if sometimes we gather manna easily and without labour, and given, as it
were, freely to our hands, yet of which also, many portions are to be cultivated
with pains and toil ere they will yield food for the use of man. This bread of life
also is to be eaten in the wholesome sweat of our brow.—*Richard Chenevix French,
1807—.*

Verse 98.—*"Thou through thy commandments hast made me wiser than mine
enemies."* Now he praiseth the word for the singular profit and fruit which he reaped
by it ; to wit, that he learned wisdom by it. And this he amplifies, by comparing
himself with three sorts of men ; his enemies, his teachers, and the ancients. And
this he doth, not of vain glory (for bragging is far from him who is governed by
the Spirit of grace) ; but to commend the word of the Lord, and to allure others
to love it, by declaring to them what manifold good he found in it.

"Wiser than mine enemies." But how can this be, seeing that our Saviour
saith that the men of this world are wiser in their own generation than the children
of God ? The answer is, our Saviour doth not call worldlings wise men simply ;
but *wiser in their own generation ;* that is, wise in things pertaining to this life. Or
as Jeremy calls them, " wise to do evil " ; and when they have so done, wise to
conceal and cloak it. All which in very deed is but folly ; and therefore David,
who by the light of God's word saw that it was so, could not be moved to follow
their course. Well ; there is a great controversy between the godly and the wicked :
either of them in their judgment accounts the other to be fools ; but it is the light
of God's word which must decide it.—*William Cowper.*

Verse 98.—*"Wiser than mine enemies."* They are wiser than their enemies
as to security against their attempts, and that enmity and opposition that they
carry on against them ; they are far more safe by walking under the covert of God's
protection than their enemies can possibly be, who have all manner of worldly
advantages. A godly-wise man is careful to keep in with God : he is more prepared
and furnished, can have a higher hope, more expectation of success, than others
have ; or, if not, he is well enough provided for, though all things fall out never
so cross to his desires. As to success, who hath made wiser provision, think you,
he that hath made God his friend, or he that is borne up with worldly props and
dependences ? they that are guided by the Spirit of God, or they that are guided
by Satan ? those that make it their business to walk with God step by step, or those

that not only forsake him, but provoke him to his face? those that break with men, and keep in with God, or those that break with God? Surely, a child of God hath more security by piety than his enemies can have by secular policy, whereby they think to overreach and ruin him. The safety of a child of God lieth in two things: 1. God is his friend. 2. As long as God hath work for him to do, he will maintain him, and bear him out in it.—*Thomas Manton.*

Verse 98.—"*They are ever with me.*" The meaning of the last clause is not merely, "*it is ever with me,*" but "*it is for ever to me,*" i.e., mine, my inalienable, indefeasible possession.—*Joseph Addison Alexander.*

Verse 98.—"*They are ever with me.*" God gives knowledge to whom he pleaseth; but those that meditate most, thrive most. This may imply also that the word should be a ready help. Such as derive their wisdom from without cannot have their counsellers always with them to give advice. But, when a man hath gotten the word in his heart, he finds a ready help: he hath a seasonable word to direct him in all difficulties, in all straits, and in all temptations, to teach him what to do against the burden of the present exigence; to teach him what to do and what to hope for.—*Thomas Manton.*

Verse 98.—"*They are ever with me.*" A good man, wherever he goes, carries his Bible along with him, if not in his hands, yet in his head and in his heart.—*Matthew Henry.*

Verses 98, 99, 100.—Three sorts of men he mentioneth, "*enemies,*" "*teachers,*" "*ancients*"; the enemies excel in policy, teachers in doctrine, and ancients in counsel; and yet by the word was David made wiser than all these. Malice sharpens the wit of enemies, and teacheth them the arts of opposition; teachers are furnished with learning because of their office; and ancients grow wise by experience; yet David, by the study of the word, excelled all these.—*Thomas Manton.*

Verse 99.—"*I have more understanding than all my teachers.*" Even where the preacher is godly, partaker of that grace himself, whereof he is an ambassador to others, it falls out oftentimes that greater measure of light and grace is communicated by his ministry to another than is given to himself; as Augustine first illuminated and converted by Ambrose did far excel, both in knowledge and spiritual grace, him that taught him. And herein God wonderfully shows his glory, that, whoever be the instrument, he is the dispenser of light and glory, giving more by the instrument than it hath in itself. And this is so far from being to a godly teacher a matter of grief, that it is rather a matter of glory.—*William Cowper.*

Verse 99.—"*I have more understanding than all my teachers.*" It is no reflection upon my teachers, but rather an honour to them, for me to improve so as to excel them, and no longer to need them. By *meditation* we preach to ourselves, and so we come to *understand more than our teachers,* for we come to understand our hearts, which they cannot.—*Matthew Henry.*

Verse 100.—"*I understand . . . because I keep.*" Would we know the Lord? let us keep his commandments. "By thy precepts," saith David, that is, by the observance of thy precepts, "I get understanding." "If any man do my will" (saith our blessed Saviour, John vii. 17), "he shall know my doctrine." Βούλει θεόλογος γενέσθαι? τὰς ἐντογὰς φύλασσε, saith Nazienzen: Wouldst thou be a divine? do the commandments; for action is (as it were) the basis of contemplation. It is St. Gregory's observation concerning the two disciples who, whilst Christ talked with them, knew him not; but in performing an act of hospitality towards him, to wit, breaking bread with him, they knew him, that they were enlightened, not by hearing him, but by doing divine precepts, *Quisquis ergo vult audita intelligere; festinet ea quæ jam audire potuit, opere implere,* Whosoever therefore will understand, let him first make haste to do what he heareth.—*Nathanael Hardy,* 1618—1670.

Verse 100.—"*I understand more than the ancients.*" The ordinary answer of ignorant people is, "What! must we be wiser than our forefathers?" And yet those same people would be richer than their forefathers were. The *maximum quod sic* of a Christian is this,—he must grow in grace, till his head reach up to heaven, till grace is perfected in glory.—*Christopher Love,* 1618—1651.

Verse 100.—"*More than the ancients.*" Understanding gotten by the precepts of the word is better than understanding gotten by long experience. It is better in four regards. First, It is *more exact.* Our experience reacheth but to a few things; but the word of God reacheth to all cases that concern true happiness.

The word is the result of God's wisdom, who is the Ancient of days ; therefore exceeds the wisdom of the ancients, or experience of any men, or all men.   Secondly, as it is more exact, so a *more sure* way of learning wisdom, whereas experience is more uncertain.   Many have much experience, yet have not a heart to see and to gather wisdom from what they feel : Deut. xxix. 2—4.   Thirdly, It is a *safer and cheaper* way of learning, to learn by rule, than to come home by weeping cross, and to learn wisdom by our own smart.   Experience is too expensive a way ; and, if we had nothing else to guide us, into how many thousand miseries should we run ?   Fourthly, It is *shorter.*   The way by age and experience is a long way ; and so, for a long time, all a man's younger age must needs be miserable and foolish. Now, here you may come betimes to be wise by studying the word of God.   It concerns a man, not only to be wise at length, but to be wise betimes.   The foolish virgins were wise too late ; but never were any wise too soon.—*Condensed from Thomas Manton.*

Verse 100.—If this way [the Word of God] were thus perfect in David's time, what is it by the addition of so many parcels of Scripture since ?   If it then gave wisdom to the simple (Ps. xix. 7) ; if it made David, being brought up but as a shepherd, *wiser than* his enemies, than *his ancients,* than his teachers ; as an angel of God in discerning right from wrong (2 Sam. xiv. 17) ; able to guide the people by the skilfulness of his hands (Ps. lxxviii, 72) ; what kind of wisdom is there which we may not now gather from thence ?   What depth of natural philosophy have we in Genesis and Job !   what flowers of rhetoric in the prophets !   what force of logic in Saint Paul's epistles !   what art of poetry in the Psalms !   what excellent moral precepts, not only for private life, but for the regulation of families and commonwealths in the Proverbs and Ecclesiastes !   to which may be added in a second rank as very useful, though apocryphal, the Book of Wisdom and Ecclesiasticus. What reasonable and just laws have we in Leviticus and Deuteronomy, which moved the great Ptolemy to hire the Septuagints to translate them into Greek : what unmatchable antiquity, variety, and wonderful events, and certainty of story, in the books of Moses, Joshua, the Judges, Samuel, the Kings, and Chronicles, together with Ruth and Esther, Ezra and Nehemiah, and, since Christ, in the sacred Gospels and Acts of the Apostles.   And, lastly, what profound mysteries have we in the prophecies of Ezekiel and Daniel, and the Revelation of Saint John.   But in this it infinitely exceeds the wisdom of all human writings, that it is alone " able to make a man wise unto salvation " (2 Tim. iii. 15).   Upon these considerations, Charles the Fifth of France, surnamed *The Wise,* not only caused the Bible to be translated into French, but was himself very studious in the Holy Scriptures.   And Alphonsus, King of Arragon, is said to have read over the whole Bible fourteen several times, with Lyra's notes upon it ; though he were otherwise excellently well learned, yet was the law of God his delight, " more desired of him than gold, yea, than much fine gold, sweeter also than honey and the honeycomb."—*George Hakewell, 1579—1649.*

Verse 101.—"*I have refrained my feet,*" etc.   1. We have David's practice : "*I have refrained my feet from every evil way.*"   2. His end or motive : "*That I might keep thy word ; "* that he might be exact and punctual with God in a course of obedience.

First, In his practice.   You may note the seriousness of it : "*I have refrained my feet.*"   By the *feet* are meant the affections : " Keep thy foot when thou goest to the house of God," Eccl. v. 1.   Our affections which are the rigorous bent of the soul, do engage us to practice ; therefore fitly resembled by the feet, by which we walk to any place that we do desire : so that, "*I have refrained my feet,*" the meaning is, I keep a close and strict hand over my affections, that they might not lead me to sin.   Then you may note the extent of it ; he doth not only say, I refrained from evil, but universally, "*from every evil way.*"   But how could David say this is truth of heart, if conscious of his offence in the matter of Uriah ?   Answer : This was the usual frame and temper of his soul, and the course of his life ; and such kind of assertions concerning the saints are to be interpreted, *voce et canatu, licet non semper eventu.*   This was his errand and drift, his purpose and endeavour, his usual course, though he had his failings.

Secondly, What was his end and motive in this ?   " That I might keep thy word " ; that I might be exact and punctual with God in a course of obedience, and adhere to his word universally, impartially.—*Thomas Manton.*

Verse 101.—*"I have refrained my feet,"* etc. Where there is real holiness, there is a holy hatred, detestation, and indignation against all ungodliness and wickedness, and that upon holy accounts : *" I have refrained my feet from every evil way."* But why ? *"That I may keep thy word."* *"* Through thy precepts I get understanding; therefore I hate every false way ; " ver. 104. The good that he got by divine precepts stirred up his hatred against every false way : verse 128, " Therefore I esteem all thy precepts concerning all things to be right ; and I hate every false way." His high esteem of every precept raised up in him a holy indignation against every evil way. A holy man knows that all sin strikes at the holiness of God, the glory of God, the nature of God, the being of God, and the law of God ; and therefore his heart rises against all ; he looks upon every sin as the Scribes and Pharisees that accused Christ ; and as that Judas that betrayed Christ ; and as that Pilate that condemned Christ ; and as those soldiers that scourged Christ ; and as those spears that pierced Christ ; and therefore his heart cries out for justice upon all.—*Thomas Brooks.*

Verse 101.—*"Refrained . . that I might keep."* By doing what is right we come both to know right and to be better able to do it.—*"Plain Commentary."*

Verse 101.—*"I have refrained my feet,"* etc. The word *"refrained"* warns us that we are naturally borne by our feet into the path of every kind of sin, and are hurried along it by the rush of human passions, so that even the wise and understanding need to check, recall, and retrace their steps, in order that they may keep God's word, and not become castaways. And further note that the Hebrew verb here translated *"refrained"* is even stronger in meaning, and denotes, " I *fettered,* or *imprisoned,* my feet," whereby we may learn that no light resistance is enough to prevent them from leading us astray.—*Agellius and Genebrardus, in Neale and Littledale.*

Verse 102.—By *misphalim, "judgments,"* is meant God's law ; for thereby he will judge the world. And the word *"departed not "* intimateth both his exactness and constancy : his exactness, that he did not go a hair's-breadth from his direction ; " Ye shall observe to do therefore as the Lord your God hath commanded you : ye shall not turn aside to the right hand or to the left " (Deut. v. 32) ; and his constancy is implied in it, for then we are said to depart from God and his law, when we fall off from him in judgment and practice. Jer. xxxii. 40.—*Thomas Manton.*

Verse 102.—*"Thou hast taught me."* God teacheth two ways :—1. By common illumination. 2. By special operation.

1. By common illumination, barely enlightening the mind to know or understand what he propoundeth by his messengers : so God showed it to the heathen : Rom. i. 20.

But then, 2. By way of special operation, effectually inclining the will to embrace and prosecute duties so known : " I will put my law in their inward parts, and write it in their hearts " : Jer. xxxi. 33. This way of teaching is always effectual and persuasive. Now, in this sense they are taught of God, so that they do not only get an ear to hear, but a heart to understand, learn, and practise.

This teaching is the ground of constancy, because, (1) They that are thus taught of God see things more clearly than others do ; God is the most excellent teacher. (2) They know things more surely, and with certainty of demonstration, whereas others have but dubious conjectures, and loose and wavering opinions about the things of God. (3) This teaching is so efficacious and powerful, as that the effect followeth : " Teach me thy way, O Lord, I will walk in thy truth " (Ps. lxxxvi. 11.) (4) God reneweth this teaching, and is always at hand to guide us, and give counsel to us, which is the cause of our standing.—*Thomas Manton.*

Verse 102.—*"For thou hast taught me."* Lest it should seem that David ascribed the praise of godliness to himself, or that it came from any goodness in him that he did refrain his feet from every evil way, he gives here all the glory to God, protesting, that because God did teach him, therefore he declined not. Wherefrom we learn, that if at any time we stand, or if when we have fallen we rise and repent, it is ever to be imputed to God that teacheth us ; for there is no evil so abominable, but it would soon become plausible to us, if God should leave us to ourselves. David was taught by his ordinary teachers, and he did reverence them ; but that he profited by them he ascribes unto God. Paul may plant, and Apollos water ; God must give the increase.—*William Cowper.*

Verse 103.—*"How sweet are thy words unto my taste!"* Even the words of a fellow-creature of earth, how inexpressibly sweet sometimes, how beyond all calculation precious! All gold and silver would be despised in comparison with them. They come freighted with love, and the heart is enriched with them as though the breath of God had come into it. But does not this rainbow of earthly joy die gradually out? Do not the enrapturing words sooner or later become exsiccated in the memory, and may they not meet with contemptuous treatment as remembrancers of an earthly illusion? Indeed they do; indeed they may.

Nevertheless the heart may find its happiness, its true and undying happiness, *in words.* At this moment there is nothing in the whole world so much to be desired as certain words. Words of love. Words expressive of infinite love. Treasures, pleasures, honours, of earth, what are they? My unsatisfied soul cries out, Give me words. Words whereby I may know the love that God has towards me. Words declaring the unchangeable attachment of the Saviour. Words purifying my heart. Emboldening me in prayer. Exhibiting to me the blissful future. Words that shall give life to my dead powers, and change me from glory to glory, as by the Spirit of the Lord.—*George Bowen, in "Daily Meditations,"* 1873.

Verse 103.—*"How sweet are thy words unto my taste!"* etc. There is given to the regenerated a new, supernatural sense, a certain divine, spiritual taste. This is in its whole nature diverse from any of the other five senses, and something is perceived by a true saint in the exercise of this new sense of mind, in spiritual and divine things, as entirely different from any thing that is perceived in them by natural men, as the sweet taste of honey is diverse from the ideas men get of honey by looking on it or feeling of it. Now the beauty of holiness is that which is perceived by this spiritual sense, so diverse from all that natural men perceive in them; or, this kind of beauty is the quality that is the immediate object of this spiritual sense; this is the sweetness that is the proper object of this spiritual taste. The Scripture often represents the beauty and sweetness of holiness as the grand object of a spiritual taste and a spiritual appetite. This was the sweet food of the holy soul of Jesus Christ, John iv. 32, 34. "I have meat to eat that ye know not of . . . My meat is to do the will of him that sent me, and to finish his work." I know of no part of the Holy Scriptures where the nature and evidence of true and sincere godliness are so fully and largely insisted on and delineated, as in the 119th Psalm. The Psalmist declares his design in the first verses of the Psalm, keeps his eye on it all along, and pursues it to the end. The excellency of holiness is represented as the immediate object of a spiritual taste and delight. *God's law,* that grand expression and emanation of the holiness of God's nature, and prescription of holiness to the creature, is all along represented as the great object of the love, the complacence, and rejoicing of the gracious nature, which prizes God's commandments *above gold, yea, the finest gold,* and to which they are *sweeter than honey, and the honey-comb;* and that upon account of their holiness. The same Psalmist declares that this is the sweetness that a spiritual taste relishes in God's law: Ps. xix. 7—10.—*Jonathan Edwards,* 1703—1758.

Verse 103.—*"How sweet are thy words unto my taste!"* Why does he not rather say, How pleasant are thy words to my ears? than that they are sweet to his taste and his mouth? I answer: It is most meet that when God speaks by the mouth of his ministers we should be hearers, and the words of God should be the most joyous of all to our ears. But it is also the practice of the godly to converse about the words of God, and their words are so sweet to their own taste that they are more pleased and delighted than by any honey from the comb. And this is most necessary when either there is a scarcity of teachers, as with David in the wilderness or dwelling among the Philistines; or when those who hold the office of teaching, adulterate and vitiate the pure word of God.—*Wolfgang Musculus.*

Verse 103.—That which is here called, *"word,"* I take rather for *"judgments,"* partly because in the proper tongue the word is left out, and partly because he had used this word *"judgments"* in the verse immediately going before. But some will say, How can the judgments of God be *"sweet,"* which are so troublesome, fearful, and grievous? I answer, that the godly have no greater joy than when they feel either the mercies of God accomplished towards them that fear him, or his judgments showered upon the reprobates.—*Richard Greenham.*

Verse 103.—*"Unto my taste." "To my mouth."* That is, I take as great pleasure in talking, conferring, and persuading, thy judgments, as my mouth, or the mouth of any that loveth honey, delighteth therewith.—*Richard Greenham.*

Verse 103.—*"Sweeter."* As there are always among violets some that are very much sweeter than others, so among texts there are some that are more precious to us than others.—*Henry Ward Beecher*, 1879.

Verse 103.—An affectionate wife often says, " My husband ! your words are sweeter to me than honey ; yea, they are sweeter than the sugar-cane." " Alas ! my husband is gone," says the widow : " how sweet were his words ! Honey dropped from his mouth : his words were ambrosia."—*Joseph Roberts.*

Verse 104.—*"Through thy precepts I get understanding : therefore I hate every false way."* In this sentence the prophet seems to invert the order set down in verse 101. He had said, " I have refrained my feet from every evil way, that I might keep thy word," where the avoiding of evil is made the means of profiting by the word ; here his profiting by the word is made the cause of avoiding evil. In the one verse you have an account of his beginning with God ; in the other, of his progress.—*Thomas Manton.*

Verse 104.—*"I hate every false way,"* David saith, *"I hate every false way" ;* I hate not only the way, when I have been misled into it, but I hate to go in it ; and he professeth at the 163rd verse, *"I hate and abhor lying, but thy law do I love."* To abstain from and forbear lying is a sign of a gracious heart, much more to hate and abhor it. A godly man not only doth that which is good, but he delights to do it, his soul cleaves to it ; he is in his element when he is doing it, nothing comes more suitably to him than the business of his duty, he loveth to do it, yea, he loveth it when he cannot do it ; Rom. vii. 22. Paul complained much that his corruptions clogged, hindered and shackled him ; he was in lime twigs as to the doing of good, yet (saith he) " I delight in the law of God after the inward man " ; that is, the inward man delightfully moves after the law of God, when I am basely moved by my corrupt heart, and stirred by temptation against it. Now, as a godly man not only chooseth to do the holy will of God, but delights and rejoiceth to do it, and hath sweet content in doing it ; so likewise a godly man not only refuseth to do the will of the flesh, or to follow the course of the world, but hates to do it, and is never so discontented with himself as when through carelessness and neglect of his watch he hath been overtaken and hath fallen. A carnal man may forbear the doing of evil, and do what is materially good, but he never abhors what is evil, nor delights in what is good. Though he abstain from acting those things which God forbids, yet he doth not say, with Job, " God forbid, I should act them.". . . . To delight in good is better than the doing of it, and to abhor evil is better than abstaining from it. And if we compare the nature of sin with the new nature of a godly man, we may see clear grounds why his abstinence from sin is joined with an abhorrence of it.—*Joseph Caryl.*

Verse 104.—*"Through thy precepts I get understanding."* Spiritual understanding is connected with the taste of spiritual sweetness. (Compare Proverbs ii. 10, 11.) " The sweetness of the lips "—as the wise man observes—" increaseth learning. The heart of the wise teacheth his mouth, and addeth learning to his lips." Prov. xvi. 21, 23. Thus having learned " the principles of the doctrine of Christ," we are encouraged to " go on to perfection "—" growing *in grace* and in the knowledge of Christ." For the connexion between " grace and knowledge " is clearly manifested.—*Charles Bridges.*

Verse 104.—*"I hate every false way."* Universality in this is a sure sign of sincerity. Herod spits out some sins, when he rolls others as sweet morsels in his mouth. A hypocrite ever leaves the devil some nest-egg to sit upon, though he take many away. Some men will not buy some commodities, because they cannot have them at their own price, but they lay out the same money on others ; so hypocrites forbear some sins, yea, are displeased at them, because they cannot have them without disgrace or disease, or some other disadvantage ; but they lay out the same love upon other sins which will suit better with their designs. Some affirm that what the sea loseth in one place it gaineth in another ; so what ground the corruption of the unconverted loseth one way, it gaineth another. There is in him some one lust especially which is his favourite ; some king sin, like Agag, which must be spared when others are destroyed. " In this the Lord be merciful to thy servant," saith Naaman. But now the regenerate laboureth to cleanse himself from all pollutions, both of flesh and spirit. 2 Cor. vii. 1.—*George Swinnock.*

Verse 104.—*"I hate."* The Scriptures place religion very much in the affection of *love ;* love to God, and the Lord Jesus Christ ; love to the people of God, and to mankind.   The texts in which this is manifest, both in the Old Testament and the New, are innumerable.   The contrary affection of *hatred* also, as having sin for its object, is spoken of in Scripture as no inconsiderable part of true religion.   It is spoken of as that by which true religion may be known and distinguished.   Prov. viii. 13.   "The fear of the Lord is to hate evil."   Accordingly, the saints are called upon to give evidence of their sincerity by this, Psalm xcvii. 10.   "Ye that love the Lord, hate evil."   And the Psalmist often mentions it as an evidence of his sincerity : Ps. ci. 2, 3, "I will walk within my house with a perfect heart.   I will set no wicked thing before mine eyes ; I *hate* the work of them that turn aside." So Ps. cxix., verse 128, and the present place.   Again, Ps. cxxxix. 21 : "Do not I *hate* them, O Lord, that hate thee ? "—*Jonathan Edwards.*

Verse 104.—"*I hate.*"   Hatred is a stabbing, murdering affection, it pursues sin with a hot heart to death, as an avenger of blood, that is to say, of the blood of the soul which sin would spill, and of the blood of Christ which sin hath shed. Hate sin perfectly and perpetually and then you will not spare it but kill it presently. Till sin be hated it cannot be mortified ; you will not cry against it, as the Jews did against Christ, Crucify it !   Crucify it !   but shew indulgence to it as David did to Absalom and say, Deal gently with the young man,—with this or that lust, for my sake.   Mercy to sin is cruelty to the soul.—*Edward Reyner,* 1600—1670.

Verse 104.—"*False way.*"   It is not said, "evil way," but "false way" : or, as it is in the original, every path of lying and falsehood.   Falsehood is either in point of opinion or practice.   If you take it in the first sense, for falsehood in opinion or error in judgment, or false doctrine, or false worship, this sentence holds good. Those that get understanding by the word are established against error, and not only established against error, or against the embracing or possession of it, but they hate it.—*Thomas Manton.*

Verse 104.—"*False way.*"   All sin is a *lie.*   By it we attempt to cheat God. By it we actually cheat our souls : Prov. xiv. 12.   There is no delusion like the folly of believing that a course of sin will conduce to our happiness.—*William S. Plumer.*

EXPOSITION OF VERSES 105 TO 112.

THY word *is* a lamp unto my feet, and a light unto my path.

106 I have sworn, and I will perform *it*, that I will keep thy righteous judgments.

107 I am afflicted very much : quicken me, O LORD, according unto thy word.

108 Accept, I beseech thee, the freewill offerings of my mouth, O LORD, and teach me thy judgments.

109 My soul *is* continually in my hand : yet do I not forget thy law.

110 The wicked have laid a snare for me : yet I erred not from thy precepts.

111 Thy testimonies have I taken as an heritage for ever : for they *are* the rejoicing of my heart.

112 I have inclined mine heart to perform thy statutes alway, *even unto* the end.

105. "*Thy word is a lamp unto my feet.*" We are walkers through the city of this world, and we are often called to go out into its darkness ; let us never venture there without the light-giving word, lest we slip with our feet. Each man should use the word of God personally, practically, and habitually, that he may see his way and see what lies in it. When darkness settles down upon all around me, the word of the Lord, like a flaming torch, reveals my way. Having no fixed lamps in eastern towns, in old time each passenger carried a lantern with him that he might not fall into the open sewer, or stumble over the heaps of ordure which defiled the road. This is a true picture of our path through this dark world : we should not know the way, or how to walk in it, if the Scripture, like a blazing flambeau, did not reveal it. One of the most practical benefits of Holy Writ is guidance in the acts of daily life ; it is not sent to astound us with its brilliance, but to guide us by its instruction. It is true the head needs illumination, but even more the feet need direction, else head and feet may both fall into a ditch. Happy is the man who personally appropriates God's word, and practically uses it as his comfort and counsellor,—a lamp to his own feet. "*And a light unto my path.*" It is a lamp by night, a light by day, and a delight at all times. David guided his own steps by it, and also saw the difficulties of his road by its beams. He who walks in darkness is sure, sooner or later, to stumble ; while he who walks by the light of day, or by the lamp of night, stumbleth not, but keeps his uprightness. Ignorance is painful upon practical subjects ; it breeds indecision and suspense, and these are uncomfortable : the word of God, by imparting heavenly knowledge, leads to decision, and when that is followed by determined resolution, as in this case, it brings with it great restfulness of heart.

This verse converses with God in adoring and yet familiar tones. Have we not something of like tenor to address to our heavenly Father ?

Note how like this verse is to the first verse of the first octave, and the first of the second and other octaves. The seconds also are often in unison.

106. "*I have sworn, and I will perform it, that I will keep thy righteous judgments.*" Under the influence of the clear light of knowledge he had firmly made up his mind and solemnly declared his resolve in the sight of God. Perhaps mistrusting his own fickle mind, he had pledged himself in sacred form to abide faithful to the determinations and decisions of his God. Whatever path might open before him, he was sworn to follow that only upon which the lamp of the word was shining. The Scriptures are God's judgments, or verdicts, upon great moral questions ; these are all righteous, and hence righteous men should be resolved to keep them at all hazards, since it must always be right to do right. Experience shows that the less of covenanting and swearing men formally enter upon the better, and the genius of our Saviour's teaching is against all supererogatory pledging and swearing ; and yet under the gospel we ought to feel ourselves as much bound to

obey the word of the Lord as if we had taken an oath so to do. The bonds of love are not less sacred than the fetters of law. When a man has vowed he must be careful to " perform it," and when a man has not vowed in so many words to keep the Lord's judgments, yet is he equally bound to do so by obligations which exist apart from any promise on our part,—obligations founded in the eternal fitness of things, and confirmed by the abounding goodness of the Lord our God. Will not every believer own that he is under bonds to the redeeming Lord to follow his example, and keep his words ? Yes, the vows of the Lord are upon us, especially upon such as have made profession of discipleship, have been baptized into the thrice-holy name, have eaten of the consecrated memorials, and have spoken in the name of the Lord Jesus. We are enlisted, and sworn in, and are bound to be loyal soldiers all through the war. Thus having taken the word into our hearts by a firm resolve to obey it, we have a lamp within our souls as well as in the Book, and our course will be light unto the end.

107. "*I am afflicted very much.*" According to the last verse he had been sworn in as a soldier of the Lord, and in this next verse he is called to suffer hardness in that capacity. Our service of the Lord does not screen us from trial, but rather secures it for us. The Psalmist was a consecrated man, and yet a chastened man ; nor were his chastisements light ; for it seemed as if the more he was obedient the more he was afflicted. He evidently felt the rod to be cutting deep, and this he pleads before the Lord. He speaks not by way of murmuring, but by way of pleading ; from the very much affliction he argues for very much quickening.

"*Quicken me, O LORD, according unto thy word.*" This is the best remedy for tribulation ; the soul is raised above the thought of present distress, and is filled with that holy joy which attends all vigorous spiritual life, and so the affliction grows light. Jehovah alone can quicken : he has life in himself, and therefore can communicate it readily ; he can give us life at any moment, yea, at this present instant ; for it is of the nature of quickening to be quick in its operation. The Lord has promised, prepared, and provided this blessing of renewed life for all his waiting servants : it is a covenant blessing, and it is as obtainable as it is needful. Frequently the affliction is made the means of the quickening, even as the stirring of a fire promotes the heat of the flame. In their affliction some desire death, let us pray for life. Our forebodings under trial are often very gloomy, let us entreat the Lord to deal with us, not according to our fears, but according to his own word. David had but few promises to quote, and probably these were in his own Psalms, yet he pleads the word of the Lord ; how much more should we do so, since to us so many holy men have spoken by the Spirit of the Lord in that wonderful library which is now our Bible. Seeing we have more promises, let us offer more prayers.

108. "*Accept, I beseech thee, the freewill offerings of my mouth, O Lord.*" The living praise the living God, and therefore the quickened one presents his sacrifice. He offers prayer, praise, confession, and testimony—these, presented with his voice in the presence of an audience, were the tribute of his mouth unto Jehovah. He trembles lest these should be so ill uttered as to displease the Lord, and therefore he implores acceptance. He pleads that the homage of his mouth was cheerfully and spontaneously rendered ; all his utterances were freewill offerings. There can be no value in extorted confessions : God's revenues are not derived from forced taxation, but from freewill donation. There can be no acceptance where there is no willingness ; there is no work of free grace where there is no fruit of free will. Acceptance is a favour to be sought from the Lord with all earnestness, for without it our offerings are worse thon useless. What a wonder of grace that the the Lord will accept anything of such unworthy ones as we are !

"*And teach me thy judgments.*" When we render unto the Lord our best, we become all the more concerned to do better. If, indeed, the Lord shall accept us, we then desire to be further instructed, that we may still be more acceptable. After quickening we need teaching : life without light, or zeal without knowledge, would be but half a blessing. These repeated cries for teaching show the humility of the man of God, and also discover to us our own need of similar instruction. Our judgment needs educating till it knows, agrees with, and acts upon, the judgments of the Lord. Those judgments are not always so clear as to be seen at once ; we need to be taught in them till we admire their wisdom and adore their goodness as soon as ever we perceive them.

109. "*My soul is continually in my hand.*" He lived in the midst of danger. He had to be always fighting for existence—hiding in caves, or contending in

battles. This is a very uncomfortable and trying state of affairs, and men are apt to think any expedient justifiable by which they can end such a condition : but David did not turn aside to find safety in sin, for he says,"*Yet do I not forget thy law.*" They say that all things are fair in love and war ; but the holy man thought not so : while he carried his life in his hand, he also carried the law in his heart. No danger of body should make us endanger our souls by forgetting that which is right. Trouble makes many a man forget his duty, and it would have had the same effect upon the Psalmist if he had not obtained quickening (verse 107) and teaching (verse 108). In his memory of the Lord's law lay his safety ; he was certain not to be forgotten of God, for God was not forgotten of him. It is a special proof of grace when nothing can drive truth out of our thoughts, or holiness out of our lives. If we remember the law even when death stares us in the face, we may be well assured that the Lord is remembering us.

110. "*The wicked have laid a snare for me.*" Spiritual life is the scene of constant danger : the believer lives with his life in his hand, and meanwhile all seem plotting to take it from him, by cunning if they cannot by violence. We shall not find it an easy thing to live the life of the faithful. Wicked spirits and wicked men will leave no stone unturned for our destruction. If all other devices fail, and even hidden pits do not succeed, the wicked still persevere in their treacherous endeavours, and, becoming craftier still, they set snares for the victim of their hate. The smaller species of game are usually taken by this method, by gin, or trap, or net, or noose. Wicked men are quite indifferent as to the manner in which they can destroy the good man—they think no more of him than if he were a rabbit or a rat : cunning and treachery are always the allies of malice, and everything like a generous or chivalrous feeling is unknown among the graceless, who treat the godly as if they were vermin to be exterminated. When a man knows that he is thus assailed, he is too apt to become timorous, and rush upon some hasty device for deliverance, not without sin in the endeavour ; but David calmly kept his way, and was able to write, "*Yet I erred not from thy precepts.*" He was not snared, for he kept his eyes open, and kept near his God. He was not entrapped and robbed for he followed the King's highway of holiness, where God secures safety to every traveller. He did not err from the right, and he was not deterred from following it, because he referred to the Lord for guidance, and obtained it. If we err from the precepts, we part with the promises ; if we get away from God's presence, we wander into the wilds where the fowlers freely spread their nets. From this verse let us learn to be on our guard, for we, too, have enemies both crafty and wicked. Hunters set their traps in the animals' usual runs, and our worst snares are laid in our own ways. By keeping to the ways of the Lord we shall escape the snares of our adversaries, for his ways are safe and free from treachery.

111. "*Thy testimonies have I taken as an heritage for ever.*" He chose them as his lot, his portion, his estate ; and what is more, he laid hold upon them and made them so,—taking them into possession and enjoyment. David's choice is our choice. If we might have our desire, we would desire to keep the commands of God perfectly. To know the doctrine, to enjoy the promise to practise the command,—be this a kingdom large enough for me. Here we have an inheritance which cannot fade and cannot be alienated ; it is for ever, and ours for ever, if we have so taken it. Sometimes, like Israel at the first coming into Canaan, we have to take our heritage by hard fighting, and, if so, it is worthy of all our labour and suffering ; but always it has to be taken by a decided choice of the heart and grip of the will. What God gives we must take. "*For they are the rejoicing of my heart.*" The gladness which had come to him through the word of the Lord had caused him to make an unalterable choice of it. All the parts of Scripture had been pleasing to David, and were so still, and therefore he stuck to them, and meant to stick to them for ever. That which rejoices the heart is sure to be chosen and treasured. It is not the head-knowledge but the heart-experience which brings the joy.

In this verse, which is the seventh of its octave, we have reached the same sweetness as in the last seventh (103) : indeed, in several of the adjoining sevenths, delight is evident. How good a thing it is when experience ripens into joy, passing up through sorrow, prayer, conflict, hope, decision, and holy content into rejoicing ! Joy fixes the spirit : when once a man's heart rejoices in the divine word, he greatly values it, and is for ever united to it.

112. "*I have inclined mine heart to perform thy statutes alway, even unto the end.*"

He was not half inclined to virtue, but heartily inclined to it. His whole heart was bent on practical, persevering godliness. He was resolved to keep the statutes of the Lord with all his heart, throughout all his time, without erring or ending. He made it his end to keep the law unto the end, and that without end. He had by prayer, and meditation, and resolution made his whole being lean towards God's commands ; or as we should say in other words—the grace of God had inclined him to incline his heart in a sanctified direction. Many are inclined to preach, but the Psalmist was inclined to practise ; many are inclined to perform ceremonies, but he was inclined to perform statutes ; many are inclined to obey occasionally, but David would obey alway ; and, alas, many are inclined for temporary religion, but this godly man was bound for eternity, he would perform the statutes of his Lord and King even unto the end. Lord, send us such a heavenly inclination of heart as this : then shall we show that thou hast quickened and taught us. To this end create in us a clean heart, and daily renew a right spirit within us, for only so shall we incline in the right direction.

NOTES ON VERSES 105 TO 112.

Verse 105.—*"Thy word is a lamp unto my feet, and a light,"* etc. David was a man of very good wit and natural understanding ; but he gives to God the glory of his wisdom, and owns that his best light was but darkness when he was not lightened and ruled by the word of God. Oh that we would consider this, that in all our ways wherein the word of God shines not unto us to direct us, we do but walk in darkness, and our ways without it can lead us to none other end but utter darkness. If we hearken not to the word of God, if we walk not by the rule thereof, how is it possible we can come to the face of God ?—*William Cowper.*

Verse 105.—*"Thy word is a lamp unto my feet, and a light unto my path."* The use of a *lamp* is by night, while the *light* of the sun shineth by day. Whether it be day or night with us, we clearly understand our duty by the Word of God. The *night* signifieth adversity, and the *day* prosperity. Hence we may learn how to behave ourselves in all conditions. The word *" path "* noteth our general choice and course of life ; the word *" feet "* our particular actions. Now whether the matter, wherein we would be informed, concerneth our choice of the way that leadeth to true happiness, or our dexterous prosecution of the way, still the word of God will direct a humble and well-disposed mind.—*Thomas Manton.*

Verse 105.—*"Thy word is a lamp unto my feet,"* etc. Basil the Great, interpreting the *" word "* as God's will revealed in Holy Scriptures, observes that the Old Testament, and in especial the Law, was only a *lantern* (*lamp* or *candle*) because an artificial light, imperfectly illumining the darkness, whereas the Gospel, given by the Lord Jesus himself, is a *light* of the Sun of Righteousness, giving brightness to all things. Ambrose, going yet deeper, tells us that Christ is himself both *lamp* and *light*. He, the Word of God, is a great light to some, to others he is a lamp. To me he is a lamp ; to angels a light, He was a light to Peter, when the angel stood by him in the prison, and the light shined about him. He was a light to Paul when the light from heaven shined round about him, and he heard Christ saying to him, " Saul, Saul, why persecutest thou me ? " And Christ is truly a lamp to me when I speak of him with my mouth. He shineth in clay, he shineth in a potter's vessel : he is that treasure which we bear in earthen vessels.—*Neale and Littledale.*

Verse 105.—*"Thy word is a lamp . . . and a light."* Except the *" lamp "* be lighted—except the teaching of the Spirit accompany the word—all is *"darkness, gross darkness "* still. Did we more habitually wait to receive, and watch to improve, the light of the word, we should not so often complain of the perplexity of our path.—*Charles Bridges.*

Verse 105.—*"Thy word is a lamp unto my feet,"* etc. What we all want, is not to see wonders that daze us, and to be rapt in ecstatic visions and splendours, but a little light on the dark and troubled path we have to tread, a lamp that will burn steadfastly and helpfully over the work we have to do. The stars are infinitely more sublime, meteors infinitely more superb and dazzling ; but the lamp shining in a dark place is infinitely closer to our practical needs.—*From "The Expositor,"* 1864.

Verse 105.—*"Thy word is a lamp unto my feet."* Going two miles into a neighbourhood where very few could read, to spend an evening in reading to a company who were assembled to listen, and about to return by a narrow path through the woods where paths diverged, I was provided with a torch of light wood, or " pitch pine." I objected ; it was too small, weighing not over half a pound. *"It will light you home,"* answered my host. I said, " The wind may blow it out." He said, " It will light you home." " But if it should rain ? " I again objected. " It will light you home," he insisted.

Contrary to my fears, it gave abundant light to my path all the way home, furnishing an apt illustration, I often think, of the way in which doubting hearts would be led safely along the " narrow way." If they would take the Bible as their guide, it would be a lamp to their feet, leading to the heavenly home. One man had five objections to the Bible. If he would take it as a lamp to his feet, it would " light him home." Another told me he had two faults to find with the Bible. I answered him in the words of my good friend who furnished the torch, " It will light you home."—*From the American Messenger,"* 1881.

Verse 105.—*"A lamp unto my feet,"* etc. All depends on our way of using the lamp. A man tells that when a boy he was proud to carry the lantern for his Sabbath school teacher. The way to their school led through unlit, muddy streets. The boy held the lantern far too high, and both sank in the deep mud. "Ah! you must hold the lamp lower," the teacher exclaimed, as they gained a firm footing on the farther side of the slough. The teacher then beautifully explained our text, and the man declares that he never forgot the lesson of that night. You may easily hold the lamp too high; but you can hardly hold it too low.—*James Wells, in "Bible Images," 1882.*

Verse 105.—"*Light.*"

> Lead, kindly light, amid the encircling gloom,
>   Lead thou me on.
> The night is dark, and I am far from home,
>   Lead thou me on.
> Keep thou my feet; I do not ask to see
> The distant scene; one step enough for me.
>
> *John Henry Newman* (1801—).

Verses 105, 106.—"*A light unto my path. I have sworn, and I will perform it,*" etc. I have looked upon thy word as a lamp to my own feet, as a thing nearly concerning myself, and then I have sworn, and I will perform it, that I will keep thy righteous judgments. It is a mighty means to stir up a man's spirit and quicken him to obedience, to look upon the word as written to himself, as a lamp and a light for him. When you come to hear out of God's Word, and God directs the minister so that you apprehend the truth as spoken to you, it will stir and awaken you, and you will say, "Oh methought this day every word the minister spoke was directed to me; I must take heed thereto." And so every word in the Scripture that concerns thee, God writes to thee; and if thou wilt take it so, it will be a mighty means to stir thee up to obedience.—*Jeremiah Burroughs, 1599—1646.*

Verse 106.—"*I have sworn,*" etc. Patrick's paraphrase is, "I have solemnly resolved and bound myself by the most sacred ties, which I will never break, but do now confirm."

Verse 106.—"*I have sworn.*" I would now urge you to make a solemn surrender of yourself unto the service of God. Do not only form such a purpose in your heart, but expressly declare it in the Divine presence. Such solemnity in the manner of doing it is certainly very reasonable in the nature of things; and sure it is highly expedient, for binding to the Lord such a treacherous heart, as we know our own to be. It will be pleasant to reflect upon it, as done at such and such a time, with such and such circumstances of place and method, which may serve to strike the memory and the conscience. The sense of the vows of God which are upon you will strengthen you in an hour of temptation; and the recollection may encourage your humble boldness and freedom in applying to him under the character and relation of your covenant God and Father, as future exigencies may require.

Do it therefore, but do it deliberately. Consider what it is that you are to do: and consider how reasonable it is that it should be done, and done cordially and cheerfully, "not by constraint, but willingly"; for in this sense, and every other, "God loveth a cheerful giver." . . . . . .

Let me remind you that this surrender must be perpetual. You must give yourself up to God in such a manner, as never more to pretend to be your own; for the rights of God are, like his nature, eternal and immutable; and with regard to his rational creatures, are the same yesterday, to-day, and for ever.

I would further advise and urge, that this dedication may be made with all possible solemnity. Do it in express words. And perhaps it may be in many cases most expedient, as many pious divines have recommended, to do it in writing. Set your hand and seal to it, "that on such a day of such a month and year, and at such a place, on full consideration and serious reflection, you came to this happy resolution, that whatever others might do, you would serve the Lord."—*Philip Doddridge (1702—1751) in "The Rise and Progress of Religion in the Soul."*

Verse 106.—Frequently renew settled and holy resolutions. A soldier unresolved to fight may easily be defeated. True and sharpened courage tread down those difficulties which would triumph over a cold and wavering spirit. Resolution in a weak man will perform more than strength in a coward. The weakness of our graces, the strength of our temptations, and the diligence of our spiritual enemies, require strong resolutions. We must be "steadfast and unmoveable," and this will make us "abound in the work of the Lord": 1 Cor. xv. 58. Abundant exercise in God's work will strengthen the habit of grace, increase our skill in the contest, and make the victory more easy and pleasant to us. Let us frame believing, humble resolutions in the strength of God's grace, with a fear of ourselves, but a confidence in God. David bound himself to God with a hearty vow, depending upon his strength: "*I have sworn, and I will perform it, that I will keep thy righteous judgments.*" This was not in his own strength, for, ver. 107, he desires God to quicken him, and to "accept the freewill offerings of his mouth," ver. 108, namely, the oath which proceeded from a free and resolved will. God will not slight, but strengthen the affectionate resolutions of his creature. We cannot keep ourselves from falling unless we first keep our resolutions from flagging.—*Stephen Charnock.*

Verse 106.—"*I have sworn, and I will perform it.*" Theodoricus, Archbishop of Cologne, when the Emperor Sigismund demanded of him the directest and most compendious way how to attain true happiness, made answer in brief, thus: "Perform when thou art well what thou promisedst when thou wast sick." David did so; he made vows in war, and paid them in peace; and thus should all good men do; not like the cunning devil, of whom the epigrammatist writeth:

> "The devil was sick, the devil a monk would be;
> The devil was well, the devil a monk was he."

Nor like unto many now-a-days, that, if God's hand do but lie somewhat heavy upon them, oh, what promises, what engagements are there for amendment of life! How like unto marble against rain do they seem to sweat and melt but still retain their hardness! Let but the rod be taken off their backs, or health restored, then, as their bodies live, their vows die; all is forgotten: nay, many times it so falleth out, that they are far worse than ever they were before.—*From John Spencer's "Things New and Old," 1658.*

Verse 106.—"*Thy righteous judgments.*" So David styles the word of God, because it judgeth most righteously between right and wrong, truth and falsehood. And, secondly, because according to the judgment given therein, God will act towards men. Let us take heed unto it; for the word contains God's judgment of men and hath a catalogue of such as shall not inherit the kingdom of God, and another of such as shall dwell in God's tabernacle: let us read and see in which of the two catalogues our two selves are; for according to that word will the judgment go.—*William Cowper.*

Verse 107.—"*I am afflicted very much,*" etc. Whence learn, 1. It is no strange thing for the most holy men to be acquainted with the saddest sort of affliction, bodily and spiritual: "*I am afflicted very much.*" 2. From whence soever affliction doth come, faith goeth to God only for comfort, as here: "*Quicken me, O LORD.*" 3. When God is pleased to make the word of promise lively, or to perform what the promise alloweth us to expect, such a consolation is a sufficient antidote to the heaviest affliction: "*Quicken me, O LORD, according unto thy word.*"—*David Dickson.*

Verse 107.—"*I am afflicted very much.*" We can recommend so persuasively the cheerful drinking of the cup of sorrow when in the hand of others, but what wry faces we make when it is put into our own.—*Alfred John Morris, 1814—1869.*

Verse 107.—"*I am afflicted . . . quicken me.*" The Christian lives in the midst of crosses, as the fish lives in the sea.—*Jean-Baptiste-Marie Vianney, 1786—1859.*

Verse 107.—"*Quicken me, O LORD.*" How doth God quicken us? By reviving our suffering graces, such as our hope, patience, and faith. Thus he puts life into us again, that we may go on cheerfully in our service, by infusion of new comforts. He revives the heart of his contrite ones, so the prophet saith (Isa. lvii. 15). This is very necessary, for the Psalmist saith elsewhere, "Quicken us, and we will call upon thy name" (Ps. lxxx. 18). Discomfort and discouragement weaken our hands in calling upon God. Until the Lord cheers us again we have no life in prayer. By two things especially doth God quicken us in affliction, by reviving our sense of his love, and by reviving our hope of glory.—*Thomas Manton.*

Verse 107.—"*According unto thy word.*" David goes often over with that phrase, which imports that David lay under the sense of some promise which God had made for the quickening of his heart when it was out of frame, and acordingly he recounts the gracious influence of God's Spirit, and professeth that he will never forget his precepts, because by them he had quickened him : ver. 93.

Thus, lay your dead hearts at Christ's feet, and plead in this manner : Lord, my heart is exceedingly dull and distracted ; I feel not these enlarging, melting influences which thy saints have felt ; but are they not chief material mercies of the covenant ? dost thou not promise a spirit of illumination, conviction, and humiliation ? is not holiness of heart and life a main branch of it ? dost thou not promise therein to write thy law in my heart ? to give me oneness of heart, to put thy fear within me, to subdue my corruptions, to help my infirmities in prayer ? Now, Lord, these are the mercies my soul wants and waits for, fill my soul with these animating influences, revive thy work of grace in my soul, draw out my heart towards thee, increase my affection for thee, repair thine image, call forth grace into lively exercise. Doth not that gracious word intend such a mercy when thou sayest thou wilt not only give a new heart, but " put a new spirit within me " (Ezek. xxxvi. 26), to make my soul lively, active, and spiritual in duties and exercises ? Dear Lord, am not I in covenant with thee ? and are not these covenant mercies ? why, then, my God, is my heart thus hardened from thy fear ? why dost thou leave me in all this deadness and distraction ? Remember thy word unto thy servant in which thou hast caused me to hope, and which thou hast helped me to plead ; O quicken my dull heart, according to thy word.—*Oliver Heywood.*

Verse 107.—*"According unto thy word."* David, when he begs for quickening, he is encouraged so to do by a promise. The question is, where this promise should be ? Some think it was that general promise of the law, if thou do these things thou shalt live in them (Lev. xviii. 5), and that from thence David drew this particular conclusion, that God would give life to his people. But rather, it was some other promise, some word of God he had, to bear him out in this request. The Lord has made many promises to us of sanctifying our affliction. The fruit of all shall be the taking away of sin (Isa. xxvii. 9) ; of bettering and improving us by it (Heb. ii. 10), of moderating our affliction, that he will stay his rough wind in the day of the east wind (Isa. xxvii. 8) ; that he will lay no more upon us than he will enable us to bear (1 Cor. x. 13). He hath promised he will moderate our affliction so that we shall not be tempted above our strength. He hath promised he will deliver us from it, that the rod of the wicked shall not always rest on the lot of the righteous (Ps. cxxv. 3) ; that he will be with us in it, and never fail us (Heb. xiii. 5). Now, I argue thus : if the people of God could stay their hearts upon God's word, when they had but such obscure hints to work upon that we do not know where the promise lies, ah ! how should our hearts be stayed upon God, when we have so many promises ! When the Scriptures are enlarged for the comfort and enlarging of our faith, surely we should say now as Paul, when we got a word, " I believed God " (Acts xxvii. 25) ; I may expect God will do thus for me, when his word speaks it everywhere.—*Thomas Manton.*

Verse 108.—*"The freewill offerings of the mouth,"* may be the offerings which the mouth had promised and vowed. And who can lay claim to these as the Lord ? His are all things.—*John Stephen.*

Verse 108.—*"The freewill offerings of my mouth."* This place makes known that species of sacrifices, which neither tribulations nor poverty of means can hinder, and which does not require an external temple, but in desert places and among heathen may be offered by a godly man. And these sacrifices of the mouth God himself makes more of than if all the flocks of the whole earth had been offered to him, and all the treasures of gold, and of silver, and of precious stones.—*Wolfgang Musculus.*

Verse 108.—*"Freewill offerings."* This expression is often used in the law (Lev. xxii. 18 ; Numb. xxix. 39 ; 2 Chron. xxxi. 14 ; Amos iv. 5). What are these freewill offerings ? They are distinguished from God's stated worship, and distinguished from that service which fell under a vow. Besides the stated peace-offerings, there were certain sacrifices performed upon certain occasions, to testify God's general goodness, and upon receipt of some special mercy ; and you will find these sacrifices to be expressly distinguished from such services as men bound themselves to by vow (Lev. vii. 16) . . . . . These serve to teach us two things. 1st. They are to teach us how ready we should be to take all occasions of thankfulness and spiritual worship ; for, besides their vowed services and instituted sacrifices, they had their freewill offerings, offered to God in thankfulness for some special blessing received, or for deliverance from danger. 2ndly. It shows with what voluntariness and cheerfulness we should go about God's worship in the Gospel, and what a free disposition of heart there should be, and edge upon our affections, in all things that we offer to God ; in this latter sense our offerings to God—prayer and praise —should be freewill offerings, come from us not like water out of a still forced by the fire, but like water out of a fountain with native freeness, readily and freely.— *Thomas Manton.*

Verse 108.—*"Offerings."* All God's people are made priests unto God ; for every offering supposeth a priest : so it is said, that Christ Jesus hath made us kings and priests (Rev. i. 6). All Christians have a communion with Christ in all his offices ; whatever Christ was, that certainly they are in some measure and degree.— *Thomas Manton.*

Verse 108.—*"Accept . . . . . the freewill offerings of my mouth, O Lord."* It is a great grace that the Lord should accept anything from us, if we consider these three things : First, who the Lord is ; next, what we are ; thirdly, what it is we have to give unto him.

As for the Lord, he is all-sufficient, and stands in need of nothing we can give him. Our goodness extends not to the Lord (Ps. xvi).

As for us, we are poor creatures, living by his liberality ; yea, begging from all the rest of his creatures ; from the sun and moon ; from the air, the water, and the earth ; from fowls and fishes ; yea, from the worms : some give us light, some meat, some clothes ; and are such beggars as we meet to give to a king ?

And, thirdly, if we well consider, What is it that we give ? Have we anything to give but that which we have received from him ? and whereof we may say with David, " O Lord, all things are of thee, and of thine own have we given thee again " (1 Chron. xxix. 14). Let this humble us, and restrain us from that vain conceit of meriting at God's hand.

David at this time, in his great necessity, having no other sacrifice to offer unto the Lord, offers him the calves of his lips ; but no doubt, when he might, he offered more.

There is nothing so small, but if it come from a good heart, God will accept it : the widow's mite, a cup of cold water ; yea, and the praise of our lips, although it has no other external oblation joined with it : but where men may do more, and will not, it is an argument that their heart is not sincerely affected toward him, and their praises are not welcome to him.—*William Cowper.*

Verse 108.—*"Accept . . . . the freewill offerings of my mouth, O LORD, and teach me thy judgments."* Two things we are here taught to pray for in reference to our religious performances.

1. Acceptance of them : this we must aim at in all we do in religion, that whether present or absent we may be accepted of the Lord. That which David here earnestly prays for the acceptance of is " *the freewill offerings,*" not of his purse, but of his " *mouth,*" his prayers and praises ; "the calves of our lips " (Hosea xiv. 2) ; " the fruit of our lips " (Heb. xiii. 15) ; these are the spiritual offerings which all Christians, as spiritual priests, must offer to God ; and they must be " *freewill offerings ;* " for we must offer them abundantly and cheerfully ; and it is this willing mind that is accepted. The more there is of freeness and willingness in the service of God, the more pleasing it is to him.

2. Assistance in them : *"Teach me thy judgments."* We cannot offer anything to God which we have reason to think he will accept of, but what he is pleased to instruct us in the doing of ; and we must be earnest for the grace of God in us as for the favour of God toward us.—*Matthew Henry.*

Verse 108.—*"Teach me thy judgments."* As if the man of God should say, This is one thing whereunto I will give over myself, even to see how thou dost punish the wicked, and conduct thy children. So that we must learn, that as it is necessary to understand the law and the gospel, so is it requisite to discern God's judgments. For as we cannot learn the one without observing God's mercy ; so we cannot attain to the other without marking his vengeance. We must see always by the peculiar teaching of God's Spirit, how the Lord punisheth in justice, and yet in mercy ; in wrath, and yet in love ; in rigour and hatred of our sin, humbling us with one hand ; in pity and compassion to our salvation, comforting us with the other hand. We see then how the prophet prayeth, both to see them and to mark them : we need teach this often, because we dream so much of fatal necessity, and of the connections of natural causes, or else because we cannot discern between the crosses of the godly and the ungodly . . . This is then a singular gift of God, to discern how by the self-same means the Lord both humbleth the good and over-throweth the wicked.—*Richard Greenham.*

Verse 109.—*"My soul is continually in my hand."* He had his soul in his hand, ready to give whenever God should take it. And this is to be observed, that there is no trouble so ready to take away the life of God's children, as they are ready to give it. As Elijah came out to the mouth of his cave to meet with the Lord; and Abraham stood in the door of his tent to speak to the angel; so the soul of the godly stands ready in the door of the tabernacle of this body to remove when the Lord shall command it; whereas the soul of the wicked lies back, hiding itself, as Adam among the bushes, and is taken out of the body perforce; as was the soul of that worldling; "This night thy soul shall be required of thee;" but they never sacrifice their souls willingly to the Lord.—*William Cowper.*

Verse 109.—*"My soul is continually in my hand."* If any one carry in the hand a fragile vessel, made of glass or any other similar material, filled with a precious liquor, especially if the hand be weak, or if from other causes dangers be threatening, he will scarcely be able to avoid the breaking of the vessel and the running out of the liquor. Such is the condition of my life, which I, set upon by various enemies, carry as it were in my hand; which, therefore, is exposed to such a great danger, as that I always have death present before my sight, my life hanging on the slenderest thread.—*Andreas Rivetus, 1572—1651.*

Verse 109.—*"My soul is continually in my hand."* The believer is always in the very jaws of death. He lives with wings outstretched to fly away. Paul testified, "I die daily." In the extremity of persecution, the fervent desire was to know what God would have him to do.—*Henry Law.*

Verse 109.—*"My soul is continually in my hand."* I make no more of life than a child doth of his bird which he carrieth in the palm of his hand held open.—*John Trapp.*

Verse 109.—*"My soul is continually in my hand,"* etc. Why doth David say, "My soul is in mine hand"; had he called it out of the hand of God, and taken the care of it upon himself? Nothing less. His meaning is only this,—I walk in the midst of dangers and among a thousand deaths continually; I am in deaths often, my life is exposed to perils every day, yet do I not forget thy law: I keep close to thee, and will keep close to thee whatsoever comes of it. Augustine upon that place doth ingeniously confess that he understood not what David meant, by having his soul in his hands; but Jerome, another of the ancients, teacheth us, that it is an Hebraism, signifying a state of extremest peril. The Greeks also have drawn it into a proverb speaking the same thing.

But why doth the holding or putting the life in the hand signify the exposing of the life to peril? There is a twofold reason of it.

First. Because those things which are carried openly in the hand are apt to fall out of the hand, and being carried in sight, they are apt to be snatched or wrested out of the hand. And, therefore, though to be in the hand of God signifies *safety*, because his hand is armed with irresistible power to protect us; yet for a man to carry a thing in his own hand is to carry it in danger, because his hand is weak, and there are safer ways of carrying or conveying a thing than openly in the hand. If a man be to ride a long journey with any treasure about him, he doth not carry it in his hand, but puts it in some secret and close place where it may be hidden, and so be more secure. The Chaldee paraphrast, to express the elegancy of that place forecited out of the Psalm, gives it thus, *"My life is in as much danger as if it stood upon the very superficies or outside of my hand,"* as if he had no hold of it, but it stood barely upon his hand; for that which is set upon the palm of the hand, and not grasped, is in greater danger. Things safe kept are hidden or held fast.

Secondly. There is another reason of that speech, because when a man is about to deliver a thing or to give it up, he takes it in his hand. They that put themselves upon great perils and dangers for God and his people, deliver up their lives and their all to God. Hence that counsel of the Apostle (1 Pet. iv. 19): "Let them that suffer according to the will of God commit the keeping of their souls to him in well doing, as unto a faithful Creator." So here, the life of men in danger is said to be put in the hand, because such are, as it were, ready to deliver and commit their lives unto God, that he would take care of their lives to preserve them from the danger, or to take them to himself if they lose them in his service.—*Joseph Caryl.*

Verse 110.—"*The wicked.*" He calls them *wicked men ;* which importeth three things. First, they work wickedness. Secondly, they love it. Thirdly, they persevere in it.—*William Cowper.*

Verse 110.—"*A snare.*" One manner of catching wild animals, such as lions, bears, jackals, foxes, hart, roebuck, and fallow-deer, was by a trap (*pach*), which is the word used in this place ; this was set under ground (Job xviii. 10), in the run of the animal (Prov. xxii. 5), and caught it by the leg (Job xviii. 9).—*William Latham Bevan, in Smith's Dictionary of the Bible,* 1863.

Verse 110.—"*The wicked have laid a snare for me.*" In eating, he sets before us gluttony ; in love he impels to lust ; in labour, sluggishness ; in conversing, envy ; in governing, covetousness ; in correcting, anger ; in honour, pride ; in the heart, he sets evil thoughts ; in the mouth, evil words ; in actions, evil works ; when awake, he moves us to evil actions ; when asleep, to filthy dreams.—*Girolamo Savonarola,* 1452—1498.

Verse 110.—"*Laid a snare for me : yet I erred not,*" etc. It is not the laying the bait hurts the fish, if the fish do not bite.—*Thomas Watson.*

Verse 111.—"*Thy testimonies have I taken,*" etc. The Scripture is called " testimonies " in respect to God himself, because it doth give a testimony to him, and makes God known to us : it gives a testimony of all those attributes that are himself, of his wisdom, of his power, of his justice, of his goodness, of his truth. The declaration of these, we have them all in the various books of the Scriptures : there is never a book, but there is a testification of these attributes. In the book of Genesis we have a testimony of his *power* in making the world, of his *justice* in drowning the world, and of his *goodness* in saving Noah. In the book of Exodus we have a testimony of his *providence* in leading the people of Israel through the Red Sea, in bringing them out of Egypt ; we have a testimony of his *wisdom* in giving them his law. What should I name more ? In the *New* Testament, in the Gospel, all is testimony. As the *Old* gave testimony to *God,* so the *New* to *Christ :* " To him gave all the prophets witness ; " not only the *Old,* but the *New :* " These are they that testify of me." Everywhere there is testimony of Christ,— of his *humility,* in taking our nature ; of his *power,* in working miracles ; of his *wisdom,* in the parables that he spoke ; of his *patience* and *love,* in the torments that he suffered for us. Both Law and Gospel—the whole book of Scripture, and every part of it in these regards is fitly called " *the testimonies of the Lord.*" And the holy Psalmist made choice of this name when he was to speak to the honour and glory of it ; because it was that name from which he sucked a great deal of comfort, because it was the testimony of God's *truth* and *goodness* and *wisdom* and *power* to him ; thereupon he makes so precious esteem of it as to account it his " *heritage.*"—*Richard Holdsworth* (1590—1649), *in* "*The Valley of Vision.*"

Verse 111.—"*Thy testimonies.*" By " *testimonies* " is meant the covenant between God and his people ; wherein he bindeth himself to them, and them to him. Some think that the excellency of the word is here set out by many names ; but we must look to the propriety of every word : as before by " judgments," so by this word " *testimonies,*" is meant the covenant : not the commandments, because they cannot be an inheritance, for they cannot comfort us, because we cannot fulfil them, but fail in them, and cannot therefore take comfort in them. It is the gospel that bringeth peace and comfort. "*The law,*" when it is taken generally, containeth all the word, particularly the commandments ; so " *the word* " generally containeth both law and gospel, but particularly the promises, as Rom. x. So likewise by the " *testimonies,*" when they are opposed to the law, is meant the promise of the covenant, as Isaiah viii., and this testimony is confirmed to us by the sacraments, as to them by sacrifices.—*Richard Greenham.*

Verse 111.—"*As an heritage.*" Why the divine testimonies should be called by the Psalmist an *inheritance ;* why he brings them within the compass of this notion, may not so easily be understood ; for the word of God points out the inheritance, but it is not the inheritance itself. Yes, there is good reason to be given for the expression, were there no more than this, that we consider the inestimable comfort, and heavenly treasure that is to be found in the word of God ; it is a rich mine of all celestial treasure, it is a storehouse of all good things, of all saving knowledge.

All privileges whatsoever they are that we can expect on earth or heaven, they are all contained in the word of God : here is ground enough why it is called an *inheritance ;* he hath a good *heritage* that hath all these.

Yet there is a better reason than this ; for if it be so that heaven is our inheritance, then the word of God is ; because it is the word that points out heaven, that gives the *assurance* of heaven : we have in the word of God all the evidences of heaven. Whatsoever *title* any saint hath to heaven, he hath it in and out of the word of God. There are the evidences in the word of God ; both the evidence of *discovery*, it is the holy terrier of the celestial Canaan, and the evidence of *assurance*, it is as a sacred bond or indenture between God and his creature. St. Gregory said wittily, when he called it God's epistle that he sent to man for the declaration of his will and pleasure, he might as well have called it God's deed of gift, whereby he makes over and conveys to us all those hopes that we look for in heaven. Whatsoever interest we have in God, in Christ, whatsoever hope of bliss and glory, whatsoever comfort of the Spirit, whatsoever proportion of grace, all are made over to us in the promises of the gospel, in the word of God.

Now put this together, look as in human affairs, *evidences*, though they be not properly the inheritance itself, yet they are called the inheritance, and are the inheritance, though not actually, yet virtually so ; because all the title we have to an inheritance is in the deeds and evidences ; therefore evidences are precious things. Though it be but a piece of paper, or parchment full of dust and worm-eaten, yet it is as much worth sometimes as a county, as much worth as all a man's possessions besides. So likewise it is with the Scriptures ; they are not actually and properly the inheritance itself, but they are *via*, the way to the kingdom. It is called the gospel of the kingdom, nay more, the kingdom itself : " The kingdom of God is come among you," or " to you." Why the kingdom ? Why the inheritance ? By the same reason, both, because here we have the *conveyance*, here we have the *deed*, here we have the *assurance* of whatsoever title or claim we make to heaven.—*Richard Holdsworth.*

Verse 111.—*"They are the rejoicing of my heart."* He saith not that God's testimonies bring joy, but that they are joy, there is no other joy but the delight in the law of the Lord. For all other joy, the wise king said of laughter, " thou art mad," and of joy, " what is it that thou dost ?" Eccles. ii. True joy is the earnest which we have of heaven, it is the treasure of the soul, and therefore should be laid up in a safe place ; and nothing in this world is safe to place it in. And therefore with the spouse we say, " We will be glad in thee, we will remember thy love more than wine." Let others seek their joy in wine, in society, in conversation, in music ; for me, thou hast put gladness in my heart, more than in the time that their corn and their wine increased. These indeed are the precious fruits of the earth, but they seal not up special favour ; a man may have together with them, an empty, husky, and chaffy soul. And therefore these are not the joys of the saints ; they must have God, or else they die for sorrow ; his law is their life.—*Abraham Wright.*

Verse 112.—*"I have inclined my heart to perform thy statutes alway,"* etc. In the former verse he showed his faith, and his joy which came thereof ; now he showeth that here in this joy he will keep the commandments ; whereby he showeth that this was a true joy, because it wrought a care to do good. For if we believe the promises truly, then we also love the commandments, otherwise faith is vain ; a care to live a godly life nourisheth faith in God's promises. Here is the cause then why many regard not the word and sacraments ; or if they do a little, it is to no purpose, because they labour not to keep the commandments. For unless they have care to do this, the word of God to them cannot be profitable, nor the sacraments sacred.—*Richard Greenham.*

Verse 112.—*"I have inclined my heart to perform,"* etc. Observe. In the 36th verse he prayed to God, saying, *"Incline my heart unto thy testimonies."* And here he speaks about himself, saying, *"I have inclined mine heart to perform thy statutes alway even unto the end."* What need, then, was there to ask from God that which he in another place glories to have done himself ? I answer : These things are not contrary the one to the other. God inclines, and the godly man inclines. Man inclines by striving ; God inclines by effecting. Neither is that which the man attempts, nor that which he by striving achieves goodwards, from the man, but from God, who gives, ' *both to will and to do of his good pleasure :* " Phil. ii. 13.—*Wolfgang Musculus.*

Verse 112.—The sinful heart of itself will run any way ; upon earthly things, upon evil things, or upon impertinent and unseasonable things ; but it will not come to or keep upon that which it should mind ; therefore it must be taken as by strong hand, and set upon spiritual things, set on musing and meditation of heavenly things. A carnal heart is like the loadstone, it cleaves to nothing but steel or iron, and both of them easily unite : but the heart must be of another property, and act in a higher way. And a good heart, though it thinks too much earthward, and runs often wrong, yet it will set itself in its thinkings on right objects, and make itself and them to meet and unite. David tells us how he did ; he *inclined his heart to God's commandments,* both to keep them and to meditate on them. He took and *bent his heart,* as a thing bending too much to other things ; set his mind on musing on it. He found his heart and the law of God too far asunder, and so would continue, unless he brought them together and made them one. If he had not brought his heart to the word, he had never meditated : the object cannot apply itself to the mind, but the mind must bring itself to the object. No holy duties will come to us, we must come to them.—*Nathanael Ranew, in "Solitude Improved by Divine Meditation,"* 1670.

Verse 112.—"*I have inclined mine heart to perform,*" etc. In this work he was determined to *continue.* 1. "*I have inclined my heart.*" The counsel of the soul is like a balance ; and the mind, which hath the commanding power over the affections, inclines the balance to that which it judges best. 2. It was to *perform it,* that he thus *inclined his heart.* 3. And this not for a *time,* or some *particular occasion,* but *always,* and unto *the end.* Then *the end of life* would be the *beginning of glory.*—*Adam Clarke.*

Verse 112.—"*I have inclined my heart.*" The prophet, in order briefly to define what it is to serve God, asserts that he applied not only his hands, eyes, or feet, to the keeping of the law, but that he began with the affection of the heart.—*John Calvin.*

Verse 112.—"*Unto the end.*" Our life on earth is a race ; in vain begins he to run swiftly, that fainteth, and gives over before he come to the end. And this was signified (saith Gregory) when in the law the tail of the beast was sacrificed with the rest : perseverance crowneth all. It is good we have begun to do well ; let us also strive to persevere to the end.—*William Cowper.*

EXPOSITION OF VERSES 113 TO 120.

I HATE *vain* thoughts : but thy law do I love.

114 Thou *art* my hiding place and my shield : I hope in thy word.

115 Depart from me, ye evildoers : for I will keep the commandments of my God.

116 Uphold me according unto thy word, that I may live : and let me not be ashamed of my hope.

117 Hold thou me up, and I shall be safe : and I will have respect unto thy statutes continually.

118 Thou hast trodden down all them that err from thy statutes : for their deceit *is* falsehood.

119 Thou puttest away all the wicked of the earth *like* dross : therefore I love thy testimonies.

120 My flesh trembleth for fear of thee ; and I am afraid of thy judgments.

Verse 113. "I hate vain thoughts : but thy law do I love." In this paragraph the Psalmist deals with thoughts and things and persons which are the opposite of God's holy thoughts and ways. He is evidently in great fear of the powers of darkness, and of their allies, and his whole soul is stirred up to stand against them with a determined opposition. Just as he began the octave, verse 97, with " O how I love thy law," so here he begins with a declaration of hatred against that which breaks the law. The opposite of the fixed and infallible law of God is the wavering, changing opinion of men : David had an utter contempt and abhorrence for this ; all his reverence and regard went to the sure word of testimony. In proportion to his love to the law was his hate of men's inventions. The thoughts of men are vanity ; but the thoughts of God are verity. We hear much in these days of " men of thought," " thoughtful preachers," and " modern thought " : what is this but the old pride of the human heart ? Vain man would be wise. The Psalmist did not glory in his thoughts ; and that which was called " thought " in his day was a thing which he detested. When man thinks his best, his highest thoughts are as far below those of divine revelation as the earth is beneath the heavens. Some of our thoughts are specially vain in the sense of vain-glory, pride, conceit, and self-trust ; others in the sense of bringing disappointment, such as fond ambition, sinful dreaming, and confidence in man ; in the sense of emptiness and frivolity, such as the idle thoughts and vacant romancings in which so many indulge ; and, yet once more, too many of our thoughts are vain in the sense of being sinful, evil, and foolish. The Psalmist is not indifferent to evil thoughts as the careless are ; but upon them he looks with a hate as true as was the love with which he clung to the pure thoughts of God.

The last octave was practical, this is thoughtful ; there the man of God attended to his feet, and here to his heart : the emotions of the soul are as important as the acts of the life, for they are the fountain and spring from which the actions proceed. When we love the law it becomes a law of love, and we cling to it with our whole heart.

114. *"Thou art my hiding place and my shield."* To his God he ran for shelter from vain thoughts ; there he hid himself away from their tormenting intrusions, and in solemn silence of the soul he found God to be his hiding-place. When called into the world, if he could not be alone with God as his hiding-place, he could have the Lord with him as his shield, and by this means he could ward off the attacks of wicked suggestions. This is an experimental verse, and it testifies to that which the writer knew of his own personal knowledge : he could not fight with his own thoughts, or escape from them, till he flew to his God, and then he found deliverance. Observe that he does not speak of God's word as being his double defence, but he ascribes that to God himself. When we are beset by very spiritual assaults, such as those which arise out of vain thoughts, we shall do well to fly distinctly to the person of our Lord, and to cast ourselves upon his real presence. Happy is he who can truly say to the triune God, " Thou art my hiding-place." He has beheld

God under that glorious covenant aspect which ensures to the beholder the surest consolation. "*I hope in thy word.*" And well he might, since he had tried and proved it : he looked for protection from all danger, and preservation from all temptation to him who had hitherto been the tower of his defence on former occasions. It is easy to exercise hope where we have experienced help. Sometimes when gloomy thoughts afflict us, the only thing we can do is to hope, and, happily, the word of God always sets before us objects of hope and reasons for hope, so that it becomes the very sphere and support of hope, and thus tiresome thoughts are overcome. Amid fret and worry a hope of heaven is an effectual quietus.

115. "*Depart from me, ye evildoers.*" Those who make a conscience of their thoughts are not likely to tolerate evil company. If we fly to God from vain thoughts, much more shall we avoid vain men. Kings are all too apt to be surrounded by a class of men who flatter them, and at the same time take liberty to break the laws of God : David purged his palace of such parasites ; he would not harbour them beneath his roof. No doubt they would have brought upon him an ill name, for their doings would have been imputed to him, since the acts of courtiers are generally set down as acts of the court itself ; therefore the king sent them packing bag and baggage, saying,—" Depart from me." Herein he anticipated the sentence of the last great day, when the Son of David shall say, " Depart from me, ye workers of iniquity." We cannot thus send all malefactors out of our houses, but it will often become a duty to do so where there is right and reason for it. A house is all the better for being rid of liars, pilferers, lewd talkers, and slanderers. We are bound at all hazards to keep ourselves clear of such companions as come to us by our own choice if we have any reason to believe that their character is vicious. Evildoers make evil counsellors. Those who say unto God, " Depart from us," ought to hear the immediate echo of their words from the mouths of God's children, " Depart from us. We cannot eat bread with traitors."

"*For I will keep the commandments of my God.*" Since he found it hard to keep the commandments in the company of the ungodly, he gave them their marching orders. He *must* keep the commandments, but he did not need to keep their company. What a beautiful title for the Lord this verse contains ! The word *God* only occurs in this one place in all this lengthened Psalm, and then it is attended by the personal word " my "—" my God."

> " My God ! how charming is the sound !
> How pleasant to repeat !
> Well may that heart with pleasure bound,
> Where God hath fix'd his seat."

Because Jehovah is our God therefore we resolve to obey him, and to chase out of our sight those who would hinder us in his service. It is a grand thing for the mind to have come to a point, and to be steadfastly fixed in the holy determination, —" I will keep the commandments." God's law is our pleasure when the God of the law is our God.

116. "*Uphold me according unto thy word, that I may live.*" It was so necessary that the Lord should hold up his servant, that he could not even live without it. Our soul would die if the Lord did not continually sustain it, and every grace which makes spiritual life to be truly life would decay if he withdrew his upholding hand. It is a sweet comfort that this great necessity of upholding is provided for in the word, and we have not to ask for it as for an uncovenanted mercy, but simply to plead for the fulfilment of a promise, saying, " Uphold me according to thy word." He who has given us eternal life hath in that gift secured to us all that is essential thereto, and as gracious upholding is one of the necessary things we may be sure that we shall have it. "*And let me not be ashamed of my hope.*" In verse 114 he had spoken of his hope as founded on the word, and now he begs for the fulfilment of that word that his hope might be justified in the sight of all. A man would be ashamed of his hope if it turned out that it was not based upon a sure foundation ; but this will never happen in our case. We may be ashamed of our thoughts, and our words, and our deeds, for they spring from ourselves ; but we never shall be ashamed of our hope, for that springs from the Lord our God. Such is the frailty of our nature that unless we are continually upheld by grace, we shall fall so foully as to be ashamed of ourselves, and ashamed of all those glorious hopes which are now the crown and glory of our life. The man of God had uttered the most positive resolves, but he felt that he could not trust in his own solemn determination : hence

these prayers. It is not wrong to make resolutions, but it will be useless to do so unless we salt them well with believing cries to God. David meant to keep the law of the Lord, but he first needed the Lord of the law to keep him.

117. *"Hold thou me up "*: as a nurse holds up a little child. *"And I shall be safe,"* and not else ; for unless thou hold me up I shall be falling about like an infant that is weak upon its knees. We are saved by past grace, but we are not safe unless we receive present grace. The Psalmist had vowed to keep the Lord's commands, but here he pleads with the Lord to keep him : a very sensible course of procedure. Our version reads the word " uphold," and then " hold up ; " and truly we need this blessing in every shape in which it can come, for in all manner of ways our adversaries seek to cast us down. To be safe is a happy condition ; there is only one door to it, and that is to be held up by God himself ; thank God, that door is open to the least among us. *"And I will have respect unto thy statutes continually."* In obedience is safety ; in being held up is obedience. No man will outwardly keep the Lord's statutes for long together unless he has an inward respect for them, and this will never be unless the hand of the Lord perpetually upholds the heart in holy love. Perseverance to the end, obedience continually, comes only through the divine power ; we start aside as a deceitful bow unless we are kept right by him that first gave us grace. Happy is the man who realizes this verse in his life ; upheld through his whole life in a course of unswerving integrity, he becomes a safe and trusted man, and maintains a sacred delicacy of conscience which is unknown to others. He feels a tender respect for the statutes of the Lord, which keeps him clear of inconsistencies and conformities to the world that are so common among others, and hence he is a pillar in the house of the Lord. Alas, we know some professors who are not upright, and therefore they lean to sin till they fall over, and though they are restored they are never safe or reliable, neither have they that sweet purity of soul which is the charm of the more sanctified who have been kept from falling into the mire.

118. *"Thou hast trodden down all them that err from thy statutes."* There is no holding up for them ; they are thrown down and then trodden down, for they choose to go down into the wandering ways of sin. Sooner or later God will set his foot on those who turn their foot from his commands : it has always been so, and it always will be so to the end. If the salt has lost its savour, what is it fit for but to be trodden under foot ? God puts away the wicked like dross, which is only fit to be cast out as road-metal to be trodden down.

"For their deceit is falsehood." They call it far-seeing policy, but it is absolute falsehood, and it shall be treated as such. Ordinary men call it clever diplomacy, but the man of God calls a spade a spade, and declares it to be falsehood, and nothing less, for he knows that it is so in the sight of God. Men who err from the right road invent pretty excuses with which to deceive themselves and others, and so quiet their consciences and maintain their credits ; but their mask of falsehood is too transparent. God treads down falsehoods ; they are only fit to be spurned by his feet, and crushed into the dust. How horrified must those be who have spent all their lives in contriving a confectionery religion, and then see it all trodden upon by God as a sham which he cannot endure !

119. *"Thou puttest away all the wicked of the earth like dross."* He does not trifle with them, or handle them with kid gloves. No, he judges them to be the scum of the earth, and he treats them accordingly by putting them away. He puts them away from his church, away from their honours, away from the earth, and at last away from himself. " Depart," saith he, " ye cursed." If even a good *man* feels forced to put away the evil-doers from him, much more must the thrice holy God put away the wicked. They looked like precious metal, they were intimately mixed up with it, they were laid up in the same heap ; but the Lord is a refiner, and every day he removes some of the wicked from among his people, either by making a shameful discovery of their hypocrisy or by consuming them from off the earth. They are put away as dross, never to be recalled. As the metal is the better for losing its alloy, so is the church the better for having the wicked removed. These wicked ones are " of the earth,"—" the wicked of the earth," and they have no right to be with those who are not of the world ; the Lord perceives them to be out of place and injurious, and therefore he puts them away, *all* of them, leaving none of them to deteriorate his church. The process will one day be perfect ; no dross will be spared, no gold will be left impure. Where shall we be when that great work is finished ?

"Therefore I love thy testimonies." Even the severities of the Lord excite the

love of his people. If he allowed men to sin with impunity, he would not be so fully the object of our loving admiration; he is glorious in holiness because he thus rids his kingdom of rebels, and his temple of them that defile it. In these evil days, when God's punishment of sinners has become the butt of proud sceptical contentions, we may regard as a mark of the true man of God that he loves the Lord none the less, but a great deal the more, because of his condign judgment of the ungodly.

120. *"My flesh trembleth for fear of thee."* Such was his awe in the presence of the Judge of all the earth, whose judgment he had just now been considering, that he did exceedingly fear and quake. Even the grosser part of his being,—his flesh felt a solemn dread at the thought of offending one so good and great, who would so effectually sever the wicked from among the just. Alas, poor flesh, this is the highest thing to which thou canst attain! *"And I am afraid of thy judgments."* God's words of judgment are solemn, and his deeds of judgment are terrible; they may well make us afraid. At the thought of the Judge of all,—his piercing eye, his books of record, his day of assize, and the operations of his justice,—we may well cry for cleansed thoughts, and hearts, and ways, lest his judgments should light on us. When we see the great Refiner separating the precious from the vile, we may well feel a godly fear, lest we should be put away by him, and left to be trodden under his feet.

Love in the previous verse is quite consistent with fear in this verse: the fear which hath torment is cast out, but not the filial fear which leads to reverence and obedience.

NOTES ON VERSES 113 TO 120.

The fifteenth letter, SAMECH, denotes a *prop* or *pillar*, and this agrees well with the subject matter of the strophe, in which God is twice implored to uphold his servant (verses 16, 17), while the utter destruction of those who make light of his law, or encourage scepticism regarding it, may be compared to the fate of the Philistine lords, on whom Samson brought down the roof of the house where they were making merry, by overthrowing the pillars which supported it.—*Neale and Littledale.*

Verses 112, 113.—When David had an inclination in his heart to God's statutes, the immediate effect of it was to "*hate vain thoughts.*" We read, "*I have inclined mine heart to perform thy statutes* "; and it follows, "*I hate vain thoughts.*" The vanity of his heart was a burden to him. A new creature is as careful against wickedness in the head or heart, as in the life. A godly man would be purer in the sight of God than in the view of man. He knows none but God can see the wanderings of his heart or the thoughts of his head, yet he is as careful that sins should not rise up as that they should not break out.—*Stephen Charnock.*

Verse 113.—"*I hate vain thoughts,*" or, the evil devices ; or, the double-hearted imaginations ; or, the intermeddling, counter-coursing thoughts : that is to say, that kind of practice of some men, that sail with every wind, and seek still to have two strings to their bow. The Hebrew word doth properly signify boughs or branches, which shoot up perplexedly or confusedly in a tree.—*Theodore Haak, 1618—1657.*

Verse 113.—"*I hate vain thoughts.*" In those vacant hours which are spared from business, pleasure, company, and sleep, and which are spent in solitude, at home or abroad ; unprofitable, proud, covetous, sensual, envious, or malicious imaginations, occupy the minds of ungodly men, and often infect their very dreams. These are not only sinful in themselves, indicating the state of their hearts, and as such will be brought into the account at the day of judgment ; but they excite the dormant corruptions, and lead to more open and gross violations of the holy law. The carnal mind welcomes and delights to dwell upon these congenial imaginations, and to solace itself by ideal indulgences, when opportunity of other gratification is not presented, or when a man dares not commit the actual transgression. But the spiritual mind recoils at them ; such thoughts will intrude from time to time, but they are unwelcome and distressing, and are immediately thrust out ; while other subjects, from the word of God, are stored up in readiness to occupy the mind more profitably and pleasantly during the hours of leisure and retirement. There is no better test of our true character, than the habitual effect of "*vain thoughts*" upon our minds—whether we love and indulge them, or abhor, and watch and pray against them.—*Thomas Scott, 1747—1821.*

Verse 113.—"*I hate vain thoughts.*" A godly man may have roving thoughts in duty. Sad experience proves this ; the thoughts will be dancing up and down in prayer. The saints are called stars ; but many times in duty they are wandering stars. The heart is like quicksilver which will not fix. It is hard to tie two good thoughts together ; we cannot lock our hearts so close, but that distracting thoughts, like wind, will get in. Hierom complains of himself; " Sometimes," saith he, " when I am about God's service, I am walking in the galleries, or casting up accounts." But these wandering thoughts are not allowed : "*I hate vain thoughts,*" they come as unwelcome guests, which are no sooner spied, but turned out of doors.—*Thomas Watson.*

Verse 113.—"*I hate.*" Every dislike of evil is not sufficient ; but perfect hatred is required of us against all sorts and degrees of sin.—*David Dickson.*

Verse 113.—"*Vain thoughts.*" The word is used for the *opinions* of men ; and may be applied to all heterodox opinions, human doctrines, damnable heresies ; such as are inconsistent with the perfections of God, derogate from his grace, and from the person and offices of Christ ; and are contrary to the word, and which are therefore rejected and abhorred by good men.—*John Gill.*

Verse 113.—"*Vain thoughts.*" Hebrew, *seäphim,* haltings between two opinions. See 1 Kings xviii. 21. Hence it signifies *sceptical doubts.*—*Christopher Wordsworth.*

Verse 113.—"*Vain thoughts.*" Our thoughts are set upon trifles and frivolous things, neither tending to our own profit nor the benefit of others : " The heart of the wicked is little worth ; " all their debates, conceits, musings, are of no value : for all their thoughts are taken up about childish vanity and foolish conceits. " The thought of foolishness is sin " (Prov. xxiv. 9) ; not only the thought of wickedness, but foolishness. Thoughts are the first-born of the soul, the immediate issues of the mind ; yet we lavish them away upon every trifle. Follow men all the day long, and take account of their thoughts. Oh ! what madness and folly are in all the musings they are conscious of : " The Lord knoweth the thoughts of man, that they are vanity " (Ps. xciv. 11). If we did judge as God judges, all the thoughts, reasonings, discourses of the mind, if they were set down in a table, we might write at the bottom, Here is the sum and total account of all,—nothing but vanity.

The sins that do most usually engross and take up our thoughts are,

1st. Uncleanness. Speculative wickedness makes way for active : " Hath committed adultery . . . . in his heart " (Matt. v. 28). There is a polluting ourselves by our thoughts, and this sin usually works that way.

2ndly. Revenge. Liquors are soured when long kept ; so, when we dwell upon discontents, they turn to revenge. Purposes of revenge are most sweet and pleasant to carnal nature : " Frowardness is in his heart, he deviseth mischief continually " (Prov. vi. 14), that is to say, he is full of revengeful and spiteful thoughts.

3rdly. Envy. It is a sin that feeds upon the mind. Those songs of the women, that Saul had slain his thousands, but David his ten thousands, they ran in Saul's mind, therefore he hated David (1 Sam. xviii. 9). Envy is an evil disease that dwelleth in the heart, and betrays itself mostly in thoughts.

4thly. Pride. Either pride in the desires or pride in the mind, either vain-glory or self-conceit ; this is entertaining our hearts with whispers of vanity : there-fore it is said, " He hath scattered the proud in the imagination of their hearts " (Luke i. 51) : proud men are full of imaginations.

5thly. Covetousness, which is nothing but vain musings and exercises of the heart : " A heart they have exercised with covetous practices " (2 Peter ii. 14). And it withdraws the heart in the very time of God's worship : " Their heart goeth after their covetousness " (Ezek. xxxiii. 31).

6thly. Distrust is another thing which usually takes up our thoughts—distracting motions against God's providence.—*Thomas Manton.*

Verse 113.—"*Vain thoughts.*" Let us see what *vanity* is. Take it in all the acceptations of it, it is true of our thoughts that they are "*vain.*"

1. It is taken for *unprofitableness.* So, Eccles. i. 2, 3, " All is vain," because there is " no profit in them under the sun." Such are our thoughts by nature ; the wisest of them will not stand us in any stead in time of need, in time of temptation, distress of conscience, day of death or judgment : 1 Cor. ii. 6, " All the wisdom of the wise comes to nought " ; Prov. x. 20, " The heart of the wicked is little worth," not a penny for them all.

2. Vanity is taken for *lightness.* " Lighter than vanity " is a phrase used, Ps. lxii. 9 ; and whom is it spoken of ? Of men ; and if anything in them be lighter than other, it is their *thoughts,* which swim in the uppermost parts, float at the top, are as the scum of the heart. When all the best, and wisest, and deepest, and solidest thoughts in Belshazzar, a prince, were weighed, they were found too light, Dan. v. 27.

3. Vanity is put for *folly.* So, Prov. xii. 11, " vain men " is made all one with men " void of understanding." Such are our thoughts. Among other evils which are said to " come out of the heart" (Mark vii. 22), ἀφροσύνη is reckoned as one, " foolishness " ; that is, thoughts that are such as madmen have, and fools—nothing to the purpose of which there can be made no use.

4. Vanity is put for *inconstancy* and frailty ; therefore vanity and a shadow are made synonymous, Ps. cxliv. 4. Such are our thoughts, flitting and perishing, as bubbles : Ps. cxlvi. 4, " All their thoughts perish."

5. Lastly, they are *wicked and sinful.* Vanity is [Jer. iv. 14] yoked with wicked-ness, and vain men and sons of Belial are all one, 2 Chron. xiii. 7. And such are our thoughts by nature : Prov. xxiv. 9, " The thought of foolishness is sin." And therefore a man is to be humbled for a proud thought.—*Thomas Goodwin.*

Verse 113.—"*But thy law do I love.*" Ballast your heart with a love to God. Love will, by a pleasing violence, bind down our thoughts : if it doth not establish our minds, they will be like a cork, which, with a light breath, and a short curl of water, shall be tossed up and down from its station. Scholars that love learning will be continually hammering upon some notion or other which may further their progress, and as greedily clasp it as the iron will its beloved loadstone. He that is " winged with a divine love " to Christ will have frequent glances and flights toward him, and will start out from his worldly business several times in a day to give him a visit. Love, in the very working, is a settling grace ; it increaseth our delight in God, partly by the sight of his amiableness, which is cleared to us in the very act of loving ; and partly by the recompences he gives to the affectionate carriage of his creature ; both which will prevent the heart's giving entertainment to such loose companions as evil thoughts.—*Stephen Charnock.*

Verses 113, 114.—When David was able to vouch his love to the command, he did not question his title to the promise. Here he asserts his sincere affection to the precepts : *"I hate vain thoughts : but thy law do I love."* Mark, he doth not say he is *free* from vain thoughts, but he " hates " them, he likes their company no better than one would a pack of thieves that break into his house. Neither saith he that he *fully kept* the law, but he *"loved"* the law even when he failed of exact obedience to it. Now from this testimony his conscience brought in for his love to the law, his faith acts clearly and strongly on the promise in the next words, *"Thou art my hiding place and my shield : I hope in thy word."*—*William Gurnall.*

Verse 114.—*"Thou art my hiding place and my shield,"* etc. From vain thoughts and vain persons the Psalmist teaches us to fly, by prayer, to God, as our Refuge and Protector. This course a believer will as naturally take, in the hour of temptation and danger, as the offspring of the hen, on perceiving a bird of prey hovering over their heads, retire to their *"hiding-place,"* under the wings of the dam ; or as the warrior opposeth his *" shield "* to the darts which are aimed at him.—*George Horne.*

Verse 114.—*"Thou art my hiding place."* Christ hath all qualifications that may fit him for this work [of being a *hiding-place* to believers].

1. He hath *strength.* A hiding-place must be *locus munitissimus.* Paper houses will never be good hiding-places. Houses made of reeds or rotten timber will not be fit places for men to hide themselves in. Jesus Christ is a place of strength. He is the Rock of Ages : His name is " the Mighty God," Isaiah ix. 6.

2. He hath *height.* A hiding-place must be *locus excelsissimus.* Your low houses are soon scaled. Jesus Christ is a high place ; he is as high as heaven. He is the Jacob's ladder that reacheth from earth to heaven : Gen. xxviii. 12. He is too high for men, too high for devils ; no creature can scale these high walls.

3. He hath *secret places.* A hiding-place must be *locus abditissimus.* The more secret, the more safe. Now, Jesus Christ hath many secret chambers that no creatures can ever find : Cant. ii. 14, " O my dove, that art in the secret places of the stairs ! " As Christ hath hidden comforts which no man knows but he that receiveth them ; so he hath hidden places of secresy which none can find out but he that dwells in them. " Come, my people, enter into thy chambers, and shut the doors upon thee " (Isaiah xxvi. 20).

4. Christ is *faithful.* He that will hide others had need be very faithful. A false-hearted protector is worse than an open pursuer. " Will the men of Keilah deliver me up ? " saith David ; " They will deliver thee up," saith the Lord. But now Christ is faithful : Rev. iii. 14, he is " the faithful witness ; " he cannot be bribed to surrender up any creature that comes to hide himself with him. Christ will die before he will betray his trust.

5. Christ is *diligent.* Diligence is as necessary in those that will hide others, as faithfulness. A sleepy guard may betray a castle or garrison as well as a faithless guard. But Jesus Christ is very diligent and watchful, he hath his intelligencers abroad ; yea, his own eyes run to and fro in the earth, to see what contrivances are made and set on foot against those who are hid with him : Ps. cxxi. 3, 4, " He that keepeth Israel neither slumbereth nor sleepeth."—*Ralph Robinson* (1614—1655) *in "Christ All in All."*

Verse 114.—*"Hiding place."* The first word in the verse means properly a secret, or a secret place.—*Joseph Addison Alexander.*

Verse 114.—*"My shield."* Good people are safe under God's protection ; he is their " strength and their shield " ; their " shield and their great reward " ; and here, their *"hiding place and their shield."*—*Matthew Henry.*

Verse 114.—*"Shield."* The excellency and properties of a shield lie in these things :—1. In the largeness and breadth of it, in that it hides and covers the person that weareth it from all darts that are flung at him, so as they cannot reach him : Thou, Lord, wilt bless the righteous ; with favour wilt thou compass him as with a shield (Ps. v. 12). 2. The excellence of a shield lies in that it is hard and impenetrable. So this answers to the invincible power of God's providence, by which he can break the assaults of all enemies ; and such a shield is God to his people : " My shield, and he in whom I trust " (Ps. cxliv. 2). 3. Shall I add one thing more ? Stones and darts flung upon a hard shield are beaten back upon him that flings them ; so God beats back the evil upon his enemies and the enemies of his people : " Bring them down, O Lord, our shield " (Ps. lix. 11).—*Thomas Manton.*

Verse 114.—*"I hope in thy word."* Of all the ingredients that sweeten the cup of human life, there is none more rich or powerful than hope. Its absence embitters the sweetest lot ; its presence alleviates the deepest woe. Surround me with all the joys which memory can awaken or possession bestow,—without hope it is not enough. In the absence of hope there is sadness in past and present joys—sadness in the thought that the past is past, and that the present is passing too. But though you strip me of all the joys the past or the present can confer, if the morrow shineth bright with hope, I am glad amid my woe. Of all the busy motives that stir this teeming earth, hope is the busiest. It is the sweetest balm that soothes our sorrows, the brightest beam that gilds our pleasures. Hope is the noblest offspring, the first born, the last buried child of foreseeing and forecasting man. Without it the unthinking cattle may be content amid present plenty. But without it reflecting man should not, cannot be truly happy.—*William Grant* (1814—1876), *in "Christ our Hope, and other Sermons."*

Verses 114, 115.—*"Thou art my hiding place." "Depart from me, ye evil-doers."* Safe and quiet in his hiding-place, David deprecates all attempts to disturb his peace. The society, therefore, of the ungodly is intolerable to him, and he cannot forbear frowning them from his presence. He had found them to be opposed to his best interests ; and he feared their influence in shaking his determination of obedience to his God. Indeed, when have the Lord's people failed to experience such society to be a prevailing hindrance alike to the enjoyment and to the service of God ?—*Charles Bridges.*

Verse 115.—*"Depart from me, ye evildoers,"* etc. As if he had said, Talk no more of it, save your breath, I am resolved on my course, I have sworn, and am steadfastly purposed to keep the commandments of my God ; with God's help, there will I hold me, and all the world shall not wrest me from it.—*Robert Sanderson,* 1587—1662-3.

Verse 115.—*"Depart from me, ye workers of iniquity,"* etc. It is common to sin for company, and that cup usually goeth round, and is handed from one to another. It is therefore wise to quit the company which is infected by sin. It can bring thee no benefit. At least evil company will abate the good in thee. The herb of grace will never thrive in such a cold soil. How poorly doth the good corn grow which is compassed about with weeds ! Cordials and restoratives will do little good to the natural body, whilst it aboundeth with ill-humours. Ordinances are little effectual to souls which are distempered with such noxious inmates. It is said of the mountain Kadish, that whatsoever vine be planted near it, it causeth it to wither and die : it is exceeding rare for saints to thrive near such pull-backs. It is difficult, even to a miracle, to keep God's commandments and evil company too ; therefore when David would marry himself to God's commands, to love them, and live with them, for better for worse, all his days, he is forced to give a bill of divorce to wicked companions, knowing that otherwise the match could never be made : *"Depart from me, ye workers of iniquity, for I will keep the commandments of my God."* As if he had said, Be it known unto you, O sinners, that I am striking a hearty covenant with God's commands ; I like them so well, that I am resolved to give myself up to them, and to please them well in all things, which I never do unless ye depart ; ye are like a strumpet, which will steal away the love from the true wife. I cannot, as I ought, obey my God's precepts, whilst ye abide in my presence ; therefore depart from me, ye workers of iniquity, for I will keep the commandments of my God.—*George Swinnock.*

Verse 115.—*"Depart from me, ye evildoers."* Woe be to the wicked man, and woe to those who adhere to him and associate with him, saith *Ben Sira.* And even the pagans of old thought that a curse went along with those who kept evil company.

To inhabit, or to travel with an impious man, and one not beloved of the gods, was held by them to be unlucky and unfortunate.

> Vetabo qui Cereris sacrum
> Vulgavit, sub isdem
> Sit trabibus, fragilemque mecum
> Solvat phaselum,

as Horace speaks.*

To dwell under the same roof, or to sail in the same yacht or pleasure-boat with profane persons was deemed unsafe and dangerous by men of Pagan principles. How much more, then, ought Christians to be thoroughly persuaded of the mischief and danger of conversing with wicked men? It can no ways be safe to hold correspondence with them. Yea, we are in great danger all the while we are with them. You have heard, I suppose, who it was that would not stay in the bath so long as an arch-heretic was there. It was St. John the Evangelist; he would not (as *Irenæus* acquaints us) remain in that place because *Cerinthus*, who denied the divinity of Christ, was then present there. That holy man thought no place was safe where such persons are.

Therefore be mindful of the Apostle's exhortation, and " Come out from among them " (2 Cor. vi. 17); listen to that voice from heaven: " Come out, that ye be not partakers of their sins, and that ye receive not of their plagues." Separate yourselves from them, lest you not only indamage your souls, but your bodies, lest some remarkable judgment arrest you here, and lest the divine vengeance more furiously assault you hereafter. The fanciful poets tell us that *Theseus* and *Perithous* (a pair of intimate friends) loved one another so well that they went down to hell together. I am sure it is no poetical fiction that many do thus; that is to say, that they perish together, and descend into the bottomless pit for company's sake.—*John Edwards* (1637—1716), *in "Theologia Reformata."*

Verse 115.—Depart from them that depart from God.—*T. Manton.*

Verse 115.—*"Of my God."* As a man can esteem of anything which he knows is his own; so if once he know that God is his, he cannot but love him, and carefully obey him: neither is it possible that any man can give to God hearty and permanent service, who is not persuaded to say with David, *He is my God.* All the pleasures, all the terrors of the world cannot sunder that soul from God, who can truly say, *The Lord is my God.—W. Cowper.*

Verse 116.—*"Uphold me."* A kite soaring on high is in a situation quite foreign to its nature; as much as the soul of man is when raised above this lower world to high and heavenly pursuits. A person at a distance sees not how it is kept in its exalted situation: he sees not the wind that blows it, nor the hand that holds it, nor the string by whose instrumentality it is held. But all of these powers are necessary to its preservation in that preternatural state. If the wind were to sink it would fall. It has nothing whatever in itself to uphold itself; it has the same tendency to gravitate towards the earth that it ever had; and if left for a moment to itself it would fall. Thus it is with the soul of every true believer. It has been raised by the Spirit of God to a new, a preternatural, a heavenly state; and in that state it is upheld by an invisible and Almighty hand, through the medium of faith. And upheld it shall be, but not by any power in itself. If left for a moment it would fall as much as ever. Its whole strength is in God alone; and its whole security is in the unchangeableness of his nature, and in the efficacy of his grace. In a word, " It is kept by the power of God, through faith, unto salvation."—*From "The Book of Illustrations," by H. G. Salter,* 1840.

Verse 116.—*"That I may live."* The life of a Christian stands in this, to have his soul quickened by the spirit of grace. For as the presence of the soul quickens the body, and the departure thereof brings instant death; and the body without it is but a dead lump of clay: so it is the presence of God's Spirit which giveth life to the soul of man. And this life is known by these two notable effects; for first, it brings a joyful sense of God's mercy; and next, a spiritual disposition to spiritual exercises. And without this, pretend a man what he will, he is but the image of a Christian, looking somewhat like him, but not quickened by his life.— *William Cowper.*

---

* They who mysteries reveal
Beneath my roof shall never live,
Shall never hoist with me the doubtful sail.

Verse 116.—"*That I may live.*" The children of God think they have no life if they live not in God's life. For if we think we are alive, because we see, so do the brute beasts ; if we think we are alive because we hear, so do the cattle ; if we think we are alive because we eat and drink, or sleep, so do beasts ; if we think we live because we do reason and confer, so do the heathen. The life of God's children is the death of sin ; for where sin is alive, there that part is dead unto God. . . . . God's children, finding themselves dull and slow to good things, when they cannot either rejoice in the promises of God, or find their inward man delighted with the law of God, think themselves to be dead.—*Richard Greenham.*

Verse 117.—"*Hold thou me up, and I shall be safe.*" Not only the consciousness of my weakness, but the danger of the slippery path before me, reminds me, that the safety of every moment depends upon the upholding power of my faithful God. The ways of temptation are so many and imperceptible—the influence of it so appalling—the entrance into it so deceitful, so specious, so insensible—and my own weakness and unwatchfulness are so unspeakable—that I can do nothing but go on my way, praying at every step, "*Hold thou me up, and I shall be safe.*"—*Charles Bridges.*

Verse 117.—"*Hold thou me up.*" Three things made David afraid. First, great temptation without ; for from every air the wind of temptation blows upon a Christian. Secondly, great corruption within. Thirdly, examples of other worthy men that had fallen before him, and are written for us : not that we should learn to fall, but to fear lest we fall. These three should alway hold us humble, according to that warning, "Let him that thinketh he standeth take heed lest he fall."—*William Cowper.*

Verse 117.—"*Up,*" up above the littlenesses in which I have lived too long,—above the snares which have so often caught me,—above the stumbling-blocks upon which I have so often fallen,—above the world,—above myself,—higher than I have ever reached yet,—above the level of my own mortality : worthy of thee,—worthy of the blood, with which I have been bought,—nearer to heaven,—nearer to thee,—"*hold thou me up.*"

God's methods of holding his people up are many. Sometimes it is by the preacher's word, when the word comes fitly spoken to the heart and conscience. May God, in his infinite condescension, enable his servants in this church so to hold you up. Sometimes it is by the ordained means and sacraments which his grace commanded. Sometimes it is by the efficacy of the Holy Scriptures, when some passages in your own room strikes the mind, just in season ; or the stay of some sweet promise comes in sustainingly to your spirit. Sometimes by the simple inworking of the Holy Ghost in a man's own thoughts, as he will work,—"Uphold me with thy free Spirit." Sometimes by the ministration of angels,—"They shall hold thee up in their hands, lest thou dash thy foot against a stone." Sometimes by putting you very low indeed, making you feel that the safe place is the valley. There is no elevation like the elevation of abasement. Sometimes by severe discipline to brace up the heart, and strengthen it, and make it independent of external things. Sometimes by heavy affliction, which is the grasp of his hand, that he may hold you tighter. Sometimes by putting into your heart to think the exact thing that you need,—to pray the very prayer which he intends at the moment to grant. Sometimes by appearing to let you go, and forsake you, while at the same time—like the Syro-Phœnician woman—he is giving you the wish to hold on that he may give you the more at the last.—*James Vaughan, of Brighton,* 1877.

Verse 117.—"*I will have respect unto thy statutes continually.*" I will employ myself, so some ; I will delight myself, so others ; in thy statutes. If God's right hand uphold us, we must in his strength go on in our duty, both with diligence and with pleasure.—*Matthew Henry.*

Verse 118.—"*Thou hast trodden down,*" etc. David here, by a new meditation, confirms himself in the course of godliness : for considering the judgments of God, executed according to his word in all ages upon the wicked, he resolves so much the more to fear God and keep his testimonies. Thus the judgments of God, executed on others, should be awe-bands to keep us from sinning after their similitude.

The Lord in chastening his own children takes them in hand like a father to correct them ; but when his wrath is kindled against the wicked he tramples them under his feet, as vile creatures which are no account with him.—*William Cowper.*

Verse 118.—"*Thou hast trodden down.*" The Septuagint, ἐξουδένωσας, *ad nihil deduxisti ;* thou hast brought to nothing ; Aquila, *confixisti,* thou hast stricken through : Symmachus, ἀπήλεγξας, *reprobasti,* thou hast disproved ; the Vulgate, *sprevisti,* thou hast contemned ; Apollinarius, ἀθέριξας, *parvi pependisti,* thou hast little esteemed : all to the same purpose. The phrase of treading under foot, used by us, implies, 1. A full punishment ; 2. A disgraceful one. 1. A full punishment. God will pull them down from their altitudes, even to the dust, though never so high and proudly exalting themselves against God. A full conquest of enemies is thus often expressed in Scripture. The Assyrian is said " to take the prey, and to tread them down like the mire of the streets " (Isa. x. 6). 2. It implies a disgraceful punishment : " Until I make thine enemies thy footstool " (Ps. cx. 1) ; an expression used to show the ignominy and contempt God will put upon them. Thus Sapores, the king of Persia, trampled upon Valentinian the emperor, and Tamerlane made Bajazet his footstool. The meaning is, God will not only bring them under, but reduce them to an abject and contemptible condition. So Chrysostom on the text expoundeth this phrase, that God will make them ἐπονειδίστους καὶ καταγελάστους, ignominious and contemptible. They shall not go off honourably, but with scorn and confusion of face, miserably broken.—*Thomas Manton.*

Verse 118.—"*Thou hast trodden down,*" etc. There is a disposition to merge all the characterictics of the Divinity into one ; and while with many of our most eminent writers, the exuberant goodness, the soft and yielding benignity, the mercy that overlooks and makes liberal allowance for the infirmities of human weakness, have been fondly and most abundantly dwelt upon—there has been what the French would call, if not a studied, at least an actually observed *reticence,* on the subject of his truth and purity and his hatred of moral evil. There can be no government without a law ; and the question is little entertained—how are the violations of that law to be disposed of ? Every law has its sanctions—the hopes of proffered reward on the one hand, the fears of threatened vengeance on the other. Is the vengeance to be threatened only, but never to be executed ? Is guilt only to be dealt with by proclamations that go before, but never by punishments that are to follow ? . . . . Take away from jurisprudence its penalties, or, what were still worse, let the penalties only be denounced but never exacted ; and we reduce the whole to an unsubstantial mockery. The fabric of moral government falls to pieces ; and, instead of a great presiding authority in the universe, we have a subverted throne and a degraded Sovereign. . . . . If there is only to be the parade of a judicial economy, without any of its power or its performance ; if the truth is only to be kept in the promises of reward, but as constantly to be receded from in the threats of vengeance ; if the judge is thus to be lost in the overweening parent —there is positively nothing of a moral government over us but the name, we are not the subjects of God's authority ; we are the fondlings of his regard. Under a system like this, the whole universe would drift, as it were, into a state of anarchy ; and, in the uproar of this wild misrule, the King who sitteth on high would lose his hold on the creation that he had formed.—*Thomas Chalmers.*

Verse 118.—"*For their deceit is falsehood.*" The true sense of the passage is, " for their cunning hath been fallacious," that is, it hath deceived themselves and brought on their ruin.—*Samuel Horsley,* 1733—1806.

Verse 118.—"*Their deceit is falsehood.*" He means not here of that deceit whereby the wicked deceive others, but that whereby they deceive themselves. And this is two-fold : first, in that they look for a good in sin, which sin deceitfully promiseth, but they shall never find. Next, that they flatter themselves with a vain conceit to escape judgment, which shall assuredly overtake them.—*William Cowper.*

Verse 119.—"*Thou puttest away all the wicked of the earth like dross.*" The godly and the wicked live together in the visible Church, as dross and good metal ; but God, who is the purger of his church, will not fail by diversity of trials and judgments to put difference between them, and at last will make a perfect separation of them, and cast away the wicked as refuse.—*David Dickson.*

Verse 119.—God's judgments upon others may be a necessary act of love to us. They are purged out as "*dross,*" that they may not infect us by their example, or molest us by their persecutions or oppressions. Now, the more we are befriended in this kind, the more we are bound to serve God cheerfully : " That we being delivered out of the hand of our enemies might serve him without fear, in holiness and righteousness before him all the days of our life ": Luke i. 74, 75. The world is one of those enemies, or the wicked of the earth ; therefore we should serve him faithfully.—*Thomas Manton.*

Verse 119.—*"Thou puttest away all the wicked."* Many ways are wicked men taken away ; sometime by the hand of other men, sometime by their own hand. The Philistines slew not Saul, but forced him to slay himself ; yet the eye of faith ever looks to the finger of God, and sees that the fall of the wicked is the work of God.—*William Cowper.*

Verse 119.—*"The wicked of the earth."* Why are they thus characterized ? Because here they flourish ; their names "shall be written in the earth " (Jer. xvii. 13) ; they grow great and of good reckoning and account here. Judas had the bag ; they prosper in the world : "Behold, these are the ungodly, who prosper in the world " (Ps. lxxiii. 12). Here they are respected : "They are of the world, therefore speak they of the world, and the world heareth them " (1 John iv. 5). Their hearts and minds are in the world (Matt. vi. 19, 20). It is their natural frame to be worldly, they only savour the things of the world ; preferment, honour, greatness, it is their *unum magnum ;* here is their pleasure, and here is their portion, their hope, and their happiness. A child of God looketh for another inheritance, immortal and undefiled.—*Thomas Manton.*

Verse 119.—*"Like dross."* The men of this world esteem God's children as the offscourings of the earth ; so Paul (a chosen vessel of God) was disesteemed of men ; but ye see here what the wicked are, in God's account, but dross indeed, which is the refuse of gold and silver. Let this confirm the godly against the contempt of men : only the Lord hath in his own hand the balance which weigheth men according as they are.—*William Cowper.*

Verse 119.—*"Dross."* 1. The *dross* obscures the lustre and glory of the metal, yea, covers it up, so that it appears not ; rust and filth compass and hide the gold, so that neither the nature nor lustre of it can be seen. 2. *Dross* is a deceiving thing. It is like metal, but is not metal ; the dross of silver is like it, and so the dross of gold is like gold, but the dross is neither silver nor gold. 3. *Dross* is not bettered by the fire : put it into the fire time after time, it abides so still. 4. *Dross* is a worthless thing. It is of no value—base, vile, contemptible. 5. It is useless, and to be rejected. 6. *Dross* is an offensive thing : rust eats into the metal, endangers it, and makes the goldsmith to kindle the fire, to separate it from the gold and silver.—*Condensed from William Greenhill.*

Verse 119.—*"Thy testimonies."* So, very frequently, he calleth God's word, wherein there are both commands and promises : the commandments of God appertain to all, his testimonies belong to his children only ; whereby more strictly, I understand his promises containing special declarations of his love and favour toward his own in Christ Jesus.—*William Cowper.*

Verse 120.—*"My flesh trembleth for fear of thee."* Instead of exulting over those who fell under God's displeasure he humbleth himself. What we read and hear of judgments of God upon wicked people should make us (1) Te reverence his terrible majesty, and to stand in awe of him. Who is able to stand before this holy Lord God ? 1 Sam. vi. 20. (2) To fear lest we offend him, and become obnoxious to his wrath. Good men have need to be restrained from sin by the terrors of the Lord ; especially when judgment begins at the house of God, and hypocrites are discovered, and put away as dross.—*Matthew Henry.*

Verse 120.—*"My flesh trembleth for fear of thee,"* etc. At the presence of Jehovah, when he appeareth in judgment, the earth trembled and is still. His best servants are not exempted from an awful dread, upon such occasions ; scenes of this kind, shown in vision to the prophets, cause their flesh to quiver, and all their bones to shake. Encompassed with a frail body, and a sinful world, we stand in need of every possible tie ; and the affections both of fear and love must be employed, to restrain us from transgression ; we must, at the same time, "love God's testimonies, and fear his judgments."—*George Horne.*

Verse 120.—*"My flesh trembleth for fear of thee,"* etc. In prayer, in the evening, I had such near and terrific views of God's judgments upon sinners in hell, that my flesh trembled for fear of them. . . . . I flew trembling to Jesus Christ as if the flames were taking hold of me ! Oh ! Christ will indeed save me or else I perish. —*Henry Martyn,* 1781—1812.

Verse 120.—*"My flesh trembleth for fear of thee."* Familiarity with men breeds contempt ; familiarity with God, not so : none reverence the Lord more than they who know him best and are most familiar with him.—*William Cowper.*

Verse 120 *with* 116.—*"My flesh trembleth for fear of thee ; I am afraid."* . . . . *"Let me not be ashamed of my hope."* True religion consists in a proper mixture of *fear* of God, and of *hope* in his mercy ; and wherever either of these is entirely wanting, there can be no true religion. God has joined these things, and we ought by no means to put them asunder. He cannot take pleasure in those who fear him with a slavish fear, without hoping in his mercy, because they seem to consider him as a cruel and tyrannical being, who has not mercy or goodness in his nature ; and, besides, they implictly charge him with falsehood, by refusing to believe and hope in his invitations and offers of mercy. On the other hand, he cannot be pleased with those who pretend to hope in his mercy without fearing him ; for they insult him by supposing that there is nothing in him which ought to be feared ; and, in addition to this, they make him a liar, by disbelieving his awful threatenings denounced against sinners, and call in question his authority, by refusing to obey him. Those only who both fear him and hope in his mercy, give him the honour that is due to his name.—*Edward Payson.*

Verse 120.—*"Trembleth"* or shuddereth, strictly used of the hair **as standing erect in terror (comp. Job iv. 15).—***J. J. Stewart Perowne.*

EXPOSITION OF VERSES 121 TO 128.

I HAVE done judgment and justice : leave me not to mine oppressors.

122 Be surety for thy servant for good : let not the proud oppress me.

123 Mine eyes fail for thy salvation, and for the word of thy righteousness.

124 Deal with thy servant according unto thy mercy, and teach me thy statutes.

125 I *am* thy servant ; give me understanding, that I may know thy testimonies.

126 *It is* time for *thee*, LORD, to work : *for* they have made void thy law.

127 Therefore I love thy commandments above gold ; yea, above fine gold.

128 Therefore I esteem all *thy* precepts *concerning* all *things to be* right ; *and* I hate every false way.

121. *"I have done judgment and justice."* This was a great thing for an Eastern ruler to say at any time, for these despots mostly cared more for gain than justice. Some of them altogether neglected their duty, and would not even do judgment at all, preferring their pleasures to their duties ; and many more of them sold their judgments to the highest bidders by taking bribes, or regarding the persons of men. Some rulers gave neither judgment nor justice, others gave judgment without justice, but David gave judgment and justice, and saw that his sentences were carried out. He could claim before the Lord that he had dealt out even-handed justice, and was doing so still. On this fact he founded a plea with which he backed the prayer—*"Leave me not to mine oppressors."* He who, as far as his power goes, has been doing right, may hope to be delivered from his superiors when attempts are made by them to do him wrong. If I will not oppress others, I may hopefully pray that others may not oppress me. A course of upright conduct is one which gives us boldness in appealing to the Great Judge for deliverance from the injustice of others. Nor is this kind of pleading to be censured as self-righteous : when we are dealing with God as to our shortcomings, we use a very different tone from that with which we face the censures of our fellow-men ; when they are in the question, and we are guiltless towards them, we are justified in pleading our innocence.

122. *"Be surety for thy servant for good."* Answer for me. Do not leave thy poor servant to die by the hand of his enemy and thine. Take up my interests and weave them with thine own, and stand for me. As my Master, undertake thy servants' cause, and represent me before the faces of haughty men till they see what an august ally I have in the Lord my God.

"Let not the proud oppress me." Thine interposition will answer the purpose of my rescue : when the proud see that thou art my advocate they will hide their heads. We should have been crushed beneath our proud adversary the devil if our Lord Jesus had not stood between us and the accuser, and become a surety for us. It is by his suretiship that we escape like a bird from the snare of the fowler. What a blessing to be able to leave our matters in our Surety's hands, knowing that all will be well, since he has an answer for every accuser, a rebuke for every reviler.

Good men dread oppression, for it makes even a wise man mad, and they send up their cries to heaven for deliverance ; nor shall they cry in vain, for the Lord will undertake the cause of his servants, and fight their battles against the proud. The word " servant " is wisely used as a plea for favour for himself, and the word " proud " as an argument against his enemies. It seems to be inevitable that proud men should become oppressors, and that they should take most delight in oppressing really gracious men.

123. *"Mine eyes fail for thy salvation."* He wept, waited, and watched for God's saving hand, and these exercises tried the eyes of his faith till they were almost ready to give out. He looked to God alone, he looked eagerly, he looked long, he looked till his eyes ached. The mercy is, that if our eyes fail, God does not fail, nor do *his* eyes fail. Eyes are tender things, and so are our faith, hope and expectancy : the Lord will not try them above what they are able to bear. *"And for the word of thy righteousness :"* a word that would silence the unrighteous words

of his oppressors. His eyes as well as his ears waited for the Lord's word : he looked to see the divine word come forth as a fiat for his deliverance. He was " waiting for the verdict "—the verdict of righteousness itself. How happy are we if we have righteousness on our side ; for then that which is the sinners' terror is our hope, that which the proud dread is our expectation and desire. David left his reputation entirely in the Lord's hand, and was eager to be cleared by the word of the Judge rather than by any defence of his own. He knew that he had done right, and, therefore, instead of avoiding the supreme court, he begged for the sentence which he knew would work out his deliverance. He even watched with eager eyes for the judgment and the deliverance, the word of righteousness from God which meant salvation to himself.

124. *"Deal with thy servant according unto thy mercy."* Here he recollects himself : although before men he was so clear that he could challenge the word of righteousness, yet before the Lord, as his servant, he felt that he must appeal to mercy. We feel safest here. Our heart has more rest in the cry, " God be merciful to me," than in appealing to justice. It is well to be able to say, " I have done judgment and justice," and then to add in all lowliness, yet " deal with thy servant according unto thy mercy." The title of servant covers a plea ; a master should clear the character of his servant if he be falsely accused, and rescue him from those who would oppress him ; and, moreover, the master should show mercy to a servant, even if he deal severely with a stranger. The Lord condescendingly deals, or has communications with his servants, not spurning them, but communing with them ; and this he does in a tender and merciful way, for in any other form of dealing we should be crushed into the dust. *"And teach me thy statutes."* This will be one way of dealing with us in mercy. We may expect a master to teach his own servant the meaning of his own orders. Yet since our ignorance arises from our own sinful stupidity, it is great mercy on God's part that he condescends to instruct us in his commands. For our ruler to become our teacher is an act of great grace, for which we cannot be too grateful. Among our mercies this is one of the choicest.

125. *"I am thy servant."* This is the third time he has repeated this title in this one section : he is evidently fond of the name, and conceives it to be a very effective plea. We who rejoice that we are sons of God are by no means the less delighted to be his servants. Did not the firstborn Son assume the servant's form and fulfil the servant's labour to the full ? What higher honour can the younger brethren desire than to be made like the Heir of all things ?

"Give me understanding, that I may know thy testimonies." In the previous verse he sought teaching ; but here he goes much further, and craves for understanding. Usually, if the instructor supplies the teaching, the pupil finds the understanding ; but in our case we are far more dependent, and must beg for understanding as well as teaching : this the ordinary teacher cannot give, and we are thrice happy that our Divine Tutor can furnish us with it. We are to confess ourselves fools, and then our Lord will make us wise, as well as give us knowledge. The best understanding is that which enables us to render perfect obedience and to exhibit intelligent faith, and it is this which David desires,—" understanding, that I may know thy testimonies." Some would rather not know these things ; they prefer to be at ease in the dark rather than possess the light which leads to repentance and diligence. The servant of God longs to know in an understanding manner all that the Lord reveals of man and to man ; he wishes to be so instructed that he may apprehend and comprehend that which is taught him. A servant should not be ignorant concerning his master, or his master's business ; he should study the mind, will, purpose, and aim of him whom he serves, for so only can he complete his service ; and as no man knows these things so well as his master himself, he should often go to him for instructions, lest his very zeal should only serve to make him the greater blunderer.

It is remarkable that the Psalmist does not pray for understanding through acquiring knowledge, but begs of the Lord first that he may have the gracious gift of understanding, and then may obtain the desired instruction. All that we know before we have understanding is apt to spoil us and breed vanity in us ; but if there be first an understanding heart, then the stores of knowledge enrich the soul, and bring neither sin nor sorrow therewith. Moreover, this gift of understanding acts also in the form of discernment, and thus the good man is preserved from hoarding up that which is false and dangerous : he knows what are and what are not the testimonies of the Lord.

126. *"It is time for thee, LORD, to work: for they have made void thy law."* David was a servant, and therefore it was always his time to work : but being oppressed by a sight of man's ungodly behaviour, he feels that his Master's hand is wanted, and therefore he appeals to him to work against the working of evil. Men make void the law of God by denying it to be his law, by promulgating commands and doctrines in opposition to it, by setting up tradition in its place, or by utterly disregarding and scorning the authority of the lawgiver. Then sin becomes fashionable, and a holy walk is regarded as a contemptible puritanism ; vice is styled pleasure, and vanity bears the bell. Then the saints sigh for the presence and power of their God : Oh for an hour of the King upon the throne and the rod of iron ! Oh for another Pentecost with all its wonders, to reveal the energy of God to gainsayers, and make them see that there is a God in Israel ! Man's extremity, whether of need or sin, is God's opportunity. When the earth was without form and void, the Spirit came and moved upon the face of the waters ; should he not come when society is returning to a like chaos ? When Israel in Egypt were reduced to the lowest point, and it seemed that the covenant would be void, then Moses appeared and wrought mighty miracles ; so, too, when the church of God is trampled down, and her message is derided, we may expect to see the hand of the Lord stretched out for the revival of religion, the defence of the truth, and the glorifying of the divine name. The Lord can work either by judgments which hurl down the ramparts of the foe ; or by revivals which build up the walls of his own Jerusalem. How heartily may we pray the Lord to raise up new evangelists, to quicken those we already have, to set his whole church on fire, and to bring the world to his feet. God's work is ever honourable and glorious ; as for our work, it is as nothing apart from him.

127. *"Therefore I love thy commandments above gold ; yea, above fine gold."* As it was God's time to work so it was David's time to love. So far from being swayed by the example of evil men, so as to join them in slighting the Scriptures, he was the rather led into a more vehement love of them. As he saw the commandments slighted by the ungodly, his heart was in sympathy with God, and he felt a burning affection for his holy precepts. It is the mark of a true believer that he does not depend upon others for his religion, but drinks water out of his own well, which springs up even when the cisterns of earth are all dried. Our holy poet amid a general depreciation of the law felt his own esteem of it rising so high that gold and silver sank in comparison. Wealth brings with it so many conveniences that men naturally esteem it, and gold as the symbol of it is much set by ; and yet, in the judgment of the wise, God's laws are more enriching, and bring with them more comfort than all the choicest treasures. The Psalmist could not boast that he always kept the commands ; but he could declare that he loved them ; he was perfect in heart, and would fain have been perfect in life. He judged God's holy commands to be better than the best earthly thing, yea, better than the best sort of the best earthly thing ; and this esteem was confirmed and forced into expression by those very oppositions of the world which drive hypocrites to forsake the Lord and his ways.

> " The dearer, for their rage,
> Thy words I love and own,—
> A wealthier heritage
> Than gold and precious stone "

128. *"Therefore I esteem all thy precepts concerning all things to be right."* Because the ungodly found fault with the precepts of God, therefore David was all the more sure of their being right. The censure of the wicked is a certificate of merit ; that which they sanction we may justly suspect, but that which they abominate we may ardently admire. The good man's delight in God's law is unreserved, he believes in all God's precepts concerning all things.

"And I hate every false way." Love to truth begat hatred of falsehood. This godly man was not indifferent to anything, but that which he did not love he hated. He was no chip in the porridge without flavour ; he was a good lover or a good hater, but he was never a waverer. He knew what he felt, and expressed it. He was no Gallio, caring for none of the things. His detestation was as unreserved as his affection ; he had not a good word for any practice which would not bear the light of truth. The fact that such large multitudes follow the broad road had no influence upon this holy man, except to make him more determined to avoid every form of error and sin. May the Holy Spirit so rule in our hearts that our affections may be in the same decided condition towards the precepts of the word.

NOTES ON VERSES 121 TO 128.

Verse 121.—This commences a new division of the Psalm indicated by the Hebrew letter *Ain*—a letter which cannot well be represented in the English alphabet, as there is, in fact, no letter in our language exactly corresponding with it. It would be best represented probably by what are called "*breathings*" in Greek.—*Albert Barnes.*

Verse 121.—"*I have done judgment*" against the wicked, "and *justice*" towards the good.—*Simon de Muis*, 1587—1644.

Verse 121.—"*I have done judgment and justice.*"—Here the view of David in his judicial capacity might present itself to us ; and if so, we have David in the midst of large experiences ; for the words would take in a large portion of his life. How blessed were their reflections, if, after a long reign, all sovereign rulers could thus appeal unto God. It should be so ; for to him all shall be accountable at last. Even although we only conceive of David as speaking in the character of a private man, the sentiment is worthy of all consideration. . . . . For parents to say this of their dealings with their children, masters of servants, a man of his neighbours, is very excellent.—*John Stephen.*

Verse 121.—"*Judgment*" and "*justice*" are often put in Scripture for the same, and when put together, the latter is as an epithet to the former. "*I have done judgment and justice,*" that is, I have done judgment *justly*, exactly, to a hair.—*Joseph Caryl.*

Verse 121.—

> Do right and be a king,
> Be this thy brazen bulwark of defence,
> Still to preserve thy conscious innocence,
> Nor e'er turn pale with guilt.
>
> —*Francis's Horace.*

Verse 121.—" If our heart condemn us not, then have we confidence before God : " 1 John iii. 21. This " testimony of conscience " has often been " the rejoicing " of the Lord's people, when suffereng under unmerited reproach or "proud oppression." They have been enabled to plead it without offence in the presence of their holy, heart-searching God ; nay, even when, in the near prospect of the great and final account, they might well have been supposed to shrink from the strict and unerring scrutiny of their Omniscient Judge. Perhaps, however, we are not sufficiently aware of the importance of moral integrity in connexion with our spiritual comfort. Mark the boldness which it gave David in prayer : "*I have done judgment and justice : leave me not to mine oppressors.*"—*Charles Bridges.*

Verse 121.—"*Leave me not to mine oppressors.*" That is, maintain me against those who would wrong me, because I do right ; interpose thyself between me and my enemies, as if thou wert my pledge. Impartial justice upon oppressors sometimes lays judges open to oppression ; but yet they who run greatest hazards in zeal for God shall find God ready to be their surety, when they pray, " be surety for thy servant," as in the next verse.—*Abraham Wright.*

Verses 121, 122.—"*I have done judgment and justice ;* " but, that I may always do it, and never fail in doing it, "*uphold thy servant unto good,*" by directing him, so that he may always relish what is good, and then the consequence will be that " *the proud will not calumniate me ;* " for he that is well established " unto good," and so made up that nothing but what is good and righteous will be agreeable to him, he will so persevere that he will have no reason for fearing " *the proud that calumniate him.*"—*Robert Bellarmine.*

Verse 122.—"*Be surety for thy servant for good.*" What David prays to God to be for him, that Christ is for all his people : Heb. vii. 22. He drew nigh to God, struck hands with him, gave his word and bond to pay the debts of his people ; put himself in their law-place and stead, and became responsible to law and justice for them ; engaged to make satisfaction for their sins, to bring in everlasting righteousness for their justification, and to preserve and keep them, and bring them safe to eternal glory and happiness ; and this was being *a surety for them for good.*—*John Gill.*

Verse 122.—"*Be surety for thy servant for good.*" There are three expositions of this clause, as noting the end, the cause, the event. 1. Undertake for me, *ut* *sim bonus et justus*, so Rabbi Arama on the place ; " Be surety for me *that I may be good*." Theodoret expounds it, " Undertake that I shall make good my resolution of keeping thy law." He that joineth, undertaketh ; though we have precepts and promises, without God's undertaking we shall never be able to perform our duty. 2. Undertake for me to help me *in doing good ;* so some read it : God would not take his part in an evil cause. To commend a wrong cause to God's protection, is to provoke him to hasten our punishment, to make us serve under our oppressors ; but, when we have a good cause, and a good conscience, he will own us. We cannot expect he should maintain us and bear us out in the Devil's service, wherein we have entangled ourselves by our own sin.

3. *Be with me for good :* so it is often rendered : " Shew me a token for good " (Ps. lxxxvi. 17) ; " Pray not for this people for good " (Jer. xiv. 11) ; so, " Remember me, O my God, for good " (Neh. xiii. 31). So here ; "*Be surety for thy servant for good.*"—*Thomas Manton.*

Verse 122.—"*Be surety for thy servant for good.*" It is the prayer of Hezekiah in his trouble, " O Lord, I am oppressed, undertake for me " (Isa. xxxviii. 14) ; it is the prayer of Job for a " daysman " to stand between him and God (Job ix. 33) ; it is the cry of the church before the Incarnation for the appearance of a Divine Mediator ; it is the confidence of every faithful soul since that blessed time in the perpetual intercession of our great High Priest in heaven, which is to us the pledge of future blessedness.—*Agellius and Cocceius, in Neale and Littledale.*

Verse 122.—"*Be surety for thy servant for good.*" His meaning is, Lord, thou knowest how unjustly I am calumniated and evil spoken of in many parts : where I am not present or where I may not answer for myself, Lord, answer thou for me.—*William Cowper.*

Verse 122.—"*Be surety for thy servant for good.*" The keen eye of the world may possibly not be able to affix any blot upon my outward profession ; but, " if thou, Lord, shouldst mark iniquities ; O Lord, who shall stand ? " The debt is continually accumulating, and the prospect of payment as distant as ever. I might well expect to be " left to my oppressors," until I should pay all that was due unto my Lord. But behold ! " Where is the fury of the oppressor ? " Isa. li. 13. The surety is found—the debt is paid—the ransom is accepted—the sinner is free. There was a voice heard in heaven—" Deliver him from going down to the pit : I have found a ransom," Job xxxiii. 24. The Son of God himself became " Surety for a stranger," and " smarted for it," Prov. xi. 15. At an infinite cost—the cost of his own precious blood—he delivered me from " *mine oppressors* "—sin—Satan —the world—death—hell.—*Charles Bridges.*

Verse 122.—Some observe that this is the only verse throughout the whole Psalm wherein the Word is not mentioned under the name of " law," " judgments," " statutes," or the like terms, and they make this note upon it,—" Where the Law faileth, there Christ is a surety of a better testament." There are that render the words thus,—"*Dulcify, or, delight thy servant in good,*" that is, make him joyful and comfortable in the pursuit and practice of that which is good.—*John Trapp.*

Verse 123.—"*Mine eyes fail for thy salvation.*" In times of great sorrow, when the heart is oppressed with care, and when danger threatens on every side, the human eye expresses with amazing accuracy the distressed and anguished emotions of the soul. The posture here described is that of an individual who perceives himself surrounded with enemies of the most formidable character, who feels his own weakness and insufficiency to enter into conflict with them, but who is eagerly looking for the arrival of a devoted and powerful friend who has promised to succour him in the hour of his calamity. As his friend delays the hour of his coming, his fears and anxieties multiply, till he finds himself in the condition of one whose eyes fail and grow dim in looking for the approach of his great deliverer. In this condition was the suppliant here described,—his enemies were ready to swallow him up, and except from heaven he had no hope of final extrication. To the promises of God he betook himself, and while waiting their accomplishment, and looking with the utmost eagerness to the word of God's righteousness, he gives utterance to the desponding sentiment, "*Mine eyes fail for thy salvation.*" O for such warm and anxious desires for that great salvation, which will realize the victory over all our spiritual enemies, and enable us to shout triumphantly through all eternity in the name of our almighty Deliverer !—*John Morison.*

Verse 123.—"*Mine eyes fail . . . . . for the word of thy righteousness.*" Albeit the words of promise be neither performed, nor the like to be performed, yet faith should justify the promise, for true and faithful.—*David Dickson.*

Verse 123.—*"For the word of thy righteousness."* This would be the word of promised salvation, which the Lord had given in righteousness. What an amazing plea—God on the ground of his own righteousness appealed to for deliverance—and yet how true ! Or this might be the word of his justice, the issuing of justice, the exercising of a righteous decision between him and his oppressors. He looked for the Lord to interpose between them, and so to fulfil all he had promised on behalf of the believer. The Lord will vindicate his own. Are any in great difficulty ; and are they waiting for the Lord to interpose, to whom they have committed their concerns ? . . . . Wait on ; he will not disappoint a gracious hope.—*John Stephen.*

Verse 123.—*"For the word of thy righteousness,"* or, " the word of thy *justice ;* " that is to say, for the sentence of justice on my oppressors, as the first part of the verse teaches ; for the passing this sentence will be equivalent to the granting the salvation which the Psalmist so earnestly desired.—*George Phillips.*

Verse 124.—*"Deal with thy servant according unto thy mercy."* If I am a " servant " of God, I can bring my services before him only upon the ground of " mercy " ; feeling that for my best performances I need an immeasurable world of mercy—pardoning—saving—everlasting mercy ; and yet I am emboldened by the blood of Jesus to plead for my soul—*"Deal with thy servant according unto thy mercy."*

But then I am ignorant as well as guilty ; and yet I dare not pray for divine teaching, much and hourly as I need it, until I have afresh obtained mercy. *"Mercy"* is the first blessing, not only in point of importance, but in point of order. I must seek the Lord, and know him as a Saviour, before I can go to him with any confidence to be my teacher. But when once I have found acceptance to my petition—*"Deal with thy servant according unto thy mercy "*—my way will be opened to follow on my petition—*"Teach me thy statutes. Give me understanding, that I may know thy testimonies "*—that I may know, walk, yea, " run in the way of thy commandments " with an enlarged heart, ver. 32. My plea is the same as I have urged with acceptance (ver. 94)—*"I am thy servant."*—*Charles Bridges.*

Verse 124.—*"Thy mercy."* All the year round, every hour of every day, God is richly blessing us ; both when we sleep and when we wake, his mercy waits upon us. The sun may leave off shining, but our God will never cease to cheer his children with his love. Like a river, his loving-kindness is always flowing, with a fulness inexhaustible as his own nature, which is its source. Like the atmosphere which always surrounds the earth, and is always ready to support the life of man, the benevolence of God surrounds all his creatures ; in it, as in their element, they live, and move, and have their being. Yet as the sun on summer days appears to gladden us with beams more warm and bright than at other times, and as rivers are at certain seasons swollen with the rain, and as the atmosphere itself on occasions is fraught with more fresh, more bracing, or more balmy influences than heretofore, so is it with the mercy of God ; it hath its golden hours, its days of overflow, when the Lord magnifieth his grace and lifteth high his love before the sons of men.—*C. H. S.*

Verse 124.—*"Teach me."* David had Nathan and Gad the prophets ; and beside them, the ordinary Levites to teach him. He read the word of God diligently, and did meditate in the law night and day ; but he acknowledgeth all this was nothing unless God speaks to the heart : so Paul preached to Lydia, but God opened her heart. Let us pray for this grace.—*William Cowper.*

Verse 125.—*"I am thy servant ; give me understanding,"* etc. I am not a stranger to thee, but thine own domestic servant ; let me want no grace which may enable me to serve thee.—*William Cowper.*

Verse 125.—*"I am thy servant."* That thou art the servant *of God,* thou shouldst regard as thy chiefest glory and blessedness.—*Martin Geier.*

Verse 126.—*"It is time for thee, LORD, to work."* Was ever vessel more hopelessly becalmed in mid-ocean ? or did crew ever cry with more frenzy for some favouring breeze than those should cry who man the Church of the living God ? If God work not, it is certain there is nothing before the Church but the prospect of utter discomfiture and overthrow. Greater is the world than the Church if God be not in her. But if God be in her, she shall not be moved. May he help her, and that right early !

When he arises to work we know not what may be the form and fashion of his operations. He worketh according to the counsel of his own will ; and who knows but that when once he wakes, and puts on his strength, it may not be confined in its results to the immediate and exclusive quickening of the spiritual life of the Church ; but may be associated with providential upheavals and convulsions which will fill the heart of the world with astonishment and dismay. His spiritual kingdom does not stand in isolation. It has relations which closely involve it with the material universe, and with human society and national life. There have been times when God has worked, and the signs of his presence have been seen, in terrible shakings of the nations, in the ploughing up from their foundations of hoary injustice, in the smiting of grinding tyrannies, and in the emancipation of peoples whose life had been a long and hopeless moan. There have been times, too, and many, when he has worked through the elements of nature —through blasting and mildew, through floods and famine, through locust, caterpillar and palmer-worm ; through flagging commerce, with its machinery rusting in the mill and its ships rotting in the harbour. All these things are his servants. Sometimes the sleep of the world, and the Church too, is so profound that it can be broken only by agencies like the wind, or fire, or earthquake, which made the prophet shiver at the mouth of the cave, and without which the voice that followed, so still, so small and tender, would have lost much of its melting and subduing power. When society has become drugged with the Circean cup of wordliness, and the voices that come from eternity are unheeded, if not unheard, even terror has its merciful mission. The frivolous and superficial hearts of men have to be made serious, their idols have to be broken, their nests have to be stoned, or tossed from the trees where they had been made with so much care, and they have to be taught that if this life be all, it is but a phantom and a mockery. When the day of the Lord shall come, in which he shall begin to work, let us not marvel if it " shall be upon every one that is proud and lofty, and upon every one that is lifted up ; and he shall be brought low ; and upon all the cedars of Lebanon, that are high and lifted up, and upon every high tower, and upon every fenced wall, and upon all the ships of Tarshish, and upon all the pleasant pictures. And the loftiness of man shall be bowed down, and the haughtiness of men shall be made low : and the Lord alone shall be exalted in that day." But this working of God will also take other shapes. Will it not be seen in the inspiration of the Church with faith in its own creed, so far as that creed has the warrant of the Divine word ? Does the Church believe its creed ? It writes it, sets it forth, sings it, defends it ; but does it believe it, at least with a faith which begets either enthusiasm in itself, or respect from the world ? Have not the truths which form the methodized symbols of the Church become propositions instead of living powers ? Do they not lie embalmed with superstitious reverence in the ark of tradition, tenderly cherished for what they have been and done ? But is it not forgotten that if they be truths they are not dead and cannot die ? They are true now, or they were never true ; living now, or they never lived. Time cannot touch them, nor human opinion, nor the Church's sluggishness or unbelief, for they are emanations from the Divine essence, instinct with his own undecaying life. They are not machinery which may become antiquated and obsolete and displaced by better inventions ; they are not methods of policy framed for conditions which are transient, and vanishing with them ; they are not scaffolding within which other and higher truth is to be reared from age to age. They are like him who is the end of our conversation, " Jesus Christ, the same yesterday, to-day, and for ever." There is not one of them which, if the faith it awakens were but commensurate with its intrinsic worth, would not clothe the Church with a new and wondrous power. But what would be that power if that faith were to grasp them all ? It would be life from the dead.—*Enoch Mellor* (1823 —1881), *in "The Hem of Christ's Garment, and other Sermons."*

Verse 126.—*"It is time for thee, Lord, to work."* עֵת expresses emphatically *the proper time* for the Lord to do his own work ; as if the Psalmist had said, " It is not for us to prescribe the time and occasion for God to exercise his power, and to vindicate the authority of his own law ; he does every thing at the proper time, and he will at the proper season punish those ' *who have made void his law,*' and who have become notorious for their impiety and wickedness."—*George Phillips.*

Verse 126.—"*It is time to work*," just as when the attack of some illness is becoming more severe, you hurry to the physician, that he may come more quickly, lest he should later be unable to do any good. So when the prophet saw in the Holy Spirit the rebellion of the people, their luxury, pleasures, deceits, frauds, avarice, drunkenness, he runs, for our help, to Christ, whom he knew to be alone able to remedy, such sins; implores him to come, and admits of no delay.—*Ambrose, in Neale and Littledale.*

Verse 126.—"*It is time for thee, Lord, to work*."—Infidelity was never more subtle, more hurtful, more plausible, perhaps more successful, than in the day in which we live. It has left the low grounds of vulgarity, and coarseness and ribaldry, and entrenched itself upon the lofty heights of criticism, philology, and even science itself. It pervades to a fearful extent our popular literature; it has invested itself with the charms of poetry, to throw its spell over the public mind; it has endeavoured to enweave itself with science; and he must be little acquainted with the state of opinion in this land, who does not know that it is espoused by a large portion of the cultivated mind of this generation. " It is time for thee, Lord, to work." —*John Angell James, 1785—1859.*

Verse 126.—"*It is time for thee, Lord, to work*," etc. To send the Messiah, to work by righteousness, to fulfil the law and vindicate the honour of it, broken by men. It was always a notion of the Jews that the time of the Messiah's coming would be when it was a time of great wickedness in the earth; and which seems to agree with the word of God, and was true in fact. See Mal. ii. 17, and iii. 1, 2, 3, 15, 16, and iv. 2.—*John Gill.*

Verse 126.—"*It is time for thee, Lord, to work*," etc. True it is, Lord, that we are not to appoint thee thy times and limits, for thou art the Ancient of Days, Time's Creator and destinator. Neither do we presume to press in at the portal of thy privy chamber, to " know the times and seasons " which thou our Father hast reserved in thine own power; yet, Lord, thou hast taught us, as to discern the face of the sky, so to descry the signs of the times, and from the cause to expect the effect which necessarily doth ensue. " Thou art a God full of compassion and mercy, slow to anger, and of great kindness " (Ps. ciii. 8); and thou dost sustain many wrongs of the sons of men, being crushed with their sins as a cart is laden with sheaves : but if still they continue to load thee, thou wilt ease thyself of that burden, and cast it on the ground of confusion. Thou art " slow to anger, but great in power, and wilt not surely clear the wicked " (Nahum i. 3). Thou dost for a long space hold thy peace at men's sins, and art still, and dost restrain thyself. But if men will not turn, thou wilt whet thy sword and bend thy bow, and make it ready. Patient thou art, and for a long time dost forbear thine hand; but when the forehead of sin beginneth to lose the blush of shame, when the beadroll of transgressions doth grow in score from East to West, when the cry of them pierceth above the clouds, when the height of wickedness is come unto the top, and the fruits thereof are ripe and full, then it is time for thee, Lord, to take notice of it, to awake like a giant, and to put to thine all-revenging hand.

But our sins are already ripe, yea, rotten ripe, the measure of our iniquities is full up to the brim. Doubtless our land is sunken deep in iniquity; our tongues and works have been against the Lord, to provoke the eyes of his glory; the trial of our countenance doth testify against us (Isaiah iii. 8, 9), yea, we declare our sins as Sodom; we hide them not, the cry of our sins is exceeding grievous, the clamours of them pierce the skies, and with a loud voice roar, saying : " How long, Lord, holy and true ? How long ere thou come to avenge thyself on such a nation as this ? " Rev. vi. 10 ; Jer. ix. 9.—*George Webbe, in "A Posie of Spiritual Flowers,"* 1610.

Verse 126.—"*It is time for thee, Lord*." Some read it, and the original will bear it, "*It is time to work for thee, O Lord ;* " it is time for every one in his place to appear on the Lord's side, against the threatening growth of profaneness and immorality. We must do what we can for the support of the sinking interests of religion, and after all, we must beg of God to take the work into his own hands. —*Matthew Henry.*

Verse 126.—"*They have made void thy law*." In the second verse of this section he complained that the proud would oppress him, now he complaineth that they destroyed the law of God. Who, then, are David's enemies, who seek to oppress him ? Only such as are enemies to God, and seek to destroy his law. A great comfort have we in this, that if we love the Lord, and study in a good conscience

to serve him, we can have no enemies but such as are enemies to God.—
William Cowper.

Verse 126.—*"They have made void thy law."* As if they would not only sin against
the Law, but sin away the Law, not only withdraw themselves from the obedience
of it, but drive it out of the world ; they would make void and repeal the holy acts
of God, that their own wicked acts might not be questioned ; and lest the Law should
have a power to punish them, they will deny it a power to rule them ; that's the
force of the simple word here used, as applied to highest transgressing against the
Law of God.—*Joseph Caryl.*

Verses 126, 127.—Everything betters a saint. Not only ordinances, word,
sacraments, holy society, but even sinners and their very sinning. Even these draw
forth their graces into exercise, and put them upon godly, broken-hearted mourning.
A saint sails with every wind. As the wicked are hurt by the best things, so the
godly are bettered by the worst. Because *" they have made void thy law, therefore
do I love thy commandments."* Holiness is the more owned by the godly, the more
the world despiseth it. The most eminent saints were those of Cæsar's (Nero's)
house (Phil. iv. 22) ; they who kept God's name were they who lived where Satan's
throne was (Rev. ii. 13). Zeal for God grows the hotter by opposition ; and thereby
the godly most labour to give the glory of God reparation.—*William Jenkyn* (1612
—1685), *in "The Morning Exercises."*

Verse 127.—*"Therefore I love thy commandments above gold,"* etc. Partly,
because it is one evidence of their excellency, that they are disliked by the vilest
of men. Partly, out of just indignation and opposition against my sworn enemies ;
and partly, because the great and general apostasy of others makes this duty more
necessary to prevent their own and other men's relapses.—*Matthew Pool.*

Verse 127.—*"I love thy commandments above gold ; yea, above fine gold."* The
image employed brings before us the picture of the miser ; his heart and his treasure
are in his gold. With what delight he counts it ! with what watchfulness he keeps
it ! hiding it in safe custody, lest he should be despoiled of that which is dearer
to him than life. Such should Christians be, spiritual misers, counting their treasure
which is *" above fine gold " ;* and *" hiding it in their hearts,"* in safe keeping, where
the great despoiler shall not be able to reach it. Oh, Christians ! how much more
is your portion to you than the miser's treasure ! Hide it ; watch it ; retain it.
You need not be afraid of covetousness in spiritual things : rather " covet earnestly "
to increase your store ; and by living upon it and living in it, it will grow richer in
extent, and more precious in value.—*Charles Bridges.*

Verse 127.—*"I love thy commandments."* He professeth not that he fulfilled
them, but that he *loved* them ; and truly it is a great progress in godliness, if we
become thus far, as from our heart to love them. The natural man hates the
commandments of God ; they are so contrary to his corruption ; but the regenerate
man, as he hates his own corruption, so he loves the word, because according to it
he desires to be reformed. And here is our comfort, that, albeit we cannot do what
is commanded, yet if we love to do it, it is an argument of grace received. *"Above
gold,"* etc. It is lawful to love those creatures which God hath appointed for our
use ; with these conditions : the one is, that the first seat in our affection of love
be reserved to God ; and any other thing we love, that we love it in him and for
him, and give it only the second room. Thus David, being a natural man, loved
his natural food ; but he protesteth he loved the law of the Lord more than his
appointed food ; and here he loves the commandments of God above all gold.—
William Cowper.

Verse 128.—*"I esteem all thy precepts concerning all things to be right."* It is no
compromising testimony to the integrity and value of the Lord's precepts with
which the Psalmist concludes, *"I esteem all thy precepts concerning all things to be
right "*—every command, however hard ; every injunction, however distasteful ;
every precept, however severe ; even cut off thy right hand, pluck out thy right
eye ; forget thine own people and thy father's house ; take up thy cross daily ;
sell all that thou hast—yea, Lord, even so, *" all* thy precepts concerning ALL
things are right." What a blessed truth to arrive at, and find comfort in !—*Barton
Bouchier.*

Verse 128.—*"I esteem all thy precepts,"* etc. We must not only respect all God's
commandments, but also respect them all alike, and give them all the like respect.

Obedience must be universal.—*R. Mayhew, in "The death of Death in the Death of Christ,"* 1679.

Verse 128.—*"All."* The many *alls* in this verse used (not unlike that in Ezekiel xliv. 30) showeth the integrity and universality of his obedience. *"All"* is but a little word, but of large extent.—*John Trapp.*

Verse 128.—*"All thy precepts concerning all things to be right."* He had a high estimate of God's precepts; he thought them just in all things; just, because they prescribe nothing but that which is exactly just; and just, because they bring a just punishment on the transgressors, and a reward to the righteous.—*William Nicholson.*

Verse 128.—The upright man squares all his actions by a right rule: carnal reason cannot bias him, corrupt practice cannot sway him, but God's sacred word directs him. Hence it is that his respect is universal to all divine precepts, avoiding all evil, performing all good without exception. Thus David's upright man here *esteems God's precepts concerning all things to be right,* and therefore is careful to observe them. Hence it is, that he is the same man at all times, in all places; because at all times, and in all societies, he acts by one and the same rule. 'Tis a good saying of S. Cyprian, *ea non est religio, sed dissimulatio, quæ per omnia non constat sibi,* that is not piety, but hypocrisy, that is not in all things like itself, since the upright man measures every action by the straight line of divine prescript. —*Abraham Wright.*

Verse 128.—*"I hate every false way."* The best trial of our love to God and his word is the contrary—hatred of sin and impiety: " Ye that love the Lord, hate evil." He that loves a tree, hates the worm that consumes it; he that loves a garment, hates the moth that eats it; he that loveth life, abhorreth death; and he that loves the Lord hates every thing that offends him. Let men take heed to this, who are in love of their sins: how can the love of God be in them?

Religion binds us not only to hate one way of falsehood, but all the ways of it. As there is nothing good, but in some measure a godly man loves it; so there is nothing evil, but in some measure he hates it. And this is the perfection of the children of God; a perfection not of degrees; for we neither love good nor hate evil as we should; but a perfection of parts; because we love every good, and we hate every evil in some measure.—*William Cowper.*

Verse 128.—*"And I hate."* The Being who loves the good with infinite intensity must hate evil with the same intensity. So far from the incompatibility between this love and this hatred, they are the counterparts of each other,—opposite poles of the same moral emotion.—*John W. Haley, in "An Examination of the alleged Discrepancies of the Bible,"* 1875.

Verse 128.—*"I hate every false way."* If Satan get a grip of thee by any one sin, is it not enough to carry thee to damnation? As the butcher carries the beast to the slaughter, sometime bound by all the four feet, and sometime by one only; so it is with Satan. Though thou be not a slave to all sin; if thou be a slave to one, the grip he hath of thee, by that one sinful affection, is sufficient to captive thee.—*William Cowper.*

EXPOSITION OF VERSES 129 TO 136.

THY testimonies *are* wonderful : therefore doth my soul keep them.

130 The entrance of thy words giveth light ; it giveth understanding unto the simple.

131 I opened my mouth, and panted : for I longed for thy commandments.

132 Look thou upon me, and be merciful unto me, as thou usest to do unto those that love thy name.

133 Order my steps in thy word : and let not any iniquity have dominion over me.

134 Deliver me from the oppression of man : so will I keep thy precepts.

135 Make thy face to shine upon thy servant ; and teach me thy statutes.

136 Rivers of waters run down mine eyes, because they keep not thy law.

129. *"Thy testimonies are wonderful."* Full of wonderful revelations, commands and promises. Wonderful in their nature, as being free from all error, and bearing within themselves overwhelming self-evidence of their truth ; wonderful in their effects as instructing, elevating, strengthening, and comforting the soul. Jesus the eternal Word is called Wonderful, and all the uttered words of God are wonderful in their degree. Those who know them best wonder at them most. It is wonderful that God should have borne testimony at all to sinful men, and more wonderful still that his testimony should be of such a character, so clear, so full, so gracious, so mighty. *"Therefore doth my soul keep them."* Their wonderful character so impressed itself upon his mind that he kept them in his memory : their wonderful excellence so charmed his heart that he kept them in his life. Some men wonder at the words of God, and use them for their speculation ; but David was always practical, and the more he wondered the more he obeyed. Note that his religion was soul work ; not with head and hand alone did he keep the testimonies ; but his soul, his truest and most real self, held fast to them.

130. *"The entrance of thy words giveth light."* No sooner do they gain admission into the soul than they enlighten it : what light may be expected from their prolonged indwelling ! Their very entrance floods the mind with instruction, for they are so full, so clear ; but, on the other hand, there must be such an "entrance," or there will be no illumination. The mere hearing of the word with the external ear is of small value by itself, but when the words of God enter into the chambers of the heart then light is scattered on all sides. The word finds no entrance into some minds because they are blocked up with self-conceit, or prejudice, or indifference ; but where due attention is given, divine illumination must surely follow upon knowledge of the mind of God. Oh, that thy words, like the beams of the sun, may enter through the window of my understanding, and dispel the darkness of my mind ! *"It giveth understanding unto the simple."* The sincere and candid are the true disciples of the word. To such it gives not only knowledge, but understanding. These simple-hearted ones are frequently despised, and their simplicity has another meaning infused into it, so as to be made the theme of ridicule ; but what matters it ? Those whom the world dubs as fools are among the truly wise if they are taught of God. What a divine power rests in the word of God, since it not only bestows light, but gives that very mental eye by which the light is received —" It giveth understanding." Hence the value of the words of God to the simple, who cannot receive mysterious truth unless their minds are aided to see it and prepared to grasp it.

131. *"I opened my mouth, and panted."* So animated was his desire that he looked into the animal world to find a picture of it. He was filled with an intense longing, and was not ashamed to describe it by a most expressive, natural, and yet singular symbol. Like a stag that has been hunted in the chase, and is hard pressed, and therefore pants for breath, so did the Psalmist pant for the entrance of God's word into his soul. Nothing else could content him. All that the world

could yield him left him still panting with open mouth. *"For I longed for thy commandments."* Longed to know them, longed to obey them, longed to be conformed to their spirit, longed to teach them to others. He was a servant of God, and his industrious mind longed to receive orders ; he was a learner in the school of grace, and his eager spirit longed to be taught of the Lord.

132. *"Look thou upon me."* A godly man cannot long be without prayer. During the previous verses he had been expressing his love to God's word, but here he is upon his knees again. This prayer is specially short, but exceedingly sententious, " Look thou upon me." While he stood with open mouth panting for the commandments, he besought the Lord to look upon him, and let his condition and his unexpressed longings plead for him. He desires to be known of God, and daily observed by him. He wishes also to be favoured with the divine smile which is included in that word—" look." If a look from us to God has saving efficacy in it, what may we not expect from a look from God to us. *"And be merciful unto me."* Christ's look at Peter was a look of mercy, and all the looks of the heavenly Father are of the same kind. If he looked in stern justice his eyes would not endure us, but looking in mercy he spares and blesses us. If God looks and sees us panting, he will not fail to be merciful to us. *"As thou usest to do unto those that love thy name."* Look on me as thou lookest on those who love thee ; be merciful to me as thou art accustomed to be towards those who truly serve thee. There is a use and wont which God observes towards them that love him, and David craved that he might experience it. He would not have the Lord deal better or worse with him than he was accustomed to deal with his saints—worse would not save him, better could not be. In effect he prays, " I am thy servant ; treat me as thou treatest thy servants. I am thy child ; deal with me as with a son." Especially is it clear from the context that he desired such an entering in of the word, and such a clear understanding of it as God usually gives to his own, according to the promise, " All thy children shall be taught of the Lord."

Reader, do you love the name of the Lord ? Is his character most honourable in your sight ? most dear to your heart ? This is a sure mark of grace, for no soul ever loved the Lord except as the result of love received from the Lord himself.

133. *"Order my steps in thy word."* This is one of the Lord's customary mercies to his chosen,—" He keepeth the feet of his saints." By his grace he enables us to put our feet step by step in the very place which his word ordains. This prayer seeks a very choice favour, namely, that every distinct act, every step, might be arranged and governed by the will of God. This does not stop short of perfect holiness, neither will the believer's desires be satisfied with anything beneath that blessed consummation. *"And let not any iniquity have dominion over me."* This is the negative side of the blessing. We ask to do all that is right, and to fall under the power of nothing that is wrong. God is our sovereign, and we would have every thought in subjection to his sway. Believers have no choice, darling sins to which they would be willing to bow. They pant for perfect liberty from the power of evil, and being conscious that they cannot obtain it of themselves, they cry unto God for it.

134. *"Deliver me from the oppression of man."* David had tasted all the bitterness of this great evil. It had made him an exile from his country, and banished him from the sanctuary of the Lord : therefore he pleads to be saved from it. It is said that oppression makes a wise man mad, and no doubt it has made many a righteous man sinful. Oppression is in itself wicked, and it drives men to wickedness. We little know how much of our virtue is due to our liberty ; if we had been in bonds under haughty tyrants we might have yielded to them, and instead of being confessors we might now have been apostates. He who taught us to pray, " Lead us not into temptation," will sanction this prayer, which is of much the same tenor, since to be oppressed is to be tempted. *"So will I keep thy statutes."* When the stress of oppression was taken off he would go his own way, and that way would be the way of the Lord. Although we ought not to yield to the threatenings of men, yet many do so ; the wife is sometimes compelled by the oppression of her husband to act against her conscience : children and servants, and even whole nations have been brought into the same difficulty. Their sins will be largely laid at the oppressor's door, and it usually pleases God ere long to overthrow those powers and dominions which compel men to do evil. The worst of it is that some persons, when the pressure is taken off from them, follow after unrighteousness of their own accord. These give evidence of being sinners in grain. As for the righteous, it happens

to them as it did to the apostles of old, " Being let go, they went to their own company."
When saints are freed from the tyrant they joyfully pay homage to their king.

135. *"Make thy face to shine upon thy servant."* Oppressors frown, but do thou
smile. They darken my life, but do thou shine upon me, and all will be bright.
The Psalmist again declares that he is God's servant, and he seeks for no favour
from others, but only from his own Lord and Master. *"And teach me thy statutes."*
This is the favour which he considers to be the shining of the face of God upon
him. If the Lord will be exceeding gracious, and make him his favourite, he will
ask no higher blessing than still to be taught the royal statutes. See how he craves
after holiness ; this is the choicest of all gems in his esteem. As we say among
men that a good education is a great fortune, so to be taught of the Lord is a gift
of special grace. The most favoured believer needs teaching ; even when he walks
in the light of God's countenance he has still to be taught the divine statutes or he
will transgress.

136. *"Rivers of waters run down mine eyes, because they keep not thy law."* He
wept in sympathy with God to see the holy law despised and broken. He wept
in pity for men who were thus drawing down upon themselves the fiery wrath of
God. His grief was such that he could scarcely give it vent ; his tears were not
mere drops of sorrow, but torrents of woe. In this he became like the Lord Jesus
who beheld the city, and wept over it ; and like unto Jehovah himself, who hath
no pleasure in the death of him that dieth, but that he turn unto him and live. The
experience of this verse indicates a great advance upon anything we have had before :
the Psalm and the Psalmist are both growing. That man is a ripe believer who
sorrows because of the sins of others. In verse 120 his flesh trembled at the presence
of God, and here it seems to melt and flow away in floods of tears. None are so
affected by heavenly things as those who are much in the study of the word, and
are thereby taught the truth and essence of things. Carnal men are afraid of brute
force, and weep over losses and crosses ; but spiritual men feel a holy fear of the
Lord himself, and most of all lament when they see dishonour cast upon his holy
name.

> " Lord, let me weep for nought but sin,
> And after none but thee,
> And then I would, O that I might !
> A constant weeper be."

NOTES ON VERSES 129 TO 136.

All the verses of this section begin with the seventeenth letter of the Hebrew alphabet; but each verse with a different word.—*William S. Plumer.*

This seventeenth letter is the letter P. The section is precious, practical, profitable, powerful: peculiarly so.—*C. H. S.*

Verse 129.—*"Thy testimonies are wonderful."* The Scriptures are *"wonderful,"* with respect to the matter which they contain, the manner in which they are written, and the effects which they produce. They contain the sublimest spiritual truths, veiled under external ceremonies and sacraments, figurative descriptions, typical histories, parables, similitudes, etc. When properly opened and enforced, they terrify and humble, they convert and transform, they console and strengthen. Who but must delight to study and to "observe" these "testimonies" of the will and the wisdom, the love and the power of God Most High! While we have these holy writings, let us not waste our time, mis-employ our thoughts, and prostitute our admiration, by doating on human follies, and wondering at human trifles.—*George Horne.*

Verse 129.—*"Thy testimonies are wonderful."* God's testimonies are "wonderful" (1) in their *majesty* and *composure*, which striketh reverence into the hearts of those that consider; the Scripture speaketh to us at a God-like rate. (2) It is "wonderful" for the *matter* and *depth of mystery*, which cannot be found elsewhere, concerning God, and Christ, the creation of the world, the souls of men, and their immortal and everlasting condition, the fall of man, etc. (3) It is "wonderful" for *purity* and *perfection*. The Decalogue in ten words compriseth the whole duty of man, and reacheth to the very soul, and all the motions of the heart. (4) It is "wonderful" for the *harmony* and *consent* of all the parts. All religion is of a piece, and one part doth not interfere with another, but conspireth to promote the great end, of subjection of the creature to God. (5) It is "wonderful" for the *power* of it. There is a mighty power which goeth along with the word of God, and astonisheth the hearts of those that consider it and feel it. 1 Thess. i. 5.—*Thomas Manton.*

Verse 129.—*"Thy testimonies are wonderful."* The Bible itself is an astonishing and standing miracle. Written fragment by fragment, through the course of fifteen centuries, under different states of society, and in different languages, by persons of the most opposite tempers, talents, and conditions, learned and unlearned, prince and peasant, bond and free; cast into every form of instructive composition and good writing; history, prophecy, poetry, allegory, emblematic representation, judicious interpretation, literal statement, precept, example, proverbs, disquisition, epistle, sermon, prayer—in short, all rational shapes of human discourse, and treating, moreover, on subjects not obvious, but most difficult; its authors are not found like other men, contradicting one another upon the most ordinary matters of fact and opinion, but are at harmony upon the whole of their sublime and momentous scheme.—*J. Maclagan*, 1853.

Verse 129.—Highly prize the Scriptures, or you will not obey them. David said, "*therefore doth my soul keep them*"; and why was this, but that he counted them to be wonderful? Can *he* make a proficiency in any art, who doth slight and deprecate it? Prize this book of God above all other books. St. Gregory calls the Bible "the heart and soul of God." The rabbins say, that there is a mountain of sense hangs upon every *apex* and tittle of Scripture. "The law of the Lord is perfect" (Ps. xix. 7). The Scripture is the library of the Holy Ghost; it is a pandect of divine knowledge, an exact model and platform of religion. The Scripture contains in it the *credenda*, "the things which we are to believe," and the *agenda*, "the things which we are to practise." It is "able to make us wise unto salvation" 2 Tim. iii. 15. "The Scripture is the standard of truth," the judge of controversies; it is the pole-star to direct us to heaven (Isa. viii. 20). "The commandment is a lamp": Prov. vi. 23. The Scripture is the compass by which the rudder of our will is to be steered; it is the field in which Christ, the Pearl of price, is hid; it is a rock of diamonds, it is a sacred *collyrium*, or "*eye-salve;*" it mends *their* eyes *that* look upon it; it is a spiritual optic-glass in which the glory of God is resplendent; it is the panacea or "universal medicine" for the soul. The leaves of Scripture are like the leaves of the tree of life, "for the healing of the nations": Rev. xxii. 2. The Scripture is both the breeder and feeder of grace. How is the

convert born, but by "the word of truth"?   James i. 18.   How doth he grow,
but by "the sincere milk of the word"?   1 Pet. ii. 2.   The word written is the
book out of which our evidences for heaven are fetched; it is the sea-mark which
shows us the rocks of sin to avoid; it is the antidote against error and apostasy,
the two-edged sword which wounds the old serpent.   It is our bulwark to withstand the force of lust; like the Capitol of Rome, which was a place of strength and
ammunition.   The Scripture is the "tower of David," whereon the shields of our
faith hang: Canticles iv. 4.   "Take away the word, and you deprive us of the
sun," said Luther.   The word written is above an angelic embassy, or voice from
heaven.   "This voice which came from heaven we heard.   We have also," βεβαιότερον
λογον "a more sure word": 2 Peter i. 18, 19.   O, prize the word written; prizing
is the way to profiting.   If Cæsar so valued his Commentaries, that for preserving
them he lost his purple robe, how should we estimate the sacred oracles of God?
"I have esteemed the words of his mouth more than any necessary food": Job
xxiii. 12.   King Edward the Sixth, on the day of his coronation, had presented
before him three swords, signifying that he was monarch of three kingdoms.   The
king said, there was one sword wanting; being asked what that was, he answered,
"The Holy Bible, which is the sword of the Spirit, and is to be preferred before
these ensigns of royalty."   Robert King of Sicily did so prize God's word, that,
speaking to his friend Petrarcha, he said, "I protest, the Scriptures are dearer
to me than my kingdom; and if I must be deprived of one of them, I had rather
lose my diadem than the Scriptures."—*Thomas Watson, in "The Morning Exercises."*

Verse 129.—The word contains matter to exercise the greatest minds.   Many
men cannot endure to spend their thoughts and time about trivial matters; whereas
others think it happiness enough if they can, by the meanest employments, procure
subsistence.   Oh, let all those of high aspirations exercise themselves in the law
of God; here are objects fit for great minds, yea, objects that will elevate the
greatest: and indeed none in the world are truly great but the saints, for they
exercise themselves in the great counsels of God.   We account those men the greatest
that are employed in state affairs: now the saints are lifted up above all things
in the world, and regard them all as little and mean, and are exercised in the great
affairs of the kingdom of Jesus Christ.   Hence the Lord would have the kings and
the judges to have the book of the law written, Deut. xvii. 18, 19; and it is reported
of Alphonsus, king of Arragon, that in midst of all his great and manifold occupations,
he read over the Scriptures fourteen times with commentaries.   How many have
we, men of great estates, and claiming to be of great minds, that scarce regard the
law of God: they look upon his law as beneath them.   Books of history and war
they will peruse with diligence; but for the Scripture, it is a thing that has little
in it.   It is a special means to obedience to have high thoughts of God's law.   That
is the reason why the prophet speaks thus, "I have written to him the great things
of my law, but they were counted as a strange thing": Hos. viii. 12.   As if he
should say, if they had had the things of my law in their thoughts, they would
never so have acted.   Ps. cxix. 129, *"Thy testimonies are wonderful, therefore doth
my soul keep them."*   He saith not, therefore do I keep them; but, therefore doth
my soul keep them; my very soul is in this, in keeping thy testimonies, for I look
upon them as wonderful things.   It is a good sign that the spirit of the great God
is in a man, when it raises him above other things, to look upon the things of his
word as the only great things in the world.   "All flesh is grass, and all the goodliness thereof is as the flower of the field: the grass withereth, the flower fadeth:
but the word of our God shall stand for ever:" Isa. xl. 6, 8.   There is a vanity in
all things of the world; but in that which the word reveals, in that there is an
eternity: we should therefore admire at nothing so as at the word, and we should
greatly delight in God's commandments; an ordinary degree of admiration or
delight is not sufficient, but great admiration and great delight there should be in
the law of God.   And all arguments drawn from God's law should powerfully prevail with you.—*Jeremiah Burroughs.*

Verse 129.—*"Thy testimonies are wonderful."*   Wonders will never cease.   Air,
earth, water, the world above, the world beneath, time, eternity, worms, birds,
fishes, beasts, men, angels are all full of wonders.   The more all things are studied,
the more do wonders appear.   It is idle, therefore, to find fault with the mysteries
of Scripture, or to deny them.   Inspiration glories in them.   He who rejects the
mysteries of love, grace, truth, power, justice and faithfulness of God's word, rejects
salvation.   It has marvels in itself, and marvels in its operation.   They are good

cause of love, not of offence ; of *keeping*, not of breaking God's precepts.—*William S. Plumer.*

Verse 129.—"*My soul*," not merely I, but I with all my heart and soul.—*Joseph Addison Alexander.*

Verse 129.—I have completed reading the whole Bible through since January last. I began it on the first day of the present year, and finished it on the the 26th of October. I have read it in that space four times, and not without real profit to myself. I always find in it something new ; it being, like its Author, infinite and inexhaustible.—*Samuel Eyles Pierce*, 1841.

Verse 129.—What do I not owe to the Lord for permitting me to take a part in the translation of his word ? Never did I see such wonders, and wisdom, and love, in the blessed book, as since I have been obliged to study every expression ; and it is a delightful reflection, that death cannot deprive us of the pleasure of studying its mysteries.—*Henry Martyn.*

Verse 130.—"*The opening of thy words enlightens, making the simple understand.*" The common version of the first word (*entrance*) is inaccurate, and the one here given, though exact, is ambiguous. The clause does not refer to the mechanical opening of the book by the reader, but to the spiritual opening of its true sense by divine illumination, to the mind which naturally cannot discern it.—*Joseph Addison Alexander.*

Verse 130.—"*Entrance*," lit. *opening*, i.e. unfolding or unveiling.—*J. J. Stewart Perowne.*

Verse 130.—"*The entrance of thy words giveth light.*" The first entrance, or vestibule : for the Psalmist wishes to point out that only the beginnings are apprehended in this life ; and that these beginnings are to be preferred to all human wisdom.—*Henricus Mollerus.*

Verse 130.—"*The entrance of thy words giveth light,*" etc. The beginning of them ; the first three chapters in Genesis, what light do they give into the origin of all things ; the creation of man, his state of innocence ; his fall through the temptations of Satan, and his recovery and salvation by Christ, the seed of the woman ! The first principles of the oracles of God, the rudiments of religion, the elements of the world, the rites of the ceremonial law gave great light unto the Gospel mysteries.—*John Gill.*

Verse 130.—"*The entrance of thy words giveth light.*" A profane shopman crams into his pocket a leaf of a Bible, and reads the last words of Daniel : " Go thou thy way, till the end be, for thou shalt rest and stand in thy lot at the end of the days," and begins to think what his own lot will be when days are ended. A Göttingen Professor opens a big printed Bible to see if he has eyesight enough to read it, and alights on the passage, "I will bring the blind by a way that they knew not," and in reading it the eyes of his understanding are enlightened. Cromwell's soldier opens his Bible to see how far the musket-ball has pierced, and finds it stopped at the verse : " Rejoice, O young man, in thy youth, and let thy heart cheer thee in the days of thy youth ; and walk in the ways of thine heart and the sight of thine eyes ; but know thou that for all these things God will bring thee into judgment." And in a frolic the Kentish soldier opens the Bible which his broken-hearted mother had sent him, and the first sentence that turns up is the text so familiar in boyish days : " Come unto me, all ye that labour and are heavy laden," and the weary profligate repairs for rest to Jesus Christ.—*James Hamilton*, 1814—1867.

Verse 130.—He amplifies his praise of the word of God when he saith that the entrance thereof, the first opening of the door of the word, gives light : for if the first entrance to it give light, what will the progress and continuance thereof do ? This accuseth the age wherein we live, who now of a long time hath been taught by the word of God so clearly, that in regard of time they might have been teachers of others, yet are they but children in knowledge and understanding. But to whom doth the word give understanding ? David saith to the " *simple* ": not to such as are high-minded, or double in heart, or wise in their own eyes, who will examine the mysteries of godliness by the quickness of natural reason. No : to such as deny themselves, as captive their natural understanding, and like humble disciples submit themselves, not to ask, but to hear ; not to reason, but to believe. And if for this cause, naturalists who want this humility cannot profit by the word ; what marvel that Papists far less become wise by it, who have their hearts so full of prejudices concerning it, that they spare not to utter blasphemies against it, calling it not unprofitable, but pernicious to the simple and to the idiots.

And again, where they charge it with difficulty, that simple men and idiots should not be suffered to read it, because it is obscure ; all these frivolous allegations of men are annulled by this one testimony of God, that *it gives light to the simple.*—*William Cowper.*

Verse 130.—*"Light."* This " *light* " hath excellent properties. 1. It is *lux manifestans*, it manifesteth itself and all things else. How do I see the sun, but by the sun, by its own light ? How do I know the Scripture to be the word of God, but by the light that shineth in it, commending itself to my conscience ! So it manifests all things else ; it layeth open all the frauds and impostures of Satan, the vanity of wordly things, the deceits of the heart, the odiousness of sin 2. It is *lux dirigens*, a directing light, that we may see our way and work. As the sun lighteth man to his labour, so doth this direct us in all our conditions : verse 105. It directs us how to manage ourselves in all conditions. 3. It is *lux vivificans,* a quickening light. " I am the light of the world : he that followeth me shall not walk in darkness, but shall have the light of life " : John viii. 12. "Awake thou that sleepest, and arise from the dead, and Christ shall give thee light " : Eph. v. 14. That light was the life of men : so is this spiritual life ; it not only discovereth the object, but helpeth the faculty, filleth the soul with life and strength. 4. It is *lux exhilarans*, a comforting, refreshing, cheering light ; and that in two respects. (1) Because it presents us with excellent grounds of comfort. (2) Because it is a soul-satisfying light.—*Condensed from Manton.*

Verse 130.—*"It giveth understanding."* If all the books in the world were assembled together, the Bible would as much take the lead in disciplining the understanding as in directing the soul. It will not make astronomers, chemists, or linguists, but there is a great difference between strengthening the mind and storing it with information.—*Henry Melvill.*

Verse 130.—*"It giveth understanding to the simple."* There are none so knowing that God cannot blind ; none so blind and ignorant whose mind and heart his spirit cannot open. He who, by his incubation upon the waters at the creation, hatched that rude mass into the beautiful form we now see, and out of that dark chaos made the glorious heavens, and garnished them with so many orient stars, can move upon thy dark soul and enlighten it, though it be as void of knowledge as the evening of the world's first day was of light. The schoolmaster sometimes sends home the child, and bids his father to put him to another trade, because not able, with all his art, to make a scholar of him ; but if the Spirit of God be master, thou shalt learn, though a dunce : *"The entrance of thy word giveth light, it giveth understanding to the simple."* No sooner is the soul entered into the Spirit's school, than he becomes a proficient.—*William Gurnall.*

Verse 130.—*"To the simple."* He does not say, *" giveth understanding "* to the wise and prudent, and to learned men, and to those skilled in letters ; but to the " simple."—*Wolfgang Musculus.*

Verse 130.—*"To the simple."* This is one great characteristic of the word of God,—however incomprehensible to the carnal mind, it is adapted to every grade of enlightened intelligence.—*W. Wilson.*

Verse 130.—*"To the simple."* The word is used sometimes in a good sense, and sometimes in a bad sense. It is used in a good sense, First, for the sincere and plain-hearted : " The Lord preserveth the simple : I was brought low, and he helped me " : Ps. cxvi. 6. " For our rejoicing is this, the testimony of our conscience, that in simplicity and godly sincerity, not with fleshly wisdom, but by the grace of God, we have had our conversation in the world, and more abundantly to you-ward " : 2 Cor. i. 12. Secondly, for those that do not oppose the presumption of carnal wisdom to the pure light of the word : so we must all be simple, or fools, that we may be wise : " If any man among you seemeth to be wise in this world, let him become a fool, that he may be wise " (1 Cor. iii. 18) ; that is, in simplicity of heart submitting to God's conduct, and believing what he hath revealed.—*Thomas Manton*

Verse 131.—*"I opened my mouth, and panted."* By this manner of speech, David expresses, as Basil thinks, *animi propensionem*, that the inclination of his soul was after God's word. For, this opened mouth, Ambrose thinks, is *os interioris hominis*, the mouth of the inward man, which in effect is his heart ; and the speech notes *vehementem animi intensionem*, a vehement intension of his spirit, saith Euthymius. Yet shall it not be amiss to consider here how the mind of the godly earnestly affected moves the body also. The speech may be drawn from travellers, who being very desirous to attain to their proposed ends, enforce their strength thereunto ; and finding a weakness in their body to answer their will, they pant and open their mouth, seeking refreshment from the air to renew their strength : or as Vatablus thinks, from men exceeding hungry and thirsty, who open their mouth as if they would draw in the whole air, and then pant and sigh within themselves when they find no full refreshment by it. So he expresseth it : " My heart burns with so ardent a longing for thy commandments, that I am forced ever and anon to gasp by reason of my painful breathing."

However it be, it lets us see how the hearing, reading, or meditating of God's word wakened in David a most earnest affection to have the light, joy, grace, and comfort thereof communicated to his own heart. For in the godly, knowledge of good increaseth desires ; and it cannot be expressed how vehemently their souls long to feel that power and comfort which they know is in the word ; and how sore they are grieved and troubled when they find it not.

And happy were we, if we could meet the Lord with this like affection ; that when he opens his mouth, we could also open our heart to hear. as David here doth. *Christus aperit os, ut daret aliis spiritum ; David aperuit ut acciperet ;* offering his heart to receive the spirit of grace, when God openeth his mouth in his word to give it. For it is his promise to us all—" Open thy mouth wide, and I will fill it." Let us turn it into a prayer, that the Lord, who opened the heart of Lydia, would open our heart to receive grace when he offers by his word to give it.—*William Cowper.*

Verse 131.—*"I opened my mouth, and panted,"* etc. There are two ways in which these words may be understood. They may be considered as expressing the very earnest longing of the Psalmist for greater acquaintance with God in spiritual things ; and then, in saying, *"I opened my mouth, and panted,"* he merely asserts the vehemence of his desire. Or you may separate the clauses : you may regard the first as the utterance of a man utterly dissatisfied with the earth and earthly things, and the second as the expression of a consciousness that God, and God only, could meet the longings of his soul. *"I opened my mouth, and panted."* Out of breath, with chasing shadows, and hunting after baubles, I sit down exhausted, as far off as ever from the happiness which has been earnestly but fruitlessly sought. Whither, then, shall I turn ? Thy commandments, O Lord, and these alone, can satisfy the desires of an immortal being like myself ; and on these, therefore, henceforward shall my longings be turned.—*Henry Melvill.*

Verse 131.—*"I opened my mouth, and panted."* A metaphor taken from men scorched and sweltered with heat, or from those that have run themselves out of breath in following the thing which they would overtake. The former metaphor expressed the vehemency of his love ; the other the earnestness of his pursuit ; he was like a man gasping for breath, and sucking in the cool air.—*Thomas Manton.*

Verse 131.—*"I longed for thy commandments."* This is a desire which God will satisfy. " Open thy mouth wide, and I will fill it " : Ps. lxxxi. 10.—*Thomas Manton.*

Verse 132.—*"Look thou upon me, and be merciful unto me,"* etc. *"Look upon me,"* stripped by thieves of my virtues, and then wounded with sins, and *"be merciful unto me,"* showing compassion on me, taking care of me in the inn of the Church universal, that I fall not again among thieves, nor be harmed by the wolves which howl about this fold, but dare not enter in. *"Look upon me,"* no longer worthy to be called thy son, and *"be merciful unto me,"* not as the jealous elder brother would treat me, but let me join the glad song and banquet of them that love thy name. Look upon me the publican, standing afar off in thy temple the Church, and be merciful unto me, not after the Pharisee's judgment, but *"as thou usest to do unto them that love thy name,"* which is the gracious God. Look on me as on weeping Peter, and be merciful unto me as thou wast to him, who so loved thy name as by his triple confession of love to wash out his threefold denial, saying, " Lord, thou knowest that I love thee." *"Look upon me,"* as on the sinful woman, penitent and weeping, and be merciful unto me, not according to the judgment of the Pharisee who murmured at her, as Judas who was indignant at her, but forgiving me as thou didst her, " because she loved much," telling me also, " Thy faith hath saved thee, go in peace."—*Neale and Littledale.*

Verse 132.—*"Look thou upon me."* Lord ! since our looks to thee are often so slight, so cold, so distant, that no impression is made upon our hearts, do thou condescend continually to look upon us with mercy and with power. Vouchsafe us such a look, as may bring us to ourselves, and touch us with tenderness and contrition in the remembrance of that sin, unbelief, and disobedience, which pierced the hands, the feet, the heart of our dearest Lord and Saviour. Comp. Luke xxii. 61. —*Charles Bridges.*

Verse 132.—*"As thou usest to do,"* etc. David would not lose any privilege that God hath by promise settled on his children. Do with me, saith he, *"as thou usest to do."* This is no more than family fare, what thou promisest to do for all that love thee ; and let me not go worse clad than the rest of my brethren.—*William Gurnall.*

Verse 132.—*"As thou usest to do unto those,"* etc. We should be content if God deals with us as he has always dealt with his people. While he could not be satisfied with anything less than their portion, David asks for nothing better ; he implores no singular dispensation in his favour, no deviation from the accustomed methods of his grace. . . . It is always a good proof that your convictions and desires are from the operation of the Spirit when you are willing to conform to God's order. What is this order ? It is to dispense his blessings connectedly. It is never to justify without sanctifying ; never to give a title to heaven without a meetness for it. Now the man that is divinely wrought upon will not expect nor desire the one without the other. Therefore he will not expect the blessing of God without obedience ; because it is always God's way to connect the comforts of the Holy Ghost with the fear of the Lord ; and if his children transgress his laws, to visit their transgressions with a rod. Therefore he will neither expect nor desire his blessing without exertion ; for it has always been God's way to crown only those that run the race that is set before them, and fight the good fight of faith. Therefore he will not expect nor desire the Divine blessing without prayer ; for it has always been God's way to make his people sensible of their wants, and to give an answer to prayer. Therefore he will not expect nor desire to reach heaven without difficulties ; for his people have always had to deny themselves, and take up their cross. If they have not been chosen in the furnace of affliction, they have been purified. God had one Son without sin, but he never had one without sorrow : " he scourgeth every son whom he receiveth." " Yes," says the suppliant before us, " secure me their everlasting portion, and I am willing to drink of the cup they drank of, and to be baptized with the baptism they were baptized with. I want no new, no by-path to glory. I am content to keep the King's high road. *'Be merciful unto me, as thou usest to do unto those that love thy name.'* I ask no more."—*William Jay,* 1769—1853.

Verse 133.—*"Order my steps in thy word."* As before he sought mercy, so now he seeks grace. There are many that seek mercy to forgive sin, who seek not grace to deliver them from the power of sin : this is to abuse God's mercy, and turn his grace into wantonness. He that prayeth for mercy to forgive the guilt of sin only, seeks not that by sin he should not offend God ; but that he may sin and not hurt himself : but he who craves deliverance also from the commanding power and deceit of sin, seeks not only a benefit to himself, but grace also to please and serve the Lord his God. The first is but a lover of himself ; the second is a lover of God, more than of himself. And truly he never knew what it was to seek mercy for sin past, who with it also earnestly sought not grace to keep him from sin in time to come. These benefits cannot be divided : he who hath not the second (howsoever he flatter himself) may be assured that he hath not gotten the first.—*William Cowper.*

Verse 133.—*"Order my steps in thy word."* It is written of Boleslaus, one of the kings of Poland, that he still carries about him the picture of his father, and when he was to do any great work or set upon any design extraordinary, he would look on the picture and pray that he might do nothing unworthy of such a father's name. Thus it is that the Scriptures are the picture of God's will, therein drawn out to the very life. Before a man enter upon or engage himself in any business whatsoever, let him look there, and read there what is to be done ; what to be undone ; and what God commands, let that be done ; what he forbids, let that be undone ; let the balance of the sanctuary weigh all, the oracles of God decide all, the rule of God's word be the square of all, and his glory the ultimate of all intendments whatsoever.—*From Spencer's "Things New and Old."*

Verse 133.—*"Order my steps."* הכן *hachen*; make them *firm ;* let me not walk with a halting or unsteady step.—*Adam Clarke.*

Verse 133.—"*Order my steps,*" etc. The people of God would not only have their path right, but their *steps ordered ;* as not their general course wrong (as those who walk in the way of everlasting perdition), so not a step awry ; they would not miss the way to heaven, either in whole or in part.—*Thomas Manton.*

Verse 133.—"*My steps.*" Speaking of the steps of the Temple, Bunyan says, " These steps, whether cedar, gold, or stone, yet that which added to their adornment, was the wonderment of a Queen. And whatever they were made of, to be sure, they were a shadow of those steps, which we should take to, and in the house of God. 'Steps of God,' Ps. lxxxv. 13. 'Steps ordered by him,' Ps. xxxvii. 23. 'Steps ordered in his word,' Ps. cxix. 133. 'Steps of faith,' Rom. iv. 12. 'Steps of the spirit,' 2 Cor. xii. 18. 'Steps of truth,' 3 John 4. 'Steps washed with butter,' Job xxix. 6. 'Steps taken before, or in the presence of God.' Steps butted and bounded by a divine rule. These are steps indeed."—*John Bunyan, in "Solomon's Temple Spiritualized."*

Verse 133.—"*Let not any iniquity,*" etc. True obedience to God is inconsistent with the dominion of any one lust, or corrupt affection. I say, though a man out of some slender and insufficient touch of religion upon his heart, may go right for a while, and do many things gladly ; yet that corruption which is indulged, and under the power of which a man lieth, will at length draw off from God ; and therefore no one sin should have dominion over us. When doth sin reign, or have dominion over us ? When we do not endeavour to mortify it, and to cut off the provisions that may feed that lust. Chrysostom's observation is, the apostle does not say, let it not tyrannize over you, but, let it not reign over you ; that is, when you suffer it to have a quiet reign in your hearts.—*Thomas Manton.*

Verse 133.—"*Let not any iniquity have dominion over me.*" I had rather be a prisoner to man all my life than be a bondage to sin one day. He says not, Let not this and the other man rule over me ; but "let not *sin* have dominion over me." Well said ! There is hope in such a man's condition as long as it is so.—*Michael Bruce,* 1666.

Verse 134.—"*Deliver me from the oppression of man.*" 1. "*Man*" by way of *distinction.* There is the oppression and tyranny of the Devil and sin ; but the Psalmist doth not mean that now : *Hominum non dæmonum,* saith Hugo. 2. "*Man*" by way of *aggravation. Homo homini lupus :* no creatures so ravenous and destructive to one another as man. It is a shame that one man should oppress another. Beasts do not usually devour those of the same kind ; but, usually, a man's enemies are those of his own household : Matt. x. 36. The nearer we are in bonds of alliance, the greater the hatred. 3. "*Man*" by way of *diminution.* And to lessen the fear of this evil, this term Adam is given them, to show their weakness in comparison of God. Thou art God ; but they that are so ready and forward to oppress and injure us are but men : thou canst easily overrule their power and break the yoke. I think this consideration chiefest, because of other places. " Who art thou, that thou shouldst be afraid of a man that shall die, and of the son of man which shall be made as grass ; and forgettest the Lord thy maker, that hath stretched forth the heavens, and laid the foundations of the earth ; and hast feared continually every day because of the fury of the oppressor, as if he were ready to destroy ? and where is the fury of the oppressor ? " Isa. li. 12, 13.—*Thomas Manton.*

Verse 134.—"*From the oppression of man.*" Some render it, "*from the oppression of Adam ;* " as Jarchi observes ; and Arama interprets it of the sin of Adam, and as a prayer to be delivered or redeemed from it ; as the Lord's people are by the blood of Christ.—*John Gill.*

Verse 135.—"*Make thy face to shine upon thy servant.*" The face of God shines upon us, when, in his providence, we are guided and upheld ; also when we are made to share in the good things of his providence, and when we are placed in a position wherein we can do much good. Much more does the face of God shine upon us, when we are favoured with tokens of his gracious favour ; for then we grow under the consciousness of a loving God, with rich supplies of his grace and Spirit. —*John Stephen.*

Verse 135.—"*Make thy face to shine upon thy servant.*" Oftentimes the wrongful dealings of men, of others, and of ourselves, like a cloud of smoke arising from the earth and obscuring the face of the sun, hide from us for a while the light of the countenance of God : but he soon clears it all away, and looks down upon us in loving mercy as before, lighting for us the path of obedience, and brightening our way unto himself.—*"Plain Commentary,"* 1859.

Verse 135.—*"Make thy face to shine upon thy servant."* The believer's incessant cry is, Let me see "the King's face." This is a blessing worth praying for. It is his heart's desire, his present privilege, and what is infinitely better, his sure, everlasting prospect—*"They shall see his face."* Rev. xxii. 4.—*Charles Bridges.*

Verse 135.—*"Make thy face to shine . . . and teach me."* Blessed is the man whom eternal Truth teacheth, not by obscure figures and transient sounds, but by direct and full communication. The perceptions of our senses are narrow and dull, and our reason on those perceptions frequently misleads us. He whom the eternal Word condescendeth to teach is disengaged at once from the labyrinth of human opinions. For "of one word are all things"; and all things without voice or language speak of him alone : he is that divine principle which speaketh in our hearts, and without which there can be neither just apprehension nor rectitude of judgment.

O God, who art the truth, make me one with thee in everlasting life ! I am often weary of reading, and weary of hearing ; in thee alone is the sum of my desire ! Let all teachers be silent, let the whole creation be dumb before thee, and do thou only speak unto my soul !

Thy ministers can pronounce the words, but cannot impart the spirit ; they may entertain the fancy with the charms of eloquence, but if thou art silent they do not inflame the heart. They administer the letter, but thou openest the sense ; they utter the mystery, but thou revealest its meaning ; they point out the way of life, but thou bestowest strength to walk in it ; they water, but thou givest the increase. Therefore do thou, O Lord my God, Eternal Truth ! speak to my soul ! lest, being outwardly warmed, but not inwardly quickened, I die, and be found unfruitful. "Speak, Lord, for thy servant heareth." "Thou only hast the words of eternal life."—*Thomas à Kempis,* 1380—1471.

Verse 135.—*"Make thy face to shine . . . . teach me,"* etc. God hath many ways of teaching ; he teaches by book, he teaches by his fingers, he teaches by his rod ; but his most comfortable and effectual teaching is by the light of his eye : *"O send out thy light and thy truth ; let them lead me : let them bring me unto thy holy hill :"* Ps. xlii. 3.—*Richard Alleine* (1611—1681), in *"Heaven Opened."*

Verse 135.—*"Make thy face to shine . . . . teach me thy statutes."* God's children, when they beg comfort, also beg grace to serve him acceptably. For by teaching God's statutes is not meant barely a giving us a speculative knowledge of God's will ; for so David here ; *"Make thy face to shine";* and *"Teach me thy statutes."*—*Thomas Manton.*

Verse 136.—*"Rivers of waters run down my eyes."* Most of the easterns shed tears much more copiously than the people of Europe. The Psalmist said *rivers of waters* ran down his eyes ; and though the language is beautifully figurative, I have no doubt it was also literally true. I have myself seen Arabs shed tears like streams.—*John Gadsby.*

Verse 136.—*"Rivers of waters run down mine eyes,"* etc. Either *because mine eyes keep not thy law,* so some. The eye is the inlet and outlet of a great deal of sin, and therefore it ought to be a weeping eye. Or rather, *they,* i.e., those about me : ver. 139. Note, the sins of sinners are the sorrows of saints. We must mourn for that which we cannot mend.—*Matthew Henry.*

Verse 136.—*"Rivers of waters run down mine eyes,"* etc. David's afflictions drew not so many tears from him as the sins of others ; not his banishment by his son, as the breach of God's law by the wicked. Nothing went so to his heart as the dishonour of God, whose glory shining in his word and ordinances, is dearer to the godly than their lives. Elijah desired to die when he saw God so dishonoured by Ahab and Jezebel. The eye is for two things, sight and tears : if we see God dishonoured, presently our eyes should be filled with tears.—*William Greenhill,* 1591—1677.

Verse 136.—*"Rivers of waters run down mine eyes,"* etc. Godly men are affected with deep sorrow for the sins of the ungodly.

Let us consider the *nature* of this affection. 1. It is not a stoical apathy, and affected carelessness ; much less a delightful partaking with sinful practices. 2. Not a proud setting off of their own goodness, with marking the sin of others as the

Pharisee did in the gospel. 3. Not the derision and mocking of the folly of men, with that "laughing philosopher": it comes nearer to the temper of the *other* who *wept* always for it. 4. It is not a bitter, bilious anger, breaking forth into railings and reproaches, nor an upbraiding insultation. 5. Nor is it a vindictive desire of punishment, venting itself in curses and imprecations, which is the rash temper of many, but especially of the vulgar sort. The disciples' motion to Christ was far different from that way, and yet he says to them, " Ye know not of what spirit ye are." They thought they had been of Elijah's spirit, but he told them they were mistaken, and did not know of what a spirit they were in that motion. Thus heady zeal often mistakes and flatters itself. We find not here a desire of fire to come down from heaven upon the breakers of the law, but such a grief as would rather bring water to quench it, if it were falling on them. *"Rivers of waters run down mine eyes."—Robert Leighton.*

Verse 136.—*"Rivers of waters run down mine eyes,"* etc. The Lord requireth this [mourning bitterly for other men's sins] to keep our hearts the more tender and upright ; it is an act God useth to make us more careful of our own souls, to be troubled at the sins of others, at sin in a third person. It keepeth us at a great distance from temptation. This is like quenching of fire in a neighbour's house : before it comes near thee, thou runnest with thy bucket. There is no way to keep us free from the infection, so much as mourning. The soul will never agree to do that which it grieved itself to see another do. And, as it keepeth us upright, so also humble, fearful of Divine judgment, tender lest we ourselves offend, and draw down the wrath of God. He that shruggeth when he seeth a snake creeping upon another, will much more be afraid when it cometh near to himself. In our own sins we have the advantage of conscience scourging the soul with remorse and shame ; in bewailing the sins of others, we have only the reasons of duty and obedience. They that fight abroad out of love to valour and exploits, will certainly fight at home out of love to their own safety.—*Thomas Manton.*

Verse 136.—*"Rivers of waters run down mine eyes,"* etc. Thus uniformly is the character of God's people represented—not merely as those who are *free from* —but as *"those that sigh and cry for—all the abominations that are done in the midst of the land"* : Ezek. ix. 4. And who does not see what an enlarged sphere still presents itself on every side for the unrestrained exercise of Christian compassion ? The appalling spectacle of a world apostatized from God, of multitudes sporting with everlasting destruction—as if the God of heaven were " a man that he should lie " is surely enough to force *"rivers of waters"* from the hearts of those that are concerned for his honour. What a mass of sin ascends as a cloud before the Lord, from a single heart ! Add the aggregate of a village—a town—a country—a world ! every day—every hour—every moment. Well might the *"rivers of waters"* rise to an overflowing tide, ready to burst its barriers.—*Charles Bridges.*

Verse 136.—*"Rivers of waters run down mine eyes, because they keep not thy law."* —The vices of the religious are the shame of religion : the sight of this hath made the stoutest champions of Christ melt into tears. David was one of those great worthies of the world, not matchable in his times ; yet he weeps. Did he tear in pieces a bear like a kid ? Rescue a lamb with the death of a lion ? Foil a mighty giant, that had dared the whole army of God ? Did he like a whirlwind, bear and beat down his enemies before him ; and now, does he, like a child or a woman, fall a-weeping ? Yes, he had heard the name of God blasphemed, seen his holy rites prophaned, his statutes vilipended, and violence offered to the pure chastity of that holy virgin, religion ; this resolved that valiant heart into tears : *"Rivers of waters run down mine eyes."—Thomas Adams.*

Verse 136.—My soul frequently spent itself in such breathings after conformity to the law of God as the one hundred and nineteenth Psalm is filled with throughout : " O that my ways were directed to keep thy statutes ! My heart breaketh through the longing it hath to thy commands at all times ; incline my heart that I may keep them alway unto the end," and the like. This appeared further in a fixed dislike of the least inconformity to the law, either in myself or others. Now ; albeit I was always suitably affected with my own or others' breaches, yet this was my burden ; I wished always that rivers of tears might run down mine eyes, because I, or other transgressors, kept not God's law.—*Thomas Halyburton, 1674—1712.*

Verse 136.—If we grieve not for others, their sin may become ours. Ezek. ix. 8 ; 1 Cor. v. 2.—*William Nicholson.*

EXPOSITION OF VERSES 137 TO 144.

R IGHTEOUS *art* thou, O LORD, and upright *are* thy judgments.

138 Thy testimonies *that* thou hast commanded *are* righteous and very faithful.

139 My zeal hath consumed me, because mine enemies have forgotten thy words.

140 Thy word *is* very pure : therefore thy servant loveth it.

141 I *am* small and despised : *yet* do not I forget thy precepts.

142 Thy righteousness *is* an everlasting righteousness, and thy law *is* the truth.

143 Trouble and anguish have taken hold on me : *yet* thy commandments *are* my delights.

144 The righteousness of thy testimonies *is* everlasting : give me understanding, and I shall live.

This passage deals with the perfect righteousness of Jehovah and his word, and expresses the struggles of a holy soul in reference to that righteousness. The initial letter with which every verse commences sounds like the Hebrew word for *righteousness :* our keynote is righteousness.

137. *"Righteous art thou, O LORD."* The Psalmist has not often used the name of Jehovah in this vast composition. The whole Psalm shows him to have been a deeply religious man, thoroughly familiar with the things of God ; and such persons never use the holy name of God carelessly, nor do they even use it at all frequently in comparison with the thoughtless and the ungodly. Familiarity begets reverence in this case. Here he uses the sacred name in worship. He praises God by ascribing to him perfect righteousness. God is always right, and he is always actively right, that is, righteous. This quality is bound up in our very idea of God. We cannot imagine an unrighteous God. *"And upright are thy judgments."* Here he extols God's word, or recorded judgments, as being right, even as their Author is righteous. That which comes from the righteous God is itself righteous. Jehovah both saith and doth that which is right, and that alone. This is a great stay to the soul in time of trouble. When we are most sorely afflicted, and cannot see the reason for the dispensation, we may fall back upon this most sure and certain fact, that God is righteous, and his dealings with us are righteous too. It should be our glory to sing this brave confession when all things around us appear to suggest the contrary. This is the richest adoration—this which rises from the lips of faith when carnal reason mutters about undue severity, and the like.

138. *"Thy testimonies that thou hast commanded are righteous and very faithful."* All that which God hath testified in his word is right and truthful. It is righteous, and may be relied upon for the present ; it is faithful, and may be trusted in for the future. About every portion of the inspired testimonies there is a divine authority, they are issued and published by God's *command*, and they bear the impress of the royal style which carries omnipotence about it. Not only the precepts but the promises also are commanded of the Lord, and so are all the teachings of Scripture. It is not left to our choice whether we will accept them or no ; they are issued by royal command, and are not to be questioned. Their characteristic is that they are like the Lord who has proclaimed them, they are the essence of justice and the soul of truth. God's word is righteous and cannot be impeached ; it is faithful and cannot be questioned ; it is true from the beginning, and it will be true unto the end.

Dwell upon that sweet word—*"very faithful."* What a mercy that we have a God to deal with who is scrupulously faithful, true to all the items and details of his promises, punctual to time, steadfast during all time. Well may we risk all upon a word which is " ever faithful, ever sure."

139. In the last two verses David spoke concerning his God and his law ; here he speaks of himself, and says, *"My zeal hath consumed me, because mine enemies have forgotten thy words"* : this was no doubt occasioned by his having so clear a sense of the admirable character of God's word. His zeal was like a fire burning

within his soul. The sight of man's forgetfulness of God acted as a fierce blast to excite the fire to a more vehement flame, and it blazed until it was ready to consume him. David could not bear that men should forget God's words. He was ready to forget himself, ay, to consume himself, because these men forgot God. The ungodly were David's enemies: his enemies because they hated him for his godliness; his enemies, because he abhorred them for their ungodliness. These men had gone so far in iniquity that they not only violated and neglected the commands of God, but they appeared actually to have forgotten them. This put David into a great heat; he burned with indignation. How dare they trample on sacred things! How could they utterly ignore the commands of God himself! He was astonished, and filled with holy anger.

140. *"Thy word is very pure."* It is truth distilled, holiness in its quintessence. In the word of God there is no admixture of error or sin. It is pure in its sense, pure in its language, pure in its spirit, pure in its influence, and all this to the very highest degree—*"very* pure." *"Therefore thy servant loveth it,"* which is a proof that he himself was pure in heart, for only those who are pure love God's word because of its purity. His heart was knit to the word because of its glorious holiness and truth. He admired it, delighted in it, sought to practise it, and longed to come under its purifying power.

141. *"I am small and despised: yet do not I forget thy precepts."* That fault of forgetfulness which he condemned in others (verse 139) could not be charged upon himself. His enemies made no account of him, regarded him as a man without power or ability, and therefore looked down upon him. He appears to accept the situation and humbly take the lowest room, but he carries God's word with him. How many a man has been driven to do some ill action in order to reply to the contempt of his enemies: to make himself conspicuous he has either spoken or acted in a manner which he could not justify. The beauty of the Psalmist's piety was that it was calm and well-balanced, and as he was not carried away by flattery, so was he not overcome by shame. If small, he the more jealously attended to the smaller duties; and if despised, he was the more in earnest to keep the despised commandments of God.

142. *"Thy righteousness is an everlasting righteousness."* Having in a previous verse ascribed righteousness to God, he now goes on to declare that that righteousness is unchanging and endures from age to age. This is the joy and glory of the saints, that what God is he always will be, and his mode of procedure towards the sons of men is immutable: having kept his promise, and dealt out justice among his people, he will do so world without end. Both the righteousnesses and the unrighteousnesses of man come to an end, but the righteousness of God is without end. *"And thy law is the truth."* As God is love, so his law is the truth, the very essence of truth, truth applied to ethics, truth in action, truth upon the judgment-seat. We hear great disputes about, "What is truth?" The holy Scriptures are the only answer to that question. Note, that they are not only true, but the truth itself. We may not say of them that they contain the truth, but that they are the truth: "thy law is the truth." There is nothing false about the law or preceptory part of Scripture. Those who are obedient thereto shall find that they are walking in a way consistent with fact, while those who act contrary thereto are walking in a vain show.

143. *"Trouble and anguish have taken hold on me."* This affliction may have arisen from his circumstances, or from the cruelty of his enemies, or from his own internal conflicts, but certain it is that he was the subject of much distress, a distress which apprehended him, and carried him away a captive to its power. His griefs, like fierce dogs, had taken hold upon him; he felt their teeth. He had double trouble: trouble without and anguish within, as the apostle Paul put it, "without were fightings and within were fears." *"Yet thy commandments are my delights."* Thus he became a riddle; troubled, and yet delighted; in anguish, and yet in pleasure. The child of God can understand this enigma, for well he knows that while he is cast down on account of what he sees within himself he is all the more lifted up by what he sees in the word. He is delighted with the commandments, although he is troubled because he cannot perfectly obey them. He finds abundant light in the commandments, and by the influence of that light he discovers and mourns over his own darkness. Only the man who is acquainted with the struggles of the spiritual life will understand the expression before us. Let the reader herein find a balance in which to weigh himself. Does he find even when he is begirt with

sorrow that it is a delightful thing to do the will of the Lord ? Does he find more
joy in being sanctified than sorrow in being chastised ? Then the spot of God's
children is upon him.

144. *"The righteousness of thy testimonies is everlasting."* First he had said
that God's testimonies were righteous, then that they were everlasting, and now
that their righteousness is everlasting. Thus he gives us a larger and more detailed
account of the word of God the longer he is engaged in writing upon it. The more
we say in praise of holy writ, the more we may say and the more we can say. God's
testimonies to man cannot be assailed, they are righteous from beginning to end ;
and though ungodly men have opposed the divine justice, especially in the plan
of salvation, they have always failed to establish any charge against the Most High.
Long as the earth shall stand long as there shall be a single intelligent creature
in the universe it will be confessed that God's plans of mercy are in all respects
marvellous proofs of his love of justice : even that he may be gracious Jehovah
will not be unjust. *"Give me understanding and I shall live."* This is a prayer
which he is constantly praying, that God would give him understanding. Here
he evidently considers that such a gift is essential to his living. To live without
understanding is not to live the life of a man, but to be dead while we live. Only
as we know and apprehend the things of God can we be said to enter into life. The
more the Lord teaches us to admire the eternal rightness of his word, and the more
he quickens us to the love of such rightness, the happier and the better we shall
be. As we love life, and seek many days that we may see good, it behoves us to
seek immortality in the everlasting word which liveth and abideth for ever, and
to seek good in that renewal of our entire nature which begins with the enlightenment
of the understanding and passes on to the regeneration of the entire man. Here
is our need of the Holy Spirit, the Lord and giver of life, and the guide of all the
quickened ones, who shall lead us into all truth. O for the visitations of his grace
at this good hour !

NOTES ON VERSES 137 TO 144.

S. Jerome, whom most of the mediævalists follow, explains *Tsaddi* as meaning *justice* or *righteousness*, which, however, is צֶדֶק, *tsedek*. But he is so far right that there is a play in this strophe on the sound of the initial letter, as in the case of *Gemol;* for the very first word, righteous, is צַדִּיק, *tsaddik*, and the whole scope of the strophe is the strong grasp which even the young and inexperienced soul can have of righteousness amidst the troubles of the world.—*Neale and Littledale.*

All these verses begin wth *Tzaddi*, the eighteenth letter of the Hebrew alphabet; 137, 142, 144, with some form of the word which we render *righteous*, or *righteousness;* each of the remainder with a wholly different word.—*William S. Plumer.*

Verse 137.—*"Righteous art thou, O Lord,"* etc. Here David, sore troubled with grief for the wickedness of his enemies, yea, tempted greatly to impatience and distrust, by looking to their prosperous estate, notwithstanding their so gross impiety, doth now show unto us a three-fold ground of comfort, which in this dangerous temptation upheld him. The first is, a consideration of that which God is in himself; namely, just and righteous: the second, a consideration of the equity of his word; the third, a view of his constant truth, declared in his working and doing according to his word. When we find ourselves tempted to distrust by looking to the prosperity of the wicked, let us look up to God, and consider his nature, his word, his works, and we shall find comfort.

"Righteous art thou." This is the first ground of comfort—a meditation of the righteousness of God's nature; he alters not with times, he changes not with persons, he is, alway and unto all, one and the same righteous and holy God. Righteousness is essential to him, it is himself; and he can no more defraud the godly of their promised comforts, nor let the wicked go unpunished in their sins, than he can deny himself to be God, which is impossible.—*William Cowper.*

Verse 137.—*"Righteous art thou, O Lord,"* etc. Essentially, originally, and of himself; naturally, immutably and universally, in all his ways and works of nature and grace; in his thoughts, purposes, counsels, and decrees; in all the dispensations of his providence; in redemption, in the justification of a sinner, in the pardon of sin, and in the gift of eternal life through Christ. *"And upright are thy judgments."* They are according to the rules of justice and equity. He refers to the precepts of the word, the doctrines of the gospel, as well as the judgments of God inflicted on wicked men, and all the providential dealings of God with his people, and also the final judgment.—*John Gill.*

Verse 137.—*"Righteous art thou, O Lord,"* etc. Here is much to keep the children of God in awe. The Lord is a righteous God: though they have found mercy and taken sanctuary in his grace, the Lord is impartial in his justice. God that did not spare the angels when they sinned, nor his Son when he was a sinner by imputation, will not spare you, though you are the dearly beloved of his soul: Prov. xi. 31. The sinful courses of God's children occasion bitterness enough; they never venture upon sin, but with great loss. If Paul give way to a little pride, God will humble him. If any give way to sin, their pilgrimage will be made uncomfortable. Eli falls into negligence and indulgence, then is the ark of God taken, his two sons are slain in battle, his daughter-in-law dies, he himself breaks his neck. Oh! the wonderful tragedies that sin works in the houses of the children of God! David, when he intermeddled with forbidden fruit, was driven from his palace, his concubines defiled, his own son slain; a great many calamities did light upon him. Therefore the children of God have cause to fear; for the Lord is a just God, and they will find it so. Here upon earth he hath reserved liberty to visit their iniquity with rods, and their transgression with scourges. I must press you to imitate God's righteousness: "If ye know that he is righteous, ye know that every one that doeth righteousness is born of him": 1 John ii. 29. You have a righteous God; and this part of his character you should copy out.—*Thomas Manton.*

Verse 137.—David's great care, when he was under the afflicting hand of God, was to clear the Lord of injustice. Oh! Lord, saith he, there is not the least show, spot, stain, blemish, or mixture of injustice, in all the afflictions thou hast brought upon me. I desire to take shame to myself, and to set to my seal, that the Lord is righteous, and that there is no injustice, no cruelty, nor no extremity in all that the Lord hath brought upon me. He sweetly and readily subscribes unto the righteousness of God in those sharp and smart afflictions that God exercised him with. "*Righteous art thou, O Lord, and upright are thy judgments.*" God's judgments are always just ; he never afflicts but in faithfulness. His will is the rule of justice ; and therefore a gracious soul dares not cavil nor question his proceedings. —*Thomas Brooks.*

Verse 137.—The hundred and thirty-seventh verse, like the twenty-fifth, is associated with the sorrows of an Imperial penitent.* When the deposed and captive Emperor Maurice was led out for execution by the usurper Phocas, his five sons were previously murdered one by one in his presence ; and at each fatal blow he patiently exclaimed, "*Righteous art thou, O Lord, and upright are thy judgments.*"— *Neale and Littledale.*

Verse 138.—"*Thy testimonies that thou hast commanded are righteous and very faithful.*" The force of this expression is much feebler than that of the original, which literally may be rendered, "Thou hast commanded righteousness, thy testimonies, and truth exceedingly." So the Septuagint hath it. Righteousness and truth were his testimonies ; the testimonies were one with his righteousness and truth. The English translation gives *the quality of the testimonies ;* the Hebrew gives *that which is commanded ;* as if we might say, Thou hast enjoined righteousness to be thy testimonies, and truth exceedingly.—*John Stephen.*

Verse 138.—"*Thy testimonies.*" The word of God is called his *testimony,* both because it testifies his will, which he will have us to do ; as also because it testifies unto men truly what shall become of them, whether good or evil. Men by nature are curious to know their end, rather than careful to mend their life ; and for this cause seek answers where they never get good : but if they would know, let me go to the word and testimony ; they need not to seek any other oracle. If the word of God testify good things unto them, they have cause to rejoice ; if otherwise it witnesseth evil unto them, let them haste to prevent it, or else it will assuredly overtake them.—*William Cowper.*

Verse 138.—"*Righteous and very faithful.*" Literally, "faithfulness exceedingly." Harsh and severe as they may seem, they are all thoroughly for man's highest good.—*William Kay.*

Verse 139.—"*My zeal hath consumed me.*" "*Zeal*" is a high degree of love ; and when the object of that love is ill treated, it venteth itself in a mixture of grief and indignation which are sufficient to wear and "consume" the heart. This will be the case where men rightly conceive of that dishonour which is continually done to God by creatures whom he hath made and redeemed. But never could the verse be uttered with such fulness of truth and propriety by any one as by the Son of God, who had such a sense of his Father's glory, and of man's sin, as no person else ever had. And, accordingly, when his zeal had exerted itself in purging the temple, St. John tells us, "his disciples remembered that it was written, The zeal of thine house hath eaten me up." The place where it is so written is Psalm lxix. 9, and the passage is exactly parallel to this before us.— *George Horne.*

Verse 139.—"*My zeal hath consumed me,*" etc. Zeal is the heat or intension of the affections ; it is a holy warmth, whereby our love and anger are drawn out to the utmost for God, and his glory. Now, our love to God and his ways, and our hatred of wickedness, should be increased, because of ungodly men. Cloudy and dark colours in a table, make those that are fresh and lively to appear more beautiful ; others' sin should make God and godliness more amiable in thine eyes. Thy heart should take fire by striking on such cold flints. David by a holy antiperistasis did kindle from others' coldness : "*My zeal hath consumed me, because mine enemies have forgotten thy words.*" Cold blasts make a fire to flame the higher, and burn the hotter.—*George Swinnock.*

Verse 139.—"*My zeal hath consumed me.*" The fire of zeal, like the fire which consumed Solomon's sacrifice, cometh down from heaven ; and true zealots are not those salamanders that always live in the fire of hatred and contention ; but seraphims, burning with the spiritual fire of divine love. And there true zeal inflames the desires and affections of the soul. If it be true zeal, then tract of time, multitude of discouragements, falseness of men deserting the cause, strength of oppositions, will not tire out a man's spirit. Zeal makes men resolute, difficulties are but whetstones to their fortitude, it steels men's spirits with an undaunted resolution.

---

* Gibbon. Decline and Fall ; ch. xlvi.

This was the zeal that burned in the disciples (Luke xxiv.), that consumed David here, and dried up the very marrow of Christ: John ii. 17.—*Abraham Wright.*

Verse 139.—*"My zeal hath consumed me."* There are divers kinds of zeal: there is a zeal of the world, there is a zeal of the flesh, there is a zeal of false religion, there is a zeal of heresy, and there is a zeal of the true word of God. First, we see the zeal of the world maketh men to labour day and night to get a transitory thing. The zeal of the flesh tormenteth men's minds early and late for a momentary pleasure. The zeal of heresy maketh men travel and compass sea and land, for the maintaining and increasing of their opinion. Thus we see every man is eaten up with some kind of zeal. The drunkard is consumed with drunkenness, the whore-monger is spent with his whoredom, the heretic is eaten with heresies. Oh, how ought this to make us ashamed, who are so little eaten, spent, and consumed with the zeal of the word! And so much the rather, because godly zeal leaveth in us an advantage and a recompence, which the worldly and carnally zealous men have not. For when they have spent all the strength of their bodies, and powers of their mind, they have no gain or comfort left, but torment of conscience; and when they are outwardly spent, they are inwardly never the better: whereas the godly being concerned for a good thing, and eaten up with the zeal of God's glory, have this notable privilege and profit, that howsoever their outward man perisheth and decayeth, yet their inward man is still refreshed and nourished to everlasting life. Oh, what a benefit it is to be eaten up with the love and zeal of a good thing!—*Richard Greenham.*

Verse 139.—*"Have forgotten thy words."* A proper phrase to set forth those in the bosom of the visible church who do not wholly deny and reject the word and rule of Scripture, but yet live on as though they had forgotten it: they do not observe it; as if God had never spoken any such thing, or given them any such rule. They that reject and condemn such things as the word enforceth, surely do not remember to do them.—*Thomas Manton.*

Verse 140.—*"Thy word is very pure."* In the original, "tried, refined, purified like gold in the furnace," absolutely perfect, without the dross of vanity and fallibility, which runs through human writings. The more we try the promises, the surer we shall find them. Pure gold is so fixed, that Boerhaave informs us of an ounce of it set in the eye of a glass furnace for two months, without losing a single grain.—*George Horne.*

Verse 140.—*"Thy word is very pure; therefore,"* etc. The word of God is not only *"pure,"* free from all base admixture, but it is a *purifier;* it cleanses from sin and guilt every heart with which it comes into contact. "Now ye are clean," said Jesus Christ to his disciples, "by the word which I have spoken unto you": John xv. 3. It is this its pure quality combined with its tendency to purify every nature that yields to its holy influence, that endears it to every child of God. Here it is that he finds views of the divine character, those promises, those precepts, those representations of the deformity of sin, of the beauty of holiness, which lead him, above all things, to seek conformity to the divine image. A child of God in his best moments does not wish the word of God brought down to a level with his own imperfect character, but desires rather that his character may be gradually raised to a conformity to that blessed word. Because it is altogether pure, and because it tends to convey to those who make it their constant study a measure of its own purity, the child of God loves it, and delights to meditate in it day and night.—*John Morison.*

Verse 140.—*"Thy word is very pure."* Before I knew the word of God in spirit and in truth, for its great antiquity, its interesting narratives, its impartial biography, its pure morality, its sublime poetry, in a word, for its beautiful and wonderful variety, I preferred it to all other books; but since I have entered into its spirit, like the Psalmist, I love it above all things for its purity; and desire, whatever else I read, it may tend to increase my knowledge of the Bible, and strengthen my affection for its divine and holy truths.—*Sir William Jones,* 1746—1794.

Verse 140.—*"Thy word."* Let us refresh our minds and our memories with some of the Scripture adjuncts connected with "the word," and realize, in some degree at least, the manifold relations which it bears both to God and our souls. It is called "the word of Christ," because much of it was given by him, and it all bears testimony to him . . . . It is called "the word of his grace," because the glorious theme on which it loves to expatiate is *grace*, and especially grace as it is seen in Christ's dying love for sinful men. It is called ὁ λόγος τοῦ σταυροῦ, " the word of the cross " (1 Cor. i. 18), because in the crucifixion of the divine Redeemer we see eternal mercy in its brightest lustre. It is called " the word of the gospel," because it brings glad tidings of great joy to all nations. It is called " the word of the kingdom," because it holds out to all believers the hope of an everlasting kingdom of righteousness and peace. It is called " the word of salvation," because the purpose for which it was given is the salvation of sinners. It is called " the word of truth," because, as Chillingworth says, it has God for its author, salvation for its end, and truth without mixture of error for its contents. And we will only add, it is called " the word of life," because it reveals to a sinful, perishing world the doctrines of life and immortality.—*W. Graham, in "A Commentary on the First Epistle of John,"* 1857.

Verse 140.—*"Therefore thy servant loveth it."* Love in God is the fountain of all his benefits extended to us ; and love in man is the fountain of all our service and obedience to God. He loved us first to do us good ; and hereof it comes that we have grace to love him next to do him service. Love is such a duty that the want thereof cannot be excused in any ; for the poorest both may and should love God : yet without it all the rest thou canst do in his service is nothing ; nay, not if thou shouldst give thy goods to the poor, and offer thy body to be burned. Small sacrifices, flowing from faith and love, are welcome to him, where greater without these are but abomination to him. Proofs of both we have in the widow's mite and Cain's rich oblation ; whereof the one was rejected, the other received. Happy are we though we cannot say, " We have done as God commands," if out of a good heart we can say,—" We love to do what he commands."—*William Cowper.*

Verse 140.—*"Therefore thy servant loveth it."* Of all our grounds and reasons of love to the word of God, the most noble and excellent is to love the word for its purity. This showeth indeed that we are made partakers of the Divine nature : 2 Pet. i. 4. For I pray you mark, when we hate evil as evil, and love good as good, we have the same love and hatred that God hath. When once we come to love things because they are pure, it is a sign that we have the same love that God hath.— *Thomas Manton.*

Verse 140.—*"Thy servant loveth it."* Otherwise, indeed, the Psalmist would not have been the Lord's servant at all. But he glories in the title because he delights in the pure service.—*John Stephen.*

Verses 140, 141.—God's own utterance is indeed without spot, and therefore not to be carped at ; it is pure, fire-proved, noblest metal, therefore he loves it, and does not, though young and lightly esteemed, care for the remonstrances of his proud opponents who are older and more learned than himself.—*Franz Delitzsch.*

Verse 141.—*"I am small and despised,"* or, *I have been.* Some versions render it *young* ; as if it had respect to the time of his anointing by Samuel, when he was overlooked and despised in his father's family (1 Sam. xvi. 11, and xvii. 28) ; but the word here used is not expressive of age, but of state, condition, and circumstances ; and the meaning is, that he was little in his own esteem, and in the esteem of men, and was despised ; and that on account of religion, in which he was a type of Christ (Ps. xxii. 6, and Isa. liii. 3), and which is the common lot of good men, who are treated by the world as the filth of it, and the offscouring of all things.— *John Gill.*

Verse 141.—*"I am small."* They that love God may be reduced to a mean, low, and afflicted condition ; the Lord seeth it meet for divers reasons : 1. That they may know their happiness is not in this world, and so the more long for heaven, and delight in heavenly things. 2. It is necessary to cut off the provisions of the flesh and the fuel of their lusts. A rank soil breedeth weeds ; and when we sail with a full stream we are apt to be carried away with it. 3. That they may be more sensible of his displeasure against their sins and scandalous carriage by which they have dishonoured him, and provoked the pure eyes of his glory. 4. That they may learn to live upon the promises, and learn to exercise suffering graces ; especially dependence upon God, who can support us without a temporal, visible interest. 5. That God may convince the enemies that there is a people that do sincerely serve him, and not for carnal, selfish ends : Job i. 6. That his glory may be more seen in their deliverance ; and therefore, before God doth appear for his children, he bringeth them very low.—*Thomas Manton.*

Verse 141.—*"Small."* This applies to David in his early days of trouble and persecution. It is difficult to find any other individual to whom it is so suitable.—*James G. Murphy.*

Verse 141.—A notable example to the shame of them, that perhaps will serve and praise God in their prosperity, and when they are increased; but let affliction or want come, and then they have little heart to do it.—*Abraham Wright.*

Verse 141.—*"Yet do not I forget thy precepts."* God observeth what we do in our trouble: "If we have forgotten the name of our God, or stretched out our hands to a strange god; shall not God search this out? for he knoweth the secrets of the heart"; Ps. xliv. 20, 21. If we slacken our service to God, or fall off to any degree of apostasy, the Judge of hearts knoweth all: God knoweth whether we would have depraved and corrupt doctrine, worship, or ordinances; or whether we will faithfully adhere to him, to his word, and worship, and ordinances, whatever it cost us.

In our poor and despicable condition we see more cause to love the word than we did before; because we experience supports and comforts which we have thereby: "Knowing that tribulation worketh patience," etc. (Rom. v. 3); "For as the sufferings of Christ abound in us, so our consolation also aboundeth by Christ": 2 Cor. i. 5. God hath special consolations for his afflicted and despised people, and makes their consolation by Christ to run parallel with, and keep pace with, their sufferings for Christ.—*Thomas Manton.*

Verse 141.—*"Yet do not I forget thy precepts."* We see by experience that our affection leaves anything from the time it goes out of our remembrance. We cease to love when we cease to remember; but earnest love ever renews remembrance of that which is beloved. The first step of defection is to forget what God hath commanded, and what we are obliged in duty to do to him; and upon this easily follows the offending of God by our transgression. Such beasts as did not chew their cud, under the law were accounted unclean, and not meet to be sacrificed unto God: that was but a figure, signifying unto us that a man who hath received good things from God, and doth not think upon them, cannot feel the sweetness of them, and so cannot be thankful to God.—*William Cowper.*

Verse 142.—*"Thy righteousness is an everlasting righteousness."* Here the law of God is honoured by the additional encomium, that it is everlasting righteousness and truth; as if it had been said, that all other rules of life, with whatever attractions they may appear to be recommended, are but a shadow, which quickly vanishes away. The Psalmist, no doubt, indirectly contrasts the doctrine of the law with all the human precepts which were ever delivered, that he may bring all the faithful in subjection to it, since it is the school of perfect wisdom. There may be more of plausibility in the refined and subtle disquisitions of men; but there is in them nothing firm or solid at bottom, as there is in God's law. This firmness of the divine law he proves in the following verse from one instance—the continual comfort he found in it when grievously harassed with temptations. And the true test of the profit we have reaped from it is, when we oppose to all the distresses of whatever kind which may straiten us, the consolation derived from the word of God, that thereby all sadness may be effaced from our minds. David here expresses something more than he did in the preceding verse; for there he only said that he reverently served God, although from his rough and hard treatment he might seem to lose his labour; but now when distressed and tormented, he affirms that he finds in the law of God the most soothing delight, which mitigates all griefs, and not only tempers their bitterness, but also seasons them with a certain sweetness. Assuredly when this taste does not exist to afford us delight, nothing is more natural than for us to be swallowed up of sorrow.—*John Calvin.*

Verse 142.—*"Thy righteousness is an everlasting righteousness."* Not only righteous at the first giving out, but righteous in all ages and times; and should we slight this rule that will hold for ever? In the world new lords, new laws; men vary and change their designs and purposes; privileges granted to-day may be repealed to-morrow; but this word will hold true for ever. Our justification by Christ is irrevocable; that part of righteousness is everlasting. Be sure you are justified now upon terms of the gospel, and you shall be justified for ever: your forgiveness is an everlasting forgiveness, and your peace is an everlasting peace: "I will remember their sin no more": Jer. xxxi. 34. So the other righteousness of sanctification, it is for ever; approve yourselves to God now, and you will approve yourselves at the day of judgment.—*Thomas Manton.*

Verse 142.—*"Thy righteousness is an everlasting righteousness,"* etc. The original is better expressed thus, "Thy righteousness is righteousness everlastingly, and thy law is truth." So the Septuagint. The English translation expresses the *perpetuity* of the righteousness, the original expresses also the *character* of it. . . . God's righteousness is essentially and eternally righteousness. The expressions are absolute ; there is only this righteousness, and only this truth.—*John Stephen.*

Verse 142.—*"Thy law is the truth."* 1. It is the *chief* truth. There is some truth in the laws of men and the writings of men, even of heathens ; but they are but sorry fragments and scraps of truth, that have escaped since the fall. 2. It is the *only* truth ; that is, the only revelation of the mind of God that you can build upon. It is the rule of truth. 3. It is the *pure* truth. In it there is nothing but the truth, without the mixture of falsehood ; every part is true as truth itself. It is true in the promises, threatenings, doctrines, histories, precepts, prohibitions. 4. It is *the whole* truth. It containeth all things necessary for the salvation of those that yield up themselves to be instructed by it.—*Thomas Manton.*

Verse 143.—*"Trouble and anguish have taken hold on me : yet thy commandments are my delights."* This is strange, that in the midst of anguish David had *delight :* but indeed the sweetness of God's word is best perceived under the bitterness of the cross. The joy of Christ and the joy of the world cannot consist together. A heart delighted with worldly joy cannot feel the consolations of the Spirit ; the one of these destroys the other ; but in sanctified trouble, the comforts of God's word are felt and perceived in a most sensible manner. Many a time hath David protested this delight of his in the word of God ; and truly it is a great argument of godliness, when men come not only to reverence it, but to love it, and delight in it. Let this be considered by those unhappy men who hear it of custom, and count it but a weariness.—*Abraham Wright.*

Verse 143.—*"Trouble and anguish have taken hold on me,"* or *"found me,"* etc. We need not take pains, as many do, "to find trouble and anguish ; " for they will, one day, "find us." In that day the revelations of God must be to us instead of all worldly "delights" and pleasures, which will then have forsaken us ; and how forlorn and desolate will be our state if we should have no other delights, no other pleasures, to succeed them, and to accompany us into eternity ! Let our study be then in the Scriptures, if we expect our comfort in them in time to come.—*George Horne.*

Verse 143.—*"Trouble and anguish have taken hold on me."* You may conceive a bold figure here, as if Trouble and Anguish were being sent out against the helpless sons of men. These, like enemies, were going round. Instead of seizing upon the wicked, they had found the righteous man. So it was by the ordering of God. I suppose many of us have remarked, that the believer is never long at ease. He is in the world ; he is in the flesh ; there is indwelling sin ; there are enemies around ; there is the great enemy ; besides all this, the Lord, for wise purposes, hides his face. Then the believer is in trouble and anguish.—*John Stephen.*

Verse 143.—*"Have taken hold on me."* Hebrew, *found me.* Like dogs tracking out a wild beast hiding or fleeing.—*A. R. Fausset.*

Verse 143.—*"Thy commandments are my delights."* Delight in moral things (saith Aquinas) is the rule by which we may judge of men's goodness or badness. *Delectatio est quies voluntatis in bono.* Men are good and bad, as the objects of their delight are : they are good who delight in good things, and they are evil who delight in evil things.—*Thomas Manton.*

Verse 144.—*"The righteousness of thy testimonies is everlasting."* Thy *moral law* was not made for one people, or for one particular time ; it is as imperishable as thy nature, and of endless obligation. It is that law by which all the children of Adam shall be judged. *"Give me understanding."* To know and practise it. *"And I shall live."* Shall glorify thee, and live eternally ; not for the *merit* of having done it, but because thou didst fulfil the work of the law in my heart, having saved me from condemnation by it.—*Adam Clarke.*

Verse 144.—*"Give me understanding, and I shall live."* I read it in connection with the preceding clause ; for although David desires to have his mind enlightened by God, yet he does not conceive of any other way by which he was to obtain an enlightened understanding than by his profiting aright in the study of the law. Further, he here teaches that men cannot, properly speaking, be said to live when they are destitute of the light of heavenly wisdom ; and as the end for which men are created is not that, like swine or asses, they may stuff their bellies, but that they may exercise themselves in the knowledge and service of God, when they turn away from such employment their life is worse than a thousand deaths. David therefore protests that for him to live was not merely to be fed with meat and drink, and to enjoy earthly comforts, but to aspire after a better life, which he could not do save under the guidance of faith. This is a very necessary warning ; for although it is universally acknowledged that man is born with this distinction, that he excels the lower animals in intelligence, yet the great bulk of mankind, as if with deliberate purpose, stifle whatever light God pours into their understandings. I indeed admit that all men desire to be sharp-witted ; but how few aspire to heaven, and consider that the fear of God is the beginning of wisdom. Since, then, meditation upon the celestial life is buried by earthly care, men do nothing else than plunge into the grave, so that while living to the world, they die to God. Under the term life, however, the prophet denotes the utmost he could wish. Lord, as if he had said, although I am already dead, yet if thou art pleased to illumine my mind with the knowledge of heavenly truth, this grace alone will be sufficient to revive me.—*John Calvin.*

Verse 144.—*"Give me understanding, and I shall live."* The saving knowledge of God's testimonies is the only way to live. There is a threefold life. 1. Life natural. 2. Life spiritual, and, 3. Life eternal. In all these considerations may the point be made good.

First. Life is taken for the *life of nature,* or the life of the body, or life temporal, called " this life " in Scripture : 1 Cor. xv. 19 ; 1 Tim. iv. 8. Life is better preserved in a way of obedience than by evil-doing ; that provoketh God to cast us off, and exposes us to dangers. It is not in the power of the world to make us live or die a day sooner or longer than God pleaseth. If God will make us happy, they cannot make us miserable : therefore, *"Give me understanding, and I shall live" ;* that is, lead a comfortable and happy life for the present. Prevent sin, and you prevent danger. Obedience is the best way to preserve life temporal : as great a paradox as it seems to the world, it is a Scripture truth, " Keep my commandments, and live " (Prov. iv. 4) ; and, " Take fast hold of instruction ; let her not go : keep her ; for she is thy life " (verse 13) ; and, " Length of days is in her right hand ; and in her left hand riches and honour " (Prov. iii. 16) ; and, " She is a tree of life " (verse 18). The knowledge and practice of the word is the only means to live comfortably and happily here, as well as for ever hereafter.

Secondly. *Life spiritual ;* that is twofold, the life of justification, and the life of sanctification.

1. The life of justification : " The free gift came upon all men unto justification of life " : Rom. v. 18. He is dead, not only on whom the hangman hath done his work, but also he on whom the judge hath passed sentence, and the law pronounceth him dead. In this sense we were all passed, and justification is called justification to life ; there is no living in this sense without knowledge : " By his knowledge shall my righteous servant justify many " : Isa. liii. 11. We live by faith, and faith cometh by hearing, and hearing doeth no good unless the Lord giveth understanding ; as meats nourish not unless received and digested.

2. The life of sanctification : " And you hath he quickened, who were dead in trespasses and sins " : Eph. ii. 1. And men live not properly till they live the life of grace ; they live a false, counterfeit life, not a blessed, happy, certain, and true life. Now this life is begun and carried on by saving knowledge : *"*The new man which is renewed in knowledge*"*: Col. iii. 10. Again, men are said to be " alienated from the life of God through the ignorance that is in them : " Eph. iv. 18. They that are ignorant are dead in sin : life spiritual cometh by knowledge. Hence beginneth the change of the inward man, and thenceforth we live. *"Give me understanding,"* ut vere in te vivam, that the true life begun in me may grow and increase daily, but never be quenched by sin.

Thirdly. *Life everlasting,* or our blessed estate in heaven. So it is said of the saints departed, they all live unto God : Luke xx. 38. And this is called the water of life, the tree of life, the crown of life ; properly this is life. What is the present life in comparison of everlasting life ? The present life, it is *mors vitalis,* a living death ; or *mortalis vita,* a dying life, a kind of death ; it is always *in fluxu,* like a stream : it runneth from us as fast as it cometh to us : " He fleeth also as a shadow and continueth not " : Job. xiv. 2. We die as fast as we live : it differeth but as the point from the line where it terminateth. It is not one and the same, no permanent thing; it is like the shadow of a star in a flowing stream. Its contentments are base and low, called " the life of thine hand " : Isa. lvii. 10. It is patched up of several creatures, fain to ransack the storehouses of nature to support a ruinous fabric. And compare it with the life of grace here, it doth not exempt us from sin, nor miseries. Our capacities are narrow. We are full of fears, and doubts, and dangers ; but in the life of glory we shall neither sin nor sorrow any more. This is meant here : *"The righteousness of thy testimonies is everlasting: give me understanding and I shall live " ;* it is chiefly meant of the life of glory. This is the fruit of saving knowledge, when we so know God and Christ as to come to God by him.—*Thomas Manton.*

Verse 144.—*"I shall live."* I shall be kept from those sins which deserve and bring death.—*Matthew Pool.*

EXPOSITION OF VERSES 145 TO 152.

I CRIED with *my* whole heart ; hear me, O LORD : I will keep thy statutes.

146 I cried unto thee ; save me, and I shall keep thy testimonies.

147 I prevented the dawning of the morning, and cried : I hoped in thy word.

148 Mine eyes prevent the *night* watches, that I might meditate in thy word.

149 Hear my voice according unto thy lovingkindness : O LORD, quicken me according to thy judgment.

150 They draw nigh that follow after mischief : they are far from thy law.

151 Thou *art* near, O LORD ; and all thy commandments *are* truth.

152 Concerning thy testimonies, I have known of old that thou hast founded them for ever.

This section is given up to memories of prayer. The Psalmist describes the time and the manner of his devotions, and pleads with God for deliverance from his troubles. He who has been with God in the closet will find God with him in the furnace. If we have cried we shall be answered. Delayed answers may drive us to importunity ; but we need not fear the ultimate result, since God's promises are not uncertain, but are " founded for ever." The whole passage shows us : How he prayed (verse 145). What he prayed for (146). When he prayed (147). How long he prayed (148). What he pleaded (149). What happened (150). How he was rescued (151). What was his witness as to the whole matter (152).

145.—"*I cried with my whole heart.*" His prayer was a sincere, plaintive, painful, natural utterance, as of a creature in pain. We cannot tell whether at all times he used his voice when he thus cried ; but we are informed of something which is of much greater consequence, he cried with his heart. Heart-cries are the essence of prayer. He mentions the unity of his heart in this holy engagement. His whole soul pleaded with God, his entire affections, his united desires all went out towards the living God. It is well when a man can say as much as this of his prayers : it is to be feared that many never cried to God with their whole heart in all their lives. There may be no beauty of elocution about such prayers, no length of expression, no depth of doctrine, nor accuracy of diction ; but if the whole heart be in them they will find their way to the heart of God. "*Hear me, O LORD.*" He desires of Jehovah that his cries may not die upon the air, but that God may have respect to them. True supplicants are not satisfied with the exercise itself, they have an end and object in praying, and they look out for it. If God does not hear prayer we pray in vain. The term " hear " is often used in Scripture to express attention and consideration. In one sense God hears every sound that is made on earth, and every desire of every heart ; but David meant much more ; he desired a kindly, sympathetic hearing, such as a physician gives to his patient when he tells him his pitiful story. He asked that the Lord would draw near, and listen with friendly ear to the voice of his complaint, with the view of pitying him and helping him. Observe, that his whole-hearted prayer goes to the Lord alone ; he has no second hope or help. " Hear me, O LORD," is the full range of his petition and expectation. "*I will keep thy statutes.*" He could not expect the Lord to hear him if he did not hear the Lord, neither would it be true that he prayed with his whole heart unless it was manifest that he laboured with all his might to be obedient to the divine will. His object in seeking deliverance was that he might be free to fulfil his religion and carry out every ordinance of the Lord. He would be a free man that he might be at liberty to serve the Lord. Note well that a holy resolution goes well with an importunate supplication : David is determined to be holy, his whole heart goes with that resolve as well as with his prayers. He will keep God's statutes in his memory, in his affections, and in his actions. He will not wilfully neglect or violate any one of the divine laws.

146.—*"I cried unto thee."* Again he mentions that his prayer was unto God alone. The sentence imports that he prayed vehemently, and very often ; and that it had become one of the greatest facts of his life that he cried unto God. *"Save me."* This was his prayer ; very short, but very full. He needed saving, none but the Lord could save him, to him he cried, " Save me " from the dangers which surround me, from the enemies that pursue me, from the temptations which beset me, from the sins which accuse me. He did not multiply words, and men never do so when they are in downright earnest. He did not multiply objects, and men seldom do so when they are intent upon the one thing needful : " save me " was his one and only prayer. *"And I shall keep thy testimonies."* This was his great object in desiring salvation, that he might be able to continue in a blameless life of obedience to God, that he might be able to believe the witness of God, and also to become himself a witness for God. It is a great thing when men seek salvation for so high an end. He did not ask to be delivered that he might sin with impunity ; his cry was to be delivered from sin itself. He had vowed to keep the statutes or laws, here he resolves to keep the testimonies or doctrines, and so to be sound of head as well as clean of hand. Salvation brings all these good things in its train. David had no idea of a salvation which would allow him to live in sin, or abide in error : he knew right well that there is no saving a man while he abides in disobedience and ignorance.

147.—*"I prevented the dawning of the morning, and cried."* He was up before the sun, and began his pleadings before the dew began to leave the grass. Whatever is worth doing is worth doing speedily. This is the third time that he mentions that he cried. He cried, and cried, and cried again. His supplications had become so frequent, fervent, and intense, that he might hardly be said to be doing anything else from morning to night but crying unto his God. So strong was his desire after salvation that he could not rest in his bed ; so eagerly did he seek it that at the first possible moment he was on his knees. *"I hoped in thy word."* Hope is a very powerful means of strengthening us in prayer. Who would pray if he had no hope that God would hear him ? Who would not pray when he has a good hope of a blessed issue to his entreaties ? His hope was fixed upon God's word, and this is a sure anchorage, because God is true, and in no case has he ever run back from his promise, or altered the thing that has gone forth from his mouth. He who is diligent in prayer will never be destitute of hope. Observe that as the early bird gets the worm, so the early prayer is soon refreshed with hope.

148.—*"Mine eyes prevent the night watches."* Or rather, *the watches.* Before the watchman cried the hour, he was crying to God. He did not need to be informed as to how the hours were flying, for every hour his heart was flying towards heaven. He began the day with prayer, and he continued in prayer through the watches of the day, and the watches of the night. The soldiers changed guard, but David did not change his holy occupation. Specially, however, at night did he keep his eyes open, and drive away sleep, that he might maintain communion with his God. He worshipped on from watch to watch as travellers journey from stage to stage. *"That I might meditate in thy word."* This had become meat and drink to him. Meditation was the food of his hope, and the solace of his sorrow : the one theme upon which his thoughts ran was that blessed " word " which he continually mentions, and in which his heart rejoices. He preferred study to slumber ; and he learned to forego his necessary sleep for much more necessary devotion. It is instructive to find meditation so constantly connected with fervent prayer : it is the fuel which sustains the flame. How rare an article is it in these days.

149.—*"Hear my voice according unto thy lovingkindness."* Men find it very helpful to use their voices in prayer ; it is difficult long to maintain the intensity of devotion unless we hear ourselves speak ; hence David at length broke through his silence, arose from his quiet meditations, and began crying with voice as well as heart unto the Lord his God. Note, that he does not plead his own deservings, nor for a moment appeal for payment of a debt on account of merit ; he takes the free-grace way, and puts it, " according unto thy lovingkindness." When God hears prayer according to his lovingkindness he overlooks all the imperfections of the prayer, he forgets the sinfulness of the offerer, and in pitying love he grants the desire though the suppliant be unworthy. It is according to God's lovingkindness to answer speedily, to answer frequently, to answer abundantly, yea, exceeding abundantly above all that we ask or even think. Lovingkindness is one of the sweetest words in our language. Kindness has much in it that is most precious, but lovingkindness is doubly dear ; it is the cream of kindness. *"O LORD, quicken me according to thy judgment."* This is another of David's wise and ardent prayers. He first cried, " Save me ; " then, " Hear me ; " and now, " Quicken me." This is often the very best way of delivering us from trouble,—to give us more life that we may escape from death ; and to add more strength to that life that we may not be overloaded with its burdens. Observe, that he asks to receive quickening according to God's judgment, that is, in such a way as should be consistent with infinite wisdom and prudence. God's methods of communicating greater vigour to our spiritual life are exceedingly wise ; it would probably be in vain for us to attempt to understand them ; and it will be our wisdom to wish to receive grace, not according to our notion of how it should come to us, but according to God's heavenly method of bestowing it. It is his prerogative to make alive as well as to kill, and that sovereign act is best left to his infallible judgment. Hath he not already given us to have life more and more abundantly ? " Wherein he hath abounded toward us in all wisdom and prudence."

150.—*"They draw nigh that follow after mischief."* He could hear their footfalls close behind him. They are not following him for his benefit, but for his hurt, and therefore the sound of their approach is to be dreaded. They are not prosecuting a good object, but persecuting a good man. As if they had not enough mischief in their own hearts, they are hunting after more. He sees them going a steeple-chase over hedge and ditch in order to bring mischief to himself, and he points them out to God, and entreats the Lord to fix his eyes upon them, and deal with them to their confusion. They were already upon him, and he was almost in their grip, and therefore he cries the more earnestly. *"They are far from thy law."* A mischievous life cannot be an obedient one. Before these men could become persecutors of David they were obliged to get away from the restraints of God's law. They could not hate a saint and yet love the law. Those who keep God's law neither do harm to themselves nor to others. Sin is the greatest mischief in the world. David mentions this to the Lord in prayer, feeling some kind of comfort in the fact that those who hated him hated God also, and found it needful to get away from God before they could be free to act their cruel parts towards himself. When we know that our enemies are God's enemies, and ours because they are his, we may well take comfort to ourselves.

151. *"Thou art near, O LORD."* Near as the enemy might be, God was nearer : this is one of the choicest comforts of the persecuted child of God. The Lord is near to hear our cries, and to speedily afford us succour. He is near to chase away our enemies, and to give us rest and peace. *"And all thy commandments are truth."* God neither commands a lie, nor lies in his commands. Virtue is truth in action, and this is what God commands. Sin is falsehood in action, and this is what God forbids. If all God's commands are truth, then the true man will be glad to keep near to them, and therein he will find the true God near him. This sentence will be the persecuted man's protection from the false hearts that seek to do him mischief: God is near and God is true, therefore his people are safe. If at any time we fall into danger through keeping the commands of God we need not suppose that we have acted unwisely : we may, on the contrary, be quite sure that we are in the right way ; for God's precepts are right and true. It is for this very reason that wicked men assail us : they hate the truth, and therefore hate those who do the truth. Their opposition may be our consolation ; while God's presence upon our side is our glory and delight.

152. *"Concerning thy testimonies, I have known of old that thou hast founded them for ever."* David found of old that God had founded them of old, and that they would stand firm throughout all ages. It is a very blessed thing to be so early taught of God that we know substantial doctrines even from our youth. Those who think that David was a young man when he wrote this Psalm will find it rather difficult to reconcile this verse with the theory ; it is much more probable that he was now grown grey, and was looking back upon what he had known long before. He knew at the very first that the doctrines of God's word were settled before the world began, that they had never altered, and never could by any possibility be altered. He had begun by building on a rock, by seeing that God's testimonies

were " founded," that is, grounded, laid as foundations, settled and established ; and that with a view to all the ages that should come, during all the changes that should intervene. It was because David knew this that he had such confidence in prayer, and was so importunate in it. It is sweet to plead immutable promises with an immutable God. It was because of this that David learned to hope : a man cannot have much expectation from a changing friend, but he may well have confidence in a God who cannot change. It was because of this that he delighted in being near the Lord, for it is a most blessed thing to keep up close intercourse with a Friend who never varies. Let those who choose follow at the heels of the modern school and look for fresh light to break forth which will put the old light out of countenance ; we are satisfied with the truth which is old as the hills and as fixed as the great mountains. Let " cultured intellects " invent another god, more gentle and effeminate than the God of Abraham ; we are well content to worship Jehovah, who is eternally the same. Things everlastingly established are the joy of established saints. Bubbles please boys, but men prize those things which are solid and substantial, with a foundation and a bottom to them which will bear the test of ages.

NOTES ON VERSES 145 TO 152.

Verse 145.—"I cried with my whole heart." As a man cries most loudly when he cries with all his mouth opened ; so a man prays most effectually when he prays with his whole heart. Neither doth this speech declare only the fervency of his affection ; but it imports also that it was a great thing which he sought from God. And thou, when thou prayest, pray for great things ; for things enduring, not for things perishing : pray not for silver, it is but rust ; nor for gold, it is but metal ; nor for possessions, they are but earth. Such prayer ascends not to God. He is a great God, and esteems himself dishonoured when great things with great affection are not sought from him.—*William Cowper*

Verse 145.—"I cried with my whole heart." In all your closet duties God looks first and most to your *hearts :* " My son, give me thine heart " : Prov. xxiii. 26. It is not a piece, it is not a corner of the heart, that will satisfy the Maker of the heart ; the heart is a treasure, a bed of spices, a royal throne wherein he delights. God looks not at the elegancy of your prayers, to see how neat they are ; nor yet at the geometry of your prayers, to see how long they are ; nor yet at the arithmetic of your prayers, to see how many they are ; nor yet at the music of your prayers, nor yet at the sweetness of your voice, nor yet at the logic of your prayers ; but at the sincerity of your prayers, how hearty they are. There is no prayer acknowledged, approved, accepted, recorded, or rewarded by God, but that wherein the heart is sincerely and wholly. The true mother would not have the child divided. God loves a broken and a contrite heart, so he loathes a divided heart : Ps. li. 17 ; James i. 8. God neither loves halting nor halving ; he will be served truly and totally. The royal law is, " Thou shalt love and serve the Lord thy God with all they heart, and with all thy soul." Among the heathens, when the beasts were cut up for sacrifice, the first thing the priest looked upon was the heart, and if the heart was naught, the sacrifice was rejected. Verily, God rejects all those sacrifices wherein the heart is not. Prayer without the heart is but as sounding brass or a tinkling cymbal. Prayer is only lovely and weighty, as the heart is in it, and no otherwise. It is not lifting up of the voice, nor the wringing of the hands, nor the beating of the breasts, nor an affected tone, nor studied motions, nor seraphical expressions, but the strrings of the heart, that God looks at in prayer. God hears no more than the heart speaks. If the heart be dumb, God will certainly be deaf. No prayer takes with God, but that which is the travail of the heart.—*Thomas Brooks.*

Verse 146.—"I cried unto thee." The distressed soul expresses itself in strong cries and tears. Of old they cried unto the Lord, and he heard them in their distress. So Israel at the Red Sea. The men of the Reformation thus expressed themselves in earnest prayer, and found relief. Luther at the Diet of Worms, when remanded for another day, spent the long night in the loud utterance of prayer that he might appear for his Lord before an august earthly assembly. Our reading of the covenanting times will remind us of many instances of the same. We may think of John Welch, going into his garden night after night, in a night covering, and crying to the Lord to grant him Scotland. The expression of prayer, however, is manifold as the frame of the spirit. Intense feeling will beget strong cries in prayer ; but prayer that is uttered under realizing views of our gracious God will be mild, and often delivered as it were in whispers. So was Alexander Peden accustomed to pray, as if he had been engaged in calm converse with a friend. . . . . But when the feeling is intense, when wrath lies heavy upon us, when danger is apprehended as near, when the Lord is conceived to be at a distance, or when there is eager desire after immediate attainment—in all these cases there will be the strong cries. Such seems to have been the state of the Psalmist's mind when he poured forth the expressive utterance of this part.—*John Stephen.*

*Verse 146.—*Brief as are the petitions, the whole compass of language could not make them more comprehensive. *"Hear me."* The Soul is in earnest, *the whole heart* is engaged in the " cry." *"Save me "*—includes a sinner's whole need— pardon, acceptance, access, holiness, strength, comfort, heaven,—all in one word— Christ. The way of access *is not indeed mentioned* in these short ejaculations. But *it is always implied* in every moment's approach and address to the throne of grace. *"Hear me "* in the name of my all-prevailing Advocate. *"Save me "* through him, whose name is Jesus the Saviour.—*Charles Bridges.*

Verse 146.—*"I cried unto thee."* A crying prayer pierces the depths of heaven. We read not a word that Moses spake, but God was moved by his cry. Exod. xiv. 15. It means not an obstreperous noise, but melting moans of heart. Yet sometimes the sore and pinching necessities and distresses of spirit extort even vocal cries not displeasant to the inclined ears of God. " I cried unto God with my voice," says David, " and he heard me out of his holy hill " : Ps. iii. 4. And this encourages to a fresh onset : " Hearken unto the voice of my cry, my King, and my God " : Ps. v. 2. " Give ear unto my cry : hold not thy peace at my tears " : Ps. xxxix. 12. Another time he makes the cave echo with his cries. " I cried, I cried. Attend unto my cry, for I am brought very low."—*Samuel Lee* (1625—1691), *in "The Morning Exercises."*

Verse 146.—*"I cried unto thee ; save me."* In our troubles, we must have recourse to God, and sue to him by prayer and supplication for help and deliverance in due time ; because he is the author of our trouble. In mercies and afflictions, our business lieth not with men, but God ; by humble dealing with him we stop wrath at the fountain-head : he that bindeth us must loose us ; he is at the upper end of causes, and whoever be the instruments of our trouble, and how malicious soever, God is the party with whom we are to make our peace ; for he hath the absolute disposal of all creatures, and will have us to acknowledge the dominion of his providence and our dependence upon him. In treaties of peace between two warring parties, the address is not made to private soldiers, but to their chief : " The Lord hath taken away," saith Job ; " When he giveth quietness, who then can make trouble ? " Job. xxxiv. 29.—*Thomas Manton.*

Verse 146.—*"Save me, and I shall keep thy testimonies."* The servants of God regard life itself as chiefly desirable on account of the opportunity which it affords for serving God : " *Save me that I might keep thy testimonies,*" is the prayer of the believer in the day of trouble and conflict. " To me to live," says he, " is Christ, and to die is gain." How unlike is this to the wicked ! Their whole desire in the day of trouble is expended on the wish to escape calamity ; they have no desire to be delivered from sin, no wish to be conformed to God !—*John Morison.*

Verse 146.—*"Save me."* From my sins, my corruptions, my temptations, all the hindrances that lie in my way, that I may *"keep thy testimonies."* We must cry for salvation, not that we may have the ease and comfort of it, but that we may have the opportunity of serving God the more cheerfully.—*Matthew Henry.*

Verse 146.—God hears us, that we should hear him.—*Thomas Manton.*

Verse 147.—*"I prevented the dawning of the morning."* The manner of speech is to be marked. He saith he prevented the morning watch, thereby declaring that he lived, as it were, in a strife with time, careful that it should nor overrun him. He knew that time posts away, and in running by wearieth man to dust and ashes. But David pressed to get before it, by doing some good in it, before that it should spur away from him. And this care which David had of every day, alas, how may it make them ashamed who have no care of a whole life ! He was afraid to lose a day ; they take no thought to lose months and years without doing good in them : yea, having spent the three ages of their life in vanity and licentiousness, scarce will they consecrate their old and decrepit age to the Lord.—*William Cowper.*

Verse 147.—*"I prevented the dawning of the morning,"* etc. Those that make a business of prayer will use great vigilancy and diligence therein. I say, that make a business of prayer ; others that use it as a compliment and customary formality, will not be thus affected ; they do it as a thing by-the-by, or a work that might well be spared, and do not look upon it as a necessary duty ; but if a man's heart be in it, he will be early at work, and follow it close, morning and night : his business is to maintain communion with God, his desires will not let him sleep, and he gets up early to be calling upon God. " But unto thee have I cried, O Lord : and in the morning shall my prayer prevent thee." Ps. lxxxviii. 13. Thus will good men even break their sleep to give themselves to prayer, and calling upon the name of God.—*Thomas Manton.*

Verse 147.—*"I prevented the dawning of the morning."* It is a grievous thing if the rays of the rising sun find thee lazy and ashamed in thy bed, and the bright light strike on eyes still weighed down with slumbering sloth. Knowest thou not, O man, that thou owest the daily first-fruits of thy heart and voice to God ? Thou hast a daily harvest, a daily revenue. The Lord Jesus remained all night in prayer, not that he needed its help, but putting an example before thee to imitate. He spent the night in prayer for thee, that thou mightest learn how to ask for thyself. Give him again, therefore, what he paid for thee.—*Ambrose.*

Verse 147.—"*I prevented the dawning of the morning.*" David was a good husband, up early at it : at night he was late at this duty : " At midnight will I rise to give thanks unto thee " : verse 62. This surely was his meaning when he said he should dwell in the house of the Lord for ever ; he would be ever in the house of prayer. . . . . I wish that when I first open my eyes in the morning, I may then, in soul ejaculatory prayer, open my heart to my God, that at night prayer may make my bed soft, and lay my pillow easy ; that in the day-time prayer may perfume my clothes, sweeten my food, oil the wheels of my particular vocation, keep me company upon all occasions, and gild over all my natural, civil, and religious actions. I wish that, after I have poured out my prayer in the name of Christ, according to the will of God, having sowed my seed, I may expect a crop, looking earnestly for the springing of it up, and believing assuredly that I shall reap in time if I faint not.—*George Swinnock.*

Verse 147. "*I prevented the dawning of the morning.*" Early prayers are undisturbed by the agitating cares of life, and resemble the sweet melody of those birds which sing loudest and sweetest when fewest ears are open to listen to them. O my soul, canst thou say that thou hast thus "*prevented the dawning of the morning*" in thy approaches to God ? Has the desire of communion with heaven raised thee from thy slumbers, shaken off thy sloth, and carried thee to thy knees ?—*John Morison.*

Verse 147.—"*And cried.*" Here is a repetition of the same prayer, "*I cried*" ; yea, again I cried, and a third time, " I prevented the dawning of the morning, and cried." We use to knock at a door thrice, and then depart. Our Lord Jesus " prayed the third time, saying the same words " (Matt. xxvi. 44), " Father, if it be possible, let this cup pass from me." So the apostle Paul : " For this thing I besought the Lord thrice, that it might depart from me " : 2 Cor. xii. 8. So, " And he stretched himself upon the child three times, and cried unto the Lord, and said, O Lord my God, I pray thee, let this child's soul come into him again " : 1 Kings xvii. 21. This, it seemeth, was the time in which they expected an answer in weighty cases ; and yet I will not confine it to that number ; for here we are to reiterate our petitions for one and the same thing as often as occasion requireth, till it be granted.—*Thomas Manton.*

Verse 147.—Poets have delighted to sing of the morning as " Mother of the Dews," " sowing the earth with orient pearl " ; and many of the saints upstarting from their beds at the first blush of dawn have found the poetry of nature to be the reality of grace as they have felt the dews of heaven refreshing their spirit. Hence morning exercises have ever been dear to the enlightened, heaven-loving souls, and it has been their rule, never to see the face of man till they have first seen the face of God. The breath of morn redolent of the smell of flowers is incense offered by earth to her Creator, and living men should never let the dead earth excel them ; truly living men tuning their hearts for song, like the birds, salute the radiant mercy which reveals itself in the east. The first fresh hour of every morning should be dedicated to the Lord whose mercy gladdens it with golden light. The eye of day openeth its lids, and in so doing opens the eyes of hosts of heaven-protected slumberers ; it is fitting that those eyes should first look up to the great Father of Lights, the fount and source of all the good upon which the sunlight gleams. It augurs for us a day of grace when we begin betimes with God ; the sanctifying influence of the season spent upon the mount operates upon each succeeding hour. Morning devotion anchors the soul so that it will not very readily drift far away from God during the day ; it perfumes the heart so that it smells fragrant with piety until nightfall ; it girds up the soul's garments so that it is less apt to stumble, and feeds all its powers so that it is not permitted to faint. The morning is the gate of the day, and should be well guarded with prayer. It is one end of the thread on which the day's actions are strung, and should be well knotted with devotion. If we felt more the majesty of life we should be more careful of its mornings. He who rushes from his bed to his business and waiteth not to worship, is as foolish as though he had not put on his clothes, or cleansed his face, and as unwise as though he dashed into battle without arms or armour. Be it ours to bathe in the softly flowing river of communion with God, before the heat of the wilderness and the burden of the way begin to oppress us.—*C. H. S.*

Verse 147.—"*I hoped in thy word.*" Even if there should not be actual enjoyment, at least let us honour God by the spirit of expectancy.—*Charles Bridges.*

Verses 147, 148.—The student of theology and the minister of the word should begin the day with prayer, and this chiefly to seek from God, that he may rightly understand the word of God, and be able to teach others.—*Solomon Gesner.* Brethren, note this!—*C. H. S.*

Verses 147, 148.—See here: 1. That David was an early riser, which perhaps contributed to his eminency. He was none of those that say, "Yet a little sleep." 2. That he began the day with God; the first thing he did in the morning, before he admitted any business, was to pray; when his mind was most fresh and in the best frame. If our first thoughts in the morning be of God, it will help to keep us in his fear all the day long. 3. That his mind was so full of God and the cares and delights of his religion, that a little sleep served his turn, even in "*the night-watches,*" when he awaked from his first sleep, he would rather meditate and pray, than turn him and go to sleep again. He esteemed the words of God's mouth more than his necessary repose, which we can as ill want as our food: Job xxiii. 21. 4. That he would redeem time for religious exercises; he was full of business all day, but that will excuse no man from secret devotion; it is better to take time from sleep, as David did, than not find time for prayer. And this is our comfort when we pray in the night, that we can never come unseasonably to the throne of grace, if we may have access to it at all hours. Baal may be asleep, but Israel's God never slumbers, nor are there any hours in which he may not be spoken with.—*Matthew Henry.*

Verse 148.—"*Mine eyes prevent the night watches, that I might meditate in thy word.*" You will all admit that this is the language of an ardent, earnest, and painstaking student. David represents himself as "rising early, and late taking rest," on purpose that he might employ himself in the study of God's word. "He *meditates* in this word," the expression implying close and patient thought; as if there were much in the word which was not to be detected by a cursory glance, and which required the strictest application both of the head and the heart.

The Bible is a book in which we may continually meditate, and yet not exhaust its contents. When David expressed himself in the language of our text, Holy Writ—the word of God—was of course a far smaller volume than it now is, though, even now, the Bible is far from a large book. Yet David could not, so to speak, get to the end of the book. He might have been studying the book for years,—nay, we are sure that he had been,—and yet, as though he were just entering on a new course of reading, with volume upon volume to peruse, he must rise before day to prosecute the study. "*Mine eyes prevent the night watches, that I might meditate in thy word.*"

The same remark may be made upon precepts which enjoin continued study of the Bible. Is there material for that study? Unless there be, the precepts will become out of place; the Scriptural student will have exhausted the Scriptures; and what is he to do then? He can no longer obey the precepts, and the precepts will prove that they cannot have been made for perpetuity—for the men of all ages and all conditions. . . . .

Here is a servant of God, who, from his youth upward, has been diligent in the study of the Bible. Year after year he has devoted to that study, and yet the Bible is but a single volume, and that not a large volume. "Well, then," you might be inclined to say, "the study must surely by this time have exhausted the book! There can be nothing new for him to bring out; nothing which he has not investigated and fathomed." Ah, how you mistake the Bible! What a much larger book it must be than it seems! In place of having exhausted it, the royal student speaks as though there were more work before him than he knew how to compass. "*Mine eyes prevent the night watches, that I might mediate in thy word.*"—*Henry Melvill.*

Verse 148.—"*Mine eyes prevent the night watches.*" The Hebrew word means a *watch*—a part of the night, so called from military watches, or a dividing of the night to keep guard. The idea of the Psalmist here is, that he *anticipated* these regular divisions of the night in order that he might engage in devotion. Instead of waiting for their return, he arose for prayer before they recurred; so much did his heart delight in the service of God. The language would seem to be that of one who was accustomed to pray in these successive "*watches*" of the night; the early, the middle, and the dawn. This may illustrate what occurs in the life of all who love God. They will have regular seasons of devotion, but they will often *anticipate* those seasons. They will be in a state of mind which prompts them to pray ; when nothing will meet their state of mind *but* prayer ; and when they cannot wait for the regular and ordinary season of devotion ; like a hungry man, who cannot wait for the usual and regular hour of his meals. The meaning of the phrase, *"Mine eyes prevent,"* is that he awoke before the usual time for devotion.— *Albert Barnes.*

Verse 148.—*"Mine eyes prevent the night watches,"* etc. His former purpose is yet continued, declaring his indefatigable perseverance in prayer. Oh, that we could learn of him to use our time well ! At evening he lay down with prayers and tears ; at midnight he rose to give thanks ; he got up before the morning light to call upon the Lord. This is to imitate the life of angels, who ever are delighted to behold the face of God, singing alway a new song without wearying. This is to begin our heaven upon earth : Oh, that we could alway remember it !—*William Cowper.*

Verse 148.—*"Night watches."* The Jews, like the Greeks and Romans, divided the night into military watches instead of hours, each watch representing the period for which sentinels or pickets remained on duty. The proper Jewish reckoning recognised only three such watches, entitled the first, or " beginning of the watches " (Lam. ii. 19), " the middle watch " (Judg. vii. 19), and " the morning watch " (Exod. xiv. 24 ; 1 Sam. xi. 11). These would last respectively from sunset to 10 p.m. ; from 10 p.m. to 2 a.m. ; and from 2 a.m. to sunrise. It has been contended by Lightfoot that the Jews really reckoned four watches, three only of which were in the dead of the night, the fourth being in the morning. This, however, is rendered improbable by the use of the term " middle," and is opposed to Rabbinical authority. Subsequently to the establishment of Roman supremacy, the number of watches was increased to four, which were described either according to their numerical order, as in the case of the " fourth watch " (Matt. xiv. 25), or by the terms " even, midnight, cock-crowing, and morning " (Mark xiii. 35), These terminated respectively at 9 p.m., midnight, 3 a.m., and 6 a.m. Conformably to this, the guard of soldiers was divided into four relays (Acts xii. 4), showing that the Roman régime was followed in Herod's army. Watchmen appear to have patrolled the streets of the Jewish towns (Cant. iii. 3 ; v. 7 ; Ps. cxxvii. 1, where for " maketh " we should substitute " watcheth " ; Ps. cxxx. 6).—*William Latham Bevan, in Smith's Dictionary of the Bible,* 1863.

Verse 149.—*"Quicken me."* By *quickening* some understand restitution to happiness ; for a calamitous man is as one dead and buried under deep and heavy troubles, and his recovery is a life from the dead, or a reviving from the grave : so quickening seemeth to be taken in Psalm lxxi. 20 : " Thou, which hast shewed me great and sore troubles, shalt quicken me again and shalt bring me up again from the depths of the earth."

Others understand by *quickening,* the renewing and increasing in him the vigour of his spiritual life. That he beggeth that God would revive, increase, and preserve that life, which he had already given, that it might be perfected and consummated in glory. That he might be ever ready to bring forth the habits of grace into acts. —*Thomas Manton.*

Verse 149.—*"Judgment"* is sometimes taken for the execution of God's threatenings against transgressors ; and this David declares : " Enter not into judgment with thy servant " : Ps. cxliii. 2. Sometime it is taken for the performance of his promises, according to his word ; and this David desires as in this verse.—*William Cowper.*

Verse 150.—*"They are far from thy law."* Truly it should greatly comfort all the godly, to remember that such as are their enemies are God's enemies also. Since they are far from the obedience of God's law, what marvel they be also far from the duty of love which they owe us ? It may content us to want that comfort in men which otherwise we might and would have, when we consider that God wants his glory in them. Let this sustain us when we see that godless men are enemies unto us.—*William Cowper.*

Verse 150.—If we can get a carnal pillow and bolster under our heads, we sleep and dream many a golden dream of ease and safety. Now, God, who is jealous of our trust, will not let us alone, and therefore will put us upon sharp trials. It is not faith, but sense, we live upon before ; that is faith, if we can depend upon God when " they draw near that follow after mischief : " " I will not be afraid of ten thousands of people, that have set themselves against me round about " : Ps. iii. 6. A danger at a distance is but imagined, it worketh otherwise when it is at hand. Christ himself had other thoughts of approaching danger than danger at a distance : " Now is my soul troubled " : John xii. 27. This vessel of pure water was troubled, though he discovered no dross.—*Thomas Manton.*

Verses 150, 151.—Our spiritual enemies, like David's earthly persecutors, are ever present and active. The devouring " lion," or the insinuating " serpent " is *"nigh to follow after mischief"*; and so much the more dangerous, as his approaches are invisible. Nigh also is a tempting ensnaring world ; and nearer still, a lurking world of sin within, separating us from communion with our God. But in turning habitually and immediately to our stronghold, we can enjoy the confidence—*"Thou art near, O Lord."* Though " the High and Lofty One, whose name is Holy "— though the just and terrible God, yet art thou made nigh to thy people, and they to thee, " by the blood of the cross." And thou dost manifest thy presence to them in " the Son of thy love."—*Charles Bridges.*

Verses 150, 151.—They are *"nigh"* to persecute and destroy me ; thou art nigh, O Lord, to help me.—*J. J. Stewart Perowne.*

Verses 150, 151.—*"They draw nigh."* . . . . *"Thou art near."* From the meditation of his enemies' malice he returns again to the meditation of God's mercy ; and so it is expedient for us to do, lest the number and greatness and maliciousness of our enemies make us to faint when we look unto them. It is good that we should cast our eyes upward to the Lord ; then shall we see that they are not so near to hurt us as the Lord our God is near to help us ; and that there is no evil in them which we have cause to fear, but we shall find in our God a contrary good sufficient to preserve us. Otherwise we could not endure, if when Satan and his instruments come near to pursue us, the Lord were not near to protect us.—*William Cowper.*

Verse 151.—*"Thou art near, O Lord."*—How sweetly and how often has this thought been brought home to some forsaken and forgotten one ! " When my father and my mother forsake me, the Lord will take me up," was the comfort of one in that deep affliction. And in the first outbreaking of the heart, how sweetly has the conviction come, like some whisper of peace, " I am with thee ! " And I have no doubt that many and many a time in those hours of solitary prayer, when before the dawning of the morning, and before the night watches, or the Psalmist arose at midnight to commune with God, when no voice broke on the stillness, and every sound was hushed save the beating of his own heart, then had David heard the whisper of God's Holy Spirit, *"I am near,"* " Fear not, I am with thee."—*Barton Bouchier.*

Verse 151.—*"Thou art near, O Lord."* This was *once* man's greatest blessing, and source of sweetest consolation. It was the fairest flower which grew in Paradise ; but sin withered it, the flower faded, it drooped, it died. Gen. iii. 8 ; iv. 16. It must be so *once more ;* the flower must once again bloom, again it must revive ; even upon earth must it blossom, or in heaven it will never put forth its fragrance.

"Thou art near." Even in thy works of *creation*, in the sun in his glory, in the moon in her softness, gleaming in the firmament, I see thee. In the balm of this fragrant air, in the light of this cheerful day, in the redolence of these shrubs around me, whose flowery tops, as they drink in the soft and gentle shower as it falls, seem to breathe forth a fresh perfume in gratitude to him who sends it. In the melody of these birds which fill the air with their songs, thou, O Lord, art near. I perceive thee not with my bodily eyes, although by these I discern thy workmanship, and with the eye of the mind behold thee in thy works, *a present God.*

"Thou art near." Even in the book of thy providence, dark and mysterious though it be, I see thee. There do I read thy *wisdom*, as developed in thy world, thy church, thy saints, thy servant before thee ; the wisdom that guides, the wisdom that guards, the wisdom that bestows, the wisdom that encourages, the wisdom that corrects, that kills and makes alive. There do I read thy *power*, thy *justice*, thy *faithfulness*, thy *holiness*, thy *love*.

But it is in thy *Son*, thy beloved Son, that I most clearly and distinctly see thee as near. If in creation, if in providence, thou art near, in him thou art very near, O Lord. Near as a sin-forgiving God. Rom. viii. 1. Near as a promise-keeping God.   2 Cor. i. 20.   Near as a prayer-hearing God.   John xvi. 20 ; Ps. cxlv. 18.   Near as a covenant-keeping God.   Heb. viii. 10.   Near as a gracious, tender Father.   John xx. 17.

"*Thou art near, O Lord.*"   O that I might live in the constant sense of thy nearness to me !   How often, far too often, alas, do I seem quite to forget it !

Art thou near ?   Then may I realizingly remember, that *by the blood of thy dear Son,* and by that alone, have I been brought nigh (Eph. ii. 13) ; that it required nothing less than the stoop of Deity, and the sufferings and death of his perfect humanity, to remove those hindrances which interposed between a holy God and an unholy creature.   Oh, to walk before thee with a grateful spirit, and with a broken, contrite heart !

Art thou near ?   Then may I walk as before thee, *as seeing thee,* in holy fear, in filial love, in simple faith, in child-like confidence.   Gen. xvii. 1.   When *sin* would tempt and solicit indulgence, when the *world* presents some new allurement, when *Satan* would take advantage of constitution, society, circumstances, oh, that I may ever remember "*Thou art near.*"

If my dearest comforts droop and die, if friends are cool, if the bonds once the firmest, the closest, the tenderest, are torn asunder, and dissevered, yet may I still remember, "*Thou* art near, O Lord," and not afar off.   And when the solemn moment shall come, when heart and flesh shall fail, when all earthly things are seen with a dying eye, when I hear thee say, " Thou must die, and not live," then, oh then may I remember, with all the composedness of faith, and all the liveliness of hope, and all the ardour of love, "*Thou art near, O Lord.*"—*James Harrington Evans,* 1785—1849.

Verse 151.—"*All thy commandments are truth.*"   His meaning is,—Albeit, O Lord, the evil will of wicked men follows me because I follow thee ; yet I know thy commandments are true, and that it is not possible that thou canst desert or fail thy servants who stand to the maintenance of thy word.   Then, ye see, David's comfort in trouble was not in any presumptuous conceit of his own wisdom or strength but in the truth of God's promises, which he was persuaded could not fail him.   And here also he makes a secret opposition between the word of the Lord and the word of his enemies.   Sometimes men command, but without reason ; sometimes they threaten, but without effect.   Herod's commanding, Rabshakeh's railing, Jezebel's proud boasting against Elijah, may prove this.   But as to the Lord our God he is alway better than his word, and his servants shall find more in his performance hereafter than now they can perceive in his promise : like as his enemies should find more weight in his judgments than now they can apprehend in his threatenings. —*William Cowper.*

Verse 152.—This portion of our Psalm endeth with the triumph of faith over all dangers and temptations.   "*Concerning thy testimonies,*" the revelations of thy will, thy counsels for the salvation of thy servants, "*I have known of old,*" by faith, and by my own experience, as well as that of others, "*that thou hast founded them for ever*" ;   they are unalterable and everlasting as the attributes of their great Author, and can never fail those who rely upon them, in time or in eternity.—*George Horne.*

Verse 152.—"*I have known of old.*"   It was not a late persuasion, or a thing that he was now to learn ; he always knew it since he knew anything of God, that God had owned his word as the constant rule of his proceedings with creatures, in that God had so often made good his word to him, not only by present and late, but by old and ancient experiences.   Well, then, David's persuasion of the truth and unchangeableness of the word was not a sudden humour or a present fit, or a persuasion of a few days' standing ; but he was confirmed in it by long experience. One or two experiences had been no trial of the truth of the word, they might seem but a good hit ; but his word ever proveth true, not once or twice, but always ; what we say " of old," the Septuagint reads κατ αρχὰς, " from the beginnings " ; that is, either—1. From my tender years.   Timothy knew the Scriptures from a child (2 Tim. iii. 15) ; so David very young was acquainted with God and his truth. 2. Or, from the first time that he began to be serious, or to mind the word in good earnest, or to be a student either in God's word or works, by comparing providences and promises, he found concerning his testimonies that "*God had founded them for ever.*"   3. Lastly, "*of old*" may be what I have heard of all foregoing ages, their experience as well as mine :   " Our fathers trusted in thee : they trusted, and thou didst deliver them. They cried unto thee, and were delivered : they trusted in thee, and were not confounded : " Ps. xxii. 4, 5.—*Thomas Manton.*

Verse 152.—Let us mark this eternal basis of " the testimonies of God." The whole plan of redemption was emphatically *"founded for ever "* : the Saviour was *"foreordained before the foundation of the world."* The people of God were *"chosen in Christ before the world began ! "* The great Author *"declares the end from the beginning,"* and thus clears his dispensations from any charge of mutability or contingency. Every event in the church is fixed, permitted, and provided for— not in the passing moment of time, but in the counsels of eternity. When, therefore, the testimonies set forth God's faithful engagements with his people of old, the recollection that they are *"founded for ever "* gives us a present and unchangeable interest in them. And when we see that they are grounded upon the oath and promise of God—the two " immutable things, in which it is impossible for God to lie "—we may truly " have strong consolation " in venturing every hope for eternity upon this rock ; nor need we be dismayed to see all our earthly dependencies— " the world, and the lust, and the fashion of it—passing away " before us.—*Charles Bridges.*

EXPOSITION OF VERSES 153 TO 160.

CONSIDER mine affliction, and deliver me: for I do not forget thy law.

154 Plead my cause, and deliver me: quicken me according to thy word.

155 Salvation is far from the wicked: for they seek not thy statutes.

156 Great are thy tender mercies, O LORD: quicken me according to thy judgments.

157 Many are my persecutors and mine enemies; yet do I not decline from thy testimonies.

158 I beheld the transgressors, and was grieved; because they kept not thy word.

159 Consider how I love thy precepts: quicken me, O LORD, according to thy lovingkindness.

160 Thy word is true from the beginning: and every one of thy righteous judgments endureth for ever.

In this section the Psalmist seems to draw still nearer to God in prayer, and to state his case and to invoke the divine help with more of boldness and expectation. It is a pleading passage, and the key-word of it is, "Consider." With much boldness he pleads his intimate union with the Lord's cause as a reason why he should be aided. The special aid that he seeks is personal *quickening*, for which he cries to the Lord again and again.

153. "*Consider mine affliction, and deliver me.*" The writer has a good case, though it be a grievous one, and he is ready, yea anxious, to submit it to the divine arbitration. His matters are right, and he is ready to lay them before the supreme court. His manner is that of one who feels safe at the throne. Yet there is no impatience: he does not ask for hasty action, but for consideration. In effect he cries—" Look into my grief, and see whether I do not need to be delivered. From my sorrowful condition judge as to the proper method and time for my rescue." The Psalmist desires two things, and these two things blended: first, a full consideration of his sorrow; secondly, deliverance; and, then, that this deliverance should come with a consideration of his affliction. It should be the desire of every gracious man who is in adversity that the Lord should look upon his need, and relieve it in such a way as shall be most for the divine glory, and for his own benefit. The words, " mine affliction," are picturesque; they seem to portion off a special spot of woe as the writer's own inheritance: he possesses it as no one else had ever done, and he begs the Lord to have that special spot under his eye: even as a husbandman looking over all his fields may yet take double care of a certain selected plot. His prayer is eminently practical, for he seeks to be delivered; that is, brought out of the trouble and preserved from sustaining any serious damage by it. For God to consider is to act in due season: men consider and do nothing; but such is never the case with out God. "*For I do not forget thy law.*" His affliction was not sufficient, with all its bitterness, to drive out of his mind the memory of God's law; nor could it lead him to act contrary to the divine command. He forgot prosperity, but he did not forget obedience. This is a good plea when it can be honestly urged. If we are kept faithful to God's law we may be sure that God will remain faithful to his promise. If we do not forget his law the Lord will not forget us. He will not long leave that man in trouble whose only fear in trouble is lest he should leave the way of right.

154.—"*Plead my cause, and deliver me.*" In the last verse he had prayed, " Deliver me," and here he specifies one method in which that deliverance might be vouchsafed, namely, by the advocacy of his cause. In providence the Lord has many ways of clearing the slandered of the accusations brought against them. He can make it manifest to all that they have been belied, and in this way he can practically plead their cause. He can, moreover, raise up friends for the godly who will leave no stone unturned till their characters are cleared ; or he can smite their enemies with such fearfulness of heart that they will be forced to confess their falsehood, and thus the righteous will be delivered without the striking of a blow. Alexander reads it, " Strive my strife, and redeem me "—that is, stand in my stead, bear my burden, fight my fight, pay my price, and bring me out to liberty. When we feel ourselves dumb before the foe, here is a prayer made to our hand. What a comfort that if we sin we have an advocate, and if we do *not* sin the same pleader is engaged on our side. *"Quicken me."* We had this prayer in the last section, and we shall have it again and again in this. It is a desire which cannot be too often felt and expressed. As the soul is the centre of everything, so to be quickened is the central blessing. It means more love, more grace, more faith, more courage, more strength, and if we get these we can hold up our heads before our adversaries. God alone can give this quickening ; but to the Lord and giver of life the work is easy enough, and he delights to perform it. *"According to thy word."* David had found such a blessing among the promised things, or at least he perceived that it was according to the general tenor of God's word that tried believers should be quickened and brought up again from the dust of the earth ; therefore he pleads the word, and desires the Lord to act to him according to the usual run of that word. What a mighty plea is this—" according to thy word." No gun in all our arsenals can match it.

155.—*"Salvation is far from the wicked."* By their perseverance in evil they have almost put themselves out of the pale of hope. They talk about being saved, but they cannot have known anything of it or they would not remain wicked. Every step they have taken in the path of evil has removed them further from the kingdom of grace : they go from one degree of hardness to another till their hearts become as stone. When they fall into trouble it will be irremediable. Yet they talk big, as if they either needed no salvation or could save themselves whenever their fancy turned that way. *"For they seek not thy statutes."* They do not endeavour to be obedient, but quite the reverse ; they seek themselves, they seek evil, and therefore they never find the way of peace and righteousness. When men have broken the statutes of the Lord their wisest course is by repentance to seek forgiveness, and by faith to seek salvation : then salvation is near them, so near them that they shall not miss it ; but when the wicked continue to seek after mischief, salvation is set further and further from them. Salvation and God's statutes go together : those who are saved by the King of grace love the statutes of the King of glory.

156. This verse is exceedingly like verse one hundred and forty-nine, and yet it is no vain repetition. There is such a difference in the main idea that the one verse stands out distinct from the other. In the first case he mentions his prayer, but leaves the method of its accomplishment with the wisdom or judgment of God ; while here he pleads no prayer of his own, but simply the mercies of the Lord, and begs to be quickened by judgments rather than to be left to spiritual lethargy. We may take it for granted that an inspired author is never so short of thought as to be obliged to repeat himself : where we think we have the same idea in this Psalm we are mislead by our neglect of careful study. Each verse is a distinct pearl. Each blade of grass in this field has its own drop of heavenly dew. *"Great are thy tender mercies, O LORD."* Here the Psalmist pleads the largeness of God's mercy, the immensity of his tender love ; yea, he speaks of *mercies*—mercies many, mercies tender, mercies great ; and with the glorious Jehovah he makes this a plea for his one leading prayer, the prayer for quickening. Quickening is a great and tender mercy ; and it is many mercies in one. Shall one so greatly good permit his servant to die ? Will not one so tender breathe new life into him? *"Quicken me according to thy judgments."* A measure of awakening comes with the judgments of God ; they are startling and arousing ; and hence the believer's quickening thereby. David would have every severe stroke sanctified to his benefit, as well as every tender mercy. The first clause of this verse may run, " Many," or, " manifold are thy compassions, O Jehovah." This he remembers in connection with the " many persecutors " of whom he will speak in the next verse. By all these many mercies he pleads for enlivening grace, and thus he has many strings to his bow. We shall never be short of arguments if we draw them from God himself, and urge both his mercies and his judgments as reasons for our quickening.

157.—*"Many are my persecutors and mine enemies."* Those who actually assail me, or who secretly abhor me, are many. He sets this over against the many tender mercies of God. It seems a strange thing that a truly godly man, as David was, should have many enemies ; but it is inevitable. The disciple cannot be loved where his Master is hated. The seed of the serpent must oppose the seed of the woman : it is their nature. *"Yet do I not decline from thy testimonies."* He did not deviate from the truth of God, but proceeded in the straight way, however many adversaries might endeavour to block up his path. Some men have been led astray by one enemy, but here is a saint who held on his way in the teeth of many persecutors. There is enough in the testimonies of God to recompense us for pushing forward against all the hosts that may combine against us. So long as they cannot drive or draw us into a spiritual decline our foes have done us no great harm, and they have accomplished nothing by their malice. If we do not decline they are defeated. If they cannot make us sin they have missed their mark. Faithfulness to the truth is victory over our enemies.

158.—*"I beheld the transgressors."* I saw the traitors ; I understood their character, their object, their way, and their end. I could not help seeing them, for they pushed themselves into my way. As I was obliged to see them I fixed my eyes on them, to learn what I could from them. *"And was grieved."* I was sorry to see such sinners. I was sick of them, disgusted with them, I could not endure them. I found no pleasure in them, they were a sad sight to me, however fine their clothing or witty their chattering. Even when they were most mirthful a sight of them made my heart heavy ; I could not tolerate either them or their doings. *"Because they kept not thy word."* My grief was occasioned more by their sin against God than by their enmity against myself. I could bear their evil treatment of my words, but not their neglect of thy word. Thy word is so precious to me that those who will not keep it move me to indignation ; I cannot keep the company of those who keep not God's word. That they should have no love for me is a trifle ; but to despise the teaching of the Lord is abominable.

159.—*"Consider,"* or see, *"how I love thy precepts."* A second time he asks for consideration. As he said before, " Consider mine affliction," so now he says, " Consider mine affection." He loved the precepts of God—loved them unspeakably —loved them so as to be grieved with those who did not love them. This is a sure test : many there are who have a warm side towards the promises, but as for the precepts, they cannot endure them. The Psalmist so loved everything that was good and excellent that he loved all God had commanded. The precepts are all of them wise and holy, therefore the man of God loved them extremely, loved to know them, to think of them, to proclaim them, and principally to practise them. He asked the Lord to remember and consider this, not upon the ground of merit, but that it should serve as an answer to the slanderous accusations which at this time were the great sting of his sorrow. *"Quicken me, O LORD, according to thy lovingkindness."* Here he comes back to his former prayer, " Quicken me " (v. 154), " quicken me " (v. 156). " Quicken me." He prays again the third time, using the same words. We may understand that David felt like one who was half stunned with the assaults of his foes, ready to faint under their incessant malice. What he wanted was revival, restoration, renewal ; therefore he pleaded for more life, O thou who didst quicken me when I was dead, quicken me again that I may not return to the dead ! Quicken me that I may outlive the blows of my enemies, the faintness of my faith, and the swooning of my sorrow. This time he does not say, " Quicken me according to thy judgments," but " Quicken me, O Lord, according to thy lovingkindness." This is the great gun which he brings up last to the conflict : it is his ultimate argument, if this succeed not he must fail. He has long been knocking at mercy's gate, and with this plea he strikes his heaviest blow. When he had fallen into great sin this was his plea, " Have mercy upon me, O God, according to thy lovingkindness," and now that he is in great trouble he flies to the same effectual reasoning. Because God is love he will give us life ; because he is kind he will again kindle the heavenly flame within us.

160. The sweet singer finishes up this section in the same way as the last by dwelling upon the sureness of the truth of God. It will be well for the reader to note the likeness between verses 144, 152, and the present one. *"Thy word is true."* Whatever the transgressors may say, God is true, and his word is true. The ungodly are false, but God's word is true. They charge us with being false, but our solace is that God's true word will clear us. *"From the beginning."* God's word has been

true from the first moment in which it was spoken, true throughout the whole of history, true to us from the instant in which we believed it, ay, true to us before we were true to it. Some read it, " Thy word is true from the head ; " true as a whole, true from top to bottom. Experience had taught David this lesson, and experience is teaching us the same. The Scriptures are as true in Genesis as in Revelation, and the five books of Moses are as inspired as the four Gospels. *"And every one of thy righteous judgments endureth for ever."* That which thou hast decided remains irreversible in every case. Against the decisions of the Lord no writ of error can be demanded, neither will there ever be a repealing of any of the acts of his sovereignty. There is not one single mistake either in the word of God or in the providential dealings of God. Neither in the book of revelation nor of providence will there be any need to put a single note of *errata*. The Lord has nothing to regret or to retract, nothing to amend or to reverse. All God's judgments, decrees, commands, and purposes are righteous, and as righteous things are lasting things, every one of them will outlive the stars. "Till heaven and earth pass, one jot or one tittle shall in no wise pass from the law, till all be fulfilled." God's justice endureth for ever. This is a cheering thought, but there is a much sweeter one, which of old was the song of the priests in the temple ; let it be ours, " His mercy endureth for ever."

NOTES ON VERSES 153 TO 160.

Verse 153.—*"Consider mine affliction, and deliver me."* God looks upon or considers man in various ways, and for different ends. To give him light ; for " as Jesus passed by, he saw a man which was blind from his birth " (John ix. 1). To convert him ; " He saw a man, named Matthew, sitting at the receipt of custom : and he saith unto him, Follow me " (Matt. ix. 9). To restore him ; " And the Lord turned, and looked upon Peter " (Luke xxii. 61). To deliver him ; " I have surely seen the affliction of my people which are in Egypt " (Exod. iii. 7). To advance him ; " He hath regarded the low estate of his handmaiden " (Luke i. 48) : and to reward him ; " The Lord had respect unto Abel and to his offering " (Gen. iv. 4).—*Hugo (circa* 1120), *in Neale and Littledale.*

Verse 153.—*"Consider mine affliction, and deliver me."* We must pray that God will help and deliver us, not after the device of our own brains, but after such wise as seemeth best unto his tender wisdom, or else that he will mitigate our pain, that our weakness may not utterly faint. Like as a sick person, although he doubt nothing of the faithfulness and tenderness of his physician, yet, for all that, desireth him to handle his wound as tenderly as possible, even so may we call upon God, that, if it be not against his honour and glory, he will vouchsafe to give some mitigation of the pain.—*Otho Wermullerus.*

Verse 153.—*"Consider mine affliction."* These prayers of David are penned with such heavenly wisdom that they are convenient for the state of the whole church, and every member thereof. The church is the bush that burneth with fire, but cannot be consumed ; every member thereof beareth a part of the cross of Christ ; they are never without some affliction, for which they have need to pray with David, *"Behold mine affliction."*

We know that in afflictions it is some comfort to us to have our crosses known to those of whom we are assured that they love us : it mitigates our dolour when they mourn with us, albeit they be not able to help us. But the Christian hath a more solid comfort ; to wit, that in all his troubles the Lord beholds him ; like a king, rejoicing to see his own servant wrestle with the enemy. He looks on with a merciful eye, pitying the infirmity of his own, when he sees it ; and with a powerful hand ready to help them. But because many a time the cloud of our corruption cometh between the Lord and us, and lets us not see his helping hand, nor his loving face looking upon us, we have need to pray at such times with David, *"Behold mine affliction."*—*William Cowper.*

Verse 154.—*"Plead my cause, and deliver me,"* etc. Albeit the godly under persecution have a good cause, yet they cannot plead it except God the Redeemer show himself as Advocate for them ; therefore prayeth the Psalmist, *"Plead my cause."*

When God the Redeemer pleadeth a man's cause, he doth it to purpose and effectually : *"Plead my cause, and deliver me."*

Except the Lord's clients shall find new influence from God from time to time in their troubles, they are but as dead men in their exercise ; for, *"Quicken me"* importeth this.

Till we find lively encouragement given to us in trouble we must adhere to the word of promise : *"Quicken me according to thy word."*

What the believer hath need of, that God hath not only a will to supply, but also an office to attend it, and power to effectuate it, as here he hath the office of an Advocate and of a powerful Redeemer also, wherein the believer may confidently give him daily employment, as he needeth : *"Plead my cause, and deliver me : quicken me according to thy word."*—*David Dickson.*

Verse 154.—*"Plead my cause, and deliver me,"* etc. He now supposes himself to be arraigned before the tribunal of men, as he certainly was in their general charges against him ; arraigned, too, in his helplessness, without a name, without state ; in such way as one disowned would be arraigned. He prays the Lord to come in and plead his cause ; so should he be redeemed ; for this is the import of the original. As it were, he regards himself as one sold to corrupt judges, or at all events, as one that has lost his standing in society in the estimation of men. But if the Lord will come, and maintain the cause of his servant, his servant shall be redeemed indeed. There is good confidence in this prayer ; the man of God is acquainted with the way of the Lord, and he makes his believing application. O how much do we need to know the Lord's righteous character in our seasons of great distress! Now the Lord pleads the cause of his own by the power of the truth; he pleads it also in his providences of divers kinds; he acts upon the hearts, and the hopes, and the fears of men; and in many wondrous ways he pleads his people's cause. He redeems his saints from all evil; and if not altogether from all evil in this world, certainly from all evil as concerns the world to come.—*John Stephen.*

Verse 154.—*"Plead my cause, and deliver me,"* etc. In this verse are three requests, and all backed with one and the same argument. In the first, he intimateth the right of his cause, and that he was unjustly vexed by wicked men; therefore, as burdened with their calumnies, he desireth God to undertake his defence: *"Plead my cause."* In the second, he representeth the misery and helplessness of his condition; therefore, as oppressed by violence, he saith, *"Deliver me;"* or, as the words will bear, Redeem me. In the third, his own weakness, and readiness to faint under this burden; therefore he saith, *"Quicken me."*

Or, in short, with respect to the injustice of his adversaries, *"Plead my cause;"* with respect to the misery of his condition, *"Deliver me:"* with respect to the weakness and imbecility of his own heart, *"Quicken me."* . . .

The reason and ground of asking, *"According to thy word."* This last clause must be applied to all the branches of the prayer: *"Plead my cause,"* "according to thy word;" "deliver me," "according to thy word;" "quicken me," "according to thy word:" for God in his word engageth for all: to be advocate, Redeemer, and fountain of life. The word that David buildeth upon was found either in the general promises made to them that kept the law, or in some particular promise made to himself by the prophets of that time.—*Thomas Manton.*

Verse 154.—*"Plead my cause, and deliver me."* A wicked woman once brought against Dr. Payson an accusation, under circumstances which seemed to render it impossible that he should escape. She was in the same packet, in which, many months before, he had gone to Boston. For a time, it seemed almost certain that his character would be ruined. He was cut off from all resource except the throne of grace. He felt that his only hope was in God; and to him he addressed his fervent prayer. He was heard by the Defender of the innocent. A "compunctious visiting" induced the wretched woman to confess that the whole was a malicious slander.—*From Asa Cummings' Memoir of Edward Payson.*

Verse 154.—*"Plead my cause."* I do not know that David meant, by calling upon God to plead his cause, anything more than that he should vindicate his innocence, and make it manifest to all, by delivering him out of the hand of all his enemies; but whether he had an ulterior reference or no, the word powerfully and sweetly recalls to every Christian heart him who was indeed to be the Advocate for poor sinners, even Jesus Christ the righteous, who is the propitiation for our sins.—*Barton Bouchier.*

Verse 154.—*"Plead my cause."* The children of this world are wiser in their generation than the children of God. Which made David here pray to God that *he* would *plead his cause,* and be his Advocate against all their policies. He trusted not to the equity of his own cause, but to the Lord. From whence we gather, that the cause why our oppressors prevail oft against us is, because we trust too much in our own wits, and lean too much upon our own inventions; opposing subtilty to subtilty, one evil device to another, matching and maintaining policy by policy, and not committing our cause to God.—·*Abraham Wright.*

Verse 154.—*"Deliver."* Not as in verse 153, but a word meaning to *redeem* or to save by avenging. The corresponding particle is rendered redeemer, avenger, revenger, kinsman, near kinsman, next kinsman.—*William S. Plumer.*

Verse 154.—*"Quicken me."* Here, again, we are called to consider the bearing of the pious mind. Ever and anon, the great desire of the man of God is to advance in the divine life. He makes spiritual gain of everything. He seeks his goodly pearls out of strange conditions; the reason is, his heart is in these things. Deliverance from temporal evil, deliverance from spiritual evil, both were sought; but along with these, ever does the man of God take up the prayer to be quickened. Certainly we may understand him as seeking life. Such is the import of the phraseology; but in a man like David, the life he seeks must be the highest. He desires spiritual life above all things; he wants to get more into a blessed assimilation to God, that so he may enjoy the highest good. So pants the heaven-born soul. . . . Give the believer this, and this will set him above all the ills of life. And this and all good had been promised in the word. So he prays, *"Quicken me according to thy word."* He goes upon the word for everything ; he cannot be self-deceived there. Judge of yourselves, my brethren, by your spiritual aspirations. Nothing less will prove you to be of the Lord's redeemed.—*John Stephen.*

Verses 154, 156, 159.—*"Quicken me."* Pray to be *quickened*, as the Psalmist often does, and look unto Jesus, who is a quickening spirit : 1 Cor. xv. 45. " The first man Adam was made a living soul ; the last Adam was made a quickening spirit." As he has given you life, so he is ready to give it more and more abundantly ; this will make you to live to him, and to be unweariedly active for him.— *Nathanael Vincent, in " A Present for such as have been Sick and Recovered," 1693.*

Verse 155.—*"Salvation is far from the wicked."* The Lord is almighty to pardon ; but he will not use it for thee an impenitent sinner. Thou hast not a friend on the bench, not an attribute in all God's name will speak for thee. Mercy itself will sit and vote with the rest of its fellow-attributes for thy damnation. God is able to save and help in a time of need, but upon what acquaintance is it that thou art so bold with God, as to expect his saving arm to be stretched forth for thee ? Though a man rise at midnight to let in a child that cries and knocks at his door, yet he will not take so much pains for a dog that lies howling there. This presents thy condition, sinner, sad enough, yet this is to tell thy story fairest ; for that almighty power of God which is engaged for the believer's salvation, is as deeply obliged to bring thee to thy execution and damnation. What greater tie than an oath ? God himself is under an oath to be the destruction of every impenitent soul. That oath which God sware in his wrath against the unbelieving Israelites, that they should not enter into his rest, concerns every unbeliever to the end of the world. In the name of God consider, were it but the oath of a man, or a company of men that, like those in the Acts, should swear to be the death of such an one, and thou wert the man, would it not fill thee with fear and trembling, night and day, and take away the quiet of thy life, till they were made thy friends ? What then are their pillows stuffed with, who can sleep so soundly without any horror or amazement, though they be told that the almighty God is under an oath of damning them body and soul, without timely repentance ?—*William Gurnall.*

Verse 155.—*"Salvation "* ! What music is there in that word, music that never tires, but is always new, that always rouses yet always rests us ! It holds in itself all that our hearts would say. It is sweet vigour to us in the morning, and in the evening it is contented peace. It is a song that is always singing itself deep down in the delighted soul. Angelic ears are ravished by it up in heaven ; and our Eternal Father himself listens to it with adorable complacency. It is sweet even to him out of whose mind is the music of a thousand worlds. To be saved ! What is it to be saved in the fullest and utmost meaning ? Who can tell ? Eye hath not seen, nor ear heard. It is a rescue, and from such a shipwreck ! It is a rest, and in such an unimaginable home ! It is to lie down for ever in the bosom of God, in an endless rapture of insatiable contentment.—*Frederick William Faber,* 1853.

Verses 155, 156.—*"Salvation is far from the wicked."* *"Great are thy tender mercies, O LORD."* When the godly do think and speak of the damnable condition of the wicked, they should not be senseless of their own ill deserving, nor of God's grace which hath made the difference between the wicked and them.—*David Dickson.*

Verse 156.—*"Great are thy tender mercies, O LORD."* Two epithets he ascribes to God's mercies ; first, he calls them *"great,"* and then he calls them *"tender "* mercies. They are great in many respects : for continuance, they endure for ever ; for largeness, they reach unto the heavens, and are higher than they ; yea, they are above all the works of God. And this is for the comfort of poor sinners, whose sins are many and great : let them not despair ; his mercies are greater and more ; for since they are greater than all his works, how much more greater than thou and all thy sinful works ! . . . . . The other epithet he gives them is, that they are *"tender "* mercies ; because the Lord is easy to be entreated ; for he is slow unto wrath, but ready to show mercy. S. James saith that the wisdom which is from above is "gentle, peaceable, easy to be entreated." If his grace in his children make them gentle and easy to be entreated, what shall we think of himself ? Since he will have such pity in us poor creatures, that seventy times seven times in the day he will have us to forgive the offences of our brethren ; Oh, what pity and compassion abound in himself ! Thus we see our comfort is increased ; that as his mercies are great, so are they tender ; easily obtained, where they are earnestly craved.—*William Cowper.*

Verse 156.—The Psalmist, when speaking of the wretched condition of *"the wicked,"* is naturally led to adore the mercies of the Lord which had " made him to differ." For indeed to this source alone must we trace the distinction between us and them.—*Charles Bridges.*

Verse 157.—*"Persecutors."* A participle from the verb rendered *pursue, chase.* *"Enemies,"* as in verse 139, the authors of my distress. Until men are hunted and hounded by many enemies, who for the time have power, and are withal fierce and to some extent unscrupulous, they can have but a faint conception of the anguish of the prophet when he experienced the evils noted in this verse. Yet they did not move him from his constancy and integrity.—*William S. Plumer.*

Verse 158.—*"I beheld the trangressors, and was grieved."* Celerinus in Cyprian's Epistles, acquaints a friend with his great grief for the apostasy of a woman through fear of persecution ; which afflicteth him so much, that at the feast of Easter (the Queen of feasts in the primitive church) he wept night and day, and resolved never to know a moment's delight, till through the mercy of God she should be recovered. —*Charles Bridges.*

Verse 158.—*"I beheld the transgressors, and was grieved."* Oh, if you have the hearts of Christians or of men in you, let them yearn towards your poor ignorant, ungodly neighbours. Alas, there is but a step betwixt them and death and hell : many hundred diseases are waiting ready to seize on them, and if they die unregenerate they are lost for ever. Have you hearts of rock, that cannot pity men in such a case as this ? If you believe not the word of God, and the danger of sinners, why are you Christians yourselves ? If you do believe it, why do you not bestir yourself to the helping of others ? Do you not care who is damned, so you be saved ? If so, you have sufficient cause to pity yourselves, for it is a frame of spirit utterly inconsistent with grace : should you not rather say, as the lepers of Samaria, Is it not a day of glad tidings, and do we sit still and hold our peace ? 2 Kings vii. 9. Hath God had so much mercy on you, and will you have no mercy on your poor neighbours ? You need not go far to find objects for your pity : look but into your streets, or into the next house to you, and you will probably find some. Have you never an ignorant, an unregenerate neighbour that sets his heart on things below, and neglecteth eternity ? What blessed place do you live in, where there is none such ? If there be not some of them in thine own family, it is well ; and yet art thou silent ? Dost thou live close by them, or meet them in the streets, or labour with them, or travel with them, or sit and talk with them, and say nothing to them of their souls, or the life to come ? If their houses were on fire, thou wouldst run and help them ; and wilt thou not help them when their souls are almost at the fire of hell ? If thou knewest but a remedy for their diseases thou wouldst tell it them, or else thou wouldst judge thyself guilty of their death.—*Richard Baxter* (1615—1691), *in "The Saints' Everlasting Rest."*

Verse 158.—*"Grieved, because they kept not thy law."* I never thought the world had been so wicked, when the Gospel began, as now I see it is ; I rather hoped that every one would have leaped for joy to have found himself freed from the filth of the Pope, from his lamentable molestations of poor troubled consciences, and that through Christ they would by faith obtain the celestial treasure they sought after before with such vast cost and labour, though in vain. And especially I thought the bishops and universities would with joy of heart have received the true doctrines ; but I have been lamentably deceived. Moses and Jeremiah, too, complained they had been deceived.—*Martin Luther.*

Verse 158.—*"Grieved."* The word that is here translated *"grieved"* is from *katat,* that signifies to loathe, abhor, and contend. I beheld the transgressors, and I loathed them ; I beheld the transgressors, and I abhorred them ; I beheld the transgressors, and I contended with them ; but not so much because they were mine enemies, as because they were thine.—*Thomas Brooks.*

Verse 158.—The day when I first met Colonel Gardiner at Leicester, I happened to preach a lecture from Ps. cxix. 158 : *"I beheld the transgressors, and was grieved ; because they kept not thy word."* I was large in describing that mixture of indignation and grief, strongly expressed by the original word there, with which a good man looks on the varying transgressors of the divine law; and in tracing the causes of that grief, as arising from a regard to the divine honour, and the interest of a Redeemer, and a compassionate concern for the misery such offenders bring on themselves, and for the mischief they do to the world about them. I little thought how exactly I was drawing Colonel Gardiner's character under each of those heads; and I have often reflected upon it as a happy providence, which opened a much speedier way than I could have expected, to the breast of one of the most amiable and useful friends which I ever expect to find upon earth. We afterwards sung a hymn, which brought over again some of the leading thoughts in the sermon, and struck him so strongly, that on obtaining a copy of it, he committed it to his memory, and used to repeat it with so forcible an accent, as showed how much every line expressed of his very soul. In this view the reader will pardon my inserting it; especially as I know not when I may get time to publish a volume of these serious though artless compositions, which I sent him in manuscript some years ago, and to which I have since made very large additions :—

> Arise, my tenderest thoughts, arise,
> To torrents melt my streaming eyes;
> And thou, my heart, with anguish feel
> Those evils which thou canst not heal.
>
> See human nature sunk in shame;
> See scandals pour'd on Jesu's name;
> The Father wounded through the Son;
> The world abused, and souls undone.
>
> See the short course of vain delight
> Closing in everlasting night;
> In flames that no abatement know,
> Though briny tears for ever flow.
>
> My God, I feel the mournful scene;
> My bowels yearn o'er dying men,
> And fain my pity would reclaim,
> And snatch the firebrands from the flame.
>
> But feeble my compassion proves,
> And can but weep where most it loves;
> Thy own all-saving arm employ,
> And turn these drops of grief to joy.

Philip Doddridge, in "The Life of Colonel Gardiner."

Verse 159.—*"Consider how I love thy precepts."* Search me. Behold the evidence of my attachment to thy law. This is the confident appeal of one who was conscious that he was truly attached to God; that he really loved his law. It is similar to the appeal of Peter to the Saviour (John xxi. 17), " Lord, thou knowest all things; thou knowest that I love thee." A man who truly loves God *may* make this appeal without impropriety. He may be so confident, so certain, that he has true love for the character of God, that he may make a solemn appeal to him on the subject, as he might appeal to a friend, to his wife, to his son, to his daughter, with the utmost confidence that he loved them. A man *ought* to have such love for *them*, that he could affirm this without hesitation or doubt; a man *ought* to have such love for *God*, that he could affirm this with equal confidence and propriety.—*Albert Barnes.*

Verse 159.—*"Consider how I love thy precepts."* He saith not, consider how I *perform* thy precepts; but how I *love* them. The comfort of a Christian militant, in this body of sin, is rather in the sincerity and fervency of his affections than in the absolute perfection of his actions. He fails many times in his obedience to God's precepts, in regard of his action; but love in his affection still remains; so that both before the temptation to sin, and after it, there is a grief in his soul, that he should find in himself any corrupt will or desire, contrary to the holy will of the Lord his God; and this proves an invincible love in him to the precepts of God.—*William Cowper.*

Verse 159.—*"Consider,"* etc. Translate (the Hebrew being the same as in verse 158) *"Behold* how I love thy precepts," as is evinced in that when " I *beheld* the transgressors I was grieved." He begs to God to behold this, not as meritorious of grace, but as a distinctive mark of a godly man.—*A. R. Fausset.*

Verse 159.—"*I love thy precepts : quicken me.*" The love wherewith he loved God came from that love wherewith God first loved him. For by seeing the great love wherewith God loved him, he was moved and inforced to love God again. So that his meaning is thus much : Thou seest, Lord, that I am an enemy to sin in myself, for I forget not thy law ; thou seest that I am an enemy to sin in others, for I am grieved to see them transgress thy law ; wherefore, O Lord, "*quicken me,*" and let thy loving mercy whereby thou hast created me and redeemed me in Christ, whereby thou hast delivered me from so many troubles, and enriched me with so many and continual benefits, renew, revive, quicken, and restore me.—*Richard Greenham.*

Verse 159.—"*Quicken me.*" Often as the Psalmist had repeated his prayer for quickening grace,* it was not a "*vain repetition,*" or an empty sound. Each time was it enlivened with abundant faith, intense feeling of his necessity, and the vehemency of most ardent affection. If the consciousness of the faintness of our strength and the coldness of our affections should lead us to offer this petition a hundred times a day in this spirit, it would never fail of acceptance.—*Charles Bridges.*

Verse 159.—"*According to thy lovingkindness.*" We need not desire to be quickened any further than God's lovingkindness will quicken us.—*Matthew Henry.*

Verse 160.—"*Thy word is true from the beginning.*" Literally, "The beginning of thy word is truth," in antithesis to the "enduring for ever," in the future, in the next clause. Cocceius and Hengstenberg take it, "The sum of thy word is true," as in Numbers xxvi. 2 ; xxxi. 26. But the antithesis noticed above in the English version is thus lost ; and the old versions support the English version. Also, if it were "*the sum,*" the plural ought to follow, viz., "of thy *words,*" not "*word.*"—*A. R. Fausset.*

Verse 160.—"*Thy word is true from the beginning,*" etc. As if he should say, I believe that thou wilt thus quicken me, because the very beginning of thy word is most just and true ; and when thou didst enter into covenant with me, I did find that thou didst not deceive me, nor beguile me. And when by thy Spirit thou madest me believe thy covenant, thou meanedst truth ; and I know that as thou didst promise, thou wilt perform, for thou art no more liberal in promising than faithful and just in performing, and thy judgment will be as righteous as thy promise is true. I know that as soon as thou speakest, truth proceedeth from thee ; and even so I know thou wilt defend and preserve me, that thy judgments may shine as righteous in thee.—*Richard Greenham.*

Verse 160.—"*Thy word is true from the beginning,*" etc. God's commandment and promise is exceeding broad, reaching to all times. Was a word of command "the guide of thy youth"? I assure thee it will be as good a staff of thine age. A good promise is a good nurse, both to the young babe and to the decrepid old man. Your apothecaries' best cordials in time will lose their spirits, and sometimes the stronger they are, the sooner. But hath a promise cheered thee, say, twenty, thirty, forty years ago? Taste it but now afresh, and thou shalt find it as fresh, and as full of refreshment as ever. If it hath been thy greatest joy in thy joyful youth, I tell thee, it hath as much joy in it for thy sad old age. That may be said of God's word, which the prophet saith of God himself (Isa. xlvi. 4) : "And even to your old age I am he ; and even to hoar hairs will I carry you." Doth not the Psalmist say as much here, "*Thy word is true from the beginning*"? It's well, it begins well. But will it last as well? Yes : he adds, "*and every one of thy righteous judgments endureth for ever.*" Answerable to which is that other expression (verse 152), "*Concerning thy testimonies, I have known of old that thou hast founded them for ever.*" "For ever," and "founded for ever." O sweet expression ! O grounded comfort ! Brethren, get acquainted with God's word and promise as soon as you can, and maintain that acquaintance everlastingly ; and your knowledge of it shall not either go before, or go beyond its truth. Know it as soon and as long as you will or can, and you shall never find it tripping or failing ; but you may after long experience of God say of it, "*I have known of old that thou hast founded it for ever.*"—*Anthony Tuckney, 1599—1670.*

---

* Nine times is this petition urged, verses 25, 37, 40, 88, 107, 149, 154, 156, 159.

EXPOSITION OF VERSES 161 TO 168.

PRINCES have persecuted me without a cause : but my heart standeth in awe of thy word.

162 I rejoice at thy word, as one that findeth great spoil.

163 I hate and abhor lying : *but* thy law do I love.

164 Seven times a day do I praise thee because of thy righteous judgments.

165 Great peace have they which love thy law : and nothing shall offend them.

166 LORD, I have hoped for thy salvation, and done thy commandments.

167 My soul hath kept thy testimonies ; and I love them exceedingly.

168 I have kept thy precepts and thy testimonies ; for all my ways *are* before thee.

161. *"Princes have persecuted me without a cause."* Such persons ought to have known better ; they should have had sympathy with one of their own rank. A man expects a fair trial at the hand of his peers : it is ignoble to be prejudiced. Moreover, if honour be banished from all other breasts it should remain in the bosom of kings, and honour forbids the persecution of the innocent. Princes are appointed to protect the innocent and avenge the oppressed, and it is a shame when they themselves become the assailants of the righteous. It was a sad case when the man of God found himself attacked by the judges of the earth, for eminent position added weight and venom to their enmity. It was well that the sufferer could truthfully assert that this persecution was without cause. He had not broken their laws, he had not injured them, he had not even desired to see them injured, he had not been an advocate of rebellion or anarchy, he had neither openly nor secretly opposed their power, and therefore, while this made their oppression the more inexcusable, it took away a part of its sting, and helped the brave-hearted servant of God to bear up. *"But my heart standeth in awe of thy word."* He might have been overcome by awe of the princes had it not been that a greater fear drove out the less, and he was swayed by awe of God's word. How little do crowns and sceptres become in the judgment of that man who perceives a more majestic royalty in the commands of his God. We are not likely to be disheartened by persecution, or driven by it into sin, if the word of God continually has supreme power over our minds.

162. *"I rejoice at thy word, as one that findeth great spoil."* His awe did not prevent his joy ; his fear of God was not of the kind which perfect love casts out, but of the sort which it nourishes. He trembled at the word of the Lord, and yet rejoiced at it. He compares his joy to that of one who has been long in battle, and has at last won the victory and is dividing the spoil. This usually falls to the lot of princes, and though David was not one with them in their persecutions, yet he had his victories, and his spoil was equal to their greatest gains. The profits made in searching the Scriptures were greater than the trophies of war. We too have to fight for divine truth ; every doctrine costs us a battle, but when we gain a full understanding of it by personal struggles it becomes doubly precious to us. In these days godly men have a full share of battling for the word of God ; may we have for our spoil a firmer hold upon the priceless word. Perhaps, however, the Psalmist may have rejoiced as one who comes upon hidden treasure for which he had not fought, in which case we find the analogy in the man of God who, while reading the Bible, makes grand and blessed discoveries of the grace of God laid up for him,—discoveries which surprise him, for he looked not to find such a prize. Whether we come by the truth as finders or as warriors fighting for it, the heavenly treasure should be equally dear to us. With what quiet joy does the ploughman steal home with his golden find ! How victors shout as they share the plunder ! How glad should that man be who has discovered his portion in the promises of holy writ, and is able to enjoy it for himself, knowing by the witness of the Holy Spirit that it is all his own.

163. *"I hate and abhor lying."* A double expression for an inexpressible loathing.

Falsehood in doctrine, in life, or in speech, falsehood in any form or shape, had become utterly detestable to the Psalmist. This was a remarkable state for an Oriental, for generally lying is the delight of Easterns, and the only wrong they see in it is a want of skill in its exercise so that the liar is found out. David himself had made much progress when he had come to this. He does not, however, alone refer to falsehood in conversation ; he evidently intends perversity in faith and teaching. He set down all opposition to the God of truth as lying, and then he turned his whole soul against it in the intensest form of indignation. Godly men should detest false doctrine even as they abhor a lie. *"But thy law do I love,"* because it is all truth. His love was as ardent as his hate. True men love truth, and hate lying. It is well for us to know which way our hates and loves run, and we may do essential service to others by declaring what are their objects. Both love and hate are contagious, and when they are sanctified the wider their influence the better.

164. *"Seven times a day do I praise thee because of thy righteous judgments."* He laboured perfectly to praise his perfect God, and therefore fulfilled the perfect number of songs. Seven may also intend frequency. Frequently he lifted up his heart in thanksgiving to God for his divine teachings in the word, and for his divine actions in providence. With his voice he extolled the righteousness of the Judge of all the earth. As often as ever he thought of God's ways a song leaped to his lips. At the sight of the oppressive princes, and at the hearing of the abounding falsehood around him, he felt all the more bound to adore and magnify God, who in all things is truth and righteousness. When others rob us of our praise it should be a caution to us not to fall into the same conduct towards our God, who is so much more worthy of honour. If we praise God when we are persecuted our music will be all the sweeter to him because of our constancy in suffering. If we keep clear of all lying, our song will be the more acceptable because it comes out of pure lips. If we never flatter men we shall be in the better condition for honouring the Lord. Do we praise God seven times a day ? Do we praise him once in seven days ?

165. *"Great peace have they which love thy law."* What a charming verse is this ! It deals not with those who perfectly keep the law, for where should such men be found ? but with those who love it, whose hearts and hands are made to square with its precepts and demands. These men are ever striving, with all their hearts, to walk in obedience to the law, and though they are often persecuted they have peace, yea, *great* peace ; for they have learned the secret of the reconciling blood, they have felt the power of the comforting Spirit, and they stand before the Father as men accepted. The Lord has given them to feel his peace, which passed all understanding. They have many troubles, and are likely to be persecuted by the proud, but their usual condition is that of deep calm—a peace too great for this little world to break. *"And nothing shall offend them,"* or, " shall really injure them." " All things work together for good to them that love God, to them who are the called according to his purpose." It must needs be that offences come, but these lovers of the law are peacemakers, and so they neither give nor take offence. That peace which is founded upon conformity to God's will is a living and lasting one, worth writing of with enthusiasm, as the Psalmist here does.

166. *"Lord, I have hoped for thy salvation, and done thy commandments."* Here we have salvation by grace, and the fruits thereof. All David's hope was fixed upon God, he looked to him alone for salvation ; and then he endeavoured most earnestly to fulfil the commands of his law. Those who place least reliance upon good works are very frequently those who have the most of them ; that same divine teaching which delivers us from confidence in our own doings leads us to abound in every good work to the glory of God. In times of trouble there are two things to be done, the first is to hope in God, and the second is to do that which is right. The first without the second would be mere presumption : the second without the first mere formalism. It is well if in looking back we can claim to have acted in the way which is commanded of the Lord. If we have acted rightly towards God we are sure that he will act kindly with us.

167. *"My soul hath kept thy testimonies."* My outward life has kept thy precepts, and my inward life—my soul, has kept thy testimonies. God has borne testimony to many sacred truths, and these we hold fast as for life itself. The gracious man stores up the truth of God within his heart as a treasure exceedingly dear and precious —he keeps it. His secret soul, his inmost self, becomes the guardian of these divine teachings which are his sole authority in soul matters. *"And I love them exceedingly."* This was why he kept them, and having kept them this was the result of the keeping.

He did not merely store up revealed truth by way of duty, but because of a deep, unutterable affection for it. He felt that he could sooner die than give up any part of the revelation of God. The more we store our minds with heavenly truth, the more deeply shall we be in love with it : the more we see the exceeding riches of the Bible the more will our love exceed measure, and exceed expression.

168. *"I have kept thy precepts and thy testimonies."* Both the practical and the doctrinal parts of God's word he had stored up, and preserved, and followed. It is a blessed thing to see the two forms of the divine word, equally known, equally valued, equally confessed : there should be no picking and choosing as to the mind of God. We know those who endeavour to be careful as to the precepts, but who seem to think that the doctrines of the gospel are mere matters of opinion, which they may shape for themselves. This is not a perfect condition of things. We have known others again who are very rigid as to the doctrines, and painfully lax with reference to the precepts. This also is far from right. When the two are " kept " with equal earnestness then have we the perfect man. *"For all my ways are before thee."* Probably he means to say that this was the motive of his endeavouring to be right both in head and heart, because he knew that God saw him, and under the sense of the divine presence he was afraid to err. Or else he is thus appealing to God to bear witness to the truth of what he has said. In either case it is no small consolation to feel that our heavenly Father knows all about us, and that if princes speak against us, and worldlings fill their mouths with cruel lies, yet he can vindicate us, for there is nothing secret or hidden from him.

We are struck with the contrast between this verse, which is the last of its octave, and verse 176, which is similarly placed in the next octave. This is a protest of innocence, " I have kept thy precepts," and that a confession of sin, " I have gone astray like a lost sheep." Both were sincere, both accurate. Experience makes many a paradox plain, and this is one. Before God we may be clear of open fault and yet at the same time mourn over a thousand heart-wanderings which need his restoring hand.

NOTES ON VERSES 161 TO 168.

Verse 161.—"Princes have persecuted me." The evil is aggravated from the consideration that it is the very persons who ought to be as bucklers to defend us, who employ their strength in hurting us. Yea, when the afflicted are stricken by those in high places, they in a manner think that the hand of God is against them. There was also this peculiarity in the case of the prophet, that he had to encounter the grandees of the chosen people—men whom God had placed in such honourable stations, to the end they might be the pillars of the Church.—*John Calvin.*

Verse 161.—"Without a cause." I settle it as an established point with me, that the more diligently and faithfully I serve Christ, the greater reproach and the more injury I must expect. I have drank deep of the cup of slander and reproach of late, but I am in no wise discouraged ; no, nor by, what is much harder to bear, the unsuccessfulness of my endeavours to mend this bad world.—*Philip Doddridge.*

Verse 161.—"Without a cause." We know what persecutions the body of Christ, that is, the holy Church, suffered from the kings of the earth. Let us therefore here also recognize the words of the Church : *"Princes have persecuted me without a cause."* For how had the Christians injured the kingdoms of the earth ? Although their King promised them the kingdom of heaven, how, I ask, had they injured the kingdoms of earth ? Did their King forbid his soldiers to pay and to render due service to the kings of the earth ? Saith he not to the Jews who were striving to calumniate him, " Render therefore unto Cæsar the things which are Cæsar's ; and unto God the things that are God's " ? Matt. xxii. 21. Did he not even in his own person pay tribute from the mouth of a fish ? Did not his forerunner, when the soldiers of this kingdom were seeking what they ought to do for their everlasting salvation, instead of replying, " Loose your belts, throw away your arms, desert your king, that ye may wage war for the Lord," answer, " Do violence to no man, neither accuse any falsely ; and be content with your wages " ? Luke iii. 14. Did not one of his soldiers, his most beloved companion, say to his fellow soldiers, the provincials, so to speak, of Christ, " Let every soul be subject unto the higher powers " ? and a little lower he addeth, " Render therefore to all their dues : tribute to whom tribute is due ; custom to whom custom ; fear to whom fear ; honour to whom honour. Owe no man anything, but to love one another." Rom. xiii. 1, 7, 8. Does he not enjoin the Church to pray even for kings themselves ? How, then, have the Christians offended against them ? What due have they not rendered ? In what have not Christians obeyed the monarchs of earth ? The kings of the earth therefore have persecuted the Christians *without a cause.*—*Augustine.*

Verse 161.—"But my heart standeth in awe of thy word." If there remains any qualm of fear on thy heart, fear from the wrath of bloody men threatening thee for thy profession of the truth, then to a heart inflamed with the love of truth, labour to add a heart filled with the fear of that wrath which God hath in store for all that apostatize from the truth. When you chance to burn your finger, you hold it to the fire, which being a greater fire draws out the other. Thus, when thy thoughts are scorched, and thy heart scared with the fire of man's wrath, hold them a while to hell fire, which God hath prepared for the fearful (Rev. xxi. 8), and all that run away from truth's colours (Heb. x. 39), and thou wilt lose the sense of the one for fear of the other. *Ignosce imperator,* saith the holy man, *tu carcerem, Deus gehennam minatur ;* " Pardon me, O Emperor, if I obey not thy command ; thou threatenest a prison, but God a hell." Observable is that of David : " Princes have persecuted me without a cause : but my heart standeth in awe of thy word." He had no cause to fear them that had no cause to persecute him. One threatening out of the word, that sets the point of God's wrath to his heart, scares him more than the worst that the greatest on earth can do to him. Man's wrath, when hottest, is but a temperate climate to the wrath of the living God. They who have felt both have testified as much. Man's wrath cannot hinder the access of God's love to the creature, which hath made the saints sing in the fire, in spite of their enemies' teeth. But the creature under God's wrath is like one shut up in a close oven, no crevice is open to let any of the heat out, or any refreshing in to him.—*William Gurnall.*

Verse 161.—"My heart standeth in awe of thy word." There is an *awe* of the word, not that maketh us shy of it, but tender of violating it, or doing anything contrary to it. This is not the fruit of slavish fear, but of holy love ; it is not afraid of the word, but delighteth in it, as it discovereth the mind of God to us ; as in the next verse it is written, " I rejoice at thy word." This awe is called by a proper name, reverence, or godly fear ; when we consider whose word it is, namely, the word of the Lord, who is our God, and hath a right to command what he pleaseth ; to whose will and word we have already yielded obedience, and devoted ourselves to walk worthy of him in all well-pleasing ; who can find us out in all our failings, as knowing our very thoughts afar off (Ps. cxxxix. 2), and having all our ways before him, and being one of whom we read,—" He is a holy God ; he is a jealous God ; he will not forgive your transgressions nor your sins " (Josh. xxiv. 19), that is to say, if we impenitently continue in them. Considering these things we receive the word with that trembling of heart which God so much respects.—*Thomas Manton.*

Verse 161.—*"In awe of thy word."* I would advise you all, that come to the reading or hearing of this book, which is the word of God, the most precious jewel, and most holy relic that remaineth upon earth, that ye bring with you the fear of God, and that ye do it with all due reverence, and use your knowledge thereof, not to vain glory of frivolous disputation, but to the honour of God, increase of virtue, and edification both of yourselves and others.—*Thomas Cranmer, 1489—1555.*

Verse 161.—*"Awe of thy word."* They that tremble at the convictions of the word may triumph in the consolations of it.—*Matthew Henry.*

Verse 162.—*"I rejoice at thy word, as one that findeth great spoil."* He never came to an ordinance but as a soldier to the spoil, after a great battle, as having a constant warfare with his corruptions that fought against his soul. Now he comes to see what God will say to him, and he will make himself a saver [or gainer], and get a booty out of every commandment, promise, or threatening he hears.—*John Cotton (1585—1652), in "The way of life."*

Verse 162.—*"I rejoice at thy word."* " Euripides," saith the orator, " hath in his well-composed tragedies more sentiments than sayings ; " and Thucydides hath so stuffed every syllable of his history with substance, that the one runs parallel along with the other ; Lysias's works are so well couched that you cannot take out the least word but you take away the whole sense with it ; and Phocion had a special faculty of speaking much in a few words. The Cretians, in Plato's time (however degenerated in St. Paul's), were more weighty than wordy ; Timanthes was famous in this, that in his pictures more things were intended than deciphered ; and of Homer it is said that none could ever peer him for poetry. Then how much more apt and apposite are these high praises to the book of God, rightly called *the Bible* or *the book*, as if it were, as indeed it is, both for fitness of terms and fulness of truth, the only book to which (as Luther saith) all the books in the world are but waste paper. It is called *the word*, by way of eminency, because it must be the butt and boundary of all our words ; and *the scripture*, as the lord paramount above all other words or writings of men collected into volumes, there being, as the Rabbins say, a mountain of sense hanging upon every tittle of it, whence may be gathered flowers and phrases to polish our speeches with, even sound words, that have a healing property in them, far above all filed phrases of human elocution.—*Thomas Adams.*

Verse 162.—*"As one that findeth great spoil."* This expressive image may remind us of the inward conflict to be endured in acquiring the spoils of this precious word. It is so contrary to our natural taste and temper, that habitual self-denial and struggle with the indisposition of the heart can alone enable us to *"find the spoil."* But what *"great spoil"* is divided as the fruit of the conflict ! How rich and abundant is the recompense of the " good soldier of Jesus Christ," who is determined through the power of the Spirit to " endure hardness," until he overcome the reluctance of his heart to this spiritual duty. He shall *"rejoice"* in *"finding great spoil."* Sometimes—as the spoil with which the lepers enriched themselves in the Syrian camp—it may be found unexpectedly. Sometimes we see the riches and treasures contained in a passage or doctrine, long before we can make it our own. And often when we gird ourselves to the conflict with indolence, and wanderings, under the weakness of our spiritual perceptions and the power of unbelief, many a prayer, and many a sigh is sent up for Divine aid, before we are crowned with victory, and are enabled, as the fruit of our conquest joyfully to appropriate the word to our present need and distress.—*Charles Bridges.*

Verse 163.—*"I hate and abhor lying,"* etc. One sees here how the light on David's soul was increasing more and more unto the perfect day. In the earlier part of this Psalm, David in the recollection of his own sin had prayed, " Remove from me the way of lying," and the Lord had indeed answered his prayer, for he now declares his utter loathing of every false way : *"I hate and abhor lying."* And we see, in some measure, the instrument by which the Holy Spirit wrought the change : *"Thy law do I love"* ; nay, as he adds in a later verse, " I love them exceedingly." And so it ever must be, the heart must have some holier object of its affection to fill up the void, or there will be no security against a relapse into sin. I might talk for ever on the sin, the disgrace, and the danger of lying, and though at the time and for a time my words might have some influence, yet, unless the heart be filled with the love of God and of God's law, the first temptation would prove too powerful. The Bible teaches us this in a variety of ways. God says to Israel, not only " cease to do evil," but, " learn to do well." And still more pointedly does the apostle, when he was warring against drunkenness, say, " Be not drunk with wine, wherein is excess,—but be filled with the Spirit."—*Barton Bouchier.*

Verse 163.—*"I hate and abhor lying."* *"Lying,"* according to Scripture usage, not only signifies speaking contrary to what one thinks, but also thinking contrary to the truth of things, and, particularly, the giving to any other of that worship and glory which are due to the true God alone. It is to think and act aside from God's truth. The men who persecuted that godly man thought of earthly prosperity and power as they should not have thought ; they judged God's servant falsely, and they thought wickedly of God himself. The man of God took a view of these things ; he saw the wickedness and the vileness of them, and he continued—*"Falsehood I hate and abhor : thy law do I love."* From all the false and delusive ways of men, from all the pride and pomp that surround courts, from the sinful pleasures and pursuits of worldly men, as well as from the ostentatious idolatry of heathen nations, he could turn with heart delight to the contemplation of Jehovah, in that wonderful ritual which manifested the divine mercy in vicarious sacrifices, and observances, and festivals ; and to that holy law which was given as man's rule of duty and grateful obedience, and all these he loved as the manifestations of God's grace.—*John Stephen.*

Verse 163.—*"I hate and abhor lying"* : not only *"hate"* it, nor simply I *"abhor"* it, but *"hate and abhor,"* to strengthen and increase the sense, and make it more vehement. Where the enmity is not great against the sin, the matter may be compounded and taken up ; but David will have nothing to do with it, for he saith,— I loathe and abhor it, and hate it with a deadly hatred. Slight hatred of a sinful course is not sufficient to guard us against it.—*Thomas Manton.*

Verse 163.—Sin seemeth to have its name from the Hebrew word *sana, to hate,* the word here used, because it is most of all to be hated, as the greatest evil, as that which setteth us furthest from God the greatest good. None can hate it but those that love the law of God ; for all hatred comes from love. A natural man may be angry with his sin, but hate it he cannot ; nay, he may leave it, but not loathe it ; if he did, he would loathe all sin as well as any one sin.—*Abraham Wright.*

Verse 163.—*"Lying."* All injustice is abominable : to do any sort of wrong is a heinous crime, but lying is that crime which, above all others, tendeth to the dissolution of society and disturbance of human life ; which God therefore doth most loathe, and men have reason especially to detest. Of this the slanderer is most deeply guilty. "A witness of Belial scorneth judgment, and the mouth of the wicked devoureth iniquity," saith the wise man : Prov. xix. 28. He is indeed, according to just estimation, guilty of all kinds of injury, breaking all the second table of commands respecting our neighbour. Most distinctly he beareth false witness against his neighbour : he doth covet his neighbour's goods, for 'tis constantly out of such an irregular desire, for his own presumed advantage, to dispossess his neighbour of some good, and transfer it on himself, that the slanderer uttereth his tale : he is also a thief and robber of his good name, a deflowerer and defiler of his reputation, an assassin and murderer of his honour. So doth he violate all the rules of justice, and perpetrateth all sorts of wrong against his neighbour.—*Isaac Barrow.*

Verse 164.—*"Seven times a day do I praise thee."* Affections of the soul cannot long be kept secret ; if they be strong they will break forth in actions. The love of God is like a fire in the heart of man, which breaks forth, and manifests itself in the obedience of his commandments, and praising him for his benefits ; and this is it which David now protests, that the love of God was not idle in his heart, but made him fervent and earnest in praising God, so that *"seven times a day"* he did praise God. For by this number the carefulness of holy devotion is expressed, and the fervency of his love. In praising God he could not be satisfied, saith Basil.—*William Cowper.*

Verse 164.—*"Seven times a day do I praise thee."* "As every grace," says Sibbes, "increaseth by exercise of itself, so doth the grace of prayer. By prayer we learn to pray." And thus it was with the Psalmist; he oftentimes anticipated the dawning of the morning for his exercise of prayer; and at midnight frequently arose to pour out his soul in prayer; now he adds that *"seven times in a day,"* or as we might express it, "at every touch and turn," he finds opportunity for and delight in praise. Oh for David's spirit and David's practice!—*Barton Bouchier.*

Verse 164.—*"Seven times a day do I praise thee."* A Christian ought to give himself up eminently to this duty without limits.—*Walter Marshall.*

Verse 164.—*"Seven times a day do I praise thee."* Not as if he had seven set hours for this duty every day, as the Papists would have it, to countenance their seven canonical hours, but rather a definite number is put for an indefinite, and so amounts to this,—he did very often in a day praise God; his holy heart taking the hint of every providence to carry him to heaven on this errand of prayer and praise.—*William Gurnall.*

Verse 164.—*"Seven times a day."* Some of the Jewish Rabbis affirm that David is here to be understood literally, observing, that the devout Hebrews were accustomed to praise God twice in the morning, before reading the ten commandments, and once after; twice in the evening before reading the same portion of inspiration, and twice after; which makes up the number of seven times a day.—*James Anderson's note to Calvin in loc.*

Verse 165.—*"Great peace have they which love thy law."* Amidst the storms and tempests of the world, there is a perfect calm in the breasts of those, who not only do the will of God, but *"love"* to do it. They are at peace with God, by the blood of reconciliation; at peace with themselves, by the answer of a good conscience, and the subjection of those desires which war against the soul; at peace with all men, by the spirit of charity; and the whole creation is so at peace with them that all things work together for their good. No external troubles can rob them of this *"great peace,"* no "offences" or stumbling blocks, which are thrown in their way by persecution, or temptation, by the malice of enemies, or by the apostasy of friends, by anything which they see, hear of, or feel, can detain, or divert them from their course. Heavenly love surmounts every obstacle, and runs with delight the way of God's commandments.—*George Horne.*

Verse 165.—*"Great peace have they which love thy law."* There have been Elis trembling for the ark of God, and Uzzahs putting out their hand in fear that it was going to fall; but in the midst of the deepest troubles through which the church has passed, and the fiercest storms that have raged about it, there have been true, faithful men of God who have never despaired. In every age there have been Luthers and Latimers, who have not only held fast their confidence, but whose peace has deepened with the roaring of the waves. The more they have been forsaken of men, the closer has been their communion with God. And with strong hold of him and of his promises, and hearts that could enter into the secret place of the Most High, although there has been everything without to agitate, threaten, and alarm, they have been guided into perfect peace.—*James Martin, in "The Christian Mirror, and other Sermons,"* 1878.

Verse 165.—*"Great peace have they which love thy law."* Clearness of conscience is a help to comfortable thoughts. Yet observe, that peace is not so much affected as preserved by a good conscience and conversation; for though joy in the Holy Ghost will make its nest nowhere but in a holy soul, yet the blood of Christ only can speak peace; "being justified by faith, we have peace:" Rom. v. 1. An exact life will not make, but keep conscience quiet; an easy shoe does not heal a sore foot, but it keeps a sound one from hurt. Walking with God according to gospel rules hath peace entailed upon it, and that peace is such a treasure, as thereby a Christian may have his rejoicing from himself. Gal. vi. 4, 16. His own heart sings him a merry tune, which the threats and reproaches of the world cannot silence. The treasure of comfort is not expended in affliction; death itself doth not exhaust but increase and advance it to an eternal triumph. O the excellency and necessity of it! Paul laid it up for a death-bed cordial: "Our rejoicing is this, the testimony of our conscience:" 2 Cor. i. 12. And Hezekiah dares hold it up to God, as well as cheer himself up with it on approaching death. A conscience good in point of integrity will be good also in point of tranquillity: "The righteous are bold as a lion": they have great peace that love and keep God's commandments: Prov. xxviii. 1; Ps. cxix. 165. And saith the apostle, "If our heart condemn us not, then have we confidence towards God" (1 John iii. 2), and I may add also, towards men. Oh! what comfort and solace hath a clear conscience! A conscientious man hath something within to answer accusations without; he hath such a rich treasure as will not fail in greatest straits and hazards. I shall conclude this with a notable saying of Bernard:—"The pleasures of a good conscience are the Paradise of souls, the joy of angels, a garden of delights, a field of blessing, the temple of Solomon, the court of God, the habitation of the Holy Spirit."—*Oliver Heywood.*

Verse 165.—"*Great peace.*" Note that for "*peace*" the Hebrew word is שלום *shâlom:* it signifies not only "*peace*," but also *perfection, wholeness, prosperity, tranquillity, healthfulness, safety,* the *completion* and *consummation* of every good thing, and so it is frequently taken by the Hebrews; hence in salutations wishing one the other well, they say, שלום לך, *shâlom lekha, i.e.,* "peace be with thee"; as if one should say, "may all things be prosperous with thee."—*Thomas Le Blanc.*

Verse 165.—"*They which love thy law.*" To *love* a law may seem strange; but it is the only true divine life. To keep it because we are afraid of its penalties is only a form of fear or prudential consideration. To keep it to preserve a good name may be propriety and respectability. To keep it because it is best for society may be worldly self-interest. To keep it because of physical health may be the policy of epicurean philosophy. To keep it because we love it is to show that it is already part of us—has entered into the moral texture of our being. Sin then becomes distasteful, and temptations lose their power.—*W. M. Statham, quoted in "A Homiletic Commentary on the Psalms,"* 1879.

Verse 165.—"*And nothing shall offend them.*" Hebrew, "they shall have no stumblingblock." 1 John ii. 10, "There is none *occasion of stumbling* in him" who abides in the *light,* which makes him to see and avoid such stumblingblocks. Wealth, tribulation, temptation, which are the occasion to many of falling (Isa. viii. 14, 15; Ezek. iii. 20; vii. 19; xiv. 3, 4, 7), are not so to him.—*A. R Faussett.*

Verse 165.—Learn the true wisdom of those of you who are new creatures, and who love God's holy law. All of you who are really brought to Christ are changed into his image, so that you love God's holy law. "I delight in the law of God after the inward man." "The statutes of the Lord are right, rejoicing the heart": Ps. xix. The world says: What a slave you are! you cannot have a little amusement on the Sabbath—you cannot take a Sabbath walk, or join a Sabbath tea-party; you cannot go to a dance or a theatre; you cannot enjoy the pleasures of sensual indulgence—you are a slave. I answer: Christ had none of these pleasures. He did not want them; nor do we. He knew what was truly wise, and good, and happy, and he chose God's holy law. He was the freest of all beings, and yet he knew no sin. Only make me free as Christ is free—this is all I ask. "Great peace have they which love thy law: and nothing shall offend them."—*Robert Murray M'Cheyne,* 1813—1843.

Verse 165.—"*Nothing shall offend them.*" They that have this character of God's children, will not be stumbled at God's dispensations, let them be never so cross to their desires, because they have a God to fly unto in all their troubles, and a sure covenant to rest upon. Therefore the reproaches cast upon them, and on the way of God, do not scandalize them; for they have found God in that very way which others speak evil of; they are not so offended by anything that attends the way of God, as to dislike or forsake that way. Nevertheless we must take heed that we be not offended.—*John Bunyan.*

Verse 166.—"*LORD, I have hoped for thy salvation,*" etc. This is the true posture in which all the servants of God should desire to be found—hoping in his mercy, and doing his commands. How easy were it to demonstrate the connection between the mental feeling here recognized, and the obedience with which it is here associated! It is the hope of salvation which is the great and pervading motive to holiness, and it is the consciousness of obedience to the will of God which strengthens our hope of interest in the divine mercy.—*John Morison.*

Verse 166.—"*LORD, I have hoped for thy salvation.*" This saying he borrowed from good old Jacob. Gen. xlix. 18.—*John Trapp.*

Verse 166.—"*I have done thy commandments.*" Set upon the practice of what you read. A student in physic doth not satisfy himself to read over a system or body of physic, but he falls upon practising physic : the life-blood of religion lies in the practical part. Christians should be walking Bibles. Xenophon said, " Many read Lycurgus's laws, but few observe them." The word written is not only a rule of knowledge, but a rule of obedience ; it is not only to mend our sight, but to mend our pace. David calls God's word " a lamp unto his feet " (verse 105). It was not only a light to his eyes to see by, but to his feet to walk by. By practice we trade with the talent of knowledge, and turn it to profit. This is a blessed reading of Scripture, when we fly from the sins which the word forbids, and espouse the doctrines which the word commands. Reading without practice will be but a torch to light men to hell.—*Thomas Watson.*

Verses 166, 167, 168.—He that casts the commands behind his back is very presumptuous in applying the promises to himself. That hope which is not accompanied with obedience will make a man ashamed. He that has learned the word of God knows that the law is not made void by faith, but established : Rom. iii. 31. Christ the Church's Head and Prophet, in his sermon upon the mount shows the extent of the law, requiring purity in the heart and thoughts, as well as in the life and actions, and condemns them " who shall break the least of these commands and shall teach men so "; but " those that teach and do them," he owns as great in his kingdom : Matt. v. 19. The law spoken on Mount Sinai is established by the Legislator Christ in Mount Zion as a rule of righteousness. And they who are rightly instructed, " which walk according to this rule," will have both heart and conversation ordered according to his direction, and " peace and mercy will be upon them," and hereby they will show themselves to be indeed the Israel of God.—*Nathanael Vincent.*

Verse 167.—*My soul hath kept thy testimonies ; and I love them exceedingly.*" Should he not have said, first, I have loved thy commandments, and so have kept them ? Doubtless he did so ; but he ran here in a holy and most heavenly circle, I have kept them and loved them, and loved them and kept them. If we love Christ, we shall also live the life of love in our measure, and his commandments will be most dear when himself is most precious.—*Thomas Shepard, in "The Sound Believer,"* 1671.

Verse 167.—*"My soul."* It is a usual phrase among the Hebrews, when they would express their affection to anything, to say, *"My soul"* : as Ps. ciii. 1 and civ. 1, *"My soul,* praise thou the Lord," and Luke i. *"My soul* doth magnify the Lord."—*Richard Greenham.*

Verse 167.—*"I love them exceedingly."* It is only a reasonable return to God ; for the Father loved me so *exceedingly* as not to spare his own Son, but to give him up for me ; and the Son loved me so *exceedingly* that he gave himself to me, and gave me back to myself when I was lost in my sins, original and actual.—*Gerhohus* (1093—1169), *in Neale and Littledale.*

Verses 167, 168.—Let not our consciousness of daily failures make us shrink from this strong expression of confidence. It is alleged as an evidence of grace, not as a claim of merit, and therefore the most humble believer need not hesitate to adopt it as the expression of Christian sincerity before God. David aspired to no higher character than that of a poor sinner : but he was conscious of spirituality of obedience, " *exceeding love* " to the divine word, and an habitual walk under the eye of his God—the evidences of a heart (often mentioned in the Old Testament) " perfect with him."—*Charles Bridges.*

Verse 168.—*"I have kept thy precepts, for all my ways are before thee."* When men are some way off in a king's eye they will be comely in their carriage ; but when they come into his presence-chamber to speak with him they will be most careful. Because saints are always in God's sight, their constant deportment must be pious and seemly.—*George Swinnock.*

Verse 168.—*"I have kept thy precepts,* etc. The Hebrew word שמר, *shamar,* that is here rendered " *kept,*" signifies to keep carefully, diligently, studiously, exactly. It signifies to keep as men keep prisoners, and to keep as a watchman keeps the city or the garrison ; yea, to keep as a man would keep his very life. But now mark what was the reason that David kept the precepts and the testimonies of the Lord so carefully, so sincerely, so diligently, so studiously, and so exactly. Why, the reason you have in the latter part of the verse, " *for all my ways are before thee.*" O sirs ! it is as necessary for him that would be eminent in holiness, to set the Lord always before him, as it is necessary for him to breathe. In that 31st of Job you have a very large narrative of that height and perfection of holiness that Job had attained to, and the great reason that he gives you, for this is in the 4th verse, " Doth not he see my way, and count all my steps ? " The eye of God had so strong an influence upon his heart and life, that it wrought him up to a very high pitch of holiness.—*Thomas Brooks.*

Verse 168.—*"All my ways are before thee."* That God seeth the secrets of our heart, is a point terrible to the wicked but joyful to the godly. The wicked are sorry that their heart is so open : it is a boiling pot of all mischief, a furnace and forge-house for evil. It grieveth them that man should hear and see their words and actions ; but what a terror is this—that their Judge, whom they hate, seeth their thought ! If they could deny this, they would. But so many of them as are convinced and forced to acknowledge a God, are shaken betimes with this also—that he is All-seeing. Others proceed more summarily, and at once deny the Godhead in their heart, and so destroy this conscience of his All-knowledge. But it is in vain : the more they harden their heart by this godless thought, the more fear is in them ; while they choke and check their conscience that it crow not against them it checketh them with foresight of fearful vengeance, and for the present convinceth them of the omniscience of God, the more they press to suppress it. But the godly rejoice herein ; it is to them a rule to square their thoughts by ; they take no liberty of evil thinking, willing, wishing, or affecting, in their hearts. Where that candle shineth, all things are framed as worthy of him and of his sight, whom they know to be seeing their heart.—*William Struther,* 1633.

Verse 168.—*"All my ways are before thee."* Walk Christian, in the view of God's omniscience ; say to thy soul, *cave, videt Deus ;* take heed God seeth. It is under the rose, as the common phrase is, that treason is spoken, when subjects think they are far enough from their king's hearing ; but did such know the prince to be under the window, or behind the hangings, their discourse would be more loyal. This made David so upright in his walking : *"I have kept thy precepts, for all my ways are before thee."* If Alexander's empty chair, which his captains, when they met in counsel, set before them, did awe them so as to keep them in good order ; how helpful would it be to set before ourselves the fact that God is looking upon us ! The Jews covered Christ's face, and then buffeted him : Mark xiv. 65. So does the hypocrite ; he first says in his heart, God sees not, or at least forgets that he sees, and then he makes bold to sin against him ; like that foolish bird, which runs her head among the reeds, and thinks herself safe from the fowler, as if because she did not see her enemy, therefore he could not see her. *Te mihi abscondam, non me tibi* (Augustine). I may hide thee from my eye, but not myself from thine eye.— *William Gurnall.*

NOTES ON VERSES 169 TO 176.

LET my cry come near before thee, O LORD : give me understanding according to thy word.

170 Let my supplication come before thee : deliver me according to thy word.

171 My lips shall utter praise, when thou hast taught me thy statutes.

172 My tongue shall speak of thy word : for all thy commandments *are* righteousness.

173 Let thine hand help me ; for I have chosen thy precepts.

174 I have longed for thy salvation, O LORD ; and thy law *is* my delight.

175 Let my soul live, and it shall praise thee ; and let thy judgments help me.

176 I have gone astray like a lost sheep ; seek thy servant : for I do not forget thy commandments.

The Psalmist is approaching the end of the Psalm, and his petitions gather force and fervency; he seems to break into the inner circle of divine fellowship, and to come even to the feet of the great God whose help he is imploring. This nearness creates the most lowly view of himself, and leads him to close the Psalm upon his face in deepest self-humiliation, begging to be sought out like a lost sheep.

169. *"Let my cry come near before thee, O LORD."* He is tremblingly afraid lest he should not be heard. He is conscious that his prayer is nothing better than the cry of a poor child, or the groan of a wounded beast. He dreads lest it should be shut out from the ear of the most High, but he very boldly prays that it may come before God, that it may be in his sight, under his notice, and looked upon with his acceptance ; yea, he goes further, and entreats, " Let my cry come near before thee, O Lord." He wants the Lord's attention to his prayer to be very close and considerate. He uses a figure of speech and personifies his prayer. We may picture his prayer as Esther, venturing into the royal presence, entreating an audience, and begging to find favour in the sight of the blessed and only Potentate. It is a very sweet thing to a suppliant when he knows of a surety that his prayer has obtained audience, when it has trodden the sea of glass before the throne, and has come even to the footstool of the glorious seat around which heaven and earth adore. It is to Jehovah that this prayer is expressed with trembling earnestness —our translators, filled with holy reverence, translate the word, " O LORD." We crave audience of none else, for we have confidence in none beside. " *Give me understanding according to thy word.*" This is the prayer about which the Psalmist is so exceedingly anxious. With all his gettings he would get understanding, and whatever he misses he is resolved not to miss this priceless boon. He desires spiritual light and understanding as it is promised in God's word, as it proceeds from God's word, and as it produces obedience to God's word. He pleads as though he had no understanding whatever of his own, and asks to have one given to him. " Give me understanding." In truth, he had an understanding according to the judgment of men, but what he sought was an understanding according to God's word, which is quite another thing. To understand spiritual things is the gift of God. To have a judgment enlightened by heavenly light and conformed to divine truth is a privilege which only grace can give. Many a man who is accounted wise after the manner of this world is a fool according to the word of the Lord. May we be among those happy children who shall all be taught of the Lord.

170. " *Let my supplication come before thee.*" It is the same entreaty with a slight change of words. He humbly calls his cry a supplication, a sort of beggar's petition ; and again he asks for audience and for answer. There might be hindrances in the way to an audience, and he begs for their removal—let it come. Other believers are heard—let my prayer come before thee. " *Deliver me according to thy word.*" Rid me of mine adversaries, clear me of my slanderers, preserve me from my tempters, and bring me up out of all my afflictions even as thy word has led me to expect thou wilt do. It is for this that he seeks understanding. His enemies would succeed through his folly, if they succeeded at all ; but if he exercised a sound discretion they would be baffled, and he would escape from them. The

Lord in answer to prayer frequently delivers his children by making them wise as serpents as well as harmless as doves.

171. "*My lips shall utter praise, when thou hast taught me thy statutes.*" He will not always be pleading for himself, he will rise above all selfishness, and render thanks for the benefit received. He promises to praise God when he has obtained practical instruction in the life of godliness : this is something to praise for, no blessing is more precious. The best possible praise is that which proceeds from men who honour God, not only with their lips, but in their lives. We learn the music of heaven in the school of holy living. He whose life honours the Lord is sure to be a man of praise. David would not only be grateful in silence, but he would express that gratitude in appropriate terms : his lips would utter what his life had practised. Eminent disciples are wont to speak well of the master who instructed them, and this holy man, when taught the statutes of the Lord, promises to give all the glory to him to whom it is due.

172. "*My tongue shall speak of thy word.*" When he had done singing he began preaching. God's tender mercies are such that they may be either said or sung. When the tongue speaks of God's word it has a most fruitful subject ; such speaking will be as a tree of life, whose leaves shall be for the healing of the people. Men will gather together to listen to such talk, and they will treasure it up in their hearts. The worst of us is that for the most part we are full of our own words, and speak but little of God's word. Oh, that we could come to the same resolve as this godly man, and say henceforth, "My tongue shall speak of thy word." Then should we break through our sinful silence ; we should no more be cowardly and half-hearted, but should be true witnesses for Jesus. It is not only of God's works that we are to speak, but of his word. We may extol its truth, its wisdom, its preciousness, its grace, its power ; and then we may tell of all it has revealed, all it has promised, all it has commanded, all it has effected. The subject gives us plenty of sea-room ; we may speak on for ever : the tale is for ever telling, yet untold. "*For all thy commandments are righteousness.*" David appears to have been mainly enamoured of the preceptive part of the word of God, and concerning the precept his chief delight lay in its purity and excellence. When a man can speak this from his heart, his heart is indeed a temple of the Holy Ghost. He had said aforetime (verse 138), "Thy testimonies are righteous," but here he declares that they are righteousness itself. The law of God is not only the standard of right, but it is the essence of righteousness. This the Psalmist affirms of each and every one of the precepts without exception. He felt like Paul—"The law is holy, and the commandment holy and just good." When a man has so high an opinion of God's commandments it is little wonder that his lips should be ready to extol the ever-glorious One.

173. "*Let thine hand help me.*" Give me practical succour. Do not entrust me to my friends or thy friends, but put thine own hand to the work. Thy hand has both skill and power, readiness and force : display all these qualities on my behalf. I am willing to do the utmost that I am able to do ; but what I need is thine help, and this is so urgently required that if I have it not I shall sink. Do not refuse thy succour. Great as thy hand is, let it light on me, even me. The prayer reminds us of Peter walking on the sea and beginning to sink ; he, too, cried, "Lord, help me," and the hand of his Master was stretched out for his rescue. "*For I have chosen thy precepts.*" A good argument. A man may fitly ask help from God's hand when he has dedicated his own hand entirely to the obedience of the faith. "I have chosen thy precepts." His election was made, his mind was made up. In reference to all earthly rules and ways, in preference even to his own will, he had chosen to be obedient to the divine commands. Will not God help such a man in holy work and sacred service ? Assuredly he will. If grace has given us the heart with which to will, it will also give us the hand with which to perform. Whenever, under the constraints of a divine call, we are engaged in any high and lofty enterprise, and feel it to be too much for our strength, we may always invoke the right hand of God in words like these.

174. "*I have longed for thy salvation, O LORD.*" He speaks like old Jacob on his deathbed ; indeed, all saints, both in prayer and in death, appear as one, in word, and deed, and mind. He knew God's salvation, and yet he longed for it ; that is to say, he had experienced a share of it, and he was therefore led to expect something yet higher and more complete. There is a salvation yet to come, when we shall be clean delivered from the body of this death, set free from all the turmoil

and trouble of this mortal life, raised above the temptations and assaults of Satan, and brought near unto our God, to be like him and with him for ever and ever. " I have longed for thy salvation, O Jehovah ; *and thy law is my delight."* The first clause tells us what the saint longs for, and this informs us what is his present satisfaction. God's law, contained in the ten commandments, gives joy to believers. God's law, that is, the entire Bible, is a well-spring of consolation and enjoyment to all who receive it. Though we have not yet reached the fulness of our salvation, yet we find in God's word so much concerning a present salvation that we are even now delighted.

175. *"Let my soul live."* Fill it full of life, preserve it from wandering into the ways of death, give it to enjoy the indwelling of the Holy Ghost, let it live to the fulness of life, to the utmost possibilities of its new-created being. *"And it shall praise thee."* It shall praise thee for life, for new life, for thou art the Lord and Giver of Life. The more it shall live, the more it shall praise, and when it shall live in perfection it shall praise thee in perfection. Spiritual life is prayer and praise. *"And let thy judgments help me."* While I read the record of what thou hast done, in terror or in love, let me be quickened and developed. While I see thy hand actually at work upon me, and upon others, chastening sin, and smiling upon righteousness, let me be helped both to live aright and to praise thee. Let all thy deeds in providence instruct me, and aid me in the struggle to overcome sin and to practise holiness. This is the second time he has asked for help in this portion ; he was always in need of it, and so are we.

176. This is the *finale*, the conclusion of the whole matter : *"I have gone astray like a lost sheep"*—often, wilfully, wantonly, and even hopelessly, but for thine interposing grace. In times gone by, before I was afflicted, and before thou hadst fully taught me thy statutes, "I went astray" from the practical precepts, from the instructive doctrines, and from the heavenly experiences which thou hadst set before me. I lost my road, and I lost myself. Even now I am apt to wander. and, in fact, have roamed already ; therefore, Lord, restore me. *"Seek thy servant."* He was not like a dog, that somehow or other can find its way back ; but he was like a lost sheep, which goes further and further away from home ; yet still he was a sheep, and the Lord's sheep, his property, and precious in his sight, and therefore he hoped to be sought in order to be restored. However far he might have wandered he was still not only a sheep, but God's " servant," and therefore he desired to be in his Master's house again, and once more honoured with commissions for his Lord. Had he been only a lost sheep he would not have prayed to be sought ; but being also a " servant " he had the power to pray. He cries, " Seek thy servant," and he hopes to be not only sought, but forgiven, accepted, and taken into work again by his gracious Master.

Notice this confession ; many times in the Psalm David has defended his own innocence against foul-mouthed accusers, but when he comes into the presence of the Lord his God he is ready enough to confess his transgressions. He here sums up, not only his past, but even his present life, under the image of a sheep which has broken from its pasture, forsaken the flock, left the shepherd, and brought itself into the wild wilderness, where it has become as a lost thing. The sheep bleats, and David prays, " Seek thy servant." His argument is a forcible one,— *" for I do not forget thy commandments."* I know the right, I approve and admire the right, what is more, I love the right, and long for it. I cannot be satisfied to continue in sin, I must be restored to the ways of righteousness. I have a home-sickness after my God, I pine after the ways of peace ; I do not and I cannot forget thy commandments, nor cease to know that I am always happiest and safest when I scrupulously obey them, and find all my joy in doing so. Now, if the grace of God enables us to maintain in our hearts the loving memory of God's commandments it will surely yet restore us to practical holiness. That man cannot be utterly lost whose heart is still with God. If he be gone astray in many respects, yet still, if he be true in his soul's inmost desires, he will be found again, and fully restored. Yet let the reader remember the first verse of the Psalm while he reads the last : the major blessedness lies not in being restored from wandering, but in being upheld in a blameless way even to the end. Be it ours to keep the crown of the causeway, never leaving the King's highway for By-path Meadow, or any other flowery path of sin. May the Lord uphold us even to the end. Yet even then we shall not be able to boast with the Pharisee, but shall still pray with the publican, " God be merciful to me a sinner ; " and with the Psalmist, " Seek thy servant."

EXPOSITION OF VERSES 169 TO 176.

This commences a new division of the Psalm, indicated by the last letter of the Hebrew alphabet, the letter *Tau*, corresponding to our *t*, or *th*.—*Albert Barnes.*

Verse 169.—*"Let my cry come near before thee, O LORD."* That is, as some will have it, Let this whole preceding Psalm, and all the petitions (whereof we have here a repetition) therein contained, be highly accepted in heaven.—*John Trapp.*

Verse 169.—*"Let my cry come near before thee, O LORD."* We are now come to the last section of this Psalm, wherein we see David more fervent in prayer than he was in the first, as ye shall easily observe by comparing them both together. The godly, the longer they speak to God, are the more fervent and earnest to speak to him ; so that unless necessity compel them, they desire never to intermit conference with him.

Many prayers hath he made to God in this Psalm : now in the end he prays for his prayers, that the Lord would let them come before him. Some men send out prayers, but God turns them into sin, and puts them away back from him : therefore David seeks favour to his prayers.—*William Cowper.*

Verse 169.—*"Give me understanding."* This was the prayer of Solomon (1 Kings iii. 9), and we are told that it pleased the Lord, and as a reward he added temporal prosperity, which the young king had not asked. Yet Solomon meant less by his prayer than his father David did ; for we see in him little trace of the deep devotion for which his father was so remarkable. The Psalmist here prays a deep prayer which can only be answered by the Holy Ghost himself enlightening the soul. The understanding is a most important member of our spiritual frame. Conscience is the understanding exercised upon moral questions, and if that be not right, where shall we be ? Our understanding of the word of God comes by teaching, but also through experience we understand hardly anything till we experience it. Such an enlightening experience is the gift of God, and to him we must look for it in prayer.—*C. H. S.*

Verse 169.—*"Give me understanding."* The especial work of the Holy Spirit in the illumination of our minds unto the understanding of the Scripture is called *"understanding."* The Psalmist prays *"Give me understanding, and I shall keep thy law"* (verse 34). So the apostle speaks to Timothy " Consider what I say ; and the Lord give thee understanding in all things " 2 Tim. ii. 7. Besides his own consideration of what was proposed unto him, which includes the due and diligent use of all outward means, it was moreover necessary that God *should give him understanding* by an inward effectual work of his Spirit, that he might comprehend the things wherein he was instructed. And the desire hereof, as of that without which there can be no saving knowledge of the word, nor advantage by it, the Psalmist expresseth emphatically, with great fervency of spirit in verse 144 : " The righteousness of thy testimony is everlasting give me understanding, and I shall live." Without this he knew that he could have no benefit by the everlasting righteousness of the testimonies of God. All understanding, indeed, however it be abused by the most, is the work and effect of the Holy Ghost , for " the inspiration of the Almighty giveth understanding " Job xxxii. 8. So is this spiritual understanding in an especial manner the gift of God. In this " understanding " both the ability of our mind and the due exercise of it is included. This one consideration, that the saints of God have with so much earnestness prayed that God would *give them understanding* as to his mind and will as revealed in the word, with his reiterated promises that he would so do, is of more weight with me than all the disputes of men to the contrary. No farther argument is necessary to prove that men do not understand the mind of God in the Scripture in a due manner, than their supposal and confidence that so they can do without the communication of a spiritual understanding unto them by the Holy Spirit. This self-confidence is directly contrary unto the plain, express testimonies of the word.—*John Owen.*

Verse 169.—*"Give me understanding."* Why should the man of God here pray for *understanding?* Had he not often prayed for it before ? Was he a novice in knowledge, being a prophet ? Doth not our Saviour Christ reprehend repetitions and babbling in prayer ? True it is our Saviour Christ doth reprehend that babbling which is without faith and knowledge and a feeling of our wants ; but he speaketh not against those serious repetitions which proceed from a plentiful knowledge, abundant faith, and lively feeling of our necessities. Again, although it cannot be denied but he was a man of God, and had received great grace, yet God giveth knowledge to his dearest saints in this life but in part, and the most which we see and know is but little. Besides, when we have knowledge, and knowledge must be brought into practice, we shall find such difficulties, such waywardness, such forgetfulness, such wants, that although we have had with the prophet a very good direction in the general things of the word, which are universal and few, yet we shall find many distractions in our practices, which must be particular and many ; and we shall either fail in memory by forgetfulness, or in judgment by blindness, or in affection by dulness. So easily may we slip when we think we may hold our journey on. Wherefore the man of God, through that examination which he took of his heart and affections, seeing those manifold straits and difficulties, prayeth in the verse following, not for the renewing of men in general in their troubles, but for the considering of his own particular condition.—*Richard Greenham.*

Verse 169.—"According to thy word." David here seeks understanding not carnally, for the wisdom of the flesh is death : but he seeks understanding *according to God's word.* Without this the wisdom of man is foolishness ; and the more subtil he seems to be in his ways, the more deeply he involves himself in the snare of the devil. " They have rejected the word of the Lord ; and what wisdom is in them ? " Jer. viii. 9. But seeing he was an excellent prophet, and protested before that he had more understanding than the ancients, yea, than his teachers ; how is it that he still prays for understanding ? In answer to this we are to know, that there is a great difference between the gifts of nature and grace. Nature ofttimes gives to man very excellent gifts, as rare memory, knowledge, quick wit, strength, external beauty ; but therewithal it teacheth not man to consider that in which he is wanting ; whereof it comes to pass, that he waxeth proud of that which he hath. This is a common thing to men in the state of nature, that of small gifts they conceive a great pride : but grace, as it gives to man more excellent gifts than nature can afford, so it teacheth him to look unto that which he wants, that he be not puffed up by considering that which he hath, but carried in all humility of heart to pray for that which he wants.—*Abraham Wright.*

Verse 170.—"Let my supplication come before thee," etc. The sincere worshipper cannot be contented with anything short of actual intercourse with God. The round of duty cannot please where the spirit of grace and supplication has not been vouchsafed. A filial disposition will pour itself forth in earnest longings after communion with God. Nor will the hope of gracious audience be founded on any other plea save that of the sure word of Jehovah's promise. It is in accordance with that word, and not in opposition to it, that the child of God expects to be heard. All his deliverance he feels to be from the Lord, and all that he looks for from heaven he anticipates in answer to prayer. O for more of that faith which makes its appeal to the divine veracity, and which looks with steadfast eye to the promise of a covenant-keeping God.—*John Morison.*

Verse 170.—"Let my supplication come before thee." Observe the order of the words here and in the preceding verse. First we had, " Let my cry come near ; " then " Give me understanding," and that " according to thy word," and now we have *"Let my prayer enter in* (LXX., Syr., Arb., Vulg.,) *before thee."* Just so, if you wish for an interview with a man of very high rank, first you come near his house, then you ask for information and instruction as to his intentions, then you ask permission to enter, lest you should be driven away and refused admittance. Knock therefore at the door of the heavenly palace : knock, not with your bodily hand, but with the right hand of prayer. For the voice can knock as well as the hand, as it is written, " It is the voice of my Beloved that knocketh " : Cant. v. 2. And when you have knocked, see how you go in, lest after entering you should not get the sight of the King. For there are many who make their way into palaces, and do not at once get an audience of an earthly sovereign, but have to watch constantly to obtain an interview at last. Nor have they the choice of the opportunity, they come when they are sent for, and then present their petition, if they wish to be favourably received.—*Ambrose, in Neale and Littledale.*

Verse 171.—"My lips shall utter praise." You have stood at the fountain head of a stream of water, and admired while it bubbled up, and ran down in a clear rivulet, till at length it swelled the mighty river. Such is the allusion here.

The heart taught of God cannot contain itself, but breaks out in praise and singing. This would be the effect of divine illumination, and this would be felt to be a privilege, yea, and a high duty. Have you not found so, believers, specially on communion occasions ? Be assured, such utterances are the sign of a renewed heart ; yea, of a heart filled with all gratitude of right feeling.—*John Stephen.*

Verse 171.—*"My lips shall utter praise,"* etc.

> O make me, Lord, thy statutes learn !
>   Keep in thy ways my feet,
> Then shall my lips divinely burn ;
>   Then shall my songs be sweet.
>
> Each sin I cast away shall make
>   My soul more strong to soar ;
> Each deed of holiness shall wake
>   A strain divine the more.
>
> My voice shall more delight thine ear
>   The more I wait on thee ;
> Thy service bring my song more near
>   The angelic harmony.

T. H. Gill, in *"Breathings of the Better Life"* [1881].

Verse 172.—*"My tongue shall speak of thy word."* One duty of thankfulness promised by David is, *to speak of God's words* for the edification of others. Every Christian man, as he is a priest to offer sacrifice unto God, so is he a prophet to teach his brethren ; for unto us all stands that commandment, " Edify one another in their most holy faith." But, alas, ye shall see many Christians now, who at their tables, and in their companies, can speak freely upon any subject ; only for spiritual matters, which concern the soul, there they are dumb, and cannot say with David, *"My tongue shall speak of thy word."*—*William Cowper.*

Verse 173.—*"Let thine hand help me."* David having before made promises of thankfulness, seeks now help from God, that he may perform them. Our sufficiency is not of ourselves, but of God ; to will and to do are both from him. In temporal things men ofttimes take great pains with small profit ; first, because they seek not to make their conscience good ; next, because they seek not help from God : therefore they speed no better than Peter, who fished all night and got nothing till he cast his net in the name of the Lord. But in spiritual things we may far less look to prosper, if we call not for God's assistance : the means will not profit us unless God's blessing accompany them. There is preaching, but for the most part without profit ; there is prayer, but it prevails not ; there is hearing of the word, but without edifying ; and all because in spiritual exercises instant prayer is not made unto God, that his hand may be with us to help us.—*Abraham Wright.*

Verse 173.—*"I have chosen thy precepts."* Hath God given you a heart to make choice of his ways ? O bless God ! There was a time when you went on in giving pleasure to the flesh, and you saw then no better thing than such a kind of life, and the Lord hath been pleased to discover better things to you, so as to make you renounce your former ways, and to make choice of another way, in which your souls have found other manner of comforts, and satisfactions, and contentments than ever you did before. Bless God as David did : " Blessed be the Lord who hath given me counsel " . . . . Seeing God hath thus inclined your heart to himself, be for ever established in your *choice :* seeing God hath shown to you his ways, as Pilate said in another case, " That I have written I have written " : so say you, " That I have chosen I have chosen."—*Jeremiah Burroughs,* in *"Moses his Choice."*

Verses 173, 174.—*"I have chosen." "My delight."* Cheerfulness accompanies election of a thing. Lumpishness is a sign we never chose it, but were forced to it. Such cheerfulness in service procures cheerfulness in mercies : Isa. lxiv. 5, " Thou meetest him that rejoiceth and worketh righteousness." He puts to his hand to help such an one. Christ loves not melancholy and phlegmatic service ; such a temper in acts of obedience is a disgrace to God and to religion : to God, it betrays us to have jealous thoughts of God, as though he were a hard master ; to religion it makes others think duties are drudgeries, and not privileges.—*Stephen Charnock.*

Verse 174.—"I have longed for thy salvation, O Lord," etc. The thing which we learn hence out of David's joining these two together, *I long for salvation,* and *thy law is my delight,* is this, that it is not enough for a man to say, he longs and desires to be saved, unless he makes a conscience to use the appointed means to bring him thereunto. It had been but hypocrisy in David to say he longed for salvation, if his conscience had not been able to witness with him that *the law was his delight.* It is mere mockery for a man to say he longeth for bread, and prayeth to God every day to give him his daily bread, if he yet walk in no calling, or else seek to get it by fraud and rapine, not staying himself at all upon God's providence. Who will imagine that a man wisheth for health, who either despiseth or neglecteth the means of his recovery ? God hath in his own wisdom appointed a lawful means for every lawful thing ; this means, being obediently used, the comfortable obtaining of the end may be confidently looked for ; the means being not observed, to think to attain to the end is mere presumption. God will deliver Noah from the flood, but Noah must be *"moved with reverence,"* and *"prepare the ark"* (Heb. xi. 7), or else he could not have escaped. He would save Lot from Sodom, but yet Lot must hie him out quickly, and not look behind him till he have entered Zoar : Gen. xix. 17. He was pleased to cure Hezekiah of the plague, but yet Hezekiah must take " a lump of figs, and lay it upon his boil : ". Isa. xxxviii. 21. He vouchsafed to preserve Paul and company at sea, yet the sailors must " abide in the ship," else ye cannot be saved, saith Paul : Acts xxvii. 31.—*Samuel Hieron, 1572—1617.*

Verse 174.—"I have longed for thy salvation." It is God's salvation proper that he must desire—*"thy salvation"*—for nothing else could satisfy his pure mind—perfect peace with God, perfect purity and perfect hope. Now if you ask what was God's way of delivering, and what was his way of salvation, the answer is, it was set forth in his word, and was what the Psalmist calls his *"law."* God's salvation and his law were discerned to be one. *"I have longed for thy salvation, O Lord ; and thy law is my delight."*—*John Stephen.*

Verse 174.—"I have longed for thy salvation, O Lord." *"Salvation,"* by the " hand," or arm of Jehovah (which is often in scripture a title of Messiah), hath been the object of the hopes, the desires, and " longing " expectations of the faithful, from Adam to this hour, and will continue so to be until he, who hath already visited us in great humility, shall come again in glorious majesty to complete our redemption and take us to himself.—*George Horne.*

Verse 174.—"I have longed for thy salvation, O Lord." For a present salvation from the guilt and power of sin, and for future salvation, in the full and everlasting enjoyment of God in heaven. David had the happiness to be a partaker, both of pardoning mercy and of sanctifying grace ; yet still he longed for more of this salvation, that is, for a more assured faith of pardoning mercy, and larger measures of sanctifying grace. A gracious soul is insatiable ; the more it hath received, the more it desires to receive. Enjoyment, instead of surfeiting, sharpens the appetite. Nay, so sweet is the relishing of spiritual things, that every renewed taste of them quenches the thirst for other things.

"Thy law is my delight." Here David chooses the term *"law"* for denoting the whole revelation of God's will, to remind us of the inseparable connexion between privilege and duty, faith and obedience, holiness and comfort ; and to teach us that we ought to be thankful to God for the direction he hath given us in the road to heaven no less than for the promises by which we are assured of the possession of it.—*Robert Walker, 1716—1783.*

Verse 174.—"Thy law is my delight." Religion will decay or flourish as it is our *duty* or our *delight.* The mind is incapable of continued exertion *for duty ;* but it readily falls in *with "delight."* Thus our duties become our privileges, while Christ is their source and life. Every step of progress is progress in happiness. This verse (of which experience is the best interpreter) is the believer's language in his lively, as well as in his fainting state. For the more he knows and enjoys of the Divine presence, the more he longs to know and enjoy it.—*Charles Bridges.*

Verse 174.—"Delight," in the plural, " *delights,"* as in verses 24, 77, 92, 143. God's word is an abundant source of pleasure to his people.—*William S. Plumer.*

Verse 175.—"Let my soul live, and it shall praise thee," etc. This verse containeth three things, 1st. David's petition for life : *"Let my soul live."* *"My soul ; "* that is, myself : the soul is put for the whole man. The contrary : " Let me die with the Philistines," said Samson (Judges xxi. 30) ; Hebrew, margin, " Let my soul die." His life was sought after by the cruelty of his enemies; and he desireth God to keep him alive.

2ndly. His argument from the aim of his life; *"And it shall praise thee."* The glorifying of God was his aim. The fruit of all God's benefits is to profit us, and praise God. David professeth that all the days of his life he would live in the sense and acknowledgment of such a benefit.

3rdly. The ground of his hope and confidence in the last clause: *"And let thy judgments help me."* Our hopes of help are grounded on God's judgments, whereby is meant his word. There are judgments decreed, and judgments executed; doctrinal judgments, and providential judgments. That place intimateth the distinction: " Because sentence against an evil work is not executed speedily, therefore the heart of the sons of men is fully set in them to do evil : " Eccl. viii. 11. There is *sententia lata et dilata.* Here God's judgments are put for the sentence pronounced; and chiefly for one part of them, the promises of grace. As also, " I have hoped in thy judgments : " Ps. cxix. 43. Promises are the objects of hope.—*Thomas Manton.*

Verse 175.—*"Let my soul live."* What is the life that the Psalmist is now praying for, but the salvation for which he had just expressed his longing? The taste that he has received makes him hunger for a higher and more continued enjoyment—not for selfish gratification, but that he might employ himself in the praise of his God. Indeed, as we have drawn towards the close of this Psalm, we cannot but have observed that character of praise to pervade his experience, which has been generally remarked in the concluding Psalms of this sacred book. Much do we lose of spiritual strength for want of occupying ourselves more in the exercise of praise.—*Charles Bridges.*

Verse 175.—*"Live and praise."* The saint improves his earthly things for an heavenly end. Where layest thou up thy treasure? Dost thou bestow it on thy voluptuous appetite, thy hawks and thy hounds; or lockest thou it up in the bosom of Christ's poor members? What use makest thou of thy honour and greatness? To strengthen the hands of the godly or the wicked? And so of all thy other temporal enjoyments. A gracious heart improves them for God; when a saint prays for these things, he hath an eye to some heavenly end. If David prays for life, it is not that he may live, but *"live and praise God."* When he was driven from his regal throne by the rebellious arms of Absalom, see what his desire and hope were, 2 Sam. xv. 25 : " The king said unto Zadok, Carry back the ark of God into the city : if I shall find favour in the eyes of the Lord, he will bring me again, and shew me both it, and his habitation." Mark, not shew me my crown, my palace, but the ark, the house of God.—*William Gurnall.*

Verse 175.—*"Live and praise."* Liveliness of soul is the Spirit's gift, and it will show itself in abounding praises.—*Henry Law.*

Verse 175.—*"Let thy judgments help me."* In the second clause it would be harsh to understand the word *"judgments"* of the commandments, to which it does not properly belong to give help. It seems, then, that the prophet, perceiving himself liable to numberless calamities—even as the faithful, by reason of the unbridled license of the wicked, dwell in this world as sheep among wolves,—calls upon God to protect him in the way of restraining, by his secret providence, the wicked from doing him harm. It is a very profitable doctrine, when things in the world are in a state of great confusion, and when our safety is in danger amidst so many and varied storms, to lift up our eyes to the judgments of God, and to seek a remedy in them.—*John Calvin.*

Verses 175, 176—

> Though like a sheep estranged I stray,
> Yet have I not renounced thy way.
> Thine hand extend ; thine own reclaim ;
> Grant me to live, and praise thy name.
>
> *Richard Mant.*

Verse 176.—*"I have gone astray like a lost sheep."* Though a sheep go astray, yet it is soon called back by the voice of the shepherd : " My sheep hear my voice." Thus David when he went against Nabal was called back by the Lord's voice in a woman ; and when he had slain Uriah he was brought again by Nathan. And therefore if we will be sheep, then though we sometimes go astray, yet we must be easily reclaimed.—*Richard Greenham.*

Verse 176.—"*I have gone astray like a lost sheep,*" driven out by storm, or dark day, or by the hunting of the dogs chased out from the rest of the flock.—*David Dickson.*

Verse 176.—"*I have gone astray like a lost sheep,*" etc.   And this is all the conclusion—"*a lost sheep*" !   This long Psalm of ascriptions, praises, avowals, resolves, high hopes, ends in this, that he is a perishing sheep.   But, stay, there is hope— "*Seek thy servant.*"   "*I have gone astray like a lost sheep.*"   The original is of the most extensive range, comprehending all time past, and also the habitual tendencies of the man.   The believer feels that he had gone astray when the grace of God found him ; that he had gone astray many times, had not the grace of God prevented it.   He feels that he went astray on such and such unhappy occasions.   He also feels that he hath gone astray in all that he hath done ; and indeed that he is astray now.   But the word expresses the habitual tendency likewise—I go astray like a lost sheep, and this rendering is in keeping with the prayer, "*Seek thy servant.*"   The third member is also properly rendered in keeping with it : " I go astray like a lost sheep ; seek thy servant ; for I do not forget thy commandments."   All this is descriptive of the remaining corruption that is in the believer.   He is not unmindful of the Lord ; he has the root of the matter in him, the seed of divine life ; yet he does go astray ; whence the necessity of the prayer : "*Seek thy servant.*"   Isaiah's description of men, although conveyed in the same terms, is evidently more sweeping as the context words show : " All we like sheep have gone astray ; we have turned every one to his own way ; and the Lord hath laid on him the iniquity of us all." This would seem to apply to the race of man.   Rather is the experience of the Psalmist similar to that described by the apostle Paul : " I find a law, that when I would do good, evil is present with me.   For I delight in the law of God, after the inward man : But I see another law in my members, warring against the law of my mind, and bringing me into captivity to the law of sin which is in my members." And the Psalmist had the same remedy at the early period, as had the apostle in the later times ; for God's salvation is one.   The Psalmist's remedy was, "*Seek thy servant ;*" the apostle's, " O wretched man that I am ! who shall deliver me from the body of this death?   I thank God through Jesus Christ our Lord."—*John Stephen.*

Verse 176.—"*I have gone astray.*"   The original word signifies either the turning of the foot, or the turning of the heart, or both, out of the way.   "*I have gone astray like a lost sheep ;*" that is, I have been deceived, and so have gone out of the way of thy holy commandments.   Satan is an ill guide, and our hearts are no better : he that follows either, quickly loseth himself ; and until God seeketh us (as David prays in the next words), we cannot find our way when we are once out of it.— *Joseph Caryl.*

Verse 176.—"*I have gone astray.*"   Gotthold one day saw a farmer carefully counting his sheep as they came from the field.   Happening at the time to be in an anxious and sorrowful mood, he gave vent to his feelings and said : Why art thou cast down, my soul ? and why disquieted with vexing thoughts ? Surely thou must be dear to the Most High as his lambs are to this farmer.   Art thou not better than many sheep ? Is not Jesus Christ thy shepherd ? Has not he risked his blood and life for thee ?   Hast thou no interest in his words : " I give unto my sheep eternal life, and they shall never perish, neither shall any pluck them out of my hand " ?   John x. 28.   This man is numbering his flock ; and thinkest thou that God does not also count and care for his believing children and elect, especially as his beloved Son has averred, that the very hairs of our head are all numbered ? Matt. x. 30.   During the day, I may perhaps have gone out of the way, and heedlessly followed my own devices ; still, at the approach of evening, when the faithful Shepherd counts his lambs, he will mark my absence, and graciously seek and bring me back.   Lord Jesus, "*I have gone astray like a lost sheep ; seek thy servant ; for I do not forget thy commandments.*"—*Christian Scriver* (1629—1693), *in Gotthold's Emblems.*

Verse 176.—"*I have gone astray,*" etc.   Who is called " the man after God's own heart " ?   David, the Hebrew king, had fallen into sins enough—blackest crimes— there was no want of sin.   And, therefore, unbelievers sneer, and ask, " Is this your man after God's own heart ? "   The sneer, it seems to me, is but a shallow one. What are faults, what are the outward details of a life, if the inner secret of it, the remorse, temptations, the often-baffled, never-ended struggle of it, be forgotten ? . . . . David's life and history, as written for us in those Psalms of his, I consider to be the truest emblem ever given us of a man's moral progress and warfare here below. All earnest souls will ever discover in it the faithful struggle of an earnest human soul towards what is good and best. Struggle often baffled—sore baffled—driven as into entire wreck ; yet a struggle never ended, ever with tears, repentance, true unconquerable purpose begun anew.—*Thomas Carlyle* (1795—1881), *in "Heroes and Hero-Worship."*

Verse 176.—*"For I do not forget thy commandments."* In all my wandering ; with my consciousness of error ; with my sense of guilt ; I still *do* feel that I love thy law, thy service, thy commandments. They are the joy of my heart, and I desire to be recalled from all my wanderings, that I may find perfect happiness in thee and in thy service evermore. Such is the earnest wish of every regenerated heart. For as such a one may have wandered from God, yet he is conscious of true attachment to him and his service ; he desires and earnestly prays that he may be " sought out," brought back, and kept from wandering any more.—*Albert Barnes.*

Verses 176.—*"For I do not forget thy commandments."* The godly never so fall but there remains in them some grace, which reserves a hope of medicine to cure them : so David here. Albeit he transgressed some of God's commandments, yet he fell not into any full oblivion of them.—*William Cowper.*

Verse 176.—I do not think that there could possibly be a more appropriate conclusion of such a Psalm as this, so full of the varied experience and the ever-changing frames and feelings even of a child of God, in the sunshine and the cloud, in the calm and in the storm, than this ever-clinging sense of his propensity to wander, and the expression of his utter inability to find his way back without the Lord's guiding hand to restore him ; and at the same time with it all, his fixed and abiding determination never to forget the Lord's commandments. What an insight into our poor wayward hearts does this verse give us—not merely liable to wander, but ever wandering, ever losing our way, ever stumbling on the dark mountains, even while cleaving to God's commandments ! But at the same time what a prayer does it put into our mouths, *"Seek thy servant,"*—" I am thine, save me." Yes, blessed be God ! there is One mighty to save. " Kept by the power of God through faith unto salvation."—*Barton Bouchier.*

As far as I have been able, as far as I have been aided by the Lord, I have treated throughout, and expounded, this great Psalm. A task which more able and learned expositors have performed, or will perform better ; nevertheless, my services were not to be withheld from it on that account, when my brethren earnestly required it of me.—*Augustine.*

HINTS TO PREACHERS.

Outlines upon Keywords of the Psalm, by Pastor C. A. Davis.

A good memory.—I. What it should retain : God's *"name"* (ver. 55) ; God's *"word"* (ver. 16) ; God's *"law"* (ver. 109). The law is dilated upon under various names, *"statutes"* (ver. 83) ; *"precepts"* (ver. 141) ; *"commandments"* (ver. 176) ; *"judgments"* (ver. 52). II. How its retentive power may be fostered. By effort of will (ver. 16 ; 93). By delight in the theme (ver. 16). By a consideration of blessings received (ver. 93). III. Hindrances that must be overcome. Such as arise from severe affliction (ver. 83) ; from personal danger (ver. 109) ; and from insignificance and relative contempt (ver. 141). IV. Reasons for its cultivation. Former blessings derived (ver. 93). It furnishes ground of appeal to God (ver. 153 ; 176). V. The good that will spring from it. Consistent fidelity (ver. 55) ; or, if necessary, restoration from backsliding (ver. 176). Divine consideration (ver. 153) ; comfort (ver. 52) ; delight (ver. 16). And now the believer may appeal to the remembrance of God (ver. 49).

The believer in affliction.—I. His distress (ver. 92). II. His support (ver. 92). III. His submission (ver. 75). IV. His prayer (ver. 107 ; 153). V. Its answer (ver. 50). VI. His review (ver. 71).

Spiritual understanding.—I. Is the gift of God. Jehovah (the only wise), 169. Creator (who has endowed us with our other faculties, therefore with this), 73. Master (who allots our service and therefore our qualification), 125. II. Must be sought from God. With deep sense of need, 169. With faith, 169. With perseverance and importunity, 27, 34, 73, 125, 144, 169. III. Pleas to be used in the prayer for understanding. That I may *learn*, 73, and *know* thy commandments, 125. That thus I may live, 144. Hating every false way, 104. Rendering whole-hearted obedience, 34, and engaging in godly conversation, 27. IV. When obtained it must be improved by exercise in the Word of God. The entrance of the word into the heart is its dawn, 130. It increases by meditation in the word, 99. Is brought to perfection by faithful observance of the precepts of the word, 100. John vii. 17.

The Ten Titles of the Word of God.—" Way " (ver. 1, etc.). " Law " (ver. 1). " Testimonies " (ver. 2). " Precepts " (ver. 4). " Statutes " (ver. 5). " Commandments " (ver. 6). " Judgments " (ver. 7). " Word " (ver. 9). " Truth " (ver. 30). " Righteousness " (ver. 40).
Show the particular shade of meaning in each of these titles, and the light they cast on the divine law and on the duty of the believer.

Holy meditation.—I. Its theme : The revealed will of God in its varied aspects ; *i.e.* " precepts " ; " statutes " ; " law " ; " testimonies " ; " word." II. The spirit which prompts it : Love (vers. 48 and 97). Love to God will induce meditation. Neglect of meditation argues want of love. III. Its times : By " day " (ver. 97). By " night " (ver. 148) ; when maltreated by the world (ver. 78) ; when falsely accused (ver. 23). IV. Its results : A holy walk (ver. 15). Proficiency in understanding (ver. 99). Support in trial (ver. 23, 78).
If you would gladden your nights and days and your times of trial, if you would excel in heavenly wisdom, and hallow your life, abundantly occupy yourself with sacred meditation.

The Psalm treated in its Sections, by C. A. Davis.

The subject of each portion is indicated in its first verse. Each section may serve as the subject for a discourse.
Verses 1—8.—*The undefiled ;* described, in vers. 1—3. Such a life commanded by God is prayed for in ver. 5, and with its attendant happiness is anticipated in ver. 6—7, and resolved upon in ver. 8.

Verses 9—16.—*Sanctification by the word*, declared generally (ver. 9) ; sought personally (ver. 10—12) ; published to others (ver. 13) ; personally rejoiced in (ver. 14—16).

Verses 17—24.—*Divine bounties desired.* Life, for godly service (ver. 17). Illumination (ver. 18). Guidance homeward for the stranger (" thy commandments ") (ver. 19—20), and, glancing at the proud who err from this guidance (ver. 21), the Psalmist prays for removal of the " reproach " entailed by fidelity to God (ver. 22—24).

Verses 25—32.—*Quickening.* Prayed for with confession (ver. 25, 26). When obtained shall be talked of (ver. 27). Desired for the sake of strength (ver. 28), of truthfulness (ver. 29—31), and of activity (ver. 32).

Verses 33—40.—*Faithfulness secured by divine inworking.* Prayer for divine teaching, understanding, constraint, and control of heart and eyes, to ensure persevering and whole-hearted faithfulness (ver. 33—37). The Psalmist, thus established in the word, prays for the establishment of the word to himself (ver. 38) ; deprecates the reproach of unfaithfulness (ver. 39) ; and enforces the whole prayer by the vehemence of the desire which prompts it (ver. 40).

Verses 41—48.—*Promised mercies.* Desired (ver. 41), as an answer to " him that reproacheth " (ver. 42, 43) ; as a means of faithfulness (ver. 44) ; liberty (ver. 45) ; boldness (ver. 46) ; delight (ver. 47), and eager longing (ver. 48).

Verses 49—56.—*Hope in affliction.* It arises from God's word (ver. 49). It produces comfort (ver. 50), even in trouble caused by the wicked (ver. 51—53). It gladdens the believer's pilgrimage and his holy night-seasons (ver. 54—56).

Verses 57—64.—*The believer's portion.* The Lord is the believer's portion (ver. 57) ; heartily sought (ver. 58—60) ; remaining though all else be taken away (ver. 61) ; causing joy even at midnight (ver. 62), and the selection of congenial company (ver. 63, 64).

Verses 65—72.—*The Lord's dealings.* Gratefully acknowledged (ver. 65), and their instructiveness still desired (ver. 66), even affliction from him is " good " (ver. 67, 68), and with its beneficial result is preferred to the prosperity of the wicked (ver. 69—72).

Verses 73—80.—*Natural and spiritual creation.* The Psalmist prays to the Creator for spiritual life or " understanding " (ver. 73), he will then be welcomed by the spiritual (ver. 74). He submissively receives affliction for spiritual training (vers. 75—77), deprecates the hostility of the proud (ver. 78), craves the company of the spiritual (ver. 79), and prays for heart-soundness (ver. 80).

Verses 81—88.—*Hope in depression.* In the depression arising from mortal frailness (ver. 81—84), and from unjust persecution (ver. 85—87), the word of God is the source of joy and comfort.

Verses 89—96.—*The immutable word of God.* Is enthroned in heaven (ver. 89), and on earth (ver. 90, 91), is the salvation of the believer in affliction (ver. 92—94), his resource in danger (ver. 95), and the embodiment of perfection (ver. 96).

Verses 97—104.—*The profitableness of holy meditation.* Its theme—" thy law " (ver. 97), its effect—" wisdom " (ver. 98—100), practically shown in daily life (ver. 101, 102), its sweetness (ver. 103), and hallowing influence (ver. 104).

Verses 105—112.—*The word a lamp.* For guidance (ver. 105, 106). For life in affliction (ver. 107). For preservation in peril of enemies (ver. 109, 110). For joy of heart (ver. 111, 112).

Verses 113—120.—*Vain thoughts contrasted with God's law.* The believer takes sides (ver. 113—115) ; prays for upholding in the law (ver. 116, 117) ; contemplates the fate of the followers of vain thoughts (ver. 118, 119) ; and expresses the godly fear thereby inspired (ver. 120).

Verses 121—128.—*The just man's prayer against injustice.* Out of the prison of oppression he appeals to God to be his surety (ver. 121, 122) ; utters his weary longing for deliverance (ver. 123—125) ; points to the " time " (ver. 126) ; and professes his supreme love for God's law in contrast to the oppressors' contempt of it (ver. 127, 128).

Verses 129—136.—*The wonderfulness of God's testimonies.* Declared (ver. 129), instanced as light-giving (ver. 130), pantingly longed for (ver. 131). An appeal for divine ordering in the word (ver. 132—135). Grief at its rejection by others (ver. 136).

Verses 137—144.—*The righteousness of God and his word.* Declared (ver. 137, 138). Indignation at the forgetfulness of the enemies (ver. 139). The purity of the word (ver. 140, 141). This righteousness of God and of his testimonies is everlasting (ver. 142—144).

Verses 145—152.—*The believer's cry.* The reiterated cry (ver. 145—148). An appeal for audience (ver. 149). The nearness of the enemy perceived (ver. 150). But, in response to the cry, God is also near (ver. 151).

Verses 153—160.—*Divine consideration besought.* "Consider my affliction" (ver. 153); my cause (ver. 154); "for thy mercies' sake" (ver. 156). Consider my persecutors (ver. 157—158), and my love to thy precepts (ver. 160), and act accordingly.

Verses 161—168.—*What the word is to the believer.* The object of awe (ver. 161), joy (ver. 162), love (ver. 163), praise (ver. 164), the producer of peace (ver. 165), and hope (166); therefore exceedingly loved (ver. 167), and faithfully kept (ver. 168).

Verses 169—176.—*The concluding cry.* Bespeaking audience for his cry, the Psalmist asks for understanding and deliverance (ver. 169, 170); promises to praise God (ver. 171), and to speak of God (ver. 172), and again cries for help (ver. 173), salvation (ver. 174), life (ver. 175), and restoration (ver. 176).

HINTS TO PREACHERS.

Verse 1.—*"Blessed."* True blessedness lies in—I. Defilement avoided by the word. II. Delight experienced in the word.

Verse 1.—Spiritual pedestrians are often mentioned in this Psalm. Model travellers are described in this passage. Observe,—I. *Their Character :* " Undefiled." They are so (1) *in Christ :* found in him ; complete ; accepted. They are so (2) *by Christ :* His spirit, truth, and grace are in them. " Chosen generation," " peculiar people." II. *Their path :* " the law of the Lord." This path is (1) *Conspicuous*—high, visible, distinguished from every other. (2) *Ancient.* The old path. Holiness is older than sin, wisdom than folly, life than death, joy than sorrow. (3) *Safe.* Christ has repaired it. Apart from his work none can pass safely over. He has brought down mountains, raised up valleys, made crooked places straight, and rough places smooth. He has driven away the lion. (4) *Narrow.* It has a fence of commands on one side, and of prohibitions on the other. It is entered by a strait gate, which renders it necessary for the great to become as little children. III. *Their progress :* " walk." Not only talk, but step in the footprints of Jesus. Follow the law-fulfiller. They proceed in the exercise of his graces, in the exhibition of his virtues, in the fulfilment of his injunctions, and in the enjoyment of his favours. IV. *Their happiness :* " Blessed." They have unfailing help, suitable company, animating prospects on the way.—*W. Jackson,* 1882.

Verses 1, 2, 3.—I. Positive and Negative Beatitudes of Being.—II. Six Conditions of Peace with God. 1. Purity. 2. Obedience. 3. Fidelity. 4. Seeking. 5. Integrity. 6. Following.—*William Durban,* 1882.

Verse 2.—*"Blessed are they that keep his testimonies, and that seek him with the whole heart."* I. *The sacred Quest :* " Seek him." He has been sought among the trees, the hills, the planets, the stars. He has been sought in his own defaced image, man. He has been sought amid the mysterious wheels of Providence. But these quests have often been prompted simply by intellect, or compelled by conscience, and have therefore resulted but in a cold, faint light. He has been sought in the word which this Psalm so highly extols, when it has led up the smoke-covered and gleaming peaks of Sinai. It has been followed, when it has led beneath the olives of Gethsemane to witness a mysterious struggle in blood-sweating and anguish ; to Calvary, where, in the place of a skull, life and immortality are brought to light. The sacred quest but there begins. II. *The Conduct of the Quest.* Seekers might be mistakenly dejected by so literal an interpretation of the " whole heart." We do not hesitate to say a stream is in its whole volume flowing toward sea while there are little side creeks in which the water eddies backward ; or to say the tide is coming despite receding waves ; or that spring is upon us despite hail-storm and biting wind. Indication of, 1. Unity. 2. Intensity. 3. Determination. No one conducts this quest aright who is not prompted to or sustained in it by the gracious Spirit. III. *Blessedness both in the pursuit and issue.* 1. Blessedness in the bitterness of penitence. The door-handle touched by him drops of myrrh. The rising sun sends kindling beams upon the highest peaks. 2. Blessedness in the gladsome findings of salvation and adoption. 3. Blessedness in the perpetual pursuit.—*William Anderson,* 1882.

Verse 2.—The double blessing. I. On keeping the testimonies. II. On seeking the Lord.

Verse 2.—*"That seek him with the whole heart."* I. Seek what ? God himself. No peace until he is found. II. Seek where ? In his testimonies. 1. By studying them. 2. By keeping to them. III. Seek how ? With the whole heart.—*George Rogers.*

Verse 2. — *Seeking for God.* I. The Psalmist's way of seeking God. 1. He sought God *with the heart.* Only the heart can find God. Sight fails. " The scientific method " fails. All reason fails. Only love and trust can succeed. Love sees much where all other perception finds nothing. Faith generally goes with discovery, and nowhere so much as in finding God. 2. He sought God *with all his heart.* (1) Half-heartedness seldom finds anything worth having. (2) Half-heartedness shows contempt for God. (3) God will not reveal himself to half-heartedness. It would be putting the highest premium possible upon indifference. II. The Psalmist's plea in seeking God : " Let me not wander from thy commandments." 1. God's commandments lead, presently, into his own presence. If we take even the moral law, every one of the ten commandments leads away from the world, and sin, into that seclusion of holiness in which he hides. It is thus with all the commandments of the Scriptures. 2. The earnestness of the soul's search for God becomes, in itself, a plea with God that he will be found of us. God, who loves importunity in prayer, loves it no less when it takes the form of searching with all the heart. He who seeks with all the heart finds special encouragement to pray : " Let me not wander from thy commandments."—*F. G. Marchant.*

Verse 2.—*"That seek him."* We must remember six conditions required in them who would seek the Lord rightly. I. We must seek him in Christ the Mediator. John xiv. 6. II. We must seek him in truth. Jer. x. 10 ; John iv. 24 ; Ps. vii. 6. III. We must seek him in holiness. 2 Tim. ii. 19 ; Heb. xii. 14 ; 1 John iii. IV. We must seek him above all things and for himself. V. We must seek him by the light of his own word. VI. We must seek him diligently and with perseverance, never resting till we find him, with the spouse in the Canticles.—*William Cowper.*

Verses 2, 4, 5, 8.—" Blessed are they that *keep.*" " Thou hast commanded us to *keep.*" " O that my ways were directed to *keep.*" " I will *keep.*" The blessedness of *keeping* God's precepts—displayed (2), commanded (4), prayed for (5), resolved upon (8).—*C. A. D.*

Verse 3.—*"They also do no iniquity."* They work no iniquity with—1. Purpose of heart ; 2. Delight ; 3. Perseverance ; 4. Nor at all when the heart is fully sanctified unto God ; Christ dwelling in it by faith, and casting out sin.—*Adam Clarke.*

Verse 3.—The relation between negative and positive virtue. Or walking with God the best preventive of iniquity.

Verse 4.—I. Take notice of the law-giver : " Thou." Not thy equal, or one that will be baffled, but the great God. II. He hath interposed his authority : " hast commanded." III. The nature of this obedience, or the thing commanded : " To keep thy precepts."—*T. Manton.*

Verse 4.—*The supplementary commandment.* God having ordained the moral law, supplements it with a commandment prescribing the manner of keeping it. Hence : I. God is not indifferent to men's treatment of his law—whether they observe, neglect, or defy it. II. When observed, God discriminates the spirit of its observance, whether slavish, partial, careless, or diligent. III. There is but one spirit of obedience, whether slavish, partial, careless, or diligent. III. There is but one spirit of obedience which satisfies God's requirements. " Diligently " implies an obedience which is,—careful to ascertain the law—prompt to fulfil it (ver. 60)—unreserved—love-inspired (" diligently," old meaning, through the Latin, " lovingly," ver. 47, 97, 113). IV. Does our obedience come up to this standard ?—*C. A. D.*

Verse 4.—Not only is service commanded, but the manner of it. Heartiness, care, perseverance required, because without these it will not be true, uniform, or victorious over difficulty.

Verse 4.—How to obey : *"Diligently."* 1. Not partially, but fully. 2. Not doubtfully, but confidently. 3. Not reluctantly, but readily. 4. Not slovenly, but carefully. 5. Not coldly, but earnestly. 6. Not fitfully, but regularly.—*W. J.*

Verses 4, 5, 6.—A willing recognition (ver. 4). An ardent aspiration (ver. 5). A happy consequence (ver. 6).—*W. D.*

Verse 5.—The prayer of the gracious. I. Suggested by each preceding clause of blessing. II. By a consciousness of failure. III. By a loving clinging to the Lord.

Verse 5.—I. The end desired : " To keep thy statutes." Not to be safe merely, or happy, but holy. II. The help implored. 1. To understand the divine precepts. 2. To keep them.—*G. R.*

Verse 5.—Longing to obey. 1. *It is a noble aspiration.* There is nothing grander than the desire to do this except the doing of it. 2. *It is a spiritual aspiration.* Not the offspring of our carnal nature. It is the heart of God in the new creature. 3. *It is a practicable aspiration.* We sometimes sigh for the impossible. But this may be attained by divine grace. 4. *It is an intense aspiration.* It is the " Oh ! " of a burning wish. 5. *It is an influential aspiration.* It does not evaporate in sighs. It is a mighty incentive implanted by grace which will not let us rest without holiness.—*W. J.*

Verse 6.—See " Spurgeon's Sermons," No. 1443 : " A Clear Conscience."

Verse 6.—Holy confidence the offspring of universal obedience.

Verse 6.—*The armour of proof.* I. Universal obedience will give unabashed confidence—1. Before the criticising world. 2. In the court of conscience. 3. At the throne of grace. 4. In the day of judgment. II. But our obedience is far from universal, and leaves us open to—1. The world's shafts. 2. The rebukes of conscience. 3. It paralyses our prayers, and, 4. It dares not appear for us at the bar of God. III. Then let us by faith wrap ourselves in the perfect righteousness of Christ. Our answer to the world's cavil. We are not faultless, and for salvation we rest wholly on another. This righteousness is—1. The salve of our wounded conscience. 2. Our mighty plea in prayer. 3. Our triumphant vindication in the judgment day.—*C. A. D.*

Verse 6.—Topic :—Self-respect depends on respect for one greater than self.—*W. D.*

Verse 7.—The best of praise, the best of learning, the best of blendings, viz., praise and holiness.

Verse 7.—I. The professor of sacred music : " I will praise." II. The subject of his song : " Thee." III. The instrument : " Heart." IV. The instrument tuned : " Uprightness of heart." V. The musician's training academy : " Judgments."—*W. D.*

Verse 7.—Learning and praising. I. They are *two spiritual exercises.* It is possible for learners and singers to be carnal and sensual ; but in this case they are employed about the righteous ends, works, and ways of the Lord. II. They are *two appropriate exercises.* What can be more seemly than to learn of God and to praise him ? III. They are *two profitable exercises.* The expectations of the most utilitarian are surpassed. The pleasure and the profit yield abundant reward. Heart, head, life are all benefited. IV. They are *two mutually-assisting exercises.* In the one we are receptive, and in the other communicative. By the one we are fitted to do the other. By the former we are stimulated to do the latter. How wonderfully the lesson is turned into a song, and the learner into a singer.—*W. J.*

Verse 7.—I. Deficiency confessed : " When I shall have learned." This is essential to growth. It is an admission all can truly make. II. Progress anticipated. He gave his heart to the work of learning. He sought divine help. III. Praise promised. He promised it to God alone. He vowed it should be sincere : " with upright heart."—*W. Williams,* 1882.

Verse 8.—I. A hopeful resolve for life. II. A dreadful fear. III. A series of considerations removing the fear.

Verse 8.—I. The resolution : " I will keep," etc. II. The petition : " O forsake me not utterly." 1. Filial submission. I deserve it occasionally. 2. Filial confidence. " Not utterly." III. The connection between the two. Obedience without prayer and prayer without obedience are equally in vain. To make headway both oars must be applied. God cannot abide lazy beggars, who while they can get anything by asking will not work.—*G. R.*

Verse 8.—*"O forsake me not utterly."* Divine desertion deprecated. I. The anguished prayer. 1. Sovereign forsakings. Sovereignty is not arbitrariness or capriciousness ; perhaps its right definition is mysterious kingly love ; unknown now, but justified when revealed. 2. Vicarious forsakings. 3. Forsakings on account of sin. David, Jonah, and Peter. The seven churches of Asia ; the Jews. But to know what *"utter"* both in regard to degree and time means, we must go to hell. Like one trembling on the very verge of hell, he prays. Like belated traveller, in vast wood and surrounded by beasts of prey, sighs at day's departure. Like the watch on the raft, seeing the sail that he has shouted himself hoarse to stop fading away in the sky line. II. Its doctrinal foundation. Where he condescendeth to dwell, his abode is perpetual. He can only utterly forsake us because he was deceived in us. He can only utterly forsake because baffled. Both imply blasphemy. Thou who hatest putting away, thou who hast never yet *utterly* forsaken any saint, make not me the solitary exception. III. Historical certainty of answer. The saint and the church in all time delivered. It may tarry till " eventide," as in Cowper's case. His face bore after death an expression of delighted surprrise.—*W. A.*

Verse 9.—I. The young man's question. II. The wise man's reply.

Verse 9.—In the word of God, when applied to the heart by the Spirit of God, there is, I. A sufficiency of light to discover to men the need of cleansing their way. II. Sufficiency of energy for the cleansing their way. III. A sufficiency of pleasure to encourage them to choose to cleanse their way. IV. A sufficiency of support to sustain them in their cleansed way.—*Theophilus Jones, in a* "Sermon to the Young," 1829.

Verse 9.—The word of God provides for the cleansing of the way, I. By pointing out to the young man the evil of the way. II. By discovering an infallible remedy for the disorders of his nature—the salvation that is by Jesus Christ. III. By becoming a directory in all the paths of duty to which he may be called.—*Daniel Wilson*, 1828.

Verse 9.—The Psalmist's rules for the attainment of holiness deduced from his own experience. 1. Seek God with thy " whole heart " (ver. 2). Be truly sensible of your wants. 2. Keep and remember what God says (ver. 11): " Thy word have I hidden," etc. 3. Reduce all this to practice (ver. 11): " That I might not sin against thee." 4. Bless God for what he has given (ver. 12): " Blessed art thou," etc. 5. Ask more (ver. 12): " Teach me thy statutes." 6. Be ready to communicate his knowledge to others (ver. 13): " With my lips have I declared." 7. Let it have a due effect on thy own heart (ver. 14): " I have rejoiced," etc. 8. Meditate frequently upon them (ver. 15): " I will meditate," etc. 9. Deeply reflect on them (ver. 16): " I will have respect," etc. As food undigested will not nourish the body, so the word of God not considered with deep meditation and reflection will not feed the soul. 10. Having pursued the above course he should continue in it, and then his happiness would be secured (ver. 16): " I will not forget thy word : I will (in consequence) delight myself in thy statutes."—*Adam Clarke*.

Verse 9.—A question and answer for the young. The Bible is a book for young people. Here it intimates, I. That the young man's way *needs to be cleansed*. His way of thinking, feeling, speaking, acting. II. That *he must take an active part in the work*. The efficient cause in the operation is God. Other good influences are also at work. But the young man must be in hearty and practical sympathy with the work. III. That *he must use the Bible for the purpose*. This records facts, presents incitations, enjoins precepts, utters promises, and sets up examples, all which are adapted to make a young man holy. By reading, studying, and imitating the Scriptures in a lowly and prayerful spirit the young shall escape pollution and ornament society.—*W. J.*

Verse 9.—A word to the young. I. Show how the young man is in special danger of defiling his way. Through, 1. His strong passions. 2. His immature judgment. 3. His inexperience. 4. His rash self-sufficiency. 5. His light companions, and, 6. His general heedlessness. II. The circumspection he should use to cleanse his way. "*Taking heed*," 1. Of his evil propensities. 2. Of his companions. 3. Of his pursuits. 4. Of the tendencies of all he does. III. The infallible guide by which his circumspection is to be regulated : "*according to thy word* "—that is to say, 1. Its precepts. 2. Its examples. 3. Its motives. 4. Its warnings. 5. Its allurements.—*C. A. D.*

Verse 10.—I. A grateful review. II. An anxious forecast. III. A commendable prayer.

Verse 10.—The believer's two great solicitudes. 1. What he is anxious to find : " I have sought thee." 2. What he is afraid of losing : " Thy commandments."—*W. D.*

Verse 10.—*Sincerity not self-sufficiency.* I. The believer must be conscious of whole-heartedness in seeking God. II. But consciousness of sincerity does not warrant self-sufficiency. III. The most whole-hearted seeker must still look to divine grace to keep him from wandering.—*C. A. D.*

Verse 11.—The best thing, in the best place, for the best of purposes.

Verse 12.—The blessedness of God, and the mode of entering into it.

Verse 12.—I. David gives glory to God : "*Blessed art thou, O* LORD." II. He asks grace from God.—*Matthew Henry*.

Verse 12.—I. What it is, or how God doth teach us. 1. God doth teach us outwardly ; by his ordinances, by the ministry of men. 2. Inwardly ; by the inspiration and work of the Holy Ghost. II. The necessity of his teaching. III. The benefit and utility of it.—*T. Manton*.

Verse 12.—*Desire for Divine Teaching excited by the Recognition of Divine Blessedness.* I. Unveil in some inadequate degree the happiness of the ever blessed God, arising from his purity, benevolence, love. II. Show the way in which man may become partaker of that blessedness by conformity to his precepts. III. Utter the prayer of the text.—*C. A. D.*

Verse 13.—Speech fitly employed. It is occupied with a choice subject, a full subject, a subject profitable to men, and glorifying to God.

Verse 14.—Practical religion, the source of a comfort surpassing riches. It gives a man ease of mind, independence of carriage, weight of influence, and other matters supposed to arise out of wealth.

Verse 14.—I. The subject of rejoicing. Not the "testimonies" merely, but their observances, "the way of," etc. II. The rejoicing in that subject. 1. In its inward peace. 2. In its external consequences. III. The degree of the rejoicing : " as much as," etc.—*G. R.*

Verse 14.—*The two scales of the balance.* Whatever riches are good for, God's testimonies are good for. I. Riches are desirable as the means of procuring the necessaries of life ; but God's testimonies supply the necessities of the soul. II. Riches are desirable as a means of procuring personal enjoyment ; but God's testimonies produce the highest joy. III. Riches are desirable as a means of attaining personal improvement ; but God's testimonies are the highest educators. IV. Riches are desirable as a means of doing good ; but God's testimonies work the highest good.—*C. A. D.*

Verse 15.—The contemplative and active life ; their common food, object, and reward.

Verse 16.—I. What there is to be delighted in. II. What comes of such delight : ' I will never forget." III. What comes of such memory—more delight.

Verse 17.—I. A bountiful master. II. A needy servant—begging for very life. III. A suitable recompense : " and keep thy word."

Verse 17.—We are here taught, I. That we owe our lives to God's mercy. II. That therefore we ought to spend our lives in God's service.—*Matthew Henry.*

Verse 18.—I. The precious casket : " thy law." II. The invisible treasure : " wondrous things." III. The miraculous eyesight : " that I may behold." IV. The divine oculist : " Open thou mine eyes."

Verse 18.—*The hidden wonders of the gospel.* There are many hidden things in nature ; many in our fellow men ; so there are many in the Bible. The things of the Bible are hidden because of the blindness of man. I. *The blind man's sorrow :* " Open mine eyes." I cannot see. I have eyes and see not. The pain of this conscious blindness when a man really feels it. II. *The blind man's conviction :* " That I may behold wondrous," etc. There are wondrous things there to be seen. I am sure of it. There is a wonderful view,—(1) of sin ; (2) of hell, as its desert ; (3) of One ready to save ; (4) of perfect pardon ; (5) of God's love ; (6) of all-sufficient grace ; (7) of heaven. III. *The blind man's wisdom.* The fault is in my eyes, not in thy word. " Open my eyes," and all will be well. The reason for not seeing is because the eyes are blinded by sin. There is nothing wanting in the Bible. IV. *The blind man's prayer :* " Open *thou* mine eyes." 1. I cannot open them. 2. My dearest friends cannot. 3. Only thou canst. " Lord, I pray thee, now open them." Many seek to stop such praying. Be like Bartimeus who *"cried so much the more."* V. *The blind man's anticipation :* " That I may behold." 1. The joy of a cured blind man when he is about to behold, for the first time, the beauties of nature. **2.** The joy of the spiritually healed when they begin " looking unto Jesus." 3. The personal character of the joy : " Open thou *mine* eyes, that I may behold." I have hitherto had to see through the eyes of others. I would depend on other eyes no longer. The glad anticipation of Job : " Whom I shall see for myself, and mine eyes shall behold, and not another."—*Frederick G. Marchant,* 1882.

Verse 18.—God's word suited to man's sense of wonder. I. We shall make some remarks on the sense of wonder in man, and what generally excites it. One of the first causes of wonder is the *new or unexpected.* The second source is to be found in things *beautiful and grand.* A third source is the *mysterious* which surrounds man— there are things *unknowable.* II. God has made provision for this sense of wonder in his revealed word. The Bible addresses our sense of wonder by constantly presenting the *new and unexpected* to us ; it sets before us things *beautiful and grand.* If we come to the third source of wonder, that which raises it to *awe,* it is the peculiar province of the Bible to deal with this. III. The means we are to use in order to have God's word thus unfolded—the prayer of the Psalmist may be our guide— " Open thou mine eyes, that I may behold wondrous things out of thy law."— *John Ker, of Glasgow,* 1877.

Verse 18.—*Wondrous sights for opened eyes.* I. The wondrous things in God's law. A wondrous rule of life. A wondrous curse against transgression. A wondrous redemption from the curse shadowed forth in the ceremonial law. II. Special eyesight needed to behold them. They are spiritual things. Men are spiritually blind. 1 Cor. ii. 14. III. Personal prayer to the Great Opener of eyes.—*C. A. D.*

Verse 19.—An insight into the divine will, the best assistance in our journey through the earth. Or, what I am ; where I am ; where I am going ; how am I to get there ?

Verse 19 (first clause).—The stranger in the earth. I. A short exposition. The text means,—1. That the saint is not born of the earth. 2. That the saint is not known on earth. 3. The saint's portion is not upon the earth. 4. The saint is compassed with sorrows and trials upon earth. 5. The saint is soon to leave the earth. II. A short application. 1. Do not be like the world. 2. Be prepared to be a sufferer on the earth. 3. Sit loose to the world. 4. Correspond with home. 5. Cherish brotherly love for your fellow-strangers on the earth. 6. Hasten home. 7. Press others to come with you.—*Duncan Macgregor's Sermon in "The Shepherd in Israel,"* 1869.

Verse 19.—*The stranger's prayer.* I. How he came to be a stranger in the earth. He was born again. He learned the manners of his foreign home. He spoke the language of his Fatherland ; and so was misunderstood and rejected on earth. II. How he longed after everything homelike. Home rules : " thy commandments." Home teaching : " hide not." Specially his Father's voice. III. How in his loneliness he solaced himself by communication with his Father. IV. Would you not like to be a stranger ?—*C. A. D.*

Verse 20.—I. The word sought, and sought at all times. II. The word sought, and sought with intense desire. III. The word sought, and sought the more intensely the more it is found. It was because he had found so much in the word of the Lord already, that the soul of the Psalmist was breaking to find more. Those who have been once admitted to " the secret of the Lord " find their highest joy in knowing that secret still more fully. It is to those who know that secret that the promise is given : " He will shew them his covenant : " Ps. xxv. 14.— *F. G. M.*

Verse 20.—One of the best tests of character and prophecies of what a man will be, are his longings. I. The saint's absorbing object : " Thy judgments." The word here is synonymous with the " word " of God. 1. The Psalmist greatly reverenced the word. 2. He intensely desired to know its contents. 3. He wishes to feed upon God's word. 4. He longed to obey it. 5. He longed to feel the power of God's judgments in his own heart. II. The saint's ardent longings. 1. They constitute a living experience. 2. The expression used in the text represents a humble sense of imperfection. 3. It indicates an advanced experience. 4. It is an experience which we may term a bitter sweet. 5. These longings may become very wearying to a man's soul. III. Cheering reflections. 1. God is at work in your soul. 2. The result of God's work is very precious. 3. It is leading on to something more precious. 4. The desire itself is doing you good. 5. It makes Christ precious. See " Spurgeon's Sermons," No. 1586 : " Holy Longings."

Verse 21.—I. The character of the proud. II. God's dealings with them. III. Our own relation to them.

Verse 21.—I. The sin ; " Err from the commandments." 1. By neglect ; or, 2. By abuse of them. II. Its origin—pride : pride of reason, of heart, of life. III. Its punishment. 1. Rebuke. 2. Condemnation.—*G. R.*

Verse 23.—Meditation. I. Our best employment while others slander. II. Our best comfort under their falsehood. III. Our best preservative from a spirit of revenge. IV. Our best mode of showing our superiority to their attacks.

Verse 24.—I. He reverenced them as God's testimonies. II. He revelled in them as his delight. III. He referred to them as his counsellors.

Verse 25.—I. Nature and its tendency. II. Grace and its mode of operation. III. Both truths in their personal application.

Verse 25.—"Quicken thou me," etc. I. There are many reasons why we should seek quickening. 1. Because of the deadening influence of the world. " My soul cleaveth," etc. 2. The influence of vanity (see ver. 37). 3. Because we are surrounded by deceivers (see ver. 87, 88). 4. Because of the effect of seasons of affliction upon us (see ver. 7). II. Some of the motives for seeking quickening. 1. Because of what you are—a Christian ; life seeks more life. 2. Because of what you ought to be. 3. Because of what we shall be. 4. In order to obedience (see ver. 88). 5. For your comfort (ver. 107 and 50). 6. As the best security against the attacks of enemies (ver. 87 and 88). 7. To invigorate our memories (ver. 93). 8. Consider (as a motive to seek this quickening) the terrible consequences of losing spiritual life or, in other words, lacking it in its manifest display. III. Some of the ways in which the quickening may be brought to us. 1. It must be by the Lord himself.

" Quicken me, O Lord." 2. By the turning of the eyes (ver. 37). 3. By the word (ver. 50). 4. By the precepts (ver. 93). 5. By affliction (ver. 107). 6. By divine comforts. IV. Enquire where are our pleas when we come before God to ask for quickening. 1. Our necessity (ver. 107, etc.). 2. Our earnest desire (ver. 40). 3. Appeal to God's righteousness (ver. 40). 4. To his lovingkindness (ver. 88, 149, 156). 5. The plea in the text : " according to thy word " (ver. 28 and 107). See " Spurgeon's Sermons," No. 1350 : " Enlivening and Invigorating."

Verse 26.—Confession. Absolution. Instruction.

Verse 26.—I. The duty : " I have declared my ways "—made known my experience of thy word to others. II. Its notice by God : " Thou heardest me." III. Its reward. More knowledge will be given : " Teach me," etc.—G. R.

Verse 27.—I. A student's prayer. 1. It deals with the main subject of the conversation which is to be that student's occupation—" the way of God's precepts." 2. A confession is implied : " Make me," etc. 3. A great boon is asked—to understand, to know, thy statutes. 4. The Fountain of all wisdom is applied to. II. The occupation of the instructed man. 1. He testifies of God's works—his wondrous works—Christ's work for us ; the Holy Spirit's work in us. The wonderful character of these works of God, a wide field for devout study. 2. He speaks very plainly : " I will talk," etc. 3. He will speak very frequently : " I will talk." 4. He will speak to the point : " So "—i.e., according to understanding. III. The intimate relation between the prayer of the student and the pursuit that he subsequently followed. See " Spurgeon's Sermons," No. 1344 : " The Student's Prayer."

Verse 27.—Education for the ministry. I. The student at college : " Make me to understand." His lesson. His instructor. His application. II. The preacher at his work : " So shall I talk," etc. His qualification. His theme. His manner.— C. A. D.

Verse 28.—Heaviness, its cause, curse, and cure.

Verse 29.—The way of lying. I. Describe the way of lying. Various paths, e.g., erroneous views of doctrine : false grounds of faith : looseness of practice : shrinking from the daily cross. II. Show why it is thus named. It does not furnish its promised pleasures. It does not lead to its professed goal. It lies through the territory of the father of lies. III. Notice the peculiarity in the prayer against it. Not remove me from, but remove from me : for the way of lying is within us. IV. Our deliverance from the way of lying lies with God.—C. A. D.

Verses 29, 30.—I. The way of lying, our wish to have it removed, and the method of answer. II. The way of truth, our choice, and the method of carrying it out.

Verse 31.—Reasons for sticking to the Divine testimonies.

Verse 31.—A wholesome mixture. I. Sturdy fidelity. II. Self-distrust, and, III. Importunate prayer.—C. A. D.

Verse 32.—The Fettered Racer set free. I. The course that invited him. II. The shackles that bound him. III. The impatience that prompted him. IV. The Lord that freed him. V. Now let him go.—C. A. D.

Verse 32.—I. Liberty desired. II. Liberty rightly used. Or, the effect of the heart upon the feet.

Verse 32.—The text will give us occasion to speak, 1. Of the benefit of an enlarged heart. The necessary precedency of this work on God's part, before there can be any serious bent or motion of heart towards God on our part. 3. The subsequent resolution of the saints to engage their hearts to live to God. 4. With what earnestness, alacrity and vigour of spirit this work is to be carried on : " I will run."— T. Manton.

Verse 32.—I. The way of obedience : " Thy commandments." II. The duty of obedience : " I will run "—not stand still—not loiter—not creep—not walk, but run. III. The life of obedience. 1. Where it lies—in the heart. 2. Whence it comes : " When thou shalt," etc. 3. What it does—enlarges the heart.—G. R.

Verse 33.—In this prayer for grace observe, 1. The person to whom he prays : "O Lord." 2. The person for whom : " teach me." 3. The grace for which he prayeth : to be taught. 4. The object of this teaching : " The way of thy statutes." The teaching which he beggeth, is not speculative, but practical, to learn how to walk in the way of God.—T. Manton.

Verse 33.—The superior efficacy of divine teaching : it secures holy practice and insures its perpetuity.

Verses 33, 34.—Light from above. I. The blinding power of sin. " Teach me," i.e., " point out to me." " Give me understanding." Whatever may have been the original amount of light which came from eating from the tree of knowledge of good and evil, that light has long been insufficient. 1. Men need light to discern the right way from the wrong. 2. Men need light to understand the beauties of the right way. Such beauties line the way of truth on either hand, but only the God-taught mind appreciates them. Even Jesus, who is the way, the truth, and the life, is as a root out of a dry ground, till the mind is taught of the Lord. Sin is the cause of this blindness. The farther any man walks in the way of sin, the less can he see of the beauties of holiness. II. The enlightening grace of the Lord. " Teach me." " Give me understanding." This grace, 1. May be boldly asked : " If any man lack wisdom let him ask of God." 2. Will be freely given. " Who giveth to all men liberally." " Ask, and it shall be given." 3. Will be amply sufficient. " I shall keep it unto the end." " I shall keep Thy law." To see is to follow. III. The stimulating power of clearly revealed truth. " I shall observe it with my whole heart." To see is not only to follow, but to follow with love and gladness. It is written of the light which will come before the throne, " We shall be like him, *for* we shall see him as he is." " O thou, that dwellest between the Cherubim, shine forth," even here, on the way that leads to thy presence.—*F. G. M.*

Verses 33—35.—Alpha and Omega. I. God, the giver of spiritual instruction : ver. 33. II. Of spiritual understanding, without which this instruction is in vain : ver. 34. III. Of grace for practical obedience when thus instructed : ver. 35. IV. For whole-hearted obedience : ver. 34. V. For final perseverance : ver. 33.— *C. A. D.*

Verses 33—36.—Human Dependence on Divine help. I. There can be no steady keeping in the way of the Lord without the Lord's guidance : ver. 33. II. There can be no observing of the way with the heart without Divine light for the mind : ver. 34. III. There can be no diligent pursuit of the way till divine energy be given to the will : ver. 35. IV. There can be no true love of the way unless the heart be constrained by the love of God : ver. 36. He who said, " Without me ye can do nothing," is necessary for us to see the way, to understand the way, to walk in the way, and to love the way.—*F. G. M.*

Verse 34.—The influence of the understanding upon the heart, and the united power of understanding and heart over the life.

Verse 34.—Seeing and loving. I. When men see they love (the whole verse). II. When men love they see. Only the loving heart would have seen enough to write such a verse.—*F. G. M.*

Verse 35.—The prayer of a child, and the delight of a child. Or, Our pleasure in holiness a plea for grace.

Verse 35.—I. Delight avowed. II. Disinclination implied. III. Constraint implored.—*W. W.*

Verse 36.—Holiness a cure for covetousness.

Verses 36, 112.—The Co-operation of the Divine and the Human in Salvation. I. It is God that worketh in you : ver. 36. II. Therefore work out your own salvation with fear and trembling : ver. 112.—*C. A. D.*

Verse 37.—"Quicken thou me in thy way." This brief prayer—1. Deals with the believer's frequent need. II It directs us to the sole worker of quickening: "Thou." III. It describes the sphere of renewed vigour : " in thy way." IV. It denotes that there may be special reasons and special seasons for this prayer—times of temptation : ver. 37 ; seasons of affliction : ver. 107 ; when called to some extraordinary service. See " Spurgeon's Sermons," No. 1073 : " A Honeycomb."

Verse 37.—Here is, I. Conversion *from*—" vanity." II. Conversion *to*—" thy way. III. Conversion *by*—" Quicken thou me."—*G. R.*

Verse 37.—David prays, (1) for *restraining* grace that he might be prevented and kept back from that which would hinder him in the way of his duty : " Turn away mine eyes from beholding vanity." He prays (2) for *constraining* grace, that he might not only be kept from everything that would obstruct his progress heaven-ward, but that he might have that grace which was necessary to forward him in that progress : " Quicken thou me in thy way."—*M. Henry.*

Verse 38.—Confirmation. What ? " Thy word established." To whom ? " Unto thy servant." Why ? " Who is devoted," etc.

Verse 38.—Fear of God evidences itself, 1. By a dread of his displeasure. 2. Desire of his favour. 3. Regard for his excellencies. 4. Submission to his will. 5. Gratitude for his benefits. 6. Conscientious obedience to his com-mands.—*Charles Buck.*

Verse 38.—The four kinds of fear. 1. The fear of man, by which we are led rather to do wrong than to suffer evil. 2. Servile fear, through which we are induced to avoid sin only from the dread of hell. 3. Initial fear, in which we avoid sin partly from the fear of hell, but partly also from the love of God, which is the fear of ordinary Christians. 4. Filial fear, when we are afraid to disobey God only and altogether from the love we bear him. Jer. xxxii. 40.—*Ayguan, in J. Edward Vaux's "Preacher's Storehouse,"* 1878.

Verse 39.—I. Man's judgment dreaded. II. God's judgment approved.

Verse 39.—*The reproach of inconsistency.* I. The dishonour caused by it (2 Sam. xii. 14). II. The danger of incurring it. III. The prayer against it.—*C. A. D.*

Verse 40.—I. Gracious longings experienced. II. Great necessity felt—more life needed. III. Wise petition offered.

Verse 41.—See "Spurgeon's Sermons," No. 1524 : "Your Personal Salvation."

Verse 41.—I. God's mercies come to us unsought continually. His sparing mercies, temporal mercies, etc. II. The chief outcome of God's mercies is his salvation. It is our greatest need ; it is his greatest gift. III. We should have a personal interest in this salvation : "Let thy mercies come also unto me." IV. When we seek God's salvation, we may plead his promise : "according to thy word."—*Horatio Wilkins,* 1882.

Verse 41.—"Even me." I. In me there is need of mercy. II. To me mercy can come. III. Thy salvation suits me. IV. Special difficulties would daunt me. V. Thy word encourages me.

Verse 41.—I. Salvation is all of mercy. II. All mercies are in salvation. III. All men should be anxious for salvation to come to them. IV. It can only come according to God's word.—*W. W.*

Verses 41—43.—*A Comprehensive Prayer.* I. The possession of salvation, ver. 41. II. Is the power for defence : ver. 42. III. And the qualification for usefulness : ver. 43.—*C. A. D.*

Verse 42.—Faith's answer to reproach found in the fact that she trusts God's word.

Verses 42, 43, 47.—Faith, hope, and love. "I trust." "I have hoped." "I have loved." Faith warring, hope testifying, love obeying.

Verse 43.—How the true preacher could be silenced, and his plea that he may not be so.

Verse 44.—The perpetuity of gracious living. On what it is conditioned : "So." How entirely it is consistent with free agency : "I keep." How continuous it is, and how eternal.

Verse 44.—*Heaven begun below.* I. The present life of the believer—keeping God's law. II. The continual care of the believer—to keep God's law. III. The eternal prospect of the believer—keeping God's law for ever and ever.—*C. A. D.*

Verses 45—47.—Liberty of walk. Liberty of speech. Liberty of heart.

Verses 45—48.—The true freeman enjoys—1. *Free walk* with God. 2. *Free talk* about God. 3. *Free love* unto God. 4. *Free exercise* of soul, (1) in holy practice ; (2) in heavenly meditation.—*W. Durban.*

Verses 45—48.—Five things the Psalmist promiseth himself here in the strength of God's grace. 1. That he should be free and easy in his duty : "I will walk at liberty." 2. That he should be bold and courageous in his duty : "I will speak of thy testimonies also before kings." 3. That he should be cheerful and pleasant in his duty : "I will delight myself in thy commandments." 4. That he should be diligent and vigorous in his duty : "I will delight myself in thy commandments." 5. That he should be thoughtful and considerate in his duty : "I will meditate in thy statutes."—*M. Henry.*

Verses 46—48.—*Lips, heart, and hands.* I. Public profession of God's word ("I will speak," ver. 46) must be warranted by—II. Private delight in God's word ("I will delight myself," ver. 47), which must result in—III. Practical obedience to God's word ("I will lift up my hands," ver. 48).

Verse 46.—I. The truly earnest must speak. II. They are at no loss for good subjects : "Thy testimonies." The range is boundless—the variety endless. III. They never fear any audience : "before kings."—*W. W.*

Verse 48.—I. Love renewing its activity. II. Love refreshing itself with spiritual food.

Verse 48.—I. Scripture in the hand for reading. Often in the hand. II. In the mind for meditation: " I will meditate," etc. III. In the heart for love: " Which I have loved."—*G. R.*

Verse 48.—Religion engaged the whole manhood of David : hands, heart, head. I. The uplifted hands. 1. *Taking an oath of allegiance to God's word.* Gen. xiv. 22 ; Ezek. xx. 28. To receive its doctrines, obey its precepts, regard its warnings, uphold its honour. 2. *Imploring a blessing upon God's word.* Gen. xlviii. 14 ; Lev. ix. 22 ; Luke xxiv. 50. That its light might spread : " Fly abroad, thou mighty gospel ; " that its influence may become universal. II. The loyal heart. 1. *This accounts for uplifted hands.* He had loved the word himself. Religion is inward first, then outward. We must love it before we are anxious to spread it. 2. *But what accounts for the loyal heart?* The word had brought him salvation, yielded him sustenance, afforded him guidance. We love the word for its joyous effects upon ourselves. III. The studious mind. 1. Devout meditation the best employment. 2. The word of God affords a grand field for it. 3. To meditate in it learn to love it : " have loved," " will meditate."—*W. W.*

Verse 48.—I. God's commandments loved. We love the law when we love the Lawgiver. We love his will only when our hearts are reconciled and renewed. Hence the need of spiritual renewal. II. God's commandments the subject of prayer : " My hands also will I lift up." Perowne says, " The expression denotes the act of prayer." We may pray for a fuller knowledge, a deeper experience, a readier and more perfect obedience. III. A theme for meditation. Amidst the hurry of outward activities we must not forget the need of quiet meditation. —*H. W.*

Verse 49.—I. The personality of the word : " the word unto thy servant." II. The application of the word : " upon which thou hast caused me to hope." III. The pleading of the word : " Remember the word," etc.

Verse 49.—*The word of hope.* I. God's word the foundation of human hope. (The fact of a revelation. The substance of the revelation.) II. Particular words of God which have been found peculiarly hope-enkindling. III. The pleading of such words at the throne of grace.—*C. A. D.*

Verse 50.—Each man has his own affliction and his own consolation. Quickened piety the best comfort. The word the means of it.

Verse 50.—I. The need of consolation. II. The consolation needed.—*G. R.*

Verse 51.—The proud man's contumely, and the gracious man's constancy.

Verse 51.—*Fidelity in the face of contempt.* I. The proud deride the believer's subjection to God's law. II. They ridicule the believer's delight in God's service. III. They are met by the believer's resolution to cleave to God. 2 Sam. vi. 20, 22. —*C. A. D.*

Verse 52.—Comfort derived from a review of the ancient doings of the Lord towards the wicked and his people.

Verse 52.—I. The dead speaking to the living. II. The living listening to the dead.—*G. R.*

Verse 52.—*Sweet water from a dark well.* I. God's judgments are calculated to inspire terror. II. But they prove God's superintending care over the world. III. They are ever against sin, and for holiness. IV. In all times of judgment God delivers his people. Noah, Lot, etc. V. Therefore God's judgments are a source of comfort to the believer.—*C. A. D.*

Verse 53.—The sensations of godly men at the sight of sinners : horror at their crime, their perseverance in it, their rejection of grace, and their end.

Verse 53.—*Horror-stricken.* I. The guilt and danger of impenitent sinners. II. The horror and concern of godly spectators. III. The prayer and labour which such concern should dictate.—*C. A. D.*

Verse 54.—Here is—I. Light in darkness. II. Companionship in solitude. III. Activity in rest : " house of pilgrimage."—*G. R.*

Verse 54.—The cheerful pilgrim. I. A good man views his residence in this world as only the house of his pilgrimage. II. The situation, however disadvantageous, admits of cheerfulness. III. The sources of his joy are derived from the Scriptures.—*W. Jay.*

Verse 54.—See " Spurgeon's Sermons," No. 1652 : " The Singing Pilgrim."

Verse 55 with 49.—" Remember." " I have remembered."

Verse 55.—Night memories. Day duties. How they act and react upon each other.

Verse 55.—Dark nights. Bright memories. Right results.—*C. A. D.*

Verse 55.—I. Happy though restless night. II. Happy though busy day.—*W. D.*

Verse 56.—The gains of godliness ; or, what a man gets through holy living.

Verse 56.—I. The duty : " I kept thy precepts." II. Its reward : " This I had," etc. Protection : " this I had." Guidance : " this I had." Prosperity : " this I had." Consolation : " this I had."—*G. R.*

Verse 57.—I. The infinite possession : " Thou art my portion, O LORD." Notice—1. A clear distinction made by the Psalmist between his portion and that of the ungodly here and hereafter : See Ps. lxxiii. 2. A positive claim : " Thou art my portion, O LORD." This " portion " is boundless, abiding, appropriate, satisfying, elevating, all of grace. II. The appropriate resolution : " I have said that I would keep thy words." 1. Notice the preface : " I have said." 2. The link between the portion possessed and the resolution made. 3. The work of keeping God's words. Keep him who is the *Word*—Christ Jesus. Keep the word of the gospel—doctrines, precepts, promises (kept in the heart to comfort the believer). This blessed subject suggests a solemn contrast. See the portion of that servant who did not keep his Lord's word : Matt. xxix. 48—51. See " Spurgeon's Sermons," No. 1372 : " God our Portion, and his Word our Treasure."

Verse 57 (*first clause*).—The believer's portion. I. Show the validity of his claim : " my." 1. A gift by covenant : Heb. viii. 10—13. 2. Involved in joint heirship with Christ : Rom. viii. 17. 3. Confirmed by the experience of faith. II. Survey. the superlative value of his possession : " The Lord." 1. Absolutely good. 2. Infinitely precious. 3. Inexhaustibly full. 4. Everlastingly sure. III. Suggest a method of deriving the greatest *present* advantage from it. 1. Meditate much upon God, under the conviction that he is your portion. 2. Carry all cares to him, and cast every burden on him. 3. Refer every temptation to the word of his law, and every doubt to the word of his promise. 4. Draw largely upon his riches to meet every need as it arises.—*John Field*, 1882.

Verses 57, 58.—The believer's estate, profession, and petition.

Verse 58.—*The soul's sunshine.* I. God's favour the one thing needful. II. Whole-heartedness the one mode of entreating it. III. Covenant mercy the one plea for obtaining it.—*C. A. D.*

Verse 58.—We may learn how a seeker may come to enjoy saving favour, by a careful study of—I. The Profession : " I intreated thy favour with my whole heart." 1. What he did : " I intreated." *Heb.* " I painfully sought thy face." Earnest desire. Importunate supplication. Painful sorrow for sin. 2. How he did it : " With my whole heart." The intellect, affections, will, all engaged and concentrating effort. Otherwise, seeking is solemn trifling. This only worthy of our purpose, pleasing to God, and successful. 3. The evidence that we are doing it. Frequent prayer, searching the word, often enquiring. The first and main business —Giving up for Christ. II. The Petition : " Be merciful unto me." 1. God's favour to be expected on the terms of mercy only. 2. Happily, this is a prayer every sinner can and should use. 3. Blessedly true it is, that it never fails. III. The Plea : " According to thy word." 1. A plea that cannot be gainsaid is a great thing in an entreaty. 2. The promise of God is just such a plea. 3. Seek it out, lay hold of it, and urge it.—*J. F.*

Verse 59.—I. Self-examination : " I thought on " my private " ways "—my social ways—my sacred ways—my public ways. II. Its advantages : " And turned my feet," etc.—*G. R.*

Verse 59.—I. Unthinking and straying. II. Thinking and turning.—*C. A. D.*

Verse 59.—I. Conviction. II. Conversion.—*W. D.*

Verse 59.—*Thinking on our own ways.* Enquire, I. Why so generally neglected ? 1. Want of courage. 2. Occupied too much. 3. Unpleasant, and therefore the chief care of many is to banish it. II. When is it wisely conducted ? 1. When honestly engaged in. 2. When thoroughly carried out. 3. When Scripture is made the referee and standard. 4. When Divine help is sought. III. What end will it serve ? 1. Turn us from our own ways with shame and penitence. 2. Turn us to God's testimonies with earnestness, reverence, and hopefulness.—*J. F.*

Verse 59.—I. Right thinking : " I thought on my ways." 1. That this thought upon his ways caused the Psalmist dissatisfaction is evident. 2. Right thinking upon our ways will suggest a practical change. 3. The retrospect we take of our life should suggest that any turn we make should be Godward : " Unto thy testimonies." 4. Right thinking also suggests that such a turning is possible. II. Right turning. The turn was—1. Complete. 2. Practical. 3. Spiritual.

4. Immediate. 5. It must be a divine work. See "Spurgeon's Sermons," No. 1181: " Thinking and Turning."

Verse 60.—The dangers of delay. The reasons for prompt action.

Verse 60.—*A sermon to loiterers.* I. Reflection. Keeping God's commandments is my duty ; is my welfare. Commandments delayed may be never kept. Delay is in itself disobedience. Alacrity is the soul of obedience. II. Resolve. I will make haste and delay not.—*C. A. D.*

Verse 60.—I. Quick. II. Sure.—*W. D.*

Verse 60.—Procrastination considered in its most important application ; that is, to religion. I. This procrastination is irrational. II. It is unpleasant, disagreeable, painful. III. It is disgraceful. IV. It is sinful, and that is the highest degree. V. It is dangerous.—*John Angell James.*

Verse 61.—I. Spiritual highway-robbery. II. The traveller keeping his road. Or, what enemies can do, and what they cannot do.

Verse 62.—I. The duty of gratitude : " give thanks." II. The subject for gratitude : " thy righteous judgments." III. The season for gratitude : at night as well as in the day.—*G. R.*

Verse 62.—Up in the night. Singing in the night. Reasons for such singular conduct.

Verse 62.—*The nightingale.* I. A natural association of thought : " midnight " and " judgments." Exod. xii., etc. II. An incongruous association of feeling : " thanks " and " judgments." III. A full justification of this apparent incongruity : "*thanks* because of thy *righteous* judgments." IV. A vigorous performance of an incumbent duty : " at midnight I will rise to give thanks."—*C. A. D.*

Verse 63.—I. True religion is friendly. II. Our friendliness should be catholic. III. Our friendliness should be discriminating. IV. Such friendliness is most useful.

Verse 63.—Of good and bad company. How to avoid the one, and improve the other. See W. Bridge's Sermon, in his works, vol. v., p. 90. Tegg's edition, 1845.

Verse 63.—The believer's choice of companions. I. Ought to be decided by their piety : " Them that fear thee." II. Is directed by their conduct : " Them that keep thy precepts." III. Should be extended as far as possible : " All." IV. Involves reciprocal obligation : " I am a companion."—*J. F.*

Verse 64.—The sum and substance of this verse will be comprised in these five propositions :—I. That saving knowledge is a benefit that must be asked of God. II. That this benefit cannot be too often or sufficiently enough asked : it is his continual request. III. In asking, we are encouraged by the bounty or mercy of God. IV. That God is merciful all his creatures declare. V. That his goodness to all his creatures should confirm us in hoping for saving grace or spiritual good things—*T. Manton.*

Verse 64.—I. Observations in the school of nature. II. Supplications to enter the school of grace.

Verse 64.—The mercy of God in nature and his mercy as revealed in the word. I. The one excellent ; the other super-excellent. II. The one easily given ; the other coming through a great sacrifice. III. The one may be enjoyed, and even increase condemnation ; the other, if enjoyed, is sure salvation. IV. The one should lead to repentance ; the other is specially adapted for the penitent's restoration to holiness.—*J. F.*

Verse 65.—The servant giving his master a character ; or, experience tallying with Scripture : two fruitful themes.

Verse 65.—I. Experience confirmed by the word. II. The word confirmed by experience.—*G. R.*

Verse 65.—A servant's story. I. Although he knew my faults he engaged me. II. Although I am so far beneath him, yet he familiarly teaches me. III. Although I am always ailing, he is very kind to me in my afflictions. IV. Although I am one of the meanest of his servants, he permits me to feast at his own table. V. Although I do little work, he will pay me good wages. VI. Although I am to have such great wages, I have very many perquisites. VII. Although my Master is all this to me (can you believe it ?) I murmur and repine at him if he crosses me in anything. Application :—1. Does not the word " servant " sound like a misnomer ?—" not servants. . . . but I have called you friends." 2. Though he calls me " friend," I shall never cease to call him " Master."—*Richard Andrew Griffin, in "Stems and Twigs."*

Verse 66.—I. Singular faith : " I have believed thy commandments."
II. Special petition based upon it : " Teach me."

Verse 66.—The value of a good judgment to sound knowledge.   I. It carefully
discriminates between truth and error.   II. It puts each truth in its proper relation
to other truths.   III. It holds every truth firmly, but has the greater care for the
more important.   IV. It rather avoids the curious and the speculative, but really
loves the plain and useful.   V. Knowing that truths are rightly held only, when
applied, it turns all to practical account.   VI. Knowing also, that good food may,
under some circumstances, become poisonous, it is careful in its selection and use
of truths.—*J. F.*

Verse 67.—I. The dangers of prosperity.   II. The benefits of adversity.
—*G. R.*

Verse 67.—The restraining power of affliction.

Verses 67, 71, 75.—*Affliction thrice viewed and thrice blessed.*   I. Before affliction :
straying.   II. In affliction : learning.   III. After affliction : knowing.—*C. A. D.*

Verse 68.—The double plea for a choice blessing.   The goodness of God the
hope of our ignorance.

Verse 68.—"*Thou art good and doest good.*"   The nature and work of God are
manifest in nature, providence, grace, and glory.   They are morally good ; bene-
ficially good ; perfectly good ; immeasurably good ; immutably good ; experimentally
good ; satisfactorily good.—*W. J.*

Verse 68 (*first clause*).—A sermon on God's goodness.   I. The perfectness of it.
II. The proofs of it.   III. The power it should have over us.—*J. F.*

Verse 69.—Whole-hearted obedience the best solace under slander ; the best
answer to it ; and the best way of converting the slanderers.

Verse 70.—I. Fatty degeneration of the heart.   II. Thorough regeneration of
the heart.

Verse 70.—*A fatty heart.*   I. The diagnosis of the disease.   II. Its symptoms.
Pride ; no delight in God, nor in his law ; dislike to his people ; readiness to lie :
ver. 69.   III. Its fatal character.   IV. Its only cure.   Psa. li. 10 ; Ezek. xxxvi. 26.
—*C. A. D.*

Verse 71.—I. David knew what was good for him.   II. David learned what is
good essentially.   Active obedience is learned by passive obedience.

Verse 71.—Affliction an instructor.   I. Never welcomed : " Have been."
II. Often impatiently endured.   III. Always gratefully remembered : " It is
good," etc.   IV. Efficient for a perverse scholar : " That I might learn."   V. Indispensable in the education of all.—*J. F.*

Verse 71.—*The school of affliction.*   I. The reluctant scholar sent to school.
II. The scholar's hard lesson.   III. The scholar's blessed learning.   IV. The
scholar's sweet reflection.—*C. A. D.*

Verse 72.—The advantages of riches far excelled by the blessings of the word.

Verse 72.—*A valuation.*   I. The saints' high estimate of God's law.   II. Show
when it was formed : in affliction : ver. 71.   III. Vindicate its truth—by illustrating
the hollowness of riches, and the satisfaction found in godliness.—*C. A. D.*

Verse 72.—The word, better than gold and silver.   I. It gives what gold and
silver cannot purchase.   II. Without what it gives, gold and silver may be a curse.
III. Without gold and silver, it may yield its treasure more freely and fully than
with them.   IV. The word and what it gives shall rejoice the heart when gold
and silver shall be useless to their disappointed worshippers.—*J. F.*

Verse 72.—"*The law of thy mouth is better,*" etc.   I. It is more refining, and
makes me a better man.   II. It is more enriching, and makes me a wealthier man.
III. It is more distinguishing, and makes me a greater man.   IV. It is more
sustaining, and makes me a stronger man.   V. It is more preserving, and makes
me a safer man.   VI. It is more satisfying and makes me a happier man.   VII. It
is more lasting, and better suited to me as an immortal man.—*W. J.*

Verse 73.—I. Consider the Lord's great care in our creation.   II. See in it a
reason for his perfecting the new creation within us.   III. Observe the method of
this perfecting.

Verse 74.—I. The encouraging influence of good men upon others.   II. The
instructive influence of others upon them.—*G. R.*

Verse 74.—Converse with a tried but steadfast believer is a source of gladness
to the children of God.   I. He has a thrilling tale of experience to tell.   II. He
has valuable counsels and cautions to give.   III. He is a monument of God's

faithfulness, confirming the hope of others. IV. He is an epistle of Christ, written expressly to illustrate the preciousness and the power of the gospel.—*J. F.*

Verse 75.—Experimental knowledge : positive, personal, glorifying to God, consoling to the saints.

Verse 76.—Comfort. I. May be a matter of prayer. II. Is provided for in the Lord. III. Is promised in the word. IV. Is of great value to the believer.

Verse 76.—I. The need of comfort. II. The source of comfort : " Thy merciful kindness " III. The rule of comfort : " According to thy word."—*G. R.*

Verse 77.—I. Visitors invited. II. Boon expected. III. Welcome guaranteed : " for thy law," etc.

Verse 77.—*Divine life*—It is born, sustained, increased, by God's tender mercies. —*W. W.*

Verse 78.—I. A hard thing—to make the proud ashamed. II. A cruel thing— " they dealt perversely with me," etc. III. A wise thing—" but I will meditate," etc.

Verse 79.—Restoration to church fellowship. I. Good men may be in such a case as to need to be restored. II. They should not be ashamed to seek it. III. They should pray about it.

Verse 79.—*Select society.* I. Sociableness is an instinct of human nature. II. Sociableness is helpful to a wholesome Christian life. III. The choice of society should be a subject of prayer.—*C. A. D.*

Verse 80.—I. David's prayer for sincerity—that his heart might be brought to God's statutes, and that it might be sound in them, not rotten or deceitful. II. His dread of the consequences of hypocrisy : " that I be not ashamed." Shame is the portion of hypocrites, here or hereafter.—*M. Henry.*

Verse 80.—I. The heart in religion. II. The necessity of its being sound in it. III. The result of such sound-heartedness.

Verse 81.—Text suitable for a missionary sermon. I. The condition of the heathen world, enough to make the Christian faint for the salvation of God to visit it. 1. The grossness of its darkness. 2. Its wide area. 3. Its long continuance. 4. The limited character and effort of mission labour. 5. The opposing influences. II. This condition, though exceedingly sad, is not hopeless. Because—1. Of the intention, adaptation, and universal call of the gospel. 2. Of Christ's commission to his church. 3. Of the compassionate character of the spiritually enlightened, produced by their faith in the word. 4. Of the prophecies and promises. Thus, there is hope in the word. III. If Christians are fainting for the salvation, but hoping in the word, their interest in mission work will be intense, and will show itself. 1. In earnest prayer for more labourers, and greater results. 2. In devoting themselves, if possible, to the work. 3. In free and generous giving, to help on the work.—*J. F.*

Verse 81.—*"My soul fainteth,"* etc. Men faint for health, provision, rest, promotion, success, and in some instances for salvation. David fainted. I. For his own salvation. 1. From guilt : " Deliver me from all my transgressions ; " " from bloodguiltiness." 2. From defilement : " Create in me a clean heart." " Wash me." 3. From formality : " Let the words of my mouth," etc. 4. From darkness : " Why hidest thou thyself ? " " Lift up," etc. " Say unto my soul," etc. 5. From unhappiness : " Out of the depths," etc. II. For the salvation of others. 1. He talked about it : " Time for thee to work, Lord." 2. He prayed for it : " Oh that the salvation," etc. " Let thy work," etc. " God be merciful unto us : " " Save now, I beseech thee." 3. He laboured for it : " I will make mention of thy righteousness : " " I will teach transgressors thy ways."—*W. J.*

Verse 81.—I. Eagerness of expectation. II. Energy of hope. III. Establishment of promise : " in thy word."

Verse 81.—*"Salvation,"* in Scripture, hath divers acceptations : it is put— 1. For that temporal deliverance which God giveth, or hath promised to give to his people : so it is taken. Exod. xiv. 13. 2. For the exhibition of Christ in the flesh. Ps. xcviii. 2, 3 ; Luke ii. 29, 30. 3. For the benefits which we have by Christ on this side of heaven ; as the pardon of sin, and the renovation of our natures. Matt. i. 21 ; Titus iii. 5 ; Ps. li. 12. 4. For everlasting life : " Receiving the end of your faith, even the salvation of your souls " (1 Pet. i. 9) ; meaning thereby our final reward.—*T. Manton.*

Verse 81.—I. Faint. II. Pursuing.—*W. D.*

Verse 82.—Answer to the enquiry—" When wilt thou comfort me ? " 1. When your grief has answered its purpose. 2. When you believe. 3. When you leave sin. 4. When you obey. 5. When you submit to my will. 6. When you seek my glory.

Verse 82.—I. How longingly the believer turns to God for comfort in his affliction : "When wilt thou comfort me ? " II. How intently he gazes upon the Divine promises : " My eyes fail for thy word." III. How the weariness of waiting cannot wear out his patience, while hope increases his importunity : " When wilt thou ? " —*J. F.*

Verse 82.—*The pleading of the eyes.* I. How the eyes speak. By " expression " of the moods of the soul, as—longing, Isa. viii. 17 ; faith, Isa. xlv. 22 ; Heb. xii. 2 ; expectation, Ps. v. 3 ; Phil. iii. 20 ; Tit. ii. 13 ; love, 2 Cor. iii. 18 ; John i. 14. II. What the eyes say. " When wilt *thou* comfort me ? Brushing aside all other comforters, thou art my sun : my life : my love : my all." III. How the pleading eyes shall meet the responsive Eye of the Lord : Heb. ix. 18. In the look of the recognition of grief, Ex. ii. 25 ; in the look of pardon, Luke xxiii. 61 ; of strength-giving, Jud. vi. 14 ; of complacent love, Isa. lxvi. 2.—*C. A. D.*

Verse 83.—I. The outward man in ill case. II. Character blackened. III. Constantly exposed to discomfort. IV. Contents maturing.

Verse 83.—"*A bottle in the smoke.*" I. God's people have their trials. 1. From the poverty of their condition. 2. Our trials frequently result from our comforts. 3. The ministry hath made much smoke with it. 4. The poor bottle in the smoke keeps there for a long time, till it gets black. II. Christian men feel their troubles ; they are like " bottles " in the smoke. 1. The trial that we do not feel is no trial at all. 2. Trials which are not felt are unprofitable trials. A bottle in the smoke gets very black, becomes very useless, is an empty bottle. III. Christians do not, in their troubles, forget God's statutes of command, the statutes of promise. Why was it that David still held fast by God's statutes ? 1. He was not a bottle in the fire, or he would have forgotten them. 2. Jesus Christ was in the smoke with him, and the statutes were in the smoke with him too. 3. The statutes were in the soul, where the smoke does not enter.—*From "Spurgeon's Sermons,"* No. 71.

Verse 84.—A solemn question pointing to the shortness of life, the severity of sorrow, the necessity of industry, the nearness of the reward.

Verse 85.—Pits ; or, the secret schemes of wicked men against the godly.

Verse 86 (last clause).—A prayer for all occasions. See the many cases in which it is used in Scripture.

Verse 87.—I. What the good man loses by gaining. II. What he gains by losing.—*G. R.*

Verse 87.—I. "Almost," but not altogether. II. The saving clause: " I forsook not thy precepts."

Verse 87.—Passing through fires, and the asbestos covering.

Verse 88.—I. New life is the cause of new obedience. II. New obedience is the effect of new life.—*G. R.*

Verse 88.—Quickening. I. Our greatest need. II. God's most gracious boon. III. The guarantee of our steadfastness ; and so, IV. The promotor of God's glory.

Verse 88.—1. He closes with a frequent petition : "*Quicken thou me*—make me alive." All true religion consists in the LIFE *of God* in the SOUL *of man.* 2. The *manner* in which he wishes to be quickened : "*After thy lovingkindness.*" He wishes not to be raised from the *death of sin by God's thunder*, but by the *loving voice* of a *tender Father.* 3. The *effect* it should have upon him : "*So shall I keep the testimony of thy mouth.*" Whatever thou *speakest* I will *hear, receive, love, and obey.*—*Adam Clarke.*

Verses 89—92.—The Psalmist here tells us the prescription which soothed his pains and sustained his spirits. Here we have strong consolation. I. In certain facts which he remembered. 1. The eternal existence of God. 2. The immutability of his word. 3. The faithfulness of the fulfilment of that word. 4. The perpetuity of the word in nature. 5. The perpetuity of the word in experience. II. The delights which he experienced in the time of his trouble. In bereavements ; when everything seemed shifting and inconstant ; when his own faith failed him ; when all helpers failed him ; he fell back upon the eternal settlements : " O Lord, thy word is settled," etc. See " Spurgeon's Sermons," No. 1656 : " My Solace in my Affliction."

Verse 89.—Eternal settlements, or, heavenly certainties.

Verse 89.—God's eternal calm (in contrast with earth's mutations) imaged in the starry heavens.—*William Bickle Haynes*, 1882.

Verse 89.—Consider, I. The term, " thy word." 1. A word is a revealed thought. The Scriptures are just this : the thoughts and purposes of God made intelligible to man. 2. But a " word " also marks specially unity (it is one word) and wholeness or completeness, a word, not a syllable. The Scriptures are one and complete. II. The statement, " for ever settled in heaven." 1. " Settled in heaven " before it came to earth ; therefore it could come as a continuous unfolding, through various dispensations, without the shadow of hesitation or contradiction manifest in it. 2. Abides " settled in heaven," for its central revelation ; the atonement is a completed fact, and Christ is now in heaven a perfected Saviour ; thus the word is unalterable. 3. "For ever settled in heaven." Not only because God in heaven is of one mind and cannot be turned ; but because righteousness itself, the righteousness of heaven, demands that an atonement by suffering shall be fully and everlastingly answered by its due reward. III. The lessons. 1. If settled in heaven, men on earth can never unsettle it. 2. The wicked may not indulge a future hope arising from any new dispensation beyond the grave ; God's present word to us cannot then be unsettled. 3. The godly may rely on a settled word amidst the unsettled experiences and feelings incident to earth.—*J. F.*

Verse 90.—The stability of the earth a present picture of everlasting faithfulness.

Verses 90, 91.—Consider, I. The steadfastness of nature as dependent upon the divine decree : " according to thy ordinances." II. The subserviency of nature to the divine will : " for all are thy servants." III. The fixedness of nature's laws, together with their subserviency to God's purposes, as a confirmation of the Christian's faith in the written word, in the care of a divine providence, and in the sureness of spiritual and heavenly things. " Thy faithfulness is," etc.—*J. F.*

Verse 91.—Our starry monitors. They teach us, I. To serve : though we cannot shine with their brightness. II. To do all with strict regard to God's will. III. To " continue "—" according to thine ordinances."—*W. B. H.*

Verse 91.—The service of nature. I. Universal : " all are thy servants." II. Obedient : " according to thy ordinances." III. Perpetual : " they continue." IV. Derived : " thou hast established the earth."

Verse 92.—The sustaining power of joy in God.

Verse 92.—The word of God as a sustaining power amid the greater sorrows of life. I. Its necessity. 1. For want of it, men have become drunkards to drown their sorrows, have become suicides because life was unbearable, have become broken and hopeless because they had no strength to struggle against misfortune, have become atheists in creed as, alas, they were before in practice ; all, in fact, become subject to sorrow's worst bitterness and calamity's worst effects. 2. Nothing can supply the place of God's word. Nature throws no light on the mystery of suffering. Human philosophy is at best cold comfort, and when most needed most fails. II. Its efficiency. Proved—1. In the experience of those who have tried it. 2. By the character of its promises. 3. By the discovery it makes of a beneficent providence working through calamity and sorrow. 4. By the revelation it gives of the pity of God and the sympathy of Christ. 5. By its record of the " Man of sorrows," who through suffering wrought out man's salvation, and entered into glory. 6. By its teaching concerning the Incarnate Word ; thus showing a suffering God, which may well be a solace to suffering men. 7. By displaying the glory of heaven and the eternal felicity awaiting those who overcome through the blood of the Lamb.—*J. F.*

Verse 92.—The Godly Man's Ark ; or, City of Refuge in the day of his Distress. Discovered in divers (five) Sermons . . . . By Edmund Calamy, B. D. . . . . . Eighteenth edition. 1709. 12mo.

Verse 92.—We have here set before us by the Psalmist, I. The case which he had been in, and which he now refers to—one sad and sinking. He was under such affliction that he was ready to perish ; which seems to include inward and outward trouble at once ; trials without and pressure within. II. What it was that gave him relief, and this when nothing else could, etc., the law of God. III. How he looked back upon this relief received, namely, with thankfulness to God, to whom he speaks, and records it for the encouragement and direction of others : " Unless thy law had been my delights, I should then have perished in mine affliction."—*Daniel Wilcox*, 1676—1733.

Verse 92.—*The life-buoy*. Under the form of the narrative of a shipwrecked mariner, describe the experience of the soul struggling in the sea of affliction; almost overwhelmed: yet buoyed up over each successive billow: and finally saved by clinging to the Word of God.—*C. A. D.*

Verse 92.—The Psalmist's shudder at recollected danger. I. Sore peril: affliction tending to despair and ruin. II. Fearful crisis: "then." III. Many-handed help: "thy law my delights."—*W. B. H.*

Verse 93.—Experience fixes the word upon the memory.

Verse 93.—I. A good resolve: "I will never forget thy precepts." 1. The precepts are worth remembering. 2. Safety lies in remembering them. 3. Fidelity to God cannot be without remembering them. 4. Not to remember them is shameful ingratitude. II. An excellent reason for making it: "For with them thou hast quickened me." 1. A reason founded upon personal experience: "me." 2. A reason appreciative of the benefit received: "quickened." 3. A reason indicative of gratitude to God: "thou."—*J. F.*

Verse 93.—"Never forget"; an often-uttered phrase. Here golden. I. Something that *could* not be forgotten: life and pardon received. How could it? II. Something that *should* not be forgotten: the precious instrumentality.—*W. B. H.*

Verse 93.—I. The instrumental power of truth. 1. Used by God in our regeneration: James i. 18; Ps. xix. 7. 2. Used in our liberation: John viii. 32. 3. Used in our sanctification: John xvii. 7. II. Our consequent affection for it. We cannot forget. 1. Our past obligations to it. 2. Our present dependence upon it. 3. Our future needs of it.—*W. W.*

Verse 94.—1. David claims relation to God: "I am thine"—devoted to thee, and owned by thee, thine in covenant. 2. He proves his claim: "I am thine, save me; for I have sought thy precepts"; *i.e.*, I have carefully enquired concerning my duty, and diligently endeavoured to do it. 3. He improves his claim: "I am thine, save me." Save me from sin, save me from ruin.—*M. Henry.*

Verse 94.—I. A great prayer: "Save me." II. A grand prayer: "I am thine." III. A gracious experience: "I have sought," etc.

Verse 94.—I. Relation: "I am thine." II. Preservation: "save me." III. Obligation: "I have sought," etc.—*G. R.*

Verse 94.—God's child humbly points out to him his responsibility: "I am thine." II. Ventures to urge his own sincerity: he has at least "sought." III. With these two hands extended, he utters a sharp cry for help: "save me."—*W. B. H.*

Verse 94.—*Multum in parvo.* I. A profession. II. A prayer. III. A plea.—*C. A. D.*

Verse 94.—I. God's interest in us. II. Our interest in God.—*W. D.*

Verse 94.—The characteristics of personal religion. I. Personal devotedness to God: "I am thine." II. Personal obedience rendered: "I have sought thy precepts." III. Personal expectation cherished; "save me."—*J. F.*

Verse 94.—The courage obedience gives. I. It emboldens us to a firm assurance: "I am thine, for I have," etc. 1. We become God's by faith alone. 2. But the assurance of being his cannot exist without obedience; obedience proves the faith to ourselves; satisfies us concerning grace received. 3. Poor obedience always interferes with assurance. II. It emboldens us to pray, and in prayer: "Save me." 1. The Christian's prayers are only of faith and offered in faith. 2. Yet disobedience makes him shrink from approaching God in prayer, and renders him feeble in petitioning. 3. Obedience is humble but bold. The middle clause of the text applies equally to the first and third clauses.—*J. F.*

Verse 95.—Wicked men patient in carrying out their evil designs. Good men patient in considering the ways of the Lord.

Verse 95.—The hatred of the wicked towards the righteous. I. Show that it ever has been, and still is. 1. Select Scriptural instances, beginning with Abel. 2. Notice the persecutions of the church. 3. Treatment in the workshop. 4. Often in the home. 5. The contemptuous manner the "saints" are spoken of, etc. II. Enquire as to why it is so. 1. The enmity of the carnal heart to God. 2. The jealousy excited by the Christian's assurance of eternal blessedness. 3. The consciousness of being rebuked by a holy life. 4. Excited to it by Satan. 5. The restless mischievousness of sin which, if it cannot hinder holiness, will maliciously hurt its advocates. III. Direct how to act when exposed to it: "I will consider thy testimonies." That means—1. Be the more obedient to God. 2. Have the more watchful control over words and feelings. 3. Love your enemies. 4. Pray for those who hate you.   5. Do good to them on every opportunity.   6. Be thankful that you are among the hated and not the haters.   7. Especially consider the holy testimony of Christ's forbearing patience.—*J. F.*

Verse 95.—Waiting counterwrought by waiting. I. Temptations in ambush. II. The saint with his Lord.—*W. B. H.*

Verse 95.—*Immunity.* I. I am in danger. II. I will attend to my duty. III. I will trust. thee to deliver me.—*C. A. D.*

Verse 96.—I. An end :—" seen "; seen by one man where it should not have been ; seen where there was no end of boasting ; seen in *all* perfection.   II. No end :—to the extent, spirituality, perpetuity, and perfectness of the law.

Verse 96.—I. The Finite explored.   II. The Infinite unexplored.—*W. D.*

Verse 96.—Perfectionism disproved by experience and inspiration.—*W. B. H.*

Verse 96.—*Perfection—perfect and imperfect.* I. Loud professions of perfection arise from ignorance (of self, or of God's requirements).   II. Are peculiarly liable to collapse : " I have seen an end."   III. Are best corrected by a survey of the breadth of the divine law.—*C. A. D.*

Verse 97.—I. Unusual Exclamation.   II. Unusual Application.—*W. D.*

Verse 97.—Indescribable love and insatiable thought. The action and reaction of affection and meditation.

Verse 97.—I. The object of love : " thy law." II. The degree of that love : " oh, how love I," etc.   III. The evidence of that love : " it is my meditation," etc.—*G. R.*

Verse 97.—*Love to the law.* I. An ardent confession of love. II. An unanswerable evidence of love.—*C. A. D.*

Verse 97 (*first clause*).—Vehemency of love for God's word. I. Its recognisable marks. 1. Profound reverence for the authority of the word. 2. Admiration for its holiness. 3. Jealousy for its honour ; God's servant feels acute pain when men show it any slight. 4. Respect for its wholeness ; he would not divorce precepts from promises, nor ignore a single statement in it. 5. Indefatigability in its study. 6. Eager desire to obey it. 7. Forwardness in praising it. 8. Activity in spreading it abroad. II. Its reasonableness. 1. The word well deserves it. 2. It is a proof of true intelligence. 3. It is not less than a regard for our own interest demands. III. Its requisiteness to the true worship of God. Men sneeringly call such an affection bibliolatry, as though it were the worship of a book. In truth, it is an essential element in the due worship of God. For—1. Without it there cannot be the faith which honours God. 2. It is involved in that love to God which constitutes the very essence of worship. 3. It is itself an act of homage that a worshipper dare not withhold.—*J. F.*

Verses 97—100.—*Spiritual wisdom.* I. God's word the source of surpassing wisdom—excelling that of " mine enemies," " my teachers," " the ancients." II. The three methods of acquiring this wisdom—love, meditation, practice. III. The one Giver of this wisdom : " Thou : " ver. 98.—*C. A. D.*

Verse 98.—Constant communion with truth the student's road to proficiency.

Verses 98, 99, 100.—The truly wise man. 1. *The source of his wisdom.* The word of " the only wise God," here described as (1) Thy commandments. (2) Thy testimonies.   (3) Thy precepts.   2. *The increase of his wisdom.* It arises from (1) The abiding indwelling of the word : " ever with me," ver. 98. (2) Meditation upon the word, ver. 99. (3) Obedience to the word, ver. 100. 3. *The measure of his wisdom.* (1) Wiser than his enemies, whose wisdom was " not from above, but earthly, sensual, devilish." (2) Wiser than his teachers, whose wisdom was " of this world." (3) Wiser than the ancients, whose wisdom was that of unsanctified age and experience.—*W. H. J. Page*, 1882.

Verse 99.—The surest way to excellence. I. A good subject : " thy testimonies." II. A good method : " are my meditations."

Verse 100.—Antiquity no security for truth as contrasted with revelation : old age no proof of wisdom as contrasted with holy living : open confession no evidence of boasting as contrasted with sullen pride.

Verse 100.—Obedience the high road to understanding.—*W. B. H.*

Verse 100.—Obedience the key of knowledge. John vii. 17.

Verse 100.—Self-restraint needful to piety.

Verse 102.—Divine teaching necessary to secure perseverance, and effectual to that end.

Verse 102.—Consider,—I. The path appointed for men to walk in : " Thy judgments." 1. Right path. 2. Clean path. 3. Pleasant path. 4. Safe path. 5. The end—eternal glory. II. The persistent pursuit of it : " I have not departed." 1. Persecution would drive from it. 2. Pleasures would allure from it. 3. The flesh would weary in it. 4. But the true believer determines to hold on his way to the end. 5. And carefully watches his steps lest they depart. III. The preserving power that holds the traveller to it : " For thou hast taught me." 1. The traveller walks with God, and receives instruction by the special illumination of the Holy Spirit. 2. The choice property of this teaching is, not only that it makes wise, but that it captivates the soul, strengthens it, and holds it to a holy obedience.—*J. F.*

Verse 103.—Experience in religion the source of enjoyment in it ; or, I. Tasting the word : its sweetness. II. Declaring the word with the mouth : its greater sweetness.

Verse 103.—I. The word is positively sweet : " sweet to my taste." II. Comparatively sweet : " sweeter than honey." III. Superlatively sweet : " how sweet," etc.—*G. R.*

Verse 103.—The comparison, setting forth the precious property of sweetness in the word : " Sweeter than honey." " Better than honey," would not do as well. It is—1. The purest sweetness ; even precepts and rebukes. 2. Uncloying sweetness. 3. Always a beneficial sweetness. 4. A specially grateful sweetness—in affliction, in the hour of death.—*J. F.*

Verse 103.—*Spiritual delicacy.* I. The taste needed to relish it. II. The life that alone is nourished by it. III. The rare enjoyment derived from it.—*C. A. D.*

Verse 103.—I. It is sweet. II. Let us enjoy it. III. The best effects will follow. George Herbert says :—

> " O Book ! infinite sweetness ! let my heart
> Suck every letter, and a honey gain,
> Precious for any grief in any part ;
> To clear the breast, to mollify all pain."

Verse 103.—If we would taste the honey of God, we must have the palate of faith.—*A. R. Fausset.*

Verse 104.—The influence of the precepts. I. Upon the understanding. II. Upon the affections. III. Upon the life.

Verse 104.—I. The intellectual effect of the Scriptures : " I get understanding." II. Their moral effect : " I hate," etc.—*G. R.*

Verse 104.—The understanding derived from God's precepts begets holy hatred, I. To the false ways of conventional morality. II. To the false ways of a formal religiousness. III. To the false ways of an erring theology. IV. To the false ways of hypocritical practice. V. To the false ways of sinful suggestions. VI. To the false ways of one's own deceitful heart.—*J. F.*

Verses 105—108.—I. Illumination (ver. 105). II. Decision (ver. 106). III. Testing : " I am afflicted " (ver. 107). IV. Consecration (ver. 108). V. Education : " teach me," etc. (ver. 108).

Verse 105.—The practical, personal, everyday use of the word of God.

Verse 105.—*Lamp-light.* I. The believer's dangerous night-journey through the world. II. The lamp that illumines his path. III. The eternal day towards which he travels (when the lamp will be laid aside) : Rev. xxii. 5).—*C. A. D.*

Verse 106.—Decision for God, and fit modes of expressing it.

Verse 106.—I. Veneration for the word. II. Consecration to the word. III. Fidelity to the word.—*G. R.*

Verse 106.—*Swearing and performing.* I. The usefulness of religious vows. To quicken perception ; to rouse conscience ; (seen in Jewish nation : Ex. xxiv. 37 ; 2 Chr. xv. 12—15 ; Neh. x. 28, 29 ; in Scottish nation—Solemn League and Covenant). II. The danger of religious vows. A vow unfulfilled, or receded from, is a moral injury : Eccl. v. 4—7. III. The safeguard of religious vows : dependence on the Spirit of God : Ezek. xi. 19, 20 ; 2 Cor. iv. 5.—*C. A. D.*

Verse 107.—I. A good man greatly afflicted. II. A sure cure for the ills of affliction : " Quicken me." III. A safe rule to pray by when afflicted : " according unto thy word."

Verse 107.—I. The " very much " afflicted. 1. The world has such—widows, orphans, etc, etc. 2. Most take their turn. II. But there is " very much " grace. 1. God's word promises the needed quickening. 2. Himself very much greater than all our needs. 3. Christ tried " in all points " has all help. III. Therefore bring " very much " faith, as the Psalmist here. 1. Keen-eyed for promises. 2. Fervent in pleading them. 3. Strong in expectation.—*W. B. H.*

Verse 108.—Consider,—I. The instructive title given to prayer and praise : " The free-will offerings of my mouth." 1. It shows the believer to be a priest : " offerings." 2. It shows the peculiarity of his service : " free-will." 3. It implies whole-hearted consecration. II. The humility portrayed in the prayer : " Accept, I beseech thee." 1. Here is no pharisaic boasting. 2. Even the free-will offering is felt to need an " I beseech thee." III. The longing desire for further instruction in order to a more perfect obedience : " Teach me thy judgments."—*J. F.*

Verse 108.—Free will seeking free grace.—*W. D.*

Verse 108.—Work for Free-willers. I. Offerings of Prayer—for each of the blessings of salvation. II. Offerings of Repudiation—of all claim to unassisted good. III. Offerings of Praise—for sovereign grace.—*W. B. H.*

Verse 109.—The soul's life in jeopardy. The life of the soul secured.

Verses 109, 110.—Here is—I. David in danger of losing his life. There is but a step between him and death ; for " the wicked have laid a snare " for him. Wherever he was he found some design or other laid against him ; which made him say, " My soul is continually in my hand." It was not so only as a man—it is true of us all that we are exposed to the strokes of death—but as a man of war, and especially as " a man after God's own heart." II. David in no danger of losing his religion through this peril ; for, 1. He " doth not forget the law," and therefore is likely to persevere. 2. He hath not yet erred from God's precepts, and therefore it is to be hoped he will not.—*M. Henry.*

Verse 110.—Various kinds of snares, and the one way of escaping them.

Verse 110.—Consider,—I. Some of the snares set for saints by sinners. 1. Doctrinal snares, by intellectual sinners. 2. False accusations, by malignant sinners. 3. False flatteries, by deceitful sinners. 4. False charity, by a large number of sinners nowadays. II. The secure safeguard for a saint's safety : " I erred not from thy precepts." Obedience to God gives security, because—1. The snares are then suspected and watched against. 2. The feet cannot become entangled by them. 3. God keeps him who keeps his word.—*J. F.*

Verse 111.—I. Estate. II. Entering upon it. III. Entail upon it. IV. Enjoyment of it.

Verse 111.—Notice,—I. How rich the Psalmist was determined to be : " Thy testimonies have I taken as a heritage." Rich,—1. In knowledge. 2. In holiness. 3. In comfort. 4. In companionship, for God's company goes with his word. 5. In hope. II. How he clung to his wealth : " For ever." 1. He hurt none by so doing ; he could give generously his portion, and yet not waste. 2. He was right ; for he had the only wealth of which an everlasting possession is possible. 3. He was wise. III. How he rejoiced in his wealth : " They are the rejoicing of my heart." 1. Here is internal and deep joy ; not always possible to the possession of wealth. 2. Pure, unalloyed joy ; it is never so with other wealth. 3. Safe joy ; other joy is dangerous. 4. Unlosable joy.—*J. F.*

Verse 112.—Heart-leanings. Personality, pressure, inclination, performance, constancy, perpetuity.

Verse 112.—The godly man's obedience. I. Its reality. 1. " To perform " ; not words or feelings merely ; but deeds. 2. " Thy statutes " ; not human inventions, nor self conceits, nor conventional maxims. II. Its cordiality : " inclined my heart." 1. Heart inclination is requisite for pleasing a heart-searching God. 2. And to make obedience easy and even delightful. 3. " I have," he says ; was it therefore his doing ? Yes. Was it his work alone ? No. See verse 36. 4. The proofs. (1) Universality : " statutes," the whole of them. (2) Uniformity : " alway." III. Its constancy : " even unto the end." 1. Though a man should be cautious when planning for the future, yet this life-long purpose is right, wise, and safe. 2. Nor can he purpose less, if holy fervency fill the heart. 3. It is no more than what God and consistency demand.—*J. F.*

Verse 113.—The thought of the age, and the truth of all ages.

Verse 113.—I. The object of hatred. II. The object of love. Or—I. Love the cause of hatred. II. Hatred the effect of love.—*G. R.*

Verse 113.—" *Vain thoughts.*" What they are. Whence they arise. The mischief they cause. How they should be treated.—*W. H. J. P.*

Verse 113.—How the believer—1. Is troubled by vain thoughts. A frequent and painful experience. 2. Does not tolerate vain thoughts. Some suffer them to lodge within; he is anxious to expel them. 3. Triumphs over vain thoughts. By his love to the law of God. His prayer is—

> "With thoughts of Christ and things divine,
> Fill up this foolish heart of mine."
>
> *W. H. J. P.*

Verse 114. — Our protection *from* danger—" hiding-place "; *in* danger — " shield "; *before* danger—" I hope."

Verse 114.—"*Hiding-place.*" Secrecy to conceal us. Capacity to hold us. Safety. Comfort.—*T. Manton.*

Verse 114.—*Hiding and hoping.* I. A hiding-place needed. II. A hiding-place provided (Isa. xxv. 14; xxxii. 2). III. A hiding-place used.—*C. A. D.*

Verse 114.—I. The refuge provided : " Thou art," etc. II. The refuge revealed : " In thy word." III. The refuge found : " I hope," etc.—*G. R.*

Verse 114.—"*Thou art my hiding place.*" I. In thy grace, from condemnation. II. In thy compassion, from sorrow. III. In thy succour, from temptation. IV. In thy power, from opposition. V. In thy fulness, from want.—*W. J.*

Verse 115.—I. Ill company hinders piety. II. Piety quits ill company. III. Piety, in compelling this departure, acts as God will do at the last.

Verse 115.—Evil companionships incompatible with genuine righteousness. I. They necessitate concealment and compromise. II. They destroy the capability of communion with God, and the relish for spiritual things. III. They blunt the sensitiveness of conscience. IV. They involve deliberate disobedience to God.— *J. F.*

Verse 116.—I. Upholding promised. II. Needful for holy living. III. The preventive of shameful acts.

Verse 116.—"*Uphold me according unto thy word,*" etc. 1. The Psalmist pleads the promise of God, his dependence upon the promise, and his expectation from it : "*Uphold me according unto thy word,*" which word I hope in, and if it be not performed I shall be " ashamed of my hope." 2. He pleads the great need he had of God's grace, and the great advantage it would be to him : " Uphold me, that I may live "; intimating that he could not live without the grace of God.—*M. Henry.*

Verse 117.—I. Upholding—God's holding us up. It implies a danger, and that danger takes many forms. The believer's life may be described as walking in uprightness; he is a pilgrim. He needs upholding, for—1. The way is slippery. 2. Our feet make the danger as well as the way. 3. Cunning foes seek to trip us up. 4. Sometimes the difficulty is not caused by the way, but by the height to which God may elevate us. 5. The prayer is all the more needful because the most of people do not keep upright. II. Two blessed things that come out of this holding up. 1. We shall be safe for ourselves, as examples, and as pillars of the church. 2. We shall be watchful and sensitive : " I will have respect unto thy statutes continually." Without this no man is safe. See " Spurgeon's Sermons," No. 1657 : " My Hourly Prayer."

Verse 117.—"*Hold thou me up,*" etc. I. The good man is up. II. The good man wishes to keep up. III. The good man prays to be held up. IV. The good man knows that divine support is abundantly sufficient.—*W. J.*

Verse 117.—I. Dependence for the future : " Hold," etc. II. Resolution for the future : " I will have," etc.—*G. R.*

Verse 118.—Sin and falsehood : their connection, punishment, and cure.

Verse 118.—I. Hearken to the tramp of God's armies. In nature; providence; angelic hosts of last day. II. The mangled victims. Cunning deceivers specially obnoxious to God. Examples : Balaam, Pharaoh, Rome, the deceiver of the nations. III. The warnings to us of this Aceldama. Repent. Avoid deceit. Mind God's landmarks. Hide in Christ.—*W. B. H.*

Verse 118.—God's punishment of the wicked though awfully severe is just and necessary. I. It is due as the merited wages of iniquity. II. It is demanded by the position of God as moral governor, and by his character as righteous. III. It is necessary to mark the real worth of righteousness and its reward. If the wicked are not punished, the full worth of righteousness cannot appear. IV. In the nature of the case, it is absolutely unavoidable, except upon one condition, namely, the gift of genuine repentance and holiness after death; *that* no man has any right to expect, nor has God given the slightest intimation that he will bestow it. V. Hell lies in the bosom of sin ; and if the wicked were taken to heaven, they would carry hell thither. Heaven supplies not the things in which the wicked delight while it abounds in those they can neither understand nor sympathise with.—*J. F.*

Verse 118 (*second clause*).—The deceits of the wicked are all falsehoods. I. The world they embrace is a false Delilah. II. The pleasure they enjoy is a Satanic snare. III. Their formal religiousness is a vain delusion. IV. Their conceits of God are self-invented lies.—*J. F.*

Verses 118—120.—*Saved by fear.* I. The wrath of God revealed against sin. II. The judgment of God executed upon sinners. III. The fear of God created in the heart.—*C. A. D.*

Verse 119.—The saint's acquiescence in God's judgments.—*W. B. H.*

Verse 119.—I. Comparison of the wicked to dross. II. Comparison of their doom to the putting away of dross. III. The saint's admiration of divine justice as seen in the rejection of the wicked.

Verse 119.—God's putting away the wicked like dross. I. God's judgments are a searching and separating fire. II. The final judgment of the great day will complete the separating process. III. The great result will be, the true metal and the dross, each gathered to its *own* place.—*J. F.*

Verse 120.—The judgments of God on the wicked cause in the righteous, I. Love. II. Awe. III. Fear.

Verse 120.—I. Describe the true character of the fear. 1. It is the fear of reverence for God's authority and power. 2. It is the fear of horror against sin as meriting judgment. II. Show its compatibility with filial love. 1. The more we love God the more firmly we believe in the certainty and awfulness of his judgments. 2. The more we love God the more will we fear to arouse his chastising rod against ourselves. 3. In fact, if we love not God, we shall have no fear lest sin should involve us in judgment. III. Commend it. 1. As it proves a just sense of sin's desert. 2. As it shows a true appreciation of God's righteousness. 3. As it is not a fear that hath torment, but a fear which increases watchfulness, and walks hand in hand with perfect confidence in saving grace.—*J. F.*

Verses 121, 122.—*The double appeal.* I. Of conscious integrity : " I have done judgment," etc. II. Of conscious deficiency : " Be surety for thy servant for good."—*C. A. D.*

Verse 122.—I. Suretyship entreated. II. Good expected. III. Obligation acknowledged : " thy servant."

Verse 122 (*first clause*).—After explaining the Psalmist's meaning as shown in the preceding verse, this sentence may be used for a sermon upon the Suretyship of Christ, by a reference to Heb. vii. 22. I. A Surety for good wanted—the deeply felt, though, perhaps, undefined want of a sin-burdened soul. 1. The mere statement of a gratuitous pardon on the part of God is not thoroughly believable to such a soul, nor, if it could be believed in, would it give peace to the conscience. For, on the one hand, the pardon could not be perceived as just, nor as consistent with God's necessary hatred of sin, yet the conscience demands this perception ; on the other hand, mere pardon does not show how the obligation to a perfect fulfilment of God's law, as righteousness, can be met, yet the conscience demands to see this before it can be satisfied to realize peace. Luther's experience. 2. Now the Scriptures tell us that God " justifies the ungodly," and that his " righteousness " is declared in his justifying sinners : Rom. iii. 25. He can forgive sins with justice. He can treat sinners as righteous persons, and yet be righteous in doing so. How ? By a Surety. Therefore, a Surety is the real want. II. A Surety existent. Jesus is the Surety. 1. He undertook to bear our obligation to the law's penalty, and fulfilled it in death. Thus pardon, though mercy to us, is an act of justice to Christ. 2. He undertook our obligation to a perfect obedience, and satisfied for that in his fulfilment of the law ; thus for God to treat us as righteous is only just to Christ. 3. God has shown his satisfaction with the office of Christ, and with his work, by the resurrection and glorification of Christ. Hence a well-accredited and efficient Surety exists. III. A Surety nigh at hand. 1. In the gospel, Christ as Surety comes to the sinner as truly as though he himself left his throne and came in his own person. 2. Thus, he is so close that a sinner has but to receive the gospel into his heart and he receives Christ. 3. Christ received as a Surety is the Surety for whosoever receives him.—*J. F.*

Verse 123.—Holy expectation—long maintained, in danger of failing ; this fact pleaded ; reasons for never renouncing it.

Verses 124, 125.—*The servant of God.* I. Making profession : " I am thy servant." II. Making confession—of guilt, dulness, ignorance. III. Making petition—for mercy, understanding, and teaching.—*C. A. D.*

Verse 124.—Heavenly instruction a great mercy.

Verse 124.—I. His confidence in divine mercy. II. His submission to divine authority. III. His prayer for divine teaching.—*G. R.*

Verse 124.—A Perfect Prayer, I. As to the matter of it. 1. Here is nothing superfluous ; no petition for wealth, nor for honours, nor for anything the worldling covets. 2. Here is nothing wanting ; " Deal with thy servant according to thy mercy " comprehends everything the guilty soul needs ; " Teach me thy statutes " comprehends all a saint needs to be anxious for. II. As to the manner of it. 1. It is direct and definite. 2. It is simple and fervent. 3. It is reverent yet bold. III. As to the spirit of it. 1. " Deal with thy *servant* " *;* a sense of obligation ; a feeling of devotedness ; a spirit of consecration to holy work. 2. " Deal . . . . according to thy mercy " ; a sense of unworthiness ; becoming humility ; submissiveness to the divine will as to what form the mercy shall take ; great faith in the mercy, its freeness and sufficiency. 3. " Teach me thy statutes." Longing for holiness, sense of ignorance, of weakness, of dependence upon special divine spiritual influence.—*J. F.*

Verse 125.—I. An office accepted. II. Fitness requested. III. Discernment desired.

Verse 125.—I. A cheerful acknowledgment : " I am thy servant." II. A desire implied—to serve more perfectly. III. A need recognized—Divine instruction in holy service. IV. A plea urged : " I am thy servant," therefore " Teach me," etc.—*W. H. J. P.*

Verses 126—128.—I. A terrible fact : " They have made void thy law " : ver. 126. II. Two blessed inferences : " Therefore," " Therefore," etc : verses 127, 128.

Verses 126.—They make void the law, by denying inspiration, by exalting tradition, by antinomianism, by scepticism, by indifference, etc.

Verse 126.—1. There are times when sin is specially active and dominant. 2. Such times reveal the dependence of the church upon God. 3. Such times awaken the desires of the church for the intervention of God. 4. Such times are the times when God does arise to plead his own cause.—*W. H. J. P.*

Verse 126.—I. The work anticipated—the vindication of the divine law. II. The work delayed. III. The work executed : " It is time," etc.—*G. R.*

Verse 127.—The world's assault upon the truth a reason for our loving it.

Verse 127.—I. The object of love : " Thy commandments." II. The degree of love : " above gold," etc. III. The reason of this love : " therefore," etc., because its object must ultimately prevail.—*G. R.*

Verse 127.—God's will *versus* the golden idol. I. God's commandments are better than gold. II. The love of them is proportionably nobler. III. The unmeasurable superiority of character they produce.—*W. B. H.*

Verse 128 (*first clause*).—This view should be taken of all divine precepts in their bearing, I. Christ-ward. II. Self-ward. III. World-ward. IV. Church-ward. V. Heaven-ward.—*W. J.*

Verse 128.—The Bible right. I. Its science is correct. II. Its history is true. III. Its promises are genuine. IV. Its morality is perfect. V. Its doctrines are divine.—*W. W.*

Verse 128.—Learn four lessons,—I. It is a good thing when wicked men do not praise the truth they cannot love. II. It is a suspicious circumstance when they are found speaking well of any part of it ; it is a Judas' kiss in order to betray its interests. III. It must be right to accept and love what the wicked oppose. IV. It is always safe to be on the opposite side to them.—*J. F.*

Verses 129—136.—In this division the Psalmist—I. Praises God's word. II. Shows his affection to it. III. Prays for grace to keep it. IV. Mourns for those who do not.—*Adam Clarke.*

Verse 129.—The wonderful character of the word a reason for obedience. So wonderfully pure, just, balanced, elevating. So much for our own benefit, for the good of society, and for the divine glory.

Verse 129.—I. What is wonderful in God's word should be believed. II. What is believed should be obeyed.—*G. R.*

Verse 129.—"*Thy testimonies are wonderful.*" 1. The *facts* which they record are wonderful—so wonderful, that if the book recording them were now published for the first time, there would be no bounds to the avidity and curiosity with which it would be sought and perused. 2. The *morality* which they inculcate is wonderful. 3. If you turn from the morality to the *doctrines* of the Bible, your admiration will rather increase than diminish at the contents of the singular book. 4. These testimonies are wonderful for *the style* in which they are written. 5. They are wonderful for *their preservation* in the world. 6. They are wonderful for the *effects* which they have produced.—*Hugh Hughes*, 1838.

Verse 129.—*"Thy testimonies are wonderful."* The *ceremonial law* is wonderful, because the mystery of our redemption by the blood of Christ is pointed out in it. 2. The *prophecies* are wonderful, as predicting things, humanly speaking, so uncertain, and at such great distance of time, with so much accuracy. 3. The *decalogue* is wonderful, as containing in a very few words all the principles of justice and charity. 4. Were we to go to the *New Testament*, here wonders rise on wonders ! All is astonishing ; but the Psalmist could not have had this in view.—*Adam Clarke*.

Verse 129 (first clause).—I. Let us look at five of the wonders of the Bible. 1. Its authority. It prefaces every statement with a " Thus saith the Lord." 2. Its light. 3. Its power—it has a convincing, awakening, drawing, life-giving power. 4. Its depth. 5. Its universal adaptation. II. Indicate three practical uses. 1. Study the Bible daily. 2. Pray for the Spirit to grave it on your heart with a pen of iron. 3. Practise it daily.—*D. Macgregor*.

Verse 129.—To whom and in what respects are God's testimonies wonderful ? I. To whom ? To those, and those only, who through grace do know, believe, and experience the truth and power of them for themselves. II. In what respects wonderful, *i.e.*, astonishingly pleasing, delightful, and profitable (see ver. 174). 1. In respect of the Author and origin of them, whose they are and from whence they come. 2. In respect of the subject matter of them, which they contain and reveal. 3. In respect of the manner of language in which they are revealed and declared. 4. In respect of the multitude and variety of them suited to every case. 5. In respect of the usefulness of them, and the great benefit and advantage he received from them. 6. In the respect of the pleasure and delight he finds in them (see ver. 111). 7. In respect of the final design, intent, and end of them : viz., eternal life, salvation, and glory.—*Samuel Medley*, 1738—1799.

Verse 130.—I. The essential light of the word. II. The dawn of it in the soul. III. The great benefit of its advancing day.

Verse 130.—I. The source of divine light to man : " Thy words." II. Its force. It forces an entrance into the heart. III. Its direction : " unto the simple." IV. Its effect : " it giveth understanding."—*G. R.*

Verse 130.—*A Bible Society Sermon.* I. Evidence from history and from personal experience that God's word has imparted the light of civilization, liberty, holiness. II. Argument drawn from hence for the further spread of the word of God.—*C. A. D.*

Verse 130.—The Self-evidencing Virtue of God's Word. I. Prove it. " The entrance of thy word giveth light." If this be true, God's word is light ; for only light can give light. But light is self-evidencing ; it needs nothing to show its presence and its value but itself ; so the word of God, to show its own truth and divinity to the believer. I. His conscience proves it ; in its conviction of sin ; in its peace through the atoning blood. 2. His heart proves it ; in its outgoings of love to the God, the Christ, and the righteousness revealed. 3. His experience in affliction and temptation proves it ; in the solace and in the strength given by the word. II. Answer an objection. " If God's word were self-evidencing as light is, then everyone would acknowledge it to be truth." Answer, No ; for the law holds good in universal experience, that the " entrance " only of light gives light. Light cannot enter a blind man. 1. The Scriptures teach that men by nature are blind. 2. If all men did perceive, by merely reading and hearing the word, that it was light and truth, paradoxical as it may seem, the word would not be truth. 3. Hence the want of universal acknowledgment is not an objection, but a confirmation. III. Show its importance. 1. It makes the believer independent of church authority for his faith. 2. He need not trouble to examine books of evidence ; his faith is valid enough without them. 3. He who receives the word into his soul shall be satisfied of its truth and value.—*J. F.*

Verse 131.—Panting for holiness. A rare hunger ; the evidence of much grace, and the pledge of glory.

Verse 132.—I. Look. II. Love. III. Use and wont.

Verse 132.—Fellowship with the righteous. I. There are some who love God's name. II. His mercy is the source of all the goodness they experience. III. The Lord has been always accustomed to deal mercifully with them. IV. His mercy towards them should encourage us to implore mercy for ourselves. V. We should be anxious to secure the mercy that is peculiar to them. VI. We should be content if God deals with us as he has always dealt with his people.—*W. Jay.*

Verse 132.—*Divine use and wont.* I. God is accustomed to look upon and be merciful toward his people. II. We are stirred up to specially desire such merciful dealings in time of affliction. III. Love to God qualifies us for these loving looks and merciful dealings.—*C. A. D.*

Verse 132.—Notice,—I. The mark of true believers: "Those that love thy name." II. God's custom of dealing with them: "Be merciful as thou usest to do." III. Their individual and earnest solicitude: "Look thou upon me." —*J. F.*

Verse 133.—I. A holy life is no work of chance, it is a masterpiece of *order*— the order of conformity to the prescribed rule; there is arithmetical and geometrical order: the proportional order; the order of relation; an order of period: holiness, as to the order, is seasonable, suitable. II. The rule of this order: "in thy word." III. The director chosen. See "Spurgeon's Sermons," No. 878: "A Well-ordered Life."

Verse 133.—I. Order in outward life desired. II. Order according to the divine idea. III. Order in the government within.

Verse 133.—I. Help needed. 1. To avoid sin. 2. To be holy. II. Help sought. 1. From below: "thy word." 2. From above: "order," etc., and "let not," etc.—*G. R.*

Verse 133.—Sin's sway in the soul. I. Fervently deprecated. 1. Realization of the horrors of its rule. 2. Recognition of the better power. 3. Thorough exclusion sought. II. Wisely combated. 1. Practicalness as well as prayerfulness. 2. Regard had to little "steps." 3. Steps to be governed by divine rule. 4. System not trusted apart from God.—*W. B. H.*

Verse 133.—Notice,—I. The right path for human feet: "In thy word." II. The needed help to control the steps: "Order my steps." III. The perverting power of a dominant sin: "Let not any," etc.—*J. F.*

Verse 134.—What sins may be produced by oppression. What obedience ought to come from those who are set free.

Verse 134.—I. The course to be pursued: "thy precepts." II. The opposition to that course: "the oppression of men." 1. Human opinions. 2. Human examples. 3. Human sympathies. 4. Interests. 5. Persecutions. III. The resistance to that opposition: "Deliver me, so will I," etc.—*G. R.*

Verse 134.—*Hindrances removed.* I. The impeding influence of persecution. II. The prayer of the persecuted one. III. The conduct of the delivered one (Luke i. 74, 75).—*C. A. D.*

Verse 134.—I. How some men oppress their fellows. By the laws they make— as statesmen. By the books they write—as authors. By the tyranny they exercise —as masters. By the lives they live—as professors. By the sermons they deliver —as *ministers!* II. How the prayer of the oppressed may be answered. By the gift of wise and good statesmen. By increase of sound literature. By the conversion or removal of hard masters. By a baptism of the Spirit on the church.—*W. W.*

Verse 135.—I. A choice position: "thy servant." II. A choice delight: "thy face to shine." III. A choice privilege: "teach me thy statutes."

Verse 135.—I. God *in* the word: "Thy word." II. God *for* the word: "Teach me," etc. III. God *with* the word: "Make thy face," etc.—*G. R.*

Verse 135 —*Sunshine.* I. The light in which we can best learn our lessons —God's favour shown in pardon, justification, adoption, assurance, etc. II. The lessons we should learn in the light—grace is productive of holiness.—*C. A. D.*

Verse 135.—I. A rich historic promise (Num. vi. 25). Its sublime origin and associations. II. The *new* prayer born of it. 1. Looks up for the face Divine; the same in its majestic sweetness that has watched generations decay since the word was first spoken. 2. Asks to know its shinings. Light of fatherhood, etc. III. The *old* prayer repeated: "Teach me thy statutes." Last time in the Psalm. 1. Our need of teaching—oft-repeated prayer. 2. The intimate connection between obedience and the shinings of God's face.—*W. B. H.*

Verse 136.—Abundant sorrow for abounding sin. Other men's sins the saint's own sorrows. He thinks of the good God provoked, of the sinners themselves debased, of their death, and their perdition.

Verse 136.—I. Occasion of his grief: " they keep not thy law." II. Extent of his grief: " rivers," etc. See examples in Jeremiah, Ezra, Paul, Christ himself. III. Effect of his grief. To warn, teach, invite, and exhort them—as in his Psalms. —*G. R.*

Verse 136.—*Sacred tears.* I. The world sinning. II. The church weeping. III. It is time the world began to weep for itself.—*C. A. D.*

Verse 136.—I weep, because, 1. Of the dishonour done to the Law-giver. 2. Of the injury done to the law-breaker. 3. Of the wrong done to the law-abiding.

" That kingly prophet, that wept so plentifully for his own offences (Psalm vi. 6), had yet floods of tears left to bewail his people's " (Psalm cxix. 136).—*Thomas Adams.* " Bendetti, a Franciscan monk, author of the *Stabat Mater*, one day was found weeping, and when asked the reason of his tears, he exclaimed, ' I weep because Love goes about unloved.' "—*W. H. J. P.*

Verses 137, 138.—*Solemn contemplation.* I. The contemplation of the deep and awful display of the divine character is good for the soul. II. It will lead to a conviction of the righteousness of God's character and administration. III. It will result in loyal submission.—*C. A. D.*

Verse 137.—A consideration of divine righteousness. Convinces us of sin, reconciles us to trying providences, excites a desire to imitate, arouses to reverent adoration.

Verse 137.—God is righteous. I. In his commands. II. In his threatenings. III. In his chastisements. IV. In his judgments. V. In his promises.—*G. R.*

Verse 138.—"*Very faithful.*" Based on a faithful covenant ; confirmed by faithful promises ; carried out by a faithful Redeemer ; enjoyed hitherto ; relied on for the future. " Though we believe not, yet he abideth faithful."

Verse 139.—"*Zeal.*" I. Consuming self. II. Inflamed by that which would naturally quench it. III. Fed upon God's words.

Verse 139.—"*Zeal.*" I. Flourishing in an uncompromising atmosphere. II. Attaining an astonishing growth. III. Accomplishing a blessed work—the consumption of self.—*C. A. D.*

Verse 139.—I. The object of his zeal: " Thy words." II. The occasion of his zeal : " Mine enemies," etc. III. The fervour of his zeal : " My zeal hath consumed me."—*G. R.*

Verse 140.—I. An awakened sinner adoring the holy law. II. A saint loving it because the pure love the pure. III. A saint among sinners loving the law all the more for its contrast.

Verse 140.—I. The crystal stream. 1. Flows from under the throne. 2. Mirrors heaven. 3. Undefiled through the ages. 4. Nourishes holiness as it flows. II. The enraptured pilgrim. 1. Keeping by its brink. 2. Delighted with its lucid depths. 3. Pleased with its mirrored revelations—self, heaven, God. 4. Cleansed and refreshed by its waters.—*W. B. H.*

Verse 140.—I. *The purity of God's word.* 1. It proceeds from a perfectly pure source : "*Thy* word." 2. It reveals a purity otherwise unknown. 3. It treats impure subjects with absolute purity. 4. It inculcates the most perfect purity. 5. It produces such purity in those who are subject to its power. II. *The love which its purity inspires in gracious souls.* 1. They love it because, while it reveals their natural impurity, it shows them how to escape from it. 2. They love it because it conforms them to its own purity. 3. They love it because to a pure heart the purity of the word is one of its chief commendations. III. *The evidences of this love to the pure word.* 1. Desire to possess it in its purity. 2. Subjection to its spirit and teachings. 3. Zeal for its honour and diffusion.—*W. H. J. P.*

Verses 141—144.—*A mournful song and a joyful refrain.* Stanza I. " I am small and despised." Refrain. The everlasting righteousness of God. Stanza II. " Trouble and anguish have seized me." Refrain. The everlasting righteousness of God.—*C. A. D.*

Verse 141.—Here is—1. David pious, and yet poor. He was a man after God's own heart, and yet " small and despised " in his own account and in account of many others. 2. David poor and yet pious ; " small and despised " for his strict and serious godliness ; yet his conscience can witness for him, that he " did not forget God's precepts."—*M. Henry.*

Verse 141.—I. The source of man's littleness is in himself. II. The source of his greatness is in the Divine word. Hence the greatest philosopher is a small man compared with the most uneducated whose delight is in the law of God, and who meditates, etc.—*G. R.*

Verse 141.—I. A little scholar. II. A quick learner. III. A firm remembrancer.

Verse 141.—"*Unknown, yet well known.*" I. The estimate formed of the believer by the world. II. The estimate formed of the believer by himself. III. The profession made by the believer to God. IV. On a review, a revised estimate of the believer : 1 Cor. i. 27 ; James ii. 5.—*C. A. D.*

Verse 142.—Righteousness, immutability, and truth combined in the revelation of God.

Verse 143.—Mingled emotions.

Verse 143.—I. The dark cloud. Trouble, etc. II. His silver lining. Yet, etc.

Verse 143.—I. The saint cast into prison. 1. The jailers : "Trouble and anguish." 2. Their proceeding : "take hold" and make him fast. II. Songs in the night. 1. Blessed theme : "thy commandments." 2. Ecstatic melodies : "delights." III. Let the prisoners hear them. 1. Pain-held, sin-held, despair held. 2. It is matter and melody to open prisons.—*W. B. H.*

Verse 143.—Consider,—I. The excellency of the word, in that it gives delight when trouble and anguish oppress. II. The great kindness of God in so framing his word that it can give delight at such a time, and under such circumstances. III. The disposition of the believer to resort to the word for delight, when others give themselves over to vain grief and despondency. IV. The blessed position of the believer, in that he need never be without joy.—*J. F.*

Verse 144.—Everlasting righteousness revealed in the word, and producing everlasting life in believers.

Verse 144.—I. Eternal truths. II. Eternal life dependent upon them. III. A cry from amid these everlasting hills.—*W. B. H.*

Verse 144 (*last clause*).—I. Consider the prayer in its simplicity. 1. It is suitable for the awakened sinner. 2. For the Christian struggling against temptation. 3. For the suffering believer. 4. For the worker. 5. For aspiring minds in the church of God. 6. For expiring saints. II. The prayer more fully opened up. 1. Here is want confessed. 2. The prayer is evidently put upon the footing of free grace : "Give." III. Lay bare the argument in the prayer. 1. The word of God, when practically and experimentally understood, is a pledge of life. 2. The word of God is the incorruptible "seed" which liveth and abideth for ever. 3. It is the food of life. 4. It is the very flower and crown and glory of true life. 5. It is righteous. 6. It is everlasting. See "Spurgeon's Sermons," No. 1572 : "Alive."

Verses 145—148.—*The cry.* I. Whence it came : from my heart. II. Whither it went : to the Lord. III. When it was heard : at dawn and dark. IV. What it sought : hearing, salvation. V. What it promised : obedience. VI. How it was sustained : by hope in God's word.—*C. A. D.*

Verses 145, 146.—The soul's cry. I. The depth from which it rose. II. The height it reached.

Verses 145, 146.—*Childlike prayer.* I. In its ring : "I cried." II. In its directness : "to thee." III. In its outburst : "whole heart." IV. In its outcries : "hear me"; "save me." V. In its promise of better behaviour : "I *will* keep thy statutes."—*W. B. H.*

Verse 145.—I. The model of prayer : "I cried with my whole heart." II. The object of prayer : "Hear me, O Lord." III. The accompaniment of prayer : "I will keep thy statutes."

Verse 146.—I. Prayer remembered. II. Prayer continued : "Save me." III. Prayer yielding fruit : "I shall keep," etc.

Verse 146.—*Salvation.* I. A likely path to it—prayer : cry on. II. The proper place for it : "unto thee"; not man, not the heart. III. A sound view of it : "keep thy testimonies." Not to escape hell, or gain heaven, but to please and love God.—*W. B. H.*

Verses 147, 148.—I. The heavenly companions : prayer and meditation. Inseparable. Mutually helpful. II. Their favourite seasons : times of stillness ; night ; the hour before day. III. Their volume and night-lamp : "Thy word ;" "Hope." Or—I. A grand plea : "Thy lovingkindness." Who can match it ?

Who can measure it ? Who can mar it ? II. An insignificant pleader : "my voice." What can "my voice" ever say to keep step with "thy lovingkindness"? Asking too much out of the question. III. A clever petition (" according to thy judgment ") ; requesting life ; stolen from God's mouth. God's lovingkindness is matched by God's own promise.—*W. B. H.*

Verse 147.—Observe in this David's diligence. I. That it was a personal, closet, or secret prayer ; " I cried " ; I alone, with thee in secret. II. That it was an early morning prayer : " I prevented the dawning of the morning." III. That it was a vehement and earnest prayer ; for it is expressed by crying.— *T. Manton.*

Verse 147.—*Early rising commended.* I. A fit time for prayer. II. For reading the word. III. For indulging the emotions excited by it : " I hoped in thy word."

Verse 148.—" The Inexhaustibleness of the Bible." A sermon by Harry Melvill, at " The Golden Lecture." 1850.

Verse 148.—*Meditation.* Appropriate time, and fruitful subject.

Verse 148.—Meditation in the word well worth self-denial and care on the part of the Christian. I. Without meditation reading is a waste of time and an indignity offered to the word. II. Meditation with prayer, but not prayer without meditation, will discover the sense of the word, when all other means fail ; and it has this advantage, that the meaning sinks into the mind. III. Meditation extracts sweetness from the promises, and nourishment from the whole truth. IV. Meditation makes a wise teacher and an efficient worker of one who has little natural skill or learning. V. Meditation subjects the soul to the sanctifying power of the word. VI. Meditation is an invitation to the Holy Spirit to bless the soul, for he is closely associated with the truth, and delights to see the truth honoured. —*J. F.*

Verse 149.—Prayer—hearing the result of love ; prayer—answering ruled by wisdom.

Verse 149.—*Quickening.* I. A prayer of unquestionable necessity : " quicken me." II. Twin pleas of irresistible power : " thy lovingkindness : " " thy judgment."—*C. A. D.*

Verse 149.—The two accordings. I. The " according," to which a believer hopes to be heard by God : " Hear my voice according unto thy lovingkindness." 1. The believer is fully aware of his own unworthiness, and the imperfections of his prayers, therefore he would have God to accept him and interpret them after the rule of his own lovingkindness. 2. Nor does he hope in vain ; God's lovingkindness overlooks the imperfections, and supplies the omissions. 3. What a blessed thing it is, that while the Holy Spirit helps our infirmities, the groanings that cannot be uttered are read in their true meaning by divine lovingkindness ! II. The " according" to which he expects to be answered by God: " Quicken me according to thy judgment." " Judgment " here may mean the revealed word. Then—1. He expects to be answered certainly. 2. He expects to be answered wisely. 3. He expects to be answered fully, as all his needs require. 4. He expects that every answer should quicken spiritual life, making him holy.—*J. F.*

Verses 150, 151.—*Against mischief-makers.* I. They press as near as they can to harm us. II. They get far from right to get more liberty to injure us. III. The Lord is nearer than they. IV. God's truth is our shield and sword.

Verses 150, 151.—*Foes near : the Friend nearer.* I. The believer viewing with alarm the *approach* of his foes : " They draw near." II. The believer viewing with comfort the *presence* of his friend : " Thou art near : " Gen. xv. 1 ; 2 Kings vi. 14—17.—*C. A. D.*

Verses 150, 151.—Two beleaguering hosts. I. The host of evil : NEAR— 1. Demons, godless men, spiritual foes of world and heart. 2. Mischief in their van. 3. Law and truth left far behind. 4. Seeking to narrow their lines. 5. Thus are all saints beset. II. The host of God : NEARER—Jehovah, his angels, and battalions of truths holy and immortal : " Thou and all thy commandments. 1. Entrenched in the reason : " are truth." 2. Camped in the heart's pavilion : " near." 3. Forming impregnable lines within those of the foe.—*W. B. H.*

Verse 150.—Consider—I. Whether the description here given does not apply, more or less, to all believers in Christ : " They that follow after mischief." 1. Some men undoubtedly and of set purpose do follow after mischief ; they make themselves the tempters of others, and delight in it. 2. Others, who do not delight in it, yet cannot help the mischievous effect of their example. 3. The very morality of many unbelievers enables them to carry the pernicious influence of their unbelief where the immorally wicked cannot come. 4. Even regular attendants at public worship may by their indecision encourage others in delay. II. The dangerous position of all to whom the description, in any measure, belongs : " They are far from thy law." 1. They are so, in that they are unbelievers ; for " this is his commandment, that we shall believe," etc. 2. They are so, in that they are a cause of evil to others ; for we are commanded to love and do good. 3. To be far from God's law is to be nigh unto God's righteous wrath. 4. For the sake of others, as well as their own, men should believe in Christ, and through faith become sanctified.—*J. F.*

Verse 151 (*last clause*).—The commandments of the Lord are true in principle ; they lead to true living, if carried out ; they truly reward the obedient ; they never lead to falsehood, nor cause to be deluded.

Verse 152.—Knowledge of the word. I. It is well to know it as God's own word. II. As founded in truth. III. As founded for ever. IV. The earlier we know this the better.

Verses 153—159.—The two considers. The subjects, the prayers, the arguments.

Verses 153, 154—Here—I. David prays for succour in distress. " Is any afflicted ? let him pray " ; let him pray as David doth here. 1. He hath an eye to God's pity and prays, "*Consider mine affliction*"; take it unto thy thoughts, and all the circumstances, and sit not by as one unconcerned. God is never unmindful of his people's afflictions, but he will have us to " put him in remembrance " (Isa. xliii. 26), to spread our case before him, and then leave it to his compassionate consideration to do in it as in his wisdom he shall think fit, in his own time and way. 2. He has an eye to God's power, and prays, "*Deliver me*," and again, "*Deliver me.*" Consider my troubles and bring me out of them. God has promised deliverance (Ps. l. 15), and we may pray for it with submission to his will, and with regard to his glory, that we may serve him the better. 3. He has an eye to God's righteousness, and prays, "*Plead my cause*": be thou my patron and advocate, and take me for thy client. David had a just cause, but his adversaries were many and mighty, and he was in danger of being run down by them: he therefore begs of God to clear his integrity, and silence their false accusations. If God do not plead his people's cause, who will ? He is righteous, and they commit themselves to him, and therefore he will do it, and do it effectually : Isa. li. 22 ; Jer. i. 34. 4. He has an eye to God's grace, and prays, "*Quicken me.*" Lord, I am weak, and unable to bear my troubles ; my spirit is apt to droop and sink : Oh, that thou wouldst revive and comfort me, till the deliverance is wrought ! II. He pleads his dependence upon the word of God, and his devotedness to his conduct. "*Quicken*" and "*deliver me according to thy word*"of promise ; " *for I do not forget thy precepts.*" The closer we cleave to the word of God, both as our rule and as our stay, the more assurance we may have of deliverance in due time.—*M. Henry.*

Verse 153.—*The sick man's prayer.* I. The medicine remembered. II. The physician sent for. III. The physician considering the case. IV. The healing wrought.—*C. A. D.*

Verse 153.—I. Lord, do not forget my sorrow. II. I do not forget thy law.

Verses 154, 156, 159.—The threefold quickening. A capital subject, if the contexts are carefully considered.

Verse 154.—Intercession, deliverance, quickening, and all in faithfulness to the word.

Verse 154.—A prayer. I. For promisd defence. II. For promised deliverance. III. For promised revival.—*G. R.*

Verse 154.—*The advocate.* I. The soul hard-pressed by the accuser—in the conscience (1 John iii. 20) ; before the world ; at the throne of grace (Zech. iii.) ; at the bar of judgment. II. The accused soul commiting its case to the Advocate : 1 John ii. 2 ; 2 Tim. i. 12. III. How the case will go. He never lost one yet. —*C. A. D.*

Verse 155.—I. An awful distance. II. A distance never decreased by seeking. III. A distance increased by sinning.

Verse 155.—I. When salvation is far off. II. When it is near. Or—I. When the word is far off salvation is far off. II. When the word is near salvation is near.—*G. R.*

Verse 155.—*How to avoid salvation.* I. Salvation is inseparable from conformity to God's law: Lev. xviii. 5; Luke x. 25—28; Matt. xix. 17. II. Salvation is brought to law-breakers by the Law-giver condescending to become the Law-keeper and the Law-victim. Salvation is avoided by those who refuse to be conformed to the eternal law or will of God. They perish themselves: their own sin punishes them: necessity punishes them.—*C. A. D.*

Verse 155.—A syllogism on salvation. I. Salvation and obedience go together. 1. Have a common centre—God, his *arm* and his *lips*. 2. A mutual relation: we are saved in order to obedience. In obeying we are being saved. Without obedience there is no salvation. 3. An identical aim—our good and God's glory. 4. Obedience and salvation are inseparable for ever. II. The godless are far from obedience. 1. Commands avoided. 2. Submission excluded. III. Therefore they are far from salvation. They *will* not have the one; they *cannot* have the other.—*W. B. H.*

Verse 156.—I. A great need. II. Laid before a great Lord. III. Great favours pleaded. IV. A great mercy sought: "Quicken me."

Verse 156.—*Just, and the Quickener.* I. Spiritual life is the gift of God's mercy. II. Its continuance depends on the exercise of God's power. III. We may therefore plead for quickening on the ground of God's justice.—*C. A. D.*

Verse 156.—The saint, I. Lost in admiration. 1. Of God's tender mercies. 2. He cries out at their greatness. They are numerous. Greatly tender. Great *and* tender; (exquisite combination!). II. Filled with animation. The child of his admiration. 1. The arrow-like prayer: "Quicken me." To be like, to be true to, such a God. 2. The bow in the hand: "according to thy judgments."—*W. B. H.*

Verse 156.—I. The tenderness of God's greatness. II. The greatness of God's tenderness. III. The stimulus to life found in his great and tender presence.

Verse 157.—I. A word of multitude: "many." II. A tendency of dread, viz., a tendency to decline. III. A note of consolation: "yet do I not decline."

Verse 158.—*A grievous sight.* I. Transgressors beyond God's bounds. II. Bounds so kindly set: "thy word." III. Transgressions so wantonly ungrateful, so terribly dangerous, so fatal.

Verse 158.—*Sorrow over sinners.* I. A sight we cannot avoid seeing. II. A sorrow we ought not to avoid feeling. (See Lot: 2 Pet. ii. 7, 8. Moses: Deut. ix. 18, 19. Samuel: 1 Sam. xv. 11; Jeremiah ix. 1. Paul: Phil. iii. 18. Christ: Luke xix. 41.) III. A reason we will not avoid endorsing.

Verse 158.—A righteous man cannot but be grieved at the sins of the wicked. He sees in them,—I. The violation of the divine law which he loves. II. Ungrateful rebellion against the God he worships. III. Contempt for the gospel of salvation and the blood of Christ. IV. The dominion of Satan, the enemy of his God. V. The degradation of souls which might have been sacred temples. VI. Prophetic signs of an awful, everlasting retribution.—*J. F.*

Verse 159.—I. His own love avowed. II. God's love pleaded. III. Renewed life implored.

Verse 159.—I. Attention invited: "Consider how." II. Profession made: "I love thy precepts." III. Petition offered: "Quicken me," etc. IV. Plea suggested: "according to," etc.—*G. R.*

Verse 159.—*My love and thy lovingkindness.* The saint's love. I. Avowed. "Thou knowest all things," etc. II. Submitted. In humble insistance on its sincerity. In sense of its insufficiency. In prayer to God not to overlook it. III. Lost sight of in the sudden glory of God's lovingkindness. Where is my love now? IV. Recovered and humbly brought for quickening. Lord, I'll say no more about it: "Quicken me."—*W. B. H.*

Verse 159.—*Quicken me for love's sake.* I. A prayer for quickened life. II. Awakened by love to the divine rule of life. III. Enforced by the plea of that love. IV. Addressed to the God of love.—*C. A. D.*

Verse 159.—Consider,—I. The holy unsatisfiedness of the believer: "Quicken me" etc. 1. A prayer frequently occurring in the Psalm, and always urged with great earnestness. 2. Its importunity proves the possession of spiritual life; in fact, none but the living ones crave quickening. 3. The most earnest feel the most acutely their indwelling sin, and appreciate most highly thorough sanctification. 4. Thus, this is, perhaps, the only unsatisfiedness perfectly pure in its character. II. The assuring Divine attribute to which he can appeal: "According to thy lovingkindness." 1. An attribute, not only made known in the word, but made manifest to us in our experience of its gentle dealing. 2. An attribute that covers sin, and is touched with a feeling of our infirmities. 3. An attribute that must be affected with the cry for quickening grace. III. The consideration he ought to be able to lay before God : " Consider how I love thy precepts." 1. Because from the word he learnt of the lovingkindness, and through it received life. 2. Without it the prayer cannot be genuine. 3. It is a good reason for expecting more grace ; for " whosoever hath, to him shall be given," etc.—*J. F.*

Verse 160.—I. Early : " true from the beginning." II. Late : " endureth for ever." Or, Truth and immutability the believer's Jachin and Boaz.

Verses 161, 162.—God's word, the object of godly fear and godly joy. 1. It makes the heart quake by its purity and power. 2. It makes the heart rejoice by its grace and truth.—*W. H. J. P.*

Verse 161.—I. Wrong without cause. II. Right with abundant cause.

Verse 161 (*second clause*).—Awe of God's word—its propriety, its hallowed influence, the evil of its absence.

Verse 161.—*Restrained by awe.* I. The causelessness of persecution. II. The temptations to evil occasioned thereby—to revenge : to apostasy. III. The safeguard against falling : awe of God's word. 1 Sam. xxiv. 6 ; Dan. iii. 16—18 ; Acts iv. 19 ; v. 29.—*C. A. D.*

Verse 162.—I. The treasure hid : " great spoil " hidden in the divine word. II. The treasure found : " as one that findeth," etc. 1. By reading. 2. By meditation. 3. By prayer. III. The treasure enjoyed : " I rejoice," etc.—*G. R.*

Verse 162.—David's joy over God's word he compares to the joy of the warrior when he finds great spoil. I. This great joy is sometimes aroused by the fact that there is a word of God. 1. The Scriptures are a revealing of God. 2. The guide of our life. 3. A sure pledge of mercy. 4. The beginning of communion with God. 5. The instrument of usefulness. II. Frequently the joy of the believer in the word arises out of his having had to battle to obtain a grasp of it. 1. We have had to fight over certain doctrines before we could really come at them. 2. The same may be said of the promises. 3. Of the precepts. 4. Of the threatenings. 5. Even about the word which reveals Christ. III. At times the joy of the believer lies in enjoying God's word without any fighting at all : " One that findeth." IV. There is a joy arising out of the very fact that Holy Scripture may be considered to be a spoil. 1. A spoil is the end of uncertainty. 2. It is the weakening of the adversary for any future attacks. 3. It gives a sense of victory. 4. There is, in dividing the spoil, profit, pleasure, and honour. 5. The spoiling of the enemy is a prophecy of rest. See " Spurgeon's Sermons," No. 1641 : " Great Spoil."

Verse 163.—*Opposite poles of the Christian character.* I. Why I hate lying, because it comes from the devil (Pro. viii. 44, Acts v. 3) : it leads to the devil (Rev. xxi. 8, xxii. 15) : it is base, dangerous, degrading (Prov. xix. 5, 1 Tim. iv. 2, 2 Tim. iii. 13) : it is hated by the Lord (Prov. vi. 16, 17, xii. 22). II. Why I love the law. Because it emanates from God ; is the reflection of his character ; is the ideal of my character. III. How I came thus to hate and love. By the grace of God : ver. 29.—*C. A. D.*

Verse 163.—I. Opposite things. II. Opposite feelings.

Verse 164.—Praise rendered. Frequently, statedly, heartily, intelligently.

Verse 164.—*Perpetual praise.* I. True praise is ever warranted. II. True praise is ever welcome. III. True praise is never weary.—*C. A. D.*

Verse 164.—1. Some never praise thee ; but, " seven times a day," etc. ; for I delight to do so. " Thy righteous judgments " are a terror to them, a joy to me. 2. Some feebly and coldly praise thee, while, " seven times," etc. My warm devotion must frequently express itself in praise. 3. Some are content with occasionally praising thee, but, " seven times," etc. They think it enough to begin and end the day with praise, while all the day long I am in the spirit of praise. 4. Some soon cease to praise thee, but, " seven times," etc. Not seven times only, but " unto seventy times seven." Even without ceasing, will I praise thee.—*W. H. J. P.*

Verse 165.—I. Great love to a great law. II. Great peace under great disquietude. III. Great upholding from all stumbling blocks.

Verse 165.—*Perfect peace.* I. The law of God should be regarded with love. II. Love to the law is productive of great peace. Peace with God through the blood of reconciliation : peace with self by good conscience and suppression of evil desires : peace with men by charity. III. The peace which springs from love to the law is a security against stumbling : " nothing shall offend them ; " neither the daily cross (Mark x. 21, 22) ; nor the fiery trial (Mark iv. 7) ; nor the humbling doctrine (John vi. 60, 66, etc.).—*C. A. D.*

Verse 165.—I. The characters described : " they which love thy law." II. The blessing they enjoy : " great peace." III. The evils they escape : " nothing shall offend them."—*G. R.*

Verse 165.—The peace and security of the godly. I. *Their peace.* It arises from—1. Freedom from an accusing conscience. 2. Conformity to the requirements of the law. 3. Enjoyment of the privileges revealed in the law. 4. Assurance of divine approval and benediction. II. *Their security.* 1. They are prepared for every duty. 2. They are proof against every temptation. 3. They are pledged to final perseverance. 4. They have the promise of divine protection.—*W. H. J. P.*

Verse 165.—I. An honourable title : " They which love thy law." II. A good possession : " Great peace have they." III. A blessed immunity : " Nothing shall offend them."—*J. F.*

Verse 166.—I. A hope which is not ashamed. II. A life which is not ashamed. III. A God of whom he is not ashamed.

Verse 166.—*A good hope through grace.* I. Salvation is God's gift : " thy salvation." II. Is apprehended by hope : " I have hoped." III. Is accompanied by obedience : " and done thy commandments." Heb. vi. 9.—*C. A. D.*

Verse 167.—Past and present.

Verse 167.—I. The more we keep God's testimonies the more we shall love them. II. The more we love them the more we shall keep them.—*G. R.*

Verse 167.—I. The jewels : " Thy testimonies." 1. Rare ; none like them. 2. Rich ; surpassing valuation. 3. Beautifying those who wear them. 4. Glittering with an internal and essential splendour, in the darkness of this world. 5. Realising in truth the old superstitions regarding precious stones having medicinal and magic virtues. II. The cabinet : " My soul." 1. Exactly made to receive the jewels. 2. A wonderful piece of divine workmanship ; but all ruined and marred unless applied to the use designed. 3. The only receptacle out of which the genuine beauty of God's testimonies can so shine as to excite the admiration of beholders. III. The lock that keeps all safe : " I love them exceedingly." 1. Love is the strongest holdfast in the universe. 2. It is needed, for ten thousand thieves prowl around to steal from us the treasure. 3. A love " exceedingly " is a heavenly patent ; no ingenuity can pick it ; it is fire-proof and burglar-proof against hell itself.—*J. F.*

Verse 168.—I. The claim of God's word upon our utmost obedience. " I have kept thy precepts and thy testimonies." He does not mean that he had kept them perfectly ; for that were to contradict other expressions in the Psalm. He means that he kept them sincerely and strove to keep them perfectly, as one who realized their claim upon him. 1. The whole word is divine : an equal authority pervades every precept ; no distinction should be made of more or less obligation. 2. The whole word is pure and right ; expediency, or making the measure and manner of obedience suitable to our own purpose, is a false principle ; to be carefully distinguished from righteous expediency, which is the foregoing of a personal right in consideration of another's benefit. 3. The moral code of the word is a unity ; obedience is like a connected chain, a wilful flaw in one link renders all useless. II. The consciousness which greatly helps obedience : " For all my ways are before thee." 1. " Are before thee," as plainly seen by thee. 2. " Are before thee," constantly observed. 3. " Are before thee ; " deliberately placed before thee by me, that they may be corrected and directed.—*J. F.*

Verse 168.—"*All my ways are before thee.*" I. The saint's delight. II. The sinner's distress.—*W. W.*

Verse 168 (second clause).—1. *Necessarily so :* for thou art the omniscient God : Psalm cxxxix. 3. 2. *Voluntarily so :* for I choose to walk in thy sight. See Psalm cxvi. 9. 3. *Consciously and blessedly so :* for the light of thy countenance inspires and gladdens me. See Psalm lxxxix. 15.—*W. H. J. P.*

Verse 168 (second clause).—Living in the sight of God. Actually the case with all ; designedly the case of the godly ; happily the case of the favoured ; pre-eminently the case of those who abide in fellowship.

Verse 168.—I. The practical and doctrinal teachings of God before us. II. All our ways before him. III. The sort of conduct which these two causes will produce.

Verses 169, 170.—I. The singular dignity of prayer. We are on earth, but our prayers pass the seraphim and " come near before God." II. The powerful right of prayer—to urge with God his own word : "according to thy word." III. The triumphant possibilities of prayer. Blessing us in mind and estate. For time and eternity. "Give me understanding." "Deliver me." IV. The amazing license accorded to prayer. To double and reiterate its requests (as here).—*W. B. H.*

Verse 169.—I. Admission to the royal court. II. Instruction from the royal throne. III. Reliance on the royal word.

Verses 170—174.—The pleader : ver. 170. The singer : ver. 171. The preacher : ver. 172. The worker : ver. 173. The waiter : ver. 174.

Verse 170.—I. Access sought. II. Answer entreated. III. Argument employed.

Verse 171.—Taught ; taught to praise ; praising ; praising for being taught.

Verse 171.—Learning to sing by learning to obey.

Verse 171.—*The Happy Scholar.* I. He rejoices in the lesson he has learnt. II. In the Teacher who has taught him. III. Looks forward to the end of his lesson as the time for the full singing of his song.—*C. A. D.*

Verse 171.—Lessons in Praise.—I. It is saints' work. II. It is sacred work, not to be hurriedly rushed into. III. It needs Spirit-instructed singers.—*W. B. H.*

Verse 172.—I. The orator : "My tongue shall speak." II. His chosen theme : "of thy word." III. His inward impulse : "for all thy commandments are righteousness."

Verse 172.—*Savoury Speech.* I. A resolution all believers should make. II. The qualification all believers should seek (Psalm xlv. 1 ; Mat. xii. 34, 35). III. The edification believers would thus secure.—*C. A. D.*

Verse 173.—I. "To will is present with me." II. "How to perform that which I would, I find not." III. "Help, Lord."

Verse 173.—I. Help needed to keep the divine precepts. II. Help sought : "Let thy hand," etc. We should choose nothing and do nothing in which we cannot ask help from God.—*G. R.*

Verse 173.—I. God's Hand. 1. Its warm hold (John x. 29). 2. Its wealth of contents (Ps. civ. 28). 3. Its heavy blow (Ps. xxxix. 10). 4. Its weight (1 Sam. v. 11). 5. Its saving reach (Isa. lix. 1). 6. Its sweet shadow (Isa. xlix. 2), etc. II. The saint plucks him by the sleeve : "Let thy hand help me." 1. His humble representation. 2. His down-drawing of the hand of God.—*W. B. H.*

Verse 173.—"*Let thy hand help me.*" I. Thy reconciling hand : "stretched out." II. Thy comforting hand ; like that which touched Daniel and John. III. Thy supplying hand. "Thou openest thy hand," etc. IV. Thy protecting hand : "all his saints are in thy hand" : Deut. xxxiii. 3. "Great Shepherd of the sheep." V. Thy supporting hand : "I will uphold thee." VI. Thy governing hand : "all my times are in thy hand." VII. Thy chastening hand : "thy hand was heavy upon me." VIII. Thy prospering hand : "the hand of the Lord was with," etc.—*W. J.*

Verse 174.—I. Jacob's longings. II. Moses' choice.

Verse 174.—God's servant drinking at salvation's well, but unsated. I. Longing yielding to delight. 1. At God's salvation. 2. At the rich Scripture inventory. II. Delight bringing forth further longing. 1. For deeper discoveries in the word. 2. Richer experiences in the life. 3. Heaven's consummation.—*W. B. H.*

Verse 174.—I. Sighings for heaven. Holiness, happiness, God. II. Sips by the way. The word of God, the will of God, service of God, the God in all.—*W. B. H.*

Verse 174.—"*I have longed for thy salvation.*" Thy holy salvation. Thy full salvation. Thy free salvation. Thy present salvation. Thy permanent salvation.—*W. J.*

Verse 174.—"*I have longed,*" etc. This longing arises, 1. From a painful consciousness of the need of salvation. 2. From a perception of the glories of God's salvation. 3. From the promises which give assurance of the possibility of obtaining this salvation. 4. From the gracious promptings of the Holy Ghost.—*W. H. J. P.*

Verse 175.—I. The highest life. II. The highest occupation. III. Both dependent on the highest aid.

Verse 175.—*Praise.* I. The noblest employment of life—to praise God. II. The noblest presentation of praise—the holy life. III. The noblest application of divine judgments—to inspire praise.

Verse 176.—I. My confession : "I have gone astray." II. My profession : "thy servant." III. My petition : "seek thy servant." IV. My plea : "for I do not forget," etc.

Verse 176.—I. The confession : " I have gone astray." II. The petition : " Seek thy servant." III. The plea : " For I do not," etc.—*G. R.*

Verse 176.—The last verse *as such*. *The closing minor cadence.* I. The highest flights of human devotion must end in confession of sin : " I have gone astray." II. The sincerest professions of human fidelity must give place to the acknowledgment of helplessness : " seek thy servant." III. The loftiest human declarations of love to God's law must come down to the mournful acknowledgment that we have only not forgotten it.—*C. A. D.*

THE
TREASURY OF DAVID

PREFACE.

AT the end of all these years the last page of this Commentary is printed, and the final preface is requested. The demand sounds strangely in my ears. A preface when the work is done? It can be only nominally a preface, for it is really a farewell. I beg to introduce my closing volume, and then to retire with many apologies for having trespassed so much upon my reader's patience.

A tinge of sadness is on my spirit as I quit "The Treasury of David," never to find on this earth a richer storehouse, though the whole palace of revelation is open to me. Blessed have been the days spent in meditating, mourning, hoping, believing, and exulting with David! Can I hope to spend hours more joyous on this side of the golden gate. Perhaps not; for the seasons have been very choice in which the harp of the great poet of the sanctuary has charmed my ears. Yet the training which has come of these heavenly contemplations may haply go far to create and sustain a peaceful spirit which will never be without its own happy psalmody, and never without aspirations after something higher than it yet has known. The Book of Psalms instructs us in the use of wings as well as words: it sets us both mounting and singing. Ofter have I ceased my commenting upon the text, that I might rise with the Psalm, and gaze upon visions of God. If I may only hope that these volumes will be as useful to other hearts in the reading as to mine in the writing, I shall be well rewarded by the prospect.

The former volumes have enjoyed a singular popularity. It may be questioned if in any age a commentary so large, upon a single book of the Bible, has enjoyed a circulation within measurable distance of that which has been obtained by this work. Among all orders of Christians "The Treasury" has found its way unrestrained by sectarian prejudice—another proof of the unity of the spiritual life, and the oneness of the food upon which it delights to feed. The author may not dare to be proud of the generous acknowledgments which he has received from men of all sections of the church; but, on the other hand, he cannot pass over them in ungrateful silence. Conscious as he is of his many literary sins of omission and of commission in these volumes, he is yet glad to have been permitted to do his best, and to have received abundant encouragement in the doing of it. Of all its good the glory is the Lord's; of all its weakness the unworthy author must bear the blame.

This last portion of the Psalms has not been the easiest part of my gigantic task. On the contrary, with the exception of *The Songs of Degrees*, and one or two other Psalms, these later hymns and hallelujahs have not been largely expounded, nor frequently referred to, by our great divines. Failing the English, a larger use has been made of the Latin authors; and my esteemed friend, W. DURBAN, B.A., has rendered me great service in their translation. It would astonish our readers if they could see what tomes have been read, what folios have been covered with translations, and in the end what tiny morsels have been culled from the vast mass for incorporation with this Treasury. Heaps of earth have been sifted and washed, and have yielded only here and there a little "dust of gold." No labour has been spared; no difficulty has been shirked. May the good Lord accept my service, and enrich his church by it this day, and when I am gathered to my fathers!

My friend and amanuensis, Mr. J. L. KEYS, has continued to search the British Museum and public Libraries for me; and to him and many other kind friends I owe many a quotation which else might have been overlooked. Of the extracts I am editor in chief, and not much more; for brethren such as Mr. HENSON, of Kingsgate Street, have at sundry times, of their own accord, sent me material more or less useful. In the homiletical department my obligations are exceedingly great, and are duly acknowledged under initials. My venerable friend, the Rev. GEORGE ROGERS, leads the way; but several other brethren, hailing from the Pastors' College, follow with almost equal steps. Thanks are hereby tendered to them all, and to the multitude of authors from whom I have gathered flowers and fruits, fragrant and nourishing.

And now the colossal work is done! To God be all glory. More than twenty years have glided away while this pleasant labour has been in the doing; but the wealth of mercy which has been lavished upon me during that time my grateful heart is unable to measure. Surely goodness and mercy have followed me all those years, and made my heart to sing new Psalms for new mercies. There is none like the God of Jeshurun. To him be all glory for ever and ever.

In these busy days, it would be greatly to the spiritual profit of Christian men if they were more familiar with the Book of Psalms, in which they would find a complete armoury for life's battles, and a perfect supply for life's needs. Here we have both delight and usefulness, consolation and instruction. For every condition there is a Psalm, suitable and elevating. The Book supplies the babe in grace with penitent cries, and the perfected saint with triumphant songs. Its breadth of experience stretches from the jaws of hell to the gate of heaven. He who is acquainted with the marches of the Psalm-country knows that the land floweth with milk and honey, and he delights to travel therein. To such I have aspired to be a helpful companion.

Reader, I beseech David's God to bless thee; and I pray thee, when it is well with thee, breathe a like prayer for

Thine heartily,

C. H. Spurgeon

INDEX

OF AUTHORS QUOTED OR REFERRED TO.

C. H. SPURGEON IN HIS LIBRARY AT WESTWOOD.

Specially drawn for "The Treasury of David" by E. H. Fitchew.

THE

SONGS OF DEGREES,

OR,

THE GRADUAL PSALMS.

PSALM CXX. TO CXXXIV.

THE SONGS OF DEGREES AS A WHOLE.

This little Psalter within the Psalter consists of fifteen brief songs. Why they are grouped together and what is meant by their generic name it would be hard to tell. The conjectures are very many, but they are mere suppositions. Out of them all the conjecture of Dr. Jebb best commends itself to my own mind, though it would be quite consistent with this suggestion to believe that the series of songs arranged by David became the Pilgrim Psalms of after ages, and were chanted by the Lord's people as they went up to the temple. They are " Songs of the Goings Up ; " so some read the word. Those who delight to spiritualize everything find here Ascents of the Soul, or language fitted to describe the rising of the heart from the deepest grief to the highest delight. I have thought it well to indicate the methods by which learned men have tried to explain the term " Songs of Degrees," but the reader must select his own interpretation.—*C. H. S.*

In the thirteenth chapter of the First Book of Chronicles, it is related, that David brought up the Ark from Kirjath-jearim to the house of Obed-edom. The word (עלמה) used in the seventh verse, for " bringing up " the Ark, is of the same etymology with, and cognate to that which is translated *"degrees."* And upon this occasion the great event was celebrated by the accompaniment of sacred music. " And David and all Israel played before God with all their might, and with singing, and with harps, and with psalteries, and with timbrels, and with cymbals, and with trumpets." Again, in the fifteenth chapter of the same book, in the fourteenth verse, the same term is employed for bringing up the Ark to Jerusalem ; and the choral services of the Levites are mentioned in immediate connection. And in the fifth chapter of the Second Book of Chronicles (fifth verse), we are told that Solomon assembled the people at the dedication of the Temple, to bring up the Ark from Sion to the Temple of the Lord.—*John Jebb.*

I abide in the simple and plain sense as much as I may, and judge that these Psalms are called The Psalms of Degrees because the Levites or priests were wont to sing them upon the stairs or some high place ; even as with us he that beginneth the Psalms or preacheth, standeth in a place above the rest, that he may be the better seen and heard. For it seemeth not that these Psalms were sung of the multitude which were in the Temple, or of the rest of the choir, but of certain which were appointed to sing them, or at least to begin them on the stairs to the rest, and so have their name ; like as some other of the Psalms have their name and title from the singer. But how should a man know all their rites and ceremonies, especially after so long a time, whereby they are now clean worn out of the memory of all men ? Seeing therefore among such a multitude of Psalms, when the law was yet in his full force and power, some were wont to be sung with one manner of ceremony, and some with another, according to the time and place, as the use and custom then was, let this suffice us to think that this title pertaineth to no point of doctrine, but only to the ceremony of the singers, what manner of ceremony soever it was.—*Martin Luther, in "A Commentarie upon the Psalmes of Degrees,"* 1577.

There were *fifteen steps* by which the priests ascended into the Temple, on each of which they sang one of these *fifteen* Psalms.—*David Kimchi.*

Whatever view of the *Songs of Degrees* you may take besides, you cannot leave out some association of them with the steps, without ignoring the unanimous belief about them handed down from time immemorial amongst the people who gave them to us ; without, in fact, implying that at some epoch or other this strange association of the steps with the Psalms was gratuitously invented, and, being invented, secured general acceptance in the sacred literature of the Hebrew nation. It is quite impossible to believe such a thing, when we are dealing with a people so jealous of precedent and authority in religion as the Hebrews have always been. I see, in fact, no sufficient reason why we should not follow the leading of the Mischna and feel that Songs of Degrees, Songs of the Steps, is as much as to say Songs in the sacred Orchestra.—*H. T. Armfield, in "The Gradual Psalms,"* 1874.

The great Carmelite expositor, Michael Ayguan, alleges that the fifteen Psalms were divided by the Jews into three portions of five, with prayers intercalated, much as the Gregorian division of matins into three nocturns ; and that each of the three grades of advance in the spiritual life is betokened by each quinary ; the beginners, the progressors, and the perfect ; or, in other terms, those who are severally in the purgative, the illuminative, and the unitive way. And thus it will be noticed that in Psalms cxx.—cxxiv. there is constant reference to trouble and danger ; in cxxv.—cxxix. to confidence in God ; in cxxx.—cxxxiv. to direct communion with him in his house. And Genebrardus, a later commentator, defines the fifteen degrees of going up out of the valley of weeping to the presence of God to be (1) affliction, (2) looking to God, (3) joy in communion, (4) invocation, (5) thanksgiving, (6) confidence, (7) patient waiting for deliverance, (8) God's grace and favour, (9) fear of the Lord, (10) martyrdom, (11) hatred of sins, (12) humility, (13) desire for the coming of Christ, (14) concord and charity, (15) constant blessing of God.—*Neale and Littledale.*

No trace in history, or authentic tradition, can be found of these *steps*, which owe their construction solely to the accommodating fancy of the Rabbins, who, as usual, imagined facts, in order to support their preconceived theories.—*John Jebb.*

It is an additional objection to this Rabbinical conceit, that David, whose name several of these Psalms bear—and others of which have evident reference to his time and circumstances—lived in the time of the tabernacle which had no steps.—*James Anderson's Note to Calvin in loc.*

In the version of Theodotian, executed in the early part of the second century, with the express view of correcting the errors of the Septuagint, as well as in the translations by Aquila and by Symmachus, these Psalms are rightly described as songs for the journeys up, and are thus at once referred to the stated pilgrimages to the Temple. The expressions, " Thou shalt *go up* to appear before the Lord thy God thrice in the year " (Exod. xxxiv. 24), " If this people *go up* to do sacrifice " (1 Kings xii. 27)—a form of expression constantly employed as often as these sacred journeys are mentioned—is precisely that which the Psalms themselves exhibit : " I was glad when it was said unto me, Go up unto the house of the Lord " ; and while we may well adopt this view, for the additional reason that it is in harmony with the whole spirit and sentiment which they breathe throughout, we shall find these Psalms to form at the same time one of the most admirable and instructive manuals of devotion with which the love of our heavenly Father, through the grace of the Holy Spirit, has been pleased to bless us.—*Robert Nisbet, in "The Songs of the Temple Pilgrims,"* 1863.

If the traditionary interpretation of the title, Song of Degrees, be accepted, that they were sung by devout pilgrims on their way to Jerusalem to keep the great feasts of the Lord, we may suppose that companies toiling up this long ascent would relieve the tedium of the way by chanting some of them.

From the customs of Orientals still prevalent, I think it highly probable that such an explanation of the title may be substantially correct. Nothing is more common than to hear individuals and parties of natives, travelling together through the open country and along mountain-paths, especially during the night, break out into singing some of their favourite songs. Once, descending from the top of Sunnîn, above Beirût, with a large company of natives, they spontaneously began to sing in concert. The moon was shining brightly in the clear sky, and they kept up their chanting for a long time. I shall not soon forget the impression made by that moonlight concert, as we wound our way down the eastern side of Lebanon to the Bukâ'a, on the way to Ba'albek. Through the still midnight air of that lofty region the rough edge of their stentorian voices, softened into melody, rang out full and strong, waking the sleeping echoes far and wide down the rocky defiles of the mountain. Something like this may have often rendered vocal this dreary ascent to Jerusalem. It is common in this country to travel in the night during the summer, and we know that the Hebrew pilgrims journeyed in large companies. On his ascent along this road from Jericho to the Holy City, Jesus was attended not only by the twelve apostles, but by others, both men and women ; and it would be strange indeed if sometimes they did not seek relief from this oppressive solitude by singing the beautiful songs of Zion.—-*William M. Thomson, in "The Land and the Book,"* 1881.

When we consider the place in the Psalter which these *"Songs of Degrees,* or *of the goings up* " occupy, we see good reason to accept the statement (of the Syriac version, and of S. Chrysostom, Theodoret, Euthymius, and other Fathers, and also of Symmachus, Aquila, and of Hammond, Ewald, and many moderns), that these Psalms describe the feelings of those Israelites who *went up* with Zerubbabel and Jeshua, and afterwards with Ezra, and still later with Nehemiah, from the land of their captivity and dispersion at Babylon, Susa, and other regions of the East, to the home of their fathers, Jerusalem. Hence, in some of the foregoing Psalms, we have seen a reference to the dedication of the Second Temple (Ps. cxviii.), and of the walls of Jerusalem (Ps. cii.), and to the building up of the nation itself on the old foundation of the law of God, given to their fathers at Sinai (Ps. cxix.)—*Christopher Wordsworth.*

Gesenius has the merit of having first discerned the true meaning of the questioned inscription, inasmuch as first in 1812, and frequently since that time, he has taught that the fifteen songs have their name from the step-like progressive rhythm of their thoughts, and that consequently the name, like the triolet (roundelay) in Western poetry, does not refer to the liturgical usage, but to the technical structure. The correctness of this view has been duly appraised more particularly by De Wette, who adduces this rhythm of steps or degrees, too, among the more artificial rhythms. The songs are called Songs of Degrees or Gradual Psalms as being songs that move onward towards a climax, and that by means of πλοκή (ἐπιπλοκή), *i.e.*, a taking up again of the immediately preceding word by way of giving intensity to the expression ; and they are placed together on account of this common characteristic, just like the *Michtammim*, which bear that name from a similar characteristic.—*Franz Delitzsch.*

" Go up, go up, my soul ! " must be the motto of one who would enter into the meaning of these Psalms. They are a Jacob's ladder whose foot is fixed on the earth, but the top reaches up to the " heavenly Jerusalem."

The rhythmical structure of these Psalms (in which one line is built up upon another stair-wise) is a suitable outward accompaniment of the interior character of the Psalms. Short, pointed lines fall in well with the flow of mystico-allegorical thought :—as in " Nearer, my God, to thee," or, " Jerusalem the golden."—*William Kay.*

We may notice the following characteristics of nearly all these Psalms : sweetness and tenderness ; a sad pathetic tone ; brevity ; an absence generally of the ordinary parallelism ; and something of a quick, trochaic rhythm.—"*The Speaker's Commentary.*"

Though it may be they are so called because Of their excellency ; a song of degrees being an *excellent* song, as an excellent man is called a man of high degree (1 Chron. xvii. 17) ; these being excellent ones for the matter of them, their manner of composure, and the brevity of them.—*John Gill.*

This being a matter of small moment, I am not disposed to make it the subject of elaborate investigation ; but the probable conjecture is, that this title was given to these Psalms because they were sung on a higher key than others. The Hebrew word for *degrees* being derived from the word, אלצ, *tsalah, to ascend* or *go up*, I agree with those who are of opinion that it denotes the different musical notes rising in succession.—*John Calvin.*

Hezekiah liveth, these fifteen years, in safety and prosperity, having humbled himself before the Lord for his pride to the ambassadors of Babel. The degrees of the sun's reversing, and the fifteen years of Hezekiah's life prolonging, may call to our minds the fifteen Psalms of Degrees ; viz. from Psalm cxx. and forward. There were Hezekiah's songs that were sung to the stringed instruments in the house of the Lord (Isa. xxxviii. 20) : whether these were picked out by him for that purpose may be left to conjecture.—*John Lightfoot,* 1602—1675.

PSALM CXX.

Suddenly we have left the continent of the vast Hundred and Nineteenth Psalm for the islands and islets of the Songs of Degrees. It may be well to engage in protracted devotion upon a special occasion, but this must cast no slur upon the sacred brevities which sanctify the godly life day by day. He who inspired the longest Psalm was equally the author of the short compositions which follow it.

TITLE.—A SONG OF DEGREES.—*We have already devoted a sufficient space to the consideration of this title in its application to this Psalm and the fourteen compositions which succeed it. These appear to us to be Pilgrim Psalms, but we are not sure that they were always sung in company ; for many of them are in the first person singular. No doubt there were solitary pilgrims as well as troops who went to the house of God in company, and for these lonely ones hymns were prepared.*

SUBJECT.—*A certain author supposes that this hymn was sung by an Israelite upon leaving his house to go up to Jerusalem. He thinks that the good man had suffered from the slander of his neighbours, and was glad to get away from their gossip, and spend his time in the happier engagements of the holy feasts. It may be so, but we hope that pious people were not so foolish as to sing about their bad neighbours when they were leaving them for a few days. If they wished to leave their houses in safety, and to come home to kind surroundings, it would have been the height of folly to provoke those whom they were leaving behind by singing aloud a Psalm of complaint against them. We do not know why this ode is placed first among the Psalms of Degrees, and we had rather hazard no conjecture of our own. We prefer the old summary of the translators—" David prayeth against Doeg "—to any far-fetched supposition : and if this be the scope of the Psalm, we see at once why it suggested itself to David at the station where the ark abode, and from which he had come to remove it. He came to fetch away the ark, and at the place where he found it he thought of Doeg, and poured out his plaint concerning him. The author had been grievously calumniated, and had been tortured into bitterness by the false charges of his persecutors, and here is his appeal to the great Arbiter of right and wrong, before whose judgment-seat no man shall suffer from slanderous tongues.*

EXPOSITION.

IN my distress I cried unto the LORD, and he heard me.

2 Deliver my soul, O LORD, from lying lips, *and* from a deceitful tongue.

3 What shall be given unto thee ? or what shall be done unto thee, thou false tongue ?

4 Sharp arrows of the mighty, with coals of juniper.

5 Woe is me, that I sojourn in Mesech, *that* I dwell in the tents of Kedar !

6 My soul hath long dwelt with him that hateth peace.

7 I *am for* peace : but when I speak, they *are* for war.

1. "*In my distress.*" Slander occasions distress of the most grievous kind. Those who have felt the edge of a cruel tongue know assuredly that it is sharper than the sword. Calumny rouses our indignation by a sense of injustice, and yet we find ourselves helpless to fight with the evil, or to act in our own defence. We could ward off the strokes of a cutlass, but we have no shield against a liar's tongue. We do not know who was the father of the falsehood, nor where it was born, nor where it has gone, nor how to follow it, nor how to stay its withering influence. We are perplexed, and know not which way to turn. Like the plague of flies in Egypt, it baffles opposition, and few can stand before it. Detraction touches us in the tenderest point, cuts to the quick, and leaves a venom behind which it is difficult to extract. In all ways it is a sore distress to come under the power of " slander, the foulest whelp of sin." Even in such distress we need not hesitate to cry unto the Lord. Silence to man and prayer to God are the best cures for the evil of slander.

"*I cried unto the LORD* " (or Jehovah). The wisest course that he could follow. It is of little use to appeal to our fellows on the matter of slander, for the more we stir in it the more it spreads ; it is of no avail to appeal to the honour of the slanderers, for they have none, and the most piteous demands for justice will only increase their malignity and encourage them to fresh insult.   As well plead with panthers and wolves as with black-hearted traducers.   However, when cries to man would be our weakness, cries to God will be our strength.   To whom should children cry but to their father ?   Does not some good come even out of that vile thing, falsehood, when it drives us to our knees and to our God ?   *"And he heard me."*   Yes, Jehovah hears.   He is the living God, and hence prayer to him is reasonable and profitable. The Psalmist remembered and recorded this instance of prayer-hearing, for it had evidently much affected him ; and now he rehearses it for the glory of God and the good of his brethren.   " The righteous cry and the Lord heareth them."   The ear of our God is not deaf, nor even heavy.   He listens attentively, he catches the first accent of supplication ; he makes each of his children confess,—" he heard *me*." When we are slandered it is a joy that the Lord knows us, and cannot be made to doubt our uprightness : he will not hear the lie against us, but he will hear our prayer against the lie.

If these Psalms were sung at the ascent of the ark to Mount Zion, and then afterwards by the pilgrims to Jerusalem at the annual festivals and at the return from Babylon, we shall find in the life of David a reason for this being made the first of them.   Did not this servant of God meet with Doeg the Edomite when he enquired of the oracle by Abiathar, and did not that wretched creature belie him and betray him to Saul ?   This made a very painful and permanent impression upon David's memory, and therefore in commencing the ark-journey he poured out his lament before the Lord, concerning the great and monstrous wrong of " that dog of a Doeg," as Trapp wittily calls him.   The poet, like the preacher, may find it to his advantage to " begin low," for then he has the more room to rise : the next Psalm is a full octave above the present mournful hymn.   Whenever we are abused it may console us to see that we are not alone in our misery : we are traversing a road upon which David left his footprints.

2.   *"Deliver my soul, O Lord, from lying lips."*   It will need divine power to save a man from these deadly instruments.   Lips are soft ; but when they are *lying* lips they suck away the life of character and are as murderous as razors.   Lips should never be red with the blood of honest men's reputes, nor salved with malicious falsehoods.   David says, " Deliver my soul " : the soul, the life of the man, is endangered by lying lips ; cobras are not more venomous, nor devils themselves more pitiless.   Some seem to lie for lying sake, it is their sport and spirit : their lips deserve to be kissed with a hot iron ; but it is not for the friends of Jesus to render to men according to their deserts.   Oh for a dumb generation rather than a lying one !   The faculty of speech becomes a curse when it is degraded into a mean weapon for smiting men behind their backs.   We need to be delivered from slander by the Lord's restraint upon wicked tongues, or else to be delivered out of it by having our good name cleared from the liar's calumny.   *"And from a deceitful tongue."*   This is rather worse than downright falsehood.   Those who fawn and flatter, and all the while have enmity in their hearts, are horrible beings ; they are the seed of the devil, and he worketh in them after his own deceptive nature.   Better to meet wild beasts and serpents than deceivers : these are a kind of monster whose birth is from beneath, and whose end lies far below.   It should be a warning to liars and deceivers when they see that all good men pray against them, and that even bad men are afraid of them.   Here is to the believer good cause for prayer. " Deliver us from evil," may be used with emphasis concerning this business.   From gossips, talebearers, writers of anonymous letters, forgers of newspaper paragraphs, and all sorts of liemongers, good Lord deliver us !

3.   *"What shall be given unto thee ?"*   What is the expected guerdon of slander ? It ought to be something great to make it worth while to work in so foul an atmosphere and to ruin one's soul.   Could a thousand worlds be bribe enough for such villainous deeds ?   The liar shall have no welcome recompense : he shall meet with his deserts ; but what shall they be ?   What punishment can equal his crime ?   The Psalmist seems lost to suggest a fitting punishment.   It is the worst of offences—this detraction, calumny, and slander.   Judgment sharp and crushing would be measured out to it if men were visited for their transgressions.   But what punishment could be heavy enough ?   What form shall the chastisement take ?   O liar, " what shall be given unto thee ? "

"Or what shall be done unto thee, thou false tongue ?"   How shalt thou be visited ?

The law of retaliation can hardly meet the case, since none can slander the slanderer, he is too black to be blackened ; neither would any of us blacken him if we could. Wretched being ! He fights with weapons which true men cannot touch. Like the cuttlefish, he surrounds himself with an inky blackness into which honest men cannot penetrate. Like the foul skunk, he emits an odour of falsehood which cannot be endured by the true ; and therefore he often escapes, unchastised by those whom he has most injured. His crime, in a certain sense, becomes his shield ; men do not care to encounter so base a foe. But what will God do with lying tongues ? He has uttered his most terrible threats against them, and he will terribly execute them in due time.

4. "*Sharp arrows of the mighty.*" Swift, sure, and sharp shall be the judgment Their words were as arrows, and so shall their punishment be. God will see to it that their punishment shall be comparable to an arrow keen in itself, and driven home with all the force with which a mighty man shoots it from his bow of steel,— "sharp arrows of the mighty." Nor shall one form of judgment suffice to avenge this complicated sin. The slanderer shall feel woes comparable to *coals of juniper*, which are quick in flaming, fierce in blazing, and long in burning. He shall feel sharp arrows and sharper fires. Awful doom ! All liars shall have their portion in the lake which burneth with fire and brimstone. Their worm dieth not, and their fire is not quenched. Juniper-coals long retain their heat, but hell burneth ever, and the deceitful tongue may not deceive itself with the hope of escape from the fire which it has kindled. What a crime is this to which the All-merciful allots a doom so dreadful ! Let us hate it with perfect hatred. It is better to be the victim of slander than to be the author of it. The shafts of calumny will miss the mark, but not so the arrows of God : the coals of malice will cool, but not the fire of justice. Shun slander as you would avoid hell.

5. "*Woe is me, that I sojourn in Mesech, that I dwell in the tents of Kedar !*" Gracious men are vexed with the conversation of the wicked. Our poet felt himself to be as ill-at-ease among lying neighbours as if he had lived among savages and cannibals. The traitors around him were as bad as the unspeakable Turk. He cries "Woe is me ! " Their sin appalled him, their enmity galled him. He had some hope from the fact that he was only a sojourner in Mesech ; but as years rolled on the time dragged heavily, and he feared that he might call himself a dweller in Kedar. The wandering tribes to whom he refers were constantly at war with one another ; it was their habit to travel armed to the teeth ; they were a kind of plundering gipsies, with their hand against every man and every man's hand against them ; and to these he compared the false-hearted ones who had assailed his character. Those who defame the righteous are worse than cannibals ; for savages only eat men after they are dead, but these wretches eat them up alive.

> " Woe's me that I in Mesech am
> A sojourner so long ;
> That I in tabernacles dwell
> To Kedar that belong.
>
> My soul with him that hateth peace
> Hath long a dweller been ;
> I am for peace ; but when I speak,
> For battle they are keen.
>
> My soul distracted mourns and pines
> To reach that peaceful shore,
> Where all the weary are at rest,
> And troublers vex no more."

6. "*My soul hath long dwelt with him that hateth peace.*" Long, long enough, too long had he been an exile among such barbarians. A peace-maker is a blessing, but a peace-hater is a curse. To lodge with such for a night is dangerous, but to dwell with them is horrible. The verse may apply to any one of the Psalmist's detractors : he had seen enough of him and pined to quit such company. Perhaps the sweet singer did not at first detect the nature of the man, for he was a deceiver ; and when he did discover him he found himself unable to shake him off, and so was compelled to abide with him. Thoughts of Doeg, Saul, Ahithophel, and the sons of Zeruiah come to our mind,—these last, not as enemies, but as hot-blooded soldiers who were often too strong for David. What a change for the man of God from the quietude

of the sheepfold to the turmoil of court and the tumult of combat ! How he must have longed to lay aside his sceptre, and to resume his crook. He felt the time of his dwelling with quarrelsome spirits to be long, too long ; and he only endured it because, as the Prayer-book version has it, he was *constrained* so to abide.

7. "*I am for peace.*" Properly, " I am peace " ; desirous of peace, peacefu̇, forbearing,—in fact, peace itself. "*But when I speak, they are for war.*" My kindest words appear to provoke them, and they are at daggers drawn at once. Nothing pleases them ; if I am silent they count me morose, and if I open my mouth they cavil and controvert. Let those who dwell with such pugilistic company console themselves with the remembrance that both David and David's Lord endured the same trial. It is the lot of the saints to find foes even in their own households. Others besides David dwelt in the place of dragons. Others besides Daniel have been cast into a den of lions. Meanwhile, let those who are in quiet resting-places and peaceful habitations be greatly grateful for such ease. *Deus nobis hæc otia fecit :* God has given us this tranquillity. Be it ours never to inflict upon others that from which we have been screened ourselves.

EXPLANATORY NOTES AND QUAINT SAYINGS.

Title.—"*A Song of Degrees.*" A most excellent song, Tremellius rendereth it ; and so indeed this and the fourteen following are, both for the matter, and for the form or manner of expression, which is wondrous short and sweet, as the very epigrams of the Holy Ghost himself, wherein each verse may well stand for an oracle. And in this sense, *adam hammahalah,* or, a man of degrees, is put for an eminent or excellent man : 1 Chron. xvii. 17. Others understand it otherwise ; wherein they have good leave to abound in their own sense ; an error here is not dangerous.—*John Trapp.*

Whole Psalm.—In the interpretation of these Psalms, which sees in them the " degrees " of Christian virtues, this Psalm aptly describes the first of such steps— the renunciation of the evil and vanity of the world. It thus divides itself into two parts. 1. The Psalmist, in the person of one beginning the grades of virtue, finds many opponents in the shape of slanderers and ill advisers. 2. He laments the admixture of evil—" Woe is me."—*H. T. Armfield.*

Whole Psalm.—It is a painful but useful lesson which is taught by this first of the Pilgrim Psalms, that all who manifest a resolution to obey the commands and seek the favour of God, may expect to encounter opposition and reproach in such a course. . . . This these worshippers of old found when preparing to seek the Lord in his Temple. They were watched in their preparation by malignant eyes ; they were followed to the house of prayer by the contempt and insinuations of bitter tongues. But their refuge is in him they worship ; and, firmly convinced that he never can forsake his servants, they look up through the cloud of obloquy to his throne, and implore the succour which they know that his children shall ever find there. "*O* Lord, *in this my trouble deliver my soul.*"—*Robert Nisbet.*

Whole Psalm.—The pilgrims were leaving home ; and lying lips commonly attack the absent. They were about to join the pilgrim caravan ; and in the excitements of social intercourse their own lips might easily deviate from truth. The Psalm, moreover, breathes an intense longing for peace ; and in this world of strife and confusion, when is that longing inappropriate ? Is it any marvel that a Hebrew, with a deep spiritual longing for peace, should as he started for the Temple, " Let me get out of all *that*, at least for a time. Let me be quit of this fever and strain, free from the vain turbulence and conflicting noises of the world. Let me rest and recreate myself a while in the sacred asylum and sanctuary of the God of peace. God of peace, grant me thy peace as I worship in thy presence ; and let me find a bettered world when I come back to it, or at least bring a bettered and more patient heart to its duties and strifes."—*Samuel Cox.*

Verse 1.—"*In my distress I cried unto the* Lord," etc. See the wondrous advantage of trouble,—that it makes us call upon God ; and again see the wondrous readiness of mercy, that when we call he heareth us ! Very blessed are they that mourn while they are travelling the long upward journey from the Galilee of the Gentiles of this lower world to the heavenly Jerusalem, the high and holy city of the saints of God.— *J. W. Burgon, in "A Plain Commentary."*

Verse 1.—*"In my distress."* God's help is seasonable; it comes when we need it. Christ is a seasonable good. . . . For the soul to be dark, and for Christ to enlighten it ; for the soul to be dead, and Christ to enliven it ; for the soul to be doubting, and for Christ to resolve it ; and for the soul to be distressed, and for Christ to relieve it ; is not this in season ? For a soul to be hard, and for Christ to soften it ; for a soul to be haughty, and for Christ to humble it ; for a soul to be tempted, and for Christ to succour it ; and for a soul to be wounded, and for Christ to heal it ? Is not this in season ?—*R. Mayhew,* 1679.

Verse 1.—*"Cried." "Heard."* The verbs are in the past tense, but do not refer merely to a past occasion. Past experience and present are here combined. From the past he draws encouragement for the present.—*J. J. Stewart Perowne.*

Verse 1.—*"And he heard me."* The effectual fervent prayer of a righteous man availeth much : James v. 16 ; Zech. xiii. 9. He that prayeth ardently, speedeth assuredly (Ps. xci. 15) ; and the unmiscarrying return of prayer should be carefully observed and thankfully improved : Ps. lxvi. 20.—*John Trapp.*

Verse 2.—*"Deliver my soul, O Lord, from lying lips,"* etc. An unbridled tongue is *vehiculum Diaboli,* the chariot of the Devil, wherein he rides in triumph. Mr. Greenham doth describe the tongue prettily by contraries, or diversities : " It is a little piece of flesh, small in quantity, but mighty in quality ; it is soft, but slippery ; it goeth lightly, but falleth heavily ; it striketh soft, but woundeth sore ; it goeth out quickly, but burneth vehemently ; it pierceth deep, and therefore not healed speedily ; it hath liberty granted easily to go forth, but it will find no means easily to return home ; and being once inflamed with Satan's bellows, it is like the fire of hell." The course of an unruly tongue is to proceed from evil to worse, to begin with foolishness, and go on with bitterness, and to end in mischief and madness. See Eccles. x. 13. The Jew's conference with our Saviour began with arguments : " We be Abraham's seed," said they, etc. ; but proceeded to blasphemies : " Say we not well that thou art a Samaritan, and hast a devil ? " and ended in cruelty : " Then took they up stones to cast at him." John viii. 33, 48, 59. This also is the base disposition of a bad tongue to hate those whom it afflicts : Prov. xxvi. 28.

The mischief of the tongue may further appear by the mercy of being delivered from it, for, 1. So God hath promised it (Job v. 15, 21). " God saveth the poor from the sword, from their mouth, and from the hand of the mighty," and " thou shalt be hid from the scourge of the tongue," or from being betongued, as some render it, that is, from being, as it were, caned or cudgelled with the tongues of others. " Thou shalt hide them in the secret of thy presence from the pride of man : thou shalt keep them secretly in a pavilion from the strife of tongues " (Ps. xxxi. 20) ; that is, from all calumnies, reproaches, evil speakings of all kinds. God will preserve the good names of his people from the blots and bespatterings of malicious men, as kings protect their favourites against slanders and clamours. 2. So the saints have prayed for it, as David : *"Deliver my soul, O Lord, from lying lips, and from a deceitful tongue."*—*Edward Reyner.*

Verse 2.—*"Deliver my soul, O Lord, from lying lips,"* etc. In the drop of venom which distils from the sting of the smallest insect, or the spike of the nettle-leaf, there is concentrated the quintessence of a poison so subtle that the microscope cannot distinguish it, and yet so virulent that it can inflame the blood, irritate the whole constitution, and convert day and night into restless misery ; so it is sometimes with the words of the slanderer.—*Frederick William Robertson.*

Verse 2.—*"Lying lips "* bore false witness against him, or with a *"deceitful tongue "* tried to ensnare him, and to draw something from him, on which they might ground an accusation.—*George Horne.*

Verse 3.—*"What shall be given unto thee ? or what shall be done unto thee, thou false tongue ?"* What dost thou expect, *"thou false tongue,"* in pleading a bad cause ? What fee or reward hast thou for being an accuser instead of an advocate ? What shall it profit thee (as we put it in the margin) ; what shalt thou gain by thy deceitful tongue ? or (as our margin hath it again), *"What shall the deceitful tongue give unto thee,"* that thou goest about slandering thy brother, and tearing his good name ? Hath thy deceitful tongue houses or lands to give thee ? hath it any treasures of gold and silver to bestow upon thee ? Surely, as itself is, so it gives only "*Sharp arrows of the mighty, with coals of juniper,*" as the next verse intimates. . . . The tongue indeed will speak often in these cases *gratis*, or without a fee ; but it never doth without danger and damage to the speaker. As such speakers shoot arrows, like the arrows of the mighty, and as they scatter coals, like the coals of juniper, so they usually get an arrow in their own sides, and not only burn their fingers, but heap coals of fire upon their own heads. Ungodly men will do mischief to other men purely for mischief's sake : yet when once mischief is done it proves most mischievous to the doers of it ; and while they hold their brethren's heaviness a profit, though they are never the better, they shall feel and find themselves in a short time much the worse.—*Joseph Caryl.*

Verses 3, 4.—"*What shall be given ?*" Intimating that his enemy expected some great reward for his malice against David ; but, saith the Psalmist, he shall have "*sharp arrows of the Almighty, with coals of juniper*"; as if he had said, " Whatever reward he have from men, this shall be his reward from God."—*John Jackson, in "The Morning Exercises,"* 1661.

Verses 3, 4.—The victim of slander, in these heavy complaints he has just uttered, may be indulging in excess, which pious friends are represented as coming forward to reprove by reminding him how little a true servant of God can be really injured by slander. Hence, as in the margin of our Bibles, the Psalm assumes the dramatic form, and represents his fellow-worshippers as asking the complainer : What evil, O servant of God, *can the false tongue give to thee !* Nursling of Omnipotence, *what can it do to thee !* . . . . The answer of suffering nature and bleeding peace still returns : "*It is like the sharp arrows of the mighty, like coals of juniper.*" An arrow from the bow of a mighty warrior, that flies unseen and unsuspected to its mark, and whose presence is only known when it quivers in the victim's heart, not unaptly represents the silent and deadly flight of slander ; while the fire which the desert pilgrim kindles on the sand, from the dry roots of the juniper, a wood which, of all that are known to him, throws out the fiercest and most continued heat, is not less powerfully descriptive of the intense pain and the lasting injury of a false and malicious tongue.— *Robert Nisbet.*

Verses 3, 4.—"*Coals of juniper,*" these "*shall be given unto thee.*" As if he had said, thou shalt have the hottest coals, such coals as will maintain heat longest, implying that the hottest and most lasting wrath of God should be their portion. Some naturalists say that coals of juniper raked up in the ashes will keep fire a whole year ; but I stay not upon this.—*Joseph Caryl.*

Verse 4.—"*Sharp arrows of the mighty, with coals of juniper.*" The world's sin is the world's punishment. A correspondence is frequently observed between the transgression and the retribution. . . . This law of correspondence seems to be here indicated. Similar figures are employed to express the offence and the punishment of the wicked. "*They bend their tongue like a bow for lies.*" " *Who whet their tongue like a sword, and bend their bows to shoot in secret at the perfect.*" But let the slanderer be upon his guard. There is another bow besides that in his possession. The arrows are sharp and burning ; and when they are sent from the bow by the arm of Omnipotence, nothing can resist their force, and in mortal agony his enemies bite the dust. " He hath bent his bow, and made it ready. He hath also prepared for him the instruments of death : he ordaineth his arrows against the persecutors." " God shall shoot at them with an arrow ; suddenly shall they be wounded ; so shall they make their own tongue fall upon themselves." This train of thought is also pursued in the illustration of fire. James compares the tongue of slander to fire. " And the tongue is a fire, a world of iniquity : so is the tongue among the members, that it defileth the whole body, and setteth on fire the course of nature ; and it is set on fire of hell." Such is the tongue, and here is the punishment : "*Coals of juniper,*" remarkable for their long retention of heat. And yet what a feeble illustration of the wrath of God, which burns down to the lowest hell ! " His lips are full of indignation, and his tongue as a devouring fire." Liars are excluded from heaven by a special enactment of the Sovereign ; and all of them "shall have their part in the lake which burneth with fire and brimstone, which is the second death." " Who among us shall dwell with the devouring fire ? Who among us shall dwell with everlasting burnings ? " With what solemn awe should we not cry out to the Lord,

" Gather not my soul with sinners, nor my life with bloody men ! "—*N. McMichael, in "The Pilgrim Psalms,"* 1860.

Verse 4.—"Sharp arrows of the mighty." He compareth wicked doctrine to an *arrow* which is not blunt, but *sharp ;* and moreover which is cast, not of him that is weak and feeble, but that is strong and *mighty ;* so that there is danger on both sides, as well of the arrow which is sharp and able to pierce, as also of him which with great violence hurleth the same.—*Martin Luther.*

Verse 4.—"Arrows." "Coals of juniper." When the *tongue* is compared to *"arrows,"* there is a reference (according to the Midrash), to the irrevocableness of the tongue's work. Even the lifted sword may be stayed, but the shot arrow may not. The special point to be drawn out in the mention of " coals of *juniper,"* is the unextinguishableness of such fuel. There is a marvellous story in the Midrash which illustrates this very well. Two men in the desert sat down under a juniper tree, and gathered sticks of it wherewith they cooked their food. After a year they passed over the same spot where was the dust of what they had burned ; and remarking that it was now twelve months since they had the fire, they walked fearlessly upon the dust, and their feet were burned by the " coals " beneath it, which were still unextinguished.—*H. T. Armfield.*

Verse 4.—"Coals of juniper." The fire of the *rothem* burns for a very long time covered with its ashes ; like malignant slander. But the secret malignity becomes its own terrible punishment.—*William Kay.*

Verse 4.—"Coals of juniper." We here [at Wádi Kinnah] found several Bedouins occupied in collecting brushwood, which they burn into charcoal for the Cairo market ; they prefer for this purpose the thick roots of the shrub Retham, *Genista rætam* of Forskal, which grows here in abundance.—*Johann Ludwig Burckhardt,* 1784—1817.

Verse 4.—"Coals of juniper." At this time we spoke four " ships of the desert," bound for Cairo, and loaded with *"coals of juniper,"* or, in other words, with charcoal made from the roots or branches of the *ratam,* or white broom of the desert, the identical bush referred to by the sacred writer.—*John Wilson, in "The Lands of the Bible visited and described,"* 1847.

*Verse 4.—*By *"coals of juniper,"* we understand arrows made of this wood, which when heated possesses the property of retaining the heat for a long time : and consequently, arrows of this kind, after having been placed in the fire, would in the hands of the warrior do terrible execution.

Some persons think that this verse is not to be understood as a figurative description of calumny, but rather of the punishment which God will inflict upon the calumniator. They therefore regard this as an answer to the question in the preceding verse : *"What shall he give ?"* etc.—*George Phillips.*

Verse 5.—"Woe is me, that I sojourn in Mesech, that I dwell in the tents of Kedar !" Mesech was a son of Japheth ; and the name here signifies his descendants, the Mosques, who occupied that wild mountain region which lies between the Caspian Sea and the Black Sea. Kedar, again, was a son of Ishmael ; and the name here signifies his descendants, the wandering tribes, whose " hand is against every man, and every man's hand against them." There is no geographical connection between those two nations : the former being upon the north of Palestine, and the latter upon the south. The connection is a moral one. They are mentioned together, because they were fierce and warlike barbarians. David had never lived on the shores of the Caspian Sea, or in the Arabian wilderness ; and he means no more than this, that the persons with whom he now dwelt were as savage and quarrelsome as Mesech and Kedar. After a similar fashion, we call rude and troublesome persons Turks, Tartars, and Hottentots. David exclaims, I am just as miserable among these haters of peace, as if I had taken up my abode with those savage and treacherous tribes.—*N. McMichael.*

Verse 5.—"Woe is me, that I sojourn in Mesech," etc. David exclaims, *Alas for me !* because, dwelling amongst false brethren and a bastard race of Abraham, he was wrongfully molested and tormented by them, although he had behaved himself towards them in good conscience. Since then, at the present day, in the church of Rome, religion is dishonoured by all manner of disgraceful imputations, faith torn in pieces, light turned into darkness, and the majesty of God exposed to the grossest mockeries, it will certainly be impossible for those who have any feeling of true piety within them to lie in the midst of such pollutions without great anguish of spirit.—*John Calvin.*

Verse 6.—The Arabs are naturally thievish and treacherous; and it sometimes happens, that those very persons are overtaken and pillaged in the morning who were entertained the night before with all the instances of friendship and hospitality. Neither are they to be accused for plundering strangers only, and attacking almost every person whom they find unarmed and defenceless, but for those many implacable and hereditary animosities which continually subsist among them; literally fulfilling the prophecy of Hagar, that " Ishmael should be a wild man ; his hand should be against every man, and every man's hand against him."—*Thomas Shaw,* 1692—1751.

Verse 6.—Our Lord was with the wild beasts in the wilderness. There are not a few who would rather face even these than the angry spirits which, alas, are still to be found even in Christian Churches.—*Wesleyan Methodist Magazine,* 1879.

Verses 6, 7.—What holy and gentle delight is associated with the very name of *peace !* Peace resting upon our bosom, and soothing all its cares : peace resting upon our households, and folding all the members in one loving embrace : peace resting upon our country, and pouring abundance from her golden horn : peace resting upon all nations, and binding them together with the threefold cord of a common humanity, a common interest, and a common religion ! The man who hates peace is a dishonour to the race, an enemy to his brother, and a traitor to his God. He hates Christ, who is the Prince of peace. He hates Christians, who are men of peace.—*N. McMichael.*

Verse 7.—"*I am for peace,*" etc. Jesus was a man of peace ; he came into our world, and was worshipped at his nativity as the Prince of peace : there was universal peace throughout the world at the time of his birth ; he lived to make peace " by the blood of his cross : " he died to complete it. When he was going out of the world, he said to his disciples, " Peace I leave with you, my peace I give unto you : not as the world giveth, give I unto you. Let not your heart be troubled, neither let it be afraid " : John xiv. 27. When he was risen from the dead, and made his first appearance to his disciples, he said unto them, " Peace be unto you " : he is the peace-maker : the Holy Ghost is the peace-maker : his gospel is the gospel of peace ; it contains the peace of God which passeth all understanding. "*I am for peace : but when I speak, they are for war.*" The bulk of the Jewish nation abhorred Christ, they were for putting him to death ; to avenge which, the Lord brought the Roman army against them, and many of them were utterly destroyed. So David literally was for peace with Saul ; yet, when opportunities made way for any negotiations, it was soon discovered Saul was for war, instead of peace, with him.

May we see how this, which is the introductory Psalm to those fourteen which follow, styled *Songs of Degrees,* hath a concern with our Lord Jesus Christ ; and that David the son of Jesse was in many cases a type of him, and several of his enemies, sorrows, and griefs, forerunning figures of what would befall Messiah, and come upon him. Amen.—*Samuel Eyles Pierce.*

Verse 7.—"*I am for peace.*" Good men love peace, pray for it, seek it, pursue it, will give anything but a good conscience for it. Compare Matt. v. 9 ; Heb. xii. 14 : *W. S. Plumer.* " It is a mark of a pious man, as far as in him is, to seek peace " : *Amesius.* " I would not give one hour of brotherly love for a whole eternity of contention."—*Dr. Ruffner.*

Verse 7.—"*When I speak, they are for war.*" He spoke with all respect and kindness that could be ; proposed methods of accommodation ; spoke reason, spoke love ; but they would not so much as hear him patiently ; but cried out, To arms ! To arms ! so fierce and implacable were they, and so bent on mischief. Such were Christ's enemies : for his love they were his adversaries ; and for his good words and good works they stoned him ; and if we meet with such enemies we must not think it strange, nor love peace the less for our seeking it in vain. " Be not overcome of evil," no, not of such evil as this ; " but," even when thus tried, still try to " overcome evil with good."—*Matthew Henry.*

HINTS TO PREACHERS.

Verse 1.—*A reminiscence.* I. It is threefold ; distress, prayer, deliverance. II. It has a threefold bearing : it excites my hope, stimulates my petitions, and arouses my gratitude.

Verse 1.—I. Special trouble : " In my distress." II. Special prayer : " I cried unto the Lord." III. Special favour : " He heard me."—*G. R.*

Verse 2.—The unjustly slandered have, besides the avenging majesty of their God to protect them, many other consolations, as—1. The consciousness of innocence to sustain them. 2. The promise of divine favour to support them : " I will hide thee from the scourge of the tongue." 3. There is the consideration to soothe : " Blessed are ye when men shall revile you and persecute you," etc. 4. That a lie has not usually a long life. 5. There is, lastly, for comfort, the repairing influence of time.—*R. Nisbet.*

Verse 2.—*A prayer against slander.* We are liable to it ; it would do us great injury and cause us great pain ; yet none but the Lord can protect us from it, or deliver us out of it.

Verse 3.—*The rewards of calumny.* What can they be ? What ought they to be ? What have they been ?.

Verse 3.—I. What the reviler does for others. II. What he does to himself. III. What God will do with him.

Verse 4.—The nature of slander and the punishment of slander.

Verse 4.—I. The tongue is sharper than an arrow. 1. It is shot in private. 2. It is tipped with poison. 3. It is polished with seeming kindness. 4. It is aimed at the tenderest part. II. The tongue is more destructive than fire. Its scandals spread with greater rapidity. They consume that which other fires cannot touch, and they are less easily quenched. " The tongue," says an Apostle, " is a fire . . . and setteth on fire the course of nature ; and it is set on fire of hell." A fiery dart of the wicked one.—*G. R.*

Verse 5.—*Bad lodgings.* Only the wicked can be at home with the wicked. Our dwelling with them is trying, and yet it may be useful (1) to them, (2) to us : it tries our graces, reveals our character, abates our pride, drives us to prayer, and makes us long to be home.

Verse 5.—I. None but the wicked enjoy the company of the wicked. II. None but the worldly enjoy the company of worldlings. III. None but the righteous enjoy the company of the righteous.—*G. R.*

Verse 6.—I. Trying company. II. Admirable behaviour. III. Undesirable consequences : " When I speak they are for war."

Verse 7.—*The character of the man of God.* He is at peace. He is for peace. He is peace. He shall have peace.

Verse 7.—I. Piety and peace are united. II. So are wickedness and war.—*G. R.*

PSALM CXXI.

TITLE, ETC.—*This bears no other title than " A song of degrees." It is several steps in advance of its predecessor, for it tells of the peace of God's house, and the guardian care of the Lord, while Psalm cxx. bemoans the departure of peace from the goodman's abode, and his exposure to the venomous assaults of slanderous tongues. In the first instance his eyes looked around with anguish, but here they look up with hope. From the constant recurrence of the word* keep, *we are led to name this song " a Psalm to the keeper of Israel." Were it not placed among the Pilgrim Psalms we should regard it is a martial hymn, fitted for the evensong of one who slept upon the tented field. It is a soldier's song as well as a traveller's hymn. There is an ascent in the Psalm itself which rises to the greatest elevation of restful confidence.*

EXPOSITION.

I WILL lift up mine eyes unto the hills, from whence cometh my help.

2 My help *cometh* from the LORD, which made heaven and earth.

3 He will not suffer thy foot to be moved : he that keepeth thee will not slumber.

4 Behold, he that keepeth Israel shall neither slumber nor sleep.

5 The LORD *is* thy keeper : the LORD *is* thy shade upon thy right hand.

6 The sun shall not smite thee by day, nor the moon by night.

7 The LORD shall preserve thee from all evil : he shall preserve thy soul.

8 The LORD shall preserve thy going out and thy coming in from this time forth, and even for evermore.

1. "*I will lift up mine eyes unto the hills, from whence cometh my help.*" It is wise to look to the strong for strength. Dwellers in valleys are subject to many disorders for which there is no cure but a sojourn in the uplands, and it is well when they shake off their lethargy and resolve upon a climb. Down below they are the prey of marauders, and to escape from them the surest method is to fly to the strongholds upon the mountains. Often before the actual ascent the sick and plundered people looked towards the hills and longed to be upon their summits. The holy man who here sings a choice sonnet looked away from the slanderers by whom he was tormented to the Lord who saw all from his high places, and was ready to pour down succour for his injured servant. Help comes to saints only from above, they look elsewhere in vain : let us lift up our eyes with hope, expectancy, desire and confidence. Satan will endeavour to keep our eyes upon our sorrows that we may be disquieted and discouraged ; be it ours firmly to resolve that we will look out and look up, for there is good cheer for the eyes, and they that lift up their eyes to the eternal hills shall soon have their hearts lifted up also. The purposes of God ; the divine attributes ; the immutable promises ; the covenant, ordered in all things and sure ; the providence, predestination, and proved faithfulness of the Lord—these are the hills to which we must lift our eyes, for from these our help must come. It is our resolve that we will not be bandaged and blindfolded, but will lift up our eyes.

Or is the text in the interrogative ? Dose he ask, " Shall I lift up mine eyes to the hills ? " Does he feel that the highest places of the earth can afford him no shelter ? Or does he renounce the idea of recruits hastening to his standard from the hardy mountaineers ? and hence does he again enquire, " Whence cometh my help ? " If so, the next verse answers the question, and shows whence all help must come.

2. "*My help cometh from the LORD, which made heaven and earth.*" What we need is help,—help powerful, efficient, constant : we need a very present help in trouble. What a mercy that we have it in our God. Our hope is in Jehovah, for our help comes from him. Help is on the road, and will not fail to reach us in due time, for he who sends it to us was never known to be too late. Jehovah who created all things is equal to every emergency ; heaven and earth are at the disposal of him who made them, therefore let us be very joyful in our infinite helper. He

will sooner destroy heaven and earth than permit his people to be dstroyed, and the perpetual hills themselves shall bow rather than he shall fail whose ways are everlasting. We are bound to look beyond heaven and earth to him who made them both : it is vain to trust the creatures : it is wise to trust the Creator.

3. *"He will not suffer thy foot to be moved."* Though the paths of life are dangerous and difficult, yet we shall stand fast, for Jehovah will not permit our feet to slide; and if he will not suffer it we shall not suffer it. If our foot will be thus kept we may be sure that our head and heart will be preserved also. In the original the words express a wish or prayer,—" May he not suffer thy foot to be moved." Promised preservation should be the subject of perpetual prayer ; and we may pray believingly ; for those who have God for their keeper shall be safe from all perils of the way. Among the hills and ravines of Palestine the literal keeping of the feet is a great mercy ; but in the slippery ways of a tried and afflicted life, the boon of upholding is of priceless value, for a single false step might cause us a fall fraught with awful danger. To stand erect and pursue the even tenor of our way is a blessing which only God can give, which is worthy of the divine hand, and worthy also of perennial gratitude. Our feet shall move in progress, but they shall not be moved to their overthrow. *"He that keepeth thee will not slumber,"*—or " thy keeper shall not slumber." We should not stand a moment if our keeper were to sleep ; we need him by day and by night ; not a single step can be safely taken except under his guardian eye. This is a choice stanza in a pilgrim song. God is the convoy and body-guard of his saints. When dangers are awake around us we are safe, for our Preserver is awake also, and will not permit us to be taken unawares. No fatigue or exhaustion can cast our God into sleep ; his watchful eyes are never closed.

4. *"Behold, he that keepeth Israel shall neither slumber nor sleep."* The consoling truth must be repeated : it is too rich to be dismissed in a single line. It were well if we always imitated the sweet singer, and would dwell a little upon a choice doctrine, sucking the honey from it. What a glorious title is in the Hebrew—*"The keeper of Israel,"* and how delightful to think that no form of unconsciousness ever steals over him, neither the deep slumber nor the lighter sleep. He will never suffer the house to be broken up by the silent thief ; he is ever on the watch, and speedily perceives every intruder. This is a subject of wonder, a theme for attentive consideration, therefore the word *"Behold"* is set up as a waymark. Israel fell asleep, but his God was awake. Jacob had neither walls, nor curtains, nor body-guard around him ; but the Lord was in that place though Jacob knew it not, and therefore the defenceless man was safe as in a castle. In after days he mentioned God under this enchanting name—" The God that led me all my life long " : perhaps David alludes to that passage in this expression. The word " keepeth " is also full of meaning : he keeps us as a rich man keeps his treasures, as a captain keeps a city with a garrison, as a royal guard keeps his monarch's head. If the former verse is in strict accuracy a prayer, this is the answer to it; it affirms the matter thus, " Lo, he shall not slumber nor sleep—the Keeper of Israel." It may also be worthy of mention that in verse three the Lord is spoken of as the personal keeper of one individual, and here of all those who are in his chosen nation, described as Israel : mercy to one saint is the pledge of blessing to them all, Happy are the pilgrims to whom this Psalm is a safe-conduct ; they may journey all the way to the celestial city without fear.

5. *"The LORD is thy keeper."* Here the preserving One, who had been spoken of by pronouns in the two previous verses, is distinctly named—Jehovah is thy keeper. What a mint of meaning lies here : the sentence is a mass of bullion, and when coined and stamped with the king's name it will bear all our expenses between our birthplace on earth and our rest in heaven. Here is a glorious person—*Jehovah*, assuming a gracious office and fulfilling it in person,—Jehovah is thy *keeper*, in behalf of a favoured individual—*thy* and a firm assurance of revelation that it is even so at this hour—Jehovah *is* thy keeper. Can we appropriate the divine declaration ? If so, we may journey onward to Jerusalem and know no fear ; yea, we may journey through the valley of the shadow of death and fear no evil. *"The LORD is thy shade upon thy right hand."* A shade gives protection from burning heat and glaring light. We cannot bear too much blessing even divine goodness, which is a right-hand dispensation, must be toned down and shaded to suit our infirmity, and this the Lord will do for us. He will bear a shield before us, and guard the right arm with which we fight the foe. That member which

has the most of labour shall have the most of protection. When a blazing sun pours down its burning beams upon our heads the Lord Jehovah himself will interpose to shade us, and that in the most honourable manner, acting as our right-hand attendant, and placing us in comfort and safety. "The Lord at thy right hand shall smite through kings." How different this from the portion of the ungodly ones who have Satan standing at their right hand, and of those of whom Moses said "their defence has departed from them." God is as near us as our shadow, and we are as safe as angels.

6. "*The sun shall not smite thee by day, nor the moon by night.*" None but the Lord could shelter us from these tremendous forces. These two great lights rule the day and the night, and under the lordship of both we shall labour or rest in equal safety. Doubtless there are dangers of the light and of the dark, but in both and from both we shall be preserved—literally from excessive heat and from baneful chills; mystically from any injurious effects which might follow from doctrine bright or dim; spiritually from the evils of prosperity and adversity; eternally from the strain of overpowering glory and from the pressure of terrible events, such as judgment and the burning of the world. Day and night make up all time: thus the ever-present protection never ceases. All evil may be ranked as under the sun or the moon, and if neither of these can smite us we are indeed secure. God has not made a new sun or a fresh moon for his chosen, they exist under the same outward circumstances as others, but the power to *smite* is in their case removed from temporal agencies; saints are enriched, and not injured, by the powers which govern the earth's condition; to them has the Lord given "the precious things brought forth by the sun, and the precious things put forth by the moon," while at the same moment he has removed from them all bale and curse of heat or damp, of glare or chill.

7. "*The LORD shall preserve thee from all evil,*" or *keep* thee from all evil. It is a great pity that our admirable translation did not keep to the word *keep* all through the Psalm, for all along it is one. God not only keeps his own in all evil times but from all evil influences and operations, yea, from evils themselves. This is a far-reaching word of covering: it includes everything and excludes nothing: the wings of Jehovah amply guard his own from evils great and small, temporary and eternal. There is a most delightful double personality in this verse: Jehovah keeps the believer, not by agent, but by himself; and the person protected is definitely pointed out by the word *thee*,—it is not our estate or name which is shielded, but the proper personal man. To make this even more intensely real and personal another sentence is added, "*The LORD shall preserve thee from all evil: he shall preserve thy soul,*"—or Jehovah will keep thy soul. Soul-keeping is the soul of keeping. If the soul be kept all is kept. The preservation of the greater includes that of the less so far as it is essential to the main design: the kernel shall be preserved, and in order thereto the shell shall be preserved also. God is the sole keeper of the soul. Our soul is kept from the dominion of sin, the infection of error, the crush of despondency, the puffing up of pride; kept from the world, the flesh and the devil; kept for holier and greater things; kept in the love of God; kept unto the eternal kingdom and glory. What can harm a soul that is kept of the Lord?

8. "*The LORD shall preserve thy going out and thy coming in from this time forth, and even for evermore.*" When we go out in the morning to labour, and come home at eventide to rest, Jehovah shall keep us. When we go out in youth to begin life, and come in at the end to die, we shall experience the same keeping. Our exits and our entrances are under one protection. Three times have we the phrase, "Jehovah shall keep," as if the sacred Trinity thus sealed the word to make it sure: ought not all our fears to be slain by such a threefold flight of arrows? What anxiety can survive this triple promise? This keeping is eternal; continuing from this time forth, even for evermore. The whole church is thus assured of everlasting security: the final perseverance of the saints is thus ensured, and the glorious immortality of believers is guaranteed. Under the ægis of such a promise we may go on pilgrimage without trembling, and venture into battle without dread. None are so safe as those whom God keeps; none so much in danger as the self-secure. To goings out and comings in belong peculiar dangers, since every change of position turns a fresh quarter to the foe, and it is for these weak points that an especial security is provided: Jehovah will keep the door when it opens and closes, and this he will perseveringly continue to do so long as there is left a single man that trusteth in him, as long as a danger survives, and, in fact, as long as time

endures. Glory be unto the Keeper of Israel, who is endeared to us under that title, since our growing sense of weakness makes us feel more deeply than ever our need of being kept. Over the reader we would breathe a benediction, couched in the verse of Keble.

> "God keep thee safe from harm and sin,
> Thy spirit keep; the Lord watch o'er
> Thy going out, thy coming in,
> From this time, evermore."

EXPLANATORY NOTES AND QUAINT SAYINGS.

Title, "A song of degrees."—It has been ingeniously pointed out that these *"degrees"* or *" steps "* consist in the reiteration of a word or thought occurring in one clause, verse, or stanza, which in the next verse or stanza is used, as it were, as a *step* (or degree) by which to ascend to another and higher truth. Thus in our Psalm, the idea of *" my help,"* expressed in verse 1, is repeated in verse 2. This has now become a step by which in verse 3 we reach the higher truth or explanation of *" my help,"* as : *"He that keepeth thee will not slumber,"* the same idea being with slight modification re-embodied in verse 4. Another *" degree "* is then reached in verse 5, when *" He who slumbers* not " is designated as *Jehovah,* the same idea once more enlarged upon being (the *word* occurring twice in verse 5) in verse 6. The last and highest degree of this song is attained in verse 7, when the truth implied in the word *Jehovah* unfolds itself in its application to our *preservation,* which, with further enlargement, is once more repeated in verse 8. *Perhaps* some internal connexion might be traced between all the fifteen Psalms of Degrees. At any rate, it will not be difficult to trace the same structure in each of the Psalms "of Degrees," making allowance for occasional devotions and modifications.—*Alfred Edersheim, in "The Golden Diary,"* 1877.

Whole Psalm.—According to verse 1 this Psalm was designed to be sung in view of the mountains of Jerusalem, and is manifestly an evening song for the sacred band of pilgrims, to be sung in the last night-watch, the figures of which are also peculiarly suitable for a pilgrim song ; and with Ps. cxxii. which, according to the express announcement in the introduction, was sung, when the sacred pilgrim trains had reached the gates of Jerusalem, and halted for the purpose of forming in order, for the solemn procession into the Sanctuary, Ps. cxxxiv. . . . .

The idea is a very probable one, that the Psalm was the evening song of the sacred pilgrim band, sung on retiring to rest upon the last evening, when the long wished-for termination of their wandering, the mountains of Jerusalem, had come into view in the distance. In this we obtain a suitable connection with the following Psalm, which would be sung *one* station further on when the pilgrims were at the gates of Jerusalem. In this case we find an explanation of the fact, that in the middle point of the Psalm there stands the Lord as the *" keeper "* of Israel, with reference to the declaration, " I keep thee," which was addressed to the patriarch as he slept on his pilgrimage : and in this case also " he neither slumbereth nor sleepeth " is seen in its true light.—*E. W. Hengstenberg.*

It has been said Mr. Romaine read this Psalm every day ; and sure it is, that every word in it is calculated to encourage and strengthen our faith and hope in God.—*Samuel Eyles Pierce.*

Verse 1.—*"I will lift up mine eyes,"* etc. Since we, being burthened with the effects of worldly pleasures, and also with other cares and troubles, can by no means ascend to thee that art on the top of so high a mountain, accompanied with so many legions of angels that still attend upon thee, we have no remedy, but with thy prophet David now to lift up the eyes of our hearts and minds toward thee, and to cry for help to come down from thee to us, thy poor and wretched servants.—*Sir Anthony Cope, in "Meditations on Twenty Select Psalms,"* 1547.

Verse 1.—*"I will lift up mine eyes,"* etc. In thy agony of a troubled conscience always look upwards unto a gracious God to keep thy soul steady ; for looking downward on thyself thou shalt find nothing but what will increase thy fear, infinite sins, good deeds few, and imperfect: it is not thy faith, but God's faithfulness thou must rely upon; casting thine eyes downwards on thyself, to behold the great distance betwixt what thou deservest and what thou desirest, is enough to make thee giddy, stagger, and reel into despair. Ever therefore *lift up thine eyes unto the hills, from whence cometh thy help,* never viewing the deep dale of thy own unworthiness, but to abate thy pride when tempted to presumption.—*Thomas Fuller* (1608—1661), *in "The cause and Cure of a Wounded Conscience."*

Verse 1.—"*The hills.*" There can be no doubt that in Palestine we are in the " Highlands " of Asia. This was the more remarkable in connection with the Israelites, because they were the only civilized nation then existing in the world, which dwelt in a mountainous country. . . . . The Hebrew people was raised above the other ancient states, equally in its moral and in its physical relations. From the Desert of Arabia to Hebron is a continual ascent, and from that ascent there is no descent of any importance, except to the plains of the Jordan, Esdraelon, and the coast. From a mountain sanctuary, as it were, Israel looked over the world. . . . . It was to the " mountains " of Israel that the exile lifted up his eyes, as the place *from whence his help came.—Arthur Penrhyn Stanley.*

Verse 1.—"*The hills, from whence cometh my help.*" See no riches but in grace, no health but in piety, no beauty but in holiness, no treasure but in heaven, no delight but in " the things above."—*Anthony Farindon.*

Verse 1.—"*From whence cometh my help.*" The natives of India used to say that when Sir Henry Lawrence looked twice to heaven and then to earth he knew what to do.

> To Heaven I lift mine eye,
> To Heaven, Jehovah's throne,
> For there my Saviour sits on high,
> And thence shall strength and aid supply
> To all He calls His own.
>
> He will not faint nor fail,
> Nor cause thy feet to stray:
> For him no weary hours assail,
> Nor evening darkness spreads her veil
> O'er his eternal day.
>
> Beneath that light divine
> Securely shalt thou move;
> The sun with milder beams shall shine,
> And eve's still queen her lamp incline
> Benignant from above.
>
> For he, thy God and Friend,
> Shall keep thy soul from harm,
> In each sad scene of doubt attend,
> And guide thy life, and bless thy end,
> With his almighty arm.
>
> *John Bowdler*, 1814.

Verses 1, 2.—Faint at the close of life's journey, a Christian pilgrim repeated the line,—

> " Will he not his help afford ? "

She quoted it several times, trying to recall the song in which it occurs, and asked that the once familiar hymn, part of the voice of which she caught, might be all fetched home to her mind again; and she was greatly refreshed and comforted when we read at her bedside Charles Wesley's spirited paraphrase, beginning,—

> " To the hills I lift mine eyes,
> The everlasting hills;
> Streaming thence in fresh supplies,
> My soul the Spirit feels.
>
> Will he not his help afford ?
> Help, while yet I ask, is given:
> God comes down; the God and Lord
> That made both earth and heaven."

Edward Jewitt Robinson, in "The Caravan and the Temple," 1878.

Verses 1—3.—

Look away to Jesus,
  Look away from all !
Then we need not stumble,
  Then we shall not fall.
From each snare that lureth,
  Foe or phantom grim,
Safety this ensureth,
  Look away to him !

Frances Ridley Havergal.

Verse 2.—"*My help cometh from the Lord.*" I require to remember that *my help cometh from the Lord*, not only when seemingly there is no *outward* help from men or otherwise, but also and especially when all seems to go well with me,—when abundance of friends and help are at hand. For then, surely, I am most in danger of making an arm of flesh my trust, and thus reaping its curse ; or else of saying to my soul, " Take thine ease," and finding the destruction which attends such folly.—*Alfred Edersheim.*

Verse 2.—"*Maker of heaven and earth,*" and therefore mighty to help.—*James G. Murphy.*

Verse 3.—"*He will not suffer thy foot to be moved.*" The sliding of the foot is a frequent description of misfortune, for example, Ps. xxxviii. 16, lxvi. 9, and a very natural one in mountainous Canaan, where a single slip of the foot was often attended with great danger. The language here naturally refers to complete, lasting misfortune.—*E. W. Hengstenberg.*

Verse 3.—"*He will not suffer thy foot to be moved.*" A man cannot go without moving his feet ; and a man cannot stand whose feet are moved. The foot by a *synechdoche* is put for the whole body, and the body for the whole outward estate ; so that, " *he will not suffer thy foot to be moved,*" is, he will not suffer thee or thine to be moved or violently cast down. The power of thine opposers shall not prevail over thee, for the power of God sustains thee. Many are striking at thy heels, but they cannot strike them up while God holds thee up. If the will of thine enemies might stand, thou shouldst quickly fall; but God " *will not suffer thy foot to be moved.*"—*Joseph Caryl.*

Verses 3—8.—There is something very striking in the assurance that the Lord will not suffer the foot even of the most faint and wearied one to be moved. The everlasting mountains stand fast, and we feel as if, like Mount Zion, they could not be removed for ever ; but the step of man—how feeble in itself, how liable to stumble or trip even against a pebble in the way ! Yet that foot is as firm and immoveable in God's protection as the hills themselves. It is one of his own sweet promises, that he will give his angels charge over every child of his, that he come to no harm by the way. But, oh, how immeasurably beyond even the untiring wings of angels is the love promised here ! that love which engages to protect from every danger, as a hen gathereth her chickens under her wings. In the hours of occupation and hurry, in the conflicts and perils of the day, in the helplessness of sleep, in the glare and heat of the noon-day, amid the damps and dews of night, that unslumbering eye is still over every child for his good. Man, indeed, goeth forth to his work and to his labour till the evening ; but alike as he goes forth in the morning, and as he returns in the evening, the Lord still holds him up in all his goings forth and his comings in ; no manner of evil shall befall him. And oh ! what a sweet addition is it to the promise. " He shall preserve *thy soul.*" It is the very argument of the apostle, and the very inference he draws, " The eyes of the Lord are upon the righteous, and his ears are open unto their cry,"—" He neither slumbereth nor sleepeth,"—and then he asks, " Who is he that will harm you, if ye be followers of that which is good ? " From the very dawn of life to its latest close, even for evermore, " He will preserve thee from all evil ; he will preserve thy soul."—*Barton Bouchier.*

Verses 3, 4, 5.—A great practical difficulty is to find a " keeper " who will remain *awake during the whole night*. The weariness of those who keep a faithful watch, and their longing for day during the tedious lonely hours of darkness, is alluded to in a graphic and beautiful figure of the Psalmist—

" My soul waiteth for the Lord
More than keepers for the morning,
More than keepers for the morning."

The usual method adopted to secure due vigilance is to require the man to call out loudly, or to blow a whistle, every quarter of an hour. . . . . Yet, notwithstanding all precautions, as soon as sleep falls on the tired camp, it is too often the case that the hireling keeper lies down on the ground, wraps around him his thick *abaiyeh*, or cloak, and, careless of his charge, or overcome with weariness, yields himself up to his drowsy propensities.

Viewed in the light of these facts, how full of condescension and cheer is the assurance of God's never-ceasing care—

" He who keepeth thee will not slumber.
Behold, he who keepeth Israel
Doth not slumber or sleep.
Jehovah is thy keeper."

While the services of the keeper constitute at all times a marked feature of life in Palestine, they are perhaps more needed when travelling through the country than at any other time. Then, when the moving camp is nightly pitched in strange fields, it becomes absolutely necessary to apply to the nearest authorities for a nocturnal guardian, before one can safely lie down to rest. Now this Psalm cxxi. being one of "the Songs of Degrees," was probably composed to be sung on the way to Jerusalem, as a pilgrim hymn, when the Israelites were coming up annually to keep the three great feasts. As a journeying Psalm, it would therefore have peculiar significance in its allusion to *the keeper by night.—James Neil, in "Palestine Explored,"* 1882.

Verses 3, 4.—When one asked Alexander how he could sleep so soundly and securely in the midst of danger, he told him that Parmenio watched. Oh, how securely may they sleep over whom *he* watcheth that never slumbers nor sleeps !— *From "The Dictionary of Illustrations,"* 1873.

Verses 3, 4.—A poor woman, as the Eastern story has it, came to the Sultan one day, and asked compensation for the loss of some property. "How did you lose it ? " said the monarch. " I fell asleep," was the reply, " and a robber entered my dwelling." "Why did you fall asleep ?" " I fell asleep because I believed that you were awake." The Sultan was so much delighted with the answer of the woman, that he ordered her loss to be made up. But what is true, only by a legal fiction, of human governments, that they never sleep, is true in the most absolute sense with reference to the divine government. We can sleep in safety because our God is ever awake. We are safe because he never slumbers. Jacob had a beautiful picture of the ceaseless care of Divine Providence on the night when he fled from his father's house. The lonely traveller slept on the ground, with the stones for his pillow, and the sky for his canopy. He had a wondrous vision of a ladder stretching from earth to heaven, and on which angels were seen ascending and descending. And he heard Jehovah saying to him, " Behold, I am with thee, and will keep thee in all places whither thou goest."—*N. McMichael.*

Verse 4.—It is necessary, observes S. Bernard, that *"he who keepeth Israel"* should *"neither slumber nor sleep,"* for he who assails Israel neither slumbers nor sleeps. And as the One is anxious about us, so is the other to slay and destroy us, and his one care is that he who has once been turned aside may never come back.— *Neale and Littledale.*

Verse 4.—*"Slumber." "Sleep."* There is no climax in these words, as some have supposed. Etymologically, the first is the stronger word, and it occurs in Ps. lxxvi. 5 [6] of the sleep of death. In this instance there is no real distinction between the two. Possibly there may be an allusion to the nightly encampment, and the sentries of the caravan.—*J. J. Stewart Perowne.*

Verse 4.—*"He . . . shall neither slumber nor sleep."* This form of expression, *he will not slumber nor sleep,* would be improper in other languages, according to the idiom of which it should rather be, *He will not sleep, yea, he will not slumber :* but when the Hebrews invert this order, they argue from the greater to the less. The sense then is, that as God never slumbers even in the smallest degree, we need not be afraid of any harm befalling us while he is asleep.—*John Calvin.*

Verse 4.—*"He that keepeth Israel."* With an allusion to Jacob, who slept at Bethel, and to whom the promise of God took this form, " And, behold, I am with thee, and will *keep* thee in all places whither thou goest " : Gen. xxviii. 15.—*Aben Ezra, quoted by H. T Armfield.*

Verse 4.—"*Shall neither slumber nor sleep.*" Man sleeps ; a sentinel *may* slumber on his post by inattention, by long-continued wakefulness, or by weariness ; a pilot *may* slumber at the helm ; even a mother *may* fall asleep by the side of the sick child ; but God is never exhausted, is never weary, is never inattentive. He never closes his eyes on the condition of his people, on the wants of the world.—*Albert Barnes.*

Verse 4.—A number of years ago Captain D. commanded a vessel sailing from Liverpool to New York, and on one voyage he had all his family with him on board the ship.

One night, when all were quietly asleep, there arose a sudden squall of wind, which came sweeping over the waters until it struck the vessel, and instantly threw her on her side, tumbling and crashing everything that was moveable, and awaking the passengers to a consciousness that they were in imminent peril.

Everyone on board was alarmed and uneasy, and some sprang from their berths and began to dress, that they might be ready for the worst.

Captain D. had a little girl on board, just eight years old, who, of course, awoke with the rest.

" What's the matter ? " said the frightened child.

They told her a squall had struck the ship.

" Is father on deck ? " said she.

" Yes ; father's on deck."

The little thing dropped herself on her pillow again without a fear, and in a few moments was sleeping sweetly in spite of winds or waves.

> Fear not the windy tempests wild,
> Thy bark they shall not wreck ;
> Lie down and sleep, O helpless child !
> Thy Father's on the deck.

" The Biblical Treasury," 1873.

Verses 4, 5.—The same that is the protector of the church in general, is engaged for the preservation of every particular believer ; the same wisdom, the same power, the same promises. *"He that keepeth Israel"* (verse 4), *"is thy keeper"* (verse 5). The Shepherd of the flock is the Shepherd of every sheep, and will take care that not one, even of the little ones, shall perish.—*Matthew Henry.*

Verse 5.—"*The Lord is thy keeper.*" Two principal points are asserted in these previous words. 1. Jehovah, and Jehovah alone, the omnipotent and self-existent God, is the Keeper, and Preserver of his people. 2. The people of God are kept, at all times and in all circumstances, by his mighty power unto everlasting salvation ; they are preserved even " for evermore." In the first particular, the divinity of the great Keeper is declared ; and, in the second, the eternal security of his people through his omnipotence and faithfulness. This was the Psalmist's gospel. He preached it to others, and he felt it himself. He did not speculate upon what he did not understand ; but he had a clear evidence, and a sweet perception, of these two glorious doctrines, which he delivered to the people. . . . This character, under the name of Jehovah, is the character of Christ. Just such a one is Jesus, the Shepherd of Israel. He says of himself to the Father, " Those that thou gavest me *I have kept*, and *none of them is lost*, but the Son of Perdition, that the Scripture might be fulfilled." . . . . From what has been premised, it seems evident, that the keeper of the faithful is no other than Jehovah. This the Psalmist has proved. It appears equally evident that Christ is their Keeper and Preserver.)This he hath declared himself ; and his apostles have repeatedly declared it of him. It follows, therefore, that Christ is truly and essentially Jehovah. All the sophistry in the world cannot elude this conclusion ; nor all the heretics in the world destroy the premises. And, if Christ be Jehovah, he is all that supreme, eternal, omnipotent being, which Arians, Socinians, and others deny him to be.—*Ambrose Serle, in "Horæ Solitariæ,"* 1815.

Verse 5.—"*Keeper.*" "*Shade.*" The titles of God are virtually promises— when he is called a sun, a shield, a strong tower, a hiding-place, a portion. The titles of Christ, light of the world, bread of life, the way, the truth, and life ; the titles of the Spirit, the Spirit of truth, of holiness, of glory, of grace, and supplication, the sealing, witnessing Spirit ; faith may conclude as much out of these as out of promises. Is the Lord a sun ? then he will influence me, etc. Is Christ life ? then he will enliven me, etc.—*David Clarkson,* 1621—1686.

Verse 5.—"*Thy shade upon thy right hand.*" That is, always present with thee; or, as the Jewish Arab renders it, " Nigher than thy shadow at, or from thy right hand."—*Thomas Fenton, in "Annotations on the Book of Job and the Psalms,"* 1732.

Verse 5.—"*Thy shade.*" In eastern countries the sun's burning rays are often arrows by which premature death is inflicted; and when the Psalmist speaks of Jehovah as a shady covert for the righteous, that imagery suggests the idea of the "coup de soleil" or sunstroke as the evil avoided.—*J. F., in "The Baptist Magazine,"* 1831.

Verse 5.—"*Shade.*" The Hebrew word is לצ, *tsel,* " a shadow," and hence it has been supposed that the words, " thy shadow at thy right hand," are a figurative expression, referring to the protection afforded by the shade of a tree against the scorching rays of the sun or to the custom which prevails in tropical climates especially, of keeping off the intense heat of the sun by a portable screen, such as an umbrella or parasol. The word is often put for *defence* in general. Compare Num. xiv. 9; Isaiah xxx. 2; Jer. xlviii. 45.—*James Anderson.*

Verses 5—8.—How large a writ or patent of protection is granted here! No time shall be hurtful, neither "*day nor night,*" which includes all times. Nothing shall hurt, neither *sun nor moon,* nor heat nor cold. These should include all annoyances. Nothing shall be hurt, "*Thy soul shall be preserved, thy outgoings and thy comings in shall be preserved.*" These include the whole person of man, and him in all his just affairs and actions. Nothing of man is safe without a guard, and nothing of man can be unsafe which is thus guarded. They should be kept who can say, " The Lord is our keeper "; and they cannot be kept, no, not by legions of angels, who have not the Lord for their keeper. None can keep us but he, and he hath promised to keep us "*for evermore.*"—*Joseph Caryl.*

Verse 6.—"*The sun shall not smite thee.*" חפה of the sun signifies to smite injuriously (Isa. xlix. 10), plants, so that they wither (Ps. cii. 5), and the head (Jonah iv. 8), so that symptoms of sunstroke (2 Kings iv. 19; Judith viii. 2 seq.) appear. The transferring of the word to the moon is not zeugmatic. Even the moon's rays may become insupportable, may affect the eyes injuriously, and (more particularly in the equatorial regions) produce fatal inflammation of the brain. From the hurtful influences of nature that are round about him the promise extends in verses 7, 8 in every direction. Jahve, says the poet to himself, will keep (guard) thee against all evil, of whatever kind it may be and whencesoever it may threaten; he will keep thy soul, and thereafter thy life both inwardly and outwardly; he will keep thy going out and coming in, *i.e.,* all thy business and intercourse of life . . . . . . everywhere and at all times; and that from this time forth even for ever.—*Franz Delitzsch.*

Verse 6.—"*The sun shall not smite thee by day,*" etc. A promise made with allusion unto, and application of that care which God had over his people, when he brought them out of Egypt through the wilderness, when he guarded them from the heat of the sun by a cloud by day, and from the cold and moistness of the night and moon by a pillar of fire by night.—*David Dickson.*

Verse 6.—"*Nor the moon by night.*"

> The moon, the governess of floods,
> Pale in her anger, washes all the air,
> That rheumatic diseases do abound.

William Shakespeare (1564—1616), *in "The Midsummer Night's Dream."*

Verse 6.—Joseph Hart in one of his hymns speaks of some who " travel much by night." To such this promise is precious.—"*Biblical Treasury.*"

Verse 6.—"*Nor the moon by night.*" The effect of the moonlight on the eyes in this country is singularly injurious. . . . The moon here really strikes and affects the sight, when you sleep exposed to it, much more than the sun, a fact of which I had a very unpleasant proof one night, and took care to guard against it afterwards; indeed, the sight of a person who should sleep with his face exposed at night would soon be utterly impaired or destroyed.—*John Carne, in " Letters from the East,"* 1826.

Verse 6.—"*Nor the moon by night.*" In the cloudless skies of the East, where the moon shines with such exceeding clearness, its effects upon the human frame have been found most injurious. The inhabitants of these countries are most careful in taking precautionary measures before exposing themselves to its influence. Sleeping much in the open air, they are careful to cover well their heads and faces. It has been proved beyond a doubt that the moon smites as well as the sun, causing blindness for a time, and even distortion of the features.

Sailors are well aware of this fact ; and a naval officer relates that he has often, when sailing between the tropics, seen the commanders of vessels waken up young men who have fallen asleep in the moonlight. Indeed, he witnessed more than once the effects of a moonstroke, when the mouth was drawn on one side and the sight injured for a time. He was of opinion that, with long exposure, the mind might become seriously affected. It is supposed that patients suffering under fever and other illnesses are affected by this planet, and the natives of India constantly affirm that they will either get better or worse, according to her changes.—*C. W., in "The Biblical Treasury."*

Verse 7.—*"The Lord shall preserve thee from all evil."* Lawyers, when they are drawing up important documents, frequently conclude with some general terms to meet any emergency which may possibly occur. They do this on the principle, that what is not in may be supposed to be intentionally left out. In order to guard against this inference, they are not content with inserting a number of particular cases ; they conclude with a general statement, which includes everything, whether expressed or not. A similar formula is inserted here. It is of great importance that the feet of travellers be kept from sliding, as they pursue their journey. It is of great importance that they be preserved from heat by day, and from cold by night. But other dangers await them, from which they require protection ; and lest the suspicion be entertained, that no provision is made for these being surmounted, they are all introduced in the saving and comprehensive clause. No matter what may be their character, no matter from what quarter they may appear, no matter when they may come, and no matter how long they may continue, the declaration covers them all. Divine grace changes the nature of everything it handles, and transforms everything it touches into gold. Afflictions are overruled for good ; and the virtues of the Christian life are developed with unusual lustre. *"The Lord shall preserve thee from all evil."*—*N. McMichael.*

Verse 7.—*"The Lord shall preserve thee from all evil,"* etc. It is an absolute promise, there are no conditions annexed ; it honours God for us simply to believe it, and rest on the Lord for the performance of it. As we view it, what have we to fear ? The mouth of the Lord hath spoken it, his word is immutable. Jesus preserves body and soul, he is the Saviour of the body as well as of the soul.—*Samuel Eyles Pierce.*

Verses 7, 8.—The threefold expression, "shall keep *thee . . . thy soul . . . thy going out* and *thy coming in,"* marks the completeness of the protection vouchsafed, extending to all that the man is and that he does.—*J. J. Stewart Perowne.*

Verses 7, 8.—It is of importance to mark the reason why the prophet repeats so often what he had so briefly and in one word expressed with sufficient plainness. Such repetition seems at first sight superfluous ; but when we consider how difficult it is to correct our distrust, it will be easily perceived that he does not improperly dwell upon the commendation of the divine providence. How few are to be found who yield to God the honour of being a *"keeper,"* in order to their being thence assured of their safety, and led to call upon him in the midst of their perils ! On the contrary, even when we seem to have largely experienced what this protection of God implies, we yet instantly tremble at the noise of a leaf falling from a tree, as if God had quite forgotten us. Being then entangled in so many unholy misgivings, and so much inclined to distrust, we are taught from the passage that if a sentence couched in a few words does not suffice us, we should gather together whatever may be found throughout the whole Scriptures concerning the providence of God, until this doctrine—" That God always keeps watch for us "—is deeply rooted in our hearts ; so that, depending upon his guardianship alone, we may bid adieu to all the vain confidences of the world.—*John Calvin.*

Verse 8.—*"The Lord shall preserve."* The word *shamar* imports a most tender preservation ; from it comes *shemuroth*, signifying the eyelids, because they are the keepers of the eye, as the Lord is called in the verse preceding—*shomer Ishrael, "the keeper of Israel."* If the lids of the eye open, it is to let the eye see ; if they close, it is to let it rest, at least to defend it ; all their motion is for the good of the eye. O, what a comfort is here! The Lord calleth his Church " the apple of his eye": " he that toucheth you, touches the apple of mine eye." The Church is the apple of God's eye, and the Lord is the covering of it. O, how well are they kept whom " the keeper of Israel " keepeth! The Lord was a buckler to Abraham, none of his enemies could harm him; for his buckler covered him throughly. The Lord was a hedge unto Job; Satan himself confessed he could not get through it, howsoever many a time he assayed it, to have done evil unto Job. . . . . . .

But seeing this same promise of preservation was made before (for from the third verse to the end of the Psalm, six sundry times, is the word of keeping or preserving repeated), why is it now made over again? Not without cause; for this doubling and redoubling serves, first, for a remedy of our ignorance. Men, if they be in any good estate, are ready to " sacrifice to their own net," or " to cause their mouth to kiss their own hand," as if their own hand had helped them: thus to impute their " deliverance " to their " calf," and therefore often is this resounded, " The Lord," " The Lord." Is thy estate advanced? The Lord hath done it. Hast thou been preserved from desperate dangers? Look up to the Lord, thy help is from on high, and to him let the praise be returned. Secondly, it is for a remedy for our natural diffidence: the word of the Lord in itself is as sure when it is spoken, as when it is sworn; as sure spoken once, as when it is oftener repeated; yet is not the Lord content to speak only, but to swear also; nor to speak once, but often, one and the selfsame thing. The reason is showed us by the apostle, that hereby he may " declare to the heirs of promise the stability of his counsel." Heb. vi.; Gen. xxi. 32. As Joseph spake of Pharaoh his vision, " It was doubled, because the thing is established by God, and God hasteth to perform it"; so is it with every word of the Lord, when it is repeated; it is because it is established, and God hastens to perform it.—*From a Sermon by Bishop Cowper, entitled "His Majesties Comming in," 1623.*

Verse 8.—*"The Lord shall preserve thy going out and thy coming in."* All actions being comprehended under one of these two sorts, *"going out"* to more public, and *"coming in"* to more private affairs; or again, *" going out "* to begin, and *"coming in "* at the end of the work. But by this expression may here perhaps be more particularly signified that God would protect David, even to the end of his days, whenever he marched out with his armies, or brought them home.—*Thomas Fenton.*

Verse 8.—*"From this time forth and even for evermore."* He has not led me so tenderly thus far to forsake me at the very gate of heaven.—*Adoniram Judson.*

HINTS TO PREACHERS.

Verse 1.—The window opened towards Jerusalem. I. The hills we look to. II. The help we look for. III. The eyes we look with.

Verse 1.—*"Whence cometh my help?"* A grave question; for, I. I need it, greatly, in varied forms, constantly, and now. II. In few directions can I look for it, for men are feeble, changeable, hostile, etc. III. I must look above. To Providence, to Grace, to my God.

Verse 2.—The Creator the creature's helper.

Verse 2.—I. God is his people's "help." II. He helps them in proportion as they feel their need of his help. III. His help is never in vain. " My help cometh," not from the earth merely, or the skies, but " from the Lord, which made heaven and earth." Isa. xl. 26—31.—*G. R.*

Verse 3 (*first clause*).—The preservation of saintly character the care of the Creator.

Verse 3.—Comfort for a pilgrim along the *mauvais pas* of life. We have a Guide omniscient, omnipotent, unsleeping, unchanging.

Verse 3.—*"He that keepeth thee will not slumber."* I. The Lord's care is personal in its objects. The keeper of Israel is the keeper of the individual. God deals with us individually. 1. This is implied in his care of the church, which is composed of individuals. 2. It is involved in the nature of our religion, which is a **personal** thing. 3. It is affirmed in Scripture. Examples; promises; experiences. " He loved *me*," etc., etc. 4. It is confirmed by experience. II. The Lord's care is unwearied in its exercise : " Will not slumber." 1. He is never unacquainted with our condition. 2. He is never indifferent to it. 3. He is never weary of helping us. We sometimes think he sleeps, but this is our folly.—*Frederick J. Benskin,* 1882.

Verse 4.—I. The suspicion—that God sleeps. II. The denial. III. The implied opposite—he is ever on the watch to bless.

Verse 4.—He keepeth Israel, 1. As his chief treasure, most watchfully. 2. As his dearest spouse, most tenderly. 3. As the apple of his eye, most charily and warily.—*Daniel Featly,* 1582—1645.

Verse 5.—The Lord Keeper. I. Blessings included in this title. II. Necessities which demand it. III. Offices which imply it,—Shepherd, King, Husband, Father, etc. IV. Conduct suggested by it.

Verse 5 (*last clause*).—God as near us, and as indivisible from us as our shadow.

Verse 5.—"*The* LORD *is thy keeper*," not angels. I. He is *able* to keep thee. He has infinite knowledge, power, etc. II. He has *engaged* to keep thee. III. He *has* kept thee. IV. He *will* keep thee. In his love ; in his covenant, etc., as his sheep, his children, his treasures, as the apple of his eye, etc.—*F. J. B.*

Verse 5.—"*The* LORD *is thy keeper*." I. Wakeful : " Will not slumber." II. Universal : " Thy going out and thy coming in:" " From all evil." III. Perpetual: " Day:" " night:" " evermore." IV. Special: " Thy:" " Israel."—*W. J.*

Verse 6.—The highest powers, under God, prevented from hurting believers, and even made to serve them.

Verse 6.—Our Horoscope. I. Superstitious fears removed. II. Sacred assurances supplied.

Verse 7.—I. Personal agency of God in providence. II. Personal regard of providence to the favoured individual. III. Special care over the centre of the personality—" thy soul."

Verse 8.—Who ? " The Lord." What ? " Shall preserve thee." When ? " Going out and coming in from this time forth." How long ? " For evermore." What then ? " I will lift up mine eyes."

Verse 8.—I. Changing—going out and coming in. II. Unchanging—" The Lord shall preserve," etc.

PSALM CXXII.

TITLE AND SUBJECT.—*This brief but spirited Psalm is entitled " A Song of Degrees of David," and thus we are informed as to its author, and the occasion for which it was designed : David wrote it for the people to sing at the time of their goings up to the holy feasts at Jerusalem. It comes third in the series, and appears to be suitable to be sung when the people had entered the gates, and their feet stood within the city. It was most natural that they should sing of Jerusalem itself, and invoke peace and prosperity upon the Holy City, for it was the centre of their worship, and the place where the Lord revealed himself above the mercy-seat. Possibly the city was not all built in David's day, but he wrote under the spirit of prophecy, and spoke of it as it would be in the age of Solomon : a poet has license to speak of things, not only as they are, but as they will be when they come to their perfection. Jerusalem, or the Habitation of Peace, is used as the key-word of this Psalm, wherein we have in the original many happy allusions to the salem, or peace, which they implored upon Jerusalem. When they stood within the triple walls, all things around the pilgrims helped to explain the words which they sang within her ramparts of strength. One voice led the Psalm with its personal "I," but ten thousand brethren and companions united with the first musician and swelled the chorus of the strain.*

EXPOSITION.

I WAS glad when they said unto me, Let us go into the house of the LORD.

2 Our feet shall stand within thy gates, O Jerusalem.

3 Jerusalem is builded as a city that is compact together :

4 Whither the tribes go up, the tribes of the LORD, unto the testimony of Israel, to give thanks unto the name of the LORD.

5 For there are set thrones of judgment, the thrones of the house of David.

6 Pray for the peace of Jerusalem : they shall prosper that love thee.

7 Peace be within thy walls, *and* prosperity within thy palaces.

8 For my brethren and companions' sakes, I will now say, Peace be within thee.

9 Because of the house of the LORD our God I will seek thy good.

1. *"I was glad when they said unto me, Let us go into the house of the LORD."* Good children are pleased to go home, and glad to hear their brothers and sisters call them thither. David's heart was in the worship of God, and he was delighted when he found others inviting him to go where his desires had already gone : it helps the ardour of the most ardent to hear others inviting them to a holy duty. The word was not " go," but " let us go"; hence the ear of the Psalmist found a double joy in it. He was glad *for the sake of others :* glad that they wished to go themselves, glad that they had the courage and liberality to invite others. He knew that it would do them good ; nothing better can happen to men and their friends than to love the place where God's honour dwelleth. What a glorious day shall that be when many people shall go and say, " Come ye, and let us go up to the mountain of the Lord, to the house of the God of Jacob, and he will teach us of his ways, and we will walk in his paths." But David was glad *for his own sake :* he loved the invitation to the holy place, he delighted in being called to go to worship in company, and, moreover, he rejoiced that good people thought enough of him to extend their invitation to him. Some men would have been offended, and would have said, " Mind your own business. Let my religion alone ; " but not so King David, though he had more dignity than any of us, and less need to be reminded of his duty. He was not teased but pleased by being pressed to attend holy services. He was glad to go into the house of the Lord, glad to go in holy company, glad

to find good men and women willing to have him in their society. He may have been sad before, but this happy suggestion cheered him up : he pricked up his ears, as the proverb puts it, at the very mention of his Father's house. Is it so with us ? Are we glad when others invite us to public worship, or to church fellowship ? Then we shall be glad when the spirits above shall call us to the house of the Lord not made with hands, eternal in the heavens.

> " Hark ! they whisper : angels say,
> Sister spirit, come away."

If we are glad to be called by others to our Father's house, how much more glad shall we be actually to go there. We love our Lord, and therefore we love his house, and pangs of strong desire are upon us that we may soon reach the eternal abode of his glory. An aged saint, when dying, cheered herself with this evidence of grace, for she cried, " I have loved the habitation of thine house, and the place where thine honour dwelleth," and therefore she begged that she might join the holy congregation of those who for ever behold the King in his beauty. Our gladness at the bare thought of being in God's house is detective as to our character, and prophetic of our being one day happy in the Father's house on high. What a sweet Sabbath Psalm is this ! In prospect of the Lord's day, and all its hallowed associations, our soul rejoices. How well, also, may it refer to the church ! We are happy when we see numerous bands ready to unite themselves with the people of God. The pastor is specially glad when many come forward and ask of him assistance in entering into fellowship with the church. No language is more cheering to him than the humble request, " Let us go into the house of the Lord."

2. *"Our feet shall stand within thy gates, O Jerusalem ; "* or, better, " our feet are standing." The words imply present and joyous standing within the walls of the city of peace ; or perhaps the pilgrims felt so sure of getting there that they antedated the joy, and spoke as if they were already there, though they were as yet only on the road. If we are within the church we may well triumph in the fact. While our feet are standing in Jerusalem our lips may well be singing. Outside the gates all is danger, and one day all will be destruction; but within the gates all is safety, seclusion, serenity, salvation, and glory. The gates are opened that we may pass in, and they are only shut that our enemies may not follow us. The Lord loveth the gates of Zion, and so do we when we are enclosed within them. What a choice favour, to be a citizen of the New Jerusalem ! Why are *we* so greatly favoured ? Many feet are running the downward road, or kicking against the pricks, or held by snares, or sliding to an awful fall ; but our feet, through grace divine, are " standing "—an honourable posture, " within thy gates, O Jerusalem "—an honourable position, and there shall they stand for ever—an honourable future.

3. *"Jerusalem is builded as a city that is compact together."* David saw in vision the city built ; no more a waste, or a mere collection of tents, or a city upon paper, commenced but not completed. God's mercy to the Israelitish nation allowed of peace and plenty, sufficient for the uprise and perfecting of its capital : that city flourished in happy times, even as the church is only built up when all the people of God are prospering. Thanks be to God, Jerusalem is builded : the Lord by his glorious appearing has built up Zion. Furthermore, it is not erected as a set of booths, or a conglomeration of hovels, but as a city, substantial, architectural, designed, arranged, and defended. The church is a permanent and important institution, founded on a rock, builded with art, and arranged with wisdom. The city of God had this peculiarity about it, that it was not a long, straggling street, or a city of magnificent distances (as some mere skeleton places have been styled), but the allotted space was filled, the buildings were a solid block, a massive unity : this struck the dwellers in villages, and conveyed to them the idea of close neighbourhood, sure standing, and strong defence. No quarter could be surprised and sacked while other portions of the town were unaware of the assault : the ramparts surrounded every part of the metropolis, which was singularly one and indivisible. There was no flaw in this diamond of the world, this pearl of cities. In a church one of the most delightful conditions is the compactness of unity : " one Lord, one faith, one baptism." A church should be one in creed and one in heart, one in testimony and one in service, one in aspiration and one in sympathy. They greatly injure our Jerusalem who would build dividing walls within her ; she needs compacting, not dividing. There is no joy in going up to a church which is rent with internal dissension : the gladness of holy men is aroused by the adhesiveness

of love, the unity of life ; it would be their sadness if they saw the church to be a house divided against itself. Some bodies of Christians appear to be periodically blown to fragments, and no gracious man is glad to be in the way when the explosions take place : thither the tribes do not go up, for strife and contention are not attractive forces.

4. *"Whither the tribes go up, the tribes of the* LORD*."* When there is unity within there will be gatherings from without : the tribes go up to a compact centre. Note that Israel was one people, but yet it was in a sense divided by the mere surface distinction of tribes ; and this may be a lesson to us that all Christendom is essentially one, though from various causes we are divided into tribes. Let us as much as possible sink the tribal individuality in the national unity, so that the church may be many waves, but one sea ; many branches, but one tree ; many members, but one body. Observe that the tribes were all of them the Lord's ; whether Judah or Benjamin, Manasseh or Ephraim, they were all the Lord's. Oh that all the regiments of the Christian army may be all and equally the Lord's own, alike chosen, redeemed, accepted, and upheld by Jehovah. *"Unto the testimony of Israel."* They went up to the holy city to hear and to bear testimony. Everything in the temple was a testimony unto the Lord, and the annual journeys of the tribes to the hallowed shrine partook of the same testifying character, for these journeys were Israel's open avowal that Jehovah was their God, and that he was the one only living and true God. When we assemble on the Sabbath a large part of our business is giving out and receiving testimony : we are God's witnesses ; all the tribes of the one church of Jesus Christ bear witness unto the Lord. *"To give thanks unto the name of the* LORD*."* Another part of our delightful duty is to praise the Lord. Sacred praise is a chief design of the assembling of ourselves together. All Israel had been fed by the fruit of the field, and they went up to give thanks unto the name of their great Husbandman : we, too, have countless mercies, and it becomes us unitedly in our solemn gatherings to magnify the name of our loving Lord. Testimony should be mingled with thanks, and thanks with testimony, for in combination they bless both God and man, and tend to spread themselves over the hearts of our companions ; who, seeing our joyful gratitude, are the more inclined to hearken to our witness-bearing.

Here, then, was part of the cause of the gladness of the pious Israelite when he had an invitation to join the caravan which was going to Zion : he would there meet with representatives of all the clans of his nation, and aid them in the double object of their holy assemblies, namely, testimony and thanksgiving. The very anticipation of such delightful engagements filled him to overflowing with sacred gladness.

5. *"For there are set thrones of judgment."* If discontented with the petty judgments of their village lords, the people could bring their hard matters to the royal seat, and the beloved King would be sure to decide aright ; for the judgment-thrones were *"The thrones of the house of David."* We who come to the church and its public worship are charmed to come to the throne of God, and to the throne of the reigning Saviour.

> " He reigns ! Ye saints, exalt your strains :
> Your God is King, your Father reigns :
> And he is at the Father's side,
> The Man of love, the Crucified."

To a true saint the throne is never more amiable than in its judicial capacity : righteous men love judgment, and are glad that right will be rewarded and iniquity will be punished. To see God reigning in the Son of David and evermore avenging the just cause is a thing which is good for weeping eyes, and cheering for disconsolate hearts. They sang of old as they went towards the throne, and so do we. " The Lord reigneth, let the earth rejoice." The throne of judgment is not removed, but firmly *"set,"* and there it shall remain till the work of justice is accomplished, and truth and right are set on the throne with their King. Happy people to be under so glorious a rule.

6. *"Pray for the peace of Jerusalem."* Peace was her name, pray that her condition may verify her title. Abode of Peace, peace be to thee. Here was a most sufficient reason for rejoicing at the thought of going up to the house of the Lord, since that sacred shrine stood in the centre of an area of peace : well might Israel pray that such peace should be continued. In a church peace is to be desired,

expected, promoted, and enjoyed. If we may not say " Peace at any price," yet we may certainly cry " Peace at the highest price." Those who are daily fluttered by rude alarms are charmed to reach their nest in a holy fellowship, and abide in it. In a church one of the main ingredients of success is internal peace : strife, suspicion, party-spirit, division,—these are deadly things. Those who break the peace of the church deserve to suffer, and those who sustain it win a great blessing. Peace in the church should be our daily prayer, and in so praying we shall bring down peace upon ourselves ; for the Psalmist goes on to say, "*They shall prosper that love thee.*" Whether the passage be regarded as a promise or as a prayer matters not, for prayer pleads the promise, and the promise is the ground of prayer. Prosperity of soul is already enjoyed by those who take a deep interest in the church and cause of God : they are men of peace, and find peace in their holy endeavours : God's people pray for them, and God himself delights in them. Prosperity of worldly condition often comes to the lovers of the church if they are able to bear it : many a time the house of Obed-edom is blessed because of the ark of the Lord. Because the Egyptian midwives feared the Lord, therefore the Lord made them houses. No man shall ever be a permanent loser by the house of the Lord : in peace of heart alone, if in nothing else, we find recompense enough for all that we can do in promoting the interests of Zion.

7. "*Peace be within thy walls.*" See how the poet personifies the church, and speaks to it ; his heart is with Zion, and therefore his conversation runs in that direction. A second time is the sweet favour of peace earnestly sought after : " There is none like it, give it me." Walls were needed to keep out the foe, but it was asked of the Lord that those walls might prove sufficient for her security. May the munitions of rock so securely defend the city of God that no intruder may ever enter within her enclosure. May her ramparts repose in safety. Three walls environed her, and thus she had a trinity of security. "*And prosperity within thy palaces,*" or " Repose within thy palaces." Peace is prosperity ; there can be no prosperity which is not based on peace, nor can there long be peace if prosperity be gone, for decline of grace breeds decay of love. We wish for the church rest from internal dissension and external assault : war is not her element, but we read of old, " Then had the churches rest ; and walking in the fear of the Lord, and in the comfort of the Holy Ghost, were multiplied." The bird of Paradise is not a stormy petrel : her element is not the hurricane of debate, but the calm of communion.

Observe that our Jerusalem is a city of palaces : kings dwell within her walls, and God himself is there. The smallest church is worthy of higher honour than the greatest confederacies of nobles. The order of the New Jerusalem is of more repute in heaven than the knights of the Golden Fleece. For the sake of all the saintly spirits which inhabit the city of God we may well entreat for her the boons of lasting peace and abounding prosperity.

8. "*For my brethren and companions' sakes, I will now say, Peace be within thee.*" It is to the advantage of all Israel that there should be peace in Jerusalem. It is for the good of every Christian, yea, of every man, that there should be peace and prosperity in the church. Here our humanity and our common philanthropy assist our religious prayer. By a flourishing church our children, our neighbours, our fellow-countrymen are likely to be blest. Moreover, we cannot but pray for a cause with which our dearest relatives and choicest friends are associated : if they labour for it, we must and will pray for it. Here peace is mentioned for the third time. Are not these frequent threes some hint of the Trinity ? It would be hard to believe that the triple form of so many parts of the Old Testament is merely accidental. At least, the repetition of the desire displays the writer's high valuation of the blessing mentioned ; he would not again and again have invoked peace had he not perceived its extreme desirableness.

9. "*Because of the house of the LORD our God I will seek thy good.*" He prays for Jerusalem because of Zion. How the church salts and savours all around it. The presence of Jehovah, our God, endears to us every place wherein he reveals his glory. Well may we seek her good within whose walls there dwells God who alone is good. We are to live for God's cause, and to be ready to die for it. First we love it (verse 6) and then we labour for it, as in this passage : we see its good, and then seek its good. If we can do nothing else we can intercede for it. Our covenant relation to Jehovah as our God binds us to pray for his people,—they are " the house of the Lord our God." If we honour our God we desire the prosperity of the church which he has chosen for his indwelling.

Thus is the poet glad of an invitation to join with others in the Lord's service. He goes with them and rejoices, and then he turns his delight into devotion, and intercedes for the city of the great King. O church of the living God, we hail thine assemblies, and on bended knee we pray that thou mayest have peace and felicity. May our Jehovah so send it. Amen.

EXPLANATORY NOTES AND QUAINT SAYINGS.

Whole Psalm.—Foxe, in his "Acts and Monuments," relates of Wolfgang Schuch, the martyr, of Lothareng in Germany, that upon hearing the sentence that he was to be burned pronounced upon him, he began to sing the hundred and twenty-second Psalm, *Lætus sum in his quæ dicta sunt mihi,* etc.

Whole Psalm.—An introduction of two verses stands instead of a *Title,* announcing the object of the Psalm. The preceding Psalm was intended to be sung in sight of Jerusalem, and this one at the gates of the city, where the pilgrim train had halted for the purpose of arranging the solemn procession to the sanctuary.—*E. W. Hengstenberg.*

Verse 1.—"*I was glad when they said unto me,*" etc. Gregory Nazianzen writeth that his father being a heathen, and often besought by his wife to become a Christian, had this verse suggested unto him in a dream, and was much wrought upon thereby. —*John Trapp.*

Verse 1.—"*I was glad when they said,*" etc. These words seem to be very simple, and to contain in them no great matter ; but if you look into the same with spiritual eyes, there appeareth a wonderful great majesty in them ; which because our Papists cannot see, they do so coldly and negligently pray, read, and sing this Psalm and others, that a man would think there were no tale so foolish or vain, which they would not either recite or hear with more courage and delight. These words, therefore, must be unfolded and laid before the eyes of the faithful : for when he saith, "*We will go into the house of the* LORD," what notable thing can we see in these words, if we only behold the stones, timber, gold, and other ornaments of the material temple ? But to go into the house of the Lord signifieth another manner of thing ; namely, to come together where we may have God present with us, hear his word, call upon his holy name, and receive help and succour in our necessity. Therefore it is a false definition of the temple which the Papists make ; that it is a house built with stones and timber to the honour of God. What this temple is they themselves know not ; for the temple of Solomon was not therefore beautiful because it was adorned with gold and silver, and other precious ornaments ; but the true beauty of the temple was, because in that place the people heard the word of the Lord, called upon his name, found him merciful, giving peace and remission of sins, etc. This is rightly to behold the temple, and not as the visored bishops behold their idolatrous temple when they consecrate it.—*Martin Luther.*

Verse 1.—"*I was glad when they said unto me, Let us* (or, *We will*) *go,*" etc. You have here, I. David's delight. II. The object or reason of it. I. In the object there are circumstances enough to raise his joy to the highest note. First, *A company,* either a tribe or many of, or all, the people : " They said unto me." So, in another place, he speaketh of " walking to the house of God in company : " Ps. lv. 14. A glorious sight, a representation of heaven itself, of all the angels crying aloud, the Seraphim to the Cherubim, and the Cherubim echoing back again to the Seraphim, " Holy, holy, holy, Lord God of Sabaoth." Secondly, *Their resolution* to serve the Lord : *Dixerunt,* " They said it : " and " to say " in Scripture is to resolve. " We will go," is either a lie, or a resolution. Thirdly, *Their agreement* and joint consent : " We." This is as a circle, and taketh in all within its compass. If there be any dissenting, unwilling person, he is not within this circumference, he is none of the " We." A Turk, a Jew, and a Christian cannot say, " We will serve the Lord ; " and the schismatic or separatist shutteth himself out of the house of the Lord. " We " is a bond of peace, keepeth us at unity, and maketh many as one. Fourthly, *Their cheerfulness* and alacrity. They speak like men going out of a dungeon into the light, as those who had been long absent from what they loved, and were now approaching unto it, and in fair hope to enjoy what they most earnestly desired : " We will go ; " we will make haste, and delay no longer. *Ipsa festinatio tarda est ;* " Speed itself is but slow paced." We cannot be, there soon enough. Fifthly and lastly : *The place where they will serve God :* not one of their own choosing ; not the groves, or hills, or high places ; no oratory which pride, or malice, or faction had erected ; but a place appointed and set apart by God himself. *Servient Domino in domo suâ :* " They will serve the Lord in his own house." They said unto me, " We will go into the house of the Lord."—*Anthony Farindon.*

Verse 1.—*"Let us go into the house of the LORD."* *"Let us go,"* spoken by one hundred men in any city to those over whom they have influence, would raise a monster meeting. . . . But who among those who thus single out the working classes, have gone to them and said, " Let us go—let us go together into the house of the Lord " ? The religious adviser, standing at a distance from the multitude, has advised, and warned, and pleaded, saying " Go, or you will not escape perdition ; " " Why don't you go ? " The Christian visitor has likewise used this kind of influence ; but how few have taken the working man by the hand, and said, " Let us go together " ? You can *bring* multitudes whom you never can send. Many who would never come alone would come most willingly under the shadow of your company. Then, brethren, to your non-attending neighbours say, " Let us go "; to reluctant members of your own family say, " Let us go " ; to those who once went to the house of God in your company, but who have backslidden from worship say, " Let us go " ; to all whose ear, and mind, and heart, you can command for such a purpose say, " Let us go—let us go together into the house of the Lord."— *Samuel Martin* (1817—1878), *in a Sermon entitled " Gladness in the Prospect of Public Worship."*

Verse 1.—*"I was glad when they said unto me,"* etc. Such in kind, but far greater in degree, is the gladness, which the pious soul experiences when she is called hence ; when descending angels say unto her, Thy labour and sorrow are at an end, and the hour of thy enlargement is come ; put off immortality and misery at once ; quit thy house of bondage, and the land of thy captivity ; fly forth, and " let us go together into the house of the Lord, not made with hands, eternal in the heavens."—*George Horne.*

Verses 1, 2.—This is a mutual exhortation. The members of the church invite each other : " Let us go into the house of the Lord." It is not enough to say, Go you to church, and I shall stop at home. That will never do. We must invite by example as well as by precept. Mark the plural forms : " Let *us* go into the house of God. *Our* feet shall stand within thy gates, O Jerusalem." We are to speak as Moses did to Hobab, his brother-in-law, " Come thou with us, and we will do thee good ; for the Lord hath spoken good concerning Israel." The same duty is binding upon us, with regard to those who make no profession of religion, and whose feet never stand in the house of God. Zechariah, in an animated picture of the future glories of the church, describes the new-born zeal of the converts as taking this direction. They cannot but speak of what they have seen and heard, and others must share in their joy. " And the inhabitants of one city shall go to another, saying, Let us go speedily to pray before the Lord, and to seek the Lord of hosts : I will go also."—*N. M'Michael.*

Verse 2.—With what a blessed hope do they, while they are here in this mortal life, lift up their affections, desires, and thoughts to the heavenly country, because they are able to say with the prophet, *"Our feet stand within thy gates, O Jerusalem."* Like those who haste to any place, they are said to be always thinking as if they were already there, and in reality they are there in mind though not in body, and are able greatly to comfort others. What wonder, if a righteous man, wishing to comfort others, should thus speak, *"Our feet stand,"* i.e., our desires, our contemplations, shall be fixed and stable in thy courts, O Jerusalem ; i.e., in the mansions of the heavenly kingdom, so that our conversation shall be in heaven, and all our works be done in relation to eternal life, for which we long with greatest intensity of desire. This is not that Jerusalem which killed the prophets and stoned those that were sent unto her, but that where the perfect vision of peace reigns.—*Paulus Palanterius.*

Verse 2.—*"Our feet shall stand within thy gates, O Jerusalem."* Dr. Clarke, in his travels, speaking of the companies that were travelling from the East to Jerusalem, represents the procession as being very long, and, after climbing over the extended and heavy ranges of hills that bounded the way, some of the foremost at length reached the top of the last hill, and, stretching up their hands in gestures of joy, cried out, " The Holy City ! The Holy City ! "—and fell down and worshipped ; while those who were behind pressed forward to see. So the dying Christian, when he gets on the last summit of life, and stretches his vision to catch a glimpse of the heavenly city, may cry out of its glories, and incite those who are behind to press forward to the sight.—*Edward Payson*, 1783—1827.

Verse 2.—*"O Jerusalem."* The celestial city is full in my view. Its glories beam upon me, its breezes fan me, its odours are wafted to me, its sounds strike upon my ears, and its spirit is breathed into my heart. Nothing separates me from it but the river of death, which now appears but as an insignificant rill, that may be crossed at a single step, whenever God shall give permission. The Sun of Righteousness has been gradually drawing nearer and nearer, appearing larger and brighter as he approached, and now he fills the whole hemisphere ; pouring forth a flood of glory, in which I seem to float like an insect in the beams of the sun ; exulting, yet almost trembling, while I gaze on this excessive brightness, and wondering, with unutterable wonder, why God should deign thus to shine upon a sinful worm.—*Edward Payson's dying experience.*

Verse 2.—*"O Jerusalem"*—

> Lo, towered Jerusalem salutes the eyes !
> A thousand pointing fingers tell the tale ;
> " Jerusalem ! " a thousand voices cry,
> " All hail, Jerusalem ! " hill, down, and dale
> Catch the glad sounds, and shout " Jerusalem, all hail."

> *Torquato Tasso*, 1544—1595.

Verse 3.—*"Jerusalem is builded as a city that is compact together."* The deep depressions which secured the city must have always acted as its natural defence. But they also determined its natural boundaries. The city, wherever else it spread, could never overleap the valley of the Kedron or of Hinnom ; and those two fosses, so to speak, became accordingly, as in the analogous case of the ancient towns of Etruria, the Necropolis of Jerusalem. . . . The compression between these valleys probably occasioned the words of the Psalmist : *"Jerusalem is built as a city that is at unity in itself."* It is an expression not inapplicable even to the modern city, as seen from the east. But it was still more appropriate to the original city, if, as seems probable, the valley of Tyropœon formed in earlier times a fosse within a fosse, shutting in Zion and Moriah into one compact mass not more than half a mile in breadth.—*Arthur Penrhyn Stanley* (1815—1881), *in "Sinai and Palestine."*

Verse 3.—*"Jerusalem."* It matters not how wicked or degraded a place may have been in former times, when it is sanctified to the use and service of God it becomes honourable. Jerusalem was formerly Jebus—a place where the Jebusites committed their abominations, and where were all the miseries of those who hasten after another God. But now, since it is devoted to God's service, it is a city—*"compact together," "the joy of the whole earth."*—*William S. Plumer.*

Verse 3.—*"Compact."* Jerusalem was compactly built ; every rood of ground, every foot of frontage, was valuable ; house was joined to house ; those who had gardens had them beyond the city walls, among the " paradises " of the valley of Jehoshaphat.—*Samuel Cox.*

Verse 3.—*"Compact together."* Methinks Philadelphia, the name of one of the seven golden candlesticks (Rev. i.), is a very proper fitting name for a church, which signifies brotherly love ; and every congregation ought to be in a good sense the family of love. Breaches and divisions, distractions and heart-burnings, may happen in other kingdoms which are without God in the world and strangers to the covenant of grace ; yet let Jerusalem, the Church of God, be always like a city which is at unity within itself.—*John Pigot*, 1643.

Verse 3.—*"As a city that is compact together."* Can we say of the great universal church throughout the world, what the pilgrims said of Jerusalem when gazing on its splendour, from the surrounding hills, that it is built *"as a city that is compact together "* ? A stately capital, throned on a base of rock, its spacious streets and noble edifices, beautiful in themselves, deriving added splendour from the taste and regularity of their arrangement, appears, both to the scoffing unbeliever and grieving Christian, a singularly inappropriate emblem of the divided and distracted, the jarring and warring church. If the church may be compared to a city in respect of magnitude, it is one in which every one builds on his own plan ; in which the various masses which should embellish and support each other are studiously kept apart, suggesting less the idea of a compact and united capital than of detached and isolated forts, held by persons who keep themselves jealously aloof from each other, save when mutual hatred and heart-burnings bring them together for conflict. There is some truth in the picture ; alas ! for the proud, foolish builders who give occasion to it, and who, instead of praying for and seeking the peace of Jerusalem, rejoice in exhibiting, perpetuating, and fomenting strife ! But, blessed be God, there is yet more of falsehood than truth in it. With all our divisions the Christian Jerusalem *is compact in itself together.* What occupies the hearts and tongues of the myriads of worshippers that assemble themselves weekly in the sanctuaries of our beloved land, and of the millions that assemble beyond the Atlantic billows, but the one glorious gospel of the grace of God ? Leave out from the computation the priest with his mass-book, the cold Socinian without his Saviour, and the deluded orthodox professor who holds the truth in unrighteousness ; still yonder and yonder and yonder, whatever their name, their place, or their outward worship, are myriads of true hearts, beating with one pulse, gazing on one hope, possessed of one conviction, and praying and pressing forward to one blessed home.—*Robert Nisbet.*

Verses 3, 4.—He commendeth Jerusalem, the figure of the church of God and of the corporation of his people. First, as a city for a community. Secondly, as the place of God's public assemblies for religious worship. Thirdly, as the place of public judicature, for governing the Lord's people under David, the type of Christ. Wh nce learn, 1. The church of God is not without cause compared to a city, and especially to Jerusalem, because of the union, concord, community of laws, mutual commodities, and conjunction of strength which should be among God's people : *"Jerusalem is builded as a city that is compact together."* 2. That which commendeth a place most of anything is the erecting of the Lord's banner of love in it, and making it a place for his people to meet together for his worship : *"Jerusalem is a city whither the tribes go up."* 3. Whatsoever civil distinction God's children have among themselves, and howsoever they dwell scattered in several places of the earth, yet as they are the Lord's people, they should entertain a communion and conjunction among themselves as members of one universal church, as the signification of the peoples meeting thrice in the year at Jerusalem did reach : *"Whither the tribes did go up, the tribes of the Lord."* 4. As the tribes, so all particular churches, how far soever scattered, have one Lord, one covenant, one law and Scripture, signified by the tribes going up to *" the testimony of Israel,"* or to the Ark of the Covenant or testimony where the whole ordinances of God were to be exercised. 5. The end of the ordinances of God, of holy covenanting and communion, and joining in public worship, is to acknowledge the grace and goodness of God, and to glorify him ; for the tribes did go up *" to give thanks unto the name of the Lord."*—*David Dickson.*

Verse 4.—"*The tribes* " are " the tribes of the Lord," as being the keepers of his commandments.—*H. T. Armfield.*

Verse 4.—"*Unto the testimony of Israel, and to give thanks unto the name of the Lord.*" These two mean nothing else than that in Jerusalem was the appointed place where the word was to be taught and prayer offered. But these ought to be written in golden letters, because David says nothing about the other services, but only of these two. He does not say that the Temple was divinely appointed, that there the victims should be sacrificed ; that there incense should be offered ; that oblations and sacrifices should be brought ; that each one should by his gifts show his gratitude. He says nothing about these things, although only in the Temple were they commanded to be done. He makes mention only of prayer and of thanksgiving.—*Martin Luther.*

Verse 4.—"*The testimony of Israel.*" The object which is represented in the Psalm as having power to attract all hearts, and command the ready attendance of the tribes, is *" the testimony of Israel,"* the revelation, in other words, which God made to that people of his character, feelings, and purposes, as most holy, yet ready to forgive, a just God and the Saviour. This discovery of the nature of that great Being before whom all must appear, is justly regarded as a ground of joy.—*Robert Nisbet.*

Verses 4, 5.—Observe what a goodly sight it was to see *"the testimony of Israel"* and the *"thrones of judgment"* such near neighbours ; and they are good neighbours, which may greatly befriend one another. Let *"the testimony of Israel"* direct the *"thrones of judgment,"* and the *"thrones of judgment"* protect *"the testimony of Israel."* —*Matthew Henry.*

Verse 5.—*"Thrones of judgment."* On a throne of ivory, brought from Africa or India, the throne of many an Arabian legend, the kings of Judah were solemnly seated on the day of their accession. From its lofty seat, and under that high gateway, Solomon and his successors after him delivered their solemn judgments. That " porch " or " gate of justice," still kept alive the likeness of the old patriarchal custom of sitting in judgment at the gate ; exactly as the Gate of Justice still recalls it to us at Granada, and the Sublime Porte—" the Lofty Gate " at Constantinople. He sate on the back of a golden bull, its head turned over its shoulder, probably the ox or bull of Ephraim ; under his feet, on each side of the steps, were six golden lions, probably the lions of Judah. This was " the seat of judgment." This was the throne of the house of David.—*Arthur Penrhyn Stanley, in "Lectures on the History of the Jewish Church."*

Verse 5.—It was a worthy commendation that David uttered in the praise of Jerusalem when he said, *"There is the seat for judgment ; "* the which appointing of that seat for judgment was an argument that they loved justice. And first, the place wherein it was set assureth us hereof, for it was set in the gate, where-through men might have passage to and from the judgment seat. Secondly, the manner of framing the seat in the gate, namely, that the judges of force must sit with their faces towards the rising of the sun, in token that then judgment should be as pure from corruption, as the sun was clear in his chiefest brightness. Oh happy house of David, whose seat was set so conveniently, whose causes were heard so carefully, and matters judged so justly !—*Henry Smith, 1560—1591.*

Verse 6.—*"Pray for the peace of Jerusalem."* By praying for Jerusalem's peace is meant such serene times wherein the people of God might enjoy his pure worship without disturbance. The Church has always had her vicissitudes, sometimes fair, and sometimes foul weather ; but her winter commonly longer than her summer ; yea, at the same time that the Sun of peace brings day to one part of it, another is wrapped up in the night of persecution. Universal peace over all the churches is a great rarity.—*William Gurnall.*

Verse 6.—*"Pray for the peace of Jerusalem."* When the Wesleyan Methodists opened a chapel at Painswick, near his own meeting, the late excellent Cornelius Winter prayed three times publicly the preceding Sabbath for their encouragement and success. When Mr. Hoskins, of Bristol, the Independent minister of Castle-green, opened a meeting in Temple Street ; what did the incomparable Easterbrooke, the Vicar of the parish ? The morning it was opened, he was almost the first that entered it. He seated himself near the pulpit. When the service was over, he met the preacher at the foot of the stairs, and shaking him with both hands, said aloud : " I thank you cordially, my dear brother, for coming to my help—here is room enough for us both ; and work enough for us both ; and much more than we can both accomplish : and I hope the Lord will bless our co-operation in this good cause."—*William Jay.*

Verse 6.—*"Pray* (with this princely prophet) *for the peace of Jerusalem."* I wish I could express the incomparable sweetness of this little *hemistichium.* I guess, the Holy Ghost was pleased to let the Psalmist play the poet here : the Psalms are holy poetry. The original words have such elegancy here, as (I think) all the Scripture cannot parallel this verse. It is in English unexpressible. For the point in hand only, he bids us pray for the peace of *Jerusalem.* Peace denominates *Jerusalem,* 'tis the etymon of the word, it means *the vision of peace.* David by that term most sweetly alludes to the name of the city, yet conceals his wit ; which could have been made more open : he said, שַׁאֲלוּ שְׁלוֹם שָׁלֵם, *"Pray for the peace of Salem."* For so it was called too, called first so, called still so (Ps. lxxvi.) : " At Salem is his tabernacle." That word merely sounds *peace :* God would have his Church the house of peace ; and his temple there David might not build because he was a man of war ; but Solomon his son, who had his name of peace, must build it. Christ, whose the church is, she his spouse, would not be born in Julius Cæsar's reign ; he was a warrior too : but in Augustus's days, who reigned in peace. And this may be a reason too, if you please, why David bids pray but for peace only, an earthly blessing. That word most fitted his art here, and sounded best. But under that word, by poetical *synecdoche*, lie couched all heavenly blessings.—*Richard Clerke*, 1634.

Verse 6.—*"Pray,"* etc. Our praying for the church giveth us a share in all the church's prayers ; we have a venture in every ship of prayer that maketh a voyage for heaven, if our hearts be willing to pray for the church ; and if not, we have no share in it.

Let no man flatter himself : they that *pray not* for the church of God *love not* the church of God. *"Let them prosper that love thee"* ; that is, that *pray* for thee, the one is the counterpart of the other. If we do not love it, we will not pray for it ; and if we do not pray for it, we do not love it. Yea, if we pray not for the church, *we lose* our share in the prayers of the church. You will say that man hath a great estate that hath a part in every ship at sea ; and yet to have an adventure in all the prayers that are made to heaven is better than all the world. All the church's prayers are for all the living members of it, viz.—the blessings will be to them, for a man to have a venture in every ship of prayer of all the churches throughout all the world. I would not (for my part) leave my share in it for all the world ; and that man hath no share in it that will not afford a prayer for the church.—*John Stoughton*, 1640.

Verse 6.—*"They shall prosper that love thee."* The word *"prosper"* conveys an idea which is not in the original. The Hebrew word means *to be secure, tranquil, at rest,* spoken especially of one who enjoys quiet prosperity : Job iii. 26 ; xii. 6. The essential idea is that of quietness or rest ; and the meaning here is, that those who love Zion *will* have peace ; or, that the tendency of that love is to produce peace. See Rom. v. 1. The prayer was for " peace " ; the thought in connexion with that was naturally that those who loved Zion *would* have peace. It is indeed true, in general, that they who love Zion, or who serve God, *will* " prosper " ; but that is not the truth taught here. The idea is that they will have *peace :*—peace with God ; peace in their own consciences ; peace in the prospect of death and of the future world ; peace amidst the storms and tempests of life ; peace in death, in the grave, and for ever.—*Albert Barnes.*

Verse 6.—*"They shall prosper that love thee."* Seeing they prosper that love and bear affection to Jerusalem, let men learn to show good will unto Christ's church, though as yet they be no ripe scholars themselves in Christ's school : though they be not grown to perfection let them express a good affection. A good will and inclination, where strength yet faileth, is accepted, and a ready disposition is not rejected : though thou be not yet of the saints, yet love the saints. If thou likest and lovest that thou wouldst be, thou must be that hereafter which yet thou art not. The little bird before she flieth fluttereth with her wings in the nest : the child creepeth before he goeth : so religion beginneth with affection, and devotion proceedeth from desire. A man must first love that he would be, before he can be that which he loveth. It is a good sign when a man affecteth that which he expecteth, and doth favour that which he would more fully favour. He that loveth Sion shall prosper : he that loveth virtue shall increase and prosper in it. The day of small things shall not be despised (Zech. iv. 10), neither shall the smoking flax be quenched (Matt. xii. 20) ; but the smoke shall bring forth fire, and fire shall break forth into a flame.—*Andrew Willett* (1562—1621), *in "Certaine Fruitfull Meditations upon the 122. Psalme."*

Verse 6.—*"They shall prosper that love thee."* The reverse is also true. " None ever took a stone out of the Temple, but the dust did fly into his eyes."—*Jewish Proverb.*

Verses 6—9.—In this cordial and even impassioned invocation, it is curious to find one of those puns, or plays on words, which are characteristic of Hebrew poetry. The leading words of the strophe are *"peace"* and *"prosperity."* Now the Hebrew word for *"peace"* is shâlōm, and the Hebrew word for *"prosperity"* is shalvah, while the Hebrew form of " Jerusalem," which means " City of Peace," is Yeru-*shalaim.* So that, in effect, the poet wishes shâlōm and shalvah on shalaim—" peace " and " prosperity " on " the City of Peace." Such an use of words may not strike us as indicating any very subtle or profound sense of humour, or any remarkable artistic skill. But we must always remember that it is always difficult for one race to appreciate the humour, or wit, of another race. We must also remember that this art of playing on words and the sound of words—an art of which we are growing weary—was very novel and surprising to men not surfeited with it as we are, and who were themselves for the most part quite incapable of the simplest dexterities of speech.—*Samuel Cox*

Verse 7.—"Peace be within thy walls." The Church is a war-town, and a walled-town, which is situated among enemies, and may not trust them who are without, but must be upon its keeping, as the type thereof, Jerusalem, with her walls and towers, did shadow forth.—*David Dickson.*

Verse 7.—"Within thy walls." Or, *To thy outward wall.* Josephus tells us (Book V.) that there were at Jerusalem three ranges or rows of walls. The sense here is, Let no enemy approach so much as to thy out-works to disturb thee.—*Thomas Fenton.*

Verse 8.—"For my brethren and companions' sakes." Because they dwell there or, because they go up there to worship ; or, because they love thee, and find their happiness in thee ; or, because they are unconverted, and all my hope of their salvation is to be derived from thee,—from the church, from the influence of religion.—*Albert Barnes.*

Verse 8.—"My brethren." On another occasion, an elderly native, formerly a cannibal, addressing the Church members, said, " Brethren ! " and, pausing for a moment, continued, " Ah ! that is a new name ; we did not know the true meaning of that word in our heathenism. It is the ' Evangelia a Jesu ' that has taught us the meaning of ' brethren.' "—*William Gill, in "Gems from the Coral Islands,"* 1869.

Verse 9.—"Because of the house of the Lord." The city that was the scene of so immense assemblies had necessarily a peculiar character of its own. It existed for them, it lived by them. There were priests needed for the conduct of the worship, twenty-four courses of them and 20,000 men. There were Levites, their servants, in immense numbers, needed to watch, maintain, clean the temple—to do the menial and ministering work necessary to its elaborate service and stupendous acts of worship. There were scribes needed for the interpretation of the law, men skilled in the Scriptures and tradition, with names like Gamaliel, so famed for wisdom as to draw young men like Saul from distant Tarsus, or Apollos from rich Alexandria. There were synagogues, 480 of them at least, where the rabbis read and the people heard the word which God had in past times spoken unto the fathers by the prophets. The city was indeed in a sense the religion of Israel, incorporated and localized, and the man who loved the one turned daily his face toward the other, saying, " My soul longeth, yea, even fainteth for the courts of Jahveh."—*A. M. Fairbairn, in "Studies in the Life of Christ,"* 1881.

Verse 9.—"I will seek thy good." It is not a cold wish ; it is not a careless, loose seeking after it, that is the phrase in my text—*"I will seek thy good."* It is not a careless, loose seeking after it, almost as indifferently as a woman seeks after a pin which she has dropped ; no, no ; effort is implied. *"I will seek"* ; I will throw my energies into it ; my powers, my faculties, my property, my time, my influence, my connections, my family, my house, all that I have under my command shall, as far as I have power to command, and as far as God gives me ability to turn them to such a use, be employed in an effort to promote the interests of Zion.—*Joseph Irons,* 1786—1852.

HINTS TO PREACHERS.

Whole Psalm.—Observe, I. The joy with which they were to go up to Jerusalem : verses 1, 2. II. The great esteem they were to have of Jerusalem : verses 3—5. III. The great concern they were to have for Jerusalem, and the prayers they were to put up for its welfare.—*M. Henry.*

Verse 1.—I. David was glad to go to the house of the Lord. It was the house of the Lord, therefore he desired to go. He preferred it to his own house. II. He was glad when others said to him, " Let us go." The distance may be great, the weather may be rough, still, " Let us go." III. He was glad to say it to others, " Let us go," and to persuade others to accompany him.—*G. R.*

Verse 1.—I. Joy in prospect of religious worship. 1. Because of the instruction we receive. 2. Because of the exercises in which we engage. 3. Because of the society in which we mingle. 4. Because of the sacred interests we promote. II. Joy in the invitation to religious worship. 1. Because it shows others are interested in the service of God. 2. Because it shows their interest in us. 3. Because it furthers the interests of Zion.—*F. J. B.*

Verse 1.—Gladness of God's house. Are you " glad when," etc. ? Why glad ? I. That I have a house of the Lord to which I may go. II. That any feel enough interest in me to say, " Let us go," etc. III. That I am able to go to God's house. IV. That I am disposed to go.—*J. G. Butler, in "The Preacher's Monthly,"* 1882.

Verse 1.—"*I was glad,*" etc. So says, I. *The devout worshipper,* who is glad to be invited *to God's earthly house.* It is his home, his school, his hospital, his bank. II. *The adhesive Christian, who is glad to be invited to God's spiritual house.* Church is builded together, etc. There would he find a settled rest. Has no sympathies with religious gipsies, or no-church people. III. *The dying saint, who is glad to be invited to God's heavenly house.* Simeon—Stephen—Peter—Paul.—*W. J.*

Verse 1.—1. The duty of attending the services of God's house. 2. The duty of exciting one another to go. 3. The benefit of being thus excited.—*F. J. B.*

Verse 2. — Here is, I. Personal attendance : "*My* feet shall stand," etc. II. Personal security : " My feet shall *stand.*" III. Personal fellowship : " O Jerusalem."—*G. R.*

Verse 2.—The inside of the church. The honour, privilege, joy, and fellowship of standing there.

Verse 3. — I. A type of the New Jerusalem. 1. As chosen by God. 2. As founded upon a rock. 3. As taken from an enemy. II. A type of its prosperity : " Builded as a city." III. A type of its perfection : " Compact together."—*G. R.*

Verse 3.—The unity of the church. 1. Implied in all covenant dealings. 2. Suggested by all Scriptural metaphors. 3. Prayed for by our Lord. 4. Promoted by the gifts of the Spirit. 5. To be maintained by us all.

Verses 3, 4.—The united church the growing church.

Verse 4.—I. The duty of public worship. 1. In one place : "*Whither* the tribes go up." 2. In one company, though of many tribes : " Whither the *tribes* go up." II. The design. 1. For instruction : " Unto the testimony of Israel." 2. For praise : " To give thanks unto the name of the Lord."—*G. R.*

Verse 5.—I. There are thrones of judgment in the sanctuary. Men are judged there. 1. By the law. 2. By their own consciences. 3. By the gospel. II. There are thrones of grace : " Of the house of David." 1. Of David's Son in the hearts of his people. 2. Of his people in David's Son.—*G. R.*

Verse 6.—I. The prayer. 1. " For Jerusalem : " not for ourselves merely, or for the world ; but for the church. For the babes in grace ; for the young men, and for the fathers. For the pastors, with the deacons and elders. 2. For the " peace " of Jerusalem. Inward peace and outward peace. II. The promise. 1. To whom given : " They that love thee." 2. The promise itself : " They shall prosper "—individually and collectively. Or, I. Love to Jerusalem is the effect of true piety. II. Prayer for Jerusalem is the effect of that love. III. The peace of Jerusalem is the effect of that prayer ; and, IV. The prosperity of Jerusalem is the effect of that peace.—*G. R.*

Verse 6.—God has connected giving and receiving, scattering and increasing, sowing and reaping, praying and prospering. I. What we must do if we would prosper—" Pray for the peace of Jerusalem." 1. Comprehensively : " Peace "—spiritual, social, ecclesiastical, national. 2. Supremely : " Prefer Jerusalem above," etc. 3. Practically : " Let peace rule in your hearts." " Seek peace and pursue it." II. What we shall gain if we pray thus—" Prosperity." 1. Temporal prosperity may thus come. God turned again the captivity of Job when he prayed for his friends. 2. Spiritual prosperity shall thus come. Affairs of soul—holy exercises and services. 3. Numerical prosperity will thus come. " Increased with men as a flock."—*W. J.*

Verses 6—9.—I. The blessings desired for the church. 1. Peace. 2. Prosperity. Notice the order and connection of these two. II. The way to secure them. 1. Prayer : " Pray for the peace of Jerusalem." 2. Delight in the service of God : " I was glad," etc. 3. Practical effort : " I will seek thy good." III. Reasons for seeking them. 1. For our own sake : " They shall prosper," etc. 2. For our " companions' " sake. 3. For the sake of the " house of the Lord."—*F. J. B.*

Verse 7.—I. Where peace is most desirable : "Within thy walls." Within town walls, within house walls, but principally within temple walls. II. Where prosperity is most desirable. 1. In the closet. 2. In the church. These are the palaces of the Great King ; "The ivory palaces whereby they have made thee glad."—*G. R.*

Verse 7.—The connection between peace and prosperity.

Verse 7.—"*Thy walls.*" 1. Enquire why the church needs walls. 2. Enquire what are the walls of a church. 3. Enquire on which side of them we are.

Verse 7.—The church a palace. 1. Intended for the great King. 2. Inhabited by the royal family. 3. Adorned with regal splendour. 4. Guarded by special power. 5. Known as the court of the blessed and only potentate.

Verses 8, 9.—Two great principles are here laid down why we should pray for the church,—I. Love to the brethren : " For my brethren and companions' sakes." II. Love to God : " Because of the house of the Lord our God I will seek thy good."—*N. M'Michael.*

Verse 9.—"*I will seek thy good.*" 1. By prayer for the church. 2. By service in the church. 3. By bringing others to attend. 4. By keeping the peace. 5. By living so as to commend religion.

PSALM CXXIII.

TITLE.—A Song of degrees. *We are climbing.* The first step (Ps. cxx.) saw us *lamenting our troublesome surroundings, and the next saw us lifting our eyes to the hills and resting in assured security ; from this we rose to delight in the house of the Lord ; but here we look to the Lord himself, and this is the highest ascent of all by many degrees.* The eyes are now looking above the hills, and above Jehovah's footstool on *earth, to his throne in the heavens.* Let us know it as " the Psalm of the eyes." *Old authors call it* Oculus Sperans, *or the eye of hope.* It is a short Psalm, written with *singular art, containing one thought, and expressing it in a most engaging manner. Doubtless it would be a favourite song among the people of God.* It has been conjectured *that this brief song, or rather sigh, may have first been heard in the days of Nehemiah, or under the persecutions of Antiochus.* It may be so, but there is no evidence of it ; *it seems to us quite as probable that afflicted ones in all periods after David's time found this Psalm ready to their hand.* If it appears to describe days remote from David, it *is all the more evident that the Psalmist was also a prophet, and sang what he saw in vision.*

UNTO thee will I lift up mine eyes, O thou that dwellest in the heavens.

2 Behold, as the eyes of servants *look* unto the hand of their masters, *and* as the eyes of a maiden unto the hand of her mistress ; so our eyes *wait* upon the LORD our God, until that he have mercy upon us.

3 Have mercy upon us, O LORD, have mercy upon us : for we are exceedingly filled with contempt.

4 Our soul is exceedingly filled with the scorning of those that are at ease, *and* with the contempt of the proud.

EXPOSITION.

1. *"Unto thee lift I up mine eyes."* It is good to have some one to look up to. The Psalmist looked so high that he could look no higher. Not to the hills, but to the God of the hills he looked. He believed in a personal God, and knew nothing of that modern pantheism which is nothing more than atheism wearing a figleaf. The uplifted eyes naturally and instinctively represent the state of heart which fixes desire, hope, confidence, and expectation upon the Lord. God is everywhere, and yet it is most natural to think of him as being above us, in that glory-land which lies beyond the skies. *"O thou that dwellest in the heavens,"* just sets forth the unsophisticated idea of a child of God in distress ; God is, God is in heaven, God resides in one place, and God is evermore the same, therefore will I look to him. When we cannot look to any helper on a level with us it is greatly wise to look above us ; in fact, if we have a thousand helpers, our eyes should still be toward the Lord. The higher the Lord is the better for our faith, since that height represents power, glory, and excellence, and these will be all engaged on our behalf. We ought to be very thankful for spiritual eyes ; the blind men of this world, however much of human learning they may possess, cannot behold our God, for in heavenly matters they are devoid of sight. Yet we must use our eyes with resolution, for they will not go upward to the Lord of themselves, but they incline to look downward, or inward, or anywhere but to the Lord : let it be our firm resolve that the heavenward glance shall not be lacking. If we cannot see God, at least we will look towards him. God is in heaven as a king in his palace ; he is there revealed, adored, and glorified : thence he looks down on the world and sends succours to his saints as their needs demand ; hence we look up, even when our sorrow is so great that we can do no

more. It is a blessed condescension on God's part that he permits us to lift up our eyes to his glorious high throne ; yea, more, that he invites and even commands us so to do. When we are looking to the Lord in hope, it is well to tell him so in prayer : the Psalmist uses his voice as well as his eye. We need not speak in prayer : a glance of the eye will do it all ; for—

> " Prayer is the burden of a sigh,
> The falling of a tear,
> The upward glancing of an eye
> When none but God is near."

Still, it is helpful to the heart to use the tongue, and we do well to address ourselves in words and sentences to the God who heareth his people. It is no small joy that our God is always at home : he is not on a journey, like Baal, but he dwells in the heavens. Let us think no hour of the day inopportune for waiting upon the Lord ; no watch of the night too dark for us to look to him.

2. *"Behold"*—for it is worthy of regard among men, and O that the Majesty of heaven would also note it, and speedily send the mercy which our waiting spirits seek. See, O Lord, how we look to thee, and in thy mercy look on us. This *Behold* has, however, a call to us to observe and consider. Whenever saints of God have waited upon the Lord their example has been worthy of earnest consideration. Sanctification is a miracle of grace ; therefore let us behold it. For God to have wrought in men the spirit of service is a great marvel, and as such let all men turn aside and see this great sight. *"As the eyes of servants* (or slaves) *look unto the hand of their masters."* They stand at the end of the room with their hands folded watching their lord's movements. Orientals speak less than we do, and prefer to direct their slaves by movements of their hands ; hence, the domestic must fix his eyes on his master, or he might miss a sign, and so fail to obey it : even so, the sanctified man lifts his eyes unto God, and endeavours to learn the divine will from every one of the signs which the Lord is pleased to use. Creation, providence, grace ; these are all motions of Jehovah's hand, and from each of them a portion of our duty is to be learned ; therefore should we carefully study them, to discover the divine will. *"And as the eyes of a maiden unto the hand of her mistress ; "* this second comparison may be used because Eastern women are even more thorough than the men in the training of their servants. It is usually thought that women issue more commands, and are more sensitive of disobedience, than the sterner sex. Among the Roman matrons female slaves had a sorry time of it, and no doubt it was the same among the generality of Eastern ladies. *"Even so our eyes wait upon the* LORD *our God."* Believers desire to be attentive to each and all of the directions of the Lord ; even those which concern apparently little things are not little to us, for we know that even for idle words we shall be called to account, and we are anxious to give in that account with joy, and not with grief. True saints, like obedient servants, look to the Lord their God *reverentially :* they have a holy awe and inward fear of the great and glorious One. They watch, *obediently,* doing his commandments, guided by his eye. Their constant gaze is fixed *attentively* on all that comes from the Most High ; they give earnest heed, and fear lest they should let anything slip through inadvertence or drowsiness. They look *continuously,* for there never is a time when they are off duty ; at all times they delight to serve in all things. Upon the Lord they fix their eyes *expectantly,* looking for supply, succour, and safety from his hands, waiting that he may have mercy upon them. To him they look *singly,* they have no other confidence, and they learn to look *submissively,* waiting patiently for the Lord, seeking both in activity and suffering to glorify his name. When they are smitten with the rod they turn their eyes *imploringly* to the hand which chastens, hoping that mercy will soon abate the rigour of the affliction. There is much more in the figure than we can display in this brief comment ; perhaps it will be most profitable to suggest the question—Are we thus trained to service ? Though we are sons, have we learned the full obedience of servants ? Have we surrendered self, and bowed our will before the heavenly Majesty ? Do we desire in all things to be at the Lord's disposal ? If so, happy are we. Though we are made joint-heirs with Christ, yet for the present we differ little from servants, and may be well content to take them for our model.

Observe the covenant name, *"Jehovah our God" :* it is sweet to wait upon a covenant God. Because of that covenant he will show mercy to us ; but we may have to wait for it. *"Until that he have mercy upon us : "* God hath his time and season, and we must wait *until* it cometh. For the trial of our faith our blessed Lord may for awhile delay, but in the end the vision will be fulfilled. Mercy is that which we need, that which we look for, that which our Lord will manifest to us. Even those who look to the Lord, with that holy look which is here described, still need mercy, and as they cannot claim it by right they wait for it till sovereign grace chooses to vouchsafe it. Blessed are those servants whom their Master shall find so doing. Waiting upon the Lord is a posture suitable both for earth and heaven : it is, indeed, in every place the right and fitting condition for a servant of the Lord. Nor may we leave the posture so long as we are by grace dwellers in the realm of mercy. It is a great mercy to be enabled to wait for mercy.

3. *"Have mercy upon us, O LORD, have mercy upon us."* He hangs upon the word " mercy," and embodies it in a vehement prayer : the very word seems to hold him, and he harps upon it. It is well for us to pray about everything, and turn everything into prayer ; and especially when we are reminded of a great necessity we should catch at it as a keynote, and pitch our tune to it. The reduplication of the prayer before us is meant to express the eagerness of the Psalmist's spirit and his urgent need : what he needed speedily he begs for importunately. Note that he has left the first person singular for the plural. All the saints need mercy ; they all seek it ; they shall all have it, therefore we pray—" have mercy upon *us*." A slave when corrected looks to his master's hand that the punishment may cease, and even so we look to the Lord for mercy, and entreat for it with all our hearts. Our contemptuous opponents will have no mercy upon us ; let us not ask it at their hands, but turn to the God of mercy, and seek his aid alone.

"For we are exceedingly filled with contempt," and this is an acid which eats into the soul. Observe the emphatic words. *Contempt* is bitterness, wormwood mingled with gall ; he that feels it may well cry for mercy to his God. *Filled* with contempt, as if the bitter wine had been poured in till it was up to the brim. This had become the chief thought of their minds, the peculiar sorrow of their hearts. Excluding all other feelings, a sense of scorn monopolized the soul and made it unutterably wretched. Another word is added adverbially—*exceedingly* filled. Filled even to running over, as if pressed down and then heaped up. A little contempt they could bear, but now they were satiated with it, and weary of it. Do we wonder at the threefold mention of mercy when this master evil was in the ascendant ? Nothing is more wounding, embittering, festering than disdain. When our companions make little of us we are far too apt to make little of ourselves and of the consolations prepared for us. Oh to be filled with communion, and then contempt will run off from us, and never be able to fill us with its biting vinegar.

4. *"Our soul is exceedingly filled with the scorning of those that are at ease."* Knowing no troubles of their own, the easy ones grow cruel and deride the people of the Lord. Having the godly already in secret contempt, they show it by openly scorning them. Note those who do this : they are not the poor, the humble, the troubled, but those who have a merry life of it. and are self-content. They are in easy circumstances ; they are easy in heart through a deadened conscience and so they easily come to mock at holiness ; they are easy from needing nothing, and from having no severe toil exacted from them ; they are easy as to any anxiety to improve, for their conceit of themselves is boundless. Such men take things easily, and therefore they scorn the holy carefulness of those who watch the hand of the Lord. They say, Who is the Lord that we should obey his voice ? and then they turn round with a contemptuous look and sneer at those who fear the Lord. Woe unto them that are at ease in Zion ; their contempt of the godly shall hasten and increase their misery. The injurious effect of freedom from affliction is singularly evident here. Place a man perfectly at ease and he derides the suffering godly, and becomes himself proud in heart and conduct. *"And with the contempt of the proud."* The proud think so much of themselves that they must needs think all the less of those who are better than themselves. Pride is both contemptible and contemptuous. The contempt of the great ones of the earth is often peculiarly acrid : some of them, like a well-known statesman, are " masters of gibes and flouts and sneers," and never do they seem so much at home in their acrimony as when a servant of the Lord is the victim of their venom. It is easy enough to write upon this subject, but to be selected as the target of contempt is quite another matter. Great hearts have been broken and brave spirits have been withered beneath the accursed power of falsehood, and the horrible blight of contempt. For our comfort we may remember that our divine Lord was despised and rejected of men, yet he ceased not from his perfect service

till he was exalted to dwell in the heavens. Let us bear our share of this evil which still rages under the sun, and let us firmly believe that the contempt of the ungodly shall turn to our honour in the world to come : even now it serves as a certificate that we are not of the world, for if we were of the world the world would love us as its own.

EXPLANATORY NOTES AND QUAINT SAYINGS.

Whole Psalm.—This Psalm (as ye see) is but short, and therefore a very fit example to show the force of prayer not to consist in many words, but in fervency of spirit. For great and weighty matters may be comprised in a few words, if they proceed from the spirit and the unspeakable groanings of the heart, especially when our necessity is such as will not suffer any long prayer. Every prayer is long enough if it be fervent and proceed from a heart that understandeth the necessity of the saints.—*Martin Luther.*

Whole Psalm.—The change of performers in this Psalm is very evident ; the pronoun in the first distich is in the first person *singular*, in the rest of Psalm the first *plural* is used.—*Stephen Street.*

Whole Psalm.—This Psalm has one distinction which is to be found in " scarcely any other piece in the Old Testament." In the Hebrew it has many rhymes. But these rhymes are purely accidental. They result simply from the fact that many words are used in it with the same inflexions, and therefore with the same or similar terminations. Regularly recurring and intentional rhymes are not a characteristic of Hebrew poetry, any more than they were of Greek or Latin poetry.—*Samuel Cox.*

Verse 1.—*"Unto thee lift I up mine eyes."* He who previously lifted his eyes unto the hills, now hath raised his heart's eyes to the Lord himself.—*The Venerable Bede* (672—735), *in Neale and Littledale.*

Verse 1.—*"Unto thee lift I up mine eyes,"* etc. This is the sigh of the pilgrim who ascendeth and loveth, and ascendeth because he loveth. He is ascending from earth to heaven, and while he is ascending, unto whom shall he lift his eyes, but unto him that dwelleth in heaven ? We ascend to heaven each time we think of God. In that ascent lies all goodness : if we would repent, we must look not on ourselves, but on him ; if we would be humble, we must look not on ourselves, but on him ; if we would truly love, we must look not on ourselves, but on him who dwelleth in the heavens. If we would have him turn his eyes from our sins, we must turn our eyes unto his mercy and truth.—*"Plain Commentary."*

Verse 1.—*"Unto thee lift I up mine eyes."* Praying by the glances of the eye rather than by words ; mine afflictions having swollen my heart too big for my mouth.—*John Trapp.*

Verse 1.—*"Unto* THEE *do I lift up mine eyes."* You feel the greatness of the contrast these words imply. Earth and heaven, dust and deity ; the poor, weeping, sinful children of mortality, the holy, ever-blessed, eternal God : how wide is the interval of separation between them ! But over the awful chasm, broader than ocean though it be, love and wisdom in the person of Jesus Christ, have thrown a passage, by which the most sinful may repair unterrified to his presence, and find the shame and the fears of guilt exchanged for the peace of forgiveness and the hope that is full of immortality.—*Robert Nisbet.*

Verse 1.—There are many testimonies in *the lifting up of the eyes to heaven.* 1. It is the testimony of a *believing*, humble heart. *Infidelity* will never carry a man above the earth. *Pride* can carry a man no higher than the earth either. 2. It is the testimony of an *obedient* heart. A man that lifts up his eye to God, he acknowledgeth thus much,—Lord, I am thy servant. 3. It is the testimony of a *thankful* heart ; acknowledging that every good blessing, every perfect gift, is from the hand of God. 4. It is the testimony of a *heavenly* heart. He that lifts up his eyes to heaven acknowledgeth that he is weary of the earth ; his heart is not there ; his hope and desire is above. 5. It is the testimony of a *devout* heart : there is no part of the body besides the tongue that is so great an agent in prayer as the *eye.*—*Condensed from Richard Holdsworth.*

Verse 1.—"*O thou that dwellest in the heavens.*" "*That sittest.*" The Lord is here contemplated as enthroned in heaven, where he administers the affairs of the universe executes judgment, and hears prayer.—*James G. Murphy.*

Verses 1, 2.—The lifting up the eyes, implies faith and confident persuasion that God is ready and willing to help us. The very lifting up of the bodily eyes towards heaven is an expression of this inward trust : so David in effect saith, From thee, Lord, I expect relief, and the fulfilling of thy promises. So that there is faith in it, that faith which is the evidence of things not seen. How great soever the darkness of our calamities be, though the clouds of present troubles thicken about us, and hide the Lord's care and loving-kindness from us, yet faith must look through all to his power and constancy of truth and love. The eye of faith is a clear, piercing, eagle eye : Moses " endured, as seeing him who is invisible : " Heb. xi. 27. . . . Faith seeth things afar off in the promises (Heb. xi. 13), at a greater distance than the eye of nature can reach to. Take it either for the eye of the body, or the mind, faith will draw comfort not only from that which is invisible, but also from that which is future as well as invisible ; its supports lie in the other world, and in things which are yet to come.—*Thomas Manton.*

Verses 1, 2.—In the first strophe the poet places himself before us as standing in the presence of the Majesty of Heaven, with his eyes fixed on the hand of God, absorbed in watchful expectation of some sign or gesture, however slight, which may indicate the Divine will. He is like a slave standing silent but alert, in the presence of the Oriental " lord," with hands folded on his breast, and eyes fixed on his master, seeking to read, and to anticipate, if possible, his every wish. He is like a maiden in attendance on her mistress, anxiously striving to see her mind in her looks, to discover and administer to her moods and wants. The grave, reserved Orientals, as we know, seldom speak to their attendants, at least on public occasions. They intimate their wishes and commands by a wave of the hand, by a glance of the eye, by slight movements and gestures which might escape notice were they not watched for with eager attention. Their slaves "*hang* upon their faces ; " they "*fasten* their eyes " on the eyes of their master ; they watch and obey every turn of his hand, every movement of his finger. Thus the Psalmist conceives of himself as waiting on God, looking to him alone, watching for the faintest signal bent on catching and obeying it.—*Samuel Cox.*

Verse 2.—"*Behold.*" An ordinary word, but here it hath an extraordinary position. Ordinarily it is a term of *attention*, used for the awakening of man, to stir up their admiration and audience ; but here it is a word not only prefixed for the exciting of men, but of God himself. David is speaking to God in his meditations. " Behold," saith he. As we take it with respect to God, so it is a *precatory* particle : he beseecheth God to look *down* upon him, while he looks *up* unto God : Look on us, as we look to thee ; "*Behold, Lord, as the eyes of servants,*" etc. If we take it as it hath respect to *man*, so it is an *exemplary* particle, to stir them up to do the like. "*Behold*" what we do, and do likewise ; let your eyes be like ours. " Behold, as the eyes of servants are to the hand of their masters, so are our eyes to the Lord our God." Let yours have the same fixing. So it is a word that draws all eyes after it to imitation.—*Richard Holdsworth.*

Verse 2.—"*Behold, as the eyes of servants look,*" etc. For direction, defence, maintenance, mercy in time of correction, help when the service is over-hard, etc., " *so do our eyes wait upon the Lord our God,*" viz., for direction and benediction. —*John Trapp.*

Verse 2.—"*Eyes of servants unto the hand,*" etc. Our eyes ought to be to the hand of the Lord our God :—First, that we may admire his works. Secondly, that we may show that our service is pleasant to us ; and to show our dependence on such a benign, mighty, and bountiful hand. Thirdly, that we may evince to him our love, and devoted willingness to do all things which he shall command by the slightest movement of a finger. Fourthly, that from him we may receive food, and all things necessary for sustenance. Fifthly, that he may be a defence for us against the enemies that molest us, either by smiting them with the sword, or by shooting of arrows ; or by repelling others by the movement of a finger ; or, at least, by covering us with the shield of his good-will. Sixthly and lastly, that, moved by mercy, he would cease from chastisement.—*Condensed from Le Blanc.*

Verse 2.—"*As the eyes of servants look unto the hand of their masters,*" etc. A traveller says, " I have seen a fine illustration of this passage in a gentleman's house at Damascus. The people of the East do not speak so much or so quick as those in the West, and a sign of the hand is frequently the only instructions given to the servants in waiting. As soon as we were introduced and seated on the divan, a wave of the master's hand indicated that sherbet was to be served. Another wave brought coffee and pipes; another brought sweetmeats. At another signal dinner was made ready. The attendants watched their master's eye and hand, to know their will and do it instantly." Such is the attention with which we ought to wait upon the Lord, anxious to fulfil his holy pleasure,—our great desire being, "Lord, what wilt thou have me to do?" An equally pointed and more homely illustration may be seen any day, on our own river Thames, or in any of our large seaport towns, where the call-boy watches attentively the hand of the captain of the boat, and conveys his will to the engine-men.—*"The Sunday at Home."*

Verse 2.—*"As the eyes of slaves,"* watching anxiously the least movement, the smallest sign of their master's will. The image expresses complete and absolute dependence. Savary (in his *Letters on Egypt*, p. 135), says, "The slaves stand silent at the bottom of the rooms with their hands crossed over their breasts. *With their eyes fixed upon their master* they seek to anticipate every one of his wishes." . . . . In the Psalm the eye directed to the hand of God is the *oculus sperans*, the eye which waits, and hopes, and is patient, looking only to him and none other for help.—*J. J. Stewart Perowne.*

Verse 2.—*"As the eyes of servants,"* etc. The true explanation, I should apprehend, is this: As a slave, ordered by a master or mistress to be chastised for a fault, turns his or her imploring eyes to that superior, till that motion of the hand appears that puts an end to the bitterness that is felt; so our eyes are up to thee, our God, till thy hand shall give the signal for putting an end to our sorrows: for our enemies, O Lord, we are sensible, are only executing thy orders, and chastening us according to thy pleasure.—*Thomas Harmer.*

Verse 2.—*"Servants."* Note how humbly the faithful think of themselves in the sight of God. They are called and chosen to this dignity, to be the heirs and children of God, and are exalted above the angels, and yet, notwithstanding, they count themselves no better in God's sight than "*servants*." They say not here, Behold, like as children look to the hand of their fathers, but "as servants" to the hand of their masters. This is the humility and modesty of the godly, and it is so far off that hereby they lose the dignity of God's children, to the which they are called, that by this means it is made to them more sure and certain.—*Martin Luther.*

Verse 2.—From the everyday conduct of domestic servants we should learn our duty Godwards. Not without cause did our Saviour take his parables from common, everyday things, from fields, vines, trees, marriages, etc., that thus we might have everywhere apt reminders.—*Martin Geier.*

Verse 2.—*"Servants."* *"A maiden."* Consider that there be two sorts of servants set down here, man-servants and maid-servants; and this is to let us know that both sexes may be confident in God. Not only may men be confident in the power of God, but even women also, who are more frail and feeble. Not only may women mourn to God for wrongs done to them, and have repentance for sin, but they may be confident in God also. And therefore see, in that rehearsal of believers and cloud of witnesses, not only is the faith of men noted and commended by the Spirit of God, but also the faith of women: and among the judges, Deborah, Jael, etc., are commended as worthies, and courageous in God. And the women also in the New Testament are noted for their following of Christ—even when all fled from him, then they followed him.—*From a sermon by Alexander Henderson,* 1583—1646.

Verse 2.—*"Servants."* *"A maiden."* We know how shamefully servants were treated in ancient times, and what reproaches must be cast upon them, whilst yet they durst not move a finger to repel the outrage. Being therefore deprived of all means of defending themselves, the only thing which remained for them to do was, what is here stated, to crave the protection of their masters. The same explanation is equally applicable to the case of *handmaids*. Their condition was indeed shameful and degrading; but there is no reason why we should be ashamed of, or offended at, being compared to slaves, provided God is our defender, and takes our lives under his guardianship; God, I say, who purposely disarms us and strips us of all worldly aid, that we may learn to rely upon his grace, and to be contented with it alone. It having been anciently a capital crime for bondmen to carry a sword or any other weapon about them, and as they were exposed to injuries of every description, their masters were wont to defend them with so much the more spirit, when anyone causelessly did them violence. Nor can it be doubted that God, when he sees us placing an exclusive dependence upon his protection, and renouncing all confidence in our own resources, will, as our defender, encounter and shield us from all the molestation that shall be offered to us.—*John Calvin.*

Verse 2.—*"Hand."* With the *hand* we demand, we promise, we call, dismiss, threaten, entreat, supplicate, deny, refuse, interrogate, admire, reckon, confess, repent; express fear, express shame, express doubt; we instruct, command, unite, encourage, swear, testify, accuse, condemn, acquit, insult, despise, defy, disdain, flatter, applaud, bless, abase, ridicule, reconcile, recommend, exalt, regale, gladden, complain, afflict, discomfort, discourage, astonish; exclaim, indicate silence, and what not? with a variety and a multiplication that keep pace with the tongue.—*Michael de Montaigne,* 1533—1592.

Verse 2.—*"Masters."* It is said of Mr. George Herbert, that divine poet, that, to satisfy his independency upon all others, and to quicken his diligence in God's service, he used in his ordinary speech, when he made mention of the blessed name of Jesus, to add, "my Master." And, without any doubt, if men were unfeignedly of his mind, their respects would be more to Christ's command, to Christ's will, to Christ's pleasure.—*From Spencer's "Things New and Old."*

Verse 2.—*"Our eyes wait."* Here the Psalmist uses another word: it is the eye *waiting.* What is the reason of the second word? Now he leaves the similitude in the first line; for in the first line it is thus,—"As the eyes of servants *look,* and the eyes of a maiden *look* "; here it is the eye *waits.* There is good reason: to *wait* is more than to *look* : to *wait* is to look constantly, with patience and submission, by subjecting our affections and wills and desires to God's will; that is to *wait.* David in the second part, in the second line, gives a *better* word, he betters his copy. There is the duty of a Christian, to better his example; the eyes of servants *look,* David's eyes shall *wait:* "So our eyes wait." It is true indeed this word is not in the original, therefore you may observe it is in a small letter in your Bibles, to note that it is a word of necessity, added for the supply of the sense, because the Holy Ghost left it not imperfect, but more perfect, that he put not in the verb; because it is left to every man's heart to supply a verb to his own comfort, and a better he cannot than this. And that this word must be added appears by the next words: " *until that he have mercy upon us.*" To look till he have mercy on us is to *wait;* so there is good reason why this word is added. If we look to the thing begged—"*mercy*"—it is so precious that we may *wait* for it. It was "servants" that he mentioned, and it is their duty to *wait* upon their masters; they wait upon their trenchers at meat; they wait when they go to bed and when they rise; they wait in every place. Therefore, because he had mentioned the first word, he takes the proper duty; there is nothing more proper to servants than waiting, and if we are the servants of God we must *wait.* There is good reason in that respect, because it is a word so significant, therefore the Spirit of God varies it; he keeps not exactly to the line, " So do our eyes *look,*" but he puts it, " So do our eyes *wait.*" —*Richard Holdsworth.*

Verse 3.—*"Have mercy upon us, O LORD, have mercy upon us!"* Note how a godly man speaks. He does not say, "*Have mercy upon me, O LORD, have mercy upon me!* because I am disgraced;" but, "*Have mercy upon us, O LORD, for we are filled with contempt!*" The godly man is not so grieved for his own and individual contempt as he is for the general contempt of the good and faithful. There is an accord of the godly, not only in the cross, but also in groanings, and in the invocation of divine grace.—*Wolfgang Musculus.*

Verse 3.—*"For we are exceedingly filled."* The Hebrew word here used means "*to be saturated* "; to have the appetite fully satisfied—as applied to one who is hungry or thirsty. Then it comes to mean to be entirely full, and the idea here is, that as much contempt had been thrown upon them as could be; they could experience no more.—*Albert Barnes.*

Verse 3.—*"We are exceedingly filled with contempt."* Men of the world regard the Temple Pilgrims and their religion with the quiet smile of disdain, wondering that those who have so much to engage them in a present life should be weak enough to concern themselves about frames and feelings, about an unseen God, and unknown eternity; and this is a trial they find hard to bear. *Their soul, too, is filled exceedingly with the scorning of those that are at ease.* The prosperous of their neighbours declare that they have found the world a generous and happy scene to all who deserve its gifts. Poverty and sorrow they attribute to unworthiness alone. " Let them exert themselves," is the unfeeling cry ; " let them bestir themselves instead of praying, and with them as with us it will soon be well;" and these words of harsh and unfeeling ignorance are like poison to the wounds of the bleeding heart. They have further " *the contempt of the proud* " to mourn ; of those who give expression to their fierce disdain by assailing them with words of contumely, and who seek to draw them by reproaches both from peace and from piety. These are still the trials of Zion's worshippers : silent contempt, open misrepresentation, fierce opposition. Religion, their last comfort, is despised ; peace, their first desire, is denied. Anxious to devote themselves in the spirit of humble and earnest piety to the duties of their appointed sphere, they find enemies in open outcry and array against them. But God is their refuge, and to him they go.—*Robert Nisbet.*

Verses 3, 4.—The second strophe takes up the " have mercy upon us," as it were in echo. It begins with a *Kyrie eleison*, which is confirmed in a *crescendo* manner after the form of steps.—*Franz Delitzsch.*

Verse 4.—"*Exceedingly filled,*" or perhaps, " *has long been filled.*" (Compare cxx. 6). This expression, together with the earnestness of the repeated prayer, " Be gracious unto us," shows that the " scorn " and " contempt " have long pressed upon the people, and their faith has accordingly been exposed to a severe trial. The more remarkable is the entire absence of anything like impatience in the language of the Psalm.—*J. J. Stewart Perowne.*

Verse 4.—"*The scorning of those that are at ease.*" When men go on prosperously, they are apt wrongfully to trouble others, and then to shout at them in their misery, and to despise the person and cause of God's people. This is the sure effect of great arrogancy and pride. They think they may do what they please ; they have no changes, therefore they fear not God, but put forth their hands against such as be at peace with them (Ps. lv. 19, 20) ; whilst they go on prosperously and undisturbedly, they cannot abstain from violence and oppression. This is certainly pride, for it is a lifting up of the heart above God and against God and without God. And they do not consider his providence, which alternately lifts up and casts down, that adversity may not be without a cordial, nor prosperity without a curb and bridle. When men sit fast, and are well at ease, they are apt to be insolent and scornful. Riches and worldly greatness make men insolent and despisers of others, and not to care what burdens they impose upon them ; they are intrenched within a mass of wealth and power and greatness, and so think none can call them to an account.—*Thomas Manton.*

Verse 4.—"*Those that are at ease.*" The word always means such as are reck-lessly at their ease, *the careless ones,* such as those whom Isaiah bids, " rise up, tremble, be troubled ; " for " many days and years shall ye be troubled " (ch. xxxii. 9—11). It is that luxury and ease which sensualize the soul, and make it dull, stupid, hard-hearted.—*Edward Bouverie Pusey (1800—), in "The Minor Prophets."*

Verse 4.—"*Those that are at ease,*" who are regardless of the troubles of others, and expect none of their own.—*James G. Murphy.*

HINTS TO PREACHERS.

Whole Psalm.—We have here, I. The prayer of *dependence,* verse 2. II. The prayer of *apprehension :* " Unto *thee,*" etc. III. The spirit of *obedience :* " As the eyes of servants," etc. IV. The *patience* of the saints : "*Until* he have mercy upon us."—*R. Nisbet.*

Whole Psalm.—Eyes and no eyes. I. EYES. 1. *Upward,* in confidence, in prayer, in thought. 2. "*Unto,*" in reverence, watchfulness, obedience. 3. *Inward,* producing a cry for mercy. II. NO EYES. 1. No sight of the excellence of the godly. 2. No sense of their own danger : " at ease." 3. No humility before God : " proud." 4. No uplifted eyes in hope, prayer, expectation.

Verse 1.—*The eyes of faith.* I. Need uplifting. II. See best upward. III. Have always something to see upward. IV. Let us look up, and so turn our eyes from too much introspection and retrospection.

Verse 1.—I. The language of Adoration: " Thou that dwellest in the heavens." II. The language of Confession. 1. Of need. 2. Of helplessness. III. The language of Supplication : " Unto thee," etc. IV. The language of Expectation ; as shown in verse 2.—*G. R.*

Verse 2.—(Psalm cxxi. 4 with this verse.) Two beholds. I. God's watchful eye over us. II. The saint's watchful eye upon God.

Verse 2.—"*Our eyes wait upon the Lord our God.*" I. What it is to wait with the eye. II. What peculiar aspect of the Lord suggests such waiting : " Jehovah our God." The covenant God is the trusted God. III. What comes of such waiting —" mercy."

Verse 2.—The guiding hand. I. A beckoning hand—to go near. II. A directing hand—to go here and there. III. A quiescent hand—to remain where we are. —*G. R.*

Verse 2.—Homely metaphors, or what may be learned from maids and their mistresses.

Verse 3 (*first portion*).—The Sinner's Litany. The Saint's Entreaty.

Verse 3 (*second portion*).—The world's contempt, the abundance of it, the reason of it, the bitterness of it, the comfort under it.

Verses 3, 4.—I. The occasion of the prayer : the contempt of men. This is often the most difficult to bear. 1. Because it is most unreasonable. Why ridicule men for yielding to their own convictions of what is right ? 2. Most undeserved. True religion injures no man, but seeks the good of all. 3. Most profane. To reproach the people of God because they are his people is to reproach God himself. II. The subject of the prayer. 1. The prayer : is not for justice, which might be desired, but for mercy. 2. The plea : " For we are," etc. The reproaches of men are an encouragement to look for special help from God. The harp hung upon the willows sends forth its sweetest tones. The less it is in human hands the more freely it is played upon by the Spirit of God.—*G. R.*

Verse 4.—"*Those that are at ease.*" I. Explain their state : " at ease." II. Show their ordinary state of mind : " proud." III. Denounce their frequent sin : scorn of the godly. IV. Exhibit their terrible danger.

PSALM CXXIV.

TITLE.—A Song of degrees of David. *Of course the superfine critics have pounced upon this title as inaccurate, but we are at liberty to believe as much or as little of their assertions as we may please. They declare that there are certain ornaments of language in this little ode which were unknown in the Davidic period. It may be so ; but in their superlative wisdom they have ventured upon so many other questionable statements that we are not bound to receive this dictum. Assuredly the manner of the song is very like to David's, and we are unable to see why he should be excluded from the authorship. Whether it be his composition or no, it breathes the same spirit as that which animates the unchallenged songs of the royal composer.*

DIVISION.—*This short Psalm contains an acknowledgment of favour received by way of special deliverance (1—5), then a grateful act of worship in blessing Jehovah (6, 7), and, lastly, a declaration of confidence in the Lord for all future time of trial. May our experience lead us to the same conclusion as the saints of David's time. From all confidence in man may we be rescued by a holy reliance upon our God.*

EXPOSITION.

IF it had not been the LORD who was on our side, now may Israel say ;

2 If it had not been the LORD who was on our side, when men rose up against us :

3 Then they had swallowed us up quick, when their wrath was kindled against us :

4 Then the waters had overwhelmed us, the stream had gone over our soul :

5 Then the proud waters had gone over our soul.

1. *"If it had not been the LORD who was on our side, now may Israel say."* The opening sentence is abrupt, and remains a fragment. By such a commencement attention was aroused as well as feeling expressed : and this is ever the way of poetic fire—to break forth in uncontrollable flame. The many words in italics in our authorized version will show the reader that the translators did their best to patch up the passage, which, perhaps, had better have been left in its broken grandeur, and it would then have run thus :—

" Had it not been Jehovah ! He was for us, oh let Israel say !
Had it not been Jehovah ! He who was for us when men rose against us.

The glorious Lord became our ally ; he took our part, and entered into treaty with us. If Jehovah were not our protector where should we be ? Nothing but his power and wisdom could have guarded us from the cunning and malice of our adversaries ; therefore, let all his people say so, and openly give him the honour of his preserving goodness. Here are two " ifs," and yet there is no " if " in the matter. The Lord was on our side, and is still our defender, and will be so from henceforth, even for ever. Let us with holy confidence exult in this joyful fact. We are far too slow in declaring our gratitude, hence the exclamation which should be rendered, " O let Israel say." We murmur without being stirred up to it, but our thanksgiving needs a spur, and it is well when some warm-hearted friend bids us say what we feel. Imagine what would have happened if the Lord had left us, and then see what has happened because he has been faithful to us. Are not all the materials of a song spread before us ? Let us sing unto the Lord.

2. *"If it had not been the LORD who was on our side, when men rose up against us."* When all men combined, and the whole race of men seemed set upon stamping out the house of Israel, what must have happened if the covenant Lord had not interposed ? When they stirred themselves, and combined to make an assault upon our quietude and safety, what should we have done in their rising if the Lord had not also risen ? No one who could or would help was near, but the bare arm

of the Lord sufficed to preserve his own against all the leagued hosts of adversaries. There is no doubt as to our deliverer, we cannot ascribe our salvation to any second cause, for it would not have been equal to the emergency ; nothing less than omnipotence and omiscience could have wrought our rescue. We set every other claimant on one side, and rejoice because the Lord was on our side.

3. *"Then they had swallowed us up quick when their wrath was kindled against us."* They were so eager for our destruction that they would have made only one morsel of us, and have swallowed us up alive and whole in a single instant. The fury of the enemies of the church is raised to the highest pitch, nothing will content them but the total annihilation of God's chosen. Their wrath is like a fire which is kindled, and has taken such firm hold upon the fuel that there is no quenching it. Anger is never more fiery than when the people of God are its objects. Sparks become flames, and the furnace is heated seven times hotter when God's elect are to be thrust into the blaze. The cruel world would make a full end of the godly seed were it not that Jehovah bars the way. When the Lord appears, the cruel throats cannot swallow, and the consuming fires cannot destroy. Ah, if it were not Jehovah, if our help came from all the creatures united, there would be no way of escape for us : it is only because the Lord liveth that his people are alive.

4. *"Then the waters had overwhelmed us."* Rising irresistibly, like the Nile, the flood of opposition would soon have rolled over our heads. Across the mighty waste of waters we should have cast an anxious eye, but looked in vain for escape. The motto of a royal house is, " Tossed about but not submerged " : we should have needed an epitaph rather than an epigram, for we should have been driven by the torrent and sunken, never to rise again. *"The stream had gone over our soul."* The rushing torrent would have drowned our soul, our hope, our life. The figures seem to be the steadily-rising flood, and the hurriedly-rushing stream. Who can stand against two such mighty powers ? Everything is destroyed by these unconquerable forces, either by being submerged or swept away. When the world's enmity obtains a vent it both rises and rushes, it rages and rolls along, and spares nothing. In the great water-floods of persecution and affliction who can help but Jehovah ? But for him where would we be at this very hour ? We have experienced seasons in which the combined forces of earth and hell must have made an end of us had not omnipotent grace interfered for our rescue.

5. *"Then the proud waters had gone over our soul."* The figure represents the waves as proud, and so they seem to be when they overleap the bulwarks of a frail bark, and threaten every moment to sink her. The opposition of men is usually embittered by a haughty scorn which derides all our godly efforts as mere fanaticism or obstinate ignorance. In all the persecutions of the church a cruel contempt has largely mingled with the oppression, and this is overpowering to the soul. Had not God been with us our disdainful enemies would have made nothing of us, and dashed over us as a mountain torrent sweeps down the side of a hill, driving every-thing before it. Not only would our goods and possessions have been carried off, but our soul, our courage, our hope would have been borne away by the impetuous assault, and buried beneath the insults of our antagonists. Let us pause here, and as we see what might have been, let us adore the guardian power which has kept us in the flood, and yet above the flood. In our hours of dire peril we must have perished had not our Preserver prevailed for our safe keeping.

6 Blessed *be* the LORD, who hath not given us *as* a prey to their teeth.

7 Our soul is escaped as a bird out of the snare of the fowlers : the snare is broken, and we are escaped.

6. *"Blessed be the LORD, who hath not given us as a prey to their teeth."* Leaving the metaphor of a boiling flood, he compares the adversaries of Israel to wild beasts who desired to make the godly their prey. Their teeth are prepared to tear, and they regard the godly as their victims. The Lord is heartily praised for not permitting his servants to be devoured when they were between the jaws of the raging ones. It implies that none can harm us till the Lord permits : we cannot be their prey unless the Lord gives us up to them, and that our loving Lord will never do. Hitherto he has refused permission to any foe to destroy us, blessed be his name. The more imminent the danger the more eminent the mercy which would not permit the soul to perish in it. God be blessed for ever for keeping us from the curse. Jehovah be praised for checking the fury of the foe, and saving his own. The

verse reads like a merely negative blessing, but no boon can be more positively precious. He has given us to his Son Jesus, and he will never give us to our enemies.

7. *"Our soul is escaped as a bird out of the snare of the fowlers."* Our soul is like a bird for many reasons ; but in this case the point of likeness is weakness, folly, and the ease with which it is enticed into the snare. Fowlers have many methods of taking small birds, and Satan has many methods of entrapping souls. Some are decoyed by evil companions, others are enticed by the love of dainties ; hunger drives many into the trap, and fright impels numbers to fly into the net. Fowlers know their birds, and how to take them ; but the birds see not the snare so as to avoid it, and they cannot break it so as to escape from it. Happy is the bird that hath a deliverer strong, and mighty, and ready in the moment of peril ; happier still is the soul over which the Lord watches day and night to pluck its feet out of the net. What joy there is in this song, " our soul is escaped." How the emancipated one sings and soars, and soars and sings again. Blessed be God many of us can make joyous music with these notes, " our soul is escaped." Escaped from our natural slavery ; escaped from the guilt, the degradation, the habit, the dominion of sin ; escaped from the vain deceits and fascinations of Satan ; escaped from all that can destroy ; we do indeed experience delight. What a wonder of grace it is ! What a miraculous escape that we who are so easily misled should not have been permitted to die by the dread fowler's hand. The Lord has heard the prayer which he taught us to pray, and he hath delivered us from evil. *"The snare is broken, and we are escaped."* The song is worth repeating ; it is well to dwell upon so great a mercy. The snare may be false doctrine, pride, lust, or a temptation to indulge in policy, or to despair, or to presume ; what a high favour it is to have it broken before our eyes, so that it has no more power over us. We see not the mercy while we are in the snare ; perhaps we are so foolish as to deplore the breaking of the Satanic charm ; the gratitude comes when the escape is seen, and when we perceive what we have escaped from, and by what hand we have been set free. Then our Lord has a song from our mouths and hearts as we make heaven and earth ring with the notes, " the snare is broken, and we are escaped." We have been tempted, but not taken ; cast down, but not destroyed ; perplexed, but not in despair ; in deaths oft, but still alive : blessed be Jehovah !

This song might well have suited our whole nation at the time of the Spanish Armada, the church in the days of the Jesuits, and each believer among us in seasons of strong personal temptation.

8 Our help *is* in the name of the LORD, who made heaven and earth.

8. *"Our help,"* our hope for the future, our ground of confidence in all trials present and to come. *"Is in the name of the LORD."* Jehovah's revealed character is our foundation of confidence, his person is our sure fountain of strength. *"Who made heaven and earth."* Our Creator is our preserver. He is immensely great in his creating work ; he has not fashioned a few little things alone, but all heaven and the whole round earth are the works of his hands. When we worship the Creator let us increase our trust in our Comforter. Did he create all that we see, and can he not preserve us from evils which we cannot see ? Blessed be his name, he that has fashioned us will watch over us ; yea, he has done so, and rendered us help in the moment of jeopardy. He is our help and our shield, even he alone. He will to the end break every snare. He made heaven for us, and he will keep us for heaven ; he made the earth, and he will succour us upon it until the hour cometh for our departure. Every work of his hand preaches to us the duty and the delight of reposing upon him only. All nature cries, " Trust ye in the Lord for ever, for in the Lord Jehovah there is everlasting strength." " Wherefore comfort one another with these words."

The following versification of the sense rather than the words of this Psalm is presented to the reader with much diffidence :—

> Had not the Lord, my soul may cry,
> Had not the Lord been on my side ;
> Had he not brought deliverance nigh,
> Then must my helpless soul have died.
>
> Had not the Lord been on my side,
> My soul had been by Satan slain ;
> And Tophet, opening large and wide,
> Would not have gaped for me in vain.

Lo, floods of wrath, and floods of hell,
In fierce impetuous torrents roll ;
Had not the Lord defended well,
The waters had o'erwhelm'd my soul.

As when the fowler's snare is broke,
The bird escapes on cheerful wings ;
My soul, set free from Satan's yoke,
With joy bursts forth, and mounts, and sings.

She sings the Lord her Saviour's praise ;
Sings forth his praise with joy and mirth ;
To him her song in heaven she'll raise,
To him that made both heaven and earth

EXPLANATORY NOTES AND QUAINT SAYINGS.

Title.—The title informs us that this sacred march was composed by king David ; and we learn very clearly from the subject, that the progression referred to was the triumphant return of the king and his loyal army to Jerusalem, upon the overthrow of the dangerous rebellion to which the great mass of the people had been excited by Absalom and his powerful band of confederates.—*John Mason Good.*

Whole Psalm.—This Psalm is ascribed to David.   No reference is made to any specific danger and deliverance.   There is a delightful universality in the language which suits it admirably for an anthem of the redeemed, in every age and in every clime.   The people of God still live in a hostile territory.   Traitors are in the camp, and there are numerous foes without.   And the church would soon be exterminated, if the malice and might of her adversaries were not restrained and defeated by a higher power.   Hence this ode of praise has never become obsolete.   How frequently have its strains of adoring gratitude floated on the breeze !   What land is there, in which its outbursting gladness has not been heard !   It has been sung upon the banks of the Jordan and the Nile, the Euphrates and the Tigris.   It has been sung upon the banks of the Tiber and the Rhine, the Thames and the Forth.   It has been sung upon the banks of the Ganges and the Indus, the Mississippi and the Irrawady.   And we anticipate a period when the church, surmounting all her difficulties, and victory waving over her banners, shall sing this Psalm of praise in every island and continent of our globe.   The year of God's redeemed must come. The salvation of Christ shall extend to the utmost extremities of earth.   And when this final emancipation takes place, the nations will shout for joy, and praise their Deliverer in Psalms, and hymns, and spiritual songs.—*N. McMichael.*

Whole Psalm.—In the year 1582, this Psalm was sung on a remarkable occasion in Edinburgh.   An imprisoned minister, John Durie, had been set free, and was met and welcomed on entering the town by two hundred of his friends.   The number increased till he found himself in the midst of a company of two thousand, who began to sing, as they moved up the long High Street, "*Now Israel may say,*" etc. They sang in four parts with deep solemnity, all joining in the well-known tune and Psalm.   They were much moved themselves, and so were all who heard ; and one of the chief persecutors is said to have been more alarmed at this sight and song than at anything he had seen in Scotland.—*Andrew A. Bonar, in "Christ and His Church in the Book of Psalms,"* 1859.

Verse 1. "The LORD . . . . on our side."   Jehovah is on the side of his people in a spiritual sense, or otherwise it would be bad for them.   God the Father is on their side ;   his love and relation to them engage him to be so ;   hence all those good things that are provided for them and bestowed on them ;   nor will he suffer any to do them hurt, they being as dear to him as the apple of his eye ;   hence he grants them his gracious presence, supports them under all their trials and exercises, supplies all their wants, and keeps them by his power, and preserves them from all their enemies ;   so that they have nothing to fear from any quarter.   Christ is on their side ; he is the Surety for them, the Saviour of them ; has taken their part against all their spiritual enemies, sin, Satan, the world, and death ; has engaged with them and conquered them ; he is the Captain of their salvation, their King at the head of them, that protects and defends them here, and is their friend in the court of heaven ; their Advocate and interceding High-priest there, who pleads their cause against Satan, and obtains every blessing for them. The Spirit of Jehovah is on their side, to carry on his work in them ; to assist them in their prayers and supplications ; to secure them from Satan's temptations ; to set up a standard for them when the enemy comes in like a flood upon them ; and to comfort them in all their castings down ; and to work them up for, and bring them safe to heaven : but were this not the case, what would become of them ?—*John Gill.*

Verse 1.—"*Israel.*" The "*Israel*" spoken of in this Psalm may be Israel in the house of Laban, in whose person the Midrash Tehillim imagines the Psalm to be said. There are certainly some of its phrases which acquire an appropriate meaning from being interpreted in this connection.—*H. T. Armfield.*

Verses 1—4.—Such abrupt and unfinished expressions in the beginning of the Psalm indicate the great joy and exultation that will not suffer the speaker to finish his sentences.—*Robert Bellarmine.*

Verses 1, 2.—The somewhat paraphrastic rendering of these verses (with the unnecessary interpolation of the words in italics in the Authorised Version) greatly weaken their force and obscure their meaning. There is far more meant and expressed than simply that God gave the Israelites the victory over their enemies. The Psalm is typico-prophetic. It sets forth the condition of the church in this world, surrounded by enemies, implacable in their hatred, maddened by rage, and bent on her destruction. It gives assurance of her preservation, and continuous triumph, because Jehovah is her God. It foretells the future, full, and final destruction of all her enemies. It re-echoes the song sung on the shores of the Red Sea. In it are heard the notes of the New Song before the great white throne. The praise and thanksgiving are to יְהֹוָה, the revealed אֱלֹהִים, whose "*eternal power and Godhead are understood by the things that are made :*"—*to* יְהֹוָה, the revealed אֵל שַׁדַּי, whom the fathers knew as the Almighty, from the great things which he did for them :—to יְהֹוָה, the God who has made a covenant with his people, the Redeemer. It is יִשְׂרָאֵל, the chosen people of God, the holy nation, the peculiar treasure to him above all peoples, and thus become as the Rabbins say, "*Odium generis humani,*" against whom אָדָם (not *men,* but *man* collectively) rose up, and sought to destroy. It is יִשְׂרָאֵל, God's chosen, the people of the covenant, that with the " full delight of a personal ' my,' " joys in God and sings, "*But that Jehovah was* לָֽנוּ, ours ! " Tame and frigid is the rendering—"*was on our side.*" Jehovah was theirs: *that,* their safety: *that,* their blessedness : *that,* their joy.—*Edward Thomas Gibson,* 1818—1880.

Verses 1, 2.—1. God was on our side ; he took our part, espoused our cause and appeared for us. He was our helper, and a very present help, a help on our side, nigh at hand. He was with us ; not only for us, but among us, and commander-in-chief of our forces. 2. That God was Jehovah ; there the emphasis lies. " If it had not been Jehovah himself, a God of infinite power and perfection, that had undertaken our deliverance, our enemies would have overpowered us. Happy the people therefore whose God is Jehovah, a God all-sufficient. Let Israel say this to his honour, and resolve never to forsake him.—*Matthew Henry.*

Verses 1, 2, 8.—These three things will I bear on my heart, O Lord : " The Lord *was* on our side," this for the *past ;* " The snare is broken," for the *present ;* " Our help is in the name of the Lord," this for the *future.* I will not and I cannot be fainthearted, whether in my contest with Satan, in my intercourse with the world, or in the upheavings of my wicked heart, so long as I hold this " threefold cord " in my hand, or rather, am held by it.—*Alfred Edersheim.*

Verse 2.—"*If it had not been the Lord,*" etc. This repetition is not in vain. For whilst we are in danger, our fear is without measure ; but when it is once past, we imagine it to have been less than it was indeed. And this is the delusion of Satan, to diminish and obscure the grace of God. David therefore with this repetition stirreth up the people to more thankfulness unto God for his gracious deliverance, and amplifieth the dangers which they had passed. Whereby we are taught how to think of our troubles and afflictions past, lest the sense and feeling of God's grace vanish out of our minds.—*Martin Luther.*

Verse 2.—"*Men rose up against us.*" It may seem strange that these wicked and wretched enemies, monsters rather than men, should be thus moderately spoken of, and have no other name than this of *men* given them, which of all others they least deserved, as having in them nothing of man but outward show and shape, being rather beasts, yea, devils in the form and fashion of men, than right men. But hereby the church would show that she did leave the further censuring of them unto God their righteous Judge ; and would also further amplify their wickedness, who being men, did yet in their desires and dispositions bewray a more than beastly immanity and inhumanity.—*Daniel Dyke* (—1614 ?) *in "Comfortable Sermons upon the cxxiiii. Psalme,"* 1617.

Verse 3.—*" Then they had swallowed us up quick."* The metaphor may be taken from famished wild beasts attacking and devouring men (comp. v. 5) ; or the reference may be to the case of a man shut up alive in a sepulchre (Prov. i. 12) and left there to perish, or (Numb. xvi. 30) swallowed up by an earthquake.—*Daniel Cresswell.*

Verse 3.—*"Then they had swallowed us up."* The word implieth eating with insatiable appetite ; every man that eateth must also swallow ; but a glutton is rather a swallower than an eater. He throws his meat whole down his throat, and eats (as we may say) without chewing. The rod of Moses, turned into a serpent, " swallowed up " the rods of the Egyptian sorcerers. The word is often applied to express oppression (Ps. xxxv. 25) : " Let them not say in their hearts, Ah, so would we have it : let them not say, We have swallowed him up " : that is, we have made clear riddance of him ; he is now a gone man for ever. The ravenous rage of the adversary is described in this language.—*Joseph Caryl.*

Verse 3.—*"Quick."* Not an adverb, *"quickly,"* but an adjective, *alive.* As greedy monsters, both of the land and of the deep, sometimes swallow their food before the life is out of it, so would the enemies of the Church have destroyed her as in a moment, but for divine interposition.—*William S. Plumer.*

Verse 3.—Objection. But what may the reason thereof be ? May a man say, thus the godly shall always prevail and be never overthrown by their enemies, but overcome them rather ? Experience doth teach us that they are fewer in number than the wicked are, that they are weaker for power and strength, that they are more simple for wit and policy, and that they are more careless for diligence and watchfulness than their adversaries be : how, then, comes it to pass that they have the upper hand ?

Answer. The Prophet Esay doth declare it unto us in the 8th chapter of his prophecy, and the 10th verse thereof, it is in few words " because the Lord is with them and for them."

For, first, he is stronger than all, being able to resist all power that is devised against him and his, and to do whatsoever he will both in heaven and in earth.

2. He is wiser than all, knowing how to prevent them in all their ways, and also how to bring matters to pass for the good of his people.

3. He is diligenter than all, to stand, as it were, upon the watch, and to take his advantage when it is offered him, for " He that keepeth Israel doth neither slumber nor sleep."

4. Lastly, he is happier than all to have good success in all his enterprizes, for he doth prosper still in all things which he doth take in hand and none can resist a thought of his ; yea, the very " word which goeth out of his mouth doth accomplish that which he wills, and prosper in the thing whereunto he doth send it." In war, all these four things are respected in a captain that will still overcome : first, that he be strong ; secondly, that he be wise ; thirdly, that he be diligent ; and, lastly, that he be fortunate ; for the victory goeth not always with the strong, nor always with the wise, nor always with the diligent, nor always with the fortunate ; but sometimes with the one of them, and sometimes with the other : but look, where all four do concur together there is always the victory, and therefore seeing all of them are in God, it is no marvel though those whose battles he doth fight, do always overcome and get the victory.—*Thomas Stint,* 1621.

Verses 4, 5.—A familiar, but exceedingly apt and most significant figure. Horrible is the sight of a raging conflagration ; but far more destructive is a river overflowing its banks and rushing violently on : for it is not possible to restrain it by any strength or power. As, then, he says, a river is carried along with great impetuosity, and carries away and destroys whatever it meets with in its course ;

thus also is the rage of the enemies of the church, not to be withstood by human strength. Hence, we should learn to avail ourselves of the protection and help of God. For what else is the church but a little boat fastened to the bank, which is carried away by the force of the waters? or a shrub growing on the bank, which without effort the flood roots up? Such was the people of Israel in the days of David compared with the surrounding nations. Such in the present day is the church compared with her enemies. Such is each one of us compared with the power of the malignant spirit. We are as a little shrub, of recent growth and having no firm hold: but he is like the Elbe, overflowing, and with great force overthrowing all things far and wide. We are like a withered leaf, lightly holding to the tree; he is like the north wind, with great force rooting up and throwing down the trees. How, then, can we withstand or defend ourselves by our own power?—*Martin Luther.*

Verses 4, 5.—First the *"waters"*; then *"the stream"* or *torrent;* then *" the proud waters,"* lifting up their heads on high. First the waters overwhelm us; then the torrent goes over our soul; and then the proud waters go over our soul. What power can resist the rapid floods of waters, when they overspread their boundaries, and rush over a country? Onward they sweep with resistless force, and men and cattle, and crops and houses, are destroyed. Let the impetuous waters break loose, and, in a few minutes, the scene of life, and industry, and happiness, is made a scene of desolation and woe. Perhaps, there is an allusion here to the destruction of the Egyptians in the Red Sea. The floods fell upon them, the depths covered them: they sank into the bottom as a stone. Had God not stretched forth his hand to rescue the Israelites, their enemies would have overwhelmed them. Happy they who, in seasons of danger, have Jehovah for a hiding-place.—*N. McMichael.*

Verse 5.—*"Then the proud waters had gone over our soul."* The same again, to note the greatness both of the danger and of the deliverance. And it may teach us not lightly to pass over God's great blessings, but to make the most of them.—*John Trapp.*

Verse 5.—

" When winds and seas do rage,
    And threaten to undo me,
Thou dost their wrath assuage,
    If I but call unto thee.

A mighty storm last night
    Did seek my soul to swallow
But by the peep of light
    A gentle calm did follow.

What need I then despair
    Though ills stand round about me;
Since mischiefs neither dare
    To bark or bite without thee ? "

Robert Herrick, 1591—1674.

Verses 6, 7.—Two figures are again employed, in order to show how imminent was the destruction, had there been no divine interposition. The first is that of a savage beast, which was formerly used. But an addition is made, to describe the urgency of the danger. The wild beast was not only lying in wait for them; he was not merely ready to spring upon his prey, he had already leaped upon it: he had actually seized it: it was even now between his teeth. What a graphic description! A moment's delay, and all help would have been in vain. But Jehovah appears on the ground. He goes up to the ferocious beast, and takes out the trembling prey from between his bloody jaws. The danger is imminent; but nothing is too hard for the Lord. " My soul is among lions." " What time I am afraid I will trust in thee." " He shall send from heaven, and save me from the reproach of him that would swallow me up." The second figure is that of a fowler. The fowler has prepared his snare in a skilful manner. The bird enters it, unconscious of danger: the net is thrown over it; and in an instant its liberty is lost. There it lies, the poor bird, its little heart throbbing wildly, and its little wings beating vainly against the net. It is completely at the mercy of the fowler, and escape is impossible. But again the Lord appears, and his presence is safety. He goes up to the net, lifts it from the ground ; the bird flies out, lights on a neighbouring tree, and sings among the branches. " Surely he shall deliver thee from the snare of the fowler." God rescues his people from the craft and subtlety of their enemies, as he does from their open violence.—*N. McMichael.*

Verses 6, 7.—We were delivered, 1. Like a *lamb* out of the very jaws of a beast of prey : God "*hath not given us as a prey to their teeth*"; intimating that they had no power against God's people, but what was given them from above. They could not be a prey to their teeth unless God gave them up, and therefore they were rescued, because God would not suffer them to be ruined. 2. Like "*a bird*," a *little* bird, the word signifies a sparrow, "*out of the snare of the fowler.*" The enemies are very subtle and spiteful, they lay snares for God's people, to bring them into sin and trouble, and to hold them there. Sometimes they seem to have prevailed so far as to gain their point, the children of God are taken in the snare, and are as unable to help themselves out as any weak and silly bird is ; and then is God's time to appear for their relief ; when all other friends fail, then God breaks the snare, and turns the counsel of the enemies into foolishness : "*The snare is broken, and so we are delivered.*"—*Matthew Henry.*

Verse 7.—"*Our soul is escaped as a bird out of the snare of the fowlers,*" etc. Various snares are placed for birds, by traps, bird-lime, guns, etc. : who can enumerate all the dangers of the godly, threatening them from Satan, and from the world ? Psalm xci. 3 : Hosea v. 1. — "*We are delivered,*" not by our own skill or cunning, but by the grace and power of God only : so that every device is made vain, and freedom is preserved.—*Martin Geier.*

Verse 7.—"*Our soul is escaped as a bird out of the snare of the fowlers,*" etc. I am quite sure that there is not a day of our lives in which Satan does not lay some snare for our souls, the more perilous because unseen ; and if seen, because perhaps unheeded and despised. And of this, too, I am equally sure, that if any one brings home with him at night a conscience void of offence towards God and man, it is in no might nor strength of his own, and that if the Lord had not been his guide and preserver he would have been given over, nay, he would have given himself over, as a prey to the devourer's teeth. I believe there are few even of God's saints who have not had occasion, in some season of sore temptation, when Satan has let loose all his malice and might, and poured in suggestion upon suggestion and trial upon trial, as he did on Job, and they have been ready to faint, if not to fall by the way—then, perhaps, in a moment when they looked not for it, Satan has departed, foiled and discomfited, and with his prey snatched out of his hands, and they, too, have had gratefully to own, "*Our soul is escaped as a bird out of the snare of the fowlers ; the snare is broken, and we are escaped.*" Yes ! depend upon it, our best and only hope "*is in the name of the Lord, who made heaven and earth.*"—*Barton Bouchier.*

Verse 7.—"*Our soul is escaped as a bird.*" The snare of the fowler was the lime-twigs of this world ; our soul was caught in them by the feathers, our affections : now, indeed, we are escaped ; but the Lord delivered us.—*Thomas Adams.*

Verse 7.—"*As a bird out of the snare of the fowlers.*" The soul is surrounded by many dangers. 1. *It is ensnared by worldliness.* One of the most gigantic dangers against which God's people have specially to guard—an enemy to all spirituality of thought and feeling. 2. *It is ensnared by selfishness*—a foe to all simple-hearted charity, to all expansive generosity and Christian philanthropy. 3. *It is ensnared by unbelief*—the enemy of prayer, of ingenuous confidence, of all personal Christian effort. These are not imaginary dangers. We meet them in everyday life. They threaten us at every point, and often have we to lament over the havoc they make in our hearts.—*George Barlow, in a "Homiletic Commentary on the Book of Psalms," 1879.*

Verse 7.—"*The snare is broken.*" It is as easy for God to deliver his people out of their enemies' hands, even when they have the godly in their power, as to break a net made of thread or yarn, wherewith birds are taken.—*David Dickson.*

Verse 7.—"*The snare is broken, and we are escaped.*" Our life lieth open always to the snares of Satan, and we as silly birds are like at every moment to be carried away, notwithstanding the Lord maketh a way for us to escape ; yea, when Satan seemeth to be most sure of us, by the mighty power of God the snares are broken and we are delivered. Experience we have hereof in those who are inwardly afflicted and with heaviness of spirit grievously oppressed, that when they seem to be in utter despair, and ready now, as you would say, to perish, yet even at the last pinch, and in the uttermost extremity cometh the sweet comfort of God's Holy Spirit and raiseth them up again. When we are most ready to perish, then is God most ready to help. "Except the Lord had holpen me," saith David, "my soul had almost dwelt in silence." And this again do we mark for the comfort of the weak conscience. It is Satan's subtlety whereby commonly he disquiets many, that because carnal corruption is in them he would therefore bear them in hand that they are none of Christ's. In this he plays the deceiver ; he tries us by the wrong rule of perfect sanctification ; this is the square that ought to be laid to Christ's members triumphant in heaven, and not to those who are militant on earth. Sin remaining in me will not prove that therefore I am not in Christ, otherwise Christ should have no members upon earth ; but grace working that new disposition which nature could never effect proves undoubtedly that we are in Christ Jesus.— *Thomas Stint.*

Verse 8.—"*Our help is in the name of the* LORD, *who made heaven and earth.*" He hath made *the earth* where the snare lies, so that he can rightfully destroy the snare as laid unlawfully in his domain ; he hath made the *heaven,* the true sphere of the soaring wings of those souls which he has delivered, so that they may fly upwards from their late prison, rejoicing. He came down to earth himself, the Lord Jesus in whose name is our help, that he might break the snare ; he returned to heaven, that we might fly " as the doves to their windows " (Isa. lx. 8), following where he showed the way.—*Richard Rolle, of Hampole* (1340), *in* "*Neale and Little-dale.*"

Verse 8.—"*Our help is in the name of the* LORD." The fairest fruits of our by-past experience is to glorify God by confidence in him for time to come, as here.—*David Dickson.*

Verse 8.—"*The* LORD *who made heaven and earth.*" As if the Pslamist had said, As long as I see heaven and earth I will never distrust. I hope in that God which made all these things out of nothing ; and therefore as long as I see those two great standing monuments of his power before me, heaven and earth, I will never be discouraged. So the apostle : 1 Peter iv. 19, " Commit the keeping of your souls to him in well-doing, as unto a faithful Creator." O Christian ! remember when you trust God you trust an almighty Creator, who is able to help, let your case be never so desperate. God could create when he had nothing to work *upon,* which made one wonder ; and he could create when he had nothing to work *with,* which is another wonder. What is become of the tools wherewith he made the world ? Where is the trowel wherewith he arched the heaven ? and the spade wherewith he digged the sea ? What had God to work upon, or work withal when he made the world ? He made it out of nothing. Now you commit your souls to the same faithful Creator.—*Thomas Manton.*

Verse 8.—The Romans in a great distress were put so hard to it, that they were fain to take the weapons out of the temples of their gods to fight with them ; and so they overcame. And this ought to be the course of every good Christian, in times of public distress, to fly to the weapons of the church, prayers and tears. The Spartans' walls were their spears, the Christians' walls are his prayers. His help standeth in the name of the Lord who hath made both heaven and earth.— *Edmund Calamy.*

Verse 8.—The French Protestants always begin their public worship with the last verse of this Psalm, and there is no thought more encouraging and comfortable. —*Job Orton,* 1717—1783.

Verse 8.—"*Our help is in the name of the* LORD," etc. These are the words of a triumphing and victorious faith, "*Our help standeth in the name of the* LORD, *which made heaven and earth* " : as if he said, the Maker of heaven and earth is my God and my helper. Ye see whither he flieth in his great distress. He despaireth not, but crieth unto the Lord, as one yet hoping assuredly to find relief and comfort. Rest thou also in this hope, and do as he did. David was not tempted to the end he should despair ; think not thou, therefore, that thy temptations are sent unto thee that thou shouldest be swallowed up with sorrow and desperation : if thou be brought down to the very gates of hell, believe that the Lord will surely raise thee up again. If so thou be bruised and broken, know it is the Lord that will help thee again. If thy heart be full of sorrow and heaviness, look for comfort from him, who said, that a troubled spirit is a sacrifice unto him: (Ps. li. 17.) Thus he setteth the eternal God, the Maker of heaven and earth, against all troubles and dangers, against the floods and overflowings of all temptations, and swalloweth up, as it were, with one breath all the raging furies of the whole world, and of hell itself, even as a little drop of water is swallowed up by a mighty flaming fire: and what is the world with all its force and power, in respect of him that made heaven and earth!—*Thomas Stint.*

HINTS TO PREACHERS.

Verse 1.—"The LORD *who was on our side."* Who is he? Why on our side? How does he prove it? What are we bound to do?

Verses 1—3.—Regard the text, I. From the life of Jacob or Israel. II. From the history of the nation. III. From the annals of the church. IV. From our personal biography.

Verses 1—5.—I. What might have been. II. Why it has not been.

Verses 1—5.—I. What the people of God would have been if the Lord had not been on our side. 1. What if left to their enemies? verses 2, 3. Israel left to Pharaoh and his host in the time of Moses: left to the Canaanites in the time of Joshua: to the Midianites in the time of Gideon: Judah to the Assyrians in the time of Hezekiah: "Then they had swallowed us up," etc. 2. What if left to themselves? "The stream had gone over our soul": verses 4, 5. II. What the people of God are with the Lord on their side. 1. All the designs of their enemies against them are frustrated. 2. Their inward sorrow is turned into joy. 3. Both their inward and their outward troubles work together for their good.—*G. R.*

Verses 2, 3.—I. To swallow us alive—the desire of our wrathful enemies. II. To save us alive—the work of our faithful God.

Verses 4, 5.—Perils of waters: a number of thoughts may be worked out from the likeness between afflictions and torrents.

Verse 6.—I. The Lamb. II. The Lion. III. The Lord.

Verse 6.—I. They would gladly devour us. II. They cannot devour unless the Lord will. III. God is to be praised since he does not permit them to injure us.

Verse 6.—I. The ill-will of men against the righteous. 1. For their spoliation. 2. For their destruction: "As a prey to their teeth." II. The goodwill of God. "Blessed be the Lord," etc. 1. What it supposes—that good men, in a measure and for a time, may be given into the hands of the wicked. 2. What it affirms— that they are not given entirely into their hands—*G. R.*

Verse 7.—I. The soul ensnared. 1. By whom? Wicked men are fowlers. By Satan.

> "Satan, the fowler, who betrays
> Unguarded souls a thousand ways."

2. How? By temptations—to pride, worldliness, drunkenness, error, or lust, according to the tastes and habits of the individual. II. The soul escaped: "Our soul is escaped," etc. "The snare is broken," not by ourselves, but by the hand of God.—*G. R.*

Verse 7.—I. A bird. II. A snare. III. A capture. IV. An escape.

Verse 8.—Our Creator, our Helper. Special comfort to be drawn from creation in this matter.

Verse 8.—I. The Helper: "The LORD, who made heaven and earth," who in his works has given ample proofs of what he can do. II. The helped. "Our help" is, 1. Promised in his name. 2. Sought in his name: these make it ours. —*G. R.*

Verse 8.—I. We have help. As troubled sinners, as dull scholars, as trembling professors, as inexperienced travellers, as feeble workers. II. We have help in God's name. In his perfections—"They shall put my name upon the children of Israel." In his gospel—"A chosen vessel to bear my name." In his authority —"In the name of Jesus Christ rise up," etc. III. Therefore we exert ourselves. —*W. J.*

PSALM CXXV.

TITLE.—A Song of Degrees. *Another step is taken in the ascent, another station in the pilgrimage is reached : certainly a rise in the sense is here perceptible, since full assurance concerning years to come is a higher form of faith than the ascription of former escapes to the Lord. Faith has praised Jehovah for past deliverances, and here she rises to a confident joy in the present and future safety of believers. She asserts that they shall for ever be secure who trust themselves with the Lord. We can imagine the pilgrims chanting this song when perambulating the city walls.*

We do not assert that David wrote this Psalm, but we have as much ground for doing so as others have for declaring that it was written after the captivity. It would seem probable that all the Pilgrim Psalms were composed, or, at least, compiled by the same writer, and as some of them are certainly by David, there is no conclusive reason for taking away the rest from him.

DIVISION.—*First we have a song of holy confidence* (1, 2) *; then a promise,* 3 *; followed by a prayer,* 4 *; and a note of warning.*

EXPOSITION.

THEY that trust in the LORD *shall be* as mount Zion, *which* cannot be removed, *but* abideth for ever.

2 *As* the mountains *are* round about Jerusalem, so the LORD *is* round about his people from henceforth even for ever.

3 For the rod of the wicked shall not rest upon the lot of the righteous ; lest the righteous put forth their hands unto iniquity.

4 Do good, O LORD, unto *those that be* good, and to *them that are* upright in their hearts.

5 As for such as turn aside unto their crooked ways, the LORD shall lead them forth with the workers of iniquity : *but* peace *shall be* upon Israel.

1. *"They that trust in the LORD shall be as mount Zion."* The emphasis lies upon the object of their trust, namely, Jehovah the Lord. What a privilege to be allowed to repose in God ! How condescending is Jehovah to become the confidence of his people ! To trust elsewhere is vanity ; and the more implicit such misplaced trust becomes the more bitter will be the ensuing disappointment ; but to trust in the living God is sanctified common sense which needs no excuse, its result shall be its best vindication. There is no conceivable reason why we should not trust in Jehovah, and there is every possible argument for so doing ; but, apart from all argument, the end will prove the wisdom of the confidence. The result of faith is not occasional and accidental ; its blessing comes, not to some who trust, but to all who trust in the Lord. Trusters in Jehovah shall be as fixed, firm, and stable as the mount where David dwelt, and where the ark abode. To move mount Zion was impossible : the mere supposition was absurd. *"Which cannot be removed, but abideth for ever."* Zion was the image of eternal steadfastness,—this hill which, according to the Hebrew, " sits to eternity," neither bowing down nor moving to and fro. Thus doth the trusting worshipper of Jehovah enjoy a restfulness which is the mirror of tranquillity ; and this not without cause, for his hope is sure, and of his confidence he can never be ashamed. As the Lord sitteth King for ever, so do his people sit enthroned in perfect peace when their trust in him is firm. This is, and is to be our portion ; we are, we have been, we shall be as steadfast as the hill of God. Zion cannot be removed, and does not remove ; so the people of God can neither be moved passively nor actively, by force from without or fickleness from within. Faith in God is a settling and establishing virtue ; he who by his strength setteth fast the mountains, by that same power stays the hearts of them that trust in him. This steadfastness will endure " for ever," and we may be assured

therefore that no believer shall perish either in life or in death, in time or in eternity. We trust in an eternal God, and our safety shall be eternal.

2. "*As the mountains are round about Jerusalem, so the* LORD *is round about his people from henceforth even for ever.*" The hill of Zion is the type of the believer's constancy, and the surrounding mountains are made emblems of the all-surrounding presence of the Lord. The mountains around the holy city, though they do not make a circular wall, are, nevertheless, set like sentinels to guard her gates. God doth not enclose his people within ramparts and bulwarks, making their city to be a prison; but yet he so orders the arrangements of his providence that his saints are as safe as if they dwelt behind the strongest fortifications. What a double security the two verses set before us! First, we are established, and then entrenched: settled, and then sentinelled: made like a mount, and then protected as if by mountains. This is no matter of poetry, it is so in fact; and it is no matter of temporary privilege, but it shall be so for ever. Date when we please, "from henceforth" Jehovah encircles his people: look on us as far as we please, the protection extends "even for ever." Note, it is not said that Jehovah's power or wisdom defends believers, but he himself is round about them: they have his personality for their protection, his Godhead for their guard. We are here taught that the Lord's people are those who trust him, for they are thus described in the first verses: the line of faith is the line of grace, those who trust in the Lord are chosen of the Lord. The two verses together prove the eternal safety of the saints: they must abide where God has placed them, and God must for ever protect them from all evil. It would be difficult to imagine greater safety than is here set forth.

3. "*For the rod of the wicked shall not rest upon the lot of the righteous.*" The people of God are not to expect immunity from trial because the Lord surrounds them, for they may feel the power and persecution of the ungodly. Isaac, even in Abraham's family, was mocked by Ishmael. Assyria laid its sceptre even upon Zion itself. The graceless often bear rule and wield the rod; and when they do so they are pretty sure to make it fall heavily upon the Lord's believing people, so that the godly cry out by reason of their oppressors. Egypt's rod was exceeding heavy upon Israel, but the time came for it to be broken. God has set a limit to the woes of his chosen: the rod may light on their portion, but it shall not *rest* upon it. The righteous have a lot which none can take from them, for God has appointed them heirs of it by gracious entail: on that lot the rod of the wicked may fall, but over that lot it cannot have lasting sway. The saints abide for ever, but their troubles will not. Here is a good argument in prayer for all righteous ones who are in the hands of the wicked.

"*Lest the righteous put forth their hands unto iniquity.*" The tendency of oppression is to drive the best of men into some hasty deed for self-deliverance or vengeance. If the rack be too long used the patient sufferer may at last give way; and therefore the Lord puts a limit to the tyranny of the wicked. He ordained that an Israelite who deserved punishment should not be beaten without measure: forty stripes save one was the appointed limit. We may therefore expect that he will set a bound to the suffering of the innocent, and will not allow them to be pushed to the uttermost extreme. Especially in point of time he will limit the domination of the persecutor, for length adds strength to oppression, and makes it intolerable: hence the Lord himself said of a certain tribulation, "except those days should be shortened, there should no flesh be saved; but for the elect's sake those days shall be shortened."

It seems that even righteous men are in peril of sinning in evil days, and that it is not the will of the Lord that they should yield to the stress of the times in order to escape from suffering. The power and influence of wicked men when they are uppermost are used to lead or drive the righteous astray; but the godly must not accept this as an excuse, and yield to the evil pressure; far rather must they resist with all their might till it shall please God to stay the violence of the persecutor, and give his children rest. This the Lord here promises to do in due time.

4. "*Do good, O* LORD, *unto those that be good, and to them that are upright in their hearts.*" Men to be good at all must be good at heart. Those who trust in the Lord are good; for faith is the root of righteousness, and the evidence of uprightness. Faith in God is a good and upright thing, and its influence makes the rest of the man good and upright. To such God will do good: the prayer of the text is but another form of promise, for that which the Lord prompts us to ask he virtually promises to give. Jehovah will take off evil from his people, and in the place thereof

will enrich them with all manner of good. When the rod of the wicked is gone his own rod and staff shall comfort us. Meanwhile it is for us to pray that it may be well with all the upright who are now among men. God bless them, and do them good in every possible form. We wish well to those who do well. We are so plagued by the crooked that we would pour benedictions upon the upright.

5. "*As for such as turn aside unto their crooked ways, the* LORD *shall lead them forth with the workers of iniquity.*" Two kinds of men are always to be found, the upright and the men of crooked ways. Alas, there are some who pass from one class to another, not by a happy conversion, turning from the twisting lanes of deceit into the highway of truth, but by an unhappy declension leaving the main road of honesty and holiness for the bypaths of wickedness. Such apostates have been seen in all ages, and David knew enough of them ; he could never forget Saul, and Ahithophel, and others. How sad that men who once walked in the right way should turn aside from it ! Observe the course of the falsehearted : first, they look out for crooked ways ; next, they choose them and make them "*their* crooked ways " ; and then they turn aside into them. They never intend to go back unto perdition, but only to make a curve and drop into the right road again. The straight way becomes a little difficult, and so they make a circumbendibus, which all along aims at coming out right, though it may a little deviate from precision. These people are neither upright in heart, nor good, nor trusters in Jehovah, and therefore the Lord will deal otherwise with them than with his own people : when execution day comes these hypocrites and time-servers shall be led out to the same gallows as the openly wicked. All sin will one day be expelled the universe, even as criminals condemned to die are led out of the city ; then shall secret traitors find themselves ejected with open rebels. Divine truth will unveil their hidden pursuits, and lead them forth, and to the surprise of many they shall be set in the same rank with those who avowedly wrought iniquity.

"*But peace shall be upon Israel.*" In fact the execution of the deceivers shall tend to give the true Israel peace. When God is smiting the unfaithful not a blow shall fall upon the faithful. The chosen of the Lord shall not only be like Salem, but they shall have salem, or peace. Like a prince, Israel has prevailed with God, and therefore he need not fear the face of man ; his wrestlings are over, the blessing of peace has been pronounced upon him. He who has peace with God may enjoy peace concerning all things. Bind the first and last verses together : Israel trusts in the Lord (verse 1), and Israel has peace (verse 5).

EXPLANATORY NOTES AND QUAINT SAYINGS.

Whole Psalm.—In the degrees of Christian virtue, this Psalm represents the sixth step—the confidence which the Christian places in the Lord. " It teacheth us, while we ascend and raise our minds unto the Lord our God in loving charity and piety, not to fix our gaze upon men who are prosperous in the world with a false happiness."*—*H. T. Armfield, in "The Gradual Psalms,"* 1874.

Whole Psalm.—This short Psalm may be summed up in those words of the prophet (Isaiah iii. 10, 11), " Say ye to the righteous, that it shall be well with him. Woe unto the wicked ! it shall be ill with him." Thus are life and death, the blessing and the curse, set before us often in the Psalms, as well as in the law and in the prophets.—*Matthew Henry,* 1662—1714.

Verse 1.—"*They that trust in the* LORD." Note how he commandeth no work here to be done, but only speaketh of trust. In popery in the time of trouble men were taught to enter into some kind of religion, to fast, to go on pilgrimage, and to do such other foolish works of devotion, which they devised as an high service unto God, and thereby thought to make condign satisfaction for sin and to merit eternal life. But here the Psalmist leadeth us the plain way unto God, pronouncing this to be the chiefest anchor of our salvation,—only to hope and trust in the Lord ;

---

* Augustine

and declaring that the greatest service that we can do unto God is to trust him. For this is the nature of God—to create all things of nothing. Therefore he createth and bringeth forth in death, life ; in darkness, light. Now to believe this is the essential nature and most special property of faith. When God then seeth such a one as agreeth with his own nature, that is, which believeth to find in danger help, in poverty riches, in sin righteousness, and that for God's own mercy's sake in Christ alone, him can God neither hate nor forsake.—*Martin Luther* (1483—1546), *in* "A Commentary on the Psalms of Degrees."

Verse 1.—*"They that trust in the* LORD." All that deal with God must deal upon trust, and he will give comfort to those only that give credit to him, and make it appear they do so by quitting other confidences, and venturing to the utmost for God. The closer our expectations are confined to God, the higher our expectations may be raised.—*Matthew Henry.*

Verse 1.—*"They that trust,"* etc. Trust, therefore, in the Lord, *always, altogether, and for all things.*—*Robert Nisbet, in "The Songs of the Temple Pilgrims,"* 1863.

Verse 1.—*"Shall be as mount Zion."* Some persons are like the sand—ever shifting and treacherous. See Matthew vii. 26. Some are like the sea—restless and unsettled. See Isaiah lvii. 20 ; James i. 6. Some are like the wind—uncertain and inconstant. See Ephesians iv. 14. Believers are like a mountain—strong, stable, and secure. To every soul that trusts him the Lord says, " Thou art Peter."— *W. H. J. Page,* 1883.

Verse 1.—*"As mount Zion,"* etc.—Great is the stability of a believer's felicity.— *John Trapp,* 1601—1669.

Verse 1.—*"Mount Zion, which cannot be removed,"* etc. Lieutenant Conder, reviewing Mr. Maudslay's important exploration, says, " It is especially valuable as showing that, however the masonry may have been destroyed and lost, we may yet hope to find indications of the ancient enceinte *in the rock scarps which are imperishable."* This is very true ; for, while man can destroy what man has made, the everlasting hills smile at his rage. Yet who can hear of it without perceiving the force and sublimity of that glorious description of the immobility of believers.

> " They that trust in Jehovah are as mount Zion,
> Which shall not be moved, it abideth for ever."

James Neil, in "Palestine Explored," 1882.

Verse 1.—*"Cannot be removed,"* etc. They can never be removed from the Lord, though they may be removed from his house and ordinances, as sometimes David was ; and from his gracious presence, and sensible communion with him ; and out of the world by death : yet never from his heart's love, nor out of the covenant of his grace, which is sure and everlasting ; nor out of his family, into which they are taken ; nor from the Lord Jesus Christ, nor out of his hands and arms, nor from off his heart ; nor from off him, as the foundation on which they are laid ; nor out of a state of grace, either regeneration or justification ; but such abide in the love of God, in the covenant of his grace, in the hands of his Son, in the grace wherein they stand, and in the house of God for evermore.—*John Gill,* 1697—1771.

Verse 1.—*"Abideth for ever."* So surely as *"Mount Zion"* shall never be *"removed,"* so surely shall the church of God be preserved. Is it not strange that wicked and idolatrous powers have not joined together, dug down this mount, and carried it into the sea, that they might nullify a promise in which the people of God exult ! Till ye can carry Mount Zion into the Mediterranean Sea, the church of Christ shall grow and prevail. Hear this, ye murderous Mohammedans !—*Adam Clarke,* 1760—1832.

Verse 1.—*"Abideth."* Literally, *sitteth ;* as spoken of a mountain, " lieth " or " is situated " ; but here with the following *"for ever,"* used in a still stronger sense.— *J. J. Stewart Perowne,* 1868.

Verses 1, 2.—That which is here promised the saints is a perpetual preservation of them in that condition wherein they are ; both on the part of God, " he is round about them from henceforth even for ever " ; and on their parts, *"they shall not be removed,"*—that is, from the condition of acceptation with God wherein they are supposed to be,—but they shall abide for ever, and continue therein immovable unto the end. This is a plain promise of their continuance in that condition wherein they are, with their safety from thence, and not a promise of some other good thing provided that they continue in that condition. Their being compared to mountains, and their stability, which consists in their being and continuing so, will admit no other sense. As mount Zion abides in its condition, so shall they; and as the mountains about Jerusalem continue, so doth the Lord continue his presence unto them.

That expression which is used, verse 2, is weighty and full to this purpose, *"The Lord is round about his people from henceforth even for ever."* What can be spoken more fully, more pathetically ? Can any expression of men so set forth the safety of the saints ? The Lord is round about them, not to save them from this or that incursion, but from all; not from one or two evils, but from every one whereby they are or may be assaulted. He is with them, and round about them on every side that no evil shall come nigh them. It is a most full expression of universal preservation, or of God's keeping his saints in his love and favour, upon all accounts whatsoever; and that not for a season only, but it is *"henceforth,"* from his giving this promise unto their souls in particular, and their receiving of it, throughout all generations, *"even for ever."*—*John Owen*, 1616—1683.

Verse 2.—*"As the mountains are round about Jerusalem."* This image is not realised, as most persons familiar with our European scenery would wish and expect it to be realised. Jerusalem is not literally shut in by mountains, except on the eastern side, where it may be said to be enclosed by the arms of Olivet, with its outlying ridges on the north-east and south-west. Anyone facing Jerusalem westward, northward, or southward, will always see the city itself on an elevation higher than the hills in its immediate neighbourhood, its towers and walls standing out against the sky, and not against any high back-ground such as that which encloses the mountain towns and villages of our own Cumbrian or Westmoreland valleys. Nor, again, is the plain on which it stands enclosed by a continuous though distant circle of mountains, like that which gives its peculiar charm to Athens and Innspruck. The mountains in the neighbourhood of Jerusalem are of unequal height, and only in two or three instances—Neby-Samwil, Er-Rain, and Tuleil el-Ful—rising to any considerable elevation. Even Olivet is only a hundred and eighty feet above the top of Mount Zion. Still they act as a shelter : they must be surmounted before the traveller can see, or the invader attack, the Holy City ; and the distant line of Moab would always seem to rise as a wall against invaders from the remote east. It is these mountains, expressly including those beyond the Jordan, which are mentioned as " standing round about Jerusalem," in another and more terrible sense, when, on the night of the assault of Jerusalem by the Roman armies, they " echoed back " the screams of the inhabitants of the captured city, and the victorious shouts of the soldiers of Titus.*—*Arthur Penrhyn Stanley* (1815—1881), *in "Sinai and Palestine."*

Verse 2.—*"As the mountains are round about Jerusalem."* Jerusalem is situated in the centre of a mountainous region, whose valleys have drawn around it in all directions a perfect net-work of deep ravines, the perpendicular walls of which constitute a very efficient system of defence.—*William M. Thomson, in "The Land and the Book,"* 1881.

Verse 2.—*"As the mountains are round about Jerusalem,"* etc. The mountains most emphatically stand *"round about Jerusalem,"* and in doing so must have greatly safeguarded it in ancient times. We are specially told that when Titus besieged the city, he found it impossible to invest it completely until he had built a wall round the entire sides of these mountains, nearly five miles long, with thirteen places at intervals in which he stationed garrisons, which added another mile and a quarter to these vast earthworks. " The whole was completed," says the Jewish historian, " in three days ; so that what would naturally have required some months was done in so short an interval as is incredible."† Assaults upon the city, even then, could only be delivered effectively upon its level corner to the north-west, whence every hostile advance was necessarily directed in all its various sieges. To those familiar with these facts, beautifully bold, graphic, and forceful is the Psalmist's figure of the security of the Lord's people—

> " The mountains are round about Jerusalem ;
> And Jehovah is round about his people,
> Henceforth, even for evermore."

---

* Josephus. Bell. Jud. **vi. 5,** 1.
† Josephus. Wars of the Jews. Book **v.** chap **xii.** section 2.

These words must have been in Hebrew ears as sublime as the were comforting, and, when sung on the heights of Zion, inspiring in the last degr.—*James Neil.*

Verse 2.—*"The* LORD *is round about his people."* It is not ough that we are compassed about with fiery walls, that is, with the sure custody, t continual watch and ward of the angels ; but the Lord himself is our wall : so t every way we are defended by the Lord against all dangers. Above us is his aven, on both sides he is as a wall, under us he is as a strong rock whereupon we nd : so are we everywhere sure and safe. Now if Satan through these munition ists his darts at us, it must needs be that the Lord himself shall be hurt befor take harm. Great is our incredulity if we hear all these things in vain.—*Martii ther.*

Verse 2.—*"From henceforth, even for ever."* This amplification he promise taken from time or duration, should be carefully noted ; for it shows the promises made to the people of Israel pertain generally to the Church in ever promises not to expire with that polity. Thus it expressly declares, that th and are continuously endure in this life ; which is most sweet consolation for rch will especially in great dangers and public calamities, when everything appear minds, ruin and destruction.—*D. H. Mollerus,* 1639. eaten

Verse 3.—*"The rod of the wicked."* It is *their* rod, made for them ; if G his children a little with it, he doth but borrow it from the immediate an ge use for which it was ordained ; their rod, their judgment. So it is called t al " This is the portion " and potion " of their cup." Ps. xi. 6.—*Thomas.* in *"An Exposition of the Second Epistle of Peter,"* 1633.

Verse 3.—*"For the rod of the wicked,"* etc. According to Gussetius, th be understood of a measuring rod ; laid not on persons, but on lands and e and best agrees with the lot, inheritance, and estate of the righteous ; and signify that though wicked men unjustly seize upon and retain the farms, posses and estates of good men, as if they were assigned to them by the measuring yet they shall not hold them long, or always.—*John Gill.*

Verse 3.—*"For the rod of the wicked shall not rest upon the lot of the righteou* No tyranny, although it appear firm and stable, is of long continuance : inasmu as God does not relinquish the sceptre. This is manifest from the example of Phara of Saul, of Sennacherib, of Herod, and of others. Rightly, therefore, says Athanasi of Julian the Apostate, " That little cloud has quickly passed away." And ho quickly beyond all human expectation the foundations of the ungodly are overthrown is fully declared in Psalm xxxvii.—*Solomon Gesner,* 1559—1605.

Verse 3.—*"Shall not rest,"* that is to say, " lie heavy," so as to oppress, as in Isa. xxv. 10, with a further sense of *continuance* of the oppression.—*J. J. Stewart Perowne.*

Verse 3.—*"Shall not rest,"* etc. The wrath of man, like water turned upon a mill, shall come on them with no more force than shall be sufficient for accomplishing God's gracious purposes on their souls : the rest, however menacing its power may be, shall be made to pass off by an opened sluice. Nevertheless the trouble shall be sufficient to try every man, and to prove the truth and measure of his integrity.— *Charles Simeon* (1759—1836) *in "Horæ Homileticæ."*

Verse 3.—*"The lot of the righteous."* There is a fourfold lot belonging to the faithful. 1. The lot of the saints is the sufferings of the saints. " All that will live godly in Christ Jesus shall suffer persecution : " 2 Tim. iii. 12. 2. The lot of the saints is also that light and happiness they have in this world. The lot is " fallen unto me in pleasant places ; yea, I have a goodly heritage : " Ps. xvi. 6. When David sat at the sheepfold, which was his lot, he was thus prepared for the kingdom of Israel which was given him by lot from God. 3. But more specially faith, grace, and sanctification ; which give them just right and title to the inheritance of glory. Heaven is theirs now ; though not in possession, yet in succession. They have the earnest of it ; let them grow up to stature and perfection, and take it. 4. Lastly, they have the lot of heaven. Hell is the lot of the wicked : " Behold at eveningtide trouble ; and before the morning he is not. This is the portion of them that spoil us, and the lot of them that rob us "; Isa. xvii. 14. Therefore it is said of Judas, that he went " to his own place ": Acts i. 25. " Upon the wicked he shall rain snares, fire and brimstone, and an horrible tempest ; this shall be the portion of their cup " : Ps. xi. 6. But the lot of the righteous is faith, and the end of their faith the salvation of their souls. God gives them heaven, not for any foreseen worthiness in the receivers, for no worthiness of our own can make us our father's heirs ; but for hi own mercy and favour in Christ, preparing heaven for us, and us for heaven. So iat upon his decree it is allotted to us ; and unless heaven could lose God, we ca ot lose heaven.

Here, then, nsider how the lottery of Canaan may shadow out to us that blessed land of promi est whereof the other was a type.—*Thomas Adams.*

Verse 3.— est the righteous put forth their hands unto iniquity." Lest overcome by impatien or drawn aside by the world's *allurements* or *affrightments*, they should yiel d comply with the desires of the wicked, or seek to help themselves out of tro by sinister practices. God (saith Chrysostom) acts like a lutanist, who will et the strings of his lute be too slack, lest it mar the music, nor suffer them to o hard stretched or screwed up, lest they break.—*John Trapp, 1601—1669.*

—"*Lest the righteous put forth their hands,*" etc. The trial is to prove Ve o endanger it by too sharp a pressure ; *lest,* overcome by this, even faith, l put forth a hand (as in Gen. iii. 22), to forbidden pleasure ; or (as in the fi 8), to contamination : through force of custom gradually persuading Ex compliance, or through despair of good, as the Psalmist (see Ps. xxxvii. t iii.) lescribes some in his day who witnessed the prosperity of wicked men.— *eake 's Commentary, 1871—1881.*

erse 4.—"*Do good, O LORD, unto those that be good.*" The Midrash here calls ind a Talmudic riddle :—There came a good one (Moses, Ex. ii. 2) and received ood thing (the Tôra, or Law, Prov. iv. 2) from the good One (God, Ps. cxlv. 9) the good ones (Israel, Ps. cxxv. 4).—*Franz Delitzsch, 1871.*

Verse 4.—"*Do good, O LORD, unto those that be good.*" A favourite thought vith Nehemiah. See Nehemiah ii. 8, 18 ; v. 19 ; xiii. 14, 31 : " Remember me, O my God, for *good,*" the concluding words of his book.—*Christopher Wordsworth, 1872.*

Verse 4.—"*Do good, O LORD, unto those that be good.*" They consult their own good best, who do most good. I may say these three things of *those who do good* (and what is serving God but doing of good ? or what is doing good but serving God ?). First, they shall receive true good. Secondly, they shall for ever hold the best good, the chief good ; they shall not only spend their days and years in good ; but when their days and years are spent, they shall have good, and a greater good than any they had, in spending the days and years of this life. They shall have good in death, they shall come to a fuller enjoyment of God, *the chief good,* when they have left and let fall the possession of all earthly goods. Thirdly, they that do good shall find all things working together for their good ; if they have a loss they shall receive good by it ; if they bear a cross, that cross shall bear good to them.—*Joseph Caryl, 1602—1673.*

Verse 4.—"*Do good, O LORD, unto those that be good,*" etc. Perhaps it may not prove unprofitable to enquire, with some minuteness, who are the persons for whom prayer is presented, and who have an interest in the Divine promises. They are brought before us under different denominations. In the first verse, they are described as trusting in the Lord : in the second verse, they are described as the Lord's people : in the third verse, they are called the righteous : in the fourth verse, they are called good and upright in heart : and in the fifth verse, they are called Israel. Let us collect these terms together, and endeavour to ascertain from them, what is their true condition and character, for whose security the Divine perfections are pledged. And while a rapid sketch is thus drawn, let each breathe the silent prayer, " Search me, O God, and know my heart ; try me, and know my thoughts ; and see if there be any wicked way in me, and lead me in the way everlasting."— *N. M'Michael, in "The Pilgrim Psalms," 1860.*

Verse 4.—" *Do good, O LORD, unto those that be good.*" Believers are described as "*good.*" The name is explained by the Spirit as implying the indwelling of the Holy Ghost and of faith. It is proof that no guile is harboured in their hearts. Prayer is made that God would visit them with goodness. This prayer indited by the Spirit amounts to a heavenly promise that they shall receive such honour.— *Henry Law, in "Family Devotion," 1878.*

Verse 4.—"*Them that be good.*" Oh, brethren, the good in us is God in us. The inwardness makes the outwardness, the godliness the beauty. It is indisputable that it is Christ in us that makes all our Christianity. Oh, Christians who have no Christ in them—such Christians are poor, cheap imitations, and hollow shams—

and Christ will, with infinite impatience, even infinite love, fling them away.—
Charles Stanford, in a Sermon preached before the Baptist Union, 1876.

Verse 4.—*"Upright in their hearts."* All true excellence has its seat here. It is not the good action which makes the good man : it is the good man who does the good action. The merit of an action depends entirely upon the motives which have prompted its performance ; and, tried by this simple test, how many deeds, which have wrung from the world its admiration and its glory, might well be described in old words, as nothing better than splendid sins. When the heart is wrong, all is wrong. When the heart is right, all is right.—*N. M'Michael.*

Verse 4.—*"Upright."* Literally, *straight*, straightforward, as opposed to all moral obliquity whatever.—*Joseph Addison Alexander (1809—1860), in "The Psalms Translated and Explained."*

Verse 5.—*"Such as turn aside unto their crooked ways."* This is the anxiety of the pastor in this pilgrim song. The shepherd would keep his sheep from straggling. His distress is that all in Israel are not true Israelites. Two sorts of people, described by the poet, have ever been in the church. The second class, instead of being at the trouble to " withstand in the evil day," will " put forth their hands unto iniquity." Rather than feel, they will follow the rod of the wicked. They will " turn aside unto their crooked ways," sooner than risk temporal and material interests.—*Edward Jewitt Robinson, in "The Caravan and the Temple," 1878.*

Verse 5.—*"Such as turn aside unto their crooked ways."* All the ways of sin are called *"crooked ways,"* and they are our own ways. The Psalmist calls them *"their* crooked ways"* ; that is, the ways of their own devising ; whereas the way of holiness is the Lord's way. To exceed or do more ; to be deficient or do less, than God requires, both these are *"crooked ways."* The way of the Lord lies straight forward, right before us. " Whoso walketh uprightly shall be saved ; but he that is perverse (or *crooked*) in his ways shall fall at once": Prov. xxviii. 18. The motion of a godly man is like that of the kine that carried the ark: "Who took the straight way to the way of Beth-shemesh, and went along the highway, lowing as they went, and turned not aside to the right hand or to the left": 1 Sam. vi. 12.—*Joseph Caryl.*

Verse 5.—*"Crooked ways."* The ways of sinners are *"crooked "* ; they shift from one pursuit to another, and turn hither and thither to deceive ; they wind about a thousand ways to conceal their base intentions, to accomplish their iniquitous projects, or to escape the punishment of their crimes ; yet disappointment, detection, confusion, and misery, are their inevitable portion.—*Thomas Scott, 1747—1821.*

Verse 5.—*The* LORD *shall lead them forth with the workers of iniquity."* They walked according to the prince of the air, and they shall go where the prince of the air is. God will bring forth men from their hiding-places. Though they walk among the drove of his children, in procession now, yet if they also walk in by-lanes of sin, God will rank them at the latter day, yea, often in this world, with the workers of iniquity. They walk after workers of iniquity here before God, and God will make manifest that it is so before he hath done with them. The reason, my brethren, why they are to be reckoned among workers of iniquity, and as walkers among them, though they sever themselves from them in respect of external conversation, is, because they agree in the same internal principle of sin. They walk in their lusts : every unregenerate man doth so. Refine him how you will, it is certain he doth in heart pursue *"crooked ways."*—*Thomas Goodwin, 1600—1679.*

Verse 5.—Sometimes God takes away a barren professor by permitting him to fall into open profaneness. There is one that hath taken up a profession of the worthy name of the Lord Jesus Christ, but this profession is only a cloak ; he secretly practiseth wickedness ; he is a glutton, or a drunkard, or covetous, or unclean. Well, saith God, I will loose the reins of this professor, I will give him up to his vile affections. I will loose the reins of his sins before him, he shall be entangled with his filthy lusts, he shall be overcome of ungodly company. Thus they that turn aside to their own crooked ways, *"the Lord shall lead them forth with the workers of iniquity."*—*John Bunyan, 1628—1688.*

Verse 5.—*"But peace shall be upon Israel."* Do you ask, What is the peace upon Israel ? I answer :—First, the peace of Israel, that is, of a believing and holy soul, is *from above*, and is higher than all the disturbances of the world ; it rests upon him, and makes him calm and peaceful, and lifts him above the world : for upon him rests the Holy Spirit, who is the Comforter ; who is essential love and uncreated peace. Secondly, the peace of a believing and holy soul is *internal ;* for it is sent down from heaven upon his head, flows into his heart, and dwells there, and stills all agitations of mind. Thirdly, the peace of a believing and holy soul, is also *external*. It is a fountain of Paradise watering all the face of the earth ; Gen. ii. 6 : you see it in the man's face and life. Fourthly, the peace of a believing and holy soul is *divine :* for chiefly, it maintains peace with God. Fifthly, the peace of a believing and holy soul is *universal :* to wit, with neighbours, with God, with himself : in the body, in the eyes, in the ears, in tasting, smelling, feeling, in all the members, and in all the appetites. This peace is not disturbed by devils, the world, and the flesh, setting forth their honours, riches, pleasures. Sixthly, the peace of a believing and holy soul is peace *eternal* and never interrupted ; for it flows from an eternal and exhaustless fountain, even from God himself.—*Condensed from Le Blanc*, 1599 —1669.

Verse 5.—"*Israel.*" The Israelites derived their joint names from the two chief parts of religion : Israelites, from Israel, whose prayer was his " strength " (Hosea xii. 3), and Jews, from Judah, whose name means " praise."—*George Seaton Bowes, in "Illustrative Gatherings,"* 1869.

HINTS TO PREACHERS.

Whole Psalm.—I. The mark of the covenant : " They that trust." II. The security of the covenant (verses 1, 2). III. The rod of the covenant (verse 3). IV. The tenor of the covenant (verse 4). V. The spirit of the covenant,—" peace."

Verse 1.—See " Spurgeon's Sermons," No. 1,450 : " The Immortality of the Believer."

Verses 1, 2.—I. The believer's singularity : he trusts in Jehovah. II. The believer's stability : " abideth for ever." III. The believer's safety : " As the mountains," etc.

Verse 2.—The all-surrounding presence of Jehovah the glory, safety, and eternal blessedness of his people. Yet this to the wicked would be hell.

Verse 2.—See " Spurgeon's Sermons," Nos. 161-2 : " The Security of the Church."

Verse 2.—The endurance of mercy : " From henceforth even for ever."

Verse 2.—Saints hemmed-in by infinite love. I. *The City and the Girdle,* or *the symbols separated.* 1. Jerusalem imaging God's people. Anciently chosen ; singularly honoured ; much beloved ; the shrine of Deity. 2. The Mountain Girdle setting forth Jehovah : Strength ; All-sidedness ; Sentinel through day and night. II. *The City within the Girdle,* or *the symbols related.* 1. Delightful Entanglement. The view from the windows ! (Jehovah " round about.") To be lost must *break through God !* Sound sleep and safe labour. 2. Omnipotent Circumvallation, suggesting—God's determination ; Satan's dismay. This mountain ring immutable. —*W. B. Haynes.*

Verse 3.—Observe, I. The Permission implied. The rod of the wicked may come upon the lot of the righteous. Why ? 1. That wickedness may be free to manifest itself. 2. That the righteous may be made to hate sin. 3. That the righteousness of God's retribution may be seen. 4. That the consolations of the righteous may abound. 2 Cor. i. 5. II. The Permanency denied : " The rod . . . shall *not rest,*" etc. Illustrate by history of Job, Joseph, David, Daniel, Christ, martyrs, etc. III. The Probity tried and preserved : " Lest the righteous put forth," etc., by rebelling, sinful compromise, etc. 1. God will have it tried, to prove its worth, beauty, etc. 2. But no more than sufficiently tried.—*John Field.*

Verses 3, 4.—I. The good defined : " The upright in heart ; " such as do not " turn aside," and are not " workers of iniquity." II. The good distressed : by " the rod of the wicked." III. The good delivered : " Do good "; fulfil thy promise (verse 3).—*W. H. J. Page.*

Verse 4.—I. What it is to be good. II. What it is for God to do us good.

Verse 5.—Temporary Professors. I. The crucial test : " They turn aside." II. The crooked policy : they make crooked ways their own. III. The crushing doom : " led forth with workers of iniquity."

Verse 5.—Hypocrites. I. Their ways: "crooked." 1. Like the way of a winding stream, seeking out the fair level, or the easy descent. 2. Like the course of a tacking ship, which skilfully makes every wind to drive her forward. 3. Ways constructed upon no principle but that of pure selfishness. II. Their conduct under trial. They "turn aside." 1. From their religious profession. 2. From their former companions. 3. To become the worst scorners of spiritual things, and the most violent calumniators of spiritually-minded men. III. Their doom: "The Lord shall," etc. 1. In the judgment they shall be classed with the most flagrant sinners; "with the workers of iniquity." 2. They shall be exposed by an irresistible power: "The Lord shall lead them forth." 3. They shall meet with terrible execution with the wicked in hell.—*J. Field.*

Verse 5 (last clause).—To whom peace belongs. To "Israel"; the chosen, the once wrestler, the now prevailing prince. Consider Jacob's life after he obtained the name of Israel; note his trials, and his security under them as illustrating this text. Then take the text as a sure promise.

Verse 5 (last clause).—Enquire, I. Who are the Israel? 1. Covenanted ones. 2. Circumcised in heart. 3. True worshippers. II. What is the peace? 1. Peace of conscience. 2. Of friendship with God. 3. Of a settled and satisfied heart. 4. Of eternal glory, in reversion. III. Why the certainty ("shall be")? 1. Christ has made peace for them. 2. The Holy Spirit brings peace to them. 3. They walk in the way of peace.—*J. Field.*

PSALM CXXVI.

Title.—A Song of Degrees. *This is the seventh step, and we may therefore expect to meet with some special perfection of joy in it; nor shall we look in vain. We see here not only that Zion abides, but that her joy returns after sorrow. Abiding is not enough, f uitfulness is added. The pilgrims went from blessing to blessing in their Psalmody as they proceeded on their holy way. Happy people to whom every ascent was a song, every halt a hymn. Here the truster becomes a sower : faith works by love, obtains a present bliss, and secures a harvest of delight.*

There is nothing in this Psalm by which we can decide its date, further than this,— that it is a song after a great deliverance from oppression. "Turning captivity" by no means requires an actual removal into banishment to fill out the idea ; rescue from any dire affliction or crushing tyranny w uld be fitly described as "captivity turned." Indeed, the passage is not applicable to captives in Babylon, for it is Zion itself which is in captivity, and not a part of her citizens : the holy city was in sorrow and distress ; though it could not be removed, the prosperity could be diminished. Some dark cloud lowered over the beloved capital, and its citizens prayed "Turn again our captivity, O Lord."

This Psalm is in its right place and most fittingly follows its predecessor, for as in Psalm cxxv. we read that the rod of the wicked shall not rest upon the lot of the righteous, we here see it removed from them to their great joy. The word "turn" would seem to be the key-note of the song ; it is a Psalm of conversion—conversion from captivity ; and it may well be used to set forth the rapture of a pardoned soul when the anger of the Lord is turned away from it. We will call it, "Leading captivity captive."

The Psalm divides itself into a narrative (1, 2), a song (3), a prayer (4), and a promise (5 and 6).

EXPOSITION.

WHEN the Lord turned again the captivity of Zion, we were like them that dream.

2 Then was our mouth filled with laughter, and our tongue with singing : then said they among the heathen, The Lord hath done great things for them.

3 The Lord hath done great things for us ; *whereof* we are glad.

4 Turn again our captivity, O Lord, as the streams in the south.

5 They that sow in tears shall reap in joy.

6 He that goeth forth and weepeth, bearing precious seed, shall doubtless come again with rejoicing, bringing his sheaves *with him*.

1. "*When the Lord turned again the captivity of Zion, we were like them that dream.*" Being in trouble, the gracious pilgrims remember for their comfort times of national woe which were succeeded by remarkable deliverances. Then sorrow was gone like a dream, and the joy which followed was so great that it seemed too good to be true, and they feared that it must be the vision of an idle brain. So sudden and so overwhelming was their joy that they felt like men out of themselves, ecstatic, or in a trance. The captivity had been great, and great was the deliverance ; for the great God himself had wrought it : it seemed too good to be actually true : each man said to himself,—

"Is this a dream ? O if it be a dream,
Let me sleep on, and do not wake me yet."

It was not the freedom of an individual which the Lord in mercy had wrought, but of all Zion, of the whole nation ; and this was reason enough for overflowing gladness. We need not instance the histories which illustrate this verse in connection with literal Israel ; but it is well to remember how often it has been true to ourselves. Let us look to the prison-houses from which we have been set free. Ah, me, what captives we have been ! At our first conversion what a turning again of captivity we experienced. Never shall that hour be forgotten. Joy! Joy! Joy! Since then, from multiplied troubles, from depression of spirit, from miserable backsliding, from grievous doubt, we have been emancipated, and we are not able to describe the bliss which followed each emancipation.

> " When God reveal'd his gracious name
> And changed our mournful state,
> Our rapture seem'd a pleasing dream,
> The grace appeared so great."

This verse will have a higher fulfilment in the day of the final overthrow of the powers of darkness when the Lord shall come forth for the salvation and glorification of his redeemed. Then in a fuller sense than even at Pentecost our old men shall see visions, and our young men shall dream dreams : yea, all things shall be so wonderful, so far beyond all expectation, that those who behold them shall ask themselves whether it be not all a dream. The past is ever a sure prognostic of the future ; the thing which has been is the thing that shall be : we shall again and again find ourselves amazed at the wonderful goodness of the Lord. Let our hearts gratefully remember the former lovingkindnesses of the Lord : we were sadly low, sorely distressed, and completely past hope, but when Jehovah appeared he did not merely lift us out of despondency, he raised us into wondering happiness. The Lord who alone turns our captivity does nothing by halves : those whom he saves from hell he brings to heaven. He turns exile into ecstasy, and banishment into bliss.

2. *"Then was our mouth filled with laughter, and our tongue with singing."* So full were they of joy that they could not contain themselves. They must express their joy and yet they could not find expression for it. Irrepressible mirth could do no other than laugh, for speech was far too dull a thing for it. The mercy was so unexpected, so amazing, so singular that they could not do less than laugh ; and they laughed much, so that their mouths were full of it, and that because their hearts were full too. When at last the tongue could move articulately, it could not be content simply to talk, but it must needs sing ; and sing heartily too, for it was full of singing. Doubtless the former pain added to the zest of the pleasure : the captivity threw a brighter colour into the emancipation. The people remembered this joy-flood for years after, and here is the record of it turned into a song. Note the *when* and the *then*. God's *when* is our *then*. At the moment when he turns our captivity, the heart turns from its sorrow ; when he fills us with grace we are filled with gratitude. We were made to be as them that dream, but we both laughed and sang in our sleep. We are wide awake now, and though we can scarcely realize the blessing, yet we rejoice in it exceedingly.

"Then said they among the heathen, The Lord hath done great things for them." The heathen heard the songs of Israel, and the better sort among them soon guessed the cause of their joy. Jehovah was known to be their God, and to him the other nations ascribed the emancipation of his people, reckoning it to be no small thing which the Lord had thus done ; for those who carried away the nations had never in any other instance restored a people to their ancient dwelling-place. These foreigners were no dreamers ; though they were only lookers-on, and not partakers in the surprising mercy, they plainly saw what had been done, and rightly ascribed it to the great Giver of all good. It is a blessed thing when saints set sinners talking about the lovingkindness of the Lord : and it is equally blessed when the saints who are hidden away in the world hear of what the Lord has done for his church, and themselves resolve to come out from their captivity and unite with the Lord's people. Ah, dear reader, Jehovah has indeed done marvellous things for his chosen, and these " great things " shall be themes for eternal praise among all intelligent creatures.

3. *"The Lord hath done great things for us ; whereof we are glad."* They did not deny the statement which reflected so much glory upon Jehovah : with exultation they admitted and repeated the statement of Jehovah's notable dealings with them. To themselves they appropriated the joyful assertion ; they said " The Lord hath done great things *for us,*" and they declared their gladness at the fact. It is a poor modesty which is ashamed to own its joy in the Lord. Call it rather a robbery of God. There is so little of happiness abroad that if we possess a full share of it we ought not to hide our light under a bushel, but let it shine on all that are in the house. Let us avow our joy, and the reason of it, stating the " whereof " as

well as the fact. None are so happy as those who are newly turned and returned from captivity ; none can more promptly and satisfactorily give a reason for the gladness that is in them. The Lord himself has blessed us, blessed us greatly, blessed us individually, blessed us assuredly ; and because of this we sing unto his name. I heard one say the other day in prayer " whereof we desire to be glad." Strange dilution and defilement of Scriptural language ! Surely if God has done great things for us we are glad, and cannot be otherwise. No doubt such language is meant to be lowly, but in truth it is loathsome.

4. *"Turn again our captivity, O Lord."* Remembering the former joy of a past rescue they cry to Jehovah for a repetition of it. When we pray for the turning of our captivity, it is wise to recall former instances thereof : nothing strengthens faith more effectually than the memory of a previous experience. " The Lord hath done" harmonizes well with the prayer, " Turn again." The text shows us how wise it is to resort anew to the Lord who in former times has been so good to us. Where else should we go but to him who has done such great things for us ? Who can turn again our captivity but he who turned it before ?

"As the streams in the south." Even as the Lord sends floods adown the dry beds of southern torrents after long droughts, so can he fill our wasted and wearied spirits with floods of holy delight. This the Lord can do for any of us, and he can do it at once, for nothing is too hard for the Lord. It is well for us thus to pray, and to bring our suit before him who is able to bless us exceeding abundantly. Do not let us forget the past, but in the presence of our present difficulty let us resort unto the Lord, and beseech him to do that for us which we cannot possibly do for ourselves,—that which no other power can perform on our behalf. Israel did return from the captivity in Babylon, and it was even as though a flood of people hastened to Zion. Suddenly and plenteously the people filled again the temple courts. In streams they shall also in the latter days return to their own land, and replenish it yet again. Like mighty torrents shall the nations flow unto the Lord in the day of his grace. May the Lord hasten it in his own time.

5. *"They that sow in tears shall reap in joy."* Hence, present distress must not be viewed as if it would last for ever : it is not the end, by any means, but only a means to the end. Sorrow is our sowing, rejoicing shall be our reaping. If there were no sowing in tears there would be no reaping in joy. If we were never captives we could never lead our captivity captive. Our mouth had never been filled with holy laughter if it had not been first filled with the bitterness of grief. We must sow : we may have to sow in the wet weather of sorrow ; but we shall reap, and reap in the bright summer season of joy. Let us keep to the work of this present sowing time, and find strength in the promise which is here so positively given us. Here is one of the Lord's shalls and wills ; it is freely given both to workers, waiters, and weepers, and they may rest assured that it will not fail : " in due season they *shall* reap."

This sentence may well pass current in the church as an inspired proverb. It is not every sowing which is thus insured against all danger, and guaranteed a harvest ; but the promise specially belongs to sowing *in tears.* When a man's heart is so stirred that he weeps over the sins of others, he is elect to usefulness. Winners of souls are first weepers for souls. As there is no birth without travail, so is there no spiritual harvest without painful tillage. When our own hearts are broken with grief at man's transgression we shall break other men's hearts : tears of earnestness beget tears of repentance : " deep calleth unto deep."

6. *"He."* The general assurance is applied to each one in particular. That which is spoken in the previous verse in the plural—"they," is here repeated in the singular—" he." *"He that goeth forth and weepeth, bearing precious seed, shall doubtless come again with rejoicing, bringing his sheaves with him."* He leaves his couch to go forth into the frosty air and tread the heavy soil ; and as he goes he weeps because of past failures, or because the ground is so sterile, or the weather so unseasonable, or his corn so scarce, and his enemies so plentiful and so eager to rob him of his reward. He drops a seed and a tear, a seed and a tear, and so goes on his way. In his basket he has seed which is precious to him, for he has little of it, and it is his hope for the next year. Each grain leaves his hand with anxious prayer that it may not be lost : he thinks little of himself, but much of his seed, and he eagerly asks, " Will it prosper ? shall I receive a reward for my labour ? " Yes, good husbandman, *doubtless* you will gather sheaves from your sowing. Because the Lord has written *doubtless,* take heed that you do not doubt. No

reason for doubt can remain after the Lord has spoken. You will return to this field—not to sow, but to reap ; not to weep, but to rejoice ; and after awhile you will go home again with nimbler step than to-day, though with a heavier load, for you shall have sheaves to bear with you. Your handful shall be so greatly multiplied that many sheaves shall spring from it ; and you shall have the pleasure of reaping them and bringing them home to the place from which you went out weeping.

This is a figurative description of that which was literally described in the first three verses. It is the turning of the worker's captivity, when, instead of seed buried beneath black earth, he sees the waving crops inviting him to a golden harvest.

It is somewhat singular to find this promise of fruitfulness in close contact with return from captivity ; and yet it is so in our own experience, for when our own soul is revived the souls of others are blessed by our labours. If any of us, having been once lonesome and lingering captives, have now returned home, and have become longing and labouring sowers, may the Lord, who has already delivered us, soon transform us into glad-hearted reapers, and to him shall be praise for ever and ever. Amen.

EXPLANATORY NOTES AND QUAINT SAYINGS.

Title.—Augustine interprets the title, " A Song of Degrees, i.e. a Song of drawing upwards," of the drawing (going) up to the heavenly Jerusalem. This is right, inasmuch as the deliverance from the captivity of sin and death should in an increased measure excite those feelings of gratitude which Israel must have felt on being delivered from their corporeal captivity ; in this respect again is the history of the outward theocracy a type of the history of the church.—*Augustus F. Tholuck*, 1856.

Whole Psalm.—In its Christian aspect the Psalm represents the seventh of the " degrees " in our ascent to the Jerusalem that is above. The Christian's exultation at his deliverance from the spiritual captivity of sin.—*H. T. Armfield.*

Whole Psalm.—In mine opinion they go near to the sense and true meaning of the Psalm who do refer it to that great and general captivity of mankind under sin, death and the devil, and to the redemption purchased by the death and blood-shedding of Christ, and published in the Gospel. For this kind of speech which the Prophet useth here is of greater importance than that it may be applied only to Jewish particular captivities. For what great matter was it for these people of the Jews, being, as it were, a little handful, to be delivered out of temporal captivity, in comparison of the exceeding and incomparable deliverance whereby mankind was set at liberty from the power of their enemies, not temporal but eternal, even from death, Satan and hell itself ? Wherefore we take this Psalm to be a prophecy of the redemption that should come by Jesus Christ, and the publishing of the gospel, whereby the kingdom of Christ is advanced, and death and the devil with all the powers of darkness are vanquished.—*Thomas Stint, in An Exposition on Psalms cxxiv—cxxvi,* 1621.

Whole Psalm.—I believe this Psalm is yet once more to be sung in still more joyous strain ; once more will the glad tidings of Israel's restoration break upon her scattered tribes, like the unreal shadow of a dream ; once more will the inhabitants of the various lands from among whom they come forth exclaim in adoring wonder, " The Lord hath done great things for them," when they see Israelite after Israelite and Jew after Jew, as on that wondrous night of Egypt, with their loins girded, their shoes on their feet, and their staff in their hand, hasting to obey the summons that recalls them to their own loved land !—*Barton Bouchier* (1794—1865), *in "Manna in the Heart."*

Whole Psalm.—

> When, her sons from bonds redeeming,
>   God to Zion led the way,
> We were like to people dreaming
>   Thoughts of bliss too bright to stay.

Fill'd with laughter, stood we gazing,
  Loud our tongues in rapture sang ;
Quickly with the news amazing
  All the startled nations rang.

" See Jehovah's works of glory !
  Mark what love for them he had ! "
" Yes, FOR US ! Go tell the story.
  This was done, and we are glad."

Lord ! thy work of grace completing
  All our exiled hosts restore,
As in thirsty channels meeting
  Southern streams refreshing pour.

They that now in sorrow weeping
  Tears and seed commingled sow,
Soon, the fruitful harvest reaping,
  Shall with joyful bosoms glow.

Tho' the sower's heart is breaking,
  Bearing forth the seed to shed,
He shall come, the echoes waking,
  Laden with his sheaves instead.

William Digby, in "The Hebrew Psalter. A New Metrical Translation," 1882.

Verse 1.—*"When the Lord turned again the captivity."* As by the Lord's permission they were led into captivity, so only by his power they were set at liberty.
When the Israelites had served in a strange land four hundred years, it was not
Moses, but Jehovah, that brought them out of the land of Egypt, and out of the house
of bondage.   In like manner it was he and not Deborah that freed them from Jabin
after they had been vexed twenty years under the Canaanites.   It was he and not
Gideon that brought them out of the hands of the Midianites, after seven years'
servitude.   It was he and not Jephthah that delivered them from the Philistines
and Amorites after eighteen years' oppression.   Although in all these he did employ
Moses and Deborah, Gideon and Jephthah, as instruments for their deliverance ;
and so it was not Cyrus's valour, but the Lord's power ; not his policy, but God's
wisdom, that, overthrowing the enemies, gave to Cyrus the victory, and put it into
his heart to set his people at liberty ; for he upheld his hands to subdue nations.
He did weaken the loins of kings, and did open the doors before him, he did go
before him and made the crooked places straight ; and he did break the brazen
doors, and burst the iron bars. Isaiah xlv. 1, 2.—*John Hume, in "The Jewes
Deliverance," 1628.*
    Verse 1.—*"In Jehovah's turning (to) the turning of Zion."* Meaning to return
to the return, or meet those returning, as it were, half way.   The Hebrew noun
denotes *conversion*, in its spiritual sense, and the verb God's gracious condescension
in accepting or responding to it.—*Joseph Addison Alexander.*
    Verse 1.—*"The captivity of Zion."* I ask, first, Why of *Zion?* why not the
captivity of Jerusalem, Judah, Israel ?   Jerusalem, Judah, Israel, were led away
captives, no less than Zion.   They, the greater and more general ; why not *the
captivity* of them, but of *Zion?*   It should seem there is more in Zion's captivity
than in the rest, that choice is made of it before the rest.   Why ? what was Zion ?
We know it was but a hill in Jerusalem, on the north side.   Why is that hill so
honoured ?   No reason in the world but this,—that upon it the Temple was built ;
and so, that Zion is much spoken of, and much made of, it is only for the Temple's
sake.   For whose sake it is (even for his church), that " the Lord loveth the gates
of Zion more than all the dwellings of Jacob " (Ps. lxxxvii. 2) ; loveth her more,
and so her captivity goeth nearer him, and her deliverance better pleaseth him,
than all Jacob besides.   This maketh *Zion's captivity* to be mentioned chiefly,
as chiefly regarded by God, and to be regarded by his people.   As we see it was :
when they sat by the waters of Babylon, that which made them weep was, " When
we remembered thee, O Zion "; that was their greatest grief.   That their greatest
grief, and this their greatest joy ; *Lætati sumus,* when news came (not, saith the
Psalm, *in domos nostras,* We shall go everyone to his own house, but) in *domum
Domini ibimus,* "We shall go to the house of the Lord, we shall appear before the
God of gods in Zion."—*Lancelot Andrewes, 1555—1626.*

Verse 1.—"We were like them that dream." That is, they thought it was but mere fantasy and imagination.—*Sydrach Simpson,* 1658.

Verse 1.—"We were like them that dream." Here you may observe that God doth often send succour and deliverance to the godly in the time of their affliction, distress, and adversity; that many times they themselves do doubt of the truth thereof, and think that in very deed they are not delivered, but rather that they have dreamed. Peter, being imprisoned by Herod, when he was delivered by an angel, for all the light that did shine in the prison; though the angel did smite him on the side and raised him up; though he caused the chains to fall off his hands; though he spake to him three several times, *Surge, cinge, circunda;* "Arise quickly, gird thyself, and cast thy garment about thee"; though he conducted him safely by the watches; and though he caused the iron gates to open willingly; yet for all this he was like unto them that dream. "For he wist not that it was true which was done by the angel; but thought he saw a vision": Acts xii. 9. When old Jacob was told by his sons that his son Joseph was alive, his heart failed, and he believed them not; but when he had heard all that Joseph had said, and when he saw the chariots that Joseph had sent, then, as it were, raised from a sleep, and awakened from a dream, his spirit revived, then, and, rejoicing, he cried out, " I have enough; Joseph my son is yet alive."

Lorinus seems to excuse this their distrust, because they were so over-ravished with joy, that they misdoubted the true cause of their joy : like the Apostles, who having Christ after his resurrection standing before them, they were so exceedingly joyed, that rejoicing they wondered and doubted ; and like the two Marys, when the angel told them of our Saviour Christ's resurrection, they returned from the sepulchre rejoicing, and yet withal fearing. It may be they feared the truth of so glad news, and doubted lest they were deceived by some apparition.—*John Hume.*

Verse 1.—"We were like them that dream." We thought that we were dreaming ; we could hardly believe our eyes, when at the command of Cyrus, king of the Persians, we had returned to our own land. The same thing happened to the Greeks, when they heard that their country, being conquered by the Romans, had been made free by the Roman consul, P. Quinctius Flaminius. Livy says that when the herald had finished there was more good news than the people could receive all at once. They could scarcely believe that they had heard aright. They were looking on each other wonderingly, like sleepers on an empty dream.—*John Le Clerc [Clericus],* 1657—1736.

Verse 1.—"We were like them that dream," etc. In the lapse of seventy years the hope of restoration to their land, so long deferred, had mostly gone out in despair, save as it rested (in some minds) on their faith in God's promise. The policy of those great powers in the East had long been settled, viz., to break up the old tribes and kingdoms of Western Asia ; take the people into far eastern countries, and *never let them return.* No nation known to history, except the Jews, ever did return to rebuild their ancient cities and homes. Hence this joyous surprise.—*Henry Cowles, in "The Psalms ; with Notes."* 1872.

Verse 1.—"Like them that dream." It was no dream ; it was Jacob's dream become a reality. It was the promise, " I will bring thee back into this land " (Gen. xxviii. 15), fulfilled beyond all their hope.—*William Kay, in "The Psalms, with Notes, chiefly exegetical,"* 1871.

Verse 1.—"We were like them that dream." The words should rather be translated, *"We are like unto those that are restored to health."* The Hebrew word signifies to recover, or, to be restored to health. And so the same word is translated in Isa. xxxviii., when Hezekiah recovered, he made a Psalm of praise, and said, " O Lord, by these things men live, and in all these things is the life of my spirit : so wilt thou recover me, and make me to live." It is the same word that is used here. Thus Cajetan, Shindler, and others would have it translated here ; and it suits best with the following words, " Then were our mouths filled with laughter, and our tongues with praise." When a man is in a good dream, his mouth is not filled with laughter, nor his tongue with praise ; if a man be in a bad dream, his mouth is not filled with laughter, nor his tongue with praise ; but when a man is restored to health after a great sickness, it is so.—*William Bridge,* 1600—1670.

Verse 2.—"Then was our mouth filled with laughter," etc. We must earnestly endeavour to learn this practice, or at least to attain to some knowledge thereof ; and we must raise up ourselves with this consideration—that the gospel is nothing else but laughter and joy. This joy properly pertaineth to captives, that is, to those that feel the captivity of sin and death ; to the fleshy and tender hearts, terrified with the feeling of the wrath and judgment of God. These are the disciples in whose hearts should be planted laughter and joy, and that by the authority of the Holy Ghost, which this verse setteth forth. This people was in Zion, and, after the outward show of the kingdom and priesthood, did mightily flourish ; but if a man consider them according to the spirit, he shall see them to be in miserable captivity, and that their tongue is full of heaviness and mourning, because their heart is terrified with the sense of sin and death. This is Moses' tongue or Moses' mouth, full of wormwood and of bitterness of death ; wherewith he designs to kill none but those which are too lively and full of security. But they who feel their captivity shall have their mouths filled with laughter and joy : that is, redemption and deliverance from sin and death shall be preached unto them. This is the sense and meaning of the Holy Ghost, that the mouth of such shall be filled with laughter, that is, their mouth shall show forth nothing else but great gladness through the inestimable consolations of the gospel, with voices of triumph and victory by Christ, overcoming Satan, destroying death, and taking away sins. This was first spoken unto the Jews ; for this laughter was first offered to that people, then having the promises. Now he turneth to the Gentiles, whom he calleth to the partaking of this laughter.—*Martin Luther.*

Verse 2.—*"Then was our mouth filled with laughter,"* etc. It was thus in the valley of Elah, where Goliath fell, and Philistia fled. It was thus at Baal-Perazim. It was thus when one morning, after many nights of gloom, Jerusalem arose at dawn of day, and found Sennacherib's thousands a camp of the dead. And it has all along been the manner of our God.

> " The Lord has wrought mightily
> In what he has done for us ;
> And we have been made glad."

Ever do this till conflict is over ! Just as thou dost with the streams of the south, year by year, so do with us—with all, with each. And we are confident thou wilt ; we are sure that we make no vain boast when we sing this Psalm as descriptive of the experience of all thy pilgrims and worshippers.—*Andrew A. Bonar, in "Christ and his Church in the Book of Psalms,"* 1859.

Verse 2.—*"Then was our mouth filled with laughter."*—They that were laughed at, now laugh, and a new song is put into their mouths. It was a laughter of joy in God, not scorn of their enemies.—*Matthew Henry.*

Verse 2.—*"Mouth" ; "tongue."* Lorinus, the Jesuit, hath observed that the Psalmist nominates the *mouth* and *tongue* in the singular, not *mouths* and *tongues* in the plural ; because all the faithful and the whole congregation of the Jews *univocè*, with one voice, with one consent, and, as it were, with one mouth, did praise and glorify the Lord.—*John Hume.*

Verse 2.—*"And our tongue with singing."* Out of the abundance of the heart the mouth speaks ; and if the heart be glad the tongue is glib. Joy cannot be suppressed in the heart, but it must be expressed with the tongue.—*John Hume.*

Verse 2.—*"Then said they among the heathen."* And what is it they said ? It is to the purpose. In this (as in many others) the heathens' saying cannot be mended. This they say : 1. That they were no quotidian, or common things ; but " *great.*" 2. Then, these great things they ascribe not to *chance ;* that they happened not, but were " *done.*" 3. Then, " done " *by God himself :* they see God in them. 4. Then, not done by God at random, without any particular aim ; but *purposely* done *for them.* 5. And yet, there is more in *magnificavit facere* (if we look well). For, *magna fecit* would have served all this ; but in saying *magnificavit facere*, they say *magnifecit illos, ut magna faceret pro illis.* He magnified them, or set greatly by them, for whom he would bring to pass so great a work. This said they among the " heathen."

And it is a pity the " *heathen* " said it, and that the Jews themselves spake not these words first. But now, finding the " *heathen* " so saying ; and finding it was all true that they said, they must needs find themselves bound to say at least as much ; and more they could not say ; for more cannot be said. So much then, and no less than they. And this addeth a degree to the *dicebant*,—that the sound of it was so great among *the heathen* that it made an *echo* even in Jewry itself.—*Lancelot Andrewes.*

Verse 2.—*"The* Lord *hath done great things."* He multiplied to do great things ;

so the Chaldee, Syriac, and Arabic versions render it; and the history of this deliverance makes it good.—*Thomas Hodges, in a Sermon entitled "Sion's Hallelujah,"* 1660.

Verses 2, 3.—There is this great difference between the praise which the heathen are forced to give to God, and that which the Lord's people heartily offer unto him : the one doth speak as having no interest nor share in the mercy ; the other do speak as they to whom the mercy is intended, and wherein they have their portion with others : *"He hath done great things for them,"* say the heathen : but, *" he hath done great things for us,"* say the Lord's people.—*David Dickson,* 1583—1662.

Verse 3.—*"The* LORD *hath done great things for us,"* etc. This verse is the marrow of the whole Psalm, occasioned by the return of God's people out of Babel's captivity into their own country. Their deliverance was so great and incredible that when God brought it to pass they were *as men in a dream,* thinking it rather a dream, and a vain imagination, than a real truth. 1. Because it was so great a deliverance from so great and lasting a bondage, it seemed too good to be true. 2. It was sudden and unexpected, when they little thought or hoped for it. . . . . 3. All things seemed desperate, nothing more unlikely, or impossible rather. 4. The manner was so admirable (without the counsel, help, or strength of man : nay, it was beyond and against all human means) ; that they doubt whether these things be not the dreams of men that are awake.—*Thomas Taylor* (1576—1632) *in "A Mappe of Rome."*

Verse 3.—*"For us."* What were we, might Sion say (who were glad to lick the dust of the feet of our enemies), that the Lord of heaven and earth should look so graciously upon us ? The meanness of the receiver argueth the magnificence of the giver. " Who am I, that the mother of my Lord should visit me ? " this was a true and religious compliment of devout Elizabeth. The best of men are but the children of dust, and grand-children of nothing. And yet for the Lord to do " *great things* " for us ! this yet *greatens* those *"great things."* Was it because *we were his church ?* It was his superabounding grace to select us out of others, as it was our greater gracelessness, above all others, so to provoke him, as to force him to throw us into captivity. Or was it because *our humiliation,* in that disconsolate condition, did move him to so great compassion ? Alas ! there was a choice of nations whom he might have taken in our room, that might have proved far more faithful than we have been for the one half of those favours we have enjoyed. Or was it for *his covenant's sake* with our forefathers ? Alas ! we had forfeited that long since, again and again, we know not how often. Wherefore, when we remember ourselves, we cannot but make this an aggravation of God's *"great things,"* that he should do them *for us,* FOR US, so very, very unworthy.—*Malachiah [or Matthew] Harris, in a Sermon entitled "Brittaines Hallelujah,"* 1639.

Verse 4.—*"Turn again our captivity, O* LORD.*"* A prayer for the perfecting of their deliverance. Let those that are returned to their own land be eased of their burdens which they are yet groaning under. Let those that remain in Babylon have their hearts stirred up, as ours were, to take the benefit of the liberty granted. The beginnings of mercy are encouragements to us to pray for the completing of it. While we are here in this world, there will still be matter for prayer, even when we are most furnished with matter for praise. When we are free, and in prosperity ourselves, we must not be unmindful of our brethren that are in trouble and under restraint.—*Matthew Henry.*

Verse 4.—*"Turn again our captivity."* As Israel of old prayed that he would bring all their brethren scattered abroad in captivity back to their own land in one full stream, multitudinous, joyous, mighty, like the waters of Nile or Euphrates pouring over the parching fields of the south in the hot, dry summer-tide ; so now should the members of Christ's church ever pray " that all that profess and call themselves Christians may be led into the way of truth, and hold the faith in unity of spirit, in the bond of peace, and in righteousness of life."—*J. W. Burgon, in "A Plain Commentary,"* 1859.

Verse 4.—The Psalmist cries—

" Turn our captivity, O Jehovah,
As aqueducts in the Negeb."

This Negeb, or South Country, the region stretching below Hebron, being comparatively dry and waterless, was doubtless irrigated by a system of small artificial channels. The words of the Psalmist imply that it is as easy for God to turn Israel back from Babylonian bondage to their own land, as for the horticulturist to direct the waters of the spring to any part of the land he chooses along the channels of the aqueducts.—*James Neil.*

Verse 4.—"*As the streams in the south.*" Then shall our captivity be perfectly changed even as *the rivers* or *waters in the south*, which by the mighty work of God were dried up and utterly consumed. Whether ye understand here the Red Sea, or else the river of Jordan, it mattereth little. The similitude is this : Like as by thy mighty hand thou broughtest to pass miraculously that the waters were dried up and consumed, so dry up, O Lord, and bring to nothing all our captivity. Some do interpret this verse otherwise ; that is, Turn our captivity, O Lord, as the rivers in the south, which in the summer are dried up in the desert places by the heat of the sun, but in the winter are filled up again with plenty of water.—*Martin Luther.*

Verse 4.—"*Streams.*" The Hebrew word for "*streams*" means strictly a river's bed, the channel which holds water when water is there, but is often dry. Naturally there is joy for the husbandmen when those valley-beds are filled again with flowing waters. So, the prayer is, let thy people return joyfully to their father-land.—*Henry Cowles.*

Verse 4.—"*As the streams in the south.*" Some render it, *As the mighty waters in the south.* Why would they have their captivity turned like those mighty floods in the south ? The reason is this, because the south is a dry country, where there are few springs, scarce a fountain to be found in a whole desert. What, then, are the waters they have in the south, in those parched countries ? They are these mighty strong torrents, which are caused by the showers of heaven : so the meaning of that prayer in the Psalm is, that God would suddenly turn their captivity. Rivers come suddenly in the south : where no spring appears, nor any sign of a river, yet in an hour the water is up and the streams overflow. As when Elijah sent his servant toward the sea, in the time of Ahab, he went and looked, and said, "there is nothing"; that is, no show of rain, not the least cloud to be seen ; yet presently the heavens grew black, and there was a great rain : 1 Kings xviii. 44. Thus let our captivity be turned thus speedily and suddenly, though there be no appearance of salvation, no more than there is of a fountain in the sandy desert, or of rain in the clearest of heavens, yet bring salvation for us. We used to say of things beyond our supply, Have we a spring of them ? or can we fetch them out of the clouds ? So though no ground appears whence such rivers should flow, yet let our salvation be as rivers in the south, as rivers fetched out of the clouds, and dropped in an instant immediately from the heavens.—*Joseph Caryl,* 1602 —1673.

Verses 4, 5, 6.—The saints are oft feeding their hopes on the carcases of their slain fears. The time which God chose and the instrument he used to give the captive Jews their gaol delivery and liberty to return home were so incredible to them when it came to pass (like Peter whom the angel had carried out of prison, Acts xii.), it was some time before they could come to themselves and resolve whether it was real truth, or but a pleasing dream. Now see, what effect this strange disappointment of their fears had upon their hope for afterward. It sends them to the throne of grace for the accomplishment of what was so marvellously begun. "The Lord hath done great things for us ; whereof we are glad. Turn again our captivity, O Lord" : verses 3, 4. They have got a hand-hold by this experiment of his power and mercy, and they will not now let him go till they have more ; yea, their hope is raised to such a pitch of confidence, that they draw a general conclusion from this particular experience for the comfort of themselves or others in any future distress : "They that sow in tears shall reap in joy," etc., verses 5, 6.— *William Gurnall,* 1617—1679.

Verse 5.—"*They that sow in tears.*" I never saw people sowing in tears exactly, but have often known them to do it in fear and distress sufficient to draw them from any eye. In seasons of great scarcity, the poor peasants part in sorrow with every measure of precious seed cast into the ground. It is like taking bread out of the mouths of their children ; and in such times many bitter tears are actually shed over it. The distress is frequently so great that government is obliged to furnish seed, or none would be sown. Ibrahim Pasha did this more than once within my remembrance, copying the example, perhaps, of his great predecessor in Egypt when the seven years' famine was ended.

The thoughts of this Psalm may likewise have been suggested by the extreme danger which frequently attends the farmer in his ploughing and sowing. The calamity which fell upon the husbandmen of Job when the oxen were ploughing, and the asses feeding beside them, and the Sabeans fell upon them and took them away, and slew the servants with the edge of the sword (Job i. 14, 15), is often repeated in our day. To understand this you must remember what I have just told you about the situation of the arable lands in the open country ; and here again we meet that verbal accuracy : the sower *"goes forth "*—that is, from the village. The people of Ibel and Khiem, in Merj' Aiyûn, for example, have their best grain-growing fields down in the 'Ard Hûleh, six or eight miles from their homes, and just that much nearer the lawless border of the desert. When the country is disturbed, or the government weak, they cannot sow these lands except at the risk of their lives. Indeed, they always *go forth* in large companies, and completely armed, ready to drop the plough and seize the musket at a moment's warning ; and yet, with all this care, many sad and fatal calamities overtake the men who must thus sow in tears. And still another origin may be found for the thoughts of the Psalm in the extreme difficulty of the work itself in many places. The soil is rocky, impracticable, overgrown with sharp thorns ; and it costs much painful toil to break up and gather out the rock, cut and burn the briars, and to subdue the stubborn soil, especially with their feeble oxen and insignificant ploughs. Join all these together, and the sentiment is very forcibly brought out, that he who labours hard, in cold and rain, in fear and danger, in poverty and in want, casting his precious seed into the ground, will surely come again, at harvest-time, with rejoicing, and bearing his sheaves with him.—*W. M. Thomson.*

Verse 5.—*"They that sow in tears shall reap in joy,"* etc. This promise is conveyed under images borrowed from the instructive scenes of agriculture. In the sweat of his brow the husbandman tills his land, and casts the seed into the ground, where for a time it lies dead and buried. A dark and dreary winter succeeds, and all seems to be lost ; but at the return of spring universal nature revives, and the once desolate fields are covered with corn which, when matured by the sun's heat, the cheerful reapers cut down, and it is brought home with triumphant shouts of joy. Here, O disciple of Jesus, behold an emblem of thy present labour and thy future reward! Thou " sowest," perhaps, in "tears"; thou doest thy duty amidst persecution, and affliction, sickness, pain, and sorrow ; thou labourest in the Church, and no account is made of thy labours, no profit seems likely to arise from them. Nay, thou must thyself drop into the dust of death, and all the storms of that winter must pass over thee, until thy form shall be perished, and thou shalt see corruption. Yet the day is coming when thou shalt " reap in joy," and plentiful shall be thy harvest. For thus thy blessed Master " went forth weeping," a man of sorrows and acquainted with grief, " bearing precious seed " and sowing it around him, till at length his own body was buried, like a grain of wheat, in the furrow of the grave. But he arose, and is now in heaven, from whence he shall " doubtless come again with rejoicing," with the voice of the archangel and the trump of God, " bringing his sheaves with him." Then shall every man receive the fruit of his works, and have praise of God.—*George Horne* (1730—1792), *in "A Commentary on the Psalms."*

Verse 5.—*"They that sow in tears shall reap in joy."* They sow *in faith ;* and God will bless that seed : it shall grow up to heaven, for it is sown in the side of Jesus Christ who is in heaven. " He that believeth on God," this is the seed ; " shall have everlasting life " (John v. 24) ; this is the harvest. *Qui credit quod non videt, videbit quod credit,*—he that believes what he doth not see ; this is the seed : shall one day see what he hath believed ; this is the harvest.

They sow *in obedience :* this is also a blessed seed, that will not fail to prosper wheresoever it is cast. " If ye keep my commandments "; this is the seed : " ye shall abide in my love " (John xv. 10) ; this is the harvest. (Rom. vi. 22), " Ye are become servants to God, and have your fruit unto holiness " ; this is the sowing : " and the end everlasting life " ; this is the reaping. *Obedientia in terris, regnabit in cælis,*—he that serves God on earth, and sows the seed of obedience, shall in heaven reap the harvest of a kingdom.

They sow *in repentance ;* and this seed must needs grow up to blessedness. . . . Many saints have now reaped their crop in heaven, that sowed their seed in tears. David, Mary Magdalene, Peter ; as if they had made good the proverb, " No coming to heaven with dry eyes." Thus nature and God differ in their proceedings. To have a good crop on earth, we desire a fair seedtime ; but here a wet time of sowing shall bring the best harvest in the barn of heaven. " Blessed are they that mourn " ; this is the seeding : " for they shall be comforted " (Matt. v. 4) ; this is the harvest.

They sow *in renouncing the world*, and adherence to Christ ; and they reap a great harvest. " Behold," saith Peter to Christ, " we have forsaken all, and followed thee " (Matt. xix. 27) ; this is the seeding. " What shall we have therefore ? " What ? " You shall sit on twelve thrones, judging the twelve tribes of Israel " (verses 28, 29) ; all that you have lost shall be centupled to you : " and you shall inherit everlasting life " ; this is the harvest. " Sow to yourselves in righteousness and reap in mercy " : Hos. x. 12.

They sow *in charity*. He that sows this seed shall be sure of a plentiful crop. " Whosoever shall give to drink to one of these little ones a cup of cold water only "— a little refreshing—" in the name of a disciple ; verily I say unto you, he shall in no wise lose his reward : " Matt. x. 42. But if he that giveth a little shall be thus recompensed, then " he that soweth bountifully shall reap bountifully " : 2 Cor. ix. 6. Therefore sparse abroad with a full hand, like a seedsman in a broad field, without fear. Doth any think he shall lose by his charity ? No worldling, when he sows his seed, thinks he shall lose his seed ; he hopes for increase at harvest. Darest thou trust the ground and not God ? Sure God is a better paymaster than the earth : grace doth give a larger recompense than nature. Below thou mayest receive forty grains for one ; but in heaven, (by the promise of Christ,) a hundred-fold : a " measure heapen, and shaken, and thrust together, and yet running over." " Blessed is he that considereth the poor " ; this is the seeding : " the Lord shall deliver him in the time of trouble " (Ps. xli. 1) ; this is the harvest.—*Thomas Adams.*

Verse 5.—"*They that sow in tears,*" etc. Observe two things here. I. That the afflictions of God's people are as sowing in tears. 1. In sowing ye know there is great pains. The land must be first tilled and dressed ; and there is pains in casting the seed into it ; and then it takes a great dressing all the year, before it be set in the barn-yard. 2. It requires great charges, too, and therefore it is called " precious seed." For ye know that seed corn is aye dearest. 3. There is also great hazard ; for corn, after it is sown, is subject to many dangers. And so it is with the children of God in a good cause. II. Then after the seed-time follows the harvest, and that comes with joy. There be three degrees of the happiness of God's children, in reaping of fruits. 1. In the first-fruits. Even when they are enduring anything for the Gospel of Christ, it carries contentment and fruit with it. 2. After the first-fruits, then come sheaves to refresh the husbandman, and to assure him that the full harvest is coming. The Lord now and then gives testimony of a full deliverance to his own people, especially of the deliverance of Sion, and lets them taste of the sheaves which they have reaped. 3. And lastly, they get the full harvest ; and that is gotten at the great and last day. Then we get peace without trouble, joy without grief, profit without loss, pleasure without pain ; and then we have a full sight of the face of God.—*Alexander Henderson.*

Verse 5.—"*They that sow in tears shall reap in joy.*" Gospel tears are not lost ; they are seeds of comfort : while the penitent doth pour out tears, God pours in joy. If thou wouldst be cheerful, saith Chrysostom, be sad. It was the end of Christ's anointing and coming into the world, that he might comfort them that mourn : Isaiah lxi. 3. Christ had the oil of gladness poured on him, as Chrysostom saith, that he might pour it on the mourner ; well then might the apostle call it " a repentance not to be repented of " : 2 Cor. vii. 10. . . . Here is sweet fruit from a bitter stock : Christ caused the earthen vessels to be filled with water, and then turned the water into wine : John ii. 9. So when the eye, that earthen vessel, hath been filled with water brim full, then Christ will turn the water of tears into the wine of joy. Holy mourning, saith St. Basil, is the seed out of which the flower of eternal joy doth grow.—*Thomas Watson* (—1690 ?), *in "The Beatitudes."*

Verse 5.—"*They that sow in tears shall reap.*" We must take notice of the reapers : "*They* shall reap." Which *they* ? They that did sow ; they shall, and none but they shall. They shall ; and good reason they should, because it was they that did sow. And though some that have sown in tears do complain of the lateness or thinness of the harvest, that they have not reaped in joy, as is here promised ; know that some grounds are later than others, and in some years the harvest falleth later than in others, and that God, who is the Lord of the harvest, in his good time will ripen thy joy, and thou shalt reap it : and in the meantime, if we try it narrowly, we shall find the cause in ourselves, both of the lateness of our joy, because we were too late in sowing our tears ; and of the thinness of our joy, because we did sow our tears too thin. And if after our sowing of tears we find no harvest of joy at all, we may be well assured that either our seed was not good, or else some of the mischances are come upon them, which came upon the seed that came to no good in the thirteenth of Matthew.—*Walter Balcanqual, in "a Sermon preached at St. Maries Spittle,"* 1623.

Verse 5.—*"They that sow in tears,"* etc. I saw in seedtime a husbandman at plough in a very rainy day. Asking him the reason why he would not rather leave off than labour in such foul weather, his answer was returned me in their country rhythm :—

> " Sow beans in the mud,
> And they'll come up like a wood.'

This could not but remind me of David's expression, *"They that sow in tears shall reap in joy,"* etc.—*Thomas Fuller* (1608—1661), *in "Good Thoughts in Worse Times."*

Verse 5.—*"Sow in tears."* There are tears which are themselves the seed that we must sow ; tears of sorrow for sin, our own and others' ; tears of sympathy with the afflicted church ; and tears of tenderness in prayer and under the word.— *Matthew Henry.*

Verse 5.—*"Shall reap in joy."* This spiritual harvest comes not alike soon to all, no more than the other which is outward doth. But here's the comfort, whoever hath a seed-time of grace pass over his soul shall have his harvest-time also of joy : this law God hath bound himself to as strongly as to the other, which " is not to cease while the earth remaineth " (Gen. viii. 22) ; yea, more strongly ; for that was to the world in general, not to every country, town, or field in particular, for some of these may want a harvest, and yet God may keep his word : but God cannot perform his promise if any one particular saint should everlastingly go without his reaping time. And therefore you who think so basely of the gospel and the professors of it, because at present their peace and comfort are not come, should know that it is on the way to them, and comes to stay everlastingly with them ; whereas your peace is going from you every moment, and is sure to leave you without any hope of returning to you again. Look not how the Christian begins, but ends. The Spirit of God by his convictions comes into the soul with some terrors, but it closeth with peace and joy. As we say of the month of March, it enters like a lion, but goes out like a lamb. " Mark the perfect man, and behold the upright : for the end of that man is peace " : Psalm xxxvii. 37.—*William Gurnall.*

Verses 5, 6.—In my little reading and small experience, I have found that corn sown in dear years and times of scarcity hath yielded much more increase than at other times ; so that presently after much want, there hath followed great plenty of grain, even beyond expectation.—*Humphrey Hardwick, in a Sermon entitled "The Difficulty of Sion's Deliverance and Reformation,"* 1644.

Verses 5, 6.—Mind we the undoubted certainty of our harvest verified by divers absolute positive asseverations in the text : " *he shall reap* " ; " *he shall come again* " ; "*he shall bring his sheaves with him.*" Here's no item of contingency or possibility, but all absolute affirmations ; and you know heaven and earth shall pass away, but a jot of God's word shall not fail. Nothing shall prevent the harvest of a labourer in Sion's vineyard.—*Humphrey Hardwick.*

Verses 5, 6.—In a fuller, deeper sense, the sower in tears is the Man of sorrows himself. Believers know him thus. He has accomplished, in the sore travail of his soul, the seed time of affliction which is to bear its satisfying harvest when he shall again appear as the reaper of his own reward. He will fill his bosom with sheaves in that day of joy. The garner of his gladness will be filled to overflowing. By how much his affliction surpassed the natural measure of human grief, when he underwent for our sakes the dread realities of death and judgment ; by so much shall the fulness of his pure delight as the eternal blesser of his people excel their joy (yet what a measure, too, is there !) whose sum of blessedness is to be for ever with the Lord.—*Arthur Pridham, in "Notes and Reflections on the Psalms,"* 1869.

Verse 6.—*"He that goeth forth and weepeth, bearing precious seed,"* etc. This is very expressive of a gospel minister's life ; he goeth forth with the everlasting gospel which he preaches ; he sows it as precious seed in the church of God ; he waters it with tears and prayers ; the Lord's blessing accompanies it ; the Lord crowns his labours with success ; he has seals to his ministry ; and at the last day he shall doubtless come again with joy from the grave of death *"bringing his sheaves with* him"; and will, in the new Jerusalem state, be addressed by his Lord with, "Well done, good and faithful servant, enter thou into the joy of thy Lord."—*Samuel Eyles Pierce* (1746—1829 ?), *in "The Book of Psalms, an Epitome of the Old Testament Scripture."*

Verse 6.—*"He may go forth, he may go forth, and weep, bearing (his) load of seed. He shall come, he shall come with singing, bearing sheaves."* The emphatic combination of the finite tense with the infinitive is altogether foreign from our idiom, and very imperfectly represented, in the ancient and some modern versions, by the active participle (*venientes venient,* coming they shall come), which conveys neither the peculiar form nor the precise sense of the Hebrew phrase. The best approximation to the force of the original is Luther's repetition of the finite tense, *he shall come, he shall come,* because in all such cases the infinitive is really defined or determined by the term which follows, and in sense, though not in form, assimilated to it.—*Joseph Addison Alexander.*

Verse 6.—

> " Though he go, though he go, and be weeping,
>   While bearing some handfuls of seed ;
> He shall come, he shall come with bright singing,
>   While bearing his plentiful sheaves."

Ben-Tehillim, in "The Book of Psalms, in English Blank Verse," 1883.

Verse 6.—*"Goeth forth."* The church must not only keep this seed in the store-house, for such as come to enquire for it ; but must send her sowers forth to cast it among those who are ignorant of its value, or too indifferent to ask it at her hands. She must not sit weeping because men will not apply to her, but must go forth and bear the precious seed to the unwilling, the careless, the prejudiced, and the profligate. —*Edwin Sidney, in "The Pulpit,"* 1840.

Verse 6.—*Weeping* must not hinder sowing : when we suffer ill we must be doing well.—*Matthew Henry.*

Verse 6.—*"Precious seed."* Seed-corn is always dearest ; and when other corn is dear, then it is very dear ; yet though never so dear, the husbandman resolves that he must have it ; and he will deprive his own belly, and his wife and children of it, and will sow it, going out *"weeping "* with it. There is also great hazard ; for corn, after it is sown, is subject to many dangers. And so is it, indeed, with the children of God in a good cause. Ye must resolve to undergo hazards also, in life, lands, moveables, or whatsoever else ye have in this world : rather hazard all these before either religion be in hazard, or your own souls.—*Alexander Henderson.*

Verse 6.—*"Precious seed."* Aben Ezra, by the words rendered *precious seed,* or, as they may be, *a draught of seed,* understands the vessel in which the sower carries his seed, the seed basket, from whence he draws and takes out the seed, and scatters it ; see Amos ix. 13 : so the Targum, " bearing a tray of sowing corn."— *John Gill.*

Verse 6.—*"Precious seed."* Faith is called *"precious seed " : quod rarum est charum est.* Seed was accounted precious when all countries came unto Egypt to buy corn of·Joseph, and truly faith must needs be precious, seeing that when Christ comes he shall hardly "find faith upon the earth " : Luke xviii. 8. The necessity of faith is such, that therefore it must need be precious ; for as the material seed is the only instrumental means to preserve the life of man ; for all the spices, honey, myrrh, nuts, and almonds, gold and silver, that were in Canaan, were not sufficient for Jacob and his children's sustenance ; but they were forced to repair unto Egypt for corn, that they might live and not die ; even so, without faith the soul is starved ; it is the food of it ; for, " the just man liveth by his faith " : Gal. iii. 11.—*John Hume.*

Verse 6.—*"Sheaves."* The Psalm which begins with " dream " and ends with " sheaves " invites us to think of Joseph ; Joseph, " in whom," according to S. Ambrose's beautiful application, " there was revealed the future resurrection of the Lord Jesus, to whom both his eleven disciples did obeisance when they saw him gone into Galilee, and to whom all the saints shall on their resurrection do obeisance, bringing forth the fruit of good works, as it is written, ' He shall doubtless come again with rejoicing, bringing his sheaves with him.' "—*H. T. Armfield.*

HINTS TO PREACHERS.

Verse 1.—I. Sunny memories of what the Lord did, "he turned again the captivity," etc. II. Singular impressions,—we could not believe it to be true. III. Special discoveries—it was true, abiding, etc.

Verse 1.—A comparison and a contrast. I. The saved like them that dream. 1. In the strangeness of their experience. 2. In the ecstasy of their joy. II. The saved unlike them that dream. 1. In the reality of their experience. Dreams are unsubstantial things, but "the Lord turned"—an actual fact. 2. In their freedom from disappointment. No awakening to find it "but a dream": see Isaiah xxix. 8. 3. In the endurance of their joy. The joy of dreams is soon forgotten, but this is "everlasting joy."—*W. H. J. P.*

Verse 2.—Saintly laughter. What creates it, and how it is justified.

Verse 2.—*Recipe for holy laughter.*—1. Lie in prison a few weeks. 2. Hear the Lord turning the key. 3. Follow him into the high-road. 4. Your sky will burst with sunshine, and your heart with song and laughter. 5. If this recipe is thought too expensive, try *keeping in the high-road.*—*W. B. H.*

Verses 2, 3.—I. Reports of God's doings. II. Experience of God's doings.

Verses 2, 3.—I. The Lord does great things for his people. II. These great things command the attention of the world. III. They inspire the joyful devotion of the saints.—*W. H. J. P.*

Verse 3.—"*The LORD hath done great things for us.*" In this acknowledgment and confession there are three noteworthy points of thankfulness. I. That they were "*great things*" which were done. II. Who it was who did them: "*the Lord.*" III. That they are done, not *against* us, but "*for us.*"—*Alexander Henderson, 1583—1646.*

Verse 4.—Believers, rejoicing in their own deliverance, solicitous for a flood of prosperity to overflow the church. See the connection, verses 1—3. Remark, I. The doubting and despondent are too concerned about themselves, and too busy seeking comfort, to have either solicitude or energy to spare for the church's welfare; but the joyful heart is free to be earnest for the church's good. II. Joyful believers, other things being equal, know more of the constraining power of Christ's love, which makes them anxious for his glory and the success of his cause. III. The joyful can appreciate more fully the contrast of their condition to that of the undelivered, and for their sake cannot fail to be anxious for the church through whose ministry their deliverance comes. IV. The joyful are, in general, the most believing and the most hopeful; their expectation of success leads them to prayer, and impels them to effort.—*J. F.*

Verse 4.—I. The dried-up Christian. II. His unhappy condition. III. His one hope. IV. Result when realized.

Verse 5. — *The Christian Husbandman.* I. Illustrate the metaphor. The husbandman has a great variety of work before him; every season and every day brings its proper business. So the Christian has duties in the closet, in the family, in the church, in the world, etc., etc. II. Whence it is that many Christians sow in tears. 1. It may be owing to the badness of the soil. 2. The inclemency of the season. 3. The malice and opposition of enemies. 4. Past disappointments. III. What connection there is between sowing in tears and reaping in joy. 1. A joyful harvest, by God's blessing, is the natural consequence of a dripping seed-time. 2. God, who cannot lie, hath promised it. IV. When this joyful harvest may be expected. It must not be expected in our wintry world, for there is not sun enough to ripen it. Heaven is the Christian's summer. When you come to reap the fruits of your present trials, you will bless God who made you sow in tears. *Improvement.* 1. How greatly are they to blame who in this busy time stand all the day idle! 2. How greatly have Christians the advantage of the rest of the world! 3. Let the hope and prospect of this joyful harvest support us under all the glooms and distresses of this vale of tears.—*Outline of a Sermon by Samuel Lavington, 1726—1807.*

Verse 5.—Two pictures. The connecting "shall."

Verse 5.—I. There must be sowing before reaping. II. What men sow they will reap. If they sow precious seed, they will reap precious seed. III. In proportion as they sow they will reap. "He that soweth sparingly," etc. IV. The sowing may be with sorrow, but the reaping will be with joy. V. In proportion to the sorrow of sowing will be the joy of reaping.—*G. R.*

Verse 6.—In the two parts of this verse we may behold a threefold antithesis or opposition ; in the *progress*, 1. A sojourning : " He that now goeth on his way." 2. A sorrowing : " weeping." 3. A sowing : " and beareth forth good seed." In the *regress* there are three opposites unto these. 1. Returning : " He shall doubtless come again." 2. A Rejoicing : " with joy." 3. A Reaping : " and bring his sheaves with him."—*John Hume.*

Verse 6.—"*Doubtless.*" Or the reasons why our labour cannot be in vain in the Lord.

Verse 6.—"*Bringing his sheaves with him.*" The faithful sower's return to his Lord. Successful, knowing it, personally honoured, abundantly recompensed.

Verse 6.—See " Spurgeon's Sermon," No. 867 : " Tearful Sowing and Joyful Reaping."

Verse 6.—I. The sorrowful sower. 1. His activity—" he goeth forth." 2. His humility—" and weepeth." 3. His fidelity—" bearing precious seed." II. The joyful reaper. 1. His certain harvest-time—" shall doubtless come again." 2. His abundant joy—" with rejoicing." 3. His rich rewards—" bringing his sheaves with him."—*W. H. J. P.*

PSALM CXXVII.

TITLE.—A Song of Degrees for Solomon. *It was meet that the builder of the holy house should be remembered by the pilgrims to its sacred shrine. The title probably indicates that David wrote it for his wise son, in whom he so greatly rejoiced, and whose name Jedidiah, or "beloved of the Lord," is introduced into the second verse. The spirit of his name, "Solomon, or peaceable," breathes through the whole of this most charming song. If Solomon himself was the author, it comes fitly from him who reared the house of the Lord. Observe how in each of these songs the heart is fixed upon Jehovah only. Read the first verses of these Psalms, from Psalm cxx. to the present song, and they run thus: "I cried unto the Lord," "I will lift up mine eyes to the hills," "Let us go unto the house of the Lord," "Unto thee will I lift up mine eyes," "If it had not been the Lord," "They that trust in the Lord," "When the Lord turned again the captivity." The Lord and the Lord alone is thus lauded at each step of these songs of the ascents. O for a life whose every halting-place shall suggest a new song unto the Lord !*

SUBJECT.—*God's blessing on his people as their one great necessity and privilege is here spoken of. We are here taught that builders of houses and cities, systems and fortunes, empires and churches all labour in vain without the Lord ; but under the divine favour they enjoy perfect rest. Sons, who are in the Hebrew called "builders," are set forth as building up families under the same divine blessing, to the great honour and happiness of their parents. It is* THE BUILDER'S PSALM. *"Every house is builded by some man, but he that built all things is God," and unto God be praise.*

EXPOSITION.

EXCEPT the LORD build the house, they labour in vain that build it : except the LORD keep the city, the watchman waketh *but* in vain.

2 *It is* vain for you to rise up early, to sit up late, to eat the bread of sorrows : *for* so he giveth his beloved sleep.

3 Lo, children *are* an heritage of the LORD : *and* the fruit of the womb *is his* reward.

4 As arrows *are* in the hand of a mighty man ; so *are* children of the youth.

5 Happy *is* the man that hath his quiver full of them : they shall not be ashamed, but they shall speak with the enemies in the gate.

1. *"Except the* LORD *build the house, they labour in vain that build it."* The word *vain* is the key-note here, and we hear it ring out clearly three times. Men desiring to build know that they must labour, and accordingly they put forth all their skill and strength ; but let them remember that if Jehovah is not with them their designs will prove failures. So was it with the Babel builders ; they said, " Go to, let us build us a city and a tower "; and the Lord returned their words into their own bosoms, saying, " Go to, let us go down and there confound their language." In vain they toiled, for the Lord's face was against them. When Solomon resolved to build a house for the Lord, matters were very different, for all things united under God to aid him in his great undertaking : even the heathen were at his beck and call that he might erect a temple for the Lord his God. In the same manner God blessed him in the erection of his own palace ; for this verse evidently refers to all sorts of house-building. Without God we are nothing. Great houses have been erected by ambitious men ; but like the baseless fabric of a vision they have passed away, and scarce a stone remains to tell where once they stood. The wealthy builder of a Non-such Palace, could he revisit the glimpses of the moon, would be perplexed to find a relic of his former pride : he laboured in vain, for the place of his travail knows not a trace of his handiwork. The like may be said of the builders of castles and abbeys : when the mode of life indicated by these piles ceased to be

endurable by the Lord, the massive walls of ancient architects crumbled into ruins, and their toil melted like the froth of vanity. Not only do we now spend our strength for nought without Jehovah, but all who have ever laboured apart from him come under the same sentence. Trowel and hammer, saw and plane are instruments of vanity unless the Lord be the Master-builder.

"Except the LORD keep the city, the watchman waketh but in vain." Around the wall the sentinels pace with constant step ; but yet the city is betrayed unless the unsleeping Watcher is with them. We are not safe because of watchmen if Jehovah refuses to watch over us. Even if the guards are wakeful, and do their duty, still the place may be surprised if God be not there. " I, the Lord, do keep it," is better than an army of sleepless guards. Note that the Psalmist does not bid the builder cease from labouring, nor suggest that watchmen should neglect their duty, nor that men should show their trust in God by doing nothing : nay, he supposes that they will do all that they can do, and then he forbids their fixing their trust in what they have done, and assures them that all creature effort will be in vain unless the Creator puts forth his power, to render second causes effectual. Holy Scripture endorses the order of Cromwell—" Trust in God, and keep your powder dry " : only here the sense is varied, and we are told that the dried powder will not win the victory unless we trust in God. Happy is the man who hits the golden mean by so working as to believe in God, and so believing in God as to work without fear.

In Scriptural phrase a dispensation or system is called a house. Moses was faithful as a servant over all his house ; and as long as the Lord was with that house it stood and prospered ; but when he left it, the builders of it became foolish and their labour was lost. They sought to maintain the walls of Judaism, but sought in vain : they watched around every ceremony and tradition, but their care was idle. Of every church, and every system of religious thought, this is equally true : unless the Lord is in it, and is honoured by it, the whole structure must sooner or later fall in hopeless ruin. Much can be done by man ; he can both labour and watch ; but without the Lord he has accomplished nothing, and his wakefulness has not warded off evil.

2. *"It is vain for you to rise up early, to sit up late, to eat the bread of sorrows."* Because the Lord is mainly to be rested in, all carking care is mere vanity and vexation of spirit. We are bound to be diligent, for this the Lord blesses ; we ought not to be anxious, for that dishonours the Lord, and can never secure his favour. Some deny themselves needful rest ; the morning sees them rise before they are rested, the evening sees them toiling long after the curfew has tolled the knell of parting day. They threaten to bring themselves into the sleep of death by neglect of the sleep which refreshes life. Nor is their sleeplessness the only index of their daily fret ; they stint themselves in their meals, they eat the commonest food, and the smallest possible quantity of it, and what they do swallow is washed down with the salt tears of grief, for they fear that daily bread will fail them. Hard earned is their food, scantily rationed, and scarcely ever sweetened, but perpetually smeared with sorrow ; and all because they have no faith in God, and find no joy except in hoarding up the gold which is their only trust. Not thus, not thus, would the Lord have his children live. He would have them, as princes of the blood, lead a happy and restful life. Let them take a fair measure of rest and a due portion of food, for it is for their health. Of course the true believer will never be lazy or extravagant ; if he should be he will have to suffer for it ; but he will not think it needful or right to be worried and miserly. Faith brings calm with it, and banishes the disturbers who both by day and by night murder peace.

"For so he giveth his beloved sleep." Through faith the Lord makes his chosen ones to rest in him in happy freedom from care. The text may mean that God gives blessings to his beloved in sleep, even as he gave Solomon the desire of his heart while he slept. The meaning is much the same : those whom the Lord loves are delivered from the fret and fume of life, and take a sweet repose upon the bosom of their Lord. He rests them ; blesses them while resting ; blesses them more in resting than others in their moiling and toiling. God is sure to give the best thing to his beloved, and we here see that he gives them sleep—that is a laying aside of care, a forgetfulness of need, a quiet leaving of matters with God : this kind of sleep is better than riches and honour. Note how Jesus slept amid the hurly-burly of a storm at sea. He knew that he was in his Father's hands, and

therefore he was so quiet in spirit that the billows rocked him to sleep : it would be much oftener the same with us if we were more like HIM.

It is to be hoped that those who built Solomon's temple were allowed to work at it steadily and joyfully.   Surely such a house was not built by unwilling labourers. One would hope that the workmen were not called upon to hurry up in the morning nor to protract their labours far into the night ; but we would fain believe that they went on steadily, resting duly, and eating their bread with joy.   So, at least, should the spiritual temple be erected ; though, truth to tell, the workers upon its walls are all too apt to grow cumbered with much serving, all too ready to forget their Lord, and to dream that the building is to be done by themselves alone.   How much happier might we be if we would but trust the Lord's house to the Lord of the house !   What is far more important, how much better would our building and watching be done if we would but confide in the Lord who both builds and keeps his own church !

3. *"Lo, children are an heritage of the LORD."*   This points to another mode of building up a house, namely, by leaving descendants to keep our name and family alive upon the earth.   Without this what is a man's purpose in accumulating wealth ?   To what purpose does he build a house if he has none in his household to hold the house after him ?   What boots it that he is the possessor of broad acres if he has no heir ?   Yet in this matter a man is powerless without the Lord.   The great Napoleon, with all his sinful care on this point, could not create a dynasty. Hundreds of wealthy persons would give half their estates if they could hear the cry of a babe born of their own bodies.   Children are a heritage which Jehovah himself must give, or a man will die childless, and thus his house will be unbuilt.

"And the fruit of the womb is his reward," or a reward from God.   He gives children, not as a penalty nor as a burden, but as a favour.   They are a token for good if men know how to receive them, and educate them.   They are " doubtful blessings " only because we are doubtful persons.   Where society is rightly ordered children are regarded, not as an incumbrance, but as an inheritance ; and they are received, not with regret, but as a reward.   If we are over-crowded in England, and so seem to be embarrassed with too large an increase, we must remember that the Lord does not order us to remain in this narrow island, but would have us fill those boundless regions which wait for the axe and the plough.   Yet even here, with all the straits of limited incomes, our best possessions are our own dear offspring, for whom we bless God every day.

4. *"As arrows are in the hand of a mighty man ; so are children of the youth."* Children born to men in their early days, by God's blessing become the comfort of their riper years.   A man of war is glad of weapons which may fly where he cannot : good sons are their father's arrows speeding to hit the mark which their sires aim at.   What wonders a good man can accomplish if he has affectionate children to second his desires, and lend themselves to his designs !   To this end we must have our children in hand while they are yet children, or they are never likely to be so when they are grown up ; and we must try to point them and straighten them, so as to make arrows of them in their youth, lest they should prove crooked and unserviceable in after life.   Let the Lord favour us with loyal, obedient, affectionate offspring, and we shall find in them our best helpers.   We shall see them shot forth into life to our comfort and delight, if we take care from the very beginning that they are directed to the right point.

5. *"Happy is the man that hath his quiver full of them."*   Those who have no children bewail the fact ; those who have few children see them soon gone, and the house is silent, and their life has lost a charm ; those who have many gracious children are upon the whole the happiest.   Of course a large number of children means a large number of trials ; but when these are met by faith in the Lord it also means a mass of love, and a multitude of joys.   The writer of this comment gives it as his own observation, that he has seen the most frequent unhappiness in marriages which are unfruitful ; that he has himself been most grateful for two of the best of sons ; but as they have both grown up, and he has no child at home, he has without a tinge of murmuring, or even wishing that he were otherwise circumstanced, felt that it might have been a blessing to have had a more numerous family : he therefore heartily agrees with the Psalmist's verdict herein expressed. He has known a family in which there were some twelve daughters and three sons, and he never expects to witness upon earth greater domestic felicity than fell to the lot of their parents, who rejoiced in all their children, as the children also rejoiced

in their parents and in one another. When sons and daughters are arrows, it is well to have a quiver full of them ; but if they are only sticks, knotty and useless, the fewer of them the better. While those are blessed whose quiver is full, there is no reason to doubt that many are blessed who have no quiver at all ; for a quiet life may not need such a warlike weapon. Moreover, a quiver may be small and yet full ; and then the blessing is obtained. In any case we may be sure that a man's life consisteth not in the abundance of children that he possesseth.

"They shall not be ashamed, but they shall speak with the enemies in the gate." They can meet foes both in law and in fight. Nobody cares to meddle with a man who can gather a clan of brave sons about him. He speaks to purpose whose own sons make his words emphatic by the resolve to carry out their father's wishes. This is the blessing of Abraham, the old covenant benediction, " Thy seed shall possess the gate of his enemies"; and it is sure to all the beloved of the Lord in some sense or other. Doth not the Lord Jesus thus triumph in his seed ? Looked at literally, this favour cometh of the Lord : without his will there would be no children to build up the house, and without his grace there would be no good children to be their parent's strength. If this must be left with the Lord, let us leave every other thing in the same hands. He will undertake for us and prosper our trustful endeavours, and we shall enjoy a tranquil life, and prove ourselves to be our Lord's beloved by the calm and quiet of our spirit. We need not doubt that if God gives us children as a reward he will also send us the food and raiment which he knows they need.

He who is the father of a host of spiritual children is unquestionably happy. He can answer all opponents by pointing to souls who have been saved by his means. Converts are emphatically the heritage of the Lord, and the reward of the preacher's soul travail. By these, under the power of the Holy Ghost, the city of the church is both built up and watched, and the Lord has the glory of it.

EXPLANATORY NOTES AND QUAINT SAYINGS.

Title.—*"A Song of Degrees for Solomon."* This Psalm has Solomon's name prefixed to the title, for the purpose that the very builder of the Temple may teach us that he availed nothing to build it without the help of the Lord.—*The Venerable Bede (672–3—735), in Neale and Littledale.*

Whole Psalm.—Viewed as one of the " Degrees " in Christian virtue, the ninth, the Psalm is directed against self-reliance.—*H. T. Armfield.*

Whole Psalm.—The steps or degrees in this Psalm, though distinctly marked, are not so regular as in some others.

The twice repeated *"in vain"* of verse 1 may be regarded as the motto or " degree " for verse 2. The correspondence between the two clauses in verse 1 is also very striking. It is as if, on entering on some spiritual undertaking, or even in referring to the present state of matters, the Psalmist emphatically disclaimed as *vain* every other interposition or help than that of Jehovah. And of this *"in vain"* it is well constantly to remind ourselves, especially in seasons of activity and in times of peace ; for then we are most liable to fall into the snare of this *vanity.*

The next " degree " is that of success and prosperity (verses 3, 4), which is ascribed to the same Jehovah whose help and protection constituted the commencement and continuance, as now the completion of our well-being. Hence also verse 5 goes not beyond this, but contemplates the highest symbol of full security, influence, and power, in the figurative language of the Old Testament, which St. Augustine refers to " spiritual children, shot forth like arrows into all the world."—*Alfred Edersheim, in "The Golden Diary of Heart Converse with Jesus in the Book of Psalms,"* 1877.

Whole Psalm.—Solomon, the wisest and richest of kings, after having proved, both from experience and careful observation, that there was nothing but vanity in the life and labours of man, comes to this conclusion, that there is nothing better for a man in this life than that he should moderate his cares and labours, enjoy what he has, and fear God and keep his commandments : to this end he directs all that is debated in the Book of Ecclesiastes. Very similar are the argument and intention of the Psalm ; the authorship of which is ascribed to Solomon in the Inscription, and which there is no reason to doubt. Nor would it be safe, either to call in doubt any inscription without an urgent reason, or to give any other sense to the letter ל than that of *authorship*, unless it be meant that all the inscriptions are uncertain. Again, if the collectors of the Psalms added *titles* according to their own opinion and judgment, there would be no reason why they should have left so many Psalms without any title. This Psalm, therefore, is *Solomon's*, with whose genius and condition it well agrees, as is clear from *Ecclesiastes*, with which it may be compared, and from many *proverbs* on the same subject. . . . The design is, to drawn men away from excessive labours and anxious cares ; and to excite godliness and faith in Jehovah. To this the Psalm manifestly tends : for since men, desirous of the happiness and stability of their houses, are unable to secure this by their own endeavours, but need the blessing of God, who gives prosperity with even lighter labours to those that fear him ; it is their duty to put a limit to their labours and cares, and to seek the favour of God, by conforming their life and conduct to his will, and confiding in him.—*Herman Venema*, 1697—1787.

Verse 1.—*"Except the LORD build."* It is a fact that בן, *ben, a son*, and בת, *bath, a daughter*, and בית, *beith, a house*, come from the same root, בנה, *banah, to build ;* because sons and daughters build up a household, or constitute a *family*, as much and as really as stones and timber constitute a *building*. Now it is true that unless the good hand of God be upon us we cannot prosperously build a place of worship for his name. Unless we have his blessing, a dwelling-house cannot be comfortably erected. And if his blessing be not on our children, the house (the family) may be built up ; but instead of its being the house of God, it will be the synagogue of Satan. All marriages that are not under God's blessing will be a private and public curse.—*Adam Clarke*.

Verse 1.—*"Except the LORD build the house,"* etc. He does not say, Unless the Lord consents and is willing that the house should be built and the city kept : but, " Unless the Lord *build ;* unless he *keep*." Hence, in order that the building and keeping may be prosperous and successful, there is necessary, not only the consent of God, but also his working is required : and that working without which nothing can be accomplished, that may be attempted by man. He does not say, Unless the Lord help ; but unless the Lord build, unless he keep ; *i.e.*, Unless he do all himself. He does not say, To little purpose he labours and watches ; but to no purpose he labours, both the builder and the keeper. Therefore, all the efficacy of labours and cares is dependent on the operation and providence of God ; and all human strength, care, and industry is in itself vain.

It should be noticed, that he does not say, Because the Lord builds the house he labours in vain who builds it, and, because the Lord keeps the city the watchman waketh in vain : but, If the Lord do not build the house, if he do not keep the city ; he labours in vain who builds the house , he waketh in vain who keeps the city. He is far from thinking that the care and human labour, which is employed in the building of houses and keeping of cities, is to be regarded as useless, because the Lord builds and keeps ; since it is then the more especially useful and effectual when the Lord himself is the builder and keeper. The Holy Spirit is not the patron of lazy and inert men ; but he directs the minds of those who labour to the providence and power of God.—*Wolfgang Musculus*, 1497—1563.

Verse 1.—*"Except the LORD build the house."* On the lintel of the door in many an old English house, we may still read the words, *Nisi Dominus frustra*—the Latin version of the opening words of the Psalm. Let us also trust in him, and inscribe these words over the portal of " the house of our pilgrimage " ; and beyond a doubt all *will* be well with us, both in this world and in that which is to come.—*Samuel Cox, in* "The Pilgrim Psalms," 1874.

Verse 1.—*"Except the LORD build the house,"* etc. In the beginning of the contest with Britain, when we were sensible of danger, we had daily prayers in this room for the Divine protection. Our prayers, sir, were heard, and they were graciously answered. All of us who were engaged in the struggle must have observed frequent instances of a superintending Providence in our favour. To that kind Providence we owe this happy opportunity of consulting in peace on the means of establishing our future national felicity. And have we now forgotten this powerful Friend ?

or do we imagine we no longer need his assistance ?   I have lived for a long time [81 years] ; and the longer I live the more convincing proofs I see of this truth, that God governs in the affairs of man.   And if a sparrow cannot fall to the ground without his notice, is it probable that an empire can rise without his aid ?   We have been assured, sir, in the sacred writings, that "Except the LORD build the house, they labour in vain that build it."   I firmly believe this ; and I also believe that without his concurring aid we shall proceed in this political building no better than the builders of Babel : we shall be divided by our little, partial, local interests ; our prospects will be confounded ; and we ourselves shall become a reproach and a by-word down to future ages.   And what is worse, mankind may hereafter, from this unfortunate instance, despair of establishing government by human wisdom, and leave it to chance, war, or conquest.   I therefore beg leave to move that henceforth prayers, imploring the assistance of Heaven and its blessings on our deliberations, be held in this assembly every morning before we proceed to business ; and that one or more of the clergy of this city be requested to officiate in that service.—*Benjamin Franklin : Speech in Convention for forming a Constitution for the United States*, 1787.

Verse 1.—Note, how he puts first the building of the house, and then subjoins the keeping of the city.   He advances from the part to the whole ; for the city consists of houses.—*Wolfgang Musculus.*

Verse 1.—"*Except the* LORD *keep the city,*" etc.   Fires may break out in spite of the watchmen ; a tempest may sweep over it ; bands of armed men may assail it ; or the pestilence may suddenly come into it, and spread desolation through its dwellings.—*Albert Barnes* (1798—1870), *in "Notes on the Psalms."*

Verse 1.—One important lesson which Madame Guyon learned from her temptations and follies was that of her entire dependence on Divine grace.   " I became," she says, " deeply assured of what the prophet hath said, '*Except the* LORD *keep the city, the watchman waketh but in vain.*'   When I looked to thee, O my Lord ! thou wast my faithful keeper ; thou didst continually defend my heart against all kinds of enemies.   But, alas ! when left to myself, I was all weakness.   How easily did my enemies prevail over me !   Let others ascribe their victories to their own fidelity : as for myself, I shall never attribute them to anything else than thy paternal care.   I have too often experienced, to my cost, what I should be without thee, to presume in the least on any wisdom or efforts of my own.   It is to thee, O God, my Deliverer, that I owe everything !   And it is a source of infinite satisfaction, that I am thus indebted to thee."—*From the Life of Jeanne Bouvier de la Mothe Guyon*, 1648—1717.

Verse 1.—

> If God build not the house, and lay
>   The groundwork sure—whoever build,
> It cannot stand one stormy day.
> If God be not the city's shield,
> If he be not their bars and wall,
> In vain is watch-tower, men, and all.
>
> Though then thou wak'st when others rest,
>   Though rising thou prevent'st the sun,
> Though with lean care thou daily feast,
>   Thy labour's lost, and thou undone ;
> But God his child will feed and keep,
> And draw the curtains to his sleep.
>
>   *Phineas Fletcher*, 1584—1650.

Verse 2.—"*It is vain for you to rise up early, to sit up late,*" etc.   The Psalmist is exhorting to give over undue and anxious labour to accomplish our designs.   The phrases in the Hebrew are " making early to rise " and " making late to sit "— not " up," but *down*.   This means an artificial lengthening of the day.   The law of work is in our nature.   The limitations of effort are set forth in nature.   In order that all may be accomplished by the human race which is necessary to be done for human progress, all men must work.   But no man should work beyond his physical and intellectual ability, nor beyond the hours which nature allots.   No net result of good to the individual or to the race comes of any artificial prolonging of the day at either end.   Early rising, eating one's breakfast by candlelight, and prolonged vigils, the scholar's "midnight oil," are a delusion and a snare. Work while it is day. When the night comes, rest. The other animals do this, and, as races, fare as well as this anxious human race.

"*The bread of sorrows*" means the bread of toil, of wearisome effort. Do what you ought to do, and the Lord will take care of that which you cannot do. Compare Prov. x. 22 : " The blessing of the Lord, it maketh rich, and he addeth no sorrow with it," which means, " The blessing of Jehovah maketh rich, and toil can add nothing thereto." Compare also Matt. vi. 25 : " Take no thought [be not anxious] for your life," etc.

"*For so he giveth his beloved sleep.*" The "*for*" is not in the original. "*So*" means " with just the same result " or " all the same," or "without more trouble." That is the signification of the Hebrew word as it occurs. "*His beloved*" may work and sleep ; and what is needed will be provided just as certainly as if they laboured unduly, with anxiety. It has been suggested that the translation should be "*in sleep.*" While they are sleeping, the Heavenly Father is carrying forward his work for them. Or, while they wake and work, the Lord giveth to them, and so he does when they rest and sleep.—*Charles F. Deems, in "The Study," 1879.*

Verse 2.—The Lord's Temple was built without any looking unto or dependence on man ; all human wisdom and confidence was rejected on the whole ; the plan was given by the Lord God himself ; the model of it was in Solomon's possession ; nothing was left to the wit or wisdom of men ; there was no reason to rise up early, to sit up late, to eat the bread of sorrows, whilst engaged in the good work ; no, I should conceive it was a season of grace to such as were employed in the building ; somewhat like what it was with you and me when engaged in God's holy ordinances. I should conceive the minds of the workmen at perfect peace, their conversation together much on the grand subject of the Temple, and its intention as referring to the glorious Messiah, its grand and glorious antitype. I should conceive their minds were wholly disencumbered from all carking cares. They did not rise early without being refreshed in body and mind ; they did not sit up late as though they wanted ; they were not careful how they should provide for their families ; they were, as the beloved of the Lord, perfectly contented ; they enjoyed sweet sleep and refreshment by it, this was from the Lord ; he giveth his beloved ones sleep.— *Samuel Eyles Pierce.*

Verse 2.—"*It is vain,*" etc. Some take this place in a more particular and restrained sense ; as if David would intimate that all their agitations to oppose the reign of Solomon, though backed with much care and industry, should be fruitless ; though Absalom and Adonijah were tortured with the care of their own ambitious designs, yet God would give Jedidiah, or his beloved, rest ; that is, the kingdom should safely be devolved upon Solomon, who took no such pains to court the people, and to raise himself up into their esteem as Absalom and Adonijah did. The meaning is, that though worldly men fare never so hardly, beat their brains, tire their spirits, rack their consciences, yet many times all is for nothing ; either God doth not give them an estate, or not the comfort of it. But his beloved, without any of these racking cares, enjoy contentment ; if they have not the world, they have sleep and rest ; with silence submitting to the will of God, and with quietness waiting for the blessing of God. Well, then, acknowledge the providence that you may come under the blessing of it : labour *without God* cannot prosper ; *against God* and against his will in his word, will surely miscarry.—*Thomas Manton,* 1620—1677.

Verse 2.—"*It is vain for you to rise up early, to sit up late, to eat the bread of sorrows :* *for so he giveth his beloved sleep.*" No prayer without work, no work without prayer.—

> By caring and fretting,
> By agony and fear,
> There is of God no getting,
> But prayer he will hear.
>
> *From J. P. Lange's Commentary on James,* 1862.

Verse 2.—"*Eat the bread of sorrows.*" Living a life of misery and labours, fretting at their own disappointments, eaten up with envy at the advancement of others, afflicted overmuch with losses and wrongs. There is no end of all their labours. Some have died of it, others been distracted and put out of their wits ; so that you are never like to see good days as long as you cherish the love of the world, but will still lie under self-tormenting care and trouble of mind, by which a man grateth on his own flesh.—*Thomas Manton.*

Verse 2.—*"So he giveth his beloved sleep."* כֵּן יִתֵּן לִידִידוֹ שֵׁנָה. These latter words are variously rendered, and sufficiently obscurely, because all take this כֵּן as a particle of comparison, which does not seem to be in place here: some even omit it altogether. But כֵּן also signifies *" well," " rightly " :* 2 Kings vii. 9 ; Num. xxvii. 7. Why should we not render it here, *" He giveth to His beloved to sleep well " : i.e.,* While those who, mistrusting God, attribute all things to their own labour, do not sleep well; for truly they *"rise early and sit up late "* ; he gives to his beloved this grace, that reposing in his fatherly care and goodness, they fully enjoy their sleep, as those who know that such anxious labour is not necessary for them : or, *"Truly, he giveth to his beloved sleep ; "* as כֵּן may be the same as אָכֵן. But שֵׁנָה may be taken for בְּשֵׁנָה, and rendered, *"Truly, he giveth to his beloved in sleep ; "* viz., that he should be refreshed by this means.—*Louis De Dieu,* 1590—1642.

Verse 2 (last clause).—The sentence may be read either, *he will give sleep to his beloved,* or, *he will give in sleeping ;* that is, he will give them those things which unbelievers labour to acquire by their own industry. The particle כֵּן, *ken, thus,* is put to express certainty ; for with the view of producing a more undoubted persuasion of the truth—that God gives food to his people without any great care on their part—which seems incredible and a fiction, Solomon points to the thing as it were with the finger. He indeed speaks as if God nourished the slothfulness of his servants by his gentle treatment ; but as we know that men are created with the design of their being occupied, and as in the subsequent Psalm we shall find that the servants of God are accounted happy when they eat the labour of their hands, it is certain that the word *sleep* is not to be understood as implying slothfulness, but a placid labour, to which true believers subject themselves by the obedience of faith. Whence proceeds this so great ardour in the unbelieving, that they move not a finger without a tumult or bustle, in other words, without tormenting themselves with superfluous cares, but because they attribute nothing to the providence of God ! The faithful, on the other hand, although they lead a laborious life, yet follow their vocations with composed and tranquil minds. Thus their hands are not idle, but their minds repose in the stillness of faith, as if they were asleep.—*John Calvin,* 1509—1564.

Verse 2.—*"He giveth his beloved sleep."* It is *a peculiar rest,* it is a rest peculiar to sons, to saints, to heirs, to beloved ones. " So he gives *his beloved* rest," or as the Hebrew hath it, dearling, or dear beloved, quiet rest, without care or sorrow. The Hebrew word שׁנא, *shena,* is written with א, a quiet, dumb letter, which is not usual, to denote the more quietness and rest. This rest is a crown that God sets only upon the head of saints ; it is a gold chain that he only puts about his children's necks ; it is a jewel that he only hangs between his beloved's breasts ; it is a flower that he only sticks in his darlings' bosoms. This rest is a tree of life that is proper and peculiar to the inhabitants of that heavenly country ; it is children's bread, and shall never be given to dogs.—*Thomas Brooks,* 1608—1680.

Verse 2 (last clause).—As the Lord *gave* a precious gift to his *beloved,* the first Adam, while he *slept,* by taking a rib from his side, and by *building* therefrom a woman, Eve his bride, the Mother of all living ; so, while Christ, the Second Adam, the true Jedidiah, the Well-beloved Son of God, was sleeping in death on the cross, God formed for him, in his death, and by his death,—even by the life-giving streams flowing from his own precious side,—the Church, the spiritual Eve, the Mother of all living ; and gave her to him as his bride. Thus he *built* for him in his *sleep* the spiritual Temple of his Church.—*Christopher Wordsworth.*

Verse 2.—Quiet sleep is the gift of God, and it is the love of God to give quiet sleep.

1. *'Tis God's gift* when we have it : quiet sleep does revive nature as the dew or small rain does refresh the grass. Now, as the prophet speaks (Jer. xiv. 22), " Are there any of the gods of the heathen can cause rain, or can the heavens give showers ? " so it may be said : Are there any of the creatures in earth or heaven that can give sleep ? That God which gives showers of rain must give hours of rest : peaceable repose is God's peculiar *gift.*

2. *'Tis God's love* when he gives it, *"for so he giveth his beloved sleep ";* that is, sleep with quietness : yea, the Hebrew word, *shena,* being with *aleph,* a quiet or resting letter, otherwise than is usual, it signifies the greater quietness in time of sleep. And whereas some apply the peace only to Solomon, who was called Jedidiah, the beloved of the Lord, to whom God gave sleep ; the Septuagint turns the Hebrew word plurally, *" so God giveth his beloved ones sleep ";* to his saints in general God

gives quiet sleep as a token of his love ; yea, in the times of their greatest peril. Thus Peter in prison when he was bound with chains, beset with soldiers, and to die the next day, yet see how fast he was found asleep (Acts xii. 6, 7) : " The same night Peter was sleeping, and behold the angel of the Lord came upon him, and a light shined in the prison," yet Peter slept till the angel smote him on the side and raised him up : so God " gives his beloved sleep," and let his beloved give him the honour ; and the rather because *herein God answers our prayer, herein God fulfils his promise.*

Is it not *our prayer* that God would prevent affrighting, and afford refreshing sleep ? and is it not God's answer when in sleep he doth sustain us ? " I cried (says David) unto the Lord with my voice, and he heard me out of his holy hill. I laid me down and slept, for the Lord sustained me " : Ps. iii. 4, 5.

Is it not *God's promise* to vouchsafe sleep free from frights ? " When thou liest down, thou shalt not be afraid : yea, thou shalt lie down, and thy sleep shall be sweet " : Prov. iii. 24. Hence God's servants while they are in the wilderness and woods of this world, they sleep safely, and devils as wild beasts can do them no harm. Ezek. xxxiv. 25. Have we through God's blessing this benefit, let us abundantly give praise and live praise unto God hereupon. Yea, large praise belongs to the Lord for quiet sleep from men of all sorts.—*Philip Goodwin, in "The Mystery of Dreams,"* 1658.

Verse 2.—*"So he giveth his beloved sleep."* The world would give its favourites power, wealth, distinction ; God gives *"sleep."* Could he give anything better ? To give sleep when the storm is raging ; to give sleep when conscience is arraying a long catalogue of sins ; to give sleep when evil angels are trying to overturn our confidence in Christ ; to give sleep when death is approaching, when judgment is at hand—oh ! what gift could be more suitable ? what more worthy of God ? or what more precious to the soul ?

But we do not mean to enlarge upon the various senses which might thus be assigned to the gift. You will see for yourselves that sleep, as denoting repose and refreshment, may be regarded as symbolising " the rest which remaineth for the righteous," which is the gift of God to his chosen. " Surely he giveth his beloved sleep," may be taken as parallel to what is promised in Isaiah—" Thou wilt keep him in perfect peace whose mind is stayed on thee." Whatever you can understand by the " peace " in the one case, you may also understand by the *"sleep"* in the other. But throughout the Old and New Testaments, and especially the latter, sleep, as you know, is often put for death. " He slept with his fathers " is a common expression in the Jewish Scriptures. To " sleep in Jesus " is a common way of speaking of those who die in the faith of the Redeemer.

Suppose, then, we take the *"sleep"* in our text as denoting death, and confine our discourse to an illustration of the passage under this one point of view. *"Surely he giveth his beloved sleep."* What an aspect will this confer on death—to regard it as God's gift—a gift which he vouchsafes to those whom he loves !

It is not " he *sendeth* his beloved sleep," which might be true whilst God himself remained at a distance ; it is " he *giveth* his beloved sleep " ; as though God himself brought the sleep, and laid it on the eyes of the weary Christian warrior. And if God himself have to do with the dissolution, can we not trust him that he will loosen gently the silver cord, and use all kindness and tenderness in " taking down the earthly house of this tabernacle " ? I know not more comforting words than those of our text, whether for the being uttered in the sick-room of the righteous, or breathed over their graves. They might almost take the pain from disease, as they certainly do the dishonour from death. What is bestowed by God as a " gift on his beloved " will assuredly occupy his care, his watchfulness, his solicitude ; and I conclude, therefore, that he is present, in some special and extraordinary sense when the righteous lie dying ; ay, and that he sets his seal, and plants his guardianship where the righteous lie dead. "O death, where is thy sting ? O grave, where is thy victory?" Let the saint be but constant in the profession of godliness, and his last hours shall be those in which Deity himself shall stand almost visibly at his side, and his last resting-place that which he shall shadow with his wings. Sickness may be protracted and distressing ; " earth to earth, ashes to ashes, dust to dust," may be plaintively breathed over the unconscious dead ; but nothing in all this lengthened struggle, nothing in all this apparent defeat, can harm the righteous man—nay, nothing can be other than for his present good and his eternal glory, seeing that death with all its accompaniments is but joy—God's gift to his beloved. Dry your tears, ye that stand around the bed of the dying believer, the parting moment is almost at hand—a cold damp is on the forehead—the eye is fixed—the pulse too feeble to be felt—are you staggered at such a spectacle ? Nay ! let faith do its part ! The chamber is crowded with glorious forms ; angels are waiting there to take charge of the disembodied soul ; a hand gentler than any human is closing those eyes ; and a voice sweeter than any human is whispering—"*Surely the Lord giveth his beloved sleep.*"—*Henry Melvill* (1798—1871), *in a Sermon entitled "Death the Gift of God."*

Verse 2.—"*For so he giveth his beloved sleep.*" One night I could not rest, and in the wild wanderings of my thoughts I met this text, and communed with it : "*So he giveth his beloved sleep.*" In my reverie, as I was on the border of the land of dreams, methought I was in a castle. Around its massive walls there ran a deep moat. Watchmen paced the walls both day and night. It was a fine old fortress, bidding defiance to the foe ; but I was not happy in it. I thought I lay upon a couch ; but scarcely had I closed my eyes, ere a trumpet blew, " To arms ! To arms ! " and when the danger was overpast, I lay me down again. " To arms ! To arms ! " once more resounded, and again I started up. Never could I rest. I thought I had my armour on, and moved about perpetually clad in mail, rushing each hour to the castle top, aroused by some fresh alarm. At one time a foe was coming from the west ; at another from the east. I thought I had a treasure somewhere down in some deep part of the castle, and all my care was to guard it. I dreaded, I feared, I trembled lest it should be taken from me. I awoke, and I thought I would not live in such a tower as that for all its grandeur. It was the castle of discontent, the castle of ambition, in which man never rests. It is ever, " To arms ! To arms ! " There is a foe here, or a foe there. His dear-loved treasure must be guarded. Sleep never crossed the drawbridge of the castle of discontent. Then I thought I would supplement it by another reverie. I was in a cottage. It was in what poets call a beautiful and pleasant place, but I cared not for that. I had no treasure in the world, save one sparkling jewel on my breast : and I thought I put my hand on that and went to sleep, nor did I wake till morning light. That treasure was a quiet conscience and the love of God—" the peace that passeth all understanding." I slept, because I slept in the house of content, satisfied with what I had. Go, ye overreaching misers ! Go, ye grasping, ambitious men ! I envy not your life of inquietude. The sleep of statesmen is often broken ; the dream of the miser is always evil ; the sleep of the man who loves gain is never hearty ; but God "*giveth,*" by contentment, " *his beloved sleep.*"—*C. H. S.*

Verse 2.—"*He giveth his beloved sleep.*"

> Of all the thoughts of God that are
> Borne inward unto souls afar,
>   Along the Psalmist's music deep,
> Now tell me if that any is,
> For gift or grace surpassing this—
> "*He giveth his beloved sleep.*"
>
>   *Elizabeth Barrett Browning*, 1809—1861.

Verse 3.—"*Lo, children are an heritage of the Lord.*" There is no reason, therefore, why you should be apprehensive for your families and country ; there is no reason why you should weary yourselves with such great and such restless labour. God will be with you and your children, since they are his heritage.—*Thomas Le Blanc.*

Verse 3.—"*Lo, children are an heritage of the LORD.*" That is, to many God gives children in place of temporal good. To many others he gives houses, lands, and thousands of gold and silver, and with them the womb that beareth not ; and these are their inheritance. The poor man has from God a number of children, without lands or money ; these are his inheritance ; and God shows himself their father, feeding and supporting them by a chain of miraculous providences. Where is the *poor man* who would give up his *six children* with the prospect of having *more*, for the *thousands* or *millions* of him who is the *centre* of his *own existence*, and has neither *root* nor *branch* but his forlorn solitary self upon the face of the earth ? Let the fruitful family, however poor, lay this to heart · "*Children are an heritage of the Lord : and the fruit of the womb is his reward.*" And he who gave them will feed them ; for it is a fact, and the *maxim* formed on it has never failed, " Wherever God sends mouths, he sends meat." " Murmur not," said an Arab to his friend,

" because thy family is large ; know that it is for *their sakes* that God feeds *thee*."—*Adam Clarke.*

Verse 3.—"*Children are an heritage of the Lord.*" The Hebrew seems to imply that children are an heritage belonging to the Lord, and not an heritage given by the Lord, as most English readers appear to take it. The Targum likewise bears this out.—*H. T. Armfield.*

Verse 3.—"*Children are an heritage of the* LORD," etc. The Psalmist speaks of what children are unto godly and holy parents, for unto such only is any blessing given by God as a reward, and the Psalmist expressly speaks of blessings which God gives his beloved ones, and this blessing of children he makes to be the last and greatest. It is also as certain that he speaks of children as supposed to be holy and godly ; for otherwise they are not a reward, but a curse, and a sorrow to him that begat them. The Psalm was made, as appears by the title of it, "*of* or *for Solomon*," and therefore, as it is more than probable, was penned, as that other Psalm, the 72nd, which bears the same title, by David the father, of and for Solomon his son, who was, for his father's sake, " the beloved of God " (2 Sam. xii. 24, 25), and upon whom the sure covenant and mercies of David were entailed, together with his kingdom. And what is said in this Psalm, in the verse before, fitly agrees to him, for he it was who was to build God's house, to keep, and preserve Jerusalem the city, and the kingdom in peace, and to have rest, or as the Psalmist calls it (verse 3), quiet sleep given him by God, from all his enemies round about him. And for this, compare the prophecy of him (1 Chron. xxii. 9, 10) with the instructions here given him in the three first verses of this Psalm, and ye will see how fitly this Psalm concerns him.—*Thomas Goodwin.*

Verse 3.—"*Children are an heritage of the Lord.*" Hence note, 'tis one of the greatest outward blessings to have a family full of dutiful children. To have many children is the next blessing to much grace. To have many children about us is better than to have much wealth about us. To have store of these olive plants (as the Psalmist calls them) round about our table is better than to have store of oil and wine upon our table. We know the worth of dead, or rather lifeless treasures, but who knows the worth of living treasures ? Every man who hath children hath not a blessing in them, yet children are a blessing, and some have many blessings in one child. Children are chiefly a blessing to the children of God. "*Lo, children are an heritage of the* LORD : *and the fruit of the womb is his reward.*" But are not houses and lands, gold and silver, an heritage bestowed by the Lord upon his people ? Doubtless they are, for the earth is his, and the fulness of it, and he gives it to the children of men. But though all things are of God, yet all things are not alike of him : children are more of God than houses and lands.—*Joseph Caryl.*

Verse 3.—Children !—might one say as the word was uttered—I left mine in my distant home, in poverty, their wants and numbers increasing. with the means of providing for their comfort daily narrowing. Even should my life be prolonged, they will be children of want, but with sickness and warnings of death upon me, they will soon be helpless and friendless orphans. Yes! but will God be neglectful of his own heritage ? will he turn a gift into a sorrow ? Poor as thou art, repine not at the number of thy children. Though lions lack thou shalt not, if thou seekest him ; and know that it may be even for their sakes that he feedeth thee. If even thou wouldst not part with one of them for thousands of gold and silver, believe that he who is the fountain of all tenderness regards them with yet deeper love, and will make them now, in thy hour of trial, a means of increasing thy dependence on him, and soon thy support and pride.

Children !—might another say, as the Psalm referred to them—on their opening promise the breath of the destroyer has been poured. They are ripening visibly for the grave, and their very smile and caress cause my wounded heart to bleed anew. Yes, mourner ; but *God's heritage !* may he not claim his own ? They are in safe keeping when in his, and will soon be restored to thee in the better land, where death will make them ministering angels at his throne ; nay, they will be the first to welcome thee to its glories, to love and worship with thee throughout eternity.

Children ! this word to a third, of an even sadder and more anxious spirit, might seem like the planting of a dagger in his heart. His children have forsaken their father's God. Their associates were the vain and vicious ; their pleasures were the pleasures of folly and shame ; their lives barren of all promise, their souls destitute of all purpose, and steeled against all reproof. True, but *the heritage of the Lord still.* Hast thou, sorrowing parent, asked him for wisdom to keep it for him ?

Have due thought, prayer, watchful and holy living been expended on that heritage of God ?   No culture, no harvest in the soil ; no prayer, no blessing from the soul. " Train up a child in the way he should go, and when he is old he will not depart from it," is a promise that though sometimes, yet but seldom has missed fulfilment. Bring them to Jesus, and, unchanged in his tenderness, he will still lay his hands upon them and bless them.—*Robert Nisbet.*

Verse 3.—*"The fruit of the womb is his reward."*   John Howard Hinton's daughter said to him as she knelt by his death-bed :—" There is no greater blessing than for children to have godly parents."   "And the next," said the dying father, with a beam of gratitude, " for parents to have godly children."—*Memoir in Baptist Handbook,* 1875.

Verse 4.—*"As arrows."*   Well doth David call children *"arrows"*; for if they be well bred, they shoot at their parents' enemies ; and if they be evil bred, they shoot at their parents.—*Henry Smith,* 1560—1591.

Verse 4.—*"As arrows."*   Children are compared to *"arrows."*   Now, we know that sticks are not by nature arrows ; they do not grow so, but they are made so ; by nature they are knotty and rugged, but by art they are made smooth and handsome.   So children by nature are rugged and untoward, but by education are refined and reformed, made pliable to the divine will and pleasure.—*George Swinnock,* 1627—1673.

Verse 4.—*"As arrows."*   " Our children are what we make them.   They are represented '*As arrows in the hand of a mighty man,*' and *arrows* go the way we aim them."

Verse 4.—*"As arrows."*   In a collection of *Chinese Proverbs and Apophthegms,* subjoined to *Hau Kiou Choaan,* or, *The Pleasing History,* I find a proverb cited from *Du Halde,* which seems full to our purpose.   It is this :—" When a son is born into a family, a bow and arrow are hung before the gate."   To which the following note is added :   " As no such custom appears to be literally observed, this should seem to be a metaphorical expression, signifying that a new protector is added to the family," equivalent to that of the Psalms,—*"as arrows,"* etc.—*James Merrick* (1720—1769), *in "Annotations on the Psalms."*

Verse 4.—*"Children of the youth "* are *"arrows in the hand,"* which, with prudence, may be directed aright to the mark, God's glory, and the service of their generation ; but afterwards, when they are gone abroad in the world, they are arrows out of the hand ; it is too late to bend them then.   But these *"arrows in the hand "* too often prove arrows in the heart, a constant grief to their godly parents, whose grey hairs they bring with sorrow to the grave.—*Matthew Henry.*

Verse 4.—*"Children of the youth."*   Sons of youth, *i.e.,* born while their parents are still young.   See Gen. xxxvii. 2 ; Isa. liv. 6.   The allusion is not only to their vigour (Gen. xlix. 3), but the value of their aid to the parent in declining age.—*Joseph Addison Alexander.*

Verse 4.—*"Children of the youth."*   If the right interpretation is commonly given to this phrase, this Psalm greatly encourages early marriages.   It is a growing evil of modern times that marriages are so often deferred till it is highly improbable that in the course of nature the father can live to mould his offspring to habits of honour and virtue.—*William Swan Plumer* (1802—1880), *in "Studies in the Book of Psalms."*

Verse 5.—*"Happy is the man that hath his quiver full of them."*   Dr. Guthrie used to say, " I am rich in nothing but children."   They were eleven in number.

Verse 5.—*"Quiver full."*   Many children make many prayers, and many prayers bring much blessing.—*German Proverb.*

Verse 5.—The Rev. Moses Browne had twelve children.   On one remarking to him, " Sir, you have just as many children as Jacob," he replied, " Yes, and I have Jacob's God to provide for them."—*G. S. Bowes.*

Verse 5.—I remember a great man coming into my house, at Waltham, and seeing all my children standing in the order of their age and stature, said, " These are they that make rich men poor."   But he straight received this answer, " Nay, my lord, these are they that make a poor man rich ; for there is not one of these whom we would part with for all your wealth."   It is easy to observe that none are so gripple and hardfisted as the childless ; whereas those, who, for the maintenance of large families, are inured to frequent disbursements, find such experience of Divine providence in the faithful management of their affairs, as that they lay out with more cheerfulness what they receive. Wherein their care must be abated when God takes it off from them to himself ; and, if they be not wanting to themselves, their faith gives them ease in casting their burden upon him, who hath more power and more right to it, since our children are more his than our own. He that feedeth the young ravens, can he fail the best of his creatures ?—*Joseph Hall, 1574— 1656.*

Verse 5.—*"They shall not be ashamed,"* etc. Able enough he shall be to defend himself, and keep off all injuries, being fortified by his children ; and if it happen that he hath a cause depending in the gate, and to be tried before the judges, he shall have the patronage of his children, and not suffer in his plea for want of advocates ; his sons will stand up in a just cause for him.—*William Nicholson* (——1671), *in "David's Harp Strung and Tuned."*

Verse 5.—*"But they shall speak."* *"But destroy"* is the marginal version, and is here much more emphatical than the rendering *"speak."* For this sense see 2 Chron. xxii. 10. Others refer it to litigation, when they shall successfully defend the cause of their parents. But as I do not see how their number or vigour could add weight to their evidence in a judicial cause, I prefer the sense given.—*Benjamin Boothroyd, 1768—1836.*

Verse 5.—*"With the enemies in the gate."* Probably the Psalmist alludes here to the defence of a besieged city ; the gate was very commonly the point of attack, and the taking of it rendered the conquest of the place easy : compare Gen. xxii. 17 ; xxiv. 60.—*Daniel Cresswell (1776—1844), in "The Psalms . . . . with Critical and Explanatory Notes,"* 1843.

Verse 5.—

This is the pride, the glory of a man,
To train obedient children in his house,
Prompt on his enemies t' avenge his wrongs,
And with the father's zeal in honour high
To hold his friends.

Sophocles' "Antigone." R. Potter's Translation.

HINTS TO PREACHERS.

Verse 1.—I. The human hand without the hand of God is in vain. II. The human eye without the eye of God is in vain. Or, I. God is to be acknowledged in all our works. 1. By seeking his direction before them. 2. By depending upon his help in them. 3. By giving him the glory of them. II. In all our cares. 1. By owning our short sight. 2. By trusting to his foresight.—*G. R.*

Verse 1 (first part).—Illustrate the principles : I. In building up character. II. In constructing plans of life and of work. III. In framing schemes of happiness. IV. In rearing a hope of eternal life. V. In raising and enlarging the church.—*J. F.*

Verses 1, 2.—I. What we may not expect : namely, God to work without our building, watching, etc. II. What we may expect : Failure if we are without God. III. What we should not do : Fret, worry, etc. IV. What we may do : So trust as to rest in peace.

Verse 2 (with Psalm cxxvi. 2).—The labour of the law contrasted with the laughter of the gospel.

Verse 2.—*"The bread of sorrows."* I. When God sends it, it is good to eat it. II. When we bake it ourselves, it is vain to eat it. III. When the devil brings it, it is deadly meat.

Verse 2 (last clause).—Blessings that come to us in sleep. 1. Renewed health and vigour of body. 2. Mental repose and refreshment. 3. Sweeter thoughts and holier purposes. 4. Providential gifts. The rains fall, the fruits of the earth grow and ripen, the mill wheel goes round, the ship pursues her voyage, etc., while we slumber. Often when we are doing nothing for ourselves God is doing most.—*W. H. J. P.*

Verse 2 (*last clause*).—See " Spurgeon's Sermons," No. 12 : " The Peculiar Sleep of the Beloved."

Verse 3.—Sermon by Thomas Manton. Works : vol. xviii. pp. 84—95. [Nichol's Edition.]

Verses 3—5.—Children. Consider : I. The effects of receiving them as a heritage from the Lord. 1. Parents will trust in the Lord for their provision and safety. 2. Will regard them as a sacred trust from the Lord of whose care they must render an account. 3. Will train them up in the fear of the Lord. 4. Will often consult God concerning them. 5. Will render them up uncomplainingly when the Lord calls them to himself by death. II. The effects of their right training. 1. They become the parents' joy. 2. The permanent record of the parents' wisdom. 3. The support and solace of the parents' old age. 4. The transmitters of their parents' virtues to another generation ; for well-trained children become, in their turn, wise parents.—*J. F.*

Verse 4.—The spiritual uses of children. I. When they die in infancy, awakening parents. II. When they go home from Sunday-school carrying holy influences. III. When they become converted. IV. When they grow up and become useful men and women.

Verses 4, 5.—I. The dependence of children upon parents. 1. For safety. They are in their quiver. 2. For direction. They are sent forth by them. 3. For support. They are in the hands of the mighty. II. The dependence of parents upon children. 1. For defence. Who will hear a parent spoken against ? 2. For happiness. " A wise son maketh," etc. Children elicit some of the noblest and tenderest emotions of human nature. Happy is the Christian minister who with a full quiver can say, " Here am I, and the children which thou hast given me."—*G. R.*

Verse 6.—" The Reward of Well-doing Sure." Sermon by Henry Melvill, in " The Pulpit," 1856.

PSALM CXXVIII.

TITLE.—A Song of Degrees. *There is an evident ascent from the last Psalm : that did but hint at the way in which a house may be built up, but this draws a picture of that house built, and adorned with domestic bliss through the Lord's own benediction. There is clearly an advance in age, for here we go beyond children to children's children ; and also a progress in happiness, for children which in the last Psalm were arrows are here olive plants, and instead of speaking "with the enemies in the gate" we close with "peace upon Israel." Thus we rise step by step, and sing as we ascend.*

SUBJECT.—*It is a family hymn,—a song for a marriage, or a birth, or for any day in which a happy household has met to praise the Lord. Like all the songs of degrees, it has an eye to Zion and Jerusalem, which are both expressly mentioned, and it closes like Psalms cxxv., cxxx., and cxxxi., with an allusion to Israel. It is a short Psalm, but exceedingly full and suggestive. Its poetry is of the highest order. Perhaps in no country can it be better understood than in our own, for we above all nations delight to sing of "Home, sweet home."*

EXPOSITION.

BLESSED *is* everyone that feareth the LORD ; that walketh in his ways.

2 For thou shalt eat the labour of thine hands : happy *shalt* thou *be,* and *it shall be* well with thee.

3 Thy wife *shall be* as a fruitful vine by the sides of thine house : thy children like olive plants round about thy table.

4 Behold, that thus shall the man be blessed that feareth the LORD.

5 The LORD shall bless thee out of Zion : and thou shalt see the good of Jerusalem all the days of thy life.

6 Yea, thou shalt see thy children's children, *and* peace upon Israel.

1. *"Blessed is every one that feareth the LORD."* The last Psalm ended with a blessing,—for the word there translated "happy" is the same as that which is here rendered "blessed": thus the two songs are joined by a catch-word. There is also in them a close community of subject. The fear of God is the corner-stone of all blessedness. We must reverence the ever-blessed God before we can be blessed ourselves. Some think that this life is an evil, an infliction, a thing upon which rests a curse ; but it is not so ; the God-fearing man has a present blessing resting upon him. It is not true that it would be to him "something better not to be." He is happy now, for he is the child of the happy God, the ever-living Jehovah ; and he is even here a joint-heir with Jesus Christ, whose heritage is not misery, but joy. This is true of every one of the God-fearing, of all conditions, in all ages : each one and every one is blessed. Their blessedness may not always be seen by carnal reason, but it is always a fact, for God himself declares that it is so ; and we know that those whom he blesses are blessed indeed. Let us cultivate that holy filial fear of Jehovah which is the essence of all true religion ;—the fear of reverence, of dread to offend, of anxiety to please, and of entire submission and obedience. This fear of the Lord is the fit fountain of holy living : we look in vain for holiness apart from it : none but those who fear the Lord will ever walk in his ways.

"That walketh in his ways." The religious life, which God declares to be blessed, must be practical as well as emotional. It is idle to talk of fearing the Lord if we act like those who have no care whether there be a God or no. God's ways will be our ways if we have a sincere reverence for him : if the heart is joined unto God, the feet will follow hard after him. A man's heart will be seen in his walk, and the blessing will come where heart and walk are both with God. Note that the first Psalm links the benediction with the walk in a negative way, "Blessed is the man that walketh *not*," etc. ; but here we find it in connection with the positive form of our conversation. To enjoy the divine blessing we must be active, and walk :

we must be methodical, and walk in certain ways; and we must be godly, and walk in the Lord's ways. God's ways are blessed ways; they were cast up by the Blessed One, they were trodden by him in whom we are blessed, they are frequented by the blessed, they are provided with means of blessing, they are paved with present blessings, and they lead to eternal blessedness: who would not desire to walk in them?

2. "*For thou shalt eat the labour of thine hands.*" The general doctrine of the first verse here receives a personal application: note the change to the second person: "*thou* shalt eat," etc. This is the portion of God's saints,—to work, and to find a reward in so doing. God is the God of labourers. We are not to leave our worldly callings because the Lord has called us by grace: we are not promised a blessing upon romantic idleness or unreasonable dreaming, but upon hard work and honest industry. Though we are in God's hands we are to be supported by our own hands. He will give us daily bread, but it must be made our own by labour. All kinds of labour are here included; for if one toils by the sweat of his brow, and another does so by the sweat of his brain, there is no difference in the blessing; save that it is generally more healthy to work with the body than with the mind only. Without God it would be vain to labour; but when we are labourers together with God a promise is set before us. The promise is that labour shall be fruitful, and that he who performs it shall himself enjoy the recompense of it. It is a grievous ill for a man to slave his life away and receive no fair remuneration for his toil: as a rule, God's servants rise out of such bondage and claim their own, and receive it: at any rate, this verse may encourage them to do so. "The labourer is worthy of his hire." Under the Theocracy the chosen people could see this promise literally fulfilled; but when evil rulers oppressed them their earnings were withheld by churls, and their harvests were snatched away from them by marauders. Had they walked in the fear of the Lord they would never have known such great evils. Some men never enjoy their labour, for they give themselves no time for rest. Eagerness to get takes from them the ability to enjoy. Surely, if it is worth while to labour, it is worth while to eat of that labour. "*Happy shalt thou be,*" or, *Oh, thy happiness.* Heaped up happinesses in the plural belong to that man who fears the Lord. He is happy, and he shall be happy in a thousand ways. The context leads us to expect family happiness. Our God is our household God. The Romans had their Lares and Penates, but we have far more than they in the one only living and true God. "*And it shall be well with thee,*" or *good for thee.* Yes, good is for the good; and it shall be well with those who do well.

> "What cheering words are these!
> Their sweetness who can tell?
> In time, and to eternal days,
> 'Tis with the righteous well."

If we fear God we may dismiss all other fear. In walking in God's ways we shall be under his protection, provision, and approval; danger and destruction shall be far from us: all things shall work our good. In God's view it would not be a blessed thing for us to live without exertion, nor to eat the unearned bread of dependence: the happiest state on earth is one in which we have something to do, strength to do it with, and a fair return for what we have done. This, with the divine blessing, is all that we ought to desire, and it is sufficient for any man who fears the Lord and abhors covetousness. Having food and raiment, let us be therewith content.

3. "*Thy wife.*" To reach the full of earthly felicity a man must not be alone. A helpmeet was needed in Paradise, and assuredly she is not less necessary out of it. He that findeth a wife findeth a good thing. It is not every man that feareth the Lord who has a wife; but if he has, she shall share in his blessedness and increase it.

"*Shall be as a fruitful vine.*" To complete domestic bliss children are sent. They come as the lawful fruit of marriage, even as clusters appear upon the vine. For the grapes the vine was planted; for children was the wife provided. It is generally well with any creature when it fulfills its purpose, and it is so far well with married people when the great design of their union is brought about. They must not look upon fruitfulness as a burden, but as a blessing. Good wives are also fruitful in kindness, thrift, helpfulness, and affection: if they bear no children, they are by no means barren if they yield us the wine of consolation and the clusters of comfort. Truly blessed is the man whose wife is fruitful in those good works which are suitable to her near and dear position.

"*By the sides of thine house.*" She keeps to the house : she is a home bird. Some imagine that she is like a vine which is nailed up to the house wall ; but they have no such custom in Palestine, neither is it pleasant to think of a wife as growing up by a wall, and as bound to the very bricks and mortar of her husband's dwelling. No, she is a fruitful vine, and a faithful house-keeper ; if you wish to find her, she is within the house : she is to be found both inside and outside the home, but her chief fruitfulness is in the inner side of the dwelling, which she adorns. Eastern houses usually have an open square in the centre, and the various rooms are ranged around the sides,—there shall the wife be found, busy in one room or another, as the hour of the day demands. She keeps at home, and so keeps the home. It is her husband's house, and she is her husband's ; as the text puts it—" thy wife," and " thy house " ; but by her loving care her husband is made so happy that he is glad to own her as an equal proprietor with himself, for he is hers, and the house is hers too.

"*Thy children like olive plants round about thy table.*" Hundreds of times have I seen the young olive plants springing up around the parent stem, and it has always made me think of this verse. The Psalmist never intended to suggest the idea of olive plants round a table, but of young people springing up around their parents, even as olive plants surround the fine, well-rooted tree. The figure is very striking, and would be sure to present itself to the mind of every observer in the olive country. How beautiful to see the gnarled olive, still bearing abundant fruit, surrounded with a little band of sturdy successors, any one of which would be able to take its place should the central olive be blown down, or removed in any other way. The notion of a table in a bower may suit a cockney in a tea-garden, but would never occur to an oriental poet ; it is not the olive plants, but the children, that are round about the table. Moreover, note that it is not olive *branches*, but *plants*,—a very different thing. Our children gather around our table to be fed, and this involves expenses : how much better is this than to see them pining upon beds of sickness, unable to come for their meals ! What a blessing to have sufficient to put upon the table ! Let us for this benefit praise the bounty of the Lord. The wife is busy all over the house, but the youngsters are busiest at meal-times ; and if the blessing of the Lord rest upon the family, no sight can be more delightful. Here we have the vine and the olive blended—joy from the fruitful wife, and solid comfort from the growing family ; these are the choicest products earth can yield : our families are gardens of the Lord. It may help us to value the privileges of our home if we consider where we should be if they were withdrawn. What if the dear partner of our life were removed from the sides of our house to the recesses of the sepulchre ? What is the trouble of children compared with the sorrow of their loss ? Think, dear father, what would be your grief if you had to cry with Job, " Oh that I were as in months past, as in the days when God preserved me ; when my children were about me."

4. "*Behold, that thus shall the man be blessed that feareth the* LORD." Mark this. Put a *Nota Bene* against it, for it is worthy of observation. It is not to be inferred that all blessed men are married, and are fathers ; but that this is the way in which the Lord favours godly people who are placed in domestic life. He makes their relationships happy and profitable. In this fashion does Jehovah bless God-fearing households, for he is the God of all the families of Israel. We have seen this blessing scores of times, and we have never ceased to admire in domestic peace the sweetest of human felicity. Family blessedness comes from the Lord, and is a part of his plan for the preservation of a godly race, and for the maintence of his worship in the land. To the Lord alone we must look for it. The possession of riches will not ensure it ; the choice of a healthy and beautiful bride will not ensure it ; the birth of numerous comely children will not ensure it : there must be the blessing of God, the influence of piety, the result of holy living.

Verse 5. "*The* LORD *shall bless thee out of Zion.*" A spiritual blessing shall be received by the gracious man, and this shall crown all his temporal mercies. He is one among the many who make up God's inheritance ; his tent is part and parcel of the encampment around the tabernacle ; and therefore when the benediction is pronounced at the centre it shall radiate to him in his place. The blessing of the house of God shall be upon his house. The priestly benediction which is recorded in Numbers vi. 24—26, runs thus : " The Lord bless thee, and keep thee : the

Lord make his face shine upon thee, and be gracious unto thee : the Lord lift up his countenance upon thee, and give thee peace." This is it which shall come upon the head of the God-fearing man. Zion was the centre of blessing, and to it the people looked when they sought for mercy : from the altar of sacrifice, from the mercy-seat, from the Shekinah-light, yea, from Jehovah himself, the blessing shall come to each one of his holy people. *"And thou shalt see the good of Jerusalem all the days of thy life."* He shall have a patriot's joy as well as a patriarch's peace. God shall give him to see his country prosper, and its metropolitan city flourish. When tent-mercies are followed by temple-mercies, and these are attended by national mercies,—the man, the worshipper, the patriot is trebly favoured of the Lord. This favour is to be permanent throughout the good man's life, and that life is to be a long one, for he is to see his sons' sons. Many a time does true religion bring such blessings to men ; and when these good things are denied them, they have a greater reward as a compensation.

6. *"Yea, thou shalt see thy children's children."* This is a great pleasure. Men live their young lives over again in their grandchildren. Does not Solomon say that " children's children are the crown of old men " ? So they are. The good man is glad that a pious stock is likely to be continued ; he rejoices in the belief that other homes as happy as his own will be built up wherein altars to the glory of God shall smoke with the morning and evening sacrifice. This promise implies long life, and that life rendered happy by its being continued in our offspring. It is one token of the immortality of man that he derives joy from extending his life in the lives of his descendants.

"And peace upon Israel." With this sweet word Psalm cxxv. was closed. It is a favourite formula. Let God's own heritage be at peace, and we are all glad of it. We count it our own prosperity for the chosen of the Lord to find rest and quiet. Jacob was sorely tossed about ; his life knew little of peace ; but yet the Lord delivered him out of all his tribulations, and brought him to a place of rest in Goshen for a while, and afterwards to sleep with his fathers in the cave of Machpelah. His glorious Seed was grievously afflicted and at last crucified ; but he has risen to eternal peace, and in his peace we dwell. Israel's spiritual descendants still share his chequered conditions, but there remains a rest for them also, and they shall have peace from the God of peace. Israel was a praying petitioner in the days of his wrestling, but he became a prevailing prince, and therein his soul found peace. Yes, all around it is true—" Peace upon Israel ! Peace upon Israel."

EXPLANATORY NOTES AND QUAINT SAYINGS.

Whole Psalm.—Psalm cxxviii. follows Psalm cxxvii. for the same reason as Psalm ii. follows Psalm i. In both instances they are Psalms placed together, of which one begins with *ashrê* (happy, very happy), and the other ends with *ashrê*. In other respects Psalms cxxviii. and cxxvii. supplement one another. They are related to one another much as the New Testament parables of the treasure in the field and the one pearl are related. That which makes man happy is represented in Psalm cxxvii. as a gift coming as a blessing, and in Psalm cxxviii. as a reward coming as a blessing, that which is briefly indicated in the word שָׂכָר, *sakar, reward*, in cxxvii. 3 being here expanded and unfolded. There it appears as a gift of grace in contrast to the God-estranged self-activity of man ; here as a fruit of the *ora et labora.*—*Franz Delitzsch.*

Whole Psalm.—It is to be observed, that here all men are spoken to as wedded ; because this is the ordinary estate of most people. See 1 Cor. vii. 1, 2. At this day every Jew is bound to marry at about eighteen years of age, or before twenty ; else he is accounted as one that liveth in sin.—*John Trapp.*

Whole Psalm.—This Psalm is an ἐπιθαλάμιος λόγος, written for the commendation, instruction, and consolation of those who are either already married or are about to enter on that kind of life. It enumerates, therefore, at the commencement, as is usual in songs of this kind, all those things which are regarded as burdens in the married life, such as the labours in seeking to provide for the whole family ;

the spouse, and that marriage bond, which, as it were, binds a man and seems to make him a slave, just as that character says in the comedy, " I have taken a wife ; I have sold my liberty : " lastly, the education of the children, which certainly is most laborious, and requires the largest expenditure. To lighten the burden of all these things, there is added to each a blessing, or a promise, so that they might appear slight. And at the close, it subjoins in general, a spiritual promise, which easily makes light of all the labours and disquiets of the married life ; even if they should be the very heaviest. The blessing comes from Zion or the Church : for there is nothing so burdensome and difficult, but what it can be easily borne by those who are members of the true Church, and know the sources of true consolation.—*D. H. Mollerus.*

Verse 1.—"Blessed is every one that feareth the LORD," etc. Here we have the living fountain of the blessing which rests upon the conjugal and domestic state. When worldly prudence attempts to choose a wife and form a household, it can apply its hand only to so much of the work as has its seat upon earth, and is visible to the eye of sense. It builds, so to speak, the first and the second story, adds cornice and pediment, and the fabric presents a fair appearance—but it has no foundation. Whenever you see the household of a married pair continuing to defy every storm, you may be sure that it rests upon a sure foundation, lying beyond the reach of human sense, and that that foundation is *the fear of the Lord*. To the fear of the Lord, therefore, the holy Psalmist has wisely given a place in front of this beautiful Psalm. which celebrates the blessing that descends upon conjugal and domestic life.—*Augustus F. Tholuck, in "Hours of Christian Devotion,"* 1870.

Verse 1.—"Blessed is every one that feareth the LORD." There is a fear of the Lord which hath terror in it and not blessedness. The apprehension with which a warring rebel regards his triumphant and offended soverign, or the feelings of a fraudulent bankrupt towards a stern creditor, or, a conscience-striken criminal to a righteous judge, are frequently types of men's feelings in regard to God. This evidently cannot be the fear which the *" blessed "* of this Psalm feel. Nor can theirs, on the other hand, be the tormenting fear of self-reproach.

Their fear is that which the believed revelations given of him in his Word produce. It is the fear which a child feels towards an honoured parent,—a fear to offend : it is that which they who have been rescued from destruction feel to the benefactor who nobly and at the vastest sacrifice interposed for their safety,—a fear to act unworthily of his kindness : it is that which fills the breast of a pardoned and grateful rebel in the presence of a venerated sovereign at whose throne he is permitted to stand in honour,—a fear lest he should ever forget his goodness, and give him cause to regret it. Such is the fear of the Christian now : a fear which reverence for majesty, gratitude for mercies, dread of displeasure, desire of approval, and longing for the fellowship of heaven, inspire ; the fear of angels and the blessed Son ; the fear not of sorrow but of love, which shrinks with instinctive recoil from doing aught that would tend to grieve, or from denying aught that would tend to honour. Religion is the grand and the only wisdom ; and since the beginning, the middle, and the end of it, is the fear of the Lord, blessed is every man that is swayed by it.—*Robert Nisbet, in "The Songs of the Temple Pilgrims,"* 1863.

Verse 1.—"Blessed is every one that feareth the LORD." Let us take a little of the character of the blessed man. Who is it that is undaunted ? *"The man that feareth God."* Fear sounds rather contrary to blessedness ; hath an air of misery ; but add whom. He that feareth *the LORD";* that touch turns it into gold. He that so fears, fears not : he shall not be afraid ; all petty fears are swallowed up in this great fear ; and this great fear is as sweet and pleasing as little fears are anxious and vexing. Secure of other things, he can say—" If my God be pleased, no matter who is displeased ; no matter who despise me, if he account me his. Though all forsake me, though my dearest friends grow estranged, if he reject me not, that is my only fear ; and for that I am not perplexed, I know he will not." A believer hath no fear but of the displeasure of heaven, the anger of God to fall upon him ; he accounts that only terrible ; but yet he doth not fear it, doth not apprehend it will fall on him, is better persuaded of the goodness of God. So this fear is still joined with trust :—" Behold the eye of the Lord is upon them that fear him, upon them that hope in his mercy " ; Ps. xxxiii. 18.—*Robert Leighton,* 1611—1684.

Verse 1.—"Blessed is every one," etc. There is a stress on *all* (" *every one* "), teaching that no disparity of sex or condition, of rank or wealth, affects the degree of happiness granted by God to every one of his true servants in their several stations. It is to be observed, further, that whenever the fear of the Lord is mentioned in Holy Writ, it is never set by itself, as though sufficient for the consummation of our faith, but always has something added or prefixed, by which to estimate its due proportion of perfection, according as it is stated by Solomon in the Proverbs (ii. 3—5).—*J. M. Neale and R. F. Littledale, in "A Commentary on the Psalms from Primitive and Mediæval Writers," 1860.*

Verse 1.—*"Blessed is every one"* etc. It is a precious promise, but perhaps thou art tempted to say in thy heart, not meant for everyone. Wilt thou answer against the Lord ? Hear him speak in the song. He says, *" every one." "Blessed is every one that feareth the LORD."* None are excluded but those who will not walk in his ways.—*Edward Jewitt Robinson.*

Verse 1.—*"Blessed,"* etc. The adage, " That it is best not to be born at all, or to die as soon as possible," has certainly been long since received by the common consent of almost all men. Carnal reason judges either that all mankind without exception are miserable, or that fortune is more favourable to ungodly and wicked men than to the good. To the sentiment that those are blessed who fear the Lord, it has an entire aversion. So much the more requisite, then, is it to dwell upon the consideration of this truth. Farther, as this blessedness is not apparent to the eye, it is of importance, in order to our being able to apprehend it, first to attend to the definition which will be given of it by-and-bye ; and secondly, to know that it depends chiefly upon the protection of God. Although we collect together all the circumstances which seem to contribute to a happy life, surely nothing will be found more desirable than to be kept hidden under the guardianship of God. If this blessing is, in our estimation, to be preferred, as it deserves, to all other good things, whoever is persuaded that the care of God is exercised about the world and human affairs, will at the same time unquestionably acknowledge that what is here laid down is the chief point of happiness.—*John Calvin.*

Verse 1.—*"That feareth the LORD ; that walketh in his ways."* The fear of the Lord is the internal principle ; but unless there be a corresponding expression in the outward life, what reason is there to suppose that it has any existence at all ?
Observe also, that there is no walking in the ways of the Lord, until his fear is established in the heart. There can be no genuine morality apart from the fear of God. How can a man obey God while his affections are alienated from him ? —*N. M'Michael.*

Verse 1.—*"That walketh in his ways."* God makes blessed those that walk in his ways, because he himself walks with them. This is said concerning David, and it is explained how that companionship blessed him, 2 Sam. v. 10 : " And David went on, and grew great, and the Lord God of hosts was with him " : where the " and " may be taken as the causal particle " because." That God does indeed join himself to those who walk in his ways as companion and leader we have in 2 Chron. xvii. 3, 4 : " And the Lord was with Jehoshaphat, because he walked in the first ways of his father David, and sought not unto Baalim ; but sought to the Lord God of his father."—*Thomas Le Blanc.*

Verse 2.—*"For thou shalt eat the labour of thine hands,"* etc. There is a fourfold literal sense here : Thou shalt live by honest, peaceful labour, not by rapine and violence on that produced by the toil of others, nor yet indolently and luxuriously ; thou shalt *"eat,"* and not penuriously stint thyself and others ; thy crops shall not be blighted, but shall bring forth abundantly ; and no enemy shall destroy or carry off thy harvest. And these two latter interpretations accord best with the converse punishments threatened to the disobedient by Moses. *"Thou shalt eat the labour of thine hands."* But he who hates labour does not eat of it, nor can he say, " My meat is to do the will of him that sent me, and to finish his work " : John iv. 34. On the other hand, he to whom such labour is a delight, does not merely look forward in hope to the future fruits or rewards of labour, but even here and now finds sustenance and pleasure in toiling for God ; so that it is *"well"* with him in the world, even amidst all its cares and troubles, and he *" shall be happy"* in that which is to come, whence sorrow is banished for ever, as it is written in the gospel : " Blessed is he that shall eat bread in the kingdom of God " : Luke xiv. 15.—*Neale and Littledale.*

Verse 2.—*"Thou shalt eat the labour of thine hands,"* etc. This must they learn also which are married, that they must labour. For the law of nature requireth that the husband should sustain and nourish his wife and his children. For after that man and wife do know that they ought to fear God their Creator, who not only made them, but gave his blessing also unto his creature ; this secondly must they know, that something they must do that they consume not their days in ease and idleness. Hesiod, the poet, giveth his counsel, that first thou shouldst get thee a house, then a wife, and also an ox to till the ground. . . . For albeit that our diligence, care, and travail is not able to maintain our family, yet God useth such as a means by the which he will bless us.—*Martin Luther.*

Verse 2.—*"Thou shalt eat the labour of thine hands."* Men have dreamed fascinating dreams of removing the disabilities and limitations of the world and the evils of life, without sorrow. Poets have pictured earthly paradises, where life would be one long festival,—

"Summer isles of Eden lying in dark purple spheres of sea."

But vain are all such dreams and longings. They are of human, not of Divine origin, and spring from a root of selfishness and not of holiness. They cannot be realized in a fallen world, full of sorrow because full of sin. All blessings in man's economy are got from pains. Happiness is the flower that grows from a thorn of sorrow transformed by man's cultivation. The beautiful myth which placed the golden apples of the Hesperides in a garden guarded by dragons, is an allegory illustrative of the great human fact, that not till we have slain the dragons of selfishness and sloth can we obtain any of the golden successes of life. Supposing it were possible that we could obtain the objects of our desire without any toil or trouble, we should not enjoy them. To benefit us really, they must be the growths of our own self-denial and labour. And this is the great lesson which the miracles of our Lord, wrought in the manner in which they were, unfolded. They teach us that, in both temporal and spiritual things, we should not so throw ourselves upon the providence or grace of God as to neglect the part we have ourselves to act,—that God crowns every honest and faithful effort of man with success : *"Blessed is every one that feareth the LORD ; that walketh in his ways. For thou shalt eat the labour of thine hands : happy shalt thou be, and it shall be well with thee."*—*Hugh Macmillan, in "The Ministry of Nature,"* 1871.

Verse 2 (*first clause*).—

Labour, the symbol of man's punishment ;
Labour, the secret of man's happiness.

James Montgomery, 1771—1854.

Verse 2.—*"Happy shalt thou be."* Oh trust in the Lord for happiness as well as for help ! All the springs of happiness are in him. Trust " in him who giveth us all things richly to enjoy " ; who, of his own rich and free mercy, holds them out to us, as in his own hand, that, receiving them as his gifts, and as pledges of his love, we may enjoy all that we possess. It is his love gives a relish to all we taste, puts life and sweetness into all ; while every creature leads us up to the great Creator, and all earth is a scale to heaven. He transfuses the joys that are at his own right hand into all that he bestows on his thankful children, who, having fellowship with the Father and his Son Jesus Christ, enjoy him in all and above all.—*John Wesley,* 1703—1791.

Verse 2.—*"Happy shalt thou be."* Mr. Disraeli puts these remarkable words into the mouth of one of his characters :—" Youth is a blunder ; manhood a struggle ; old age a regret." A sad and cheerless view of life's progress that ! It may be true, in measure, of a life separated from godliness ; it certainly is not true of a life allied with godliness. Let there be " life and godliness," and then youth is not a blunder, but a wise purpose and a glowing hope ; manhood is not a struggle only, but a conquest and a joy ; old age is not a regret, but a rich memory and a glorious prospect.—*R. P. Macmaster, in "The Baptist Magazine,"* 1878.

Verse 3.—*"Thy wife shall be as a fruitful vine,"* etc. The comparison would perhaps be brought out more clearly by arranging the verse as follows :—

" Thy wife shall be in the inner part of thy house
Like a fruitful vine ;
Thy children round about thy table
Like the shoots of the olive."

In the inner part, literally, *"the sides of thy house,"* as in Amos vi. 10, *i.e.,* the women's apartments, as marking the proper sphere of the wife engaged in her domestic duties, and also to some extent her seclusion, though this was far less amongst the Jews than amongst other Orientals.

The *" vine "* is an emblem chiefly of *fruitfulness,* but perhaps also of dependence, as needing support ; the *"olive,"* of vigorous, healthy, joyous life. The same figure is employed by Euripides, *Herc. Fur.,* 839. *Med.* 1098.—*J. J. Stewart Perowne.*

Verse 3.—*"Thy wife shall be as a fruitful vine,"* etc. We do not remember to have met with a single instance, in the East, of vines trained *against the walls of a house,* or of olives near or about a house. Neither have we read of such instances. The passage doubtless derives its figures from the fertility of the vine, and from the appearance of the olive, or the order in which olive trees are planted. The construction would then be : " Thy wife, in the sides (interior apartments) of thy house, shall be as the fruitful vine, and thy children round about thy table, like olive plants."—*John Kitto* (1804—1854), *in "The Pictorial Bible."*

Verse 3.—*"Thy wife shall be as a fruitful vine by the sides of thine house."* The wife is likened not to thorns or briers, nor even to oaks or to other fruits and trees, but to the vine ; and also to a vine neither in a vineyard nor in a garden, but set by the walls of the house ; also not barren, but fertile and fruit-bearing. This admonishes husbands as well as wives of their duties. For as the walls support the vine, and defend it against the force of winds and tempests, so ought husbands, as far as is in their power, to defend their wives by their godly conversation and wholesome teachings and institutions against the pestilential wind of the old serpent ; also against the injuries of evil-disposed men. " He that loveth his wife loveth himself. For no man ever yet hated his own flesh ; but nourisheth and cherisheth it, even as the Lord the Church " : Ephes. v. 28, 29.

Further, the vine is exceedingly fragile wood, and not meet for any work, Ezek. xv. 4. Husbands, therefore, should remember that they ought to behave towards their wives patiently and prudently, as with the weaker vessel ; not keeping in mind the fragility of the wood, but the abundance and sweetness of the fruit. If husbands observe this, that will happen to them which Scripture says concerning the peaceful time of Solomon, " And Judah and Israel dwelt safely, every man under his vine and under his fig-tree " : 1 Kings iv. 25. Such was the married life of Abraham with Sarah, Isaac with Rebecca, Jacob with Leah and Rachel.—*Solomon Gesner.*

Verse 3.—*"A fruitful vine by the sides of thine house."* It does not say *on* the sides of the house, but *by* the sides. The passage probably refers to the trellissed bowers which often lead up to the houses, and are covered with vines, the grapes hanging over head. Sitting in these bowers is sitting under our own vines : Micah iv. 4. I have seen in Constantinople grapes hanging over the people's heads in the principal streets, the vines being trained from one side of the street to the other.—*John Gadsby, in "My Wanderings,"* 1860.

Verse 3.—*"By the sides of thine house."* Not on the roof, nor on the floor ; the one is too high, she is no ruler ; the other too low, she is no slave : but in the sides, an equal place between both.—*Thomas Adams.*

Verse 3.—*"By the sides of thine house."* The house is her proper place ; for she is " the beauty of the house " ; there her business lies, there she is safe. The ancients painting them with a snail under their feet, and the Egyptians denying their women shoes, and the Scythians burning the bride's chariot axle-tree at her door, when she was brought to her husband's house, and the angel's asking Abraham where Sarah was (though he knew well enough), that it might be observed, she was " in the tent," do all intimate, that, by the law of nature, and by the rules of religion, the wife ought to keep at home, unless urgent necessity do call her abroad.—*Richard Steele* (—1692), *in "The Morning Exercises."*

Verse 3.—As it is visible that the good man's sons being *" like olive plants round about his table,"* means not that they should be like the olive plants which grew round his table, it being, I presume, a thought in Bishop Patrick that will not be defended, that the Psalmist refers to a table spread in an arbour composed of young olive trees, for we find no such arbours in the Levant, nor is the tree very proper for such a purpose ; so in like manner the first clause must signify, thy wife *shall be in the sides,* or private apartments, *of thy house, fruitful as a thriving vine :* the place here mentioned (the sides of the house) referring to the wife, not to the vine ; as

the other (the table) refers to the children, not to the olives.
thought, it is a remark that Musculus and other interpreters h
The Hebrew word, translated *sides*, is very well known to sig
apartments of a house, as they have also remarked; and he th
description of an Eastern house, must immediately see the prop
private apartments *its sides*. Such a house consists of a squar
doctor observes, is called *the midst* of the house: and private ap't,
which may as properly be called *its sides* in consequence: into its
house, or this quadrangle, company, he tells us, are sometimes r
other authors tell us their *wives* remain concealed at such times.—
1719—1788.

Verse 3.—"*Thy children like olive plants*," etc. Follow me into
will show you what may have suggested the comparison. Here we
a beautiful illustration. This aged and decayed tree is surrounde
by several young and thrifty shoots, which spring from the root of
parent. They seem to uphold, protect, and embrace it, we may ev
they now bear that load of fruit which would otherwise be demanded
parent. Thus do good and affectionate children gather round the
righteous. Each contributes something to the common wealth an
the whole—a beautiful sight, with which may God refresh the eyes of
of mine.—*W. M. Thomson.*

Verse 3.—Man by nature, uninfluenced by grace, is "a wild olive
the object of most parents is merely to cultivate this wild olive tree. Wh
is there about accomplishments which, how attractive soever, are but
blossoms of this wild olive tree!—*Richard Cecil, 1748—1810.*

Verse 3.—Although the world is carried away by irregular desires afte
objects, between which it is perpetually fluctuating in its choice, God gi
this Psalm a description of what he considers to be a blessing beyond al
and therefore we ought to hold it in high estimation. If a man has a wife of
manners as the companion of his life, let him set no less value upon this l
than Solomon did, who, in Prov. xix. 14, affirms that it is God alone who g
good wife. In like manner, if a man be a father of a numerous offspring, let
receive that goodly boon with a thankful heart.—*John Calvin.*

Verse 3.—Before the fall Paradise was man's home; since the fall home ha
been his Paradise.—*Augustus William Hare (1792—1834), and Julius Charles Hare*
(1795—1855), *in "Guesses at Truth."*

Verse 4.—As Haman caused it to be proclaimed (Esther vi. 9), "Thus shall it
be done to the man whom the king delighteth to honour"; so here, "*Behold, that
thus shall the man be blessed that feareth the* LORD." He shall be blessed in his wife,
and blessed in his children; so blessed in both that the Psalmist calls all to behold
it, as a rare, beautiful, yea, wonderful sight: "*Behold, thus shall the man be blessed.*"
And yet the man fearing God shall be blessed more than *thus :* his blessing shall
come in the best way (verse 5): "*The* LORD *shall bless thee out of Zion*"; his temporal
mercies shall come in a spiritual way, yea, he shall have spiritual blessings: "*He
shall bless thee out of Zion*"; and he shall have blessings beyond his own walls:
"*Thou shalt see the good of Jerusalem all the days of thy life. Yea, thou shalt see thy
children's children, and peace upon Israel.*" Sometimes a good man can take no
content in his family mercies because of the church's afflictions; he "prefers
Jerusalem above his chief joy" (Ps. cxxxvii. 6), and while that is mourning he cannot
but be sorrowing, though his own house be full of joy. Sometimes a man's own
family is so afflicted, and his house so full of sorrow, that he cannot but mourn,
even when Jerusalem rejoiceth and Zion is glad. But when a good man looks home
to his own house and sees good there; when also he looks abroad to Jerusalem
and sees good there too, how full is his joy! how complete is his blessedness! and,
"*Behold, thus the man is blessed that feareth the* LORD."—*Joseph Caryl.*

Verse 4.—"*Behold, that thus shall the man be blessed*," etc. It is asserted with a
note commanding attention: *behold* it by faith in the promise; *behold* it by
observation in the performance of the promise; *behold* it with assurance that it shall
be so, for God is faithful; and with admiration that it should be so; for we merit
no favour, no blessing from him.—*Matthew Henry.*

Verse 5.—"*Thou shalt see the good of Jerusalem*," etc. What is added concerning
"*the good of Jerusalem*" is to be regarded as enjoining upon the godly the duty not

Nor is this a new
made.
the more private
ads Dr. Shaw's
of calling the
which the
round it,
ddle of the
in which
Harmer,

and I
upon
see,
ble
at

only of seeking t^r own individual welfare, or of being devoted to their own peculiar interests; but _{ti}er of having it as their chief desire to see the church of God in a flourishing c_fion. It would be a very unreasonable thing for each member to desire what me profitable for itself, while in the meantime the body was neglected. From our ne proneness to err in this respect, the prophet, with good reason, recomme_dtitude about the public welfare; and he mingles together domestic blessing_{gs}ne common benefits of the church in such a way as to show us that they as joined together, and which it is unlawful to put asunder.—*John Calvi*

Lord, let thy blessing so accompany my endeavours in their breedings, sons may be Benaiahs, the Lord's building, and then they will all be eir father's light; and that all my daughters may be Bethias, the Lord's t; and then they will all be Abigails, their father's joy.—*George Swinnock*.

6.—Religion is as favourable for long life as for happiness. She promotes by destroying those evils, the tendency of which is to limit the duration in existence. War sweeps millions into a premature grave. Men live longer stian than in heathen countries. They live longer in Protestant than in n Catholic countries. The direct effect of true religion is to increase the d of human life. "Length of days is in her right hand."—*N. M'Michael*.

erse 6.—Connecting this with the next Psalm we find the following in a famous ch divine:—"'*Peace upon Israel.*' The great blessing of peace, which the Lord h promised to his people even in this life, (for where the Lord gives mercy to y, he gives them peace also, peace and grace are inseparably joined together,) his peace, I say, does not consist in this, that the people of God shall have no enemies; o, for there is an immortal and endless enmity against them. Neither does their peace consist in this, that their enemies shall not assault them; neither does it consist in this, that their enemies shall not molest or afflict them. We do but deceive ourselves if so be that we imagine, so long as we are in this our pilgrimage, and in our warfare here, if we promise to ourselves a peace of this kind; for while we live in this world, we shall still have enemies, and these enemies shall assault us, and persecute and afflict us."—*Alexander Henderson*.

HINTS TO PREACHERS.

Verse 1.—The universality of the blessedness of God-fearing men. Circumstances, personal or relative, cannot alter the blessing; nor age, nor public opinion, nor even their own sense of unworthiness.

Verse 1.—Consider: I. The union of a right fear with a right walk. 1. There is a wrong fear, because slavish; this never can lead to genuine obedience, which must be willingly and cheerfully rendered. 2. But the fear of reverence and filial love will surely turn the feet to God's ways, keep them steadfast therein, and wing them with speed. II. The blessedness of him in whom they are united. 1. It is blessedness of life; for that is prospered. 2. It is blessedness of domestic happiness; for where the head of a family is holy, the family is the home of peace. 3. It is the blessedness of a holy influence in every sphere of his activity. 4. It is deep-felt heart-blessedness in walking with God. 5. And all is but a prelude to the everlasting blessedness of heaven.—*J. F.*

Verse 2.—The blessednesses of the righteous are first generalized, then particularized. Here they are divided into three particulars. I. The fruit of past labours. II. Present enjoyment. III. Future welfare: "It shall be well with thee." Well in time; well in death; well at the last judgment; well for ever.—*G. R.*

Verse 2.—I. Labour a blessing to him who fears God. II. The fruits of labour the result of God's blessing. III. The enjoyment of the fruits of labour a further blessing from God.—*W. H. J. P.*

Verse 2 (*first clause*).—Success in life. I. Its source—God's blessing. II. Its channel—our own labour. III. The measure in which it is promised—as much as we can eat.   More is above the promise.   IV. The enjoyment.   We are permitted to eat or enjoy our labour.

Verse 2 (second clause).—Godly happiness.   I. Follows upon God's blessing. II. Grows out of character : " feareth the Lord."   III. Follows labour : see preceding sentence.   IV. It is supported by well-being : see following sentence.

Verse 2 (last clause).—I. It shall be well with thee while thou livest.   II. It shall be better with thee when thou diest.   III. It shall be best of all with thee in eternity.—*Adapted from Matthew Henry.*

Verse 3.— The blessing of children.   I. They are round our table—expense, anxiety, responsibility, pleasure.   II. They are like olive plants—strong, planted in order, coming on to succeed us, fruitful for God—as the olive provided oil for the lamp.

Verse 3.—A complete family picture.   Here are the husband, the wife, the children, the house, the rooms in the side, the table.   We should ask a blessing upon each, bless God for each, and use each in a blessed manner.

Verse 4.—Domestic happiness the peculiar blessing of piety.   Show how it produces and maintains it.

Verse 5.—The blessing out of Zion.   See Numbers vi. 24—26.

Verse 5.—Two priceless mercies.   I. The house of God a blessing to our house. It is connected with our own salvation, edification, consolation, etc.   It is our hope for the conversion of our children and servants, etc.   It is the place of their education, and for the formation of helpful friendship, etc.   II. Our house a blessing to God's house.   Personal interest in the church, hospitality, generosity, service, etc.   Children aiding holy work.   Wife useful, etc.

Verse 6.—Old age blessed when—I. Life has been spent in the fear of God. II. When it is surrounded to its close by human affection.   III. When it maintains its interest in the cause of God.—*W. H. J. P.*

Verse 6 (last clause).—Church peace—its excellence, its enemies, its friends, its fruits.

PSALM CXXIX.

TITLE.—A Song of Degrees. *I fail to see how this is a step beyond the previous Psalm; and yet it is clearly the song of an older and more tried individual, who looks back upon a life of affliction in which he suffered all along, even from his youth. Inasmuch as patience is a higher, or at least more difficult, grace than domestic love, the ascent or progress may perhaps be seen in that direction. Probably if we knew more of the stations on the road to the Temple we should see a reason for the order of these Psalms; but as that information cannot be obtained, we must take the songs as we find them, and remember that, as we do not now go on pilgrimages to Zion, it is our curiosity and not our necessity which is a loser by our not knowing the cause of the arrangement of the songs in this Pilgrim Psalter.*

AUTHOR, ETC.—*It does not seem to us at all needful to ascribe this Psalm to a period subsequent to the captivity: indeed, it is more suitable to a time when as yet the enemy had not so far prevailed as to have carried the people into a distant land. It is a mingled hymn of sorrow and of strong resolve. Though sorely smitten, the afflicted one is heart-whole, and scorns to yield in the least degree to the enemy. The poet sings the trials of Israel, verses 1—3; the interposition of the Lord, verse 4; and the unblessed condition of Israel's foes, verses 5—8. It is a rustic song, full of allusions to husbandry. It reminds us of the books of Ruth and Amos.*

EXPOSITION.

MANY a time have they afflicted me from my youth, may Israel now say:

2 Many a time have they afflicted me from my youth: yet they have not prevailed against me.

3 The plowers plowed upon my back: they made long their furrows.

4 The LORD is righteous: he hath cut asunder the cords of the wicked.

5 Let them all be confounded and turned back that hate Zion.

6 Let them be as the grass *upon* the housetops, which withereth afore it groweth up:

7 Wherewith the mower filleth not his hand; nor he that bindeth sheaves his bosom.

8 Neither do they which go by say, The blessing of the LORD *be* upon you: we bless you in the name of the LORD.

1. "*Many a time have they afflicted me from my youth, may Israel now say.*" In her present hour of trial, she may remember her former afflictions and speak of them for her comfort, drawing from them the assurance that he who has been with her for so long will not desert her in the end. The song begins abruptly. The poet has been musing, and the fire burns, therefore speaks he with his tongue: he cannot help it, he feels that he must speak, and therefore " may now say " what he has to say. The trials of the church have been repeated again and again, times beyond all count: the same afflictions are fulfilled in us as in our fathers. Jacob of old found his days full of trouble; each Israelite is often harassed; and Israel as a whole has proceeded from tribulation to tribulation. " Many a time," Israel says, because she could not say how many times. She speaks of her assailants as " they," because it would be impossible to write or even to know all their names. They had straitened, harassed, and fought against her from the earliest days of her history— from her youth; and they had continued their assaults right on without ceasing. Persecution is the heirloom of the church, and the ensign of the elect. Israel among the nations was peculiar, and this peculiarity brought against her many restless foes, who could never be easy unless they were warring against the people of God. When in Canaan, at the first, the chosen household was often severely tried; in

Egypt it was heavily oppressed ; in the wilderness it was fiercely assailed ; and in the promised land it was often surrounded by deadly enemies. It was something for the afflicted nation, that it survived to *say*, " Many a time have they afflicted me." The affliction began early—" from my youth " ; and it continued late. The earliest years of Israel and of the church of God were spent in trial. Babes in grace are cradled in opposition. No sooner is the man-child born than the dragon is after it. " It is," however, " good for a man that he bear the yoke in his youth," and he shall see it to be so when in after days he tells the tale.

2. *"Many a time have they afflicted me from my youth."* Israel repeats her statement of her repeated afflictions. The fact was uppermost in her thoughts, and she could not help soliloquizing upon it again and again. These repetitions are after the manner of poetry : thus she makes a sonnet out of her sorrows, music out of her miseries. *"Yet they have not prevailed against me."* We seem to hear the beat of timbrels and the clash of cymbals here : the foe is derided ; his malice has failed. That *"yet"* breaks in like the blast of trumpets, or the roll of kettledrums. " Cast down, but not destroyed," is the shout of a victor. Israel has wrestled, and has overcome in the struggle. Who wonders ? If Israel overcame the angel of the covenant, what man or devil shall vanquish him ? The fight was oft renewed and long protracted : the champion severely felt the conflict, and was at times fearful of the issue ; but at length he takes breath, and cries, " Yet they have not prevailed against me." " Many a time ; " yes, " many a time," the enemy has had his opportunity and his vantage, but not so much as once has he gained the victory.

3. *"The plowers plowed upon my back."* The scourgers tore the flesh as ploughmen furrow a field. The people were maltreated like a criminal given over to the lictors with their cruel whips ; the back of the nation was scored and furrowed by oppression. It is a grand piece of imagery condensed into few words. A writer says the metaphor is muddled, but he is mistaken : there are several figures, like wheel within wheel, but there is no confusion. The afflicted nation was, as it were, lashed by her adversaries so cruelly that each blow left a long red mark, or perhaps a bleeding wound, upon her back and shoulders, comparable to a furrow which tears up the ground from one end of the field to the other. Many a heart has been in like case ; smitten and sore wounded by them that use the scourge of the tongue ; so smitten that their whole character has been cut up and scored by calumny. The true church has in every age had fellowship with her Lord under his cruel flagellations : his sufferings were a prophecy of what she would be called hereafter to endure, and the foreshadowing has been fulfilled. Zion has in this sense been ploughed as a field.

"They made long their furrows :"—as if delighting in their cruel labour. They missed not an inch, but went from end to end of the field, meaning to make thorough work of their congenial engagement. Those who laid on the scourge did it with a thoroughness which showed how hearty was their hate. Assuredly the enemies of Christ's church never spare pains to inflict the utmost injury : they never do the work of the devil deceitfully, or hold back their hand from blood. They smite so as to plough into the man ; they plough the quivering flesh as if it were clods of clay ; they plough deep and long with countless furrows ; until they leave no portion of the church unfurrowed or unassailed. Ah me ! Well did Latimer say that there was no busier ploughman in all the world than the devil : whoever makes short furrows, he does not. Whoever baulks and shirks, he is thorough in all that he does. Whoever stops work at sundown, he never does. He and his children plough like practised ploughmen ; but they prefer to carry on their pernicious work upon the saints behind their backs, for they are as cowardly as they are cruel.

4. *"The LORD is righteous."* Whatever men may be, Jehovah remains just, and will therefore keep covenant with his people and deal out justice to their oppressors. Here is the hinge of the condition : this makes the turning point of Israel's distress. The Lord bears with the long furrows of the wicked, but he will surely make them cease from their ploughing before he has done with them. *"He hath cut asunder the cords of the wicked."* The rope which binds the oxen to the plough is cut ; the cord which bound the victim is broken ; the bond which held the enemies in cruel unity has snapped. As in Psalm cxxiv. 7 we read, " the snare is broken ; we are escaped," so here the breaking of the enemies' instrument of oppression is Israel's release. Sooner or later a righteous God will interpose, and when he does so, his action will be most effectual ; he does not unfasten, but cuts asunder, the harness which the ungodly use in their labour of hate. Never has

God used a nation to chastise his Israel without destroying that nation when the chastisement has come to a close : he hates those who hurt his people even though he permits their hate to triumph for a while for his own purpose. If any man would have his harness cut, let him begin to plough one of the Lord's fields with the plough of persecution. The shortest way to ruin is to meddle with a saint : the divine warning is, " He that toucheth you toucheth the apple of his eye."

5. *"Let them all be confounded and turned back that hate Zion."* And so say we right heartily : and in this case *vox populi* is *vox Dei*, for so it shall be. If this be an imprecation, let it stand ; for our heart says " Amen " to it. It is but justice that those who hate, harass, and hurt the good should be brought to naught. Those who confound right and wrong ought to be confounded, and those who turn back from God ought to be turned back. Loyal subjects wish ill to those who plot against their king.

> " Confound their politics,
> Frustrate their knavish tricks,"

is but a proper wish, and contains within it no trace of personal ill-will. We desire their welfare as men, their downfall as traitors. Let their conspiracies be confounded, their policies be turned back. How can we wish prosperity to those who would destroy that which is dearest to our hearts ? This present age is so flippant that if a man loves the Saviour he is styled a fanatic, and if he hates the powers of evil he is named a bigot. As for ourselves, despite all objectors, we join heartily in this commination ; and would revive in our heart the old practice of Ebal and Gerizim, where those were blessed who bless God, and those were cursed who make themselves a curse to the righteous. We have heard men desire a thousand times that the gallows might be the reward of the assassins who murdered two inoffensive men in Dublin, and we would never censure the wish ; for justice ought to be rendered to the evil as well as to the good. Besides, the church of God is so useful, so beautiful, so innocent of harm, so fraught with good, that those who do her wrong are wronging all mankind and deserve to be treated as the enemies of the human race. Study a chapter from the " Book of Martyrs," and see if you do not feel inclined to read an imprecatory Psalm over Bishop Bonner and Bloody Mary: It may be that some wretched nineteenth century sentimentalist will blame you : if so, read another *over him*.

6. *"Let them be as the grass upon the housetops, which withereth afore it groweth up."* Grass on the housetop is soon up and soon down. It sprouts in the heat, finds enough nutriment to send up a green blade, and then it dies away before it reaches maturity, because it has neither earth nor moisture sufficient for its proper development. Before it grows up it dies ; it needs not to be plucked up, for it hastens to decay of itself. Such is and such ought to be the lot of the enemies of God's people. Transient is their prosperity ; speedy is their destruction. The height of their position, as it hastens their progress, so it hurries their doom. Had they been lower in station they had perhaps been longer in being. " Soon ripe, soon rotten," is an old proverb. Soon plotting and soon rotting, is a version of the old adage which will suit in this place. We have seen grass on the rustic thatch of our own country cottages which will serve for an illustration almost as well as that which comes up so readily on the flat roofs and domes of eastern habitations. The idea is—they make speed to success, and equal speed to failure. Persecutors are all sound and fury, flash and flame ; but they speedily vanish—more speedily than is common to men. Grass in the field withers, but not as speedily as grass on the housetops. Without a mower the tufts of verdure perish from the roofs, and so do opposers pass away by other deaths than fall to the common lot of men ; they are gone, and none is the worse. If they are missed at all, their absence is never regretted. Grass on the housetop is a nonentity in the world : the house is not improverished when the last blade is dried up : and, even so, the opposers of Christ pass away, and none lament them. One of the fathers said of the apostate emperor Julian, " That little cloud will soon be gone "; and so it was. Every sceptical system of philosophy has much the same history ; and the like may be said of each heresy. Poor, rootless things, they are and are not : they come and go, even though no one rises against them. Evil carries the seeds of dissolution within itself. So let it be.

7. *"Wherewith the mower filleth not his hand ; nor he that bindeth sheaves his bosom."* When with his sickle the husbandman would cut down the tufts, he found

nothing to lay hold upon : the grass promised fairly enough, but there was no fulfilment, there was nothing to cut or to carry, nothing for the hand to grasp, nothing for the lap to gather. Easterns carry their corn in their bosoms, but in this case there was nothing to bear home. Thus do the wicked come to nothing. By God's just appointment they prove a disappointment. Their fire ends in smoke : their verdure turns to vanity ; their flourishing is but a form of withering. No one profits by them, least of all are they profitable to themselves. Their aim is bad, their work is worse, their end is worst of all.

8. *"Neither do they which go by say, The blessing of the* LORD *be upon you : we bless you in the name of the* LORD.*"* In harvest times men bless each other in the name of the Lord ; but there is nothing in the course and conduct of the ungodly man to suggest the giving or receiving of a benediction. Upon a survey of the sinner's life from beginning to end, we feel more inclined to weep than to rejoice, and we feel bound rather to wish him failure than success. We dare not use pious expressions as mere compliments, and hence we dare not wish God-speed to evil men lest we be partakers of their evil deeds. When persecutors are worrying the saints, we cannot say, " The blessing of the Lord be upon you." When they slander the godly and oppose the doctrine of the cross, we dare not bless them in the name of the Lord. It would be infamous to compromise the name of the righteous Jehovah by pronouncing his blessing upon unrighteous deeds.

See how godly men are roughly ploughed by their adversaries, and yet a harvest comes of it which endures and produces blessing ; while the ungodly, though they flourish for a while and enjoy a complete immunity, dwelling, as they think, quite above the reach of harm, are found in a short time to have gone their way and to have left no trace behind. Lord, number me with thy saints. Let me share their grief if I may also partake of their glory. Thus would I make this Psalm my own, and magnify thy name, because thine afflicted ones are not destroyed, and thy persecuted ones are not forsaken.

EXPLANATORY NOTES AND QUAINT SAYINGS.

Whole Psalm.—In the " degrees " of Christian virtue the Psalm corresponds to the tenth step, which is patience in adversity.—*H. T. Armfield.*

Whole Psalm.—The following incident in connection with the glorious return of the Vaudois under Henri Arnaud is related in Muston's " Israel of the Alps " :—" After these successes the gallant patriots took an oath of fidelity to each other, and celebrated divine service in one of their own churches, for the first time since their banishment. The enthusiasm of the moment was irrepressible ; they chanted the seventy-fourth Psalm to the clash of arms ; and Henri Arnaud, mounting the pulpit with a sword in one hand and a Bible in the other, preached from the Hundred and twenty-ninth Psalm, and once more declared, in the face of heaven, that he would never resume his pastoral office in patience and peace, until he should witness the restoration of his brethren to their ancient and rightful settlements."

Verse 1.—*"Many a time have they afflicted me from my youth."* 1. How *old* these afflictions are : *"From my youth."* Ay, from my infancy, birth and conception. 2. There is the *frequency* and *iteration* of these afflictions. They were *oft* and *many* : *"many a time."* 3. There is the *grievousness* of these afflictions, expressed by a comparison. " The plowers plowed upon my back : they made long their furrows." So these were *old* afflictions—*from her youth.* They were *many a time :* more times than can be numbered. And then they were *grievous*, even like iron ploughs, drawing deep and long furrows on their back.—*Alexander Henderson.*

Verse 1.—*"Many a time have they afflicted me,"* etc. God had one Son, and but one Son, without sin ; but never any without sorrow. We may be God's children, and yet still under persecution : his Israel, and afflicted from our youth up. We may feel God's hand as a Father upon us when he strikes us as well as when he strokes us. When he strokes us, it is lest we faint under his hand ; and when he strikes us, it is that we should know his hand.—*Abraham Wright* (1611—1690), *in "A Practical Commentary upon the Psalms."*

Verse 1.—"*They.*" The persecutors deserve not a name. The rich man is not named (as Lazarus is) because not worthy : Luke xvi. "They shall be written in the earth" : Jeremiah xvii. 13.—*John Trapp.*

Verse 1.—"*They.*" In speaking of the enemies of Israel simply by the pronoun "*they,*" without being more specific, the Psalmist aggravates the greatness of the evil more than if he had expressly named the Assyrians or the Egyptians. By not specifying any particular class of foes, he tacitly intimates that the world is filled with innumerable bands of enemies, whom Satan easily arms for the destruction of good men, his object being that new wars may arise continually on every side. History certainly bears ample testimony that the people of God had not to deal with a few enemies, but that they were assaulted by almost the whole world ; and further, that they were molested not only by external foes, but also by those of an internal kind, by such as professed to belong to the Church.—*John Calvin.*

Verse 1.—"'*They afflicted me.*" Why are these afflictions of the righteous ? Whence is it that he who has given up his Son to death for them, should deny them earthly blessings ? Why is faith a mourner so frequently here below, and with all that heroic firmness in her aspect, and hope of glory in her eye, why needs she to be painted with so deep a sorrow on her countenance, and the trace of continual tears on her cheek ? First, we reply, *for her own safety.* Place religion out of the reach of sorrow, and soon she would pine and perish. God is said to choose his people in the furnace, because they oftenest choose him there.

It is ever from the cross that the most earnest "My God" proceeds, and never is the cry heard but he speeds forth at its utterance, who once hung there, to support, to comfort, and to save.

As it is only in affliction God is *sought*, so by many it is only in affliction God is *known*. This, one of the kings of these worshippers of the Temple found. "When Manasseh was brought to affliction, *then* he knew that the Lord he was God " : 2 Chronicles xxxiii. 12, 13.

But, further, it is only by affliction *we ourselves are known*. What is the source of that profound and obstinate indifference to divine truth which prevails among men of the world, except the proud conviction that they may dispense with it ? It is only when they are crushed as the worm they are made to feel that the dust is their source ; only when earthly props are withdrawn will they take hold of that arm of omnipotence which Jesus offers, and which he has offered so long in vain.

While men know themselves, they *know their sin* also in affliction. What is the natural course and experience of the unbelieving of mankind ? Transgression, remorse, and then forgetfulness ; new transgression, new sorrow, and again forget-fulness. How shall this carelessness be broken ? How convince them that they stand in need of a Saviour as the first and deepest want of their being, and that they can only secure deliverance from wrath eternal by a prompt and urgent application to him ? By nothing so effectually as by affliction. God's children, who had forgotten him, arise and go to their Father when thus smitten by the scourge of sorrow ; and no sooner is the penitent "*Father, I have sinned* " spoken, than they are clasped in his arms, and safe and happy in his love.

It is, further, by affliction that the *world* is known to God's children. God's great rival is the world. The lust of the flesh, pleasure ; the lust of the eye, desire ; the pride of life, the longing to be deemed superior to those about us,—comprise everything man naturally covets. Give us ease, honour, distinction, and all life's good will seem obtained. *But what wilt thou do, when he shall judge thee ?* This is a question fitted to alarm the happiest of the children of prosperity.

What so frequently and effectually shows the necessity of piety as the sharp teachings of affliction ? They show what moralists and preachers never could, that riches profit not in the day of death, that pleasures most fully enjoyed bring no soothing to the terrors which nearness to eternity presents, and that friends, however affectionate, cannot plead for and save us at the bar of God. "Miserable comforters are they all," and it is for the very purpose of inspiring this conviction, along with a belief that it is Jesus alone who can comfort in the hour of need, that affliction is sent to God's children.—*Robert Nisbet.*

Verse 1.—"*From my youth.*" The first that ever died, died for religion ; so early came martyrdom into the world.—*John Trapp.*

Verses 1, 2.—1. The visible Church from the beginning of the world is one body, and, as it were, one man, growing up from infancy to riper age ; for so speaketh the church here : "*Many a time have they afflicted me from my youth.*" 2. The wicked enemies of the church, they also are one body, one adverse army, from the beginning of the world continuing war against the church : *"Many a time have they afflicted me from my youth."* 3. As the former injuries done to the church are owned by the church, in after-ages, as done against the same body, so also the persecution of former enemies is imputed and put upon the score of present persecutors : *"Many a time have they afflicted me from my youth, may Israel now say."* 4. New experience of persecution, when they call to mind the exercise of the church in former ages, serves much for encouragement and consolation in troubles : *"Many a time have they afflicted me from my youth, may Israel now say."* 5. Albeit this hath been the endeavour of the wicked in all ages to destroy the church, yet God hath still preserved her from age to age : *"Yet they have not prevailed."*—*David Dickson.*

Verses 1, 2.—When the prophet says twice, *"They have afflicted me,"* *"they have afflicted me,"* the repetition is not superfluous, it being intended to teach us that the people of God had not merely once or twice to enter the conflict, but that their patience had been tried by continual exercises.—*John Calvin.*

Verse 2.—*"Many a time,"* etc. The Christian Church may adopt the language of the Hebrew Church : " Many a time have they afflicted me from my youth : yet they have not prevailed against me." What afflictions were endured by the Christian Church from her youth up ! How feeble was that youth ! How small the number of the apostles to whom our Lord gave his gospel in charge ! How destitute were they of human learning, of worldly influence, of secular power ! To effect their destruction, and to frustrate their object—the glory of God and the salvation of men—the dungeon and the mine, the rack and the gibbet, were all successively employed. The ploughers ploughed their back, and made long their furrows. Their property was confiscated ; their persons were imprisoned ; their civil rights were taken from them ; their heads rolled on the scaffold ; their bodies were consumed at the burning pile ; they were thrown, amidst the ringing shouts of the multitude, to the wild beasts of the amphitheatre. Despite, however, of every opposition, our holy religion took root and grew upward. Not all the fury of ten persecutions could exterminate it from the earth. The teeth of wild beasts could not grind it to powder ; the fire could not burn it ; the waters could not drown it ; the dungeon could not confine it. Truth is eternal, like the great God from whose bosom it springs, and therefore it cannot be destroyed. And because Christianity is the truth, and no lie, her enemies have never prevailed against her.—*M. M'Michael.*

Verse 2.—*"Yet they have not prevailed against me."* The words are the same as in Gen. xxxii. 28. The blessing won by Jacob, when he wrestled with the angel, remained on his descendants. During the long night of the Captivity the faithful had wrestled in faithful prayer ; now the morning had appeared, and Israel was raised to a higher stage of privilege.—*W. Kay.*

Verse 2.—*"Yet they have not prevailed against me."* Israel prevailed with God in wrestling with him, and therefore it is that he prevails with men also. If so be that we will wrestle with God for a blessing, and prevail with him, then we need not to fear but we shall wrestle the enemies out of it also. If we be the people of God, and persist in wrestling against his enemies, we need not fear but that we shall be victorious.—*Alexander Henderson.*

Verse 3.—*"The plowers plowed,"* etc. There does not seem to be any need to look for an interpretation of this in scourging or any other bodily infliction of pain ; it seems to be " a figurative mode of expressing severe oppression." Roberts informs us that when, in the East, a man is in much trouble through oppressors, he says, " How they plough me and turn me up."—*Ingram Cobbin,* 1839.

Verse 3.—*"The plowers plowed,"* etc. The great Husbandman who owns this plough (at least by whose permission this plough goes), is God. Not only is it God who makes your common ploughs to gang, and sends the gospel into a land, but it is God also who disposes and overrules this same plough of persecution. For without his licence the plough cannot be yoked ; and being yoked, cannot enter to gang till he direct ; and he tempers the irons, so that they cannot go one inch deeper than he thinks meet. When he thinks it time to quit work, then presently he cuts their cords, so that they cannot go once about after he thinks it time to quit work. Albeit when they yoke, they resolve to have all the land upside down, yet he will let them plough no more of it than he sees meet. Now for the ploughmen of this plough, they are Satan and the evil angels ; they hold the plough, and are goad-men to it ; and they yoke in the oxen into the plough, and drive them up with their goads. And they have a sort of music also, which they whistle into their ears, to make them go the faster ; and that is the allurements and provocations of the world. And for the oxen who draw into this plough, it may be princes when they turn persecutors of the kirk ; it may be prelates ; it may be politicians in the world : these are the oxen, Satan and the ill spirits inciting them, and stirring them up to go forward in their intended course. Then consider here that the plough and the ploughmen and oxen go about as God thinks meet ; but what is it that they are doing in the meantime ? Nothing else but preparing the ground for seed, and so the Lord employs them to prepare his people better to receive the seed of his word and of his Spirit.—*Alexander Henderson.*

Verse 3.—God fails not to sow blessings in the furrows, which the plowers plow upon the back of the church.—*Jeremy Taylor,* 1613—1667.

Verse 3.—*"The plowers plowed upon my back : they made long their furrows."* When the Lord Jesus Christ was in his suffering state, and during his passion, these words here predicted of him were most expressly realized. Whilst he remained in the hands of the Roman soldiers they stript him of his raiment ; they bound him with cords to a pillar ; they flogged him. This was so performed by them, that they made ridges in his back and sides ; they tore skin and flesh, and made him bare even to the bone, so that his body was like a ploughed field ; the gashes made in it were like ridges made in a ploughed field ; these were on his back. *"The plowers plowed upon my back : they made long their furrows."* Whilst every part of our Lord's sorrows and sufferings is most minutely set forth in the sacred hymns, Psalms, and songs, contained in what we style the Book of Psalms, yet we shall never comprehend what our most blessed Lord, in every part of his life, and in his passion and death, underwent for us : may the Lord the Spirit imprint this fresh expression used on this subject effectually upon us. Our Lord's words here are very expressive of the violence of his tormentors and their rage against him, and of the wounds and torments they had inflicted on him.

What must the feelings of our Lord have been when they made such furrows on his back, that it was all furrowed and welted with such long wounds, that it was more like a ploughed field than anything else. Blessings on him for his grace and patience, it is " with his stripes we are healed."—*Samuel Eyles Pierce.*

Verse 3.—*"They made long their furrows."* The apparent harshness of this figure will disappear if it be considered to refer to severe public scourgings. To those who have been so unhappy as to witness such scourgings this allusion will then appear most expressive. The long weals or wounds which the scourge leaves at each stroke may most aptly be compared either to *furrows* or (as the original admits) to the *ridges between the furrows.* The *furrows* made by the plough in the East are very superficial, and (although straight) are usually carried to a great length, the fields not being enclosed as in this country.—*John Kitto, in "The Pictorial Bible."*

Verse 4.—*"The LORD is righteous : he hath cut asunder the cords of the wicked ;"* i.e., he has put an end to their domination and tyranny over us. In the Hebrew word which is rendered *"cords"* there is a reference to the *harness* with which the oxen were fastened to the plough ; and so to the *involved machinations* and *cruelties* of the enemy. The Hebrew word properly denotes thick *twisted cords ;* figuratively, intertwined wickedness ; Micah vii. 3. *"The cords of the wicked,"* therefore, signify their *power, dominion, tyranny,* wickedness, and violence. These cords God is said *"to have cut,"* so that *he should have made an end ;* and, therefore, *"to have cut"* for ever, so that they should never be reunited.—*Hermann Venema.*

Verse 4.—*"He hath cut asunder the cords of the wicked."* The enemies' power has been broken ; *God has cut asunder the cords of the wicked,* has cut their gears, their traces, and so spoiled their ploughing ; has cut their scourges, and so spoiled their lashing ; has cut the bands of union, by which they were combined together ; he has cut the bands of captivity, in which they held God's people. God has many ways of disabling wicked men to do the mischief they design against his church, and shaming their counsels.—*Matthew Henry.*

Verse 4.—*"He hath cut asunder the cords of the wicked."* He repeateth the same praise of God in delivering his church from oppression of the enemy, under the similitude of cutting the cords of the plough, which tilleth up another man's field. Whence learn, 1. The enemies of the church do no more regard her than they do the earth under their feet, and do seek to make their own advantage of her, as usurpers use to do in possessing and labouring of another man's field. *"The plowers plowed upon my back."* 2. The Lord useth to suffer his enemies to break up the fallow ground of his people's proud and stiff hearts with the plough of persecution, and to draw deep and long furrows on them : *"They made long their furrows."* 3. What the enemies do against the church the Lord maketh use of for manuring the church, which is his field, albeit they intend no good to God's church, yet they serve in God's wisdom to prepare the Lord's people for receiving the seed of God's word ; for the similitude speaketh of their tilling of the church, but nothing of their sowing, for that is reserved for the Lord himself, who is owner of the field. 4. When the wicked have performed so much of God's husbandry as he thinketh good to suffer them, then he stoppeth their design, and looseth their plough. *"He hath cut asunder the cords of the wicked."—David Dickson.*

Verse 5.—If any one be desirous to accept these words, *"Let them be confounded and turned backward,"* as they sound, he will devoutly explain the imprecation : that is to say, it may be an imprecation of good confusion, which leads to repentance, and of turning to God from sin ; thus Bellarmine. There is a confounding by bringing grace, glory, and turning from the evil way. Thus some enemies and persecutors of the Christians have been holily confounded and turned to the faith of Christ ; as St. Paul, who full of wrath and slaughter was going to Damascus that he might afflict the believers, but was graciously confounded on the road.—*Thomas Le Blanc.*

Verse 5.—*"Let them all be confounded."* Mr. Emerson told a convention of rationalists once, in this city, that the morality of the New Testament is scientific and perfect. But the morality of the New Testament is that of the Old. " Yes," you say ; " but what of the imprecatory Psalms ? " A renowned professor, who, as Germany thinks, has done more for New England theology than any man since Jonathan Edwards, was once walking in this city with a clergyman of a radical faith, who objected to the doctrine that the Bible is inspired, and did so on the ground of the imprecatory Psalms. The replies of the usual kind were made ; and it was presumed that David expressed the Divine purpose in praying that his enemies might be destroyed, and that he gave utterance only to the natural, righteous indignation of conscience against unspeakable iniquity. But the doubter would not be satisfied. The two came at last to a newspaper bulletin, on which the words were written,—" Baltimore to be shelled at twelve o'clock." " I am glad of it," said the radical preacher ; " I am glad of it." " And so am I," said his companion, " but I hardly dare say so, for fear you should say that I am uttering an imprecatory Psalm."—*Joseph Cook, in Boston Monday Lectures. "Transcendentalism."*

Verse 5.—*"And turned back ; "* from pursuing their designs and accomplishing them ; as the Assyrian monarch was, who had a hook put into his nose, and a bridle in his lips, and was turned back by the way he came : Isaiah xxxvii. 29. —*John Gill.*

Verse 5.—*"All those who hate Zion."* Note that he does not say, All who hate me ; but " all who hate Zion." Thus the saints are not led to this from the desire of revenge, but from zeal for the people of God, so that they pray for the confusion and repression of the ungodly.—*Wolfgang Musculus.*

Verse 6.—*" Let them be as the grass upon the housetops."* They are rightly compared to *"grass on the housetops ; "* for more contemptuously the Holy Ghost could not speak of them. For this grass is such, that it soon withereth away before the sickle be put into it. Yea, no man thinketh it worthy to be cut down, no man regardeth it, every man suffereth it to brag for a while, and to show itself unto men from the housetops as though it were something when it is nothing. So the wicked persecutors in the world, which are taken to be mighty and terrible according to the outward show, are of all men most contemptible. For Christians do not once think of plucking them up or cutting them down ; they persecute them not, they revenge not their own injuries, but suffer them to increase, to brag and glory as much as they list. For they know that they cannot abide the violence of a vehement wind. Yea, though all things be in quietness, yet as grass upon the housetops, by little and little, withereth away through the heat of the sun, so tyrannies upon small occasions do perish and soon vanish away. The faithful, therefore, in suffering do prevail and overcome ; but the wicked in doing are overthrown, and miserably perish, as all the histories of all times and ages do plainly witness.—*Martin Luther.*

Verse 6.—*"Like grass upon the housetops."* The flat roofs of the Eastern houses " are plastered with a composition of mortar, tar, ashes, and sand," in the crevices of which grass often springs. The houses of the poor in the country were formed of a plaster of mud and straw, where the grass would grow still more freely : as all the images are taken from country life, it is doubtless to country dwellings that the poet refers.—*J. J. Stewart Perowne.*

Verse 6.—*" Like grass upon the housetops."* The enemies of Zion may have an elevated position in the nation, they may seem to promise growth, but having no root in themselves, like the hearers on the stony ground, give no promise of fruit. Their profession dies away and leaves no benefit to the church, as it claims no blessing from others.—*William Wilson* (1783—1873), *in "The Book of Psalms, with an Exposition."*

Verse 6.—*"Grass upon the housetops."* In the morning the master of the house laid in a stock of earth, which was carried up, and spread evenly on the top of the house, which is flat. The whole roof is thus formed of mere earth, laid on and rolled hard and flat. On the top of every house is a large stone roller, for the purpose of hardening and flattening this layer of rude soil, so that the rain may not penetrate ; but upon this surface, as may be supposed, grass and weeds grow freely, but never come to maturity. It is to such grass the Psalmist alludes as useless and bad.—*William Jowett, in "Christian Researches in Syria and the Holy Land,"* 1825.

Verse 7.—*"The mower filleth not his hand,"* etc. The grain was rather pulled than cut, and as each handful was taken the reaper gave it a flourishing swing up into his bosom.—*Mrs. Finn, in "Home in the Holy Land,"* 1866.

Verse 7.—*"He that bindeth sheaves his bosom."* A practice prevails in hot climates of sending out persons into the woods and other wild places to collect the grass, which would otherwise be wasted ; and it is no uncommon thing in the evening to see groups of grass-cutters in the market, waiting to dispose of their bundles or sheaves, which are often so large that one is disposed to wonder how they could have been conveyed from the woods upon one man's shoulders.—*Maria Calcott, in "A Scripture Herbal,"* 1842.

Verse 8.—The latter expressions are most refreshingly Arabic. Nothing is more natural than for them, when passing by a fruit-tree or corn-field loaded with a rich crop to exclaim, *"Barak Allah !"* God bless you ! We bless you in the name of the *Lord !*—*W. M. Thomson.*

HINTS TO PREACHERS.

Verse 1.—Affliction as it comes to saints from men of the world. I. Reason for it—enmity of the serpent's seed. II. Modes of its display—persecution, ridicule, slander, disdain, etc. III. Comfort under it. So persecuted they the prophets: so the Master. It is their nature. They cannot kill the soul. It is but for a time, etc.

Verses 1 and 2.—I. How far persecution for righteousness' sake may go. 1. It may be great : " afflicted " " afflicted." 2. It may be frequent : " Many a time." 3. It may be early : " From my youth." II. How far it cannot go. 1. It may seem to prevail. 2. It may prevail in some degree. 3. It cannot ultimately prevail. 4. It shall cause that to which it is opposed increasingly to prevail.—*G. R.*

Verses 1—4.—Israel persecuted but not forsaken. Persecution. I. Whence it came : " they." II. How it came : " Many a time," " from my youth," severely : " afflicted," " ploughed." III. Why it came. Human and Satanic hatred, and Divine permission. IV. What came of it: " not prevailed"—to destroy, to drive to despair, to lead to sin. God's righteousness manifested in upholding his people, baffling their foes, etc.

Verses 1—4. The enemies of God's church. I. Their violence: "The plowers plowed," etc. II. Their persistency: "Many a time . . . . from my youth." III. Their failure: "Yet they have not prevailed." IV. Their great opponent: "The Lord . . . . hath cut asunder."—*J. F.*

Verse 3.—I. Literally fulfilled. 1. In Christ. Matt. xxvii. 26; xx. 19; Mark xv. 15; Luke xviii. 33; John xix. 1. 2. In his followers. Matt. x. 17; Acts xvi. 23; 2 Cor. vi. 5; xi. 23, 24; Heb. xi. 36. And frequently in subsequent persecutions. II. Figuratively. In secret calumnies both in Christ and his followers.—*G. R.*

Verse 4.—Israel's song of triumph. I. The Lord is righteous in permitting these afflictions to come upon his people. II. He is righteous in keeping his promise of deliverance to his people. III. He is righteous in visiting the enemies of his people with judgment.—*W. H. J. P.*

Verse 5.—I. An inexcusable hatred described: "hate Zion," God's church and cause. For, 1. Her people are righteous. 2. Her faith is a gospel. 3. Her mission is peace. 4. Her very existence is the world's preservation. II. An inveterate sinfulness indicated: "Them that hate Zion." For, whatever moral virtues they may boast of, they must be, 1. Enemies to the human race. 2. In defiant opposition to God. 3. Perversely blind, as Saul, or radically vile. 4. Devil-like. III. An instinctive feeling of a good man expressed: "Let them all be," etc. Prompted by, 1. His love to God. 2. Love to man. 3. Love to righteousness. Hence, its existence is in itself a pledge that the righteous God will respect and comply with it.—*J. F.*

Verses 5—8.—I. The characters described. 1. They do not love Zion. They say not, "Lord, I have loved the habitation of thine house," etc. 2. They hate Zion—both its King and its subjects. II. Their prosperity: "As the grass," etc. III. Their end. 1. Shame: "Let them be confounded." 2. Loss: "Turned back." 3. Disappointment. No mowing; no reaping. 4. Dishonour. Unblessed by others as well as in themselves.—*G. R.*

Verses 6—9.—The wicked flourishing and perishing. I. Eminent in position. II. Envied in prosperity. III. Evanescent in duration. IV. Empty as to solidity. V. Excepted from blessing.

PSALM CXXX.

TITLE.—*A Song of Degrees. It would be hard to see any upward step from the preceding to the present Psalm, and therefore it is possible that the steps or ascents are in the song itself : certainly it does rise rapidly out of the depths of anguish to the heights of assurance. It follows well upon cxxix. : when we have overcome the trials which arise from man we are the better prepared to meet those sharper sorrows which arise out of our matters towards God. He who has borne the scourges of the wicked is trained in all patience to wait the dealings of the Holy Lord. We name this the* DE PROFUNDIS PSALM : *"Out of the depths" is the leading word of it : out of those depths we cry, wait, watch, and hope. In this Psalm we hear of the pearl of redemption, verses 7 and 8 : perhaps the sweet singer would never have found that precious thing had he not been cast into the depths. "Pearls lie deep."*

DIVISION.—*The first two verses reveal an intense desire ; and the next two are a humble confession of repentance and faith, verses 3 and 4. In verses 5 and 6 waiting watchfulness is declared and resolved upon ; and in the last two verses joyful expectation, both for himself and all Israel, finds expression.*

EXPOSITION.

OUT of the depths have I cried unto thee, O LORD.

2 Lord, hear my voice : let thine ears be attentive to the voice of my supplications.

3 If thou, LORD, shouldest mark iniquities, O Lord, who shall stand ?

4 But *there is* forgiveness with thee, that thou mayest be feared.

5 I wait for the LORD, my soul doth wait, and in his word do I hope.

6 My soul *waiteth* for the Lord more than they that watch for the morning : *I say, more than* they that watch for the morning.

7 Let Israel hope in the LORD : for with the LORD *there is* mercy, and with him *is* plenteous redemption.

8 And he shall redeem Israel from all his iniquities.

1. *"Out of the depths have I cried unto thee, O LORD."* This is the Psalmist's statement and plea : he had never ceased to pray even when brought into the lowest state. The depths usually silence all they engulf, but they could not close the mouth of this servant of the Lord ; on the contrary, it was in the abyss itself that he cried unto Jehovah. Beneath the floods prayer lived and struggled ; yea, above the roar of the billows rose the cry of faith. It little matters where we are if we can pray ; but prayer is never more real and acceptable than when it rises out of the worst places. Deep places beget deep devotion. Depths of earnestness are stirred by depths of tribulation. Diamonds sparkle most amid the darkness. Prayer *de profundis* gives to God *gloria in excelsis*. The more distressed we are, the more excellent is the faith which trusts bravely in the Lord, and therefore appeals to him, and to him alone. Good men may be in the depths of temporal and spiritual trouble ; but good men in such cases look only to their God, and they stir themselves up to be more instant and earnest in prayer than at other times. The depth of their distress moves the depths of their being ; and from the bottom of their hearts an exceeding great and bitter cry rises unto the one living and true God. David had often been in the deep, and as often had he pleaded with Jehovah, his God, in whose hand are all deep places. He prayed, and remembered that he had prayed, and pleaded that he had prayed ; hoping ere long to receive an answer. It would be dreadful to look back on trouble and feel forced to own that we did not cry unto the Lord in it ; but it is most comforting to know that whatever we did not do, or could not do, yet we did pray, even in our worst times. He that prays in the depth will not sink out of his depth. He that cries out of the depths shall soon sing in the heights.

2. "*Lord, hear my voice.*" It is all we ask ; but nothing less will content us. If the Lord will but hear us we will leave it to his superior wisdom to decide whether he will answer us or no. It is better for our prayer to be heard than answered. If the Lord were to make an absolute promise to answer all our requests it might be rather a curse than a blessing, for it would be casting the responsibility of our lives upon ourselves, and we should be placed in a very anxious position : but now the Lord hears our desires, and that is enough ; we only wish him to grant them if his infinite wisdom sees that it would be for our good and for his glory. Note that the Psalmist spoke audibly in prayer : this is not at all needful, but it is exceedingly helpful ; for the use of the voice assists the thoughts. Still, there is a voice in silent supplication, a voice in our weeping, a voice in that sorrow which cannot find a tongue : that voice the Lord will hear if its cry is meant for his ear. "*Let thine ears be attentive to the voice of my supplication.*" The Psalmist's cry is a beggar's petition ; he begs the great King and Lord to lend an ear to it. He has supplicated many times, but always with one voice, or for one purpose ; and he begs to be noticed in the one matter which he has pressed with so much importunity. He would have the King hearken, consider, remember, and weigh his request. He is confused, and his prayer may therefore be broken, and difficult to understand ; he begs therefore that his Lord will give the more earnest and compassionate heed to the voice of his many and painful pleadings. When we have already prayed over our troubles it is well to pray over our prayers. If we can find no more words, let us entreat the Lord to hear those petitions which we have already presented. If we have faithfully obeyed the precept by praying without ceasing, we may be confident that the Lord will faithfully fulfil the promise by helping us without fail. Though the Psalmist was under a painful sense of sin, and so was in the depth, his faith pleaded in the teeth of conscious unworthiness ; for well he knew that the Lord's keeping his promise depends upon his own character and not upon that of his erring creatures.

3. "*If thou, Lord, shouldest mark iniquities, O Lord, who shall stand ?*" If JAH, the all-seeing, should in strict justice call every man to account for every want of conformity to righteousness, where would any one of us be ? Truly, he does record all our transgressions ; but as yet he does not act upon the record, but lays it aside till another day. If men were to be judged upon no system but that of works, who among us could answer for himself at the Lord's bar, and hope to stand clear and accepted ? This verse shows that the Psalmist was under a sense of sin, and felt it imperative upon him not only to cry as a suppliant but to confess as a sinner. Here he owns that he cannot stand before the great King in his own righteousness, and he is so struck with a sense of the holiness of God, and the rectitude of the law, that he is convinced that no man of mortal race can answer for himself before a Judge so perfect, concerning a law so divine. Well does he cry, "O Lord, who shall stand ?" None can do so : there is none that doeth good, no, not one. Iniquities are matters which are not according to equity : what a multitude we have of these ! Jehovah, who sees all, and is also our *Adonai*, or Lord, will assuredly bring us into judgment concerning those thoughts, and words, and works which are not in exact conformity to his law. Were it not for the Lord Jesus, could we hope to stand ? Dare we meet him in the dread day of account on the footing of law and equity ? What a mercy it is that we need not do so, for the next verse sets forth another way of acceptance to which we flee.

4. "*But there is forgiveness with thee.*" Blessed *but*. Free, full, sovereign pardon is in the hand of the great King : it is his prerogative to forgive, and he delights to exercise it. Because his nature is mercy, and because he has provided a sacrifice for sin, therefore forgiveness is with him for all that come to him confessing their sins. The power of pardon is permanently resident with God : he has forgiveness ready to his hand at this instant. "*That thou mayest be feared.*" This is the fruitful root of piety. None fear the Lord like those who have experienced his forgiving love. Gratitude for pardon produces far more fear and reverence of God than all the dread which is inspired by punishment. If the Lord were to execute justice upon all, there would be none left to fear him ; if all were under apprehension of his deserved wrath, despair would harden them against fearing him : it is grace which leads the way to a holy regard of God, and a fear of grieving him.

5. "*I wait for the Lord, my soul doth wait.*" Expecting him to come to me in love, I quietly wait for his appearing ; I wait *upon* him in service, and *for* him in faith. For God I wait and for him only : if he will manifest himself I shall have nothing more to wait for ; but until he shall appear for my help I must wait on,

hoping even in the depths. This waiting of mine is no mere formal act, my very soul is in it,—" my soul doth wait." I wait and I wait—mark the repetition! " My soul waits," and then again, " My soul waits " ; to make sure work of the waiting. It is well to deal with the Lord intensely. Such repetitions are the reverse of vain repetitions. If the Lord Jehovah makes us wait, let us do so with our whole hearts ; for blessed are all they that wait for him. He is worth waiting for. The waiting itself is beneficial to us : it tries faith, exercises patience, trains submission, and endears the blessing when it comes. The Lord's people have always been a waiting people : they waited for the First Advent, and now they wait for the Second. They waited for a sense of pardon, and now they wait for perfect sanctification. They waited in the depths, and they are not now wearied with waiting in a happier condition. They have cried and they do wait ; probably their past prayer sustains their present patience.

"And in his word do I hope." This is the source, strength, and sweetness of waiting. Those who do not hope cannot wait ; but if we hope for that we see not, then do we with patience wait for it. God's word is a true word, but at times it tarries ; if ours is true faith it will wait the Lord's time. A word from the Lord is as bread to the soul of the believer ; and, refreshed thereby, it holds out through the night of sorrow expecting the dawn of deliverance and delight. Waiting, we study the word, believe the word, hope in the word, and live on the word ; and all because it is *"his* word,"—the word of him who never speaks in vain. Jehovah's word is a firm ground for a waiting soul to rest upon.

6. *"My soul waiteth for the Lord more than they that watch for the morning."* Men who guard a city, and women who wait by the sick, long for daylight. Worshippers tarrying for the morning sacrifice, the kindling of the incense and the lighting of the lamps, mingle fervent prayers with their holy vigils, and pine for the hour when the lamb shall smoke upon the altar. David, however, waited more than these, waited longer, waited more longingly, waited more expectantly. He was not afraid of the great Adonai before whom none can stand in their own righteousness, for he had put on the righteousness of faith, and therefore longed for gracious audience with the Holy One. God was no more dreaded by him than light is dreaded by those engaged in a lawful calling. He pined and yearned after his God. *"I say, more than they that watch for the morning."* The figure was not strong enough, though one can hardly think of anything more vigorous : he felt that his own eagerness was unique and unrivalled. Oh to be thus hungry and thirsty after God ! Our version spoils the abruptness of the language ; the original runs thus—" My soul for the Lord more than those watching for the morning—watching for the morning." This is a fine poetical repeat. We long for the favour of the Lord more than weary sentinels long for the morning light which will release them from their tedious watch. Indeed this is true. He that has once rejoiced in communion with God is sore tried by the hidings of his face, and grows faint with strong desire for the Lord's appearing,

" When wilt thou come unto me, Lord ?
Until thou dost appear,
I count each moment for a day,
Each minute for a year."

7. *"Let Israel hope in the LORD."* Or, " Hope thou, Israel, in Jehovah." Jehovah is Israel's God ; therefore, let Israel hope in him. What one Israelite does he wishes all Israel to do. That man has a just right to exhort others who is himself setting the example. Israel of old waited upon Jehovah and wrestled all the night long, and at last he went his way succoured by the Hope of Israel : the like shall happen to all his seed. God has great things in store for his people ; they ought to have large expectations. *"For with the LORD there is mercy."* This is in his very nature, and by the light of nature it may be seen. But we have also the light of grace, and therefore we see still more of his mercy. With us there is sin ; but hope is ours, because " with the Lord there is mercy." Our comfort lies not in that which is with us, but in that which is with our God. Let us look out of self and its poverty to Jehovah and his riches of mercy. *"And with him is plenteous redemption."* He can and will redeem all his people out of their many and great troubles ; nay, their redemption is already wrought out and laid up with him, so that he can at any time give his waiting ones the full benefit thereof. The attribute of mercy, and the fact of redemption, are two most sufficient reasons for hoping in Jehovah ; and the fact that there is no mercy or deliverance elsewhere should effectually wean the

soul from all idolatry. Are not these deep things of God a grand comfort for those who are crying out of the depths? Is it not better to be in the deeps with David, hoping in God's mercy, than up on the mountain-tops, boasting in our own fancied righteousness?

8. *"And he shall redeem Israel from all his iniquities."* Our iniquities are our worst dangers: if saved from these, we are saved altogether; but there is no salvation from them except by redemption. What a blessing that this is here promised in terms which remove it out of the region of question: the Lord shall certainly redeem his believing people from all their sins. Well may the redemption be plenteous since it concerns all Israel and all iniquities! Truly, our Psalm has ascended to a great height in this verse: this is no cry out of the depths, but a chorale in the heights. Redemption is the top of covenant blessings. When it shall be experienced by all Israel, the latter-day glory shall have come, and the Lord's people shall say, "Now, Lord, what wait we for?" Is not this a clear prophecy of the coming of our Lord Jesus the first time? and may we not now regard it as the promise of his second and more glorious coming for the redemption of the body? For this our soul doth wait: yea, our heart and our flesh cry out for it with joyful expectation.

EXPLANATORY NOTES AND QUAINT SAYINGS.

Whole Psalm.—The Psalm is the eleventh in the order of the gradual Psalms, and treats of the eleventh step in the spiritual ascent, viz., penitential prayer.—*H. T. Armfield.*

Whole Psalm.—Of the Psalms which are called Penitential this is the chiefest. But, as it is the most excellent, so it has been perverted to the most disgraceful abuse in the Popedom: *e.g.*, that it should be mumbled in the lowest voice by slow bellies, in the sepulchral vigils for their liberation of souls from purgatory: as if David were here treating of the dead, when he has not even spoken a word about them; but says that he himself, a living man, was calling upon God; and exhorts the Israelites, living men also, to do the same. But leaving the buffooneries of the Papists we will rather consider the true meaning and use of the Psalm. It contains the most ardent prayer of a man grievously distressed by a sense of the Divine anger against sin: by earnest turning to God and penitence, he is seeking the forgiveness of his iniquities.—*Solomon Gesner.*

Whole Psalm.—The Holy Ghost layeth out here two opposite passions most plainly—*fear*, in respect of evil-deserving sins, and *hope*, in regard of undeserved mercies.—*Alexander Roberts, 1610.*

Whole Psalm.—The passionate earnestness of the Psalm is enhanced by the repetition eight times in it of the Divine Name.—*The Speaker's Commentary, 1873.*

Whole Psalm.—This Psalm, perhaps more than any other, is marked by its mountings: depth; prayer; conviction; light; hope; waiting; watching; longing; confidence; assurance; universal happiness and joy. . . . Just as the barometer marks the rising of the weather, so does this Psalm, sentence by sentence, record the progress of the soul. And you may test yourself by it, as by a rule or measure, and ask yourself at each line, "Have I reached to this? Have I reached to this?" and so take your spiritual gauge.—*James Vaughan, in "Steps to Heaven," 1878.*

Whole Psalm.—Whosoever he was that wrote this Psalm, he maketh mention and rehearsal of that prayer that he made to his God in the time of his great danger, and this he doth to the fifth verse: then finding in experience a comfortable answer, and how good a thing it was to pray to God, and to wait on him, he professeth, that, as before, he had awaited on him, so still in time coming he would await on him, and this he doeth to the seventh verse. In the third and last part, he turneth him to Israel, to the church, and exhorteth them to await on God, as he had done, promising them mercy and redemption from all their iniquities if they would await on him.—*Robert Rollock, 1555—1599.*

Whole Psalm.—Luther being once asked which were the best Psalms, replied, *Psalmi Paulini;* and when his companions at table pressed him to say which these were, he answered: Psalms xxxii., li., cxxx., and cxliii.—*Franz Delitzsch.*

Whole Psalm.—Luther, when he was buffeted by the devil at Coburg, and in great affliction, said to those about him, *Venite, in contemptum Diaboli, Psalmum, De Profundis, quatuor vocibus cantemus ;* " Come, let us sing that Psalm, ' Out of the depths,' etc., in derision of the devil."—*John Trapp.*

Whole Psalm.—The circumstances in which Dr. John Owen's Exposition of Psalm cxxx. originated are peculiarly interesting. Dr. Owen himself, in a statement made to Mr. Richard Davis, who ultimately became pastor of a church in Rowel, Northamptonshire, explains the occasion which led him to a very careful examination of the fourth verse in the Psalm. Mr. Davis, being under religious impressions, had sought a conference with Owen. In the course of the conversation, Dr. Owen put the question, " Young man, pray in what manner do you think to go to God?" " Through the Mediator, sir," answered Mr. Davis. " That is easily said," replied the doctor, " but I assure you it is another thing to go to God through the Mediator than many who make use of the expression are aware of. I myself preached Christ," he continued, " some years, when I had but very little, if any, experimental acquaintance with access to God through Christ ; until the Lord was pleased to visit me with sore affliction, whereby I was brought to the mouth of the grave, and under which my soul was oppressed with horror and darkness ; but God graciously relieved my spirit by a powerful application of Psalm cxxx. 4, '*But there is forgiveness with thee, that thou mayest be feared,*' from whence I received special instruction, peace and comfort, in drawing near to God through the Mediator, and preached thereupon immediately after my recovery."—*William H. Goold, editor of Owen's Collected Works,* 1851.

Verse 1.—"*Out of the depths have I cried unto thee, O Lord.*" Is there not a depth of sin, and a depth of misery by reason of sin, and a depth of sorrow by reason of misery ? In all which, both David was, and I, God help me, am deeply plunged ; and are not these depths enough out of which to cry ? And yet, perhaps, none of these depths is that which David means ; but there are depths of danger—a danger of body and a danger of soul, and out of these it seems that David cried ; for the danger of his body was so deep that it had brought him to death's door, and the danger of his soul so deep that it had almost brought him to the gates of despair ; and had he not just cause then to say, "*Out of the depths have I cried to thee, O God* " ? And yet there is a depth besides these that must help to lift us out of these—a depth of devotion, without which depth our crying out of other depths will never be heard. For devotion is a fire that puts a heat into our crying, and carries it up into *cœlum empyræum*—the heaven of fire, where God himself is. And now join all these depths together—the depth of sin, of misery, of sorrow, the depth of danger, and the depth of devotion,—and then tell me if David had not, if I have not, as just cause as ever Jonah had to say, " Out of the depths have I cried to thee, O God." Indeed, to cry out of the depths hath many considerable circumstances to move God to hear : it acknowledgeth his infinite power when no distance can hinder his assistance ; it presents our own faith when no extremity can weaken our hope ; it magnifies God's goodness when he, the Most High, regards the most low ; it expresseth our own earnestness, seeing crying out of depths must needs be a deep cry ; and if each of these singly, and by itself, be motive sufficient to move God to hear, how strong must the motive needs be when they are all united ? and united they are all in crying out of the depths ; and therefore now that I cry to thee out of the depths, be moved, O God, in thy great mercy to "*hear my voice.*"

It is cause enough for God not to hear some because they do not cry—cause enough not to hear some that cry because not out of the depths ; but when crying and out of the depths are joined together, it was never known that ever God refused to hear ; and therefore now that I cry to thee out of the depths, be pleased, O God, in thy great mercy to hear my voice.—*Sir Richard Baker, in "Meditations and Dis-quisitions upon the Three last Psalmes of David,*" 1639.

Verse 1.—"*Out of the depths.*" By the deep places (as all the ancients consent) is meant the deep places of afflictions, and the deep places of the heart troubled for sin. Afflictions are compared to deep waters. Ps. xviii. 16 : " He drew me out of many waters." " Save me, O God, for the waters are come in unto my soul." And surely God's children are often cast into very desperate cases, and plunged into deep miseries, to the end that they may send out of a contrite and feeling heart such prayers as may mount aloft and pierce the heavens. When we are in prosperity our prayers come from our lips ; and therefore the Lord is forced to cast us down, that our prayers may come from our hearts, and that our senses may be wakened from the security in which they are lying. Albeit the throne of God be most high, yet he delighteth to hear the petition of hearts that are most low, that are most cast down by the sight of sin. There is no affliction, neither any place so low (yea, if as low as the belly of the whale wherein Jonah lay) which can separate us from the love of the Lord, or stay our prayers from coming before him. Those that are farthest cast down, are not farthest from God, but are nearest unto him. God is near to a contrite heart, and it is the proper seat where his Spirit dwelleth : Isai. lxvi. 2. And thus God dealeth with us, as men do with such houses that they are minded to build sumptuously and on high ; for then they dig deep grounds for the foundation. Thus God purposing to make a fair show of Daniel, and the three children in Babel ; of Joseph in Egypt ; of David in Israel ; he first threw them into the deep waters of afflictions. Daniel is cast into the den of lions ; the three children are thrown into the fiery furnace ; Joseph is imprisoned ; David exiled. Yet all those he exalted and made glorious temples to himself. Mark hereby the dulness of our nature, that is such, that God is forced to use sharp remedies to awaken us. Jonah lay sleeping in the ship, when the tempest of God's wrath was pursuing him : God therefore threw him into the belly of the whale, and the bottom of the deep, that from those deep places he might cry to him.

When, therefore, we are troubled by heavy sickness, or poverty, or oppressed by the tyranny of men, let us make profit and use thereof, considering that God hath cast his best children into such dangers for their profit ; and that it is better to be in deep dangers praying, than on high mountains of vanity playing.—*Archibald Symson, in "A Sacred Septenarie."* 1638.

Verse 1.—*"Out of the depths."* " Depths ! " oh ! into what " *depths* " men can sink ! How far from happiness, glory, and goodness men can fall.

There is the depth of *poverty*. A man can become utterly stripped of all earthly possessions and worldly friends ! Sometimes we come upon a man, still living, but in such abject circumstances, that it strikes us as a marvel that a human being can sink lower than the beasts of the field.

Then there is the depth of *sorrow*. Billow after billow breaks over the man, friend after friend departs, lover and friend are put into darkness. All the fountains of his nature are broken up. He is like a water-logged ship, from the top waves plunging down as if into the bottom of the sea. So often in such depths, sometimes like Jonah in the whale's belly, the monster carrying him down, down, down, into darkness.

There are depths after depths of *mental darkness*, when the soul becomes more and more sorrowful, down to that very depth which is just this side of *despair*. Earth hollow, heaven empty, the air heavy, every form a deformity, all sounds discord, the past a gloom, the present a puzzle, the future a horror. One more step down, and the man will stand in the chamber of despair, the floor of which is blisteringly hot, while the air is biting cold as the polar atmosphere. To what depths the spirit of a man may fall !

But the most horrible depth into which a man's soul can descend is *sin*. Sometimes we begin on gradual slopes, and slide so swiftly that we soon reach great depths ; depths in which there are horrors that are neither in poverty, nor sorrow, nor mental depression. It is sin, it is an outrage against God and ourselves. We feel that there is no bottom. Each opening depth reveals a greater deep. This is really the bottomless pit, with everlasting accumulations of speed, and perpetual lacerations as we descend. Oh, depths below depths ! Oh, falls from light to gloom, from gloom to darkness ! Oh, the hell of sin !

What can we do ? We can simply *cry*, CRY, CRY ! But, let us cry to God. Useless, injurious are other cries. They are mere expressions of impotency, or protests against imaginary fate. But the cry of the spirit to the Most High is a manful cry. Out of the depths of all poverty, all sorrow, all mental depression, all sin, *cry unto God !—From "The Study and the Pulpit,"* 1877.

Verse 1.—*"Out of the depths have I cried."*

> Up from the deeps, O God, I cry to thee !
> Hear my soul's prayer, hear thou her litany,
> O thou who sayest, " Come, wanderer, home to me."

> Up from the deeps of sorrow, wherein lie
> Dark secrets veil'd from earth's unpitying eye,
> My prayers, like star-crown'd angels, Godward fly.

From the calm bosom when in quiet hour
God's Holy Spirit reigns with largest power,
Then shall each thought in prayer's white blossom flower.

Not from life's shallows, where the waters sleep,
A dull, low marsh where stagnant vapours creep,
But ocean-voiced, deep calling unto deep.

As he of old, King David, call'd to thee,
As cries the heart of poor humanity,
" Clamavi, Domine, exaudi me ! "

C. S. Fenner.

Verse 1.—But when he crieth from the deep, he riseth from the deep, and his very cry suffereth him not to be long at the bottom.—*Augustine.*

Verse 1.—It has been well said that the verse puts before us six conditions of true prayer : it is lowly, "*out of the deep*"; fervent, "*have I called*"; direct to God himself, "*unto thee*"; reverent, "*O Lord*"; awed, "*Lord*," a solemn title, is again used ; one's very own, " hear *my voice.*"—*Neale and Littledale.*

Verse 1.—"*Have I cried.*" There are many kinds and degrees of prayer in the world ; from the coldest form to the intensest agony. Every one prays ; but very few " cry." But of those who do " cry to God," the majority would say,— "*I owe it to the depths.* I learnt it there. I often prayed before ; but never—till I was carried down very deep— did I *cry.*" " Out of the depths have I cried unto thee, O Lord." It is well worth while to go down into any " depth " to be taught to " cry."

It is not too much to say that we do not know what prayer may be till we have "*cried.*" And we seldom rise till we have gone very deep. " I die ! I perish ! I am lost ! Help, Lord ! Help me ! Save me now ! Do it *now*, Lord, or I am lost. O Lord, hear ! O Lord, forgive ! O Lord, hearken and do ; defer not, for thine own sake, O my God ! "

In mid-day, if you are taken from the bright and sunny scenes of light, and go down into the bottom of a pit, you may see the stars, which were invisible to you in the upper air. And how many could say that things they knew not in life's noon, they have found in life's midnight, and that they owe their glimpses of glory, and their best avenues of thought, and the importunacy of prayer, and the victories of faith, to seasons when they walked in very dark places. "*Out of the depths* have I cried unto thee, O Lord."—*James Vaughan.*

Verse 1.—"*Have I cried unto thee, Jehovah.*" God gave out that name Jehovah to his people to confirm their faith in the stability of his promises : Exod. iii. He who is Being himself will assuredly give being and subsistence to his promises. Being to deal with God about the promises of grace, he makes his application to him under this name : "*I call upon thee, Jehovah.*"—*John Owen, in "A practical Exposition upon Psalm cxxx."*

Verse 2.—"*Lord, hear my voice,*" etc. Every prayer should have its reverent invocation, as every temple its porch. The two greatest prayers in the Old Testament—Solomon's prayer and Daniel's prayer—both have it very emphatically. And it is a very distinct part of our own perfect model : " Our Father, which art in heaven, hallowed be thy name." On our part it is deferential, and puts the mind into its proper form ; while it places the great God, whom it addresses, where he ought to be,—in the awe of his glory ; in the magnitude of his power ; in the infinitude of his wisdom and love.

Never think little of that part of your prayer : never omit, never hurry over the opening address. Do not go into his presence without a pause, or some devout ascription. "*Lord, hear my voice : let thine ears be attentive to the voice of my supplications.*" True, he is always listening and waiting for his children's " cry," —far more prepared to answer, than we are to ask. And the very fact that we are praying is a proof of his attention,—for who but he put it into our hearts to make that prayer ? Nevertheless, it becomes us, and honours him, to establish, at the outset, the right relationship between a creature and his Creator ; between a child and his father : " Lord, hear my voice : let thine ears be attentive to the voice of my supplication."—*James Vaughan.*

Verse 2.—"*Lord.*" Hebrew, *Adonai.* As *Jehovah* marks his unchangeable faithfulness to his promises of delivering his people, so *Adonai* his *Lordship* over all hindrances in the way of his delivering them.—*Andrew Robert Fausset, in "A Commentary, Critical, Experimental and Practical," 1866.*

Verse 2.—*"Lord, hear my voice,"* etc. The expressions are metaphorical, and borrowed from the carriage of a parent to a child, and upon the matter his suit is this,—Lord, notice me when I pray, as a parent will notice his distressed child's cry when he is like to ruin. *"Let thine ears be attentive to the voice of my supplications;"* that goes a little further; that as a parent knowing a child to be in hazard, he will listen and hearken attentively if he can here him cry, and notice and ponder that cry, and what he cries for ; so he pleaded with God, that he would be waiting on and attentive, to see and hear if a cry should come from him, and that he would affectionately ponder and notice it when he hears it.—*George Hutcheson,—1678.*

Verse 3.—*"If thou, Lord, shouldest mark iniquities,"* etc. But doth not the Lord mark iniquity ? Doth not he take notice of every sin acted by any of the children of men, especially by his own children ? Why, then, doth the Psalmist put it upon an *if?* *"If thou, Lord, shouldest mark iniquity."* 'Tis true, the Lord marks all iniquity to know it, but he doth not mark any iniquity in his children to condemn them for it : so the meaning of the Psalm is, that if the Lord should mark sin with a strict and severe eye, as a judge, to charge it upon the person sinning, no man could bear it.

The word rendered *to mark* notes, first, to watch, or to observe with strictest diligence, and is therefore in the noun rendered *a watch-tower,* upon which a man is placed to take observation of all things that are done, and of all persons that pass by, or approach and come near. A watchman placed upon a high tower is bound industriously and critically to observe all passengers and passages, all that his eye can reach. So saith the text, —If thou shouldst mark as a watchman, and eye with rigour everything that passeth from us, *"who will stand?"* that is, make good his cause in the day of his judgment and trial before thee ?

Secondly, the word signifieth to keep in mind, to lay up, to have, as it were, a store and stock, a memorial or record, of such and such things by us. In that sense it is said (Gen. xxxvii. 11), "Joseph's brethen envied him ; but his father observed the saying " : he marked what Joseph spake about his dreams, he laid it up, and did not let it pass away as a dream, or as a vision of the night. Thus, by *"If the Lord should mark iniquity."* we understand—if he should treasure up our sins in his memory, and keep them by him, *" who were able to stand when accounted with ? "* The Lord, in a way of grace, seeth as if he saw not, and winks at us oftentimes when we do amiss.—*Joseph Caryl.*

Verse 3.—Let thine ears be attentive to the voice of my supplication, but let not thine eyes be intentive to the stains of my sin ; for *"If thou, Lord, shouldest mark iniquities, O Lord, who shall stand ?"* or who shall be able to abide it ? Did not the angels fall when thou markedst their follies ? Can flesh, which is but dust, be clean before thee, when the stars, which are of a far purer substance, are not ? Can anything be clean in thy sight which is not as clean as thy sight ? and can any cleanness be equal to thine ? Alas ! O Lord, we are neither angels nor stars, and how then can we stand when those fell ? how can we be clean when these be impure ? If thou shouldest mark what is done amiss, there would be marking-work enough for thee as long as the world lasts ; for what action of man is free from stain of sin, or from defect of righteousness ? Therefore, mark not anything in me, O God, that I have done, but mark that only in me which thou hast done thyself. Mark in me thine own image ; and then thou mayest look upon me, and yet say still, as once thou saidst, *Et erant omnia valde bona* [" And all things were very good "].—*Sir Richard Baker.*

Verse 3 (*whole verse*).—We are introduced at once into all the solemnities of a criminal court. The judge is seated on the bench : the culprit is standing at the bar, charged with a capital offence : the witnesses are giving their evidence against him. The judge is listening attentively to everything which is said ; and in order to assist his memory, he takes notes of the more important parts. If the Lord were to try us after this fashion, what would be the result ? Suppose him seated on his throne of inflexible righteousness, taking notes, with a pen in his hand, of the transgressions which are proven against us. Nothing is omitted. Every sin is marked down with its peculiar aggravations. There is no possibility of escape from the deserved condemnation. The evidence against us is clear, and copious, and overwhelming. A thousandth part of it is sufficient to determine our doom.

The judge has no alternative but to pronounce the awful sentence. We must die a felon's death. *"If thou, LORD, shouldest mark iniquities, O Lord, who shall stand ?"* —N. M'Michael.

Verse 3.—*"If thou, LORD, shouldest mark."* If thou shouldst inquire and scrutinize, and then shouldst retain and impute : (for the Hebrew word imports both :) if thou shouldst inquire, thou wouldst find something of iniquity in the most righteous of mankind : and when thou hast found it, if thou shouldst retain it, and call him to an account for it, he could by no means free himself of the charge, or expiate the crime. Inquiring, thou wouldst easily find iniquity ; but the sinner by the most diligent inquiry will not be able to discover a ransom, and therefore will be unable to stand, will have no place on which to rest his foot, but will fall by the irresistible judgments of thy law, and the sentence of thy justice.—*Robert Leighton.*

Verse 3.—*"If thou, LORD."* He here fixes on another name of God, which is Jah : a name, though from the same root as the former, yet seldom used but to intimate and express the terrible majesty of God : "He rideth on the heavens, and is extolled by his name JAH :" Ps. lxviii. 4. He is to deal now with God about the guilt of sin : and God is represented to the soul as great and terrible, that he may know what to expect and look for, if the matter must be tried out according to the demerit of sin,—*John Owen.*

Verse 3.—*"If thou, LORD . . . O Lord."* Mark here that in this third verse he two times nameth God by *the Lord* (as he doth also in the ninth verse), showing to us hereby his earnest desire to take hold of God with both his hands. He nameth not only *Adonai,* but also *Jah* (which two signify his nature and power) ; all the qualities of God must be conjoined and concur together for us : although he be *Adonai,* yet if he be not also *Jah* we are undone.—*Archibald Symson.*

Verse 3.—*"LORD . . . Lord."* If God should show himself as JAH, no creature would be able to stand before him, who is *Adonai,* and can therefore carry out his judicial will or purpose.—*Franz Delitzsch.*

Verse 3.—*"Iniquities."* The literal meaning of the word "iniquity" is "a thing which is not equal," or "not fair." Whatever breaks a command of God is "not equal." It does not match with what man is, nor with what God is. It does not keep the high level of the law. It is altogether out of proportion to all that God has done. It destroys the harmony of creation. It does not rise even to the height of conscience. Still more, it mars and makes a flaw in the divine government. Therefore sin is an unequal thing, fitting nothing, disarranging everything. And it is *not fair.* It is not fair to that God upon whose empire it is a tresspass. It is not fair to your fellow-creatures, to whom it may be a very great injury. It is not fair to yourself, for your happiness lies in obedience. Therefore we call sin "iniquity" Or, as the Prayer-Book Version expresses the same idea, "a thing amiss," missing its proper mark. "If thou shouldest be extreme to mark what is *done amiss."*—*James Vaughan.*

Verse 3.—*"O Lord, who shall stand ?"* As soon as God manifests signs of anger, even those who appear to be the most holy adopt this language. If God should determine to deal with them according to justice, and call them to his tribunal, not one would be able to stand ; but would be compelled to fly for refuge to the mercy of God. See the confessions of Moses, Job, David, Nehemiah, Isaiah, Daniel, Paul, and others of the apostles. Hear Christ teaching his disciples to cry to the Father who is in heaven, *"Forgive us our trespasses !"* If before God the Patriarchs, Prophets, and Apostles, although possessing unusual holiness, nevertheless fell down, and as suppliants prayed for forgiveness, what shall be done with those who add sin to sin ?—*D. H. Mollerus.*

Verses 3, 4.—These two verses contain the sum of all the Scriptures. In the third is the form of repentance, and in the fourth the mercies of the Lord. These are the two mountains, Gerizim and Ebal, mentioned in Deut. xxvii. 12, 13. These are the pillars in Solomon's Temple (1 Kings vii. 21), called Jachin and Boaz. We must, with Paul, persuade ourselves that we are come from Mount Sinai to Mount Zion, where mercy is, although some sour grapes must be eaten by the way. Jeremy tasted in his vision first a bitter fig out of one basket, then a sweet fig out of the other. In the days of Moses the waters were first bitter, then sweetened by the sweet wood. And Elisha cast in salt into the pottage of the sons of the prophets, then it became wholesome.—*Archibald Symson.*

Verses 3, 4.—As I was thus in musing and in my studies, considering how to love the Lord, and to express my love to him, that saying came in upon me : *"If thou, LORD, shouldest mark iniquities, O Lord, who shall stand ? But there is forgiveness with thee, that thou mayest be feared."* These were good words to me, especially the latter part thereof ; to wit, that there is forgiveness with thee that thou mayest be feared ; that is, as then I understood it, that he might be loved and had in reverence ; for it was thus made out to me, that the great God did set so high an esteem upon the love of his poor creatures, that rather than he would go without their love he would pardon their transgressions.—*John Bunyan.*

Verse 4.—*"But there is forgiveness with thee, that thou mayest be feared."* One would think that punishment should procure fear, and forgiveness love ; but *nemo majus diligit, quam qui maxime veretur offendere*—no man more truly loves God than he that is most fearful to offend him. " Thy mercy reacheth to the heavens, and thy faithfulness to the clouds "—that is, above all sublimities. God is glorious in all his works, but most glorious in his works of mercy ; and this may be one reason why St. Paul calls the gospel of Christ a " glorious gospel " : 1 Tim. i. 11. Solomon tells us, " It is the glory of a man to pass by an offence." Herein is God most glorious, in that he passeth by all the offences of his children. Lord, who can know thee and not love thee, know thee and not fear thee ? We fear thee for thy justice, and love thee for thy mercy ; yea, fear thee for thy mercy, and love thee for thy justice ; for thou art infinitely good in both.—*Thomas Adams.*

Verse 4.—*"But there is forgiveness with thee, that thou mayest be feared."* But is this not a mistaking in David to say, There is mercy with God, that he may be feared ; all as one to say, There is severity with him, that he may be loved ? for if we cannot love one for being severe, how should we fear him for being merciful ? Should it not, therefore, have been rather said, There is justice with thee, that thou mayest be feared ? seeing it is justice that strikes a terror and keeps in awe ; mercy breeds a boldness, and boldness cannot stand with fear, and therefore not fear with mercy. But is there not, I may say, an active fear, not to offend God, as well as a passive fear for having offended him ? and with God's mercy may well stand the active fear, though not so well, perhaps, the passive fear which is incident properly to his justice.

There is a common error in the world, to think we may be the bolder to sin because God is merciful ; but, O my soul, take heed of this error, for God's mercy is to no such purpose ; it is not to make us bold, but to make us fear : the greater his mercy is, the greater ought our fear to be, for there is mercy with him that he may be feared. Unless we fear, he may choose whether he will be merciful or no ; or rather, we may be sure he will not be merciful, seeing he hath mercy for none but for them that fear him ; and there is great reason for this, for to whom should mercy show itself but to them that need it ? and if we think we need it we will certainly fear. Oh, therefore, most gracious God, make me to fear thee ; for as thou wilt not be merciful to me unless I fear thee, so I cannot fear thee unless thou first be merciful unto me.—*Sir Richard Baker.*

Verse 4.—*"But there is forgiveness with thee, that thou mayest be feared."* Even Saul himself will lift up his voice and weep when he seeth a clear testimony of the love and undeserved kindness of David. Hast thou never beheld a condemned prisoner dissolved in tears upon the unexpected and unmerited receipt of a pardon, who all the time before was as hard as a flint ? The hammer of the law may break the icy heart of man with terrors and horrors, and yet it may remain ice still, unchanged ; but when the fire of love kindly thaweth its ice, it is changed and dissolved into water—it is no longer ice, but of another nature.—*George Swinnock.*

Verse 4.—*"But there is forgiveness with thee, that thou mayest be feared."* The Evangelical doctrine of the gratuitous forgiveness of sins does not of itself beget carelessness, as the Papists falsely allege ; but rather a true and genuine fear of God ; like as the Psalmist here shows that this is the final cause and effect of the doctrine.—*Solomon Gesner.*

Verse 4.—*"But there is forgiveness with thee,"* etc. His judgments and his wrath may make us astonished and stupefied ; but, if there be no more, they will never make us to come to God. Then if this be not sufficient, what more is requisite ? Even a sight of the Lord's mercy, for that is most forcible to allure, as the prophet saith here, and as the church of God sayeth (Cant. i. 3), " Because of the savour of thy good ointments, therefore the virgins love thee." This only is forcible to allure the sinner : for all the judgments of God, and curses of the law, will never allure

him. What was the chief thing that moved the prodigal son to return home to
his father? Was it chiefly the distress, the disgrace and poverty wherewith he was
burdened, or the famine that almost caused him to starve? No, but the chief
thing was this, he remembered that he had a loving father. That maketh him
to resolve with an humble confession to go home. Luke xv. Even so it is with
the sinner; it is not terrors and threatenings that chiefly will move him to come
to God, but the consideration of his manifold and great mercies.—*Robert Rollock.*

Verse 4.—"*But.*" How significant is that word "*but!*" As if you heard justice
clamouring, "Let the sinner die," and the fiends in hell howling, "Cast, him
down into the fires," and conscience shrieking, "Let him perish," and nature
itself groaning beneath his weight, the earth weary with carrying him, and the
sun tired with shining upon the traitor, the very air sick with finding breath for
one who only spends it in disobedience to God. The man is about to be destroyed,
to be swallowed up quick, when suddenly there comes this thrice-blessed "*but,*"
which stops the reckless course of ruin, puts forth its strong arm bearing a golden
shield between the sinner and destruction, and pronounces these words, "*But there
is forgiveness with God, that he may be feared.*"—*C. H. S.*

Verse 4.—"*There is a propitiation with thee,*" so some read it: Jesus Christ is
the great propitiation, the ransom which God has found; he is ever with him, as
advocate for us, and through him we hope to obtain forgiveness.—*Matthew Henry.*

Verse 4.—"*Forgiveness,*" Hebrew, *selichah,* a word used only here and by
Daniel once (ix. 9), and by Nehemiah (ix. 17).—*Christopher Wordsworth.*

Verse 4.—"*That thou mayest be feared.*" This forgiveness, this smile of God,
binds the soul to God with a beautiful fear. Fear to lose one glance of love. Fear
to lose one word of kindness. Fear to be carried away from the heaven of his
presence by an insidious current of wordliness. Fear of slumber. Fear of error.
Fear of not enough pleasing him. Our duty, then, is to drink deep of God's forgiving love. To be filled with it is to be filled with purity, fervency, and faith.
Our sins have to hide their diminished heads, and slink away through crevices,
when forgiveness—when Christ—enters the soul.—*George Bowen, in "Daily Meditations,"* 1873.

Verses 4, 5, 7, 8.—David puts his soul out of all fear of God's taking this course
[reckoning strictly] with poor penitent souls, by laying down this comfortable
conclusion, as an indubitable truth: "*But there is forgiveness with thee, that thou
mayest be feared.*" That is, there is forgiveness in thy nature, thou carriest a
pardoning heart in thy bosom; yea, there is forgiveness in thy promise; thy
merciful heart doth not only incline thee to thoughts of forgiving; but thy faithful
promise binds thee to draw forth the same unto all that humbly and seasonably
lay claim thereunto. Now, this foundation laid, see what superstructure this holy
man raiseth (verse 5): "*I wait for the LORD, my soul doth wait, and in his word do
I hope.*" As if he had said, Lord, I take thee at thy word, and am resolved by
thy grace to wait at the door of thy promise, never to stir thence till I have my
promised dole (forgiveness of my sins) sent out unto me. And this is so sweet
a morsel, that he is loth to eat it alone, and therefore he sends down the dish, even
to the lower end of the table, that every godly person may taste with him of it
(verses 7, 8): "*Let Israel hope in the LORD: for with the LORD there is mercy, and
with him is plenteous redemption. And he shall redeem Israel from all his iniquities.*"
As if he had said, That which is a ground of hope to me, notwithstanding the clamour
of my sins, affords as solid and firm a bottom to any true Israelites or sincere soul
in the world, did he but rightly understand himself, and the mind of God in his
promise. Yea, I have as strong a faith for such as [for] my own soul, and I durst
pawn the eternity of my happiness upon this principle,—that God should redeem
every sincere Israelite from all his iniquities.—*William Gurnall.*

Verse 5.—"*I wait for the LORD,*" etc. We pronounce this a most blessed posture
of the believer. It runs counter to everything that is natural, and, therefore, it
is all the more a supernatural grace of the gracious soul. In the first place it is
the posture of faith. Here is the gracious soul hanging in faith upon God in Christ
Jesus; upon the veracity of God to fulfil his promise, upon the power of God to
help him in difficulty, upon the wisdom of God to counsel him in perplexity, upon
the omniscience of God to guide him with his eye, and upon the omnipresence of
God to cheer him with his presence, at all times and in all places, his sun and shield.
Oh, have faith in God.

It is also a *prayerful posture.* The soul waiting *for* God, is the soul waiting *upon* God. The Lord often shuts us up to this waiting for his interposition on our behalf, that he may keep us waiting and watching at the foot of his cross, in earnest, believing, importunate prayer. Oh, it is the waiting *for* the Lord that keeps the soul waiting *upon* the Lord !

It is also *the posture of a patient waiting* for the Lord. There is not a more God-honouring grace of the Christian character than *patience*—a patient waiting on and for the Lord. It is that Christian grace, the fruit of the Spirit which will enable you to bear with dignity, calmness, and submission the afflictive dealings of your Heavenly Father, the rebuke of the world, and the wounding of the saints.

It is *the posture of rest.* A soul-waiting for the Lord is a soul-resting in the Lord. Waiting and resting ! Wearied with traversing in vain the wide circle of human expedients ; coming to the end of all your own wisdom, strength, and resources ; your uneasy, jaded spirit is brought into this resting posture of waiting on, and waiting for, the Lord ; and thus folds its drooping wings upon the very bosom of God. Oh, how real and instant is the rest found in Jesus ! Reposing in him, however profound the depth of the soul, however dark the clouds that drape it, or surging the waters that overwhelm it, all is sunshine and serenity within.—*Condensed from "Soul-Depths and soul-heights," by Octavius Winslow, 1874.*

Verse 5.—"*I wait for the* Lord." Waiting is a great part of life's discipline, and therefore God often exercises the grace of waiting. *Waiting* has four purposes. It practises the patience of faith. It gives time for preparation for the coming gift. It makes the blessing the sweeter when it arrives. And it shows the sovereignty of God,—to give just *when* and just *as* he pleases. It may be difficult to define exactly what the Psalmist had in his mind when he said, " I wait *for the Lord,* my soul doth wait, and in his word do I hope. My soul waiteth *for the Lord* more than they that watch for the morning." It may have been the Messiah, whose coming was a thing close at hand to the mind of the ancient Jews, just as the Second Advent is to us.

It may have been some special interposition of divine Providence. But more probably, looking at the place which it occupies, and at the whole tenor of the Psalm, and its line of thought, " The Lord " he waited for so intently was that full sense of safety, peace, and love which God's felt presence gives, and which is, indeed, nothing else but the coming of the Lord most sensibly and palpably into an anxious and longing heart.

The picture of *the waiting man* is a striking one. It is as one on the ridge of a journey, looking onward on his way, standing on tiptoe, and therefore needing something to lean on, and to support him. "*I wait for the Lord,*"—spiritually, with my deepest thoughts—in the very centre of my being—"*I wait for the Lord, my soul doth wait.*" And I rest, I stay myself on what thou, O Lord, hast said, " My soul doth wait, and *in his word* do I hope."

In all your *waitings* remember two things : Let it not be so much the event which you wait for, as the Lord *of* the event ; the Lord *in* the event. And take care that you have a promise underneath you.—" In his word do I hope,"—else " waiting " will be too much for you, and after all it may be in vain.—*James Vaughan.*

Verse 5.—"*I wait . . . I hope.*" Waiting and hoping ever attend the same thing. No man will wait at all for that which he hath no hope of, and he who hath hope will wait always. He gives not over waiting, till he gives over hoping. The object of hope is some future good, but the act of hoping is a present good, and that is present pay to bear our charges in waiting. The word implies both a patient waiting and a hopeful trusting. So Christ expounds it (Matt. xii. 21), rendering that of the prophet (Isa. xlii. 4), " The isles shall wait for his law," thus, " In his name shall the Gentiles trust."—*Joseph Caryl.*

Verses 5, 6.—In these two verses he doth four times make mention of his hope, and attendance upon God and his word, to let us see how sure a hold we should take on God, and with how many temptations our faith is assaulted, when we can see no reason thereof. Nothing will bear us up but hope. *Spero meliora.* What encourageth husbandmen and mariners against the surges and waves of the sea, and evil weather, but hope of better times ? What comforteth a sick man in time of sickness, but hope of health ? or a poor man in his distress, but hope of riches ? or a prisoner, but hope of liberty ? or a banished man, but hope to come home ? All these hopes may fail, as oftentimes wanting a warrant. Albeit a physician may encourage a sick man by his fair words, yet he cannot give him an assurance of his recovery, for his health dependeth on God : friends and courtiers may promise poor men relief, but all men are liars ; only God is faithful who hath promised. Therefore let us fix our faith on God, and our hope in God ; for he will stand by his promise. No man hath hoped in him in vain, neither was ever any disappointed of his hope.— *Archibald Symson.*

Verses 5, 7.—Faith doth ultimately centre in the Deity. God himself in his glorious nature, is the ultimate object whereunto our faith is resolved. The promise, simply considered, is not the object of trust, but God in the promise ; and from the consideration of that we ascend to the Deity, and cast our anchor there. " Hope in the word " is the first act, but succeeded by hoping in the Lord : *"In his word do I hope"* : that is not all ; but, *"Let Israel hope in the Lord."* That is the ultimate object of faith, wherein the essence of our happiness consists, and that is God. God himself is the true and full portion of the soul.—*Stephen Charnock,* 1628—1680.

Verse 6.—*"My soul waiteth for the* LORD." And now, my soul, what do I live for but only to wait upon God, and to wait for God ? To wait upon him, to do him service, to wait for him, to be enabled to do him better service ; to wait upon him, as being Lord of all ; and to wait for him, as being the rewarder of all ; to wait upon him whose service is better than any other command, and to wait for him whose expectation is better than any other possession. Let, others, therefore, wait upon the world, wait for the world ; I, O God, will wait upon thee, for thee, seeing I find more true contentment in this waiting than all the world can give me in enjoying ; for how can I doubt of receiving reward by my waiting for thee when my waiting for thee is itself the reward of my waiting upon thee ? And therefore my soul waiteth ; for if my soul did not wait, what were my waiting worth ? no more than I were worth myself, if I had not a soul ; but my soul puts a life into my waiting, and makes it become a living sacrifice. Alas, my frail body is very unfit to make a waiter : it rather needs to be waited upon itself : it must have so much resting, so often leave to be excused from waiting, that if God should have no other waiters than bodies, he would be left oftentimes to wait upon himself ; but my soul is *Divinæ particula auræ* [a portion of the Divine breath], endued with all qualities fit for a waiter : and hath it not received its abilities, O God, from thee ? And therefore my soul waiteth, and is so intentive in the service that it waits *"more than they that watch for the morning."*—*Sir Richard Baker.*

Verse 6.—Hammond thus renders the verse :—" My soul hasteneth to the Lord from the guards in the morning, the guards in the morning."

Verse 6.—*"More than they that watch for the morning."* Look, as the weary sentinel that is wet and stiff with cold and the dews of the night, or as the porters that watched in the Temple, the Levites, were waiting for the daylight, so " more than they that watch for the morning " was he waiting for some glimpse of God's favour. Though he do not presently ease us of our smart or gratify our desires, yet we are to wait upon God. In time we shall have a good answer. God's delays are not denials. Day will come at length, though the weary sentinel or watchman counts it long first ; so God will come at length ; he will not be at our beck. We have deserved nothing, but must wait for him in the diligent use of means ; as Benhadad's servants watched for the word " brother," or anything of kindness to drop from the king of Israel.—*Thomas Manton.*

Verse 6.—*"More than they that watch for the morning."* How many in the hallowed precincts of the Temple turned with anxious eye to the east, for the first red streak over Moab's mountains that gave intimation of approaching day ; yet it was not for deliverance they waited, but for the accustomed hour when the morning sacrifice could be offered, and the soul be relieved of its gratitude in the hymn of thanksgiving, and of the burden of its sorrows and sins by prayer, and could draw that strength from renewed intercourse with heaven, that would enable it in this world to breathe the spirit and engage in the beneficent and holy deeds of a better.—*Robert Nisbet.*

Verse 6.—*"I say, more than they that watch for the morning,"* for must there not be a proportion between the cause and effect ? If my cause of watching be more than theirs, should not my watching be more than theirs ? They that watch for the morning have good cause, no doubt, to watch for it, that it may bring them the light of day ; but have not I more cause to watch, who wait for the light that lighteth every one that comes into the world ? They that watch for the morning wait but for the rising of the sun to free them from darkness, that hinders their sight ; but I wait for the rising of the Sun of righteousness to dispel the horrors of darkness that affright my soul. They watch for the morning that they may have light to walk by ; but I wait for the Dayspring from on High to give light to them that sit in darkness and in the shadow of death, and to guide our feet into the way of peace. But though there may be question made of the intentiveness of our watching, yet of the extensiveness there can be none, for they that watch for the morning watch at most but a piece of the night ; but I have watched whole days and whole nights, and may I not then justly say, I wait *more* than they that watch for the morning ?— *Sir Richard Baker.*

Verse 6.—Holy men like Simeon, and devout priests like Zacharias, there were, amidst this seething people, who, brooding, longing, waiting, chanted to themselves day by day the words of the Psalmist, *"My soul waiteth for the Lord more than they that watch for the morning."* As lovers that watch for the appointed coming, and start at the quivering of a leaf, the flight of a bird, or the humming of a bee, and grow weary of the tense strain, so did the Jews watch for their Deliverer. It is one of the most piteous sights of history, especially when we reflect that he came,—and they knew him not.—*Henry Ward Beecher, in his "Life of Jesus the Christ."*

Verse 6.—*"Watch."* We do injustice to that good and happy word, *"watch,"* when we take it as watching against ; against a danger ; against a coming evil. It will bear that interpretation ; but it is a far higher, and better, and more filial thing to watch *for* a coming good than to watch *against* an approaching evil.

So, *"watching for,"* we send up our arrows of prayer, and then look trustingly to see where they are coming down again. So, *"watching for,"* we listen, in silence, for the familiar voice we love. So, *"watching for,"* we expect the Bridegroom !

Take care, that as one always standing on the eve,—not of danger, but of happiness,—your *"watch"* be the *"watch"* of love, and confidence, and cheerful hope.— *James Vaughan.*

Verse 6.—In the year 1830, on the night preceding the 1st of August, the day the slaves in our West Indian Colonies were to come into possession of the freedom promised them, many of them, we are told, never went to bed at all. Thousands, and tens of thousands of them, assembled in their places of worship, engaging in devotional duties, and singing praises to God, waiting for the first streak of the light of the morning of that day on which they were to be made free. Some of their number were sent to the hills, from which they might obtain the first view of the coming day, and, by a signal, intimate to their brethren down in the valley the dawn of the day that was to make them men, and no longer, as they had hitherto been, mere goods and chattels,—men with souls that God had created to live for ever. How eagerly must these men have watched for the morning.—*T. W. Aveling, in "The Biblical Museum,"* 1872.

Verse 7.—*"Let Israel hope in the* LORD." This title is applied to all the Lord's people ; it sets forth *their dignity*—they are PRINCES ; it refers to *their experience*— they wrestle with God in prayer, and they prevail. Despondency does not become a prince, much less a Christian. Our God is " THE GOD OF HOPE"; and we should hope in him. Israel should hope in his mercy, in his patience, in his provision, in his plenteous redemption. They should hope for light in darkness ; for strength in weakness ; for direction in perplexity ; for deliverance in danger ; for victory in conflict ; and for triumph in death.

They should hope in God confidently, because he hath promised ; prayerfully, for he loves to hear from us ; obediently, for his precepts are to be observed by us ; and constantly, for he is always the same.—*James Smith* (1802—1862), *in "The Believer's Daily Remembrancer."*

Verse 7.—*"Let Israel hope in the* LORD." Whereas, in all preceding verses of the Psalm, the thoughts, the sorrows, the prayer, the penitence, the awe, the waiting, the watching, were all personal and confined to himself ; here a great change has taken place, and it is no longer *"I,"* but *"Israel"* ; all Israel. " Let *Israel* hope in the Lord : for with the Lord there is mercy, and with him is plenteous redemption. And he shall redeem *Israel* from all his iniquities." This is as it always ought to be. . . . It is the genius of our religion to go forth to multitudes.—*James Vaughan.*

Verse 7.—*"For with the* LORD *there is mercy."* Mercy has been shown to us, but it dwells in God. It is one of his perfections. The exercise of it is his delight. There is mercy with the Lord in all its *fulness ;* he never was more merciful than now, neither will he ever be. There is mercy with the Lord in all its *tenderness,* he is full of compassion, his bowels are troubled for us, his tender mercies are over us. There is mercy with him in all its *variety*, it suits every case.

Here is mercy that receives sinners, mercy that restores backsliders, mercy that keeps believers. Here is the mercy that pardons sin, that introduces to the enjoyment of all gospel privileges, and that blesses the praying soul far beyond its expectations. With the Lord there is mercy, and he loves to display it, he is ready to impart it, he has determined to exalt and glorify it.

There is mercy with the Lord ; this should encourage the miserable to approach him ; this informs the fearful that they need bring nothing to induce him to bless them ; this calls upon backsliders to return to him ; and this is calculated to cheer the tried Christian, under all his troubles and distresses. Remember, mercy is like God, it is infinite and eternal. Mercy is always on the throne. Mercy may be obtained by any sinner.—*James Smith.*

Verse 7.—"*With him is plenteous redemption.*" This plenteous redemption leaves behind it no more relics of sin than Moses left hoofs of beasts behind him in Egypt. It redeems not only from the fault, but from the punishment ; not only *a tanto*, but *a toto* [not only from such, but also from all sin and penalty] ; not only from the sense but from the fear of pain ; and in the fault, not only from the guilt, but from the stain ; not only from being censured, but from being questioned. Or is it meant by a plenteous redemption that not only he leads captivity captive, but gives gifts unto men ? For what good is it to a prisoner to have his pardon, if he be kept in prison still for not paying his fees ? but if the prince, together with the pardon, sends also a largess that may maintain him when he is set at liberty, this, indeed, is a plenteous redemption ; and such is the redemption that God's mercy procures unto us. It not only delivers us from a dungeon, but puts us in possession of a palace ; it not only frees us from eating bread in the sweat of our brows, but it restores us to Paradise, where all fruits are growing of their own accord ; it not only clears us from being captives, but endears us to be children ; and not only children, but heirs ; and not only heirs, but co-heirs with Christ ; and who can deny this to be a plenteous redemption ? Or is it said a plenteous redemption in regard of the price that was paid to redeem us ? for we are redeemed with a price, not of gold or precious stones, but with the precious blood of the Lamb slain before the foundation of the world. For God so loved the world that he gave his only Son to be a ransom for us ; and this I am sure is a plenteous redemption.—*Sir Richard Baker.*

Verse 7.—"*Plenteous redemption,*" or more literally, "redemption plenteously." He calls it plenteous, as Luther says, because such is the straitness of our heart, the slenderness of our hopes, the weakness of our faith, that it far exceeds all our capacity, all our petitions and all our desires.—*J. J. Stewart Perowne.*

Verses 7, 8.—This Psalm containeth an evident prophecy of the Messias ; in setting forth his plentiful redemption, and that he should redeem Israel, that is, the Church, from all their sins. Which words in their full sense were used by an angel to Joseph, in telling him that the child's name should be JESUS, " because he should save his people from their sins " : Matt. i. 21.—*Sir John Hayward* (1560—1627), *in "David's Tears."* 1623.

Verse 8.—"*He will redeem.*" HE emphatic, He alone, for none other can.— J. J. Stewart Perowne.

Verse 8.—"*From his iniquities.*" Not only from the punishment (as Ewald and Hupfeld). The redemption includes the forgiveness of sins, the breaking of the power and dominion of sin, and the setting free from all the consequences of sin.— J. J. Stewart Perowne.

Verse 8.—"*Iniquities.*" Iniquities of *eye*—has conscience no voice there ? Is no iniquity ever practised by your eye ? Let conscience speak. Iniquity of *ear*— is there no iniquity that enters into your heart through the ear ? You cannot listen to a conversation in the street without iniquity entering into your heart through what Bunyan calls "Ear-gate." Iniquity of *lip*—do you always keep your tongue as with a bridle ? Do your lips never drop anything unbecoming the gospel ? Is there no carnal conversation, no angry word at home, no expression that you would not like the saints of God to hear ? What ! your lips always kept so strictly that there is never a single expression dropped from them which you would be ashamed to utter before an assembly of God's people ? Iniquity of *thought*—if your eyes, ears, and lips are clean, is there no iniquity of thought ? What ! in that workshop within, no iniquitous suggestions, no evil workings? Oh, how ignorant must we be of ourselves, if we feel that we have no iniquity of thought! Iniquity of *imagination*—does not fancy sometimes bring before you scenes of sensuality in which your carnal nature is vile enough to revel? Iniquity of *memory*—does not memory sometimes bring back sins you formerly committed, and your evil nature is perhaps base enough to desire they had been greater? Iniquity of *feeling*—no enmity against God's people ever working? no pride of heart? no covetousness? no hypocrisy? no self-righteousness? no sensuality? no base thought that you cannot disclose even to your bosom friend? But here is the blessed promise—a promise only suited to Israel: for all but Israel lose sight of their iniquities, and justify themselves in self-righteousness. None but Israel feel and confess their iniquities, and therefore to Israel is the promise of redemption limited: "He shall redeem *Israel* from all his iniquities." What! *all?* Yes. Not *one* left? No, not a trace, not a shade, not the shadow of a shade; all buried, all gone, all swallowed up, all blotted out, all freely pardoned, all cast behind God's back.—*Joseph C. Philpot*, 1802—1869.

Verse 8.—What a graceful and appropriate conclusion of this comprehensive and instructive Psalm! Like the sun, it dawns veiled in cloud, it sets bathed in splendour; it opens with soul-depth, it closes with soul-height. Redemption from all iniquity! It baffles the most descriptive language, and distances the highest measurement. The most vivid imagination faints in conceiving it, the most glowing image fails in portraying it, and faith droops her wing in the bold attempt to scale its summit. "*He shall redeem Israel from all his iniquities.*" The verse is a word-painting of man restored, and of Paradise regained.—*Octavius Winslow*.

HINTS TO PREACHERS

Verse 1.—The assertion of an experienced believer. I. I have cried—that is, I have earnestly, constantly, truthfully prayed. II. I have cried only unto thee. Nothing could draw me to other confidences, or make me despair of thee. III. I have cried in distress. At my worst, temporally or spiritually, I have cried out of the depths. IV. I therefore infer—that I am thy child, no hypocrite, no apostate; and that thou hast heard and wilt hear me evermore.

Verse 1.—I. What we are to understand by "the depths." Great misery and distress. II. How men get into "the depths." By sin and unbelief. III. What gracious souls do when in "the depths." Cry unto the Lord. IV. How the Lord lifts praying souls out of "the depths": "He shall redeem," etc., verse 8.—*W. H. J. P*

Verse 1.—I. In the pit. II. The morning-star seen: "Thee, O Lord." III. Prayer flutters up "out of the depths."—*W. B. H.*

Verses 1, 2.—I. The depths from which prayer may rise. 1. Of affliction. 2. Of conviction. 3. Of desertion. II. The height to which it may ascend. 1. To the hearing of God. 2. To a patient hearing. "Hear my voice." 3. To an attentive hearing.

Or, I. We should pray at all times. II. We should pray that our prayers may be heard. III. We should pray until we know we are heard. IV. We should pray in faith that when heard we have the thing we have asked. "That which thou hast prayed to me against the King of Assyria I have heard." God had heard. That was enough. It was the death of Sennacherib and the overthrow of his host.—*G. R.*

Verses 1, 2.—Consider, I. The Psalmist's condition in the light of a warning. Evidently, through sin, he came into the depths; see verses 3 and 4. Learn, 1. The need of watchfulness on the part of all. 2. That backsliding will, sooner or later, bring great trouble of soul. II. His sometime continuance in that condition, in the light of a Divine judgment: "I *have* cried." Certainly his first cry had not brought deliverance. 1. The realization of pardon is a Divine work, dependent upon God's pleasure. Ps. lxxxv. 8. 2. But he will not always nor often speak pardon at the first asking; for He will make His people reverence his holiness, feel the bitterness of sinning, learn caution, etc.   III. His conduct while in that condition in the light of a direction. He, 1. Seeks deliverance only of God. 2. Is intensely earnest in his application : " I cried." 3. Is importunate in his pleading : " Hear my voice," etc.—*J. F.*

Verse 2.—Attention from God to us—how to gain it.   I. Let us plead the name which commands attention.   II. Let us ourselves pay attention to God's word. III. Let us give earnest attention to what we ask, and how we ask.   IV. Let us attentively watch for a reply.

Verse 2.—*"Lord, hear my voice."*   I. Though it be faint by reason of distance— hear it.   II. Though it be broken because of my distress—hear it.   III. Though it be unworthy on account of my iniquities—hear it.—*W. H. J. P.*

Verse 3.—I. The supposition : " If thou, Lord, shouldst mark iniquities." 1. It is scriptural.   2. It is reasonable.   If God is not indifferent towards men, he must observe their sins.   If he is holy, he must manifest indignation against sin. If he is the Creator of conscience, he must certainly uphold its verdict against sin. If he is not wholly on the side of sin, how can he fail to avenge the mischiefs and miseries sin has caused ?   II. The question it suggests : " Who shall stand ? " A question, 1. Not difficult to answer.   2. Of solemn import to all.   3. Which ought to be seriously pondered without delay.   III. The possibility it hints at.   " If thou, Lord." The " if " hints at the possibility that God may not mark sin.   The possibility, 1. Is reasonable, providing it can be without damage to God's righteous- ness ; for the Creator and Preserver of men cannot delight in condemning and punishing.   2. Is a God-honouring reality, through the blood of Christ, Rom. iii. 21—26.   3. Becomes a glorious certainty in the experience of penitent and believing souls.—*J. F.*

Verses 3, 4.—I. The Confession.   He could not stand.   II. The Confidence. " There is forgiveness."   III. The Consequence.   " That thou mayest be feared."

Verses 3, 4.—I. The fearful supposition.   II. The solemn interrogation.   III. The Divine consolation.—*W. J.*

Verse 4. — *Forgiveness with God.*   I. The proofs of it.   1. Divine declarations. 2. Invitations and promises, Isa. i. 18.   3. The bestowment of pardon so effectually as to give assurance and joy. 2 Sam. xii. 13.   Ps. xxxii. 5.   Luke vii. 47-8.   1 John ii. 12.   II. The reason of it.   1. In God's nature there is the desire to forgive ; the gift of Christ is sufficient evidence for it.   2. But, the text speaks not so much of a desire as it asserts the existence of a forgiveness being " with " God, therefore ready to be dispensed.   The blood of Christ is the reason (Col. i. 14) ; by it the disposition to forgive righteously manifests itself in the forgiving act : Rom. iii. 25, 26. 3. Hence, forgiveness for all who believe is sure : Rom. iii. 25 ; 1 John ii. 1, 2. III. The result of its realization : " That thou mayest be feared " : with a reverential fear, and spiritual worship.   1. The possibility of forgiveness begets in an anxious soul true penitence, as opposed to terror and despair.   2. The hope of receiving it begets earnest seeking and prayerfulness.   3. A believing reception of it gives peace and rest, and, exciting grateful love, leads to spiritual worship and filial service.— *J. F.*

Verse 4.—*"There is forgiveness."*   I. It is needed.   II. God alone can give it. III. It may be had.   IV. We may know that we have it.

Verse 4.—I. A most cheering announcement : " There is forgiveness with thee." 1. A fact certain.   2. A fact in the present tense.   3. A fact which arises out of God himself.   4. A fact stated in general terms.   5. A fact to be meditated upon with delight.   II. A most admirable design : " That thou mayest be feared." 1. Very contrary to the abuse made of it by rebels, triflers, and procrastinators. 2. Very different from the pretended fears of legalists.   3. No pardon, no fear of God—devils, reprobates.   4. No pardon, none survive to fear him.   5. But the means of pardon encourage faith, repentance, prayer ; and the receipt of pardon creates love, suggests obedience, inflames zeal.

Verse 4.—See " Spurgeon's Sermons," No. 351 : " Plenteous Redemption."

Verse 4.—Tender Light.   I. The Angel by the Throne : " Forgiveness with Thee."   II. The shadow that enhances his sweet majesty : " If," " But."   III. The homage resultant from his ministry ; universal from highest to least.—*W. B. H.*

Verses 5, 6.—Three postures : Waiting, Hoping, Watching.

Verses 5, 6.—1. The seeking sinner.   2. The Christian mourner.   3. The loving intercessor.   4. The spiritual labourer.   5. The dying believer.—*W. J.*

Verses 5, 6.—I. We are to wait on God.   1. By faith : " In his word do I hope."

2. By prayer. Prayer can wait when it has a promise to rest upon.   II. We are to wait for God: "I wait for the Lord."   "My soul waiteth for the Lord more," etc.   1. Because he has his own time for giving.   2. Because what he gives is worth waiting for.—*G. R.*

Verse 6.—"*More than they.*"   I. For the darker sorrow his absence causes. II. For the richer splendour his coming must bring.   III. For the greater might of our indwelling love.—*W. B. H.*

Verse 6.—I. A long, dark night: The Lord absent.   II. An eager, hopeful watcher: Waiting the Lord's return.   III. A bright, blessed morning: The time of the Lord's appearing.—*W. H. J. P.*

Verse 7.—Redeeming grace the sole hope of the holiest.—*W. B. H.*

Verse 7.—I. A divine exhortation: "Let Israel hope in the Lord."   II. A spiritual reason: "For with the Lord there is mercy," etc.   III. A gracious promise: "He shall redeem Israel from all his iniquities."—*J. C. Philpot.*

Verses 7, 8.—It is our wisdom to have personal dealings with God.   I. The first exercise of faith must be upon the Lord himself.   This is the natural order, the necessary order, easiest, wisest, and most profitable order.   Begin where all begins. II. Exercises of faith about other things must still be in connection with the Lord. Mercy—"with the Lord."   Plenteous redemption "with him."   III. Exercises of faith, whatever their object, must *all* settle on him.   "He shall redeem," etc.

Verse 8.—I. The Redemption: "From all iniquities."   II. The Redeemer: "The Lord."   See Titus ii. 14.   III. The Redeemed: "Israel."—*W. H. J. P.*

PSALM CXXXI.

TITLE.—A Song of Degrees of David. *It is both by David and of David : he is the author and the subject of it, and many incidents of his life may be employed to illustrate it. Comparing all the Psalms to gems, we should liken this to a pearl : how beautifully it will adorn the neck of patience. It is one of the shortest Psalms to read, but one of the longest to learn. It speaks of a young child, but it contains the experience of a man in Christ. Lowliness and humility are here seen in connection with a sanctified heart, a will subdued to the mind of God, and a hope looking to the Lord alone. Happy is the man who can without falsehood use these words as his own ; for he wears about him the likeness of his Lord, who said, "I am meek and lowly in heart." The Psalm is in advance of all the Songs of Degrees which have preceded it ; for lowliness is one of the highest attainments in the divine life. There are also steps in this Song of Degrees : it is a short ladder, if we count the words ; but yet it rises to a great height, reaching from deep humility to fixed confidence. Le Blanc thinks that this is a song of the Israelites who returned from Babylon with humbled hearts, weaned from their idols. At any rate, after any spiritual captivity let it be the expression of our hearts.*

EXPOSITION.

LORD, my heart is not haughty, nor mine eyes lofty : neither do I exercise myself in great matters, or in things too high for me.

2 Surely I have behaved and quieted myself, as a child that is weaned of his mother : my soul *is* even as a weaned child.

3 Let Israel hope in the LORD from henceforth and for ever.

1. *"LORD, my heart is not haughty."* The Psalm deals with the Lord, and is a solitary colloquy with him, not a discourse before men. We have a sufficient audience when we speak with the Lord, and we may say to him many things which were not proper for the ears of men. The holy man makes his appeal to Jehovah, who alone knows the heart : a man should be slow to do this upon any matter, for the Lord is not to be trifled with ; and when anyone ventures on such an appeal he should be sure of his case. He begins with his heart, for that is the centre of our nature, and if pride be there it defiles everything ; just as mire in the spring causes mud in all the streams. It is a grand thing for a man to know his own heart so as to be able to speak before the Lord about it. It is beyond all things deceitful and desperately wicked, who can know it ? Who can know it unless taught by the Spirit of God ? It is a still greater thing if, upon searching himself thoroughly, a man can solemnly protest unto the Omniscient One that his heart is not haughty : that is to say, neither proud in his opinion of himself, contemptuous to others, nor self-righteous before the Lord ; neither boastful of the past, proud of the present, nor ambitious for the future. *"Nor mine eyes lofty."* What the heart desires the eyes look for. Where the desires run the glances usually follow. This holy man felt that he did not seek after elevated places where he might gratify his self-esteem, neither did he look down upon others as being his inferiors. A proud look the Lord hates ; and in this all men are agreed with him ; yea, even the proud themselves hate haughtiness in the gestures of others. Lofty eyes are so generally hateful that haughty men have been known to avoid the manners natural to the proud in order to escape the ill-will of their fellows. The pride which apes humility always takes care to cast its eyes downward, since every man's consciousness tells him that contemptuous glances are the sure ensigns of a boastful spirit. In Psalm cxxi. David lifted up his eyes to the hills ; but here he declares that they were not lifted up in any other sense. When the heart is right, and the eyes are right, the whole man is on the road to a healthy and happy condition. Let us take care that we do not use the language of this Psalm unless, indeed, it be true as to ourselves ; for there is no worse pride than that which claims humility when it does not possess it.

"Neither do I exercise myself in great matters." As a private man he did not usurp the power of the king or devise plots against him : he minded his own business, and left others to mind theirs. As a thoughtful man he did not pry into things unrevealed ; he was not speculative, self-conceited or opinionated. As a secular person he did not thrust himself into the priesthood as Saul had done before him, and as Uzziah did after him. It is well so to exercise ourselves unto godliness that we know our true sphere, and diligently keep to it. Many through wishing to be great have failed to be good : they were not content to adorn the lowly stations which the Lord appointed them, and so they have rushed at grandeur and power, and found destruction where they looked for honour. *"Or in things too high for me."* High things may suit others who are of greater stature, and yet they may be quite unfit for us. A man does well to know his own size. Ascertaining his own capacity, he will be foolish if he aims at that which is beyond his reach, straining himself, and thus injuring himself. Such is the vanity of many men that if a work be within their range they despise it, and think it beneath them : the only service which they are willing to undertake is that to which they have never been called, and for which they are by no means qualified. What a haughty heart must he have who will not serve God at all unless he may be trusted with five talents at the least ! His looks are indeed lofty who disdains to be a light among his poor friends and neighbours here below, but demands to be created a star of the first magnitude to shine among the upper ranks, and to be admired by gazing crowds. It is just on God's part that those who wish to be everything should end in being nothing. It is a righteous retribution from God when every matter turns out to be too great for the man who would only handle great matters, and every thing proves to be too high for the man who exercised himself in things too high for him. Lord, make us lowly, keep us lowly, fix us for ever in lowliness. Help us to be in such a case that the confession of this verse may come from our lips as a truthful utterance which we dare make before the Judge of all the earth.

2. *"Surely I have behaved and quieted myself."* The original bears somewhat of the form of an oath, and therefore our translators exhibited great judgment in introducing the word " surely "; it is not a literal version, but it correctly gives the meaning. The Psalmist had been upon his best behaviour, and had smoothed down the roughnesses of his self-will ; by holy effort he had mastered his own spirit, so that towards God he was not rebellious, even as towards man he was not haughty. It is no easy thing to quiet yourself : sooner may a man calm the sea, or rule the wind, or tame a tiger, than quiet himself. We are clamorous, uneasy, petulant ; and nothing but grace can make us quiet under afflictions, irritations, and disappointments. *"As a child that is weaned of his mother."* He had become as subdued and content as a child whose weaning is fully accomplished. The Easterns put off the time of weaning far later than we do, and we may conclude that the process grows none the easier by being postponed. At last there must be an end to the suckling period, and then a battle begins : the child is denied his comfort, and therefore frets and worries, flies into pets, or sinks into sulks. It is facing its first great sorrow, and it is in sore distress. Yet time brings not only alleviations, but the ending of the conflict ; the boy ere long is quite content to find his nourishment at the table with his brothers, and he feels no lingering wish to return to those dear fountains from which he once sustained his life. He is no longer angry with his mother, but buries his head in that very bosom after which he pined so grievously : he is weaned *on* his mother rather than *from* her.

> " My soul doth like a weanling rest,
>   I cease to weep ;
> So mother's lap, though dried her breast,
>   Can lull to sleep."

To the weaned child his mother is his comfort though she has denied him comfort. It is a blessed mark of growth out of spiritual infancy when we can forego the joys which once appeared to be essential, and can find our solace in him who denies them to us : then we behave manfully, and every childish complaint is hushed. If the Lord removes our dearest delight we bow to his will without a murmuring thought ; in fact, we find a delight in giving up our delight. This is no spontaneous fruit of nature, but a well-tended product of divine grace : it grows out of humility and lowliness, and it is the stem upon which peace blooms as a fair flower. *"My soul is even as a weaned child"*; or it may be read, "as a weaned child on me my soul," as if his soul leaned upon him in mute submission, neither boasting nor complaining. It is not every child of God who arrives at this weanedness speedily. Some are sucklings when they ought to be fathers ; others are hard to wean, and cry, and fight, and rage against their heavenly parent's discipline. When we think ourselves safely through the weaning, we sadly discover that the old appetites are rather wounded than slain, and we begin crying again for the breasts which we had given up, It is easy to begin shouting before we are out of the wood, and no doubt hundreds have sung this Psalm long before they have understood it. Blessed are those afflictions which subdue our affections, which wean us from self-sufficiency, which educate us into Christian manliness, which teach us to love God not merely when he comforts us, but even when he tries us. Well might the sacred poet repeat his figure of the weaned child ; it is worthy of admiration and imitation ; it is doubly desirable and difficult of attainment. Such weanedness from self springs from the gentle humility declared in the former verse, and partly accounts for its existence. If pride is gone, submission will be sure to follow ; and, on the other hand, if pride is to be driven out, self must also be vanquished.

3. *"Let Israel hope in the Lord from henceforth and for ever."* See how lovingly a man who is weaned from self thinks of others ! David thinks of his people, and loses himself in his care for Israel. How he prizes the grace of hope ! He has given up the things which are seen, and therefore he values the treasures which are not seen except by the eyes of hope. There is room for the largest hope when self is gone, ground for eternal hope when transient things no longer hold the mastery of our spirits. This verse is the lesson of experience : a man of God who had been taught to renounce the world and live upon the Lord alone, here exhorts all his friends and companions to do the same. He found it a blessed thing to live by hope, and therefore he would have all his kinsmen do the same. Let all the nation hope, let all their hope be in Jehovah, let them at once begin hoping " from henceforth," and let them continue hoping " for ever." Weaning takes the child out of a temporary condition into a state in which he will continue for the rest of his life : to rise above the world is to enter upon a heavenly existence which can never end. When we cease to hanker for the world we begin hoping in the Lord. O Lord, as a parent weans a child, so do thou wean me, and then shall I fix all my hope on thee alone.

EXPLANATORY NOTES AND QUAINT SAYINGS.

Whole Psalm.—This little song is inscribed לְדָוִד because it is like an echo of the answer (2 Sam. vi. 21 sq.) with which David repelled the mocking observation of Michal when he danced before the Ark in a linen ephod, and therefore not in kingly attire, but in the common raiment of the priests. *I esteem myself still less than I now show it, and I appear base in mine own eyes.* In general David is the model of the state of mind which the poet expresses here. He did not push himself forward, but suffered himself to be drawn forth out of seclusion. He did not take possession of the throne violently ; but after Samuel has anointed him, he willingly and patiently traverses the long, thorny, circuitous way of deep abasement, until he receives from God's hand that which God's promise had assured to him. The persecution by Saul lasted about ten years, and his kingship in Hebron, at first only incipient, seven years and a half. He left it entirely to God to remove Saul and Ishbosheth. He let Shimei curse. He left Jerusalem before Absalom. Submission to God's guidance, resignation to his dispensations, contentment with that which was allotted to him, are the distinguishing traits of his noble character. —*Franz Delitzsch.*

Whole Psalm.—Psalm cxxx. is a Song of Forgiveness ; Psalm cxxxi. is a Song of Humility : the former celebrates the blessedness of the man whose transgressions are pardoned ; the latter celebrates the blessedness of the man who is of a meek and lowly spirit. Forgiveness *should* humble us. Forgiveness implies sin ; and should not the sinner clothe himself with humility ? and when not for any desert of his, but simply by the free grace of Heaven, his sins have been pardoned, should he not bind the garments of humility still more closely about him ? The man who is of a nature at once sincere and sweet, will be even more humbled by the sense of an undeserved forgiveness than by the memory of the sins from which it has cleansed him. Very fitly, therefore, does the Psalm of humility follow the Psalm which sings of the Divine lovingkindness and tender mercy.—*Samuel Cox.*

Whole Psalm.—This Psalm, which records the meek and humble spirit of those who are the true worshippers of the Temple, doubtless belongs, as its title announces, to the time of David. It is exactly in the spirit of that humble thanksgiving made by him, after the divine revelation by Nathan of the future blessings of his posterity (1 Chron. xxii. 9—11); and forms a most appropriate introduction to the following Psalm, the theme of which is evidently the dedication of the Temple.—*John Jebb.*

Verse 1.—"*Lord, my heart is not haughty.*" For the truth of his plea he appealeth to God; and from all those who are affected like David, God will accept of the appeal.

Firstly. He could in truth of heart appeal to God: "*Lord, my heart is not haughty.*" He appealeth to him who knoweth all things. "Lord, from whom nothing is hid, thou knowest that this is the very disposition of my soul. If I have anything, it is from thee; it is thy providence which brought me from following the ewes great with young to feed and govern thy people." Such a holy man would not rashly invoke God, and take his holy name in vain; but knowing his integrity, durst call God to witness. The saints are wont to do so upon like occasions; as Peter (John xxi. 17); "Lord, thou knowest all things; thou knowest that I love thee." They know they have a God that will not be deceived with any shows, and that he knoweth and approveth them for such as he findeth them to be.

Secondly. From those that are affected like David, God will accept the appeal; for in the account of God we are that which we sincerely desire and endeavour to be, and that which is the general course and tenor of our lives, though there be some intermixture of failing. David saith, "*Lord, my heart is not haughty*"; and yet he was not altogether free from pride. His profession respecteth his sincere purpose and constant endeavour, and the predominant disposition of his soul. God himself confirmeth such appeals by his own testimony: 1 Kings xv. 5, "My servant David did that which was right in the eyes of the Lord, neither departed from all that which he had commanded him, save only in the matter of Uriah " . . . . . By all this it is shown that the plea of sincerity is allowed by God, though there be some mixture of failings and weaknesses.

Thirdly. Is not this boasting like the Pharisee? Luke xviii. 9, "God, I thank thee, I am not like other men." If David were thus humble, why doth he speak of it? Is he not guilty of pride while he seemeth to speak against pride?

This is spoken either as, (1) A necessary vindication; or (2) A necessary instruction. 1. As a necessary vindication against the censures and calumnies of his adversaries. Saul's courtiers accused him as aspiring after the kingdom; yea, his own brother taxed him with pride when he came first abroad: 1 Sam. xvii. 28, " I know thy pride, and the naughtiness of thine heart; for thou art come down that thou mightest see the battle." If his brother would calumniate his actions, much more might others. Now it is for the honour of God that his children, as they would not commit a fault, so they should not be under the suspicion of it; therefore he appealeth to God. 2. A necessary instruction; for whatsoever David said or wrote here, he said or wrote by the inspiration of the Holy Ghost, that Israel may learn how to hope in God. Herein David is a notable pattern of duty both to superiors and inferiors.—*Thomas Manton.*

Verse 1.—"*My heart is not haughty.*" Albeit pride is a common vice, which attendeth vain man in every degree of excellency and supposed worth in him, yet the grace of God is able to keep humble a wise, rich, and potent man, yea, to keep humble a king and conqueror; for it is no less a person than David who saith here, "*Lord, my heart is not haughty.*"—*David Dickson.*

Verse 1.—"*Nor mine eyes lofty.*" Pride has its seat in the heart; but its principal expression is in the eye. The eye is the mirror of the soul; and from it mental and moral characteristics may be ascertained, with no small degree of precision. What a world of meaning is sometimes concentrated in a single glance! But of all the passions, pride is most clearly revealed in the eyes. There can scarcely be a mistake here. We are all familiar with a class of phrases, which run in pairs. We speak of sin and misery; holiness and happiness; peace and prosperity; war and desolation. Among these may be numbered, the proud heart and the haughty

look. " There is a generation, Oh, how lofty are their eyes ! and their eyelids
are lifted up."   " Him that hath an high look and a proud heart I will not suffer."
. . . A proud look is one of the seven things which are an abomination unto the
Lord.   It is said of him, " Thou wilt save the afflicted people ; but wilt bring down
high looks."   And hence David makes the acknowledgment : Lord, thou knowest
all things ; thou knowest that pride has no existence in my heart. Thou knowest
that no pride flashes forth from mine eyes.—*N. M'Michael.*

Verse 1.—*"Nor mine eyes lofty."* He had neither a scornful nor an aspiring
look. *"My eyes are not lofty,"* either to look with envy upon those that are above
me, or to look with disdain upon those that are below me.   Where there is a proud
heart, there is commonly a proud look (Prov. vi. 17) ; but the humble publican
will not so much as lift up his eyes.—*Matthew Henry.*

Verse 1.—*"Neither have I occupied myself,"* etc.   One cannot admire enough
the prayer of Anselm, a profound divine of our own country, in the eleventh century.
" I do not seek, O Lord, to penetrate thy depths.   I by no means think my intellect
equal to them : but I long to understand in some degree thy truth, which my heart
believes and loves.   For I do not seek to understand that I may believe ; but I
believe, that I may understand."—*N. M'Michael.*

Verse 1.—*"Great matters . . . things too high for me."* The great and wonderful
things meant are God's secret purposes, and sovereign means for their accomplishment,
in which man is not called to co-operate, but to acquiesce.   As David practised
this forbearance by the patient expectation of the kingdom, both before and after
the death of Saul, so he here describes it as a characteristic of the chosen people.—
Joseph Addison Alexander.

Verses 1, 2.—Our Father is our superior ; it is fit therefore that we be resigned
to his will.   " Honour thy father and thy mother " (Exod. xx. 12) ; how much
more our heavenly Father ! (Heb. xii. 9).   See David's spirit in the case : *"Lord,
my heart is not haughty,"* etc. : Ps. cxxxi. 1, 2.   As if he had said, " I will keep
within my own sphere ; I will not stretch beyond my line, in prescribing to God ;
but submit to his will, *'as a weaned child,'* taken from its dear breasts": intimating
that he would wean himself from whatever God removed from him.   How patiently
did Isaac permit himself to be bound and sacrificed by Abraham ! Gen. xxii. 9.
And yet he was of age and strength sufficient to have struggled for his life, being
twenty-five years old ; but that holy young man abhorred the thought of striving
with his father.   And shall not we resign ourselves to our God and Father in Christ
Jesus ?—*John Singleton (— 1706), in "The Morning Exercises."*

Verses 1, 2.—It has always been my aim, and it is my prayer, to have no plan
as regards myself ; well assured as I am that the place where the Saviour sees
meet to place me must ever be the best place for me.—*Robert Murray M'Cheyne,
1813—1843.*

Verse 2.—*"Surely I have behaved and quieted myself,"* etc.   Oh, how sapless
and insipid doth the world grow to the soul that is making meet for heaven !   " I
am crucified to the world, and this world to me."   Gal. vi. 14.   In vain doth this
harlot think to allure me by her attractions of profit and pleasure.   " Surely I
have behaved and quieted myself, as a child that is weaned of his mother : my soul
is even as a weaned child."   There is no more relish in these gaudy things to my
palate, than in the white of an egg ; everything grows a burden to me, were it not
my duty to follow my calling, and be thankful for my enjoyments.   Methinks
I have my wife, husband, and dearest relations, as if I had none ; I weep for outward
losses, as if I wept not ; rejoice in comforts below as if I rejoiced not (1 Cor. vii.
29, 30) ; my thoughts are taken up with other objects.   The men of the world
slight me, many seem to be weary of me, and I am as weary of them.   It is none
of these earthly things that my heart is set upon ; my soul is set on things above,
my treasure is in heaven, and I would have my heart there also : I have sent before
me all my goods into another country, and am shortly for removing ; and when
I look about me, I see a bare, empty house, and am ready to say with Monica, What
do I here ? my father, husband, mother (Jerusalem above), my brethren, sisters,
best friends are above.   Methinks, I grudge the world any portion of my heart,
and think not these temporal visible things worth a cast of my eye compared with
things invisible and eternal : 2 Cor. iv. 18.—*Oliver Heywood, 1629—1702.*

Verse 2 (*first clause*).—*"If I have not restrained,"* or quieted, and compelled
to silence, *" my soul."*   It is a Hebrew phrase of asseveration and of swearing: as

if he would say, I have thoroughly imposed silence on my soul, that it should be tranquil, and should bear patiently the divinely imposed cross. Just as in the following Psalm we hear a like form of asseveration : " If I will come into the tabernacle of my house," meaning " I will not come," etc.—*Solomon Gesner.*

Verse 2.—"*I have behaved and quieted myself, as a child that is weaned.*" Weaned from what ? Self-sufficiency, self-will, self-seeking. From creatures and the things of the world—not, indeed, as to their use, but as to any dependence upon them for his happiness and portion. . . . . Yet this experience is no easy attainment. The very form of expression—" I have behaved and *quieted* myself," reminds us of some risings which were with difficulty subdued. There is a difference here between Christ and Christians. In him the exercise of grace encountered no adverse principles ; but in them it meets with constant opposition. The flesh lusteth against the spirit ; and when we would do good, evil is present with us ; hence the warfare within. So it is with "the child that is weaned." The task to the mother is trying and troublesome. The infant cries, and seems to sob out his heart. He thinks it very hard in her, and knows not what she means by her seeming cruelty, and the mother's fondness renders all her firmness necessary to keep her at the process ; and sometimes she also weeps at the importunity of his dear looks, and big tears, and stretched-out hands. But it must be done, and therefore, though she pities, she perseveres ; and after a while he is soothed and satisfied, forgets the breast, and no longer feels even a hankering after his former pleasure. But how is the weaning of the child accomplished ? By embittering the member to his lips ; by the removal of the object in the absence and concealment of the mother ; by the substitution of other food ; by the influence of time. So it is with us. We love the world, and it deceives us. We depend on creatures, and they fail us, and pierce us through with many sorrows. We enter forbidden paths, and follow after our lovers ; and our way is hedged up with thorns ; and we then say, " Return unto thy rest, O my soul ; and now, Lord, what wait I for ? My hope is in thee." The enjoyment of a greater good subdues the relish of a less. What are the indulgences of sin, or the dissipations of the world to one who is abundantly satisfied with the goodness of God's house, and is made to drink of the river of his pleasures ? —*William Jay* (1769—1853), *in "Evening Exercises for the Closet."*

Verse 2.—"*As a child that is weaned of his mother.*" Though the weaned child has not what it would have, or what it naturally most desireth, the milk of the breast—yet it is contented with what the mother giveth—it rests upon her love and provision. So are we to be content with what providence alloweth us : Heb. xiii. 5, " Let your conversation be without covetousness, and be content with such things as ye have"; and Phil. iv. 11, " I have learned, in whatsover state I am, therewith to be content." Whatever pleaseth our heavenly Father should please us. The child that is put from the breast to a harder diet is yet contented at last. The child doth not prescribe what it will eat, drink or put on. Children are in no care for enlarging possessions, heaping up riches, aspiring after dignities and honours ; but meekly take what is provided for them. The child, when it has lost the food which nature provideth for it, is not solicitous, but wholly referreth itself to the mother, hangeth upon the mother. So for everything whatsoever should we depend upon God, refer ourselves to God, and expect all things from him : Ps. lxii. 5, " My soul, wait thou only upon God ; for my expectation is from him." With such a simplicity of submission should we rest and depend upon God. Let us take heed of being over wise and provident for ourselves, but let us trust our Father which is in heaven, and refer ourselves to his wise and holy government.— *Thomas Manton.*

Verse 2.—"*As a child that is weaned of his mother.*" Weaned from the world, the riches, honours, pleasures, and profits of it ; as well as from nature, from self, from his own righteousness, and all dependence upon it ; and as a child that is weaned from the breast wholly depends on its nurse for sustenance, so did he wholly depend upon God, his providence, grace, and strength ; and as to the kingdom, he had no more covetous desires after it than a weaned child has to the breast, and was very willing to wait the due time for the enjoyment of it. The Targum has it, " as one weaned on the breasts of its mother, I am strengthened in the law." This is to be understood not of a child whilst weaning, when it is usually peevish, fretful, and froward, but when it is weaned, and is quiet and easy in its mother's arms without the breast.—*John Gill.*

Verse 2.—"*My soul is even as a weaned child.*" In its *nature*, weanedness of soul differs essentially from that disgust with the world, to which its ill-usage and meanness sometimes give rise. It is one thing to be angry with the world, or ashamed of it, and another to be weaned from it. Alter the world, ennoble it, and many a proud mind that now despises, would court it. It is different also from that weariness of spirit which generally follows a free indulgence in earthly enjoyments. There is such a thing as wearing out the affections. Solomon appears to have done this at one period of his life. " I have not a wish left," said a well-known sensualist of our own country, who had drunk as deeply as he could drink of the world's cup. " Were all the earth contains spread out before me, I do not know a thing I would take the trouble of putting out my hand to reach."

This weanedness of soul presupposes a power left in the soul of loving and desiring. It is not the destruction of its appetite, but the controlling and changing of it. A weaned child still hungers, but it hungers no more after the food that once delighted it ; it is quiet without it ; it can feed on other things : so a soul weaned from the world, still pants as much as ever for food and happiness, but it no longer seeks them in worldly things, or desires to do so. There is nothing in the world that it feels necessary for its happiness. This thing in it it loves, and that thing it values ; but it knows that it can do without them, and it is ready to do without them whenever God pleases.

Let us inquire now into *the sources of this frame of mind*—how we get it. One thing is certain—it is not our work. We do not bring ourselves to it. No infant weans itself. The truth is, it is God that must wean us from the world. We shall never leave it of our own accord. It is God's own right hand that must draw us from it. And how ? The figure in the text will partly tell us. 1. *By embittering the world to us.* 2. At other times *the Lord removes from us the thing we love.* 3. But he weans us most from the earth *by giving us better food.*—*Condensed from a Sermon by Charles Bradley, entitled* "*Weanedness of Soul,*" 1836.

Verse 2.—"*As a weaned child.*" That is, meek, modest, humble, submissive, simple, etc. See Matt. xviii. 1, 2, 3, 4.—*Henry Ainsworth,* —1622.

Verse 2.—Here is David's picture of himself . . . Observe, the "*child*"—which is drawn for us to copy—is "*weaned*": the process is complete ; it has been truly disciplined ; the lesson is learned ; and now it rests in its " weaning." The whole image expresses a repose which follows a struggle. "*Surely I have behaved and quieted myself, as a child that is weaned of his mother*"; or, more literally, " *on* his mother"; now content to lie still on the very place of its privation,—" as a child that is weaned on his mother."

·That obedience would be a tame and valueless thing, which was not the consequence of quiet control. A mere apathetic state is the very opposite of obedience that may be truly so called. But this is the point of the similitude,—there has been a distress, and a battle, and a self-victory ; and now the stilled will is hushed into submission and contentment ; ready to forego what is most liked, and to take just whatever is given it—"*a weaned child.*"

I do not believe that it was ever the intention of God that any man should so merge and lose his will in the Divine, that he should have no distinct will of his own. There have been many who have tried to attain this annihilation of will ; and they have made it the great aim and end of life. But the character of the dispensation does not allow it. I do not believe it to be a possible thing ; and if it were possible, I do not believe that it would be after the mind of God. It is not man's present relation to his Maker. None of the saints in the Bible did more than submit a strong existing will. The Lord Jesus Christ himself did no more. " What shall I say ? Father, save me from this hour ; but for this cause came I unto this hour. Father, glorify thy name. Not my will, but thine be done." Evidently two things—" My will," " Thy will." It was an instantly and perfectly subjugated will,—nevertheless, a will.

And this is what is required of us ; and what the nature of our manhood, and the provisions of our religion have to assume. A will, decidedly a will: the more decided the will, the stronger the character, and the greater the man. But a will that is always being given up, separated, conformed, constantly, increasingly conformed. The unity of the two wills is heaven.—*Condensed from a Sermon by James Vaughan.*

Verse 3.—"*Let Israel hope in the* LORD." After the example, therefore, of the King of Israel, who thus demeaned himself in his afflictions, lowly, contented, and resigned, casting all his care upon the Father who cared for him, and patiently waiting his time for deliverance and salvation ; after this their example and pattern, let his faithful people hope and trust, not in themselves, their wisdom, or their power, but in Jehovah alone, who will not fail to exalt them, as he hath already exalted their Redeemer, if they do but follow his steps.—*George Horne.*

Verse 3.—*"Let Israel hope in the* LORD." Though David could himself wait patiently and quietly for the crown designed him, yet perhaps Israel, the people whose darling he was, would be ready to attempt something in favour of him before the time ; he therefore endeavours to quiet them too, and bids them " *hope in the* LORD " that *they* should see a happy change of the face of affairs in due time. Thus " it is good to hope, and quietly to wait for the salvation of the Lord."—*Matthew Henry.*

Verse 3.—*"Let Israel hope in the* LORD," etc. Remember that he is *Jehovah.* 1. Wise to plan. 2. Good to purpose. 3. Strong to execute, and that he will withhold no good thing from them that walk uprightly. 4. Trust *"from hence-forth."* If you have not begun before, begin now. 5. And do not be weary ; trust *"for ever."* Your case can never be out of the reach of God's power and mercy.—*Adam Clarke.*

HINTS TO PREACHERS.

Verse 1.—*Humility.* I. A profession which ought to befit every child of God. II. A profession which nevertheless many children of God cannot truthfully make. Point out the prevalence of pride and ambition even in the church. III. A profession which can only be justified through the possession of the spirit of Christ (Matt. xi. 29, 30 ; xviii. 1—5).—*C. A. D.*

Verse 2.—The soul is as a weaned child : I. In conversion. II. In sanctification, which is a continual weaning from the world and sin. III. In bereavement. IV. In affliction of every kind. V. In death.—*G. R.*

Verse 2.—I. The soul has to be weaned as well as the body. 1. It is first nourished by others. 2. It is afterwards thrown upon its own resources. II. The soul is weaned from one thing by giving its attention to another. 1. From worldly things by heavenly. 2. From self-righteousness by the righteousness of another. 3. From sin to holiness. 4. From the world to Christ. 5. From self to God.—*G. R.*

Verse 2.—I. A desirable condition : " As a weaned child." II. A difficult task—to subdue and quiet self. III. A delightful result : " Surely . . . . my soul is as a weaned child."—*W. H. J. P.*

Verse 2. — I. Soul - fretfulness : weak, dishonourable, rebellious. II. Soul-government ; throne often abdicated ; God gives each the sceptre of self-rule ; necessary to successful life. III. Soul-quiet ; its sweetness ; its power. Come, Holy Spirit, breathe it upon us !—*W. B. H.*

Verse 2.—See " Spurgeon's Sermons," No. 1,210 : " The Weaned Child."

Verses 2, 3.—The weaned child hoping in the Lord : I. The first weaning of the soul, the grand event of a man's history. II. The joy in the Lord that springs up in every weaned soul : " My soul is even as a weaned child ; let Israel hope in the Lord from henceforth and for ever." III. The daily weaning of the soul through life. IV. The earnest desires and the fruitful work of every weaned soul. —*A. Moody Stuart.*

Verse 3.—I. The encouragement to hope in God. 1. As a covenant God, "the God of Israel." 2. As a covenant-keeping God : " From henceforth," etc. II. The effect of this hope. 1. The humility and dependence in the first verse. 2. The contentment and weaning in the second verse. Would Israel be thus humble and obedient as a little child ? " Let Israel hope," etc.—*G. R.*

Verse 3.—*The Voice of Hope heard in the Calm.* I. Calmed souls appreciate God. Quiet favours contemplation. God's majesty, perfection, and praise so discovered. II. Calmed souls confide in God ; seen to be so worthy of trust. III. Calmed souls look fearlessly into eternity ; " from henceforth and for ever."—*W. B. H.*

Verse 3.—*Hope on, hope ever.* I. For the past warrants such confidence. II. For the present demands such confidence. III. For the future will justify such confidence.—*W. H. J. P.*

PSALM CXXXII.

TITLE.—A Song of Degrees. *A joyful song indeed : let all pilgrims to the New Jerusalem sing it often. The degrees or ascents are very visible ; the theme ascends step by step from " afflictions " to a " crown," from " remember David," to "I will make the horn of David to bud." The latter half is like the over-arching sky bending above " the fields of the wood " which are found in the resolves and prayers of the former portion.*

DIVISION.—*Our translators have rightly divided this Psalm. It contains a statement of David's anxious care to build a house for the Lord (verses 1 to 7) ; a prayer at the removal of the ark (verses 8 to 10) ; and a pleading of the divine covenant and its promises (verses 11 to 18).*

EXPOSITION.

LORD, remember David, *and* all his afflictions :
2 How he sware unto the LORD, *and* vowed unto the mighty *God* of Jacob ;
3 Surely I will not come into the tabernacle of my house, nor go up into my bed ;
4 I will not give sleep to mine eyes, *or* slumber to mine eyelids,
5 Until I find out a place for the LORD, an habitation for the mighty *God* of Jacob.
6 Lo, we heard of it at Ephratah ; we found it in the fields of the wood.
7 We will go into his tabernacles ; we will worship at his footstool.

1. "*LORD, remember David, and all his afflictions.*" With David the covenant was made, and therefore his name is pleaded on behalf of his descendants, and the people who would be blessed by his dynasty. Jehovah, who changes not, will never forget one of his servants, or fail to keep his covenant ; yet for this thing he is to be entreated. That which we are assured the Lord will do must, nevertheless, be made a matter of prayer. The request is that the Lord would *remember*, and this is a word full of meaning. We know that the Lord remembered Noah, and assuaged the flood ; he remembered Abraham, and sent Lot out of Sodom ; he remembered Rachel, and Hannah, and gave them children ; he remembered his mercy to the house of Israel, and delivered his people. That is a choice song wherein we sing, " He *remembered us* in our low estate : for his mercy endureth for ever "; and that is a notable prayer, " Lord, remember me." The plea is urged with God that he would bless the family of David for the sake of their progenitor ; how much stronger is our master-argument in prayer that God would deal well with us for Jesus' sake ! David had no personal merit ; the plea is based upon the covenant graciously made with him : but Jesus has deserts which are his own, and of boundless merit—these we may urge without hesitation. When the Lord was angry with the reigning prince, the people cried, " Lord, remember David " ; and when they needed any special blessing, again they sang, " Lord, remember David." This was good pleading, but it was not so good as ours, which runs on this wise, " Lord, remember *Jesus*, and all his afflictions."

The *afflictions* of David here meant were those which came upon him as a godly man in his endeavours to maintain the worship of Jehovah, and to provide for its decent and suitable celebration. There was always an ungodly party in the nation, and these persons were never slow to slander, hinder, and molest the servant of the Lord. Whatever were David's faults, he kept true to the one, only, living, and true God ; and for this he was a speckled bird among monarchs. Since he zealously delighted in the worship of Jehovah, his God, he was despised and ridiculed by those who could not understand his enthusiasm. God will never forget what his people suffer for his sake. No doubt innumerable blessings descend upon families and nations through the godly lives and patient sufferings of the saints. We cannot be saved by the merits of others, but beyond all question we are benefited by their virtues. Paul saith, " God is not unrighteous to forget your work and labour of love, which ye have showed toward his name." Under the New Testament dispensation, as well as under the Old, there is a full reward for the righteous. That reward frequently comes upon their descendants rather than upon themselves : they sow, and their successors reap. We may at this day pray—Lord, remember the martyrs and confessors of our race, who suffered for thy name's sake, and bless our people and nation with gospel grace for our fathers' sakes.

2. *"How he sware unto the* LORD, *and vowed unto the mighty God of Jacob."* Moved by intense devotion, David expressed his resolve in the form of a solemn vow, which was sealed with an oath. The fewer of such vows the better under a dispensation whose great Representative has said, " swear not at all." Perhaps even in this case it had been wiser to have left the pious resolve in the hands of God in the form of a prayer ; for the vow was not actually fulfilled as intended, since the Lord forbade David to build him a temple. We had better not swear to do anything before we know the Lord's mind about it, and then we shall not need to swear. The instance of David's vow shows that vows are allowable, but it does not prove that they are desirable. Probably David went too far in his words, and it is well that the Lord did not hold him to the letter of his bond, but accepted the will for the deed, and the meaning of his promise instead of the literal sense of it. David imitated Jacob, that great maker of vows at Bethel, and upon him rested the blessing pronounced on Jacob by Isaac, " God Almighty bless thee " (Gen. xxviii. 3), which was remembered by the patriarch on his death-bed, when he spoke of " the mighty God of Jacob." God is mighty to hear us, and to help us in performing our vow. We should be full of awe at the idea of making any promise to the Mighty God : to dare to trifle with him would be grievous indeed. It is observable that affliction led both David and Jacob into covenant dealings with the Lord : many vows are made in anguish of soul. We may also remark that if the votive obligations of David are to be remembered of the Lord, much more are the suretiship engagements of the Lord Jesus before the mind of the great Lord, to whom our soul turns in the hour of our distress.

Note, upon this verse, that Jehovah was the God of Jacob, the same God evermore ; that he had this for his attribute, that he is mighty—mighty to succour his Jacobs who put their trust in him, though their afflictions be many. He is, moreover, specially *the Mighty One* of his people ; he is the God of Jacob in a sense in which he is not the God of unbelievers. So here we have three points concerning our God :—*name*, Jehovah ; *attribute*, mighty ; *special relationship*, "mighty God of Jacob." He it is who is asked to remember David and his trials, and there is a plea for that blessing in each one of the three points.

3. *"Surely I will not come into the tabernacle of my house, nor go up into my bed."* Our translators give the meaning though not the literal form, of David's vow, which ran thus, " If I go "—" If I go up," etc. This was an elliptical form of imprecation, implying more than it expressed, and having therefore about it a mystery which made it all the more solemn. David would not take his ease in his house, nor his rest in his bed, till he had determined upon a place for the worship of Jehovah. The ark had been neglected, the Tabernacle had fallen into disrespect ; he would find the ark, and build for it a suitable house ; he felt that he could not take pleasure in his own palace till this was done. David meant well, but he spake more than he could carry out. His language was hyperbolical, and the Lord knew what he meant : zeal does not always measure its terms, for it is not thoughtful of the criticisms of men, but is carried away with love to the Lord, who reads the hearts of his people. David would not think himself housed till he had built a house for the Lord, nor would he reckon himself rested till he had said, "Arise, O Lord, into thy rest." Alas, we have many around us who will never carry their care for the Lord's worship too far ! No fear of their being indiscreet ! They are housed and bedded, and as for the Lord, his people may meet in a barn, or never meet at all, it will be all the same to them. Observe that Jacob in his vow spoke of the stone being God's house, and David's vow also deals with a house for God.

4. *"I will not give sleep to mine eyes, or slumber to mine eyelids."* He could not enjoy sleep till he had done his best to provide a place for the ark. It is a strong expression, and it is not to be coolly discussed by us. Remember that the man was all on fire, and he was writing poetry also, and therefore his language is not

that which we should employ in cold blood. Everybody can see what he means, and how intensely he means it. Oh, that many more were seized with sleeplessness because the house of the Lord lies waste ! They can slumber fast enough and not even disturb themselves with a dream, though the cause of God should be brought to the lowest ebb by their covetousness. What is to become of those who have no care about divine things, and never give a thought to the claims of their God ?

5. *"Until I find out a place for the LORD, an habitation for the mighty God of Jacob."* He resolved to find a place where Jehovah would allow his worship to be celebrated, a house where God would fix the symbol of his presence, and commune with his people. At that time, in all David's land, there was no proper place for that ark whereon the Lord had placed the mercy-seat, where prayer could be offered, and where the manifested glory shone forth. All things had fallen into decay, and the outward forms of public worship were too much disregarded ; hence the King resolves to be first and foremost in establishing a better order of things.

Yet one cannot help remembering that the holy resolve of David gave to a place and a house much more importance than the Lord himself ever attached to such matters. This is indicated in Nathan's message from the Lord to the king—" Go and tell my servant David, Thus saith the Lord, Shalt thou build me an house for me to dwell in ? Whereas I have not dwelt in any house since the time that I brought up the children of Israel out of Egypt, even to this day, but have walked in a tent and in a tabernacle. In all the places wherein I have walked with all the children of Israel, spake I a word with any of the tribes of Israel, whom I commanded to feed my people Israel, saying, Why build ye not me an house of cedar ? " Stephen in his inspired speech puts the matter plainly : " Solomon built him an house. Howbeit the Most High dwelleth not in temples made with hands." It is a striking fact that true religion never flourished more in Israel than before the temple was built, and that from the day of the erection of that magnificent house the spirit of godliness declined. Good men may have on their hearts matters which seem to them of chief importance, and it may be acceptable with God that they should seek to carry them out ; and yet in his infinite wisdom he may judge it best to prevent their executing their designs. God does not measure his people's actions by their wisdom or want of wisdom, but by the sincere desire for his glory which has led up to them. David's resolution, though he was not allowed to fulfil it, brought a blessing upon him : the Lord promised to build the house of David, because he had desired to build the house of the Lord. Moreover, the King was allowed to prepare the treasure for the erection of the glorious edifice which was built by his son and successor. The Lord shows the acceptance of what we desire to do by permitting us to do something else which his infinite mind judges to be fitter for us, and more honourable to himself.

6. Meanwhile, where was the habitation of God among men ? He was wont to shine forth from between the cherubim, but where was the ark ? It was like a hidden thing, a stranger in its own land. *"Lo, we heard of it at Ephratah."* Rumours came that it was somewhere in the land of Ephraim, in a temporary lodging ; rather an object of dread than of delight. Is it not wonderful that so renowned a symbol of the presence of the Lord should be lingering in neglect—a neglect so great that it was remarkable that we should have heard of its whereabouts at all ? When a man begins to think upon God and his service it is comforting that the gospel is heard of. Considering the opposition which it has encountered it is marvellous that it should be heard of, and heard of in a place remote from the central city ; but yet we are sorrowful that it is only in connection with some poor despised place that we do hear of it. What is Ephratah ? Who at this time knows where it was ? How could the ark have remained there so long ?

David instituted a search for the ark. It had to be hunted for high and low ; and at last at Kirjath-jearim, the forest-city, he came upon it. How often do souls find Christ and his salvation in out-of-the-way places ! What matters where we meet with him so long as we do behold him, and find life in him ? That is a blessed Eureka which is embedded in our text—" *we found it.*" The matter began with hearing, led on to a search, and concluded in a joyful find. *"We found it in the fields of the wood."* Alas that there should be no room for the Lord in the palaces of kings, so that he must needs take to the woods. If Christ be in a wood he will yet be found of those who seek for him. He is as near in the rustic home, embowered among the trees, as in the open streets of the city ; yea, he will answer prayer offered from the heart of the black forest where the lone traveller seems out of all hope of hearing. The text presents us with an instance of one whose heart was set upon finding the place where God would meet with him ; this made him quick of hearing, and so the cheering news soon reached him. The tidings renewed his ardour, and led him to stick at no difficulties in his search ; and so it came to pass that, where he could hardly have expected it, he lighted upon the treasure which he so much prized.

7. *"We will go into his tabernacles."* Having found the place where he dwells we will hasten thereto. He has many dwellings in one in the various courts of his house, and each of these shall receive the reverence due : in each the priest shall offer for us the appointed service ; and our hearts shall go where our bodies may not enter. David is not alone, he is represented as having sought for the ark with others, for so the word *" we "* implies ; and now they are glad to attend him in his pilgrimage to the chosen shrine, saying, *"We* found it, *we* will go." Because these are the Lord's courts we will resort to them. *"We will worship at his footstool."* The best ordered earthly house can be no more than the footstool of so great a King. His ark can only reveal the glories of his feet, according to his promise that he will make the place of his feet glorious : yet thither will we hasten with joy, in glad companionship, and there will we adore him. Where Jehovah is, there shall he be worshipped. It is well not only to go to the Lord's house, but to *worship* there : we do but profane his tabernacles if we enter them for any other purpose.

Before leaving this verse let us note the ascent of this Psalm of degrees—" we heard. . . . we found . . . we will go . . . we will worship."

8 Arise, O LORD, into thy rest ; thou, and the ark of thy strength.

9 Let thy priests be clothed with righteousness ; and let thy saints shout for joy.

10 For thy servant David's sake turn not away the face of thine anointed.

8. In these three verses we see the finders of the ark removing it to its appointed place, using a formula somewhat like to that used by Moses when he said, " Rise up, Lord," and again, " Return, O Lord, unto the many thousands of Israel." The ark had been long upon the move, and no fit place had been found for it in Canaan, but now devout men have prepared a temple, and they sing, *"Arise, O LORD, into thy rest ; thou, and the ark of thy strength."* They hoped that now the covenant symbol had found a permanent abode—a rest, and they trusted that Jehovah would now abide with it for ever. Vain would it be for the ark to be settled if the Lord did not continue with it, and perpetually shine forth from between the cherubim. Unless the Lord shall rest with us there is no rest for us ; unless the ark of his strength abide with us we are ourselves without strength. The ark of the covenant is here mentioned by a name which it well deserved ; for in its captivity it smote its captors, and broke their gods, and when it was brought back it guarded its own honour by the death of those who dared to treat it with disrespect. The power of God was thus connected with the sacred chest. Reverently, therefore did Solomon pray concerning it as he besought the living God to consecrate the temple by his presence. It is the Lord and the covenant, or rather say the covenant Jehovah whose presence we desire in our assemblies, and this presence is the strength of his people. Oh that the Lord would indeed abide in all the churches, and cause his power to be revealed in Zion.

9. *"Let thy priests be clothed with righteousness."* No garment is so resplendent as that of a holy character. In this glorious robe our great High-priest is evermore arrayed, and he would have all his people adorned in the same manner. Then only are priests fit to appear before the Lord, and to minister for the profit of the people, when their lives are dignified with goodness. They must ever remember that they are God's priests, and should therefore wear the livery of their Lord, which is holiness : they are not only to have righteousness, but to be clothed with it, so that upon every part of them righteousness shall be conspicuous. Whoever looks upon God's servants should see holiness if they see nothing else. Now, this righteousness of the ministers of the temple is prayed for in connection with the presence of the Lord ; and this instructs us that holiness is only to be found among those who commune with God, and only comes to them through his visitation of their spirits. God will dwell among a holy people : and on the other hand, where God is the people become holy.

"And let thy saints shout for joy." Holiness and happiness go together ; where the one is found, the other ought never to be far away. Holy persons have a right

to great and demonstrative joy : they may shout because of it. Since they are saints, and thy saints, and thou hast come to dwell with them, O Lord, thou hast made it their duty to rejoice, and to let others know of their joy. The sentence, while it may read as a permit, is also a precept : saints are commanded to rejoice in the Lord. Happy religion which makes it a duty to be glad ! Where righteousness is the clothing, joy may well be the occupation.

10. "*For thy servant David's sake turn not away the face of thine anointed.*" King Solomon was praying, and here the people pray for him that his face may not be turned away, or that he may not be refused an audience. It is a dreadful thing to have our face turned away from God, or to have his face turned away from us. If we are anointed of the Spirit the Lord will look upon us with favour. Specially is this true of HIM who represents us, and is on our behalf the *Christ*—the truly anointed of the Lord. Jesus is both our David and God's anointed ; in him is found in fulness that which David received in measure. For his sake all those who are anointed in him are accepted. God blessed Solomon and succeeding kings, for David's sake ; and he will bless us for Jesus' sake. How condescending was the Son of the Highest to take upon himself the form of a *servant*, to be anointed for us, and to go in before the mercy-seat to plead on our behalf ! The Psalm sings of the ark, and it may well remind us of the going in of the anointed priest within the veil : all depended upon his acceptance, and therefore well do the people pray, " Turn not away the face of thine anointed."

Thus, in these three verses, we have a prayer for the temple, the ark, the priests, the Levites, the people, and the king : in each petition there is a fulness of meaning well worthy of careful thought. We cannot plead too much in detail ; the fault of most prayers is their indefiniteness. In God's house and worship everything needs a blessing, and every person connected therewith needs it continually. As David vowed and prayed when he was minded to house the ark, so now the prayer is continued when the temple is consecrated, and the Lord deigns to fill it with his glory. We shall never have done praying till we have done needing.

11 The LORD hath sworn *in* truth unto David ; he will not turn from it ; Of the fruit of thy body will I set upon thy throne.

12 If thy children will keep my covenant and my testimony that I shall teach them, their children shall also sit upon thy throne for evermore.

13 For the LORD hath chosen Zion ; he hath desired *it* for his habitation.

14 This *is* my rest for ever : here will I dwell ; for I have desired it.

15 I will abundantly bless her provision : I will satisfy her poor with bread.

16 I will also clothe her priests with salvation : and her saints shall shout aloud for joy.

17 There will I make the horn of David to bud : I have ordained a lamp for mine anointed.

18 His enemies will I clothe with shame : but upon himself shall his crown flourish.

11. Here we come to a grand covenant pleading of the kind which is always prevalent with the Lord. "*The LORD hath sworn in truth unto David.*" We cannot urge anything with God which is equal to his own word and oath. Jehovah swears that our faith may have strong confidence in it : he cannot forswear himself. He swears *in truth*, for he means every word that he utters ; men may be perjured, but none will be so profane as to imagine this of the God of truth. By Nathan this covenant of Jehovah was conveyed to David, and there was no delusion in it. "*He will not turn from it.*" Jehovah is not a changeable being. He never turns from his purpose, much less from his promise solemnly ratified by oath. He turneth never. He is not a man that he should lie, nor the son of man that he should repent. What a rock they stand upon who have an immutable oath of God for their foundation ! We know that this covenant was really made with Christ, the spiritual seed of David, for Peter quotes it at Pentecost, saying, " Men and brethen, let me freely speak unto you of the patriarch David, that he is both dead and buried, and his sepulchre is with us unto this day. Therefore being a prophet, and knowing that God had sworn with an oath to him, that of the fruit of his

loins, according to the flesh, he would raise up Christ to sit on his throne ; he seeing this before spake of the resurrection of Christ." Christ therefore sits on a sure throne for ever and ever, seeing that he has kept the covenant, and through him the blessing comes upon Zion, whose poor are blessed in him. *"Of the fruit of thy body will I set upon thy throne."* Jesus sprang from the race of David, as the evangelists are careful to record ; he was " of the house and lineage of David " : at this day he is the King of the Jews, and the Lord has also given him the heathen for his inheritance. He must reign, and of his kingdom there shall be no end. God himself has set him on the throne and no rebellion of men or devils can shake his dominion. The honour of Jehovah is concerned in his reign, and therefore it is never in danger ; for the Lord will not suffer his oath to be dishonoured.

12. *"If thy children will keep my covenant and my testimony that I shall teach them."* There is a condition to the covenant so far as it concerned kings of David's line before the coming of the true Seed ; but *he* has fulfilled that condition, and made the covenant indefeasible henceforth and for ever as to himself and the spiritual seed in him. Considered as it related to temporal things it was no small blessing for David's dynasty to be secured the throne upon good behaviour. These monarchs held their crowns from God upon the terms of loyalty to their superior Sovereign, the Lord who had elevated them to their high position. They were to be faithful to the covenant by obedience to the divine law, and by belief of divine truth. They were to accept Jehovah as their Lord and their Teacher, regarding him in both relations as in covenant with him. What a condescension on God's part to be their teacher ! How gladly ought they to render intelligent obedience ! What a proper, righteous, and needful stipulation for God to make that they should be true to him when the reward was the promise, *"Their children shall also sit upon thy throne for evermore."* If they will sit at his feet God will make them sit on a throne ; if they will keep the covenant they shall keep the crown from generation to generation.

The kingdom of Judah might have stood to this day had its kings been faithful to the Lord. No internal revolt or external attack could have overthrown the royal house of David : it fell by its own sin, and by nothing else. The Lord was continually provoked, but he was amazingly long-suffering, for long after seceding Israel had gone into captivity, Judah still remained. Miracles of mercy were shown to her. Divine patience exceeded all limits, for the Lord's regard for David was exceeding great. The princes of David's house seemed set on ruining themselves, and nothing could save them ; justice waited long, but it was bound at last to unsheathe the sword and strike. Still, if in the letter man's breach of promise caused the covenant to fail, yet in spirit and essence the Lord has been true to it, for Jesus reigns, and holds the throne for ever. David's seed is still royal, for he was the progenitor according to the flesh of him who is King of kings and Lord of lords.

This verse shows us the need of family piety. Parents must see to it that their children know the fear of the Lord, and they must beg the Lord himself to teach them his truth. We have no hereditary right to the divine favour : the Lord keeps up his friendship to families from generation to generation, for he is loth to leave the descendants of his servants, and never does so except under grievous and long-continued provocation. As believers we are all in a measure under some such covenant as that of David : certain of us can look backward for four generations of saintly ancestors, and we are now glad to look forward to see our children, and our children's children, walking in the truth. Yet we know that grace does not run in the blood, and we are filled with holy fear lest in any of our seed there should be an evil heart of unbelief in departing from the living God.

13. *"For the LORD hath chosen Zion."* It was no more than any other Canaanite town till God chose it, David captured it, Solomon built it, and the Lord dwelt in it. So was the church a mere Jebusite stronghold till grace chose it, conquered it, rebuilt it, and dwelt in it. Jehovah has chosen his people, and hence they are his people. He has chosen the church, and hence it is what it is. Thus in the covenant David and Zion, Christ and his people, go together. David is for Zion, and Zion for David : the interests of Christ and his people are mutual. *"He hath desired it for his habitation."* David's question is answered. The Lord has spoken : the site of the temple is fixed : the place of the divine manifestation is determined. Indwelling follows upon election, and arises out of it : Zion is chosen, chosen for a habitation of God. The desire of God to dwell among the people whom he has

chosen for himself is very gracious and yet very natural : his love will not rest apart from those upon whom he has placed it. God desires to abide with those whom he has loved with an everlasting love ; and we do not wonder that it should be so, for we also desire the company of our beloved ones. It is a double marvel, that the Lord should choose and desire such poor creatures as we are : the indwelling of the Holy Ghost in believers is a wonder of grace parallel to the incarnation of the Son of God. God in the church is the wonder of heaven, the miracle of eternity, the glory of infinite love.

14. *"This is my rest for ever."* Oh, glorious words ! It is God himself who here speaks. Think of rest for God ! A Sabbath for the Eternal and a place of abiding for the Infinite. He calls Zion *my rest.* Here his love remains and displays itself with delight. " He shall rest in his love." And this *for ever.* He will not seek another place of repose, nor grow weary of his saints. In Christ the heart of Deity is filled with content, and for his sake he is satisfied with his people, and will be so world without end. These august words declare a distinctive choice—*this* and no other ; a certain choice—*this* which is well known to me ; a present choice— *this* which is here at this moment. God has made his election of old, he has not changed it, and he never will repent of it : his church was his rest and *is* his rest still. As he will not turn from his oath, so he will never turn from his choice. Oh, that we may enter into *his* rest, may be part and parcel of his church, and yield by our loving faith a delight to the mind of him who taketh pleasure in them that fear him, in them that hope in his mercy. *"Here will I dwell ; for I have desired it."* Again are we filled with wonder that he who fills all things should dwell in Zion—should dwell in his church. God does not unwillingly visit his chosen ; he desires to dwell with them ; he desires them. He is already in Zion, for he says *here,* as one upon the spot. Not only will he occasionally come to his church, but he will dwell in it, as his fixed abode. He cared not for the magnificence of Solomon's temple, but he determined that at the mercy-seat he would be found by suppliants, and that thence he would shine forth in brightness of grace among the favoured nation. All this, however, was but a type of the spiritual house, of which Jesus is foundation and cornerstone, upon which all the living stones are builded together for an habitation of God through the Spirit. Oh, the sweetness of the thought that God *desires* to dwell in his people and rest among them ! Surely if it be his desire he will cause it to be so. If the desire of the righteous shall be granted much more shall the desire of the righteous God be accomplished. This is the joy of our souls, for surely we shall rest in God, and certainly our desire is to dwell in him. This also is the end of our fears for the church of God ; for if the Lord dwell in her, she shall not be moved ; if the Lord desire her, the devil cannot destroy her.

15. *"I will abundantly bless her provision."* It must be so. How can we be without a blessing when the Lord is among us ? We live upon his word, we are clothed by his charity, we are armed by his power : all sorts of provision are in him, and how can they be otherwise than blessed ? The provision is to be *abundantly blessed ;* then it will be abundant and blessed. Daily provision, royal provision, satisfying provision, overflowingly joyful provision the church shall receive ; and the divine benediction shall cause us to receive it with faith, to feed upon it by experience, to grow upon it by sanctification, to be strengthened by it to labour, cheered by it to patience, and built up by it to perfection. *"I will satisfy her poor with bread."* The citizens of Zion are poor in themselves, poor in spirit, and often poor in pocket, but their hearts and souls shall dwell in such abundance that they shall neither need more nor desire more. Satisfaction is the crown of experience. Where God rests his people shall be satisfied. They are to be satisfied with what the Lord himself calls " bread," and we may be sure that he knows what is really bread for souls. He will not give us a stone. The Lord's poor shall " have food convenient for them " : that which will suit their palate, remove their hunger, fill their desire, build up their frame, and perfect their growth. The bread of earth is " the bread that perisheth," but the bread of God endureth to life eternal. In the church where God rests his people shall not starve ; the Lord would never rest if they did. He did not take rest for six days till he had prepared the world for the first man to live in ; he would not stay his hand till all things were ready ; therefore, we may be sure if the Lord rests it is because " it is finished," and the Lord hath prepared of his goodness for the poor. Where God finds his desire his people shall find theirs ; if he is satisfied, they shall be.

Taking the two clauses together, we see that nothing but an abundant blessing in the church will satisfy the Lord's poor people : they are naked and miserable till that comes. All the provision that Solomon himself could make would not have satisfied the saints of his day : they looked higher, and longed for the Lord's own boundless blessing, and hungered for the bread which came down from heaven. Blessed be the Lord, they had in this verse two of the " I wills " of God to rest upon, and nothing could be a better support to their faith.

16. More is promised than was prayed for. See how the ninth verse asks for the priests to be clad in righteousness, and the answer is, *"I will also clothe her priests with salvation."* God is wont to do exceeding abundantly, above all that we ask or even think. Righteousness is but one feature of blessing, salvation is the whole of it. What cloth of gold is this ! What more than regal array ! Garments of salvation ! we know who has woven them, who has dyed them, and who has given them to his people. These are the best robes for priests and preachers, for princes and people ; there is none like them ; give them me. Not every priest shall be thus clothed, but only *her* priests, those who truly belong to Zion, by faith which is in Christ Jesus, who hath made them priests unto God. These are clothed by the Lord himself, and none can clothe as he does. If even the grass of the field is so clothed by the Creator as to outvie Solomon in all his glory, how must his own children be clad ? Truly he shall be admired in his saints ; the liveries of his servants shall be the wonder of heaven. *"And her saints shall shout aloud for joy."* Again we have a golden answer to a silver prayer. The Psalmist would have the " saints shout for joy." " That they shall do," saith the Lord, " and *aloud* too " ; they shall be exceedingly full of delight ; their songs and shouts shall be so hearty that they shall sound as the noise of many waters, and as great thunders. These joyful ones are not, however, the mimic saints of superstition, but *her* saints, saints of the Most High, " sanctified in Christ Jesus." These shall be so abundantly blessed and so satisfied, and so apparelled that they can do no otherwise than shout to show their astonishment, their triumph, their gratitude, their exultation, their enthusiasm, their joy in the Lord. Zion has no dumb saints. The sight of God at rest among his chosen is enough to make the most silent shout. If the morning stars sang together when the earth and heavens were made, much more will all the sons of God shout for joy when the new heavens and the new earth are finished, and the New Jerusalem comes down out of heaven from God, prepared as a bride for her husband. Meanwhile, even now the dwelling of the Lord among us is a perennial fountain of sparkling delight to all holy minds. This shouting for joy is guaranteed to Zion's holy ones : God says they *shall* shout aloud, and depend upon it they will : who shall stop them of this glorying ? The Lord hath said by his Spirit, " let them shout," and then he has promised that " they shall shout aloud " : who is he that shall make them hold their peace ? The Bridegroom is with them, and shall the children of the bride-chamber fast ? Nay, verily, we rejoice, yea and will rejoice.

17. *"There will I make the horn of David to bud."* In Zion David's dynasty shall develop power and glory. In our notes from other authors we have included a description of the growth of the horns of stags, which is the natural fact from which we conceive the expression in the text to be borrowed. As the stag is made noble and strong by the development of his horns, so the house of David shall advance from strength to strength. This was to be by the work of the Lord—" there will I make," and therefore it would be sure and solid growth. When God makes us to bud none can cause us to fade. When David's descendants left the Lord and the worship of his house, they declined in all respects, for it was only through the Lord, and in connection with his worship that their horn would bud.

"I have ordained a lamp for mine anointed." David's name was to be illustrious, and brilliant as a lamp ; it was to continue shining like a lamp in the sanctuary ; it was thus to be a comfort to the people, and an enlightenment to the nations. God would not suffer the light of David to go out by the extinction of his race : his holy ordinances had decreed that the house of his servant should remain in the midst of Israel. What a lamp is our Lord Jesus ! A light to lighten the Gentiles, and the glory of his people Israel. As the anointed—the true Christ, he shall be the light of heaven itself. Oh for grace to receive our illumination and our consolation from Jesus Christ alone.

18. *"His enemies will I clothe with shame."* They shall be utterly defeated, they shall loathe their evil design, they shall be despised for having hated the Ever Blessed One. Their shame they will be unable to hide, it shall cover them : God

will array them in it for ever, and it shall be their convict dress to all eternity. *"But upon himself shall his crown flourish."* Green shall be his laurels of victory. He shall win and wear the crown of honour, and his inherited diadem shall increase in splendour. Is it not so to this hour with Jesus ? His kingdom cannot fail, his imperial glories cannot fade. It is *himself* that we delight to honour ; it is to himself that the honour comes, and upon himself that it flourishes. If others snatch at his crown their traitorous aims are defeated ; but he in his own person reigns with ever growing splendour.

> " Crown him, crown him,
> Crowns become the victor's brow."

EXPLANATORY NOTES AND QUAINT SAYINGS.

Whole Psalm.—Lightfoot ascribes this Psalm to David, and supposes it to have been composed on the second removal of the ark from the house of Obed-edom : 1 Chron. xv. 4, etc. But the mention of David's name in the tenth verse in the third person, and the terms there employed, militate against his being the author. Others ascribe it to Solomon, who, they think, wrote it about the time of the removing of the ark into the Temple which he had built for it : 2 Chron. v. 2, etc. Others are of opinion, that it was composed by Solomon for the solemn services that were celebrated at the dedication of the Temple.—*James Anderson's note to Calvin in loc.*

Whole Psalm.—The Psalm is divided into four stanzas of ten lines, each of which contains the name of David. The first part begins with speaking of David's vow to the Lord ; the third with the Lord's promise to David.—*William Kay.*

Whole Psalm.—The parallelisms need to be traced with some care. Verses 1, 2, 3, 4, 5, 6 are answered by verse 12 ; verse 7 by verse 13 ; verse 8 by verse 14 ; verse 9 by verses 15, 16 ; verse 10 by verses 17, 18.

An attention to these parallelisms is often necessary to bring out the meaning of Scripture.—*Joseph Angus, in "The Bible Handbook,"* 1862.

Verse 1.—*" Lord, remember."* It is a gracious privilege to be permitted to be God's remembrancers. Faith is encouraged to remind him of his covenant, and of his precious promises. There is, indeed, no forgetfulness with him. The past, as also the future, is a present page before his eye. But by this exercise we impress on our own minds invaluable lessons.—*Henry Law.*

Verse 1.—*"Remember David, and all his afflictions."* Solomon was a wise man, yet pleads not any merit of his own ;—I am not worthy, for whom thou shouldst do this, but, " Lord, remember David," with whom thou madest the covenant ; as Moses prayed (Exod. xxxii. 13), *"Remember Abraham,"* the first trustee of the covenant ; remember *"all his afflictions,"* all the troubles of his life, which his being anointed was the occasion of ; or his care and concern about the ark, and what an uneasiness it was to him that the ark was in curtains (2 Sam. vii. 2). *Remember all his humility and weakness,* so some read it ; all that pious and devout affection with which he had made the following vow.—*Matthew Henry.*

Verse 1.—*"Remember . . . all his afflictions."* The sufferings of believers for the cause of truth are not meritorious, but neither are they in vain ; they are not forgotten by God. .Matt. v. 11, 12.—*Christopher Starke,* 1740.

Verse 1.—*"Afflictions."* The Hebrew word for *"afflictions"* is akin to the word for " trouble " in 1 Chron. xxii. 14 : " Now, behold, in my *trouble* I have prepared for the house of the Lord an hundred thousand talents of gold."—*H. T. Armfield.*

Verses 1, 2.—If the Jew could rightly appeal to God to show mercy to his church and nation for the sake of that shepherd youth whom he had advanced to the kingdom, much more shall we justly plead our cause in the name of David's son (called *David* four times in the prophets), and of *all his trouble,* all the sorrows of his birth and infancy, his ministry and passion and death, which he bore as a consequence of his self-dedication to his Father's will, when his priesthood, foreordained from all eternity, was confirmed with an oath, " for those [Levitical] priests were made without [swearing] an oath ; but this with an oath by him that said unto him, The

Lord sware and will not repent, Thou art a priest for ever after the order of Melchizedek ": Heb. vii. 21 ; Ps. cx. 4.—*Theodoret and Cassiodorus, in Neale and Littledale.*

Verse 2.—*"And vowed."* The history does not record the time nor the occasion of this vow ; but history does record how it was ever in David's thoughts and on David's heart. David, indeed, in the first verse, asks of God to remember his afflictions, and then records his vow ; and you may, perhaps, think that the vow was the consequence of his afflictions, and that he made it contingent on his deliverance. . . . It is far more consistent with the character of David to look upon the affliction to which he alludes as resulting from the Lord's not permitting him to carry out his purpose of erecting an earthly habitation for the God of heaven, inasmuch as he had shed blood abundantly. And if, as is more than probable, amid that blood which he had shed, David's conscience recalled the blood of Uriah as swelling the measure, he could not but be deeply afflicted, even while he acknowledged the righteousness of the sentence.

But though not permitted of God to execute his purpose, we cannot but feel and own that it was a noble resolution which David here makes ; and though recorded in all the amplification of Oriental imagery, it expresses the holy determination of the Psalmist to forego every occupation and pursuit, and not to allow a single day to elapse till he had at least fixed on the site of the future temple.—*Barton Bouchier.*

Verse 2.—*"He vowed."* He who is ready to vow on every occasion will break his vow on every occasion. It is a necessary rule, that " we be as sparing in making our vows as may be " ; there being many great inconveniences attending frequent and multiplied vows. It is very observable, that the Scripture mentioneth very few examples of vows, compared with the many instances of very great and wonderful providences ; as if it would give us some instances, that we might know what we have to do, and yet would give us but few, that we might know we are not to do it often. You read Jacob lived seven score and seven years (Gen. xlvii. 28) ; but you read, I think, but of one vow that he made. Our extraordinary exigencies are not many ; and, I say, our vows should not be more. Let this, then, be the first necessary ingredient of a well-ordered vow. Let it be no oftener made than the pressing greatness of an evil to be removed, or the alluring excellency of a blessing extraordinary to be obtained, will well warrant. Jephthah's vow was so far right ; he had just occasion ; there was a great and pressing danger to be removed ; there was an excellent blessing to be obtained : the danger was, lest Israel should be enslaved ; the blessing was victory over their enemies. This warranted his vow, though his rashness marred it. It was in David's troubles that David sware, and vowed a vow to the Most High ; and Jacob forbare to vow until his more than ordinary case bade him vow, and warranted him in so doing : Gen. xxviii. 20. Let us do as he did,—spare to vow, until such case puts us on it.—*Henry Hurst* (1629 ?— 1690), *in "The Morning Exercises."*

Verse 2.—*"Vowed unto the mighty God of Jacob."* The first holy votary that ever we read of was Jacob here mentioned in this text, who is therefore called the father of vows : and upon this account some think David mentions God here under the title of *"the mighty God of Jacob,"* rather than any other, because of his vow.— *Abraham Wright.*

Verse 2.—*"The mighty God of Jacob."* The title *strong one of Jacob*, by which God is here designated, first used by Jacob himself, Gen. xlix. 24, and thence more generally used as is clear from Isaiah i. 24, xlix. 26, and other places, here sets forth God both as the *most mighty* who is able most severely to punish perjury, and with whom no one may dare to contend, and also as the *defender* and most mighty vindicator of Israel, such as Jacob had proved him, and all his descendants, in particular David, who frequently rejoiced and gloried in this mighty one and defender. Such a mighty one of Jacob was worthy to have a temple built for him, and was so great that he would not suffer perjury.—*Hermann Venema.*

Verse 2.—Where the interpreters have translated, *"the God of Jacob,"* it is in the Hebrew, *"the mighty in Jacob."* Which name is sometimes attributed unto the angels, and sometimes it is also applied to other things wherein are great strength and fortitude ; as to a lion, an ox, and such like. But here it is a singular word of faith, signifying that God is the power and strength of his people ; for only faith ascribeth this unto God. Reason and the flesh do attribute more to riches, and such other worldly helps as man seeth and knoweth. All such carnal helps are very

Idols, which deceive men, and draw them to perdition ; but this is the strength and fortitude of the people, to have God present with them. . . . So the Scripture saith in another place : " Some trust in chariots, and some in horses, but we will remember the name of the Lord." Likewise Paul saith : " Be strong in the Lord, and in the power of his might." For this power is eternal, and deceiveth not. All other powers are not only deceitful, but they are transitory, and continue but for a moment.—*Martin Luther.*

Verse 3.—*"Surely I will not come into the tabernacle of my house,"* etc. To avoid the absurdity of thinking that David should make such a rash and unwarrantable vow as this might seem to be, that till he had his desire satisfied in that which is afterwards expressed he would abide in the open air, and never go within his doors, nor ever take any rest, either by day or by night, some say that David spake this with reference to his purpose of taking the fort of Zion from the Jebusites (2 Sam. v. 6), where by revelation he knew that God meant to have the ark settled, and which he might probably think would be accomplished within some short time. And then others again say, that he meant it only of that stately cedar house, which he had lately built for himself at Jerusalem (2 Sam. vii. 1, 2), to wit, that he would not go into that house ; and so also that he would not go up unto his bed, nor (verse 4) give any sleep to his eyes, nor slumber to his eyelids, to wit, in that house. But neither of these expositions give me any satisfaction. I rather take these to be hyperbolical expressions of the continual, exceeding great care wherewith he was perplexed about providing a settled place for the ark to rest in, like that in Prov. vi. 4, 5 : " Give not sleep to thine eyes, nor slumber to thine eyelids ; deliver thyself as a roe from the hand of the hunter," etc. Neither is it any more in effect than if he had said, I will never lay by this care to mind myself in anything whatsoever : I shall never with any content abide in mine own house, nor with any quiet rest in my bed, until, etc.—*Arthur Jackson,* 1593—1666.

Verse 3.—*"Surely I will not come into the tabernacle of my house,"* etc. When he had built himself a palace (1 Chron. xv. 1), it appears by the context, that he did not *bless* it (ch. xvi. 43), nor consequently live in it (for that he might not do till it were blest) until he had first prepared a place, and brought up the ark to it.—*Henry Hammond.*

Verse 3.—*"Surely I will not come,"* etc. Our translation of the verse is justified by Aben Ezra, who remarks that אם is here to be translated not in its usual sense of " if,"—" if I shall come "—but as introducing a vow, " I will not come." This idiom, it may be observed, is more or less missed by our existing translation of Hebrews iv. 5 : " And in this place again, If they shall enter into my rest "—a translation which is the more curious from the fact that the idiom in the present Psalm is hit off exactly in the preceding chapter, Hebrews iii. 11 : " So I sware in my wrath, They shall not enter into my rest."—*H. T. Armfield.*

Verse 3.—*"I will not come into the tent which is my house."* What does this singular form of expression denote ? Is it " an instance of the way in which the associations of the old patriarchal tent life fixed themselves in the language of the people," as Perowne suggests ? or does David deliberately select it to imply that even his palace is but a tent as compared with the house that he will rear for God ?—*Samuel Cox.*

Verse 3.—*"Nor go up into my bed."* From the expression of the Psalmist it would seem that a lofty bed was not only a necessary luxury, but a sign of superior rank. This idea was very prevalent in the period of the revival of the arts on the Continent, where the state bed, often six feet high, always stood on a dais in an alcove, richly curtained off from the saloon. In the East the same custom still continues, and a verse in the Koran declares it to be one of the delights of the faithful in paradise that " they shall repose themselves on lofty beds " (Cap. 56, " The Inevitable "). Frequently these state beds were composed of the most costly and magnificent materials. The prophet Amos speaks of ivory beds (Amos vi. 4) ; Nero had a golden one ; that of the Mogul Aurungzeebe was jewelled ; and, lastly, in the privy purse expenses of our own profligate Charles II., we read of a " silver bedstead for Mrs. Gwynn." And to this day the state bedsteads in the viceregal palace at Cairo are executed in the same metal, and are supposed to have cost upwards of £3,000 each.—*From "The Biblical Museum,"* 1879.

Verses 3—5.—*"Surely I will not come,"* etc. These were all types and figures of Christ, the true David, who, in his desire of raising a living temple, and an everlasting tabernacle to God, spent whole nights in prayer, and truly, neither entered his house, nor went up into his bed, nor gave slumber to his eyelids, nor rest to his temples, and presented to himself " a glorious church, not having spot, nor wrinkle, nor any such thing," nor built " with corruptible gold or silver," but with his own precious sweat and more precious blood ; it was with them he built that city in heaven that was seen by St. John in the Apocalypse, and " was ornamented with all manner of precious stones."   Hence, we can all understand the amount of care, cost, and labour we need to erect a becoming temple in our hearts to God.—*Robert Bellarmine (1542—1621), in "A Commentary on the Book of Psalms."*

Verses 3—5.—This admirable zeal of this pious king condemns the indifference of those who leave the sacred places which are dependent upon their care in a condition of shameful neglect, while they lavish all their care to make for themselves sumptuous houses.—*Pasquier Quesnel (1634—1719), dans "Les Pseaumes, avec des Reflexions,"* 1700.

Verse 5.—"*An habitation for the mighty God of Jacob.*"   Jacob " vowed a vow," when he declared, " this . . . shall be God's house " : Gen. xxviii. 20—22.   David accordingly preserved a reminiscence of the fact, when he vowed a vow in connection with a similar object.—*H. T. Armfield.*

Verse 6.—"*We heard of it at Ephratah.*"   This is commonly understood of Bethlehem, as that place had this name.   But the ark never was at Bethlehem, at least we read of no such thing.   There was a district called by this name, or one closely resembling it, where Elkanah, Samuel's father, lived, and whence Jeroboam came, both of whom are called Ephrathites.   1 Sam. i. 1 ; 1 Kings xi. 26.   This was in the tribe of Ephraim, and is probably the place meant by the Psalmist.   Now the ark had been for a long series of years at Shiloh, which is in Ephraim, when it was taken to be present at the battle with the Philistines, in which Hophni and Phinehas, the sons of Eli, were slain, and when thirty thousand of the Israelites lost their lives, together with the capture of the ark.   The frightful report of this calamity was brought to Eli, and occasioned his instant death.   This appears to be the event referred to in the words, "*We heard of it at Ephratah*" ;   and a grievous report it was, not likely to be soon forgotten.

"*We found it in the fields of Jaar.*"   After the ark had been for some time in the land of the Philistines, they sent it away, and it came to Bethshemesh, in the tribe of Judah.   1 Sam. vi. 12.   In the immediate vicinity of this place was also Kirjath-jearim, i.e. the city of Jaar, to which the ark was removed ; for the Bethshemites were afraid to retain it, as many thousands of them had lost their lives, for the violation of the sanctity of the ark, by looking into it.   As this slaughter took place close by, if not in the fields of Jaar, the Psalmist, with reference to it, says, "*We found it in the fields of Jaar.*"   Having glanced at these two afflictive and memorable events, he goes on with his direct design, of encouraging the people to perform due honour to the ark, and to the temple, by contrasting with the sad occurrences to which he had adverted their present joy and prosperity.—*William Walford, in "The Book of Psalms.   A New Translation, with Notes."   1837.*

Verse 6.—"*We heard of it at Ephratah,*" etc.   Either of the ark which David and others had heard of, that it formerly was at Shiloh (Josh. xviii. 1), here called Ephratah, as some think ; so the Ephraimites are called Ephrathites (Jud. xii. 5) ; and Elkanah of Ramathaim-zophim, of Mount Ephraim, is said to be an Ephrathite (1 Sam. i. 1) ; but this tribe the Lord chose not, but the tribe of Judah, for his habitation ; and rejected the tabernacle of Shiloh, and removed it from thence (Ps. lxxviii. 60, 67, 68).   "*We found it in the fields of the wood ;*" at Kirjath-jearim, which signifies *the city of woods ;* being built among woods, and surrounded with them : here the ark was twenty years, and here David found it ; and from hence he brought it to the house of Obed-edom, and from thence to Zion.

Christ has been *found in the fields of the wood ;* in a low, mean, abject state, as this phrase signifies : Ezek. xvi. 5.   The shepherds found him rejected from being in the inn, there being no room for him, and lying in a manger (Luke ii. 7, 16) ; the angels found him in the wilderness, among the wild beasts of the field (Mark i. 13) ; nor had he the convenience even of foxes and birds of the air ; he had no habitation or place where to lay his head : Matt. viii. 20.   And he is to be found in the field of the Scriptures, where this rich treasure and pearl of great price lies hid : Matt. xiii. 44.—*John Gill.*

Verse 6.—"We heard of it at Ephratah."　The only explanation, equally agreeable to usage and the context, is that which makes Ephratah the ancient name of Bethlehem (Gen. xlviii. 7), here mentioned as the place where David spent his youth, and where he used to hear of the ark, although he never saw it till long afterwards, when he found it in the fields of the wood, in the neighbourhood of *Kirjath-jearim*, which name means Forest-town, or City of the Woods.　Compare 1 Sam vii. 1 with 2 Sam. vi. 3, 4.—*Joseph Addison Alexander.*

Verse 6.—"We heard of it at Ephratah," etc.　Having prepared a sumptuous tabernacle, or tent, for the ark on Mount Zion, in the "City of David," a great national assembly was summoned, at which all the tribes were invited to attend its removal to this new sanctuary.　The excitement spread over all Israel.　"We heard men say at Ephratah [Bethlehem], in the south of the land, and we found them repeat it in the woody Lebanon," sings the writer of the 132nd Psalm, according to Ewald's rendering.　"Let us go into his tabernacle; let us worship at his footstool."　The very words of the summons were fitted to rouse the deepest feelings of the nation, for they were to gather at Baalah, of Judah, another name for Kirjath-jearim, to "bring up thence" to the mountain capital "the Ark of God, called by the name, the name of Jehovah of Hosts that dwelleth between the cherubim": 2 Sam. vi. 2.　It "had not been enquired at in the days of Saul": but, when restored, the nation would have their great palladium once more in their midst, and could "appear before God in Zion," and be instructed and taught in the way they should go.—*Cunningham Geikie, in "Hours with the Bible,"* 1881.

Verse 6.—"Ephratah."　The Psalmist says, that David himself, even when a youth in Bethlehem-Ephratah, heard of the sojourn of the ark in Kirjath-jearim, and that it was a fond dream of David's boyhood to be permitted to bring up the ark to some settled habitation, which he desired *to find* (verse 5).—*Christopher Wordsworth.*

Verse 6.—"We found it."　The church can never long be hid.　The sun reappears after a short eclipse.—*Henry Law.*

*Verse 6.—*It is not always where we first seek God that he is to be found.　"We *heard* of it at Ephratah: we *found* it in the fields of the wood."　We must not be governed by hearsay in seeking for God in Christ; but seek for ourselves until we find.　It is not in every house of prayer that God in Christ can be found: after seeking him in gorgeous temples we may find him "in the fields of the woods."　"If any man shall say unto you, Lo, here is Christ, or lo, there; believe it not" upon his own testimony, but seek him for yourselves.—*George Rogers,* 1883.

Verse 7.—"We will go . . . we will worship."　Note their agreement and joint consent, which is visible in the pronoun *"we"*: "We will go."　"We" taketh in a whole nation, a whole people, the whole world, and maketh them one.　*"We"* maketh a commonwealth; and *"we"* maketh a church.　We go up to the house of the Lord together, and we hope to go to heaven together.　Note their alacrity and cheerfulness in going.　Their long absence rendered the object more glorious. For, what we love and want, we love the more and desire the more earnestly.　When Hezekiah, having been "sick unto death," had a longer lease of life granted him, he asketh the question, "What is the sign" (not, *that I shall live,* but) "that I shall go up to the house of the Lord?"　Isaiah xxxviii. 1—22.　Love is on the wing, cheerful to meet its object; yea, it reacheth it at a distance, and is united to it while it is afar off. . . . *"We will go."*　We long to be there.　We will hasten our pace.　We will break through all difficulties in the way.—*Condensed from Anthony Farindon.*

Verse 7 (first clause).—"Tabernacles" are spoken of in the plural number, and this it may be (though we may doubt whether the Psalmist had such minute distinctions in his eye) because there was in the Temple an inner sanctuary, a middle apartment, and then the court.　It is of more importance to attend to the epithet which follows, where the Psalmist calls the Ark of the Covenant *God's footstool,* to intimate that the sanctuary could never contain the immensity of God's essence, as men were apt absurdly to imagine.　The mere outward Temple with all its majesty being no more than his footstool, his people were called upon to look upwards to the heavens, and fix their contemplations with due reverence upon God himself.— *John Calvin.*

*Verse 7.—*The Lord's *"footstool"* here mentioned was either *the Ark of the Testimony* itself, or the place at least where it stood, called *Debir,* or the *Holy of*

Holies, towards which the Jews in their temple used to worship. The very next words argue so much : *"Arise, O LORD, into thy rest ; thou, and the ark of thy strength " ;* and it is plain out of 1 Chron. xxviii. 2, where David saith concerning his purpose to have built God an house, " I had in mine heart to build an house of rest for the ark of the covenant of the Lord, and for the *footstool* of our God," where the conjunction *and* is exegetical, and the same with *that is.* According to this expression the prophet Jeremy also, in the beginning of the second of his Lamentations, bewaileth that " the Lord had cast down the beauty of Israel " (that is, his glorious Temple), " and remembered not his *footstool* " (that is, the Ark of the Covenant), " in the day of his wrath " ; as Isaiah lx. 7, and lxiv. 11 ; Ps. xcvi. 6.

That this is the true and genuine meaning of this phrase of *worshipping the Lord towards his footstool*, besides the confessed custom of the time, is evidently confirmed by a parallel expression of this worshipping posture (Ps. xxviii. 2) : " Hear the voice of my supplications when I cry unto thee, when I lift up mine hands אֶל־דְּבִיר קָדְשֶׁ towards thy *holy oracle"* ; that is, towards the Most Holy place where the ark stood, and from whence God gave his answers. For that דביר *Debir*, which is here translated *"oracle"*, was the *Sanctum Sanctorum* or Most Holy place, is clear out of the sixth and eighth chapters of the First Book of Kings ; where in the former we read (verse 19) that " Solomon prepared the *oracle* or *Debir*, to set the ark of the covenant of the Lord there " : in the latter (verse 6), that " the priests brought in the ark of the covenant of the Lord unto his place, into the oracle of the house, to the most holy place, even under the wings of the cherubims." Wherefore the authors of the translation used in our Liturgy rendered this passage of the Psalm, " When I hold up my hands toward the mercy seat of thy holy temple " ; namely, having respect to the meaning thereof. Thus you see that one of the two must needs be this *scabellum pedum*, or *"footstool"* of God, either *the ark* or *mercy-seat* itself, or the *adytum Templi*, the Most Holy place, where it stood. For that it is not the whole Temple at large (though it might be so called), but some thing or part of those that are within it, the first words of my text (*"We will go into his tabernacles "*) do argue. If, then, it be *the ark* (whose *cover* was that which we call the *mercy-seat*), it seems to have been so called in respect of God's sitting upon the cherubims, under which the ark lay, as it were his footstool : whence sometimes it is described, " The ark of the covenant of the Lord of Hosts, which sitteth upon the cherubims " : 1 Sam iv. 4. If the *ark*, with the *cover* thereof (*the mercy-seat*), be considered as God's *throne*, then the place thereof, the *Debir*, may not unfitly be termed his *"footstool."* Or, lastly, if we consider heaven to be the throne of God, as indeed it is, then whatsoever place or monument of presence he hath here on earth is in true esteem no more than his *"footstool."*—*Joseph Mede*, 1586—1638.

Verse 8.—*"Arise, O LORD, into thy rest ; thou, and the ark of thy strength."* Whenever the camp was about to move, Moses used the language found in the first part of this verse. *"Arise (or rise up), O Jehovah."*—*William Swan Plumer.*

Verse 8.—*"Thou, and the ark of thy strength."* " Both he that sanctifieth and they who are sanctified are all of one " : Heb. ii. 11. Now Christ, our Great High Priest, is gone up into the holy resting-place. Of him it is said, " Arise " : for he arose from the dead, and ascended into heaven. And to his *"ark,"* the church, it is said, " Arise " : because he lives, all in him shall live also.—*Edward Simms, in "A Spiritual Commentary on the Book of Psalms,"* 1882.

Verse 8.—*"The ark of thy strength."* The historical records of the ark are numerous, and deeply interesting. Miracles were often wrought at its presence. At the passage of the Jordan, no sooner were the feet of the priests which bare this holy vessel dipped in the brim of the river, than the waters rose up upon an heap, and the people of God passed over on dry ground—" clean over Jordan " : Joshua iii. 14—17. At the siege of Jericho, the ark occupied a most prominent position in the daily procession of the tribes around the doomed city. . . . It was, however, captured by the Philistines, and Hophni and Phineas, Eli's wicked sons, in whose care it was placed, slain. Thus the Lord " delivered his strength into captivity and his glory into the enemy's hand " : Ps. lxxviii. 61.—*Frank H. White, in "Christ in the Tabernacle,"* 1877.

Verse 9 (first clause).—The chief badge and cognizance of the Lord's minister is the true doctrine of justification and obedience of faith in a holy conversation : *"Let thy priests be clothed with righteousness."*—*David Dickson.*

Verse 9.—*"Let thy priests be clothed with righteousness."*

Holiness on the head,
Light and perfections on the breast,
Harmonious bells below, raising the dead
To lead them unto life and rest.
Thus are true *Aarons* drest, etc.

George Herbert, 1593—1633.

Verse 9.—*"Saints."* If the very names given by God's prophets to his people are such as *saints, gracious ones, merciful ones,* surely his professed people ought to see to it that they are not cruel, untender, or *unholy.*—*William Swan Plumer.*

Verses 9, 16.—Let us notice the prayer, verse 9, with the answer, verse 16. The prayer asks in behalf of the priests *"righteousness" :* the answer is, " I will clothe her priests with *salvation,"* *i.e.*, with what shows forth God's *gracious character.* Caring for the interest of God, the worshipper finds his own interest fully cared for. And now, after spreading the Lord's pledged word (verses 11, 12) before him, the worshipper hears the Lord himself utter the reply, *q.d.*, " I will do all that has been sought."—*A. A. Bonar.*

Verse 10.—*" For thy servant David's sake."* Solomon's plea for the divine blessing to rest upon him as king, *"For thy servant David's sake,"* was justified in its use by God: Is. xxxvii. 35. It gives no countenance to the idea of intercession on the part of deceased saints ; for it is not a prayer to David, but a pleading with God for the sake of David. Nor does it support the idea of works of supererogation on the part of David ; it only implies a special divine delight in David, on account of which God was pleased to honour David's name during succeeding generations ; and if the delight itself is pure grace, the expression of it, in any way, must be grace. Nor does it even give countenance to the idea that God's converting and saving grace may be expected by any man because his parents or ancestors were delighted in by God ; for a plea of this character is in Scripture strictly confined to two instances, Abraham and David, with both of whom a special covenant was made, including their descendants, and it was just this covenant that authorised the use of the plea by those who by promise were specially interested, and by none others, and for the ends contemplated by the covenant. But it did prefigure the great Christian plea, " For Christ Jesus' sake"; just as God's selection of individual men and making them centres of revelation and religion, in the old time, prefigured " The man Christ Jesus " as the centre and basis of religion for all time. Hence in the plea, " For Christ's sake," the old pleas referred to are abolished, as the Jewish ritual is abolished. Christ bids us use His name : John xiv. 13, 14 ; xvi. 26, etc. To believe the false notions mentioned above, or to trust in any other name for divine, gracious favour, is to dishonour the name of Christ. " For Christ's sake " is effective on account of the great covenant, the merits of Christ, and his session in heaven.—*John Field*, 1883.

Verse 10.—*"For thy servant David's sake."* The frequency with which God is urged to hear and answer prayer *for David's sake* (1 Kings xi. 12, 13 ; xv. 4 ; 2 Kings viii. 19, etc.), is not to be explained by making *David* mean the promise to David, nor from the personal favour of which he was the object, but for his historical position as the great theocratical model, in whom it pleased God that the old economy should reach its culminating point, and who is always held up as the type and representative of the Messiah, so that all the intervening kings are mere connecting links, and their reigns mere repetitions and continuations of the reign of David, with more or less resemblance as they happened to be good or bad. Hence the frequency with which his name appears in the later Scriptures, compared with even the last of his successors, and the otherwise inexplicable transfer of that name to the Messiah himself.—*Joseph Addison Alexander.*

Verse 10.—*"For thy servant David's sake."* When Sennacherib's army lay around Jerusalem besieging it, God wrought deliverance for Israel partly out of regard to the prayer of the devout Hezekiah, but partly also out of respect for the pious memory of David, the hero-king, the man after God's own heart. The message sent through Isaiah to the king concluded thus : " Therefore thus saith the Lord concerning the king of Assyria, he shall not come into this city, nor shoot an arrow there, not come before it with shield, nor cast a bank against it. By the way that he came, by the same shall he return, and shall not come into this city, saith the Lord. For I will defend this city, to save it, for mine own sake, and for my servant

David's sake " : 2 Kings xix. 32—4. What a respect is shown to David's name by its being thus put on a level with God ! *Mine own sake, and David's sake.—Alexander Balmain Bruce, in "The Galilean Gospel,"* 1882.

Verse 10.—*"Turn not away the face,"* etc. As if in displeasure, or in forgetfulness.—*Albert Barnes.*

Verse 10.—*"Thine anointed."* What is meant by *"thine anointed"?* Is it David himself ; or some definite king among his merely human descendants ; or does it apply to each or any of them as they come into office to bear the responsibilities of this line of anointed kings ? I incline to the latter construction, under which the petition is applicable to any one or to all the anointed successors of David. For David's sake let every one of them be admitted to free audience before thee, and his prayer be evermore availing. The context contemplates a long line of kings descended from David. It was pertinent to make them all the subjects of this prayer.—*Henry Cowles.*

Verse 11.—*"The* LORD *hath sworn."* The most potent weapon with God is his own word. They remind him, therefore, as did Ethan in Psalm lxxxix. 20, etc., of the solemn words which he had spoken by Nathan, and which must at that time have been still fresh in the memory of all. Solomon, too, made mention of those glorious words of comfort in his prayer at the dedication of the temple.—*Augustus F. Tholuck.*

Verses 11, 12.—This Psalm is one of those fifteen which are called Psalms of Degrees ; of which title whatsoever reason can be given fitting the rest, surely if we consider the argument of this, it may well import the excellency thereof, and why ? It is nothing else but a sacred emulation, wherein God and a king contend ; the king in piety, God in bounty. The king declares himself to be a most eminent pattern of zeal, and God himself to be a most magnificent rewarder of his servants. The king debarreth himself of all worldly content, while he is busily providing to entertain God ; and God, who filleth heaven and earth, vouchsafeth to lodge in that place which was provided by the king. The king presents his supplication not only for himself, but also for his charge, the priests, the people ; and God restraineth not his blessing to the king, but also at his suit enlargeth it to church and commonweal. Finally, the king bindeth himself to make good his duty with a votive oath, and God restipulateth with an oath that which he promised both to king and kingdom : to the kingdom in the words that follow ; but to the king in those that I have now read to you.

This speech, then, is directed unto the king, unto David ; but it containeth a blessing which redounds unto his issue, *"the fruit of his body."* This blessing is no less than a royal succession in the throne of David : David's sons shall inherit it, but it is God that states them in it. They shall sit, but *I will set* them, yea, so set them that they shall never fall ; they shall sit for ever ; the succession shall be perpetual. And hitherto the promise runs absolute : it is qualified in that which followeth.

The king was busy to build God's house ; and see how God answers him, promising the building of the king's house ! God requites a building with a building. There is a very apt allusion in the word, upon which the son of Syrach also plays, when he saith, that children and the building of a city make a perpetual name ; how much more if they be a royal offspring, that are destined to sit upon a throne ? And God promiseth David sons for this honourable end—*"to sit upon his throne."—Arthur Lake,* —1626.

Verse 12.—*"If thy children will keep my covenant,"* etc. Lest David's sons, if they be left without law, should live without care, they must know that the succession shall be perpetual ; but the promise is conditional ; if David's sons conform themselves to God, *"if thou keep my covenant,"* whereof they cannot pretend ignorance. And they have an authentical record : the record, *"my testimonies " ;* authentical, *"I myself will teach them."* You see the king's blessing, it is very great ; but lest the promise thereof be thought too good to be true, God secures the king with a most unchangeable warrant. The warrant is his oath, *"The Lord sware" ;* and this warrant is, 1. Unchangeable, because sincere ; he swore in truth. 2. Stable, *he will not turn from it.* And what could king David desire more for his own house than a promise of such a blessing, and such a warrant of that promise ? Yes, he might, and no doubt he did desire [more] ; and God also intended to him more than the letter of this promise doth express, even the accomplishment of the truth whereof this was but a type. And what is that? The establishment of the kingdom of Jesus Christ.—*Arthur Lake.*

Verse 12.—"*That I shall teach them.*" Here is to be noted that he addeth, "*which I will teach them*"; for he will be the teacher and will be heard. He wills not that church councils should be heard, or such as teach that which he hath not taught. . . . God giveth no authority unto man above the word. So should he set man, that is to say, dust and dung, above himself; for what is the word, but God himself? This word they that honour, obey, and keep, are the true church indeed, be they never so contemptible in the world: but they which do not, are the church of Satan, and accursed of God. And this is the cause why it is expressly set down in the text, "*The testimonies which I will teach them.*" For so will God use the ministry of teachers and pastors in the church, that he notwithstanding will be their chief Pastor, and all other ministers and pastors whatsoever, yea, the church itself, shall be ruled and governed by the word.—*Martin Luther.*

Verse 12.—"*Their children shall also sit upon thy throne for evermore.*" As if he had said, this promise as touching Christ will I accomplish, and will undoubtedly establish the throne unto my servant David; but do not ye, which in the meantime sit on this throne, and govern this kingdom, presume upon the promise, and think that you cannot err, or that I will wink at your errors, and not rather condemn and severely punish them. Therefore either govern your kingdom according to my word, or else I will root you out and destroy you for ever. This promise he now amplifieth, and setteth forth more at large.—*Martin Luther.*

Verse 13.—"*For the* Lord *hath chosen Zion,*" etc. The Lord's pitching upon any place to dwell there cometh not of the worthiness of the place, or persons, but from God's good pleasure alone. The Lord having chosen his church, resteth in his love to her: he smelleth a sweet savour of Christ, and this maketh his seat among his people steadfast.—*David Dickson.*

Verse 13.—"*For the* Lord *hath chosen Zion.*" Here, of a singular purpose, he useth the same word which Moses used (Deut. xvi. 6): "As the place which the Lord thy God *shall choose* to place his name in." For at the beginning there was no certain place appointed wherein the tabernacle should remain; but it wandered, not only from place to place, but also from tribe to tribe, as Ephraim, Manasseh, Dan, etc.

Moreover, by the word, "*hath chosen,*" he overthroweth all kinds of worship and religion of men's own devising and choosing, whereof there was an infinite number among the Jews. Election or choice belongeth not unto us; but we must yield obedience to the voice of the Lord. Else shall that happen unto us which Jeremiah threateneth: "That they have chosen will I reject." These things destroy and confound the inventions, the devices and devotions, the false and counterfeit religions, which we have seen in the papacy. . . . God is not served but when that is done which he hath commanded. Wherefore election or choice pertaineth not to us, so that what God hath commanded, that we must do.—*Martin Luther.*

Verse 14.—"*This is my rest for ever.*" Of the Christian church we may affirm with undoubted certainty, that it is *God's rest for ever*: after this dispensation of his will, there will never succeed another; Christianity closes and completes the Divine communication from God to man; nothing greater, nothing better can or will be imparted to him on this side eternity; and even in heaven itself we shall, through an everlasting duration, be employed in contemplating and adoring the riches of that grace, the brightest glories of which have been realized in the consummations of Calvary, the ascension of the Messiah, the breaking down of all national peculiarity, and the gift and mission of the Divine Spirit. Let the argument of the apostle to the Hebrews be fully weighed, and the conclusion of every mind must be, that God has "removed those things that are shaken, as of things that are made, that those things which cannot be shaken may remain:" Heb. xii. 27.—*John Morison, in "An Exposition of the Book of Psalms," 1829.*

Verse 14.—"*This is my rest for ever.*" The heart of the saints is the dwelling-place of God. He rests in those who rest in him. He rests when he causes us to rest.—*Pasquier Quesnel.*

Verse 14.—"*Dwell.*" The word translated "*dwell*" means originally to *sit*, and especially to sit enthroned, so that this idea would be necessarily suggested with the other to a Hebrew reader.—*Joseph Addison Alexander.*

Verses 14—18.—Now that he might apparently see how near the Lord is to all them that call upon him in faithfulness and truth, he waiteth not long for an answer, but carries it away with him before he departs. For to David's petition, *"Return, O LORD, unto thy resting-place, thou, and the ark of thy strength";* God's answer is this,—" This shall be my resting-place, here will I dwell, for I have a delight therein. I will bless her victuals with increase, and will satisfy her poor with bread." To David's petition, *"Let thy priests be clothed with righteousness, and let thy saints sing with joyfulness,"* God's answer is this : " I will clothe her priests with salvation : and her saints shall rejoice and sing." Lastly, to David's petition, *"For thy servant David's sake turn not away the face of thine anointed,"* God's answer is this : " There will I make the horn of David to flourish : I have ordained a light for mine anointed. As for his enemies, I will clothe them with shame ; but upon himself shall his crown flourish." As if he should have said,—Turn away the face of mine anointed ? Nay, that will I never do ; I will indeed turn away the face of the enemies of mine anointed ; their face shall be covered with confusion, and clothed with shame. But contrariwise, I have ordained a light for mine anointed. He shall even have a light in his face and a crown upon his head. " As for his enemies, I will clothe them with shame ; but upon himself shall his crown flourish."—*Thomas Playfere,* 1633.

Verse 15.—*"I will abundantly bless her provision,"* etc. The *provision* of Zion, the church of God, the word and ordinances, of which Christ is the sum and substance ; the gospel is milk for babes, and meat for strong men ; the ordinances are a feast of fat things ; Christ's flesh is meat indeed, and his blood drink indeed ; the whole provision is spiritual, savoury, salutary, strengthening, satisfying, and nourishing, when the Lord blesses it ; as he does to those who hunger and thirst after it, and feed upon it by faith ; so that their souls grow thereby, and they become fat and flourishing ; grace increases in them, and they are fruitful in every good work ; and this the Lord promises to do *abundantly,* in a very large way and manner ; or *certainly,* for it is, in the original text, " in blessing I will bless," that is, will surely bless, as this phrase is sometimes rendered.

"I will satisfy her poor with bread." Zion has her poor ; persons may be poor and yet belong to Zion, belong to Zion and yet be poor ; there are poor in all the churches of Christ ; our Lord told his disciples that they had the poor, and might expect to have them, always with them ; and particular directions are given to take care of Zion's poor under the gospel dispensation, that they may not want bread in a literal sense : though by the *poor* are chiefly designed the Lord's afflicted and distressed ones ; or those who in a spiritual sense are poor, sensible of their spiritual poverty, and seeking after the true riches ; or are poor in spirit, to whom the kingdom of heaven belongs ; these the Lord promises to satisfy, to fill them to the full with the bread of the gospel, made of the finest of the wheat, of which there is enough and to spare in his house ; and with Christ the bread of life, of which those that eat shall never die, but live for ever.—*John Gill.*

Verse 15.—*"Her provision I will bless, I will bless."* The repetition of the verb may express either certainty or fulness. *I will surely bless,* or *I will bless abundantly.* —*Joseph Addison Alexander.*

Verse 15.—*"I will abundantly bless her provision."* Believe it, a saint hath rare fare, gallant cheer, and rich diet, and all at free cost. He is feasted all the day long ; he is brought oft into the banqueting-house, and hath the rarest, the costliest, the wholesomest diet, that which is most hearty and strengthening, that which is most dainty and pleasant, and the greatest variety, and nothing is wanting, that may make his state happy, except a full enjoyment of glory itself. The Lord gives him all the experiences of his power and goodness to his Church in former ages to feed his hopes upon ; nay, many choice providences, many answers of prayer, many foretastes of glory, many ordinances, especially that great one of the Lord's Supper, at which Christ and all his benefits are served up in a royal dish to refresh and feast the faith, hope, and love of the saints. And that which sweetens all this—he knows that all this is but a little to what he shall shortly live upon when he comes to the marriage-supper ; then he shall always be feasted and never surfeited. And beside all this, he hath the sweet and refreshing incomes of the Spirit, filling him with such true pleasure, that he can easily spare the most sumptuous banquet, the noblest feast, and highest worldly delights, as infinitely short of one hour's treatment in his

Friend's chamber. And, if this be his entertainment in the inn, what shall he have at the court ? If this heavenly manna be his food in the wilderness, at what rate is he like to live when he comes into Canaan ? If this be the provision of the way, what is that of the country ?—*John Janeway, about* 1670.

Verse 15.—"*I will satisfy her poor with bread.*" Christ is a satisfying good. A wooden loaf, a silver loaf, a golden loaf will not satisfy a hungry man ; the man must have bread. The dainties and dignities of the world, the grandeur and glory of the world, the plenty and prosperity of the world, the puff and popularity of the world, will not satisfy a soul sailing by the gates of hell, and crying out of the depths ; it must be a Christ. " Children, or I die," was the cry of the woman ; a Christ, or I die—a Christ, or I am damned, is the doleful ditty and doleful dialect of a despairing or desponding soul. " He that loveth silver shall not be satisfied therewith ; nor he that loveth abundance with increase : " Eccles. v. 10. It is a good observation that the world is round, but the heart of man is triangular. Now, all the globe of the world will not fill the triangular heart of man. What of the world and in the world can give quietness, when Christ, the Sun of Righteousness, goes down upon the soul ? The heart is a three-square, and nothing but a trinity in unity and a unity in trinity will satisfy this. Not riches, nor relations, nor barns, nor bags, will satisfy a convinced and deserted soul. This person can say concerning his bags as a great person upon a sick, if not a dying, bed, did concerning his bags,— Away, and away for ever. Though there be bag upon bag, yet they are altogether insignificant in a dying hour ; these bags, they are but as so many ciphers before a figure. This is the cry of despairing and desponding souls : " O satisfy us early with thy mercy ; that we may rejoice and be glad all our days : " Ps. xc. 14.—*Richard Mayhew,* 1679.

Verse 15.—"*I will satisfy her poor with bread.*" Dainties I will not promise them ; a *sufficiency,* but not a *superfluity :* poor they may be, but not destitute ; bread they shall have, and of that *God's plenty,* as they say ; enough to bring them to their Father's house, " where there is bread enough." Let not, therefore, the poor Israelite fear to bring his offerings, or to disfurnish himself for God's worship, etc.— *John Trapp.*

Verse 16.—"*I will clothe her priests with salvation.*" Their salvation shall be evident and conspicuous, just as a garment is.—*Aben-Ezra.*

Verse 16.—God's presence is an earnest of all good ; for all this follows upon " here will I dwell." By it he giveth meat to the hungry, and comfort to the poor, even the Bread of Life to the believing and repenting soul ; by it he himself is the sanctification of his priests, and his righteousness and salvation is their most glorious vesture ; and by his presence he maketh his elect ever glad, filling their hearts with joy and their mouths with songs.—*J. W. Burgon.*

Verse 16.—"*Her saints shall shout aloud for joy.*" It would astonish and amuse a European stranger to hear these natives sing. They have not the least idea either of harmony or melody ; noise is what they best understand, and he that sings the loudest is considered to sing the best. I have occasionally remonstrated with them on the subject ; but the reply I once received silenced me for ever after. " Sing softly, brother," I said to one of the principal members. " Sing softly ! " he replied, " is it you, our father, who tells us to sing softly ? Did you ever hear us sing the praises of our Hindoo gods ? how we threw our heads backward, and with all our might shouted out the praises of those who are no gods ! And now do you tell us to *whisper* the praises of Jesus ? No, sir, we cannot—we must express in loud tones our gratitude to him who loved us, and died for us ! " And so they continued to sing with all their might, and without further remonstrance.— *G. Gogerly, in* "*The Pioneers : a Narrative of the Bengal Mission,*" 1870.

Verse 17.—" *There will I make the horn of David to bud,*" etc. A metaphor taken from those goodly creatures, as stags, and such like ; whose chiefest beauty and strength consisteth in their horns, especially when they bud and branch abroad. —*Thomas Playfere.*

Verse 17.—" *The horn of David.*" This image of *a horn* is frequent in the Old Testament. . . The explanation must be found neither in the horns of the altar on which criminals sought to lay hold, nor in the horns with which they ornamented their helmets ; the figure is taken from the horns of the bull, in which the power of this animal resides. It is a natural image among an agricultural people. . . .

Just as the strength of the animal is concentrated in its horn, so all the delivering power granted to the family of David for the advantage of the people will be concentrated in the Messiah.—*F. Godet, in " A Commentary on the Gospel of St. Luke,"* 1875.

Verse 17.—*" Make the horn to bud."* In the beginning of the month of March the common stag, or red deer, is lurking in the sequestered spots of his forest home, harmless as his mate, and as timorous. Soon a pair of prominences make their appearance on his forehead, covered with a velvety skin. In a few days these little prominences have attained some length, and give the first indication of their true form. Grasp one of these in the hand and it will be found burning hot to the touch, for the blood runs fiercely through the velvety skin, depositing at every touch a minute portion of bony matter. More and more rapidly grow the horns, the carotid arteries enlarging in order to supply a sufficiency of nourishment, and in the short period of ten weeks the enormous mass of bony matter has been completed. Such a process is almost, if not entirely, without parallel in the history of the animal kingdom.—*J. G. Wood, in " The Illustrated Natural History,"* 1861.

Verse 17.—*" The horn."* My friend, Mr. Graham, of Damascus, says, concerning the horns worn by eastern women, " This head-dress is of dough, tin, silver, or gold, according to the wealth of the different classes. The rank is also indicated by the length of it. The nobler the lady, the longer the horn. Some of them are more than an English yard." I procured at Damascus an ancient gem, representing a *man* wearing the horn. In the present day, its use is confined to the women.— *John Wilson, in " The Lands of the Bible,"* 1847.

Verse 17.—*" I have ordained a lamp for mine anointed."* This clause contains an allusion to the law, which cannot be preserved in any version. The word translated *" lamp "* is used to designate the several burners of the golden candlesticks (Ex. xxv. 37 ; xxxv. 14 ; xxxvii. 23 ; xxxix. 37), and the verb here joined with it is the one applied to the ordering or tending of the sacred lights by the priests (Ex. xxvii. 21 ; Lev. xxvii. 3). The meaning of the whole verse is, that the promise of old made to David and to Zion should be yet fulfilled, however dark and inauspicious present appearances.—*Joseph Addison Alexander.*

Verse 17.—*"I have ordained a lamp for mine anointed."* We here remark, 1. The designation given unto Christ by God his Father ; he is *"mine anointed."* Though he be despised and rejected of men ; though an unbelieving world see no form or comeliness in him, why he should be desired, yet I own him, and challenge him as mine Anointed, the Prophet, Priest, and King of my church. " I have found David my servant : with my holy oil have I anointed him : with whom my hand shall be established : mine arm also shall strengthen him " : Ps. lxxxix. 20, 21. 2. The great means of God's appointment for manifesting the glory of Christ to a lost world ; he has provided *" a lamp "* for his Anointed. The use of a lamp is to give light to people in the darkness of the night ; so the word of God, particularly the gospel, is a light shining in a dark place, until the day of glory dawn, when the Lord God and the Lamb will be the light of the ransomed for endless evermore. 3. The authority by which this lamp is lighted and carried through this dark world ; it is *"ordained"* of God ; and by his commandment it is that we preach and spread the light of the gospel (Mark xvi. 15, 20).—*Ebenezer Erskine,* 1680—.

Verse 17.—*"I have ordained a lamp for mine anointed."* That is, I have ordained prosperity and blessings for him ; blessings upon his person, and especially the blessing of posterity. Children are as a *lamp* or *candle* in their father's house, making the name of their ancestors conspicuous ; hence in Scripture a child given to succeed his father is called a *lamp.* When God by Ahijah the prophet told Jeroboam that God would take the kingdom out of the hand of Solomon's son, and give it unto him, even ten tribes ; he yet adds (1 Kings xi. 36), " And unto his son will I give one tribe, that David my servant may have a light (*lamp* or *candle*) alway before me in Jerusalem, the city which I have chosen me to put my name there." And again (1 Kings xv. 4), when Abijam the son of Rehoboam proved wicked, the text saith, " Nevertheless for David's sake did the Lord his God give him a *lamp* (or *candle*) in Jerusalem, to set up his son after him."—*Joseph Caryl.*

Verses 17, 18.—God having chosen David's family, he here promiseth to bless that also with suitable blessings.

1. Growing power : *"There* (in Zion) *will I make the horn of David to bud."* The royal dignity should increase more and more, and constant additions be made to the lustre of it. Christ is the "horn of salvation," noting a plentiful and powerful

salvation, which God hath raised up and made to bud " in the house of his servant David." David had promised to use his power for God's glory, to cut off the horns of the wicked, and to exalt the horns of the righteous (Ps. lxxv. 10) ; and in recompense for it, God here promises to make his horn to bud ; for to them that have power and use it well, more shall be given.

2. Lasting honour : *"I have ordained a lamp for mine anointed."* Thou wilt "light my candle" (Ps. xviii. 28): that lamp is likely to burn brightly which God ordains. A lamp is a successor ; for when a lamp is almost out, another may be lighted by it : it is a succession ; for by this means David shall not want a man to stand before God. Christ is the lamp and the light of the world.

3. Complete victory. *"His enemies,"* that have formed designs against him, *"will I clothe with shame,"* when they shall see their designs baffled. Let the enemies of all good governors expect to be clothed with shame, and especially the enemies of the Lord Jesus and his government, who shall rise in the last great day " to everlasting shame and contempt."

4. Universal prosperity : *"Upon himself shall his crown flourish,"* i.e., his government shall be more and more his honour. This was to have its full accomplishment in Christ Jesus, whose crown of honour and power shall never fade, nor the flowers of it wither. The crowns of earthly princes " endure not to all generations " (Prov. xxvii. 24) ; but Christ's crown shall endure to all eternity, and the crowns reserved for his faithful subjects are such as " fade not away."— *Matthew Henry.*

Verse 18.—*"His enemies will I clothe with shame."* That is, *shame* shall so inseparably cover them, that as wheresoever a man goeth, he carrieth his clothes with him ; so wheresoever they go they shall carry their *shame* with them. And that which is strangest of all, they which are ashamed use to clothe or cover their shame, and then think themselves well enough ; but David's enemies shall be so ashamed, that even the very covering of their shame shall be a discovering of it ; and the clothing or cloaking of their ignominy shall be nothing else but a girding of it more closely and more inseparably unto them.—*Thomas Playfere.*

Verse 18.—*"Upon himself shall the crown flourish."* This idea seems to be taken from the nature of the ancient crowns bestowed upon conquerors. From the earliest periods of history, the laurel, olive, ivy, etc., furnished crowns to adorn the heads of heroes, who had conquered in the field of battle, gained the prize in the race or performed some other important service to the public. These were the dear bought rewards of the most heroic exploits of antiquity. This sets the propriety of the phrase in full view. The idea of a crown of gold and jewels flourishing, is at least unnatural ; whereas, flourishing is natural to laurels, oaks, etc. These were put upon the heads of the victors in full verdure, and their merit seemed to make them flourish on their heads, in fresher green. The literal crown which Jesus wore was also of the vegetable kind, and the thorn of sorrow never flourished in such vigour as on his head. Now he has got the crown of life, which shall not fade away, like the perishing verdure of the crowns of other heroes. It shall flourish for ever, with all the vigour of immortality, and bring forth all the olive-fruits of peace for his people. Its branches shall spread, and furnish crowns for all the victors in the spiritual warfare.—*Alexander Pirie,* —1804.

HINTS TO PREACHERS.

Verse 1.—I. The Lord remembers Jesus, our David : he loves him, he delights in him, he is with him. II. In that memory his griefs have a prominent place— " all his afflictions." III. Yet the Lord would be put in remembrance by his people.

Verses 1, 2.—Concerning his people, I. The Lord remembers, 1. Their persons. 2. Their afflictions. 3. Their vows. II. The Lord remembers them, 1. To accept them. 2. To sympathise with them. 3. To assist them.

Verses 1, 2.—I. God remembers his people, each one : " Remember David."

The Spirit maketh intercession within us according to the will of God. II. He remembers their afflictions : " David and all his afflictions." " I know thy works and thy tribulation." III. He remembers their vows, especially, 1. Those which relate to his service. 2. Those which are solemnly made. 3. Those which are faithfully performed.—*G. R.*

Verses 1—5.—Notice, I. How painfully David felt what he conceived to be a dishonouring of God, which he thought he might be able to remedy. Consider " his afflictions,"—because the ark dwelt within curtains, while he himself dwelt in a house of cedar : 2 Sam. vii. 2. Consider, 1. Its singularity. Most find affliction in personal losses ; very few suffer from a cause like this. 2. The little sympathy such a feeling meets with from the most of men. " If God means to convert the heathen, he can do it without you, young man," was said to Dr., then Mr. Carey, when heathenism was an affliction to him. 3. Its fittingness to a really God-fearing man. 4. Its pleasingness to God : 1 Sam. ii. 30. II. How earnestly he set himself to remedy the evil he deplored : " He sware," etc. There cannot be the least doubt that he would have foregone the enjoyment of temporal luxuries until he had accomplished the work dear to his heart, if he had been permitted of God. Remark, 1. There is little zeal for God's honour when self-denial is not exercised for the sake of his cause. 2. Were a like zeal generally shown by God's people, there would be more givers and more liberal gifts ; more workers, and the work more heartily and better done. 3. It would be well to astonish the world, and deserve the commendations of the righteous by becoming enthusiasts for the honour of God.—*J. F.*

Verses 3—5.—I. We should desire a habitation for God more than for ourselves. God should have the best of everything. " See, now, I dwell in a house of cedar, but the ark of God dwelleth within curtains." II. We should be guided by the house of God in seeking a house for ourselves : " Surely I will not come," etc. III. We should labour for the prosperity of God's house even more than of our own. Nothing should make sleep more sweet to us than when the church of God prospers ; nothing keep us more awake then when it declines : " I will not give sleep," etc. (verse 4) ; " Is it time for you, O ye, to dwell in your ceiled houses, and this house lie waste ? "—*G. R.*

Verse 5.—Something to live for—to find fresh habitations for God. I. The Condescension implied : God *with us.* II. The Districts explored : hearts, homes, " dark places of the earth." III. The Royalty of the Work. It makes King David busy, and is labour worthy of a king.—*W. B. H.*

Verse 5.—"*A place for the* LORD." In the heart, the home, the assembly, the life. Everywhere we must find or make a place for the Lord.

Verse 5.—"*The mighty God of Jacob.*" I. Mighty, and therefore he joined heaven and earth at Bethel. II. Mighty, and therefore brought Jacob back from Mesopotamia. III. Mighty, and yet wrestled with him at Jabbok. IV. Mighty, and yet allowed him to be afflicted. V. Mighty and therefore gave him full deliverance.

Verses 6, 7.—We shall use this for practical purposes. A soul longing to meet with God. God has appointed a meeting place. I. *We know what it is.* A mercy-seat, a throne of grace, a place of revealed glory. Within it the law preserved. Heavenly food—pot of manna. Holy rule—Aaron's rod. II. *We desire to find it.* Intensely. Immediately. Reverently. Longing to receive it. III. *We heard of it.* In our young days. We almost forget where. From ministers, from holy men, from those who loved us. IV. *We found it.* Where we least expected it. In a despised place. In a lonely place. Where we lost ourselves. Very near us— where we hid like Adam among the trees. V. *We will go.* To God in Christ. For all he gives. To dwell with him. To learn of him. VI. *We will worship.* Humbly. Solemnly. Gratefully. Preparing for heaven.

Verse 7.—I. The Place : " His tabernacles." 1. Built for God. 2. Accepted by God : present everywhere, he is especially present here. II. The Attendance : " We will go," etc. There God is present to meet us, and there we should be present to meet him. III. The Design : 1. For adoration. 2. For self-consecration : " We will worship at his footstool."—*G. R.*

Verses 8, 9.—I. The Presence of God desired—1. That it may be signally manifested : " Arise " and enter. 2. That it may be gracious : " Thou and the ark "—that he may be present on the mercy-seat. 3. That it may be felt : accompanied with power : " The ark of thy strength." 4. That it may be abiding :

" Arise into thy rest." II. The reasons for this desire. 1. With respect to the priests or ministers : " Let thy priests," etc. : not their own righteousness, but as a clothing : let them speak of " garments of salvation " and " robes of righteousness." 2. With respect to the worshippers : " And let thy saints," etc. Let ministers preach the gift of righteousness ; not that which grows out of man's nature, but that which is " unto all and upon all them that believe," and saints will shout for joy.—*G. R.*

Verse 9.—Consider, I. The importance of a righteous ministry in the church. II. The connection between such a ministry and a joyous people. III. The dependence of both on the gracious working of God.—*J. F.*

Verse 9 (second clause).—I. Saints. II. Shouting. III. Explaining—" for joy." IV. Encouraging—" Let thy saints shout."

Verse 9 (second clause).—The connection between holiness and joy.

Verses 9, 16.—*The Spiritual Vestry.* I. The Vestments : 1. Righteousness ; for which the costliest stole is a poor substitute. 2. Salvation : learning, oratory, etc., of small account in comparison. II. The Procuring of the vestments : 1. Must be from God. 2. Earnest prayer should constantly arise from all saints. III. The Robing : 1. By God's own hand ! 2. Their beauty and power who are so invested. 3. The persons are " thy priests."—*W. B. H.*

Verses 9, 16.—I. Priests and Saints. II. Vestments. III. " Hymns Ancient and Modern." IV. The Real Presence : God giving the garments and the joy.

Verse 10.—I. An evil to be deprecated : " Turn not away the face "—so that he cannot see thee, or be seen of thee, or accepted, or allowed to hope. II. A plea to be employed, " for thy servant David's sake "—thy covenant with him, his zeal, his consecration, his afflictions, his service. Good gospel pleading, such as may be used on many occasions.

Verse 11.—I. The divine oath. II. Its eternal stability. III. The everlasting Kingship.

Verse 11 (middle clause).—Our confidence : " He will not turn from it." He is not a changing God. He foreknew everything. He is able to carry out his purpose. His honour is bound up in it. His oath can never be broken.

Verse 12.—Family favour may be perpetual, but the conditions must be observed.

Verse 13.—I. Sovereign choice. II. Condescending indwelling. III. Eternal rest. IV. Gracious reason—" I have desired it."

Verse 14.—I. *God finding rest in his church.* 1. The three persons honoured. 2. The divine nature exercised. 3. Eternal purposes fulfilled. 4. Almighty energies rewarded. 5. Tremendous sacrifices remembered. 6. Glorious attributes extolled. 7. Dearest relationships indulged. II. *This rest enduring for ever.* 1. There will always be a church. 2. That church will always be such as God can rest in. 3. That church will therefore be secure on earth. 4. That church will be glorified eternally in heaven.

Verse 15.—I. Blessed provision. II. Satisfied people—" satisfy her poor." III. Glorified God—" I will." IV. Happy place—Zion.

Verses 16, 18.—Two forms of clothing : salvation and shame, prepared for his priests and his enemies. Which will you wear ?

Verse 17.—A Lamp ordained for God's Anointed. Being the Substance of Two Sermons, by Ebenezer Erskine. [Works, Vol. 3, pp. 3—41.]

Verses 17, 18.—I. The budding horn of growing power. II. The perpetual lamp of constant brightness. III. The sordid array of defeated foes. IV. The unfading wreath of glorious sovereignty.

Verse 18.—I. *His enemies clothed.* 1. Who are they ? The openly profane. The moral but irreligious. The self-righteous. The hypocritical. 2. How clothed with shame ? In repentance, in disappointment, in remorse, in destruction. Sin detected. Self defeated. Hopes scattered. 3. Who clothes them ? The Lord. He will shame them thoroughly. II. *Himself crowned.* 1. His crown : his dominion and glory. 2. Its flourishing. Glory extending. Subjects increasing. Wealth growing. Foes fearing, etc.

Verse 18 (last clause).—The Lord Jesus himself the source, sustenance, and centre of the prosperity of his kingdom.

PSALM CXXXIII.

TITLE.—A Song of Degrees of David. *We see no reason for depriving David of the authorship of this sparkling sonnet. He knew by experience the bitterness occasioned by divisions in families, and was well prepared to celebrate in choicest psalmody the blessing of unity for which he sighed. Among the " songs of degrees," this hymn has certainly attained unto a good degree, and even in common literature it is frequently quoted for its perfume and dew. In this Psalm there is no wry word, all is " sweetness and light,"—a notable ascent from Psalm cxx. with which the pilgrims set out. That is full of war and lamentation, but this sings of peace and pleasantness. The visitors to Zion were about to return, and this may have been their hymn of joy because they had seen such union among the tribes who had gathered at the common altar. The previous Psalm, which sings of the covenant, had also revealed the centre of Israel's unity in the Lord's anointed and the promises made to him. No wonder that brethren dwell in unity when God dwells among them, and finds his rest in them. Our translators have given to this Psalm an admirable explanatory heading, " The benefit of the communion of saints." These good men often hit off the meaning of a passage in a few words.*

EXPOSITION.

BEHOLD, how good and how pleasant *it is* for brethren to dwell together in unity!

2 *It is* like the precious ointment upon the head, that ran down upon the beard, *even* Aaron's beard : that went down to the skirts of his garments ;

3 As the dew of Hermon, *and as the dew* that descended upon the mountains of Zion : for there the LORD commanded the blessing, *even* life for evermore.

1. *"Behold."* It is a wonder seldom seen, therefore behold it ! It may be seen, for it is the characteristic of real saints,—therefore fail not to inspect it ! It is well worthy of admiration; pause and gaze upon it ! It will charm you into imitation, therefore note it well ! God looks on with approval, therefore consider it with attention. *"How good and how pleasant it is for brethren to dwell together in unity ! "* No one can tell the exceeding excellence of such a condition ; and so the Psalmist uses the word " how " twice ;—Behold how good ! and how pleasant ! He does not attempt to measure either the good or the pleasure, but invites us to behold for ourselves. The combination of the two adjectives " good " and " pleasant," is more remarkable than the conjunction of two stars of the first magnitude : for a thing to be " good " is good, but for it also to be pleasant is better. All men love pleasant things, and yet it frequently happens that the pleasure is evil ; but here the condition is as good as it is pleasant, as pleasant as it is good, for the same *" how "* is set before each qualifying word.

For *brethren* according to the flesh to dwell together is not always wise ; for experience teaches that they are better a little apart, and it is shameful for them to dwell together in disunion. They had much better part in peace like Abraham and Lot, than dwell together in envy like Joseph's brothers. When brethren can and do dwell together *in unity*, then is their communion worthy to be gazed upon and sung of in holy psalmody. Such sights ought often to be seen among those who are near of kin, for they are brethren, and therefore should be united in heart and aim ; they dwell together, and it is for their mutual comfort that there should be no strife ; and yet how many families are rent by fierce feuds, and exhibit a spectacle which is neither good nor pleasant !

As to brethren in spirit, they ought to dwell together in church fellowship, and in that fellowship one essential matter is unity. We can dispense with uniformity if we possess unity : oneness of life, truth, and way ; oneness in Christ Jesus ; oneness of object and spirit—these we must have, or our assemblies will be synagogues of contention rather than churches of Christ. The closer the unity the better; for the more of the good and the pleasant there will be. Since we are imperfect beings, somewhat of the evil and the unpleasant is sure to intrude; but this will readily be neutralized and easily ejected by the true love of the saints, if it really exists. Christian unity is good in itself, good for ourselves, good for the brethren, good for our converts, good for the outside world; and for certain it is pleasant; for a loving heart must have pleasure and give pleasure in associating with others of like nature. A church united for years in earnest service of the Lord is a well of goodness and joy to all those who dwell round about it.

2. *"It is like the precious ointment upon the head."* In order that we may the better behold brotherly unity David gives us a resemblance, so that as in a glass we may perceive its blessedness. It has a *sweet perfume* about it, comparable to that precious ointment with which the first High Priest was anointed at his ordination. It is *a holy thing*, and so again is like the oil of consecration which was to be used only in the Lord's service. What a sacred thing must brotherly love be when it can be likened to an oil which must never be poured on any man but on the Lord's high-priest alone! It is a *diffusive* thing: being poured on his head the fragrant oil flowed down upon Aaron's head, and thence dropped upon his garments till the utmost hem was anointed therewith; and even so doth brotherly love extend its benign power and bless all who are beneath its influence. Hearty concord brings a benediction upon all concerned; its goodness and pleasure are shared in by the lowliest members of the household; even the servants are the better and the happier because of the lovely unity among the members of the family. *It has a special use* about it; for as by the anointing oil Aaron was set apart for the special service of Jehovah, even so those who dwell in love are the better fitted to glorify God in his church. The Lord is not likely to use for his glory those who are devoid of love; they lack the anointing needful to make them priests unto the Lord. *"That ran bown upon the beard, even Aaron's beard."* This is a chief point of comparison, that as the oil did not remain confined to the place where it first fell, but flowed down the High Priest's hair and bedewed his beard, even so brotherly love descending from the head distils and descends, anointing as it runs, and perfuming all it lights upon. *"That went down to the skirts of his garments."* Once set in motion it would not cease from flowing. It might seem as if it were better not to smear his garments with oil, but the sacred unguent could not be restrained, it flowed over his holy robes; even thus does brotherly love not only flow over the hearts upon which it was first poured out, and descend to those who are an inferior part of the mystical body of Christ, but it runs where it is not sought for, asking neither leave nor license to make its way. Christian affection knows no limits of parish, nation, sect or age. Is the man a believer in Christ? Then he is in the one body, and I must yield him an abiding love. Is he one of the poorest, one of the least spiritual, one of the least lovable? Then he is as the skirts of the garment, and my heart's love must fall even upon him. Brotherly love comes from the head, but falls to the feet. Its way is downward. It "ran down," and it "went down": love for the brethren condescends to men of low estate, it is not puffed up, but is lowly and meek. This is no small part of its excellence: oil would not anoint if it did not flow down, neither would brotherly love diffuse its blessing if it did not descend.

3. *"As the dew of Hermon, and as the dew that descended upon the mountains of Zion."* From the loftier mountains the moisture appears to be wafted to the lesser hills: the dews of Hermon fall on Zion. The Alpine Lebanon ministers to the minor elevation of the city of David; and so does brotherly love descend from higher to the lower, refreshing and enlivening in its course. Holy concord is as dew, mysteriously blessed, full of life and growth for all plants of grace. It brings with it so much benediction that it is as no common dew, but as that of Hermon which is specially copious, and far-reaching. The proper rendering is, "As the dew of Hermon that descended upon the mountains of Zion," and this tallies with the figure which has been already used; and sets forth by a second simile the sweet descending diffusiveness of brotherly unity. *"For there the LORD commanded the blessing, even life for evermore."* That is, in Zion, or better still, in the place where brotherly love abounds. Where love reigns God reigns. Where love wishes blessing, there God commands the blessing. God has but to command, and it is done. He is so pleased to see his dear children happy in one another that he fails not to make them happy in himself. He gives especially his best blessing of eternal life, for love is life; dwelling together in love we have begun the enjoyments of eternity,

and these shall not be taken from us. Let us love for evermore, and we shall live for evermore. This makes Christian brotherhood so good and pleasant ; it has Jehovah's blessing resting upon it, and it cannot be otherwise than sacred like "the precious ointment," and heavenly like " the dew of Hermon."

O for more of this rare virtue ! Not the love which comes and goes, but that which dwells ; not that spirit which separates and secludes, but that which dwells together ; not that mind which is all for debate and difference, but that which dwells together in unity. Never shall we know the full power of the anointing till we are of one heart and of one spirit ; never will the sacred dew of the spirit descend in all its fulness till we are perfectly joined together in the same mind ; never will the covenanted and commanded blessing come forth from the Lord our God till once again we shall have " one Lord, one faith, one baptism." Lord, lead us into this most precious spiritual unity, for thy Son's sake. Amen.

EXPLANATORY NOTES AND QUAINT SAYINGS.

Whole Psalm.—This Psalm is an effusion of holy joy occasioned by the sight of the gathering of Israel as one great household at the yearly feasts. . . . There might likewise be an allusion to the previous jealousies and alienations in the family of Israel, which seemed to be exchanged for mutual concord and affection, on David's accession to the throne of the whole nation.—*Joseph Addison Alexander.*

Verse 1.—"*Behold how good and how pleasant it is,*" etc. There are three things wherein it is very pleasant to behold the people of God joining in one.

1. When they join or are *one in opinion* and judgment, when they all think the same thing, and are of one mind in the truth.

2. When they join together and are *one in affection,* when they are all of one heart, though possibly they are not all of one mind ; or, when they meet in affection, though not in opinion. When David had spoken admiringly of this goodly sight, he spoke declaratively concerning the goodness of it (verse 2) : "*It is like the precious ointment upon the head.*" 'Tis so, first, for the sweetness of it ; 'tis so, secondly· for the diffusiveness of it (as followeth), "*that ran down upon the beard, even Aaron's beard : that went down to the skirts of his garments.*"

3. It is a blessed thing to see them joining *together in duty,* either as duty is considered—First, *in doing that which is good ;* or, when, as the apostle's word is (2 Cor. vi. 1), they are, among themselves, " workers together " in any good work : we say (to fill up the text), " workers together with God." That's a blessed sight indeed, when we join with God, and God joineth with us in his work. It is also a blessed sight when all the ministers of Jesus Christ, and many as members of Jesus Christ, join in any good work, in this especially, to beseech all we have to do with " that they receive not the grace of God in vain." Secondly, *in turning from evil,* and putting iniquity far from them ; in praying for the pardon of sin, and making their peace with God. 'Tis a good work to turn away from evil, especially when all who are concerned in it join in it . . . . As to join in sin, and to be brethren in iniquity, is the worst of unions, indeed, a combination against God ; so to join as brethren in mourning for sin and repenting of our iniquities is a blessed union, and highly pleasing to God.—*Joseph Caryl.*

Verse 1.—"*How good and how pleasant it is,*" etc. The terms of this praise and commendation, or the particulars whereof it consists, is taken from a twofold qualification.

1. Brotherly concord and the improvement of it in all occasional expressions is a very great good. This is, and will appear to be so in sundry considerations.

As, *First,* in regard of the *Author* and *owner* of it, which is *God Himself,* who lays special claim hereunto. Therefore in Scripture we find him to be from hence denominated and intitled. 1 Cor. xiv. 33. " God is not the author of confusion (or of unquietness), but the author of peace. 2 Cor. xiii. 11. " The God of peace and love." Peace is called " the peace of God :" Phil. iv. 7. And God is called the "God of peace;" each of which expressions does refer it and reduce it to him, and does thereby advance it. Look, then, how far forth God himself is said to be good, so far forth is this dwelling in unity good also, as it is commanded and owned by him, as it appears thus to be.

Secondly. It is good in the *nature* of it; it is good, as any grace is good. It is good morally. Love is a fruit of the Spirit: Gal. v. 22. And so to dwell in love and unity one with another is a goodness reducible thereunto. It is good spiritually; it is not only such a good as is taught by moral philosophy, and practised by the students thereof, but it is taught by the *Holy Ghost himself*, and is a part of the work of regeneration and of the new creature in us, especially if we take it in the full latitude and extent of it, as it becomes us to do.

Thirdly. It is good in the *effects* and *consequences* and *concomitants* of it: it has much good. It is *bonum utile.* A great deal of advantage comes by brethren's dwelling together in unity, especially *spiritual advantage*, and for the doing and receiving of good.

2. The second qualification is, the sweetness of it, because it is *"pleasant:"* it is not only *bonum utile*, and *bonum honestum*, but it is also *bonum jucundum;* it has a great deal of pleasure in it. Pleasure is such a kind of goodness, especially to some kind of persons, as that they care not almost what they do or part with to obtain it, and all other good besides is nothing to them, if it be devoid of this. Therefore for the further commendation of this fraternal unity to us, there is this also to be considered, that it is *"pleasant."* Thus it is with respect to all sorts of persons whatsoever, that are made sensible of it.

First. It is *pleasant to God*, it is such as is very acceptable to him; it is that which he much delights in, wheresoever he observes it; being himself a God of peace, he does therefore so much the more delight in peaceable Christians, and such as do relate to himself. How much do natural parents rejoice in the agreement of their children, to see them loving and friendly and kind and courteous to one another, oh, it pleases them and joys them at their very heart! and so it is likewise with God to those who are truly his.

Secondly. This brotherly unity is also *pleasant to ourselves*, who accordingly shall have so much the greater pleasure in it and from it.

Thirdly. It is also *pleasing to others*, indeed to all men else besides, that are standers-by and spectators of it. *"Behold, how pleasant it is,"* etc. It is pleasant to all beholders: "He that in these things serveth Christ is acceptable to God, and approved of men," says the apostle: Rom. xiv. 18.—*Thomas Horton,—*1673.

Verse 1.—"Pleasant." It is a pleasant thing for the saints and people of God to agree together; for the same word which is used here for *"pleasant,"* is used also in the Hebrew for a harmony of music, such as when they rise to the highest strains of the viol, when the strings are all put in order to make up a harmony; so pleasant is it, such pleasantness is there in the saints' agreement. The same word is used also in the Hebrew for the pleasantness of a corn field. When a field is clothed with corn, though it be cut down, yet it is very pleasant, oh, how pleasant is it; and such is the saints' agreement. The same word in the Psalmist is used also for the sweetness of honey, and of sweet things in oppostion to bitter things. And thus you see the pleasantness of it, by its being compared to the harmony of music, to the corn field, to the sweetness of honey, to the precious ointment that ran down Aaron's beard, and to the dew that fell upon Hermon and the hills of Zion: and all this to discover the pleasantness, profitableness, and sweetness of the saints' agreement. It is a pleasant thing to behold the sun, but it is much more pleasant to behold the saints' agreement and unity among themselves.—*William Bridge.*

Verse 1.—"Brethren." Abraham made this name, *"brethren,"* a mediator to keep peace between Lot and him: "Are we not brethren?" saith Abraham. As if he should say, Shall brethren fall out for trifles, like infidels? This was enough to pacify Lot, for Abraham to put him in mind that they were brethren; when he heard the name of brethren, straight his heart yielded, and the strife was ended. So this should be the lawyer to end quarrels between Christians, to call to mind that they are brethren. And they which have spent all at law wished that they had taken this lawyer, to think, with Lot, whether it were meet for brethren to strive like enemies.—*Henry Smith.*

Verse 1.—"Brethren." Some critics observe that the Hebrew word for a *brother* is of near brotherhood or alliance with two other words, whereof the first signifies *one*, and the other *alike* or *together*, to show that *"brethren"* ought to be as *one*, and *alike*, or *together ;* which latter is by an elegant *paranomasia* joined with it : " Behold, how good and how pleasant it is for *brethren to dwell together in unity,*" or, as we put it in the margin, *"to dwell even together."* So then, the very word whereby *"brethren"* are expressed notes that there ought to be a *nearness*, a *similitude*, yea, a *oneness* (if I may so speak) between them in their affections and actions.— *Joseph Caryl.*

Verse 1.—To dwell is a word of residence, and abode, and continuation. There is also pertaining to the love and concord of brethren a perseverance and persistency in it ; not only to be together, or to come together, or to meet together for some certain time ; but *to dwell* together in unity, this is which is here so extolled and commended unto us. It seems to be no such great matter, nor to carry any such great difficulty in it, for men to command themselves to some expresions of peace and friendship for some short space of time (though there are many now and then who are hardly able to do that) ; but to hold out in it, and to continue so long, this endurance is almost impossible to them. Yet this is that which is required of them as *Christians* and as *"brethren"* one to another, even to *"dwell together in unity ; "* to follow peace, and love, and concord, and mutual agreement, not only upon some occasional meetings, but all along the whole course of their lives, whilst they converse and live together.—*Thomas Horton.*

Verse 1.—"Together in unity." If there be but one God, as God is one, so let them that serve him be one. This is what Christ prayed so heartily for. " That they may be one ": John xvii. 21. Christians should be one, 1. *In judgment.* The apostle exhorts to be all of one mind. 1 Cor. i. 10. How sad is it to see religion wearing a coat of divers colours ; to see Christians of so many opinions, and going so many different ways ! It is Satan that has sown these tares of division. Matt. xiii. 39. He first divided men from God, and then one man from another. 2. One *in affection.* They should have one heart. " The multitude of them that believed were of one heart and of one soul ": Acts iv. 32. As in music, though there be several strings of a viol, yet all make one sweet harmony ; so, though there are several Christians, yet there should be one sweet harmony of affection among them. There is but one God, and they that serve him should be one. There is nothing that would render the true religion more lovely, or make more proselytes to it, than to see the professors of it tied together with the heart-strings of love. If God be one, let all that profess him be of one mind, and one heart, and thus fulfil Christ's prayer, " that they all may be one."—*Thomas Watson.*

Verse 2.—"Precious ointment upon the head." Though every priest was anointed, yet only the high priest was anointed on the *head*, and there is a tradition that this rite was omitted after the Captivity, so that there is a special stress on the name of Aaron.—*Neale and Littledale.*

Verse 2.—"The precious ointment . . . that ran down upon the beard . . . that went down to the skirts of his garments." Magnificence, misnamed by churls extravagance and waste, is the invariable attribute of all true love. David recognised this truth when he selected the profuse anointing of Aaron with the oil of consecration at his installation into the office of High Priest as a fit emblem of brotherly love. There was waste in that anointing, too, as well as in the one which took place at Bethany. For the oil was not *sprinkled* on the head of Aaron, though that might have been sufficient for the purpose of a mere ceremony. The vessel was emptied on the High Priest's person, so that its contents flowed down from the head upon the beard, and even to the skirts of the sacerdotal robes. In that very waste lay the point of the resemblance for David. It was a feature that was very likely to strike his mind, for he, too, was a wasteful man in his way. He had loved God in a manner which exposed him to the charge of extravagance. He had danced before the Lord, for example, when the ark was brought up from the house of Obed-edom to Jerusalem, forgetful of his dignity, exceeding the bounds of decorum, and, as it might seem, without excuse, as a much less hearty demonstration would have served the purpose of a religious solemnity.—*Alexander Balmain Bruce, in* "The Training of the Twelve," 1877.

Verse 2.—"The precious ointment . . . that ran down." Of the Hebrew perfumes an immense quantity was annually manufactured and consumed, of which we have a very significant indication in the fact that the holy anointing oil of the tabernacle and temple was never made in smaller quantities than 750 ounces of solids compounded with five quarts of oil, and was so profusely employed that when applied to Aaron's head it flowed down over his beard and breast, to the very skirts of his garments.—*Hugh Macmillan, in "The Ministry of Nature,"* 1871.

Verse 2.—*"That ran down . . . . that went down,"* etc. Christ's grace is so diffusive of itself, that it conveys holiness to us, "running down from the head to the skirts," to all his members. He was not only anointed himself, but he is our anointer. Therefore it is called "the oil of gladness," because it rejoiceth our hearts, by giving us spiritual gladness, and peace of conscience.—*Thomas Adams.*

Verse 2.—*"Down upon the beard, even Aaron's beard : that went down to the skirts of his garments."* Not the extremity of them, as our version inclines to ; for not so great a quantity of oil was poured upon him ; nor would it have been decent to have his clothes thus greased from top to bottom ; but the upper part of his garment, the top of his coat, on which the beard lay, as Zarchi ; the neck or collar of it, as Kimchi and Ben Melech ; the hole in which the head went through when it was put on, about which there was a band, that it might not be rent : Exod. xxviii. 32, and xxxix. 23 ; where the Septuagint use the same word as here.—*John Gill.*

Verses 2, 3.—In this prayer and song of the unity of the church, it is noteworthy how, commencing with the fundamental idea of *"brethren,"* we rise to the realization of the Elder Brother, who is our common anointed High Priest. It is the bond of his priesthood which joins us together as brethren. It is the common anointing which flows down even to the skirts of the garment of our High Priest which marks our being brethren. Whether we dwell north or south, meeting in Zion, and sharing in the blessings of that eternal Priesthood of Christ, we form in reality, and before our Father, but one family—"the whole family in earth and heaven." Our real bond of union consists in the "flowing down," the "running down," or "descending" of the common blessing, which marks the steps in this Psalm of Degrees (verses 2, 3). And if " the dew of Hermon " has descended upon " the mountains of Zion," long after the sun has risen shall gladsome fruit appear—in some twenty, in some thirty, and in some a hundredfold.—*Alfred Edersheim.*

Verse 3.—*"As the dew of Hermon,"* etc. " What we read in the 133rd Psalm of the dew of Hermon descending upon the mountains of Zion," says Van de Velde in his " Travels " (Bd. i. S. 97), " is now become quite clear to me. Here as I sat at the foot of Hermon, I understood how the water-drops which rose from its forest-mantled heights, and out of the highest ravines, which are filled the whole year round with snow, after the sun's rays have attenuated them and moistened the atmosphere with them, descend at evening-time as a heavy dew upon the lower mountains which lie round about as its spurs. One sought to have seen Hermon with its white-golden crown glistening aloft in the blue sky, in order to be able rightly to understand the figure. Nowhere in the whole country is so heavy a dew perceptible as in the districts near to Hermon." To this dew the poet likens brotherly love. This is *"as the dew of Hermon"* : of such pristine freshness and thus refreshing, possessing such pristine power and thus quickening, thus born from above (cx. 3), and in fact like the dew of Hermon which comes down upon the mountains of Zion—a feature in the picture which is taken from the natural reality ; for an abundant dew, when warm days have preceded, might very well be diverted to Jerusalem by the operation of the cold current of air sweeping down from the north over Hermon. We know, indeed, from our own experience how far off a cold air coming from the Alps is perceptible, and produces its effects. The figure of the poet is therefore as true to nature as it is beautiful. When brethren bound together in love also meet together in one place, and, in fact, when brethren of the north unite with brethren in the south in Jerusalem, the city which is the mother of all, at the great Feasts, it is as when the dew of Mount Hermon, which is covered with deep, almost eternal snow, descends upon the bare, unfruitful—and therefore longing for such quickening—mountains round about Zion. In Jerusalem must love and all that is good meet.—*Franz Delitzsch.*

Verse 3.—*"As the dew of Hermon,"* etc. As touching this similitude, I think the prophet useth the common manner of speaking. For whereas the mountains oftentimes seem to those that behold them afar off, to reach up even unto heaven, the dew which cometh from heaven seemeth to fall from the high mountains unto the hills which are under them. Therefore he saith that the dew descendeth from Hermon unto the mount Sion, because it so seemeth unto those that do behold it afar off.—*Martin Luther.*

Verse 3.—*"As the dew of Hermon."* The dews of the mists that rose from the watery ravines, or of the clouds that rested on the summit of Hermon, were perpetual witnesses of freshness and coolness—the sources, as it seemed, of all the moisture, which was to the land of Palestine what the fragrant oil was to the garments of the High Priest ; what the influence of brotherly love was to the whole community.— *Arthur Penrhyn Stanley (1815–1881), in "Sinai and Palestine."*

Verse 3.—*"Dew of Hermon."*   We had sensibly proof at Rasheiya of the copiousness of the *"dew of Hermon,"* spoken of in Ps. cxxxiii. 3, where " Zion " is only another name for the same mountain.   Unlike most other mountains which gradually rise from lofty table-lands and often at a distance from the sea, Hermon starts at once to the height of nearly ten thousand feet, from a platform scarcely above the sea level.   This platform, too—the upper Jordan valley, and marshes of Merom— is for the most part an impenetrable swamp of unknown depth, whence the seething vapour, under the rays of an almost tropical sun, is constantly ascending into the upper atmosphere during the day.   The vapour, coming in contact with the snowy sides of the mountain, is rapidly congealed, and is precipitated in the evening in the form of a dew, the most copious we ever experienced.   It penetrated everywhere, and saturated everything.   The floor of our tent was soaked, our bed was covered with it, our guns were dripping, and dewdrops hung about everywhere.   No wonder that the foot of Hermon is clad with orchards and gardens of such marvellous fertility in this land of droughts.—*Henry Baker Tristram*, 1867.

Verse 3.—*"As the dew of Hermon that descended upon the mountain of Zion."*—

> So the dews on Hermon's hill
> Which the summer clouds distil,
> Floating southward in the night,
> Pearly gems on Zion light.

William Digby Seymour.

Verse 3.—*" There the* Lord *commanded the blessing."*   God commands his blessing where peace is cultivated ; by which is meant, that he testifies how much he is pleased with concord amongst men, by showering down blessings upon them.   The same sentiment is expressed by Paul in other words, (2 Cor. xiii. 11 ; Phil. iv. 9) " Live in peace, and the God of peace shall be with you."—*John Calvin.*

Verse 3.—*"The* Lord *commanded the blessing."*   By a bare word of command he blesseth :   *"there he commands the blessing,"* that blessing of blessings, *"even life for evermore"*;   like as it is said, " he commanded, and they were created " : Ps. cxlviii. 5.   So he commands and we are blessed."—*Thomas Goodwin.*

Verse 3.—*"The* Lord *commanded the blessing."*   It is an allusion possibly to great persons, to a general, or an emperor : " Where the word of a king is, there is power."   The centurion said, " I say to one soldier, Go, and he goeth ; to another, Come, and he cometh ; to a third, Do this, and he doth it."   So God commandeth one ordinance, " Go and build up such a saint," and it goeth ; he saith to another ordinance, " Come, and call home such a sinner," and it doth it ;   God's words and work go together.   Men cannot enable others, or give them power to obey them ; they may bid a lame man walk, or a blind man see ; but they cannot enable them to walk or see :   God with his word giveth strength to do the thing commanded ; as in the old, so in the new creation, " He spake, and it was done ; he commanded, and it stood fast : " Ps. xxxiii. 9.   But there the Lord commands his blessing, *" even life for evermore."*   The stream of regeneration, or a spiritual life, which shall never cease, but still go forward and increase, till it swell to, and be swallowed up in the ocean of eternal life, *"even life for evermore."*—*George Swinnock.*

HINTS TO PREACHERS.

Verse 1.—Christian unity. I. Its admirable excellences. II. The signs of its existence. III. The causes of its decay. IV. The means of its renewal.

Verse 1.—The saints are here contemplated, I. In their brotherhood. II. In their concord. III. In their felicity.—*W. J.*

Verses 1—3.—Six blessings which dwell with unity. 1. Goodness. 2. Pleasure. 3. Anointing. 4. Dew. 5. God's blessing. 6. Eternal life.

Verses 1—3.—I. The contemplation: brethren dwelling together in unity. 1. In a family. 2. In a Christian church. 3. Brethren of the same denomination. 4. Of different denominations. II. Its commendation. 1. Literally: " good and pleasant." 2. Figuratively: fragrant as the priestly anointing; fruitful as the dew on Hermon. 3. Spiritually, it has a blessing from God, that gives life, and continues for evermore !—*G. R.*

Verses 1—3.—On Christians dwelling together in unity as a church. 1. *Its propriety,* on account of fraternal relationship: *"For brethren."* The Christian brotherhood is so unique, sacred and lasting, that a lack of unity is a disgrace. They are brethren, 1. Because born of God, who is " the God of peace." Their claim to the brotherhood is dependent upon likeness to Him: Matt. v. 9. 2. Because united to Christ, who as elder brother desires unity: John xvii. 20, 21. Not to seek it is virtually to disown Him. 3. Because " by one Spirit are we all baptized into one body " (1 Cor. xii. 13), wherein unity must be kept : Eph. iv. 3. 4. Because destined to " dwell together in unity," for ever in heaven ; therefore we should aim at it here. II. *Its peculiar excellency :* both " good and pleasant." 1. Good, in respect of church work and influence ; of mutual edification and growth in grace (2 Cor. xiii. 11) ; of the success of prayer (Mat. xviii. 19) ; of recommending the gospel to others. 2. Pleasant, as productive of happiness : as pleasing to God. III. *Its promotion* and maintenance. 1. Seeking the glory of God unites ; in opposition to self-honour which divides. 2. Love to Christ as a constraining power unites each to the other as it binds all closely to Christ. 3. Activity in ministering to others, rather than desiring to be ministered unto, binds heart to heart.—*J. F.*

Verse 2.—There must have been special reasons why a priestly anointing should be selected for the comparison, and why that of Aaron, rather than of any other of the high priests. They are these—I. *The ointment was "holy,"* prepared in accordance with the Divine prescription : Ex. xxx. 23—25. Church union is sacred. It must spring from the love commanded by God ; be based on the principles laid down by God ; and exist for the ends appointed of God. II. *The anointing was from God through Moses,* who acted on behalf of God in the matter. Church unity is of the Holy Spirit (1 Cor. xiii. 13), through Jesus as Mediator. Therefore it should be prayed for, and thankfully acknowledged. III. *By the anointing, Aaron became consecrated,* and officially qualified to act as priest. By unity the Church, as a whole, lives its life of consecration, and effectively ministers in the priesthood assigned it. IV. *The oil was diffusive ;* it rested not on Aaron's head, but flowed down to the skirts of his garments. Unity will, in time, make its way from a few to the whole, especially from the leaders in a church to the rest of its members. Hence, it is a personal matter. Each should realize it, and by love and wise conduct diffuse it.—*J. F.*

Verses 2, 3.—Christian love scatters blessing by the way of down-coming : " ran down," " went down," " descended." I. God to his saints. II. Saint to saint. III. Saint to sinner.

Verse 3.—The chosen place for blessing. A church ; a church united, a church bedewed of the Spirit. What a blessing for the world that there is a commanded place of blessing !

Verse 3 (first clause).—This should be rendered, " As the dew of Hermon, that cometh down on the mountains of Zion." From the snows upon the lofty Hermon, the moisture raised by the sun is carried in the form of vapour, by the wind towards the lesser elevations of Zion, upon which it falls as a copious dew. Thus, Christian concord in church-fellowship—I. Despises not the little ones, *i.e.* the mean, poor, and less gifted. It, 1. Recognises that God is the Father, and Christ is the Redeemer of all believers alike. 2. Acknowledges oneness of faith as the true basis of fellowship ; not wealth, social position or talent. 3. Believes that the least member is essential to the completeness of Christ's body. 4. Realises that everything which renders one in any way superior to another is the gift of God. II. Distributes of its abundance to the needy : Acts iv. 32—37. 1. The wealthy to the poor : 1 John iii. 17. 2. The learned to the ignorant. 3. The joyful to the sorrowing. 4. The steadfast to the erring : Jas. v. 19. III. Displays its value more by loving generosity, than by a conspicuous appearance before the world. As Hermon was more valuable to Zion for its dew than for its adornment of the landscape. 1. A generous activity exhibits and requires more real grace than showy architecture or ornate worship does. 2. Through it, godliness flourishes more than by a vaunted respectability. Zion was fertilized by the dew, not by the grandeur of Hermon. 3. By it the heart of Christ is touched and his reward secured : Mark ix. 40, 42.— J. F.

Verse 3.—*Commanded Mercy.* Elsewhere goodness is bestowed, but in Zion it is commanded. I. Commanded mercy implies that it must necessarily be given. II. Commanded mercy attends commanded unity. III. Commanded mercy secures life more abundantly, " life for evermore."—*W. B. H.*

PSALM CXXXIV.

Title.—A Song of Degrees. *We have now reached the last of the Gradual Psalms. The Pilgrims are going home, and are singing the last song in their Psalter. They leave early in the morning, before the day has fully commenced, for the journey is long for many of them. While yet the night lingers they are on the move. As soon as they are outside the gates they see the guards upon the temple wall, and the lamps shining from the windows of the chambers which surround the sanctuary ; therefore, moved by the sight, they chant a farewell to the perpetual attendants upon the holy shrine. Their parting exhortation arouses the priests to pronounce upon them a blessing out of the holy place : this benediction is contained in the third verse. The priests as good as say, " You have desired us to bless the Lord, and now we pray the Lord to bless you."*

The Psalm teaches us to pray for those who are continually ministering before the Lord, and it invites all ministers to pronounce benedictions upon their loving and prayerful people.

EXPOSITION.

BEHOLD, bless ye the LORD, all *ye* servants of the LORD, which by night stand in the house of the LORD.

2 Lift up your hands *in* the sanctuary, and bless the LORD.

3 The LORD that made heaven and earth bless thee out of Zion.

1. *"Behold."* By this call the pilgrims bespeak the attention of the night-watch. They shout to them—Behold ! The retiring pilgrims stir up the holy brotherhood of those who are appointed to keep the watch of the house of the Lord. Let them look around them upon the holy place, and everywhere " behold " reasons for sacred praise. Let them look above them at night and magnify him that made heaven and earth, and lighted the one with stars and the other with his love. Let them see to it that their hallelujahs never come to an end. Their departing brethren arouse them with the shrill cry of " Behold ! " Behold !—see, take care, be on the watch, diligently mind your work, and incessantly adore and bless Jehovah's name.

"Bless ye the Lord." Think well of Jehovah, and speak well of him. Adore him with reverence, draw near to him with love, delight in him with exultation. Be not content with praise, such as all his works render to him ; but, as his saints, see that ye " bless " him. He blesses you ; therefore, be zealous to bless him. The word " bless " is the characteristic word of the Psalm. The first two verses stir us up to bless Jehovah, and in the last verse Jehovah's blessing is invoked upon the people. Oh to abound in blessing ! May *blessed* and *blessing* be the two words which describe our lives. Let others flatter their fellows, or bless their stars, or praise themselves ; as for us, we will bless Jehovah, from whom all blessings flow. *"All ye servants of the Lord."* It is your office to bless him ; take care that you lead the way therein. Servants should speak well of their masters. Not one of you should serve him as of compulsion, but all should bless him while you serve him ; yea, bless him for permitting you to serve him, fitting you to serve him, and accepting your service. To be a servant of Jehovah is an incalculable honour, a blessing beyond all estimate. To be a servant in his temple, a domestic in his house, is even more a delight and a glory : if those who are ever with the Lord, and dwell in his own temple, do not bless the Lord, who will ? *"Which by night stand in the house of the Lord."* We can well understand how the holy pilgrims half envied those consecrated ones who guarded the temple, and attended to the necessary offices thereof through the hours of night. To the silence and solemnity of night there was added the awful glory of the place where Jehovah had ordained that his worship should be celebrated ; blessed were the priests and Levites who were ordained to a service so sublime. That these should bless the Lord throughout

their nightly vigils was most fitting : the people would have them mark this, and never fail in the duty. They were not to move about like so many machines, but to put their hearts into all their duties, and worship spiritually in the whole course of their duty. It would be well to watch, but better still to be " watching unto prayer " and praise.

When night settles down on a church the Lord has his watchers and holy ones still guarding his truth, and these must not be discouraged, but must bless the Lord even when the darkest hours draw on. Be it ours to cheer them, and lay upon them this charge—to bless the Lord at all times, and let his praise be continually in their mouths.

2. *"Lift up your hands in the sanctuary."* In the holy place they must be busy, full of strength, wide-awake, energetic, and moved with holy ardour. Hands, heart, and every other part of their manhood must be upraised, elevated, and consecrated to the adoring service of the Lord. As the angels praise God day without night, so must the angels of the churches be instant in season and out of season. *"And bless the* LORD.*"* This is their main business. They are to bless men by their teaching, but they must yet more bless Jehovah with their worship. Too often men look at public worship only from the side of its usefulness to the people ; but the other matter is of even higher importance : we must see to it that the Lord God is adored, extolled, and had in reverence. For a second time the word " bless " is used, and applied to Jehovah. Bless the Lord, O my soul, and let every other soul bless him. There will be no drowsiness about even midnight devotion if the heart is set upon blessing God in Christ Jesus, which is the gospel translation of God in the sanctuary.

3. This last verse is the answer from the temple of the pilgrims preparing to depart as the day breaks. It is the ancient blessing of the high-priest condensed, and poured forth upon each individual pilgrim. " *The* LORD *that made heaven and earth bless thee out of Zion.*" Ye are scattering and going to your homes one by one ; may the benediction come upon you one by one. You have been up to Jehovah's city and temple at his bidding ; return each one with such a benediction as only he can give—divine, infinite, effectual, eternal. You are not going away from Jehovah's works or glories, for he made the heaven above you and the earth on which you dwell. He is your Creator, and he can bless you with untold mercies ; he can create joy and peace in your hearts, and make for you a new heaven and a new earth. May the Maker of all things make you to abound in blessings.

The benediction comes from the City of the Great King, from his appointed ministers, by virtue of his covenant, and so it is said to be " out of Zion." To this day the Lord blesses each one of his people through his church, his gospel, and the ordinances of his house. It is in communion with the saints that we receive untold benisons. May each one of us obtain yet more of the blessing which cometh from the Lord alone. Zion cannot bless us ; the holiest ministers can only wish us a blessing ; but Jehovah can and will bless each one of his waiting people. So may it be at this good hour. Do we desire it ? Let us then bless the Lord ourselves. Let us do it a second time. Then we may confidently hope that the third time we think of blessing we shall find ourselves conscious receivers of it from the Ever-blessed One. Amen.

EXPLANATORY NOTES AND QUAINT SAYINGS.

Whole Psalm.—It is a beautiful little ode, equally full of sublimity and simplicity. It is commonly supposed to be the work of David. With what admiration should we contemplate the man whose zeal in the cause of religion thus urged him to embrace every opportunity that could occur to him, among the lowest as well as the highest ranks of life, of promoting the praise and glory of his Creator ; now composing penitential hymns for his own closet ; now leading the temple service in national eulogies of the sublimest pitch to which human language can reach ; and now descending to the class of the watchman and patrol of the temple and the city, and tuning their lips to a reverential utterance of the name and the service of God !—*John Mason Good* (1764—1827), *in "An Historical Outline of the Book of Psalms."*

Whole Psalm.—This Psalm consists of a greeting, verses 1, 2, and the reply thereto. The greeting is addressed to those priests and Levites who have the night-watch in the Temple ; and this antiphon is purposely placed at the end of the collection of Songs of Degrees in order to take the place of a final beracha.* In this sense Luther styles the Psalm *epiphonema superiorum.*† It is also in other respects an appropriate finale.—*Franz Delitzsch.*

Whole Psalm.—The last cloud of smoke from the evening sacrifice has mixed with the blue sky, the last note of the evening hymn has died away on the ear. The watch is being set for the night. The twenty-four Levites, the three priests, and the captain of the guard, whose duty it was to keep ward from sunset to sunrise over the hallowed precincts, are already at their several posts, and the multitude are retiring through the gates, which will soon be shut, to many of them to open no more. But they cannot depart without one last expression of the piety that fills their hearts ; and turning to the watchers on tower and battlement, they address them in holy song, in what was at once a brotherly admonition and a touching prayer : "*Behold, bless ye the LORD, all ye servants of the LORD, which by night stand in the house of the LORD. Lift up your hands in the sanctuary, and bless the LORD.*" The pious guard are not unprepared for the appeal, and from their lofty heights, in words that float over the peopled city and down into the quiet valley of the Kedron, like the melody of angels, they respond to each worshipper who thus addressed them with a benedictory farewell : "*The LORD bless thee out of Zion, even he who made heaven and earth.*"—*Robert Nisbet.*

Whole Psalm.—The tabernacle and temple were served by priests during the *night* as well as the day. Those priests renewed the altar fire, fed the lamps, and guarded the sacred structure from intrusion and from plunder. The Psalm before us was prepared for the priests who served the sacred place by night. They were in danger of slumbering ; and they were in danger of idle reverie. Oh, how much time is wasted in mere reverie—in letting thought wander, and wander, and wander ! The priests were in danger, we say, of slumbering, of idle reverie, of vain thoughts, of useless meditation, and of profitless talk ; and therefore it is written,—"*Behold, bless ye the LORD, all ye servants of the LORD, which by night stand in the house of the LORD.*" Is it your duty to spend the night in watching ? then spend the night in worship. Do not let the time of watching be idle, wasted time ; but when others are slumbering and sleeping, and you are necessarily watchful, sustain the praises of God's house ; let there be praise in Zion—still praise by night as well as by day ! "*Lift up your hands in the sanctuary, and bless the LORD.*"

We may suppose these words to be addressed to the sacred sentinels, by the head of their course, or by the captain of the guard, or even by the high priest. We can imagine the captain of the guard coming in during the night watches, and saying to the priests who were guarding the temple, "*Behold, bless ye the LORD, all ye servants of the LORD, which by night stand in the house of the LORD.*" Or we could imagine the high priests, when the watch was set for the first part of the night, going to the priests who were under his control, and addressing to them these same soul-stirring words. Now our text is the response of these sacred sentinels. As they listened to the captain of the guard, or to the high priest, telling them to worship by night in the courts of the Lord—to lift up their hands in the sanctuary, and bless the Lord—they answered him, "*The LORD that made heaven and earth bless thee out of Zion.*" So that here you have brought before you the interesting and instructive subject of mutual benediction—the saints blessing each other.—*Samuel Martin,* 1817—1878.

Verse 1.—The Targum explains the first verse of the Temple watch. " The custom in the Second Temple appears to have been this. After midnight the chief of the door-keepers took the key of the inner Temple, and went with some of the priests through the small postern of the Fire Gate. In the inner court this watch divided itself into two companies, each carrying a burning torch ; one company turned west, the other east, and so they compassed the court to see whether all

---

* Blessing.

† " I take this Psalm to be a conclusion of those things which were spoken of before."—*Luther.*

were in readiness for the Temple service on the following morning. In the bake-house, where the *Mincha* (' meat-offering ') of the High Priest was baked, they met with the cry, ' All well.' Meanwhile the rest of the priests arose, bathed them-selves, and put on their garments. They then went into the stone chamber (one half of which was the hall of session of the Sanhedrim), and there, under the superintendence of the officer who gave the watchword, and one of the Sanhedrim, surrounded by the priests clad in their robes of office, their several duties for the coming day were assigned to each of the priests by lot. Luke i. 9."—*J. J. Stewart Perowne.*

Verse 1.—*"Behold."* The Psalm begins with the demonstrative adverb *Behold!* setting the matter of their duty before their eyes, for they were to be stimulated to devotion by looking constantly to the Temple. We are to notice the Psalmist's design in urging the duty of praise so earnestly upon them. Many of the Levites, through the tendency which there is in all men to abuse ceremonies, considered that nothing more was necessary than standing idly in the Temple, and thus over-looked the principal part of their duty. The Psalmist would show that merely to keep nightly watch over the Temple, kindle the lamps, and superintend the sacrifices, was of no importance, unless they served God spiritually, and referred all outward ceremonies to that which must be considered the main sacrifice—the celebration of God's praises. You may think it a very laborious service, as if he had said, to stand at watch in the Temple, while others sleep in their own houses ; but the worship which God requires is something more excellent than this, and demands of you to sing his praises before all the people.—*John Calvin.*

Verse 1.—*"Behold."* The first word in this verse, *"Behold,"* seemeth to point at the reasons which the priests in the Temple had to bless Jehovah ; as if it had been said, Behold, the house of God is built, the holy services are appointed, and the Lord hath given you rest from your enemies, that you may serve him acceptably ; set about it, therefore, with gratitude and alacrity. We read (1 Chron. ix. 33) that the Levitical singers were " employed in their work day and night " ; to the end, doubtless, that the earthly sanctuary might bear some resemblance to that above, where St. John tells us, the redeemed " are before the throne of God, and serve him day and night in his temple " : Rev. vii. 15.—*George Horne.*

Verse 1.—*"Behold, bless ye the Lord, all ye servants of the Lord."* From the exhortation to the Lord's ministers, learn, that the public worship of God is to be carefully looked unto ; and all men, but especially ministers, had need to be stirred up to take heed to themselves, and to the work of God's public worship, when they go about it ; for so much doth *"behold"* in this place import.—*David Dickson.*

Verse 1.—*"By night."* Even by night the Lord is to be remembered, and his praises are to be rehearsed.—*Martin Geier,* 1614—1681.

Verse 1.—*"Stand in the house of the Lord."* The Rabbins say, that the high priest only sat in the sanctuary (as did Eli, 1 Sam. i. 9) ; the rest stood, as ready pressed to do their office.—*John Trapp.*

Verse 1.—*"Which stand in the house of the Lord."* You who have now a per-manent house, and no longer, like pilgrims, have to dwell in tents.—*Robert Bellarmine.*

Verse 1.—*"Which stand in the house of the Lord."* Let not this your frequent being in his presence breed in you contempt ; as the saying is, " Too much familiarity breedeth contempt ; " but bless him always, acknowledge, and with reverence praise his excelllency.—*John Mayer,* 1653.

Verse 2.—*"Lift up your hands,"* etc. The lifting up of the hands was a gesture in prayer, it was an intimation of their expectation of receiving blessings from the Lord, and it was also an acknowledgment of their having received the same.—*Samuel Eyles Pierce.*

Verse 2.—*"In the sanctuary."* The Hebrew word signifying *holiness* as well as the *holy place* may here be taken in the former sense, the latter having been sufficiently expressed (verse 1) by " the house of the Lord " . . . . The priests (which are here spoken to) before their officiating, which is here expressed by *lifting up their hands,* were obliged to wash their hands.—*Henry Hammond.*

Verse 3.—*"The Lord that made heaven and earth bless thee out of Zion."* He doth not say, the Lord that made the earth bless thee out of heaven ; nor, the Lord that made heaven bless thee out of heaven ; but *"bless thee out of Zion."* As if he would teach us that all blessings come as immediately and primarily from heaven, so mediately and secondarily from *Zion*, where the Temple stood. If ever, therefore, we would have blessings outward, inward, private, public, secular, spiritual ; if ever we would have blessing in our estate, blessing in our land, blessing in our souls, we must pray for it, and pray for it here, in *Zion*, in God's house : for from the piety there exercised all blessings flow, as from a fountain that can never be drawn dry.—*Abraham Wright.*

Verse 3.—*"The* LORD *that made heaven and earth,"* etc. The priestly benediction brings God before us in a twofold character. He is described first as the Creator of the universe. He is described, in the second place, as dwelling "in Zion." In the first aspect, he is represented as the God of nature; in the second, as the God of grace. When I contemplate him as the Creator of the universe, there is abundant proof that he *can* bless me. When I contemplate him as dwelling in the Church, there is abundant proof that he *will* bless me. Both of these elements are essential to our faith.—*N. M'Michael.*

Verse 3.—*"The* LORD *that made heaven and earth,"* etc. As the priests were called upon to bless God in behalf of the people, so here they bless the people in behalf of God. Between the verses we may suppose the previous request to be complied with. The priests, having blessed God, turn and bless the people. The obvious allusion to the sacerdotal blessing (Num. vi. 23—27), favours the optative construction of this verse, which really includes a prediction—the Lord will bless thee. —*Joseph Addison Alexander.*

Verse 3.—*"The* LORD *bless thee."* All men lie under the curse, till God brings them into the fellowship of his church, and pronounce them blessed by his word, as *"The* LORD *bless thee"* doth import.—*David Dickson.*

Verse 3.—*"The* LORD *bless thee out of Zion."* The Church is the conservator of Divine revelation ; the Church is the offerer on earth of true worship ; it consists of a company of priests, a royal priesthood, part of whose mission is " to offer up spiritual sacrifices acceptable to God by Jesus Christ." The Church is the heritor of the covenants. God's covenants are made with his Church, and his promises are addressed chiefly to his Church. The Church is the scene of special Divine ministrations, God shows himself to his Church as he does not to that which is called the world. It is also the scene of special heavenly influences : and in a sense next to that in which God is said to reside in heaven, the Church is the dwelling-place of the Most High. Now, what is it to be *blessed out of Zion?* It is surely to be blessed with Zion's blessings, and to have Zion's endowments and gifts rendered sources of advantage and profit to us.—*Samuel Martin.*

Verse 3.—*"Bless thee."* The singular instead of the plural " bless you," because the words are taken from the form used by the High Priest in blessing the people. Num. vi. 24.—*J. J. Stewart Perowne.*

Verse 3.—*"Bless thee."* It is addressed to the church as one person, and to each individual in this united, unit-like church.—*Franz Delitzsch.*

HINTS TO PREACHERS.

Whole Psalm.—There are two things in this Psalm. I. Our blessing God : verses 1, 2. 1. How ? By gratitude, by love, by obedience, by prayer, by praise. 2. Where ? " In the house of the Lord," " in the sanctuary." 3. When ? Not in the day merely, but at night. Some of old spent the whole night, others part of the night, in the temple, praising God. As Christ spent whole nights in prayer for his people, they should not think it too much occasionally to spend whole nights in praise of him. Evening services should not be neglected on the Sabbath, nor on other days of the week.

II. God blessing us : verse 3. 1. The persons blessed : " bless thee "—every one who blesses him. 2. The condition : " out of Zion." In the fulfilment of religious duties, not in the neglect of them. 3. The blessing itself : of the Lord. They are blessed whom he blesses.—*G. R.*

Whole Psalm.—I. God—Jehovah—the fountain of blessing. II. The heavens and the earth, evidence of divine capacity to bless. III. The church, a channel of blessing. IV. The saints, the means of spreading blessing, through the spirit of blessing. V. The riches involved in the divine benediction.—*Samuel Martin.*

Whole Psalm.—I. Unique service: temple watching, night-sentinelship. II. Sublime society: the awful things of the sanctuary. III. Holy uplifting: hands, hearts, eyes. IV. Praise in the darkness heard far up in the light. V. Response from the stars fulfilling the prayer: "The Creator Lord bless *thee.*"—*W. B. H.*

Verse 1.—I. Night settles on the holy place: dark periods of church story. II. But God has his guards: Wycliffe and his band watching for the Reformation; Waldenses, etc. Never a night so dark but God is praised and served. III. Be it night or day, let the Levites fulfil their courses.—*W. B. H.*

Verse 1.—The Lord's servants exhorted to be, 1. Devout and joyful in their service. Sing at your work, though it be in the dark. 2. Zealous to employ every season of service aright. "By night," as by day, "bless the Lord." 3. Careful to avoid all hindrances to devotion in their service. When tempted to indolence and drowsiness, say—

> "Wake, and lift up thyself, my heart,
> And with the angels bear thy part,
> Who all night long, unwearied, sing
> High praise to the Eternal King."
>
> *W. H. J. P.*

Verse 1.—Directions for worship. I. It should be with great care: "Behold." II. With grateful joy: "Bless ye the Lord." III. Unanimously: "all ye." IV. With holy reverence, as by "servants of the Lord." V. With unflagging constancy: "stand by night."

Verse 1.—"Ye that stand by night." The night-watchman of the Lord's house, their value, their obscurity, their danger-slumber, their consolation, their dignity, their reward.

Verse 2.—Ingredients of worship. I. Uplifted hands. Energy, courage, prayer, aspiration. II. Uplifted hearts. Thank, praise, adore, and love the Lord.

Verse 3.—The Divine Benediction. I. From the Creator: ample, new, varied, boundless, enduring—all illustrated by his making heaven and earth. II. From the Redeemer: blessings most needful, rich, effectual, abiding,—all illustrated and guaranteed by his dwelling among men, purchasing a church, building an abode, revealing his glory, reigning on his throne

PSALM CXXXV.

GENERAL REMARKS.—*This Psalm has no title. It is mainly made up of selections from other Scriptures. It has been called a mosaic, and compared to a tessellated pavement. At the outset, its first two verses are taken from Ps. cxxxiv; while the latter part of verse 2 and the commencement of verse 3 put us in mind of Ps. cxvi. 19; and verse 4 suggests Deut. vii. 6. Does not verse 5 remind us of Ps. xcv. 3? As for verse 7, it is almost identical with Jer. x. 13, which may have been taken from it. The passage contained in verse 13 is to be found in Ex. iii. 15, and verse 14 in Deut. xxxii. 36. The closing verses, 8 to 12, are in Ps. cxxxvi. From verse 15 to the end the strain is a repetition of Ps. cxv. This process of tracing the expressions to other sources might be pushed further without straining the quotations; the whole Psalm is a compound of many choice extracts, and yet it has all the continuity and freshness of an original poem. The Holy Spirit occasionally repeats himself; not because he has any lack of thoughts or words, but because it is expedient for us that we hear the same things in the same form. Yet, when our great Teacher uses repetition, it is usually with instructive variations, which deserve our careful attention.*

DIVISION.—*The first fourteen verses contain an exhortation to praise Jehovah for his goodness (verse 3), for his electing love (verse 4), his greatness (5—7), his judgments (8—12), his unchanging character (13), and his love towards his people. This is followed by a denunciation of idols (verses 15 to 18), and a further exhortation to bless the name of the Lord. It is a song full of life, vigour, variety, and devotion.*

EXPOSITION.

PRAISE ye the LORD. Praise ye the name of the LORD; praise *him*, O ye servants of the LORD.

2 Ye that stand in the house of the LORD, in the courts of the house of our God,

3 Praise the LORD; for the LORD *is* good: sing praises unto his name; for *it is* pleasant.

4 For the LORD hath chosen Jacob unto himself, *and* Israel for his peculiar treasure.

5 For I know that the LORD *is* great, and *that* our Lord *is* above all gods.

6 Whatsoever the LORD pleased, *that* did he in heaven, and in earth, in the seas, and all deep places.

7 He causeth the vapours to ascend from the ends of the earth; he maketh lightnings for the rain; he bringeth the wind out of his treasuries.

8 Who smote the firstborn of Egypt, both of man and beast.

9 *Who* sent tokens and wonders into the midst of thee, O Egypt, upon Pharaoh, and upon all his servants.

10 Who smote great nations, and slew mighty kings;

11 Sihon king of the Amorites, and Og king of Bashan, and all the kingdoms of Canaan;

12 And gave their land *for* an heritage, an heritage unto Israel his people.

13 Thy name, O LORD, *endureth* for ever; *and* thy memorial, O LORD, throughout all generations.

14 For the LORD will judge his people, and he will repent himself concerning his servants.

1. "*Praise ye the LORD,*" or, *Hallelujah.* Let those who are themselves full of holy praise labour to excite the like spirit in others. It is not enough for us

to praise God ourselves, we are quite unequal to such a work ; let us call in all our friends and neighbours, and if they have been slack in such service, let us stir them up to it with loving exhortations. *"Praise ye the name of the LORD."* Let his character be extolled by you, and let all that he has revealed concerning himself be the subject of your song ; for this is truly his *name*. Specially let his holy and incommunicable name of " Jehovah " be the object of your adoration. By that name he sets forth his self-existence, and his immutability ; let these arouse your praises of his Godhead. Think of him with love, admire him with heartiness, and then extol him with ardour. Do not only magnify the Lord because he is God ; but study his character and his doings, and thus render intelligent, appreciative praise. *"Praise him, O ye servants of the LORD."* If others are silent, you must not be ; you must be the first to celebrate his praises. You are " servants," and this is part of your service ; his " name " is named upon you, therefore celebrate his name with praises ; you know what a blessed Master he is, therefore speak well of him. Those who shun his service are sure to neglect his praise ; but as grace has made you his own personal servants, let your hearts make you his court-musicians. Here we see the servant of the Lord arousing his fellow-servants by three times calling upon them to praise. Are we then, so slow in such a sweet employ ? Or is it that when we do our utmost it is all too little for such a Lord ? Both are true. We do not praise enough ; we cannot praise too much. We ought to be always at it ; answering to the command here given—Praise, Praise, Praise. Let the three-in-one have the praises of our spirit, soul, and body. For the past, the present, and the future, let us render three-fold hallelujahs.

2. *"Ye that stand in the house of the LORD, in the courts of the house of our God."* You are highly favoured ; you are the domestics of the palace, nearest to the Father of the heavenly family, privileged to find your home in his house ; therefore you must, beyond all others, abound in thanksgiving. You " stand," or abide in the temple ; you are constant occupants of its various courts ; and therefore from you we expect unceasing praise. Should not ministers be celebrated for celebrating the praises of Jehovah ? Should not church-officers and church-members excel all others in the excellent duty of adoration ? Should not all of every degree who wait even in his outer courts unite in his worship ? Ought not the least and feeblest of his people to proclaim his praises, in company with those who live nearest to him ? Is it not a proper thing to remind them of their obligations ? Is not the Psalmist wise when he does so in this case and in many others ? Those who can call Jehovah *"our God"* are highly blessed, and therefore should abound in the work of blessing him. Perhaps this is the sweetest word in these two verses. " This God is our God for ever and ever." " Our God " signifies possession, communion in possession, assurance of possession, delight in possession. Oh the unutterable joy of calling God our own !

3. *"Praise the LORD."* Do it again ; continue to do it ; do it better and more heartily ; do it in growing numbers ; do it at once. There are good reasons for praising the Lord, and among the first is this—*" for the LORD is good."* He is so good that there is none good in the same sense or degree. He is so good that all good is found in him, flows from him, and is rewarded by him. The word God is brief for good ; and truly God is the essence of goodness. Should not his goodness be well spoken of ? Yea, with our best thoughts, and words, and hymns let us glorify his name. *"Sing praises unto his name ; for it is pleasant."* The adjective may apply to the singing and to the name—they are both pleasant. The vocal expression of praise by sacred song is one of our greatest delights. We were created for this purpose, and hence it is a joy to us. It is a charming duty to praise the lovely name of our God. All pleasure is to be found in the joyful worship of Jehovah ; all joys are in his sacred name as perfumes lie slumbering in a garden of flowers. The mind expands, the soul is lifted up, the heart warms, the whole being is filled with delight when we are engaged in singing the high praises of our Father, Redeemer, Comforter. When in any occupation goodness and pleasure unite, we do well to follow it up without stint : yet it is to be feared that few of us sing to the Lord at all in proportion as we talk to men.

4. *"For the LORD hath chosen Jacob unto himself."* Jehovah hath chosen Jacob. Should not the sons of Jacob praise him who has so singularly favoured them ? Election is one of the most forcible arguments for adoring love. Chosen ! chosen unto himself !—who can be grateful enough for being concerned in this privilege ? " Jacob have I loved," said Jehovah, and he gave no reason for his love except that

he chose to love. Jacob had then done neither good nor evil, yet thus the Lord determined, and thus he spake. If it be said that the choice was made upon foresight of Jacob's character, it is, perhaps, even more remarkable ; for there was little enough about Jacob that could deserve special choice. By nature Jacob was by no means the most lovable of men. No, it was sovereign grace which dictated the choice. But, mark, it was not a choice whose main result was the personal welfare of Jacob's seed : the nation was chosen by God *unto himself,* to answer the divine ends and purposes in blessing all mankind. Jacob's race was chosen to be the Lord's own, to be the trustees of his truth, the maintainers of his worship, the mirrors of his mercy. Chosen they were ; but mainly for this end, that they might be a peculiar people, set apart unto the service of the true God.

"And Israel for his peculiar treasure." God's choice exalts ; for here the name is changed from Jacob, the supplanter, to Israel, the prince. The love of God gives a new name and imparts a new value ; for the comparison to a royal treasure is a most honourable one. As kings have a special regalia, and a selection of the rarest jewels, so the Lord deigns to reckon his chosen nation as his wealth, his delight, his glory. What an honour to the spiritual Israel that they are all this to the Lord their God ! We are a people near and dear unto him ; precious and honourable in his sight. How can we refuse our loudest, heartiest, sweetest music ? If *we* did not extol him, the stones in the street would cry out against us.

5. *"For I know that the* LORD *is great, and that our Lord is above all gods."* The greatness of God is as much a reason for adoration as his goodness, when we are once reconciled to him. God is great positively, great comparatively, and great superlatively—" above all gods." Of this the Psalmist had an assured personal persuasion. He says positively, "I know." It is knowledge worth possessing. He knew by observation, inspiration, and realization ; he was no agnostic, he was certain and clear upon the matter. He not only knows the greatness of Jehovah, but that as the Adonai, or Ruler, " our Lord " is infinitely superior to all the imaginary deities of the heathen, and to all great ones besides.

> " Let princes hear, let angels know,
>   How mean their natures seem ;
> Those gods on high, and gods below,
>   When once compared with him."

Many have thought to worship Jehovah, and other gods with him ; but this holy man tolerated no such notion. Others have thought to combine their religion with obedience to the unrighteous laws of tyrannical princes ; this, also, the sweet singer of Israel denounced ; for he regarded the living God as altogether above all men, who as magistrates and princes have been called gods. Observe here the fourth of the five " fors." Verses 3, 4, 5, and 14 contain reasons for praise, each set forth with " for." A fruitful meditation might be suggested by this.

6. *"Whatsoever the* LORD *pleased, that did he in heaven, and in earth, in the seas, and all deep places."* His will is carried out throughout all space. The king's warrant runs in every portion of the universe. The heathen divided the great domain ; but Jupiter does not rule in heaven, nor Neptune on the sea, nor Pluto in the lower regions ; Jehovah rules over all. His decree is not defeated, his purpose is not frustrated : in no one point is his good pleasure set aside. The word " whatsoever " is of the widest range and includes all things, and the four words of peace which are mentioned comprehend all space ; therefore the declaration of the text knows neither limit nor exception. Jehovah works his will : he pleases to do, and he performs the deed. None can stay his hand. How different this from the gods whom the heathen fabled to be subject to all the disappointments, failures, and passions of men ! How contrary even to those so-called Christian conceptions of God which subordinate him to the will of man, and make his eternal purposes the football of human caprice. Our theology teaches us no such degrading notions of the Eternal as that he can be baffled by man. " His purpose shall stand, and he will do all his pleasure." No region is too high, no abyss too deep, no land too distant, no sea too wide for his omnipotence : his divine pleasure travels post over all the realm of nature, and his behests are obeyed.

7. *"He causeth the vapours to ascend from the ends of the earth."* Here we are taught the power of God in creation. The process of evaporation is passed by unnoticed by the many, because they see it going on all around them ; the usual ceases to be wonderful to the thoughtless, but it remains a marvel to the instructed.

When we consider upon what an immense scale evaporation is continually going on, and how needful it is for the existence of all life, we may well admire the wisdom and the power which are displayed therein. All around us from every point of the horizon the vapour rises, condenses into clouds, and ultimately descends as rain. Whence the vapours originally ascended from which our showers are formed it would be impossible to tell ; most probably the main part of them comes from the tropical regions, and other remote places at " the ends of the earth." It is the Lord who causes them to rise, and not a mere law. What is law without a force at the back of it ? *"He maketh lightnings for the rain."* There is an intimate connection between lightning and rain, and this would seem to be more apparent in Palestine than even with ourselves ; for we constantly read of thunderstorms in that country as attending heavy down-pours of rain. Lightning is not to be regarded as a lawless force, but as a part of that wonderful machinery by which the earth is kept in a fit condition : a force as much under the control of God as any other, a force most essential to our existence. The ever-changing waters, rains, winds, and electric currents circulate as if they were the life-blood and vital spirits of the universe. *"He bringeth the wind out of his treasuries."* This great force which seems left to its own wild will is really under the supreme and careful government of the Lord. As a monarch is specially master of the contents of his own treasure, so is our God the Lord of the tempest and hurricane ; and as princes do not spend their treasure without taking note and count of it, so the Lord does not permit the wind to be wasted, or squandered without purpose. Everything in the material world is under the immediate direction and control of the Lord of all. Observe how the Psalmist brings before us the personal action of Jehovah : " he causeth," " he maketh," " he bringeth." Everywhere the Lord worketh all things, and there is no power which escapes his supremacy. It is well for us that it is so : one bandit force wandering through the Lord's domains defying his control would cast fear and trembling over all the provinces of providence. Let us praise Jehovah for the power and wisdom with which he rules clouds, and lightnings, and winds, and all other mighty and mysterious agencies.

8. *"Who smote the firstborn of Egypt, both of man and beast."* Herein the Lord is to be praised ; for this deadly smiting was an act of justice against Egypt, and of love to Israel. But what a blow it was ! All the firstborn slain in a moment ! How it must have horrified the nation, and cowed the boldest enemies of Israel ! Beasts because of their relationship to man as domestic animals are in many ways made to suffer with him. The firstborn of beasts must die as well as the firstborn of their owners, for the blow was meant to astound and overwhelm, and it accomplished its purpose. The firstborn of God had been sorely smitten, and they were set free by the Lord's meting out to their oppressors the like treatment.

9. *"Who sent tokens and wonders into the midst of thee, O Egypt, upon Pharaoh, and upon all his servants."* The Lord is still seen by the Psalmist as sending judgments upon rebellious men ; he keeps before us the personal action of God, " who sent tokens, etc." The more distinctly God is seen the better. Even in plagues he is to be seen, as truly as in mercies. The plagues were not only terrible wonders which astounded men, but forcible tokens or signs by which they were instructed. No doubt the plagues were aimed at the various deities of the Egyptians, and were a grand exposure of their impotence : each one had its own special significance. The judgments of the Lord were no side blows, they struck the nation at the heart ; he sent his bolts " into the midst of thee, O Egypt ! " These marvels happened in the centre of the proud and exclusive nation of Egypt, which thought itself far superior to other lands ; and many of these plagues touched the nation in points upon which it prided itself. The Psalmist addresses that haughty nation, saying, " O Egypt," as though reminding it of the lessons which it had been taught by the Lord's right hand. Imperious Pharaoh had been the ringleader in defying Jehovah, and he was made personally to smart for it ; nor did his flattering courtiers escape, upon each one of them the scourge fell heavily. God's servants are far better off than Pharaoh's servants : those who stand in the courts of Jehovah are delivered, but the courtiers of Pharaoh are smitten all of them, for they were all partakers in his evil deeds. The Lord is to be praised for thus rescuing his own people, and causing their cruel adversaries to bite the dust. Let no true Israelite forget the song of the Red Sea, but anew let us hear a voice summoning us to exulting praise : " Sing unto the Lord, for he hath triumphed gloriously."

10. *"Who smote great nations, and slew mighty kings."* The nations of Canaan

joined in the desperate resistance offered by their monarchs, and so they were smitten ; while their kings, the ringleaders of the fight, were slain. Those who resist the divine purpose will find it hard to kick against the pricks. The greatness of the nations and the might of the kings availed nothing against the Lord. He is prepared to mete out vengeance to those who oppose his designs : those who dream of him as too tender to come to blows have mistaken the God of Israel. He intended to bless the work through his chosen people, and he would not be turned from his purpose : cost what it might, he would preserve the candle of truth which he had lighted, even though the blood of nations should be spilt in its defence. The wars against the Canaanite races were a price paid for the setting up of a nation which was to preserve for the whole world the lively oracles of God.

11. *"Sihon king of the Amorites, and Og king of Bashan."* These two kings were the first to oppose, and they were among the most notable of the adversaries : their being smitten is therefore a special object of song for loyal Israelites. The enmity of these two kings was wanton and unprovoked, and hence their overthrow was the more welcome to Israel. Sihon had been victorious in his war with Moab, and thought to make short work with Israel, but he was speedily overthrown : Og was of the race of the giants,. and by his huge size inspired the tribes with dread ; but they were encouraged by the previous overthrow of Sihon, and soon the giant king fell beneath their sword. *"And all the kingdoms of Canaan."* Many were these petty principalities, and some of them were populous and valiant ; but they all fell beneath the conquering hand of Joshua, for the Lord was with him. Even so shall all the foes of the Lord's believing people in these days be put to the rout : Satan and the world shall be overthrown, and all the hosts of sin shall be destroyed, for our greater Joshua leads forth our armies, conquering and to conquer.

Note that in this verse we have the details of matters which were mentioned in the bulk in the previous stanza : it is well when we have sung of mercies in the gross to consider them one by one, and give to each individual blessing a share in our song. It is well to preserve abundant memorials of the Lord's deliverance, so that we not only sing of mighty kings as a class, but also of " Sihon king of the Amorites, and Og king of Bashan " as distinct persons.

12. *"And gave their land for an heritage, an heritage unto Israel his people."* Jehovah is Lord Paramount, and permits men to hold their lands upon lease, terminable at his pleasure. The nations of Canaan had become loathsome with abominable vices, and they were condemned by the great Judge of all the earth to be cut off from the face of the country which they defiled. The twelve tribes were charged to act as their executioners, and as their fee they were to receive Canaan as a possession. Of old the Lord had given this land to Abraham and his seed by a covenant of salt, but he allowed the Amorites and other tribes to sojourn in it till their iniquity was full, and then he bade his people come and take their own out of the holders' hands. Canaan was their heritage beeause they were the Lord's heritage, and he gave it to them actually because he had long before given it to them by promise.

The Lord's chosen still have a heritage from which none can keep them back. Covenant blessings of inestimable value are secured to them ; and, as surely as God has a people, his people shall have a heritage. To them it comes by gift, though they have to fight for it. Often does it happen when they slay a sin or conquer a difficulty that they are enriched by the spoil : to them even evils work for good, and trials ensure triumphs. No enemy shall prevail so as to really injure them, for they shall find a heritage where once they were opposed by " all the kingdoms of Canaan."

13. *"Thy name, O Lord, endureth for ever."* God's name is eternal, and will never be changed. His character is immutable ; his fame and honour also shall remain to all eternity. There shall always be life in the name of Jesus, and sweetness and consolation. Those upon whom the Lord's name is named in verity and truth shall be preserved by it, and kept from all evil, world without end. Jehovah is a name which shall outlive the ages, and retain the fulness of its glory and might for ever. *"And thy memorial, O Lord, throughout all generations."* Never shall men forget thee, O Lord. The ordinances of thine house shall keep thee in men's memories, and thine everlasting gospel and the grace which goes therewith shall be abiding remembrancers of thee. Grateful hearts will for ever beat to thy praise, and enlightened minds shall continue to marvel at all thy wondrous works. Men's memorials decay, but the memorial of the Lord abideth evermore. What a comfort

to desponding minds, trembling for the ark of the Lord! No, precious Name, thou shalt never perish! Fame of the Eternal, thou shalt never grow dim!

This verse must be construed in its connection, and it teaches us that the honour and glory gained by the Lord in the overthrow of the mighty kings would never die out. Israel for long ages reaped the benefit of the *prestige* which the divine victories had brought to the nation. Moreover, the Lord in thus keeping his covenant which he made with Abraham, when he promised to give the land to his seed, was making it clear that his memorial contained in promises and covenant would never be out of his sight. His name endures in all its truthfulness, for those who occupied Israel's land were driven out that the true heirs might dwell therein in peace.

14. *"For the LORD will judge his people."* He will exercise personal discipline over them, and not leave it to their foes to maltreat them at pleasure. When the correction is ended he will arise and avenge them of their oppressors, who for a while were used by him as his rod. He may seem to forget his people, but it is not so; he will undertake their cause and deliver them. The judges of Israel were also her deliverers, and such is the Lord of hosts: in this sense—as ruling, preserving, and delivering his chosen—Jehovah will judge his people. *"And he will repent himself concerning his servants."* When he has smitten them, and they lie low before him, he will pity them as a father pitieth his children, for he doth not afflict willingly. The Psalm speaks after the manner of men: the nearest description that words can give of the Lord's feeling towards his suffering servants is that he repents the evil which he inflicted upon them. He acts as if he had changed his mind and regretted smiting them. It goes to the heart of God to see his beloved ones oppressed by their enemies: though they deserve all they suffer, and more than all, yet the Lord cannot see them smart without a pang. It is remarkable that the nations by which God has afflicted Israel have all been destroyed as if the tender Father hated the instruments of his children's correction. The chosen nation is here called, first, " his people," and then " his servants:" as his people he judges them, as his servants he finds comfort in them, for so the word may be read. He is most tender to them when he sees their service; hence the Scripture saith, " I will spare them, as a man spareth his own son that serveth him." Should not the " servants " of God praise him? He plagued Pharaoh's servants; but as for his own he has mercy upon them, and returns to them in love after he has in the truest affection smitten them for their iniquities. " Praise him, O ye servants of the Lord."

Now we come to the Psalmist's denunciation of idols, which follows most naturally upon his celebration of the one only living and true God.

15 The idols of the heathen *are* silver and gold, the work of men's hands.

16 They have mouths, but they speak not; eyes have they, but they see not;

17 They have ears, but they hear not; neither is there *any* breath in their mouths.

18 They that make them are like unto them: *so is* every one that trusteth in them.

15. *"The idols of the heathen are silver and gold, the work of men's hands."* Their essential material is dead metal, their attributes are but the qualities of senseless substances, and what of form and fashion they exhibit they derive from the skill and labour of those who worship them. It is the height of insanity to worship metallic manufactures. Though silver and gold are useful to us when we rightly employ them, there is nothing about them which can entitle them to reverence and worship. If we did not know the sorrowful fact to be indisputable, it would seem to be impossible that intelligent beings could bow down before substances which they must themselves refine from the ore, and fashion into form. One would think it less absurd to worship one's own hands than to adore that which those hands have made. What great works can these mock deities perform for man when they are themselves the works of man? Idols are fitter to be played with, like dolls by babes, than to be adored by grown-up men. Hands are better used in breaking than in making objects which can be put to such an idiotic use. Yet the heathen love their abominable deities better than silver and gold: it were well if we could say that some professed believers in the Lord had as much love for *him*.

16. *"They have mouths."* For their makers fashioned them like themselves. An opening is made where the mouth should be, and yet it is no mouth, for they eat not, *they speak not.* They cannot communicate with their worshippers; they are dumb as death. If they cannot even speak, they are not even so worthy of worship as our children at school. Jehovah speaks, and it is done; but these images utter never a word. Surely, if they could speak, they would rebuke their votaries. Is not their silence a still more powerful rebuke? When our philosophical teachers deny that God has made any verbal revelation of himself they also confess that their god is dumb.

"Eyes have they, but they see not." Who would adore a blind man—how can the heathen be so mad as to bow themselves before a blind image? The eyes of idols have frequently been very costly; diamonds have been used for that purpose; but of what avail is the expense, since they see nothing? If they cannot even see us, how can they know our wants, appreciate our sacrifices, or spy out for us the means of help? What a wretched thing, that a man who can see should bow down before an image which is blind! The worshipper is certainly physically in advance of his god, and yet mentally he is on a level with it; for assuredly his foolish heart is darkened, or he would not so absurdly play the fool.

17. *"They have ears,"* and very large ones too, if we remember certain of the Hindoo idols. *"But they hear not."* Useless are their ears; in fact, they are mere counterfeits and deceits. Ears which men make are always deaf: the secret of hearing is wrapped up with the mystery of life, and both are in the unsearchable mind of the Lord. It seems that these heathen gods are dumb, and blind, and deaf— a pretty bundle of infirmities to be found in a deity! *"Neither is there any breath in their mouths;"* they are dead, no sign of life is perceptible; and breathing, which is of the essence of animal life, they never know. Shall a man waste his breath in crying to an idol which has no breath? Shall life offer up petitions to death? Verily, this is a turning of things upside down.

18. *"They that make them are like unto them:"* they are as blockish, as senseless, as stupid as the gods they have made, and, like them they are the objects of divine abhorrence, and shall be broken in pieces in due time. *"So is every one that trusteth in them."* The idol-worshippers are as bad as the idol-makers; for if there were none to worship, there would be no market for the degrading manufacture. Idolaters are spiritually dead, they are the mere images of men, their best being is gone, they are not what they seem. Their mouths do not really pray, their eyes see not the truth, their ears hear not the voice of the Lord, and the life of God is not in them. Those who believe in their own inventions in religion betray great folly, and an utter absence of the quickening Spirit. Gracious men can see the absurdity of forsaking the true God and setting up rivals in his place; but those who perpetrate this crime think not so: on the contrary, they pride themselves upon their great wisdom, and boast of " advanced thought " and " modern culture." Others there are who believe in a baptismal regeneration which does not renew the nature, and they make members of Christ and children of God who have none of the spirit of Christ, or the signs of adoption. May we be saved from such mimicry of divine work lest we also become like our idols.

19 Bless the LORD, O house of Israel : bless the LORD, O house of Aaron :

20 Bless the LORD, O house of Levi : ye that fear the LORD, bless the LORD.

21 Blessed be the LORD out of Zion, which dwelleth at Jerusalem. Praise ye the LORD.

19. *"Bless the LORD, O house of Israel."* All of you, in all your tribes, praise the one Jehovah. Each tribe, from Reuben to Benjamin, has its own special cause for blessing the Lord, and the nation as a whole has substantial reasons for pouring out benedictions upon his name. Those whom God has named " the house of Israel," a family of prevailing princes, ought to show their loyalty by thankfully bowing before their sovereign Lord. *"Bless the LORD, O house of Aaron."* These were elected to high office and permitted to draw very near to the divine presence ; therefore they beyond all others were bound to bless the Lord. Those who are favoured to be leaders in the church should be foremost in adoration. In God's house the house of Aaron should feel bound to speak well of his name before all the house of Israel.

20. *"Bless the LORD, O house of Levi."* These helped the priests in other things, let them aid them in this also. The house of Israel comprehends all the chosen seed ; then we come down to the smaller but more central ring of the house of Aaron, and now we widen out to the whole tribe of Levi. Let reverence and adoration spread from man to man until the whole lump of humanity shall be leavened. The house of Levi had choice reasons for blessing God : read the Levite story and see. Remember that the whole of the Levites were set apart for holy service, and supported by the tribes allotted to them ; therefore they were in honour bound above all others to worship Jehovah with cheerfulness.

"Ye that fear the LORD, bless the LORD." These are the choicer spirits, the truly spiritual : they are not the Lord's in name only, but in heart and spirit. The Father seeketh such to worship him. If Aaron and Levi both forget and fail, these will not. It may be that this verse is intended to bring in God-fearing men who were not included under Israel, Aaron, and Levi. They were Gentile proselytes, and this verse opens the door and bids them enter. Those who fear God need not wait for any other qualification for sacred service ; godly fear proves us to be in the covenant with Israel, in the priesthood with Aaron, and in the service of the Lord with Levi. Filial fear, such as saints feel towards the Lord, does not hinder their praise ; nay, it is the main source and fountain of their adoration.

21. *"Blessed be the LORD out of Zion, which dwelleth at Jerusalem."* Let him be most praised at home. Where he blesses most, let him be blessed most. Let the beloved mount of Zion, and the chosen city of Jerusalem echo his praises. He remains among his people : he is their dwelling-place, and they are his dwelling-place : let this intimate communion ensure intense gratitude on the part of his chosen. The temple of holy solemnities which is Christ, and the city of the Great King, which is the church, may fitly be regarded as the head-quarters of the praises of Jehovah, the God of Israel. *"Praise ye the LORD."* Hallelujah. Amen, and Amen.

EXPLANATORY NOTES AND QUAINT SAYINGS.

Whole Psalm.—This glorious Psalm of universal praise, placed at the end of the " Songs of Up-goings," which flow into it, and find their response in it, may be likened to a large and beautiful lake, into which rivers discharge their waters, and lose themselves in its calm expanse.—*Chr. Wordsworth.*

Whole Psalm.—This Psalm differs from that which went before. Its drift is not only to stir up the priests and Levites, as it was in the former, to this duty of praising God, but *the people* also : and that, 1. Because the arguments which here he brings to press this duty, did in common concern both priests and people ; and, 2. Because that clause, which is here added, " *in the courts of the house of our God,*" may be extended to the people, as well as to the priests, seeing there were some courts in the Temple which were for the people to worship God in.—*Arthur Jackson.*

Whole Psalm.—This is a song of praise to the Lord for his goodness as the Lord of creation, in seven verses ; for his grace as the deliverer of his people, in seven more : and for his unity as the only true and living God, in seven more.—*James G. Murphy.*

Whole Psalm.—This seems to have been the morning hymn which the Levites were called upon to sing at the opening of the gates of the Temple ; and, as some think, the one before was used at shutting them in the evening.—*John Kitto, in "The Pictorial Bible."*

Verse 1.—This verse and the following are word for word with the first verse of the last Psalm, and are now repeated, with the view of keeping up the praise then and there commenced.—*Robert Bellarmine.*

Verse 1.—*"Praise ye the LORD."* Hallelujah is the Hebrew word. It signifies " *Praise ye the LORD.*" By this the faithful do provoke one another to give thanks unto God, and they cheer up their hearts and tune their spirits to perform this duty in the best manner, by making this preface as it were thereunto. True joy of the

Holy Ghost will not endure to be kept and cooped up in any one man's breast and bosom, but it striveth to get companions both for the pouring out and imparting of itself unto them, that they may be filled and refreshed out of this spring of joy ; as also that itself may be the more increased and inflamed by the united rejoicing of many good hearts together, that are all baptized in one spirit, and are thereby made able to inflame and to edify one another.—*Thomas Brightman* (1557—1607), *in "The Revelation of St. John Illustrated."*

Verse 1.—*"Praise ye the name of the* LORD*."* That is, the Lord himself, and the perfections of his nature; his greatness, goodness, grace, and mercy; his holiness, justice, power, truth, and faithfulness. Also his word, by which he makes known himself : this is a distinguishing blessing to his people, for which he is to be praised : see Ps. xlviii. 1, and Ps. cxlvii. 19, 20.—*John Gill.*

Verse 1.—*"The name of the* LORD*."*—The first discovery of the name I AM, which signifies the Divine eternity, as well as immutability, was for the comfort of the oppressed Israelites in Egypt : Exodus iii. 14, 15. It was then published from the secret place of the Almighty, as the only strong cordial to refresh them. It hath not yet, it shall not ever, lose its virtue in any of the miseries that have or shall successively befall the church. 'Tis as durable as the God whose name it is : he is still I AM and the same to the church as he was then to his Israel. His spiritual Israel have a greater right to the glories of it than the carnal Israel could have. No oppression can be greater than theirs ; what was a comfort suited to that distress hath the same suitableness to every other oppression. It was not a temporary name, but a name for ever, his " memorial to all generations " (verse 15), and reacheth to the church of the Gentiles, with whom he treats as the God of Abraham, ratifying that covenant by the Messiah, which he made with Abraham the father of the faithful.—*Stephen Charnock.*

Verse 1.—*"The name of the* LORD*."* Jehovah is called *" the name "* as far exceeding all other names, and as being proper and peculiar only to the true God. Other things are sometimes called gods, but nothing is or can be called Jehovah but only the Almighty Creator of the world. " That men may know," saith David, " that thou, whose name is Jehovah, art the Most High over all the earth " : Ps. lxxxiii. 18. From his calling himself JEHOVAH the LORD, we may easily gather what kind of thoughts he would have us, his creatures, entertain in our minds concerning him. When we think of him, we must raise our thoughts above all things else, and think of him as the Universal Being of the world, that gives essence and existence to all things in it : as Jehovah, the Being in whom we particularly, as well as other things, live and move, and have our being : as Jehovah, the Lord paramount over the whole world, to whom all angels and archangels in heaven, with all the kings and kingdoms upon earth, are entirely subject : as Jehovah, in whom all perfections are so perfectly united that they are all but one infinite perfection : as Jehovah, knowledge itself, always actually knowing all things that ever were, or are, or will be, or can be known : as Jehovah, wisdom itself, always contriving, ordering, and disposing of all, and everything, in the best order, after the best manner, and to the best possible end : as Jehovah, power, omnipotence itself, continually doing what he wills, only by willing it should be done, and always working either with means or without means, as he himself sees good : as Jehovah, light and glory itself, shining forth in and by and through everything that is made or done in the whole world. as Jehovah, holiness, purity, simplicity, greatness, majesty, eminency, super-eminency itself, infinitely exalted above all things else, existing in, and of himself, and having all things else continually subsisting in him : as Jehovah, goodness itself, doing and making all things good, and so communicating his goodness to all his creatures as to be the only fountain of all the goodness that is in any of them : as Jehovah, justice and righteousness itself, giving to all their due, and exacting no more of any man than what is absolutely due to him : as Jehovah, mercy itself, pardoning and forgiving all the sins that mankind commit against him, as soon as they repent and turn to him : as Jehovah, patience and longsuffering itself, bearing a long time, even with those who continue in their rebellions against him, waiting for their coming to a due sense of their folly and madness, that he may be gracious and merciful to them ; as Jehovah, love and kindness, and bounty itself, freely distributing his blessings among all his creatures, both good and bad, just and unjust, those that love him, and those that love him not : as Jehovah, truth and faithfulness itself, always performing what he promiseth to his people : as Jehovah, infinitude, immensity itself, in all things, to all things, beyond all things, everywhere, wholly, essentially, continually present : as Jehovah, constancy, immutability, eternity itself, without any variableness, or shadow of change ; yesterday, to-day, and for ever the same. In a word, when we think of the Most High God, Father, Son, and Holy Ghost, we should think of him as Jehovah, Unity in Trinity, Trinity in Unity, Three Persons, One Being, One Essence, One Lord, One Jehovah, blessed for ever. This is that glorious, that Almighty being, which the Psalmist here means when he saith, *"Praise ye the name of the Lord."*—*William Beveridge, 1636—1708.*

Verse 1.—*"Praise him, O ye servants of the Lord."* For ye will do nothing out of place by praising your Lord *as servants.* And if ye were to be for ever only servants, ye ought to praise the Lord ; how much more ought those servants to praise the Lord who have obtained the privilege of sons ?—*Augustine.*

Verse 1.—*"Praise," "praise," "praise."* When duties are thus inculcated, it noteth the necessity and excellency thereof ; together with our dulness and backwardness thereunto.—*John Trapp.*

Verses 1, 2, 21.—*"Praise."* To prevent any feeling of weariness which might arise from the very frequent repetition of this exhortation to praise God, it is only necessary to remember that there is no sacrifice in which he takes greater delight than in the expression of praise. Thus (Ps. l. 14), " Sacrifice unto the Lord thanksgiving, and pay thy vows unto the Most High ; " and (Ps. cxvi. 12, 13), " What shall I render unto the Lord for all his benefits toward me ? I will take the cup of salvation, and call upon the name of the Lord." Particular attention is to be paid to those passages of Scripture which speak in such high terms of that worship of God which is spiritual ; otherwise we may be led, in the exercise of a misguided zeal, to spend our labour upon trifles, and in this respect imitate the example of too many who have wearied themselves with ridiculous attempts to invent additions to the service of God, while they have neglected what is of all other things most important. That is the reason why the Holy Spirit so repeatedly inculcates the duty of praise. It is that we may not undervalue, or grow careless in this devotional exercise. It implies, too, an indirect censure of our tardiness in proceeding to the duty ; for he would not reiterate the admonition were we ready and active in the discharge of it.—*John Calvin.*

Verses 1, 2, 3.—As *Gotthold* was one day passing a tradesman's house, he heard the notes of a Psalm, with which the family were concluding their morning meal. He was deeply affected, and, with a full heart, said to himself : O my God, how pleasing to my ears is the sound of thy praise, and how comforting to my soul the thought that there are still a few who bless thee for thy goodness. Alas, the great bulk of mankind have become brutalized, and resemble the swine, which in harvest gather and fatten upon the acorns beneath the oak, but show to the tree, which bore them, no other thanks than rubbing off its bark, and tearing up the sod around it. In former times, it was the law in certain monasteries, that the chanting of the praise of God should know no interruption, and that one choir of monks should, at stated intervals, relieve another in the holy employment. To the superstition and trust in human works, of which there may have been here a mixture, we justly assign a place among the wood, hay, and stubble (1 Cor. iii. 12). At the same time it is undeniably right that thy praise should never cease ; and were men to be silent, the very stones would cry out. We must begin eternal life here below, not only in our conscience, but also with our praise. Our soul ought to be like a flower, not merely receiving the gentle influence of heaven, but, in its turn, and as if in gratitude, exhaling also a sweet and pleasant perfume. It should be our desire, as it once was that of a pious man, that our hearts should melt and dissolve like incense in the fire of love, and yield the sweet fragrance of praise ; or we should be like the holy martyr who professed himself willing to be consumed, if from his ashes a little flower might spring and blossom to the glory of God. We should be ready to give our very blood to fertilize the garden of the church, and render it more productive of the fruit of praise.

Well, then, my God, I will praise and extol thee with heart and mouth to the utmost of my power. Oh, that without the interruptions which eating, and drinking, and sleep require, I could apply myself to this heavenly calling ! Every mouthful of air which I inhale is mixed with the goodness which preserves my life ; let every breath which I exhale be mingled at least with a hearty desire for thy honour and praise.

Hallelujah ! Ye holy angels, ye children of men, and all ye creatures, praise the Lord with me, and let us exalt his name together.—*Christian Scriver [Gotthold]*, 1629—1693.

Verse 3.—"*Praise the* LORD." *Hallelujah* (praise to Jah !) *for good (is) Jehovah, Make music to his name, for it is lovely.* The last words may also be translated, *he is lovely,* i.e. an object worthy of supreme attachment.—*Joseph Addison Alexander.*

Verse 3.—"*Praise the* LORD ; *for the* LORD *is good.*" That is, originally, transcendently, effectively ; he is good, and doeth good (Ps. cxix. 68), and is therefore to be praised with mind, mouth, and practice.—*John Trapp.*

Verse 3.—"*Sing praises unto his name ; for it is pleasant.*" The work of praising God hath a sort of reward joined with it. When we praise God most we get much benefit by so doing : it is so comely in itself, so pleasant unto God, and profitable to the person that offereth praises, so fit to cheer up his spirit, and strengthen his faith in God, whose praises are the pillars of the believer's confidence and comfort, that a man should be allured thereunto : "*Sing praises unto his name ; for it is pleasant ;*" and this is the second motive or reason to praise God [the first being that "the Lord is good"].—*David Dickson.*

Verse 4.—"*For the* LORD *hath chosen,*" etc. God's distinguishing grace should make his elect lift up many a humble, joyful, and thankful heart to him.—*John Trapp.*

Verse 4.—"*Jacob,*" "*Israel.*" Praise the Lord for enrolling you in this company. To quicken you in this work of praise, consider what you were ; you were not a people, God raised you up from the very dunghill to this preferment ; remember your past estate. Look, as old Jacob considered what he had been when God preferred him (Gen. xxxii. 10) ; " With my staff I passed over this Jordan, and now I am become two bands ; " so do you say, I am a worthless creature, it is God that hath taken me into his grace, praised be the Lord that hath chosen me. Then consider how many are left to perish in the wide world. Some live out of the church's pale that never heard of Christ, and many others have only a loose general form of Christianity. Oh ! blessed be God that hath chosen me to be of the number of his peculiar people. It is said (Zech. xiii. 8), " And it shall come to pass in all the land, saith the Lord, that two parts shall be cut off and die, but the third shall be left therein." We pass through many bolters before we come to be God's peculiar people, as the corn is ground, bolted, searched before it comes to be fine flour. Many have not the knowledge of God, and others live in the church but are carnal ; and for me to be one of his peculiar people, a member of Christ's mystical body, oh ! what a privilege is this ! And then what moved him to all this ? Nothing but his own free grace. Therefore praise the Lord.—*Thomas Manton.*

Verse 4.—"*His peculiar treasure.*" The Hebrew word *segullah* signifieth God's special jewels, God's proper ones, or God's secret ones, that he keeps in store for himself, and for his own special service and use. Princes lock up with their own hands in secret their most precious and costly jewels ; and so doth God his : "*For the* LORD *hath chosen Jacob unto himself, and Israel for his peculiar treasure,*" or for his secret gain.—*Thomas Brooks.*

Verse 4.—"*His peculiar treasure.*" Will not a man that is not defective in his prudentials secure his jewels ? " They shall be mine in that day when I make up my jewels, and I will spare them as a father his son that serveth him : " Malachi iii. 17. If a house be on fire, the owner of it will first take care of his wife and children, then of his jewels, and last of all, of his lumber and rubbish. Christ secures first his people, for they are his jewels ; the world is but lumber and rubbish.—*Richard Mayhew.*

Verse 5. -"*For I know.*" The word "*I*" is made emphatic in the original. Whatever may be the case with others, I have had personal and precious experience of the greatness of Jehovah's power, and of his infinite supremacy above all other gods. The author of the Psalm may either speak for all Israel as a unit, or he may have framed his song so that every worshipper might say this for himself as his own testimony.—*Henry Cowles.*

Verse 5.—"*For I know that the* LORD *is great,*" etc. On what a firm foundation does the Psalmist plant his foot—"*I know !*" One loves to hear men of God speaking in this calm, undoubting, and assured confidence, whether it be of the Lord's goodness or of the Lord's greatness. You may perhaps say, that it required no great stretch of faith or knowledge, or any amount of bravery, to declare that God was great ; but I think that not many wise nor mighty had in the Psalmist's days attained unto his knowledge or made his confession, that Jehovah, the God of Israel, was *"above all gods."*   Baal and Chemosh, and Milcom and Dagon, claimed the fealty of the nations round about ; and David, in the Court of Achish, would have found his declaration as unwelcome, as it would have been rejected as untrue. Moses once carried a message from Jehovah to the king of Egypt, and his reply was, " Who is the Lord, that I should obey his voice ?   I know not the Lord ; " and even of Jehovah's peculiar treasure, all were not Israel that were of Israel.

There is a knowledge that plays round the head, like lightning on a mountain's summit, that leaves no trace behind ; and there is a knowledge that, like the fertilizing stream, penetrates into the very recesses of the heart, and issues forth in all the fruits of holiness, of love, and peace, and joy for evermore.—*Barton Bouchier.*

Verse 6.—*"Whatsoever the* Lord *pleased, that did he,"* etc.   He was not forced to make all that he made, but *all that he willed he made.*   His will was the cause of all things which he made.   Thou makest a house, because if thou didst not make it thou wouldest be left without a habitation : necessity compels thee to make a home, not free-will.   Thou makest a garment, because thou wouldest go about naked if thou didst not make it ; thou art therefore led to making a garment by necessity, not by free-will.   Thou plantest a mountain with vines, thou sowest seed, because if thou didst not do so, thou wouldest not have food ; all such things thou doest of necessity.   God has made all things of his goodness.   He needed nothing that he made ; and therefore he hath made all things that he willed.

He did whatsoever he willed in the heaven and earth : dost thou do all that thou willest even in thy field ?   Thou willest many things, but canst not do all thou wishest in thy own house.   Thy wife, perchance, gainsays thee, thy children gainsay thee, sometimes even thy servant contumaciously gainsays thee, and thou doest not what thou willest.   But thou sayest, I do what I will, because I punish the disobedient and gainsayer.   Even this thou doest not when thou willest.—*Augustine.*

Verse 6.—*"Whatsoever the* Lord *pleased, that did he,"* etc.   God's will obtains and hath the upper hand everywhere.   Down man, down pope, down devil ; you must yield ; things shall not be as you will, but as God will !   We may well say, " Who hath resisted his will ? " Rom. ix. 19.   Many, indeed, disobey, and sin against the will of his precept ; but none ever did, none ever shall, frustrate or obstruct the will of his purpose ; for he will do all his pleasure, and in his way mountains shall become a plain.—*William Slater* (—1704), *in "The Morning Exercises."*

Verse 6.—Upon the Arminian's plan (if absurdity can deserve the name of a plan), the glorious work of God's salvation, and the eternal redemption of Jesus Christ, are not complete, unless a dying mortal lends his arm ; that is, unless he, who of himself can do nothing, vouchsafe to begin and accomplish that which all the angels in heaven cannot do ; namely, to convert the soul from Satan to God. How contrary is all this to the language of Scripture—how repugnant to the oracles of truth !   " Whatsoever the Lord pleased, that did he in heaven and in earth."—*Ambrose Serle* (—1815), *in "Horæ Solitariæ."*

Verse 6.—*"In heaven and in the earth,"* etc.   His power is infinite.   He can do what he will do everywhere ; all places are there named but purgatory ; perhaps he can do nothing there, but leaves all that work for the Pope.—*Thomas Adams.*

Verse 6.—*"In the seas, and all deep places."*   He did wonders in the mighty waters : more than once he made the boisterous sea a calm, and walked upon the surface of it ; and as of old he broke up the fountains of the great deep, and drowned the world ; and at another time dried up the sea, and led his people through the depths, as through a wilderness ; so he will hereafter bind the old serpent, the devil, and cast him into the abyss, into the great deep, the bottomless pit, where he will continue during the thousand years' reign of Christ with his saints.—*John Gill.*

Verse 6.—The word *"pleaseth"* limits the general note or particle *"all"* unto all works which in themselves are good, or else serve for good use, and so are pleasing to the Lord for the use sake.   He doth not say that the Lord doth all things which are done, but all things which he pleaseth, that is, he doth not make men sinful and wicked, neither doth he work rebellion in men, which is displeasing unto him ;

but he doth whatsoever is pleasing, that is, all things which are agreeable to his nature. And whatsoever is according to his will and good pleasure, that he doth, for none can hinder it. This is the true sense and meaning of the words.—*George Walker, in "God made visible in his Works,"* 1641.

Verse 6.—*"Whatsoever the* LORD *pleased, that did he,"* etc. With reference to the government of Providence, it is said of God, that " he doeth according to his will in the army of heaven, and among the inhabitants of the earth." Even insensible matter is under his control. Fire and hail, snow and vapour, and stormy wind, fulfil his word : and with reference to intelligent agents, we are told that he maketh the most refractory, even the wrath of man, to praise him, and the remainder of wrath he restrains. The whole Bible exhibits Jehovah as so ordering the affairs of individuals, and of nations, as to secure the grand purpose he had in view in creating the world,—viz., the promotion of his own glory, in the salvation of a multitude which no man can number, of all nations, and kindreds, and tribes, and peoples, and tongues. One of the most prominent distinctions between divine revelation and ordinary history is, that when the same general events are narrated, the latter exhibits—(it is its province so to do—it is not able indeed to do more,) the agency of man, the former, the agency of God. Profane history exhibits the instruments by which Jehovah works ; the finger of divine revelation points to the unseen but almighty hand which wields and guides the instrument, and causes even Herod and Pontius Pilate, together with the Jews and the people of Israel, to do what the hand and the counsel of God determined before to be done.—*George Payne, in "Lectures on Christian Theology,"* 1850.

Verse 7.—*"He causeth the vapours to ascend,"* etc. Dr. Halley made a number of experiments at St. Helena as to the quantity of water that is daily evaporated from the sea, and he found that ten square inches of the ocean's surface yielded one cubic inch of water in twelve hours—a square mile therefore yields 401,448,960 cubic inches, or 6,914 tons of water. From the surface of the Mediterranean Sea during a summer's day there would pass off in invisible vapour five thousand millions of tons of water. This being only for one day, the quantity evaporated in a year would be 365 times greater, and in two thousand years it would amount to four thousand billions of tons, which evaporation would in time empty the Mediterranean Sea ; but we have good reason for believing that there is as much water there now as in the time of the Romans, therefore the balance is kept up by the downpour of rain, the influx of the rivers, and the currents from the Atlantic.

Now let us consider the amount of power required for all this evaporation. Mr. Joule, whose experiments have given to the world so much valuable information, says that if we had a pool of water one square mile and six inches in depth to be evaporated by artificial heat, it would require the combustion of 30,000 tons of coal to effect it ; therefore to evaporate all the water that ascends from the earth it would take 6,000,000,000,000 (six billion) tons, or more than all the coal that could be stowed away in half-a-dozen such worlds as this ; and yet silently and surely has the process of evaporation been going on for millions of years.—*Samuel Kinns, in "Moses and Geology,"* 1882.

Verse 7.—*"He causeth the vapours to ascend,"* etc. There is no physical necessity that the boiling-point of water should occur at two hundred and twelve degrees of the Fahrenheit scale. As far as we know, it might have been the same with the boiling-points of oil of turpentine, alcohol or ether. We shall see the benevolence of the present adjustment by noticing some of the consequences which would follow if any change were made.

The amount of vapour given off at ordinary temperatures by any liquid depends on the temperature at which it boils. If the boiling-point of water were the same as that of alcohol, the vapour given off by the ocean would be two and a half times as much as at present. Such an excess of aqueous vapour would produce continual rains and inundations, and would make the air too damp for animal, and too cloudy for vegetable life. If water boiled at the same temperature as ether, the vapour rising from the ocean would be more than twenty-five times as much as at present. In such a state of things no man could see the sun on account of the clouds ; the rain would be so excessive as to tear up the soil and wash away plants ; inundations would be constant, and navigation would be impossible in the inland torrents which would take the place of our rivers. In winter the snow of one day might bury the houses. If, on the other hand, water boiled at the same temperature with oil of turpentine, the vapour given off by the ocean would be less than one-fourth of its present amount. In this case rain would be a rarity, like an eclipse of the sun, the dryness of the desert of Sahara would be equalled in a large part of the globe, which would, therefore, be bare of vegetation, and incapable of sustaining animal life. Plants would be scorched by unclouded sunshine, springs and rivulets would be dry, and inland navigation would cease ; for nearly all the rain would be absorbed by the porous earth.

We see, then, that the boiling-point of water has been adjusted to various relations. It is adjusted to the capacity of space to contain aqueous vapour in a transparent state ; if it were higher than two hundred and twelve degrees, the earth would be scorched by an unclouded sun ; if it were lower, it would droop under continual shade. It is suited to the demand of plants for water ; if it were higher, they would suffer from drought ; if it were lower, they would be torn up by floods. It is in harmony with the texture of the soil ; if it were higher, the earth would absorb all the rain which falls ; if it were lower, the soil would often be washed away by the surface torrents after a shower. It is adapted to the elevation of the continents above the sea ; if it were higher, rivers with their present inclination would be so shallow as to be often dry ; if it were lower, most rivers would be so deep as to be torrents, while the land would be covered with floods.—*Professor Hemholtz.*

Verse 7.—*"To ascend from the ends of the earth."* Rains in England are often introduced by a south-east wind. "Vapour brought to us by such a wind must have been generated in countries to the south and east of our island. It is therefore, probably, in the extensive valleys watered by the Meuse, the Moselle, and the Rhine, if not from the more distant Elbe, with the Oder and the Weser, that the water rises, in the midst of sunshine, which is soon afterwards to form *our* clouds, and pour down *our* thunder-showers." "Drought and sunshine in one part of Europe may be necessary to the production of a wet season in another."*—*William Whewell* (1795—1866), *in "The Bridgwater Treatise" [Astronomy and General Physics]*, 1839.

Verse 7.—*"From the surface of the earth raising the vapours."* The whole description is beautifully exact and picturesque. Not " the ends," or even " the summits " or " extreme mountains," for the original is in the singular number (נשא), but from the whole of the *extreme layer*, the *superficies* or *surface* of the earth ; from every point of which the great process of exhalation is perpetually going on to supply the firmament with refreshing and fruitful clouds.—*John Mason Good.*

Verse 7.—*"He maketh lightnings for the rain."* When the electrical clouds are much agitated, the rain generally falls heavily, and if the agitation is excessive, it hails. As the electricity is dissipated by the frequent discharges the cloud condenses and there comes a sudden and heavy rain ; but the greater the accumulation of electricity, the longer is the rain delayed. Thus connected as the electrical phenomena of the atmosphere are with clouds, vapour, and rain, how forcibly are we struck with these appropriate words in the Scriptures.—*Edwin Sidney, in "Conversations on the Bible and Science,"* 1866.

Verse 7.—*"He maketh lightnings for the rain."* Dr. Russell, in his description of the weather at Aleppo, in September, tells us, that seldom a night passes without much *lightning* in the north-west quarter, but not attended with *thunder ;* and that when this *lightning* appears in the west or south-west points, it is a *sure sign* of the approaching rain, which is *often followed* with thunder. This last clause, which is not perfectly clear, is afterwards explained in his more enlarged account of the weather of the year 1746, when he tells us that though it began to be cloudy on the 4th of September, and continued so for a few days, and *even thundered*, yet no rain fell till the 11th, which shows that his meaning was, that the *lightning* in the west or south-west points, which is often followed with thunder, is a sure sign of the approach of rain. I have before mentioned that a squall of wind and clouds of dust are the usual forerunners of these first rains. Most of these things are taken notice of in Ps. cxxxv. 7 ; Jer. x. 13 ; li. 16 ; and serve to illustrate them. Russell's account determines, I think, that the Nesiim, which our translators render *vapours*, must mean, as they elsewhere translate the word, *clouds.* It shows that God *"maketh lightnings for the rain,"* they, in the west and south-west points, being at Aleppo the sure *prognostics* of rain. The squalls of wind bring on these refreshing

---

* Howard on the Climate of London.

showers, and are therefore " precious things " of the " treasuries " of God.—
Thomas Harmer.

Verse 7.—*"He maketh lightnings for the rain."* The Psalmist mentions it as
another circumstance calling for our wonder, that *lightnings are mixed with rain,*
things quite opposite in their nature one from another. Did not custom make us
familiar with the spectacle, we would pronounce this mixture of fire and water to
be a phenomenon altogether incredible. The same may be said of the phenomena
of the winds. Natural causes can be assigned for them, and philosophers have
pointed them out ; but the winds, with their various currents, are a wonderful
work of God. He does not merely assert the power of God, be it observed, in the
sense in which philosophers themselves grant it, but he maintains that not a drop
of rain falls from heaven without a divine commission or dispensation to that effect.
All readily allow that God is the author of rain, thunder, and wind, in so far as he
originally established the order of things in nature ; but the Psalmist goes farther
than this, holding that when it rains, this is not effected by a blind instinct of nature,
but is the consequence of the decree of God, who is pleased at one time to darken
the sky with clouds, and at another to brighten it again with sunshine.—*John Calvin.*

Verse 7.—*"He maketh lightnings for the rain."* It is a great instance of the
divine wisdom and goodness, that lightning should be accompanied by rain, to
soften its rage, and prevent its mischievous effects. Thus, in the midst of judgment, does God remember mercy. The threatenings in his word against sinners
are like lightning ; they would blast and scorch us up, were it not for his promises
made in the same word to penitents, which, as a gracious rain, turn aside their fury,
refreshing and comforting our affrighted spirits.—*George Horne.*

Verse 7.—*"He bringeth the wind out of his treasuries."* That is, say some, out
of the caves and hollow places of the earth ; but I rather conceive that because
the wind riseth many times on a sudden, and as our Saviour saith (John iii. 8), "we
cannot tell whence it cometh," therefore God is said here to bring it forth, as if he
had it locked up in readiness in some secret and hidden treasuries or storehouses.—
Arthur Jackson.

Verse 7.—*"He bringeth the wind."* The winds are with great beauty, represented
as laid up by him as jewels in a treasure house. Indeed, few verses better express
creative control, than those in which the winds, which make sport of man's efforts
and defy his power, are represented as thus ready to spring forth at God's bidding
from the quarters where they quietly sleep. The occasion comes, the thoughts
of Jehovah find expression in his providence, and his ready servants leap suddenly
forth : *"He bringeth the winds out of his treasuries."* But this bringing forth is not
for physical purposes only ; it is for great moral and spiritual ends also. Take
one illustration out of many. His people were on the edge of deepest and most
brutish idolatry. They were ready to fall into a most degraded form of idol worship,
when he offered to them that ever yearning heart of Fatherly love : " Thus saith
the Lord, Learn not the way of the heathen." Their God is only " the tree cut
out of the forest," silvered over, or decked with gold ; " upright as the palm tree,
but speaks not ; the stock is a doctrine of vanities ; but the Lord is the true God ;
he maketh lightnings with rain ; he bringeth the wind out of his treasures." Jer.
x. 2—16. Thus, too, the words of Agur to Ithiel and Ucal, " He hath gathered
the wind in his fists." Prov. xxx. 4.—*John Duns, in "Science and Christian Thought,"*
1868.

Verse 8.—*"Who smote the firstborn of Egypt."* The firstborn only were smitten ;
these were singled out in every family with unerring precision, the houses of the
Israelites, wherever the blood of the lamb was sprinkled on the door-posts, being
passed over. The death of all those thousands, both of man and beast, took place
at the same instant—" at midnight."

Is God unrighteous, then, that taketh vengeance ? No ; this is an act of
retribution. The Egyptians had slain the children of the Israelites, casting their
infants into the river. Now the affliction is turned upon themselves ; the delight
of their eyes is taken from them ; all their firstborn are dead, from the firstborn
of Pharaoh that sat upon his throne, unto the the firstborn of the captive that was
in the dungeon.—*Thomas S. Millington, in "Signs and Wonders in the Land of Ham,"*
1873.

Verse 8.—*"And beast."* The Egyptians worshipped many animals, and when
the firstborn of the sacred animals died the circumstance greatly increased the

impressiveness of the plague as an assault upon the gods of Egypt.—*C. H. S. Suggested by Otto Von Gerlach.*

Verses 8, 9, 10—12.—Worthy is Jahve to be praised, for he is the Redeemer out of Egypt. Worthy is he to be praised, for he is the Conqueror of the Land of Promise.—*Franz Delitzsch.*

Verse 9.—*"Who sent tokens and wonders."*—*"Tokens,"* that is, signs or evidences of the Divine power. *"Wonders,"* things fitted to impress the mind with awe; things outside of the ordinary course of events; things not produced by natural laws, but by the direct power of God. The allusion here is, of course, to the plagues of Egypt, as recorded in Exodus.—*Albert Barnes.*

Verse 10.—*"Who smote great nations,"* etc. It is better that the wicked should be destroyed a hundred times over than that they should tempt those who are as yet innocent to join their company. Let us but think what might have been our fate, and the fate of every other nation under heaven at this hour, had the sword of the Israelites done its work more sparingly. Even as it was, the small portions of the Canaanites who were left, and the nations around them, so tempted the Israelites by their idolatrous practices that we read continually of the whole people of God turning away from his service. But, had the heathen lived in the land in equal numbers, and, still more, had they intermarried largely with the Israelites, how was it possible humanly speaking, that any sparks of the light of God's truth should have survived to the coming of Christ? Would not the Israelites have lost all their peculiar character; and if they had retained the name of Jehovah as of their God, would they not have formed as unworthy notions of his attributes, and worship him with a worship as abominable as that which the Moabites paid to Chemosh or the Philistines to Dagon?

But this was not to be, and therefore the nations of Canaan were to be cut off utterly. The Israelites, sword, in its bloodiest executions, wrought a work of mercy for all the countries of the earth to the very end of the world. They seem of very small importance to us now, these perpetual contests with the Canaanites, and the Midianites, and the Ammonites, and the Philistines, with which the Books of Joshua and Judges and Samuel are almost filled. We may half wonder that God should have interferred in such quarrels, or have changed the course of nature, in order to give one of the nations of Palestine the victory over another. But in these contests, on the fate of one of these nations of Palestine the happiness of the human race depended. The Israelites fought not for themselves only, but for us. It might follow that they should thus be accounted the enemies of all mankind, —it might be that they were tempted by their very distinctness to despise other nations; still they did God's work,—still they preserved unhurt the seed of eternal life, and were the ministers of blessing to all other nations, even though they themselves failed to enjoy it.—*Thomas Arnold, 1795—1842.*

Verse 10.—*"Who smote great nations,"* etc. Let us not stand in fear of any enemies that rise up against us, and conspire to hinder the peace of the church, and stop the passage of the gospel; when God beginneth to take the cause of his people into his own hand, and smitteth any of his enemies on the jaw-bone, the rest are reserved to the like destruction. For wherefore doth God punish his adversaries, and enter into judgment with them? Wherefore doth he visit them, and strike them down with his right hand! Is it only to take vengeance, and to show his justice in their confusion? No, it serveth for the comfort and consolation of his servants, that howsoever God be patient, yet in the end they shall not escape.—*William Attersoll, 1618.*

Verse 11.—*"Sihon king of the Amorites, and Og."* Notice is taken of two kings, Sihon and Og, not as being more powerful than the rest, but because shutting up the entrance to the land in front they were the most formidable enemies met with, and the people, besides, were not as yet habituated to war.—*John Calvin.*

Verse 11.—*"Sihon king of the Amorites."* When Israel arrived on the borders of the promised Land they encountered Sihon. (Numb. xxi. 21.) He was evidently a man of very great courage and audacity. Shortly before the time of Israel's arrival he had dispossessed the Moabites of a splendid territory, driving them south of the natural bulwark of the Arnon with great slaughter and the loss of a great number of captives (xxi. 26—29). When the Israelite host appears, he does not hesitate or temporize like Balak, but at once gathers his people together and attacks them.   But the battle was his last.   He and all his host were destroyed, and their district from Arnon to Jabbok became at once the possession of the conqueror.

Josephus (Ant. iv. 5, § 2) has preserved some singular details of the battle, which have not survived in the text either of the Hebrew or LXX.   He represents the Amorite army as containing every man in the nation fit to bear arms.   He states that they were unable to fight when away from the shelter of their cities, and that being especially galled by the slings and arrows of the Hebrews, and at last suffering severely from thirst, they rushed to the stream and to the recesses of the ravine of the Arnon.   Into these recesses they were pursued by their active enemy and slaughtered in vast numbers.

Whether we accept these details or not, it is plain, from the manner in which the name of Sihon fixed itself in the national mind, and the space which his image occupies in the official records, and in the later poetry of Israel, that he was a truly formidable chieftain.—*George Grove, in Smith's Dictionary of the Bible,* 1863.

Verse 11.—*Sihon,* although conqueror of Moab, and much more formidable than the Canaanites whom Israel had feared at Kadesh, fell easily because Israel fought in faith.   There is no adversary that can really offer any effectual opposition to our onward march if assailed in the strength of Christ with a cheerful courage.

Og the king of Bashan was much more formidable even than *Sihon,* but he seems to have fallen yet more easily, judging from the brief notice of the conquest.   Even so, when once we have overcome a difficulty or conquered an evil habit in the strength of faith, other conquests open out before us readily and naturally which we should not have dared to contemplate before.   It is most true in religion that "nothing succeeds like success."—*R. Winterbotham, in "The Pulpit Commentary,"* 1881.

Verse 11.—*"Og king of Bashan."*   The task was not an easy one, for Edrei—"*the strong*"—Og's capital, was in ordinary circumstances almost unassailable, since it was, strange to say, built in a hollow artificially scooped out of the top of a hill, which the deep gorge of the Hieromax isolates from the country round.   Its streets may be still seen running in all directions beneath the present town of Adraha.   But Kenath, in the district called Argob—"*the stony*"—was still stronger, for it was built in the crevices of a great island of lava which has split, in cooling, into innumerable fissures, through whose labyrinth no enemy could safely penetrate.   In these were its streets and houses, some of which, of a later date, with stone doors, turning on hinges of stone, remain till this day. . . . .   Nor were these the only fastnesses.   No fewer than sixty cities "fenced with high walls, gates, and bars" (Deut. iii. 5), had to be taken ; but they all fell, sooner or later, before the vigorous assaults of the invaders, and, long afterwards, there might be seen, in the capital of their allies, the Ammonites, one of the trophies of the campaign—the gigantic iron bedstead of King Og, or as some think, the huge sarcophagus he had prepared for himself, as was the custom with Canaanite kings.—*Cunningham Geikie, in "Hours with the Bible,"* 1881.

Verse 12.—*"Their land for an heritage."*   The land was given to them to be transmitted from father to son, by hereditary right and succession.—*Joseph Addison Alexander.*

Verse 13. — *"Thy name, O Lord, endureth for ever,"* etc.   Immutability is a glory belonging to all the attributes of God.   It is not a single perfection of the Divine nature, nor is it limited to particular objects thus and thus disposed.   Mercy and justice have their distinct objects and distinct acts : mercy is conversant about a penitent, justice about an obstinate sinner.   In our conceptions of the Divine perfections, his perfections are different.   The wisdom of God is not his power, nor his power his holiness ; but immutability is the centre wherein they all unite.   There is not one perfection which may not be said to be, and truly is, immutable ; none of them will appear so glorious about this beam, the sun of immutability, which renders them highly excellent, without the least shadow of imperfection.   How cloudy would his blessedness be, if it were changeable ; how dim his wisdom, if it might be obscured ; how feeble his power, if it were capable of becoming sickly and languishing ; how would mercy lose much of its lustre, if it could change into wrath, and justice much of its dread, if it could be turned into mercy ; while the object of justice remains unfit for mercy, and one that hath need of mercy continues only fit for the Divine fury? But unchangeableness is the thread that runs through the whole web ; it is the enamel of all the rest ; none of them without it could look with a triumphant aspect.—*Stephen Charnock.*

Verse 13.—*"Thy name, O LORD, endureth for ever."* God is, and will be always the same to his church, a gracious, faithful, wonder-working God ; and his church is, and will be the same to him, a thankful, praising people ; and thus his name *endures for ever.—Matthew Henry.*

Verse 13.—*"Thy memorial, O LORD, throughout all generations ; "* or, *the remembrance of them to generation and generation;* to every age. The love of Christ is remembered by his people in every age, as they enjoy the blessings of his grace in redemption, justification, pardon, etc. It cannot be forgotten as long as the gospel is preached, the ordinances of Baptism and the Lord's Supper administered, and the Lord has a people in the world ; all which will be as long as the sun and moon endure, and there will therefore always be a memorial of him.—*John Gill.*

Verse 14.—*"For the LORD will judge his people,"* etc. Is it so, that all providence is for the good of the church? This is comfort in the low estate of the church at any time. God's eye is upon his people even whilst he seems to have forsaken them. If he seems to be departed, it is but in some other part of the earth, to show himself strong for them ; wherever his eye is fixed in any part of the world, his church hath his heart, and his church's relief is his end. Though the church may sometimes lie among the pots in a dirty condition, yet there is a time of resurrection, when God will restore it to its true glory, and make it as white as a dove with its silver wings : Ps. lxviii. 13. The sun is not always obscured by a thick cloud, but it will be freed from the darkness of it. *"God will judge his people, and he will repent himself concerning his servants "* [the original is, *Comfort himself*]. It is a comfort to God to deliver his people, and he will do it when it shall be most comfortable to his glory and to their hearts.—*Stephen Charnock.*

Verse 14.—*"He will repent himself."* The original word *" repent himself"* here has a very extensive signification, which cannot be expressed by any one English rendering. It implies taking compassion upon them, with the intention of being comforted in their future, and of taking vengeance on their oppressors. Such are the several meanings in which the word is used. Language fails to express the mind of God toward his faithful people. How dear ought his counsels to be to us, and the consideration of all his ways ! This reflection was continually urged upon the nation of Israel, so liable as they were to fall away to idolatory.—*W. Wilson.*

Verse 15.—*"The idols of the heathen."* The shrines on the hill-tops were very rude affairs, enclosures formed by rough stone walls, and containing ragamuffin gods—stocks of weather-beaten wood, blocks of battered stone, and lumps of rusty old iron. The carved wooden gods were so much the worse for the weather, that their features, if they ever had any, were altogether defaced. One, not made of a single piece, like the rest, but built together by joiner work, had fared worse than its more humble neighbours. His arms were gone, and his breast, heart, and stomach had all fallen out ; strange to say, his head remained, and it was laughable to see such a hollow mockery stare at you with a solemn face. The stone images were sadly battered by tumbling about among the rubbish, and the cast-metal gods mostly had their heads broken off and set carefully on again, to stand there till the next storm would send them rolling. Thus God is not only robbed in the valley, but men climb up as near to heaven as they can, and insult him to his face. —*James Gilmour, in "Among the Mongols," 1883.*

Verse 15.—*"The idols,"* etc. Herodotus telleth us that Amasis had a large laver of gold, wherein both he and his guests used to wash their feet. This vessel he brake and made a god of it, which the Egyptians devoutly worshipped. And the like idolomania is at this day found among Papists, what distinction soever they would fain make betwixt an *idol* and an *image,* which indeed (as they use them) are all one.—*John Trapp.*

Verse 15.—*"Silver and gold."* By singling out these metals, the most precious materials of which the idols were framed, and pouring contempt upon even these costly images, the Psalmist heightens the scorn which he implies for such as were of inferior price, and which had not the one element of costliness in their favour. And when we bear in mind the Apostles saying that covetousness is idolatry we shall be warned that we, too, may need this lesson against worshipping silver and gold, or the worldly wisdom and specious eloquence which may be compared to these metals.—*Neale and Littledale.*

Verse 15.—"*The work of men's hands.*" Therefore they should rather, if it were possible, worship man, as their creator and lord, than be worshipped by him.—*Matthew Pool,* 1624—1679.

Verses 15, 16, 17.—The Rev. John Thomas, a missionary in India, was one day travelling alone through the country, when he saw a great number of people waiting near an idol temple. He went up to them, and as soon as the doors were opened, he walked into the temple. Seeing an idol raised above the people, he walked boldly up to it, held up his hand, and asked for silence. He then put his fingers on its eyes, and said, " It has eyes, but it cannot see ! It has ears, but it cannot hear ! It has a nose, but it cannot smell ! It has hands, but it cannot handle ! It has a mouth, but it cannot speak ! Neither is there any breath in it ! " Instead of doing injury to him for affronting their god and themselves, the natives were all surprised; and an old Brahmin was so convinced of his folly by what Mr. Thomas said, that he also cried out, " It has feet, but cannot run away ! " The people raised a shout, and being ashamed of their stupidity, they left the temple, and went to their homes—*From "The New Cyclopædia of Illustrative Anecdote,"* 1875.

Verses 16, 17.—"*Mouths,*" " *eyes,*" " *ears.*" So many members as the images have, serving to represent perfections ascribed to them, so many are the lies.—*David Dickson.*

Verses 16—17.—They can neither *speak* in answer to your prayers and enquiries, nor *see* what you do or what you want, nor *hear* your petitions, nor *smell* your incenses and sacrifices, nor use their *hands* either to take anything from you, or to give anything to you ; nor so much as *mutter,* nor give the least sign of apprehending your condition or concerns.—*Matthew Pool.*

Verses 16—17.—"*Mouths, but they speak not :*" " *ears, but they hear not.*"

A heated fancy or imagination
May be mistaken for an inspiration.
True ; but is this conclusion fair to make
That inspiration must be all mistake ?
A pebble-stone is not a diamond : true ;
But must a diamond be a pebble too ?
To own a God who does not speak to men,
Is first to own, and then disown again ;
Of all idolatry the total sum
Is having gods that are both deaf and dumb.

John Byrom, 1691—1763.

Verse 18.—"*Like them shall be those making them, every one who (is) trusting in them.*" If the meaning had been simply, those who make them *are* like them, Hebrew usage would have required the verb to be suppressed. Its insertion, therefore, in the future form (יהיו) requires it to be rendered strictly *shall be,* i.e., in fate as well as character. Idolaters shall perish with their perishable idols. See Isa. i. 31.—*Joseph Addison Alexander.*

Verse 18.—People never rise above the level of their gods, which are to them their better nature.—*Andrew Robert Faussett.*

Verse 18.—"*They that make them are like unto them.*" Idolatry is a benumbing sin, which bereaveth the idolater of the right use of his senses.—*David Dickson.*

Verse 18.—"*They that make them,*" etc. Teacheth us, that the idol, the idol-maker, and all such also as serve idols, are not only beastly and blockish before men, but shall before God, in good time, come to shame and confusion.—*Thomas Wilcocks,* 1549—1608.

Verse 18.—"*Like unto them.*" A singular phenomenon, known as the Spectre of the Brocken, is seen on a certain mountain in Germany. The traveller who at dawn stands on the topmost ridge beholds a colossal shadowy spectre. But in fact it is only his own shadow projected upon the morning mists by the rising sun ; and it imitates, of course, every movement of its creator. So heathen nations have mistaken their own image for Deity. Their gods display human frailties and passions and scanty virtues, projected and magnified upon the heavens, just as the small figures on the slide of a magic-lantern are projected, magnified, and illuminated upon a white sheet.—*From Elan Foster's New Cyclopædia of Illustrations*, 1870.

Verse 18.—*"Like unto them."* How many are like idol-images, when they have eyes, ears, and mouths as though they had none : that is, when they do not use them when and how they should !—*Christoph Starke*.

Verse 19.—*"Bless the* LORD." Blessing of God is to wish well to, and speak well of God, out of good-will to God himself, and a sense of his goodness to ourselves. God loves your good word, that is, to be spoken of well by you ; he rejoiceth in your well-wishes, and to hear from you expressions of rejoicings in his own independent blessedness. Though God hath an infinite ocean of all blessedness, to which we can add nothing, and he is therefore called by way of eminency, " The Blessed One " (Mark xiv. 61), a title solely proper and peculiar to him, yet he delights to hear the *amen* of the saints, his creatures, resounding thereto ; he delights to hear us utter our " so be it."—*Thomas Goodwin*.

Verse 19.—*"Bless the* LORD." And not an idol (Isa. lxvi. 3), as the Philistines, did their Dagon and as Papists still do their he-saints and she-saints.—*John Trapp*.

Verse 20.—*"Bless the* LORD, *O house of Levi."* In Ps. cxv. the exhortation given is to *trust* or *hope* in the Lord ; here, to *bless* him. The *Levites* are mentioned in addition to the house of Aaron, there being two orders of priesthood. Everything else in the two Psalms is the same, except that, in the last verse, the Psalmist here joins himself, along with the rest of the Lord's people, in blessing God.—*Franz Delitzsch*.

Verse 20.—*" Ye that fear the* LORD, *bless the* LORD." These are distinct from the Israelites, priests, and Levites, and design the proselytes among them of other nations that truly feared God, as Jarchi notes ; and all such persons, whoever and wherever they are, have reason to bless the Lord for the fear of him they have, which is not from nature but from grace ; and for the favours shown them, the blessings bestowed upon them, the good things laid up for them, and the guard that is about them, which the Sriptures abundantly declare, and experience confirms.—*John Gill*.

Verse 20.—*" Ye that fear the* LORD, *bless the* LORD." In Scripture it is quite common to find this *"fear "* put for holiness itself, or the sum of true religion. It is not, therefore, such a fear as seized the hearts of our first parents when, hearing the voice of the Lord God, they hid themselves amongst the trees of the garden ; nor such as suddenly quenched the noise of royal revelry in the night of Babylon's overthrow ; nor such as, on some day yet future, shall drive desparing sinners to the unavailing shelter of the mountains and rocks. It is not the fear of guilty distrust, or of hatred, or of bondage—that fear which hath torment, and which perfect love casteth out ; but a fear compatible with the highest privileges, attainments, and hopes of the Christian life. It is the fear of deep humility and reverence, and filial subjection, and adoring gratitude ; the fear which " blesseth the Lord," saying, *"His mercy endureth for ever."*—*John Lillie* (1812—1867), *in "Lectures on the Epistles of Peter."*

Verse 21.—The conclusion, verse 21, alludes to the conclusion of the preceding Psalm. There, the Lord blesses thee out of Zion ; here, let him be blessed out of Zion. The praise proceeds from the same place from which the blessing issues. For Zion is the place where the community dwells with God.—*E. W. Hengstenberg*.

Verse 21.—*"Praise ye the* LORD." When the song of praise is sung unto God, the work of his praise is not ended, but must be continued, renewed, and followed still : *"Praise ye the* LORD."—*David Dickson*.

Verse 21.—*"Bless," " Praise."* We are not only to bless God, but to praise him : " All thy works shall praise thee, O LORD ; and thy saints shall bless thee." Blessing relateth to his benefits, praise to his excellencies. We bless him for what he is to us, we praise him for what he is in himself. Now, whether we bless him, or praise him ; it is still to increase our love to him, and delight in him ; for God is not affected with the flattery of empty praises ; yet this is an especial duty, which is of use to you, as all other duties are. It doth you good to consider him as an infinite and eternal Being, and of glorious and incomprehensible majesty. It is pleasant and profitable to us.—*Thomas Manton*.

HINTS TO PREACHERS.

Verses 1—4.—I. The Employment. Praise three times commended, and in three respects. 1. With respect to God: not his works merely, but himself. 2. With respect to ourselves: it is pleasant and profitable. 3. With respect to others: it best recommends our religion to all who hear it. All others are religions of fear, ours of joy and praise. II. The Persons: servants in attendance at his house, who stand there by appointment, ready to hear, ready to obey. III. The Motives. 1. In general. It is due to God, because he is good; and it is pleasant to us: verse 3. 2. In particular. Those who are specially privileged by God should specially praise him: verse 4. "This people have I formed for myself; they shall show forth my praise."—*G. R.*

Verse 1.—"*Praise ye the* LORD." I. The Lord ought to be praised. II. He ought to be praised *by you.* III. He ought to be praised *now:* let us remember his present favours. IV. He ought to be praised in everything for ever.

Verse 1.—"*Praise him, O ye servants of the* LORD." I. Praise him for the privilege of serving him. II. Praise him for the power to serve him. III. Praise him for the acceptance of your service. IV. Praise him as the chief part of your service. V. Praise him that others may be induced to engage in his service.—*W. H. J. P.*

Verse 2.—What is at this day "the house of the Lord"? Who may be said to stand in it? What special reasons have they for praise?

Verse 2.—The nearer to God, the dearer to God; and the better our place, the sweeter our praise.—*W. B. H.*

Verses 2—5.—"*Our God,*" "*Our Lord.*" Sweet subject. See our Exposition.

Verse 3.—Praise the Lord, I. For the excellence of his nature. II. For the revelation of his name. III. For the pleasantness of his worship.

Verse 4.—It is a song of praise, and therefore election is mentioned because it is a motive for song. I. *The Choice*—"The Lord hath chosen." Divine. Sovereign. Gracious. Immutable. II. *The Consecration*—"Chosen Jacob to himself." To know him. To preserve his truth. To maintain his worship. To manifest his grace. To keep alive the hope of the Coming One. III. *The Separation* —implied in the special choice. By being taken into covenant: Abraham and his seed. By receiving the covenant inheritance: Canaan. By redemption. By power and by blood out of Egypt. Wilderness separation. Settled establishment in their own land. IV. *The Elevation.* In name—from Jacob to Israel. In value—from worthless to precious. In purpose and use—crown jewels. In preservation—kept as treasures. In delight—God rejoices in his people as his heritage.

Verse 5.—"*I know that the* LORD *is great.*" I. By observing nature and providence. II. By reading his word. III. By my own conversion, comfort, and regeneration. IV. By my after-experience. V. By my overpowering communion with him.

Verse 5.—Delicious dogmatism. "*I know,*" etc. I. What I know. 1. The Lord. 2. That he is great. 3. That he is above all. II. Why I know it. 1. Because he is "our Lord." 2. By his operations in nature, providence, and grace (vers. 6—13) III. My incorrigible obstinacy in this regard is proof against worshippers of all other gods: which gods are effeminate; without sovereignty; no god, or any god.—*W. B. H.*

Verse 6.—"*Whatsoever the* LORD *pleased, that did he.*" *God's good pleasure in the work of grace.* Seen, *not* in the death of the wicked, Ezek. xxxiii. 11; but in the election of his people, 1 Sam. xii. 22; in the infliction of suffering on the substitute, Isa. liii. 10; in the provision of all fulness for his people in Christ, Col. i. 19, in the arrangement of salvation by faith in Christ, John vi. 39; in instituting preaching as the means of salvation, 1 Cor. i. 21; in the adoption of believers as his children, Eph. i. 5; in their sanctification, 1 Thess. iv. 3; in their ultimate triumph and reign, Luke xii. 32.—*C. A. D.*

Verse 6 (*last words*).—The power of God in places of trouble, change, and danger —*seas;* and in conditions of sin, weakness, despair, perplexity—in all *deep places.*

Verses 6—12.—The Resistless Pleasure of Jehovah. I. Behold it as here exemplified: 1. Ruling all nature. 2. Overturning a rebellious nation. 3. Making sport of kings and crowns. 4. Laying a fertile country at the feet of the chosen. II. Be wise in view thereof. 1. Submit to it: it sweeps the seas, and lays hands on earth and heaven. 2. Think not to hide from it: the "ends of the earth" and " all deep places " are open to it ; it is swifter than its own lightnings. 3. Be awed by its majesty : God's way is strewn with crowns and the bones of kings. 4. Seek its protection : its mightiest efforts are in defence of those it favours. 5. Let the Lord's people fear not with so great a God, and so exhaustless an armoury.— W. B. H.

Verse 13.—"*Thy name, O Lord, endureth for ever.*" I. As *the embodiment of perfection :* God's attributes and glory. II. As *the object of veneration :* " Holy and reverend is his name." III. As *the cause of salvation :* " For my name's sake," etc. IV. As *the centre of attraction :* " In his name shall the Gentiles trust." " Our desire is to the remembrance of thy name." " Where two or three are gathered in my name," etc. V. As *a plea in supplication :* " For thy name's sake, pardon," etc. " Hitherto ye have asked nothing in my name." VI. As *a warrant for action :* " Whatsoever ye do, do all in the name," etc. VII. As *a refuge in tribulation :* " The name of the Lord is a strong tower : the righteous runneth into it, and is safe." " I have kept them in thy name." VIII. As *a mark of glorification :* " I will write upon him the name of my God." IX. As *a terror to transgressors :* " My name is dreadful among the heathen."—*W. J.*

Verse 14.—"*The Lord will judge his people.*" Others would like to do it, but must not. The world has seven judgment-days in every week, but shall not be able to condemn the saints. He himself will judge. How will he judge them ? 1. Their persons, as to whether they are in or out of Christ. 2. Their principles, as to whether they are genuine or spurious. 3. Their prayers, as to whether they are availing or useless. 4. Their profession, as to whether it is true or false. 5. Their procedure, as to whether it is good or bad.—*W. J.*

Verse 14.—I. The position of believers—"his people," "his servants." II. The discipline of God's family. III. The tenderness of the Lord to them. IV. The safety of believers : they are still the Lord's.

Verse 15.—"*Silver and gold.*" These are idols in our own land, among worldlings, and with some professors. Show the folly and wickedness of loving riches, and the evils which come of it.

Verses 16, 17.—The Portrait of many. I. "*Mouths, but they speak not.*" No prayer, praise, confession. II. "*Eyes, but they see not.*" Discern not, understand not, take no warning ; do not look to Christ. III. "*Ears, but they hear not.*' Attend no ministry, or are present but unaffected ; hear not God. IV. "*Neither is there any breath in their mouths.*" No life, no tokens of life, no prayer and praise which are the breath of spiritual life.

Verse 18.—I. Men make idols like themselves. II. The idols make their makers like themselves. Describe both processes.

Verse 19.—"*House of Israel.*" The Lord's great goodness to all his people, perceived and proclaimed, and the Lord praised for it.

Verse 19.—"*House of Aaron.*" God's blessing on Aaron's house typical of his grace to those who are priests unto God.

Verses 19—21.—I. The Exhortation. 1. To bless the Lord. 2. To bless him in his own house. II. To whom it is addressed. 1. To the house of Israel, or the whole church. 2. To the house of Aaron, or ministers of the sanctuary. 3. To the house of Levi, or the attendants upon ministers, and assistants in the services. 4. To all who fear God, wherever they may be. Even they who fear God are invited to praise him, which is a sure sign that he delighteth in mercy.—*G. R.*

Verse 20.—The Levites, their history, duties, rewards, and obligations to bless God.

Verse 20 (*second clause*).—I. The fear of God includes all religion. II. The fear of the Lord suggests praise. III. The fear of the Lord renders praise acceptable.

Verse 21.—I. The double fact. 1. Blessing perpetually ascending from Zion to God. 2. God perpetually blessing his people by dwelling with them in Zion. II. The double reason for praise, which is found in the double fact, and concerns every member of the church.

PSALM CXXXVI.

We know not by whom this Psalm was written, but we do know that it was sung in Solomon's temple (2 Chron. vii. 3, 6), and by the armies of Jehoshaphat when they sang themselves into victory in the wilderness of Tekoa. From the striking form of it we should infer that it was a popular hymn among the Lord's ancient people. Most hymns with a solid, simple chorus become favourites with congregations, and this is sure to have been one of the best beloved. It contains nothing but praise. It is tuned to rapture, and can only be fully enjoyed by a devoutly grateful heart.

It commences with a three-fold praise to the Triune Lord (1—3), then it gives us six notes of praise to the Creator (4—9), six more upon deliverance from Egypt (10—15), and seven upon the journey through the wilderness and the entrance into Canaan. Then we have two happy verses of personal gratitude for present mercy (23 and 24), one (verse 25) to tell of the Lord's universal providence, and a closing verse to excite to never-ending praise.

EXPOSITION.

O GIVE thanks unto the LORD ; for *he is* good : for his mercy *endureth* for ever.

2 O give thanks unto the God of gods : for his mercy *endureth* for ever.

3 O give thanks to the Lord of lords : for his mercy *endureth* for ever.

1. *"O give thanks unto the LORD."* The exhortation is intensely earnest : the Psalmist pleads with the Lord's people with an " O," three times repeated. Thanks are the least that we can offer, and these we ought freely to give. The inspired writer calls us to praise Jehovah for all his goodness to us, and all the greatness of his power in blessing his chosen. We thank our parents, let us praise our heavenly Father ; we are grateful to our benefactors, let us give thanks unto the Giver of all good. *"For he is good."* Essentially he is goodness itself, practically all that he does is good, relatively he is good to his creatures. Let us thank him that we have seen, proved, and tasted that he is good. He is good beyond all others ; indeed, he alone is good in the highest sense ; he is the source of good, the good of all good, the sustainer of good, the perfecter of good, and the rewarder of good. For this he deserves the constant gratitude of his people. *"For his mercy endureth for ever."* We shall have this repeated in every verse of this song, but not once too often. It is the sweetest stanza that a man can sing. What joy that there is mercy, mercy with Jehovah, enduring mercy, mercy enduring for ever. We are ever needing it, trying it, praying for it, receiving it : therefore let us for ever sing of it.

> " When all else is changing within and around,
> In God and his mercy no change can be found."

2. *"O give thanks unto the God of gods,"* If there be powers in heaven or on earth worthy of the name of gods he is the God of them ; from him their dominion comes, their authority is derived from him, and their very existence is dependent upon his will. Moreover, for the moment assuming that the deities of the heathen were gods, yet none of them could be compared with our Elohim, who is infinitely beyond what they are fabled to be. Jehovah is our God, to be worshipped and adored, and he is worthy of our reverence to the highest degree. If the heathen cultivate the worship of their gods with zeal, how much more intently should we seek the glory of the God of gods—the only true and real God. Foolish persons have gathered from this verse that the Israelites believed in the existence of many gods, at the same time believing that their Jehovah was the chief among them ; but this is an absurd inference, since gods who have a God over them cannot possibly be gods themselves. The words are to be understood after the usual manner of human speech, in which things are often spoken of not as they really are, but as they profess to be. God as God is worthy of our warmest thanks, *"for his mercy endureth*

for ever." Imagine supreme Godhead without everlasting mercy ! It would then have been as fruitful a source of terror as it is now a fountain of thanksgiving. Let the Highest be praised in the highest style, for right well do his nature and his acts deserve the gratitude of all his creatures.

> Praise your God with right good will,
> For his love endureth still.

3. *"O give thanks to the Lord of lords."* There are lords many, but Jehovah is the Lord of them. All lordship is vested in the Eternal. He makes and administers law, he rules and governs mind and matter, he possesses in himself all sovereignty and power. All lords in the plural are summed up in this Lord in the singular : he is more lordly than all emperors and kings condensed into one. For this we may well be thankful, for we know the superior Sovereign will rectify the abuses of the underlings who now lord it over mankind. He will call these lords to his bar, and reckon with them for every oppression and injustice. He is as truly the Lord of lords as he is Lord over the meanest of the land, and he rules with a strict impartiality, for which every just man should give heartiest thanks. *"For his mercy endureth for ever."* Yes, he mingles mercy with his justice, and reigns for the benefit of his subjects. He pities the sorrowful, protects the helpless, provides for the needy, and pardons the guilty ; and this he does from generation to generation, never wearying of his grace, " because he delighteth in mercy." Let us arouse ourselves to laud our glorious Lord ! A third time let us thank him who is our Jehovah, our God, and our Lord ; and let this one reason suffice us for three thanksgivings, or for three thousand—

> For his mercy shall endure,
> Ever faithful, ever sure.

4 To him who alone doth great wonders : for his mercy *endureth* for ever.

5 To him that by wisdom made the heavens : for his mercy *endureth* for ever.

6 To him that stretched out the earth above the waters : for his mercy *endureth* for ever.

7 To him that made great lights : for his mercy *endureth* for ever :

8 The sun to rule by day : for his mercy *endureth* for ever :

9 The moon and stars to rule by night : for his mercy *endureth* for ever.

4. *" To him who alone doeth great wonders."* Jehovah is the great Thaumaturge, the unrivalled Wonderworker. None can be likened unto him, he is alone in wonderland, the Creator and Worker of true marvels, compared with which all other remarkable things are as child's play. His works are all great in wonder even when they are not great in size ; in fact, in the minute objects of the microscope we behold as great wonders as even the telescope can reveal. All the works of his unrivalled skill are wrought by him alone and unaided, and to him, therefore, must be undivided honour. None of the gods or the lords helped Jehovah in creation, or in the redemption of his people : his own right hand and his holy arm wrought for him these great deeds. What have the gods of the heathen done ? If the question be settled by doings, Jehovah is indeed " alone." It is exceedingly wonderful that men should worship gods who can do nothing, and forget the Lord who alone doeth great wonders. Even when the Lord uses men as his instruments, yet the wonder of the work is his alone ; therefore let us not trust in men, or idolize them, or tremble before them. Praise is to be rendered to Jehovah, *"for his mercy endureth for ever."* The mercy of the wonder is the wonder of the mercy ; and the enduring nature of that mercy is the central wonder of that wonder. The Lord causes us often to sit down in amazement as we see what his mercy has wrought out and prepared for us : " wonders of grace to God belong," yea, great wonders and unsearchable. Oh the depth ! Glory be to his name world without end !

> Doing wondrous deeds alone,
> Mercy sits upon his throne.

5. *"To him that by wisdom made the heavens."* His goodness appears in creating the upper regions. He set his wisdom to the task of fashioning a firmament, or

an atmosphere suitable for a world upon which mortal men should dwell. What a mass of wisdom lies hidden in this one creating act ! The discoveries of our keenest observers have never searched out all the evidences of design which are crowded together in this work of God's hands. The lives of plants, animals, and men are dependent upon the fashioning of our heavens : had the skies been other than they are we had not been here to praise God. Divine foresight planned the air and the clouds, with a view to the human race. *"For his mercy endureth for ever."* The Psalmist's details of mercy begin in the loftiest regions, and gradually descend from the heavens to " our low estate " (verse 23) ; and this is an ascent, for mercy becomes greater as its objects become less worthy. Mercy is far-reaching, long-enduring, all-encompassing. Nothing is too high for its reach, as nothing is beneath its stoop.

> High as heaven his wisdom reigns,
> Mercy on the throne remains.

6. *"To him that stretched out the earth above the waters."* Lifting it up from the mingled mass, the dank morass, the bottomless bog, of mixed land and sea ; and so fitting it to be the abode of man. Who but the Lord could have wrought this marvel ? Few even think of the divine wisdom and power which performed all this of old ; yet, if a continent can be proved to have risen or fallen an inch within historic memory, the fact is recorded in the " transactions " of learned societies, and discussed at every gathering of philosophers. *"For his mercy endureth for ever,"* as is seen in the original upheaval and perpetual upstanding of the habitable land, so that no deluge drowns the race. By his strength he sets fast the mountains and consolidates the land upon which we sojourn.

> From the flood he lifts the land :
> Firm his mercies ever stand.

7. *"To him that made great lights."* This also is a creating miracle worthy of our loudest thanks. What could men have done without light ? Though they had the heavens above them, and dry land to move upon, yet what could they see, and where could they go without light ? Thanks be to the Lord, who has not consigned us to darkness. In great mercy he has not left us to an uncertain, indistinct light, floating about fitfully, and without order ; but he has concentrated light upon two grand luminaries, which, as far as we are concerned, are to us " great lights." The Psalmist is making a song for common people, not for your critical savans,—and so he sings of the sun and moon as they appear to us,—the greatest of lights. These the Lord created in the beginning ; and for the present age of man made or constituted them light-bearers for the world. *"For his mercy endureth for ever."* Mercy gleams in every ray of light, and it is most clearly seen in the arrangement by which it is distributed with order and regularity from the sun and moon.

> Lamps he lit in heaven's heights,
> For in mercy he delights.

8. *"The sun to rule by day."* We cannot be too specific in our praises ; after mentioning great lights, we may sing of each of them, and yet not outwear our theme. The influences of the sun are too many for us to enumerate them all, but untold benefits come to all orders of beings by its light, warmth, and other operations. Whenever we sit in the sunshine, our gratitude should be kindled. The sun is a great ruler, and his government is pure beneficence, because by God's mercy it is moderated to our feebleness ; let all who rule take lessons from the sun which rules to bless. By day we may well give thanks, for God gives cheer. The sun rules because God rules ; it is not the sun which we should worship, like the Parsees ; but the Creator of the sun, as he did who wrote this sacred song. *"For his mercy endureth for ever."* Day unto day uttereth speech concerning the mercy of the Lord ; every sunbeam is a mercy, for it falls on undeserving sinners who else would sit in doleful darkness, and find earth a hell. Milton puts it well :

> He, the golden tressèd sun
> Caused all day his course to run;
> For his mercy shall endure
> Ever faithful, ever sure.

9. *"The moon and stars to rule by night."* No hour is left without rule. Blessed be God, he leaves us never to the doom of anarchy. The rule is one of light and

benediction. The moon with her charming changes, and the stars in their fixed spheres gladden the night. When the season would be dark and dreary because of the absence of the sun, forth come the many minor comforters. The sun is enough alone ; but when he is gone a numerous band cannot suffice to give more than a humble imitation of his radiance. Jesus, the Sun of Righteousness, alone, can do more for us than all his servants put together. He makes our day. When he is hidden, it is night, and remains night, let our human comforters shine at their full. What mercy is seen in the lamps of heaven gladdening our landscape at night ! What equal mercy in all the influences of the moon upon the tides, those life-floods of the earth ! The Lord is the Maker of every star, be the stars what they may ; he calleth them all by their names, and at his bidding each messenger with his torch enlightens our darkness. *"For his mercy endureth for ever."* Let our thanks be as many as the stars, and let our lives reflect the goodness of the Lord, even as the moon reflects the light of the sun. The nightly guides and illuminators of men on land and sea are not for now and then, but for all time. They shone on Adam, and they shine on us. Thus they are tokens and pledges of undying grace to men ; and we may sing with our Scotch friends—

> For certainly
> His mercies dure
> Most firm and sure
> Eternally.

10 To him that smote Egypt in their firstborn : for his mercy *endureth* for ever :

11 And brought out Israel from among them : for his mercy *endureth* for ever :

12 With a strong hand, and with a stretched out arm : for his mercy *endureth* for ever.

13 To him which divided the Red sea into parts : for his mercy *endureth* for ever :

14 And made Israel to pass through the midst of it : for his mercy *endureth* for ever :

15 But overthrew Pharaoh and his host in the Red sea : for his mercy *endureth* for ever.

10. We have heard of the glory of the world's creation, we are now to praise the Lord for the creation of his favoured nation by their Exodus from Egypt. Because the monarch of Egypt stood in the way of the Lord's gracious purposes it became needful for the Lord to deal with him in justice ; but the great design was mercy to Israel, and through Israel mercy to succeeding ages, to all the world. *"To him that smote Egypt in their firstborn."* The last and greatest of the plagues struck all Egypt to the heart. The sorrow and the terror which it caused throughout the nation it is hardly possible to exaggerate. From king to slave each one was wounded in the tenderest point. The joy and hope of every household was struck down in one moment, and each family had its own wailing. The former blows had missed their aim compared with the last ; but that " smote Egypt." The Lord's firstborn had been oppressed by Egypt, and at last the Lord fulfilled his threatening, " I will slay thy son, even thy firstborn." Justice lingered but it struck home at last. *"For his mercy endureth for ever."* Yes, even to the extremity of vengeance upon a whole nation the Lord's mercy to his people endured. He is slow to anger, and judgment is his strange work ; but when mercy to men demands severe punishments he will not hold back his hand from the needful surgery. What were all the firstborn of Egypt compared with those divine purposes of mercy to all generations of men which were wrapt up in the deliverance of the elect people ? Let us even when the Lord's judgments are abroad in the earth continue to sing of his unfailing grace.

> For evermore his love shall last
> For ever sure, for ever fast.

11. *"And brought out Israel from among them."* Scattered as the tribes were up and down the country, and apparently held in a grasp which would never be

relaxed, the Lord wrought their deliverance, and severed them from their idolatrous task-masters. None of them remained in bondage. The Lord brought them out ; brought them out at the very hour when his promise was due ; brought them out brought them all out ; despite their being mingled among the Egyptians ; brought them out never to return. Unto his name let us give thanks for this further proof of his favour to the chosen ones, *"For his mercy endureth for ever."* Once the Israelites did not care to go out, but preferred to bear the ills they had rather than risk they knew not what ; but the Lord's mercy endured that test also, and ceased not to stir up the nest till the birds were glad to take to their wings. He turned the land of plenty into a house of bondage, and the persecuted nation was glad to escape from slavery. The unfailing mercy of the Lord is gloriously seen in his separating his elect from the world. He brings out his redeemed, and they are henceforth a people who show forth his praise.

> For God doth prove
> Our constant friend ;
> His boundless love
> Shall never end.

12. *"With a strong hand, and with a stretched out arm."* Not only the matter but the manner of the Lord's mighty acts should be the cause of our praise. We ought to bless the Lord for adverbs as well as adjectives. In the Exodus the great power and glory of Jehovah were seen. He dashed in pieces the enemy with his right hand. He led forth his people in no mean or clandestine manner. " He brought them forth also with silver and gold, and there was not one feeble person in all their tribes." Egypt was glad when they departed. God worked with great display of force, and with exceeding majesty ; he stretched out his arm like a workman intent on his labour, he lifted up his hand as one who is not ashamed to be seen. Even thus was it in the deliverance of each one of us from the thraldom of sin : " according to the working of his mighty power which he wrought in Christ when he raised him from the dead and set him at his own right hand in the heavenly places." *"For his mercy endureth for ever "*—therefore his power is put forth for the rescue of his own. If one plague will not set them free there shall be ten ; but free they shall all be at the appointed hour ; not one Israelite shall remain under Pharaoh's power. God will not only use his hand but his arm—his extraordinary power shall be put to the work sooner than his purpose of mercy shall fail.

> See he lifts his strong right hand,
> For his mercies steadfast stand.

13. *"To him which divided the Red sea into parts."* He made a road across the sea-bottom, causing the divided waters to stand like walls on either side. Men deny miracles ; but, granted that there is a God, they become easy of belief. Since it requires me to be an atheist that I may logically reject miracles, I prefer the far smaller difficulty of believing in the infinite power of God. He who causes the waters of the sea ordinarily to remain as one mass can with equal readiness divide them. He who can throw a stone in one direction can with the same force throw it another way : the Lord can do precisely what he wills, and he wills to do anything which is for the deliverance of his people. *"For his mercy endureth for ever,"* and therefore it endures through the sea as well as over the dry land. He will do a new thing to keep his old promise. His way is in the sea, and he will make a way for his people in the same pathless region.

> Lo, the Red Sea he divides
> For his mercy sure abides.

14. *"And made Israel to pass through the midst of it."* He gave the people courage to follow the predestined track through the yawning abyss, which might well have terrified a veteran host. It needed no little generalship to conduct so vast and motley a company along a way so novel and apparently so dangerous. He made them to pass, by the untrodden road ; he led them down into the deep and up again on the further shore in perfect order, keeping their enemies back by the thick darkness of the cloudy pillar. Herein is the glory of God set forth, as all his people see it in their own deliverance from sin. By faith we also give up all reliance upon works and trust ourselves to pass by a way which we have not known, even by the way of reliance upon the atoning blood : thus are we effectually sundered from

the Egypt of our former estate, and our sins themselves are drowned. The people marched dry shod through the heart of the sea. Hallelujah ! *"For his mercy endureth for ever."* Mercy cleared the road, mercy cheered the host, mercy led them down, and mercy brought them up again. Even to the depth of the sea mercy reaches,—there is no end to it, no obstacle in the way of it, no danger to believers in it, while Jehovah is all around. "Forward !" be *our* watchword as it was that of Israel of old, for mercy doth compass us about.

> Through the fire or through the sea
> Still his mercy guardeth thee.

15. *"But overthrew Pharaoh and his host in the Red sea."* Here comes the thunder-clap. Though we hear them sounding peal upon peal, yet the judgments of the Lord were only loud-mouthed mercies speaking confusion to the foe, that the chosen might tremble before him no longer. The chariots were thrown over, the horses were overthrown. The King and his warriors were alike overwhelmed ; they were hurled from their chariots as locusts are tossed to and fro in the wind. Broken was the power and conquered was the pride of Egypt. Jehovah had vanquished the enemy. "Art thou not it which cut Rahab and wounded the crocodile ?" None are too great for the Lord to subdue, none too high for the Lord to abase. The enemy in his fury drove after Israel into the sea, but there his wrath found a terrible recompense beneath the waves. *"For his mercy endureth for ever."* Yes, mercy continued to protect its children, and therefore called in the aid of justice to fulfil the capital sentence on their foes. Taken red-handed, in the very act of rebellion against their sovereign Lord, the audacious adversaries met the fate which they had themselves invited. He that goes down into the midst of the sea asks to be drowned. Sin is self-damnation. The sinner goes downward of his own choice, and if he finds out too late that he cannot return, is not his blood upon his own head ? The finally impenitent, however terrible their doom, will not be witnesses against mercy ; but rather this shall aggravate their misery, that they went on in defiance of mercy, and would not yield themselves to him whose mercy endureth for ever. To the Israelites as they sung this song their one thought would be of the rescue of their fathers from the fierce oppressor. Taken like a lamb from between the teeth of the lion, Israel justly praises her Deliverer and chants aloud :

> Evermore his love shall reign ;
> Pharaoh and his host are slain.

16 To him which led his people through the wilderness : for his mercy *endureth* for ever.

17 To him which smote great kings : for his mercy *endureth* for ever :

18 And slew famous kings : for his mercy *endureth* for ever :

19 Sihon king of the Amorites : for his mercy *endureth* for ever :

20 And Og the king of Bashan : for his mercy *endureth* for ever :

21 And gave their land for an heritage : for his mercy *endureth* for ever :

22 *Even* an heritage unto Israel his servant : for his mercy *endureth* for ever.

16. *"To him which led his people through the wilderness."* He led them into it, and therefore he was pledged to lead them through it. They were "his people," and yet they must go into the wilderness, and the wilderness must remain as barren as ever it was ; but in the end they must come out of it into the promised land. God's dealings are mysterious, but they must be right, simply because they are his. The people knew nothing of the way, but they were led ; they were a vast host, yet they were all led ; there were neither roads nor tracks, but being led by unerring wisdom they never lost their way. He who brought them out of Egypt, also led them through the wilderness. By Moses, and Aaron, and Jethro, and the pillar of cloud he led them. What a multitude of mercies are comprehended in the conduct of such an enormous host through a region wherein there was no provision even for single travellers ; yet the Lord by his infinite power and wisdom conducted a whole nation for forty years through a desert land, and their feet did not swell, neither did their garments wax old in all the journey. *"For his mercy endureth for ever."* Their conduct in the wilderness tested his mercy most severely, but it bore the

strain; many a time he forgave them; and though he smote them for their transgressions, yet he waited to be gracious and speedily turned to them in compassion. *Their* faithfulness soon failed, but *his* did not: the fiery, cloudy pillar which never ceased to lead the van was the visible proof of his immutable love—

> For his mercy, changing never,
> Still endureth, sure for ever.

17. *"To him which smote great kings."* Within sight of their inheritance Israel had to face powerful enemies. Kings judged to be great because of the armies at their back blocked up their road. This difficulty soon disappeared, for the Lord smote their adversaries, and a single stroke sufficed for their destruction. He who had subdued the really mighty ruler of Egypt made short work of these petty sovereigns, great though they were in the esteem of neighbouring princes. *"For his mercy endureth for ever."* Mercy, which had brought the chosen tribes so far, would not be baulked by the opposition of boastful foes. The Lord who smote Pharaoh at the beginning of the wilderness march, smote Sihon and Og at the close of it. How could these kings hope to succeed when even mercy itself was in arms against them.

> Evermore his mercy stands
> Saving from the foeman's hands.

18. *"And slew famous kings."* What good was their fame to them? As they opposed God they became infamous rather than famous. Their deaths made the Lord's fame to increase among the nations while their fame ended in disgraceful defeat. *"For his mercy endureth for ever."* Israelitish patriots felt that they could never have too much of this music; God had protected their nation, and they chanted his praises with unwearied iteration.

> Kings he smote despite their fame,
> For his mercy's still the same.

19. *"Sihon king of the Amorites."* Let the name be mentioned that the mercy may be the better remembered. Sihon smote Moab, but he could not smite Israel, for the Lord smote *him.* He was valiant and powerful, so as to be both great and famous; but as he wilfully refused to give a peaceful passage to the Israelites, and fought against them in malice, there was no choice for it but to let him run into that destruction which he courted. His fall was speedy and final, and the chosen people were so struck with it that they sung of his overthrow in their national songs. *"For his mercy endureth for ever."* His mercy is no respecter of persons, and neither the greatness nor the fame of Sihon could protect him after he had dared to attack Israel. The Lord will not forsake his people because Sihon blusters.

> Come what may
> By night or day,
> Still most sure,
> His love shall dure.

20. *"And Og the king of Bashan."* He was of the race of the giants, but he was routed like a pigmy when he entered the lists with Israel's God. The Lord's people were called upon to fight against him, but it was God who won the victory. The fastnesses of Bashan were no defence against Jehovah. Og was soon ousted from his stronghold when the captain of the Lord's host led the war against him. He had to exchange his bedstead of iron for a bed in the dust, for he fell on the battlefield. Glory be to the divine conqueror, *"for his mercy endureth for ever."*

> Giant kings before him yield,
> Mercy ever holds the field.

If Sihon could not turn the Lord from his purpose we may be sure that Og could not. He who delivers us out of one trouble will rescue us out of another, and fulfil all the good pleasure of his grace in us.

21. *"And gave their land for an heritage."* As Lord of the whole earth he transferred his estate from one tenant to another. The land did not become the property of the Israelites by their own sword and bow, but by a grant from the throne. This was the great end which all along had been aimed at from Egypt to Jordan. He who brought his people out also brought them in. He who had promised the and

to the seed of Abraham also saw to it that the deed of gift did not remain a dead letter. Both our temporal and our spiritual estates come to us by royal charter. What God gives us is ours by the best of titles. Inheritance by God's gift is a tenure which even Satan cannot dispute. *"For his mercy endureth for ever."* Faithful love endures without end, and secures its own end. " Thou wilt surely bring them in," said the prophet poet ; and here we see the deed complete.

> Till they reach the promised land
> Mercy still the same must stand.

22. *"Even an heritage unto Israel his servant."* Repetitions are effective in poetry, and the more so if there be some little variation in them, bringing out into fuller light some point which else had not been noticed. The lands of the heathen kings were given to " Israel," the name by which the chosen seed is here mentioned for the third time in the Psalm, with the addition of the words, " his servant." The leasehold of Canaan to Israel after the flesh was made dependent upon suit and service rendered to the Lord-of-the-manor by whom the lease was granted. It was a country worth singing about, richly justifying the two stanzas devoted to it. The division of the country by lot, and the laws by which the portions of ground were reserved to the owners and their descendants for a perpetual inheritance were fit subjects for song. Had other nations enjoyed land-laws which ensured to every family a plot of ground for cultivation, much of the present discontent would never have arisen, beggary would soon have become uncommon, and poverty itself would have been rare. *"For his mercy endureth for ever."* Yes, mercy fights for the land, mercy divides the spoil among its favoured ones, and mercy secures each man in his inheritance. Glory be to God the faithful One.

> For his mercy full and free,
> Wins us full felicity.

23 Who remembered us in our low estate : for his mercy *endureth* for ever :

24 And hath redeemed us from our enemies : for his mercy *endureth* for ever.

23. *"Who remembered us in our low estate."* Personal mercies awake the sweetest song—" he remembered *us*." Our prayer is, " Lord remember me," and this is our encouragement—he has remembered us. For the Lord even to think of us is a wealth of mercy. Ours was a sorry estate,—an estate of bankruptcy and mendicancy. Israel rested in its heritage, but we were still in bondage, groaning in captivity : the Lord seemed to have forgotten us, and left us in our sorrow ; but it was not so for long : he turned again in his compassion, bethinking himself of his afflicted children. Our state was once so low as to be at hell's mouth ; since then it has been low in poverty, bereavement, despondency, sickness, and heart-sorrow, and we fear, also, sinfully low in faith, and love, and every other grace ; and yet the Lord has not forgotten us as a dead thing out of mind ; but he has tenderly remembered us still. We thought ourselves too small and too worthless for his memory to burden itself about us, yet he remembered us. *"For his mercy endureth for ever."* Yes, this is one of the best proofs of the immutability of his mercy, for if he could have changed towards any, it would certainly have been towards us who have brought ourselves low, kept ourselves low, and prepared ourselves to sink yet lower. It is memorable mercy to remember us in our low estate : in our highest joys we will exalt Jehovah's name, since of this we are sure,—he will not now desert us—

> For his mercy full and free
> Lasteth to eternity.

24. *"And hath redeemed us from our enemies."* Israel's enemies brought the people low ; but the Lord intervened, and turned the tables by a great redemption. The expression implies that they had become like slaves, and were not set free without price and power ; for they needed to be " *redeemed*." In our case the redemption which is in Christ Jesus is an eminent reason for giving thanks unto the Lord. Sin is our enemy, and we are redeemed from it by the atoning blood ; Satan is our enemy, and we are redeemed from him by the Redeemer's power ; the world is our

enemy, and we are redeemed from it by the Holy Spirit. We are ransomed, let us enjoy our liberty ; Christ has wrought our redemption, let us praise his name.

"*For his mercy endureth for ever.*" Even to redemption by the death of his Son did divine mercy stretch itself. What more can be desired ? What more can be imagined ? Many waters could not quench love, neither could the floods drown it.

> E'en to death upon the tree
> Mercy dureth faithfully.

25 Who giveth food to all flesh : for his mercy *endureth* for ever.

25. "*Who giveth food to all flesh.*" Common providence, which cares for all living things, deserves our devoutest thanks. If we think of heavenly food, by which all saints are supplied, our praises rise to a still greater height ; but meanwhile the universal goodness of God in feeding all his creatures is as worthy of praise as his special favours to the elect nation. Because the Lord feeds all life therefore we expect him to take special care of his own family. "*For his mercy endureth for ever.*" Reaching downward even to beasts and reptiles, it is, indeed, a boundless mercy, which knows no limit because of the meanness of its object.

> All things living he doth feed,
> His full hand supplies their need ;
> For his mercy shall endure,
> Ever faithful, ever sure.

26 O give thanks unto the God of heaven : for his mercy *endureth for* ever.

26. "*O give thanks unto the God of heaven.*" The title is full of honour. The Lord is God in the highest realms, and among celestial beings. His throne is set in glory, above all, out of reach of foes, in the place of universal oversight. He who feeds ravens and sparrows is yet the glorious God of the highest realms. Angels count it their glory to proclaim his glory in every heavenly street. See herein the greatness of his nature, the depth of his condescension, and the range of his love. Mark the one sole cause of his bounty—"*For his mercy endureth for ever.*" He hath done all things from this motive ; and because his mercy never ceases, he will continue to multiply deeds of love world without end. Let us with all our powers of heart and tongue give thanks unto the holy name of Jehovah for ever and ever.

> Change and decay in all around I see,
> O thou who changest not, abide with me.

EXPLANATORY NOTES AND QUAINT SAYINGS.

Whole Psalm.—This Psalm was very probably composed by David, and given to the Levites to sing every day : 1 Chron. xvi. 41. Solomon his son followed his example, and made use of it in singing at the dedication of the Temple (2 Chron. vii. 3—6) ; as Jehoshaphat seems to have done when he went out to war against his enemies (2 Chron. xx. 21).—*John Gill.*

Whole Psalm.—The grand peculiarity of form in this Psalm . . . . is the regular recurrence, at the close of every verse, of a burden or *refrain*. . . . It has been a favourite idea with interpreters that such repetitions necessarily imply alternate or responsive choirs. But the other indications of this usage in the Psalter are extremely doubtful, and every exegetical condition may be satisfied by simply supposing that the singers, in some cases, answered their own questions, and that in others, as in that before us, the people united in the burden or chorus, as they were wont to do in the Amen.—*Joseph Addison Alexander.*

Whole Psalm.—The Psalm is called by the Greek church *Polyeleos*, from its continual mention of the mercy of God.—*Neale and Littledale.*

Whole Psalm.—In the liturgical language this Psalm is called *par excellence* the great Hallel, for according to its broadest compass the great Hallel comprehends Ps. cxx. to cxxxvi., whilst the Hallel which is absolutely so called extends from Ps. cxiii. to cxviii.—*Franz Delitzsch.*

Whole Psalm.—"*Praise ye* (הוֹדוּ) *Jehovah*"; not as in Ps. cxxxv. 1, "Hallelujah," but varying the words,—"Be ye *Judahs* to the Lord !"

Praise him for what he is (ver. 1—3).
Praise him for what he is able to do (ver. 4).
Praise him for what he has done in creation (ver. 5—9).
Praise him for what he did in redeeming Israel from bondage (ver. 10—15).
Praise him for what he did in his providence toward them (ver. 16—22).
Praise him for his grace in times of calamity (ver. 23, 24).
Praise him for his grace to the world at large (ver. 25).
Praise him at the remembrance that this God is the God of heaven (ver. 26).—*Andrew A. Bonar.*

Whole Psalm.—When, in the time of the Emperor Constantius, S. Athanasius was assaulted by night in his church at Alexandria by Syrianus and his troops, and many were wounded and murdered, the Bishop of Alexandria sat still in his chair, and ordered the deacon to begin this Psalm, and the people answered in prompt alternation, "*For his mercy endureth for ever.*"—*Christopher Wordsworth.*

Verse 1.—"*O give thanks unto the LORD.*" When we have praised God for reasons offered unto us in one Psalm, we must begin again, and praise him for other reasons; and even when we have done this, we have not overtaken our task, the duty lieth still at our door, to be discharged afresh, as this Psalm doth show.—*David Dickson.*

Verse 1.—"*For he is good.*" Observe what we must give thanks for : not as the Pharisee that made all his thanksgivings terminate in his own goodness—"God, I thank thee" that I am so and so—but directing them all to God's glory : "*for he is good.*"—*Matthew Henry.*

Verse 1.—"*His mercy endureth for ever.*" This appears four times in Ps. cxviii. 1—4. This sentence is the wonder of Moses, the sum of revelation, and the hope of man.—*James G. Murphy.*

Verse 1.—"*His mercy.*" Many sweet things are in the word of God, but the name of mercy is the sweetest word in all the Scriptures, which made David harp upon it twenty-six times in this Psalm : "*For his mercy endureth for ever.*" It was such a cheerful note in his ears when he struck upon mercy, that, like a bird that is taught to pipe, when he had sung it, he sang it again, and when he had sung it again, he recorded it again, and made it the burden of his song : "*For his mercy endureth for ever.*" Like a nightingale which, when she is in a pleasant vein, quavers and capers, and trebles upon it, so did David upon his mercy : "*For his mercy endureth for ever.*"—*Henry Smith.*

Verse 1.—"*Mercy.*" By "*mercy*" we understand the Lord's disposition to compassionate and relieve those whom sin has rendered miserable and base ; his readiness to forgive and to be reconciled to the most provoking of transgressors, and to bestow all blessings upon them ; together with all the provision which he has made for the honour of his name, in the redemption of sinners by Jesus Christ.—*Thomas Scott.*

Verse 1.—"*His mercy endureth for ever.*" It is everlasting. Everlastingness, or eternity, is a perfect possession, all at once, of an endless life (saith Boëthius). Everlasting mercy, then, is perfect mercy, which shuts out all the imperfections of time, beginning, end, succession, and such is God's mercy. First, his *essential mercy* is everlastingness itself ; for it is himself, and God hath not, but *is*, things. He is beginning, end, being ; and that which is of himself and even himself is eternity itself. Secondly, his *relative mercy* (which respects us, and makes impression on us), is everlasting, too, in a sense ; for the creatures, ever since they had being in him, or existence in their natural causes, ever did and ever will need mercy, either preserving or conserving. Preventing or continuing mercy in the first sense is *negatively endless*, that is, incapable of end, because unboundable for being : in the second sense, it is *privatively endless*, it shall never actually take end, though in itself it may be, and in some ways is, bounded ; the first is included in the latter, but the latter is chiefly here intended ; and therefore the point arises to be this,—*God's mercy* (*chiefly to his church*) *is an endless mercy* ; it knows no end, receives no interruption. Reasons hereof from the word are these (for as touching testimony this Psalm shall be our security), first, from *God's nature, "he is good."* Mercy pleaseth him. It is no trouble for him to exercise mercy. It is his delight : we are never weary of receiving, therefore he cannot be of giving ; for it is a more blessed thing to give than to receive ; so God takes more content in the one than we in the other.— *Robert Harris*, 1578—1658.

Verse 1.—*"His mercy endureth-for ever."* God's goodness is a fountain ; it is never dry. As grace is from the world's beginning (Ps. xxv. 6), so it is to the world's end, *à seculo in seculum*, from one generation to another. Salvation is no termer ; grace ties not itself to times. Noah as well as Abel, Moses as well as Jacob, Jeremy as well as David, Paul as well as Simeon hath part in this salvation. God's gracious purpose the Flood drowned not, the smoke of Sinai smothered not, the Captivity ended not, the ends of the world (Saint Paul calls them so) determined not. For Christ, by whom it is, was slain from the beginning,—Saint John saith so. He was before Abraham, he himself saith so. And *Clemens Alexandrinus* [tom. v. page 233] doth Marcion wrong, though otherwise an heretic, in blaming him for holding that Christ saved those also that believed in him before his incarnation. The blood of the beasts under the law was a type of his. And the scars of his wounds appear yet still, and will for ever, till he cometh to judgment. The Apostle shall end this : he is *heri*, and *hodi*, and *semper idem :* Christ is the same yesterday and to-day and for ever.—*Richard Clerke,*—1634.

Verses 1—3.—The three first verses of this Psalm contain the three several names of the Deity, which are commonly rendered *Jehovah, God,* and *Lord,* respectively ; the first having reference to his essence as *self-existent,* and being his proper name ; the second designating him under the character of *a judge* or of an all-powerful being, if Aleim be derived from *Al ;* and the third, *Adondi,* representing him as *exercising rule.*—*Daniel Cresswell.*

Verses 1—3.—*"O give thanks."*

What ! give God thanks for everything.
    Whatever may befall—
Whatever the dark clouds may bring ?
    Yes, give God thanks for all ;
For safe he leads thee, hand in hand,
To thy blessèd Fatherland.

What ! thank him for the lonely way
    He to me hath given—
For the path which, day by day
    Seems farther off from heaven ?
Yes, thank him, for he holds thy hand
And leads thee to thy Fatherland.

Close, close he shields thee from all harm ;
    And if the road be steep,
Thou know'st his everlasting arm
    In safety doth thee keep,
Although thou canst not understand
The windings to thy Fatherland.

What blessing, thinkest thou, will he,
    Who knows the good and ill,
Keep back, if it is good for thee,
    While climbing up the hill ?
Then trust him, and keep fast his hand,
He leads thee to thy Fatherland.

                              B. S., in "The Christian Treasury," 1865.

Verses 1—9.—Like the preceding Psalm, this Psalm allies itself to the Book of Deuteronomy. The first clauses of verses 2 and 3 (*"God of gods"* and *"Lord of lords"*) are taken from Deut. x. 17 ; verse 12, first clause (*"with a strong hand and stretched out arm"*) from Deut. iv. 34, and v. 15. Verse 16, first clause, is like Deut. viii. 15 (cf. Jer. ii. 6).—*Franz Delitzsch.*

Verses 1—26.—All repetitions are not vain, nor is all length in prayer to be accounted babbling. For repetitions may be used, 1. When they express *fervency* and *zeal :* and so we read, Christ prayed over the same prayer thrice (Matt. xxvi. 44) ; "O my Father, if it be possible, let this cup pass from me." And another evangelist showeth that he did this out of special fervency of spirit (Luke xxii. 44) ; "Being in an agony, he prayed more earnestly." 2. This repetition is not to be disapproved when there is *a special emphasis*, and spiritual elegancy in it, as in Psalm cxxxvi. you have it twenty-six times repeated, *"For his mercy endureth for ever,"* because there was a special reason in it, the Psalmist's purpose there being to show the unweariedness, and the unexhausted riches of God's free grace ; that notwithstanding all the former experiences they had had, God is where he was at first. We waste by giving, our drop is soon spent ; but God is not wasted by bestowing, but hath the same mercy to do good to his creatures, as before. Though he had done all those wonders for them, yet his mercy was as ready to do good to them still. All along God saved and blessed his people, *"For his mercy endureth for ever."—Thomas Manton.*

Verse 2.—"The God of gods." *"God of gods"* is an Hebrew superlative, because he is far above all gods, whether they be so reputed or deputed.—*Robert Harris.*

Verse 2.—"The God of gods." One, as being Creator, infinitely higher than all others, his creatures, who have at any time been regarded as gods.—*French and Skinner*, 1842.

Verses 2, 3.—Before proceeding to recite God's works, the Psalmist declares his supreme Deity, and dominion : not that such comparative language implies that there is anything approaching Deity besides him, but there is a disposition in men, whenever they see any part of his glory displayed, to conceive of a God separate from him, thus impiously dividing the Godhead into parts, and even proceeding so far as to frame gods of wood and stone. There is a depraved tendency in all to take delight in a multiplicity of gods. For this reason, apparently, the Psalmist uses the plural number not only in the word *Elohim* but in the word *Adonim,* so that it reads literally, *Praise ye the Lords of lords :* he would intimate, that the fullest perfection of all dominion is to be found in the one God.—*John Calvin.*

Verse 3.—"The Lord of lords." The meaning of the title *"Lord,"* as distinct from " Jehovah " and " God," is " GOVERNOR." And in this view also he is eminently entitled to praise and thanksgiving, in that his rule and government of the world are also eminently marked by *"mercy"* and *"goodness : "* not the display of power only, but of power declared chiefly in showing mercy and pity : as again all subject to that rule are witnesses. Such is God *in himself.* Nor is it without intention that the doxology is threefold, indicating, doubtless, like the threefold invocation of the Name of the Lord in the blessing of the people (Num. vi. 24—26)—God in Trinity, " Father, Son, and Holy Ghost," as now fully revealed.—*William De Burgh.*

Verse 4.—"To him who alone doeth great wonders." God hath preserved to himself the power of miracles, as his prerogative : for the devil does no miracles ; the devil and his instruments do but hasten nature or hinder nature, antedate nature or postdate nature, bring things sooner to pass or retard them ; and however they pretend to oppose nature, yet still it is but upon nature and by natural means that they work. Only God shakes the whole frame of nature in pieces, and in a miracle proceeds so, as if there were no creation yet accomplished, no course of nature yet established. *Facit mirabilia magna solus,* says David here. There are *mirabilia parva,* some lesser wonders, that the devil and his instruments, Pharaoh's sorcerers, can do ; but when it comes to *mirabilia magna,* great wonders, so great that they amount to the nature of a miracle, *facit solus,* God and God only does them.—*Abraham Wright.*

Verse 4.—"To him who alone doeth great wonders." Does he *"alone"* do great wonders ? that means, he does so by himself, unaided, needing nothing from others, asking no help from his creatures. As the Nile from Nubia to the Mediterranean rolls on 1,300 miles in solitary grandeur, receiving not one tributary, but itself alone dispensing fertility and fatness wherever it comes ; so our God " alone " does wonders. (See Deut. xxxii. 12 ; Ps. lxxii. 18, etc.) No prompter, no helper ; spontaneously he goes forth to work, and all he works is worthy of God. Then we have no need of any other ; we are independent of all others ; all our springs are in him.—*Andrew A. Bonar.*

Verse 4.—"Who alone doeth great wonders." There are three things here declared of God ; that he doeth *wonders,* that the wonders he doeth are *great ;* that he *only* doeth them.—*Augustine, in Neale and Littledale.*

Verse 4.—"Who alone doeth great wonders." Whatsoever instruments the Lord is pleased to use in any of his wonderful works, he alone is the worker, and will not share the glory of the work with any creature.—*David Dickson.*

Verse 4.—It becomes the great God to grant great things. *"To him who alone doeth great wonders."* When you ask great things, you ask such as it becomes God to give, *"* whose mercy is great above the heavens !*"* Nothing under heaven can be too great for him to give. The greater things he bestows, the greater glory redounds to his Name.—*David Clarkson,* 1622—1686.

Verse 4.—Christians should not be ashamed of the mysteries and *miracles* of their religion. Sometimes of late years there has been manifested a disposition to recede from the defence of the supernatural in religion. This is a great mistake. Give up all that is miraculous in true religion and there is nothing left of power sufficient to move any heart to worship or adore ; and without worship there is no piety.—*William Swan Plumer.*

Verse 4.—The longer I live, O my God, the more do I wonder at all the works of thy hands. I see such admirable artifice in the very least and most despicable of all thy creatures, as doth every day more and more astonish my observation. I need not look so far as heaven for matter of marvel, though therein thou art infinitely glorious ; while I have but a spider in my window, or a bee in my garden, or a worm under my feet : every one of these overcomes me with a just amazement : yet can I see no more than their very outsides ; their inward form, which gives their being and operations, I cannot pierce into. The less I can know, O Lord, the more let me wonder ; and the less I can satisfy myself with marvelling at thy works, the more let me adore the majesty and omnipotence of thee, that wroughtest them.—*Joseph Hall.*

Verse 5.—*"To him that by wisdom made the heavens."* We find that God has built the heavens in wisdom, to declare his glory, and to show forth his handiwork. There are no iron tracks, with bars and bolts, to hold the planets in their orbits. Freely in space they move, ever changing, but never changed ; poised and balancing ; swaying and swayed ; disturbing and disturbed, onward they fly, fulfilling with unerring certainty their mighty cycles. The entire system forms one grand complicated piece of celestial machinery ; circle within circle, wheel within wheel, cycle within cycle ; revolutions so swift as to be completed in a few hours ; movements so slow, that their mighty periods are only counted by millions of years.—*From "The Orbs of Heaven,"* 1859.

Verse 5.—*"To him that by wisdom made the heavens."* Not only the firmament, but the third heavens, too, where all is felicity, where is the throne of glory. Then, I infer, that if the *mercy* which visits earth is from the same Jehovah who built that heaven and filled it with glory, there must be in his *mercy* something of the same *"understanding"* or *"wisdom."* It is wise, prudent mercy ; not rashly given forth ; and it is the mercy of him whose love has filled that heaven with bliss. The same architect, the same skill, the same love !—*Andrew A. Bonar.*

Verse 6.—*"Stretched out the earth above the waters."* The waters of the great deep (Gen. vii. 11) are meant ; above which the crust of the earth is outspread. In Prov. viii. 27 the great deep encircles the earth.—*"Speaker's Commentary."*

Verse 7.—*"Great lights."* The luminaries of heaven are unspeakable blessings to the children of men. The sun, in the greatness of his strength, measures their day, and exerts an influence over animal and vegetable life, which surrounds them with innumerable comforts ; and the moon and stars walking forth in their brightness, give direction to them amidst the sable hours of night, and both by land and sea proclaim the wisdom, and benignity, and gracious arrangement of the adorable Creator. By these luminaries, day and night, heat and cold, summer and winter are continually regulated ; so that God's covenant with the earth is maintained through their medium. How truly, then, may we exclaim, " His mercy endureth for ever !*"*—*John Morison.*

Verse 7.—*"To him that made great lights."* Light is the life and soul of the universe, the noblest emblem of the power and glory of God, who, in the night season, leaves not himself without witness, but gives us some portion of that light reflected, which by day we behold flowing from its great fountain in the heart of heaven. Thy church and thy saints, O Lord, " are the moon and the stars," which, by the communication of doctrine, and the splendour of example, guide our feet, while we travel on in the night that hath overtaken us, waiting for the dawn of everlasting day. Then we shall behold thy glory, and see thee as thou art.—*George Horne.*

Verse 8.—"*The sun to rule by day.*" This verse showeth that the sun shineth in the day, by the order which God hath set, and not for any natural cause alone, as some imagine and conjecture.—*Thomas Wilcocks.*

Verse 8.—"*The Sun.*" The *lantern of the world* (*lucerna Mundi*), as Copernicus names the sun, enthroned in the centre—according to Theon of Smyrna, the all-vivifying, pulsating *heart of the universe*, is the primary source of light and of radiating heat, and the generator of numerous terrestrial, electro-magnetic processes, and indeed of the greater part of the organic vital activity upon our planet, more especially that of the vegetable kingdom. In considering the expression of solar force, in its widest generality, we find that it gives rise to alterations on the surface of the earth, —partly by gravitative attraction,—as in the ebb and flow of the ocean (if we except the share taken in the phenomenon by lunar attraction), partly by light and heat-generating transverse vibrations of ether, as in the fructifying admixture of the aerial and aqueous envelopes of our planet, from the contact of the atmosphere with the vaporizing fluid element in seas, lakes, and rivers. The solar action operates, moreover, by differences of heat, in exciting atmospheric and oceanic currents ; the latter of which have continued for thousands of years (though in an inconsiderable degree) to accumulate or waste away alluvial strata, and thus change the surface of the inundated land ; it operates in the generation and maintenance of the electro-magnetic activity of the earth's crust, and that of the oxygen contained in the atmosphere ; at one time calling forth calm and gentle forces of chemical attraction, and variously determining organic life in the endosmose of cell-walls and in tissue of muscular and nervous fibres ; at another time evoking light processes in the atmosphere, such as the coloured coruscations of the polar light, thunder and lightning, hurricanes and waterspouts.

Our object in endeavouring to compress in one picture the *influences of solar action*, in as far as they are independent of the orbit and the position of the axis of our globe, has been clearly to demonstrate, by an exposition of the connection existing between great, and at first sight heterogeneous, phenomena, how physical nature may be depicted in the *History of the Cosmos* as a whole, moved and animated by internal and frequently self-adjusting forces. But the waves of light not only exert a decomposing and combining action on the corporeal world ; they not only call forth the tender germs of plants from the earth, generate the green colouring matter (chlorophyll) within the leaf, and give colour to the fragrant blossom—they not only produce myriads of reflected images of the Sun in the graceful play of the waves, as in the moving grass of the field—but the rays of celestial light, in the varied gradations of their intensity and duration, are also mysteriously connected with the inner life of man, his intellectual susceptibilities, and the melancholy or cheerful tone of his feelings. This is what Pliny the elder referred to in these words, "*Cæli tristram discutit sol, et humani nubila animi serenat.*" [" The sun chases sadness from the sky, and dissipates the clouds which darken the human heart."]—*F. H. Alexander Von Humboldt (1769—1859), in "Cosmos."*

Verse 8.—"*The sun.*"

O sun ! what makes thy beams so bright ?
The word that said, " Let there be light."

James Montgomery.

Verse 9.—"*The moon and stars to rule by night.*" While the apparent revolution of the sun marks out the year and the course of the seasons, the revolution of the moon round the heavens marks out our months ; and by regularly changing its figure at the four quarters of its course, subdivides the months into two periods of weeks, and thus exhibits to all the nations of the earth a " watch-light," or signal, which every seven days presents a form entirely new, for marking out the shorter periods of duration. By its nearness to the earth, and the consequent increase of its gravitating power, it produces currents in the atmosphere, which direct the course of the winds, and purify the aerial fluid from noxious exhalations ; it raises the waters of the ocean, and perpetuates the regular returns of ebb and flow, by which the liquid element is preserved from filth and putrefaction. It extends its sway even over the human frame, and our health and disorders are sometimes partially dependent on its influence. Even its eclipses, and those it produces of the sun, are not without their use. They tend to arouse mankind to the study of astronomy, and the wonders of the firmament ; they serve to confirm the deductions of chronology, to direct the navigator, and to settle the geographical position of towns and countries ; they assist the astronomer in his celestial investigations, and exhibit an agreeable variety of phenomena in the scenery of the heavens. In short, there are terrestrial scenes presented in moon-light, which, in point of solemnity, grandeur, and picturesque beauty, far surpass in interest, to a poetic imagination, all the brilliancy and splendours of noon-day. Hence, in all ages, a moonlight scene has been regarded, by all ranks of men, with feelings of joy and sentiments of admiration. The following description of Homer, translated into English verse by Pope, has been esteemed one of the finest night-pieces in poetry :—

> " Behold the moon, refulgent lamp of night,
> O'er Heaven's clear azure spreads her sacred light,
> When not a breath disturbs the deep serene,
> And not a cloud o'ercasts the solemn scene ;
> Around her throne the vivid planets roll,
> And stars unnumbered gild the glowing pole ;
> O'er the dark trees a yellower verdure shed,
> And tip with silver every mountain's head ;
> Then shine the vales ; the rocks in prospect rise ;
> A flood of glory bursts from all the skies ;
> The conscious swains, rejoicing in the sight,
> Eye the blue vault, and bless the useful light."

Without the light of the moon, the inhabitants of the polar regions would be for weeks and months immersed in darkness. But the moon, like a kindly visitant, returns at short intervals, in the absence of the sun, and cheers them with her beams for days and weeks together. So that, in this nocturnal luminary, as in all the other arrangements of nature, we behold a display of the paternal care and beneficence of that Almighty Being who ordained " the moon and the stars to rule by night," as an evidence of his superabundant goodness, and of " his mercy which endureth for ever."—*Thomas Dick (1774—1857), in "Celestial Scenery."*

Verse 9.—*"Stars to rule by night."* The purpose of the sacred narrative being to describe the adaptation of the earth to the use of man, no account is taken of the nature of the stars, as suns or planets, but merely as signs in the heavens.—*"Speaker's Commentary."*

Verse 9.—*"Stars."* The stars not only adorn the roof of our sublunary mansion, they are also in many respects *useful* to man. Their influences are placid and gentle. Their rays, being dispersed through spaces so vast and immense, are entirely destitute of heat by the time they arrive at our abode ; so that we enjoy the view of a numerous assemblage of luminous globes without any danger of their destroying the coolness of the night or the quiet of our repose. They serve to guide the traveller both by sea and land ; they direct the navigator in tracing his course from one continent to another through the pathless ocean. They serve " for signs and for seasons, and for days and years." They direct the labours of the husbandman, and determine the return and conclusion of the seasons. They serve as a magnificent "time piece," to determine the true length of the day and of the year, and to mark with accuracy all their subordinate divisions. They assist us in our commerce, and in endeavouring to propagate religion among the nations, by showing us our path to every region of the earth. They have enabled us to measure the circumference of the globe, to ascertain the *density* of the materials of which it is composed, and to determine the exact position of all places upon its surface. They cheer the long nights of several months in the polar regions, which would otherwise be overspread with impenetrable darkness. Above all, they open a prospect into the regions of other worlds, and tend to amplify our views of the Almighty Being who brought them into existence by his power, and " whose kingdom ruleth over all." In these arrangements of the stars in reference to our globe, the Divine wisdom and goodness may be clearly perceived. We enjoy all the advantages to which we have alluded as much as if the stars had been created solely for the use of our world, while, at the same time, they serve to diversify the nocturnal sky of other planets, and to diffuse their light and influence over ten thousands of other worlds with which they are more immediately connected, so that, in this respect, as well as in every other, the Almighty produces the most sublime and diversified effects by means the most simple and economical, and renders every part of the universe subservient to another, and to the good of the whole.—*Thomas Dick.*

Verse 9.—"Stars." When the First Consul crossed the Mediterranean on his Egyptian expedition, he carried with him a cohort of *savans*, who ultimately did good service in many ways. Among them, however, as might be expected at that era, were not a few philosophers of the Voltaire-Diderot school. Napoleon, for his own instruction and amusement on shipboard, encouraged disputation among these gentlemen ; and on one occasion they undertook to show, and, according to their own account, *did* demonstrate, by infallible logic and metaphysic, that there is no God. Bonaparte, who hated all idealogists, abstract reasoners, and logical demonstrators, no matter what they were demonstrating, would not fence with these subtle dialecticians, but had them immediately on deck, and, pointing to the stars in the clear sky, replied, by way of counter-argument, " Very good, messieurs ! but who made all these ? "—*George Wilson, in "Religio Chemici,"* 1862.

Verse 10.—"To him that smote Egypt in their first-born." The Egyptians are well said to have been *smitten in their first-born ;* because they continued in their outrageous obstinacy under the other plagues, though occasionally terrified by them, but were broken and subdued by this last plague, and submitted.—*John Calvin.*

Verse 10.—"To him that smote Egypt in their first-born, for his mercy," etc. Remember his sovereign grace, when righteousness would show itself upon the guilty. There was mercy even then to Israel—drops of that mercy that for ever endureth—at the very time when judgment fell on others. Should not this give emphasis to our praises ? The dark background makes the figures in the foreground more prominent.—*Andrew A. Bonar.*

Verse 11.—"And brought out Israel from among them." Such an emigration as this the world never saw. On the lowest computation, the entire multitude must have been above two millions, and in all probability the number exceeded three millions. Is the magnitude of this movement usually apprehended ? Do we think of the emigration of the Israelites from Egypt as of the emigration of a number of families twice as numerous as the population of the principality of Wales, or considerably more than the whole population of the British Metropolis (in 1841), with all their goods, property, and cattle ? The collecting together of so immense a multitude—the arranging the order of their march—the provision of the requisite food even for a few days, must, under the circumstances, have been utterly impossible, unless a very special and overruling Providence had graciously interfered to obviate the difficulties of the case. To the most superficial observer it must be evident, that no man, or number of men, having nothing but human resources, could have ventured to undertake this journey. Scarcely any wonder, wrought by Divine power in Egypt, appears greater than this emigration of a nation, when fairly and fully considered.—*George Smith, in "Sacred Annals,"* 1850.

Verse 12.—"With a stretched out arm." The figure of *an outstretched arm* is appropriate, for we stretch out the arm when any great effort is required ; so that this implies that God put forth an extraordinary and not a common or slight display of his power in redeeming his people.—*John Calvin.*

Verse 13.—"Divided the Red Sea into parts." The entire space between the mountains of Ataka and Abon Deradj was dry. At the former point the gulf is eight miles across, at the latter more than double that distance. The waters that had filled this broad and deep chasm stood in two huge mounds on the right hand and on the left. The light of God shone brightly on the astonished multitude. The word was given, they advanced abreast ; awe-stricken, but quiet and confident. . . . " Then the Egyptians pursued and went in after them into the midst of the sea, all Pharaoh's horses, even his chariots and his fleet horses " : Exod. xiv. 23.—*William Osburn, in "Israel in Egypt,"* 1856.

Verse 14.—"And made Israel to pass through the midst of it," etc. Willingly, without reluctance ; with great spirit and courage, fearless of danger, and with the utmost safety, so that not one was lost in the passage ; see Ps. lxxviii. 53 ; and thus the Lord makes his people willing to pass through afflictions, he being with them ;

and able to bear them, he putting underneath the everlasting arms, even when in the valley of the shadow of death. He carries them safely through them, so that they are not hurt by them ; the waters do not overflow them, nor the flames kindle upon them ; nor are any suffered to be lost : but all come safe to land.—*John Gill.*

Verse 14.—*"And made Israel to pass through the midst of it."* It is a work of no less mercy and power to give his people grace to make use of an offered means of delivery, than to prepare the deliverance for them ; but the constancy of God's mercy doth not only provide the means, but also giveth his people grace to make use thereof in all ages.—*David Dickson.*

Verse 14.—*"And made Israel to pass through the midst of it."* It is many times *hail* with the saints, when *ill* with the wicked. Abraham from the hill seeth Sodom on fire.—*John Trapp.*

Verse 15.—*"But overthrew Pharaoh,"* etc. Thus fell Sethos II. It was his terrible destiny to leave to after-times the strongest exemplification of daring wickedness and mad impiety in his life, and of the vengeance of God in his death, that ever was enacted on the earth. Never had such a judgment befallen any nation, as his reign in Egypt. Accordingly the memory of this fearful event has never departed from among men. The gulf in which he perished is named Bahr-Kolzoum, " the sea of destruction," to this day.

The memory and name of Sethos II. were infamous in Egypt. His tomb was desecrated, and his sarcophagus publicly and judicially broken. The vault seems to have been used as a burying-place for slaves. The distinctive title of his name, *Sethos*, has been mutilated on all the monuments of Egypt. In Lower Egypt the mutilation has even been extended to the same title in the rings of his great-grandfather (Sethos I.), such was the deep abhorrence in which the name had fallen, after it had been borne by this wicked king. His is the only one in the whole range of the kings of Egypt which has suffered this mark of public infamy.—*William Osburn.*

Verse 15.—*"But overthrew Pharaoh,"* etc. Margin, as in Hebrew, *shaked off.* The word is applicable to a tree shaking off its foliage, Isa. xxxiii. 9. The same word is used in Ex. xiv. 27 : " And the Lord overthrew (Margin, *shook off*) the Egyptians in the midst of the sea." He shook them off as if he would no longer protect them. He left them to perish.—*Albert Barnes.*

Verse 15.—*"But shook off Pharaoh."* This translation gives an image of locusts. They fell into the sea like a swarm of locusts.—*Zachary Mudge*—1769.

Verse 15.—*"But overthrew Pharaoh,"* etc. I know that the Gospel is a book of mercy ; I know likewise that in the prophets there are many expressions of mercy ; I know likewise that in the ten commandments, which are the ministration of death, there is made express mention of mercy, " I will have mercy on thousands ": yet, notwithstanding all this, if every leaf, and every line, and every word in the Bible were nothing but mercy, it would nothing avail the presumptuous sinner. Our God is not an impotent God with one arm ; but as he is slow to anger, so is he great in power. And therefore though in this Psalm there is nothing but *"his mercy endureth for ever,"* which is twenty-six times in twenty-six verses : yet mark what a rattling thunder-clap is here in this verse. In our addresses therefore unto God, let us so look upon him as a just God as well as a merciful ; and not either despair of or presume upon his mercy.—*Abraham Wright.*

Verse 16.—*"Led his people through the wilderness."*

> When Israel, of the Lord beloved,
>   Out of the land of bondage came,
> Her father's God before her moved,
>   An awful guide, in smoke and flame.
> By day, along the astonished lands,
>   The cloudy pillar glided slow ;
> By night Arabia's crimsoned sands
> Returned the fiery column's glow.

Sir Walter Scott, 1711—1832.

Verse 16.—*"He led his people through the wilderness."* It was an astonishing miracle of God to support so many hundreds of thousands of people in a wilderness totally deprived of all necessaries for the life of man, and that for the space of forty years.—*Adam Clarke.*

Verse 16.—*"He led his people through the wilderness,"* etc. It is a very sweet truth which is enunciated in this verse, and one which I think we need very much to realize. His own people, his peculiar people, his chosen, loved, and favoured ones, whom he cherished as the apple of his eye, who were graven on the palms of his hands, and loved with an everlasting love, even these he led through the wilderness; and all this *because* " His mercy endureth for ever." In another Psalm it is said, " He leadeth them beside the still waters, he maketh them to lie down in green pastures "; but the barren wilderness has no green pastures, the parched and arid desert has no still waters. And yet " in the wilderness shall waters break out, and streams in the desert, and an highway shall be there; and the ransomed of the Lord shall return, and come to Zion with songs and everlasting joy upon their heads." " Who is this that cometh up from the wilderness, leaning upon her beloved ? " It is one of the Lord's sweet truths that so perplex those that are without, but which are so full of consolation to his own children, that the wilderness and mercy are linked together of God in indissoluble union here. " I will allure her," saith the Lord, " and bring her into the wilderness, and speak comfortably unto her."—*Barton Bouchier.*

Verse 16.—"*Who led his people.*" Note that in what precedes this, in this verse itself, and in what follows, God's three ways of leading are set forth. He leads *out*, he leads *through*, and he leads *into ;* out of sin, through the world, into heaven ; out by faith, through by hope, into by love.—*Michael Ayguan* (1416), *in Neale and Littledale.*

Verse 17.—"*Great kings.*" *Great,* as those times accounted them, when every small city almost had her king. Canaan had thirty and more of them. *Great* also in regard of their stature and strength ; for they were of the giants' race. Deut. iii. ; Amos ii.—*John Trapp.*

Verses 18, 20.—The profane of our times may hence learn to take heed how they wrong the faithful. God is " wise in heart and mighty in strength : " Job ix. 4. Who ever waxed fierce against his people and hath prospered ? For their sakes he hath destroyed great kings and mighty, "*Sihon king of the Amorites, and Og the king of Bashan.*" He can pluck off thy chariot wheels, strike thee in the hinder parts, cause thy heart to fail thee for fear, and in a moment fetch thy soul from thee : better were it for thee to have a millstone hanged about thy neck, and thou to be cast into the bottom of the sea, than to offend the least of these faithful ones ; they are dear in his sight, tender to him, as the apple of his eye.—*John Barlow,* 1632.

Verse 19.—"*Sihon* " occupied the whole district between the Arnon and Jabbok, through which the approach to the Jordan lay. He had wrested it from the predecessor of Balak, and had established himself, not in the ancient capital of Moab-Ar, but in the city still conspicuous to the modern traveller from its wide prospect and its cluster of stone pines—Heshbon. The recollection of his victory survived in a savage war-song, which passed into a kind of proverb in after-times :—

> " Come home to Heshbon ;
> Let the city of Sihon be built and prepared,
> For there is gone out a fire from Heshbon,
> A flame from the city of Sihon.
> It hath consumed Ar of Moab,
> And the lords of the high places of Arnon :
> Woe to thee, Moab ; thou art undone, thou people of Chemosh !
> He hath given his sons that escaped, and his daughters, into captivity
> To the king of the Amorites, Sihon."*

The decisive battle between Sihon and his new foes took place at Jahaz, probably on the confines of the rich pastures of Moab and the desert whence the Israelites emerged. It was the first engagement in which they were confronted with the future enemies of their nation. The slingers and archers of Israel, afterwards so renowned, now first showed their skill. Sihon fell ; the army fled † (so ran the later tradition), and devoured by thirst, like the Athenians in the Assinarus on their flight from Syracuse, were slaughtered in the bed of one of the mountain streams. The memory of this battle was cherished in triumphant strains, in which, after reciting, in bitter

---

* Num. xxi. 27–29, repeated, as is well known, in Jer. xlviii. 45, 46.
† Joseph. Ant. iv. 5, § 2.

irony, the song just quoted of the Amorites' triumph, they broke out into an exulting contrast of the past greatness of the defeated chief and his present fall :—

> " We have shot at them : Heshbon is perished :
> We have laid them waste : even unto Nophah :
> With fire : even unto Medeba."*

Arthur Penrhyn Stanley, in "The History of the Jewish Church."

Verse 20.—"*Og the king of Bashan.*" There is continued victory. The second hindrance disappears after the first. "*Og, king of Bashan,*" last of the giants (Deut. iii. 11), fared no better for all his strength than *Sihon.* It was not some peculiar weakness of Sihon that overthrew him. All enemies of God, however different in resource they may appear when they measure themselves among themselves, are alike to those who march in the strength of God. The power by which the Christian conquers one foe will enable him to conquer all. And yet because *Og* did *look* more formidable than Sihon, God gave his people special encouragement in meeting him : Numb. xxi. 34. God remembers that even the most faithful and ardent of his people cannot get entirely above the deceitfulness of outward appearances.—*Pulpit Commentary.*

Verse 20.—When "*Og king of Bashan* " took the field—a giant, a new and more terrific foe—he, too, fell. And the *mercy* that thus dealt with enemies so great, enemies so strong, one after another, "*endureth for ever.*" When Antichrist raises up his hosts in the latter days, one after another—when the great, the famous, the mighty, the noble, the gigantic men, in succession assail the Church, they shall perish : " For his *mercy* endureth for ever.—*Andrew A. Bonar.*

Verse 22.—"*Israel his servant.*" He speaks of all that people as of one man, because they were united together in one body, in the worship of one and the same God. Thus God calleth them all his " first-born ": Exod. iv. 22.—*Matthew Pool.*

Verse 23.—"*Who remembered us.*" We should echo in our thankfulness the first intimation that God gives in his providence of an approaching mercy. If you do but hear when the king is on his road towards your town you raise your bells to ring him in, and stay not till he be entered the gates. The birds rise betimes in the morning, and are saluting the rising sun with their sweet notes in the air. Thus should we strike up our harps in praising God at the first appearance of a mercy.—*William Gurnall.*

Verse 23.—"*Who remembered us.*" The word "*remembered*" is a pregnant word, it bears twins twice told, it is big of a six-fold sense, as so many degrees of mercy in it. 1. *To remember* signifies to think upon, in opposition to forgetfulness. We may dwell in man's thoughts and not be the better for it, but we cannot be in God's remembering thoughts but we shall be the better for it. 2. To remember (as the second degree of the mercy) signifies to take notice of a thing, in opposition to neglect ; so it is used in Exod. xx. 8 : "*Remember* the Sabbath-day, to keep it holy : " take notice, that is, neglect it not, " remember " to keep holy the Sabbath-day. So God " remembered " us in our low estates : how ? Why, he did not barely think upon us, but he did observe and take notice of us, and considered what our case was. But, 3. It signifies (as the third degree of mercy), to lay to heart, to pity and compassionate persons in such a case. What am I better for anybody's thinking of me, if he do not take notice of me, so as to pity me in my low estate ? So God doth, as in Jer. xxxi. 20. 4. *To remember,* signifies yet more (as the fourth degree of mercy) to be well pleased with a person in such a case, to accept of a person in such a case ; so the word is used in Ps. xx. 3 : " The Lord *remember* all thy offerings, and accept thy burnt sacrifice"; remember, that is accept. 5. *To remember* signifies (as the fifth degree of mercy) to hear and to grant a request ; so it is used in 1 Sam. i. 19, 20, 27 : " God *remembered* Hannah," and the next word is, " He gave her what she asked." 6. *To remember* signifies (as the sixth degree of mercy) to help and succour, or to redeem and deliver from that which we were appointed to, from the low estate ; and so it is in Gal. ii. 10 : " Only they would that we should *remember* the poor." Remembering the poor is not barely a thought, but a relieving thought ; therefore saith the Psalmist in the following verse, " who hath redeemed us from our enemies : " this was the *remembrance* of God, *redemption* from enemies.

---

* Numb. xxi. 30.

I might draw considerations [for thanksgiving] from the *Author* of the mercy, *God;* a God that was offended by us, a God that needed us not, and a God that gains nothing by us ; and yet this God remembered us in our low estate ; that should engage us. I might also draw obligations from *the objects*, and that is *us* that were not only an undeserving but an ill-deserving, and are not a suitable returning people. I might draw arguments from *the mercy*, itself,—that God *remembered* us. . . . and I might draw arguments from *the season*, " in our low estate," and from *the excellency of the duty* of thanksgiving ; 'tis a comely thing ; it makes us like the angels, whose whole employment and liturgy is to give and live praise to God. And from this also I might enlarge the discoveries of the obligation, that " *his mercy endureth* for ever."

"*For his mercy endureth for ever.*" There is no reason to be given for grace but grace ; there is no reason to be given for mercy but mercy ; who remembered us : " *for his mercy endureth for ever.*"—*Ralph Venning* (1620—1673), *in "Mercies Memorial."*

Verse 24.—"*And.*" If the end of one mercy were not the beginning of another, we were undone.—*Philip Henry*, 1631—1696.

Verse 24.—"*And hath redeemed us.*" Or, *broken us off*, pulled us away, as by violence ; for they would never else have loosed us.—*John Trapp.*

Verse 25.—"*Who giveth food to all flesh,*" etc. The very air we breathe in, the bread we eat, our common blessings, be they never so mean, we have them all from grace, and all from the tender mercy of the Lord. Ps. cxxxvi. 25, you have there the story of the notable effects of God's mercy, and he concludes it thus : "*Who giveth food to all flesh : for his mercy endureth for ever.*" Mark, the Psalmist doth not only ascribe those mighty victories, those glorious instances of his love and power, to his unchangeable mercy, but he traces our daily bread to the same cause. In eminent deliverances of the church we will acknowledge mercy ; yea, but we should do it in every bit of meat we eat ; for the same reason is rendered all along. What is the reason his people smote Sihon king of the Amorites, and Og the king of Bashan, and that they were rescued so often out of danger ? " For his mercy endureth for ever." And what is the reason he giveth food to all flesh ? " For his mercy endureth for ever." It is not only mercy which gives us Christ, and salvation by Christ, and all those glorious deliverances and triumphs over the enemies of the church ; but it is mercy which furnisheth our tables, it is mercy that we taste with our mouths and wear at our backs. It is notable, our Lord Jesus, when there were but five barley loaves and two fishes (John vi. 11), " He lift up his eyes and gave thanks." Though our provision be never so homely and slender, yet God's grace and mercy must be acknowledged.—*Thomas Manton.*

Verse 25.—"*Who giveth food to all flesh.*" We might fancy that they who have so much to sing of in regard to themselves, so much done for their own souls, would have little care for others. We might fear that they would be found selfish. But not so ; the love of God felt by a man makes the man feel as God does toward men ; and as God's love is ever going forth to others, so is the heart of the man of God. We see how it is even as to patriotism—a man's intensest patriotic feelings do not necessarily make him indifferent to the good of other countries, but rather make him wish all countries to be like his own ; so it is, much more certainly and truly, with the Lord's people in their enjoyment of blessing. Their heart expands towards others ; they would fain have all men share in what they enjoy. They therefore cannot close their song without having this other clause—Praise him who is " *the giver of bread to all flesh.*" Not to Israel only does he give blessing. Israel had their manna ; but, at the same time, the earth at large has its food. So in spiritual things. Israel's God is he who giveth himself as the Bread of Life to the world. Perhaps at this point the Psalmist's eye may be supposed to see *earth in its state of blessedness*, after Israel is for the last time redeemed from all enemies, and become " life from the dead " to the world—when Christ reigns and dispenses the bread of life to the New Earth, as widely as he gave common food—" the feast of fat things to all nations," (Isa. xxv. 6.) ; for his mercy will not rest till this is accomplished.—*Andrew A. Bonar.*

Verse 25.—"*Who giveth food to all flesh.*" In the close the Psalmist speaks of the paternal providence of God as extending not only to all mankind, but to every living creature, suggesting that we have no reason to feel surprise at his sustaining the character of a kind and provident father to his own people, when he condescends to care for the cattle, and the asses of the field, and the crow, and the sparrow.　Men are much better than brute beasts, and there is a great difference between some men and others, though not in merit, yet as regards the privilege of the divine adoption, and the Psalmist is to be considered as reasoning from the less to the greater and enhancing the incomparably superior mercy which God shows to his own children.—*John Calvin.*

Verse 25.—"*Who giveth food to all flesh.*"　Of Edward Taylor, better known as "Father Taylor," the Sailor Preacher of Boston, it is said that his prayers were more like the utterances of an Oriental, abounding in imagery, than a son of these colder western climes.　The Sunday before he was to sail for Europe, he was entreating the Lord to care well for his church during his absence.　All at once he stopped and ejaculated, "What have I done ?　Distrust the providence of heaven ! A God that gives a whale a ton of herrings for a breakfast, will he not care for my children ? " and then went on, closing his prayer in a more confiding strain.— *C. H. Spurgeon, in "Eccentric Preachers,"* 1880.

Verse 26.—"*The God of heaven.*"　The phrase *"God of heaven"* is not found in the earlier Scriptures.　We meet it nowhere else in the Psalms ; but we meet it in 2 Chron. xxxvi. 23 ; Ezra i. 2 ; v. 11, 12 ; vi. 9 ; vii. 12, 23 ; Neh. i. 4 ; ii. 4 ; Dan. ii. 18, 19, 44 ; Jonah i. 9.　It is twice found in the Apocalypse, Rev. xi. 13 ; xvi. 11.　It is a sublime and appropriate designation of the true God, expressive of his glorious elevation above the passions and perturbations of earth.　To him all flesh should give thanks, for all receive his mercy in many forms and ways.　His favours come down on generation after generation, and to his willing, obedient people they shall flow on during eternal ages.—*William Swan Plumer.*

Verse 26.—My brethen, God's mercies are from everlasting ; and it is a treasure that can never be spent, never exhausted, unto eternity.　In Isa. lxiv. 5, we read, " In thy mercy is continuance."　If God will but continue to be merciful to me, will a poor soul say, I have enough.　Why, saith he, " in his mercies is continuance, and we shall be saved."　Hath God pardoned thee hitherto ? but hast thou sinned again ?　Can he stretch his goodness and mercy a little further ?　Why, he will stretch them out unto eternity, unto everlasting ; and if one *everlasting* be not enough, there are twenty-six everlastings in this one Psalm.　In Isa. liv. 8, " In a little wrath I hid my face from thee, but with everlasting kindness will I have mercy on thee."—*Thomas Goodwin.*

Verse 26.—"*O give thanks unto the God of heaven.*"　His mercy in providing heaven for his people is more than all the rest.—*John Trapp.*

HINTS TO PREACHERS.

Verse 1.—I. Consider his name—" Jehovah."　II. Carry out your joyful duty : " O give thanks."　III. Contemplate the two reasons given—goodness and enduring mercy.

Verse 1.—I. Many subjects for praise.　1. For the goodness of God : " He is good " (verse 1).　2. For his supremacy : " God of gods ; Lord of lords " (verses 2, 3).　3. For his works in general (verse 4).　4. For his works of creation in particular (verses 5—9).　5. For his works of Providence (verses 10—26).　II. The chief subject for praise :—" For his mercy endureth for ever."　1. For mercy. This is the sinner's principal need.　2. For mercy in God.　This is the sinner's attribute, and is as essential to God as justice.　3. For mercy enduring for ever. If they who have sinned need mercy for ever, they must exist for ever ; and their guilt must be for ever.—*G. R.*

Verse 1.—"*The LORD is good.*"　God is originally good—good of himself.　He is infinitely good.　He is perfectly good, because infinitely good.　He is immutably good.—*Charnock.*

Verses 1—3.—I. The triplet of names : " Jehovah," " the God of gods," " the Lord of lords."　II. The threefold adjuration, " O give thanks."　III. The irrepressible attribute and argument—" for his mercy," etc.—*W. B. H.*

Verses 1—26.—" For his mercy endureth for ever." See " Spurgeon's Sermons," No. 787 : " A Song, a Solace, a Sermon, and a Summons."

Verse 4.—I. The Lord does great wonders of mercy. II. He does them unaided. III. He does them as none else can do. IV. He should have unique praise.

Verse 4.—*The great lone Wonderworker.* I. God was alone in the wonderwork of Creation : Gen. i. II. Alone in the wonderwork of redemption : Isa. lxiii. 5. III. Is alone in the wonderwork of Providence : Ps. civ. 27, 28. IV. Alone in the wonderwork of Sanctification : 1 Thess. v. 23, 24. V. Will be alone in the wonderwork of Universal Triumph : 1 Cor. xv. 25.—*C. A. D.*

Verse 4.—The merciful in the wonderful. The wonderful in the merciful.

Verse 7.—The mercy which dwells in the creation and distribution of light.

Verses 7—9.—I. The constancy of rule. II. The association of light with rule. III. The perpetuity of mercy in this matter.

Verses 8, 9.—I. The glory of the day of joy. II. The comforts of the night of sorrow. III. The hand of God in each.

Verse 10.—Mercy and judgment. In the stroke that filled Egypt with anguish there was conspicuous mercy.—I. Even to Egypt ; the sharp stroke should have wrought repentance. So God still strives with men. II. Evidently to Israel ; they being thus delivered ; their firstborn saved. III. Emphatically to the whole world : power made known, Christ foreshadowed, an important link in the chain of redemption.—*W. B. H.*

Verse 11.—The bringing out of God's people from their natural state, from their misery, and from association with the ungodly, a great marvel of everlasting mercy.

Verse 11.—Effectual calling ; the intervention at the determined moment of the mercy of infinite ages.—*W. B. H.*

Verse 12.—Displays of divine power in the history of the saints a reason for song.

Verses 13, 14.—God to be praised not only, I. For clearing our way ; but also, II. For giving faith to traverse it. The last as great a mercy as the first.

Verses 13—15.—Mercy queen of the Exodus. I. Her sceptre upon the sea. What cannot Love divine conquer for its chosen ! II. Her standard in the van. Whither shall saints fear to follow her ? III. Her frown upon the pursuers ; life to the beloved, fatal to the foe. IV. To her let there be brought the chaplet of our praises.—*W. B. H.*

Verse 15.—Final victory. I. Battalions of evil annihilated. II. Love unharmed mounting immortal above the wave : " for his mercy endureth for ever." III. Heaven resonant with the song of Moses and the Lamb, to him give thanks. —*W. B. H.*

Verse 16.—I. Personal care : " To him which led." II. Peculiar interest : " His people." III. Persevering goodness : " Through the wilderness."

Verse 16.—*Led through the wilderness.* I. God's people must enter the wilderness for trial, for self knowledge, for development of graces, for preparation for Canaan. II. God leads his people while in the wilderness. Their route, their provision, their discipline, their protection. III. God will bring his people out of the wilderness.—*C. A. D.*

Verses 17—22.—See " Spurgeon's Sermons," No. 1285 : " Sihon and Og ; or, Mercies in Detail."

Verse 21.—I. Our portion, a heritage. II. Our title-deed, a royal grant : " And gave." III. Our praise, due to enduring mercy.

Verse 23.—Prayer of the dying thief turned into a song.

Verses 23, 24.—The gracious remembrance and the glorious redemption.— *C. A. D.*

Verse 24.—Our enemies, our accomplished redemption, the author of it, and his reason for effecting it.

Verse 24.—The multiplied redemptions of the Christian life, and their inexhaustible spring.—*W. B. H.*

Verse 25.—Divine housekeeping. I. The Royal Commissariat. II. Its spiritual counterpart : God's august provisioning for our immortal nature. III. The queenly grace that hath the keeping of the keys : " for his mercy," etc.—*W. B. H.*

Verse 26.—Consider, I. How he rules in heaven. II. How he rules earth from heaven. III. How mercy is the eternal element of that rule, and therefore he is the eternal object of praise.

PSALM CXXXVII.

This plaintive ode is one of the most charming compositions in the whole Book of Psalms for its poetic power. If it were not inspired it would nevertheless occupy a high place in poesy, especially the former portion of it, which is tender and patriotic to the highest degree. In the later verses (7, 8, 9), we have utterances of burning indignation against the chief adversaries of Israel,—an indignation as righteous as it was fervent. Let those find fault with it who have never seen their temple burned, their city ruined, their wives ravished, and their children slain; they might not, perhaps, be quite so velvet-mouthed if they had suffered after this fashion. It is one thing to talk of the bitter feeling which moved captive Israelites in Babylon, and quite another thing to be captives ourselves under a savage and remorseless power, which knew not how to show mercy, but delighted in barbarities to the defenceless. The song is such as might fitly be sung in the Jews' wailing-place. It is a fruit of the Captivity in Babylon, and often has it furnished expression for sorrows which else had been unutterable. It is an opalesque Psalm within whose mild radiance there glows a fire which strikes the beholder with wonder.

EXPOSITION.

BY the rivers of Babylon, there we sat down, yea, we wept, when we remembered Zion.

2 We hanged our harps upon the willows in the midst thereof.

3 For there they that carried us away captive required of us a song; and they that wasted us *required of us* mirth, *saying*, Sing us *one* of the songs of Zion.

4 How shall we sing the LORD's song in a strange land?

5 If I forget thee, O Jerusalem, let my right hand forget *her cunning*.

6 If I do not remember thee, let my tongue cleave to the roof of my mouth; if I prefer not Jerusalem above my chief joy.

1. *"By the rivers of Babylon, there we sat down."* Water-courses were abundant in Babylon, wherein were not only natural streams but artificial canals: it was a place of broad rivers and streams. Glad to be away from the noisy streets, the captives sought the river side, where the flow of the waters seemed to be in sympathy with their tears. It was some slight comfort to be out of the crowd, and to have a little breathing room, and therefore they sat down, as if to rest a while and solace themselves in their sorrow. In little groups they sat down and made common lamentation, mingling their memories and their tears. The rivers were well enough, but, alas, they were the rivers of Babylon, and the ground whereon the sons of Israel sat was foreign soil, and therefore they wept. Those who came to interrupt their quiet were citizens of the destroying city, and their company was not desired. Everything reminded Israel of her banishment from the holy city, her servitude beneath the shadow of the temple of Bel, her helplessness under a cruel enemy; and therefore her sons and daughters sat down in sorrow.

"*Yea, we wept, when we remembered Zion.*" Nothing else could have subdued their brave spirits; but the remembrance of the temple of their God, the palace of their king, and the centre of their national life, quite broke them down. Destruction had swept down all their delights, and therefore they wept—the strong men wept, the sweet singers wept! They did not weep when they remembered the cruelties of Babylon; the memory of fierce oppression dried their tears and made their hearts burn with wrath: but when the beloved city of their solemnities came into their minds they could not refrain from floods of tears. Even thus do true believers mourn when they see the church despoiled, and find themselves unable to succour her: we could bear anything better than this. In these our times the

Babylon of error ravages the city of God, and the hearts of the faithful are grievously wounded as they see truth fallen in the streets, and unbelief rampant among the professed servants of the Lord. We bear our protests, but they appear to be in vain; the multitude are mad upon their idols. Be it ours to weep in secret for the hurt of our Zion: it is the least thing we can do; perhaps in its result it may prove to be the best thing we can do. Be it ours also to sit down and deeply consider what is to be done. Be it ours, in any case, to keep upon our mind and heart the memory of the church of God which is so dear to us. The frivolous may forget, but Zion is graven on our hearts, and her prosperity is our chief desire.

2. *"We hanged our harps upon the willows in the midst thereof.* The drooping branches appeared to weep as we did, and so we gave to them our instruments of music; the willows could as well make melody as we, for we had no mind for minstrelsy. In the midst of the willows, or in the midst of the rivers, or in the midst of Babylon, it matters little which, they hung their harps aloft—those harps which once in Zion's halls the soul of music shed. Better to hang them up than to dash them down: better to hang them on willows than profane them to the service of idols. Sad indeed is the child of sorrow when he grows weary of his harp, from which in better days he had been able to draw sweet solaces. Music hath charms to give unquiet spirits rest; but when the heart is sorely sad it only mocks the grief which flies to it. Men put away their instruments of mirth when a heavy cloud darkens their souls.

3. *"For there they that carried us away captive required of us a song."* It was ill to be a singer at all when it was demanded that this talent should go into bondage to an oppressor's will. Better be dumb than be forced to please an enemy with forced song. What cruelty to make a people sigh, and then require them to sing! Shall men be carried away from home and all that is dear to them, and yet chant merrily for the pleasure of their unfeeling captors? This is studied torture: the iron enters into the soul. It is indeed "woe to the conquered" when they are forced to sing to increase the triumph of their conquerors. Cruelty herein reached a refinement seldom thought of. We do not wonder that the captives sat them down to weep when thus insulted. *"And they that wasted us required of us mirth."* The captives must not only sing but smile, and add merriment to their music. Blind Samson in former days must be brought forth to make sport for Philistines, and now the Babylonians prove themselves to be loaves of the same leaven. Plundered, wounded, fettered, carried into captivity and poverty, yet must the people laugh as if it were all a play, and they must sport as if they felt no sorrow. This was wormwood and gall to the true lovers of God and his chosen land. *"Saying, Sing us one of the songs of Zion."* Nothing would serve their turn but a holy hymn, and a tune sacred to the worship of Jehovah. Nothing will content the Babylonian mockers but one of Israel's Psalms when in her happiest days she sang unto the Lord whose mercy endureth for ever: this would make rare fun for their persecutors, who would deride their worship and ridicule their faith in Jehovah. In this demand there was an insult to their God, as well as a mockery of themselves, and this made it the more intensely cruel. Nothing could have been more malicious, nothing more productive of grief. These wanton persecutors had followed the captives into their retirement, and had remarked upon their sorrowful appearance, and "there" and then they bade the mourners make mirth for them. Could they not let the sufferers alone? Were the exiles to have no rest? The daughter of Babylon seemed determined to fill up her cup of iniquity, by torturing the Lord's people. Those who had been the most active agents of Israel's undoing must needs follow up their ferocities by mockeries. "The tender mercies of the wicked are cruel." Worse than the Egyptians, they asked not labour which their victims could have rendered, but they demanded mirth which they could not give, and holy songs which they dared not profane to such a purpose.

4. *"How shall we sing the LORD's song in a strange land?"* How shall they sing at all? sing in a strange land? sing Jehovah's song among the uncircumcised? No, that must not be; it shall not be. With one voice they refuse, but the refusal is humbly worded by being put in the form of a question. If the men of Babylon were wicked enough to suggest the defiling of holy things for the gratification of curiosity, or for the creation of amusement, the men of Zion had not so hardened their hearts as to be willing to please them at such a fearful cost. There are many things which the ungodly could do, and think nothing of the doing thereof, which gracious men cannot venture upon. The question "How can I?" or "How shall

we ? " comes of a tender conscience and denotes an inability to sin which is greatly to be cultivated.

5. *"If I forget thee, O Jerusalem, let my right hand forget her cunning."* To sing Zion's songs for the pleasure of Zion's foes, would be to forget the Holy City. Each Jew declares for himself that he will not do this ; for the pronoun alters from " we " to " I." Individually the captives pledge themselves to fidelity to Jerusalem, and each one asserts that he had sooner forget the art which drew music from his harp-strings than use it for Babel's delectation. Better far that the right hand should forget its usual handicraft, and lose all its dexterity, than that it should fetch music for rebels out of the Lord's instruments, or accompany with sweet skill a holy Psalm desecrated into a common song for fools to laugh at. Not one of them will thus dishonour Jehovah to glorify Belus and gratify his votaries. Solemnly they imprecate vengeance upon themselves should they so false, so faithless prove.

6. *"If I do not remember thee, let my tongue cleave to the roof of my mouth."* Thus the singers imprecate eternal silence upon their mouths if they forget Jerusalem to gratify Babylon. The players on instruments and the sweet songsters are of one mind : the enemies of the Lord will get no mirthful tune or song from them. *"If I prefer not Jerusalem above my chief joy."* The sacred city must ever be first in their thoughts, the queen of their souls ; they had sooner be dumb than dishonour her sacred hymns, and give occasion to the oppressor to ridicule her worship. If such the attachment of a banished Jew to his native land, how much more should we love the church of God of which we are children and citizens. How jealous should we be of her honour, how zealous for her prosperity. Never let us find jests in the words of Scripture, or make amusement out of holy things, lest we be guilty of forgetting the Lord and his cause. It is to be feared that many tongues have lost all power to charm the congregations of the saints because they have forgotten the gospel, and God has forgotten *them*.

7 Remember, O LORD, the children of Edom in the day of Jerusalem ; who said, Rase *it*, rase *it*, *even* to the foundation thereof.

8 O daughter of Babylon, who art to be destroyed ; happy *shall he be*, that rewardeth thee as thou hast served us.

9 Happy *shall he be*, that taketh and dasheth thy little ones against the stones.

7. *"Remember, O LORD, the children of Edom in the day of Jerusalem."* The case is left in Jehovah's hands. He is a God of recompenses, and will deal out justice with impartiality. The Edomites ought to have been friendly with the Israelites, from kinship ; but there was a deep hatred and cruel spite displayed by them. The elder loved not to serve the younger, and so when Jacob's day of tribulation came, Esau was ready to take advantage of it. The captive Israelites being moved by grief to lodge their plaints with God, also added a prayer for his visitation of the nation which meanly sided with their enemies, and even urged the invaders to more than their usual cruelty. *"Who said, Rase it, rase it, even to the foundation thereof."* They wished to see the last of Jerusalem and the Jewish state ; they would have no stone left standing, they desired to see a clean sweep of temple, palace, wall, and habitation. It is horrible for neighbours to be enemies, worse for them to show their enmity in times of great affliction, worst of all for neighbours to egg others on to malicious deeds. Those are responsible for other men's sins who would use them as the tools of their own enmity. It is a shame for men to incite the wicked to deeds which they are not able to perform themselves. The Chaldeans were ferocious enough without being excited to greater fury ; but Edom's hate was insatiable. Those deserve to be remembered by vengeance who in evil times do not remember mercy ; how much more those who take advantage of calamities to wreak revenge upon sufferers. When Jerusalem's day of restoration comes Edom will be remembered and wiped out of existence.

8. *"O daughter of Babylon, who art to be destroyed."* Or the destroyer, let us accept the word either way, or both ways : the destroyer would be destroyed, and the Psalmist in vision saw her as already destroyed. It is usual to speak of a city as a virgin daughter. Babylon was in her prime and beauty, but she was already doomed for her crimes. *"Happy shall he be that rewardeth thee as thou hast served us."* The avenger would be fulfilling an honourable calling in overthrowing a power so brutal, so inhuman. Assyrian and Chaldean armies had been boastfully

brutal in their conquests ; it was meet that their conduct should be measured back into their own bosoms. No awards of punishment can be more unanswerably just than those which closely follow the *lex talionis,* even to the letter. Babylon must fall, as she caused Jerusalem to fall ; and her sack and slaughter must be such as she appointed for other cities. The patriot-poet sitting sorrowfully in his exile, finds a solace in the prospect of the overthrow of the empress city which holds him in bondage, and he accounts Cyrus right happy to be ordained to such a righteous work. The whole earth would bless the conqueror for ridding the nations of a tyrant ; future generations would call him blessed for enabling men to breathe again, and for once more making liberty possible upon the earth.

We may rest assured that every unrighteous power is doomed to destruction, and that from the throne of God justice will be measured out to all whose law is force, whose rule is selfishness, and whose policy is oppression. Happy is the man who shall help in the overthrow of the spiritual Babylon, which, despite its riches and power, is " to be destroyed." Happier still shall he be who shall see it sink like a millstone in the flood, never to rise again. What that spiritual Babylon is none need enquire. There is but one city upon earth which can answer to the name.

9. *"Happy shall he be, that taketh and dasheth thy little ones against the stones."* Fierce was the heart of the Jew who had seen his beloved city the scene of such terrific butchery. His heart pronounced like sentence upon Babylon. She should be scourged with her own whip of wire. The desire for righteous retribution is rather the spirit of the law than of the gospel ; and yet in moments of righteous wrath the old fire will burn ; and while justice survives in the human breast it will not lack for fuel among the various tyrannies which still survive. We shall be wise to view this passage as a prophecy. History informs us that it was literally fulfilled : the Babylonian people in their terror agreed to destroy their own offspring, and men thought themselves happy when they had put their own wives and children to the sword. Horrible as was the whole transaction, it is a thing to be glad of if we take a broad view of the world's welfare ; for Babylon, the gigantic robber, had for many a year slaughtered nations without mercy, and her fall was the rising of many people to a freer and safer state. The murder of innocent infants can never be sufficiently deplored, but it was an incident of ancient warfare which the Babylonians had not omitted in their massacres, and, therefore, they were not spared it themselves. The revenges of providence may be slow, but they are ever sure ; neither can they be received with regret by those who see God's righteous hand in them. It is a wretched thing that a nation should need an executioner ; but yet if men will commit murder tears are more fitly shed over their victims than over the assassins themselves. A feeling of universal love is admirable, but it must not be divorced from a keen sense of justice.

The captives in Babylon did not make music, but they poured forth their righteous maledictions, and these were far more in harmony with their surroundings than songs and laughter could have been. Those who mock the Lord's people will receive more than they desire, to their own confusion : they shall have little enough to make mirth for them, and more than enough to fill them with misery. The execrations of good men are terrible things, for they are not lightly uttered, and they are heard in heaven. " The curse causeless shall not come ; " but is there not a cause ? Shall despots crush virtue beneath their iron heel and never be punished ? Time will show.

EXPLANATORY NOTES AND QUAINT SAYINGS.

Whole Psalm.—Observe that this very Psalm in which the question is asked, " How can we sing ? " is itself a song, one of the Lord's songs, still. Nothing can be more sad, more desponding. It speaks of weeping in the remembrance of Zion ; it speaks of harps hung upon the willows by exiles who have no heart to use them ; and yet the very telling of these sorrows, of this incapacity for song, is a song still.

We chant it in our congregations now, hundreds and thousands of years after its composition, as one of the Church's melodies, as one of the Lord's songs. It gives us a striking example of the variety, of the versatility of worship, even in that department which might seem to be all joyous, all praise. The very refusal to sing may be itself a song. Any real utterance of good thoughts, whether they be thoughts of gladness or thoughts of sorrow, may be a true hymn, a true melody for the congregation, even though it may not breathe at every moment the very thought of all the worshippers. "How shall we sing?" is itself a permanent hymn, an inspired song, for all the churches.—*C. J. Vaughan.*

Whole Psalm.—This Psalm is composed of two parts. The first is, an heavy complaint of the church, unto verse 7. The other is an heavy imprecation and a prophetical denunciation against the enemies of the church, unto the end of the Psalm.—*Robert Rollock.*

Whole Psalm.—What a wonderful mixture is the Psalm of soft melancholy and fiery patriotism! The hand which wrote it must have known how to smite sharply with the sword, as well as how to tune the harp. The words are burning words of a heart breathing undying love to his country, undying hate to his foe. The poet is indeed

> "Dower'd with the hate of hate, the scorn of scorn,
>   The love of love."
>   *J. J. Stewart Perowne.*

Whole Psalm.—Several of the Psalms obviously refer to the time of the Babylonian captivity . . . . The captives' mournful sentiments of pensive melancholy and weary longing during its long and weary continuance constitute the burden of the hundred and thirty-seventh. It was probably written by some gifted captive Levite at the time. Some suppose it to have been composed by Jeremiah, the prophet of tears, and sent to his countrymen in the land of their exile, in order to awaken fond memories of the past and sustain a lively hope for the future; and certainly the ode is worthy even of his pen, for it is one of the sweetest, most plaintive, and exquisitely beautiful elegies in any language. It is full of heart-melting, tear-bringing pathos. The moaning of the captive, the wailing of the exile, and the sighing of the saints are heard in every line.—*W. Ormiston, in "The Study,"* 1874

Whole Psalm.—Here, I. The melancholy captives cannot enjoy themselves, verses 1, 2. II. They cannot humour their proud oppressors, verses 3, 4. III. They cannot forget Jerusalem, verses 5, 6. IV. They cannot forget Edom and Babylon, verses 7, 8, 9.—*Matthew Henry.*

Verse 1.—"*By the rivers of Babylon.*" The canals of Babylon itself, probably (comp. verse 2).—*William Kay.*

Verse 1.—"*By the rivers.*" Euphrates, Tigris, Chaboras, etc., and the canals which intersected the country. The exiles would naturally resort to the banks of the streams as shady, cool and retired spots, where they could indulge in their sorrowful remembrances. The prophets of the exile saw their visions by the river, Ezek. i. 1; Dan. viii. 2; x. 4.—"*Bibliotheca Sacra and Theological Review,*" 1848

Verse 1.—"*By the rivers.*" The bank of a river, like the seashore, is a favourite place of sojourn of those whom deep grief drives forth from the bustle of men into solitude. The boundary line of the river gives to solitude a safe back; the monotonous splashing of the waves keeps up the dull, melancholy alternation of thoughts and feelings; and at the same time the sight of the cool, fresh water exercises a soothing influence upon the consuming fever within the heart.—*Franz Delitzsch.*

Verse 1.—"*By the rivers.*" The peculiar reason for the children of Israel being represented as sitting at the streams is the *weeping.* An internal reference of the weeping to the streams, must therefore have been what gave rise to the representation of the sitting. Nor is this reference difficult to be discovered. All languages know of brooks, or streams of tears, compare in Scripture, Lam. ii. 18; "Let tears run down like a river day and night"; iii. 48; also Job xxviii. 11; also inversely the gushing of the floods is called *weeping* (Marg.). The children of Israel placed themselves beside the streams of Babel because they saw in them the image and symbol of their floods of tears.—*E. W. Hengstenberg.*

Verse 1.—"*We sat down.*" Among the poets, sitting on the ground is a mark of misery or captivity.

Multos illa dies incomtis mœsta capillis
Sederat.—*Propertius.*

With locks unkempt, mournful, for many days
She sat.

O utinam ante tuos sedeam captiva penates.—*Propertius*
O might I sit a captive at thy gate!

You have the same posture in an old coin that celebrates a victory of Lucius Verus over the Parthians.

We find Judea on several coins of Vespasian and Titus in the posture that denotes sorrow and captivity.—*From Joseph Addison's Dialogues on Medals.*

Verse 1.—*"Sat down"* implies that the burst of grief was a long one, and also that it was looked on by the captives as some relaxation and repose.—*Chrysostom.*

Verse 1.—*"We wept when we remembered Zion."* A godly man lays to heart the miseries of the church. I have read of certain trees, whose leaves if cut or touched, the other leaves contract and shrink up themselves, and for a space hang down their heads; such a spiritual sympathy is there among Christians; when other parts of God's church suffer, they feel themselves, as it were, touched in their own persons. Ambrose reports, that when Theodosius was sick unto death, he was more troubled about the church of God than about his own sickness. When Æneas would have saved Anchises' life, saith he, " Far be it from me that I should desire to live when Troy is buried in its ruins." There are in music two unisons; if you strike one, you shall perceive the other to stir, as if it were affected : when the Lord strikes others a godly heart is deeply affected, Isa. xv. 11 : " My bowels shall sound like an harp." Though it be well with a child of God in his own particular, and he dwells in an house of cedar, yet he grieves to see it go ill with the public. Queen Esther enjoyed the king's favour, and all the delights of the court, yet when a bloody warrant was signed for the death of the Jews she mourns and fasts, and ventures her own life to save theirs.—*Thomas Watson.*

Verse 1.—For *Sion* only they wept, unlike many who weep with the weeping and rejoice with the joy of Babylon, because their whole interests and affections are bound up in the things of this world.—*Augustine.*

Verse 1.—Let us weep, because in this life we are forced to sit by the waters of Babylon, and are yet strangers and as it were banished and barred from being satisfied with the pleasures of that river which gladdeth the city of God. Alas, if we did consider that our country were heaven, and did apprehend this place here below to be our prison, or place of banishment, the least absence from our country would draw tears from our eyes and sighs from our hearts, with David (Ps. cxx. 5) : " Woe is me that I sojourn in Mesech, and am constrained to dwell in the tents of Kedar."

Do you remember how the Jews behaved themselves in the time of their exile and captivity, while they sat by the rivers and waters of Babylon ? They wept, would not be comforted; hanged up their harps and instruments. What are the waters of Babylon but the pleasures and delights of the world, the waters of confusion, as the word signifies ? Now when the people of God sit by them, that is to say, do not carelessly, but deliberately, with a settled consideration, see them slide by and pass away, and compare them with Sion, that is to say, with the inconceivable rivers of pleasure, which are permanent in the heavenly Jerusalem ; how can they choose but weep, when they see themselves sitting by the one, and sojourning from the other ? And it is worthy your observing, that notwithstanding the Jews had many causes of tears, the Chaldeans had robbed them of their goods, honours, countries, liberty, parents, children, friends : the chief thing, for all this, that they mourn for is their absence from Sion,—*"We wept when we remembered thee, O Sion"* —for their absence from Jerusalem. What should we then do for our absence from another manner of Jerusalem ? Theirs was an earthly, old, robbed, spoiled, burned, sacked Jerusalem ; ours a heavenly, new one, into which no arrow can be shot, no noise of the drum heard, nor sound of the trumpet, nor calling unto battle : who would not then weep, to be absent from hence ? "—*Walter Balcanqual, in "A Sermon Preached at St. Maries Spittle," 1623.*

Verse 1.—*"We remembered Zion."* It necessarily implies they had *forgot*, else how could they now remember ? In their peace and plenty they had but little regard of Zion then.—*John Whincop, in a Sermon entitled, "Israel's Tears for Distressed Zion," 1645.*

Verse 1.—Nothing could present a more striking contrast to their native country than the region into which the Hebrews were transplanted. Instead of their irregular and picturesque mountain city, crowning its unequal heights, and looking down into its deep and precipitous ravines, through one of which a scanty stream wound along, they entered the vast, square, and level city of Babylon, occupying both sides of the broad Euphrates ; while all around spread immense plains, which were intersected by long, straight canals, bordered by rows of willows. How unlike their national temple—a small but highly finished and richly adorned fabric, standing in the midst of its courts on the brow of a lofty precipice—the colossal temple of the Chaldean Bel, rising from the plain, with its eight stupendous stories or towers, one above the other, to the perpendicular height of a furlong : The palace of the Babylonian kings was more than twice the size of their whole city ; it covered eight miles, with its hanging gardens built on arched terraces, each rising above the other, and rich in all the luxuriance of artificial cultivation. How different from the sunny cliffs of their own land, where the olive and the vine grew spontaneously, and the cool, shady, and secluded valleys, where they could always find shelter from the heat of the burning noon ! No wonder then that, in the pathetic words of their own hymn, *"by the waters of Babylon they sat down and wept, when they remembered thee, O Zion."* Of their general treatment as captives we know little. The Psalm above quoted seems to intimate that the Babylonians had taste enough to appreciate the poetical and musical talent of the exiles, and that they were summoned occasionally to amuse the banquets of their masters, though it was much against their will that they sang the songs of Zion in a strange land. In general it seems that the Jewish exiles were allowed to dwell together in considerable bodies, not sold as household or personal or prædial slaves, at least not those of the better order of whom the Captivity chiefly consisted. They were colonists rather than captives, and became by degrees possessed of considerable property. They had taken the advice of the prophet Jeremiah (who gave them no hopes of speedy return to their homes) : they had built houses, planted gardens, married and brought up children, submitted themselves as peaceful subjects to the local authorities : all which implies a certain freedom, a certain degree of prosperity and comfort. They had free enjoyment of their religion, such at least as adhered faithfully to their belief in Jehovah. We hear of no special and general religious persecution.—*Henry Hart Milman* (1791—1868), *in "The History of the Jews."*

Verse 1.—They sat in silence ; they remembered in silence ; they wept in silence. —*J. W. Burgon.*

Verses 1—6.—Israel was a typical people. 1. They were typical of God's church in all ages of the world. And, 2. They were typical of the soul of every individual believer.

This Psalm is composed for Israel in her captivity. Let us go over it, taking its typical meaning.

I. *When a believer is in captivity he has a sorrowful remembrance of Zion.* So it was with God's ancient people : " By the rivers of Babylon, there we sat down, yea, we wept, when we remembered Zion " (verse 1). In the last chapter of 2 Chron. (14—20,) we find the melancholy tale of Judah's captivity. Many of their friends had been slain by the sword—the house of God was burned—the walls of Jerusalem were broken down—and they themselves were captives in a foreign land. No wonder that they sat down and wept when they remembered Zion.

So it is often with the believer when led captive by sin—he sits down and weeps when he remembers Zion. Zion is the place where God makes himself known. When a poor awakened sinner is brought to know the Saviour, and to enter through the rent veil into the holiest of all, then he becomes one of the people of Zion : " A day in thy courts is better than a thousand." He dwells in Zion ; and the people that dwell therein are forgiven their iniquity. But when a believer falls into sin he falls into darkness—he is carried a captive away from Zion. No more does he find entrance within the veil ; no more is he glad when they say to him, " Let us go up to the house of the Lord." He sits down and weeps when he remembers Zion.

II. *The world derides the believer in his captivity.* So it was with ancient Israel. The Chaldeans were cruel conquerors. God says by his prophet,—" I was but a little displeased, and they helped forward the affliction." Not only did they carry them away from their temple, their country, and their homes, but they made a mock of their sorrows. When they saw them sit down to shed bitter tears by the rivers of Babylon, they demanded mirth and a song, saying, " Sing us one of the songs of Zion."

So is it with the world and the captive Christian. There are times when the world does not mock at the Christian. Often the Christian is filled with so strange a joy that the world wonders in silence. Often there is a meek and quiet spirit in the Christian, which disarms opposition. The soft answer turneth away wrath ; and his very enemies are forced to be at peace with him. But stop till the Christian's day of darkness comes—stop till sin and unbelief have brought him into captivity —stop till he is shut out from Zion, and carried afar off, and sits and weeps ; then will the cruel world help forward the affliction—then will they ask for mirth and song ; and when they see the bitter tear trickling down the cheek, they will ask with savage mockery, " Where is your Psalm-singing now ? " " Sing us one of the songs of Zion." Even Christ felt this bitterness when he hung upon the cross.

III. *The Christian cannot sing in captivity.* So it was with ancient Israel. They were peculiarly attached to the sweet songs of Zion. They reminded them of the times of David and Solomon—when the temple was built, and Israel was in its greatest glory. They reminded them, above all, of their God, of their temple, and the services of the sanctuary. Three times a year they came up from the country in companies, singing these sweet songs of Zion—lifting their eyes to the hills whence came their help. But now, when they were in captivity, they hanged their harps upon the willows ; and when their cruel spoilers demanded mirth and a song, they said : " How shall we sing the Lord's song in a strange land ? " So is it with the believer in darkness. He hangs his harp upon the willows, and cannot sing the song of the Lord. Every believer has got a harp. Every heart that has been made new is turned into a harp of praise. The mouth is filled with laughter—the tongue with divinest melody. Every true Christian loves praise—the holiest Christians love it most. But when the believer falls into sin and darkness, his harp is on the willows, and he cannot sing the Lord's song, for he is in a strange land.

1. *He loses all sense of pardon.* It is the sense of pardon that gives its sweetest tones to the song of the Christian. But when a believer is in captivity he loses this sweet sense of forgiveness, and therefore cannot sing.

2. *He loses all sense of the presence of God.* It is the sweet presence of God with the soul that makes the believer sing. But when that presence is away, the Lord's house is but a howling wilderness ; and you say, " How can we sing the Lord's song in a strange land ? "

3. *He loses sight of the heavenly Canaan.* The sight of the everlasting hills draws forth the heavenly melodies of the believing soul. But when a believer sins, and is carried away captive, he loses this hope of glory. He sits and weeps—he hangs his harp upon the willows, and cannot sing the Lord's song in a strange land.

4. *The believer in darkness still remembers Zion, and prefers it above his chief joy.* He often finds, when he has fallen into sin and captivity, that he has fallen among worldly delights and worldly friends. A thousand pleasures tempt him to take up his rest here ; but if he be a true child of Zion he will never settle down in a strange land. He will look over all the pleasures of the world and the pleasures of sin, and say, " A day in thy courts is better than a thousand "—" If I forget thee, O Jerusalem, let my right hand forget her cunning."—*Condensed from Robert Murray M'Chayne*, 1813—1843.

Verses 1, 2.—The Psalm is universally admired. Indeed, nothing can be more exquisitely beautiful. It is written in a strain of sensibility that must touch every soul that is capable of feeling. It is remarkable that Dr. Watts, in his excellent versification, has omitted it. He has indeed some verses upon it in his Lyrics ; and many others have written on this ode. We have seen more than ten productions of this kind ; the last, and perhaps the best, of which is Lord Byron's. But who is satisfied with any of these attempts ? Thus it begins : " By the rivers of Babylon, there we sat down, yea, we wept, when we remembered Zion." These rivers were probably some of the streams branching off from the Euphrates and Tigris. Here it is commonly supposed these captive Jews were placed by their task-masters, to preserve or repair the water-works. But is it improper to conjecture that the Psalmist refers to their being here ; not constantly, but occasionally ; not by compulsion, but choice ? Hither I imagine their retiring, to unbend their oppressed minds in solitude. " Come," said one of these pious Jews to another, " come, let us for a while go forth, from this vanity and vileness. Let us assemble together by ourselves under the refreshing shade of the willows by the watercourses. And let us take our harps with us, and solace ourselves with some of the songs of Zion." But as soon as they arrive, and begin to touch the chords, the notes—such is the power of association—awaken the memory of their former privileges and pleasures. And, overwhelmed with grief, they sit down on the grass ; and weep when they remember Zion ; their dejected looks, averted from each other, seeming to say, " If I forget thee, O Jerusalem, let my right hand forget her cunning. If I do not remember thee, let my tongue cleave to the roof of my mouth ; if I prefer not Jerusalem above my chief joy." But what do they with their harps ? The voice of mirth is heard no more, and all the daughters of music are brought low. Melody is not in season to a distressed spirit. " Is any afflicted ? Let him pray. Is any merry ? Let him sing Psalms." " As he that taketh away a garment in cold weather, and as vinegar upon nitre, so is he that singeth songs to a heavy heart." They did not, however, break them to pieces, or throw them into the stream—but *hanged* them up only. They hoped that what they could not use at present they might be able to resume at some happier period. To be cast down is not to be destroyed. Distress is not despondency.

> " Beware of desperate steps : the darkest day,
> Live till to-morrow, will have passed away."

"*We hanged our harps upon the willows in the midst thereof.*" Let us pass from the Jew to the Christian ; and let us survey the Christian in his SPIRITUAL SORROWS. He who would preach well, says Luther, must distinguish well. It is peculiarly necessary to discriminate, when we enter upon the present subject. For all the sorrows of the Christian are not of the same kind or descent. Let us consider four sources of his moral sadness. I. The first will be *physical*. II. The second will be *criminal*. III. The third will be *intellectual*. IV. The fourth will be *pious.—William Jay, in "The Christian Contemplated.*"

Verse 2.—"*Our harps.*" Many singers were carried captives : Ezra ii. 41. These would of course carry their instruments with them, and be insulted, as here. Their songs were sacred, and unfit to be sung before idolaters.—*From "Anonymous Notes" in James Merrick's Annotations*, 1768.

Verse 2.—"*Willows.*" All the flat, whereon Babylon stood, being by reason of so many rivers and canals running through it made in many places marshy, especially near the said rivers and canals, this caused it to abound much in *willows*, and therefore it is called in Scripture the " Valley of Willows " ; for so the words in Isaiah xv. 7, which we translate " the brook of the willows," ought to be rendered. —*Humphrey Prideaux (1648—1724), in "The Old and New Testament Connected,*" etc.

Verse 2.—"*Willows.*" The *Weeping Willow* of Babylon will grow to be a large tree ; its branches being long, slender, and pendulous, makes it proper to be planted upon the banks of rivers, ponds, and over springs ; the leaves, also, are long and narrow ; and when any mist or dew falls, a drop of water is seen hanging at their extremities, which, together with their hanging branches, cause a most lugubrious appearance. Lovers' garlands are said to have been made of a species of this willow, the branches of which are very slender and pliable ; and the plant itself has always been sought after for ornamental plantations, either to mix with others of the like growth in the largest quarters, or to be planted out singly over springs, or in large opens, for the peculiar variety occasioned by its mournful look.—*John Evelyn (1620— 1706), in "Silva ; or, A Discourse of Forest-Trees.*"

Verse 2.—"*Willows.*" It is a curious fact, that during the Commonwealth of England, when Cromwell, like a wise politician, allowed them to settle in London and to have synagogues, the Jews came hither in sufficient numbers to celebrate the feast of Tabernacles in booths, among the *Willows* on the borders of the Thames. The disturbance of their comfort from the innumerable spectators, chiefly London apprentices, called for some protection from the local magistrates. Not that any insult was offered to their persons, but a natural curiosity, excited by so new and extraordinary a spectacle, induced many to press too closely round their camp, and perhaps intrude upon their privacy.—*Maria Callcott (1788–1842), in "A Scripture Herbal,*" 1842.

Verse 2.—"*Willows.*" There is a pretty story told about the way in which the

Weeping Willow was introduced into England.* Many years ago, the well-known poet, Alexander Pope, who resided at Twickenham, received a basket of figs as a present from Turkey. The basket was made of the supple branches of the Weeping Willow, the very same species under which the captive Jews sat when they wept by the waters of Babylon. *"We hanged our harps upon the willows."* The poet valued highly the small slender twigs as associated with so much that was interesting, and he untwisted the basket, and planted one of the branches on the ground. It had some tiny buds upon it, and he hoped he might be able to rear it, as none of this species of willow was known in England. Happily the willow is very quick to take root and grow. The little branch soon became a tree, and drooped gracefully over the river, in the same manner that its race had done over the waters of Babylon. From that one branch all the Weeping Willows in England are descended.—*Mary and Elizabeth Kirby, in "Chapters on Trees,"* 1873.

Verse 2.—*"In the midst thereof."* This is most naturally understood of the *city* of Babylon ; which was nearly as large as Middlesex, and had parks and gardens inside it.—*William Kay.*

Verse 3.—*"They that carried us away captive required of us a song" ;* or rather, as it should be rendered, *"the words* of a song." They see no inconsistency in a religion which freely mixes with the world. In their ignorance they only require *"the words* of a song"; its heavenly strain they have never caught. "They that *wasted us* required of us mirth." Remember, it is this worldly element which wasteth, or lays on heaps, whether so far as our own hearts or the church of God is concerned. But, true to his spiritual instincts, the child of God replies, "How shall we sing *Jehovah's* song in the land of a *stranger ?"* and then, so far from being utterly cast down or overcome, rises with fresh outburst of resolution and intenseness of new vigour, to utter the vows of verses 5 and 6. For, after having passed through such a spiritual conflict, we come forth, not wearied, but refreshed ; not weaker, but stronger. It is one of the seeming contradictions of the gospel, that the cure of weariness, and the relief of heavy-ladenness, lies in this—*to take the cross upon ourselves.* After the night-long conflict of Israel, " as he passed over Peniel, *the sun rose upon him,"* and that though " he halted upon his thigh."—*Alfred Edersheim.*

Verse 3.—*"Sing us one of the songs of Zion."* It is variously set down as simple curiosity to hear something of the famous melodies of the Hebrew people ; as well-meaning counsel to the exiles to reconcile themsleves to their inevitable situation, and to resume their former habits in social harmony with the inhabitants of the land ; or, most generally as a fresh aggravation of their misery, in requiring them to make sport for their new masters.—*Genebrardus, Chrysostom, and Cocceius, in Neale and Littledale.*

Verse 3.—*"Sing us one of the songs of Zion."* No music will serve the epicures in the prophet but temple music : Amos. vi. 5, " They invent to themselves instruments of music like David." As choice and excellent as David was in the service of the temple, so would they be in their private feasts. Belshazzar's draughts are not half so sweet in other vessels as in the utensils of the temple : Dan. v. 2, " He commanded to bring forth the golden and silver vessels that were taken out of the house of God." So the Babylonian humour is pleased with nothing so much as with " *one of the songs of Zion;"* not an ordinary song, but " Sing us *one of your songs of Zion."* No jest relisheth with a profane spirit so well as when Scripture is abused, and made to lackey to their sportive jollity. Vain man thinketh he can never put honour enough upon his pleasures, and scorn enough upon God and holy things.—*Thomas Manton.*

Verse 3.—*"Sing us one of the songs of Zion."* The insulting nature of the demand will become the more conspicuous, if we consider, that the usual subjects of these songs were the omnipotence of Jehovah, and his love towards his chosen people.—*William Keatinge Clay,* 1839.

Verse 3.—The Babylonians asked them in derision for one of the songs of Zion. They loaded with ridicule their pure and venerable religion, and aggravated the sufferings of the weary and oppressed exiles by their mirth and their indecency. We are sorry to say that the resemblance still holds betwixt the Jews in a state of captivity and the Christians in the state of their pilgrimage. We have also

---

* The two preceding extracts would seem to prove that this story is not true ; at least Evelyn's willow is evidently the weeping willow, and would seem to have long been known.

to sustain the mockery of the profane and the unthinking. Ridicule and disdain are often the fate of sincere piety in this world. Fashion and frivolity and false philosophy have made a formidable combination against us ; and the same truth, the same honesty, the same integrity of principle, which in any other cause would be esteemed as manly and respectable, is despised and laughed at when attached to the cause of the gospel and its sublime interests.—*Thomas Chalmers.*

Verses 3, 4.—St. John Chrysostom observes the improvement such tribulation effected in the Jews, who previously derided, nay, even put to death, some of the prophets ; but now that they were captives in a foreign land, they would not attempt to expose their sacred hymns to the ridicule of the Gentiles.—*Robert Bellarmine.*

Verse 4.—"*How shall we sing the* LORD'S *song in a strange land?*" Now, is it not true that, in many senses, we, like the Jewish exiles, have to sing the Lord's song in a strange land ? If not a land strange to *us*, then, all the more strange to *it*—a land foreign, so to say, and alien to the Lord's song. The very life which we live here in the body is a life of sight and sense. Naturally we walk by sight ; and to sing the Lord's song is possible only to faith. Faith is the soul's sight : faith is seeing the Invisible : this comes not of nature, and without this we cannot sing the Lord's song, because we are in a land strange to it.

Again, the feelings of the present life are often adverse to praise. The exiles in Babylon could not sing because they were in heaviness. God's hand was heavy upon them. He had a controversy with them for their sins. Now the feelings of many of us are in like manner adverse to the Lord's song. Some of us are in great sorrow. We have lost a friend ; we are in anxiety about one who is all to us ; we know not which way to turn for to-morrow's bread or for this day's comfort. How can we sing the Lord's song ?

And there is another kind of sorrow, still more fatal, if it be possible, to the lively exercise of adoration. And that is, a weight and burden of unforgiven sin. Songs may be heard from the prison-cell of Philippi ; songs may be heard from the calm death-bed, or by the open grave ; but songs cannot be drawn forth from the soul on which the load of God's displeasure, real or imagined, is lying, or which is still powerless to apprehend the grace and the life for sinners which is in Christ Jesus. That, we imagine, was *the* difficulty which pressed upon the exile Israelite ; that certainly is an impediment now, in many, to the outburst of Christian praise. And again, there is a land yet more strange and foreign to the Lord's song even than the land of unforgiven guilt—and that is the land of unforsaken sin.—*Condensed from C. J. Vaughan.*

Verse 4.—"*The Lord's song—in a strange land.*" It was the contrast, it was the incongruity which perplexed them. The captives in Babylon—that huge, unwieldy city, with its temple of the Chaldean Bel towering aloft on its eight stupendous stories to the height of a furlong into the sky—the Israelite exiles, bidden there to an idolatrous feast, that they might make sport for the company by singing to them one of the far-famed Hebrew melodies, for the gratification of curiosity or the amusement of the ear—how could it be done ? *The Lord's song*— one of those inspired compositions of Moses or David, in which the saintly soul of the king or the prophet poured itself forth in lowliest, loftiest adoration, before the one Divine Creator, Redeemer, and Sanctifier—how *could* it be sung, they ask, in a scene so incongruous ? The words would languish upon the tongue, the notes would refuse to sound upon the disused harp. Such Psalmody requires its accompaniment and its adaptation—if not actually in the Temple-courts of Zion, yet at least in the balmy gales of Palestine and the believing atmosphere of Israel.— *C. J. Vaughan, in "The Family Prayer and Sermon Book."*

Verse 4.—"*The Lord's song.*" These songs of old, to distinguish them from heathenish songs, were called God's songs, the Lord's songs ; because taught by him, learned of him, and commanded by him to be sung to his praise.—*John Bunyan.*

Verse 4.—Many were the sad thoughts which the remembrance of Zion would call up : the privileges they had there enjoyed ; the solemn feasts and happy meetings of their tribes to worship there before the Lord ; the Temple—" the beautiful house where their fathers had worshipped "—now laid waste.

But the one embittering thought that made them indeed heavy at heart, silenced their voices, and unstrung their harps, was the cause of this calamity—their sin. Paul and Silas could sing in a dungeon, but it was not their sin brought them there :

and so the saints suffering for the name of Christ could say, " we are exceeding joyful in all our tribulation." There is no real sorrow in any circumstances into which God brings us, or where he leads and goes with us ; but where sin is, and suffering is felt to be—not persecution, but—judgment, there is and can be no joy ; the soul refuses to be comforted. Israel cannot sing beside the waters of Babylon.—*William De Burgh.*

Verse 4.—There is a distinction between us and God's ancient people ; for at that time the worship of God was confined to one place ; but now he has his temple wherever two or three are met together in Christ's name, if they separate themselves from all idolatrous profession, and maintain purity of Divine worship.—*John Calvin.*

Verse 4.—It is one of the pathetic touches about the English captivity of King John II. of France, that once sitting as a guest to see a great tournament held in his honour, he looked on sorrowfully, and being urged by some of those about him to be cheerful and enjoy the splendid pageant, he answered with a mournful smile, *"How shall we sing the LORD'S song in a strange land ? "—Polydore Virgil,* —1555.

Verse 5.—*"If I forget thee, O Jerusalem."* Calvary, Mount of Olives, Siloam, how fragrant are ye with the Name that is above every name ! *"If I forget thee, O Jerusalem ! "* Can I forget where he walked so often, where he spake such gracious words, where he died ? Can I forget that his feet shall stand on that " Mount of Olives, which is before Jerusalem, on the east ? " Can I forget that there stood the Upper Room, and there fell the showers of Pentecost ?—*Andrew A. Bonar.*

Verse 5.—*"Let my right hand forget her cunning."* There is a striking and appropriate point in this, which has been overlooked. It is, that, as it is customary for people in the East to swear by their professions, so one who has no profession —who is poor and destitute, and has nothing of recognized value in the world— swears by his right hand, which is his sole stake in society, and by the *"cunning "* of which he earns his daily bread. Hence the common Arabic proverb (given by Burckhardt) reflecting on the change of demeanour produced by improved circumstances :—" He was wont to swear ' by the cutting off of his right hand ! ' He now swears ' by the giving of money to the poor.' " The words, " *her cunning,*" are supplied by the translators, in whose time *cunning* (from the Saxon *cannan,* Dutch *konnen,* " to know ") meant " skill ; " and a cunning man was what we should now call a skilful man. In the present case the skill indicated is doubtless that of playing on the harp, in which particular sense it occurs so late as Prior :—

> " When Pedro does the lute command,
> She guides the cunning artist's hand."

Modern translators substitute " skill ; " but perhaps a term still more general would be better—such as, " May my right hand lose its power."—*John Kitto, in "The Pictorial Bible."*

Verse 5.—*"Let my right hand forget."* Something must be supplied from the context . . . . the playing on the stringed instrument, verse 2, whether the right hand should be applied to the purpose or not, was the point in question. Then, the punishment also perfectly accords with the misdeed, as in Job xxxi. 22 : If I, misapplying my right hand to the playing of joyful strains on my instrument, forget thee, Jerusalem, let my right hand, as a punishment, forget the noble art ; and then also verse 6 fits admirably to what goes before : May my misemployed hand lose its capacity to play, and my tongue, misemployed in singing cheerful songs, its capacity to sing.—*E. W. Hengstenberg.*

Verse 6.—*"If I do not remember thee."* Either our beds are soft, or our hearts hard, that can rest when the church is at unrest, that feel not our brethren's hard cords through our soft beds.—*John Trapp.*

Verse 6.—*"If I prefer not Jerusalem above my chief joy."* Literally, *"if I advance not Jerusalem above the head of my joy."* If I set not Jerusalem as a diadem on the head of my rejoicing, and crown all my happiness with it.—*Christopher Wordsworth.*

Verse 7.—*"Remember, O LORD, the children of Edom,"* etc. The Jews were their brethren : Obad. 10 ; Amos i. 11. They were their neighbours, Idumea and Judea bordered upon one another : Mark iii. 8. They were confederates with the Jews (Jer. xxvii. 3 : an Edomitish ambassador was at Jerusalem), who, together with the ambassadors of the other kings there mentioned, were strengthening themselves with Zedekiah against Nebuchadnezzar ; see Obad. 7. For them, therefore, to revenge themselves for former wrongs done them upon the Jews, and that in the day of their calamity, this made their sin exceeding sinful.—*William Greenhill*, 1591—1677.

Verse 7.—*"Remember, O Lord, the children of Edom,"* etc. Of all kinds of evil speaking against our brother, this sin of Edom, to sharpen an enemy against our brother in the day of his sorrow and distress, this opening of the mouth wide against him, to insult over him in his calamity, is most barbarous and unchristian. . . . Observe how the cruelty of the Edomites is aggravated by the time ; the wofullest time that ever Jerusalem had, called therefore *"the day of Jerusalem."* When all things conspired to make their sorrow full, then, in the anguish and fit of their mortal disease, then did Edom arm his eye, his tongue, his heart, his hand, and join all those with the enemy against his brother. Learn, that God taketh notice not only *what* we do against another, but *when ;* for he will set these things in order before us ; for the God of mercy cannot abide cruelty.—*Edward Marbury*, 1649.

Verse 7.—*"Remember, O Lord, the children of Edom."* Edom shall be remembered for the mischievous counsel he gave ; and the daughter of Babylon shall be for ever razed out of memory for razing Jerusalem to the ground. And let all the secret and open enemies of God's church take heed how they employ their tongues and hands against God's secret ones : they that presume to do either may here read their fatal doom written in the *dust* of Edom, and in the *ashes* of Babylon.—*Daniel Featley* (1582—1645), *in "Clavis Mystica."*

Verse 7.—In Herod, the Idumean, Edom's hatred found its concentrated expression. *His* attempt was to destroy him whom God had laid in Zion as the " sure foundation."—*William Kay.*

Verse 7.—It may be observed that the Jews afterward acted the same part toward the Christian church which the Edomites had acted toward them, encouraging and stirring up the Gentiles to persecute and destroy it from off the face of the earth. And God " remembered " them for the Christians' sakes, as they prayed him to " remember Edom " for their sakes. Learn we hence, what a crime it is, for Christians to assist the common enemy, or call in the common enemy to assist them, against their brethren.—*George Horne.*

Verse 7.—We are not to regard the imprecations of this Psalm in any other light than as prophetical. They are grounded on the many prophecies which had already gone forth on the subject of the destruction of Babylon, if, as we may admit, the Psalm before us was written after the desolation of Jerusalem. But these prophecies have not yet been fulfilled in every particular, and remain to be accomplished in mystic Babylon, when the dominion of Antichrist shall be for ever swept away, and the true church introduced into the glorious liberty of the sons of God, at the appearing of their Lord and Saviour Jesus Christ in his own kingdom.—*William Wilson.*

Veres 7.—Edom's hatred was the hatred with which the carnal mind in its natural enmity against God always regards whatever is the elect object of his favour. Jerusalem was the city of *God.* " Rase it, rase it even to the ground," is the mischievous desire of every unregenerate mind against every building that rests on the elect Stone of Divine foundation. For God's election never pleases man until, through grace, his own heart has become an adoring receiver of that mercy which while in his natural state he angrily resented and refused to own in its effects on other men. From Cain to Antichrist this solemn truth holds always good.—*Arthur Pridham.*

Verse 7—9.—I do not know if the same feeling has occurred to others, but I have often wished the latter verses of this Psalm had been disjoined from this sweet and touching beginning. It sounds as if one of the strings on their well-tuned harps was out of melody, as if it struck a jarring note of discord. And yet I know the feeling is wrong, for it is no more than what the Lord himself had foretold and declared should be the final desolation of proud Babylon itself : yet one longs more intensely for the period when the nations of the earth shall learn war no more ; and every harp and every voice, even those of the martyred ones beneath God's altar loudest and sweetest of all, shall sing the Lord's songs, the song of Moses, and the Lamb, in that pleasant land, where no sighing and no tears are seen.—*Barton Bouchier.*

Verse 8.—*"O daughter of Babylon, who art to be destroyed."* In the beginning of the fifth year of Darius happened the revolt of the Babylonians which cost him the trouble of a tedious siege again to reduce them . . . . he besieged the city with all his forces . . . . As soon as the Babylonians saw themselves begirt by such an army as they could not cope with in the field, they turned their thoughts wholly to the supporting of themselves in the siege ; in order whereto they took a resolution, the most desperate and barbarous that ever any nation practised. For to make their provisions last the longer, they agreed to cut off all unnecessary mouths among them, and therefore drawing together all the women and children, they strangled them all, whether wives, sisters, daughters, or young children useless for the wars, excepting only that every man was allowed to save one of his wives, which he best loved, and a maid-servant to do the work of the house.—*Humphrey Prideaux.*

Verse 8.—*"Who art to be destroyed."* הַשְּׁדוּדָה has been explained in a variety of ways. Seventy : ἡ ταλαίπωρος ; Vulg. *misera :* others, *destroyer, powerful, violent,* or *fierce.* Perhaps it best suits the context to regard it as expressing what is already accomplished : it is so certain, in the view of the Psalmist, that the ruin will come, that he uses the past participle, as if the work were now completed. " O daughter of Babylon, the destroyed ! "—*"Bibliotheca Sacra and Theological Review."*

Verse 8.—He that sows evil shall reap evil ; he that soweth the evil of sin, shall reap the evil of punishment. So Eliphaz told Job that he had seen (Job iv. 8), " they that plough iniquity, and sow wickedness, reap the same." And that either in kind or quality, proportion or quantity. In kind, the very same that he did to others shall be done to him ; or in proportion, a measure answerable to it. So he shall reap what he hath sown, in quality or in quantity ; either in portion the same, or in proportion the like. The prophet cursing Edom and Babel saith thus, " O daughter of Zion, happy shall he be that rewardeth thee as thou hast served us." The original is, " that recompenseth to thee thy deed which thou didst to us." . . . Thus is wickedness recompensed *suo genere,* in its own kind. So often the transgressor is against the transgressor, the thief robs the thief, *proditoris proditor ;* as in Rome many unchristened emperors, and many christened popes, by blood and treason got the sovereignty, and by blood and treason lost it. Evil men drink of their own brewing, are scourged with their own rod, drowned in the pit which they digged for others, as Haman was hanged on his own gallows, Perillus tormented in his own engine !—*Thomas Adams.*

Verses 8, 9.—The subject of these two verses is the same with that of many chapters in Isaiah and Jeremiah ; namely, the vengeance of heaven executed upon Babylon by Cyrus, raised up to be king of the Medes and Persians, united under him for that purpose. The meaning of the words, *"Happy shall he be,"* is, He shall go on and prosper, for the Lord of hosts shall go with him, and fight his battles against the enemy and oppressor of his people, empowering him to recompense upon the Chaldeans the works of their hands, and to reward them as they served Israel.—*George Horne.*

Verses 8, 9.—It needs no record to tell us that, in the siege and carrying away of Jerusalem, great atrocities were committed by the conquerors. We may be quite sure that

" Many a childing mother then
And new-born baby died."

for the wars of the old world were always attended by such barbarous cruelties. The apostrophe of verses 8, 9, consequently merely proclaims the certainty of a just retribution—of the same retribution that the prophets had foretold (Isa. xiii. 16 ; xlvii. ; Jer. l. ; compare, " who art to be destroyed, verse 8), and the happiness of those who should be its ministers ; who should mete out to her what she had measured to the conquered Jew. It was the decree of Heaven that their " children " should " be dashed to pieces before their eyes." The Psalmist simply recognizes the decree as just and salutary ; he pronounces the terrible vengeance to have been deserved. To charge him with vindictiveness, therefore, is to impugn the justice and mercy of the Most High. And there is nothing to sustain the charge, for his words are simply a prediction, like that of the prophet, " As thou hast done, it shall be done unto thee : thy reward shall return upon thine own head :" Obad. 15. —*Joseph Hammond, in "The Expositor,"* 1876.

Verse 9.—*"Happy shall he be that taketh,"* etc. That is, so oppressive hast thou been to all under thy domination, as to become universally hated and detested ; so that those who may have the last hand in thy destruction, and the total extermination of thy inhabitants, shall be reputed *"happy"*—shall be *celebrated* and *extolled* as those who have rid the world of a curse so grievous. These prophetic declarations contain no excitement to any person or persons to commit acts of cruelty and barbarity ; but are simply *declarative* of what would take place in the order of the retributive providence and justice of God, and the general opinion that should in consequence be expressed on the subject ; therefore *praying for the destruction of our enemies* is totally out of the question.—*Adam Clarke.*

Verse 9.—*"Happy shall he be,"* etc. With all possible might and speed oppose the very first risings and movings of the heart to sin ; for these are the buds that produce the bitter fruit ; and if sin be not nipped in the very bud, it is not imaginable how quickly it will shoot forth. . . . Now these sins, though they may seem small in themselves, yet are exceedingly pernicious in their effects. These little foxes destroy the grapes as much or more than the greater, and therefore are to be diligently sought out, hunted, and killed by us, if we would keep our hearts fruitful. We should deal with these first streamings out of sin as the Psalmist would have the people of God deal with the brats of Babylon : *"Happy shall he be, that taketh and dasheth thy little ones against the stones."* And without doubt most happy and successful will that man prove in his spiritual welfare, who puts on no bowels of pity even to his infant corruptions, but slays the small as well as the great ; and so not only conquers his enemies by opposing their present force, but also by extinguishing their future race. The smallest children, if they live, will be grown men ; and the first motions of sin, if they are let alone, will spread into great, open, and audacious presumptions.—*Robert South*, 1633—1716.

Verse 9.—*"Against the stones."* That סלע signifies *a rock*, is undubitable, from the concurrent testimony of all the best Hebrew lexicographers Hence it follows, because there is no rock, nor mountain, nor hill, either in the city or in the province of ancient Babylonia, that the locality, against which the malediction of this Psalm is hurled, cannot be the metropolis of the ancient Assyrian empire, but must be apocalyptic Babylon, or Papal Rome, built upon seven hills, one of which is the celebrated Tarpeian Rock. But the eighth verse emphatically declares that the retributive justice of God will visit upon apocalyptic Babylon, the same infliction which Assyrian Babylon, and also Pagan Rome, inflicted upon Jerusalem. As therefore Nebuchadnezzar as well as Titus " burnt the house of the Lord, and the king's house, and all the houses of Jerusalem, and every great man's house burnt he with fire " (2 Kings xxv. 9) so " the ten horns shall hate the whore, and shall make her desolate and naked, and shall eat her flesh, and burn her with fire ; and she shall be utterly burned with fire " (Rev. xvii. 16 ; xviii. 8). When the Canaanites had filled up the measure of their iniquity, Israel received a divine commission to exterminate the guilty nation. When Papal Rome shall have filled up the measure of her iniquity, then " a mighty angel will take up a stone, like a great millstone, and will cast it into the sea, saying, Thus with violence shall that great city Babylon be thrown down " : " For her sins have reached unto heaven, and God hath remembered her iniquities. Reward her even as she rewarded you, and double unto her double according to her works : in the cup which she hath filled fill to her double " (Rev. xviii. 5, 6). Then shall issue the divine proclamation : " Rejoice over her, thou heaven, and ye holy apostles and prophets ; for God hath avenged you on her" (Rev. xviii. 20).—*John Noble Coleman, in "The Book of Psalms, with Notes,"* 1863.

Verse 9.—*"He that taketh and dasheth thy little ones against the stones."*

> My heroes slain, my bridal bed o'erturned,
> My daughters ravish'd, and my city burn'd,
> My bleeding infants dash'd against the floor ;
> These have I yet to see, perhaps yet more.

Homer's Iliad, Pope's Translation, Book xxii. 89—91.

HINTS TO PREACHERS.

Verse 1.—I. A duty once the source of joy: " remember Zion." II. Circumstances which make the remembrances sorrowful. III. Peculiar persons who feel this joy or sorrow : " we."

Verse 1.—I. Zion forsaken in prosperity. Its services neglected ; its priests demoralized ; the worship of Baal and of Ashtaroth preferred to the worship of the true God. II. Zion remembered in adversity. In Babylon more than in Jerusalem ; on the banks of the Euphrates more than on the banks of Jordan ; with tears when they might have remembered it with joy. " I spake unto thee in thy prosperity, and thou saidst, I will not hear." " Lord, in trouble they have visited thee. They poured out a prayer when thy chastening was upon them."— *G. R.*

Verse 2.—I. Harps—or capacities for praise. II. Harps on willows, or song suspended. III. Harps retuned, or joys to come.

Verse 2.—I. A confession of joy being turned into sorrow : " we hanged," etc. The moaning of their harps upon weeping willows better harmonized with their feelings than any tunes which they had been accustomed to play. II. A hope of sorrow being turned into joy. They took their harps with them into captivity, and hung them up for future use.—*G. R.*

Verse 2.—"*We hanged our harps,*" etc. I. In remembrance of lost joys. Their harps were associated with a glorious past. They could not afford to forget that past. They kept up the good old custom. There are always means of remembrance at hand. II. In manifestation of present sorrow. They could not play on account of, 1. Their sinfulness. 2. Their circumstances. 3. Their home. III. In anticipation of future blessing. They did not dash their harps to pieces. Term of exile limited. Return expressly foretold. We shall want our harps in the good times coming. Sinners play their harps now, but must soon lay them aside for ever.— *W. J.*

Verse 3 (last clause).—Taken away from the text this is a very pleasant and praiseworthy request. Why do we wish for such a song ? 1. It is sure to be pure. 2. It will certainly be elevating. 3. It will probably be gladsome. 4. It will comfort and enliven us. 5. It will help to express our gratitude.

Verses 3, 4.—I. The cruel demand. 1. A song when we are captives. 2. A song to please our adversaries. 3. A holy song for unholy purposes. II. The motive for it. Sometimes mere ridicule ; at others, mistaken kindness seeking by sharpness to arouse us from despondency ; often mere levity. III. The answer to it, " How can ? " etc.

Verses 3, 4.—I. When God calls for joy we ought not to sorrow. The songs of Zion should be sung in Zion. II. When God calls for sorrow we ought not to rejoice. " How shall we sing ? " etc. See Is. v. 12.—*G. R.*

Verses 3, 4.—I. The unreasonable request : " Sing us one of the songs of Zion." This was—1. A striking testimony to the joyful character of Jehovah's worship. Even the heathen had heard of " the songs of Zion." 2. A severe trial of the fidelity of captive Israel. It might have been to their present advantage to have complied with the request. 3. A cruel taunt of the sad and desponding condition of the captives. II. The indignant refusal. " How shall we sing the Lord's song in a strange land ? " There is no singing this song by true Israelites—1. When the heart is out of tune, as it must necessarily be when in " a strange land." 2. In uncongenial society—amongst unsympathetic strangers. 3. For unsanctified purposes—to make mirth for the heathen. Many so-called sacred concerts pain devout Christians as much as the demand to sing the Lord's song did the devout Israelites. The Lord's song must be sung only " to the Lord;"—*W. H. J. P.*

Verses 3, 4.—The burlesque of holy things. I. The servants of God are in an unsympathetic world. II. The demand to be amused and entertained. Temple songs to pass an idle hour ! Such the popular demand to-day. Men would have us burlesque religion to tickle them. III. The justly indignant reply of all true men, " How shall we ? " Christian workers have more serious if less popular business on hand.—*W. B. H.*

Verse 5.—The person who remembers ; the thing remembered ; the solemn imprecation.

Verse 5.—No harp but for Jesus.
   I. The harp consecrated. At conversion.

> "One sword, at least, thy rights shall guard,
> One faithful harp shall praise thee."

   II. The harp silent:

> "Thy songs were made for the brave and free,
> They shall never sound in slavery."

   III. The harp re-strung above:

> "And I heard the voice of harpers
> Harping with their harps."

W. B. H.

Verses 5, 6.—I. To rejoice with the world is to forget the church. II. To love the church we must prefer her above-everything. III. To serve the church we must be prepared to suffer anything.

Verse 7.—The hatred of the ungodly to true religion. I. Its cause. II. Its extent. "Rase it," etc. III. Its season for display: "in the day of Jerusalem" —trouble, etc. IV. Its reward: "Remember, O Lord."

PSALM CXXXVIII.

TITLE.—*A Psalm of David. This Psalm is wisely placed. Whoever edited and arranged these sacred poems, he had an eye to apposition and contrast; for if in Ps. cxxxvii. we see the need of silence before revilers, here we see the excellence of a brave confession. There is a time to be silent, lest we cast pearls before swine; and there is a time to speak openly, lest we be found guilty of cowardly non-confession. The Psalm is evidently of a Davidic character, exhibiting all the fidelity, courage, and decision of that King of Israel and Prince of Psalmists. Of course the critics have tried to rend the authorship from David on account of the mention of the temple, though it so happens that in one of the Psalms which is allowed to be David's the same word occurs. Many modern critics are to the word of God what blow-flies are to the food of men: they cannot do any good, and unless relentlessly driven away they do great harm.*

DIVISION.—*In full confidence David is prepared to own his God before the gods of the heathen, or before angels or rulers (1—3); he declares that he will instruct and convert kings and nations, till on every highway men shall sing the praises of the Lord (4 and 5). Having thus spoken, he utters his personal confidence in Jehovah, who will help his lowly servant, and preserve him from all the malice of wrathful foes.*

EXPOSITION.

I WILL praise thee with my whole heart: before the gods will I sing praise unto thee.

2 I will worship toward thy holy temple, and praise thy name for thy lovingkindness and for thy truth: for thou hast magnified thy word above all thy name.

3 In the day when I cried thou answeredst me, *and* strengthenedst me *with* strength in my soul.

1. *"I will praise thee with my whole heart."* His mind is so taken up with God that he does not mention his name: to him there is no other God, and Jehovah is so perfectly realized and so intimately known, that the Psalmist, in addressing him, no more thinks of mentioning his name than we should do if we were speaking to a father or a friend. He sees God with his mind's eye, and simply addresses him with the pronoun "thee." He is resolved to praise the Lord, and to do it with the whole force of his life, even with his whole heart. He would not submit to act as one under restraint, because of the opinions of others; but in the presence of the opponents of the living God he would be as hearty in worship as if all were friends and would cheerfully unite with him. If others do not praise the Lord, there is all the more reason why we should do so, and should do so with enthusiastic eagerness. We need a broken heart to mourn our own sins, but a whole heart to praise the Lord's perfections. If ever our heart is whole and wholly occupied with one thing, it should be when we are praising the Lord. *"Before the gods will I sing praise unto thee."* Why should these idols rob Jehovah of his praises? The Psalmist will not for a moment suspend his songs because there are images before him, and their foolish worshippers might not approve of his music. I believe David referred to the false gods of the neighbouring nations, and the deities of the surviving Canaanites. He was not pleased that such gods were set up; but he intended to express at once his contempt of *them*, and his own absorption in the worship of the living Jehovah by continuing most earnestly to sing wherever he might be. It would be paying these dead idols too much respect to cease singing because they were perched aloft. In these days when new religions are daily excogitated, and

new gods are set up, it is well to know how to act. Bitterness is forbidden, and controversy is apt to advertise the heresy ; the very best method is to go on personally worshipping the Lord with unvarying zeal, singing with heart and voice his royal praises. Do they deny the Divinity of our Lord ? Let us the more fervently adore him. Do they despise the atonement ? Let us the more constantly proclaim it. Had half the time spent in councils and controversies been given to praising the Lord, the church would have been far sounder and stronger than she is at this day. The Hallelujah Legion will win the day. Praising and singing are our armour against the idolatries of heresy, our comfort under the depression caused by insolent attacks upon the truth, and our weapons for defending the gospel. Faith when displayed in cheerful courage, has about it a sacred contagion : others learn to believe in the Most High when they see his servant

> " Calm 'mid the bewildering cry,
> Confident of victory."

2. *"I will worship toward thy holy temple,"* or the place of God's dwelling, where the ark abode. He would worship God in God's own way. The Lord had ordained a centre of unity, a place of sacrifice, a house of his indwelling ; and David accepted the way of worship enjoined by revelation. Even so, the true-hearted believer of these days must not fall into the will-worship of superstition, or the wild worship of scepticism, but reverently worship as the Lord himself prescribes. The idol gods had their temples ; but David averts his glance from them, and looks earnestly to the spot chosen of the Lord for his own sanctuary. We are not only to adore the true God, but to do so in his own appointed way : the Jew looked to the temple, we are to look to Jesus, the living temple of the Godhead. *"And praise thy name for thy lovingkindness and for thy truth."* Praise would be the main part of David's worship ; the name or character of God the great object of his song ; and the special point of his praise the grace and truth which shone so conspicuously in that name. The person of Jesus is the temple of the Godhead, and therein we behold the glory of the Father, " full of grace and truth." It is upon these two points that the name of Jehovah is at this time assailed—his grace and his truth. He is said to be too stern, too terrible, and therefore " modern thought " displaces the God of Abraham, Isaac, and Jacob, and sets up an effeminate deity of its own making. As for us, we firmly believe that God is love, and that in the summing up of all things it will be seen that hell itself is not inconsistent with the beneficence of Jehovah, but is, indeed, a necessary part of his moral government now that sin has intruded into the universe. True believers hear the thunders of his justice, and yet they do not doubt his lovingkindness. Especially do we delight in God's great love to his own elect, such as he showed to Israel as a race, and more especially to David and his seed when he entered into covenant with him. Concerning this there is abundant room for praise. But not only do men attack the lovingkindness of God, but the truth of God is at this time assailed on all sides ; some doubt the truth of the inspired record as to its histories, others challenge the doctrines, many sneer at the prophecies ; in fact, the infallible word of the Lord is at this time treated as if it were the writing of imposters, and only worthy to be carped at. The swine are trampling on the pearls at this time, and nothing restrains them ; nevertheless, the pearls are pearls still, and shall yet shine about our Monarch's brow. We sing the lovingkindness and truth of the God of the Old Testament,—" the God of the whole earth shall he be called." David before the false gods first sang, then worshipped, and then proclaimed the grace and truth of Jehovah ; let us do the same before the idols of the New Theology.

"For thou hast magnified thy word above all thy name." The word of promise made to David was in his eyes more glorious than all else that he had seen of the Most High. Revelation excels creation in the clearness, definiteness, and fulness of its teaching. The name of the Lord in nature is not so easily read as in the Scriptures, which are a revelation in human language, specially adapted to the human mind, treating of human need, and of a Saviour who appeared in human nature to redeem humanity. Heaven and earth shall pass away, but the divine word will not pass away, and in this respect especially it has a pre-eminence over every other form of manifestation. Moreover, the Lord lays all the rest of his name under tribute to his word : his wisdom, power, love, and all his other attributes combine to carry out his word. It is his word which creates, sustains, quickens, enlightens, and comforts. As a word of command it is supreme ; and in the person of the

incarnate Word it is set above all the works of God's hands. The sentence in the text is wonderfully full of meaning. We have collected a vast mass of literature upon it, but space will not allow us to put it all into our notes. Let us adore the Lord who has spoken to us by his word, and by his Son ; and in the presence of unbelievers let us both praise his holy name and extol his holy word.

3. *"In the day when I cried thou answeredst me."* No proof is so convincing as that of experience. No man doubts the power of prayer after he has received an answer of peace to his supplication. It is the distinguishing mark of the true and living God that he hears the pleadings of his people, and answers them ; the gods hear not and answer not, but Jehovah's memorial is—"the God that heareth prayer." There was some special day in which David cried more vehemently than usual ; he was weak, wounded, worried, and his heart was wearied ; then like a child he " cried,"—cried unto his Father. It was a bitter, earnest, eager prayer, as natural and as plaintive as the cry of a babe. The Lord answered it ; but what answer can there be to a cry ?—to a mere inarticulate wail of grief ? Our heavenly Father is able to interpret tears, and cries, and he replies to their inner sense in such a way as fully meets the case. The answer came in the same day as the cry ascended : so speedily does prayer rise to heaven, so quickly does mercy return to earth.' The statement of this sentence is one which all believers can make, and as they can substantiate it with many facts, they ought boldly to publish it, for it is greatly to God's glory. Well might the Psalmist say, " I will worship " when he felt bound to say "thou answeredst me." Well might he glory before the idols and their worshippers when he had answers to prayer to look back upon. This also is our defence against modern heresies : we cannot forsake the Lord, for he has heard our prayers.

"And strengthenedst me with strength in my soul." This was a true answer to his prayer. If the burden was not removed, yet strength was given wherewith to bear it, and this is an equally effective method of help. It may not be best for us that the trial should come to an end ; it may be far more to our advantage that by its pressure we should learn patience. Sweet are the uses of adversity, and our prudent Father in heaven will not deprive us of those benefits. Strength imparted to the soul is an inestimable boon ; it means courage, fortitude, assurance, heroism. By his word and Spirit the Lord can make the trembler brave, the sick whole, the weary bright. This soul-might will continue : the man having been strengthened for one emergency remains vigorous for life, and is prepared for all future labours and sufferings ; unless, indeed, he throw away his force by unbelief, or pride, or some other sin. When God strengthens, none can weaken. Then is our soul strong indeed when the Lord infuses might into us.

4 All the kings of the earth shall praise thee, O LORD, when they hear the words of thy mouth.

5 Yea, they shall sing in the ways of the LORD : for great *is* the glory of the LORD.

4. *"All the kings of the earth shall praise thee, O LORD, when they hear the words of thy mouth."* Kings have usually small care to hear the word of the Lord ; but King David feels assured that if they do hear it they will feel its power. A little piety goes a long way in courts ; but brighter days are coming, in which rulers will become hearers and worshippers : may the advent of such happy times be hastened. What an assembly !—" all the kings of the earth ! " What a purpose ! Gathered to hear the words of Jehovah's mouth. What a preacher ! David himself rehearses the words of Jehovah. What praise ! when they all in happy union lift up their songs unto the Lord. Kings are as gods below, and they do well when they worship the God above. The way of conversion for kings is the same as for ourselves : faith to them also cometh by hearing, and hearing by the word of God. Happy are those who can cause the word of the Lord to penetrate palaces ; for the occupants of thrones are usually the last to know the joyful sounds of the gospel. David, the king, cared for kings' souls, and it will be wise for each man to look first after those who are of his own order. He went to his work of testimony with full assurance of success : he meant to speak only the words of Jehovah's mouth, and he felt sure that the kings would hear and praise Jehovah.

5. *"Yea, they shall sing in the ways of the LORD."* Here is a double wonder— kings in God's ways, and kings singing there. Let a man once know the ways of

Jehovah, and he will find therein abundant reason for song ; but the difficulty is to bring the great ones of the earth into ways so little attractive to the carnal mind. Perhaps when the Lord sends us a King David to preach, we shall yet see monarchs converted and hear their voices raised in devout adoration. *"For great is the glory of the Lord."* This glory shall overshadow all the greatness and glory of all kings : they shall be stirred by a sight of it to obey and adore. O that Jehovah's glory were revealed even now ! O that the blind eyes of men could once behold it, then their hearts would be subdued to joyful reverence. David, under a sense of Jehovah's glory, exclaimed, " I will sing " (verse 1), and here he represents the kings as doing the same thing.

6 Though the Lord *be* high, yet hath he respect unto the lowly : but the proud he knoweth afar off.

7 Though I walk in the midst of trouble, thou wilt revive me : thou shalt stretch forth thine hand against the wrath of mine enemies, and thy right hand shall save me.

8 The Lord will perfect *that which* concerneth me : thy mercy, O Lord, *endureth* for ever : forsake not the works of thine own hands.

6. *"Though the Lord be high."* In greatness, dignity, and power, Jehovah is higher than the highest. His nature is high above the comprehension of his creatures, and his glory even exceeds the loftiest soarings of imagination. *"Yet hath he respect unto the lowly."* He views them with pleasure, thinks of them with care, listens to their prayers, and protects them from evil. Because they think little of themselves he thinks much of them. They reverence him, and he respects them. They are low in their own esteem, and he makes them high in his esteem. *"But the proud he knoweth afar off."* He does not need to come near them in order to discover their utter vanity : a glance from afar reveals to him their emptiness and offensiveness. He has no fellowship with them, but views them from a distance ; he is not deceived, but knows the truth about them, despite their blustering ; he has no respect unto them, but utterly abhors them. To a Cain's sacrifice, a Pharaoh's promise, and a Rab-shakeh's threat, and a Pharisee's prayer, the Lord has no respect. Nebuchadnezzar, when far off from God, cried, " Behold this great Babylon which I have builded ; " but the Lord knew him, and sent him grazing with cattle. Proud men boast loudly of their culture and " the freedom of thought," and even dare to criticize their Maker : but he knows them from afar, and will keep them at arm's length in this life, and shut them up in hell in the next.

7. *"Though I walk in the midst of trouble, thou wilt revive me."* If I am walking there now, or shall be doing so in years to come, I have no cause for fear ; for God is with me, and will give me new life. When we are somewhat in trouble it is bad enough, but it is worse to penetrate into the centre of that dark continent and traverse its midst : yet in such a case the believer makes progress, for he walks ; he keeps to a quiet pace, for he does no more than walk ; and he is not without the best of company, for his God is near to pour fresh life into him. It is a happy circumstance that, if God be away at any other time, yet he is pledged to be with us in trying hours : " when thou passest through the rivers I will be with thee." He is in a blessed condition who can confidently use the language of David,—" thou wilt revive me." He shall not make his boast of God in vain : he shall be kept alive, and made more alive than ever. How often has the Lord quickened us by our sorrows ! Are they not his readiest means of exciting to fulness of energy the holy life which dwells within us ? If we receive reviving, we need not regret affliction. When God revives us, trouble will never harm us. *"Thou shalt stretch forth thine hand against the wrath of mine enemies, and thy right hand shall save me."* This is the fact which would revive fainting David. Our foes fall when the Lord comes to deal with them ; he makes short work of the enemies of his people,—with one hand he routs them. His wrath soon quenches their wrath ; his hand stays their hand. Adversaries may be many, and malicious, and mighty ; but our glorious Defender has only to stretch out his arm and their armies vanish. The sweet singer rehearses his assurance of salvation, and sings of it in the ears of the Lord, addressing him with this confident language. He will be saved,—saved dexterously, decidedly, divinely ; he has no doubt about it. God's right hand cannot forget its cunning ; Jerusalem is his chief joy, and he will defend his own elect.

8. *"The* LORD *will perfect that which concerneth me."* All my interests are safe in Jehovah's hands.

> " The work which his goodness began,
> The arm of his strength will complete ;
> His promise is yea and Amen,
> And never was forfeited yet."

God is concerned in all that concerns his servants. He will see to it that none of their precious things shall fail of completion ; their life, their strength, their hopes, their graces, their pilgrimage, shall each and all be perfected. Jehovah himself will see to this ; and therefore it is most sure. *"Thy mercy, O* LORD, *endureth for ever."* The refrain of the former Psalm is in his ears, and he repeats it as his own personal conviction and consolation. The first clause of the verse is the assurance of faith, and this second one reaches to the full assurance of understanding. God's work in us will abide unto perfection because God's mercy towards us thus abideth. *"Forsake not the works of thine own hands."* Our confidence does not cause us to live without prayer, but encourages us to pray all the more. Since we have it written upon our hearts that God will perfect his work in us, and we see it also written in Scripture that his mercy changeth not, we with holy earnestness entreat that we may not be forsaken. If there be anything good in us, it is the work of God's own hands : will he leave it ? Why has he wrought so much in us if he means to give us up ?—it will be a sheer waste of effort. He who has gone so far will surely persevere with us to the end. Our hope for the final perseverance of the believer lies in the final perseverance of the believer's God. If the Lord begins to build, and does not finish, it will not be to his honour. He will have a desire to the work of his hands, for he knows what it has cost him already, and he will not throw away a vessel upon which he has expended so much of labour and skill. Therefore do we praise him with our whole heart, even in the presence of those who depart from his Holy Word, and set up another God and another gospel ; which are not another, but there be some that trouble us.

EXPLANATORY NOTES AND QUAINT SAYINGS.

*Psalms cxxxviii.—cxlv.—*These eight Psalms are composed in the *first* person, and they follow very happily after the fifteen " Songs of Up-goings," and the three Psalms of praise uttered by the chorus of those who have *gone up* to Sion. Those Psalms were the united utterances of national devotion. These eight Psalms are the devout Israelite's Manual of *private* prayer and praise.—*Christopher Wordsworth.*

*Whole Psalm.—*This is the first of a series of eight Psalms (cxxxviii.—cxlv.), probably the last composed by David, a kind of commentary on the great Messianic promise in 2 Sam. vii. They are found in this part of the Psalter, in consequence of having been made the basis, or rather the body, of a system or series (cxxxv.--cxlvi.) by a later writer.—*Joseph Addison Alexander.*

*Whole Psalm.—*If this Psalm refers to the promise in 2 Sam. vii., there can be no doubt of the correctness of the superscription, which ascribes it to David. For he, on whom the promise has been conferred, himself stands forth as the speaker. Proof also of David's authorship is found in the union, so characteristic of him, of bold courage, see especially verse 3, and deep humility, see verse 6. And in proof of the same comes, finally, the near relationship in which it stands with the other Psalms of David, especially those which likewise refer to the promise of the everlasting kingdom ; and with David's thanksgiving in 2 Sam. vii., the conclusion of which remarkably agrees with the conclusion of our Psalm : " And now, Lord God, the word which thou hast spoken upon thy servant and upon his house, that fulfil even to eternity, and do as thou hast spoken."—*E. W. Hengstenberg.*

Verse 1.—"I will praise thee with my whole heart." It is a part of our thankfulness to engage our heart to praise God in time to come, since we find that all the thanks we can give for the present are short of our duty or desire to praise him : *"I will praise thee,"* saith David. Sometimes the believer will find his heart set at liberty in God's worship, which at another time he will find to be in bands, and then he should take the opportunity of an enlarged heart to run in the way of God's service, as David doth here : *"I will praise thee with my whole heart."*—*David Dickson.*

Verse 1.—*"I will praise thee."* Up, dear soul ! What though thou hast once complained like Israel of thy captivity in Babylon, Ps. cxxxvii. 1, yet now sing once more a song of joy to the Lord. Thou hast been pressed like a cluster of grapes, now give forth thy ripe juice.—*Christoph Starke.*

Verse 1.—*"I will praise thee."* Alas, for that capital crime of the Lord's people— barrenness in praises ! Oh, how fully I am persuaded that a line of praises is worth a leaf of prayer, and an hour of praises is worth a day of fasting and mourning !— *John Livingstone,* 1603—1672.

Verse 1.—*"With my whole heart."* This expression, as in Ps. ix. 1, points to the surpassing greatness of the benefit received, which filled the whole heart with thankfulness, and did not proceed, as it were, from some particular corner of it. It corresponds also to the greatness of the benefaction, in the expression, *"before the gods,"*—demanding of these, whether they would verify their godhead by pointing to any such boon conferred by them on their servants. The benefit which could afford such a demonstration, and give occasion and ground for raillery, must have been a surpassingly great one.—*E. W. Hengstenberg.*

Verse 1.—*"Before the gods."* There is much diversity in the meaning assigned to *"gods"* in this verse. It may mean literally in an idolatrous country, in the very temples of false gods, as so many Christian martyrs bore testimony to the faith. The LXX., Vulgate, Ethiopic, and Arabic translate *angels.* The Chaldee has *judges,* the Syriac *kings,* and the earlier Greek fathers explain it as a reference to the choirs of *Priests and Levites* in the Temple.—*Zigabenus, in Neale and Littledale.*

Verse 1.—*"Before the gods."* Some (LXX., Luther, Calvin, etc.) interpret these words of the angels, and compare Ps. xxix. 1 ; but it is doubtful if the Hebrew word Elohim, used nakedly and without any explanation, can have this meaning : it is also, as it would seem, in this connection, pointless : others (Rabbins, Flamin., Delitzsch, etc.) interpret " the great ones of the earth," and compare verse 4 below, and Pss. lxxxii. 1, cxix. 46, etc. ; but this interpretation, too, seems to give no special force to the passage. Probably (Aq., Symm., Jer., etc.) the meaning is, " Before, or in the presence of, the gods of the heathen, *i.e.,* in scorn of, in sight of, the idols, who can do nothing, I will praise Jehovah, who does miracles for me and his people." For a similar expression, see Ps. xxiii. 5, Heb. : see also Pss. xcv. 3, xcvi. 5, for places in which the Hebrew word *"gods"* is used probably for idols.— *Speaker's Commentary.*

Verse 1.—*"Before the gods,"* etc. The Vulgate hath, *in conspectu angelorum,* " before the angels " ; their presence should awe men and women, and keep them from all dishonesty, evil words, acts, gestures, secret grudging, all discontents and distempers. For as they are rejoiced to discern a good frame of spirit in you, to see you keep that order God hath set in the church and state, to walk as Christians to the honour of God ; so they are grieved to see the contrary, and you must answer for your sins against these great officers in the great family of heaven and earth.— *William Greenhill.*

Verse 2.—*"I will worship toward thy holy temple."* The holy temple was a type and figure of the Lord Jesus Christ. Therefore we find Daniel opening his windows toward the temple, where he prayed three times a day ; and we find Jonah saying, " Yet will I look again toward thy holy temple." So looking to Jesus, he is our temple. There is no acceptable worship except through him ; but we can offer spiritual sacrifices acceptable to God through Jesus Christ. Then, set the Lord Jesus Christ before your eyes, that you may worship God and draw near to the footstool of mercy through him, that you may offer an acceptable sacrifice, and praise his name for his lovingkindness and for his truth.—*Joseph C. Philpot,* 1802— 1869.

Verse 2.—*"Thy holy temple."* This Psalm is entitled " a Psalm of David," and Calvin considers him to be its author agreeably to the title ; but the mention of " the temple " in this verse seems to render such an opinion doubtful. If, however, we translate this word by " mansion," which is the proper rendering of the original— *"the mansion of thy sanctity,"*—this objection to its composition by David falls to the ground.—*James Anderson's Note to Calvin in loc.*

Verse 2.—*"I will . . . . praise thy name for thy lovingkindness."* There are two beautiful thoughts brought out here ; one is, " God's condescension in thought ; " the other, " his tenderness in action." These are both included in "*lovingkindness.*" And both of these are shown by God to his own people. He humbleth himself to behold the things of the children of men ; he condescends to men of low estate. Of the blessed Jesus it is said, that " though he was rich, yet for your sakes he became poor, that ye through his poverty might be rich : " 2 Cor. viii. 9. Who can tell the depths to which God condescends in loving thought ? We are told that the very hairs of our head are all numbered ; and if the hairs of our head, then surely all else beside. God, as the Heavenly Father, takes an interest in everything about his people ; he takes this interest in matters which they think beneath his notice, or of which they, from their ignorance, do not know the importance. The mother may draw whole stores of comfort from a realization of the *condescending thoughtfulness of God.* He will be interested about her babe ; if she commit it to him, he who made the universe will, with his infinite mind, think upon her cradle and the helpless creature that is rocked to sleep therein. The sick man may draw whole stores of comfort from the same source, for he can believe the ONE by whom the body was fearfully and wonderfully made will think over the sufferings of that body, and alleviate them, or give strength for the endurance of them if they must be borne. Condescension of thought marks all the dealings of God with his people. And hard following upon it comes *tenderness in action.* Now this " tenderness in action " is a great part of the lovingkindness of God ; it is meet that a thoughtful mind and tender hand should go together in the perfection of love. God is not only energetic, but tender also in action ; he is the God of the dew-drops, as well as the God of the thunder showers ; the God of the tender grass blade, as much as of the mountain oak. We read of great machines, which are able to crush iron bars, and yet they can touch so gently as not to break the shell of the smallest egg ; as it is with them, so is it with the hand of the Most High ; he can crush a world, and yet bind up a wound. And great need have we of tenderness in our low estate ; a little thing would crush us : we have such bruised and feeble souls, that unless we had One who would deal tenderly with us we must soon be destroyed.—*Philip Bennett Power, in "The 'I Wills' of the Psalms,"* 1861.

Verse 2.—"*Thou hast magnified thy word above all thy name.*" His "*word*" being here annexed to "*lovingkindness* and *truth,*" must needs be that part of his word to which these two are applicable, *i.e.*, his promise, the matter whereof is *mercy* or *lovingkindness,* and in the performance of which is *truth* or *fidelity.* And then to " magnify " this " word " of promise seems to signify two things ; 1, the making very great and excellent promises, and then, 2, the performing them most punctually ; and the doing it *above all his name* is promising and performing most superlative mercies above all that is famed or spoken or believed of God. Then thus it will run ; *I will worship,* etc., *and praise thy name above thy lovingkindness and above thy truth ;* i.e., it will be too low, too short a compellation, to call thee merciful or veracious, or style thee after any other of thy attributes ; thou art all these, and more than so, " *thou hast magnified thy word,*" given and performed most glorious promises, "*above all thy name,*" above all that men have apprehended or spoken of thee.

This verse and Psalm may easily be interpreted of God's mercies in Christ, so far above what could be famed, or said, or believed, or apprehended of him.—*Condensed from H. Hammond.*

Verse 2.—"*Thou hast magnified thy word above all thy name.*" Beyond all question there are higher and clearer manifestations of himself, of his being, of his perfection, of his purposes in the volume of revelation, than any which his works have disclosed or can disclose. There are very many points in relation to God, of the highest interest to mankind, on which the disclosures of science shed no light ; there are many things which it is desirable for man to know, which cannot be learned in the schools of philosophy ; there are consolations which man needs in a world of trouble which cannot be found in nature ; there is especially a knowledge of the method by which sin may be pardoned, and the soul saved, which can never be disclosed by the blow-pipe, the telescope, or the microscope. These things, if learned at all, must be learned from revelation, and these are of more importance to man as a traveller to another world than all the learning which can be acquired in the schools of philosophy—valuable as that learning is.—*Albert Barnes.*

Verse 2.—"*For thou hast magnified thy word above all thy name,*" etc. This is a dark sentence at the first view, but as a judicious expositor upon the place well observes, the words may be thus read, and will better agree with the Hebrew; "*thou hast magnified thy name above all things, in thy word*," that is, in fulfilling thy word thou hast magnified thy name above all things, in that thou hast fulfilled thy word. What thou freely promisedst, thou hast faithfully performed; what thou hast spoken with thy mouth thou hast fulfilled with thy hand; for which thy name is wonderfully to be magnified.—*James Nalton*, 1664.

Verse 2.—"*Thou hast magnified thy word above all thy name.*" Every creature bears the name of God; but in his word and truth therein contained it is written at length, and therefore he is more choice of this than of all his other works; he cares not much what becomes of the world and all in it, so that he keeps his word, and saves his truth. Ere long we shall see the world in flames; the heavens and earth shall pass away, "but the word of the Lord endures for ever." When God will, he can make more such worlds as this; but he cannot make another truth, and therefore he will not lose one jot thereof. Satan, knowing this, sets all his wits on work to deface this and disfigure it by unsound doctrine. The word is the glass in which we see God, and seeing him are changed into his likeness by his Spirit. If this glass be cracked, then the conceptions we have of God will misrepresent him unto us; whereas the word, in its native clearness, sets him out in all his glory unto our eye.—*William Gurnall.*

Verse 2.—"*Thou hast magnified thy word above all thy name.*" Thou hast bestowed the promise of perpetuity to my house and to my kingdom, which rises in grandeur and goodness above all thy past manifestations of thyself in behalf of thy people (2 Sam. vii. 10, 12, 13, 15, 16, 21, 22, 24—26, 29: ver. 21 especially, "For thy *Word's* sake . . . hast thou done all these *great* things"; ver. 26, "And let thy name be *magnified* for ever"—an undesigned coincidence of language between the history and the Psalm). In the Messiah alone the greatness of the promise finds, and shall hereafter more fully find, its realization for Israel and the whole world.—*Andrew Robert Fausset.*

Verse 2.—"*Thou hast magnified thy word above all thy name.*" God has sent his word to us,

1. As *a mirror*, to reflect his glory. "The heavens declare the glory of God; and the firmament sheweth his handy-work"; from them may his eternal power and Godhead be clearly seen. Ps. xix. 1, 3, 4. In his providential dealings, also, is much of his wisdom and goodness exhibited. But of his perfections, generally, we can form no idea from these things; of his purposes we can know nothing. The state of the Heathen world clearly attests this; for they behold the wonders of Creation and Providence, as well as we: "There is no speech nor language where *their* voice is not heard. Their line is gone out through all the earth, and their words to the end of the world": Ps. xix. 3, 4. But in the sacred volume all the glory of the Godhead shines: there we are admitted, so to speak, even to the council-chamber of the Most High; to hear the covenant entered into between the Father and the Son; the Father engaging to give to him a seed, whom he should have for his inheritance, if he, on his part, would "make his soul an offering for their sins," and in their nature, expiate the guilt of their iniquities. This mysterious transaction having taken place in the incarnation and death of the Lord Jesus Christ, we behold all the perfections of God united and harmonizing in a way that they never did, or could, by any other means: we see justice more inexorable, than if it had executed vengeance on the whole human race; and mercy more abundant, than if it had spared the whole human race without any such atonement. There, as it is well expressed, "Mercy and truth are met together; righteousness and peace have kissed each other": Ps. lxxxv. 10. Of this great mystery we find not a trace in the whole creation besides: but in the word it is reflected, as in a mirror (2 Cor. iii. 18); and it shines so brightly, that the very angels around the throne are made wiser by the revelation of it to the Church: Eph. iii. 10.

2. As *a standard*, to which everything may be referred. Of God's will we know nothing, but from the word: "we know neither good nor evil from all that is before us." What God requires of us, nothing in Creation or Providence can inform us: what he will do for us, we cannot ascertain: how he will deal with us, we cannot ascertain. But, in the sacred volume, all is written as with a sunbeam. There is nothing which God expects us to do for him, which is not there most explicitly declared: nothing which he engages to do for us, that does not form the subject of a distinct promise. The whole of his procedure in the day of judgment is there laid open: the laws by which we shall be judged; the manner in which the testimony,

whether against us or in our favour, shall be produced ; the grounds on which the sentence of condemnation or acquittal shall be passed ; yea, the very state to which every person, either as acquitted or condemned, shall be consigned ; all is so clearly made known, that every person, who will judge himself with candour now, may assuredly anticipate his fate. There is nothing left to conjecture. Every man has a standard to which he may refer, for the rectifying of his judgment in every particular : so that nothing can be added for the instruction of our minds, or the regulation of our future expectations.

3. As *a fountain*, from whence all his blessings emanate. Great blessings, beyond all doubt, flow down to us through the works of Creation and Providence : in fact, they are incessantly administering to our welfare ; for " God opens his hands, and fills all things living with plenteousness." Still, however, the benefits derived from them are only temporal ; whereas those which the inspired volume imparts are spiritual and eternal ; from whence we derive all our knowledge of Divine truth, and all our hopes of everlasting salvation. Nor is it the knowledge only of truth that we obtain, but the operation and efficacy of it on our souls. There is in Divine truth, when applied by the Holy Spirit, a power to wound, to sanctify, to save : Ps. xix. 7—11. When it comes to the soul with power, the stoutest heart in the universe is made to tremble : when it is poured out as balm, the most afflicted creature under heaven is made to leap for joy. Look over the face of the globe, and see how many, who were once under the unrestrained dominion of sin, are now transformed into the image of their God. And then ascend to heaven, and behold the myriads of the redeemed around the throne of God, uniting their hallelujahs to God and to the Lamb ; to this state were they all brought by that blessed word, which alone could ever prevail for so great a work. Thus it is that God has magnified his word ; and thus it is that he *will* magnify it, to the end of time ; yea, through eternity will it be acknowledged as the one source of all blessings that shall ever be enjoyed.—*Charles Simeon, in Horæ Homileticæ.*

Verse 2.—*"For thou hast magnified thy word above all thy name."* This is one of those expressions of Scripture that seem so comprehensive, and yet so amazing. To my mind it is one of the most remarkable expressions in the whole book of God. *"Thou hast magnified thy word above all thy name."* The *name* of God includes all the perfections of God ; everything that God is, and which God has revealed himself as having—his justice, majesty, holiness, greatness, and glory, and whatever he is in himself, that is God's name. And yet he has *"magnified"* something *"above his name "*—his *word*—his *truth.* This may refer to the Incarnate Word, the Son of God, who was called *"the Word."* " There are three that bear record in heaven, the Father, the *Word*, and the Holy Ghost, and these three are one " 1 John v. 7, " In the beginning was the *Word*, and the *Word* was with God " : John i. 1. You may take the words either as meaning that God has magnified his *Word*, his eternal Son—above all his great name, that is, he has set Jesus on high above all the other perfections of his majesty ; or take it as meaning his written word, which is written in the sacred Scriptures. So, in that case, not only the Incarnate *Word* in the person of Jesus ; but also the written word in the Scriptures of truth. He has magnified it above all his name in the fulfilment of it : God's faithfulness being so dear to him, he has exalted his faithfulness above all his other perfections. We see this in nature. Here is a man so to be depended upon, so faithful to his word, that he will sacrifice anything sooner than depart from it : that man will give up his property, or life itself, rather than forfeit his word. So God has spoken of magnifying his word above all his name. He would sooner allow all his other perfections to come to naught, than for his faithfulness to fail. He has so magnified his faithfulness, that his love, his mercy, his grace, would all sooner fail than his faithfulness—the word of his mouth and what he has revealed in the Scripture. What a firm salvation, then, is ours, which rests upon his word, when God has magnified that word above all his name ! What volumes of blessedness and truth are contained therein ! so that, if God has revealed his truth to your soul, and given you faith to anchor in the word of promise, sooner than that should fail, he would suffer the loss of all ; for, he has magnified his word above all his name.— *Joseph C. Philpot.*

Verse 2.—*"Thou hast magnified thy word above all thy name."* God has a *greater* regard unto the words of his mouth, than to the works of his hand : heaven and earth shall pass away, but one jot or tittle of what he hath spoken shall never fall to the ground. Some do understand this of Christ the essential Word, in whom he has set his name, and whom he has so highly exalted, that he has given him " a name above every name."—*Ebenezer Erskine*, 1680—1754.

Verse 2.—*"Thou hast magnified thy word above all thy name."* Meaning that his word or promise shall have, as it were, and exercise a kind of sovereignty over all his prerogatives and attributes, wisdom, justice, power, etc. So that men need not fear that any of them shall at any time, or in any case whatsoever, move in the least contrariety thereunto.—*John Goodwin*, 1593—1665.

Verse 2.—*"Thou hast magnified thy word above all thy name."* It may be when there are some extraordinary works of God in the world, thunder and lightning, etc., we are ready to be afraid, and oh ! the great God that doth appear in these great works ! Were our hearts as they ought to be when we read the *Word*, we would tremble at that more than at any manifestation of God since the world began in all his works ; and if so be thou dost not see more of the glory of God in his *Word* than in his works, it is because thou hast little light in thee.—*Jeremiah Burroughs*, 1599—1646.

Verse 2.—*"Thou hast magnified thy word above all thy name."* " By the word of the Lord were the heavens made, and all the host of them by the breath of his mouth." But mightier far is the word by which a lost world is redeemed. This is the *"word"* that he hath *"magnified above all his name,"* as displaying at once the exceeding greatness of his power, the resources of his manifold wisdom, and the blended glories of holiness and love.—*John Lillie.*

Verse 2.—It is not with the truth merely excogitated, but with the truth expressed, that we have any concern ; not with the truth as seen by our inspired teacher, but with the truth as by him spoken to us. It is not enough that the Spirit hath made him to see it aright—this is not enough if he have not also made him to speak it aright. A pure influx into the mind of an apostle is no sufficient guarantee for the instruction of the world, unless there be a pure efflux also ; for not the doctrine that has flowed in, but the doctrine that has flowed out, is truly all that we have to do with. Accordingly, it is to the doctrine in efflux, that is to the *word*, that we are bidden to yield ourselves. It is the word that is a light unto our feet and a lamp unto our path ; it is his word that God hath exalted above all his name ; it is the word that he hath settled fast in heaven, and given to it a stability surer and more lasting than to the ordinances of nature. We can take no cognizance of the doctrine that is conveyed from heaven to earth, when it has only come the length of excogitation in the mind of an apostle ; and it is not till brought the farther length of expression, either by speech or by writing, that it comes into contact with us. In short our immediate concern is with, not what apostles conceive inwardly, but what they bring forth outwardly not with the schemes or the systems which they have been made to apprehend, but with the books which they have written ; and had the whole force and effect of this observation been sufficiently pondered, we feel persuaded that the advocates of a mitigated inspiration would not have dissevered, as they have done, the inspiration of sentiment from the inspiration of language.—*Thomas Chalmers.*

Verse 2.—*"Thy word,"* or *"Thy promise."* So great are God's promises, and so faithful and complete is his performance of them, as even to surpass the expectations which the greatness of his name has excited.—*Annotated Paragraph Bible.*

Verse 3.—*"In the day when I cried,"* etc. God granted him a speedy answer : for it was in the very day that he cried that he was heard : and it was a spiritual answer ; he was *strengthened with strength in his soul.* Would you have soul strength for the work you have in view ? then cry unto him who is the " strength of Israel " for it ; for " he giveth power to the faint, and he increaseth strength to them that have no might."—*Ebenezer Erskine.*

Verse 3.—*"In the day when I cried thou answeredst me,"* etc. That part of an army which is upon action in the field is sure to have their pay, if their masters have any money in their purse, or care of them ; yea, sometimes when their fellows left in their quarters are made to wait. I am sure there is more gold and silver (spiritual joy, I mean, and comfort) to be found in Christ's camp, among his suffering ones, than their brethren at home in peace and prosperity ordinarily can show. What are the promises but vessels of cordial wine, tunned on purpose against a groaning hour, when God usually broacheth them ! " Call upon me," saith God, " in the day of trouble." Ps. l. 15. And may we not do so in the day of peace ? Yes ; but he would have us most bold with him in the day of trouble. None find such quick despatch at the throne of grace as suffering saints. *"In the day that I cried,"* said David, *"thou answeredst me, and strengthenedst me with strength in my soul."* He was now in a strait, and God comes in haste to him. Though we may keep a well friend waiting should he send for us, yet we will give a sick friend leave to call us up at midnight. In such extremities we usually go with the messenger that comes for us; and so doth God with the prayer. Peter knocked at their gate, who were assembled to seek God for him, almost as soon as their prayer knocked at heaven gate in his behalf. And truly it is no more than needs, if we consider the temptations of our afflicted condition; we are prone then to be suspicious that our best friends forget us, and to think every stay a delay, and neglect of us; therefore God chooseth to show himself most kind at such a time. "As the sufferings of Christ abound in us, so our consolation also aboundeth by Christ:" 2 Cor. i. 5. As man laid on trouble, so Christ laid in consolation: both tides rose and fell together; when it was spring-tide with him in affliction, it was so with him in his joy. We relieve the poor as their need increaseth; so Christ comforts his people as their troubles multiply. And now, Christian, tell me, doth not thy dear Lord deserve a ready spirit in thee to meet any suffering with, for, or from him, who gives his sweetest comforts where his people are put to bear their saddest sorrows? Well may the servant do his work, cheerfully when his master is so careful of him as with his own hands to bring him his breakfast into the fields. The Christian stays not till he comes to heaven for all his comfort. There indeed shall be the full supper, but there is a breakfast, Christian, of previous joys, more or less, which Christ brings to thee into the field, to be eaten on the place where thou endurest thy hardship.—*William Gurnall.*

Verse 3.—*"Thou answeredst me, and strengthenedst me with strength in my soul."* It is one gracious way of answering our prayers when God doth bestow upon us spiritual strength in our souls; if he do not give the things we desire, yet if he gives us strength in our souls, he graciously answers our prayers. What is this spiritual strength? I answer, it is a work of the Spirit of God, enabling a man to do and suffer what God would have him without fainting or backsliding.—*James Nalton.*

Verse 3.—*"Thou strengthenedst me with strength in my soul."* Other masters cut out work for their servants, but do not help them in their work; but our Master in heaven doth not only give us work, but strength. God bids us serve him, and he will enable us to serve him, Ezek. xxxvi. 27: "I will cause you to walk in my statutes." The Lord doth not only fit work for us, but fits us for our work; with his command he gives power.—*Thomas Watson.*

Verse 3.—*"Thou makest me brave in my soul (with) strength."* The common version of this clause (*"strengthenedst me with strength in my soul"*) contains a paronomasia not in the original, where the verb and noun have not even a letter in common. The verb is by some translated *made me proud, i.e.,* elated me, not with a vain or selfish pride, but with a lofty and exhilarating hope.—*Joseph Addison Alexander.*

Verse 4.—*"All the kings of the earth shall praise thee."* In a sense sufficiently striking this promise was fulfilled to David, and to the nation of Israel, as surrounding monarchs beheld the wonderful dispensations of divine providence which attended their steps (2 Sam. v. 11; viii. 10); but in its completest sense, it shall realize its accomplishment in the future conquests of Messiah, when the princes and potentates of the earth receive his word, learn by divine grace to celebrate the glorious methods of his love, and see in the light of faith the greatness of Jehovah's glory as the God of salvation. *"All the kings of the earth"* shall yet praise the Lord, and shall hasten with their numerous subjects to hail the triumphs of his grace.—*John Morison.*

Verse 5.—*"Yea, they shall sing in the ways of the LORD."* There will come a time when the praise of Jahve, which according to cxxxvii. 4 was obliged to be dumb in the presence of the heathen, will be sung by the kings of the heathen themselves.—*Franz Delitzsch.*

Verse 5.—*"Yea, they shall sing in the ways of the LORD."* Walking with God is a pleasant walk: the ways of wisdom are called "ways of pleasantness": Prov. iii. 17. Is not the light pleasant? Ps. lxxxix. 15: "They shall walk, O LORD, in the light of thy countenance." Walking with God is like walking among beds of spices, which send forth a fragrant perfume. This is it which brings peace,

Acts ix. 31 : " Walking in the fear of the Lord, and in the comfort of the Holy Ghost." While we walk with God, what sweet music doth the bird of conscience make in our breast ! *"They shall sing in the ways of the Lord."—Thomas Watson.*

Verse 6.—"Though the Lord *be high."* We have here God's transcendent greatness ; he is the *high Lord,* or Jehovah : he is " the high and lofty One, who inhabits eternity, and who dwells in the high and lofty place, to which no man can approach." Who can think or speak of his highness in a suitable manner ? It dazzles the eyes of sinful mortal worms to behold " the place where his honour dwells." Oh how infinite is the distance between him and us ! " There are none of the sons of the mighty that can be compared unto him ; " yea, " the inhabitants of the earth are before him but as the drop in the bucket, and the small dust in the balance." He is not only *"high"* above men, but above angels : cherubims and seraphims are his ministering spirits. He is *"high"* above the heavens ; for " the heaven, yea, the heaven of heavens cannot contain him " ; and he " humbleth himself " when " he beholds things that are in heaven." Oh, sirs, study to entertain high and admiring thoughts and apprehensions of the glorious majesty of God ; for " honour and majesty are before him ; strength and beauty are in his sanctuary." *—Ebenezer Erskine.*

Verse 6.—"The Lord *hath respect unto the lowly."* God has such a respect unto the lowly, not as if this frame of soul were meritorious of any good at his hand, but because,—

1. This is a disposition that best serves God's great design of lifting up and glorifying his free grace. What think you, sirs, was God's design in election, in redemption, in the whole of the gospel dispensation, and in all the ordinances thereof ? His grand design in all was to rear up a glorious high throne, from which he might display the riches of his free and sovereign grace ; this is that which he will have magnified through eternity above all his other name. Now, this lowliness and humility of spirit suits best unto God's design of exalting the freedom of his grace. It is not the legalist, or proud Pharisee, but the poor humble publican, who is smiting on his breast, and crying, " God be merciful to me, a sinner," that submits to the revelation of grace.

2. God has such respect unto the humble soul because it is a fruit of the Spirit inhabiting the soul, and an evidence of the soul's union with the Lord Jesus Christ, in whom alone we are accepted.

3. This is a disposition that makes the soul like Christ ; and the like that a person is to Christ, God loves him ay the better. We are told that Christ was " meek and lowly " ; " he did not cry, nor lift up, nor cause his voice to be heard in the streets " ; though he was " the brightness of his Father's glory," yet he was content to appear " in the form of a servant" ; though he was rich, yet he was content to become poor, that we through his poverty might be rich. Now, the humble soul, being the image of Christ, who is the express image of his Father, God cannot but have a regard unto him.—*Ebenezer Erskine.*

Verse 6.—"He hath respect unto the lowly." Give me the homely vessel of humility, which God shall preserve, and fill with the wine of his grace ; rather than the varnished cup of pride, which he will dash in pieces, like a potter's vessel. Where humility is the corner stone, there glory shall be the topstone.—*William Secker, in "The Nonsuch Professor in his Meridian Splendour,"* 1660.

Verse 6.—"The proud he knoweth afar off." He that meets a spectacle or person which he cannot endure to look upon, avoids it, or turns from it while he is yet afar off ; whereas, if the object be delightful, he draweth near and comes as close as he can. When therefore it is said, *the Lord knoweth a proud man afar off,* it shows his disdain of him : he will scarce touch him with a pair of tongs (as we say) ; he cannot abide to come near him. He knows well enough how vile he is even at the greatest distance.—*Joseph Caryl.*

Verse 6.—"The proud he knoweth afar off." By punishing them in hell.—*Richard Rolle,* 1340.

Verse 7.—"Though I walk in the midst of trouble, thou wilt revive me." So as to the three youths in the fiery furnace, their persecutor, Nebuchadnezzar, said, " Lo, I see four men loose, *walking in the midst of the fire,* and they have no hurt, and the form of the fourth is like the Son of God."—*Andrew Robert Fausset.*

Verse 7.—"In the midst of trouble thou wilt revive me." The wisdom of God is seen in helping in desperate cases. God loves to show his wisdom when human help and wisdom fail. Exquisite lawyers love to wrestle with niceties and difficulties in the law, to show their skill the more. God's wisdom is never at a loss ; but when providences are darkest, then the morning star of deliverance appears. Sometimes God melts away the spirits of his enemies. Josh. ii. 24. Sometimes he finds them other work to do, and sounds a retreat to them, as he did to Saul when he was pursuing David. " The Philistines are in the land." " In the mount God will be seen." When the church seems to be upon the altar, her peace and liberty ready to be sacrificed, then the angel comes.—*Thomas Watson.*

Verse 7.—*"Thou shalt stretch forth thine hand,"* etc. Thou shalt interpose thine help betwixt me and them, and save me harmless ; as the poets feign their gods did those whom they favoured. *Thou shalt strike them with thy left hand, and save me with thy right ;* so Tremellius senseth it.—*John Trapp.*

Verse 8.—*"The LORD will perfect,"* etc. God's work is perfect, man's is clumsy and incomplete. God does not leave off till he has finished. When he rests, it is because, looking on his work, he sees it all " very good." His Sabbath is the Sabbath of an achieved purpose, of a fulfilled counsel. The palaces which we build are ever like that in the story, where one window remains dark and unjewelled, while the rest blaze in beauty. But when God builds none can say, " He was not able to finish." In his great palace he makes her " windows of agates," and *all* her " borders of pleasant stones."

I suppose that if the mediæval dream had ever come true, and an alchemist had ever turned a grain of lead into gold, he could have turned all the lead in the world, in time, and with crucibles and furnaces enough. The first step is all the difficulty, and if you and I have been changed from enemies into sons, and had one spark of love to God kindled in our hearts, that is a mightier change than any that yet remains to be effected in order to make us perfect. One grain has been changed, the whole mass will be in due time.—*Alexander Maclaren, Sermon in " Wesleyan Methodist Magazine,"* 1879.

Verse 8.—*"Forsake not the works of thine own hands."* When we are under such afflictions as threaten to ruin us, 'tis seasonable to tell the Lord he made us. David strengthens prayer upon this argument : *"Forsake not the works of thine own hands."* All men love their own works, many dote upon them : shall we think God will forsake his ? See how the people of God plead with God in greatest distress. (Isa. lxiv. 8) : " But now, O LORD, thou art our father ; we are the clay, and thou our potter ; and we are all the work of thy hand. Be not wroth very sore, O LORD." —*Joseph Cary.*

Verse 8.—*"Forsake not the works of thine own hands."* Look upon the wounds of thine hands, and forsake not the works of thine hands, prayed Queen Elizabeth. And Luther's usual prayer was, Confirm, O God, in us that thou hast wrought, and perfect the work that thou hast begun in us, to thy glory. So be it.—*John Trapp.*

Verse 8.—*"Forsake not the works of thine own hands."* Behold in me thy work, not mine : for mine, if thou seest, thou condemnest ; thine, if thou seest, thou crownest. For whatever good works there be of mine, from thee are they to me ; and so they are more thine than mine. For I hear from thine apostle, " By grace are ye saved through faith ; and that not of yourselves : it is the gift of God : Not of works, lest any man should boast. For we are his workmanship, created in Christ Jesus : " Eph. ii. 8—10.—*Augustine.*

Verse 8.—*"Thine own hands."* His creating hands formed our souls at the beginning ; his nail-pierced hands redeemed them on Calvary ; his glorified hands will hold our souls fast and not let them go for ever. Unto his hands let us commend our spirits, sure that even though the works of our hands have made void the works of his hands, yet his hands will again make perfect all that our hands have unmade. —*J. W. Burgon.*

HINTS TO PREACHERS.

Verses 1, 2, 3.—David vexed with rival gods, as we are with rival gospels. How will he act? I. *Sing with whole-hearted praise.* 1. It would generously show his contempt of the false. 2. It would evince his strong faith in the true. 3. It would declare his joyful zeal for God. 4. It would shield him from evil from those about him. II. *Worship by the despised rule.* 1. Quietly ignoring all will-worship. 2. Looking to the person of Christ, which was typified by the temple. 3. Trusting in sacrifice. 4. Realizing God himself, for it is to God he speaks. III. *Praise the questioned attributes.* 1. Lovingkindness in its universality, in its speciality. Grace in everything. 2. Truth. Historic accuracy. Certainty of promises. Correctness of prophecies. Assured of the love of God and the truth of his word, let us cling the closer to these. IV. *Reverence the honoured word.* It is beyond all revelation by creation and providence, for it is—1. More clear. 2. More sure. 3. More sovereign. 4. More complete, unique. 5. More lasting. 6. More glorifying to God. V. *Prove it by experience.* 1. By offering prayer. 2. By narrating the answer. 3. By exhibiting the strength in soul which was given in answer to prayer.

Verse 2.—The Christward position. I. Worship and praise are to be blended. II. They are to be presented with an eye to God in Christ, for he is the temple: the place of divine indwelling, sacrifice, intercession, priesthood, oracle, and manifestation.

Verse 2 (*first clause*).—I. The soul's noblest attitude: "Toward thy holy temple." II. The soul's noblest exercise: "worship," "praise."—*W. W.*

Verse 2.—I. *The worshipper's contemplation.* Gaze fixed on Holy Temple. Material temple not yet built. Christ the sanctuary. Heb. viii. 2. All worship through him. Eye of worshippers fixed on him. II. *The worshipper's song.* Love and truth. Note the combination. Truth by Moses. Grace and truth by Jesus Christ. III. *The worshipper's argument.* Because Christ "The Word" is the embodiment and most glorious manifestation of God. Heb. i. 2, 3.—*Archibald G. Brown.*

Verse 3.—I. Prayer answered *in* the day. II. Prayer answered by giving strength *for* the day. See 2 Cor. xii. 8, 9.—*A. G. B.*

Verse 3.—I. Answers to prayer should be noted and acknowledged: "Thou answeredst me." II. Speedy answers should have special praise: "In the day when I cried, thou," etc. III. A strengthened soul is sometimes the best answer to prayer: "Strengthened me with strength."—*J. F.*

Verse 3.—Remarkable answer to prayer. I. The prayer: feeble, earnest, sorrowful, inarticulate. II. The answer: prompt, divine, effectual, certain. III. The praise deserved by such grace. See preceding verses.

Verse 3.—I. A special day. II. A specific form of prayer: "I cried." III. A special method of response.—*W. W.*

Verse 4.—I. A royal audience. II. A royal orchestra.

Verses 4, 5.—I. They who hear the words of God will know God. II. They who know God will praise him, however exalted they may be amongst men: "All the kings," etc. III. They who praise God will walk in his ways. IV. They who walk in the ways of the Lord will glorify him, and he will be glorified in them.—*G. R.*

Verse 5.—See "Spurgeon's Sermons," No. 1615: "Singing in the Ways of the Lord."

Verse 5.—This is spoken of kings, but it is true of the humblest pilgrims. The Lord hath respect unto the lowly, and will make them sing. I. *They shall sing in the ways.* 1. They take pleasure in them. 2. They do not go out of them to find pleasure. 3. They sing as they proceed in service, in worship, in holiness, in suffering. 4. They are in a case for singing. They have strength, safety, guidance, provision, comfort. II. *They sing of the ways of the Lord.* 1. Of God's ways to them. 2. Of their way to God. They know whence they came out. They know where they are going. It is a good road; prophets went by it, and the Lord of the prophets. Therein we have good company, good accommodation, good prospects, good daylight. III. *They sing of the Lord of the way.* His lovingkindness. His truth. Answers to prayer. His condescension. His reviving us in trouble. His delivering us. His perfecting us. His everlasting mercy. IV. *They shall sing to the Lord of the way.* 1. To his honour. 2. To the extending of that honour. 3. As a preparation to eternally honouring him.

Verse 6.—Divine inversions. I. Lowliness honoured to its great surprise. II. Pride passed by to its eternal mortification.—*W. B. H.*

Verse 7 (*first clause*).—I. The Psalmist's dismal excursion : walking " in the midst of trouble ; " this is not a spectator, but one assailed. Troubles—personal, social, ecclesiastical, national. II. His cheering anticipation—of revival, defence, deliverance.—*W. J.*

Verse 7.—I. Good men are sometimes in the midst of troubles : these are many, and continue long. II. They interfere not with their progress. They " walk in the midst " of them ; faint, yet pursuing ; sometimes they " run with patience," etc. III. They have comfort in them : " Though I walk," etc., " thou wilt revive me." IV. They are benefited by them. 1. Their enemies are overthrown. 2. Their deliverance is complete.—*G. R.*

Verse 7.—The child of God often revived *out* of trouble ; more frequently *in* trouble ; not seldom *through* trouble. Delivered from, sustained in, sanctified through, trouble.—*A. G. B.*

Verse 7.—An incident of the road to the city. I. Pilgrim beset by thieves and struck down. II. The arrival of Greatheart and flight of the enemy. III. The flask to the lips : " thou wilt revive me." Sweet awakening to know the beauty of his face and strength of his hand !—*W. B. H.*

Verse 7 (*third clause*).—Right-hand salvation. I. It shall be wrought of God. II. He shall throw his strength into the deed. III. His utmost dexterity shall be displayed.

Verse 8 (*first clause*).—I. A wide subject—" That which concerneth me." Not necessarily that which gives me concern. II. A promise that covers it : " the Lord will perfect."—*A. G. B.*

Verse 8 (*first and last clauses*).—Faith in divine purpose no hindrance to prayer, but rather an encouragement in it : " The Lord will perfect." " Forsake not."—*A. G. B.*

Verse 8.—See " Spurgeon's Sermons," Nos. 231 and 1506 : " Faith in Perfection," and, " Choice Comfort for a Young Believer."

Verse 8.—The grace of God makes a man thoughtful, and leads him to concern about himself, his life, his future, and the completeness of the work of grace. This might lead us to sadness and despair, but the Lord worketh in us for other ends. I. *He fills us with assurance.* 1. That the Lord will work for us. 2. That he will complete his work. 3. That he will do this in providence ; if it be properly a concern of ours. 4. That he will do this within us. Our graces shall grow. Our soul shall become Christly. Our whole nature perfect. 5. That he will do this with our work for him. II. *He gives us rest in his mercy.* 1. Thou wilt forgive my sins. 2. Thou wilt bear with my nature. 3. Thou wilt support me in suffering. 4. Thou wilt supply me in need. 5. Thou wilt succour me in death. III. *He puts prayer into our hearts.* 1. That he will not forsake me. 2. That he will not leave his own work in me undone. 3. Nor his work by me unfinished. Why did he begin ? Why carry so far ? Why not complete ?

Verse 8.—I. Faith's full assurance : " The Lord will perfect that which concerneth me." II. Faith's firm foundation : " Thy mercy, O Lord, endureth for ever." III. Faith's fervent prayer : " Forsake not the works of thine own hands." —*W. H. J. P.*

PSALM CXXXIX.

One of the most notable of the sacred hymns. It sings the omniscience and omnipresence of God, inferring from these the overthrow of the powers of wickedness, since he who sees and hears the abominable deeds and words of the rebellious will surely deal with them according to his justice. The brightness of this Psalm is like unto a sapphire stone, or Ezekiel's "terrible crystal"; it flames out with such flashes of light as to turn night into day. Like a Pharos, this holy song casts a clear light even to the uttermost parts of the sea, and warns us against that practical atheism which ignores the presence of God, and so makes shipwreck of the soul.

TITLE.—To the Chief Musician. *The last time this title occurred was in Psalm cix. This sacred song is worthy of the most excellent of the singers, and is fitly dedicated to the leader of the Temple psalmody, that he might set it to music, and see that it was devoutly sung in the solemn worship of the Most High.* A Psalm of David. *It bears the image and superscription of King David, and could have come from no other mint than that of the son of Jesse. Of course the critics take this composition away from David, on account of certain Aramaic expressions in it. We believe that upon the principles of criticism now in vogue it would be extremely easy to prove that Milton did not write Paradise Lost. We have yet to learn that David could not have used expressions belonging to "the language of the patriarchal ancestral house." Who knows how much of the antique speech may have been purposely retained among those nobler minds who rejoiced in remembering the descent of their race? Knowing to what wild inferences the critics have run in other matters, we have lost nearly all faith in them, and prefer to believe David to be the author of this Psalm, from internal evidences of style and matter, rather than to accept the determination of men whose modes of judgment are manifestly unreliable.*

EXPOSITION.

O LORD, thou hast searched me, and known *me*.

2 Thou knowest my downsitting and mine uprising, thou understandest my thought afar off.

3 Thou compassest my path and my lying down, and art acquainted *with* all my ways.

4 For *there is* not a word in my tongue, *but*, lo, O LORD, thou knowest it altogether.

5 Thou hast beset me behind and before, and laid thine hand upon me.

6 *Such* knowledge *is* too wonderful for me; it is high, I cannot *attain* unto it.

1. "*O LORD, thou hast searched me, and known me.*" He invokes in adoration Jehovah the all-knowing God, and he proceeds to adore him by proclaiming one of his peculiar attributes. If we would praise God aright we must draw the matter of our praise from himself—"O Jehovah, thou hast." No pretended god knows aught of us; but the true God, Jehovah, understands us, and is most intimately acquainted with our persons, nature, and character. How well it is for us to know the God who knows us! The divine knowledge is extremely thorough and searching; it is as if he had searched us, as officers search a man for contraband goods, or as pillagers ransack a house for plunder. Yet we must not let the figure run upon all fours, and lead us further than it is meant to do: the Lord knows all things naturally and as a matter of course, and not by any effort on his part. Searching ordinarily implies a measure of ignorance which is removed by observation; of course this is not the case with the Lord; but the meaning of the Psalmist is, that the Lord knows us as thoroughly as if he had examined us minutely, and had pried into the most secret corners of our being. This infallible knowledge has always existed—"Thou hast searched me"; and it continues unto this day, since God

cannot forget that which he has once known. There never was a time in which we were unknown to God, and there never will be a moment in which we shall be beyond his observation. Note how the Psalmist makes his doctrine personal : he saith not, " O God, thou knowest all things "; but, " thou hast known *me.*" It is ever our wisdom to lay truth home to ourselves. How wonderful the contrast between the observer and the observed ! Jehovah and me ! Yet this most intimate connection exists, and therein lies our hope. Let the reader sit still a while and try to realize the two poles of this statement,—the Lord and poor puny man—and he will see much to admire and wonder at.

2. *"Thou knowest my downsitting and mine uprising."* *Me* thou knowest, and all that comes of me. I am observed when I quietly sit down, and marked when I resolutely rise up. My most common and casual acts, my most needful and necessary movements, are noted by thee, and thou knowest the inward thoughts which regulate them. Whether I sink in lowly self-renunciation, or ascend in pride, thou seest the motions of my mind, as well as those of my body. This is a fact to be remembered every moment : sitting down to consider, or rising up to act, we are still seen, known, and read by Jehovah our Lord. *"Thou understandest my thought afar off."* Before it is my own it is foreknown and comprehended by thee. Though my thought be invisible to the sight, though as yet I be not myself cognizant of the shape it is assuming, yet thou hast it under thy consideration, and thou perceivest its nature, its source, its drift, its result. Never dost thou misjudge or wrongly interpret me : my inmost thought is perfectly understood by thine impartial mind. Though thou shouldst give but a glance at my heart, and see me as one sees a passing meteor moving afar, yet thou wouldst by that glimpse sum up all the meanings of my soul, so transparent is everything to thy piercing glance.

3. *"Thou compassest my path and my lying down."* My path and my pallet, my running and my resting, are alike within the circle of thine observation. Thou dost surround me even as the air continually surrounds all creatures that live. I am shut up within the wall of thy being ; I am encircled within the bounds of thy knowledge. Waking or sleeping I am still observed of thee. I may leave thy path, but thou never leavest mine. I may sleep and forget thee, but thou dost never slumber, nor fall into oblivion concerning thy creature. The original signifies not only surrounding, but winnowing and sifting. The Lord judges our active life and our quiet life ; he discriminates our action and our repose, and marks that in them which is good and also that which is evil. There is chaff in all our wheat, and the Lord divides them with unerring precision. *"And art acquainted with all my ways."* Thou art familiar with all I do ; nothing is concealed from thee, nor surprising to thee, nor misunderstood by thee. Our paths may be habitual or accidental, open or secret, but with them all the Most Holy One is well acquainted. This should fill us with awe, so that we sin not ; with courage, so that we fear not ; with delight, so that we mourn not.

4. *"For there is not a word in my tongue, but lo, O LORD, thou knowest it altogether."* The unformed word, which lies within the tongue like a seed in the soil, is certainly and completely known to the Great Searcher of hearts. A negative expression is used to make the positive statement all the stronger : not a word is unknown is a forcible way of saying that every word is well known. Divine knowledge is perfect, since not a single word is unknown, nay, not even an unspoken word, and each one is " altogether " or wholly known. What hope of concealment can remain when the speech with which too many conceal their thoughts is itself transparent before the Lord ? O Jehovah, how great art thou ! If thine eye hath such power, what must be the united force of thine whole nature !

5. *"Thou hast beset me behind and before."* As though we were caught in an ambush, or besieged by an army which has wholly beleaguered the city walls, we are surrounded by the Lord. God has set us where we be, and beset us wherever we be. Behind us there is God recording our sins, or in grace blotting out the remembrance of them ; and before us there is God foreknowing all our deeds, and providing for all our wants. We cannot turn back and so escape him, for he is behind ; we cannot go forward and outmarch him, for he is before. He not only beholds us, but he besets us ; and lest there should seem any chance of escape, or lest we should imagine that the surrounding presence is yet a distant one, it is added,—*"And laid thine hand upon me."* The prisoner marches along surrounded by a guard, and gripped by an officer. God is very near ; we are wholly in his power ; from that power there is no escape. It is not said that God *will* thus beset

us and arrest us, but it is done—"Thou hast beset me." Shall we not alter the figure, and say that our heavenly Father has folded his arms around us, and caressed us with his hand? It is even so with those who are by faith the children of the Most High.

6. "*Such knowledge is too wonderful for me.*" I cannot grasp it. I can hardly endure to think of it. The theme overwhelms me. I am amazed and astounded at it. Such knowledge not only surpasses my comprehension, but even my imagination. "*It is high, I cannot attain unto it.*" Mount as I may, this truth is too lofty for my mind. It seems to be always above me, even when I soar into the loftiest regions of spiritual thought. Is it not so with every attribute of God? Can we attain to any idea of his power, his wisdom, his holiness? Our mind has no line with which to measure the Infinite. Do we therefore question? Say, rather, that we therefore believe and adore. We are not surprised that the Most Glorious God should in his knowledge be high above all the knowledge to which we can attain: it must of necessity be so, since we are such poor limited beings; and when we stand a-tip-toe we cannot reach to the lowest step of the throne of the Eternal.

7 Whither shall I go from thy spirit? or whither shall I flee from thy presence?

8 If I ascend up into heaven, thou *art* there: if I make my bed in hell, behold, thou *art there.*

9 *If* I take the wings of the morning, *and* dwell in the uttermost parts of the sea;

10 Even there shall thy hand lead me, and thy right hand shall hold me.

11 If I say, Surely the darkness shall cover me; even the night shall be light about me.

12 Yea, the darkness hideth not from thee; but the night shineth as the day: the darkness and the light *are* both alike *to thee.*

Here omnipresence is the theme,—a truth to which omniscience naturally leads up. "*Whither shall I go from thy spirit?*" Not that the Psalmist wished to go from God, or to avoid the power of the divine life; but he asks this question to set forth the fact that no one can escape from the all-pervading being and observation of the Great Invisible Spirit. Observe how the writer makes the matter personal to himself—"Whither shall *I* go?" It were well if we all thus applied truth to our own cases. It were wise for each one to say—The spirit of the Lord is ever around *me:* Jehovah is omnipresent *to me.* "*Or whither shall I flee from thy presence?*" If, full of dread, I hastened to escape from that nearness of God which had become my terror, which way could I turn? "Whither?" "Whither?" He repeats his cry. No answer comes back to him. The reply to his first "Whither?" is its echo,—a second "Whither?" From the sight of God he cannot be hidden, but that is not all,—from the immediate, actual, constant presence of God he cannot be withdrawn. We must be, whether we will it or not, as near to God as our soul is to our body. This makes it dreadful work to sin; for we offend the Almighty to his face, and commit acts of treason at the very foot of his throne. Go from him, or *flee* from him we cannot: neither by patient travel nor by hasty flight can we withdraw from the all-surrounding Deity. His mind is in our mind; himself within ourselves. His spirit is over our spirit; our presence is ever in his presence.

8. "*If I ascend up into heaven, thou art there.*" Filling the loftiest region with his yet loftier presence, Jehovah is in the heavenly place, at home, upon his throne. The ascent, if it were possible, would be unavailing for purposes of escape; it would, in fact, be a flying into the centre of the fire to avoid the heat. There would he be immediately confronted by the terrible personality of God. Note the abrupt words—"THOU, THERE." "*If I make my bed in hell, behold, thou art there.*" Descending into the lowest imaginable depths among the dead, there should we find the Lord. THOU! says the Psalmist, as if he felt that God was the one great Existence in all places. Whatever Hades may be, or whoever may be there, one thing is certain, Thou, O Jehovah, art there. Two regions, the one of glory and the other of darkness, are set in contrast, and this one fact is asserted of both —"thou art there." Whether we rise up or lie down, take our wing or make our

bed, we shall find God near us. A *"behold"* is added to the second clause, since it seems more a wonder to meet with God in hell than in heaven, in Hades than in Paradise. Of course the presence of God produces very different effects in these places, but it is unquestionably in each ; the bliss of one, the terror of the other. What an awful thought, that some men seem resolved to take up their night's abode in hell, a night which shall know no morning.

9. *"If I take the wings of the morning, and dwell in the uttermost parts of the sea."*— If I could fly with all swiftness, and find a habitation where the mariner has not yet ploughed the deep, yet I could not reach the boundaries of the divine presence. Light flies with inconceivable rapidity, and it flashes far afield beyond all human ken ; it illuminates the great and wide sea, and sets its waves gleaming afar ; but its speed would utterly fail if employed in flying from the Lord. Were we to speed on the wings of the morning breeze, and break into oceans unknown to chart and map, yet there we should find the Lord already present. He who saves to the uttermost would be with us in the uttermost parts of the sea.

10. *"Even there shall thy hand lead me."* We could only fly from God by his own power. The Lord would be leading, covering, preserving, sustaining us even when we were fugitives from him. *"And thy right hand shall hold me."* In the uttermost parts of the sea my arrest would be as certain as at home : God's right hand would there seize and detain the runaway. Should we be commanded on the most distant errand, we may assuredly depend upon the upholding right hand of God as with us in all mercy, wisdom, and power. The exploring missionary in his lonely wanderings is led, in his solitary feebleness he is held. Both the hands of God are with his own servants to sustain them, and against rebels to overthrow them ; and in this respect it matters not to what realms they resort, the active energy of God is around them still.

11. *"If I say, Surely the darkness shall cover me."* Dense darkness may oppress me, but it cannot shut me out from thee, or thee from me. Thou seest as well without the light as with it, since thou art not dependent upon light, which is thine own creature, for the full exercise of thy perceptions. Moreover, thou art present with me whatever may be the hour ; and being present thou discoverest all that I think, or feel, or do. Men are still so foolish as to prefer night and darkness for their evil deeds ; but so impossible is it for anything to be hidden from the Lord that they might just as well transgress in broad daylight.

> Darkness and light in this agree ;
> Great God, they're both alike to thee.
> Thine hand can pierce thy foes as soon
> Through midnight shades as blazing noon.

A good man will not wish to be hidden by the darkness, a wise man will not expect any such thing. If we were so foolish as to make sure of concealment because the place was shrouded in midnight, we might well be alarmed out of our security by the fact that, as far as God is concerned, we always dwell in the light ; for even the night itself glows with a revealing force,—*"even the night shall be light about me."* Let us think of this if ever we are tempted to take license from the dark—it is light about us. If the darkness be light, how great is that light in which we dwell ! Note well how David keeps his song in the first person ; let us mind that we do the same as we cry with Hagar, " Thou God seest *me*."

12. *"Yea,"* of a surety, beyond all denial. *"The darkness hideth not from thee ; "* it veils nothing, it is not the medium of concealment in any degree whatever. It hides from men, but not from God. *"But the night shineth as the day : "* it is but another form of day : it shines, revealing all ; it " shineth as the day,"—quite as clearly and distinctly manifesting all that is done. *"The darkness and the light are both alike to thee."* This sentence seems to sum up all that went before, and most emphatically puts the negative upon the faintest idea of hiding under the cover of night. Men cling to this notion, because it is easier and less expensive to hide under darkness than to journey to remote places ; and therefore the foolish thought is here beaten to pieces by statements which in their varied forms effectually batter it. Yet the ungodly are still duped by their grovelling notions of God, and enquire, " How doth God know ? " They must fancy that he is as limited in his powers of observation as they are, and yet if they would but consider for a moment they would conclude that he who could not see in the dark could not be God, and he who is not present everywhere could not be the Almighty Creator. Assuredly

God is in all places, at all times, and nothing can by any possibility be kept away from his all-observing, all-comprehending mind. The Great Spirit comprehends within himself all time and space, and yet he is infinitely greater than these, or aught else that he has made.

13 For thou hast possessed my reins : thou hast covered me in my mother's womb.

14 I will praise thee ; for I am fearfully *and* wonderfully made : marvellous *are* thy works ; and *that* my soul knoweth right well.

15 My substance was not hid from thee, when I was made in secret, *and* curiously wrought in the lowest parts of the earth.

16 Thine eyes did see my substance, yet being unperfect ; and in thy book all *my members* were written, *which* in continuance were fashioned, when *as yet there was* none of them.

17 How precious also are thy thoughts unto me, O God ! how great is the sum of them !

18 *If* I should count them, they are more in number than the sand : when I awake, I am still with thee.

13. *"For thou hast possessed my reins."* Thou art the owner of my inmost parts and passions : not the indweller and observer only, but the acknowledged lord and possessor of my most secret self. The word " reins " signifies the kidneys, which by the Hebrews were supposed to be the seat of the desires and longings ; but perhaps it indicates here the most hidden and vital portion of the man ; this God doth not only inspect, and visit, but it is his own ; he is as much at home there as a landlord on his own estate, or a proprietor in his own house. *"Thou hast covered me in my mother's womb."* There I lay hidden—covered by thee. Before I could know thee, or aught else, thou hadst a care for me, and didst hide me away as a treasure till thou shouldst see fit to bring me to the light. Thus the Psalmist describes the intimacy which God had with him. In his most secret part—his reins, and in his most secret condition—yet unborn, he was under the control and guardianship of God.

14. *"I will praise thee :"* a good resolve, and one which he was even now carrying out. Those who are praising God are the very men who *will* praise him. Those who wish to praise have subjects for adoration ready to hand. We too seldom remember our creation, and all the skill and kindness bestowed upon our frame : but the sweet singer of Israel was better instructed, and therefore he prepares for the chief musician a song concerning our nativity and all the fashioning which precedes it. We cannot begin too soon to bless our Maker, who began so soon to bless us : even in the act of creation he created reasons for our praising his name. *"For I am fearfully and wonderfully made."* Who can gaze even upon a model of our anatomy without wonder and awe ? Who could dissect a portion of the human frame without marvelling at its delicacy, and trembling at its frailty ? The Psalmist had scarcely peered within the veil which hides the nerves, sinews, and blood-vessels from common inspection ; the science of anatomy was quite unknown to him ; and yet he had seen enough to arouse his admiration of the work and his reverence for the Worker. *"Marvellous are thy works."* These parts of my frame are all *thy* works ; and though they be home works, close under my own eye, yet are they wonderful to the last degree. They are works within my own self, yet are they beyond my understanding, and appear to me as so many miracles of skill and power. We need not go to the ends of the earth for marvels, nor even across our own threshold ; they abound in our own bodies.

"And that my soul knoweth right well." He was no agnostic—he knew ; he was no doubter—his soul knew ; he was no dupe—his soul knew right well. Those know indeed and of a truth who first know the Lord, and then know all things in him. He was made to know the marvellous nature of God's work with assurance and accuracy, for he had found by experience that the Lord is a master-worker, performing inimitable wonders when accomplishing his kind designs. If we are marvellously wrought upon even before we are born, what shall we say of the Lord's dealings with us after we quit his secret workshop, and he directs our pathway through the pilgrimage of life ? What shall we not say of that new birth which

is even more mysterious than the first, and exhibits even more the love and wisdom of the Lord.

15. *"My substance was not hid from thee."* The substantial part of my being was before thine all-seeing eye ; the bones which make my frame were put together by thine hand. The essential materials of my being before they were arranged were all within the range of thine eye. I was hidden from all human knowledge, but not from thee : thou hast ever been intimately acquainted with me. *"When I was made in secret."* Most chastely and beautifully is here described the formation of our being before the time of our birth. A great artist will often labour alone in his studio, and not suffer his work to be seen until it is finished ; even so did the Lord fashion us where no eye beheld us, and the veil was not lifted till every member was complete. Much of the formation of our inner man still proceeds in secret ; hence the more of solitude the better for us. The true church also is being fashioned in secret, so that none may cry, " Lo, here ! " or " Lo, there ! " as if that which is visible could ever be identical with the invisibly growing body of Christ. *"And curiously wrought it in the lowest parts of the earth."* " Embroidered with great skill," is an accurate poetical description of the creation of veins, sinews, muscles, nerves, etc. What tapestry can equal the human fabric ? This work is wrought as much in private as if it had been accomplished in the grave, or in the darkness of the abyss. The expressions are poetical, beautifully veiling, though not absolutely concealing, the real meaning. God's intimate knowledge of us from the beginning, and even before it, is here most charmingly set forth. Cannot he who made us thus wondrously when we were not, still carry on his work of power till he has perfected us, though we feel unable to aid in the process, and are lying in great sorrow and self-loathing, as though cast into the lowest parts of the earth ?

16. *"Thine eyes did see my substance, yet being unperfect."* While as yet the vessel was upon the wheel the Potter saw it all. The Lord knows not only our shape, but our substance : this is substantial knowledge indeed. The Lord's observation of us is intent and intentional,—" Thine eyes did see." Moreover, the divine mind discerns all things as clearly and certainly as men perceive by actual eye-sight. His is not hearsay acquaintance, but the knowledge which comes of sight. *"And in thy book all my members were written, which in continuance were fashioned, when as yet there was none of them."* An architect draws his plans, and makes out his specifications ; even so did the great Maker of our frame write down all our members in the book of his purposes. That we have eyes, and ears, and hands, and feet, is all due to the wise and gracious purpose of heaven : it was so ordered in the secret decree by which all things are as they are. God's purposes concern our limbs and faculties. Their form, and shape, and everything about them were appointed of God long before they had any existence. God saw us when we could not be seen, and he wrote about us when there was nothing of us to write about. When as yet there were none of our members in existence, all those members were before the eye of God in the sketch-book of his foreknowledge and predestination.

This verse is an exceedingly difficult one to translate, but we do not think that any of the proposed amendments are better than the rendering afforded us by the Authorized Version. The large number of words in italics will warn the English reader that the sense is hard to come at, and difficult to express, and that it would be unwise to found any doctrine upon the *English* words ; happily there is no temptation to do so.

The great truth expressed in these lines has by many been referred to the formation of the mystical body of our Lord Jesus. Of course, what is true of man, as man, is emphatically true of Him who is the representative man. The great Lord knows who belong to Christ ; his eye perceives the chosen members who shall yet be made one with the living person of the mystical Christ. Those of the elect who are as yet unborn, or unrenewed, are nevertheless written in the Lord's book. As the form of Eve grew up in silence and secrecy under the fashioning hand of the Maker, so at this hour is the Bride being fashioned for the Lord Jesus ; or, to change the figure,—a body is being prepared in which the life and glory of the indwelling Lord shall for ever be displayed. The Lord knoweth them that are his : he has a specially familiar acquaintance with the members of the body of Christ ; he sees their substance, unperfect though they be.

17. *"How precious also are thy thoughts unto me, O God ! "* He is not alarmed at the fact that God knows all about him ; on the contrary, he is comforted, and even feels himself to be enriched, as with a casket of precious jewels. That God

should think upon him is the believer's treasure and pleasure. He cries, " How costly, how valued are thy thoughts, how dear to me is thy perpetual attention! " He thinks upon God's thoughts with delight ; the more of them the better he is pleased. It is a joy worth worlds that the Lord should think upon us who are so poor and needy : it is a joy which fills our whole nature to think upon God ; returning love for love, thought for thought, after our poor fashion. *"How great is the sum of them!"* When we remember that God thought upon us from old eternity, continues to think upon us every moment, and will think of us when time shall be no more, we may well exclaim, " How great is the sum ! " Thoughts such as are natural to the Creator, the Preserver, the Redeemer, the Father, the Friend, are evermore flowing from the heart of the Lord. Thoughts of our pardon, renewal, upholding, supplying, educating, perfecting, and a thousand more kinds perpetually well up in the mind of the Most High. It should fill us with adoring wonder and reverent surprise that the infinite mind of God should turn so many thoughts towards us who are so insignificant and so unworthy ! What a contrast is all this to the notion of those who deny the existence of a personal, conscious God ! Imagine a world without a thinking, personal God ! Conceive of a grim providence of machinery !—a fatherhood of law ! Such philosophy is hard and cold. As well might a man pillow his head upon a razor edge as seek rest in such a fancy. But a God always thinking of us makes a happy world, a rich life, a heavenly hereafter.

18. *"If I should count them, they are more in number than the sand."* This figure shows the thoughts of God to be altogether innumerable ; for nothing can surpass in number the grains of sand which belt the main ocean and all the minor seas. The task of counting God's thoughts of love would be a never-ending one. If we should attempt the reckoning we must necessarily fail, for the infinite falls not within the line of our feeble intellect. Even could we count the sands on the sea-shore, we should not then be able to number God's thoughts, for they are " more in number than the sand." This is not the hyperbole of poetry, but the solid fact of inspired statement : God thinks upon us infinitely : there is a limit to the act of creation, but not to the might of divine love.

"When I am awake I am still with thee." Thy thoughts of love are so many that my mind never gets away from them, they surround me at all hours. I go to my bed, and God is my last thought ; and when I wake I find my mind still hovering about his palace-gates ; God is ever with me, and I am ever with him. This is life indeed. If during sleep my mind wanders away into dreams, yet it only wanders upon holy ground, and the moment I wake my heart is back with its Lord. The Psalmist does not say, " When I awake, I return to thee," but, " I am still with thee " ; as if his meditations were continuous, and his communion unbroken. Soon we shall lie down to sleep for the last time : God grant that when the trumpet of the archangel shall waken us we may find ourselves still with him.

19 Surely thou wilt slay the wicked, O God : depart from me therefore, ye bloody men.

20 For they speak against thee wickedly, *and* thine enemies take *thy name* in vain.

21 Do not I hate them, O LORD, that hate thee ? and am not I grieved with those that rise up against thee ?

22 I hate them with perfect hatred : I count them mine enemies.

23 Search me, O God, and know my heart : try me, and know my thoughts.

24 And see if *there be any* wicked way in me, and lead me in the way everlasting.

19. *"Surely thou wilt slay the wicked, O God."* There can be no doubt upon that head, for thou hast seen all their transgressions, which indeed have been done in thy presence ; and thou hast long enough endured their provocations, which have been so openly manifest before thee. Crimes committed before the face of the Judge are not likely to go unpunished. If the eye of God is grieved with the presence of evil, it is but natural to expect that he will remove the offending object. God who sees all evil will slay all evil. With earthly sovereigns sin may go unpunished for lack of evidence, or the law may be left without execution from lack of vigour in the judge ; but this cannot happen in the case of God, the living God. He beareth not the sword in vain. Such is his love of holiness and hatred of wrong,

that he will carry on war to the death with those whose hearts and lives are wicked. God will not always suffer his lovely creation to be defaced and defiled by the presence of wickedness : if anything is sure, this is sure, that he will ease him of his adversaries. *"Depart from me therefore, ye bloody men."* Men who delight in cruelty and war are not fit companions for those who walk with God. David chases the men of blood from his court, for he is weary of those of whom God is weary. He seems to say—If God will not let you live with him I will not have you live with me. You would destroy others, and therefore I want you not in my society. You will be destroyed yourselves, I desire you not in my service. Depart from me, for you depart from God. As we delight to have the holy God always near us, so would we eagerly desire to have wicked men removed as far as possible from us. We tremble in the society of the ungodly lest their doom should fall upon them suddenly, and we should see them lie dead at our feet. We do not wish to have our place of intercourse turned into gallows of execution, therefore let the condemned be removed out of our company.

20. *"For they speak against thee wickedly."* Why should I bear their company when their talk sickens me ? They vent their treasons and blasphemies as often as they please, doing so without the slightest excuse or provocation ; let them therefore begone, where they may find a more congenial associate than I can be. When men speak against God they will be sure to speak against us, if they find it serve their turn ; hence godless men are not the stuff out of which true friends can ever be made. God gave these men their tongues, and they turn against their Benefactor, wickedly, from sheer malice, and with great perverseness. *"And thine enemies take thy name in vain."* This is their sport : to insult Jehovah's glorious name is their amusement. To blaspheme the name of the Lord is a gratuitous wickedness in which there can be no pleasure, and from which there can be no profit. This is a sure mark of the " enemies " of the Lord, that they have the impudence to assail his honour, and treat his glory with irreverence. How can God do other than slay them ? How can we do other than withdraw from every sort of association with them ? What a wonder of sin it is that men should rail against so good a Being as the Lord our God ! The impudence of those who talk wickedly is a singular fact, and it is the more singular when we reflect that the Lord against whom they speak is all around them, and lays to heart every dishonour which they render to his holy name. We ought not to wonder that men slander and deride us, for they do the same with the Most High God.

21. *"Do not I hate them, O Lord, that hate thee ?"* He was a good hater, for he hated only those who hated good. Of this hatred he is not ashamed, but he sets it forth as a virtue to which he would have the Lord bear testimony. To love all men with benevolence is our duty ; but to love any wicked man with complacency would be a crime. To hate a man for his own sake, or for any evil done to us, would be wrong ; but to hate a man because he is the foe of all goodness and the enemy of all righteousness, is nothing more nor less than an obligation. The more we love God the more indignant shall we grow with those who refuse him their affection. " If any man love not the Lord Jesus Christ let him be Anathema Maranatha." Truly, " jealousy is cruel as the grave." The loyal subject must not be friendly to the traitor. *"And am not I grieved with those that rise up against thee ?"* He appeals to heaven that he took no pleasure in those who rebelled against the Lord ; but, on the contrary, he was made to mourn by a sight of their ill behaviour. Since God is everywhere, he knows our feelings towards the profane and ungodly, and he knows that so far from approving such characters the very sight of them is grievous to our eyes.

22. *"I hate them with perfect hatred."* He does not leave it a matter of question. He does not occupy a neutral position. His hatred to bad, vicious, blasphemous men is intense, complete, energetic. He is as whole-hearted in his hate of wickedness as in his love of goodness. *"I count them mine enemies."* He makes a personal matter of it. They may have done him no ill, but if they are doing despite to God, to his laws, and to the great principles of truth and righteousness, David proclaims war against them. Wickedness passes men into favour with unrighteous spirits ; but it excludes them from the communion of the just. We pull up the drawbridge and man the walls when a man of Belial goes by our castle. His character is a *casus belli ;* we cannot do otherwise than contend with those who contend with God.

23. *"Search me, O God, and know my heart."* David is no accomplice with traitors. He has disowned them in set form, and now he appeals to God that he

does not harbour a trace of fellowship with them. He will have God himself search him, and search him thoroughly, till every point of his being is known, and read, and understood ; for he is sure that even by such an investigation there will be found in him no complicity with wicked men. He challenges the fullest investigation, the innermost search : he had need be a true man who can put himself deliberately into such a crucible. Yet we may each one desire such searching ; for it would be a terrible calamity to us for sin to remain in our hearts unknown and undiscovered. *"Try me, and know my thoughts."* Exercise any and every test upon me. By fire and by water let me be examined. Read not alone the desires of my heart, but the fugitive thoughts of my head. Know with all-penetrating knowledge all that is or has been in the chambers of my mind. What a mercy that there is one being who can know us to perfection ! He is intimately at home with us. He is graciously inclined towards us, and is willing to bend his omniscience to serve the end of our sanctification. Let us pray as David did, and let us be as honest as he. We cannot hide our sin : salvation lies the other way, in a plain discovery of evil, and an effectual severance from it.

24. *"And see if there be any wicked way in me."* See whether there be in my heart, or in my life, any evil habit unknown to myself. If there be such an evil way, take me from it, take it from me. No matter how dear the wrong may have become, nor how deeply prejudiced I may have been in its favour, be pleased to deliver me therefrom altogether, effectually, and at once, that I may tolerate nothing which is contrary to thy mind. As I hate the wicked in their way, so would I hate every wicked way in myself. *"And lead me in the way everlasting."* If thou hast introduced me already to the good old way, be pleased to keep me in it, and conduct me further and further along it. It is a way which thou hast set up of old, it is based upon everlasting principles, and it is the way in which immortal spirits will gladly run for ever and ever. There will be no end to it world without end. It lasts for ever, and they who are in it last for ever. Conduct me into it, O Lord, and conduct me throughout the whole length of it. By thy providence, by thy word, by thy grace, and by thy Spirit, lead me evermore.

EXPLANATORY NOTES AND QUAINT SAYINGS.

Whole Psalm.—Aben Ezra observes, that this is the most glorious and excellent Psalm in all the book : a very excellent one it is ; but whether the most excellent, it is hard to say.—*John Gill.*

Whole Psalm.—There is one Psalm which it were well if Christians would do by it as Pythagoras by his Golden Precepts,—every morning and evening repeat it. It is David's appeal of a good conscience unto God, against the malicious suspicions and calumnies of men, in Psalm cxxxix.—*Samuel Annesley* (1620—1696), *in "The Morning Exercises."*

Whole Psalm.—This Psalm is one of the sublimest compositions in the world. How came a shepherd boy to conceive so sublime a theme, and to write in so sublime a strain ? Holy men of God spake as they were moved by the Holy Ghost. What themes are more sublime than the Divine attributes ? And which of these attributes is more sublime than Omnipresence ? Omniscience, spirituality, infinity, immutability and eternity are necessarily included in it.—*George Rogers.*

Whole Psalm.—Let the modern wits, after this, look upon the honest shepherds of Palestine as a company of *rude and unpolished clowns ;* let them, if they can, produce from profane authors thoughts that are more sublime, more delicate, or better turned ; not to mention the sound divinity and solid piety which are apparent under these expressions.—*Claude Fleury,* 1640—1723.

Whole Psalm.—Here the poet inverts his gaze, from the blaze of suns, to the strange atoms composing his own frame. He stands shuddering over the precipice of himself. Above is the All-encompassing Spirit, from whom the morning wings cannot save ; and below, at a deep distance, appears amid the branching forest of his animal frame, so fearfully and wonderfully made, the abyss of his spiritual existence, lying like a dark lake in the midst. How, between mystery and mystery his mind, his wonder, his very reason, seem to rock like a little boat between the sea and sky. But speedily does he regain his serenity; when he throws himself, with childlike haste and confidence, into the arms of that Fatherly Spirit, and murmurs in his bosom, " How precious also are thy thoughts unto *me*, O God; how great is the sum of them "; and looking up at last in his face, cries—" Search me, O Lord. I cannot search thee; I cannot search myself; I am overwhelmed by those dreadful depths; but search me as thou only canst; see if there be any wicked way in me, and lead me in the way everlasting."—*George Gilfillan* (1813—1878), *in "The Bards of the Bible."*

Whole Psalm.—The Psalm has an immediately practical aim, which is unfolded near the close. It is not an abstract description of the Divine attributes, with a mere indirect purpose in view. If God is such a being, if his vital agency reaches over all his creation, pervades all objects, illumines the deepest and darkest recesses; if his knowledge has no limits, piercing into the mysterious processes of creation, into the smallest and most elemental germs of life; if his eye can discern the still more subtle and recondite processes of mind, comprehending the half-formed conception, the germinating desire " afar off "; if, anterior to all finite existence, his predetermining decree went forth; if in those ancient records of eternity man's framework, with all its countless elements and organs, in all the ages of his duration, were inscribed—then for his servant, his worshipper on earth, two consequences follow, most practical and momentous : *first*, the ceasing to have or feel any complacency with the wicked, any sympathy with their evil ways, any communion with them as such; and, *secondly*, the earnest desire that God would search the Psalmist's soul, lest in its unsounded depths there might be some lurking iniquity, lest there might be, beyond the present jurisdiction of his conscience, some dark realm which the Omniscient eye only could explore.—*Bela B. Edwards* (1802–1852), *in H. C. Fish's "Masterpieces of Pulpit Eloquence."*

Whole Psalm.—

Searcher of hearts! to thee are known
The inmost secrets of my breast;
At home, abroad, in crowds, alone,
Thou mark'st my rising and my rest,
My thoughts far off, through every maze,
Source, stream, and issue—all my ways.

How from thy presence should I go,
Or whither from thy Spirit flee,
Since all above, around, below,
Exist in thine immensity ?
If up to heaven I take my way,
I meet thee in eternal day.

If in the grave I make my bed
With worms and dust, lo! thou art there!
If, on the wings of morning sped,
Beyond the ocean I repair,
I feel thine all-controlling will,
And thy right hand upholds me still.

" Let darkness hide me," if I say,
Darkness can no concealment be;
Night, on thy rising, shines like day;
Darkness and light are one with thee:
For thou mine embryo-form didst view,
Ere her own babe my mother knew.

In me thy workmanship display'd,
A miracle of power I stand :
Fearfully, wonderfully made,
And framed in secret by thine hand;
I lived, ere into being brought,
Through thine eternity of thought.

How precious are thy thoughts of peace,
O God, to me! how great the sum!
New every morn, they never cease;
They were, they are, and yet shall come,
In number and in compass more
Than ocean's sands or ocean's shore.

Search me, O God! and know my heart,
Try me, my inmost soul survey;
And warn thy servant to depart
From every false and evil way:
So shall thy truth my guidance be
To life and immortality.

James Montgomery.

Whole Psalm.—The Psalm may be thus summarized. Verse 1. *"O Lord, thou hast searched me, and known me."*—As though he said, " O Lord, thou art the heart-searching God, who perfectly knowest all the thoughts, counsels, studies, endeavours, and actions of all men, and therefore mine." Verse 2. *"Thou knowest my downsitting and mine uprising, thou understandest my thought afar off."*—As if he had said, " Thou knowest my rest and motion, and my plodding thoughts of both." Verse 3. *"Thou compassest my path and my lying down, and art acquainted with all my ways."*—As if he had said, " Thou fannest and winnowest me," that is, " Thou discussest and triest me to the utmost." Verse 4. *"For there is not a word in my tongue, but, lo, O Lord, thou knowest it altogether."*—As if he had said, "I cannot speak a word, though never so secret, obscure, or subtle, but thou knowest what, and why, and with what mind it was uttered." Verse 5. *" Thou hast beset me behind and before, and laid thine hand upon me."*—As if he had said, " Thou keepest me within the compass of thy knowledge, like a man that will not let his servant go out of his sight. I cannot break away from thee." Verse 6. *" Such knowledge is too wonderful for me ; it is high, I cannot attain unto it."*—As if he had said, " The knowledge of thy great and glorious majesty and infiniteness is utterly past all human comprehension." Verse 7. *" Whither shall I go from thy spirit ? or whither shall I flee from thy presence ? "*—As if he had said, " Whither can I flee from thee, whose essence, presence, and power is everywhere ? " Verse 8. *"If I ascend up into heaven, thou art there : if I make my bed in hell, behold, thou art there."*—As if he had said, " There is no height above thee, there is no depth below thee." Verse 9. *"If I take the wings of the morning, and dwell in the uttermost parts of the sea."*—As if he had said, " If I had wings to fly as swift as the morning light, from the east to the west, that I could in a moment get to the furthest parts of the world." Verse 10. *"Even there shall thy hand lead me, and thy right hand shall hold me."*—As if he had said, " Thence shall thy hand lead me back, and hold me fast like a fugitive." Verse 11. *"If I say, Surely the darkness shall cover me ; even the night shall be light about me."*—As if he had said, " Though darkness hinders man's sight, it doth not thine." In a word, look which way you will, there is no hiding-place from God. " For his eyes are upon the ways of man, and he seeth all his goings. There is no darkness nor shadow of death, where the workers of iniquity may hide themselves " : Job xxxiv. 21, 22. Therefore, Christians, do nothing but what you are willing God should take notice of ; and judge in yourselves whether this be not the way to have a good and quiet conscience.—*Samuel Annesley.*

Whole Psalm.—In this Aramaizing Psalm what the preceding Psalm says in verse 6 comes to be carried into effect, viz. : *"For Jahve is exalted and he seeth the lowly, and the proud he knoweth from afar."* This Psalm has manifold points of contact with its predecessor.—*Franz Delitzsch.*

" To the Chief Musician."—As a later writer could have no motive for prefixing the title, " To the Chief Musician," it affords an incidental proof of antiquity and genuineness.—*Joseph Addison Alexander.*

"A Psalm of David."—How any critic can assign this Psalm to other than David I cannot understand. Every line, every thought, every turn of expression and transition, is his, and his only. As for the arguments drawn from the two Chaldaisms which occur, this is really nugatory. These Chaldaisms consist merely in the substitution of one letter for another, very like it in shape, and easily to be mistaken by a transcriber, particularly by one who had been used to the Chaldee idiom ; but the moral arguments for David's authorship are so strong as to overwhelm any such verbal, or rather *literal* criticism, were even the objections more formidable than they actually are.—*John Jebb.*

Verse 1.—*"O Lord, thou hast searched me, and known (me)."* There is no *" me "* after " known " in the Hebrew ; therefore it is better to take the object after " known " in a wider sense. The omission is intentional, that the believing heart of all who use this Psalm may supply the ellipsis. Thou hast known and knowest *all that concerns the matter in question*, as well whether I and mine are guilty or innocent

(Ps. xliv. 21) ; also my exact circumstances, my needs, my sorrows, and the precise time when to relieve me.—*A. R. Fausset.*

Verse 1.—*"O LORD, thou hast searched me, and known me."* The godly may sometimes be so overclouded with calumnies and reproaches as not to be able to find a way to clear themselves before men, but must content and comfort themselves with the testimony of a good conscience and with God's approbation of their integrity, as here David doth.—*David Dickson.*

Verse 1.—*"O LORD, thou hast searched me, and known me."* David here lays down the great doctrine, that God has a perfect knowledge of us, First, *in the way of an address to God :* he saith it to him, acknowledging it to him, and giving him the glory of it. Divine truths look full as well when they are prayed over as when they are preached over : and much better than when they are disputed over. When we speak of God to him himself, we find ourselves concerned to speak with the utmost degree both of sincerity and reverence, which will be likely to make the impressions the deeper. Secondly, he lays it down *in a way of application to himself :* not thou hast known all, but " thou hast known *me* " ; that is it which I am most concerned to believe, and which it will be most profitable for me to consider. Then we know things for our good when we know them for ourselves. Job v. 27. . . . David was a king, and " the hearts of kings are unsearchable " to their subjects (Prov. xxv. 3), but they are not so to their sovereign.—*Matthew Henry.*

Verse 1.—*"O LORD, thou hast searched me."* I would have you observe how thoroughly in the very first verse he brings home the truth to his own heart and his own conscience : " O LORD, thou hast searched *me.*" He does not slur it over as a general truth, in which such numbers shared that he might hope to escape or evade its solemn appeal to himself ; but it is, " Thou hast searched *me.*"—*Barton Bouchier.*

Verse 1.—*"Searched."* The Hebrew word originally means *to dig,* and is applied to the search for precious metals (Job xxviii. 3), but metaphorically to a moral inquisition into guilt.—*Joseph Addison Alexander.*

Verses 1—5.—God knows everything that passes in our inmost souls better than we do ourselves : he reads our most secret thoughts : all the cogitations of our hearts pass in review before him ; and he is as perfectly and entirely employed in the scrutiny of the thoughts and actions of an individual, as in the regulation of the most important concerns of the universe. This is what we cannot comprehend ; but it is what, according to the light of reason, must be true, and, according to revelation, is indeed true. God can do nothing imperfectly ; and we may form some idea of his superintending knowledge, by conceiving what is indeed the truth, that all the powers of the Godhead are employed, and solely employed, in the observation and examination of the conduct of one individual. I say, this is indeed the case, because all the powers of the Godhead are employed upon the least as well as upon the greatest concerns of the universe ; and the whole mind and power of the Creator are as exclusively employed upon the formation of a grub as of a world. God knows everything perfectly, and he knows everything perfectly at once. This, to a human understanding, would breed confusion ; but there can be no confusion in the Divine understanding, because confusion arises from imperfection. Thus God, without confusion, beholds as distinctly the actions of every man, as if that man were the only created being, and the Godhead were solely employed in observing him. Let this thought fill your mind with awe and with remorse.—*Henry Kirke White,* 1785—1806.

Verses 1—12.—

O Lord, in me there lieth nought
But to thy search revealed lies ;
For when I sit
Thou markest it ;
No less thou notest when I rise ;
Yea, closest closet of my thought
Hath open windows to thine eyes.

Thou walkest with me when I walk,
When to my bed for rest I go,
I find thee there,
And everywhere :
Not youngest thought in me doth grow,
No, not one word I cast to talk
But, yet unuttered, thou dost know.

If forth I march, thou goest before;
If back I turn, thou com'st behind:
        So forth nor back
        Thy guard I lack;
Nay, on me, too, thy hand I find.
Well, I thy wisdom may adore,
But never reach with earthy mind.

To shun thy notice, leave thine eye,
    O whither might I take my way?
        To starry sphere?
        Thy throne is there.
    To dead men's undelightsome stay?
There is thy walk, and there to lie
Unknown, in vain I should assay.

O sun, whom light nor flight can match!
Suppose thy lightful flightful wings
        Thou lend to me,
        And I could flee
As far as thee the evening brings:
Ev'n led to west he would me catch,
    Nor should I lurk with western things.

Do thou thy best, O secret night,
    In sable veil to cover me:
        Thy sable veil
        Shall vainly fail:
With day unmasked my night shall be;
For night is day, and darkness light,
    O Father of all lights, to thee.

Sir Philip Sidney, 1554—1586.

Verse 2.—"Thou." David makes the personal pronoun the very frontispiece of the verse, and so says expressly and distinctly to Jehovah, *"Thou* knowest;" thus marking the difference between God and all others, as though he said, "Thou, and thou alone, O God, in all the universe, knowest altogether all that can be known concerning me, even to my inmost thought, as well as outward act."—*Martin Geier.*

Verse 2.—"Thou knowest my downsitting and mine uprising." Does God care? *Is* he our Friend? Even in such little matters as these, does he watch over us "to do us good"? . . . When we "sit down" he sees; when we rise up he is there. Not an action is lost or a thought overlooked. No wonder that, as these tiny miracles of care are related by David, he adds the words, *"Such knowledge is too wonderful for me; it is high, I cannot attain unto it."* We get accustomed to the thought that God made the sun and sky, the "moon and stars which he hath ordained," and we bow to the fact that they are "the work of his fingers." Let us go further! The *"coming in"* and *"going out"* of the Christian is mentioned several times in Scripture as though it were very important. So much hinges on these little words. "David went out and came in before the people. And David behaved himself wisely in all his ways; and the Lord was with him": 1 Sam. xviii. 13, 14. "The Lord shall preserve thy going out and thy coming in from this time forth, and even for evermore": Ps. cxxi. 8. David was given both *preservation* and *wisdom* in his "goings out" and "comings in." Perhaps the latter was both cause and effect of the first. It was needed, for many eyes were upon him, and many eyes are upon us: are they not? Perhaps more than we think.—*Lady Hope, in "Between Times,"* 1884.

Verse 2.—"Downsitting and uprising." *"Uprising"* following *"downsitting"* is in the order of right sequence; for action ought to follow meditation. Jacob saw the angels ascending to God before they descended to service among mortals. Hence we are taught first to join ourselves to God by meditation, and afterwards to repair to the aid of our fellows.—*Thomas Le Blanc.*

Verse 2.—"Uprising" may respect either rising *from bed*, when the Lord knows whether the heart is still with him (ver. 18); what sense is had of the Divine protection and sustentation, and what thankfulness there is for the mercies of the night past; and whether the voice of prayer and praise is directed to him in the morning, as it should be (Ps. iii. 5; v. 3); or else rising *from the table*, when the Lord knows whether a man's table has been his snare, and with what thankfulness he rises from it for the favours he has received.   The Targum interprets this of rising up to go to war ; which David did, in the name and strength, and by the direction of the Lord.—*John Gill.*

Verse 2.—*"Thou understandest my thought afar off."*   *"My thought :"* that is, every thought, though innumerable thoughts pass through me in a day.   The divine knowledge reaches to their source and fountain, before they are our thoughts.   If the Lord knows them before their existence, before they can be properly called ours, much more doth he know them when they actually spring up in us ; he knows the tendency of them, where the bird will alight when it is in flight ; he knows them exactly ; he is therefore called a " discerner " or criticiser of the heart : Heb. iv. 2.—*Stephen Charnock.*

Verse 2.—*"Thou understandest my thought afar off."*   Not that God is at a distance from our thoughts ; but he understands them while they are far off from us, from our knowledge, while they are potential, as gardeners know what weeds such ground will bring forth, when nothing appears.   Deut. xxxi. 21.   " I know their imagination which they go about, even now, before I have brought them into the land which I sware " : God knew their thoughts before they came into Canaan, what they would be there.   And how can it be, but that God should know all our thoughts, seeing he made the heart, and it is in his hand (Prov. xxi. 1), seeing, " we live, and move, and have our being " in God (Acts xvii. 28) ; seeing he is through us all, and in us all (Eph. iv. 6).   Look well to your hearts, thoughts, risings, whatever comes into your mind ; let no secret sins, or corruptions, lodge there ; think not to conceal anything from the eye of God.—*William Greenhill.*

Verse 2.—*"Thou understandest my thought afar off."*   Though my thoughts be never so foreign and distant from one another, thou understandest the chain of them, and canst make out their connexion, when so many of them slip my notice that I myself cannot.—*Matthew Henry.*

Verse 2.—*"My thought."*   The רֵעַ, *rea*, which we have rendered *"thought,"* signifies also a *friend* or *companion*, on which account some read—*thou knowest what is nearest me afar off*, a meaning more to the point than any other, if it could be supported by example.   The reference would then be very appropriately to the fact that the most distant objects are contemplated as near by God.   Some for *"afar off"* read *beforehand*, in which signification the Hebrew word is elsewhere taken ; as if he had said, O Lord, every thought which I conceive in my heart is already known to thee beforehand.—*John Calvin.*

Verse 2.—*"Thought."*   In all affliction, in all business, a man's best comfort is this, that all he does and even all he thinks, God knows.   In the Septuagint we read διαλογισμοὺς, that is, " reasonings."   God knows all our inner ratiocination, all the dialogues, all the colloquies of the soul with itself.—*Thomas Le Blanc.*

Verse 2.—*"Thou understandest my thought."*   Before men we stand as opaque bee-hives.   They can see the thoughts go in and out of us, but what work they do inside of a man they cannot tell.   Before God we are as glass bee-hives, and all that our thoughts are doing within us he perfectly sees and understands.—*Henry Ward Beecher.*

Verse 2.—*"Thou understandest my thought afar off."*

> Man may not see thee do an impious deed ;
> But God thy very inmost thought can read."
>
> *Plutarch.*

Verse 2.—*"Afar off."*   This expression is, as in Ps. cxxxviii. 6, to be understood as contradicting the delusion (Job xxii. 12—14) that God's dwelling in heaven prevents him from observing mundane things.—*Lange's Commentary.*

Verse 2.—*"Afar off."*   Both in distance, however far off a man may seek to hide his thoughts from God ; and in time, for God knows the human thought before man conceives it in his heart, in his eternal prescience.   The Egyptians called God the " eye of the world."—*Thomas Le Blanc.*

Verses 2—4.—Do not fancy that your demeanour, posture, dress, or deportment are not under God's providence.   You deceive yourself.   Do not think that your thoughts pass free from inspection.   The Lord understands them afar off.   Think not that your words are dissipated in the air before God can hear.   Oh, no !   He knows them even when still upon your tongue.   Do not think that your ways are so private and concealed that there is none to know or censure them.   You mistake.   God knows all your ways.—*Johann David Frisch*, 1731.

Verse 3.—*"Thou compassest my path and my lying down,"* etc. The words that I have read unto you, seem to be a metaphor, taken from soldiers surrounding the ways with an ambush, or placing scouts and spies in every corner, to discover the enemy in his march ; *"Thou compassest my path" :* thou hast (as it were) thy spies over me, wheresoever I go. By *"path"* is meant the outward actions and carriage of his ordinary conversation. By *"lying down"* is signified to us the private and close actions of his life ; such as were attended only by darkness and solitude. In Ps. xxxvi. verse 4, it is said of the wicked that " he deviseth mischief upon his bed," to denote not only his perverse diligence, but also his secresy in it : and God is said to " hide his children in the secret of his pavilion," so that these places of rest and lying down are designed for secresy and withdrawing. When a man retires into his chamber, he does in a manner, for a while, shut himself out of the world. And that this is the fine sense of that expression of *lying down* appears from the next words, *"Thou art acquainted with all my ways"*; where he collects in one word what he had before said in two ; or, it may come in by way of entrance and deduction, from the former. As if he should say, Thou knowest what I do in my ordinary converse with men, and also how I behave myself when I am retired from them ; therefore thou knowest *all* my actions, since a man's actions may be reduced either to his public or private deportment. By the other expression of *"my ways"* is here meant the total of a man's behaviour before God, whether in thoughts, words, or deeds, as is manifest by comparing this with other verses.—*Robert South.*

Verse 3.—*"Thou compassest my path."*   This is a metaphor either from huntsmen watching all the motions and lurking-places of wild beasts, that they may catch them ; or from soldiers besieging their enemies in a city, and setting round about them.—*Matthew Pool.*

Verse 3.—*"Thou compassest,"* or *fannest,* or *winnowest, "my path" ;* that is, discussest or triest out to the utmost, even tracing the footsteps, as the Greek signifieth. Compare Job xxxi. 4.—*Henry Ainsworth.*

Verse 3.—*"Thou art acquainted with all my ways."*   God takes notice of every step we take, every right step, and every by-step. He knows what rule we walk by, what end we walk toward, what company we walk with.—*Religious Tract Society's Commentary.*

Verse 3.—*"Art acquainted,"* as by most familiar intercourse, as if thou hadst always lived with me [Hebrew] and thus become entirely familiar with my ways.—*Henry Cowles.*

Verse 3.—The Psalmist mentions four modes of human existence ; *stationis, sessionis, itionis, cubationis ;* because man never stayeth long in one mood, but in every change the eyes of the Lord cease not to watch him.—*Geier.*

Verse 4.—*"For there is not a word in my tongue,"* etc. The words admit a double meaning. Accordingly some understand them to imply that God knows what we are about to say before the words are formed on our tongue ; others, that though we speak not a word, and try by silence to conceal our secret intentions, we cannot elude his notice. Either rendering amounts to the same thing, and it is of no consequence which we adopt. The idea meant to be conveyed is, that while the tongue is the index of thought to man, being the great medium of communication, God, who knows the heart, is independent of words. And use is made of the demonstrative particle *lo !* to indicate emphatically that the innermost recesses of our spirit stand present to his view.—*John Calvin.*

Verse 4.—*"For there is not a word in my tongue,"* etc. How needful it is to set a watch before the doors of our mouth, to hold that unruly member of ours, the tongue, as with bit and bridle. Some of you feel at times that you can scarcely say a word, and the less you say the better. Well, it may be as well ; for great talkers are almost sure to make slips with their tongue. It may be a good thing that you cannot speak much ; for in the multitude of words there lacketh not sin. Wherever you go, what light, vain, and foolish conversations you hear ! I am glad not to be thrown into circumstances where I can hear it. But with you it may be different. You may often repent of speaking, you will rarely repent of silence. How soon angry words are spoken ! How soon foolish expressions drop from the mouth ! The Lord knows it all, marks it all, and did you carry about with you a more solemn recollection of it you would be more watchful than you are.—*Joseph C. Philpot.*

Verse 4.—*"When there is not a word in my tongue, O* LORD, *thou knowest all ;"* so some read it ; for thoughts are words to God.—*Matthew Henry.*

Verse 4.—*"Thou knowest it."* The gods know what passes in our minds without the aid of eyes, ears, or tongues ; on which divine omniscience is founded the feeling of men that, when they wish in silence, or offer up a prayer for anything, the gods hear them.—*Cicero.*

Verse 5.—*"Thou hast beset me behind and before,"* etc. There is here an insensible transition from God's omniscience to his omnipresence, out of which the Scriptures represent it as arising. *"Behind and before,"* i.e. on all sides. The idea of *above* and *below* is suggested by the last clause. *"Beset,"* besiege, hem in, or closely surround. *"Thy hand,"* or the palm of thy hand, as the Hebrew word strictly denotes.—*Joseph Addison Alexander.*

Verse 5.—*"Thou hast beset me behind and before."* What would you say if, wherever you turned, whatever you were doing, whatever thinking, whether in public or private, with a confidential friend telling your secrets, or alone planning them—if, I say, you saw an eye constantly fixed on you, from whose watching, though you strove ever so much, you could never escape. . . . that could perceive your every thought ? The supposition is awful enough. There is such an Eye.—*De Vere.*

Verse 5.—*"Thou hast beset me behind and before."* One who finds the way blocked up turns back ; but David found himself hedged in *behind* as well as *before.* —*John Calvin.*

Verse 5.—*"Thou hast . . . . laid thine hand upon me."* As by an arrest ; so that I am thy prisoner, and cannot stir a foot from thee.—*John Trapp.*

Verse 5.—*"And laid thine hand upon me."* To make of me one acceptable to thyself. To rule me, to lead me, to uphold me, to protect me ; to restore me ; in my growth, in my walk, in my failures, in my affliction, in my despair.—*Thomas Le Blanc.*

Verse 6.—*"Such knowledge is too wonderful for me,"* etc. When we are about to look upon God's perfections, we should observe our own imperfections, and thereby learn to be the more modest in our searching of God's unsearchable perfection : *"Such knowledge,"* saith David, *"is too high for me, I cannot attain unto it."* Then do we see most of God, when we see him incomprehensible, and do see ourselves swallowed up in the thoughts of his perfection, and are forced to fall in admiration of God, as here. *"Such knowledge is too wonderful for me ; it is high, I cannot attain unto it."*—*David Dickson.*

Verse 6.—*"Such knowledge is too wonderful for me."* Compared with our stinted knowledge, how amazing is the knowledge of God ! As he made all things, he must be intimately acquainted, not only with their properties, but with their every essence. His eye, at the same instant, surveys all the works of his immeasurable creation. He observes, not only the complicated system of the universe, but the slightest motion of the most microscopic insect ;—not only the sublimest conception of angels, but the meanest propensity of the most worthless of his creatures. At this moment he is listening to the praises breathed by grateful hearts in distant worlds, and reading every grovelling thought which passes through the polluted minds of the fallen race of Adam. . . . At one view, he surveys the past, the present, and the future. No inattention prevents him from observing ; no defect of memory or of judgment obscures his comprehension. In his remembrance are stored not only the transactions of this world, but of all the worlds in the universe ; not only the events of the six thousand years which have passed since the earth was created, but of a duration without beginning. Nay, things to come, extending to a duration without end, are also before him. An eternity past and an eternity to come are, at the same moment, in his eye ; and with that eternal eye he surveys infinity. How amazing ! How inconceivable !—*Henry Duncan* (1774—1846), *in "Sacred Philosophy of the Seasons."*

Verse 6.—*" Such knowledge is too wonderful for me."* There is a mystery about the Divine Omnipresence, which we do not learn to solve, after years of meditation. As God is a simple spirit, without dimensions, parts, or susceptibility of division, he is equally, that is, fully, present at all times in all places. At any given moment he is not present partly here and partly in the utmost skirt of the furthest system which revolves about the dimmest telescopic star, as if like a galaxy of perfection he stretched a sublime magnificence through universal space, which admitted of separation and partition ; but he is present, with the totality of his glorious properties in every point of space. This results undeniably from the simple spirituality of the Great Supreme. All that God is in one place he is in all places. All there is of God is in every place. Indeed, his presence has no dependence on space or matter. His attribute of essential presence were the same if universal matter were blotted out. Only by a figure can God be said to be in the universe ; for the universe is comprehended by him. All the boundless glory of the Godhead is essentially present at every spot in his creation, however various may be the manifestations of this glory at different times and places.

Here we have a case which ought to instruct and sober those, who, in their shallow philosophy, demand a religion without mystery. It would be a religion without God ; for "who by searching can find out God?"—*James W. Alexander, in "The [American] National Preacher,"* 1860.

Verse 7.—*"Whither shall I go from thy spirit?"* By the *"spirit of God"* we are not here, as in several other parts of Scripture, to conceive of his power merely, but his understanding and knowledge. In man the spirit is the seat of intelligence, and so it is here in reference to God, as is plain from the second part of the sentence, where by *"the face of God"* is meant his knowledge or inspection.—*John Calvin.*

Verse 7.—*"Whither shall I go from thy spirit?"* That is, either from thee, who art a spirit, and so canst pierce and penetrate me ; be as truly and essentially in the very bowels and marrow of my soul, as my soul is intimately and essentially in my body : *"from thy spirit;"* that is, from thy knowledge and thy power ; thy knowledge to detect and observe me, thy power to uphold or crush me.—*Ezekiel Hopkins,* 1633—1690.

Verse 7.—We may elude the vigilance of a human enemy and place ourselves beyond his reach. God fills all space—there is not a spot in which his piercing eye is not on us, and his uplifted hand cannot find us out. Man must strike soon if he would strike at all ; for opportunities pass away from him, and his victim may escape his vengeance by death. There is no passing of opportunity with God, and it is this which makes his longsuffering a solemn thing. God can wait, for he has a whole eternity before him in which he may strike. "All things are open and naked to him with whom we have to do."—*Frederick William Robertson,* 1816—1853.

Verse 7.—*"Whither shall I go,"* etc. A heathen philosopher once asked, "Where is God?" The Christian answered, "Let me first ask you, Where is he not?"—*John Arrowsmith,* 1602—1659.

Verse 7.—*"Whither shall I flee from thy presence?"* That exile would be strange that could separate us from God. I speak not of those poor and common comforts, that in all lands and coasts it is his sun that shines, his elements of earth or water that bear us, his air we breathe ; but of that special privilege, that his gracious presence is ever with us ; that no sea is so broad as to divide us from his favour ; that wheresoever we feed, he is our host ; wheresoever we rest, the wings of his blessed providence are stretched over us. Let my soul be sure of this, though the whole world be traitors to me.—*Thomas Adams.*

Verse 7.—*"Whither shall I flee?"* etc. Surely no whither : they that attempt it, do but as the fish which swimmeth to the length of the line, with a hook in the mouth.—*John Trapp.*

Verse 7.—*"Thy presence."* The presence of God's glory is in heaven ; the presence of his power on earth ; the presence of his justice in hell ; and the presence of his grace with his people. If he deny us his powerful presence, we fall into nothing ; if he deny us his gracious presence, we fall into sin ; if he deny us his merciful presence, we fall into hell.—*John Mason.*

Verse 7.—*"Thy presence."* The celebrated Linnæus testified in his conversation, writings, and actions, the greatest sense of God's presence. So strongly indeed was he impressed with the idea, that he wrote over the door of his library : *"Innocuè vivite, Numen adest—Live innocently : God is present."*—*George Seaton Bowes, in "Information and Illustration,"* 1884.

Verses 7—11.—You will never be neglected by the Deity, though you were so small as to sink into the depths of the earth, or so lofty as to fly up to heaven ; but you will suffer from the gods the punishment due to you, whether you abide here, or depart to Hades, or are carried to a place still more wild than these.—*Plato.*

Verses 7—12.—The Psalm was not written by a Pantheist. The Psalmist speaks of God as a Person everywhere present in creation, yet distinct from creation. In these verses he says, "*Thy spirit . . . thy* presence *. . . thou* art there *. . . thy* hand *. . . thy* right hand *. . .* darkness hideth not from *thee.*" God is everywhere, but he is not everything.—*William Jones, in "A Homiletic Commentary on the Book of Psalms,"* 1879.

Verse 8.—"*If I make my bed.*" Properly, " If I strew or spread my couch." If I should seek that as a place to lie down.—*Albert Barnes.*

Verse 8.—"*Hell* " in some places in Scripture signifies the lower parts of the earth, without relation to punishment : "*If I ascend up into heaven, thou art there ; if I make my bed in hell, behold, thou art there.*" By "*heaven*" he means the upper region of the world, without any respect to the state of blessedness ; and "*hell*" is the most opposite and remote in distance, without respect to misery. As if he had said, Let me go whither I will, thy presence finds me out.—*Joseph Caryl.*

Verse 8.—"*Thou art there.*" Or, more emphatically and impressively in the original, "*Thou !*" That is, the Psalmist imagines himself in the highest heaven, or in the deepest abodes of the dead,—and lo ! God is there also ; he has not gone from *him !* he is still in the presence of the same God !—*Albert Barnes.*

Verse 8.—"*Thou art there.*" This is not meant of his knowledge, for that the Psalmist had spoken of before : verses 2, 3, " Thou understandest my thought afar off : thou art acquainted with all my ways." Besides, " thou art there " not thy wisdom or knowledge, but *thou,* thy essence, not only thy virtue. For having before spoken of his omniscience, he proves that such knowledge could not be in God unless he were present in his essence in all places, so as to be excluded from none. He fills the depths of hell, the extension of the earth, and the heights of the heavens. When the Scripture mentions the power of God only, it expresseth it by hand or arm ; but when it mentions the spirit of God, and doth not intend the third person of the Trinity, it signifies the nature and essence of God ; and so here, when he saith, "*Whither shall I go from thy spirit ?* " he adds exegetically, "*whither shall I flee from thy presence?*" or Hebrew, "*face*" *;* and the face of God in Scripture signifies the essence of God : Exod. xxxiii. 20, 23, " Thou canst not see my face," and " my face shall not be seen"; the effects of his power, wisdom, providence, are seen, which are his back-parts, but not his face. The effects of his power and wisdom are seen in the world, but his essence is invisible, and this the Psalmist elegantly expresseth.—*Stephen Charnock.*

Verse 9.—"*The wings of the morning,*" is an elegant metaphor ; and by them we may conjecture is meant the sunbeams, called "*wings*" because of their swift and speedy motion, making their passage so sudden and instantaneous, as that they do prevent the observation of the eye ; called "*the wings of the morning*" because the dawn of the morning comes flying in upon these wings of the sun, and brings light along with it ; and, by beating and fanning of these wings, scatters the darkness before it. " Now," saith the Psalmist, " if I could pluck these wings of the morning," the sunbeams, if I could imp [graft] my own shoulders with them, if I should fly as far and as swift as light, even in an instant, to the uttermost parts of the sea ; yea, if in my flight I should spy out some solitary rock, so formidable and dismal as if we might almost call in question whether ever a Providence had been there, if I could pitch there on the top of it, where never anything had made its abode, but coldness, thunders, and tempests ; yet there shall thy hand lead me, and thy right hand shall hold me."—*Ezekiel Hopkins.*

Verse 9.—"*The wings of the morning.*" This figure to a Western is not a little obscure. For my part, I cannot doubt that we are to understand certain beautiful light clouds as thus poetically described. I have observed invariably, that in the late spring-time, in summer, and yet more especially in the autumn, white clouds are to be seen in Palestine. They only occur at the earliest hours of morning, just previous to and at the time of sunrise. It is the total absence of clouds at all other parts of the day, except during the short period of the winter rains, that lends such striking solemnity and force to those descriptions of the Second Advent where our Lord is represented as coming in the clouds. This feature of his majesty loses all its meaning in lands like ours, in which clouds are of such common occurrence that they are rarely absent from the sky. The morning clouds of summer and autumn are always of a brilliant silvery white, save at such times as they are dyed with the delicate opal tints of dawn. They hang low upon the mountains of Judah, and produce effects of undescribable beauty, as they float far down in the valleys, or rise to wrap themselves around the summit of the hills. In almost every instance, by about seven o'clock the heat has dissipated these fleecy clouds, and to the vivid Eastern imagination morn has folded her outstretched wings.— *James Neil.*

Verse 9.—"*If I take the wings of the morning.*" The point of comparison appears to be the incalculable velocity of light.—*Joseph Addison Alexander.*

Verses 9, 10.—When we think that we fly from God, in running out of one place into another, we do but run from one hand to the other ; for there is no place where God is not, and whithersoever a rebellious sinner doth run, the hand of God will meet with him to cross him, and hinder his hoped-for good success, although he securely prophesieth never so much good unto himself in his journey. What! had Jonah offended the winds or the waters, that they bear him such enmity ? The winds and the waters and all God's creatures are wont to take God's part against Jonah, or any rebellious sinner. For though God in the beginning gave power to man over all creatures to rule them, yet when man sins, God giveth power and strength to his creatures to rule and bridle man. Therefore even he that now was lord over the waters, now the waters are lord over him.—*Henry Smith.*

Verses 9, 10.—

> Should fate command me to the farthest verge
> Of the green earth, to distant barbarous climes,
> Rivers unknown to song ; where first the sun
> Gilds Indian mountains, or his setting beam
> Flames on the Atlantic isles ; 'tis nought to me :
> Since GOD is ever present, ever felt,
> In the void waste as in the city full ;
> And where he vital breathes, there must be joy,
> When e'en at last the solemn hour shall come,
> And wing my mystic flight to future worlds,
> I cheerful will obey ; there with new powers,
> Will rising wonders sing : I cannot go
> Where universal love smiles not around,
> Sustaining all yon orbs, and all their sons :
> From seeming evil still deducing good,
> And better thence again, and better still,
> In infinite progression.
>
> *James Thomson, 1700—1748.*

Verse 11.—"*If I say, Surely the darkness shall cover me,*" etc. The foulest enormities of human conduct have always striven to cover themselves with the shroud of night. The thief, the counterfeiter, the assassin, the robber, the murderer, and the seducer, feel comparatively safe in the midnight darkness, because no human eye can scrutinize their actions. But what if it should turn out that sable night, to speak paradoxically, is an unerring photographist ! What if wicked men, as they open their eyes from the sleep of death, in another world, should find the universe hung round with faithful pictures of their earthly enormities, which they had supposed for ever lost in the oblivion of night ! What scenes for them to gaze at for ever ! They may now, indeed, smile incredulously at such a suggestion ; but the disclosures of chemistry may well make them tremble. Analogy does make it a scientific probability that every action of man, however deep the darkness in which it was performed, has imprinted its image on nature, and that there may be tests which shall draw it into daylight, and make it permanent so long as materialism endures.—*Edward Hitchcock, in "The Religion of Geology,"* 1851.

Verse 12.—"*The darkness hideth not from thee.*" Though the place where we sin be to men as dark as Egypt, yet to God it is as light as Goshen.—*William Secker.*

Verse 13.—"*Thou hast possessed my reins.*" From the sensitiveness to pain of this part of the body, it was regarded by the Hebrews as the seat of sensation and feeling, as also of desire and longing (Ps. lxxii. 21 ; Job xvi. 13 ; xix. 27). It is sometimes used of the inner nature generally (Ps. xvi. 7 ; Jer. xx. 12), and specially of the judgment or direction of reason (Jer. xi. 20 ; xii. 2).—*William Lindsay Alexander, in Kitto's Cyclopædia.*

Verse 13.—"*Thou hast possessed my reins.*" The *reins* are made specially prominent in order to mark them, the seat of the tenderest, most secret emotions, as the work of him who trieth the heart and the reins.—*Franz Delitzsch.*

Verse 13.—"*Thou hast covered me in my mother's womb.*" The word here rendered *cover* means properly to interweave; to weave; to knit together, and the literal translation would be, "Thou hast *woven* me in my mother's womb," meaning that God had put his parts together, as one who weaves cloth, or who makes a basket. So it is rendered by De Wette and by Gesenius (*Lex.*). The original word has however, also the idea of protecting, as in a booth or hut, woven or knit together, —to wit, of boughs and branches. The former signification best suits the connection; and then the sense would be, that as God had made him—as he had formed his members, and united them in a bodily frame and form before he was born— he must be able to understand all his thoughts and feelings. As he was not concealed from God before he saw the light, so he could not be anywhere.—*Albert Barnes.*

Verse 14.—"*I will praise thee,*" etc. All God's works are admirable, man wonderfully wonderful. "Marvellous are thy works; and that my soul knoweth right well." What infers he on all this? Therefore "*I will praise thee.*" If we will not praise him that made us, will he not repent that he made us? Oh that we knew what the saints do in heaven, and how the sweetness of that doth swallow up all earthly pleasures! They sing honour and glory to the Lord. Why? Because he hath created all things: Rev. iv. 11. When we behold an exquisite piece of work, we presently enquire after him that made it, purposely to commend his skill: and there is no greater disgrace to an artist, than having perfected a famous work, to find it neglected, no man minding it, or so much as casting an eye upon it. All the works of God are considerable, and man is bound to this contemplation. "When I consider the heavens," etc., I say, "What is man?" Ps. viii. 3, 4. He admires the heavens, but his admiration reflects upon man. *Quis homo?* There is no workman but would have his instruments used, and used to that purpose for which they were made . . . . Man is set like a little world in the midst of the great, to glorify God; this is the scope and end of his creation.—*Thomas Adams.*

Verse 14.—"*I am fearfully and wonderfully made.*" The term "*fearful*" is sometimes to be taken subjectively, for our being possessed of fear. In this sense it signifies the same as timid. Thus the prophet was directed to say to them that were of a "fearful heart, be strong." At other times it is taken objectively, for that property in an object the contemplation of which excites fear in the beholder. Thus it is said of God that he is "fearful in praises," and that it is "a fearful thing to fall into the hands of the living God." In this sense it is manifestly to be understood in the passage now under consideration. The human frame is so admirably constructed, so delicately combined, and so much in danger of being dissolved by innumerable causes, that the more we think of it the more we tremble, and wonder at our own continued existence.

> "How poor, how rich, how abject, how august,
> How complicate, how wonderful is man!
> How passing wonder he who made him such,
> Who mingled in our make such strange extremes
> Of different natures, marvellously mixed!
> Helpless immortal, insect infinite,
> A worm, a god—I tremble at myself!"

To do justice to the subject, it would be ncessary to be well acquainted with anatomy. I have no doubt that a thorough examination of that "substance which God hath curiously wrought" (verse 15), would furnish abundant evidence of the justness of the Psalmist's words; but even those things which are manifest to common observation may be sufficient for this purpose. In general it is observable that the human frame abounds with avenues at which enter every thing conducive to preservation and comfort, and every thing that can excite alarm. Perhaps there is not one of these avenues but what may become an inlet to death, nor one of the blessings of life but what may be the means of accomplishing it. We live by inhalation, but we also die by it. Diseases and death in innumerable forms are conveyed by the very air we breathe. God hath given us a relish for divers aliments, and rendered them necessary to our subsistence : yet, from the abuse of them, what a train of disorders and premature deaths are found amongst men ! And, when there is no abuse, a single delicious morsel may, by the evil design of another, or even by mere accident, convey poison through all our veins, and in one hour reduce the most athletic form to a corpse.

The elements of fire and water, without which we could not subsist, contain properties which in a few moments would be able to destroy us ; nor can the utmost circumspection at all times preserve us from their destructive power. A single stroke on the head may divest us of reason or of life. A wound or a bruise of the spine may instantly deprive the lower extremities of all sensation. If the vital parts be injured, so as to suspend the performance of their mysterious functions, how soon is the constitution broken up ! By means of the circulation of the blood, how easily and suddenly are deadly substances diffused throughout the frame ! The putridity of a morbid subject has been imparted to the very hand stretched out to save it. The poisoned arrow, the envenomed fang, the hydrophobic saliva, derive from hence their fearful efficacy. Even the pores of the skin, necessary as they are to life, may be the means of death. Not only are poisonous substances hereby admitted, but, when obstructed by surrounding damps, the noxious humours of the body, instead of being emitted, are retained in the system, and become productive of numerous diseases, always afflictive, and often fatal to life.

Instead of wondering at the number of premature deaths that are constantly witnessed, there is far greater reason to wonder that there are no more, and that any of us survive to seventy or eighty years of age.

> " Our life contains a thousand springs,
>   And dies if one be gone :
> Strange that a harp of thousand strings
>   Should keep in tune so long."

Nor is this all. If we are *"fearfully made"* as to our animal frame, it will be found that we are much more so considered as moral and accountable beings. In what relates to our animal nature, we are in most instances constructed like other animals ; but, in what relates to us as moral agents, we stand distinguished from all the lower creation. We are made for eternity. The present life is only the introductory part of our existence. It is that, however, which stamps a character on all that follows. How fearful is our situation ! What innumerable influences is the mind exposed to from the temptations which surround us ! Not more dangerous to the body is the pestilence that walketh in darkness than these are to the soul. Such is the construction of our nature that the very word of life, if heard without regard, becomes a savour of death unto death. What consequences hang upon the small and apparently trifling beginning of evils ! A wicked thought may issue in a wicked purpose, this purpose in a wicked action, this action in a course of conduct, this course may draw into its vortex millions of our fellow-creatures, and terminate in perdition, both to ourselves and them. The whole of this process was exemplified in the case of Jeroboam, the son of Nebat. When placed over the ten tribes, he first *said in his heart*, " If this people go up to sacrifice at Jerusalem, their hearts will turn to Rehoboam ; and thus shall the kingdom return to the house of David." 1 Kings xii. 26—30. On this he took counsel, and made the calves of Dan and Bethel. This engaged him in a course of wickedness, from which no remonstrances could reclaim him. Nor was it confined to himself ; for he " made all Israel to sin." The issue was, not only their destruction as a nation, but, to all appearance, the eternal ruin of himself, and great numbers of his followers. Such were the fruits of an evil thought !

Oh, my soul, tremble at thyself ! Tremble at the fearfulness of thy situation ; and commit thine immortal all into his hands " who is able to keep thee from falling, and to present thee faultless before the presence of his glory with exceeding joy."—*Andrew Fuller.*

Verse 14.—*"I am fearfully and wonderfully made."* Never was so terse and expressive a description of the physical conformation of man given by any human being. So *"fearfully"* are we made, that there is not an action or gesture of our bodies, which does not, apparently, endanger some muscle, vein, or sinew, the rupture of which would destroy either life or health. We are so *"wonderfully"* made, that our organization infinitely surpasses, in skill, contrivance, design, and adaptation of means to ends, the most curious and complicated piece of mechanism, not only ever executed " by art and man's device," but ever conceived by human imagination.—*Richard Warner*, 1828.

Verse 14.—"*I am wonderfully made.*" Take notice of the curious frame of the body. David saith, "*I am wonderfully made*"; *acu pictus sum*, so the Vulgate rendereth it, " painted as with a needle," like a garment of needlework, of divers colours, richly embroidered with nerves and veins. What shall I speak of the eye, wherein there is such curious workmanship, that many upon the first sight of it have been driven to acknowledge God? Of the hand made to open and shut, and to serve the labours and ministries of nature without wasting and decay for many years? If they should be of marble or iron, with such constant use they would soon wear out; and yet now they are of flesh they last so long as life lasteth. Of the head? fitly placed to be the seat of the senses, to command and direct the rest of the members. Of the lungs? a frail piece of flesh, yet, though in continual action, of a long use. It were easy to enlarge upon this occasion; but I am to preach a sermon, not to read an anatomy lecture. In short, therefore, every part is so placed and framed, as if God had employed his whole wisdom about it.

But as yet we have spoken but of the casket wherein the jewel lieth. The soul, that divine spark of blast, how quick, nimble, various, and indefatigable in its motions! how comprehensive in its capacities! how it animateth the body, and is like God himself, all in every part! Who can trace the flights of reason? What a value hath God set upon the soul! He made it after his image, he redeemed it with Christ's blood.—*Thomas Manton.*

Verse 14.—What is meant by saying that the soul is *in* the body, any more than saying that a thought or a hope is in a stone or a tree? *How* is it joined to the body? what keeps it one with the body? what keeps it in the body? what prevents it any moment from separating from the body? When two things which we see are united, they are united by some connexion which we can understand. A chain or cable keeps a ship in its place; we lay the foundation of a building in the earth, and the building endures. But what is it which unites soul and body? how do they touch? how do they keep together? how is it we do not wander to the stars or the depths of the sea, or to and fro as chance may carry us, while our body remains where it was on earth? So far from its being wonderful that the body one day dies, how is it that it is made to live and move at all? how is it that it keeps from dying a single hour? Certainly it is as uncomprehensible as anything can be, how soul and body can make up one man; and, unless we had the instance before our eyes, we should seem in saying so to be using words without meaning. For instance, would it not be extravagant and idle to speak of time as deep or high, or of space as quick or slow? Not less idle, surely, it perhaps seems to some races of spirits to say that thought and mind have a body, which in the case of man they have, according to God's marvellous will.—*John Henry Newman, in Parochial Sermons,* 1839.

Verse 14.—Moses describes the creation of man (Gen. ii. 7): " The Lord God formed man of the dust of the ground, and breathed into his nostrils the breath of life; and man became a living soul." Now what God did then immediately, he doth still by means. Do not think that God made man at first, and that ever since men have made one another. No (saith Job), " he that made me in the womb made him: " ch. xxxi. 15. David will inform us: "*I am fearfully and wonderfully made: marvellous are thy works,*" etc. As if he had said, Lord, I am wonderfully made, and thou hast made me. I am a part or parcel of thy marvellous works, yea, the breviate or compendium of them all. The frame of the body (much more the frame of the soul, most of all the frame of the new creature in the soul) is God's work, and it is a wonderful work of God. And therefore David could not satisfy himself in the bare affirmation of this, but enlargeth in the explication of it in verses 15 and 16. David took no notice of father or mother, but ascribed the whole efficiency of himself to God. And indeed David was as much made by God as Adam; and so is every son of Adam. Though we are begotten and born of our earthly parents, yet God is the chief parent and the only fashioner of us all. Thus graciously spake Jacob to his brother Esau, demanding, " Who are those with thee? And he said, The children which God hath graciously given thy servant ": Gen. xxxiii. 5. Therefore, as the Spirit of God warns, " Know ye that the Lord he is God: it is he that hath made us, and not we ourselves " (Ps. c. 3); which as it is true especially of our spiritual making, so 'tis true also of our natural.—*Joseph Caryl.*

Verse 14.—Those who were skilful in Anatomy among the ancients, concluded, from the outward and inward make of a human body, that it was the work of a Being transcendently wise and powerful. As the world grew more enlightened in this art, their discoveries gave them fresh opportunities of admiring the conduct of Providence in the formation of a human body. Galen was converted by his dissections, and could not but own a Supreme Being upon a survey of this his handiwork. There are, indeed, many parts, of which the old anatomists did not know the certain use ; but as they saw that most of those which they examined were adapted with admirable art to their several functions, they did not question but those whose uses they could not determine, were contrived with the same wisdom for respective ends and purposes. Since the circulation of the blood has been found out, and many other great discoveries have been made by our modern anatomists, we see new wonders in the human frame, and discern several important uses for those parts, which uses the ancients knew nothing of. In short, the body of man is such a subject as stands the utmost test of examination. Though it appears formed with the nicest wisdom upon the most superficial survey of it, it still mends upon the search, and produces our surprise and amazement in proportion as we pry into it.—*The Spectator.*

Verses 14—16.—The subject, from the 14th verse to the 16th inclusive, might have been much more particularly illustrated ; but we are taught, by the peculiar delicacy of expression in the Sacred Writings, to avoid, as in this case, the entering too minutely into *anatomical* details.—*Adam Clarke.*

Verse 15.—"*My substance was not hid from thee,*" etc. What deeper solitude, what state of concealment more complete, than that of the babe as yet unborn ? Yet the Psalmist represents the Almighty as present even there. "*My substance was not hid from thee, when I was made in secret, and curiously wrought in the lowest parts of the earth.*" The whole image and train of thought is one of striking beauty. We see the wonderful work of the human body, with all its complex tissue of bones, and joints, and nerves, and veins, and arteries growing up, and fashioned, as it had been a piece of rich and curious embroidery under the hand of the manufacturer. But it is not the work itself that we are now called on to admire. The contexture is indeed fearful and wonderful ; but how much more when we reflect that the divine Artificer wrought within the dark and narrow confines of the womb. Surely the darkness is no darkness with him who could thus work. Surely the blackest night, the closest and most artificial recess, the subtlest disguises and hypocrisies are all seen through, are all naked and bare before him whose "*eyes did see our substance yet being imperfect.*" The night is as clear as the day ; and secret sins are set in the light of his countenance, no less than those which are open and scandalous, committed before the sun or on the house-top. And if " in his book all our members are written, which day by day were fashioned, when as yet there was none of them," surely the actions of these members, now that they are grown, or growing, to maturity, and called upon to fulfil the functions for which they were created, shall be all noted down ; and none be contrived so secretly, but that when the books are opened at the last day, it shall be found written therein to justify or to condemn us. Such is the main lesson which David himself would teach us in this Psalm,—the *omnipresence* and *omniscience* of Almighty God. My brethren, let us reflect for a little upon this deep mystery ; that he, " the High and Lofty One that inhabiteth eternity," is about our path and about our bed, and spieth out all our ways ; that go whither we will he is there ; that say what we will, there is not a word on our tongue but he knoweth it altogether. The reflection is, indeed, mysterious, but it is also most profitable.—*Charles Wordsworth, in "Christian Boyhood,"* 1846.

Verse 15.—"*My substance was not hid from thee.*" Should an artizan intend commencing a work in some dark cave where there was no light to assist him, how would he set his hand to it ? in what way would he proceed ? and what kind of workmanship would it prove ? But God makes the most perfect work of all in the dark, for he fashions man in the mother's womb.—*John Calvin.*

Verse 15.—"*When I was made in secret,*" etc. The author uses a metaphor derived from the most subtle art of the Phrygian workman :

" When I was formed in the secret place,
When I was wrought with a needle in the depths of the earth.

Whoever observes this (in truth he will not be able to observe it in the common translations), and at the same time reflects upon the wonderful mechanism of the human body ; the various implications of the veins, arteries, fibres, and membranes ; the " undescribable texture " of the whole fabric—may, indeed, feel the beauty and gracefulness of this well-adapted metaphor, but will miss much of its force and sublimity, unless he be apprised that the art of designing in needlework was wholly dedicated to the use of the sanctuary, and, by a direct precept of the divine law, chiefly employed in furnishing a part of the sacerdotal habit, and the vails for the entrance of the Tabernacle. Exod. xxviii. 39 ; xxvi. 36 ; xxvii. 16. Thus the poet compares the wisdom of the divine Artificer with the most estimable of human arts—that art which was dignified by being consecrated altogether to the use of religion ; and the workmanship of which was so exquisite, that even the sacred writings seem to attribute it to a supernatural guidance. See Exod. xxxv. 30—35.—*Robert Lowth* (1710—1787), *in "Lectures on the Sacred Poetry of the Hebrews."*

Verse 15.—"Curiously wrought in the lowest parts of the earth," that is, in the womb : as curious workmen, when they have some choice piece in hand, they perfect it in private, and then bring it forth to light for men to gaze at. What a wonderful piece of work is man's head (God's masterpiece in this little world), the chief seat of the soul, that *cura Divini ingenii*, as Favorinus calls it. Many locks and keys argue the value of the jewel that they keep, and many papers wrapping the token within them, the price of the token. The tables of the testament, first laid up in the ark, secondly, the ark bound about with pure gold ; thirdly, over-shadowed with cherubim's wings ; fourthly, enclosed within the vail of the Tabernacle ; fifthly, with the compass of the Tabernacle ; sixthly, with a court about all ; seventhly, with a treble covering of goats' rams', and badgers' skins above all ; they must needs be precious tables. So when the Almighty made man's head (the seat of the reasonable soul) and overlaid it with hair, skin, and flesh, like the threefold covering of the Tabernacle, and encompassed it with a skull and bones like boards of cedar, and afterwards with divers skins like silken curtains ; and lastly, enclosed it with the yellow skin that covers the brain (like the purple veil), he would doubtless have us to know it was made for some great treasure to be put therein. How and when the reasonable soul is put into this curious cabinet philosophers dispute many things, but can affirm nothing of certainty.—*Abraham Wright.*

Verse 15.—"In the lowest parts of the earth." From this remarkable expression which, in the original, and as elsewhere used, denotes the region of the dead—*Sheol,* or *Hades*—it would appear that it is not only his formation in the womb the Psalmist here contemplates, but also—regarding the region of the dead as the womb of resurrection life—the refashioning of the body hereafter, and its new birth to the life immortal, which will be no less " marvellous " a work, but rather more so, than the first fashioning of man's " substance." Confirmed by the words of verse 18—"When I awake, I am still with thee "—the same language before employed to express the resurrection hope, Ps. xvii. 15 : when there shall be a further illustration of God's mindfulness of his purposes and " precious counsels " with respect to his redeemed, in anticipation of which they may repeat this Psalm with renewed feelings of wonder and admiration.—*William De Burgh.*

*Verses 15, 16.—*The word *"substance"* represents different words in these verses. In verse 15 it is " my strength," or " my bones ; " in verse 16 the word is usually rendered " embryo " : but " clew " (life a ball yet to be unwound) finds favour with great scholars.

"In the lowest parts of the earth" denotes no subterranean limbo or workshop ; but is a poetical parallel to " in secret."

"Which in continuance were fashioned" is wrong. The margin, though also wrong, indicates the right way : " my days were determined before one of them was."—*David M'Laren, in "The Book of Psalms in Metre,"* 1883.

Verse 16.—"Thine eyes did see my substance, yet being unperfect," etc. From whence we may learn, first, not to be proud of what we are ; all's the work of God. How beautiful or comely, how wise or holy soever you are, 'tis not of yourselves. What hath any man, either in naturals or supernaturals, which he hath not received ? Secondly, despise not what others are or have, though they are not such exact pieces, though they have not such excellent endowments as yourselves ; yet they are what God hath made them. Thirdly, despise not what yourselves are. Many are ashamed to be seen as God made them ; few are ashamed to be seen what the devil hath made them. Many are troubled at small defects in the outward man ; few are troubled at the greatest deformities of the inward man : many buy artificial beauty to supply the natural ; few spiritual, to supply the defects of the supernatural beauty of the soul.—*Abraham Wright.*

Verse 16.—*"My substance yet being unperfect."* One word in the original, which means strictly anything *rolled together* as a ball, and hence is generally supposed to mean here the fœtus or embryo. Hupfeld, however, prefers to understand it of the ball of life, as consisting of a number of different threads (" the days " of verse 16—see margin) which are first a compact mass as it were, and which are then unwound as life runs on.—*J. J. Stewart Perowne.*

Verse 16.—A skilful architect before he builds draws a model, or gives a draught of the building in his book, or upon a table ; there he will show you every room and contrivance : in his book are all the parts of the building written, while as yet there are none of them, or before any of them are framed and set up. In allusion to architects and other artisans, David speaks of God, *"In thy book all my members were written"*; that is, Thou hast made me as exactly as if thou hadst drawn my several members and my whole proportion with a pen or pencil in a book, before thou wouldst adventure to form me up. The Lord uses no book, no pen to decipher his work. He had the perfect idea of all things in himself from everlasting ; but he may well be said to work as by pattern, whose work is the most perfect pattern. —*Joseph Caryl.*

Verse 17.—*"How precious also are thy thoughts unto me,"* etc. So far from thinking it a hardship to be subject to this scrutiny, he counts it a most valuable privilege. However others may regard this truth, *"to me,"* my judgment and my feelings, *"how costly,"* valuable *"are thy thoughts,"* i.e. thy perpetual attention to me.—*Joseph Addison Alexander.*

Verse 17.—*"How precious also are thy thoughts unto me, O God!"* How cold and poor are *our* warmest thoughts towards God ! How unspeakably loving and gloriously rich are *his* thoughts towards us ! Compare Eph. i. 18 : " The riches of the glory of his inheritance in the saints."—*A. R. Fausset.*

Verse 17.—*"How precious . . . how great is the sum of them!"* Our comforts vie with the number of our sorrows, and win the game. The mercies of God passed over in a gross sum breed no admiration ; but cast up the particulars, and then arithmetic is too dull an art to number them. As many dusts as a man's hands can hold, is but his handful of so many dusts ; but tell them one by one, and they exceed all numeration. It was but a crown which king Solomon wore ; but weigh the gold, tell the precious stones, value the richness of them, and what was it then ? —*Thomas Adams.*

Verses 17, 18.—Behold David's love to God ; sleeping and waking his mind runs upon him. There needs no arguments to bring those to our remembrance whom we love. We neglect ourselves to think upon them. A man in love wastes his spirits, vexes his mind, neglects his meat, regards not his business, his mind still feeds on that he loves. When men love that they should not, there is more need of a bridle to keep them from thinking of it, than of spurs to keep them to it. Try thy love of God by this. If thou thinkest not often of God, thou lovest him not. If thou canst not satisfy thyself with profits, pleasures, friends, and other worldly objects, but thou must turn other businesses aside, that thou mayest daily think of God, then thou lovest him.—*Francis Taylor, in "God's Glory in Man's Happiness,"* 1654.

Verses 17, 18.—Mercies are either ordinary or extraordinary—our common necessaries, or the remarkable supplies which we receive now and then at the hand of God. Thou must not only praise him for some extraordinary mercy, that comes with such pomp and observation that all thy neighbours take notice of it with thee, as the mercy which Zacharias and Elizabeth had in their son, that was noised about all the country (Luke i. 65) ; but also for ordinary, every-day mercies : for first, we are unworthy of the least mercy (Gen. xxxii. 10), and therefore God is worthy of praise for the least, because it is more than he owes us. Secondly, these common, ordinary mercies are many. Thus David enhanceth the mercies of this kind,— *"O God, how great is the sum of them!* If I should count them, they are more in number than the sand ; when I wake I am still with thee." As if he had said,

There is not a point of time wherein thou art not doing me good ; as soon as I open my eyes in the morning I have a new theme, in some fresh mercies given since I closed them over-night, to employ my praiseful meditations. Many little items make together a great sum. What is lighter than a grain of sand, yet what is heavier than the sand upon the sea-shore ? As little sins (such as vain thoughts and idle words), because of their multitude, arise to a great guilt, and will bring in a long bill, a heavy reckoning at last ; so, ordinary mercies, what they want in their size of some other great mercies, have compensated it in their number. Who will not say that a man shows greater kindness in maintaining one at his table with ordinary fare all the year than in entertaining him at a great feast twice or thrice in the same time ?—*William Gurnall.*

Verse 18.—*"They are more in number than the sand."* Pindar says, that sand flies number (*Olymp. Ode* 2). The Pythian oracle indeed boastingly said, I know the number of the sand, and the measure of the sea (*Herodot. Clio.* l. i. c. 47). It is to this that Lucan may refer when he says, measure is not wanting to the ocean, or number to the sand (*Pharsal.* l. 5, v. 182).—*Samuel Burder.*

Verse 18.—*"If I should count them, they are more in number than the sand."*

> If all his glorious deeds my song would tell,
> The shore's unnumbered stones I might recount as well.
>
> *Pindar,* B.C. 518—442.

Verse 18.—*"When I awake, I am still with thee."* It is the great advantage of a Christian, which he has above other men, that he has his friends always about him, and (if the fault be not his own) need never to be absent from them. In the friendship and converse of the world, we use to say, " Friends must part," and those who have delight and satisfaction in one another's society must be content to leave it, and to be taken off from it. But this is the privilege of a believer that undertakes communion with God, that it is possible for him always to be with him. Again, in human converse and society we know it is ordinary for friends to dream that they are in company with one another ; but when they awake they are a great way off. But a Christian that converses with God, and has his thoughts fastened upon him, when he awakes he is still with him, which is that which is here exhibited to us in the example of the prophet David.

A godly soul should fall asleep in God's arms, like a child in the mother's lap ; it should be sung and lulled to sleep with " songs of the night." And this will make him the fitter for converse with God the next day after. This is the happiness of a Christian that is careful to lie down with God, that he finds his work still as he left it, and is in the same disposition when he rises as he was at night when he lay down to rest. As a man that winds up his watch over night, he finds it going the next morning ; so is it also, as I may say, with a Christian that winds up his heart. This is a good observation to be remembered, especially in the evening afore the Sabbath.—*Thomas Horton,* —1673.

Verse 18.—*"When I awake, I am still with thee."* It is no small advantage to the holy life to " begin the day with God." The saints are wont to leave their hearts with him over night, that they may find them with him in the morning. Before earthly things break in upon us, and we receive impressions from abroad, it is good to season the heart with thoughts of God, and to consecrate the early and virgin operations of the mind before they are prostituted to baser objects. When the world gets the start of religion in the morning, it can hardly overtake it all the day ; and so the heart is habituated to vanity all the day long. But when we begin with God, we take him along with us to all the business and comforts of the day ; which, being seasoned with his love and fear, are the more sweet and savoury to us.—*Thomas Case* (1598—1682), *in the Epistle Dedicatory to "The Morning Exercise."*

Verse 18.—*"When I awake."* Accustom yourself to a serious meditation every morning. Fresh airing our souls in heaven will engender in us a purer spirit and nobler thoughts. A morning seasoning will secure us for all the day. Though other necessary thoughts about our calling will and must come in, yet when we have dispatched them, let us attend to our morning theme as our chief companion. As a man that is going with another about some considerable business, suppose to Westminster, though he meets with several friends on the way, and salutes some, and with others with whom he has some affairs he spends some little time, yet he quickly returns to his companion, and both together go to their intended stage.

Do thus in the present case. Our minds are active and will be doing something, though to little purpose ; and if they be not fixed upon some noble object, they will, like madmen and fools, be mightily pleased in playing with straws. The thoughts of God were the first visitors David had in the morning. God and his heart met together as soon as he was awake, and kept company all the day after.—*Stephen Charnock.*

Verse 19.—"*Depart from me therefore, ye bloody men.*" The expression, "*bloody men,*" or "*men of blood,*" includes not only homicides, who shed human blood, but all other wicked and evil doers, who injure, or seek to injure others, or who slay their own souls by sin, or the souls of others by scandal ; all of whom may be truly called homicides ; for hatred may be called the mainspring of homicide, and thus St. John says, "Whoso hateth his brother is a homicide."—*Robert Bellarmine.*

Verse 19.—"*Therefore.*" When we have a controversy with the wicked we should take heed that private spleen do not rule us, but that only our interest in God's quarrel with them doth move us, as the Psalmist doth here.—*David Dickson.*

Verse 20.—"*Thine enemies take thy name in vain.*" In every action three things are considerable,—the *end*, the *agent*, the *work*. These three duly weighed, we shall soon see what it is to take God's name in vain.

I. That which hath no end proposed, or is done to no end, may truly be said to be done in vain. As the sowing of seed without reaping the fruit, the planting a vineyard without a vintage, or feeding a flock without eating the milk of it. These are labours in vain. So he that taketh the name of God to no end, neither to God's glory, nor the private or public good, taketh it in vain. *Cui bono ?* is a question in all undertakings. If to no good, as good and better not undertaken at all ; it is to no end, it is in vain. If a man have well-fashioned legs, and they be lame, *frustra pulchras habet tibia claudus,* the lame man hath them in vain. The chief end, therefore, in taking this name must be, 1. The glory of God, otherwise we open our mouths in vain, as it is in Job. God is willing to impart all his blessings to us, and requires nothing of us again but glory, which if we return not, he may say, as David did of Nabal, for whom he had done many good turns, in securing his shepherds and flocks, etc. ; and when he desired nothing but a little meat for the young men he denied it : All that I have done for this fellow is in vain ; in vain have I kept all he hath. So, God having done so much for us, and expecting nothing but the glory of his name, if we be defective herein, he may well say all that he hath done for us is in vain.

2. Next to God's glory is the good of ourselves and others ; and so to take God's name without reference to this end, if we neither promote our own good nor the good of others, it is in vain, *ex privatione finis*, because it wants a right end ; therefore Saint Paul rejoiced, having by his preaching laboured for the saving of souls, I rejoice, saith he, that I have not run in vain, neither laboured in vain.

II. In the *agent* the heart and soul is to be considered, which in the person acting is the chief mover. If the soul be *Rachah*, vain and light, as when we take God's name without due advice and reverence, though we propound a right end, yet we take his name in vain. Therefore the wise man advises "not to be rash with our mouth" (Eccl. v. 2) ; and the Psalmist professeth that his heart was fixed when he praised God (Ps. lvii. 7) : the heart ought to be fixed and stablished by a due consideration of God's greatness when we speak of him. This is opposed to rashness, inconstancy, and lightness, such as are in chaff and smoke, which are apt to be carried away with every blast, and such as are so qualified do take God's name in vain.

III. In the *work* itself may be a twofold vanity, which must be avoided. Firstly. Falsehood. Secondly, Injustice.

1. If it be *false*, then is it also vain, as theirs in Isaiah (ch. xxviii. 15) : "We have made a covenant with death, and with hell are we at agreement ; when the overflowing scourge shall pass through, it shall not come unto us : for we have made lies our refuge, and under falsehood have we hid ourselves." And this is that *actio erroris*, work of error, of which Jeremiah speaketh. *Vanitas opponitur veritati*, vanity is opposed to verity and truth ; therefore a thing is said to be vain when it is false or erroneous. "They are vanity, the work of errors," saith the prophet (Jer. x. 15) ; and as there is truth in natural things, so is there a truth in moral things, which if it be wanting, our speech is vain.

2. If *unjust* it is vain too. " If I be wicked, why then labour I in vain ? " saith holy Job (ch. ix. 29) ; " The very hope of unjust men perisheth," saith the wise man (Prov. xi. 7) ; and, " They walk in a vain shadow, and disquiet themselves in vain " (Ps. xxxix. 6). If justice be wanting in our actions, or truth in our assertions and promises, they are vain ; and to use God's name in either is to take his name in vain. So that if either we take the name of God to no end, but make it common, and take it up as a custom till it come to a habit, not for any good end ; or if our hearts be not stable or fixed, but light and inconstant when we take it ; or if we take it to colour or bolster up any falsehood or any unjust act, we take it in vain, and break the commandment.—*Lancelot Andrews.*

Verse 21.—*"Do not I hate them, O Lord, that hate thee ? "* The simple future in the first clause comprehends several distinct shades of meaning. Do I not, may I not, must I not, hate those hating thee ? Hate them, not as man hates, but as God hates.—*Joseph Addison Alexander.*

Verse 21.—*"Do not I hate them, O Lord, that hate thee ? "* Can he who thinks good faith the holiest thing in life, avoid being an enemy to that man who, as quæstor, dared to despoil, desert, and betray ? Can he who wishes to pay due honours to the immortal gods, by any means avoid being an enemy to that man who has plundered all their temples ?—*Cicero.*

Verse 21.—*"And am not I grieved with those that rise up against thee ? "* The expression here—*"grieved "*—explains the meaning of the word *"hate "* in the former member of the verse. It is not that hatred which is followed by malignity or ill-will ; it is that which is accompanied with grief, pain of heart, pity, sorrow. So the Saviour looked on men : Mark iii. 5 : " And when he had looked round about on them with *anger*, being *grieved* for the hardness of their hearts." The Hebrew word used here, however, contains *also* the idea of being disgusted with ; of loathing ; of nauseating. The feeling referred to is anger—conscious disgust—at such conduct ; grief, pain, sorrow, that men should evince such feelings towards their Maker.—*Albert Barnes.*

Verse 21.—*"Am not I grieved ? "* etc. Acted upon by mingled feelings of sorrow for them, and loathing at their evil practices. Thus our Lord " looked round about on them with *anger*, being *grieved* for the hardness of their hearts " : Mark iii. 5.—*French and Skinner.*

Verse 21.—It is said that Adam Smith disliked nothing more than that moral apathy—that obtuseness of moral perception—which prevents man from not only seeing clearly, but feeling strongly, the broad distinction between virtue and vice, and which, under the pretext of liberality, is all indulgent even to the blackest crimes. At a party at Dalkeith Palace, where Mr. ——, in his mawkish way, was finding palliations for some villainous transactions, the doctor waited in patient silence until he was gone, then exclaimed : " Now I can breathe more freely. I cannot bear that man ; he has no indignation in him."

Verses 21, 22.—A faithful servant hath the same interests, the same friends, the same enemies, with his master, whose cause and honour he is, upon all occasions, in duty bound to support and maintain. A good man hates, as God himself doth ; he hates not the persons of men, but their sins ; not what God made them, but what they have made themselves. We are neither to hate the men, on account of the vices they practise ; nor to love the vices, for the sake of the men who practise them. He who observeth invariably this distinction, fulfilleth the perfect law of charity, and hath the love of God and of his neighbour abiding in him.—*George Horne.*

Verses 21, 22.—First, we must hate the company and society of manifest and obstinate sinners, who will not be reclaimed. Secondly, all their sins, not communicating with any man in his sin, we must have no fellowship (as with the workers so) with the unfruitful works of darkness. Thirdly, all occasions and inducements unto these sins. Fourthly, all appearances of wickedness (1 Thess. v. 22), that is, which men in common judgment account evil ; and all this must proceed from a good ground, even from a good heart hating sin perfectly, that is all sin, as David, *"I hate them with perfect hatred ; "* and not as some, who can hate some sin, but cleave to some other : as many can hate pride, but love covetousness or some other darling sin : but we must attain to the hatred of all, before we can come to the practice of this precept [Jude 23] ; besides that, all sins are hateful even in themselves.—*William Perkins,* 1558—1602.

Verses 21, 24.—The temper of mourning for public sins, for the sins of others, is the greatest note of sincerity. When all other signs of righteousness may have their exceptions, this temper is the utmost term, which we cannot go beyond in our self-examination. The utmost prospect David had of his sincerity, when he was upon a diligent enquiry after it, was his anger and grief for the sin of others. When he had reached so far, he was at a stand, and knew not what more to add : " Am not I grieved with those that rise up against thee ? I hate them with perfect hatred : I count them mine enemies. Search me, O God, and know my heart : try me, and know my thoughts : and see if there be any wicked way in me." If there be anything that better can evidence my sincerity than this, Lord, acquaint me with it ; " know my heart," *i.e.*, make me to know it. He whose sorrow is only for matter confined within his own breast, or streams with it in his life, has reason many times to question the truth of it ; but when a man cannot behold sin as sin in another without sensible regret, it is a sign he hath savingly felt the bitterness of it in his own soul. It is a high pitch and growth, and a consent between the Spirit of God and the soul of a Christian, when he can lament those sins in others whereby the Spirit is grieved ; when he can rejoice with the Spirit rejoicing, and mourn with the Spirit mourning. This is a clear testimony that we have not self-ends in the service of God ; that we take not up religion to serve a turn ; that God is our aim, and Christ our beloved.—*Stephen Charnock.*

Verse 22.—"*I hate them with perfect hatred.*" What is "*with a perfect hatred* " ? I hated in them their iniquities, I loved thy creation. This it is to hate with a perfect hatred, that neither on account of the vices thou hate the men, nor on account of the men love the vices. For see what he addeth, "*They became my enemies.*" Not only as God's enemies, but as his own too doth he now describe them. How then will he fulfil in them both his own saying, "*Have not I hated those that hated thee, Lord,*" and the Lord's command, "*Love your enemies* " ? How will he fulfil this, save with that perfect hatred, that he hate in them that they are wicked, and love that they are men ? For in the time even of the Old Testament, when the carnal people was restrained by visible punishments, how did Moses, the servant of God, who by understanding belonged to the New Testament, how did he hate sinners when he prayed for them, or how did he not hate them when he slew them, save that he "*hated them with a perfect hatred* " ? For with such perfection did he hate the iniquity which he punished, as to love the manhood for which he prayed.—*Augustine.*

Verse 23.—"*Try me.*" True faith is precious ; it is like gold, it will endure a trial. Presumption is but a counterfeit, and cannot abide to be tried : 1 Pet. i. 7. A true believer fears no trial. He is willing to be tried by God. He is willing to have his faith tried by others, he shuns not the touchstone. He is much in testing himself. He would not take anything upon trust, especially that which is of such moment. He is willing to hear the worst as well as the best. That preaching pleases him best which is most searching and distinguishing : Heb. iv. 12. He is loath to be deluded with vain hopes. He would not be flattered into a false conceit of his spiritual state. When trials are offered, he complies with the apostle's advice, 2 Cor. xiii. 5.—*David Clarkson.*

Verse 23.—What fearful dilemma have we here ? The Holiest changeth not when he comes a visitant to a human heart. He is the same there that he is in the highest heaven. He cannot look upon sin ; and how can a human heart welcome him into its secret chambers ? How can the blazing fire welcome the quenching water ? It is easy to commit to memory the seemly prayer of an ancient penitent, "*Search me, O God, and know my heart ; try me, and know my thoughts.*" The dead letters, worn smooth by frequent use, may drop freely from callous lips, leaving no sense of scalding on the conscience ; and yet, truth of God, though they are, they may be turned into a lie in the act of utterance. The prayer is not true, although it is borrowed from the Bible, if the suppliant invite the All-seeing in, and yet would give a thousand worlds, if he had them, to keep him out for ever.

Christ has declared the difficulty, and solved it : " I am the way, the truth, and the life : no man cometh unto the Father, but by me." When the Son has made the sinner free, he is free indeed. The dear child, pardoned and reconciled, loves and longs for the Father's presence. What ! is there neither spot nor wrinkle now upon the man, that he dares to challenge inspection by the Omniscient, and to offer his heart as Jehovah's dwelling-place ?　He is not yet so pure ; and well he knows it. The groan is bursting yet from his broken heart : " O wretched man that I am ! who shall deliver me from the body of this death ? "　Many stains defile him yet ; but he loathes them now, and longs to be free.　The differcnce between an unconverted and a converted man is not that the one has sins, and the other has none ; but that the one takes part with his cherished sins against a dreaded God, and the other takes part with a reconciled God against his hated sins.　He is out with his former friends, and in with his former adversary.　Conversion is a turning, and it is one turning only ; but it produces simultaneously and necessarily two distinct efforts.　Whereas his face was formerly turned away from God, and toward his own sins ; it is now turned away from his own sins, and toward God.　This one turning, with its twofold result, is in Christ the Mediator, and through the work of the Spirit.

As long as God is my enemy, I am his.　I have no more power to change that condition than the polished surface has to refrain from reflecting the sunshine that falls upon it.　It is God's love, from the face of Jesus shining into my dark heart, that makes my heart open to him, and delight to be his dwelling-place.　The eyes of the just Avenger I cannot endure to be in this place of sin ; but the eye of the compassionate Physician I shall gladly admit into this place of disease ; for he comes from heaven to earth that he may heal such sin-sick souls as mine.　When a disciple desires to be searched by the living God, he does not thereby intimate that there are no sins in him to be discovered : he intimates rather that his foes are so many and so lively, that nothing can subdue them except the presence and power of God.— *William Arnot* (—1875), *in "Laws from Heaven for Life on Earth."*

Verses 23, 24.—There are several things worthy of notice in the Psalmist's appeal, in the words before us.　First, notice *the Psalmist's intrepidity.*　Here is a man determined to explore the recesses of his own heart.　Did Buonaparte, did Nelson, did Wellington, ever propose to do this ?　Were all the renowned heroes of antiquity present, I would ask them all if they ever had courage to enter into their own hearts. David was a man of courage.　When he slew a lion in the way, when he successfully encountered a bear, when he went out to meet the giant Goliath, he gave undoubted proofs of courage ; but never did he display such signal intrepidity as when he determined to look into his own heart.　If you stood upon some eminence, and saw all the ravenous and venomous creatures that ever lived collected before you, it would not require such courage to combat them as to combat with your own heart. Every sin is a devil, and each may say, " My name is Legion, for we are many." Who knows what it is to face himself ?　And yet, if we would be saved, this must be done.

Secondly, notice *the Psalmist's integrity.*　He wished to know all his sins, that he might be delivered from them.　As every individual must know his sins at some period, a wise man will seek to know them here, because the present is the only time in which to glorify God, by confessing, by renouncing, by overcoming them.　One of the attributes of sin is to hide man from himself, to conceal his deformity, to prevent him from forming a just conception of his true condition.　It is a solemn fact, that there is not an evil principle in the bosom of the devil himself which does not exist in ours, at the present moment, unless we are fully renewed by the power of the Holy Spirit.　That these evil principles do not continually develop themselves, in all their hideous deformity, is entirely owing to the restraining and forbearing mercy of God.

Thirdly, notice *the Psalmist's wisdom.*　He presents his prayer to God himself. God is the only Being in the universe that knows himself—that peruses himself in his own light.　In the same light he sees all other beings ; and hence it follows that, if other beings see themselves truly, it must be in the light of God.　If the sun were an intelligent being, I would ask him, " How do you see yourself ?　In your own light ? "　And he would reply, " Yes."　"And how do you see the planets that are continually revolving around you ? "　" In my own light also, for all the light that is in them is borrowed from me."

You will observe that the Psalmist begins with his principles : his desire is to have these tried by a competent judge, and to have every thing that is evil removed from them.　This is an evidence of his wisdom.　The heart and its thoughts must be made right, before the actions of the life can be set right.　Those who are most eminent for piety are most conversant with God ; and, for this reason, they become most conversant with themselves.　David says, elsewhere, " Who can understand his errors ?   Cleanse THOU me from *secret* faults."   And Job says, " If I wash myself with snow water, and make me never so clean, yet shalt THOU plunge me in the ditch, and mine own clothes shall abhor me."   When these holy men perused themselves in God's light, they saw their sins of omission and commission, and prayed earnestly to be delivered from all.—*William Howels*, 1832.

Verses 23, 24.—The text is a prayer, and it indicates, as we think, three great facts in regard to the suppliant : the first, that David thoroughly wished to become acquainted with himself ; the second, that he felt conscious that God could see through all disguises ; and the third, that he desired to discover, in order that by Divine help he might correct, whatsoever was wrong in his conduct.

Now, the first inference which we draw from the text, when considered as indicating the feelings of the petitioner is, that he was thoroughly honest, that it was really his wish to become acquainted with his own heart.   And is there, you may say, anything rare or remarkable in this ?   Indeed we think there is.   It would need, we believe, a very high degree of piety to be able to put up with sincerity the prayers of our text.   For, will you tell me that it does not often happen, that even whilst men are carrying on a process of self-examination, there is a secret wish to remain ignorant of certain points, a desire not to be proved wrong when interest and inclination combine in demanding an opposite verdict ? . . .   In searching into yourselves, you know where the tender points are, and those points you will be apt to avoid, so as not to put yourselves to pain, nor make it evident how much you need the caustic and the knife.   Indeed, we may be sure that we state nothing but what experience will prove, when we declare it a high attainment in religion to be ready to know how bad we are. . . .   And this had evidently been reached by the Psalmist, for he pleads very earnestly with God that he would leave no recess of his spirit unexplored, that he would bring the heart and all its thoughts, the life and all its ways, under a most searching examination, so that no form and no degree of evil might fail to be detected.—*Henry Melvill.*

Verses 23, 24.—Self-examination is not the simple thing which, at first sight, it might appear.   No Christian who has ever really practised it has found it easy. Is there any exercise of the soul which any one of us has found so unsatisfactory, so almost impossible, as self-examination ?   The fact is this, that the heart is so exceedingly complicated and intricate, and it is so very near the eye which has to investigate it, and both it and the eye are so restless and so shifting, that its deep anatomy baffles our research.   Just a few things, here and there, broad and open, and floating upon the surface, a man discovers ; but there are chambers receding within chambers, in that deepest of all deep things, a sinner's heart, which no mere human investigation ever will reach, . . . it is the prerogative of God alone to "*search*" the human heart.

To the child of God—the most intimate with himself in all the earth—I do not hesitate to say—" There are sins latent at this moment in you, of which you have no idea ; but it only requires a larger measure of spiritual illumination to impress and unfold them.   You have no idea of the wickedness that is now in you."   But while I say this, let every Christian count well the cost before he ventures on the bold act of asking God to " search " him.   For be sure of this, if you do really and earnestly ask God to "*search*" you, he will do it.   And he will search you most searchingly ; and if you ask him to "*try*" you, he will try you,—and the trial will be no light matter !

I am persuaded that we often little calculate what we are doing—what we are asking God to do—when we implore him to give us some spiritual attainment, some growth in grace, some increase in holiness, or peace.   To all these things there is a condition, and that condition lies in a discipline, and that discipline is generally proportionate to the strength and the measure of the gift that we ask.

I do not know what may have been the state of the Psalmist at the period when he indited this Psalm ; but I should think either one of Saul's most cruel persecutions, or the rebellion of his son Absalom, followed quick upon the traces of that prayer,— "*Search me, O God, and know my heart : try me, and know my thoughts,*" etc.

Still, whatever his attainment, every child of God will desire, at any sacrifice, to know his own exact state before God ; for, as he desires in all things to have a mind conformed to the mind of God, so he is especially jealous lest he should, by any means, be taking a different view, or estimate, of his own soul from that which God sees it.—*Condensed from James Vaughan.*

Verses 23, 24.—Hypocrisy at the fashionable end of the town is very different from hypocrisy in the city. The modish hypocrite endeavours to appear more vicious than he really is, the other kind of hypocrite more virtuous. The former is afraid of everything that has the show of religion in it, and would be thought engaged in many criminal gallantries and amours which he is not guilty of. The latter assumes a face of sanctity, and covers a multitude of vices under a seeming religious deportment.

But there is another kind of hypocrisy, which differs from both these ; I mean that hypocrisy by which a man does not only deceive the world, but very often imposes on himself ; that hypocrisy which conceals his own heart from him, and makes him believe he is more virtuous than he really is, and either not attend to his vices, or mistake even his vices for virtues. It is this fatal hypocrisy and self-deceit which is taken notice of in those words, " Who can understand his errors ? cleanse thou me from secret faults."

These two kinds of hypocrisy, namely, that of deceiving the world, and that of imposing on ourselves, are touched with wonderful beauty in the hundred and thirty-ninth Psalm. The folly of the first kind of hypocrisy is there set forth by reflections on God's omniscience and omnipresence, which are celebrated in as noble strains of poetry as any other I ever met with, either sacred or profane. The other kind of hypocrisy, whereby a man deceives himself, is intimated in the two last verses, where the Psalmist addresses himself to the great Searcher of hearts in that emphatical petition ; " Try me, O God, and seek the ground of my heart : prove me, and examine my thoughts. Look well if there be any way of wickedness in me, and lead me in the way everlasting."—*Joseph Addison* (1672—1719), *in "The Spectator."*

Verses 23, 24.—How beautiful is the humility of David ! He cannot speak of the wicked but in terms of righteous indignation ; he cannot but hate the haters of his God ; yet, he seems immediately to recollect, and to check himself—" Try *me*, O Lord, and seek the ground of *my* heart." Precisely in the same spirit of inward humility and self-recollection, Abraham, when pleading before God in prayer for guilty depraved Sodom, fails not to speak of *himself*, as being dust and ashes : Gen. xviii. 27.—*James Ford*, 1871.

Verses 23, 24.—Why did David pray thus to God, "*Search me, O God, and know my heart*," having said before, in the first verse, "*Thou hast searched me, and known me*" ? Seeing David knew that God had searched him, what needed he to pray that God would search him ? why did he beg God to do that which he had done already ? The answer is at hand. David was a diligent self-searcher, and therefore he was so willing to be searched, yea, he delighted to be searched by God ; and that not (as was said) because himself had done it already, but also because he knew God could do it better. He knew by his own search that he did not live in any way of wickedness against his knowledge, and yet he knew there might be some way of wickedness in him that he knew not of. And therefore he doth not only say, "*Search me, O God, and know my thoughts*"; but he adds, "*See if there be any wicked way* (or *any way of pain and grief*) *in me*"; (the same word signifies both, because wicked ways lead in the end to pain and grief); "*and lead me in the way everlasting.*" As if he had said, Lord, I have searched myself, and can see no wicked way in me ; but, Lord, thy sight is infinitely clearer than mine, and if thou wilt but search me thou mayest see some wicked way in me which I could not see, and I would fain see and know the worst of myself, that I might amend and grow better ; therefore, Lord, if there be any such way in me, cause me to know it also. O take that way out of me, and take me out of that way ; "*lead me in the way everlasting.*" David had tried himself, and he would again be tried by God, that he, being better tried, might become yet better. He found himself gold upon his own trial, and yet he feared there might be some dross in him that he had not found ; and now he would be re-tried that he might come forth purest gold. Pure gold fears neither the furnace nor the fire, neither the test nor the touchstone ; nor is weighty gold afraid of the balance. He that is weight will be weight, how often soever he is weighed ; he that is gold will be gold, how often soever he is tried, and the oftener he is tried the purer gold he will be ; what he is he will be, and he would be better than he is.—*Joseph Caryl.*

Verse 24.—"*See if there be any wicked way in me.*" This is a beautiful and impressive *prayer* for the commencement of every day. It is, also, a great sentiment to *admonish* us at the beginning of each day.

There is the way of *unbelief* within, to which we are very prone. There is the way of *vanity* and pride, to which we often accustom ourselves. There is the way of *selfishness* in which we frequently walk. There is the way of *worldliness* we often pursue—empty pleasures, shadowy honours, etc. There is the way of *sluggishness*. What apathy in prayer, in the examination and application of God's Word, we manifest! There is the way of *self-dependence*, by which we often dishonour God and injure ourselves. There is, unhappily, the way of *disobedience*, in which we often walk. At any rate, our obedience is cold, reluctant, uncertain—not simple, entire, fervent.

How necessary is it, then, to go to God at once, and earnestly to prefer the petition, "*Lord, see if there be any wicked way in me.*" Let nothing that is wrong, that is opposed to thy character, repugnant to thy word, or injurious and debasing to ourselves, remain, or be harboured within us.—*Condensed from T. Wallace, in* "*Homiletic Commentary.*"

Verse 24.—"*See if there be any wicked way in me.*" To what a holiness must David have attained ere he could need, if we may so speak, Divine scrutiny, in order to his being informed of errors and defects! Is there one of us who can say that he has corrected his conduct up to the measure of his knowledge, and that now he must wait the being better informed before he can do more towards improving his life? I do not know how to define a higher point in religious attainment than supposing a man warranted in offering up the prayer of our text. I call upon you to be cautious in using this prayer. It is easy to mock God, by asking him to search you whilst you have made but little effort to search yourselves, and perhaps still less to act upon the result of the scrutiny.—*Henry Melvill.*

Verse 24.—"*See if there be any wicked way in me,*" etc.—

> Think and be careful what thou art within,
> For there is sin in the desire of sin:
> Think and be thankful, in a different case,
> For there is grace in the desire of grace.
>
> *John Byrom, 1691—1763.*

Verse 24.—"*The way everlasting.*" *Way of eternity,* or *of antiquity, the old way,* as Jer. vi. 16; meaning the way of faith and godliness, which God taught from the beginning, and which continueth for ever; contrary to "the way of the wicked," which perisheth: Ps. i. 6.—*Henry Ainsworth.*

HINTS TO PREACHERS.

Verses 1 and 23.—A matter of fact made a matter of prayer.

Verse 1.—1. A cheering thought for sinners. If God knew them not perfectly, how could he have prepared a perfect salvation for them? 2. A comfortable truth for saints. "Your heavenly Father knoweth that ye have need of all these things."—*G. R.*

Verses 1—5.—In these verses we have God's Omniscience, I. Described. 1. As observing minute and comparatively unimportant actions: "My downsitting and uprising." 2. As taking note of our thoughts and the motives behind them: "Understandest my thought." 3. As investigating all our ways: "Thou compassest," etc.; better rendered, "Thou triest my walking and lying down," *i.e.*, my activities and restings. 4. Accurately estimating every word at the instant of its utterance: "For there is not a word," etc. 5. As being "behind" men, remembering their past, and "before" men, acquainted with their future: "Thou hast beset me," etc. 6. As every instant holding men under watchful scrutiny: "And laid," etc. II. Personally realized and pondered: "Thou hast searched *me.*" *Me* and *my* run through the whole set of statements. Thus felt and used, the fact of God's omniscience. 1. Begets reverence. 2. Inspires confidence. 3. Produces carefulness of conduct.—*J. F.*

Verses 2—4.—The knowledge of God extends, I. To our movements, our "downsitting and uprising"—when we sit down to read, write, or converse, and when we rise up to active service. II. To our thoughts: "Thou understandest my thoughts afar off." What they have been, what they now are, what they will be, what under all circumstances they would have been. He who made minds knows what their thoughts will be at all times, or he could not predict future events, or govern the world. He can know our thoughts without being the Author of them. III. To our actions : verse 3. Every step we take by day, and all we purpose to do in wakeful hours of the night : all our private, social, and public ways, are compassed or sifted by him, to distinguish the good from the bad, as wheat from the chaff. IV. To our words : verse 4. It has been said that the words of all men and from all time are registered in the atmosphere, and may be faithfully recalled. Whether it be so or not, they are phonographed in the mind of God.—*G. R.*

Verse 2 (first clause).—The importance of the commonest acts of life.

Verse 2 (second clause).—The serious nature of thoughts. Known to God ; seen through, their drift perceived ; and attention given to them while as yet in the distance.

Verse 3.—The encircling Presence, in our activities, meditations, secrecies, and movements.

Verse 4.—I. Words on the tongue first *in* it, and in that stage known to God. II. Words on the tongue very numerous, yet all known. III. Words on the tongue have wide meaning, yet known " altogether." Lesson : Take heed of your words not yet spoken.

Verse 5.—A soul captured. Stopped, overtaken, arrested. What has it done ? What shall it do ?

Verse 6.—I. God imperfectly known to man. II. Man perfectly known to God. It has been said that wise men never wonder ; to us it appears they are always wondering.—*G. R.*

Verse 6.—Theme : the facts of our religion, too wonderful to understand, are just those in which we have most reason to rejoice. I. Prove it. 1. The incomprehensible attributes of God give unspeakable value to his promises. 2. The Incarnation is at once the most complete and most endearing manifestation of God we possess, yet it is the most inexplicable. 3. Redemption by the death of Christ is the highest guarantee of salvation we can conceive ; but who can explain it ? 4. Inspiration makes the Bible the word of God, though none can give an account of its mode of operation in the minds of those " moved by the Holy Ghost." 5. The resurrection of the body, and its glorification, satisfy the deepest yearning of our soul (Rom. viii. 23 ; 2 Cor. v. 2—4) ; but none can conceive the how. II. Apply its lessons. 1. Let us not stumble at doctrines simply because they are mysterious. 2. Let us be thankful God has not kept back the great mysteries of our religion simply because there would be some offended at them. 3. Let us readily receive all the joy which the mysteries bring, and calmly wait the light of heaven to make them better understood.—*J. F.*

Verses 7—10.—I. God is wherever I am. I fill but a small part of space ; he fills all space. II. He is wherever I shall be. He does not move with me, but I move in him. " In him we live, and move," etc. III. God is wherever I could be. " If I ascend to heaven," etc. " If I descend to Sheol," etc. If I travel with the sunbeams to the most distant part of the earth, or heavens, or the sea, I shall be in thy hand. No mention is here made of annihilation, as though that were possible ; which would be the only escape from the Divine Presence ; for he is not the God of the dead, of the annihilated, in the Sadducean meaning of the word, but of the living. Man is always somewhere, and God is always everywhere.—*G. R.*

Verse 8.—The glory of heaven and the terror of hell : " THOU."

Verses 9, 10.—I. The greatest security and encouragement to a sinner supposed. 1. The place—the remotest part of the sea ; by which you are to understand the most obscure nook in the creation. 2. His swift and speedy flight after the commission of sin, to this supposed refuge and sanctuary : " If I take the wings of the morning." II. This supposed security and encouragement is utterly destroyed (verse 10).—*See Flavel's "Seaman's Preservative in Foreign Countries."*

Verses 11, 12.—Darkness and light are both alike to God. I. Naturally. " I form the light, and I create the darkness." II. Providentially. Providential dispensations that are dark to us are light to him. We change with respect to him, not he to us. III. Spiritually. " Let him that walketh in darkness," etc. " Yea, though I walk," etc. He went before them in a pillar of cloud to guide them by day, and a pillar of fire to guide them by night. It was the same God in the day-cloud and in the night-light.—*G. R.*

Verse 14.—" I am fearfully and wonderfully made." This is true of man in his fourfold state. I. In his primitive integrity. II. In his deplorable depravity. III. In his regeneration. IV. In his fixed state in hell or heaven.—*W. W.*

Verses 17, 18.—The Psalm dilates upon the omniscience of God. In no mournful manner, but the reverse. I. *God's thoughts of us.* 1. How certain. 2. How numerous. 3. How condescending. 4. How tender. 5. How wise. 6. How practical. 7. How constant. II. *Our thoughts upon his thoughts.* 1. How rare and yet how due to the subject. 2. How delightful. 3. How consoling. 4. How strengthening to faith. 5. How arousing to love. III. *Our thoughts upon God himself.* 1. They place us near God. 2. They keep us near God. 3. They restore us to him. We are with God when we awake from sleep, from lethargy, from death.

Verses 17, 18.—I. The saint precious to God. He thinks of him tenderly ; in countless ways ; perpetually. II. God precious to the saints. Noting God's loving-kindnesses, numbering them, newly awakening to them. III. The mingling of these loves : " I am still with thee."—*W. B. H.*

Verse 18.—"*When I awake I am still with thee.*" Awaking is sometimes, yea, most commonly, taken in the *natural signification*, for the recovery from bodily sleep. 2. *Morally*, for recovery from sin. 3. *Mystically ;* " when I shall awake," that is, from the sleep of death.—*T. Horton.*

Verse 18.—" A Christian on Earth still in Heaven " [an Appendix to "A Christian on the Mount ; or, A Treatise concerning Meditation "], by *Thomas Watson,* 1660.

Verse 18.—"*I am still with thee.*" 1. By way of meditation. 2. In respect to communion. 3. In regard of action, and the businesses which are done by us.— *T. Horton.*

Verse 19.—I. The doctrine of punishment the necessary outcome of omniscience. II. Inevitable judgment an argument for separation from sinners.—*W. B. H.*

Verse 20.—Two scandalous offences against God. I. To speak slanderously of him. II. To speak irreverently of him. These are committed only by his enemies.

Verses 21, 22.—I. Such hatred one need not be ashamed of. II. Such hatred one should be able to define : " grieved." III. Such hatred one must labour to keep right. " Perfect hatred " is a form of hate consistent with all the virtues.

Verses 23, 24.—The language, I. Of self-examination. 1. As in the sight of God. 2. With a desire for the help of God : verse 23. Look me through and through, and tell me what thou thinkest of me. II. Of self-renunciation : " See if," etc. (verse 24) ; any sin unpardoned, any evil disposition unsubdued, any evil habit unrestrained, that I may renounce it. III. Of self-dedication : " Lead me," etc. : a submission entirely to divine guidance in the future.—*G. R.*

Verse 24.—I. The evil way. Naturally in us ; may be of different kinds ; must be removed ; removal needs Divine help. II. The everlasting way. There is but one, we need leading in it. It is the good old way, it does not come to an end ; it leads to blessedness without end.

Verse 24 (*last clause*).—See " Spurgeon's Sermons," No. 903 : " The Way Everlasting."

PSALM CXL.

This Psalm is in its proper place, and so fitly follows cxxxix. that you might almost read right on, and make no break between the two. Serious injury would follow to the whole Book of Psalms if the order should be interferred with as certain wiseacres propose. It is THE CRY OF A HUNTED SOUL, *the supplication of a believer incessantly persecuted and beset by cunning enemies, who hungered for his destruction. David was hunted like a partridge upon the mountains, and seldom obtained a moment's rest. This is his pathetic appeal to Jehovah for protection, an appeal which gradually intensifies into a denunciation of his bitter foes. With this sacrifice of prayer he offers the salt of faith ; for in a very marked and emphatic manner he expresses his personal confidence in the Lord as the protector of the oppressed, and as his own God and Defender. Few short Psalms are so rich in the jewelry of precious faith.*

" To the Chief Musician."—The writer wished this experimental hymn to be under the care of the chief master of song, that it might neither be left unsung, nor chanted in a slovenly manner. Such trials and such rescues deserved to be had in remembrance, and to be set up among the choicest memorials of the Lord's goodness. We too, have our songs which are of no ordinary kind, and these must be sung with our best powers of heart and tongue. We will offer them to the Lord by no other hand than that of " the Chief Musician."

" A Psalm of David."—The life of David wherein he comes in contact with Saul and Doeg is the best explanation of this Psalm ; and surely there can be no reasonable doubt that David wrote it, and wrote it in the time of his exile and peril. The tremendous outburst at the end has in it the warmth which was so natural to David, who was never lukewarm in anything ; yet it is to be noticed that concerning his enemies he was often hot in language through indignation, and yet he was cool in action, for he was not revengeful. His was no petty malice, but a righteous anger : he foresaw, foretold, and even desired the just vengeance of God upon the proud and wicked, and yet he would not avail himself of opportunities to revenge himself upon those who had done him wrong. It may be that his appeals to the great King cooled his anger, and enabled him to leave his wrongs unredressed by any personal act of violence. "Vengeance is mine ; I will repay, saith the Lord"; and David when most wounded by undeserved persecution and wicked falsehood was glad to leave his matters at the foot of the throne, where they would be safe with the King of kings.

EXPOSITION.

DELIVER me, O LORD, from the evil man : preserve me from the violent man ;

2 Which imagine mischiefs in *their* heart ; continually are they gathered together *for* war.

3 They have sharpened their tongues like a serpent ; adders' poison *is* under their lips. Selah.

1. *"Deliver me, O LORD, from the evil man."* It reads like a clause of the Lord's prayer, " Deliver us from evil." David does not so much plead against an individual as against the species represented by him, namely, the being whose best description is— " the evil man." There are many such abroad ; indeed we we shall not find an unregenerate man who is not in some sense an evil man, and yet all are not alike evil. It is well for us that our enemies are evil : it would be a horrible thing to have the good against us. When " the evil man " bestirs himself against the godly he is as terrible a being as a wolf, or a serpent, or even a devil. Fierce, implacable, unpitying, unrelenting, unscrupulous, he cares for nothing but the indulgence of his malice. The persecuted man turns to God in prayer ; he could not do a wiser thing. Who can meet the evil man and defeat him save Jehovah himself, whose infinite goodness is more than a match for all the evil in

the universe ? We cannot of ourselves baffle the craft of the enemy, but the Lord knoweth how to deliver his saints. He can keep us out of the enemy's reach, he can sustain us when under his power, he can rescue us when our doom seems fixed, he can give us the victory when defeat seems certain ; and in any and every case, if he do not save us from the man he can keep us from the evil. Should we be at this moment oppressed in any measure by ungodly men, it will be better to leave our defence with God than to attempt it ourselves.

"*Preserve me from the violent man.*" Evil in the heart simmers in malice, and at last boils in passion. Evil is a raging thing when it getteth liberty to manifest itself ; and so "the evil man" soon develops into "the violent man." What watchfulness, strength, or valour can preserve the child of God from deceit and violence ? There is but one sure Preserver, and it is our wisdom to hide under the shadow of his wings. It is a common thing for good men to be assailed by enemies : David was attacked by Saul, Doeg, Ahithophel, Shimei, and others ; even Mordecai sitting humbly in the gate had his Haman ; and our Lord, the Perfect One, was surrounded by those who thirsted for his blood. We may not, therefore, hope to pass through the world without enemies, but we may hope to be delivered out of their hands, and preserved from their rage, so that no real harm shall come of their malignity. This blessing is to be sought by prayer, and expected by faith.

2. "*Which imagine mischiefs in their heart.*" They cannot be happy unless they are plotting and planning, conspiring and contriving. They seem to have but one heart, for they are completely agreed in their malice ; and with all their heart and soul they pursue their victim. One piece of mischief is not enough for them ; they work in the plural, and prepare many arrows for their bow. What they cannot actually do they nevertheless like to think over, and to rehearse on the stage of their cruel fancy. It is an awful thing to have such a heart-disease as this. When the imagination gloats over doing harm to others, it is a sure sign that the entire nature is far gone in wickedness. "*Continually are they gathered together for war.*" They are a committee of opposition in permanent session : they never adjourn, but perpetually consider the all-absorbing question of how to do the most harm to the man of God. They are a standing army always ready for the fray : they not only go to the wars, but dwell in them. Though they are the worst of company, yet they put up with one another, and are continually in each other's society, confederate for fight. David's enemies were as violent as they were evil, as crafty as they were violent, and as persistent as they were crafty. It is hard dealing with persons who are only in their element when they are at daggers-drawn with you. Such a case calls for prayer, and prayer calls on God.

3. "*They have sharpened their tongues like a serpent.*" The rapid motion of a viper's tongue gives you the idea of its sharpening it ; even thus do the malicious move their tongues at such a rate that one might suppose them to be in the very act of wearing them to a point, or rubbing them to a keen edge. It was a common notion that serpents inserted their poison by their tongues, and the poets used the idea as a poetical expression, although it is certain that the serpent wounds by his fangs and not by his tongue. We are not to suppose that all authors who used such language were mistaken in their natural history any more than a writer can be charged with ignorance of astronomy because he speaks of the sun's travelling from east to west. How else can poets speak but according to the appearance of things to an imaginative eye. The world's great poet puts it in " King Lear " :

> " She struck me with her tongue,
> Most serpent-like, upon the very heart."

In the case of slanderers, they so literally sting with their tongues, which are so nimble in malice, and withal so piercing and cutting, that it is by no means unjust to speak of them as sharpened. "*Adders' poison is under their lips.*" The deadliest of all venom is the slander of the unscrupulous. Some men care not what they say so long as they can vex and injure. Our text, however, must not be confined in its reference to some few individuals, for in the inspired epistle to the Romans it is quoted by the apostle as being true of us all. So depraved are we by nature that the most venomous creatures are our fit types. The old serpent has not only inoculated us with his venom, but he has caused us to be ourselves producers of the like poison : it lies under our lips, ready for use, and, alas, it is all too freely used when we grow angry, and desire to take vengeance upon any who have caused us vexation. It is sadly wonderful what hard things even good men will say when provoked ; yea, even such as call themselves " perfect " in cool blood are not quite as gentle as doves when their claims to sinlessness are bluntly questioned. This poison of evil-speaking would never fall from our lips, however much we might be provoked, if it were not there at other times ; but by nature we have as great a store of venomous words as a cobra has of poison. O Lord, take the poison-bags away, and cause our lips to drop nothing but honey. "*Selah.*" This is heavy work. Go up, go up, my heart ! Sink not too low. Fall not into the lowest key. Lift up thyself to God.

4 Keep me, O LORD, from the hands of the wicked ; preserve me from the violent man ; who have purposed to overthrow my goings.

5 The proud have hid a snare for me, and cords ; they have spread a net by the wayside ; they have set gins for me. Selah.

4. "*Keep me, O* LORD, *from the hands of the wicked.*" To fall into their hands would be a calamity indeed. David in his most pitiable plight chose to fall into the hand of a chastising God rather than to be left in the power of men. No creature among the wild beasts of the wood is so terrible an enemy to man as man himself when guided by evil, and impelled by violence. The Lord by providence and grace can keep us out of the power of the wicked. He alone can do this, for neither our own watchfulness nor the faithfulness of friends can secure us against the serpentine assaults of the foe. We have need to be preserved from the smooth as well as the rough hands of the ungodly, for their flatteries may harm us as much as their calumnies. The hands of their example may pollute us, and so do us more harm than the hands of their oppression. Jehovah must be our keeper, or evil hands will do what evil hearts have imagined and evil lips have threatened. "*Preserve me from the violent man.*" His intense passion makes him terribly dangerous. He will strike anyhow, use any weapon, smite from any quarter : he is so furious that he is reckless of his own life if he may accomplish his detestable design. Lord, preserve us by thine omnipotence when men attack us with their violence. This prayer is a wise and suitable one. "*Who have purposed to overthrow my goings.*" They resolve to turn the good man from his resolve, they would defeat his designs, injure his integrity, and blast his character. Their own goings are wicked, and therefore they hate those of the righteous, seeing they are a standing rebuke to them. This is a forcible argument to use in prayer with God : he is the patron of holiness, and when the pure lives of his people are in danger of overthrow, he may be expected to interpose. Never let the pious forget to pray, for this is a weapon against which the most determined enemy cannot stand.

5. "*The proud have hid a snare for me.*" Proud as they are, they stoop to this mean action : they use a snare, and they hide it away, that their victim may be taken like a poor hare who is killed without warning—killed in its usual run, by a snare which it could not see. David's enemies wished to snare him in his path of service, the usual way of his life. Saul laid many snares for David, but the Lord preserved him. All around us there are snares of one sort or another, and he will be well kept, ay, divinely kept, who never falls into one of them. "*And cords.*" With these they pull the net together and with these they bind their captive. Thus fowlers do, and trappers of certain large animals. The cords of love are pleasant, but the cords of hate are cruel as death itself. "*They have spread a net by the wayside.*" Where it will be near their prey ; where the slightest divergence from the path will bring the victim into it. Surely the common wayside ought to be safe : men who go out of the way may well be taken in a net, but the path of duty is proverbially the path of safety ; yet it is safe nowhere when malicious persons are abroad. Birds are taken in nets, and men are taken by deceit. Satan instructs his children in the art of fowling, and they right speedily learn how to spread nets : perhaps they have been doing that for us already ; let us make our appeal to God concerning it. "*They have set gins for me.*" One instrument of destruction is not enough ; they are so afraid of missing their prey that they multiply their traps, using differing devices, so that one way or another they may take their victim. Those who avoid the snare and the net may yet be caught in a gin, and accordingly gins are placed in all likely places. If a godly man can be cajoled, or bribed, or cowed, or made angry, the wicked will make the attempt. Ready are they to twist his words, misread his intentions, and misdirect his efforts ; ready to fawn, and lie, and make themselves mean to the last degree so that they

may accomplish their abominable purpose. *"Selah."* The harp needs tuning after such a strain, and the heart needs lifting up towards God.

6 I said unto the LORD, Thou *art* my God : hear the voice of my supplications, O LORD.

7 O GOD the Lord, the strength of my salvation, thou hast covered my head in the day of battle.

8 Grant not, O LORD, the desires of the wicked : further not his wicked device ; *lest* they exalt themselves. Selah.

6. *"I said unto the LORD, thou art my God."* Here was David's stay and hope. He was assured that Jehovah was his God, he expressed that assurance, and he expressed it before Jehovah himself. That had need be a good and full assurance which a man dares to lay before the face of the heart-searching Lord. The Psalmist when hunted by man, addressed himself to God. Often the less we say to our foes, and the more we say to our best Friend the better it will fare with us : if we say anything, let it be said unto the Lord. David rejoiced in the fact that he had already said that Jehovah was his God : he was content to have committed himself, he had no wish to draw back. The Lord was David's own by deliberate choice, to which he again sets his seal with delight. The wicked reject God, but the righteous receive him as their own, their treasure, their pleasure, their light and delight. *"Hear the voice of my supplications, O LORD."* Since thou art mine, I pray thee hear my cries. We cannot ask this favour of another man's god, but we may seek it from our own God. The prayers of saints have a voice in them ; they are expressive pleadings even when they sound like inarticulate moanings. The Lord can discern a voice in our wailings, and he can and will hearken thereto. Because he is God he can hear us ; because he is *our* God he will hear us. So long as the Lord doth but hear us we are content : the answer may be according to his own will, but we do entreat to be heard : a soul in distress is grateful to any one who will be kind and patient enough to hearken to its tale, but specially is it thankful for an audience with Jehovah. The more we consider his greatness and our insignificance, his wisdom and our folly, the more shall we be filled with praise when the Lord attends unto our cry.

7. *"O GOD the Lord, the strength of my salvation, thou hast covered my head in the day of battle."* When he looked back upon past dangers and deliverances, the good man felt that he should have perished had not the Lord held a shield over his head. In the day of the clash of arms, or of putting on of armour (as some read it), the glorious Lord had been his constant protector. Goliath had his armour-bearer, and so had Saul, and these each one guarded his master ; yet the giant and the king both perished, while David, without armour or shield, slew the giant and baffled the tyrant. The shield of the Eternal is better protection than a helmet of brass. When arrows fly thick and the battle-axe crashes right and left, there is no covering for the head like the power of the Almighty. See how the child of providence glorifies his Preserver ! He calls him not only his salvation, but the strength of it, by whose unrivalled force he had been enabled to outlive the cunning and cruelty of his adversaries. He had obtained a deliverance in which the strength of the Omnipotent was clearly to be seen. This is a grand utterance of praise, a gracious ground of comfort, a prevalent argument in prayer. He that has covered our head aforetime will not now desert us. Wherefore let us fight a good fight, and fear no deadly wound : the Lord God is our shield, and our exceeding great reward.

8. *"Grant not, O LORD, the desires of the wicked."* Even they are dependent upon thee ; they can do no more than thou dost permit. Thou dost restrain them ; not a dog of them can move his tongue without thy leave and license. Therefore I entreat thee not to let them have their way. Even though they dare to pray to thee, do not hear their prayers against innocent men. Assuredly the Lord Jehovah will be no accomplice with the malevolent ; their desires shall never be his desires ; if they thirst for blood he will not gratify their cruelty. *"Further not his wicked device."* They are so united as to be like one man in their wishes ; but do not hear their prayers. Though hand join in hand, and they desire and design as one man, yet do not thou lend them the aid of thy providence. Do not permit their malicious schemes to succeed. The Lord may allow success to attend the policy of the wicked

for a time for wise reasons unknown to us, but we are permitted to pray that it be not so. The petition " Deliver us from evil " includes and allows such supplication. *"Lest they exalt themselves."* If successful, the wicked are sure to grow proud, and insult the righteous over whom they have triumphed, and this is so great an evil, and so dishonouring to God, that the Psalmist uses it in his pleading as an argument against their being allowed to prosper. The glory of the wicked is opposed to the glory of God. If God seems to favour them they grow too high for this world, and their heads strike against the heavens. Let us hope that the Lord will not suffer this to be. *"Selah."* Here let us exalt our thoughts and praises high over the heads of self-exalting sinners. The more they rise in conceit the higher let us rise in confidence.

9 As *for* the head of those that compass me about, let the mischief of their own lips cover them.

10 Let burning coals fall upon them; let them be cast into the fire; into deep pits, that they rise not up again.

11 Let not an evil speaker be established in the earth: evil shall hunt the violent man to overthrow *him*.

9. *"As for the head of those that compass me about, let the mischief of their own lips cover them."* To the Lord who had covered his head amid the din of arms the Psalmist appeals against his foes, that their heads may be covered in quite another sense—covered with the reward of their own malice. David's foes were so many that they hemmed him in, encircling him as hunters do their prey. It is little wonder that he turns to the Lord in his dire need. The poet represents his adversaries as so united as to have but one head; for there is often a unanimity among evil spirits which makes them the more strong and terrible for their vile purposes. The *lex talionis*, or law of retaliation, often brings down upon violent men the evil which they planned and spoke of for others: their arrows fall upon themselves. When a man's lips vent curses they will probably, like chickens, come home to roost. A stone hurled upward into the air is apt to fall upon the thrower's head.

David's words may be read in the future as a prophecy; but in this verse, at any rate, there is no need to do so in order to soften their tone. It is so just that the mischief which men plot and the slander which they speak should recoil upon themselves that every righteous man must desire it: he who does not desire it may wish to be considered humane and Christlike, but the chances are that he has a sneaking agreement with the wicked, or is deficient in a manly sense of right and wrong. When evil men fall into pits which they have digged for the innocent we believe that even the angels are glad; certainly the most gentle and tender of philanthropists, however much they pity the sufferers, must also approve the justice which makes them suffer. We suspect that some of our excessively soft-spoken critics only need to be put into David's place, and they would become a vast deal more bitter than he ever was.

10. *"Let burning coals fall upon them."* Then will they know that the scattering of the firebrands is not the sport they thought it to be. When hailstones and coals of fire descend upon them, how will they escape? Even the skies above the wicked are able to deal out vengeance upon them. *"Let them be cast into the fire."* They have kindled the flames of strife, and it is fair that they should be cast therein. They have heated the furnace of slander seven times hotter than it was wont to be heated, and they shall be devoured therein. Who would have pitied Nebuchadnezzar if he had been thrown into his own burning fiery furnace? *"Into deep pits, that they rise not up again."* They made those ditches or fosses for the godly, and it is meet that they should themselves fall into them and never escape. When a righteous man falls he rises again; but when the wicked man goes down " he falls like Lucifer, never to hope again." The Psalmist in this passage graphically depicts the Sodom of the wicked persecutor: fire falls upon him from heaven; the city blazes, and he is cast into the conflagration; the vale of Siddim is full of slime-pits, and into these he is buried. Extraordinary judgment overtakes the extraordinary offender: above, around, beneath, all is destruction. He would have consumed the righteous, and now he is consumed himself. So shall it be: so let it be.

11. *"Let not an evil speaker be established in the earth."* For that would be an established plague, a perpetual curse. Men of false and cruel tongues are of most use when they go to fatten the soil in which they rot as carcasses: while they are alive they are the terror of the good, and the torment of the poor. God will not allow the specious orators of falsehood to retain the power they temporarily obtain by their deceitful speaking. They may become prominent, but they cannot become permanent. They shall be disendowed and disestablished in spite of all that they can say to the contrary. All evil bears the element of decay within itself; for what is it but corruption? Hence the utmost powers of oratory are insufficient to settle upon a sure foundation the cause which bears a lie within it. *"Evil shall hunt the violent man to overthrow him."* He hunted the good, and now his own evil shall hunt him. He tried to overthrow the goings of the righteous, and now his own unrighteousness shall prove his overthrow. As he was violent, so shall he be violently assaulted and hunted down. Sin is its own punishment; a violent man will need no direr doom than to reap what he has sown. It is horrible for a huntsman to be devoured by his own hounds; yet this is the sure fate of the persecutor.

12 I know that the LORD will maintain the cause of the afflicted, *and* the right of the poor.

13 Surely the righteous shall give thanks unto thy name: the upright shall dwell in thy presence.

12. *"I know that the LORD will maintain the cause of the afflicted, and the right of the poor."* All through the Psalm the writer is bravely confident, and speaks of things about which he had no doubt: in fact, no Psalm can be more grandly positive than this protest against slander. The slandered saint knew Jehovah's care for the afflicted, for he had received actual proofs of it himself. " I will maintain it " is the motto of the great Defender of the rights of the needy. What confidence this should create within the bosoms of the persecuted and poverty-stricken! The prosperous and wealthy can maintain their own cause, but those who are otherwise shall find that God helps those who cannot help themselves. Many talk as if the poor had no rights worth noticing, but they will sooner or later find out their mistake when the judge of all the earth begins to plead with them.

13. *"Surely the righteous shall give thanks unto thy name."* The former Psalm had its " surely," but this is a more pleasing one. As surely as God will slay the wicked he will save the oppressed, and fill their hearts and mouths with praises. Whoever else may be silent, the righteous will give thanks; and whatever they may suffer, the matter will end in their living through the trial, and magnifying the Lord for his delivering grace. On earth ere long, and in heaven for ever, the pure heart shall sing unto the Lord. How loud and sweet will be the songs of the redeemed in the millennial age, when the meek shall inherit the earth, and delight themselves in the abundance of peace!

"The upright shall dwell in thy presence." Thus shall they give thanks in the truest and fullest manner. This abiding before the Lord shall render to him " songs without words," and therefore all the more spiritual and true. Their living and walking with their God shall be their practical form of gratitude. Sitting down in holy peace, like children at their father's table, their joyful looks and language shall speak their high esteem and fervent love to him who has become their dwelling-place. How high have we climbed in this Psalm—from being hunted by the evil man to dwelling in the divine presence; so doth faith upraise the saint from the lowest depths to heights of peaceful repose. Well might the song be studded with Selahs, or uplifters.

EXPLANATORY NOTES AND QUAINT SAYINGS.

Whole Psalm.—Another Psalm " *of David*," to be sung by all saints, even as it was used by their Head, David's Son. In it we have (verses 1—3) the *picture of the wicked*, with a "*Selah*," that bids us pause over its dark colours. Then we have (verses 4, 5) *a view of the snares spread by the wicked*, with another " Selah "-pause. Thereafter, we see a soul in *the attitude of faith* (verses 6—8). They are laying the snares, but calm as Elisha beholding the Syrian host assembling (2 Kings v. 15), the stayed soul sings—

"*I have said to the Lord, My God art thou ;*"

and then he prays, putting a "*Selah*" at the close, that we may again pause and survey the scene.—*Andrew A. Bonar.*

Whole Psalm.—There is no doubt that this Psalm expresses the feelings of David on the first intelligence of Saul's setting out *anew* in pursuit of him (comp. verse 2). And then, in Psalm cxli. we have his supplication at the time when this danger was ever approaching nearer. Various things are said in this Psalm (according to the Hebrew) primarily of a single person, (Saul:) thus *e.g.*, verses 1, 4; and the numerous tongues of which David complains (verse 3) are just the tongues of traitors who again informed Saul of this new place of residence in the wilderness of Engedi, where he might have imagined himself so secure. The laying of snares (verse 5) agrees perfectly in part with this treachery, and in part with the search after David by Saul and his numerous army, mentioned in 1 Sam. xxiv. 2. In the same way might the burning coals, spoken of in verse 10, and likewise the deep pits (German, floods) mentioned there, have suggested themselves most naturally to David upon the rocks of Engedi, where he had the Dead Sea just before him. Verse 10 seems also to allude to the events which happened on the night before the destruction of Sodom.—*T. C. Barth, in "The Bible Manual."*

Whole Psalm.—As in Psalm cxxxviii. David set before his seed God's promise as the anchor of hope (2 Sam. vii.) ; and in Psalm cxxxix., God's omniscience as our consolation in danger and motive for shunning evil ; so in this Psalm he sets forth the danger from calumnious enemies, and our only safety in Jehovah, our strength.—*Andrew Robert Fausset.*

Verses 1, 4, 6, 8.—Good men live by prayer. He who gets to the throne of grace is covered by the cloud of glory, through which no sun can smite by day, nor moon by night.—*William Swan Plumer.*

Verses 1, 7—11.—On the first reading of this Psalm one is inclined to think that there is somewhat of fierceness and bitterness in it, which is hardly consistent with the character of a child of God, and therefore unbecoming in David . . . . And yet I really think that a little more examination of the language of this Psalm will lead us to believe that we are doing David wrong in affixing anything like a meaning or desire of vindictiveness to his words.

Assuredly we can find no fault with one who takes his wrongs in prayer to God ; who, like Hezekiah, takes the roll of his cares, and sorrows, and trials, and spreads it before the Lord. And this is what David does in the very first verse: "*Deliver me, O LORD, from the evil man ; preserve me from the violent man.*" I do not think a person who does this, who, when smarting under a sense of injury and wrong, goes at once to God and lays open his heart to him, is likely to go very far wrong ; for even though he may have begun in somewhat of an unkindly spirit, yet prayer opens before us such a sight and sense of our own guiltiness and wrongs towards God, and thereby exercises such an abasing, as well as healing and soothing, influence over our feelings towards others, that we might almost be assured that he whose prayer might begin even with a vehement enumeration of his own wrongs, would end with something very like a determination to bless them that cursed, and to do good to them that hated him.

You will observe, too, how, from first to last, David leaves his cause in God's hands ; it is not " my sword and my bow that shall help me ; " he counted them vain things to help a man ; and therefore, as he had so often said in other Psalms ; " The Lord was his shield and his defence," and as God had already shielded his head in the day of battle, so he prays for the same protection against his enemies now.—*Barton Bouchier.*

Verses 1, 11.—Three special forms of Satanic energy are individualized. The *evil* or wicked man, the *violent* man, and the *man of tongue* are severally appealed from by the suppliant speaker of the prayer of faith.—*Arthur Pridham.*

Verse 2.—"*Continually are they gathered together for war.*" Literally, this clause reads, "*who gather wars*," and so some understand it. But it is well known that the prepositions are often omitted in the Hebrew, and no doubt he means that they stirred up general enmity by their false information which acted as a trumpet sounding to battle.—*John Calvin.*

Verses 2, 3.—The wicked assault the righteous with three weapons—with the heart, by conspiracy; with the tongue, by lying; and with the hand, by violence. —*John Lorinus,* 1569—1634.

Verse 3.—*They have sharpened their tongues like a serpent.*" To sharpen or whet the tongue imports the keenest and extremest kind of talkativeness, much more to sharpen the tongue "*like a serpent.*" Naturalists tell us that no living creature stirs his tongue so swiftly as a serpent, and serpents are therefore said to have a treble tongue, because, moving their tongues so fast, they seem to have three tongues. The Psalmist means—the wicked speak thick and threefold, they sting and poison me with their tongues.—*Joseph Caryl.*

Verse 3.—"*They have sharpened their tongues like a serpent.*" This is an exact description of the way in which a serpent darts out his tongue before he inflicts the wound. See him: his head is erect, and his piercing eye is wildly and fiercely fixed on the object; the tongue rapidly appears and disappears, as if by that process it would be sharpened for the contest. Thus were the enemies of David making sharp their tongues for his destruction.—*Joseph Roberts, in "Oriental Illustrations of the Sacred Scriptures,"* 1835.

Verse 3.—"*They have sharpened their tongues like a serpent,*" etc. Is it not a fact, that there are many men, the very existence of whom is a baneful poison, as it were? They dart their livid tongue like the tongue of a serpent; and the venom of their disposition corrodes every object upon which it concentrates itself; ever vilifying and maligning, like the ill-omened bird of night.—*Pliny.*

Verse 3.—"*They have sharpened their tongues like a serpent.*" As the adder skilfully prepares herself for her work of death, so do the unhappy children of slander and falsehood prepare themselves, by every possible effort, for injuring their unoffending victims.—*John Morison.*

Verse 3.—In St. James's day, as now, it would appear that there were idle men and idle women, who went about from house to house, dropping slander as they went, and yet you could not take up that slander and detect the falsehood there. You could not evaporate the truth in the slow process of the crucible, and then show the residuum of falsehood glittering and visible. You could not fasten upon any word or sentence, and say that it was calumny; for in order to constitute slander, it is not necessary that the word spoken should be false—half-truths are often more calumnious than whole falsehoods. It is not even neccessary that a word should be distinctly uttered; a dropped lip, an arched eyebrow, a shrugged shoulder, a significant look, an incredulous expression of countenance, nay, even an emphatic silence, may do the work; and when the light and trifling thing which has done the mischief has fluttered off, the venom is left behind, to work and rankle, to inflame hearts, to fever human existence, and to poison human society at the fountain springs of life. Very emphatically was it said by one whose whole being had smarted under such affliction, "*Adders' poison is under their lips.*" —*Frederick Wiliam Robertson.*

Verse 3.—Slander and calumny must always precede and accompany perse-cution, because malice itself cannot excite people against a good man, as such; to do this, he must first be represented as a bad man. What can be said of those who are busied in this manner, but that they are a "generation of vipers," the brood of the old "Serpent," that grand accuser and calumniator of the brethren, having under their tongues a bag of "poison," conveying instant death to the reputation on which they fasten. Thus David was hunted as a rebel, Christ was crucified as a blasphemer, and the primitive Christians were tortured as guilty of incest and murder.—*George Horne.*

Verse 3.—Man consists of soul and body; the body is but the shadow, or at best but the bearer of the soul: it's the soul that bears God's image; it's the soul especially for which Christ died. Now, by how much the soul is more precious than the body, by so much are the helps more excellent, and the enemies more dangerous than the body's. The body is fed with meat; but it is perishing meat (1 Cor. vi. 13); but the food of the soul is the heavenly manna (John vi. 27). Answerably, the enemies are more hurtful, for that that hurts or kills the body toucheth not the soul; but what hurts or kills the soul kills the body with it, and destroys the whole man. The conclusion is, that therefore the bane or poison of the soul is much more hideous, horrible and hateful than that of the body; and of that poison speaks the present Scripture: "*adders' poison is under their lips.*"

A strange text some may say, and 'tis true; but it is the fitter for these strange times, wherein the poison both of soul and body so far prevails. The words do describe in part the malignant and malicious nature of the unregenerate and sinful man; and to that purpose are they cited by the apostle to the Romans (ch. iii. 13). The *asp* is but a little creature; but not a little poisonful. So little a creature hath been the bane and death of many a great person; let one suffice for all. That royal and renowned Cleopatra, queen of Egpyt, chose rather to die by the biting of two asps than to be carried in triumph at Rome by Augustus. The manner of their poisoning is this,—he that is bitten by the asp falls forthwith into a gentle sweat and a sweet sleep, and his strength and vital spirits decay and weaken by little till he die; thus the present pain is little, but the stroke is deadly. And even such stings are the tongues, and such swords the words of wicked men. And no marvel; for what can come but poisonful words and actions from them whose very inward nature is all poison within!

The poison of the soul is only *sin*, and this is like to poison in many respects. Poison, wherever it enters, stays not there, but diffuseth itself all over the body, and never ceaseth till it has infected all. Such is the nature of sin; enter where it will it creeps from one member of the body to another, and from the body to the soul, till it has infected the whole man; and then from man to man, till the whole family; and stays not there, but runs like a wildfire, from family to family, till it has poisoned a whole town, and so a whole country, and a whole kingdom. Woeful experience proves this true, both for Popish opinions, idle fashions, vain customs, and ill-examples of all sorts, which once set on foot, spread themselves over the politic body of church and commonwealth, like a gangrene or a leprosy over the natural body or like a poison through all the blood. Poison, having entered anywhere, as it seeks to creep presently over all, so desires it especially to seize upon the heart; such a malice and pride lies in the malignant nature of it, that it aspires to the heart; and such a craft and cunning lurks in it, that having once entered, it creeps closely and unfelt till it gets to the heart; but having possessed itself of that sovereign part of man, then like a tyrant it reigns and rages, and infecting first the vital blood and noble parts, it diffuseth itself over all and every part. And such is the nature of sin, the spiritual poison of the soul; enter where it will, it is the heart it aims at, and it will never stay till it come there. The truth of this is so clear that proofs are needless; for who knows not that the senses are but the doors or windows, but the heart is the throne, and the soul itself the seat of sin: and hence it is that Solomon adviseth,—"My son, keep thy heart with all diligence": Prov. iv. 23. —*William Crashaw, in "The Parable of Poyson," 1618.*

Verse 3.—"*Adders' poison is under their lips."* The word rendered "*adder,*" עַכְשׁוּב, *achsub*, occurs here only; and it is perhaps impossible to determine what species is intended. As the word, in its proper signification, seems to express coiling, or bending back—an act common to most serpents—the name has perhaps no determinate reference; or it may be another name for the *pethen*, mentioned under Job xx.; which seems also to have been the opinion of the Seventy, as they render both words by ἀσπίς, and are followed by the Vulgate (*aspis*).

As to the *poison*, it will be observed, that in the venomous serpents there is a gland under the eye secreting the poisonous matter, which is conveyed, in a small tube or canal, to the end of a fang which lies concealed at the roof of the mouth. This fang is moveable at the pleasure of the serpent, and is protruded when it is about to strike at an antagonist. The situation of this poison, which is, in a manner, behind the upper lip, gives great propriety to the expression, "*adders' poison is under their lips.*" The usage of the Hebrew language renders it by no means improbable that the fang itself is called לָשׁוֹן *lashon*, a tongue, in the present text; and a serpent might then be said to sharpen its tongue, when, in preparing to strike, it protruded its fangs. We do not see any explanation by which a more consistent meaning may be extracted from the expression here employed.—*John Kitto, in the "Pictorial Bible."*

Verse 3.—Often the tongue of the serpent is spoken of as the seat of its venom. This is popular, not scientific language.—*William Swan Plumer.*

Verse 3.—*"Adder."* The word *acshub* (pronounced ăk-shoob), only occurs in this one passage. The precise species represented by this word, is unknown. Buxtorf, however, explains the word as the Spitter, "*illud genus quod venenum procul exspuit.*" Now, if we accept this derivation, we must take the word *acshub* as a synonym for *pethen.* We have already identified the Pethen with the Naja haje, a snake which has the power of expelling the poison to some distance, when it is out of reach of its enemy. Whether the snake really intends to eject the poison, or whether it is merely flung from the hollow fangs by the force of the sudenly-checked stroke, is uncertain. That the Haje cobra can expel its poison is an acknowledged fact, and the Dutch colonists of the Cape have been so familiarly acquainted with this habit, that they have called this reptile by the name of Spuugh-Slange, or Spitting-Snake, a name which, if we accept Buxtorf's etymology, is precisely equivalent to the word *acshub.*—*J. G. Wood, in "Bible Animals."*

Verses 3, 5, 8.—*"Selah."* We meet with *Selah* here for the first time since Psalm lxxxix. From Psalm xc. to Psalm cxl. no *Selah* occurs. Why omitted in these fifty we cannot tell any more than why so often recurring in others. However, there are only about forty Psalms in all in which it is used.—*Andrew A. Bonar.*

Verse 4.—*"Keep me,"* etc. From doing as they do, or as they would have me do, or as they promise themselves I will do.—*Matthew Henry.*

Verse 4.—*"Preserve me from the violent man."* The second clause of the first versicle of this verse is the same as the second versicle of verse 1, which seems the burden of the song.—*"Speaker's Commentary."*

Verse 4.—*"To overthrow my goings."* To take my feet from under me, to destroy the basis of belief, the power of advance in good works, that we may turn back from the way of salvation, or fall upon it, or, at any rate, may go very slowly along it.—*Neale and Littledale.*

Verse 5.—*"The proud have hid a snare for me, and cords."* The following story illustrates how *cords* have been used by thieves so lately as the year 1822 :—" Two skilful leaders of Dacoits, having collected some forty followers, and distributed among them ten matchlocks, ten swords, and twenty-five spears, waylaid a treasure going from the native Collector's treasury at Budrauna to Goruckpore. The prize consisted of £1,200, and was guarded by a Naik, or corporal, with four sepoys and five troopers. It had to pass through a dense jungle, and it was settled—said one of them in after years—' that the attack should take place there ; that we should have strong ropes tied across the road in front and festooned to trees on both sides, and, at a certain distance behind, similar ropes festooned to trees on one side, and ready to be fastened on the other, as soon as the escort of horse and foot should get well in between them.' Having completed these preparations the gang laid down on either side of the road patiently awaiting their prey. ' About five in the morning,' continued the narrator, ' we heard a voice as if calling upon the name of God (Allah), and one of the gang started up at the sound and said, " Here comes the treasure ! " We put five men in front with their matchlocks loaded—not with ball but shot, that we might, if possible, avoid killing anybody. When we got the troopers, infantry, and treasure all within the space, the hind ropes were run across the road, and made fast to the trees on the opposite side, and we opened a fire in upon the party from all sides. The foot soldiers got into the jungle at the sides of the road, and the troopers tried to get over the ropes at both ends, but in vain.' The corporal and a horse were killed ; two troopers wounded, and the treasure carried off in spite of a hot pursuit."—*From James Hutton's "Popular Account of the Thugs and Dacoits of India,"* 1857.

Verse 5.—*"The proud have hid a snare for me, and cords."* There was " a trap hidden for him with cords ;" a trap being sunk into some frequented path, and always covered over with grass or brushwood, and having long cords attached to each side, by which the hunter, lurking at a little distance, might close it whenever he saw the game stepping on the spot. But the net spread for him by his enemies extended to the very " side of the encampment," which indicates, that even among the soldiers lying around him, there were some who had been bribed and persuaded to watch and betray him.—*Benjamin Weiss, in "A New Translation of the Psalms, with Notes,"* 1858.

Verse 5.—*"Snare." "Net." "Gins."* The several uses to which the contrivances denoted by the Hebrew words thus rendered were respectively applied, do not appear to be well ascertained. In general the Psalmist alludes to the artifices employed for capturing birds or beasts. It is, however, a curious circumstance, as noticed by Thevenot, that artifices of this kind are literally employed against men as well as other animals by some of the Orientals. " The cunningest robbers in the world," says he, " are in this country. They use a certain slip with a running noose, which they cast with so much sleight about a man's neck when they are within reach of him, that they never fail, so that they strangle him in a trice."— *Richard Mant.*

Verse 6.—*"The voice of my supplications."* The one safety for simple and unlearned people when assailed by the crafty arguments of heretics and infidels is not controversy, but prayer, a weapon their adversaries seldom use, and cannot understand—*Bruno of Aste,* 1123.

Verse 7.—*"Thou hast covered my head in the day of battle."* Hebrew, *of armour.* For David had never indeed any battle with Saul, but declined it ; but Saul often armed against him ; but then God's providence covered him as a shield : but the *head* is only spoken of to set forth his whole body, because that is chiefly aimed at by the enemy, as where the life principally lieth.—*John Meyer.*

Verse 7.—*"Thou hast covered my head,"* etc. That is, I had no other helmet or armour but thy Almighty power in the day when I fought with Goliath. 1 Sam. xvii. 39, 40. 50.—*Thomas Fenton.*

Verse 7.—*"Thou hast covered my head in the day of battle."* A captain or prince had always beside him in battle an armour-bearer, whose duty it was " to cover his master's head," that is, to ward off with the shield the blows aimed at his head, and which, in the heat of the fight, had escaped his own notice.—*Benjamin Weiss.*

Verse 8.—*"His wicked device"* ; which is to destroy me. *"Exalt themselves"* ; not only against me, but against thee also, as if by their power and policy they had frustrated thy design and promise made to me.—*M. Pool.*

Verse 9.—*"As for the head of those that compass me about,"* etc. God, he saith, had covered his head in the day of battle : now contrariwise he showeth what should cover the head of his enemies, viz., it should come to them as with their lips they had maliciously spoken against him ; for it may be thus rendered—"The head of my besieger, let the trouble of his lips cover it " : for cursing, let him be covered with cursing as with a cloak.—*John Mayer.*

Vere 9.—*"Those that compass me about."* For an explanation of this expression we would refer the reader to "The Treasury of David," vol. i., p. 343—344, where he will find two very pertinent extracts from J. Stevenson and Dr. Shaw.

Verse 9.—*"The mischief of their own lips."* The pride and hauteur of the Jews in our Lord's day brought the Roman arms upon them, and caused them to fall into irremediable ruin. They evoked their own fate by exposing themselves to an invasion from Rome at all ; but they did it still more in that terrific cry—" His blood be upon us and on our children."—*William Hill Tucker, in "The Psalms, with Notes, shewing their Prophetic and Christian Character,"* 1840.

Verses 9, 10.—Such passages admit of translation in the future, and are rather predictions than imprecations.—*Ingram Cobbin,* 1839.

Verses 9—11.—The prophet, in these three verses, predicted those just judgments which heaven will inflict on the slanderers and persecutors of the righteous. Their lips, which uttered mischief against others, shall be the means of covering themselves with confusion, when out of their own mouths they shall be judged. Those tongues which have contributed to set the world on fire, shall be tormented with the hot burning coals of eternal vengeance : and they, who, with so much eagerness and diligence have prepared pits for the destruction of their brethren, shall be cast into a deep and bottomless pit, out of which they will not rise up again any more for ever. Evil speakers and false accusers shall gain no lasting establishment, but punishment shall hunt sin through all its doubles, and seize it at last as its legal prey. Let these great truths be firmly rooted in our hearts, and they will keep us steady in the worst of times.—*George Horne.*

Verse 10.—*"Let burning coals fall upon them,"* etc. The Psalmist seems here to allude to the destruction of the Sodomites. In these imprecations he considered his enemies as the enemies of God, rather than as his own ; and he thus cursed them, as knowing, in the quality of a prophet, that God himself had cursed them : and therefore these sorts of imprecations do not authorize other persons to curse their enemies.—*Thomas Fenton.*

Verse 10.—*"Let burning coals fall upon them,"* etc. An imprecation which (with the similar previous one, Psalm ix. 6, etc.), is a prophecy ; and one which, while it has had no fulfilment in the case of David's enemies, or any persecutors of the church in times past, brings again vividly before the mind the fiery judgment of the Lord's coming, and the awful sentence already pronounced against " the beast and false prophet," the leaders of the confederation of the kings of the earth and their armies, then " gathered together to make war against him "—" these were cast alive into the lake of fire burning with brimstone"; Rev. xix. 19, 20. So before, Psalm lv. 15 ; lxiii. 9.—*William De Burgh.*

Verse 11.—*"Let not an evil speaker [a man full of tongue] be established,"* etc. The man given to talk, the liar, the flatterer, the detractor, the scold, the brawler, *"shall not be established in the earth,"* for such people are abhorred by the wicked as well as by the good.—*Robert Bellarmine.*

Verse 11.—*"Let not an evil speaker be established,"* etc. The positions laid down in this verse will find abundant illustration in every age of the church. *"An evil speaker,"* who takes delight in wounding the reputation of others, is seldom established or prospered in the earth. Providence fights against such an unhappy wretch. *"The violent man,"* the Ishmaelite whose hand is against every man, is in general overthrown by the very same weapons which he wields against others.—*John Morison.*

Verse 11.—*"An evil speaker."* By " a man of the tongue," as the original has it, the Hebrews express a *detractor* or *sycophant ;* one who gives his tongue the liberty to vent what mischief he pleases. The Chaldee here expresses it by *a delator* or vile informer with a *threefold* or *three-forked tongue ;* because such a man wounds *three* at once ; the receiver, the sufferer, and himself.—*Thomas Fenton.*

Verse 11.—*"Evil shall hunt the violent man to overthrow him."* 'Tis an allusion to hounds that are of a quick scent, and pursue the game with pleasure ; they do not see the deer or the hare, yet they follow upon the scent ; and though they have sometimes a very cold and dead scent, yet they will follow and work it out. Thus *"evil shall hunt the violent man to overthrow him";* and though sometimes he hath, as it were, got out of the view or sight of evil, and thinks himself under covert, yet these evils, like a company of greedy hounds, will pursue till they have overtaken and overthrown him.—*Joseph Caryl.*

Verse 12.—*"I know."* For I have a promise of it, and that's infallible.—*John Trapp.*

Verses 12, 13.—*"I know that the LORD will maintain the cause,"* etc. Why, how comes the Psalmist so confident ? *"Surely the righteous shall give thanks unto thy name " :* as if he had said, Thou hast a name for a gracious and faithful God in thy promise, and this thou wilt never suffer to be blotted by failing in thy word. Christian, thou mayest venture all thou art worth on the public faith of Heaven : " His words are pure, as silver tried seven times in a furnace." He that will not suffer a liar or covenant-breaker to set foot on his holy hill, will much less suffer any one thought of falseness or unfaithfulness to enter into his own most holy heart.—*William Gurnall.*

Verse 13.—*"Surely the righteous shall give thanks unto thy name,"* etc. Teacheth us two things, first, that it becometh the godly to show themselves continually thankful, because God is continually merciful to them ; secondly, what is the excellent estate and condition of God's children, which, though it do not yet appear, yet shall it in the end break forth with fulness of glory."—*Thomas Wilcocks.*

Verse 13.—*"The upright shall dwell in thy presence."* *"Sit in thy presence,"* as thy friends or guests or favoured servants. Perhaps it may mean *sit (enthroned) before thee.* Compare Matt. xix. 28. Some understand the sense to be *shall dwell (in the land) before thee,* i.e., under thy protection and inspection.—*Joseph Addison Alexander.*

HINTS TO PREACHERS.

Verses 1—5.—I. The particular source of David's affliction : it was from men. In this he was a type of Christ. 1. Their wickedness : " the evil man." 2. Their violence : " the violent man." 3. Their malicious designs : " which imagine mischiefs in their heart." 4. Their confederacy : " continually are they gathered together for war." 5. Their false accusations : " They have sharpened their tongues like a serpent," etc. (verse 3). 6. Their avowed design : " they have purposed to overthrow my goings " (verse 4). 7. Their intrigues (verse 5). II. His universal remedy : " Deliver me, O LORD "; " preserve " and help me. His defence is, 1. In God. 2. In prayer to God.—*G. R.*

Verses 1—5.—In our position, age, and country, we are not in danger of violence from men, as was David; still, no man is absolutely safe from the danger. I. Mention some cases not yet impossible. 1. A Christian workman, because he cannot comply with unrighteous customs, excites the animosity of his fellow workers. They will do him mischief, spoil his work, steal his tools, speak evil of him, until his employer discharges him to restore peace in the factory. 2. A Christian clerk or shop assistant, because his presence is a check upon his sinful companions, may have snares laid for him, etc. II. Suggest advice, useful, should such a case arise. 1. Resort to God with a " Deliver me," and a " Preserve me." 2. Maintain integrity and uprightness. 3. Should the mischievous ones succeed, still trust in God, who can make their mischief lead to your profit, and make his goodness outwit their devices.—*J. F.*

Verse 3.—The depraved state of the natural man as to his speech.

Verse 4 (*first clause*).—A wise prayer. The wicked will slander, and oppress, or mislead, flatter and defile. No one can keep us but the Lord.

Verse 5.—The Dangers of Society. I. The secrecy of the attacks of the ungodly : " hid a snare." II. The variety of their weapons : " and cords." III. The cunning choice of position : " by the wayside." IV. The object of their designs : " for me " : they desire to destroy the man himself.

Verse 5.—" The Net by the Wayside," or, covert temptations ; temptations brought near, and made applicable to daily life.

Verse 6.—I. The language of assurance. II. The plea for acceptance in prayer.

Verses 6, 7.—David comforted himself, 1. In his interest in God : " I said . . . thou art my God." 2. In his access to God : he had leave to speak to him, and might expect an answer of peace : " Hear," etc. 3. In the assurance he had of help from God, and happiness in him (verse 7). 4. In the experience he had formerly of God's care of him : " Thou hast covered my head in the day of battle."—*Matthew Henry.*

Verses 6—8.—Three arguments to be pleaded in a prayer for protection. I. The believer's covenanted property in God. " I said . . . thou art my God." II. The past mercies of God. " Thou hast covered," etc. III. The impropriety of the wicked being encouraged in their wickedness, ver. 8.—*J. F.*

Verses 6, 7—12.—The Consolations of the Believer in Time of Trouble. I. What he can say. II. What he can remember. III. What he is assured of.

Verses 6, 7, 12, 13.—Times of Assault, Slander, and Temptation should be special times of Prayer and Faith. David here makes prominent five things. I. *Possession asserted.* 1. The Possession : " My God." Opposed to idols. Beloved by self. 2. The Claim published. 3. The Witness selected. Secret. Sacred. Searching. 4. The Occasion chosen. II. *Petition presented.* 1. His prayers were frequent. 2. His prayers were full of meaning. 3. His prayers were meant for God. 4. His prayers needed divine attention. III. *Preservation experienced.* 1. God had been his Armour-bearer. 2. God had guarded his most vital part. 3. God had saved him. 4. God's strength had been displayed. IV. *Protection expected.* 1. God is a righteous Judge. 2. God is a compassionate Friend. 3. God is a well-known Guardian. V. *Praise predicted.* 1. Praise assured by gratitude. 2. Praise expressed by words. 3. Praise implied in confidence. 4. Praise practised by communion.

Verse 9.—How the sin of evil-speakers comes home to them.—*W. B. H.*

Verse 11 (*first clause*).—I. Notice a few varieties of evil speakers, 1. Liars the common liar, the trade liar, the stock-exchange liar, the political liar, etc. 2. Scandal-mongers. 3. Blasphemers and swearers. 4. Libertines and seducers.

5. Sceptics and new theology inventors.　II. The propriety of the prayer.　1. Because evil speaking is intrinsically an evil thing.　2. It is an extensively injurious thing. 3. He who would have God's truth established must needs desire that evil speaking must fail.　III. The limitation of the prayer : " In the earth."　1. It is certain an evil speaker cannot be established in heaven, nor in hell.　2. The earth is the only sphere of his influence ; but, alas ! men on the earth are too prone to be influenced by him.　3. Then, become righteous and true, by faith in the Righteous One and the " Truth."—*J. F.*

Verse 11 (*second clause*).—The Cruel Hunter pursued by his own Dogs.

Verse 11 (*second clause*).—Theme—Sins committed, and not repented of, pursue men to their ruin.　I. Illustrate.　1. They may raise a force of opposition from men.　Tarquin, Napoleon, etc.　2. They may precipitate ruin, as Haman was hunted by his own sin to the gallows.　3. They may arouse destructive remorse, as in Judas.　4. Certainly they will pursue to the judgment-seat, and hunt the soul into hell.　II. Apply.　1. How fearful a thing must sin be.　2. The more terrible because self-created.　3. Flee from the avenging pursuers to Christ, the only and safe refuge.—*J. F.*

Verse 11 (*second clause*).—The hunt and pursuit of the violent sinner.　I. The progress of the chase.　1. At first the victim is ignorant of it.　2. But ere long he finds Scripture, conscience, God, Death, at his heels.　3. His own sins cry loudest after him.　II. The issue of the hunt.　Hemmed in, overthrown, lost for ever, unless he repent.　III. Another Huntsman.　" The Son of man is come to seek and save that which was lost."—*W. B. H.*

Verse 12.—I. The known fact.　II. The reasons for being so assured of it. III. The conduct arising out of the knowledge.

Verse 12.—Something worth knowing.　I. By the afflicted and the poor who trust in the Lord.　II. By the oppressors who afflict and do the wrong.　III. By all men, that they may trust in the Lord, and praise him for his compassion towards the needy, and for his even-handed justice.—*J. F.*

Verses 12, 13.—I. Trust under all circumstances (verse 12).　II. Gratitude for all things : " The righteous shall give thanks unto thy name."　III. Safety at all times : " The upright shall dwell in thy presence."—*G. R.*

Verse 13.—One of the noblest forms of praise,—dwelling in the presence of God. Or, reverent regard to God's presence, holy communion with the Lord, confiding rest in God's dealings, obedient doing of the heavenly will—the best way of giving thanks to God.

Verse 13.—Two assertions beyond contradiction.　I. The righteous are sure to give thanks to God, let others be as thankless as they will.　For, 1. They recognise all their good as coming from God.　2. They realise themselves as unworthy of the good they receive.　3. They are anxious to do right, because they are righteous ; and that involves thanksgiving.　4. Thankfulness is a part of the joy derived from what they enjoy.　II. The upright are sure to dwell in God's presence.　1. In the sense of setting the Lord before them.　2. In the sense of an abiding, present fellowship with God.　3. In the sense of enjoying God's approval.　4. In the sense of dwelling in heaven for ever.—*J. F.*

PSALM CXLI

TITLE.—A Psalm of David. *Yes, David under suspicion, half afraid to speak lest he should speak unadvisedly while trying to clear himself; David slandered and beset by enemies; David censured even by saints, and taking it kindly; David deploring the condition of the godly party of whom he was the acknowledged head; David waiting upon God with confident expectation. The Psalm is one of a group of four, and it bears a striking likeness to the other three. Its meaning lies so deep as to be in places exceedingly obscure, yet even upon its surface it has dust of gold. In its commencement the Psalm is lighted up with the evening glow as the incense rises to heaven; then comes a night of language whose meaning we cannot see; and this gives place to morning light in which our eyes are unto the Lord.*

DIVISION.—*The Psalmist cries for acceptance in prayer (verses 1, 2); then he begs to be kept as to his speech, preserved in heart and deed, and delivered from every sort of fellowship with the ungodly. He prefers to be rebuked by the gracious rather than to be flattered by the wicked, and consoles himself with the confident assurance that he will one day be understood by the godly party, and made to be a comfort to them (verses 3—6). In the last verses the slandered saint represents the condition of the persecuted church, looks away to God and pleads for rescue from his cruel enemies, and for the punishment of his oppressors.*

EXPOSITION.

LORD, I cry unto thee: make haste unto me; give ear unto my voice, when I cry unto thee.

2 Let my prayer be set forth before thee *as* incense; *and* the lifting up of my hands *as* the evening sacrifice.

1. "*LORD, I cry unto thee.*" This is my last resort: prayer never fails me. My prayer is painful and feeble, and worthy only to be called a cry; but it is a cry unto Jehovah, and this ennobles it. I have cried unto thee, I still cry to thee, and I always mean to cry to thee. To whom else could I go? What else can I do? Others trust to themselves, but I cry unto thee. The weapon of all prayer is one which the believer may always carry with him, and use in every time of need. "*Make haste unto me.*" His case was urgent, and he pleaded that urgency. God's time is the best time, but when we are sorely pressed we may with holy importunity quicken the movements of mercy. In many cases, if help should come late, it would come too late; and we are permitted to pray against such a calamity. "*Give ear unto my voice, when I cry unto thee.*" See how a second time he talks of crying: prayer had become his frequent, yea, his constant exercise: twice in a few words he says, " I cry; I cry." How he longs to be heard, and to be heard at once! There is a voice to the great Father in every cry, and groan, and tear of his children: he can understand what they mean when they are quite unable to express it. It troubles the spirit of the saints when they fear that no favourable ear is turned to their doleful cries: they cannot rest unless their " unto thee " is answered by an " unto me." When prayer is a man's only refuge, he is deeply distressed at the bare idea of his failing therein.

> " That were a grief I could not bear,
>   Didst thou not hear and answer prayer;
>   But a prayer-hearing, answering God
>   Supports me under every load."

2. "*Let my prayer be set forth before thee as incense.*" As incense is carefully prepared, kindled with holy fire, and devoutly presented unto God, so let my prayer

be. We are not to look upon prayer as easy work requiring no thought, it needs to be " set forth " ; what is more, it must be set forth " before the Lord," by a sense of his presence and a holy reverence for his name : neither may we regard all supplication as certain of divine acceptance, it needs to be set forth before the Lord " as incense," concerning the offering of which there were rules to be observed, otherwise it would be rejected of God. "*And the lifting up of my hands as the evening sacrifice.*" Whatever form his prayer might take his one desire was that it might be accepted of God. Prayer is sometimes presented without words by the very motions of our bodies : bended knees and lifted hands are the tokens of earnest, expectant prayer. Certainly work, or the lifting up of the hands in labour, is prayer if it be done in dependence upon God and for his glory : there is a hand-prayer as well as a heart-prayer, and our desire is that this may be sweet unto the Lord as the sacrifice of eventide. Holy hope, the lifting up of hands that hang down, is also a kind of worship : may it ever be acceptable with God. The Psalmist makes a bold request : he would have his humble cries and prayers to be as much regarded of the Lord as the appointed morning and evening sacrifices of the holy place. Yet the prayer is by no means too bold, for, after all, the spiritual is in the Lord's esteem higher than the ceremonial, and the calves of the lips are a truer sacrifice than the calves of the stall.

So far we have a prayer about prayer ; we have a distinct supplication in the two following verses.

3 Set a watch, O LORD, before my mouth ; keep the door of my lips.

4 Incline not my heart to *any* evil thing, to practise wicked works with men that work iniquity : and let me not eat of their dainties.

5 Let the righteous smite me ; *it shall be* a kindness : and let him reprove me ; *it shall be* an excellent oil, *which* shall not break my head : for yet my prayer also *shall be* in their calamities.

6 When their judges are overthrown in stony places, they shall hear my words ; for they are sweet.

3. "*Set a watch, O LORD, before my mouth.*" That mouth had been used in prayer, it would be a pity it should ever be defiled with untruth, or pride, or wrath ; yet so it will become unless carefully watched, for these intruders are ever lurking about the door. David feels that with all his own watchfulness he may be surprised into sin, and so he begs the Lord himself to keep him. When Jehovah sets the watch the city is well guarded : when the Lord becomes the guard of our mouth the whole man is well garrisoned. "*Keep the door of my lips.*" God has made our lips the door of the mouth, but we cannot keep that door of ourselves, therefore do we entreat the Lord to take the rule of it. O that the Lord would both open and shut our lips, for we can do neither the one nor the other aright if left to ourselves. In times of persecution by ungodly men we are peculiarly liable to speak hastily, or evasively, and therefore we should be specially anxious to be preserved in that direction from every form of sin. How condescending is the Lord ! We are ennobled by being door-keepers for him, and yet he deigns to be a door-keeper for us.

4. "*Incline not my heart to any evil thing.*" It is equivalent to the petition, " Lead us not into temptation." O that nothing may arise in providence which would excite our desires in a wrong direction. The Psalmist is here careful of his heart. He who holds the heart is lord of the man ; but if the tongue and the heart are under God's care all is safe. Let us pray that he may never leave us to our own inclinings, or we shall soon decline from the right.

"*To practise wicked works with men that work iniquity.*" The way the heart inclines the life soon tends : evil things desired bring forth wicked things practised. Unless the fountain of life is kept pure the streams of life will soon be polluted. Alas, there is great power in company : even good men are apt to be swayed by association ; hence the fear that we may practise wicked works when we are with wicked workers. We must endeavour not to be with them lest we sin with them. It is bad when the heart goes the wrong way alone, worse when the life runs in the evil road alone ; but it is apt to increase unto a high degree of ungodliness when the backslider runs the downward path with a whole horde of sinners around him. Our practice will be our perdition if it be evil ; it is an aggravation of sin rather than an excuse for it to say that it is our custom and our habit. It is God's practice to punish all who make a practice of iniquity. Good men are horrified at the thought of sinning as others do ; the fear of it drives them to their knees. Iniquity, which, being interpreted, is a want of equity, is a thing to be shunned as we would avoid an infectious disease. *"And let me not eat of their dainties."* If we work with them we shall soon eat with them. They will bring out their sweet morsels, and delicate dishes, in the hope of binding us to their service by the means of our palates. The trap is baited with delicious meats that we may be captured and become meat for their malice. If we would not sin with men we had better not sit with them, and if we would not share their wickedness we must not share their wantonness.

5. *"Let the righteous smite me ; it shall be a kindness."* He prefers the bitters of gracious company to the dainties of the ungodly. He would rather be smitten by the righteous than feasted by the wicked. He gives a permit to faithful admonition, he even invites it—" let the righteous smite me." When the ungodly smile upon us their flattery is cruel ; when the righteous smite us their faithfulness is kind. Sometimes godly men rap hard ; they do not merely hint at evil, but hammer at it ; and even then we are to receive the blows in love, and be thankful to the hand which smites so heavily. Fools resent reproof ; wise men endeavour to profit by it. *"And let him reprove me ; it shall be an excellent oil, which shall not break my head."* Oil breaks no heads, and rebuke does no man any harm ; rather, as oil refreshes and perfumes, so does reproof when fitly taken sweeten and renew the heart. My friend must love me well if he will tell me of my faults : there is an unction about him if he is honest enough to point out my errors. Many a man has had his head broken at the feasts of the wicked, but none at the table of a true-hearted reprover. The oil of flattery is not excellent ; the oil so lavishly used at the banquet of the reveller is not excellent ; head-breaking and heart-breaking attend the anointings of the riotous ; but it is otherwise with the severest censures of the godly : they are not always sweet, but they are always excellent ; they may for the moment bruise the heart, but they never break either it or the head. *"For yet my prayer also shall be in their calamities."* Gracious men never grow wrathful with candid friends so as to harbour an ill-feeling against them ; if so, when they saw them in affliction, they would turn round upon them and taunt them with their rebukes. Far from it ; these wisely grateful souls are greatly concerned to see their instructors in trouble, and they bring forth their best prayers for their assistance. They do not merely pray for them, but they so closely and heartily sympathize that their prayers are " in their calamities," down in the dungeon with them. So true is Christian brotherhood that we are with our friends in sickness or persecution, suffering their griefs ; so that our heart's prayer is in their sorrows. When we can give good men nothing more, let us give them our prayers, and let us do this doubly to those who have given us their rebukes.

6. This is a verse of which the meaning seems far to seek. Does it refer to the righteous among the Israelites ? We think so. David surely means that when their leaders fell never to rise again, they would then turn to him and take delight in listening to his voice. *"When their judges are overthrown in stony places, they shall hear my words ; for they are sweet."* And so they did : the death of Saul made all the best of the nation look to the son of Jesse as the Lord's anointed ; his words became sweet to them. Many of those good men who had spoken severely of David's quitting his country, and going over to the Philistines, were nevertheless dear to his heart for their fidelity, and to them he returned nothing but good-will, loving prayers, and sweet speeches, knowing that by-and-by they would overlook his faults, and select him to be their leader. They smote him when he erred, but they recognized his excellences. He, on his part, bore no resentment, but loved them for their honesty. He would pray for them when their land lay bleeding at the feet of their foreign enemies ; he would come to their rescue when their former leaders were slain ; and his words of courageous hopefulness would be sweet in their ears. This seems to me to be a good sense, consistent with the context. At the same time, other and more laboured interpretations have their learned admirers, and to these we will refer in our notes from other authors.

7 Our bones are scattered at the grave's mouth, as when one cutteth and cleaveth *wood* upon the earth.

8 But mine eyes *are* unto thee, O GOD the Lord : in thee is my trust ; leave not my soul destitute.

9 Keep me from the snares *which* they have laid for me, and the gins of the workers of iniquity.

10 Let the wicked fall into their own nets, whilst that I withal escape.

7. David's case seemed hopeless : the cause of God in Israel was as a dead thing, even as a skeleton broken, and rotten, and shovelled out of the grave, to return as dust to its dust. *"Our bones are scattered at the grave's mouth."* There seemed to be no life, no cohesion, no form, order, or headship among the godly party in Israel : Saul had demolished it, and scattered all its parts, so that it did not exist as an organized whole. David himself was like one of these dried bones, and the rest of the godly were in much the same condition. There seemed to be no vitality or union among the holy seed ; but their cause lay at death's door. *"As when one cutteth and cleaveth wood upon the earth."* They were like wood divided and thrown apart : not as one piece of timber, nor even as a bundle, but all cut to pieces, and thoroughly divided. Leaving out the word " wood," which is supplied by the translators, the figure relates to cleaving upon the earth, which probably means ploughing, but may signify any other form of chopping and splitting, such as felling a forest, tearing up bushes, or otherwise causing confusion and division. How often have good men thought thus of the cause of God ! Wherever they have looked, death, division, and destruction have stared them in the face. Cut and cloven, hopelessly sundered ! Scattered, yea, scattered at the grave's mouth ! Split up and split for the fire ! Such the cause of God and truth has seemed to be. " Upon the earth " the prospect was wretched ; the field of the church was ploughed, harrowed, and scarified : it had become like a wood-chopper's yard, where everything was doomed to be broken up. We have seen churches in such a state, and have been heart-broken. What a mercy that there is always a place above the earth to which we can look ! There lives One who will give a resurrection to his cause, and a reunion to his divided people. He will bring up the dead bones from the grave's mouth, and make the dried faggots live again. Let us imitate the Psalmist in the next verse, and look up to the living God.

8. *"But mine eyes are unto thee, O God the Lord."* He looked upward and kept his eyes fixed there. He regarded duty more than circumstances ; he considered the promise rather than the external providence ; and he expected from God rather than from men. He did not shut his eyes in indifference or despair, neither did he turn them to the creature in vain confidence, but he gave his eyes to his God, and saw nothing to fear. Jehovah his Lord is also his hope. Thomas called Jesus Lord and God, and David here speaks of his God and Lord. Saints delight to dwell upon the divine names when they are adoring or appealing. *"In thee is my trust."* Not alone in thine attributes or in thy promises, but in thyself. Others might confide where they chose, but David kept to his God : in him he trusted always, only, confidently, and unreservedly. *"Leave not my soul destitute"*; as it would be if the Lord did not remember and fulfil his promise. To be destitute in circumstances is bad, but to be destitute in soul is far worse ; to be left of friends is a calamity, but to be left of God would be destruction. Destitute of God is destitution with a vengeance. The comfort is that God hath said, " I will never leave thee nor forsake thee."

9. *"Keep me from the snares which they have laid for me."* He had before asked, in verse 3, that the door of his mouth might be kept ; but his prayer now grows into " Keep *me*." He seems more in trouble about covert temptation than concerning open attacks. Brave men do not dread battle, but they hate secret plots. We cannot endure to be entrapped like unsuspecting animals ; therefore we cry to the God of wisdom for protection. *"And the gins of the workers of iniquity."* These evil workers sought to catch David in his speech or acts. This was in itself a piece of in-equity, and so of a piece with the rest of their conduct. They were bad themselves, and they wished either to make him like themselves, or to cause him to seem so. If they could not catch the good man in one way, they would try another ; snares and gins should be multiplied, for anyhow they were determined to work his ruin. Nobody could preserve David but the Omniscient and Omnipotent One : he also will preserve us. It is hard to keep out of snares which you cannot see, and to escape gins which you cannot discover. Well might the much-hunted Psalmist cry, " Keep me."

10. *"Let the wicked fall into their own nets, whilst that I withal escape."* It may not be a Christian prayer, but it is a very just one, and it takes a great deal of grace

to refrain from crying *Amen* to it ; in fact, grace does not work towards making us wish otherwise concerning the enemies of holy men. Do we not all wish the innocent to be delivered, and the guilty to reap the result of their own malice ? Of course we do, if we are just men. There can be no wrong in desiring that to happen in our own case which we wish for all good men. Yet is there a more excellent way.

EXPLANATORY NOTES AND QUAINT SAYINGS.

Whole Psalm.—This Psalm, like the one before it, is distinguished by a pregnant brevity and the use of rare expressions, while at the same time it is full of verbal and real coincidences with the other Psalms of David. These indications are so clear and undeniable, that a sceptical critic of great eminence (De Wette) pronounces it one of the oldest Psalms in the collection.—*Joseph Addison Alexander.*

Whole Psalm.—Few Psalms in so small a compass crowd together so many gems of precious and holy truth.—*Barton Bouchier.*

Whole Psalm.—Many commentators are strongly of opinion that this Psalm was written as a memorial of that very interesting scene in the life of David recorded in 1 Sam. xxiv., relating to his generous treatment of Saul. Though he had an opportunity of putting his cruel persecutor to death in the cave of Engedi, yet he spared his life, only cutting off his skirt, and not suffering his followers to touch him ; and when Saul had gone out of the cave, David, going out after him, remonstrated with him from some distance in the gentlest and most respectful language in regard to the injustice of his conduct towards him. It is thought that the sixth verse contains so express a reference to this very remarkable occurrence in David's history, as to leave little doubt that it was the occasion on which the Psalm was composed.—*James Anderson's Note to Calvin, in loc.*

Whole Psalm.—The imagery and allusions of the Psalm are in keeping ; viz., the oil which had lately anointed him ; and the watch before his mouth, etc., suggested by the watching at the mouth of the cave, though ultimately referring to the tabernacle service.—*John Jebb.*

Verse 1.—"*Lord, I cry unto thee.*" Misbelief doth seek many ways for delivery from trouble ; but faith hath but one way,—to go to God, to wit, by prayer, for whatsoever is needful.—*David Dickson.*

Verse 1.—"*Lord, I cry unto thee.*" No distress or danger, how great soever, shall stifle my faith or stop my mouth, but it shall make me more earnest, and my prayers, like strong streams in narrow straits, shall bear down all before them.— *John Trapp.*

Verse 1.—"*Unto thee . . . . unto me.*" Our prayer and God's mercy are like two buckets in a well ; while the one ascends, the other descends.—*Ezekiel Hopkins.*

Verse 1.—Note that the difference of tense, "*I have cried*" (Heb., LXX., and Vulgate) followed by "*when I cry,*" signifies the earnest perseverance of the saint in prayer, never ceasing, so long as trouble lasts. And trouble does last so long as we are in the world ; wherefore the apostle teaches us to " Pray without ceasing." —*Augustine and Bruno, in Neale and Littledale.*

Verses 1—5.—That the Psalmist was now in some distress, whereof he was deeply sensible, is evident from the vehemency of his spirit, which he expresseth in the reiteration of his request or supplication (verse 1) ; and by his desire that his " prayer might come before the Lord like incense, and the lifting up of his hands as the evening sacrifice " (verse 2). The Jewish expositors guess, not improbably, that in that allusion he had regard unto his present exclusion from the holy services of the tabernacle, which in other places he deeply complains of.

For the matter of his prayer in this beginning of the Psalm, it respecteth himself, and his deportment under his present condition, which he desireth may be harmless and holy, becoming himself, and useful to others. And whereas he was two ways liable to miscarry ; first, by too high an exasperation of spirit against his oppressors and persecutors ; and, secondly, by a fraudulent and pusillanimous compliance with them in their wicked courses ;—which are the two extremes which men are apt sinfully to run into in such conditions : he prays earnestly to be delivered from them both. The first he hath respect unto in verse 3, *"Set a watch, O Lord, before my mouth ; keep the door of my lips"* : namely, that he might not, under those great provocations which were given him, break forth into an unseemly intemperance of speech against his unjust oppressors, which sometimes fierce and unreasonable cruelties will wrest from the most sedate and moderate spirits. But it was the desire of this holy Psalmist, as in like cases it should be ours, that his heart might be always preserved in such a frame, under the conduct of the Spirit of God, as not to be surprised into an expression of distempered passion in any of his words or sayings. The other he regards in his earnest supplication to be delivered from it, verse 4 : *"Incline not my heart to any evil thing, to practise wicked works with men that work iniquity : and let me not eat of their dainties."* There are two parts of his request unto the purpose intended. 1. That by the power of God's grace influencing his mind and soul, his heart might not be inclined unto any communion or society with his wicked adversaries in their wickedness. 2. That he might be preserved from a liking of, or a longing after those things, which are the baits and allurements whereby men are apt to be drawn into societies and conspiracies with the workers of iniquity ; *"And let me not eat of their dainties."* See Prov. i. 10—14. For he here describeth the condition of men prospering for a season in a course of wickedness ; they firstly give up themselves unto the practice of iniquity, and then together solace themselves in those satisfactions of their lusts, with which their power and interest in the world do furnish them.

These are the *"dainties,"* for which an impotent longing and desire do betray the minds of unstable persons unto a compliance with ways of sin and folly : for I look on these *"dainties"* as comprising whatever the lust of the eyes, the lust of the flesh, or the pride of life can afford. All these David prays to be delivered from any inclination unto ; especially when they are made the allurements of a course of sin. In the enjoyment of these *"dainties,"* it is the common practice of wicked men to soothe up, and mutually encourage one another in the way and course wherein they are engaged. And this completes that poor felicity which in this world so many aspire unto, and whereof alone they are capable. The whole of it is but a society in perishing sensual enjoyments, without control, and with mutual applauses from one another. This the Psalmist had a special regard unto when casting his eye towards another communion and society which he longed after (verse 5). He saw there not dainties but rebukes : he discerned that which is most opposite unto those mutual applauses and rejoicings in one another, which is the salt and cement of all evil societies, for he noticed rebukes and reproofs for the least miscarriages that shall be observed. Now whereas the dainties which some enjoy in a course of prosperous wickedness, are that alone which seems to have anything in it amongst them that is desirable, and on the other side rebukes and reproofs are those alone which seem to have any sharpness, or matter of uneasiness and dislike in the society of the godly, David balanceth that which seemeth to be sharpest in the one society, against that which seems to be sweetest in the other, and, without respect unto other advantages, prefers the one above the other. Hence, some read the beginning of the words, " Let the righteous *rather* smite me," meaning, " rather than that I should eat of the dainties of the ungodly." —*John Owen.*

Verse 2.—*"Let my prayer be set forth before thee."* Margin, *directed.* The Hebrew word means to fit ; to establish ; to make firm. The Psalmist desires that his prayer should not be like that which is feeble, languishing, easily dissipated ; but that it should be like that which is firm and secure.—*Albert Barnes.*

Verse 2.—*"Let my prayer be set forth before thee as incense."* Literally, Let my prayer, incense, be set in order before Thee,—implying that prayer was in the reality what incense was in the symbol. . . . Passing to New Testament Scripture, though still only to that portion which refers to Old Testament times, we are told of the people without being engaged in prayer, while Zacharias was offering incense within the Sanctuary (Luke i. 10) ; they were in spirit going along with the priestly service. And in the book of Revelation the prayers of saints are once and again identified with the offering of incense on the golden altar before the throne. Rev. v. 8 ; viii. 3, 4.—*Patrick Fairbairn, in "The Typology of Scripture."*

Verse 2.—*"Set forth."* Prayer is knowing work, believing work, thinking work, searching work, humbling work, and nothing worth if heart and hand do not join in it.—*Thomas Adam*, 1701—1784.

Verse 2.—"*Set forth before thee as incense*," whose fragrant smoke still ascends upwards. But many times in the very ascent, whilst it strives up higher and higher, *infimo phantasmate verberatur*, saith Gregory, " it is beaten back again by earthly imaginations which intervene," and then is extenuated by degrees, and vanisheth to nothing. Therefore the prophet prays *ut dirigatur oratio*, " that his prayer may be set before God," *ut stabiliatur ;* so some render it out of the Hebrew, " that it may be established," that it may neither evaporate itself nor be whiffed about with the wind of vain and contrary imaginations, which come *ab extrinseco* [from without], and may corrupt it.—*Anthony Farindon*.

Verse 2.—"*As incense.*" That in general by *incense* prayer is signified, the Scripture expressly testifieth. And there is a fourfold resemblance between them : 1. In that *it was beaten and pounded* before it was used. So doth acceptable prayer proceed from a broken and contrite heart : Ps. li. 17. 2. *It was of no use until fire was put under it*, and that taken from the altar. Nor is that prayer of any virtue or efficacy which is not kindled by the fire from above, the Holy Spirit of God, which we have from our altar, Christ Jesus. 3. *It naturally ascended upwards towards heaven*, as all offerings in the Hebrew are called נֹיבֹּ, " ascensions," risings up. And this is the design of prayer, to ascend unto the throne of God : " I will direct unto thee, and will look up " ; that is, pray : Ps. v. 3. 4. *It yielded a sweet savour ;* which was one end of it in temple services, wherein there was so much burning of flesh and blood. So doth prayer yield a sweet savour unto God ; a savour of rest, wherein he is well pleased.—*John Owen*.

Verse 2.—"*As incense . . . . as the evening sacrifice.*" Though this address of mine must necessarily want all that solemnity of preparation required in the service of thy holy Tabernacle, the cloud of incense and perfume, etc., the mincha or oblation of fine flour, etc., yet let the purity and fervour of my heart, and the innocency of my hands, now lifted up to thee in this sad hour of my distress, be accepted instead of all these, and prevail for deliverance and a safe retreat to me and my companions.—*Charles Peters* (—1777), *in "A Critical Dissertation on the Book of Job,"* 1751.

Verse 2.—"*As the evening sacrifice.*" This should be our daily service, as a lamb was offered up morning and evening for a sacrifice. But, alas ! how dull and dead are our devotions ! Like Pharaoh's chariots, they drive on heavily. Some, like Balaam's ass, scarce ever open their mouths twice.—*Thomas Adams*.

Verse 2.—"*My hands.*" Spreading forth our hands in believing and fervent prayer is the only way of grasping mercy.—*F. E.*, in "*The Saints Ebenezer*," 1667.

Verse 2.—In the gorgeous ceremonial worship of the Hebrews, none of the senses were excluded from taking part in the service. . . . . The sense of smell occupied, perhaps, the most prominent place ; for the acceptance of the worship was always indicated by a symbol borrowed from this sense : " The Lord smelled a sweet savour." The prayer of the people ascended as incense, and the lifting up of their hands as the evening sacrifice. The offering of incense formed an essential part of the religious service. The altar of incense occupied one of the most conspicuous and honoured positions in the tabernacle and temple. . . . On this altar a censer full of incense poured forth its fragrant clouds every morning and evening ; and yearly, as the day of atonement came round, when the high priest entered the holy of holies, he filled a censer with live coals from the sacred fire on the altar of burnt-offerings, and bore it into the sanctuary, where he threw upon the burning coals the " sweet incense beaten small," which he had brought in his hand. Without this smoking censer he was forbidden, on pain of death, to enter into the awful shrine of Jehovah. Notwithstanding the washing of his flesh, and the linen garments with which he was clothed, he dare not enter the holiest of all with the blood of atonement, unless he could personally shelter himself under a cloud of incense.

It has been supposed by some writers that incense was invented for the purpose of concealing or neutralizing the noxious effluvia caused by the number of beasts slaughtered every day in the sanctuary. Other writers have attached a mystical import to it, and believed that it was a symbol of the breath of the world arising in praise to the Creator, the four ingredients of which it was composed representing the four elements. While a third class, looking upon the tabernacle as the palace of God, the theocratic King of Israel, and the ark of the covenant as his throne, regarded the incense as merely corresponding to the perfume so lavishly employed about the person and appointments of an Oriental monarch. It may doubtless have been intended primarily to serve these purposes and convey these meanings, but it derived its chief importance in connection with the ceremonial observances of the Mosaic ritual from the fact of its being the great symbol of prayer. It was offered at the time when the people were in the posture and act of devotion; and their prayers were supposed to be presented to God by the priest, and to ascend to him in the smoke and odour of that fragrant offering. Scripture is full of allusions to it, understood in this beautiful symbolical sense. Acceptable, prevailing prayer was a sweet-smelling savour to the Lord; and prayer that was unlawful, or hypocritical, or unprofitable, was rejected with disgust by the organ of smell.

Doubtless the Jews felt, when they saw the soft white clouds of fragrant smoke rising slowly from the altar of incense, as if the voice of the priest were silently but eloquently pleading in that expressive emblem in their behalf. The association of sound was lost in that of smell, and the two senses were blended in one. And this symbolical mode of supplication, as Dr. George Wilson has remarked, has this one advantage over spoken or written prayer, that it appealed to those who were both blind and deaf, a class that are usually shut out from social worship by their affliction. Those who could not hear the prayers of the priest could join in devotional exercises symbolized by incense, through the medium of their sense of smell; and the hallowed impressions shut out by one avenue were admitted to the mind and heart by another.

The altar of incense stood in the closest connection with the altar of burnt-offerings. The blood of the sin-offering was sprinkled on the horns of both on the great day of annual atonement. Morning and evening, as soon as the sacrifice was offered, the censer poured forth its fragrant contents, so that the perpetual incense within ascended simultaneously with the perpetual burnt-offering outside. Without the live coals from off the sacrificial altar, the sacred incense could not be kindled; and without the incense previously filling the holy place, the blood of atonement from the altar of burnt-offering could not be sprinkled on the mercy-seat. Beautiful and expressive type of the perfect sacrifice and the all-prevailing intercession of Jesus—of intercession founded upon atonement, of atonement preceded and followed by intercession! Beautiful and expressive type, too, of the prayers of believers kindled by the altar-fire of Christ's sacrifice, and perfumed by his merits!—*Hugh Macmillan, in "The Ministry of Nature," 1871.*

Verse 3.—"Set a watch, O Lord, before my mouth," etc. 1. A man would never use this language without a conviction of *the importance of the subject.* . . . Everything is transacted by speech, in natural, civil, and religious concerns: how much, therefore, depends on the good or evil management of the tongue! What an ardour of holy love and friendship, or of anger and malice, may a few words fan into a flame! The tongue is the principal instrument in the cause of God; and it is the chief engine of the devil; give him this, and he asks no more—there is no mischief or misery he will not accomplish by it. The use, the influence of it, therefore, is inexpressible; and words are never to be considered only as *effects*, but as *causes*, the operation of which can never be fully imagined. Let us suppose a case, I fear, but too common. You drop, in the thoughtlessness of conversation, or for the sake of argument or wit, some irreligious, sceptical expression—it lodges in the memory of a child, or a servant—it takes root in a soil favourable to such seed—it gradually springs up, and brings forth fruit, in the profanation of the Sabbath; the neglect of the means of grace; in the reading of improper books; in the choice of dangerous companions;—who can tell where it will end? But there is a Being who knows where it began. It will be acknowledged that some have it in their power, by reason of their office, talents, and influence, to do much more injury than others; but none are so insignificant as to be harmless.

2. A man would never use this language without a conviction that *he is in danger of transgression.* And if David was conscious of a liableness to err, shall we ever presume on our safety? Our danger arises from the depravity of our nature. "The heart is deceitful above all things, and desperately wicked"; and "who can bring a clean thing out of an unclean?" Our danger arises from the contagion of example. There is nothing in which mankind are more universally culpable than in the disorders of speech. Yet with these we are constantly surrounded; and to these we have been accustomed from our impressible infancy. We are in danger from the frequency of speech. "In the multitude of words there wanteth not sin."

We must of necessity speak often ; but we often speak without necessity. Duty calls us to intermingle much with our fellow-creatures ; but we are too little in the closet, and too much in the crowd—and when we are in company we forget the admonition, " Let every man be swift to hear, and slow to speak."

3. A man would never use this language without a conviction of *inability to preserve himself.* The Bible teaches us this truth, not only doctrinally, but historically. The examples of good men, and men eminent in godliness, confirm it in the very article before us. Moses, the meekest man in the earth, " spake unadvisedly with his lips." You have heard of the patience of Job, but he " cursed the day of his birth " ; and Jeremiah, the prophet of the Lord, did the same. Peter said, " Though all men should be offended because of thee, I will never be offended ; though I should die with thee, yet will I not deny thee." But how did he use his tongue a few hours after ? Then " began he to curse and to swear, saying, I know not the man ! "

4. A man would never use this language without a conviction of *the wisdom of applying to God for the assistance he needs.* Prayer is the effect of our weakness, and the expression of our dependence. It confesses the agency of God. 1. In the first place—God is equal to our preservation. 2. His succours are not to be obtained without prayer. 3. Prayer always brings the assistance it implores.— *Condensed from W. Jay's Sermon on "The Regulation of the Tongue."*

Verse 3.—"*Set a watch, O Lord, before my mouth,*" etc. Watching and prayer are often joined together. We are best kept when recommended into God's hand. I do observe here, First, That unadvised and passionate speeches do easily drop from us in our troubles, especially in our persecution. Secondly, That a godly, conscientious man is very tender of these, as of all evil. He that would live in communion with God for the present, and hope to appear with comfort before him hereafter, is sensible of the least thing that tends to God's displeasure, and God's dishonour : this is the true spirit of one that will be owned by Christ at the last day. Thirdly, There is no way to prevent being provoked to impatience and rashness of speech, or any evil, but by keeping a watch, and renewing our obligations to God. Fourthly, Whoever would keep a watch must call in the aid and assistance of God's grace ; "*Lord, set a watch before my mouth.*"—*Thomas Manton.*

Verse 3.—"*Set a watch, O Lord, before my mouth,*" etc. Thus holy men have kept the sessions at home, and made their hearts the foremen of the jury, and examined themselves as we examine others. The fear of the Lord stood at the door of their souls, to examine every thought before it went in, and at the door of their lips, to examine every word before it went out, whereby they escaped a thousand sins which we commit, as though we had no other work.—*Henry Smith.*

Verse 3.—"*Set a watch, O Lord, before my mouth.*" Nature having made my lips to be a door to my words, let grace keep that door, that no word may be suffered to go out which may any way tend to the dishonour of God, or the hurt of others.— *Matthew Henry.*

Verse 3.—"*Set a watch,*" etc. Let a seal for words not to be spoken lie on the tongue. A watch over words is better than over wealth.—*Lucian.*

Verse 3.—"*Keep the door of my lips.*" That it move not creaking and complaining, as on rusty hinges, for want of the oil of joy and gladness. David had somewhat to do with his tongue, as we see (Ps. xxxix. 1, 3) ; and when he had carted the ark, how untowardly he spake, as if the fault were more in God than himself, that there was such a breach made in Uzzah (1 Chron. xiii. 12). It was but need thus to pray. —*John Trapp.*

Verse 4.—"*Incline not my heart to any evil thing,*" etc. The present pleasure and commodity of sin is in high estimation with the sinner, and much sweeter to him than what he may lawfully enjoy ; the pleasures of sin are his delicates. No man can keep himself from being taken with the allurements of a sinful course, except the Lord preserve him : "*Let me not eat of their dainties.*" The holiest men in Scripture have been most sensible of the impotency of their own free will, and of their inability to resist temptations, or to bring the principles of grace into action ; most diffident of themselves, most dependent upon God, most careful to make use of means, and conscientious in following of ordinances, as their prayers do testify : "*Incline not my heart to any evil thing,*" etc.—*David Dickson.*

Verse 4.—"*Incline not my heart.*" Heb. Let not be inclined my heart.— *John Jebb.*

Verse 4.—"*My heart.*" That man is like Esau which had an inheritance, which had a heart but now he hath not possession of his own ; therefore, give God thy heart, that he may keep it ; and not a piece of thy heart, not a room in thy heart, but thy heart. The heart divided, dyeth. God is not like the mother which would have the child divided, but like the natural mother, which said, rather than it should be divided, let her take all. Let the devil have all, if he which gave it be not worthy of it. God hath no cope-mate, therefore he will have no parting of stakes, but all or none ; and therefore he which asks here thy heart, in the sixth of Deuteronomy and the fifth verse, asketh " all thy heart, all thy soul, and all thy strength " ; thrice he requireth *all*, lest we should keep a thought behind. Yet it is *thy* heart, that is, a vain heart, a barren heart, a sinful heart, until thou give it unto God, and then it is the spouse of Christ, the temple of the Holy Ghost, and the image of God, so changed, and formed, and refined, that God calls it a new heart.

There is such strife for the heart as there was for Moses's body. " Give it me," saith the Lord ; " give it me," saith the tempter ; " give it me," saith the pope ; " give it me," saith riches ; " give it me," saith pleasure ; as though thou must needs give it to some one. Now here is the choice, whether thou wilt give it to God or the devil ; God's heart or the devil's heart ; whose wilt thou be ?—*Henry Smith.*

Verse 4.—"*Let me not eat of their dainties.*" Sin is not only meat, but sweet meat ; not only bread, but pleasant bread to an evil heart. Daniel for some weeks ate no pleasant bread ; he ate bread to keep life and soul together, but he forbare feasting or good cheer. Sin is a feast to a carnal man, it is his good cheer, yea, it is "*dainties*" to him. David, speaking of wicked men says, "*Incline not my heart to any evil thing, to practise wicked works with men that work iniquity : and let me not eat of their dainties.*" These "*dainties*" may be expounded either for the prosperity that comes in by wicked practices (some by wicked ways get not only their ordinary food but "*dainties*") ; or those "*dainties*" are sin itself : they feasted themselves in doing evil : "LORD, *let me not eat of their dainties.*" If that be their food I had rather starve than eat with them.—*Joseph Caryl.*

Verse 4.—"*Their dainties.*" The enemies of David were sensual and luxurious ; and they would have gladly admitted him to share in their banquets, if his character had resembled their own. He entreats to be preserved from inducement so to do.—*William Walford.*

Verse 5.—"*Let the righteous smite me,*" etc. This verse is so obscure as to be almost unintelligible. According to the English versions, it expresses his willingness to be rebuked by good men for his benefit. But this sense is not only hard to be extracted from the words, but foreign from the context. Of the many contradictory interpretations which have been proposed the most probable is that which makes the sentence mean, that the sufferings endured by the good man, even at the hand of the wicked, are chastisements inflicted by a righteous God in justice and with mercy, and as such may be likened to a festive ointment, which the head of the sufferer should not refuse, as he will still have need of consolation and occasion to invoke God, in the midst of trials and of mischiefs yet to be experienced.—*Joseph Addison Alexander.*

Verse 5.—"*Let the righteous smite me.*" The word הלם is seldom used in Scripture but to signify a severe stroke which shakes the subject smitten, and causeth it to tremble ; see Prov. xxiii. 35 ; 1 Sam. xiv. 16 ; Ps. lxxiv. 6 ; and it is used for the stroke of the hammer on the anvil in fashioning of the iron (Isa. xli. 7). Wherefore the word חסד following may be taken adverbially, as a lenitive of that severity which this word importeth : " Let him smite me, but " *leniter, benignè, misericorditer,* " gently, kindly, friendly, mercifully : " and so some translations read the words, " Let the righteous smite me friendly, or kindly."—*John Owen.*

Verse 5.—"*Let the righteous smite me ; it shall be a kindness,*" etc. Grace will teach a Christian to take those potions which are wholesome, though they be not toothsome. Faithful reproof is a token of love, and therefore may well be esteemed a kindness. Such wounding of a friend is healing, and so David might well call it " *an excellent oil.*" And he did not only say so, which is easy and ordinary, but acted accordingly. He did not as the papists, who highly commend holy water, but turn away their faces when it comes to be sprinkled on them. When he had by sin, and continuance in it, so gangrened his flesh, and corrupted himself, that he was in danger of death, he suffered his sores to be thoroughly searched without regret. Nathan was the chirurgeon whom God employed to search that wound

which had divers mouths for festering in his soul; and truly he did not dally with his patient, though he were a prince, but thrust his instrument to the bottom; yet whatever pain it put him to, he took it patiently, and was so far from being angry with the prophet, that he made him one of his privy council.   It is a sign of a polluted nature for a man, like a serpent, if he be but touched, to gather poison and vomit it up at the party.   "Rebuke a wise man, and he will love thee ": Prov. ix. 8.
—*George Swinnock.*

Verse 5.—"*Let the righteous smite me,*" etc.   If the righteous smite us by reproofs, it must be taken as a kindness, and as a precious balsam, which doth not break our head, but heal us.   Not that we are bound to belie ourselves in compliance with every man's censorious humour that will accuse us; but we must be readier to censure ourselves than others, and readier to confess a fault than to expect a confession from others whom we reprove.   Sincerity and serious repentance will be honourable in that person who is most careful to avoid sin, and most ready penitently to confess it when he hath been overcome, and truly thankful to those that call him to repentance; as being more desirous that God and his laws and religion should have the glory of their holiness, than that he himself should have the undue glory of innocency, and escape the deserved shame of sin.

It is one of the most dangerous diseases of professors, and one of the greatest scandals of this age, that persons taken for eminently religious are more impatient of pain, though just, reproof than many a drunkard, swearer, or fornicator; and when they have spent hours or days in the seeming earnest confession of their sin, and lament before God and man that they cannot do it with more grief and tears, yet they take it for a heinous injury in another that will say half so much against them, and take him for a malignant enemy of the godly who will call them as they call themselves.—*Richard Baxter* (1615—1691),   in "*The Morning Exercises.*"

Verse 5.—"*Let the righteous smite me.*"   If a righteous or a right-wise man smite and reprove, he will do it, 1. *Sine felle,* without gall, without bitterness. 2. *Sine publicatione,* without publishing, divulging, or telling it to the world.   3. *Sine contumelia,* without disgrace—to reform his friend, not to disgrace him.   4. *Sine adulatione,* without flattery.   5. *Non sine Deo,* not without God.—*John Gore, in a Sermon entitled "Unknowne Kindnesse,"* 1635.

Verse 5.—"*The righteous,*" etc.   The minister cannot be always preaching; two or three hours, may be, in a week, he spends among his people in the pulpit, holding the glass of the gospel before their faces; but the lives of professors, these preach all the week long: if they were but holy and exemplary, they would be as a repetition of the preacher's sermon to their families and neighbours among whom they converse, and keep the sound of his doctrine continually ringing in their ears.   This would give Christians an amiable advantage in doing good to their carnal neighbours by counsel and reproof, which now is seldom done, and when done it proves to little purpose, because not backed with their own exemplary walking.   " It behoves him," saith Tertullian, " that would counsel or reprove another, to guard his speech with the authority of his own conversation, lest, wanting that, what he says puts himself to the blush."   We do not love one that hath a stinking breath to come very near us; such, therefore, had need have a sweet-scented life.

Reproofs are a good physic, but they have an unpleasant reception; it is hard for men not to throw them back on the face of them that gives them.   Now nothing is more powerful to keep a reproof from thus coming back than the holiness of the person that reproves.   "*Let the righteous smite me.*" saith David, " *it shall be a kindness: and let him reprove me; it shall be an excellent oil, which shall not break my head.*" See how well it is taken from such a hand, from the authority that holiness carries with it.   None but a vile wretch will smite a righteous man with reproach for smiting him with a reproof, if softly laid on, and like oil fomented, and wrought into him, as it should, with compassion and love to his soul!   Thus we see how influential the power of holiness would be unto the wicked, neither would it be less upon our brethren and fellow-Christians.   Holy David professed he would take it as a kindness for the righteous to smite him; yea, as kindly as if he broke a box of precious oil upon his head, which was amongst the Jews a high expression of love.—*William Gurnall.*

Verse 5.—"*It shall be a kindness* "   1. It is a kindness *reducere erratum,* to bring back the wandering.   2. *Sanare ægrotum,* to recover the sick.   3. *Suscitare lethargum,* to awake, to stir up the lethargic, the sleepy.   4. *Ligare insanum,* to bind a madman. 5. *Liberare perditum*, to save a lost man, one in imminent danger.—*John Gore*.

Verse 5.—"*It shall be an excellent oil, which shall not break my head.*" Some persons pride themselves on being blunt, or, as they call it, "honest"; but very blunt people do little good to others, and get little love to themselves. The Scriptures recommend gentleness and kindness. Reproof should fall like the dew, and not like the rushing hail-storm. The "*oil*" insinuates itself; the stone wounds and then rebounds. Christians should take heed of getting fond of the work of "rebuking." Such "spiritual constables" do a great deal of mischief without intending it. They are in a church what a very witty and sarcastic person is in society, or what a tell-tale is in school; and approximate very closely to that class which the apostle terms "busybodies in other men's matters." Our manner must be tender and winning. The nail of reproof, says an old writer, must be well oiled in kindness before it is driven home. Meddling with the faults of others is like attempting to move a person afflicted with the rheumatic gout: it must be done slowly and tenderly, nor must we be frightened by an outcry or two. The great thing is to show the person that you really love him; and if you manifest this in the sight of God, he will bless your efforts, and give you favour in the sight of an erring brother.—*Christian Treasury*.

Verse 5.—"*It shall be an excellent oil.*" Certain oils are said to have a most salutary effect on the head; hence in fevers, or any other complaints which effect the head, the medical men always recommend oil. I have known people who were deranged, cured in a very short time by nothing more than the application of a peculiar kind of oil to the head. There are, however, other kinds which are believed, when thus applied, to produce delirium. Thus the reproofs of the righteous were compared to "*excellent oil*," which produced a most salutary effect on the head. So common is this practice of anointing the head, that all who can afford it do it every week.

But, strange as it may appear, the crown of their heads is the place selected for the chastisement; thus owners of slaves, or husbands, or schoolmasters, beat the heads of the offenders with their knuckles. Should an urchin come late to school, or forget his lesson, the pedagogue says to some of the other boys, "Go, beat his head!" "Begone, fellow! or I will beat thy head." Should a man be thus chastised by an inferior, he quotes the old proverb: "If my head is to be beaten, let it be done with the fingers that have rings on"; meaning a man of rank. "Yes, yes; let a holy man smite my head! and what of that? it is an excellent oil." "My master has been beating my head, but it has been good oil for me."—*Joseph Roberts*.

Verse 5.—"*Oil, which shall not break my head.*" When I first took this text in hand, this seemed unto me a very strange and uncouth expression. If the Psalmist had said, It shall be a stone that shall not break my head, etc., we had easily understood him; but to speak of an oil, or a balm, which we know to be so soft, so supple, so lithe and gentle an ointment, that he should speak of breaking his head with oil, it is strange. I confess it troubled me a while, till at length I conceived it might be spoken by contraries; as when a physician gives a patient some pectoral, or cordial, and saith, Take this, it will not hurt you; his meaning is, it will help and do him good. So this oil *shall not break my head;* that is, it shall heal it, being broken by my own corruption, by Satan's temptations, and by the evil influence of such as flatter me in my sins.—*John Gore*.

Verse 5.—If David could say of his enemy that cursed him, "Let him alone, for God hath bidden him to curse"; much more safely mayest thou say of thy friend that reproves thee, "Let him alone, for God hath bidden him to smite." And as the apostle saith of ministers, that God "doth entreat you by us"; so persuade yourselves that God doth reprove you by them.—*John Gore*.

Verse 5.—It was the saying of a heathen, though no heathenish saying, "That he who would be good, must either have a faithful friend to instruct him, or a watchful enemy to correct him." Should we murder a physician because he comes to cure us; or like him worse, because he would make us better? The flaming sword of *reprehension* is but to keep us from the forbidden fruit of *transgression*. "*Let the righteous smite me; it shall be a kindness: and let him reprove me; it shall be an excellent oil, which shall not break my head.*" Let him smite me as with a hammer, for so the word signifies. A Boanerges is as necessary as a Barnabas.—*William Secker*.

Verse 5.—"*Yet my prayer also shall be in their calamities.*" That is, if ever they who are my reprovers fall into calamity, though they may think they provoked me so by reproving me, that they have lost my love, and have cast themselves out of my prayers, or that I will never speak well of them or for them again ; yet I will pray for them with all my heart, as their matter shall require. I will pray for them when they have most need of prayer, even "*in their calamities.*" Some heighten the sense thus,—The more they sharpen their reproof, the more I think myself bound to pray for them. It shows an excellent spirit, not to be hindered from doing good to others by anything they do or speak against us, nor their sharpest (though perhaps mistaken) reproofs of us. Thus it was that that good man Job "*prayed for his friends,*" who had spoken much against him, and not only reproved him without cause, but reproached him without charity.—*Joseph Caryl.*

Verse 6.—"*When their judges are overthrown,*" etc. When the judgments in reserve for the leaders of my enemies shall come upon them, they will perceive too late how reasonble are my words, and wish that they had hearkened to them sooner. —*Joseph Addison Alexander.*

Verse 6.—"*Overthrown.*" The verb rendered "*overthrown*" is used of Jezebel in 2 Kings ix. 33 ; "Throw her down. So they threw her down."—*Speaker's Commentary.*

Verse 6.—"*They shall hear my words ; for they are sweet.*" This is especially true of all the words which David spake by inspiration, or the Spirit of God spake to him ; particularly in his book of Psalms, concerning the Messiah, the covenant of grace, and the blessings of it ; of the rich experiences of grace he had, and the several doctrines of the gospel declared by him ; which were sweet, delightful, and entertaining to those who have ears to hear such things ; or those ears are opened to hear them, so as to understand them and distinguish them, but to others not. —*John Gill.*

Verse 6.—"*They shall hear my words ; for they are sweet.*" Those that slighted the word of God before, will relish it and be glad of it when they are in affliction ; for that opens the ear to instruction. When the world is bitter the word is sweet. Oppressed innocency cannot gain a hearing with those that live in pomp and pleasure ; but when they come to be overthrown themselves, they will have more compassionate thoughts of the afflicted.—*Matthew Henry.*

Verse 6.—"*For they are sweet.*" They shall be pleasant ; mild ; gentle ; equitable ; just. After the harsh and severe enactments of Saul, after enduring his acts of tyranny, the people will be glad to welcome me, and to live under the laws of a just and equal administration. The passage, therefore, expresses confidence that Saul and his hosts would be overthrown, and that the people of the land would gladly hail the accession to the throne of one who had been anointed to reign over them.—*Albert Barnes.*

Verses 6, 7.—The mild and dutiful behaviour of David towards Saul and his friends are set together by way of contrast, in the strongest light, from the instances of each sort here produced. The first is, David's humanity towards Saul, in giving him his life at two several times, when he had it in his power to destroy him as he pleased. "*Their judges have been dismissed in the rocky places ; and have heard my words that they are sweet* " ; that is, "Their princes have been dismissed in safety, when I had them at an advantage in those rocky deserts ; and only heard me expostulate with them in the gentlest words."

The other is, Saul's barbarity and cruelty towards David (or his friends, which is much the same) in the horrid massacre of Ahimelech and the priests, by the hand of Doeg the Edomite, done in such a savage manner, that he compares it to the chopping and cleaving wood ; "*Like as when one cutteth and cleaveth, so have our bones been scattered on the earth at the command of Saul* " ; for so I read the Hebrew words, *le-pi Saul, at the mouth,* that is, the command *of Saul.*

Should we suppose this passage to refer to the first time of David's sparing Saul, viz., when he had him in his power in the cave of *Engedi* (here called *jedé selay*), the sides of the rock, or the rocky places, the speech he made on this occasion when he called after Saul (and which is recorded in 1 Sam. xxiv., from the eighth to the sixteenth verse) might well be called *sweet* or *pleasant words.* For they set his own innocence and the king's unjust behaviour to him in so strong a light, and with all that gentleness and mildness, and even this hard-hearted prince could not forbear being greatly affected with it for the present ; and we are told (verses 16, 17) that " he lifted up his voice and wept."—*Charles Peters*.

Verse 7.—"*Our bones are scattered at the grave's mouth,*" etc. The primary reference may be to the slaughter of the priests by the command of Saul, 1 Sam. xxii. 16—19. The language, however, may be illustrative of the many massacres like that on the eve of St. Bartholomew, so numerous as to be scattered on the face of the earth, marking the passage of pious martyrs from this world to a better, and testifying where the blood of the slain shall be disclosed for the judgment of their murderers.—*W. Wilson*.

Verse 7.—"*Our bones are scattered at the grave's mouth,*" etc. Assuming the very extreme, it is a look of hope into the future : should his bones and the bones of his followers be even scattered about the mouth of Sheôl (cf. the Syrian picture of Sheôl : " the dust upon its threshold, '*al-escûfteh,*" *Deutsche Morgenländ. Zeitschrift,* xx. 513), their soul below, their bones above—it would nevertheless be only as when one in ploughing cleaves the earth ; *i.e.,* they do not lie there in order that they may continue lying, but that they may rise up anew, as the seed that is sown sprouts up out of the upturned earth.—*Franz Delitzsch*.

Verse 7.—"*Our bones are scattered at the grave's mouth.*" That is to say, I and my company are in a dying condition, free among the dead ; yea, if taken we should be put to most cruel deaths, hewn in pieces, or pulled limbmeal, and left unburied ; and our dead bodies mangled by a barbarous inhumanity, as wood-cleavers make the shivers fly hither and thither. This is the perilous case of me and my partisans. —*John Trapp*.

Verse 7.—"*Our bones are scattered at the grave's mouth.*"—This seems to be strong eastern painting, and almost figurative language ; but that it may be strictly true, the following extract demonstrates : " At five o'clock we left Garigana, our journey being still to the eastward of north ; and, at a quarter past six in the evening, arrived at the village of that name, whose inhabitants had all perished with hunger the year before; their wretched bones being all unburied, and scattered upon the surface of the ground, where the village formerly stood. We encamped among the bones of the dead, as no space could be found free from them ; and on the 23rd, at six in the morning, full of horror at this miserable spectacle, we set out for Teawa." —(*James Bruce's Travels.*) To the Jews such a spectacle must have been very dreadful, as the want of burial was esteemed one of the greatest calamities which could befall them.—*Burder's "Oriental Customs."*

Verse 7.—"*Like one ploughing and cleaving in the earth.*" This clause may be explained not of cleaving wood but ploughing, to which the first verb is applied in Arabic. *Like (one) ploughing and cleaving* (making furrows) *in the earth,* not for the sake of mangling its surface, but to make it fruitful and productive, (so) *our bones are scattered at the mouth of hell,* as the necessary means of a glorious resurrection.—*Joseph Addison Alexander*.

Verse 7.—Who can attend the digging of a grave, and view the ruins then disclosed, without exclaiming, "*Our bones are scattered at the grave's mouth, as when one cutteth and cleaveth wood upon the earth*" ?—*George Horne*.

Verse 8.—"*Mine eyes are unto thee, O GOD the Lord.*" If you would keep your mind fixed in prayer, keep your *eye* fixed. Much vanity comes in at the eye. When the eyes wander in prayer the heart wanders. To think to keep the heart fixed in prayer, and yet let the eyes gaze abroad, is as if one should think to keep his house safe, yet let the windows be open.—*Thomas Watson*.

Verse 8.—"*Leave not my soul destitute.*" The literal Hebrew is, *Pour not out my soul,* but keep it in thy cup of salvation.—*Agellius*. [Compare Isa. liii. 12 : " He hath poured out his soul unto death."]

Verse 8.—"*Leave not my soul destitute,*" or, "*Cast not out my soul.*" That is, cast not my life away, as water, which is of no account, is cast out of a vessel containing it.—*Daniel Cresswell*.

Verse 8.—"*Leave not my soul destitute.*" His soul knew what it was to be " destitute " ; he had known the misery of spiritual beggary and soul poverty. It was not with him as natural poverty is with the rich, a matter of speculation, a mere matter of theory ; but a matter of personal and painful experience. . . . It is in the margin "*Make not my soul bare*" ; Strip me not of every hope ; leave me not completely naked ; abandon me not to nature's beggary and misery ; let me not go down into the pit with all my sins upon my head ; leave not my soul destitute of pardon and peace.—*Joseph C. Philpot.*

Verses 8—10.—

> O pour not out my soul, I pray,
> From the dark snare preserve my way,
> The chambers of the blind entangling net,
> Which by my path the powers of evil set.
>
> Behold them laid, the godless crew,
> Low in the toils they darkly drew :
> The while, with gathering heart and watchful eye,
> I wait mine hour to pass victorious by.

John Keble.

Verse 9. 10.—"*Snares,*" "*Gins,*" "*Nets.*" The usual method of capturing or killing the lion in Palestine was by pitfalls or nets, to both of which there are many references in the Scriptures. The mode of hunting the lion with the nets was identical with that which is practised in India at the present time. The precise locality of the lion's dwelling-place having been discovered, a circular wall of net is arranged round it, or if only a few nets can be obtained, they are set in a curved form, the concave side being towards the lion. They then send dogs into the thicket, hurl stones and sticks at the den, shoot arrows into it, fling burning torches at it, and so irritate and alarm the animal that it rushes against the net, which is so made that it falls down and envelops the animal in its folds. If the nets be few, the drivers go to the opposite side of the den, and induce the lion to escape in the direction where he sees no foes, but where he is sure to run against the treacherous net. Other large and dangerous animals were also captured by the same means. Another and more common, because an easier and a cheaper method, was, by digging a deep pit, covering the mouth with a slight covering of sticks and earth, and driving the animal upon the treacherous covering. It is an easier method than the net, because after the pit is once dug, the only trouble lies in throwing the covering over its mouth. But it is not so well adapted for taking beasts alive, as they are likely to be damaged, either by the fall into the pit, or by the means used in getting them out again. Animals, therefore, that are caught in pits are generally, though not always, killed before they are taken out. The net, however, envelops the animal so perfectly, and renders it so helpless, that it can be easily bound and taken away, The hunting net is very expensive, and requires a large staff of men to work it, so that none but a rich man could use the net in hunting.

Besides the net, several other modes of bird-catching were used by the ancient Jews, just as is the case at the present day. Boys, for example, who catch birds for their own consumption, and not for the market, can do so by means of various traps, most of which are made on the principle of the noose, or snare. Sometimes a great number of hair-nooses are set in places to which the birds are decoyed, so that in hopping about, many of them are sure to be entangled in the snares. Sometimes the noose is ingeniously suspended in a narrow passage which the birds are likely to traverse, and sometimes a simple fall-trap is employed.—*J. G. Wood.*

Verse 10.—"*Into their own nets.*" The word rendered " *nets* " occurs only in this place, as the closely corresponding word in Ps.cxl. 10, which is rendered " *deep pits,*" occurs there only.—*Speaker's Commentary.*

HINTS TO PREACHERS.

Verse 1.—I. The Perpetuity of Prayer : " I cry, I cry." II. The Personality : " unto thee," " unto me." II. The Practicalness : " Make haste ; give ear."

Verse 1.—Holy haste. I. The saint hasting to God. II. The saint hastening God. III. God's sure hastening to his help.—*W. B. H.*

Verses 1, 2.—I. Prayer put forth : 1. With urgency : " Make haste unto me." 2. With fervency : " Give ear," etc. II. Prayer set forth : " Let my prayer be set forth," etc. When hearing is obtained there is composure and order in prayer.

When the fire is kindled the incense rises. III. Prayer held forth : " The lifting up of my hands as the evening sacrifice," as constant and accepted.—*G. R.*

Verse 2.—True prayer acceptable as incense and as the evening sacrifice. It is spiritual, solemn, ordained of God, brings Christ to remembrance.

Verse 3.—I. The mouth a door. II. A watchman needed. III. The Lord fulfilling that office.

Verse 4.—Total abstinence from evil desires, practices, and delights.

Verse 4.—A prayer, I. For the repression of every evil tendency in the heart : " Incline not my heart," etc. II. For the prevention of any association with the wicked in their sinful works : " To practise," etc. III. For a holy contempt of the temporal pleasure or profit placed in our way through the sin of others : " Let me not eat," etc. Note, many who will not engage in a wicked act do not object to participate in its gains.—*J. F.*

Verse 4.—Deprecation of, I. Devil's desires. II. Devil's deeds. III. Devil's dainties.—*W. B. H.*

Verse 5.—Rebukes of good men. I. Invited. II. Appreciated : " it shall be a kindness." III. Utilized : " an excellent oil." IV. Cheerfully endured : " not break my head." V. Repaid, by our prayers for them in time of trouble.

Verse 5 (*last clause*).—" Intercessory Prayer." See " Spurgeon's Sermons," No. 1,049,

Verse 6.—I. Times of trouble will come to the careless. II. Then they will be more ready to hear the gospel. III. Then they will find sweetness in that which they formerly refused.

Verse 6.—A Desert Oasis. I. The world is a stony place, hard, barren. II. Often pride and self-trust suffer overthrowing there. III. Then words of God by his sent servant make an oasis in the desert.—*W. B. H.*

Verses 7, 8.—A cemetery scene. I. Dry bones of the dead about the grave. II. Weary bones of the aged and sick around the grave. III. all bones being from day to day made ready for the grave. IV. Bones finding rest in God : " mine eyes are unto thee, O God," etc.

Verse 8.—Expectation. Supplication.

Verse 9.—The snares. Who lay them ? Why ? Who so many ? How are we to escape ? " Keep me."

Verses 9, 10.—David prays, 1. That he may see God in his deliverance from his enemies, and 2. That they may see God in the frustration of their designs.—*G. R.*

Verse 10.—Great pains to little purpose. I. The making of nets, etc. II. The taking of God's antagonists in their own nets. III. The invariable escape of God's friends. **Lesson**: Nothing can prosper sin, or hurt godliness.—*W. B. H.*

PSALM CXLII.

TITLE.—Maschil of David. *This Maschil is written for our instruction. It teaches us principally by example how to order our prayer in times of distress. Such instruction is among the most needful, practical, and effectual parts of our spiritual education. He who has learned how to pray has been taught the most useful of the arts and sciences. The disciples said unto the Son of David, "Lord, teach us to pray"; and here David gives us a valuable lesson by recording his own experience as to supplication from beneath a cloud.*

A Prayer when he was in the cave. He was in one of his many lurking places, either Engedi, Adullam, or some other lone cavern wherein he could conceal himself from Saul and his bloodhounds. Caves make good closets for prayer; their gloom and solitude are helpful to the exercise of devotion. Had David prayed as much in his palace as he did in his cave, he might never have fallen into the act which brought such misery upon his later days.

SUBJECT.—*There can be little doubt that this song dates from the days when Saul was sorely persecuting David, and David himself was in soul-trouble, probably produced by that weakness of faith which led him to associate with heathen princes. His fortunes were evidently at their lowest, and, what was worse, his repute had fearfully fallen; yet he displayed a true faith in God, to whom he made known his pressing sorrows. The gloom of the cave is over the Psalm, and yet as if standing at the mouth of it the prophet-poet sees a bright light a little beyond.*

EXPOSITION.

I CRIED unto the LORD with my voice; with my voice unto the LORD did I make my supplication.

2 I poured out my complaint before him; I shewed before him my trouble.

3 When my spirit was overwhelmed within me, then thou knewest my path. In the way wherein I walked have they privily laid a snare for me.

4 I looked on *my* right hand, and beheld, but *there was* no man that would know me: refuge failed me; no man cared for my soul.

5 I cried unto thee, O LORD: I said, Thou *art* my refuge *and* my portion in the land of the living.

6 Attend unto my cry; for I am brought very low: deliver me from my persecutors; for they are stronger than I.

7 Bring my soul out of prison, that I may praise thy name: the righteous shall compass me about; for thou shalt deal bountifully with me.

1. *"I cried unto the LORD with my voice."* It was a cry of such anguish that he remembers it long after, and makes a record of it. In the loneliness of the cave he could use his voice as much as he pleased; and therefore he made its gloomy vaults echo with his appeals to heaven. When there was no soul in the cavern seeking his blood, David with all his soul was engaged in seeking his God. He felt it a relief to his heart to use his voice in his pleadings with Jehovah. There was a voice *in* his prayer when he used his voice *for* prayer: it was not *vox et præterea nihil.* It was a prayer *vivo corde* as well as *vivâ voce.* *"With my voice unto the LORD did I make my supplication."* He dwells upon the fact that he spoke aloud in prayer; it was evidently well impressed upon his memory, hence he doubles the word and says, "with my voice; with my voice." It is well when our supplications are such that we find pleasure in looking back upon them. He that is cheered by the memory of his prayers will pray again. See how the good man's appeal was to Jehovah only: he did not go round about to men, but he ran straight forward to Jehovah, his God. What true wisdom is here! Consider how the Psalmist's prayer grew into shape as he proceeded with it. He first poured out his natural longings,—

" I cried ; " and then he gathered up all his wits and arranged his thoughts,—" I made supplication." True prayers may differ in their diction, but not in their direction : an impromptu cry and a preconceived supplication must alike ascend towards the one prayer-hearing God, and he will accept each of them with equal readiness. The intense personality of the prayer is noteworthy : no doubt the Psalmist was glad of the prayers of others, but he was not content to be silent himself. See how everything is in the first person,—"*I* cried with *my* voice ; with *my* voice did *I* make *my* supplication." It is good to pray in the plural—" Our Father," but in times of trouble we shall feel forced to change our note into " Let this cup pass from *me*."

2. "*I poured out my complaint before him.*" His inward meditation filled his soul : the bitter water rose up to the brim ; what was to be done ? He must pour out the wormwood and the gall, he could not keep it in ; he lets it run away as best it can, that so his heart may be emptied of the fermenting mixture. But he took care *where* he outpoured his complaint, lest he should do mischief, or receive an ill return. If he poured it out before man he might only receive contempt from the proud, hard-heartedness from the careless, or pretended sympathy from the false ; and therefore he resolved upon an outpouring before God alone, since *he* would pity and relieve. The word is scarcely " complaint " ; but even if it be so we may learn from this text that our complaint must never be of a kind that we dare not bring before God. We may complain *to* God, but not *of* God. When we complain it should not be before men, but before God alone. "*I shewed before him my trouble.*" He exhibited his griefs to one who could assuage them : he did not fall into the mistaken plan of so many who publish their sorrows to those who cannot help them. This verse is parallel with the first ; David first pours out his complaint, letting it flow forth in a natural, spontaneous manner, and then afterwards he makes a more elaborate show of his affliction ; just as in the former verse he began with crying, and went on to " make supplication." Praying men pray better as they proceed. Note that we do not show our trouble before the Lord that *he* may see *it*, but that *we* may see *him*. It is for *our* relief, and not for his information that we make plain statements concerning our woes : it does us much good to set out our sorrow in order, for much of it vanishes in the process, like a ghost which will not abide the light of day ; and the rest loses much of its terror, because the veil of mystery is removed by a clear and deliberate stating of the trying facts. Pour out your thoughts and you will see what they are ; show your trouble and the extent of it will be known to you : let all be done before the Lord, for in comparison with his great majesty of love the trouble will seem to be as nothing.

3. "*When my spirit was overwhelmed within me, then thou knewest my path.*" The bravest spirit is sometimes sorely put to it. A heavy fog settles down upon the mind, and the man seems drowned and smothered in it ; covered with a cloud, crushed with a load, confused with difficulties, conquered by impossibilities. David was a hero, and yet his spirit sank : he could smite a giant down, but he could not keep himself up. He did not know his own path, nor feel able to bear his own burden. Observe his comfort : he looked away from his own condition to the ever-observant, all-knowing God ; and solaced himself with the fact that all was known to his heavenly Friend. Truly it is well for us to know that God knows what we do not know. We lose our heads, but God never closes his eyes : our judgments lose their balance, but the eternal mind is always clear.

"*In the way wherein I walked have they privily laid a snare for me.*" This the Lord knew at the time, and gave his servant warning of it. Looking back, the sweet singer is rejoiced that he had so gracious a Guardian, who kept him from unseen dangers. Nothing is hidden from God ; no secret snare can hurt the man who dwells in the secret place of the Most High, for he shall abide under the shadow of the Almighty. The use of concealed traps is disgraceful to our enemies, but they care little to what tricks they resort for their evil purposes. Wicked men must find some exercise for their malice, and therefore when they dare not openly assail they will privately ensnare. They watch the gracious man to see where his haunt is, and there they set their trap ; but they do it with great caution, avoiding all observation, lest their victim being forewarned should escape their toils. This is a great trial, but the Lord is greater still, and makes us to walk safely in the midst of danger, for he knows us and our enemies, our way and the snare which is laid in it. Blessed be his name.

4. "*I looked on my right hand and beheld, but there was no man that would know*

me." He did not miss a friend for want of looking for him, nor for want of looking in a likely place. Surely some helper would be found in the place of honour ; some one would stand at his right hand to undertake his defence. He looked steadily, and saw all that could be seen, for he " beheld " ; but his anxious gaze was not met by an answering smile. Strange to say, all were strange to David. He had known many, but none would know him. When a person is in ill odour it is wonderful how weak the memories of his former friends become : they quite forget, they refuse to know. This is a dire calamity. It is better to be opposed by foes than to be forsaken by friends. When friends look for us they affect to have known us from our birth, but when we look for friends it is wonderful how little we can make them remember : the fact is that in times of desertion it is not true that no man did know us, but no man *would* know us. Their ignorance is wilful. *"Refuge failed me."* Where in happier days I found a ready harbour I now discovered none at all. My place of flight had taken to flight. My refuge gave me a refusal. *"No man cared for my soul."* Whether I lived or died was no concern of anybody's. I was cast out as an outcast. No soul cared for my soul. I dwelt in No-man's land, where none cared to have me, and none cared about me. This is an ill-plight—no place where to lay our head, and no head willing to find us a place. How pleased were his enemies to see the friend of God without a friend ! How sad was he to be utterly deserted in his utmost need ! Can we not picture David in the cave, complaining that even the cave was not a refuge for him, for Saul had come even there ? Hopeless was his looking out, we shall soon see him looking up.

5. *"I cried unto thee, O LORD."* As man would not regard him, David was driven to Jehovah, his God. Was not this a gain made out of a loss ? wealth gained by a failure ? Anything which leads us to cry unto God is a blessing to us. This is the second time that in this short Psalm we find the same record, " I cried unto thee, O LORD": the saintly man is evidently glad to remember his cry and its results. We hear often of the bitter cry of outcast London, here is another bitter cry, and it comes from an outcast, in wretched lodgings, forgotten by those who should have helped him. *"I said, Thou art my refuge and my portion in the land of the living."* There is a sort of progressive repetition all through this sacred song ; he *cried* first, but he *said* afterwards : his cry was bitter, but his saying was sweet ; his cry was sharp and short, but his saying was fresh and full. It gives a believer great pleasure to remember his own believing speeches : he may well desire to bury his unbelieving murmurings in oblivion, but the triumphs of grace in working in him a living faith, he will not dream of forgetting. What a grand confession of faith was this ! David spoke to God, and of God—" THOU art my refuge." Not thou hast provided me a refuge, but thou, thyself, art my refuge. He fled to God alone ; he hid himself beneath the wings of the Eternal. He not only believed this, but said it, and practised it. Nor was this all ; for David, when banished from his portion in the promised land, and cut off from the portion of goods which he by right inherited, found his portion in God, yea, God *was* his portion. This was so not only in reference to a future state, but here among living men. It is sometimes easier to believe in a portion in heaven than in a portion upon earth : we could die more easily than live, at least we think so. But there is no living in the land of the living like living upon the living God. For the man of God to say these precious things in the hour of his dire distress was a grand attainment. It is easy to prate bravely when we dwell at ease, but to speak confidently in affliction is quite another matter.

Even in this one sentence we have two parts, the second rising far above the first. It is something to have Jehovah for our refuge, but it is everything to have him for our portion. If David had not *cried* he would not have *said ;* and if the Lord had not been his *refuge* he would never have been his *portion.* The lower step is as needful as the higher ; but it is not necessary always to stop on the first round of the ladder.

6. *"Attend unto my cry."* Men of God look upon prayer as a reality, and they are not content without having an audience with God ; moreover, they have such confidence in the Lord's condescending grace, that they hope he will even attend to that poor broken prayer which can only be described as a cry. *"For I am brought very low,"* and therefore all the prayer I can raise is a mournful cry. This is his argument with God : he is reduced to such a sad condition that if he be not rescued he will be ruined. Gracious men may not only be low, but very low ; and this should not be a reason for their doubting the efficacy of their prayers, but rather a plea

with the Lord why they should have special attention. *"Deliver me from my persecutors."* If he did not get out of their hands, they would soon kill him out of hand, and as he could not himself effect an escape, he cried to God, " deliver me." *"For they are stronger than I."* As he before found a plea in his sadness, so now in his feebleness : Saul and his courtiers were in power, and could command the aid of all who sought royal favour ; but poor David was in the cave, and every Nabal girded at him. Saul was a monarch, and David a fugitive ; Saul had all the forms of law on his side, while David was an outlaw : so that the prayer before us comes from the weak, who proverbially go to the wall,—a good place to go to if they turn their faces to it in prayer, as Hezekiah did in his sickness. The Lord is wont to take the side of the oppressed, and to show his power by baffling tyrants ; David's supplication was therefore sure to speed. In these sentences we see how explicitly the man of God described his case in his private communings with his Lord : in real earnest he poured out his complaint before him, and showed before him his trouble.

7. *"Bring my soul out of prison, that I may praise thy name."* That God may be glorified is another notable plea for a suppliant. Escaped prisoners are sure to speak well of those who give them liberty. Soul-emancipation is the noblest form of liberation, and calls for the loudest praise : he who is delivered from the dungeons of despair is sure to magnify the name of the Lord. We are in such a prison that only God himself can bring us out of it, and when he does so he will put a new song into our mouths. The cave was not half such a dungeon to David's body as persecution and temptation made for his soul. To be exiled from the godly is worse than imprisonment, hence David makes it one point of his release that he would be restored to church fellowship—*"The righteous shall compass me about."* Saints gather around a child of God when his Father smiles upon him ; they come to hear his joyful testimony, to rejoice with him, and to have their own faith encouraged. All the true believers in the twelve tribes were glad to rally to David's banner when the Lord enlarged his spirit ; they glorified God for him and with him and through him. They congratulated him, consorted with him, crowned him, and championed him. This was a sweet experience for righteous David, who had for awhile come under the censure of the upright. He bore their smiting with patience, and now he welcomes their sanction with gratitude. *"For thou shalt deal bountifully with me."* God's bountiful dealing is sure to bring with it the sympathy and alliance of all the favourites of the Great King. What a change from looking for a friend and finding none to this enthusiastic concourse of allies around the man after God's own heart ! When we can begin a Psalm with crying, we may hope to close it with singing. The voice of prayer soon awakens the voice of praise.

EXPLANATORY NOTES AND QUAINT SAYINGS.

Title.—He calls this prayer *Maschil*, " a Psalm of instruction," because of the good lessons he had himself learned in the cave, learned on his knees, and so learned that he desired to teach others.—*Matthew Henry.*

Title.—*"A prayer when he was in the cave."* Every part of this Psalm shows the propriety of its inscription or title. He expressly mentions his being in a place where he was entirely shut up, where he saw no possible method of escaping, as having no friends that dared to own him and appear for his deliverance, and when every one seemed to desert him, and to have abandoned all care of his safety and life. This he pathetically describes, and in such terms as cannot fail to move the tender affections of every one who considers them. On the first sense of his danger, shut up in a cave, surrounded by three thousand chosen soldiers, closely observed by a watchful enemy who would spare no art or pains to apprehend him, he seems almost to have despaired of himself, and declares that his spirit is quite overwhelmed with the greatness of his distress. At length, recollecting his principles, and the promises that God had made him, he earnestly supplicates the protection of God, and assures himself that he should yet praise God for his deliverance, and that good men should share his joy, and encompass the altar of God with thanksgiving for the mercy that he had shown him.—*Samuel Chandler.*

Title.—*"The cave."* Leaving our horses in charge of some Arabs, and taking one for our guide, we started for the cave now known as Mughâret Khureitûn, which is believed to be the cave Adullam, having a fearful gorge below, gigantic cliffs above, and the path winding along a narrow shelf of the rock. At length, from a great rock hanging on the edge of the shelf, we entered by a long leap a low window which opened into the perpendicular face of the cliff. We were then within the traditional hold of David, and, creeping half doubled through a narrow crevice for a few rods, we stood beneath the dark vault of the first grand chamber of this mysterious and oppressive cavern, 1 Sam. xxii. 1, 2 ; 2 Sam. xxiii. 13—17. Our whole collection of lights did little more than make the damp darkness visible. After groping about as long as we had time to spare, we returned to the light of day, fully convinced that, with David and his lion-hearted followers inside, all the strength of Israel under Saul could not have forced an entrance—would not have even attempted it.—*William M. Thompson.*

Verse 1.—"*I cried unto the LORD.*" Thou hast posted me over to no deputy for the hearing of my prayer, neither dost thou require that I should bring a spokesman for the presenting of it ; but thou hast commanded me to come myself, and to come to thee thyself.—*Sir Richard Baker on the Lord's Prayer.*

Verse 1.—"*With my voice.*" The Lord needs not the tongue to be an interpreter between him and the hearts of his children. He that hears without ears can interpret prayers though not uttered by the tongue. Our desires are cries in the ears of the Lord of hosts. The vehemency of the affections may sometimes cause the outcrying of the voice ; but alas ! without this it is but a tinkling cymbal . . . . There is a use of words in prayer, to excite, and convey, and give vent to, affection : Hosea xiv. 2, " Take with you words, and turn to the LORD : say unto him, Take away all iniquity, and receive us graciously." The prophet doth not only prescribe that they should take affections, but take with them words.—*Thomas Manton.*

Verse 2.—"*I poured out my complaint before him.*" Literally, my meditation ; that is—what so much occupied my thoughts at the time I expressed aloud. The word "*complaint*" does not express the idea. The meaning is, not that he *complained* of God or of man ; but that his mind *meditated* on his condition.—*Albert Barnes.*

Verse 2.—"*I poured out,*" etc. I did it fully, and fervently, and confidently.—*Matthew Henry.*

Verse 2.—"*Poured out . . . before him.*" Those words teach us that in prayer we should not try to keep anything back from God, but should show him all that is in our hearts, and that in his presence in our closet, with the door shut, but not before men. The Carmelite adds that there is much force in the words "*with my voice,*" twice repeated (as in Heb., A.V., Vulgate, etc.) to show us that we ought to pray to God directly for ourselves, and in person, and not to be contented with an *Ora pro me* addressed to some one else.—*Cassiodorus and Ayguan, in Neale and Littledale.*

Verse 2.—"*I shewed before him my trouble.*" Be very particular in secret prayer, both as to sins, wants, and mercies . . . Be not ashamed to open out all thy necessities. David argues because he is " poor and needy ; " four several times he presses his wants and exigencies before God, like an earnest but holy beggar (Ps. xl. 17 ; lxx. 5 ; lxxxvi. 1 ; cix. 22). He "*shewed before him*" his trouble. He presents "*before*" God his ragged condition, and spreads open his secret wounds ; as Job said, he ' would order " his " cause before him ": Job xxiii. 4. . . . Before God we may peak out our minds fully, and name the persons that afflict, affront, and trouble s ; and woe to them that a child of God upon a mature judgment names in prayer ! find not that such a prayer in Scripture ever returned empty . . . A great reason y we reap so little benefit in prayer, is because we rest too much in generals ; and ve have success, it is but dark, so that often we cannot tell what to make of the es of prayer. Besides, to be particular in our petitions would keep the spirit h from wandering when we are intent upon a weighty cause, and the progress e soul in grace would manifest its gradual success in prayer.—*Samuel Lee* (1625 1), *in "The Morning Exercises."*

rse 2.—The committing of our cause to God is at once our duty, our safety, ur ease.—*Abraham Wright.*

se 3.—"*When my spirit was overwhelmed within me.*" "*When even my spirit her faculty) is wrapped in darkness upon me ;* " that is, when even my spirit (*ruach*), which ought to elevate my *soul* (*nephesh*) falls heavily upon me, as in a swoon.

> " When heavy, like a veil of woe,
> My spirit on me lay."

What is here said of the *spirit*, is oftener predicated of the *soul*, the seat of the passions. See Psalms xlii. 6 ; xliii. 5 ; cxxxi. 2. The dejection of the *spirit* represents a still more sorrowful and downcast condition, than the fainting of the *soul*. See Psalm cxliii. 3, 4, and compare our Lord's words, " My *soul* is troubled " (John xii. 27) with the Evangelist's statement, " Jesus was troubled in spirit " (John xiii. 21 ; xi. 33).—*Christopher Wordsworth.*

Verse 3.—*"When my spirit was overwhelmed within me."* Literally, *in the muffling upon me of my spirit.* When my spirit was so wrapped in trouble and gloom, so " muffled round with woe," that I could not see the path before me, was distracted and unable to choose a line of conduct, *"Thou* (emphatic) knewest my path."— *A. S. Aglen, in "An Old Testament Commentary for English Readers,"* 1884.

Verse 3.—I wish you much comfort from David's thought : *"When my spirit was overwhelmed within me, then thou knewest my path."* The Lord is not withdrawn to a great distance, but his eye is upon you. He sees you not with the indifference of a mere spectator ; but he observes with attention, he knows, he considers your path : yea, he appoints it, and every circumstance about it is under his direction. Your trouble began at the hour he saw best,—it could not come before ; and he has marked the degree of it to a hair's breadth, and its duration to a minute. He knows likewise how your spirit is affected ; and such supplies of grace and strength, and in such seasons as he sees needful, he will afford in due season. So that when things appear darkest, you shall still be able to say, Though chastened, not killed. Therefore hope in God, for you shall yet praise him.—*John Newton (1725—1807), in "Cardiphonia."*

Verse 3.—*"Thou knewest."*

> From human eyes 'tis better to conceal
> Much that I suffer, much I hourly feel ;
> But, oh, this thought can tranquillize and heal,
> All, all is known to thee.

> Nay, all by thee is ordered, chosen, planned,
> Each drop that fills my daily cup, thy hand
> Prescribes for ills, none else can understand,
> All, all is known to thee.
> *Charlotte Elliott.*

Verse 3.—Although we as Christians possess the full solution of the problem of suffering, yet we frequently find ourselves in the position of Job, in regard to this or that particular affliction. There are sorrows so far reaching, so universal ; there are losses so absolute, and blows so terrible and inexplicable, that it seems for a time as if we were wrapped in thickest gloom, and as if the secret of the Lord had not been revealed. Why was this man stricken, and that man spared ? Why was such and such a being, in whom so many hopes centred, or who had already realised so many pleasant expectations, why was he withdrawn ? Why was th other person left, a useless encumbrance to earth ? Why was that voice, which fou echo in so many hearts, suddenly silenced ? Why have I been smitten ? V have I lost that which rendered my moral life beautiful and useful ? Often the soul seems lost for awhile in thoughts which overwhelm it, it loses its foo it tumbles about helplessly amid the deep waters of affliction. It seems a were over. Do not believe it. Remember Job ; you cannot go to greater of despair than he, and yet God had pity on him. There is much comfor in this example of indescribable suffering, exasperated to the highest de yet pardoned and consoled. Cling to the memory of this blessed fact a of deliverance, a board or a plank amidst the shipwreck. And the that affliction forms part of God's plan, and that he also asks you to m and absolute confidence in him.—*E. De Pressensé, D.D., in "Tl Suffering,"* 1869.

Verse 3.—*"They have privily laid a snare for me."* Snares on and snares on the left : snares on the right hand, worldly prosp the left hand, worldly adversity ; snares on the right hand, fl the left hand, alarm. Do thou walk in the midst of the snares : depart not from the way : let neither flattery ensnare thee, nor alarm drive thee off it.—*Augustine.*

Verse 4.—"*I looked on my right hand, and beheld.*" The first two verbs must be translated as imperatives, as in the margin of the English Bible. [" Look on the right hand, and see."] The right hand is mentioned as the post of a protector.—*Joseph Addison Alexander.*

Verse 4.—"*I looked on my right hand.*" The allusion here, it is supposed, is to the observance of the ancient Jewish courts of judicature, in which the advocate, as well as the accuser, stood on the *right hand* of the accused (Psalm cx. 5). The Psalmist felt himself in the condition of one who had nobody to plead his cause, and to protect him in the dangerous circumstances in which he was placed.—*James Anderson's Note to Calvin in loc.*

Verse 4.—"*There was no man that would know me.*" The fact that David, although surrounded by a band of loyal subjects, confesses to having no true friend, is to be understood similarly to the language of Paul when he says in Phil. ii. 20 : " I have no man like-minded." All human love, since sin has taken possession of humanity, is more or less selfish, and all fellowship of faith and of love imperfect ; and there are circumstances in life in which these dark sides make themselves felt overpoweringly, so that a man seems to himself to be perfectly isolated, and turns all the more urgently to God, who alone is able to supply the soul's want of some object to love, whose love is absolutely unselfish, and unchangeable, and unbeclouded, to whom the soul can confide without reserve whatever burdens it, and who not only honestly desires its good, but is able also to compass it in spite of every obstacle. Surrounded by bloodthirsty enemies, and misunderstood, or at least not thoroughly understood by his friends, David feels himself broken off from all created beings.—*Franz Delitzsch.*

Verse 4.—"*There was no man that would know me.*" Teacheth us of what little estimation God's children be, with the world and worldly men.—*Thomas Wilcocks.*

Verse 4.—"*There was no man that would know me.*" Persecution from the side of our enemies presses sorely, but abandonment by our friends, who should have stood by one's side as helpers and defenders, presses more sorely still.—*Taube, in Lange's Commentary.*

Verse 4.—Observe the beautiful opposition between " Thou knewest " (verse 3) and " no man would know me." "*Refuge failed me,*"—literally "*perished*" from me (Jer. xxv. 35 ; Amos ii. 14). But " thou hast been my *refuge* in the day of my trouble " ; Ps. lix. 16.—*Andrew Robert Fausset.*

Verses 4, 5.—"*Refuge failed me. . . Thou art my refuge.*" Travellers tell us that they who are at the top of the Alps can see great showers of rain fall under them, but not one drop of it falls on them. They who have God for their portion are in a high tower, and thereby safe from all troubles and showers. A drift-rain of evil will beat in at the creature's windows, be they never so well pointed ; all the garments this world can make up cannot keep them that travel in such weather from being wet to the skin. No creature is able to bear the weight of its fellow-creature ; but as reeds, they break under the pressure, and as thorns, they run into the sides of those who lean on them. The bow drawn beyond its compass breaks in sunder, and the string wound above its strength snaps in pieces. Such are outward helps to all that trust to them in hardships.—*George Swinnock.*

Verses 4, 5.—"*Refuge failed me. . . Thou art my refuge.*" Are there any among us to whom the world's face is quite changed, and the brooks of comfort in it are dried up, and they are so tossed, chased, and harassed in it that they have forgotten their resting-place ? Are any of you " become a stranger unto your brethren and an alien unto your mother's children " ? Ps. lxix. 8. Is it grown such a strange world, that even " your own familiar friend, in whom you trusted, which did eat of your bread, hath lifted up his heel against you " ? (Ps. xli. 9) ; and that wherever you turn yourselves in it, to find rest and refuge, the door is shut in your face ? Here is refuge for you ; here is one open door ; come in, thou blessed of the Lord : " the Lord gathereth the outcasts of Israel " : Ps. cxlvii. 2. It seems the Lord minds to have you in : he is doing with you as a father with a stubborn son who ran away from his father's house, thinking to shift for himself among his friends, and not come back : the father sends peremptory word through them all, saying, " In whosesoever house my son is skulking, presently turn him out of doors, and let none of you take him in ; and if he come to you give him not one night's lodging, nay, let him not eat in your house." Wherefore is all this but just to get him back again to his father's house ?—*Thomas Boston*, 1676—1732.

Verses 4, 5.—When all slighted him, when none took care of him ; what doth David in this case ? The words in verse 5 tell us what. "*I cried unto thee, O LORD : I said, Thou art my refuge and my portion in the land of the living.*" As if he had said, Upon these unkindnesses, disrespects, and slightings which I found in the world, I took occasion, yea, I was stirred in my spirit to cry unto thee, O Lord, and to say, "*Thou art my refuge,*" that is, then I made thee my refuge more than ever. Having made thee my choice in my best times, when men honoured and embraced me, I am much encouraged in these evil times when men regard me not, to shelter my weather-beaten self in thy name and power. When we have most friends in the world, then God is our best friend, but when the world hates us, and frowns upon us, especially when (as the prophet speaks of some, Isa. lxvi. 5) " our brethren hate us, and cast us out for the name's sake of God himself," saying, " Let the Lord be glorified," when 'tis thus with us (I say) our souls are even forced into the presence of God, to renew our interests in his love, and to assure our souls that we are accepted with him.—*Joseph Caryl.*

Verse 5.—"*I have cried unto thee, Jehovah, I have said,*" etc. I have cried and still cry ; I have said and still say.—*Joseph Addison Alexander.*

Verse 5.—"*I said.*" This imports, I. A REMEMBRANCE OF THE SOLEMN TRANSACTION, Ps. ciii. 18. This is a deed never to be forgotten, but always to be kept in remembrance. But, O ye who have said this, remember, 1. *What* you said. You said that God in Christ should be your refuge, that under the shade of his wings you hid yourselves, and that, renouncing all other refuges, as refuges of lies, you did betake yourselves to the covert of Christ's righteousness, and that there ye would abide for your portion ; which was a formal acceptance of and laying hold on the covenant. 2. *To whom* you said it. To God in Christ speaking to you in the gospel-offer, and inviting you into the refuge. What men say to their superiors, they think themselves specially concerned to mind. And surely what ye have said to God, ye ought in a peculiar manner to remember, and awe your hearts with the consideration of the majesty of the party to whom ye said it, Ps. xvi. 2 : " O my soul, thou hast said unto the Lord, Thou art my Lord "; for he is not one with whom we may deal falsely. 3. *How* ye said it. Did ye not say it in your hearts, while God in Christ was held out as a refuge for you ? And the language of the heart is plain language with a heart-searching God. Did not some of you say it with your mouths ? and did not all communicants say it solemnly before the world, angels, and men, by their receiving the elements of bread and wine ? 4. *Upon what grounds* you said it. Did you not see a necessity of a refuge for you, and a necessity of taking God in Christ for your refuge ? Ye had rational grounds for it, and lasting grounds that can never fail ; so that ye can never have ground to retract, nor shift about for another refuge. Jer. ii. 31. 5. *Where* ye said it. Remember the spot of ground where ye said it in prayer, where ye said it at the communion-table. Ps. xlii. 6. The stones of the place will be witnesses of your saying it. Josh. xxiv. 27.

II. A STANDING TO IT, without regretting that we said it, remembering what is said, John vi. 66—69 ; " From that time many of his disciples went back, and walked no more with him. Then said Jesus unto the twelve, Will ye also go away ? Then Simon Peter answered him, Lord, to whom shall we go ? thou hast the words of eternal life. And we believe and are sure that thou art that Christ, the Son of the living God." Men often repent what they have said, and therefore will not own that they have said it. But gracious souls will not repent their saying this, but will abide by it. If they were to make their choice a thousand times, having chosen God in Christ for their refuge and portion, they would not alter ; Jer. iii. 19 : " I said, Thou shalt call me, My Father ; and shalt not turn away from me." Many alterations may be in men's circumstances in the world, but there can never be one that will afford ground for retracting this saying.

III. AN OWNING OF THE OBLIGATION OF IT : " *I said,*" and am obliged thereby to stand to it, " For I have opened my mouth unto the Lord, and I cannot go back," Judg. xi. 35. God in Christ is yours, and ye are his by his own consent ; ye are no more your own ; ye have said the word, and must own that it is binding on you ; and ye must beware that after vows ye make not enquiry. Whoever may pretend they have their choice yet to make of a refuge and portion to themselves, ye cannot :

ye are engaged already, and ye are not at liberty to hearken to ar other proposals, any more than a woman who has already signed her contract wit ne man.

IV. A PROFESSING OF IT CONFIDENTLY without being ashamed it: as though you should say, " I own it before all men, and am not ashame my choice." Antichrist allows some of his vassals to carry his mark in their ri hand. Rev. xiii. 16. But all the followers of the Lamb have their mark on foreheads, where it will not hide, Rev. xiv. 1. The world would put the p of God to shame on the head of their refuge and portion, as if they had made a bargain of it, Psa. xiv. 6 : " Ye have shamed the counsel of the poor, bech LORD is his refuge." But sincerity will make men despise that shame the said, " And I will yet be more vile than thus, and will be base in mine own id

V. A SATISFACTION OF HEART IN IT : as though you should say and, Oh, but I am well pleased that ever I said it ; it was the best sa it, ever say. Ps. xvi. 2, 5, 6, 7. And this is in effect to say it over again. uld reason there is for them who have sincerely said it to be well satisfied in od and to rejoice in their portion. The reflecting upon it may afford solid e, content of heart. Ye who have taken the Lord for your refuge may ve, satisfaction reflect upon what you have done.—*Thomas Boston.*

Verse 6.—*"Attend unto my cry."*—

Can I see another's woe,
And not be in sorrow too ?
Can I see another's grief,
And not seek for kind relief ?

Can I see a falling tear,
And not feel my sorrow's share ?
Can a father see his child
Weep, nor be with sorrow filled ?

Can a mother sit and hear
An infant groan, an infant fear ?
No, no ; never can it be !
Never, never can it be !

And can he, who smiles on all,
Hear the wren, with sorrows small—
Hear the small bird's grief and care,
Hear the woes that infants bear,

And not sit beside the nest,
Pouring pity in its breast ?
And not sit the cradle near,
Weeping tear on infant's tear ?

And not sit both night and day
Wiping all our tears away ?
Oh, no ! never can it be !
Never, never can it be !

He doth give his joy to all ;
He becomes an infant small ;
He becomes a man of woe ;
He doth feel the sorrow too.

Think not thou canst sigh a sigh,
And thy Maker is not by ;
Think not thou canst weep a tear,
And thy Maker is not near.

Oh ! he gives to us his joy,
That our grief he may destroy :
Till our grief is fled and gone,
He doth sit by us and moan.

William Blake (1757—1828), *in "Songs of Innocence,"* 1789.

Verse 6.—*"I am brought very low,"* etc. However true this may have been David lurking in a cave, while his enemy, Saul, was at the head of a powerful literally true of Christ, who could truly say, "*I am brought very low*," army, it is mor-self became obedient unto death, even to the death of the cross." because "he *rought very low*," when he, that had the right of sitting on the He was also between two robbers. Truly also were his enemies "*stronger than* cherubim, 'eir hour came," and "power was given to darkness," so as to appear, he" when eclipse the sun of justice itself.—*Robert Bellarmine*.

for awhil"*For they are stronger than I*." But they are not stronger than THOU. Ver-make us "stronger than our enemies": Ps. cv. 24. He who is stronger Thou ,rong man armed (Luke xi. 22), Israel's oppressor, and whose very than is stronger than men" (1 Cor. i. 25), shall "ransom" her "from him "w stronger than" she: Jer. xxxi. 11; Ps. xviii. 17.—*Andrew Robert* th

e 7.—"*Bring my soul out of prison*," etc. As if he should say, O Lord, ss I am a poor prisoner to sin and Satan, I would fain be set at liberty to believe ord, and to do thy will; but, alas, I cannot. I find many a door fast shut me in this prison, and many a lock upon the doors, many lets and impediments h I am never able to remove; and therefore, gracious Lord, do that for me, ch neither I myself nor all the friends I can make are ever able to do for me; y the debts of thy poor prisoner in my blessed Surety, and set open the prison ors: "*Bring my soul out of prison, O LORD, that I may praise thy name!*"—*Matthew* Lawrence, in "*The Use and Practice of Faith*," 1657.

Verse 7.—"*The righteous shall compass me about.*" In a circle, like a crown, as the word signifies; when delivered they should flock to him and come about him to see him and look at him, as a miracle of mercy, whose deliverance was marvellous; and to congratulate him upon it, and to join with him in praise unto God for it. The Targum is, "For my sake the righteous will make to thee a crown of praise."—*John Gill*.

Verse 7.—"*For thou shalt deal bountifully with me.*" Others' mercies ought to be the matter of our praises to God; and others' praises to God on our behalf ought to be both desired and rejoiced in by us.—*Matthew Henry*.

HINTS TO PREACHERS.

Verse 1.—I. A vivid memory—of what he did, and how, and when. II. A public declaration; from which we infer that his prayer cheered him, brought him succour in trouble, and deliverance out of it. III. A reasonable inference: he prays again.

Verses 1, 2.—I. Special seasons for prayer: times of complaint and trouble. II. Special prayer on such occasions; "I cried," "I make my supplication." "I poured out my complaint," "I showed before him my trouble." Spread the whole case before God, as Hezekiah did the letter from Sennacherib.—*G. R.*

Verse 2.—I. The true place for prayer—"before him." II. The freedom of prayer—"poured out." III. The unveiling of the heart in prayer—"shewed before him my trouble."

Verse 3 (first clause).—I. When. II. Then.

Verse 3 (latter clause).—Temptations. I. What form they take?—"snares." II. Who lay them?—"they." III. How do they lay them? Secretly, craftily —"in the way," frequently. IV. What becomes of the tempted believer? He lives to tell the tale, to warn others to glorify God.

Verse 4 (last clause).—The soul considered of no value. I. Consider the worth of the soul. 1. The soul will continue for ever. 2. The righteous will grow more happy, and the wicked more miserable. 3. A great price has been paid for it. II. Contrast the care we take of our souls, and our anxiety about worldly objects. 1. The solicitude we manifest for riches. 2. Our care in educating the intellects of our children. 3. Eagerness in pursuit of business, honour—even trifles. 4. How anxious about a human life! Describe the search for a lost child. 5. Contrast our care for souls and our Saviour's care for them: Paul's, Luther's, Whitefield's. III. Remember some things which show that this care does not exist. 1. If you do not statedly observe secret prayer.   2. If your soul is not burdened with the souls of others.   3. If you neglect family prayer, or observe it as a mere form.   4. If you do not regularly go to prayer-meetings.   Remark : The great responsibility resting upon every Christian.—*Jacob Knapp, in "The Homiletic Monthly,"* 1882.

Verse 4 (last clause).—The burden of souls.   I.   What is meant by care for souls ?   1. To have a firm conviction of their value   2. To cherish tender solicitude for their welfare.   3. To feel alarming apprehensions of their danger.   4. To make zealous exertions for their salvation.   II.   Who ought specially to exercise this care ?   1. Parents.   2. Teachers.   3. Ministers.   4. Members.   III.   The criminality of neglect.   1. It is ungrateful.   2. It is cruel.   3. It is fatal.—*W. W. Wythe, in "The Pulpit Analyst,"* 1870.

Verses 4, 5.—I. A terrible plight ; no friend, no helper, no pitying heart.   II. A touching prayer.   A cry and a saying.

Verses 4, 5.—I. Human help fails most when most needed.   1. In outward troubles : " I looked," etc.   2. In soul troubles : " No man cared for my soul."   II. Divine help is most given when most needed.   A refuge and a portion when all others fail.   Man has many friends in prosperity, one only in adversity.—*G. R.*

Verses 4, 5.—I. Why the saints make God their refuge, and the object of their faith and hope in their greatest afflictions.   1. God has given himself to the saints, in the covenant of grace, to be their God, and has promised that they shall be his people.   2. God stands in a most near relation to the saints, and condescends to sustain many endearing characters of love, which he fulfils to their advantage.   3. The saints, through the power of God's grace upon their souls, have chosen him for their portion, and their highest felicity.   II.   What perfections there are in God that render him a safe refuge for the saints, and a proper object of their confidence.   1. God is infinite in mercy.   2. God is infallible in wisdom.   3. God is boundless in power.   4. God is omniscient and omnipresent.   5. God is a Being whose love never changes.   6. God is an independent Being, and the Governor and Director of all things.   III.   The many sweet advantages, arising to the saints, from this practice of making God their refuge, in their greatest troubles.   1. They have been preserved from fainting under their heavy burdens.   2. They have derived from God new and seasonable supplies of divine grace and strength for service.   3. God has refreshed his saints with divine consolations for the future.—*John Farmer,* 1744.

Verse 5.—The soul choosing God.   I.   Deliberately : " I cried unto thee, I said."   II.   For all in all : " refuge," " portion."   III.   Before every other " in the land of the living."—*W. B. H.*

Verse 5.—" How we may bring our Hearts to bear Reproofs."   See John Owen's Sermon in " The Morning Exercises," vol. ii. page 600, etc. ; and in his " Works," vol. xvi. p. 23, etc.

Verse 6.—Two petitions and two arguments.

Verses 6, 7.—I. The language of Despondency.   " I am brought very low."   " My enemies are stronger than I."   " My soul is in prison."   II. Of Prayer.   " Attend unto me."   " Deliver me."   " Bring me out of prison."   III. Of Praise.   1. For the congratulation of others.   2. For his own deliverance and prosperity.   —*G. R.*

Verse 6.—Low and Lowly.   Here is David, I. In a low place ; the depth of a cave.   II. In a low way : " very low " ; " stronger than I."   III. But see,—" with the lowly is wisdom " (Prov. xi. 2) ; he prays.   IV. The Lord " hath respect to the lowly," Ps. cxxxviii. 6.   He will not pray in vain.—*W. B. H.*

Verse 7.—A prisoner.   A freed-man.   A singer.   A centre.   A wonder.

Verse 7.—Prison Dreams.   I.   What we image in our fetters.   1. Christ's brow girt about with rare praise.   2. Christ's people compassing and companying us in costliest service.   3. A new life of bounty and blessing when we get out.   II.   How far do our dreamings come true ?   Before peril and after ; under conviction, and after conversion ;   sick room, and active service.   III.   The duty of fidelity to prison vows and lessons.—*W. B. H.*

Verse 7 (middle clause).—A Queen Bee.   An under-shepherd.   A warm hearth.   A Museum of wonders.   Or, they shall surround me, interested in my story—" out of prison " ;   drawn by my song—" praise thy name " ;   attracted by likeness of character, and admiring the goodness of the Lord."

Verse 7 (last clause).—Take this with Ps. cxvi. 7.   " The Lord hath dealt bountifully with thee."   Infer the future from the past.

PSALM CXLIII.

TITLE.—*A Psalm of David. It is so much like other Davidic Psalms that we accept the title without a moment's hesitation. David's history illustrates it, and his spirit breathes in it. Why it has been set down as one of the seven Penitential Psalms we can hardly tell; for it is rather a vindication of his own integrity, and an indignant prayer against his slanderers, than a confession of fault. It is true the second verse proves that he never dreamed of justifying himself before the Lord; but even in it there is scarcely the brokenness of penitence. It seems to us rather martial than penitential, rather a supplication for deliverance from trouble than a weeping acknowledgment of transgression. We suppose that seven penitentials were needed by ecclesiastical rabbis, and therefore this was impressed into the service. In truth, it is a mingled strain, a box of ointment composed of divers ingredients, sweet and bitter, pungent and precious. It is the outcry of an overwhelmed spirit, unable to abide in the highest state of spiritual prayer, again and again descending to bewail its deep temporal distress; yet evermore struggling to rise to the best things. The singer moans at intervals; the petitioner for mercy cannot withhold his cries for vindication. His hands are outstretched to heaven, but at his girdle hangs a sharp sword, which rattles in its scabbard as he closes his Psalm.*

DIVISION.—*This Psalm is divided by the Selah. We prefer to follow the natural cleavage, and therefore have made no other dissection of it. May the holy Spirit lead us into its inner meaning.*

EXPOSITION.

HEAR my prayer, O LORD, give ear to my supplications: in thy faithfulness answer me, *and* in thy righteousness.

2 And enter not into judgment with thy servant: for in thy sight shall no man living be justified.

3 For the enemy hath persecuted my soul; he hath smitten my life down to the ground; he hath made me to dwell in darkness, as those that have been long dead.

4 Therefore is my spirit overwhelmed within me; my heart within me is desolate.

5 I remember the days of old; I meditate on all thy works; I muse on the work of thy hands.

6 I stretch forth my hands unto thee: my soul *thirsteth* after thee, as a thirsty land. Selah.

1. "*Hear my prayer, O LORD, give ear to my supplication.*" In the preceding Psalm he began by declaring that he had cried unto the Lord; here he begs to be favourably regarded by Jehovah the living God, whose memorial is that he heareth prayer. He knew that Jehovah did hear prayer, and therefore he entreated him to hear his supplication, however feeble and broken it might be. In two forms he implores the one blessing of gracious audience:—"hear" and "give ear." Gracious men are so eager to be heard in prayer that they double their entreaties for that boon. The Psalmist desires to be heard and to be considered; hence he cries, "hear," and then "give ear." Our case is difficult, and we plead for special attention. Here it is probable that David wished his suit against his adversaries to be heard by the righteous Judge; confident that if he had a hearing in the matter whereof he was slanderously accused, he would be triumphantly acquitted. Yet while somewhat inclined thus to lay his case before the Court of King's Bench, he prefers rather to turn it all into a petition, and present it before the Court of Requests, hence he cries rather "hear my prayer" than "hear my suit." Indeed David is specially earnest that he himself, and the whole of his life, may not become the

subject of trial, for in that event he could not hope for acquittal. Observe that he offered so much pleading that his life became one continual *prayer ;* but that petitioning was so varied in form that it broke out in many *supplications.*

"*In thy faithfulness answer me, and in thy righteousness.*" Saints desire to be answered as well as heard : they long to find the Lord faithful to his promise and righteous in defending the cause of justice. It is a happy thing when we dare appeal even to righteousness for our deliverance ; and this we can do upon gospel principles, for " if we confess our sins he is faithful and just to forgive us our sins." Even the sterner attributes of God are upon the side of the man who humbly trusts, and turns his trust into prayer. It is a sign of our safety when our interests and those of righteousness are blended. With God's faithfulness and righteousness upon our side we are guarded on the right hand and on the left. These are active attributes, and fully equal to the answering of any prayer which it would be right to answer. Requests which do not appeal to either of these attributes it would not be for he glory of God to hear, for they must contain desires for things unpromised, and unrighteous.

2. "*And enter not into judgment with thy servant.*" He had entreated for audience at the mercy-seat, but he has no wish to appear before the judgment-seat. Though clear before men, he could not claim innocence before God. Even though he knew himself to be the Lord's servant, yet he did not claim perfection, or plead merit ; for even as a servant he was unprofitable. If such be the humble cry of a servant, what ought to be the pleading of a sinner ? "*For in thy sight shall no man living be justified.*" None can stand before God upon the footing of the law. God's sight is piercing and discriminating ; the slightest flaw is seen and judged ; and therefore pretence and profession cannot avail where that glance reads all the secrets of the soul. In this verse David told out the doctrine of universal condemnation by the law long before Paul had taken his pen to write the same truth. To this day it stands true even to the same extent as in David's day : no man living even at this moment may dare to present himself for trial before the throne of the Great King on the footing of the law. This foolish age has produced specimens of a pride so rank that men have dared to claim perfection in the flesh ; but these vain-glorious boasters are no exception to the rule here laid down : they are but men, and poor specimens of men. When their lives are examined they are frequently found to be more faulty than the humble penitents before whom they vaunt their superiority.

3. "*For the enemy hath persecuted my soul.*" He has followed me up with perseverance, and has worried me as often as I have been within his reach. The attack was upon the soul or life of the Psalmist : our adversaries mean us the worst possible evil, their attacks are no child's play, they hunt for the precious life. "*He hath smitten my life down to the ground.*" The existence of David was made bitter by the cruelty of his enemy ; he was as one who was hurled down and made to lie upon the ground, where he could be trampled on by his assailant. Slander has a very depressing effect upon the spirits ; it is a blow which overthrows the mind as though it were knocked down with the fist. "*He hath made me to dwell in darkness, as those that have been long dead.*" The enemy was not content with felling his life to the ground—he would lay him lower still, even in the grave ; and lower than that if possible, for the enemy would shut up the saint in the darkness of hell if he could. David was driven by Saul's animosity to haunt caverns and holes, like an unquiet ghost ; he wandered out by night, and lay hid by day like an uneasy spirit which had long been denied the repose of the grave. Good men began to forget him, as though he had been long dead ; and bad men made ridicule of his rueful visage, as though it belonged not to a living man, but was dark with the shadow of the sepulchre. Poor David ! He was qualified to bless the house of the living, but he was driven to consort with the dead ! Such may be our case, and yet we may be very dear to the Lord. One thing is certain, the Lord who permits us to dwell in darkness among the dead, will surely bring us into light, and cause us to dwell with those who enjoy life eternal.

4. "*Therefore is my spirit overwhelmed within me ; my heart within me is desolate.*" David was no stoic : he felt his banishment, and smarted under the cruel assaults which were made upon his character. He felt perplexed and overturned, lonely and afflicted. He was a man of thought and feeling, and suffered both in spirit and in heart from the undeserved and unprovoked hostility of his persecutors. Moreover, he laboured under the sense of fearful loneliness : he was for a while forsaken of his God, and his soul was exceeding heavy, even unto death. Such

words our Lord Jesus might have used : in this the Head is like the members, and the members are as the Head.

5. *"I remember the days of old."* When we see nothing new which can cheer us, let us think upon old things. We once had merry days, days of deliverance, and joy and thanksgiving ; why not again ? Jehovah rescued his people in the ages which lie back, centuries ago ; why should he not do the like again ? We ourselves have a rich past to look back upon ; we have sunny memories, sacred memories, satisfactory memories, and these are as flowers for the bees of faith to visit, from whence they may make honey for present use. *"I meditate on all thy works."* When my own works reproach me, thy works refresh me. If at the first view the deeds of the Lord do not encourage us, let us think them over again, ruminating and considering the histories of divine providence. We ought to take a wide and large view of *all* God's works ; for as a whole they work together for good, and in each part they are worthy of reverent study. *"I muse on the work of thy hands."* This he had done in former days, even in his most trying hours. Creation had been the book in which he read of the wisdom and goodness of the Lord. He repeats his perusal of the page of nature, and counts it a balm for his wounds, a cordial for his cares, to see what the Lord has made by his skilful hands. When the work of our own hand grieves us, let us look to the work of God's hands. Memory, meditation, and musing are here set together as the three graces, ministering grace to a mind depressed and likely to be diseased. As David with his harp played away the evil spirit from Saul, so does he here chase away gloom from his own soul by holy communion with God.

6. *"I stretch forth my hands unto thee."* He was eager for his God. His thoughts of God kindled in him burning desires, and these led to energetic expressions of his inward longings. As a prisoner whose feet are bound extends his hands in supplication when there is hope of liberty, so does David. *"My soul thirsteth after thee, as a thirsty land."* As the soil cracks, and yawns, and thus opens its mouth in dumb pleadings, so did the Psalmist's soul break with longings. No heavenly shower had refreshed him from the sanctuary : banished from the means of grace, his soul felt parched and dry, and he cried out, " My soul to thee "; nothing would content him but the presence of his God. Not alone did he extend his hands, but his heart was stretched out towards the Lord. He was athirst for the Lord. If he could but feel the presence of his God he would no longer be overwhelmed or dwell in darkness ; nay, everything would turn to peace and joy.

Selah.—It was time to pause, for the supplication had risen to agony point. Both harp-strings and heart-strings were strained, and needed a little rest to get them right again for the second half of the song.

7 Hear me speedily, O LORD : my spirit faileth : hide not thy face from me, lest I be like unto them that go down into the pit.

8 Cause me to hear thy lovingkindness in the morning ; for in thee do I trust : cause me to know the way wherein I should walk ; for I lift up my soul unto thee.

9 Deliver me, O LORD, from mine enemies : I flee unto thee to hide me.

10 Teach me to do thy will ; for thou *art* my God : thy spirit *is* good ; lead me into the land of uprightness.

11 Quicken me, O LORD, for thy name's sake : for thy righteousness' sake bring my soul out of trouble.

12 And of thy mercy cut off mine enemies, and destroy all them that afflict my soul : for I *am* thy servant.

7. *"Hear me speedily, O LORD : my spirit faileth."* If long delayed, the deliverance would come too late. The afflicted suppliant faints, and is ready to die. His life is ebbing out ; each moment is of importance ; it will soon be all over with him. No argument for speed can be more powerful than this. Who will not run to help a suppliant when his life is in jeopardy ? Mercy has wings to its heels when misery is in extremity. God will not fail when our spirit fails, but the rather he will hasten his course and come to us on the wings of the wind. *"Hide not thy face from me, lest I be like unto them that go down into the pit."* Communion with God is so dear to a true heart that the withdrawal of it makes the man

feel as though he were ready to die and perish utterly. God's ῾hdrawals reduce
the heart to despair, and take away all strength from the mir Moreover, his
absence enables adversaries to work their will without restraint ῾nd thus, in a
second way, the persecuted one is like to perish. If we have G῾countenance
we live, but if he turns his back upon us we die. When the Lord ῾with favour
upon our efforts we prosper, but if he refuses to countenance th῾labour in
vain.

8. *"Cause me to hear thy lovingkindness in the morning ; for in ι* ῾I trust."
Lord, my sorrow makes me deaf,—cause me to hear : there is but ῾ce that
can cheer me—cause me to hear thy lovingkindness ; that music I wc῾enjoy
at once—cause me to hear it in the morning, at the first dawning h῾sense
of divine love is to the soul both dawn and dew ; the end of the nigh῾ing,
the beginning of the morning of joy. Only God can take away fron῾ry
ears the din of our care, and charm them with the sweet notes of hi῾ιr
plea with the Lord is our faith ; if we are relying upon him, he canno῾ιr
us : " in thee do I trust " is a sound and solid argument with God. He῾ιr
the ear will cause us to hear : he who is love itself will have the kindne῾
his lovingkindness before our minds. *"Cause me to know the way whereiι
walk ; for I lift up my soul unto thee."* The Great First Cause must ca
hear and to know. Spiritual senses are dependent upon God, and heaven.
ledge comes from him alone. To know the way we ought to take is exc
needful, for how can we be exact in obedience to a law with which we
acquainted ? or how can there be an ignorant holiness ? If we know not tl
how shall we keep in it ? If we know not wherein we should walk, how sl
be likely to follow the right path ? The Psalmist lifts up his soul ; faith is
at a dead lift : the soul that trusts will rise. We will not allow our hope to
but we will strive to get up and rise out of our daily griefs. This is wise. ῾
David was in any difficulty as to his way he lifted his soul towards God him,
and then he knew that he could not go very far wrong. If the soul will not ῾
of itself we must lift it, lift it up unto God. This is good argument in prayer
surely the God to whom we endeavour to lift up our soul will condescend to show
us what he would have us to do. Let us attend to David's example, and when our
heart is low, let us heartily endeavour to lift it up, not so much to comfort as to
the Lord himself.

9. *"Deliver me, O LORD, from mine enemies."* Many foes beset us, we cannot
overcome them, we cannot even escape from them ; but Jehovah can and will
rescue us if we pray to him. The weapon of all-prayer will stand us in better stead
than sword and shield. *"I flee unto thee to hide me."* This was a good result from
his persecutions. That which makes us flee to our God may be an ill wind, but it
blows us good. There is no cowardice in such flight, but much holy courage. God
can hide us out of reach of harm, and even out of sight of it. He is our hiding-
place ; Jesus has made himself the refuge of his people : the sooner, and the more
entirely we flee to him the better for us. Beneath the crimson canopy of our Lord's
atonement believers are completely hidden ; let us abide there and be at rest. In
the seventh verse our poet cried, " Hide not thy face," and here he prays, " Hide
me." Note also how often he uses the words " unto thee " ; he is after his God ;
he must travel in that direction by some means, even though he may seem to be
beating a retreat ; his whole being longs to be near the Lord. It is possible that
such thirstings for God will be left unsupplied ? Never, while the Lord is love.

10. *"Teach me to do thy will."* How childlike—" teach me " ! How practical
—" Teach me to do " ! How undivided in obedience—" to do thy will " ! To
do all of it, let it be what it may. This is the best form of instruction, for its source
is God, its object is holiness, its spirit is that of hearty loyalty. The man is hidden
in the Lord, and spends his peaceful life in learning the will of his Preserver. A
heart cannot long be desolate which is thus docile. *"For thou art my God."* Who
else can teach me as thou canst ? Who else will care to do it but my God ? Thou
hast given me thyself, thou wilt surely give me thy teaching. If I have thee, may
I not ask to have thy perfect mind ? When the heart can sincerely call Jehovah
" my God," the understanding is ready to learn of him, the will is prepared to obey
him, the whole man is eager to please him. *"Thy spirit is good."* God is all spirit
and all good. His essence is goodness, kindness, holiness : it is his nature to do
good, and what greater good can he do to us than to hear such a prayer as that
which follows—*"Lead me into the land of uprightness"* ? David would fain be among

...nd of another sort from that which had cast him out. He sighed
the godly, in ...eadows of grace, the table-lands of peace, the fertile plains of
for the uplan... could not reach them of himself; he must be led there. God,
communion... best conduct us to the goodly land. There is no inheritance like
who is gone land of promise, the land of precept, the land of perfectness. He
a portio...s must put us into leading-strings, and guide and conduct us to his
who te...-place in the country of holiness. The way is long, and steep, and
own ...s delightful to follow, and there is neither stumbling nor wandering.
he ...uicken me, O LORD, for thy name's sake." Oh for more life as well as
to ...! Teaching and leading call for invigoration, or we shall be dull scholars
pilgrims. Jehovah, the Lord and giver of life, is the only one from whom
...come to renew and revive us;—hence, the prayer is to him only. Perchance
...nt might teach and lead, but only the Master can enliven. We are often
...o death, and hence each one may fitly cry, " Quicken *me* "; but what is
...in us which we can plead as a reason for such a favour? Nothing, literally
...ing. We must beg it for his name's sake. He must quicken us because he
...e living God, the loving God, the Lord who delighteth in mercy. What blessed
...uments lie clustered together in his glorious name! We need never cease praying
...r want of acceptable pleas; and we may always fall back upon the one before us
...—" thy name's sake." It will render the name of Jehovah the more glorious in
...he eyes of men if he creates a high degree of spiritual life in his servants; and
this is a reason for his doing so, which we may urge with much confidence.

"For thy righteousness' sake bring my soul out of trouble." Let men see that
thou art on the side of the right, and that thou wilt not allow the wicked to ride
rough-shod over those who trust in thee. Thou hast promised to succour thy
people; thou art not unrighteous to forget their work of faith; thou art, on the
contrary, righteous in answering sincere prayer, and in comforting thy people.
David was heavily afflicted. Not only was there trouble in his soul, but his soul
was in trouble; plunged in it as in a sea, shut up in it as in a prison. God could
bring him out of it, and especially he could at once lift up his soul or spirit out of
the ditch. The prayer is an eager one, and the appeal a bold one. We may be
sure that trouble was soon over when the Lord heard such supplications.

12. *"And of thy mercy cut off mine enemies, and destroy all them that afflict my
soul."* He believes that it will be so, and thus prophesies the event; for the words
may be read as a declaration, and it is better so to understand them. We could
not *pray* just so with our Christian light; but under Old Testament arrangements
the spirit of it was congruous to the law. It is a petition which justice sanctions,
but the spirit of love is not at home in presenting it. *We*, as Christians, turn the
petition to spiritual use only. Yet David was of so generous a mind, and dealt
so tenderly with Saul, that he could hardly have meant all that his words are made
in our version to say. *"For I am thy servant;"* and therefore I hope that my Master
will protect me in his service, and grant me victory while I fight his battles. It is
a warrior's prayer, and smells of the dust and smoke of battle. It was heard, and
therefore it was not asking amiss. Still there is a more excellent way.

EXPLANATORY NOTES AND QUAINT SAYINGS.

Whole Psalm.—This Psalm of David most aptly answereth to that Psalm which
precedeth it; for in Ps. cxlii. he showeth that he prayed, repeating it twice (verse 1);
and here he twice saith, " Hear my prayer, give ear to my supplication." In Psalm
cxlii. (verse 3) he saith, " When my spirit was overwhelmed within me "; here
(verse 4), " My spirit is overwhelmed within me."—*John Mayer.*

Whole Psalm.—The promise referred to throughout this octave of Psalms
[cxxxviii—cxlv.] is that recorded in 2 Sam. vii. 12, etc., " When thy days be
fulfilled . . . . . I will set up thy seed after thee . . . . . and I will establish
his kingdom . . . . . If he commit iniquity, I will chasten him . . . . . But my
mercy shall not depart away from him; and thine house and thy kingdom shall

be established for ever." What fixes the connection of the Psalm with the history is the frequent application of the term *"Thy* (Jehovah's) *servant,"* by David to himself in the latter, as in verses 2 and 12 of the former. Jehovah had first used it of David, " Tell to my servant, to David ; " David therefore fastens on it as his plea again and again (2 Sam. vii. 5, 9—21, 25—29). David's plea, " For I am thy servant," is no boast of his service, but a magnifying of God's electing grace : " Who am I, O Lord God ? and what is my house, that thou hast brought me hitherto ? " 2 Sam. vii. 18.

The cry (verse 6) *"My soul thirsteth after thee as a thirsty land,"* answers to David's own words in Psalm lxiii. 1, when he was fleeing from Absalom, and still in the wilderness of Judah (title, Ps. lxiii.) on the near side of Jordan : " My soul *thirsteth* for thee." The history here again is an undesigned agreement with the Psalm : (2 Sam. xvi. 2, 14,) " The King, and all the people with him, came *weary,* and refreshed themselves " with Ziba's fruits ; also xvii. 2. The Hebrew for *"thirsty"* in Psalm cxliii. is the same as for *"weary"* in lxiii. 1, and in 2 Sam. xvi. 14, and means " panting," " weary," " thirsting."—*Andrew Robert Fausset, in "Studies in the CL. Psalms,"* 1876.

Whole Psalm.—At the making of this Psalm (as it plainly appeareth) David was cast into some desperate danger ; whether by Saul when he was forced to flee into the cave, as in the former Psalm, or by Absalom his son, or by any other, it is uncertain. Howsoever, in this he complaineth grievously to God of the malice of his enemies, and desireth God to hear his prayers, he acknowledgeth that he suffereth those things by God's just judgment, most humbly craving mercy for his sins ; desiring not only to be restored, but also to be governed by God's Spirit, that he may dedicate and consecrate the rest of his life to God's service. This worthy Psalm, then, containeth these three things. First, a confession of his sins. Secondly, a lamentation over his injuries. Thirdly, a supplication for temporal deliverance and spiritual graces.—*Archibald Symson.*

Whole Psalm.—It is not without some use to observe in this Psalm how the heart of its devout composer turned alternately from spiritual to temporal, and again from temporal to spiritual subjects. He first complains of *his sins,* and begs for *mercy ;* then of *his enemies,* and prays for *deliverance.* Then he laments his darkness and pleads for the light of God's countenance, and for wisdom, and understanding. After this, the thought of his enemies rushes in again upon his soul, and he flees to God for protection. Lastly, he again puts up his prayer for wisdom and holiness : " Teach me to do thy will ; for thou art my God : thy spirit is good ; lead me into the land of uprightness." This is a peculiarly important petition : before he had prayed to know the way in which he should walk, he now prays that he may walk in it.—*John Fawcett,* 1769—1851.

Whole Psalm.—This is appointed by the Church for Ash-Wednesday, and is the seventh and last of the Penitential Psalms. These seven Penitential Psalms are also sometimes called " the Special Psalms," and have long been used in the Church as the completest and most spiritual acts of repentance which she possesses. They have sometimes been considered as directed against the seven deadly sins ; as, for instance, Psalm vi. against Wrath ; Ps. xxxii. against Pride ; Ps. xxxviii. against Gluttony ; Ps. li. against Impurity ; Ps. cii. against Covetousness ; Ps. cxxx. against Envy ; and the present Psalm against Indifference, or Carelessness.— *J. W. Burgon.*

Verse 1.—*"Hear my prayer, O LORD,"* etc. Alas, O Lord, if thou hear not my prayer, I were as good not pray at all ; and if thou hear it, and give not ear unto it, it were as good thou didst not hear it at all. O, therefore, *"hear my prayer, O God, and give ear to my supplications ";* that neither my praying may be lost for want of thy hearing it, nor thy hearing it be lost for want of thy attending it. When I only make a prayer to God, it seems enough that he hear it ; but when I make a supplication, it requires that he give ear unto it ; for seeing a supplication hath a greater intention in the setting out, it cannot without a greater attention be entertained.

But what niceness of words is this ? as though it were not all one *" to hear "* and *" to give ear "?* or as though there were any difference between a prayer and a supplication ? Is it not perhaps so indeed ? for hearing sometimes may be only passive, where giving ear is always active ; and seeing Christ, we doubt not, heard the woman of Canaan's first cry, while it was a prayer ; but gave no ear till her second cry, when it was grown to a supplication. However it be, as thy hearing, O God, without giving ear would be to no purpose, so thy giving ear without giving answer would do me no good; O, therefore, *"answer me,"* O God; for if thou answer not my prayer, how canst thou answer my expectation? My prayer is but the seed; it is thy answer that makes the harvest. If thou shouldst not answer me at all, I could not hope for any harvest at all; and if thou shouldst answer me, and not *"in thy righteousness,"* that would be a harvest indeed, but nothing but of blasted corn. Therefore, answer me, O God, but " in thy righteousness"; for thy righteousness never made an unpleasing answer. It was an answer in thy righteousness which thou madest to Noah: " My spirit shall not always strive with man; for the imagination of man's heart is evil from his infancy." It was an answer in thy righteousness which thou madest to Abraham: " Fear not; I will be thy shield, and thy exceeding great reward." It was an answer in thy righteousness which thou madest to the thief upon the cross : " This day thou shalt be with me in paradise." Oh, then, answer me also in thy righteousness, O God, and then the harvest of my hope will be as plentiful as the seven years of plenty foretold by Joseph.—*Sir Richard Baker.*

Verse 1.—*"Hear my prayer,"* . . . *"give ear to my supplications,"* . . . *"answer me."* He doth here three times repeat his earnest desire to be heard, as in the fifth Psalm four times he doubleth and ingeminateth this same suit to be heard. . . . When he doubleth his request of hearing, he would have God hear him with both his ears, that is, most attentively and readily : so instant is a troubled mind that he desireth the prayer he putteth up to be remembered, as was said by the angel to the centurion : " Thy prayer and almsdeeds are come up before God": Acts x. 4. —*Archibald Symson.*

Verse 1.—*"In thy faithfulness answer me, and in thy righteousness."* It was thy righteousness that thou didst make the promise, but it is thy faithfulness that thou wilt keep thy promise : and seeing I am certain of thy making it, how can I be doubtful of thy keeping it ? If thou shouldst not answer me in thy righteousness, yet thou shouldst be righteous still ; but if thou shouldst not answer me in thy faithfulness, thou shouldst not be faithful still.—*Sir Richard Baker.*

Verse 1.—*"Answer me in thy righteousness."* Forgiveness is not inconsistent with the truth or righteousness, and the pardon which in mercy God bestows upon the sinner is bestowed in justice to the well-beloved Son who accepted and discharged the sinner's obligations. This is an infinitely precious truth, and the hearts of thousands in every age have been sustained and gladdened by it. A good old Christian woman in humble life so fully realized this, that when a revered servant of God asked her, as she lay on her dying pillow, the ground of her hope for eternity, she replied, with great composure, " I rely on the justice of God"; adding, however, when the reply excited surprise, " justice, not to me, but to my Substitute, *in whom I trust.*—*Robert Macdonald, in "From Day to Day ; or, Helpful Words for Christian Life,"* 1879.

Verse 2.—*"Enter not into judgment with thy servant."* The Divine justice has just been invoked in the first verse ; and now the appellant suddenly seems to deprecate it. These verses really sum up the apparent paradox of the Book of Job (See Job iv. 17, ix. 2, 32, xiv. 3, *seq.,* xv. 14, xxii. 4, etc.) In one breath Job frequently pours forth pathetic protestations of his innocence, and a dread lest God should take him at his word, and arraign him for trial. The godly man, in his desire to have his character vindicated before man, appeals to the just Judge, but instantly falls back with a guilty sense that before his tribunal none can stand :

> " For merit lives from man to man,
> And not from man, O Lord, to thee."

A. S. Aglen.

Verse 2.—He doth not pray absolutely that God " would not enter into judgment with him," for this were to forego his government of the world; but that he would not do so on account of his own duties and obedience. But if so be these duties and obedience did answer, in any sense or way, what is required of us as a righteousness unto justification, there was no reason why he should deprecate a trial by them, or upon them.—*John Owen.*

Verse 2.—He doth not say, " with an enemy, a rebel, a traitor, an impenitent sinner ; " but " *with thy servant,*" one that is devoted to thy fear, one that is consecrated to thy service, one that is really and indeed "wholly thine, as much and as fully as he can be." As if he had said, " Lord, if the holiest, purest, best of men should come and stand before thee in judgment, or plead with thee, they must needs be cast in their cause. ' If thou, Lord, shouldest mark iniquities,' alas ! ' O Lord, who shall stand ? ' " Psalm cxxx. 3.—*Thomas Lye* (1621—1684), *in "The Morning Exercises."*

Verse 2.—"Enter not into judgment with thy servant," for thou hast already entered into judgment with thy Son, and laid upon him the iniquity of us all. *"Enter not into judgment with thy servant,"* for thy servant enters into judgment with himself ; and " if we will judge ourselves we shall not be judged."—*Matthew Henry.*

Verse 2.—Not the proudest philosopher among the Gentiles, nor the most precise Pharisee among the Jews ; we may go yet further and say, not the holiest saint that ever lived, can stand righteous before that bar. God hath nailed that door up, that none can for ever enter by a law-righteousness into life and happiness. This way to heaven is like the northern passage to the Indies, whoever attempts it is sure to be frozen up before he gets half way thither.—*William Gurnall.*

Verse 2.—"Enter not into judgment," &c. Some years ago I visited a poor young woman dying with consumption. She was a stranger in our town, and had been there a few weeks before, some time in her girlhood, and had attended my Sabbath-school class. What did I find was her only stay, and hope, and comfort in the view of the dark valley of the shadow of death, which was drawing down upon her ? One verse of a Psalm she had learned at the class, and never forgot. She repeated it with clasped hands, piercing eyes, and thin voice trembling from her white lips :

> " Thy servant also bring thou not
> In judgment to be tried :
> Because no living man can be
> In thy sight justify'd."

No—no sinner can endure sight of thee, O God, if he tries to be self-justified. —*James Comper Gray, in "The Biblical Museum,"* 1879.

Verse 2.—"Enter not into judgment with thy servant." We read of a certain Dutch divine, who being to die, was full of fears and doubts. And when some said to him, " You have been so active and faithful, why should you fear ? " Oh, said he, the judgment of man and the judgment of God are different.—*John Trapp.*

Verse 2.—"Enter not into judgment." A metaphor taken from the course pursued by those who seek to recover the very utmost to which they are entitled by strict legal process. Compare Job xxii. 4, 5. In a similar sense we are commanded to pray to God that he will forgive us our debts.—*Daniel Cresswell.*

Verse 2.—There is probably here a tacit reference to the great transgression, the consequences of which followed David all his days.—*William Walford.*

Verse 2.—"Thy servant." A servant is one who obeys the will of another. . . . . There were these four ways in which one might come to be a servant,—by birth, by purchase, by conquest, and by voluntary engagement. Some were servants in one of the ways, and some in another. There were servants who were born in the master's house, servants who were bought with the master's money, servants who were the captives of his sword and bow, and servants who had freely engaged themselves to do his work. . . . In the case of the believer there is something that is peculiar and remarkable. He is God's servant by birth. But he is more—he is God's servant by purchase. And that is not all : he is God's servant by conquest. Yes, and by voluntary engagement too. He is the servant of God, not in some ne of the four ways, but in all of them together.—*Andrew Gray* (1805—1861), *"Gospel Contrasts and Parallels."*

Verse 2.—Not only the worst of my sins, but the best of my duties speak me a ild of Adam.—*William Beveridge.*

Verse 2.—So far from being able to answer for my sins, I cannot answer even my righteousness.—*Bernard of Clairvaux,* 1091—1153.

Verse 2.—A young man once said to me : " I do not think I am a sinner." ked him if he would be willing his mother or sister should know all he had done, id, or thought,—all his motions and all his desires. After a moment he said : indeed, I should not like to have them know ; no, not for the world." " Then ou dare to say, in the presence of a holy God, who knows every thought of your ' I do not commit sin ' ? "—*John B. Gough, in "Sunlight and Shadow,"*

Verse 3.—"*For the enemy,*" etc. If ever trouble be just cause for calling upon thee, how can mine but be most just, when "*the enemy hath persecuted my soul, hath smitten my life down to the ground, and hath made me to dwell in darkness, as those that have been long dead*"? All this "*the enemy*" hath done unto me: but what enemy? Is it not the enemy of all mankind, who hath singled me out, as it were to a duel? And can *I* resist him myself alone, whom the whole army of mankind cannot? But it is not the enemy of thyself, O God, who is but my enemy because I am thy servant? And wilt thou see thy servants persecuted—in thy cause persecuted —and not protect them? Shall I suffer, grievously suffer, for thy sake, and wilt thou forsake me? Alas, O Lord; if they were but some light evils that are inflicted upon me I would bear them without complaining, and never make my moan to thee about them; but they are the three greatest miseries that can be thought of; the greatest persecution, the greatest overthrow, and the greatest captivity. For what persecution so grievous as to be persecuted in my soul? for he plays no less a game than for souls: he casts indeed at the body sometimes, and sometimes at goods, yet these are but the bye; the main of his aim is at the soul; for if he can otherwise win the soul he cares not much for either body or goods, but rather makes use of them to keep men in security; for whatsoever he doth, whatsoever he leaves undone, it is all done but in persecution of the soul; and he can persecute as well with prosperity as with adversity, and knows how to fit their several application. It seems as if he takes me for another Job; he sees he can do no good upon me with fawning and clawing, and therefore falls now to quarrelling and striking; and he strikes no light blows; for "*he hath stricken my life down to the ground*"; and lower would have struck it, if thou, God, hadst not broken his blow. He strikes me downward, to keep me from heaven, as much as he can: and now that he sees me down, he lets not me rest so neither; but seizeth upon me, and being himself the prince of darkness, hath kept me in darkness; not for a night or two, as men stay at their inn, but for a much longer time, as at their dwelling: and it is no ordinary darkness that he hath made me to dwell in, but even the darkness of dead men; and that in the highest degree, as those that have been long dead. They that have been dead but a while are yet remembered sometimes, and sometimes talked of; but they that have been long dead are as quite forgotten as if they had never been; and such, alas, am I. So long have I been made to dwell in darkness, as if I had been dead many years ago, that he that would seek to find me out must be fain to look for me amongst the tombs and monuments. Indeed, to dwell in darkness is no better than the house of death: for as long as we are in life, if we want sometimes the light of the sun, yet the light of a candle will serve to supply it; but I, alas, am kept in such darkness that neither the sunshine of thy gospel nor the lantern of thy law gives any light unto me. I cannot with confidence say, as once I did, "Thou, O Lord, shalt light my candle for me"; and as a body being dead grows cold and stiff, and is not to be bowed, so my soul with continuance in sinning is grown hardened, and, as it were, stiff in sin; that it is as hard a matter to make me flexible to any goodness as to bring a body long dead to life again.—*Sir Richard Baker.*

Verse 3.—"*To dwell in darkness.*" To seek my safety in holes and obscure places in the wilderness. See 2 Sam. xvii. 16. "*As those that have been long dead.*" That is, where I seem to be buried alive, and to have no more hopes of being restore to a happy condition in this world than those that have been long dead have living again in it.—*Thomas Fenton.*

Verse 4.—"*Therefore is my spirit overwhelmed,*" etc. David was not o great saint, but a great soldier, and yet even he was sometimes ready to faint day of adversity. "Howl, fir trees, if the cedars be shaken."—*Matthew Hen*

Verse 4 (*second clause*). — "*Within me*" — literally, "*in the midst o* implying how *deeply* the feeling had penetrated. "*Is desolate,*" or ra *stupefied,*" in a similar sense to that of the Hebrew (Isa. lix. 16; lxiii. viii. 27). So the Chaldaic, The LXX., Vulgate, Arabic, and Syriac, "*i* —*Andrew Robert Fausset.*

Verse 4.—"*Is desolate.*" Or rather, "is full of amazement," literall itself"; seeks to comprehend the mystery of its sufferings, and is eve upon itself in its perplexity: such is the full force of the reflexive co employed.—*J. J. Stewart Perowne.*

Verses 4, 5.—How poor a man's judgment can be formed of a

the considerations of comfort only. A holy man, we clearly see, may be void of comfort; his spirit may be overwhelmed, and his heart desolate. Nay, was it not so even with the holy Jesus himself? was he not very heavy, and his soul exceeding sorrowful even unto death? But never did the Saviour's faith and submission to his Father's will shine more brightly than in that hour of darkness. And David's faith also rises to meet the occasion. His trial is great, and his faith is great also. Hardly when he is on the mount of praise, and singing his songs of Zion in the most triumphant strain, does he appear more admirable than when struggling through this painful conflict. He is troubled on every side, yet not removed; perplexed, but not in despair; persecuted, but not forsaken; cast down, but not destroyed. He has no arm of flesh to trust to, and nothing within himself to support his hope; but with what simplicity, and energy of trust, does he betake himself to God, revolving in his memory past seasons of deliverance, and staying his mind on the power and truth of Jehovah! " I remember the days of old; I meditate on all thy works; I muse on the work of thy hands."—*John Fawcett.*

Verse 5.—*"I remember the days of old; I meditate,"* etc. This meditation gives an ease to the overwhelming of my spirits, a comfort to the desolateness of my heart; for I am thinking sometimes upon Jonah, how he was overwhelmed with waters and swallowed up of a whale, and yet at last delivered; sometimes I am thinking of Joseph, how he was bound and left desolate in a pit, and yet at last relieved; and then I meditate thus with myself,—Is God's power confined to persons? could he deliver them in their extremities, and can he not deliver me in mine?— *Sir Richard Baker.*

Verse 5.—*"I meditate on all thy works."* Let us look for God in the future more earnestly than we have done in the past,—look for him in vineyards and orchards and harvest fields,—in the bright plumage of birds, and the delicate bloom of fruit, and the sweet gracefulness of flowers,—in the dense foliage of the forest, and the sparse heather of the moor,—in the rich luxuriance of fertile valleys, and the rugged grandeur of the everlasting hills,—in the merry dance of the rivulet, and the majestic tides of the ocean,—in the gay colours of the rainbow, and the splendour of the starry heavens,—in the gentle radiance of the moon, and the gorgeous light of setting suns,—in the clear azure sky, and the weird pageantry of clouds,—in the snow-mantled wintry landscape, and the brilliant effulgence of a summer's noon,—in the virgin loveliness of spring, and in the pensive fading beauty of autumn,—let us look for him with an earnest, eager, and unwearied gaze, till we see him to be a God of wisdom as well as power, of love as well as sovereignty, of beauty as well as glory.—*A. W. Momerie, in "The Origin of Evil, and other Sermons,"* 1881.

Verses 5, 6.—*"I meditate." "I stretch forth my hands."* Meditation is prayer's handmaid to wait on it, both before and after the performance of supplication. It is as the plough before the sower, to prepare the heart for the duty of prayer; and as the harrow after the sower, to cover the seed, when 'tis sown. As the hopper feeds the mill with grist, so does meditation supply the heart with matter for prayer. —*William Gurnall.*

Verse 6.—*"I stretch forth my hands unto thee."* As a poor beggar for an alms. Beggary here is not the easiest and poorest trade, but the hardest and richest of all other.—*John Trapp.*

Verse 6.—*"I stretch forth my hands unto thee,"* as if I were in hope thou wouldst take me by the hand and draw me to thee.—*Sir Richard Baker.*

Verse 6.—*"My soul thirsteth after thee,"* etc. Alas! this thirst is rare to be found. Worldly thirsts there are in many: the drunkard's thirst, Deut. xxix. 19; the worldling's thirst, Hab. ii. 5; the epicure's thirst, whose belly is his god, Phil. iii. 19; the ambitious man's thirst—Diotrephes, 3 John 9; and the malicious man's thirst, the blood thirsty, Ps. v. 6. Thirst after these things doth keep away that thirst after grace without which we shall never escape Dives' thirst in hell, Luke xvi. 24. If we have a godly thirst, it will appear by diligence in frequenting the place and means of grace, Prov. viii. 34; brute beasts for want of water will break through hedges, and grace-thirsty souls will make their ways through all encumbrances to come where they may have satisfaction.—*Thomas Pierson,* 1570— 1633.

Verse 6.—*"My soul thirsteth after thee, as a thirsty land."* He declareth his vehement affection to God by a very pretty similitude, taken from the ground which is thirsty by the long drought of summer, wherein the earth, rent in pieces, as it were, and with open mouth through long thirst, seeketh drink from heaven. By which he showeth that he came to God as destitute of natural substance, and therefore seeketh from above that which he lacked. So in all his extremities he looked ever upward ; from above he seeketh help and comfort. Albeit we be in extremity, and as it were rent asunder, yet here is comfort,—there are waters in heaven which will refresh us, if we gape after them. Here is a blessing—those that thirst shall be satisfied. If we thirst for mercy, for deliverance, for spiritual or temporal comfort, we shall be satisfied therewith ; for if God heard the prayers of Hagar and Ishmael being athirst in the wilderness, and opened unto them a fountain (Gen. xxi. 17, 19), will he forsake Isaac, the child of promise ? If he heard Samson in the bitterness of his heart, when he said, " I die from thirst," and opened a spring out of the jawbone of an ass (Jud. xv. 19), will he forsake us in time of our distress, if we thirst aright ?—*Archibald Symson.*

Verse 6.—"*My soul thirsteth after thee, as a thirsty land.*" Sir John Chardin, in his MSS. says :—" The lands of the East, which the great dryness there causes to crack, are the ground of this figure, which is certainly extremely beautiful ; for these dry lands have chinks too deep for a person to see the bottom of : this may be observed in the Indies more than anywhere, a little before the rains fall, and wherever the lands are rich and hard."—*Harmer's Observations.*

Verse 6.—"*I stretch forth my hands unto thee,*" etc. It is not a strange thing, then, for the soul to find its life in God. This is its native air : God as the Environment of the soul has been from the remotest age the doctrine of all the deepest thinkers in religion. How profoundly Hebrew poetry is saturated with this high thought will appear when we try to conceive of it with this left out. True poetry is only science in another form. And long before it was possible for religion to give scientific expression to its greatest truths, men of insight uttered themselves in Psalms which could not have been truer to Nature had the most modern light controlled the inspiration. " As the hart panteth after the water-brooks, so panteth my soul after thee, O God." What fine sense of the natural analogy of the natural and spiritual does not underlie these words. As the hart after its environment, so man after his ; as the water-brooks are fitly designed to meet the natural wants, so fitly does God implement the spiritual need of man. It will be noticed that in the Hebrew poets the longing for God never strikes one as morbid, or unnatural to the men who uttered it. It is as natural for them to long for God as for the swallow to seek her nest. Throughout all their images no suspicion rises within us that they are exaggerating. We feel how truly they are reading themselves, their deepest selves. No false note occurs in all their aspiration. There is no weariness even in their ceaseless sighing, except the lover's weariness for the absent—if they would fly away, it is only to be at rest. Men who have no soul can only wonder at this. Men who have a soul, but with little faith, can only envy it. How joyous a thing it was to the Hebrews to seek their God ! How artlessly they call upon him to entertain them in his pavilion, to cover them with his feathers, to hide them in his secret place, to hold them in the hollow of his hand, or stretch around them the everlasting arms ! These men were true children of nature. As the humming-bird among its own palm-trees, as the ephemera in the sunshine of a summer evening, so they lived their joyous lives. And even the full share of the sadder experiences of life which came to all of them but drove them the further into the secret place, and led them with more consecration to make, as they expressed it, "*the Lord their portion.*" All that has been said since from Marcus Aurelius to Swedenborg, from Augustine to Schleiermacher, of a besetting God as the full complement of humanity is but a repetition of the Hebrew poets' faith. And even the New Testament has nothing higher to offer man than this. The Psalmist's " God is our refuge and strength " is only the earlier form, less defined, less practicable, but not less noble, of Christ's " Come unto me, and I will give you rest."—*Henry Drummond, in* "*Natural Law in the Spiritual World,*" 1884.

Verses 6, 7.—"*I stretch forth my hands. . . . . Hear me,*" etc. So will the weary hands be raised yet again, through faith in him who stretched forth his hands upon the cross. So will the fainting soul wait and long for the outpouring of his grace, who upon the cross said, " I thirst." We shall thirst for our salvation, even as the parched-up fields and dying herbs seem to gasp and pant like living things for the sweet and cheering showers in the fierce heat of summer. So will the soul cry to be heard, and that soon, lest its faith grow faint with delay ; and the hiding of God's face, the denying of his smile of pardon, will press on the spirit like sickness, and weigh it down like the heaviness of death.—*J. W. Burgon.*

Verse 7.—*"Hear me speedily."* David is in trouble, and he betakes himself to prayer. Prayer is the sovereign remedy the godly fly to in all their extremities. The saints in sorrows have fled for comfort and healing unto prayers and supplications. Heaven is a shop full of all good things—there are stored up blessings and mercies ; this the children of God know who fly to this shop in their troubles, begging for help from this holy sanctuary. " In the day of my trouble I sought the Lord": Ps. lxxvii. 2. When any vexation makes our life grievous unto us, what should we seek but help ? of whom should we seek, but of the Lord ? how should we seek, but by prayer ? . . . . *"Speedily."* His request is not only for hearing, but for speedy hearing : *"Hear me, and hear me speedily ; "* answer, and answer quickly. This is the tone and tune of men in distress. Man in misery earnestly sues for speedy delivery. In our afflictions and troubles, deliverance, though it should come with wings, we never think it comes soon enough. Weak man cannot content himself to know he shall have help, unless it be present help.—*Thomas Calvert, 1647.*

Verse 7.—*"My spirit faileth."* This is David's first reason to move the Lord ; he is at the last cast and even giving up the ghost with long waiting for help : from his low condition we may see what is often the condition of God's children,—and the best of God's servants have waited for comfort and the feelings of his Spirit, to the very failing of their own spirit. David, a man after God's own heart, is yet brought low with the faintness and failing of his heart, in waiting for help from God. " In the sweat of thy face shalt thou eat bread " (Gen. iii. 19) ; this lies upon the sons of men. But here, not sweat of face only, that were but small ; but sighs and fainting of the heart lie upon the sons of God, in seeking and hungering after a taste of God's bread of life, inward comfort, assurance, and joy of the Holy Ghost. Thus the Church was brought to this sick bed ere her comfort came : " For these things I weep ; mine eye, mine eye runneth down with water, because the comforter that should relieve my soul is far from me : " Lam. i. 16. The disciples' spirits were even failing in the tempest, when Christ slept and seemed to neglect them, as if he cared not though they perished. How should our spirits do other but fail, when our Comforter sleeps, when our only friend seems to be our enemy ?

Failing of spirit is both a motive which God means to yield unto and to be won by withal ; and it is also his opportunity, when he usually helps. It is a strong motive in our prayers to move him, for he is pitiful, and will not let his children utterly fail and perish ; he is a pitiful Spirit to failing spirits. " I will not contend (saith the Lord) for ever, neither will I be always wroth ; " why ? we deserve his wrath should last and take fire for ever against us ; yea, but (saith the Lord) this is the reason, " The spirit should fail before me, and the souls which I have made " (Isaiah lvii. 16) : I love and pity the fainting souls and spirits of men ; I will help my children ; how can I see my creatures whom I made and do love, to perish for want of my help ? David knew the Lord's nature, and that this was a speeding argument in prayer, which made him here and elsewhere so often use it. A pitiful father will not see the spirit of his children utterly fail. It is his opportunity ; he usually helps when all other helps fail, that we may the more strongly cleave to him, and ground ourselves upon him, as knowing how infirm we are, if he confirm us not. When man's cruse of oil is dry, and fails, and can drop no more, then is God's time to prepare his. Thus helped he the Israelites at the Red Sea, when all man's strength and wisdom was at a stand. He loves to be seen in the mount, in extremities.—*Condensed from Thomas Calvert.*

Verse 7.—The prayer of David becomes, as he proceeds, both more spiritual and more fervent. In the sixth verse we find him thirsting after God ; and now that thirst is become so intense that it admits of no delay. In the beginning of the Psalm he was content to say, " Hear my prayer ; " but now he cries, " Hear me *speedily."* This is not the language of sinful impatience : it is, indeed, good that a man should both hope and quietly wait for the salvation of God ; yet a man may desire, not only an answer, but also a speedy answer, without incurring the charge of impatience. Whatever a man desires to have he desires to have soon ; nor can be be otherwise than grieved at anything which delays the accomplishment of his wishes. In such desire or grief there is nothing sinful, provided it do not lead to murmuring or distrust of God. Hence this petition for *speedy* relief, and manifestation of God's presence and favour is very frequent with the Psalmist. He often prays, " Make haste, O Lord, to deliver ; make haste to help me, O Lord." Nay, if a man does not desire the light of God's countenance soon, it is a certain proof that he does not desire it at all. If the natural language of his heart be not, " hear me speedily," delay is to him no exercise of patience. The very idea of patience implies that something is contrary to our wish ; and the stronger the desire is, the more difficult will that exercise of patience become.

" Hope deferred maketh the heart sick ; " and therefore David adds, " my spirit faileth." He believed verily to see the goodness of the Lord in the land of the living ; yet so intense was his desire, that faith could hardly keep his spirit from fainting, while the blessing, which he so eagerly pursued, seemed still distant, and fled before him. He is afraid lest if God should long delay, and withdraw himself, faith and hope could hold out no longer. He therefore pleads, " hide not thy face from me, lest I become like them that go down into the pit ; " and urges the failing of his spirit before him who " will not contend for ever, lest the spirit should fail before him."—*John Fawcett.*

Verses 7, 8, 10, 11.—Observe how David mixes together prayers for joy, for guidance, and for sanctification—" Hide not thy face from me." " Cause me to know the way wherein I should walk." " Teach me to do thy will." " Cause me to hear thy loving-kindness in the morning." " Quicken me, O Lord, for thy name's sake." Now this is exactly right : our prayers, as well as our other obedience, must be without partiality ; nay, we should desire comfort for the sake of holiness, rather than holiness for the sake of comfort.—*John Fawcett.*

Verse 8.—"*Cause me to hear thy lovingkindness.*" Here he craveth God's favour and kindness, as he doth in many other Psalms. Because in his favour is life, wealth, and grace, all good things, and pleasure for evermore, so that if he look kindly to us we need be afraid of nothing. But how shall he be assured of his favour ? Even by *hearing* it, as he saith in the fifty-first Psalm : " Make me to hear joy and gladness." The voice which is heard is the word of God, which, being apprehended by faith, is able to comfort our souls in whatsoever temptation. It is no marvel that such atheists and papists who altogether refuse the word of God, live comfortless and die without comfort, because they refuse that instrument which should carry joy to them. Good reason they die athirst, since they reject that vessel, the word of God, by which they might be refreshed. Therefore since faith cometh by hearing of God's word, and all our comfort cometh by it, let us pray God to bore our ears and our hearts, that we may receive the glad tidings of reconciliation from God.

"*Cause me to know the way wherein I should walk.*" The second petition ariseth very well from the first. For when we have obtained an assurance of God's favour, as he is reconciled to us in Jesus Christ, it followeth next that we should desire to conform our lives to the obedience of his commandments. For no man will frame himself to walk in God's ways till he be assured of God's favour. Therefore faith in God's promises is the most effectual cause to bring forth good works ; and an assurance of justification the surest means to produce sanctification.

"*For I lift up my soul unto thee.*" Behold what a wonderful effect God worketh by afflictions : they depress and cast down the outward man, and our inward man by them is elevated and raised aloft ; yea, the more we are afflicted, the more we are stirred up. The oftener the messenger of Satan is sent to buffet us, the more earnestly (with Paul) we cry unto the Lord to be delivered (2 Cor. xii. 8). So if we be cast down to hell in our feelings, what the worse are we if by that we be raised up to heaven ?—*Archibald Symson.*

Verse 8.—"*Cause me to hear thy lovingkindness in the morning,*" etc. To hear thy lovingkindness in the morning makes my waking to be saluted, as it were, with music ; makes my troubles seem as if they were but dreams ; makes me find it true that though " weeping may endure for a night, yet joy cometh in the morning : " Ps. xxx. 5. . . . It may well be said we hear this lovingkindness in the morning, seeing it makes it morning to us whensoever we hear it.—*Sir Richard Baker.*

Verse 8.—"*Cause me to hear thy lovingkindness in the morning.*" If evil fall upon us in the night, we would have it removed ere the morning ; if in the morning, we would not have it our bed-fellow in the evening. We would have the Lord's promise run thus,—Your sorrows shall not endure the whole night, your joy shall come long before the morning. The luxurious Emperor (? Smyndirides the Sybarite) and his drunken mates sat and drank all the night, and slept all the day, insomuch that it was said of them, they never saw sun-set nor sun-rise. Such would we have the evils we suffer—of so short continuance that neither sun-set nor sun-rise might see us in our misery. This makes me wonder at that strange Egyptian beast called Pharaoh, who being demanded of Moses when he would have God's plague of the frogs removed, answered, "*To-morrow.*" Surely, here he spake not as a man, to whom one hour's trouble is accounted a day, a day a month, a month a year. For in leaving of two things we change our desires, and are much different.

1. In leaving of sin, then we procrastinate and put off; and when God says, "To-day hear my voice," we answer, "To-morrow," and are like the Levite's wife's father (Judg. xix. 6), too kind hosts to such bad guests : saying to our sins "tarry till the morning." Our pace to repentance is slow, we are far from haste in that matter.

2. But for afflictions to leave us, then we wish they had feet like hinds' feet, to run away from us, or we the wings of a dove to fly away from them, and be at rest. . . . . What prisoner desires not to be presently set free, and that liberty's soft hand may loose his iron knots ? What mariner wishes a long storm ? What servant sighs not over his hard apprenticeship ? Yea, who is he, that if there were an appearance of an offering to take the cup of calamity from his mouth, saying, "Thou shalt drink no more," would answer, "This cup shall not yet pass from me, I delight to carouse and drink deeply of these bitter waters"? Yea, this desire extends so far that it comes to the Son of Man, the blessed Seed of the woman, who was so clad with human weakness that he earnestly prayed for speedy help from his heavy anguish; and that not once, but often,—"Oh, my Father, if it be possible," etc. ; and when his Father answers not, he cries like one ready to fall under the burden, "My God, my God, why hast thou forsaken me ?" The reason for Christ's thus complaining is to be fetched from thence, whence his flesh came ; even from us. It was our human flesh, not his Divine spirit, which was so weary of suffering ; his spirit was willing, it was our flesh that was so weak.—*Thomas Calvert.*

Verse 8.—"*Cause me to hear thy lovingkindness in the morning.*" This is a short and sweet morning prayer. God hears early prayer, and lovingly responds to it. The smiles of his face, the sweetness of his voice, the gifts of his hand, bless the morning, bless all the day. Do we write and read experimentally? Then we know the blessedness of divine love. The subject is truly pleasant and precious. "*Lovingkindness*" is a favourite expression, is a choice theme of David's. It is used more in the Book of Psalms than in any other book in the Scriptures. Lovingkindness is love showing kindness ; it is the sun of love shining with rays of kindness ; the river of love sending forth streams of kindness ; it is the heart of love uttering itself by words of kindness, doing deeds, and giving gifts of kindness.

Here it is the *voice* of the lovingkindness of the Lord that David desires to hear. This voice is the music of heaven, the joyful sound of the gospel, and it makes a jubilee in the Christian's heart. To him there is beauty, sweetness, fulness in the theme ; it is his joy and rejoicing. This is the voice that speaks *pardon.* Pardon is through Jesus the medium of this kindness. Apart from this there is no hope of forgiveness. We plead this and realize pardon. "Have mercy upon me, O God, according to thy lovingkindness : according unto the multitude of thy tender mercies blot out my transgressions": Ps. li. 1. It is the Lord's lovingkindness that pardons me. This voice speaks *peace :* "The Lord will speak peace unto his people." Precious peace is the result of pardoning kindness. This voice also speaks *joy.* This is the alone and all-sufficient source of joy. It is sought elsewhere, but found only here. It sweetens every bitter, and makes sweeter every sweet. It is a balsam for every wound, a cordial for every fear. The present is but a taste, but a drop of the future fulness of joy. How sweetly refreshing is the joy of the Lord's lovingkindness. This voice speaks *hope.* With the sweet music of this voice falling upon our ears, the night of hopelessness passes away, and the morning of expectation opens upon us. It assures us of supplies for our wants, of safety in danger, of endurance to the end, and of a glorious portion in eternity.

"*The morning*" is the season in which David desires to hear the voice of the lovingkindness of the Lord. The morning is a season often mentioned by him, and as a time of devotion is much prized by him. "My voice shalt thou hear in the morning, O LORD ; in the morning will I direct my prayer unto thee, and will look up": Ps. v. 3. "*Cause me to hear thy lovingkindness in the morning*": let it engage my thoughts and affections. It is well to have a subject like this to occupy our waking thoughts, and to take hold of our first desires. If other thoughts get into our hearts in the morning, we may not be able to turn them out all the day. Prayer and praise, reading and meditation, will be sweet with such a subject occupying and influencing our minds. They will be exercises of cheerfulness, freedom, and blessedness.

"*Cause me to hear*" this voice. It speaks every morning, but many ears are deaf to it. But while others are indifferent to it, cause me to hear it ; let me not lose the opportunity : waken my ear morning by morning, so that I may hail the season and enjoy the privilege. And when the morning of eternity shall come, " cause me to hear the voice of thy lovingkindness " welcoming me to its joys.— *W. Abbot, in "The Baptist Messenger,"* 1870.

Verse 8.—"*Cause me to know the way wherein I should walk.*" The whole valley is surrounded by ranges of regal crags ; but the mountain of the Gemmi, apparently absolutely inaccessible, is the last point to which you would turn for an outlet. A side gorge that sweeps up to the glaciers and snowy pyramids flashing upon you in the opposite direction is the route which you suppose your guide is going to take ; and visions of pedestrians perilously scaling icy precipices, or struggling up to the middle through ridges of snow, begin to surround you, as the prospect of your own experience in this day's expedition. So convinced was I that the path *must* go in that direction, that I took a short cut, which I conceived would bring me again into the mule path at a point under the glaciers ; but after scaling precipices and getting lost in a wood of firs in the valley, I was glad to rejoin my friend with the guide, and to clamber on in pure ignorance and wonder. . . . Now what a striking symbol is this of things that sometimes take place in our spiritual pilgrimage. We are often brought to a stand, hedged up and hemmed in by the providence of God so that there seems no way out. A man is sometimes thrown into difficulties in which he sits down beginning to despair, and says to himself, " Well, this time it is all over with me " ; like Sterne's starling, or, worse, like Bunyan's man in the cage, he says, " I cannot get out." Then when God has drawn him from all self-confidence and self-resource, a door opens in the wall and he rises up, and walks at liberty, praising God.—*George Barrell Cheever*, 1807—.

Verses 8—10.—After thou hast prayed, observe what God doth towards thee ; especially how he doth guide thy feet and heart after prayer ; there is much in that. That which was the spirit of supplication in a man when he prayed, rests upon him as the spirit of obedience in his course. That dependence which he hath upon God for the mercy he seeks for is a special motive and means to keep him fearful of offending, and diligent in duty. He looks to his paths, and endeavours to behave himself as becomes a suitor, as well as to pray as a suitor. David walked by this principle when he said (Ps. lxvi. 18), " If I regard iniquity in my heart, the Lord will not hear me " ; that consideration still came in as a curb unto sin. Therefore David, in these verses, when he was to pray, even as for his life, for deliverance from his enemies, he specially prays God to direct him and keep him, that he might not sin against him ; for he knew that by sinning he should enervate and spoil all his prayers. He cries not only "*Hear me speedily,*" but also, "*Cause me to know the way wherein I should walk ; teach me to do thy will.*" This he especially prays for, more than for deliverance, for else he knew God would not hear him. Therefore when thou art in treaty with God for any mercy, observe, doth God still after praying keep thee in a more obedient frame of spirit ? If so, it is a sign he intends to answer thee. The same is true when he keeps thee from using ill means, etc. When he meant to give David the kingdom, he kept him innocent, and made his heart tender, so that it smote him but for cutting off the lap of Saul's garment.—*Thomas Goodwin.*

Verse 9.—"*Deliver me, O LORD, from mine enemies.*" In the former verse he desireth God's mercy and lovingkindness, and that he might be showed the way wherein he should walk : now he desireth to be free of temporal danger. This is a good method in prayer, first to seek the kingdom of God and spiritual graces, for then all other things shall be added to us. We seek in vain temporal deliverances of God if we neglect to seek spiritual graces, which are most necessary for us.

As for *enemies*, the church and her members neither have wanted nor shall want innumerable foes, against whom we can only oppose God's protection. In number, in power, in policy and subtilty they are ever above us. There is no help for us against them all but our gracious God. Esau came with four hundred against Jacob, a naked man, with his wife, children, and droves of cattle. But

Mahanaim was with him; he was guarded by God's angels. And, therefore, since the church of God in France, Germany, and elsewhere is in danger of the Leviathan and the sons of Anak, let us run to the Lord, and cry unto him,—O God Jehovah, who art one against all, deliver thy church from her enemies, who likewise are thy enemies.—*Archibald Symson.*

Verse 9.—"*I flee unto thee to hide me.*" Is David's valour come to this, that he is come now to be glad to fly? Had he not done better to have died valiantly than to fly basely? O my soul, to fly is not always a sign of baseness; it is not always a point of valour to stand to it; but then to fly when we feel our own weakness, and to him to fly, in whom is our strength—this is, if not valour, at least wisdom, but it is, to say true, both wisdom and true valour. And now, O God, seeing I find my own weakness, and know thy strength, what should I do but fly, and whither fly but only to thee?—to thee, a strong fortress to all that build upon thee; to thee, a safe sanctuary to all that fly unto thee.—*Sir Richard Baker.*

Verse 9.—"*I flee unto thee to hide me.*" This implies, 1. *Danger :* the Christian may be in danger from sin, self, foes. 2. *Fear :* his fears may be groundless, but they are often very painful. 3. *Inability*—to defend himself or overcome his opposers. 4. *Foresight :* he sees the storm in the distance, and looks out for the covert. 5. *Prudence :* he hides before the storm, ere the enemy comes upon him. 6. A laudable *concern* for safety and comfort. The believer, if wise, will at all times flee to Jehovah. Jacob flies to Laban; the manslayer to the refuge; the bird to his mountain; and the Christian to his God. Asa may seek to physicians; Ephraim to king Jareb; and Saul to the witch; but the believer looks to his God. The Lord receives, befriends, and secures him. Let us flee to him by prayer, in faith, with hope, for salvation; and he will receive us, shelter us, and be our refuge and strength. Flee from sin, from self, from the world; but flee to Jesus. His heart is ever toward us, his ear is open to us, and his hand is ready to help, protect, and deliver us. His throne is our asylum. His promise is our comfort, and his omnipotence is our guard.

> Happy soul, that, free from harms
> Rests within his Shepherd's arms!
> Who his quiet shall molest?
> Who shall violate his rest?
> He who found the wandering sheep,
> Loves, and still delights to keep.

James Smith, in "The Believer's Daily Remembrancer."

Verse 9.—"*I flee unto thee to hide me.*" The Lord hid the prophets so that Ahab could not find them out : 1 Kings xviii. 13. If we will creep under his wings he will surely keep us.—*Archibald Symson.*

Verse 9.—"*I flee unto thee to hide me.*" It may be rendered, "*With thee have I hid*"; that is, myself : so Arama gives the sense. "*I have hid myself with thee.*" Jarchi, Aben Ezra, and Kimchi interpret it to this purpose, "I have hid my affairs, my straits and troubles, my difficulties and necessities, from men, and have revealed them unto thee, who alone can save." The Targum is, "I have appointed thy Word to be (my) Redeemer.—*John Gill.*

Verses 9, 10.—Be persuaded actually to hide yourselves with Jesus Christ. To have a hiding-place and not to use it is as bad as to want one : fly to Christ; run into the holes of this rock. Three things must be done by all those that would hide themselves with Christ.

1. You must put away sin by repentance. Jesus Christ will not be a sanctuary for rebels, he will not protect evil-doers. Christ will never hide the devil, nor any of his servants. Isa. lv. 6, 7 : "Let the ungodly forsake his ways," etc. David knew this, therefore he prays that God would teach him to do his will : "*Deliver me, etc. I flee unto thee to hide me. Teach me to do thy will.*" He that will not do the will of Christ shall receive no protection from Christ. *Protectio sequitur allegiantiam.* You must be his liege people if you will have him to defend you. Job xxii. 23, 25.

2. You must pray that he would hide you. The promise is made to prayer : Isa. lxv. 10, "Sharon shall be a fold of flocks, and the valley of Achor a place for the herds to lie down in, for my people that have sought me." He that prays most fervently is like to be hid most securely. And then,

3. You must believe in him. Faith is the key that opens the door of this

hiding-place, and locks it again.   One word in the Hebrew signifies to trust and to make a refuge.   Ps. lvii. 1.   He that doth not make Christ his trust shall not have Christ for his hiding-place ; he will hide none but those that commit themselves to him : " I will set him on high, because he hath known my name " : Ps. xci. 9, 14. —*Ralph Robinson.*

Verse 10.—*"Teach me to do thy will."*   He saith not, Teach me to *know* thy will, but to *do* thy will.   God teaches us in three ways.   First, by his word. Secondly, he illuminateth our minds by the Spirit.   Thirdly, he imprinteth it in our hearts, and maketh us obedient to the same ; for the servant who knoweth the will of his master, and doeth it not, shall be beaten with many stripes : Luke xii. 47.—*Archibald Symson.*

Verse 10.—*"Teach me to do thy will."*   We are to pray that God would teach us to know, and then teach us to do, his will.   Knowledge without obedience is lame, obedience without knowledge is blind ; and we must never hope for acceptance if we offer the blind and the lame to God.—*Vincent Alsop (—1703), in "The Morning Exercises."*

Verse 10.—*"Teach me to do thy will."*   The Lord doth no sooner call his people to himself, but as soon as ever he hath thus crowned them with these glorious privileges, and given them any sense and feeling of them, then they immediately cry out, O Lord, what shall I now do for thee ?   How shall I now live to thee ? They know now that they are no more their own, but his ; and therefore should now live to him.

It is true indeed, obedience to the law is not required of us now as it was of Adam ; it was required of him as a condition antecedent to life, but of those that be in Christ it is required only as a duty consequent to life, or as a rule of life, that seeing he hath purchased our lives in redemption, and actually given us life in vocation and sanctification, we should now live unto him, in all thankful and fruitful obedience, according to his will revealed in the moral law.   It is a vain thing to imagine that our obedience is to have no other rule but the Spirit, without an attendance to the law : the Spirit is indeed the efficient cause of our obedience, and hence we are said to be " led by the Spirit " (Rom. viii. 14) ; but it is not properly the rule of our obedience, but the will of God revealed in his word, especially in the law, is the rule ; the Spirit is the wind that drives us in our obedience ; the law is our compass, according to which it steers our course for us : the Spirit and the law, the wind and the compass, can stand well together.   *"Teach me to do thy will ; for thou art my God "* (there is David's rule, viz., God's will revealed) ; *"Thy Spirit is good "* (there is David's wind, that enabled him to steer his course according to it).   The Spirit of life doth free us from the law of sin and death ; but not from the holy, and pure, and good, and righteous law of God.   Rom. viii. 1—3.—*Thomas Shepard, in "The Sound Believer," 1671.*

Verse 10.—*"Teach me to do thy will,"* etc.   We are inclined and enabled [to good] by the sanctifying Spirit.   In the Christian religion, not only the precepts are good, but there goeth along with them the power of God to make us good.   *"Teach me to do thy will ; for thou art my God : thy Spirit is good."*   The Spirit's direction hath strength joined with it.   And he is a good Spirit, as he doth incline us to good. The Spirit is the only fountain of all goodness and holiness : Neh. ix. 20, " Thou gavest also thy good Spirit to instruct them."   Why is he so often called the good Spirit, but that all his operations tend to make men good and holy ?   Eph. v. 9, " The fruit of the Spirit is in all goodness and righteousness and truth."—*Thomas Manton.*

Verse 10.—*"Thy Spirit is good ; lead me,"* says the Psalmist.   And therefore it is a usual phrase in Rom. viii. and Gal. iv., our being *led* by the Spirit.—*Thomas Goodwin.*

Verse 10.—*"Lead me into the land of uprightness,"* into the communion of saints, the pleasant land of the upright ; or into a settled course of holy living, which will lead to heaven, that land of uprightness, where holiness will be in perfection, and he that is holy will be holy still.   We should desire to be led and kept safe to heaven, not only because it is a land of blessedness, but because it is a land of uprightness ; it is the perfection of grace.—*Matthew Henry.*

Verse 10.—*"Lead me."*   Man by nature is as a cripple and blind, he cannot go upright unless he be led by a superior spirit ; yea, he must be carried as an eagle carrieth her little ones, or as a mother her tender child.   Think not that we can step one right step to heaven but by the conduct and convoy of God's Holy Spirit. Miserable are those who go without his conduction.—*Archibald Symson.*

Verse 10.—*"The land of uprightness."* *Mishor* is the name for the smooth upland downs of Moab (Deut. iii. 10 ; Josh. xiii. 17 ; xx. 8 ; Jer. xlviii. 8, 21). Derived from the root *yashar,* " even, level plain," it naturally came to be used figuratively for equity, right, righteous, and uprightness.   Mal. ii. 6 ;   Isa. xi. 4 ; Ps. xlv. 7 ; lxvii. 5 ; cxliii. 10.—*Cunningham Geikie, in "Hours with the Bible,"* 1884.

Verse 10.—*"The land of uprightness."*   The land of plainness, a land where no wickedness of men, and malice of Satan, vex the soul from day to day ; a land where no rough paths and crooked turns lengthen out the traveller's weary journey (see verse 5) ; but where all is like the smooth pasture-lands of Reuben (Deut. iii. 10 ; Josh. xiii. 9), a fit place for flocks to lie down.—*Andrew A. Bonar.*

Verse 11.—*"Quicken me, O Lord, for thy name's sake."*   For the sake of thine own glory, that thou mayest show thyself to be the God of lovingkindness and power which thou art esteemed to be.—*Andrew Robert Fausset.*

Verse 11.—*"For thy righteousness' sake."*   It is worthy of observation that the Psalmist pleads God's righteousness as the foundation on which he bases his supplication for the deliverance of his soul from trouble, and God's lovingkindness or mercy as that on which he grounds his prayer, or his conviction, that God will destroy his enemies.   This is not the language of a revengeful and bloodthirsty spirit.—*Speaker's Commentary.*

Verse 11.—*"Bring my soul out of trouble."*   I can bring it in, but thou only canst bring it out.—*John Trapp.*

Verses 11, 12.—*"Thy name's sake . . . thy righteousness' sake . . . And of thy mercy."*   Mark here, my soul, with what three cords David seeks to draw God to grant him his suits : for his name's sake, for his righteousness' sake, and for his mercy's sake,—three such motives, that it must be a very hard suit that God will deny, if either of them be used.   But though all the three strong motives, yet as David riseth in his suits, so he may seem also to rise in his motives ; and by this account ; for his righteousness' sake will prove a motive of a higher degree than for his name's sake, and for his mercy's sake the highest of them all—as indeed his mercy-seat is the highest part of all his ark, if it be not rather that as the attributes of God, so these motives, that are drawn from the attributes, are of equal pre-eminence.   But if the three motives be all of them so strong, being each of them single, how strong would they be if they were all united, and twisted, I may say, into one cord ?   And united they are all, indeed, into a motive, which God hath more clearly revealed to us than he did to David (although it be strange, seeing it was his Lord ;   and yet not strange, seeing it was his son) ;   and this is the motive : for thy Son Christ Jesus' sake ; for he is the *verbum abbreviatum* [the Word in brief], in whom are included all the motives—all the powerful motives—that can be used to God for obtaining our suits.—*Sir Richard Baker.*

Verses 11, 12.—The verbs in these two last verses, as Dr. Hammond hath noted, should be rendered in the future ; *"Thou shalt quicken,"* etc., and then the Psalm will end, as usual, with an act of faith and assurance, that all those mercies, which have been asked, shall be obtained ; that God, for the sake of his *" name,"* and his *" righteousness,"* of his glory, and his faithfulness in the performance of his promises, will not fail to be favourable and gracious to his servants, *" quickening "* them, even when dead in trespasses and sins, and bringing them, by degrees, *" out of all their troubles "* : going forth with them to the battle against their spiritual *" enemies,"* and enabling them to vanquish the authors of their *" affliction "* and misery, to mortify the flesh, and to overcome the world ; that so they may triumph with their Redeemer, in the day when he shall likewise quicken their mortal bodies, and put all enemies under their feet.—*George Horne.*

Verse 12.—*"Of thy mercy cut off mine enemies."*   He desireth God to slay his enemies in his mercy, when rather their destruction was a work of his justice ? I answer that the destruction of the wicked is a mercy to the church.   As God showed great mercy and kindness to his church by the death of Pharaoh, Sennacherib, Herod, and other troublers thereof.—*Archibald Symson.*

Verse 12.—*"Cut off mine enemies,"* etc.   When you find these imprecations to be prophecies of events which the Psalmist himself could not understand ; but were to be fulfilled in persons whom the Psalmist could not know, as they were to live in distant future ages,—for instance, Judas, and the Romans, and leaders of the Jewish nation,—who would make these imprecations proofs of a revengeful spirit ?—*James Bennett* (1774—1862), *in "Lectures on the Acts of the Apostles,"* 1847.

Verse 12.—*"I am thy servant."* David the king professeth himself one of God's pensioners. Paul, when he would blaze his coat of arms, and set forth his best heraldry, he doth not call himself Paul, an Hebrew of the Hebrews, or Paul of the tribe of Benjamin, but Paul " a servant of Christ " : Rom. i. 1. Theodosius thought it a greater dignity to be God's servant than to be an emperor. Christ himself, who is equal with his Father, yet is not ashamed of the title *servant :* Isa. liii. 11. Every servant of God is a son, every subject a prince : it is more honour to serve God than to have kings to serve us : the angels in heaven are servitors to the saints.—*Thomas Watson.*

HINTS TO PREACHERS.

Verse 1.—Three threes. I. As to his devotions,—prayers, supplications, requests. II. As to his success,—hear, give ear, answer me. III. As to his argument,— because thou art Jehovah, faithful, righteous.

Verses 1, 2.—A suitable prayer for a believer who has reason to suppose that he is suffering chastening for sin. I. Here is earnest importunity, as of one depending entirely upon divine favour for a hearing. II. Here is believing fervency laying hold of divine faithfulness and justice ; see 1 John i. 9. III. Here is a deep consciousness of the vanity of self-justification pleading for pure mercy, ver. 2. —*J. F.*

Verse 2.—I. Who he is. " Thy servant." II. What he knows. " In thy sight shall no man living be justified." III. What he asks. " Enter not into judgment."

Verses 3—6.—Consider, I. The great lengths God may sometimes permit the enemy to go, ver 3. The case of Job a good illustration. II. The deep depression of spirit he may even permit his saints to experience, ver. 4. III. The good things he has provided for their meditation when even at their worst, ver. 5. IV. The two things his grace will never suffer to die, whose existence is a pledge of near approaching joy,—1. The thirsting after himself. 2. The practice of prayer. The whole is a good text for a lecture on the life and experience of Job.—*J. F.*

Verses 4, 5, 6.—I. Down in Despondency. II. Deep in Meditation. III. Determined in Supplication.

Verses 5, 6.—*"I muse on the work of thy hands. I stretch forth my hands unto thee."* Hand in hand : or the child of God admiring the work of God's hands, and praying with uplifted hands to be wrought upon by the like power.

Verse 5.—David's method. I. He gathered materials ; facts and evidence concerning God : " I remember." II. He thought out his subject and arranged his matter : " I meditate." III. He discoursed thereon, and was brought nearer to God : " I muse "—discourse. IV. Let us close by viewing all this as an example for preachers and others.—*W. B. H.*

Verse 6.—God alone the desire of his people.

Verse 6.—Deep calling to deep. I. The insatiable craving of the heart. II. The vast riches in glory. III. The rushing together of these as : " My soul is to thee." —*W. B. H.*

Verse 7.—Reasons for speedy answers.

Verse 7.—Never despair. I. Because you have the Lord to plead with. Because you may freely tell him the desperateness of your case. III. Because you may be urgent with him for deliverance.—*J. F.*

Verse 7.—Cordial for the swooning heart. I. God's beloved fainting. II. The best restorative ; her Lord's face. III. She has the presence of mind to call him as she falls.—*W. B. H.*

Verse 8.—The two prayers—*"Cause me to hear,"* and *"Cause me to know."* The two pleas—*"In thee do I trust,"* and *"I lift up my soul unto thee."*

Verse 8, Ps. cxlii. 3.—*"Thou knewest my path."* Ps. cxliii. 8.—*"Cause me to know the way."*   I. Trusting Omniscience in everything.   II. Following conscience in everything.

Verse 8.—On fixing a time for the answering of our prayer.   I. By whom it may be done.   Not by all believers, but by those who through dwelling with God have attained to a holy boldness.   II. When it may be done.   1. When the case is specially urgent.   2. When God's honour is concerned.   III. What renders it pleasing to God when done.   Great faith.   "For in thee do I trust."—*J. F.*

Verse 8.—Listening for Lovingkindness.   I. Where to listen.   At the gates of Scripture ; in the halls of meditation ; nigh the footsteps of Jesus.   II. When to listen.   "In the morning ;" as early and as often as possible.   III. How to listen.   In trustful dependence : "Cause me to hear thy lovingkindness in the morning, for in thee do I trust."   IV. Why to listen.   To "know the way wherein I should walk."—*W. B. H.*

Verse 9.—Admirable points in this prayer to be imitated by us.   There is, I. A sense of danger.   II. A confession of weakness.   III. A prudent foresight. IV. A solid confidence : —he expects to be hidden from his foes.

Verse 9.—I. Looking up.   II. Lying close.—*W. B. H.*

Verse 10.—Two childlike requests—" Teach me. . . . lead me."

Verse 10.—See "Spurgeon's Sermons," No. 1519, " At School,"

Verse 10 (*first half*).—I. The best instructions : "Teach me to do thy will." Not merely to know, but "to do."   II. The only efficient Instructor.   III. The best reason for asking and expecting instruction : " For thou art my God."—*J. F.*

Verse 10.—"*Teach me to do thy will.*"   We may call this sentence a description of David's school ; and it is a very complete one ; at least, it hath in it the three best things that belong to a school.   I. The best teacher.   II. The best scholar. III. The best lesson ; for who so good a teacher as God ? who so good a scholar as David ? what so good a lesson as to do God's will ?—*Sir Richard Baker.*

Verse 10 (*latter half*).—I. Utopia—" the land of uprightness."   Describe it, and declare its glories.   II. The difficult paths to that upland country.   III. The divine Guide,—" thy Spirit is good."

Verse 11 (*first clause*).—I. What is this blessing ? " Quicken me."   II. In what way will it glorify God, so that we may plead for the sake of his name ?

Verse 11 (*second clause*).—How is the righteousness of God concerned in our deliverance from trouble ?

Verse 12.—I. To the Master : " I am thy servant."   II. For the servant : he seeks protection because he belongs to his master.

PSALM CXLIV.

Albeit that this Psalm is in some measure very similar to Psalm xviii., yet it is a new song, and in its latter portion it is strikingly so. Let the reader accept it as a new Psalm, and not as a mere variation of an old one, or as two compositions roughly joined together. It is true that it would be a complete composition if the passage from verse 12 to the close were dropped; but there are other parts of David's poems which might be equally self-contained if certain verses were omitted; and the same might be said of many uninspired sonnets. It does not, therefore, follow that the latter part was added by another hand, nor even that the latter part was a fragment by the same author, appended to the first song merely with the view of preserving it. It seems to us to be highly probable that the Psalmist, remembering that he had trodden some of the same ground before, felt his mind moved to fresh thought, and that the Holy Spirit used this mood for his own high purposes. Assuredly the addendum is worthy of the greatest Hebrew poet, and it is so admirable in language, and so full of beautiful imagery, that persons of taste who were by no means overloaded with reverence have quoted it times without number, thus confessing its singular poetical excellence. To us the whole Psalm appears to be perfect as it stands, and to exhibit such unity throughout that it would be a literary Vandalism, as well as a spiritual crime, to rend away one part from the other.

TITLE.—Its title is " Of David," and its language is of David, if ever language can belong to any man. As surely as we could say of any poem, This is of Tennyson, or of Longfellow, we may say, This is of David. Nothing but the disease which closes the eye to manifest fact and opens it to fancy, could have led learned critics to ascribe this song to anybody but David. Alexander well says, "The Davidic origin of this Psalm is as marked as that of any in the Psalter."

It is to God the devout warrior sings when he extols him as his strength and stay (verses 1 and 2). Man he holds in small account, and wonders at the Lord's regard for him (verses 3 and 4); but he turns in his hour of conflict to the Lord, who is declared to be " a man of war," whose triumphant interposition he implores (verses 5 to 8). He again extols and entreats in verses 9, 10, and 11; and then closes with a delightful picture of the Lord's work for his chosen people, who are congratulated upon having such a God to be their God.

EXPOSITION.

BLESSED *be* the LORD my strength, which teacheth my hands to war, *and* my fingers to fight:

  2 My goodness, and my fortress; my high tower, and my deliverer; my shield, and *he* in whom I trust; who subdueth my people under me.

1. *"Blessed be the LORD my strength."* He cannot delay the utterance of his gratitude, he bursts at once into a loud note of praise. His best word is given to his best friend—" Blessed be Jehovah." When the heart is in a right state it must praise God, it cannot be restrained; its utterances leap forth as waters forcing their way from a living spring. With all his strength David blesses the God of his strength. We ought not to receive so great a boon as strength to resist evil, to defend truth, and to conquer error, without knowing who gave it to us, and rendering to him the glory of it. Not only does Jehovah give strength to his saints, but he is their strength. The strength is made theirs because God is theirs. God is full of power, and he becomes the power of those who trust him. In him our great strength lieth, and to him be blessings more than we are able to utter. It may be read, "My Rock," but this hardly so well consorts with the following words: "Which teacheth my hands to war and my fingers to fight." The word *rock* is the Hebrew way of expressing strength: the grand old language is full of such suggestive symbols. The Psalmist in the second part of the verse sets forth the Lord as teacher in the arts of war. If we have strength we are not much the better unless we have skill also. Untrained force is often an injury to the man who possesses it, and it even becomes a danger to those who are round about him; and therefore the

Psalmist blesses the Lord as much for teaching as for strength. Let us also bless Jehovah if he has in anything made us efficient. The tuition mentioned was very practical, it was not so much of the brain as of the hands and fingers ; for these were the members most needful for conflict. Men with little scholastic education should be grateful for deftness and skill in their handicrafts. To a fighting man the education of the hands is of far more value than mere book-learning could ever be ; he who has to use a sling or a bow needs suitable training, quite as much as a scientific man or a classical professor. Men are too apt to fancy that an artisan's efficiency is to be ascribed to himself ; but this is a popular fallacy. A clergyman may be supposed to be taught of God, but people do not allow this to be true of weavers or workers in brass ; yet these callings are specially mentioned in the Bible as having been taught to holy women and earnest men when the tabernacle was set up at the first. All wisdom and skill are from the Lord, and for them he deserves to be gratefully extolled. This teaching extends to the smallest members of our frame : the Lord teaches fingers as well as hands ; indeed, it sometimes happens that if the finger is not well trained the whole hand is incapable.

David was called to be a man of war, and he was eminently successful in his battles ; he does not trace this to his good generalship or valour, but to his being taught and strengthened for the war and the fight. If the Lord deigns to have a hand in such unspiritual work as fighting, surely he will help us to proclaim the gospel and win souls ; and then we will bless his name with even greater intensity of heart. We will be pupils, and he shall be our Master, and if we ever accomplish anything we will give our instructor hearty blessing.

This verse is full of personality ; it is mercy shown to David himself which is the subject of grateful song. It has also a presentness about it ; for Jehovah is now his strength, and is still teaching him ; we ought to make a point of presenting praise while yet the blessing is on the wing. The verse is also pre-eminently practical, and full of the actual life of every day ; for David's days were spent in camps and conflicts. Some of us who are grievously tormented with rheumatism might cry, " Blessed be the Lord, my Comforter, who teacheth my knees to bear in patience, and my feet to endure in resignation " ; others who are on the look out to help young converts might say, " Blessed be God who teaches my eyes to see wounded souls, and my lips to cheer them " ; but David has his own peculiar help from God, and praises him accordingly. This tends to make the harmony of heaven perfect when all the singers take their parts ; if we all followed the same score, the music would not be so full and rich.

2. Now our royal poet multiplies metaphors to extol his God. *"My goodness, and my fortress."* The word for *goodness* signifies *mercy.* Whoever we may be, and wherever we may be, we need mercy such as can only be found in the infinite God. It is all of mercy that he is any of the other good things to us, so that this is a highly comprehensive title. O how truly has the Lord been mercy to many of us in a thousand ways ! He is goodness itself, and he has been unbounded goodness to us. We have no goodness of our own, but the Lord has become goodness to us. So is he himself also our *fortress* and safe abode : in him we dwell as behind impregnable ramparts and immovable bastions. We cannot be driven out, or starved out ; for our fortress is prepared for a siege ; it is stored with abundance of food, and a well of living water is within it. Kings usually think much of their fenced cities, but King David relies upon his God, who is more to him than fortresses could have been. *"My high tower, and my deliverer."* As from a lofty watch-tower the believer, trusting in the Lord, looks down upon his enemies. They cannot reach him in his elevated position ; he is out of bow-shot ; he is beyond their scaling ladders ; he dwells on high. Nor is this all ; for Jehovah is our Deliverer as well as our Defender. These different figures set forth the varied benefits which come to us from our Lord. He is every good thing which we can need for this world or the next. He not only places us out of harm's way full often, but when we must be exposed, he comes to our rescue, he raises the siege, routs the foe, and sets us in joyous liberty. *"My shield, and he in whom I trust."* When the warrior rushes on his adversary, he bears his targe upon his arm, and thrusts death aside ; thus doth the believer oppose the Lord to the blows of the enemy, and finds himself secure from harm. For this and a thousand other reasons our trust rests in our God for everything ; he never fails us, and we feel boundless confidence in him. *'Who subdueth my people under me."* He keeps my natural subjects subject, and my conquered subjects peaceful under my sway. Men who rule others should

thank God if they succeed in the task. Such strange creatures are human beings, that if a number of them are kept in peaceful association under the leadership of any one of the Lord's servants, he is bound to bless God every day for the wonderful fact. The victories of peace are as much worthy of joyful gratitude as the victories of war. Leaders in the Christian church cannot maintain their position except as the Lord preserves to them the mighty influence which ensures obedience and evokes enthusiastic loyalty. For every particle of influence for good which we may possess let us magnify the name of the Lord.

Thus has David blessed Jehovah for blessing him. How many times he has appropriated the Lord by that little word *My !* Each time he grasps the Lord, he adores and blesses him ; for the one word *Blessed* runs through all the passage like a golden thread. He began by acknowledging that his strength for fighting foreign enemies was of the Lord, and he concluded by ascribing his domestic peace to the same source. All round as a king he saw himself to be surrounded by the King of kings, to whom he bowed in lowly homage, doing suit and service on bended knee, with grateful heart admitting that he owned everything to the Rock of his salvation.

3 LORD, what *is* man, that thou takest knowledge of him ! *or* the son of man, that thou makest account of him !

4 Man is like to vanity : his days *are* as a shadow that passeth away.

3. *"LORD what is man, that thou takest knowledge of him !"* What a contrast between Jehovah and man ! The Psalmist turns from the glorious all-sufficiency of God to the insignificance and nothingness of man. He sees Jehovah to be everything, and then cries, " Lord, what is man ! " What is man in the presence of the Infinite God ? ʼWhat can he be compared to ? He is too little to be described at all : only God, who knows the most minute object, can tell what man is. Certainly he is not fit to be the rock of our confidence : he is at once too feeble and too fickle to be relied upon. The Psalmist's wonder is that God should stoop to know him, and indeed it is more remarkable than if the greatest archangel should make a study of emmets, or become the friend of mites. God knows his people with a tender intimacy, a constant, careful observation : he foreknew them in love, he knows them by care, he will know them is acceptance at last. Why and wherefore is this ? What has man done ? What has he been ? What is he now that God should know him, and make himself known to him as his goodness, fortress, and high tower ? This is an unanswerable question. Infinite condescension can alone account for the Lord stooping to be the friend of man. That he should make man the subject of election, the object of redemption, the child of eternal love, the darling of infallible providence, the next of kin to Deity, is indeed a matter requiring more than the two notes of exclamation found in this verse.

"Or the son of man, that thou makest account of him !" The son of man is a weaker being still,—so the original word implies. He is not so much *man* as God made him, but man as his mother bore him ; and how can the Lord think of him, and write down such a cipher in his accounts ? The Lord thinks much of man, and in connection with redeeming love makes a great figure of him : this can be believed, but it cannot be explained. Adoring wonder makes us each one cry out, Why dost thou take knowledge of me ? We know by experience how little man is to be reckoned upon, and we know by observation how greatly he can vaunt himself, it is therefore meet for us to be humble and to distrust ourselves ; but all this should make us the more grateful to the Lord, who knows man better than we do, and yet communes with him, and even dwells in him. Every trace of the misanthrope should be hateful to the believer ; for if God makes account of man it is not for us to despise our own kind.

4. *"Man is like to vanity."* Adam is like to Abel. He is like that which is nothing at all. He is actually vain, and he resembles that unsubstantial empty thing which is nothing but a blown-up nothing,—a puff, a bubble. Yet he is not vanity, but only like it. He is not so substantial as that unreal thing ; he is only the likeness of it. Lord, what is a man ? It is wonderful that God should think of such a pretentious insignificance. *"His days are as a shadow that passeth away."* He is so short-lived that he scarcely attains to years, but exists by the day, like the ephemera, whose birth and death are both seen by the self-same sun. His life is only like to a shadow, which is in itself a vague resemblance, an absence of something

rather than in itself an existence. Observe that human life is not only as a shade, but as a shade which is about to depart. It is a mere mirage, the image of a thing which is not, a phantasm which melts back into nothing. How is it that the Eternal should make so much of mortal man, who begins to die as soon as he begins to live ?

The connection of the two verses before us with the rest of the Psalm is not far to seek : David trusts in God and finds him everything ; he looks to man and sees him to be nothing ; and then he wonders how it is that the great Lord can condescend to take notice of such a piece of folly and deceit as man.

5 Bow thy heavens, O LORD, and come down : touch the mountains, and they shall smoke.

6 Cast forth lightning, and scatter them : shoot out thine arrows, and destroy them.

7 Send thine hand from above ; rid me, and deliver me out of great waters, from the hand of strange children ;

8 Whose mouth speaketh vanity, and their right hand *is* a right hand of falsehood.

5. *"Bow thy heavens, O LORD, and come down."* The heavens are the Lord's own, and he who exalted them can bow them. His servant is struggling against bitter foes, and he finds no help in men, therefore he entreats Jehovah to come down to his rescue. It is, indeed, a coming down for Jehovah to interfere in the conflicts of his tried people. Earth cries to heaven to stoop ; nay, the cry is to the Lord of heaven to bow the heaven, and appear among the sons of earth. The Lord has often done this, and never more fully than when in Bethlehem the Word was made flesh and dwelt among us : now doth he know the way, and he never refuses to come down to defend his beloved ones. David would have the real presence of God to counterbalance the mocking appearance of boastful man : eternal verity could alone relieve him of human vanity. *"Touch the mountains, and they shall smoke."* It was so when the Lord appeared on Sinai ; the strongest pillars of earth cannot bear the weight of the finger of God. He is a consuming fire, and his touch kindles the peaks of the Alps, and makes them smoke. If Jehovah would appear, nothing could stand before him ; if the mighty mountains smoke at his touch, then all mortal power which is opposed to the Lord must end in smoke. How long-suffering he is to his adversaries, whom he could so readily consume. A touch would do it ; God's finger of flame would set the hills on fire, and consume opposition of every kind.

6. *"Cast forth lightning, and scatter them."* The Eternal can hurl his lightnings wheresoever he pleases, and effect his purpose instantaneously. The artillery of heaven soon puts the enemy to flight : a single bolt sets the armies running hither and thither in utter rout. *"Shoot out thine arrows, and destroy them."* Jehovah never misses the mark ; his arrows are fatal to his foes when he goes forth to war. It was no common faith which led the poet-king to expect the Lord to use his thunderbolts on behalf of a single member of that race which he had just now described as " like to vanity." A believer in God may without presumption expect the Almighty Lord to use on his behalf all the stores of his wisdom and power : even the terrible forces of tempest shall be marshalled to the fight, for the defence of the Lord's chosen. When we have once mastered the greater difficulty of the Lord's taking any interest in us, it is but a small thing that we should expect him to exert his great power on our behalf. This is far from being the only time in which this believing warrior had thus prayed : the eighteenth Psalm is specially like the present ; the good man was not abashed at his former boldness, but here repeats himself without fear.

7. *"Send thine hand from above."* Let thy long and strong arm be stretched out till thine hand seizes my foes, and delivers me from them. *"Rid me, and deliver me out of great waters."* Make a Moses of me,—one drawn out of the waters. My foes pour in upon me like torrents, they threaten to overwhelm me ; save me from their force and fury ; take them from me, and me from them. *"From the hand of strange children."* From foreigners of every race ; men strange to me and thee, who therefore must work evil to me, and rebellion against thyself. Those against whom he pleaded were out of covenant with God ; they were Philistines and Edomites ; or else they were men of his own nation of black heart and traitorous

spirit, who were real strangers, though they bore the name of Israel. Oh to be rid of those infidel, blaspheming beings who pollute society with their false teachings and hard speeches! Oh to be delivered from slanderous tongues, deceptive lips, and false hearts! No wonder these words are repeated, for they are the frequent cry of many a tried child of God;—"*Rid me and deliver me.*" The devil's children are strange to us: we can never agree with them, and they will never understand us, they are aliens to us, and we are despised by them. O Lord, deliver us from the evil one, and from all who are of his race.

8. "*Whose mouth speaketh vanity.*" No wonder that men who are vanity speak vanity. "When he speaketh a lie, he speaketh of his own." They cannot be depended upon, let them promise as fairly as they may: their solemn declarations are light as the foam of the sea, in no wise to be depended upon. Good men desire to be rid of such characters: of all men deceivers and liars are among the most disgusting to true hearts. "*And their right hand is a right hand of falsehood.*" So far their hands and their tongues agree, for they are vanity and falsehood. These men act as falsely as they speak, and prove themselves to be all of a piece. Their falsehood is right-handed, they lie with dexterity, they deceive with all their might. It is a dreadful thing when a man's expertness lies more in lies than in truth; when he can neither speak nor act without proving himself to be false. God save us from lying mouths, and hands of falsehood.

9 I will sing a new song unto thee, O God: upon a psaltery *and* an instrument of ten strings will I sing praises unto thee.

10 *It is he* that giveth salvation unto kings: who delivereth David his servant from the hurtful sword.

11 Rid me, and deliver me from the hand of strange children, whose mouth speaketh vanity, and their right hand *is* a right hand of falsehood:

9. "*I will sing a new song unto thee, O God.*" Weary of the false, I will adore the true. Fired with fresh enthusiasm, my gratitude shall make a new channel for itself. I will sing as others have done; but it shall be a new song, such as no others have sung. That song shall be all and altogether for my God: I will extol none but the Lord, from whom my deliverance has come. "*Upon a Psaltery and an instrument of ten strings will I sing praises unto thee.*" His hand should aid his tongue, not as in the case of the wicked, co-operating in deceit; but his hand should unite with his mouth in truthful praise. David intended to tune his best instruments as well as to use his best vocal music: the best is all too poor for so great a God, and therefore we must not fall short of our utmost. He meant to use many instruments of music, that by all means he might express his great joy in God. The Old Testament dispensation abounded in types, and figures, and outward ritual, and therefore music dropped naturally into its place in the "worldly sanctuary"; but, after all, it can do no more than represent praise, and assist our expression of it; the real praise is in the heart, the true music is that of the soul. When music drowns the voice, and artistic skill takes a higher place than hearty singing, it is time that instruments were banished from public worship; but when they are subordinate to the song, as here, it is not for us to prohibit them, or condemn those who use them, though we ourselves greatly prefer to do without them, since it seems to us that the utmost simplicity of praise is far more congruous with the spirit of the gospel than pomp of organs. The private worshipper, singing his solo unto the Lord, has often found it helpful to accompany himself on some familiar instrument, and of this David in the present Psalm is an instance, for he says, "I will sing praise unto thee,"—that is, not so much in the company of others as by himself alone. He saith not "we," but "I."

10. "*It is he that giveth salvation unto kings.*" Those whom the Lord sets up he will keep up. Kings, from their conspicuous position, are exposed to special danger, and when their lives and their thrones are preserved to them they should give the Lord the glory of it. In his many battles David would have perished had not almighty care preserved him. He had by his valour wrought salvation for Israel, but he lays his laurels at the feet of his Lord and Preserver. If any men need salvation kings do, and if they get it the fact is so astonishing that it deserves a verse to itself in the Psalm of praise. "*Who delivereth David his servant from the hurtful sword.*" He traces his escape from death to the delivering hand of God. Note, he speaks in the present tense—*delivereth*, for this was an act which covered

his whole life. He puts his name to the confession of his indebtness : it is David who owns without demur to mercy given to himself. He styles himself the Lord's servant, accepting this as the highest title he had attained or desired.

11. Because of what the Lord had done, David returns to his pleading. He begs deliverance from him who is ever delivering him. *"Rid me, and deliver me from the hand of strange children."* This is in measure the refrain of the song, and the burden of the prayer. He desired to be delivered from his open and foreign adversaries, who had broken compacts, and treated treaties as vain things. *"Whose mouth speaketh vanity, and their right hand is a right hand of falsehood."* He would not strike hands with those who carried a lie in their right hand : he would be quit of such at once, if possible. Those who are surrounded by such serpents know not how to deal with them, and the only available method seems to be payer to God for a riddance and deliverance. David in the seventh verse, according to the original, had sought the help of both the Lord's hands, and well he might for his deceitful enemies with remarkable unanimity, were with one mouth and one hand seeking his destruction.

12 That our sons *may be* as plants grown up in their youth ; *that* our daughters *may be* as corner stones, polished *after* the similitude of a palace :

13 *That* our garners *may be* full, affording all manner of store : *that* our sheep may bring forth thousands and ten thousands in our streets :

14 *That* our oxen *may be* strong to labour ; *that there be* no breaking in, nor going out ; that *there be* no complaining in our streets.

15 Happy *is that* people, that is in such a case : *yea*, happy *is that* people, whose God *is the* LORD.

Riddance from the wicked and the gracious presence of the Lord are sought with a special eye to the peace and prosperity which will follow thereupon. The sparing of David's life would mean the peace and happiness of a whole nation. We can scarcely judge how much of happiness may hang upon the Lord's favour to one man.

12. God's blessing works wonders for a people. " *That our sons may be as plants grown up in their youth."* Our sons are of first importance to the state, since men take a leading part in its affairs ; and what the young men are the older men will be. He desires that they may be like strong, well rooted, young trees, which promise great things. If they do not grow in their youth, when will they grow ? If in their opening manhood they are dwarfed, they will never get over it. O the joys which we may have through our sons ! And, on the other hand, what misery they may cause us ! Plants may grow crooked, or in some other way disappoint the planter, and so may our sons. But when we see them developed in holiness, what joy we have of them ! *"That our daughters may be as corner stones, polished after the similitude of a palace."* We desire a blessing for our whole family, daughters as well as sons. For the girls to be left out of the circle of blessing would be unhappy indeed. Daughters unite families as corner stones join walls together, and at the same time they adorn them as polished stones garnish the structure into which they are builded. Home becomes a palace when the daughters are maids of honour, and the sons are nobles in spirit ; then the father is a king, and the mother a queen, and royal residences are more than outdone. A city built up of such dwellings is a city of palaces, and a state composed of such cities is a republic of princes.

13. *"That our garners may be full, affording all manner of store."* A household must exercise thrift and forethought : it must have its granary as well as its nursery. Husbands should husband their resources ; and should not only furnish their tables but fill their garners. Where there are happy households. there must needs be plentiful provision for them, for famine brings misery even where love abounds. It is well when there is plenty, and that plenty consists of " all manner of store." We have occasionally heard murmurs concerning the abundance of grain, and the cheapness of the poor man's loaf. A novel çalamity ! We dare not pray against it. David would have prayed for it, and blessed the Lord when he saw his heart's desire. When all the fruits of the earth are plentiful, the fruits of our lips should be joyful worship and thanksgiving. Plenteous and varied may our products be, that every form of want may be readily supplied. *"That our sheep may bring forth thousands and ten thousands in our streets,"* or rather in the open places, the fields, and

sheep-walks where lambs should be born. A teeming increase is here described. Adam tilled the ground to fill the garner, but Abel kept sheep, and watched the lambs. Each occupation needs the divine blessing. The second man who was born into this world was a shepherd, and that trade has ever held an important part in the economy of nations. Food and clothing come from the flock, and both are of first consideration.

14. *"That our oxen may be strong to labour ; "* so that the ploughing and cartage of the farm may be duly performed, and the husbandman's work may be accomplished without unduly taxing the cattle, or working them cruelly. *"That there be no breaking in, nor going out ; "* no irruption of marauders, and no forced emigration ; no burglaries and no evictions. *"That there be no complaining in our streets ; "* no secret dissatisfaction, no public riot ; no fainting of poverty, no clamour for rights denied, nor concerning wrongs unredressed. The state of things here pictured is very delightful : all is peaceful and prosperous ; the throne is occupied efficiently, and even the beasts in their stalls are the better for it. This has been the condition of our own country, and if it should now be changed, who can wonder ? for our ingratitude well deserves to be deprived of blessings which it has despised.

These verses may with a little accommodation be applied to a prosperous church, where the converts are growing and beautiful, the gospel stores abundant, and the spiritual increase most cheering. There ministers and workers are in full vigour, and the people are happy and united. The Lord make it so in all our churches evermore.

15. *"Happy is that people, that is in such a case."* Such things are not to be overlooked. Temporal blessings are not trifles, for the miss of them would be a dire calamity. It is a great happiness to belong to a people so highly favoured. *" Yea, happy is that people, whose God is the Lord."* This comes in as an explanation of their prosperity. Under the Old Testament Israel had present earthly rewards for obedience ; when Jehovah was their God they were a nation enriched and flourishing. This sentence is also a sort of correction of all that had gone before; as if the poet would say—all these temporal gifts are a part of happiness, but still the heart and soul of happiness lies in the people being right with God, and having a full possession of him. Those who worship the happy God become a happy people. Then if we have not temporal mercies literally we have something better : if we have not the silver of earth we have the gold of heaven, which is better still.

In this Psalm David ascribes his own power over the people, and the prosperity which attended his reign, to the Lord himself. Happy was the nation which he ruled ; happy in its king, in its families, in its prosperity, and in the possession of peace ; but yet more in enjoying true religion and worshipping Jehovah, the only living and true God.

EXPLANATORY NOTES AND QUAINT SAYINGS.

Whole Psalm.—The Psalm, in its mingled tones of prayer and praise, is a fit connecting link between the supplicatory Psalms which go before, and the strains of thanksgiving which follow it.—*Speaker's Commentary.*

Whole Psalm.—After six Psalms of sorrowful prayer in distress, we have now a Psalm of praise and thanksgiving for God's gracious answer to supplications ; and also a Psalm of intercession. The present Psalm bears a strong resemblance to David's last song in 2 Sam. xxii. and to Ps. xviii. Here we have a vision of Christ rejoicing ;—after his passion—risen in glory, and having ascended in triumph, and pleading for us at the right hand of God.—*Christopher Wordsworth.*

Whole Psalm.—This Psalm is ruled by the numbers ten and seven. Ten verses complete the first part of the Psalm, which falls into two divisions. The first portion contains, in verses 1 and 2, ten attributes of God,—three and seven, the seven divided into four and three. In like manner it contains ten requests to God in verses 5—7, divided precisely as the attributes. To this significance of the number ten for the first part, allusion is pointedly made in verse 9. Seven blessings are prayed for in the second part, four in verses 12, 13 (valiant sons, beautiful daughters, full store-houses, numerous flocks), and three in verse 14 (labouring oxen, no breach and diminution, no cry). The whole contains, apart from the closing epiphonem, which, as usual, stands outside the formal arrangement, seven strophes, each of two verses.

An objection has been brought against the Davidic authorship from the "traces of reading" it contains. But one would require to consider more exactly, what sort of reading is here to be thought of. It is only the Psalms of David which form the ground-work of this new Psalm. But that it is one of David's peculiarities to derive from his earlier productions a foundation for new ones, is evident from a variety of facts, which, if any doubt must still be entertained on the subject, would obtain a firm ground to stand upon in this Psalm, which *can* only have been composed by David. The way and manner of the use made of such materials is to be kept in view. This is always of a spirited and feeling nature, and no trace anywhere exists of a dead borrowing. That we cannot think here of such a borrowing; that the appropriation of the earlier language did not proceed from spiritual impotence, but rested upon deeper grounds, is manifest from the consideration of the second part, where the dependence entirely ceases, and where even the opponents of the Davidic authorship have not been able to overlook the strong poetical spirit of the time of David. They betake themselves to the miserable shift of affirming that the Psalmist borrowed this part of the Psalm from a much older poem now lost.—*E. W. Hengstenberg.*

Verse 1.—*"Blessed be the Lord."* A prayer for further mercy is fitly begun with a thanksgiving for former mercy ; and when we are waiting upon God to bless us, we should stir up ourselves to bless him.—*Matthew Henry.*

Verse 1.—*"The Lord my strength,"* etc. Agamemnon says to Achilles—

> If thou hast strength, 'twas heaven that strength bestowed ;
> For know, vain man ! thy valour is from God.
>
> *Homer.*

Verse 1.—*"My strength"* [Heb. *" my rock "*]. The climax should be noted ; the rock, or cliff, comes first as the place of refuge, then the fortress or *fastness*, as a place carefully fortified, then the personal deliverer, without whose intervention escape would have been impossible.—*Speaker's Commentary.*

Verse 1.—*"The Lord . . . teacheth" :* and not as man teacheth. Thus he taught Gideon to fight with the innumerable host of Midian by sending to their homes two-and-twenty thousand, and retaining but ten thousand of his soldiers : and then again by reducing that remnant to the little band of three hundred who lapped when brought down to the water. Thus he taught Samson by abstaining from strong drink, and by suffering no razor to pass over his head. Thus he taught the three kings in the wilderness to war against their enemies, not by any strength of their armies, but by making ditches in the desert. Thus he taught David himself by waiting for the sound of the going in the tops of the mulberry trees. And so he taught the arms of the True David to fight when stretched on the cross : nailed, to human sight, to the tree of suffering, but, in reality, winning for themselves the crown of glory : helpless in the eyes of scribes and Pharisees ; in those of archangels, laying hold of the two pillars, sin and death, whereon the house of Satan rested, and heaving them up from their foundation.—*Ayguan, in Neale and Littledale.*

Verse 1.—*" The Lord my strength, which teacheth my hands to war."* There were three qualities of a valiant soldier found in Christ, the Captain of our salvation, in his war against Satan, which his followers are bound to emulate : boldness in attack, skill in defence, steadiness in conflict, all which he teaches by his example (Matt. iv. 1, 4, 7, 10, 11). He was *bold in attack,* for he began the combat by going up into the wilderness to defy the enemy. So we, too, should be always beforehand with Satan : ought to fast, even if not tempted to gluttony, and be humble, though not assailed by pride, and so forth. He was *skilful in defence,* parrying every attack with Holy Writ ; where we, too, in the examples of the saints, may find lessons for the combat. He was *steadfast in conflict,* for he persevered to the end, till the devil left him, and angels came and ministered unto him ; and we, too, should not be content with repelling the first attack, but persevere in our resistance until evil thoughts are put to flight, and heavenly resolutions take their place.—*Neale and Littledale.*

Verse 1.—*"Teacheth my hands."* Used to the hook and harp, and not to the sword and spear ; but God hath apted and abled them to feats of arms and warlike exploits. It is God that giveth skill and success, saith Solomon (Prov. viii.) ; wisdom

and ability, saith Daniel (chap. ii.).   And as in the spiritual warfare, so here ; our
weapons are " mighty through God " (2 Cor. x. 4), who promiseth that no weapon
formed against his people shall prosper (Isa. liv. 17).—*John Trapp.*

Verse 1.—"*To war, . . . to fight.*" I want to speak of a great defect among us,
which often prevents the realization of going " from strength to strength " ; viz.,
the *not using, not trading with*, the strength given.   We should not think of going
to God for money only to keep it in the bank.   But are we not doing this with
regard to strength ?   We are constantly asking for strength for service ; but if
we are not putting this out in hearty effort, it is of no use to us.   Nothing comes
of hoarded strength.

   " Blessed be the Lord my strength, *which teacheth my hands to war, and my fingers
to fight.*"   David, you see, was looking for strength for a purpose.   Some people
seem to expect strength, but never attempt to put forth their hands to war, and
their fingers to fight—there is so little venturing upon God, so little use of grace
given, partly from fear of man, partly from indolence and worldly-mindedness . . .
It is not for us to be merely luxuriating in the power which God supplies.   Action
strengthens, and before we have a right to ask for an increase, we must use that
already given.—*Catherine Pennefather, in " Service," 1881.*

Verse 1.—Is not the spiritual victory of every believer achieved by God ?   Truly
it is he who teaches his *hands to war and his fingers to fight* : and when the final
triumph shall be sung in heaven, the victor's song will be, " Not unto me, O Lord,
not unto me, but unto thy name give glory, for thy mercy and for thy truth's sake."—
John Morison.

Verse 1.—"*My hands for fight, my fingers for war.*" *Fight* and *war* are both
verbs and nouns in English, but the Hebrew words are nouns with the article prefixed.
—*Joseph Addison Alexander.*

Verse 1.—"*My fingers to fight.*" Probably the immediate reference here is
to the use of the bow,—placing the arrow, and drawing the string.—*Albert Barnes.*

Verse 2.—"*My goodness,*" etc.   This way of using the word in a passive sense,
as in the Hebrew, sounds harshly ; just as elsewhere (Ps. xviii. 50) he calls himself
" God's king," not in the sense of his having dominion over God, but being made
and appointed king by him.   Having experienced God's kindness in so many ways,
he calls him "*his goodness,*" meaning that whatever good he possessed flowed from
him.   The accumulation of terms, one upon another, which follows, may appear
unnecessary, yet it tends greatly to strengthen faith.   We know how unstable men's
minds are, and especially how soon faith wavers, when they are assailed by some
trial of more than usual severity.—*John Calvin.*

Verse 2.—"*My fortress.*"   David calls God by names connected with the chief
deliverances of his life.   The Psalms abound in local references and descriptive
expressions, *e.g.* Ps. xviii. 2 [and in this place].   The word translated "*fortress*"
is *metzudah* or *masada*.   From 1 Sam. xxiii. 29, I have no doubt that he is speaking
of Masada, an isolated peak 1,500 feet high, on which was a stronghold.—*James
Wareing Bardsley, in "Glimpses through the Veil," 1883.*

Verse 2.—"*My high tower.*"   Such *towers* were erected on mountains, on rocks,
or on the walls of a city, and were regarded as safe places mainly because they were
inaccessible.   So the old castles in Europe,—as that at Heidelberg, and generally
those along the Rhine,—were built on lofty places, and in such positions as not to
be easily accessible.—*Albert Barnes.*

Verse 2.—"*My shield.*"   The Hebrew word signifies, not the huge shield which
was carried by an armour-bearer, but the handy target with which heroes entered
into hand-to-hand conflicts.   A warrior took it with him when he used his bow
or his sword.   It was often made of metal, but still was portable, and useful, and
was made to serve as an ornament, being brightened or anointed with oil.   David
had made abundant use of the Lord, his God, from day to day, in battles many and
murderous.—*C. H. S.*

Verse 2.—"*Who subdueth my people under me.*"   David, accordingly, having
ascribed the victories he had gained over foreign enemies to God, thanks him at
the same time for the settled state of the kingdom.   Raised indeed as he was from
an obscure station, and exposed to hatred from calumnious charges, it was scarcely
to have been believed that he would ever obtain a peaceable reign.   The people
had suddenly, and beyond expectation, submitted to him ; and so surprising a
change was eminently God's work.—*John Calvin.*

Verse 3.—*"Lord, what is man,"* etc.

> Now what is man, when grace reveals
> The virtues of a Saviour's blood ?
> Again a life divine he feels,
> Despises earth, and walks with God.

> And what in yonder realms above,
> Is ransomed man ordained to be ?
> With honour, holiness, and love,
> No seraph more adorned than he.

> Nearest the throne, and first in song.
> Man shall his hallelujahs raise,
> While wondering angels round him throng,
> And swell the chorus of his praise.

> *John Newton, in Olney Hymns.*

Verse 3.—*"Lord, what is man ?"* Take him in his four elements, of earth, air, fire, and water. In the *earth*, he is as fleeting dust ; in the *air*, he is as disappearing vapour ; in the *water*, he is as a breaking bubble ; and in the *fire*, he is as consuming smoke.—*William Secker, in "The Nonsuch Professor."*

Verses 3, 4.—*"Lord, what is man,"* etc. There is no book so well worthy reading as this living one. Even now David spake as a king of men, of *people subdued under him !* now he speaks as a humble vassal to God : *"Lord, what is man that thou takest knowledge of him ?"* In one breath is both sovereignty and subjugation : an absolute sovereignty over his people ; *"My people are subdued under me"* ; an humble subjection to the God of kings ; *"Lord, what is man ?"* Yea, in the very same word wherein is the profession of that sovereignty, there is an acknowledgment of subjection : *"Thou hast subdued my people."* In that he had a people, he was a king : that they might be his people, a subjection was requisite ; and that subjugation was God's and not his own : *"Thou* hast subdued." Lo, David, had not subdued his people, if God had not subdued them for him. He was a great king, but they were a stiff people : the God that made them swayed them to a due subjection. The great conquerors of worlds could not conquer hearts, if he, that moulded hearts, did not temper them. " By me kings reign," saith the Eternal Wisdom ; and he that had courage enough to encounter a bear, a lion, Goliath, yet can say, *"Thou hast subdued my people."*

Contrarily, in the lowliest subjection of himself, there is an acknowledgment of greatness. Though he abused himself with, *"What is man ?"* yet, withal he adds, *"Thou takest knowledge of him, thou makest account of him"*: and this knowledge, this account of God, doth more exalt man than his own vanity can depress him. My text, then, ye see, is David's rapture, expressed in an ecstatical question of sudden wonder ; a wonder at God and at man : MAN'S VILENESS ; *"What is man ?"* GOD'S MERCY AND FAVOUR, in his knowledge, in his estimation of man. Lo, there are but two lessons that we need to take out here, in the world, God and man ; man, in the notion of his wretchedness ; God, in the notion of his bounty.

Let us, if you please, take a short view of both ; and, in the one, see cause of our humiliation ; of our joy and thankfulness in the other : and if, in the former, there be a sad Lent of mortification ; there is, in the latter, a cheerful Easter of our raising and exaltation.

Many a one besides David wonders at himself : one wonders at his own honour ; and, though he will not say so, yet thinks, " What a great man am I ! Is not this great Babel, which I have built ? " This is Nebuchadnezzar's wonder. Another wonders at his person, and finds, either a good face, or a fair eye, or an exquisite hand, or a well-shaped leg, or some gay fleece, to admire in himself : this was Absalom's wonder. Another wonders at his wit and learning : " How came I by all this ? *Turba hæc !* This vulgar, that knows not the law, is accursed " : this was the Pharisee's wonder. Another wonders at his wealth ; " Soul, take thine ease " ; as the epicure in the gospel. David's wonder is as much above, as against all these : he wonders at his *vileness :* like as the Chosen Vessel would boast of nothing but his infirmities : *"Lord, what is man ?"*

How well this hangs together ! No sooner had he said, *"Thou hast subdued my people under me,"* then he adds, *"Lord, what is man ?"* Some vain heart would have been lifted up with a conceit of his own eminence ; " Who am I ? I am not as other men. I have people under me ; and people of my own, and people subdued to me ; " this is to be more than a man. I know who hath said, " I said ye are gods."—*Joseph Hall.*

Verse 3.—Dr. Hammond refers this Psalm to the slaying of Goliath, and thus understands the appellation *"son of man,"*—" David was but a young stripling, the youngest and most inconsiderable of all the sons of Jesse, who also was himself an ordinary man."

Verse 3.—*"Thou takest knowledge of him."* It is a great word. Alas! what knowledge do we take of the gnats that play in the sun ; or the ants, or worms, that are crawling in our grounds ? Yet the disproportion betwixt us and them is but finite ; infinite betwixt God and us. Thou, the Great God of Heaven, to take knowledge of such a thing as man ! If a mighty prince shall vouchsafe to spy and single out a plain homely swain in a throng, as the Great Sultan did lately a tankard-bearer ; and take special notice of him, and call him but to a kiss of his hand and nearness to his person ; he boasts of it as a great favour : for thee, then, O God, who abasest thyself to behold the things in heaven itself, to cast thine eye upon so poor a worm as man, it must needs be a wonderful mercy.—*Exigua pauperibus magna ;* as Nazianzen to his Amphilochius.—*Joseph Hall.*

Verse 4.—*"Man is like to vanity."* As he that goeth to a fair, with a purse full of money, is devising and debating with himself how to lay it out—possibly thinking that such and such commodities will be most profitable, and bring him in the greatest gain—when on a sudden a cut-purse comes and easeth him both of his money and how to dispose of it. Surely thou mightst have taken notice how some of thy neighbours or countrymen, when they have been busy in their contrivances, and big with many plots and projects how to raise their estate and names and families, were arrested by death in a moment, returned to their earth, and in that day all their gay, their great thoughts perished, and came to nothing. The heathen historian could not but observe how Alexander the Great, when he had to carry on his great designs, summoned a parliament before him of the whole world, he was himself summond by death to appear in the other world. The Dutch, therefore, very wittily to express the world's vanity, picture at Amsterdam a man with a full-blown bladder on his shoulders, and another standing by pricking the bladder with a pin, with this motto, QUAM SUBITO, How soon is all blown down ! —*George Swinnock.*

Verse 4.—*"Man is like to vanity."* When Cain was born, there was much ado about his birth ; " I have gotten a man-child from God," saith his mother ; she looked upon him as a great possession, and therefore called his name *Cain,* which signifies " a possession." But the second man that was born unto the world bare the title of the world, *" vanity" ;* his name was *Abel,* that is, *" vanity."* A premonition was given in the name of the second man what would or should be the condition of all men. In Psalm cxliv. 4 there is an allusion unto those two names. We translate it, *"Man is like to vanity" ;* the Hebrew is, *"Adam is as Abel" ; Adam,* you know, was the name of the first man, the name of Abel's faither ; but as Adam was the proper name of the first, so it is an appellative, or common to all men, now *Adam,* that is, man or all men, are *Abel,* vain, and walking in a vain show. —*Joseph Caryl.*

Verse 4.—*"Man is like to vanity,"* etc. The occasion of the introduction of these sentiments here is not quite clear. It may be the humility of the warrior who ascribes all success to God instead of to human prowess, or it may be a reflection uttered over the corpses of comrades, or, perhaps a blending of the two.—*A. S. Aglen.*

Verse 4.—*"Man is like to vanity,"* etc. With what idle dreams, what foolish plans, what vain pursuits, are men for the most part occupied ! They undertake dangerous expeditions and difficult enterprises in foreign countries, and they acquire fame ; but what is it ?—*Vanity !* They pursue deep and abstruse speculations, and give themselves to that " much study which is a weariness to the flesh," and they attain to literary renown, and survive in their writings ; but what is it ?— *Vanity !* They rise up early and sit up late, and eat the bread of anxiety and care, and thus they amass wealth ; but what is it ?—*Vanity !* They frame and execute plans and schemes of ambition—they are loaded with honours and adorned with titles—they afford employment for the herald, and form a subject for the historian ; but what is it ?—*Vanity !* In fact, all occupations and pursuits are worthy of no other epithet, if they are not preceded by, and connected with, a deep and paramount regard to the salvation of the soul, the honour of God, and the interests of eternity. . . . . Oh, then, what phantoms, what airy nothings are those things that wholly absorb the powers and occupy the days of the great mass of mankind around us! Their most substantial good perishes in the using, and their most enduring realities are but " the fashion of this world that passeth away."—*Thomas Raffles*, 1788—1863.

Verse 4.—"*A shadow that passeth away.*" The shadows of the mountains are constanly shifting their position during the day, and ultimately disappear altogether on the approach of night : so is it with man, who is every day advancing to the moment of his final departure from this world.—*Bellarmine*.

Verse 5.—"*Bow thy heavens.*" This expression is derived from the appearance of the clouds during a tempest : they hang low, so as to obscure the hills and mountains, and seem to mingle earth and heaven together, Such an appearance is figuratively used to depict the coming of God, to execute vengeance upon the enemies of his people. See Ps. xviii. 10, and other instances.—*William Walford*.

Verse 5.—"*Bow thy heavens, O LORD, and come down,*" etc. This was never so remarkably fulfilled as in the incarnation of Jesus Christ, when heaven and earth were, as it were, brought together. Heaven itself was, as it were, made to bow that it might be united to the earth. God did, as it were, come down and bring heaven with him. He not only came down to the earth, but he brought heaven down with him to men and for men. It was a most strange and wonderful thing. But this will be more remarkably fulfilled still by Christ's second coming, when he will indeed bring all heaven down with him—viz., all the inhabitants of heaven. Heaven shall be left empty of its inhabitants to come down to the earth ; and then the mountains shall smoke, and shall indeed flow down at his presence, as in Isa. lxiv. 1.—*Jonathan Edwards*.

Verse 5.—"*Touch the mountains, and they shall smoke.*" The meaning is, when God doth but lay his hand upon great men, upon the mightiest of the world, he makes them smoke or fume, which some understand of their anger ; they are presently in a passion, if God do but touch them. Or we may understand it of their consumption. A *smoking* mountain will soon be a *burnt* mountain. In our language, to make a man smoke is a proverbial expression for destroying or subduing.—*Joseph Caryl*.

Verses 5, 6.—

> Bow thy heavens, Jehovah,
> 　Come down in thy might ;
> Let the rays of thy glory
> 　The mountain-tops light.
>
> With the bolts of thy thunder
> 　Discomfit my foe,
> With the flash of thine arrows
> 　Their force overthrow.
>
> *William Digby Seymour.*

Verse 6.—"*Cast forth lightning.*" The Hebrew here is, " Lighten lightning ; " that is, Send forth lightning. The word is used as a verb nowhere else.—*Albert Barnes*.

Verse 7.—"*Send thine hand from above.*" Hebrew, *hands*, both hands, all thy whole power, for I need it.—*John Trapp*.

Verse 7.—"*Rid me, and deliver me.*" Away, you who theorize about suffering, and can do no more than descant upon it, away ! for in the time of weeping we cannot endure your reasonings. If you have no means of delivering us, if you have nothing but sententious phrases to offer, put your hands on you mouths ; enwarp yourselves in silence ! It is enough to suffer ; but to suffer and listen to you is more than we can bear. If Job's mouth was nigh unto blasphemy, the blame is yours, ye miserable comforters, who talked instead of weeping. If I must suffer, than I pray for suffering without fine talk !—*E. De Pressensé*.

Verse 7.—"*Rid me, and deliver me . . . from the hand of strange children.*" We must remember that as the Grecians (conceiting themselves the best bred people in the world) called all other nations " barbarians ; " so the people of Israel, the stock of Abraham (being God's peculiar covenant people), called all other nations "aliens" or "*strangers;*" and because they were hated and maligned by all other nations, therefore they called all professed strangers *enemies;* so the word is used (Isa. i. 7), "Your land strangers shall devour"; that is, enemies shall invade and prevail over you. "*Deliver me out of the hand of strange children,*" or out of the hand of strangers; that is, out of the hand of mine enemies. The Latin word *alienus* is often put for *hostis,* and the Roman orator [Cicero] telleth us that "he who is now called a stranger was called an enemy by our ancestors." The reason was because strangers proved unkind to, yea, turned enemies against those that entertained them.—*Joseph Caryl.*

Verse 7.—"*Strange children.*" He calls them *strangers,* not in respect of generic origin, but character and disposition.—*John Calvin.*

Verse 7.—The "*strange children,*" now the enemies of David, shall be either won to willing subjection, or else shall be crushed under the triumphant Messiah (Ps. ii.). The Spirit by David spake things the deep significance of which reached further than even he understood (1 Pet. i. 11, 12).—*Andrew Robert Fausset.*

Verse 8.—"*Whose mouth speaketh vanity,*" etc. Two things go naturally together in the verse—the lying tongue and deceitful hand. The meaning is that upon the matter in hand nothing was to be looked for from any of their promises, since it was only to deceive that they flattered with their mouth and gave the hand.—*John Calvin.*

Verse 8.—"*Their right hand is a right hand of falsehood.*" The pledge of the right hand, which used to be a witness of good faith, was violated by treachery and wickedness.—*Cicero. Philip. xi. c.* 2.

Verse 9.—"*Psaltery—an instrument of ten strings.*" *Nebel-azor.* We are led to the conclusion that the *nebel* was the veritable *harp* of the Hebrews. It could not have been large, because it is so frequently mentioned in the Bible as being carried in processions. . . . . The English translators render *nebel* (apparently without any special reason) by no less than four words ; (1) Psaltery, (2) Psalm, (3) lute, (4) viol. The first of these is by far the most common in the Authorised Version, and is no doubt the most correct translation if the word be understood in its true sense as a *portable harp. Nebels* were made of fir-wood, and afterwards of almug, or algum, which was, perhaps, the red sandal-wood of India. . . . . With *nebel* is often associated the word *azor,* which is traced to a root signifying *ten,* and which has therefore been rendered in the Septuagint by ἐν δεκαχόρδῳ or as ψαλτηριον δεκάχορδον (*psalterium decem chordarum*), or in *dechachordo psalterio* in the Vulgate. In the Chaldee, Syriac, and Arabic versions also are found words implying the existence of ten strings in the *nebel-azor.* The word *azor* may therefore be considered as qualifying or describing the special kind of *nebel* to be used, much in the same way as we now speak of a *trichord* pianoforte. It is in our English version always rendered by the words "*ten-stringed.*"—*John Stainer in "The Music of the Bible,*" 1882.

Verse 10.—"*It is he that giveth salvation unto kings.*" Ferdinand, king of Aragon, sending his son against the Florentines, thus bespake him: Believe me, son, victories are not gotten by art or subtlety, but given of God.—*John Trapp.*

Verse 10.—"*It is he that giveth salvation unto kings.*" What a doctrine this for the kings and great men of the earth to remember ! Could they be brought to feel and acknowledge it, they would not trust to the sagacity of their own councils, nor to the strength of their own arm ; but would ever remember that the Most High is the ruler among the nations, and that he putteth down one and raiseth up another according to the dictates of his own all-perfect will. Such remembrances as this would stain the pride of all human glory, and would lead men to feel that the Lord alone is to be exalted.—*John Morison.*

Verse 11.—This Psalm is the language of a prince who wished his people's prosperity : that their "garners might be full of all manner of stores" ; that their "sheep might bring forth thousands and ten thousands in their streets"; that their "oxen" might be fat for slaughter, or "strong for labour" ; that there might be neither robbery nor beggary in their streets : no oppressive magistrates, nor complaining people : and as if all these blessings were to be derived from the character of the people, and the character of the people from the education they had received, our text is a prayer for the youth of Judea.—*Robert Robinson* (1735—1790), *in "The Nature and Necessity of Early Piety."*

Verse 12.—The reminiscences or imitations of Ps. xvii. suddenly cease here, and are followed by a series of original, peculiar, and for the most part no doubt antique expressions. On the supposition that the title is correct in making David the author, this is natural enough. On any other supposition, it is unaccountable, unless by the gratuitous assumption, that this is a fragment of an older composition, a mode of reasoning by which anything may be either proved or disproved.—*Joseph Addison Alexander.*

Verse 12.—*"That our sons may be as plants,"* etc. They who have ever been employed in the cultivation of plants of any kind, are continually tempted to wish that the human objects of their care and culture would grow up as rapidly, as straight, as flourishingly, would as uniformly fulfil their specific idea and purpose, as abundantly reward the labour bestowed on them. . . . . If our sons are indeed to grow up as young plants, like our English oaks, which according to the analogies of Nature, furnish no inappropriate type of our national character, they must not be stunted or dwarfed or pollarded, for the sake of being kept under the shade of a stranger. They should grow up straight toward heaven, as God had ordained them to grow. . . . There is something so palpable and striking in this type, that five-and-twenty years ago, in speaking of the gentlemanly character, I was led to say, " If a gentleman is to grow up he must grow like a tree : there must be nothing between him and heaven."—*Julius Charles Hare, in a Sermon entitled "Education the Necessity of Mankind,"* 1851.

Verse 12.—*"That our sons may be as plants grown up in their youth,"* etc. Thus David prays for the rising generation. Metaphors seem generally unsuitable to prayer, but they do not wear this aspect in the prayers recorded in the Scriptures. The language of the text is tropical, but the metaphors are suitable and seasonable. *Roots* of vegetables are necessarily invisible. *Tender* plants are insignificant. A plant *grown up,* having height in its stem, width in its branches, abundance in its foliage, and fulness in its bloom, is conspicuous. David prays that the sons of that generation might be in their youth *"as plants grown up,"* that is, that their piety might not only live, but that their godliness might be fully expressed. The stones of a *foundation* are concealed. The stones in the *mid-wall* of a building are also necessarily hid. The stones on the *surface* of a wall are visible, but they are not distinguished. The *corner-stone* of buildings in that day was prominent and eminent. Placed at the angle of the structure, where two walls met, on the top of the walls, and being richly ornamented and polished, it attracted attention. David prays that the daughters of that day might make an open and lovely profession of religion—that both sons and daughters might not only *have* piety but *show* it.—*Samuel Martin, in "Cares of Youth."*

Verse 12.—*"Plants grown up." "Corner-stones polished."* These processes of growth and polish can be carried on in one place only, the church of Christ.—*Neale and Littledale.*

Verse 12.—*"That our daughters may be as corner stones,"* etc. *"The polished corners of the temple,"* rather " *the sculptured angles, the ornament, of a palace."* Great care and much ornament were bestowed by the ancients upon the angles of their splendid palaces. It is remarkable that the Greeks made use of pilasters, called Caryatides (carved after the figure of a woman dressed in long robes), to support the entablatures of their buildings.—*Daniel Cresswell.*

Verse 12.—*"That our daughters may be as corner stones, polished after the similitude of a palace "* or temple. By daughters families are united and connected to their mutual strength, as the parts of a building are by the corner-stones ; and when they are graceful and beautiful both in body and mind, they are then polished after the similitude of a nice and curious structure. When we see our daughters well established, and stayed with wisdom and discretion, as corner-stones are fastened in the building ; when we see them by faith united to Christ, as the chief corner-stone, adorned with the graces of God's Spirit, which are the polishing of that which is naturally rough, and " become women professing godliness " ; when we see them purified and consecrated to God as living temples, we think ourselves happy in them.—*Matthew Henry.*

Verse 12.—*"That our daughters may be as corner stones,"* etc. One might perhaps at the first glance have expected that the *daughters* of a household would be as the graceful ornament of the clustering foliage or the fruit-bearing tree, and the *sons* as the corner-stones upholding the weight and burden of the building, and yet it is the reverse here. And I think one may read the love and tenderness of the Lord in this apparently casual but intended expression, and that he meant the nations of the earth to know and understand how much of their happiness, their strength, and their security was dependent on the female children of a family. It has not been so considered in many a nation that knew not God : in polished Greece in times of old, and in some heathen nations even to this day, the female children of a family have been cruelly destroyed, as adding to the burdens and diminishing the resources of a household ; and alas ! too, even in Christian countries, if not destroyed, they are with equal pitiless and remorseless cruelty cut off from all the solace and ties and endearments of life, and immured in that living mockery of a grave, the cloister, that they may not prove incumbrances and hindrances to others ! How contrary all this to the loving purpose of our loving God ! whose Holy Spirit has written for our learning that sons and daughters are alike intended to be the ornament and grace, the happiness and blessing of every household.—*Barton Bouchier.*

Verse 12.—*"After the similitude of a palace."* Most interpreters give the last word the vague sense of *" a palace."* There is something, however, far more striking in the translation *temple*, found in the Prayer Book and the ancient versions. The omission of the article is a poetic license of perpetual occurrence. The temple was the great architectural model and standard of comparison, and particularly remarkable for the great size and skilful elaboration of its foundation-stones, some of which, there is reason to believe, have remained undisturbed since the time of Solomon.— *Joseph Addison Alexander.*

Verses 12—15.—In the former part of the Psalm he speaks of such things as concern *his own* happiness : " Blessed be the Lord my strength " (verse 1) ; " Send thine hand from above ; and deliver me out of great waters " (verse 7) ; " Rid me, and deliver me from the hand of strange children " (verse 11). And he might as easily have continued the same strain in the clauses following : " That *my* sons may grow up as plants, *my* daughters may be as the polished corners of the temple, *my* sheep fruitful, *my* oxen strong, *my* garners full and plenteous " ; and accordingly he might have concluded it also—" Happy shall *I* be, if *I* be in such a case." This, I say, he might have done ; nay, this he would have done, if his desires had reflected only upon himself. But being of a diffusive heart, and knowing what belonged to the neighbourhoods of piety, as loth to enjoy this happiness alone, he alters his style, and (being in the height of well-wishes to himself) he turns the singular into a plural—*our sheep, our oxen, our garners, our sons and daughters,* that he might compendiate all in this,—*"Happy are the people."* Here is a true testimony both of a religious and generous mind, who knew in his most retired thoughts to look out of himself, and to be mindful of the public welfare in his privatest meditations. S. Ambrose observes it as a clear character of a noble spirit, to do what tends to the public good, though to his own disadvantage.—*Richard Holdsworth* (1590—1649), *in "The Valley of Vision."*

Verses 12—15.—These words contain a striking picture of a prosperous and happy nation. We are presented with a view of the *masculine youth* of the nation by the oaks of the forest, become great in the early period of the vigour and excellency of the soil. They are represented in the distinguishing character of their sex, standing abroad the strength of the nation, whence its resources for action must be derived. On the other hand, the *young females* of a nation are exhibited under an equally just and proper representation of their position and distinguishing character. They are not exhibited by a metaphor derived from the hardier tenants of the forest, but they are shown to us by a representation taken from the perpetual accompaniments of the dwelling ; they are the supports and the ornaments of domestic life. *Plenty* of every kind is represented to us in possession and in reasonable expectation. *"No breaking in,"* no invasion by a furious foe, oppresses the inhabitants of this happy country with terror ; neither is there any *" going out."* The barbarous practice employed by Sennacherib, and other ancient conquerors, of transporting the inhabitants of a vanquished country to some distant, unfriendly, and hated land, —the practice at this moment employed, to the scandal of the name and the sorrow of Europe—they dread not : they fear no *"going out."* Under circumstances of such a nature causes of distress or complaint exist not ; or, if they do, they are capable of being so modified, and alleviated, and remedied, that *there is no complaining in the streets.* "Happy, then, is that people, that is in such a case."—*John Pye Smith*, 1775—1851.

Verse 13.—*"That our sheep may bring forth thousands,"* etc. The surprising fecundity of the sheep has been celebrated by writers of every class. It has not escaped the notice of the royal Psalmist, who, in a beautiful ascription of praise to the living and the true God, entreats that the sheep of his chosen people might *" bring forth thousands and ten thousands in our streets."* In another song of Zion, he represents, by a very elegant metaphor, the numerous flocks covering like a garment the face of the field :—" The pastures are clothed with flocks ; the valleys also are covered over with corn ; they shout for joy, they also sing " : Ps. lxv. 13. The bold figure is fully warranted by the prodigious numbers of sheep which whitened the extensive pastures of Syria and Canaan. In that part of Arabia which borders on Judea, the patriarch Job possessed at first seven thousand, and after the return of his prosperity, fourteen thousand sheep ; and Mesha, the king of Moab, paid the king of Israel " a yearly tribute of a hundred thousand lambs, and an equal number of rams with the wool " : 2 Kings iii. 4. In the war which the tribe of Reuben waged with the Hagarites, the former drove away " two hundred and fifty thousand sheep " : 1 Chron. v. 21. At the dedication of the temple, Solomon offered in sacrifice " an hundred and twenty thousand sheep." At the feast of the passover, Josiah, the king of Judah, " gave to the people, of the flock, lambs and kids, all for the passover offerings, for all that were present, to the number of thirty thousand, and three thousand bullocks : these were of the king's substance " : 2 Chron. xxxv. 7. The ewe brings forth her young commonly once a year, and in more ungenial climes, seldom more than one lamb at a time. But twin lambs are as frequent in the oriental regions, as they are rare in other places ; which accounts in a satisfactory manner for the prodigious numbers which the Syrian shepherd led to the mountains. This uncommon fruitfulness seems to be intimated by Solomon in his address to the spouse :—" Thy teeth are like a flock of sheep that are even shorn, which came up from the washing ; whereof every one bear twins, and none is barren among them " : Cant. iv. 2.—*George Paxton* (1762—1837), *in "Illustrations of Scripture."*

Verses 13, 14.—*"Streets,"* though not incorrect, is an inadequate translation of the Hebrew word, which means external spaces, streets as opposed to the inside of houses, fields or country as opposed to a whole town. Here it includes not only roads but fields.—*Joseph Addison Alexander.*

Verse 14.—*"That our oxen may be strong to labour."* [Margin : *"able to bear burdens,"* or, *loaded* with flesh]. As in the verse before he had ascribed the fruitfulness of the herds and flocks to God's goodness, so now the fattening of their oxen, to show that there is nothing relating to us here which he overlooks.—*John Calvin.*

Verse 14.—*"That our oxen may be strong to labour."* Oxen were not only used for ploughing, thrashing, and drawing, but also for bearing burdens ; compare 1 Chron. xii. 40, which passage is peculiarly fitted to throw light on the verse before us. Laden oxen presuppose a rich abundance of produce.—*E. W. Hengstenberg.*

Verse 14.—*"That there be no complaining in our streets."* Rather, " and no cry of sorrow " (comp. Isaiah xxiv. 11 ; Jer. xiv. 2 ; xlvi. 12) " in our open places," *i.e.*, the places where the people commonly assembled near the gate of the city (comp. 2 Chron. xxxii. 6 ; Neh. viii. 1). The word rendered " *complaining* " does not occur elsewhere in the Psalter.—*Speaker's Commentary.*

Verse 14.—*"No complaining."* No outcries but " Harvest-homes."—*John Trapp.*

Verse 15.—*"Happy is that people,"* etc. We have in the text happiness with an echo, or ingemination ; " *happy* " and " *happy*." From this ingemination arise the parts of my text ; the same which are the parts both of the greater world and the less. As the heaven and earth in the one, and the body and soul in the other ; so are the passages of this Scripture in the two veins of happiness. We may range them as Isaac does the two parts of his blessing (Gen. xxvii. 28) ; the vein of civil happiness, in " the fatness of the earth ; " and the vein of Divine happiness, in " the fatness of heaven." Or (if you will have it out of the gospel), here's Martha's portion in the " many things " of the body ; and Mary's better part in the *unum necessarium* of the soul. To give it yet more concisely, here's the path of *prosperity* in outward comforts, *"Happy is that people that is in such a case"* ; and the path of *piety* in comforts spiritual : *"Yea, happy is that people, whose God is the LORD."*

In the handling of the first, without any further subdivision, I will only show what it is the Psalmist treats of ; and that shall be by way of gradation, in these three particulars. It is *De* FELICITATE ; *De Felicitate* POPULI ; *De* HAC *Felicitate Populi :* of *happiness ;* of the *people's* happiness ; of the people's happiness, as *in such a case.*

Happiness is the general, and the first : a noble argument, and worthy of an inspired pen, especially the Psalmist's. Of all other there can be none better to speak of *popular* happiness than such a *king ;* nor of *celestial,* than such a *prophet.* Yet I mean not to discourse of it in the full latitude, but only as it hath a peculiar positure in this Psalm, very various and different from the order of other Psalms. In this Psalm it is reserved to the *end,* as the close of the foregoing meditations. In other Psalms it is set in the *front,* or first place of all ; as in the xxxii., in the cxii., in the cxix., and in the cxxviii. Again, in this the Psalmist ends with *our* happiness and begins with God's. " Blessed be the LORD my strength." In the 41st Psalm, contrary, he makes his *exordium* from *man's ;* " Blessed is he that considereth the poor"; his *conclusion* with *God's ;* " Blessed be the LORD God of Israel." I therefore observe these variations, because they are helpful to the understanding both of the *essence* and *splendour* of true happiness. To the knowledge of the *essence* they help, because they demonstrate how our own happiness is enfolded in the glory of God, and subordinate unto it. As we cannot begin with *beatus* unless we end with *benedictus :* so we must begin with *benedictus* that we may end with *beatus.* The reason is this,—because the glory of God is as well the *consummation* as the *introduction* to a Christian's happiness. Therefore as in the other Psalm he begins below and ends upwards ; so in this, having begun from above with that which is principal, " Blessed be the LORD"; he fixeth his second thoughts upon the subordinate, " Blessed, or happy, are the people." He could not proceed in a better order : he first looks up to *God's* kingdom, then reflects upon his own, as not meaning to *take* blessedness before he had *given* it.—*Richard Holdsworth.*

Verse 15.—*"Happy is that people, that is in such a case,"* etc. The first part of this text hath relation to temporal blessings, *"Blessed is the people that be so" :* the second to spiritual, *"Yea, blessed is the people whose God is the LORD."* "His left hand is under my head," saith the spouse (Cant. ii. 6) ; that sustains me from falling into murmuring, or diffidence of his providence, because out of his left hand he hath given me a competency of his temporal blessings ; " But his right hand doth embrace me," saith the spouse there ; his spiritual blessings fill me, possess me so that no rebellious fire breaks out within me, no outward temptation breaks in upon me. So also Solomon says again, " In her left hand is riches and glory," (temporal blessings) " and in her right hand length of days " (Prov. iii. 16), all that accomplishes and fulfils the eternal joys of the saints of heaven. The person to whom Solomon attributes this right and left hand is Wisdom ; and a wise man may reach out his right and left hand, to receive the blessings of both sorts. And the person whom Solomon represents by Wisdom there, is Christ himself. So that not only a wordly wiseman, but a Christian wiseman may reach out both hands, to both kinds of blessings, right and left, spiritual and temporal.

Now, for this blessedness, as no philosophers could ever tell us amongst the Gentiles what true blessedness was, so no grammarian amongst the Jews, amongst the Hebrews, could ever tell us what the right signification of this word is, in which David expresses blessedness here ; whether *asherei,* which is the word, be a plural noun, and signify *beatitudines,* blessednesses in the plural, and intimate thus much, that blessedness consists not in any one thing, but in a harmony and consent of many ; or whether this *asherei* be an adverb, and signify *beate,* and so be an acclamation, O how happily, how blessedly are such men provided for that are so ; they cannot tell. Whatsoever it be, it is the very first word with which David begins his Book of Psalms ; *beatus vir ;* as the last word of that book is *laudate Dominum ;* to show that all that passes between God and man, from first to last, is blessings from God to man, and praises from man to God ; and that the first degree of blessedness is to find the print of the hand of God even in his temporal blessednesses, and to praise and glorify him for them in the right use of them. A man that hath no land to hold by it, nor title to recover by it, is never the better for finding, or buying, or having a fair piece of evidence, a fair instrument, fairly written, duly sealed, authentically testified ; a man that hath not the grace of God, and spiritual blessings too, is never the nearer happiness, for all his abundances of temporal blessedness. Evidences are evidences to them who have title.   Temporal blessings are evidences to them who have a testimony of God's spiritual blessings in the temporal.   Otherwise, as in his hands who hath no title, it is a suspicious thing to find evidences, and he will be thought to have embezzled and purloined them, he will be thought to have forged and counterfeited them, and he will be called to an account for them, how he came by them, and what he meant to do with them : so to them who have temporal blessings without spiritual, they are but useless blessings, they are but counterfeit blessings, they shall not purchase a minute's peace here, nor a minute's refreshing to the soul hereafter ; and there must be a heavy account made for them, both how they were got, and how they were employed.—*John Donne.*

Verse 15.—"*Happy is that people,*" etc.   It is only a narrow and one-sided religion that can see anything out of place in this beatitude of plenty and peace. If we could rejoice with the Psalms fully and without misgiving, in the temporal blessings bestowed by heaven, we should the more readily and sincerely enter into the depths of their spiritual experience.   And the secret of this lies in the full comprehension and contemplation of the beautiful and pleasant as the gift of God.—*A. S. Aglen.*

Verse 15.—" *Yea, happy is that people, whose God is the LORD.*"   " *Yea, happy.*" This is the best wine, kept to the last, though all men be not of this opinion.   You shall hardly bring a worldly man to think so.   The world is willing enough to misconstrue the order of the words, and to give the priority to civil happiness, as if it were first in dignity, because 'tis first named : they like better to hear of the *cui sic* than the *cui Dominus.*   To prevent this folly, the Psalmist interposeth a caution in this corrective particle, " *yea, happy.*"   It hath the force of a revocation, whereby he seems to retract what went before, not simply and absolutely, but in a certain degree, lest worldly men should wrest it to a misinterpretation.   It is not an *absolute* revocation, but a *comparative ;* it does not simply deny that there is some part of popular happiness in these outward things, but it prefers the spirituals before them : " *Yea,*" that is, *Yea more,* or, *Yea rather ;* like that of Christ in the Gospel, when one in the company blessed the womb that bare him, he presently replies, " Yea, rather blessed are they that hear the word of God and keep it : " Luke xi. 28.   In like manner, the prophet David, having first premised the inferior part and outside of a happy condition ; fearing lest they should of purpose mistake his meaning, and, hearing the first proposition, should either there set up their rest, and not at all take up the second ; or if they take it in, do it preposterously, and give it the precedence before the second, according to the world's order, *Virtus post nummos.*   In this respect he puts in the clause of revocation, whereby he shows that these outward things, though *named* first, yet they are not to be *reputed* first. The particle "*Yea* " removes them to the second place ; it tacitly transposeth the order ; and the path of piety, which was *locally* after, it placeth *virtually* before. 'Tis as if he said, Did I call them *happy* who are in such a case ?   Nay, miserable are they if they be only in such a case : the temporal part cannot make them so without the spiritual.   Admit the windows of the visible heaven were opened, and all outward blessings poured down upon us ; admit we did perfectly enjoy whatsoever the vastness of the earth contains in it ; tell me, What will it profit to gain all and lose God ?   If the earth be bestowed upon us, and not heaven ; or the material heaven be opened, and not the beatifical ; or the whole world made ours, and God not ours ; we do not arrive at happiness.   All that is in the first proposition is nothing unless this be added, "*Yea, happy are the people which have the Lord for their God.*"—*Richard Holdsworth.*

Verse 15.—

> Thrice happy nations, where with look benign
> Thine aspect bends ; beneath thy smile divine
> The fields are with increasing harvests crown'd,
> The flocks grow fast, and plenty reigns around,
> Nor sire, nor infant son, black death shall crave,
> Till ripe with age they drop into the grave ;
> Nor fell suspicion, nor relentless care,
> Nor peace-destroying discord enter there,
> But friends and brothers, wives and sisters, join
> The feast in concord and in love divine.
>
> *Callimachus.*

Verse 15.—David having prayed for many temporal blessings in the behalf of the people from verse 12 to verse 15, at last concludes, *"Blessed are the people that are in such a case "*; but presently he checks and corrects himself, and eats, as it were, his own words, but rather, *" happy is that people whose God is the Lord."* The Syriac rendereth it question wise, " Is not the people [happy] that is in such a case ? " The answer is, *"No,"* except they have God to boot : Ps. cxlvi. 5. Nothing can make that man truly miserable that hath God for his portion, and nothing can make that man truly happy that wants God for his portion. God is the author of all true happiness ; he is the donor of all true happiness ; he is the maintainer of all true happiness, and he is the centre of all true happiness ; and, therefore, he that hath him for his God, and for his portion, is the only happy man in the world.—*Thomas Brooks.*

Verse 15.—*"Whose God is JEHOVAH."* A word or name well-known to us English, by our translators now often retaining that name in the mention of God in our English Bibles, and therefore we do well to retain it. *Lord* was a lower word, in common acceptation, than *God.* But JEHOVAH is a higher name than either, and more peculiar, incommunicable, and comprehensive. Exod. vi. 3 : " I appeared " (saith the Lord) " unto Abraham, unto Isaac, and unto Jacob, by the name *God Almighty,* but by my name JEHOVAH was I not known to them."

To have God to be our *Jehovah* is the insurance of happiness to us. For of many, observe but these two things in the name *Jehovah :* First, God's absolute *independency*—that he is of himself omnipotent, Exod. iii. 14 : " And God said, I AM THAT I AM." Secondly, God's *faithfulness,* that he cannot but be as good as his word, Exod. vi. 2, 3, 4, 6 : " And I have also established my covenant with them ; wherefore say unto the children of Israel, I am JEHOVAH (so in the Hebrew), and I will bring you out from under the burdens of the Egyptians." So that this name is our *security* of God's performance. Examine we therefore our bonds, and bills, that is, his promises to us ; behold, they are all the promises of Jehovah ; they must stand good, for they bear his name ; they must reflect his name, and promote both our good and God's grand design.—*Nathanael Homes,* 1678.

With this prayer of Jehovah's anointed One end the prayers of the Book of Psalms. The remaining six Psalms consist exclusively of praise and high Hallelujahs.—*Lord Congleton, in "The Psalms : a new Version, with Notes,"* 1875.

HINTS TO PREACHERS.

Verse 1.—I. Two things needful in our holy war—strength and skill ; for the hands and the fingers, for the difficult and the delicate. II. In what way God supplies us with both. He is the one, and teaches the other. Impartation and Instruction. The teaching comes by illumination, experience, distinct guidance.

Verse 1.—Things not to be forgotten by the Christian Soldier. I. The true source of his strength : " The Lord my strength." If remembered, 1. He will not be found trusting in self. 2. He will never be wanting in courage. 3. He will always anticipate victory. 4. He will never be worsted in the conflict. II. His constant need of instruction, and the Teacher who never forgets him : " Which teacheth my hands," etc. If remembered, 1. He will gird on the armour provided and commended by God. 2. He will select for his weapon the sword of the Spirit. 3. He will study the divinely-given text-book of military tactics and discipline, that he may learn (1) the devices of the enemy ; (2) methods of attack and defence ; (3) how to bear himself in the thick of the fight. 4. He will wait upon God for understanding. III. The praise due to God, both for victories won and skill displayed : " Blessed be," etc. If remembered, 1. He will wear his honours humbly. 2. Glorify the honour of his King. 3. Twice taste the sweets of victory in the happiness of gratitude.—*J. F.*

Verse 2.—Double flowers. I. Good preserved from evil : goodness " and " fortress." II. Safety enlarged into liberty: " tower," " deliverer." III. Security attended with rest : " shield, in whom I trust." IV. Sufficiency to maintain superiority : " subdueth my people under me." View God as working all.

Verse 2.—A Group of Titles. Notice, I. Which comes first. " Goodness." *Heb.* " Mercy." 1. It is right and natural that a saved sinner should make the most of " mercy," and place it in the foreground. 2. Mercy is the ground and reason of the other titles named. For whatever God is to us, it is a special manifestation of his mercy. 3. It is a good thing to see a believer ripe in experience making mercy the leading note in his song of praise. II. Which comes last : " He in whom I trust." It suggests, 1. That what God is makes him worthy of trust. 2. That meditation upon what he is strengthens our trust. III. What peculiar force the word " my " gives to each. It makes, 1. A record of experience. 2. An ascription of praise. 3. A blessed boasting. 4. An incentive, enough to set others longing.—*J. F.*

Verse 3.—A note of interrogation, exclamation, and admiration.

Verse 3.—The question, I. Denies any right in man to claim the regard of God. II. Asserts the great honour God has nevertheless put upon him. III. Suggests that the true reason of God's generous dealings is the graciousness of his own heart. IV. Implies the becomingness of gratitude and humility. V. Encourages the most unworthy to put their confidence in God.—*J. F.*

Verse 3.—I. What was man as he came from the hands of his Creator ? 1. Rational. 2. Responsible. 3. Immortal. 4. Holy and happy. II. What is man in his present condition ? 1. Fallen. 2. Guilty. 3. Sinful. 4. Miserable, and helpless in his misery. III. What is man when he has believed in Christ ? 1. Restored to a right relation to God. 2. Restored to a right disposition toward God. 3. He enjoys the influences of the Holy Spirit. 4. He is in process of preparation for the heavenly world. IV. What shall man be when he is admitted into heaven ? 1. Free from sin and sorrow. 2. Advanced to the perfection of his nature. 3. Associated with angels. 4. Near to his Saviour and his God.— *George Brooks, in "The Homiletic Commentary,"* 1879.

Verse 3.—Worthless man much regarded by the mighty God. Sermon by Ebenezer Erskine. Works iii., pp. 141—162.

Verse 3.—It is a wonder above all wonders, that ever the great God should make such account of such a thing as man. I. It will appear if you consider what a great God the Lord is. II. What a poor thing man is. III. What a great account the great God hath of this poor thing, man.—*Joseph Alleine.*

Verse 4.—He is nothing, he pretends to be something, he is soon gone, he ends in nothing as to this life ; yet there is a light somewhere.

Verse 4.—The Shadow-World. I. Our lives are like shadows. II. But God's light casts these shadows. Our being is of God. The brevity and mystery of life are a part of providence. III. The destiny of the shadows ; eternal night ; or eternal light.—*W. B. H.*

Verse 4.—The brevity of our earthly life. 1. A profitable subject for meditation. II. A rebuke to those who provide for this life alone. III. A trumpet-call to prepare for eternity. IV. An incentive to the Christian to make the best of this life for the glory of God.—*J. F.*

Verse 5.—Condescension, visitation, contact, and conflagration.

Verses 7, 8, 11.—Repetitions, not vain. Repetitions in prayer are vain when they result from form, thoughtlessness, or superstition ; but not, *e.g.,* I. When they are the utterance of genuine fervour. II. When the danger prayed against is imminent. III. When the fear which prompts the prayer is urgent. IV. When the repetition is prompted by a new motive, verses 7, 8 ; by God's condescension, verses 3, 11 ; by God's former deliverance, verse 10 ; and by the results which will flow from the answer, verses 12—14.—*C. A. D.*

Verse 8.—What is " a right hand of falsehood " ? Ask the hypocrite, the schemer, the man of false doctrine, the boaster, the slanderer, the man who forgets his promise, the apostate.

Verse 9.—For God's Ear. I. The Singer. A grateful heart. II. The Song. Praiseful. New. III. The Accompaniment : " Psaltery." Helps to devotion. Give God the best. IV. The Auditor and Object of the eulogium : " Thee, O God."—*W. B. H.*

Verse 11.—Persons from whom it is a mercy to escape : those alien to God, vain in conversation, false in deed.

Verses 11, 12.—The Nature and Necessity of early Piety. A Sermon preached to a Society of Young People, at Willingham, Cambridgeshire, on the First Day of the Year M.DCC.LXXII.—*Robert Robinson.*

Verse 12.—Youth attended with development, stability, usefulness, and spiritual health.

Verse 12 (*first clause*).—To Young Men. Consider, 1. What is desired on your behalf : " Sons may be as plants," etc. 1. That you may be respected and valued. 2. That you may have settled principles and virtues. Plants are not blown hither and thither. 3. That you may be vigorous and strong in moral power. II. What is requisite on your part to the accomplishment of this desire. 1. A good rootage in Christ. 2. Constant nourishment from the word of God. 3. The dews of divine grace obtained by prayer. 4. A resolute tendency within to answer the God-appointed purpose of your existence.—*J. F.*

Verse 12 (*second clause*).—To Young Women. Consider, 1. The important position you may occupy in the social fabric : " As corner-stones." 1. The moral and religious tone of society is determined more by your character and influence than by those of men. 2. The complexion of home life will be a reflex of your conduct and character, either as daughters, sisters, or wives. 3. The moulding of the character of the next generation, remember, begins with the mother's influence. 4. Let these facts weigh with you as a motive in seeking the grace of God, without which you can never fulfil your mission worthily. II. The beauty which ought to belong to you in your position. " Polished after," etc. The beauty of, 1. Heart purity : " The King's daughter is all glorious within." 2. A noble and modest conduct : " wrought gold," no imitation ; real gold. 3. Gracious and gentle demeanour. III. How both the right position and right beauty are obtained. 1. By yielding yourselves to God. 2. By Christ dwelling in your heart. 3. By becoming living stones and polished stones under the workmanship of the Holy Spirit.—*J. F.*

Verse 14.—A prayer for our ministers, and for the security, unity, and happiness of the church.

Verse 14.—The prosperous Church. There—I. Labour is cheerfully performed. II. The enemy is kept without the gate. III. There are few or no departures. IV. Faith and content silence complaint. V. Pray that such may be our case as a church.—*W. B. H.*

Verse 15.—The peculiar happiness of those whose God is the Lord.

PSALM CXLV.

This is one of the alphabetical Psalms, composed with much art, and, doubtless, so arranged that the memory might be aided. The Holy Spirit condescends to use even the more artificial methods of the poet, to secure attention, and impress the heart.

TITLE.—DAVID'S PSALM OF PRAISE. *It is David's, David's very own, David's favourite. It is David's Praise just as another (Psalm lxxxvi.) is David's Prayer. It is altogether praise, and praise pitched in a high key. David had blessed God many a time in other Psalms, but this he regarded as his peculiar, his crown jewel of praise. Certainly David's praise is the best of praise, for it is that of a man of experience, of sincerity, of calm deliberation, and of intense warmth of heart. It is not for any one of us to render David's praise, for David only could do that; but we may take David's Psalm as a model, and aim at making our own personal adoration as much like it as possible: we shall be long before we equal our model. Let each Christian reader present his own praise unto the Lord, and call it by his own name. What a wealth of varied praise will thus be presented through Christ Jesus!*

DIVISION.—*The Psalm does not fall into any marked divisions, but is one and indivisible. Our own translators have mapped out this song with considerable discernment. It is not a perfect arrangement, but it will suit our convenience in exposition. David praiseth God for his fame or glory (1—7), for his goodness (8—10), for his kingdom (11—13), for his providence (14—16), for his saving mercy (17—21).*

EXPOSITION.

I WILL extol thee, my God, O king; and I will bless thy name for ever and ever.

2 Every day will I bless thee; and I will praise thy name for ever and ever.

3 Great *is* the LORD, and greatly to be praised; and his greatness *is* unsearchable.

4 One generation shall praise thy works to another, and shall declare thy mighty acts.

5 I will speak of the glorious honour of thy majesty, and of thy wondrous works.

6 And *men* shall speak of the might of thy terrible acts; and I will declare thy greatness.

7 They shall abundantly utter the memory of thy great goodness, and shall sing of thy righteousness.

1. "*I will extol thee, my God, O king.*" David as God's king adores God as his king. It is well when the Lord's royalty arouses our loyalty, and our spirit is moved to magnify his majesty. The Psalmist has extolled his Lord many a time before, he is doing so still, and he will do so in the future: praise is for all tenses. When we cannot express all our praise just now, it is wise to register our resolution to continue in the blessed work, and write it down as a bond, "I will extol thee." See how David testifies his devotion and adherence to his God by the pronoun "my," how he owns his allegiance by the title "king," and how he goes on to declare his determination to make much of him in his song.

"*And I will bless thy name for ever and ever.*" David determined that his praise should rise to blessing, should intelligently spend itself upon the name or character of God, and should be continued world without end. He uses the word "bless" not merely for variation of sound, but also for the deepening and sweetening of the sense. To bless God is to praise him with a personal affection for him, and a wishing well to him; this is a growingly easy exercise as we advance in experience and grow in grace. David declares that he will offer every form of praise, through every form of existence. His notion of duration is a full one—"for ever" has no end, but when he adds another " ever " to it he forbids all idea of a close. Our praise of God shall be as eternal as the God we praise.

2. *"Every day will I bless thee."* Whatever the character of the day, or of my circumstances and conditions during that day, I will continue to glorify God. Were we well to consider the matter we should see abundant cause in each day for rendering special blessing unto the Lord. All before the day, all in the day, all following the day should constrain us to magnify our God every day, all the year round. Our love to God is not a matter of holy days : every day is alike holy to holy men. David here comes closer to God than when he said, " I will bless thy name ": it is now, " I will bless *thee*." This is the centre and kernel of true devotion : we do not only admire the Lord's words and works, but himself. Without realizing the personality of God, praise is well-nigh impossible ; you cannot extol an abstraction. *"And I will praise thy name for ever and ever."* He said he would bless that name, and now he vows to praise it ; he will extol the Lord in every sense and way. Eternal worship shall not be without its variations ; it will never become monotonous. Heavenly music is not harping upon one string, but all strings shall be tuned to one praise. Observe the personal pronouns here : four times he says " *I* will ": praise is not to be discharged by proxy : there must be your very self in it, or there is nothing in it.

3. *"Great is the LORD, and greatly to be praised."* Worship should be somewhat like its object—great praise for a great God. There is no part of Jehovah's greatness which is not worthy of great praise. In some beings greatness is but vastness of evil : in him it is magnificence of goodness. Praise may be said to be great when the song contains great matter, when the hearts producing it are intensely fervent, and when large numbers unite in the grand acclaim. No chorus is too loud, no orchestra too large, no Psalm too lofty for the lauding of the Lord of Hosts.

"And his greatness is unsearchable."

> " Still his worth your praise exceeds,
> Excellent are all his deeds."

Song should be founded upon search ; hymns composed without thought are of no worth, and tunes upon which no pains have been spent are beneath the dignity of divine adoration. Yet when we meditate most, and search most studiously, we shall still find ourselves surrounded with unknowable wonders, which will baffle all attempts to sing them worthily. The best adoration of the Unsearchable is to own him to be so, and close the eyes in reverence before the excessive light of his glory. Not all the minds of all the centuries shall suffice to search out the unsearchable riches of God: he is past finding out ; and, therefore, his deserved praise is still above and beyond all that we can render to him.

4. *"One generation shall praise thy works to another."* There shall be a tradition of praise : men shall hand on the service, they shall make it a point to instruct their descendants in this hallowed exercise. We look back upon the experience of our fathers, and sing of it ; even thus shall our sons learn praise from the Lord's works among ourselves. Let us see to it that we praise God before our children, and never make them think that his service is an unhappy one. *"And shall declare thy mighty acts."* The generations shall herein unite : together they shall make up an extraordinary history. Each generation shall contribute its chapter, and all the generations together shall compose a volume of matchless character. David began with " I," but he has in this verse soon reached to an inconceivable multitude, comprehending all the myriads of our race of every age. The praise of the Lord enlarges the heart, and as it grows upon us our minds grow with it. God's works of goodness and acts of power make up a subject which all the eras of human story can never exhaust. A praiseful heart seems to live in all the centuries in delightful companionship with all the good. We are not afraid that the incense will ever cease to burn upon the altars of Jehovah : the priests die, but the adoration lives on. All glory be unto him who remains the same Lord throughout all generations.

5. *"I will speak of the glorious honour of thy majesty."* 'Tis fit a king should speak of the majesty of the King of kings. David cannot give over the worship of God into the hands of others, even though all generations should undertake to perpetuate it : he must have his own individual share in it, and so he saith, " I will speak." What a speaker ! for he no sooner begins than he heaps up words of honour—" the glorious honour of thy majesty," or " the beauty of the honour

of thy majesty." His language labours to express his meaning ; he multiplies the terms by which he would extol Jehovah, his King. Everything which has to do with the Great King is majestic, honourable, glorious. His least is greater than man's greatest, his lowest is higher than man's highest. There is nothing about the infinite Lord which is unworthy of his royalty ; and, on the other hand, nothing is wanting to the splendour of his reign : his majesty is honourable, and his honour is glorious : he is altogether wonderful.

"*And of thy wondrous works.*" All the works of God among men are Godlike, but certain of them are specially calculated to create surprise. Many works of power, of justice, of wisdom, are wonderful ; and his work of grace is wondrous above all. This specially, and all the rest proportionately, should be spoken of by holy men, by experienced men, and by men who have the ability to speak with power. These things must not be permitted to pass away in silence ; if others do not remember them, representative men like David must make a point of conversing upon them in private, and speaking of them in public. Let it be the delight of each one of us according to our position to speak lovingly of our Lord.

6. "*And men shall speak of the might of thy terrible acts.*" If unobservant of other matters these acts of judgment shall seize their attention and impress their minds so that they must talk about them. Did not men in our Saviour's day speak of the falling tower of Siloam and the slaughtered Galileans ? Are there not rumours of wars, when there are not even whispers of other things ? Horrible news is sure to spread : under mercies men may be dumb, but concerning miseries they raise a great outcry. The force of dread is a power which loosens the tongue of the multitude : they are sure to talk of that which makes the ear to tingle and the hair to stand upright.

While they are thus occupied with " fearsome facts," such as the drowning of a world, the destruction of the cities of the plain, the plagues of Egypt, the destruction at the Red Sea, and so forth, David would look at these affairs in another light, and sing another tune. "*And I will declare thy greatness.*" Those acts which were terrible deeds to most men were mighty deeds, or *greatnesses* to our holy poet : these he would publish like a herald, who mentions the titles and honours of his royal master. It is the occupation of every true believer to rehearse the great doings of his great God. We are not to leave this to the common converse of the crowd, but we are personally to make a declaration of what we have seen and known. We are even bound in deep solemnity of manner to warn men of the Lord's greatness in his terrible acts of justice : thus will they be admonished to abstain from provoking him. To fulfil this duty we are already bound by solemn obligations, and we shall do well to bind ourselves further by resolutions, " I will—God helping me, I will."

7. "*They shall abundantly utter the memory of thy great goodness.*" They shall pour forth grateful memories even as springs gush with water, plenteously, spontaneously, constantly, joyously. The Lord's redeemed people having been filled with his great goodness, shall retain the happy recollection of it, and shall be moved often and often to utter those recollections. Not content with a scanty mention of such amazing love, they shall go on to an abundant utterance of such abundant favour. It shall be their delight to speak with one another of God's dealings with them, and to compare notes of their experiences. God has done nothing stintedly ; all his goodness is great goodness, all worthy to be remembered, all suggestive of holy discourse. Upon this subject there is no scarcity of matter, and when the heart is right there is no need to stop from want of facts to tell. Oh, that there were more of these memories and utterances, for it is not meet that the goodness of the living God should be buried in the cemetery of silence, in the grave of ingratitude.

"*And shall sing of thy righteousness.*" They shall say and then sing. And what is the theme which impels them to leave the pulpit for the orchestra ? What do they sing of ? They sing of that righteousness which is the sinner's terror, which even good men mention with deep solemnity. Righteousness received by gospel light is in reality the secret foundation of the believer's hope. God's covenant of grace is our strong consolation, because he who made it is righteous, and will not run back from it. Since Jesus died as our substitute, righteousness requires and secures the salvation of all the redeemed. This attribute is our best friend, and therefore we sing of it.

Modern thinkers would fain expunge the idea of righteousness from their notion of God ; but converted men would not. It is a sign of growth in sanctification when we rejoice in the justice, rectitude, and holiness of our God. Even a rebel may rejoice in mercy, which he looks upon as laxity ; but a loyal subject rejoices when he learns that God is so just that not even to save his own elect would he consent to violate the righteousness of his moral government. Few men will shout for joy at the righteousness of Jehovah, but those who do so are his chosen, in whom his soul delighteth.

8 The LORD *is* gracious, and full of compassion ; slow to anger, and of great mercy.

9 The LORD *is* good to all : and his tender mercies *are* over all his works.

10 All thy works shall praise thee, O LORD ; and thy saints shall bless thee.

8. "*The LORD is gracious.*" Was it not in some such terms that the Lord revealed himself to Moses ? Is not this Jehovah's glory ? To all living men this is his aspect : he is gracious, or full of goodness and generosity. He treats his creatures with kindness, his subjects with consideration, and his saints with favour. His words and ways, his promises and his gifts, his plans and his purposes all manifest his grace, or free favour. There is nothing suspicious, prejudiced, morose, tyrannical, or unapproachable in Jehovah,—he is condescending and kind. "*And full of compassion.*" To the suffering, the weak, the foolish, the despondent, he is very pitiful : he feels for them, he feels with them : he does this heartily, and in a practical manner. Of this pitifulness he is full, so that he compassionates freely, constantly, deeply, divinely, and effectually. In God is fulness in a sense not known among men, and this fulness is all fragrant with sympathy for human misery. If the Lord be full of compassion there is no room in him for forgetfulness or harshness, and none should suspect him thereof. What an ocean of compassion there must be since the Infinite God is full of it. "*Slow to anger.*" Even those who refuse his grace yet share in long-suffering. When men do not repent, but, on the contrary, go from bad to worse, he is still averse to let his wrath flame forth against them. Greatly patient and extremely anxious that the sinner may live, he " lets the lifted thunder drop," and still forbears. " Love suffereth long and is kind," and God is love. "*And of great mercy.*" This is his attitude towards the guilty. When men at last repent, they find pardon awaiting them. Great is their sin, and great is God's mercy. They need great help, and they have it though they deserve it not ; for he is greatly good to the greatly guilty.

9. "*The LORD is good to all.*" No one, not even his fiercest enemy, can deny this ; for the falsehood would be too barefaced, since the very existence of the lips which slander him is a proof that it is slander. He allows his enemies to live, he even supplies them with food, and smooths their way with many comforts ; for them the sun shines as brightly as if they were saints, and the rain waters their fields as plentifully as if they were perfect men. Is not this goodness to all ? In our own land the gospel sounds in the ears of all who care to listen ; and the Scriptures are within reach of the poorest child. It would be a wanton wresting of Scripture to limit this expression to the elect, as some have tried to do : we rejoice in electing love, but none the less we welcome the glorious truth, " Jehovah is good to all."

"*And his tender mercies are over all his works.*" Not " his new-covenant works," as one read it the other day who was wise above that which is written, yea, contrary to that which is written. Kindness is a law of God's universe : the world was planned for happiness ; even now that sin has so sadly marred God's handiwork, and introduced elements which were not from the beginning, the Lord has so arranged matters that the fall is broken, the curse is met by an antidote, and the inevitable pain is softened with mitigations. Even in this sin-stricken world, under its disordered economy, there are abundant traces of a hand skilful to soothe distress and heal disease. That which makes life bearable is the tenderness of the great Father. This is seen in the creation of an insect as well as in the ruling of nations. The Creator is never rough, the Provider is never forgetful, the Ruler is never cruel. Nothing is done to create disease, no organs are arranged to promote misery ; the incoming of sickness and pain is not according to the original design, but a result of our disordered state. Man's body as it left the Maker's hand was neither framed for disease, decay, nor death, neither was the purpose of it discomfort and anguish ; far otherwise, it was framed for a joyful activity, and a peaceful enjoyment of God. Jehovah has in great consideration laid up in the world cures for our ailments, and helps for our feebleness, and if many of these have been long in their discovery, it is because it was more for man's benefit to find them out himself, than to have them labelled and placed in order before his eyes. We may be sure of this, that Jehovah has never taken delight in the ills of his creatures, but has sought their good, and laid himself out to alleviate the distresses into which they have guiltily plunged themselves.

The duty of kindness to animals may logically be argued from this verse. Should not the children of God be like their Father in kindness ?

10. "*All thy works shall praise thee, O LORD.*" There is a something about every creature which redounds to the honour of God. The skill, kindness, and power manifested in the formation of each living thing is in itself to the praise of God, and when observed by an intelligent mind the Lord is honoured thereby. Some works praise him by their being, and others by their well-being ; some by their mere existence, and others by their hearty volition. "*And thy saints shall bless thee.*" These holy ones come nearer, and render sweeter adoration. Men have been known to praise those whom they hated, as we may admire the prowess of a warrior who is our foe ; but saints lovingly praise, and therefore are said to " bless." They wish well to God ; they would make him more blessed, if such a thing were possible ; they desire blessings upon his cause and his children, and invoke success upon his work and warfare. None but blessed men will bless the Lord. Only saints or holy ones will bless the thrice holy God. If we praise Jehovah because of his works around us, we must go on to bless him for his works within us. Let the two " shalls " of this verse be fulfilled, especially the latter one.

11 They shall speak of the glory of thy kingdom, and talk of thy power ;

12 To make known to the sons of men his mighty acts, and the glorious majesty of his kingdom.

13 Thy kingdom *is* an everlasting kingdom, and thy dominion *endureth* throughout all generations.

11. "*They shall speak of the glory of thy kingdom.*" Excellent themes for saintly minds. Those who bless God from their hearts rejoice to see him enthroned, glorified, and magnified in power. No subject is more profitable for humility obedience, hope, and joy than that of the reigning power of the Lord our God. His works praise him, but they cannot crown him : this remains for holy hands and hearts. It is their high pleasure to tell of the glory of his kingdom in its justice, kindness, eternity, and so forth. Kingdoms of earth are glorious for riches, for extent of territory, for victories, for liberty, for commerce, and other matters ; but in all true glories the kingdom of Jehovah excels them. We have seen a palace dedicated " to all the glories of France " ; but time, eternity, and all space are filled with the glories of God : on these we love to speak. "*And talk of thy power.*" This power supports the kingdom and displays the glory, and we are sure to talk of it when the glory of the divine kingdom is under discussion. God's power to create or to destroy, to bless or to punish, to strengthen or to crush, is matter for frequent rehearsal. All power comes from God. Apart from him the laws of nature would be inoperative. His power is the one source of force—mechanical, vital, mental, spiritual. Beyond the power of God which has been put forth, infinite force lies latent in himself. Who can calculate the reserve forces of the Infinite ? How, then, can his kingdom fail ? We hear talk of the five great powers, but what are they to the One Great Power ? The Lord is " the blessed and only Potentate." Let us accustom ourselves to think more deeply and speak more largely of th' power which ever makes for righteousness and works for mercy.

12. "*To make known to the sons of men his mighty acts.*" These glorious deeds ought to be known to all mankind ; but yet few reckon such knowledge to be an essential part of education. As the State cannot teach these holy histories the people of God must take care to do it themselves. The work must be done for every age, for men have short memories in reference to their God, and the doings of his power. They inscribe the deeds of their heroes upon brass, but the glorious acts of Jehovah are written upon the sand, and the tide of time washes them from present memory ; therefore we must repeat the lesson, and yet again repeat it. The saints are the religious instructors of the race ; they ought to be not only the historians of the past, but the bards of the present, whose duty it is to keep the sons of men in memory of the great deeds which the Lord did in the days of their fathers

and in the old time before them. Note the contrast between the great deeds of God and the puny sons of Adam, who have even degenerated from their father, though he was as nothing compared with his Maker.

"*And the glorious majesty of his kingdom.*" What a grand subject! Yet this we are to make known ; the publication of it is left to us who bless the Lord. " The glory of the majesty of his reign." What a theme! Jehovah's reign as sovereign Lord of all, his majesty in that dominion, and the glory of that majesty! The threefold subject baffles the most willing mind. How shall we make this known to the sons of men ? Let us first labour to know it ourselves, and then let us make it a frequent subject of discourse, so shall men know it from us, the Holy Spirit attending our word.

13. "*Thy kingdom is an everlasting kingdom.*" His meditation has brought him near to God, and God near to him : he speaks to him in adoration, changing the pronoun from " his " to " thy." He sees the great King, and prostrates himself before him. It is well when our devotion opens the gate of heaven, and enters within the portal to speak with God face to face, as a man speaketh with his friend. The point upon which the Psalmist's mind rests is the eternity of the divine throne, —" thy reign is a reign of all eternities." The Lord's kingdom is without beginning, without break, without bound, and without end. He never abdicates his throne, neither does he call in a second to share his empire. None can overthrow his power, or break away from his rule. Neither this age, nor the age to come, nor ages of ages shall cause his sovereignty to fail. Herein is rest for faith. " The Lord sitteth King for ever." "*And thy dominion endureth throughout all generations.*" Men come and go like shadows on the wall, but God reigneth eternally. We distinguish kings as they succeed each other by calling them first and second ; but this King is Jehovah, the First and the Last. Adam in his generation knew his Creator to be King, and the last of his race shall know the same. All hail, Great God! Thou art ever Lord of lords!

These three verses are a reverent hymn concerning " the kingdom of God " : they will be best appreciated by those who are in that kingdom in the fullest sense, and are most truly loyal to the Lord. It is, according to these verses, a kingdom of glory and power ; a kingdom of light which men are to know, and of might which men are to feel ; it is full of majesty and eternity ; it is the benediction of every generation. We are to speak of it, talk of it, and make it known, and then we are to acknowledge it in the homage directed distinctly to the Lord himself—as in verse thirteen.

14 The LORD upholdeth all that fall, and raiseth up all *those that be* bowed down.

15 The eyes of all wait upon thee ; and thou givest them their meat in due season.

16 Thou openest thine hand, and satisfiest the desire of every living thing.

In these three verses Jehovah is adored for his gracious providence towards men and all other creatures ; this fitly follows the proclamation of his royalty, for we here see how he rules his kingdom, and provides for his subjects.

14. "*The LORD upholdeth all that fall.*" Read this verse in connection with the preceding and admire the unexpected contrast : he who reigns in glorious majesty, yet condescends to lift up and hold up those who are apt to fall. The form of the verb shows that he is always doing this ; he is Jehovah upholding. His choice of the fallen, and the falling, as the subjects of his gracious help is specially to be noted. The fallen of our race, especially fallen women, are shunned by us, and it is peculiar tenderness on the Lord's part that such he looks upon, even those who are at once the chief of sinners and the least regarded of mankind. The falling ones among us are too apt to be pushed down by the strong : their timidity and dependence make them the victims of the proud and domineering. To them also the Lord gives his upholding help. The Lord loves to reverse things,—he puts down the lofty, and lifts up the lowly.

"*And raiseth up all those that be bowed down.*" Another deed of condescension. Many are despondent, and cannot lift up their heads in courage, or their hearts with comfort ; but these he cheers. Some are bent with their daily load, and these he strengthens. Jesus loosed a daughter of Abraham whom Satan had so bound that she was bowed down, and could by no means lift up herself. In this he proved himself to be the true Son of the Highest. Think of the Infinite bowing to lift up the bowed, and stooping to be leaned upon by those who are ready to fall. The two "alls" should not be overlooked: the Lord has a kindly heart towards the whole company of the afflicted.

15. *"The eyes of all wait upon thee."* They have learned to look to thee: it has become their nature to turn to thee for all they want. As children look to a father for all they need, so do the creatures look to God, the all-sufficient Provider. It were well if all men had the eye of faith, and if all waited therewith upon the Lord. *"And thou givest them their meat in due season."* They wait, and God gives. The thought of this brings God so near to our poet-prophet that he is again speaking with God after the style of thee and thou. Is it to be wondered at when the Lord is feeding the hungry all around us,—giving food to all creatures, and to ourselves among them? Like a flock of sheep the creatures stand around the Lord as their great Shepherd; all eyes are to his hand expecting to receive their food; nor are they disappointed, for when the hour comes suitable provender is ready for each creature. Observe the punctuality of the Lord in giving food at meal-time,—in the season when it is due. This he does for all, and each living thing has its own season, so that the Lord of heaven is feeding his great flock both by day and by night, during every moment of time.

16. *"Thou openest thine hand, and satisfiest the desire of every living thing."* Thou alone providest, O Jehovah! Thou doest it liberally, with open hand; thou doest it easily, as if it were only to open thine hand; thou doest this at once as promptly as if all supplies were ready to hand. Living things have needs, and these create desires; the living God has suitable supplies at hand, and these he gives till inward satisfaction is produced, and the creature sighs no longer. In spiritual things, when God has raised a desire, he always gratifies it; hence the longing is prophetic of the blessing. In no case is the desire of the living thing excited to produce distress, but in order that it may seek and find satisfaction.

These verses refer to natural providence; but they may equally well apply to the stores of grace, since the same God is king in both spheres. If we will but wait upon the Lord for pardon, renewing, or whatever else we need, we shall not wait in vain. The hand of grace is never closed while the sinner lives.

17 The LORD *is* righteous in all his ways, and holy in all his works.

18 The LORD *is* nigh unto all them that call upon him, to all that call upon him in truth.

19 He will fulfil the desire of them that fear him: he also will hear their cry, and will save them.

20 The LORD preserveth all them that love him: but all the wicked will he destroy.

21 My mouth shall speak the praise of the LORD: and let all flesh bless his holy name for ever and ever.

In these verses we behold our God in the realm of his free grace dealing well with his believing people.

17. *"The LORD is righteous in all his ways, and holy in all his works."* His ways and works are both worthy to be praised. Jehovah cannot be unjust or impure. Let his doings be what they may, they are in every case righteous and holy. This is the confession of the godly who follow his ways, and of the gracious who study his works. Whatever God is or does must be right. In the salvation of his people he is as righteous and holy as in any other of his ways and works: he has not manifested mercy at the expense of justice, but the rather he has magnified his righteousness by the death of his Son.

18. *"The LORD is nigh unto all them that call upon him."* Not only near by his omnipresence, but to sympathize and favour. He does not leave praying men, and men who confess his name, to battle with the world alone, but he is ever at their side. This favour is not for a few of those who invoke him; but for each one of the pious company. "All" who place themselves beneath the shield of his glorious name by calling themselves by it, and by calling upon it in supplication, shall find him to be a very present help in trouble. *"To all that call upon him in truth:"* for there are many whose formal prayers and false professions will never bring them into communion with the Lord. To pray in truth, we must have a true

heart, and the truth in our heart ; and then we must be humble, for pride is a falsehood ; and be earnest, or else prayer is a lie. A God of truth cannot be nigh to the spirit of hypocrisy ; this he knows and hates ; neither can he be far removed from a sincere spirit, since it is his work, and he forsakes not the work of his own hands.

19. *"He will fulfil the desire of them that fear him :"* that is, those who reverence his name and his law. Inasmuch as they have respect unto his will, he will have respect unto their will. They shall have their way for they have his way in their hearts. A holy heart only desires what a holy God can give, and so its desire is filled full out of the fulness of the Lord. *"He also will hear their cry, and will save them."* Divinely practical shall his nearness be, for he will work their deliverance. He will listen to their piteous cry, and then will send salvation from every ill. This he will do himself personally ; he will not trust them to angels or saints.

20. *"The LORD preserveth all them that love him."* They keep him in their love, and he keeps them by his love. See how these favoured ones have advanced from fearing the Lord and crying to him, even to loving him, and in that love they are secure from all danger. Mark the number of " alls " in these later verses of the Psalm. In each of these God is all in all. *"But all the wicked will he destroy."* Wickedness is an offence to all holy beings, and therefore those who are determined to continue in it must be weeded out. As good sanitary laws remove all creators of pest and plague, so does the moral government of God mark every evil thing for destruction ; it cannot be tolerated in the presence of a perfectly holy God. What ruins wicked men frequently become in this life ! What monuments of wrath will they be in the world to come ! Like Nineveh and Babylon, and other destroyed places, they shall only exist to declare how thoroughly God fulfils his threatenings.

21. *"My mouth shall speak the praise of the LORD."* Whatever others may do, I will not be silent in the praise of the Lord : whatever others may speak upon, my topic is fixed once for all : I will speak the praise of Jehovah. I am doing it, and I will do it as long as I breathe. *"And let all flesh bless his holy name for ever and ever."* Praise is no monopoly for one, even though he be a David ; others are debtors, let them also be songsters. All men of every race, condition, or generation should unite to glorify God. No man need think that he will be rejected when he comes with his personal note of praise ; all are permitted, invited, and exhorted to magnify the Lord. Specially should his holiness be adored : this is the crown, and in a certain sense the sum, of all his attributes. Only holy hearts will praise the holy name, or character of the Lord ; oh, that all flesh were sanctified, then would the sancity of God be the delight of all. Once let the song begin and there will be no end to it. It shall go on for ever and a day, as the old folks used to say. If there were two for-evers, or twenty for-evers, they ought all to be spent in the praises of the ever-living, ever-blessing, ever-blessed JEHOVAH. Blessed be the Lord for ever for having revealed to us his name, and blessed be that name as he has revealed it ; yea, blessed be he above all that we can know, or think, or say. Our hearts revel in the delight of praising him. Our mouth, our mind, our lip, our life shall be our Lord's throughout this mortal existence, and when time shall be no more.

EXPLANATORY NOTES AND QUAINT SAYINGS.

This has been happily characterized as the " new song " promised in Ps. cxliv. 9. In other words, it is the song of praise, corresponding to the didactic, penitential, and supplicatory Psalms of this series.—*Joseph Addison Alexander.*

The ancient Hebrews declare him happy whoever, in after times, utters this Psalm thrice each day with the mouth, heart, and tongue.—*Victorinus Bythner,*—1670.

The last six or seven Psalms are the Beulah of the book, where the sun shineth night and day, and the voice of the turtle is heard in the land. Coming at the close after all the mournful, plaintive, penitential, prayerful, varying notes, they unconsciously typify the joy and rest of glory.—*George Gilfillan.*

Title.—The Praise of David. Psalms are the praises of God accompanied with song ; Psalms are songs containing the praise of God. If there be praise, but not of God, it is not a Psalm. If there be praise, and praise of God, if it is not sung, it is not a Psalm. To make a Psalm there go these three—praise, God's praise, and song.—*Augustine.*

Title.—It is observable concerning David's entitling the Psalm *"The Praise of David,"* that in the original no Psalm else beareth such a title. It is appropriated to it, because this wholly consists of praise ; he was elevated therein to a frame of spirit made up of the pure praise of God, without any touch of what was particular to himself. It was not thanks, but altogether praise, and wholly praise.—*Thomas Goodwin.*

Title.—This Psalm, which is designated a *Tehillah,* or a Psalm of *praise,*— a name which has passed from this Psalm to the whole Psalter, which is commonly called *Sepher Tehillim,* or *"Book of Praises,"*—is the last of the Psalms ascribed to David.

It is remarkable, that although that is the name given to the Psalter (which is entitled in Hebrew *Sepher Tehillim,* or *Book of Praises*), this is the only Psalm in the whole number which is designated in the title as a *Tehillah*—a word derived from the same root as *Hallelujah.* It seems as if this name *Tehillah* had been studiously reserved for the *last* of David's Psalms, in order to mark more emphatically that all his utterances are consummated in *praise.* And this view is more clearly manifested by the circumstance that the word *Tehillah* is introduced into the *last* verse of this Psalm, " My soul shall speak the *praise"* (*tehillah*) " of the Lord," (observe this preparation for Hallelujah, *Praise ye* the Lord) ; " and let all flesh bless his holy name for ever and ever." As much as to say, that though David's voice was now about to be hushed in this life, yet it would never be silent in the world to come, and would ever " praise the Lord " ; and as much, also, as to say that his last exhortation should be to all nations to praise him, " Let all flesh bless his holy name for ever and ever."—*Christopher Wordsworth.*

Title.—This Psalm is entitled *"David's praise."* For howsoever the prayers and the praises (all) in this book, are (for the most part) of David's penning : yet two there are he hath singled out from the rest, and set his own mark on them as proper to himself : the lxxxvi. Psalm, his *Tephilla, David's* own *Prayer ;* and there is here his *Tehilla,* his own *Praise* or thanksgiving. As if he had made the rest for all in common, but reserved these peculiarly for himself.—*Lancelot Andrewes.*

Whole Psalm.—In regard to its alphabetic structure, it has one peculiarity, *viz.,* the *nun* is omitted ; the reason of which may be, that (as we have seen in some others Psalms of this structure) by means of that or some other such omission, we might be kept from putting stress on the mere form of the composition.—*Andrew A. Bonar.*

Whole Psalm.—Cassiodorus quaintly remarks that the Psalms in which the alphabetital order is complete, are especially fitted for the righteous in the Church Triumphant, but those in which one letter is missing, are for the Church Militant here on earth, as still imperfect, and needing to be purified from defect.—*Neale and Littledale.*

Verse 1.—"I will extol thee, my God, O King." To extol is to set pre-eminently on high ; to exalt above all others ; it is the expression of the greatest possible admiration ; it is letting others know our high opinion of a person, and endeavouring to win them over to it. The man who has such a high opinion of another as to induce him to extol him, will not be likely to rest without bringing forth into prominent observation the object of his praise.—*Philip Bennett Power.*

Verse 1.—"O King"; or *the King,* by way of eminency ; the King of kings, the God by whom kings reign, and to whom I and all other kings owe subjection and obedience.—*Matthew Pool.*

Verse 1.—"O king." The Psalmist in rapt ecstasy seems as though he saw God incarnate in Christ present to inspire his praise. Christ is our God and King, to be extolled in the heart, with the mouth, and by the life.—*Thomas Le Blanc.*

Verse 1.—"King." God is King in verity ; others are called kings in vanity.— *Martin Geier.*

Verse 1.—"I will bless thy name for ever and ever." The name of God in Scripture is taken, first, for *God himself.* The name of a thing is put for the thing named, Ps. xliv. 5 : " Through thee will we push down our enemies : through thy name will we tread them under that rise up against us." " Through thy *name*," that is, through *thee.* Secondly, the name of God is often in Scripture put for *the attributes of God.* Thirdly, the name of God is put for *his ordinances or worship.* " Go ye now unto my place which was in Shiloh, where I set my name at the first " (Jer. vii. 12), that is, where I first set up my public worship ; because, as a man is known by his proper name, so is God by his proper worship. Fourthly, the name of God is *that reverence, esteem and honour which angels and men give unto God.* As we know amongst us, the report and reputation that a man hath among men is a man's name ; what men speak of him, that is his name ; such an one hath a good name, we say ; such an one hath an ill name, that is, men speak or think well or ill of such persons. So Gen. vi. 4. When Moses describes the giants, he saith, " They, were men of renown "; the Hebrew is, " They were men of *name*," because the name of a man is the character he hath amongst men ; as a man is esteemed, so his name is carried, and himself is accepted in the world. So the name of God is that high esteem, those honourable apprehensions, which angels and men have of God ; such as the thoughts and speeches of men are for the celebration of God's glory and praise, such is his name in the world.—*Joseph Caryl.*

Verse 1.—*"For ever and ever."* עוֹלָם וָעֶד, *leolam vaed, for ever and onward,* in this and the coming world. Expressions of this sort are very difficult to be translated, but they are, on the whole, well interpreted by those words of Mr. Addison :—

> " Through all eternity to thee,
> A joyful song I'll raise ;
> But oh, eternity's too short
> To utter all thy praise ! "

Adam Clarke.

Verse 1.—*"For ever and ever."* Praise is the only part of duty in which we at present engage, which is lasting. We pray, but there shall be a time when prayer shall offer its last litany ; we believe, but there shall be a time when faith shall be lost in sight ; we hope, and hope maketh not ashamed, but there shall be a time when hope lies down and dies, lost in the splendour of the fruition that God shall reveal. But praise goes singing into heaven, and is ready without a teacher to strike the harp that is waiting for it, to transmit along the echoes of eternity the song of the Lamb. In the party-coloured world in which we live, there are days of various sorts and experiences, making up the aggregate of the Christian's life. There are waiting days, in which, because Providence fences us round, and it seems as if we cannot march, we cannot move, as though we must just wait to see what the Lord is about to do in us and for us ; and there are watching days, when it behoves us never to slumber, but to be always ready for the attacks of our spiritual enemy ; and there are warring days, when with nodding plume, and with ample armour, we must go forth to do battle for the truth ; and there are weeping days, when it seems as if the fountains of the great deep within us were broken up ; and as though, through much tribulation, we had to pass to heaven in tears. But these days shall all pass away by-and-by—waiting days all be passed, warring days all be passed, watching days all be passed ; but

> " Our days of praise shall ne'er be past
> While life, and thought, and being last,
> And immortality endures."

William Morley Punshon, 1824—1881.

Verse 1.—*"For ever and ever."* To praise God now does not satisfy devout aspiration, for in this age the worshipper's devotion is interrupted by sin, fear, sickness, etc. ; but in eternity praise will proceed in unbroken procession.—*John Lorinus.*

Verses 1, 2.—*"I will bless thee for ever and ever,"* and again, verse 2. This intimates, 1. That he resolved to continue in this work *to the end of his life,* throughout his " for ever " in this world. 2. That the Psalms he penned should be made use of in praising God by the church *to the end of time.* 2 Chron. xxix. 30. 3. That he hoped to be praising God *to all eternity* in the other world : they that make it their constant work on earth, shall have it their everlasting bliss in heaven.— *Matthew Henry.*

Verse 2.—*"Every day."* Then God is to be blessed and praised in dark as well as bright days.—*Johannes Paulus Palanterius,* 1600.

Verse 2.—*"Every day (in the week) will I bless thee,"* the Psalmist seems to signify. As there are " seven spirits " peculiarly existing in nearness to God, David holds the seven days of the week like seven stars in his hand, or like a seven-branched candlestick of gold, burning every day with his devotion. He calls the seven days to be as seven angels with trumpets.—*Thomas Le Blanc.*

Verse 2.—*"I will bless thee : I will praise thy name."* The repetition intimates the fervency of his affection to this work, the fixedness of his purpose to abound in it, and the frequency of his performances therein.—*Matthew Henry.*

Verse 2.—*"Praise."* If we are to define it in words, we may say that *praise* is thankful, lowly, loving worship of the goodness and majesty of God. And therefore we often find the word " praise " joined with " blessing " and " thanksgiving": but though all three are akin to each other, they are not all alike. They are steps in a gradual scale—a song of degrees. Thanksgiving runs up into blessing, and blessing ascends into praise ; for praise comprehends both, and is the highest and most perfect work of all living spirits.—*Henry Edward Manning,* 1850.

Verse 3.—*"Great is the Lord."* If *"great"* here be referred to God as a king, then a *great* king he is in respect of the breadth of his empire, for all creatures, from the highest angel to the poorest worm, are under him. " Great " for length ; for " his kingdom is an everlasting kingdom." " Great " for depth ; for he rules even in the hearts of kings, of all men, overrules their thoughts, affections, nothing is hid from him. And " great " again for height ; being " a great King above all gods," ruling by his own absolute power and authority ; whereas all other kings have their sword from him, and rule by a delegated and vicarious power.—*William Nicholson.*

Verse 3.—*"His greatness is unsearchable."* God is so great, that till Christ revealed the Father, Deity was lost in its own infinity to the perception of men. He who attempts to navigate an infinite ocean must come back to his starting point, never being able to cross. So the ancient philosophers, disputing as to the Divine Nature, were baffled by their own ingenuity, they had to confess that they comprehended nothing of God except that he was incomprehensible. Without Christ, men can only find out about God that they can never find him.—*Thomas Le Blanc.*

Verse 3 (last clause).—The Vulgate renders thus, " Of his greatness no *end*." The Hebrew is, " Of his greatness no investigation." As the classic Greeks would say, ἀνεξιχνίαστος, *not to be traced out.*—*Simon de Muis,* 1587—1644.

Verse 3.—God had searched David through and through (Ps. cxxxix. 1), but David proved he could not search God's greatness.—*Martin Geier.*

Verses 3—6.—Verses 3 and 4 contain the material of praise, and verses 5 and 6 the praise itself. Verse 3 states a proposition, and verse 4 gives the amplification. —*Hermann Venema.*

Verse 4.—*"One generation shall praise thy works to another,"* etc. Deut. iv. 9, and vi. 7. Fathers teaching their sons the goodness and glory of God. This was a legal ordinance. The church and its worshippers are *collecting praises* of successive generations for the final Hallelujah celebration.—*Martin Geier.*

Verse 4.—*"One generation shall praise thy works to another."* Singular is exchanged for plural in the Hebrew, " One generation shall praise (sing) thy works to another, and shall declare (plural) thy mighty acts." Here is melody first, the antiphony of the choirs responding to each other ; then harmony ; all generations will burst into chorus together.—*Hermann Venema.*

Verse 4.—*"One generation to another."* The *tradition* of praise ! Each generation catches the strains from the last, echoes it, and passes it along to the next. One generation declares what it has seen, and passes on the praise to the generation which has not seen as yet the wonders celebrated.—*Simon de Muis.*

Verse 4.—*"One generation shall praise thy works to another,"* etc. Thus God provides for his Church. When Elijah is carried into heaven, Elisha must follow in the power and spirit of Elias. When one stream is slid and shed into the ocean, another circulates from the same ocean through the bowels of the earth into the springs under the mountains, and refreshes the scorched plains. When one star sets, another rises to guide the wandering traveller, and at length the bright morning lamp glitters in the east, and then the glorious Sun of Righteousness. While the Church sits fainting under a juniper-tree in the wilderness, there shall fly prophets to feed her till the blessed resurrection of the witnesses. It's our high duty to study present work, and prize present help, and greatly rejoice when the Lord sends forth, as once he did, both Boanerges and Barnabas together. Pray for the mantle, girdle, and blessing of Elijah, for the love of John, and the zeal of Paul, to twine hands together to draw souls to heaven ; till the Beloved comes like a roe or a young hart upon the mountains of spices ; till the shadows flee away ; till the day dawn, and the Day-star arise in your hearts.—*Samuel Lee, in his Preface to Row's "Emmanuel,"* 1679.

Verse 4.—*"One generation shall praise thy works to another."* There is no phenomenon of human life more solemn than its succession of generations. " One generation passeth away, another generation cometh." And, as if to put this in a light as affecting and indelible as possible, the Psalmist immediately adds, " but the earth abideth for ever." A thought that gleams like a lightning flash across this panorama of life, burning it into the beholder's brain for ever. Even the rude, gross, material earth, which we were created to subdue, and upon which we so proudly tread, is represented as having to the palpable sense this advantage over us. The abiding earth constitutes a little eternity, compared with the duration of its changing inhabitants. We come into it, and pass over it, obliterating, perhaps, some footprints in its dust by the impress of our own, to be in their turn effaced, and then leave it with amazing rapidity, as a hireling man accomplishes his days.—*Henry Allon*, 1852.

Verse 5.—*"I will speak of the glorious honour,"* etc. The word which we here translate *"speak,"* is considered by Hebrew critics to include also the idea of " expatiating," " speaking at large"; not merely " alluding to incidentally," but " entering into particulars " ; as though one took delight in speaking upon the matter in hand. Now there is something very satisfactory in entering into particulars ; we can often gather light upon a great truth by having had set before us some of the particulars connected with it ; we can often understand what is too high for us, *in* itself and *by* itself, by some examples which bring it within reach of our dull understandings. We are like men who want to attain a height, who have not wings to fly up to it, but who can reach it by going up a ladder step by step. Particulars are often like the rounds of a ladder, little, it may be, in themselves, but very helpful to us ; and to dwell upon particulars is often of use to ourselves ; it certainly is to many with whom we converse.

Let us remember, that circumstanced as we are in our present state, we have no faculties for grasping in its simple grandeur the glorious honour of the majesty of God. We know most of God from what we know of his doings amongst the children of men. Hereafter, the Lord's people shall, no doubt, have much revealed to them of the glorious honour of the majesty of God, which they could now neither bear nor understand ; meanwhile they have to know him chiefly by what he has said and done ; and if only our eyes be open, we shall be at no loss to recognise in these the glorious honour of his majesty.—*Philip Bennett Power.*

Verse 5.—*"I will speak,"* etc. " I will *muse* " is better than " speak," as being the primary and more usual sense of the Hebrew word. It suggests that these glorious qualities of God's character and deeds should be not merely talked about and extolled in song, but be deeply pondered, laid close upon our very heart, so that the legitimate impression may be wrought into our very soul, and may mould our whole spirit and character into God's own moral image.—*Henry Cowles.*

Verse 5.—With what a cumulus of glowing terms does Holy Writ seek to display the excellence of Deity ! By these descriptions, those attributes which are feebly imitated or reflected in what we call *good* among created things are declared to exist in God, infinitely, immutably, ineffably.—*Martin Geier.*

Verse 5.—*"Thy wonderful works."*—Heb. : " *the words of thy wonderful works."* Thus the Psalmist declares that the records left of God's olden doings in the history of Israel are very precious. He has heard them. Moses and Aaron and others spoke them. He delights in them ; he will sing them again on his own harp.—*Hermann Venema.*

Verses 5 and 6.—Verse 5 speaks of God's *opera mirabilia ;* verse 6 of his *opera terribilia.* The former delight his saints ; the latter terrify the wicked.—*John Lorinus.*

Verse 6.—"*And men shall speak of the might of thy terrible acts.*" When men do not mark his works of mercy and bounty, the Lord will show unto them works of justice, that is, terrible works, and give them matter of talking upon this account. —*David Dickson.*

Verse 6 (*last clause*).—To "*declare*" here means either in speech or song ; not merely to *predicate* as a fact, but to *proclaim* in praise. The Hebrew word has this width of meaning ; not merely to declare in cold utterance, concerning mere history.—*Hermann Venema.*

Verse 6.—"*Thy greatness.*" All men are enamoured of greatness. Then they must seek it *in* God, and get it *from* God. David did both. All history shows the creature aspiring after this glory. Ahasuerus, Astyages, Cyrus, Cambyses, Nebuchadnezzar, were all called *the great.* Alexander the Great, when he came to the Ganges, ordered his statue to be made of more than life size, that posterity might believe him to have been of nobler stature. In Christ alone does man attain the greatness his heart yearns for—the glory of perfect goodness.—*Thomas Le Blanc.*

Verse 6.—"*Thy greatness.*" Or, according to the written text, *greatnesses.* So Aquila and Jerome. The parallelism is decidedly in favour of the plural.— *A. S. Aglen.*

Verse 7.—There is an extensive and an intensive greatness, and both must be found in our praises of God. First, an extensive greatness in regard of their number ; we must be frequent and plentiful in the duty : we must "*Abundantly utter the memory of God's great goodness.*" Secondly, there must be an intensive greatness in our praises, in regard of the degree, fervour and heat of them. They must be high, and vehement, fervent, flaming, zealous and affectionate, full of life and vigour ; our spirits must be raised, our hearts and tongues enlarged in the performance of this duty. God's glorious name, as it is in Nehem. ix. 5, " is exalted above all blessing and praise," above our devoutest and most zealous praises ; and therefore surely faint, heartless, and lifeless praises are so far from reaching him, as that they may seem to be meant of another, and a lower object. God then is not praised at all if he be not greatly praised. Weak and dull praises are dispraises ; for a person or thing is not honoured or praised, unless there be some proportion between the honour and praise and the worthiness of the person or thing honoured and praised.—*Henry Jeanes, in "The Works of Heaven upon Earth,"* 1649.

Verse 7.—"*Abundantly utter.*" The word contains the idea of boiling or bubbling-up like a fountain. It signifies, a holy fluency about the mercy of God. We have quite enough fluent people about, but they are many of them idlers for whom Satan finds abundant work to do. The Lord deliver us from the noise of fluent women ; but it matters not how fluent men and women are if they will be fluent on the topic now before us. Open your mouths ; let the praise pour forth let it come, rivers of it. Stream away ! Gush away, all that you possibly can. "*They shall abundantly utter the memory of thy great goodness.*" Do not stop the joyful speakers, let them go on for ever. They do not exaggerate, they cannot. You say they are enthusiastic, but they are not half up to the pitch yet ; bid them become more excited and speak yet more fervently. Go on, brother, go on ; pile it up ; say something greater, grander, and more fiery still ! You cannot exceed the truth. You have come to a theme where your most fluent powers will fail in utterance. The text calls for a sacred fluency, and I would exhort you liberally to exercise it when you are speaking on the goodness of God.—*C. H. S.*

Verse 7.—Too many witnesses of God's goodness are silent witnesses. Men do not enough speak out the testimonies that they might bear in this matter. The reason that I love the Methodists—good ones—is, that they have a tongue to their piety. They fulfil the command of God,—to be fervent in spirit.—*Henry Ward Beecher.*

Verse 7.—

> The thought of our past years in me doth breed
> Perpetual benedictions.
>
> *William Wordsworth,* 1770—1805.

Verse 7.—"*They shall sing of thy righteousness,*" or *justice.* To sing of goodness, mercy, forgiveness, is natural ; but a *song of justice* is singular. Here is the beauty of David's praise, that he sees subject of delight as much in the righteousness of God as in his mercy.—*John Lorinus.*

Verse 7.—*"They shall sing of thy righteousness."* The righteousness of God, whereby he justifieth sinners, and sanctifieth the justified, and execu eth judgment for his reconciled people, is the sweetest object of the church's joy.—*David Dickson.*

Verse 7.—*"Thy righteousness"* (read in connection with next verse). It is an easy thing to conceive the glory of the Creator, manifested in the good of an innocent creature ; but the glory of the righteous Judge, manifested in the good of the guilty criminal, is the peculiar, mysterious wisdom of the Cross. It is easy to perceive God's righteousness declared in the punishment of sins ; the Cross alone declares " His righteousness for the remission of sins." It magnifies justice in the way of pardoning sin, and mercy in the way of punishing it.—*John M'Laurin,* 1693—1754.

Verse 8.—*"The LORD is gracious,"* etc. The proclamation of the Lord to Moses (Exod. xxxiv. 6) is the fountain-head of these epithets.—*James G. Murphy.*

Verse 8.—In God there is no passion, only compassion.—*Richard Rothe,* 1799—1867.

Verse 8.—*"Of great mercy."* Mercy hath misery for its object, and is that attribute towards which the eyes of a fallen world must necessarily be turned. The Psalmist hath, accordingly, introduced her last with great pomp and splendour, seated in her triumphal chariot, and invested with a supremacy over all the works of God. She is above the heavens, and over all the earth, so that the whole creation findeth that refuge under the shadow of her wings of which, by reason of man's transgression, it standeth in need.—*Samuel Burder.*

Verse 9.—*"The LORD is good to all,"* etc. According to the doctrine of Christianity, we are not the creatures of a God who takes no care of his beings, and leaves them to themselves ; not the offspring of a father who disowns his children, who does not concern himself about them, and is indifferent to their happiness and their misery. No ; never has God, according to that comfortable doctrine, left himself unwitnessed to man ; never withdrawn from him his fatherly providence and love ; never abandoned the fortunes of his feeble, helpless, untutored children, to blind chance or to their own ignorance. No; from their first progenitor, to his latest posterity, he has himself provided for their support, their instruction, their guidance, their progress to higher attainments. He has constantly revealed himself to them in various ways; constantly shed innumerable benefits on them; sometimes lovingly correcting, and sometimes bountifully blessing them ; has constantly been nigh to them, and has left them in want of no means for becoming wiser and better.—*George Joachim Zollikofer,* 1730—1788.

Verse 9.—*"The LORD is good to all,"* etc. God's pity is not as some sweet cordial, poured in dainty drops from a golden phial. It is not like the musical water-drops of some slender rill, murmuring down the dark side of Mount Sinai. It is wide as the whole scope of heaven. It is abundant as all the air. If one had art to gather up all the golden sunlight that to-day falls wide over the continent, falling through every silent hour ; and all that is dispersed over the whole ocean, floating from every wave ; and all that is poured refulgent over the northern wastes of ice, and along the whole continent of Europe, and the vast outlying Asia and torrid Africa—if we could in any wise gather up this immense and incalculable outflow and treasure that falls down through the bright hours, and runs in liquid ether about the mountains, and fills all the plains, and sends innumerable rays through every secret place, pouring over and filling every flower, shining down the sides of every blade of grass, resting in glorious humility upon the humblest things—on sticks, and stones, and pebbles—on the spider's web, the sparrow's nest, the threshold of the young foxes' hole, where they play and warm themselves—that rests on the prisoner's window, that strikes radiant beams through the slave's tear, and puts gold upon the widow's weeds, that plates and roofs the city with burnished gold, and goes on in its wild abundance up and down the earth, shining everywhere and always, since the day of primal creation, without faltering, without stint, without waste or diminution ; as full, as fresh, as overflowing to-day as if it were the very first day of its outlay—if one might gather up this boundless, endless, infinite treasure, to measure it, then might he tell the height, and depth, and unending glory of the pity of God ! That light, and the sun, its source, are God's own figure of the immensity and copiousness of his mercy and compassion.—*Henry Ward Beecher,* 1873.

Verse 9.—Even the worst taste of God's mercy ; such as fight against God's mercy taste of it ; the wicked have some crumbs from mercy's table. *"The Lord is good to all."* Sweet dewdrops are on the thistle as well as on the rose. The diocese where mercy visits is very large. Pharaoh's head was crowned though his heart was hardened.—*Thomas Watson.*

Verse 9.—*"His tender Mercies are over all his works."* When the sensible sinner is seeking faith of God, he may plead the *largeness* of mercy. God's mercy is like the firmament spread over all this lower world ; and every infirm creature partakes more or less of its influence, according to its exigence and capacity. True, may he say, I have made myself, by sin, the vilest of all creatures ; I am become worse than the beasts that perish ; as vile as a worm, as loathsome as a toad, by reason of the venomous corruption that is in my heart, and my woeful contrariety to the nature of a holy God. But there is *" mercy over all,"* even over such vile and loathsome creatures as these ; there may be some over me, though wrath do now abide on me. Oh, let that mercy, whose glory it is to stretch itself over all, reach my soul also ! Oh, that the blessed and powerful influence thereof would beget faith in my heart !—*David Clarkson.*

Verse 9.—*"His tender mercies."* The nature and force of the word רחמים, is properly the *bowels ;* that is, there are *tender mercies in God* (so we term it in the *Benedictus*). Not of the ordinary sort, slight, and such as pierce not deep, come not far ; but such as come *de profundis,* from the very *bowels* themselves, that affect that part, make the *bowels* relent. And what *bowels ?* Not the *bowels* of the common man (for then מעים had been the right word,) but רחם are the *bowels* of a *parent* (so, we said, the word signifies), and this adds much ; adds to *mercy* στοργὴ, *natural love ;* to one strong affection another as strong or stronger than it.

And what *parent ?* the more pitiful of the twain, the *mother.* For רחם (the singular of this word) is Hebrew for the *womb.* So as this, to the two former addeth the sex ; the sex holden to be the more compassionate. Of all mercies, those of the *bowels ;* and of the bowels, the bowels of a *parent ;* and of the two parents, those of the *mother :* such pity as the mother takes of the children of her womb. *Mercies* are in God ; *such mercies* are in God.

"Over all." It is good news for us that these mercies are in God ; but, better yet, that they are in him with a *super—" over."* But, best of all, that that *super* is a *super omnia—" over all."* Much is said in few words to mercy's praise when 'tis said, *super omnia. Nihil supra* were much, none above it : but it is written *super omnia, above all.* He that saith this, leaves no more to say : there is no higher degree ; *super omnia* is the superlative.

All that are *above* are not *over.* It is not *above* only, as an obelisk or Maypole, higher than all about them, but have neither shadow nor shelter ; no good they do ! Mercy hath a broad top, spreading itself *over* all. It is so *above* all, as it is *over* them, too. As the vault of this chapel is *over* us, and the great vault of the firmament *over* that ; the *super* of latitude and expansion, no less than of altitude and elevation. And this to the end that all may retire to it, and take covert : it *over* them, and they *under* it. Under it, under the *shadow* of it, as of Esay's " great rock in the wilderness," from the *heat :* under the *shelter* of it as of Daniel's " great tree," from the tempest. (Isa. xxxii. 2 ; Dan. iv, 11, 12).—*Lancelot Andrewes.*

Verse 10.—*"All thy works shall praise thee, O LORD."* It is a poor philosophy and a narrow religion which does not recognise God as all in all. Every moment of our lives, we breathe, stand, or move in the temple of the Most High ; for the universe is that temple. Wherever we go, the testimony to his power, the impress of his hand, are there. Ask of the bright worlds around us, as they roll in the everlasting harmony of their circles, and they shall tell you of him whose power launched them on their courses ; ask of the mountains, that lift their heads among and above the clouds, and the bleak summit of one shall seem to call aloud to the snow-clad top of another, in proclaiming their testimony to the Agency which has laid their deep foundations. Ask of ocean's waters ; and the roar of their boundless waves shall chant from shore to shore a hymn of ascription to that Being, who hath said, " Hitherto shall ye come and no further." Ask of the rivers ; and, as they roll onward to the sea, do they not bear along their ceaseless tribute to the ever-working Energy, which struck open their fountains and poured them down through the valleys ? Ask of every region of the earth, from the burning equator to the icy pole, from the rock-bound coast to the plain covered with its luxuriant vegetation ; and will you not find on them all the record of the Creator's presence ? Ask of the countless tribes of plants and animals : and shall they not testify to the action of the great Source of Life ?   Yes, from every portion, from every department of nature, comes the same voice ;   everywhere we hear thy name, O God !   everywhere we see thy love !   Creation, in all its length and breadth, in all its depth and height, is the manifestation of thy Spirit, and without thee the worlds were dark and dead.   The universe is to us as the burning bush which the Hebrew leader saw :   God is ever present in it, for it burns with his glory, and the ground on which we stand is always holy.—*"Francis" (Viscount Dillon).*

Verse 10.—Marvellous is it that man is not always praising, since everything amidst which he dwells is continually inviting praise.—*Gregory the Great.*

Verse 10.—*"All thy works shall praise thee, O Lord,"* etc.   *"All"* God's *"works"* do *"praise"* him, as the beautiful building praiseth the builder, or the well-drawn picture praiseth the painter :   but his *"saints bless"* him, as the children of prudent and tender parents rise up and call them blessed.   Of all God's works, his saints, the workmanship of his grace, the first-fruits of his creatures, have most reason to bless him.—*Matthew Henry.*

Verse 10.—*"All thy works shall praise thee, O Lord,"* etc.   There are two words by which our thankfulness to God is expressed, *praising* and *blessing.*   What is the difference ?   Praise respecteth God's excellences, and blessing respecteth God's benefits.   We may praise a man that never hath done us good, if he be excellent and praiseworthy ;   but blessing respecteth God's bounty and benefits ;   yet they are often used promiscuously.—*Thomas Manton.*

Verse 10.—*"And thy saints shall bless thee."*   The lily lifts itself upon its slender stem, and displays its golden petals and its glittering ivory leaves ;   and by its very existence it praises God.   Yonder deep and booming sea rolls up in storm and tempest, sweeping everything before it ;   and every dash of its waves praises God.   The birds in the morning, and some of them all through the night, can never cease from praising ;   uniting with the ten thousand other voices which make ceaseless concert before the throne.   But observe, neither the flower, nor the sea, nor the bird, praises with intent to praise.   To them it is no exercise of intellect, for they do not know God, and cannot understand his worthiness ;   nor do they even know that they are praising him.   They exhibit his skill, and his goodness, and so forth, and in so doing they do much ;   but we must learn to do more.   When you and I praise God, there is the element of will, of intelligence, of desire, of intent ;   and in the saints of God there is another element, namely, that love to him, of reverent gratitude towards him, and this turns the praise into blessing.   A man is an eminent painter, and you exclaim, " His pencil is instinct with life."   Still, the man is no friend of yours, you pronounce no blessings on his name.   It may be that your feeling towards him is that of deep regret that such abilities should be united with so ill a character.   A certain person is exceedingly skilful in his profession, but he treats you unjustly, and therefore, though you often praise him for his extraordinary performances, you cannot bless him, for you have no cause to do so.   I am afraid that there might be such a feeling as that of admiration of God for his great skill, his wonderful power, his extraordinary justness, and yet no warmth of love in the heart towards him :   but in the saints the praise is sweetened with love, and is full of blessing.—*C. H. S.*

Verses 10, 11.—If not only irrational, but inanimate creatures praise God by giving occasion for his praise ;   then how much more should men set forth his praise, who are not only living, but reasonable creatures !   And if creatures without life and reason should provoke mankind in general, as having life and reason, to praise God ;   how much more should godly men be provoked by them to sing his praise, they having not only life, which stars have not ;   and reason, which birds and beasts have not ;   but grace, which the most of men have not !   Among visible creatures, men have most reason (because they have reason) to praise God ;   and among men gracious men have most reason to praise God, because they have grace.   And therefore as soon as ever David had said, *"All thy works shall praise thee, O Lord,"* he adds in the next words, *"and thy saints shall bless thee.   They shall speak of the glory of thy kingdom, and talk of thy power."*   As if he had said, As all thy works, O Lord, praise thee, so saints (who are the choicest pieces of thy workmanship) have cause to do it above all :   they cannot but be speaking and talking of thy kingdom and power, which are very glorious.—*Joseph Caryl.*

Verse 11.—*"They shall speak of the glory of thy kingdom,"* etc.   The glory of a kingdom is synonymous with its power.   The power of a kingdom consists in the number of its subjects, and the sufficiency of its revenues to maintain them. Now, the glory, or the power of God's kingdom, may be inferred from the difference between it and that of man.   There are four points of difference.   First, the kings of this world have but *few subjects*, with but little wealth,—not more than the population and riches of one kingdom, or one province, while God reigns over all angels, all men, all demons ; and all wealth on land, in the sea, or in the air, belongs to him.   There is another difference, that while the kings of this world rule their subjects, they are still ruled by them, they are *dependent on them*, could do nothing without them ; and, however abundant their revenues may be, they are generally in want, nay, even in debt, and, consequently, always calling for fresh tributes and taxes ; but God, while he governs all, is subject to none, because he needs nobody's help or assistance.   Instead of being in want, he abounds in everything, because he could, in one moment, bring from nothing much more than he now beholds or enjoys.   The third difference is a consequence of the second, while the kings of this world seem so to enjoy their honours and dignities, they are, at the same time, *suffering acutely from interior fears*, doubts, and cares, which have some-times been so burdensome, as to cause them to abdicate altogether.   God never suffers such pressure, is subject to no fear, no misgivings, but reigns absolutely in perfect tranquillity.   The fourth difference, an essential one, is, that the kings of the world *reign but for a time ;* but God reigneth for ever.—*Robert Bellarmine.*

Verse 11.—*"They shall speak . . . and talk."* Joy and sorrow are hard to conceal ; as from the countenance, so from the tongue. There is so much corres-pondence betwixt the heart and tongue that they will move at once : every man therefore speaks of his own pleasure and care ; the hunter and falconer of his game ; the ploughman of his team ; the soldier of his march and colours. If the heart were as full of God, the tongue could not refrain from talking of him : the rareness of Christian communication argues the common poverty of grace. If Christ be not in our hearts, we are godless ; if he be there without our joy, we are senseless ; if we rejoice in him and speak not of him, we are shamefully unthankful. Every man taketh, yea, raiseth occasion, to bring in speech of what he liketh. As I will think of thee always, O Lord, so it shall be my joy to speak of thee often ; and if I find not opportunity, I will make it,—*Joseph Hall.*

Verse 13.—The Kingdom of God is his government of the world. The glory of it becomes especially conspicuous in this, that he raises the dominion of his anointed over all the kingdoms of the world : comp. Ps. lxxxix. 27. *"Thy kingdom is a kingdom of all eternities "* (verse 13), and so must also the kingdom of thine anointed be an eternal one, and will survive all the transitory kingdoms of this world, however highly they may puff themselves up.—*E. W. Hengstenberg.*

Verse 13.—On the door of the old mosque in Damascus, which was once a Christian church, but for twelve centuries has ranked among the holiest of the Mahomedan sancturies, are inscribed these memorable words : " Thy kingdom, O Christ, is an everlasting kingdom, and thy dominion endureth throughout all generations." Though the name of Christ has been regularly blasphemed, and the disciples of Christ regularly cursed for twelve hundred years within it, the inscription has, nevertheless, remained unimpaired by time, and undisturbed by man. It was unknown during the long reign of Mahomedan intolerance and oppression ; but when religious liberty was partially restored, and the missionaries were enabled to establish a Christian church in that city, it was again brought to light, encouraging them in their work of faith and labour of love.—*From John Bate's "Cyclopædia of Illustrations,"* 1865.

Verses 13, 14.—What we admire in these verses, is their combining the mag-nificence of unlimited power with assiduity of unlimited tenderness. It is this combination which men are apt to regard as well-nigh incredible, supposing that a Being so great as God can never concern himself with beings so inconsiderable as themselves. Tell them that God lifteth up those that be bowed down, and they cannot imagine that his kingdom and dominion are unbounded ; or tell them, on the other hand, of the greatness of his empire, and they think it impossible that he should uphold all that fall.—*Henry Melvill.*

Verse 14.—*"The LORD upholdeth all that fall,"* etc. It is noteworthy how the Psalmist proceeds to exhibit the mightiness of God's kingdom, not by its power " to break in pieces and bruise," like the iron legs of the statue in Nebuchadnezzar's vision (Dan. ii. 40), but by the King's readiness to aid the weak. Even a heathen could see that this was the noblest use of power.

> Regia (crede mihi) res est succurrere lapsis.
> Ovid., Ep. de Panto, ii. 9, 11.
> It is a kingly thing to help the fallen.
>
> *Neale and Littledale.*

Verse 14.—*"The LORD upholdeth all that fall,"* etc. נֹפְלִים, *nophelim,* the *falling,* or those who are not able to keep their feet ; the weak. He *shores* them up ; he is their *prop.* No man falls through his own weakness merely ; if he rely on God, the strongest foe cannot shake him.—*Adam* Clarke.

Verse 14.—*"And raiseth up all those that be bowed down,"* incurvatos. Many who do not actually fall are reduced to distress that may be even more painful ; for the struggling are greater sufferers than the actually passive. Men are *bowed down* physically by infirmity ; mentally, by care ; spiritually, by remorse ; some are even crushed by all three burdens. For all such there is help in a Mighty One. But none can help themselves alone : none are raised but by supernatural interposition—*non nisi opitulante Domino.*—*Martin Geier.*

Verse 14.—*"The LORD upholdeth all that fall."* The word here used is a participle, literally, *"The Lord sustaining"*; that is, the Lord *is* a Sustainer or Upholder of all that fall.—*Albert Barnes.*

Verse 14.—*"And raiseth up all those that he bowed down."* Alphonsus, King of Arragon, is famous for helping with his own hand one of his subjects out of a ditch. Of Queen Elizabeth it is recorded, to her eternal praise, that she hated (no less than did Mithridates) such as sought to crush virtue forsaken of fortune. Christ bruiseth not the broken reed, but upholdeth it, he quencheth not the smoking wick, but cherisheth it.—*John Trapp.*

Verses 14—19.—The Psalmist sets up a splendid argument. Having praised the kingdom, he goes on to display *seven glories* peculiar to kings, and shows that in Jehovah these shine supremely. Verses 14 to 19 contain each a royal virtue.—*John Lorinus.*

Verse 15.—*"The eyes of all wait upon thee."* God cannot be overmastered by what is great and enormous, so neither can he overlook what is small and insignificant. God is that being to whom the only great thing is himself ; and, therefore, when " the eyes of all wait upon him," the seraph gains not attention by his gaze of fire, and the insect loses it not through the feebleness of vision. Archangels, and angels, and men, and beasts of the field, and fowls of the air, and fish of the sea, draw equally the regard of him, who, counting nothing great but himself, the Creator, can pass over as small no fraction of the creature.—*Henry Melvill.*

Verse 15.—Doth not nature teach you to pray ? Ask the brutes, the ravens, lions, etc. (Job xxxviii. 41 ; Ps. cxlvii. 9 ; civ. 27 ; cxlv. 15) ; not as if these unreasonable creatures could know and worship God, but because nature hath taught them so much of this duty as they are capable of and can bear ; they have some sense of their burdens and wants, they groan and cry, and desire to be eased ; and the Lord hearkeneth to this voice and saith, " Now the poor creature is crying to me, and I will pity it." Ah ! shall the beasts in their own way cry to God, and wilt thou be silent ? Hath the Lord elevated thee so far above these inferior creatures, and fitted thee for the immediate acts of his worship, and for a higher communion with himself, and wilt thou not serve him accordingly ? Hath he given thee a heart and a spiritual soul, as he hath given the brutes a sensitive appetite and natural desires, and shall they cry to God with the one, and not thou with the other ?—*Alexander Pitcairne,* 1664.

Verse 15.—*"Eyes . . . wait upon thee."* Many dumb beggars have been relieved at Christ's gate by making signs.—*William Secker.*

Verse 15.—In agony nature is no atheist, the mind which knows not where to fly, flies to God.—*Hannah More,* 1745—1833.

Verse 15.—The creatures are his, and therefore to be received with thanksgiving ; this our Saviour performed with great vigour and zeal ; thus teaching us, when " looking up to heaven," that *"the eyes of all"* ought, in the most literal sense, *"to wait"* upon that Lord *"who gives them their meat in due season."* . . . A secret sense of God's goodness is by no means enough. Men should make solemn and outward expressions of it, when they receive his creatures for their support ;

a service and homage not only due to him, but profitable to themselves.—*George Stanhope*, 1660—1728.

Verse 15.—While atheism, in its strict signification, namely, that of total denial of God's existence, is scarcely, if at all, to be found on earth ; atheism, as regards the denial of God's providence, is the espoused creed of hundreds amongst us. . . . Providence, which is confessed in great things, is rejected in small things ; and even if you can work up men to an easy confession that God presideth over national concerns, you will find them withdrawing individuals from his scrutiny. We bring against this paring down of God's providence a distinct charge of atheism. If we confess the existence of a God at all, we read it in the workmanship of the tiniest leaf, as well as the magnificent pinnacles of Andes and Alps ; if we believe in the providence of God at all, we must confess that he numbers the hairs of our heads, as well as marshals the stars of the firmament ; and that providence is not universal, and therefore cannot be godlike, if a sparrow, any more than a seraph, flit away unregarded.

Now, the words before us set themselves most strenuously against this popular atheism. The whole creation is represented as fastening its gaze on the universal Parent, and as drawing from his fulness the supply of every necessity. *"The eyes of all wait upon thee ; and thou givest them their meat in due season."* There is made, you observe, no exception whatever ; the exhibition is simply that of every rank and order of beings looking to the Almighty, confessing dependence upon him, and standing environed by his guardianship. So that, in place of anything which approximates to the abandonment of our creation, the Psalmist asserts a ceaseless attention to its wants, the suspension of which for an instant would cause chill and darkness throughout the whole universe.—*Henry Melvill.*

Verse 15.—*"Thou givest them their meat in due season."* The meat which endures to everlasting life ; the flesh of Christ, which is meat indeed ; the doctrines of the gospel, which, as some of them are milk for babes, others are meat for strong men, or strong meat for experienced believers ; and these are given forth under Christ's direction, by his ministering servants, who are his wise and faithful stewards, that give to everyone of the family their portion of meat in due season, which is the word fitly spoken ; and, when it is so, how good it is ! Luke xii. 42 ; Prov. xv. 23. This is food convenient for them, given out *in his time*, as in the original ; either in the Lord's time, when he sees best, or in *their* time, as the Syriac version, when they most need it, and it will do them most good.—*John Gill.*

Verse 15.—(*second clause.*) It is said that God gives them *"their food,"* and *"in its season,"* for the very variety of it serves more to illustrate the providence of God. Each has its own way of feeding, and the different kinds of aliment are designed and adapted for different uses. David therefore speaks of the food which is particular to them. The pronoun is not in the plural, and we are not to read *in their* season, as if it applied to the animals. The food he notices as given in its season ; for here also we are to notice the admirable arrangements of divine providence, that there is a certain time appointed for harvest, vintage, and hay crop, and that the year is so divided into intervals, that the cattle are fed at one time on grass, at another on hay, or straw, or acorns, or other products of the earth. Were the whole supply poured forth at one and the same moment, it could not be gathered together so conveniently ; and we have no small reason to admire the seasonableness with which the different kinds of fruit and aliment are yearly produced.—*John Calvin.*

Verse 15.—Mr. Robertson told of a poor child who was accustomed to see unexpected provision for his mother's wants arrive in answer to prayer. The meal-barrel in Scotland is everything to a hungry boy : so he said, "Mither, I think God aye hears when we're scraping the bottom o' the barrel."—*"The Christian."*

Verses 15—17.—Who can fear that, because God's ways are unsearchable, they may not be all tending to the final good of his creatures, when he knows that with the tenderness of a most affectionate parent this Creator and Governor ministers to the meanest living thing ? Who can be disquieted by the mysteriousness of the Divine dealings when he remembers that they are those of one who never ceases for a solitary moment to consult the happiness of whatsoever he hath formed ? Who, in short, can distrust God because clouds and darkness are round about him, when there is light enough to show that he is the vigilant guardian of every tenant of this earth, that his hand upholds, and his breath animates, and his bounty nourishes, the teeming hordes of the city, and the desert, and the ocean ? It seems that there is thus a beautiful, though tacit process of reasoning in our text, and that the seventeenth verse is set in its proper connection.   It is as though David had said, " Come, let us muse on the righteousness of God.   He would not be God if he were not righteous in all his ways and holy in all his works ; and therefore we may be sure that whatsoever he does is the best that could be done, whether or not we can discover its excellence."

Yes, this may be true, but when we look on the divine dealings what an abyss of dark waters there is !   How unsearchable, how unfathomable are God's judgments ! We admit it ; but being previously convinced of God's righteousness, we ought not to be staggered by what is dark in his dispensations.

"True," you reply, " but the mind does not seem satisfied by this reasoning ; it may be convincing to the intellect, but it does not address itself to the feelings." Well, then, pass from what is dark in God's dealing to what is clear.   He is about your path and about your bed ; he " preserveth man and beast " ; " his tender mercies are over all his works."   Is this a God of whom to be suspicious ?   Is this a God to mistrust ?   Oh ! surely if you will fortify yourselves by such facts as these—" Thou, O Lord, satisfiest the desire of every living thing," "*The eyes of all wait upon thee ; and thou givest them their meat in due season* "—if, I say, you will fortify your minds by such facts as these, you will be able at all times and in all circumstances to join heartily in the acknowledgment of the Psalmist—"*The Lord is righteous in all his ways and holy in all his works*."—*Henry Melvill.*

Verse 16.—

Thou openest thy hand of grace
And thou dost satisfy
The wants of all in every place
Who for thy presence cry.

Thomas MacKellar, 1883.

Verse 16.—"*Thou openest thy hand.*"   This seems as if depicted from a house-keeper's habit of feeding a brood of chickens and other creatures.   She flings abroad with full and open hand a large supply, not measuring to a grain just what might be enough.—*Martin Geier.*

Verse 16.—"*Thou openest thy hand.*"   What an idea does this convey of the *paternal goodness* of the great Father of his creation !   How opposite to the conduct of many of his creatures one to another, whose hands and hearts are *shut !*   What an idea also does it convey of the *ease* with which the wants of the whole creation are supplied !   Let me pause a moment and think of their wants.   What a quantity of vegetable and animal food is daily consumed in one town : what a quantity in a large city like London : what a quantity in a nation : in the whole world ! But *men* do not compose a hundredth part of "every living thing" !   What innumerable wants throughout all animate nature ; in the earth, in the air, in the waters !   Whence comes their supply ?   " Thou openest thy hand," and all are satisfied.   And can all these wants be supplied by only *the opening of his hand* ? What then must sin be, and salvation from it ?   That is a work of wonderful expense.   God openeth his hand and satisfieth all creation, but he must purchase the Church *with his blood*. . . . .   In what a *variety of ways* are our wants supplied. The earth is fruitful, the air is full of life, the clouds empty themselves upon the earth, the sun pours forth its genial rays ; but the operation of all these second causes is only *the opening of his hand !*   Nay further : look we to *instruments* as well as means ?   Parents feed us in our childhood, and supply our youthful wants ; ways are opened for our future subsistence ; connexions are formed, which prove sources of comfort ; friends are kind in seasons of extremity ; supplies are presented from quarters that we never expected.   What are all these but *the opening of his hand* ?   If his hand were shut, what a world would this be !   The heavens brass, the earth iron ; famine, pestilence, and death must follow.   See Ps. civ. 27—29.

Consider next the term "*hand.*"   There is a difference between the *hand* and the *heart.*   God opens his hand, in the way of providence, towards his worst enemies. He gave Nebuchadnezzar all the kingdoms of the earth.   But he opens his *heart* in the gospel of his Son.   This is the better portion of the two.   While we are thankful for the one, let us not rest satisfied in it : it is merely a *hand* portion. Rather let us pray with Jabez to be blessed *indeed ;* and that we might have a Joseph's portion ; not only the precious things of the earth and the fulness thereof, but " the good will of him that dwelt in the bush ! "

"Thou satisfiest the desire," etc. God does not give grudgingly. It seems to be a characteristic of the divine nature, both in the natural and moral world, to raise desires, not with a view to disappoint, but to satisfy them. O what a consoling thought is this ! If there be any desires in us which are not satisfied, it is through their being self-created ones, which is our own fault ; or through artificial scarcity from men's luxury, which is the fault of our species. God raises no desires as our Creator, but he gives enough to satisfy them ; and none as our Redeemer and Sanctifier but what shall be actually satisfied. O the wonderful munificence of God ! " How great is his goodness, and how great is his beauty ! "—*Andrew Fuller.*

Verse 16 (*second clause*).—The word רצון, *ratson*, some render *"desire,"* as though he meant that God supplies each kind of animal with food according to its wish. And a little afterwards we do indeed find it used in that sense. Others, however, refer it rather to God's feeding them of his mere good pleasure and kindness ; it is not enough to say that our food is given us by God, unless we add, as in the second clause of the verse, that his kindness is gratuitous, and that there is no extrinsic cause whatever moving him to provide so liberally for every living creature. In that case the cause is put for the effect ; the various kinds of provision being effects of his good pleasure—χαρισματα της χαριτος.—*John Calvin.*

Verse 17.—*"The* LORD *is righteous in all his ways,"* etc. The ground upon which praise is here ascribed to God may seem a common one, being in every one's mouth ; but in nothing is wisdom shown more than in holding fast the truth, that God is just in all his ways, so as to retain in our hearts an unabated sense of it amidst all troubles and confusions. Though all acknowledge God to be just, most men are no sooner overtaken by affliction than they quarrel with his severity : unless their wishes are immediately complied with, they are impatient, and nothing is more common than to hear his justice impeached. As it is everywhere abused by the wicked imputations men cast upon it, here it is very properly vindicated from such ungrateful treatment, and asserted to be constant and unfailing, however loudly the world may disparage it. It is expressly added, *"in all his ways and works"* ; for we fail to give God due honour unless we recognise a constant tenor of righteousness in the whole progress of his operation. Nothing is more difficult in the time of trouble, when God has apparently forsaken us, or afflicts us without cause, than to restrain our corrupt feelings from breaking out against his judgments ; as we are told of the Emperor Mauricius in a memorable passage of history, that seeing his sons murdered by the wicked and perfidious traitor Phocas, and being about to be carried out himself to death, he cried out—" Thou art righteous, O God, and just are thy judgments."—*John Calvin.*

Verse 17.—*"Holy in all his works."* God is good, the absolute and perfect ; and from good nothing can come but good : and therefore all which God has made is good, as he is ; and therefore if anything in the world seems to be bad, one of two things must be true of it.

Either it is *not* bad, though it seems so to us ; and God will bring good out of it in his good time, and justify himself to men, and show us that he is holy in all his works, and righteous in all his ways. Or else—

If the thing be really bad, then God did not make it. It must be a disease, a mistake, a failure, a man's making, or some person's making, but not of God's making. For all that he has made he sees eternally ; and behold, it is very good.— *Charles Kingsley, in "The Good News of God,"* 1878.

Verse 18.—*"The* LORD *is nigh."* The nearness or remoteness of a friend is very material and considerable in our troubles, distresses, wants, dangers, etc. I have such a friend and he would help me, but he lives so far off ; and I have another friend that has a great love for me, that is able to counsel me, and to speak a word in season to me, and that in my distress would stand close to me, but he is so remote. I have a special friend, that did he know how things stand with me would make my burdens his, and my wants his, and my sorrows his ; but he is in a far country, he is at the Indies, and I may be undone before I can hear from him. But it is not thus with you, O Christians ! who have a God so nigh unto you, who have the signal presence of God in the midst of you, yea, who have a God always standing by you, " The Lord stood by me," etc. : 2 Tim. iv. 17.—*Thomas Brooks.*

Verse 18.—*"Them that call upon him."* To call upon the name of the Lord implies *right faith,* to call upon him as he *is* ; *right trust* in him, leaning upon him, *right devotion*, calling upon him as he has appointed ; *right life*, ourselves who call upon him being, or becoming by his grace, what he wills. They *"call"* not *" upon the Lord,"* but upon some idol of their own imagining, who call upon him as other than he has revealed himself, or remaining themselves other than those whom he has declared that he will hear. For such *deny* the very primary attribute of God, his truth. *Their* God is not a God of truth.—*Edward Bouverie Pusey,* 1800—1882.

Verse 18.—*"To all that call upon him in truth."* Because there is a counterfeit and false sort of worshipping, and calling upon God, which is debarred from the benefit of this promise, to wit, when the party suppliant is not reconciled, nor seeking reconciliation through Christ the Mediator, or is seeking something not promised, or something for a carnal end, that he may bestow it on his lusts ; therefore he who hath right unto this promise must be a worshipper of God in faith, and sincere intention ; and to such the Lord will show himself *"nigh."*—*David Dickson.*

Verse 18.—To call upon God in truth is, first, to repose an implicit confidence in the faithfulness of his promise, and to look for unlimited answers to prayer from the riches of his grace in Christ Jesus. But it is also, in the next place, to feel our own urgent need of the things for which we supplicate, and to realize an earnest and unfeigned concern to obtain them. " What things ye desire when ye pray," said the Lord, " believe that ye receive them, and ye shall have them ; " and hence we gather, that the hearty desire, arising out of the consciousness of need, is an integral and inseparable part of genuine and effectual prayer.—*Thomas Dale,* 1853.

Verses 18, 19.—God's people are a praying people, a generation of seekers, and such commonly are speeders. God never said to the seed of Jacob, Seek ye my face in vain. They seek his face, righteousness and strength, and he is found of them. . . . The saints alone betake themselves to God and his help, run to him as their sanctuary ; others fly from God's presence, run to the rocks, and the tops of the ragged rocks, call to the hills and the mountains ; but a child of God goes only and tells his Father, and before him lays open his cause ; as good Hezekiah did, when Rabshakeh came out against him ; " O Lord, I am oppressed, undertake for me "; or the Church (Isa. xxxiii. 2), " Be thou our arm every morning, and our salvation in time of trouble." They only sensibly need, and so alone crave and implore divine succour ; and God will not suffer his people to lose the precious treasure of their prayers. *"The Lord is nigh unto all them that call upon him ; he will fulfil their desire, he will hear their cry,"* etc. That God who prepares his people's heart to pray, prepares also his own ear to hear ; and he that promiseth to hear before we call, will never deny to hearken when we cry unto him. As Calvin saith : " Oppressions and afflictions make man cry, and cries and supplications make God hear."—*F. E., in " The Saint's Ebenezer,"* 1667.

Verse 19.—*"He will fulfil the desire of them that fear him."* This is for comfort for all poor broken hearts in whom God hath ingendered the true desire of grace. Let such know that the first step to grace is to see they have no grace ; and the first degree of grace is the *desire* of grace. It is not with the body as with the soul, if you will be healed you shall be healed. A man may desire to be healed corporally, and yet his disease continue upon him ; but it is not so with the soul : if thou wilt say, " Christ heal me," thou shalt be made whole. If a man have but the true desire of grace it shall be given him : " Lord, thou hast heard the desire of the humble " (Ps. x. 17) : when the poor soul is humbled before God in the sense of the want of grace, and breathes and desires after it, the Lord will grant such desires : *"He will fulfil the desire of them that fear him : he also will hear their cry, and will save them."* One said, " The greatest part of Christianity is to desire to be a Christian." And another said, " The total sum of a man's religion in this life consists in the true desires of saving grace." This was the perfection Saint Paul attained unto (Rom. vii. 18) : " To will is present with me ; but how to perform that which is good I find not." Saint Paul we know was the child of God, and one dearly beloved of God ; yet that was the pitch of his godliness ; it consisted more in desire than accomplishment. Canst thou approve by evident and sound arguments that thou hast the true desires of grace ? Then know for thy comfort that the Lord's spirit of grace hath been moving and stirring in thee : " It is God that worketh in you both the will and the deed " (Phil. ii. 13), and that of his good pleasure, not only of his bounty, from whence he hath bestowed many graces, even upon such as he will damn afterwards for their accursed abuse of them, with the neglect of the power thereof. But if God hath set thy will, and the stream of thy affections and desires, to himself and to grace, it is an evidence of God's good pleasure from which he did at first elect thee, and gave his Son to redeem thee.—*William Fenner* (1560—1640), *in "The Riches of Grace."*

Verse 19.—*"He will fulfil the desire of them that fear him."* God will not grant us every desire, that is our mercy ; for, 1. Some of them are *sinful.* David desired to be revenged on Nabal and his innocent family. Jonah desired Nineveh's ruin. 2. Others would *not be for our good.* David desired the life of the child he had by Bathsheba ; David also desired the life of Jonathan; neither of which would have been for his good. Nay, not every *righteous* desire. It is a righteous desire for a minister to desire the salvation of those that hear him. So Paul declared, " I would to God that all that are here present were altogether such as I am"; Acts xxvi. 29. So again, " I could wish that myself were accursed from Christ for my brethren, my kinsmen according to the flesh " : Rom. ix. 1. David *desired* to build a house for God, and it was a righteous desire, for God took it well at his hands ; yet he did not grant it. Kings and prophets desired to see the Lord Messiah, and yet did not see him. How then are we to understand it ? Answer. The sum or substance of their desires shall be fulfilled. What is the main desire of a seaman ? that he may arrive at the haven. So saints will be brought to their desired haven. What of a pilgrim ? See Heb. xi. 16. So all the desires of a Christian are summed up in this, *That he may eternally enjoy God and be like him.* Doubtless there is great mystery in these things. However I think it is certain that, when God raises a spiritual desire in a person, it is *often,* though not *always,* with an intention to bestow the object desired.—*Andrew Fuller.*

Verse 19 (*first clause*).—God will fulfil the will of those who fear to disobey *his* will.—*Simon de Muis.*

Verse 19.—*"Desire "* is the largest and most comprehensive word that can be used ; it contains all things in it . . . . Nothing good, nothing necessary, nothing profitable, but comes under this word *"desire."* When God promises to *"fulfil the desires of them that fear him,"* he doth promise all good things ; desire comprehends all that can be desired.—*Ralph Robinson.*

Verse 19.—*"He will hear their cry,"* etc. A mark of a great king—he gives willing audience to suppliants.—*Johannes Paulus Palanterius.*

Verse 19.—*"He will hear and save."* How true a description of Christ in his constant office. He heard Mary Magdalene and saved her. He heard the Canaanitish woman, and saved her daughter. He heard the cry of the two blind men and enlightened them. He heard the lepers and cleansed them. He heard the cry of the dying thief and promised him Paradise. Never has one yet cried to King Jesus who has not been heard and delivered.—*Thomas Le Blanc.*

Verse 20.—*"The Lord preserveth,"* etc. God's mercy and God's justice ; he preserves and he destroys. Philip IV. of France, surnamed the Beautiful, on his escutcheon emblazoned a sword and an olive branch, with the motto, *Utrumque,* i.e. " one or the other." A truly great king is master of either art—war and peace. —*Thomas Le Blanc.*

Verse 20.—Those who were called " them that *fear* him " are now denominated " them that *love* him."—*Simon de Muis.*

Verse 20. — *"All the wicked will he destroy."* God has so many different, unsearchable ways of taking wicked men out of the world, and sending them to hell, that there is nothing to make it appear that God had need to be at the expense of a miracle, or go out of the ordinary course of his providence, to destroy any wicked man at any moment.—*Jonathan Edwards.*

Verse 20.—*"All the wicked will he destroy."* It must not be overlooked that this declaration occurs in a song of praise. The whole of the context is utterly inconsistent with the expression of emotions of anger or revenge.—*Speaker's Commentary.*

Verse 20.—*"All the wicked will he destroy."* [Prayer-Book Version, *"scattereth abroad."*] Like the ruins of a demolished building ; or rather, like an army, which the enemy has completely routed.—*William Keatinge Clay.*

Verse 20.—*"Preserveth" . . . " destroy."* Notice this recurrent thought, that the guardianship of the good implies the destruction of the wicked.—*A. S. Aglen.*

HINTS TO PREACHERS.

Verses 1, 2.—Praise. 1. Personal Praise. 2. Daily praise. 3. Enthusiastic praise. 4. Perpetual praise. Or : I. The attractive theme of the song. II. The increasing fulness of the song. III. The unending life of the singer.—*C. A. D.*

Verses 1 & 2.—The four " I wills " of praise. Praise to the King ; praise to the divine character ; praise for all time ; praise for all eternity.

Verse 2.—*Every day ; for ever.* I. Day by day for ever God and I will endure. II. Day by day for ever our present relations will continue. He the God, I the creature ; he the Father, I the child ; he the blessing, I the blest. III. Day by day for ever he shall have my homage.—*W. B. H.*

Verse 3.—I. The dignity of man is here implied in his capacity for praising God greatly. II. His immortality in his capacity for praising his unsearchable greatness.—*G. R.*

Verse 3 (*last clause*).—The unsearchable greatness of God. Consider it, I. As a fact amply demonstrated. II. As a rebuke to despondency : see Isaiah xl. 28. III. As the stay of a soul oppressed by mysteries. IV. As indicating a subject for our everlasting study.—*J. F.*

Verse 4.—I. Our obligation to past generations. II. Our duty to generations to come.—*G. R.*

Verses 5—7.—The Antiphon. I. To praise God is a personal duty : " I will." II. Its right performance will excite others to engage in it ; " And men shall." III. The accompaniment of others in praise will re-act upon ourselves. " And I will " ; " And they shall abundantly," etc. IV. Such praise widens and expands as it rolls along. Beginning with God's majesty and works, it extends to his acts, greatness, goodness, and righteousness.—*C. A. D.*

Verses 5—7.—I. Subjects for praise. 1. Divine majesty. 2. Divine works. 3. Divine judgments. 4. Divine greatness. 5. Divine goodness. 6. Divine righteousness. II. Of whom is it required. 1. Personal ; " I will speak." 2. Universal ; " men shall speak."—*G. R.*

Verses 6, 7.—I. *The awe-struck talk.* Silent as to mercies and promises, men must speak when God's terrible acts are among them. II. *The bold avowal.* One individual declares God's greatness in power, wisdom, truth and grace. This leads others to the same conclusion, and hence—III. *The grateful outpouring.* Many bless the Lord's great goodness in a song fresh, free, constant, joyous, refreshing, abundant, like the gush of a spring. IV. *The select song.* They *utter* goodness but *sing* of righteousness. This is a noteworthy topic for a discourse.

Verse 7.—See " Spurgeon's Sermons," No. 1468 : " The Philosophy and Propriety of Abundant Praise."

Verse 8.—I. Grace to the unworthy. II. Compassion to the afflicted. II. Forbearance to the guilty. IV. Mercy to the penitent.—*G. R.*

Verse 9.—The universal goodness of God in no degree a contradiction to the special election of grace.

Verse 10.—See " Spurgeon's Sermons," No. 1796 : " Concerning Saints."

Verse 11.—The glory of Christ's kingdom. The glory of this kingdom is manifested,—I. In its origin. II. In the manner and spirit of its administration. III. In the character of its subjects. IV. In the privileges that are attached to it.—*Robert Hall,*

Verses 11, 12.—Talk transfigured. I. The faculty of talk is extensively possessed II. Is commonly misused. III. May be nobly employed. IV. Will then be gloriously useful.—*C. A. D.*

Verses 11—13.—To show the greatness of God's kingdom, David observes, 1. *The pomp of it.* Would we by faith look within the veil, we should " speak of the glory of his kingdom " (verse 11) ; " and the glorious majesty of it " (verse 12). 2. *The power of it.* When " they speak of the glory of God's kingdom," they must " talk of his power," the extent of it, the efficacy of it. 3. *The perpetuity of it* (verse 13). The thrones of earthly princes totter, and the flowers of their crowns wither, monarchs come to an end ; but, Lord, " thy kingdom is an everlasting kingdom."—*Matthew Henry.*

Verse 14.—The grace of God in his kindness to the undeserving and the miserable, who look to him for help. I. He " upholdeth all that fall." 1. A description, embracing (1) Sinners who have fallen lowest : (2) Backsliders who have tripped most foully.   2. An act implying (1) Pity which draws nigh ; (2) Power which places the fallen upon their feet ; (3) Preservation which keeps them standing. II. He " raiseth up all those that are bowed down." Consolation for those who are —1. Bowed down with shame and penitence.   2. Oppressed with perplexities and cares.   3. Weighed with a sense of weakness in the presence of onerous duties. 4. Depressed because of prevailing error and sin around them.—*J. F.*

Verse 14.—Help for the fallible.   I. Whatever our present position we are liable to fall.   Sickness.   Loss.   Friendlessness.   Sin.   II. However low we fall we are not below the reach of God's hand.   III. Within the reach of God's hand we shall experience the action of God's love.   "Upholdeth."   "Raiseth up."— *C. A. D.*

Verses 15, 16.—Universal dependence and divine support.   The Psalmist here teaches—I. The Universality of Dependence amongst creatures :   " The eyes of all wait upon thee."   We depend upon God for " life, and breath, and all things." Entire dependence should beget deep humility.   II. The Infinitude of the Divine Resources :   " And thou givest them their meat."   His resources must be, 1. Infinitely vast.   2. Infinitely various.   Both sufficient and adapted for all.   III. The Timeliness of the Divine Communications :   " In due season."   A reason for patience if his gifts seem delayed.   IV. The Sublime Ease of the Divine Communications : " Thou openest thine hand," and the countless needs of the universe are satisfied. An encouragement to believing prayer.   V. The Sufficiency of the Divine Communications :   " And satisfiest the desire of every living thing."   " God giveth to all liberally."   Our subject urges all men to, 1. Gratitude.   Constant provision should lead to constant thankfulness and consecration.   2. Trust. (1) For temporal supplies.   " Grace to help in time of need " will surely be given to all who look to him.—*William Jones, in "The Homiletic Quarterly,"* 1878.

Verse 17.—I. What God declares himself to be.   II. What his people find him to be.   III. What all creatures will ultimately acknowledge him to be.—*G. R.*

Verses 18—20.—Gather from these verses the character of God's people.   I. They call upon God.   II. They fear God.   III. They have desires towards God. IV. They have answers from God.   V. They love God.

Verse 18 (last clause).—True prayer, in what it differs essentially from mere formalism.

Verse 18.—At the palace gates.   I. Directions to callers.   1. " Call upon *him* "; let the repetition suggest pertinacity.   2. Call " in truth " ; sincerely, with promises, in appointed way.   II. Encouragement for callers.   Jehovah is nigh, with his ready ear, sympathizing heart, and helpful hand.—*W. B. H.*

Verses 18, 19.—The blessedness of prayer.   I. Definition of prayer :   " calling upon God."   II. Variety in prayer :   " call, desire, cry."   III. Essential characteristic of prayer :   " truth."   IV. God's nearness in prayer.   V. Assured success of prayer.   " He will fu. l, hear, save."—*C. A. D.*

Verse 20.—Those who love God are preserved *from* excessive temptation, falling into sin, despair, apostasy, remorse, famishing ; preserved *in* trial, persecution, depression, death ; preserved *to* activity, holiness, victory, glory.

Verse 20.—Solemn Contrasts.   1. Between human characters.   " Them that love him."   " The wicked."   2. Between human destinies.   " Preserveth." " Destroy."—*C. A. D.*

Verse 20.—How the love of God is the opposite of wickedness, and wickedness inconsistent with the love of God.

Verse 21.—Individual praise suggests the desire for universal praise.   We like company in a good deed ; we perceive the inadequacy of our own song ; we desire others to be happy ; we long to see that done which is right and good.

PSALM CXLVI.

DIVISION, ETC.—*We are now among the Hallelujahs. The rest of our journey lies through the Delectable Mountains. All is praise to the close of the book. The key is high-pitched : the music is upon the high-sounding cymbals. O for a heart full of joyful gratitude, that we may run, and leap, and glorify God, even as these Psalms do.*

Alexander thinks that this song may be regarded as composed of two equal parts ; in the first we see the happiness of those who trust in God, and not in man (1—5), while the second gives the reason drawn from the Divine perfections (5—10). This might suffice for our purpose ; but as there is really no break at all, we will keep it entire. It is "one pearl," a sacred censer of holy incense, pouring forth one sweet perfume.

EXPOSITION.

PRAISE ye the LORD. Praise the LORD, O my soul.

2 While I live will I praise the LORD : I will sing praises unto my God while I have any being.

3 Put not your trust in princes, *nor* in the son of man, in whom *there is* no help.

4 His breath goeth forth, he returneth to his earth ; in that very day his thoughts perish.

5 Happy *is he* that *hath* the God of Jacob for his help, whose hope *is* in the LORD his God :

6 Which made heaven, and earth, the sea, and all that therein *is :* which keepeth truth for ever :

7 Which executeth judgment for the oppressed : which giveth food to the hungry. The LORD looseth the prisoners :

8 The LORD openeth *the eyes of* the blind : the LORD raiseth them that are bowed down : the LORD loveth the righteous :

9 The LORD preserveth the strangers ; he relieveth the fatherless and widow : but the way of the wicked he turneth upside down.

10 The LORD shall reign for ever, *even* thy God, O Zion, unto all generations. Praise ye the LORD.

1. *"Praise ye the LORD,"* or, Hallelujah. It is saddening to remember how this majestic word has been trailed in the mire of late. Its irreverent use is an aggravated instance of taking the name of Jehovah our God in vain. Let us hope that it has been done in ignorance by the ruder sort ; but great responsibility lies with leaders who countenance and even copy this blasphemy. With holy awe let us pronounce the word HALLELUJAH, and by it summon ourselves and all others to adore the God of the whole earth. Men need to be called to praise ; it is important that they should praise ; and there are many reasons why they should do it at once. Let all who hear the word *Hallelujah* unite immediately in holy praise.

"Praise the LORD, O my soul." He would practise what he had preached. He would be the leader of the choir which he had summoned. It is a poor business if we solely exhort others, and do not stir up our own soul. It is an evil thing to say, " Praise ye," and never to add, " Praise, O my soul." When we praise God let us arouse our innermost self, our central life : we have but one soul, and if it be saved from eternal wrath, it is bound to praise its Saviour. Come heart, mind, thought ! Come my whole being, my soul, my all, be all on flame with joyful adoration ! Up, my brethren ! Lift up the song ! " Praise ye the Lord." But what am I at ? How dare I call upon others, and be negligent myself ? If ever man was under bonds to bless the Lord I am that man, wherefore let me put my

soul into the centre of the choir, and then let my better nature excite my whole manhood to the utmost height of loving praise. " O for a well-tuned harp ! " Nay, rather, O for a sanctified heart. Then if my voice should be of the poorer sort, and somewhat lacking in melody, yet my soul without my voice shall accomplish my resolve to magnify the Lord.

2. *"While I live I will praise the LORD."* I shall not live here for ever. This mortal life will find a finis in death ; but while it lasts I will laud the Lord my God. I cannot tell how long or short my life may be ; but every hour of it shall be given to the praises of my God. While I live I'll love ; and while I breathe I'll bless. It is but for a while, and I will not wile that time away in idleness, but consecrate it to that same service which shall occupy eternity. As our life is the gift of God's mercy, it should be used for his glory. *"I will sing praises unto my God while I have any being."* When I am no longer in being on earth, I hope to have a higher being in heaven, and there I will not only praise, but *sing* praises. Here I have to sigh and praise, but there I shall only sing and praise. This " while I have any being " will be a great while, but the whole of it shall be filled up with adoration ; for the glorious Jehovah is my God, my own God by covenant, and by blood relationship in Christ Jesus. I have no being apart from my God, therefore, I will not attempt to enjoy my being otherwise than by singing to his honour. Twice the Psalmist says " I will " ; here first thoughts and second thoughts are alike good. We cannot be too firm in the holy resolve to praise God, for it is the chief end of our living and being that we should glorify God and enjoy him for ever.

3. *"Put not your trust in princes."* If David be the author this warning comes from a prince. In any case it comes from the Spirit of the living God. Men are always far too apt to depend upon the great ones of earth, and forget the Great One above ; and this habit is the fruitful source of disappointment. Princes are only men, and men with greater needs than others ; why, then, should we look to them for aid ? They are in greater danger, are burdened with greater cares, and are more likely to be misled than other men ; therefore, it is folly to select them for our confidence. Probably no order of men have been so false to their promises and treaties as men of royal blood. So live as to deserve *their* trust, but not burden them with your trust. *"Nor the son of man, in whom there is no help."* Though you should select one son of man out of the many, and should imagine that he differs from the rest and may be safely depended on, you will be mistaken. There is none to be trusted, no, not one. Adam fell ; therefore lean not on his sons. Man is a helpless creature without God ; therefore, look not for help in that direction. All men are like the few men who are made into princes, they are more in appearance than in reality, more in promising than in performing, more apt to help themselves than to help others. How many have turned away heart-sick from men on whom they once relied ! Never was this the case with a believer in the Lord. He is a very present help in time of trouble. In man there is no help in times of mental depression, in the day of sore bereavement, in the night of conviction of sin, or in the hour of death. What a horror when most in need of help to read those black words, NO HELP !

4. *"His breath goeth forth, he returneth to his earth."* His breath goes from his body, and his body goes to the grave. His spirit goes one way, and his body another. High as he stood, the want of a little air brings him down to the ground, and lays him under it. Man who comes from the earth returns to the earth : it is the mother and sister of his body, and he must needs lie among his kindred as soon as the spirit which was his life has made its exit. There is a spirit in man, and when that goes the man goes. The spirit returns to God who gave it, and the flesh to the dust out of which it was fashioned. This is a poor creature to trust in : a dying creature, a corrupting creature. Those hopes will surely fall to the ground which are built upon men who so soon lie under ground.

"In that very day his thoughts perish." Whatever he may have proposed to do, the proposal ends in smoke. He cannot think, and what he had thought of cannot effect itself, and therefore it dies. Now that he has gone, men are ready enough to let his thoughts go with him into oblivion ; another thinker comes, and turns the thoughts of his predecessor to ridicule. It is a pitiful thing to be waiting upon princes or upon any other men, in the hope that they will think of us. In an hour they are gone, and where are their schemes for our promotion ? A day has ended their thoughts by ending *them ;* and our trusts have perished, for

their thoughts have perished. Men's ambitions, expectations, declarations, and boastings all vanish into thin air when the breath of life vanishes from their bodies. This is the narrow estate of man : his breath, his earth, and his thoughts ; and this is his threefold climax therein,—his breath goeth forth, to his earth he returns, and his thoughts perish. Is this a being to be relied upon ? Vanity of vanities, all is vanity. To trust it would be a still greater vanity.

5. *"Happy is he that hath the God of Jacob for his help."* Heaped up is his happiness. He has happiness indeed : the true and the real delight is with him. The God of Jacob is the God of the covenant, the God of wrestling prayer, the God of the tried believer ; he is the only living and true God. The God of Jacob is Jehovah, who appeared unto Moses, and led the tribes of Jacob out of Egypt, and through the wilderness. Those are happy who trust him, for they shall never be ashamed or confounded. The Lord never dies, neither do his thoughts perish : his purpose of mercy, like himself, endures throughout all generations. Hallelujah ! *"Whose hope is in the Lord his God."* He is happy in help for the present and in hope for the future, who has placed all his confidence in Jehovah, who is his God by a covenant of salt. Happy is he when others are despairing ! Happiest shall he be in that very hour when others are discovering the depths of agony. We have here a statement which we have personally tried and proved : resting in the Lord, we know a happiness which is beyond description, beyond comparison, beyond conception. O how blessed a thing it is to know that God is our present help, and our eternal hope. Full assurance is more than heaven in the bud, the flower has begun to open. We would not exchange with Cæsar ; his sceptre is a bauble, but our bliss is true treasure.

In each of the two titles here given, namely, " the God of Jacob," and " Jehovah his God," there is a peculiar sweetness. Either one of them has a fountain of joy in it ; but the first will not cheer us without the second. Unless Jehovah be his God no man can find confidence in the fact that he was Jacob's God. But when by faith we know the Lord to be ours, then we are " rich to all the intents of bliss."

6. *"Which made heaven, and earth, the sea, and all that therein is."* Wisely may we trust our Creator : justly may we expect to be happy in so doing. He who made heaven can make a heaven for us, and make us fit for heaven. He who made the earth can preserve us while we are on earth, and help us to make good use of it while we sojourn upon it. He who made the sea and all its mysteries can steer us across the pathless deeps of a troubled life, and make it a way for his redeemed to pass over. This God who still makes the world by keeping it in existence is assuredly able to keep us to his eternal kingdom and glory. The making of the worlds is the standing proof of the power and wisdom of that great God in whom we trust. It is our joy that he not only made heaven but the sea ; not only things which are bright and blessed, but things which are deep and dark. Concerning all our circumstances, we may say the Lord is there. In storms and hurricanes the Lord reigneth as truly as in that great calm which rules the firmament above. *"Which keepeth truth for ever."* This is a second and most forcible justification of our trust the Lord will never permit his promise to fail. He is true to his own nature, true to the relationships which he has assumed, true to his covenant, true to his Word, true to his Son. He keeps true, and is the keeper of all that is true. Immutable fidelity is the character of Jehovah's procedure. None can charge him with falsehood or vacillation.

7. *"Which executeth judgment for the oppressed."* He is a swift and impartial administrator of justice. Our king surpasses all earthly princes because he pays no deference to rank or wealth, and is never the respecter of persons. He is the friend of the down-trodden, the avenger of the persecuted, the champion of the helpless. Safely may we trust our cause with such a Judge if it be a just one : happy are we to be under such a Ruler. Are we " evil entreated " ? Are our rights denied us ? Are we slandered ? Let this console us, that he who occupies the throne will not only think upon our case, but bestir himself to execute judgment on our behalf. *"Which giveth food to the hungry."* Glorious King art thou, O Jehovah ! Thou dost not only mete out justice but thou dost dispense bounty ! All food comes from God ; but when we are reduced to hunger, and providence supplies our necessity, we are peculiarly struck with the fact. Let every hungry man lay hold on this statement, and plead it before the mercy-seat, whether he suffer bodily-hunger or heart-hunger. See how our God finds his special clients

among the lowest of mankind : the oppressed and the starving find help in the God of Jacob *"The LORD looseth the prisoners."* Thus he completes the triple blessing : justice, bread, and liberty. Jehovah loves not to see man pining in dungeons, or fretting in fetters ; he brought up Joseph from the round-house, and Israel from the house of bondage. Jesus is the Emancipator, spiritually, providentially, and nationally. Thy chains, O Africa ! were broken by his hand. As faith in Jehovah shall become common among men freedom will advance in every form, especially will mental, moral, and spiritual bonds be loosed, and the slaves of error, sin, and death shall be set free. Well might the Psalmist praise Jehovah, who is so kind to men in bonds ! Well may the loosened ones be loudest in the song !

8. *"The LORD openeth the eyes of the blind."* Jesus did this very frequently, and hereby proved himself to be Jehovah. He who made the eye can open it, and when he does so it is to his glory. How often is the mental eye closed in moral night ! And who can remove this dreary effect of the fall but the Almighty God ? This miracle of grace he has performed in myriads of cases, and it is in each case a theme for loftiest praise. *"The LORD raiseth them that are bowed down."* This also Jesus did literally, thus doing the work peculiar to God. Jehovah consoles the bereaved, cheers the defeated, solaces the despondent, comforts the despairing. Let those who are bowed to the ground appeal to him, and he will speedily upraise them. *"The LORD loveth the righteous."* He gives to them the love of complacency, communion, and reward. Bad kings affect the licentious, but Jehovah makes the upright to be his favoured ones. This is greatly to his glory. Let those who enjoy the inestimable privilege of his love magnify his name with enthusiastic delight. Loved ones, you must never be absent from the choir ! You must never pause from his praise whose infinite love has made you what you are.

9. *"The LORD preserveth the strangers."* Many monarchs hunted aliens down, or transported them from place to place, or left them as outlaws unworthy of the rights of man ; but Jehovah made special laws for their shelter within his domain. In this country the stranger was, a little while ago, looked upon as a vagabond, —a kind of wild beast to be avoided if not to be assaulted ; and even to this day there are prejudices against foreigners which are contrary to our holy religion. Our God and King is never strange to any of his creatures, and if any are left in a solitary and forlorn condition he has a special eye to their preservation. *"He relieveth the fatherless and widow."* These excite his compassion, and he shows it in a practical way by upraising them from their forlorn condition. The Mosaic law made provision for these destitute persons. When the secondary fatherhood is gone the child falls back upon the primary fatherhood of the Creator ; when the husband of earth is removed the godly widow casts herself upon the care of her Maker. *"But the way of the wicked he turneth upside down."* He fills it with crooked places ; he reverses it, sets it down, or upsets it. That which the man aimed at he misses, and he secures that for himself which he would gladly have avoided. The wicked man's way is in itself a turning of things upside down morally, and the Lord makes it so to him providentially : everything goes wrong with him who goes wrong.

10. *"The LORD shall reign for ever."* Jehovah is King, and his kingdom can never come to an end. Neither does he die, nor abdicate, nor lose his crown by force. Glory be to his name, his throne is never in jeopardy. As the Lord ever liveth, so he ever reigneth. *"Even thy God, O Zion, unto all generations."* Zion's God, the God of his worshipping people, is he who in every age shall reign. There will always be a Zion ; Zion will always have Jehovah for her King ; for her he will always prove himself to be reigning in great power. What should we do in the presence of so great a King, but enter into his courts with praise, and pay to him our joyful homage ? *"Praise ye the LORD."* Again they said Hallelujah. Again the sweet perfume arose from the golden vials full of sweet odours. Are we not prepared for an outburst of holy song ? Do not we also say—Hallelujah ? Here endeth this gladsome Psalm. Here endeth *not* the praise of the Lord, which shall ascend for ever and ever. Amen.

EXPLANATORY NOTES AND QUAINT SAYINGS.

Psalms cxlvi.—cxlviii.—At the dedication of the second Temple, in the beginning of the seventh year of Darius, Psalms cxlvii., cxlvi. and cxlviii., seem to have been sung ; for in the Septuagint Version they are styled the Psalms of Haggai and Zechariah, as if they had been composed by them for this occasion. This, no doubt, was from some ancient tradition ; but in the original Hebrew these Psalms have no such title prefixed to them, neither have they any other to contradict it.— *Humphrey Prideaux.*

Psalms cxlvi.—cl.—We do not know who put together these different sacred compositions, or whether they were arranged on any particular principle. This, however, is obvious,—that the last series, those that close the whole, are full of praise. Though we meet frequently with grief and shame and tears in the former part, a great deal that presses upon the spirit,—and in the centre a great many references to the various vicissitudes and fortunes through which the church or the individual has passed,—yet, as we get towards the end, and as the book closes, it is *Hallelujah—praise.* As the ancient church ceases to speak to us, as she lays down her lyre, and ceases to touch it, the last tones are tones of heaven ; as if the warfare were done, the conflict accomplished, and she were anticipating either the revelations which are to make her glorious here, the " new thing " which God is about to " create " when he places her under another dispensation, or as you and I (I trust) shall do when we come to die, anticipating the praise and occupation of that eternity and rest for which we hope in the bosom of God.—*Thomas Binney,* 1798—1874.

Whole Psalm.—This Psalm gives in brief the Gospel of Confidence. It inculcates the elements of Faith, Hope, and Thanksgiving.—*Martin Geier.*

Verse 1.—*"Praise ye the* LORD.*"* The word here used is *Alleluia,* and this is very proper to be constantly used by us who are dependent creatures, and under such great obligations to the Father of mercies. We have often heard of prayer doing great wonders ; but instances also are not wanting of praise being accompanied with signal events. The ancient Britons, in the year 420, obtained a victory over the army of the Picts and Saxons, near Mold, in Flintshire, The Britons, unarmed, having Germanicus and Lupus at their head, when the Picts and Saxons came to the attack, the two commanders, Gideon-like, ordered their little army to shout *Alleluia* three times over, at the sound of which the enemy, being suddenly struck with terror, ran away in the greatest confusion, and left the Britons masters of the field. A stone monument to perpetuate the remembrance of this Alleluia victory, I believe, remains to this day, in a field near Mold.—*Charles Buck,* 1771—1815.

Verse 1.—*"Praise the* LORD, *O my soul."* The Psalmist calls upon the noblest element of his being to exercise its noblest function.—*Hermann Venema.*

Verse 2.—*"While I live will I praise the* LORD.*"* Mr. John Janeway on his death-bed cried out thus,—" Come, help me with praises, yet all is too little. Come, help me, all ye mighty and glorious angels, who are so well skilled in the heavenly work of praise ! Praise him, all ye creatures upon earth ; let every thing that hath being help me to praise God. Hallelujah ! Hallelujah ! Hallelujah ! Praise is now my work, and I shall be engaged in this sweet work now and for ever. Bring the Bible ; turn to David's Psalms, and let us sing a Psalm of praise. Come, let us lift up our voices in the praises of the Most High. I will sing with you as long as my breath doth last, and when I have none, I shall do it better."

Verse 2.—*"While I live will I praise the* LORD.*"*—George Carpenter, the Bavarian martyr, being desired by some godly brethren, that when he was burning in the fire he would give them some sign of his constancy, answered, " Let this be a sure sign unto you of my faith and perseverance in the truth, that so long as I am able to hold open my mouth, or to whisper, I will never cease to praise God, and to profess his truth " ; the which also he did, saith mine author ; and so did many other martyrs besides.—*John Trapp.*

Verse 2.—*"I will sing praises unto my God while I have my being."* He had consecrated his entire earthly existence to the exercise of praise. And not only so, but he adds, *"I will sing praises unto my God while I have any being."* In which expression we may fairly conclude that the Psalmist stretches his thoughts beyond the limits of time, and contemplates that scene of eternal praise which shall succeed the less perfect songs of the church below.—*John Morison.*

Verse 2.—*"Unto my God."* Then praise is most pleasant, when in praising God we have an eye to him as ours, whom we have an interest in, and stand in relation to.—*Matthew Henry.*

Verse 2.—*"While I have any being."* Praise God for deliverance constantly. Some will be thankful while the memory of a deliverance is fresh, and then leave off. The Carthaginians used, at first, to send the tenth of their yearly revenues to Hercules ; and then by degrees they grew weary, and left off sending ; but we must be constant in our eucharistic sacrifice, or thankoffering. The motion of our praise must be like the motion of our pulse, which beats as long as life lasts.— *Thomas Watson.*

Verse 3.—*"Put not your trust in princes,"* etc. Through some kind of weakness, the soul of man, whensoever it is in tribulation here, despaireth of God, and chooseth to rely on man. Let it be said to one when set in some affliction, " There is a great man by whom thou mayest be set free ; " he smileth, he rejoiceth, he is lifted up. But if it is said to him, " God freeth thee," he is chilled, so to speak, by despair. The aid of the mortal is promised, and thou rejoicest ; the aid of the Immortal is promised, and art thou sad ? It is promised thee that thou shalt be freed by one who needeth to be freed with thee, and thou exultest as at some great aid : thou art promised that great Liberator, who needeth none to free him, and thou despairest, as though it were but a fable. Woe to such thoughts : they wander far ; truly there is sad and great death in them.—*Augustine.*

Verse 3.—*"Put not your trust in princes."* The word rendered " princes " signifieth liberal, bountiful ones, εὐεργέται, so princes would be accounted ; but there's no trusting to them without God, or against him.—*John Trapp.*

Verse 3.—*"Put not your trust in princes."* King Charles had given the Earl of Strafford a solemn pledge, on the word of a king, that he should not suffer in " life, honour, or fortune," yet with singular baseness and ingratitude, as well as short-sighted policy, gave his assent to the bill of attainder, On learning that this had been done, Strafford, laying his hand on his heart, and raising his eyes to heaven, uttered the memorable words, " Put not your trust in princes, nor in the sons of men, for in them there is no salvation."—*James Taylor, in the "Imperial Dictionary of Universal Biography,"* 1868.

Verse 3.—*"Put not your trust in princes."* Shakespeare puts this sentiment into Wolsey's mouth :—

> " O how wretched
> Is that poor man that hangs on princes' favour !
> There is, betwixt that smile we would aspire to,
> That sweet aspect of princes, and their ruin,
> More pangs and fears than wars and women have :
> And when he falls, he falls like Lucifer,
> Never to hope again."

Verse 3.—*"Put not your trust in princes,"* etc. True, may some say, it were a folly to trust in weak princes, to trust in them for help who have no power to help ; but we will apply to mighty princes ; we hope there is help in them. No ; those words, *"in whom there is no help,"* are not a distinction of weak princes from strong, but a conclusion that there is no help in the strongest. That's strange. What ? No help in strong princes ! If he had said, no help in mean men, carnal reason would have consented ; but when he saith, *"Trust not in princes, nor in any son of man,"* one or other, who can believe this ? Yet this is divine truth ; we may write *insufficiency, insufficiency,* and a third time, *insufficiency,* upon them all ; the close of this verse may be their motto, *"There is no help in them."*—*Joseph Caryl.*

Verse 3.—*"Princes."* Earthly princes offer baubles to allure the soul from the pursuit of an eternal prize. Princes themselves have pronounced their principality to be their own greatest peril. Pope Pius V. said, " When I was a monk I had hope of my salvation ; when I became Cardinal I began to fear ; when I was made Pope I all but despaired of eternity."—*Thomas Le Blanc.*

Verse 3.—*"Nor in the son of man."* All sons of man are like the man they are sprung of, who, being in honour, did not abide.—*Matthew Henry.*

Verse 3.—For one man to put confidence in another, is as if one beggar should ask an alms of another, or one cripple should carry another, or the blind lead the blind.—*Anthony Farindon.*

Verses 3, 4.—You see the first and the last, highest and lowest, of all the sons of Adam, they may be made honourable *"princes,"* but they are born sinful, *"the sons of men" ;* born weak, *"there is no help in them" ;* born mortal, *"their breath departeth ; "* born corruptible, *"they return to their earth " ;* and lastly, the mortality and corruption is not only in their flesh, but in some part or remnant of their spirits, for *"their thoughts perish."* The prophet (if you mark it) climbeth up by degrees to the disabling of the best men amongst us, and in them of all the rest. For if princes deserve not confidence, the argument must needs hold by comparison, much less do meaner men deserve it. The order of the words is so set that the members following are evermore either the reason or some confirmation to that which went before. *"Trust not in princes."* Why? Because they are *"the sons of men."* Why not in *"the sons of men" ?* Because there is *no help in them.* Why is there no help in them? Because when *"their breath goeth forth, they turn again to their earth."* What if their flesh be corrupted? Nay, *"their thoughts"* also *"come to nothing."*

For, first, this first order and rank which the prophet hath here placed, the princes and gods of the earth, are by birth *men ;* secondly, *weak* men, and such in whom *no help is ;* thirdly, not only weak, but *dying,* their breath goeth out ; fourthly, not only dying, but subject to dissolution, *they turn to the earth ;* fifthly, if their bodies only were dissolved, and their intentions and actions might stand, there were less cause to distrust them ; but their *thoughts* are as transitory as their bodies.—*John King* (1559 ?—1621), *in a Funeral Sermon.*

Verses 3, 4.—The Psalmist inscribes an antithesis. Princes, though masters of armies, possessors of riches, loaded with honours, revelling in pleasures, are at the mercy of a ruthless Black Prince. Death is tyrant over prince and peasant alike. The very pleasures which are envied are often ministers of death to voluptuous princes.—*Thomas Le Blanc.*

Verse 4.—*"He returneth to his earth."* The earth—the dust—*is* *"his."* 1. It is *"his"* as that from which he was made: he turns back to what he was, Genesis iii. 19. "Dust thou art, and unto dust shalt thou return." 2. The earth—the dust—the grave is *"his,"* and it is his home—the place where he will abide. 3. It is *"his"* as it is the only property which he has in reversion. All that a man— a prince, a nobleman, a monarch, a millionaire—will soon have will be his grave, his few feet of earth. *That* will be his by right of possession, by the fact that for the time being he will occupy it, and not another man ! But that, too, may soon become another man's grave, so that even there he is a tenant only for a time ; he has no permanent possession *even of a grave.*—*Albert Barnes.*

Verse 4.—*"His breath goeth forth."* There is the death's-head, the mortality of man indeed, that a breath is as much as his being is worth. Our soul, that *spiraculum vitarum* (breath of lives), the Lord inspired it, not into Adam's eye, or ear, or mouth, but into his nostrils, which may show to man his imbecility, *cujus anima in naribus,* whose soul is in his nostrils, and dependeth upon a breath, as it were ; for the very soul must away if but breath expires ; soul and breath go forth together.

Now hear this, all ye people, ponder it high and low ; your castle is built upon the very air, the subsistence is in your nostrils, in a breath that is gone in the twinkling of an eye. Wherefore David maketh a question, saying, " Lord, what is man ? " He answereth himself also : " Man is a vanishing shadow " (Ps. cxliv. 3, 4), a shadow of smoke, or the dream of a shadow rather, as the poet speaketh. Blessed therefore are the poor in spirit ; this advantage have all afflicted ones, that they have checks enough to call them home, and make them see they be but men. The curtain of honour, profit, or pleasure, hard it is and rare to draw aside when it is spread over us : " man in honour understandeth not " (Ps. xlix. 20). To great ones therefore be it spoken ; the Psalm intendeth it of very princes : *"His breath goeth forth."*

See we now the continuedness, *exit,* *"it goeth" ;* as if it were now presently in its passage : showing this, that *Homo vivens continuè moritur,* that life is a

continued death ; our candle lightens, consumes, and dies : as in the passing of
an hour-glass, every minute some sand falleth, and the glass once turned, no creature
can intreat the sands to stay, but they continue to fall till all are gone : so is our
life, it shortens and dies every minute, and we cannot beg a minute of time back,
and that which we call death is but the termination, or consummation of it.—
*Thomas Williamson ; in a Sermon, entitled, "A Comfortable Meditation of Humane
Frailtie and Divine Mercie,"* 1630.

Verse 4.—The primary idea of *breath* and the secondary one of *spirit* run into
each other in the usage of the Hebrew word רוח, so that either may be expressed
in the translation without entirely excluding the other.—*Joseph Addison Alexander.*

Verse 4.—"*His breath* (or spirit) *goeth forth.*" Now I come to the liberty of
the spirit, that it recedes inviolate ; 1. In Act ; "*it goeth :*" 2. In Essence ; "*it
goeth forth.*"

1. Our spirit is *free in the act ;* it is not snatched out, as it were ; "*it goeth.*"
A soul in life sealed to eternity by the first fruits of the Spirit hath its good issue,
its free passing, its hopes even in death ; for let this breath fade, *fidelis Deus,* God
who cannot lie, will stand nigh us in that exigency, and begin to help where man
leaveth. The Holy Spirit, whose name is the Comforter, will not omit and leave
off his own act or office in the great needs of death. Hence good Hilarion, having
served the Lord Christ seventy years, checks his soul that it was so loth at the last
to go forth, saying, *Egredere, O anima mea, egredere,* " Go forth, my soul, go forth."
Devout Simeon sueth for a manumission : " Lord, now lettest thou thy servant
depart in peace, according to thy word." The spirit goeth forth ; it passes freely ;
because it taketh up or embraceth the cross of Christ, as he commandeth us to
do. But is the act at our will and liberty ? Not simply. We may not *projicere
animam,* thrust or cast forth our breath or spirit ; *spiritus exit,* it goeth forth.
Strive, we must, to cast the world out of us ; we may not cast ourselves out of
the world. Saint Paul dareth not dissolve himself, though he could wish to be
dissolved : God must part that which he joins ; God giveth, and God taketh away ;
and if God say, as he doth to Lazarus, *Exi foras,* Come forth ; with faithful Stephen
we must resign our spirit and all into his hands. When God biddeth us yoke, he
is the wisest man that yieldeth his neck most willingly. When our great Captain
recalls us, we must take the retreat in good part. But it is heathenish to force
out the soul ; for when the misdeeming flesh, amidst our disasters, will not listen
with patience for God's call, but rather shake off the thought of divine providence
quite, then are we ready to curse God, and die, and that is probably to leap *e fumo
in flammam,* out of the sin of self-murder into hell. No, but God will have our
spirits to pass forth upon good terms. *Spiritus exit, "the spirit goeth forth."*

2. Secondly, the spirit goeth *free or inviolate in essence ;* death is not the end,
but the outgoing of the soul, a transmigration or journey from one place to another.
"*It goeth forth ;*" so the character of our weakness we see in the issue ; it is an
argument of our eternity ; for man indeed is perishing, but so is not his spirit. The
phœnix goes forth or out of his ashes, " the spirit returneth to God who gave it "
(Eccl. xii. 7) ; that is, it abides still ; and as in the body it pleased God to inclose
the soul for a season, so it may as well exist elsewhere without it, if God will ; for
it hath no rise at all from the clay, yea, it bears in it immortality, an image of that
breast whence it is breathed. The separate and very abstract acts of the spirit,
even while it is in the body, the wondrous visions of the Lord to his prophets, usually
when their bodies were bound up in sleep ; Saint Paul's rapture when he knew not
whether he was in the body or out of it ; the admirable inventions and arts of men,
manifest the soul's self-consisting. Not Socrates, and Cato, and the civilised heathen
only, but the very savages believe this, and so entertain death, *ut exitum, non ut
exitium,* as a dissolution, not as a destruction : *spiritus exit, "his spirit goeth forth."*
—*Thomas Williamson.*

Verse 4.—"*His breath goeth forth,*" etc. The Hebrew gives the idea not that
the *spirit,* but the mortal part of man will return to the dust. " His *soul* (fem. רוח)
goeth forth," *i.e.,* returneth to God : "returneth *he* (masc. שׁב) to his earth." As
in Eccl. xii. 7 : "*He* " is the mortal man of clay, but " his *breath* " (*soul*) is the real
immortal man.—*Simon de Muis.*

Verse 4.—"*He returneth to his earth.*" Returning, in its proper notion, is a-going
back to that place from whence we came, so that in this clause here is a threefold
truth, implied, expressed, inferred.

1. That which is *implied* in this phrase of returning is, that man in respect of his body came from the earth ; and as it is here implied, so it is expressed concerning the first man by Moses (Gen. ii. 7). " The Lord God formed man " (that is, the *body* of man) " of the dust " ; or according to the Hebrew, " dust of the ground " ; and by St. Paul (1 Cor. xv. 47), where he saith, " The first man is of the earth, earthy." True it is, we are formed in our mother's womb ; but yet inasmuch as we all came from the first man, we are truly said to come from *the earth ;* only with this difference, that he immediately, we mediately are framed out of the earth. This truth was engraven in full characters upon the name of the first man, who is called *Adam,* from a word that signifieth *red earth,* and that very word is here used, perhaps to mind us of that earth whereof man was first made ; yea, according to the usual etymology, the name *homo,* which in the Latin is a common name to both sexes, is derived *ab humo,* from *the ground.* For this reason it is that the earth is called by the poet *magna parens,* the great parent of all mankind, and in the answer of the Oracle, *our mother ;* and in this respect we are said by Eliphaz " to dwell in houses of clay, whose foundation is in the dust," Job iv. 19.

2. That which is *expressed* is, that man (when he dieth) returneth to the earth, πάντες λυόμενοι κόνις ἐσμέν, saith the poet, " We are all dust when dissolved." As the white snow when melted is black water ; so flesh and blood when bereaved of the soul become dust and ashes : in which respect St. Paul giveth this epithet of " vile " to our bodies. Phil. iii. 21. Indeed, man's original being from the earth, he had a natural propensity to earth ; according to the maxim, *Omne principiatum sequitur naturam principiorum,* " Everything hath an aptitude of returning to the principle whence it cometh " ; but yet had he not *turned away* from God he had never actually *returned* thither. It is sin which hath brought upon man a necessity of dying, and that dying brings a necessity of returning to the earth : in which respect it is observable, that the threat, " thou shalt die the death " (Gen. ii. 17), which was denounced against man before his fall, being afterwards renewed (iii. 19), is explained (as to temporal death) by these words, " to dust thou shalt return " ; so that now the motion of the little world man is like that of the great, *Circulare ab eodem puncto ad idem,* from the same to the same ; and that as in his *soul* from God to God, so in his *body* from the earth to the earth. The rivers come from the sea, and they return thither. The sun ariseth out of the east, and thither it returneth. Man is formed of the earth, and into earth he is again transformed : with which agreeth that of the poet Lucretius :

> Cedit item retro de terra quod fuit ante.

3. That which is *inferred* in the emphatical pronoun *"his,"* which is annexed to the noun *"earth,"* is that the earth to which man returneth is *his ;* this being that which ariseth out of both the former conclusions ; since it is therefore *his earth* because he cometh from and returneth to it. Earth is man's Genesis and Analysis, his composition and resolution, his Alpha and Omega, his first and last ; *Ortus pulvis, finis cinis ;* earth is his both originally and finally. So that our bodies can challenge no alliance with, or property in any thing so much as earth. For if we call those things *ours* which had only an external relation to us, as our friends, our horses, our goods, our lands ; much more may we call that *our earth* whereof we are made and into which we shall moulder ; no wonder it is here said to be *"his" ;* so elsewhere he is said to *be earth,* as being called by that name.—*Nathanael Hardy, in a Funeral Sermon entitled,* "*Man's Last Journey to His Long Home,*" 1659.

Verse 4.—"In that very day his thoughts perish." The thoughts which the Psalmist here, no doubt, especially intends are those *purposes* which are in the minds of great men of doing good to those who are under, and depend upon them. The Hebrew word here used is derived from a verb that signifieth *to be bright : cogitationes serenæ,* those candid, serene, benign, benevolent thoughts which they have of advancing their allies, friends and followers. These thoughts are said to *"perish"* in *"that day"* wherein they are conceived ; so Tremellius glosseth. In which sense the instability of great men's favour is asserted, whose smiles are quickly changed into frowns, love into hatred, and so in a moment their mind being changed, their wellwishing thoughts vanish. But more rationally, " their thoughts perish in that day " wherein their *persons die,* because there is no opportunity of putting their purposes into execution. They perish like the child which comes to the birth, and there is no strength to bring forth ; or like the fruit which is plucked off before it be ripe. Whilst they live we may be deceived in our expectations by the alteration of their minds ; but, however, their condition is mortal, and when that great change by death comes, their designs (how well soever meant) must want success.

From hence it followeth, which is by some looked upon as a part of the meaning of the words, that the *"thoughts"* or *hopes of them who trust in them perish.* It is a true apothegm, *Major pars hominum expectando moritur ;* the greatest part of men perish by expectation. And good reason, inasmuch as their expectation, being misplaced, perisheth. How strongly this argument serveth to press the Psalmist's caution against confidence in man, though never so great, is obvious. It is true, princes and nobles being invested with honour, wealth and authority, have power in their hands, and perhaps they may have thoughts in their hearts to do thee good ; but, alas, how uncertain is the execution of those intentions, and therefore how foolish is it to depend upon them. "Trust in the Lord Jehovah" (saith the prophet), " for with him is everlasting strength." Ay, and with him is unchangeable goodness. It is safe building upon the rock, trusting upon God, whose thoughts of mercy are (like himself) from everlasting to everlasting ; but nothing is more foolish than to build on the sand, trust to men, whose persons, together with their thoughts, perish in a moment. Therefore let our resolution be that of David : " It is better to trust in the Lord than to put confidence in man ; it is better to trust in the Lord than to put confidence in princes," Psalm cxviii. 8, 9.—*Nathanael Hardy.*

Verse 4.—"*In that very day his thoughts perish.*" At death a man sees all those thoughts which were not spent upon God to be fruitless. All worldly, vain thoughts, in the day of death perish and come to nothing. What good will the whole globe of the world do at such a time ? Those who have revelled out their thoughts in impertinences will but be the more disquieted ; it will cut them to the heart to think how they have spun a fool's thread. A Scythian captain having, for a draught of water, yielded up a city, cried out : " What have I lost ? What have I betrayed ? " So will it be with that man when he comes to die, who hath spent all his meditations upon the world ; he will say, What have I lost ? What have I betrayed ? I have lost heaven, I have betrayed my soul. Should not the considera- tion of this fix our minds upon the thoughts of God and glory ? All other meditations are fruitless ; like a piece of ground which hath much cost laid out upon it, but it yields no crop.—*Thomas Watson.*

Verse 4.—I would have you take this passage and illustrate it as applying to purposes, projects, and intentions. That, I think now, is precisely the idea intended to be conveyed. "*In that very day his thoughts perish*"; his purposes, his projects— what he intended to do. These cherished thoughts are gone. My dear brethren, there is something here for us. You find many beautiful passages and instances in Scripture in which this idea is embodied and realised, sometimes with great beauty and poetic effect, in relation to the enemies of the church. " The enemy said, I will pursue, I will overtake, I will divide the spoil, my hand shall destroy them ; thou didst blow with thy wind, the sea covered them, they sank as lead in the mighty waters." In that very day their thoughts perished. " Have they not sped ? have they not divided the prey ? to every man a damsel or two ? to Sisera a prey of divers colours of needlework ? So let all thine enemies perish, O Lord." The sacred poet does not even suggest that they had perished ; but feeling that it was a fact, only lifts up her heart to God. " So let all thine enemies perish, O Lord." And so you will find in many parts of Scripture beautiful ideas like this concerning the purposes and intentions that were in men's hearts utterly " perishing " by God's just laying his hand upon them—the purposes that were in their hearts against the church.—*Thomas Binney.*

Verse 4.—"*In that very day his thoughts perish.*" In the case of the rich fool (Luke xii. 16, 20), his " thoughts " of building larger barns, and of many years of ease and prosperity,—all his selfish and worldly schemes,—" perished " in that self-same night.—*John W. Haley, in "An Examination of the Alleged Discrepancies of the Bible,"* 1875.

Verse 4.—"*His thoughts perish.*" The science, the philosophy, the statesmanship of one age is exploded in the next. The men who are the masters of the world's intellect to-day are discrowned to-morrow. In this age of restless and rapid change they may survive their own thoughts ; their thoughts do not survive them.—*J. J. Stewart Perowne.*

Verse 4.—"*His thoughts perish.*" As the purposes of all about worldly things perish in the approaches of death, so do the purposes of some about spiritual and heavenly things. How many have had purposes to repent, to amend their lives and turn to God, which have been prevented and totally broken off by the extremity of pain and sickness, but chiefly by the stroke of death when they have (as they thought) " been about to repent," and (as we say) " turn over a new leaf " in their lives ; they have been turned into the grave by death, and into hell by the just wrath of God.—*Joseph Caryl.*

Verse 4.—*"His thoughts."* Rather, " his false, deceitful show"; literally, " his glitterings."—*Samuel Horsley, 1733—1806.*

Verse 4.—To trust man is to lean not on a pillar but on a little heap of dust. The proudest element in man is his thought. In the thoughts of his heart he is lifted up if nowhere else ; but, behold, even his proudest thoughts, says the Psalmist, will be degraded and perish in that dust to which he will return. Poor, perishing pride ! Who should trust it ?—*Johannes Paulus Palanterius.*

Verse 5.—*"Happy is he."* This is the last of the twenty-five places (or twenty-six, if Psalm cxxviii. 2 be included) in which the word *ashre*, with which the Psalter begins, is found.—*Speaker's Commentary.*

Verse 5.—Alas, how often do we trust when we should be afraid, and become afraid when we should trust !—*Lange's Commentary.*

Verse 5.—*"The God of Jacob."* A famous and significant description of God ; and that, First, *in respect of his nature,* or the verity and reality of his being and excellence. He is styled here by way of elegancy or emphasis, *"The God of Jacob,"* saith Mollerus, to discern and distinguish the true God of Israel from all Heathenish deities, and to explode all fictitious gods and all worships thereof. As the true God is the God of Jacob, so the God of Jacob is the true God. He is God alone, and there is no other besides him. . . . Secondly. This title or appellation serves also to describe him *in his special relation to his people.* We find him called by our Psalmist, " The mighty God of Jacob " : Ps. cxxxii. 5. He is indeed the God of the whole earth, but in a peculiar manner " the God of *Israel* " : Matt. xv. 31. . . . It is observable in Scripture that he styles not himself so frequently, in his revelations of himself to them, " the God of heaven and earth " (though that also is a title full of encouragement), but " the God of Abraham, Isaac, and Jacob " ; as if he had borne such choice goodwill, and had such a peculiar care for these three men, as to overlook all the world besides them. So near and intimate relation have God's people to him, that their interests are mutually involved, and twisted in a reciprocal and covenant bond. They are his, he is their portion ; their Beloved is theirs and they are his : they are called by his name, the saints are styled his " holy ones," and the Church is termed expressly " Christ." Yea, he condescends to be called by their name ; he assumes the name of *Jacob,* Ps. xxiv. 6 : " This is the generation of them that seek him, that seek thy face, O Jacob."—*From "The Saints' Ebenezer," by F. E.,* 1667.

Verse 5.—*"The God of Jacob."* This verse aptly warrants us to apply to all believers all the illustrations of *help* and *hope* furnished by Jacob in his exile when none but God could help him.—*Simon de Muis.*

Verses 5, 6.—*"The God of Jacob . . . . which made heaven and earth, the sea, and all that therein is."* It is a characteristic of these Psalms, to proclaim to all nations which worshipped idols that " the God of Jacob," " the God of Zion," is the Creator and Governor of all things ; and to make an appeal to all nations to turn to him. All these Psalms have a *missionary character* and an *evangelical function.* We may compare here the apostolic prayer at Jerusalem, after the descent of the Holy Ghost at Pentecost ; " They lifted up their voices to God with one accord, and said, Lord, thou art God, *that made heaven and earth, and the sea, and all that in them is* " (where the words are the same as in the Septuagint in this place): " Who by the mouth of thy servant David hast said, Why do the heathen rage ? " Acts iv. 24, 25. The office of these Psalms is to declare to the universe, that Jehovah, and he alone, is *Elohim ;* and to invite all to worship him as such, by their oft repeated *Hallelujah.*—*Christopher Wordsworth.*

Verse 6.—*"Which keepeth truth for ever."* Stored in his inexhaustible treasury as the most costly jewel ever there. And that because the *truth* which he so keeps, and which is the sustaining power which preserves the fabric of creation, is the Eternal Word, his only begotten Son, Jesus Christ.—*Dionysius the Carthusian, and Ayguan, in Neale and Littledale.*

Verse 6.—*"Which keepeth truth for ever."* God does indeed keep the truth from age to age—how else would the Book of God have lived ?—*John Lorinus.*

Verses 6—9.—The LORD, is an *Almighty* God, as the Creator of the universe ; next, he is a *faithful* God " who keepeth truth for ever " ; further, he is a *righteous* God (verse 7), a *bountiful* God (*ib.*) a *gracious* God (verses 7—9).—*J. J. Stewart Perowne.*

Verse 7.—*"Giveth food to the hungry."* We learn from this that he is not always so indulgent to his own as to load them with abundance, but occasionally withdraws his blessing, that he may succour them when reduced to hunger. Had the Psalmist said that God fed his people with abundance, and pampered them, would not any of those under want or in famine have immediately desponded ? The goodness of God is therefore properly extended farther to the feeding of the hungry.—*John Calvin.*

Verse 7.—*"Giveth food to the hungry."* Now, that Jesus was that Lord of whom the Psalmist in this place, and in Ps. cxlv. 16, speaketh, was fully testified by the miracles which he wrought, in feeding many thousands with some few loaves and two small fishes, and in filling so many baskets with the fragments or relics of that provision wherewith he had filled thousands. From these miracles, the people which had seen him do them, and tasted of his bounty, did rightly infer that he was the prophet which was to come into the world, as you may read, John vi. 14 ; and being supposed to be the prophet, they consequently presumed that he was likewise to be the King of Israel ; and out of this concert or presumption they would have enforced him to be their king, verse 15.—*Thomas Jackson,* 1579—1640.

Verse 7.—*"The LORD looseth the prisoners."* As in that place of Isaiah (lxi. 1) the phrase of " opening the prison to them that are bound," is by the learned thought to be a prophetic elegance, to signify the cure of those that are deaf and dumb, whose souls consequently were shut up from being able to express themselves, as language enables others to do ; so here also it may be used poetically, and then it will be directly parallel to that part of Christ's answer, " the deaf hear " (Matt. xi. 5). At the curing of such, Christ's form of speech was, Ephphatha, " be opened," as to the door of a prison, when those which were under restraint therein were to be let loose out of it, their fetters being shaken off from them. But then, 'tis further manifest, that those that were under any sore disease or lameness, etc., are said to be " bound by Satan " (Luke xiii. 16), and be " loosed " by Christ, when they were cured by him. So saith Christ (verse 12), " Woman, thou art loosed from thine infirmity : and immediately she was made straight." Her being " made straight " was her being loosed out of her restraint, or bonds, or prison. And in this latitude of the poetic or prophetic expression, the Lord's *loosing the prisoners* here will comprehend the walking of the lame, the lepers being cleansed, the hearing of the deaf, yea, and the raising up of the dead ; for those of all others are fastest bound, and so when they were raised, the style is as proper as to Lazarus in respect of the graveclothes, " loose them, and let him go."—*Henry Hammond.*

Verses 7, 8.—It ought not to pass without remark that the name Jehovah is repeated here five times in five lines, to intimate that it is an almighty power, that of Jehovah, that is engaged and exerted for the relief of the oppressed ; and that it is as much to the glory of God to succour them that are in misery, as it is to ride on the heavens by his name JAH, Ps. lxviii. 4.—*Matthew Henry.*

Verse 8.—*"Openeth the eyes of the blind."* Literally, *"openeth the blind"*—*i.e.*, maketh them to see. The expression may be used figuratively, as a remedy applied either to physical helplessness, as Deut. xxviii. 29 ; Isa. lix. 9, 10 ; Job xii. 25 ; or to spiritual want of discernment, as Isa. xxix. 18 ; xlii. 7, 18 ; xliii. 8. Here the context favours the former.—*J. J. Stewart Perowne.*

Verse 8.—*"The LORD openeth the eyes of the blind."* The Hebrew does not mention *the eyes* of the blind. Hilary renders it *sapientificat.* The Arabic version follows the same. Jehovah by his *wisdom illumines dark minds.* It is *mental* blindness which is the common affliction of men.—*John Lorinus.*

Verse 8.—*"The blind."* The large number of blind persons to be seen feeling their way along the streets in Cairo and Alexandria has been noticed by Volney. " Walking in the streets of Cairo," he says, " out of a hundred persons whom I met, there were often twenty blind, eighteen one eyed, and twenty others with eyes red, purulent, or spotted. Almost every one wears bandages, indicating that they either have or are recovering from ophthalmia." Ophthalmia is, in fact, one of the scourges of Egypt, as all physicians know. Its prevalence must be attributed in a great degree to the sand which the wind blows into the eyes ; but one can understand how in Oriental countries in general the excessive heat of the sun must make blindness much commoner than it is with us.

It is not therefore surprising to any one who knows the East to find the blind so often mentioned in the gospel history, and to meet in Scripture with so many allusions to this infirmity. Of the twelve maledictions of the Levites there is one against him " who maketh the blind to go out of the way " : Deut. xxvii. 18. " The spirit of God hath anointed me," said Jesus, quoting from Isaiah, " to preach the gospel to the poor, and recovery of sight to the blind " : Luke iv. 19. " The Lord," says David, " setteth at liberty them that are bound ; the Lord giveth sight to the blind."—*Felix Bovet* (1824—), *in "Egypt, Palestine, and Phœnicia,"* 1882.

Verse 9.—*"The* Lord *preserveth the strangers."* God has peculiar love for wanderers and pilgrims (Deut. x. 18), and Jacob was a stranger in a strange land when God showed himself to be the God of Jacob as his elect servant.—*Thomas Le Blanc.*

Verse 9.—*"The* Lord *preserveth the strangers."* They who do not belong to Babylon, nor to this world, but the true pilgrims in a strange land.—*Robert Bellarmine.*

Verse 9.—*"He relieveth the fatherless and widow."* The olive tree is not to be twice shaken, the vineyard is not to be twice gathered, nor are the sheaves of corn left in the fields to be gleaned ; all that belongs to the poor, to the widow and the orphan. It was allowable to pluck with the hand the ears of corn while passing through a neighbour's field (Deut. xxiii. 25), though a sickle might not be used. The law cares most anxiously for widows and orphans, for " God is a father of the fatherless and a judge of the widows " (Ps. lxviii. 5). A widow's raiment might not be taken in pledge, and both widows and orphans were to be invited to their feasts. An institution specially designed for the protection and relief of the poor was the second tithe, the so-called poor's-tithe. The first tithe belonged to the Levites. What remained over was again tithed, and the produce of this second tithe, devoted in the first two years to a feast in the sanctuary at the offering of first-fruits, was devoted in the third year to a feast in the dwelling-house, to which the Levites and the strangers, the widows and the orphans, were invited (Deut. xiv. 28, 29 ; xxvi. 12, 13.)—*G. Uhlhorn, in "Christian Charity in the Ancient Church,"* 1883.

Verse 9.—*"The way of the wicked he turneth upside down."* He overturns their plans, defeats their schemes ; makes their purposes accomplish what they did not intend they should accomplish. The Hebrew word here means to bend, to curve, to make crooked, to distort ; then, to overturn, to turn upside down. The same word is applied to the conduct of the wicked, in Ps. cxix. 78 : " They dealt perversely with me." The idea here is that the path is not a straight path ; that God makes it a crooked way ; that they are diverted from their design ; that through them he accomplishes purposes which they did not intend ; that he prevents their accomplishing their own designs ; and that he will make their plans subservient to a higher and better purpose than their own. This is the eleventh reason why those who put their trust in God are happy. It is that God is worthy of confidence and love, because he has all the plans of wicked men entirely under his control.—*Albert Barnes.*

Verse 9.—*"The way of the wicked he turneth upside down."* As the potter's clay, when the potter hath spent some time and pains in tempering and forming it upon the wheel, and now the vessel is even almost brought to its shape, a man that stands by may, with the least push, put it clean out of shape, and mar all on a sudden that he hath been so long a-making : so is it that all the plots and contrivances of wicked men, all their turning of things upside down shall be but as the potter's clay ; for when they think they have brought all to maturity, ripeness, and perfection, when they look upon their business as good as done, all on a sudden all their labour is lost ; for God, who stands by all the while and looks on, will, with one small touch, with the least breath of his wrath, blast and break all in pieces.—*Edlin,* 1656.

Verse 9.—*"The way of the wicked he turneth upside down."* All the ten clauses preceding lift up the poor saint step by step, higher and higher. At one word suddenly, like Satan falling as lightning from heaven, the wicked are shown dashed down the whole way from the summit of pride to the depths of hell.—*Johannes Paulus Palanterius.*

Verse 9.—*"The way of the wicked he turneth upside down."* A striking illustration of the folly of counting God out of one's plans for life, is given in the course of William M. Tweed, whose death is recently announced. Here was a man who sought wealth and power, and who for a time seemed successful in their pursuit. Apparently he did not propose to obey God or to live for a life to come. What he wanted was worldly prosperity. He thought he had it. He went to congress. He gathered his millions. He controlled the material interests of the metropolis of his country. He openly defied public sentiment and courts of justice in the prosecution of his plans. He was a brilliant and therefore a dangerous example of successful villainy. But the promise of prosperity for the life which now is, is only to the godly. As William M. Tweed lay dying in a prison-house in the city he once ruled, his confession of bitter disappointment was, " My life has been a failure in everything. There is nothing I am proud of." If any young man wants to come to an end like this, the way to it is simple and plain. " The great God that formed all things both rewardeth the fool, and rewardeth transgressors." *"The way of the wicked he turneth upside down."—American Sunday School Times,* 1878.

HINTS TO PREACHERS.

Verse 1.—I. An exhortation : it is addressed to ourselves : " Praise ye the Lord." II. An example : the Psalmist cries to himself, " Praise the Lord." III. An echo : " Praise the Lord, O my soul." Let us say this to our own souls.

Verse 1.—Whom should I praise ? And why ? And when ? And how ?

Verse 1.—Public worship. I. Should be with a sense of fellowship : " Praise *ye* " : pleasures of communion in praise. II. Should never lose its individuality : " O my soul." God is only praised by individual hearts. Temptations to wandering in public services. III. Should be full of Jehovah's felt presence : each and all should worship *him* alone.—*W. B. H.*

Verse 2.—Work for here and hereafter. I. " While I live " ; or a period of uncertainty and mystery. II. " I will praise the Lord " ; or a service definite, determined, due, and delightful. Certainty amid uncertainty. III. " While I have any being " ; or an enthusiastic pre-engagement of eternity.—*W. B. H.*

Verse 3.—I. It dishonours God. II. It degrades you. III. It disappoints in every case.

Verse 4.—Decease, Decay, Defeat.

Verse 4 (*second clause*). The failure of man's projects, the disappearance of his philosophies, the disproving of his boastings.

Verse 5.—The secret of true happiness. I. *What it is not.* The man here mentioned has his work and warfare, for he needs help ; and he has not all he desires, for he is a man of hope. II. *What it is.* It lies in the *hath,* the *help,* and the *hope,* and these are all in God.

Verses 6, 7.—The God of our hope is, I. Creator. II. Truth-keeper. III. Vindicator. IV. Provider. V. Deliverer.

Verse 7 (*last clause*).—See " Spurgeon's Sermons," No. 484 : " The Lord—the Liberator."

Verse 7.—The People's Rights. I. Three rights of humanity. Justice, Bread, Freedom. II. God's interventions in their behalf. Revolutions, Reforms, Regenerations. Christ's war with Satan. III. The magnificent supply of the three blessings in Christ's kingdom. IV. The men who are fashioned and trained under this *régime.—W. B. H.*

Verse 8 (*first clause*).—Spiritual blindness, its curse, cause, and cure.

Verse 8 (*second clause*).—Who are the people ? Who raises them ? How he does it. And what then ?

Verse 8 (*third clause*).—God's love to the righteous. I. He made them righteous. II. They are like him. III. They love him. IV. Their purposes are one with his own.

Verse 9.—Observe the provision made in the Jewish law for the stranger. The way in which strangers were received by God. The truth that his chosen are strangers in the world. His design to gather in strangers in the latter days.

Verse 9 (*centre clause*).—The claims of orphans and widows upon the people of God.

Verse 9 (*last clause*).—Illustrated by Joseph's brethren, Haman, and others.

Verse 10.—I. A cause for praise—" The Lord shall reign for ever." II. A centre of praise : " O Zion." III. A cycle of praise : " all generations." IV. A call to praise : " Praise ye the Lord."

PSALM CXLVII.

SUBJECT.—*This is a specially remarkable song. In it the greatness and the condescending goodness of the Lord are celebrated. The God of Israel is set forth in his peculiarity of glory as caring for the sorrowing, the insignificant, and forgotten. The poet finds a singular joy in extolling one who is so singularly gracious. It is a Psalm of the city and of the field, of the first and the second creations, of the commonwealth and of the church. It is good and pleasant throughout.*

DIVISION.—*The song appears to divide itself into three portions. From 1 to 6, Jehovah is extolled for building up Zion, and blessing his mourners; from 7 to 11, the like praise is given because of his provision for the lowly, and his pleasure in them; and then, from 12 to 20, he is magnified for his work on behalf of his people, and the power of his word in nature and in grace. Let it be studied with joyful gratitude.*

EXPOSITION.

PRAISE ye the LORD : for *it is* good to sing praises unto our God ; for *it is* pleasant ; *and* praise is comely.

2 The LORD doth build up Jerusalem : he gathereth together the outcasts of Israel.

3 He healeth the broken in heart, and bindeth up their wounds.

4 He telleth the number of the stars ; he calleth them all by *their* names.

5 Great *is* our Lord, and of great power : his understanding *is* infinite.

6 The LORD lifteth up the meek : he casteth the wicked down to the ground.

1. "*Praise ye the LORD,*" or Hallelujah. The flow of the broad river of the Book of Psalms ends in a cataract of praise. The present Psalm begins and ends with Hallelujah. Jehovah and happy praise should ever be associated in the mind of a believer. Jove was dreaded, but Jehovah is beloved. To one and all of the true seed of Israel the Psalmist acts as choir-master, and cries, " Praise *ye* the Lord." Such an exhortation may fitly be addressed to all those who owe anything to the favour of God ; and which of us does not ? Pay him we cannot, but praise him we will, not only now, but for ever. "*For it is good to sing praises unto our God.*" It is good because it is right ; good because it is acceptable with God, beneficial to ourselves, and stimulating to our fellows. The goodness of an exercise is good argument with good men for its continual practice. Singing the divine praises is the best possible use of speech : it speaks of God, for God, and to God, and it does this in a joyful and reverent manner. Singing in the heart is good, but singing with heart and voice is better, for it allows others to join with us. Jehovah is *our* God, our covenant God, therefore let him have the homage of our praise ; and he is so gracious and happy a God that our praise may best be expressed in joyful song.

"*For it is pleasant ; and praise is comely.*" It is pleasant and proper, sweet and suitable to laud the Lord Most High. It is refreshing to the taste of the truly refined mind, and it is agreeable to the eye of the pure in heart : it is delightful both to hear and to see a whole assembly praising the Lord. These are arguments for song-service which men who love true piety, real pleasure, and strict propriety will not despise. Please to praise, for praise is pleasant : praise the Lord in the beauty of holiness, for praise is comely. Where duty and delight, benefit and beauty unite, we ought not to be backward. Let each reader feel that he and his family ought to constitute a choir for the daily celebration of the praises of the Lord.

2. "*The LORD doth build up Jerusalem.*" God appears both in the material and spiritual world as a Builder and Maker, and therein he is to be praised. His grace, wisdom, and power are all seen in the formation and establishment of the chosen seat of his worship ; once a city with material walls, but now a church

composed of spiritual stones. The Jews rejoiced in the uprising of their capital from its ruins, and we triumph in the growth of the church from among a godless world. *"He gathereth together the outcasts of Israel"*; and thus he repairs the waste places, and causes the former desolations to be inhabited. This sentence may relate to Nehemiah and those who returned with him; but there is no reason why it should not with equal fitness be referred to David, who, with his friends, was once an outcast, but ere long became the means of building up Jerusalem. In any case, the Psalmist ascribes to Jehovah all the blessings enjoyed; the restoration of the city and the restoration of the banished he equally traces to the divine hand. How clearly these ancient believers saw the Lord present, working among them and for them ! Spiritually we see the hand of God in the edification of the church, and in the ingathering of sinners. What are men under conviction of sin but outcasts from God, from holiness, from heaven, and even from hope ? Who could gather them from their dispersions, and make citizens of them in Christ Jesus save the Lord our God ? This deed of love and power he is constantly performing. Therefore let the song begin at Jerusalem our home, and let every living stone in the spiritual city echo the strain ; for it is the Lord who has brought again his banished ones, and builded them together in Zion.

3. *"He healeth the broken in heart, and bindeth up their wounds."* This the Holy Spirit mentions as a part of the glory of God, and a reason for our declaring his praise : the Lord is not only a Builder, but a Healer ; he restores broken hearts as well as broken walls. The kings of the earth think to be great through their loftiness ; but Jehovah becomes really so by his condescension. Behold, the Most High has to do with the sick and the sorry, with the wretched and the wounded ! He walks the hospitals as the good Physician ! His deep sympathy with mourners is a special mark of his goodness. Few will associate with the despondent, but Jehovah chooses their company, and abides with them till he has healed them by his comforts. He deigns to handle and heal broken hearts : he himself lays on the ointment of grace, and the soft bandages of love, and thus binds up the bleeding wounds of those convinced of sin. This is compassion like a God. Well may those praise him to whom he has acted so gracious a part. The Lord is always healing and binding : this is no new work to him, he has done it of old ; and it is not a thing of the past of which he is now weary, for he is still healing and still binding, as the original hath it. Come, broken hearts, come to the Physician who never fails to heal : uncover your wounds to him who so tenderly binds them up !

4. *"He telleth the number of the stars."* None but he can count the mighty host, but as he made them and sustains them he can number them. To Jehovah stars are as mere coins, which the merchant tells as he puts them into his bag. *"He calleth them all by their names."* He has an intimate acquaintance with each separate orb, so as to know its name or character. Indeed, he gives to each its appropriate title, because he knows its constitution and nature. Vast as these stars are, they are perfectly obedient to his bidding ; even as soldiers to a captain who calls their names, and allots them their stations. Do they not rise, and set, and move, or stand, precisely according to his order ? What a change is here from the preceding verse ! Read the two without a break, and feel the full force of the contrast. From stars to sighs is a deep descent ! From worlds to wounds is a distance which only infinite compassion can bridge. Yet he who acts a surgeon's part with wounded hearts, marshals the heavenly host, and reads the muster-roll of suns and their majestic systems. O Lord, it is good to praise thee as ruling the stars, but it is pleasant to adore thee as healing the broken in heart !

5. *"Great is our Lord."* Our Lord and King is great—magnanimous, infinite, inconceivably glorious. None can describe his majesty, or reckon up the number of his excellences. *"And of great power."* Doing as he wills, and willing to do mighty deeds. His acts reveal something of his might, but the mass of his power is hidden, for all things are possible with God, even the things impossible with men. *"His understanding is infinite."* There is no fathoming his wisdom, or measuring his knowledge. He is infinite in existence, in power, and in knowledge, as these three phrases plainly teach us. The gods of the heathen are nothing, but our God filleth all things. And yet how condescending ! For this is he who so tenderly nurses the sick souls, and waits to be gracious to sinful men. He brings his boundless power and infinite understanding to bear upon human distress for its assuagement and sanctification. For all these reasons let his praise be great : even could it be infinite, it would not exceed his due. In the building of his church and the salvation of

souls, his greatness, power, and wisdom are all displayed : let him be extolled because of each of these attributes.

6. *"The LORD lifteth up the meek : he casteth the wicked down to the ground."* He reverses the evil order of things. The meek are down, and he lifts them up ; the wicked are exalted, and he hurls them down to the dust. The Lord loves those who are reverent to himself, humble in their own eyes, and gentle to their fellow-men : these he lifts up to hope, to peace, to power, to eternal honour. When God lifts a man, it is a lift indeed. Proud men are, in their own esteem, high enough already ; only those who are low will care to be lifted up, and only such will Jehovah upraise. As for the wicked, they must come down from their seats of vain glory. God is accustomed to overthrow such ; it is his way and habit. None of the wicked shall in the end escape. To the earth they must go ; for from the earth they came, and for the earth they live. It is one of the glories of our God for which his saints praise him, that he hath put down the mighty from their seats, and hath exalted them of low degree. Well may the righteous be lifted up in spirit and the wicked be downcast as they think of the judgments of the Lord God.

In this verse we see the practical outcome of that character of Jehovah, which leads him to count and call the stars as if they were little things, while he deals tenderly with sorrowful men, as if they were precious in his esteem. He is so great that nothing is great to him, and he is so condescending that nothing is little to him : his infinite majesty thus naturally brings low the lofty and exalts the lowly.

7 Sing unto the LORD with thanksgiving ; sing praise upon the harp unto our God :

8 Who covereth the heaven with clouds, who prepareth rain for the earth, who maketh grass to grow upon the mountains.

9 He giveth to the beast his food, *and* to the young ravens which cry.

10 He delighteth not in the strength of the horse : he taketh not pleasure in the legs of a man.

11 The LORD taketh pleasure in them that fear him, in those that hope in his mercy.

7. In this paragraph the contrast announced in the former section is enlarged upon from another point of view, namely, as it is seen in nature and in providence.

"Sing unto the LORD with thanksgiving ;" or rather, "respond to Jehovah." He speaks to us in his works, let us answer him with our thanks. All that he does is gracious, every movement of his hand is goodness ; therefore let our hearts reply with gratitude, and our lips with song. Our lives should be responses to divine love. Jehovah is ever engaged in giving, let us respond with thanksgiving.

"Sing praise upon the harp unto our God." Blend music with song. Under a dispensation of ritual the use of music was most commendable, and suitable in the great congregation : those of us who judge it to be less desirable for public worship, under a spiritual economy, because it has led to so many abuses, nevertheless rejoice in it in our privacy, and are by no means insensible to its charms. It seems a profanation that choice minstrelsy should so often be devoted to unworthy themes : the sweetest harmonies should be consecrated to the honour of the Lord. He is *our* God, and this fact is one choice joy of the song. We have chosen him because he has chosen us ; and we see in him peculiarities which distinguish him from all the pretended deities of those among whom we dwell. He is *our* God in covenant relationship for ever and ever, and to him be praise in every possible form.

8. *"Who covereth the heaven with clouds."* He works in all things, above as well as below. Clouds are not caused by accident, but produced by God himself, and made to assume degrees of density by which the blue firmament is hidden. A sky-scape might seem to be a mere fortuitous concourse of vapours, but it is not so : the Great Artist's hand thus covers the canvas of the heavens. *"Who prepareth rain for the earth."* The Lord prepares clouds with a view to rain, and rain with an eye to the fields below. By many concurrent circumstances all things are made ready for the production of a shower ; there is more of art in the formation of a rain-cloud and in the fashioning of a rain-drop, than appears to superficial observers. God is in the vapour, and in the pearly drop which is born of it. *"Who maketh grass to grow upon the mountains."* By the far-reaching shower he produces vegetation where the hand of man is all unknown. He cares not only for Goshen's fertile plains,

but for Carmel's steep ascents. God makes the heavens the servants of the earth, and the clouds the irrigators of the mountain meadows. This is a kind of evolution about which there can be no dispute. Nor does the Lord forget the waste and desolate places, but causes the lone hills to be the first partakers of his refreshing visitations. This is after the manner of our God. He not only causes rain to descend from the heavens to water the grass, and thus unites the skies and the herbs by a ministry of mercy; but he also thinks of the rocky ledges among the hills, and forgets not the pastures of the wilderness. What a God is this !

> " Passing by the rich and great,
> For the poor and desolate."

9. *"He giveth to the beast his food."* By causing the grass to grow on the hills the Lord feeds the cattle. God careth for the brute creation. Men tread grass under foot as though it were nothing, but God causeth it to grow; too often men treat their cattle with cruelty, but the Lord himself feedeth them. The great God is too good, and, indeed, too great to overlook things that are despised. Say not, " Doth God care for oxen ? " Indeed he does, and he permits himself to be here described as giving them their food as husbandmen are wont to do. *"And to the young ravens which cry."* These wild creatures, which seem to be of no use to man ; are they therefore worthless ? By no means ; they fill their place in the economy of nature. When they are mere fledgelings, and can only clamour to the parent birds for food, the Lord does not suffer them to starve, but supplies their needs. Is it not wonderful how such numbers of little birds are fed ! A bird in a cage under human care is in more danger of lacking seed and water than any one of the myriads that fly in the open heavens, with no owner but their Creator, and no provider but the Lord. Greatness occupied with little things makes up a chief feature of this Psalm. Ought we not all to feel special joy in praising One who is so specially remarkable for his care of the needy and the forgotten ? Ought we not also to trust in the Lord ? for he who feeds the sons of the raven will surely nourish the sons of God ! Hallelujah to him who both feeds the ravens and rules the stars ! What a God art thou, O Jehovah !

10. *"He delighteth not in the strength of the horse."* Not to great and strong animals doth the Creator in any measure direct his special thought ; but in lesser living things he has equal pleasure. If man could act the Creator's part, he would take peculiar delight in producing noble quadrupeds like horses, whose strength and speed would reflect honour upon their maker ; but Jehovah has no such feeling ; he cares as much for helpless birds in the nest as for the war-horse in the pride of its power. *"He taketh not pleasure in the legs of a man."* These are the athlete's glory, but God hath no pleasure in them. Not the capacities of the creature, but rather its weakness and necessity, win the regard of our God. Monarchs trust in their cavalry and infantry ; but the King of kings exults not in the hosts of his creatures as though they could lend power to him. Physical or material greatness and power are of no account with Jehovah ; he has respect to other and more precious qualities. Men who boast in fight the valour of gigantic might, will not find themselves the favourites of God : though earthly princes may feast their eyes upon their Joabs and their Abners, their Abishais and Asahels, the Lord of hosts has no pleasure in mere bone and muscle. Sinews and thews are of small account, either in horses or in men, with Him who is a spirit, and delights most in spiritual things. The expression of the text may be viewed as including all creature power, even of a mental or moral kind. God does not take pleasure in us because of our attainments, or potentialities : he respects character rather than capacity.

11. *"The* LORD *taketh pleasure in them that fear him, in those that hope in his mercy."* While the bodily powers give no content to God, spiritual qualities are his delight. He cares most for those emotions which centre in himself : the fear which he approves is fear *of him,* and the hope which he accepts is hope *in his mercy.* It is a striking thought that God should not only be at peace with some kinds of men, but even find a solace and a joy in their company. Oh ! the matchless condescension of the Lord, that his greatness should take pleasure in the insignificant creatures of his hand. Who are these favoured men in whom Jehovah takes pleasure ? Some of them are the least in his family, who have never risen beyond hoping and fearing. Others of them are more fully developed, but still they exhibit a blended character composed of fear and hope : they fear God with holy awe and filial reverence, and they also hope for forgiveness and blessedness because of the divine mercy. As a father takes pleasure in his own children, so doth the Lord solace himself in his own

beloved ones, whose marks of new birth are fear and hope. They fear, for they are sinners ; they hope, for God is merciful. They fear him, for he is great ; they hope in him, for he is good. Their fear sobers their hope ; their hope brightens their fear : God takes pleasure in them both in their trembling and in their rejoicing.

Is there not rich cause for praise in this special feature of the divine character ? After all, it is a poor nature which is delighted with brute force ; it is a diviner thing to take pleasure in the holy character of those around us. As men may be known by the nature of the things which give them pleasure, so is the Lord known by the blessed fact that he taketh pleasure in the righteous, even though that righteousness is as yet in its initial stage of fear and hope.

12 Praise the LORD, O Jerusalem ; praise thy God, O Zion.

13 For he hath strengthened the bars of thy gates ; he hath blessed thy children within thee.

14 He maketh peace *in* thy borders, *and* filleth thee with the finest of the wheat.

15 He sendeth forth his commandment *upon* earth : his word runneth very swiftly.

16 He giveth snow like wool : he scattereth the hoarfrost like ashes.

17 He casteth forth his ice like morsels : who can stand before his cold ?

18 He sendeth out his word, and melteth them : he causeth his wind to blow, *and* the waters flow.

19 He sheweth his word unto Jacob, his statutes and his judgments unto Israel.

20 He hath not dealt so with any nation : and *as for his* judgments, they have not known them. Praise ye the LORD.

12. *"Praise the* LORD, *O Jerusalem ; praise thy God, O Zion."* How the poet insists upon praise ; he cries *praise, praise,* as if it were the most important of all duties. A peculiar people should render peculiar praise. The city of peace should be the city of praise ; and the temple of the covenant God should resound with his glories. If nowhere else, yet certainly in Zion there should be joyful adoration of Zion's God. Note, that we are to praise the Lord in our own houses in Jerusalem as well as in his own house in Zion. The holy city surrounds the holy hill, and both are dedicated to the holy God, therefore both should ring with hallelujahs.

13. *"For he hath strengthened the bars of thy gates."* Her fortifications were finished, even to the fastenings of the gates, and God had made all sound and strong, even to her bolts and bars : thus her security against invading foes was guaranteed. This is no small mercy. Oh, that our churches were thus preserved from all false doctrine and unholy living ! This must be the Lord's doing ; and where he has wrought it his name is greatly to be praised. Modern libertines would tear down all gates and abolish all bars ; but so do not we, because of the fear of the Lord. *"He hath blessed thy children within thee."* Internal happiness is as truly the Lord's gift as external security. When the Lord blesses " thy sons in the midst of thee," thou art, O Zion, filled with a happy, united, zealous, prosperous, holy people, who dwell in communion with God, and enter into the joy of their Lord. When God makes thy walls salvation thy gates must be praise. It would little avail to fortify a wretched, starving city ; but when the walls are strengthened, it is a still greater joy to see that the inhabitants are blessed with all good gifts. How much our churches need a present and abiding benediction.

14. *"He maketh peace in thy borders."* Even to the boundaries quiet extends ; no enemies are wrangling with the borderers. If there is peace there, we may be sure that peace is everywhere. " When a man's ways please the Lord he maketh even his enemies to be at peace with him." Peace is from the God of peace. Considering the differing constitutions, conditions, tastes, and opinions of men, it is a work of God when in large churches unbroken peace is found year after year ; and it is an equal wonder if worldlings, instead of persecuting the godly, treat them with marked respect. He who builds Zion is also her Peace-maker, the Lord and Giver of peace. *"And filleth thee with the finest of the wheat."* Peace is attended with plenty,—plenty of the best food, and of the best sort of that food. It is a great reason for thanksgiving when men's wants are so supplied that they are filled :

it takes much to fill some men : perhaps none ever are filled but the inhabitants of Zion ; and they are only to be filled by the Lord himself. Gospel truth is the finest of the wheat, and those are indeed blessed who are content to be filled therewith, and are not hungering after the husks of the world. Let those who are filled with heavenly food fill their mouths with heavenly praise.

15. *"He sendeth forth his commandment upon the earth."* His messages fly throughout his dominions : upon earth his warrants are executed as well as in heaven. From his church his word goes forth ; from Zion he missions the nations with the word of life. *"His word runneth very swiftly "* : his purposes of love are speedily accomplished. Oriental monarchs laboured hard to establish rapid postal communication ; the desire, will, and command of the Lord flash in an instant from pole to pole, yea, from heaven to earth. We who dwell in the centre of the Lord's dominions may exceedingly rejoice that to the utmost extremity of the realm the divine commandment speeds with sure result, and is not hindered by distance or time. The Lord can deliver his people right speedily, or send them supplies immediately from his courts above. God's commands in nature and providence are fiats against which no opposition is ever raised ; say, rather, to effect which all things rush onward with alacrity. The expressions in the text are so distinctly in the present that they are meant to teach us the present mission and efficiency of the word of the Lord, and thus to prompt us to present praise.

16. Here follow instances of the power of God upon the elements. *"He giveth snow like wool."* As a gift he scatters the snow, which falls in flakes like fleecy wool. Snow falls softly, covers universally, and clothes warmly, even as wool covers the sheep. The most evident resemblance lies in the whiteness of the two substances ; but many other likenesses are to be seen by the observant eye. It is wise to see God in winter and in distress as well as in summer and prosperity. He who one day feeds us with the finest of the wheat, at another time robes us in snow : he is the same God in each case, and each form of his operation bestows a gift on men. *"He scattereth the hoarfrost like ashes."* Here again the Psalmist sees God directly and personally at work. As ashes powder the earth when men are burning up the rank herbage ; and as when men cast ashes into the air they cause a singular sort of whiteness in the places where they fall, so also does the frost. The country people talk of a black frost and a white frost, and the same thing may be said of ashes, for they are both black and white. Moreover, excessive cold burns as effectually as great heat, and hence there is an inner as well as an outer likeness between hoarfrost and ashes. Let us praise the Lord who condescends to wing each flake of snow and scatter each particle of rime. Ours is no absent or inactive deity : he worketh all things, and is everywhere at home.

17. *"He casteth forth his ice like morsels."* Such are the crumbs of hail which he casts forth, or the crusts of ice which he creates upon the waters. These morsels are *his* ice, and *he* casts them abroad. The two expressions indicate a very real presence of God in the phenomena of nature. *"Who can stand before his cold ? "* None can resist the utmost rigours of cold any more than they can bear the vehemence of heat. God's withdrawals of light are a darkness that may be felt, and his withdrawals of heat are a cold which is absolutely omnipotent. If the Lord, instead of revealing himself as a fire, should adopt the opposite manifestation of cold, he would, in either case, consume us should he put forth all his power. It is ours to submit to deprivations with patience, seeing the cold is *his* cold. That which God sends, whether it be heat or cold, no man can defy with impunity, but he is happy who bows before it with child-like submission. When we cannot stand before God we will gladly lie at his feet, or nestle under his wings.

18. *"He sendeth out his word, and melteth them."* When the frost is sharpest, and the ice is hardest, the Lord intervenes ; and though he doth no more than send his word, yet the rocks of ice are dissolved at once, and the huge bergs begin to float into the southern seas. The phenomena of winter are not so abundant in Palestine as with us, yet they are witnessed sufficiently to cause the devout to bless God for the return of spring. At the will of God snow, hoar-frost, and ice disappear, and the time of the opening bud and the singing of birds has come. For this let us praise the Lord as we sun ourselves amid the spring flowers. *"He causeth his wind to blow, and the waters flow."* The Lord is the great first cause of everything ; even the fickle, wandering winds are caused by him. Natural laws are in themselves mere inoperative rules, but the power emanates directly from the Ever-potent One. The soft gales from the south, which bring a general thaw, are from the Lord, as

were those wintry blasts which bound the streams in icy bonds.   Simple but effectual
are the methods of Jehovah in the natural world ; equally so are those which he
employs in the spiritual kingdom ; for the breath of his Holy Spirit breathes upon
frozen hearts, and streams of penitence and love gush forth at once.

Observe how these two sentences the word and the wind go together in nature.
They attend each other in grace ; the gospel and the Holy Spirit co-operate in
salvation.   The truth which the Spirit breathed into prophets and apostles he
breathes into dead souls, and they are quickened into spiritual life.

19. *"He sheweth his word unto Jacob, his statutes and his judgments unto Israel."*
He who is the Creator is also the Revealer.   We are to praise the Lord above all
things for his manifesting himself to us as he does not unto the world.   Whatever
part of his mind he discloses to us, whether it be a word of instruction, a statute
of direction, or a judgment of government, we are bound to bless the Lord for it.
He who causes summer to come in the place of winter has also removed the coldness
and death from our hearts by the power of his word, and this is abundant cause
for singing unto his name.   As Jacob's seed of old were made to know the Lord,
even so are we in these latter days ; wherefore, let his name be magnified among
us.   By that knowledge Jacob is ennobled into Israel, and therefore let him who
is made a prevailing prince in prayer be also a chief musician in praise.   The elect
people were bound to sing hallelujahs to their own God.   Why were they so specially
favoured if they did not, above all others, tell forth the glory of their God ?

20. *"He hath not dealt so with any nation."*   Israel had clear and exclusive
knowledge of God, while others were left in ignorance.   Election is the loudest call
for grateful adoration.   *"And as for his judgments, they have not known them";* or,
" and judgments, they had not known them," as if not knowing the laws of God,
they might be looked upon as having no laws at all worth mentioning.   The nations
were covered with darkness, and only Israel sat in the light.   This was sovereign
grace in its fullest noontide of power.   *"Praise ye the Lord."*   When we have
mentioned electing, distinguishing love, our praise can rise no higher, and therefore
we close with one more hallelujah.

EXPLANATORY NOTES AND QUAINT SAYINGS.

Whole Psalm.—The whole Psalm is an invitation unto praising of God.
Arguments therein are drawn, First, from God's *general goodness* to the world (verses
4, 8, 9, 16—18) : Secondly, from his *special mercy to his Church*.   1. In *restoring*
it out of a sad and broken condition (verses 2, 3).   2. In *confirming* it in a happy
and prosperous estate, both temporal, in regard of strength, peace, and plenty
(verses 12—14) ;   and spiritual, in regard of his word, statutes, and judgments,
made known unto them (verses 19, 20).   Lastly, these mercies are all commended
by the *manner* of bestowing them—*powerfully* and *swiftly*.   He doth it by a word
of command, and by a word of speed :   " He sendeth forth his commandment
upon earth :   his word runneth very swiftly " (verse 15).

The temporal part of this happy estate, together with the manner of bestowing
it, is herein described, but we must by no means exclude the spiritual meaning.
And what can be wanting to a nation which is " strengthened " with walls, " blessed "
with multitudes, hath " peace " in the border, " plenty " in the field, and, what
is all in all, God in the sanctuary :   God the bar of the " gate," the Father of the
children, the crown of the " peace," the staff of the " plenty " ?   They have a " gate "
restored, a" city " blessed, a " border " quieted, a " field " crowned, a " sanctuary "
beautified with the oracles of God.   What can be wanting to such a people, but
a mouth filled, a heart enlarged, a spirit exalted in the praises of the Lord ?   " Praise
the Lord, O Jerusalem ;   praise thy God, O Zion," etc. (verse 12).—*Edward
Reynolds, in a Sermon entitled "Sion's Praises,"* 1657.

Whole Psalm.—The God of Israel, what he has done, what he does, what he
can do—this is the *"Hallelujah"* note of his song.   So gladsome is the theme, that
in verse 1 we find a contribution for it levied on Ps. xxxiii. 1, xcii. 1, and cxxxv. 3 ;
each must furnish its quota of testimony to the desirableness of giving praise to such
a God.—*Andrew A. Bonar.*

Verse 1.—*"Praise ye the Lord." Alleluia.* An expression in sound very similar to this seems to have been used by many nations, who can hardly be supposed to have borrowed it from the Jews. Is it impossible that this is one of the most ancient expressions of devotion? From the Greeks using ἐλελεῦ ἰή, as a solemn beginning and ending of their hymns to Apollo, it should seem that they knew it; it is said to have been heard among the Indians in America, and *Alla, Alla,* as the name of God, is used in great part of the East: also in composition. What might be the primitive stock which has furnished such spreading branches?— *Augustine Calmet,* 1672—1757.

Verse 1.—*"It is good to sing praises unto our God."* Singing is necessarily included and recognised in the praise of the Psalms. That the joyful should sing is as natural as that the afflicted should pray—rather more natural. Song as the expression of cheerfulness is something universal in human nature; there were always, both in Israel and among all other nations, songs of joy. Hence it is constantly mentioned in the prophets, by whom joyous singing is used as a frequent figure, even as they threaten that God will take away the song of the bridegroom and the bride, and so forth. The *singing* of men is in itself good and noble. The same God who furnished the birds of heaven with the notes wherein they unconsciously praise their Creator, gave to man the power to sing. We all know how highly Luther, for example, estimated the gift and the art of song. Let him to whom it is granted rejoice therein; let him who lacks it seek, if possible, to excite it; for it is a good gift of the Creator. Let our children learn to sing in the schools, even as they learn to read. Our fathers sang more in all the affairs of life than we do; our tunes are in this respect less fresh, and artless, and joyous. There are many among us who never sing, except when adding their voices to the voice of the church, —and therefore they sing so badly there. Not that a harsh song from a good heart is unacceptable to God; but he should have our best. As David in his day took care that there should be practised singers for the sanctuary, we should also make provision for the church's service of song, that God may have in all respects a perfect offering. How gracious and lovely is the congregation singing with the heart acceptable songs!—*Rudolf Stier, in "The Epistle of James Expounded,"* 1859.

Verse 1.—The translation here is doubtful. It may either be rendered, " Praise the Lord for *he* is good," or, " for *it* (*praise*) is good." Why is it declared to be " *pleasant* " and " *comely*" to praise the Deity? Not only because if we glorify him he will also glorify us, but because he is so infinitely glorious that we are infinitely honoured simply in being reckoned worthy to worship One so great.— *John Lorinus.*

Verse 1.—*"It is good to sing praises unto our God ; for it is pleasant ; and praise is comely."* These points are worthy of careful consideration.

I. To praise God is " *good* " for divers reasons. 1. That is good which God commands (Mic. vi. 8). So that thanksgiving is no indifferent action, no will-worship, but it is *cultus institutus,* not to be neglected. 2. It raiseth the heart from earth to heaven; and being the work of angels and saints in heaven, joins us with that choir above. 3. It is good, again, because by it we pay, or at least acknowledge, a debt, and this is common justice. 4. Good, because for it we are like to receive a good and a great reward; for if he that prays to God is like to be rewarded (Matt. vi, 6), much more that man who sings praises to him; for in prayer we consult with our own necessities, in our praises we honour God, and bless him for his gifts.

II. To praise God is " *pleasant.*" 1. Because it proceeds out of love; for nothing is more pleasant to him that loves, than to make sonnets in the praise of that party he loves. 2. Because it must needs please a man to perform that duty for which he was created; for to that end God created men and angels, that they should praise him. 3. Because God is delighted with it, as the sweetest sacrifice (Ps. l. 23). 4. It is pleasant to God, because he is delighted with those virtues which are in us,—faith, hope, charity, religion, devotion, humility, etc., of all which our praises are a manifestation and exercise.

III. To praise God is " *comely* " ; for there is no greater stain than ingratitude ; it is made up of a lie and injustice. There is, then, all the decency in the world in praise, and it is comely that a man be thankful to his God, who freely gives him all things,—*William Nicholson.*

Verse 1.—David, to persuade all men to thankfulness, saith, *"It is a good and pleasant thing "* to be thankful. If he had said no more but " *good,*" all which love goodness are bound to be thankful ; but when he saith not only " *good*," but " *pleasant* " too, all which love pleasure are bound to be thankful ; and therefore, as Peter's mother-in-law, so soon as Christ healed her of a fever, rose up immediately to minister unto him (Matt. viii. 15), so we, so soon as Christ hath done anything for us, should rise up immediately to serve him.—*Henry Smith.*

Verse 1.—There is no heaven, either in this world, or the world to come, for people who do not praise God. If you do not enter into the spirit and worship of heaven, how should the spirit and joy of heaven enter into you ? Selfishness makes long prayers, but love makes short prayers, that it may continue longer in praise.—*John Pulsford*, 1857.

Verse 1.—"*Praise.*" There is one other thing which is a serious embarrassment to praising through the song-service of the Church, and that is, that we have so few hymns of praise. You will be surprised to hear me say so ; but you will be more surprised if you take a real specimen of praising and search for hymns of praise. You shall find any number of hymns that talk about praise, and exhort you to praise. There is no lack of hymns that say that God ought to be praised. But of hymns that praise, and say nothing about it, there are very few indeed. And for what there are we are almost wholly indebted to the old churches. Most of them came down to us from the Latin and Greek Churches . . . . There is no place in human literature where you can find such praise as there is in the Psalms of David. —*Henry Ward Beecher.*

Verse 2.—"*The Lord doth build up Jerusalem,*" etc. If this Psalm were written on occasion of the return from Babylon, and the rebuilding of the earthly city, the ideas are to be transferred, as in other Psalms of the same kind, to a more important restoration from a much worse captivity, and to the building up of the church under the gospel, when Christ " gathered together in one the children of God that were scattered abroad " (John xi. 52) ; that is, in the words of our Psalm, he "*gathered together the outcasts of Israel.*" So shall he again, at the resurrection, " gather together his elect from the four winds " (Matt. xxiv. 31), and "build up a Jerusalem," in which they shall serve and praise him for ever.—*George Horne.*

Verse 2.—"*The Lord doth build up Jerusalem,*" etc.

> Jerusalem ! Jerusalem ! the blessing lingers yet
> On the city of the chosen, where the Sabbath seal was set
> And though her sons are scattered, and her daughters weep apart,
> While desolation, like a pall, weighs down each faithful heart ;
> As the plain beside the waters, as the cedar on the hills,
> She shall rise in strength and beauty when the Lord Jehovah wills :
> He has promised her protection, and the holy pledge is good,
> 'Tis whispered through the olive groves, and murmured by the flood,
> As in the Sabbath stillness the Jordan's flow is heard,
> And by the Sabbath breezes the hoary trees are stirred.
>
> *Mrs. Hale, in "The Rhyme of Life."*

Verse 2.—"*He gathereth together the outcasts of Israel.*" Wonder not that God calls together "*the outcasts*," and singles them out from every corner for a return ; why can he not do this, as well as " tell the number of the stars, and call them all by their names " ? There are none of his people so despicable in the eye of man, but they are known and regarded by God. Though they are clouded in the world, yet they are the stars of the world ; and shall God number the inanimate stars in the heavens, and make no account of his living stars on the earth ? No ; wherever they are dispersed, he will not forget them : however they are afflicted, he will not despise them. The stars are so numerous that they are innumerable by man ; some are visible and known by men, others lie more hid and undiscovered in a confused light, as those in the milky way ; a man cannot see one of them distinctly. God knows all his people. As he can do what is above the power of man to perform, so he understands what is above the skill of man to discover.—*Stephen Charnock.*

Verse 2.—"*He gathereth together the outcasts of Israel.*" David might well have written feelingly about the "*outcasts*," for he had himself been one ; and even from Jerusalem, in his age, when driven forth from thence by his unnatural son, he went up by the ascent of Olivet, weeping and barefooted, and other "*outcasts* " with him weeping also as they went.—*Barton Bouchier.*

Verse 3.—"*He healeth the broken in heart,*" etc. Here are two things contained in this text ; the *patients* and the *physician*. The patients are the broken in heart. The physician is Christ ; it is he who bindeth up their wounds.

The patients here are felt and discerned to have two wounds or maladies ; brokenness of heart, and woundedness : he binds up such. Brokenness of heart presupposeth a former wholeness of heart. Wholeness of heart is twofold ; either wholeness of heart *in sin,* or wholeness of heart *from sin.* First, wholeness of heart *from sin* is when the heart is *without sin ;* and so the blessed angels have whole hearts, and so Adam and Eve, and we in them, before the fall, had whole hearts. Secondly, wholeness of heart *in sin ;* so the devils have whole hearts, and all men since the fall, from their conception till their conversion, have whole hearts ; and these are they that our Saviour intends,—" The whole need not the physician, but they that are sick."

Brokenness of heart may be considered two ways ; first, *in relation to wholeness of heart in sin :* so brokenness of heart is not a malady, but the commencement of the cure of a desperate disease. Secondly, *in relation to wholeness of heart from sin ;* and so it is a malady or sickness, and yet peculiar to one blood alone, namely, God's elect ; for though the heart be made whole in its desire towards God, yet it is broken for its sins. As a man that hath a barbed arrow shot into his side, and the arrow is plucked out of the flesh, yet the wound is not presently healed ; so sin may be plucked out of the heart, but the scar that was made with plucking it out is not yet cured. The wounds that are yet under cure are the plagues and troubles of conscience, the sighs and groans of a hungering soul after grace, the stinging poison that the serpent's fang hath left behind it ; these are the wounds.

Now the heart is broken three ways. First, *by the law ;* as it breaks the heart of a thief to hear the sentence of the law, that he must be hanged for his robbery ; so it breaks the heart of the soul, sensibly to understand the sentence of the law,—Thou shalt not sin ; if thou do, thou shalt be damned. If ever the heart come to be sensible of this sentence,—" Thou art a damned man," it is impossible to stand out under it, but it must break. " Is not my word like a hammer, that breaketh the rock in pieces ? " (Jer. xxiii. 29). Can any rock-heart hold out and not be broken with the blows of it ? Indeed, thus far a man may be broken, and yet be a reprobate ; for they shall all be thus broken in hell, and therefore this breaking is not enough.

Secondly, *by the Gospel ;* for if ever the heart come to be sensible of the love of the Gospel, it will break all to shatters. " Rend your heart ; for the Lord is gracious," etc. : Joel ii. 13. When all the shakes of God's mercy come, they all cry " Rend." Indeed, the heart cannot stand out against them, if it once feel them. Beat thy soul upon the gospel : if any way under heaven can break it, this is the way.

Thirdly, the heart is broken *by the skill of the minister* in the handling of these two, the law and the gospel : God furnisheth him with skill to press the law home, and gives him understanding how to put the gospel, and by this means doth God break the heart : for, alas, though the law be never so good a hammer, and although the gospel be never so fit an anvil, yet if the minister lay not the soul upon it the heart will not break : he must fetch a full stroke with the law, and he must set the full power of the gospel at the back of the soul, or else the heart will not break.

"*He healeth the broken in heart.*" Hence observe, that *Christ justifies and sanctifies ;* for that is the meaning.

1. First, because *God hath given Christ grace to practise for the sake of the broken in heart ;* and therefore if this be his grace, to heal the broken-hearted, certainly he will heal them. " The Spirit of the Lord is upon me," etc. He hath sent me to heal the broken-hearted," etc. : Luke iv. 18. If he be *created* master of this art, even for this purpose, to heal the broken in heart, he will verily heal them, and none but them. He is not like Hosander and Hippocrates, whose father appointed them both to be physicians : he appointed his son Hippocrates to be a physician of horses, yet he proved a physician for men ; he appointed Hosander to be a physician for men, and he proved a physician for horses. Jesus is not like these ; no, no ; he will heal those whom he was appointed to heal.

2. Because *Christ hath undertaken to do it.* When a skilful physician hath undertaken a cure, he will surely do it : indeed, sometimes a good physician may fail, as Trajan's physician did, for he died under his hands ; on whose tomb this was written, " Here lies Trajan the emperor, that may thank his physician that he died." But if Christ undertake it, thou mayest be sure of it ; for he tells thee that art broken in heart that he hath undertaken it, he hath felt thy pulse already. Isa. lvii. 15. He

doth not only undertake it, but he saith he will go *visit* his sick patient, he will come to thy bedside, yea, he will come and dwell with thee all the time of thy sickness ; thou shalt never want anything, but he will be ready to help thee : thou needest not complain and say, " Oh, the physician is too far off, he will not come at me." I dwell in the high places indeed, saith God, but yet I will come and dwell with thee that art of an humble spirit. Thou needest not fear, saying, " Will a man cure his enemies ? I have been an enemy to God's glory, and will he yet cure me ? " Yea, saith Christ, if thou be *broken in heart* I will bind thee up.

3. Thirdly, because *this is Christ's charge*, and he will look to his own calling : " The Lord hath sent me to bind up the broken-hearted " (Isa. lxi. 1). . . . Neither needest thou fear thine own poverty, because thou hast not a fee to give him ; for thou mayest come to him by way of begging ; he will look to thee for nothing for, " To him will I look that is poor," etc. : Isa. lxvi. 2.

4. Fourthly, *none but the broken in heart will take physic of Christ.* Now this is a physician's desire, that his patient would cast himself upon him ; if he will not, the physician hath no desire to meddle with him. Now none but the broken in heart will take such physic as Christ gives, and therefore he saith, " To him will I look that is of a broken heart, and trembles at my words" : Isa. lxv. 2. When I bid him take such a purge, saith God, he trembles, and he takes it.— *William Fenner, in a Sermon entitled "The Sovereign Virtue of the Gospel,"* 1647.

Verse 3.—

> O thou who dry'st the mourner's tear,
>   How dark this world would be,
> If, when deceived and wounded here,
>   We could not fly to Thee !
> The friends, who in our sunshine live,
>   When winter comes are flown ;
> And he who has but tears to give
>   Must weep those tears alone.
> But Thou wilt heal that broken heart,
>   Which, like the plants that throw
> Their fragrance from the wounded part,
>   Breathes sweetness out of woe.
>
> When joy no longer soothes or cheers,
>   And e'en the hope that threw
> A moment's sparkle o'er our tears
>   Is dimmed and vanished too ;
> Oh ! who would bear life's stormy doom,
>   Did not thy wing of love
> Come, brightly wafting through the gloom
>   Our peace-branch from above ?
> Then sorrow, touched by Thee, grows bright
>   With more than rapture's ray ;
> As darkness shows us worlds of light
>   We never saw by day !
>
> *Thomas Moore,* 1779—1852.

Verse 3.—"*He healeth the broken in heart.*" The broken in heart is one whose heart is affected with the evil of sin, and weeps bitter tears on account of it ; one who feels sorrow, shame, and anguish, on the review of his past sinful life, and his base rebellion against a righteous God. Such a one has a broken heart. His heart is broken at the sight of his own ingratitude —the despite done by him to the strivings of the Holy Spirit. His heart is broken when he considers the numberless invitations made to him in the Scriptures, all of which he has wickedly slighted and despised. His heart is broken at the recollection of a thousand kind providences to him and to his family, by day and by night, all sent by God, and intended for his moral, spiritual, and eternal benefit, but by him basely and wantonly abused. His heart is broken at the consideration of the love and compassion of the adorable Redeemer; the humiliation of his birth ; the devotedness of his life ; the reproach, the indignity of his sufferings ; the ignominy and anguish of his death. His heart is broken when his conscience assures him that all this humiliation, this suffering, this death, was for him, who had so deliberately and repeatedly refused the grace which the blood and righteousness of Christ has purchased. It is the sight of Calvary that fills him with anguish of spirit, that overwhelms him with confusion and self-abasement. While he contemplates the amazing scene, he stands, he weeps, he

prays, he smites upon his breast, he exclaims, " God be merciful to me a sinner ! "
And adds, " O wretched man that I am, who shall deliver me from the body of
this death ? "

The broken in heart must further be understood as one who seeks help from God
alone, and will not be comforted till he speaks peace to his soul.

The act of God, in the scripture before us, is the moral and spiritual health of
man—of man, who had brought disease on himself—of man, by his own rebellion
against his Creator—of man, who had, in ten thousand ways, provoked the justice
of heaven, and deserved only indignation and eternal wrath—the health of man,
whom, in an instant, he could hurl to utter destruction. The saving health here
proposed is the removal of all guilt, however contracted, and of all pollution, however rooted. It is the communication of God's favour, the riches of his grace, the
implantation of his righteousness.

To effect the healing of the broken heart, God has, moreover, appointed a
Physician, whose skill is infallible, whose goodness and care are equal to his skill.
That Physician is none other than the Son of God. In that character he has been
made known to us. " They that be whole need not a physician, but they that
be sick." The prophet Isaiah introduces his advent in the most sublime language :
" He hath sent me to bind up the broken-hearted, to proclaim liberty to the captives,
and the opening of the prison to them that are bound."

The health, the moral and spiritual soundness of the soul, my brethen, is derived
from the atoning sacrifice of Christ. The grace of God flows to the broken in heart
through his manhood, his godhead, his righteousness, his truth ; through his patience,
his humility, his death and passion ; through his victory over sin, his resurrection,
and ascension into heaven. Here, thou broken in heart, thou sorrowing, watching
penitent ; here is the medicine, here the Physician, here the cure, here the health
thou art seeking.

The healing of the broken in heart must be further understood as effected through
the agency of the Holy Spirit. It is done by the Spirit of God, that it may be done,
and that it may be well done ; and that all the praise, the glory of that which is
done, may be ascribed to the plenitude, the freeness, the sovereignty of his grace.
The Spirit of God, however, uses means. The means of grace are appointed expressly
for this purpose ; the blessing of health is there applied. There, under the sound
of the everlasting gospel, while looking by faith to Christ, and appropriating his
merits, he healeth the broken in heart. There, while commemorating the dying
love of Christ, and applying its benefits by faith to the soul, he healeth the broken
in heart. There, while the soul, sensible of his goodness, is offering up the song
of praise, and trusting alone in his mercy, he healeth the broken in heart. There,
while prostrate at his footstool, supplicating his grace, resting on his finished
redemption, he healeth the broken in heart. In the private acts of devotion the
Spirit of God also is near to bless and save. There, while reading and believing
his holy Word, while meditating on its meaning ; there, while in secret, solemn
prayer, the soul takes hold on God in Christ Jesus ; he healeth the broken in heart.
—*Condensed from a Sermon by Thomas Blackley,* 1826.

Verse 3.—*"He healeth the broken in heart."* I do indeed most sincerely sympathise
with you in this fresh sorrow. " Thy breaking waves pass over me." The trial,
so much the heavier that it is not the first breaking in, but the waters continuing
still, and continuing to rise, until deep calleth unto deep at the noise of God's
water-spouts, " Yea, and thy billows all." In such circumstances we are greatly
tempted to wonder if it be true, of the Holy One in the midst of us, that a bruised
reed he will not break, that the smoking flax he will not quench. We may not,
however, doubt it, nor even in the day of our grief and our desperate sorrow, are
we at liberty to call it in question. Our God is the God of the broken heart.
The deeper such a heart is smitten, and the more it bleeds, the more precious
it is in his sight, the nearer he draws to it, the longer he stays there. " I dwell
with him who is of a contrite heart." The more abundantly will he manifest the
kindness and the glory of his power, in tenderly carrying it in his bosom, and at
last binding up its painful wounds. " He healeth the broken in heart." " O thou
afflicted, tossed with tempest, and not comforted, behold, I will lay thy stones
with fair colours, and lay thy foundations with sapphires." Weeping Naomi said,
" Call me Mara, for the Lord hath dealt very bitterly with me." Afterwards,
happy Naomi took the child of her own Ruth, and laid it in her bosom, and sweetly
found that the days of her mourning were ended.

My dear friend, this new gash of deep sorrow was prepared for you by the Ancient of Days. His Son—and that Son is love—watched over the counsels of old, to keep and to perform them to the minutest circumstance.—*John Jameson*, 1838.

Verse 4.—"*He telleth the number of the stars,*" etc. In which similitude he showeth, that albeit Abraham could not comprehend the multitude of the children, either of his faith or of his flesh, more than he could count the number of the stars ; yet the Lord knoweth every believer by name, as he knoweth every star and can call everyone by its name.—*David Dickson.*

Verse 4.—"*He telleth the number of the stars,*" etc. Among the heathen every constellation represented some God. But the Scriptures show Jehovah, not as one of many starry gods, but as the one God of all the stars. He is, too, as he taught his people by Abraham, the God of a firmament of nobler stars. His people are scattered and trodden as the sands of the sea-shore. But he turns dust and dirt to stars of glory. He will make of every saint a star, and Heaven is his people's sky, where broken-hearted sufferers of earth are glorified into glittering galaxies. —*Hermann Venema.*

Verse 4.—"*He calleth them all by their names.*" Literally, " calleth names to all of them," an expression marking not only God's power in marshalling them all as a host (Isa. xl. 26), but also the most intimate knowledge and watchful care, as that of a shepherd for his flock. John x. 3.—*J. J. Stewart Perowne.*

Verse 4.—"*He calleth them all by their names.*" They render a due obedience to him, as servants to their master. When he singles them out and calls them by name to do some official service, he calls them out to their several offices, as the general of an army appoints the station of every regiment in a battalion ; or, " *he calls them by name,*" *i.e.* he imposeth names upon them, a sign of dominion, the giving names to the inferior creatures being the first act of Adam's derivative dominion over them. These are under the sovereignty of God. The stars by their influences fight against Sisera (Jud. v. 20) ; and the sun holds in its reins, and stands stone-still to light Joshua to a complete victory : Josh. x. 12. They are all marshalled in their ranks to receive his word of command, and fight in close order, as being desirous to have a share in the ruin of the enemies of their sovereign. —*Stephen Charnock.*

Verse 4.—The immense distance at which the nearest stars are known to be placed, proves that they are bodies of a prodigious size, not inferior to our own sun, and that they shine, not by reflected rays, but by their own native light. But bodies encircled with such refulgent splendour, would be of little use in Jehovah's enpire, unless surrounding worlds were cheered by their benign influence, and enlightened by their beams. Every star is therefore concluded to be a sun surrounded by planetary globes. Nearly a thousand of these luminaries may be seen in a clear winter's night by the naked eye. But these do not form the eighty-thousandth part of what may be descried by the help of telescopes. While Dr. Herschel was exploring the most crowded part of the milky way, in one quarter of an hour's time no less than 116,000 stars passed through the field of view of his telescope. It has been computed, that nearly one hundred millions of stars might be perceived by our most perfect instruments, if all the regions of the sky were thoroughly explored. But immeasurable regions of space lie beyond the utmost boundaries of human vision, even thus assisted, into which imagination itself can scarcely penetrate, but which are doubtless filled with operations of divine wisdom and divine omnipotence.—*Thomas Dick, in "The Christian Philosopher."*

Verse 5.—"*His understanding is infinite.*" Hebrew : "*Of his understanding there is no number.*" God is incomprehensible. In *place ;* in *time ;* in *understanding ;* in *love.* First, in *place ;* because no place, no space, can be imagined so great, but God exceeds it, and may be found beyond it. Secondly, in *time ;* because he exceeds all time : for he was before all time that can be conceived, and shall be after all time. Time is a created thing, to attend upon the creation and continuance of all things created and continued by God. Thirdly, in *understanding ;* because no created understanding can comprehend him so that nothing of God may be hid from it. Fourthly, in *love ;* because God doth exceed all love : no creature can love God according to his worth. All these ways of incomprehensibleness follow upon his infiniteness.—*Thomas Larkham in "The Attributes of God Unfolded, and Applied,"* —1656.

Verse 5.—"His understanding is infinite." The Divine wisdom is said to be *"without number";* that is, the objects of which this wisdom of God can take cognisance are innumerable.—*Simon de Muis.*

Verse 5.—In this verse we have three of God's attributes, his greatness, his power, and his knowledge; and though only the last of these be expressly said to be *infinite,* yet is the same implied also of the two former; for all the perfections of God being essential to him, must need be infinite as he himself is; and therefore what is affirmed of one must, by a parity of reason, be extended to the rest.—*John Conant,* 1608—1693.

Verse 6.—"The LORD *lifteth up the meek,"* etc. The meek need not envy the lofty who sweep the earth with their gay robes, any more than real royalty is jealous of the kingly hero who struts his hour upon the stage. They shall be princes and rulers long after these actors have laid aside their tinselled crowns.

How wonderful shall be the reversal when God shall place the last first and the first last! Moralists have often pointed us to the ruler of a hundred broad kingdoms lying down at last in six feet of imprisoning clay; but God shall show us the wayside cottager lifted into the inheritance of the universe.—*Evangelical Magazine.*

Verses 7—9.—God creates, and then fails not to supply. Analogically, the Lord buildeth Jerusalem, and provides for the wants of the inhabitants : by spiritual inference, the saints argue that Christ establishes his church and gives all the gracious gifts which are needed in that institution.—*John Lorinus.*

Verses 8, 9.—"Mountains . . . ravens." Wonderful Providence which takes cognisance of the mountainous and the minute alike. The All-Provider descends from august and sublime heights to save the meanest creature from starvation—extending constant care to the wants of even those abject little objects, the young ravens, Heb. " the sons of the raven."—*Martin Geier.*

Verse 8.—"Clouds . . . rain . . . grass." There is a mutual dependence and subordination between all second causes. The creatures are serviceable to one another by mutual ministries and supplies; the earth is cherished by the heat of the heavens, moistened by the water, and by the temperament of both made fruitful; and so sendeth forth innumerable plants for the comfort and use of living creatures, and living creatures are for the supply of man. It is wonderful to consider the subordination of all causes, and the proportion they bear to one another. The heavens work upon the elements, the elements upon the earth, and the earth yieldeth fruits for the use of man. The prophet taketh notice of this admirable gradation : " I will hear the heavens, and the heavens shall hear the earth ; and the earth shall hear the corn, and the wine, and the oil ; and the corn, and the wine, and the oil, shall hear Jezreel " (Hosea ii. 21, 22). We look to the fields for the supplies of corn, wine, and oil ; but they can do nothing without clouds, and the clouds can do nothing without God. The creatures are beholden to one another, and all to God. In the order of the world there is an excellent chain of causes, by which all things hang together, that so they may lead up the soul to the Lord.—*Thomas Manton.*

Verse 8.—"Who prepareth rain?" The rain-cloud parts with its contents only when God commands it, and *as* he commands, whether in the soft gentle shower or in the drenching downpour that floods the fields and obstructs the labours of the husbandman.—*Thomas Robinson, in "Homiletical Commentary on the Book of Job,"* 1876.

Verse 8.—"Who maketh grass to grow upon the mountains." The wild grasses are taken, as it were, under the special providence of God. In the perennial verdure in regions above the zone of man's cultivation, we have a perpetual proof of God's care of the lower animals that neither sow nor reap. The mountain grasses grow spontaneously ; they require no culture but such as the rain and the sunshine of heaven supply. They obtain their nourishment directly from the inorganic soil, and are independent of organic materials. Nowhere is the grass so green and vigorous as on the beautiful slopes of lawn-like pasture high up in the Alps, radiant with the glory of wild flowers, and ever musical with the hum of grasshoppers, and the tinkling of cattle-bells. Innumerable cows and goats browse upon them ; the peasants spend their summer months in making cheese and hay from them for winter consumption in the valleys. This exhausting system of husbandry has been carried on during untold centuries ; no one thinks of manuring the Alpine pastures ; and yet no deficiency has been observed in their fertility, though the soil is but a thin covering spread over the naked rocks. It may be regarded as a part of the same wise and gracious arrangement of Providence, that the insects which devour the grasses on the *Kuh* and *Schaf Alpen*, the pasturages of the cows and sheep, are kept in check by a predominance of carnivorous insects. In all the mountain meadows it has been ascertained that the species of carnivorous are at least four times as numerous as the species of herb-eating insects. Thus, in the absence of birds, which are rare in Switzerland, the pastures are preserved from a terrible scourge. To one not aware of this check, it may seem surprising how the verdure of the Alpine pastures should be so rich and luxuriant considering the immense development of insect life. The grass, whenever the sun shines, is literally covered with them—butterflies of gayest hues, and beetles of brightest iridescence ; and the air is filled with their loud murmurs. I remember well the vivid feeling of God's gracious providence, which possessed me when passing over the beautiful Wengern Alp at the foot of the Jungfrau, and seeing, wherever I rested on the green turf, alive with its tiny inhabitants, the balance of nature so wonderfully preserved between the herb which is for man's food and the moth before which he is crushed. Were the herbivorous insects allowed to multiply to their full extent, in such favourable circumstances as the warmth of the air and the verdure of the earth in Switzerland produce, the rich pastures which now yield abundant food for upwards of a million and a half of cattle would speedily become bare and leafless deserts. Nor only in their power of growing without cultivation, but also in the peculiarities of their structure, the mountain grasses proclaim the hand of God. Many of them are viviparous. Instead of producing flowers and seed, as the grasses in the tranquil valleys do, the young plants spring from them perfectly formed. They cling round the stem and form a kind of blossom. In this state they remain until the parent stalk withers and falls prostrate on the ground, when they immediately strike root and form independent grasses. This is a remarkable adaptation to circumstances ; for it is manifest that were seeds instead of living plants developed in the ears of the mountain grasses, they would be useless in the stormy regions where they grow. They would be blown away far from the places they were intended to clothe, to spots foreign to their nature and habits, and thus the species would speedily perish.

The more we think of it, the more we are struck with the wise foresight which suggested the creative fiat, " Let the earth bring forth grass." It is the most abundant and the most generally diffused of all vegetation. It suits almost every soil and climate.—*Hugh Macmillan, in "Bible Teachings in Nature," 1868.*

Verses 8, 9.—The Hebrews had no notion of what we denominate " secondary laws," but believed that God acted directly upon matter, and was the immediate, efficient cause of the solemn order, and the varied and wonderful phenomena of nature. Dispensing thus with the whole machinery of cause and effect, as we employ those terms in philosophical language, their minds were brought into immediate contact with God in his manifold works, and this gave, both to devotion and the spirit of poetry, the liveliest inspiration and the freest scope of action. Heaven and earth were governed by his commands ; the thunder was his " voice," the lightning his " arrows." It is he who " causeth the vapour to ascend from the ends of the earth." When the famished city should call upon the corn, the wine, and the oil, and those should call upon the earth for nourishment, and the parched earth should call upon the heavens for moisture, and the heavens should call upon the Lord for permission to refresh the earth, then Jehovah would hear and supply. He gave the rain, and he sent the drought and famine. The clouds were not looked upon merely as sustained by a law of specific gravity, but God spread them out in the sky ; these clouds were God's chariot, the curtains of his pavilion, the dust of his feet. Snow and hail were fearful manifestations of God, often sent as the messengers of his wrath.—*F. G. Hubbard, in "Bate's Encyclopædia," 1865.*

Verses 8, 9.—God by his special providence prepares *"food"* for those who have no other care taken for them. *"Beasts"* that live among men are by men taken care of ; they enrich the ground with manure, and till the ground ; and that brings forth corn for the use of these cattle as well as men. But the *wild beasts* that live upon the *mountains*, and in woods and desert places, are fed only from the heavens : the *"rain"* that from thence distils enricheth those dry hills and *"maketh grass to grow"* there, which else would not, and so God giveth to these *wild beasts* their food after the same manner of Divine Providence as in the end of the verse he is said to provide for the "*young ravens.*"—*Henry Hammond.*

Verse 9.—"*The young ravens cry.*" The strange stories told by Jewish and Arabian writers, on the raven's cruelty to its young, in driving them out of their nests before they are quite able to provide for themselves, are entirely without foundation, as no bird is more careful of its young ones than the raven. To its habit of flying restlessly about in search of food to satisfy its own appetite and that of its young ones, may perhaps be traced the reason of its being selected by the sacred writers as an especial object of God's protecting care.—*W. Houghton, in "The Bible Educator."*

Verse 9.—"*The young ravens cry.*" While still unfledged the young ravens have a strange habit of falling out of their nests, and flapping their wings heavily to the ground. Next morning they are found by the shepherds sitting croaking on the ground beneath their former homes, and are then captured and taken away with comparative ease.—*J. G. Wood, in "The Illustrated Natural History,"* 1869.

Verse 9.—"*The young ravens cry.*" The evening proceedings and manœuvres of the rooks are curious and amusing in the autumn. Just before dusk they return in long strings from the foraging of the day, and rendezvous by thousands over Selbourne-down, where they wheel round in the air, and sport and dive in a playful manner, all the while exerting their voices, and making a loud cawing, which, being blended and softened by the distance that we at the village are below them, becomes a confused noise or chiding ; or rather a pleasing murmur, very engaging to the imagination, and not unlike the cry of a pack of hounds in hollow, echoing woods, or the rushing of the wind in tall trees, or the tumbling of the tide upon a pebbly shore. When this ceremony is over, with the last gleam of day, they retire for the night to the deep beechen woods of Tisted and Ropley. We remember a little girl, who, as she was going to bed used to remark on such an occurrence, in the true spirit of physico-theology, that the rooks were saying their prayers, and yet this child was much too young to be aware that the Scriptures had said of the Deity that " He feedeth the ravens that call upon him."—*Gilbert White (1720—1793), in "The Natural History of Selbourne."*

Verse 9.—

> Behold, and look away your low despair ;
> See the light tenants of the barren air :
> To them, nor stores, nor granaries belong,
> Nought but the woodlands and the pleasing song ;
> Yet, your kind heavenly Father bends his eye
> On the least wing that flits along the sky.
> To him they sing when Spring renews the plain ;
> To him they cry in Winter's pinching reign ;
> Nor is the music, nor their plaint, in vain.
> He hears the gay, and the distressful call,
> And with unsparing bounty fills them all.
> Will he not care for you, ye faithless, say ?
> Is he unwise ? Or, are ye less than they ?
>
> *James Thomson, 1700—1748.*

Verse 9.—It is related of Edward Taylor, the sailor-preacher of Boston, that on the Sunday before he was to sail for Europe, he was entreating the Lord to care well for his church during his absence. All at once he stopped, and ejaculated, " What have I done ? Distrust the Providence of heaven ! A God that gives a whale a ton of herrings for a breakfast, will he not care for my children ? " and then went on, closing his prayer in a more confiding manner.—*From "Eccentric Preachers," by C. H. S.*

Verse 10.—The two clauses of this verse are probably intended to describe *cavalry* and *infantry*, as forming the military strength of nations. It is not to those who trust in such resources that Jehovah shows favour, but to those who rely on his protection (verse 11).—*Annotated Paragraph Bible.*

Verses 10, 11.—When a sinner is brought upon his knees, and becomes a suppliant, when as he is laid low by affliction, so he lieth low in prayer and supplication, then the Lord will be favourable to him, and show his delight in him. "*The Lord delighteth not in the strength of the horse ; he taketh not pleasure in the legs of a man.*" No man is favoured by God because of his outward favour, because he hath a beautiful face, or strong, clean limbs ; yea, not only hath the Lord no pleasure in any man's legs, but not in any man's brains, how reaching soever, nor in any man's wit how quick soever, nor in any man's judgment how deep soever, nor in any man's tongue how eloquent or well spoken soever ; but *"The Lord taketh pleasure in them that fear him, in those that hope in his mercy,"* in those that walk humbly with him, and call upon him. . . All the beauties and rarities both of persons and things are dull and flat, yea, wearisome and loathsome to God, in comparison of a gracious, honest, humble soul. Princes have their favourites (Job. xxxiii. 26) : they are favourable to some above many, either because they are beautiful and goodly persons, or because they are men of excellent speech, prudence and deportment. All godly men are God's favourites ; he is favourable to them not only above many men in the world, but above all the men of this world, who have their portion in this life ; and he therefore favours them, because they are the purchase of his Son and the workmanship of his Spirit, convincing them of, and humbling them for, their sins, as also creating them after God in righteousness and true holiness. Such shall be his favourites. —*Joseph Caryl.*

Verse 11.—*"Them that fear him, those that hope in his mercy."* Patience and fear are the fences of hope. There is a beautiful relation between hope and fear. The two are linked in this verse. They are like the cork in a fisherman's net, which keeps it from sinking, and the lead, which prevents it from floating. Hope without fear is in danger of being too sanguine ; fear without hope would soon become desponding.—*George Seaton Bowes, in "In Prospect of Sunday,"* 1880.

Verse 11.—*"Them that fear him, those that hope in his mercy."* A sincere Christian is known by both these ; a fear of God, or a constant obedience to his commands, and an affiance, trust, and dependence upon his mercies. Oh, how sweetly are both these coupled, a uniform, sincere obedience to him, and an unshaken, constant reliance on his mercy and goodness ! The whole perfection of the Christian life is comprised in these two—believing God and fearing him, trusting in his mercy and fearing his name ; the one maketh us careful in avoiding sin, the other diligent to follow after righteousness ; the one is a bridle from sin and temptations, the other a spur to our duties. Fear is our curb, and hope our motive and encouragement ; the one respects our duty, the other our comfort ; the one allayeth the other. God is so to be feared, as also to be trusted ; so to be trusted, as also to be feared ; and as we must not suffer our fear to degenerate into legal bondage, but hope in his mercy, so our trust must not degenerate into carnal sloth and wantonness, but so hope in his word as to fear his name. Well, then, such as both believe in God and fear to offend him are the only men who are acceptable to God and his people. God will take pleasure in them, and they take pleasure in one another.—*Thomas Manton.*

Verse 11.—*"Fear"* and *"Hope"* are the great *vincula* of Old Testament theology, bracketing and including in their meaning all its ideas.—*Thomas Le Blanc.*

Verse 11.—*Fear* and *hope* are passions of the mind so contrary the one to the other, that with regard to the same object, it is strange they should meet in the same laudable character ; yet here we see they do so, and it is the praise of the same persons, that they both fear God, and hope in him. Whence we may gather this doctrine : That in every concern that lies upon our hearts, we should still endeavour to keep the balance even between hope and fear.

We know how much the health of the body depends upon a due temperament of the humours, such as preserves any one from being predominant above the rest ; and how much the safety and peace of the nations result from a due balance of trade and power, that no one grow too great for its neighbours ; and so necessary is it to the health and welfare of our souls, that there be a due proportion maintained between their powers and passions, and that the one may always be a check upon the other, to keep it from running into extremes ; as in these affections mentioned in the text. A holy fear of God must be check upon our hope, to keep that from swelling into presumption ; and a pious hope in God must be a check upon our fear, to keep that from sinking into despondency. This balance must, I say, by a wise and steady hand, be kept even in every concern that lies upon our hearts, and that we have thoughts about. I shall enumerate those that are of the greatest importance. We must keep up both hope and fear. 1. As to the concerns of our souls, and our spiritual and eternal state. 2. As to our outward concerns, relating to the body and the life that now is. 3. As to the public concerns of the church of God, and our own land and nation.

In reference to each of these, we must always study and strive to support that affection, whether it be hope or fear, which the present temper of our minds and circumstances of our case make necessary to preserve us from an extreme.—*Matthew Henry.*

Verse 12.—That all Creation must involuntarily praise the Lord, and that the primary duty of conscious intelligence is the willing praise of the same Deity, are the two *axioms* of the Psalmist's theology. He has in the first part of this Psalm been stating the first, and now he is about to announce the second.—*Martin Geier.*

Verse 13.—"*He hath strengthened the bars of thy gates.*"—Blessed is the city whose gates God barreth up with his power, and openeth again with his mercy. There is nothing can defend where his justice will strike ; and there is nothing can offend where his goodness will preserve.—*Thomas Adams.*

Verses 13, 14.—The Psalmist recites four arguments from which he would have Zion sing praises. 1. Security and defence. 2. Benediction. 3. Peace. 4. Sustenance or provision.

1. *Security.* Jerusalem is a city secure, being defended by God : "*For he hath strengthened the bars of thy gates.*" Gates and bars do well to a city, but then only is the city secure when God makes them strong. The true munition of a city is God's defence of it. Arms, laws, wealth, etc., are the bars, but God must put strength into them.

2. *Benediction.* Jerusalem is a happy city, for "*he hath blessed thy children within thee,*" thy kings, princes, magistrates, etc., with wisdom, piety, etc.

3. *Peace.* Jerusalem is a peaceable city. "*He maketh peace in thy borders,*" the very name intimates so much ; for Jerusalem interpreted is *visio pacis*—Vision of peace.

4. *Abundance.* Jerusalem is a city provided by God with necessary food and provision ; for "*He filleth thee with the finest of the wheat.*"—*William Nicholson.*

Verse 14.—"*He maketh peace in thy borders,*" etc. There is a political peace—peace in city and country ; this is the fairest flower of a Prince's crown ; peace is the best blessing of a nation. It is well with bees when there is a noise ; but it is best with Christians when, as in the building of the Temple, there is no noise of hammer heard. Peace brings plenty along with it ; how many miles would some go on pilgrimage to purchase this peace ! Therefore the Greeks made Peace to be the nurse of Pluto, the God of wealth. Political plants thrive best in the sunshine of peace. "*He maketh peace in thy borders, and filleth thee with the finest of the wheat.*" The ancients made the harp the emblem of peace : how sweet would the sounding of this harp be after the roaring of the cannon ! All should study to promote this political peace. The godly man, when he dies, " enters into peace " (Isa. lvii. 2) ; but while he lives, peace must enter into him.—*Thomas Watson.*

Verse 14.—"*He maketh peace.*" The Hebrews observe that all the letters in the name of God are *literæ quiescentes*, letters of rest. God only is the centre were the soul may find rest : God only can speak peace to the conscience.—*John Stoughton,* —1639.

Verse 14.—"*Finest of the wheat.*" If men give much it is in cheap and coarse commodity. Quantity and quality are only possible with human production *in inverse ratio ;* but the Lord gives the *most* and *best* of all supplies to his pensioners. How truly the believer under the gospel knows the inner spirit of the meaning here ! The Lord Jesus Christ says, " My peace I give unto you." And when he sets us at rest and all is reconciliation and peace, then he feeds us with *himself*—his body, the finest wheat, and his blood, the richest wine.—*Johannes Paulus Palanterius.*

Verse 15.—"*His word runneth very swiftly.*" There is not a moment between the shooting out of the arrow and the fastening of it in the mark ; both are done in the very same atom and point of time. Therefore we read in the Scripture of the immediate effects of the word of Christ. Saith he to the leprous man, " Be thou clean. And immediately his leprosy was cleansed " : Matt. viii. 3. And to the blind man, " Go thy way ; thy faith hath made thee whole. And immediately he received his sight " : Mark x. 52. No arrow makes so immediate an impression in the mark aimed at as the arrow of Christ's word. No sooner doth Christ say to the soul, Be enlightened, be quickened, be comforted, but the work is done.— *Ralph Robinson.*

Verse 16.—"*He giveth snow like wool.*" There are three things considerable in snow, for which it is compared to wool. First, for the *whiteness* of it. Snow is white as wool; snow is so exceeding white that the whiteness of a soul cleansed by pardoning grace, in the blood of Christ, is likened unto it (Isa. i. 18); and the latter part of the same verse intimates that the whiteness of snow bears resemblance to that of wool. The whiteness of snow is caused by the abundance of air and spirits that are in that pellucid body, as the naturalists speak. Any thing that is of a watery substance, being frozen or much wrought upon by cold, appears more white; and hence it is that all persons inhabiting cold climates or countries, are of a whiter complexion than they who inhabit hot. Secondly, snow is like wool for *softness*, 'tis pliable to the hand as a lock or fleece of wool. Thirdly, snow is like wool (which may seem strange) with respect to the *warmness* of it. Though snow be cold in itself, yet it is to the earth as wool, or as a woollen cloth or blanket that keeps the body warm. Snow is not warm formally, yet it is warm effectively and virtually; and therefore is it compared to wool.—*Joseph Caryl.*

Verse 16.—"*Like wool.*" Namely, curled and tufted, and as white as the snow in those countries. Isa. i. 18, Rev. i. 14.—*John Diodati.*

Verse 16.—"*Snow like wool.*" The ancients used to call snow εριωδες υδωρ, *woolly water* (Eustathius, in Dionys. Perieget. p. 91). Martial gives it the name of *densum vellus aquarum, a thick fleece of waters* (Epigram. l. iv. Ep. 3). Aristophanes calls clouds, *flying fleeces of wool* (Nubes, p. 146). Pliny calls it *the froth of the celestial waters* (Nat. His. lib. xvii. cap. 2).—*Samuel Burder.*

Verse 16.—"*He giveth snow like wool.*" In Palestine snow is not the characteristic feature of winter as it is in northern latitudes. It is merely an occasional phenomenon. Showers of it fall now and then in severer seasons on the loftier parts of the land, and whiten for a day or two the vineyards and cornfields: but it melts from the green earth as rapidly as its sister vapours vanish from the blue sky. . . . . But the Psalmist seized the occasional snow, as he seized the fleeting vapour, and made it a text of his spiritual meditations. Let us follow his example.

"*He giveth snow like wool,*" says the Psalmist. This comparison expressly indicates one of the most important purposes which the snow serves in the economy of nature. It covers the earth like a blanket during that period of winter sleep which is necessary to recruit its exhausted energies, and prepare it for fresh efforts in the spring; and being, like wool, a bad conductor, it conserves the latent heat of the soil, and protects the dormant life of plant and animal hid under it from the frosty rigour of the outside air. Winter-sown wheat, when defended by this covering, whose under surface seldom falls much below 32° Fahr., can thrive even though the temperature of the air above may be many degrees below the freezing-point. Our country, enjoying an equable climate, seldom requires this protection; but in northern climates, where the winter is severe and prolonged, its beneficial effects are most marked. The scanty vegetation which blooms with such sudden and marvellous loveliness in the height of summer, in the Arctic regions and on mountain summits, would perish utterly were it not for the protection of the snow that lies on it for three quarters of a year.

But it is not only to Alpine plants and hybernating animals that God gives snow like wool. The Esquimaux take advantage of its curious protective property, and ingeniously build their winter huts of blocks of hardened snow; thus, strangely enough, by a homœopathic law, protecting themselves against cold by the effects of cold. The Arctic navigator has been often indebted to walls of snow banked up around his ship for the comparative comfort of his winter quarters, when the temperature without has fallen so low that even chloric ether became solid. And many a precious life has been saved by the timely shelter which the snow-storm itself has provided against its own violence. But while snow thus warms in cold regions, it also cools in warm regions. It sends down from the white summits of equatorial mountains its cool breath to revive and brace the drooping life of lands sweltering under a tropic sun; and from its lofty, inexhaustible reservoirs it feeds perennial rivers that water the plains when all the wells and streams are white and silent in the baking heat. Without the perpetual snow of mountain regions the earth would be reduced to a lifeless desert.

And not only does the Alpine snow thus keep always full rivers that water the plains, but, by its grinding force as it presses down the mountains, it removes particles from the rocks, which are carried off by the rivers and spread over the plains. Such is the origin of a large part of the level land of Europe. It has been formed out of the ruins of the mountains by the action of snow. It was by the snow of far-off ages that our valleys and lake-basins were scooped out, the form of our landscapes sculptured and rounded, and the soil formed in which we grow our harvests. Who would think of such a connection? And yet it is true! Just as each season we owe the bloom and brightness of our summer fields to the gloom and blight of winter, so do we owe the present summer beauty of the world to the great secular winter of the glacial period. And does not God bring about results as striking by agencies apparently as contradictory in the human world? He who warms the tender latent life of the flowers by the snow, and moulds the quiet beauty of the summer landscape, by the desolating glacier, makes the cold of adversity to cherish the life of the soul, and to round into spiritual loveliness the harshness and roughness of a carnal, selfish nature. Many a profitable Christian life owes its fairness and fruitfulness to causes which wrecked and wasted it for a time. God giveth snow like wool; and chill and blighting as is the touch of sorrow, it has a protective influence which guards against greater evils; it sculptures the spiritual landscape within into forms of beauty and grace, and deepens and fertilises the soil of the heart, so that in it may grow from God's own planting the peaceable fruits of righteousness.

And now let us look at the Giver of the snow. "*He* giveth snow like wool." " The snow-flake," as Professor Tyndall strikingly says, " leads back to the sun "—so intimately related are all things to each other in this wonderful universe. It leads further and higher still—even to him who is our sun and shield, the light and heat of all creation. The whole vast realm of winter, with its strange phenomena, is but the breath of God—the Creative Word—as it were, congealed against the blue transparency of space, like the marvellous frost-work on a window-pane. The Psalmist had not the shadow of a doubt that God formed and sent the annual miracle of snow, as he had formed and sent the daily miracle of manna in the desert. It was a common-place thing; it was a natural, ordinary occurrence; but it had the Divine sign upon it, and it showed forth the glory and goodness of God as strikingly as the most wonderful supernatural event in his nation's history. When God would impress Job with a sense of his power, it was not to some of his miraculous, but to some of his ordinary works that he appealed. And when the Psalmist would praise God for the preservation of Israel and the restoration of Jerusalem—as he does in the Psalm from which my subject is taken—it is not to the wonderful, miraculous events with which the history of Israel abounded that he directs attention, but to the common events of Providence and the ordinary appearances and processes of nature. He cannot think enough of the Omnipotent Creator and Ruler of the Universe entering into familiar relations with his people, and condescending to their humblest wants. It is the same God that "giveth snow like wool," who "shows his word unto Jacob, and his statutes and commandments unto Israel." And the wonder of the peculiarity is enhanced by thoughts borrowed from the wonders of nature. We know a thousand times more of the nature, formation, and purpose of the snow than the Psalmist did. But that knowledge is dearly earned if our science destroys our faith. What amount or precision of scientific knowledge can compensate us for the loss of the spiritual sensibility, which in all the wonders and beauties of the Creation brings us into personal contact with an infinitely wise mind and an infinitely loving heart?—*Hugh Macmillan, in "Two Worlds are Ours,"* 1880.

Verse 16.—"*Snow.*" It is worth pausing to think what wonderful work is going on in the atmosphere during the formation and descent of every snow shower; what building power is brought into play! and how imperfect seem the productions of human minds and hands when compared with those formed by the blind forces of nature! But who ventures to call the forces of nature blind? In reality, when we speak thus, we are describing our own condition. The blindness is ours; and what we really ought to say, and to confess, is that our powers are absolutely unable to comprehend either the origin or the end of the operations of nature.—*John Tyndall, in "The Forms of Water,"* 1872.

Verses 16, 17.—The Lord takes the ice and frost and cold to be his; it is not only *his* sun, but *his* ice, and *his* frost: " he scattereth *his hoar frost* like ashes." The frost is compared to ashes in a threefold respect. First, because the hoarfrost gives a little interruption to the sight. If you scatter ashes into the air, it darkens the light, so doth the hoar frost. Secondly, the hoary frost is like ashes because near in colour to ashes. Thirdly, 'tis like, because there is a kind of burning in it : frost burns the tender buds and blossoms, it nips them and dries them up. The hoar frost hath its denomination in the Latin tongue from *burning*, and it differs but very little from that word which is commonly used in Latin for a coal of fire. The cold frost hath a kind of scorching in it, as well as the hot sun. Unseasonable frosts in the spring scorch the tender fruits, which bad effect of frost is usually expressed by *carbunculation* or blasting.—*Joseph Caryl.*

Verse 17.—*"He casteth forth his ice like morsels."* Or, *shivers of bread.* It is a worthy saying of one from this text,—The ice is bread, the rain is drink, the snow is wool, the frost a fire to the earth, causing it inwardly to glow with heat ; teaching us what to do for God's poor.—*John Trapp.*

Verse 17.—*"He casteth forth his ice like morsels."* The word here translated *"morsels,"* means, in most of the places where it occurs in the Bible, *pieces of bread,* exactly the LXX. ψωμούς ; for this very ice, this wintry cold, is profitable to the earth, to fit it for bearing future harvests, and thus it matures the *morsels of bread* which man will yet win from the soil in due season.—*Genebrardus, in Neale and Littledale.*

Verse 17.—*"Morsels."* Or, *crumbs.* Gen. xviii. 5 ; Judges xix. 5. Doubtless the allusion is to hail.—*A. S. Aglen.*

Verse 17.—" It is extremely severe," said his sister to Archbishop Leighton one day, speaking of the season. The good man only said in reply, " But thou, O God, hast made summer and winter."—*From J. N. Pearson's Life of Archbishop Leighton,* 1830.

Verse 18.—*"He sendeth out his word, and melteth them."* Israel in the captivity had been ice-bound, like ships of Arctic voyagers in the Polar Sea ; but God sent forth the vernal breeze of his love, and the water flowed, the ice melted, and they were released. God turned their captivity, and, their icy chains being melted by the solar beams of God's mercy, they flowed in fresh and buoyant streams, like " rivers of the south," shining in the sun. See Ps. cxxvi. 4.

So it was on the day of Pentecost. The winter of spiritual captivity was thawed and dissolved by the soft breath of the Holy Ghost, and the earth laughed and bloomed with spring-tide flowers of faith, love, and joy.—*Christopher Wordsworth.*

Verse 19.—Here we see God in compassion bending down, in order to communicate to the deeply fallen son of man something of a blessed secret, of which without his special enlightment, the eye would never have seen anything, nor the ear ever have heard.—*J. J. Van Oosterzee, on "The Image of Christ."*

Verses 19, 20.—If the publication of the law by the ministry of angels to the Israelites were such a privilege that it is reckoned their peculiar treasure—*"He hath shewed his statutes unto Israel ; he hath not dealt so with any nation"*—what is the revelation of the gosel by the Son of God himself ? For although the law is obscured and defaced since the fall, yet there are some ingrafted notions of it in human nature ; but there is not the least suspicion of the gospel. The law discovers our misery, but the gospel alone shows the way to be delivered from it. If an advantage so great and so precious doth not touch our hearts ; and, in possessing it with joy, if we are not sensible of the engagements the Father of mercies hath laid upon us ; we shall be the ungratefulest wretches in the world.—*William Bates.*

Verses 19, 20.—That some should have more means of knowing the Creator, others less, it is all from the mercy and will of God. His church hath a privilege and an advantage above other nations in the world ; the Jews had this favour above the heathens, and Christians above the Jews ; and no other reason can be assigned but his eternal love.—*Thomas Manton.*

Verse 20.—*"He hath not dealt so with any nation . . . . Praise ye the Lord."* The sweet Psalmist of Israel, a man skilful in praises, doth begin and end this Psalm with *Hallelujah.* In the body of the Psalm he doth set forth the mercy of God, both towards all *creatures* in general in his common providence, and towards his *church* in particular. So in this close of the Psalm : " He sheweth his word unto Jacob, and his statutes to Israel. He hath not dealt so with any nation." In the original 'tis, " He hath not dealt so with *every* nation : " that is, with *any* nation.

In the text you may observe *a position* and *a conclusion*. *A position ;* and that is, that God deals in a singular way of mercy with his people above all other people. And then the *conclusion* : "*Praise ye the Lord.*" Doctrine. That God deals in a singular way of mercy with his people, and therefore expects singular praises from his people.—*Joseph Alleine* (1663—1668), *in "A Thanksgiving Sermon.*"

Verse 20.—See the wonderful goodness of God, who besides the light of nature, has committed to us the sacred Scriptures. The heathen are enveloped in ignorance. "*As for his judgments, they have not known them.*" They have the oracles of the Sybils, but not the writings of Moses and the apostles. How many live in the region of death, where the bright star of Scripture has never appeared ! We have the blessed Book of God to resolve all our doubts, and to point out a way of life to us. " Lord, how is it thou wilt manifest thyself unto us, and not unto the world ? "—John xiv. 22.—*Thomas Watson.*

HINTS TO PREACHERS.

Verse 1.—Praise. Its profit, pleasure, and propriety.—*J. F.*

Verse 1.—The Reasonable Service. I. The methods of praise : by word, song, life ; individually, socially. II. The offerers of praise : " ye." III. The object of praise : " the Lord, our God." IV. The reasons for praise : it is " good," " pleasant," " becoming."—*C. A. D.*

Verses 1—3.—I. The Privilege of Praising God. 1. It is good. 2. Pleasant. 3. Becoming. II. The Duty of Praising God. 1. For gathering a church for himself among men : " The Lord doth build up Jerusalem." 2. For the materials of which it is composed : " The outcasts," etc. 3. For the preparation of those materials for his purpose : " He healeth," etc., verse 3.—*G. R.*

Verse 2.—The Lord is Architect, Builder, Sustainer, Restorer, and Owner of the Church. In each relation let him be praised.

Verse 2.—The Great Gatherer. I. Strange persons sought for. II. Special search and means made use of. III. Selected centre to which he brings them. IV. Singular exhibition of them for ever and ever in heaven.

Verse 2.—First the church built and then the sinners gathered into it. A prosperous state of the church within necessary to her increase from without.

Verse 2.—See " Spurgeon's Sermons," No. 1302 : " Good Cheer for Outcasts."

Verse 2.—Upbuilding and In gathering. I. The church may be in a fallen condition. II. Its upbuilding is the Lord's work. III. He accomplishes it by gathering together its outcast citizens.—*C. A. D.*

Verse 3.—See " Spurgeon's Sermons," No. 53 : " Healing for the Wounded."

Verse 3.—God a true physician, and a tender nurse.—*J. F.*

Verses 3, 4.—Heaven's Brilliants, and Earth's Broken Hearts. I. The Proprietor of the Stars with the Wounded. The stars left kingless for broken hearts. Jehovah ! with lint and liniment and a woman's hand. Who binds together the stars, shall bind firmly grieved hearts. II. The Gentle Heart-healer with the Stars. Be all power entrusted to such tenderness. Its comely splendour. God guides the stars with an eye on wounded hearts. The hopefulness of prayer. III. Hearts, Stars, and Eternity. Some hearts shall " shine as the stars." Some stars shall expire in " blackness of darkness." God's hand and eye are everywhere making justice certain. Trust and sing.—*W. B. H.*

Verses 3, 4.—God's Compassion and Power. I. Striking diversity of God's cares : " hearts " and " stars." II. Wonderful variety of God's operations. Gently caring for human hearts. Preserving the order, regularity, and stability of creation. III. Blessed results of God's work. Broken hearts healed ; wounds bound up. Light, harmony, and beauty in the heavens. IV. Mighty encouragement to trust in God. God takes care of the universe ; may I not entrust my life, my soul, to him ? Where he rules unquestioned there is light and harmony ; let me not resist his will in my life.—*C. A. D.*

Verse 5.—A contemplation of God's greatness. I. Great in his essential nature. II. Great in power. III. Great in wisdom. Let us draw inferences concerning the insignificance of man, &c.

Verse 6.—Reversal. I. In the estimate of the world the meek are cast down and the wicked lifted up. II. In the judgment of heaven the meek are lifted up and the wicked cast down. III. The judgment of heaven will, in the end, be found the true one.—*C. A. D.*

Verse 7.—The use and benefit of singing.

Verse 8.—God in all. The unity of his plan ; the co-operation of divine forces ; the condescending mercy of the result.

Verse 9.—See " Spurgeon's Sermons," No. 672 : " The Ravens' Cry."

Verse 11.—The singularity of our God, and of his favour. For which he is to be praised. I. *The objects of that favour distinguished.* 1. From physical strength. 2. From mental vigour. 3. From self-reliance. 4. From mere capacity for service. II. *The objects of that favour described.* 1. By emotions relating to God. 2. By the weakest forms of spiritual life. 3. By the highest degrees of it ; for the maturest saint fears and hopes. 4. By the sacred blend of it. Fear of our guilt, hope of his mercy. Fear of self, confidence in God. Hope of perseverance, fear of sinning. Hope of heaven, fear of coming short. Hope of perfection, mourning defects. III. *The blessing of that favour implied.* 1. God loves to think of them. 2. To be with them. 3. To minister to them. 4. To meet them in their fears and their hopes. 5. To reward them for ever.

Verse 11.—He takes pleasure in their persons, emotions, desires, devotions, hopes, and characters.—*W. W.*

Verse 12.—I. The Lord whom we praise. II. His praise in our houses— Jerusalem. III. Our praise in his house—Zion.

Verse 13.—A Strong Church. I. The utility and value of a strong church. II. The marks which distinguish it. 1. Gates well kept. 2. Increase of membership. 3. The converts blessed to others. III. The important care of a strong church : to trace all blessing to Zion's God.—*W. B. H.*

Verses 14, 15.—See " Spurgeon's Sermons,''' No. 425 : " Peace at Home, and Prosperity Abroad."

Verses 14, 15.—Church blessings. I. Peace. II. Food. III. Missionary energy. IV. The presence of God : the source of all blessing.

Verse 15 (*second clause*).—See " Spurgeon's Sermons," No. 1607 : " The Swiftly Running Word."

Verse 16.—The unexpected results of adversity : snow acting as wool.

Verses 16—18.—See " Spurgeon's Sermons," No. 670 : " Frost and Thaw."

Verse 19.—I. God's people. II. God's Word. III. God's revelation to the soul. IV. God's praise for this special revelation.

Verse 20.—Electing Grace inspires the Heart with Praise. I. God's love has chosen us. Hallelujah. II. God has entrusted us with his truth. Hallelujah. III. God has made us almoners of his bounty. Hallelujah. IV. God through us is to save the world. Hallelujah.—*W. B. H.*

PSALM CXLVIII.

The song is one and indivisible. It seems almost impossible to expound it in detail, for a living poem is not to be dissected verse by verse. It is a song of nature and of grace. As a flash of lightning flames through space, and enwraps both heaven and earth in one vestment of glory, so doth the adoration of the Lord in this Psalm light up all the universe and cause it to glow with a radiance of praise. The song begins in the heavens, sweeps downward to dragons and all deeps, and then ascends again, till the people near unto Jehovah take up the strain. For its exposition the chief requisite is a heart on fire with reverent love to the Lord over all, who is to be blessed for ever.

EXPOSITION.

Praise ye the Lord. Praise ye the Lord from the heavens : praise him in the heights.

2 Praise ye him, all his angels : praise ye him, all his hosts.

3 Praise ye him, sun and moon : praise him, all ye stars of light.

4 Praise him, ye heavens of heavens, and ye waters that *be* above the heavens.

5 Let them praise the name of the Lord : for he commanded, and they were created.

6 He hath also stablished them for ever and ever : he hath made a decree which shall not pass.

7 Praise the Lord from the earth, ye dragons, and all deeps :

8 Fire, and hail ; snow, and vapours ; stormy wind fulfilling his word :

9 Mountains, and all hills ; fruitful trees, and all cedars :

10 Beasts, and all cattle ; creeping things, and flying fowl :

11 Kings of the earth, and all people ; princes, and all judges of the earth :

12 Both young men, and maidens ; old men, and children :

13 Let them praise the name of the Lord : for his name alone is excellent ; his glory *is* above the earth and heaven.

14 He also exalteth the horn of his people, the praise of all his saints ; *even* of the children of Israel, a people near unto him. Praise ye the Lord.

1. *"Praise ye the Lord."* Whoever ye may be that hear this word, ye are invited, entreated, commanded, to magnify Jehovah. Assuredly he has made you, and, if for nothing else, ye are bound, upon the ground of creatureship, to adore your Maker. This exhortation can never be out of place, speak it where we may ; and never out of time, speak it when we may. *"Praise ye the Lord from the heavens."* Since ye are nearest to the High and lofty One, be ye sure to lead the song. Ye angels, ye cherubim and seraphim, and all others who dwell in the precincts of his courts, praise ye Jehovah. Do this as from a starting-point from which the praise is to pass on to other realms. Keep not your worship to yourselves, but let it fall like a golden shower from the heavens on men beneath. *"Praise him in the heights."* This is no vain repetition ; but after the manner of attractive poesy the truth is emphasized by reiteration in other words. Moreover, God is not only to be praised *from* the heights, but *in* them : the adoration is to be perfected in the heavens from which it takes its rise. No place is too high for the praises of the most High. On the summit of creation the glory of the Lord is to be revealed, even as the tops of the highest Alps are tipped with the golden light of the same sun which glads the valleys. Heavens and heights become the higher and the more heavenly as they are made to resound with the praises

of Jehovah. See how the Psalmist trumpets out the word " PRAISE." It sounds forth some nine times in the first five verses of this song. Like minute-guns, exultant exhortations are sounded forth in tremendous force—*Praise! Praise! Praise!* The drum of the great King beats round the world with this one note—*Praise! Praise! Praise!* "Again they said, Hallelujah." All this praise is distinctly and personally for Jehovah. Praise not his servants nor his works ; but praise HIM. Is he not worthy of all possible praise ? Pour it forth before HIM in full volume ; pour it only there !

2. *"Praise ye him all his angels."* Living intelligences, perfect in character and in bliss, lift up your loudest music to your Lord, each one of you. Not one bright spirit is exempted from this consecrated service. However many ye be, O angels, ye are all *his* angels, and therefore ye are bound, all of you, to render service to your Lord. Ye have all seen enough of him to be able to praise him, and ye have all abundant reasons for so doing. Whether ye be named Gabriel, or Michael, or by whatever other titles ye are known, praise ye the Lord. Whether ye bow before him, or fly on his errands, or desire to look into his covenant, or behold his Son, cease not, ye messengers of Jehovah, to sound forth his praise while ye move at his bidding. *"Praise ye him, all his hosts."* This includes angelic armies, but groups with them all the heavenly bodies. Though they be inanimate, the stars, the clouds, the lightnings, have their ways of praising Jehovah. Let each one of the countless legions of the Lord of hosts show forth his glory ; for the countless armies are all *his*, his by creation, and preservation, and consequent obligation. Both these sentences claim unanimity of praise from those in the upper regions who are called upon to commence the strain—" *all* his angels, *all* his hosts." That same hearty oneness must pervade the whole orchestra of praising ones ; hence, further on, we read of all stars of light, all deeps, all hills, all cedars, and all people. How well the concert begins when all angels, and all the heavenly host, strike the first joyful notes ! In that concert our souls would at once take their part.

3. *"Praise ye him, sun and moon : praise him, all ye stars of light."* The Psalmist enters into detail as to the heavenly hosts. As all, so each, must praise the God of each and all. The sun and moon, as joint rulers of day and night, are paired in praise : the one is the complement of the other, and so they are closely associated in the summons to worship. The sun has his peculiar mode of glorifying the Great Father of lights, and the moon has her own special method of reflecting his brightness. There is a perpetual adoration of the Lord in the skies : it varies with night and day, but it ever continues while sun and moon endure. There is ever a lamp burning before the high altar of the Lord. Nor are the greater luminaries allowed to drown with their floods of light the glory of the lesser brilliants, for all the stars are bidden to the banquet of praise. Stars are many, so many that no one can count the host included under the words, " all ye stars " ; yet no one of them refuses to praise its Maker. From their extreme brilliance they are fitly named " stars of light "; and this light is praise in a visible form twinkling to true music. Light is song glittering before the eye instead of resounding in the ear. Stars without light would render no praise, and Christians without light rob the Lord of his glory. However small our beam, we must not hide it : if we cannot be sun or moon we must aim to be one of the " stars of light," and our every twinkling must be to the honour of our Lord.

4. *"Praise him, ye heavens of heavens."* By these are meant those regions which are heavens to those who dwell in our heavens ; or those most heavenly of abodes where the most choice of spirits dwell. As the highest of the highest, so the best of the best are to praise the Lord. If we could climb as much above the heavens as the heavens are above the earth, we could still cry out to all around us, " Praise ye the Lord." There can be none so great and high as to be above praising Jehovah. *"And ye waters that be above the heavens."* Let the clouds roll up volumes of adoration. Let the sea above roar, and the fulness thereof, at the presence of Jehovah, the God of Israel. There is something of mystery about these supposed reservoirs of water ; but let them be what they may, and as they may, they shall give glory to the Lord our God. Let the most unknown and perplexing phenomena take up their parts in the universal praise.

5. *"Let them praise the name of the LORD ; for he commanded, and they were created."* Here is good argument : The Maker should have honour from his works, they should tell forth *his* praise ; and thus they should praise his *name*—by which his character is intended. The name of JEHOVAH is written legibly upon his works,

so that his power, wisdom, goodness, and other attributes are there made manifest to thoughtful men, and thus his name is praised. The highest praise of God is to declare what he is. We can invent nothing which would magnify the Lord : we can never extol him better than by repeating his name, or describing his character. The Lord is to be extolled as creating all things that exist, and as doing so by the simple agency of his word. He cretead by a command ; what a power is this ! Well may he expect those to praise him who owe their being to him. Evolution may be atheistic ; but the doctrine of creation logically demands worship ; and hence, as the tree is known by its fruit, it proves itself to be true. Those who were created by command are under command to adore their Creator. The voice which said " Let them be," now saith " Let them praise."

6. *"He hath also stablished them for ever and ever."* The continued existence of celestial beings is due to the supporting might of Jehovah, and to that alone. They do not fail because the Lord does not fail them. Without his will these things cannot alter ; he has impressed upon them laws which only he himself can change. Eternally his ordinances are binding upon them. Therefore ought the Lord to be praised because he is Preserver as well as Creator, Ruler as well as Maker. *"He hath made a decree which shall not pass."* The heavenly bodies are ruled by Jehovah's decree : they cannot pass his limit, or trespass against his law. His rule and ordination can never be changed except by himself, and in this sense his decree " shall not pass " : moreover, the highest and most wonderful of creatures are perfectly obedient to the statutes of the Great King, and thus his decree is not passed over. This submission to law is praise. Obedience is homage ; order is harmony. In this respect the praise rendered to Jehovah from the " bodies celestial " is absolutely perfect. His almighty power upholds all things in their spheres, securing the march of stars and the flight of seraphs ; and thus the music of the upper regions is never marred by discord, nor interrupted by destruction. The eternal hymn is for ever chanted ; even the solemn silence of the spheres is a perpetual psalm.

7. *"Praise the LORD from the earth."* The song descends to our abode, and so comes nearer home to us. We who are " bodies terrestial," are to pour out our portion of praise from the golden globe of this favoured planet. Jehovah is to be praised not only *in* the earth but *from* the earth, as if the adoration ran over from this planet into the general accumulation of worship. In the first verse the song was " from the heavens " ; here it is going " from the earth " ; songs coming down from heaven are to blend with those going up from earth. The " earth " here meant is our entire globe of land and water : it is to be made vocal everywhere with praise. *"Ye dragons, and all deeps."* It would be idle to enquire what special sea-monsters are here meant ; but we believe all of them are intended, and the places where they abide are indicated by " all deeps." Terrible beasts or fishes, whether they roam the earth or swim the seas, are bidden to the feast of praise. Whether they float amid the teeming waves of the tropics, or wend their way among the floes and bergs of polar waters, they are commanded by our sacred poet to yield their tribute to the creating Jehovah. They pay no service to man ; let them the more heartily confess their allegiance to the Lord. About " dragons " and " deeps " there is somewhat of dread, but this may the more fitly become the bass of the music of the Psalm. If there be aught grim in mythology, or fantastic in heraldry, let it praise the incomprehensible Lord.

8. *"Fire and hail."* Lightning and hailstones go together. In the plagues of Egypt they co-operated in making Jehovah known in all the terrors of his power. Fire and ice-morsels are a contrast in nature, but they are combined in magnifying the Lord. *"Snow and vapours."* Offsprings of cold, or creations of heat, be ye equally consecrated to his praise. Congealed or expanded vapours, falling flakes or rising clouds, should, rising or falling, still reveal the praises of the Lord. *"Stormy winds fulfilling his word."* Though rushing with incalculable fury, the storm-wind is still under law, and moves in order due, to carry out the designs of God. It is a grand orchestra which contains such wind-instruments as these ! He is a great leader who can keep all these musicians in concert, and direct both time and tune.

9. *"Mountains and all hills."* Towering steeps and swelling knolls alike declare their Creator. " All hills " are to be consecrated ; we have no longer Ebal and Gerizim, the hill of the curse and the hill of the blessing, but all our Ebals are turned to Gerizims. Tabor and Hermon, Lebanon and Carmel, rejoice in the name of the Lord. The greater and the lesser mounts are one in their adoration. Not

only the Alps and the mountains of the Jura thunder out his praise ; but our own Cotswolds and Grampians are vocal with songs in his honour. *"Fruitful trees and all cedars."* Fruit trees and forest trees, trees deciduous or evergreen, are equally full of benevolent design, and alike subserve some purpose of love ; therefore for all and by all let the great Designer be praised. There are many species of cedar, but they all reveal the wisdom of their Maker. When kings fell them, that they may make beams for their palaces, they do but confess their obligation to the King of trees, and to the King of kings, whose trees they are. Varieties in the landscape are produced by the rising and falling of the soil, and by the many kinds of trees which adorn the land : let all, and all alike, glorify their one Lord. When the trees clap their hands in the wind, or their leaves rustle in the gentle breath of Zephyr, they do to their best ability sing out unto the Lord.

10. *"Beasts, and all cattle."* Animals fierce or tame ; wild beasts and domestic cattle ; let all these show forth the praises of Jehovah. Those are worse than beasts who do not praise our God. More than brutish are those who are wilfully dumb concerning their Maker. *"Creeping things, and flying fowl."* The multitudes that throng the earth and the air ; insects of every form and birds of every wing are called upon to join the universal worship. No one can become familiar with insect and bird life without feeling that they constitute a wonderful chapter in the history of divine wisdom. The minute insect marvellously proclaims the Lord's handiwork : when placed under the microscope it tells a wondrous tale. So, too, the bird which soars aloft displays in its adaptation for an aerial life an amount of skill which our balloonists have in vain attempted to emulate. True devotion not only hears the praises of God in the sweet song of feathered ministrels, but even discovers it in the croaking from the marsh or in the buzz of "the bluefly which singeth in the window-pane." More base than reptiles, more insignificant than insects, are songless men.

11. *"Kings of the earth, and all people : princes, and all judges of the earth."* Now the poet has reached our own race, and very justly he would have rulers and subjects, chieftains and magistrates, unite in worshipping the sovereign Lord of all. Monarchs must not disdain to sing, nor must their people refrain from uniting with them. Those who lead in battle and those who decide in courts must neither of them allow their vocations to keep them from reverently adoring the Chief and Judge of all. All people, and all judges, must praise the Lord of all. What a happy day it will be when it is universally acknowledged that through our Lord Jesus, the incarnate Wisdom, " kings reign and princes decree justice " ! Alas, it is not so as yet ! kings have been patrons of vice, and princes ringleaders in folly. Let us pray that the song of the Psalmist may be realized in fact.

12. *"Both young men, and maidens ; old men, and children."* Both sexes and all ages are summoned to the blessed service of song. Those who usually make merry together are to be devoutly joyful together : those who make up the ends of families, that is to say, the elders and the juveniles, should make the Lord their one and only end. Old men should by their experience teach children to praise ; and children by their cheerfulness should excite old men to song. There is room for every voice at this concert : fruitful trees and maidens, cedars and young men, angels and children, old men and judges—all may unite in this oratorio. None, indeed, can be dispensed with : for perfect Psalmody we must have the whole universe aroused to worship, and all parts of creation must take their parts in devotion.

13. *"Let them praise the name of the Lord."* All that is contained in the name or character of Jehovah is worthy of praise, and all the objects of his creating care will be too few to set it forth in its completeness. *"For his name alone is excellent."* It alone deserves to be exalted in praise, for alone it is exalted in worth. There is none like unto the Lord, none that for a moment can be compared unto him. His unique name should have a monopoly of praise. *"His glory is above the earth and heaven : "* it is therefore alone because it surpasses all others. His royal splendour exceeds all that earth and heaven can express. He is himself the crown of all things, the excellency of the creation. There is more glory in him personally than in all his works united. It is not possible for us to exceed and become extravagant in the Lord's praise : his own natural glory is infinitely greater than any glory which we can render to him.

14. *"He also exalteth the horn of his people."* He hath made them strong, famous, and victorious. His goodness to all his creatures does not prevent his having a

special favour to his chosen nation : he is good to all, but he is God to his people. He lifts up the down-trodden, but he in a peculiar manner lifts up his people. When they are brought low he raises up a horn for them by sending them a deliverer ; when they are in conflict he gives them courage and strength, so that they lift up their horn amid the fray ; and when all is peaceful around them, he fills their horn with plenty, and they lift it up with delight. *"The praise of all his saints."* He is their glory : to him they render praise ; and he by his mercy to them evermore gives them further reasons for praise, and higher motives for adoration. He lifts up their horn, and they lift up his praise. He exalts them, and they exalt him. The Holy One is praised by holy ones. He is their God, and they are his saints ; he makes them blessed, and they bless him in return. *"Even of the children of Israel."* The Lord knoweth them that are his. He knows the name of him with whom he made a covenant, and how he came by that name, and who his children are, and where they are. All nations are bidden in verse 11 to praise the Lord ; but here the call is specially addressed to his elect people, who know him beyond all others. Those who are children of privilege should be children of praise. *"A people near unto him,"* near by kin, and near by care ; near as to manifestation and near as to affection. This is a highly honourable description of the beloved race ; and it is true even more emphatically of the spiritual Israel, the believing seed. This nearness should prompt us to perpetual adoration. The Lord's elect are the children of his love, the courtiers of his palace, the priests of his temple, and therefore they are bound beyond all others to be filled with reverence for him, and delight in him. *"Praise ye the LORD,"* or, *Hallelujah.* This should be the Alpha and Omega of a good man's life. Let us praise God to the end, world without end. The field of praise which lies before us in this Psalm is bounded at beginning and end by land-marks in the form of Hallelujahs, and all that lieth between them is every word of it to the Lord's honour. Amen.

EXPLANATORY NOTES AND QUAINT SAYINGS.

Psalms cxlviii.—cl.—The last three Psalms are *a triad of wondrous praise,* ascending from praise to higher praise, until it becomes " joy unspeakable and full of glory "—exultation which knows no bounds. The joy overflows the soul, and spreads throughout the universe ; every creature is magnetized by it, and drawn into the chorus. Heaven is full of praise, the earth is full of praise, praises rise from under the earth, " every thing that hath breath " joins in the rapture. God is encompassed by a loving, praising creation. Man, the last in creation, but the first in song, knows not how to contain himself. He dances, he sings, he commands all the heavens, with all their angels, to help him, "beasts and all cattle, creeping things and flying fowl " must do likewise, even "dragons" must not be silent, and " all deeps " must yield contributions. He presses even dead things into his service, timbrels, trumpets, harps, organs, cymbals, high-sounding cymbals, if by any means, and by all means, he may give utterance to his love and joy.—*John Pulsford.*

Whole Psalm.—In this splendid anthem the Psalmist calls upon the whole creation, in its two great divisions (according to the Hebrew conception) of heaven and earth, to praise Jehovah : things with and things without life, beings rational and irrational, are summoned to join the mighty chorus. This Psalm is the expression of the loftiest devotion, and it embraces at the same time the most comprehensive view of the relation of the creature to the Creator. Whether it is exclusively the utterance of a heart filled to the full with the thought of the infinite majesty of God, or whether it is also an anticipation, a prophetic forecast, of the final glory of creation, when at the manifestation of the sons of God, the creation itself also shall be redeemed from the bondage of corruption (Rom. viii. 18—23), and the homage of praise shall indeed be rendered by all things that are in heaven and earth and under the earth, is a question into which we need not enter.—*J. J. Stewart Perowne.*

Whole Psalm.—Milton, in his Paradise Lost (Book V., line 153, etc.), has elegantly imitated this Psalm, and put it into the mouth of Adam and Eve as their morning hymn in a state of innocency.—*James Anderson.*

Whole Psalm.—Is this universal praise never to be realized ? is it only the longing, intense desire of the Psalmist's heart, which will never be heard on earth, and can only be perfected in heaven ? Is there to be no jubilee in which the mountains and the hills shall break forth into singing, and all the trees of the field shall clap their hands ? If there is to be no such day, then is the word of God of none effect ; if no such universal anthem is to swell the chorus of heaven, and to be re-echoed by all that is on earth, then is God's promise void. It is true, in this Psalm our translation presents it to us as a call or summons for everything that hath or hath not breath to praise the Lord—or as a petition that they may praise ; but it is in reality a prediction that they *shall* praise. . . . This Psalm is neither more nor less than a glorious prophecy of that coming day, when not only shall the knowledge of the Lord be spread over the whole earth, as the waters cover the sea, but from every created object in heaven and in earth, animate and inanimate, from the highest archangel through every grade and phase of being, down to the tiniest atom—young men and maidens, old men and children, and all kings and princes, and judges of the earth, shall unite in this millennial anthem to the Redeemer's praise.—*Barton Bouchier.*

Verse 1.—"*Praise ye the Lord,*" etc. All things praise, and yet he says, "*Praise ye.*" Wherefore doth he say, "*Praise ye,*" when they are praising ? Because he delighteth in their praising, and therefore it pleaseth him to add, as it were, his own encouragement. Just as, when you come to men who are doing any good work with pleasure in their vineyard or in their harvest-field, or in some other matter of husbandry, you are pleased at what they are doing, and say, " Work on," " Go on " ; not that they may begin to work, when you say this, but, because you are pleased at finding them working, you add your approbation and encouragement. For by saying, " Work on," and encouraging those who are working, you, so to speak, work with them in wish. In this sort of encouragement, then, the Psalmist, filled with the Holy Ghost, saith this.—*Augustine.*

Verse 1.—The thrice-repeated exhortation, "*Praise . . Praise . . Praise,*" in this first verse is not merely imperative, nor only hortative, but it is an exultant hallelujah.—*Martin Geier.*

Verse 1.—"*From the heavens : praise him in the heights.*" Or, high places. As God in framing the world begun above, and wrought downward, so doth the Psalmist proceed in this his exhortation to all creatures to praise the Lord.—*John Trapp.*

Verse 1.—"*Praise him in the heights.*" The principle applied in this verse is this, that those who have been exalted to the highest honours of the created universe, should proportionately excel in their tribute of honour to him who has exalted them. —*Hermann Venema.*

Verse 1.—Bernard, in his sermon on the death of his brother Gerard, relates that in the middle of his last night on earth his brother, to the astonishment of all present, with a voice and countenance of exultation, broke forth in the words of the Psalmist—"*Praise the Lord of heaven, praise him in the heights !*"

Verse 2.—"*Praise ye him, all his angels.*" Angels are first invoked, because they can praise God with humility, reverence, and purity. The highest are the humblest, the leaders of all created hosts are the most ready themselves to obey.— *Thomas Le Blanc.*

Verse 2.—"*Praise ye him, all his angels.*" The angels of God were his first creatures ; it has even been thought that they existed prior to the inanimate universe. They were already praising their Maker before the light of day, and they have never ceased their holy song. Angels praise God best in their holy service. They praised Christ as God when they sang their *Gloria in Excelsis* at the Incarnation, and they praised him as man when they ministered to him after his temptation and before his crucifixion. So also now angels praise the Lord by their alacrity in ministering to his saints.—*John Lorinus.*

Verse 2.—"*Praise ye him, all his hosts.*" That is, his creatures (those above especially which are as his *cavalry*) called his "hosts," for, 1, Their number ; 2, their order ; 3, their obedience.—*John Trapp.*

Verse 3.—"*Praise ye him, sun and moon,*" etc. How does the *sun* specially praise Jehovah ? 1. By its beauty. Jesus son of Sirach calls it the " globe of beauty." 2. By its fulness. Dion calls it " the image of the Divine capacity."

3. By its exaltation. Pliny calls it *cæli rector*, "the ruler of heaven." 4. By its perfect brightness. Pliny adds that it is "the mind and soul of the whole universe." 5. By its velocity and constancy of motion. Martian calls it "the Guide of Nature."

God the Supreme was depicted by the ancients holding in his hand a wreath of stars, to show the double conception, that they both obey and adorn him.—*Thomas Le Blanc.*

Verses 3, 4.—Let the sun, the fount of light, and warmth, and gladness, the greater light which rules the day, the visible emblem of the Uncreated Wisdom, the Light which lighteth every man, the centre round whom all our hopes and fears, our wants and prayers, our faith and love, are ever moving,—let the moon, the lesser light which rules the night, the type of the Church, which giveth to the world the light she gains from the Sun of Righteousness,—let the stars, so vast in their number, so lovely in their arrangement and their brightness, which God hath appointed in the heavens, even as he hath appointed his elect to shine for ever and ever,—let all the heavens with all their wonders and their worlds, the depths of space above, and the waters which are above the firmament, the images of God's Holy Scripture and of the glories and the mysteries contained therein,—let these ever praise him who made and blessed them in the beginning of the creation.—*J. W. Burgon.*

Verses 3, 4.—

> Praise him, thou golden-tressèd sun;
> Praise him, thou fair and silver moon,
>   And ye bright orbs of streaming light;
> Ye floods that float above the skies,
> Ye heav'ns, that vault o'er vault arise,
>   Praise him, who sits above all height.
>
> Richard Mant.

Verse 4.—"*Praise him, ye heavens of heavens,*" etc. From the heavenly inhabitants the poetic strain passes in transition to the *heavens* themselves. There are orders of heavens, ranks and heights supreme, and stages and degrees of lower altitude. This verse sublimely traverses the immensities which are the home of the most exalted dignities who wait on Deity, and then it descends to the firmament where the meteors flash forth, and where the heavens stoop to lift the clouds that aspire from earth. And the idea sustained is that all these vast realms, higher and lower, are one temple of unceasing praise.—*Hermann Venema.*

Verse 4.—The ancients thought there was an ethereal and lofty ocean in which the worlds floated like ships in a sea.—*Thomas Le Blanc.*

Verses 5, 6.—This is the account of creation in a word—He spake; it was done. When Jesus came, he went everywhere showing his Divinity by this evidence, that his word was omnipotent. These verses declare two miracles of God's Will and Word, viz., the creation and consolidation of the earth. Jehovah first produced matter, then he ordered and established it.—*John Lorinus.*

Verse 6.—"*He hath also stablished them for ever and ever,*" etc. Here two things are set before us, the permanence and the cosmic order of creation. Each created thing is not only formed to endure, in the type or the development, if not in the individual, but has its place in the universe fixed by Gods decree, that it may fulfil its appointed share of working out his will. They raise a question as to the words "*for ever and ever,*" how they can be reconciled with the prophecy, Isaiah lxv. 17: "Behold, I create new heavens and a new earth: and the former shall not be remembered, nor come into mind"; a prophecy confirmed by the Lord himself, saying, "Heaven and earth shall pass away," and seen fulfilled in vision by the beloved disciple. Matt. v. 18; Rev. xxi. 1. And they answer that just as man dies and rises again to incorruption, having the same personality in a glorified body, so will it be with heaven and earth. Their qualities will be changed, not their identity, in that new birth of all things.—*Neale and Littledale.*

Verse 6.—"*For ever and ever.*"

> My heart is awed within me, when I think
> Of the great miracle which still goes on,
> In silence, round me—the perpetual work
> Of thy creation, finished, yet renewed,
> For ever.
>
> William Cullen Bryant, 1794—1878.

Verse 6.—*"He hath made a decree,"* etc. Rather, *He hath made an ordinance, and will not trangress it.* This is more obvious and natural than to supply a new subject to the second verb, " and none of them transgress it." This anticipates, but only in form, the modern scientific doctrine of the inviolability of natural order. It is the imperishable faithfulness of God that renders the law invariable.—*A. S. Aglen.*

Verse 7.—*"Dragons."* The word *tanninim*, rendered *"dragons,"* is a word which may denote whales, sharks, serpents, or sea-monsters of any kind (Job vii. 1 ; Ezek. xxix. 3).—*John Morison.*

Verse 7.—*"Sea-monsters,"* in Revised Version. Fishes constrain our admiration, as a created wonder, by the perfection of their form, their magnitude, their adaptation to the element they inhabit, and their multitude. Thus their very nature praises the Creator.—*Thomas Le Blanc.*

Verses 7, 8.—He calls to the *deeps, fire, hail, snow, mountains, and hills,* to bear a part in this work of praise. Not that they are able to do it actively, but to show that man is to call in the whole creation to assist him passively, and should have so much charity to all creatures as to receive what they offer, and so much affection to God as to present to him what he receives from him. *Snow* and *hail* cannot bless and praise God, but man ought to bless God for those things, wherein there is a mixture of trouble and inconvenience, something to molest our sense, as well as something that improves the earth for fruit.—*Stephen Charnock.*

Verses 7—10.—Here be many things easy to be understood, they are clear to every eye ; as when David doth exhort " kings " and " princes," " old men " and " babes " to praise God ; that is easy to be done, and we know the meaning as soon as we look on it ; but here are some things again that are hard to be understood, dark and obscure, and they are two :—

First, in that David doth exhort *dumb, unreasonable, and senseless creatures* to praise God, such as cannot hear, at least cannot understand. Doth the Holy Ghost in the gospel bid us avoid impertinent speeches, and vain repetitions, and shall we think he will use them himself ? No, no. But,

Secondly, not only doth he call upon these creatures, but also he calls upon the *"deeps"* and the *"seas"* to praise God ; these two things are hard to be conceived. But to give you some reasons.

The first reason may be this, why David calls upon the unreasonable creatures to perform this duty,—*He doth his duty like a faithful preacher,* whether they will hear or no that he preaches to, yet he will discharge his soul : a true preacher, he speaks forth the truth, and calls upon them to hear, though his auditors sleep, are careless, and regard it not. So likewise doth David, in this sense, with these creatures ; he doth his duty, and calls upon them to do it, though they understand not, though they comprehend it not. And likewise he doth it to show his vehement desire for all creatures to praise God.

The second reason may be this : *he doth it craftily,* by way of policy, to incite others to perform this duty, that if such creatures as they ought to do this, then those that are above them in degree have more cause, and may be ashamed to neglect it ; as an ill-governed master, though he stay himself at home, yet he will send his servants to church : so David, being conscious of his own neglect, yet he calls upon others not to be slack and negligent : though he came infinitely short of that he should do, yet he shows his own desire for all creatures to perform this duty.

But if these reasons will not satisfy you, though they have done many others, a third reason may be this : *to set forth the sweet harmony that is among all God's creatures ;* to show how that all the creatures being God's family, do with one consent speak and preach aloud God's praise ; and therefore he calls upon some above him, some below him, on both sides, everywhere, to speak God's praise ; for every one in their place, degree, and calling, show forth, though it be in a dumb sense and way, their Creator's praise.

Or, fourthly, and lastly, which I think to be a good reason : *zeal makes men speak and utter things impossible ;* the fire of zeal will so transport him that it will make him speak things unreasonable, impossible, as Moses in his zeal desired God, for the safety of Israel, " to blot his name out of his book " ; and Paul wished himself " anathema," accursed or separate from Christ, for his brethren's salvation, which was a thing impossible, it could not be.—*John Everard, in "Some Gospel Treasures,"* 1653.

Verses 7—10.—The ox and the ass acknowledge their master. The winds and the sea obey him. It should seem that as there is a religion above man, the religion of angels, so there may be a religion beneath man, the religion of dumb creatures. For wheresoever there is a service of God, in effect it is a religion. Thus according to the several degrees and difference of states—the state of nature, grace, and glory —religion may likewise admit of degrees.—*G. G., in a sermon entitled "The Creatures Praysing God,"* 1662.

Verse 8.—This verse arrays in striking order three elements that are ever full of movement and power—*ignea, aquea, aërea ;* fire (or caloric), water (or vapour), and air (or wind). The first includes meteors, lightnings and thunders ; the second, snow, hoar-frost, dew, mist and rain; the third breezes, tempests and hurricanes. —*Hermann Venema.*

Verse 8.—*"Fire and hail."* These are contrasted with one another. *"Snow and mist."* The mist is the vapour raised by the heat of the sun, and therefore suitably contrasted with the snow, which is the effect of cold. *"Stormy wind "* (Ps. cvii. 25), which accompanies the changes of temperature in the air.—*James G. Murphy.*

Verse 8.—*"Snow."* As sure as every falling flake of winter's snow has a part in the great economy of nature, so surely has every Word of God which falls within the sanctuary its end to accomplish in the moral sphere. I have stood on a winter's day, and seen the tiny flakes in little clouds lose themselves one by one in the rushing river. They seemed to die to no purpose—to be swallowed up by an enemy which ignored both their power and their existence. And so have I seen the Word of God fall upon human hearts. Sent of God, from day to day and from year to year, I have seen it dropping apparently all resultless into the fierce current of unbelief—into the fiercer gulf-stream of worldliness which was sweeping through the minds and the lives of the hearers. But as I stood upon the river's bank and looked upon what seemed to be the death of the little fluttering crystal, a second thought assured me that it was but death into life, and that every tiny flake which wept its life away in the rushing waters, became incorporate with the river's being. So when I have seen the Word of God fall apparently fruitless upon the restless, seething, rushing current of human life, a recovered faith in the immutable declaration of God has assured me that what I looked upon was not a chance or idle death, but rather the falling of the soldier, after that he had wrought his life-force into the destiny of a nation and into the history of a world. And so it must ever be. The Word of God ever reaches unto its end.—*S. S. Mitchell, in a Sermon entitled "The Coming of the Snow and the Coming of the Word,"* 1884.

Verse 8.—The *"stormy wind "* is the swift messenger of God, Ps. cxlvii. 15. The hurricane fulfils the divine command. See Matt. viii. 27. " Even the winds and the sea obey him." The *"wind "* is the minister of judgment. See Ezek. xiii. 13. The words of this verse have special use ; for men are exceedingly apt to ascribe the violence of tempests to blind chance.—*Martin Geier.*

Verse 8.—The half-learned man is apt to laugh at the simple faith of the clown or savage, who tells us that rain comes from God. The former, it seems, has discovered that it is the product of certain laws of air, water, and electricity. But truly the peasant is the more enlightened of the two, for he has discovered the main cause, and the real Actor, while the other has found only the second cause, and the mere instrument. It is as if a friend were to send us a gift of ingenious and beautiful workmanship, and just as our gratitude was beginning to rise to the donor, some bystanders were to endeavour to damp it all, by telling us that the gift is the product of certain machinery he had seen.—*James MacCosh,* 1811.

Verse 9.—*"Mountains and all hills,"* etc.—The diversifying of the face of the earth with higher and lower parts, with mountains, hills, and valleys, and the adorning of the face thereof with trees of varied sorts, contributeth much to the praise of God. —*David Dickson.*

Verse 9.—*"Mountains and all hills."* What voices have the hills ! How solemn the sounds of the mountains from their sublime solitudes ! The mountains thunder, and the hills re-echo ; but they speak peace and send down plenty to the vales in running rivulets.—*Thomas Le Blanc.*

Verse 9.—*"Fruitful trees and all cedars."* The praise of God is in the rustling voices of the trees. They fulfil his purpose in giving fruit to refresh, and shelter and shadow for a covert, and their murmur is the soft cadence that chants mercy and grace. In India, the ancients reported that the trees were worshipped as divine, and death was a penalty awarded to those who cut them down. In classic mythology the groves were the homes of gods. Jehovah decreed that an ark of safety for man, and also a temple for himself, should be constructed of wood. Thus more than any other created things, the trees of the wood have redounded to his glory.—*Le Blanc.*

Verse 9.—*"Fruitful trees."* Rather *fruit trees;* the fruit-bearing tree being representative of one division of the vegetable world, planted and reared by man; the "cedars" of the other, which are (Ps. civ. 16) of God's own plantation. So in verse 10 we have *wild* animals and *domesticated* animals.—*A. S. Aglen.*

Verse 9.—*"Trees."*

> All creatures of the eternal God but man,
> In several sorts do glorify his name;
> Each tree doth seem ten thousand tongues to have,
> With them to laud the Lord omnipotent;
> Each leaf that with wind's gentle breath doth wave,
> Seems as a tongue to speak to that intent,
> In language admirably excellent.
> The sundry sorts of fragrant flowers do seem
> Sundry discourses God to glorify,
> And sweetest volumes may we them esteem;
> For all these creatures in their several sort
> Praise God, and man unto the same exhort.
>
> *Peter Pett,* 1599.

Verse 9.—*"All cedars."* Beautiful indeed is the pine forest in all seasons: in the freshness of spring, when the gnarled boughs are penetrated and mollified by the soft wind and the warm sun, and, thrilled with new life, burst out into fringes and tassels of the richest green, and cones of the tenderest purple; beautiful in the sultry summer, when among its cool, dim shadows the heated hours all day sing vespers, while the open landscape is palpitating in the scorching heat; beautiful in the sadness of autumn, when its unfading verdure stands out in striking relief amid changing scenes, that have no sympathy with anything earthly save sorrow and decay, and directs the thoughts to the imperishableness of the heavenly Paradise; beautiful exceedingly in the depth of winter, when the tiers of branches are covered with pure, unsullied wreaths of snow, sculptured by the wind into curves of exquisite grace. It is beautiful in calm, when the tree-tops scarce whisper to each other, and the twitter of the golden wren sounds loud in the expectant hush; it is more than beautiful in storm, when the wild fingers of the wind play the most mournful music on its great harp-strings, and its full diapason is sublime as the roar of the ocean on a rock-bound shore. I do not wonder that the northern imagination in heathen times should have invested it with awe and fear as the favourite haunt of Odin and Thor; or that, in after times, its long rows of trunks, vanishing in the dim perspective, should have furnished designs for the aisles of Christian temples, and the sunset, burning among its fretted branches, should have suggested the gorgeous painted window of the cathedral. It looks like a place made for worship, all its sentiments and associations seem of a sacred and solemn character. Nature, with folded hands, as Longfellow says, seems kneeling there in prayer. It certainly reminds us in various ways of the power, wisdom, and goodness of him who thus spake by the mouth of his prophet: "I will plant in the wilderness the cedar, the fir tree, and the pine, and the box tree together: that they may see, and know, and consider, and understand together, that the hand of the Lord hath done this, and the Holy One of Israel hath created it."—*Hugh Macmillan, in "Bible Teachings in Nature,"* 1867.

Verse 10.—*"Creeping things."* In public worship all should join. The little strings go to make up a concert, as well as the great.—*Thomas Goodwin.*

Verse 10.—*"Flying fowl."* Thus the air is vocal. It has a hallelujah of its own. The *"flying fowl"* praise him; whether it be "the stork that knoweth her appointed time" (Jer. viii. 7), or "the sparrow alone upon the housetop" (Ps. cii. 7), or "the raven of the valley" (Prov. xxx. 17), or the eagle "stirring up her nest, and fluttering over her young" (Deut. xxxii. 11), or the turtle making its voice to be heard in the land (Song. ii. 12), or the dove winging its way to the wilderness (Ps. lv. 6). This is creation's harp (truer and sweeter than Memnon's), which each sunrise awakens, "turning all the air to music."—*Horatius Bonar, in "Earth's Morning; or, Thoughts on Genesis,"* 1875.

Verse 11.—"*Kings of the earth, and all people; princes.*" As kings and princes are blinded by the dazzling influence of their station, so as to think the world was made for them, and to despise God in the pride of their hearts, he particularly calls them to this duty; and, by mentioning them first, he reproves their ingratitude in withholding their tribute of praise when they are under greater obligations than others. As all men originally stand upon a level as to condition, the higher persons have risen, and the nearer they have been brought to God, the more sacredly are they bound to proclaim his goodness. The more intolerable is the wickedness of kings and princes who claim exemption from the common rule, when they ought rather to inculcate it upon others, and lead the way. He could have addressed his exhortation at once summarily to all men, as indeed he mentions *people* in general terms; but by thrice specifying *princes* he suggests that they are slow to discharge the duty, and need to be urged to it.—*John Calvin.*

Verse 11.—"*Kings of the earth*"; "*judges of the earth*"; these are not proud but humiliating titles; for *earthly* kings and *earthly* judges will not be kings and judges long.

Verse 12.—"*Both young men, and maidens; old men, and children.*" The parties are mentioned by couples, being tied two and two together. "*Young men and maidens; old men and children.*" And here is a double *caveat;* first, against presumption; and secondly, against despair. First, that the younger sort might desire to praise God, they are exhorted to address themselves to the service of God, to remember their Creator in the days of their youth. Secondly, for aged men, that they might not doubt of the acceptation of their service, our Prophet exhorts them also. For the first, you know, David calls upon the sun and the moon to praise God. Should the sun reply, I will not do it in the morning, or at noon time, but when I am about to set? or the moon reply, I will not in the full, but in the wane? or the tree, not in the spring time, or in the summer, but at the fall of the leaf? So likewise, thou young man, defer not the time of praising God: take the swing of thy youth, and do not defer to apply thyself to the service of God till thy old age; but remember that for all these things thou shalt come to judgment. He that styles himself by the title *I AM,* cares not for I will be, or I have been, but he that is at this present: take heed, therefore, thou strong and lusty young man: the Devil that holds thee now will every day tie a new cord about thee. Consider this, you that are yet young, whom the morning sun of light adorns with his glorious rays: everyone doth not live to be old. Let us not procrastinate in God's service; for the longer we defer to serve God, the farther God's grace is distant from us, and the dominion of Satan is more strengthened in our hearts; the more we delay, the more is our debt, the greater our sin, and the less our grace. I will commend this lesson unto all. He that doth not repent to-day hath a day more to repent of, and a day less to repent in. I shall conclude with a hearty exhortation for us all, of what sex, age, and degree soever; I could wish that all our lives might end like this book of Psalms, in blessing and praising Almighty God.—*Thomas Cheshire, in "A Sermon preached in Saint Paule's Church,"* 1641.

Verse 12.—"*Old men.*" Think not, ye who are now near the end of life, that your tongues may without blame be silent in the praises of the Lord, because you are come to those years in which men say, they "have no pleasure in them." Were you not frequently praising God when you were children and young men? Have you less, or have you not greater, reason now to praise God than in those early days of life?

Old men ought to be better qualified than young persons to show forth the glory both of the perfections and works of God, because they have enjoyed more time, and more abundant opportunities than their juniors, for attaining the knowledge of God, and of those glorious perfections and works which furnish us with endless materials for praise. "Days should speak, and the multitude of years should teach wisdom."

The heavens are constantly declaring "the glory of God, and the firmament showeth forth his handy work. Day unto day uttereth speech, and night unto night showeth knowledge." Have you, then, lived twenty thousand days and twenty thousand nights? What deep impressions ought to be made upon your spirits, of those wonders which have been preached in your ears or eyes, ever since you could use your bodily senses as ministers to your intellectual powers! All the works of God praise him, by showing forth how wonderful in power, and goodness, and wisdom, the Creator is. Your tongues are indeed inexcusable, if they are silent in the praises of him whose glory is proclaimed by every object above or around them, and even by every member of their own bodies, and every faculty of their souls. But old men are doubly inexcusable, if they are inattentive to those precious instructions which are given them by all the works of God which they have seen, or of which they have been informed, every day since the powers of their rational natures began to operate.

But old men in this highly favoured land have been blessed with more excellent instructions than those which are given them by the mountains and fruitful valleys, by the dragons of the desert or the deep, or by the fowls of heaven and the beasts of the earth, or by the sun and stars of heaven. For many more years than young men or maidens you have been learners, or you are very blamable if you have not been at the school of Christ. You were early taught to read the Word of God. In the course of fifty or sixty years, you have probably heard six thousand religious discourses from the ministers of Christ, not to mention other excellent means you have enjoyed for increasing in the knowledge of God. " For the time," says Paul to the Hebrew Christians, " ye might have been teachers." May I not say the same to all aged Christians, who have had the Bible in their possession, and have enjoyed opportunities of frequenting the holy assemblies from their earliest days ? May it not be expected that your hearts and your mouths will be filled with the praises of God, not only as your Maker, but as your Redeemer ?

But there are many things more especially relating to themselves, which should induce the aged to abound in this duty of praise to God.

Consider how long you have lived. Is not every day of life, and even every hour, and every moment, an undeserved mercy ? You might have been cut off from the breast and the womb, for you were conceived in iniquity and born in sin. How many of your race have been cut off before they could distinguish between their right hand and their left, before they could do good or evil ! Since you were moral agents, not a day has passed in which you were not chargeable with many sins. What riches of long-suffering is manifested in a life of sixty or seventy years ! If you have lived in a state of sin all that time, have you not reason to be astonished, that you are not already in a condition which would for ever render it impossible for you to utter the voice of praise ? Give glory, therefore, to that God who has still preserved you alive.

Consider with what mercies your days have been filled up. God's mercies have been new to you every morning, although every day you have sinned against him.

Reflections on your own conduct through life will suggest to you many reasons for praise and thanksgiving. But on this part of the subject it is proper to put you in mind of the two great classes into which men are divided : saints and sinners. If you belong to the former class, who is it that has made you to differ from others ? Give thanks to him who delivered you from the power of darkness, and translated you into the kingdom of his dear Son. Have you been enabled to do some good works in the course of your lives ? For every one of them bless God, who wrought " in you both to will and to do of his good pleasure." Have any of your endeavours been successful to bring about the reformation of any of your fellow-men, or to promote their spiritual welfare ? What sufficient thanks can you render to God for making you the humble ministers of his grace ?

But there are too many of the old who have no reason to think that they have yet passed from death to life. These, certainly, are very unfit to praise God, and will not be able to praise him with their hearts, unless that change pass upon them, without which no man shall ever enter into the kingdom of heaven. Yet, surely, they have great reason to praise the Lord ; and they may see good reason for it, although they cannot carry their knowledge into practice. You have, indeed, greater reason to praise God that you are in the land of the living than those who are in a better state ; because, if you were deprived of your present life, nothing is left for you but the terrors of eternal death. Bless God, ye who have lived fifty or sixty years in sin, and have been all along spared in a world so full of mercy. You are still called by the gospel to receive that salvation which you have long treated with contempt.—*Condensed from a Sermon by George Lawson* (1749—1820), *entitled, "The Duty of the Old to praise God."*

Verse 12.—*"Old men and children."* It is interesting always to see a friendship between the old and the young. It is striking to see the aged one retaining so much of freshness and simplicity as not to repel the sympathies of boyhood. It is surprising to see the younger one so advanced and thoughtful, as not to find dull the society of one who has outlived excitability and passion. – *Frederick William Robertson.*

Verses 12, 13.—The Psalms are church songs, and all who belong to the church are to sing them. *"Both young men, and maidens; old men, and children; let them praise the name of the LORD."* The ripe believer who can triumph in the steadfast hope of God's glory, is to lend his voice to swell the song of the church when she cries to God out of the depths ; and the penitent, who is still sitting in darkness, is not to refrain his voice when the church pours out in song her sense of God's love. The whole church has fellowship in the Psalms.—*William Binnie, in "The Psalms, their History, Teachings, and Use,"* 1870.

Verses 12, 13.—*"Old men . . . Let them praise the name of the LORD."* It is a favourite speculation of mine that if spared to sixty we then enter on the seventh decade of human life, and that this, if possible, should be turned into the Sabbath of our earthly pilgrimage and spent sabbatically, as if on the shores of an eternal world, or in the outer courts, as it were, of the temple that is above, the tabernacle in heaven.—*Thomas Chalmers.*

Verse 13.—*"Let them praise."* Exactly as at the close of the first great division of the anthem (verse 5), and, in the same way as there, the reason for the exhortation follows in the next clause. But it is a different reason. It is no longer because he has given them a decree, bound them as passive, unconscious creatures by a law which they cannot transgress. (It is the fearful mystery of the reasonable will that it can transgress the law.) It is because his name is exalted, so that the eyes of men can see, and the hearts and tongues of men confess it ; it is because he has graciously revealed himself to, and mightily succoured, the people whom he loves, the nation who are near to him. If it be said that what was designed to be a Universal Anthem is thus narrowed at its close, it must be remembered that, however largely the glory of God was written on the visible creation, it was only to the Jew that any direct revelation of his character had been made.—*J. J. Stewart Perowne.*

Verse 13.—*"The name of Jehovah."* Jehovah is a name of great power and efficacy, a name that hath in it five vowels, without which no language can be expressed ; a name that hath in it also three syllables, to signify the Trinity of Persons, the eternity of God, One in Three, and Three in One ; a name of such dread and reverence amongst the Jews, that they tremble to name it, and therefore they use the name *Adonai* (Lord) in all their devotions. And thus ought every one to stand in awe, and sin not by taking the name of God in vain ; but to sing praises, to honour, to remember, to declare, to exalt, and bless it ; for holy and reverend, only worthy and excellent is his name.—*Rayment,* 1630.

Verse 14.—*"His people, the praise of all his saints."* But among all, one class in particular is called on to praise him, for they have an additional motive for so doing, namely, *"his people,"* and *"his saints."* As man above all the creatures, so among men his elect or chosen, who are the objects of his special grace, and, above all, of his redeeming love. *"He also exalteth the horn of his people "*—exalts them, one and all, from the death of sin to the life of righteousness, and consequent on this, from the dust of earth to the glory of heaven. *"The praise of all his saints " ;* and, yet again, among them, of one people in particular—*"even of the children of Israel, a people near unto him."* *"Near to him "* of old, and yet again to be—yea, nearest of all the peoples of the earth—when he recalls them from their dispersion, and again places his name and his throne among them. HALLELUJAH—PRAISE YE THE LORD.—*William De Burgh.*

Verse 14.—*"A people near unto him."* Jesus took our nature, and became one with us ; thus he is *"near "* unto us ; he gives us his Holy Spirit, brings us into union with himself, and thus we are near to him. This is our highest honour, an unfailing source of happiness and peace. We are near to him in point of *relation,* being his children ; near to him in point of *affection,* being loved with an everlasting love ; we are near to him in point of *union,* being members of his body, of his flesh, and of his bones ; we are near to him in point of *fellowship,* walking with him as a man walketh with his friend ; we are near to him in point of *attention,* being the objects of his daily, hourly, tender care ; we shall soon be near to him in point of *locality,* when our mansion is prepared, for we shall depart to be with Christ, which is far better. We are near to him when poor, and when deeply tried ; and if ever nearer at one time than another, we shall be nearest to him in death. If we are near unto him, he will sympathize with us in all our sorrows, assist us in all our trials, protect us in all our dangers, hold intercourse with us in all our lonely hours, provide for us in all seasons of necessity, and honourably introduce us to glory. Let us realize this fact daily—we are near and dear to our God.—*James Smith.*

HINTS TO PREACHERS.

Whole Psalm.—I. What is implied in the invitation to the natural creation to praise God. 1. That praise is due to God on its account. 2. That it is due from those for whose benefit it was created. 3. That it is a reproof to those who do not praise God who are actually capable of it. "If these should hold their peace, the stones would immediately cry out." II. What is implied in the invitation to innocent beings to praise God. "Praise ye the Lord from the heavens. Praise ye him all his angels, praise ye him all his hosts : " verses 1, 2.—1. That they owe their creation in innocence to God. 2. That they owe their preservation in innocence to him. 3. That they owe the reward of their innocence to him. III. What is implied in the invitation to fallen beings to praise God : "Kings of the earth and all people," etc. : verses 11—13.—1. That God is merciful and ready to forgive. "Not willing that any should perish," etc. They would not be called upon to praise God if they were irrecoverably lost. Our Lord would not when on earth accept praise from an evil spirit. 2. That means of restoration from the fall are provided by God for men. Without this they would have no hope, and could offer no praise. IV. What is implied in the invitation to the redeemed to praise God : verse 14.—1. That God is their God. 2. That all his perfections are engaged for their present and eternal welfare.—*G. R.*

Verse 1.—"*Praise ye the Lord.*" I. The Voice—of Scripture. of nature, of grace, of duty. II. The Ear on which it rightly falls—of saints and sinners, old and young, healthy and sick. It falls on our ear. III. The Time when it is heard. Now, ever, yet also at special times. IV. The Response which we will give. Let us now praise with heart, life, lip.

Verse 1 (second and third clauses).—I. The character of the praises of heaven. II. How far they influence us who are here below. III. The hope which we have of uniting in them.

Verse 2.—I. The angels as praiseful servants. II. The other hosts of God, and how they praise him. III. The rule without exception : "*all—all.*" Imagine one heavenly being living without praising the Lord !

Verse 3.—I. God's praise continual both day and night. II. Light the leading fountain of this praise. III. Life behind all, calling for the praise.

Verses 5, 6.—Creation and conversation, two chief reasons for praise.

Verse 7.—God's praise from dark, deep, and mysterious things.

Verse 8.—Canon Liddon preached in St. Paul's on Sunday afternoon, December 23, 1883, and took for his text Ps. cxlviii. 8, "*Wind and storm fulfilling his word.*" He spoke of the divine use of destructive forces. I. In the physical world we see wind and storm fulfilling God's word. 1. The Bible occasionally lifts the veil, and shows us how destructive forces of Nature have been the servants of God. 2. Modern history illustrates this vividly. II. In the human, spiritual, and moral world, we find new and rich application of the words of the text. 1. In the State we see the storm of invasion and the storm of revolution fulfilling God's word. 2. In the Church we see the storm of persecution and the storm of controversy fulfilling God's word. 3. In the experience of individual life we see outward troubles, and inward storms of religious doubts fulfilling God's word.—*The Contemporary Pulpit*, 1884.

Verse 9.—"*Trees.*" The glory of God as seen in trees.

Verse 10.—The wildest, the quietest, the most depressed, and the most aspiring should each have its song.

Verses 11—13.—I. The universal King. Alone in excelling. Supreme in glory.

II. The universal summons.   Of all nations, ranks, classes and ages.   Foreshadowing the Judgment.   III. The universal duty : praise,—constant, emphatic, growing. —*W. B. H.*

Verse 12.—God to be served by strength and beauty, experience and expectation.

Verse 12.—"*And children.*"   A Children's Address.   I. Where the children are found (verses 11 and 12).   In royal and distinguished society : yet not lost or overlooked.   II. What they are called to.   "Praise the Lord."   Even they have abundant reason.   III. What are the lessons of the subject ?   1. Children should come up with their parents on the Sabbath.   2. Children should unite in heart and voice in God's praises.   3. Children should seek fitness for this praise by believing in Christ.—*W. B. H.*

Verse 14.—The Favoured People and their God.   I. What he does for them. II. What he makes them : "Saints."   III. Who they are : "Children of Israel." IV. Where they are : "Near unto him."   V. What they do for him : "Praise ye the Lord."

PSALM CXLIX.

We are almost at the last Psalm, and still among the Hallelujahs. This is "a new song," evidently intended for the new creation, and the men who are of new heart. It is such a song as may be sung at the coming of the Lord, when the new dispensation shall bring overthrow to the wicked and honour to all the saints. The tone is exceedingly jubilant and exultant. All through one hears the beat of the feet of dancing maidens, keeping time to the timbrel and harp.

EXPOSITION.

PRAISE ye the LORD. Sing unto the LORD a new song, *and* his praise in the congregation of saints.

2 Let Israel rejoice in him that made him : let the children of Zion be joyful in their King.

3 Let them praise his name in the dance : let them sing praises unto him with the timbrel and harp.

4 For the LORD taketh pleasure in his people : he will beautify the meek with salvation.

5 Let the saints be joyful in glory : let them sing aloud upon their beds.

6 *Let* the high *praises* of God *be* in their mouth, and a two-edged sword in their hand ;

7 To execute vengeance upon the heathen, *and* punishments upon the people ;

8 To bind their kings with chains, and their nobles with fetters of iron ;

9 To execute upon them the judgment written : this honour have all his saints. Praise ye the LORD.

1. *"Praise ye the LORD."* Specially you, ye chosen people, whom he has made to be his saints. You have praised him aforetime, praise him yet again ; yea, for ever praise him. With renewed zeal and fresh delight lift up your song unto Jehovah. *"Sing unto the Lord a new song."* Sing, for it is the fittest method for expressing reverent praise. Sing a hymn newly composed, for you have now a new knowledge of God. He is ever new in his manifestations ; his mercies are new every morning ; his deliverances are new in every night of sorrow ; let your gratitude and thanksgivings be new also. It is well to repeat the old ; it is more useful to invent the new. Novelty goes well with heartiness. Our singing should be "unto the Lord" ; the songs we sing should be of him and to him, "for of him, and to him, and through him are all things." Among our novelties there should be new songs : alas ! men are fonder of making new complaints than new Psalms. Our new songs should be devised in Jehovah's honour ; indeed all our newest thoughts should run towards him. Never can we find a nobler subject for a song than the Lord, nor one more full of fresh matter for a new song, nor one which we are personally so much bound to sing as a new song "unto the Lord." *"And his praise in the congregation of saints."* Saints are precious, and a congregation of saints is a treasure house of jewels. God is in the midst of saints, and because of this we may well long to be among them. They are so full of his praise that we feel at home among them when we are ourselves full of praise. The sanctuary is the house of praise as well as the house of prayer. All saints praise God : they would not be saints if they did not. Their praise is sincere, suitable, seasonable, and acceptable. Personal praise is sweet unto God, but congregated praise has a multiplicity of sweetnesses in it. When holy ones meet, they adore the Holy One. Saints do not gather to amuse themselves with music, nor to extol one another, but to sing his praise whose

saints they are.   A congregation of saints is heaven upon earth : should not Jehovah, the Lord of saints, have all the praise that can come from such an assembly ?   Yet at times even saintly conclaves need to be stirred up to thanksgiving ; for saints may be sad and apprehensive, and then their spirits require to be raised to a higher key, and stimulated to happier worship.

2. *"Let Israel rejoice in him that made him."*   Here is that new creation which calls for the new song.   It was Jehovah who made Israel to be Israel, and the tribes to become a great nation : therefore let the Founder of the nation be had in perpetual honour.   Joy and rejoicing are evidently to be the special characteristics of the new song.   The religion of the dead in sin is more apt to chant dirges than to sing hallelujahs ; but when we are made new in the spirit of our minds we joy and rejoice in him that made us.   Our joy is in our God and King : we choose no lower delight. *"Let the children of Zion be joyful in their King."*   Those who had seen the tribes formed into a settled kingdom as well as into a united nation should rejoice.   Israel is the nation, Zion is the capital of the kingdom : Israel rejoices in her Maker, Zion in her King.   In the case of our God we who believe in him are as glad of his Government as we are of his Creation : his reign is as truly the making of us as was his divine power.   The children of Israel are happy to be made a people ; the children of Zion are equally happy to be ruled as a people.   In every character our God is the source of joy to us : this verse issues a permit to our joy, yea it lays an injunction upon us to be glad in the Lord.

3. *"Let them praise his name in the dance : let them sing praises unto him with the timbrel and harp."*   Thus let them repeat the triumph of the Red Sea, which was ever the typical glory of Israel.   Miriam led the daughters of Israel in the dance when the Lord had triumphed gloriously ; was it not most fit that she should ? The sacred dance of devout joy is no example, nor even excuse, for frivolous dances, much less for lewd ones.   Who could help dancing when Egypt was vanquished, and the tribes were free ?   Every mode of expressing delight was bound to be employed on so memorable an occasion.   Dancing, singing, and playing on instruments were all called into requisition, and most fitly so.   There are unusual seasons which call for unusual expressions of joy.   When the Lord saves a soul its holy joy overflows, and it cannot find channels enough for its exceeding gratitude : if the man does not leap, or play, or sing, at any rate he praises God, and wishes for a thousand tongues with which to magnify his Saviour.   Who would wish it to be otherwise ?   Young converts are not to be restrained in their joy.   Let them sing and dance while they can.   How can they mourn now that their Bridegroom is with them ?   Let us give the utmost liberty to joy.   Let us never attempt its suppression, but issue in the terms of this verse a double license for exultation. If any ought to be glad it is the children of Zion ; rejoicing is more fit for Israel than for any other people : it is their own folly and fault that they are not oftener brimming with joy in God, for the very thought of him is delight.

4. *"For the LORD taketh pleasure in his people ; "* and therefore they should take pleasure in him.   If our joy be pleasing to him let us make it full.   What condescension is this on Jehovah's part, to notice, to love, and to delight in his chosen !   Surely there is nothing in our persons, or our actions, which could cause pleasure to the Ever-blessed One, were it not that he condescends to men of low estate.   The thought of the Lord's taking pleasure in us is a mine of joy never to be exhausted. *"He will beautify the meek with salvation."*   They are humble, and feel their need of salvation ; he is gracious, and bestows it upon them.   They lament their deformity and he puts a beauty upon them of the choicest sort.   He saves them by sanctifying them, and thus they wear the beauty of holiness, and the beauty of a joy which springs out of full salvation.   He makes his people meek, and then makes the meek beautiful.   Herein is grand argument for worshipping the Lord with the utmost exultation : he who takes such a pleasure in us must be approached with every token of exceeding joy.

God taketh pleasure in all his children as Jacob loved all his sons ; but the meek are his Josephs, and upon these he puts the coat of many colours, beautifying them with peace, content, joy, holiness, and influence.   A meek and quiet spirit is called " an ornament," and certainly it is " the beauty of holiness."   When God himself beautifies a man, he becomes beautiful indeed and beautiful for ever.

The verse may be read, " He shall beautify the meek with salvation," or " He shall beautify the afflicted with deliverance," or, " He shall beautify the meek with victory " ;   and each of these readings gives a new shade of meaning, well worthy of quiet consideration. Each reading also suggests new cause for joyful adoration. " O come, let us sing unto the Lord."

5. *"Let the saints be joyful in glory."* God has honoured them, and put a rare glory upon them ; therefore let them exult therein. Shall those to whom God is their glory be cast down and troubled ? Nay, let their joy proclaim their honourable estate. *"Let them sing aloud upon their beds."* Their exultation should express itself in shouts and songs, for it is not a feeling of which they have any need to be ashamed. That which is so fully justified by fact, may well be loudly proclaimed. Even in their quietest retreats let them burst into song ; when no one hears them, let them sing aloud unto God. If confined by sickness let them joy in God. In the night watches let them not lie awake and weep, but like nightingales let them charm the midnight hours. Their shouts are not now for the battlefield, but for the places of their rest : they can peacefully lie down and yet enjoy the victory with which the Lord has beautified them. Without fighting, faith wins and sings the victory. What a blessing to have our beds made into thrones, and our retirements turned into triumphs !

6. *"Let the high praises of God be in their mouth, and a two-edged sword in their hand."* It seems they are not always on their beds, but are ready for deeds of prowess. When called to fight, the meek are very hard to overcome ; they are just as steady in conflict as they are steadfast in patience. Besides, their way of fighting is of an extraordinary sort, for they sing to God but keep their swords in their hands. They can do two things at a time : if they do not wield the trowel and the sword, at least they sing and strike. In this Israel was not an example, but a type : we will not copy the chosen people in making literal war, but we will fulfil the emblem by carrying on spiritual war. We praise God and contend with our corruptions ; we sing joyfully and war earnestly with evil of every kind. Our weapons are not carnal, but they are mighty, and wound with both back and edge. The word of God is all edge ; whichever way we turn it, it strikes deadly blows at falsehood and wickedness. If we do not praise we shall grow sad in our conflict ; and if we do not fight we shall become presumptuous in our song. The verse indicates a happy blending of the chorister and the crusader.

Note how each thing in the believer is emphatic : if he sings, it is high praises, and praises deep down in his throat, as the original hath it ; and if he fights, it is with the sword, and the sword is two-edged. The living God imparts vigorous life to those who trust him. They are not of a neutral tint : men both hear them and feel them. Quiet is their spirit, but in that very quietude abides the thunder of an irresistible force. When godly men give battle to the powers of evil each conflict is high praise unto the God of goodness. Even the tumult of our holy war is a part of the music of our lives.

7. *"To execute vengeance upon the heathen, and punishments upon the people."* This was once literally the duty of Israel : when they came into Canaan they fulfilled the righteous sentence of the Lord upon guilty nations. At this hour, under the gentler dispensation of grace, we wrestle not with flesh and blood ; yet is our warfare none the less stern, and our victory none the less sure. All evil shall eventually be overthrown : the Lord shall display his justice against evil-doers, and in that warfare his servants shall play their parts. The saints shall judge the world. Both the conflict and the victory at the end of it shall cause glory to God, and honour to his holy ones.

8. *"To bind their kings with chains, and their nobles with fetters of iron."* Thus are the greatest enemies of Jehovah and his people reduced to shame, rendered helpless, and themselves punished. This was Israel's boast in actual fact, it is ours spiritually. The chief powers of evil shall be restrained and ultimately destroyed. Those who made captives of the godly shall themselves be made captive. The powers of evil cannot bind *our* King, but by his power *their* king shall be bound with a great chain, and shut up in the bottomless pit, that he may at length be trodden under the feet of saints.

9. *"To execute upon them the judgment written."* Israel as a nation had this to do, and did it, and then they rejoiced in the God who gave success to their arms. *We* praise our God after another fashion ; we are not executioners of justice, but heralds of mercy. It would be a sad thing for any one to misuse this text : lest any warlike believer should be led to do so, we would remind him that the execution must not go beyond the sentence and warrant ; and we have received no warrant of execution against our fellow men. Christians have no commission of vengeance ;

it is theirs to execute the command of mercy, and that alone. *"This honour have all his saints."* All the godly shared in the triumphs of the Lord when he smote Israel's foes. We have like honour, but it is shown in victories of another sort. All the holy ones are sent upon errands by their holy Lord. The honours described in this Psalm are common to all the family of grace; and such service as the Lord appoints is to be undertaken by every one of them, without exception. The Lord honours all his chosen here, and he will glorify them all hereafter: this rule is without exception. Surely in this we have the best argument for glorifying the Lord, wherefore we close our new song with another Hallelujah, *"Praise ye the Lord."*

EXPLANATORY NOTES AND QUAINT SAYINGS.

Whole Psalm.—The foregoing Psalm was a hymn of praise to the Creator; this is a hymn to the Redeemer.—*Matthew Henry.*

Whole Psalm.—The New Testament spiritual church cannot pray as the Old Testament national church here prays. Under the illusion that it must be used as a prayer without any spiritual transmutation, Psalm cxlix. has become the watchword of the most horrible errors. It was by means of this Psalm that Caspar Scloppius, in his *Classicum Belli Sacri,* which, as Bakius says, is written, not with ink, but with blood, inflamed the Roman Catholic princes to the Thirty Years' Religious War. And in the Protestant church Thomas Müntzer stirred up the War of the Peasants by means of this Psalm. We see that the Christian cannot make such a Psalm directly his own, without disavowing the apostolic warning, "The weapons of our warfare are not carnal" (2 Cor. x. 4). The praying Christian must therefore transpose the letter of this Psalm into the spirit of the New Covenant.—*Franz Delitzsch.*

Verse 1.—*"A new song"*; for this Psalm is a song of renovation. If Israel when restored and renewed had new cause for rejoicing, much more should the New Covenant Israel feel constrained to strike the new note of triumph. Infidels blaspheme, the ungrateful murmur, the thoughtless are silent, the mournful weep, all acting according to their old nature; but new men take up a new mode, which is the divinely-inspired song of peace, charity, and joy in the Lord.—*Johannes Paulus Palanterius.*

Verse 1.—*"A new song."*—The old man hath an old song, the new man a new song. The Old Testament is an old song, the New Testament is a new song. . . . . Whoso loveth earthly things singeth an old song: let him that desireth to sing a new song love the things of eternity. Love itself is new and eternal; therefore is it ever new, because it never groweth old.—*Augustine.*

Verse 1.—*"Saints."*—A title not to be restricted to the godly of the first times, but common to all that are saved in all after-times also, as Eph. iv. 12. This name putteth mere morality and formal profession out of countenance, as the sun doth a glow-worm. Saintship is a matter of Divine workmanship, and therefore it is far more remarkable than human excellence. We should keep up the name of "saints," that the reality of the true religion be not lowered by avoiding this title; for in these times it is to be feared that the name is out of use, because holiness itself is out of fashion.—*Thomas Goodwin.*

Verse 2.—*"Let Israel rejoice,"* etc. Give us, oh, give us the man who sings at his work! Be his occupation what it may, he is equal to any of those who follow the same pursuit in silent sullenness. He will do more in the same time—he will do it better—he will persevere longer. One is scarcely sensible of fatigue whilst he marches to music. The very stars are said to make harmony as they revolve in their spheres. Wondrous is the strength of cheerfulness, altogether past calculation its powers of endurance. Efforts to be permanently useful must be uniformly joyous—a spiritual sunshine—graceful from very gladness—beautiful because bright.—*Thomas Carlyle.*

Verse 2.—*"Rejoice in him that made him: let the children of Zion be joyful."*

You are never right until you can be heartily merry in the Lord, nor until you can enjoy mirth in connection with holiness.—*Walter Marshall.*

Verse 2.—*"Him that made him."* Jehovah is called *Maker*, as one who formed Israel as a nation, and constituted the people a kingdom, though they had been a race of slaves. This is more than a general creation of men.—*Hermann Venema.*

Verse 2.—Literally the Hebrew here brings forward the mystic doctrine of the Trinity, for it reads, " Let Israel rejoice in God *his Makers.*"—*Simon de Muis.*

Verse 2.—*"Joyful in their King."* I beg the reader to remark with me, here is nothing said of Israel being joyful in what their king had done for them. These things in their proper place, became sweet subjects of praise. But the subject of praise in which Israel is now to be engaged is Jesus himself. Reader, pause over this apparently small, but most important, distinction. The Lord is gracious in his gifts, gracious in his love, gracious in his salvation. Every thing he gives, it is from his mercy, and ever to be so acknowledged. But Jesus' gifts are not himself: I cannot be satisfied with his gifts, while I know that to others he gives his *Person*. It is Jesus himself I want. Though he give me all things that I need, yet if he be to me himself all things that I need, in him I have all things. Hence, therefore, let us see that Jesus not only gives us all, but that he is our all.—*Robert Hawker.*

Verse 3.—*"The dance"* was in early times one of the modes of expressing religious joy (Ex. xv. 20 ; 2 Sam. vi. 16). When from any cause men's ideas shall undergo such a revolution as to lead them to do the same thing for the same purpose, it will be time enough to discuss that matter. In our time, dancing has no such use, and cannot, therefore, in any wise be justified by pleading the practice of pious Jews of old.—*William Swan Plumer.*

Verse 3.—*"Let them sing praises unto him with the timbrel and harp."* They who from hence urge the use of music in religious worship, must, by the same rule, introduce dancing, for they went together, as in David's dancing before the ark (Judges xxi. 21). But whereas many Scriptures in the New Testament keep up singing as a gospel ordinance, none provide for the keeping up of music and dancing ; the gospel canon for Psalmody is to " sing with the spirit and with the understanding." —*Matthew Henry.*

Verse 2.—*"Timbrel."* The *toph* was employed by David in all the festivities of religion (2 Sam. vi. 5). The occasions on which it was used were mostly joyful, and those who played upon it were generally females (Psalm lxviii. 25), as was the case among most ancient nations, and is so at the present day in the East. The usages of the modern East might adequately illustrate all the scriptural allusions to this instrument, but happily we have more ancient and very valuable illustration from the monuments of Egypt. In these we find that the tambourine was a favourite instrument, both on sacred and festive occasions. There were three kinds, differing, no doubt, in sound as well as in form ; one was circular, another square or oblong, and the third consisted of two squares separated by a bar. They were all beaten by the hand, and often used as an accomplishment to the harp and other instruments. The tambourine was usually played by females, who are represented as dancing to its sound without the accompaniment of any other instrument.—*John Kitto.*

Verse 3.—*"Harp."* Of the *kinnor* the Scripture affords little further information than that it was composed of the sounding parts of good wood, and furnished with strings. Josephus asserts that it was furnished with ten strings, and played with a *plectrum ;* which, however, is not understood to imply that it never had any other number of strings, or was always played with the *plectrum.* David certainly played it with the hand (1 Sam. xvi. 23 ; xviii. 10 ; xix. 9) ; and it was probably used in both ways, according to its size. That this instrument was really a *harp* is now very generally denied (*Kitto*). The reader will, by this time, have balanced the probabilities as to the nature and construction of the *kinnor ;* and most likely he will be led to think that it was either a *guitar* or *lyre*, a belief which seems to be gaining ground, on account of the aptitude of such instruments for the uses to which the *kinnor* was devoted.—*J. Stainer.*

Verse 4.—*"For the Lord taketh pleasure in his people."* In the text there are two causes assigned why the saints should be excited to praise the Lord, and to be joyful in their King.

I.—THE DELIGHT WHICH THE LORD HAS IN THE SAINTS. " He taketh pleasure

in his people." In this statement there are three subjects for inquiry, namely :
1. *Who* are the Lord's people ? 2. *Why* he takes pleasure in them ? 3. *In what respects* he takes pleasure in them ?

1. *Who are the Lord's people ?* Many are the names and titles given to them in Scripture. We find one in the second clause of the text ; but it equally belongs to the first. " He will beautify *the meek.*" The scriptural term " *meekness* " is one which singularly characterizes and distinguishes the true Christian. It, in fact, contains in itself a combination of graces, which are most evidently the fruit of the Spirit, and can grow on no other tree than on the Christian vine. *Meekness,* as a Christian grace, may be considered as it respects both God and man. As it respects God, it implies poverty of spirit ; humiliation of heart arising from a sense of guilt and a feeling of corruption ; submission to God's will ; silence and patience under his rod ; acquiescence with his dispensations ; and a surrender of our own natural desires and inclinations to his overruling appointments. As it respects man, meekness comprehends lowliness of mind, and a readiness to prefer others before ourselves ; gentleness of disposition and behaviour ; forbearance under provocations ; forgiveness of injuries ; quietness of spirit, and moderation in pushing forward our own interest and benefit. These are the qualities which distinguish " *the meek.*" Are not these, my brethen, the graces and tempers and dispositions which characterize and adorn true Christians ? *They* are, in an especial manner, " *the meek* upon earth.*" In fact, there are, and can be, no others to whom this title really belongs. No man in his natural state can be *meek,* in the Scriptural sense of the word.

2. But *why* does the Lord " take pleasure " in them ? Is there anything in them of *their own,* which he can regard with complacency and delight ? No : they know and feel that they have no pretensions of this kind. It is not for their sake, but for his own sake ; for his name's, his truth's, and his mercy's sake, that he has now a favour unto them. The Lord " taketh pleasure in his people," because they are his people ; those whom he has purchased by his blood, renewed by his Spirit, and redeemed by his power. He " taketh pleasure in them," because in them he is himself honoured and glorified ; because he sees in them the travail of his soul, the fruit of his suffering and mediation ; because of the work which he has already begun in them ; because they already exhibit some traces of his own image, some transcript of that mind which was in him, who was " meek and lowly in heart."

3. *In what respects* the Lord takes pleasure in his people. First : the Lord takes pleasure in them, inasmuch as he delights in *the exercise of their graces towards him.* They all believe in him, and have faith in his word and promises ; they rely on his truth and power ; they hope in his mercy ; they fear his displeasure ; they love his person and name. Secondly : the Lord hath pleasure in *the services* of his people. It is true, that they can do but little for him, and that little is nothing worth. At the best they can but render to him of his own again. But he regards their services, not with an eye to their intrinsic value in themselves, but for the sake of the willing mind from which they flow. He takes pleasure in their poor attempts to please him, because they are attempts. He weighs not the worth or merit of the action, but the principle and motive from which it springs. Thirdly : the Lord hath pleasure in the *prosperity* of his people. His name is love ; his nature is goodness ; and can we doubt but that he loves to see his people happy ? Nay, we are expressly told that " he rejoiceth over them with joy " ; that " he rejoiceth over them to do them good." Even in those dispensations which in themselves are grievous and painful he is seeking their good, and in the end promoting their happiness. What consolations do these reflections furnish to the *meek* and suffering servants of the Lord !

II.—Let us now consider THE LORD'S GRACIOUS DESIGNS concerning his people :
"*He will beautify them with salvation.*" He designs not only to save, but to adorn and honour his people. Those " whom he justifies, them he also glorifies." He " will *beautify* them with salvation*" ; a promise relating both to the present life and to the future one.

1. *To the present life.* It is the purpose of God to beautify his people with salvation in this world. There are many passages in the Scripture which intimate this purpose, and lead us to this view of the happy effects of religion, even in the present life. When the prodigal returned home to his father's house, contrite, penitent, and reformed, he was not only received with kindness, assured of forgiveness,

and welcomed as a son, but he was *adorned* and *beautified* (Luke xv. 22). So in the forty-fifth Psalm, the Church, the bride of Christ, is thus described : " The king's daughter is all glorious within : her clothing is of wrought gold. She shall be brought unto the king in raiment of needlework." " So shall he greatly desire thy *beauty*." See also Eph. v. 25—27.

But what is the glory, the beauty, which is here meant in these passages, with which Christ will adorn and beautify his people ? It is " the beauty of holiness." We have already seen that the meek and quiet spirit by which the Christian is distinguished is an " ornament " to him ; and we read in another place that he is " adorned " with good works. It is the great object of the gospel to sanctify all who embrace it, to restore them to the image of God which they have lost through sin.

2. We may now consider this promise as it relates *to the future world.* Lovely and glorious as are the saints on earth, their beauty falls far short of the perfection to which it will attain hereafter. They are " predestinated to be conformed to the image of his Son " ; and when they awake up in another world, it will be after his likeness, without any remaining blemish, defect or spot. Carry forward your thoughts to the morning of the resurrection, when this corruption shall have put on incorruption, this mortal immortality ; when the body, raised in honour and glory, shall be clothed in its beauteous apparel, and being made like unto Christ's glorious body, shall shine as the sun in the firmament ; when now, once more united to its kindred and sanctified spirit, it shall no longer be a weight, and a clog, and a hindrance, but become a furtherer of its joy, and a sharer and a helper in its spiritual happiness. This is the meaning of the text, this is the *beauty* which he has designed for his people, and for which he is now preparing them. In the contemplation of these, with reason may it be said to them, " Praise ye the Lord." —*Condensed from a Sermon by Edward Cooper,* 1826.

Verse 4.—Here in *ratio propositionis,* the important reason of the proposed praising of the Lord. Those who know that they are objects of Divine complacency are likely to act on the principle of reciprocity. God takes pleasure in sanctifying, justifying and glorifying them ; they must surely take pleasure in extolling him as Friend, Protector, Law-giver, Leader, King, God !—*Simon de Muis.*

Verse 4.—"*He will beautify the meek with salvation.*" Meekness not only gives great peace of mind, but often adds a lustre to the countenance. We only read of three in Scripture whose faces shone remarkably —viz., Christ, Moses, and Stephen —and they were eminent for meekness.—*Matthew Henry.*

Verse 4.—"*The meek.*" In the Hebrew עֲנָוִים, *anavim,* means *poor and afflicted ones ;* but the term came afterwards to be applied to *merciful persons,* as bodily afflictions have a tendency to subdue pride, while abundance begets cruelty.— *John Calvin.*

Verse 5.—" *Let the saints be joyful,*" etc. Here begins a beautiful exegesis of the former passage. A protected people may rejoice with confidence. An anxious and fearful people could not sing aloud on their couches of repose.—*Simon de Muis.*

Verse 5.—"*Let the saints be joyful in glory : let them sing aloud upon their beds.*" At what time soever God is pleased to inspire his grace and comfort into us, we ought to rejoice therein, and by night on the bed to seek him whom our soul loveth ; abridging that time of rest and ease, that it may become as beneficial unto us as the day itself. David was not satisfied by offering the sacrifice of thanksgiving in the courts of the Lord's house, and paying his vows in the presence of all the people ; but in the night also he would continue his song of God's mercy. Like that excellent bird, the nightingale, which is never weary nor spent by continuing her delightful notes, so this sweet singer of Israel was incessant in praising the Lord ; not giving sleep to his eyes until he had blessed his holy name. In time of affliction he made his bed to swim, praying unto the Lord to return and deliver his soul. Now in prosperity he gives thanks for the blessings he doth receive. When our bones are vexed, and our sleep departeth from us, we pray unto God to deal mercifully with us ; but when our diseases are healed, we do not return thanks, being soon overtaken with heaviness and security. And yet David did endeavour to watch in the night, that he might sing praise unto the Lord. He did not then only meditate in the law of God, when he could not take any rest (as Ahasuerus had the book of the records of the Chronicles read before him, when he could not sleep) ; for now he might lie down in peace, and sleep, when God made him to dwell in safety.

Much less did he intend to procure sleep by a sinister performance of any good duty, like those who, by singing, or reading, or hearing, or meditating will have an unworthy aim to bring themselves asleep. David saith, *"Let the saints sing aloud upon their beds"*: thereby to testify their cheerful devotion, and also to chase away the spirit of slumber.—*William Bloys, in "Meditations upon the xlii. Psalm,"* 1632.

Verse 5.—*"The saints in glory"* shall rest from their labours, but not from their praises.—*Robert Bellarmine.*

Verse 5.—*"Upon their beds,"* where before in the loneliness of night they consumed themselves with grief for their shame. Comp. Hosea vii. 14.—*E. W. Hengstenberg.*

Verse 5.—The saints of God know most of domestic joy and peace. As the word of Jesus in John xiv. records, they have sorrows in plenty, but the more of these, the greater will be their joy, because their sorrows are to be transmuted into joys. They are to sing aloud *" on their beds,"* or rather couches, for on these the Orientals not only sleep, but also dine, and feast. So this verse calls on the saints to hold a banquet, a feast of fat things. They are, as David sings in Ps. xxiii., to sit at the table prepared by the Lord in the presence of their enemies. —*Johannes Paulus Palanterius.*

Verse 5.—This verse has been fulfilled in solemn crises of saintly life. On beds of death, and at the scaffold and the stake, joy and glory have been kindled in the hearts of Christ's faithful witnesses.—*Thomas Le Blanc.*

Verse 5.—How I long for my bed ! Not that I may sleep—I lie awake often and long ! but to hold sweet communion with my God. What shall I render unto him for all his revelations and gifts to me ? Were there no historical evidence of the truth of Christianity, were there no well-established miracles, still I should believe that the religion propagated by the fishermen of Galilee is divine. The holy joys it brings to me must be from heaven Do I write this boastingly, brother ? Nay, it is with tears of humble gratitude that I tell of the goodness of the Lord. —*From a private letter from Bapa Padmanji, in "Feathers for Arrows,"* 1870.

Verse 6.—*"Let the high praises of God be in their mouth and a two-edged sword in their hand."* Praise and power go ever hand in hand. The two things act and react upon each other. An era of spiritual force in the Church is always one of praise ; and when there comes some grand outburst of sacred song, we may expect that the people of God are entering upon some new crusade for Christ. Cromwell's Ironsides were sneeringly called Psalm-singers ; but God's Psalm-singers are always Ironsides. He who has a " new song in his mouth " is ever stronger, both to suffer " and to labour, than the man who has a dumb spirit and a hymnless heart. When he sings at his work, he will both do more and do it better than he would without his song. Hence, we need not be surprised that all through its history the Church of God has travelled " along the line of music "—*William Taylor, in "The Study,"* 1873.

Verse 6.—*"The high praises of God."* This expression needs a little explication, because so variously rendered by most interpreters ; some rendering it only, exaltations of God ; others, praisings exalting God ; others, sublime praises of God ; others, prasies highly uttered unto God : the reason whereof is, because the word *romemoth* in the text signifies sometimes actively, and then it notes the height, exaltation, and lifting up of anything to the observation of others ; and sometimes passively, and then it notes the height, worth, excellency of the thing that is exalted, or lifted up, in itself. But the scope and nature of the duty prescribed in the text necessarily comprehends both—as well the high acts for which God is to be praised, as the high praises to be given unto God for those high acts ; but especially the latter, namely, the height and excellency of the duty of praise to be performed for those high acts of God. This appears from the whole argument of the Psalm, which is entirely laudatory, as also from the instrument wherewith these high praises are to be performed, namely, the " mouth," *" the high praises of God in their mouth"*; showing that the height herein mentioned is a property of man's work in praising God, and not only for the work of God, for which he is to be praised. In my observations I shall comprehend both, and all the particulars in the duty prescribed besides, which is this—

The duty of praising God is a high duty, which must exalt and lift up the high God in it.

This truth I shall labour to demonstrate, 1. From the Object. 2. The Effect.

3. Their Price. 4. Their Performance; or, to use the School terms, they are "high": 1. Objectivè. 2. Effectivè. 3. Appreciativè. 4. Perfectivè.

1. The praises of God are "*high*" in relation to their *Object*, which is none other but the Most High God, and that in the consideration of his transcendent height and sublimity over and above all other things or persons : so the Psalmist's resolution intimates (Ps. vii. 17), "I will praise the LORD according to his righteousness," which he expresseth in the following words, "To sing praise to the name of the Lord most high"; and Ps. xcii. 1 : "It is a good thing to give thanks unto the LORD, and to sing praises unto thy name, O most High." In which places, and very many more in the Scriptures, it is evident that the Lord, considered in his highest sublimity, is the object of high praise, and that by most special and peculiar appropriation of it unto himself, and none other (Isa. xlii. 8).

2. In the second place, the praises of God will appear to be of a high, sublime nature, from the high *effect*, the genuine and proper fruit they produce, viz., that although their object to whom they are peculiarly appropriate (I mean the Lord himself) be in his own nature, and of himself, most infinitely high and transcendent, yet by the attribution and performance of praise unto him, doth he account his name, his power, his wisdom, and justice, and himself to be exalted thereby. What else do those expressions in Scripture imply wherein it is asserted, that by this high duty of praise the high Jehovah is exalted (Ps. cviii. 32); His sublime perfections are extolled and lifted up (Ps. lxviii. 4) : His great Name is magnified (Luke i. 64); His infinite majesty is glorified (Ps. l. 23)? Oh how high must be that duty, that adds height to the high God, that magnifies the great God, and glorifies the God of glory, and makes him higher, greater, and more glorious than he was before!

3. Thirdly, the praises of God are of a high nature, *appreciativè*, in respect of *the high estimation the Lord himself hath of them*, which appears two ways : (1) By the high price wherewith he purchaseth them; (2) By the high delight he takes in them, after he hath procured them.

First. The *price* wherewith God is willing to purchase them is very high, for not only the expense of all his wisdom, power, and goodness, put forth in creation, not only the layings out of all his counsel, care, love, and faithfulness in providence and preservation; but also the rich treasure of his promises, covenant, grace, yea, the precious blood of his own Son, in our redemption, is given freely, absolutely, intentionally, and ultimately, for no other thing but the purchase of high praises to God (Eph. i. 5, 6). All that God doth and giveth; all that Christ doth and suffereth, is for the praise of the glory of his grace. I confess, consider men's highest praises of God, as they are man's performance, they are poor and inconsiderable things; but consider them as they are the testimonies and expressions of a believing heart, declaring and making known the unspeakable wisdom, faithfulness, bounty, and excellencies of God, exercised in his works; in this notion the Scripture declares the heart of God to be so taken with the desire of them, that he is willing to give heaven, earth, Himself, and Son to poor men for the praises of their hearts, hands, and tongues; and accounts himself abundantly satisfied. Therefore, when his people will speak good of his name, they speak of him in the dialect of angels' notes, "*the high praises of God.*"

Secondly. The high value that God hath of "high praises" will be evident by the *high delight and pleasure* God takes in them thus purchased; for skilful artists, and high-principled, elevated understandings, never take pleasure or delight in any thing or work which is not answerable to their highest principles, and proportionable to their uttermost skill and desire. Now the Lord, who is of the most perfect understanding, and deepest skill and knowledge, declares himself to take infinite delight in his people's praises. It is his solace and pleasure to be attended with them, either in earth or in heaven, by men or angels; and his soul is ravished with the thoughts and contemplation of them.

4. In the fourth place, the praises of God are high, and of a high nature *perfectivè*, that is, in respect of the high measure of grace they are to be attended withal in *their performance :* the Lord requiring the duty of high praise to be performed with a great measure of Scripture-light, with a high degree of effectual faith, and with a more ample proportion of practical holiness than any other of the most solemn exercises of his public worship.—*Condensed from a Sermon by Samuel Fairclough, entitled "The Prisoner's Praise,"* 1650.

Verse 8.—"*To bind their kings with chains,*" etc. Agrippa was captive to Paul.

The word had him in bands like a prisoner, and made him confess against himself before Festus that he was " almost persuaded to be a Christian." Then it was verified which before was prophesied, *"They shall bind kings in chains, and nobles in fetters of iron."* Oh, the majesty and force of the word !—*Henry Smith.*

Verse 8.—It was once the saying of Pompey, that with one stamp of his foot he could raise all Italy up in arms ; and the mighty men of the world may have nations, kingdoms, and commonwealths at their command, but yet God is more powerful than they all. If he do but arise, they shall all of them fly before him. If he once fall to fettering of princes, it shall be done so sure, that no flesh shall be able to knock off their bolts again.—*Stephen Gosson,* 1554—1623.

Verse 9.—*"This honour have all his saints."* All other glories and honours are but feminine, weak, poor things to it. God is their glory ; honoured they are with his blessed presence, honoured with his sight, with his embraces ; they see him and enjoy him. This is the very glory of their honour, the height and pitch of all, for " in thy presence is joy, and at thy right hand there is pleasure for evermore," honour advanced into eternal glory ; and *"this honour"* also *"have all his saints"* ; some *in spe,* and some *in re,* some *in hope,* and some *in deed ;* all either in promise or in possession.—*Mark Frank.*

Verse 9.—*"This honour have all his saints."* *"His* saints " emphatically ; Divine providence foreseeing that in after ages some would usurp the title of saintship to whom it did not belong. " His saints " exclusively ; casting out saint traitors, as Beckett and Garnet ; saint hypocrites, and many others ; who, in the same sense as *auri sacra fames,* may be termed *sacri,* or *sancti,* saints. But, what honour have all his saints ? Mark what went before—" as it is written " ; but by whom, and where ? Though chapters and verses be of later date, the Holy Spirit might have cited the book. O no ! He, to quicken our industry, refers us to the Word at large. However, " search the Scriptures," and therein we shall meet with many honours afforded to the saints ; both whilst they were living, and when they were dead.

Honour to their memories is sometimes paid them very abundantly, even by those who formerly were so niggardly and covetous as not to afford them a good word in their lifetime.

Many are made converts by the godly ends of good men ; as the centurion himself, who attended and ordered the crucifying of Christ, after his expiring broke forth into that testimony of him,—" Verily, this was the Son of God." So, such as rail at, revile, curse, condemn, persecute, execute pious people, speak other language of them when such men have passed the purgation of death, and confess them faithful and sincere servants of God.

The last *"honour"* is imitation of their virtuous examples. The Papists brag that Stapleton, their great controversial divine, was born on that very day whereon Sir Thomas More was put to death ; but Providence so ordereth it that out of the ashes of dead saints many living ones do spring and sprout, by following the pious precedents of such godly persons deceased.—*Thomas Fuller, in "Abel Redivivus."*

HINTS TO PREACHERS.

Verse 1.—*"Praise ye the Lord."* I. The one work of a life. II. The work of the truly living of all degrees. III. Their work in many and various forms. IV. A work for which there is abundant cause, reason, and argument.

Verse 1.—I. A wonderful gift—to be a saint. II. A wonderful people—who are saints. III. A wonderful assembly—a congregation of saints. IV. A wonderful God—the object of their song.

Verses 1, 2.—*The new song of the saints.* I. The saints are God's children by the new birth. II. The new birth has given them a new heart. III. The new heart utters itself in a new song.—*C. A. D.*

Verses 1, 5.—I. We must praise God in public, " in the congregation of the saints " : the more the better ; it is like to heaven. II. We must praise him in private. "Let the saints" be so transported with their joy in God as to "sing aloud upon their beds," when they awake in the night, as David ; Ps. cxix. 62. —*Matthew Henry.*

Verse 2.—The duty, reasonableness, and benefit of holy joy.

Verse 2.—A peculiar people, their peculiar God, and their peculiar joy in him.

Verse 2 (second clause).—Christ's people may well rejoice :—I. In the majesty of his person. II. In the righteousness of his rule. III. In the extent of his conquests. IV. In the protection they enjoy under him. V. In the glory to which he will raise them.—*From "The Homiletical Library,"* 1882.

Verses 2, 4.—The cause given to God's Israel for Praise. Consider, I. God's doings for them. They have reason to rejoice in God, and employ themselves in his service ; for it is he that "made" them. II. God's dominion over them. This follows upon the former : if he made them he is their King. III. God's delight in them. He is a King that rules by love, and therefore to be praised. IV. God's designs concerning them. Besides the present complacency he hath in them, he hath prepared for their future glory. "He will beautify the meek," etc.—*Matthew Henry.*

Verse 4.—The text bears other renderings. Read as in Authorized Version. I. *The character to be aimed at—"the meek."* 1. Submissive to God. To his truth. To his dealings. 2. Gentle towards men. Bearing with patience. Forgiving with heartiness. Loving with perseverance. 3. Lowly in ourselves. II. *The favour to be enjoyed—"beautify."* 1. The beauty of gentleness. 2. The beauty of peace. 3. The beauty of content. 4. The beauty of joy. 5. The beauty of holiness. 6. The beauty of respect and influence. III. *The good results to be expected.* 1. God will be glorified and Christ manifested. 2. Men will be attracted. 3. Heaven will be anticipated.

Verse 4 (first clause).—The Lord's taking pleasure in his people is, I. A wonderful evidence of his grace. II. The highest honour they can desire. III. Their security for time and eternity.—*J. F.*

Verse 5.—*Saintly joy.* I. The state to which God has lifted the saints : "glory," in contrast with sin, reproach, affliction. II. The emotion which accordingly befits the saints : "be joyful." III. The utterance of that emotion incumbent on the saints : "sing aloud."—*C. A. D.*

Verse 5 (second clause).—Let them praise God—I. Upon their beds of *rest*, upon their *nightly* couch. 1. Because of what God has done for them during the day. 2. Because sleep is the gift of God. 3. Because they have a bed to lie upon. 4. Because the Lord is their keeper (Psalm iv. 5, 8). II. Upon their beds of *sickness*. 1. Because it is God's will they should suffer. 2. Because affliction is often a proof of God's love. 3. Because, if sanctified, sickness is a great blessing. 4. Because praise offered upon a bed of sickness is a testimony to the power of religion. III. Upon their beds of *death*. 1. Because the sting of death is removed. 2. Because their Lord has passed through death. 3. Because Christ is with them while they suffer. 4. Because of what awaits them. 5. Because they have the glorious hope of resurrection.—*C. W. Townsend.*

Verse 6.—I. The Christian life a combination of adoration and conflict. II. In each case it should be at its best : "high praises," "two-edged sword." III. In each case holiness should be conspicuous : it is of saints that the text speaks.

Verse 8.—The restraining and subduing power of the gospel.

Verse 9.—The honour common to all saints.

PSALM CL.

We have now reached the last summit of the mountain chain of Psalms. It rises high into the clear azure, and its brow is bathed in the sunlight of the eternal world of worship. It is a rapture. The poet-prophet is full of inspiration and enthusiasm. He stays not to argue, to teach, to explain: but cries with burning words, "Praise him, Praise him, Praise ye the LORD."

EXPOSITION.

PRAISE ye the LORD. Praise God in his sanctuary: praise him in the firmament of his power.

2 Praise him for his mighty acts: praise him according to his excellent greatness.

3 Praise him with the sound of the trumpet: praise him with the psaltery and harp.

4 Praise him with the timbrel and dance: praise him with stringed instruments and organs.

5 Praise him upon the loud cymbals: praise him upon the high sounding cymbals.

6 Let everything that hath breath praise the LORD. Praise ye the LORD.

1. *"Praise ye the LORD."* Hallelujah! The exhortation is to all things in earth or in heaven. Should they not all declare the glory of him for whose glory they are, and were created? Jehovah, the one God, should be the one object of adoration. To give the least particle of his honour to another is shameful treason; to refuse to render it to him is heartless robbery. *"Praise God in his sanctuary."* Praise El, or the strong one, in his holy place. See how power is mentioned with holiness in this change of names. Praise begins at home. "In God's own house pronounce his praise." The holy place should be filled with praise, even as of old the high-priest filled the *sanctum sanctorum* with the smoke of sweet-smelling incense. In his church below and in his courts above hallelujahs should be continually presented. In the person of Jesus God finds a holy dwelling or sanctuary, and there he is greatly to be praised. He may also be said to dwell in holiness, for all his ways are right and good; for this we ought to extol him with heart and with voice. Whenever we assemble for holy purposes our main work should be to present praises unto the Lord our God. *"Praise him in the firmament of his power."* It is a blessed thing that in our God holiness and power are united. Power without righteousness would be oppression, and righteousness without power would be too weak for usefulness; but put the two together in an infinite degree and we have God. What an expanse we have in the boundless firmament of divine power! Let it all be filled with praise. Let the heavens, so great and strong, echo with the praise of the thrice holy Jehovah, while the sanctuaries of earth magnify the Almighty One.

2. *"Praise him for his mighty acts."* Here is a reason for praise. In these deeds of power we see himself. These doings of his omnipotence are always on behalf of truth and righteousness. His works of creation, providence, and redemption all call for praise; they are his acts, and his acts of might, therefore let him be praised for them. *"Praise him according to his excellent greatness."* His being is unlimited, and his praise should correspond therewith. He possesses a multitude or a plenitude of greatness, and therefore he should be greatly praised. There is nothing little about God, and there is nothing great apart from him. If we were always careful to make our worship fit and appropriate for our great Lord how much better should we sing! How much more reverently should we adore! Such excellent deeds should have excellent praise.

3. *"Praise him with the sound of the trumpet."* With the loudest, clearest note

call the people together.　Make all men to know that we are not ashamed to worship. Summon them with unmistakable sound to bow before their God.　The sound of trumpet is associated with the grandest and most solemn events, such as the giving of the law, the proclamation of jubilee, the coronation of Jewish kings, and the raging of war.　It is to be thought of in reference to the coming of our Lord in his second advent and the raising of the dead.　If we cannot give voice to this martial instrument, at least let our praise be as decided and bold as if we could give a blast upon the horn.　Let us never sound a trumpet before us to our own honour, but reserve all our trumpeting for God's glory.　When the people have been gathered by blast of trumpet, then proceed to *"praise him with the psaltery and harp."* Stringed instruments are to be used as well as those which are rendered vocal by wind.　Dulcet notes are to be consecrated as well as more startling sounds.　The gospel meaning is that all powers and faculties should praise the Lord—all sorts of persons, under all circumstances, and with differing constitutions, should do honour unto the Lord of all.　If there be any virtue, if there be any talent, if there be any influence, let all be consecrated to the service of the universal Benefactor.　Harp and lyre—the choicest, the sweetest, must be all our Lord's.

4. *"Praise him with the timbrel and dance."*　Associated with the deliverance at the Red Sea, this form of worship set forth the most jubilant and exultant of worship.　The hands, and the feet were both employed, and the entire body moved in sympathy with the members.　Are there not periods of life when we feel so glad that we would fain dance for joy ?　Let not such exhilaration be spent upon common themes, but let the name of God stir us to ecstasy.　Let us exult as we cry,—

> " In the heavenly Lamb thrice happy I am,
> And my heart it doth dance at the sound of his name."

There is enough in our holy faith to create and to justify the utmost degree of rapturous delight.　If men are dull in the worship of the Lord our God they are not acting consistently with the character of their religion.　*"Praise him with stringed instruments and organs."*　We have here the three kinds of musical instruments : timbrels, which are struck, and strings, and pipes : let all be educated to praise the Lord.　Nothing is common and unclean : all may be sanctified to highest uses. Many men, many minds, and these as different as strings and pipes ; but there is only one God, and that one God all should worship.　The word translated " organs " signifies pipe—a simpler form of wind instrument than the more modern and more elaborate organ.　Doubtless many a pious shepherd has poured out gracious pastorals from a reed or oaten pipe, and so has magnified his God.

5. *"Praise him upon the loud cymbals : praise him upon the high sounding cymbals."*　Let the clash of the loudest music be the Lord's : let the joyful clang of the loftiest notes be all for him.　Praise has beaten the timbrel, swept the harp, and sounded the trumpet, and now for a last effort, awakening the most heavy of slumberers, and startling the most indifferent of onlookers, she dashes together the disks of brass, and with sounds both loud and high proclaims the glories of the Lord.

6. *"Let everything that hath breath praise the Lord."*　" Let all breath praise him " : that is to say, all living beings.　He gave them breath, let them breathe his praise.　His name is in the Hebrew composed rather of breathings than of letters, to show that all breath comes from him : therefore let it be used for him.　Join all ye living things in the eternal song.　Be ye least or greatest, withhold not your praises.　What a day will it be when all things in all places unite to glorify the one only living and true God !　This will be the final triumph of the church of God.

"Praise ye the Lord."　Once more, Hallelujah !　Thus is the Psalm rounded with the note of praise ; and thus is the Book of Psalms ended by a glowing word of adoration.　Reader, wilt not thou at this moment pause a while, and worship the Lord thy God ?　Hallelujah !

EXPLANATORY NOTES AND QUAINT SAYINGS.

Whole Psalm.—Each of the last five Psalms begins and ends with *Hallelujah !*—*"Praise ye the Lord."* And each Psalm increases in praise, love, and joy, unto the last, which is praise celebrating its ecstasy. The elect soul, the heir of God, becomes " eaten up " with the love of God. He begins every sentence with *Hallelujah ;* and his sentences are very short, for he is in haste to utter his next *Hallelujah,* and his next, and his next. He is as one out of breath with enthusiasm, or as one on tiptoe, in the act of rising from earth to heaven. The greatest number of words between any two Hallelujahs is four, and that only once : in every other instance, between one Hallelujah and another there are but two words. It is as though the soul gave utterance to its whole life and feeling in the one word, *Hallelujah !* The words, " Praise ye the Lord ! " or, " Praise him ! " " Praise him ! " " Praise him ! " are reiterated no fewer than twelve times in a short Psalm of six short verses.—*John Pulsford, in "Quiet Hours,"* 1857.

Whole Psalm.—And now, in the last Psalm of all, we see an echo to the first Psalm. The first Psalm began with " Blessed," and it ended with " Blessed,"—" Blessed are all they that meditate on God's law and do it." Such was the theme of the first Psalm ; and now the fruit of that blessedness is shown in this Psalm, which begins and ends with Hallelujah.—*Christopher Wordsworth.*

Whole Psalm.—In his *Cours de Littérature,* the celebrated Lamartine, probably regarding the last four Psalms (the Hallelujah Psalms) as one whole (as Hengstenberg also does), thus speaks :—" The last Psalm ends with a chorus to the praise of God, in which the poet calls on all people, all instruments of sacred music, all the elements, and all the stars to join. Sublime finale of that opera of sixty years sung by the shepherd, the hero, the king, and the old man ! In this closing Psalm we see the almost inarticulate enthusiasm of the lyric poet ; so rapidly do the words press to his lips, floating upwards towards God, their source, like the smoke of a great fire of the soul wafted by the tempest ! Here we see David, or rather the human heart itself with all its God-given notes of grief, joy, tears, and adoration—poetry sanctified to its highest expression ; a vase of perfume broken on the step of the temple, and shedding abroad its odours from the heart of David to the heart of all humanity ! Hebrew, Christian, or even Mohammedan, every religion, every complaint, every prayer has taken from this vase, shed on the heights of Jerusalem, wherewith to give forth their accents. The little shepherd has become the master of the sacred choir of the Universe. There is not a worship on earth which prays not with his words, or sings not with his voice. A chord of his harp is to be found in all choirs, resounding everywhere and for ever in unison with the echoes of Horeb and Engedi ! David is the Psalmist of eternity ; what a destiny—what a power hath poetry when inspired by God ! As for myself, when my spirit is excited, or devotional, or sad, and seeks for an echo to its enthusiasm, its devotion, or its melancholy, I do not open Pindar or Horace, or Hafiz, those purely Academic poets ; neither do I find within myself murmurings to express my emotion. I open the Book of Psalms, and there I find words which seem to issue from the soul of the ages, and which penetrate even to the heart of all generations. Happy the bard who has thus become the eternal hymn, the personified prayer and complaint of all humanity ! If we look back to that remote age when such songs resounded over the world ; if we consider that while the lyric poetry of all the most cultivated nations only sang of wine, love, blood, and the victories of coursers at the games of Elidus, we are seized with profound astonishment at the mystic accents of the shepherd prophet, who speaks to God the Creator as one friend to another, who understands and praises his great works, admires his justice, implores his mercy, and becomes, as it were, an anticipative echo of the evangelic poetry, speaking the soft words of Christ before his coming. Prophet or not, as he may be considered by Christian or sceptic, none can deny in the poet-king an inspiration granted to no other man. Read Greek or Latin poetry after a Psalm, and see how pale it looks."—*William Swan Plumer.*

Whole Psalm.—The first and last of the Psalms have both the same number of verses, are both short and very memorable ; but the scope of them is very different ; the first Psalm is an elaborate instruction in our duty, to prepare us for the comforts of our devotion ; this is all rapture and transport, and perhaps was penned on purpose to be the conclusion of those sacred songs, to show what is the design of them all, and that is, to assist us in praising God.—*Matthew Henry.*

Whole Psalm.—Thirteen hallelujahs, according to the number of the tribes (Levi, Ephraim and Manasseh making three), one for each.—*John Henry Michaëlis,* 1668—1738.

Whole Psalm.—Some say this Psalm was sung by the Israelites, when they came with the first fruits into the sanctuary, with the baskets on their shoulders. *Thirteen* times in this short Psalm is the word *praise* used ; not on account of thirteen perfections or properties in God, as Kimchi thinks ; but it is so frequently, and in every clause used, to show the vehement desire of the Psalmist that the Lord might be praised ; and to express his sense of things, how worthy he is of praise ; and that all ways and means to praise him should be made use of, all being little enough to set forth his honour and glory.—*John Gill.*

Whole Psalm.—There is an interesting association connected with this Psalm which deserves to be recorded : that in former times, when the casting of church bells was more of a religious ceremony, this Psalm was chanted by the brethren of the guild as they stood ranged around the furnace, and while the molten metal was prepared to be let off into the mould ready to receive it. One may picture these swarthy sons of the furnace with the ruddy glow of the fire upon their faces as they stand around, while their deep voices rung forth this Hymn of Praise.— *Barton Bouchier.*

Verse 1.—"*Praise ye the* LORD." Praise God with a strong faith ; praise him with holy love and delight ; praise him with an entire confidence in Christ ; praise him with a believing triumph over the powers of darkness ; praise him with an earnest desire towards him, and a full satisfaction in him ; praise him by a universal respect to all his commands ; praise him by a cheerful submission to all his disposals ; praise him by rejoicing in his love, and solacing yourselves in his great goodness ; praise him by promoting the interests of the kingdom of his grace ; praise him by a lively hope and expectation of the kingdom of his glory.—*Matthew Henry.*

Verse 1.—"*In his sanctuary.*" בְּקָדְשׁוֹ. Many have been the notions of the commentators as to the shade of meaning here ; for the word differs from the form in Ps. xx. 2. מִקֹּדֶשׁ (*from the sanctuary*). The Vulgate adopts the plural rendering, *in sanctis ejus,* " in his holy places." Campensis renders it, *ob insignem sanctitatem ipsius,* " because of his excellent holiness." Some see under the word an allusion to the holy tabernacle of Deity, the flesh of Christ. Luther, in his German version, translates thus *in seinem Heiligthum,* " in his holiness." The same harmony of comparative thought appears in the two clauses of this verse as in such passages as 1 Kings viii. 13, 49 ; Isa. lvii. 15. The place of worship where God specially hears prayer and accepts praise, and the firmament where angels fly at his command, and veil their faces in adoration, are each a sanctuary. The sanctuary is manifestly here looked at as the temple of grace, the firmament as the temple of power. So the verse proclaims both grace and glory.—*Martin Geier.*

Verse 1.—" *Praise God in his sanctuary.*" The Septuagint, Vulgate Latin, and the eastern versions, render it, "*in his holy ones*" ; among his saints, in the assembly of them, where he is to be feared and praised : it may be translated, "*in his holy One,*" and be understood of Christ, as it is by Cocceius. . . . Some render it, "*for*" or "*because of his holiness.*" The perfection of holiness in him ; in which he is glorious and fearful in the praises of, and which appears in all his works of providence and grace.—*John Gill.*

Verse 1.—"*Praise God.*" In many places we have the compound word, הללו־יה, *halelujah,* praise ye Jehovah ; but this is the first place in which we find, הללו־אל, *halelu-el,* praise God, or the strong God. Praise him who is Jehovah, the infinite and self-existent Being ; and praise him who is God, *El,* or *Elohim,* the great God in covenant with mankind, to bless and save them unto eternal life.—*Adam Clarke.*

Verse 1.—Psalm cl. gives the full praise to Jehovah in a double character, *the sanctuary and the firmament of his power,* for his ways which come from the firmament of his power were always according to the sanctuary in which he governed Israel, and made good the revelation of himself there.—*John Nelson Darby,* 1800—1882.

Verse 2.—"*Praise him for his mighty acts,*" etc. The reasons of that praise which it becomes all intelligent creatures, and especially redeemed men, to render to Jehovah, are here assigned. We are to praise Jehovah " in his sanctuary," in the place where his glory dwells, where his holiness shines forth with ineffable splendour ; we are to praise him in the wide expanse over which he has spread the tokens of his power, whether in the heaven above, or in the earth beneath ; we are to praise him for those omnipotent acts whereby he hath shown himself to be above all gods ; we are to praise him in a manner suited to the excellent majesty of a Being whom all the heavens adore, and who is wonderful in counsel and excellent in working. His holiness, the infinity of his operations, the miraculous power which he has displayed, the unspotted excellence of his administration, call for loudest songs of praise from all whose reason enables them to rise to the contemplation of the great Supreme.—*John Morison.*

Verse 2.—*"Praise him according to his excellent greatness."* There is required special understanding and knowledge of the nature and worth of the mercy for which the duty of praise is undertaken ; for God will not be praised confusedly, but distinctly and proportionably to his dispensation : *"Praise him according to his wondrous works";* which is to be the prime and proper matter of their high praises, even his more proper and peculiar high acts, then to be remembered, as is largely expressed in Moses' praise for the particular mercy of coming safe through the Red Sea (Exod. xv.) ; and Deborah's high praise for deliverance from the host of Sisera (Judges v.) ; where the chiefest and highest part of the celebration and exaltation of God in his praise consists in the declaration and commemoration of the particulars of God's special goodness in their present deliverance. Thus, you see, the first thing that God looks for is proportionable praise, great praise for a great God, doing great things, and high praises for a high God, doing high things. —*Samuel Fairclough.*

Verse 2.—*"Praise him according to his excellent greatness,"* or, as the words may bear, " according to his *muchness of greatness* "; for when the Scripture saith " God is great," this positive is to be taken as a superlative. " God is great," that is, he is greatest, he is greater than all ; so great that all persons and all things are little, yea, nothing before him. Isaiah xl. 15 : " Behold, the nations are (to him but) as a drop of a bucket, and are counted as the small dust of the balance : behold, he taketh up the isles as a very little thing. And Lebanon is not sufficient to burn, nor the beasts thereof sufficient for a burnt offering. All nations before him are as nothing ; and they are counted to him less than nothing, and vanity." How great is God, in comparison of whom the greatest things are little things, yea, the greatest things are nothing !—*Joseph Caryl.*

Verse 3.—*Trumpets* and *horns* are the only instruments concerning which any directions are given in the law.—*James Anderson.*

Verse 3.—*"Trumpet."* Of natural horns and of instruments in the shape of horns the antiquity and general use are evinced by every extensive collection of antiquities. . . . The Hebrew word *shophar,* rendered " trumpet," seems, first to denote horns of the straighter kind, including, probably, those of neat-cattle, and all the instruments which were eventually made in imitation of and in improvement upon such horns. The name *shophar* means *bright* or *clear,* and the instrument may be conceived to have been so called from its clear and shrill sound, just as we call an instrument a " clarion," and speak of a musical tone as " brilliant " or " clear." In the service of God this *shophar* or *trumpet,* was only employed in making announcements, and for calling the people together in the time of the holy solemnities, of war, of rebellion, or of any other great occasion. The strong sound of the instrument would have confounded a choir of singers, rather than have elevated their music. (*John Kitto.*) The *shophar* is especially interesting to us as being the only Hebrew instrument whose use on certain solemn occasions seems to be retained to this day. Engel, with his usual trustworthy research, has traced out and examined some of those in modern synagogues. Of those shown in our engraving, one is from the synagogue of Spanish and Portugese Jews, Bevis Marks, and is, he says, one foot in length ; the other is one used in the Great Synagogue, St. James's place, Aldgate, twenty-one inches in length. Both are made of horn.—*James Stainer.*

Verse 3.— The *"Psaltery"* was a ten-stringed instrument. It is constantly mentioned with the " harp." The *Psaltery* was struck with a plectrum, the *harp* more gently with the fingers. *"Psaltery and harp"* speak to us in figure of " law and gospel."—*Thomas Le Blanc*

Verse 3.—On *"Psaltery"* (*nebel*) see Note on Ps. cxliv. 9, and on " *harp* " see Note on Ps. cxlix. 3.

Verses 3, 4, 5.—As St. Augustine says here, " No kind of faculty is here omitted.

All are enlisted in praising God." The breath is employed in blowing the trumpet ; the fingers are used in striking the strings of the psaltery and the harp ; the whole hand is exerted in beating the timbrel ; the feet move in the dance ; there are stringed instruments (literally *strings*) ; there is the organ (the *'ugab, syrinx*) composed of many pipes, implying *combination*, and the cymbals clang one upon another.— *C. Wordsworth.*

Verses 3, 4, 5.—The variety of musical instruments, some of them made use of in the camp, as trumpets ; some of them more suitable to a peaceable condition, as psalteries and harps ; some of them sounding by blowing wind in them ; some of them sounding by lighter touching of them, as stringed instruments ; some of them by beating on them more sharply, as tabrets, drums and cymbals ; some of them sounding by touching and blowing also, as organs : all of them giving some certain sound, some more quiet, and some making more noise : some of them having a harmony by themselves ; some of them making a concert with other instruments, or with the motions of the body in dancings, some of them serving for one use, some of them serving for another, and all of them serving to set forth God's glory, and to shadow forth the duty of worshippers, and the privileges of the saints. The plurality and variety (I say) of these instruments were fit to represent divers conditions of the spiritual man, and of the greatness of his joy to be found in God, and to teach what stirring up should be of the affections and powers of our soul, and of one another, unto God's worship ; what harmony should be among the worshippers of God, what melody each should make in himself, singing to God with grace in his heart, and to show the excellency of God's praise, which no means nor instrument, nor any expression of the body joined thereunto, could sufficiently set forth in these exhortations to praise God with trumpet, psaltery, etc.—*David Dickson.*

Verses 3, 4, 5.—Patrick has an interesting note on the many instruments of music in Psalm cxlix., which we quote here : " The ancient inhabitants of Etruria used the trumpet ; the Arcadians, the whistle ; the Sicilians, the pectid ; the Cretians, the harp ; the Thracians, the cornet ; the Lacedemonians, the pipe ; the Egyptians, the drum ; the Arabians, the cymbal. (Clem. Pædag. ii. 4.) May we not say that in this Psalm's enumeration of musical instruments, there is a reference to the variety which exists among men in the mode of expressing joy, and exciting to feeling ?—*Andrew A. Bonar.*

Verse 4.—"*Stringed instruments.*" *Minnim* [which is derived from a root signifying " division," or " distribution," hence *strings*] occurs in Ps. xlv. 8, and cl. 4, and is supposed by some to denote a stringed instrument, but it seems merely a poetical allusion to the *strings* of any instrument. Thus, in Ps. xlv. 8, we would read, " Out of the ivory palaces *the strings* (*i.e.* concerts of music) have made thee glad " ; and so in Ps.cl. 4, " Praise him with *strings* (stringed instruments), and *'ugabs.*"—*John Kitto.*

Verse 4.—"*Organs.*" עוּגָב, *'ugab* is the word rendered " organ " in our version. The Targum renders the word simply by אבּוּבָא, *a pipe ;* the Septuagint varies, it has κιθάρα in Genesis, ψάλμος in Job, and ὄργανον in the Psalms. The last is the sense which the Arabic, Syriac, Latin, English, and most other versions have adopted. The *organon* simply denotes a double or manifold pipe, and hence, in particular, the Pandæan or shepherd's pipe, which is at this day called a " mouth organ," among ourselves. (*Kitto.*) A collection of tubes of different sizes, stopped at one end and blown at the other, forms the musical instrument, known as Pan's pipes, in the Greek *syrinx*, σύρυγξ . . . . Was the *'ugab* a *syrinx* or an organ ? As the former seems to have been the more ancient of the two, and as *'ugab* is included in the very first allusion to musical instruments in the Bible, it would seem reasonable to say at once that it was *syrinx*, especially as this instrument was, and is to this day, commonly met with in various parts of Asia. Yet it would, indeed, be strange if such an instrument were selected for use in divine worship ; and that the *ugab* was so used is proved beyond a doubt by its mention in Ps. cl. : " Praise him with the *minnim* and *'ugab.* " Its mention here in antithesis to a collective name for stringed instruments, surely points to the fact of its being a more important instrument than a few river-reeds fixed together with wax. Let us not forget that we have but one and the same name for the single row of about fifty pipes, placed, perhaps, in a little room, and the mighty instrument of five thousand pipes, occupying as much space as an ordinary dwelling-house. . . . Each is an organ. May it not have been the case that the *'ugab*, which in Gen. iv. 21 is mentioned as the simply-constructed *wind*-instrument, in contrast to the simple *stringed*-instrument, the *kinnor*, was a greatly inferior instrument to that which in Ps. cl. is thought worthy of mention by the side of a term for the whole string power ?—*J. Stainer.*

Verse 5.—*"Loud cymbals . . . . high-sounding cymbals."* This important passage clearly points to two instruments under the same name, and leaves us to conclude that the Hebrews had both hand-cymbals and finger-cymbals (or castanets), although it may not in all cases be easy to say which of the two is intended in particular texts.—*John Kitto.*

Verse 5. (Prayer Book Version).—*"Praise him upon the well-tuned cymbals: praise him upon the loud cymbals."* As I have heard these words read monthly in our churches, it has often come into my thoughts that when we intend to glorify God with our cymbals, it should not be our only care to have them loud enough, but our first care should be to have them well tuned, else the louder the worse. Zeal does very well—there is great, yea, necessary use for it in every part of God's service. The cymbal will be flat, it will have no life or spirit in it, it will not be loud enough without it. But if meekness, peaceableness, and moderation do not first put the cymbal into good tune, the loudness will but make it the more ungrateful in the player, the more ungrateful to the hearer.—*Robert Sanderson,* 1587—1662.

Verse 6.—*"Praise ye the LORD."* As the life of the faithful, and the history of the church, so also the Psalter, with all its cries from the depths, runs out into a Hallelujah.—*E. W. Hengstenberg.*

Verse 6.—*"Praise ye the LORD."* When we have said all we are able to say for God's praise, we are but to begin anew ; for this are we taught by the renewing of the exhortation, in the close of sundry Psalms, and here also at the end of all the Psalms : *"Praise ye the LORD."*—*David Dickson.*

Verse 6.—*"Let all breath praise Jah ! Hallelujah."* The very ambiguity of *"all breath"* gives extraordinary richness of meaning to this closing sentence. From the simple idea of wind instruments, mentioned in the context, it leads us, by a beautiful transition, to that of vocal, articulate, intelligent praise, uttered by the breath of living men, as distinguished from mere lifeless instruments. Then, lastly, by a natural association, we ascend to the idea expressed in the common version, *"everything that hath breath,"* not merely all that lives, but all that has a voice to praise God. There is nothing in the Psalter more majestic or more beautiful than this brief but most significant *finale*, in which solemnity of tone predominates, without however in the least disturbing the exhilaration which the close of the Psalter seems intended to produce, as if in emblematical allusion to the triumph which awaits the church and all its members, when through much tribulation they shall enter into rest.—*Joseph Addison Alexander.*

HINTS TO PREACHERS.

Verse 1.—*"Praise God in his sanctuary."* I. In his personal holiness. II. In the person of his Son. III. In heaven. IV. In the assembly of saints. V. In the silence of the heart.

Verses 1—6.—God should be praised. Where ? (*verse 1*). Wherefore ? (*verse 2*). Wherewith ? (*verses 3—5*). By whom ? (*verse 6*).—*C. A. D.*

Verse 2.—*"His excellent greatness."* Wherein the greatness of God is specially excellent, and where it is best seen.

Verse 2.—*"Praise him for his mighty acts."* I. For us. Election. Redemption. Inspiration. II. In us. The work of enlightenment in the understanding ; purification in the heart ; quickening in the conscience, subjugation in the will. III. By us. Thought through us ; felt through us, spoken through us ; worked through us. To him be all the glory !—*W. J.*

Verse 2.—*"Praise him according to his excellent greatness."* I. Reverently according to the greatness of his being. II. Gratefully, according to the greatness of his love. III. Retrospectively, according to the greatness of his gifts. IV. Prospectively, according to the greatness of his promises—*W. J.*

Verse 2.—What the exhortation requires. I. That men should study God's works, and observe the glory of God in them. II. That they should meditate on his greatness till they realize its excellence. III. That they should openly proclaim the honour due to him. IV. That they should not contradict in their life the praise they speak.—*J. F.*

Verse 3.—*"Praise him with the sound of the trumpet."* I. When you fight. II. When you conquer. III. When you assemble. IV. When you proclaim his Word. V. When you welcome Jubilee.

Verses 3—6.—I. The variety of the ancient service of worship necessitating serious expenditure ; consecration of high talent ; hard and constant toil. II. The lessons of such service. 1. God should be worshipped loyally. 2. The efforts of the best genius are his rightful tribute. 3. All human ability cannot place a worthy offering at his feet. III. The soul and essential of true worship. IV. God's requirements as to worship in these present times.—*W. B. H.*

Verse 6.—I. The august Giver of " life, and breath, and all things." II. The due and true use of the gifts of life. III. The resultant swathing of earth in consecrated atmosphere, and millennial hallelujahs.—*W. B. H.*

Verse 6.—A fitting close to the Psalter, considered as a desire, a prayer, or an exhortation. I. As a desire, it realizes the glory due to God, the worship ennobling to man, the disposition of heart which would make all the world into a holy brotherhood. II. As a prayer, it seeks the downfall of every superstition, the universal spread of the truth, the conversion of every soul. III. As an exhortation it is plain, pertinent, pure in its piety, perfect in its charity.—*J. F.*

HALLELUJAH!

THE RESTING-PLACE OF C. H. SPURGEON IN NORWOOD CEMETERY.

Specially drawn for "The Treasury of David" by E. H. Fitchew.